ERIC IDENTIFIER CATEGORIES (STATISTICS FOR DEC 94)

CATEGORY NUMBER	CATEGORY NAME	NUMBER OF IDENTIFIERS IN CATEGORY	PERCENT OF IDENTIFIER AUTHORITY FILE
02	CONFERENCES/MEETINGS	379	.8
03	CURRICULUM AREAS	626	1.3
04	EQUIPMENT (INCLUDING COMPUTER PROGRAMS)	1,608	3.2
05	FACILITIES	599	1.2
07	GEOGRAPHIC LOCATIONS	2,785	5.5
08	GROUPS (ETHNIC)	447	.9
09	GROUPS (OCCUPATIONS)	755	1.5
10	GROUPS (OTHER)	551	1.1
11	HEALTH-RELATED (INCLUDING PSYCHOLOGY)	2,220	4.4
12	HISTORICAL/SPECIAL EVENTS	316	.6
13	LANGUAGES/LINGUISTICS	1,607	3.2
14	LAWS/LEGISLATION	1,472	3.0
15	METHODS/THEORIES	4,499	9.0
16	MISCELLANEOUS	3,667	7.3
17	ORGANIZATIONS/ INSTITUTIONS	10,586	21.0
18	PERSONAL NAMES	3,374	6.7
19	PROJECTS/PROGRAMS	5,091	10.1
20	SCIENCE & TECHNOLOGY	2,162	4.3
21	TESTS/TESTING	6,014	12.0
22	TITLES (LITERARY AND ARTISTIC)	1,453	2.9
	TOTAL	50,211	100.0%

*Categories 01 (Acronyms) and 06 (Foreign Words/Phrases) have been abandoned; their entries were integrated into other categories.

ERIC®

Identifier Authority List (IAL)

1995

ERIC®
Identifier Authority List (IAL)

1995

Edited by James E. Houston,
Carolyn R. Weller, and Carol A. Patt

ERIC Processing and Reference Facility
Systems Engineering Division
Computer Sciences Corporation

ORYX PRESS

The rare Arabian Oryx is believed to have inspired the myth of the unicorn. This desert antelope became virtually extinct in the early 1960s. At that time, several groups of international conservationists arranged to have nine animals sent to the Phoenix Zoo to be the nucleus of a captive breeding herd. Today the Oryx population is over 1,000, and 500 have been returned to reserves in the Middle East.

4041 North Central at Indian School Road
Phoenix, Arizona 85012-3397

The material contained herein was generated under contracts with the Office of Educational Research and Improvement, Department of Education. However, the contents do not necessarily reflect the position or policy of that agency, and no U.S. Government endorsement is to be inferred.

Published simultaneously in Canada

Printed and Bound in the United States of America

∞ The paper used in this publication meets the minimum requirements of American National Standard for Information Science—Permanence of Paper for Printed Library Materials, ANSI Z39.48, 1984.

ISBN 0-89774-890-5
ISSN 1062-0508

Contents

Introduction

The *ERIC Identifier Authority List (IAL),* first produced in March 1980, was the culmination of a multiyear, systemwide editorial project to consolidate Identifiers and systematize their use in ERIC indexing and searching. Over the years, continuing interest in the *IAL* has been stimulated by the product's general utility for anyone involved in building and accessing the ERIC database. The *IAL* was first made available in a commercially published edition by The Oryx Press in 1992, and the 1995 printing marks the second published edition of this product.

The discussion that follows will attempt to put ERIC Identifiers and the *IAL* into a meaningful context within the attributes and purposes of the ERIC database.[1]

Users are invited to direct questions and comments about the *IAL,* Identifiers, or the ERIC vocabulary in general to Jim Houston, Lexicographer, ERIC Facility, Computer Sciences Corporation, 1301 Piccard Drive, Suite 300, Rockville, MD 20850-4305. Telephone: (301) 258-5500. Fax: (301) 948-3695. Internet: jhouston@inet.ed.gov

IDENTIFIERS—DEFINITION AND FUNCTION

Identifiers are semicontrolled retrieval terms, intended to add a depth to indexing that is not always possible with Descriptors alone. Descriptors are *controlled* vocabulary terms appearing in structured database thesauri.[2] An Identifier is usually the name of a specific entity, e.g., project, piece of legislation, person, place, organization, test, group, item of equipment. There are a nearly infinite number of specific entities, and it would not be appropriate to burden a thesaurus with such multiplicity. Also, Identifiers, being so specific, are often transitory, or represented in the literature infrequently, further arguing for separate treatment.

An Identifier may also be a new concept, under consideration for Descriptor status once its scope, definition, authoritativeness, and "staying power" have been established. Candidate Descriptors, awaiting approval for admission to the *ERIC Thesaurus,* are first introduced as Identifiers.[3]

IDENTIFIERS—GUIDELINES

Identifiers are neither structured nor formally defined (as Descriptors are); however, some control must be exercised in order to eliminate proliferation of variant forms of the same concept. Such control is achieved by imposing format standards, particularly for such entities as geographic locations, organization names, and specific ethnic and occupational groups.

Guidelines and rules for the creation and use of Identifiers have been compiled in the *ERIC Processing Manual,*[4] Section VIII (Part 2): "Vocabulary Development and Maintenance—Identifiers." A synopsis of important "Identifier Rules" for indexers concludes this introduction.

IDENTIFIER AUTHORITY LIST

The *ERIC Identifier Authority List* is a total list of the *preferred* Identifier forms, developed according to standards, which can be used to achieve consistency in indexing and searching alike. In printed form, it serves as a companion volume or supplement to the *Thesaurus of ERIC Descriptors.* Just as the *Thesaurus* controls Descriptor usage, the *IAL* provides control over Identifiers to the extent that variant forms of the same concept are eliminated.

The *IAL* is produced in two displays:

1. The main "Alphabetical Display," with all approved Identifiers arranged alphabetically together with a category number and a postings count for each term; some cross-references and Scope Notes are provided.
2. The supplemental "Category Display," consisting of 20 separate lists of Identifiers, arranged alphabetically within each of the broad categories. For the names of categories, see right front endsheet of this publication.

Both printed and computerized versions of the *IAL* are used. Indexers contributing to the ERIC database should consult the printed *IAL* before adding any index terms to the Identifier fields of *RIE* and *CIJE.*[5] The *IAL* in computerized form[6] is used as an automatic validation file for all incoming ERIC resumes (citations).

Origins

First published in 1980, the *IAL* was the result of an Identifier editorial project that reviewed the Identifiers in the file from the beginning of

---

1. The organizational entities that regularly contribute to building the Educational Resources Information Center (ERIC) database are listed in the "ERIC Network Components" section on pp. xi–xiv. The ERIC system components are displayed graphically on the right back endsheet of this publication.

2. ERIC's Descriptors appear in the *Thesaurus of ERIC Descriptors, 13th edition*—1995, available from The Oryx Press, 4041 North Central at Indian School Rd., Phoenix, AZ 85012-3397. Telephone: (800) 279-ORYX. Fax: (800) 279-4663. Internet: info@oryxpress.com. Prices (subject to change) are $69.50 (North America) and $83.40 (elsewhere). The 13th edition lists 10,363 vocabulary terms, of which 5,759 are main-entry Descriptors and 4,604 are nonindexable USE references and "dead" terms.

3. The left back endsheet of this publication contains a flowchart of the procedure by which Identifiers are elevated to *Thesaurus* Descriptors. Since mid-1993, *ERIC Thesaurus* vocabulary evaluations have occurred via an Internet listserv, resulting in a simplified input and a shortened disposition cycle. Users, both internal and external to the ERIC system, are encouraged to participate in vocabulary development and to recommend vocabulary additions and changes to the appropriate subject-oriented ERIC Clearinghouses or directly to the ERIC Facility Lexicographer, Jim Houston, 1301 Piccard Drive, Suite 300, Rockville, MD 20850-5305, (301) 258-5500. Fax: (301) 948-3695. Internet: jhouston@inet.ed.gov

4. The *ERIC Processing Manual* (1992 edition) is available for $75.00 from the ERIC Processing and Reference Facility, 1301 Piccard Dr., Suite 300, Rockville, MD 20851-4305. Sections relevant to indexing and vocabulary—*Section 7: Indexing* (Jun92); *Section 8/Part 1: Descriptors* (May92); *Section 8/Part 2: Identifiers* (Jun92); *Appendix C: ERIC Indexing Handbook* (Jun92)—may be purchased for $7.50 each from the ERIC Facility. The manual also appears in the ERIC Microfiche Collection (entire manual, ED 348 055; Indexing Section, ED 348 062; Descriptor Section, ED 348 063; Identifier Section, ED 348 064; Indexing Handbook Appendix, ED 348 069) and is available from the ERIC Document Reproduction Service.

5. ERIC essentially consists of two subfiles: *Resources in Education* (*RIE*); and *Current Index to Journals in Education* (*CIJE*). *RIE* covers the "document" literature and is designated by the "ED" accession number series. *CIJE* is reserved for the journal article literature, whose entries are identified by "EJ" accession numbers.

6. For the availability of computerized ERIC files, contact the ERIC Processing and Reference Facility (see p. xiv).

ERIC in 1966 through April 1976. The project ultimately reduced the number of Identifiers on the file for that period from approximately 46,000 to 25,000. The cumulation of this large number of Identifiers over ERIC's first 10 years occurred as the system evolved from a manual, print-oriented database to a system accessible via computer in a variety of different ways. As the number of entry points increased and the file expanded, it became necessary to reduce the number of ways single subjects could be accessed.

The approximately 25,000 edited Identifiers, known as "preferred terms," became the basis for the *IAL* as it now exists. The other 21,000 "nonpreferred terms" were either variant Identifier forms transferred to one of the preferred forms, variants (or duplicates) of Descriptors and eventually transferred to the appropriate Descriptors, or unnecessary or ambiguous items that could simply be purged.

Since the creation of the *IAL* in March 1980, additional Identifiers continue to be added to the *IAL* as a result of the regular monthly *RIE* and *CIJE* input to the database. Items are purged from the *IAL* as they are upgraded to Descriptor status and shifted to the *ERIC Thesaurus.*

Present Status

The 1995 *IAL* contains more than 50,000 Identifiers. This issue of the *IAL* is matched with the 1995 *Thesaurus of ERIC Descriptors, 13th Edition;* all Identifiers and their synonyms that have "graduated" to the *ERIC Thesaurus* have been deleted from the *IAL.*

Recent examples of former Identifiers that now appear in the *Thesaurus* as Descriptors are[7]

- Active Learning
- Aesthetics
- Bus Drivers
- Computer Security
- Corporations
- Decision Support Systems
- Discipline Based Art Education
- Econometrics
- Freedom
- Global Education
- Happiness
- Information Policy
- Melody
- Negligence
- Professional Development Schools
- Recess Breaks
- Reflective Teaching
- Wilderness

Identifiers in the *IAL* versus in the Database

Searchers are cautioned not to depend entirely on the *IAL* for retrieving all forms of a particular concept. Many Identifiers added to *RIE* or *CIJE* during the period of the mid-1976 to mid-1980 Identifier editorial project are *not* yet reflected in the *IAL.* These Identifiers are being gradually integrated through the normal updates as their usage recurs. (Around 10 percent of all Identifiers occurring in the current input that are not already in the *IAL* had been used for the first time in the period from mid-1976 to mid-1980.) Additionally, variant Identifier forms generated since December 1980 (when the last general reload of ERIC by the database vendors occurred) remain in the searchable ERIC files. Although ERIC provides postings transfers from variant to preferred Identifiers, such conversions are not available in commercial searchable files until general reloads are performed.

Alphabetical Display

An entry in the *Identifier Authority List* "Alphabetical Display" may either be an authorized Identifier or a cross-reference to an authorized Identifier. For sample *IAL* entries, see left front endsheet of this publication. Each authorized Identifier is followed by 2 postings counts and a category number. The numbers designated "CIJE:" and "RIE:" represent total numbers of postings in *CIJE (Current Index to Journals in Education)* and *RIE (Resources in Education),* respectively, at the time the *IAL* is produced. Postings in this particular *IAL* edition reflect the ERIC file as of the December 1994 issues of *CIJE* and *RIE.* The two-digit code following "CAT:" indicates the broad category to which the term belongs. For the names of categories, see right front endsheet of this publication.

Identifiers that show zero postings are generally newly authorized terms that were revised after publication of either *RIE* or *CIJE.*

While Identifiers do not have the complex cross-reference structure accorded ERIC Descriptors, the *Identifier Authority List* does include two elements of structure: (1) Used For (UF) cross-references; and (2) Scope Notes (SN). Either or both of these elements may be added on an "as needed" basis to any given Identifier.

1. **"Used For" (UF) Cross-References**

   Used For (UF) cross-references are used to indicate nonpreferred synonyms or variant forms of preferred Identifiers. They display reciprocally as USE references, e.g.:

   State University of New York Empire State Coll
   UF Empire State College NY

   Lung Diseases
   UF Pulmonary Diseases

   Empire State College NY
   USE State University of New York Empire State Coll

   Pulmonary Diseases
   USE Lung Diseases

2. **Scope Notes**

   The Scope Note (SN) field explains indexing or searching distinctions and clarifications, e.g.:

   Higher Education General Information Survey
   SN See add'l listings under "HEGIS..."

   Gypsies
   SN See also "Roma"

   Piraha
   SN Amazonian language of central Brazil (Mura family)

   Horaces Compromise
   SN "Horace's Compromise: The Dilemma of the American High School"

7. List taken from Lynn Barnett's "ERIC's Indexing and Retrieval: 1995 Update" in the introductory material of the 13th edition, 1995 *ERIC Thesaurus* (see footnote 2 for availability).

Infrastructure

SN Use a more specific term if possible, e.g., "Building Infrastructure," "Communications Infrastructure," "Information Infrastructure," "National Information Infrastructure," "Research Infrastructure," "Technological Infrastructure," "Telecommunications Infrastructure," "Urban Infrastructures"

Germany

SN See "West Germany" and "East Germany" for the 1945–1990 time frame

In general, Identifier Scope Notes are *not* used simply to define a term, as is done frequently in the *Thesaurus*. It is not ERIC's intention to provide definitions for the many thousands of relatively obscure Identifiers.

Identifier Format

The maximum length of Identifiers and their Used For cross-references is 50 characters (including spaces). All standard alphanumeric characters may be used, as well as left and right parentheses (to qualify homographs). Other punctuation marks are not permitted, except in Scope Notes.

The "Alphabetical Display" is sequenced in word-by-word order. Parentheses sort before alphabetic characters, e.g.:

Massachusetts
Massachusetts (Amherst)
Massachusetts Advisory Council on Education

Identifier Categories

It is helpful to group Identifiers into meaningful categories for the purpose of bringing like terms together. The table "ERIC Identifier Categories (Statistics for Dec 94)" on the right front endsheet of this publication depicts the current set of Identifier categories used by ERIC, and the number of Identifiers, as well as the percentage of total Identifiers, in each category as of the present. Categories are useful in subdividing the Identifier file for particular indexing and searching applications. Editors find categories helpful for determining quickly the available options among particular types of terms. Lexicographers use them for spotting omissions and commissions that are not as apparent in a cumulated Identifier listing such as the "Identifier Alphabetical Display."

The "Identifier Category Display" is a companion section to the main "Alphabetical Display." (A category number, e.g., CAT:04, accompanies each main entry in the "Alphabetical Display," providing a convenient cross-reference to the entry's location in the "Category Display.")

Page headers in the "Category Display" identify the particular category. Within the category, Identifiers are listed in alphabetical order using a word-by-word sort.

When using the "Category Display," it is important to keep in mind that alphabetically related terms may be separated if they do not belong to the same category. For example, "Lapland" will be found in the Geographic Locations category (07); "Lappish" will be found in the Languages/Linguistics category (13); "Lapps" will be found in the Groups (Ethnic) category (08). For this reason, indexers are encouraged to always index from the main "Alphabetical Display" and not from the "Category Display."

The individual category lists are useful in that they enable indexers and searchers to scan relatively brief lists for terms of a particular type instead of having to scan the entire 50,000 or so Identifiers listed in the "Alphabetical Display." In addition, the assignment of an Identifier to a specific category provides further information about that Identifier's proper use in ERIC. For example, "Washington (Everett)" is listed under the Geographic Locations category, thus identifying it clearly as a city rather than a person. Searchers will also find the category lists helpful in detecting a specific indexing term when the exact word form for that concept is unknown. And lastly, the "Category Display" can be a rich source of index terms other than the relatively familiar ones in the *Thesaurus*. For example, the Languages/Linguistics category includes a large number of little-known languages that have been indexed in the ERIC database but are not in the *ERIC Thesaurus*.

IDENTIFIER RULES

Here is a synopsis of the most important ERIC Identifier rules for indexers contributing to the ERIC database. They are reproduced from the *ERIC Indexing Handbook*.[8]

Most Important Rules

1. ***IAL.*** Use the *Identifier Authority List*! Try every possible way to correlate a new concept with already existing terms.
2. **UFs.** Don't use *Thesaurus* UFs as Identifiers.
3. **Majors.** Assign a maximum of 2 major Identifiers (with up to 5 major Descriptors), or only one if the maximum 6 major Descriptors are used. Major terms appear in the printed indexes of *RIE* and *CIJE*.
4. **Format.** Use *IAL* precedents rather than creating or inventing unnecessary new Identifiers.

   When creating necessary new Identifiers, follow the *IAL* format for similar terms. Use the *IAL* "Category Display" to find parallel terms.

   Remember the 50-character limit (including spaces).

   No punctuation is allowed except left and right parentheses (do not use apostrophes). Examples:

   Adams v Richardson
   Americas Competitive Challenge
   Bennett (William J)
5. **Acronyms.** Acronyms are not allowed as a rule. Some exceptions: ERIC, UNESCO, USSR.

Potential Identifiers

Don't be reluctant to use Identifiers! Always index the following when they're the subjects of documents/articles:

- Institution or association names (don't index them if they merely prepared the report, unless it is an official position paper or similar statement).
  (*Ed. note*: If an institution or association is the preparer, its name may be: (a) cataloged in the *RIE* Institution field; or (b) mentioned in the *CIJE* Annotation.)
- School district names (use in lieu of public school names, unless the latter are particularly significant)
- College or university names

8. The *ERIC Indexing Handbook: Clearinghouse Indexing Practices* (rev. ed., Jun92) is "Appendix C" of the *ERIC Processing Manual (EPM). EPM Appendix C* may be obtained for $7.50 from the ERIC Processing and Reference Facility or seen as ED 348 069 in the ERIC Microfiche Collection.

- Languages not in the *Thesaurus*
- Tribes not in the *Thesaurus*
- Persons
- Laws (enacted, not proposed)
  (*Ed. note:* see "Legislation" below.)
- Geographic regions
- Foreign country names (coordinated with the minor Descriptor Foreign Countries—watch out for ERIC's idiosyncrasies for Canada and the U.K.)
  (*Ed. note*: see "Country Names" below.)
- Test names
- Computers/computer programs
- Specific methods, theories, ideas, etc., not in the *Thesaurus*
- New terms in the field not in the *Thesaurus*

Country Names

Use DESC_Foreign Countries (minor) and IDEN_name of country (major or minor, followed by city or other geopolitical subdivision, if appropriate, in parentheses).

Refer to *IAL* for proper citation.

Example: North Korea or South Korea, not Korea

Use IDEN_United States sparingly—usually for various subdivisions, e.g., United States (South), or for overall comparisons with other countries. Otherwise, it is implied by its absence.

Don't index Canada or United Kingdom alone unless you mean the entire country. Identifiers for Canada name the province, e.g., Alberta (Edmonton). Identifiers for the United Kingdom name the individual country, e.g., England (London), Scotland (Edinburgh), Northern Ireland (Belfast). Don't index Great Britain unless you mean England, Scotland, and Wales, but not Northern Ireland.

Don't use Africa (continent) in lieu of more specific African countries.

Geographic Attribution

Organization names are generally followed by U.S. state or Canadian province postal abbreviations, or by other country names in parentheses.

Examples: American University of Beirut (Lebanon)
Harvard University MA
University of Victoria BC

Note the Canadian abbreviations:

Alberta	AB
British Columbia	BC
Labrador	LB
Manitoba	MB
New Brunswick	NB
Newfoundland	NF
Northwest Territories	NT
Nova Scotia	NS
Ontario	ON
Prince Edward Island	PE
Quebec	PQ
Saskatchewan	SK
Yukon Territory	YT

United Kingdom organizations are followed by one of the four principal divisions, if appropriate, i.e., (England), (Scotland), (Wales), (Northern Ireland).

School System or City?

If the focus of a document is on a particular public school system, use the school district name as an Identifier.

Example: New York City Board of Education

If the focus is more on the school system's general locale, use the location itself as the Identifier.

Example: New York (New York)

Such Identifiers are majored (asterisked) when crucial to the content of the document.

Note: Names of specific public grade or high schools should not be indexed unless they're particularly important; instead, index the school district's name.

Coordinate with Descriptors

To index a specific concept, both a Descriptor and an Identifier may be needed.

Example: DESC_Games and IDEN_*Card Games

Collections of Documents

Sometimes unique Identifiers are assigned to a collection of documents important to retrieve as a group.

Examples: *AAUP Contracts—for collective bargaining contracts collected for ERIC by the American Association of University Professors

National Diffusion Network Programs—for descriptions of programs sponsored by NDN

Legislation

Use *Proposed Legislation* for legislation that hasn't passed yet.

Use name and date for legislation that has passed.

Example: Missing Children Act 1982

Use public law numbers only as a last resort. The name is preferable.

Example: Public Law 87 276

Include the number of the Congressional sessions on documents like House and Senate hearings.

Example: Congress 102nd

*An asterisk indicates a major index term; no asterisk indicates a minor index term.

ERIC® NETWORK COMPONENTS

The ERIC network of organizations is comprised of the following major components:

- **ERIC Program Office**

The central funding and monitoring unit within the U.S. Department of Education, Office of Educational Research and Improvement (OERI). Responsible for overall management of the ERIC network.

Educational Resources Information Center (ERIC)
Office of Educational Research and Improvement (OERI)
U.S. Department of Education
555 New Jersey Avenue, NW
Washington, DC 20208-5720

Telephone:	202-219-2289
FAX:	202-219-1817
Internet:	eric@inet.ed.gov

- **ERIC Clearinghouses**

Sixteen contractors from the academic and not-for-profit sectors, each responsible for collecting the significant educational literature within their particular scope of interest area (e.g., career education), selecting the highest quality and most relevant material, processing (i.e., cataloging, indexing, abstracting) the selected items for input to the database, and also for synthesizing the literature and providing information analysis products (e.g., Digests) and various user services. (See list on p. 2-3.)

- **Adjunct ERIC Clearinghouses**

Various organizations that cooperate with ERIC Clearinghouses at no cost to ERIC to cover a particular specialized area of education in which they have a special interest, e.g., consumer education. (See list on p. 4.)

- **ERIC Support Components**

Four components providing various specialized technical services in support of the ERIC Program Office, ERIC Clearinghouses, and each other: e.g., centralized database management and abstract journal production, document delivery and micrographics, outreach and user services, and commercial publishing (*Current Index to Journals in Education* (CIJE) and ERIC *Thesaurus*). (See list on p.4.)

ERIC Clearinghouse on ADULT, CAREER, AND VOCATIONAL EDUCATION (CE)
Ohio State University
Center on Education and Training for Employment
1900 Kenny Road
Columbus, Ohio 43210-1090
Telephone: 614-292-4353; **800:** 800-848-4815
FAX: 614-292-1260
Internet: ericacve@magnus.acs.ohio-state.edu

All levels of adult and continuing education from basic literacy training through professional skill upgrading. The focus is upon factors contributing to the purposeful learning of adults in a variety of life situations usually related to adult roles (e.g., occupation, family, leisure time, citizenship, organizational relationships, retirement, and so forth). Includes input from Adjunct ERIC Clearinghouse on Consumer Education.

ERIC Clearinghouse on ASSESSMENT AND EVALUATION (TM)
Catholic University of America
210 O'Boyle Hall
Washington, DC 20064-4035
Telephone: 202-319-5120; **800:** 800-464-ERIC (3742)
FAX: 202-319-6692
Internet: eric_ae@cua.edu

All aspects of tests and other measurement devices. The design and methodology of research, measurement, and evaluation. The evaluation of programs and projects. The application of tests, measurement, and evaluation devices/instrumentation in education projects and programs. Includes input from Adjunct ERIC Clearinghouse for the Test Collection.

ERIC Clearinghouse for COMMUNITY COLLEGES (JC)
University of California at Los Angeles (UCLA)
3051 Moore Hall
405 Hilgard Avenue
Los Angeles, California 90024-1564
Telephone: 310-825-3931; **800:** 800-832-8256
FAX: 310-206-8095
Internet: eeh3usc@mvs.oac.ucla.edu

Development, administration, and evaluation of two-year public and private community and junior colleges, technical institutes,and two-year branch university campuses. Two-year college students, faculty, staff, curricula, programs, support services, libraries, and community services. Linkages between two-year colleges and business/industrial/community organizations. Articulation of two-year colleges with secondary and four-year postsecondary institutions.

ERIC Clearinghouse on COUNSELING AND STUDENT SERVICES (CG)
University of North Carolina at Greensboro
School of Education
101 Park Building
Greensboro, North Carolina 27412-5001
Telephone: 910-334-4114; **800:** 800-414-9769
FAX: 910-334-4116
Internet: ericcass@iris.uncg.edu

Preparation, practice, and supervision of counselors at all educational levels and in all settings. Theoretical development of counseling and guidance, including the nature of relevant human characteristics. Use and results of personnel practices and procedures. Group process (counseling, therapy, dynamics) and case work.

ERIC Clearinghouse on DISABILITIES AND GIFTED EDUCATION (EC)
Council for Exceptional Children (CEC)
1920 Association Drive
Reston, Virginia 22091-1589
Telephone: 703-264-9474; **800:** 800-328-0272
FAX: 703-264-9494
Internet: ericec@inet.ed.gov

All aspects of the education and development of persons (of all ages) who have disabilities or who are gifted, including the delivery of all types of education-related services to these groups. Includes prevention, identification and assessment, intervention, and enrichment for these groups, in both regular and special education settings.

ERIC Clearinghouse on EDUCATIONAL MANAGEMENT (EA)
University of Oregon
1787 Agate Street
Eugene, Oregon 97403-5207
Telephone: 503-346-5043; **800:** 800-438-8841
FAX: 503-346-2334
Internet: ppiele@oregon.uoregon.edu

All aspects of the governance, leadership, administration, and structure of public and private educational organizations at the elementary and secondary levels, including the provision of physical facilities for their operation.

ERIC Clearinghouse on ELEMENTARY AND EARLY CHILDHOOD EDUCATION (PS)
University of Illinois
805 West Pennsylvania Avenue
Urbana, Illinois 61801-4897
Telephone: 217-333-1386; **800:** 800-583-4135
FAX: 217-333-3767
Internet: ericeece@ux1.cso.uiuc.edu

All aspects of the physical, cognitive, social, emotional, educational, and cultural development of children, from birth through early adolescence. Among the topics covered are: prenatal and infant development and care; parent education; home and school relationships; learning theory research and practice related to children's development; preparation of early childhood teachers and caregivers; and educational programs and community service for children.

ERIC Clearinghouse on HIGHER EDUCATION (HE)
George Washington University
One Dupont Circle, N.W., Suite 630
Washington, DC 20036-1183
Telephone: 202-296-2597; **800:** 800-773-ERIC (3742)
FAX: 202-296-8379
Internet: eriche@inet.ed.gov

All aspects of the conditions, programs, and problems at colleges and universities providing higher education (i.e., four-year degrees and beyond). This includes: governance and management; planning; finance; inter-institutional arrangements; business or industry programs leading to a degree; institutional research at the college/university level; Federal programs; legal issues and legislation; professional education (e.g., medicine, law, etc.) and professional continuing education.

ERIC Clearinghouse on INFORMATION & TECHNOLOGY (IR)
Syracuse University
Center for Science and Technology, 4th Floor, Room 194
Syracuse, New York 13244-4100
Telephone: 315-443-3640
800: 800-464-9107
FAX: 315-443-5448
Internet: eric@ericir.syr.edu

AskERIC (Question-answering service via Internet): askeric@ericir.syr.edu
Telephone: 315-443-9114

Educational technology and library/information science at all academic levels and with all populations, including the preparation of professionals. The media and devices of educational communication, as they pertain to teaching and learning (in both conventional and distance education settings). The operation and management of libraries and information services. All aspects of information management and information technology related to education.

ERIC Clearinghouse on LANGUAGES AND LINGUISTICS (FL)
Center for Applied Linguistics (CAL)
1118 22nd Street, N.W.
Washington, DC 20037-0037
Telephone: 202-429-9292; **800:** 800-276-9834
FAX: 202-659-5641
Internet: eric@cal.org

Languages and language sciences. All aspects of second language instruction and learning in all commonly and uncommonly taught languages, including English as a second language. Bilingualism and bilingual education. Cultural education in the context of second language learning, including intercultural communication, study abroad, and international educational exchange. All areas of linguistics, including theoretical and applied linguistics, sociolinguistics, and psycholinguistics. Includes input from Adjunct ERIC Clearinghouse on ESL Literacy Education.

ERIC Clearinghouse on READING, ENGLISH, AND COMMUNICATION (CS)
Indiana University
Smith Research Center, Suite 150
2805 East 10th Street
Bloomington, Indiana 47408-2698
Telephone: 812-855-5847; **800:** 800-759-4723
FAX: 812-855-4220
Internet: ericcs@ucs.indiana.edu

Reading and writing, English (as a first language), and communications skills (verbal and nonverbal), kindergarten through college. Includes family or intergenerational literacy. Research and instructional development in reading, writing, speaking, and listening. Identification, diagnosis, and remediation of reading problems. Speech communication (including forensics), mass communication (including journalism), interpersonal and small group interaction, oral interpretation, rhetorical and communication theory, and theater/drama. Preparation of instructional staff and related personnel in all the above areas.

ERIC Clearinghouse on RURAL EDUCATION AND SMALL SCHOOLS (RC)
Appalachia Educational Laboratory (AEL)
1031 Quarrier Street, P.O. Box 1348
Charleston, West Virginia 25325-1348
Telephone: 304-347-0465; **800:** 800-624-9120
FAX: 304-347-0487
Internet: u56d9@wvnvm.wvnet.edu

Curriculum and instructional programs and research/evaluation efforts that address the education of students in rural schools or districts, small schools wherever located, and schools of districts wherever located that serve American Indian and Alaskan natives, Mexican Americans, and migrants, or that have programs related to outdoor education. Includes the cultural, ethnic, linguistic, economic, and social conditions that affect these educational institutions and groups. Preparation programs, including related services, that train education professionals to work in such contexts.

ERIC Clearinghouse for SCIENCE, MATHEMATICS, AND ENVIRONMENTAL EDUCATION (SE)
Ohio State University
1929 Kenny Road
Columbus, Ohio 43210-1080
Telephone: 614-292-6717; **800:** 800-276-0462
FAX: 614-292-0263
Internet: ericse@osu.edu

Science, mathematics, engineering/technology, and environmental education at all levels. The following topics when focused on any of the above broad scope areas: applications of learning theory; curriculum and instructional materials; teachers and teacher education; educational programs and projects; research and evaluative studies; applications of educational technology and media.

ERIC Clearinghouse for SOCIAL STUDIES/ SOCIAL SCIENCE EDUCATION (SO)
Indiana University
Social Studies Development Center
2805 East 10th Street, Suite 120
Bloomington, Indiana 47408-2698
Telephone: 812-855-3838; **800:** 800-266-3815
FAX: 812-855-0455
Internet: ericso@ucs.indiana.edu

All aspects of Social Studies and Social Science Education, including values education (and the social aspects of environmental education and sex education), international education, comparative education, and cross-cultural studies in all subject areas (K-12). Ethnic heritage, gender equity, aging, and social bias/discrimination topics. Also covered are music, art, and architecture as related to the fine arts. Includes input from Adjunct ERIC Clearinghouses for U.S.-Japan Studies, Art Education, and Law-Related Education.

ERIC Clearinghouse on TEACHING AND TEACHER EDUCATION (SP)
American Association of Colleges for Teacher Education (AACTE)
One Dupont Circle, N.W., Suite 610
Washington, DC 20036-1186
Telephone: 202-293-2450; **800:** 800-822-9229
FAX: 202-457-8095
Internet: ericsp@inet.ed.gov

School personnel at all levels. Teacher recruitment, selection, licensing, certification, training, preservice and inservice preparation, evaluation, retention, and retirement. The theory, philosophy, and practice of teaching. Organization, administration, finance, and legal issues relating to teacher education programs and institutions. All aspects of health, physical, recreation, and dance education. Includes input from Adjunct ERIC Clearinghouse on Clinical Schools.

ERIC Clearinghouse on URBAN EDUCATION (UD)
Teachers College, Columbia University
Institute for Urban and Minority Education
Main Hall, Room 303, Box 40
525 West 120th Street
New York, New York 10027-9998
Telephone: 212-678-3433; **800:** 800-601-4868
FAX: 212-678-4048
Internet: eric-cue@columbia.edu

The educational characteristics experiences of the diverse racial, ethnic, social class, and linguistic populations in urban (and suburban) schools. Curriculum and instruction of students from these populations and the organization of their schools. The relationship of urban schools to their communities. The social and economic conditions that affect the education of urban populations, with particular attention to factors that place urban students at risk educationally, and ways that public and private sector policies can improve these conditions.

ADJUNCT ERIC CLEARINGHOUSES

Adjunct ERIC Clearinghouse for Art Education
Indiana University
Social Studies Development Center
2805 East 10th Street, Suite 120
Bloomington, India 47408-2373
Telephone: 812-855-3838
Fax: 812-855-0455
Internet: —

Adjunct ERIC Clearinghouse on Chapter 1 (Compensatory Education)
Chapter 1 Technical Assistance Center
PRC Inc.
2601 Fortune Circle East
One Park Fletcher Building, Suite 300-A
Indianapolis, Indiana 46241-2237
Telephone: 317-244-8160; **800:** 800-456-2380
Fax: 317-244-7386
Internet: prcinc@delphi.com

Adjunct ERIC Clearinghouse on Clinical Schools
American Association of Colleges for Teacher Education (AACTE)
One Dupont Circle, NW, Suite 610
Washington, DC 20036-1186
Telephone: 202-293-2450; **800:** 800-822-9229
Fax: 202-457-8095
Internet: iabdalha@inet.ed.gov

Adjunct ERIC Clearinghouse on Consumer Education
National Institute for Consumer Education (NICE)
207 Rackham Building, West Circle Drive
Eastern Michigan University
Ypsilanti, Michigan 48197-2237
Telephone: 313-487-2292; **800:** 800-336-6423
Fax: 313-487-7153
Internet: nice@emuvax.emich.edu

Adjunct ERIC Clearinghouse for ESL Literacy Education
National Clearinghouse for Literacy Education (NCLE)
Center for Applied Linguistics (CAL)
1118 22nd Street, NW
Washington, DC 20037-0037
Telephone: 202-429-9292, Ext. 200
Fax: 202-659-5641
Internet: ncle@cal.org

Adjunct ERIC Clearinghouse for Law-Related Education
Indiana University
Social Studies Development Center
2805 East 10th Street, Suite 120
Bloomington, Indiana 47408-2373
Telephone: 812-855-3838
Fax: 812-855-0455
Internet: patrick@ucs.indiana.edu

Adjunct ERIC Clearinghouse for the Test Collection
Educational Testing Service (ETS)
ETS Test Collection
Rosedale and Carter Roads
Princeton, New Jersey 08541
Telephone: 609-734-5737
Fax: 609-683-7186
Internet: mhalpern@rosedale.org

Adjunct ERIC Clearinghouse for United States-Japan Studies
Indiana University
Social Studies Development Center
3805 East 10th Street, Suite 120
Bloomington, Indiana 47408-2698
Telephone: 812-855-3838
Fax: 812-855-0455
Internet: eabrooks@ucs.indiana.edu

ERIC SUPPORT COMPONENTS

CENTRALIZED DATABASE MANAGEMENT (And Abstract Journal Production)

ERIC Processing and Reference Facility
Computer Sciences Corporation
Systems Engineering Division
1301 Piccard Drive, Suite 300
Rockville, Maryland 20850-4305
Telephone: 301-258-5500
800: 800-799-ERIC (3742)
FAX: 301-948-3695
Internet: ericfac@inet.ed.gov

OUTREACH AND USER SERVICES

ACCESS ERIC
Aspen Systems Corporation
1600 Research Boulevard
Rockville, Maryland 20850-3172
Telephone: 301-251-5506
800: 800-LET-ERIC (538-3742)
FAX: 301-251-5767
Internet: acceric@inet.ed.gov

DOCUMENT DELIVERY AND MICROGRAPHICS

ERIC Document Reproduction Service (EDRS)
7420 Fullerton Road, Suite 110
Springfield, Virginia 22153-2852
Telephone: 703-440-1400
800: 800-443-ERIC (3742)
FAX: 703-440-1408
Internet: edrs@gwuvm.gwu.edu

CIJE AND THESAURUS PUBLISHING

Oryx Press
4041 North Central Avenue at Indian School
Suite 700
Phoenix, Arizona 85012-3397
Telephone: 602-265-2651
800: 800-279-ORYX (6799)
FAX: 800-279-4663; 602-265-6250
Internet: info@oryxpress.com

Identifier Alphabetical Display

0 1 Linear Programming Model
CIJE: 0 RIE: 1 CAT: 15

1 RM Chin Test
CIJE: 1 RIE: 0 CAT: 21

2 4 Dinitrophenol
CIJE: 1 RIE: 0 CAT: 20

2 Plus 2 Articulation Plan
CIJE: 0 RIE: 7 CAT: 15

2 Plus 2 Plus 2 Plus 1 Programs
CIJE: 0 RIE: 1 CAT: 19

2 Plus 2 Plus 2 Programs
CIJE: 0 RIE: 4 CAT: 19

2 Plus 2 Plus 2 Tech Prep Programs
CIJE: 0 RIE: 1 CAT: 19

2 Plus 2 Tech Prep Associate Degrees
CIJE: 0 RIE: 15 CAT: 19

2 Plus 2 Tech Prep Programs
CIJE: 1 RIE: 4 CAT: 19

3 2 1 Contact
CIJE: 6 RIE: 2 CAT: 22

3 2 1 Contact Extras
CIJE: 0 RIE: 1 CAT: 22

3 Phase Version Code Transformation Task
CIJE: 1 RIE: 0 CAT: 15

3M Factory Training Center
CIJE: 1 RIE: 0 CAT: 17

3M Optical Videodisc Project
CIJE: 1 RIE: 0 CAT: 19

3P COTRAN
CIJE: 1 RIE: 0 CAT: 15

3RIP Search System
CIJE: 0 RIE: 5 CAT: 04

3RIP Text Data Base System
CIJE: 0 RIE: 1 CAT: 04

3Rs
CIJE: 0 RIE: 4 CAT: 03
UF Three Rs

3Rs Abilities and Achievement Tests
CIJE: 0 RIE: 1 CAT: 21

3Rs Achievement Test
CIJE: 1 RIE: 0 CAT: 21

3Rs Program
CIJE: 0 RIE: 1 CAT: 19

4 1 4 Calendar
CIJE: 7 RIE: 8 CAT: 15

4 H Clubs
CIJE: 52 RIE: 149 CAT: 17

4 H Debate Project
CIJE: 0 RIE: 1 CAT: 19

4 H National Center
CIJE: 1 RIE: 2 CAT: 17

4 H Programs
CIJE: 20 RIE: 70 CAT: 19

4 Plus 2 Plus 2 Tech Prep Programs
CIJE: 0 RIE: 1 CAT: 19

4MAT System
CIJE: 13 RIE: 6 CAT: 15

6 S Paradigm
CIJE: 0 RIE: 2 CAT: 15

6PQ Method for Discovery Learning
CIJE: 0 RIE: 1 CAT: 15

9p Trisomy
CIJE: 2 RIE: 0 CAT: 11

10 Cents To Save a Life
CIJE: 0 RIE: 1 CAT: 19

12 Step Programs
CIJE: 0 RIE: 2 CAT: 19
UF Twelve Step Programs

20 20 Analysis
CIJE: 0 RIE: 1 CAT: 15

21st Century Schools Pilot Project IN
CIJE: 0 RIE: 1 CAT: 19

45 15 Plan
CIJE: 4 RIE: 12 CAT: 15

60 Minutes (Title)
CIJE: 1 RIE: 4 CAT: 22

80 Percent Rule
CIJE: 0 RIE: 1 CAT: 21

100 Good Schools
CIJE: 0 RIE: 1 CAT: 22
UF One Hundred Good Schools

120 Years of American Educ Statistical Portrait
CIJE: 0 RIE: 1 CAT: 22

310 Project
CIJE: 0 RIE: 222 CAT: 19

353 Project
CIJE: 0 RIE: 172 CAT: 19

401(k) Plans
CIJE: 0 RIE: 1 CAT: 16

1202 Commissions
CIJE: 1 RIE: 20 CAT: 17

1880s
CIJE: 0 RIE: 2 CAT: 12

1930s
CIJE: 6 RIE: 4 CAT: 12

1960s
CIJE: 10 RIE: 5 CAT: 12

1970s
CIJE: 8 RIE: 1 CAT: 12

1980s
CIJE: 1 RIE: 7 CAT: 12

1984 (Title)
CIJE: 4 RIE: 9 CAT: 22

1985 Resolution (American Nurses Association)
CIJE: 2 RIE: 1 CAT: 16

1990s
CIJE: 3 RIE: 6 CAT: 12

2001 A Space Odyssey
CIJE: 1 RIE: 0 CAT: 22

70001 Ltd
CIJE: 2 RIE: 2 CAT: 17

A B Therapist Scales
CIJE: 5 RIE: 0 CAT: 21

A Better Chance Inc
CIJE: 7 RIE: 8 CAT: 17

A M Consolidated Schools TX
CIJE: 0 RIE: 1 CAT: 17

A M L Behavior Rating Scale
CIJE: 0 RIE: 2 CAT: 21

A Picture Choice
CIJE: 0 RIE: 1 CAT: 21

A Posteriori Index
CIJE: 0 RIE: 3 CAT: 21

A Priori Tests
CIJE: 5 RIE: 11 CAT: 21

A T and T
USE American Telephone and Telegraph Company

A T and T Alliance for Tomorrows Teachers
CIJE: 0 RIE: 1 CAT: 19

A T and T Communications Inc
CIJE: 0 RIE: 1 CAT: 17

A T and T Learning Network
CIJE: 3 RIE: 1 CAT: 20

A T and T Long Distance Learning Network
USE Long Distance Learning Network

AAAS Project 2061
USE Project 2061 (AAAS)

AAAS Study Guides on Contemporary Problems
CIJE: 0 RIE: 10 CAT: 22

AACC Commission to Improve Minority Education
USE Commission to Improve Minority Education (AACC)

AACTE Media Project
USE Teacher Education and Media Project

AACTE RATE Project
USE Research About Teacher Education Project

AAHE Assessment Forum
CIJE: 0 RIE: 53 CAT: 02

AAHPER Cooperative Health Education Tests
CIJE: 0 RIE: 1 CAT: 21

AAHPER Cooperative Physical Education Tests
CIJE: 0 RIE: 1 CAT: 21

AAHPER Physical Fitness Tests
CIJE: 2 RIE: 0 CAT: 21

AAHPER Youth Fitness Test
CIJE: 2 RIE: 5 CAT: 21

AAHPERD
CIJE: 15 RIE: 12 CAT: 17
UF American Alliance for Health Phys Ed Rec and Dance

AAHPERD Physical Fitness Tests
CIJE: 6 RIE: 1 CAT: 21

AAMD Adaptive Behavior Scales
USE Adaptive Behavior Scales (AAMD)

AAMP Index
CIJE: 1 RIE: 0 CAT: 21

AARON (Artificial Intelligence Symbol System)
CIJE: 0 RIE: 1 CAT: 04

AAS Degrees
USE Associate in Applied Science Degrees

AASCU ERIC Model Programs Inventory Project
CIJE: 0 RIE: 204 CAT: 19

AAUP Contracts
CIJE: 0 RIE: 105 CAT: 14

ABAA Inventory
USE Alcohol Behavior Attitude and Awareness Inventory

Abacuses
CIJE: 16 RIE: 2 CAT: 04

Abandoned Children
CIJE: 1 RIE: 1 CAT: 10

Abbey Wood Schools
CIJE: 1 RIE: 0 CAT: 17

Abbott House
CIJE: 0 RIE: 1 CAT: 17

ABC (Act for Better Child Care) Bill 1988
USE Act for Better Child Care Services

ABC (Approach by Concept) Method
CIJE: 0 RIE: 3 CAT: 15

ABC Inventory (Adair and Blesch)
CIJE: 2 RIE: 0 CAT: 21

ABC Tests
CIJE: 1 RIE: 0 CAT: 21

ABC X Model (Hill)
CIJE: 0 RIE: 1 CAT: 15

ABCD Project MI
USE Accepting Behaviors for Cultural Diversity Project

Abdomen
CIJE: 3 RIE: 0 CAT: 11

ABDs of Reading
CIJE: 0 RIE: 1 CAT: 19

Abduction (Cognition)
USE Abductive Reasoning

Abductions
CIJE: 6 RIE: 8 CAT: 16
SN See also "Kidnapping"
UF Child Abductions

Abductive Reasoning
CIJE: 1 RIE: 2 CAT: 15
UF Abduction (Cognition)

ABE 321
USE Adult Education Act Section 321

ABE Assessment Instrument
CIJE: 0 RIE: 1 CAT: 21

Abe Lincoln in Illinois
CIJE: 0 RIE: 2 CAT: 22

ABE Reading Sequential Competency System
CIJE: 0 RIE: 1 CAT: 19

Abelard (Peter)
CIJE: 1 RIE: 0 CAT: 18

Abelson (Robert)
CIJE: 0 RIE: 1 CAT: 18

Abernathy Independent School District TX
CIJE: 0 RIE: 1 CAT: 17

Aberrance
CIJE: 0 RIE: 4 CAT: 21
UF Aberrant Response Patterns; Response Pattern Aberrance

Aberrant Behavior Checklist
CIJE: 7 RIE: 0 CAT: 21

Aberrant Response Patterns
USE Aberrance

ABI INFORM
CIJE: 3 RIE: 8 CAT: 17

Abilene Christian University TX
CIJE: 1 RIE: 0 CAT: 17

Ability Achievement Discrepancy
CIJE: 16 RIE: 3 CAT: 15

Ability Attributes
CIJE: 1 RIE: 1 CAT: 11

Ability Based on Older Dependable Experience
USE ABODE Program

Ability by Treatment Interaction
CIJE: 0 RIE: 1 CAT: 15

Ability Estimates
CIJE: 25 RIE: 42 CAT: 21

Ability Parameters
CIJE: 10 RIE: 10 CAT: 21

Ability to Benefit Policy
CIJE: 0 RIE: 1 CAT: 16

Abington Heights School District PA
CIJE: 1 RIE: 1 CAT: 17

Abington v Schempp
CIJE: 2 RIE: 3 CAT: 14

Abipon
CIJE: 0 RIE: 1 CAT: 13

ABLE Model Program
CIJE: 1 RIE: 8 CAT: 19

ABLEDATA Database
CIJE: 1 RIE: 1 CAT: 04

Abnormality (Test Scores)
USE Test Score Abnormality

ABODE Program
CIJE: 0 RIE: 1 CAT: 19
UF Ability Based on Older Dependable Experience

Abolitionism
CIJE: 11 RIE: 8 CAT: 15

Abood v Detroit Board of Education
CIJE: 2 RIE: 0 CAT: 14

Aboriginal Schools (Australia)
CIJE: 1 RIE: 5 CAT: 05

About My Teacher Inventory
CIJE: 1 RIE: 1 CAT: 21

About You and Your Friends
CIJE: 0 RIE: 1 CAT: 21

Abraham Baldwin Agricultural College GA
CIJE: 0 RIE: 1 CAT: 17

Abraham Jacobs Memorial Symposium
CIJE: 0 RIE: 1 CAT: 02

Abrasives
CIJE: 0 RIE: 1 CAT: 04

Abridged Scientific Literacy Instrument
CIJE: 0 RIE: 1 CAT: 21

Abridgments (Text)
CIJE: 3 RIE: 1 CAT: 16

Absalom Absalom
CIJE: 0 RIE: 1 CAT: 22

Abscam
CIJE: 1 RIE: 0 CAT: 12

Absent without Leave
CIJE: 0 RIE: 1 CAT: 16

Absolute Judgment
CIJE: 1 RIE: 0 CAT: 15

Absolute Normal Scores Test
CIJE: 0 RIE: 1 CAT: 21

Absolute Values
CIJE: 13 RIE: 0 CAT: 15

Absolutism
CIJE: 4 RIE: 2 CAT: 15

Absorption (Psychology)
CIJE: 1 RIE: 2 CAT: 11

Absorption Scale (Tellegen and Atkinson)
CIJE: 0 RIE: 1 CAT: 21

Abstat (Computer Program)
CIJE: 0 RIE: 1 CAT: 04

Abstinence
CIJE: 15 RIE: 11 CAT: 11

Abstract Algebra
CIJE: 8 RIE: 1 CAT: 20

Abstract Art
CIJE: 17 RIE: 2 CAT: 16

Abstract Reasoning Test (Myers)
CIJE: 0 RIE: 1 CAT: 21

Abstracting and Indexing Services
CIJE: 2 RIE: 0 CAT: 16
UF Indexing and Abstracting Services

Abstracts of Instructional and Research Materials
CIJE: 0 RIE: 3 CAT: 22

Absurdities
CIJE: 2 RIE: 0 CAT: 13

Abt Associates
CIJE: 2 RIE: 1 CAT: 17

Abt Study of State and Local Compliance
CIJE: 1 RIE: 0 CAT: 22

Abuse (of Disabled)
CIJE: 0 RIE: 0 CAT: 11
UF Handicap Abuse

Abwa
CIJE: 0 RIE: 1 CAT: 13

ABWA Syllabus for Letter Writing Courses
CIJE: 0 RIE: 1 CAT: 03

AC Test of Creative Ability
CIJE: 0 RIE: 1 CAT: 21

ACA Comprehensive Work Entry Program
CIJE: 0 RIE: 1 CAT: 19

Academic Ability Test
CIJE: 0 RIE: 2 CAT: 21

Academic Abstention
CIJE: 0 RIE: 1 CAT: 15

Academic Administration Internship Program
CIJE: 0 RIE: 3 CAT: 19

Academic Affairs Committees
CIJE: 1 RIE: 2 CAT: 10

Academic Alert System
CIJE: 0 RIE: 2 CAT: 15

Academic and Support Group Model
CIJE: 0 RIE: 1 CAT: 19

Academic Assessment and Placement Program TN
CIJE: 1 RIE: 0 CAT: 19

Academic Building Systems
CIJE: 0 RIE: 5 CAT: 15

Academic Challenge for Excellence
CIJE: 0 RIE: 2 CAT: 19

Academic Choice
CIJE: 2 RIE: 0 CAT: 16

Academic Community
CIJE: 21 RIE: 40 CAT: 10

Academic Competitions
CIJE: 4 RIE: 3 CAT: 16

Academic Computing
CIJE: 49 RIE: 10 CAT: 04

Academic Cooperatives
CIJE: 2 RIE: 0 CAT: 05

Academic Cross Credit
USE Cross Credit Courses

Academic Decathlon
CIJE: 1 RIE: 4 CAT: 19

Academic Development Plans
CIJE: 0 RIE: 1 CAT: 15
SN Individualized education programs for helping vocational students develop and reinforce basic academic skills

Academic Discourse
CIJE: 94 RIE: 81 CAT: 16

Academic Discourse Communities
CIJE: 19 RIE: 38 CAT: 10

Academic Discourse Theory
CIJE: 1 RIE: 2 CAT: 15

Academic Efficiency
CIJE: 0 RIE: 1 CAT: 15

Academic Enrichment for the Gifted in Summer
CIJE: 1 RIE: 0 CAT: 19

Academic Environment Inventory
CIJE: 0 RIE: 1 CAT: 21

Academic Equity for Rural Schools Program
CIJE: 1 RIE: 0 CAT: 19

Academic Excellence Program
CIJE: 0 RIE: 3 CAT: 19

Academic Facilities Loan Program
CIJE: 0 RIE: 2 CAT: 19

Academic Forgiveness
CIJE: 0 RIE: 1 CAT: 15

Academic Futility
CIJE: 0 RIE: 1 CAT: 16

Academic Growth Measurement
CIJE: 0 RIE: 2 CAT: 21

Academic Health Centers
CIJE: 8 RIE: 2 CAT: 05

Academic Instructional Measurement System
CIJE: 0 RIE: 1 CAT: 21

Academic Interest Measures
CIJE: 0 RIE: 7 CAT: 21

Academic Internship Program CA
CIJE: 0 RIE: 2 CAT: 19

Academic Language
CIJE: 3 RIE: 8 CAT: 13

Academic Learning Progress Assessment System
CIJE: 0 RIE: 0 CAT: 21

Academic Learning Time in Physical Education
CIJE: 0 RIE: 2 CAT: 21

Academic Linkage
CIJE: 0 RIE: 1 CAT: 16

Academic Load
CIJE: 0 RIE: 3 CAT: 16

Academic Misconduct
CIJE: 3 RIE: 6 CAT: 11
SN See also "Research Misconduct" and "Employee Misconduct"

Academic Misconduct Survey
CIJE: 0 RIE: 2 CAT: 21

Academic Olympiad
CIJE: 1 RIE: 1 CAT: 19

Academic Orientation
CIJE: 3 RIE: 8 CAT: 11

Academic Planning Officers
CIJE: 0 RIE: 1 CAT: 09

Academic Preparation for College
CIJE: 5 RIE: 1 CAT: 22

Academic Pressure
CIJE: 3 RIE: 8 CAT: 11

Academic Pressure Scale for Adolescents
CIJE: 1 RIE: 1 CAT: 21

Academic Professions
CIJE: 8 RIE: 7 CAT: 09

Academic Profile (ETS)
USE ETS Academic Profile

Academic Program Evaluation Paradigm
CIJE: 0 RIE: 1 CAT: 21

Academic Program Evaluation Project
CIJE: 0 RIE: 1 CAT: 19

Academic Program Evaluation Questionnaire
CIJE: 0 RIE: 1 CAT: 21

Academic Progress Report
CIJE: 0 RIE: 1 CAT: 04

Academic Progress Standards
CIJE: 0 RIE: 1 CAT: 16

Academic Promise Tests
CIJE: 1 RIE: 0 CAT: 21

Academic Qualifications Index
CIJE: 0 RIE: 1 CAT: 21

Academic Redshirting
CIJE: 2 RIE: 0 CAT: 16

Academic Remedial Training Program (Navy)
CIJE: 0 RIE: 1 CAT: 19

Academic Research Facilities Modernization Act
CIJE: 0 RIE: 1 CAT: 14
UF Public Law 100 570

Academic Self Concept
CIJE: 33 RIE: 21 CAT: 11

Academic Self Concept Scale
CIJE: 3 RIE: 3 CAT: 21

Academic Senate for California Community Colleges
CIJE: 0 RIE: 4 CAT: 17

Academic Skills
CIJE: 10 RIE: 4 CAT: 16

Academic Stress
CIJE: 3 RIE: 7 CAT: 11

Academic Structure
CIJE: 5 RIE: 1 CAT: 16

Academic Support Services
CIJE: 5 RIE: 2 CAT: 16

Academic Talent Search Program
CIJE: 0 RIE: 5 CAT: 19

Academic Tradition
CIJE: 4 RIE: 3 CAT: 16

Academic Vocational Involvement Scale
CIJE: 1 RIE: 0 CAT: 21

Academic Year Institutes
CIJE: 2 RIE: 6 CAT: 02

Academically Oriented Preschool Program
CIJE: 14 RIE: 1 CAT: 19

Academicians
CIJE: 7 RIE: 4 CAT: 10

Academics Plus Program
CIJE: 1 RIE: 1 CAT: 19

Academy Awards
CIJE: 1 RIE: 1 CAT: 16

Academy for Career Education PA
CIJE: 0 RIE: 7 CAT: 17

Academy for Educational Development
CIJE: 3 RIE: 3 CAT: 17

Academy for Effective Schools IL
CIJE: 0 RIE: 1 CAT: 17

Academy of Instruction
CIJE: 1 RIE: 0 CAT: 17

Academy of International Business
CIJE: 0 RIE: 1 CAT: 17

Academy of Pedagogical Sciences (USSR)
CIJE: 2 RIE: 3 CAT: 17

Academy of Sciences (USSR)
USE Soviet Academy of Sciences

Academy of the Hebrew Language
CIJE: 1 RIE: 0 CAT: 17

Academy Theatre GA
CIJE: 0 RIE: 1 CAT: 17

Acadia
CIJE: 1 RIE: 1 CAT: 07

Acadia University NS
CIJE: 0 RIE: 1 CAT: 17

Acadiana Consortium
CIJE: 0 RIE: 1 CAT: 17

Acadians
CIJE: 4 RIE: 19 CAT: 08

Acalanes Union High School District CA
CIJE: 0 RIE: 1 CAT: 17

Accelerated Academic Program for Low Achievers
CIJE: 1 RIE: 1 CAT: 19

Accelerated Christian Education
CIJE: 5 RIE: 3 CAT: 03

Accelerated Curriculum Classes Emphasizing Learn
USE Project ACCEL NJ

Accelerated Learning of Spanish by Satellite UT
CIJE: 0 RIE: 1 CAT: 19

Accelerated Mental Process
CIJE: 1 RIE: 0 CAT: 15

Accelerated Progressive Choice Reading Program
CIJE: 0 RIE: 2 CAT: 19

Accelerated Schools
CIJE: 4 RIE: 20 CAT: 15
SN Strategy developed by Dr. Henry M. Levin of Stanford University to accelerate the learning of at-risk students so that they are able to perform at grade level by the end of elementary school
UF Accelerated Schools Movement

Accelerated Schools Movement
USE Accelerated Schools

Accelerometers
CIJE: 1 RIE: 2 CAT: 04

Accent Extension Programme
CIJE: 1 RIE: 0 CAT: 19

Acceptability Judgments
CIJE: 3 RIE: 4 CAT: 15

Acceptance
CIJE: 25 RIE: 10 CAT: 11

Acceptance of Women Scale (Drews)
CIJE: 0 RIE: 1 CAT: 21

Accepting Behaviors for Cultural Diversity Project
CIJE: 0 RIE: 1 CAT: 19
UF ABCD Project MI

Access Control
CIJE: 3 RIE: 2 CAT: 20

ACCESS Data Center
CIJE: 1 RIE: 2 CAT: 17

ACCESS ERIC
CIJE: 0 RIE: 1 CAT: 17

ACCESS PENNSYLVANIA
CIJE: 3 RIE: 1 CAT: 19

Access to Computers
CIJE: 28 RIE: 12 CAT: 16
UF Computer Access

Access to Facilities
CIJE: 10 RIE: 6 CAT: 16

Access to Health Care
CIJE: 41 RIE: 41 CAT: 11

Access to Persons
CIJE: 0 RIE: 1 CAT: 16

Access to Services
CIJE: 1 RIE: 2 CAT: 16

Accident Compensation Act 1972 (New Zealand)
CIJE: 0 RIE: 1 CAT: 14
UF New Zealand Accident Compensation Act 1972

Accident Compensation Scheme (New Zealand)
USE New Zealand Accident Compensation Scheme

Accident Investigation
CIJE: 1 RIE: 3 CAT: 16

Accident Investigation Technicians
CIJE: 1 RIE: 2 CAT: 09

Accion Cultural Popular
CIJE: 0 RIE: 4 CAT: 16

Accommodation Theory
CIJE: 15 RIE: 8 CAT: 15
SN See also "Speech Accommodation"

Accompanists
CIJE: 2 RIE: 0 CAT: 09

Account Approach
CIJE: 1 RIE: 0 CAT: 15

Account Executives
CIJE: 1 RIE: 1 CAT: 09

Accountability Based Learning Environment
CIJE: 1 RIE: 0 CAT: 15

Accountability Index (California)
USE California Accountability Index

Accountability Models
CIJE: 2 RIE: 2 CAT: 15

Accountability Through Evaluation Institute
CIJE: 0 RIE: 1 CAT: 17

Accounting Systems
CIJE: 3 RIE: 6 CAT: 15

Accounts Receivable
CIJE: 0 RIE: 1 CAT: 16

Accounts Receivable Clerks
CIJE: 1 RIE: 2 CAT: 09

Accreditation Board for Engineering and Technology
CIJE: 6 RIE: 0 CAT: 17

Accreditation Council for Graduate Medical Educ
CIJE: 1 RIE: 0 CAT: 17

Accreditation Plus Model
CIJE: 1 RIE: 2 CAT: 15

Accreditation Standards
CIJE: 15 RIE: 12 CAT: 16

Accrediting Council Educ Journalism Mass Commun
CIJE: 3 RIE: 4 CAT: 17

Acculturation Rating Scale for Mexican Americans
CIJE: 3 RIE: 2 CAT: 21

Acculturation Scale (Hopkins)
CIJE: 0 RIE: 1 CAT: 21

Accuracy
CIJE: 135 RIE: 55 CAT: 16

Accuracy in Academia
CIJE: 6 RIE: 4 CAT: 17

Accuracy in Media
CIJE: 0 RIE: 2 CAT: 17

Accuracy Measures
CIJE: 7 RIE: 5 CAT: 21

Accuracy of Implementation Rating Scale
CIJE: 0 RIE: 2 CAT: 21

Accurate Empathy Scale (Truax)
CIJE: 4 RIE: 1 CAT: 21

ACE
USE American Council on Education

ACE Data Bank
CIJE: 0 RIE: 1 CAT: 04

ACE Institutional Research File
CIJE: 0 RIE: 1 CAT: 04

ACE UCLA Freshman Survey
CIJE: 1 RIE: 3 CAT: 19

Achebe (Chinua)
CIJE: 13 RIE: 1 CAT: 18

Achievement Anxiety Test
CIJE: 5 RIE: 3 CAT: 21

Achievement Based Curriculum
CIJE: 0 RIE: 1 CAT: 03
SN See also "I Can Achievement Based Curriculum"

Achievement Competence Training
CIJE: 1 RIE: 3 CAT: 19

Achievement Directed Leadership Program
CIJE: 0 RIE: 3 CAT: 19

Achievement Goals Program
CIJE: 0 RIE: 3 CAT: 19

Achievement Motivation Development Project
CIJE: 0 RIE: 3 CAT: 19

Achievement Motivation Inventory (Mehta)
CIJE: 0 RIE: 1 CAT: 21

Achievement Motivation Training
CIJE: 2 RIE: 1 CAT: 15

Achievement Motives Scale
CIJE: 2 RIE: 0 CAT: 21

Achievement Orientation Scale (Ray)
CIJE: 0 RIE: 1 CAT: 21

Achievement Place
CIJE: 0 RIE: 2 CAT: 17

Achievement Risk Preference Scale
CIJE: 0 RIE: 1 CAT: 21

Achievement Standards
CIJE: 3 RIE: 3 CAT: 15

Achievement Test Anxiety Scale
CIJE: 1 RIE: 0 CAT: 21

Achievement Testing Program AB
USE Alberta Achievement Testing Program

Achiever Personality Scale
CIJE: 1 RIE: 0 CAT: 21

Achieving Dialog
CIJE: 0 RIE: 1 CAT: 03

Achieving Excellence Program (McREL)
CIJE: 0 RIE: 1 CAT: 19

Achondrogenesis
CIJE: 1 RIE: 0 CAT: 11

Acid Base Equilibrium
CIJE: 5 RIE: 1 CAT: 20

Acid Free Paper
CIJE: 2 RIE: 10 CAT: 04

Acidosis
CIJE: 1 RIE: 1 CAT: 11

Acids
CIJE: 25 RIE: 2 CAT: 20

Acoma (Pueblo)
CIJE: 2 RIE: 2 CAT: 08

Acoma Reservation NM
CIJE: 0 RIE: 1 CAT: 17

ACORN
USE Association Community Organizations Reform Now

Acorns
CIJE: 0 RIE: 1 CAT: 20

ACOT
USE Apple Classrooms of Tomorrow

Acoupedics
CIJE: 2 RIE: 0 CAT: 11

Acoustic Detectors
CIJE: 0 RIE: 4 CAT: 04

Acoustic Impedance
CIJE: 2 RIE: 0 CAT: 20

Acoustic Neuroma
CIJE: 1 RIE: 0 CAT: 11

Acquaintance Rape
CIJE: 14 RIE: 8 CAT: 16

Acquainting Process
CIJE: 1 RIE: 2 CAT: 11

Acquiescence
CIJE: 7 RIE: 3 CAT: 16

Acquisition Behavior
CIJE: 5 RIE: 2 CAT: 15

Acquisition Cards
CIJE: 1 RIE: 0 CAT: 04

ACRL Bibliographic Instruction Section
CIJE: 0 RIE: 3 CAT: 17

ACRL Standards for College Libraries (1975)
CIJE: 0 RIE: 1 CAT: 22

Acrocephalosyndactylia
USE Apert Syndrome

Acroclinical Semester
CIJE: 1 RIE: 5 CAT: 16

Acrylic Materials
CIJE: 4 RIE: 0 CAT: 04

ACS Cooperative Examination in Biochemistry
CIJE: 1 RIE: 0 CAT: 21

ACS Cooperative Examination in General Chemistry
CIJE: 1 RIE: 0 CAT: 21

ACS Cooperative Examination in Inorganic Chemistry
CIJE: 0 RIE: 0 CAT: 21

ACS Cooperative Examination in Physical Chemistry
CIJE: 1 RIE: 0 CAT: 21

ACS NSTA Cooperative Examination in HS Chemistry
CIJE: 3 RIE: 0 CAT: 21

Act 84 (Pennsylvania 1986)
CIJE: 0 RIE: 1 CAT: 14

ACT 101 Programs
CIJE: 0 RIE: 2 CAT: 19

ACT Administrators for Change Training Instrument
CIJE: 0 RIE: 1 CAT: 21

ACT Adult Learner Needs Assessment
CIJE: 1 RIE: 2 CAT: 21

ACT Alumni Survey
USE American College Testing Program Alumni Survey

ACT Assessment
CIJE: 77 RIE: 223 CAT: 21
SN Use "American College Testing Program" for the organization/publisher

ACT ASSET Program
USE Assessment of Student Skills for Entry Transfer

ACT Enhanced
USE Enhanced ACT

ACT Entering Student Survey
CIJE: 0 RIE: 1 CAT: 21

ACT Evaluation Survey Service
CIJE: 0 RIE: 1 CAT: 21

Act for Better Child Care Services
CIJE: 1 RIE: 1 CAT: 14
SN See also "Alliance for Better Child Care"
UF ABC (Act for Better Child Care) Bill 1988

ACT High School Student Opinion Survey
USE High School Student Opinion Survey

ACT Interest Inventory
CIJE: 3 RIE: 9 CAT: 21

ACT Mathematics Placement Examination
CIJE: 4 RIE: 3 CAT: 21

Act of Liberty
CIJE: 0 RIE: 1 CAT: 14

ACT Proficiency Examination Program
CIJE: 3 RIE: 3 CAT: 21
UF Proficiency Examination Program (ACT)

ACT Survey of Academic Advising
CIJE: 0 RIE: 1 CAT: 21

ACT Theory
CIJE: 3 RIE: 3 CAT: 15
UF Adaptive Control of Thought system

ACT Withdrawing Nonreturning Student Surv
CIJE: 0 RIE: 1 CAT: 21

ACT Work Keys
USE Work Keys (ACT)

ACT World of Work Map
CIJE: 1 RIE: 0 CAT: 21

ACTFL
USE American Council on the Teaching of Foreign Langs

ACTFL Descriptive Scale for Reading
CIJE: 0 RIE: 1 CAT: 21

ACTFL ETS Language Proficiency Guidelines
USE ACTFL Proficiency Guidelines

ACTFL ETS Oral Proficiency Interview
USE ACTFL Oral Proficiency Interview

ACTFL ILR Oral Proficiency Guidelines
USE ACTFL Proficiency Guidelines

ACTFL Oral Proficiency Interview
CIJE: 7 RIE: 6 CAT: 21
UF ACTFL ETS Oral Proficiency Interview

ACTFL Proficiency Guidelines
CIJE: 12 RIE: 24 CAT: 22
UF ACTFL ETS Language Proficiency Guidelines; ACTFL ILR Oral Proficiency Guidelines

ACTFL Provisional Proficiency Guidelines
CIJE: 1 RIE: 1 CAT: 22

ACTION (Agency)
CIJE: 2 RIE: 14 CAT: 17

Action Agenda Project
CIJE: 2 RIE: 4 CAT: 19

Action Category System
CIJE: 0 RIE: 1 CAT: 15

Action Committee for Higher Education
CIJE: 1 RIE: 0 CAT: 17

Action Development
CIJE: 0 RIE: 1 CAT: 11

Action Femmes Project
CIJE: 0 RIE: 1 CAT: 19

Action for Boston Community Development Project
CIJE: 0 RIE: 5 CAT: 19

Action for Childrens Television
CIJE: 7 RIE: 9 CAT: 17

Action for Excellence
CIJE: 8 RIE: 5 CAT: 22

Action for Youth
CIJE: 0 RIE: 2 CAT: 19

Action Group Counseling
CIJE: 0 RIE: 1 CAT: 19

Action Library PA
CIJE: 0 RIE: 2 CAT: 17

Action Oriented Therapy
CIJE: 0 RIE: 2 CAT: 15

Action Plans
CIJE: 14 RIE: 16 CAT: 16

Action Reflection Relationship
CIJE: 0 RIE: 4 CAT: 15

Action Seminar
CIJE: 1 RIE: 0 CAT: 02

Action Studies Team Canada
CIJE: 1 RIE: 0 CAT: 17

Action Theory
CIJE: 21 RIE: 3 CAT: 15

Action Training Model
CIJE: 0 RIE: 2 CAT: 15

Actionmap
CIJE: 1 RIE: 0 CAT: 04

Activated Biofilters
CIJE: 0 RIE: 2 CAT: 20

Activation Energy
CIJE: 3 RIE: 0 CAT: 20

Active Alert Children
CIJE: 0 RIE: 1 CAT: 10

Active Audience
CIJE: 0 RIE: 1 CAT: 15

Active Listening
CIJE: 6 RIE: 1 CAT: 15

Active Mathematics Teaching
CIJE: 0 RIE: 2 CAT: 22

Active Readers
CIJE: 2 RIE: 1 CAT: 10
UF Active Reading

Active Reading
USE Active Readers

Active Staffing Process
CIJE: 0 RIE: 1 CAT: 15

Active Teaching
CIJE: 8 RIE: 3 CAT: 15

Active Teaching Behaviors
CIJE: 0 RIE: 3 CAT: 15

Activities Inventory
CIJE: 1 RIE: 2 CAT: 21

Activities Preference Questionnaire
CIJE: 5 RIE: 1 CAT: 21

Activities that Integrate Mathematics and Science
USE Project AIMS

Activity Analysis
CIJE: 3 RIE: 1 CAT: 15

Activity Based Curriculum
CIJE: 10 RIE: 4 CAT: 03

Activity Cards
CIJE: 1 RIE: 0 CAT: 04

Activity Classification
CIJE: 1 RIE: 0 CAT: 15

Activity Code and Text System
CIJE: 0 RIE: 1 CAT: 15

Activity Coordinators (Long Term Care)
CIJE: 0 RIE: 1 CAT: 09
UF Patient Activity Coordinators

Activity Group Guidance
CIJE: 2 RIE: 0 CAT: 15

Activity Oriented Classrooms
CIJE: 0 RIE: 1 CAT: 05

Activity Preferences
CIJE: 2 RIE: 3 CAT: 16

Activity Record
CIJE: 1 RIE: 1 CAT: 21

Activity Scale (Kerpelman et al)
CIJE: 0 RIE: 1 CAT: 21

Activity Segment
CIJE: 0 RIE: 3 CAT: 15

Activity Settings
CIJE: 0 RIE: 1 CAT: 16

Activity Structures
CIJE: 2 RIE: 4 CAT: 15

Activity Theory
CIJE: 6 RIE: 2 CAT: 15

Activity Vector Analysis
CIJE: 5 RIE: 0 CAT: 15

Actometers
CIJE: 2 RIE: 0 CAT: 04

Actor Observer Divergence
CIJE: 0 RIE: 1 CAT: 11

Actors Equity
CIJE: 0 RIE: 2 CAT: 17

Actualization of Mainstream Experience Skills
CIJE: 0 RIE: 3 CAT: 19
UF Project AMES

Actuarial Science
CIJE: 4 RIE: 1 CAT: 20

Acupressure
CIJE: 0 RIE: 1 CAT: 11

Acupuncture
CIJE: 10 RIE: 4 CAT: 11

Acute Care
CIJE: 4 RIE: 1 CAT: 11
UF Secondary Care

Ad Hoc Committee on Copyright Revision
CIJE: 0 RIE: 1 CAT: 17

Ad Hoc Committee on Grades and Evaluation
CIJE: 0 RIE: 1 CAT: 17

Ad Hoc Groups
CIJE: 3 RIE: 3 CAT: 10

Ad Populum Fallacy
CIJE: 0 RIE: 1 CAT: 15

Ada (Programing Language)
CIJE: 2 RIE: 3 CAT: 04

Adamantine
CIJE: 1 RIE: 0 CAT: 20

Adams (Abigail)
CIJE: 1 RIE: 1 CAT: 18

Adams (Adrienne)
CIJE: 1 RIE: 0 CAT: 18

Adams (Harriet)
CIJE: 2 RIE: 0 CAT: 18

Adams (Henry)
CIJE: 6 RIE: 0 CAT: 18

Adams (Herbert Baxter)
CIJE: 1 RIE: 0 CAT: 18

Adams (John Quincy)
CIJE: 1 RIE: 0 CAT: 18

Adams (John)
CIJE: 5 RIE: 2 CAT: 18

Adams (Richard)
CIJE: 3 RIE: 0 CAT: 18

Adams (Samuel)
CIJE: 0 RIE: 1 CAT: 18

Adams (William T)
CIJE: 1 RIE: 0 CAT: 18

Adams Chronicles
CIJE: 1 RIE: 1 CAT: 22

Adams County Public Schools CO
CIJE: 4 RIE: 1 CAT: 17

Adams School MA
CIJE: 0 RIE: 1 CAT: 17

Adams State College CO
CIJE: 3 RIE: 4 CAT: 17

Adams v Califano
CIJE: 6 RIE: 8 CAT: 14

Adams v Richardson
CIJE: 9 RIE: 9 CAT: 14

Adangme
CIJE: 0 RIE: 1 CAT: 13

Adaptability Index (Hunt)
CIJE: 1 RIE: 0 CAT: 21

Adaptability Test (Tiffin Lawshe)
CIJE: 0 RIE: 2 CAT: 21

Adaptation Concept
CIJE: 7 RIE: 1 CAT: 15

Adaptation Effect
CIJE: 5 RIE: 1 CAT: 15

Adaptation Style Theory
CIJE: 2 RIE: 0 CAT: 15

Adapted Computer Technology (for Disabled)
CIJE: 1 RIE: 0 CAT: 20
UF Adaptive Computer Technology (for Disabled)

Adapted Felt Figure Technique
CIJE: 1 RIE: 0 CAT: 15

Adapted Group Figure Attitude Technique
CIJE: 1 RIE: 0 CAT: 15

Adapted Modified Role Repertory Test
CIJE: 2 RIE: 0 CAT: 21

Adapted Physical Education Assessment Scale
CIJE: 0 RIE: 1 CAT: 21

Adapted Tests (for Disabled)
CIJE: 0 RIE: 1 CAT: 21

Adapted Thurstone Sentence Completion Form
CIJE: 1 RIE: 0 CAT: 21

Adapting Science Materials for the Blind
CIJE: 2 RIE: 0 CAT: 19

Adaptive Allocation (Testing)
CIJE: 0 RIE: 1 CAT: 21

Adaptive and Corrective Program Physical Education
CIJE: 0 RIE: 1 CAT: 19

Adaptive Behavior Assessment
CIJE: 2 RIE: 5 CAT: 21

Adaptive Behavior Checklist
CIJE: 2 RIE: 2 CAT: 21

Adaptive Behavior Inventory for Children
CIJE: 10 RIE: 7 CAT: 21

Adaptive Behavior Rating Scale
CIJE: 2 RIE: 3 CAT: 21

Adaptive Behavior Scale
CIJE: 16 RIE: 2 CAT: 21

Adaptive Behavior Scale Public School Version
CIJE: 0 RIE: 5 CAT: 21

Adaptive Behavior Scale School Edition
CIJE: 3 RIE: 1 CAT: 21

Adaptive Behavior Scales
CIJE: 30 RIE: 6 CAT: 21

Adaptive Behavior Scales (AAMD)
CIJE: 7 RIE: 0 CAT: 21
UF AAMD Adaptive Behavior Scales

Adaptive Capacity
CIJE: 4 RIE: 0 CAT: 15

Adaptive Computer Technology (for Disabled)
USE Adapted Computer Technology (for Disabled)

Adaptive Computerized Training System
CIJE: 0 RIE: 2 CAT: 19

Adaptive Concept Acquisition
CIJE: 0 RIE: 1 CAT: 15

Adaptive Control of Thought System
USE ACT Theory

Adaptive Evaluation Structure
CIJE: 0 RIE: 2 CAT: 15

Adaptive Exercise Sequencing
CIJE: 0 RIE: 1 CAT: 15

Adaptive Expertise
CIJE: 0 RIE: 1 CAT: 11

Adaptive Filtering
CIJE: 0 RIE: 1 CAT: 15

Adaptive Flexibility Inventory
CIJE: 0 RIE: 1 CAT: 21

Adaptive Instructional Management System
CIJE: 0 RIE: 2 CAT: 15

Adaptive Instructional Methods
CIJE: 0 RIE: 2 CAT: 15

Adaptive Instructional Models
CIJE: 6 RIE: 11 CAT: 15

Adaptive Instructional Systems
CIJE: 8 RIE: 6 CAT: 15

Adaptive Learning Environments Model
CIJE: 12 RIE: 7 CAT: 15

Adaptive Learning Environments Program
CIJE: 7 RIE: 2 CAT: 19

Adaptive Physical Education Consortium Project
CIJE: 0 RIE: 1 CAT: 19

Adaptive Skills Checklist
CIJE: 0 RIE: 1 CAT: 21

Add Test
CIJE: 0 RIE: 1 CAT: 21

Add Ventures for Girls
CIJE: 0 RIE: 1 CAT: 19

Addams (Jane)
CIJE: 9 RIE: 5 CAT: 18

Addiction Research Center Inventory
CIJE: 0 RIE: 1 CAT: 21

Addiction Specialists
CIJE: 0 RIE: 1 CAT: 09

Addictive Behavior
CIJE: 3 RIE: 2 CAT: 11

Additive and Multiplicative Constants
CIJE: 0 RIE: 1 CAT: 15

Additive Difference Model
CIJE: 2 RIE: 0 CAT: 15

Additive Models
CIJE: 4 RIE: 3 CAT: 15

Additive Trees
CIJE: 2 RIE: 2 CAT: 21

Additive Variance
CIJE: 2 RIE: 0 CAT: 15

Address Forms
CIJE: 11 RIE: 8 CAT: 13

Address Labels
CIJE: 0 RIE: 1 CAT: 16

Addressograph Multigraph
CIJE: 1 RIE: 0 CAT: 17

Adel DeSoto Community School District IA
CIJE: 0 RIE: 2 CAT: 17

Adelaide Coll of Arts and Education (Australia)
CIJE: 0 RIE: 2 CAT: 17

Adelante Program CA
CIJE: 0 RIE: 1 CAT: 19

Adelphi University NY
CIJE: 9 RIE: 8 CAT: 17

Adelson (J)
CIJE: 1 RIE: 0 CAT: 18

Adenosine Deaminase Enzyme Deficiency
CIJE: 2 RIE: 0 CAT: 11

Adequacy Coefficients
CIJE: 1 RIE: 0 CAT: 21

Adequate Prior Notice
CIJE: 0 RIE: 1 CAT: 14

Adhesion Bonding
CIJE: 0 RIE: 1 CAT: 20

Adipocyte Number Hypothesis
CIJE: 1 RIE: 0 CAT: 21

Adirondack Community College NY
CIJE: 0 RIE: 3 CAT: 17

Adirondack Mountains
CIJE: 7 RIE: 7 CAT: 07

Adirondack North Country Association NY
CIJE: 0 RIE: 1 CAT: 17

Adirondack Woodcraft Camps
CIJE: 1 RIE: 0 CAT: 17

Adivasi Oriya
CIJE: 0 RIE: 1 CAT: 13
SN See from "Oriya"

Adjacency Effect
CIJE: 1 RIE: 0 CAT: 15

Adjective Check List (Gough and Heilbrun)
CIJE: 44 RIE: 15 CAT: 21

Adjective Check List (Parker and Veldman)
CIJE: 0 RIE: 1 CAT: 21

Adjective Generation Technique
CIJE: 0 RIE: 3 CAT: 15

Adjective Rating Scale
CIJE: 1 RIE: 3 CAT: 21

Adjective Rating Scale for Self Description
CIJE: 0 RIE: 2 CAT: 21

Adjective Scales
CIJE: 2 RIE: 1 CAT: 21

Adjudicated Youth
CIJE: 3 RIE: 7 CAT: 10

Adjunct Aids
CIJE: 4 RIE: 9 CAT: 13

Adjunct Courses
CIJE: 3 RIE: 2 CAT: 03

Adjunct Questions
CIJE: 19 RIE: 19 CAT: 21

Adjunctive Psychiatric Therapy
CIJE: 0 RIE: 1 CAT: 11

Adjusted Agreement Index
CIJE: 1 RIE: 1 CAT: 21

Adjusted Resolution
CIJE: 0 RIE: 1 CAT: 15

Adjustment Center Management Teams
CIJE: 1 RIE: 0 CAT: 10

Adkins Life Skills Program
CIJE: 1 RIE: 0 CAT: 19

Adkins Life Skills Structured Inquiry
CIJE: 0 RIE: 1 CAT: 15

Adler (Alfred)
CIJE: 17 RIE: 16 CAT: 18

Adler (Mortimer)
CIJE: 9 RIE: 6 CAT: 18

Adlerian Psychology
CIJE: 20 RIE: 16 CAT: 15

Administering for Change Program
CIJE: 0 RIE: 1 CAT: 19

Administration by Objectives
CIJE: 0 RIE: 1 CAT: 15

Administration for Children and Families
CIJE: 0 RIE: 1 CAT: 17
SN Unit of "Department of Health and Human Services"

Administration for Children Youth and Families
CIJE: 4 RIE: 7 CAT: 17
SN Part of the "Administration for Children and Families"

Administration for Native Americans
CIJE: 1 RIE: 2 CAT: 17

Administration Native American Res Analysis Proj
CIJE: 0 RIE: 1 CAT: 19

Administration on Aging
CIJE: 5 RIE: 13 CAT: 17

Administration Supervision Natl Field Task Force
CIJE: 0 RIE: 1 CAT: 17

Administrative and Organizational Systems Model
CIJE: 0 RIE: 1 CAT: 15

Administrative Assistants
CIJE: 4 RIE: 9 CAT: 09

Administrative Attention
USE Managerial Attention

Administrative Attribution Theory
CIJE: 0 RIE: 1 CAT: 15

Administrative Communications Network
CIJE: 0 RIE: 1 CAT: 04

Administrative Compensation Survey
CIJE: 0 RIE: 4 CAT: 22

Administrative Control
CIJE: 1 RIE: 3 CAT: 15

Administrative Internship Program
CIJE: 0 RIE: 1 CAT: 19

Administrative Internship Programs
CIJE: 0 RIE: 2 CAT: 19

Administrative Management by Objective Apprais Sys
CIJE: 0 RIE: 1 CAT: 15

Administrative Q Sort
CIJE: 1 RIE: 0 CAT: 15

Administrative Routine
CIJE: 0 RIE: 1 CAT: 16

Administrative Science
CIJE: 7 RIE: 1 CAT: 20

Administrative Science Quarterly
CIJE: 1 RIE: 0 CAT: 22

Administrative Sciences Institute
CIJE: 1 RIE: 0 CAT: 17

Administrative Stress
CIJE: 2 RIE: 1 CAT: 11

Administrative Stress Index
CIJE: 0 RIE: 4 CAT: 21

Administrative Succession
CIJE: 6 RIE: 0 CAT: 16

Administrative Terminal System
CIJE: 1 RIE: 3 CAT: 15

Administrator Action Plan (Maine)
CIJE: 0 RIE: 1 CAT: 15
UF Maine Administrator Action Plan

Administrator and Teacher Survey
CIJE: 3 RIE: 2 CAT: 19

Administrator Associations
CIJE: 1 RIE: 1 CAT: 05

Administrator Bargaining
CIJE: 1 RIE: 2 CAT: 16

Administrator Certification
CIJE: 1 RIE: 4 CAT: 16

Administrator Exchange Programs
CIJE: 0 RIE: 1 CAT: 19

Administrator Involvement
CIJE: 1 RIE: 3 CAT: 15

Administrator Rights
CIJE: 4 RIE: 3 CAT: 14

Administrator Routine
CIJE: 1 RIE: 1 CAT: 16

Administrator Supply and Demand
CIJE: 2 RIE: 6 CAT: 16

Administrator Surveys
CIJE: 2 RIE: 10 CAT: 21

Administrator Task Inventory
CIJE: 0 RIE: 1 CAT: 21

Admissible Probability Testing
CIJE: 1 RIE: 4 CAT: 21

Admission Index
CIJE: 0 RIE: 1 CAT: 21

Admission Statutes (Hospitalization)
CIJE: 0 RIE: 1 CAT: 11

Admission Test for Graduate Study in Business
CIJE: 4 RIE: 4 CAT: 21

Admissions Testing Program
CIJE: 0 RIE: 9 CAT: 19

Admitted Student Questionnaire
CIJE: 0 RIE: 0 CAT: 21
UF College Board Admitted Student Questionnaire

Adolescent Alienation Index
CIJE: 1 RIE: 0 CAT: 21

Adolescent Assertion Expression Scale
CIJE: 1 RIE: 0 CAT: 21

Adolescent Attitudes
CIJE: 5 RIE: 2 CAT: 16

Adolescent Communication Screen
CIJE: 0 RIE: 1 CAT: 21

Adolescent Crisis Team and Respite House MA
CIJE: 0 RIE: 1 CAT: 17

Adolescent Drinking Index
CIJE: 1 RIE: 1 CAT: 21

Adolescent Emotional Factors Inventory
CIJE: 2 RIE: 0 CAT: 21

Adolescent Individuation Measure
CIJE: 0 RIE: 1 CAT: 21

Adolescent Infant Development Program DC
CIJE: 0 RIE: 1 CAT: 19

Adolescent Intrafamilial Perception Questionnaire
CIJE: 0 RIE: 1 CAT: 21

Adolescent Parenting Inventory
CIJE: 0 RIE: 1 CAT: 21

Adolescent Self Efficacy Scale
CIJE: 0 RIE: 1 CAT: 21

Adolescent Suicide
CIJE: 9 RIE: 39 CAT: 11
UF Teenage Suicide

Adolescent Temperament Questionnaire
CIJE: 0 RIE: 1 CAT: 21

Adolescents in Child Training
CIJE: 0 RIE: 1 CAT: 19

Adolph Coors Outward Bound Manpower Challenge Prog
CIJE: 0 RIE: 1 CAT: 19

Adopt a Grandchild Program FL
CIJE: 0 RIE: 1 CAT: 19

Adopt a School
CIJE: 12 RIE: 29 CAT: 19

Adopt a Ship Plan
CIJE: 1 RIE: 0 CAT: 19

Adoption and Guardianship Reform Organization
CIJE: 1 RIE: 0 CAT: 17

Adoption Assistance
CIJE: 2 RIE: 3 CAT: 16

Adoption Assistance and Child Welfare Act 1980
CIJE: 4 RIE: 16 CAT: 14

Adoption Bonding Program
CIJE: 0 RIE: 1 CAT: 19

Adoption Diffusion Theory (Rogers)
CIJE: 0 RIE: 1 CAT: 15

Adoption Exchange Services
CIJE: 0 RIE: 1 CAT: 05

Adoption Insights
CIJE: 4 RIE: 0 CAT: 03

Adoption of Older Children
CIJE: 0 RIE: 1 CAT: 16
UF Older Child Adoption

Adoption Resource Exchange of North America
CIJE: 1 RIE: 1 CAT: 17

Adorno (T W)
CIJE: 1 RIE: 1 CAT: 18

Adorno F Scale
CIJE: 2 RIE: 0 CAT: 21

Adrenal Hyperplasia
CIJE: 1 RIE: 0 CAT: 11

Adrenocortical Stress Reactivity
CIJE: 2 RIE: 0 CAT: 11

Adrian College MI
CIJE: 3 RIE: 1 CAT: 17

Adrian Public Library MI
CIJE: 0 RIE: 1 CAT: 17

Adult Achievement Responsibility Scale
CIJE: 0 RIE: 1 CAT: 21

Adult and Vocational Education Network
USE ADVOCNET

Adult Armchair Education Project
CIJE: 0 RIE: 1 CAT: 19

Adult Attachment Interview
CIJE: 6 RIE: 1 CAT: 21

Adult Basic Education Centre ON
CIJE: 0 RIE: 1 CAT: 17

Adult Basic Education Demonstration Project
CIJE: 0 RIE: 1 CAT: 19

Adult Basic Education Mobile Van Project
CIJE: 0 RIE: 1 CAT: 19

Adult Basic Education Outreach
CIJE: 0 RIE: 1 CAT: 19

Adult Basic Education Program
CIJE: 2 RIE: 2 CAT: 19

Adult Basic Education Teacher Competency Inventory
CIJE: 0 RIE: 6 CAT: 21

Adult Basic Learning Examination
CIJE: 0 RIE: 11 CAT: 21

Adult Behavioral Classification Project
CIJE: 0 RIE: 1 CAT: 19

Adult Bilingual Experimental School
CIJE: 1 RIE: 0 CAT: 17

Adult Career Concerns Inventory
CIJE: 3 RIE: 1 CAT: 21

Adult Career Education Counseling Project
CIJE: 0 RIE: 2 CAT: 19

Adult Career Education Resources Survey
CIJE: 0 RIE: 2 CAT: 19

Adult Child Relationship
CIJE: 67 RIE: 34 CAT: 11

Adult Children of Alcoholics
CIJE: 12 RIE: 4 CAT: 10

Adult Classroom Environment Scale
CIJE: 2 RIE: 1 CAT: 21

Adult College Career Employment Support Services
CIJE: 0 RIE: 1 CAT: 05

Adult Communication Management
CIJE: 0 RIE: 1 CAT: 15

Adult Compacts
CIJE: 0 RIE: 2 CAT: 15

Adult Competency Education Project
CIJE: 0 RIE: 19 CAT: 19

Adult Competency Training
CIJE: 0 RIE: 6 CAT: 15

Adult Cuban Immigrant Project
CIJE: 0 RIE: 2 CAT: 19

Adult Development Enrichment Program
CIJE: 2 RIE: 0 CAT: 19

Adult Developmental Decline
CIJE: 1 RIE: 0 CAT: 11

Adult Education Access Card
USE EduCard

Adult Education Act
CIJE: 3 RIE: 26 CAT: 14

Adult Education Act 1965
CIJE: 0 RIE: 2 CAT: 14

Adult Education Act 1966
CIJE: 6 RIE: 49 CAT: 14

Adult Education Act 1969
CIJE: 0 RIE: 2 CAT: 14

Adult Education Act 1978
CIJE: 0 RIE: 7 CAT: 14

Adult Education Act Amendments 1984
CIJE: 0 RIE: 1 CAT: 14

Adult Education Act Grants to States Program
USE Adult Education Act State Grant Program

Adult Education Act Section 321
CIJE: 0 RIE: 1 CAT: 14
UF ABE 321

Adult Education Act State Grant Program
CIJE: 0 RIE: 1 CAT: 19
UF Adult Education Act Grants to States Program

Adult Education Amendments 1978
CIJE: 0 RIE: 6 CAT: 14

Adult Education Association of Michigan
CIJE: 0 RIE: 1 CAT: 17

Adult Education Association of the USA
CIJE: 14 RIE: 5 CAT: 17

Adult Education for the Homeless Program
CIJE: 1 RIE: 2 CAT: 19

Adult Education Interim Steering Committee CA
CIJE: 0 RIE: 1 CAT: 17

Adult Education Research Conference
CIJE: 2 RIE: 1 CAT: 02

Adult Education Staff Development Project
CIJE: 0 RIE: 2 CAT: 19

Adult Education State Plans
CIJE: 0 RIE: 2 CAT: 15

Adult Education Survey in Finland (1972 to 1973)
CIJE: 4 RIE: 0 CAT: 19

Adult Educator Exchange Program
CIJE: 0 RIE: 1 CAT: 19

Adult Functional Reading Study
CIJE: 1 RIE: 2 CAT: 19

Adult High School Diploma
CIJE: 0 RIE: 2 CAT: 03

Adult Independent Learner Project
CIJE: 1 RIE: 1 CAT: 19

Adult Informal Reading Test
CIJE: 2 RIE: 1 CAT: 21

Adult Irrational Ideas Inventory
CIJE: 1 RIE: 0 CAT: 21

Adult Language Levels Management System
CIJE: 0 RIE: 1 CAT: 15

Adult Learning and Public Broadcasting Project
CIJE: 0 RIE: 1 CAT: 19

Adult Learning Program Service
CIJE: 1 RIE: 3 CAT: 15

Adult Learning Research Center
CIJE: 1 RIE: 0 CAT: 17

Adult Learning Specialists
CIJE: 1 RIE: 1 CAT: 09

Adult Learning Week
CIJE: 0 RIE: 1 CAT: 12

Adult Literacy and Basic Skills Unit
CIJE: 0 RIE: 2 CAT: 17
SN Located in London, England
UF ALBSU

Adult Literacy Education Program
CIJE: 0 RIE: 2 CAT: 19

Adult Literacy Initiative
CIJE: 3 RIE: 6 CAT: 19

Adult Literacy League FL
CIJE: 0 RIE: 1 CAT: 17

Adult Literacy Organization of Zimbabwe
CIJE: 0 RIE: 1 CAT: 17

Adult Literacy Resource Agency (England)
CIJE: 0 RIE: 0 CAT: 17

Adult Mental Health Abilities Test Battery
CIJE: 0 RIE: 1 CAT: 21

Adult New Readers
CIJE: 0 RIE: 3 CAT: 10

Adult Perception Scale
CIJE: 0 RIE: 1 CAT: 21

Adult Performance Level
CIJE: 14 RIE: 63 CAT: 21

Adult Protective Services
CIJE: 1 RIE: 2 CAT: 05

Adult Reading Mini Assessment (1977)
CIJE: 0 RIE: 0 CAT: 21

Adult Responses to Childrens Behavior Scale
CIJE: 0 RIE: 1 CAT: 21

Adult Science Mini Assessment (1977)
CIJE: 0 RIE: 0 CAT: 21

Adult Self Expression Scale
CIJE: 3 RIE: 0 CAT: 21

Adult Service Clubs
CIJE: 0 RIE: 1 CAT: 10

Adult Student Personnel Association
CIJE: 1 RIE: 1 CAT: 17

Adult Student Relationship
CIJE: 4 RIE: 0 CAT: 16

Adult Vocational Maturity Index (Sheppard)
CIJE: 0 RIE: 1 CAT: 21

Adults Health and Physical Developmental Program
CIJE: 1 RIE: 0 CAT: 19

Adults Learning Projects
CIJE: 0 RIE: 1 CAT: 19

Adults Molested as Children
CIJE: 0 RIE: 2 CAT: 10
UF AMACs

Advance College Project (Indiana University)
USE Indiana University Advance College Project

Advance Directives
CIJE: 11 RIE: 1 CAT: 11

Advance Notice of Employment Termination
CIJE: 0 RIE: 0 CAT: 16

Advance Teacher Preparation
CIJE: 1 RIE: 0 CAT: 15

Advanced Composition
CIJE: 48 RIE: 14 CAT: 03

Advanced Courses Development Programme (Scotland)
CIJE: 0 RIE: 2 CAT: 19

Advanced Education Projects (IBM)
CIJE: 0 RIE: 2 CAT: 19

Advanced Individual Training
CIJE: 0 RIE: 2 CAT: 15

Advanced Institutional Development Program
CIJE: 0 RIE: 12 CAT: 19

Advanced Instructional System (Air Force)
CIJE: 1 RIE: 9 CAT: 15

Advanced Learning Systems
CIJE: 0 RIE: 1 CAT: 20

Advanced Level Examination
CIJE: 3 RIE: 0 CAT: 21

Advanced Mathematics
CIJE: 0 RIE: 2 CAT: 03

Advanced Pilot Training
CIJE: 0 RIE: 5 CAT: 15

Advanced Placement Examinations (CEEB)
CIJE: 24 RIE: 34 CAT: 21

Advanced Research Projects Agency
CIJE: 2 RIE: 14 CAT: 17

Advanced Study Center OH
CIJE: 0 RIE: 1 CAT: 17

Advanced Study Guide Technique
CIJE: 0 RIE: 1 CAT: 15

Advanced Systems Incorporated
CIJE: 1 RIE: 1 CAT: 17

Advanced Technology Centers
CIJE: 4 RIE: 2 CAT: 05

Advanced Television Systems
CIJE: 0 RIE: 1 CAT: 20

Advanced Vocabulary Test II
CIJE: 1 RIE: 1 CAT: 21

Advancement Based on Competency
USE Project Advancement Based on Competency

Advancement of Librarianship
CIJE: 0 RIE: 1 CAT: 19

Advancement School NC
CIJE: 0 RIE: 1 CAT: 17

Advancement Via Individual Determination
USE AVID Program

Advantage Center LA
CIJE: 0 RIE: 1 CAT: 17

Adventure Economics
CIJE: 1 RIE: 0 CAT: 15

Adventure Games
CIJE: 5 RIE: 5 CAT: 16

Adventure Playgrounds
CIJE: 6 RIE: 6 CAT: 05

Adventure Stories
CIJE: 11 RIE: 5 CAT: 16

Adventures in Movement for the Handicapped
CIJE: 0 RIE: 1 CAT: 19

Adventures of Robinson Crusoe
CIJE: 1 RIE: 0 CAT: 22

Adverbial Modifiers
CIJE: 3 RIE: 0 CAT: 13

Adversarial Approach
USE Adversary Method

Adversary Culture
CIJE: 4 RIE: 1 CAT: 16

Adversary Evaluation Model
CIJE: 6 RIE: 6 CAT: 21

Adversary Instructional Model
CIJE: 1 RIE: 1 CAT: 15

Adversary Method
CIJE: 10 RIE: 2 CAT: 15
UF Adversarial Approach

Adversative Connectives
CIJE: 1 RIE: 1 CAT: 13

Adverse Impact
CIJE: 6 RIE: 8 CAT: 21

Advertisements
CIJE: 50 RIE: 41 CAT: 16

Advertising Agencies
CIJE: 4 RIE: 19 CAT: 05

Advertising Competitions
CIJE: 1 RIE: 2 CAT: 16

Advertising Copywriting
CIJE: 4 RIE: 11 CAT: 03

Advertising Council
CIJE: 0 RIE: 1 CAT: 17

Advertising Education
CIJE: 8 RIE: 16 CAT: 03

Advertising Effectiveness
CIJE: 27 RIE: 64 CAT: 16

Advertising Industry
CIJE: 9 RIE: 17 CAT: 10

Advertising Logos
CIJE: 0 RIE: 1 CAT: 16

Advertising Occupations
CIJE: 0 RIE: 6 CAT: 09

Advice Columns
CIJE: 5 RIE: 1 CAT: 16

Advice Seeking
CIJE: 4 RIE: 1 CAT: 11

Advisement and Graduation Information System FL
CIJE: 0 RIE: 1 CAT: 19

Advisers
CIJE: 15 RIE: 5 CAT: 10

Advisor Role
CIJE: 22 RIE: 22 CAT: 16

Advisory Approach
CIJE: 11 RIE: 5 CAT: 15

Advisory Commission on Intergovernmental Relations
CIJE: 3 RIE: 0 CAT: 17

Advisory Committee on Academic Planning
CIJE: 0 RIE: 1 CAT: 17

Advisory Committee on Mexican American Education
CIJE: 0 RIE: 1 CAT: 17

Advisory Committee on Voluntary Foreign Aid
CIJE: 0 RIE: 1 CAT: 17

Advisory Council on College Chemistry
CIJE: 4 RIE: 9 CAT: 17

Advisory Systems
CIJE: 5 RIE: 4 CAT: 15

Advocacy Communication
CIJE: 3 RIE: 1 CAT: 16

Advocacy Planning
CIJE: 3 RIE: 6 CAT: 15

Advocacy Training
CIJE: 1 RIE: 1 CAT: 15

Advocate Adversary Evaluation
CIJE: 0 RIE: 3 CAT: 21

Advocate Counseling Model
CIJE: 0 RIE: 4 CAT: 15

ADVOCNET
CIJE: 1 RIE: 0 CAT: 04
UF Adult and Vocational Education Network

AECT 76
CIJE: 0 RIE: 48 CAT: 02

AECT Research and Theory Division Meeting
CIJE: 0 RIE: 145 CAT: 02

AEL Level of Parent Involvement Questionnaire
USE Level of Parent Involvement Questionnaire

AEL Regional Exchange
CIJE: 0 RIE: 2 CAT: 22

Aeneid
CIJE: 5 RIE: 1 CAT: 22

AERA Research Training Presessions Prog
CIJE: 0 RIE: 1 CAT: 02

Aerated Lagoons
CIJE: 0 RIE: 2 CAT: 20

Aerial Combat Simulators
CIJE: 0 RIE: 1 CAT: 04

Aerial Photography
CIJE: 15 RIE: 4 CAT: 20

Aerobic Digestion
CIJE: 0 RIE: 3 CAT: 20

Aerodynamics
CIJE: 12 RIE: 3 CAT: 20

Aerographers Mates
CIJE: 0 RIE: 2 CAT: 09

Aerojet General Corporation
CIJE: 0 RIE: 1 CAT: 17

Aerometric Data
CIJE: 1 RIE: 0 CAT: 20

Aeronautical Engineering
CIJE: 0 RIE: 1 CAT: 20

Aeronautical Research
CIJE: 0 RIE: 2 CAT: 20

Aeronautics
CIJE: 4 RIE: 6 CAT: 20

Aerosols
CIJE: 7 RIE: 0 CAT: 04

Aerospace Corporation CA
CIJE: 0 RIE: 1 CAT: 17

Aerospace Education Foundation
CIJE: 1 RIE: 0 CAT: 17

Aerospace Education Resource Center
CIJE: 0 RIE: 1 CAT: 17

Aerospace Materials Information Center
CIJE: 0 RIE: 5 CAT: 17

Aerospace Medicine
CIJE: 0 RIE: 1 CAT: 11

Aeschylus
CIJE: 3 RIE: 1 CAT: 18

Aesop Fables
CIJE: 4 RIE: 1 CAT: 22

Aesthetic Communication
CIJE: 1 RIE: 2 CAT: 16

Aesthetic Education Program
CIJE: 3 RIE: 3 CAT: 19

Aesthetic Reading
CIJE: 15 RIE: 93 CAT: 03

Aesthetic Response
CIJE: 8 RIE: 7 CAT: 16

AEtna Institute for Corporate Education
CIJE: 0 RIE: 2 CAT: 17

AFCENT International School (Netherlands)
CIJE: 1 RIE: 0 CAT: 17

AFDC Unemployed Fathers Program
CIJE: 0 RIE: 1 CAT: 19

Affect Abilities Training
CIJE: 1 RIE: 0 CAT: 15

Affect Adjective Check List (Zuckerman)
CIJE: 0 RIE: 1 CAT: 21

Affect Concepts
CIJE: 1 RIE: 1 CAT: 15

Affect Effect Theory
CIJE: 0 RIE: 2 CAT: 15

Affectionate Behavior
CIJE: 0 RIE: 1 CAT: 11

Affective Cognitive Consistency
CIJE: 1 RIE: 0 CAT: 11

Affective Communication Test
CIJE: 0 RIE: 1 CAT: 21

Affective Disorders
CIJE: 3 RIE: 1 CAT: 11

Affective Domain
CIJE: 31 RIE: 20 CAT: 16

Affective Perception Inventory (Soares and Soares)
CIJE: 0 RIE: 7 CAT: 21

Affective Response
CIJE: 14 RIE: 18 CAT: 11

Affective Sensitivity Scale
CIJE: 2 RIE: 3 CAT: 21

Affective Triad Scale (MacDonell et al)
CIJE: 0 RIE: 2 CAT: 21

Affective Voice Quality
CIJE: 1 RIE: 0 CAT: 13

Affective Work Competencies Inventory
CIJE: 7 RIE: 6 CAT: 21

Affiliative Behavior
CIJE: 7 RIE: 1 CAT: 11

Affine Geometry
CIJE: 6 RIE: 0 CAT: 20

Affinity Seeking Strategies
CIJE: 4 RIE: 3 CAT: 11

Affirmation Strategy
CIJE: 0 RIE: 1 CAT: 15

Affordance (Cognition)
CIJE: 1 RIE: 1 CAT: 15

Affricates
CIJE: 1 RIE: 3 CAT: 13

Afghanistan
CIJE: 22 RIE: 68 CAT: 07

Afghans
CIJE: 2 RIE: 6 CAT: 08

AFL CIO
CIJE: 13 RIE: 15 CAT: 17

Afram Associates
CIJE: 1 RIE: 2 CAT: 17

Africa
CIJE: 630 RIE: 775 CAT: 07

Africa (Central)
CIJE: 2 RIE: 8 CAT: 07

Africa (East)
CIJE: 28 RIE: 56 CAT: 07

Africa (North)
CIJE: 4 RIE: 23 CAT: 07

Africa (Northeast)
CIJE: 1 RIE: 1 CAT: 07

Africa (South)
CIJE: 12 RIE: 47 CAT: 07

Africa (Sub Sahara)
CIJE: 36 RIE: 57 CAT: 07

Africa (Tropical)
CIJE: 1 RIE: 2 CAT: 07

Africa (West)
CIJE: 67 RIE: 56 CAT: 07

Africa South of the Sahara Survey
CIJE: 1 RIE: 0 CAT: 19

African Adult Education Association
CIJE: 1 RIE: 1 CAT: 17

African American Institute NY
CIJE: 1 RIE: 0 CAT: 17

African American Materials Project
CIJE: 0 RIE: 2 CAT: 19

African Association for Literacy and Adult Educ
CIJE: 0 RIE: 1 CAT: 17

African Diaspora
CIJE: 0 RIE: 1 CAT: 12

African Heritage Studies Association
CIJE: 2 RIE: 0 CAT: 17

African Languages (Non Bantu)
CIJE: 0 RIE: 1 CAT: 13

African Medical and Research Foundation
CIJE: 0 RIE: 1 CAT: 17

African Methodist Episcopal Church
CIJE: 1 RIE: 0 CAT: 17

African Museum of Art Frederick Douglass Institute
CIJE: 0 RIE: 1 CAT: 17

African Primary Science Programme
CIJE: 1 RIE: 0 CAT: 19

African Queen
CIJE: 1 RIE: 0 CAT: 22

African Savanna
CIJE: 1 RIE: 0 CAT: 07

African Social Studies Program
CIJE: 3 RIE: 3 CAT: 19

African Studies Association
CIJE: 2 RIE: 1 CAT: 17

Africanisms
CIJE: 3 RIE: 1 CAT: 13

Africans
CIJE: 39 RIE: 16 CAT: 08

Afrikaners
CIJE: 2 RIE: 1 CAT: 08

Afro Amerasians
CIJE: 0 RIE: 1 CAT: 08

Afro American Black History Month
USE Black History Month

Afro American Instructional Curriculum Laboratory
CIJE: 1 RIE: 0 CAT: 17

Afro American Knowledge Inventory
CIJE: 1 RIE: 0 CAT: 21

Afro American Society
CIJE: 1 RIE: 0 CAT: 17

Afro American Studies Center CA
CIJE: 0 RIE: 1 CAT: 17

Afro Asians
CIJE: 1 RIE: 1 CAT: 08

Afro Caribbeans
CIJE: 5 RIE: 1 CAT: 08

Afro Hispanics
CIJE: 1 RIE: 4 CAT: 08

Afrocentrism
CIJE: 88 RIE: 26 CAT: 16

AFSCME District Council 37 NY
CIJE: 0 RIE: 2 CAT: 17

AFT Contracts
CIJE: 0 RIE: 33 CAT: 14

After Dinner Speaking
CIJE: 1 RIE: 2 CAT: 13
UF After Dinner Speeches

After Dinner Speeches
USE After Dinner Speaking

After School Detention
CIJE: 0 RIE: 1 CAT: 15
UF Detention (After School)

Afterlife
CIJE: 4 RIE: 1 CAT: 15

Afternoon Newspapers
CIJE: 0 RIE: 1 CAT: 16

Afton Junior High School WY
CIJE: 1 RIE: 0 CAT: 17

Ag Horizons GA
CIJE: 0 RIE: 1 CAT: 19

Agam Method of Visual Education
CIJE: 0 RIE: 2 CAT: 15

Agamic Psychology
CIJE: 0 RIE: 1 CAT: 11

Agassiz (Louis)
CIJE: 4 RIE: 0 CAT: 18

Agathe (Saint)
CIJE: 0 RIE: 1 CAT: 18

Agau Languages
USE Agaw Languages

Agaw Languages
CIJE: 0 RIE: 1 CAT: 13
SN A subgroup of Cushitic languages
UF Agau Languages

Age Adjustment
CIJE: 0 RIE: 1 CAT: 15

Age Appropriateness
CIJE: 10 RIE: 34 CAT: 15

Age Bias
CIJE: 25 RIE: 12 CAT: 16

Age Dependent Measures
CIJE: 0 RIE: 2 CAT: 21

Age Differential Hypothesis
CIJE: 2 RIE: 0 CAT: 15

Age Discrimination Act 1975
CIJE: 3 RIE: 9 CAT: 14

Age Discrimination in Employment Act 1967
CIJE: 37 RIE: 28 CAT: 14

Age Discrimination in Employment Act Amend 1978
CIJE: 12 RIE: 9 CAT: 14

Age Discrimination in Employment Act Amend 1980
CIJE: 0 RIE: 5 CAT: 14

Age Discrimination in Employment Act Amend 1984
CIJE: 0 RIE: 1 CAT: 14

Age Discrimination in Employment Act Amend 1986
CIJE: 8 RIE: 0 CAT: 14

Age Grading
CIJE: 1 RIE: 1 CAT: 15

Age Independent Measures
CIJE: 0 RIE: 1 CAT: 21

Age Integrated Learning
CIJE: 0 RIE: 2 CAT: 15

Age of Enlightenment
CIJE: 2 RIE: 3 CAT: 12

Age Relevance
CIJE: 1 RIE: 2 CAT: 15

Age Segregation
CIJE: 9 RIE: 4 CAT: 16

Age Specificity
CIJE: 1 RIE: 1 CAT: 15

Agee (James)
CIJE: 3 RIE: 0 CAT: 18

AgeLink Project NC
CIJE: 0 RIE: 1 CAT: 19

Agency Client Contracting
CIJE: 0 RIE: 1 CAT: 15

Agency Fees
CIJE: 1 RIE: 7 CAT: 16

Agency for Instructional Television
CIJE: 4 RIE: 12 CAT: 17

Agency for International Development
CIJE: 29 RIE: 82 CAT: 17

Agency for Tele Education in Canada
CIJE: 0 RIE: 1 CAT: 17

Agency Provider Relationship
CIJE: 0 RIE: 2 CAT: 15

Agency Shops
CIJE: 8 RIE: 1 CAT: 05

Agency Theory
CIJE: 0 RIE: 1 CAT: 15

Agenda Control Model
CIJE: 0 RIE: 1 CAT: 15

Agenda Preparation (Meetings)
CIJE: 1 RIE: 2 CAT: 16

Agendas
CIJE: 7 RIE: 12 CAT: 16

Agent Action Objective Model
CIJE: 0 RIE: 2 CAT: 15

Agents of Innocence (Ignatius)
CIJE: 0 RIE: 1 CAT: 22

Aggravated Robbery
CIJE: 0 RIE: 1 CAT: 14

Aggregate Model
CIJE: 7 RIE: 2 CAT: 15

Aggregates (Concrete)
CIJE: 0 RIE: 1 CAT: 20

Aggregation (Data)
CIJE: 26 RIE: 40 CAT: 20

Agility
CIJE: 1 RIE: 1 CAT: 11

Aging (Library Collections)
CIJE: 0 RIE: 0 CAT: 16

Aging Out Process
CIJE: 1 RIE: 4 CAT: 16

Aging Population
USE Population Aging

Aging Sexuality Knowledge and Attitudes Scale
CIJE: 0 RIE: 2 CAT: 21

Agitated Behavior
CIJE: 0 RIE: 1 CAT: 11

Agnate Sentences Test (ODonnell)
CIJE: 0 RIE: 2 CAT: 21

Agnew (Spiro)
CIJE: 2 RIE: 2 CAT: 18

Agnews State Hospital CA
CIJE: 0 RIE: 3 CAT: 17

Agnosia
CIJE: 1 RIE: 4 CAT: 11

Agonism
USE Agonistic Behavior

Agonistic Behavior
CIJE: 2 RIE: 1 CAT: 11
UF Agonism

Agoraphobia
CIJE: 12 RIE: 5 CAT: 11

Agrarianism
CIJE: 2 RIE: 2 CAT: 16
SN The doctrine of equitable redistribution of landed property — also, a social or political movement to promote a farm economy and country way of life in contrast to that associated with an industrial economy

Agree Disagree Statements
CIJE: 0 RIE: 1 CAT: 15

Agreement (Grammar)
CIJE: 5 RIE: 3 CAT: 13

Agreement Index (Kane and Brennan)
CIJE: 1 RIE: 0 CAT: 21

Agreement Response Scale (Couch and Keniston)
CIJE: 2 RIE: 1 CAT: 21

Agreement Statistic (Subkoviak and Harris)
CIJE: 0 RIE: 1 CAT: 21

AGRICOLA
CIJE: 4 RIE: 13 CAT: 17
UF AGRICultural OnLine Access

Agricultural and Technical College at Alfred NY
USE State University of NY Agric Tech Coll Alfred

Agricultural and Technical College Morrisville NY
USE State University of NY Agric Tech Coll Morrisville

Agricultural Appropriations Act 1965
CIJE: 0 RIE: 1 CAT: 14

Agricultural Capital
CIJE: 0 RIE: 1 CAT: 20

Agricultural Change
CIJE: 11 RIE: 7 CAT: 16

Agricultural Chemicals
CIJE: 1 RIE: 6 CAT: 20

Agricultural Economics
CIJE: 7 RIE: 16 CAT: 20

Agricultural Economics Majors
CIJE: 0 RIE: 1 CAT: 10

Agricultural Education Foundation CA
CIJE: 0 RIE: 1 CAT: 17

Agricultural Education Magazine
CIJE: 0 RIE: 1 CAT: 22

Agricultural History
CIJE: 8 RIE: 1 CAT: 12

Agricultural Information
CIJE: 10 RIE: 2 CAT: 16

Agricultural Knowledge System (Israel)
CIJE: 0 RIE: 1 CAT: 15

Agricultural Literacy
CIJE: 3 RIE: 4 CAT: 03

Agricultural Manpower Needs Project
CIJE: 0 RIE: 1 CAT: 19

Agricultural Marketing
CIJE: 1 RIE: 2 CAT: 03

AGRICultural OnLine Access
USE AGRICOLA

Agricultural Policy
CIJE: 8 RIE: 5 CAT: 16

Agricultural Products
CIJE: 2 RIE: 4 CAT: 20

Agricultural Research Service
CIJE: 2 RIE: 1 CAT: 17

Agricultural Resources
CIJE: 3 RIE: 3 CAT: 20

Agricultural Sciences
CIJE: 12 RIE: 8 CAT: 03

Agricultural Specialists
CIJE: 1 RIE: 1 CAT: 09

Agricultural Technology
CIJE: 11 RIE: 3 CAT: 20

Agricultural Vocational Preference Test
CIJE: 1 RIE: 0 CAT: 21

Agricultural Work Force Survey
CIJE: 0 RIE: 1 CAT: 22
UF Current Population Survey Agric Work Force Supplt

Agriculture and Food Act 1981
CIJE: 0 RIE: 1 CAT: 14

Agriculture Industry Program
CIJE: 1 RIE: 0 CAT: 19

AgriData Network
CIJE: 1 RIE: 2 CAT: 04

Agridevelopment
CIJE: 1 RIE: 0 CAT: 20

Agta
CIJE: 0 RIE: 0 CAT: 13

Aguaruna
CIJE: 0 RIE: 1 CAT: 13
SN A language of the Jivaroan family in South America

Aguaruna (People)
CIJE: 0 RIE: 1 CAT: 08

Aguilar v Felton
CIJE: 2 RIE: 9 CAT: 14

Agusan Manobo
CIJE: 0 RIE: 1 CAT: 13
SN A Northwest Austronesian (Philippine) language
UF Manobo (Agusan)

Agusti (Ignacio)
CIJE: 1 RIE: 0 CAT: 18

Agutaynen
CIJE: 0 RIE: 1 CAT: 13
SN A Northwest Austronesian (Philippine) language (Kalamian group)

AH4 Group Test of General Intelligence
CIJE: 4 RIE: 1 CAT: 21

AHERA 1986
USE Asbestos Hazard Emergency Response Act 1986

Ahfachkee Day School
CIJE: 1 RIE: 0 CAT: 17

Ahl (David H)
CIJE: 0 RIE: 0 CAT: 18

Ahmednagar College
CIJE: 1 RIE: 0 CAT: 17

Ahtna (Tribe)
CIJE: 0 RIE: 1 CAT: 08

Ahtna Athapascan
CIJE: 0 RIE: 2 CAT: 13

Ahyokeh
CIJE: 0 RIE: 1 CAT: 18

Aid for Part Time Study Program
CIJE: 0 RIE: 1 CAT: 19
SN New York State campus-based award program
UF APTS NY

Aid to Families with Dependent Children
CIJE: 63 RIE: 181 CAT: 14

AIDA (Computer Program)
USE Apple Interactive Data Analysis

Aida (Opera)
CIJE: 0 RIE: 0 CAT: 22

AIDA Plan
USE Attention Interest Desire and Action Approach

Aiken (Conrad)
CIJE: 0 RIE: 1 CAT: 18

Aiken (George L)
CIJE: 0 RIE: 1 CAT: 18

Aiken Mathematics Interest Scale
CIJE: 1 RIE: 1 CAT: 21

Aiken v Lieuallen
CIJE: 1 RIE: 0 CAT: 14

AIME Variable
USE Amount of Invested Mental Effort

Aims Community College CO
CIJE: 2 RIE: 2 CAT: 17

Ain Shams University (Egypt)
CIJE: 0 RIE: 1 CAT: 17

Ainsworth (Mary D)
CIJE: 2 RIE: 1 CAT: 18

Ainsworth Strange Situation Procedure
CIJE: 39 RIE: 11 CAT: 15

Ainu
CIJE: 0 RIE: 1 CAT: 13

Air
CIJE: 8 RIE: 15 CAT: 20

AIR BAVTE Curriculum
CIJE: 0 RIE: 1 CAT: 03

Air Cleaners
CIJE: 0 RIE: 0 CAT: 04

Air Command and Staff College AL
CIJE: 1 RIE: 0 CAT: 17

Air Compressors
CIJE: 1 RIE: 3 CAT: 04

Air Correspondence High School (South Korea)
CIJE: 1 RIE: 0 CAT: 17

Air Emissions
CIJE: 0 RIE: 5 CAT: 20

Air Force
CIJE: 33 RIE: 321 CAT: 17

Air Force Academy CO
CIJE: 16 RIE: 36 CAT: 17

Air Force Aero Propulsion Laboratory
CIJE: 0 RIE: 1 CAT: 17

Air Force Extension Course Institute
CIJE: 0 RIE: 1 CAT: 17

Air Force Human Resources Laboratory
CIJE: 3 RIE: 9 CAT: 17

Air Force Institute of Technology
CIJE: 0 RIE: 1 CAT: 17

Air Force Junior ROTC
CIJE: 1 RIE: 26 CAT: 03

Air Force Materials Laboratory
CIJE: 0 RIE: 1 CAT: 17

Air Force Museum OH
CIJE: 1 RIE: 0 CAT: 17

Air Force Occupational Attitude Inventory
CIJE: 0 RIE: 3 CAT: 21

Air Force Officer Qualifying Test
CIJE: 0 RIE: 11 CAT: 21

Air Force Phase II Base Level System
CIJE: 0 RIE: 2 CAT: 15

Air Force Reading Abilities Test
CIJE: 0 RIE: 1 CAT: 21

Air Force Reserve
CIJE: 0 RIE: 1 CAT: 17

Air Force Reserve Officers Training Corps
CIJE: 2 RIE: 1 CAT: 17

Air Force Rocket Propulsion Laboratory
CIJE: 0 RIE: 1 CAT: 17

Air Force Specialty Code
CIJE: 0 RIE: 2 CAT: 15

AIR Forum
CIJE: 0 RIE: 505 CAT: 02

Air Gap Phenomenon
CIJE: 1 RIE: 0 CAT: 15

Air National Guard
CIJE: 0 RIE: 3 CAT: 17

Air Navigation
CIJE: 0 RIE: 1 CAT: 20

Air Pressure
CIJE: 10 RIE: 2 CAT: 20

Air Quality
CIJE: 10 RIE: 13 CAT: 20
SN See also "Indoor Air Quality"

Air Quality Standards
CIJE: 1 RIE: 1 CAT: 20

Air Rifles
CIJE: 0 RIE: 1 CAT: 04

Air Rights
CIJE: 5 RIE: 0 CAT: 20

Air Samplers
CIJE: 1 RIE: 5 CAT: 04

Air Sampling
CIJE: 1 RIE: 3 CAT: 20

Air Tracks
CIJE: 6 RIE: 0 CAT: 04

Air Training Command TX
CIJE: 1 RIE: 0 CAT: 17

Air Transportation Agents
CIJE: 0 RIE: 1 CAT: 09

Air University AL
CIJE: 1 RIE: 5 CAT: 17

Air War College AL
CIJE: 0 RIE: 1 CAT: 17

Airborne Lead
CIJE: 1 RIE: 0 CAT: 20

Airborne Radio Code Operators
CIJE: 0 RIE: 1 CAT: 09

Airborne Soldiers
CIJE: 0 RIE: 1 CAT: 09

Aircraft
CIJE: 8 RIE: 13 CAT: 04

Aircraft Assembly Occupations
CIJE: 0 RIE: 1 CAT: 09

Aircraft Design
CIJE: 1 RIE: 4 CAT: 20

Aircraft Disasters
CIJE: 0 RIE: 1 CAT: 16
UF Airplane Crashes

Aircraft Dispatchers
CIJE: 0 RIE: 1 CAT: 09
UF Flight Dispatchers

Aircraft Environmental Systems
CIJE: 0 RIE: 4 CAT: 04

Aircraft Identification
CIJE: 1 RIE: 1 CAT: 20

Aircraft Instrument Comprehension Program
CIJE: 0 RIE: 1 CAT: 19

Aircraft Instrument Comprehension Test
CIJE: 0 RIE: 2 CAT: 21

Aircraft Weapon Systems
CIJE: 0 RIE: 1 CAT: 04

Aircrew Survival Equipment Personnel
CIJE: 0 RIE: 1 CAT: 09

Aircrew Training Devices
CIJE: 0 RIE: 5 CAT: 04

Airframe Technicians
CIJE: 0 RIE: 2 CAT: 09

Airlie Conference
CIJE: 7 RIE: 0 CAT: 02

Airlie House Conference on the Classics
CIJE: 0 RIE: 1 CAT: 02

Airlie House Lifelong Learning Leaders Retreat
CIJE: 0 RIE: 1 CAT: 02

Airlines
CIJE: 5 RIE: 5 CAT: 20

Airman Qualifying Examination
CIJE: 0 RIE: 5 CAT: 21

Airman Training Line Simulator
CIJE: 0 RIE: 1 CAT: 04

Airmen Basic Resident Courses
CIJE: 0 RIE: 1 CAT: 03

Airplane Crashes
USE Aircraft Disasters

Airplane Flight Attendants
CIJE: 1 RIE: 5 CAT: 09

Airplane Flights
CIJE: 0 RIE: 5 CAT: 16

Airway Science Curriculum
CIJE: 0 RIE: 1 CAT: 03

Ak Chin (Tribe)
CIJE: 0 RIE: 1 CAT: 08

Akaike Information Criterion
CIJE: 5 RIE: 0 CAT: 15

Akbar
CIJE: 0 RIE: 0 CAT: 18
SN 1542-1605, Mogul emperor of India

Akhmatova (Anna)
CIJE: 1 RIE: 1 CAT: 18

Aklan
USE Aklanon

Aklanon
CIJE: 0 RIE: 5 CAT: 13
SN A Northwest Austronesian (Philippine) language (Bisayan group)
UF Aklan

Akron Public Schools OH
CIJE: 6 RIE: 9 CAT: 17

Akron Summit County Public Library OH
CIJE: 1 RIE: 1 CAT: 17

Akuapem
CIJE: 0 RIE: 1 CAT: 13

Akwesasne Mohawk (Tribe)
CIJE: 0 RIE: 3 CAT: 08

Al Anon
CIJE: 0 RIE: 3 CAT: 17
SN Operates to aid families who live with alcoholics, often in conjunction with Alcoholics Anonymous

Al Quds Open University (Jordan)
CIJE: 0 RIE: 1 CAT: 17

Alabama
CIJE: 158 RIE: 551 CAT: 07

Alabama (Africatown)
CIJE: 0 RIE: 1 CAT: 07

Alabama (Alexander City)
CIJE: 0 RIE: 1 CAT: 07

Alabama (Auburn)
CIJE: 1 RIE: 11 CAT: 07

Alabama (Baldwin County)
CIJE: 0 RIE: 1 CAT: 07

Alabama (Birmingham)
CIJE: 11 RIE: 23 CAT: 07

Alabama (Bullock County)
CIJE: 1 RIE: 1 CAT: 07

Alabama (Cherokee County)
CIJE: 2 RIE: 0 CAT: 07

Alabama (Conecuh County)
CIJE: 0 RIE: 4 CAT: 07

Alabama (Decatur)
CIJE: 1 RIE: 1 CAT: 07

Alabama (Etowah County)
CIJE: 1 RIE: 0 CAT: 07

Alabama (Florence)
CIJE: 0 RIE: 2 CAT: 07

Alabama (Greene County)
CIJE: 1 RIE: 2 CAT: 07

Alabama (Hale County)
CIJE: 0 RIE: 2 CAT: 07

Alabama (Huntsville)
CIJE: 1 RIE: 5 CAT: 07

Alabama (Language)
CIJE: 0 RIE: 1 CAT: 13
SN A Muskogean language

Alabama (Macon County)
CIJE: 0 RIE: 3 CAT: 07

Alabama (Marengo County)
CIJE: 0 RIE: 1 CAT: 07

Alabama (Mobile)
CIJE: 2 RIE: 6 CAT: 07

Alabama (Montgomery)
CIJE: 6 RIE: 7 CAT: 07

Alabama (Northeast)
CIJE: 0 RIE: 1 CAT: 07

Alabama (Opelika)
CIJE: 2 RIE: 1 CAT: 07

Alabama (Pike County)
CIJE: 0 RIE: 1 CAT: 07

Alabama (Selma)
CIJE: 1 RIE: 1 CAT: 07

Alabama (Soul City)
CIJE: 0 RIE: 1 CAT: 07

Alabama (Sylacauga)
CIJE: 0 RIE: 1 CAT: 07

Alabama (Tribe)
CIJE: 0 RIE: 1 CAT: 08

Alabama (Tuscaloosa County)
CIJE: 0 RIE: 5 CAT: 07

Alabama (Tuscaloosa)
CIJE: 0 RIE: 8 CAT: 07

Alabama (Tuskegee)
CIJE: 5 RIE: 4 CAT: 07

Alabama (Wilcox County)
CIJE: 1 RIE: 1 CAT: 07

Alabama A and M University
CIJE: 2 RIE: 3 CAT: 17

Alabama Aviation and Technical College
CIJE: 0 RIE: 1 CAT: 17

Alabama Basic Competency Tests
CIJE: 0 RIE: 7 CAT: 21

Alabama Commission on Higher Education
CIJE: 0 RIE: 4 CAT: 17

Alabama Education Study Commission
CIJE: 0 RIE: 1 CAT: 17

Alabama Educational Television Commission
CIJE: 0 RIE: 1 CAT: 17

Alabama Funnel Self Evaluation Interview Guide
CIJE: 0 RIE: 1 CAT: 21

Alabama High School Graduation Examination
CIJE: 1 RIE: 12 CAT: 21

Alabama Initial Certification Test
CIJE: 0 RIE: 2 CAT: 21

Alabama Interlibrary Catalog
CIJE: 0 RIE: 1 CAT: 22

Alabama Judicial College
CIJE: 0 RIE: 1 CAT: 17

Alabama Junior College Library Association
CIJE: 0 RIE: 1 CAT: 17

Alabama Lib Assn Government Documents Round Table
CIJE: 0 RIE: 1 CAT: 17

Alabama Library Information Network
CIJE: 0 RIE: 1 CAT: 17

Alabama Literacy Project
CIJE: 0 RIE: 1 CAT: 19

Alabama Lung Association
CIJE: 1 RIE: 0 CAT: 17

Alabama Model Center
CIJE: 0 RIE: 1 CAT: 17

Alabama Performance Based Accreditation Standards
CIJE: 0 RIE: 1 CAT: 21

Alabama Performance Based Career Incentive Prog
CIJE: 0 RIE: 1 CAT: 19

Alabama Polytechnic Institute
CIJE: 0 RIE: 2 CAT: 17

Alabama Public Library Service
CIJE: 0 RIE: 12 CAT: 17

Alabama Resource File
CIJE: 0 RIE: 1 CAT: 04

Alabama Resources Information Systems
CIJE: 0 RIE: 1 CAT: 15

Alabama Space and Rocket Center
CIJE: 5 RIE: 0 CAT: 17

Alabama State University
CIJE: 4 RIE: 2 CAT: 17

Alabama Student Grant Program
CIJE: 0 RIE: 1 CAT: 19

Alabama Union List of Serials
CIJE: 0 RIE: 1 CAT: 22

Alachua County School District FL
CIJE: 0 RIE: 2 CAT: 17

Alain
CIJE: 2 RIE: 0 CAT: 18

Alamance Community College NC
CIJE: 0 RIE: 1 CAT: 17

Alameda County Health Department CA
CIJE: 0 RIE: 1 CAT: 17

Alamo Community College District TX
CIJE: 1 RIE: 1 CAT: 17

Alar Controversy
CIJE: 0 RIE: 1 CAT: 11

Alas (Leopoldo)
CIJE: 4 RIE: 0 CAT: 18

Alaska
CIJE: 163 RIE: 921 CAT: 07

Alaska (Aleutian Islands)
CIJE: 1 RIE: 0 CAT: 07
SN See also "Aleutian Islands"

Alaska (Anchorage)
CIJE: 4 RIE: 28 CAT: 07

Alaska (Attu)
CIJE: 0 RIE: 1 CAT: 07

Alaska (Bethel)
CIJE: 2 RIE: 1 CAT: 07

Alaska (Bristol Bay)
CIJE: 0 RIE: 3 CAT: 07

Alaska (Chevak)
CIJE: 0 RIE: 1 CAT: 07

Alaska (Cordova)
CIJE: 0 RIE: 1 CAT: 07

Alaska (Eagle)
CIJE: 1 RIE: 1 CAT: 07

Alaska (Fairbanks)
CIJE: 3 RIE: 4 CAT: 07

Alaska (Juneau)
CIJE: 0 RIE: 11 CAT: 07

Alaska (Ketchikan)
CIJE: 0 RIE: 1 CAT: 07

Alaska (Kodiak Island)
CIJE: 0 RIE: 4 CAT: 07

Alaska (Koyuk)
CIJE: 0 RIE: 0 CAT: 07

Alaska (Manokotak)
CIJE: 1 RIE: 1 CAT: 07

Alaska (Nome)
CIJE: 2 RIE: 1 CAT: 07

Alaska (Northwest)
CIJE: 1 RIE: 1 CAT: 07

Alaska (Pribilof Islands)
CIJE: 1 RIE: 0 CAT: 07

Alaska (Sitka)
CIJE: 2 RIE: 7 CAT: 07

Alaska (South Central)
CIJE: 0 RIE: 1 CAT: 07

Alaska (Southeast)
CIJE: 0 RIE: 10 CAT: 07

Alaska (Southwest)
CIJE: 0 RIE: 3 CAT: 07

Alaska (Wainwright)
CIJE: 1 RIE: 1 CAT: 07

Alaska Advisory Council for Libraries
CIJE: 0 RIE: 1 CAT: 17

Alaska Consortium for Transition Services
CIJE: 0 RIE: 1 CAT: 19

Alaska Division of State Libraries
CIJE: 0 RIE: 2 CAT: 17

Alaska Educational Satellite Demonstration Project
CIJE: 0 RIE: 1 CAT: 19

Alaska Effective Schooling Program
CIJE: 1 RIE: 2 CAT: 19

Alaska Innovative Technology in Education Project
CIJE: 1 RIE: 0 CAT: 19

Alaska Instructional Diagnostic System
CIJE: 0 RIE: 1 CAT: 15

Alaska Knowledge Base System
CIJE: 0 RIE: 1 CAT: 04

Alaska Library Network
CIJE: 0 RIE: 1 CAT: 19

Alaska Methodist University
CIJE: 0 RIE: 2 CAT: 17

Alaska Native Claims Settlement Act 1972
CIJE: 5 RIE: 16 CAT: 14

Alaska Native Core Program
CIJE: 0 RIE: 1 CAT: 19

Alaska Native Language Center
CIJE: 0 RIE: 2 CAT: 17

Alaska Pacific University
CIJE: 1 RIE: 2 CAT: 17

Alaska Public Employment Relations Act
USE Public Employment Relations Act (Alaska 1990)

Alaska Public School Fund
CIJE: 0 RIE: 1 CAT: 17

Alaska Research on School Effectiveness Project
CIJE: 0 RIE: 9 CAT: 19

Alaska Rural School Project
CIJE: 0 RIE: 1 CAT: 19

Alaska Rural Teacher Training Corps
CIJE: 0 RIE: 4 CAT: 17

Alaska School Effectiveness Project
CIJE: 0 RIE: 1 CAT: 19

Alaska Sister Schools Network
CIJE: 0 RIE: 1 CAT: 17

Alaska Skills Center
CIJE: 0 RIE: 1 CAT: 17

Alaska State Department of Education
CIJE: 1 RIE: 11 CAT: 17

Alaska State Educational Incentive Grant Program
USE State Educational Incentive Grant Program AK

Alaska Statewide Assessment Program
CIJE: 0 RIE: 3 CAT: 19

Alaska Statewide Instructional Support System
CIJE: 0 RIE: 1 CAT: 04

Alaska Student Loan Program
CIJE: 0 RIE: 4 CAT: 19

Alaska Teleconferencing Network
CIJE: 0 RIE: 1 CAT: 04

Alaska Writing Program
CIJE: 1 RIE: 1 CAT: 19

Alaska Youth Initiative
CIJE: 0 RIE: 1 CAT: 19

Alaskan Native Needs Assessment
CIJE: 0 RIE: 9 CAT: 19

Alaskan Pipeline
CIJE: 1 RIE: 3 CAT: 04

Albania
CIJE: 4 RIE: 9 CAT: 07

Albany Librarianship Trainee Program
CIJE: 0 RIE: 1 CAT: 19

Albany Medical College NY
CIJE: 7 RIE: 1 CAT: 17

Albany State College GA
CIJE: 1 RIE: 3 CAT: 17

Albatros Club (Czechoslovakia)
CIJE: 1 RIE: 0 CAT: 17

Albee (Edward)
CIJE: 4 RIE: 1 CAT: 18

Albemarle Paper Company v Moody
CIJE: 1 RIE: 0 CAT: 14

Albemarle Report
CIJE: 0 RIE: 1 CAT: 22

Alberta
CIJE: 216 RIE: 799 CAT: 07

Alberta (Calgary)
CIJE: 12 RIE: 29 CAT: 07

Alberta (Camrose)
CIJE: 1 RIE: 1 CAT: 07

Alberta (Edmonton)
CIJE: 28 RIE: 40 CAT: 07

Alberta (Fort McMurray)
CIJE: 0 RIE: 1 CAT: 07

Alberta (Heart Lake)
CIJE: 1 RIE: 0 CAT: 07

Alberta (Lacombe County)
CIJE: 0 RIE: 1 CAT: 07

Alberta (Leduc)
CIJE: 0 RIE: 1 CAT: 07

Alberta (Lethbridge)
CIJE: 2 RIE: 1 CAT: 07

Alberta (Mission Metis)
CIJE: 0 RIE: 1 CAT: 07

Alberta (Newell County)
CIJE: 0 RIE: 1 CAT: 07

Alberta (North)
CIJE: 1 RIE: 5 CAT: 07

Alberta (Strathcona County)
CIJE: 0 RIE: 1 CAT: 07

Alberta (Vulcan County)
CIJE: 0 RIE: 1 CAT: 07

Alberta (Warner County)
CIJE: 0 RIE: 1 CAT: 07

Alberta Achievement Testing Program
CIJE: 0 RIE: 5 CAT: 19
UF Achievement Testing Program AB

ALBERTA BEST
CIJE: 0 RIE: 1 CAT: 19
SN Customer service program offered by the Alberta government

Alberta Career Develop Employment Resource Ctr
CIJE: 0 RIE: 1 CAT: 17

Alberta Catholic Education Association
CIJE: 0 RIE: 1 CAT: 17

Alberta Catholic School Trustees Association
CIJE: 0 RIE: 1 CAT: 17

Alberta Commission Educational Planning (Canada)
CIJE: 1 RIE: 0 CAT: 17

Alberta Department of Education
CIJE: 0 RIE: 1 CAT: 17

Alberta Diagnostic Reading Program
CIJE: 0 RIE: 1 CAT: 19

Alberta Distance Learning Centre
CIJE: 0 RIE: 1 CAT: 17

Alberta Essay Scales
CIJE: 1 RIE: 2 CAT: 21

Alberta Grade Twelve Diploma Examinations
CIJE: 0 RIE: 10 CAT: 21
UF Grade 12 Diploma Examinations Program AB

Alberta Initiation to Teaching Project
CIJE: 2 RIE: 2 CAT: 19
UF Initiation to Teaching Project AB

Alberta School for the Deaf
CIJE: 0 RIE: 2 CAT: 17

Alberta Vocational Centre (Edmonton)
CIJE: 0 RIE: 3 CAT: 17

Alberta Vocational College (Edmonton)
CIJE: 1 RIE: 0 CAT: 17
SN Formerly known as Alberta Vocational Centre (Edmonton)

Alberti (Rafael)
CIJE: 2 RIE: 0 CAT: 18

Albertus Magnus College CT
CIJE: 1 RIE: 2 CAT: 17

Albinos
CIJE: 3 RIE: 2 CAT: 10

Albion College MI
CIJE: 7 RIE: 4 CAT: 17

Albright College PA
CIJE: 0 RIE: 3 CAT: 17

Albrights Dystrophy
CIJE: 1 RIE: 0 CAT: 11

ALBSU
USE Adult Literacy and Basic Skills Unit

Albuquerque Indian School NM
CIJE: 3 RIE: 3 CAT: 17

Albuquerque Integration Model
CIJE: 0 RIE: 2 CAT: 15

Albuquerque Integration Outreach Project
CIJE: 0 RIE: 3 CAT: 19

Albuquerque Public Schools NM
CIJE: 4 RIE: 69 CAT: 17

Albuquerque Technical Vocational Institute NM
CIJE: 0 RIE: 5 CAT: 17

Alcatraz Island
CIJE: 3 RIE: 0 CAT: 07

Alcohol and Drug Abuse Education Act
CIJE: 0 RIE: 2 CAT: 14

Alcohol Behavior Attitude and Awareness Inventory
CIJE: 0 RIE: 1 CAT: 21
UF ABAA Inventory

Alcohol Education Discipline Program
CIJE: 0 RIE: 2 CAT: 19

Alcohol Fuels
CIJE: 0 RIE: 9 CAT: 20

Alcohol Nomograms
CIJE: 0 RIE: 1 CAT: 11

Alcohol Related Birth Defects
CIJE: 1 RIE: 3 CAT: 11

Alcohol Warning Posters
CIJE: 0 RIE: 1 CAT: 11

Alcohol Wellness
CIJE: 0 RIE: 2 CAT: 11

Alcoholic Beverage Servers
USE Bartenders

Alcoholics Anonymous
CIJE: 17 RIE: 9 CAT: 17
SN See also "Al Anon"

Alcoholism Questionnaire
CIJE: 0 RIE: 2 CAT: 21

Alcohols
CIJE: 12 RIE: 1 CAT: 20

Alcorn Agricultural and Mechanical College MS
CIJE: 0 RIE: 1 CAT: 17

Alcorn State University MS
CIJE: 0 RIE: 1 CAT: 17

Alcott (Bronson)
CIJE: 2 RIE: 1 CAT: 18

Alcott (Louisa May)
CIJE: 5 RIE: 2 CAT: 18

Alcuin
CIJE: 0 RIE: 1 CAT: 18

Aldehydes
CIJE: 2 RIE: 0 CAT: 20

Alden II Docufax
CIJE: 0 RIE: 1 CAT: 04

Aldhelm
CIJE: 0 RIE: 1 CAT: 18

Aldous Simulation of Personality
CIJE: 1 RIE: 0 CAT: 15

Aldus Pagemaker
CIJE: 1 RIE: 2 CAT: 04

Aleixandre (Vicente)
CIJE: 2 RIE: 0 CAT: 18

Alemannic Dialects
CIJE: 1 RIE: 0 CAT: 13

Alertness
CIJE: 1 RIE: 1 CAT: 11

Aleut (Tribe)
CIJE: 6 RIE: 33 CAT: 08

Aleutian Islands
CIJE: 2 RIE: 2 CAT: 07
SN See also "Alaska (Aleutian Islands)"

Aleutians East Borough School District AK
CIJE: 0 RIE: 1 CAT: 17

Alexander (F Matthias)
CIJE: 3 RIE: 0 CAT: 18

Alexander (James)
CIJE: 1 RIE: 0 CAT: 18

Alexander (Lamar)
CIJE: 11 RIE: 0 CAT: 18

Alexander (Lloyd)
CIJE: 4 RIE: 0 CAT: 18

Alexander City Schools AL
CIJE: 0 RIE: 1 CAT: 17

Alexander Graham Bell Association for the Deaf
CIJE: 3 RIE: 0 CAT: 17

Alexander the Great
CIJE: 3 RIE: 1 CAT: 18

Alexandre de Rhodes Educational TV Ctre (Vietnam)
CIJE: 1 RIE: 0 CAT: 17

Alexandria Area Technical School MN
CIJE: 1 RIE: 0 CAT: 17

Alexandria City Schools VA
CIJE: 4 RIE: 1 CAT: 17

Alexandria University (Egypt)
CIJE: 0 RIE: 1 CAT: 17

Alexandrian Library (Antiquity)
CIJE: 0 RIE: 1 CAT: 12

Alfateh University (Libya)
CIJE: 1 RIE: 0 CAT: 17

Alford (Thomas Wildcat)
CIJE: 0 RIE: 1 CAT: 18

Alford Information Technology Centre (Scotland)
CIJE: 0 RIE: 1 CAT: 17

Alfred P Sloan Foundation
CIJE: 0 RIE: 2 CAT: 17

Algae
CIJE: 23 RIE: 4 CAT: 20

Algae Purification System
CIJE: 1 RIE: 1 CAT: 16

ALGAMS Programing Language
CIJE: 0 RIE: 1 CAT: 04

Algebraic Computation
CIJE: 1 RIE: 0 CAT: 20

Algebraic Expressions
CIJE: 2 RIE: 1 CAT: 20

Algebraic Fields
CIJE: 0 RIE: 1 CAT: 20

Algebraic Fractions
CIJE: 0 RIE: 2 CAT: 20

Algebraic Geometry
CIJE: 1 RIE: 0 CAT: 20

Algebraic Interpretive Dialogue
CIJE: 0 RIE: 5 CAT: 20

Algebridge
CIJE: 0 RIE: 1 CAT: 21

Alger (Horatio)
CIJE: 5 RIE: 0 CAT: 18

Algeria
CIJE: 31 RIE: 61 CAT: 07

Algeria (Algiers)
CIJE: 1 RIE: 0 CAT: 07

ALGOL Programing Languages
CIJE: 0 RIE: 7 CAT: 04

Algonkian People
USE Algonquians

Algonquian Languages
CIJE: 1 RIE: 7 CAT: 13

Algonquians
CIJE: 0 RIE: 0 CAT: 08
UF Algonkian People

Algonquin
CIJE: 1 RIE: 2 CAT: 13
SN Dialect of Ojibwa

Algonquin (Tribe)
CIJE: 4 RIE: 13 CAT: 08

Algorithmic Processor Description Language
CIJE: 0 RIE: 1 CAT: 04

Algorithmics
CIJE: 2 RIE: 0 CAT: 20

Algorithms Process Hierarchy
CIJE: 0 RIE: 1 CAT: 20

Algren (Nelson)
CIJE: 0 RIE: 1 CAT: 18

Alhambra City School District CA
CIJE: 1 RIE: 1 CAT: 17

Alhambra High School District CA
CIJE: 0 RIE: 1 CAT: 17

Alhambra Palace
CIJE: 0 RIE: 1 CAT: 16

Alice in Wonderland
CIJE: 6 RIE: 4 CAT: 22

Alice Lloyd College KY
CIJE: 3 RIE: 0 CAT: 17

Alicias Diary (Hardy)
CIJE: 0 RIE: 1 CAT: 22

Alimony
CIJE: 2 RIE: 2 CAT: 14

Alinsky (Saul)
CIJE: 5 RIE: 5 CAT: 18

Aliteracy
CIJE: 5 RIE: 7 CAT: 11

Alkali Metals
CIJE: 2 RIE: 0 CAT: 20

Alkalosis
CIJE: 0 RIE: 1 CAT: 11

Alkanes
CIJE: 2 RIE: 3 CAT: 20

Alkenes
CIJE: 6 RIE: 4 CAT: 20

Alkyd Paints
CIJE: 1 RIE: 0 CAT: 04

All about Letters
CIJE: 1 RIE: 0 CAT: 22

All But Dissertation
CIJE: 6 RIE: 2 CAT: 16

All in the Family
CIJE: 3 RIE: 7 CAT: 22

All India Radio
CIJE: 1 RIE: 2 CAT: 17

All Indian Long Distance Runners Training Camp
CIJE: 0 RIE: 1 CAT: 17

All Indian Pueblo Coun Univ New Mex Teach Ed Prog
CIJE: 0 RIE: 1 CAT: 19

All Indian Pueblo Council NM
CIJE: 2 RIE: 1 CAT: 17

ALL Model
USE Australian Language Levels Project

All My Children
CIJE: 0 RIE: 1 CAT: 22

All Nations Church of God
CIJE: 1 RIE: 0 CAT: 17

All News Radio
CIJE: 1 RIE: 3 CAT: 16

All No Tests
CIJE: 0 RIE: 1 CAT: 21

All Russia Society for the Blind
CIJE: 0 RIE: 3 CAT: 17

All Terrain Bicycles
CIJE: 1 RIE: 0 CAT: 04

All Terrain Vehicles
CIJE: 1 RIE: 3 CAT: 04
SN See also "Off Road Vehicles"

All the Kings Men
CIJE: 1 RIE: 0 CAT: 22

All Union Ministry of Public Health (USSR)
CIJE: 1 RIE: 0 CAT: 17

All Volunteer Armed Forces
CIJE: 2 RIE: 15 CAT: 17
SN See also "Volunteer Army"

Allama Iqbal Open University (Pakistan)
CIJE: 3 RIE: 3 CAT: 17

Allan Hancock Joint Community College District CA
CIJE: 1 RIE: 1 CAT: 17

Allegany Community College MD
CIJE: 1 RIE: 2 CAT: 17

Allegheny College PA
CIJE: 6 RIE: 4 CAT: 17

Allegheny County Schools PA
CIJE: 1 RIE: 3 CAT: 17

Allegheny Ludlum Steel Corporation PA
CIJE: 1 RIE: 0 CAT: 17

Allen (James E Jr)
CIJE: 4 RIE: 1 CAT: 18

Allen (Nathaniel T)
CIJE: 0 RIE: 2 CAT: 18

Allen (Woody)
CIJE: 2 RIE: 0 CAT: 18

Allen Attitude Scale
CIJE: 0 RIE: 1 CAT: 21

Allen County Community College KS
CIJE: 0 RIE: 1 CAT: 17

Allen J Ellender Fellowship Program
CIJE: 0 RIE: 1 CAT: 19
UF Ellender Fellowships

Allen Picture Cards
CIJE: 0 RIE: 1 CAT: 21

Allen Plan
CIJE: 0 RIE: 1 CAT: 16

Allen Report
CIJE: 0 RIE: 2 CAT: 22

Allen Scale of Beliefs
CIJE: 0 RIE: 1 CAT: 21

Allen School MA
CIJE: 1 RIE: 0 CAT: 17

Allen Sentence Completion Test
CIJE: 0 RIE: 1 CAT: 21

Allen University SC
CIJE: 0 RIE: 1 CAT: 17

Allende (Salvador)
CIJE: 3 RIE: 0 CAT: 18

Allentown College of Saint Francis de Sales PA
CIJE: 2 RIE: 1 CAT: 17

Allentown School District PA
CIJE: 2 RIE: 2 CAT: 17

Allerton House IL
CIJE: 1 RIE: 0 CAT: 17

Allerton Park Institute IL
CIJE: 0 RIE: 1 CAT: 17

Alliance College PA
CIJE: 0 RIE: 1 CAT: 17

Alliance Development Committee
CIJE: 0 RIE: 1 CAT: 17

Alliance for Arts Education
CIJE: 3 RIE: 0 CAT: 17

Alliance for Better Child Care
CIJE: 1 RIE: 1 CAT: 17
SN See also "Act for Better Child Care Services"

Alliance for Career and Vocational Education
CIJE: 0 RIE: 1 CAT: 17

Alliance for Environmental Education
CIJE: 1 RIE: 2 CAT: 17

Alliance for Excellence
CIJE: 1 RIE: 1 CAT: 17
SN Affiliation of libraries at all levels for improving education in the U.S.

Alliance for Excellence VA
CIJE: 0 RIE: 1 CAT: 17
SN Partnership between black churches and community colleges for the advancement of minorities in higher education

Alliance for Progress
CIJE: 5 RIE: 0 CAT: 12

Alliance High School OH
CIJE: 1 RIE: 0 CAT: 17

Alliance to Involve Minorities in Mathematics
CIJE: 0 RIE: 1 CAT: 17

Allied Health Learning Center
CIJE: 0 RIE: 1 CAT: 17

Allied Health Professions Personnel Training Act
CIJE: 1 RIE: 2 CAT: 14

Allison Science Attitude Scale
CIJE: 0 RIE: 1 CAT: 21

Alliteration
CIJE: 4 RIE: 1 CAT: 13

Allo Centered Psychotherapy
CIJE: 0 RIE: 2 CAT: 11

Allocated Learning Time
CIJE: 1 RIE: 7 CAT: 21

Allopathic Medicine
CIJE: 1 RIE: 0 CAT: 11

Allophones
CIJE: 8 RIE: 4 CAT: 13

Alloplastic Orientation
CIJE: 0 RIE: 1 CAT: 15

Allport (Gordon W)
CIJE: 5 RIE: 5 CAT: 18

Allstate Insurance Company
CIJE: 2 RIE: 0 CAT: 17

Allyn and Bacon Reading Program
CIJE: 1 RIE: 1 CAT: 19

Alma College MI
CIJE: 4 RIE: 4 CAT: 17

Alma v Dupree
CIJE: 0 RIE: 1 CAT: 14

Almanac
CIJE: 4 RIE: 5 CAT: 22

ALOHA System
CIJE: 1 RIE: 8 CAT: 15

Alonso (Damaso)
CIJE: 5 RIE: 0 CAT: 18

ALP Ethos Instrument (Olson)
CIJE: 0 RIE: 1 CAT: 21

ALP MacProof
USE MacProof

Alpena Community College MI
CIJE: 0 RIE: 3 CAT: 17

Alpern Boll Developmental Profile
CIJE: 1 RIE: 3 CAT: 21
UF Developmental Profile (Alpern and Boll)

Alpert Haber Achievement Anxiety Test
CIJE: 10 RIE: 6 CAT: 21

Alpha Behavior (Piaget)
CIJE: 0 RIE: 1 CAT: 11

Alpha Biographical Inventory
CIJE: 0 RIE: 1 CAT: 21

Alpha Coefficient
CIJE: 32 RIE: 21 CAT: 20

Alpha Errors
USE Type I Errors

Alpha Feedback Training
CIJE: 1 RIE: 0 CAT: 11

Alpha Learning Systems
CIJE: 0 RIE: 2 CAT: 15

Alpha Plastics Printing Company
CIJE: 0 RIE: 1 CAT: 17

Alpha Tau Alpha
CIJE: 1 RIE: 0 CAT: 17

Alpha Training
CIJE: 0 RIE: 1 CAT: 11

Alphabet Boards
CIJE: 0 RIE: 1 CAT: 04

Alphabet Books
CIJE: 6 RIE: 1 CAT: 16

Alphabet Cards
CIJE: 0 RIE: 1 CAT: 04

Alphabet Recitation Test (Fletcher et al)
CIJE: 1 RIE: 0 CAT: 21

Alphabetic Principle
CIJE: 0 RIE: 1 CAT: 13

Alphabetic Writing
CIJE: 1 RIE: 0 CAT: 13

Alphanumeric Codes
CIJE: 1 RIE: 2 CAT: 16

Alphanumeric System
CIJE: 0 RIE: 1 CAT: 15

Alpine Vegetation
CIJE: 2 RIE: 0 CAT: 20

Alsatian Dialects
CIJE: 5 RIE: 3 CAT: 13

Alsea
CIJE: 0 RIE: 3 CAT: 13
SN An extinct Indian language (Yakonan group)

Altair System
CIJE: 0 RIE: 1 CAT: 04

Alterationists
CIJE: 0 RIE: 3 CAT: 09

Altered States of Consciousness Induction Devices
CIJE: 1 RIE: 0 CAT: 04

Alternance Training
CIJE: 0 RIE: 1 CAT: 15
SN Alternating schoolsite/worksite training

Alternate Choice Questions
CIJE: 2 RIE: 3 CAT: 21

Alternate Keyboards
CIJE: 0 RIE: 1 CAT: 20
UF Alternative Keyboards

Alternate Learning Project
CIJE: 1 RIE: 2 CAT: 19

Alternate Living Incorporated MD
CIJE: 0 RIE: 0 CAT: 17

Alternate Semester Program
CIJE: 0 RIE: 2 CAT: 19

Alternate State Policy Mechanism Study
CIJE: 0 RIE: 1 CAT: 19

Alternating Current
CIJE: 1 RIE: 11 CAT: 20

Alternation (Speech)
CIJE: 0 RIE: 3 CAT: 13

Alternative Administrator Certificates
CIJE: 1 RIE: 1 CAT: 21

Alternative Admissions (College)
CIJE: 0 RIE: 1 CAT: 15

Alternative Assessment
CIJE: 84 RIE: 155 CAT: 21
SN Assessment in some form other than multiple-choice standardized tests, e.g., constructed responses, open-ended essays with no single correct answer, portfolios that are collections of students' work over time, and project work that involves collaboration with peers

Alternative Assessments in Practice Data Base
CIJE: 0 RIE: 1 CAT: 04

Alternative Careers
CIJE: 13 RIE: 9 CAT: 09

Alternative Child Care Program
CIJE: 0 RIE: 1 CAT: 19

Alternative Communities
CIJE: 1 RIE: 1 CAT: 16

Alternative Community Living Arrangements
CIJE: 1 RIE: 0 CAT: 11

Alternative Conceptions
CIJE: 11 RIE: 14 CAT: 20

Alternative Educational Plan
CIJE: 2 RIE: 1 CAT: 15

Alternative Financing
CIJE: 1 RIE: 0 CAT: 16
SN See also "Financing Options"

Alternative Futures Approach to Planning Model
CIJE: 0 RIE: 0 CAT: 15

Alternative Grading
CIJE: 1 RIE: 2 CAT: 15

Alternative Justification Approach
CIJE: 0 RIE: 1 CAT: 15

Alternative Keyboards
USE Alternate Keyboards

Alternative Learning Methodologies thru Acads NY
USE Project ALMA NY

Alternative Living Arrangements
CIJE: 1 RIE: 1 CAT: 16

Alternative Media
CIJE: 0 RIE: 1 CAT: 16

Alternative Minimum Tax
CIJE: 1 RIE: 1 CAT: 14

Alternative Press
CIJE: 3 RIE: 13 CAT: 16

Alternative Program PA
CIJE: 0 RIE: 1 CAT: 19

Alternative Publishers
CIJE: 1 RIE: 3 CAT: 16

Alternative School Calendars
CIJE: 2 RIE: 0 CAT: 15

Alternative Schools Project
CIJE: 0 RIE: 1 CAT: 19

Alternative Teacher Education
CIJE: 4 RIE: 4 CAT: 15

Alternative Television
CIJE: 0 RIE: 4 CAT: 16

Alternative Training Experiment
CIJE: 0 RIE: 1 CAT: 19

Alternative Transportation Program
CIJE: 0 RIE: 1 CAT: 19

Alternative Vocational School CT
CIJE: 1 RIE: 0 CAT: 17

Alternative Youth Employment Strategies Project
CIJE: 0 RIE: 1 CAT: 19

Alternatives Prevention Program NY
CIJE: 0 RIE: 1 CAT: 19

Alternatives to Consolidation
CIJE: 0 RIE: 1 CAT: 15

Alternatives to Corporal Punishment
CIJE: 0 RIE: 2 CAT: 15

Alternatives to Standardized Testing
CIJE: 3 RIE: 27 CAT: 21

Alternatives to Suspension
CIJE: 1 RIE: 11 CAT: 16

Alternatives to the Revolving Door
USE National Project II (FIPSE)

Alternators
CIJE: 0 RIE: 5 CAT: 04

Althusser (Louis)
CIJE: 2 RIE: 0 CAT: 18

Altitude Quotient
CIJE: 1 RIE: 0 CAT: 20

Altoona Area School District PA
CIJE: 1 RIE: 2 CAT: 17

Altoona Area Vocational Technical School PA
CIJE: 0 RIE: 1 CAT: 17

Altus Independent Schools OK
CIJE: 0 RIE: 1 CAT: 17

Altus Linguistic Laboratory OK
CIJE: 0 RIE: 1 CAT: 17

Alum Rock Union School District CA
CIJE: 7 RIE: 19 CAT: 17

Aluminum
CIJE: 6 RIE: 2 CAT: 20

Aluminum Association
CIJE: 1 RIE: 0 CAT: 17

Aluminum Casting
CIJE: 3 RIE: 0 CAT: 20

Aluminum Compounds
CIJE: 3 RIE: 0 CAT: 20

Aluminum Foil
CIJE: 2 RIE: 0 CAT: 20

Aluminum Paragraph (Hunt and O Donnell)
CIJE: 0 RIE: 1 CAT: 21

Alumni Administration
CIJE: 0 RIE: 1 CAT: 16

Alumni Relations
CIJE: 32 RIE: 7 CAT: 16

Alutiiq
CIJE: 0 RIE: 2 CAT: 13

Alvares (Fernao)
CIJE: 1 RIE: 0 CAT: 18

Alverno College WI
CIJE: 16 RIE: 41 CAT: 17

Alvin Ailey American Dance Theater
CIJE: 0 RIE: 1 CAT: 17

Alvin Junior College TX
CIJE: 0 RIE: 2 CAT: 17

Alyawarra
CIJE: 0 RIE: 1 CAT: 13
SN An Arandic language (Australian Aborigine)
UF Iliaura

Alzheimers Disease Knowledge Test
CIJE: 1 RIE: 0 CAT: 21

AM (Modulation)
USE Amplitude Modulation

AMACs
USE Adults Molested as Children

Amador Valley Joint Union School District CA
CIJE: 0 RIE: 1 CAT: 17

Amalgamated Builders and Contractors of Louisiana
CIJE: 1 RIE: 0 CAT: 17

Amalgamated Clothing and Textile Workers Union
CIJE: 3 RIE: 1 CAT: 17

Amalgamated Clothing Workers of America
CIJE: 1 RIE: 1 CAT: 17

Amalgamated Day Care Center IL
CIJE: 0 RIE: 1 CAT: 17

Amana Colonies
CIJE: 0 RIE: 2 CAT: 10

Amarillo College TX
CIJE: 3 RIE: 7 CAT: 17

Amaryllis
CIJE: 3 RIE: 0 CAT: 20

Amateur Athletics
CIJE: 3 RIE: 7 CAT: 16

Amateurism
CIJE: 15 RIE: 3 CAT: 16

Amazon Basin
CIJE: 6 RIE: 4 CAT: 07

Amazonian Languages
CIJE: 0 RIE: 1 CAT: 13

Amberg (George)
CIJE: 0 RIE: 1 CAT: 18

Ambiguity Detection
CIJE: 2 RIE: 1 CAT: 13

Ambivalence (Psychology)
CIJE: 10 RIE: 3 CAT: 11

Amblyopia
CIJE: 6 RIE: 1 CAT: 11

Ambulance Equipment
CIJE: 0 RIE: 4 CAT: 04

Ambulatory Health Care
CIJE: 65 RIE: 8 CAT: 11

Ameliorative Curriculum
CIJE: 0 RIE: 4 CAT: 03

Amen Corner
CIJE: 1 RIE: 0 CAT: 22

Amendments
CIJE: 9 RIE: 24 CAT: 16

Amenorrhea
CIJE: 1 RIE: 0 CAT: 11
UF Athletic Amenorrhea; Secondary Amenorrhea

America (Song)
CIJE: 0 RIE: 0 CAT: 22

America 2000
CIJE: 94 RIE: 116 CAT: 22
SN National strategy, unveiled by President Bush in Apr91, designed to accomplish in 9 years the educational goals first articulated at the governors' Sep89 Education Summit in Charlot-

tesville, VA — see also "National Education Goals 1990" and "Education Summit 1989 (NGA)"
UF America 2000 An Education Strategy

America 2000 An Education Strategy
USE America 2000

America 2000 Library Partnership
CIJE: 0 RIE: 1 CAT: 19

America History and Life
CIJE: 0 RIE: 1 CAT: 04

America the Beautiful
CIJE: 2 RIE: 0 CAT: 22

American Academies
CIJE: 0 RIE: 1 CAT: 05

American Academy of Arts and Sciences
CIJE: 2 RIE: 2 CAT: 17

American Academy of Child Psychiatry
CIJE: 1 RIE: 0 CAT: 17

American Academy of Family Physicians
CIJE: 2 RIE: 0 CAT: 17

American Academy of Orthopaedic Surgeons
CIJE: 1 RIE: 0 CAT: 17

American Academy of Pediatrics
CIJE: 2 RIE: 4 CAT: 17

American Academy of Physical Education
CIJE: 0 RIE: 2 CAT: 17

American Academy of Physician Assistants
CIJE: 0 RIE: 1 CAT: 17

American Achievement Tests
CIJE: 1 RIE: 1 CAT: 21

American Addendum (1980)
CIJE: 0 RIE: 1 CAT: 22

American Advertising Federation
CIJE: 0 RIE: 3 CAT: 17

American Airlines
CIJE: 0 RIE: 1 CAT: 17

American Alliance for Health Phys Ed Rec and Dance
USE AAHPERD

American Alumni Council
CIJE: 1 RIE: 0 CAT: 17

American Arachnid Society
CIJE: 1 RIE: 0 CAT: 17

American Arbitration Association
CIJE: 1 RIE: 1 CAT: 17

American Assembly Collegiate Schools of Business
CIJE: 22 RIE: 5 CAT: 17

American Assn Advancement Science Academy Conf
CIJE: 0 RIE: 2 CAT: 02

American Assn Coll Registrars Admissions Officers
CIJE: 11 RIE: 1 CAT: 17

American Assn College University Business Officers
CIJE: 0 RIE: 1 CAT: 17

American Assn of Colleges of Podiatric Medicine
CIJE: 2 RIE: 0 CAT: 17

American Assn of Univ Professors v Bloomfield Coll
CIJE: 1 RIE: 0 CAT: 14

American Association for Adult Education
CIJE: 5 RIE: 1 CAT: 17

American Association for Advancement of Science
CIJE: 43 RIE: 30 CAT: 17
SN See also "AAAS..." and "American Assn Advancement Science..."

American Association for Agricultural Education
CIJE: 0 RIE: 1 CAT: 17

American Association for Agricultural Engineering
CIJE: 1 RIE: 0 CAT: 17

American Association for Counseling and Develop
CIJE: 0 RIE: 0 CAT: 17

American Association for Gifted Children
CIJE: 2 RIE: 0 CAT: 17

American Association for Higher Education
CIJE: 9 RIE: 6 CAT: 17
SN See also "AAHE..."

American Association Health Phys Educ Recreation
CIJE: 13 RIE: 3 CAT: 17
SN See also "AAHPER..."

American Association Marriage and Family Therapy
CIJE: 3 RIE: 0 CAT: 17

American Association of Bible Colleges
CIJE: 0 RIE: 1 CAT: 17

American Association of Colleges for Teacher Educ
CIJE: 15 RIE: 48 CAT: 17

American Association of Colleges of Nursing
CIJE: 7 RIE: 4 CAT: 17

American Association of Colleges of Pharmacy
CIJE: 39 RIE: 3 CAT: 17

American Association of Community and Junior Colls
CIJE: 38 RIE: 17 CAT: 17
SN Name changed to "American Association of Community Colleges," September 1, 1992

American Association of Community Colleges
CIJE: 0 RIE: 3 CAT: 17
SN See also "AACC..." — formerly "American Association of Community and Junior Colls"

American Association of Dental Schools
CIJE: 73 RIE: 1 CAT: 17

American Association of Engineering Societies
CIJE: 2 RIE: 0 CAT: 17

American Association of Instructors of the Blind
CIJE: 0 RIE: 1 CAT: 17

American Association of Jr Coll CH Comm Services
CIJE: 0 RIE: 1 CAT: 17

American Association of Junior Colleges
CIJE: 1 RIE: 42 CAT: 17

American Association of Law Libraries
CIJE: 5 RIE: 3 CAT: 17

American Association of Medical Record Librarians
CIJE: 0 RIE: 2 CAT: 17

American Association of Physics Teachers
CIJE: 15 RIE: 12 CAT: 17

American Association of Retired Persons
CIJE: 4 RIE: 0 CAT: 17

American Association of School Administrators
CIJE: 24 RIE: 22 CAT: 17

American Association of School Librarians
CIJE: 35 RIE: 3 CAT: 17

American Association of School Personnel Admins
CIJE: 0 RIE: 1 CAT: 17

American Association of Schs and Depts Journalism
CIJE: 1 RIE: 1 CAT: 17

American Association of State Colleges and Univs
CIJE: 10 RIE: 36 CAT: 17
SN See also under "AASCU..."

American Association of Teacher Educators in Agr
CIJE: 0 RIE: 1 CAT: 17

American Association of Teachers of French
CIJE: 0 RIE: 3 CAT: 17

American Association of Teachers of German
CIJE: 5 RIE: 1 CAT: 17

American Association of University Administrators
CIJE: 2 RIE: 2 CAT: 17

American Association of University Professors
CIJE: 203 RIE: 172 CAT: 17
SN See also "AAUP Contracts"

American Association of University Women
CIJE: 12 RIE: 4 CAT: 17

American Association on Mental Deficiency
CIJE: 21 RIE: 4 CAT: 17

American Association Teachers Slavic E Eur Langs
CIJE: 0 RIE: 1 CAT: 17

American Association Teachers Spanish Portuguese
CIJE: 2 RIE: 0 CAT: 17

American Astronomical Society
CIJE: 1 RIE: 0 CAT: 17

American Ballet Theatre
CIJE: 0 RIE: 1 CAT: 17

American Bankers Association
CIJE: 0 RIE: 1 CAT: 17

American Baptist Convention
CIJE: 0 RIE: 1 CAT: 17

American Bar Association
CIJE: 32 RIE: 28 CAT: 17

American Bar Association Canon 35
CIJE: 1 RIE: 3 CAT: 14

American Bar Foundation
CIJE: 1 RIE: 1 CAT: 17

American Bible Society
CIJE: 0 RIE: 0 CAT: 17

American Board of Family Practice In Training Exam
CIJE: 2 RIE: 1 CAT: 21

American Board of Surgery In Training Examination
CIJE: 0 RIE: 1 CAT: 21

American Board of Surgery Qualifying Examination
CIJE: 1 RIE: 1 CAT: 21

American Book Publishers Council
CIJE: 1 RIE: 0 CAT: 17

American Broadcasting Company
CIJE: 8 RIE: 12 CAT: 17

American Brotherhood for the Blind
CIJE: 1 RIE: 0 CAT: 17

American Bureau of Industrial Research
CIJE: 0 RIE: 1 CAT: 17

American Business
CIJE: 0 RIE: 1 CAT: 17

American Business Language Education
CIJE: 0 RIE: 1 CAT: 19

American Camping Association
CIJE: 9 RIE: 16 CAT: 17

American Can Company
CIJE: 1 RIE: 1 CAT: 17

American Cancer Society
CIJE: 3 RIE: 2 CAT: 17

American Career Training Travel School FL
CIJE: 0 RIE: 1 CAT: 17

American Chemical Society
CIJE: 78 RIE: 21 CAT: 17

American Chemical Society Cooperative Examinations
CIJE: 3 RIE: 0 CAT: 21
SN See also under "ACS..."

American Chemical Society Examinations
CIJE: 3 RIE: 0 CAT: 21

American Child Centers Inc
CIJE: 0 RIE: 1 CAT: 17

American Civil Liberties Union
CIJE: 17 RIE: 4 CAT: 17

American Classical League
CIJE: 2 RIE: 2 CAT: 17

American Coalition of Citizens with Disabilities
CIJE: 2 RIE: 0 CAT: 17

American College Health Association
CIJE: 10 RIE: 1 CAT: 17

American College of Cardiology
CIJE: 0 RIE: 1 CAT: 17

American College of Life Underwriters
CIJE: 4 RIE: 2 CAT: 17

American College PA
CIJE: 2 RIE: 1 CAT: 17

American College Personnel Association
CIJE: 11 RIE: 7 CAT: 17

American College Public Relations Association
CIJE: 1 RIE: 0 CAT: 17

American College Survey
CIJE: 0 RIE: 5 CAT: 21

American College Testing Program
CIJE: 86 RIE: 139 CAT: 17
SN See add'l listings under "ACT..." — use "ACT Assessment" for the well-known, standardized college admissions exam

American College Testing Program Alumni Survey
CIJE: 0 RIE: 2 CAT: 21
UF ACT Alumni Survey

American Community Schools (Greece)
CIJE: 1 RIE: 0 CAT: 17

American Convention on Human Rights
CIJE: 1 RIE: 0 CAT: 02

American Correctional Association
CIJE: 0 RIE: 1 CAT: 17

American Council for Construction Education
CIJE: 0 RIE: 1 CAT: 17

American Council of Learned Societies
CIJE: 9 RIE: 2 CAT: 17

American Council of Life Insurance
CIJE: 0 RIE: 1 CAT: 17

American Council of Teachers of Russian
CIJE: 0 RIE: 3 CAT: 17

American Council on Education
CIJE: 90 RIE: 35 CAT: 17
SN See add'l listings under "ACE..."
UF ACE

American Council on Education for Journalism
CIJE: 1 RIE: 0 CAT: 17

American Council on Education Psychological Exam
CIJE: 2 RIE: 1 CAT: 21

American Council on Pharmaceutical Education
CIJE: 6 RIE: 1 CAT: 17

American Council on Rural Special Education
CIJE: 1 RIE: 3 CAT: 17

American Council on the Teaching of Foreign Langs
CIJE: 11 RIE: 20 CAT: 17
SN See add'l listings under "ACTFL..."
UF ACTFL

American Counseling Association
CIJE: 3 RIE: 1 CAT: 17

American Cyanamid Company
CIJE: 1 RIE: 0 CAT: 17

American Debate Association
CIJE: 1 RIE: 2 CAT: 17

American Defense Education Act
CIJE: 1 RIE: 1 CAT: 14

American Dental Association
CIJE: 15 RIE: 5 CAT: 17

American Dental Hygienists Association
CIJE: 1 RIE: 1 CAT: 17

American Diabetes Association
CIJE: 0 RIE: 1 CAT: 17

American Dietetic Association
CIJE: 1 RIE: 1 CAT: 17

American Documentation Institute
CIJE: 4 RIE: 3 CAT: 17

American Dream
CIJE: 22 RIE: 9 CAT: 16

American Economic Association
CIJE: 7 RIE: 1 CAT: 17

American Education Week
CIJE: 1 RIE: 1 CAT: 12

American Educational Research Association
CIJE: 30 RIE: 73 CAT: 17
SN See also "AERA..."

American Educational Research Journal
CIJE: 3 RIE: 1 CAT: 22

American Educational Studies Association
CIJE: 7 RIE: 2 CAT: 17

American Educational Theatre Association
CIJE: 3 RIE: 2 CAT: 17

American Electric Power System
CIJE: 1 RIE: 0 CAT: 17

American Electronics Association
CIJE: 1 RIE: 2 CAT: 17

American Farm Bureau Federation
CIJE: 0 RIE: 1 CAT: 17

American Farm School (Greece)
CIJE: 1 RIE: 0 CAT: 17

American Fed State County Municipal Employees
CIJE: 2 RIE: 1 CAT: 17

American Federation of Labor
CIJE: 12 RIE: 5 CAT: 17

American Federation of Teachers
CIJE: 98 RIE: 133 CAT: 17
SN See also "AFT Contracts"

American Field Service
CIJE: 3 RIE: 6 CAT: 17

American Film Institute
CIJE: 3 RIE: 4 CAT: 17

American Forensic Association
CIJE: 1 RIE: 8 CAT: 17

American Foundation for the Blind
CIJE: 3 RIE: 11 CAT: 17

American Freshmen Survey
CIJE: 0 RIE: 1 CAT: 21

American Friends Service Committee
CIJE: 2 RIE: 4 CAT: 17

American Frontier Myth
CIJE: 2 RIE: 0 CAT: 16

American Geological Institute
CIJE: 11 RIE: 8 CAT: 17

American Geophysical Institute
CIJE: 1 RIE: 0 CAT: 17

American Geophysical Union
CIJE: 0 RIE: 1 CAT: 17

American Graduate School International Management
CIJE: 1 RIE: 2 CAT: 17

American Guidance Service
CIJE: 0 RIE: 1 CAT: 17

American Heart Association
CIJE: 7 RIE: 1 CAT: 17

American Heritage Dictionary
CIJE: 6 RIE: 0 CAT: 22

American Historical Association
CIJE: 15 RIE: 7 CAT: 17

American History Textbooks Project
CIJE: 0 RIE: 1 CAT: 19

American Home Economics Association
CIJE: 14 RIE: 4 CAT: 17

American Home Economics Association Convention
CIJE: 3 RIE: 0 CAT: 02

American Home Products Corporation
CIJE: 0 RIE: 1 CAT: 17

American Hospital Association
CIJE: 6 RIE: 0 CAT: 17

American Ind
CIJE: 1 RIE: 0 CAT: 13

American Independent Party
CIJE: 0 RIE: 1 CAT: 17

American Indian Achievement
CIJE: 0 RIE: 1 CAT: 16

American Indian Administrator Training Programs
CIJE: 0 RIE: 1 CAT: 19

American Indian Archaeology Program
CIJE: 0 RIE: 1 CAT: 19

American Indian Bilingual Education Center NM
CIJE: 0 RIE: 1 CAT: 17

American Indian Contributions
CIJE: 5 RIE: 9 CAT: 16

American Indian Day
CIJE: 0 RIE: 2 CAT: 12

American Indian Employment Center MN
CIJE: 0 RIE: 1 CAT: 17

American Indian Higher Education Consortium
CIJE: 2 RIE: 4 CAT: 17

American Indian Language Development Institute
CIJE: 0 RIE: 2 CAT: 02

American Indian Law Program
CIJE: 1 RIE: 0 CAT: 19

American Indian Law Students Association
CIJE: 1 RIE: 0 CAT: 17

American Indian Management Institute
CIJE: 1 RIE: 0 CAT: 02

American Indian Movement
CIJE: 11 RIE: 4 CAT: 12

American Indian Philosophy
CIJE: 3 RIE: 0 CAT: 16

American Indian Policy Review Commission
CIJE: 8 RIE: 15 CAT: 17

American Indian Policy Statement 1983
CIJE: 0 RIE: 1 CAT: 14

American Indian Program (Harvard)
CIJE: 0 RIE: 1 CAT: 19

American Indian Religious Freedom Act 1978
CIJE: 2 RIE: 2 CAT: 14

American Indian Science and Engineering Society
CIJE: 4 RIE: 2 CAT: 17

American Indian Sign
CIJE: 2 RIE: 1 CAT: 13

American Indian Students
CIJE: 3 RIE: 10 CAT: 10

American Indian Task Forces
CIJE: 0 RIE: 5 CAT: 10

American Indian Teacher Training Program
CIJE: 0 RIE: 2 CAT: 19

American Indians Into Medicine Program
CIJE: 0 RIE: 1 CAT: 19

American Industrial Arts
CIJE: 0 RIE: 1 CAT: 03

American Industrial Arts Association
CIJE: 9 RIE: 10 CAT: 17

American Industrial Arts Student Association
CIJE: 2 RIE: 7 CAT: 17
SN Became "Technology Student Association," June 1988

American Industry Project
CIJE: 3 RIE: 6 CAT: 19

American Institute for Foreign Study
CIJE: 1 RIE: 0 CAT: 17

American Institute for Research
CIJE: 0 RIE: 2 CAT: 17

American Institute of Aeronautics and Astronautics
CIJE: 0 RIE: 4 CAT: 17

American Institute of Architects
CIJE: 9 RIE: 9 CAT: 17

American Institute of Biological Sciences
CIJE: 17 RIE: 6 CAT: 17

American Institute of Cooperation
CIJE: 0 RIE: 1 CAT: 17

American Institute of Instruction
CIJE: 0 RIE: 2 CAT: 17

American Institute of Musical Studies
CIJE: 1 RIE: 1 CAT: 17

American Institute of Physics
CIJE: 13 RIE: 32 CAT: 17

American Institute of Sacred Literature
CIJE: 0 RIE: 1 CAT: 17

American Institutes for Research
CIJE: 11 RIE: 16 CAT: 17

American International School (India)
CIJE: 1 RIE: 0 CAT: 17

American Iron and Steel Institute
CIJE: 0 RIE: 1 CAT: 17

American Issues Forum
CIJE: 1 RIE: 31 CAT: 19

American Jeremiads
CIJE: 0 RIE: 1 CAT: 16
UF Puritan Jeremiads

American Jewish Committee
CIJE: 0 RIE: 4 CAT: 17

American Jewish Congress
CIJE: 0 RIE: 2 CAT: 17

American Journal of Medicine
CIJE: 0 RIE: 1 CAT: 22

American Journal of Mental Deficiency
CIJE: 1 RIE: 0 CAT: 22

American Language Institute
CIJE: 0 RIE: 3 CAT: 17

American Legion
CIJE: 1 RIE: 4 CAT: 17

American Library (France)
CIJE: 2 RIE: 0 CAT: 17

American Library Association
CIJE: 371 RIE: 66 CAT: 17

American Library Association Convention
CIJE: 15 RIE: 27 CAT: 02

American Library Association Filing Rules
CIJE: 3 RIE: 1 CAT: 16

American Library Trustee Association
CIJE: 2 RIE: 1 CAT: 17

American Management Association
CIJE: 1 RIE: 5 CAT: 17

American Marketing Association
CIJE: 0 RIE: 1 CAT: 17

American Mathematical Society
CIJE: 1 RIE: 0 CAT: 17

American Medical Association
CIJE: 17 RIE: 16 CAT: 17

American Medical College Application Service
CIJE: 4 RIE: 0 CAT: 17

American Memory Project (Library of Congress)
CIJE: 1 RIE: 3 CAT: 19

American Missionary Association
CIJE: 3 RIE: 1 CAT: 17

American Motorcyclist Association
CIJE: 0 RIE: 1 CAT: 17

American Museum of Natural History NY
CIJE: 2 RIE: 1 CAT: 17

American Musicological Society
CIJE: 0 RIE: 1 CAT: 17

American Myths
CIJE: 1 RIE: 1 CAT: 16
SN See also "American Frontier Myth"

American National Metric Council
CIJE: 1 RIE: 2 CAT: 17

American National Red Cross
USE Red Cross

American National Standards Institute
CIJE: 25 RIE: 5 CAT: 17

American Newspaper Publishers Association
CIJE: 2 RIE: 3 CAT: 17

American Nicaraguan School
CIJE: 1 RIE: 0 CAT: 17

American Nuclear Society
CIJE: 1 RIE: 1 CAT: 17

American Nurses Association
CIJE: 10 RIE: 11 CAT: 17

American Occupational Therapy Association
CIJE: 3 RIE: 4 CAT: 17

American Oil Company
CIJE: 1 RIE: 0 CAT: 17

American Open University
CIJE: 0 RIE: 1 CAT: 17

American Open University NE
CIJE: 0 RIE: 1 CAT: 17

American Optical Company Sight Screener
CIJE: 0 RIE: 1 CAT: 04

American Optical Kindergarten Chart
CIJE: 0 RIE: 1 CAT: 04

American Optometric Association
CIJE: 7 RIE: 1 CAT: 17

American Orthopsychiatric Association
CIJE: 3 RIE: 1 CAT: 17

American Outdoor Education Project
CIJE: 0 RIE: 1 CAT: 19

American Parliamentary Debate Association
CIJE: 0 RIE: 1 CAT: 17

American Personnel and Guidance Association
CIJE: 13 RIE: 11 CAT: 17

American Personnel Guidance Assn Impact Workshop
CIJE: 0 RIE: 1 CAT: 02

American Petroleum Institute
CIJE: 2 RIE: 0 CAT: 17

American Physical Society
CIJE: 6 RIE: 1 CAT: 17

American Physical Therapy Association
CIJE: 0 RIE: 3 CAT: 17

American Physiological Society
CIJE: 4 RIE: 0 CAT: 17

American Political Behavior
CIJE: 2 RIE: 3 CAT: 03

American Political Science Association
CIJE: 1 RIE: 3 CAT: 17

American Political Science Review
CIJE: 0 RIE: 1 CAT: 22

American Preceptor
CIJE: 1 RIE: 0 CAT: 13

American Printing House for the Blind
CIJE: 2 RIE: 2 CAT: 17

American Problems
CIJE: 0 RIE: 1 CAT: 03

American Production and Inventory Control Society
CIJE: 0 RIE: 2 CAT: 17

American Psychiatric Association
CIJE: 3 RIE: 1 CAT: 17

American Psychological Association
CIJE: 100 RIE: 35 CAT: 17

American Public Health Association
CIJE: 1 RIE: 1 CAT: 17

American Reading Forum
CIJE: 0 RIE: 1 CAT: 17

American Red Cross
USE Red Cross

American Registry of Radiologic Technologists
CIJE: 0 RIE: 1 CAT: 17

American Rehabilitation Counseling Association
CIJE: 4 RIE: 1 CAT: 17

American Republic Insurance Company
CIJE: 1 RIE: 0 CAT: 17

American Revolution Bicentennial Administration
CIJE: 1 RIE: 1 CAT: 17

American Revolution Bicentennial Commission
CIJE: 1 RIE: 0 CAT: 17

American River College CA
CIJE: 3 RIE: 7 CAT: 17

American Samoa
CIJE: 12 RIE: 47 CAT: 07

American Satellite Corporation
CIJE: 0 RIE: 1 CAT: 17

American School Achievement Tests
CIJE: 0 RIE: 3 CAT: 21

American School Counselor Association
CIJE: 15 RIE: 4 CAT: 17

American School Food Service Association
CIJE: 3 RIE: 0 CAT: 17

American School for the Deaf CT
CIJE: 2 RIE: 1 CAT: 17

American School Health Association
CIJE: 10 RIE: 3 CAT: 17

American School Intelligence Test
CIJE: 0 RIE: 1 CAT: 21

American Society for Aerospace Education
CIJE: 1 RIE: 0 CAT: 17

American Society for Ecological Eaucation
CIJE: 1 RIE: 0 CAT: 17

American Society for Engineering Education
CIJE: 34 RIE: 4 CAT: 17

American Society for Information Science
CIJE: 27 RIE: 5 CAT: 17

American Society for Medical Technology
CIJE: 0 RIE: 2 CAT: 17

American Society for Oceanography
CIJE: 0 RIE: 1 CAT: 17

American Society for Testing and Materials
CIJE: 2 RIE: 1 CAT: 17

American Society for Training and Development
CIJE: 37 RIE: 5 CAT: 17

American Society of Allied Health Professions
CIJE: 3 RIE: 1 CAT: 17

American Society of Clinical Pathologists
CIJE: 0 RIE: 3 CAT: 17

American Society of Journalism Administrators
CIJE: 0 RIE: 2 CAT: 17

American Society of Lubrication Engineers
CIJE: 0 RIE: 1 CAT: 17

American Society of Magazine Editors
CIJE: 0 RIE: 1 CAT: 17

American Society of Mechanical Engineers
CIJE: 0 RIE: 1 CAT: 17

American Society of Medical Technologists
CIJE: 0 RIE: 1 CAT: 17

American Society of Newspaper Editors
CIJE: 0 RIE: 4 CAT: 17

American Society of Training Directors
CIJE: 0 RIE: 1 CAT: 17

American Society of Zoologists
CIJE: 1 RIE: 0 CAT: 17

American Sociological Association
CIJE: 20 RIE: 3 CAT: 17

American Speech and Hearing Association
CIJE: 2 RIE: 1 CAT: 17

American Speech Language Hearing Association
CIJE: 5 RIE: 1 CAT: 17

American Sponsored Overseas Schools
USE Dependents Schools

American Standard Code Information Interchange
CIJE: 4 RIE: 3 CAT: 17

American Standards Association
CIJE: 0 RIE: 1 CAT: 17

American Statistical Association
CIJE: 2 RIE: 2 CAT: 17

American Student Media Association
CIJE: 0 RIE: 1 CAT: 17

American Studies Association
CIJE: 3 RIE: 1 CAT: 17

American Technical Education Association
CIJE: 0 RIE: 1 CAT: 17

American Telephone and Telegraph Company
CIJE: 45 RIE: 20 CAT: 17
SN See add'l listings under "A T and T..."
UF A T and T

American Telephone and Telegraph Long Lines
CIJE: 0 RIE: 1 CAT: 04

American Textbook Publishers Institute
CIJE: 0 RIE: 1 CAT: 17

American Theatre Association
CIJE: 7 RIE: 1 CAT: 17

American Theological Library Association
CIJE: 2 RIE: 1 CAT: 17

American Tract Society
CIJE: 0 RIE: 1 CAT: 17

American Translators Association
CIJE: 1 RIE: 0 CAT: 17

American University DC
CIJE: 18 RIE: 10 CAT: 17

American University in Cairo (Egypt)
CIJE: 2 RIE: 4 CAT: 17

American University of Beirut (Lebanon)
CIJE: 7 RIE: 1 CAT: 17

American Vacuum Society
CIJE: 1 RIE: 0 CAT: 17

American Vocational Association
CIJE: 68 RIE: 32 CAT: 17

American Vocational Association Convention
CIJE: 26 RIE: 2 CAT: 02

American Way (Magazine)
CIJE: 0 RIE: 1 CAT: 22

American Women in Radio and Television
CIJE: 0 RIE: 2 CAT: 17

American Youth Foundation
CIJE: 1 RIE: 0 CAT: 17

American Youth Hostels Inc
CIJE: 0 RIE: 2 CAT: 17

Americanism
CIJE: 3 RIE: 2 CAT: 16

Americanisms
CIJE: 0 RIE: 1 CAT: 13

Americanization
CIJE: 8 RIE: 3 CAT: 16

Americanization Classes
CIJE: 0 RIE: 1 CAT: 03

Americans (United States)
CIJE: 9 RIE: 14 CAT: 08

Americans for Indian Opportunity
CIJE: 1 RIE: 3 CAT: 17

Americans with Disabilities Act 1990
CIJE: 110 RIE: 81 CAT: 14
UF Public Law 101 336

Americas Choice High Skills or Low Wages
CIJE: 0 RIE: 1 CAT: 22

Americas Competitive Challenge
CIJE: 0 RIE: 1 CAT: 22

Americas Education Goals 1990
USE National Education Goals 1990

Americas Town Meeting of the Air
CIJE: 0 RIE: 1 CAT: 19

Americas Unidas
CIJE: 0 RIE: 1 CAT: 17

Amerika (Miniseries)
CIJE: 1 RIE: 1 CAT: 22

Amerindians
CIJE: 0 RIE: 2 CAT: 08

Ameritech
CIJE: 0 RIE: 1 CAT: 17

Ames Community School District IA
CIJE: 1 RIE: 1 CAT: 17

Ames Philosophical Belief Inventory
CIJE: 0 RIE: 1 CAT: 21

Ames Research Center
CIJE: 0 RIE: 2 CAT: 17

Ames SDI KWOK Index
CIJE: 1 RIE: 0 CAT: 22

Ames Static Trapezoidal Window Display
CIJE: 1 RIE: 0 CAT: 21

Amherst College MA
CIJE: 14 RIE: 7 CAT: 17

Amherst Project
CIJE: 0 RIE: 4 CAT: 19

Amiability Tilt
CIJE: 0 RIE: 0 CAT: 15

Amidon Flanders Interaction Scale
CIJE: 1 RIE: 2 CAT: 21

Amidon School DC
CIJE: 1 RIE: 1 CAT: 17

Amiga
CIJE: 1 RIE: 0 CAT: 04
UF Commodore Amiga

Amigos Program MA
CIJE: 0 RIE: 1 CAT: 19

Amino Acids
CIJE: 9 RIE: 0 CAT: 20

Amis
CIJE: 0 RIE: 1 CAT: 13

Amish (Old Order)
CIJE: 8 RIE: 14 CAT: 08
UF Old Order Amish

Amitosis
CIJE: 1 RIE: 0 CAT: 20

Amity School District 4J OR
CIJE: 0 RIE: 5 CAT: 17

Amityville Public Schools NY
CIJE: 0 RIE: 2 CAT: 17

AML Microwave Link
CIJE: 0 RIE: 1 CAT: 04

Ammeters
CIJE: 2 RIE: 0 CAT: 04

Ammonia
CIJE: 4 RIE: 1 CAT: 20

Ammonium Chloride
CIJE: 2 RIE: 0 CAT: 20

Ammunition
CIJE: 0 RIE: 2 CAT: 04

Amnesia
CIJE: 15 RIE: 0 CAT: 11

Amnesty
CIJE: 8 RIE: 12 CAT: 16

Amnesty Education
CIJE: 0 RIE: 1 CAT: 03

Amnesty International
CIJE: 12 RIE: 2 CAT: 17

Amniocentesis
CIJE: 3 RIE: 1 CAT: 11

Amount of Invested Mental Effort
CIJE: 2 RIE: 2 CAT: 21
UF AIME Variable; Amount of Mental Effort Investment

Amount of Mental Effort Investment
USE Amount of Invested Mental Effort

Amoy
CIJE: 2 RIE: 1 CAT: 13

Ampere (Andre)
CIJE: 1 RIE: 0 CAT: 18

Amperostats
CIJE: 1 RIE: 0 CAT: 04

Ampex Computer Products
CIJE: 1 RIE: 0 CAT: 04

Ampex Video Institute CA
CIJE: 1 RIE: 0 CAT: 17

Ampex Videotape Recorders
CIJE: 0 RIE: 4 CAT: 04

Amphetamine
CIJE: 1 RIE: 0 CAT: 11

Amphetamines
CIJE: 10 RIE: 2 CAT: 11

Amphibians
CIJE: 11 RIE: 3 CAT: 20

Amphigory
CIJE: 0 RIE: 1 CAT: 13

Amplified Telephones
CIJE: 0 RIE: 1 CAT: 04

Amplifiers
CIJE: 6 RIE: 4 CAT: 04

Amplitude Modulation
CIJE: 0 RIE: 3 CAT: 20
UF AM (Modulation)

Amsterdam News NY
CIJE: 2 RIE: 1 CAT: 17

Amuesha (People)
CIJE: 0 RIE: 1 CAT: 08

Amumara Girls Secondary School (Nigeria)
CIJE: 1 RIE: 0 CAT: 17

Amusement Parks
CIJE: 4 RIE: 1 CAT: 05

Amuzgo
CIJE: 0 RIE: 1 CAT: 13
SN An Oto-Manguean language of Mexico

Amylase
CIJE: 1 RIE: 0 CAT: 11

Anabolic Steroids
USE Steroids

Anacostia Community School Project
CIJE: 0 RIE: 3 CAT: 19

Anadolu University (Turkey)
CIJE: 2 RIE: 4 CAT: 17

Anaerobic Digestion
CIJE: 0 RIE: 5 CAT: 11

Anaerobic Power
CIJE: 1 RIE: 2 CAT: 11

Anaglyphs
CIJE: 0 RIE: 1 CAT: 04

Anagrams
CIJE: 11 RIE: 8 CAT: 13

Analog Digital Interfaces
CIJE: 5 RIE: 1 CAT: 04
UF Digital Analog Interfaces

Analog Drawing
CIJE: 0 RIE: 1 CAT: 15
SN Symbolic drawing expressing one's emotions, ideas, and feelings, often used to identify and help solve problems

Analog Television
USE Analog Transmission Systems

Analog Transmission Systems
CIJE: 3 RIE: 3 CAT: 15
UF Analog Television

Analogical Reasoning
CIJE: 55 RIE: 40 CAT: 15
SN See also "Figural Analogies"

Analogies
CIJE: 96 RIE: 68 CAT: 13

Analogue Models
CIJE: 4 RIE: 5 CAT: 15

Analogues
CIJE: 11 RIE: 1 CAT: 15

Analoguing
CIJE: 0 RIE: 1 CAT: 15

Analogy
CIJE: 92 RIE: 32 CAT: 13

Analogy Test Items
CIJE: 11 RIE: 10 CAT: 21

Analphabetic Transcription
CIJE: 0 RIE: 1 CAT: 13

Analysis of Concepts by Data Processing
CIJE: 0 RIE: 1 CAT: 15

Analysis of Patterns in Time
CIJE: 1 RIE: 0 CAT: 21
UF Nonmetric Temporal Path Analysis

Analytic Ability
CIJE: 5 RIE: 5 CAT: 11

Analytic Approach
CIJE: 21 RIE: 10 CAT: 15

Analytic Interactive Style
CIJE: 0 RIE: 1 CAT: 11

Analytic Philosophy
CIJE: 3 RIE: 1 CAT: 03

Analytic Rating Procedures
CIJE: 0 RIE: 1 CAT: 21

Analytic Rotational Methods
CIJE: 1 RIE: 0 CAT: 15

Analytic Scoring
CIJE: 7 RIE: 8 CAT: 21

Analytic Teaching
CIJE: 1 RIE: 1 CAT: 15

Analytical Balances
CIJE: 2 RIE: 1 CAT: 04

Analytical Chemistry
CIJE: 35 RIE: 2 CAT: 20

Analytical Electrochemistry
CIJE: 1 RIE: 0 CAT: 03

Analytical Ethics
CIJE: 0 RIE: 1 CAT: 03

Analytical Methods
CIJE: 14 RIE: 21 CAT: 15

Analytical Model Technique
CIJE: 0 RIE: 2 CAT: 15

Analytical Objectivity
CIJE: 1 RIE: 0 CAT: 15

Analytical Philosophy of Education
CIJE: 0 RIE: 1 CAT: 15

Analytical Reading Inventory
CIJE: 5 RIE: 1 CAT: 21

Analytical Reasoning Test (Johnson O Connor)
CIJE: 0 RIE: 1 CAT: 21

Analytical Scoring
CIJE: 3 RIE: 7 CAT: 21

Analytical Study of Teaching
CIJE: 1 RIE: 0 CAT: 19

Analytical Tests
CIJE: 2 RIE: 7 CAT: 21

Analytical Writing
CIJE: 3 RIE: 3 CAT: 13

Anansi the Spider
CIJE: 1 RIE: 0 CAT: 22

Anaphora
CIJE: 56 RIE: 44 CAT: 13

Anaphylactic Shock
CIJE: 1 RIE: 2 CAT: 11

Anarchism
CIJE: 1 RIE: 3 CAT: 15

Anarchy
CIJE: 4 RIE: 2 CAT: 14

Anasazi (Anthropological Label)
CIJE: 3 RIE: 5 CAT: 08

Anatolia College (Greece)
CIJE: 1 RIE: 0 CAT: 17

Anatomical Dolls
USE Anatomically Correct Dolls

Anatomically Correct Dolls
CIJE: 9 RIE: 3 CAT: 16
UF Anatomical Dolls; Anatomically Detailed Dolls

Anatomically Detailed Dolls
USE Anatomically Correct Dolls

Anatone School District WA
CIJE: 1 RIE: 0 CAT: 17

Ancestor Worship
CIJE: 1 RIE: 2 CAT: 16

Ancestral Language
USE Heritage Language

Anchor Effects
CIJE: 4 RIE: 0 CAT: 21

Anchor Test Study
CIJE: 6 RIE: 54 CAT: 19

Anchor Tests
CIJE: 10 RIE: 9 CAT: 21

Anchorage Community College AK
CIJE: 2 RIE: 1 CAT: 17

Anchorage School District AK
CIJE: 2 RIE: 7 CAT: 17

Anchored Assessment
CIJE: 0 RIE: 1 CAT: 15

Anchored Instruction
CIJE: 5 RIE: 9 CAT: 15

Anchoring Devices
CIJE: 2 RIE: 1 CAT: 04

ANCILLES Estimation Procedures
CIJE: 1 RIE: 3 CAT: 21

Ancona Montessori School IL
CIJE: 0 RIE: 1 CAT: 17

Andean Countries
CIJE: 1 RIE: 4 CAT: 07

Andean Languages
CIJE: 0 RIE: 2 CAT: 13

Andean Oral History Workshop
CIJE: 0 RIE: 1 CAT: 19

Andersen (Hans Christian)
CIJE: 2 RIE: 2 CAT: 18

Andersen Newman Model of Utilization
CIJE: 0 RIE: 3 CAT: 15

Anderson (John R)
CIJE: 1 RIE: 1 CAT: 18
SN Cognitive Theorist

Anderson (John)
CIJE: 5 RIE: 1 CAT: 18
SN "John B" — American politician & 1980 indep. pres. candidate

Anderson (Sherwood)
CIJE: 1 RIE: 0 CAT: 18

Anderson Adult Education Center SC
CIJE: 0 RIE: 1 CAT: 17

Anderson County School District SC
CIJE: 0 RIE: 0 CAT: 17

Anderson County Schools TN
CIJE: 1 RIE: 0 CAT: 17

Anderson Likeableness Scale
CIJE: 1 RIE: 0 CAT: 21

Anderson Mental Health Center SC
CIJE: 0 RIE: 1 CAT: 17

Anderson Public Library IN
CIJE: 0 RIE: 1 CAT: 17

Anderson School CT
CIJE: 1 RIE: 0 CAT: 17

Andes
CIJE: 1 RIE: 1 CAT: 07

Andhra Pradesh Open University (India)
CIJE: 1 RIE: 1 CAT: 17

Andioc (Rene)
CIJE: 1 RIE: 0 CAT: 18

Andover Public Schools MA
CIJE: 0 RIE: 2 CAT: 17

Andover West Junior High School MA
CIJE: 0 RIE: 1 CAT: 17

Andre (Thomas)
CIJE: 0 RIE: 1 CAT: 18

Andres Bello Agreement
CIJE: 0 RIE: 2 CAT: 16

Andrew Mellon Foundation
CIJE: 1 RIE: 0 CAT: 17

Andrew W Mellon Foundation
CIJE: 4 RIE: 2 CAT: 17

Andrews Pregibon Statistic
CIJE: 0 RIE: 2 CAT: 21

Andrews University MI
CIJE: 1 RIE: 8 CAT: 17

Andric (Ivo)
CIJE: 1 RIE: 0 CAT: 18

Androgenic Hormones
CIJE: 1 RIE: 0 CAT: 11

Andromeda Strain
CIJE: 0 RIE: 1 CAT: 22

Andrus Gerontology Center CA
CIJE: 0 RIE: 1 CAT: 17

Anecdotal Analysis
CIJE: 5 RIE: 0 CAT: 15

Anecdotal Discipline
CIJE: 1 RIE: 0 CAT: 15

Anecdotal Processing Promote Learning Experience
USE APPLE Observation System

Anecdotal Records
CIJE: 6 RIE: 8 CAT: 16

Anecdotes
CIJE: 14 RIE: 3 CAT: 16

Anemometers
CIJE: 1 RIE: 2 CAT: 04

Anencephaly
CIJE: 2 RIE: 0 CAT: 11

Angaataha
CIJE: 2 RIE: 0 CAT: 13

Angel Valente (Jose)
CIJE: 1 RIE: 0 CAT: 18

Angeles National Forest
CIJE: 1 RIE: 0 CAT: 07

Angell (James Burrill)
CIJE: 0 RIE: 1 CAT: 18

Angle of Effectiveness
CIJE: 1 RIE: 0 CAT: 21

Anglican Church
CIJE: 3 RIE: 3 CAT: 17

Anglicisms
CIJE: 6 RIE: 3 CAT: 13

Anglin Grid
CIJE: 1 RIE: 0 CAT: 15

Anglo American Cataloging Rules
CIJE: 124 RIE: 40 CAT: 22

Anglo American Corporation (Rhodesia)
CIJE: 0 RIE: 1 CAT: 17

Anglo American Historians Conference
CIJE: 1 RIE: 0 CAT: 02

Anglo American Relations
CIJE: 1 RIE: 0 CAT: 03

Anglo Saxons
CIJE: 5 RIE: 2 CAT: 08

Angoff Methods
CIJE: 27 RIE: 47 CAT: 15

Angola
CIJE: 3 RIE: 2 CAT: 07

Angular Displacement
CIJE: 2 RIE: 0 CAT: 20

Angular Momentum
CIJE: 6 RIE: 0 CAT: 20

Angular Velocity
CIJE: 2 RIE: 0 CAT: 20

Angus Journal
CIJE: 1 RIE: 1 CAT: 22

Anheuser Busch Company
CIJE: 0 RIE: 1 CAT: 17

Anhydrous Ammonia
CIJE: 0 RIE: 1 CAT: 20

Anik B Interactive Instructional TV Project
CIJE: 0 RIE: 3 CAT: 19

Anik Satellites
CIJE: 0 RIE: 1 CAT: 20

Anilines
CIJE: 1 RIE: 0 CAT: 20

Animacy
CIJE: 3 RIE: 2 CAT: 13

Animacy Inanimacy
CIJE: 1 RIE: 0 CAT: 13

Animadversion Error
CIJE: 1 RIE: 0 CAT: 15

Animal Baiting
CIJE: 1 RIE: 0 CAT: 20

Animal Communication
CIJE: 4 RIE: 6 CAT: 20

Animal Defenses
CIJE: 0 RIE: 0 CAT: 20

Animal Farm
CIJE: 5 RIE: 1 CAT: 22

Animal Operant Laboratories
CIJE: 0 RIE: 1 CAT: 05

Animal Reproduction
CIJE: 0 RIE: 0 CAT: 20

Animal Stalls Task
CIJE: 0 RIE: 1 CAT: 21

Animal Tracks
CIJE: 3 RIE: 6 CAT: 20

Animal Traction
CIJE: 0 RIE: 1 CAT: 20

Animal Traps
CIJE: 0 RIE: 1 CAT: 04
UF Traps (Animals)

Animal Welfare
CIJE: 28 RIE: 10 CAT: 20

Animal Welfare Institute
CIJE: 1 RIE: 0 CAT: 17

Animals in the Classroom Project
CIJE: 0 RIE: 1 CAT: 19

Animism
CIJE: 14 RIE: 5 CAT: 15

Anindilyakwa
CIJE: 0 RIE: 2 CAT: 13
SN An Australian Aboriginal language

Ankle Strength
CIJE: 1 RIE: 0 CAT: 11

Ankyloglossia
CIJE: 0 RIE: 1 CAT: 11

Ann Arbor Decision
CIJE: 3 RIE: 2 CAT: 14

Ann Arbor Public Schools MI
CIJE: 1 RIE: 5 CAT: 17

Ann Landers
USE Landers (Ann)

Anna Maria College MA
CIJE: 0 RIE: 1 CAT: 17

Annamese
CIJE: 0 RIE: 1 CAT: 13

Annan Committee (Great Britain)
CIJE: 1 RIE: 0 CAT: 17

Anne Arundel Community College MD
CIJE: 1 RIE: 2 CAT: 17

Anne Arundel County Community Action Agency MD
CIJE: 1 RIE: 0 CAT: 17

Anne Arundel County Public Schools MD
CIJE: 3 RIE: 8 CAT: 17

Anne Sullivan Macy Service Deaf Blind Persons NY
CIJE: 0 RIE: 1 CAT: 17

Annehurst Curriculum Classification System
CIJE: 6 RIE: 8 CAT: 04

Annehurst School OH
CIJE: 0 RIE: 1 CAT: 17

Annenberg CPB Project
CIJE: 4 RIE: 6 CAT: 19
SN Annenberg/Corporation for Public Broadcasting Project

Annenberg School of Communications DC
CIJE: 0 RIE: 1 CAT: 17

Annetts Handedness Questionnaire
CIJE: 1 RIE: 0 CAT: 21

Annie E Casey Foundation
CIJE: 0 RIE: 2 CAT: 17

Announcers
CIJE: 1 RIE: 1 CAT: 09
SN Use a more specific term if possible, e.g., "Broadcast Announcers," "Disk Jockeys," "Television Announcers"

Annual Creative Problem Solving Institute
CIJE: 1 RIE: 0 CAT: 17

Annual Funds
CIJE: 0 RIE: 2 CAT: 16

Annual High School Mathematics Examinations
CIJE: 1 RIE: 1 CAT: 21

Annual Housing Survey
CIJE: 2 RIE: 2 CAT: 16

Annual Percentage Rate
CIJE: 1 RIE: 1 CAT: 20

Annual Reading Institute
CIJE: 0 RIE: 6 CAT: 17

Annual Review Information Science and Technology
CIJE: 2 RIE: 2 CAT: 22

Annual Self Inventory for Science Teachers
CIJE: 0 RIE: 1 CAT: 21

Annual Worker Plan
CIJE: 2 RIE: 4 CAT: 16

Annuities
CIJE: 27 RIE: 9 CAT: 16

Anoka Hennepin School District MN
CIJE: 1 RIE: 2 CAT: 17

Anomia
CIJE: 10 RIE: 0 CAT: 11

Anomie Theory
CIJE: 10 RIE: 5 CAT: 15

Anonymity
CIJE: 11 RIE: 3 CAT: 16

Anonymity of Respondents
CIJE: 10 RIE: 4 CAT: 21

Anonymous Attribution
CIJE: 0 RIE: 2 CAT: 11

Anonymous Audience Response System
CIJE: 0 RIE: 1 CAT: 04

Anonymous Feedback System
CIJE: 2 RIE: 1 CAT: 15

Anorexia
CIJE: 0 RIE: 1 CAT: 11

Anouilh (Jean)
CIJE: 0 RIE: 2 CAT: 18

Anova F Test
CIJE: 4 RIE: 1 CAT: 21

Anoxia
USE Hypoxia

ANPA Foundation Newspaper Test
CIJE: 0 RIE: 2 CAT: 21

ANSER System
CIJE: 1 RIE: 0 CAT: 21

Answer Banks
CIJE: 0 RIE: 2 CAT: 21

Answer Changing (Tests)
CIJE: 14 RIE: 10 CAT: 21

Answer Constructs
CIJE: 0 RIE: 2 CAT: 21

Answer Guard Feedback Unit
CIJE: 0 RIE: 1 CAT: 21

Answer Until Correct
CIJE: 8 RIE: 10 CAT: 21

Answering Machines
CIJE: 2 RIE: 0 CAT: 04
UF Telephone Answering and Recording Devices

Answering Services
CIJE: 1 RIE: 4 CAT: 05
UF Telephone Answering Services

Antacids
CIJE: 1 RIE: 0 CAT: 11

Antagonistic Cooperation
CIJE: 1 RIE: 0 CAT: 15

Antarctic
CIJE: 2 RIE: 1 CAT: 07

Antarctica
CIJE: 12 RIE: 11 CAT: 07

Antarctica (Lake Bonney)
CIJE: 1 RIE: 0 CAT: 07

Antecedent Attributions Test
CIJE: 0 RIE: 1 CAT: 21

Antecedents
CIJE: 23 RIE: 7 CAT: 13

Antelope Valley College CA
CIJE: 0 RIE: 2 CAT: 17

Antelope Valley High School CA
CIJE: 0 RIE: 1 CAT: 17

Antelope Valley Union High School District CA
CIJE: 0 RIE: 2 CAT: 17

Antennas
CIJE: 1 RIE: 3 CAT: 04

Anthony (Susan B)
CIJE: 3 RIE: 2 CAT: 18

Anthony (W S)
CIJE: 1 RIE: 0 CAT: 18

Anthony Gadsen School District NM
CIJE: 0 RIE: 1 CAT: 17

Anthrogogy
CIJE: 0 RIE: 1 CAT: 15
SN A term for the generic set of principles that guide lifelong learning

Anthropocentrism
CIJE: 2 RIE: 2 CAT: 11

Anthropology Curriculum Project
CIJE: 2 RIE: 41 CAT: 19

Anthropology Curriculum Study Project
CIJE: 2 RIE: 14 CAT: 19

Anthropomaximology
CIJE: 1 RIE: 0 CAT: 15

Anthropometric Tests
CIJE: 3 RIE: 5 CAT: 21

Anthropometry
CIJE: 7 RIE: 5 CAT: 11

Anthropomorphism
CIJE: 15 RIE: 3 CAT: 16

Anti Americanism
CIJE: 0 RIE: 1 CAT: 16

Anti Defamation League
CIJE: 6 RIE: 2 CAT: 17

Anti Drug Abuse Act 1988
CIJE: 0 RIE: 3 CAT: 14
UF Drug Free Schools and Communities Act 1988; Public Law 100 694

Anti Federal Party
USE Antifederalists

Anti Slavery Society
CIJE: 0 RIE: 1 CAT: 17

Anti White Scale
CIJE: 0 RIE: 1 CAT: 21

Antiaircraft Weapons
CIJE: 0 RIE: 1 CAT: 04

Antibiotics
CIJE: 8 RIE: 1 CAT: 20

Antibodies
CIJE: 8 RIE: 0 CAT: 11

Antibody Responses
CIJE: 3 RIE: 0 CAT: 11

Anticipated Task Orientation Scale
CIJE: 1 RIE: 0 CAT: 21

Anticipation
CIJE: 5 RIE: 2 CAT: 11

Anticipation Interval
CIJE: 2 RIE: 0 CAT: 15

Anticipation Method
CIJE: 1 RIE: 0 CAT: 15

Anticipatory Guidance
CIJE: 6 RIE: 1 CAT: 11

Anticipatory Images
CIJE: 5 RIE: 1 CAT: 11

Anticipatory Learning
CIJE: 1 RIE: 1 CAT: 11

Anticipatory Socialization
CIJE: 3 RIE: 2 CAT: 15

Antidepressants
CIJE: 3 RIE: 2 CAT: 11
SN See also "Tricyclic Antidepressants"
UF Antidepressive Agents

Antidepressive Agents
USE Antidepressants

Antifederalists
CIJE: 5 RIE: 4 CAT: 10
UF Anti Federal Party

Antigen
CIJE: 1 RIE: 0 CAT: 11

Antigone
CIJE: 7 RIE: 4 CAT: 22

Antigone Constraint
CIJE: 0 RIE: 1 CAT: 13

Antigua
CIJE: 1 RIE: 1 CAT: 07

Antilles Consolidated School System PR
CIJE: 0 RIE: 2 CAT: 17

Antimatter
CIJE: 3 RIE: 0 CAT: 20

Antimony Trichloride
CIJE: 1 RIE: 0 CAT: 20

Antineoplastic Drugs
CIJE: 0 RIE: 1 CAT: 11

Antinuclear Movement
CIJE: 1 RIE: 1 CAT: 12

Antioch College OH
CIJE: 9 RIE: 17 CAT: 17

Antioch College Washington Baltimore Campus MD
CIJE: 0 RIE: 1 CAT: 17

Antioch College West
CIJE: 0 RIE: 1 CAT: 17

Antioch Education Abroad
CIJE: 0 RIE: 2 CAT: 19

Antioch Program on Interracial Education
CIJE: 0 RIE: 1 CAT: 19

Antioch School of Law DC
CIJE: 2 RIE: 0 CAT: 17

Antioch University WA Seattle
CIJE: 0 RIE: 1 CAT: 17

Antipoverty Study Commission
CIJE: 0 RIE: 1 CAT: 17

Antiques
CIJE: 2 RIE: 2 CAT: 16

Antitrust Laws
CIJE: 31 RIE: 7 CAT: 14

Antitrust Legislation
CIJE: 2 RIE: 2 CAT: 14

Anton Brenner Developmental Gestalt Test
CIJE: 0 RIE: 2 CAT: 21

Antonelli v Hammond
CIJE: 1 RIE: 0 CAT: 14

Antonioni (Michelangelo)
CIJE: 2 RIE: 0 CAT: 18

Antonyms
CIJE: 9 RIE: 11 CAT: 13

Ants
CIJE: 9 RIE: 0 CAT: 20

Anxiety Scale (Mendel)
CIJE: 0 RIE: 1 CAT: 21

Anxiety Scale for the Blind
CIJE: 1 RIE: 0 CAT: 21

Anxiety Self Report
CIJE: 1 RIE: 2 CAT: 21

Anyi Baoule
CIJE: 0 RIE: 1 CAT: 13

Anyuwa
USE Yanyuwa

AP NEWS
CIJE: 0 RIE: 1 CAT: 04
SN Associated Press' online database

AP Newswire
USE Associated Press

APACE Program
CIJE: 0 RIE: 1 CAT: 19

Apache (Tribe)
CIJE: 11 RIE: 34 CAT: 08

Apartments
CIJE: 5 RIE: 5 CAT: 05

Apel (Karl Otto)
CIJE: 0 RIE: 1 CAT: 18

Apell Test
CIJE: 0 RIE: 1 CAT: 21

Apert Syndrome
CIJE: 0 RIE: 1 CAT: 11
UF Acrocephalosyndactylia

Apgar Score
CIJE: 3 RIE: 2 CAT: 21

Aphesis
CIJE: 1 RIE: 0 CAT: 13

Aphorisms
CIJE: 6 RIE: 2 CAT: 13

Apiculture
CIJE: 1 RIE: 2 CAT: 20

APL Programing Language
CIJE: 19 RIE: 30 CAT: 04

Aplasia (Red Cell)
CIJE: 1 RIE: 0 CAT: 11

Apnea
CIJE: 3 RIE: 1 CAT: 11

Apocalyptic Premise (The)
CIJE: 1 RIE: 0 CAT: 22
SN ...Nuclear Arms Debated (Book Title)

Apocalypticism
CIJE: 4 RIE: 1 CAT: 15

Apolipoproteins
CIJE: 0 RIE: 1 CAT: 11
SN Protein moieties occurring in plasma lipoproteins — there are five families of apolipoproteins, designated A-E

Apollinaire (Guillaume)
CIJE: 4 RIE: 0 CAT: 18

Apollo Program
CIJE: 7 RIE: 1 CAT: 19

Apollo School LA
CIJE: 1 RIE: 0 CAT: 17

Apollo Simulation Checkout and Training System
CIJE: 0 RIE: 1 CAT: 15

Apollo Soyuz Test Project
CIJE: 1 RIE: 0 CAT: 19

Apollonianism
CIJE: 0 RIE: 1 CAT: 15

Apologia
CIJE: 1 RIE: 1 CAT: 16

Apologies
CIJE: 13 RIE: 7 CAT: 16

Apophony
CIJE: 0 RIE: 1 CAT: 13

Apothecaries Measures
CIJE: 0 RIE: 1 CAT: 11

Appalachia
CIJE: 247 RIE: 468 CAT: 07

Appalachia (Central)
CIJE: 1 RIE: 16 CAT: 07

Appalachia (Monongalia Area)
CIJE: 0 RIE: 1 CAT: 07

Appalachia (North)
CIJE: 0 RIE: 2 CAT: 07

Appalachia (South)
CIJE: 9 RIE: 19 CAT: 07

Appalachia Educational Laboratory WV
CIJE: 8 RIE: 66 CAT: 17
SN See also "AEL..."

Appalachia Improved Reference Services OH
CIJE: 0 RIE: 1 CAT: 17

Appalachia Preschool Education Program
CIJE: 0 RIE: 10 CAT: 19

Appalachian Adolescent Health Education Project
CIJE: 0 RIE: 3 CAT: 19

Appalachian Adult Education Center KY
CIJE: 0 RIE: 12 CAT: 17

Appalachian Community Impact Project
CIJE: 0 RIE: 1 CAT: 19

Appalachian Community Service Network
CIJE: 0 RIE: 3 CAT: 17

Appalachian Culture
CIJE: 0 RIE: 6 CAT: 16

Appalachian Education
CIJE: 5 RIE: 1 CAT: 16

Appalachian Education Satellite Project
CIJE: 5 RIE: 26 CAT: 19

Appalachian Literature
CIJE: 7 RIE: 10 CAT: 16

Appalachian Mountains
CIJE: 8 RIE: 6 CAT: 07

Appalachian People
CIJE: 12 RIE: 36 CAT: 08

Appalachian Power Company
CIJE: 1 RIE: 0 CAT: 17

Appalachian Preschool Test of Cognitive Skills
CIJE: 0 RIE: 4 CAT: 21

Appalachian Regional Commission DC
CIJE: 23 RIE: 26 CAT: 17

Appalachian Regional Development Act 1965
CIJE: 4 RIE: 5 CAT: 14

Appalachian Regional Development Program
CIJE: 1 RIE: 1 CAT: 19

Appalachian Regional School for Church Leaders
CIJE: 0 RIE: 2 CAT: 17

Appalachian State University NC
CIJE: 12 RIE: 18 CAT: 17

Appalachian Studies
CIJE: 2 RIE: 16 CAT: 03

Appalachian Teachers Network
CIJE: 0 RIE: 1 CAT: 17

Appalachian Trail
CIJE: 1 RIE: 1 CAT: 07

Appalachian Volunteers
CIJE: 0 RIE: 2 CAT: 17

Appalachian Whites
CIJE: 4 RIE: 3 CAT: 08

Apparatus Test
CIJE: 0 RIE: 1 CAT: 21

Appeals (Hearings)
CIJE: 4 RIE: 5 CAT: 14

Appellate Courts
CIJE: 3 RIE: 1 CAT: 05
UF Courts of Appeal

Apple (Computer)
CIJE: 16 RIE: 25 CAT: 04

Apple Cider Making
CIJE: 0 RIE: 1 CAT: 20

Apple Classrooms of Tomorrow
CIJE: 3 RIE: 26 CAT: 19
UF ACOT

Apple Computer Inc
CIJE: 17 RIE: 4 CAT: 17

Apple Corps (Georgia)
CIJE: 0 RIE: 1 CAT: 19

Apple I
CIJE: 1 RIE: 0 CAT: 04

Apple II
CIJE: 165 RIE: 106 CAT: 04

Apple II Plus
CIJE: 6 RIE: 15 CAT: 04

Apple IIc
CIJE: 5 RIE: 5 CAT: 04

Apple IIe
CIJE: 18 RIE: 50 CAT: 04

Apple IIGS
CIJE: 0 RIE: 21 CAT: 04

Apple III
CIJE: 1 RIE: 0 CAT: 04

Apple Interactive Data Analysis
CIJE: 0 RIE: 1 CAT: 04
UF AIDA (Computer Program)

Apple Macintosh
CIJE: 162 RIE: 87 CAT: 04
UF Macintosh Computers

Apple Microcomputers
CIJE: 19 RIE: 13 CAT: 04

APPLE Observation System
CIJE: 2 RIE: 2 CAT: 21
UF Anecdotal Processing Promote Learning Experience

Apple Valley Rosemount MN
CIJE: 2 RIE: 0 CAT: 17

Apple Writer
CIJE: 1 RIE: 0 CAT: 04

Apple Writer II
CIJE: 1 RIE: 0 CAT: 04

Applebee (Arthur)
CIJE: 0 RIE: 1 CAT: 18

AppleLink
CIJE: 2 RIE: 2 CAT: 04

Apples
CIJE: 4 RIE: 3 CAT: 20

Applesoft BASIC
CIJE: 3 RIE: 1 CAT: 04

Appleton Century Crofts Portable Laboratory System
CIJE: 0 RIE: 1 CAT: 15

AppleWorks
CIJE: 21 RIE: 48 CAT: 04
UF AppleWorks Software Tutorial

AppleWorks Software Tutorial
USE AppleWorks

Application Forms
CIJE: 2 RIE: 16 CAT: 04

Application Languages
CIJE: 2 RIE: 0 CAT: 04

Application Level Learning
CIJE: 0 RIE: 1 CAT: 15

Application of Principles Test
CIJE: 0 RIE: 2 CAT: 21

Applications Technology Satellite
CIJE: 9 RIE: 30 CAT: 20

Applications Transfer System
CIJE: 0 RIE: 1 CAT: 15

Applied Anthropology
CIJE: 2 RIE: 2 CAT: 03

Applied Arts
CIJE: 2 RIE: 2 CAT: 03

Applied Assessment Instrument
CIJE: 1 RIE: 0 CAT: 21

Applied Behavior Analysis
CIJE: 9 RIE: 2 CAT: 15

Applied Communication
CIJE: 4 RIE: 13 CAT: 03

Applied Developmental Psychology
CIJE: 0 RIE: 2 CAT: 11

Applied Humanities
CIJE: 0 RIE: 1 CAT: 03

Applied Mathematics
CIJE: 9 RIE: 8 CAT: 03

Applied Principles Achievement Test
CIJE: 0 RIE: 1 CAT: 21

Applied Program of Public Service
CIJE: 0 RIE: 22 CAT: 19

Applied Science Occupations
CIJE: 1 RIE: 0 CAT: 09

Applied Sociology
CIJE: 14 RIE: 4 CAT: 03

Applied Statistics
CIJE: 1 RIE: 4 CAT: 03

Applied Technical Power
CIJE: 1 RIE: 0 CAT: 20

Applying Research to Teacher Education
USE ARTE RUETE Study

Appointive Positions
CIJE: 1 RIE: 5 CAT: 16

Appointment Keeping
CIJE: 3 RIE: 3 CAT: 16

Appointments
CIJE: 2 RIE: 1 CAT: 16
SN See also beginning with "Faculty..," "Joint..," "Political..," "Term.."

Apportionment (Legislative)
CIJE: 2 RIE: 1 CAT: 14

Apprenticeship of Observation Theory
CIJE: 0 RIE: 1 CAT: 15

Apprenticeship Outreach Program
CIJE: 0 RIE: 1 CAT: 19

Approach Avoidance Conflict
CIJE: 6 RIE: 4 CAT: 11

Approach Technique
CIJE: 2 RIE: 4 CAT: 15

Approaches to Studying Inventory
CIJE: 2 RIE: 1 CAT: 21
UF Lancaster Approaches to Studying Inventory

Appropriate Technology Program KS
CIJE: 0 RIE: 2 CAT: 19

Appropriateness Measurement
CIJE: 7 RIE: 2 CAT: 21

Appropriation of New Technology
CIJE: 0 RIE: 0 CAT: 20

Approval Needs
CIJE: 13 RIE: 4 CAT: 11

Approval of Courses
USE Course Approval

Approval of Programs
USE Program Approval

Approval Order Programs
CIJE: 0 RIE: 1 CAT: 19

Approval Plans
CIJE: 21 RIE: 13 CAT: 15

Approved Program Approach
CIJE: 0 RIE: 1 CAT: 15

Approximation (Statistics)
CIJE: 15 RIE: 2 CAT: 15

Apraxia (Speech)
CIJE: 17 RIE: 3 CAT: 13

April (Month)
CIJE: 1 RIE: 0 CAT: 16

APTICOM (Computer Program)
CIJE: 0 RIE: 2 CAT: 04

Aptitude Improvement
CIJE: 0 RIE: 1 CAT: 11

Aptitude Strategies
CIJE: 0 RIE: 1 CAT: 16

Aptitudes Research Project
CIJE: 2 RIE: 1 CAT: 19

APTS NY
USE Aid for Part Time Study Program

Apuleius (Lucius)
CIJE: 1 RIE: 0 CAT: 18

Aqua Aerobics
USE Water Exercise

Aquacultural Technicians
CIJE: 1 RIE: 0 CAT: 09

Aquaculture
CIJE: 13 RIE: 25 CAT: 20

Aquatic Centers
CIJE: 5 RIE: 1 CAT: 05

Aquatic Exercise
USE Water Exercise

Aquatic Life
CIJE: 3 RIE: 6 CAT: 20

Aquatic Organisms
CIJE: 4 RIE: 4 CAT: 20

Aquatic Therapy
USE Hydrotherapy

Aquinas (Saint Thomas)
CIJE: 0 RIE: 1 CAT: 18

Aquinas College MI
CIJE: 3 RIE: 6 CAT: 17

Aquino (Corazon)
CIJE: 1 RIE: 1 CAT: 18

Arab Bureau of Education for the Gulf States
CIJE: 1 RIE: 1 CAT: 17

Arab Gulf States
CIJE: 1 RIE: 3 CAT: 07

Arab Regional Literacy Organization
CIJE: 1 RIE: 0 CAT: 17

Arab States
CIJE: 46 RIE: 66 CAT: 07

Arabia
CIJE: 3 RIE: 2 CAT: 07

Arabian American Oil Company
CIJE: 0 RIE: 1 CAT: 17
UF ARAMCO

Arabian Gulf Region
CIJE: 3 RIE: 6 CAT: 07

Arabic (Cairene)
CIJE: 1 RIE: 3 CAT: 13

Arabic (Chad)
CIJE: 0 RIE: 3 CAT: 13

Arabic (Classical)
CIJE: 2 RIE: 5 CAT: 13

Arabic (Colloquial)
CIJE: 1 RIE: 2 CAT: 13

Arabic (Egyptian)
CIJE: 1 RIE: 5 CAT: 13

Arabic (Gulf)
CIJE: 0 RIE: 4 CAT: 13

Arabic (Iraqi)
CIJE: 0 RIE: 1 CAT: 13

Arabic (Levantine)
CIJE: 0 RIE: 2 CAT: 13

Arabic (Libyan)
CIJE: 0 RIE: 0 CAT: 13

Arabic (Literary)
CIJE: 1 RIE: 2 CAT: 13

Arabic (Mauritanian)
CIJE: 0 RIE: 4 CAT: 13

Arabic (Modern Literary)
CIJE: 0 RIE: 3 CAT: 13

Arabic (Modern Standard)
CIJE: 1 RIE: 3 CAT: 13

Arabic (Moroccan)
CIJE: 9 RIE: 7 CAT: 13

Arabic (Muslim Baghdad)
CIJE: 0 RIE: 1 CAT: 13

Arabic (Palestinian)
CIJE: 0 RIE: 1 CAT: 13
UF Palestinian Arabic

Arabic (Saudi)
CIJE: 1 RIE: 2 CAT: 13

Arabic (Sudanese)
CIJE: 0 RIE: 1 CAT: 13

Arabic (Tunisian)
CIJE: 1 RIE: 1 CAT: 13

Arabic Persian Writing System
CIJE: 0 RIE: 5 CAT: 13

Arabic Picture Vocabulary Test
CIJE: 0 RIE: 2 CAT: 21

Arabic Script
CIJE: 2 RIE: 3 CAT: 13

Arabic Speaking
CIJE: 6 RIE: 2 CAT: 08

Arachnophobia
CIJE: 0 RIE: 1 CAT: 11
UF Fear of Spiders

Aragon (Louis)
CIJE: 2 RIE: 0 CAT: 18

Aramaic Languages
CIJE: 0 RIE: 1 CAT: 13
SN Subgroup of the Semitic languages

ARAMCO
USE Arabian American Oil Company

Arapaho
CIJE: 1 RIE: 1 CAT: 13
UF Atsina; Gros Ventre (Wyoming)

Arapaho (Tribe)
CIJE: 5 RIE: 5 CAT: 08
UF Gros Ventre (Wyoming) (Tribe)

Arapahoe (Tribe)
CIJE: 2 RIE: 3 CAT: 08

Arapahoe Community College CO
CIJE: 2 RIE: 9 CAT: 17

Arapahoe High School CO
CIJE: 0 RIE: 1 CAT: 17

Arapahoe School WY
CIJE: 1 RIE: 0 CAT: 17

Arbitrary Implementation Scale (Butt and Wideen)
CIJE: 0 RIE: 1 CAT: 21

Arbitrary Tightness Thought Process Scale
CIJE: 1 RIE: 0 CAT: 21

Arbitration Awards
CIJE: 1 RIE: 2 CAT: 14

Arbor Day
CIJE: 2 RIE: 1 CAT: 12

Arboriculture
CIJE: 1 RIE: 2 CAT: 20

Arc (Association for Retarded Citizens)
CIJE: 0 RIE: 4 CAT: 17
SN Formerly the "Association for Retarded Citizens," Oct92
UF The Arc

Arc Ed Curriculum
CIJE: 1 RIE: 0 CAT: 03

ARCH GRAPHIC
CIJE: 0 RIE: 1 CAT: 04

Archaeological Research Center (Denmark)
CIJE: 1 RIE: 0 CAT: 17

Archaeology and African Cultures Program NY
CIJE: 0 RIE: 1 CAT: 19

Archdiocese of Chicago IL
CIJE: 0 RIE: 1 CAT: 17

Archdiocese of Cincinnati OH
CIJE: 0 RIE: 1 CAT: 17

Archdiocese of Dubuque IA
CIJE: 1 RIE: 0 CAT: 17

Archdiocese of New York
CIJE: 0 RIE: 1 CAT: 17

Archdiocese of Omaha NE
CIJE: 0 RIE: 1 CAT: 17

Archdiocese of Philadelphia PA
CIJE: 1 RIE: 1 CAT: 17

Archetypes
CIJE: 20 RIE: 16 CAT: 16

Archibald Engine
CIJE: 1 RIE: 0 CAT: 04

Archimedes
CIJE: 3 RIE: 0 CAT: 18

Architect Role
CIJE: 4 RIE: 1 CAT: 16

Architectural Barriers Act 1968
CIJE: 2 RIE: 6 CAT: 14

Architectural Environment
CIJE: 3 RIE: 2 CAT: 05

Architectural Grammars Software
CIJE: 0 RIE: 1 CAT: 04

Architectural School Aptitude Test
CIJE: 0 RIE: 1 CAT: 21

Architectural Technology
CIJE: 0 RIE: 1 CAT: 03

Architectural Transportation Barriers Compliance
CIJE: 0 RIE: 2 CAT: 14

Archival Information Dissemination System
CIJE: 0 RIE: 1 CAT: 15

Archival Value
CIJE: 1 RIE: 4 CAT: 16

Archive Indexes
CIJE: 1 RIE: 1 CAT: 04

Archives and Records Information Coalition
CIJE: 0 RIE: 1 CAT: 17

Archives Education Services
CIJE: 0 RIE: 1 CAT: 16

Archives of Environmental Health
CIJE: 1 RIE: 0 CAT: 22

Archives of Languages of the World
CIJE: 0 RIE: 18 CAT: 22

Archivists
CIJE: 18 RIE: 16 CAT: 09

ARCS Model
CIJE: 10 RIE: 5 CAT: 15
UF ARCS Motivational Theory; Attention Relevance Confidence Satisfaction Model

ARCS Motivational Theory
USE ARCS Model

Arctic
CIJE: 8 RIE: 21 CAT: 07

Arctic National Wildlife Refuge
CIJE: 0 RIE: 1 CAT: 07

Arctic Vegetation
CIJE: 2 RIE: 0 CAT: 20

Arden (John)
CIJE: 1 RIE: 0 CAT: 18

Ardmore School District OK
CIJE: 0 RIE: 1 CAT: 17

Area Agency on Aging
CIJE: 2 RIE: 1 CAT: 17

Area Centers for Services to Deaf Blind Children
CIJE: 0 RIE: 1 CAT: 17

Area Education Agency Media Centers
CIJE: 0 RIE: 2 CAT: 05

Area Health Education Center CO
CIJE: 0 RIE: 0 CAT: 17

Area Health Education Centers
CIJE: 9 RIE: 15 CAT: 17

Area III Valley Intercultural Program
CIJE: 0 RIE: 1 CAT: 19

Area Learning Center MI
CIJE: 0 RIE: 1 CAT: 17

Area Library Councils
CIJE: 1 RIE: 0 CAT: 17

Area Redevelopment Act 1961
CIJE: 1 RIE: 5 CAT: 14

Area Redevelopment Administration CA
CIJE: 0 RIE: 1 CAT: 17

Area Resource File
CIJE: 0 RIE: 1 CAT: 22

Area Vocational Schools MI
CIJE: 0 RIE: 1 CAT: 17

Area Vocational Technical Institutes
CIJE: 0 RIE: 2 CAT: 05

Area Vocational Technical Schools
CIJE: 2 RIE: 4 CAT: 05

Area Wage Survey Program
CIJE: 1 RIE: 0 CAT: 19

Area Wide Planning Organization
CIJE: 1 RIE: 0 CAT: 17

Areal Linguistics
CIJE: 1 RIE: 0 CAT: 13

Areopagitica
CIJE: 0 RIE: 2 CAT: 22

Argentina
CIJE: 83 RIE: 79 CAT: 07

Argentina (Buenos Aires)
CIJE: 3 RIE: 5 CAT: 07

Argonne National Laboratory IL
CIJE: 2 RIE: 1 CAT: 17

Arguedas (Jose Maria)
CIJE: 1 RIE: 0 CAT: 18

Argument Research
CIJE: 7 RIE: 4 CAT: 13

Argumentation Theory
CIJE: 12 RIE: 9 CAT: 15

Argumentative Spots
CIJE: 0 RIE: 1 CAT: 16

Argumentativeness
CIJE: 26 RIE: 19 CAT: 11

Argyrian Theory
CIJE: 0 RIE: 1 CAT: 15

Arid Lands
CIJE: 1 RIE: 2 CAT: 20
UF Arid Zones

Arid Zones
USE Arid Lands

Aries (Philippe)
CIJE: 1 RIE: 3 CAT: 18

Arikara
CIJE: 0 RIE: 1 CAT: 13

Arikara (Tribe)
CIJE: 1 RIE: 4 CAT: 08

ARIMA Models
USE Autoregressive Integrated Moving Averages

ARIN Adult Learning Center
CIJE: 0 RIE: 1 CAT: 17

ARIN Adult Learning Center PA
CIJE: 0 RIE: 2 CAT: 17

Aristophanes
CIJE: 2 RIE: 3 CAT: 18

Aristotle
CIJE: 92 RIE: 43 CAT: 18

Aristotles Concept of Logos
CIJE: 1 RIE: 0 CAT: 15

Arithmetic Concepts Inventory K and 1st Grade
CIJE: 0 RIE: 1 CAT: 21

Arithmetic Mean
CIJE: 8 RIE: 2 CAT: 20

Arithmetic Reasoning
CIJE: 0 RIE: 1 CAT: 20

Arithmetic Teacher (Journal)
CIJE: 1 RIE: 2 CAT: 22

Arithmetic Test Generator
CIJE: 1 RIE: 0 CAT: 21

Arizona
CIJE: 193 RIE: 855 CAT: 07

Arizona (Black Mesa)
CIJE: 2 RIE: 1 CAT: 07

Arizona (Casa Grande)
CIJE: 0 RIE: 1 CAT: 07

Arizona (Chinle)
CIJE: 0 RIE: 5 CAT: 07

Arizona (Cochise County)
CIJE: 0 RIE: 1 CAT: 07

Arizona (Flagstaff)
CIJE: 3 RIE: 9 CAT: 07

Arizona (Fort Defiance)
CIJE: 0 RIE: 1 CAT: 07

Arizona (Fort McDowell)
CIJE: 0 RIE: 2 CAT: 07

Arizona (Ganado)
CIJE: 0 RIE: 4 CAT: 07

Arizona (Gila Crossing)
CIJE: 0 RIE: 1 CAT: 07

Arizona (Glendale)
CIJE: 1 RIE: 2 CAT: 07

Arizona (Guadalupe)
CIJE: 1 RIE: 2 CAT: 07

Arizona (Many Farms)
CIJE: 1 RIE: 0 CAT: 07

Arizona (Marana)
CIJE: 0 RIE: 1 CAT: 07

Arizona (Maricopa County)
CIJE: 1 RIE: 12 CAT: 07

Arizona (Mesa)
CIJE: 3 RIE: 32 CAT: 07

Arizona (Mohave County)
CIJE: 0 RIE: 1 CAT: 07

Arizona (Navajo County)
CIJE: 0 RIE: 3 CAT: 07

Arizona (North)
CIJE: 0 RIE: 5 CAT: 07

Arizona (Phoenix)
CIJE: 21 RIE: 74 CAT: 07

Arizona (Pima County)
CIJE: 2 RIE: 16 CAT: 07

Arizona (Rough Rock)
CIJE: 1 RIE: 4 CAT: 07

Arizona (Scottsdale)
CIJE: 4 RIE: 2 CAT: 07

Arizona (South Tucson)
CIJE: 2 RIE: 0 CAT: 07

Arizona (South)
CIJE: 1 RIE: 0 CAT: 07

Arizona (Sun City)
CIJE: 3 RIE: 1 CAT: 07

Arizona (Tempe)
CIJE: 9 RIE: 17 CAT: 07

Arizona (Tolleson)
CIJE: 1 RIE: 0 CAT: 07

Arizona (Tucson)
CIJE: 22 RIE: 55 CAT: 07

Arizona (Whiteriver)
CIJE: 0 RIE: 2 CAT: 07

Arizona (Williams)
CIJE: 0 RIE: 1 CAT: 07

Arizona (Window Rock)
CIJE: 0 RIE: 4 CAT: 07

Arizona (Yuma)
CIJE: 0 RIE: 2 CAT: 07

Arizona Agricultural Relations Act 1972
CIJE: 0 RIE: 1 CAT: 14

Arizona Archaeology Week
CIJE: 0 RIE: 1 CAT: 12

Arizona Archeological Council
CIJE: 0 RIE: 1 CAT: 17

Arizona Articulation Proficiency Scale
CIJE: 7 RIE: 0 CAT: 21

Arizona Bilingual Council
CIJE: 0 RIE: 1 CAT: 17

Arizona Career Ladder Program
CIJE: 0 RIE: 6 CAT: 19

Arizona Center for Early Childhood Education
CIJE: 0 RIE: 2 CAT: 17

Arizona Champion Coconino Sun
CIJE: 0 RIE: 1 CAT: 22

Arizona Civil Rights Act
CIJE: 0 RIE: 1 CAT: 14

Arizona Commission of Indian Affairs
CIJE: 0 RIE: 11 CAT: 17

Arizona Indian Education Association
CIJE: 0 RIE: 2 CAT: 17

Arizona Job Colleges
CIJE: 1 RIE: 1 CAT: 17

Arizona Leadership Academy
CIJE: 0 RIE: 1 CAT: 17

Arizona Principals Academy
CIJE: 0 RIE: 2 CAT: 02

Arizona Pupil Achievement Testing
CIJE: 0 RIE: 2 CAT: 21

Arizona State Assessment Programs
CIJE: 0 RIE: 7 CAT: 19

Arizona State Department of Education
CIJE: 0 RIE: 4 CAT: 17

Arizona State University
CIJE: 65 RIE: 93 CAT: 17

Arizona State University Tempe
CIJE: 0 RIE: 3 CAT: 17

Arizona Student Assessment Program
CIJE: 2 RIE: 1 CAT: 19

Arizona Teacher Proficiency Examination
CIJE: 1 RIE: 3 CAT: 21

Arkansas
CIJE: 96 RIE: 504 CAT: 07

Arkansas (Barling)
CIJE: 0 RIE: 1 CAT: 07

Arkansas (El Dorado)
CIJE: 0 RIE: 1 CAT: 07

Arkansas (Fayetteville)
CIJE: 1 RIE: 15 CAT: 07

Arkansas (Fort Smith)
CIJE: 0 RIE: 2 CAT: 07

Arkansas (Harrison)
CIJE: 0 RIE: 2 CAT: 07

Arkansas (Jonesboro)
CIJE: 1 RIE: 1 CAT: 07

Arkansas (Little Rock)
CIJE: 12 RIE: 20 CAT: 07

Arkansas (Magnolia)
CIJE: 0 RIE: 4 CAT: 07

Arkansas (Mansfield)
CIJE: 1 RIE: 0 CAT: 07

Arkansas (Nevada County)
CIJE: 0 RIE: 1 CAT: 07

Arkansas (Pine Bluff)
CIJE: 0 RIE: 2 CAT: 07

Arkansas (Pulaski County)
CIJE: 2 RIE: 2 CAT: 07

Arkansas (Texarkana)
CIJE: 2 RIE: 2 CAT: 07

Arkansas (Van Buren County)
CIJE: 0 RIE: 1 CAT: 07

Arkansas (Warren)
CIJE: 0 RIE: 1 CAT: 07

Arkansas (Wynne)
CIJE: 0 RIE: 1 CAT: 07

Arkansas Act 34
CIJE: 0 RIE: 1 CAT: 14
UF School Finance Act 1983 (Arkansas)

Arkansas Act 102
CIJE: 0 RIE: 1 CAT: 14

Arkansas Act 590
CIJE: 3 RIE: 0 CAT: 14

Arkansas Classroom Management Training Model
CIJE: 0 RIE: 1 CAT: 15

Arkansas College
CIJE: 3 RIE: 2 CAT: 17

Arkansas Community Education Development Assn
CIJE: 0 RIE: 2 CAT: 17

Arkansas Educational Assessment Program
CIJE: 0 RIE: 1 CAT: 19

Arkansas Educational Renewal Consortium
CIJE: 0 RIE: 0 CAT: 17
UF Educational Renewal Consortium AR; Education Renewal Consortium AR

Arkansas Enterprises for the Blind
CIJE: 1 RIE: 1 CAT: 17

Arkansas Governors School
CIJE: 0 RIE: 1 CAT: 17

Arkansas Minimum Performance Test
CIJE: 0 RIE: 5 CAT: 21

Arkansas Occupational Educational Information Syst
CIJE: 0 RIE: 1 CAT: 04

Arkansas Ozarks
CIJE: 0 RIE: 0 CAT: 07

Arkansas Rehabilitation Service
CIJE: 0 RIE: 1 CAT: 17

Arkansas River Education Service Cooperative
CIJE: 0 RIE: 1 CAT: 17

Arkansas Special Youth Project
CIJE: 0 RIE: 3 CAT: 19

Arkansas State Department of Education
CIJE: 1 RIE: 6 CAT: 17

Arkansas State Department of Higher Education
CIJE: 0 RIE: 1 CAT: 17

Arkansas State Technical Institute
CIJE: 0 RIE: 1 CAT: 17

Arkansas State University
CIJE: 5 RIE: 13 CAT: 17

Arkansas Technology Access Program
CIJE: 0 RIE: 1 CAT: 19
UF ARTAP

Arlin Test of Formal Reasoning
CIJE: 3 RIE: 5 CAT: 21

Arlington House VA
CIJE: 0 RIE: 1 CAT: 16
UF Custis Lee Mansion

Arlington Public Schools VA
CIJE: 3 RIE: 17 CAT: 17

Arlington School District WA
CIJE: 1 RIE: 1 CAT: 17

Arlt (Roberto)
CIJE: 1 RIE: 0 CAT: 18

Arm Ergometry
USE Ergometry

Arm Movements
CIJE: 4 RIE: 1 CAT: 11

Arm Positioning
CIJE: 2 RIE: 0 CAT: 11

Arm Swing
CIJE: 1 RIE: 1 CAT: 11

Armbands
CIJE: 2 RIE: 0 CAT: 04

ARMCO Steel Corporation
CIJE: 1 RIE: 0 CAT: 17

Armed Forces Health Prof Scholarship Program
CIJE: 0 RIE: 1 CAT: 19

Armed Forces Institute WI
CIJE: 2 RIE: 3 CAT: 17

Armed Forces Qualification Test
CIJE: 3 RIE: 28 CAT: 21

Armed Forces Staff College VA
CIJE: 0 RIE: 1 CAT: 17

Armed Forces University (West Germany)
CIJE: 1 RIE: 0 CAT: 17

Armed Forces Vision Tester
CIJE: 1 RIE: 0 CAT: 04

Armed Forces Womens Selection Test
CIJE: 0 RIE: 1 CAT: 21

Armed Services Applicant Profile
CIJE: 0 RIE: 1 CAT: 21

Armed Services Editions
CIJE: 0 RIE: 1 CAT: 16

Armed Services Materials Conversion Project
CIJE: 0 RIE: 2 CAT: 19

Armed Services Vocational Aptitude Battery
CIJE: 20 RIE: 116 CAT: 21

Armenian Americans
CIJE: 1 RIE: 4 CAT: 08

Armenians
CIJE: 7 RIE: 17 CAT: 08

Armor Crew Personnel
CIJE: 0 RIE: 1 CAT: 09

Armour and Company
CIJE: 0 RIE: 2 CAT: 17

Arms (Anatomy)
CIJE: 0 RIE: 1 CAT: 11

Armstrong Law
CIJE: 0 RIE: 2 CAT: 14

Armstrong State College GA
CIJE: 0 RIE: 3 CAT: 17

Armstrong World Industries
CIJE: 0 RIE: 1 CAT: 17

Army
CIJE: 40 RIE: 263 CAT: 17

Army Alpha Examination
CIJE: 2 RIE: 3 CAT: 21

Army Aviation Center AL
CIJE: 0 RIE: 0 CAT: 17
UF United States Army Aviation Center AL

Army Aviation School AL
CIJE: 0 RIE: 1 CAT: 17

Army Classification Battery
CIJE: 0 RIE: 6 CAT: 21

Army Engineer School VA
CIJE: 1 RIE: 0 CAT: 17

Army General Classification Test
CIJE: 0 RIE: 2 CAT: 21

Army Infantry School GA
CIJE: 1 RIE: 1 CAT: 17

Army Intern Intake Survey
CIJE: 0 RIE: 1 CAT: 21

Army Judge Advocate Generals School
CIJE: 1 RIE: 0 CAT: 17

Army Laboratories
CIJE: 0 RIE: 1 CAT: 05

Army Life 78 Study
CIJE: 0 RIE: 1 CAT: 22

Army Map Service
CIJE: 0 RIE: 1 CAT: 17

Army Medical Training Center
CIJE: 2 RIE: 0 CAT: 17

Army Natick Laboratories
CIJE: 1 RIE: 0 CAT: 17

Army National Guard
CIJE: 1 RIE: 2 CAT: 17

Army Officer Candidate School
CIJE: 0 RIE: 1 CAT: 17

Army Research Institute
CIJE: 1 RIE: 2 CAT: 17

Army Reserve
CIJE: 0 RIE: 1 CAT: 17

Army Reserve Officers Training Corps
CIJE: 0 RIE: 4 CAT: 17

Army ROTC Basic Camp Student Evaluation Report
CIJE: 0 RIE: 0 CAT: 21

Army Signal Center and School NJ
CIJE: 1 RIE: 3 CAT: 17

Army Southeastern Signal Corps School GA
CIJE: 0 RIE: 1 CAT: 17

Army Specialized Training Program
CIJE: 0 RIE: 5 CAT: 19

Army Topographic Command Library
CIJE: 1 RIE: 0 CAT: 17

Army War College Nonresident Courses
CIJE: 0 RIE: 1 CAT: 03

Army War College PA
CIJE: 0 RIE: 1 CAT: 17

Arniches (Carlos)
CIJE: 1 RIE: 0 CAT: 18

Arnim (Achim von)
CIJE: 1 RIE: 0 CAT: 18

Arnold (Matthew)
CIJE: 11 RIE: 3 CAT: 18

Arnold (Thomas)
CIJE: 1 RIE: 0 CAT: 18

Arnow (Hariette)
CIJE: 0 RIE: 1 CAT: 18

Aronfreed (J)
CIJE: 0 RIE: 1 CAT: 18

Around the Bend
CIJE: 0 RIE: 4 CAT: 22

Around the Dial (Journal)
CIJE: 0 RIE: 1 CAT: 22

Array Transformation
CIJE: 0 RIE: 1 CAT: 15

Arrays (Mathematics)
CIJE: 3 RIE: 1 CAT: 20

Arreola (Juan Jose)
CIJE: 1 RIE: 0 CAT: 18

Arrest Records
CIJE: 0 RIE: 1 CAT: 14
SN See also "Criminal Records"

Arrests
CIJE: 4 RIE: 4 CAT: 14

Arrhenius Equation
CIJE: 4 RIE: 0 CAT: 20

Arrhythmicity
CIJE: 1 RIE: 1 CAT: 11

Arrow Capron Model
CIJE: 1 RIE: 0 CAT: 15

Arrow Dot Test
CIJE: 3 RIE: 0 CAT: 21

Arrow to the Sun
CIJE: 1 RIE: 0 CAT: 22

Arrowhead Community College Region MN
CIJE: 0 RIE: 7 CAT: 17

Arrowsmith
CIJE: 1 RIE: 0 CAT: 22

Arsenic Poisoning
CIJE: 0 RIE: 1 CAT: 11

Arson
CIJE: 6 RIE: 8 CAT: 14

Art and Architecture Thesaurus
CIJE: 4 RIE: 1 CAT: 22

Art and the Built Environment Project
CIJE: 0 RIE: 0 CAT: 19

Art as Experience
CIJE: 5 RIE: 0 CAT: 22

Art Concepts
CIJE: 0 RIE: 2 CAT: 16

Art Connection
CIJE: 1 RIE: 0 CAT: 04

Art Departments
CIJE: 0 RIE: 1 CAT: 05

Art Evaluation
USE Artistic Evaluation

Art Fairs
CIJE: 1 RIE: 1 CAT: 16

Art Films
CIJE: 0 RIE: 1 CAT: 16

Art in the Mainstream (NAEA)
CIJE: 0 RIE: 1 CAT: 22

Art Librarians
CIJE: 2 RIE: 1 CAT: 09

Art Libraries
CIJE: 12 RIE: 7 CAT: 05

Art Literacy
CIJE: 1 RIE: 1 CAT: 16

Art Multimedia Kit
CIJE: 0 RIE: 1 CAT: 04

Art Museums
CIJE: 2 RIE: 0 CAT: 05

Art Observation Note Taking Form
CIJE: 0 RIE: 1 CAT: 04

Art of Teaching
USE Teaching as an Art

Art on the Air
CIJE: 1 RIE: 0 CAT: 19

Art Partnership Networks
CIJE: 1 RIE: 0 CAT: 19

Art Preference
CIJE: 2 RIE: 1 CAT: 16

Art Publications
CIJE: 2 RIE: 2 CAT: 16

Art Recognition and Talent Search
CIJE: 1 RIE: 0 CAT: 19

Art Reproductions
CIJE: 7 RIE: 1 CAT: 16

Art Research Libraries of Ohio
CIJE: 1 RIE: 0 CAT: 17

Art Skills Observation Scale
CIJE: 0 RIE: 1 CAT: 21

Art Therapists
CIJE: 1 RIE: 1 CAT: 09

Art Vocabulary Test
CIJE: 0 RIE: 1 CAT: 21

ARTAP
USE Arkansas Technology Access Program

Artaud (Antonin)
CIJE: 1 RIE: 0 CAT: 18

ARTE RUETE Study
CIJE: 0 RIE: 2 CAT: 19
UF Applying Research to Teacher Education; Research Utilization in Elementary Teacher Educ; RUETE Study

Artes Latinae
CIJE: 0 RIE: 1 CAT: 19

Arthritis
CIJE: 29 RIE: 7 CAT: 11
SN See also "Rheumatoid Arthritis"

Arthropods
CIJE: 1 RIE: 1 CAT: 20

Arthur Adaptation of Leiter Intl Performance Scale
CIJE: 1 RIE: 0 CAT: 21

Arthur Andersen and Company
CIJE: 2 RIE: 1 CAT: 17

Arthur D Little Management Education Institute MA
CIJE: 1 RIE: 1 CAT: 17

Arthur Point Scale of Performance Tests
CIJE: 0 RIE: 1 CAT: 21

Arthurdale Community School WV
CIJE: 0 RIE: 2 CAT: 17

Articles (Grammar)
CIJE: 5 RIE: 2 CAT: 13

Articles of Confederation
CIJE: 0 RIE: 1 CAT: 14

Articulated Campus Field Program
CIJE: 0 RIE: 1 CAT: 19

Articulated Faculty Concept
CIJE: 0 RIE: 1 CAT: 15

Articulated Instructional Media Program
CIJE: 1 RIE: 3 CAT: 19

Articulated Subject Indexes
CIJE: 0 RIE: 1 CAT: 04

Articulation for Career Education
CIJE: 0 RIE: 2 CAT: 19

Articulation Research System
CIJE: 0 RIE: 1 CAT: 04

Articulatory Product Score (Guttman)
CIJE: 0 RIE: 1 CAT: 21

Artifacts
CIJE: 27 RIE: 8 CAT: 04

Artifactual Evidence
CIJE: 2 RIE: 2 CAT: 14

Artificial Breeding Technicians
CIJE: 0 RIE: 1 CAT: 09

Artificial Insemination
CIJE: 4 RIE: 1 CAT: 11

Artificial Insemination Donors
CIJE: 1 RIE: 0 CAT: 10

Artificial Intelligence in Training
CIJE: 0 RIE: 1 CAT: 15

Artificial Limbs
CIJE: 0 RIE: 0 CAT: 04

Artificial Mastoid
CIJE: 1 RIE: 0 CAT: 11

Artificial Neural Networks
USE Neural Networks

Artificial Selection
CIJE: 1 RIE: 0 CAT: 20

Artificial Turf
CIJE: 3 RIE: 1 CAT: 04

Artist Residencies
CIJE: 1 RIE: 3 CAT: 16

Artistic Evaluation
CIJE: 4 RIE: 6 CAT: 21
UF Art Evaluation

Artistic Performance
CIJE: 2 RIE: 1 CAT: 16

Artistic Style
CIJE: 11 RIE: 2 CAT: 16

Artistic Teaching
USE Teaching as an Art

Artistic Thought
CIJE: 10 RIE: 3 CAT: 16

Artists in Education Program
CIJE: 1 RIE: 0 CAT: 19

Artists in Residence Program
CIJE: 2 RIE: 2 CAT: 19

Artists in Schools Program
CIJE: 19 RIE: 11 CAT: 19
UF Artists in the Schools Program

Artists in the Schools Program
USE Artists in Schools Program

Arts and Humanities Citation Index
CIJE: 2 RIE: 1 CAT: 22

Arts and Science Public Sch Teleconfer Network OK
CIJE: 1 RIE: 1 CAT: 19

Arts Council of Great Britain
CIJE: 2 RIE: 0 CAT: 17

Arts for Learning Program
CIJE: 0 RIE: 0 CAT: 19

Arts for the Basic Curriculum
CIJE: 0 RIE: 4 CAT: 03

Arts for Transition
CIJE: 0 RIE: 1 CAT: 19

Arts from the Inside Out PA
CIJE: 0 RIE: 0 CAT: 19

Arts Humanities and Cultural Affairs Act 1976
CIJE: 1 RIE: 0 CAT: 14

Arts in Education Project
CIJE: 6 RIE: 5 CAT: 19

Arts in General Education Program NY
CIJE: 0 RIE: 1 CAT: 19

Arts in Schools Basic Education Grants
CIJE: 0 RIE: 1 CAT: 19

Arts Partners Program NY
CIJE: 1 RIE: 1 CAT: 19

Arts PROPEL
CIJE: 4 RIE: 1 CAT: 19

Arts Recognition and Talent Search
CIJE: 4 RIE: 0 CAT: 19

Arvers (Felix)
CIJE: 1 RIE: 0 CAT: 18

As Parents Grow Older Model
CIJE: 0 RIE: 1 CAT: 15

As Soon As Possible Consortium
USE ASAP Consortium

As You Like It
CIJE: 2 RIE: 1 CAT: 22

Asante (Molefi K)
CIJE: 3 RIE: 1 CAT: 18

ASAP Consortium
CIJE: 0 RIE: 1 CAT: 17
UF As Soon As Possible Consortium

Asaro
CIJE: 1 RIE: 0 CAT: 13

Asbestos Abatement Act 1984 (Illinois)
CIJE: 0 RIE: 1 CAT: 14

Asbestos Hazard Emergency Response Act 1986
CIJE: 2 RIE: 6 CAT: 14
UF AHERA 1986

Asbestos School Hazard Abatement Act 1984
CIJE: 2 RIE: 2 CAT: 14

Asbestos School Hazard Detection and Control Act
CIJE: 4 RIE: 3 CAT: 14
SN ...of 1980

ASCAL Computer Program
CIJE: 2 RIE: 2 CAT: 04

ASCD Early Childhood Consortium
USE Early Childhood Consortium (ASCD)

Ascension Academy VA
CIJE: 0 RIE: 2 CAT: 17

Ascent to Excellence in Catholic Education
CIJE: 0 RIE: 1 CAT: 22

Asch (Solomon E)
CIJE: 1 RIE: 0 CAT: 18

Asch Vertical Line Scale
CIJE: 1 RIE: 3 CAT: 21

Aschner Gallagher Verbal Interaction Technique
CIJE: 1 RIE: 4 CAT: 15

Ascorbic Acid
CIJE: 4 RIE: 0 CAT: 20

ASCUS
USE Association for Sch Coll and Univ Staffing

Asensio (Eugenio)
CIJE: 1 RIE: 0 CAT: 18

Asepsis
CIJE: 1 RIE: 10 CAT: 11

Ashanti
CIJE: 1 RIE: 5 CAT: 13

Ashbury (John)
CIJE: 1 RIE: 0 CAT: 18

Ashe (Arthur)
CIJE: 0 RIE: 1 CAT: 18

ASHE Annual Meeting
CIJE: 1 RIE: 489 CAT: 02

ASHE ERIC Higher Education Course Syllabi Project
CIJE: 0 RIE: 16 CAT: 19

Ashkenazim
CIJE: 4 RIE: 3 CAT: 08

Ashland City School District OH
CIJE: 0 RIE: 1 CAT: 17

Ashland College OH
CIJE: 0 RIE: 1 CAT: 17

Ashland Community College KY
CIJE: 0 RIE: 2 CAT: 17

Ashland Federal Youth Center KY
CIJE: 0 RIE: 1 CAT: 17

Ashland University OH
CIJE: 0 RIE: 4 CAT: 17

Ashlock Welch Examination
CIJE: 1 RIE: 0 CAT: 21

Ashton Warner (Sylvia)
CIJE: 2 RIE: 4 CAT: 18

Asia
CIJE: 185 RIE: 549 CAT: 07

Asia (Central)
CIJE: 0 RIE: 8 CAT: 07

Asia (East)
CIJE: 9 RIE: 29 CAT: 07

Asia (Inner)
CIJE: 0 RIE: 2 CAT: 07

Asia (North Central)
CIJE: 0 RIE: 2 CAT: 07

Asia (South)
CIJE: 12 RIE: 36 CAT: 07

Asia (Southeast)
CIJE: 55 RIE: 142 CAT: 07

Asia (Southwest)
CIJE: 0 RIE: 1 CAT: 07

Asia (Volga Ural Region)
USE USSR (Volga Ural Region)

Asia (West)
CIJE: 2 RIE: 2 CAT: 07

Asia Pacific Economic Cooperation
CIJE: 0 RIE: 1 CAT: 17

Asia Pacific Programme of Educ Innovat for Develop
CIJE: 0 RIE: 1 CAT: 19
SN See also earlier name "Asian Programme of Educ Innovation for Development"

Asia Pacific Programme of Education for All
CIJE: 1 RIE: 4 CAT: 19

Asia Pacific Region
CIJE: 21 RIE: 107 CAT: 07
UF Asian Pacific Region; Pacific Asia

Asian African Pupil Resource Project
CIJE: 0 RIE: 1 CAT: 19

Asian American Field Survey
CIJE: 0 RIE: 1 CAT: 21

Asian American Literature
CIJE: 4 RIE: 5 CAT: 16

Asian American Students
CIJE: 15 RIE: 28 CAT: 10

Asian American Studies
CIJE: 8 RIE: 4 CAT: 03

Asian and Pacific Student Leader Project
CIJE: 1 RIE: 0 CAT: 19

Asian Blacks
CIJE: 1 RIE: 1 CAT: 08

Asian Broadcasting Union
CIJE: 1 RIE: 0 CAT: 17

Asian Development Bank
CIJE: 0 RIE: 2 CAT: 17

Asian Federation of Library Associations
CIJE: 0 RIE: 1 CAT: 17

Asian Institute of Technology
CIJE: 5 RIE: 1 CAT: 17

Asian Institute of Technology (Thailand)
CIJE: 0 RIE: 1 CAT: 17

Asian Languages
CIJE: 7 RIE: 8 CAT: 13

Asian Network for Biological Sciences
CIJE: 0 RIE: 1 CAT: 17

Asian Newcomer Parent Program
CIJE: 0 RIE: 3 CAT: 19

Asian Pacific American Heritage Week
CIJE: 0 RIE: 2 CAT: 12

Asian Pacific Region
USE Asia Pacific Region

Asian Programme of Educ Innovation for Development
CIJE: 1 RIE: 19 CAT: 19
SN See also later name "Asia Pacific Programme of Educ Innovat for Develop"

Asian South Pacific Bureau of Adult Education
CIJE: 1 RIE: 2 CAT: 17

Asian Students
CIJE: 8 RIE: 7 CAT: 10

Asian Studies Curriculum Project
CIJE: 1 RIE: 0 CAT: 19

Asian Youth Substance Abuse Project CA
CIJE: 0 RIE: 1 CAT: 19

Asians
CIJE: 52 RIE: 42 CAT: 08

AskERIC
CIJE: 1 RIE: 3 CAT: 19

Askov (Eunice N)
CIJE: 0 RIE: 1 CAT: 18

Askov Trueblood Attitude Toward Reading Scale
CIJE: 0 RIE: 1 CAT: 21
UF Attitude Toward Reading Scale (Askov Trueblood)

Asnuntuck Community College CT
CIJE: 0 RIE: 1 CAT: 17

Asolo State Theatre Company FL
CIJE: 0 RIE: 1 CAT: 17

Asolo Theater Festival of Florida
CIJE: 1 RIE: 1 CAT: 02

Asparagus Sorters
CIJE: 0 RIE: 1 CAT: 09

Aspartylglucosaminuria
CIJE: 3 RIE: 0 CAT: 11

Aspect (Verbs)
CIJE: 38 RIE: 7 CAT: 13

Aspects of Language
CIJE: 0 RIE: 1 CAT: 22

Aspects of the Theory of Syntax
CIJE: 0 RIE: 1 CAT: 22

Aspen Institute for Humanistic Studies CA
CIJE: 0 RIE: 6 CAT: 17

Aspen Middle School CO
CIJE: 2 RIE: 0 CAT: 17

Aspen Program Commun Society Govt Media Workshop
CIJE: 0 RIE: 1 CAT: 02

Aspen Program on Communications and Society
CIJE: 0 RIE: 4 CAT: 19

Aspen Project
CIJE: 1 RIE: 0 CAT: 19

Aspen Workshop on Uses of the Cable
CIJE: 0 RIE: 1 CAT: 02

Aspergers Syndrome
CIJE: 5 RIE: 1 CAT: 11

Aspergillus Niger
CIJE: 1 RIE: 0 CAT: 20

Asphyxia
CIJE: 3 RIE: 1 CAT: 11
SN See also "Hypoxia"

Aspira Inc
CIJE: 2 RIE: 6 CAT: 17

Aspira v Board of Education
CIJE: 0 RIE: 4 CAT: 14
UF Aspira v New York City Board of Education; New York City Board of Education v Aspira

Aspira v New York City Board of Education
USE Aspira v Board of Education

Aspiration (Speech)
CIJE: 2 RIE: 2 CAT: 13

Aspirations for Grade Level Completion
CIJE: 0 RIE: 1 CAT: 21

Aspirin
CIJE: 7 RIE: 0 CAT: 11

Aspy Genuineness and Respect Scales
CIJE: 1 RIE: 0 CAT: 21

Assabet Regional Vocational Sch Dist MA
CIJE: 0 RIE: 5 CAT: 17

Assassinations
CIJE: 8 RIE: 3 CAT: 16

Assaults
CIJE: 7 RIE: 5 CAT: 16

Assay Techniques
CIJE: 2 RIE: 0 CAT: 16

Assembler Languages
CIJE: 0 RIE: 4 CAT: 04

Assemblers
CIJE: 0 RIE: 7 CAT: 09

Assemblers (Dental Equipment)
CIJE: 0 RIE: 1 CAT: 09

Assemblers (Dry Cell Battery)
CIJE: 0 RIE: 1 CAT: 09

Assembly Bill 1725 (California 1989)
CIJE: 0 RIE: 8 CAT: 14

Assembly on University Goals and Governance
CIJE: 0 RIE: 1 CAT: 02

Assembly Resolution 48 (California 1963)
CIJE: 0 RIE: 2 CAT: 14

Assertion
CIJE: 6 RIE: 1 CAT: 11

Assertion Intensity
CIJE: 1 RIE: 0 CAT: 20

Assertion Structured Therapy
CIJE: 0 RIE: 1 CAT: 11

Assertive Discipline
CIJE: 18 RIE: 10 CAT: 11

Assess Test (Mosby)
USE Mosby Assess Test

Assessing Long Distance Learning via Telecommunic
USE Project ALLTEL

Assessing the Behaviors of Caregivers Scale
CIJE: 0 RIE: 3 CAT: 21

Assessment and Placement Services
CIJE: 0 RIE: 0 CAT: 21
UF College Board Assessment and Placement Services

Association of American Indian Physicians
CIJE: 2 RIE: 0 CAT: 17

Association of American Law Schools
CIJE: 19 RIE: 2 CAT: 17

Association of American Library Schools
CIJE: 23 RIE: 2 CAT: 17

Association of American Medical Colleges
CIJE: 84 RIE: 9 CAT: 17

Association of American Medical Colleges v Carey
CIJE: 1 RIE: 0 CAT: 14

Association of American Publishers
CIJE: 11 RIE: 2 CAT: 17

Association of American Universities
CIJE: 11 RIE: 8 CAT: 17

Association of British Columbia Librarians
CIJE: 1 RIE: 0 CAT: 17

Association of California School Administrators
CIJE: 0 RIE: 8 CAT: 17

Association of Canadian Community Colleges
CIJE: 1 RIE: 0 CAT: 17

Association of Chief State School AV Officers
CIJE: 1 RIE: 2 CAT: 17

Association of Child Care Workers Inc
CIJE: 0 RIE: 1 CAT: 17

Association of Christian Schools International
CIJE: 1 RIE: 1 CAT: 17

Association of Classroom Teachers
CIJE: 1 RIE: 1 CAT: 17

Association of College and Research Libraries
CIJE: 33 RIE: 14 CAT: 17
SN See also under "ACRL..."

Association of College Unions International
CIJE: 0 RIE: 2 CAT: 17
UF College Unions International

Association of Collegiate Alumnae
CIJE: 0 RIE: 1 CAT: 17

Association of Community College Trustees
CIJE: 1 RIE: 2 CAT: 17

Association of Community Orgs for Reform Now
USE Association Community Organizations Reform Now

Association of Departments of English
CIJE: 3 RIE: 3 CAT: 17

Association of Environmental Laboratories
CIJE: 1 RIE: 0 CAT: 17

Association of Farmworker Opportunity Programs
CIJE: 0 RIE: 1 CAT: 17

Association of Governing Boards of Univs and Colls
CIJE: 17 RIE: 2 CAT: 17

Association of Graduate Schools
CIJE: 0 RIE: 2 CAT: 17

Association of Head Mistresses
CIJE: 1 RIE: 0 CAT: 17

Association of Higher Education
CIJE: 0 RIE: 1 CAT: 17

Association of Information Dissemination Centers
CIJE: 1 RIE: 1 CAT: 17

Association of International Libraries
CIJE: 1 RIE: 1 CAT: 17

Association of Junior Leagues International
CIJE: 0 RIE: 0 CAT: 17
SN For local units, use the generic "Junior League"

Association of London Housing Estates
CIJE: 1 RIE: 0 CAT: 17

Association of Louisiana Evaluators
CIJE: 0 RIE: 1 CAT: 17

Association of Mexican American Educators Inc
CIJE: 0 RIE: 1 CAT: 17

Association of Modern Minority Officers
CIJE: 1 RIE: 0 CAT: 17

Association of New York Libraries for Tech Servs
CIJE: 0 RIE: 2 CAT: 17

Association of Pathology Chairmen
CIJE: 1 RIE: 0 CAT: 17

Association of Physical Plant Administrators
CIJE: 7 RIE: 4 CAT: 17

Association of Polytechnic Teachers
CIJE: 1 RIE: 0 CAT: 17

Association of Professors of Higher Education
CIJE: 1 RIE: 1 CAT: 17

Association of Records Managers and Administrators
CIJE: 0 RIE: 1 CAT: 17

Association of Research Libraries
CIJE: 74 RIE: 192 CAT: 17

Association of School Business Officials
CIJE: 16 RIE: 4 CAT: 17

Association of Schools of Public Health
CIJE: 0 RIE: 1 CAT: 17

Association of Schs of Applied Health Professions
CIJE: 1 RIE: 0 CAT: 17

Association of Scientific Inf Dissemination Ctrs
CIJE: 0 RIE: 2 CAT: 17

Association of South Central Oklahoma Governments
CIJE: 0 RIE: 1 CAT: 17

Association of Southeast Asian Nations
CIJE: 3 RIE: 2 CAT: 17

Association of State Assessment Programs
CIJE: 0 RIE: 1 CAT: 17

Association of Teacher Educators
CIJE: 18 RIE: 9 CAT: 17

Association of Teachers of Mathematics
CIJE: 1 RIE: 1 CAT: 17

Association of Teachers of Preventive Medicine
CIJE: 3 RIE: 0 CAT: 17

Association of Theological Schools
CIJE: 1 RIE: 1 CAT: 17
SN "Association of Theological Schools in the United States and Canada"

Association of Universities and Colleges of Canada
CIJE: 0 RIE: 2 CAT: 17

Association of University Evening Colleges
CIJE: 1 RIE: 7 CAT: 17

Association of Urban Universities
CIJE: 1 RIE: 1 CAT: 17

Association of World Colleges and Universities
CIJE: 1 RIE: 0 CAT: 17

Association Pennsylvania State Coll Univ Faculties
CIJE: 0 RIE: 2 CAT: 17

Association Role
CIJE: 3 RIE: 0 CAT: 16

Association Strength
CIJE: 3 RIE: 1 CAT: 11

Association Test (Otto and Koenke)
CIJE: 0 RIE: 1 CAT: 21

Association University Professors Ophthalmology
CIJE: 1 RIE: 0 CAT: 17

Associational Montage
CIJE: 0 RIE: 1 CAT: 15

Associative Clustering
CIJE: 2 RIE: 1 CAT: 20

Associative Fluency
CIJE: 1 RIE: 1 CAT: 11

Associative Group Analysis
CIJE: 2 RIE: 1 CAT: 15

Associative Grouping Strategies
CIJE: 0 RIE: 1 CAT: 15

Associative Method of Teaching
CIJE: 1 RIE: 1 CAT: 15

Associative Storage
CIJE: 2 RIE: 1 CAT: 20

Associative Symmetry
CIJE: 1 RIE: 0 CAT: 20

Assumed Similarity of Opposites
CIJE: 1 RIE: 0 CAT: 15

Assumption Recognition Index
CIJE: 0 RIE: 1 CAT: 21

Assumptions (Testing)
CIJE: 12 RIE: 3 CAT: 21

Astin (Alexander W)
CIJE: 2 RIE: 4 CAT: 18

Astin Index
CIJE: 0 RIE: 1 CAT: 21

Astor (Nancy)
CIJE: 0 RIE: 1 CAT: 18

Astor Program for Gifted Children
CIJE: 0 RIE: 3 CAT: 19

Astoria Park Elementary School FL
CIJE: 1 RIE: 0 CAT: 17

Astro Archaeology
CIJE: 1 RIE: 0 CAT: 03

Astrology
CIJE: 17 RIE: 3 CAT: 03

Astronauts
CIJE: 7 RIE: 6 CAT: 09

Astrophotography
CIJE: 2 RIE: 0 CAT: 20

Astrophysics
CIJE: 19 RIE: 5 CAT: 20

Asturias (Miguel Angel)
CIJE: 5 RIE: 0 CAT: 18

Aswan Dam
CIJE: 0 RIE: 2 CAT: 07

Asylum
CIJE: 9 RIE: 6 CAT: 14

Asymmetric Data
CIJE: 9 RIE: 1 CAT: 21

Asymmetric Relationships
CIJE: 7 RIE: 1 CAT: 15

Asymmetry (Language)
CIJE: 2 RIE: 0 CAT: 13

Asymptotic Distribution Theory
CIJE: 8 RIE: 1 CAT: 15

Asymptotic Distributions
CIJE: 13 RIE: 6 CAT: 21

Asymptotic Power
CIJE: 1 RIE: 0 CAT: 21

Asymptotic Standard Errors
CIJE: 3 RIE: 0 CAT: 21

At Home Program
CIJE: 0 RIE: 1 CAT: 19

At Risk Child Care Program
CIJE: 0 RIE: 1 CAT: 19

At Will Rule
CIJE: 0 RIE: 1 CAT: 14

At Your Service (Computer Program)
CIJE: 0 RIE: 1 CAT: 04

Atari
CIJE: 0 RIE: 1 CAT: 04

Atari 400
CIJE: 1 RIE: 0 CAT: 04

Atari 800
CIJE: 0 RIE: 1 CAT: 04

Atariwriter
CIJE: 0 RIE: 1 CAT: 04

Atcon Report 1961
CIJE: 0 RIE: 0 CAT: 22

ATE Inventory (Flynn)
CIJE: 0 RIE: 1 CAT: 21

Ateso
CIJE: 1 RIE: 0 CAT: 13

Athabasca University AB
CIJE: 14 RIE: 24 CAT: 17

Athapascan (Tribe)
CIJE: 9 RIE: 18 CAT: 08

Atheism
CIJE: 11 RIE: 3 CAT: 16

Athena Language Learning Project
CIJE: 1 RIE: 1 CAT: 19

Athens Area Vocational Technical School GA
CIJE: 0 RIE: 1 CAT: 17

Athens City School District OH
CIJE: 0 RIE: 1 CAT: 17

Athens Symposium on Child in World of Tomorrow
CIJE: 0 RIE: 1 CAT: 02

Athletes Coaching Teens (Program)
CIJE: 0 RIE: 1 CAT: 19

Athletic Ability
CIJE: 3 RIE: 2 CAT: 16

Athletic Abuses
CIJE: 4 RIE: 2 CAT: 16

Athletic Administration
CIJE: 4 RIE: 6 CAT: 16

Athletic Administrators
CIJE: 7 RIE: 1 CAT: 09

Athletic Amenorrhea
USE Amenorrhea

Athletic Departments
CIJE: 2 RIE: 2 CAT: 05

Athletic Directors
CIJE: 8 RIE: 1 CAT: 09

Athletic Draft
CIJE: 1 RIE: 0 CAT: 16

Athletic Facilities
CIJE: 1 RIE: 3 CAT: 05

Athletic Scholarships
CIJE: 0 RIE: 2 CAT: 16

Athletic Trainers
CIJE: 17 RIE: 23 CAT: 09

Atitecos
CIJE: 1 RIE: 0 CAT: 08

Atkinson (John W)
CIJE: 1 RIE: 1 CAT: 18

Atkinson (Richard C)
CIJE: 2 RIE: 1 CAT: 18

Atkinson Theory of Motivation
CIJE: 0 RIE: 1 CAT: 15

Atlanta Area School for the Deaf GA
CIJE: 1 RIE: 0 CAT: 17

Atlanta Desegregation Plan
CIJE: 0 RIE: 1 CAT: 19

Atlanta Dropout Prevention Collaborative GA
CIJE: 0 RIE: 2 CAT: 17

Atlanta Partnership of Business and Education Inc
CIJE: 2 RIE: 3 CAT: 17

Atlanta Project
CIJE: 0 RIE: 2 CAT: 19

Atlanta Public Schools GA
CIJE: 9 RIE: 89 CAT: 17

Atlanta South Metro Psychoeducational Center GA
CIJE: 0 RIE: 1 CAT: 17

Atlanta Student Manpower Project
CIJE: 0 RIE: 1 CAT: 19

Atlanta University GA
CIJE: 3 RIE: 3 CAT: 17

Atlanta World
CIJE: 0 RIE: 1 CAT: 22

Atlantic Baptist College NB
CIJE: 0 RIE: 5 CAT: 17

Atlantic Community College NJ
CIJE: 1 RIE: 3 CAT: 17

Atlantic Institute of Education NS
CIJE: 0 RIE: 1 CAT: 17

Atlantic Ocean
CIJE: 5 RIE: 2 CAT: 07

Atlantic Richfield Foundation
CIJE: 1 RIE: 0 CAT: 17

Atlantic Science Curriculum Project NS
CIJE: 1 RIE: 0 CAT: 19

Atlantic Vocational Technical Center FL
CIJE: 0 RIE: 1 CAT: 17

Atmospheres
CIJE: 8 RIE: 4 CAT: 16

Atmospheric Contaminant Sensors
CIJE: 0 RIE: 1 CAT: 04

Atmospheric Oxidants
CIJE: 1 RIE: 0 CAT: 20

Atmospheric Physics
CIJE: 1 RIE: 0 CAT: 20

Atmospheric Sciences
CIJE: 1 RIE: 2 CAT: 20

ATMs (Banking)
USE Automated Teller Machines

ATNs
USE Augmented Transition Network Grammars

Atomic Bomb
CIJE: 2 RIE: 2 CAT: 20

Atomic Bomb Casualty Commission
CIJE: 1 RIE: 0 CAT: 17

Atomic Energy Commission
CIJE: 15 RIE: 30 CAT: 17

Atomic Energy Occupations
CIJE: 1 RIE: 0 CAT: 09

Atomic Industrial Forum
CIJE: 1 RIE: 0 CAT: 02

Atonal Music
CIJE: 0 RIE: 1 CAT: 16

ATP Physics Test
USE Physics Achievement Test (ATP)

Atriums
CIJE: 4 RIE: 0 CAT: 05

ATS 1 Geosynchronous Satellite
CIJE: 0 RIE: 2 CAT: 04

Atsina
USE Arapaho

Atsugewi
CIJE: 0 RIE: 1 CAT: 13

Attachment Disorders
CIJE: 2 RIE: 2 CAT: 11

Attachment Inventory (Schaefer)
CIJE: 0 RIE: 1 CAT: 21

Attachment Security
USE Security of Attachment

Attack on Pearl Harbor Cloud of Mystery
CIJE: 0 RIE: 1 CAT: 22

Attacking the Wall
CIJE: 1 RIE: 0 CAT: 22

Attendance Improvement Plan
CIJE: 1 RIE: 11 CAT: 19

Attention Diversion
CIJE: 3 RIE: 3 CAT: 11

Attention Interest Desire and Action Approach
CIJE: 0 RIE: 1 CAT: 15
UF AIDA Plan

Attention Reduction Training
CIJE: 0 RIE: 1 CAT: 15

Attention Relevance Confidence Satisfaction Model
USE ARCS Model

Attention Test
CIJE: 1 RIE: 2 CAT: 21

Attention Theory
CIJE: 9 RIE: 7 CAT: 15

Attenuation Paradox
CIJE: 2 RIE: 1 CAT: 21

Attitude and Motivation Test Battery
CIJE: 1 RIE: 0 CAT: 21

Attitude Appreciations
CIJE: 0 RIE: 15 CAT: 21

Attitude Assessment Inventory
CIJE: 1 RIE: 0 CAT: 21

Attitude Behavior Scale Law Education
CIJE: 0 RIE: 1 CAT: 21

Attitude Discrepant Behavior
CIJE: 2 RIE: 0 CAT: 11

Attitude Flexibility
USE Flexibility (Attitude)

Attitude Information System
CIJE: 2 RIE: 0 CAT: 15

Attitude Interest Analysis Test
CIJE: 1 RIE: 0 CAT: 21

Attitude Inventory
CIJE: 4 RIE: 2 CAT: 21

Attitude Problem Questionnaire (Newman)
CIJE: 0 RIE: 1 CAT: 21

Attitude Scale
CIJE: 1 RIE: 4 CAT: 21

Attitude Story Test (Hohn and Swartz)
CIJE: 0 RIE: 1 CAT: 21

Attitude Strength
CIJE: 0 RIE: 2 CAT: 11

Attitude to School Questionnaire (Strickland)
CIJE: 1 RIE: 2 CAT: 21

Attitude Toward Blindness Questionnaire
CIJE: 0 RIE: 2 CAT: 21

Attitude Toward Cheating Scale
CIJE: 1 RIE: 1 CAT: 21

Attitude Toward Disabled Persons Scale
CIJE: 11 RIE: 3 CAT: 21

Attitude Toward Educational Research Scale
CIJE: 0 RIE: 3 CAT: 21

Attitude Toward Handicapped Individuals Scale
CIJE: 0 RIE: 2 CAT: 21
UF Attitude Towards Handicapped Individuals Scale

Attitude Toward Inservice Scale (Trueblood et al)
CIJE: 0 RIE: 1 CAT: 21

Attitude Toward Math Scale (Suydam Trueblood)
USE Suydam Trueblood Attitude Toward Mathematics Scale

Attitude Toward Programed Instruction Inventory
CIJE: 0 RIE: 1 CAT: 21

Attitude Toward Radioactivity Scale
CIJE: 1 RIE: 1 CAT: 21

Attitude Toward Reading Scale (Askov Trueblood)
USE Askov Trueblood Attitude Toward Reading Scale

Attitude Toward Reading Scale (Kux)
CIJE: 1 RIE: 0 CAT: 21

Attitude Toward School
CIJE: 4 RIE: 5 CAT: 21

Attitude Toward School Questionnaire
CIJE: 0 RIE: 1 CAT: 21

Attitude Towards Handicapped Individuals Scale
USE Attitude Toward Handicapped Individuals Scale

Attitudes Inventory for Youth
CIJE: 0 RIE: 1 CAT: 21

Attitudes of Professional Autonomy Scale
CIJE: 0 RIE: 1 CAT: 21

Attitudes to Physical Activity Inventory (Kenyon)
CIJE: 1 RIE: 0 CAT: 21

Attitudes to Science Scale
CIJE: 0 RIE: 1 CAT: 21

Attitudes Toward AIDS Scale
CIJE: 0 RIE: 1 CAT: 21

Attitudes Toward College Inventory
CIJE: 0 RIE: 1 CAT: 21

Attitudes Toward Computer Technologies
CIJE: 0 RIE: 1 CAT: 21

Attitudes toward Disabled
CIJE: 76 RIE: 20 CAT: 16

Attitudes Toward Educational Research Scale
CIJE: 1 RIE: 0 CAT: 21

Attitudes Toward Feminist Issues Scale (Elmore)
CIJE: 2 RIE: 1 CAT: 21

Attitudes Toward Love Scale (Knox and Sporakowski)
USE Knox Sporakowski Attitudes Toward Love Scale

Attitudes Toward Mainstreaming Scale
CIJE: 4 RIE: 3 CAT: 21

Attitudes Toward Men in Society Scale
CIJE: 0 RIE: 1 CAT: 21

Attitudes Toward Old People Scale
CIJE: 0 RIE: 1 CAT: 21

Attitudes Toward Parents Questionnaire
CIJE: 1 RIE: 0 CAT: 21

Attitudes Toward Reading Inventory (Hunt)
CIJE: 0 RIE: 1 CAT: 21

Attitudes Toward Reading Scale
CIJE: 0 RIE: 3 CAT: 21

Attitudes Toward Science and Scientists Scale
CIJE: 0 RIE: 0 CAT: 21

Attitudes Toward Social Issues in Medicine
CIJE: 1 RIE: 0 CAT: 21

Attitudes Toward Statistics (Wise)
CIJE: 0 RIE: 1 CAT: 21

Attitudes Toward Testing Scale
CIJE: 0 RIE: 1 CAT: 21

Attitudes Toward the Elderly Scale
CIJE: 0 RIE: 1 CAT: 21

Attitudes Toward Vocational Education Scale
CIJE: 0 RIE: 1 CAT: 21

Attitudes Toward Women Scale
CIJE: 18 RIE: 12 CAT: 21

Attitudes Toward Work and Money Questionnaire
CIJE: 1 RIE: 0 CAT: 21

Attitudes Toward Working Mothers Scale
CIJE: 2 RIE: 0 CAT: 21

Attitudes Towards the World of Work Scales
CIJE: 1 RIE: 0 CAT: 21

Attitudinal Militancy Scale (Wohnsiedler)
CIJE: 1 RIE: 0 CAT: 21

Attitudinal Reinforcing Discriminative Stimuli
CIJE: 0 RIE: 3 CAT: 11

ATTLAS Program
CIJE: 0 RIE: 1 CAT: 19
UF Augmenting Thinking Thru Lang Acquisition Skills

Attleboro Public School District MA
CIJE: 0 RIE: 1 CAT: 17

Attorney Generals Commission on Pornography
USE Meese Commission on Pornography

Attorneys Fees
USE Lawyers Fees

Attribute Blocks
CIJE: 5 RIE: 1 CAT: 04

Attribute by Treatment Interaction
CIJE: 2 RIE: 2 CAT: 15

Attribute Characteristic Curves
CIJE: 0 RIE: 1 CAT: 21

Attribute Frequency Model
CIJE: 1 RIE: 0 CAT: 15

Attribute Identification
CIJE: 16 RIE: 4 CAT: 15

Attribute Interest Form
CIJE: 0 RIE: 1 CAT: 21

Attribute Preference Attribute Description Scale
CIJE: 0 RIE: 2 CAT: 21

Attribute Requirement Inventory
CIJE: 0 RIE: 2 CAT: 21

Attributed Responsibility
CIJE: 0 RIE: 1 CAT: 15

Attribution Pattern Variable
CIJE: 1 RIE: 1 CAT: 21

Attribution Style Questionnaire
CIJE: 0 RIE: 6 CAT: 21

Attributional Feedback
CIJE: 3 RIE: 3 CAT: 11

Attributional Style Assessment Test
CIJE: 0 RIE: 1 CAT: 21

Attributive Theory of Quality
CIJE: 0 RIE: 1 CAT: 15

Atwood (Margaret)
CIJE: 5 RIE: 2 CAT: 18

Atypical Response Scale
CIJE: 0 RIE: 1 CAT: 21

Atypicality
CIJE: 4 RIE: 2 CAT: 11

Aub (Max)
CIJE: 1 RIE: 0 CAT: 18

Auburn City School District NY
CIJE: 0 RIE: 2 CAT: 17

Auburn Community College NY
CIJE: 1 RIE: 0 CAT: 17

Auburn University AL
CIJE: 30 RIE: 25 CAT: 17

Auchiah (James)
CIJE: 1 RIE: 0 CAT: 18

Auctioneers
CIJE: 0 RIE: 1 CAT: 09

Auctions
CIJE: 5 RIE: 0 CAT: 16

AUDACIOUS
CIJE: 0 RIE: 1 CAT: 15

Audiation
CIJE: 3 RIE: 1 CAT: 16

Audible Multi Imagery
CIJE: 0 RIE: 1 CAT: 15

Audience Education
CIJE: 0 RIE: 3 CAT: 16

Audience Research
CIJE: 30 RIE: 20 CAT: 15

Audience Specification
CIJE: 4 RIE: 1 CAT: 15

Audio Compression
CIJE: 0 RIE: 1 CAT: 20

Audio Cuing
CIJE: 0 RIE: 2 CAT: 11

Audio Feedback
CIJE: 0 RIE: 1 CAT: 20

Audio Intercommunication Systems
CIJE: 1 RIE: 1 CAT: 15

Audio Motor Units
CIJE: 0 RIE: 1 CAT: 15

Audio Notebook
CIJE: 0 RIE: 2 CAT: 04

Audio Reader
CIJE: 1 RIE: 1 CAT: 04

Audio Reading Progress Laboratory OH
CIJE: 0 RIE: 1 CAT: 17

Audio Tutorial Instruction
CIJE: 12 RIE: 8 CAT: 15

Audio Video Data Signals
CIJE: 0 RIE: 1 CAT: 20

Audio Video Recording
CIJE: 1 RIE: 2 CAT: 20

Audio Virtual Classrooms
CIJE: 0 RIE: 1 CAT: 05

Audio Visual Activities Commission
CIJE: 1 RIE: 0 CAT: 17

Audio Visual Education Association of California
CIJE: 0 RIE: 1 CAT: 17

Audio Visual Satellite Instruction
CIJE: 0 RIE: 1 CAT: 19

Audio Visual Structural Global Method
CIJE: 1 RIE: 0 CAT: 15

Audio Visual Tutorial Method
CIJE: 2 RIE: 1 CAT: 15

Audioanalgesia
CIJE: 0 RIE: 1 CAT: 11

Audiocups
CIJE: 1 RIE: 0 CAT: 04

Audiographic Learning Facility
CIJE: 0 RIE: 2 CAT: 17

Audiographics
CIJE: 17 RIE: 32 CAT: 04

Audioinstructional Programs
CIJE: 1 RIE: 3 CAT: 19

Audiolingual Aids
CIJE: 1 RIE: 4 CAT: 04

Audiometer Trainer Unit
CIJE: 0 RIE: 1 CAT: 04

Audiotex
CIJE: 1 RIE: 2 CAT: 20

Audiotutorial Equipment
CIJE: 1 RIE: 1 CAT: 04

Audiotutorial Minicourses
CIJE: 0 RIE: 1 CAT: 03

Audiotutorial System
CIJE: 9 RIE: 3 CAT: 15

Audiovisual Archives
CIJE: 1 RIE: 1 CAT: 16

Audiovisual Contracting
CIJE: 1 RIE: 0 CAT: 15

Audit Clerks
CIJE: 0 RIE: 1 CAT: 09

Audit Dress Rehearsal
CIJE: 0 RIE: 1 CAT: 21

Audit of Principal Effectiveness
CIJE: 0 RIE: 3 CAT: 21

Audit Trails
CIJE: 1 RIE: 3 CAT: 15

Audition (Theatrical)
CIJE: 4 RIE: 3 CAT: 15

Auditions (Music)
CIJE: 1 RIE: 0 CAT: 15

Auditors
CIJE: 11 RIE: 11 CAT: 09

Auditory Acuity
CIJE: 3 RIE: 1 CAT: 11

Auditory Analysis Test
CIJE: 3 RIE: 1 CAT: 21

Auditory Automotive Mechanics Diagnostic Achiev
CIJE: 1 RIE: 1 CAT: 21

Auditory Closure
CIJE: 1 RIE: 0 CAT: 11

Auditory Comprehension Test (Green and Kramar)
CIJE: 0 RIE: 1 CAT: 21

Auditory Conceptualization
CIJE: 0 RIE: 1 CAT: 11

Auditory Dimensional Preference Task
CIJE: 0 RIE: 1 CAT: 21

Auditory Discrimination in Depth Program
CIJE: 1 RIE: 5 CAT: 19

Auditory Figure Ground
CIJE: 0 RIE: 1 CAT: 11

Auditory Icons
CIJE: 0 RIE: 1 CAT: 15

Auditory Impulsivity Task (Kennedy and Butter)
CIJE: 2 RIE: 0 CAT: 21

Auditory Recognition Test (Brickner)
CIJE: 0 RIE: 1 CAT: 21

Auditory Sensory Memory
CIJE: 1 RIE: 1 CAT: 11

Audubon Conservation Program
CIJE: 1 RIE: 0 CAT: 19

Auerbach (Erich)
CIJE: 1 RIE: 0 CAT: 18

Auerbach Badger Discussion Group Program
CIJE: 0 RIE: 1 CAT: 19

Augmented Transition Network Grammars
CIJE: 3 RIE: 1 CAT: 20
UF ATNs

Augmenting Thinking Thru Lang Acquisition Skills
USE ATTLAS Program

Augsburg College MN
CIJE: 4 RIE: 2 CAT: 17

August (Month)
CIJE: 0 RIE: 0 CAT: 16

Augusta Unified School District 402 KS
CIJE: 0 RIE: 1 CAT: 17

Augustana College SD
CIJE: 0 RIE: 4 CAT: 17

Augustine (Saint)
CIJE: 5 RIE: 2 CAT: 18

Aumsville School District OR
CIJE: 0 RIE: 2 CAT: 17

Aunt Marthas Youth Service Center IL
CIJE: 0 RIE: 1 CAT: 17

Aural Records
CIJE: 1 RIE: 0 CAT: 04

Aural Study System
CIJE: 0 RIE: 1 CAT: 15

Auraria Higher Education Center CO
CIJE: 4 RIE: 1 CAT: 17

Auraria Library CO
CIJE: 1 RIE: 1 CAT: 17

Aurora College IL
CIJE: 1 RIE: 0 CAT: 17

Aurora PRECIS Project
CIJE: 0 RIE: 1 CAT: 19

Aurora Public Library IL
CIJE: 1 RIE: 0 CAT: 17

Aurora West Public Schools IL
CIJE: 0 RIE: 1 CAT: 17

Auscultation
CIJE: 0 RIE: 1 CAT: 11

AUSINET
CIJE: 1 RIE: 1 CAT: 17

Austen (Jane)
CIJE: 10 RIE: 3 CAT: 18

Austin (J L)
CIJE: 3 RIE: 2 CAT: 18
SN "John"

Austin College TX
CIJE: 4 RIE: 17 CAT: 17

Austin Community College TX
CIJE: 4 RIE: 8 CAT: 17

Austin Independent School District TX
CIJE: 8 RIE: 313 CAT: 17

Austin Longitudinal Research Project
CIJE: 1 RIE: 0 CAT: 19

Austin Peay State University TN
CIJE: 2 RIE: 3 CAT: 17

Austin Public Library TX
CIJE: 1 RIE: 1 CAT: 17

Austin Science and Mathematics Consortium TX
CIJE: 0 RIE: 1 CAT: 19

Austin State School TX
CIJE: 0 RIE: 1 CAT: 17

Austin State University TX
CIJE: 0 RIE: 1 CAT: 17

Austin Teacher Program TX
CIJE: 0 RIE: 1 CAT: 19

Austin Youth River Watch Program TX
CIJE: 0 RIE: 1 CAT: 19

Australasia
CIJE: 12 RIE: 3 CAT: 07

Australasian Association Institutional Research
CIJE: 0 RIE: 2 CAT: 17
SN "Australasian Association for Institutional..."

Australia
CIJE: 3282 RIE: 2236 CAT: 07

Australia (Adelaide)
CIJE: 9 RIE: 4 CAT: 07

Australia (Australian Capital Territory)
CIJE: 1 RIE: 5 CAT: 07

Australia (Brisbane)
CIJE: 14 RIE: 9 CAT: 07

Australia (East Kimberley)
CIJE: 0 RIE: 1 CAT: 07

Australia (Hallet Cove)
CIJE: 1 RIE: 0 CAT: 07

Australia (Maria Island)
CIJE: 0 RIE: 1 CAT: 07

Australia (Melbourne)
CIJE: 43 RIE: 23 CAT: 07

Australia (New South Wales)
CIJE: 115 RIE: 148 CAT: 07

Australia (Northern Territory)
CIJE: 4 RIE: 22 CAT: 07

Australia (Perth)
CIJE: 11 RIE: 3 CAT: 07

Australia (Queensland)
CIJE: 84 RIE: 135 CAT: 07

Australia (Riverina)
CIJE: 0 RIE: 1 CAT: 07

Australia (South Australia)
CIJE: 42 RIE: 44 CAT: 07

Australia (Sturt Gorge)
CIJE: 2 RIE: 0 CAT: 07

Australia (Sydney)
CIJE: 44 RIE: 39 CAT: 07

Australia (Tasmania)
CIJE: 33 RIE: 49 CAT: 07

Australia (Toomelah)
CIJE: 0 RIE: 1 CAT: 07

Australia (Torres Strait)
CIJE: 2 RIE: 1 CAT: 07
UF Torres Strait Islands

Australia (Victoria)
CIJE: 87 RIE: 118 CAT: 07

Australia (Wagga Wagga)
CIJE: 1 RIE: 0 CAT: 07

Australia (Western Australia)
CIJE: 59 RIE: 88 CAT: 07

Australia (Wycheproof)
CIJE: 0 RIE: 1 CAT: 07

Australian Association for the Teaching of English
CIJE: 1 RIE: 5 CAT: 17

Australian Association of Adult Education
CIJE: 2 RIE: 2 CAT: 17

Australian Bibliographic Network
CIJE: 2 RIE: 1 CAT: 17

Australian Broadcasting Commission
CIJE: 1 RIE: 3 CAT: 17

Australian Commonwealth Schools Commission
USE Commonwealth Schools Commission (Australia)

Australian Council for Educational Research
CIJE: 0 RIE: 17 CAT: 17

Australian Council of Trade Unions
CIJE: 1 RIE: 0 CAT: 17

Australian Culture
CIJE: 0 RIE: 1 CAT: 16

Australian Education Index Data Base
CIJE: 1 RIE: 1 CAT: 04

Australian Family Research Conference
CIJE: 0 RIE: 7 CAT: 02

Australian Frontier Incorporated
CIJE: 1 RIE: 0 CAT: 17

Australian Humanities Research Council
CIJE: 0 RIE: 1 CAT: 17

Australian Institute of Multicultural Affairs
CIJE: 0 RIE: 1 CAT: 17

Australian Language Levels Project
CIJE: 0 RIE: 5 CAT: 19
UF ALL Model

Australian National Satellite System
CIJE: 3 RIE: 1 CAT: 04

Australian National University
CIJE: 15 RIE: 4 CAT: 17

Australian Open Learning Information Network
CIJE: 2 RIE: 1 CAT: 17

Australian Outward Bound School
CIJE: 0 RIE: 1 CAT: 17

Australian Preschool Association
CIJE: 0 RIE: 1 CAT: 17

Australian Scholastic Aptitude Tests
CIJE: 6 RIE: 2 CAT: 21

Australian Science Education Project
CIJE: 39 RIE: 64 CAT: 19

Australian Science Education Research Association
CIJE: 0 RIE: 3 CAT: 17

Australian Second Language Learning Program
CIJE: 0 RIE: 1 CAT: 19

Australian Second Language Proficiency Ratings
CIJE: 0 RIE: 2 CAT: 21

Australian Sex Role Scale
CIJE: 0 RIE: 3 CAT: 21

Australian Standards of Work Performance
USE Standards of Work Performance (Australia)

Australian Studies in Student Performance
CIJE: 2 RIE: 2 CAT: 19

Australian Universities Commission
CIJE: 0 RIE: 1 CAT: 17

Australians
CIJE: 16 RIE: 17 CAT: 08

Austria
CIJE: 99 RIE: 110 CAT: 07

Austria (Molltal)
CIJE: 1 RIE: 0 CAT: 07

Austria (Vienna)
CIJE: 6 RIE: 5 CAT: 07

Austrian Broadcasting Corporation
CIJE: 0 RIE: 1 CAT: 17

Ausubel (David P)
CIJE: 57 RIE: 39 CAT: 18

Authentic Assessment
CIJE: 67 RIE: 99 CAT: 21
SN Student assessment in which knowledges and skills are measured using the real world environment, rather than standardized tests

Authentic Materials
CIJE: 73 RIE: 94 CAT: 16

Authenticity
CIJE: 32 RIE: 8 CAT: 16

Author Reader Relationship
CIJE: 38 RIE: 38 CAT: 13
UF Reader Author Relationship

Author Text Relationship
CIJE: 32 RIE: 51 CAT: 13

Authoritarian Behavior
CIJE: 9 RIE: 6 CAT: 11

Authoritarian Teaching
CIJE: 3 RIE: 2 CAT: 16

Authoritative Parenting
CIJE: 10 RIE: 6 CAT: 16

Authority
CIJE: 82 RIE: 44 CAT: 16

Authority Base
CIJE: 1 RIE: 1 CAT: 16

Authority Figures
CIJE: 15 RIE: 6 CAT: 16

Authority Files (Names)
USE Name Authority Files

Authority Social Truth Value Cluster Measure
CIJE: 0 RIE: 1 CAT: 21

Authors in the Schools
CIJE: 0 RIE: 1 CAT: 15

Authorship
CIJE: 24 RIE: 7 CAT: 16

Autism Attitude Scale for Teachers
CIJE: 0 RIE: 1 CAT: 21

Autobiographical Memory
USE Autobiographical Recall

Autobiographical Recall
CIJE: 2 RIE: 1 CAT: 11
UF Autobiographical Memory

Autobiography of Malcolm X
CIJE: 4 RIE: 0 CAT: 22

AutoCAD
CIJE: 0 RIE: 2 CAT: 04

Autoclave Operators
CIJE: 0 RIE: 1 CAT: 09

Autocoders
CIJE: 1 RIE: 1 CAT: 04

Autocorrelation
CIJE: 1 RIE: 4 CAT: 15

Autocracy
CIJE: 2 RIE: 2 CAT: 12

Autogenic Training
CIJE: 6 RIE: 1 CAT: 11

Autographs
CIJE: 2 RIE: 1 CAT: 16

Autoharps
CIJE: 0 RIE: 1 CAT: 04

Autoimmune Disease
CIJE: 3 RIE: 0 CAT: 11

Autokinetic Word Writing Technique
CIJE: 1 RIE: 0 CAT: 15

Automata Models
CIJE: 0 RIE: 1 CAT: 15

Automata Theory
CIJE: 2 RIE: 2 CAT: 15

Automated Affirmative Action System
CIJE: 0 RIE: 1 CAT: 15

Automated Braille System
CIJE: 0 RIE: 1 CAT: 15

Automated Cognitive Modeler
CIJE: 0 RIE: 2 CAT: 15

Automated Copy Editing
CIJE: 0 RIE: 1 CAT: 20

Automated Drafting Board
CIJE: 1 RIE: 0 CAT: 04

Automated Feedback
CIJE: 0 RIE: 1 CAT: 16

Automated Individualized Diagnosis System
CIJE: 0 RIE: 1 CAT: 15

Automated Instructional Management Systems
CIJE: 0 RIE: 11 CAT: 15

Automated Instructional Materials Handling System
CIJE: 0 RIE: 1 CAT: 15

Automated Instructional System
CIJE: 2 RIE: 2 CAT: 15

Automated Leadership Training Program
CIJE: 0 RIE: 1 CAT: 19

Automated Library Systems Migration
CIJE: 0 RIE: 1 CAT: 20

Automated Literature Alerting Service
CIJE: 1 RIE: 0 CAT: 17

Automated Machining
CIJE: 0 RIE: 1 CAT: 20

Automated Management Planning Control Systems
CIJE: 2 RIE: 0 CAT: 15

Automated Monitoring
CIJE: 0 RIE: 2 CAT: 15

Automated Readability Index
CIJE: 0 RIE: 2 CAT: 21

Automated Speech Recognition
USE Automatic Speech Recognition

Automated Stimulus Control System
CIJE: 0 RIE: 1 CAT: 15

Automated Teller Machines
CIJE: 2 RIE: 0 CAT: 04
UF ATMs (Banking); Automatic Tellers

Automated Tutoring
CIJE: 0 RIE: 2 CAT: 15

Automatic Content Analysis
CIJE: 2 RIE: 2 CAT: 15

Automatic Control Systems
CIJE: 1 RIE: 5 CAT: 15

Automatic Explanation of Reasoning
CIJE: 0 RIE: 1 CAT: 04

Automatic Extracting
CIJE: 2 RIE: 0 CAT: 20

Automatic Interaction Detector
CIJE: 7 RIE: 5 CAT: 04

Automatic Language Processing
CIJE: 8 RIE: 5 CAT: 20

Automatic Perceptual Processes
CIJE: 1 RIE: 1 CAT: 11

Automatic Program Synthesis
CIJE: 0 RIE: 1 CAT: 20

Automatic Speech Recognition
CIJE: 3 RIE: 6 CAT: 20
SN See also "Speech Recognition" and "Voice Recognition"
UF Automated Speech Recognition

Automatic Tellers
USE Automated Teller Machines

Automatic Vocal Transaction Analyzer
CIJE: 1 RIE: 1 CAT: 04

Automaticity Training
CIJE: 18 RIE: 4 CAT: 15

Automatization
CIJE: 7 RIE: 7 CAT: 11

Automaton Analysis
CIJE: 0 RIE: 1 CAT: 15

Automobile Adjustment
CIJE: 0 RIE: 1 CAT: 20

Automobile Alignment
CIJE: 0 RIE: 2 CAT: 20

Automobile Industry
CIJE: 43 RIE: 18 CAT: 20

Automobile Insurance
CIJE: 0 RIE: 3 CAT: 16

Automobile Painters
CIJE: 0 RIE: 1 CAT: 09

Automobile Parts
CIJE: 0 RIE: 1 CAT: 04

Automobile Service Station Attendants
USE Gas Station Attendants

Automobile Theft
CIJE: 3 RIE: 0 CAT: 14

Automobile Workers
CIJE: 5 RIE: 7 CAT: 09

Automobiles
CIJE: 16 RIE: 19 CAT: 04

Automotive Brakes
USE Brakes (Automotive)

Automotive Charging Systems
CIJE: 0 RIE: 0 CAT: 20

Automotive Clutches
USE Clutches (Automotive)

Automotive Collision Appraisal
CIJE: 1 RIE: 0 CAT: 15

Automotive Computers
CIJE: 0 RIE: 1 CAT: 04

Automotive Cooling Systems
CIJE: 0 RIE: 2 CAT: 04

Automotive Cranking Systems
CIJE: 0 RIE: 2 CAT: 20

Automotive Drive Trains
USE Drive Trains (Automotive)

Automotive Electrical Systems
CIJE: 0 RIE: 2 CAT: 04

Automotive Exhaust Systems
CIJE: 0 RIE: 4 CAT: 04

Automotive Front End Types
USE Front End Types (Automotive)

Automotive Fuel Systems
CIJE: 0 RIE: 19 CAT: 20

Automotive Service Advisors
CIJE: 0 RIE: 1 CAT: 09

Automotive Service Attendants
USE Gas Station Attendants

Automotive Supplies
CIJE: 0 RIE: 1 CAT: 04

Automotive Suspension Systems
CIJE: 0 RIE: 3 CAT: 04

Automotive Trade Association Managers
CIJE: 0 RIE: 1 CAT: 09

Automotive Transaxles
USE Transaxles (Automotive)

Automotive Transmissions
USE Transmissions (Automotive)

Automotive Tune Up
CIJE: 0 RIE: 24 CAT: 20

Automotive Tune Up Teaching System
CIJE: 1 RIE: 0 CAT: 15

Autonomic Nervous System
CIJE: 7 RIE: 5 CAT: 11

Autonomic Perception Questionnaire
CIJE: 0 RIE: 1 CAT: 21

Autonomic Responses
CIJE: 6 RIE: 0 CAT: 11

Autonomous Learner Model for Gifted and Talented
CIJE: 1 RIE: 1 CAT: 15

Autonomous Learning
CIJE: 2 RIE: 2 CAT: 15

Autonomous Technology
CIJE: 0 RIE: 1 CAT: 20

Autonomous University of Aguascalientes (Mexico)
CIJE: 0 RIE: 1 CAT: 17
UF Universidad Autonoma de Aguascalientes (Mexico)

Autonomous University of Guadalajara (Mexico)
CIJE: 0 RIE: 1 CAT: 17

Autonomous University of the North East (Mexico)
CIJE: 0 RIE: 2 CAT: 17

Autonomy and Relatedness Inventory
CIJE: 0 RIE: 1 CAT: 21

Autonomy Attitudes Inventory (Edgar and Brod)
CIJE: 0 RIE: 1 CAT: 21

Autonote
CIJE: 0 RIE: 1 CAT: 04

Autophotographic Metaphor
CIJE: 0 RIE: 1 CAT: 15

Autoplastic Orientation
CIJE: 0 RIE: 1 CAT: 15

Autoradiography
CIJE: 2 RIE: 0 CAT: 20

Autoregressive Integrated Moving Averages
CIJE: 2 RIE: 3 CAT: 15
SN See related "Box Jenkins Forecasting Model"
UF ARIMA Models

Autosegmental Phonology
USE Segmentals (Phonology)

Autotelic Responsive Environment
CIJE: 0 RIE: 5 CAT: 20

Autotronics
CIJE: 0 RIE: 1 CAT: 03

Autotutor
CIJE: 2 RIE: 4 CAT: 04

Autotutorial Techniques
CIJE: 2 RIE: 0 CAT: 15

Autumn
CIJE: 5 RIE: 2 CAT: 16
UF Fall (Season)

Auxanometers
CIJE: 1 RIE: 0 CAT: 04

Auxiliary Career Program
CIJE: 0 RIE: 1 CAT: 19

Auxiliary Loan Program
CIJE: 0 RIE: 1 CAT: 19

Auxiliary Services Act
CIJE: 0 RIE: 1 CAT: 14

Auxiliary Verbs
CIJE: 7 RIE: 11 CAT: 13

AV Communication Review
CIJE: 1 RIE: 1 CAT: 22

Availability (Programs and Services)
CIJE: 0 RIE: 1 CAT: 16

Availability Heuristic
CIJE: 1 RIE: 1 CAT: 15

Availability Rate
CIJE: 0 RIE: 4 CAT: 15

Available Motions Inventory
CIJE: 0 RIE: 1 CAT: 21

Avance San Antonio Inc
CIJE: 0 RIE: 3 CAT: 17

Avant Garde
CIJE: 0 RIE: 1 CAT: 16

Avco Day Care Center MA
CIJE: 0 RIE: 1 CAT: 17

Avellaneda (Alonso Fernandez de)
CIJE: 1 RIE: 0 CAT: 18

Average Visually Evoked Potentials
CIJE: 0 RIE: 1 CAT: 15

Averaged Electroencephalic Audiometry
CIJE: 2 RIE: 0 CAT: 15

Averaged Electroencephalic Response
CIJE: 1 RIE: 0 CAT: 15

Averaging (Mathematics)
CIJE: 21 RIE: 2 CAT: 20

Averett College VA
CIJE: 0 RIE: 1 CAT: 17

Aversion Therapy
CIJE: 16 RIE: 3 CAT: 11

Aversive Control
CIJE: 3 RIE: 0 CAT: 11

Aversive Events
CIJE: 3 RIE: 1 CAT: 11

Aversive Stimuli
CIJE: 22 RIE: 9 CAT: 11

Aversive Training
CIJE: 8 RIE: 2 CAT: 11

Avery Index to Architectural Periodicals
CIJE: 2 RIE: 0 CAT: 22

Aviation
CIJE: 10 RIE: 9 CAT: 20

Aviation College Minor
CIJE: 1 RIE: 0 CAT: 03

Aviation Data Analysts
CIJE: 0 RIE: 1 CAT: 09

Aviation Medicine
CIJE: 0 RIE: 1 CAT: 11

Aviation Occupations
CIJE: 2 RIE: 8 CAT: 09

Aviation Psychology
CIJE: 0 RIE: 1 CAT: 11

Aviation Research and Education Foundation
CIJE: 0 RIE: 1 CAT: 17

Aviation Safety
CIJE: 2 RIE: 1 CAT: 20

Aviation Weather
CIJE: 1 RIE: 0 CAT: 20

AVID Program
CIJE: 0 RIE: 2 CAT: 19
UF Advancement Via Individual Determination

Avionics
CIJE: 1 RIE: 16 CAT: 20

AVLINE
CIJE: 5 RIE: 1 CAT: 04

Avogadro Number
CIJE: 5 RIE: 0 CAT: 20

Avoidance Behavior
CIJE: 42 RIE: 17 CAT: 11

Avoidance Learning
CIJE: 3 RIE: 0 CAT: 11

Avoidance Responses
CIJE: 8 RIE: 2 CAT: 21

Avon Books
CIJE: 1 RIE: 0 CAT: 16

Avon Public Schools CT
CIJE: 0 RIE: 3 CAT: 17

Avondale Public Schools MI
CIJE: 1 RIE: 1 CAT: 17

Awalt High School CA
CIJE: 1 RIE: 0 CAT: 17

Awareness House CA
CIJE: 1 RIE: 0 CAT: 17

Axial Curve Rotator
CIJE: 0 RIE: 1 CAT: 04

Axiology
CIJE: 3 RIE: 8 CAT: 03

Axiom Systems
CIJE: 6 RIE: 1 CAT: 15

Axiomatic Geometry
CIJE: 2 RIE: 0 CAT: 20

Axiomatics
CIJE: 3 RIE: 2 CAT: 20

Axles
CIJE: 1 RIE: 1 CAT: 04

Ayacucho
CIJE: 0 RIE: 6 CAT: 13

Aydelotte (Frank)
CIJE: 1 RIE: 1 CAT: 18

Aydemir (Sevket Sureyya)
CIJE: 1 RIE: 0 CAT: 18

Ayer High School MA
CIJE: 1 RIE: 0 CAT: 17

Ayers Prognostic Test for Early Childhood Educ
CIJE: 1 RIE: 0 CAT: 21

Ayllon (Teodoro)
CIJE: 1 RIE: 0 CAT: 18

Ayres (Clarence)
CIJE: 1 RIE: 0 CAT: 18

Azana (Manuel)
CIJE: 1 RIE: 0 CAT: 18

Azande (Tribe)
CIJE: 0 RIE: 1 CAT: 08

Azides
CIJE: 1 RIE: 0 CAT: 20

Azidothymidine
USE AZT (Drug)

Azobenzene
CIJE: 1 RIE: 0 CAT: 20

Azore Islands
CIJE: 0 RIE: 0 CAT: 07

Azoreans
CIJE: 0 RIE: 1 CAT: 08

Azorin (Jose Martinez Ruiz)
CIJE: 4 RIE: 0 CAT: 18

Azrin (Nathan)
CIJE: 1 RIE: 0 CAT: 18

AZT (Drug)
CIJE: 0 RIE: 2 CAT: 11
UF Azidothymidine

Aztec (People)
CIJE: 9 RIE: 13 CAT: 08

Aztecan
CIJE: 0 RIE: 1 CAT: 13

Azuela (Mariano)
CIJE: 3 RIE: 0 CAT: 18

Azusa Pacific College CA
CIJE: 1 RIE: 2 CAT: 17

Azusa Pacific University CA
CIJE: 1 RIE: 1 CAT: 17

Azusa Unified School District CA
CIJE: 1 RIE: 0 CAT: 17

B F Goodrich
CIJE: 1 RIE: 0 CAT: 17

B Values
CIJE: 0 RIE: 2 CAT: 21

B WEST Project
USE Building Workers Entering Skilled Trades Project

Babbitt (Irving)
CIJE: 0 RIE: 1 CAT: 18

Babbling Drift Hypothesis
CIJE: 1 RIE: 0 CAT: 13

Babkin Reflex
CIJE: 2 RIE: 0 CAT: 11

Baboquivari High School AZ
CIJE: 1 RIE: 0 CAT: 17

Babson College MA
CIJE: 6 RIE: 3 CAT: 17

Baby Behavior Questionnaire
CIJE: 0 RIE: 1 CAT: 21

Baby Doe Rule
CIJE: 2 RIE: 1 CAT: 14

Baby Talk
CIJE: 10 RIE: 7 CAT: 13

Babylonia (Babylon)
CIJE: 3 RIE: 0 CAT: 07

Babylonia (Sumer)
CIJE: 1 RIE: 0 CAT: 07

Babysitters
CIJE: 9 RIE: 16 CAT: 09

Bacairi
CIJE: 1 RIE: 0 CAT: 13

Bach (Richard)
CIJE: 1 RIE: 0 CAT: 18

Bachelor Degrees for Soldiers
CIJE: 0 RIE: 1 CAT: 19

Back (Human Anatomy)
CIJE: 4 RIE: 2 CAT: 11

Back Pay
CIJE: 4 RIE: 0 CAT: 16

Back Propagation Learning
CIJE: 0 RIE: 1 CAT: 15

Backgammon
CIJE: 0 RIE: 1 CAT: 16

Background Activity Inventory
CIJE: 0 RIE: 1 CAT: 21

Background and Experience Questionnaire
CIJE: 1 RIE: 2 CAT: 21

Background Checks (Employment)
CIJE: 1 RIE: 1 CAT: 16
UF Employee Background Checks

Background Interference Procedure
CIJE: 4 RIE: 0 CAT: 15

Background Music
CIJE: 4 RIE: 2 CAT: 16

Backlash Interference
CIJE: 0 RIE: 1 CAT: 13

Backpacking
CIJE: 13 RIE: 9 CAT: 16

Backup Systems
CIJE: 6 RIE: 0 CAT: 04

Backward Conditioning
CIJE: 0 RIE: 1 CAT: 15

Backward Mapping
CIJE: 1 RIE: 3 CAT: 15

Backward Waves
CIJE: 1 RIE: 0 CAT: 20

Backwash (Tests)
USE Teaching to the Test

Bacon (Francis)
CIJE: 12 RIE: 4 CAT: 18

Bacteriology
CIJE: 4 RIE: 10 CAT: 11

Baeda
USE Bede

Baez (Joan)
CIJE: 1 RIE: 0 CAT: 18

Baffin Island
CIJE: 0 RIE: 0 CAT: 07

Bag Sealers
CIJE: 0 RIE: 1 CAT: 09

Baggers
CIJE: 0 RIE: 3 CAT: 09

Bagoong
CIJE: 0 RIE: 1 CAT: 20

Bagrooth Examinations
USE Bagrut Examinations

Bagrut Examinations
CIJE: 0 RIE: 1 CAT: 21
SN Matriculation examinations for Israeli universities
UF Bagrooth Examinations

Bahamas
CIJE: 5 RIE: 11 CAT: 07

Bahamas (Abaco Islands)
CIJE: 0 RIE: 1 CAT: 07

Bahemba People
CIJE: 0 RIE: 0 CAT: 08

Bahnar
CIJE: 1 RIE: 0 CAT: 13

Bahrain
CIJE: 12 RIE: 5 CAT: 07

Bail
CIJE: 2 RIE: 0 CAT: 14

Bailey (F Lee)
CIJE: 0 RIE: 1 CAT: 18

Bailey (Thomas A)
CIJE: 1 RIE: 0 CAT: 18

Bailyn (Bernard)
CIJE: 3 RIE: 0 CAT: 18

Bain (Alexander)
CIJE: 3 RIE: 1 CAT: 18

Baird (A Craig)
CIJE: 1 RIE: 0 CAT: 18

Baja California
CIJE: 1 RIE: 0 CAT: 07

Baker (Gwendolyn Calvert)
CIJE: 1 RIE: 0 CAT: 18

Baker (Josephine Turck)
CIJE: 0 RIE: 1 CAT: 18

Baker (Perren Earle)
CIJE: 1 RIE: 0 CAT: 18

Baker (Ray Stannard)
CIJE: 0 RIE: 1 CAT: 18

Baker Junior High School CO
CIJE: 0 RIE: 1 CAT: 17

Baker University KS
CIJE: 0 RIE: 5 CAT: 17

Baker v Owen
CIJE: 2 RIE: 3 CAT: 14

Bakers
CIJE: 0 RIE: 10 CAT: 09

Bakersfield College CA
CIJE: 2 RIE: 17 CAT: 17

Bakersfield Individualized Process
CIJE: 0 RIE: 1 CAT: 21

Bakery Products Route Personnel
CIJE: 0 RIE: 1 CAT: 09

Bakhtin (Mikhail)
CIJE: 17 RIE: 17 CAT: 18

Bakke v Regents of University of California
CIJE: 119 RIE: 72 CAT: 14

Bakker (Jim)
CIJE: 0 RIE: 1 CAT: 18

Balance
CIJE: 38 RIE: 10 CAT: 16

Balance of State Program Contractors
CIJE: 0 RIE: 2 CAT: 10

Balance Sheet Technique
CIJE: 4 RIE: 1 CAT: 15

Balance Tests
CIJE: 7 RIE: 3 CAT: 21

Balance Training
CIJE: 3 RIE: 2 CAT: 16

Balanced California F Scale (Athanasiou)
CIJE: 1 RIE: 0 CAT: 21

Balanced Designs
CIJE: 0 RIE: 2 CAT: 21

Balanced Incomplete Block Spiralling
CIJE: 1 RIE: 11 CAT: 21

Balanced Repeated Replication
CIJE: 2 RIE: 1 CAT: 15

Balangao
CIJE: 0 RIE: 1 CAT: 13

Balarat Center for Environmental Studies CO
CIJE: 0 RIE: 1 CAT: 17

Baldwin (Abraham)
CIJE: 1 RIE: 1 CAT: 18

Baldwin (James Mark)
CIJE: 3 RIE: 1 CAT: 18
SN American psychologist

Baldwin (James)
CIJE: 18 RIE: 1 CAT: 18
SN American writer

Baldwin (Simeon E)
CIJE: 0 RIE: 1 CAT: 18

Baldwin Picture Story Measure of Kindness Concept
CIJE: 1 RIE: 0 CAT: 21

Baldwin School PA
CIJE: 0 RIE: 1 CAT: 17

Baldwin Wallace College OH
CIJE: 0 RIE: 4 CAT: 17

Baldwin Whitehall School District PA
CIJE: 0 RIE: 1 CAT: 17

Bales (R F)
CIJE: 0 RIE: 2 CAT: 18

Bales Interaction Process Analysis
CIJE: 5 RIE: 2 CAT: 21

Bales Interpersonal Ratings Questionnaire
CIJE: 3 RIE: 0 CAT: 21

Bali
CIJE: 2 RIE: 2 CAT: 07

Balkan Languages
CIJE: 0 RIE: 1 CAT: 13

Balkans
CIJE: 2 RIE: 4 CAT: 07

Balke Maximum Work Capacity Test
CIJE: 1 RIE: 0 CAT: 21

Ball Aptitude Battery
CIJE: 4 RIE: 10 CAT: 21

Ball State Staff Development for Public Schools
CIJE: 0 RIE: 1 CAT: 19

Ball State University IN
CIJE: 25 RIE: 35 CAT: 17

Ball Stick Bird Reading Method
CIJE: 0 RIE: 5 CAT: 15
SN See also "Fuller Reading System"

Ballantines
CIJE: 0 RIE: 1 CAT: 15

Balling Machine Operators
CIJE: 0 RIE: 1 CAT: 09

Balloons
CIJE: 14 RIE: 3 CAT: 04

BALLOTS
CIJE: 5 RIE: 17 CAT: 04
SN Bibliographic Automation of Large Operations Using a Time-Sharing System (Stanford University)

Balls
CIJE: 1 RIE: 1 CAT: 04

Balmy Beach Community School ON
CIJE: 0 RIE: 1 CAT: 17

BALT L Discussion Group
CIJE: 0 RIE: 1 CAT: 17

Balthazar Scales of Adaptive Behavior
CIJE: 4 RIE: 2 CAT: 21

Baltic States
CIJE: 6 RIE: 2 CAT: 07
UF USSR (Baltic States)

Baltimore City Public Schools MD
CIJE: 16 RIE: 39 CAT: 17

Baltimore County Public Library MD
CIJE: 6 RIE: 1 CAT: 17

Baltimore County Public Schools MD
CIJE: 13 RIE: 6 CAT: 17

Baltimore Free University MD
CIJE: 0 RIE: 1 CAT: 17

Baltimore Longitudinal Study of Aging
CIJE: 0 RIE: 1 CAT: 19

Baltimore Museum of Art MD
CIJE: 0 RIE: 1 CAT: 17

Baltimore Teacher Training Project
CIJE: 0 RIE: 1 CAT: 19

Balto Finnic Languages
CIJE: 0 RIE: 2 CAT: 13

Balzac (Honore de)
CIJE: 5 RIE: 0 CAT: 18

Bambara
CIJE: 2 RIE: 5 CAT: 13

Bamboo
CIJE: 0 RIE: 1 CAT: 20

Bamileke
CIJE: 0 RIE: 1 CAT: 13

Band (The)
CIJE: 0 RIE: 1 CAT: 17

Band Directors
CIJE: 11 RIE: 1 CAT: 10

Bandeira (Manuel)
CIJE: 1 RIE: 0 CAT: 18

Bandura (Albert)
CIJE: 11 RIE: 9 CAT: 18

Banff Centre for Continuing Education (Canada)
CIJE: 0 RIE: 1 CAT: 17

Banff Conference 1977
CIJE: 0 RIE: 1 CAT: 02

Banff School of Fine Arts (Canada)
CIJE: 0 RIE: 1 CAT: 17

Bangalore Communicational Teaching Proj (India)
CIJE: 0 RIE: 1 CAT: 19

Bangkok Dialect
CIJE: 0 RIE: 3 CAT: 13

Bangkok Regional Education Centre (Thailand)
CIJE: 0 RIE: 1 CAT: 17

Bangladesh
CIJE: 38 RIE: 112 CAT: 07

Banjara (Lamani)
CIJE: 0 RIE: 1 CAT: 18

Bank of America
CIJE: 2 RIE: 3 CAT: 17

Bank of Canada
CIJE: 0 RIE: 1 CAT: 17

Bank Street College of Education NY
CIJE: 13 RIE: 13 CAT: 17

Bank Street Readers
CIJE: 0 RIE: 1 CAT: 22

Bank Street Writer
CIJE: 2 RIE: 3 CAT: 04

Bank Tellers
CIJE: 3 RIE: 14 CAT: 09

BankAmerica Foundation Educ Initiatives Program
CIJE: 0 RIE: 1 CAT: 19

Bankruptcy
CIJE: 27 RIE: 13 CAT: 14

Bankruptcy Reform Act 1978
CIJE: 6 RIE: 1 CAT: 14

Banks Model School Project
CIJE: 1 RIE: 0 CAT: 19

Bankson Language Screening Test
CIJE: 2 RIE: 1 CAT: 21

Bannatyne (A)
CIJE: 8 RIE: 1 CAT: 18

Bannatyne System
CIJE: 5 RIE: 2 CAT: 21

Banneker Elementary School IN
CIJE: 2 RIE: 1 CAT: 17

Banneker High School DC
CIJE: 0 RIE: 1 CAT: 17

Banneker School Project
CIJE: 0 RIE: 2 CAT: 19

Banta Replacement Puzzle
CIJE: 0 RIE: 1 CAT: 21

Bantoanon
USE Banton

Bantock (G H)
CIJE: 3 RIE: 0 CAT: 18

Banton
CIJE: 0 RIE: 1 CAT: 13
SN A Northwest Austronesian (Philippine) language, Sulic group
UF Bantoanon

Bantu Education Act 1953
CIJE: 4 RIE: 1 CAT: 14

Bantu Peoples
CIJE: 1 RIE: 0 CAT: 08

Banyankole
CIJE: 1 RIE: 0 CAT: 08

Baptist College SC
CIJE: 0 RIE: 1 CAT: 17

Baptists
CIJE: 9 RIE: 7 CAT: 10

Bar Associations
CIJE: 2 RIE: 4 CAT: 05

Bar Codes (Products)
USE Barcodes

Bar Examinations
CIJE: 2 RIE: 3 CAT: 21

Bar Graphs
CIJE: 7 RIE: 1 CAT: 15
SN See also "Histograms"

Bar Ilan University (Israel)
CIJE: 3 RIE: 3 CAT: 17

Bar Mitzvah
CIJE: 0 RIE: 1 CAT: 12

Baraka (Imamu Amiri)
CIJE: 4 RIE: 1 CAT: 18

Barat College IL
CIJE: 1 RIE: 3 CAT: 17

Baratz (Joan)
CIJE: 0 RIE: 1 CAT: 18

Barbados
CIJE: 21 RIE: 14 CAT: 07

Barbarians
CIJE: 0 RIE: 1 CAT: 10

Barber Scotia College NC
CIJE: 0 RIE: 4 CAT: 17

Barber Suggestibility Scale
CIJE: 2 RIE: 0 CAT: 21

Barbour Observer Schedule
CIJE: 0 RIE: 1 CAT: 21

Barbu (Ion)
CIJE: 1 RIE: 0 CAT: 18

Barclay Classroom Assessment System
CIJE: 1 RIE: 1 CAT: 21

Barclay Classroom Climate Inventory
CIJE: 7 RIE: 14 CAT: 21

Barclay Early Childhood Assessment System
CIJE: 0 RIE: 1 CAT: 21

Barclay Test
CIJE: 0 RIE: 1 CAT: 21

Barcode Readers
CIJE: 3 RIE: 0 CAT: 04

Barcodes
CIJE: 15 RIE: 5 CAT: 20
SN See related "Universal Product Code"
UF Bar Codes (Products); Optical Barcodes; Product Barcodes

Barcoding
CIJE: 1 RIE: 3 CAT: 15

Bard College NY
CIJE: 7 RIE: 8 CAT: 17

Barea (Arturo)
CIJE: 1 RIE: 0 CAT: 18

Barefoot Doctors
CIJE: 0 RIE: 1 CAT: 10

Bargaining
CIJE: 9 RIE: 1 CAT: 15

Bargaining in Good Faith
CIJE: 0 RIE: 2 CAT: 16
SN See also "Good Faith Requirements"

Bargy (Henry)
CIJE: 1 RIE: 0 CAT: 18

Bari University (Italy)
CIJE: 0 RIE: 1 CAT: 17

Barium
CIJE: 1 RIE: 0 CAT: 20

Barium Sulfate
CIJE: 1 RIE: 0 CAT: 20

Barkan (Manuel)
CIJE: 3 RIE: 1 CAT: 18

Barker (Joel A)
CIJE: 0 RIE: 1 CAT: 18

Barlach (Ernst)
CIJE: 2 RIE: 0 CAT: 18

Barley Sheaf Resource Center NJ
CIJE: 1 RIE: 0 CAT: 17

Barnard (Chester)
CIJE: 5 RIE: 3 CAT: 18

Barnard (Henry)
CIJE: 5 RIE: 2 CAT: 18

Barnard College NY
USE Columbia University NY Barnard College

Barnes (Harry Elmer)
CIJE: 1 RIE: 0 CAT: 18

Barnes Foundation PA
CIJE: 1 RIE: 0 CAT: 17

Barnes v Converse College
CIJE: 0 RIE: 0 CAT: 14

Barnett (Ross A)
CIJE: 0 RIE: 1 CAT: 18

Barney (Natalie Clifford)
CIJE: 0 RIE: 1 CAT: 18

Barnum Effect
CIJE: 11 RIE: 2 CAT: 16

Baroda University (India)
CIJE: 1 RIE: 0 CAT: 17

Baroja (Pio)
CIJE: 25 RIE: 0 CAT: 18

Barometers
CIJE: 2 RIE: 1 CAT: 04

Barr (A S)
CIJE: 0 RIE: 1 CAT: 18

Barr (Robert)
CIJE: 3 RIE: 1 CAT: 18

Barranquilla Rapid Survey Intelligence Test
CIJE: 1 RIE: 0 CAT: 21

Barrault (Jean Louis)
CIJE: 1 RIE: 0 CAT: 18

Barrett Lennard Relationship Inventory
CIJE: 8 RIE: 8 CAT: 21

Barrett Taxonomy
CIJE: 5 RIE: 2 CAT: 21

Barrie (J M)
CIJE: 3 RIE: 2 CAT: 18

Barrie Public Library (Canada)
CIJE: 0 RIE: 1 CAT: 17

Barrier Beaches
CIJE: 1 RIE: 1 CAT: 20

Barrier Behavior
CIJE: 5 RIE: 3 CAT: 11

Barrier Resolution Project
CIJE: 0 RIE: 1 CAT: 19

Barriers to Excellence Our Children at Risk
CIJE: 1 RIE: 0 CAT: 22

Barriers to Implementation
CIJE: 10 RIE: 6 CAT: 15

Barriers to Information
CIJE: 3 RIE: 0 CAT: 16
UF Information Barriers

Barriers to Innovation
CIJE: 3 RIE: 1 CAT: 15

Barriers to Participation
CIJE: 1 RIE: 7 CAT: 15

Barrios
CIJE: 5 RIE: 6 CAT: 16

Barrios (Eduardo)
CIJE: 2 RIE: 0 CAT: 18

Barron (Jerome)
CIJE: 1 RIE: 0 CAT: 18

Barron Ego Strength Scale
CIJE: 4 RIE: 1 CAT: 21
UF Ego Strength Scale (Barron)

Barron Welsh Art Scale
CIJE: 4 RIE: 2 CAT: 21

Barrows (Alice)
CIJE: 1 RIE: 0 CAT: 18

Barry College FL
CIJE: 1 RIE: 0 CAT: 17

Barry University FL
CIJE: 1 RIE: 5 CAT: 17

Barstow (Rosemary Shingobe)
CIJE: 0 RIE: 1 CAT: 18

Barstow College CA
CIJE: 0 RIE: 1 CAT: 17

Bartenders
CIJE: 3 RIE: 1 CAT: 09
UF Alcoholic Beverage Servers

Barter
CIJE: 7 RIE: 3 CAT: 16

Barth (James L)
CIJE: 3 RIE: 1 CAT: 18

Barth Scale
CIJE: 2 RIE: 1 CAT: 21

Barth Shermis Social Studies Preference Scale
CIJE: 3 RIE: 1 CAT: 21

Barthes (Roland)
CIJE: 5 RIE: 5 CAT: 18

Bartholdi (Frederic Auguste)
CIJE: 0 RIE: 1 CAT: 18

Bartholomae (David)
CIJE: 5 RIE: 6 CAT: 18

Bartholomew Consolidated School Corporation IN
CIJE: 0 RIE: 3 CAT: 17

Bartlett (F C)
CIJE: 1 RIE: 4 CAT: 18

Bartlett School of Architecture (England)
CIJE: 0 RIE: 1 CAT: 17

Bartletts Test of Significance in Factor Analysis
CIJE: 0 RIE: 1 CAT: 21

Bartletts Test of Sphericity
CIJE: 1 RIE: 1 CAT: 21

Bartok (Bela)
CIJE: 3 RIE: 1 CAT: 18

Barton County Community Junior College KS
CIJE: 0 RIE: 1 CAT: 17

Baruch Retrieval of Automated Info for Negotiation
CIJE: 0 RIE: 1 CAT: 04

Basal Evaluation Form
CIJE: 0 RIE: 1 CAT: 15

Basbakanlik Arsiv (Turkey)
CIJE: 0 RIE: 1 CAT: 17

BASC
USE Behavior Assessment System for Children

BASC Student Observation Scale
USE Student Observation Scale

Base Christian Communities
CIJE: 0 RIE: 1 CAT: 10
UF Basic Christian Communities; CEB Groups; Comunidades Eclesiales de Base

Base Engineer Automated Management System
CIJE: 0 RIE: 2 CAT: 15

Base Free Measure of Change
CIJE: 2 RIE: 0 CAT: 21

Base Rate Approach
CIJE: 3 RIE: 1 CAT: 15

Base Rate Information
CIJE: 0 RIE: 2 CAT: 16

BASE Rating Scale
USE Behavioral Academic Self Esteem Scale

Baseball Coaching Technical Questionnaire
CIJE: 0 RIE: 1 CAT: 21

Baseline Data
CIJE: 4 RIE: 6 CAT: 16

Baseline Statistics
CIJE: 1 RIE: 1 CAT: 16

Baser (Electrical Equipment)
CIJE: 0 RIE: 1 CAT: 09

Bases (Chemistry)
CIJE: 14 RIE: 2 CAT: 20

Bases (Mathematics)
CIJE: 4 RIE: 0 CAT: 20

Basic Achievement Skills Individual Screener
CIJE: 4 RIE: 2 CAT: 21

Basic Arithmetic Skills Evaluation
CIJE: 0 RIE: 1 CAT: 21

Basic Attitudes Toward Social Studies
CIJE: 0 RIE: 1 CAT: 16

Basic Christian Communities
USE Base Christian Communities

Basic Citizenship Competencies Project
CIJE: 0 RIE: 1 CAT: 19

Basic Color Terms
CIJE: 0 RIE: 1 CAT: 15

Basic Concept Inventory (Engelmann)
CIJE: 0 RIE: 3 CAT: 21

Basic Concept Test (Gilmer)
CIJE: 0 RIE: 1 CAT: 21

Basic Economics Simulation
CIJE: 1 RIE: 0 CAT: 15

Basic Economics Test
CIJE: 1 RIE: 2 CAT: 21

Basic Education
CIJE: 12 RIE: 23 CAT: 03

Basic Education Development Scheme (England)
CIJE: 0 RIE: 1 CAT: 19

Basic Education Student Training Program
CIJE: 0 RIE: 1 CAT: 19

Basic Education Teaching the Adult (Videotape)
CIJE: 0 RIE: 0 CAT: 22

Basic Education Test
CIJE: 0 RIE: 1 CAT: 21

Basic Educational Enrichment Program
CIJE: 0 RIE: 1 CAT: 19

Basic Educational Opportunity Grants
CIJE: 25 RIE: 131 CAT: 14
SN Changed in 1980 to Pell Grant Program

Basic Educational Skills Project
CIJE: 0 RIE: 21 CAT: 19

Basic Educational Skills Test
CIJE: 0 RIE: 1 CAT: 21

Basic Educational Skills Tutorial Program
CIJE: 0 RIE: 1 CAT: 19
UF BEST Program of San Diego

Basic English Skills Test
CIJE: 1 RIE: 6 CAT: 21

Basic English Skills Test Plus Supplement
CIJE: 0 RIE: 2 CAT: 21

Basic Facts (Mathematics)
CIJE: 12 RIE: 8 CAT: 20

Basic Human Needs
CIJE: 0 RIE: 3 CAT: 16

Basic Ideas Program
CIJE: 1 RIE: 0 CAT: 19

Basic Indian Education Act
CIJE: 0 RIE: 7 CAT: 14

Basic Instruction Programs
CIJE: 1 RIE: 2 CAT: 19
UF BIPs

Basic Interpersonal Communicative Skills
CIJE: 1 RIE: 1 CAT: 16

Basic Inventory of Natural Language
CIJE: 1 RIE: 5 CAT: 21

Basic Job Readiness Training Program (Montreal)
CIJE: 1 RIE: 0 CAT: 19

Basic Law (West Germany)
CIJE: 2 RIE: 2 CAT: 14
UF Constitution (West Germany); Grundgesetz (West Germany); West German Constitution

Basic Life Skills Mini Assessment (1977)
CIJE: 0 RIE: 0 CAT: 21

Basic Literacy for Adult Development
CIJE: 2 RIE: 0 CAT: 19
UF BLADE Program

Basic Living Skills Pupil Record Form
CIJE: 0 RIE: 1 CAT: 21

Basic Math Mastery Tests
CIJE: 0 RIE: 1 CAT: 21

Basic Medical Specialists
CIJE: 0 RIE: 1 CAT: 10

Basic Objectives Assessment Tests
CIJE: 0 RIE: 4 CAT: 21

Basic Occupational Language Training
CIJE: 1 RIE: 3 CAT: 19

Basic Occupational Literacy Test
CIJE: 0 RIE: 5 CAT: 21
UF USES Basic Occupational Literacy Test

Basic Personality Inventory
CIJE: 4 RIE: 0 CAT: 21

BASIC Programing Language
CIJE: 345 RIE: 184 CAT: 04

Basic Reading Inventory (Johns)
CIJE: 3 RIE: 2 CAT: 21

Basic School Skills Inventory
CIJE: 2 RIE: 3 CAT: 21

Basic Science Comprehensive Test
CIJE: 0 RIE: 1 CAT: 21

Basic Sight Vocabulary
CIJE: 2 RIE: 0 CAT: 21

Basic Skills Assessment Program
CIJE: 2 RIE: 18 CAT: 19
SN If appropriate, use more specific "South Carolina Basic Skills Assessment Program," "New Jersey Basic Skills Assessment Program," etc.

Basic Skills Assessment Tests
CIJE: 1 RIE: 2 CAT: 21

Basic Skills Brush Up Centers
CIJE: 0 RIE: 1 CAT: 05

Basic Skills Centers DC
CIJE: 0 RIE: 2 CAT: 05

Basic Skills Education Program
CIJE: 0 RIE: 7 CAT: 19

Basic Skills Examination
CIJE: 0 RIE: 1 CAT: 21

Basic Skills for Independent Living
CIJE: 1 RIE: 0 CAT: 03

Basic Skills Improvement Policy (Massachusetts)
CIJE: 0 RIE: 10 CAT: 14

Basic Skills Improvement Program
CIJE: 1 RIE: 3 CAT: 19
SN Project of the United States Dept. of Education

Basic Skills Improvement Program (Massachusetts)
CIJE: 0 RIE: 2 CAT: 19
UF Massachusetts Basic Skills

Basic Skills Instruction for Secondary Schools
CIJE: 1 RIE: 0 CAT: 19

Basic Skills Inventory
CIJE: 0 RIE: 1 CAT: 21

Basic Skills Learning Centers Project
CIJE: 0 RIE: 5 CAT: 19

Basic Skills Needs Assessment Project
CIJE: 0 RIE: 1 CAT: 19

Basic Skills Placement Test (New Jersey)
USE New Jersey College Basic Skills Placement Test

BASIC SKILLS Software Program
CIJE: 0 RIE: 1 CAT: 04

Basic Skills Word List
CIJE: 1 RIE: 1 CAT: 21

Basic Structure of Intellect Learning Abilits Test
USE Structure of Intellect Learning Abilities Test

Basic Studies National Field Task Force
CIJE: 0 RIE: 1 CAT: 17

Basic Training (Military)
CIJE: 0 RIE: 1 CAT: 16

Basic Trilingual Program NY
CIJE: 0 RIE: 1 CAT: 19

Basic Village Education Project (Guatemala)
CIJE: 0 RIE: 1 CAT: 19

Basic Writers
CIJE: 52 RIE: 57 CAT: 10

Basis for Choice Course
CIJE: 0 RIE: 1 CAT: 03

Basket Weaving
CIJE: 2 RIE: 6 CAT: 16

Basketball Offense
CIJE: 0 RIE: 2 CAT: 16

Basketballs
CIJE: 1 RIE: 0 CAT: 04

Basle Seminar Education Welfare of Disadvantaged
CIJE: 3 RIE: 0 CAT: 02

Bass (Saul)
CIJE: 2 RIE: 0 CAT: 18

Bass Stick Test
CIJE: 1 RIE: 1 CAT: 21

Bassa
CIJE: 0 RIE: 1 CAT: 13

Bassett (Richard)
CIJE: 0 RIE: 1 CAT: 18

Bat Mitzvah
CIJE: 0 RIE: 1 CAT: 12

Batavia School District IL
CIJE: 0 RIE: 1 CAT: 17

Batch Processing (Computer Science)
CIJE: 5 RIE: 10 CAT: 20

Bates (Daisy)
CIJE: 1 RIE: 0 CAT: 18

Before School Programs
CIJE: 2 RIE: 7 CAT: 19

Begi (Bahman)
CIJE: 1 RIE: 0 CAT: 18

Begin (Menachem)
CIJE: 1 RIE: 1 CAT: 18

Beginning Administrators
CIJE: 4 RIE: 2 CAT: 10

Beginning Competence
CIJE: 0 RIE: 14 CAT: 16

Beginning of School Year
CIJE: 3 RIE: 4 CAT: 16

Beginning Postsecondary Students Long Study
CIJE: 0 RIE: 5 CAT: 21

Beginning Principals
CIJE: 30 RIE: 22 CAT: 10

Beginning Superintendents
CIJE: 2 RIE: 1 CAT: 10

Beginning Teacher Assistance Program VA
USE Virginia Beginning Teacher Assistance Program

Beginning Teacher Computer Network
CIJE: 1 RIE: 1 CAT: 04

Beginning Teacher Evaluation Study
CIJE: 25 RIE: 14 CAT: 19

Beginning Teacher Evaluation Study Phase II
CIJE: 0 RIE: 7 CAT: 19

Beginning Teacher Program FL
USE Florida Beginning Teacher Program

Beginning Teachers Questionnaire
CIJE: 1 RIE: 0 CAT: 21

Beginning Work Rating Scale
CIJE: 0 RIE: 1 CAT: 21

Beginning Writing
CIJE: 68 RIE: 49 CAT: 13

Behavior Alteration Techniques
CIJE: 14 RIE: 7 CAT: 15

Behavior Analysis
CIJE: 31 RIE: 19 CAT: 15

Behavior Analysis Classroom
CIJE: 0 RIE: 5 CAT: 16

Behavior Analysis Follow Through
CIJE: 0 RIE: 4 CAT: 15

Behavior and Temperament Survey
CIJE: 1 RIE: 1 CAT: 21

Behavior Assessment System for Children
CIJE: 0 RIE: 2 CAT: 21
SN See also "BASC..."
UF BASC

Behavior Classification Checklist
CIJE: 0 RIE: 2 CAT: 21

Behavior Classification Proj Behav Checklist
CIJE: 0 RIE: 1 CAT: 21

Behavior Codes
CIJE: 0 RIE: 1 CAT: 11

Behavior Control Perception Theory
CIJE: 0 RIE: 2 CAT: 15

Behavior Description Index
CIJE: 0 RIE: 1 CAT: 21

Behavior Descriptions
CIJE: 2 RIE: 6 CAT: 11

Behavior Dimensions Rating Scale
CIJE: 1 RIE: 1 CAT: 21

Behavior Evaluation Scale
CIJE: 1 RIE: 1 CAT: 21

Behavior Genetics
CIJE: 7 RIE: 1 CAT: 11
SN See also "Developmental Behavioral Genetics"

Behavior Inventory (Zigler)
CIJE: 0 RIE: 1 CAT: 21

Behavior Management
CIJE: 86 RIE: 52 CAT: 11

Behavior Modeling
CIJE: 24 RIE: 2 CAT: 15

Behavior Observation Scale
CIJE: 2 RIE: 3 CAT: 21

Behavior Observation Schedule (Tannenbaum)
CIJE: 0 RIE: 1 CAT: 21

Behavior Observation Systems
CIJE: 6 RIE: 2 CAT: 15

Behavior Oriented Prescriptive Teaching Approach
CIJE: 0 RIE: 1 CAT: 15

Behavior Prediction Test (Morrison)
CIJE: 0 RIE: 1 CAT: 21

Behavior Predispositions Group Situation Inventory
CIJE: 1 RIE: 0 CAT: 21

Behavior Preference Inventory
CIJE: 1 RIE: 0 CAT: 21

Behavior Problem Checklist
CIJE: 31 RIE: 2 CAT: 21

Behavior Ranking Scale (Institute Devel Studies)
CIJE: 0 RIE: 2 CAT: 21

Behavior Rating Instrument for Autistic
CIJE: 1 RIE: 1 CAT: 21

Behavior Rating of Parents
USE Parent Behavior Rating

Behavior Rating Scale for Junior Senior High Schs
CIJE: 1 RIE: 0 CAT: 21

Behavior Settings
CIJE: 0 RIE: 1 CAT: 11

Behavior Strengths
CIJE: 0 RIE: 1 CAT: 11

Behavioral Academic Self Esteem Scale
CIJE: 0 RIE: 2 CAT: 21
UF BASE Rating Scale

Behavioral Acculturation Scale (Szapocynik)
CIJE: 0 RIE: 1 CAT: 21

Behavioral Analysis Instrument for Teachers
CIJE: 0 RIE: 1 CAT: 21

Behavioral Anchoring
CIJE: 0 RIE: 1 CAT: 15
SN See also "Behaviorally Anchored Rating Scales"

Behavioral Assessment
CIJE: 19 RIE: 4 CAT: 21

Behavioral Categories
CIJE: 1 RIE: 0 CAT: 15

Behavioral Checklist Infant Toddler Care Provider
CIJE: 0 RIE: 1 CAT: 21

Behavioral Classification Project
CIJE: 0 RIE: 1 CAT: 19

Behavioral Consistency Method
CIJE: 1 RIE: 1 CAT: 15

Behavioral Consultation
CIJE: 1 RIE: 1 CAT: 11

Behavioral Consultation Model (Bergan)
CIJE: 1 RIE: 0 CAT: 15

Behavioral Event Analysis
CIJE: 0 RIE: 1 CAT: 15

Behavioral Event Interview
CIJE: 0 RIE: 1 CAT: 21

Behavioral Expectations Scale
CIJE: 3 RIE: 2 CAT: 21

Behavioral Intention
CIJE: 0 RIE: 1 CAT: 11

Behavioral Marital Therapy
CIJE: 6 RIE: 1 CAT: 11
UF Marital Therapy (Behavioral)

Behavioral Maturity Scale (White)
CIJE: 0 RIE: 1 CAT: 21

Behavioral Measures
CIJE: 5 RIE: 1 CAT: 21

Behavioral Medicine
CIJE: 17 RIE: 2 CAT: 11

Behavioral Objectives Writing Skills Test
CIJE: 0 RIE: 1 CAT: 21

Behavioral Observation Schedule Pupils Teachers
CIJE: 0 RIE: 1 CAT: 21

Behavioral Observation Scoring System
CIJE: 0 RIE: 1 CAT: 21

Behavioral Organization
CIJE: 1 RIE: 1 CAT: 15

Behavioral Psychology
CIJE: 9 RIE: 5 CAT: 11

Behavioral Requirements Analysis Checklist
CIJE: 2 RIE: 1 CAT: 21

Behavioral Science Programing Language
CIJE: 0 RIE: 1 CAT: 04

Behavioral Science Teacher Education Program
CIJE: 0 RIE: 1 CAT: 19

Behavioral Stability
CIJE: 24 RIE: 11 CAT: 11
UF Stability (Behavior)

Behavioral Style Questionnaire
CIJE: 2 RIE: 1 CAT: 21

Behavioral Styles Inventory
CIJE: 1 RIE: 0 CAT: 21

Behavioral Systems Approach
CIJE: 4 RIE: 1 CAT: 15

Behavioral Tracking Deficits
CIJE: 0 RIE: 1 CAT: 11

Behavioral Variability
CIJE: 2 RIE: 0 CAT: 11

Behavioral Vignettes Test
CIJE: 0 RIE: 1 CAT: 21

Behaviorally Anchored Rating Scales
CIJE: 17 RIE: 7 CAT: 21
SN See also "Behavioral Anchoring"

Behaviorally Anchored Supervisor System
CIJE: 0 RIE: 1 CAT: 15

Behn (Aphra)
CIJE: 0 RIE: 1 CAT: 18

Behn (Harry)
CIJE: 1 RIE: 0 CAT: 18

Behrangi (Samad)
CIJE: 0 RIE: 1 CAT: 18

Behrens Fisher Problem
CIJE: 0 RIE: 1 CAT: 21

Behrhorst (Carroll)
CIJE: 0 RIE: 1 CAT: 18

Beijing Normal University (China)
CIJE: 0 RIE: 1 CAT: 17

Being and Time
CIJE: 1 RIE: 0 CAT: 22

Being There
CIJE: 0 RIE: 1 CAT: 22

Beirut Agreement
CIJE: 1 RIE: 1 CAT: 16

Bejar Model
CIJE: 1 RIE: 1 CAT: 15

Bekesy Audiometry
CIJE: 5 RIE: 1 CAT: 15

Belau
USE Palau

Belgian National Library
CIJE: 1 RIE: 0 CAT: 17

Belgians
CIJE: 2 RIE: 1 CAT: 08

Belgium
CIJE: 155 RIE: 193 CAT: 07

Belgium (Brussels)
CIJE: 6 RIE: 9 CAT: 07

Belgium (Flanders)
CIJE: 4 RIE: 1 CAT: 07

Belgium (Ghent)
CIJE: 1 RIE: 0 CAT: 07

Belgium (Liege)
CIJE: 0 RIE: 1 CAT: 07

Belgium (Uccle)
CIJE: 1 RIE: 0 CAT: 07

Belgium (West Flanders)
CIJE: 0 RIE: 1 CAT: 07

Belgium Colonies
CIJE: 0 RIE: 1 CAT: 07

Belief in Personal Control Scale (Revised)
CIJE: 0 RIE: 1 CAT: 21

Belief Maintenance Systems
CIJE: 1 RIE: 1 CAT: 15

Belief Perseverance
CIJE: 2 RIE: 1 CAT: 11

Beliefs About Computers Scale
CIJE: 0 RIE: 1 CAT: 21

Belize
CIJE: 11 RIE: 18 CAT: 07

Belknap (Jeremy)
CIJE: 0 RIE: 1 CAT: 18

Bell (Alexander Graham)
CIJE: 8 RIE: 2 CAT: 18

Bell (Daniel)
CIJE: 6 RIE: 2 CAT: 18

Bell (Terrel H)
CIJE: 10 RIE: 2 CAT: 18

Bell Adjustment Inventory
CIJE: 1 RIE: 1 CAT: 21

Bell and Howell
CIJE: 0 RIE: 1 CAT: 17

Bell Disability Scale of Adjustment
CIJE: 2 RIE: 0 CAT: 21

Bell Educational Resource Centre (England)
CIJE: 1 RIE: 0 CAT: 17

Bell Numbers
CIJE: 2 RIE: 0 CAT: 20

Bell School (England)
CIJE: 0 RIE: 1 CAT: 17

Bell System Center
CIJE: 1 RIE: 0 CAT: 17

Bell Telephone Communication System
CIJE: 5 RIE: 3 CAT: 17

Bell Telephone Laboratories Inc
CIJE: 11 RIE: 5 CAT: 17

Bellack (Arno)
CIJE: 1 RIE: 0 CAT: 18

Bellack System
CIJE: 1 RIE: 1 CAT: 15

Bellaks Ego Functioning Scale
CIJE: 0 RIE: 1 CAT: 21

Bellamy (Edward)
CIJE: 5 RIE: 0 CAT: 18

Bellarmine College KY
CIJE: 4 RIE: 3 CAT: 17

Belle
CIJE: 0 RIE: 1 CAT: 13

Belle Glade Infant Family Center
CIJE: 0 RIE: 1 CAT: 17

Belle Glade Project
CIJE: 1 RIE: 0 CAT: 19

Belleville Area College IL
CIJE: 0 RIE: 4 CAT: 17

Belleville School District IL
CIJE: 0 RIE: 1 CAT: 17

Belleville Union School District CA
CIJE: 1 RIE: 0 CAT: 17

Bellevue Community College WA
CIJE: 1 RIE: 4 CAT: 17

Bellevue Hospital NY
CIJE: 1 RIE: 1 CAT: 17

Bellevue Public Schools NE
CIJE: 0 RIE: 2 CAT: 17

Bellevue School District WA
CIJE: 3 RIE: 2 CAT: 17

Bellflower Unified School District CA
CIJE: 0 RIE: 1 CAT: 17

Bellingham Public Schools WA
CIJE: 1 RIE: 1 CAT: 17

Bellmore Merrick School District NY
CIJE: 0 RIE: 1 CAT: 17

Bellos (Helen)
CIJE: 1 RIE: 0 CAT: 18

Bellow (Saul)
CIJE: 3 RIE: 1 CAT: 18

Bellport High School NY
CIJE: 1 RIE: 0 CAT: 17

Belmond High School IA
CIJE: 1 RIE: 0 CAT: 17

Belmont Abbey College NC
CIJE: 0 RIE: 1 CAT: 17

Belmont Conference Training Elem Math Sci Teachers
CIJE: 0 RIE: 1 CAT: 02

Belmont Group Project
CIJE: 0 RIE: 3 CAT: 19

Belmont University TN
CIJE: 0 RIE: 1 CAT: 17

Beloit College WI
CIJE: 3 RIE: 2 CAT: 17

Belongingness
CIJE: 5 RIE: 4 CAT: 11

Beloved (Morrison)
CIJE: 0 RIE: 1 CAT: 22

Belsky (Jay)
CIJE: 5 RIE: 1 CAT: 18

Belt Filtration
CIJE: 0 RIE: 1 CAT: 20

Beltman Multi Media Traffic Safety Program
CIJE: 0 RIE: 1 CAT: 19

Belts (Mechanics)
CIJE: 0 RIE: 2 CAT: 20

Bem Sex Role Inventory
CIJE: 133 RIE: 51 CAT: 21

Bembo (Pietro)
CIJE: 0 RIE: 1 CAT: 18

Bemidji State College MN
CIJE: 0 RIE: 1 CAT: 17

Bemidji State University MN
CIJE: 0 RIE: 1 CAT: 17

Ben Gurion University (Israel)
CIJE: 7 RIE: 4 CAT: 17

Ben Hill Irwin Technical Institute GA
CIJE: 0 RIE: 1 CAT: 17

Ben Jochannan (Yosef)
CIJE: 0 RIE: 1 CAT: 18

Benavente y Martinez (Jacinto)
CIJE: 1 RIE: 1 CAT: 18

Bench Carpenters
CIJE: 0 RIE: 1 CAT: 09

Benchmark Testing
CIJE: 2 RIE: 2 CAT: 21

Benchmark Tests
CIJE: 2 RIE: 0 CAT: 21

Benchmarking
CIJE: 24 RIE: 14 CAT: 15

Benchmarks Project ON
CIJE: 0 RIE: 1 CAT: 19

Bender (Charles Albert)
CIJE: 0 RIE: 1 CAT: 18

Bender Gestalt Test
CIJE: 78 RIE: 21 CAT: 21

Bender Gestalt Test for Young Children
CIJE: 7 RIE: 2 CAT: 21

Bender v Williamsport Area School District
CIJE: 4 RIE: 1 CAT: 14

Bender Visual Memory Technique
CIJE: 1 RIE: 0 CAT: 15

Bender Visual Motor Gestalt Test
CIJE: 32 RIE: 10 CAT: 21

Bendix (Edward Herman)
CIJE: 0 RIE: 1 CAT: 18

Beneckea Natriegens
CIJE: 1 RIE: 0 CAT: 20

Benedict College SC
CIJE: 0 RIE: 1 CAT: 17

Benedum Project WV
CIJE: 0 RIE: 1 CAT: 19

Benedum Study Project
CIJE: 0 RIE: 1 CAT: 19

Benefit Forecasting Method
CIJE: 0 RIE: 1 CAT: 15

Benefit Segmentation
CIJE: 2 RIE: 2 CAT: 15

Benefit T Score
CIJE: 1 RIE: 0 CAT: 21

Benet (Stephen Vincent)
CIJE: 1 RIE: 0 CAT: 18

Benin
CIJE: 6 RIE: 7 CAT: 07

Benington (John)
CIJE: 1 RIE: 0 CAT: 18

Benjamin Bunny
CIJE: 0 RIE: 1 CAT: 22

Benjamin Franklin High School NY
CIJE: 1 RIE: 3 CAT: 17

Benjamin Franklin Intermediate School CA
CIJE: 0 RIE: 1 CAT: 17

Benjamin Franklin Street Academy NY
CIJE: 0 RIE: 1 CAT: 17

Benjamin Proverb Test
CIJE: 1 RIE: 0 CAT: 21

Benjamin Rose Institute OH
CIJE: 0 RIE: 2 CAT: 17

Bennett (Henry Garland)
CIJE: 0 RIE: 1 CAT: 18

Bennett (James Gordon)
CIJE: 0 RIE: 1 CAT: 18

Bennett (Jay)
CIJE: 0 RIE: 1 CAT: 18

Bennett (Kay)
CIJE: 0 RIE: 1 CAT: 18

Bennett (Louise)
CIJE: 1 RIE: 0 CAT: 18

Bennett (William J)
CIJE: 47 RIE: 9 CAT: 18

Bennett College NC
CIJE: 3 RIE: 3 CAT: 17

Bennett County School District SD
CIJE: 0 RIE: 1 CAT: 17

Bennett Hand Tool Test
CIJE: 0 RIE: 1 CAT: 21

Bennett Hierarchical Model
CIJE: 0 RIE: 1 CAT: 15
SN ...of Program Evaluation

Bennett Mechanical Comprehension Test
CIJE: 0 RIE: 1 CAT: 21

Bennington College VT
CIJE: 3 RIE: 4 CAT: 17

Benson Elementary School SC
CIJE: 1 RIE: 0 CAT: 17

Bentler Interview Development Scale
CIJE: 0 RIE: 1 CAT: 21

Bentley College MA
CIJE: 4 RIE: 2 CAT: 17

Benton Boutwell Reading Attitude Inventory
CIJE: 0 RIE: 1 CAT: 21

Benton Central High School IN
CIJE: 1 RIE: 0 CAT: 17

Benton Visual Retention Test
CIJE: 4 RIE: 6 CAT: 21

Bentsen (Lloyd)
CIJE: 0 RIE: 1 CAT: 18

Benzene
CIJE: 4 RIE: 1 CAT: 20

Benzhydryl Bromide
CIJE: 1 RIE: 0 CAT: 20

Benzoic Acid
CIJE: 1 RIE: 0 CAT: 20

Beowulf
CIJE: 12 RIE: 9 CAT: 22

Bequer (Gustavo)
CIJE: 1 RIE: 0 CAT: 18

Bequests
CIJE: 9 RIE: 1 CAT: 14

Berea City School District OH
CIJE: 1 RIE: 1 CAT: 17

Berea College KY
CIJE: 14 RIE: 9 CAT: 17

Berea Independent School District KY
CIJE: 0 RIE: 1 CAT: 17

Bereavement
CIJE: 65 RIE: 22 CAT: 11

Bereday (George Z F)
CIJE: 0 RIE: 1 CAT: 18

Bereiter (Carl)
CIJE: 2 RIE: 1 CAT: 18

Bereiter Engelmann Curriculum
CIJE: 5 RIE: 27 CAT: 03

Bergamo Adult Education Conference
CIJE: 0 RIE: 1 CAT: 02

Bergan Scoring Procedure
CIJE: 0 RIE: 1 CAT: 21

Bergen Community College NJ
CIJE: 4 RIE: 6 CAT: 17

Bergen County Vocational Technical Schools NJ
CIJE: 0 RIE: 6 CAT: 17

Berger (Emmanuel M)
CIJE: 0 RIE: 1 CAT: 18

Berger (Peter)
CIJE: 3 RIE: 2 CAT: 18

Berger Self Acceptance Scale
CIJE: 0 RIE: 3 CAT: 21

Berger Self Esteem Scale
CIJE: 0 RIE: 1 CAT: 21

Bergman (Ingmar)
CIJE: 3 RIE: 1 CAT: 18

Bergman (Sherrie)
CIJE: 1 RIE: 0 CAT: 18

Bergson (Henri)
CIJE: 2 RIE: 2 CAT: 18

Berke (Joel S)
CIJE: 0 RIE: 1 CAT: 18

Berkeley Adult School
CIJE: 1 RIE: 0 CAT: 17

Berkeley Center (England)
CIJE: 0 RIE: 1 CAT: 17

Berkeley Childrens Centers CA
CIJE: 0 RIE: 1 CAT: 17

Berkeley County School District SC
CIJE: 1 RIE: 1 CAT: 17

Berkeley Growth Study
CIJE: 5 RIE: 3 CAT: 19

Berkeley Guidance Project
CIJE: 3 RIE: 0 CAT: 19

Berkeley High School CA
CIJE: 3 RIE: 1 CAT: 17

Berkeley Older Generation Study
CIJE: 0 RIE: 2 CAT: 22

Berkeley Physics Course
CIJE: 1 RIE: 1 CAT: 03

Berkeley Project
CIJE: 1 RIE: 1 CAT: 19

Berkeley Reading Tests Project
CIJE: 0 RIE: 1 CAT: 19

Berkeley Unified School District CA
CIJE: 5 RIE: 8 CAT: 17

Berko (Jean)
CIJE: 1 RIE: 1 CAT: 18

Berko Test of Morphology
CIJE: 2 RIE: 1 CAT: 21

Berko Wug Test
CIJE: 1 RIE: 1 CAT: 21

Berks Vocational Technical School PA
CIJE: 0 RIE: 1 CAT: 17

Berkshire Music Center
CIJE: 1 RIE: 0 CAT: 17

Berlak (A)
CIJE: 0 RIE: 2 CAT: 18

Berlak (H)
CIJE: 0 RIE: 2 CAT: 18

Berlin (James)
CIJE: 3 RIE: 1 CAT: 18
SN "James A"

Berlin Model of Intelligence
CIJE: 0 RIE: 1 CAT: 15

Berliner (Emil)
CIJE: 1 RIE: 0 CAT: 18

Berliner Ensemble
CIJE: 1 RIE: 0 CAT: 16

Berlo (David K)
CIJE: 0 RIE: 1 CAT: 18

Berman (Ronald S)
CIJE: 1 RIE: 0 CAT: 18

Berman (Sanford)
CIJE: 0 RIE: 1 CAT: 18

Bermuda
CIJE: 5 RIE: 5 CAT: 07

Bernalillo Public Schools NM
CIJE: 0 RIE: 2 CAT: 17

Bernanos (George)
CIJE: 1 RIE: 0 CAT: 18

Bernard Baruch College NY
USE City University of New York Bernard Baruch College

Bernard Fineson Developmental Center NY
CIJE: 0 RIE: 1 CAT: 17

Bernard van Leer Foundation (Netherlands)
CIJE: 2 RIE: 16 CAT: 17

Bernardin de Saint Pierre (Jacques Henri)
CIJE: 1 RIE: 0 CAT: 18

Bernays (Doris Fleischman)
USE Fleischman (Doris E)

Bernays (Edward L)
CIJE: 1 RIE: 0 CAT: 18

Bernoulli (Daniel)
CIJE: 2 RIE: 0 CAT: 18

Bernoulli Theorem
CIJE: 9 RIE: 1 CAT: 20

Bernstein (Basil)
CIJE: 21 RIE: 11 CAT: 18

Bernstein (Leonard)
CIJE: 3 RIE: 0 CAT: 18

Bernstein Hypothesis
CIJE: 1 RIE: 3 CAT: 15

Berol Canada Inc
CIJE: 1 RIE: 0 CAT: 17

Berry (Mary)
CIJE: 3 RIE: 0 CAT: 18

Berry (Wendell)
CIJE: 3 RIE: 2 CAT: 18

Berry College GA
CIJE: 1 RIE: 4 CAT: 17

Berry Talbott Language Tests
CIJE: 2 RIE: 0 CAT: 21

Bertalanffy (Ludwig von)
CIJE: 0 RIE: 1 CAT: 18
UF Von Bertalanffy (Ludwig)

Berthoff (Ann E)
CIJE: 2 RIE: 0 CAT: 18

Beryllium
CIJE: 1 RIE: 0 CAT: 20

Berynda (Pamvo)
CIJE: 1 RIE: 0 CAT: 18

Best Evidence Synthesis
CIJE: 4 RIE: 2 CAT: 15

BEST IDEA (Career Education Model)
CIJE: 0 RIE: 1 CAT: 15

Best Interests Standards for Child Custody
CIJE: 2 RIE: 1 CAT: 21

Best Liked Least Liked
CIJE: 1 RIE: 0 CAT: 21

BEST Program of San Diego
USE Basic Educational Skills Tutorial Program

Best Short Plays (Title)
CIJE: 0 RIE: 1 CAT: 22

Best Weight Function Method
CIJE: 0 RIE: 1 CAT: 21

Bestiaries
CIJE: 0 RIE: 1 CAT: 16
SN Collections of moral fables having to do with animals

Beta Binomial Test Model
CIJE: 9 RIE: 7 CAT: 21
SN See also "Four Parameter Model"

Beta Densities
CIJE: 1 RIE: 0 CAT: 21

Beta Errors
USE Type II Errors

Beta Index
CIJE: 0 RIE: 1 CAT: 15

Beta Multinomial Test Model
CIJE: 0 RIE: 1 CAT: 15

Beta Particles
CIJE: 1 RIE: 0 CAT: 20

Beta Weights
CIJE: 3 RIE: 4 CAT: 21

BETAC
USE Bilingual Education Technical Assistance Center NY

Betalains
CIJE: 1 RIE: 0 CAT: 20

Bete
CIJE: 0 RIE: 1 CAT: 13

Betel Nut
CIJE: 0 RIE: 1 CAT: 20

Beth Israel Ambulatory Care Center MA
CIJE: 1 RIE: 0 CAT: 17

Bethany College KS
CIJE: 1 RIE: 1 CAT: 17

Bethany College WV
CIJE: 1 RIE: 2 CAT: 17

Bethany Nazarene College OK
CIJE: 0 RIE: 2 CAT: 17
SN Renamed "Southern Nazarene University OK"

Bethel College IN
CIJE: 0 RIE: 2 CAT: 17

Bethel Diagnostic Prescriptive Reading Program
CIJE: 0 RIE: 1 CAT: 19

Bethel Project
CIJE: 0 RIE: 2 CAT: 19

Bethel School District 403 v Fraser
CIJE: 3 RIE: 3 CAT: 14

Bethel School District WA
CIJE: 1 RIE: 0 CAT: 17

Bethel Theological Seminary MN
CIJE: 0 RIE: 1 CAT: 17

Bethlehem Area Chamber of Commerce PA
CIJE: 0 RIE: 1 CAT: 17

Bethlehem Area School District PA
CIJE: 1 RIE: 3 CAT: 17

Bethlehem Area Vocational Technical School PA
CIJE: 0 RIE: 1 CAT: 17

Bethune (Mary McLeod)
CIJE: 4 RIE: 2 CAT: 18

Bethune Elementary School MN
CIJE: 0 RIE: 1 CAT: 17

Bettelheim (Bruno)
CIJE: 12 RIE: 3 CAT: 18

Bettendorf Community School District IA
CIJE: 2 RIE: 0 CAT: 17

Bettendorf Middle School IA
CIJE: 0 RIE: 1 CAT: 17

Better Babies Project
CIJE: 0 RIE: 1 CAT: 17

Better Information for Student Choice
USE National Project I (FIPSE)

Better School Building Amendment (West Virginia)
CIJE: 0 RIE: 1 CAT: 14

Better Schools Program TN
CIJE: 0 RIE: 0 CAT: 19

BETTERAVEN Computer Program
CIJE: 0 RIE: 1 CAT: 04

Betts Basic Readers
CIJE: 0 RIE: 2 CAT: 22

Between Group Differences
CIJE: 5 RIE: 5 CAT: 21

Beverages
CIJE: 4 RIE: 1 CAT: 20
UF Nonalcoholic Beverages

Beverly Hills Unified School District CA
CIJE: 2 RIE: 1 CAT: 17

Bexley City Schools OH
CIJE: 0 RIE: 4 CAT: 17

Beyond Freedom and Dignity
CIJE: 3 RIE: 0 CAT: 22

Beyond Growth Next Stage Lang and Area Studies
CIJE: 0 RIE: 1 CAT: 22

Beyond New Forks
CIJE: 0 RIE: 1 CAT: 22

Beyond the Looking Glass Conference
CIJE: 0 RIE: 2 CAT: 02

Bhagavad Gita
CIJE: 2 RIE: 2 CAT: 22

Bhutan
CIJE: 0 RIE: 5 CAT: 07

Bi Factor Analysis
CIJE: 0 RIE: 1 CAT: 15

Bialer Cromwell Childrens Locus of Control Scale
CIJE: 5 RIE: 5 CAT: 21

Bias in Attitudes Survey
CIJE: 1 RIE: 1 CAT: 21

Bibb County Instructional Materials Center GA
CIJE: 1 RIE: 0 CAT: 17

Bibb County School District GA
CIJE: 1 RIE: 1 CAT: 17

Bible
CIJE: 3 RIE: 0 CAT: 22
SN Use a more specific term if possible, e.g., the Identifiers "New Testament," "Old Testament," "King James Version of the Holy Bible," "New Revised Standard Version of the Bible," etc., or the Descriptor "Biblical Literature"

Bible Belt
CIJE: 1 RIE: 0 CAT: 16
SN Areas of the U.S. characterized by ardent fundamentalism and literal interpretation of the Bible

Bible Colleges
CIJE: 0 RIE: 3 CAT: 05

Bible Study
CIJE: 1 RIE: 0 CAT: 03

Biblio Link
CIJE: 1 RIE: 0 CAT: 04

Bibliofile
CIJE: 1 RIE: 3 CAT: 04

BiblioFile Intelligent Catalog
CIJE: 1 RIE: 1 CAT: 04

Bibliographers
CIJE: 7 RIE: 1 CAT: 09

Bibliographic Access and Control System
CIJE: 1 RIE: 0 CAT: 04

Bibliographic Center for Research CO
CIJE: 0 RIE: 1 CAT: 17

Bibliographic Retrieval Services
CIJE: 17 RIE: 12 CAT: 17
SN "BRS Information Technologies" (q.v.) is currently preferred name form

Bibliographic Services
CIJE: 11 RIE: 12 CAT: 16

Bibliographic Structure
CIJE: 2 RIE: 0 CAT: 04

Bibliographic Theory
CIJE: 1 RIE: 1 CAT: 15

Bibliographical Center for Research CO
CIJE: 0 RIE: 1 CAT: 17

Bibliography of Agriculture
CIJE: 0 RIE: 4 CAT: 22

Bibliology
CIJE: 0 RIE: 1 CAT: 03

Bibliopsychology
CIJE: 0 RIE: 1 CAT: 15

BICAL Computer Program
CIJE: 1 RIE: 7 CAT: 04

Bicentennial
CIJE: 216 RIE: 177 CAT: 12

Bicentennial Ethnic Racial Coalition
CIJE: 0 RIE: 1 CAT: 17

Bichsel (Peter)
CIJE: 1 RIE: 0 CAT: 18

Bicognitive Approach
CIJE: 1 RIE: 1 CAT: 15

Bicycle Ergometer Tests
USE Ergometers

Bicycle Helmets
CIJE: 2 RIE: 1 CAT: 04

Bicycles
CIJE: 6 RIE: 17 CAT: 04

Bid Rigging
CIJE: 0 RIE: 1 CAT: 16

Bidimensional Attention
CIJE: 0 RIE: 1 CAT: 11

Bidirectionality
CIJE: 3 RIE: 1 CAT: 11

Bielefeld Centre for Interdisciplinary Research
CIJE: 0 RIE: 2 CAT: 17

Bielefeld Geometry Conference
CIJE: 1 RIE: 0 CAT: 02

Big Bang Theory
CIJE: 9 RIE: 0 CAT: 15

Big Bend National Park TX
CIJE: 0 RIE: 0 CAT: 07

Big Books
CIJE: 7 RIE: 4 CAT: 16
SN See also "Shared Book Experience"

Big Brother Big Sister Programs
CIJE: 6 RIE: 3 CAT: 19

Big Cities School Project
CIJE: 0 RIE: 1 CAT: 19

Big Eight Universities
CIJE: 0 RIE: 2 CAT: 05

Big Five Markers
CIJE: 0 RIE: 2 CAT: 11
SN See also "Factor V Personality Traits"

Big Sisters Agency
CIJE: 0 RIE: 1 CAT: 17

Big Sky Telegraph
CIJE: 0 RIE: 2 CAT: 17

Big Ten Universities
CIJE: 2 RIE: 3 CAT: 05

Biggs Learning Process Questionnaire
USE Learning Process Questionnaire (Biggs)

Biggs Study Process Questionnaire
USE Study Process Questionnaire (Biggs)

Biglan (Anthony)
CIJE: 0 RIE: 1 CAT: 18

Biglan Model
CIJE: 11 RIE: 10 CAT: 15

Bigram Strategy
CIJE: 1 RIE: 0 CAT: 21

BIGSTEPS Computer Program
CIJE: 0 RIE: 2 CAT: 04

Bilateral Agreements
CIJE: 0 RIE: 1 CAT: 14

Bildung (Concept)
CIJE: 0 RIE: 1 CAT: 15

Bildungstechnologisches Zentrum (West Germany)
CIJE: 0 RIE: 1 CAT: 17

Bilevel Dimensionality of Probability
CIJE: 2 RIE: 0 CAT: 21

Bilevel Factor Analysis
CIJE: 0 RIE: 1 CAT: 21

Bilingual Academic Career Orientation Program NY
CIJE: 0 RIE: 1 CAT: 19

Bilingual Academic Computer Technology Oriented P
USE Project COM TECH NY

Bilingual Academic Services and Intgr Career Sy NY
USE Project BASICS NY

Bilingual Academics for Special Educ Students NY
USE Project BASES NY

Bilingual Bicultural Model
CIJE: 0 RIE: 1 CAT: 15

Bilingual Catalogs
CIJE: 4 RIE: 1 CAT: 13

Bilingual Comprehensive Integrat Reading and Comp
CIJE: 0 RIE: 0 CAT: 15

Bilingual Curriculum Content Pilot Project FL
CIJE: 0 RIE: 0 CAT: 19

Bilingual Dictionaries
CIJE: 5 RIE: 3 CAT: 13

Bilingual Education Act 1968
CIJE: 37 RIE: 326 CAT: 14

Bilingual Education Act 1984
CIJE: 3 RIE: 14 CAT: 14

Bilingual Education Act Amendments 1974
CIJE: 1 RIE: 1 CAT: 14

Bilingual Education and Career Awareness Program
USE Project BECA NY

Bilingual Education Evaluation System
CIJE: 1 RIE: 3 CAT: 21

Bilingual Education Fellowship Program
CIJE: 0 RIE: 1 CAT: 19

Bilingual Education Talented Academy
USE Project BETA NY

Bilingual Education Technical Assistance Center NY
CIJE: 0 RIE: 2 CAT: 17
UF BETAC; Bilingual Technical Assistance Center NY

Bilingual Education through Architectural Math NY
USE Project BEAM NY

Bilingual Education Through the Arts NY
CIJE: 0 RIE: 1 CAT: 19
UF Project BETA (Arts)

Bilingual Evaluation Technical Assistance Project
CIJE: 0 RIE: 9 CAT: 19

Bilingual Inventory of Natural Language
CIJE: 0 RIE: 1 CAT: 21

Bilingual Language Arts Survival Training
USE Project BLAST NY

Bilingual Literature
CIJE: 3 RIE: 1 CAT: 13

Bilingual Mini School NY
CIJE: 0 RIE: 1 CAT: 17

Bilingual Oral Language Test
CIJE: 0 RIE: 1 CAT: 21

Bilingual Prediction Project
CIJE: 0 RIE: 1 CAT: 19

Bilingual Program in Auxiliary Services NY
CIJE: 0 RIE: 1 CAT: 19

Bilingual Program Surveys
CIJE: 0 RIE: 1 CAT: 21

Bilingual Pupil Services Project NY
CIJE: 0 RIE: 2 CAT: 19

Bilingual School Advisory Committees
CIJE: 1 RIE: 1 CAT: 05

Bilingual Special Education
CIJE: 14 RIE: 9 CAT: 16

Bilingual Syntax Measure
CIJE: 9 RIE: 7 CAT: 21

Bilingual Technical Assistance Center NY
USE Bilingual Education Technical Assistance Center NY

Bilingual Testing Program NJ
CIJE: 0 RIE: 1 CAT: 19

Bilingual Vocational Education
CIJE: 0 RIE: 2 CAT: 03

Bilingual Workers
CIJE: 0 RIE: 1 CAT: 10

Bilinguals
CIJE: 6 RIE: 4 CAT: 13

Biliteracy
CIJE: 13 RIE: 20 CAT: 13

Biliteracy Skills Development Program NY
CIJE: 0 RIE: 1 CAT: 19

Bill 82 (Ontario)
CIJE: 3 RIE: 2 CAT: 14
UF Education Amendment Act 1980 (Ontario); Ontario Education Amendment Act 1980

Bill 101 (Quebec)
USE Charter of the French Language (Quebec)

Bill Collectors
CIJE: 1 RIE: 0 CAT: 09

Bill of Human Rights 1960 (Canada)
CIJE: 1 RIE: 0 CAT: 14

Bill of Rights
CIJE: 80 RIE: 89 CAT: 14

Bill of Rights for Foster Children 1973
CIJE: 0 RIE: 1 CAT: 14

Bill Wilkerson Hearing and Speech Center Program
CIJE: 1 RIE: 0 CAT: 19

Billboards
CIJE: 0 RIE: 1 CAT: 04

Biller Rating Scale
CIJE: 0 RIE: 1 CAT: 21

Billets (Assignments)
CIJE: 0 RIE: 1 CAT: 16

Billiards
CIJE: 3 RIE: 0 CAT: 16

Billing
USE Invoices

Billings (Josh)
CIJE: 0 RIE: 1 CAT: 18

Billings (Nathaniel)
CIJE: 1 RIE: 0 CAT: 18

Billings School District No 2 MT
CIJE: 0 RIE: 2 CAT: 17

Bills Index of Adjustment and Values
CIJE: 2 RIE: 6 CAT: 21

Billy Budd
CIJE: 1 RIE: 1 CAT: 22

Billy Mills Indian Youth Leadership Program
CIJE: 0 RIE: 1 CAT: 19

BILOG Computer Program
CIJE: 8 RIE: 7 CAT: 04

Biloquialism
CIJE: 0 RIE: 2 CAT: 13

Bilston College (England)
CIJE: 1 RIE: 0 CAT: 17

Bimetallic Elements
CIJE: 1 RIE: 0 CAT: 20

Bimodal Theory
CIJE: 2 RIE: 3 CAT: 15

Bimultivariate Redundancy Statistic
CIJE: 1 RIE: 0 CAT: 15

Binandere Languages
CIJE: 0 RIE: 1 CAT: 13

Binary Arithmetic
CIJE: 2 RIE: 4 CAT: 20

Binary Choice Unit
CIJE: 1 RIE: 1 CAT: 20

Binary Coding
CIJE: 1 RIE: 3 CAT: 15

Binary Compounds
CIJE: 1 RIE: 0 CAT: 20

Binary Data Analysis
CIJE: 13 RIE: 2 CAT: 15

Binary Measurement Model
CIJE: 1 RIE: 1 CAT: 15

Binary Numbers
CIJE: 7 RIE: 0 CAT: 20

Binary Opposition
CIJE: 4 RIE: 0 CAT: 20

Binary Propositional Logic
CIJE: 1 RIE: 0 CAT: 15

Binary Relational Model
CIJE: 1 RIE: 1 CAT: 15

Binary Response
CIJE: 3 RIE: 3 CAT: 20

Binary Scores
CIJE: 0 RIE: 1 CAT: 21

Binary Search Scheme
CIJE: 3 RIE: 1 CAT: 15

Binary Stars
CIJE: 1 RIE: 0 CAT: 20

Binary Trees
CIJE: 7 RIE: 1 CAT: 20

Binary Vectors
CIJE: 3 RIE: 0 CAT: 20

Binational Centers
CIJE: 0 RIE: 2 CAT: 05

Bindery Workers
CIJE: 1 RIE: 7 CAT: 09

Binding Theory
CIJE: 4 RIE: 2 CAT: 13

Binet (Alfred)
CIJE: 8 RIE: 1 CAT: 18

Binet Simon Intelligence Scale
CIJE: 2 RIE: 3 CAT: 21

Binford Individualized Curriculum Analysis Project
CIJE: 0 RIE: 1 CAT: 19

Bing (Rudolf)
CIJE: 1 RIE: 0 CAT: 18

Bing Test
CIJE: 1 RIE: 0 CAT: 21

Binge Drinking
CIJE: 0 RIE: 2 CAT: 11

Binge Eating
CIJE: 14 RIE: 5 CAT: 11

Binge Eating Scale
CIJE: 0 RIE: 1 CAT: 21

Binghamton City Schools NY
CIJE: 0 RIE: 3 CAT: 17

Bingo
CIJE: 5 RIE: 0 CAT: 16

Binoculars
CIJE: 0 RIE: 1 CAT: 04

Binois Pichot Vocabulary Test
CIJE: 0 RIE: 1 CAT: 21

Binomial Coefficients
CIJE: 6 RIE: 1 CAT: 20

Binomial Distribution
CIJE: 13 RIE: 3 CAT: 21

Binomial Effect Size Display
CIJE: 2 RIE: 1 CAT: 15

Binomial Error Model
CIJE: 6 RIE: 9 CAT: 15

Binomial Test
CIJE: 3 RIE: 2 CAT: 21

Binomials
CIJE: 1 RIE: 1 CAT: 20

Binukid
USE Bukidnon

Bioassay
CIJE: 3 RIE: 1 CAT: 20
SN See also "Quantal Bioassay"

Biobehavioral State
CIJE: 4 RIE: 0 CAT: 11

Bioconversion
CIJE: 0 RIE: 0 CAT: 20

Biocybernetics
CIJE: 0 RIE: 8 CAT: 20

Biodata
CIJE: 1 RIE: 2 CAT: 16
UF Biographical Data

Biodegradation
CIJE: 1 RIE: 2 CAT: 20
UF Decay (Biology)

Bioenergetics
CIJE: 2 RIE: 1 CAT: 20

Bioengineering
CIJE: 10 RIE: 7 CAT: 20

Biofuels
CIJE: 0 RIE: 5 CAT: 20

Biofunctional Model
CIJE: 0 RIE: 1 CAT: 15

Biogeochemistry
CIJE: 1 RIE: 0 CAT: 20

Biogeography
CIJE: 5 RIE: 2 CAT: 20

Biographical Analysis
CIJE: 0 RIE: 4 CAT: 15

Biographical Data
USE Biodata

Biographical Information Blank (Cline et al)
CIJE: 0 RIE: 1 CAT: 21

Biographical Inventory (Ellison et al)
CIJE: 0 RIE: 1 CAT: 21

Biographical Inventory for Medicine
CIJE: 0 RIE: 1 CAT: 21

Biola College CA
CIJE: 1 RIE: 0 CAT: 17

Biola School of Missionary Medicine CA
CIJE: 0 RIE: 1 CAT: 17

Biolinguistics
CIJE: 0 RIE: 1 CAT: 13

Biological Abstracts
CIJE: 1 RIE: 1 CAT: 22

Biological Classification
CIJE: 3 RIE: 0 CAT: 20

Biological Control
CIJE: 2 RIE: 1 CAT: 20

Biological Determinism
CIJE: 8 RIE: 1 CAT: 15

Biological Disarmament Convention
CIJE: 1 RIE: 0 CAT: 02

Biological Diversity
CIJE: 8 RIE: 8 CAT: 20

Biological Impact
CIJE: 0 RIE: 2 CAT: 20
SN See also "Environmental Impact"

Biological Princepts Test (Shipe)
CIJE: 0 RIE: 1 CAT: 21

Biological Processes
CIJE: 4 RIE: 1 CAT: 20

Biological Sciences Communication Project
CIJE: 0 RIE: 1 CAT: 19

Biological Sciences Curr Study Biology Spec Matl
CIJE: 0 RIE: 1 CAT: 03

Biological Sciences Curr Study Blue Version
CIJE: 1 RIE: 2 CAT: 03

Biological Sciences Curr Study Green Version
CIJE: 3 RIE: 4 CAT: 03

Biological Sciences Curr Study Minicourses
CIJE: 0 RIE: 1 CAT: 03

Biological Sciences Curr Study Single Topic Films
CIJE: 0 RIE: 1 CAT: 03

Biological Sciences Curr Study Yellow Version
CIJE: 4 RIE: 1 CAT: 03

Biological Sciences Curriculum Study
CIJE: 97 RIE: 129 CAT: 03
SN See also "BSCS..."

Biological Warfare
CIJE: 2 RIE: 0 CAT: 20

Biologists
CIJE: 0 RIE: 1 CAT: 09

Biology Achievement Test (Sparks)
CIJE: 0 RIE: 1 CAT: 21

Biology Attitude Assessment Scale
CIJE: 1 RIE: 0 CAT: 21

Biology Classroom Activity Checklist
CIJE: 1 RIE: 3 CAT: 21

Biology Laboratory Activity Checklist
CIJE: 0 RIE: 1 CAT: 21

Biology Teacher Behavior Inventory (Evans)
CIJE: 1 RIE: 0 CAT: 21

Bioluminescence
CIJE: 2 RIE: 0 CAT: 20

Biomass
CIJE: 4 RIE: 11 CAT: 20

Biomedical Communications Network
CIJE: 1 RIE: 10 CAT: 17

Biomedical Computer Programs
CIJE: 5 RIE: 2 CAT: 04
UF BMDP Computer Program

Biomedical Engineering Technology
CIJE: 0 RIE: 1 CAT: 03

Biomedical Information Services
CIJE: 3 RIE: 4 CAT: 17

Biomedical Interdisciplinary Curriculum Project
CIJE: 0 RIE: 11 CAT: 19

Biomedical Model
CIJE: 3 RIE: 1 CAT: 11

Biomedical Photography
CIJE: 0 RIE: 1 CAT: 20

Biomedical Research Support Grants
CIJE: 2 RIE: 0 CAT: 19

Biomedical Sciences Preparatory Program AL
CIJE: 0 RIE: 6 CAT: 19

Biomes
CIJE: 1 RIE: 0 CAT: 20

Biometrics
CIJE: 4 RIE: 8 CAT: 20

Bioplasmic Energy
CIJE: 1 RIE: 2 CAT: 20

Biopsychosocial Model
CIJE: 3 RIE: 0 CAT: 15

Bioregions
CIJE: 1 RIE: 1 CAT: 20

Biorhythms
CIJE: 10 RIE: 3 CAT: 11

BioSciences Information Service
CIJE: 2 RIE: 0 CAT: 17
SN See also under "BIOSIS..."

BIOSIS Previews
CIJE: 1 RIE: 3 CAT: 04

Biostatistics
CIJE: 8 RIE: 3 CAT: 20

Biotelemetry
CIJE: 2 RIE: 0 CAT: 20

Biovideography
CIJE: 1 RIE: 0 CAT: 20

Bipolar Trait Ratings Scales
CIJE: 4 RIE: 3 CAT: 21

Bipolar Traits
CIJE: 0 RIE: 2 CAT: 11

BIPs
USE Basic Instruction Programs

Biracial Children
CIJE: 6 RIE: 2 CAT: 10
SN See broader "Interracial Children" — see also "Mixed Race Persons"

Biracial Family
CIJE: 0 RIE: 0 CAT: 10
SN See broader "Interracial Family" — see also "Mixed Race Persons"

Birch Bark
CIJE: 0 RIE: 1 CAT: 20

Bird Banding
CIJE: 2 RIE: 1 CAT: 20

Bird Migration
CIJE: 0 RIE: 2 CAT: 20

Bird Songs
CIJE: 1 RIE: 0 CAT: 20

Bird Watching Groups
USE Birdwatching

Birdfeeding
CIJE: 1 RIE: 0 CAT: 20

Birdhouses
CIJE: 2 RIE: 0 CAT: 05

Birdwatching
CIJE: 5 RIE: 0 CAT: 20
UF Bird Watching Groups

Birkbeck (George)
CIJE: 0 RIE: 1 CAT: 18

Birmingham Elementary Schools MI
CIJE: 1 RIE: 0 CAT: 17

Birmingham Public Schools AL
CIJE: 1 RIE: 2 CAT: 17

Birmingham Southern College AL
CIJE: 6 RIE: 2 CAT: 17

Birnbaum Models
CIJE: 2 RIE: 8 CAT: 15

Birth Attendants (Traditional)
USE Traditional Birth Attendants

Birth of a Nation
CIJE: 1 RIE: 2 CAT: 22

Birth Spacing
CIJE: 3 RIE: 8 CAT: 11

Birth Timing
CIJE: 1 RIE: 3 CAT: 11

Birthday Party (Pinter)
CIJE: 0 RIE: 1 CAT: 22

Birthdays
CIJE: 17 RIE: 2 CAT: 12

Birzeit University (Israel)
CIJE: 1 RIE: 0 CAT: 17

Bisection Procedures
CIJE: 1 RIE: 0 CAT: 21

Biserial Correlation
CIJE: 9 RIE: 6 CAT: 20

Bisexuality
CIJE: 23 RIE: 5 CAT: 11

Bishop College TX
CIJE: 2 RIE: 4 CAT: 17

Bishop Learning Center HI
CIJE: 1 RIE: 0 CAT: 17

Bishop Lowth Complex
CIJE: 1 RIE: 0 CAT: 13

Bishops Pastoral Letters
USE Pastoral Letters

Bishopswood School (England)
CIJE: 0 RIE: 1 CAT: 17

Bisociation
CIJE: 1 RIE: 0 CAT: 11

Bissell (Claude)
CIJE: 1 RIE: 0 CAT: 18

Bissell (Lewis)
CIJE: 0 RIE: 1 CAT: 18

Bistable Circuits
CIJE: 1 RIE: 0 CAT: 20

BISVUX Project (Sweden)
CIJE: 0 RIE: 1 CAT: 19

Bites and Stings
CIJE: 0 RIE: 1 CAT: 11

Biting
CIJE: 4 RIE: 1 CAT: 11

BITNET
CIJE: 23 RIE: 8 CAT: 17

Bitransitive Clauses
CIJE: 0 RIE: 1 CAT: 13

BITS Project (Sweden)
USE Child Care in the Admass Society (Sweden)

Bittersweet Farms OH
CIJE: 1 RIE: 1 CAT: 17

Bitzer (Lloyd)
CIJE: 0 RIE: 1 CAT: 18
SN "Lloyd F"

Bizet (Georges)
CIJE: 2 RIE: 0 CAT: 18

BIZQUIZ
CIJE: 0 RIE: 1 CAT: 19

Bjorklund (Eskil)
CIJE: 0 RIE: 1 CAT: 18

BK Parental Checklist (Buck and Kennealy)
CIJE: 0 RIE: 1 CAT: 21

BKR Training Program
CIJE: 1 RIE: 0 CAT: 19

Blachowicz (C Z)
CIJE: 0 RIE: 1 CAT: 18

Black (Edwin)
CIJE: 0 RIE: 1 CAT: 18

Black (Hugo)
CIJE: 1 RIE: 1 CAT: 18

Black (Word)
CIJE: 1 RIE: 0 CAT: 16

Black and White
CIJE: 0 RIE: 0 CAT: 20

Black Appalachian Commission
CIJE: 0 RIE: 1 CAT: 17

Black Body Radiation
CIJE: 2 RIE: 0 CAT: 20

Black Box Theories
CIJE: 2 RIE: 0 CAT: 15

Black Child Development Institute DC
CIJE: 1 RIE: 0 CAT: 17

Black Communication
CIJE: 6 RIE: 14 CAT: 13

Black Congressmen
CIJE: 0 RIE: 1 CAT: 10

Black Creek Watershed Project IN
CIJE: 0 RIE: 1 CAT: 19

Black Crusaders
CIJE: 1 RIE: 0 CAT: 17

Black Economic Research Center NY
CIJE: 0 RIE: 1 CAT: 17

Black Elk
CIJE: 1 RIE: 1 CAT: 18

Black Executive Exchange Program
CIJE: 1 RIE: 0 CAT: 19

Black Expressive Behavior
CIJE: 2 RIE: 1 CAT: 11

Black Folk Music
CIJE: 1 RIE: 4 CAT: 16

Black Gold Cooperative Library System PA
CIJE: 0 RIE: 2 CAT: 17

Black Hawk College IL
CIJE: 3 RIE: 11 CAT: 17

Black Hills Special Services Cooperative SD
CIJE: 0 RIE: 1 CAT: 17

Black Hills State College SD
CIJE: 0 RIE: 4 CAT: 17

Black History Month
CIJE: 11 RIE: 4 CAT: 12
UF Afro American Black History Month

Black Holes
CIJE: 9 RIE: 1 CAT: 20

Black Identity Test
CIJE: 1 RIE: 0 CAT: 21

Black Ideology Scale
CIJE: 1 RIE: 1 CAT: 21

Black in White America
CIJE: 0 RIE: 5 CAT: 22

Black Intelligence Test of Cultural Homogeneity
CIJE: 2 RIE: 3 CAT: 21

Black Jack Davy (Song)
CIJE: 0 RIE: 1 CAT: 22

Black Mesa Community School AZ
CIJE: 0 RIE: 1 CAT: 17

Black Migration
CIJE: 1 RIE: 2 CAT: 16

Black Militancy
CIJE: 3 RIE: 2 CAT: 16

Black Ministers Teachers Conference
CIJE: 0 RIE: 1 CAT: 02

Black Mountain College NC
CIJE: 2 RIE: 1 CAT: 17

Black Newspapers
CIJE: 2 RIE: 5 CAT: 16

Black Panther Party
CIJE: 3 RIE: 3 CAT: 17

Black Poetry
CIJE: 3 RIE: 1 CAT: 16

Black Press
CIJE: 3 RIE: 5 CAT: 16

Black Psychiatrists of America
CIJE: 0 RIE: 1 CAT: 17

Black Psychology
CIJE: 6 RIE: 4 CAT: 02

Black Separatism
CIJE: 1 RIE: 1 CAT: 16

Black Spirituals
CIJE: 2 RIE: 1 CAT: 16

Black Star Picture Agency
CIJE: 0 RIE: 1 CAT: 17

Black Students Union
CIJE: 1 RIE: 0 CAT: 17

Black Thunder
CIJE: 0 RIE: 1 CAT: 22

Black United Front
CIJE: 0 RIE: 1 CAT: 17

Black Womens Studies
CIJE: 3 RIE: 4 CAT: 03

Black Writers
CIJE: 10 RIE: 4 CAT: 10

Blackbird Vision Screening System
CIJE: 0 RIE: 1 CAT: 11

Blackboard Instructional Planner
CIJE: 0 RIE: 1 CAT: 04
SN See also "Dynamic Instructional Planning"

Blackfeet (Tribe)
CIJE: 2 RIE: 29 CAT: 08

Blackfeet Indian Reservation
CIJE: 1 RIE: 5 CAT: 17

Blackfoot (Language)
CIJE: 0 RIE: 7 CAT: 13
UF Siksika

Blackfoot (Tribe)
CIJE: 2 RIE: 8 CAT: 08

Blackfoot Confederacy
CIJE: 0 RIE: 2 CAT: 08

Blackhawk Technical College WI
CIJE: 0 RIE: 3 CAT: 17

Blackhawk Technical Institute WI
CIJE: 0 RIE: 2 CAT: 17

Blacklists
CIJE: 0 RIE: 3 CAT: 16

Blackout Technique
CIJE: 0 RIE: 1 CAT: 15

Blacksmiths
CIJE: 2 RIE: 1 CAT: 09

Blackstone Regional Vocational Sch Dist MA
CIJE: 0 RIE: 5 CAT: 17

Blackwater Community School AZ
CIJE: 1 RIE: 0 CAT: 17

Blackwell (Elizabeth)
CIJE: 0 RIE: 0 CAT: 18

Blackwell North America
CIJE: 1 RIE: 1 CAT: 17

Blackwolf Case
CIJE: 1 RIE: 0 CAT: 14

Blacky Pictures
CIJE: 1 RIE: 1 CAT: 22

Bladder Control
CIJE: 1 RIE: 1 CAT: 11

BLADE Program
USE Basic Literacy for Adult Development

Blade Runner (Movie)
CIJE: 0 RIE: 1 CAT: 22

Blair (David P)
CIJE: 1 RIE: 0 CAT: 18
SN "David Phillip"

Blair (Francis Preston)
CIJE: 1 RIE: 0 CAT: 18

Blair (Hugh)
CIJE: 0 RIE: 1 CAT: 18

Blair Summer School for Journalism
CIJE: 1 RIE: 0 CAT: 17

Blake (William)
CIJE: 14 RIE: 1 CAT: 18

Blalock FIRST
CIJE: 0 RIE: 2 CAT: 19
SN FIRST = Fund for the Improvement and Reform of Schools and Teaching

Blame
CIJE: 23 RIE: 23 CAT: 16

Blanchard (Brand)
CIJE: 1 RIE: 0 CAT: 18

Blanchard (Ken)
CIJE: 0 RIE: 1 CAT: 18

Blanchard Index of Scholastic Aptitude
CIJE: 1 RIE: 0 CAT: 21

Blanco (Julian C)
CIJE: 0 RIE: 1 CAT: 18

Blaney (Jack)
CIJE: 0 RIE: 1 CAT: 18

Blank (Rolf K)
CIJE: 0 RIE: 0 CAT: 18

Blank Trial Method
CIJE: 3 RIE: 1 CAT: 15

Blasco Ibanez (Vicente)
CIJE: 2 RIE: 0 CAT: 18

Blatt (Burton)
CIJE: 2 RIE: 0 CAT: 18

Blau (Peter M)
CIJE: 2 RIE: 5 CAT: 18

Blaubergs v Board of Regents Univ System Georgia
CIJE: 0 RIE: 1 CAT: 14

Blaug (Mark)
CIJE: 1 RIE: 0 CAT: 18

Bleich (David)
CIJE: 3 RIE: 2 CAT: 18

Blended Families
CIJE: 3 RIE: 5 CAT: 10

Blended Sound Sight Method of Learning
CIJE: 1 RIE: 0 CAT: 15

Blending Skills (Reading)
CIJE: 2 RIE: 1 CAT: 13

Blepharisma
CIJE: 1 RIE: 0 CAT: 11

Blind Learning Aptitude Test
CIJE: 3 RIE: 1 CAT: 21

Blind Tracing
CIJE: 1 RIE: 0 CAT: 16

Blinderman (Abraham)
CIJE: 1 RIE: 0 CAT: 18

Blindisms
CIJE: 7 RIE: 0 CAT: 11

Blindstitch Machine (Sewing)
CIJE: 0 RIE: 1 CAT: 04

Blishen Socio Economic Index
CIJE: 0 RIE: 1 CAT: 21

Bliss (Henry)
CIJE: 1 RIE: 0 CAT: 18

BLISS Programing Language
CIJE: 0 RIE: 2 CAT: 04

Bliss Symbols
CIJE: 20 RIE: 8 CAT: 04

Blizzards
CIJE: 0 RIE: 2 CAT: 20

Block Child Rearing Practices Report
CIJE: 1 RIE: 0 CAT: 21

Block Communities Inc
CIJE: 0 RIE: 1 CAT: 17

Block Counting (Bussis and Chittenden)
CIJE: 0 RIE: 1 CAT: 21

Block Design Test
CIJE: 5 RIE: 1 CAT: 21

Block Plan
CIJE: 0 RIE: 3 CAT: 03

Block Program (Indiana University)
CIJE: 0 RIE: 1 CAT: 19

Block Programs
CIJE: 0 RIE: 1 CAT: 19

Block Scheduling
CIJE: 5 RIE: 5 CAT: 15

Block Sorting (Bussis and Chittenden)
CIJE: 0 RIE: 1 CAT: 21

Block Test Mode
CIJE: 0 RIE: 2 CAT: 21

BlockAIDS
CIJE: 0 RIE: 1 CAT: 04

Blocked Careers
CIJE: 0 RIE: 1 CAT: 15

Blocker Doctrine
CIJE: 0 RIE: 1 CAT: 15

Blocking Paradigm
CIJE: 1 RIE: 0 CAT: 16

Blocks
CIJE: 17 RIE: 25 CAT: 04

Blood
CIJE: 10 RIE: 7 CAT: 11

Blood (Nation)
CIJE: 0 RIE: 1 CAT: 08
UF Kainah (Tribe)

Blood Cholesterol
USE Cholesterol

Blood Disorders
CIJE: 0 RIE: 2 CAT: 11

Blood Donation
CIJE: 3 RIE: 1 CAT: 11

Blood Pressure
CIJE: 11 RIE: 5 CAT: 11

Blood Pressure Determination
CIJE: 4 RIE: 7 CAT: 11

Blood Tests
CIJE: 5 RIE: 2 CAT: 11

Blood Transfusion
CIJE: 7 RIE: 3 CAT: 11

Bloodborne Pathogens
CIJE: 1 RIE: 1 CAT: 11

Bloom (Allan)
CIJE: 37 RIE: 8 CAT: 18

Bloom (Benjamin S)
CIJE: 43 RIE: 33 CAT: 18

Bloome (David)
CIJE: 0 RIE: 1 CAT: 18

Bloomfield (Leonard)
CIJE: 1 RIE: 4 CAT: 18

Bloomfield College NJ
CIJE: 7 RIE: 6 CAT: 17

Bloomfield Public Schools NJ
CIJE: 1 RIE: 2 CAT: 17

Bloomingdale School MA
CIJE: 0 RIE: 1 CAT: 17

Bloomingdales Department Store
CIJE: 0 RIE: 1 CAT: 17

Bloomington Curriculum Plan
CIJE: 0 RIE: 1 CAT: 03

Bloomington Normal Black History Project
CIJE: 0 RIE: 1 CAT: 19

Bloomington Public Schools MN
CIJE: 0 RIE: 2 CAT: 17

Blooms Mastery Teaching Strategy
CIJE: 1 RIE: 9 CAT: 15

Blooms Taxonomy
CIJE: 119 RIE: 133 CAT: 15
UF Taxonomy of Educational Objectives (Bloom)

Bloomsburg University PA
CIJE: 0 RIE: 8 CAT: 17

Blossers Taxonomy
CIJE: 1 RIE: 0 CAT: 21

Blouner (Robert)
CIJE: 1 RIE: 0 CAT: 18

Blount (William)
CIJE: 0 RIE: 1 CAT: 18

Bloustein (Edward J)
CIJE: 1 RIE: 0 CAT: 18

Blow Molding
CIJE: 1 RIE: 0 CAT: 04

Blox Test
CIJE: 0 RIE: 1 CAT: 21

Bloxoms Rotation Technique
CIJE: 0 RIE: 1 CAT: 15

Blue Book of the John Birch Society
CIJE: 0 RIE: 1 CAT: 22

Blue Book Series
CIJE: 0 RIE: 1 CAT: 22

Blue Hills Regional Vocational Technical School MA
CIJE: 1 RIE: 0 CAT: 17

Blue Laws
CIJE: 1 RIE: 1 CAT: 14

Blue Mountain Small Schools Consortium WA
CIJE: 0 RIE: 1 CAT: 17

Blue Ribbon Schools
CIJE: 1 RIE: 2 CAT: 05

Blue Ridge Community College NC
CIJE: 0 RIE: 2 CAT: 17

Blue Ridge Consortium DC
CIJE: 0 RIE: 1 CAT: 17

Blue Ridge Mountains
CIJE: 1 RIE: 10 CAT: 07

Blue Willow
CIJE: 0 RIE: 1 CAT: 22

Bluefield State College WV
CIJE: 1 RIE: 2 CAT: 17

Blueprint for the Future Program ON
CIJE: 0 RIE: 1 CAT: 19
SN Program of the Scarborough Board of Education

Blues Music
CIJE: 15 RIE: 3 CAT: 16

Blues Poetry
CIJE: 2 RIE: 1 CAT: 22

Bluewing Tutorial Project
CIJE: 1 RIE: 0 CAT: 19

Blumberg (Arthur)
CIJE: 2 RIE: 0 CAT: 18

Blumbergs Category System
CIJE: 0 RIE: 2 CAT: 15

Blume (Judy)
CIJE: 11 RIE: 4 CAT: 18

Blumer (Herbert)
CIJE: 2 RIE: 0 CAT: 18

Blushing
CIJE: 0 RIE: 1 CAT: 11

Blyth Second Year Algebra Test
CIJE: 0 RIE: 1 CAT: 21

Blythedale Childrens Hospital
CIJE: 1 RIE: 0 CAT: 17

Blyton (Enid)
CIJE: 4 RIE: 0 CAT: 18

BMDP Computer Program
USE Biomedical Computer Programs

Bnai Brith
CIJE: 3 RIE: 3 CAT: 17

Board Community Relationship
CIJE: 0 RIE: 1 CAT: 16

Board Games
CIJE: 2 RIE: 2 CAT: 16
UF Boardgame Use

Board of Education v Allen
CIJE: 1 RIE: 0 CAT: 14

Board of Foreign Scholarships
CIJE: 0 RIE: 2 CAT: 17

Board of Regents v Roth
CIJE: 1 RIE: 2 CAT: 14

Board of Trustees Keene State College v Sweeney
CIJE: 1 RIE: 0 CAT: 14

Board of Urban Affairs
CIJE: 1 RIE: 0 CAT: 17

Board on International Comparative Studies Educ
CIJE: 0 RIE: 1 CAT: 17

Board Parent Relationship
CIJE: 0 RIE: 2 CAT: 16

Board Student Relationship
CIJE: 1 RIE: 1 CAT: 16

Board Teacher Relationship
CIJE: 5 RIE: 5 CAT: 16

Board v Rowley
CIJE: 3 RIE: 1 CAT: 14

Boardgame Use
USE Board Games

Boarding Machine Operators
CIJE: 0 RIE: 1 CAT: 09

Boards of Cooperative Educational Services
CIJE: 18 RIE: 40 CAT: 05
UF BOCES NY

Boas (Belle)
CIJE: 0 RIE: 0 CAT: 18

Boas (Franz)
CIJE: 2 RIE: 1 CAT: 18

Boat Expeditions
CIJE: 1 RIE: 0 CAT: 20

Boat US
CIJE: 0 RIE: 1 CAT: 17

Boating
CIJE: 4 RIE: 6 CAT: 16

Boating Safety
CIJE: 2 RIE: 4 CAT: 11

Boats
CIJE: 6 RIE: 10 CAT: 04

Boatswain Mates
CIJE: 0 RIE: 3 CAT: 09

Bob Jones University SC
CIJE: 2 RIE: 2 CAT: 17

Bob Jones University v United States
CIJE: 5 RIE: 2 CAT: 14

Bobath Method
CIJE: 1 RIE: 2 CAT: 15

Bobbs Merrill Company
CIJE: 0 RIE: 1 CAT: 17

Bobbsey Twins
CIJE: 2 RIE: 0 CAT: 22

Bobitt Procedure
CIJE: 0 RIE: 1 CAT: 15

Bobsledding
CIJE: 0 RIE: 0 CAT: 16

Boccaccio (Giovanni)
CIJE: 5 RIE: 0 CAT: 18

BOCES NY
USE Boards of Cooperative Educational Services

Bochum Model
CIJE: 0 RIE: 1 CAT: 15

Bodas de Sangre
CIJE: 0 RIE: 1 CAT: 22

Bodger (Joan H)
CIJE: 2 RIE: 0 CAT: 18

Body Articulation
CIJE: 1 RIE: 0 CAT: 11

Body Awareness
CIJE: 5 RIE: 9 CAT: 11

Body Barrier Score
CIJE: 0 RIE: 1 CAT: 21

Body Builders
USE Bodybuilding

Body Contact
CIJE: 3 RIE: 3 CAT: 16
SN See also "Touching," "Physical Contact"

Body Esteem Scale
CIJE: 1 RIE: 3 CAT: 21

Body FORTRAN
CIJE: 2 RIE: 0 CAT: 11

Body Movement Style
CIJE: 2 RIE: 1 CAT: 11

Body Movement Therapy
CIJE: 1 RIE: 0 CAT: 11

Bodybuilding
CIJE: 3 RIE: 0 CAT: 11
UF Body Builders

Boehm Test of Basic Concepts
CIJE: 23 RIE: 11 CAT: 21

Boeing Company
CIJE: 4 RIE: 4 CAT: 17

Bogardus Social Distance Scale
CIJE: 5 RIE: 8 CAT: 21
UF Social Distance Scale (Bogardus)

Bogdanov Theory of Knowledge
CIJE: 0 RIE: 1 CAT: 15

Bogdanovich (Peter)
CIJE: 1 RIE: 0 CAT: 18

Boggs (Hale)
CIJE: 0 RIE: 1 CAT: 18

Boggs (Lilburn W)
CIJE: 0 RIE: 1 CAT: 18

Boggs Academy GA
CIJE: 1 RIE: 0 CAT: 17

Bogus Pipeline Technique
CIJE: 1 RIE: 0 CAT: 15
UF Generalized Bogus Pipeline

Bohm (David)
CIJE: 1 RIE: 1 CAT: 18

Bohr (Niels)
CIJE: 5 RIE: 0 CAT: 18

Boileau Despreaux (Nicolas)
CIJE: 1 RIE: 0 CAT: 18

Boilermakers
CIJE: 0 RIE: 2 CAT: 09

Boilers
CIJE: 1 RIE: 14 CAT: 04

Boise Public Schools ID
CIJE: 1 RIE: 2 CAT: 17

Boise State University ID
CIJE: 10 RIE: 3 CAT: 17

Bokmal
CIJE: 1 RIE: 1 CAT: 13

Bolinger (Dwight)
CIJE: 0 RIE: 1 CAT: 18

Bolivar (Simon)
CIJE: 1 RIE: 0 CAT: 18

Bolivia
CIJE: 34 RIE: 50 CAT: 07

Bolivia (Cochabamba)
CIJE: 1 RIE: 6 CAT: 07

Bolivia (La Paz)
CIJE: 0 RIE: 1 CAT: 07

Boll (Heinrich)
CIJE: 3 RIE: 0 CAT: 18

Bolles (Ron)
CIJE: 1 RIE: 0 CAT: 18

Bolling v Sharpe
CIJE: 0 RIE: 3 CAT: 14

Bolt Beranek and Newman Inc
CIJE: 0 RIE: 1 CAT: 17

Bolton College of Education (England)
CIJE: 1 RIE: 0 CAT: 17

Boltzmann Distribution Law
CIJE: 4 RIE: 0 CAT: 20

Bomb Threats
CIJE: 2 RIE: 4 CAT: 16

Bombs
CIJE: 2 RIE: 2 CAT: 04
SN See also "Atomic Bomb" and "Nuclear Weapons"

Bonaparte (Napoleon)
CIJE: 10 RIE: 1 CAT: 18

Bond (Edward)
CIJE: 2 RIE: 0 CAT: 18

Bond (Horace Mann)
CIJE: 4 RIE: 1 CAT: 18

Bond (Michael)
CIJE: 2 RIE: 0 CAT: 18

Bond Ratings
CIJE: 4 RIE: 1 CAT: 16

Bond Sales
CIJE: 4 RIE: 8 CAT: 16

Bone (Robert A)
CIJE: 1 RIE: 0 CAT: 18

Bone Conduction Transducers
CIJE: 0 RIE: 1 CAT: 04

Bones
CIJE: 6 RIE: 0 CAT: 20

Bonferroni Procedure
CIJE: 10 RIE: 10 CAT: 21

Bonggi
CIJE: 0 RIE: 1 CAT: 13
SN A Malaysian language

Bonham (Frank)
CIJE: 1 RIE: 0 CAT: 18

Bonnin (Gertrude Simmons)
USE Zitkala Sa

Bono
CIJE: 1 RIE: 0 CAT: 13

Bonser (Frederick)
CIJE: 2 RIE: 0 CAT: 18

Bontemps (Arna)
CIJE: 1 RIE: 0 CAT: 18

Bontoc
USE Bontok

Bontok
CIJE: 0 RIE: 3 CAT: 13
SN A Northwest Austronesian (Philippine) language
UF Bontoc

Book Availability
CIJE: 5 RIE: 1 CAT: 16

Book Awards
CIJE: 14 RIE: 2 CAT: 16

Book Binding
CIJE: 20 RIE: 18 CAT: 16

Book Binding Expenditures
CIJE: 0 RIE: 1 CAT: 16

Book Bridges MB
CIJE: 0 RIE: 1 CAT: 19

Book Clubs
CIJE: 15 RIE: 9 CAT: 05

Book Collecting
CIJE: 5 RIE: 3 CAT: 16

Book Covers
USE Book Jackets

Book Dealers
CIJE: 10 RIE: 2 CAT: 09

Book Design
CIJE: 1 RIE: 1 CAT: 16

Book Deterioration
USE Deterioration (Books)

Book Exchange
CIJE: 3 RIE: 8 CAT: 17

Book Exposure Project
CIJE: 0 RIE: 1 CAT: 19

Book Fairs
CIJE: 14 RIE: 3 CAT: 16

Book Jackets
CIJE: 6 RIE: 2 CAT: 16
UF Book Covers

Book Longevity
CIJE: 0 RIE: 1 CAT: 16

Book Losses
CIJE: 6 RIE: 5 CAT: 16

Book Mutilation
CIJE: 2 RIE: 2 CAT: 16

Book of Good Love
CIJE: 2 RIE: 0 CAT: 22

Book of Job
CIJE: 1 RIE: 1 CAT: 22

Book of Mormon
CIJE: 1 RIE: 0 CAT: 22

Book Ownership
CIJE: 3 RIE: 1 CAT: 16

Book Preservation
CIJE: 3 RIE: 15 CAT: 16

Book Production
CIJE: 4 RIE: 4 CAT: 16
UF Bookmaking (Book Production)

Book Reports
CIJE: 22 RIE: 8 CAT: 16

Book Restoration
CIJE: 5 RIE: 13 CAT: 16

Book Return Rates
USE Return Rates (Books)

Book Sales
CIJE: 9 RIE: 6 CAT: 16

Book Shelving
CIJE: 4 RIE: 2 CAT: 16

Book Storage
CIJE: 10 RIE: 8 CAT: 16

Book Talks
CIJE: 32 RIE: 6 CAT: 16

Booker T Washington Elementary School IL
CIJE: 1 RIE: 0 CAT: 17

Booker Washington Institute of Liberia
CIJE: 0 RIE: 1 CAT: 17

Bookkeeping Machine Operators
CIJE: 0 RIE: 1 CAT: 09

Bookmaking (Book Production)
USE Book Production

Bookmatch
CIJE: 1 RIE: 0 CAT: 04

Books by Mail Program
CIJE: 3 RIE: 12 CAT: 19

Books for College Libraries
CIJE: 1 RIE: 2 CAT: 22

Books for Your Children
CIJE: 2 RIE: 1 CAT: 22

Books in Print
CIJE: 5 RIE: 0 CAT: 22

Books Jobs Program
CIJE: 1 RIE: 1 CAT: 19

Booksellers
CIJE: 10 RIE: 2 CAT: 09

Bookstores
CIJE: 27 RIE: 4 CAT: 05

Boolean Algebra
CIJE: 4 RIE: 10 CAT: 20

Boolean Functions
CIJE: 7 RIE: 2 CAT: 20

Boolean Logic
CIJE: 39 RIE: 12 CAT: 20

Boolean Operators
CIJE: 16 RIE: 5 CAT: 20

Boolean Search Strategy
CIJE: 53 RIE: 9 CAT: 15

Boomerangs
CIJE: 5 RIE: 0 CAT: 04

Boone Infant Speech and Language Development Scale
CIJE: 0 RIE: 1 CAT: 21

Boorstin (Daniel)
CIJE: 3 RIE: 1 CAT: 18

Booster Clubs
CIJE: 5 RIE: 3 CAT: 10

Boosterism (Geographic)
CIJE: 0 RIE: 1 CAT: 16

Boot Camp
CIJE: 1 RIE: 0 CAT: 05

Boot Camp Corrections
USE Jail Boot Camps

Booth (Andrew)
CIJE: 1 RIE: 0 CAT: 18

Booth (David)
CIJE: 1 RIE: 0 CAT: 18

Booth (John Wilkes)
CIJE: 0 RIE: 1 CAT: 18

Booth (Philip)
CIJE: 0 RIE: 1 CAT: 18

Booth Library IL
CIJE: 0 RIE: 2 CAT: 17

Bootstrap Hypothesis
CIJE: 11 RIE: 6 CAT: 15
SN See also "Efrons Bootstrap"

Bootstrap Methods
CIJE: 14 RIE: 18 CAT: 15
SN Statistical analyses using computers to generate many more artificial data sets from sampling data than can be calculated by standard "normal distribution" equations — invented in 1977 by Bradley Efron (see also "Efrons Bootstrap")

Bophuthatswana
CIJE: 5 RIE: 2 CAT: 07

Borchert (Wolfgang)
CIJE: 1 RIE: 0 CAT: 18

Border College Consortium
CIJE: 1 RIE: 2 CAT: 17

Border Community College Consortium
CIJE: 1 RIE: 1 CAT: 17

Border Early Learning Center (South Africa)
CIJE: 0 RIE: 1 CAT: 17

Border Patrol Academy TX
CIJE: 0 RIE: 1 CAT: 17

Borderline Group Method
CIJE: 3 RIE: 5 CAT: 15

Borderline Personality Disorder
CIJE: 13 RIE: 5 CAT: 11

Boreal Institute for Northern Studies AB
CIJE: 1 RIE: 0 CAT: 17

Boredom
CIJE: 35 RIE: 5 CAT: 11
UF Tedium

Borg Warner System 80
CIJE: 0 RIE: 2 CAT: 04
UF System 80

Borges (Jorge Luis)
CIJE: 13 RIE: 2 CAT: 18

Borgese (Giuseppe Antonio)
CIJE: 1 RIE: 0 CAT: 18

Boric Acid
CIJE: 1 RIE: 0 CAT: 20

Boring Tools
CIJE: 0 RIE: 1 CAT: 04

Bork (Robert H)
CIJE: 1 RIE: 1 CAT: 18

Borland (Hal)
CIJE: 1 RIE: 1 CAT: 18

Bormann (Ernest)
CIJE: 1 RIE: 1 CAT: 18
SN "Ernest G"

Bormuth (John R)
CIJE: 0 RIE: 2 CAT: 18

Bormuth Literacy Model
CIJE: 0 RIE: 2 CAT: 15

Born Again Christians
CIJE: 0 RIE: 1 CAT: 10

Borneo
CIJE: 3 RIE: 1 CAT: 07

Bororo
CIJE: 1 RIE: 0 CAT: 13

Bororo Indians
CIJE: 0 RIE: 1 CAT: 08

Borton (Terry)
CIJE: 1 RIE: 0 CAT: 18

Bose (Subhas Chandra)
CIJE: 0 RIE: 1 CAT: 18

Boshier (Roger W)
CIJE: 0 RIE: 2 CAT: 18

Boshiers Education Participation Scale
CIJE: 2 RIE: 1 CAT: 21

Bosnia and Herzegovina
CIJE: 0 RIE: 3 CAT: 07
SN See also "Yugoslavia (Bosnia)"

Bosquet (Alain)
CIJE: 1 RIE: 0 CAT: 18

Boston Adult Literacy Fund MA
CIJE: 0 RIE: 0 CAT: 17

Boston Center for Blind Children MA
CIJE: 0 RIE: 5 CAT: 17

Boston Childrens Hospital MA
CIJE: 2 RIE: 1 CAT: 17

Boston Childrens Museum MA
CIJE: 0 RIE: 1 CAT: 17

Boston City Hospital MA
CIJE: 2 RIE: 1 CAT: 17

Boston College MA
CIJE: 26 RIE: 19 CAT: 17

Boston Compact
CIJE: 8 RIE: 15 CAT: 16

Boston Diagnostic Aphasia Examination
CIJE: 0 RIE: 1 CAT: 21

Boston Gazette
CIJE: 1 RIE: 0 CAT: 22

Boston Indian Council MA
CIJE: 0 RIE: 1 CAT: 17

Boston Massacre
CIJE: 4 RIE: 2 CAT: 12

Boston Network for Better Education MA
CIJE: 0 RIE: 1 CAT: 17

Boston Northampton Language Arts Program
CIJE: 0 RIE: 4 CAT: 19

Boston Office of Environmental Affairs MA
CIJE: 0 RIE: 2 CAT: 17

Boston Public Library MA
CIJE: 4 RIE: 3 CAT: 17

Boston Public Schools MA
CIJE: 18 RIE: 62 CAT: 17

Boston Recorder
CIJE: 0 RIE: 1 CAT: 22

Boston School for the Deaf MA
CIJE: 2 RIE: 0 CAT: 17

Boston Six MA
CIJE: 0 RIE: 1 CAT: 19

Boston State College MA
CIJE: 2 RIE: 15 CAT: 17

Boston Teachers Union
CIJE: 0 RIE: 1 CAT: 17

Boston Theological Institute MA
CIJE: 1 RIE: 1 CAT: 17

Boston TV High School MA
CIJE: 0 RIE: 1 CAT: 17

Boston University MA
CIJE: 52 RIE: 29 CAT: 17

Boswell English as a Second Language Program
CIJE: 0 RIE: 1 CAT: 19

Botanical Gardens
CIJE: 4 RIE: 2 CAT: 05

Botel Reading Inventory
CIJE: 0 RIE: 6 CAT: 21

Bothsides Thinking
CIJE: 1 RIE: 0 CAT: 11

Botswana
CIJE: 51 RIE: 85 CAT: 07

Botswana National Literacy Program
CIJE: 0 RIE: 1 CAT: 19

Bottle Feeding
CIJE: 2 RIE: 8 CAT: 16

Botwinick (J)
CIJE: 0 RIE: 0 CAT: 18

Boudinot (Elias)
CIJE: 0 RIE: 1 CAT: 18

Boulanger (Nadia J)
CIJE: 1 RIE: 0 CAT: 18

Boulder Public Library CO
CIJE: 2 RIE: 0 CAT: 17

Boulder Valley Area Vocational Technical Center CO
CIJE: 1 RIE: 0 CAT: 17

Boulder Valley Public Schools CO
CIJE: 1 RIE: 2 CAT: 17

Boulding (Elise)
CIJE: 0 RIE: 1 CAT: 18

Boundaries
CIJE: 6 RIE: 4 CAT: 16

Boundary Expansion (Psychology)
CIJE: 0 RIE: 1 CAT: 11

Boundary Spanning
CIJE: 2 RIE: 3 CAT: 16

Bourbaki (Nicolas)
CIJE: 2 RIE: 0 CAT: 18

Bourdieu (Pierre)
CIJE: 8 RIE: 2 CAT: 18

Bourdon (Raymond)
CIJE: 0 RIE: 1 CAT: 18

Bourke White (Margaret)
CIJE: 0 RIE: 2 CAT: 18

Bourkina Fasso
USE Burkina Faso

Bournemouth Teacher Center
CIJE: 1 RIE: 0 CAT: 17

Bowdler (Thomas)
CIJE: 0 RIE: 1 CAT: 18

Bowdoin College ME
CIJE: 3 RIE: 4 CAT: 17

Bowen (Howard R)
CIJE: 3 RIE: 1 CAT: 18

Bowen (Murray)
CIJE: 1 RIE: 3 CAT: 18

Bowen School DC
CIJE: 0 RIE: 1 CAT: 17

Bowers v Hardwick
CIJE: 0 RIE: 1 CAT: 14

Bowie State College MD
CIJE: 0 RIE: 16 CAT: 17

Bowie State University MD
CIJE: 0 RIE: 2 CAT: 17

Bowlby (John)
CIJE: 4 RIE: 2 CAT: 18

Bowles (Samuel)
CIJE: 1 RIE: 1 CAT: 18

Bowles Gintis Correspondence Theory
CIJE: 3 RIE: 1 CAT: 15

Bowling Green Schools Adult Learning Center Ky
CIJE: 0 RIE: 1 CAT: 17

Bowling Green State University OH
CIJE: 35 RIE: 47 CAT: 17

Bowman (Isaiah)
CIJE: 0 RIE: 1 CAT: 18

Bowman Gray School of Medicine NC
CIJE: 8 RIE: 0 CAT: 17

Bown Self Report Inventory
CIJE: 0 RIE: 1 CAT: 21

Box Cox Transformations
CIJE: 0 RIE: 1 CAT: 15

Box Jenkins Forecasting Model
CIJE: 2 RIE: 3 CAT: 15
SN See related "Autoregressive Integrated Moving Averages"

Box Scale (Harvill)
CIJE: 0 RIE: 1 CAT: 21

Box Scheffe Test
CIJE: 2 RIE: 0 CAT: 21

Box Test
CIJE: 2 RIE: 1 CAT: 15

Box World (Computer Game)
CIJE: 0 RIE: 1 CAT: 16

Boxing
CIJE: 5 RIE: 2 CAT: 16

Boy Girl Identity Task (Emmerich and Goldman)
CIJE: 0 RIE: 1 CAT: 21

Boy Scouts of America
CIJE: 13 RIE: 26 CAT: 17

Boycotts
CIJE: 11 RIE: 5 CAT: 16

Boyer (Ernest L)
CIJE: 16 RIE: 6 CAT: 18

Boyle (Richard P)
CIJE: 1 RIE: 1 CAT: 18

Boys Clubs of America
CIJE: 1 RIE: 8 CAT: 17

Boys Listening Test (Graham and Orr)
CIJE: 0 RIE: 1 CAT: 21

Boys Republic
CIJE: 0 RIE: 1 CAT: 17

Boys Town Common Sense Parenting Program
CIJE: 0 RIE: 1 CAT: 19

Boys Town NE
CIJE: 5 RIE: 2 CAT: 17
UF Nebraska (Boys Town)

Boys Town Urban Program
CIJE: 1 RIE: 1 CAT: 19

Braam Sheldon Flexibility of Reading Test
CIJE: 0 RIE: 1 CAT: 21

Bracken Basic Concept Scale
CIJE: 10 RIE: 1 CAT: 21

Brackenridge Interns in Teaching
CIJE: 1 RIE: 2 CAT: 19

Bracteacoccus Cinnabarinus
CIJE: 1 RIE: 0 CAT: 20

Bradbury (Ray)
CIJE: 8 RIE: 1 CAT: 18

Brademas (John)
CIJE: 2 RIE: 0 CAT: 18

Bradford (Leland)
CIJE: 0 RIE: 1 CAT: 18

Bradford (William)
CIJE: 2 RIE: 1 CAT: 18

Bradford Academy VT
CIJE: 1 RIE: 0 CAT: 17

Bradford College MA
CIJE: 5 RIE: 2 CAT: 17

Bradford Law of Scatter
CIJE: 44 RIE: 5 CAT: 20

Bradley Center GA
CIJE: 0 RIE: 1 CAT: 17

Bradley Commission on History in Schools
CIJE: 19 RIE: 2 CAT: 17

Bradley University IL
CIJE: 5 RIE: 3 CAT: 17

Bradshaw (Lillian)
CIJE: 1 RIE: 0 CAT: 18

Bradshaw v Rawlings
CIJE: 2 RIE: 0 CAT: 14

Bradstreet (Anne)
CIJE: 1 RIE: 1 CAT: 18

Brahmi Script
CIJE: 0 RIE: 1 CAT: 13

Braiding Machine Operators
CIJE: 0 RIE: 1 CAT: 09

Braille Book Bank
CIJE: 0 RIE: 1 CAT: 19

Braille Code
CIJE: 0 RIE: 1 CAT: 13

Braille Printers
CIJE: 1 RIE: 0 CAT: 04

Braille Tape Reader
CIJE: 0 RIE: 1 CAT: 04

Braillemboss
CIJE: 1 RIE: 0 CAT: 04

BRAILLOPHON
CIJE: 1 RIE: 0 CAT: 04

Brain
CIJE: 33 RIE: 7 CAT: 11

Brain Activity
CIJE: 6 RIE: 5 CAT: 11

Brain Based Learning
CIJE: 0 RIE: 1 CAT: 15

Brain Development
CIJE: 31 RIE: 8 CAT: 11

Brain Drain
CIJE: 22 RIE: 15 CAT: 16

Brain Event Related Potentials
USE Event Related Potentials

Brain Flow Writing Technique
CIJE: 0 RIE: 1 CAT: 15

Brain Functions
CIJE: 43 RIE: 21 CAT: 11

Brain Growth
CIJE: 13 RIE: 2 CAT: 11

Brain Link Software
CIJE: 0 RIE: 1 CAT: 04

Brain Research
CIJE: 80 RIE: 47 CAT: 11

Brain Research Bulletin
CIJE: 0 RIE: 1 CAT: 22

Brain Research Journal
CIJE: 0 RIE: 1 CAT: 22

Brain Size
CIJE: 3 RIE: 1 CAT: 11

Brain Topography
USE Topographic Brain Mapping

Brain Waves
CIJE: 9 RIE: 10 CAT: 11

Braine (Lila Ghent)
CIJE: 1 RIE: 0 CAT: 18

Brainerd Area Vocational Technical School MN
CIJE: 1 RIE: 0 CAT: 17

Brainiac
CIJE: 0 RIE: 1 CAT: 04

Brainstem Auditory Evoked Potential
CIJE: 3 RIE: 0 CAT: 11

Brainstem Auditory Evoked Response
CIJE: 4 RIE: 2 CAT: 11

Brainstem Dysfunction
CIJE: 1 RIE: 0 CAT: 11

Brake Services
CIJE: 0 RIE: 2 CAT: 16

Brakes (Automotive)
CIJE: 0 RIE: 10 CAT: 04
UF Automotive Brakes

Bramson ORT Technical Institute NY
CIJE: 0 RIE: 1 CAT: 17

Branched Chain Ketoaciduria
CIJE: 1 RIE: 0 CAT: 11

Branched Fiction
CIJE: 0 RIE: 1 CAT: 13

Branched Stories
CIJE: 1 RIE: 0 CAT: 16

Branching Algorithms
CIJE: 0 RIE: 1 CAT: 20

Brand Awareness
CIJE: 0 RIE: 1 CAT: 16

Brand Emotions Scale for Writers
CIJE: 1 RIE: 1 CAT: 21

Brand Name Products
CIJE: 0 RIE: 5 CAT: 16

Brand Names
CIJE: 5 RIE: 6 CAT: 16

Brandeis University MA
CIJE: 9 RIE: 5 CAT: 17

Brandford Analysis
CIJE: 0 RIE: 1 CAT: 16

Brandon General Hospital MB
CIJE: 0 RIE: 1 CAT: 17

Brandon University MB
CIJE: 3 RIE: 5 CAT: 17

Brandsma (Titus)
CIJE: 0 RIE: 1 CAT: 18

Brandwein (Paul)
CIJE: 1 RIE: 0 CAT: 18

Brandywine High School DE
CIJE: 0 RIE: 2 CAT: 17

Bransford (J D)
CIJE: 2 RIE: 1 CAT: 18

Bransford Franks Linear Effect
CIJE: 1 RIE: 1 CAT: 13

Branzburg v Hayes
CIJE: 0 RIE: 2 CAT: 14

Braque (Georges)
CIJE: 1 RIE: 0 CAT: 18

Brass Instruments
CIJE: 5 RIE: 0 CAT: 04

Brassens (Georges)
CIJE: 1 RIE: 0 CAT: 18

Bratt Attitude Test
CIJE: 0 RIE: 1 CAT: 21

Brattleboro Union High School VT
CIJE: 0 RIE: 2 CAT: 17

Braxton County School District WV
CIJE: 0 RIE: 2 CAT: 17

Braxton v Municipal Court
CIJE: 1 RIE: 0 CAT: 14

Bray (Thomas)
CIJE: 1 RIE: 0 CAT: 18

Braybrooke (David)
CIJE: 0 RIE: 1 CAT: 18

Brayfield Rothe Job Satisfaction Index
CIJE: 1 RIE: 1 CAT: 21

Brazelton Neonatal Assessment Scale
CIJE: 13 RIE: 12 CAT: 21

Brazelton Neonatal Behavioral Assessment Scale
CIJE: 9 RIE: 11 CAT: 21

Brazil
CIJE: 311 RIE: 279 CAT: 07

Brazil (Rio de Janeiro)
CIJE: 6 RIE: 11 CAT: 07

Brazil (Rio Grande do Sul)
CIJE: 2 RIE: 1 CAT: 07

Brazil (Salvador Bahia)
CIJE: 2 RIE: 2 CAT: 07

Brazil (Sao Paulo)
CIJE: 10 RIE: 7 CAT: 07

Brazilian Literacy Movement
CIJE: 1 RIE: 2 CAT: 19
UF MOBRAL; Movimento Brasileiro de Alfabetizacao

Brazilian Ministry of Education
USE Ministry of Education (Brazil)

Brazilian Portuguese Project
CIJE: 0 RIE: 6 CAT: 19

Brazing
CIJE: 0 RIE: 3 CAT: 20

Brazosport College TX
CIJE: 2 RIE: 1 CAT: 17

Breaching Episodes
CIJE: 0 RIE: 1 CAT: 15

Bread Loaf Writing Grants Program
CIJE: 0 RIE: 1 CAT: 19

Breads
CIJE: 0 RIE: 4 CAT: 20

Breadth of Perspective
CIJE: 0 RIE: 1 CAT: 15

Break Even Analysis
CIJE: 5 RIE: 0 CAT: 15

Breakfast Cereals
USE Cereals

Breakfast Club (The)
CIJE: 0 RIE: 1 CAT: 22

Breakthrough to Literacy Approach
CIJE: 1 RIE: 0 CAT: 15

Brearly (David)
CIJE: 0 RIE: 1 CAT: 18

Breast Cancer
CIJE: 9 RIE: 4 CAT: 11

Breast Examination
CIJE: 6 RIE: 2 CAT: 11

Breast Milk
CIJE: 1 RIE: 1 CAT: 11

Breast Milk Substitutes
CIJE: 1 RIE: 4 CAT: 11

Breaststroke
CIJE: 0 RIE: 0 CAT: 16

Breath Analyzers
CIJE: 3 RIE: 0 CAT: 04
SN See also "Random Breath Testing"
UF Breathalyzers

Breath Control Training
CIJE: 1 RIE: 0 CAT: 11
UF Breath Management Instruction

Breath Examiner Specialist Instructors
CIJE: 0 RIE: 1 CAT: 09

Breath Management Instruction
USE Breath Control Training

Breathable Liquids
CIJE: 1 RIE: 0 CAT: 20

Breathalyzers
USE Breath Analyzers

Breathing Equipment
CIJE: 1 RIE: 2 CAT: 04

Brecht (Bertolt)
CIJE: 26 RIE: 4 CAT: 18

Bredeweg (Frank)
CIJE: 0 RIE: 1 CAT: 18

Breeder Reactors
CIJE: 2 RIE: 0 CAT: 04

Brekle (Herbert Ernst)
CIJE: 1 RIE: 0 CAT: 18

Brenau College GA
CIJE: 1 RIE: 7 CAT: 17

Brennan (William J)
CIJE: 3 RIE: 2 CAT: 18

Brentano (Clemens)
CIJE: 1 RIE: 0 CAT: 18

Brentwood School District MO
CIJE: 0 RIE: 0 CAT: 17

Brentwood Union School District CA
CIJE: 0 RIE: 2 CAT: 17

Breskin Rigidity Test
CIJE: 2 RIE: 0 CAT: 21

Breton
CIJE: 7 RIE: 7 CAT: 13

Breton (Andre)
CIJE: 6 RIE: 0 CAT: 18

Breuer (Hans)
CIJE: 0 RIE: 1 CAT: 18

Brevard Community College FL
CIJE: 4 RIE: 15 CAT: 17

Brewton City School District AL
CIJE: 0 RIE: 1 CAT: 17

Brezhnev (Leonid)
CIJE: 0 RIE: 1 CAT: 18

Briar Cliff College IA
CIJE: 0 RIE: 2 CAT: 17

Brick Township Public Schools NJ
CIJE: 0 RIE: 1 CAT: 17

Brickman (William Wolfgang)
CIJE: 0 RIE: 1 CAT: 18

Bricks
CIJE: 0 RIE: 1 CAT: 04

Bride Comes to Yellow Sky (Crane)
CIJE: 0 RIE: 1 CAT: 22

Bridenthal Internship in Teaching Program
CIJE: 2 RIE: 3 CAT: 19

Bridge Independent Living Project
CIJE: 0 RIE: 2 CAT: 19

Bridge Inspectors
CIJE: 0 RIE: 1 CAT: 09

Bridge Players
CIJE: 0 RIE: 1 CAT: 10
UF Contract Bridge Players

BRIDGE Program CT
CIJE: 0 RIE: 1 CAT: 19

BRIDGE Program OR
CIJE: 0 RIE: 0 CAT: 19
SN Partnership between the Private Industry Council and Portland (Oregon) Public Schools

BRIDGE Project
CIJE: 1 RIE: 6 CAT: 19
SN Queens College (CUNY) project to prepare teachers for schools in culturally deprived neighborhoods

Bridge Youth Advocacy Program PA
CIJE: 0 RIE: 1 CAT: 19

Bridgers (Sue Ellen)
CIJE: 1 RIE: 1 CAT: 18

Bridges (Structures)
CIJE: 0 RIE: 1 CAT: 04

BRIDGES Program ON
CIJE: 0 RIE: 1 CAT: 19
SN An employment training program developed by the city of Toronto to help women move out of their traditional jobs

BRIDGES Project (Harvard University)
CIJE: 0 RIE: 4 CAT: 19
SN BRIDGES = Basic Research and Implementation in DevelopinG Education Systems

BRIDGES Project ND
CIJE: 0 RIE: 1 CAT: 19

Bridges to Leadership 2000
CIJE: 0 RIE: 1 CAT: 19
SN Howard University (DC) youth training program

Bridgewater Raritan Regional School District NJ
CIJE: 1 RIE: 0 CAT: 17

Bridgewater State College MA
CIJE: 2 RIE: 5 CAT: 17

Bridging (Reading)
CIJE: 0 RIE: 1 CAT: 11

Bridging Analogies
CIJE: 1 RIE: 1 CAT: 15

Bridging Courses (England)
CIJE: 0 RIE: 1 CAT: 03

Bridging the Gap Program
CIJE: 1 RIE: 0 CAT: 19

Bridging Vocabulary
CIJE: 0 RIE: 1 CAT: 13

Brief Polytechnic Dictionary
CIJE: 0 RIE: 1 CAT: 22

Brief Symptom Inventory
CIJE: 3 RIE: 1 CAT: 21

Brief Test of Literacy
CIJE: 0 RIE: 1 CAT: 21

Brief Therapy
CIJE: 28 RIE: 1 CAT: 11
SN See also "Solution Focused Brief Therapy"

Brigance (William Norwood)
CIJE: 1 RIE: 1 CAT: 18

Brigance CIBS
USE Comprehensive Inventory of Basic Skills (Brigance)

Brigance Diagnostic Inventories
CIJE: 0 RIE: 1 CAT: 21

Brigance Diagnostic Inventory of Basic Skills
CIJE: 2 RIE: 1 CAT: 21

Brigance K and 1 Screen
CIJE: 0 RIE: 3 CAT: 21

Brigantine National Wildlife Refuge
CIJE: 1 RIE: 0 CAT: 17

Brigdman (Percy)
CIJE: 0 RIE: 1 CAT: 18

Briggs (L)
CIJE: 1 RIE: 2 CAT: 18

Brigham (Carl C)
CIJE: 1 RIE: 1 CAT: 18

Brigham Young University Hawaii Campus
CIJE: 0 RIE: 3 CAT: 17

Brigham Young University UT
CIJE: 103 RIE: 76 CAT: 17

Brightness
CIJE: 0 RIE: 0 CAT: 20

Brighton Reading Individualized Skills Continuum
CIJE: 0 RIE: 1 CAT: 21

Brik (Osip)
CIJE: 1 RIE: 0 CAT: 18

Brill (Moshe)
CIJE: 0 RIE: 1 CAT: 18

Brim Scale
CIJE: 0 RIE: 1 CAT: 21

Bringing Out Head Start Talents
USE Project BOHST

Bringing Up Children Inventory
CIJE: 0 RIE: 1 CAT: 21

Brinkmanship
CIJE: 2 RIE: 3 CAT: 16

Bristol College of Science and Technology
CIJE: 1 RIE: 0 CAT: 17

Bristol Community College MA
CIJE: 1 RIE: 5 CAT: 17

Bristol School (England)
CIJE: 1 RIE: 1 CAT: 17

Bristol Social Adjustment Guides
CIJE: 7 RIE: 4 CAT: 22

Bristol Township School District PA
CIJE: 1 RIE: 0 CAT: 17

British
CIJE: 12 RIE: 3 CAT: 08

British Ability Scales
CIJE: 5 RIE: 1 CAT: 21

British and Foreign Bible Society
CIJE: 1 RIE: 0 CAT: 17

British Association Commercial and Industrial Educ
CIJE: 2 RIE: 0 CAT: 17

British Association for Applied Linguistics
CIJE: 1 RIE: 2 CAT: 17

British Association for the Advancement of Science
CIJE: 2 RIE: 0 CAT: 17

British Broadcasting Corporation
CIJE: 105 RIE: 42 CAT: 17

British Colonies
CIJE: 5 RIE: 5 CAT: 07

British Columbia
CIJE: 307 RIE: 437 CAT: 07

British Columbia (Alkali Lake)
CIJE: 0 RIE: 1 CAT: 07

British Columbia (Broughton Island)
CIJE: 1 RIE: 0 CAT: 07

British Columbia (Nanaimo)
CIJE: 1 RIE: 3 CAT: 07

British Columbia (Okanagan)
CIJE: 0 RIE: 2 CAT: 07

British Columbia (Vancouver Island)
CIJE: 2 RIE: 2 CAT: 07

British Columbia (Vancouver)
CIJE: 48 RIE: 55 CAT: 07

British Columbia (Victoria)
CIJE: 10 RIE: 15 CAT: 07

British Columbia (West Kootenay Region)
CIJE: 0 RIE: 1 CAT: 07

British Columbia Assessment of Written Expression
CIJE: 0 RIE: 2 CAT: 21

British Columbia Institute of Technology
CIJE: 1 RIE: 4 CAT: 17

British Columbia Learning Assessment Program
CIJE: 1 RIE: 0 CAT: 21

British Columbia Library Network
CIJE: 1 RIE: 1 CAT: 17

British Columbia Ministry of Education
CIJE: 1 RIE: 2 CAT: 17

British Columbia Reading Assessment
CIJE: 0 RIE: 1 CAT: 21

British Columbia Telephone Company
CIJE: 2 RIE: 0 CAT: 17

British Commonwealth
CIJE: 15 RIE: 30 CAT: 07
SN Official name is "Commonwealth of Nations" (q.v.)

British Commonwealth Association of Planners
CIJE: 1 RIE: 0 CAT: 17

British Commonwealth Literature
CIJE: 0 RIE: 1 CAT: 16

British Computer Society
CIJE: 1 RIE: 1 CAT: 17

British Council
CIJE: 11 RIE: 16 CAT: 17

British Education Reform Act 1988
USE Education Reform Act 1988 (England)

British Educational Administration Society
CIJE: 0 RIE: 1 CAT: 17

British European Airways
CIJE: 2 RIE: 0 CAT: 17

British Film Institute
CIJE: 2 RIE: 1 CAT: 17

British Honduras
CIJE: 3 RIE: 1 CAT: 07

British India
CIJE: 1 RIE: 1 CAT: 07

British Institute Madrid (Spain)
CIJE: 2 RIE: 0 CAT: 17

British Intelligence Scale
CIJE: 2 RIE: 1 CAT: 21

British Isles
CIJE: 2 RIE: 2 CAT: 07

British Journal of Educational Psychology
CIJE: 1 RIE: 0 CAT: 22

British Journal of Sociology
CIJE: 1 RIE: 0 CAT: 22

British Library (England)
CIJE: 33 RIE: 8 CAT: 17

British Library Lending Division
CIJE: 2 RIE: 1 CAT: 17

British Medical Journal
CIJE: 0 RIE: 1 CAT: 22

British Motor Corporation
CIJE: 1 RIE: 0 CAT: 17

British Museum (England)
CIJE: 2 RIE: 0 CAT: 17

British Museum Library (England)
CIJE: 0 RIE: 1 CAT: 17

British National Bibliography
CIJE: 6 RIE: 0 CAT: 22

British National Coal Board
CIJE: 1 RIE: 0 CAT: 17

British National Health Service
CIJE: 2 RIE: 1 CAT: 17
UF National Health Service (United Kingdom)

British North American Committee
CIJE: 0 RIE: 1 CAT: 17

British Office for Training Exchange
CIJE: 1 RIE: 0 CAT: 17

British Overseas Airways Corporation
CIJE: 1 RIE: 0 CAT: 17

British Press Council
CIJE: 0 RIE: 2 CAT: 17

British Schools Council
CIJE: 1 RIE: 1 CAT: 17

British Sign Language
CIJE: 7 RIE: 2 CAT: 13

British Solomon Islands
CIJE: 1 RIE: 0 CAT: 07

British Standards Institution
CIJE: 0 RIE: 1 CAT: 17

British Universities Film Council
CIJE: 1 RIE: 0 CAT: 17

British West Indies
CIJE: 5 RIE: 3 CAT: 07

British West Indies (Grand Cayman)
CIJE: 1 RIE: 0 CAT: 07

British West Indies Regiment
CIJE: 1 RIE: 0 CAT: 17

Brito et al v The Zia Company
CIJE: 0 RIE: 1 CAT: 14

Britting (George)
CIJE: 1 RIE: 0 CAT: 18

Brittle Books
CIJE: 2 RIE: 11 CAT: 16

Britton (James)
CIJE: 14 RIE: 17 CAT: 18

BRL Checklist of Prereading Skills
CIJE: 0 RIE: 1 CAT: 21

Broad Jump
CIJE: 3 RIE: 1 CAT: 16

Broad Range Tailored Test of Verbal Ability
CIJE: 0 RIE: 1 CAT: 21

Broadband Cable Teleservices
CIJE: 3 RIE: 23 CAT: 16

Broadcast Access Rights
CIJE: 0 RIE: 5 CAT: 14

Broadcast Announcers
CIJE: 0 RIE: 1 CAT: 09
SN Use a more specific term if possible, e.g., "Disk Jockeys," "Television Announcers"

Broadcast Content Regulation
USE Content Regulation (Broadcasting)

Broadcast Economics
CIJE: 1 RIE: 8 CAT: 16

Broadcast Education Association
CIJE: 2 RIE: 3 CAT: 17

Broadcast History
CIJE: 1 RIE: 5 CAT: 16

Broadcast Industry Conference
CIJE: 0 RIE: 3 CAT: 02

Broadcast Laboratories
CIJE: 0 RIE: 1 CAT: 05

Broadcast Licensing
CIJE: 2 RIE: 9 CAT: 14

Broadcast Regulation
CIJE: 0 RIE: 0 CAT: 14
SN If appropriate, use the more specific term "Content Regulation (Broadcasting)"

Broadcast Transmission Equipment
CIJE: 0 RIE: 3 CAT: 04

Broadcasting Act (Italy)
CIJE: 1 RIE: 0 CAT: 14

Broadcasting Curriculum
CIJE: 2 RIE: 4 CAT: 03

Broadway Plays
CIJE: 1 RIE: 3 CAT: 16

Brock University (Canada)
CIJE: 6 RIE: 8 CAT: 17

Brocki (A C)
CIJE: 0 RIE: 1 CAT: 18

Brockriede (Wayne)
CIJE: 1 RIE: 1 CAT: 18

Brockton Battery
CIJE: 0 RIE: 2 CAT: 21

Brodie (Bernard)
CIJE: 0 RIE: 1 CAT: 18

Brody Reading Method
CIJE: 0 RIE: 1 CAT: 15

Brogden (H E)
CIJE: 0 RIE: 1 CAT: 18

Broken Arrow Elementary School KS
CIJE: 1 RIE: 0 CAT: 17

Broken Squares
CIJE: 0 RIE: 1 CAT: 16

Bromates
CIJE: 1 RIE: 0 CAT: 20

Bromides
CIJE: 1 RIE: 0 CAT: 20

Bromley Heath Infant Curriculum
CIJE: 0 RIE: 1 CAT: 03

Bromthymol Blue
CIJE: 1 RIE: 0 CAT: 20

Bromwoods Residential Center MO
CIJE: 0 RIE: 1 CAT: 17

Bronchiolitis
CIJE: 1 RIE: 0 CAT: 11

Bronfenbrenner (Urie)
CIJE: 8 RIE: 7 CAT: 18

Bronnen (Arnolt)
CIJE: 0 RIE: 1 CAT: 18

Bronowski (Jacob)
CIJE: 4 RIE: 0 CAT: 18

Bronson Sonic Power Company
CIJE: 1 RIE: 0 CAT: 17

Bronte (Anne)
CIJE: 1 RIE: 2 CAT: 18

Bronte (Branwell)
CIJE: 0 RIE: 1 CAT: 18

Bronte (Charlotte)
CIJE: 1 RIE: 4 CAT: 18

Bronte (Emily)
CIJE: 4 RIE: 2 CAT: 18

Bronx Academic Bilingual Career Program
CIJE: 0 RIE: 1 CAT: 19

Bronx Community College NY
USE City University of New York Bronx Community Coll

Bronx River
CIJE: 0 RIE: 1 CAT: 07

Bronx Zoo NY
CIJE: 2 RIE: 0 CAT: 17

Brookdale Community College NJ
CIJE: 1 RIE: 8 CAT: 17

Brookings Conference on Vocational Education
CIJE: 0 RIE: 1 CAT: 02

Brookings Institution DC
CIJE: 1 RIE: 0 CAT: 17

Brookland Cayce Schools SC
CIJE: 0 RIE: 1 CAT: 17

Brookline Early Education Project
CIJE: 5 RIE: 9 CAT: 19

Brookline LOGO Project
CIJE: 1 RIE: 0 CAT: 19

Brookline Public Schools MA
CIJE: 4 RIE: 5 CAT: 17

Brooklyn College NY
USE City University of New York Brooklyn College

Brooklyn Education Task Force NY
CIJE: 0 RIE: 1 CAT: 17

Brooklyn Public Library NY
CIJE: 7 RIE: 3 CAT: 17

Brooklyn Responsive Learning Center NY
CIJE: 1 RIE: 0 CAT: 17

Brookmeade Elementary School TN
CIJE: 1 RIE: 0 CAT: 17

Brooks (Bryce)
CIJE: 1 RIE: 0 CAT: 18

Brooks (Clara Mable)
CIJE: 1 RIE: 0 CAT: 18

Brooks (Cleanth)
CIJE: 3 RIE: 1 CAT: 18

Brooks (David W)
CIJE: 1 RIE: 0 CAT: 18

Brooks (Glenwood C Jr)
CIJE: 0 RIE: 0 CAT: 18

Brooks (Gwendolyn)
CIJE: 6 RIE: 1 CAT: 18

Brooks (Walter R)
CIJE: 1 RIE: 0 CAT: 18

Brookside Park Family Life Center MA
CIJE: 1 RIE: 0 CAT: 17

Brookwood Labor College NY
CIJE: 3 RIE: 0 CAT: 17

Broome Community College NY
CIJE: 2 RIE: 6 CAT: 17

Broome Functional Behavior Checklist
CIJE: 0 RIE: 1 CAT: 21

Brophy Good Dyadic Interaction Coding System
CIJE: 6 RIE: 5 CAT: 15

Brotherhood of Railway and Airline Clerks
CIJE: 0 RIE: 1 CAT: 17

Brothers (Joyce)
CIJE: 1 RIE: 0 CAT: 18

Broudy (H S)
CIJE: 6 RIE: 0 CAT: 18

Broughal Junior High School PA
CIJE: 1 RIE: 0 CAT: 17

Brougham (Henry)
CIJE: 1 RIE: 0 CAT: 18

Broward Community College FL
CIJE: 4 RIE: 12 CAT: 17

Broward County Instructional Television Center FL
CIJE: 1 RIE: 1 CAT: 17

Broward County Public Schools FL
CIJE: 5 RIE: 20 CAT: 17

Broward County School Board FL
CIJE: 0 RIE: 1 CAT: 17

Brower (David)
CIJE: 0 RIE: 1 CAT: 18

Brown (Bob B)
CIJE: 0 RIE: 1 CAT: 18

Brown (Charlotte Hawkins)
CIJE: 1 RIE: 1 CAT: 18

Brown (John)
CIJE: 3 RIE: 0 CAT: 18

Brown (Marcia)
CIJE: 1 RIE: 0 CAT: 18

Brown (Norman O)
CIJE: 0 RIE: 1 CAT: 18

Brown (Richard H)
CIJE: 0 RIE: 1 CAT: 18

Brown Act
CIJE: 0 RIE: 1 CAT: 14

Brown Carlsen Listening Comprehension Test
CIJE: 1 RIE: 2 CAT: 21

Brown Fraser Bellgui Test of Grammatical Contrasts
CIJE: 0 RIE: 1 CAT: 21

Brown Holtzman Survey Study Habits and Attitudes
CIJE: 7 RIE: 7 CAT: 21

Brown IDS Self Concept Referents Test
CIJE: 2 RIE: 3 CAT: 21

Brown Open School
CIJE: 1 RIE: 0 CAT: 17

Brown Peterson Distractor Task
CIJE: 3 RIE: 0 CAT: 21

Brown Peterson Paradigm
CIJE: 3 RIE: 0 CAT: 21

Brown Self Report Inventory
CIJE: 1 RIE: 0 CAT: 21

Brown University Corpus of American English
CIJE: 1 RIE: 1 CAT: 22

Brown University Research Foundation RI
CIJE: 0 RIE: 0 CAT: 17

Brown University RI
CIJE: 49 RIE: 30 CAT: 17

Brown v Board of Education
CIJE: 117 RIE: 78 CAT: 14

Brown v Glines
CIJE: 0 RIE: 1 CAT: 14

Browne (Vivian)
CIJE: 1 RIE: 0 CAT: 18

Brownell (Baker)
CIJE: 1 RIE: 0 CAT: 18

Brownian Motion
CIJE: 9 RIE: 0 CAT: 20

Brownies Book
CIJE: 0 RIE: 2 CAT: 22

Browning (James)
CIJE: 0 RIE: 1 CAT: 18

Browning (Robert)
CIJE: 2 RIE: 1 CAT: 18

Brownsville Independent School District TX
CIJE: 0 RIE: 1 CAT: 17

Browsing
CIJE: 62 RIE: 4 CAT: 16

BRS After Dark
CIJE: 2 RIE: 3 CAT: 04

BRS Information Technologies
CIJE: 12 RIE: 4 CAT: 17
SN Formerly "Bibliographic Retrieval Services" (q.v.)

Bruce (Lenny)
CIJE: 2 RIE: 1 CAT: 18

Brucellosis
CIJE: 1 RIE: 0 CAT: 11

Bruch (Hilde)
CIJE: 0 RIE: 1 CAT: 18

Bruening (Stephen)
CIJE: 0 RIE: 1 CAT: 18

Bruffee (Kenneth)
CIJE: 1 RIE: 1 CAT: 18

Bruininks Oseretsky Test of Motor Proficiency
CIJE: 10 RIE: 1 CAT: 21

Brunei
CIJE: 11 RIE: 8 CAT: 07

Brunel University (England)
CIJE: 3 RIE: 0 CAT: 17

Bruner (Jerome S)
CIJE: 55 RIE: 34 CAT: 18

Bruno (Giordano)
CIJE: 1 RIE: 0 CAT: 18

Brunot (Ferdinand)
CIJE: 1 RIE: 0 CAT: 18

Brunswick County Public Schools VA
CIJE: 0 RIE: 1 CAT: 17

Brunswick Foundation Small College Program
CIJE: 0 RIE: 2 CAT: 19

Brunswick Junior College GA
CIJE: 0 RIE: 1 CAT: 17

Brunswik (Egon)
CIJE: 2 RIE: 2 CAT: 18

BRUSH (Belgium)
CIJE: 0 RIE: 1 CAT: 17
UF Brussels Support for the Handicapped (Belgium)

Brussels Satellite Convention
CIJE: 1 RIE: 0 CAT: 02

Brussels Support for the Handicapped (Belgium)
USE BRUSH (Belgium)

Bryan (Mary Edwards)
CIJE: 0 RIE: 1 CAT: 18

Bryan (William Jennings)
CIJE: 1 RIE: 1 CAT: 18

Bryan Independent School District TX
CIJE: 0 RIE: 2 CAT: 17

Bryant (Olen)
CIJE: 1 RIE: 0 CAT: 18

Bryant (Peter)
CIJE: 3 RIE: 0 CAT: 18

Bryant College of Business Administration RI
CIJE: 0 RIE: 2 CAT: 17

Bryant Woods Elementary School MD
CIJE: 1 RIE: 0 CAT: 17

Bryant Youth Educational Support Center MN
CIJE: 0 RIE: 2 CAT: 17

Bryn Mawr College PA
CIJE: 14 RIE: 8 CAT: 17

Bryngelson Glaspey Test
CIJE: 0 RIE: 1 CAT: 21

Bryson (Lyman)
CIJE: 1 RIE: 1 CAT: 18

BSCS Achievement Tests
CIJE: 0 RIE: 2 CAT: 21

BSCS Comprehensive Final Examination (Mayer)
CIJE: 0 RIE: 1 CAT: 21

Bubbles
CIJE: 7 RIE: 3 CAT: 20

Buber (Martin)
CIJE: 22 RIE: 10 CAT: 18

Buberian Learning Groups
CIJE: 3 RIE: 0 CAT: 10

Buchanan Language Program
CIJE: 0 RIE: 2 CAT: 19

Buchman (Frank)
CIJE: 0 RIE: 1 CAT: 18

Buchner (Georg)
CIJE: 3 RIE: 0 CAT: 18

Buchta (J William)
CIJE: 1 RIE: 0 CAT: 18

Buck (Gertrude)
CIJE: 0 RIE: 3 CAT: 18

Buck v Bell
CIJE: 0 RIE: 1 CAT: 14

Buckley (William F)
CIJE: 1 RIE: 0 CAT: 18

Buckley Amendment
CIJE: 26 RIE: 20 CAT: 14
SN a.k.a. "Family Educational Rights and Privacy Act 1974" (q.v.)

Buckley v Indianapolis Board School Commissioners
CIJE: 0 RIE: 1 CAT: 14

Bucknell On Line Circulation System
CIJE: 0 RIE: 1 CAT: 04

Bucknell University PA
CIJE: 5 RIE: 10 CAT: 17

Bucks County Area Vocational School PA
CIJE: 1 RIE: 0 CAT: 17

Bucks County Community College PA
CIJE: 1 RIE: 9 CAT: 17

Bucks County Public Schools PA
CIJE: 1 RIE: 1 CAT: 17

Budget Accounting Model of Mass and Energy
CIJE: 0 RIE: 1 CAT: 16

Budget Deficits
CIJE: 3 RIE: 0 CAT: 16

Budget Reconciliation Act
CIJE: 0 RIE: 3 CAT: 14

Buehler (Ezra Christian)
CIJE: 0 RIE: 2 CAT: 18

Buehrer (Huber)
CIJE: 0 RIE: 1 CAT: 18

Buem
CIJE: 0 RIE: 1 CAT: 13
SN A language of the Na branch of Central Togo family
UF Lelemi

Buena Park High School CA
CIJE: 1 RIE: 0 CAT: 17

Buena Vista City Public Schools VA
CIJE: 0 RIE: 4 CAT: 17

Buena Vista College IA
CIJE: 4 RIE: 2 CAT: 17

Buero Vallejo (Antonio)
CIJE: 3 RIE: 0 CAT: 18

Buffalo and Erie County Public Library NY
CIJE: 0 RIE: 1 CAT: 17

Buffalo English Linguistics Project
CIJE: 0 RIE: 1 CAT: 19

Buffalo Museum of Science NY
CIJE: 0 RIE: 1 CAT: 17

Buffalo Public Schools NY
CIJE: 11 RIE: 8 CAT: 17

Buffers (Chemistry)
CIJE: 8 RIE: 0 CAT: 20

Buganda
CIJE: 1 RIE: 0 CAT: 07

Buhler (Charlotte)
CIJE: 1 RIE: 0 CAT: 18

Buhler Life Goals Inventory
CIJE: 0 RIE: 2 CAT: 21

Building Better Boards Project
CIJE: 1 RIE: 0 CAT: 19

Building Block Costing
CIJE: 1 RIE: 1 CAT: 15

Building Codes
CIJE: 3 RIE: 7 CAT: 16

Building Communities (AACJC)
CIJE: 0 RIE: 2 CAT: 19

Building Construction Technicians
CIJE: 0 RIE: 1 CAT: 09

Building Consultants
CIJE: 0 RIE: 1 CAT: 09

Building Evacuation
CIJE: 0 RIE: 1 CAT: 16

Building Infrastructure
CIJE: 4 RIE: 0 CAT: 16

Building Inspectors
CIJE: 0 RIE: 1 CAT: 09

Building Maintenance
CIJE: 2 RIE: 4 CAT: 16

Building Maintenance Personnel
CIJE: 0 RIE: 5 CAT: 09

Building Managers
CIJE: 2 RIE: 0 CAT: 09

Building Memory Test (ETS)
CIJE: 0 RIE: 1 CAT: 21

Building Our American Community Program
CIJE: 0 RIE: 7 CAT: 19

Building Research Station (England)
CIJE: 0 RIE: 5 CAT: 17

Building Security
CIJE: 5 RIE: 13 CAT: 16

Building Standards
CIJE: 2 RIE: 0 CAT: 16

Building Strong Families Program
CIJE: 0 RIE: 1 CAT: 19
SN A five session parenting program

Building Workers Entering Skilled Trades Project
CIJE: 0 RIE: 4 CAT: 19
UF B WEST Project

Bukidnon
CIJE: 0 RIE: 1 CAT: 13
SN A Northwest Austronesian (Philippine) language
UF Binukid

Bulgaria
CIJE: 47 RIE: 54 CAT: 07

Bulgaria (Sophia)
CIJE: 1 RIE: 1 CAT: 07

Bulk Data Input Processor
CIJE: 0 RIE: 1 CAT: 04

Bull (William)
CIJE: 1 RIE: 2 CAT: 18

Bullen Reading Attitude Measure
CIJE: 0 RIE: 2 CAT: 21

Bulletin Kejar
CIJE: 0 RIE: 1 CAT: 22

Bulletin of Environmental Education
CIJE: 2 RIE: 0 CAT: 22

Bulloch Memorial Hospital GA
CIJE: 0 RIE: 1 CAT: 17

Bullock (Henry)
CIJE: 1 RIE: 0 CAT: 18

Bullock Report
CIJE: 10 RIE: 6 CAT: 22

Bully Pulpit Policy Strategy
CIJE: 1 RIE: 0 CAT: 15

Bullying
CIJE: 13 RIE: 8 CAT: 11

Bunche (Ralph)
CIJE: 1 RIE: 1 CAT: 18

Bundling (Television)
CIJE: 0 RIE: 1 CAT: 16
SN Packaging groups of movies and episodes of series, then selling licenses to use these packages to TV stations and cable channels

Bundy (McGeorge)
CIJE: 2 RIE: 0 CAT: 18

Bundy Aid Program
CIJE: 0 RIE: 4 CAT: 19

Bundy Report
CIJE: 1 RIE: 5 CAT: 22

Bunin (Ivan)
CIJE: 1 RIE: 0 CAT: 18

Bunker Hill Community College MA
CIJE: 2 RIE: 12 CAT: 17

Bunkyo Museum of Literature (Interactive Video)
CIJE: 0 RIE: 1 CAT: 22

Bunsen Burners
CIJE: 1 RIE: 0 CAT: 04

Bunuel (Luis)
CIJE: 1 RIE: 1 CAT: 18

Bunun
CIJE: 0 RIE: 1 CAT: 13

Burden of Proof
CIJE: 5 RIE: 3 CAT: 14

Bureau d Amenagement de l Est du Quebec (Canada)
CIJE: 0 RIE: 1 CAT: 17

Bureau for International Language Coordination
CIJE: 0 RIE: 1 CAT: 17

Bureau of Apprenticeship and Training
CIJE: 2 RIE: 6 CAT: 17

Bureau of Education for the Handicapped
CIJE: 22 RIE: 23 CAT: 17

Bureau of Educational Personnel Development
CIJE: 1 RIE: 1 CAT: 17

Bureau of Employment Security
CIJE: 0 RIE: 1 CAT: 17

Bureau of Higher Education
CIJE: 0 RIE: 1 CAT: 17

Bureau of Immigration
CIJE: 0 RIE: 1 CAT: 17

Bureau of Indian Affairs
CIJE: 88 RIE: 421 CAT: 17

Bureau of Indian Affairs Schools
CIJE: 13 RIE: 53 CAT: 05

Bureau of Labor Statistics
CIJE: 50 RIE: 29 CAT: 17

Bureau of Land Management
CIJE: 4 RIE: 2 CAT: 17

Bureau of Libraries
CIJE: 0 RIE: 1 CAT: 17

Bureau of Libraries and Educational Technology
CIJE: 3 RIE: 0 CAT: 17

Bureau of Libraries and Learning Resources
CIJE: 0 RIE: 1 CAT: 17

Bureau of Mines
CIJE: 2 RIE: 2 CAT: 17

Bureau of Occupational and Adult Education
CIJE: 1 RIE: 5 CAT: 17

Bureau of Outdoor Recreation
CIJE: 1 RIE: 4 CAT: 17

Bureau of Prisons
CIJE: 0 RIE: 4 CAT: 17

Bureau of the Budget
CIJE: 0 RIE: 3 CAT: 17

Bureau of the Census
CIJE: 44 RIE: 51 CAT: 17
UF Census Bureau

Bureau of Urban Programs Evaluation
CIJE: 0 RIE: 1 CAT: 17

Bureau Regional pour Education en Afrique
CIJE: 0 RIE: 1 CAT: 17

Bureaucratic Bargaining (Simulation)
CIJE: 0 RIE: 1 CAT: 15

Bureaucratic Language
CIJE: 4 RIE: 4 CAT: 13

Bureaucratic Orientation Scale
CIJE: 0 RIE: 1 CAT: 21

Burger (Warren E)
CIJE: 3 RIE: 2 CAT: 18

Burger Court
CIJE: 2 RIE: 4 CAT: 17

Burger King Corporation
CIJE: 1 RIE: 1 CAT: 17

Burke (C J)
CIJE: 0 RIE: 1 CAT: 18

Burke (Edmund)
CIJE: 9 RIE: 1 CAT: 18

Burke (Fred G)
CIJE: 2 RIE: 0 CAT: 18

Burke (Kenneth)
CIJE: 84 RIE: 54 CAT: 18

Burke (Yvonne B)
CIJE: 0 RIE: 1 CAT: 18

Burke County Board of Education NC
CIJE: 0 RIE: 1 CAT: 17

Burkina Faso
CIJE: 1 RIE: 2 CAT: 07
SN Country of Sub-Saharan Africa — Was "Upper Volta" (new name decreed in mid-1984)
UF Bourkina Fasso

Burks Behavior Rating Scale
CIJE: 0 RIE: 2 CAT: 21

Burks Behavior Rating Scale Organic Brain Dysfunct
CIJE: 1 RIE: 1 CAT: 21

Burlers (Textile)
CIJE: 0 RIE: 1 CAT: 09

Burlington County College NJ
CIJE: 8 RIE: 10 CAT: 17

Burlington County Special Services School Dist NJ
CIJE: 0 RIE: 1 CAT: 17

Burma
CIJE: 9 RIE: 39 CAT: 07
SN Name changed to "Myanmar," Jun89

Burmese Americans
CIJE: 0 RIE: 1 CAT: 08

Burnaby School District 41 BC
CIJE: 0 RIE: 1 CAT: 17

Burnett Reading Series Survey Test
CIJE: 0 RIE: 1 CAT: 21

Burnham Committees (England)
CIJE: 2 RIE: 0 CAT: 17

Burns (D C)
CIJE: 0 RIE: 1 CAT: 18

Burns (Injuries)
CIJE: 2 RIE: 3 CAT: 11

Burns (James MacGregor)
CIJE: 0 RIE: 2 CAT: 18

Burns (Robert)
CIJE: 0 RIE: 1 CAT: 18

Burnt Hills Ballston Lake Central Schools NY
CIJE: 1 RIE: 0 CAT: 17

Burris Laboratory School IN
CIJE: 1 RIE: 1 CAT: 17

Burroughs (John)
CIJE: 2 RIE: 0 CAT: 18

Burroughs (Nannie Helen)
CIJE: 0 RIE: 1 CAT: 18

Burroughs Computers
CIJE: 0 RIE: 4 CAT: 04

Bursley Act
CIJE: 0 RIE: 1 CAT: 14

Burt (M K)
CIJE: 1 RIE: 0 CAT: 18

Burt Word Reading Test
CIJE: 0 RIE: 1 CAT: 21

Burundi
CIJE: 7 RIE: 10 CAT: 07

Burwood Education Centre (Australia)
CIJE: 0 RIE: 1 CAT: 17

Bus Driver Trainee Aptitude Test CA
CIJE: 0 RIE: 1 CAT: 21

Busch Gardens
CIJE: 1 RIE: 0 CAT: 17

Bush (George)
CIJE: 31 RIE: 18 CAT: 18

Bush Administration
CIJE: 11 RIE: 16 CAT: 17

Bush Clinical Fellows Program
CIJE: 0 RIE: 1 CAT: 19

Bush Foundation
CIJE: 2 RIE: 2 CAT: 17

Bush Public School Executive Fellows Program
CIJE: 0 RIE: 1 CAT: 19

Bushwell John Vocabulary of Arithmetic Test
CIJE: 1 RIE: 0 CAT: 21

Business and Education Together
USE Project BET

Business and Office Career Education Curriculum
CIJE: 3 RIE: 8 CAT: 03

Business and Professional Womens Foundation
CIJE: 0 RIE: 1 CAT: 17

Business and Society
CIJE: 11 RIE: 14 CAT: 03

Business and Technician Education Council
CIJE: 0 RIE: 2 CAT: 17
SN ...of Great Britain — Name changed to "Business and Technology Education Council"

Business and Technology Education Council
CIJE: 0 RIE: 0 CAT: 17
SN ...of Great Britain — Formerly "Business and Technician Education Council"

Business Careers
CIJE: 3 RIE: 5 CAT: 09

Business Communication Teachers
CIJE: 8 RIE: 2 CAT: 09

Business Community Relationship
CIJE: 1 RIE: 1 CAT: 16
UF Community Business Relationship

Business Council for Effective Literacy
CIJE: 1 RIE: 1 CAT: 17

Business Dynamics
CIJE: 5 RIE: 1 CAT: 03

Business Education Learning System
CIJE: 0 RIE: 2 CAT: 15

Business Ethics
CIJE: 27 RIE: 12 CAT: 16

Business Executives
CIJE: 0 RIE: 2 CAT: 09
UF Corporate Executives

Business Finance
CIJE: 3 RIE: 8 CAT: 03

Business Higher Education Forum
CIJE: 4 RIE: 3 CAT: 17

Business History
CIJE: 1 RIE: 3 CAT: 12

Business Incubators
CIJE: 3 RIE: 8 CAT: 05
UF Small Business Incubators

Business Information
CIJE: 28 RIE: 7 CAT: 16

Business Law
CIJE: 16 RIE: 31 CAT: 03

Business Librarians
CIJE: 3 RIE: 2 CAT: 09

Business Literature
CIJE: 4 RIE: 3 CAT: 16

Business Loans
CIJE: 0 RIE: 1 CAT: 16

Business Management Fellowship Program
CIJE: 1 RIE: 0 CAT: 19

Business Mathematics
CIJE: 12 RIE: 24 CAT: 03

Business Media Relationship
CIJE: 2 RIE: 8 CAT: 16
UF Media Business Relationship

Business News
CIJE: 4 RIE: 6 CAT: 16

Business Partnerships
CIJE: 0 RIE: 0 CAT: 09
UF Partnerships in Business

Business Research
CIJE: 16 RIE: 6 CAT: 15

Business Revitalization
CIJE: 1 RIE: 0 CAT: 20
UF Industrial Revitalization

Business Role
CIJE: 31 RIE: 37 CAT: 16

Business Safeguards
CIJE: 0 RIE: 3 CAT: 16

Business Schools
CIJE: 9 RIE: 3 CAT: 05

Business Speech
CIJE: 1 RIE: 3 CAT: 13

Business Statistics
CIJE: 0 RIE: 1 CAT: 03

Business Technology
CIJE: 4 RIE: 1 CAT: 20

Buslayev (Fedor Ivanovich)
CIJE: 1 RIE: 0 CAT: 18

Buss (Allen R)
CIJE: 0 RIE: 0 CAT: 18

Buss (Arnold H)
CIJE: 0 RIE: 0 CAT: 18

Buss (Frances Mary)
CIJE: 1 RIE: 0 CAT: 18

Buss Durkee Hostility Inventory
CIJE: 4 RIE: 2 CAT: 21

Butler (Edith)
CIJE: 0 RIE: 1 CAT: 18

Butler (Pierce)
CIJE: 0 RIE: 1 CAT: 18

Butler (Samuel)
CIJE: 2 RIE: 0 CAT: 18

Butler County Community College PA
CIJE: 0 RIE: 1 CAT: 17

Butler Family Foundation
CIJE: 1 RIE: 0 CAT: 17

Butler Haigh Q Sort
CIJE: 0 RIE: 2 CAT: 21

Butler Hospital RI
CIJE: 0 RIE: 1 CAT: 17

Butler Manufacturing
CIJE: 0 RIE: 1 CAT: 17

Butler University IN
CIJE: 3 RIE: 9 CAT: 17

Butte Community College CA
CIJE: 0 RIE: 2 CAT: 17

Butte County Housing Authority
CIJE: 0 RIE: 1 CAT: 17

Butte County Public Library CA
CIJE: 0 RIE: 1 CAT: 17

Butterflies
CIJE: 7 RIE: 1 CAT: 20

Butterfly Catastrophe Model
CIJE: 0 RIE: 1 CAT: 15

Button Blanket
CIJE: 0 RIE: 1 CAT: 04

Butts (R Freeman)
CIJE: 1 RIE: 2 CAT: 18

Butts (William)
CIJE: 1 RIE: 0 CAT: 18

Buy Indian Act 1908
CIJE: 0 RIE: 1 CAT: 14

Buy Indian Contracting
CIJE: 0 RIE: 1 CAT: 16

Buyers
CIJE: 2 RIE: 6 CAT: 09

Buying Habits
CIJE: 1 RIE: 3 CAT: 16

Buzan Organic Study Method
CIJE: 0 RIE: 1 CAT: 15

Buzz Groups
CIJE: 0 RIE: 2 CAT: 10

Buzzard (David B)
CIJE: 0 RIE: 1 CAT: 18

Buzzatti (Dino)
CIJE: 1 RIE: 0 CAT: 18

Bylaws
CIJE: 11 RIE: 45 CAT: 14

Bylers Disease
CIJE: 1 RIE: 0 CAT: 11

Bylines
CIJE: 3 RIE: 2 CAT: 16

Byproducts
CIJE: 0 RIE: 1 CAT: 16

Byrd Scholarships
USE Robert C Byrd Honors Scholarship Program

Byrne Repression Sensitization Scale
CIJE: 9 RIE: 0 CAT: 21

Byron (Lord George Gordon)
CIJE: 0 RIE: 3 CAT: 18

Bystander Effect
CIJE: 1 RIE: 1 CAT: 11

Byte Reorganization
CIJE: 0 RIE: 1 CAT: 20

Byzantine Music
CIJE: 0 RIE: 1 CAT: 16

Bzoch Diagnostic Articulation Test
CIJE: 0 RIE: 1 CAT: 21

Bzoch League Receptive Expressive Emergent Lang
CIJE: 1 RIE: 2 CAT: 21

C Average Rule (Access to Extracurriculars)
USE No Pass No Play Rules

C BASE Test
USE College Basic Academic Subjects Examination

C LERN
USE California Local Educational Reform Network

C SPAN
CIJE: 1 RIE: 8 CAT: 17
UF Cable Satellite Public Affairs Network; CSPAN Service

C Tests
CIJE: 2 RIE: 3 CAT: 21

C W Post Center NY
CIJE: 7 RIE: 1 CAT: 17

C W Post Collegial Federation NY
CIJE: 0 RIE: 0 CAT: 17

CAB Abstracts
CIJE: 0 RIE: 0 CAT: 04

Cabaret
CIJE: 1 RIE: 0 CAT: 22
SN Musical and movie based on a story by Christopher Isherwood

Cabarets
CIJE: 0 RIE: 1 CAT: 05

Cabell County Schools WV
CIJE: 1 RIE: 0 CAT: 17

Cabeza de Baca (Fabiola)
CIJE: 0 RIE: 1 CAT: 18

Cabin John Junior High School MD
CIJE: 1 RIE: 0 CAT: 17

Cabin Leaders
CIJE: 0 RIE: 1 CAT: 10

Cabinet Committee on Cable Communications
CIJE: 0 RIE: 2 CAT: 17

Cable (George W)
CIJE: 0 RIE: 1 CAT: 18

Cable Access Centers
CIJE: 0 RIE: 1 CAT: 05

Cable Assemblers
CIJE: 0 RIE: 2 CAT: 09

Cable Libraries
CIJE: 1 RIE: 0 CAT: 05

Cable Makers
CIJE: 0 RIE: 1 CAT: 09

Cable News Network
CIJE: 5 RIE: 2 CAT: 17
SN See also "CNN..."
UF CNN

Cable Satellite Public Affairs Network
USE C SPAN

Cable Television Information Center DC
CIJE: 0 RIE: 2 CAT: 17

Cable Television Subscribers
USE Subscribers (Cable Television)

Cableshop
CIJE: 0 RIE: 1 CAT: 16

Caboclo (People)
CIJE: 0 RIE: 1 CAT: 08
SN Amerindians and mixed-blood offspring of Brazil who are acculturated in the mainstream Brazilian society

Cabot College of Applied Arts Techn Cont Educ NF
CIJE: 0 RIE: 1 CAT: 17

Cabrillo College CA
CIJE: 2 RIE: 1 CAT: 17

Cacao Farmers
CIJE: 0 RIE: 1 CAT: 09

Cacaopera
CIJE: 1 RIE: 0 CAT: 13

Cachola (Shirley)
CIJE: 0 RIE: 0 CAT: 18

CACREP
USE Council for Accred of Counsel and Relat Educ Prog

Cadalso (Jose)
CIJE: 3 RIE: 0 CAT: 18

CADAPPLE (Computer Program)
CIJE: 0 RIE: 1 CAT: 04

Cadavers
CIJE: 7 RIE: 0 CAT: 20

Caddo Parish Public Schools LA
CIJE: 1 RIE: 0 CAT: 17

Caddoan Languages
CIJE: 1 RIE: 0 CAT: 13

Cadet Corps
CIJE: 1 RIE: 2 CAT: 17

Cadman (Charles Wakefield)
CIJE: 1 RIE: 0 CAT: 18

Cadmium
CIJE: 4 RIE: 0 CAT: 20

Cadmium Sulfide
CIJE: 1 RIE: 0 CAT: 20

Cadre School (China)
CIJE: 2 RIE: 0 CAT: 17

Caesar (Julius)
CIJE: 2 RIE: 0 CAT: 18
SN Roman emperor — see also "Julius Caesar"

Caesarius (of Arles)
CIJE: 1 RIE: 0 CAT: 18

Cafeteria Monitors
CIJE: 0 RIE: 1 CAT: 09
SN See also "Lunchroom Aides"

Caffeine
CIJE: 20 RIE: 11 CAT: 11

Caffrey Isaacs Economic Impact Model
CIJE: 0 RIE: 1 CAT: 15

CAGE (Screening Test)
CIJE: 0 RIE: 1 CAT: 21
SN CAGE = Cut down, Annoyed, Guilty, Eye-opener

Cagney and Lacey
CIJE: 0 RIE: 1 CAT: 22

Cahuilla (Tribe)
CIJE: 2 RIE: 0 CAT: 08

Cain Levine Social Competency Scale
CIJE: 2 RIE: 0 CAT: 21

Cairo School District IL
CIJE: 0 RIE: 1 CAT: 17

Cairo University (Egypt)
CIJE: 0 RIE: 2 CAT: 17

CAISS
USE Community Approach to an Integrated Service System

CAISYS Programing Language
CIJE: 0 RIE: 1 CAT: 04

Cajun English
USE English (Cajun)

Cajun French
USE French (Cajun)

Cajuns
CIJE: 10 RIE: 11 CAT: 08

Cakavian Dialects
CIJE: 0 RIE: 1 CAT: 13

Cake Baking
CIJE: 1 RIE: 0 CAT: 16

Cake Finishers
CIJE: 0 RIE: 1 CAT: 09

Calcasieu Parish School System LA
CIJE: 0 RIE: 2 CAT: 17

Calcium
CIJE: 11 RIE: 2 CAT: 20

Calcium Oxide
CIJE: 1 RIE: 0 CAT: 20

Calcium Sulfates
CIJE: 1 RIE: 0 CAT: 20

Calcomp Display
CIJE: 1 RIE: 0 CAT: 04

Calculators and Mathematics Project CA
CIJE: 0 RIE: 5 CAT: 19

Calcutta Standard Dialect
CIJE: 0 RIE: 1 CAT: 13

Caldecott (Randolph)
CIJE: 0 RIE: 1 CAT: 18

Caldecott Award
CIJE: 34 RIE: 20 CAT: 19

Calderon de la Barca (Pedro)
CIJE: 12 RIE: 0 CAT: 18

Caldwell (Erskine)
CIJE: 0 RIE: 1 CAT: 18

Caldwell College NJ
CIJE: 1 RIE: 1 CAT: 17

Caldwell Community College and Technical Inst NC
CIJE: 0 RIE: 0 CAT: 17

Caldwell Inventory of Home Stimulation
CIJE: 1 RIE: 0 CAT: 21

Caldwell Soule Preschool Inventory
CIJE: 0 RIE: 3 CAT: 21

Calendar (Computer Program)
CIJE: 0 RIE: 1 CAT: 04

Calendars
CIJE: 30 RIE: 14 CAT: 04

Calexico Intercultural Design
CIJE: 0 RIE: 2 CAT: 16

Calexico Unified School District CA
CIJE: 0 RIE: 1 CAT: 17

Calgary Board of Education AB
CIJE: 0 RIE: 6 CAT: 17
UF Calgary Public Schools AB; Calgary School Board AB

Calgary Listening Inquiry Project AB
CIJE: 0 RIE: 0 CAT: 19

Calgary Public Schools AB
USE Calgary Board of Education AB

Calgary Roman Catholic Separate Sch Bd AB
CIJE: 0 RIE: 1 CAT: 17

Calgary School Board AB
USE Calgary Board of Education AB

Calhoun (John C)
CIJE: 4 RIE: 1 CAT: 18

Calhoun Elementary School CA
CIJE: 0 RIE: 1 CAT: 17

Calhoun State Community College AL
USE John C Calhoun State Community College AL

Calibration
CIJE: 13 RIE: 41 CAT: 20

California
CIJE: 1333 RIE: 4532 CAT: 07

California (Alameda County)
CIJE: 2 RIE: 11 CAT: 07

California (Alta Loma)
CIJE: 0 RIE: 1 CAT: 07

California (Alum Rock)
CIJE: 5 RIE: 5 CAT: 07

California (Anaheim)
CIJE: 0 RIE: 5 CAT: 07

California (Antelope Valley)
CIJE: 0 RIE: 1 CAT: 17

California (Arcadia)
CIJE: 0 RIE: 2 CAT: 07

California (Azusa)
CIJE: 0 RIE: 1 CAT: 07

California (Bakersfield)
CIJE: 0 RIE: 9 CAT: 07

California (Berkeley)
CIJE: 26 RIE: 114 CAT: 07

California (Beverly Hills)
CIJE: 1 RIE: 2 CAT: 07

California (Burbank)
CIJE: 0 RIE: 1 CAT: 07

California (Calexico)
CIJE: 0 RIE: 1 CAT: 07

California (Camarillo)
CIJE: 0 RIE: 2 CAT: 07

California (Campbell)
CIJE: 0 RIE: 1 CAT: 07

California (Canoga Park)
CIJE: 0 RIE: 1 CAT: 07

California (Carmichael)
CIJE: 0 RIE: 2 CAT: 07

California (Central)
CIJE: 0 RIE: 2 CAT: 07

California (Cherrywood)
CIJE: 0 RIE: 1 CAT: 07

California (Chico)
CIJE: 1 RIE: 3 CAT: 07

California (Chula Vista)
CIJE: 3 RIE: 4 CAT: 07

California (Claremont)
CIJE: 3 RIE: 3 CAT: 07

California (Coachella Valley)
CIJE: 0 RIE: 2 CAT: 07

California (Compton)
CIJE: 1 RIE: 6 CAT: 07

California (Concord)
CIJE: 2 RIE: 1 CAT: 07

California (Contra Costa County)
CIJE: 0 RIE: 13 CAT: 07

California (Costa Mesa)
CIJE: 0 RIE: 4 CAT: 07

California (Crescent City)
CIJE: 1 RIE: 0 CAT: 07

California (Culver City)
CIJE: 0 RIE: 5 CAT: 07

California (Cupertino)
CIJE: 1 RIE: 2 CAT: 07

California (Daly City)
CIJE: 0 RIE: 2 CAT: 07

California (Downey)
CIJE: 0 RIE: 2 CAT: 07

California (East Los Angeles)
CIJE: 8 RIE: 14 CAT: 07

California (East Palo Alto)
CIJE: 2 RIE: 2 CAT: 07

California (East San Jose)
CIJE: 0 RIE: 2 CAT: 07

California (El Cajon)
CIJE: 1 RIE: 4 CAT: 07

California (El Camino)
CIJE: 0 RIE: 3 CAT: 07

California (El Centro)
CIJE: 0 RIE: 2 CAT: 07

California (El Segundo)
CIJE: 0 RIE: 2 CAT: 07

California (Emeryville)
CIJE: 0 RIE: 2 CAT: 07

California (Essexville)
CIJE: 0 RIE: 3 CAT: 07

California (Eureka)
CIJE: 0 RIE: 1 CAT: 07

California (Fort Bragg)
CIJE: 1 RIE: 0 CAT: 07

California (Fort Ord)
CIJE: 0 RIE: 1 CAT: 07

California (Fort Pierce)
CIJE: 0 RIE: 1 CAT: 07

California (Fremont)
CIJE: 1 RIE: 5 CAT: 07

California (French Camp)
CIJE: 0 RIE: 1 CAT: 07

California (Fresno County)
CIJE: 5 RIE: 9 CAT: 07

California (Fresno)
CIJE: 3 RIE: 69 CAT: 07

California (Fullerton)
CIJE: 2 RIE: 4 CAT: 07

California (Garden Grove)
CIJE: 1 RIE: 2 CAT: 07

California (Glendale)
CIJE: 0 RIE: 4 CAT: 07

California (Goleta)
CIJE: 0 RIE: 1 CAT: 07

California (Grossmont)
CIJE: 0 RIE: 4 CAT: 07

California (Haight Ashbury)
CIJE: 1 RIE: 0 CAT: 07

California (Hawaiian Gardens)
CIJE: 1 RIE: 0 CAT: 07

California (Hayes Valley)
CIJE: 0 RIE: 1 CAT: 07

California (Humboldt County)
CIJE: 0 RIE: 4 CAT: 07

California (Humboldt)
CIJE: 1 RIE: 0 CAT: 07

California (Hunters Point Bayview)
CIJE: 0 RIE: 2 CAT: 07

California (Huntington Beach)
CIJE: 2 RIE: 5 CAT: 07

California (Imperial County)
CIJE: 1 RIE: 4 CAT: 07

California (Imperial Valley)
CIJE: 1 RIE: 1 CAT: 07

California (Inglewood)
CIJE: 0 RIE: 9 CAT: 07

California (Irvine)
CIJE: 2 RIE: 4 CAT: 07

California (Kern County)
CIJE: 0 RIE: 6 CAT: 07

California (La Jolla)
CIJE: 0 RIE: 1 CAT: 07

California (La Palma)
CIJE: 0 RIE: 1 CAT: 07

California (La Puente)
CIJE: 1 RIE: 0 CAT: 07

California (Lake County)
CIJE: 0 RIE: 1 CAT: 07

California (Little Canton)
CIJE: 0 RIE: 1 CAT: 07

California (Long Beach)
CIJE: 2 RIE: 11 CAT: 07

California (Los Altos)
CIJE: 0 RIE: 2 CAT: 07

California (Los Angeles County)
CIJE: 32 RIE: 40 CAT: 07

California (Los Angeles)
CIJE: 165 RIE: 413 CAT: 07

California (Madera)
CIJE: 0 RIE: 1 CAT: 07

California (Marin County)
CIJE: 4 RIE: 14 CAT: 07

California (Marysville)
CIJE: 0 RIE: 1 CAT: 07

California (Mendocino County)
CIJE: 0 RIE: 2 CAT: 07

California (Menlo Park)
CIJE: 1 RIE: 4 CAT: 07

California (Merced County)
CIJE: 0 RIE: 2 CAT: 07

California (Merced)
CIJE: 0 RIE: 1 CAT: 07

California (Mill Valley)
CIJE: 1 RIE: 0 CAT: 07

California (Millbrae)
CIJE: 0 RIE: 1 CAT: 07

California (Milpitas)
CIJE: 2 RIE: 0 CAT: 07

California (Modesto)
CIJE: 2 RIE: 14 CAT: 07

California (Monterey County)
CIJE: 2 RIE: 3 CAT: 07

California (Monterey Park)
CIJE: 0 RIE: 3 CAT: 07

California (Morgan Hill)
CIJE: 1 RIE: 0 CAT: 07

California (Mountain View)
CIJE: 1 RIE: 1 CAT: 07

California (Napa County)
CIJE: 0 RIE: 1 CAT: 07

California (North Hollywood)
CIJE: 1 RIE: 0 CAT: 07

California (North Richmond)
CIJE: 0 RIE: 1 CAT: 07

California (North)
CIJE: 5 RIE: 18 CAT: 07

California (Northeast)
CIJE: 0 RIE: 1 CAT: 07

California (Northridge)
CIJE: 0 RIE: 3 CAT: 07

California (Northwest)
CIJE: 0 RIE: 2 CAT: 07

California (Oak Glen)
CIJE: 0 RIE: 1 CAT: 07

California (Oakland Chinatown)
CIJE: 0 RIE: 0 CAT: 07
UF Chinatown Oakland

California (Oakland)
CIJE: 22 RIE: 107 CAT: 07

California (Ocean Hill Brownville)
CIJE: 5 RIE: 15 CAT: 07

California (Ocean View)
CIJE: 0 RIE: 1 CAT: 07

California (Oceanside)
CIJE: 0 RIE: 2 CAT: 07

California (Orange County)
CIJE: 4 RIE: 27 CAT: 07

California (Orange)
CIJE: 0 RIE: 1 CAT: 07

California (Oxnard)
CIJE: 0 RIE: 2 CAT: 07

California (Palm Desert)
CIJE: 1 RIE: 1 CAT: 07

California (Palo Alto)
CIJE: 6 RIE: 26 CAT: 07

California (Pasadena)
CIJE: 7 RIE: 21 CAT: 07

California (Perris)
CIJE: 0 RIE: 1 CAT: 07

California (Pico Rivera)
CIJE: 0 RIE: 1 CAT: 07

California (Pomona)
CIJE: 0 RIE: 2 CAT: 07

California (Potter Valley)
CIJE: 0 RIE: 1 CAT: 07

California (Rancho Cordova)
CIJE: 1 RIE: 1 CAT: 07

California (Redding)
CIJE: 1 RIE: 2 CAT: 07

California (Redlands)
CIJE: 0 RIE: 3 CAT: 07

California (Redwood City)
CIJE: 2 RIE: 7 CAT: 07

California (Richmond)
CIJE: 6 RIE: 2 CAT: 07

California (Rio Linda)
CIJE: 0 RIE: 1 CAT: 07

California (Riverside County)
CIJE: 3 RIE: 5 CAT: 07

California (Riverside)
CIJE: 1 RIE: 24 CAT: 07

California (Sacramento)
CIJE: 11 RIE: 93 CAT: 07

California (Saint Helena)
CIJE: 0 RIE: 1 CAT: 07

California (Salinas)
CIJE: 1 RIE: 4 CAT: 07

California (San Bernardino County)
CIJE: 0 RIE: 6 CAT: 07

California (San Bernardino)
CIJE: 2 RIE: 13 CAT: 07

California (San Bruno)
CIJE: 1 RIE: 1 CAT: 07

California (San Diego County)
CIJE: 12 RIE: 25 CAT: 07

California (San Diego)
CIJE: 42 RIE: 109 CAT: 07

California (San Fernando Valley)
CIJE: 2 RIE: 1 CAT: 07

California (San Fernando)
CIJE: 2 RIE: 0 CAT: 07

California (San Francisco Bay Area)
CIJE: 19 RIE: 50 CAT: 07

California (San Francisco Chinatown)
CIJE: 0 RIE: 1 CAT: 07
UF Chinatown San Francisco

California (San Francisco County)
CIJE: 0 RIE: 1 CAT: 07

California (San Francisco Mission District)
CIJE: 1 RIE: 0 CAT: 07

California (San Francisco Peninsula)
CIJE: 0 RIE: 3 CAT: 07

California (San Francisco)
CIJE: 96 RIE: 207 CAT: 07

California (San Jacinto)
CIJE: 1 RIE: 0 CAT: 07

California (San Joaquin County)
CIJE: 1 RIE: 2 CAT: 07

California (San Joaquin Valley)
USE San Joaquin Valley

California (San Jose)
CIJE: 13 RIE: 48 CAT: 07

California (San Luis Obispo)
CIJE: 2 RIE: 2 CAT: 07

California (San Mateo County)
CIJE: 6 RIE: 28 CAT: 07

California (San Mateo)
CIJE: 1 RIE: 14 CAT: 07

California (San Pablo)
CIJE: 0 RIE: 2 CAT: 07

California (San Rafael)
CIJE: 2 RIE: 3 CAT: 07

California (San Ramon)
CIJE: 1 RIE: 0 CAT: 07

California (Sanger)
CIJE: 0 RIE: 1 CAT: 07

California (Santa Ana)
CIJE: 0 RIE: 6 CAT: 07

California (Santa Barbara County)
CIJE: 1 RIE: 6 CAT: 07

California (Santa Barbara)
CIJE: 7 RIE: 22 CAT: 07

California (Santa Clara County)
CIJE: 6 RIE: 18 CAT: 07

California (Santa Clara)
CIJE: 1 RIE: 2 CAT: 07

California (Santa Cruz)
CIJE: 4 RIE: 13 CAT: 07

California (Santa Fe Springs)
CIJE: 0 RIE: 1 CAT: 07

California (Santa Monica)
CIJE: 3 RIE: 51 CAT: 07

California (Santa Rosa)
CIJE: 1 RIE: 2 CAT: 07

California (Sausalito)
CIJE: 2 RIE: 2 CAT: 07

California (Sequoia)
CIJE: 1 RIE: 1 CAT: 07

California (Shasta County)
CIJE: 0 RIE: 3 CAT: 07

California (Sherman Oaks)
CIJE: 0 RIE: 1 CAT: 07

California (Simi Valley)
CIJE: 1 RIE: 0 CAT: 07

California (Solano County)
CIJE: 0 RIE: 1 CAT: 07

California (Sonoma County)
CIJE: 2 RIE: 2 CAT: 07

California (South Gate)
CIJE: 0 RIE: 1 CAT: 07

California Mentally Gifted Minors Program
CIJE: 0 RIE: 1 CAT: 19
UF Mentally Gifted Minors Program CA

California Mentor Teacher Program
CIJE: 0 RIE: 10 CAT: 19

California Mexican American Educ Research Project
CIJE: 0 RIE: 1 CAT: 19

California Mini Corps
CIJE: 0 RIE: 4 CAT: 17

California Model Curriculum Computers in Education
CIJE: 0 RIE: 1 CAT: 03

California New Teacher Project
CIJE: 0 RIE: 11 CAT: 19

California Occup Prefer System Interest Inventory
CIJE: 6 RIE: 0 CAT: 21

California Occupational Survey
CIJE: 0 RIE: 1 CAT: 19

California Office of Compensatory Education
CIJE: 0 RIE: 1 CAT: 17

California Office of Private Postsecondary Educ
CIJE: 0 RIE: 1 CAT: 17

California Personality Inventory
CIJE: 6 RIE: 5 CAT: 21

California Polytechnic State University
CIJE: 13 RIE: 17 CAT: 17

California Preschool Social Competency Scale
CIJE: 1 RIE: 4 CAT: 21

California Psychological Inventory
CIJE: 77 RIE: 44 CAT: 21

California Pupil Proficiency Law
USE Pupil Proficiency Law (California)

California Roundtable
CIJE: 0 RIE: 1 CAT: 17

California School Finance Reform Act
CIJE: 0 RIE: 1 CAT: 14

California School for the Deaf
CIJE: 5 RIE: 2 CAT: 17

California School Improvement Program
CIJE: 1 RIE: 6 CAT: 19
UF School Improvement Program CA

California School Safety Center
CIJE: 0 RIE: 1 CAT: 17

California Science Framework
USE Science Framework for California Public Schools

California Short Form Test of Mental Maturity
CIJE: 2 RIE: 5 CAT: 21

California Small School Districts Association
CIJE: 0 RIE: 1 CAT: 17
UF Small School Districts Association CA

California Society of Psychiatric Technicians
CIJE: 0 RIE: 1 CAT: 17

California Spanish Language Data Base
CIJE: 1 RIE: 0 CAT: 04

California Special Education Resource Network
CIJE: 0 RIE: 2 CAT: 17

California Speech Communication Association
CIJE: 0 RIE: 1 CAT: 17

California Staff Development Study
CIJE: 0 RIE: 1 CAT: 19

California State Board of Education
CIJE: 5 RIE: 6 CAT: 17

California State College Bakersfield
CIJE: 1 RIE: 4 CAT: 17

California State College Dominguez Hills
CIJE: 0 RIE: 2 CAT: 17

California State College Long Beach
CIJE: 1 RIE: 1 CAT: 17

California State College Los Angeles
CIJE: 1 RIE: 5 CAT: 17

California State College PA
CIJE: 2 RIE: 8 CAT: 17

California State College San Bernardino
CIJE: 1 RIE: 0 CAT: 17

California State Compensatory Education Program
CIJE: 0 RIE: 1 CAT: 19

California State Department of Education
CIJE: 5 RIE: 34 CAT: 17

California State Department of Mental Health
CIJE: 0 RIE: 1 CAT: 17

California State Dept of Developmental Services
CIJE: 0 RIE: 0 CAT: 17

California State Dept of the Youth Authority
CIJE: 0 RIE: 6 CAT: 17

California State Employees Association
CIJE: 0 RIE: 1 CAT: 17

California State Employment Training Panel
USE California Employment Training Panel

California State Library
CIJE: 3 RIE: 14 CAT: 17

California State Migrant Master Plan
CIJE: 0 RIE: 1 CAT: 19

California State Polytechnic University Pomona
CIJE: 2 RIE: 8 CAT: 17

California State Postsecondary Education Comm
CIJE: 0 RIE: 22 CAT: 17

California State Preschool Program
CIJE: 0 RIE: 1 CAT: 19

California State Training Division
CIJE: 0 RIE: 1 CAT: 17

California State University
CIJE: 27 RIE: 130 CAT: 17
UF California State University System

California State University and Colleges
CIJE: 13 RIE: 50 CAT: 17
SN See add'l listings under "CSUC..." and "CSUCS..."

California State University Bakersfield
CIJE: 2 RIE: 4 CAT: 17

California State University Chico
CIJE: 16 RIE: 30 CAT: 17

California State University Dominguez Hills
CIJE: 8 RIE: 5 CAT: 17

California State University Fresno
CIJE: 10 RIE: 16 CAT: 17

California State University Fullerton
CIJE: 5 RIE: 18 CAT: 17

California State University Hayward
CIJE: 4 RIE: 8 CAT: 17

California State University Inst for Teach Learn
CIJE: 0 RIE: 24 CAT: 17

California State University Long Beach
CIJE: 15 RIE: 25 CAT: 17

California State University Los Angeles
CIJE: 8 RIE: 15 CAT: 17

California State University Northridge
CIJE: 14 RIE: 20 CAT: 17
SN See also "CSUN..."

California State University Sacramento
CIJE: 3 RIE: 12 CAT: 17

California State University San Bernardino
CIJE: 2 RIE: 3 CAT: 17

California State University San Diego
CIJE: 2 RIE: 0 CAT: 17

California State University San Jose
CIJE: 2 RIE: 0 CAT: 17

California State University System
USE California State University

California Statewide Evaluation of Migrant Educ
CIJE: 0 RIE: 1 CAT: 19

California Statewide Mathematics Advisory Com
CIJE: 0 RIE: 1 CAT: 17

California Student Aid Commission
CIJE: 2 RIE: 3 CAT: 17

California Student Opportunity and Access Program
CIJE: 0 RIE: 2 CAT: 19

California Study Activities Inventory
CIJE: 0 RIE: 1 CAT: 21

California Study Methods Survey
CIJE: 1 RIE: 3 CAT: 19

California Supreme Court
CIJE: 1 RIE: 2 CAT: 17

California Teachers Association
CIJE: 4 RIE: 19 CAT: 17

California Test Bureau
CIJE: 0 RIE: 1 CAT: 17

California Test of Basic Skills
CIJE: 5 RIE: 21 CAT: 21

California Test of Basic Skills Espanol
CIJE: 0 RIE: 2 CAT: 21

California Test of Mental Maturity
CIJE: 14 RIE: 43 CAT: 21

California Test of Personality
CIJE: 6 RIE: 18 CAT: 21

California Tomorrow Plan
CIJE: 0 RIE: 3 CAT: 19

California University of Pennsylvania
CIJE: 2 RIE: 1 CAT: 17

California Verbal Learning Test for Children
CIJE: 0 RIE: 1 CAT: 21

California Video Resource Project
CIJE: 1 RIE: 12 CAT: 19

California Visual Performing Arts Framework 1989
CIJE: 0 RIE: 1 CAT: 03

California Writing Assessment
CIJE: 0 RIE: 1 CAT: 21

California Writing Project
CIJE: 3 RIE: 4 CAT: 19

California Youth Conservation Camps
CIJE: 0 RIE: 2 CAT: 17

Calipers
CIJE: 1 RIE: 2 CAT: 04

Caliver (Ambrose)
CIJE: 1 RIE: 1 CAT: 18

Call for Change in Teacher Education
CIJE: 1 RIE: 1 CAT: 22

Call It Courage
CIJE: 1 RIE: 0 CAT: 22

Call Numbers
CIJE: 2 RIE: 4 CAT: 16

CALL Program NV
USE Computer Assisted Literacy in Libraries

CALLA
USE Cognitive Academic Language Learning Approach

Callagy Hall NY
CIJE: 0 RIE: 1 CAT: 17

Callaway Gardens Conference High School Sci Prog
CIJE: 0 RIE: 1 CAT: 02

Callendar Park College (England)
CIJE: 1 RIE: 0 CAT: 17

Callier Azusa Scale
CIJE: 1 RIE: 3 CAT: 21

Callier Center for Communication Disorders TX
CIJE: 2 RIE: 0 CAT: 17

Callier Hearing and Speech Center TX
CIJE: 1 RIE: 0 CAT: 17

Calo
CIJE: 0 RIE: 1 CAT: 13

Caloric Values (Nutrition)
CIJE: 6 RIE: 5 CAT: 11

CALTAC WILL
CIJE: 0 RIE: 1 CAT: 19
SN California Assn of Library Trustees and Commissioners, Workshops in Library Leadership

Calvin (John)
CIJE: 2 RIE: 2 CAT: 18

Calvin College MI
CIJE: 3 RIE: 3 CAT: 17

Cam Academy IL
USE Christian Action Ministry Academy IL

CaMaPe Models
CIJE: 0 RIE: 1 CAT: 15

Camarillo Childrens Treatment Center CA
CIJE: 1 RIE: 0 CAT: 17

Camarillo State Hospital CA
CIJE: 1 RIE: 1 CAT: 17

Camberwell Park Infants School (Canada)
CIJE: 1 RIE: 0 CAT: 17

Cambodia
CIJE: 14 RIE: 33 CAT: 07

Cambodian Culture
CIJE: 0 RIE: 3 CAT: 16
UF Khmer Culture

Cambria Community Adult School CA
CIJE: 1 RIE: 0 CAT: 17

Cambria County Public Library PA
CIJE: 1 RIE: 0 CAT: 17

Cambrian College (Canada)
CIJE: 1 RIE: 0 CAT: 17

Cambridge Alternative Public School MA
CIJE: 1 RIE: 1 CAT: 17

Cambridge Art Center MA
CIJE: 1 RIE: 0 CAT: 17

Cambridge Assessment of Spoken English
CIJE: 0 RIE: 1 CAT: 21

Cambridge Conference on School Mathematics MA
CIJE: 0 RIE: 14 CAT: 17

Cambridge Conference on Teacher Training
CIJE: 0 RIE: 1 CAT: 02

Cambridge Crystallographic Data Centre
CIJE: 2 RIE: 0 CAT: 17

Cambridge English Examinations
CIJE: 1 RIE: 2 CAT: 21

Cambridge Hospital MA
CIJE: 1 RIE: 0 CAT: 17

Cambridge House University Settlement (England)
CIJE: 1 RIE: 0 CAT: 17

Cambridge Job Factory Voucher Experiment MA
CIJE: 0 RIE: 1 CAT: 19

Cambridge Junior High School MN
CIJE: 0 RIE: 1 CAT: 17

Cambridge Kentucky Educ TV GED Video Series
CIJE: 0 RIE: 1 CAT: 22

Cambridge Lesley Literacy Project MA
CIJE: 0 RIE: 1 CAT: 19

Cambridge Local Examinations Syndicate (England)
USE University of Cambridge Local Exam Synd (England)

Cambridge Pilot School
CIJE: 1 RIE: 1 CAT: 17

Cambridge Public Schools MA
CIJE: 3 RIE: 6 CAT: 17

Cambridge Rindge and Latin School MA
CIJE: 0 RIE: 1 CAT: 17

Cambridge School Committee MA
CIJE: 0 RIE: 1 CAT: 17

Camden Central School District NY
CIJE: 0 RIE: 1 CAT: 17

Camden County College NJ
CIJE: 1 RIE: 1 CAT: 17

Camden County School District GA
CIJE: 0 RIE: 1 CAT: 17

Camden County Vocational and Technical School NJ
CIJE: 1 RIE: 0 CAT: 17

Camden Program for Severely Handicapped Preschool
CIJE: 0 RIE: 1 CAT: 19

Camden Public Schools NJ
CIJE: 2 RIE: 1 CAT: 17

Camelot (Computer System)
CIJE: 0 RIE: 1 CAT: 04

CAMEO
CIJE: 2 RIE: 0 CAT: 04

Camera Angles
CIJE: 1 RIE: 5 CAT: 16

Cameron Model of Organizational Effectiveness
CIJE: 0 RIE: 1 CAT: 15

Cameron University OK
CIJE: 0 RIE: 2 CAT: 17

Cameroon
CIJE: 24 RIE: 36 CAT: 07

Cameroon (East)
CIJE: 0 RIE: 1 CAT: 07

Cameroon (West)
CIJE: 0 RIE: 1 CAT: 07

Cameroonian Pidgin
CIJE: 0 RIE: 1 CAT: 13

Camino Real
CIJE: 0 RIE: 1 CAT: 07

Camp Cuyamaca CA
CIJE: 2 RIE: 0 CAT: 17

Camp David Peace Accords
CIJE: 0 RIE: 2 CAT: 12

Camp Fire Girls Inc
CIJE: 2 RIE: 3 CAT: 17

Camp Fire Inc
CIJE: 3 RIE: 1 CAT: 17

Camp Health Aid Program MI
CIJE: 0 RIE: 1 CAT: 19

Camp Kilmer
CIJE: 0 RIE: 1 CAT: 17

Camp Limberlost IL
CIJE: 0 RIE: 1 CAT: 17

Camp Logan SC
CIJE: 0 RIE: 1 CAT: 17

Camp Miniwanca MI
CIJE: 1 RIE: 6 CAT: 17

Camp Nana Mah
CIJE: 1 RIE: 0 CAT: 17

Camp Paart CT
CIJE: 0 RIE: 1 CAT: 17

Camp Partlow AL
CIJE: 0 RIE: 0 CAT: 17

Camp Riverwood MA
CIJE: 1 RIE: 0 CAT: 17

Campaign Managers
CIJE: 1 RIE: 1 CAT: 09

Campbell (Alexander)
CIJE: 0 RIE: 1 CAT: 18

Campbell (George)
CIJE: 1 RIE: 4 CAT: 18

Campbell (Helen)
CIJE: 0 RIE: 1 CAT: 18

Campbell (Joseph)
CIJE: 4 RIE: 1 CAT: 18

Campbell College NC
CIJE: 0 RIE: 3 CAT: 17

Campbell Fiske Matrix
CIJE: 4 RIE: 3 CAT: 21

Campbell Regression Continuity Analysis
CIJE: 1 RIE: 0 CAT: 21

Campbell River School District BC
CIJE: 0 RIE: 1 CAT: 17

Campbell Rose Interaction System
CIJE: 0 RIE: 1 CAT: 21

Campesinos
CIJE: 0 RIE: 1 CAT: 10

Camphill Communities
USE Camphill Villages

Camphill Villages
CIJE: 0 RIE: 1 CAT: 17
UF Camphill Communities

Campus Based Financial Aid
CIJE: 0 RIE: 5 CAT: 16

Campus Child Care
CIJE: 12 RIE: 9 CAT: 11
UF Campus Day Care

Campus Community Organizers
CIJE: 1 RIE: 1 CAT: 10

Campus Day Care
USE Campus Child Care

Campus Effectiveness Model
CIJE: 0 RIE: 1 CAT: 15

Campus Environment Study
CIJE: 0 RIE: 1 CAT: 21

Campus Free College MA
CIJE: 2 RIE: 0 CAT: 17

Campus Governance Project
CIJE: 1 RIE: 2 CAT: 19

Campus Ministry
CIJE: 1 RIE: 8 CAT: 16

Campus Radio Stations
CIJE: 0 RIE: 2 CAT: 05

Campus Safety Committee
CIJE: 1 RIE: 1 CAT: 17

Campus School Plan
CIJE: 0 RIE: 2 CAT: 19

CAMPUS Simulation Model
CIJE: 0 RIE: 3 CAT: 15

Campus Visits
CIJE: 0 RIE: 2 CAT: 16

Campuswide Information Systems
CIJE: 6 RIE: 2 CAT: 20

Camsa
CIJE: 0 RIE: 1 CAT: 13

Camus (Albert)
CIJE: 16 RIE: 5 CAT: 18

Canada
CIJE: 5247 RIE: 4131 CAT: 07

Canada (French Provinces)
CIJE: 7 RIE: 6 CAT: 07

Canada (Maritime Provinces)
CIJE: 5 RIE: 2 CAT: 07

Canada (North)
CIJE: 10 RIE: 15 CAT: 07

Canada (Prairie Provinces)
CIJE: 0 RIE: 2 CAT: 07

Canada (West)
CIJE: 15 RIE: 23 CAT: 07

Canada Assistance Plan
CIJE: 0 RIE: 2 CAT: 19

Canada China Language Centre
CIJE: 0 RIE: 0 CAT: 19

Canada College CA
CIJE: 1 RIE: 2 CAT: 17

Canada Geese
CIJE: 1 RIE: 0 CAT: 20

Canada Manpower Training Program
CIJE: 4 RIE: 1 CAT: 19

Canada Royal Commission Bilingualism Biculturalism
CIJE: 1 RIE: 0 CAT: 17

Canada Studies Foundation
CIJE: 7 RIE: 0 CAT: 17

Canada United States Free Trade Agreement 1989
CIJE: 0 RIE: 0 CAT: 14

Canadian Achievement Tests
CIJE: 0 RIE: 3 CAT: 21

Canadian Adult Achievement Test
CIJE: 0 RIE: 1 CAT: 21

Canadian Association for Adult Education
CIJE: 9 RIE: 9 CAT: 17

Canadian Association in Support of Native Peoples
CIJE: 1 RIE: 1 CAT: 17

Canadian Association of Research Libraries
CIJE: 0 RIE: 1 CAT: 17

Canadian Association of University Teachers
CIJE: 3 RIE: 1 CAT: 17

Canadian Awareness Project
CIJE: 0 RIE: 1 CAT: 19

Canadian Broadcasting Corporation
CIJE: 11 RIE: 8 CAT: 17

Canadian Census 1981
USE Census 1981 (Canada)

Canadian Centre Info Documentation on Archives
CIJE: 0 RIE: 1 CAT: 17

Canadian Charter of Rights and Freedoms
CIJE: 16 RIE: 2 CAT: 14

Canadian Child Welfare Association
CIJE: 0 RIE: 1 CAT: 17

Canadian Classification Dictionary of Occupations
CIJE: 2 RIE: 0 CAT: 22

Canadian Cognitive Abilities Test
CIJE: 2 RIE: 2 CAT: 21

Canadian Commission for the Community College
CIJE: 1 RIE: 0 CAT: 17

Canadian Construction Information System
CIJE: 0 RIE: 1 CAT: 19

Canadian Copyright Act
USE Copyright Act (Canada)

Canadian Council for Research in Education
CIJE: 1 RIE: 0 CAT: 17

Canadian Council of Ministers of Education
CIJE: 1 RIE: 1 CAT: 17

Canadian Council of Teachers of English
CIJE: 6 RIE: 0 CAT: 17

Canadian Council on Urban and Regional Research
CIJE: 0 RIE: 1 CAT: 17

Canadian Education Association
CIJE: 5 RIE: 2 CAT: 17

Canadian Education Index
CIJE: 1 RIE: 1 CAT: 21

Canadian English Language Achievement Test
CIJE: 1 RIE: 0 CAT: 21

Canadian Government
CIJE: 9 RIE: 15 CAT: 17

Canadian Guidance and Counseling Association
CIJE: 3 RIE: 0 CAT: 17

Canadian Higher Education Research Network
CIJE: 0 RIE: 1 CAT: 17

Canadian History
CIJE: 23 RIE: 2 CAT: 12

Canadian Home and School and Parent Teacher Fed
CIJE: 0 RIE: 1 CAT: 17

Canadian Home Economics Association
CIJE: 3 RIE: 1 CAT: 17

Canadian Human Rights Act
CIJE: 0 RIE: 6 CAT: 14

Canadian Human Rights Commission
CIJE: 0 RIE: 1 CAT: 17

Canadian Immigration Act 1976
USE Immigration Act 1976 (Canada)

Canadian International Development Agency
CIJE: 5 RIE: 3 CAT: 17

Canadian Jobs Strategy
CIJE: 0 RIE: 1 CAT: 19

Canadian Library Association
CIJE: 24 RIE: 2 CAT: 17

Canadian Manpower Centres
CIJE: 0 RIE: 1 CAT: 17

Canadian Manpower Consultative Service
CIJE: 0 RIE: 1 CAT: 17

Canadian Mathematics Education Study Group
CIJE: 0 RIE: 2 CAT: 17

Canadian On Line Enquiry
CIJE: 1 RIE: 2 CAT: 04

Canadian Organization for Development through Educ
CIJE: 0 RIE: 1 CAT: 17

Canadian Periodical Index
CIJE: 2 RIE: 0 CAT: 22

Canadian Postal System
CIJE: 1 RIE: 0 CAT: 17

Canadian Public Issues Project
CIJE: 2 RIE: 0 CAT: 19

Canadian Public Service Commission
USE Public Service Commission of Canada

Canadian Radio Television Commission
CIJE: 1 RIE: 2 CAT: 17

Canadian Scholastic Aptitude Test
CIJE: 0 RIE: 1 CAT: 21

Canadian School Broadcasts
CIJE: 0 RIE: 1 CAT: 16

Canadian Society for the Study of Education
CIJE: 1 RIE: 1 CAT: 17

Canadian Society for the Study of Higher Education
CIJE: 0 RIE: 1 CAT: 17

Canadian Special Committee on Poverty
CIJE: 0 RIE: 1 CAT: 17

Canadian Spelling Program
CIJE: 0 RIE: 1 CAT: 19

Canadian Standard English Achievement Test
CIJE: 1 RIE: 0 CAT: 21

Canadian Supreme Court
USE Supreme Court of Canada

Canadian Teachers Federation
CIJE: 4 RIE: 2 CAT: 17

Canadian Test of English for Scholars and Trainees
CIJE: 0 RIE: 2 CAT: 21

Canadian Tests of Basic Skills
CIJE: 2 RIE: 8 CAT: 21

Canadian University Computer Network Program
CIJE: 0 RIE: 1 CAT: 19

Canadian University Services Overseas
CIJE: 4 RIE: 0 CAT: 19

Canadian University Student Information System
USE University Student Information System (Canada)

Canadian Values Inventory
CIJE: 0 RIE: 1 CAT: 21

Canadians
CIJE: 15 RIE: 13 CAT: 08

Canal Zone
CIJE: 0 RIE: 4 CAT: 07

Canals
CIJE: 1 RIE: 1 CAT: 20

CANALS (Computer Program)
CIJE: 0 RIE: 2 CAT: 04

Canarsie School District NY
CIJE: 1 RIE: 0 CAT: 17

Canary Islands
CIJE: 1 RIE: 1 CAT: 07

Canberra College of Advanced Education (Australia)
CIJE: 0 RIE: 1 CAT: 17

Canberra Institute of Technology (Australia)
CIJE: 0 RIE: 1 CAT: 17

Candid Camera
CIJE: 1 RIE: 1 CAT: 22

Candles
CIJE: 1 RIE: 1 CAT: 04

Candy Packers
CIJE: 0 RIE: 1 CAT: 09

Candy Wrapping Machine Operators
CIJE: 0 RIE: 1 CAT: 09

Canfield Lafferty Learning Styles Inventory
CIJE: 1 RIE: 3 CAT: 21

Canfield Learning Styles Inventory
CIJE: 8 RIE: 7 CAT: 21
UF Learning Styles Inventory (Canfield)

Canfield Local School District OH
CIJE: 0 RIE: 1 CAT: 17

Caning
CIJE: 0 RIE: 1 CAT: 16

Canisius College NY
CIJE: 6 RIE: 4 CAT: 17

Cannery Mechanics
CIJE: 0 RIE: 1 CAT: 09

Cannery Workers
CIJE: 0 RIE: 1 CAT: 09

Cannes International Conference on Video Commun
CIJE: 1 RIE: 0 CAT: 02

Canning
CIJE: 0 RIE: 1 CAT: 20

Cannon v University of Chicago
CIJE: 3 RIE: 0 CAT: 14

Canoeing
CIJE: 10 RIE: 16 CAT: 16

Canon Law
CIJE: 2 RIE: 4 CAT: 14

Canoncito Navajo Reservation NM
CIJE: 0 RIE: 2 CAT: 17

Canoncito Navajos
CIJE: 0 RIE: 1 CAT: 08

Canonical Redundancy Statistic
CIJE: 5 RIE: 5 CAT: 21

Canonicality Effect
CIJE: 2 RIE: 0 CAT: 11

Cant Buy Me Love (Film)
CIJE: 0 RIE: 1 CAT: 22

Cantar de Mio Cid
CIJE: 2 RIE: 0 CAT: 22

Canter Background Interference Procedure
CIJE: 4 RIE: 0 CAT: 21

Canter Model of Assertive Discipline
CIJE: 4 RIE: 1 CAT: 15

Canterbury Tales
CIJE: 4 RIE: 0 CAT: 22

Canticle for Leibowitz
CIJE: 1 RIE: 0 CAT: 22

Canto General
CIJE: 0 RIE: 1 CAT: 22

Canton (Ray)
CIJE: 1 RIE: 0 CAT: 18

Canton Galva Unified School District KS
CIJE: 0 RIE: 1 CAT: 17

Canvas
CIJE: 0 RIE: 1 CAT: 04

Canyon High School CA
CIJE: 1 RIE: 0 CAT: 17

Capacitor Winders
CIJE: 0 RIE: 1 CAT: 09

Capacitors
CIJE: 9 RIE: 1 CAT: 04

Capacity Building
CIJE: 1 RIE: 10 CAT: 16

Capacity Building for States
USE State Capacity Building Program

Capanahua
CIJE: 0 RIE: 2 CAT: 13

Cape Croker Ojibway Indian Reserve
CIJE: 1 RIE: 0 CAT: 17

Cape Fear Community College NC
CIJE: 0 RIE: 1 CAT: 17

Cape Fear Technical Institute NC
CIJE: 0 RIE: 1 CAT: 17

Cape Hatteras
CIJE: 1 RIE: 0 CAT: 07

Cape Hatteras Lighthouse
CIJE: 0 RIE: 1 CAT: 20

Cape Verde
CIJE: 0 RIE: 3 CAT: 07
UF Cape Verde Islands

Cape Verde Islands
USE Cape Verde

Cape Verdean Language
USE Capeverdean

Cape Verdeans
CIJE: 3 RIE: 6 CAT: 08

CAPERS (Aggression Rating Scale)
CIJE: 0 RIE: 1 CAT: 21

Capeverdean
CIJE: 0 RIE: 1 CAT: 13
UF Cape Verdean Language

Capilano College BC
CIJE: 0 RIE: 1 CAT: 17

Capillary Suction Time Test
CIJE: 0 RIE: 1 CAT: 21

Capital Area Career Center
CIJE: 1 RIE: 0 CAT: 17

Capital Childrens Museum DC
CIJE: 1 RIE: 0 CAT: 17

Capital City Readout
CIJE: 0 RIE: 1 CAT: 19

Capital District Humanities Program NY
CIJE: 0 RIE: 1 CAT: 19

Capital Improvements Programming
CIJE: 0 RIE: 2 CAT: 15

Capital Investment Needs
CIJE: 2 RIE: 1 CAT: 16

Capital Punishment
CIJE: 19 RIE: 6 CAT: 14
UF Death Penalty

Capitalization (Economics)
CIJE: 1 RIE: 1 CAT: 16

Capitation of Medicare
USE Medicare Capitation

Capitation Support
CIJE: 0 RIE: 2 CAT: 16

Capitol Childrens Museum DC
CIJE: 1 RIE: 0 CAT: 17

Capitol Region Library Council
CIJE: 0 RIE: 2 CAT: 17

Caplan (Gerald)
CIJE: 2 RIE: 0 CAT: 18

Capote (Truman)
CIJE: 0 RIE: 1 CAT: 18

Capp (Al)
CIJE: 1 RIE: 0 CAT: 18

CAPPS
USE Comprehensive Assessment and Program Planning

CAPSAS Computer Program
CIJE: 0 RIE: 1 CAT: 04

Capsela (Toy)
CIJE: 0 RIE: 0 CAT: 04

Capstone Courses
CIJE: 0 RIE: 1 CAT: 03

Capstone Programs
CIJE: 8 RIE: 7 CAT: 19

Capstone Survey
CIJE: 0 RIE: 1 CAT: 19

Captain Kangaroo
CIJE: 1 RIE: 1 CAT: 22

Captain Stephen Sanislo Elementary School WA
CIJE: 1 RIE: 0 CAT: 17

Captains Courageous
CIJE: 1 RIE: 0 CAT: 22

Captioned Films
CIJE: 11 RIE: 7 CAT: 04

Captioned Films Loan Service for the Deaf
CIJE: 0 RIE: 1 CAT: 17

Captioned Media
CIJE: 12 RIE: 9 CAT: 15

Captive (The)
CIJE: 0 RIE: 1 CAT: 22

Captive Voices
CIJE: 6 RIE: 1 CAT: 22

Capuchino High School CA
CIJE: 1 RIE: 0 CAT: 17

Car Ownership
CIJE: 0 RIE: 1 CAT: 16

Car Pools
CIJE: 3 RIE: 3 CAT: 16

Caravans (Michener)
CIJE: 0 RIE: 0 CAT: 22

Carbohydrate Loading
CIJE: 0 RIE: 1 CAT: 11

Carbohydrates
CIJE: 17 RIE: 8 CAT: 20

Carbon
CIJE: 2 RIE: 3 CAT: 20

Carbon Dioxide
CIJE: 21 RIE: 4 CAT: 20

Carbon Disulfide
CIJE: 1 RIE: 0 CAT: 20

Carbon Lehigh Intermediate Unit PA
CIJE: 0 RIE: 1 CAT: 17

Carbon Monoxide
CIJE: 8 RIE: 5 CAT: 20

Carbonium Ions
CIJE: 1 RIE: 0 CAT: 20

Carbonyls
CIJE: 1 RIE: 0 CAT: 20

Carboxylic Acids
CIJE: 3 RIE: 0 CAT: 20

Carburetion Systems
CIJE: 0 RIE: 0 CAT: 20

Carburetors
CIJE: 0 RIE: 9 CAT: 04

Card Games
CIJE: 9 RIE: 5 CAT: 16

Card Sort
CIJE: 6 RIE: 2 CAT: 15

Cardboard
CIJE: 1 RIE: 4 CAT: 04

Cardboard Carpentry
CIJE: 2 RIE: 1 CAT: 03

Cardenas (Victor)
CIJE: 0 RIE: 1 CAT: 18

Cardiac Care
USE Coronary Care

Cardiac Rehabilitation
CIJE: 0 RIE: 1 CAT: 11

Cardiac Wellness Training Project
CIJE: 1 RIE: 0 CAT: 19

Cardinal Numbers
CIJE: 4 RIE: 1 CAT: 20

Cardinal Principles Report
CIJE: 2 RIE: 2 CAT: 22

Cardinal Stritch College WI
CIJE: 0 RIE: 9 CAT: 17

Cardinality
CIJE: 6 RIE: 2 CAT: 20

Carding Machine Operators
CIJE: 0 RIE: 1 CAT: 09

Cardioenergetics
CIJE: 0 RIE: 1 CAT: 11

Cardiology
CIJE: 8 RIE: 4 CAT: 11

Cardiopulmonary Function Testing
CIJE: 1 RIE: 1 CAT: 11

Cardiopulmonary Technicians
CIJE: 0 RIE: 2 CAT: 09

Cardiopulmonary Technology
CIJE: 0 RIE: 1 CAT: 11

Cardiovascular Diseases
CIJE: 1 RIE: 0 CAT: 11

Cardiovascular Technology
CIJE: 0 RIE: 3 CAT: 11

Cardozo High School DC
CIJE: 1 RIE: 2 CAT: 17

CARE Boosters Network
CIJE: 0 RIE: 1 CAT: 19
SN CARE = Care And Resources for Employees and their Dependents

CARE Inc
CIJE: 0 RIE: 1 CAT: 17

CARE Linkages Project
CIJE: 0 RIE: 4 CAT: 19

Career Abilities Interests and Values Form
CIJE: 0 RIE: 1 CAT: 21

Career Academies
CIJE: 0 RIE: 5 CAT: 05

Career Accessibility Model
CIJE: 1 RIE: 1 CAT: 15

Career Achievement Skills Training Program
CIJE: 1 RIE: 6 CAT: 19

Career Adjustment and Development Inventory
CIJE: 1 RIE: 0 CAT: 21

Career Advancement through Bilingual Educ Skills
USE Project CABES

Career Advancement Voucher Demonstration Project
CIJE: 0 RIE: 1 CAT: 19

Career Alert Planning Program
CIJE: 0 RIE: 14 CAT: 19

Career Alternatives
CIJE: 4 RIE: 4 CAT: 16

Career Alternatives for Handicapped Children
CIJE: 1 RIE: 0 CAT: 19

Career Anchors
CIJE: 6 RIE: 1 CAT: 16

Career Anchors Model
CIJE: 0 RIE: 2 CAT: 15

Career and Life Planning Model
CIJE: 0 RIE: 1 CAT: 15

Career and Life Skills Project
CIJE: 0 RIE: 1 CAT: 19

Career Area Rotation Model
CIJE: 0 RIE: 1 CAT: 15

Career Assessment Instruments
CIJE: 0 RIE: 1 CAT: 21

Career Assessment Inventory
CIJE: 3 RIE: 1 CAT: 21

Career Attitude Scale
CIJE: 2 RIE: 0 CAT: 21

Career Attitude Survey
CIJE: 0 RIE: 1 CAT: 21

Career Awareness and Resource Education prog NY
USE Project CARE NY

Career Awareness Inventory
CIJE: 1 RIE: 3 CAT: 21

Career Awareness Resources for Exceptnl Stdnts NY
USE Project CARES NY

Career Awareness Secondary Elem Students Project
CIJE: 0 RIE: 1 CAT: 19

Career Barriers
CIJE: 3 RIE: 8 CAT: 16

Career Beginnings Program
CIJE: 0 RIE: 2 CAT: 19

Career Beliefs Inventory
CIJE: 1 RIE: 2 CAT: 21

Career Business Skills Program
CIJE: 1 RIE: 0 CAT: 19

Career Centers
CIJE: 9 RIE: 23 CAT: 05

Career Commitment
CIJE: 12 RIE: 6 CAT: 16

Career Concepts Inventory
CIJE: 1 RIE: 0 CAT: 21

Career Concerns Inventory
CIJE: 0 RIE: 1 CAT: 21

Career Conscious Individual Career Education Model
CIJE: 0 RIE: 6 CAT: 15

Career Construct
CIJE: 2 RIE: 2 CAT: 03

Career Data Book
CIJE: 0 RIE: 1 CAT: 22

Career Days
CIJE: 0 RIE: 0 CAT: 12
SN See also "Career Events"

Career Decision Making Self Efficacy Scale
CIJE: 2 RIE: 0 CAT: 21

Career Decision Making System (Harrington O Shea)
USE Harrington O Shea Career Decision Making System

Career Decision Scale
CIJE: 18 RIE: 1 CAT: 21

Career Decisions
CIJE: 11 RIE: 5 CAT: 16

Career Development Attitude Inventory
CIJE: 1 RIE: 1 CAT: 21

Career Development for Children Project
CIJE: 2 RIE: 3 CAT: 19

Career Development for the Handicapped Project
CIJE: 0 RIE: 1 CAT: 19

Career Development in Global Community Health
CIJE: 0 RIE: 3 CAT: 22

Career Development Inventory
CIJE: 13 RIE: 13 CAT: 21

Career Development Modules
CIJE: 0 RIE: 1 CAT: 15

Career Development Needs Survey
CIJE: 0 RIE: 1 CAT: 21

Career Development Project for Tribal Girls
CIJE: 0 RIE: 30 CAT: 19

Career Development Responsibility Scale (Thomas)
CIJE: 0 RIE: 3 CAT: 21

Career Development Study
CIJE: 1 RIE: 0 CAT: 19

Career Doors
CIJE: 0 RIE: 1 CAT: 16

Career Ed Pre Vocational Skills Assessment Inven
CIJE: 0 RIE: 1 CAT: 21

Career Education and Learning Strat Impl Model NY
USE Project CELSIM NY

Career Education Concept Inventory
CIJE: 0 RIE: 1 CAT: 21

Career Education Directors
CIJE: 0 RIE: 1 CAT: 09

Career Education Dissemination Project
CIJE: 0 RIE: 2 CAT: 19

Career Education Document Information System
CIJE: 0 RIE: 1 CAT: 15

Career Education in the Elementary School
CIJE: 5 RIE: 1 CAT: 22

Career Education Incentive Act
CIJE: 0 RIE: 9 CAT: 14

Career Education Incentive Act 1977
CIJE: 5 RIE: 8 CAT: 14

Career Education Measurement Series Survey Test
CIJE: 0 RIE: 1 CAT: 21

Career Education PLUS Program
CIJE: 0 RIE: 1 CAT: 19

Career Education Project
CIJE: 1 RIE: 7 CAT: 19

Career Education Resource Center MO
CIJE: 0 RIE: 1 CAT: 17

Career Events
CIJE: 0 RIE: 1 CAT: 12
SN See also "Career Days"

Career Expectations
CIJE: 10 RIE: 4 CAT: 16

Career Exploration Program
CIJE: 0 RIE: 3 CAT: 19

Career Exploration Work Simulation Units
CIJE: 1 RIE: 0 CAT: 03

Career Factor Checklist
CIJE: 2 RIE: 4 CAT: 21

Career Guidance IQ Test
CIJE: 0 RIE: 1 CAT: 21

Career Guidance Program
CIJE: 0 RIE: 1 CAT: 19

Career Guidance Teams
CIJE: 0 RIE: 1 CAT: 10

Career Information
CIJE: 2 RIE: 3 CAT: 16

Career Information Centers
CIJE: 8 RIE: 1 CAT: 05

Career Information Partnership (Canada)
CIJE: 0 RIE: 1 CAT: 19

Career Information Request
CIJE: 1 RIE: 1 CAT: 16

Career Information Search Survey
CIJE: 0 RIE: 1 CAT: 22

Career Infusion
CIJE: 0 RIE: 2 CAT: 16

Career Intent Score
CIJE: 0 RIE: 1 CAT: 21

Career Interest Inventory (Thomas)
CIJE: 1 RIE: 4 CAT: 21

Career Intern Program
CIJE: 3 RIE: 18 CAT: 19

Career Key (Microcomputer System)
CIJE: 0 RIE: 1 CAT: 04

Career Ladder Program TN
USE Tennessee Career Ladder Program

Career Lattice Model
CIJE: 0 RIE: 1 CAT: 15

Career Magnet Schools
CIJE: 0 RIE: 1 CAT: 05

Career Maturity Inventory (Crites)
CIJE: 32 RIE: 14 CAT: 21

Career Motivation
CIJE: 4 RIE: 3 CAT: 16

Career Motivation Process Program
CIJE: 1 RIE: 0 CAT: 21

Career Occup Develop Mini Assess (1980)
CIJE: 0 RIE: 1 CAT: 21

Career Occupational Preference System
CIJE: 3 RIE: 2 CAT: 19

Career Opportunities Potential Evaluation
CIJE: 0 RIE: 1 CAT: 21

Career Opportunities Program
CIJE: 9 RIE: 34 CAT: 19

Career Options Research and Development
CIJE: 0 RIE: 8 CAT: 15

Career Orientation Scale
CIJE: 0 RIE: 1 CAT: 21

Career Orientations Inventory
CIJE: 1 RIE: 2 CAT: 21

Career Oriented Modules Explore Topics in Science
CIJE: 0 RIE: 1 CAT: 19

Career Passports
CIJE: 1 RIE: 1 CAT: 16

Career Paths
CIJE: 31 RIE: 10 CAT: 15

Career Pathways in Energy Conservation MA
CIJE: 0 RIE: 1 CAT: 19

Career Pattern Study
CIJE: 0 RIE: 1 CAT: 19

Career Patterns
CIJE: 24 RIE: 8 CAT: 16

Career Planning Program
CIJE: 1 RIE: 6 CAT: 19

Career Planning Support System
CIJE: 0 RIE: 18 CAT: 04

Career Planning System
CIJE: 0 RIE: 3 CAT: 04

Career Plateaus
CIJE: 4 RIE: 3 CAT: 16

Career Progression Systems
CIJE: 0 RIE: 6 CAT: 15

Career Related Skills Project
CIJE: 1 RIE: 0 CAT: 19

Career Resource Centers
CIJE: 5 RIE: 11 CAT: 05

Career Salience
CIJE: 7 RIE: 3 CAT: 15

Career Salience Questionnaire
CIJE: 0 RIE: 0 CAT: 21

Career Selection Education Project
CIJE: 0 RIE: 2 CAT: 19

Career Skills Assessment Program
CIJE: 1 RIE: 3 CAT: 19

Career Stages
CIJE: 5 RIE: 1 CAT: 16

Career Survival Skills Kit
CIJE: 0 RIE: 5 CAT: 04

Career Teacher Grant Program
CIJE: 1 RIE: 0 CAT: 19

Career Technicians
CIJE: 0 RIE: 1 CAT: 09

Career Training Center CA
CIJE: 0 RIE: 1 CAT: 17

Career Unrest
CIJE: 0 RIE: 1 CAT: 16

Career Values
CIJE: 1 RIE: 1 CAT: 16

Career Vocational Student Profile Project
CIJE: 0 RIE: 1 CAT: 19

Careers Test (Behavioral Research Associates)
CIJE: 0 RIE: 1 CAT: 21

Careful Speech
CIJE: 0 RIE: 1 CAT: 13

Caregiver Attitudes
CIJE: 4 RIE: 6 CAT: 16

Caregiver Behavior
CIJE: 10 RIE: 3 CAT: 11

Caregiver Burden
CIJE: 1 RIE: 1 CAT: 11

Caregiver Burden Inventory
CIJE: 1 RIE: 0 CAT: 21

Caregiver Child Ratio
CIJE: 6 RIE: 11 CAT: 11

Caregiver Evaluation
CIJE: 0 RIE: 0 CAT: 11

Caregiver Language Observation Instrument
CIJE: 0 RIE: 1 CAT: 21

Caregiver Observation Form and Scale
CIJE: 1 RIE: 1 CAT: 21

Caregiver Qualifications
CIJE: 0 RIE: 3 CAT: 16

Caregiver Response
CIJE: 3 RIE: 1 CAT: 11
UF Caregiving Response

Caregiver Strain Index
CIJE: 1 RIE: 0 CAT: 21

Caregiver Training
CIJE: 5 RIE: 25 CAT: 16
SN Training people to work in day care centers, facilities for the elderly, etc.

Caregivers School Readiness Inventory
CIJE: 0 RIE: 1 CAT: 21

Caregiving Hassles Scale
CIJE: 1 RIE: 0 CAT: 21

Caregiving Response
USE Caregiver Response

Carelessness
CIJE: 1 RIE: 1 CAT: 16

Careys Temperament Questionnaire
CIJE: 0 RIE: 1 CAT: 21

Cargo Handling
CIJE: 0 RIE: 1 CAT: 16

Carib
CIJE: 1 RIE: 2 CAT: 13

Caribbean
CIJE: 124 RIE: 192 CAT: 07
SN The lands bordering the Caribbean Sea, i.e., Central America, the islands of the Greater and Lesser Antilles, and the northern tier of South America
UF Caribbean Basin; Caribbean Region

Caribbean Agricultural Extension Project
CIJE: 1 RIE: 5 CAT: 19

Caribbean American Scholars Project
CIJE: 1 RIE: 0 CAT: 19

Caribbean Americans
CIJE: 2 RIE: 4 CAT: 08

Caribbean Basin
USE Caribbean

Caribbean Basin Initiative
CIJE: 1 RIE: 1 CAT: 19

Caribbean Conference for Adult Education
CIJE: 1 RIE: 0 CAT: 02

Caribbean Fishery Development Institute
CIJE: 1 RIE: 0 CAT: 17

Caribbean Fishery Development Project
CIJE: 1 RIE: 0 CAT: 19

Caribbean History
CIJE: 14 RIE: 4 CAT: 12

Caribbean Information System Economic Social Plan
USE CARISPLAN

Caribbean Islanders
CIJE: 9 RIE: 8 CAT: 08

Caribbean Islands
CIJE: 28 RIE: 32 CAT: 07
SN The island chain of the Greater and the Lesser Antilles, beginning with Cuba on the north and extending to Trinidad and Tobago on the south

Caribbean Labour Administration Center
CIJE: 0 RIE: 1 CAT: 17

Caribbean Literature (English)
CIJE: 4 RIE: 4 CAT: 16

Caribbean News Agency
CIJE: 0 RIE: 1 CAT: 17

Caribbean Region
USE Caribbean

Caring
CIJE: 96 RIE: 17 CAT: 11

CARIS
CIJE: 1 RIE: 0 CAT: 04

CARISPLAN
CIJE: 0 RIE: 1 CAT: 19
UF Caribbean Information System Economic Social Plan

Carkhuff (Robert R)
CIJE: 5 RIE: 3 CAT: 18

Carkhuff Communication Discrimination Index
CIJE: 4 RIE: 1 CAT: 21

Carkhuff Empathy Scale
CIJE: 6 RIE: 4 CAT: 21

Carkhuff Training Model
CIJE: 5 RIE: 5 CAT: 15

Carl Albert State College OK
CIJE: 0 RIE: 1 CAT: 17

Carl D Perkins Loan Program
USE Perkins Loan Program

Carl D Perkins Voc and Appl Techn Educ Act 1990
CIJE: 22 RIE: 95 CAT: 14
UF Perkins Act 1990; Public Law 101 392; Vocational and Applied Technology Educ Act 1990; Vocational Education Act 1990

Carl D Perkins Vocational Education Act 1984
CIJE: 32 RIE: 191 CAT: 14
UF Perkins Act 1984; Public Law 98 524; Vocational Education Act 1984

Carl Sandburg College IL
CIJE: 1 RIE: 2 CAT: 17

Carleton Academic English Language Assessment
CIJE: 0 RIE: 1 CAT: 21

Carleton College MN
CIJE: 20 RIE: 6 CAT: 17

Carleton Project
CIJE: 1 RIE: 0 CAT: 19

Carleton University ON
CIJE: 2 RIE: 13 CAT: 17

Carlisle Area Science Advisory Committee PA
CIJE: 1 RIE: 0 CAT: 17

Carlisle Indian School SD
CIJE: 1 RIE: 1 CAT: 17

Carlisle Institute PA
CIJE: 0 RIE: 1 CAT: 17

Carlsen (Robert G)
CIJE: 2 RIE: 0 CAT: 18

Carlson (Richard O)
CIJE: 0 RIE: 0 CAT: 18

Carlson (Robert)
CIJE: 1 RIE: 0 CAT: 18

Carlson Proposal
CIJE: 0 RIE: 1 CAT: 19

Carlyle (Thomas)
CIJE: 3 RIE: 0 CAT: 18

Carmel Clay Schools IN
CIJE: 0 RIE: 1 CAT: 17

Carmer (Carl)
CIJE: 1 RIE: 0 CAT: 18

Carmichael (Stokely)
CIJE: 0 RIE: 2 CAT: 18

Carnarvon School (Canada)
CIJE: 0 RIE: 2 CAT: 17

Carnegie (Andrew)
CIJE: 7 RIE: 1 CAT: 18

Carnegie Commission on Educational Television
CIJE: 0 RIE: 1 CAT: 17

Carnegie Commission on Higher Education
CIJE: 25 RIE: 84 CAT: 17

Carnegie Commission Report
CIJE: 15 RIE: 2 CAT: 22

Carnegie Corporation
CIJE: 9 RIE: 14 CAT: 17

Carnegie Corporation of New York
CIJE: 6 RIE: 8 CAT: 17

Carnegie Council on Adolescent Development
CIJE: 4 RIE: 1 CAT: 17

Carnegie Council on Children
CIJE: 4 RIE: 0 CAT: 17

Carnegie Council on Policy Studies in Higher Educ
CIJE: 5 RIE: 3 CAT: 17

Carnegie Foundation
CIJE: 12 RIE: 4 CAT: 17

Carnegie Foundation for Advancement of Teaching
CIJE: 37 RIE: 6 CAT: 17

Carnegie Institute of Technology PA
CIJE: 0 RIE: 4 CAT: 17

Carnegie Institution of Washington
CIJE: 1 RIE: 0 CAT: 17

Carnegie Mellon University PA
CIJE: 66 RIE: 27 CAT: 17

Carnegie Mellon University Social Studies Project
CIJE: 1 RIE: 0 CAT: 19

Carnegie Museum of Art
CIJE: 1 RIE: 1 CAT: 17

Carnegie Philosophy Project
CIJE: 0 RIE: 2 CAT: 19

Carnegie Schools
CIJE: 0 RIE: 1 CAT: 05

Carnegie Test of Social Studies Inquiry Skills
CIJE: 1 RIE: 0 CAT: 21

Carnegie Unit
CIJE: 6 RIE: 2 CAT: 17

Carnivorous Plants
CIJE: 1 RIE: 1 CAT: 20

Carnot (Hippolyte)
CIJE: 1 RIE: 0 CAT: 18

Carnot (Sadi)
CIJE: 1 RIE: 0 CAT: 18

Carnot Engine
CIJE: 2 RIE: 0 CAT: 04

Caro (M A)
CIJE: 0 RIE: 1 CAT: 18
SN "Miguel Antonio"

Carolina Abecedarian Project NC
CIJE: 4 RIE: 3 CAT: 19

Carolina Institute for Research on Early Education
CIJE: 1 RIE: 1 CAT: 17

Carolina Population Center
CIJE: 1 RIE: 1 CAT: 17

Carolinas
CIJE: 1 RIE: 0 CAT: 07

Caroline County Public Library MD
CIJE: 0 RIE: 2 CAT: 17

Caroline Islands
CIJE: 1 RIE: 1 CAT: 07
SN Comprises "Palau" and "Federated States of Micronesia"

Carpal Tunnel Syndrome
CIJE: 7 RIE: 1 CAT: 11

Carpentier (Alejo)
CIJE: 5 RIE: 0 CAT: 18

Carpinteria Unified School District CA
CIJE: 0 RIE: 1 CAT: 17

Carrascolendas (Television Series)
CIJE: 5 RIE: 13 CAT: 22

Carrier (J K)
CIJE: 1 RIE: 0 CAT: 18

Carrier Current Radio
CIJE: 0 RIE: 1 CAT: 04

Carroll (John B)
CIJE: 2 RIE: 9 CAT: 18

Carroll (Lewis G)
CIJE: 6 RIE: 0 CAT: 18

Carroll College
CIJE: 1 RIE: 1 CAT: 17

Carroll Instructional Television Consortium
CIJE: 0 RIE: 1 CAT: 17

Carroll Learning Model
CIJE: 4 RIE: 5 CAT: 15

Carroll Sapon Modern Language Aptitude Test
CIJE: 0 RIE: 1 CAT: 21

Carrollton Farmers Branch Independent Sch Dist TX
CIJE: 0 RIE: 1 CAT: 17

Carrow Auditory Test of Language Comprehension
CIJE: 1 RIE: 0 CAT: 21

Carrow Elicited Language Inventory
CIJE: 6 RIE: 0 CAT: 21

Carson (Johnny)
CIJE: 1 RIE: 1 CAT: 18

Carson (Rachel)
CIJE: 2 RIE: 1 CAT: 18

Carson Indian Agency
CIJE: 0 RIE: 1 CAT: 17

Carter (Elliott)
CIJE: 1 RIE: 0 CAT: 18

Carter (Forrest)
CIJE: 0 RIE: 2 CAT: 18

Carter (Hodding Jr)
CIJE: 0 RIE: 1 CAT: 18

Carter (Jimmy)
CIJE: 31 RIE: 23 CAT: 18

Carter Administration
CIJE: 13 RIE: 15 CAT: 17

Carter Mentor Scale
CIJE: 0 RIE: 1 CAT: 21

Carter v Rand McNally Co
CIJE: 0 RIE: 0 CAT: 14

Carteret County Public Schools NC
CIJE: 0 RIE: 1 CAT: 17

Cartesian Coordinates
CIJE: 6 RIE: 3 CAT: 20

Cartesian Diver
CIJE: 7 RIE: 0 CAT: 16

Cartesian Products
CIJE: 2 RIE: 0 CAT: 20

Carthage College WI
CIJE: 0 RIE: 1 CAT: 17

Cartographic Technicians
CIJE: 0 RIE: 6 CAT: 09

Cartoon All Stars to the Rescue
CIJE: 0 RIE: 1 CAT: 22

Cartter Ratings
CIJE: 1 RIE: 0 CAT: 21

Carver Darby Chunked Reading Test
CIJE: 1 RIE: 0 CAT: 21

Carver Elementary School DC
CIJE: 0 RIE: 1 CAT: 17

Carver Junior High School
CIJE: 1 RIE: 0 CAT: 17

Casa de La Raza
CIJE: 0 RIE: 1 CAT: 17

CASA Information Management System
USE Computerized Accountability Student Achievement

Casa Loma College CA
CIJE: 1 RIE: 0 CAT: 17

Cascade System of Special Educational Services
CIJE: 1 RIE: 1 CAT: 15

Case (R)
CIJE: 0 RIE: 2 CAT: 18

Case Abstract Vignettes (Star)
USE Stars Case Abstract Vignettes

Case Analysis
CIJE: 1 RIE: 0 CAT: 15
SN Use a more specific term if possible, e.g., "Deviant Case Analysis," "Discrepant Case Analysis," "Paradigm Case Analysis"

Case Approach (Writing)
CIJE: 9 RIE: 1 CAT: 15

Case Arguments
CIJE: 0 RIE: 1 CAT: 16

Case Conferences
CIJE: 1 RIE: 1 CAT: 02

Case Coverers
CIJE: 0 RIE: 1 CAT: 09

Case Flagging
CIJE: 0 RIE: 2 CAT: 15

Case Histories
CIJE: 4 RIE: 7 CAT: 16

Case Law
CIJE: 7 RIE: 3 CAT: 14

Case Management
CIJE: 87 RIE: 82 CAT: 16

Case Method (Teaching Technique)
CIJE: 27 RIE: 33 CAT: 15

Case Processing Systems
CIJE: 0 RIE: 1 CAT: 15

Case Reading Guides
CIJE: 0 RIE: 1 CAT: 16

CASE Reporting System
CIJE: 0 RIE: 1 CAT: 19
SN CASE = Committee on Academic Science and Engineering

Case Review Systems
CIJE: 1 RIE: 2 CAT: 15

Case Studies in Science Education
CIJE: 1 RIE: 2 CAT: 22

Case Study Simulation
CIJE: 1 RIE: 2 CAT: 15

Case Survey Method
CIJE: 1 RIE: 1 CAT: 15

Case Western Reserve University OH
CIJE: 39 RIE: 13 CAT: 17

Casework Evaluation
CIJE: 1 RIE: 2 CAT: 15

Caseworker Client Relationship
CIJE: 8 RIE: 3 CAT: 11

Cash Assistance Programs
CIJE: 0 RIE: 2 CAT: 19

Cash Flow
CIJE: 11 RIE: 4 CAT: 16

Cash Transfers
CIJE: 0 RIE: 1 CAT: 16

Cashier Checker Training
CIJE: 1 RIE: 5 CAT: 03

Cashiers
CIJE: 0 RIE: 17 CAT: 09

Cashmere School District WA
CIJE: 0 RIE: 1 CAT: 17

Casinos
CIJE: 2 RIE: 1 CAT: 05

CASPAR Database
CIJE: 0 RIE: 1 CAT: 19
UF Computer Aided Science Policy And Research System

Casper College WY
CIJE: 1 RIE: 3 CAT: 17

Casper Day Care Center WY
CIJE: 0 RIE: 1 CAT: 17

Cassette Review Program
CIJE: 0 RIE: 1 CAT: 19

Cassette Sound Filmstrip Viewers
CIJE: 1 RIE: 0 CAT: 04

CASSIP
USE Computer Assisted Study Skills Improvement Program

Castaneda (Alfredo)
CIJE: 0 RIE: 1 CAT: 18

Casting Out Nines (Mathematics)
CIJE: 1 RIE: 0 CAT: 20

Casting Techniques
CIJE: 5 RIE: 6 CAT: 16

Castleberry School District TX
CIJE: 0 RIE: 1 CAT: 17

Castles
CIJE: 1 RIE: 1 CAT: 05

Castleton State College VT
CIJE: 1 RIE: 14 CAT: 17

Castro (Americo)
CIJE: 5 RIE: 0 CAT: 18

Castro (Fidel)
CIJE: 6 RIE: 4 CAT: 18

Castro (Michel del)
CIJE: 1 RIE: 0 CAT: 18

Castro v Phoenix Union High School District 210
CIJE: 0 RIE: 1 CAT: 14

Casual Dating Dissolution
CIJE: 0 RIE: 1 CAT: 15

Caswell School NC
CIJE: 0 RIE: 1 CAT: 17

Catalan
CIJE: 33 RIE: 9 CAT: 13

Catalans
CIJE: 1 RIE: 0 CAT: 08

Catalase
CIJE: 2 RIE: 0 CAT: 20

Catalina Foothills School District AZ
CIJE: 3 RIE: 0 CAT: 17

Catalog Cards
CIJE: 10 RIE: 9 CAT: 20

Catalog of Virginia Library Resources
CIJE: 0 RIE: 1 CAT: 22

Catalogers
CIJE: 15 RIE: 2 CAT: 09

Cataloging Backlogs
CIJE: 3 RIE: 2 CAT: 16

Cataloging in Publication
CIJE: 12 RIE: 6 CAT: 16

Cataloging in Source
CIJE: 6 RIE: 2 CAT: 19

Catalysis
CIJE: 12 RIE: 0 CAT: 20

Catalysts
CIJE: 25 RIE: 1 CAT: 20

Cataracts
CIJE: 5 RIE: 1 CAT: 11

Catastrophe Models
CIJE: 2 RIE: 3 CAT: 15

Catastrophe Theory
CIJE: 12 RIE: 8 CAT: 15

Catastrophic Health Care
CIJE: 3 RIE: 3 CAT: 11

Catastrophic Health Insurance
CIJE: 1 RIE: 4 CAT: 11

Catastrophic Insurance
CIJE: 1 RIE: 11 CAT: 11

Catastrophic Phenomena
CIJE: 2 RIE: 0 CAT: 20

Catawba (Tribe)
CIJE: 1 RIE: 2 CAT: 08

Catawba River
CIJE: 0 RIE: 1 CAT: 07

Catawba Valley Community College NC
CIJE: 0 RIE: 1 CAT: 17

Catawba Valley Technical Institute NC
CIJE: 1 RIE: 0 CAT: 17

Catch 22
CIJE: 3 RIE: 0 CAT: 22

Catch Me if You Can TX
USE Project CMYC TX

Catcher in the Rye
CIJE: 6 RIE: 4 CAT: 22

Catching
CIJE: 2 RIE: 2 CAT: 16

Catechesis
CIJE: 9 RIE: 1 CAT: 16

Categorical Component
CIJE: 0 RIE: 1 CAT: 21

Categorical Data
CIJE: 36 RIE: 11 CAT: 21
UF Qualitative Data (Measurement)

Categorical Perception
CIJE: 10 RIE: 5 CAT: 21

Categorical Processing (Cognition)
CIJE: 9 RIE: 1 CAT: 11

Categorical Special Education
CIJE: 6 RIE: 3 CAT: 15

Categories Test (New Nursery School)
CIJE: 0 RIE: 1 CAT: 21

Category Clustering Procedure
CIJE: 3 RIE: 2 CAT: 21

Category Knowledge
CIJE: 13 RIE: 1 CAT: 15

Category Observation Systems
CIJE: 0 RIE: 3 CAT: 15

Category Systems
CIJE: 4 RIE: 1 CAT: 21

Category Theory
CIJE: 3 RIE: 2 CAT: 15

Caterers
CIJE: 1 RIE: 6 CAT: 09

Catering
CIJE: 0 RIE: 19 CAT: 16

Caterpillar Tractor Company
CIJE: 1 RIE: 2 CAT: 17

Caterpillars
CIJE: 3 RIE: 0 CAT: 20

Catfish Farming
CIJE: 1 RIE: 3 CAT: 20

Cathedrals
CIJE: 0 RIE: 2 CAT: 05

Cather (Willa S)
CIJE: 4 RIE: 5 CAT: 18

Catherine of Siena (Saint)
CIJE: 1 RIE: 0 CAT: 18

Catheterization (Cardiac)
CIJE: 1 RIE: 1 CAT: 11

Catheterization (Urinary)
CIJE: 5 RIE: 6 CAT: 11

Cathode Ray Tubes
CIJE: 14 RIE: 17 CAT: 04

Cathodoluminescence
CIJE: 1 RIE: 0 CAT: 20

Cathodoluminescence Apparatus
CIJE: 1 RIE: 0 CAT: 04

Catholic Bishops
CIJE: 2 RIE: 4 CAT: 10

Catholic Board of Educ Diocese of Cleveland OH
CIJE: 0 RIE: 1 CAT: 17

Catholic Church
CIJE: 15 RIE: 28 CAT: 17

Catholic International Union for Social Services
CIJE: 0 RIE: 1 CAT: 17

Catholic Interracial Council
CIJE: 1 RIE: 0 CAT: 17

Catholic Library Association
CIJE: 15 RIE: 0 CAT: 17

Catholic Radio and TV Centre for Great Britain
CIJE: 1 RIE: 0 CAT: 17

Catholic Schools Week
CIJE: 1 RIE: 0 CAT: 12

Catholic Teachers Federation
CIJE: 1 RIE: 0 CAT: 17

Catholic University Nijmegen (Netherlands)
CIJE: 3 RIE: 2 CAT: 17

Catholic University of America DC
CIJE: 15 RIE: 5 CAT: 17

Catholic University of Louvain (Belgium)
CIJE: 1 RIE: 3 CAT: 17

Catholic University of Puerto Rico
CIJE: 1 RIE: 1 CAT: 17

Catholic Worker (The)
CIJE: 0 RIE: 1 CAT: 22

Catholic Worker Movement
CIJE: 0 RIE: 1 CAT: 12

Catiline
CIJE: 0 RIE: 2 CAT: 18

Catonsville Community College MD
CIJE: 2 RIE: 2 CAT: 17

Catrileo Chiguailaf de Godo (Maria)
CIJE: 0 RIE: 1 CAT: 18

Cats
CIJE: 12 RIE: 2 CAT: 20

Cats Cradle (Vonnegut)
CIJE: 0 RIE: 1 CAT: 22

Catskill Area Project in Small School Design
CIJE: 0 RIE: 7 CAT: 19

Catskill Area School Boards Institute NY
CIJE: 0 RIE: 1 CAT: 17

Catskill Area School Study Council NY
CIJE: 0 RIE: 1 CAT: 17

Catskill Saturday Seminars
USE Saturday Seminars for Able and Ambitious Students

Cattell (Raymond B)
CIJE: 15 RIE: 6 CAT: 18

Cattell Behavior Rating Scale
CIJE: 0 RIE: 1 CAT: 21

Cattell Culture Fair Intelligence Test
CIJE: 5 RIE: 8 CAT: 21

Cattell Horn Fluid and Crystallized Ability Theory
CIJE: 1 RIE: 2 CAT: 15

Cattell Infant Intelligence Scale
CIJE: 2 RIE: 9 CAT: 21

Cattells Profile Similarity Coefficient
CIJE: 0 RIE: 1 CAT: 21

Catullus
CIJE: 2 RIE: 1 CAT: 18

CATV Operators
CIJE: 0 RIE: 1 CAT: 09

Caudill Rowlett and Scott
CIJE: 0 RIE: 1 CAT: 17

Caulfield (Holden)
CIJE: 1 RIE: 0 CAT: 18

Causal Analysis
CIJE: 18 RIE: 14 CAT: 15

Causal Connectives
CIJE: 4 RIE: 4 CAT: 16

Causal Inferences
CIJE: 48 RIE: 26 CAT: 15

Causal Influences
CIJE: 18 RIE: 7 CAT: 21

Causal Reasoning
CIJE: 32 RIE: 7 CAT: 15
UF Causal Thinking

Causal Thinking
USE Causal Reasoning

Causality Approach
CIJE: 2 RIE: 3 CAT: 19

Causatives (Grammar)
CIJE: 4 RIE: 16 CAT: 13

CAUSE
CIJE: 2 RIE: 2 CAT: 17
SN Formerly "College and University Systems Exchange"

Cause Effect Relationship
CIJE: 37 RIE: 12 CAT: 16

Cause Maps
CIJE: 1 RIE: 1 CAT: 15
UF Cognitive Cause Maps

CAUSE National Conference
CIJE: 0 RIE: 42 CAT: 02

CAUSE National Database
CIJE: 2 RIE: 1 CAT: 04

Caution Index
CIJE: 0 RIE: 1 CAT: 21

Caution Index (Sato)
CIJE: 2 RIE: 4 CAT: 21

Caution Indices
CIJE: 1 RIE: 4 CAT: 21

Cautiousness
CIJE: 3 RIE: 3 CAT: 11

Cavazos (Lauro F)
CIJE: 0 RIE: 0 CAT: 18

CAVD Verbal Intelligence Test
CIJE: 0 RIE: 1 CAT: 21

Cavendish Laboratory
CIJE: 1 RIE: 0 CAT: 17

Caves
CIJE: 6 RIE: 2 CAT: 20

Cavett (Dick)
CIJE: 0 RIE: 1 CAT: 18

CAVS
USE Computer AVersion Scale

Cawdrey (Robert)
CIJE: 0 RIE: 1 CAT: 18

CAWS
USE CUNY Association of Writing Supervisors

Cayey University College PR
USE University of Puerto Rico Cayey University College

Cayuga (Tribe)
CIJE: 1 RIE: 3 CAT: 08

Cayuga County Community College NY
CIJE: 1 RIE: 1 CAT: 17

Cayuga Onondaga Assessment for Children Handicaps
CIJE: 0 RIE: 1 CAT: 21

Cayuga Onondaga Board Coop Educ Services NY
CIJE: 0 RIE: 0 CAT: 17

Cayuse (Tribe)
CIJE: 0 RIE: 1 CAT: 08

Cazenovia College NY
CIJE: 1 RIE: 2 CAT: 17

CBS Evening News
CIJE: 0 RIE: 1 CAT: 22

CBS Incorporated
CIJE: 0 RIE: 1 CAT: 17
SN See also "Columbia Broadcasting System"

CBS News
CIJE: 3 RIE: 0 CAT: 17

CBS Reports
CIJE: 0 RIE: 2 CAT: 22

CBS Television
CIJE: 11 RIE: 1 CAT: 17

CC 30 Communications Station
CIJE: 0 RIE: 1 CAT: 04

CCC Instructional System
CIJE: 0 RIE: 1 CAT: 04
SN CCC = "Computer Curriculum Corporation"

CCCC
USE Conference on Coll Composition and Communication

CCSSO State Collaborative on Assess and Studt Stan
CIJE: 0 RIE: 1 CAT: 19

CD I Technology
USE Compact Disk Interactive

CDA
CIJE: 16 RIE: 197 CAT: 19
SN Use "CDA" (minor) and "Child Development Associate" (major, if appropriate) together — "Minor" restriction does not apply to the add'l "CDA..." listings below

CDA Competency 1
CIJE: 0 RIE: 6 CAT: 21

CDA Competency 2
CIJE: 0 RIE: 12 CAT: 21

CDA Competency 3
CIJE: 0 RIE: 7 CAT: 21

CDA Competency 4
CIJE: 0 RIE: 6 CAT: 21

CDA Competency 5
CIJE: 0 RIE: 3 CAT: 21

CDA Competency 6
CIJE: 0 RIE: 3 CAT: 21

CDA Competency Standards
CIJE: 0 RIE: 1 CAT: 21

CDA Credential
CIJE: 6 RIE: 21 CAT: 16

CDA Portfolio
CIJE: 1 RIE: 4 CAT: 16

CDA Scholarship Assistance Program
CIJE: 0 RIE: 1 CAT: 19

CDDS
USE Committee for the Development of Sport

CEB Groups
USE Base Christian Communities

Cebu Normal College (Philippines)
CIJE: 0 RIE: 1 CAT: 17

Cecil Community College MD
CIJE: 0 RIE: 1 CAT: 17

Cedar Falls Community School District IA
CIJE: 0 RIE: 1 CAT: 17

Cedar Grove High School WI
CIJE: 1 RIE: 0 CAT: 17

CEDAR Project (England)
CIJE: 0 RIE: 1 CAT: 19

Cedar Rapids Community School District IA
CIJE: 4 RIE: 3 CAT: 17

Cedar Valley College TX
CIJE: 0 RIE: 3 CAT: 17

CEDARS Model
CIJE: 0 RIE: 1 CAT: 15

Cedars Sinai Medical Center CA
CIJE: 1 RIE: 0 CAT: 17

Cedarville College OH
CIJE: 0 RIE: 1 CAT: 17

CEEB
USE College Entrance Examination Board

CEEB MAPS Placement Research Service
USE MAPS Placement Research Service

CEEB MAPS Program
USE Multiple Assessment Programs and Services

CEEPS
USE Comprehensive Early Evaluation Programming System

CEGEPs
USE Colleges of General and Professional Education PQ

Ceiling Effects
CIJE: 1 RIE: 2 CAT: 21

Cela (Camilo Jose)
CIJE: 3 RIE: 0 CAT: 18

Celan (Paul)
CIJE: 1 RIE: 0 CAT: 18

Celanese Research Company
CIJE: 1 RIE: 0 CAT: 17

Celaya (Gabriel)
CIJE: 1 RIE: 0 CAT: 18

Celebrate Life Day
CIJE: 1 RIE: 0 CAT: 12

Celebrities
CIJE: 5 RIE: 5 CAT: 10

Celestial Coordinates
CIJE: 2 RIE: 0 CAT: 20

Celiac Disease
CIJE: 2 RIE: 0 CAT: 11

Cell Membranes
CIJE: 5 RIE: 0 CAT: 20

Cellerier (Guy)
CIJE: 0 RIE: 1 CAT: 18

Cells (Biology)
CIJE: 20 RIE: 7 CAT: 20

Cellular Learning Theory
CIJE: 0 RIE: 1 CAT: 15

Cellular Radio
CIJE: 2 RIE: 1 CAT: 20

Celluloid Etching
CIJE: 1 RIE: 0 CAT: 20

Celtic Languages
CIJE: 2 RIE: 2 CAT: 13

Celts
CIJE: 2 RIE: 0 CAT: 08

Cement
CIJE: 1 RIE: 10 CAT: 04

Cement Masons
CIJE: 0 RIE: 7 CAT: 09

Cement Sealers
CIJE: 0 RIE: 1 CAT: 09

Cemeteries
CIJE: 15 RIE: 10 CAT: 05

CENFAC Computer Program
CIJE: 0 RIE: 1 CAT: 04

Censure
CIJE: 22 RIE: 1 CAT: 14

Census 1790
CIJE: 0 RIE: 1 CAT: 12

Census 1960
CIJE: 0 RIE: 2 CAT: 22

Census 1970
CIJE: 3 RIE: 5 CAT: 22

Census 1980
CIJE: 14 RIE: 47 CAT: 22
UF Census of Population and Housing 1980

Census 1981 (Canada)
CIJE: 0 RIE: 1 CAT: 22
UF Canadian Census 1981

Census 1990
CIJE: 16 RIE: 28 CAT: 22

Census Access Program
CIJE: 1 RIE: 0 CAT: 19

Census Bureau
USE Bureau of the Census

Census Bureau Current Population Survey
USE Current Population Survey

Census Data System
CIJE: 1 RIE: 27 CAT: 15

Census Employment Survey
CIJE: 0 RIE: 1 CAT: 21

Census Mapping Project
CIJE: 0 RIE: 1 CAT: 19

Census Occupational Classification
CIJE: 2 RIE: 2 CAT: 15

Census of Agriculture 1982
CIJE: 0 RIE: 3 CAT: 22

Census of Population and Housing 1980
USE Census 1980

Census Takers
CIJE: 0 RIE: 3 CAT: 09

Centennial (1876)
CIJE: 1 RIE: 0 CAT: 12

Centennial Education Program
CIJE: 1 RIE: 1 CAT: 19

Centennial Exhibition of 1876
CIJE: 1 RIE: 0 CAT: 12

Centennial High School OR
CIJE: 0 RIE: 1 CAT: 17

Centennial School District CO
CIJE: 0 RIE: 0 CAT: 17

Centennial School District MN
CIJE: 0 RIE: 1 CAT: 17

Centennial School District OR
CIJE: 0 RIE: 2 CAT: 17

Center Advanced Study Educational Admin OR
CIJE: 0 RIE: 2 CAT: 17

Center Based Programs
CIJE: 1 RIE: 5 CAT: 19
SN See also "Home Based Programs" and "Field Based Programs"

Center Environmental Communication Educ Studies WI
CIJE: 0 RIE: 1 CAT: 17

Center Facilities and Resources Inventory
CIJE: 0 RIE: 1 CAT: 21

Center for Adult Research MT
USE Kellogg Center for Adult Learning Research MT

Center for Advanced Film Studies CA
CIJE: 1 RIE: 1 CAT: 17

Center for African Afro American Affairs NC
CIJE: 1 RIE: 0 CAT: 17

Center for Agricultural and Rural Development IA
CIJE: 0 RIE: 2 CAT: 17

Center for Analysis of Public Issues NY
CIJE: 0 RIE: 1 CAT: 17

Center for Applied Linguistics VA
CIJE: 6 RIE: 9 CAT: 17

Center for Applied Research in the Apostolate DC
CIJE: 1 RIE: 0 CAT: 17

Center for Assessment Administrative Performance
CIJE: 0 RIE: 2 CAT: 17

Center for California Public Affairs
CIJE: 0 RIE: 1 CAT: 17

Center for Career and Occupational Education NY
CIJE: 0 RIE: 1 CAT: 17

Center for Citizenship Education DC
CIJE: 1 RIE: 0 CAT: 17

Center for Cognitive Studies VT
CIJE: 0 RIE: 1 CAT: 17

Center for Community Justice DC
CIJE: 1 RIE: 0 CAT: 17

Center for Computer Sciences and Technology DC
CIJE: 0 RIE: 1 CAT: 17

Center for Consumer Home Economics Education CA
CIJE: 0 RIE: 1 CAT: 17

Center for Continuing Education of Women CA
CIJE: 1 RIE: 0 CAT: 17

Center for Cooperative Research with Schools PA
CIJE: 0 RIE: 2 CAT: 17

Center for Development of Non Formal Education TX
CIJE: 0 RIE: 1 CAT: 17

Center for Distance Learning NY
CIJE: 0 RIE: 1 CAT: 17

Center for Economic Education NY
CIJE: 0 RIE: 1 CAT: 17

Center for Economic Education PA
CIJE: 0 RIE: 1 CAT: 17

Center for Education Statistics
CIJE: 2 RIE: 6 CAT: 17
SN Former name of "National Center for Education Statistics"
UF Center for Statistics

Center for Educational Design FL
CIJE: 1 RIE: 1 CAT: 17

Center for Educational Policy and Management OR
CIJE: 0 RIE: 1 CAT: 17

Center for Educational Policy Research MA
CIJE: 1 RIE: 0 CAT: 17

Center for Educational Television (Philippines)
CIJE: 0 RIE: 1 CAT: 17

Center for Employment Training
CIJE: 0 RIE: 1 CAT: 17
SN A private nonprofit corporation with training centers throughout the west

Center for English Second Language Placement Test
CIJE: 0 RIE: 1 CAT: 21

Center for Environmental Intern Programs MA
CIJE: 0 RIE: 1 CAT: 17

Center for Epidemiologic Studies Depression Scale
CIJE: 10 RIE: 1 CAT: 21

Center for Excellence in Oral Communication CO
CIJE: 0 RIE: 1 CAT: 17

Center for Family Life NY
CIJE: 0 RIE: 1 CAT: 17

Center for Gerontological Studies MO
CIJE: 0 RIE: 1 CAT: 17

Center for Gifted Education VA
CIJE: 0 RIE: 1 CAT: 17

Center for Human Development
CIJE: 1 RIE: 0 CAT: 17

Center for Human Resources TX
CIJE: 0 RIE: 1 CAT: 17

Center for Improvement of Teaching and Learning
CIJE: 0 RIE: 1 CAT: 17

Center for Independent Living
CIJE: 1 RIE: 1 CAT: 17

Center for Inner City Studies IL
CIJE: 2 RIE: 0 CAT: 17

Center for Innovation in Secondary School NC
CIJE: 1 RIE: 0 CAT: 17

Center for Innovation in Teacher Education
CIJE: 1 RIE: 0 CAT: 17

Center for Instructional Communication NY
CIJE: 1 RIE: 1 CAT: 17

Center for Instructional Development
CIJE: 1 RIE: 1 CAT: 17

Center for Interactive Techn Applications Res FL
CIJE: 0 RIE: 0 CAT: 17

Center for Intercultural Information (Mexico)
CIJE: 1 RIE: 0 CAT: 17

Center for Interdisciplinary Creativity
CIJE: 1 RIE: 0 CAT: 17

Center for International Education
CIJE: 0 RIE: 1 CAT: 17

Center for International Studies NY
CIJE: 0 RIE: 6 CAT: 17

Center for Intl Programs Comparative Studies NY
CIJE: 0 RIE: 1 CAT: 17

Center for Invention and Development
CIJE: 0 RIE: 1 CAT: 17

Center for Learning Technologies NY
CIJE: 0 RIE: 2 CAT: 17
UF New York State Center for Learning Technologies

Center for Literacy PA
CIJE: 0 RIE: 1 CAT: 17

Center for New Work of Flint MI
CIJE: 0 RIE: 1 CAT: 17

Center for Occupational Education NC
CIJE: 0 RIE: 2 CAT: 17

Center for Philosophic Exchange NY
CIJE: 0 RIE: 1 CAT: 17

Center for Population and Environmental Educ NC
CIJE: 1 RIE: 0 CAT: 17

Center for Preventive Psychiatry NY
CIJE: 0 RIE: 1 CAT: 17

Center for Preventive Therapy and Rehab DC
CIJE: 1 RIE: 0 CAT: 17

Center for Psychological Stud in the Nuc Age MA
CIJE: 0 RIE: 1 CAT: 17

Center for R and D on Educational Differences MA
CIJE: 0 RIE: 1 CAT: 17

Center for Radio and Television
CIJE: 0 RIE: 1 CAT: 17

Center for Research and Devel in Higher Educ CA
CIJE: 1 RIE: 2 CAT: 17

Center for Research for Mothers and Children
CIJE: 0 RIE: 2 CAT: 17

Center for Research Libraries IL
CIJE: 11 RIE: 5 CAT: 17

Center for Research on Educ Account Teacher Eval
CIJE: 0 RIE: 1 CAT: 17
UF CREATE (Teacher Evaluation)

Center for Research on Elementary and Middle Schs
CIJE: 1 RIE: 0 CAT: 17
UF CREMS; Johns Hopkins Center for Res on Elem and Mid Schs

Center for Research on Eval Standards Stu Test CA
CIJE: 0 RIE: 6 CAT: 17
SN "Center for Research on Evaluation Standards and Student Testing"
UF CRESST CA

Center for Research on Learning and Teaching MI
CIJE: 0 RIE: 1 CAT: 17

Center for School Improvement
CIJE: 0 RIE: 1 CAT: 17

Center for Social Organization of Schools MD
CIJE: 0 RIE: 2 CAT: 17

Center for Social Work IN
CIJE: 0 RIE: 1 CAT: 17

Center for Special Education Technology VA
CIJE: 0 RIE: 1 CAT: 17

Center for Statistics
USE Center for Education Statistics

Center for Studies in Vocational and Tech Educ
CIJE: 1 RIE: 0 CAT: 17

Center for Studies of the Person CA
CIJE: 1 RIE: 0 CAT: 17

Center for Study of Educational Innovations MA
CIJE: 0 RIE: 1 CAT: 17

Center for Study of Problems of Advanced Societies
CIJE: 1 RIE: 0 CAT: 17

Center for Successful Child Development IL
CIJE: 0 RIE: 1 CAT: 17

Center for Teacher Education Evaluation TN
CIJE: 0 RIE: 1 CAT: 17

Center for Teaching and Learning ND
CIJE: 2 RIE: 0 CAT: 17

Center for Teaching International Relations CO
CIJE: 5 RIE: 1 CAT: 17

Center for the Humanities AZ
CIJE: 0 RIE: 1 CAT: 17

Center for the Learning and Teaching of Literature
CIJE: 0 RIE: 1 CAT: 17

Center for the Study of Community Colleges CA
CIJE: 5 RIE: 17 CAT: 17

Center for the Study of Democratic Institutions CA
CIJE: 1 RIE: 1 CAT: 17

Center for the Study of Evaluation CA
CIJE: 3 RIE: 18 CAT: 17
SN See add'l listings under "CSE..."

Center for the Study of Higher Education CA
CIJE: 0 RIE: 2 CAT: 17

Center for the Study of Instruction DC
CIJE: 0 RIE: 2 CAT: 17

Center for the Study of Intergroup Relations CA
CIJE: 0 RIE: 1 CAT: 17

Center for the Study of Learning IL
CIJE: 0 RIE: 1 CAT: 17

Center for the Study of Liberal Educ for Adults MA
CIJE: 1 RIE: 9 CAT: 17

Center for the Study of Public Policy MA
CIJE: 1 RIE: 0 CAT: 17

Center for the Study of Reading IL
CIJE: 1 RIE: 47 CAT: 17

Center for the Study of Sport in Society MA
CIJE: 0 RIE: 1 CAT: 17

Center for the Study of Unemployed Youth NY
CIJE: 0 RIE: 1 CAT: 17

Center for the Study of Writing
CIJE: 0 RIE: 2 CAT: 17

Center for Urban Education NY
CIJE: 3 RIE: 4 CAT: 17

Center for Urban Minority Education FL
CIJE: 0 RIE: 0 CAT: 17

Center for Urban Research in Education OR
CIJE: 0 RIE: 1 CAT: 17

Center for Vocational and Technical Education OH
CIJE: 2 RIE: 5 CAT: 17

Center for Vocational Arts CT
CIJE: 0 RIE: 3 CAT: 17

Center for Vocational Education OH
CIJE: 1 RIE: 0 CAT: 17

Center for Vocational Technical Adult Education WI
CIJE: 0 RIE: 1 CAT: 17

Center for Young Children MD
CIJE: 2 RIE: 0 CAT: 17

Center Individually Prescribed Learn Activities PA
CIJE: 0 RIE: 1 CAT: 17

Center on Effective Elementary Middle Schools
CIJE: 0 RIE: 1 CAT: 17

Center on Innovation in Education
CIJE: 0 RIE: 1 CAT: 17

Center on New York City Affairs
CIJE: 0 RIE: 1 CAT: 17

Center on Student Testing Evaluation and Standards
CIJE: 0 RIE: 1 CAT: 17
SN "R & D Center on Student Testing, Evaluation, and Standards Setting"
UF Research and Development Center on Student Testing

Center to Improve Learning and Instruction UT
CIJE: 0 RIE: 1 CAT: 17

Centering
CIJE: 3 RIE: 3 CAT: 16

Centerprise Community Publishing Project
CIJE: 1 RIE: 0 CAT: 19

Centers for Disease Control GA
CIJE: 15 RIE: 4 CAT: 17

Centers for Independent Living Program
CIJE: 0 RIE: 4 CAT: 19
SN See also "Independent Living Centers"

Centers of Excellence in English
CIJE: 1 RIE: 2 CAT: 05
UF NCTE Centers of Excellence

Centers of Pedagogy
CIJE: 0 RIE: 1 CAT: 05
SN See also the Desc "Professional Development Schools"

Centour Analysis
CIJE: 2 RIE: 0 CAT: 15

Centra (John)
CIJE: 0 RIE: 1 CAT: 18

Central African Republic
CIJE: 1 RIE: 10 CAT: 07

Central African Republic (Bossangoa)
CIJE: 0 RIE: 1 CAT: 07

Central America
CIJE: 50 RIE: 87 CAT: 07

Central American Inst for Adult Educ (Costa Rica)
CIJE: 1 RIE: 0 CAT: 17

Central American Peace Scholarship Program
CIJE: 0 RIE: 1 CAT: 19

Central Arizona College
CIJE: 0 RIE: 0 CAT: 17

Central Arizona Inservice Consortium
CIJE: 0 RIE: 1 CAT: 17

Central Baptist College AR
CIJE: 0 RIE: 1 CAT: 17

Central Carolina Technical Institute NC
CIJE: 2 RIE: 0 CAT: 17

Central Christian College OK
CIJE: 0 RIE: 1 CAT: 17

Central Cities Project
CIJE: 1 RIE: 0 CAT: 19

Central City Head Start Day Care Center NY
CIJE: 0 RIE: 1 CAT: 17

Central College KS
CIJE: 0 RIE: 1 CAT: 17

Central Columbia High School PA
CIJE: 0 RIE: 1 CAT: 17

Central Committee Members (USSR)
CIJE: 1 RIE: 0 CAT: 17

Central Community College NE
CIJE: 0 RIE: 0 CAT: 17

Central Community College NE Platte Campus
CIJE: 0 RIE: 0 CAT: 17

Central Connecticut Business School
CIJE: 1 RIE: 0 CAT: 17

Central Connecticut State College
CIJE: 3 RIE: 1 CAT: 17

Central Connecticut State University
CIJE: 1 RIE: 1 CAT: 17

Central Control Model (Typing)
CIJE: 0 RIE: 1 CAT: 15

Central Cooperative School LA
CIJE: 1 RIE: 0 CAT: 17

Central Dynamic Store
CIJE: 1 RIE: 0 CAT: 04

Central Educational Network
CIJE: 0 RIE: 1 CAT: 17

Central Florida Community College
CIJE: 1 RIE: 8 CAT: 17

Central High School of Commerce ON
CIJE: 0 RIE: 1 CAT: 17

Central High School OK
CIJE: 3 RIE: 0 CAT: 17

Central Institute of Educ Technology (India)
CIJE: 0 RIE: 1 CAT: 17

Central Institute of Educational Research (China)
CIJE: 0 RIE: 1 CAT: 17

Central Institute of the Deaf MO
CIJE: 1 RIE: 0 CAT: 17

Central Intelligence Agency
CIJE: 20 RIE: 7 CAT: 17

Central Iowa Low Achiever Mathematics Project
CIJE: 0 RIE: 8 CAT: 19

Central Libraries Automated Network NV
CIJE: 0 RIE: 0 CAT: 17
UF CLAN NV

Central Life Interests
CIJE: 3 RIE: 4 CAT: 16

Central Limit Theorem
CIJE: 11 RIE: 4 CAT: 15

Central Luzon State University (Philippines)
CIJE: 1 RIE: 0 CAT: 17

Central Maine Interactive Telecommunications Sys
CIJE: 0 RIE: 1 CAT: 04

Central Michigan University
CIJE: 23 RIE: 35 CAT: 17

Central Midwestern Regional Educational Lab MO
CIJE: 8 RIE: 7 CAT: 17

Central Minnesota Teacher Education Council
CIJE: 0 RIE: 1 CAT: 17

Central Missouri State College
CIJE: 0 RIE: 3 CAT: 17

Central Missouri State University
CIJE: 8 RIE: 13 CAT: 17

Central Nebraska Technical Foundation
CIJE: 1 RIE: 0 CAT: 17

Central New York External High Sch Diploma Program
CIJE: 0 RIE: 1 CAT: 19

Central New York Library Resources Council
CIJE: 0 RIE: 1 CAT: 17

Central Office Administrator Relationship
CIJE: 6 RIE: 1 CAT: 16

Central Office Administrators
CIJE: 27 RIE: 11 CAT: 09

Central Office Repairers
CIJE: 0 RIE: 1 CAT: 09

Central Oregon Community College
CIJE: 1 RIE: 3 CAT: 17

Central Peel Secondary School (Canada)
CIJE: 0 RIE: 1 CAT: 17

Central Piedmont Community College NC
CIJE: 8 RIE: 7 CAT: 17

Central Place Theory
CIJE: 3 RIE: 1 CAT: 15

Central Prediction System
CIJE: 0 RIE: 2 CAT: 21

Central Processing Strategies (Cognition)
CIJE: 1 RIE: 1 CAT: 11

Central Processing Units
CIJE: 1 RIE: 2 CAT: 04

Central Radio and Television University (China)
USE Radio and Television Universities (China)

Central Registries of Child Abuse
USE Child Abuse Registries

Central Research Fund
CIJE: 0 RIE: 1 CAT: 16

Central State Colleges and Universities Seminar
CIJE: 0 RIE: 1 CAT: 02

Central State University OH
CIJE: 3 RIE: 10 CAT: 17

Central State University OK
CIJE: 0 RIE: 3 CAT: 17

Central States College Association
CIJE: 0 RIE: 1 CAT: 17

Central States Conference Teaching Foreign Lang
CIJE: 1 RIE: 0 CAT: 17

Central States Speech Association
CIJE: 2 RIE: 4 CAT: 17

Central Texas College
CIJE: 0 RIE: 2 CAT: 17

Central Texas Medical Foundation
CIJE: 1 RIE: 0 CAT: 17

Central Treaty Organization (Turkey)
CIJE: 0 RIE: 1 CAT: 17

Central Valley Microwave Network CA
CIJE: 0 RIE: 2 CAT: 17

Central Virginia Community College
CIJE: 1 RIE: 0 CAT: 17

Central Washington State College
CIJE: 1 RIE: 6 CAT: 17

Central Washington University
CIJE: 4 RIE: 11 CAT: 17

Central YMCA Community College IL
CIJE: 1 RIE: 7 CAT: 17

Centralia College WA
CIJE: 0 RIE: 2 CAT: 17

Centralized Correspondence Studies Program AK
CIJE: 1 RIE: 0 CAT: 19

Centralized Correspondence Study AK
CIJE: 1 RIE: 1 CAT: 22

Centralized Processing
CIJE: 5 RIE: 7 CAT: 16

Centration
CIJE: 3 RIE: 2 CAT: 11

Centre College KY
CIJE: 4 RIE: 1 CAT: 17

Centre d Initiation au Cinema
CIJE: 1 RIE: 0 CAT: 17

Centre for Applied Research in Ed (Great Britain)
CIJE: 1 RIE: 0 CAT: 17

Centre for Contemporary Cultural Studies (England)
CIJE: 0 RIE: 0 CAT: 17

Centre for Continuing Education (Australia)
CIJE: 1 RIE: 0 CAT: 17

Centre for Cultural Resources (India)
CIJE: 0 RIE: 1 CAT: 17

Centre for Curriculum Renewal Educ Devel (England)
CIJE: 1 RIE: 0 CAT: 17

Centre for Educ Research and Innovation (France)
CIJE: 2 RIE: 11 CAT: 17

Centre for Educational Devel Overseas (England)
CIJE: 5 RIE: 1 CAT: 17

Centre for Educational TV Overseas (England)
CIJE: 4 RIE: 2 CAT: 17

Centre for Gifted Education AB
CIJE: 0 RIE: 1 CAT: 17

Centre for Learning and Development (Canada)
CIJE: 0 RIE: 1 CAT: 17

Centre for Principal Development ON
CIJE: 0 RIE: 1 CAT: 17
SN ...at the Ontario Inst for Studies in Educ

Centre for Science Education (England)
CIJE: 1 RIE: 0 CAT: 17

Centre for Short Lived Phenomena
CIJE: 1 RIE: 0 CAT: 17

Centre for Television Research (England)
CIJE: 1 RIE: 0 CAT: 17

Centre of Entrepreneurship for the Northwest
CIJE: 0 RIE: 1 CAT: 17

Centre Universitaire de Coop Econ Soc (France)
CIJE: 0 RIE: 2 CAT: 17

Centres of Excellence
CIJE: 0 RIE: 1 CAT: 05

Centrifugal Analyzers
CIJE: 1 RIE: 0 CAT: 04

Centrifugal Force
CIJE: 4 RIE: 0 CAT: 20

Centrifuge Test
CIJE: 0 RIE: 1 CAT: 20

Centrifuges
CIJE: 1 RIE: 1 CAT: 04

Centripetal Force
CIJE: 5 RIE: 0 CAT: 20

Centro de Altos Estudios Militares
CIJE: 1 RIE: 0 CAT: 17

Centro di Telescuola
CIJE: 0 RIE: 1 CAT: 17

Centro Interamericano Libros Academicos (Mexico)
CIJE: 0 RIE: 1 CAT: 17

Centro Intercultural de Documentacion (Mexico)
CIJE: 3 RIE: 1 CAT: 17

Centroversion
CIJE: 1 RIE: 0 CAT: 16

Century 21 Shorthand
CIJE: 2 RIE: 9 CAT: 03

Century Magazine
CIJE: 0 RIE: 1 CAT: 22

Ceramic Tile
CIJE: 0 RIE: 1 CAT: 04

Cereal Boxes
CIJE: 2 RIE: 0 CAT: 16

Cereal Packers
CIJE: 0 RIE: 1 CAT: 09

Cereals
CIJE: 3 RIE: 0 CAT: 16
UF Breakfast Cereals

Cerebral Sensory Interaction
CIJE: 0 RIE: 3 CAT: 11

Cerebrovascular Disorders
CIJE: 8 RIE: 5 CAT: 11
UF Stroke (Disease)

Ceremonies
CIJE: 33 RIE: 20 CAT: 12
SN See also "Rites"

Ceremony (Title)
CIJE: 13 RIE: 0 CAT: 22

Cerenkov Radiation
CIJE: 2 RIE: 0 CAT: 20

Ceres Unified School District CA
CIJE: 0 RIE: 2 CAT: 17

CERLI Verbal Behavior Classification System
CIJE: 2 RIE: 3 CAT: 15

Cerritos College CA
CIJE: 1 RIE: 20 CAT: 17

Cerro Coso Community College CA
CIJE: 2 RIE: 0 CAT: 17

Certainty of Response Rating Technique
CIJE: 1 RIE: 1 CAT: 21

Certificate in Computer Programming
CIJE: 0 RIE: 1 CAT: 03

Certificate in Data Education
CIJE: 1 RIE: 0 CAT: 16

Certificate in Data Processing
CIJE: 0 RIE: 1 CAT: 03

Certificate in German as a Foreign Language
USE Zertifikat Deutsch als Fremdsprache

Certificate in Literacy and Learning
CIJE: 0 RIE: 1 CAT: 16
SN Developed by the Manitoba Literacy Office for adult education students

Certificate of Clinical Competence
CIJE: 1 RIE: 0 CAT: 16

Certificate of Initial Mastery
CIJE: 0 RIE: 1 CAT: 21

Certificate of Need
CIJE: 0 RIE: 2 CAT: 14

Certificate of Pre Vocational Education
CIJE: 0 RIE: 2 CAT: 16

Certificate of Secondary Education
CIJE: 17 RIE: 1 CAT: 16

Certificate Renewal
CIJE: 0 RIE: 3 CAT: 16
SN See also "License Renewal"

Certificated Employee Council
CIJE: 0 RIE: 1 CAT: 17

Certificated Personnel Perf Eval Act (Colorado)
CIJE: 0 RIE: 1 CAT: 14

Certificates in Communicative Skills in English
CIJE: 0 RIE: 1 CAT: 21

Certified Financial Planner Prof Educ Prog
CIJE: 0 RIE: 1 CAT: 19

Certified Financial Planners
CIJE: 0 RIE: 2 CAT: 09
UF Financial Planners (Certified)

Certified Mail
CIJE: 0 RIE: 1 CAT: 16
SN See also "First Class Mail"

Certified Products Seal
CIJE: 1 RIE: 0 CAT: 16

Certified Professional Secretaries
CIJE: 1 RIE: 0 CAT: 09

Certified Professional Secretary Examination
CIJE: 4 RIE: 4 CAT: 21

Certified Staff
CIJE: 0 RIE: 5 CAT: 09

Certified Trainer Systems
CIJE: 0 RIE: 2 CAT: 15

Cervantes (Lorna Dee)
CIJE: 0 RIE: 1 CAT: 18

Cervantes Saavedra (Miguel de)
CIJE: 22 RIE: 2 CAT: 18

Cervical Disease
CIJE: 3 RIE: 1 CAT: 11

Cesaire (Aime)
CIJE: 1 RIE: 1 CAT: 18

Cesium
CIJE: 2 RIE: 0 CAT: 20

Cessna Aviation Study
CIJE: 1 RIE: 0 CAT: 19

CETA
USE Comprehensive Employment and Training Act

CETA Youth Employment Program
CIJE: 4 RIE: 4 CAT: 19

Ceylon
CIJE: 15 RIE: 23 CAT: 07

Ceylon (Colombo)
CIJE: 2 RIE: 0 CAT: 07

CFK Ltd School Climate Profile (Fox et al)
CIJE: 1 RIE: 3 CAT: 21
UF Charles F Kettering School Climate Profile; Kettering School Climate Instrument

Chabacano (Cotabato)
USE Cotabato Chabacano

Chabacano (Zamboanga City)
USE Zamboangueno

Chabot College CA
CIJE: 1 RIE: 11 CAT: 17

Chabot Observatory CA
CIJE: 0 RIE: 1 CAT: 17

Chacobo
CIJE: 0 RIE: 1 CAT: 13

Chad
CIJE: 4 RIE: 11 CAT: 07

Chado Hamitic
CIJE: 0 RIE: 1 CAT: 13

Chadron State College NE
CIJE: 0 RIE: 5 CAT: 17

Chadwick (H A)
CIJE: 0 RIE: 1 CAT: 18

Chafe (Wallace)
CIJE: 1 RIE: 1 CAT: 18

Chaffey Community College CA
CIJE: 1 RIE: 1 CAT: 17

Chaga
CIJE: 0 RIE: 1 CAT: 13

Chaggas
CIJE: 1 RIE: 0 CAT: 08

Chahta Enterprise MS
CIJE: 0 RIE: 1 CAT: 17

Chain Indexing
CIJE: 2 RIE: 0 CAT: 15

Chain Reaction Forum (Technique)
CIJE: 0 RIE: 1 CAT: 15

Chain Saws
CIJE: 0 RIE: 1 CAT: 04

Chained Equipercentile Equating
CIJE: 0 RIE: 1 CAT: 21

Chains (Mechanics)
CIJE: 0 RIE: 3 CAT: 04

Chait (Richard)
CIJE: 0 RIE: 1 CAT: 18

Chaldean Americans
CIJE: 1 RIE: 1 CAT: 08

Chaldeans
CIJE: 0 RIE: 2 CAT: 08

Chalit
CIJE: 0 RIE: 1 CAT: 13

Chall (Jeanne)
CIJE: 7 RIE: 1 CAT: 18

Challe (Robert)
CIJE: 1 RIE: 0 CAT: 18

Challenge
CIJE: 1 RIE: 3 CAT: 16

Challenge Coaching
CIJE: 0 RIE: 0 CAT: 15

Challenge Courses (Outdoor Activities)
CIJE: 0 RIE: 0 CAT: 16

Challenge Examinations
CIJE: 2 RIE: 1 CAT: 21

Challenge for Change Societe Nouvelle (Canada)
CIJE: 1 RIE: 2 CAT: 17

Challenge Grants
CIJE: 1 RIE: 6 CAT: 16

Challenge of Peace (Bishops Pastoral Letter)
CIJE: 4 RIE: 0 CAT: 22

Challenge of the Unknown (Film)
CIJE: 0 RIE: 1 CAT: 22

Challenge Squared Program GA
CIJE: 0 RIE: 1 CAT: 19

Challenger Disaster
CIJE: 26 RIE: 6 CAT: 12
UF Space Shuttle Challenger Disaster

Challenging Options in Career Education
USE CHOICE (Career Education Curriculum)

Challenging Situations Task
CIJE: 0 RIE: 1 CAT: 21

Chalmers University of Technology (Sweden)
CIJE: 2 RIE: 3 CAT: 17

Chama Valley School District NM
CIJE: 0 RIE: 1 CAT: 17

Chamber Music
CIJE: 3 RIE: 0 CAT: 16

Chamber of Commerce and Industry of Paris (France)
CIJE: 0 RIE: 1 CAT: 17
UF Paris Chamber of Commerce and Industry (France)

Chamber of Commerce of the United States
CIJE: 1 RIE: 8 CAT: 17

Chamber Theater
CIJE: 3 RIE: 1 CAT: 17

Chambers (M M)
CIJE: 1 RIE: 3 CAT: 18

Chambers (Whittaker)
CIJE: 0 RIE: 1 CAT: 18

Chambers Elementary School OH
CIJE: 1 RIE: 0 CAT: 17

Chambers of Commerce
CIJE: 7 RIE: 13 CAT: 05

Chamicuro
CIJE: 0 RIE: 2 CAT: 13
SN An Arawakan language

Chamorro Materials Project
CIJE: 0 RIE: 30 CAT: 19

Chamorros
CIJE: 0 RIE: 3 CAT: 08

Champaign Community Schools IL
CIJE: 0 RIE: 2 CAT: 17

Champaign Public Library IL
CIJE: 1 RIE: 2 CAT: 17

Champlain (Samuel de)
CIJE: 1 RIE: 0 CAT: 18

Champlain Regional College PQ
CIJE: 0 RIE: 2 CAT: 17

CHAMPUS Program
CIJE: 0 RIE: 3 CAT: 17

Chana High School CA
CIJE: 0 RIE: 1 CAT: 17

Chance Level Scores
CIJE: 2 RIE: 1 CAT: 21

Chance Program
CIJE: 0 RIE: 1 CAT: 19

Chance v Board of Examiners
CIJE: 0 RIE: 2 CAT: 14

Chandler High School AZ
CIJE: 0 RIE: 1 CAT: 17

Chandler Mathis Attitude Inventory
CIJE: 0 RIE: 1 CAT: 21

Chandler Score System
CIJE: 1 RIE: 0 CAT: 20

Chandler v Florida
CIJE: 2 RIE: 2 CAT: 14

Chandrasekhar (Subrahmanyan)
CIJE: 1 RIE: 0 CAT: 18

Change Analysis
CIJE: 36 RIE: 20 CAT: 15

Change Facilitator Stages of Concern Questionnaire
CIJE: 0 RIE: 1 CAT: 21

Change Facilitator Style Questionnaire
CIJE: 0 RIE: 3 CAT: 21

Change Facilitators
USE Facilitators

Change Framework Instrument
CIJE: 0 RIE: 1 CAT: 21

Change in Liberal Education Project
CIJE: 0 RIE: 2 CAT: 19

Change Models (Havelock)
CIJE: 1 RIE: 2 CAT: 15

Change Perspectives
CIJE: 5 RIE: 2 CAT: 15

Change Ranking Questionnaire
CIJE: 0 RIE: 1 CAT: 21

Change Scores
CIJE: 16 RIE: 9 CAT: 21

Changing Criterion Design
CIJE: 2 RIE: 0 CAT: 15

Changing Face of the Soviet Union
CIJE: 1 RIE: 0 CAT: 22

Changing Old World
CIJE: 1 RIE: 0 CAT: 22

Changing Politics of Education (The)
CIJE: 0 RIE: 0 CAT: 22

Changing Teacher Practice Study
CIJE: 2 RIE: 3 CAT: 19

Channel 2000
CIJE: 2 RIE: 1 CAT: 04

Channel Capacity
CIJE: 0 RIE: 3 CAT: 20

Channel One
CIJE: 17 RIE: 24 CAT: 19

Channel Switching
CIJE: 0 RIE: 1 CAT: 20

Channel Variation
CIJE: 0 RIE: 1 CAT: 20

Chansonniers
CIJE: 1 RIE: 0 CAT: 16

Chanties
CIJE: 0 RIE: 1 CAT: 16

Chaos
CIJE: 14 RIE: 2 CAT: 16

Chaos Theory
CIJE: 38 RIE: 11 CAT: 15

Chapel Hill Alphanumeric Terminal
CIJE: 0 RIE: 1 CAT: 04

Chapel Hill City Schools NC
CIJE: 1 RIE: 1 CAT: 17

Chapel Island Indian Reserve NS
CIJE: 0 RIE: 0 CAT: 17

Chaplin (Charlie)
CIJE: 6 RIE: 1 CAT: 18

Chapman College CA
CIJE: 6 RIE: 2 CAT: 17

Chapman v Rhodes
CIJE: 0 RIE: 1 CAT: 14

Chapparal High School KS
CIJE: 1 RIE: 0 CAT: 17

Chapple Interaction Chronograph
CIJE: 0 RIE: 1 CAT: 04

Chapter 1 ECIA
USE Education Consolidation Improvement Act Chapter 1

Chapter 2 ECIA
USE Education Consolidation Improvement Act Chapter 2

Chapter 5 (Pennsylvania)
CIJE: 0 RIE: 1 CAT: 14

Chapter 53 (New York)
CIJE: 0 RIE: 1 CAT: 14

Chapter 74 (Massachusetts)
CIJE: 0 RIE: 1 CAT: 14

Chapter 97 (New Jersey)
CIJE: 0 RIE: 1 CAT: 14

Chapter 188 (Massachusetts)
CIJE: 0 RIE: 3 CAT: 14
UF Massachusetts Public School Improvement Act 1985

Chapter 241 (New Jersey)
USE High School Graduation Requirements Law (NJ)

Chapter 622 (Massachusetts)
CIJE: 0 RIE: 1 CAT: 14

Chapter 636 (Massachusetts)
CIJE: 1 RIE: 1 CAT: 14

Chapter 688 (Massachusetts)
CIJE: 0 RIE: 2 CAT: 14

Chapter 720 (New York)
CIJE: 0 RIE: 1 CAT: 14

Chapter 766 (Massachusetts)
CIJE: 2 RIE: 7 CAT: 14

Char (Rene)
CIJE: 1 RIE: 0 CAT: 18

Char Workers
CIJE: 0 RIE: 1 CAT: 09

Character Codes
CIJE: 2 RIE: 1 CAT: 04

Character Constancy
CIJE: 1 RIE: 0 CAT: 11

Character Development
CIJE: 0 RIE: 1 CAT: 11

Character Education
CIJE: 59 RIE: 13 CAT: 03
SN See also "Integrated Character Education"

Character Education Inquiry (Hartshorne and May)
CIJE: 0 RIE: 0 CAT: 22

Character Education Program
CIJE: 0 RIE: 2 CAT: 19

Character Encoding
CIJE: 1 RIE: 1 CAT: 20

Character Research Project
CIJE: 6 RIE: 0 CAT: 19

Character String Handling
CIJE: 2 RIE: 1 CAT: 13

Charades
CIJE: 0 RIE: 1 CAT: 16

Charcoal
CIJE: 1 RIE: 2 CAT: 20

Charettes
USE Charrettes

Charge Back Systems
CIJE: 4 RIE: 0 CAT: 15

Charisma
CIJE: 14 RIE: 14 CAT: 16

Charisma Potential Scale
CIJE: 0 RIE: 1 CAT: 21

Charitable Contributions
CIJE: 22 RIE: 5 CAT: 16

Charitable Organizations
CIJE: 1 RIE: 1 CAT: 16

Charitable Remainder Trusts
CIJE: 1 RIE: 1 CAT: 10

Charity Schools (England)
CIJE: 2 RIE: 0 CAT: 17

Charles Coffin Collection
CIJE: 0 RIE: 1 CAT: 16

Charles County Community College MD
CIJE: 0 RIE: 6 CAT: 17

Charles County Public Schools MD
CIJE: 0 RIE: 2 CAT: 17

Charles F Kettering Foundation
USE Kettering Foundation

Charles F Kettering School Climate Profile
USE CFK Ltd School Climate Profile (Fox et al)

Charles Law
CIJE: 4 RIE: 1 CAT: 20

Charles River School MA
CIJE: 0 RIE: 1 CAT: 17

Charles Stewart Mott Community College MI
CIJE: 1 RIE: 2 CAT: 17

Charles W Hunt Lecture 10th
CIJE: 1 RIE: 0 CAT: 02

Charleston County School District SC
CIJE: 3 RIE: 16 CAT: 17

Charleston Job Corps Center
CIJE: 1 RIE: 0 CAT: 17

Charlie Brown
CIJE: 1 RIE: 0 CAT: 22

Charlotte Florence Crittenden Home NC
CIJE: 0 RIE: 1 CAT: 17

Charlotte Mecklenburg Career Development Program
CIJE: 2 RIE: 0 CAT: 19

Charlotte Mecklenburg Public Schools NC
CIJE: 10 RIE: 12 CAT: 17

Charlottes Web
CIJE: 4 RIE: 2 CAT: 22

Charlottesville City School District VA
CIJE: 0 RIE: 1 CAT: 17

Charquin Program CA
CIJE: 0 RIE: 1 CAT: 19

Charrettes
CIJE: 3 RIE: 10 CAT: 16
UF Charettes

Chart Essays
CIJE: 0 RIE: 1 CAT: 16

Chart Method
CIJE: 0 RIE: 1 CAT: 15

Charter of the French Language (Quebec)
CIJE: 0 RIE: 1 CAT: 14
UF Bill 101 (Quebec)

Charter Schools
CIJE: 8 RIE: 14 CAT: 05
SN Independent public schools established by groups of licensed teachers under contract with local school boards, and given broad freedom from regulations in exchange for such favorable "outcomes" as improved test scores, attendance rates, dropout rates, and the like
UF Teacher Initiated Schools

Chartering Process
CIJE: 3 RIE: 5 CAT: 15

Charting
CIJE: 0 RIE: 2 CAT: 15
SN Use a more specific term if possible, e.g., "Course Charting," "Dental Charting," "Self Charting"

Chartoons
CIJE: 0 RIE: 1 CAT: 16
SN Cartoon-like informational graphics

Chase (Stuart)
CIJE: 1 RIE: 0 CAT: 18

Chase Manhattan Bank NY
CIJE: 0 RIE: 1 CAT: 17

Chase Outdoor Education Inventory
CIJE: 0 RIE: 1 CAT: 21

Chatham College PA
CIJE: 3 RIE: 1 CAT: 17

Chatsworth Avenue School NY
CIJE: 1 RIE: 0 CAT: 17

Chattanooga Hamilton County Speech Hearing Ctr TN
CIJE: 1 RIE: 0 CAT: 17

Chattanooga Public Schools TN
CIJE: 0 RIE: 4 CAT: 17

Chattanooga State Technical Community College TN
CIJE: 0 RIE: 4 CAT: 17

Chaucer (Geoffrey)
CIJE: 12 RIE: 6 CAT: 18

Chautauquas
CIJE: 16 RIE: 7 CAT: 02

Chavez (Cesar)
CIJE: 1 RIE: 2 CAT: 18

Cheaper by the Dozen
CIJE: 0 RIE: 1 CAT: 22

Chebychev Estimation
CIJE: 1 RIE: 0 CAT: 21

Cheche Konnen
CIJE: 0 RIE: 4 CAT: 19
SN Cheche Konnen = "Search for Knowledge" in Haitian Creole

Check List Desirable Characteristics Mail Surveys
CIJE: 0 RIE: 1 CAT: 21
UF Check List of Desirable Characteristics Mail Surv

Check List of Desirable Characteristics Mail Surv
USE Check List Desirable Characteristics Mail Surveys

Check Technique
CIJE: 0 RIE: 2 CAT: 15

Checkers (Occupation)
CIJE: 0 RIE: 4 CAT: 09

Checking (Mathematics)
CIJE: 1 RIE: 0 CAT: 20

Checking Accounts
CIJE: 3 RIE: 9 CAT: 16

Checklist Comprehensive Assess Instruct Scholar
CIJE: 0 RIE: 1 CAT: 21

Checklist for Assessment of Science Teachers
CIJE: 1 RIE: 0 CAT: 21

Checklist for Faculty Self Evaluation
CIJE: 0 RIE: 1 CAT: 21

Checklist for Parents of Preadolescent Children
CIJE: 0 RIE: 1 CAT: 21

Checklist of Academic Problems
CIJE: 0 RIE: 1 CAT: 21

Checklist of High School Class Activities (Scott)
CIJE: 0 RIE: 1 CAT: 21

Checklist of Instructional Characteristics
CIJE: 1 RIE: 1 CAT: 21

Checotah High School OK
CIJE: 1 RIE: 0 CAT: 17

Cheerleading
CIJE: 7 RIE: 2 CAT: 16

Cheers (Television Series)
CIJE: 0 RIE: 1 CAT: 22

Cheese Wrappers and Packers
CIJE: 0 RIE: 1 CAT: 09

Chekhov (Anton Pavlovich)
CIJE: 5 RIE: 2 CAT: 18

Chelated Calcium
CIJE: 1 RIE: 0 CAT: 20

Chelmsford Project
CIJE: 1 RIE: 0 CAT: 19

Chelmsford School System MA
CIJE: 0 RIE: 1 CAT: 17

Chelsea College of Science and Tech (England)
CIJE: 1 RIE: 0 CAT: 17

Chelsea Polytechnic (England)
CIJE: 1 RIE: 0 CAT: 17

Chelsea Public Schools MA
USE Chelsea School System MA

Chelsea School System MA
CIJE: 2 RIE: 3 CAT: 17
UF Chelsea Public Schools MA

CHEM Study
CIJE: 19 RIE: 9 CAT: 19

ChemCom
CIJE: 1 RIE: 2 CAT: 03
UF Chemistry in the Community

Chemehuevi (Tribe)
CIJE: 0 RIE: 3 CAT: 08

Chemeketa Community College OR
CIJE: 0 RIE: 7 CAT: 17

Chemical Abstracts
CIJE: 16 RIE: 7 CAT: 22

Chemical Abstracts Condensates
CIJE: 7 RIE: 2 CAT: 22

Chemical Abstracts Service
CIJE: 20 RIE: 7 CAT: 17

Chemical Addictions Prevention in Schools
CIJE: 1 RIE: 0 CAT: 19

Chemical Bond Approach
CIJE: 7 RIE: 17 CAT: 19

Chemical Calculations
CIJE: 2 RIE: 2 CAT: 20

Chemical Compounds
CIJE: 3 RIE: 1 CAT: 20

Chemical Data Processing
CIJE: 1 RIE: 0 CAT: 20

Chemical Education Materials Study
CIJE: 11 RIE: 20 CAT: 19

Chemical Educational Material Study Institutes
CIJE: 0 RIE: 1 CAT: 17

Chemical Elements
CIJE: 10 RIE: 1 CAT: 20

Chemical Energy
CIJE: 1 RIE: 2 CAT: 20

Chemical Operators
CIJE: 0 RIE: 1 CAT: 09

Chemical Process Control
CIJE: 1 RIE: 0 CAT: 20

Chemical Propulsion Information Agency
CIJE: 0 RIE: 1 CAT: 17

Chemical Registry System
CIJE: 1 RIE: 1 CAT: 16

Chemical Structure
CIJE: 14 RIE: 2 CAT: 20

Chemical Technician Curriculum Project
CIJE: 2 RIE: 5 CAT: 19

Chemical Technology
CIJE: 0 RIE: 2 CAT: 20

Chemical Titles
CIJE: 3 RIE: 0 CAT: 16

Chemical Warfare
CIJE: 2 RIE: 0 CAT: 20

Chemical Weapons
CIJE: 3 RIE: 2 CAT: 20

Chemicals
CIJE: 25 RIE: 15 CAT: 20

Chemiluminescence
CIJE: 3 RIE: 0 CAT: 20

Chemistry Between Atoms
CIJE: 1 RIE: 0 CAT: 03

Chemistry in the Community
USE ChemCom

Chemistry Modules
CIJE: 1 RIE: 0 CAT: 20

Chemists
CIJE: 8 RIE: 4 CAT: 09

Chemometrics
CIJE: 5 RIE: 0 CAT: 20

Chen (Theodore)
CIJE: 0 RIE: 1 CAT: 18

Chenowith School District OR
CIJE: 0 RIE: 1 CAT: 17

Chepang
CIJE: 0 RIE: 3 CAT: 13

Chernobyl Disaster
CIJE: 8 RIE: 3 CAT: 12

Cherokee Bilingual Education Program
CIJE: 1 RIE: 1 CAT: 19

Cherokee Nation
CIJE: 42 RIE: 21 CAT: 07
SN Cherokee homelands, including ancestral lands in the southern Alleghenies as well as areas of present-day Oklahoma and North Carolina (Note: Use the Descriptors "Cherokee" and "Cherokee (Tribe)" respectively for the language and the people)

Cherokee Nation Youth Leadership Program
CIJE: 0 RIE: 1 CAT: 19

Cherology
CIJE: 0 RIE: 1 CAT: 13

Cherry Creek School District CO
CIJE: 7 RIE: 3 CAT: 17

Cherry Creek Schools CO
CIJE: 2 RIE: 7 CAT: 17

Cherwitz (Richard A)
CIJE: 0 RIE: 1 CAT: 18

Chesapeake Bay
CIJE: 2 RIE: 8 CAT: 07

Chesapeake Bay Center for Environmental Studies MD
CIJE: 1 RIE: 0 CAT: 17

Chesapeake Bay Institute MD
CIJE: 1 RIE: 0 CAT: 17

Chesapeake College MD
CIJE: 3 RIE: 3 CAT: 17

Chess
CIJE: 11 RIE: 7 CAT: 16

Chess v Widmar
USE Florian Frederick Chess v Gary E Widmar

Chest X Rays
CIJE: 1 RIE: 0 CAT: 11

Chesterfield County Public Schools VA
CIJE: 0 RIE: 1 CAT: 17

Chesterfield County School District SC
CIJE: 0 RIE: 1 CAT: 17

Chesterton (G K)
CIJE: 1 RIE: 0 CAT: 18

Chevak Village Youth Association AK
CIJE: 0 RIE: 1 CAT: 17

Chevrolet Car Company
CIJE: 0 RIE: 1 CAT: 17

Chevy Chase Country Day School DC
CIJE: 1 RIE: 0 CAT: 17

Chewing Behavior
CIJE: 1 RIE: 0 CAT: 11

Chewing Tobacco
CIJE: 4 RIE: 3 CAT: 11

Cheyenne (Tribe)
CIJE: 10 RIE: 15 CAT: 08

Cheyenne River Community College SD
CIJE: 0 RIE: 1 CAT: 17

Cheyenne River Sioux Reservation SD
CIJE: 0 RIE: 1 CAT: 17

Cheyney State College PA
CIJE: 1 RIE: 0 CAT: 17

Cheyney University PA
CIJE: 0 RIE: 1 CAT: 17

Chi Corporation
CIJE: 1 RIE: 0 CAT: 17

Chi Research NJ
CIJE: 1 RIE: 0 CAT: 17

Chiang Mai University (Thailand)
CIJE: 1 RIE: 0 CAT: 17

Chicago Area Project
CIJE: 1 RIE: 1 CAT: 19

Chicago Attitudes Inventory
CIJE: 0 RIE: 1 CAT: 21

Chicago Bar Association IL
CIJE: 3 RIE: 0 CAT: 17

Chicago Catholic School Board IL
CIJE: 0 RIE: 1 CAT: 17

Chicago Catholic Science Teachers Association IL
CIJE: 1 RIE: 0 CAT: 17

Chicago Child Care Society
CIJE: 0 RIE: 1 CAT: 17

Chicago Child Parent Centers IL
CIJE: 0 RIE: 2 CAT: 17

Chicago City Wide College IL
USE City Colleges of Chicago IL Chicago City Wide Coll

Chicago Creativity Project
CIJE: 1 RIE: 0 CAT: 19

Chicago Criterion Referenced Record
CIJE: 0 RIE: 1 CAT: 21

Chicago Daily News IL
CIJE: 2 RIE: 1 CAT: 17

Chicago Early Assessment Remediation Lab Program
CIJE: 0 RIE: 1 CAT: 19

Chicago Effective Schools Project IL
CIJE: 1 RIE: 3 CAT: 19

Chicago Fertility Census
CIJE: 1 RIE: 0 CAT: 19

Chicago Fire 1871
CIJE: 0 RIE: 1 CAT: 12

Chicago Heights School District IL
CIJE: 0 RIE: 2 CAT: 17

Chicago Jewish Vocational Service IL
CIJE: 1 RIE: 0 CAT: 17

Chicago Latin School IL
CIJE: 1 RIE: 0 CAT: 17

Chicago Liberation School for Women IL
CIJE: 1 RIE: 0 CAT: 17

Chicago Linguistic Society IL
CIJE: 0 RIE: 1 CAT: 17

Chicago Mastery Learning Reading Program
CIJE: 2 RIE: 8 CAT: 19

Chicago Minimum Proficiency Skills Test
CIJE: 0 RIE: 1 CAT: 21

Chicago Nonverbal Examination
CIJE: 0 RIE: 2 CAT: 21

Chicago Police Department IL
CIJE: 0 RIE: 1 CAT: 17

Chicago Project
CIJE: 1 RIE: 0 CAT: 19

Chicago Public Library IL
CIJE: 13 RIE: 4 CAT: 17

Chicago Public Schools IL
CIJE: 81 RIE: 255 CAT: 17

Chicago Standard Metropolitan Statistical Area
CIJE: 1 RIE: 2 CAT: 07

Chicago State College IL
CIJE: 0 RIE: 1 CAT: 17

Chicago State University IL
CIJE: 1 RIE: 16 CAT: 17

Chicago Student Health Project
CIJE: 0 RIE: 1 CAT: 19

Chicago Times IL
CIJE: 1 RIE: 1 CAT: 17

Chicago Tribune IL
CIJE: 5 RIE: 4 CAT: 17

Chicago TV College IL
CIJE: 4 RIE: 6 CAT: 17

Chicago Urban League
CIJE: 0 RIE: 3 CAT: 17

Chicago Women in Trades
CIJE: 0 RIE: 1 CAT: 17

Chicago Youth Development Project
CIJE: 0 RIE: 1 CAT: 19

Chicanas
CIJE: 26 RIE: 52 CAT: 08

Chicano Arts
CIJE: 0 RIE: 1 CAT: 16

Chicano Cooperative History Project
CIJE: 1 RIE: 0 CAT: 19

Chicano Literature
CIJE: 18 RIE: 25 CAT: 16

Chicano Mobile Institutes
CIJE: 0 RIE: 2 CAT: 17

Chicano Movement
CIJE: 14 RIE: 10 CAT: 16

Chicano Periodical Index Project
CIJE: 0 RIE: 1 CAT: 19

Chicano Studies
CIJE: 21 RIE: 42 CAT: 03

Chicano Thesaurus
CIJE: 0 RIE: 1 CAT: 22

Chicanos
CIJE: 200 RIE: 305 CAT: 08

Chichewa
CIJE: 1 RIE: 8 CAT: 13

Chick Incubation
CIJE: 1 RIE: 0 CAT: 20

Chickasaw (Tribe)
CIJE: 1 RIE: 4 CAT: 08

Chicken Shed Theatre Workshop (England)
CIJE: 0 RIE: 1 CAT: 19

Chickens
CIJE: 3 RIE: 8 CAT: 20

Chickering (Arthur W)
CIJE: 6 RIE: 5 CAT: 18

Chickering (Arthur)
CIJE: 0 RIE: 1 CAT: 18

Chico State College CA
CIJE: 0 RIE: 1 CAT: 17

Chief Executive Officers
CIJE: 16 RIE: 13 CAT: 09
UF Chief Executives

Chief Executives
USE Chief Executive Officers

Chief Financial Officers
CIJE: 0 RIE: 1 CAT: 09

Chief Information Officers
CIJE: 7 RIE: 3 CAT: 09

Chief Planning Officers
CIJE: 0 RIE: 1 CAT: 09

Chief Storekeepers
CIJE: 0 RIE: 1 CAT: 09

Chief Student Affairs Officers
CIJE: 1 RIE: 2 CAT: 09
UF CSAOs

Chien Ou Dialect
CIJE: 0 RIE: 1 CAT: 13

Chien Yang Dialect
CIJE: 0 RIE: 1 CAT: 13

Child Abductions
USE Abductions

Child Abuse Amendments 1984
CIJE: 2 RIE: 2 CAT: 14

Child Abuse and Neglect Reporting
CIJE: 39 RIE: 23 CAT: 16
SN See also "Reporting Laws" and "Mandatory Reporting of Abuse"
UF Reporting of Child Abuse

Child Abuse Hotlines
CIJE: 0 RIE: 3 CAT: 05

Child Abuse Potential Inventory
CIJE: 20 RIE: 3 CAT: 21

Child Abuse Prevention and Treatment Act
CIJE: 1 RIE: 10 CAT: 14

Child Abuse Prevention Treatment Adoptn Reform Act
CIJE: 0 RIE: 1 CAT: 14

Child Abuse Registries
CIJE: 1 RIE: 3 CAT: 05
UF Central Registries of Child Abuse; State Registers of Child Abuse

Child Advocacy Program
CIJE: 1 RIE: 1 CAT: 19

Child and Adolescent Service System Program
CIJE: 2 RIE: 2 CAT: 19

Child and Adult Care Food Program
CIJE: 0 RIE: 2 CAT: 19

Child and Family Development Center UT
CIJE: 0 RIE: 1 CAT: 17

Child and Family Justice Project
CIJE: 1 RIE: 0 CAT: 19

Child and Family Mental Health Project
CIJE: 0 RIE: 4 CAT: 19

Child and Family Protective Services
CIJE: 0 RIE: 4 CAT: 17

Child and Family Resource Program
CIJE: 1 RIE: 34 CAT: 19

Child and the Curriculum
CIJE: 1 RIE: 0 CAT: 22

Child Assessment Scale
CIJE: 1 RIE: 0 CAT: 21

Child Assessment Schedule
CIJE: 0 RIE: 1 CAT: 21

Child Attitudes Survey
CIJE: 0 RIE: 1 CAT: 21

Child Awareness Program MO
CIJE: 1 RIE: 0 CAT: 19

Child Behavior Checklist
CIJE: 26 RIE: 5 CAT: 21
UF Child Behavior Checklist Teachers Report Form

Child Behavior Checklist Teachers Report Form
USE Child Behavior Checklist

Child Behavior Profile
CIJE: 3 RIE: 1 CAT: 21

Child Behavior Scale (Anderson and Bashaw)
CIJE: 1 RIE: 0 CAT: 21

Child Behavior Survey Instrument (Katz)
CIJE: 1 RIE: 1 CAT: 21

Child Behavior Therapy
CIJE: 0 RIE: 1 CAT: 11

Child Care Act 1979
CIJE: 0 RIE: 1 CAT: 14

Child Care Action Campaign
CIJE: 0 RIE: 1 CAT: 17

Child Care and Development Block Grants
CIJE: 5 RIE: 4 CAT: 14

Child Care Consortia
CIJE: 0 RIE: 1 CAT: 05

Child Care Coordinating Council
CIJE: 0 RIE: 1 CAT: 17

Child Care Costs
CIJE: 3 RIE: 14 CAT: 16

Child Care Dallas
CIJE: 0 RIE: 3 CAT: 17

Child Care Facility Schedule
CIJE: 0 RIE: 1 CAT: 21

Child Care Food Program
CIJE: 1 RIE: 19 CAT: 19

Child Care in the Admass Society (Sweden)
CIJE: 0 RIE: 1 CAT: 19
UF BITS Project (Sweden)

Child Care Inc NY
CIJE: 0 RIE: 0 CAT: 17

Child Care Legislation
CIJE: 18 RIE: 12 CAT: 14

Child Care Linkage Legislation
CIJE: 0 RIE: 1 CAT: 14

Child Care Needs
CIJE: 5 RIE: 31 CAT: 16

Child Care Placement
USE Child Placement

Child Care Resource Centers
CIJE: 0 RIE: 3 CAT: 05

Child Care Satisfaction
CIJE: 2 RIE: 3 CAT: 16

Child Care Services Entitlement
CIJE: 0 RIE: 1 CAT: 14

Child Care WORKS MN
CIJE: 0 RIE: 1 CAT: 17

Child Caring Reportcard
CIJE: 0 RIE: 1 CAT: 21

Child Center Our Lady of Grace MO
CIJE: 0 RIE: 1 CAT: 17

Child Centered Education
CIJE: 51 RIE: 17 CAT: 03

Child Centered Inservice Training Project NY
CIJE: 0 RIE: 5 CAT: 19

Child Count
CIJE: 1 RIE: 1 CAT: 16

Child Development Assessment Form
CIJE: 0 RIE: 1 CAT: 21

Child Development Associate
CIJE: 23 RIE: 207 CAT: 19
SN Use both "Child Development Associate" (major, if appropriate) and "CDA" (minor only) together — see add'l listings under "CDA..."

Child Development Associate Consortium
CIJE: 0 RIE: 2 CAT: 17

Child Development Associate Scholarship Assist Act
CIJE: 0 RIE: 0 CAT: 14
UF Public Law 99 425

Child Development Group of Mississippi
CIJE: 0 RIE: 2 CAT: 17

Child Development Inventory
CIJE: 0 RIE: 1 CAT: 21
SN Restandardized version of the "Minnesota Child Development Inventory" (q.v.)

Child Development Program Evaluation
CIJE: 0 RIE: 3 CAT: 21

Child Development Program Evaluation Scale
CIJE: 0 RIE: 2 CAT: 21

Child Development Programs Advisory Committee CA
CIJE: 0 RIE: 1 CAT: 17
UF California Child Development Programs Advsy Com

Child Development Project
CIJE: 3 RIE: 5 CAT: 19

Child Development Rating Scales
CIJE: 0 RIE: 1 CAT: 21

Child Development Trainer Program
CIJE: 0 RIE: 1 CAT: 19

Child Dyads
CIJE: 4 RIE: 1 CAT: 16

Child Ecology
CIJE: 0 RIE: 1 CAT: 16

Child Evaluation Centers
CIJE: 1 RIE: 0 CAT: 05

Child Expectations
CIJE: 1 RIE: 1 CAT: 11

Child Find
CIJE: 10 RIE: 31 CAT: 19

Child Growth Charts
CIJE: 0 RIE: 3 CAT: 21
UF Growth Charts (Children)

Child Guidance Movement
CIJE: 1 RIE: 1 CAT: 16

Child Health Assurance Program
CIJE: 1 RIE: 1 CAT: 19

Child Health Questionnaire
CIJE: 1 RIE: 0 CAT: 21

Child Infant Relationship
CIJE: 0 RIE: 2 CAT: 16
UF Infant Child Relationship

Child Influence
CIJE: 3 RIE: 5 CAT: 11

Child Language Data Exchange System
CIJE: 7 RIE: 3 CAT: 04

Child Life Programs
CIJE: 1 RIE: 2 CAT: 11

Child Life Specialists
CIJE: 2 RIE: 0 CAT: 09

Child Management
CIJE: 2 RIE: 1 CAT: 11

Child Mental Health Specialists
CIJE: 1 RIE: 1 CAT: 09

Child Molesters
CIJE: 3 RIE: 1 CAT: 10
SN See also "Pedophilia"
UF Molesters of Children

Child Mortality
CIJE: 1 RIE: 2 CAT: 11

Child Nutrition Act 1966
CIJE: 1 RIE: 20 CAT: 14

Child Nutrition Education Program
CIJE: 0 RIE: 1 CAT: 19

Child Nutrition Labeling Program
CIJE: 0 RIE: 2 CAT: 19

Child Nutrition Programs
CIJE: 7 RIE: 12 CAT: 19

Child Object Relationship
USE Object Child Relationship

Child Parent Centers
USE Parent Child Centers

Child Parent Relationship Scale
CIJE: 0 RIE: 1 CAT: 21

Child Placement
CIJE: 1 RIE: 2 CAT: 11
UF Child Care Placement

Child Pornography
CIJE: 1 RIE: 7 CAT: 14

Child Prodigies
CIJE: 2 RIE: 2 CAT: 10

Child Prostitution
CIJE: 0 RIE: 2 CAT: 16
SN See also "Teenage Prostitution"

Child Protection
CIJE: 24 RIE: 33 CAT: 16

Child Protection Inc
CIJE: 0 RIE: 1 CAT: 17

Child Protective Service
CIJE: 0 RIE: 11 CAT: 17

Child Protective Services
CIJE: 43 RIE: 19 CAT: 05

Child Psychiatric Day Care Unit of Univ Hosp WA
CIJE: 1 RIE: 0 CAT: 17

Child Rearing Study
CIJE: 1 RIE: 4 CAT: 19

Child Responsiveness
CIJE: 3 RIE: 6 CAT: 11

Child Safety
CIJE: 24 RIE: 22 CAT: 11

Child Self Description Scale
CIJE: 0 RIE: 1 CAT: 21

Child Service Demonstration Centers
CIJE: 5 RIE: 4 CAT: 05

Child Socialization Scale
CIJE: 0 RIE: 1 CAT: 21

Child Structured Learning in Science
CIJE: 1 RIE: 1 CAT: 22

Child Study Association of America
CIJE: 0 RIE: 3 CAT: 17

Child Study Centres (Canada)
CIJE: 0 RIE: 1 CAT: 05

Child Study Movement
CIJE: 3 RIE: 3 CAT: 16

Child Study Teams
CIJE: 4 RIE: 8 CAT: 10

Child Study Unit Screening Scales
CIJE: 0 RIE: 1 CAT: 21

Child Support Enforcement
CIJE: 0 RIE: 2 CAT: 14
SN See also "Interstate Child Support"

Child Support Enforcement Amendments 1984
CIJE: 2 RIE: 5 CAT: 14

Child Support Enforcement Program
CIJE: 0 RIE: 16 CAT: 19

Child Support Enforcement Services
CIJE: 0 RIE: 4 CAT: 14

Child Survival
CIJE: 0 RIE: 3 CAT: 11

Child Survival and Development Revolution
CIJE: 0 RIE: 2 CAT: 19

Child Survival Fair Start
CIJE: 1 RIE: 3 CAT: 19
UF Fair Start Program

Child Teacher Initiation Behaviors Checklist
CIJE: 0 RIE: 1 CAT: 21

Child Test of Esthetic Sensitivity
CIJE: 1 RIE: 0 CAT: 21

CHILD to Child Program
CIJE: 2 RIE: 7 CAT: 19

Child Welfare Act (Alberta)
CIJE: 0 RIE: 1 CAT: 14

Childs View of Himself Scale
CIJE: 0 RIE: 1 CAT: 21

Chile
CIJE: 93 RIE: 82 CAT: 07

Chile (Santiago)
CIJE: 6 RIE: 1 CAT: 07

Chilean Development Corporation
CIJE: 1 RIE: 0 CAT: 17

Chileans
CIJE: 2 RIE: 2 CAT: 08

Chillicothe City Schools OH
CIJE: 0 RIE: 1 CAT: 17

Chilocco Indian School OK
CIJE: 2 RIE: 4 CAT: 17

Chiluba
CIJE: 0 RIE: 1 CAT: 13

Chimariko (Tribe)
CIJE: 0 RIE: 1 CAT: 08

Chimpanzees
CIJE: 10 RIE: 4 CAT: 20

China
CIJE: 1175 RIE: 743 CAT: 07

China (Beijing)
CIJE: 32 RIE: 8 CAT: 07
UF China (Peking)

China (Canton)
USE China (Guangzhou)

China (Guangzhou)
CIJE: 4 RIE: 1 CAT: 07
UF China (Canton)

China (Inner Mongolia)
CIJE: 1 RIE: 3 CAT: 07

China (Manchuria)
CIJE: 0 RIE: 1 CAT: 07

China (Nanjing)
CIJE: 0 RIE: 1 CAT: 07
UF China (Nanking)

China (Nanking)
USE China (Nanjing)

China (Peking)
USE China (Beijing)

China (Shanghai)
CIJE: 17 RIE: 6 CAT: 07

China (Shanyang)
CIJE: 0 RIE: 2 CAT: 07

China (Sichuan Province)
CIJE: 1 RIE: 1 CAT: 07
UF China (Szechwan Province)

China (Szechwan Province)
USE China (Sichuan Province)

China (Tibet)
CIJE: 2 RIE: 9 CAT: 07

China (Zhuji County)
CIJE: 0 RIE: 1 CAT: 07

China a Handbook (1973)
CIJE: 1 RIE: 0 CAT: 22

China Coast
CIJE: 0 RIE: 2 CAT: 07

Chinantecan
CIJE: 1 RIE: 0 CAT: 13

Chinatown Boston
USE Massachusetts (Boston Chinatown)

Chinatown New York City
USE New York (New York Chinatown)

Chinatown Oakland
USE California (Oakland Chinatown)

Chinatown San Francisco
USE California (San Francisco Chinatown)

Chinatown Youth Services and Coordinating Ctr CA
CIJE: 0 RIE: 1 CAT: 17

Chinatowns
CIJE: 6 RIE: 3 CAT: 16

Chinese (Classical)
CIJE: 4 RIE: 2 CAT: 13

Chinese Academy of Social Sciences
CIJE: 0 RIE: 1 CAT: 17

CHinese Achievement and Mastery Program
USE Project CHAMP NY

Chinese Bilingual Education Program NY
CIJE: 0 RIE: 2 CAT: 19

Chinese Canadians
CIJE: 0 RIE: 2 CAT: 08

Chinese Character Code for Information Interchange
CIJE: 0 RIE: 1 CAT: 04

Chinese Communist Party
CIJE: 6 RIE: 6 CAT: 10

Chinese Culture University (Taiwan)
CIJE: 0 RIE: 1 CAT: 17

Chinese Enterprise Management Association
CIJE: 1 RIE: 0 CAT: 17

Chinese Language Schools
CIJE: 1 RIE: 0 CAT: 17

Chinese Letter Naming Test (Victor)
CIJE: 0 RIE: 1 CAT: 21

Chinese Literati
CIJE: 0 RIE: 1 CAT: 09
SN People from the Ming Dynasty (1368-1644) until almost the end of the Qing Dynasty (1644-1911) who were learned in the Confucian classics and took examinations based on them to serve in the government

Chinese Literature
CIJE: 13 RIE: 3 CAT: 16

Chinese Nationalists
CIJE: 1 RIE: 1 CAT: 10

Chinese Opportunities in Career Education NY
USE Project CHOICE NY

Chinese People
CIJE: 52 RIE: 82 CAT: 08

Chinese Phonetic Alphabet
CIJE: 0 RIE: 1 CAT: 13

Chinese Poetry
CIJE: 1 RIE: 1 CAT: 16

Chinese Speaking
CIJE: 2 RIE: 9 CAT: 08

Chinese Traditional Modern Scale (Dawson)
CIJE: 0 RIE: 1 CAT: 21

Chinese University of Hong Kong
CIJE: 4 RIE: 2 CAT: 17

Chinese Values Survey
CIJE: 0 RIE: 1 CAT: 21

Chinle Agency Summer Special Education Program
CIJE: 1 RIE: 1 CAT: 19

Chinning
CIJE: 1 RIE: 0 CAT: 11

Chinook (Tribe)
CIJE: 0 RIE: 2 CAT: 08

Chinook Educational Consortium (Canada)
CIJE: 0 RIE: 1 CAT: 17

Chinook Jargon
CIJE: 1 RIE: 6 CAT: 13

Chinookan (Language)
CIJE: 2 RIE: 1 CAT: 13

Chipewyan
CIJE: 2 RIE: 0 CAT: 13
UF Montagnais (Athapascan Language)

Chipewyan (Tribe)
CIJE: 0 RIE: 0 CAT: 08

Chipola Junior College FL
CIJE: 2 RIE: 3 CAT: 17

Chippewa Cree (Tribe)
CIJE: 1 RIE: 1 CAT: 08

Chiropractic Colleges
CIJE: 0 RIE: 1 CAT: 05

Chiropractic Education
CIJE: 0 RIE: 1 CAT: 03

Chiropractic Profession
CIJE: 2 RIE: 4 CAT: 10

Chiropractors
CIJE: 3 RIE: 8 CAT: 09

Chisholm (Margaret)
CIJE: 1 RIE: 0 CAT: 18

Chisholm (Shirley)
CIJE: 1 RIE: 3 CAT: 18

Chitimacha (Tribe)
CIJE: 0 RIE: 3 CAT: 08

Chitimacha Day School LA
CIJE: 0 RIE: 1 CAT: 17

Chiwere
CIJE: 0 RIE: 2 CAT: 13
SN A Siouan language

Chlordimeform
CIJE: 0 RIE: 1 CAT: 20

Chlorella
CIJE: 1 RIE: 0 CAT: 20

Chlorella Vulgaris
CIJE: 1 RIE: 0 CAT: 20

Chlorides
CIJE: 3 RIE: 0 CAT: 20

Chlorinated Hydrocarbons
CIJE: 1 RIE: 0 CAT: 20

Chlorination
CIJE: 3 RIE: 4 CAT: 20

Chlorine
CIJE: 4 RIE: 4 CAT: 20

Chlorine Dioxide
CIJE: 1 RIE: 0 CAT: 20

Chlorogalum Pomeridianum
CIJE: 1 RIE: 0 CAT: 20

Chlorophyll
CIJE: 1 RIE: 0 CAT: 20

Chlorpromazine
CIJE: 2 RIE: 0 CAT: 20

Choate (Pat)
CIJE: 1 RIE: 0 CAT: 18

Choate School CT
CIJE: 0 RIE: 1 CAT: 17

Chocho
CIJE: 0 RIE: 1 CAT: 13
SN A Tlapanecan language of Mexico
UF Tlapanec

Choctaw County School District MS
CIJE: 0 RIE: 1 CAT: 17

Chodziesner (Gertrud)
CIJE: 1 RIE: 0 CAT: 18

CHOICE (Career Education Curriculum)
CIJE: 0 RIE: 27 CAT: 03
UF Challenging Options in Career Education

Choice (Yette)
CIJE: 0 RIE: 1 CAT: 22
SN "The Choice: The Issue of Black Survival in America"

Choice Behavior
CIJE: 76 RIE: 26 CAT: 11

CHOICE Courseware
CIJE: 0 RIE: 1 CAT: 04

Choice Dilemmas Questionnaire
CIJE: 3 RIE: 2 CAT: 21

Choice Weight Scoring
CIJE: 2 RIE: 0 CAT: 21

Choices (Nuclear Issues Curriculum)
CIJE: 0 RIE: 0 CAT: 03

CHOICES (Program)
CIJE: 4 RIE: 10 CAT: 19
SN "Computerized Heuristic Occupational Information and Career Exploration System"

Choking
CIJE: 2 RIE: 4 CAT: 11

Cholesterol
CIJE: 32 RIE: 14 CAT: 11
UF Blood Cholesterol

Cholesterol HDL
USE High Density Lipoprotein Cholesterol

Cholesterol LDL
USE Low Density Lipoprotein Cholesterol

Cholinesterase
CIJE: 1 RIE: 0 CAT: 11

Cholodny Went Hypothesis
CIJE: 1 RIE: 0 CAT: 20

Chomsky (Noam)
CIJE: 75 RIE: 25 CAT: 18

Chomsky Competence Model
CIJE: 2 RIE: 1 CAT: 15

Chomsky Halle Phonological System
CIJE: 1 RIE: 2 CAT: 15

Chontal
CIJE: 3 RIE: 0 CAT: 13

Choose a Job Inventory
CIJE: 0 RIE: 1 CAT: 21

Choosing Optional Infused Career Education NY
CIJE: 0 RIE: 2 CAT: 19
UF Project CHOICE (Choosing Optionl Infusd Career Ed)

Chopin (Kate)
CIJE: 0 RIE: 1 CAT: 18

Chore Services
CIJE: 0 RIE: 1 CAT: 16

Chorea
CIJE: 1 RIE: 0 CAT: 11

Choreography
CIJE: 4 RIE: 4 CAT: 03

Choropleth Maps
CIJE: 2 RIE: 3 CAT: 04

Chorpenning (Charlotte B)
CIJE: 0 RIE: 1 CAT: 18

Chorti
CIJE: 0 RIE: 1 CAT: 13

Chosen
CIJE: 2 RIE: 0 CAT: 22

Chou En lai
USE Zhou Enlai

Christ College Irvine CA
CIJE: 0 RIE: 1 CAT: 17

Christabel
CIJE: 0 RIE: 1 CAT: 22

Christchurch College of Education (New Zealand)
CIJE: 0 RIE: 1 CAT: 17

Christensen (Francis)
CIJE: 10 RIE: 6 CAT: 18

Christensen Rhetoric Program
CIJE: 4 RIE: 1 CAT: 19

Christian Action Ministry Academy IL
CIJE: 1 RIE: 1 CAT: 17
UF Cam Academy IL

Christian Brothers
CIJE: 0 RIE: 2 CAT: 17

Christian Brothers College (Australia)
CIJE: 1 RIE: 1 CAT: 17

Christian Brothers College TN
CIJE: 0 RIE: 1 CAT: 17

Christian Brothers Colleges
CIJE: 0 RIE: 1 CAT: 17

Christian College Coalition
CIJE: 1 RIE: 3 CAT: 17

Christian College Consortium
CIJE: 1 RIE: 1 CAT: 17

Christian Democratic Party
CIJE: 1 RIE: 0 CAT: 10

Christian National Education
CIJE: 0 RIE: 1 CAT: 15

Christian Science
CIJE: 1 RIE: 1 CAT: 16

Christmas
CIJE: 31 RIE: 12 CAT: 12

Christmas Books
CIJE: 4 RIE: 2 CAT: 16

Christmas Decorations
CIJE: 3 RIE: 1 CAT: 16

Christmas Story (The)
CIJE: 1 RIE: 0 CAT: 22

Christmas Trees
CIJE: 1 RIE: 2 CAT: 16

Christopher Newport College VA
CIJE: 2 RIE: 3 CAT: 17

Christy (Arthur)
CIJE: 0 RIE: 1 CAT: 18

Chromium
CIJE: 2 RIE: 0 CAT: 20

Chromosome Abnormalities
CIJE: 10 RIE: 2 CAT: 11

Chromosomes
CIJE: 19 RIE: 4 CAT: 11

Chronemics
CIJE: 0 RIE: 3 CAT: 11

Chronicle of Higher Education
CIJE: 10 RIE: 3 CAT: 22

Chronobiology
CIJE: 4 RIE: 1 CAT: 20

Chronology
CIJE: 17 RIE: 9 CAT: 16

Chronometric Techniques
CIJE: 5 RIE: 1 CAT: 15

Chrysler Corporation
CIJE: 5 RIE: 4 CAT: 17

Chrysler Dealer Apprenticeship Program
CIJE: 0 RIE: 1 CAT: 19

Chrysler Learning Inc
CIJE: 2 RIE: 1 CAT: 17

Chu (Paul B J)
CIJE: 1 RIE: 0 CAT: 18

Chukchee
USE Chukchi

Chukchi
CIJE: 0 RIE: 1 CAT: 13
SN A Chukchee-Kamchatkan language of Siberia
UF Chukchee

Chukchi News and Information Service AK
CIJE: 0 RIE: 1 CAT: 19

Chukovsky (Kornei I)
CIJE: 1 RIE: 0 CAT: 18

Chula Vista City School District CA
CIJE: 2 RIE: 6 CAT: 17

Chulalongkorn University (Thailand)
CIJE: 2 RIE: 4 CAT: 17

Chumash
CIJE: 1 RIE: 1 CAT: 13

Chumash (Tribe)
CIJE: 1 RIE: 3 CAT: 08

Chunked Reading Test
CIJE: 2 RIE: 0 CAT: 21

Chunking
CIJE: 15 RIE: 19 CAT: 15

Chunks (Programed Instruction)
CIJE: 1 RIE: 0 CAT: 21

Church and Synagogue Library Association PA
CIJE: 1 RIE: 1 CAT: 17

Church Attendance
CIJE: 7 RIE: 3 CAT: 16

Church Based Child Care
CIJE: 0 RIE: 3 CAT: 16

Church College of Hawaii
CIJE: 1 RIE: 1 CAT: 17

Church Community Relationship
CIJE: 0 RIE: 1 CAT: 16
UF Community Church Relationship

Church Libraries
CIJE: 4 RIE: 20 CAT: 05

Church Members
CIJE: 0 RIE: 1 CAT: 10
UF Churchgoers

Church Newspapers
CIJE: 0 RIE: 2 CAT: 16

Church of England
CIJE: 4 RIE: 1 CAT: 17

Church of God
CIJE: 0 RIE: 1 CAT: 17

Church of Jesus Christ of Latter Day Saints
CIJE: 10 RIE: 5 CAT: 17

Church Records
CIJE: 1 RIE: 1 CAT: 16

Church Slavic
CIJE: 0 RIE: 1 CAT: 13

Church Women United
CIJE: 0 RIE: 1 CAT: 17

Church World Service
CIJE: 0 RIE: 2 CAT: 17

Churches Television Centre
CIJE: 2 RIE: 0 CAT: 17

Churchgoers
USE Church Members

Churchill College Conference
CIJE: 1 RIE: 0 CAT: 02

Cicero
CIJE: 13 RIE: 11 CAT: 18

Cien Anos De Soledad
CIJE: 1 RIE: 0 CAT: 22

Ciliata
CIJE: 1 RIE: 0 CAT: 20

Ciluba
CIJE: 0 RIE: 1 CAT: 13
SN A Central Western Bantu language of Zaire

Cincinnati Autonomy Test Battery
CIJE: 0 RIE: 9 CAT: 21

Cincinnati Bible College OH
CIJE: 1 RIE: 0 CAT: 17

Cincinnati Council on World Affairs OH
CIJE: 1 RIE: 0 CAT: 17

Cincinnati Mathematics Inventories
CIJE: 0 RIE: 1 CAT: 21

Cincinnati Milacron
CIJE: 0 RIE: 1 CAT: 17

Cincinnati Public Schools OH
CIJE: 13 RIE: 56 CAT: 17

Cincinnati Technical College OH
CIJE: 1 RIE: 4 CAT: 17

Cinderella
CIJE: 4 RIE: 1 CAT: 22

Cinderella Myth
CIJE: 1 RIE: 0 CAT: 16

Cinefluorography
CIJE: 2 RIE: 0 CAT: 20

Cinematographers
CIJE: 1 RIE: 1 CAT: 09

Cinerama
CIJE: 0 RIE: 1 CAT: 16

Cinquain
CIJE: 0 RIE: 1 CAT: 16

CINTERFOR
CIJE: 0 RIE: 1 CAT: 02

Cioran (E M)
CIJE: 1 RIE: 0 CAT: 18

Ciphers
CIJE: 3 RIE: 0 CAT: 20

CIPP Evaluation Model
USE Context Input Process Product Evaluation Model

CIRCA Project
CIJE: 0 RIE: 1 CAT: 19
UF Collaboration to Improve Reading in Content Areas

Circadian Activity Rhythms
CIJE: 8 RIE: 2 CAT: 11

Circle of Concern
CIJE: 0 RIE: 1 CAT: 15

Circle Test of Honesty
CIJE: 0 RIE: 1 CAT: 21

Circle Time
CIJE: 5 RIE: 2 CAT: 15

Circles
CIJE: 21 RIE: 2 CAT: 20

Circles of Knowledge
CIJE: 1 RIE: 0 CAT: 15

Circles Test
CIJE: 2 RIE: 1 CAT: 21

Circuit Riders
CIJE: 1 RIE: 1 CAT: 10

Circuit Training
CIJE: 5 RIE: 1 CAT: 03

Circular Scaling Technique
CIJE: 0 RIE: 1 CAT: 15

Circular Triad Scores
CIJE: 3 RIE: 0 CAT: 21

Circulation (Publications)
CIJE: 0 RIE: 6 CAT: 16

Circumference
CIJE: 0 RIE: 3 CAT: 20

Circumplex Model of Marital and Family Systems
CIJE: 1 RIE: 1 CAT: 15

Circumplex Models (Statistics)
CIJE: 3 RIE: 1 CAT: 21

Circus Assessment Battery
CIJE: 4 RIE: 10 CAT: 21

Circuses
CIJE: 4 RIE: 4 CAT: 10

Cisco Junior College TX
CIJE: 0 RIE: 1 CAT: 17

Ciskei
CIJE: 0 RIE: 2 CAT: 07

Cisneros (Henry G)
CIJE: 0 RIE: 0 CAT: 18

Citadel Military College of South Carolina
CIJE: 0 RIE: 4 CAT: 17
UF Citadel SC

Citadel SC
USE Citadel Military College of South Carolina

CITAR Computer Courseware Evaluation Model
CIJE: 0 RIE: 1 CAT: 15
SN CITAR = Center for Interactive Technologies, Applications, and Research (located at Univ of South Florida)
UF Computer Courseware Evaluation Model of CITAR

Citation Maps
CIJE: 7 RIE: 1 CAT: 04

Cities at Work
CIJE: 1 RIE: 0 CAT: 22

Cities in Schools
CIJE: 8 RIE: 8 CAT: 19

Citizen Bee
CIJE: 0 RIE: 1 CAT: 16

Citizen Leadership Program WI
CIJE: 0 RIE: 1 CAT: 19

Citizen Me Project TX
CIJE: 0 RIE: 14 CAT: 19

Citizens Advisory Council on Status of Women DC
CIJE: 1 RIE: 0 CAT: 17

Citizens Band Radio
CIJE: 8 RIE: 5 CAT: 04

Citizens Commission on Basic Education PA
CIJE: 0 RIE: 1 CAT: 17

Citizens Committee on Public Education PA
CIJE: 0 RIE: 1 CAT: 17

Citizens Committee to Save WEFM IL
CIJE: 0 RIE: 1 CAT: 17

Citizens Communication Ctr for Responsive Media DC
CIJE: 0 RIE: 1 CAT: 17

Citizens Conference on Man Education and Work
CIJE: 0 RIE: 1 CAT: 02

Citizens Crusade Against Poverty
CIJE: 0 RIE: 1 CAT: 17

Citizens Education Project MD
CIJE: 0 RIE: 1 CAT: 19

Citizens Forum
CIJE: 0 RIE: 4 CAT: 17

Citizens Groups
CIJE: 0 RIE: 1 CAT: 10

Citizens Learning Networks (Japan)
CIJE: 0 RIE: 1 CAT: 05

Citizenship Day
CIJE: 0 RIE: 1 CAT: 12

Citizenship in Action
CIJE: 0 RIE: 1 CAT: 19

Citizenship Knowledge Test
CIJE: 1 RIE: 1 CAT: 21

Citrus College CA
CIJE: 0 RIE: 1 CAT: 17

Citrus County School District FL
CIJE: 0 RIE: 2 CAT: 17

Citrus Farming
CIJE: 1 RIE: 2 CAT: 16

City and Country School NY
CIJE: 2 RIE: 1 CAT: 17

City and Guilds of London Institute (England)
CIJE: 4 RIE: 2 CAT: 17

City as School Program
CIJE: 2 RIE: 4 CAT: 19

City College NY
USE City University of New York City College

City College of San Francisco CA
CIJE: 1 RIE: 3 CAT: 17

City Colleges of Chicago IL
CIJE: 10 RIE: 22 CAT: 17

City Colleges of Chicago IL Chicago City Wide Coll
CIJE: 0 RIE: 3 CAT: 17
UF Chicago City Wide College IL

City Colleges of Chicago IL Harold Washington Coll
CIJE: 0 RIE: 1 CAT: 17
UF Harold Washington College IL

City Colleges of Chicago IL Kennedy King College
CIJE: 0 RIE: 1 CAT: 17
UF Kennedy King College IL

City Colleges of Chicago IL Loop College
CIJE: 1 RIE: 1 CAT: 17
UF Loop College IL

City Colleges of Chicago IL Malcolm X College
CIJE: 1 RIE: 1 CAT: 17
UF Malcolm X College IL

City Colleges of Chicago IL Olive Harvey College
CIJE: 0 RIE: 0 CAT: 17
UF Olive Harvey College IL

City Colleges of Chicago IL Richard J Daley Coll
CIJE: 0 RIE: 1 CAT: 17
UF Daley College IL; Richard J Daley College IL

City Colleges of Chicago IL Truman College
CIJE: 0 RIE: 3 CAT: 17
UF Truman College IL

City Colleges of Chicago IL Wright College
CIJE: 1 RIE: 2 CAT: 17
UF Wright College IL

City Game
CIJE: 1 RIE: 0 CAT: 15

City High School Recognition Program
CIJE: 0 RIE: 1 CAT: 19

City Magazines
CIJE: 2 RIE: 5 CAT: 16

City Managers
CIJE: 0 RIE: 4 CAT: 09

City Model Computer Simulation
CIJE: 1 RIE: 0 CAT: 15

City of God
CIJE: 1 RIE: 0 CAT: 22

City of London Polytechnic (England)
CIJE: 0 RIE: 9 CAT: 17

City of Madison Joint Sch Dist No 8 v WERC
CIJE: 0 RIE: 1 CAT: 14

City of Newport v Fact Concerts Inc
CIJE: 1 RIE: 0 CAT: 14

City Taxes
CIJE: 0 RIE: 1 CAT: 14

City Technology Colleges (England)
CIJE: 0 RIE: 3 CAT: 17

City University of New York
CIJE: 91 RIE: 185 CAT: 17
SN See add'l listings under "CUNY..."
UF CUNY

City University of New York Bernard Baruch College
CIJE: 10 RIE: 11 CAT: 17
UF Bernard Baruch College NY

City University of New York Bronx Community Coll
CIJE: 7 RIE: 18 CAT: 17
UF Bronx Community College NY

City University of New York Brooklyn College
CIJE: 20 RIE: 20 CAT: 17
UF Brooklyn College NY

City University of New York City College
CIJE: 19 RIE: 17 CAT: 17
UF City College NY

City University of New York Coll of Staten Island
CIJE: 5 RIE: 13 CAT: 17
UF College of Staten Island NY

City University of New York Hostos Community Coll
CIJE: 7 RIE: 6 CAT: 17
UF Hostos Community College NY

City University of New York Hunter College
CIJE: 16 RIE: 16 CAT: 17
UF Hunter College NY

City University of New York John Jay College
CIJE: 3 RIE: 0 CAT: 17
UF John Jay College NY

City University of New York Kingsborough Comm Coll
CIJE: 1 RIE: 3 CAT: 17
UF Kingsborough Community College NY

City University of New York La Guardia Comm Coll
CIJE: 11 RIE: 18 CAT: 17
UF La Guardia Community College NY

City University of New York Lehman College
CIJE: 16 RIE: 6 CAT: 17
UF Lehman College NY

City University of New York Manhattan Comm Coll
CIJE: 5 RIE: 11 CAT: 17
UF Manhattan Community College NY

City University of New York Mt Sinai Sch of Med
CIJE: 6 RIE: 1 CAT: 17
UF Mount Sinai School of Medicine NY

City University of New York NYC Comm Coll
CIJE: 3 RIE: 12 CAT: 17
UF New York City Community College

City University of New York NYC Technical Coll
CIJE: 1 RIE: 2 CAT: 17
UF New York City Technical College

City University of New York Queens College
CIJE: 14 RIE: 19 CAT: 17
UF Queens College NY

City University of New York Queensborough Comm C
CIJE: 13 RIE: 11 CAT: 17
UF Queensborough Community College NY

City University of New York Richmond College
CIJE: 4 RIE: 0 CAT: 17
UF Richmond College NY

City University of New York York College
CIJE: 1 RIE: 7 CAT: 17
UF York College NY

City Works Course
USE CityWorks

CityWorks
CIJE: 0 RIE: 1 CAT: 03
UF City Works Course

Civic Achievement Award Program
CIJE: 2 RIE: 1 CAT: 19
SN Citizenship education program for grades 5-8, established by Congress in 1987

Civic Center North
CIJE: 1 RIE: 0 CAT: 17

Civic Education Enhancement Project
CIJE: 0 RIE: 1 CAT: 19

Civic Institutes
CIJE: 2 RIE: 0 CAT: 05

Civic Values
CIJE: 1 RIE: 1 CAT: 16

Civic Writing
CIJE: 13 RIE: 3 CAT: 13
UF Political Writing

Civil Aeronautics Board
CIJE: 0 RIE: 1 CAT: 17

Civil Air Patrol
CIJE: 1 RIE: 2 CAT: 17

Civil Defense Adult Educ Attitude Scale (Marko)
CIJE: 0 RIE: 1 CAT: 21

Civil Defense Knowledge Scale (Marko)
CIJE: 0 RIE: 1 CAT: 21

Civil Disturbances
CIJE: 4 RIE: 3 CAT: 12

Civil Rights Act 1871
CIJE: 5 RIE: 6 CAT: 14

Civil Rights Act 1871 Section 1983
CIJE: 4 RIE: 2 CAT: 14

Civil Rights Act 1957
CIJE: 0 RIE: 1 CAT: 14

Civil Rights Act 1962 Title VII
CIJE: 0 RIE: 1 CAT: 14

Civil Rights Act 1964
CIJE: 69 RIE: 68 CAT: 14

Civil Rights Act 1964 Title IV
CIJE: 4 RIE: 43 CAT: 14

Civil Rights Act 1964 Title VI
CIJE: 35 RIE: 58 CAT: 14

Civil Rights Act 1964 Title VII
CIJE: 127 RIE: 76 CAT: 14

Civil Rights Act 1968
CIJE: 0 RIE: 1 CAT: 14

Civil Rights Act 1968 Title II
CIJE: 1 RIE: 0 CAT: 14

Civil Rights Act 1968 Title VIII
CIJE: 2 RIE: 4 CAT: 14

Civil Rights Act 1991
CIJE: 4 RIE: 2 CAT: 14
UF Public Law 102 166

Civil Rights Attorneys Fees Award Act
CIJE: 3 RIE: 0 CAT: 14

Civil Rights Evaluation Questionnaire
CIJE: 0 RIE: 1 CAT: 21

Civil Rights of Institutionalized Persons Act
CIJE: 0 RIE: 1 CAT: 14

Civil Rights Restoration Act 1987
CIJE: 3 RIE: 2 CAT: 14
UF Public Law 100 259

Civil Service
CIJE: 12 RIE: 13 CAT: 09

Civil Service Commission
CIJE: 5 RIE: 12 CAT: 17

Civil Service Reform Act 1978
CIJE: 2 RIE: 2 CAT: 14

Civil Service Retirement System
CIJE: 0 RIE: 1 CAT: 16

Civilian Affairs Training School
CIJE: 0 RIE: 1 CAT: 17

Civilian Conservation Corps
CIJE: 4 RIE: 9 CAT: 17

Civilian Employees
USE Civilian Personnel

Civilian Occupation Planning Estimates System
CIJE: 0 RIE: 1 CAT: 04
UF COPES System (Civilian Labor Stats)

Civilian Personnel
CIJE: 0 RIE: 6 CAT: 09
UF Civilian Employees

Civilian Service
CIJE: 4 RIE: 1 CAT: 16

CIVITAS
CIJE: 3 RIE: 2 CAT: 03
SN A framework for civic education

Cizek (Franz)
CIJE: 8 RIE: 0 CAT: 18

CJVS Scale of Employability
CIJE: 1 RIE: 0 CAT: 21

Clackamas Community College OR
CIJE: 4 RIE: 7 CAT: 17

Clair (Rene)
CIJE: 1 RIE: 0 CAT: 18

Clamps
CIJE: 0 RIE: 1 CAT: 04

CLAN NV
USE Central Libraries Automated Network NV

Clans
CIJE: 1 RIE: 2 CAT: 08

Clap (Thomas)
CIJE: 0 RIE: 1 CAT: 18

Clapp (Elsie Ripley)
CIJE: 0 RIE: 2 CAT: 18

Clara Barton High School Bilingual Program NY
CIJE: 0 RIE: 1 CAT: 19

Claremont Colleges CA
CIJE: 8 RIE: 13 CAT: 17

Claremont High School CA
CIJE: 1 RIE: 0 CAT: 17

Claremont Institute for the Study of Change CA
CIJE: 0 RIE: 1 CAT: 17

Claremont Mens College CA
CIJE: 2 RIE: 0 CAT: 17

Claremont Project in Anthropology and Education
CIJE: 1 RIE: 1 CAT: 19

Claremont Reading Conference
CIJE: 0 RIE: 4 CAT: 02

Claremont Univ Ctr and Grad Sch CA
CIJE: 2 RIE: 0 CAT: 17

Claremore Junior College OK
CIJE: 1 RIE: 0 CAT: 17

Clarendon (Edward Hyde 1st Earl of)
CIJE: 1 RIE: 0 CAT: 18

Clarifying Environments Program
CIJE: 1 RIE: 1 CAT: 19

Clarifying Purpose Task
CIJE: 0 RIE: 1 CAT: 15

Clarinet Performance Rating Scale
CIJE: 2 RIE: 0 CAT: 21

Clarinets
CIJE: 3 RIE: 1 CAT: 04

Clarion State College PA
CIJE: 0 RIE: 4 CAT: 17

Clarion University of Pennsylvania
CIJE: 3 RIE: 3 CAT: 17

Claris CAD
CIJE: 0 RIE: 1 CAT: 04
SN CAD = Computer Aided Drafting

Clarity
CIJE: 12 RIE: 7 CAT: 16

Clark (Ann Nolan)
CIJE: 1 RIE: 0 CAT: 18

Clark (Billy Curtis)
CIJE: 1 RIE: 0 CAT: 18

Clark (Burton R)
CIJE: 0 RIE: 1 CAT: 18

Clark (Eve)
CIJE: 2 RIE: 0 CAT: 18

Clark (George Rogers)
CIJE: 1 RIE: 2 CAT: 18

Clark (Joe)
CIJE: 1 RIE: 1 CAT: 18

Clark (Kenneth B)
CIJE: 3 RIE: 1 CAT: 18

Clark (Kenneth)
CIJE: 4 RIE: 0 CAT: 18

Clark (Mamie)
CIJE: 1 RIE: 0 CAT: 18

Clark (Richard E)
CIJE: 5 RIE: 1 CAT: 18

Clark (Solomon Henry)
CIJE: 0 RIE: 1 CAT: 18

Clark (Thomas Arkle)
CIJE: 1 RIE: 0 CAT: 18

Clark (Walter van Tilburg)
CIJE: 1 RIE: 0 CAT: 18

Clark College GA
CIJE: 4 RIE: 5 CAT: 17

Clark College WA
CIJE: 1 RIE: 1 CAT: 17

Clark County Community College NV
CIJE: 1 RIE: 5 CAT: 17

Clark County School District NV
CIJE: 3 RIE: 14 CAT: 17

Clark County Schools AL
CIJE: 1 RIE: 0 CAT: 17

Clark High School Attitude Scale
CIJE: 0 RIE: 1 CAT: 21

Clark Motor Development Scale
CIJE: 0 RIE: 1 CAT: 21

Clark State Community College OH
CIJE: 0 RIE: 1 CAT: 17

Clark Trow Ratings
CIJE: 8 RIE: 5 CAT: 21

Clark University MA
CIJE: 7 RIE: 4 CAT: 17

Clarke (Arthur C)
CIJE: 1 RIE: 1 CAT: 18

Clarke (Edward H)
CIJE: 2 RIE: 1 CAT: 18

Clarke College IA
CIJE: 1 RIE: 4 CAT: 17

Clarke School for the Deaf MA
CIJE: 4 RIE: 2 CAT: 17

Clarke Science Interests Checklist
CIJE: 1 RIE: 0 CAT: 21

Clarke Stewart Rating Scales
CIJE: 0 RIE: 1 CAT: 21

Clarkson College of Technology NY
CIJE: 5 RIE: 2 CAT: 17

Clarkson University NY
CIJE: 4 RIE: 2 CAT: 17

Class (Concept)
CIJE: 5 RIE: 1 CAT: 15

Class Achievement Test in Mathematics
CIJE: 0 RIE: 1 CAT: 21

Class Action
CIJE: 16 RIE: 2 CAT: 14

Class Action Suits
CIJE: 7 RIE: 3 CAT: 14

Class Activities Questionnaire
CIJE: 3 RIE: 5 CAT: 21

Class Analysis Chart
CIJE: 0 RIE: 1 CAT: 21

Class Conflict
CIJE: 0 RIE: 1 CAT: 16

Class Drops
CIJE: 0 RIE: 2 CAT: 16

Class Inclusion
CIJE: 36 RIE: 6 CAT: 15

Class Length
CIJE: 0 RIE: 1 CAT: 03

Class Loading and Student Scheduling Program
CIJE: 1 RIE: 0 CAT: 19

Class Means
CIJE: 3 RIE: 1 CAT: 21

Class Play
CIJE: 0 RIE: 1 CAT: 16

Class Reasoning Index
CIJE: 0 RIE: 1 CAT: 21

Class Vicariance
CIJE: 0 RIE: 1 CAT: 15

Classer (William)
CIJE: 0 RIE: 1 CAT: 18

Classical Hollywood Films
CIJE: 0 RIE: 1 CAT: 16
UF Film Classics (Hollywood); Hollywood Film Classics

Classical Music
CIJE: 20 RIE: 3 CAT: 03

Classical Period
CIJE: 2 RIE: 1 CAT: 12

Classical Rhetoric
CIJE: 54 RIE: 51 CAT: 13

Classical Studies Cambridge Project
CIJE: 1 RIE: 0 CAT: 19

Classical Test Theory
CIJE: 17 RIE: 25 CAT: 15

Classicists
CIJE: 0 RIE: 1 CAT: 09
SN People who have studied classical literature

Classics
CIJE: 12 RIE: 5 CAT: 03

Classics (Literature)
CIJE: 20 RIE: 18 CAT: 03

Classification Assessment Test
CIJE: 0 RIE: 2 CAT: 21

Classification Error
CIJE: 1 RIE: 1 CAT: 21

Classification of Instructional Programs
CIJE: 0 RIE: 11 CAT: 22

Classification of Secondary School Courses
CIJE: 0 RIE: 2 CAT: 21

Classification Questionnaire
CIJE: 1 RIE: 2 CAT: 21

Classification Research Group
CIJE: 2 RIE: 3 CAT: 17

Classification Tests
CIJE: 2 RIE: 1 CAT: 21

Classified Advertising
CIJE: 1 RIE: 5 CAT: 16

Classified Index of Occupations and Industries
CIJE: 0 RIE: 1 CAT: 22

Classified Research
CIJE: 2 RIE: 2 CAT: 16

Classified Staff
CIJE: 3 RIE: 5 CAT: 09

Classified Staff Attitudes
CIJE: 0 RIE: 2 CAT: 21

Classifiers (Language)
CIJE: 3 RIE: 1 CAT: 13

Classroom Activity Record
CIJE: 0 RIE: 1 CAT: 21

Classroom Adjustment Checklist
CIJE: 0 RIE: 2 CAT: 21

Classroom Adjustment Rating Scale
CIJE: 2 RIE: 1 CAT: 21

Classroom Assistant Program
CIJE: 1 RIE: 0 CAT: 19

Classroom Attitude Observation Schedule
CIJE: 0 RIE: 4 CAT: 21

Classroom Based Intervention
CIJE: 0 RIE: 1 CAT: 15

Classroom Behavior Description
CIJE: 0 RIE: 1 CAT: 21

Classroom Behavior Description Checklist
CIJE: 0 RIE: 1 CAT: 21

Classroom Behavior Inventory (Schaefer et al)
CIJE: 8 RIE: 8 CAT: 21

Classroom Behavior Scales (Garfunkel et al)
CIJE: 0 RIE: 1 CAT: 21

Classroom Behavior Task (Weinstein et al)
CIJE: 0 RIE: 1 CAT: 21

Classroom Boundary Questionnaire
CIJE: 1 RIE: 0 CAT: 21

Classroom Business Venture
CIJE: 0 RIE: 1 CAT: 03

Classroom Climate Questionnaire
CIJE: 0 RIE: 7 CAT: 21

Classroom Creativity Observation Schedule
CIJE: 1 RIE: 1 CAT: 21

Classroom Dimensions Observation System
CIJE: 0 RIE: 1 CAT: 21

Classroom Effectiveness
CIJE: 6 RIE: 4 CAT: 15

Classroom Environment Index
CIJE: 1 RIE: 2 CAT: 21

Classroom Environment Inventory (Stern)
CIJE: 0 RIE: 1 CAT: 21

Classroom Environment Questionnaire
CIJE: 1 RIE: 0 CAT: 21

Classroom Environment Scale (Fraser and Fisher)
CIJE: 0 RIE: 1 CAT: 21

Classroom Environment Scale (Trickett and Moos)
CIJE: 21 RIE: 8 CAT: 21

Classroom Ethos
CIJE: 3 RIE: 1 CAT: 16

Classroom Index of Individualized Instruction
CIJE: 0 RIE: 1 CAT: 21

Classroom Index of Student Needs
CIJE: 0 RIE: 1 CAT: 21

Classroom Interaction Analysis Index
CIJE: 0 RIE: 2 CAT: 21

Classroom Interaction Data
CIJE: 2 RIE: 2 CAT: 16

Classroom Learning Atmosphere Scale
CIJE: 1 RIE: 0 CAT: 21

Classroom Management Improvement Study
CIJE: 0 RIE: 2 CAT: 22

Classroom Management Observation Scale
CIJE: 0 RIE: 1 CAT: 21

Classroom Observation Form
CIJE: 0 RIE: 1 CAT: 21

Classroom Observation Instruments
CIJE: 1 RIE: 8 CAT: 04

Classroom Observation Judgment Schedule (Rummery)
CIJE: 0 RIE: 1 CAT: 21

Classroom Observation Rating Form (Ashley)
CIJE: 0 RIE: 1 CAT: 21

Classroom Observation Rating Scale
CIJE: 1 RIE: 3 CAT: 21

Classroom Observation Record
CIJE: 0 RIE: 1 CAT: 21

Classroom Observation Scales
CIJE: 1 RIE: 2 CAT: 21

Classroom Observation Schedule
CIJE: 0 RIE: 1 CAT: 21

Classroom Observations Keyed Effectiveness Res
CIJE: 3 RIE: 4 CAT: 21
SN Classroom Observations Keyed for Effectiveness Research
UF COKER

Classroom on Wheels
CIJE: 1 RIE: 1 CAT: 19

Classroom Preference Test (Koslin)
CIJE: 0 RIE: 2 CAT: 21

Classroom Reading Inventory
CIJE: 2 RIE: 6 CAT: 21

Classroom Robustness
USE Environmental Robustness

Classroom Screening Instruments
CIJE: 2 RIE: 1 CAT: 04

Classroom Simulation
CIJE: 0 RIE: 2 CAT: 15

Classroom Strategy Study
CIJE: 0 RIE: 1 CAT: 19

Classroom Strategy Survey
CIJE: 1 RIE: 0 CAT: 21

Classroom Teacher Inventory
CIJE: 1 RIE: 1 CAT: 21

Classroom Teacher Support System
CIJE: 2 RIE: 3 CAT: 15

Classroom Test of Formal Reasoning (Lawson)
USE Lawson Test of Formal Reasoning

Classroom Thoughtfulness
CIJE: 1 RIE: 2 CAT: 16

Classroom Visitors
CIJE: 2 RIE: 2 CAT: 10

ClassWorks
CIJE: 0 RIE: 1 CAT: 04

Clatsop Community College OR
CIJE: 0 RIE: 1 CAT: 17

Claudius I
CIJE: 1 RIE: 0 CAT: 18

Clauses
CIJE: 31 RIE: 33 CAT: 13

Clay (Marie)
CIJE: 4 RIE: 3 CAT: 18
SN "Marie M"

Clay Boat Project
CIJE: 0 RIE: 0 CAT: 19

Clay County Education Program KS
CIJE: 0 RIE: 1 CAT: 19

Claybrooks First Order Predicate Calculus
CIJE: 0 RIE: 1 CAT: 22

Claypit Hill School MA
CIJE: 1 RIE: 0 CAT: 17

Clayton Act
CIJE: 0 RIE: 3 CAT: 14

Clayton County Schools GA
CIJE: 1 RIE: 1 CAT: 17

Clayton Junior College GA
CIJE: 0 RIE: 3 CAT: 17

Clayton School District MO
CIJE: 1 RIE: 2 CAT: 17

Clayton State College GA
CIJE: 2 RIE: 2 CAT: 17

Clayton v Place
CIJE: 1 RIE: 0 CAT: 14

Clean Air Act 1963
CIJE: 6 RIE: 1 CAT: 14

Clean Air Amendments 1970
CIJE: 0 RIE: 3 CAT: 14

Clear Creek School District CO
CIJE: 0 RIE: 2 CAT: 17

CLEAR Oral Proficiency Exam
CIJE: 0 RIE: 1 CAT: 21
SN CLEAR = Center for Language Education and Research

CLEAR Reading Recovery Program
CIJE: 0 RIE: 10 CAT: 19
SN CLEAR = Compensatory Language Experiences And Reading

Clear Text Representation
CIJE: 0 RIE: 1 CAT: 13

Clearfield County Voc Tech School PA
CIJE: 0 RIE: 1 CAT: 17

Clearfield Job Corps Urban Center UT
CIJE: 1 RIE: 0 CAT: 17

Clearinghouse on Development Communication
CIJE: 1 RIE: 0 CAT: 17

Clearinghouse on Mastery Learning LA
CIJE: 0 RIE: 1 CAT: 17

Cleary (Beverly)
CIJE: 2 RIE: 1 CAT: 18

Cleaver (Eldridge)
CIJE: 2 RIE: 2 CAT: 18

Clemenceau (Georges)
CIJE: 1 RIE: 0 CAT: 18

Clement C Maxwell Library MA
CIJE: 0 RIE: 1 CAT: 17

Clemson University SC
CIJE: 36 RIE: 24 CAT: 17

CLEO
USE Compact for Lifelong Educational Opportunities

CLER Model
CIJE: 0 RIE: 3 CAT: 15
UF Configurations Linkages Environments Resources; Model of Planned Change (Bhola)

Clerical Perceptual Speed
CIJE: 0 RIE: 1 CAT: 11

Clerical Sector of Learning Opportunity Program
CIJE: 0 RIE: 1 CAT: 19

Clerical Skills
CIJE: 0 RIE: 2 CAT: 16

Clerical Solo Program
CIJE: 0 RIE: 1 CAT: 19

Cleveland Board of Education v Lafleur
CIJE: 3 RIE: 0 CAT: 14

Cleveland Board of Education v Loudermill
CIJE: 2 RIE: 0 CAT: 14
SN See also "Loudermill v Cleveland Board of Education"

Cleveland City Normal School OH
CIJE: 0 RIE: 1 CAT: 17

Cleveland College OH
CIJE: 0 RIE: 1 CAT: 17

Cleveland Composition Rating Scale
CIJE: 0 RIE: 1 CAT: 21

Cleveland County School District NC
CIJE: 0 RIE: 0 CAT: 17

Cleveland Foundation OH
CIJE: 0 RIE: 1 CAT: 17

Cleveland Health Sciences Library OH
CIJE: 1 RIE: 0 CAT: 17

Cleveland Institute of Art OH
CIJE: 0 RIE: 1 CAT: 17

Cleveland Major Works Classes
CIJE: 0 RIE: 1 CAT: 19

Cleveland Metropolitan Housing Authority OH
CIJE: 0 RIE: 1 CAT: 17

Cleveland Museum of Art OH
CIJE: 3 RIE: 1 CAT: 17

Cleveland Public Library OH
CIJE: 7 RIE: 1 CAT: 17

Cleveland Public Schools OH
CIJE: 12 RIE: 83 CAT: 17

Cleveland State Hospital OH
CIJE: 1 RIE: 0 CAT: 17

Cleveland State University OH
CIJE: 17 RIE: 15 CAT: 17

Cleveland Urban Learning Community OH
CIJE: 1 RIE: 1 CAT: 17

Cliches
CIJE: 0 RIE: 0 CAT: 13

Client Assistance Programs (Rehabilitation)
CIJE: 0 RIE: 1 CAT: 19

Client Attitudes
CIJE: 49 RIE: 5 CAT: 16

Client Behavior
CIJE: 21 RIE: 10 CAT: 11

Client Centered Counseling
CIJE: 8 RIE: 2 CAT: 11

Client Centered Evaluation
CIJE: 5 RIE: 2 CAT: 21

Client Centered Therapy
CIJE: 1 RIE: 1 CAT: 11

Client Cohesion of Self Schemata Scales
CIJE: 1 RIE: 0 CAT: 21

Client Engagement
CIJE: 3 RIE: 0 CAT: 11

Client Identification
CIJE: 2 RIE: 1 CAT: 11

Client Level Identification Index
CIJE: 1 RIE: 0 CAT: 21

Client Relations
CIJE: 10 RIE: 4 CAT: 16

Client Satisfaction
CIJE: 10 RIE: 2 CAT: 16

Client Tracking
CIJE: 2 RIE: 4 CAT: 15
UF Tracking (Clients)

Cliff Consistency Index
CIJE: 1 RIE: 0 CAT: 21

Cliff Hanger Problems
USE Cliffhangers

Cliffhangers
CIJE: 0 RIE: 1 CAT: 16
UF Cliff Hanger Problems

Clifford Books
CIJE: 0 RIE: 1 CAT: 22

Clifton (Lucille)
CIJE: 1 RIE: 1 CAT: 18

Climatology
CIJE: 9 RIE: 3 CAT: 20

Climax Programs
CIJE: 0 RIE: 1 CAT: 19

Climbing Trees
USE Tree Climbing

Climbing Walls
CIJE: 0 RIE: 2 CAT: 04

Clinch Powell Educ Coop Community Ed Project TN
CIJE: 0 RIE: 1 CAT: 19

Clinch Powell Educational Cooperative TN
CIJE: 2 RIE: 1 CAT: 17

Clinic on Library Applications of Data Processing
CIJE: 0 RIE: 1 CAT: 02

Clinical Analysis
CIJE: 2 RIE: 2 CAT: 15

Clinical Approach
CIJE: 0 RIE: 1 CAT: 15
SN ...for addressing idiosyncratic developmental needs in learning improvement programing

Clinical Center Associate Program
CIJE: 1 RIE: 0 CAT: 19

Clinical Competence
CIJE: 4 RIE: 0 CAT: 11

Clinical Experience (Judicial)
CIJE: 4 RIE: 0 CAT: 03

Clinical Infant Development Program
CIJE: 0 RIE: 1 CAT: 19

Clinical Interviews
CIJE: 3 RIE: 1 CAT: 15

Clinical Laboratory Occupations
CIJE: 2 RIE: 6 CAT: 09

Clinical Ladder
CIJE: 2 RIE: 0 CAT: 11

Clinical Linguistics
CIJE: 0 RIE: 2 CAT: 13

Clinical Medical Librarians
CIJE: 2 RIE: 2 CAT: 09

Clinical Nurse Specialists
USE Nurse Clinicians

Clinical Nursing Rating Scale
CIJE: 0 RIE: 1 CAT: 21

Clinical Preceptors
CIJE: 0 RIE: 2 CAT: 09

Clinical Reasoning
CIJE: 2 RIE: 2 CAT: 11

Clinical Skills Assessment Form
CIJE: 1 RIE: 0 CAT: 21

Clinical Sociology
CIJE: 0 RIE: 1 CAT: 03

Clinical Supervision Initiative
CIJE: 0 RIE: 1 CAT: 19

Clinical Supervision Model (Hunter)
USE Hunter Model of Clinical Supervision

Clinical Teacher Education
CIJE: 5 RIE: 4 CAT: 03

Clinical Teaching Model (Hunter)
USE Hunter Instructional Model

Clinical Trials
CIJE: 11 RIE: 4 CAT: 20

Clinite Center for the Hearing Impaired CA
CIJE: 0 RIE: 1 CAT: 17

Clinton (Bill)
CIJE: 11 RIE: 3 CAT: 18

Clinton (Cornelia Tappen)
CIJE: 0 RIE: 1 CAT: 18

Clinton Administration
CIJE: 22 RIE: 7 CAT: 17

Clinton Community Unit High School IL
CIJE: 1 RIE: 0 CAT: 17

Clinton County School District KY
CIJE: 0 RIE: 1 CAT: 17

Clinton Pilot Cassette Center MN
CIJE: 0 RIE: 3 CAT: 17

Clip Art
CIJE: 3 RIE: 7 CAT: 16

CLIPPT
USE Childrens Language Inst Preschool Placement Test

Cliques
CIJE: 5 RIE: 4 CAT: 10
UF Friendship Cliques

Clitic Pronouns
CIJE: 1 RIE: 0 CAT: 13

Clitics
CIJE: 4 RIE: 11 CAT: 13

Clocks
CIJE: 7 RIE: 3 CAT: 04

Clockwork Orange
CIJE: 4 RIE: 0 CAT: 22

Cloning
CIJE: 9 RIE: 1 CAT: 20

Close Ended Questions
CIJE: 0 RIE: 1 CAT: 21
UF Closed Ended Questions

Close Reading Approach
CIJE: 3 RIE: 2 CAT: 15

Close Up Foundation
USE Close Up Program

Close Up Program
CIJE: 9 RIE: 6 CAT: 19
UF Close Up Foundation

Closed Book Tests
CIJE: 1 RIE: 1 CAT: 21

Closed Captioned Television
CIJE: 12 RIE: 15 CAT: 15

Closed Captioned Television Decoders
CIJE: 0 RIE: 1 CAT: 04

Closed Catalogs
CIJE: 0 RIE: 1 CAT: 04

Closed Ended Questions
USE Close Ended Questions

Closed Loop Systems
CIJE: 1 RIE: 0 CAT: 20

Closed Sessions
CIJE: 0 RIE: 1 CAT: 16

Closeness
CIJE: 4 RIE: 1 CAT: 16

Closer Look
CIJE: 1 RIE: 0 CAT: 22

Closing of the American Mind (Bloom)
CIJE: 0 RIE: 1 CAT: 22

Clothing Care
CIJE: 0 RIE: 1 CAT: 16

Clothing Related Occupations
CIJE: 0 RIE: 3 CAT: 09

Cloud Seeding
CIJE: 1 RIE: 0 CAT: 20

Clouds
CIJE: 7 RIE: 1 CAT: 20

Clover Park School District WA
CIJE: 4 RIE: 1 CAT: 17

Clover Park Vocational Technical Institute WA
CIJE: 2 RIE: 0 CAT: 17

Cloverport Plan
CIJE: 0 RIE: 1 CAT: 19

Clovis Life Skills Materials
CIJE: 0 RIE: 1 CAT: 22

Clovis Unified School District CA
CIJE: 3 RIE: 0 CAT: 17

Cloward (Richard)
CIJE: 0 RIE: 1 CAT: 18

Clowns
CIJE: 3 RIE: 1 CAT: 09

Cloze Comprehension of Conjunctions Test
CIJE: 0 RIE: 1 CAT: 21

Club 6
CIJE: 1 RIE: 0 CAT: 17

Club Mediterrane
CIJE: 1 RIE: 0 CAT: 17

Club of Rome
CIJE: 1 RIE: 0 CAT: 17

Cluster Approach (Vocabulary)
CIJE: 1 RIE: 1 CAT: 15

Cluster Based Retrieval
CIJE: 18 RIE: 1 CAT: 20

Cluster Based Test Construction
CIJE: 0 RIE: 1 CAT: 21

Cluster Concept Program
CIJE: 1 RIE: 6 CAT: 19

Cluster Courses
CIJE: 1 RIE: 1 CAT: 03
UF Course Clusters

Cluster Districts
CIJE: 0 RIE: 1 CAT: 05

Cluster Interest Inventory (Herzog)
CIJE: 0 RIE: 2 CAT: 21

Cluster Sampling
CIJE: 3 RIE: 0 CAT: 21

Cluster Schools
CIJE: 3 RIE: 3 CAT: 05

Clustering (Learning)
CIJE: 6 RIE: 2 CAT: 11

Clustering (Reading)
CIJE: 1 RIE: 3 CAT: 13

Clutches (Automotive)
CIJE: 0 RIE: 2 CAT: 04
UF Automotive Clutches

Cluttering
CIJE: 4 RIE: 0 CAT: 16

Clyde Mood Scale
CIJE: 0 RIE: 1 CAT: 21

Clymer (Theodore)
CIJE: 0 RIE: 1 CAT: 18

Clymer Barrett Prereading Battery
CIJE: 1 RIE: 1 CAT: 21

CMS Records
CIJE: 1 RIE: 0 CAT: 17

CNN
USE Cable News Network

CNN Newsroom
CIJE: 0 RIE: 4 CAT: 19

CNN World Report
CIJE: 0 RIE: 1 CAT: 22

Co Citation Analysis
CIJE: 6 RIE: 3 CAT: 15

CO Plus Project
CIJE: 0 RIE: 1 CAT: 19

Co Workers (Employees)
USE Coworkers

Coached Clients
CIJE: 2 RIE: 0 CAT: 10

Coached Practice
CIJE: 0 RIE: 1 CAT: 15

Coaching
CIJE: 72 RIE: 26 CAT: 15

Coaching (Speech)
CIJE: 1 RIE: 3 CAT: 13
UF Speech Coaching

Coaching for Improved Teaching
CIJE: 1 RIE: 1 CAT: 19

Coaction (Speech)
CIJE: 0 RIE: 3 CAT: 13

Coahoma Junior College MS
CIJE: 0 RIE: 1 CAT: 17

Coal Employment Project
CIJE: 0 RIE: 1 CAT: 19

Coal Gasification
CIJE: 2 RIE: 0 CAT: 20

Coalcoholics
CIJE: 0 RIE: 1 CAT: 10

Coalition Concerned with Adolescent Pregnancy
CIJE: 0 RIE: 1 CAT: 17

Coalition for Better Television
CIJE: 0 RIE: 1 CAT: 17

Coalition for Education in the Outdoors
CIJE: 0 RIE: 1 CAT: 17

Coalition for National Service
CIJE: 0 RIE: 1 CAT: 17

Coalition for Public Library Research
CIJE: 0 RIE: 1 CAT: 17

Coalition of Adult Education Organizations DC
CIJE: 1 RIE: 3 CAT: 17

Coalition of Business and Educ Collaboration NY
CIJE: 0 RIE: 1 CAT: 17

Coalition of English Associations
CIJE: 1 RIE: 1 CAT: 17

Coalition of Essential Schools
CIJE: 20 RIE: 10 CAT: 17
SN See also "Essential Schools Movement"

Coalition of Indian Controlled School Bds CO
CIJE: 1 RIE: 0 CAT: 17

Coalition of Teacher Education Programs
CIJE: 0 RIE: 1 CAT: 17

Coalitions
CIJE: 30 RIE: 32 CAT: 10
SN See also the Descriptor "Partnerships in Education"

Coard (Bernard)
CIJE: 1 RIE: 0 CAT: 18

Coarticulation (Speech)
CIJE: 0 RIE: 1 CAT: 13

Coast Community College District CA
CIJE: 2 RIE: 13 CAT: 17

Coast Guard
CIJE: 5 RIE: 28 CAT: 17

Coast Guard Academy CT
CIJE: 2 RIE: 12 CAT: 17

Coast Salish (Tribe)
CIJE: 0 RIE: 1 CAT: 08

Coastal Bend Migrant Council TX
CIJE: 0 RIE: 2 CAT: 17

Coastal Carolina College SC
USE University of South Carolina Coastal Carolina Coll

Coastal Carolina Community College NC
CIJE: 0 RIE: 0 CAT: 17

Coastal Management
CIJE: 2 RIE: 3 CAT: 20

Coastal Zones
CIJE: 24 RIE: 23 CAT: 07

Coastline Community College CA
CIJE: 3 RIE: 9 CAT: 17

Coatesville Area School District PA
CIJE: 1 RIE: 0 CAT: 17

Coatsworth (Elizabeth)
CIJE: 1 RIE: 0 CAT: 18

Cobalt
CIJE: 10 RIE: 0 CAT: 20

Cobb (Stanwood)
CIJE: 1 RIE: 0 CAT: 18

Cobb County Public Schools GA
CIJE: 5 RIE: 4 CAT: 17

Cobb Douglas Function
CIJE: 3 RIE: 2 CAT: 15

COBOL Programing Language
CIJE: 15 RIE: 26 CAT: 04

COBUILD
CIJE: 1 RIE: 1 CAT: 22
UF Collins COBUILD English Language Dictionary

Coburn (Charles)
CIJE: 1 RIE: 0 CAT: 18

Coca Cola Company
CIJE: 2 RIE: 1 CAT: 17

Coca Cola Hispanic Education Fund
CIJE: 0 RIE: 1 CAT: 19

Coca Cola USA
CIJE: 1 RIE: 1 CAT: 17

Coca Paste (Drug)
CIJE: 1 RIE: 1 CAT: 11

Cocaine Freebase
CIJE: 1 RIE: 0 CAT: 11
UF Freebased Cocaine

Cochise College AZ
CIJE: 1 RIE: 4 CAT: 17

Cochlear Implants
CIJE: 24 RIE: 5 CAT: 04
UF Cochlear Prosthesis

Cochlear Prosthesis
USE Cochlear Implants

Cochrane Iroquois Falls Board of Education ON
CIJE: 0 RIE: 1 CAT: 17

Cockcroft Report
CIJE: 8 RIE: 4 CAT: 22

Cockpit Resource Management
CIJE: 0 RIE: 1 CAT: 15

Cockroaches
CIJE: 4 RIE: 3 CAT: 20

Cocoa Farmers
CIJE: 0 RIE: 1 CAT: 09

Cocteau (Jean)
CIJE: 1 RIE: 1 CAT: 18

Code Alphabet Meaning Emphasis
CIJE: 0 RIE: 1 CAT: 15

Code Emphasis Method
CIJE: 2 RIE: 0 CAT: 15

Code Enforcement Personnel
CIJE: 0 RIE: 1 CAT: 09

Code of Ethics of the Education Profession
CIJE: 1 RIE: 1 CAT: 22

Code of Ethics of the Library Profession
CIJE: 3 RIE: 0 CAT: 22

Code of Fair Testing Practices in Education
CIJE: 1 RIE: 0 CAT: 21

Code of Hammurabi
CIJE: 0 RIE: 0 CAT: 14

Code of Professional Responsibility
CIJE: 2 RIE: 1 CAT: 16

Code of Student Rights and Responsibilities
CIJE: 2 RIE: 0 CAT: 22

Coded Elaborative Outline
CIJE: 1 RIE: 1 CAT: 15

Codependency
CIJE: 9 RIE: 5 CAT: 11

Coder Drift
CIJE: 0 RIE: 1 CAT: 21

Codes of Student Conduct
CIJE: 0 RIE: 1 CAT: 14

CODIESEE
CIJE: 0 RIE: 1 CAT: 17
SN "Cooperation in Research and Development for Innovation in Education in South and Southeast Europe"

CODOC System
CIJE: 1 RIE: 0 CAT: 04

Coe College IA
CIJE: 2 RIE: 0 CAT: 17

Coed Dormitories
CIJE: 2 RIE: 0 CAT: 05

Coefficient of Association
CIJE: 6 RIE: 1 CAT: 21

Coefficient of Effective Length
CIJE: 1 RIE: 0 CAT: 21

Coefficient of Friction
CIJE: 1 RIE: 0 CAT: 20

Coefficients of Congruence
CIJE: 3 RIE: 2 CAT: 20

Coefficients of Stability
CIJE: 1 RIE: 1 CAT: 21
UF Stability Coefficients

Coenzymes
CIJE: 3 RIE: 0 CAT: 20

Coercion Theory
CIJE: 3 RIE: 2 CAT: 15

Coercive Behavior
CIJE: 8 RIE: 2 CAT: 11

Coeur d Alene (Tribe)
CIJE: 0 RIE: 2 CAT: 08

Coeur d Alene Reservation ID
CIJE: 0 RIE: 1 CAT: 07

Coffe Report
CIJE: 1 RIE: 0 CAT: 22

Coffee
CIJE: 2 RIE: 1 CAT: 20

Coffee County School District GA
CIJE: 0 RIE: 0 CAT: 17

Coffeehouses
CIJE: 2 RIE: 1 CAT: 05

Coffin Lowry Syndrome
CIJE: 1 RIE: 0 CAT: 11

Cogeneration (Energy)
CIJE: 1 RIE: 6 CAT: 20

Cognates
CIJE: 18 RIE: 23 CAT: 13

Cognition Scale of Assertiveness
CIJE: 1 RIE: 0 CAT: 21

Cognitive Abilities Test
CIJE: 6 RIE: 19 CAT: 21

Cognitive Academic Language Learning Approach
CIJE: 3 RIE: 1 CAT: 19
UF CALLA

Cognitive Academic Language Proficiency
CIJE: 3 RIE: 2 CAT: 13

Cognitive Activities Rating Scale (Steele)
CIJE: 0 RIE: 1 CAT: 21

Cognitive Affective Psychomotor Approach
CIJE: 0 RIE: 4 CAT: 15

Cognitive Anthropology
CIJE: 0 RIE: 2 CAT: 03

Cognitive Apprenticeships
CIJE: 7 RIE: 11 CAT: 15

Cognitive Aptitude
CIJE: 2 RIE: 2 CAT: 11

Cognitive Artifacts
CIJE: 0 RIE: 1 CAT: 15

Cognitive Bias Questionnaire
CIJE: 0 RIE: 1 CAT: 21

Cognitive Capacity
CIJE: 2 RIE: 0 CAT: 11

Cognitive Capacity Engagement
CIJE: 1 RIE: 0 CAT: 15

Cognitive Cause Maps
USE Cause Maps

Cognitive Code Learning Theory
CIJE: 4 RIE: 2 CAT: 15

Cognitive Competence
CIJE: 8 RIE: 0 CAT: 11

Cognitive Complexity
CIJE: 34 RIE: 9 CAT: 15

Cognitive Component Analysis
CIJE: 2 RIE: 1 CAT: 21

Cognitive Conflict
CIJE: 8 RIE: 2 CAT: 11

Cognitive Congruence Procedure
CIJE: 0 RIE: 1 CAT: 15

Cognitive Continuum Theory (Hammond)
CIJE: 0 RIE: 1 CAT: 15

Cognitive Control Battery
CIJE: 0 RIE: 2 CAT: 21

Cognitive Controls
CIJE: 8 RIE: 1 CAT: 11

Cognitive Deficit Theory
CIJE: 2 RIE: 1 CAT: 15

Cognitive Demands
CIJE: 3 RIE: 4 CAT: 15

Cognitive Developmental Grouping
CIJE: 0 RIE: 1 CAT: 15

Cognitive Distortion Task
CIJE: 1 RIE: 1 CAT: 21
UF Childrens Cognitive Distortion Task

Cognitive Domain
CIJE: 15 RIE: 18 CAT: 16

Cognitive Dumping Hypothesis
CIJE: 0 RIE: 1 CAT: 11

Cognitive Economics
CIJE: 0 RIE: 1 CAT: 15

Cognitive Engagement
CIJE: 3 RIE: 0 CAT: 11
SN See also "Cognitive Capacity Engagement"

Cognitive Engineering
CIJE: 2 RIE: 1 CAT: 15

Cognitive Enhancement
CIJE: 5 RIE: 2 CAT: 15

Cognitive Enrichment Network
CIJE: 1 RIE: 2 CAT: 19

Cognitive Entry Behaviors
CIJE: 1 RIE: 3 CAT: 11

Cognitive Environments Project
CIJE: 0 RIE: 1 CAT: 19

Cognitive Factors Scale
CIJE: 1 RIE: 1 CAT: 21

Cognitive Flexibility
CIJE: 18 RIE: 9 CAT: 11
UF Flexibility (Cognition)

Cognitive Fluency
CIJE: 0 RIE: 1 CAT: 11

Cognitive Frameworks
CIJE: 4 RIE: 3 CAT: 15

Cognitive Grammar
CIJE: 0 RIE: 1 CAT: 13

Cognitive Home Environment Scale
CIJE: 0 RIE: 2 CAT: 21

Cognitive Imaging
CIJE: 0 RIE: 1 CAT: 11

Cognitive Instructional Counseling
CIJE: 0 RIE: 1 CAT: 15

Cognitive Integration
CIJE: 6 RIE: 1 CAT: 11

Cognitive Interaction Analysis System
CIJE: 0 RIE: 2 CAT: 15

Cognitive Level
CIJE: 6 RIE: 6 CAT: 11

Cognitive Matching
CIJE: 10 RIE: 0 CAT: 15
UF Matching Procedures (Cognition)

Cognitive Mediation
CIJE: 7 RIE: 4 CAT: 11

Cognitive Mediational Paradigm
CIJE: 3 RIE: 0 CAT: 11

Cognitive Model for Assessing Portfolios
CIJE: 0 RIE: 1 CAT: 15

Cognitive Modeling
CIJE: 4 RIE: 6 CAT: 15

Cognitive Models
CIJE: 18 RIE: 6 CAT: 15

Cognitive Operation Structure
CIJE: 1 RIE: 3 CAT: 15

Cognitive Orientation Questionnaire of Curiosity
CIJE: 1 RIE: 0 CAT: 21

Cognitive Play
CIJE: 2 RIE: 1 CAT: 16

Cognitive Preference
CIJE: 13 RIE: 8 CAT: 11

Cognitive Preference Examination Chemistry
CIJE: 1 RIE: 0 CAT: 21

Cognitive Preference Inventory
CIJE: 4 RIE: 0 CAT: 21

Cognitive Press
CIJE: 1 RIE: 0 CAT: 16

Cognitive Process Theory of Writing
CIJE: 0 RIE: 2 CAT: 15

Cognitive Regression
CIJE: 2 RIE: 1 CAT: 16

Cognitive Research
CIJE: 39 RIE: 34 CAT: 11

Cognitive Research Trust
CIJE: 5 RIE: 1 CAT: 17

Cognitive Response Analysis
CIJE: 1 RIE: 1 CAT: 11

Cognitive Sciences
CIJE: 21 RIE: 21 CAT: 20

Cognitive Scripting
CIJE: 0 RIE: 1 CAT: 15

Cognitive Skills Assessment Battery
CIJE: 1 RIE: 16 CAT: 21

Cognitive Speed
CIJE: 2 RIE: 1 CAT: 11

Cognitive Strategy Instruction in Writing
CIJE: 1 RIE: 1 CAT: 15

Cognitive Stress Inoculation Training
CIJE: 0 RIE: 1 CAT: 15

Cognitive Style Interest Inventory
CIJE: 0 RIE: 3 CAT: 21

Cognitive Style Inventory
CIJE: 2 RIE: 0 CAT: 21

Cognitive Style Mapping Instrument
CIJE: 0 RIE: 1 CAT: 21

Cognitive Transition
CIJE: 0 RIE: 1 CAT: 15

Cognitive Vocational Maturity Test
CIJE: 3 RIE: 1 CAT: 21

Cognitively Guided Instruction
CIJE: 1 RIE: 2 CAT: 15

Cognitively Oriented Curriculum Model
CIJE: 3 RIE: 3 CAT: 15

Cognitively Oriented Preschool
CIJE: 1 RIE: 3 CAT: 03

Cohen (Felix)
CIJE: 0 RIE: 1 CAT: 18

Cohen (Harold L)
CIJE: 0 RIE: 1 CAT: 18

Cohen (Harold)
CIJE: 0 RIE: 1 CAT: 18
SN Modern artist

Cohen (Leonard)
CIJE: 5 RIE: 0 CAT: 18

Cohen (Michael D)
CIJE: 0 RIE: 0 CAT: 18

Cohen v Chesterfield City School Board
CIJE: 1 RIE: 1 CAT: 14

Cohesive Harmony
CIJE: 0 RIE: 2 CAT: 16

Cohesive Harmony Index
CIJE: 0 RIE: 1 CAT: 21

Cohn (Herman)
CIJE: 0 RIE: 1 CAT: 18

Cohoes City School District v Cohoes Teachers Assn
CIJE: 0 RIE: 1 CAT: 14

Cohort Change
CIJE: 2 RIE: 0 CAT: 11

Cohort Defined Tasks
CIJE: 0 RIE: 1 CAT: 15

Cohort Differences
CIJE: 7 RIE: 3 CAT: 11

Cohort Instructional Programs
CIJE: 0 RIE: 1 CAT: 19

COHORT Model
CIJE: 0 RIE: 1 CAT: 15

Cohort Size
CIJE: 3 RIE: 1 CAT: 21

Cohort Survival Procedures
CIJE: 2 RIE: 5 CAT: 15

Cohort Survival Ratio Method
CIJE: 2 RIE: 2 CAT: 15

Cohort Theory of Word Recognition
CIJE: 0 RIE: 1 CAT: 15

Coil Assemblers
CIJE: 0 RIE: 2 CAT: 09

Coil Opener and Down Ender Operators
CIJE: 0 RIE: 1 CAT: 09

Coil Winders
CIJE: 0 RIE: 1 CAT: 09

Coimbra Community Awareness Project (Portugal)
CIJE: 0 RIE: 1 CAT: 19

Coin Collecting
USE Numismatics

Coin Machine Collectors
CIJE: 0 RIE: 1 CAT: 09

Coincident Anticipation
CIJE: 3 RIE: 1 CAT: 11

Coincident Demand Metering
CIJE: 1 RIE: 0 CAT: 21

COKER
USE Classroom Observations Keyed Effectiveness Res

Colby College ME
CIJE: 3 RIE: 3 CAT: 17

Colby Community College KS
CIJE: 1 RIE: 1 CAT: 17

Colby Junior College for Women NH
CIJE: 1 RIE: 0 CAT: 17

Colby Sawyer College NH
CIJE: 1 RIE: 0 CAT: 17

Cold
CIJE: 1 RIE: 1 CAT: 20

Cold Chain
CIJE: 0 RIE: 1 CAT: 11
SN Temperature control of transported vaccines

Cold Climates
CIJE: 0 RIE: 2 CAT: 07

Cold Environment
CIJE: 1 RIE: 0 CAT: 16

Cold Injuries
CIJE: 2 RIE: 1 CAT: 11

Cold Mill Operators
CIJE: 0 RIE: 1 CAT: 09

Cold Saw Operators
CIJE: 0 RIE: 1 CAT: 09

Cold Sizing Mill Operators
CIJE: 0 RIE: 1 CAT: 09

Cold Spring Harbor Whaling Museum NY
CIJE: 1 RIE: 0 CAT: 17

Cold Type Composition (Printing)
CIJE: 2 RIE: 0 CAT: 15

Cold War
CIJE: 70 RIE: 25 CAT: 12

Cold Weather
CIJE: 1 RIE: 0 CAT: 20

Cole (Natalie Robinson)
CIJE: 2 RIE: 1 CAT: 18

Colearning
CIJE: 1 RIE: 0 CAT: 15

Colebank Health Behavior Inventory
CIJE: 0 RIE: 1 CAT: 21

Coleccion Tloque Nahuaque
CIJE: 0 RIE: 8 CAT: 17

Colegio de Mexico
CIJE: 2 RIE: 0 CAT: 17

Coleman (James S)
CIJE: 24 RIE: 18 CAT: 18

Coleman (John R)
CIJE: 1 RIE: 0 CAT: 18

Coleman (Statis)
CIJE: 1 RIE: 0 CAT: 18

Coleman II
CIJE: 7 RIE: 2 CAT: 22

Coleman Report
CIJE: 59 RIE: 67 CAT: 22

Coleman Technical Institute
CIJE: 2 RIE: 0 CAT: 17

Coleridge (Samuel Taylor)
CIJE: 10 RIE: 2 CAT: 18

Coles (William)
CIJE: 2 RIE: 1 CAT: 18

Colette (Sidonie Gabrielle)
CIJE: 2 RIE: 0 CAT: 18

Colfax Plan
CIJE: 0 RIE: 1 CAT: 19

Colgate Personal Values Inventory
CIJE: 0 RIE: 1 CAT: 21

Colgate University NY
CIJE: 9 RIE: 9 CAT: 17

Collaborating on Drug Education
USE Project CODE (Drug Education)

Collaboration for Improvement of Teacher Educ
CIJE: 0 RIE: 18 CAT: 19

Collaboration for Improving Teacher Educ SK
CIJE: 0 RIE: 1 CAT: 19

Collaboration to Improve Reading in Content Areas
USE CIRCA Project

Collaborations for Literacy
CIJE: 0 RIE: 3 CAT: 19

Collaborative Activation Based Production System
CIJE: 0 RIE: 1 CAT: 04

Collaborative Analysis Action Planning Process
CIJE: 1 RIE: 0 CAT: 15

Collaborative Bargaining
CIJE: 3 RIE: 6 CAT: 15

Collaborative Composing
CIJE: 3 RIE: 2 CAT: 13

Collaborative Consultation Support System Program
CIJE: 0 RIE: 1 CAT: 19
SN Peer cooperation and support among teachers in New York City

Collaborative Councils
CIJE: 2 RIE: 7 CAT: 10

Collaborative Evaluation
CIJE: 3 RIE: 3 CAT: 21

Collaborative Inquiry
CIJE: 7 RIE: 17 CAT: 15

Collaborative Learning
CIJE: 191 RIE: 147 CAT: 15

Collaborative Library Systems Development
CIJE: 0 RIE: 2 CAT: 15

Collaborative Network for Early Childhood Training
CIJE: 0 RIE: 1 CAT: 19
UF Project CoNECT

Collaborative Perinatal Research Project
CIJE: 2 RIE: 2 CAT: 19

Collaborative Research
CIJE: 73 RIE: 62 CAT: 16

Collaborative Research Programme (Scotland)
CIJE: 0 RIE: 1 CAT: 19

Collaborative Talk
CIJE: 1 RIE: 6 CAT: 15

Collaborative Teaching
CIJE: 22 RIE: 32 CAT: 15

Collaborative Testing
CIJE: 0 RIE: 1 CAT: 21

Collaborative Writing
CIJE: 262 RIE: 123 CAT: 13

Collars (Clothing)
CIJE: 0 RIE: 1 CAT: 16

Collateral Bar Rule
CIJE: 0 RIE: 1 CAT: 14

Collateral Informants
CIJE: 1 RIE: 0 CAT: 10

Collateral Information
CIJE: 1 RIE: 3 CAT: 16

Colleague Consultation
CIJE: 3 RIE: 1 CAT: 15

Collecting (Hobby)
CIJE: 5 RIE: 2 CAT: 16

Collection Mapping
CIJE: 6 RIE: 2 CAT: 15

Collection Overlap
CIJE: 6 RIE: 0 CAT: 16

Collection Size
CIJE: 2 RIE: 0 CAT: 16

Collections (Museum)
CIJE: 2 RIE: 1 CAT: 16

Collective Commune Schools
CIJE: 0 RIE: 1 CAT: 05

Collective Coorientation Model
CIJE: 0 RIE: 1 CAT: 15

Collective Gaining
CIJE: 1 RIE: 1 CAT: 15

Collective Intent
CIJE: 3 RIE: 1 CAT: 15

Collective Interpretation
CIJE: 0 RIE: 1 CAT: 15

Collective Security
CIJE: 0 RIE: 1 CAT: 16

Collective Violence
CIJE: 0 RIE: 5 CAT: 16

Collectivism
CIJE: 28 RIE: 7 CAT: 16

Collectivities
CIJE: 0 RIE: 1 CAT: 16

College 1
CIJE: 0 RIE: 1 CAT: 19

College Academic Self Efficacy Scale
CIJE: 0 RIE: 1 CAT: 21

College Adapter Program
CIJE: 0 RIE: 5 CAT: 19

College Advanced Placement Program
CIJE: 2 RIE: 1 CAT: 19

College Alcohol Survey
CIJE: 1 RIE: 1 CAT: 19

College and Research Libraries (Journal)
CIJE: 1 RIE: 1 CAT: 22

College and Univ Classroom Environment Inventory
USE College University Classroom Environment Inventory

College and University Environmental Scales
CIJE: 16 RIE: 25 CAT: 21

College and University Partnership Program
CIJE: 0 RIE: 2 CAT: 17

College and University Personnel Association
CIJE: 18 RIE: 2 CAT: 17

College and University Systems Exchange
CIJE: 0 RIE: 3 CAT: 17
SN Former name of "CAUSE"

College Assistance Migrant Program
CIJE: 3 RIE: 16 CAT: 19

College Assistance Program
CIJE: 0 RIE: 2 CAT: 19

College at Brockport NY
USE State University of New York Coll at Brockport

College at Buffalo NY
USE State University of New York Coll at Buffalo

College Band Directors National Association
CIJE: 2 RIE: 0 CAT: 17

College Basic Academic Subjects Examination
CIJE: 1 RIE: 2 CAT: 21
UF C BASE Test

College Behavior Questionnaire
CIJE: 0 RIE: 1 CAT: 21

College Board
USE College Entrance Examination Board

College Board Achievement Tests
CIJE: 11 RIE: 56 CAT: 21

College Board Admitted Student Questionnaire
USE Admitted Student Questionnaire

College Board Assessment and Placement Services
USE Assessment and Placement Services

College Board Computerized Placement Tests
CIJE: 0 RIE: 5 CAT: 21
UF Computerized Placement Tests (CEEB)

College Board Educational EQuality Project
USE EQuality Project

College Board Student Search Service
USE Student Search Service

College Board Validity Study Service
CIJE: 1 RIE: 2 CAT: 17

College Bound Program
CIJE: 1 RIE: 11 CAT: 19

College Cambrian College ON
CIJE: 0 RIE: 0 CAT: 17

College Center of the Finger Lakes NY
CIJE: 1 RIE: 1 CAT: 17

College Characteristics Analysis
CIJE: 0 RIE: 3 CAT: 15

College Characteristics Index (Stern and Pace)
CIJE: 5 RIE: 7 CAT: 21

College Classroom Vignettes
CIJE: 0 RIE: 1 CAT: 15

College Composition and Communication (Journal)
CIJE: 4 RIE: 1 CAT: 22

College Composition and Communication Conference
USE Conference on Coll Composition and Communication

College Consortium for International Studies
CIJE: 1 RIE: 1 CAT: 17

College Core Curriculum
CIJE: 0 RIE: 1 CAT: 19

College Costs
CIJE: 38 RIE: 86 CAT: 16

College d Enseignement Secondiere (France)
CIJE: 1 RIE: 0 CAT: 17

College Descriptive Index
CIJE: 1 RIE: 1 CAT: 21

College Development Committees
USE Development Committees

College Development Officers
USE Development Officers (College)

College Diagnostic Questionnaire
CIJE: 0 RIE: 1 CAT: 21

College Discovery and Development Program
CIJE: 1 RIE: 25 CAT: 19

College Edouard Monpetit PQ
CIJE: 0 RIE: 1 CAT: 17

College Educated
CIJE: 0 RIE: 1 CAT: 10

College Education Achievement Project
CIJE: 1 RIE: 1 CAT: 19

College English (Journal)
CIJE: 2 RIE: 1 CAT: 22

College English Association
CIJE: 1 RIE: 1 CAT: 17

College Entrance Exam Board Lang Achievement Test
CIJE: 1 RIE: 1 CAT: 21

College Entrance Exam Board Spatial Relations Test
CIJE: 2 RIE: 1 CAT: 21

College Entrance Examination Board
CIJE: 60 RIE: 82 CAT: 17
SN See add'l listings under "College Board..." — see also "Advanced Placement Examinations (CEEB)"
UF CEEB; College Board

College Executive Committees
USE Executive Committees

College Experiences Questionnaire
CIJE: 0 RIE: 1 CAT: 21

College Explorer Program
CIJE: 0 RIE: 1 CAT: 04

College Fairs
CIJE: 1 RIE: 1 CAT: 16
UF National College Fairs

College for Human Services NY
CIJE: 4 RIE: 10 CAT: 17

College for Kids
CIJE: 2 RIE: 1 CAT: 19

College for Living
CIJE: 1 RIE: 24 CAT: 19

College Freshman Adjustment Scale
CIJE: 1 RIE: 0 CAT: 21

College Guidance Placement Program
CIJE: 0 RIE: 1 CAT: 19

College Housing Loan Program
CIJE: 1 RIE: 2 CAT: 19

College Image
CIJE: 1 RIE: 6 CAT: 16

College Image Index
CIJE: 0 RIE: 1 CAT: 21

College Image Questionnaire
CIJE: 0 RIE: 1 CAT: 21

College Image Scale (Bailey)
CIJE: 0 RIE: 1 CAT: 21

College Information System
CIJE: 0 RIE: 2 CAT: 15

College Instructional Evaluation Questionnaire
CIJE: 0 RIE: 0 CAT: 21

College Investment Decision Study
CIJE: 0 RIE: 1 CAT: 19

College Language Association
CIJE: 1 RIE: 0 CAT: 17

College Level Academic Skills Test
CIJE: 7 RIE: 40 CAT: 21

College Level Examination Program
CIJE: 51 RIE: 79 CAT: 21

College Marie Victorin PQ
CIJE: 0 RIE: 2 CAT: 17

College Music Society
CIJE: 0 RIE: 1 CAT: 17

College Northern College ON
CIJE: 0 RIE: 1 CAT: 17

College of Alameda CA
CIJE: 0 RIE: 2 CAT: 17

College of Cape Breton NS
CIJE: 0 RIE: 2 CAT: 17
SN See also "University College of Cape Breton NS"

College of Charleston SC
CIJE: 6 RIE: 3 CAT: 17

College of DuPage IL
CIJE: 12 RIE: 20 CAT: 17

College of Eastern Utah
CIJE: 1 RIE: 4 CAT: 17

College of Family Physicians of Canada
CIJE: 1 RIE: 0 CAT: 17

College of Fisheries (Canada)
CIJE: 0 RIE: 1 CAT: 17

College of Ife (West Africa)
CIJE: 1 RIE: 0 CAT: 17

College of Insurance NY
CIJE: 1 RIE: 1 CAT: 17

College of Lake County IL
CIJE: 5 RIE: 11 CAT: 17

College of Marin CA
CIJE: 4 RIE: 4 CAT: 17

College of Medicine and Dentistry of New Jersey
CIJE: 4 RIE: 1 CAT: 17

College of Mount Saint Joseph OH
CIJE: 0 RIE: 2 CAT: 17

College of Mount Saint Vincent NY
CIJE: 0 RIE: 1 CAT: 17

College of New Caledonia BC
CIJE: 0 RIE: 1 CAT: 17

College of New Rochelle NY
CIJE: 9 RIE: 8 CAT: 17

College of Notre Dame CA
CIJE: 1 RIE: 1 CAT: 17

College of Notre Dame of Maryland
CIJE: 3 RIE: 1 CAT: 17

College of Osteopathic Medicine TX
CIJE: 0 RIE: 1 CAT: 17

College of Physicians of Philadelphia PA
CIJE: 2 RIE: 1 CAT: 17

College of Rock and Roll CA
CIJE: 1 RIE: 0 CAT: 17

College of Saint Benedict MN
CIJE: 1 RIE: 1 CAT: 17

College of Saint Catherine MN
CIJE: 4 RIE: 5 CAT: 17

College of Saint Elizabeth NJ
CIJE: 0 RIE: 1 CAT: 17

College of Saint Francis IL
CIJE: 0 RIE: 4 CAT: 17

College of Saint Mary NE
CIJE: 0 RIE: 1 CAT: 17

College of Saint Rose NY
CIJE: 0 RIE: 9 CAT: 17

College of Saint Scholastica MN
CIJE: 2 RIE: 7 CAT: 17

College of Saint Teresa MN
CIJE: 0 RIE: 3 CAT: 17

College of Saint Thomas MN
CIJE: 3 RIE: 5 CAT: 17

College of San Mateo CA
CIJE: 4 RIE: 4 CAT: 17

College of Santa Fe NM
CIJE: 0 RIE: 2 CAT: 17

College of Shariah (Saudia Arabia)
CIJE: 0 RIE: 1 CAT: 17

College of Southern Utah
CIJE: 1 RIE: 0 CAT: 17

College of Staten Island NY
USE City University of New York Coll of Staten Island

College of Steubenville OH
CIJE: 0 RIE: 1 CAT: 17

College of the Air OR
CIJE: 0 RIE: 4 CAT: 17

College of the Albemarle NC
CIJE: 0 RIE: 2 CAT: 17

College of the Atlantic ME
CIJE: 3 RIE: 0 CAT: 17

College of the Canyons CA
CIJE: 1 RIE: 14 CAT: 17

College of the Desert CA
CIJE: 1 RIE: 3 CAT: 17

College of the Finger Lakes NY
CIJE: 0 RIE: 1 CAT: 17

College of the Holy Cross MA
CIJE: 3 RIE: 4 CAT: 17

College of the Mainland TX
CIJE: 1 RIE: 12 CAT: 17

College of the Redwoods CA
CIJE: 0 RIE: 1 CAT: 17

College of the Sea (England)
CIJE: 0 RIE: 2 CAT: 17

College of the Sequoias CA
CIJE: 1 RIE: 5 CAT: 17

College of the Siskiyous CA
CIJE: 0 RIE: 1 CAT: 17

College of the Virgin Islands
CIJE: 2 RIE: 0 CAT: 17

College of William and Mary VA
CIJE: 10 RIE: 5 CAT: 17

College of Wooster OH
CIJE: 5 RIE: 8 CAT: 17

College Opinion Survey
CIJE: 1 RIE: 0 CAT: 19

College Opportunity Grant Program
CIJE: 0 RIE: 1 CAT: 19

College Orientation Program
CIJE: 0 RIE: 4 CAT: 19

College Orientation Program for Alaskan Natives
CIJE: 1 RIE: 2 CAT: 19

College Outcome Measures Project
CIJE: 10 RIE: 27 CAT: 19

College Outcomes Survey
CIJE: 0 RIE: 1 CAT: 21

College Parallel Program
CIJE: 1 RIE: 0 CAT: 19

College Parents Programs
CIJE: 0 RIE: 1 CAT: 19

College Placement Council
CIJE: 7 RIE: 1 CAT: 17

College Placement Council Survey 1988
CIJE: 0 RIE: 0 CAT: 19

College Preparatory Curriculum GA
CIJE: 0 RIE: 1 CAT: 03
UF Georgia College Preparatory Curriculum

College Qualification Tests
CIJE: 4 RIE: 4 CAT: 21

College Reach Out Program
CIJE: 0 RIE: 1 CAT: 19

College Readiness Program
CIJE: 0 RIE: 2 CAT: 19

College Reading and Study Skills Inventory
CIJE: 0 RIE: 1 CAT: 21

College Reading Association
CIJE: 0 RIE: 13 CAT: 17

College Reading Study Skills Program
CIJE: 0 RIE: 1 CAT: 19

College Readmission
CIJE: 0 RIE: 1 CAT: 16

College Research Center Member Colleges
CIJE: 0 RIE: 1 CAT: 17

College Retirement Equities Fund
CIJE: 33 RIE: 8 CAT: 17

College Scholarship Service NY
CIJE: 1 RIE: 2 CAT: 17

College Science Commissions
CIJE: 0 RIE: 1 CAT: 17

College Science Improvement Programs
CIJE: 1 RIE: 1 CAT: 19

College Science Instrumentation Program
CIJE: 0 RIE: 1 CAT: 19

College Seals
CIJE: 0 RIE: 1 CAT: 16
UF Seals (Colleges)

College Self Expression Scale
CIJE: 6 RIE: 3 CAT: 21

College Special Events
CIJE: 0 RIE: 3 CAT: 16
UF Special Events (College)

College Station Independent School District TX
CIJE: 1 RIE: 2 CAT: 17

College Student Experiences (Questionnaire)
CIJE: 1 RIE: 1 CAT: 21

College Student Experiences Questionnaire
CIJE: 2 RIE: 8 CAT: 21

College Student Questionnaires
CIJE: 5 RIE: 11 CAT: 21

College Student Satisfaction Questionnaire
CIJE: 1 RIE: 3 CAT: 21

College Student Value Questionnaire (Martin)
CIJE: 0 RIE: 1 CAT: 21

College Suggestor System
CIJE: 0 RIE: 6 CAT: 15

College Teacher Preparation Program
CIJE: 2 RIE: 0 CAT: 19

College Teacher Problems Q Sort (Bills)
CIJE: 0 RIE: 1 CAT: 21

College Teaching and Learning Collection
CIJE: 0 RIE: 33 CAT: 22

College to School Reporting
CIJE: 0 RIE: 1 CAT: 16

College to University Conversion
CIJE: 0 RIE: 1 CAT: 16

College Transfer Rates
USE Transfer Rates (College)

College Trustee Study
CIJE: 0 RIE: 1 CAT: 22

College Unions International
USE Association of College Unions International

College University Classroom Environment Inventory
CIJE: 0 RIE: 3 CAT: 21
UF College and Univ Classroom Environment Inventory

College Vice Presidents
CIJE: 0 RIE: 0 CAT: 09
SN See also "Vice Presidents of Academic Affairs"

College Womens Assertion Sample
CIJE: 1 RIE: 1 CAT: 21

College Work Study Program
CIJE: 0 RIE: 48 CAT: 19

Colleges d Enseignement General et Professionnel
USE Colleges of General and Professional Education PQ

Colleges of Advanced Education (Australia)
CIJE: 1 RIE: 1 CAT: 05

Colleges of Applied Arts and Technology ON
USE Ontario Colleges of Applied Arts and Technology

Colleges of Art
CIJE: 0 RIE: 1 CAT: 05

Colleges of General and Professional Education PQ
CIJE: 0 RIE: 3 CAT: 05
UF CEGEPs; Colleges d Enseignement General et Professionnel

Collegial Coaching
CIJE: 0 RIE: 1 CAT: 15

Collegial Evaluation
CIJE: 1 RIE: 1 CAT: 15

Collegial Governance Structures
CIJE: 1 RIE: 0 CAT: 15

Collegial Learning
CIJE: 2 RIE: 0 CAT: 15

Collegial Problem Solving
CIJE: 2 RIE: 1 CAT: 15

Collegial Supervision
CIJE: 0 RIE: 2 CAT: 15

Collegial Support Groups
CIJE: 0 RIE: 1 CAT: 10

Collegial Team Learning
CIJE: 1 RIE: 1 CAT: 15

Collegial Teams
CIJE: 1 RIE: 9 CAT: 10

Collegiate Assess Acad Prof Crit Think Test
CIJE: 0 RIE: 4 CAT: 21

Collegiate Assessment of Academic Proficiency
CIJE: 0 RIE: 7 CAT: 21

Collett Lester Fear of Death Scales
CIJE: 0 RIE: 1 CAT: 21

Collier (Jeremy)
CIJE: 1 RIE: 0 CAT: 18

Collier (John)
CIJE: 3 RIE: 5 CAT: 18

Collier Factor
CIJE: 0 RIE: 1 CAT: 15

Collier Macmillan English Program
CIJE: 0 RIE: 1 CAT: 19

Collinearity
CIJE: 2 RIE: 3 CAT: 16

Collings (Ellsworth)
CIJE: 1 RIE: 0 CAT: 18

Collingwood (R G)
CIJE: 3 RIE: 0 CAT: 18
SN "Robin George"

Collins (Barry)
CIJE: 1 RIE: 0 CAT: 18

Collins (Marva)
CIJE: 1 RIE: 3 CAT: 18

Collins COBUILD English Language Dictionary
USE COBUILD

Collis Romberg Mathematical Prob Solv Prof
CIJE: 0 RIE: 1 CAT: 21

Collocations (Lexical Items)
USE Lexical Collocation

Colloids
CIJE: 12 RIE: 0 CAT: 20

Colloquialisms
CIJE: 5 RIE: 2 CAT: 13

Collusion
CIJE: 1 RIE: 1 CAT: 11

Colombia
CIJE: 78 RIE: 151 CAT: 07

Colombia (Armero)
CIJE: 0 RIE: 1 CAT: 07

Colombia (Bogota)
CIJE: 5 RIE: 2 CAT: 07

Colombia (Cali)
CIJE: 1 RIE: 0 CAT: 07

Colombia (Medellin)
CIJE: 1 RIE: 0 CAT: 07

Colombian American Linguistic Institute
CIJE: 0 RIE: 1 CAT: 17

Colombian Americans
CIJE: 1 RIE: 1 CAT: 08

Colombian Institute for Advanced Training Abroad
CIJE: 0 RIE: 1 CAT: 17

Colombian Languages
CIJE: 0 RIE: 1 CAT: 13

Colombian Ministry of Education
USE Ministry of Education (Colombia)

Colombians
CIJE: 5 RIE: 5 CAT: 08

Colombo Plan
CIJE: 0 RIE: 3 CAT: 19

Colon Classification
CIJE: 2 RIE: 1 CAT: 16

Colons (Grammar)
CIJE: 0 RIE: 0 CAT: 13

Color Attending
CIJE: 2 RIE: 0 CAT: 16

Color Blindness
CIJE: 13 RIE: 6 CAT: 11

Color Categories
CIJE: 2 RIE: 2 CAT: 21

Color Coding
CIJE: 9 RIE: 5 CAT: 21

Color Discrimination
CIJE: 6 RIE: 4 CAT: 11

Color Dominance
CIJE: 2 RIE: 0 CAT: 16

Color Factor Set
CIJE: 1 RIE: 0 CAT: 20

Color Infrared Photography
CIJE: 1 RIE: 0 CAT: 20

Color Labeling Inventory
CIJE: 0 RIE: 1 CAT: 21

Color Meaning Test
CIJE: 1 RIE: 0 CAT: 21

Color Name Inventory (Institute Devel Studies)
CIJE: 0 RIE: 1 CAT: 21

Color Perception Test
CIJE: 0 RIE: 1 CAT: 21

Color Phonetic Symbol Test
CIJE: 1 RIE: 0 CAT: 21

Color Photography
CIJE: 5 RIE: 5 CAT: 20

Color Polymorphism
CIJE: 1 RIE: 0 CAT: 20

Color Preferences
CIJE: 0 RIE: 1 CAT: 11

Color Purple (The)
CIJE: 2 RIE: 2 CAT: 22

Color Pyramid Test
CIJE: 0 RIE: 1 CAT: 21

Color Rendition
CIJE: 1 RIE: 0 CAT: 20

Color Saturation
CIJE: 0 RIE: 1 CAT: 16

Color Stimuli
CIJE: 2 RIE: 3 CAT: 11

Color Theories
CIJE: 1 RIE: 2 CAT: 15

Color Vision Tests
CIJE: 0 RIE: 2 CAT: 21

Colorado
CIJE: 198 RIE: 833 CAT: 07

Colorado (Adams County)
CIJE: 5 RIE: 5 CAT: 07

Colorado (Alamosa)
CIJE: 0 RIE: 5 CAT: 07

Colorado (Aspen)
CIJE: 1 RIE: 3 CAT: 07

Colorado (Boulder County)
CIJE: 0 RIE: 1 CAT: 07

Colorado (Boulder)
CIJE: 7 RIE: 29 CAT: 07

Colorado (Colorado City)
CIJE: 0 RIE: 1 CAT: 07

Colorado (Colorado Springs)
CIJE: 10 RIE: 12 CAT: 07

Colorado (Denver)
CIJE: 38 RIE: 136 CAT: 07

Colorado (El Paso County)
CIJE: 0 RIE: 1 CAT: 07

Colorado (Fort Collins)
CIJE: 0 RIE: 17 CAT: 07

Colorado (Fort Lupton)
CIJE: 0 RIE: 2 CAT: 07

Colorado (Georgetown)
CIJE: 1 RIE: 0 CAT: 07

Colorado (Grand Junction)
CIJE: 1 RIE: 1 CAT: 07

Colorado (Greeley)
CIJE: 3 RIE: 7 CAT: 07

Colorado (Gunnison)
CIJE: 0 RIE: 2 CAT: 07

Colorado (Ignacio)
CIJE: 0 RIE: 1 CAT: 07

Colorado (Jefferson County)
CIJE: 4 RIE: 11 CAT: 07

Colorado (Lakewood)
CIJE: 0 RIE: 1 CAT: 07

Colorado (Littleton)
CIJE: 5 RIE: 1 CAT: 07

Colorado (Meeker)
CIJE: 0 RIE: 3 CAT: 07

Colorado (Mesa County)
CIJE: 0 RIE: 1 CAT: 07

Colorado (Monte Vista)
CIJE: 0 RIE: 2 CAT: 07

Colorado (Park County)
CIJE: 0 RIE: 1 CAT: 07

Colorado (Pueblo)
CIJE: 2 RIE: 3 CAT: 07

Colorado (Rocky Ford)
CIJE: 0 RIE: 1 CAT: 07

Colorado (San Luis Valley)
CIJE: 0 RIE: 3 CAT: 07

Colorado (San Luis)
CIJE: 0 RIE: 1 CAT: 07

Colorado (Sedgwick County)
CIJE: 0 RIE: 1 CAT: 07

Colorado (Sheridan)
CIJE: 0 RIE: 1 CAT: 07

Colorado (South)
CIJE: 0 RIE: 2 CAT: 07

Colorado (Vail)
CIJE: 0 RIE: 1 CAT: 07

Colorado (Weld County)
CIJE: 0 RIE: 1 CAT: 07

Colorado (West)
CIJE: 0 RIE: 4 CAT: 07

Colorado Advanced Technology Institute
CIJE: 0 RIE: 1 CAT: 17

Colorado Alliance of Research Libraries
CIJE: 7 RIE: 4 CAT: 17

Colorado Assn for Supervision and Curric Develop
CIJE: 0 RIE: 1 CAT: 17

Colorado Childrens Book Award
CIJE: 0 RIE: 1 CAT: 16

Colorado Civil Rights Commission
CIJE: 0 RIE: 1 CAT: 17

Colorado College
CIJE: 7 RIE: 9 CAT: 17

Colorado Comprehensive Health Education Act 1990
CIJE: 0 RIE: 1 CAT: 14

Colorado Conference on Stereotyping in Education
CIJE: 0 RIE: 1 CAT: 02

Colorado Consortium on Research Development
CIJE: 0 RIE: 1 CAT: 02

Colorado Council for Learning Disabilities
CIJE: 0 RIE: 1 CAT: 17

Colorado Elementary Science Project
CIJE: 0 RIE: 1 CAT: 19

Colorado Foreign Language Proficiency Sample Proj
CIJE: 0 RIE: 1 CAT: 19

Colorado Individualized Instruction
CIJE: 0 RIE: 1 CAT: 15

Colorado Migrant Council
CIJE: 0 RIE: 1 CAT: 17

Colorado Migrant Education Health Program
CIJE: 0 RIE: 0 CAT: 19

Colorado Migrant Education Resource Center
CIJE: 0 RIE: 4 CAT: 17

Colorado Migrant Health Program
CIJE: 1 RIE: 4 CAT: 19

Colorado Mountain College
CIJE: 1 RIE: 1 CAT: 17

Colorado Northwestern Community College
CIJE: 0 RIE: 1 CAT: 17

Colorado Outward Bound School
CIJE: 2 RIE: 9 CAT: 17

Colorado Program
CIJE: 0 RIE: 1 CAT: 19

Colorado River Indian Tribe
CIJE: 0 RIE: 1 CAT: 08

Colorado Rocky Mountain School
CIJE: 1 RIE: 0 CAT: 17

Colorado Rural Revitalization Project
CIJE: 0 RIE: 1 CAT: 19

Colorado School of Mines
CIJE: 6 RIE: 3 CAT: 17

Colorado Springs Public Schools CO
CIJE: 4 RIE: 4 CAT: 17

Colorado State College
CIJE: 2 RIE: 4 CAT: 17

Colorado State Department of Education
CIJE: 1 RIE: 7 CAT: 17

Colorado State Department of Social Services
CIJE: 0 RIE: 1 CAT: 17

Colorado State Library
CIJE: 0 RIE: 2 CAT: 17

Colorado State University
CIJE: 36 RIE: 51 CAT: 17

Colorado State University Fort Collins
CIJE: 2 RIE: 6 CAT: 17

Colorado Statewide Reference Network
CIJE: 0 RIE: 1 CAT: 17

Colorado Technical College
CIJE: 0 RIE: 2 CAT: 17

Colorado Training Institute
CIJE: 0 RIE: 1 CAT: 19

Colorado Video Inc
CIJE: 1 RIE: 0 CAT: 17

Colorado Western States Small Schools Project
CIJE: 0 RIE: 7 CAT: 19

Colorado Writing Project
CIJE: 1 RIE: 0 CAT: 19

Colored Farmers Alliance
CIJE: 1 RIE: 0 CAT: 17

Colorimetry
CIJE: 5 RIE: 1 CAT: 20

Coloring Books
CIJE: 4 RIE: 25 CAT: 16

Coloured Progressive Matrices
CIJE: 2 RIE: 4 CAT: 15

Colston Research Society (England)
CIJE: 0 RIE: 1 CAT: 17

Colton Unified School District CA
CIJE: 0 RIE: 1 CAT: 17

Columbia Academy (Japan)
CIJE: 1 RIE: 2 CAT: 17

Columbia Basin College WA
CIJE: 0 RIE: 3 CAT: 17

Columbia Basin School Study Council WA
CIJE: 0 RIE: 1 CAT: 17

Columbia Brazoria Independent School District TX
CIJE: 0 RIE: 1 CAT: 17

Columbia Broadcasting System
CIJE: 18 RIE: 10 CAT: 17
SN See also "CBS..."

Columbia City Joint High School IN
CIJE: 1 RIE: 0 CAT: 17

Columbia College CA
CIJE: 1 RIE: 1 CAT: 17

Columbia College IL
CIJE: 1 RIE: 1 CAT: 17
UF Columbia College of Chicago IL

Columbia College MO
CIJE: 0 RIE: 2 CAT: 17

Columbia College NY
CIJE: 1 RIE: 0 CAT: 17
SN Former name of Columbia University

Columbia College of Chicago IL
USE Columbia College IL

Columbia Communications Service Agency
CIJE: 0 RIE: 1 CAT: 17

Columbia Free Press
CIJE: 1 RIE: 0 CAT: 17

Columbia Greene Community College NY
CIJE: 1 RIE: 5 CAT: 17

Columbia Home Study Course
CIJE: 0 RIE: 1 CAT: 03

Columbia Junior College CA
CIJE: 0 RIE: 4 CAT: 17

Columbia Mental Maturity Scale
CIJE: 5 RIE: 8 CAT: 21

Columbia Public Schools MO
CIJE: 0 RIE: 2 CAT: 17

Columbia River
CIJE: 0 RIE: 2 CAT: 07

Columbia River Gorge
CIJE: 1 RIE: 1 CAT: 07

Columbia Scholastic Press Advisors Association
CIJE: 2 RIE: 0 CAT: 17

Columbia Scholastic Press Association
CIJE: 3 RIE: 4 CAT: 17

Columbia Seminar of Technology and Social Change
CIJE: 0 RIE: 1 CAT: 03

Columbia State Community College TN
CIJE: 1 RIE: 1 CAT: 17

Columbia University NY
CIJE: 82 RIE: 36 CAT: 17

Columbia University NY Barnard College
CIJE: 5 RIE: 1 CAT: 17
UF Barnard College NY

Columbia University NY Teachers College
CIJE: 20 RIE: 10 CAT: 17
SN See also "Teachers College..."
UF Teachers College Columbia University NY

Columbian Quincentenary
USE Columbus Quincentenary

Columbine Elementary School CO
CIJE: 0 RIE: 1 CAT: 17

Columbus (Christopher)
CIJE: 97 RIE: 30 CAT: 18

Columbus Board of Education v Penick
CIJE: 0 RIE: 1 CAT: 14

Columbus College GA
CIJE: 0 RIE: 3 CAT: 17

Columbus College of Art and Design OH
CIJE: 0 RIE: 1 CAT: 17

Columbus Day
CIJE: 8 RIE: 3 CAT: 12

Columbus Dispatch
CIJE: 0 RIE: 2 CAT: 22

Columbus Public Library OH
CIJE: 0 RIE: 2 CAT: 17

Columbus Public Schools OH
CIJE: 10 RIE: 77 CAT: 17

Columbus Quincentenary
CIJE: 30 RIE: 15 CAT: 12
UF Columbian Quincentenary

Columbus State School OH
CIJE: 0 RIE: 1 CAT: 17

Columbus Video Access Center IN
CIJE: 0 RIE: 2 CAT: 17

Columbus Zoo Aquarium OH
CIJE: 0 RIE: 1 CAT: 17

Colville Indian Reservation WA
CIJE: 1 RIE: 1 CAT: 17

Colville Lake
CIJE: 1 RIE: 0 CAT: 07

Comanche (Language)
CIJE: 0 RIE: 6 CAT: 13

Comanche (Tribe)
CIJE: 3 RIE: 4 CAT: 08

Combat
CIJE: 3 RIE: 2 CAT: 16

Combat Information Center CA
CIJE: 0 RIE: 1 CAT: 17

Combinatorial Skills
CIJE: 3 RIE: 1 CAT: 16

Combinatorial Verbal Written and Manipulative Test
CIJE: 0 RIE: 0 CAT: 21

Combinatorics
CIJE: 30 RIE: 4 CAT: 16

Combined Degrees
CIJE: 4 RIE: 1 CAT: 16

Combined English Language Skills Assessment Test
CIJE: 0 RIE: 2 CAT: 21
SN See also "English Language Skills Assessment"

Combined Federal Campaign
CIJE: 0 RIE: 1 CAT: 17

Combined File Search Strategy
CIJE: 1 RIE: 2 CAT: 15

Combined Health Information Database
CIJE: 0 RIE: 1 CAT: 04

Combined Immunodeficiency Disease
CIJE: 1 RIE: 0 CAT: 11

Combined Motivation Education System
CIJE: 0 RIE: 1 CAT: 15

Combined Resources for Editing Automated Teaching
CIJE: 0 RIE: 1 CAT: 19

Combs (A W)
CIJE: 1 RIE: 0 CAT: 18

Combustion
CIJE: 5 RIE: 11 CAT: 20

COMCONF
CIJE: 0 RIE: 1 CAT: 04

Comenius (Johann Amos)
CIJE: 11 RIE: 7 CAT: 18
UF Komensky (Jan Amos)

Comer (James P)
CIJE: 1 RIE: 4 CAT: 18

Comets
CIJE: 19 RIE: 6 CAT: 20

COMETS (Project)
CIJE: 0 RIE: 2 CAT: 19

COMETT
CIJE: 2 RIE: 0 CAT: 19
UF European Community Action Prog Educ Training Techn

COMETT CALLIOPE (Project)
CIJE: 0 RIE: 1 CAT: 19

Comettant (Oscar)
CIJE: 1 RIE: 0 CAT: 18

COMEX Project
CIJE: 0 RIE: 21 CAT: 19

Comfield Model Teacher Education Program
CIJE: 1 RIE: 27 CAT: 19

Comfort Index
CIJE: 0 RIE: 4 CAT: 21

Comfortability Scale in Special Education
CIJE: 0 RIE: 1 CAT: 21

Comfortable Interpersonal Distance Scale
CIJE: 3 RIE: 4 CAT: 21

Comision Nacional de Investigaciones Especiales
CIJE: 0 RIE: 1 CAT: 17

COMIT Programing Language
CIJE: 1 RIE: 4 CAT: 04

Command Action Planning System
CIJE: 0 RIE: 1 CAT: 15

Command Information Processing Systems
CIJE: 0 RIE: 1 CAT: 15

Command Language
CIJE: 28 RIE: 10 CAT: 04

Command Post Series
CIJE: 0 RIE: 1 CAT: 22

Commands
CIJE: 2 RIE: 2 CAT: 16
SN See also "Search Commands"

Commas
CIJE: 3 RIE: 3 CAT: 13

Commemorative Events
CIJE: 20 RIE: 9 CAT: 12

Commemorative Publications
CIJE: 0 RIE: 7 CAT: 16

Commemorative Stamps
CIJE: 1 RIE: 0 CAT: 16

Commercial Applications
CIJE: 6 RIE: 2 CAT: 16

Commercial Drivers
CIJE: 0 RIE: 2 CAT: 09

Commercial Educational Research
CIJE: 0 RIE: 1 CAT: 15

Commercial Generators
CIJE: 0 RIE: 1 CAT: 04

Commercial Motor Vehicle Safety Act 1986
CIJE: 1 RIE: 1 CAT: 14
UF Public Law 99 570

Commercial Recreation
CIJE: 2 RIE: 1 CAT: 16

Commercial Security
CIJE: 0 RIE: 1 CAT: 16

Commercial Update and Retrieval System
CIJE: 1 RIE: 0 CAT: 04

Commercial Zapping
CIJE: 0 RIE: 1 CAT: 16

Commercially Prepared Materials
CIJE: 15 RIE: 7 CAT: 04

Commission des Ecoles Catholiques de Montreal
CIJE: 1 RIE: 0 CAT: 17

Commission for National Education
CIJE: 1 RIE: 0 CAT: 17

Commission of Inquiry into High School Journalism
CIJE: 1 RIE: 1 CAT: 17

Commission of Professors of Adult Education
CIJE: 0 RIE: 3 CAT: 17

Commission of the European Communities
USE European Communities Commission

Commission on Academic Excellence
CIJE: 0 RIE: 1 CAT: 17

Commission on Academic Tenure
CIJE: 1 RIE: 1 CAT: 17

Commission on Accreditation for Corrections Inc
CIJE: 0 RIE: 1 CAT: 17

Commission on Campus Unrest
CIJE: 3 RIE: 0 CAT: 17

Commission on Chapter 1
CIJE: 0 RIE: 2 CAT: 17

Commission on Civil Rights
CIJE: 11 RIE: 35 CAT: 17

Commission on College Geography
CIJE: 1 RIE: 2 CAT: 17

Commission on College Physics
CIJE: 4 RIE: 6 CAT: 17

Commission on Correctional Manpower and Training
CIJE: 0 RIE: 1 CAT: 17

Commission on Dental Accreditation
CIJE: 2 RIE: 0 CAT: 17

Commission on Educ in Agric and Natural Resources
CIJE: 0 RIE: 5 CAT: 17

Commission on Education for Health Administration
CIJE: 0 RIE: 1 CAT: 17

Commission on Education of the Deaf
CIJE: 3 RIE: 2 CAT: 17

Commission on Engineering Education
CIJE: 0 RIE: 3 CAT: 17

Commission on Geography and Afro America
CIJE: 1 RIE: 0 CAT: 17

Commission on Higher Education and Adult Learner
CIJE: 0 RIE: 1 CAT: 17

Commission on Institutions of Higher Education
CIJE: 7 RIE: 8 CAT: 17

Commission on Instructional Technology
CIJE: 9 RIE: 2 CAT: 17

Commission on Language Difficulties
CIJE: 1 RIE: 0 CAT: 17

Commission on Mathematics
CIJE: 0 RIE: 1 CAT: 17

Commission on Native Education (South Africa)
CIJE: 1 RIE: 0 CAT: 17

Commission on Non Traditional Study
CIJE: 0 RIE: 2 CAT: 17

Commission on Physical Sciences Math and Resources
CIJE: 0 RIE: 1 CAT: 17

Commission on Plans for Higher Education
CIJE: 0 RIE: 1 CAT: 17

Commission on Population Growth American Future
CIJE: 2 RIE: 0 CAT: 17

Commission on Post Secondary Education in Ontario
CIJE: 0 RIE: 1 CAT: 17

Commission on Preservation and Access
CIJE: 0 RIE: 6 CAT: 17

Commission on Presidential Debates
CIJE: 0 RIE: 1 CAT: 17

Commission on Private Schools in Ontario
CIJE: 0 RIE: 1 CAT: 17

Commission on Professional Rights Responsibilities
CIJE: 0 RIE: 1 CAT: 17

Commission on Public Relations Education
CIJE: 3 RIE: 1 CAT: 17

Commission on Religion in Appalachia
CIJE: 1 RIE: 1 CAT: 17

Commission on Research Innovation and Evaluation
CIJE: 0 RIE: 1 CAT: 17

Commission on Schools
CIJE: 2 RIE: 0 CAT: 17

Commission on Science Education
CIJE: 0 RIE: 2 CAT: 17

Commission on Strengthening Presidential Leader
CIJE: 0 RIE: 1 CAT: 17

Commission on Tests
CIJE: 0 RIE: 3 CAT: 17

Commission on the Education of Teachers of Science
CIJE: 0 RIE: 1 CAT: 17

Commission on the Future
CIJE: 0 RIE: 1 CAT: 17

Commission on the Higher Education of Minorities
CIJE: 0 RIE: 2 CAT: 17

Commission on the Humanities
CIJE: 0 RIE: 1 CAT: 17

Commission on the Year 2000
CIJE: 1 RIE: 0 CAT: 17

Commission on Undergraduate Educ Biological Scis
CIJE: 10 RIE: 9 CAT: 17

Commission Seven
CIJE: 1 RIE: 0 CAT: 17

Commission to Improve Minority Education (AACC)
CIJE: 0 RIE: 1 CAT: 17
UF AACC Commission to Improve Minority Education

Commitment
CIJE: 153 RIE: 56 CAT: 16
SN Use a more specific term if possible, e.g., following such initial words as Career, Emotional, Occupational, Organizational, Outpatient, Parent, Social, Teacher, and Work

Commitment Laws
CIJE: 4 RIE: 1 CAT: 14
UF Involuntary Commitment Laws

Committee Allied Health Education Accreditation
CIJE: 0 RIE: 1 CAT: 17

Committee Evaluation Questionnaire
CIJE: 1 RIE: 0 CAT: 21

Committee for a Rational Alternative
CIJE: 1 RIE: 0 CAT: 17

Committee for Boston Public Housing MA
CIJE: 0 RIE: 1 CAT: 17

Committee for Community Research
CIJE: 0 RIE: 1 CAT: 17

Committee for Economic Development
CIJE: 10 RIE: 1 CAT: 17

Committee for Education Programs
CIJE: 0 RIE: 0 CAT: 19

Committee for Full Funding of Education Programs
CIJE: 1 RIE: 0 CAT: 17

Committee for New College
CIJE: 0 RIE: 1 CAT: 17

Committee for the Development of Sport
CIJE: 0 RIE: 1 CAT: 17
SN Subcommittee of the Council of Europe
UF CDDS

Committee in Solidarity with People of El Salvador
CIJE: 0 RIE: 0 CAT: 17

Committee Mathematics for Noncollege Bound Student
CIJE: 0 RIE: 1 CAT: 17

Committee of Adult Education Organizations
CIJE: 0 RIE: 1 CAT: 17

Committee of Social Action for Indians of Americas
CIJE: 1 RIE: 0 CAT: 17

Committee of Ten
CIJE: 5 RIE: 0 CAT: 17

Committee on Ability Testing
CIJE: 3 RIE: 0 CAT: 17

Committee on Administration of Training Programs
CIJE: 0 RIE: 1 CAT: 17

Committee on Allied Health Educ and Accreditation
CIJE: 0 RIE: 2 CAT: 17

Committee on Allied Health Education Accreditation
CIJE: 0 RIE: 1 CAT: 17

Committee on Assessing the Progress of Education
CIJE: 2 RIE: 1 CAT: 17

Committee on Basic Research in Education
CIJE: 1 RIE: 2 CAT: 17

Committee on Children of Minority Groups
CIJE: 0 RIE: 1 CAT: 17

Committee on Childrens Television
CIJE: 0 RIE: 9 CAT: 17

Committee on Economic Development
CIJE: 2 RIE: 0 CAT: 17

Committee on Economic Education
CIJE: 1 RIE: 1 CAT: 17

Committee on Education and Human Resources
CIJE: 1 RIE: 1 CAT: 17

Committee on Equal Educational Opportunity
CIJE: 0 RIE: 4 CAT: 17

Committee on Geoscience Information
CIJE: 0 RIE: 2 CAT: 17

Committee on Institutional Cooperation
CIJE: 1 RIE: 4 CAT: 17

Committee on International Education in Physics
CIJE: 2 RIE: 0 CAT: 17

Committee on Law Library Service to Prisoners
CIJE: 0 RIE: 2 CAT: 17

Committee on Physics in Secondary Education
CIJE: 1 RIE: 0 CAT: 17

Committee on Physics in Two Year Colleges
CIJE: 0 RIE: 1 CAT: 17

Committee on Public Education
CIJE: 0 RIE: 1 CAT: 17

Committee on Public Information
CIJE: 1 RIE: 2 CAT: 17

Committee on Scientific and Technical Information
CIJE: 0 RIE: 10 CAT: 17

Committee on Social and Behavioral Urban Research
CIJE: 0 RIE: 1 CAT: 17

Committee on Social Science Research
CIJE: 0 RIE: 1 CAT: 17

Committee on the Peaceful Uses of Outer Space
CIJE: 0 RIE: 1 CAT: 17

Committee on the Status of Women in Ontario Univs
CIJE: 0 RIE: 0 CAT: 17

Committee on the Undergraduate Program in Math
CIJE: 1 RIE: 14 CAT: 17

Committee on Tolerance and Understanding (Canada)
CIJE: 0 RIE: 1 CAT: 17

Committee on Vocational Educational R and D
CIJE: 0 RIE: 1 CAT: 17

Committee Public Educ Religious Liberty v Nyquist
CIJE: 0 RIE: 1 CAT: 14

Committee Role Rating Scale (Hecht)
CIJE: 0 RIE: 2 CAT: 21

Committee to Investigate Copyright Problems
CIJE: 0 RIE: 1 CAT: 17

Commodity Distribution Program
CIJE: 6 RIE: 7 CAT: 19

Commodity Futures
CIJE: 3 RIE: 2 CAT: 16

Commodore 64
CIJE: 5 RIE: 3 CAT: 04

Commodore Amiga
USE Amiga

Commodore Microcomputers
CIJE: 0 RIE: 2 CAT: 04

Commodore PET
CIJE: 0 RIE: 2 CAT: 04

Commodore VIC 20
CIJE: 2 RIE: 1 CAT: 04

Common Background Questionnaire
CIJE: 0 RIE: 1 CAT: 21

Common Basic Electronics Training
CIJE: 1 RIE: 0 CAT: 03

Common Carrier Services
CIJE: 0 RIE: 2 CAT: 16

Common College CA
CIJE: 1 RIE: 0 CAT: 17

Common Communication Format
CIJE: 1 RIE: 3 CAT: 04

Common Core of Data Program
CIJE: 0 RIE: 34 CAT: 19

Common Core of Learning (Connecticut)
CIJE: 0 RIE: 3 CAT: 03

Common Core of Learning (Kentucky)
CIJE: 0 RIE: 1 CAT: 03

Common Criterion Approach
CIJE: 0 RIE: 2 CAT: 15

Common Education
CIJE: 5 RIE: 1 CAT: 19

Common Fund
CIJE: 1 RIE: 2 CAT: 17

Common Item Effect
CIJE: 9 RIE: 3 CAT: 21

Common Law
CIJE: 19 RIE: 7 CAT: 14

Common Market (Europe)
CIJE: 11 RIE: 7 CAT: 17

Common Schools
CIJE: 5 RIE: 2 CAT: 05

Common Sense
CIJE: 9 RIE: 2 CAT: 16

Common Sense Narratives
CIJE: 0 RIE: 1 CAT: 13

Common Target Game
CIJE: 1 RIE: 0 CAT: 15

Common Threads (Film)
CIJE: 0 RIE: 1 CAT: 22
UF Common Threads Stories from the Quilt

Common Threads Stories from the Quilt
USE Common Threads (Film)

Commonality
CIJE: 2 RIE: 6 CAT: 16

Commonality Analysis
CIJE: 7 RIE: 12 CAT: 21

Commons Dilemma Choices
CIJE: 2 RIE: 3 CAT: 11

Commonwealth College
CIJE: 1 RIE: 0 CAT: 17

Commonwealth Computer Assisted Instr Consortium
CIJE: 1 RIE: 3 CAT: 02

Commonwealth Council for Educ Administration
CIJE: 0 RIE: 4 CAT: 17

Commonwealth Edison Company IL
CIJE: 2 RIE: 0 CAT: 17

Commonwealth Educational Broadcasting Conference
CIJE: 2 RIE: 0 CAT: 02

Commonwealth Fund Demonstration Clinics
CIJE: 1 RIE: 0 CAT: 02

Commonwealth Grants Commission (Australia)
CIJE: 1 RIE: 0 CAT: 17

Commonwealth Library Association (England)
CIJE: 1 RIE: 0 CAT: 17

Commonwealth of Learning
CIJE: 0 RIE: 8 CAT: 17

Commonwealth of Nations
CIJE: 0 RIE: 15 CAT: 17
SN Also called "British Commonwealth" (q.v.) — former name was British Commonwealth of Nations

Commonwealth Schools Commission (Australia)
CIJE: 0 RIE: 1 CAT: 17
UF Australian Commonwealth Schools Commission

Commonwealth Scientific Ind Res Org (Australia)
CIJE: 3 RIE: 2 CAT: 17

Commonwealth Secondary Scholarship Examination
CIJE: 1 RIE: 1 CAT: 21

Commonwealth Secretariat Reports
CIJE: 0 RIE: 2 CAT: 16

Communality
CIJE: 8 RIE: 7 CAT: 16

Communality Estimates
CIJE: 6 RIE: 0 CAT: 15

Communi Link
CIJE: 1 RIE: 1 CAT: 19

Communicability
CIJE: 0 RIE: 2 CAT: 16

Communicasting
CIJE: 1 RIE: 2 CAT: 15

Communication Accuracy
CIJE: 2 RIE: 5 CAT: 20

Communication Across the Curriculum
CIJE: 1 RIE: 7 CAT: 03

Communication Arc
CIJE: 0 RIE: 1 CAT: 16

Communication Arts
CIJE: 3 RIE: 8 CAT: 03

Communication Audit Survey Questionnaire
CIJE: 0 RIE: 2 CAT: 21

Communication Behavior
CIJE: 200 RIE: 244 CAT: 11

Communication Boards
CIJE: 14 RIE: 5 CAT: 04

Communication Channels
CIJE: 7 RIE: 8 CAT: 15

Communication Competencies
CIJE: 28 RIE: 45 CAT: 13

Communication Competency Assessment Instrument
CIJE: 3 RIE: 5 CAT: 21

Communication Consultants
CIJE: 8 RIE: 5 CAT: 09

Communication Context
CIJE: 25 RIE: 42 CAT: 16

Communication Directors
CIJE: 0 RIE: 2 CAT: 10

Communication Dominance
CIJE: 1 RIE: 5 CAT: 13

Communication in Societies
CIJE: 9 RIE: 3 CAT: 03

Communication Indicators
CIJE: 3 RIE: 3 CAT: 16

Communication Intention
USE Communicative Intention

Communication Intention Inventory
CIJE: 0 RIE: 1 CAT: 21

Communication Links
CIJE: 5 RIE: 3 CAT: 15
UF Links (Communication)

Communication Management
CIJE: 1 RIE: 0 CAT: 15
SN See also "Adult Communication Management"

Communication Openness Measure
CIJE: 0 RIE: 1 CAT: 21

Communication Patterns
CIJE: 42 RIE: 69 CAT: 16

Communication Program Survey
CIJE: 3 RIE: 1 CAT: 19

Communication Rules
CIJE: 4 RIE: 2 CAT: 15

Communication Satisfaction
CIJE: 24 RIE: 18 CAT: 13

Communication Satisfaction Questionnaire
CIJE: 1 RIE: 2 CAT: 21

Communication Satisfaction Scale (Brown)
CIJE: 0 RIE: 1 CAT: 21

Communication Satisfaction Survey
CIJE: 0 RIE: 1 CAT: 21

Communication Script Analysis
CIJE: 0 RIE: 1 CAT: 15

Communication Skills Centers Project
CIJE: 0 RIE: 4 CAT: 19

Communication Skills Through Authorship
CIJE: 3 RIE: 2 CAT: 19

Communication Strategies
CIJE: 122 RIE: 173 CAT: 15

Communication Styles
CIJE: 39 RIE: 61 CAT: 16

Communication Support
CIJE: 1 RIE: 2 CAT: 16

Communications Act 1934
CIJE: 4 RIE: 17 CAT: 14

Communications Behavior
CIJE: 4 RIE: 2 CAT: 20

Communications Curriculum
CIJE: 9 RIE: 8 CAT: 03

Communications Equipment Assemblers
CIJE: 0 RIE: 1 CAT: 09

Communications Infrastructure
CIJE: 0 RIE: 0 CAT: 20
SN See also "Telecommunications Infrastructure" and "Information Infrastructure"

Communications Network Training
CIJE: 1 RIE: 0 CAT: 15

Communications Occupations
CIJE: 6 RIE: 5 CAT: 09

Communications Protocols
CIJE: 1 RIE: 1 CAT: 15

Communications Research
CIJE: 9 RIE: 19 CAT: 15

Communications Satellite Act 1962
CIJE: 0 RIE: 4 CAT: 14

Communications Satellite Act 1969
CIJE: 0 RIE: 1 CAT: 14

Communications Satellite Corporation
CIJE: 0 RIE: 6 CAT: 17

Communications Structure
CIJE: 2 RIE: 2 CAT: 20

Communications Workers of America
CIJE: 3 RIE: 2 CAT: 17

Communicative Adaptability
CIJE: 5 RIE: 2 CAT: 16

Communicative Approach
CIJE: 17 RIE: 21 CAT: 13
UF Communicative Language Teaching

Communicative Intention
CIJE: 2 RIE: 1 CAT: 16
UF Communication Intention

Communicative Language Teaching
USE Communicative Approach

Communicator Motivation
CIJE: 0 RIE: 1 CAT: 15

Communicator Style
CIJE: 22 RIE: 61 CAT: 15

Communicology
CIJE: 1 RIE: 1 CAT: 15

Communimetrics
CIJE: 0 RIE: 1 CAT: 20

Communist Party
CIJE: 7 RIE: 8 CAT: 17

Communist Party Congress (USSR)
CIJE: 0 RIE: 1 CAT: 02

Communist Party of the Soviet Union
CIJE: 4 RIE: 3 CAT: 17

Community 70 Series
CIJE: 1 RIE: 0 CAT: 22

Community Access
CIJE: 2 RIE: 6 CAT: 16

Community Access Television
CIJE: 0 RIE: 1 CAT: 20

Community Action Agencies
CIJE: 0 RIE: 2 CAT: 10

Community Action Training Institute NJ
CIJE: 0 RIE: 1 CAT: 17

Community Adult Educationalists
CIJE: 1 RIE: 0 CAT: 16

Community Aging Project
CIJE: 3 RIE: 0 CAT: 19

Community Aide Program
CIJE: 0 RIE: 1 CAT: 19

Community Aides
CIJE: 1 RIE: 3 CAT: 09

Community Analysis Research Institute
CIJE: 0 RIE: 7 CAT: 17

Community and Continuing Educ Information Service
CIJE: 0 RIE: 2 CAT: 17

Community and Education Project for Beta Israel
CIJE: 0 RIE: 1 CAT: 19

Community Apprentice Program
CIJE: 0 RIE: 1 CAT: 19

Community Approach to an Integrated Service System
CIJE: 0 RIE: 1 CAT: 15
SN See also "Project Nexus"
UF CAISS

Community Arts Councils
CIJE: 1 RIE: 0 CAT: 05

Community Based Alternatives Program NC
CIJE: 0 RIE: 0 CAT: 19

Community Based Education
CIJE: 37 RIE: 98 CAT: 15

Community Based Organizations
CIJE: 5 RIE: 14 CAT: 05

Community Based Programing
CIJE: 1 RIE: 1 CAT: 15

Community Based Rehabilitation
CIJE: 2 RIE: 2 CAT: 11

Community Based Report
CIJE: 0 RIE: 1 CAT: 15

Community Behavioral Services AB
CIJE: 0 RIE: 0 CAT: 19

Community Boards
CIJE: 2 RIE: 2 CAT: 10

Community Bulletin Board System
CIJE: 2 RIE: 0 CAT: 04

Community Business Relationship
USE Business Community Relationship

Community Campaigns
CIJE: 1 RIE: 3 CAT: 19

Community Care Program IL
USE Illinois Community Care Program

Community Centered Learning
CIJE: 0 RIE: 1 CAT: 15

Community Centered School Support Program
CIJE: 0 RIE: 1 CAT: 19

Community Change Training Institute
CIJE: 0 RIE: 1 CAT: 17

Community Chest
CIJE: 0 RIE: 1 CAT: 17
SN Former name of the "United Way"

Community Church Relationship
USE Church Community Relationship

Community Clinical Nursery Schools MA
CIJE: 1 RIE: 0 CAT: 17

Community College Activities Survey
CIJE: 0 RIE: 1 CAT: 21

Community College Cooperative for Intl Develop
CIJE: 0 RIE: 1 CAT: 17

Community College District Twelve WA
CIJE: 0 RIE: 1 CAT: 17

Community College Goals Inventory
CIJE: 2 RIE: 4 CAT: 21

Community College Humanities Association
CIJE: 0 RIE: 6 CAT: 17

Community College Leadership Program
CIJE: 0 RIE: 1 CAT: 19

Community College Motivation Inventory
CIJE: 1 RIE: 1 CAT: 21

Community College Occupational Programs Eval Syst
CIJE: 0 RIE: 3 CAT: 15

Community College of Allegheny County PA
CIJE: 3 RIE: 10 CAT: 17

Community College of Baltimore MD
CIJE: 3 RIE: 7 CAT: 17

Community College of Beaver County PA
CIJE: 1 RIE: 2 CAT: 17

Community College of Decatur IL
CIJE: 1 RIE: 1 CAT: 17

Community College of Delaware County PA
CIJE: 0 RIE: 6 CAT: 17

Community College of Denver CO
CIJE: 2 RIE: 2 CAT: 17

Community College of Maine
CIJE: 1 RIE: 1 CAT: 17

Community College of Philadelphia PA
CIJE: 17 RIE: 15 CAT: 17

Community College of Rhode Island
CIJE: 2 RIE: 12 CAT: 17

Community College of Southern Nevada
CIJE: 0 RIE: 1 CAT: 17

Community College of the Air Force
CIJE: 1 RIE: 0 CAT: 17

Community College of the Air Force TX
CIJE: 9 RIE: 1 CAT: 17

Community College of the Finger Lakes NY
CIJE: 0 RIE: 1 CAT: 17
SN Name changed (May92) to "Finger Lakes Community College NY"

Community College of Vermont
CIJE: 7 RIE: 8 CAT: 17

Community College Satellite Network
CIJE: 1 RIE: 0 CAT: 17

Community College Student Experiences Quest
CIJE: 1 RIE: 3 CAT: 21

Community College Teachers
CIJE: 0 RIE: 5 CAT: 09

Community Colleges within Universities
USE Two Year Colleges within Universities

Community Communications Project
CIJE: 0 RIE: 1 CAT: 19

Community Concerns Report Method
USE Concerns Report Method

Community Conservation Corps CA
CIJE: 0 RIE: 1 CAT: 17

Community Controlled Education
CIJE: 1 RIE: 6 CAT: 15

Community Coordinated Child Care Program
CIJE: 1 RIE: 8 CAT: 19

Community Correctional Centers
CIJE: 0 RIE: 1 CAT: 05

Community Corrections Training Project
CIJE: 0 RIE: 1 CAT: 19

Community Councils
CIJE: 0 RIE: 1 CAT: 10

Community Counselors
CIJE: 0 RIE: 1 CAT: 09

Community Design Centers
CIJE: 2 RIE: 1 CAT: 05

Community Development Block Grant Program
CIJE: 1 RIE: 7 CAT: 19

Community Development Corporation GA
CIJE: 4 RIE: 3 CAT: 17

Community Development Foundation
CIJE: 1 RIE: 0 CAT: 17

Community Development Personnel
CIJE: 1 RIE: 2 CAT: 09

Community Development Society
CIJE: 2 RIE: 0 CAT: 17

Community Development Specialists
CIJE: 0 RIE: 4 CAT: 09

Community Disruption
CIJE: 2 RIE: 2 CAT: 16

Community Education Center Programs
CIJE: 0 RIE: 2 CAT: 19

Community Education Planning Project
CIJE: 0 RIE: 1 CAT: 19

Community Education Program on Home Rule
CIJE: 1 RIE: 0 CAT: 19

Community Educational Goals Inventory
CIJE: 1 RIE: 0 CAT: 21

Community Empowerment
CIJE: 0 RIE: 4 CAT: 15

Community Environment Scale
CIJE: 0 RIE: 1 CAT: 21

Community Exchange Systems
CIJE: 0 RIE: 1 CAT: 15

Community Family Day Care Project
CIJE: 0 RIE: 1 CAT: 19

Community Food and Nutrition Programs
CIJE: 0 RIE: 1 CAT: 19

Community Forum Concept
CIJE: 3 RIE: 2 CAT: 15

Community Forum on Financial Assistance RI
CIJE: 0 RIE: 1 CAT: 17

Community Group Health Foundation DC
CIJE: 0 RIE: 1 CAT: 17

Community Health Center Programs
CIJE: 3 RIE: 2 CAT: 19

Community Health Representatives
CIJE: 1 RIE: 1 CAT: 09

Community Helper Program
CIJE: 1 RIE: 0 CAT: 19

Community Holding Power
CIJE: 1 RIE: 4 CAT: 15

Community Hospital Industrial Rehab Placement
CIJE: 1 RIE: 0 CAT: 17

Community Human and Resources Training Program
CIJE: 0 RIE: 1 CAT: 19

Community Identity
CIJE: 1 RIE: 3 CAT: 16

Community Improvement Program
CIJE: 1 RIE: 0 CAT: 19

Community Instructional Services
CIJE: 0 RIE: 1 CAT: 05

Community Integrated Preschool
CIJE: 0 RIE: 1 CAT: 15

Community Integrated Training and Education OH
CIJE: 0 RIE: 1 CAT: 19

Community Involvement for Responsible Citizenship
CIJE: 0 RIE: 1 CAT: 19

Community Land Use Game
CIJE: 1 RIE: 1 CAT: 15

Community Language Learning
CIJE: 3 RIE: 21 CAT: 13

Community Leadership Program
CIJE: 0 RIE: 1 CAT: 19

Community Learning Center MA
CIJE: 0 RIE: 1 CAT: 17

Community Learning Centers
CIJE: 2 RIE: 6 CAT: 05

Community Literacy
CIJE: 1 RIE: 3 CAT: 13

Community Living Arrangements
CIJE: 1 RIE: 0 CAT: 16

Community Living Assessment System
CIJE: 0 RIE: 1 CAT: 15

Community Long Range Goals Project
CIJE: 0 RIE: 1 CAT: 19

Community Media Librarian Program
CIJE: 2 RIE: 0 CAT: 19

Community Medical Television System
CIJE: 0 RIE: 1 CAT: 15

Community Mental Health Centers
CIJE: 35 RIE: 13 CAT: 05

Community National Field Task Force DC
CIJE: 0 RIE: 1 CAT: 17

Community Needs
CIJE: 16 RIE: 29 CAT: 16

Community Needs Index
CIJE: 0 RIE: 1 CAT: 21

Community Newspapers
CIJE: 3 RIE: 11 CAT: 16

Community of Commitment
CIJE: 1 RIE: 0 CAT: 15

Community Options Program
CIJE: 0 RIE: 2 CAT: 19
SN State program of Wisconsin

Community Organization Curriculum Devel Project
CIJE: 0 RIE: 1 CAT: 19

Community Oriented Schools
CIJE: 2 RIE: 1 CAT: 05

Community Oriented Teacher Training Adolescents
CIJE: 0 RIE: 1 CAT: 19

Community Outreach Specialists
CIJE: 0 RIE: 1 CAT: 09

Community Peace Cultures Program
CIJE: 0 RIE: 1 CAT: 19

Community Policing
CIJE: 0 RIE: 1 CAT: 15

Community Portrait Analysis
CIJE: 0 RIE: 1 CAT: 15

Community Progress Inc CT
CIJE: 0 RIE: 2 CAT: 17

Community Radio
CIJE: 2 RIE: 3 CAT: 04

Community Relations Service
CIJE: 3 RIE: 0 CAT: 17

Community Renewal
CIJE: 1 RIE: 1 CAT: 16

Community Renewal Colleges
CIJE: 1 RIE: 2 CAT: 05

Community Research and Development Corporation CT
CIJE: 0 RIE: 1 CAT: 17

Community Resource Centers
CIJE: 2 RIE: 0 CAT: 05

Community Resource Development
CIJE: 2 RIE: 4 CAT: 15

Community Resource Development Projects
CIJE: 1 RIE: 5 CAT: 19

Community Resources Pool
CIJE: 0 RIE: 3 CAT: 15

Community School Councils
USE School Community Councils

Community School Surveys
USE School Community Surveys

Community Schools Advisory Panel TX
CIJE: 0 RIE: 1 CAT: 17

Community Service
CIJE: 24 RIE: 20 CAT: 16
SN See also "Youth Community Service," "National Service," and "National and Community Service..."

Community Service and Continuing Education Program
CIJE: 0 RIE: 2 CAT: 19

Community Service Network
CIJE: 0 RIE: 1 CAT: 17

Community Services Administration
CIJE: 1 RIE: 5 CAT: 17

Community Services Block Grant Act
CIJE: 0 RIE: 4 CAT: 14

Community Services Block Grant Program
CIJE: 0 RIE: 3 CAT: 19

Community Services Fellowship Program
CIJE: 0 RIE: 1 CAT: 19

Community Services Handbook
CIJE: 0 RIE: 1 CAT: 22

Community Services Partnerships
USE Partnerships in Human Services

Community Summer School Program
CIJE: 0 RIE: 1 CAT: 19

Community Switchboards
CIJE: 0 RIE: 1 CAT: 04

Community Talent Search
CIJE: 0 RIE: 1 CAT: 19

Community Technology
CIJE: 1 RIE: 0 CAT: 21

Community Ties
CIJE: 4 RIE: 3 CAT: 16

Community Treatment Project
CIJE: 0 RIE: 1 CAT: 19

Community Viability
CIJE: 2 RIE: 6 CAT: 16

Community Vocational Habilitation Services Model
CIJE: 0 RIE: 1 CAT: 15

Community Work and Training Program
CIJE: 0 RIE: 1 CAT: 19

Community Work Experience Program
CIJE: 0 RIE: 4 CAT: 19

Community Youth Activity Program
CIJE: 0 RIE: 1 CAT: 19

Community Zoning Plan
CIJE: 0 RIE: 1 CAT: 19

Communiversity
CIJE: 2 RIE: 3 CAT: 19

Commutativity Principle (Mathematics)
CIJE: 2 RIE: 1 CAT: 20

Commuting Patterns
CIJE: 1 RIE: 5 CAT: 16

Commuting Workers
CIJE: 4 RIE: 5 CAT: 10

Comoros
CIJE: 0 RIE: 1 CAT: 07

COMP LAB Course
CIJE: 0 RIE: 2 CAT: 03

Compact Disk Interactive
CIJE: 6 RIE: 1 CAT: 20
SN Multimedia product(s) targeted toward consumers that combine audio, video, graphic, and textual materials on compact disks and connect to standard television sets
UF CD I Technology

Compact for Education
CIJE: 2 RIE: 2 CAT: 16

Compact for Lifelong Educational Opportunities
CIJE: 3 RIE: 0 CAT: 19
UF CLEO

Compact Project (NAB)
CIJE: 0 RIE: 1 CAT: 19
SN Project of the National Alliance of Business

Companion Reading Program
CIJE: 0 RIE: 1 CAT: 19

Company Newspapers
CIJE: 1 RIE: 2 CAT: 16

Company Towns
CIJE: 1 RIE: 1 CAT: 16

Comparability
CIJE: 8 RIE: 8 CAT: 16

Comparability Coefficient
CIJE: 1 RIE: 0 CAT: 21

Comparable Cost Information
CIJE: 1 RIE: 1 CAT: 16

Comparative and International Education Society CA
CIJE: 4 RIE: 0 CAT: 17

Comparative Constructions
CIJE: 3 RIE: 1 CAT: 13

Comparative Economic Systems
CIJE: 3 RIE: 1 CAT: 15

Comparative Education Study Adapt Ctr (Nigeria)
CIJE: 1 RIE: 0 CAT: 17

Comparative Evolution
CIJE: 1 RIE: 1 CAT: 20

Comparative Guidance and Placement Program
CIJE: 5 RIE: 16 CAT: 21

Comparative Guidance and Placement Test
CIJE: 0 RIE: 2 CAT: 21

Comparative Librarianship
CIJE: 6 RIE: 2 CAT: 15

Comparative Literature
CIJE: 11 RIE: 5 CAT: 03

Comparative Method
CIJE: 2 RIE: 3 CAT: 15

Comparative Political Systems
CIJE: 8 RIE: 1 CAT: 15

Comparative Psychology
CIJE: 9 RIE: 0 CAT: 03

Comparative Reading
CIJE: 0 RIE: 1 CAT: 15

Comparative Rhetoric
CIJE: 1 RIE: 2 CAT: 13

Comparative Sentences
CIJE: 1 RIE: 0 CAT: 13

Comparative Structures
CIJE: 4 RIE: 2 CAT: 15

Comparative Stylistics
CIJE: 2 RIE: 0 CAT: 15

Comparative Systems Laboratory
CIJE: 0 RIE: 4 CAT: 17

Comparison Process
CIJE: 12 RIE: 3 CAT: 11

Compartment Flow Model Simulation Program
CIJE: 0 RIE: 1 CAT: 19

Compass Battery
CIJE: 0 RIE: 1 CAT: 21

Compass Reading
CIJE: 6 RIE: 9 CAT: 15

Compasses
CIJE: 2 RIE: 5 CAT: 04

Compassion
CIJE: 9 RIE: 2 CAT: 16

Compatibility (Computers)
CIJE: 1 RIE: 0 CAT: 20

Compatibility (Information)
CIJE: 4 RIE: 2 CAT: 20

Compatibility (Mathematical)
CIJE: 1 RIE: 0 CAT: 20

Compatibility (Social)
CIJE: 5 RIE: 4 CAT: 11

Compatibility (Software)
CIJE: 1 RIE: 0 CAT: 20

Compatibility (Systems)
CIJE: 6 RIE: 0 CAT: 20

Compatibility Index
CIJE: 1 RIE: 0 CAT: 21

Compatible Time Sharing System
CIJE: 0 RIE: 2 CAT: 15

CompEd Survey (IEA)
USE Computers in Education (IEA)

COMPENDEX
CIJE: 2 RIE: 5 CAT: 04
SN Computerized Engineering Index (of Engineering Index, Inc.)

Compensation (Communication)
CIJE: 3 RIE: 1 CAT: 13

Compensatory Models
CIJE: 1 RIE: 1 CAT: 15

Competency Assessment Profile
CIJE: 1 RIE: 0 CAT: 21

Competency Based Assessment
CIJE: 7 RIE: 11 CAT: 21

Competency Based Certification
CIJE: 4 RIE: 8 CAT: 16

Competency Based Curriculum
CIJE: 1 RIE: 9 CAT: 03

Competency Based Evaluation
CIJE: 2 RIE: 8 CAT: 21

Competency Based Guidance
CIJE: 0 RIE: 4 CAT: 15

Competency Based High School Diploma Program
CIJE: 2 RIE: 0 CAT: 19

Competency Based Principalship
CIJE: 0 RIE: 1 CAT: 16

Competency Based Teacher Education Project
CIJE: 0 RIE: 25 CAT: 19
SN Do not confuse with the Desc "Competency Based Teacher Education"

Competency Based Testing Program WI
CIJE: 0 RIE: 0 CAT: 19
UF Wisconsin Competency Based Testing Program

Competency Identification Procedures
CIJE: 2 RIE: 15 CAT: 15

Competency Lists
CIJE: 8 RIE: 28 CAT: 16

Competency Mapping
CIJE: 1 RIE: 2 CAT: 15

Competency Needs
CIJE: 4 RIE: 3 CAT: 15

Competency Rossville Model
CIJE: 0 RIE: 1 CAT: 15

Competency Tests
CIJE: 21 RIE: 28 CAT: 21

Competency Validation (Occupations)
CIJE: 0 RIE: 2 CAT: 15

Competing Values Model
CIJE: 1 RIE: 1 CAT: 15
SN See also "Competitive Values"

Competitive Argument
CIJE: 2 RIE: 5 CAT: 15

Competitive Athletic Events
CIJE: 3 RIE: 2 CAT: 16

Competitive Environment
CIJE: 6 RIE: 2 CAT: 20

Competitive Exclusion
CIJE: 1 RIE: 0 CAT: 15

Competitive Goal Structures
USE Goal Structures

Competitive Partnership Program
CIJE: 0 RIE: 2 CAT: 19

Competitive Values
CIJE: 3 RIE: 2 CAT: 15
SN See also "Competing Values Model"

Competitiveness
CIJE: 4 RIE: 1 CAT: 16
SN See also "Economic Competitiveness" and "Sport Competitiveness"

Competitiveness Policy Council
CIJE: 0 RIE: 1 CAT: 17

Competitiveness Questionnaire
CIJE: 1 RIE: 0 CAT: 21

Compilations
CIJE: 0 RIE: 5 CAT: 16

Compilers
CIJE: 2 RIE: 2 CAT: 04

Complement Abilities Pattern
CIJE: 0 RIE: 1 CAT: 15

Complementarity
CIJE: 14 RIE: 4 CAT: 16

Complementarity Symmetry Analysis
USE Symmetry Complementarity Analysis

Complementary Narcissism Theory
CIJE: 0 RIE: 1 CAT: 11

Complementary Teacher Training Program
CIJE: 0 RIE: 1 CAT: 19

Complete Assessment Battery
CIJE: 0 RIE: 2 CAT: 21

Complete Linguistic Elements Paradigm
CIJE: 0 RIE: 1 CAT: 13

Complete Procedural Review
CIJE: 0 RIE: 1 CAT: 15

Completed Research Health Physical Ed Recreation
CIJE: 1 RIE: 0 CAT: 22

Complex Adaptive Systems
CIJE: 0 RIE: 1 CAT: 20

Complex Concepts
CIJE: 2 RIE: 6 CAT: 15

Complex Instruction
CIJE: 0 RIE: 2 CAT: 15
SN An approach to cooperative learning developed at Stanford University

Complex Numbers
CIJE: 16 RIE: 9 CAT: 20

Complex Rule Learning
CIJE: 2 RIE: 0 CAT: 15

Complexity Index
CIJE: 3 RIE: 1 CAT: 21

Compliance (Counseling)
CIJE: 0 RIE: 1 CAT: 11

Compliance (Medical)
CIJE: 3 RIE: 2 CAT: 11

Compliance Gaining
CIJE: 29 RIE: 1 CAT: 11

Compliance Gaining Message Selection
CIJE: 8 RIE: 0 CAT: 15

Compliance Gaining Messages
CIJE: 2 RIE: 0 CAT: 11

Compliance Gaining Strategies
CIJE: 14 RIE: 3 CAT: 15

Compliance Training
CIJE: 4 RIE: 4 CAT: 15

Compliments (Language)
CIJE: 8 RIE: 8 CAT: 13

COMPNY Library
CIJE: 0 RIE: 1 CAT: 04
SN A LEXIS/NEXIS database of information on corporations

Component Display Theory
CIJE: 8 RIE: 3 CAT: 15

Component Theory
CIJE: 15 RIE: 2 CAT: 15

Componential Intelligence
CIJE: 6 RIE: 6 CAT: 11

COMPOSER System
CIJE: 0 RIE: 2 CAT: 04

Composers (Music)
USE Music Composers

Composing Aloud
CIJE: 0 RIE: 2 CAT: 15

Composite Direct Product Model (Browne)
CIJE: 0 RIE: 2 CAT: 15

Composite Index of Marital Satisfaction
CIJE: 1 RIE: 0 CAT: 21

Composite Indicator of Changes
CIJE: 1 RIE: 6 CAT: 21

Composite Materials
CIJE: 0 RIE: 2 CAT: 20
SN Structural materials composed of combinations of metal alloys, ceramics, or plastics, usually with the addition of strengthening agents

Composite Preprofessional Performance Score
CIJE: 0 RIE: 1 CAT: 21

Composite Scores
CIJE: 5 RIE: 15 CAT: 21

Composite Tests
CIJE: 3 RIE: 2 CAT: 21

Composition (Art)
CIJE: 3 RIE: 2 CAT: 16

Composition (Photography)
CIJE: 2 RIE: 0 CAT: 20

Composition for Personal Growth Program
CIJE: 0 RIE: 1 CAT: 19

Composition Literature Relationship
CIJE: 9 RIE: 5 CAT: 16
UF Literature Composition Relationship

Composition Rating Scale (Smith)
CIJE: 0 RIE: 1 CAT: 21

Composition Theory
CIJE: 360 RIE: 124 CAT: 15
UF Writing Theory

Compositional Syntactic Placement
CIJE: 0 RIE: 1 CAT: 15

Compositors (Printing and Publishing)
CIJE: 0 RIE: 3 CAT: 09

Composting
CIJE: 12 RIE: 11 CAT: 20

Compound Bilingualism
CIJE: 2 RIE: 2 CAT: 13

Compound Nouns
CIJE: 9 RIE: 3 CAT: 13

Compound Numbers
CIJE: 0 RIE: 1 CAT: 20

Compound Words
CIJE: 8 RIE: 3 CAT: 13

Comprehensible Input
CIJE: 2 RIE: 1 CAT: 13

Comprehensible Input Analysis
CIJE: 1 RIE: 0 CAT: 15

Comprehensible Input PLUS Language Experience
CIJE: 1 RIE: 0 CAT: 13

Comprehensible Output Analysis
CIJE: 1 RIE: 0 CAT: 15

Comprehension Monitoring
CIJE: 48 RIE: 37 CAT: 15

Comprehension Tests
CIJE: 5 RIE: 2 CAT: 21

Comprehensive Ability Battery
CIJE: 6 RIE: 1 CAT: 21

Comprehensive Achievement Monitoring
CIJE: 1 RIE: 27 CAT: 21

Comprehensive Adult Student Assessment System
CIJE: 1 RIE: 18 CAT: 15

Comprehensive Analysis of Special Education
CIJE: 1 RIE: 0 CAT: 21

Comprehensive and Cognitive Development Program MO
CIJE: 0 RIE: 1 CAT: 19

Comprehensive Area Manpower Planning System
CIJE: 1 RIE: 0 CAT: 15

Comprehensive Assessment and Program Planning
CIJE: 0 RIE: 2 CAT: 19
UF CAPPS

Comprehensive Assessment and Support System
CIJE: 0 RIE: 0 CAT: 19

Comprehensive Assessment Program
CIJE: 0 RIE: 2 CAT: 19

Comprehensive Assessment Report (New York)
CIJE: 0 RIE: 0 CAT: 15
UF New York State Comprehensive Assessment Report

Comprehensive Assistance Undergraduate Science Ed
CIJE: 1 RIE: 2 CAT: 19

Comprehensive Care for Families
CIJE: 1 RIE: 1 CAT: 19

Comprehensive Career Education Model
CIJE: 5 RIE: 22 CAT: 15

Comprehensive Career Exploration Project
CIJE: 1 RIE: 0 CAT: 19

Comprehensive Child Development Act 1971
CIJE: 1 RIE: 2 CAT: 14

Comprehensive Child Development Program (ACYF)
CIJE: 0 RIE: 2 CAT: 19
SN ACYF = Administration on Children, Youth, and Families

Comprehensive Communication Curriculum
CIJE: 0 RIE: 4 CAT: 03

Comprehensive Competencies Program
CIJE: 3 RIE: 6 CAT: 19

Comprehensive Dissertation Index
CIJE: 1 RIE: 0 CAT: 04

Comprehensive Early Childhood Education Network PA
CIJE: 0 RIE: 2 CAT: 17

Comprehensive Early Evaluation Programming System
CIJE: 0 RIE: 1 CAT: 21
UF CEEPS

Comprehensive Education Process
CIJE: 2 RIE: 0 CAT: 15

Comprehensive Education Reform Act (Tennessee)
CIJE: 8 RIE: 8 CAT: 14

Comprehensive Elementary Teacher Education Models
CIJE: 3 RIE: 67 CAT: 15

Comprehensive Employment and Training Act
CIJE: 181 RIE: 501 CAT: 14
SN See also "CETA..."
UF CETA

Comprehensive Employment and Training Act Title IV
CIJE: 1 RIE: 5 CAT: 14

Comprehensive English Language Test
CIJE: 1 RIE: 1 CAT: 21
UF Comprehensive English Language Test Speakers ESL

Comprehensive English Language Test Speakers ESL
USE Comprehensive English Language Test

Comprehensive Evaluation of Family Functioning
CIJE: 0 RIE: 1 CAT: 21

Comprehensive Evaluation System GA
USE Georgia Comprehensive Evaluation System

Comprehensive Examinations
CIJE: 18 RIE: 10 CAT: 21

Comprehensive Family Rating (Deschin)
CIJE: 0 RIE: 1 CAT: 21

Comprehensive Grammar of the English Language
CIJE: 0 RIE: 1 CAT: 22

Comprehensive Guidance
CIJE: 0 RIE: 3 CAT: 11

Comprehensive Guidance Program Model (Gysbers)
CIJE: 0 RIE: 2 CAT: 15
SN See also "Missouri Comprehensive Guidance Program Model"
UF Gysbers Model

Comprehensive Guidance Program TX
CIJE: 0 RIE: 0 CAT: 19

Comprehensive Health Manpower Training Act
CIJE: 0 RIE: 4 CAT: 14

Comprehensive Instructional Management System
CIJE: 1 RIE: 35 CAT: 03

Comprehensive Instructional Program
CIJE: 1 RIE: 14 CAT: 19

Comprehensive Inventory of Basic Skills (Brigance)
CIJE: 0 RIE: 1 CAT: 21
UF Brigance CIBS

Comprehensive Language Improvement Program
CIJE: 0 RIE: 1 CAT: 19

Comprehensive Manpower Development System
CIJE: 0 RIE: 1 CAT: 15

Comprehensive Manpower Office
CIJE: 1 RIE: 0 CAT: 17

Comprehensive Mathematics Inventory
CIJE: 1 RIE: 1 CAT: 21

Comprehensive Nursing Achievement Test
CIJE: 0 RIE: 1 CAT: 21

Comprehensive Objectives Accounting System
CIJE: 0 RIE: 1 CAT: 15

Comprehensive Occupational Data Analysis Programs
CIJE: 0 RIE: 11 CAT: 19

Comprehensive Office Laboratory Training
CIJE: 1 RIE: 0 CAT: 15

Comprehensive Program for American Schools
CIJE: 0 RIE: 3 CAT: 19

Comprehensive Reading Vocabulary Primary Level
CIJE: 1 RIE: 0 CAT: 21

Comprehensive School Health Education
CIJE: 42 RIE: 16 CAT: 03

Comprehensive School Health Programs
CIJE: 8 RIE: 32 CAT: 19

Comprehensive School Improvement Program
CIJE: 3 RIE: 5 CAT: 19

Comprehensive School Mathematics Program
CIJE: 9 RIE: 132 CAT: 19

Comprehensive Schools (Great Britain)
CIJE: 12 RIE: 1 CAT: 05

Comprehensive Service Amendments 1973
CIJE: 0 RIE: 1 CAT: 14

Comprehensive Services Program
CIJE: 3 RIE: 2 CAT: 19

Comprehensive Smoking Prevention Educ Act 1981
CIJE: 0 RIE: 2 CAT: 14

Comprehensive Special Education Law (Mass)
CIJE: 5 RIE: 6 CAT: 14

Comprehensive Student Assessment Programs
CIJE: 0 RIE: 1 CAT: 19

Comprehensive System for Personnel Development
CIJE: 0 RIE: 3 CAT: 15

Comprehensive System of Personnel Development
CIJE: 5 RIE: 9 CAT: 19

Comprehensive Tests of Basic Skills
CIJE: 61 RIE: 235 CAT: 21

Comprehensive Tests of Basic Skills Spanish
CIJE: 0 RIE: 2 CAT: 21

Comprehensive Universities
CIJE: 2 RIE: 8 CAT: 05

Comprehensive University Scheduling System
CIJE: 0 RIE: 1 CAT: 15

Comprehensive Vocational Evaluation Centers
CIJE: 0 RIE: 1 CAT: 05

Compressed Air Equipment
CIJE: 0 RIE: 2 CAT: 04

Compressed Audiotape Recordings
CIJE: 0 RIE: 2 CAT: 04

Compressed Gas Equipment
CIJE: 0 RIE: 4 CAT: 04

Compressed Motion Pictures
CIJE: 1 RIE: 1 CAT: 04

Compressed Video
CIJE: 2 RIE: 4 CAT: 20

Compressor Style Vertical Filing
CIJE: 1 RIE: 0 CAT: 04

Compromise
CIJE: 25 RIE: 8 CAT: 16

Compromise Model (Hofstee)
CIJE: 0 RIE: 2 CAT: 15

Comptometer Operators
CIJE: 0 RIE: 1 CAT: 09

Compton Bilingual Plan
CIJE: 0 RIE: 1 CAT: 19

Compton Community College CA
CIJE: 0 RIE: 2 CAT: 17

Compton Unified School District CA
CIJE: 1 RIE: 0 CAT: 17

Compucorp Model 025 Educator
CIJE: 0 RIE: 1 CAT: 04

Compulearn Career Education Program
CIJE: 0 RIE: 1 CAT: 19

Compulsive Handwashing
CIJE: 0 RIE: 0 CAT: 11

Compupoem (Computer Program)
CIJE: 0 RIE: 1 CAT: 04

CompuServe
CIJE: 13 RIE: 3 CAT: 17

Computation Centers
CIJE: 0 RIE: 3 CAT: 05

Computational Algebraic Language
CIJE: 0 RIE: 1 CAT: 04

Computational Mathematics
CIJE: 0 RIE: 1 CAT: 20

Computational Mathematics Monitoring System
CIJE: 0 RIE: 1 CAT: 15

Computational Modeling
USE Computational Models

Computational Models
CIJE: 2 RIE: 2 CAT: 20
UF Computational Modeling

Computer Access
USE Access to Computers

Computer Aided Facilities Management
CIJE: 0 RIE: 1 CAT: 15

Computer Aided Interactive Testing System
CIJE: 0 RIE: 1 CAT: 21

Computer Aided Proof
CIJE: 3 RIE: 0 CAT: 20

Computer Aided Science Policy And Research System
USE CASPAR Database

Computer Aids to Teaching Project
CIJE: 0 RIE: 7 CAT: 19

Computer Algebra
CIJE: 21 RIE: 6 CAT: 20

Computer Analysis
CIJE: 7 RIE: 5 CAT: 15

Computer and Information Science Res Center OH
CIJE: 0 RIE: 2 CAT: 17

Computer Animation
CIJE: 24 RIE: 2 CAT: 04

Computer Anxiety Index
CIJE: 1 RIE: 1 CAT: 21

Computer Anxiety Scale
CIJE: 6 RIE: 3 CAT: 21

Computer Architecture
CIJE: 33 RIE: 5 CAT: 16

Computer Art
CIJE: 3 RIE: 1 CAT: 20

Computer as Laboratory Partner Project
CIJE: 0 RIE: 1 CAT: 19

Computer Assisted Abstracting
CIJE: 3 RIE: 1 CAT: 20

Computer Assisted Advising
CIJE: 5 RIE: 1 CAT: 15

Computer Assisted Bilingual Bicultural Multiskills
CIJE: 0 RIE: 1 CAT: 19

Computer Assisted Career Guidance
CIJE: 30 RIE: 30 CAT: 15

Computer Assisted Cataloging
CIJE: 5 RIE: 1 CAT: 04

Computer Assisted College Administration
CIJE: 0 RIE: 1 CAT: 15

Computer Assisted Counseling
CIJE: 41 RIE: 38 CAT: 15

Computer Assisted Data Analysis
CIJE: 3 RIE: 4 CAT: 20

Computer Assisted Distribution and Assignment
CIJE: 0 RIE: 1 CAT: 15

Computer Assisted Engineering
CIJE: 3 RIE: 2 CAT: 20

Computer Assisted Guidance
CIJE: 33 RIE: 27 CAT: 15

Computer Assisted Instruction Test Bed
CIJE: 0 RIE: 1 CAT: 21

Computer Assisted Language Analysis System
CIJE: 6 RIE: 7 CAT: 15

Computer Assisted Language Instruction
CIJE: 17 RIE: 4 CAT: 15

Computer Assisted Language Learning
CIJE: 29 RIE: 4 CAT: 15

Computer Assisted Lesson Service
CIJE: 0 RIE: 1 CAT: 15

Computer Assisted Literacy in Libraries
CIJE: 0 RIE: 2 CAT: 19
UF CALL Program NV

Computer Assisted Machining
CIJE: 0 RIE: 0 CAT: 20

Computer Assisted Management
CIJE: 11 RIE: 1 CAT: 15

Computer Assisted Management System
CIJE: 1 RIE: 2 CAT: 15

Computer Assisted Mathematics Program
CIJE: 0 RIE: 1 CAT: 19

Computer Assisted Occupational Guidance Program
CIJE: 1 RIE: 1 CAT: 19

Computer Assisted Occupational Survey
CIJE: 0 RIE: 1 CAT: 19

Computer Assisted Patient Simulation
CIJE: 1 RIE: 1 CAT: 15

Computer Assisted Placement
CIJE: 1 RIE: 2 CAT: 15

Computer Assisted Problem Solving
CIJE: 4 RIE: 4 CAT: 15

Computer Assisted Publishing
CIJE: 5 RIE: 3 CAT: 20

Computer Assisted Reading Educational System
CIJE: 0 RIE: 1 CAT: 15

Computer Assisted Remedial Education
CIJE: 3 RIE: 13 CAT: 15

Computer Assisted Renewal Education Program
CIJE: 1 RIE: 4 CAT: 19

Computer Assisted Reporting to Parents
CIJE: 2 RIE: 1 CAT: 15

Computer Assisted Requisitioning
CIJE: 1 RIE: 0 CAT: 15

Computer Assisted Scheduling
CIJE: 6 RIE: 2 CAT: 15

Computer Assisted Spec Ed Train Small Sch Proj TX
CIJE: 0 RIE: 1 CAT: 19

Computer Assisted Study Skills Improvement Program
CIJE: 0 RIE: 1 CAT: 19
UF CASSIP

Computer Assisted Synthesizer System
CIJE: 2 RIE: 1 CAT: 15

Computer Assisted Teacher Training System
CIJE: 1 RIE: 9 CAT: 15

Computer Assisted Telephone Interviewing
CIJE: 2 RIE: 3 CAT: 15

Computer Assisted Test Construction
CIJE: 3 RIE: 9 CAT: 21

Computer Assisted Video Instruction
CIJE: 5 RIE: 1 CAT: 15

Computer Assisted Vocational Counseling System
CIJE: 1 RIE: 0 CAT: 15

Computer Assisted Writing
CIJE: 7 RIE: 7 CAT: 15

Computer Attitude Scale
CIJE: 15 RIE: 4 CAT: 21

Computer Attitudes Scale
CIJE: 1 RIE: 0 CAT: 21

Computer Augmented Lectures
CIJE: 0 RIE: 2 CAT: 15

Computer Augmented Teacher Training
CIJE: 0 RIE: 1 CAT: 15

Computer Augmented Teaching and Learning System
CIJE: 0 RIE: 1 CAT: 15

Computer AVersion Scale
CIJE: 0 RIE: 1 CAT: 21
UF CAVS

Computer Based Archives
CIJE: 0 RIE: 1 CAT: 05

Computer Based Education Project
CIJE: 1 RIE: 1 CAT: 19

Computer Based Message Switching Network
CIJE: 1 RIE: 1 CAT: 04

Computer Based Project Evaluation Media Handicap
CIJE: 0 RIE: 17 CAT: 19

Computer Based Resource Units
CIJE: 4 RIE: 4 CAT: 05

Computer Based Test Development Project
CIJE: 0 RIE: 1 CAT: 19

Computer Based Test Interpretation
CIJE: 2 RIE: 1 CAT: 21

Computer Camps
CIJE: 7 RIE: 5 CAT: 05

Computer Chips
USE Microchips

Computer Clubs
CIJE: 3 RIE: 1 CAT: 10

Computer Confidence
CIJE: 0 RIE: 1 CAT: 20

Computer Constructed Education
CIJE: 0 RIE: 1 CAT: 15

Computer Controlled Vehicles
CIJE: 1 RIE: 0 CAT: 04

Computer Coordinators
CIJE: 1 RIE: 4 CAT: 09

Computer Courseware Evaluation Model of CITAR
USE CITAR Computer Courseware Evaluation Model

Computer Crimes
CIJE: 5 RIE: 7 CAT: 14

Computer Curriculum Corporation CA
CIJE: 8 RIE: 3 CAT: 17

Computer Departments
CIJE: 1 RIE: 2 CAT: 05

Computer Directed Training Subsystem
CIJE: 0 RIE: 1 CAT: 15

Computer Discovery Project
CIJE: 0 RIE: 1 CAT: 19

Computer Engineering
CIJE: 4 RIE: 0 CAT: 03

Computer Enriched Module Project
CIJE: 0 RIE: 12 CAT: 19

Computer Equity
CIJE: 24 RIE: 15 CAT: 16

Computer Equity Training Project NY
CIJE: 2 RIE: 1 CAT: 19

Computer Ethics
CIJE: 2 RIE: 2 CAT: 03

Computer Graphics Research Group
CIJE: 1 RIE: 1 CAT: 17
UF Ohio State Univ Computer Graphics Research Group

Computer Hackers
CIJE: 1 RIE: 2 CAT: 10
UF Hackers (Computers)

Computer Image Generator
CIJE: 2 RIE: 1 CAT: 04

Computer Industry
CIJE: 62 RIE: 20 CAT: 20

Computer Integrated Instruction
CIJE: 24 RIE: 15 CAT: 20

Computer Integrated Manufacturing
CIJE: 6 RIE: 14 CAT: 20

Computer Integrated Technology
CIJE: 0 RIE: 2 CAT: 20

Computer Learning Experience Music Fundamentals
CIJE: 0 RIE: 1 CAT: 19

Computer Library System Inc
CIJE: 1 RIE: 0 CAT: 04

Computer Literacy Develop Proj Research Training
CIJE: 0 RIE: 1 CAT: 19

Computer Logic
CIJE: 5 RIE: 4 CAT: 20

Computer Maintenance
CIJE: 1 RIE: 1 CAT: 20

Computer Managed Geometry
CIJE: 3 RIE: 1 CAT: 15

Computer Managed Information
CIJE: 1 RIE: 6 CAT: 15

Computer Managed Problem Drill
CIJE: 1 RIE: 0 CAT: 04

Computer Management
CIJE: 4 RIE: 2 CAT: 20

Computer Manuals
CIJE: 1 RIE: 1 CAT: 20
UF Microcomputer Manuals

Computer Manufacturers
CIJE: 1 RIE: 1 CAT: 09

Computer Mapping
CIJE: 3 RIE: 4 CAT: 20

Computer Matching and Privacy Protection Act 1988
CIJE: 0 RIE: 1 CAT: 14

Computer Mediated Lists
CIJE: 2 RIE: 0 CAT: 20

Computer Mediated Text Systems
CIJE: 1 RIE: 0 CAT: 20

Computer Mentoring
CIJE: 0 RIE: 1 CAT: 15

Computer Models
CIJE: 27 RIE: 7 CAT: 15

Computer Museum MA
CIJE: 0 RIE: 1 CAT: 17

Computer Networking Research
CIJE: 0 RIE: 3 CAT: 20

Computer Occupations
CIJE: 3 RIE: 1 CAT: 09
SN See also "Computer Related Occupations," "Computer Service Occupatons"

Computer Operating Systems
CIJE: 12 RIE: 3 CAT: 04
UF Operating Systems (Computers)

Computer Opinion Survey (Maurer and Simonson)
CIJE: 0 RIE: 1 CAT: 21

Computer Ownership
CIJE: 7 RIE: 1 CAT: 16

Computer Performance Evaluation
CIJE: 0 RIE: 1 CAT: 20

Computer Pilot Program NY
CIJE: 0 RIE: 2 CAT: 19

Computer Piracy
CIJE: 3 RIE: 6 CAT: 16
SN See also "Software Piracy" and "Piracy of Intellectual Property"

Computer Plotters
CIJE: 0 RIE: 1 CAT: 04
SN Computer output devices that draw hard-copy graphs or pictures
UF Pen Plotters (Computers); Plotters (Computers)

Computer Presented Social Interactions
CIJE: 0 RIE: 2 CAT: 15

Computer Printouts
CIJE: 9 RIE: 2 CAT: 20

Computer Processed Sociogram
CIJE: 0 RIE: 1 CAT: 15

Computer Program Selection
CIJE: 5 RIE: 2 CAT: 15

Computer Programmer Aptitude Battery
CIJE: 1 RIE: 1 CAT: 21

Computer Related Learning Environments
CIJE: 5 RIE: 2 CAT: 15

Computer Related Occupations
CIJE: 0 RIE: 4 CAT: 09

Computer Research Avocational Guidance Program
CIJE: 1 RIE: 0 CAT: 19

Computer Resources
CIJE: 26 RIE: 10 CAT: 20

Computer Schools
CIJE: 1 RIE: 0 CAT: 05

Computer Science Education Research
CIJE: 13 RIE: 2 CAT: 20

Computer Scripts
CIJE: 0 RIE: 1 CAT: 20
UF Scripts (Computers)

Computer Searches
CIJE: 14 RIE: 12 CAT: 20

Computer Security Act 1987
CIJE: 1 RIE: 1 CAT: 14
UF Public Law 100 235

Computer Service Occupations
CIJE: 0 RIE: 1 CAT: 09

Computer Services
CIJE: 27 RIE: 9 CAT: 16

Computer Software Rental
CIJE: 0 RIE: 0 CAT: 16
UF Software Rental (Computers)

Computer Speech Recognition
CIJE: 4 RIE: 2 CAT: 20

Computer Student Ratio
USE Student Computer Ratio

Computer Supervisors
CIJE: 0 RIE: 1 CAT: 09

Computer Symbolic Mathematics
CIJE: 2 RIE: 1 CAT: 20

Computer System Simulator Program
CIJE: 0 RIE: 1 CAT: 19

Computer Tables
CIJE: 0 RIE: 1 CAT: 04

Computer Technicians
CIJE: 6 RIE: 15 CAT: 09

Computer Technology Program
CIJE: 0 RIE: 2 CAT: 19

Computer Test Scoring
CIJE: 6 RIE: 2 CAT: 21

Computer Tutor Project CA
CIJE: 1 RIE: 0 CAT: 19

Computer Tutors
CIJE: 0 RIE: 4 CAT: 04
SN Programs that interactively guide writers while they freewrite with a word processing program

Computer Typesetting
CIJE: 2 RIE: 3 CAT: 20

Computer Use
CIJE: 0 RIE: 3 CAT: 20

Computer Users
CIJE: 131 RIE: 60 CAT: 10

Computer Uses in Education CA
CIJE: 1 RIE: 1 CAT: 17

Computer Utility for Educational Systems
CIJE: 1 RIE: 1 CAT: 19

Computer Viruses
CIJE: 17 RIE: 7 CAT: 20
SN See also "Internet Worm"

Computer Writing Network
CIJE: 0 RIE: 1 CAT: 04

Computerized Academic Counseling System
CIJE: 0 RIE: 1 CAT: 15

Computerized Accountability Student Achievement
CIJE: 0 RIE: 3 CAT: 04
UF CASA Information Management System

Computerized Accounting
CIJE: 1 RIE: 1 CAT: 15

Computerized Adaptive Mathematics Locator
CIJE: 0 RIE: 1 CAT: 21

Computerized Adaptive Screening Test
CIJE: 0 RIE: 3 CAT: 21

Computerized Biofeedback Clinical Support System
CIJE: 1 RIE: 0 CAT: 11

Computerized Catalogs
CIJE: 4 RIE: 1 CAT: 04

Computerized Documentation System
CIJE: 1 RIE: 0 CAT: 04

Computerized Educational Career Information Link
CIJE: 0 RIE: 1 CAT: 04

Computerized Facilities Inventory
CIJE: 0 RIE: 1 CAT: 15

Computerized Handwriting Analysis Profiling Sys
CIJE: 0 RIE: 1 CAT: 21

Computerized Placement Tests (CEEB)
USE College Board Computerized Placement Tests

Computerized Task Inventory
USE COMTASK Database

Computerized Techniques
CIJE: 4 RIE: 10 CAT: 15

Computerized Television
CIJE: 1 RIE: 1 CAT: 04

Computerized Test Library
CIJE: 0 RIE: 1 CAT: 21

Computerized Testing Evaluative Survey
CIJE: 0 RIE: 1 CAT: 21

Computerized Understanding of Morphology Language
CIJE: 0 RIE: 1 CAT: 15

Computerized Vocational Information System
CIJE: 1 RIE: 4 CAT: 15

Computers and the Elderly Program NY
CIJE: 0 RIE: 0 CAT: 19
SN Program of Syracuse University

Computers in Bilingual Education
USE Project CIBE NY

Computers in Education (IEA)
CIJE: 5 RIE: 3 CAT: 19
UF CompEd Survey (IEA)

ComputerTown
CIJE: 1 RIE: 3 CAT: 19

Computest
CIJE: 0 RIE: 1 CAT: 21

Computing Potential in Atlanta Public School Educ
CIJE: 0 RIE: 1 CAT: 21

Comrey Personality Scales
CIJE: 8 RIE: 3 CAT: 21

Comstock (Anthony)
CIJE: 0 RIE: 1 CAT: 18

Comstock Middle School MI
CIJE: 1 RIE: 0 CAT: 17

COMTASK Database
CIJE: 0 RIE: 0 CAT: 04
UF Computerized Task Inventory

Comte (Auguste)
CIJE: 0 RIE: 1 CAT: 18

Comtois Early Childhood Rating Scales
CIJE: 0 RIE: 1 CAT: 21

Comunidades Eclesiales de Base
USE Base Christian Communities

Conant (James Bryant)
CIJE: 15 RIE: 5 CAT: 18

Conant Plan
CIJE: 1 RIE: 1 CAT: 16

Conant Report
CIJE: 3 RIE: 1 CAT: 22

Conation
CIJE: 1 RIE: 8 CAT: 11
SN Domain of behavior or mental processes associated with goal-directed action

Concealed Figures Test (Thurstone)
CIJE: 0 RIE: 2 CAT: 21

Concentrated Employment Program
CIJE: 5 RIE: 8 CAT: 19

Concentrated Study Program
CIJE: 0 RIE: 1 CAT: 19

Concentration
CIJE: 16 RIE: 6 CAT: 15

Concentration Camps
CIJE: 14 RIE: 2 CAT: 05

Concentric Curriculum
CIJE: 0 RIE: 1 CAT: 03

Concepcion Valdez (Gabriel de la)
CIJE: 1 RIE: 0 CAT: 18

Concept 6 Calendar
CIJE: 0 RIE: 2 CAT: 15

Concept Acquisition
CIJE: 29 RIE: 6 CAT: 11

Concept Assessment Kit
CIJE: 3 RIE: 1 CAT: 04

Concept Assessment Kit Conservation (Goldschmid)
CIJE: 4 RIE: 4 CAT: 21

Concept Association Attitude Scale
CIJE: 1 RIE: 0 CAT: 21

Concept Attainment Abilities Project
CIJE: 0 RIE: 1 CAT: 19

Concept Attainment Strategy
CIJE: 1 RIE: 1 CAT: 15

Concept Books
CIJE: 2 RIE: 0 CAT: 22

Concept Comparisons
CIJE: 0 RIE: 1 CAT: 11

Concept Identification
CIJE: 6 RIE: 6 CAT: 11

Concept Mapping
CIJE: 93 RIE: 52 CAT: 11

Concept Maps
CIJE: 58 RIE: 35 CAT: 20

Concept Mastery Test (Terman)
CIJE: 7 RIE: 9 CAT: 21
UF Terman Concept Mastery Test

Concept Matrices
CIJE: 1 RIE: 0 CAT: 15

Concept Networks
CIJE: 4 RIE: 1 CAT: 04

Concept of Other Sympathy
CIJE: 0 RIE: 1 CAT: 16

Concept of Reading
CIJE: 1 RIE: 1 CAT: 15

Concept Paper Approach
CIJE: 0 RIE: 1 CAT: 15

Concept Recognition
CIJE: 9 RIE: 0 CAT: 11

Concept Reinforcement
CIJE: 2 RIE: 0 CAT: 15

Concept Shift Effect
CIJE: 1 RIE: 0 CAT: 15

Concept Specific Anxiety Scale
CIJE: 1 RIE: 0 CAT: 21

Concept Structure
CIJE: 6 RIE: 2 CAT: 15

Concept Structuring Analysis Technique
CIJE: 1 RIE: 1 CAT: 15

Concept Switching
CIJE: 1 RIE: 0 CAT: 11

Concept Teaching Evaluation Form
CIJE: 0 RIE: 1 CAT: 21

Concept Tree Method
CIJE: 2 RIE: 2 CAT: 15

Concept Utilization
CIJE: 6 RIE: 1 CAT: 11

Conceptional Age
CIJE: 1 RIE: 1 CAT: 11
SN See also "Gestational Age"
UF Conceptual Age

Concepts About Print Test
CIJE: 5 RIE: 6 CAT: 21

Concepts in Political Science Project
CIJE: 0 RIE: 1 CAT: 19

Concepts in Science
CIJE: 13 RIE: 2 CAT: 22

Concepts in Secondary Mathematics Science Project
CIJE: 1 RIE: 1 CAT: 19

Concepts in Secondary School Math and Science
CIJE: 1 RIE: 0 CAT: 19

Concepts Involved Body Position Space Test
CIJE: 1 RIE: 0 CAT: 21

Conceptual Abstracting
CIJE: 0 RIE: 1 CAT: 15

Conceptual Age
USE Conceptional Age

Conceptual Analysis
CIJE: 50 RIE: 36 CAT: 15

Conceptual Approach
CIJE: 35 RIE: 11 CAT: 15

Conceptual Barriers
CIJE: 3 RIE: 2 CAT: 11

Conceptual Change
CIJE: 25 RIE: 13 CAT: 15

Conceptual Change Theory of Knowledge
CIJE: 10 RIE: 7 CAT: 15

Conceptual Comparator
CIJE: 0 RIE: 1 CAT: 15

Conceptual Dependency Theory
CIJE: 1 RIE: 1 CAT: 15

Conceptual Equivalency
CIJE: 0 RIE: 1 CAT: 15

Conceptual Frameworks
CIJE: 153 RIE: 56 CAT: 15

Conceptual Graphs
CIJE: 1 RIE: 1 CAT: 15

Conceptual Integration
CIJE: 5 RIE: 3 CAT: 15

Conceptual Language Prereading Program
CIJE: 0 RIE: 1 CAT: 19

Conceptual Level
CIJE: 7 RIE: 3 CAT: 11

Conceptual Models
CIJE: 64 RIE: 18 CAT: 15

Conceptual Parser
CIJE: 0 RIE: 1 CAT: 13

Conceptual Peg Model
CIJE: 0 RIE: 1 CAT: 15

Conceptual Styles Test
CIJE: 3 RIE: 5 CAT: 21

Conceptual Systems Test
CIJE: 2 RIE: 5 CAT: 21

Conceptual Systems Theory
CIJE: 6 RIE: 4 CAT: 15

Conceptually Oriented Program Elementary Science
CIJE: 3 RIE: 7 CAT: 19

Concerns Analysis
CIJE: 10 RIE: 6 CAT: 15

Concerns Based Adoption Model
CIJE: 22 RIE: 78 CAT: 15

Concerns Questionnaire
CIJE: 1 RIE: 1 CAT: 21

Concerns Report Method
CIJE: 0 RIE: 1 CAT: 15
UF Community Concerns Report Method

Concession Bargaining
CIJE: 2 RIE: 2 CAT: 15

Concho Indian School OK
CIJE: 0 RIE: 1 CAT: 17

Conciliation
CIJE: 4 RIE: 1 CAT: 11

Concomitant Variables
CIJE: 0 RIE: 1 CAT: 21

Concord College WV
CIJE: 0 RIE: 2 CAT: 17

Concord Lyceum MA
CIJE: 0 RIE: 1 CAT: 17

Concord VTR600
CIJE: 0 RIE: 1 CAT: 04

Concordance (Data)
CIJE: 2 RIE: 7 CAT: 20

Concordance (Twin Studies)
CIJE: 1 RIE: 0 CAT: 21

Concordia College at Moorhead MN
CIJE: 0 RIE: 3 CAT: 17

Concordia College Saint Paul MN
CIJE: 0 RIE: 2 CAT: 17

Concordia Seminary MO
CIJE: 1 RIE: 0 CAT: 17

Concordia Teachers College NE
CIJE: 0 RIE: 2 CAT: 17

Concordia Univ Sir George Williams Campus (Canada)
CIJE: 1 RIE: 2 CAT: 17

Concordia University PQ
CIJE: 6 RIE: 6 CAT: 17

Concrete Operations
CIJE: 34 RIE: 21 CAT: 16

Concrete Poetry
CIJE: 14 RIE: 5 CAT: 03

Concreteness (Language)
CIJE: 8 RIE: 2 CAT: 13

Concurrent Adaptive Measurement
CIJE: 0 RIE: 1 CAT: 15

Concurrent Enrollment
CIJE: 0 RIE: 3 CAT: 15

Condemnation (Real Estate)
CIJE: 0 RIE: 1 CAT: 16

Condensation
CIJE: 4 RIE: 1 CAT: 20

Condenser Winders
CIJE: 0 RIE: 1 CAT: 09

Condensers
CIJE: 1 RIE: 0 CAT: 04

Condillac (Abbe de)
CIJE: 0 RIE: 1 CAT: 18

Condition of Education (NCES)
CIJE: 0 RIE: 1 CAT: 22

Conditional Deregulation
CIJE: 2 RIE: 1 CAT: 14

Conditional Independence
CIJE: 2 RIE: 1 CAT: 20

Conditional Logic
CIJE: 11 RIE: 3 CAT: 20

Conditional Predicted Ordinates
CIJE: 0 RIE: 1 CAT: 21

Conditional Probability
CIJE: 3 RIE: 0 CAT: 15

Conditional Probability Functions
CIJE: 0 RIE: 1 CAT: 21

Conditionals
CIJE: 11 RIE: 19 CAT: 13

Condominiums
CIJE: 1 RIE: 2 CAT: 05

Condoms
CIJE: 39 RIE: 13 CAT: 04

Condorcet (Marie Jean Antoine Nicolas de Caritat)
CIJE: 2 RIE: 2 CAT: 18

Conductance
CIJE: 4 RIE: 0 CAT: 20

Conducting
CIJE: 1 RIE: 0 CAT: 16

Conducting (Music)
CIJE: 14 RIE: 2 CAT: 03

Conductive Education
CIJE: 9 RIE: 5 CAT: 03

CONDUIT
CIJE: 3 RIE: 0 CAT: 17

Conemaugh Valley Memorial Hospital PA
CIJE: 1 RIE: 0 CAT: 17

Conerly (James)
CIJE: 1 RIE: 0 CAT: 18

Cones (Mathematics)
CIJE: 2 RIE: 0 CAT: 20

Confederated Salish and Kootenai Tribes
CIJE: 0 RIE: 1 CAT: 08

Confederation College of Applied Arts and Techn ON
CIJE: 0 RIE: 1 CAT: 17

Conference Alternative Futures Vocational Educ
CIJE: 0 RIE: 1 CAT: 02

Conference Board Inc
CIJE: 0 RIE: 0 CAT: 17

Conference Board of the Mathematical Sciences
CIJE: 0 RIE: 2 CAT: 17

Conference Council of Associate Degree Programs
CIJE: 0 RIE: 1 CAT: 02

Conference for Human Development
CIJE: 0 RIE: 1 CAT: 02

Conference for Nursing Instructors
CIJE: 0 RIE: 1 CAT: 02

Conference Moderators
CIJE: 0 RIE: 1 CAT: 09

Conference of University Administrators (England)
CIJE: 0 RIE: 1 CAT: 17

Conference on Coll Composition and Communication
CIJE: 10 RIE: 0 CAT: 17
UF CCCC; College Composition and Communication Conference

Conference on Day Care Service 1965
CIJE: 1 RIE: 0 CAT: 02

Conference on Educ of Disadvantaged (New Mexico)
CIJE: 0 RIE: 1 CAT: 02

Conference on English Education
CIJE: 14 RIE: 2 CAT: 17

Conference on Equal Educational Opportunity
CIJE: 0 RIE: 1 CAT: 02

Conference on Interdisciplinary Activities
CIJE: 0 RIE: 1 CAT: 02

Conference on Manpower Surveys
CIJE: 0 RIE: 1 CAT: 02

Conference on Open Learning in Higher Education
CIJE: 1 RIE: 0 CAT: 02

Conference on Theatre Research (Princeton Univ)
CIJE: 0 RIE: 1 CAT: 02

Conference Role Semantic Differential (Hecht)
CIJE: 0 RIE: 3 CAT: 21

Conference Scoring (Tests)
CIJE: 0 RIE: 1 CAT: 21

Conference Search Laboratory
CIJE: 1 RIE: 0 CAT: 17

Conference Terminology
CIJE: 0 RIE: 1 CAT: 13

Conference Work Force Adjustments Private Industry
CIJE: 0 RIE: 1 CAT: 02

Confessional Poetry
CIJE: 0 RIE: 1 CAT: 16

Confessions of Zeno
CIJE: 1 RIE: 0 CAT: 22

Confidence
CIJE: 3 RIE: 0 CAT: 11
SN Psychoemotional state

Confidence Calibrations
CIJE: 0 RIE: 1 CAT: 21

Confidence Envelopes
CIJE: 1 RIE: 1 CAT: 16

Confidence in Education
CIJE: 1 RIE: 0 CAT: 16

Confidence in Interviewing Scale
CIJE: 1 RIE: 0 CAT: 21

Confidence Intervals (Statistics)
CIJE: 37 RIE: 16 CAT: 15

Confidence Scale (Cruickshank)
CIJE: 0 RIE: 1 CAT: 21

Confidential Employees
CIJE: 0 RIE: 3 CAT: 10

Configural Frequency Analysis
CIJE: 4 RIE: 1 CAT: 15

Configural Scoring Method
CIJE: 0 RIE: 2 CAT: 21

Configurational Approach
CIJE: 3 RIE: 2 CAT: 15

Configurational Theory of Innovation Diffusion
CIJE: 0 RIE: 2 CAT: 15

Configurations Linkages Environments Resources
USE CLER Model

Confined Spaces
CIJE: 0 RIE: 2 CAT: 16

Confirmation (Strategy)
CIJE: 6 RIE: 1 CAT: 15

Confirmatory Factor Analysis
CIJE: 93 RIE: 68 CAT: 15

Confirmatory Questioning Strategy
CIJE: 0 RIE: 1 CAT: 15

Conflict Analysis
CIJE: 12 RIE: 5 CAT: 15

Conflict in Marriage Scale (Hoover)
CIJE: 0 RIE: 1 CAT: 21

Conflict Management
CIJE: 34 RIE: 18 CAT: 15

Conflict Management Style
CIJE: 3 RIE: 4 CAT: 15

Conflict Matrix
CIJE: 1 RIE: 0 CAT: 15

Conflict Resolution Inventory
CIJE: 0 RIE: 1 CAT: 21

Conflict Tactics Scale
CIJE: 4 RIE: 0 CAT: 21
UF Conflict Tactics Scales

Conflict Tactics Scales
USE Conflict Tactics Scale

Conflict Theory
CIJE: 20 RIE: 8 CAT: 15

Confluence Model
CIJE: 17 RIE: 2 CAT: 15

Confluency (Second Language Instruction)
CIJE: 0 RIE: 1 CAT: 13

Conford (Ellen)
CIJE: 1 RIE: 0 CAT: 18

Confortes (Claude)
CIJE: 1 RIE: 0 CAT: 18

Confounding Variables
CIJE: 10 RIE: 5 CAT: 21

Confraternity of Christian Doctrine
CIJE: 4 RIE: 0 CAT: 22

Confrontation
CIJE: 27 RIE: 9 CAT: 11

Confucius
CIJE: 12 RIE: 7 CAT: 18

Confusion
CIJE: 5 RIE: 2 CAT: 16

Congeneric Tests
CIJE: 7 RIE: 3 CAT: 21

Congenital Cytomegalovirus
CIJE: 1 RIE: 0 CAT: 11

Congenital Toxoplasmosis
CIJE: 1 RIE: 0 CAT: 11

Congo
CIJE: 4 RIE: 15 CAT: 07

Congo (Brazzaville)
CIJE: 0 RIE: 2 CAT: 07

Congos of Panama
CIJE: 0 RIE: 0 CAT: 08

Congregate Dining
CIJE: 0 RIE: 5 CAT: 16

Congregate Housing
CIJE: 0 RIE: 2 CAT: 05

Congregate Housing Program
CIJE: 1 RIE: 4 CAT: 19

Congress
CIJE: 118 RIE: 112 CAT: 17

Congress 90th
CIJE: 0 RIE: 2 CAT: 17

Congress 91st
CIJE: 0 RIE: 1 CAT: 17

Congress 92nd
CIJE: 0 RIE: 2 CAT: 17

Congress 93rd
CIJE: 0 RIE: 2 CAT: 17

Congress 94th
CIJE: 0 RIE: 6 CAT: 17

Congress 95th
CIJE: 3 RIE: 40 CAT: 17

Congress 96th
CIJE: 3 RIE: 51 CAT: 17

Congress 97th
CIJE: 0 RIE: 115 CAT: 17

Congress 98th
CIJE: 2 RIE: 273 CAT: 17

Congress 99th
CIJE: 4 RIE: 298 CAT: 17

Congress 100th
CIJE: 4 RIE: 222 CAT: 17

Congress 101st
CIJE: 5 RIE: 174 CAT: 17

Congress 102nd
CIJE: 1 RIE: 196 CAT: 17

Congress 103rd
CIJE: 4 RIE: 81 CAT: 17

Congress of Hispanic Education CO
CIJE: 0 RIE: 1 CAT: 17

Congress of Industrial Organizations
CIJE: 5 RIE: 5 CAT: 17

Congress of Racial Equality
CIJE: 3 RIE: 3 CAT: 17

Congressional Bills
CIJE: 7 RIE: 6 CAT: 14

Congressional Black Caucus
CIJE: 2 RIE: 0 CAT: 17

Congressional Medal of Honor
CIJE: 0 RIE: 2 CAT: 16

Congressional Record
CIJE: 4 RIE: 3 CAT: 22

Congressional Research Service
CIJE: 9 RIE: 10 CAT: 17

Congressional Science Fellowship Program
CIJE: 0 RIE: 1 CAT: 19

Congreve (William)
CIJE: 3 RIE: 0 CAT: 18

Congruence Analysis Techniques
CIJE: 1 RIE: 2 CAT: 15

Congruence Coefficient (Burt)
CIJE: 0 RIE: 1 CAT: 21

Congruent Figures
CIJE: 2 RIE: 1 CAT: 21

Conics
CIJE: 12 RIE: 1 CAT: 20

Conjoint Analysis
CIJE: 5 RIE: 1 CAT: 21

Conjoint Measurement
CIJE: 10 RIE: 5 CAT: 21

Conjoint Retention Hypothesis
CIJE: 1 RIE: 2 CAT: 15
SN Notion that the dual-coding of spatial and verbal information enhances recall from either stimulus format

Conjugate Assessment of Listening
CIJE: 0 RIE: 1 CAT: 21

Conjugate Reduction (Chemistry)
CIJE: 1 RIE: 0 CAT: 20

Conjugate Reinforcement
CIJE: 0 RIE: 1 CAT: 15

Conjunction
CIJE: 2 RIE: 1 CAT: 20

Conjunctions
CIJE: 32 RIE: 16 CAT: 13

Conjunctive Item Response Functions
CIJE: 0 RIE: 1 CAT: 21

Conjunctive Transformations
CIJE: 1 RIE: 2 CAT: 13

Conjunctivitis
CIJE: 1 RIE: 0 CAT: 11

Conkling (Hilda)
CIJE: 1 RIE: 0 CAT: 18

Conlan Amendment
CIJE: 1 RIE: 0 CAT: 14

Conlingual Integrated Approach
CIJE: 1 RIE: 0 CAT: 15

Conn Keyboards
CIJE: 0 RIE: 1 CAT: 04

CONNCEPT Program
CIJE: 0 RIE: 1 CAT: 21
SN CONNCEPT = "CONNecticut Competency Examination for Prospective Teachers"

Connect Class
CIJE: 0 RIE: 1 CAT: 16

Connecticut
CIJE: 197 RIE: 726 CAT: 07

Connecticut (Bridgeport)
CIJE: 4 RIE: 15 CAT: 07

Connecticut (Canterbury)
CIJE: 0 RIE: 2 CAT: 07

Connecticut (Cheshire)
CIJE: 1 RIE: 1 CAT: 07

Connecticut (Danbury)
CIJE: 1 RIE: 4 CAT: 07

Connecticut (East Granby)
CIJE: 1 RIE: 0 CAT: 07

Connecticut (East Hartford)
CIJE: 0 RIE: 6 CAT: 07

Connecticut (Enfield)
CIJE: 0 RIE: 1 CAT: 07

Connecticut (Greenwich)
CIJE: 3 RIE: 2 CAT: 07

Connecticut (Hamden)
CIJE: 0 RIE: 6 CAT: 07

Connecticut (Hartford)
CIJE: 15 RIE: 39 CAT: 07

Connecticut (Lebanon)
CIJE: 0 RIE: 1 CAT: 07

Connecticut (Madison)
CIJE: 0 RIE: 1 CAT: 07

Connecticut (Mansfield)
CIJE: 0 RIE: 1 CAT: 17

Connecticut (Meriden)
CIJE: 1 RIE: 0 CAT: 07

Connecticut (New Britain)
CIJE: 0 RIE: 2 CAT: 07

Connecticut (New Canaan)
CIJE: 0 RIE: 1 CAT: 07

Connecticut (New Haven)
CIJE: 21 RIE: 51 CAT: 07

Connecticut (New London)
CIJE: 0 RIE: 1 CAT: 07

Connecticut (Newington)
CIJE: 0 RIE: 3 CAT: 07

Connecticut (Norwalk)
CIJE: 2 RIE: 16 CAT: 07

Connecticut (Southbury)
CIJE: 1 RIE: 0 CAT: 07

Connecticut (Southwest)
CIJE: 0 RIE: 5 CAT: 07

Connecticut (Stamford)
CIJE: 4 RIE: 13 CAT: 07

Connecticut (Storrs)
CIJE: 0 RIE: 8 CAT: 07

Connecticut (Wallingford)
CIJE: 0 RIE: 2 CAT: 07

Connecticut (Wallington)
CIJE: 0 RIE: 1 CAT: 07

Connecticut (Waterbury)
CIJE: 0 RIE: 4 CAT: 07

Connecticut (Waterford)
CIJE: 0 RIE: 2 CAT: 07

Connecticut (West Hartford)
CIJE: 4 RIE: 3 CAT: 07

Connecticut (West Haven)
CIJE: 1 RIE: 2 CAT: 07

Connecticut (Westport)
CIJE: 0 RIE: 5 CAT: 07

Connecticut (Windham)
CIJE: 0 RIE: 1 CAT: 07

Connecticut Academy for English Geography History
CIJE: 0 RIE: 1 CAT: 17

Connecticut Adult Performance Program
CIJE: 0 RIE: 1 CAT: 19

Connecticut Assessment of Educational Progress
CIJE: 2 RIE: 6 CAT: 21

Connecticut Association for Reading Research
CIJE: 1 RIE: 0 CAT: 17

Connecticut Basic Skills Proficiency Test
CIJE: 0 RIE: 2 CAT: 21

Connecticut College
CIJE: 5 RIE: 4 CAT: 17

Connecticut Commission for Higher Education
CIJE: 1 RIE: 0 CAT: 17

Connecticut Council on the Family
CIJE: 1 RIE: 0 CAT: 17

Connecticut Educational Evaluation Remedial Assist
CIJE: 0 RIE: 3 CAT: 19

Connecticut Elementary Educ Certification Exam
CIJE: 1 RIE: 0 CAT: 21
UF Elementary Education Cert Exam (Connecticut)

Connecticut Mastery Testing Program
CIJE: 1 RIE: 4 CAT: 21

Connecticut Migratory Childrens Program
CIJE: 0 RIE: 1 CAT: 19

Connecticut Ninth Grade Proficiency Test
CIJE: 1 RIE: 3 CAT: 21

Connecticut Principals Academy
CIJE: 0 RIE: 1 CAT: 17

Connecticut Regional Community Colleges
CIJE: 1 RIE: 2 CAT: 17

Connecticut Regional Medical Program
CIJE: 1 RIE: 0 CAT: 19

Connecticut River Valley
CIJE: 1 RIE: 1 CAT: 07

Connecticut School Effectiveness Project
CIJE: 0 RIE: 5 CAT: 19

Connecticut School Effectiveness Questionnaire
CIJE: 0 RIE: 2 CAT: 21

Connecticut School Interview
CIJE: 0 RIE: 5 CAT: 21

Connecticut Special Ed Computer Network Project
CIJE: 0 RIE: 1 CAT: 19

Connecticut Special Ed Network Software Evaluation
CIJE: 0 RIE: 1 CAT: 17
UF ConnSENSE

Connecticut State Act for Disadvantaged Children
USE Public Act 523 (Connecticut)

Connecticut State Department of Education
CIJE: 4 RIE: 16 CAT: 17

Connecticut State University System
CIJE: 0 RIE: 1 CAT: 17

Connecticut Valley Hospital
CIJE: 0 RIE: 1 CAT: 17

Connecticut Valley Libraries
CIJE: 0 RIE: 1 CAT: 17

Connectionism
CIJE: 20 RIE: 9 CAT: 15
UF Connectionist Approach; Connectionist Networks

Connectionist Approach
USE Connectionism

Connectionist Networks
USE Connectionism

Connections (Mathematics)
CIJE: 114 RIE: 11 CAT: 15

Connectives (Grammar)
CIJE: 19 RIE: 19 CAT: 13

Connectivity
CIJE: 8 RIE: 4 CAT: 16

Conners Abbreviated Scale
CIJE: 2 RIE: 0 CAT: 21

Conners Teacher Rating Scale
CIJE: 10 RIE: 1 CAT: 21

Connetquot Central School District NY
CIJE: 1 RIE: 0 CAT: 17

Connetquot River State Park NY
CIJE: 0 RIE: 1 CAT: 07

Connick v Myers
CIJE: 4 RIE: 3 CAT: 14

Connotations
CIJE: 9 RIE: 9 CAT: 16

ConnSENSE
USE Connecticut Special Ed Network Software Evaluation

Conrad (Joseph)
CIJE: 10 RIE: 0 CAT: 18

Conrad N Hilton Foundation
CIJE: 0 RIE: 1 CAT: 17

Conroe Independent School District TX
CIJE: 0 RIE: 4 CAT: 17

Conroy (Frank)
CIJE: 0 RIE: 1 CAT: 18

Conscience
CIJE: 10 RIE: 4 CAT: 11

Conscientious Objectors
CIJE: 4 RIE: 6 CAT: 10

Conscientiousness
CIJE: 0 RIE: 1 CAT: 11

Conscientisation
CIJE: 3 RIE: 1 CAT: 15

Conscious Processing
CIJE: 0 RIE: 1 CAT: 11

Consciousness
CIJE: 30 RIE: 22 CAT: 11

Consciousness (Physiology)
CIJE: 1 RIE: 1 CAT: 11

Consciousness Education
CIJE: 2 RIE: 0 CAT: 15

Consciousness Levels
USE Levels of Consciousness

Consciousness Research
CIJE: 1 RIE: 3 CAT: 11

Conseil des Colleges PQ
CIJE: 0 RIE: 1 CAT: 17

Consensus
CIJE: 115 RIE: 54 CAT: 15

Consensus Models
CIJE: 11 RIE: 11 CAT: 15
UF Consensus Paradigms

Consensus Moderation
CIJE: 1 RIE: 4 CAT: 15

Consensus Paradigms
USE Consensus Models

Consent
CIJE: 11 RIE: 4 CAT: 14

Consequences
CIJE: 12 RIE: 1 CAT: 16
SN Use a more specific term if possible, e.g., "Logical Consequences," "Social Consequences"

Consequential Evaluation
CIJE: 2 RIE: 2 CAT: 15

CONSER
CIJE: 9 RIE: 2 CAT: 04
SN See also "Conversion of Serials" and "Conversion of Serials Project"

Conservation and Environmental Science Center NJ
CIJE: 0 RIE: 1 CAT: 17

Conservation Centers
CIJE: 0 RIE: 2 CAT: 05

Conservation Education Association
CIJE: 0 RIE: 2 CAT: 17

Conservation Field Centres (Canada)
CIJE: 0 RIE: 1 CAT: 05

Conservation Foundation
CIJE: 0 RIE: 1 CAT: 17

Conservation of Human Resources Project
CIJE: 0 RIE: 1 CAT: 19

Conservationists
CIJE: 1 RIE: 3 CAT: 10

Conservatism Scale (Wilson and Patterson)
CIJE: 6 RIE: 0 CAT: 21

Consistency (Behavior)
CIJE: 7 RIE: 3 CAT: 11

Consistency Theory
CIJE: 8 RIE: 3 CAT: 15

Consolidated Edison Company
CIJE: 1 RIE: 0 CAT: 17

Consolidated Net Worth Statement
CIJE: 0 RIE: 1 CAT: 16

Consolidated Program Information Report
CIJE: 0 RIE: 4 CAT: 22

Consolidated Training and Education Program
CIJE: 0 RIE: 1 CAT: 19

Consolidated Youth Employment Program
CIJE: 0 RIE: 2 CAT: 19

Consonance
CIJE: 4 RIE: 3 CAT: 13

Consonant Cluster Duration
CIJE: 0 RIE: 1 CAT: 13

Consonant Clusters
CIJE: 9 RIE: 6 CAT: 13

Consonant Deletion
CIJE: 0 RIE: 1 CAT: 13

Consonant Mutation
CIJE: 0 RIE: 2 CAT: 13

Consonant Vowel Consonant Combinations
CIJE: 3 RIE: 2 CAT: 13

Consortium Committee on Latin American Studies
CIJE: 1 RIE: 0 CAT: 17

Consortium Develop Professional Materials Voc Educ
CIJE: 0 RIE: 2 CAT: 17

Consortium for Advancement Private Higher Educ
CIJE: 0 RIE: 2 CAT: 17

Consortium for International Studies Education
CIJE: 0 RIE: 1 CAT: 17

Consortium for Longitudinal Studies
CIJE: 6 RIE: 3 CAT: 16

Consortium in Educational Media and Technology
CIJE: 1 RIE: 0 CAT: 17

Consortium International Cooperation Higher Ed
CIJE: 1 RIE: 0 CAT: 17

Consortium of Professional Associations for Study
CIJE: 1 RIE: 3 CAT: 17

Consortium of States
CIJE: 0 RIE: 1 CAT: 17

Consortium on Early Childbearing and Childrearing
CIJE: 0 RIE: 10 CAT: 17

Consortium on Financing Higher Education
CIJE: 2 RIE: 5 CAT: 17

Consortium on Peace Research Education Development
CIJE: 1 RIE: 0 CAT: 17

Consortium on Research and Development
CIJE: 0 RIE: 3 CAT: 17

Consortium to Develop an Online Catalog
CIJE: 1 RIE: 0 CAT: 17

Consortium Training Program TX
CIJE: 0 RIE: 2 CAT: 17

Conspiracy
CIJE: 6 RIE: 2 CAT: 14

Conspiracy Dramas
CIJE: 0 RIE: 1 CAT: 16

Constant Comparative Method
CIJE: 0 RIE: 1 CAT: 15

Constant Information Model
CIJE: 0 RIE: 1 CAT: 15

Constant Time Delay
USE Time Delay

Constantine School District MI
CIJE: 0 RIE: 1 CAT: 17

Constellations
CIJE: 14 RIE: 5 CAT: 20

Constituency Based School Renewal Program
CIJE: 0 RIE: 1 CAT: 19

Constituency Development
CIJE: 6 RIE: 2 CAT: 16

Constitution (United States)
USE United States Constitution

Constitution (West Germany)
USE Basic Law (West Germany)

Constitution Week
CIJE: 0 RIE: 1 CAT: 12

Constitutional Amendments
CIJE: 4 RIE: 2 CAT: 14

Constitutional Convention
CIJE: 3 RIE: 1 CAT: 12
SN U.S., 1787

Constitutional Conventions
CIJE: 1 RIE: 1 CAT: 02

Constitutional Government
CIJE: 0 RIE: 1 CAT: 14

Constitutional Heritage Club
CIJE: 1 RIE: 0 CAT: 17

Constitutional Processes
CIJE: 5 RIE: 5 CAT: 16

Constitutional Ratification
CIJE: 2 RIE: 1 CAT: 14

Constitutional Rights Foundation
CIJE: 2 RIE: 1 CAT: 17

Constitutions
CIJE: 6 RIE: 11 CAT: 14

Constitutive Ethnographic Theory
CIJE: 0 RIE: 2 CAT: 15

Constraining Experiences
CIJE: 2 RIE: 1 CAT: 16

Constraint Dependency Grammar
CIJE: 0 RIE: 1 CAT: 13

Constraints
CIJE: 29 RIE: 15 CAT: 16

CONSTRUCT Programing Language
CIJE: 0 RIE: 1 CAT: 04

Constructalog
CIJE: 0 RIE: 1 CAT: 15

Constructed Listening Test
CIJE: 0 RIE: 1 CAT: 21

Construction Equipment
CIJE: 2 RIE: 1 CAT: 04

Construction Equipment Mechanics
CIJE: 0 RIE: 2 CAT: 09

Construction Grants
CIJE: 0 RIE: 1 CAT: 16

Construction Industry Interest Inventory
CIJE: 1 RIE: 1 CAT: 21

Construction Industry Training Board
CIJE: 2 RIE: 0 CAT: 17

Construction Systems Program
CIJE: 1 RIE: 3 CAT: 19

Construction Tasks
CIJE: 0 RIE: 2 CAT: 16
SN Manipulative activities indirectly associated with academic learning

Construction Test (Savoca)
CIJE: 0 RIE: 1 CAT: 21

Constructive Controversy
CIJE: 0 RIE: 1 CAT: 03

Constructive Criticism
CIJE: 3 RIE: 2 CAT: 15

Constructive Play
CIJE: 5 RIE: 2 CAT: 16

Constructive Thinking Inventory
CIJE: 0 RIE: 1 CAT: 21

Constructs
CIJE: 11 RIE: 10 CAT: 15

Consultant Linker Knowledge and Skills Inventory
CIJE: 0 RIE: 1 CAT: 21

Consultant Role
CIJE: 35 RIE: 18 CAT: 16

Consultants in Total Education
CIJE: 1 RIE: 0 CAT: 17

Consultants Workshop on Technologies
CIJE: 0 RIE: 1 CAT: 02

Consultation and Advisory Services Project
CIJE: 0 RIE: 1 CAT: 19

Consumer Complaints
CIJE: 3 RIE: 4 CAT: 16

Consumer Credit Laws
CIJE: 0 RIE: 1 CAT: 14

Consumer Education Materials Project
CIJE: 1 RIE: 0 CAT: 19

Consumer Education Resource Network
CIJE: 0 RIE: 1 CAT: 17

Consumer Evaluation
CIJE: 5 RIE: 5 CAT: 21

Consumer Expenditure Survey
CIJE: 2 RIE: 5 CAT: 19

Consumer Health Information
USE Health Information

Consumer Information
CIJE: 5 RIE: 12 CAT: 16

Consumer Law
CIJE: 3 RIE: 1 CAT: 14

Consumer Leasing Act
CIJE: 0 RIE: 1 CAT: 14

Consumer Magazines
CIJE: 1 RIE: 3 CAT: 16

Consumer Mathematics
CIJE: 8 RIE: 16 CAT: 03

Consumer Organizations
CIJE: 0 RIE: 2 CAT: 05

Consumer Price Index
CIJE: 19 RIE: 19 CAT: 21

Consumer Product Safety Commission
CIJE: 8 RIE: 7 CAT: 17

Consumer Products
CIJE: 4 RIE: 2 CAT: 16

Consumer Reports
CIJE: 3 RIE: 0 CAT: 22

Consumer Services
CIJE: 2 RIE: 4 CAT: 05

Consumer Skills
CIJE: 3 RIE: 22 CAT: 16

Consumer Skills Kit (NAEP)
CIJE: 0 RIE: 1 CAT: 22

Consumer Skills Mini Assessment (1978)
CIJE: 0 RIE: 0 CAT: 21

Consumer Validation Process
CIJE: 2 RIE: 0 CAT: 15

Consumers
CIJE: 22 RIE: 31 CAT: 10

Consumers Union of the United States
CIJE: 3 RIE: 0 CAT: 17

Consumption
CIJE: 8 RIE: 6 CAT: 16

Contact Action Space
CIJE: 0 RIE: 1 CAT: 11

Contact Hours
CIJE: 4 RIE: 3 CAT: 03

Contact Hypothesis
CIJE: 2 RIE: 2 CAT: 15

Contact Lenses
CIJE: 4 RIE: 2 CAT: 04

Contact Literature
CIJE: 2 RIE: 2 CAT: 16

Contact Narratives
CIJE: 0 RIE: 2 CAT: 16

Contact Tracing
CIJE: 2 RIE: 0 CAT: 11
UF Partner Notification (Diseases)

Container Cappers
CIJE: 0 RIE: 1 CAT: 09

Container Fillers
CIJE: 0 RIE: 1 CAT: 09

Container Makers
CIJE: 0 RIE: 1 CAT: 09

Containment
CIJE: 1 RIE: 1 CAT: 20

Containment Policy
CIJE: 5 RIE: 1 CAT: 15

Contemplation
CIJE: 4 RIE: 2 CAT: 11

Contemporaneity
CIJE: 1 RIE: 0 CAT: 16

Contemporary Image Survey
CIJE: 0 RIE: 1 CAT: 19

Contemporary Industrial Processes
CIJE: 0 RIE: 1 CAT: 15

Contemporary Literature
CIJE: 5 RIE: 4 CAT: 16

Contemporary Mathematical Vocabulary Test (Elmer)
CIJE: 1 RIE: 0 CAT: 21

Contemporary Mathematics Tests
CIJE: 1 RIE: 0 CAT: 21

Contemporary Music Project
CIJE: 6 RIE: 3 CAT: 19

Contemporary Research Inc
CIJE: 0 RIE: 1 CAT: 17

Contemporary Rhetoric
CIJE: 0 RIE: 2 CAT: 13

Contemporary Rhetorical Strategies
CIJE: 0 RIE: 1 CAT: 15

Contempt of Court
CIJE: 1 RIE: 3 CAT: 14

Contender (The)
CIJE: 0 RIE: 1 CAT: 22

Content Analysis of Textbooks for Black Students
CIJE: 0 RIE: 1 CAT: 22

Content Analysis System
CIJE: 2 RIE: 3 CAT: 15

Content Area Bilingual Education NY
USE Project CABE NY

Content Area Reading Enrichment
CIJE: 4 RIE: 0 CAT: 15

Content Area Study Experiences
CIJE: 0 RIE: 1 CAT: 15

Content Area Teaching
CIJE: 92 RIE: 254 CAT: 15
UF Content Based Teaching

Content Based Group Assessment Model
CIJE: 1 RIE: 0 CAT: 15

Content Based Teaching
USE Content Area Teaching

Content Context Words
CIJE: 1 RIE: 1 CAT: 13

Content Cues
CIJE: 2 RIE: 2 CAT: 16

Content Designators
CIJE: 0 RIE: 2 CAT: 16

Content Granularity
CIJE: 0 RIE: 1 CAT: 20

Content Learning
CIJE: 24 RIE: 7 CAT: 11

Content Mastery Examinations for Educators
CIJE: 0 RIE: 1 CAT: 21

Content Module
CIJE: 0 RIE: 1 CAT: 15

Content Referenced Tests
CIJE: 0 RIE: 2 CAT: 21

Content Regulation (Broadcasting)
CIJE: 0 RIE: 2 CAT: 14
UF Broadcast Content Regulation

Content Specific Test Items
CIJE: 0 RIE: 1 CAT: 21

Content Specificity
CIJE: 1 RIE: 1 CAT: 16

Content Structure
CIJE: 11 RIE: 4 CAT: 13

Contentment
CIJE: 0 RIE: 1 CAT: 11

Contests
CIJE: 77 RIE: 36 CAT: 16
SN Use a more specific term if possible, e.g., "Mathematics Contests," "Reading Contests," "Teaching Contests," "Writing Contests"

Context Adaptation
CIJE: 0 RIE: 1 CAT: 16

Context Dependence
CIJE: 15 RIE: 10 CAT: 13

Context Dependent Grammar
CIJE: 4 RIE: 0 CAT: 13

Context Free Tasks
CIJE: 2 RIE: 1 CAT: 15

Context Information Processing Project
CIJE: 0 RIE: 3 CAT: 19

Context Input Process Product Evaluation Model
CIJE: 10 RIE: 22 CAT: 15
UF CIPP Evaluation Model; Guba Stufflebeam CIPP Model; Stufflebeam CIPP Model

Contextual Age
CIJE: 0 RIE: 1 CAT: 11

Contextual Ambiguity Test
CIJE: 0 RIE: 1 CAT: 21

Contextual Analysis
CIJE: 35 RIE: 24 CAT: 15

Contextual Associative Method
CIJE: 0 RIE: 2 CAT: 15

Contextual Dissonance
CIJE: 2 RIE: 0 CAT: 13

Contextual Expectations
CIJE: 3 RIE: 1 CAT: 11

Contextual Interaction Theory
CIJE: 2 RIE: 1 CAT: 15

Contextual Module Analysis
CIJE: 0 RIE: 1 CAT: 15

Contextual Thinking
CIJE: 1 RIE: 5 CAT: 11

Contextualism
CIJE: 12 RIE: 3 CAT: 15

Contextualization
CIJE: 10 RIE: 13 CAT: 13
SN See also "Decontextualization"

Contextualized Apprenticeship Model
CIJE: 0 RIE: 1 CAT: 15

Contextualized Instruction
CIJE: 1 RIE: 1 CAT: 15
SN Teaching a skill within a specific or functional context — examples are "Anchored Instruction" and "Functional Context Education" (qq.v.)

Contextualized Learning Environments
CIJE: 1 RIE: 2 CAT: 20

Conti (Haroldo)
CIJE: 1 RIE: 0 CAT: 18

Contiguity Theory of Learning
CIJE: 1 RIE: 0 CAT: 15

Continental Congress
CIJE: 2 RIE: 4 CAT: 12

Continental Divide Training Center
CIJE: 1 RIE: 0 CAT: 17

Continental Drift
CIJE: 9 RIE: 5 CAT: 20

Continental Shelves
CIJE: 2 RIE: 0 CAT: 20

Continents
CIJE: 0 RIE: 1 CAT: 07

Contingency Analysis
CIJE: 4 RIE: 5 CAT: 15

Contingency Approach
CIJE: 17 RIE: 5 CAT: 15

Contingency Coefficient
CIJE: 0 RIE: 1 CAT: 15

Contingency Framework Administrator Development
CIJE: 1 RIE: 1 CAT: 15

Contingency Learning
CIJE: 2 RIE: 1 CAT: 11

Contingency Management System
CIJE: 3 RIE: 0 CAT: 15

Contingency Models
CIJE: 9 RIE: 7 CAT: 15

Contingency Power
CIJE: 0 RIE: 1 CAT: 16

Contingency Tables
CIJE: 43 RIE: 15 CAT: 15

Contingency Theories
CIJE: 21 RIE: 10 CAT: 15

Contingent Employment
CIJE: 0 RIE: 1 CAT: 16

Contingent Negative Variation
CIJE: 1 RIE: 0 CAT: 15

Continuative Verbs
CIJE: 1 RIE: 0 CAT: 13

Continued Fractions
CIJE: 3 RIE: 0 CAT: 20

Continued Voluntary Permits
CIJE: 0 RIE: 1 CAT: 19

Continuing Education Council
CIJE: 1 RIE: 0 CAT: 17

Continuing Education for Library Staffs
CIJE: 0 RIE: 4 CAT: 19

Continuing Education Needs Assessment Survey
CIJE: 0 RIE: 1 CAT: 21

Continuing Education Programmers
CIJE: 0 RIE: 3 CAT: 09

Continuing Education Systems Project (AAMC)
CIJE: 0 RIE: 1 CAT: 19

Continuing Engineering Education Directors
CIJE: 1 RIE: 0 CAT: 09

Continuing Engineering Studies
CIJE: 1 RIE: 0 CAT: 03

Continuing Library Education Network and Exchange
CIJE: 3 RIE: 8 CAT: 17

Continuing Motivation
CIJE: 6 RIE: 3 CAT: 15

Continuing Professional Education Development Proj
CIJE: 0 RIE: 1 CAT: 19

Continuing Students (Nontransfers)
USE Nontransfer Students

Continuity
CIJE: 48 RIE: 30 CAT: 16

Continuity (Mathematics)
CIJE: 3 RIE: 0 CAT: 20

Continuity Analysis
CIJE: 2 RIE: 0 CAT: 15

Continuity Theory
CIJE: 3 RIE: 0 CAT: 15

Continuous Academic Progress Program
CIJE: 1 RIE: 0 CAT: 19

Continuous Air Monitoring Program
CIJE: 1 RIE: 0 CAT: 19

Continuous Assessment
CIJE: 12 RIE: 2 CAT: 15

Continuous Attitudinal Response Technology
CIJE: 0 RIE: 2 CAT: 20

Continuous Audience Response Technology
CIJE: 0 RIE: 1 CAT: 20

Continuous Creation
CIJE: 1 RIE: 0 CAT: 15

Continuous Growth Models
CIJE: 2 RIE: 1 CAT: 15

Continuous Improvement
CIJE: 3 RIE: 1 CAT: 16

Continuous Longitudinal Manpower Survey
CIJE: 5 RIE: 1 CAT: 21

Continuous Progress Education Project
CIJE: 0 RIE: 2 CAT: 19

Continuous Progress Mathematics Program
CIJE: 0 RIE: 1 CAT: 19

Continuous Recording Techniques
CIJE: 1 RIE: 0 CAT: 15

Continuous Variables
CIJE: 7 RIE: 4 CAT: 20

Continuum Models
CIJE: 8 RIE: 12 CAT: 15

Contoocook Valley School District NH
CIJE: 0 RIE: 1 CAT: 17

Contour
CIJE: 3 RIE: 1 CAT: 11

Contour Density
CIJE: 0 RIE: 1 CAT: 11

Contour Maps
CIJE: 6 RIE: 1 CAT: 04

Contra Costa College CA
CIJE: 0 RIE: 3 CAT: 17

Contra Costa Community College District CA
CIJE: 0 RIE: 2 CAT: 17

Contra Costa County Department of Education CA
CIJE: 1 RIE: 0 CAT: 17

Contra Costa County Schools CA
CIJE: 0 RIE: 1 CAT: 17

Contra Costa Social Studies Curriculum
CIJE: 0 RIE: 2 CAT: 03

Contra Costa Social Studies Guides
CIJE: 0 RIE: 1 CAT: 22

Contract Bridge Players
USE Bridge Players

Contract Education
CIJE: 1 RIE: 4 CAT: 03

Contract Employment
CIJE: 0 RIE: 1 CAT: 16

Contract Implementation
CIJE: 0 RIE: 1 CAT: 15

Contract Item Analysis
CIJE: 1 RIE: 1 CAT: 15

Contract Law
CIJE: 5 RIE: 5 CAT: 14

Contract Management
CIJE: 12 RIE: 4 CAT: 14

Contract Officers
CIJE: 1 RIE: 2 CAT: 09

Contract Schools
CIJE: 3 RIE: 26 CAT: 05

Contract Training
CIJE: 8 RIE: 17 CAT: 15
UF Customized Contract Training

Contract Training Centers
CIJE: 0 RIE: 1 CAT: 05

Contract Vocational Education
CIJE: 0 RIE: 1 CAT: 03

Contractions (Grammar)
CIJE: 6 RIE: 2 CAT: 13

Contractors
CIJE: 14 RIE: 8 CAT: 10

Contractors (Construction Industry)
CIJE: 4 RIE: 1 CAT: 09

Contractors Association v Secretary of Labor
CIJE: 1 RIE: 0 CAT: 14

Contractual Risk Transfer
CIJE: 0 RIE: 1 CAT: 15

Contradictions
CIJE: 8 RIE: 2 CAT: 16

Contralateral Limb
CIJE: 1 RIE: 0 CAT: 11

Contralateral Routing of Signal (Hearing Aids)
CIJE: 2 RIE: 0 CAT: 20

Contrast Analysis
CIJE: 0 RIE: 3 CAT: 21

Contrast Coding
CIJE: 1 RIE: 2 CAT: 15

Contrast Sensitivity Function
CIJE: 3 RIE: 0 CAT: 11

Contrasting Groups Method
CIJE: 2 RIE: 13 CAT: 15

Contrastive Analysis Hypothesis
CIJE: 1 RIE: 0 CAT: 13
SN The claim that the best language teaching materials are based on a contrast of the two competing linguistic systems

Contrastive Rhetoric
CIJE: 6 RIE: 1 CAT: 13

Contributory Negligence
CIJE: 1 RIE: 0 CAT: 14

Control (Social Behavior)
CIJE: 31 RIE: 12 CAT: 11
UF Interpersonal Control; Social Control (Interpersonal)

Control Analysis
CIJE: 5 RIE: 4 CAT: 15

Control Assemblies
CIJE: 0 RIE: 1 CAT: 16

Control Data Basic Skills Learning System
CIJE: 0 RIE: 1 CAT: 04

Control Data Corporation
CIJE: 3 RIE: 2 CAT: 17

Control Data Corporation Computers
CIJE: 3 RIE: 8 CAT: 04

Control Factors (Administrative)
CIJE: 8 RIE: 4 CAT: 16

Control Mechanisms (Administrative)
CIJE: 1 RIE: 4 CAT: 16

Control of Outcomes
CIJE: 1 RIE: 1 CAT: 16
UF Personal Control of Outcomes

Control of Paperwork Amendments 1978
CIJE: 0 RIE: 1 CAT: 14

Control Oriented Interactive Graphic Anal Design
CIJE: 0 RIE: 2 CAT: 15

Control Perception
CIJE: 28 RIE: 8 CAT: 11

Control Systems (Mechanical)
CIJE: 6 RIE: 7 CAT: 20

Control Test AA (Peterson)
CIJE: 1 RIE: 0 CAT: 21

Control Theory
CIJE: 20 RIE: 1 CAT: 15

Controlled Choice
CIJE: 6 RIE: 1 CAT: 15

Controlled Composition
CIJE: 1 RIE: 1 CAT: 15

Controlled Compositions
CIJE: 1 RIE: 1 CAT: 13

Controlled Drinking
CIJE: 0 RIE: 2 CAT: 11

Controlled Variable Trigrams
CIJE: 1 RIE: 0 CAT: 15

Controversial Materials
CIJE: 37 RIE: 11 CAT: 16

Controversial Topics
CIJE: 58 RIE: 30 CAT: 16

Controversy
CIJE: 47 RIE: 28 CAT: 16

CONTU
USE National Comm New Tech Uses Copyrighted Works

Convalescents
CIJE: 0 RIE: 1 CAT: 10

Convection Ovens
CIJE: 1 RIE: 0 CAT: 04

Convenience Foods
CIJE: 3 RIE: 1 CAT: 16

Convenience Stores
CIJE: 0 RIE: 3 CAT: 05

Convention of American Instructors of the Deaf
CIJE: 1 RIE: 2 CAT: 02

Conventional Testing
CIJE: 1 RIE: 3 CAT: 21

Conventionalization
CIJE: 0 RIE: 1 CAT: 16
SN See also "Marital Conventionalization Scale"

Convergence (Mathematics)
CIJE: 10 RIE: 1 CAT: 20

Convergence Technique
CIJE: 1 RIE: 2 CAT: 15

Convergence Test
CIJE: 0 RIE: 1 CAT: 21

Convergence Theory
CIJE: 2 RIE: 4 CAT: 15

Convergent Communication
CIJE: 1 RIE: 2 CAT: 15

Convergent Production
CIJE: 1 RIE: 0 CAT: 16

Convergent Validation
CIJE: 33 RIE: 9 CAT: 21

Conversacion en la Catedral
CIJE: 1 RIE: 0 CAT: 22

Conversation
CIJE: 391 RIE: 168 CAT: 13

Conversation Exercises
CIJE: 4 RIE: 2 CAT: 13

Conversation Theory
CIJE: 32 RIE: 9 CAT: 15

Conversational Analysis
CIJE: 10 RIE: 4 CAT: 15

Conversational Domain
CIJE: 1 RIE: 1 CAT: 16

Conversational English Program
CIJE: 0 RIE: 1 CAT: 19

Conversational Flow
CIJE: 10 RIE: 9 CAT: 13

Conversational Management
CIJE: 13 RIE: 6 CAT: 13

Conversational Markers
CIJE: 1 RIE: 1 CAT: 13

Conversational Mode (Computers)
CIJE: 0 RIE: 1 CAT: 20

Conversational Paradigm
CIJE: 0 RIE: 1 CAT: 15

Conversational Skills Rating Scale
CIJE: 0 RIE: 1 CAT: 21

Converse College SC
CIJE: 2 RIE: 1 CAT: 17

Conversion (Linguistics)
CIJE: 0 RIE: 1 CAT: 13
SN The deliberate transfer of a word from one part of speech to another without any change in its form

Conversion (Religious)
USE Religious Conversion

Conversion of Serials
CIJE: 4 RIE: 2 CAT: 20
SN See also "CONSER" and "Conversion of Serials Project"
UF Serials Automation

Conversion of Serials Project
CIJE: 2 RIE: 2 CAT: 19

Conversion Reaction Syndrome
CIJE: 1 RIE: 0 CAT: 11

Converted Facilities
CIJE: 1 RIE: 0 CAT: 05

Converted Secondary School Rank
CIJE: 0 RIE: 2 CAT: 16

Conveyor Loaders
CIJE: 0 RIE: 1 CAT: 09

Conveyor Operators
CIJE: 0 RIE: 1 CAT: 09

Conveyors
CIJE: 0 RIE: 1 CAT: 04

Convocation of American Indian Scholars 2d
CIJE: 0 RIE: 1 CAT: 02

Convocations
CIJE: 4 RIE: 1 CAT: 02

Conway (Jill Ker)
CIJE: 0 RIE: 1 CAT: 18

Conwell Middle Magnet School PA
CIJE: 1 RIE: 1 CAT: 17

Conze (Werner)
CIJE: 1 RIE: 0 CAT: 18

Cooccurrence (Grammar)
CIJE: 2 RIE: 3 CAT: 13

Cook Books
CIJE: 3 RIE: 15 CAT: 22

Cook County Hospital IL
CIJE: 2 RIE: 0 CAT: 17

Cook Islands
CIJE: 2 RIE: 6 CAT: 07

Cook Lynn (Elizabeth)
CIJE: 0 RIE: 1 CAT: 18

Cook School AZ
CIJE: 1 RIE: 1 CAT: 17

Cooke (Janet)
CIJE: 2 RIE: 0 CAT: 18

Cookstoves
CIJE: 0 RIE: 1 CAT: 04

Coolants
CIJE: 0 RIE: 1 CAT: 20

Cooley (Charles H)
CIJE: 1 RIE: 2 CAT: 18

Cooley (William W)
CIJE: 0 RIE: 1 CAT: 18

Cooley Lohnes Evaluation Model
CIJE: 0 RIE: 2 CAT: 15

Cooleys Anemia
CIJE: 0 RIE: 1 CAT: 11

Coolidge (Archibald Cary)
CIJE: 0 RIE: 1 CAT: 18

Coolidge (Calvin)
CIJE: 1 RIE: 1 CAT: 18

Cooling Conveyor Operators
CIJE: 0 RIE: 1 CAT: 09

Cooling Out Function
CIJE: 1 RIE: 3 CAT: 20

Cooling Towers
CIJE: 1 RIE: 0 CAT: 04

Coons (John)
CIJE: 1 RIE: 3 CAT: 18

Cooper (Anthony Ashley 3rd Earl of Shaftesbury)
USE Shaftesbury (Anthony Ashley Cooper 3rd Earl of)

Cooper (Grant)
CIJE: 1 RIE: 0 CAT: 18

Cooper (Kent)
CIJE: 0 RIE: 1 CAT: 18

Cooper (Percy)
CIJE: 1 RIE: 0 CAT: 18

Cooper (Peter)
CIJE: 2 RIE: 0 CAT: 18

Cooper (Susan)
CIJE: 4 RIE: 0 CAT: 18

Cooper Union for Advancement of Science and Art NY
USE Cooper Union NY

Cooper Union NY
CIJE: 0 RIE: 1 CAT: 17
UF Cooper Union for Advancement of Science and Art NY

Cooperating Schools Program
CIJE: 0 RIE: 2 CAT: 19

Cooperative Accountability Project
CIJE: 1 RIE: 8 CAT: 19

Cooperative Advanced General Science Test
CIJE: 0 RIE: 1 CAT: 21

Cooperative Agencies Resources for Education CA
CIJE: 0 RIE: 1 CAT: 19

Cooperative Alliance for Gifted Education OH
CIJE: 0 RIE: 1 CAT: 19

Cooperative American History Test
CIJE: 0 RIE: 1 CAT: 21

Cooperative Assessment of Experiential Learning
CIJE: 4 RIE: 10 CAT: 19

Cooperative Behavior Checklist (McKinney et al)
CIJE: 0 RIE: 1 CAT: 21

Cooperative Biology Test
CIJE: 0 RIE: 2 CAT: 21

Cooperative Center for Social Science OH
CIJE: 0 RIE: 1 CAT: 17

Cooperative Centers (Vocational)
CIJE: 0 RIE: 1 CAT: 05

Cooperative Chemistry Test
CIJE: 0 RIE: 1 CAT: 21

Cooperative College Development Program
CIJE: 0 RIE: 1 CAT: 19

Cooperative College School Science Program
CIJE: 4 RIE: 6 CAT: 19

Cooperative Community Counseling
CIJE: 0 RIE: 1 CAT: 15

Cooperative Data Management Committee
CIJE: 0 RIE: 1 CAT: 17

Cooperative Demonstration Kindergarten MS
CIJE: 0 RIE: 1 CAT: 19

Cooperative Demonstration Prog (High Technology)
CIJE: 0 RIE: 3 CAT: 19

Cooperative Educ Data Collect Report Standards
CIJE: 0 RIE: 1 CAT: 19

Cooperative Education Association
CIJE: 2 RIE: 0 CAT: 17

Cooperative Education Program
CIJE: 0 RIE: 2 CAT: 19

Cooperative Educational Service Agencies
CIJE: 1 RIE: 3 CAT: 05

Cooperative Elementary Schools
CIJE: 0 RIE: 1 CAT: 05

Cooperative English Tests
CIJE: 2 RIE: 15 CAT: 21

Cooperative Eval and Develop of School Systems
CIJE: 0 RIE: 1 CAT: 15

Cooperative Extension Project for the Handicapped
CIJE: 1 RIE: 0 CAT: 19

Cooperative Extension Service
CIJE: 71 RIE: 183 CAT: 17

Cooperative Federation for Educ Experiences
USE Project COFFEE

Cooperative Goal Structures
USE Goal Structures

Cooperative Graduate Education in Nursing
CIJE: 2 RIE: 0 CAT: 19

Cooperative Industrial Education
CIJE: 0 RIE: 2 CAT: 19

Cooperative Institutional Research Program
CIJE: 34 RIE: 36 CAT: 19

Cooperative Integrated Reading and Composition
CIJE: 2 RIE: 3 CAT: 19

Cooperative Internship Program
CIJE: 0 RIE: 1 CAT: 19

Cooperative Management Information System
CIJE: 1 RIE: 0 CAT: 04

Cooperative Mathematics Tests
CIJE: 2 RIE: 3 CAT: 21

Cooperative Mathematics Tests (Algebra III)
CIJE: 1 RIE: 0 CAT: 21

Cooperative Mathematics Tests (Arithmetic)
CIJE: 0 RIE: 1 CAT: 21

Cooperative Monitoring
CIJE: 0 RIE: 1 CAT: 15

Cooperative Office Education
CIJE: 1 RIE: 1 CAT: 19

Cooperative Organization for Program Excellence VA
CIJE: 0 RIE: 1 CAT: 19
UF COPE Program (Newport News VA)

Cooperative Physics Test
CIJE: 0 RIE: 2 CAT: 21

Cooperative Play
CIJE: 3 RIE: 2 CAT: 16

Cooperative Preschool Inventory
CIJE: 2 RIE: 9 CAT: 21

Cooperative Preschool Inventory (Revised)
CIJE: 0 RIE: 1 CAT: 21

Cooperative Preschools
CIJE: 0 RIE: 5 CAT: 05

Cooperative Primary Tests
CIJE: 1 RIE: 4 CAT: 21

Cooperative Professional Education Program
CIJE: 0 RIE: 4 CAT: 19

Cooperative Program in Educational Administration
CIJE: 1 RIE: 1 CAT: 19

Cooperative Program Planning and Teaching
CIJE: 0 RIE: 1 CAT: 15
UF CPPT

Cooperative Project for Educational Development
CIJE: 1 RIE: 11 CAT: 19

Cooperative Purchasing
CIJE: 1 RIE: 1 CAT: 15

Cooperative Reading Comprehension Tests
CIJE: 1 RIE: 5 CAT: 21

Cooperative Research Act 1954
CIJE: 1 RIE: 2 CAT: 14

Cooperative Research Act 1954 Title VII
CIJE: 0 RIE: 2 CAT: 14

Cooperative School College Communication Studies
CIJE: 0 RIE: 1 CAT: 03

Cooperative Science Tests
CIJE: 0 RIE: 1 CAT: 21

Cooperative Science Tests (Chemistry)
CIJE: 0 RIE: 2 CAT: 21

Cooperative Science Tests (Physics)
CIJE: 0 RIE: 1 CAT: 21

Cooperative Teacher Education Program
CIJE: 2 RIE: 1 CAT: 19

Cooperative Test Taking
CIJE: 0 RIE: 2 CAT: 21

Cooperative Urban Teacher Education Program
CIJE: 7 RIE: 7 CAT: 19
UF CUTE Program

Cooperative Vocational Program NE
CIJE: 0 RIE: 2 CAT: 19

Coopersmith Behavior Rating Form
CIJE: 2 RIE: 1 CAT: 21

Coopersmith Self Esteem Inventory
CIJE: 54 RIE: 23 CAT: 21

COOR Intermediate School District MI
CIJE: 0 RIE: 2 CAT: 17

Coordinate Bilingualism
CIJE: 4 RIE: 2 CAT: 13

Coordinated Career Education Curriculum Project
CIJE: 0 RIE: 2 CAT: 19

Coordinated Occupational Data Analysis Program
CIJE: 0 RIE: 1 CAT: 19

Coordinated Occupational Information Network
CIJE: 0 RIE: 2 CAT: 04

Coordinated Transfer Application System
CIJE: 4 RIE: 3 CAT: 15

Coordinated Vocational Academic Education
CIJE: 2 RIE: 6 CAT: 03

Coordinates
CIJE: 3 RIE: 1 CAT: 20

Coordinating Committee on Research in Voc Ed
CIJE: 0 RIE: 1 CAT: 17

Coordinating Council for Fine Arts and Humanities
CIJE: 1 RIE: 0 CAT: 17

Coordinating Council on Higher Education
CIJE: 0 RIE: 1 CAT: 17

Coordinating Councils
CIJE: 0 RIE: 5 CAT: 10

Coordinating Information for Texas Educators
CIJE: 0 RIE: 1 CAT: 19

Coordination Complexes
CIJE: 1 RIE: 0 CAT: 15

Coorientation
CIJE: 4 RIE: 9 CAT: 15

Coos
CIJE: 1 RIE: 0 CAT: 13

Coparenting
CIJE: 6 RIE: 7 CAT: 11

COPE Model
USE Curriculum Organization and Program Evaluation

COPE Program (Newport News VA)
USE Cooperative Organization for Program Excellence VA

Copernican Plan
CIJE: 1 RIE: 1 CAT: 03

Copernicus
CIJE: 6 RIE: 1 CAT: 18

COPES System (Civilian Labor Stats)
USE Civilian Occupation Planning Estimates System

COPES Test of Science Concepts
CIJE: 0 RIE: 3 CAT: 21

Coping Analysis Schedule for Educational Settings
CIJE: 2 RIE: 10 CAT: 21

Coping Inventory
CIJE: 3 RIE: 5 CAT: 21

Coping Resources Inventory
CIJE: 1 RIE: 1 CAT: 21

Coping with Death Scale
CIJE: 1 RIE: 2 CAT: 21

Copland (Aaron)
CIJE: 1 RIE: 0 CAT: 18

Copp Clark Canadian Reading Development Series
CIJE: 0 RIE: 1 CAT: 15

Copper
CIJE: 9 RIE: 2 CAT: 20

Copper Chromate
CIJE: 1 RIE: 0 CAT: 20

Copper Complexes
CIJE: 1 RIE: 0 CAT: 20

Copper Country Intermediate School District MI
CIJE: 0 RIE: 1 CAT: 17

Copper Miners
CIJE: 0 RIE: 1 CAT: 09

Copper Oxide
CIJE: 1 RIE: 0 CAT: 20

Coppin (Fanny Jackson)
CIJE: 1 RIE: 0 CAT: 18

Coppin State College MD
CIJE: 4 RIE: 5 CAT: 17

Coppola (Francis Ford)
CIJE: 0 RIE: 1 CAT: 18

Coprincipalship
CIJE: 2 RIE: 0 CAT: 15

Copula (Grammar)
CIJE: 23 RIE: 6 CAT: 13

Copula Deletion (Grammar)
CIJE: 0 RIE: 1 CAT: 13

Copy Cat Camera
CIJE: 0 RIE: 1 CAT: 04

Copy Cataloging
CIJE: 1 RIE: 1 CAT: 16

Copy Milling
CIJE: 1 RIE: 0 CAT: 20

Copy Theory of Memory
CIJE: 1 RIE: 0 CAT: 15

Copyfitting
CIJE: 0 RIE: 1 CAT: 16

Copying Ability
CIJE: 5 RIE: 3 CAT: 16

Copying Speed
CIJE: 0 RIE: 1 CAT: 16

Copyright Act (Canada)
CIJE: 3 RIE: 0 CAT: 14
UF Canadian Copyright Act

Copyright Act 1909
CIJE: 1 RIE: 4 CAT: 14

Copyright Act 1976
USE Copyright Law 1976

Copyright Act 1978
CIJE: 2 RIE: 7 CAT: 14

Copyright Clearance Center
CIJE: 3 RIE: 0 CAT: 17

Copyright Clearinghouse
CIJE: 0 RIE: 1 CAT: 17

Copyright Compliance
CIJE: 8 RIE: 2 CAT: 14

Copyright Law 1976
CIJE: 61 RIE: 34 CAT: 14
UF Copyright Act 1976; Copyright Revision Act 1976

Copyright Law Amendments 1980
CIJE: 0 RIE: 3 CAT: 14

Copyright Office
CIJE: 3 RIE: 11 CAT: 17

Copyright Revision Act 1976
USE Copyright Law 1976

Copyright Revision Bill
CIJE: 1 RIE: 3 CAT: 14

Copyright Royalty Tribunal
CIJE: 1 RIE: 4 CAT: 17

Copywriting
CIJE: 9 RIE: 4 CAT: 16

Coral Reefs
CIJE: 1 RIE: 3 CAT: 20

Corals
CIJE: 0 RIE: 1 CAT: 20

Corbett (Ned)
CIJE: 0 RIE: 1 CAT: 18

Core Achievement Test
CIJE: 0 RIE: 1 CAT: 21

Core Alcohol and Drug Survey
CIJE: 1 RIE: 2 CAT: 21

Core Collections
CIJE: 7 RIE: 2 CAT: 16

Core Knowledge Foundation
CIJE: 0 RIE: 3 CAT: 17

Core Language
CIJE: 0 RIE: 1 CAT: 13

Core Plane Wirers
CIJE: 0 RIE: 1 CAT: 09

Core Plus Education
CIJE: 0 RIE: 1 CAT: 15

Core Skills Project
CIJE: 0 RIE: 2 CAT: 19

Coreference
CIJE: 2 RIE: 1 CAT: 13

Coreguaje
CIJE: 0 RIE: 1 CAT: 13
SN A Western Tucanoan language of Colombia
UF Correguaje

Coriolis Force
CIJE: 6 RIE: 0 CAT: 20

Cormier (Robert)
CIJE: 10 RIE: 1 CAT: 18

Corn
CIJE: 3 RIE: 5 CAT: 20

Corn Culture
CIJE: 2 RIE: 4 CAT: 08

Corn Cutting Machine Operators
CIJE: 0 RIE: 1 CAT: 09

Corn Husking Machine Operators
CIJE: 0 RIE: 1 CAT: 09

Corn Production
CIJE: 1 RIE: 1 CAT: 20

Corneal Transplants
CIJE: 1 RIE: 0 CAT: 11

Corneille (Pierre)
CIJE: 4 RIE: 0 CAT: 18

Cornelia de Lange Syndrome
USE de Lange Syndrome

Cornell Critical Thinking Test
CIJE: 9 RIE: 5 CAT: 21

Cornell Farm Account Book
CIJE: 0 RIE: 2 CAT: 04

Cornell Learning and Study Skills Inventory
CIJE: 1 RIE: 1 CAT: 21

Cornell Medical Index
CIJE: 1 RIE: 0 CAT: 22

Cornell Pilot Program
CIJE: 1 RIE: 0 CAT: 19

Cornell Studies in Intergroup Relations
CIJE: 0 RIE: 1 CAT: 15

Cornell University NY
CIJE: 99 RIE: 71 CAT: 17

Cornerstone School NY
CIJE: 0 RIE: 2 CAT: 17

Corning Community College NY
CIJE: 0 RIE: 3 CAT: 17

Corning Glassworks NY
CIJE: 0 RIE: 0 CAT: 17

Corning Museum of Glass NY
CIJE: 0 RIE: 1 CAT: 17

Cornish Test of Motor Planning
CIJE: 0 RIE: 1 CAT: 21

Cornucopians
CIJE: 0 RIE: 0 CAT: 10

Cornwell IQ Test
CIJE: 0 RIE: 1 CAT: 21

Coro Foundation NY
CIJE: 0 RIE: 1 CAT: 17

Corominas (Joan)
CIJE: 1 RIE: 0 CAT: 18

Corominas (Juan)
CIJE: 1 RIE: 0 CAT: 18

Corona Del Mar High School CA
CIJE: 1 RIE: 0 CAT: 17

Corona Unified School District CA
CIJE: 0 RIE: 3 CAT: 17

Coronary Care
CIJE: 3 RIE: 1 CAT: 11
UF Cardiac Care

Coroners
CIJE: 3 RIE: 0 CAT: 09

Corporate Athleticism
CIJE: 0 RIE: 0 CAT: 15

Corporate Community Schools of America
CIJE: 0 RIE: 3 CAT: 17
SN A not-for-profit coalition of business executives, concerned educators, and community leaders working to reform urban public education by establishing and operating business sponsored elementary schools

Corporate Culture
CIJE: 18 RIE: 7 CAT: 16

Corporate Divestiture
USE Divestiture

Corporate Excellence Rubric
CIJE: 0 RIE: 1 CAT: 16

Corporate Executives
USE Business Executives

Corporate Families
CIJE: 2 RIE: 0 CAT: 10

Corporate Higher Education Forum (Canada)
CIJE: 0 RIE: 1 CAT: 17

Corporate History
CIJE: 2 RIE: 3 CAT: 12

Corporate Libraries
CIJE: 25 RIE: 4 CAT: 05

Corporate Occupational Information System
CIJE: 1 RIE: 0 CAT: 04

Corporate Policy
CIJE: 8 RIE: 2 CAT: 16

Corporate Politics
CIJE: 10 RIE: 3 CAT: 16

Corporate Television
CIJE: 1 RIE: 1 CAT: 16

Corporate Users
CIJE: 5 RIE: 3 CAT: 10

Corporate Wellness Professionals
USE Wellness Professionals

Corporation for Economic and Industrial Research
CIJE: 0 RIE: 2 CAT: 17

Corporation for Public Broadcasting
CIJE: 26 RIE: 47 CAT: 17
SN See also "Annenberg CPB Project"

Corporation for Public Television
CIJE: 0 RIE: 1 CAT: 17

Corporatism
CIJE: 7 RIE: 4 CAT: 15

Corpsman Advisory System
CIJE: 1 RIE: 0 CAT: 15

Corpus Christi Independent School District TX
CIJE: 1 RIE: 4 CAT: 17

Corpus Christi Public Library TX
CIJE: 1 RIE: 0 CAT: 17

Corpus Christi State University TX
CIJE: 0 RIE: 1 CAT: 17

Corpuscular Theory
CIJE: 1 RIE: 0 CAT: 11

Correct English Magazine
CIJE: 0 RIE: 1 CAT: 22

Correction for Attenuation
CIJE: 4 RIE: 1 CAT: 21

Correction for Guessing
CIJE: 10 RIE: 7 CAT: 21

Correctional Education Association
CIJE: 1 RIE: 3 CAT: 17

Correctional Industries Association
CIJE: 0 RIE: 1 CAT: 17

Correctional Officers
CIJE: 15 RIE: 28 CAT: 09

Correctional Special Education Training Project
CIJE: 0 RIE: 1 CAT: 19

Corrective Feedback Paradigm
CIJE: 1 RIE: 4 CAT: 15

Correguaje
USE Coreguaje

Correlated Curriculum Program
CIJE: 0 RIE: 2 CAT: 19

Correlated Proportions
CIJE: 0 RIE: 1 CAT: 15

Correlated Science Program
CIJE: 1 RIE: 0 CAT: 19

Correlation Matrices
CIJE: 13 RIE: 7 CAT: 20

Correlation Ratio
CIJE: 1 RIE: 1 CAT: 20

Correlational Grammar
CIJE: 0 RIE: 2 CAT: 13

Correspondence Theory
CIJE: 23 RIE: 5 CAT: 15

Corridor Approach
CIJE: 0 RIE: 1 CAT: 15

Corrosion
CIJE: 3 RIE: 2 CAT: 20

Corrugator Operators
CIJE: 0 RIE: 1 CAT: 09

Corsican
CIJE: 5 RIE: 0 CAT: 13

Corsini (Raymond J)
CIJE: 0 RIE: 0 CAT: 18

Corsini Four R School System
CIJE: 1 RIE: 0 CAT: 15

Cortazar (Julio)
CIJE: 9 RIE: 0 CAT: 18

Cortes (Hernan)
CIJE: 1 RIE: 2 CAT: 18

Cortical Blindness
CIJE: 0 RIE: 1 CAT: 11

Cortical Electrical Activity
CIJE: 0 RIE: 1 CAT: 11

Cortical Visual Impairments
CIJE: 2 RIE: 0 CAT: 11

Cortisol
USE Hydrocortisone

Corvallis School District 1 MT
CIJE: 0 RIE: 1 CAT: 17

Corvallis School District OR
CIJE: 0 RIE: 1 CAT: 17

Corwin (Ronald)
CIJE: 0 RIE: 2 CAT: 18

Corwith Wesley Community School District IA
CIJE: 0 RIE: 1 CAT: 17

Cosby Show
CIJE: 4 RIE: 3 CAT: 22

Coser (Lewis)
CIJE: 1 RIE: 1 CAT: 18

Coser v Moore
CIJE: 0 RIE: 1 CAT: 14

Coshocton Public Library OH
CIJE: 0 RIE: 1 CAT: 17

Cosmetic Surgery
CIJE: 2 RIE: 0 CAT: 11

Cosmetics
CIJE: 3 RIE: 3 CAT: 16

Cosmic Approach
CIJE: 1 RIE: 1 CAT: 15

Cosmic Explorer (Computer Program)
CIJE: 0 RIE: 1 CAT: 04

Cosmic Rays
CIJE: 9 RIE: 0 CAT: 20

Cosmology
CIJE: 33 RIE: 2 CAT: 20

Cosmopolitan Local Orientation
CIJE: 3 RIE: 2 CAT: 16

Cossatot Vocational Technical School AR
CIJE: 0 RIE: 1 CAT: 17

Cost Accounting
CIJE: 6 RIE: 8 CAT: 15

Cost Allocation to Program System
CIJE: 1 RIE: 0 CAT: 15

Cost and Training Effectiveness Analysis
CIJE: 1 RIE: 1 CAT: 15

Cost Containment
CIJE: 118 RIE: 14 CAT: 15

Cost Management
CIJE: 0 RIE: 1 CAT: 16

Cost of Attaining Personnel Requirements
CIJE: 0 RIE: 1 CAT: 15

Cost of Education Indexes
CIJE: 4 RIE: 5 CAT: 21

Cost of Living
CIJE: 8 RIE: 7 CAT: 16

Cost of Living Wage Adjustment
CIJE: 5 RIE: 2 CAT: 16

Cost Plus Pricing
CIJE: 1 RIE: 1 CAT: 15

Cost Reduction Incentive Awards
CIJE: 0 RIE: 2 CAT: 19

Cost Sharing
CIJE: 1 RIE: 3 CAT: 16

Cost Sharing Awards Program
CIJE: 0 RIE: 1 CAT: 19

Cost Simulation Model
CIJE: 1 RIE: 0 CAT: 15

Costa Rica
CIJE: 47 RIE: 58 CAT: 07

Costello Comrey Anxiety Scale
CIJE: 1 RIE: 0 CAT: 21

Costing and Data Management System
CIJE: 0 RIE: 1 CAT: 04

Costs (Surgical)
CIJE: 0 RIE: 1 CAT: 11

Costs of Schools Training and Education
CIJE: 0 RIE: 1 CAT: 15

Costume History
CIJE: 0 RIE: 1 CAT: 12

Costumes
CIJE: 2 RIE: 1 CAT: 16

Costumes (Theatrical)
CIJE: 3 RIE: 2 CAT: 16

Cosumnes River College CA
CIJE: 0 RIE: 1 CAT: 17

Cotabato Chabacano
CIJE: 0 RIE: 1 CAT: 13
SN A Philippine Creole Spanish dialect
UF Chabacano (Cotabato)

Cotabato Manobo
CIJE: 0 RIE: 1 CAT: 13
SN A Northwest Austronesian (Philippine) language
UF Manobo (Cotabato)

Cottage Industry
CIJE: 1 RIE: 4 CAT: 16
SN Wage work done at home
UF Home Industry

Cotton
CIJE: 1 RIE: 3 CAT: 20

Cotton Production
CIJE: 1 RIE: 2 CAT: 20

Cotwin Control Study
CIJE: 1 RIE: 0 CAT: 19

Coulomb Law
CIJE: 5 RIE: 1 CAT: 20

Council Bluffs Community School District IA
CIJE: 0 RIE: 1 CAT: 17

Council for Accred of Counsel and Relat Educ Prog
CIJE: 0 RIE: 2 CAT: 17
UF CACREP

Council for Adult and Experiential Learning
CIJE: 1 RIE: 2 CAT: 17

Council for Advancement and Support of Education
CIJE: 51 RIE: 4 CAT: 17

Council for Advancement of Experiential Learning
CIJE: 4 RIE: 3 CAT: 17

Council for American Private Education
CIJE: 2 RIE: 3 CAT: 17

Council for Area Planning of Educational Services
CIJE: 2 RIE: 1 CAT: 17

Council for Arts and Humanities MA
CIJE: 0 RIE: 1 CAT: 17

Council for Basic Education
CIJE: 6 RIE: 3 CAT: 17

Council for Chemical Research
CIJE: 3 RIE: 0 CAT: 17

Council for Cultural Cooperation (France)
CIJE: 7 RIE: 22 CAT: 17

Council for Development of French in Louisiana
CIJE: 1 RIE: 1 CAT: 17

Council for Distributive Teacher Education
CIJE: 0 RIE: 2 CAT: 17

Council for Educational Diagnostic Services
CIJE: 0 RIE: 1 CAT: 17

Council for Elementary Science International
CIJE: 0 RIE: 1 CAT: 17

Council for Exceptional Children
CIJE: 55 RIE: 57 CAT: 17

Council for Financial Aid to Education
CIJE: 6 RIE: 1 CAT: 17

Council for International Health
CIJE: 1 RIE: 0 CAT: 17

Council for Jewish Elderly
CIJE: 0 RIE: 1 CAT: 17

Council for Learning Disabilities
CIJE: 3 RIE: 0 CAT: 17

Council for Liberal Learning
CIJE: 0 RIE: 1 CAT: 17

Council for Mutual Economic Assistance
CIJE: 0 RIE: 1 CAT: 17

Council for National Academic Awards
CIJE: 4 RIE: 0 CAT: 17

Council for National Academic Awards (England)
CIJE: 1 RIE: 2 CAT: 17

Council for Occupational Education
CIJE: 2 RIE: 0 CAT: 17

Council for Private Postsecondary Voc Educ CA
CIJE: 0 RIE: 0 CAT: 17

Council for Science and Society
CIJE: 1 RIE: 0 CAT: 17

Council for the Advancement of Small Colleges
CIJE: 1 RIE: 2 CAT: 17

Council for the Development of French in Louisiana
CIJE: 0 RIE: 1 CAT: 17

Council for Women in Independent Schools
CIJE: 1 RIE: 0 CAT: 17

Council Grove High School KS
CIJE: 1 RIE: 0 CAT: 17

Council of Administrators of Special Education
CIJE: 1 RIE: 2 CAT: 17

Council of Appalachian Governors
CIJE: 1 RIE: 0 CAT: 17

Council of Chief State School Officers
CIJE: 6 RIE: 38 CAT: 17
SN See also "CCSSO..."

Council of Counseling Psychology Training Programs
CIJE: 2 RIE: 0 CAT: 17

Council of Cultural Development (France)
CIJE: 1 RIE: 0 CAT: 17

Council of Deans
CIJE: 1 RIE: 0 CAT: 17

Council of Educators Review
CIJE: 0 RIE: 1 CAT: 16

Council of Energy Resource Tribes
CIJE: 7 RIE: 1 CAT: 17

Council of Europe (France)
CIJE: 19 RIE: 92 CAT: 17

Council of Graduate Schools
CIJE: 4 RIE: 15 CAT: 17

Council of Great City Schools
CIJE: 3 RIE: 4 CAT: 17

Council of Independent Colleges
CIJE: 2 RIE: 3 CAT: 17

Council of Learned Societies in Education
CIJE: 0 RIE: 1 CAT: 17

Council of Ministers (USSR)
CIJE: 0 RIE: 1 CAT: 17

Council of National Library and Info Associations
CIJE: 0 RIE: 1 CAT: 17

Council of National Organizations
CIJE: 1 RIE: 0 CAT: 17

Council of Ontario Universities
CIJE: 1 RIE: 4 CAT: 17

Council of Ontario Universities (Canada)
CIJE: 2 RIE: 8 CAT: 17

Council of Outdoor Educators of Ontario
CIJE: 0 RIE: 1 CAT: 17

Council of Professors of Instruction Supervision
CIJE: 0 RIE: 1 CAT: 17

Council of Scientific and Industrial Research
CIJE: 0 RIE: 1 CAT: 17

Course Prerequisites
CIJE: 1 RIE: 2 CAT: 03

Course Structure Inventory
CIJE: 1 RIE: 1 CAT: 21

Course Taking Patterns
CIJE: 2 RIE: 8 CAT: 16

Course Titles
CIJE: 1 RIE: 2 CAT: 03

Courses by Newspaper
CIJE: 4 RIE: 5 CAT: 03

Coursework Cluster Analysis Model
CIJE: 4 RIE: 1 CAT: 15

Coursewriter III
CIJE: 0 RIE: 1 CAT: 21

Coursewriter Programing Language
CIJE: 2 RIE: 34 CAT: 04

Court Appointed Special Advocate Program
CIJE: 4 RIE: 0 CAT: 19

Court Employment Project
CIJE: 0 RIE: 1 CAT: 19

Court Interpreters
CIJE: 0 RIE: 1 CAT: 09

Court Interpreters Act 1978
CIJE: 1 RIE: 2 CAT: 14

Court Interpreting
CIJE: 0 RIE: 1 CAT: 14

Court Managers
CIJE: 0 RIE: 1 CAT: 09

Court of Veterans Appeals
CIJE: 0 RIE: 1 CAT: 17

Court Review
USE Judicial Review

Court TV
CIJE: 0 RIE: 1 CAT: 17

Court Witnesses
USE Witnesses

Courtis (Stuart Appleton)
CIJE: 0 RIE: 2 CAT: 18

Courtroom Procedures
CIJE: 19 RIE: 9 CAT: 15

Courts of Appeal
USE Appellate Courts

Courts Training Project
CIJE: 0 RIE: 2 CAT: 19

Courtyards
CIJE: 2 RIE: 0 CAT: 05

Coushatta (Tribe)
CIJE: 0 RIE: 1 CAT: 08
SN See also "Koasati"

Cousin (Gabriel)
CIJE: 1 RIE: 0 CAT: 18

Cousin (Victor)
CIJE: 1 RIE: 0 CAT: 18

Cousins (Margaret)
CIJE: 0 RIE: 1 CAT: 18

Cousteau (Jacques)
CIJE: 1 RIE: 0 CAT: 18

Couzens Machine
CIJE: 0 RIE: 1 CAT: 04

Covalent Bonds
CIJE: 2 RIE: 0 CAT: 20

Covariance Structural Analysis
CIJE: 20 RIE: 6 CAT: 15

Covariance Structure Models
CIJE: 33 RIE: 4 CAT: 21

Covariation
CIJE: 19 RIE: 7 CAT: 15

Covello (Leonard)
CIJE: 1 RIE: 0 CAT: 18

Covenant Contracting
CIJE: 0 RIE: 1 CAT: 11

Covenants on Human Rights
CIJE: 2 RIE: 0 CAT: 22

Coventry College of Education (England)
CIJE: 3 RIE: 0 CAT: 17

Coverdale (Ralph)
CIJE: 1 RIE: 0 CAT: 18

Covering Machine Operators
CIJE: 0 RIE: 1 CAT: 09

Covert Communication
CIJE: 0 RIE: 1 CAT: 15

Covert Rehearsal
CIJE: 2 RIE: 2 CAT: 11

Covert Sensitization
CIJE: 3 RIE: 1 CAT: 11

Covert Verbalization
CIJE: 2 RIE: 1 CAT: 11

Covington Attitude Inventory for Problem Solving
CIJE: 0 RIE: 2 CAT: 21

Covington Catholic High School
CIJE: 1 RIE: 0 CAT: 17

Covington Junior High School
CIJE: 1 RIE: 0 CAT: 17

Cowan (William)
CIJE: 1 RIE: 0 CAT: 18

Cowboys
CIJE: 4 RIE: 6 CAT: 09

Cowles (Gardner)
CIJE: 0 RIE: 1 CAT: 18

Cowles (John)
CIJE: 0 RIE: 1 CAT: 18

Cowlitz
CIJE: 1 RIE: 1 CAT: 13

Coworker Involvement Instrument (Rusch et al)
CIJE: 0 RIE: 1 CAT: 21

Coworker Rating Blank
CIJE: 0 RIE: 2 CAT: 21

Coworkers
CIJE: 4 RIE: 1 CAT: 10
UF Co Workers (Employees)

Cowper (William)
CIJE: 1 RIE: 0 CAT: 18

Cows
CIJE: 0 RIE: 1 CAT: 20

Cox Commission Report
CIJE: 1 RIE: 0 CAT: 22

Coyotes
CIJE: 3 RIE: 0 CAT: 20

CP M Operating System
CIJE: 3 RIE: 0 CAT: 04

CPPT
USE Cooperative Program Planning and Teaching

Crabbe (George)
CIJE: 0 RIE: 1 CAT: 18

Crabs
CIJE: 4 RIE: 2 CAT: 20

Crack Babies
CIJE: 8 RIE: 7 CAT: 10

Cradleboards
CIJE: 2 RIE: 1 CAT: 04

CRAFT Project
CIJE: 2 RIE: 3 CAT: 19

Crafts Council of Great Britain
CIJE: 1 RIE: 0 CAT: 17

Craig Lipreading Inventory
CIJE: 0 RIE: 1 CAT: 21

Craig Videotape Recorder
CIJE: 0 RIE: 1 CAT: 04

Crandall (Prudence)
CIJE: 0 RIE: 1 CAT: 18

Crandall Social Desirability Scale
CIJE: 3 RIE: 1 CAT: 21

Crane (Hart)
CIJE: 1 RIE: 0 CAT: 18

Crane (Julia E)
CIJE: 1 RIE: 0 CAT: 18

Crane (Stephen)
CIJE: 3 RIE: 6 CAT: 18

Crane Normal Institute of Music
CIJE: 1 RIE: 0 CAT: 17

Cranfield Institute of Technology (England)
CIJE: 1 RIE: 1 CAT: 17

Cranfield Project
CIJE: 6 RIE: 4 CAT: 19

Cranfield School of Management (England)
CIJE: 2 RIE: 0 CAT: 17

Cranford Public Schools NJ
CIJE: 0 RIE: 2 CAT: 17

Craniofacial Dysostosis
USE Crouzon Syndrome

Craniosynostosis
CIJE: 1 RIE: 0 CAT: 11

Crankcase Breathers
CIJE: 0 RIE: 1 CAT: 04

Cransbrook Kingswood School MI
CIJE: 0 RIE: 0 CAT: 17

Crapsey (Adelaide)
CIJE: 0 RIE: 1 CAT: 18

Crary American History Test
CIJE: 0 RIE: 1 CAT: 21

Cratty Locomotor Agility Test
CIJE: 1 RIE: 0 CAT: 21

Craven (Margaret)
CIJE: 0 RIE: 2 CAT: 18

Crawford Small Parts Dexterity Test
CIJE: 1 RIE: 0 CAT: 21

Crawford v Board of Education of Los Angeles
CIJE: 0 RIE: 2 CAT: 14

Crawling
CIJE: 6 RIE: 0 CAT: 11

Crayfish
CIJE: 1 RIE: 0 CAT: 20

Crayon Resist Technique
CIJE: 2 RIE: 0 CAT: 15

CREATE (Teacher Evaluation)
USE Center for Research on Educ Account Teacher Eval

CREATE Computer System
CIJE: 0 RIE: 1 CAT: 04

Creating a Career Program
CIJE: 0 RIE: 2 CAT: 19

Creating A New Approach to Learning
USE Project CANAL

Creating Effective Schools Program
CIJE: 0 RIE: 1 CAT: 19

Creation
CIJE: 6 RIE: 3 CAT: 16

Creation Research Society CA
CIJE: 6 RIE: 0 CAT: 17

Creative Activities Checklist (Kelly)
CIJE: 0 RIE: 1 CAT: 21

Creative Alternative Games
CIJE: 0 RIE: 1 CAT: 15

Creative and Academic Thinking Skills Program TX
CIJE: 0 RIE: 1 CAT: 19

Creative Behavior Disposition Scale (Taylor et al)
CIJE: 1 RIE: 0 CAT: 21

Creative Career and Vocational Education Project
CIJE: 0 RIE: 1 CAT: 19

Creative Curriculum for Family Child Care
CIJE: 0 RIE: 2 CAT: 03

Creative Dance
CIJE: 2 RIE: 2 CAT: 03

Creative Design Test (Mkes)
CIJE: 0 RIE: 1 CAT: 21

Creative Hypothesizing
CIJE: 0 RIE: 1 CAT: 15

Creative Imagination Scale (Wilson and Barber)
CIJE: 1 RIE: 1 CAT: 21

Creative Job Search Technique
CIJE: 0 RIE: 2 CAT: 15

Creative Motivation Scale
CIJE: 1 RIE: 0 CAT: 21

Creative Play
CIJE: 4 RIE: 5 CAT: 11

Creative Problem Solving
CIJE: 9 RIE: 5 CAT: 15

Creative Problem Solving for Kids
CIJE: 0 RIE: 1 CAT: 15

Creative Problem Solving Institute
CIJE: 1 RIE: 0 CAT: 17

Creative Problem Solving Model
CIJE: 0 RIE: 1 CAT: 15

Creative Products Scale
CIJE: 0 RIE: 1 CAT: 21

Creative Resources Enriching Student Talents
CIJE: 1 RIE: 1 CAT: 19

Creative Studies Project
CIJE: 6 RIE: 0 CAT: 19

Creative Teaching Dilemma
CIJE: 0 RIE: 1 CAT: 15

Creative Visualization
CIJE: 0 RIE: 3 CAT: 15

Creativity Checklist (Ellison)
CIJE: 0 RIE: 1 CAT: 21

Creativity Project
CIJE: 1 RIE: 0 CAT: 19

Creativity Rating Scale (Ellison)
CIJE: 0 RIE: 1 CAT: 21

Creativity Training Research
CIJE: 0 RIE: 1 CAT: 19

Creches
CIJE: 5 RIE: 2 CAT: 04

Credit Accrual
CIJE: 0 RIE: 15 CAT: 16

Credit Bureaus
CIJE: 2 RIE: 2 CAT: 05

Credit Card Fraud
CIJE: 0 RIE: 3 CAT: 14

Credit Cards
CIJE: 14 RIE: 9 CAT: 16

Credit Clerks
CIJE: 1 RIE: 1 CAT: 09

Credit Collection Agents
CIJE: 0 RIE: 1 CAT: 09

Credit Investigation Agents
CIJE: 0 RIE: 1 CAT: 09

Credit Ratings
CIJE: 0 RIE: 5 CAT: 16

Credit Reports
CIJE: 0 RIE: 1 CAT: 16

Credit Transfer
CIJE: 0 RIE: 2 CAT: 16

Cree Developmental Change Project
CIJE: 0 RIE: 1 CAT: 19

Creek (Tribe)
CIJE: 4 RIE: 13 CAT: 08

Creelman (James)
CIJE: 1 RIE: 0 CAT: 18

Creighton University NE
CIJE: 5 RIE: 8 CAT: 17

Cremin (Lawrence A)
CIJE: 8 RIE: 4 CAT: 18

CREMS
USE Center for Research on Elementary and Middle Schs

CRESST CA
USE Center for Research on Eval Standards Stu Test CA

Creswell Public Schools OR
CIJE: 0 RIE: 1 CAT: 17

Crete Monee School District IL
CIJE: 0 RIE: 2 CAT: 17

Criado (Eduardo)
CIJE: 1 RIE: 0 CAT: 18

Crib Confinement
CIJE: 1 RIE: 0 CAT: 11

Crick (Francis)
CIJE: 2 RIE: 0 CAT: 18

Cricket (Magazine)
CIJE: 0 RIE: 0 CAT: 22

Cricket (Sport)
CIJE: 2 RIE: 0 CAT: 16

Crickets
CIJE: 2 RIE: 0 CAT: 20

Crilly (Lynn)
CIJE: 1 RIE: 0 CAT: 18

Crime Against Nature (Pratt)
CIJE: 0 RIE: 1 CAT: 22

Crime and Punishment
CIJE: 1 RIE: 0 CAT: 22

Crime Awareness and Campus Security Act 1990
CIJE: 1 RIE: 1 CAT: 14
UF Student Right to Know and Campus Security Title II

Crime Causation
CIJE: 4 RIE: 1 CAT: 15

Crime Detection
CIJE: 6 RIE: 2 CAT: 14

Crime Resistance Program
CIJE: 0 RIE: 1 CAT: 19

Criminal Investigations
CIJE: 5 RIE: 2 CAT: 14

Criminal Justice
CIJE: 14 RIE: 38 CAT: 14

Criminal Justice Initiative
CIJE: 0 RIE: 1 CAT: 14

Criminal Justice System
CIJE: 22 RIE: 28 CAT: 14

Criminal Justice Workers
CIJE: 0 RIE: 1 CAT: 09

Criminal Prosecution
CIJE: 8 RIE: 3 CAT: 14

Criminal Records
CIJE: 5 RIE: 7 CAT: 14
SN See also "Arrest Records"

Crisis Child Care
CIJE: 0 RIE: 12 CAT: 11
UF Crisis Nurseries

Crisis Management
CIJE: 92 RIE: 27 CAT: 15

Crisis Nurseries
USE Crisis Child Care

CRISIS Program
CIJE: 1 RIE: 2 CAT: 19

Crisis Teacher Program
CIJE: 0 RIE: 1 CAT: 19

Crisis Teachers
CIJE: 1 RIE: 0 CAT: 09

Crisis Theory
CIJE: 6 RIE: 2 CAT: 15

CRISP Computer Program
CIJE: 0 RIE: 1 CAT: 04
UF CRunch Interactive Statistical Package

Crispin System of Interaction Analysis
CIJE: 0 RIE: 1 CAT: 21

Critchton Vocabulary Scale
CIJE: 0 RIE: 1 CAT: 21

Criteria of Excellence
CIJE: 0 RIE: 1 CAT: 21

Criteria of Success in English Test (Dixon)
CIJE: 0 RIE: 1 CAT: 21

Criterial Referent Theory (Kerlinger)
CIJE: 1 RIE: 0 CAT: 15

Criterion Based Selection
CIJE: 3 RIE: 2 CAT: 21

Criterion Group Method
CIJE: 0 RIE: 1 CAT: 21

Criterion Referenced English Syntax Test
CIJE: 0 RIE: 2 CAT: 21

Criterion Referenced Language Test Development
CIJE: 0 RIE: 1 CAT: 21

Criterion Referenced Scoring
CIJE: 4 RIE: 6 CAT: 21

Criterion Referenced Supervision
CIJE: 0 RIE: 1 CAT: 15

Criterion Referenced System Achievement Tests
CIJE: 0 RIE: 1 CAT: 21

Criterion Related Validity
CIJE: 10 RIE: 10 CAT: 21

Criterion Teaching
CIJE: 0 RIE: 2 CAT: 03

Criterion Variables
CIJE: 16 RIE: 15 CAT: 21

Critical Behavior Scales
CIJE: 0 RIE: 1 CAT: 21

Critical Decision Method
CIJE: 0 RIE: 1 CAT: 15

Critical Errors
CIJE: 0 RIE: 1 CAT: 11

Critical Ethnography
CIJE: 3 RIE: 1 CAT: 03

Critical Events
CIJE: 3 RIE: 3 CAT: 11

Critical Events Interview
CIJE: 0 RIE: 1 CAT: 21

Critical Flicker Fusion Test
CIJE: 2 RIE: 0 CAT: 21

Critical Inquiry
CIJE: 2 RIE: 1 CAT: 15

Critical Languages
CIJE: 10 RIE: 1 CAT: 13

Critical Listening
CIJE: 1 RIE: 6 CAT: 16

Critical Needs Certification Program SC
CIJE: 0 RIE: 1 CAT: 19

Critical Needs in International Education
CIJE: 0 RIE: 1 CAT: 22

Critical Pedagogy
CIJE: 12 RIE: 9 CAT: 15

Critical Period
CIJE: 10 RIE: 3 CAT: 16

Critical Success Factors Method
CIJE: 3 RIE: 0 CAT: 15

Critical Television Viewing Skills Project
CIJE: 0 RIE: 8 CAT: 19

Critical Thinking in Ethics Test
CIJE: 0 RIE: 1 CAT: 21

Critical Thinking Skills Performance Assessment
CIJE: 0 RIE: 1 CAT: 21

Critical Thinking Test (Dressel)
CIJE: 0 RIE: 1 CAT: 21

Critical Writing
CIJE: 1 RIE: 1 CAT: 03

Critics
CIJE: 17 RIE: 6 CAT: 09

Critique Circle
CIJE: 0 RIE: 1 CAT: 15

Critique Sessions
CIJE: 1 RIE: 1 CAT: 16

Croasmun (Earl)
CIJE: 0 RIE: 1 CAT: 18

Croatian Americans
CIJE: 1 RIE: 3 CAT: 08

Croatians
USE Croats

Croats
CIJE: 1 RIE: 1 CAT: 08
UF Croatians

Croce (Benedetto)
CIJE: 4 RIE: 0 CAT: 18

Crocodiles
CIJE: 1 RIE: 1 CAT: 20

Crohns Disease
CIJE: 2 RIE: 0 CAT: 11

Cronbach (Lee J)
CIJE: 5 RIE: 4 CAT: 18

Cronin (Joseph)
CIJE: 1 RIE: 0 CAT: 18

Cronkite (Walter)
CIJE: 2 RIE: 2 CAT: 18

Crookes Radiometer
CIJE: 2 RIE: 0 CAT: 04

Crosby Independent School District TX
CIJE: 0 RIE: 1 CAT: 17

Cross (K Patricia)
CIJE: 0 RIE: 1 CAT: 18

Cross Ability Tutoring
CIJE: 0 RIE: 1 CAT: 15

Cross Academic Credit
USE Cross Credit Courses

Cross Angelo Classroom Assessment Model
CIJE: 0 RIE: 2 CAT: 15

Cross Burning
CIJE: 1 RIE: 1 CAT: 16

Cross Categorical Service Delivery Model
CIJE: 0 RIE: 1 CAT: 15

Cross Classification Approaches
CIJE: 4 RIE: 4 CAT: 15

Cross Comparison Chart
CIJE: 1 RIE: 0 CAT: 21

Cross Country Skiing
CIJE: 8 RIE: 1 CAT: 16

Cross Credit Courses
CIJE: 0 RIE: 7 CAT: 03
UF Academic Cross Credit; Cross Academic Credit

Cross Cultural Attitude Inventory
CIJE: 0 RIE: 2 CAT: 21

Cross Cultural Communication Packet
CIJE: 0 RIE: 2 CAT: 15

Cross Cultural Counseling
CIJE: 78 RIE: 19 CAT: 11

Cross Cultural Reentry
CIJE: 1 RIE: 0 CAT: 15

Cross Cultural Teaching
CIJE: 6 RIE: 8 CAT: 15

Cross Cultural Testing
CIJE: 2 RIE: 4 CAT: 21

Cross Discipline Education
CIJE: 4 RIE: 3 CAT: 03

Cross Examination
CIJE: 2 RIE: 5 CAT: 14

Cross Examination Debate Association
CIJE: 3 RIE: 42 CAT: 17
SN See also "National CEDA Tournament"

Cross Generational Studies
CIJE: 10 RIE: 7 CAT: 15

Cross Lagged Panel Technique
CIJE: 11 RIE: 4 CAT: 15

Cross Language Transfer
CIJE: 0 RIE: 1 CAT: 13
UF Language Transfer

Cross Level Grouping
CIJE: 3 RIE: 1 CAT: 15

Cross Linguistic Factors
USE Crosslinguistic Influence

Cross Modal Functioning
USE Crossmodal Behavior

Cross National Studies
CIJE: 15 RIE: 9 CAT: 15

Cross Over Phenomena
CIJE: 0 RIE: 1 CAT: 15

Cross Pressures Test
CIJE: 1 RIE: 0 CAT: 21

Cross Race Interaction
CIJE: 2 RIE: 6 CAT: 11

Cross Role Training
CIJE: 2 RIE: 0 CAT: 03

Cross Sex Friendship
CIJE: 8 RIE: 5 CAT: 16
SN See also "Same Sex Friendship"
UF Opposite Sex Friendship; Other Sex Friendship

Cross Sex Interaction
CIJE: 3 RIE: 7 CAT: 11
SN See also "Same Sex Interaction"
UF Opposite Sex Interaction; Other Sex Interaction

Cross Sex Peers
CIJE: 0 RIE: 0 CAT: 10
SN See also "Same Sex Peers"
UF Opposite Sex Peers; Other Sex Peers

Cross Subsidy (Programs)
CIJE: 0 RIE: 3 CAT: 19

Cross Validation
CIJE: 44 RIE: 48 CAT: 21
SN See also "Double Cross Validation"

Crossed Hand Eye Dominance
CIJE: 1 RIE: 0 CAT: 11

Crosslinguistic Influence
CIJE: 0 RIE: 1 CAT: 13
UF Cross Linguistic Factors

Crossmodal Behavior
CIJE: 11 RIE: 0 CAT: 15
UF Cross Modal Functioning

Crossover Program WI
CIJE: 0 RIE: 1 CAT: 19

Crossroads Program
CIJE: 1 RIE: 1 CAT: 19

Crossroads Rehabilitation Center IN
CIJE: 1 RIE: 0 CAT: 17

Crossroads Survey
CIJE: 0 RIE: 2 CAT: 19

Crossword Puzzles
CIJE: 18 RIE: 12 CAT: 16

Crothers (Edward)
CIJE: 1 RIE: 1 CAT: 18

Crouch (Richard Edwin)
CIJE: 1 RIE: 0 CAT: 18

Crouse Hinds Company
CIJE: 1 RIE: 0 CAT: 17

Crouzon Syndrome
CIJE: 0 RIE: 1 CAT: 11
UF Craniofacial Dysostosis; Crouzons Disease

Crouzons Disease
USE Crouzon Syndrome

Crow
CIJE: 2 RIE: 4 CAT: 13

Crow (Tribe)
CIJE: 6 RIE: 13 CAT: 08

Crow Applegate Lorane School District OR
CIJE: 0 RIE: 1 CAT: 17

Crow Report
CIJE: 0 RIE: 1 CAT: 22

Crowd Behavior
CIJE: 2 RIE: 1 CAT: 11

Crowd Control
CIJE: 5 RIE: 1 CAT: 16

Crowder (Norman)
CIJE: 1 RIE: 3 CAT: 18

Crowleys Ridge Vocational Technical School AR
CIJE: 0 RIE: 2 CAT: 17

Crown Woods Comprehensive School (England)
CIJE: 0 RIE: 1 CAT: 17

Crowne Marlowe Social Desirability Scale
USE Marlowe Crowne Social Desirability Scale

Crownpoint Institute of Technology NM
CIJE: 0 RIE: 1 CAT: 17

Croziers Law
CIJE: 0 RIE: 1 CAT: 15

Crucible
CIJE: 3 RIE: 0 CAT: 22

Cruickshank (Donald R)
CIJE: 0 RIE: 2 CAT: 18

Cruikshank (William)
CIJE: 0 RIE: 1 CAT: 18

Cruise Ships
CIJE: 1 RIE: 0 CAT: 04

CRunch Interactive Statistical Package
USE CRISP Computer Program

Crusader (The)
CIJE: 0 RIE: 1 CAT: 22

Cruse (Harold)
CIJE: 3 RIE: 0 CAT: 18

Crusher Inspectors
CIJE: 0 RIE: 1 CAT: 09

Crustacea
CIJE: 0 RIE: 0 CAT: 20

Crustal Evolution Education Project
CIJE: 15 RIE: 32 CAT: 19

Cruz (San Juan de la)
CIJE: 0 RIE: 1 CAT: 18

Cruz (Sor Juana Ines de la)
CIJE: 3 RIE: 0 CAT: 18

Cry the Beloved Country
CIJE: 1 RIE: 2 CAT: 22

Cryogenics
CIJE: 3 RIE: 0 CAT: 20

Cryotherapy
CIJE: 3 RIE: 2 CAT: 11

Cryptography
CIJE: 5 RIE: 1 CAT: 20

Cryptology
CIJE: 5 RIE: 1 CAT: 03

Crystallization (Psychology)
CIJE: 2 RIE: 3 CAT: 11

Crystallized Intelligence
CIJE: 24 RIE: 8 CAT: 11

Crystallizing Experience
CIJE: 0 RIE: 1 CAT: 16

CSAOs
USE Chief Student Affairs Officers

CSAR Interactive Item Bank System
CIJE: 0 RIE: 1 CAT: 04

CSE Alumni Survey
CIJE: 0 RIE: 1 CAT: 21

CSE Analytic Scale
CIJE: 0 RIE: 2 CAT: 21

CSE Elementary School Evaluation Kit
CIJE: 0 RIE: 1 CAT: 21

CSE Evaluation Kit
CIJE: 0 RIE: 6 CAT: 04

CSE Examination
CIJE: 9 RIE: 0 CAT: 21

CSE Research into Practice Project
CIJE: 1 RIE: 0 CAT: 19
UF Research into Practice Project (CSE)

Csikszentmihalyi (Mihaly)
CIJE: 0 RIE: 0 CAT: 18

CSLX Programing Language
CIJE: 0 RIE: 1 CAT: 04

CSPAN Service
USE C SPAN

CSRA CESA Project GA
CIJE: 0 RIE: 4 CAT: 19

CSS76 Criterion Sightsinging Test (Thostenson)
CIJE: 0 RIE: 1 CAT: 21

CSUC English Equivalency Examination
CIJE: 1 RIE: 0 CAT: 21

CSUC English Placement Test
CIJE: 0 RIE: 0 CAT: 21

CSUCS Consortium
CIJE: 1 RIE: 0 CAT: 17

CSUN Course Expectation Questionnaire
CIJE: 0 RIE: 1 CAT: 21

Cuauhtemoc Bilingual Preschool Project
CIJE: 0 RIE: 1 CAT: 19

Cuba
CIJE: 126 RIE: 50 CAT: 07

Cuba (Havana)
CIJE: 0 RIE: 2 CAT: 07

Cuban Missile Crisis
CIJE: 5 RIE: 9 CAT: 12

Cuban Refugee Program
CIJE: 1 RIE: 3 CAT: 19

Cuban Revolution
CIJE: 2 RIE: 1 CAT: 12

Cubans University of Miami FL
CIJE: 1 RIE: 0 CAT: 17

Cubberley High School CA
CIJE: 1 RIE: 0 CAT: 17

Cube Model of Attributions (Kelley)
CIJE: 0 RIE: 1 CAT: 15

Cube Roots
CIJE: 2 RIE: 0 CAT: 20

CUBE System
CIJE: 0 RIE: 7 CAT: 19

Cubic Equations
CIJE: 3 RIE: 0 CAT: 20

Cubism
CIJE: 4 RIE: 0 CAT: 15

Cue Attendance
CIJE: 0 RIE: 1 CAT: 15

Cue Controlled Relaxation
CIJE: 3 RIE: 0 CAT: 11

Cue Motor Association Theory
CIJE: 2 RIE: 0 CAT: 15

Cue Selection
CIJE: 2 RIE: 2 CAT: 11

Cuento Therapy
CIJE: 1 RIE: 1 CAT: 11

Cuervo (R J)
CIJE: 0 RIE: 1 CAT: 18
SN "Rufino Jose"

Cuesta College CA
CIJE: 0 RIE: 4 CAT: 17

Cuffs (Clothing)
CIJE: 0 RIE: 1 CAT: 16

Cuisenaire Materials
CIJE: 14 RIE: 15 CAT: 04

Cuiva (Tribe)
CIJE: 0 RIE: 1 CAT: 08

Culkin (John)
CIJE: 1 RIE: 0 CAT: 18

Cultivation Theory (Television)
CIJE: 11 RIE: 4 CAT: 15

Cults
CIJE: 30 RIE: 5 CAT: 10
SN Use a more specific term if possible, e.g., "Religious Cults," "Fertility Cults"

Cultural Adjustment
CIJE: 7 RIE: 10 CAT: 15

Cultural Anthropology
CIJE: 18 RIE: 16 CAT: 03

Cultural Arts
CIJE: 2 RIE: 4 CAT: 16

Cultural Attitude Inventory (Skeel)
CIJE: 0 RIE: 2 CAT: 21

Cultural Attitudes Repertory Technique
CIJE: 2 RIE: 1 CAT: 21

Cultural Capital
CIJE: 9 RIE: 2 CAT: 16

Cultural Change
CIJE: 24 RIE: 16 CAT: 16

Cultural Competence
CIJE: 3 RIE: 2 CAT: 15

Cultural Content
CIJE: 6 RIE: 12 CAT: 16

Cultural Contributions
CIJE: 9 RIE: 47 CAT: 16

Cultural Criticism
CIJE: 5 RIE: 1 CAT: 15

Cultural Deficit Theory
CIJE: 2 RIE: 0 CAT: 15

Cultural Democracy
CIJE: 1 RIE: 2 CAT: 16

Cultural Dependency
CIJE: 1 RIE: 3 CAT: 15

Cultural Distance Approach
CIJE: 1 RIE: 1 CAT: 15

Cultural Ecology
CIJE: 2 RIE: 2 CAT: 03

Cultural Economics
CIJE: 1 RIE: 0 CAT: 03

Cultural Education Collaborative MA
CIJE: 1 RIE: 0 CAT: 17

Cultural Environmental Achievement Project
CIJE: 0 RIE: 1 CAT: 19

Cultural Epistemology
CIJE: 0 RIE: 1 CAT: 16

Cultural Experience
CIJE: 7 RIE: 4 CAT: 16

Cultural Framing
CIJE: 0 RIE: 1 CAT: 15

Cultural Hegemony
CIJE: 16 RIE: 20 CAT: 15

Cultural Indicators Research
CIJE: 1 RIE: 1 CAT: 15

Cultural Inversion
CIJE: 0 RIE: 1 CAT: 15

Cultural Journalism
CIJE: 20 RIE: 11 CAT: 16

Cultural Jurisprudence
CIJE: 0 RIE: 1 CAT: 15

Cultural Literacy Test
CIJE: 1 RIE: 1 CAT: 21

Cultural Mistrust Inventory
CIJE: 1 RIE: 0 CAT: 21

Cultural Molding
CIJE: 0 RIE: 1 CAT: 15

Cultural Myths
CIJE: 1 RIE: 1 CAT: 16
SN See also "American Myths"

Cultural Nationalism
CIJE: 3 RIE: 0 CAT: 16

Cultural Reentry
CIJE: 0 RIE: 5 CAT: 16

Cultural Relativism
CIJE: 14 RIE: 6 CAT: 15

Cultural Relevance
CIJE: 22 RIE: 20 CAT: 16

Cultural Reproduction
CIJE: 4 RIE: 1 CAT: 15

Cultural Resources
CIJE: 6 RIE: 9 CAT: 16

Cultural Revolution
CIJE: 24 RIE: 5 CAT: 12

Cultural Revolution (China)
CIJE: 19 RIE: 13 CAT: 12

Cultural Sensitivity
CIJE: 49 RIE: 61 CAT: 16

Cultural Studies
CIJE: 19 RIE: 6 CAT: 15

Cultural Training Semester
CIJE: 0 RIE: 1 CAT: 03

Cultural Translators
CIJE: 2 RIE: 0 CAT: 11

Cultural Universal Hypothesis of Cognitive Devel
CIJE: 0 RIE: 0 CAT: 15

Cultural Universals
CIJE: 2 RIE: 3 CAT: 16

Cultural Values
CIJE: 48 RIE: 34 CAT: 16

Culturally Adapted Parent Training Project
CIJE: 0 RIE: 1 CAT: 19

Culturally Different Students
CIJE: 8 RIE: 9 CAT: 10

Culturally Relevant Curriculum
CIJE: 3 RIE: 18 CAT: 03

Culturally Responsive Education
CIJE: 7 RIE: 9 CAT: 03

Culture Area Concept
CIJE: 1 RIE: 0 CAT: 15

Culture Assimilator
CIJE: 1 RIE: 2 CAT: 15

Culture Based Curriculum
CIJE: 15 RIE: 42 CAT: 03

Culture Based Education
CIJE: 5 RIE: 5 CAT: 03

Culture Fair Intelligence Questionnaire (Dielman)
CIJE: 1 RIE: 0 CAT: 21

Culture of Information
CIJE: 0 RIE: 2 CAT: 16
SN Institutional culture or subculture that systematically collects, generates, stores, retrieves, synthesizes, interprets, and utilizes appropriate information in all processes of decision making and does so as a matter of course

Culture of Poverty
CIJE: 8 RIE: 7 CAT: 22

Culture Specific Testing
CIJE: 3 RIE: 1 CAT: 21

Culture Theory
CIJE: 0 RIE: 1 CAT: 15

Culture Transmission
CIJE: 40 RIE: 12 CAT: 16

Culturefax
CIJE: 0 RIE: 1 CAT: 22

Cultures Controversy
CIJE: 1 RIE: 0 CAT: 16

Culver City Public Schools CA
CIJE: 1 RIE: 1 CAT: 17

Cumberland College KY
CIJE: 0 RIE: 2 CAT: 17

Cumberland County College NJ
CIJE: 0 RIE: 4 CAT: 17

Cumberland County Extension Service ME
CIJE: 1 RIE: 0 CAT: 17

Cumberland Plateau
CIJE: 0 RIE: 3 CAT: 07

Cumberland Valley
CIJE: 0 RIE: 1 CAT: 07

Cummings (E E)
CIJE: 2 RIE: 0 CAT: 18

Cummings Device
CIJE: 0 RIE: 1 CAT: 04

Cummins (James)
CIJE: 1 RIE: 6 CAT: 18

Cumulative Book Index
CIJE: 2 RIE: 1 CAT: 22

Cumulative Daily Review Process
CIJE: 0 RIE: 1 CAT: 15

Cumulative Deficit
CIJE: 5 RIE: 2 CAT: 15

Cumulative Index Nursing Allied Health Literature
CIJE: 0 RIE: 1 CAT: 22

Cumulative Learning
CIJE: 6 RIE: 0 CAT: 15

Cumulative Presentation
CIJE: 2 RIE: 0 CAT: 15

Cumulative Programing
CIJE: 0 RIE: 1 CAT: 15

Cuna (Tribe)
CIJE: 1 RIE: 1 CAT: 08

Cuneiform Writing
CIJE: 2 RIE: 0 CAT: 13

Cunningham Childrens Home IL
CIJE: 1 RIE: 0 CAT: 17

CUNY
USE City University of New York

CUNY Association of Writing Supervisors
CIJE: 1 RIE: 0 CAT: 17
UF CAWS

CUNY Professional Staff Congress
USE Professional Staff Congress CUNY

CUNY Retention Exemplary Model Project
CIJE: 0 RIE: 1 CAT: 19

Cuomo (Mario M)
CIJE: 2 RIE: 0 CAT: 18

Cupeno
CIJE: 1 RIE: 0 CAT: 13

Cupertino Union School District CA
CIJE: 5 RIE: 5 CAT: 17

Cuprammonium Reagent
CIJE: 1 RIE: 0 CAT: 20

Curanderismo
CIJE: 3 RIE: 11 CAT: 11

Curators
CIJE: 10 RIE: 2 CAT: 09

Cure (The)
CIJE: 0 RIE: 1 CAT: 22

Cureton Reading Program
CIJE: 0 RIE: 1 CAT: 19

Curie Constant
CIJE: 1 RIE: 0 CAT: 20

Curie Law
CIJE: 1 RIE: 0 CAT: 20

CURMIS
CIJE: 0 RIE: 0 CAT: 04
UF Curriculum Management Information System

Currency Devaluation
CIJE: 0 RIE: 1 CAT: 16
UF Devaluation (Money)

Current Awareness in Health Education
CIJE: 0 RIE: 2 CAT: 22

Current Behavior Inventory
CIJE: 0 RIE: 1 CAT: 21

Current Biography Yearbook
CIJE: 0 RIE: 1 CAT: 22

Current Index to Journals in Education
CIJE: 11 RIE: 19 CAT: 22

Current Papers in Physics
CIJE: 0 RIE: 2 CAT: 22

Current Physics Information
CIJE: 0 RIE: 1 CAT: 22

Current Population Survey
CIJE: 35 RIE: 92 CAT: 22
UF Census Bureau Current Population Survey

Current Population Survey Agric Work Force Supplt
USE Agricultural Work Force Survey

Currere Method
CIJE: 1 RIE: 3 CAT: 15

Curricular Debate
CIJE: 3 RIE: 5 CAT: 03

Curricular Decisionmaking Questionnaire (Griffin)
CIJE: 0 RIE: 1 CAT: 21

Curricular Validity
CIJE: 3 RIE: 9 CAT: 03

Curriculum Accommodation Questionnaire
CIJE: 0 RIE: 2 CAT: 21

Curriculum Alignment
CIJE: 10 RIE: 13 CAT: 03

Curriculum Analysis Proj for Social Sciences
CIJE: 0 RIE: 1 CAT: 19

Curriculum and Evaluation Standards (NCTM)
USE NCTM Curriculum and Evaluation Standards

Curriculum and Instructional Materials Center OK
CIJE: 0 RIE: 2 CAT: 17
UF Oklahoma Curriculum and Instr Materials Center

Curriculum Assessment Planning Program
CIJE: 0 RIE: 1 CAT: 19

Curriculum Attitude Inventory
CIJE: 2 RIE: 2 CAT: 21

Curriculum Audits
CIJE: 1 RIE: 2 CAT: 15

Curriculum Balance
CIJE: 4 RIE: 5 CAT: 03

Curriculum Based Information Support System
CIJE: 1 RIE: 1 CAT: 15

Curriculum Based Staffing
CIJE: 1 RIE: 0 CAT: 15

Curriculum Choice
CIJE: 11 RIE: 6 CAT: 03

Curriculum Compacting
CIJE: 3 RIE: 2 CAT: 03

Curriculum Computers and Collaboration Project
CIJE: 1 RIE: 1 CAT: 19

Curriculum Consonance
CIJE: 2 RIE: 1 CAT: 03

Curriculum Construct Systems
CIJE: 0 RIE: 1 CAT: 15

Curriculum Coordination Centers
CIJE: 2 RIE: 3 CAT: 05

Curriculum Councils
CIJE: 1 RIE: 4 CAT: 10

Curriculum Demonstration Project
CIJE: 0 RIE: 2 CAT: 19

Curriculum Development Centre (Australia)
CIJE: 0 RIE: 3 CAT: 17

Curriculum Development Library
CIJE: 1 RIE: 0 CAT: 22

Curriculum Differentiation
CIJE: 9 RIE: 2 CAT: 03
SN If appropriate, use the more precise term "Differentiated Curriculum (Gifted)"

Curriculum Directors
CIJE: 3 RIE: 3 CAT: 09

Curriculum Duplication
CIJE: 1 RIE: 0 CAT: 03

Curriculum Embedded Tests
CIJE: 0 RIE: 3 CAT: 21

Curriculum Emphases
CIJE: 39 RIE: 63 CAT: 03

Curriculum Engineering Systems
CIJE: 0 RIE: 1 CAT: 15

Curriculum for Improving Communications Skills
CIJE: 0 RIE: 1 CAT: 22

Curriculum Implementation
CIJE: 20 RIE: 28 CAT: 03

Curriculum Information Network
CIJE: 0 RIE: 4 CAT: 17

Curriculum Leaders
CIJE: 3 RIE: 4 CAT: 10

Curriculum Leadership Hierarchy
CIJE: 0 RIE: 1 CAT: 15

Curriculum Management
CIJE: 21 RIE: 34 CAT: 03

Curriculum Management Information System
USE CURMIS

Curriculum Management Systems
CIJE: 0 RIE: 1 CAT: 03

Curriculum Mapping
CIJE: 13 RIE: 13 CAT: 03

Curriculum Materials Analysis System
CIJE: 3 RIE: 7 CAT: 15

Curriculum Matrix
CIJE: 3 RIE: 3 CAT: 15

Curriculum of Attainments
CIJE: 0 RIE: 1 CAT: 03

Curriculum Organization and Program Evaluation
CIJE: 0 RIE: 1 CAT: 15
UF COPE Model

Curriculum Reconceptualists
CIJE: 0 RIE: 1 CAT: 16

Curriculum Reduction
CIJE: 1 RIE: 1 CAT: 03

Curriculum Referenced Testing
USE Curriculum Related Testing

Curriculum Referenced Tests of Mastery
CIJE: 1 RIE: 0 CAT: 21

Curriculum Related Testing
CIJE: 4 RIE: 17 CAT: 21
SN See also the Descriptor "Curriculum Based Assessment"
UF Curriculum Referenced Testing

Curriculum Research and Development Group
CIJE: 9 RIE: 1 CAT: 17

Curriculum Restructuring Project
CIJE: 0 RIE: 1 CAT: 19

Curriculum Review Development and Implementation
CIJE: 0 RIE: 1 CAT: 15

Curriculum Specialists
CIJE: 24 RIE: 22 CAT: 09

Curriculum Standards
CIJE: 7 RIE: 8 CAT: 03

Curriculum Study and Improvement Project
CIJE: 0 RIE: 1 CAT: 19

Curriculum Test Overlap
CIJE: 2 RIE: 4 CAT: 21

Curriculum Theories
CIJE: 72 RIE: 19 CAT: 15

Curriculum Victoria
CIJE: 0 RIE: 1 CAT: 19

Currie Milonas Screening Test
CIJE: 0 RIE: 1 CAT: 21

Currie Report
CIJE: 0 RIE: 1 CAT: 22

Curry (S S)
CIJE: 2 RIE: 0 CAT: 18

Curry College MA
CIJE: 1 RIE: 2 CAT: 17

Curry Test of Critical Thinking
CIJE: 1 RIE: 0 CAT: 21

Curtis Digests
CIJE: 1 RIE: 1 CAT: 22

Curve Sketching
CIJE: 4 RIE: 0 CAT: 15

Curves
CIJE: 5 RIE: 2 CAT: 20

Curvilinear Functions
CIJE: 4 RIE: 3 CAT: 21

Curvo Strategy
CIJE: 0 RIE: 1 CAT: 15

Curwen (John)
CIJE: 3 RIE: 0 CAT: 18

Cushitic Languages
CIJE: 2 RIE: 4 CAT: 13

Custis Lee Mansion
USE Arlington House VA

Custodial Approach
CIJE: 8 RIE: 1 CAT: 15

Custodial Contracting
CIJE: 1 RIE: 2 CAT: 16

Custodian Attitudes
CIJE: 0 RIE: 1 CAT: 16

Custodians
CIJE: 9 RIE: 16 CAT: 09

Custom Publishing
CIJE: 1 RIE: 0 CAT: 16

Customary System
CIJE: 1 RIE: 0 CAT: 15

Customer Engineering Specialists
CIJE: 0 RIE: 1 CAT: 09

Customer Relations
CIJE: 8 RIE: 6 CAT: 16

Customer Satisfaction
CIJE: 1 RIE: 2 CAT: 16

Customer Service
USE Customer Services

Customer Services
CIJE: 36 RIE: 23 CAT: 16
UF Customer Service

Customized Contract Training
USE Contract Training

Customized Job Training
USE Customized Training

Customized Testing
USE Test Customization

Customized Training
CIJE: 11 RIE: 20 CAT: 15
UF Customized Job Training

Cut Score Characteristic Function
CIJE: 0 RIE: 1 CAT: 21

Cutback Management
CIJE: 2 RIE: 6 CAT: 15

CUTE Program
USE Cooperative Urban Teacher Education Program

Cutis Verticis Gyrata
CIJE: 1 RIE: 0 CAT: 11

Cutler Orosi Unified School District CA
CIJE: 0 RIE: 1 CAT: 17

Cutter (Charles)
CIJE: 2 RIE: 0 CAT: 18

Cutting Tool Assessment Battery
CIJE: 0 RIE: 1 CAT: 21

Cutting Tools
CIJE: 0 RIE: 8 CAT: 04

Cuttyhunk Island
CIJE: 1 RIE: 0 CAT: 07

Cuyahoga Community College Cleveland OH
CIJE: 6 RIE: 20 CAT: 17

Cuyahoga Community College Eastern Campus OH
CIJE: 0 RIE: 2 CAT: 17

Cuyahoga Community College OH
CIJE: 9 RIE: 25 CAT: 17

Cuyahoga Community College Western Campus OH
CIJE: 0 RIE: 1 CAT: 17

Cyberspace
CIJE: 3 RIE: 5 CAT: 20

Cyborgs
CIJE: 0 RIE: 1 CAT: 20
SN Cybernetic organisms that represent the symbiosis of technology and biology

Cyclic Method
CIJE: 2 RIE: 0 CAT: 15

Cyclical Evaluation Model
CIJE: 0 RIE: 1 CAT: 15

Cyclical Renewal (Building Operation)
CIJE: 0 RIE: 1 CAT: 20

Cymatics
CIJE: 0 RIE: 1 CAT: 20

Cypress College CA
CIJE: 1 RIE: 5 CAT: 17

Cyprus
CIJE: 14 RIE: 20 CAT: 07

Cyprus Broadcasting Corporation (Switzerland)
CIJE: 0 RIE: 2 CAT: 17

Cystic Fibrosis
CIJE: 27 RIE: 6 CAT: 11

Cytomegalovirus
CIJE: 6 RIE: 4 CAT: 11

Cytotechnology
CIJE: 0 RIE: 2 CAT: 11

Czech Americans
CIJE: 2 RIE: 4 CAT: 08

Czech Republic
CIJE: 6 RIE: 3 CAT: 07

Czechoslovakia
CIJE: 74 RIE: 97 CAT: 07
SN After 1992, divided into "Czech Republic" and "Slovakia"

Czechoslovakia (Moravia)
CIJE: 0 RIE: 1 CAT: 07

Czechoslovakia (Prague)
CIJE: 4 RIE: 0 CAT: 07

Czechoslovakia (Slovakia)
CIJE: 1 RIE: 3 CAT: 07

Czechoslovakian Academy of Sciences
CIJE: 1 RIE: 0 CAT: 17

Czechoslovakians
CIJE: 0 RIE: 2 CAT: 08

Czerniak Assessment of Science Anxiety
CIJE: 1 RIE: 1 CAT: 21

D 48
USE D48 Test

D Aulnoy (Madame)
CIJE: 1 RIE: 0 CAT: 18

D K Scale of Lateral Dominance
CIJE: 2 RIE: 0 CAT: 21

D Nealian Manuscript
CIJE: 2 RIE: 4 CAT: 15

D Nealian Method
CIJE: 1 RIE: 1 CAT: 15

D Q University CA
CIJE: 0 RIE: 3 CAT: 17

D Souza (Dinesh)
CIJE: 0 RIE: 2 CAT: 18

D Youville College NY
CIJE: 2 RIE: 2 CAT: 17

D48 Test
CIJE: 0 RIE: 4 CAT: 21
UF D 48

Dabney S Lancaster Community College VA
CIJE: 0 RIE: 1 CAT: 17

Dabrowski (Kazimierz)
CIJE: 1 RIE: 1 CAT: 18

Dabrowski Theory of Positive Disintegration
USE Positive Disintegration Theory

Dacca Dialect
CIJE: 0 RIE: 2 CAT: 13

DACUM Process
CIJE: 17 RIE: 119 CAT: 15
UF Developing a Curriculum Process

Dadaism
CIJE: 3 RIE: 0 CAT: 15

Dade County Public Schools FL
CIJE: 31 RIE: 133 CAT: 17

Dade County Tests of Language Development
CIJE: 0 RIE: 2 CAT: 21

Dade Monroe Teacher Education Center FL
CIJE: 0 RIE: 1 CAT: 17

Dag Hammarskjold Foundation (Sweden)
CIJE: 0 RIE: 1 CAT: 17

Daga
CIJE: 0 RIE: 1 CAT: 13

Dagaari
USE Dagari

Dagari
CIJE: 0 RIE: 1 CAT: 13
UF Dagaari

Dagbani
USE Dagomba

Daggett School District UT
CIJE: 0 RIE: 1 CAT: 17

Dagomba
CIJE: 0 RIE: 0 CAT: 13
UF Dagbani

Daguerreotypes
CIJE: 0 RIE: 1 CAT: 20

Dahlem Environmental Education Center MI
CIJE: 0 RIE: 1 CAT: 17

Dahomey
CIJE: 1 RIE: 5 CAT: 07

Dailey Language Facility Test
CIJE: 0 RIE: 4 CAT: 21

Dailey Vocational Tests
CIJE: 0 RIE: 2 CAT: 21

Daily Activities
CIJE: 4 RIE: 3 CAT: 16

Daily Living Literature
CIJE: 1 RIE: 0 CAT: 16

Daily Performance Grades
CIJE: 1 RIE: 0 CAT: 15

Daily Production Reports
CIJE: 1 RIE: 1 CAT: 16

Daily Routines
CIJE: 3 RIE: 3 CAT: 16

Daily Times (Pekin IL)
CIJE: 0 RIE: 1 CAT: 22

Daily Work Activities
CIJE: 0 RIE: 1 CAT: 16

Dainton Report
CIJE: 1 RIE: 0 CAT: 22

Dairy Cattle Production
CIJE: 0 RIE: 3 CAT: 20

Dairy Industry
CIJE: 3 RIE: 5 CAT: 20

Dairy Products
CIJE: 0 RIE: 5 CAT: 20

Dairy Products Route Personnel
CIJE: 0 RIE: 2 CAT: 09

Daisy Wheel Printers
CIJE: 1 RIE: 0 CAT: 04

Dakota Community Colleges
CIJE: 0 RIE: 1 CAT: 17

Dakota Parent Satisfaction Survey
CIJE: 0 RIE: 1 CAT: 21

Dakota State College SD
CIJE: 0 RIE: 1 CAT: 17

Dakota Wesleyan University SD
CIJE: 0 RIE: 3 CAT: 17

Dalcroze Method
CIJE: 7 RIE: 0 CAT: 15

Dale (Edgar)
CIJE: 1 RIE: 0 CAT: 18

Dale (R R)
CIJE: 1 RIE: 0 CAT: 18

Dale Carnegie Course
CIJE: 1 RIE: 0 CAT: 03

Dale Chall List of 3000 Familiar Words
CIJE: 0 RIE: 1 CAT: 22

Dale Chall Readability Formula
CIJE: 15 RIE: 16 CAT: 21

Daley (Richard)
CIJE: 0 RIE: 1 CAT: 18

Daley College IL
USE City Colleges of Chicago IL Richard J Daley Coll

Dalhousie University (Nova Scotia)
CIJE: 16 RIE: 1 CAT: 17

Dallas (Television Series)
CIJE: 1 RIE: 1 CAT: 22

Dallas Baptist College TX
CIJE: 2 RIE: 2 CAT: 17

Dallas Baptist University TX
CIJE: 0 RIE: 1 CAT: 17

Dallas County Boys Home TX
CIJE: 0 RIE: 1 CAT: 17

Dallas County Community College District TX
CIJE: 13 RIE: 14 CAT: 17

Dallas County Community Colleges TX
CIJE: 2 RIE: 3 CAT: 17

Dallas Family Day Care Home Observation Instrument
CIJE: 0 RIE: 1 CAT: 21

Dallas Independent School District TX
CIJE: 29 RIE: 69 CAT: 17

Dallas Preschool Screening Test
CIJE: 0 RIE: 1 CAT: 21

Dallas Project
CIJE: 0 RIE: 1 CAT: 19

Dallas Public Library TX
CIJE: 4 RIE: 11 CAT: 17

Dallas Skyline Center TX
CIJE: 1 RIE: 0 CAT: 17

Dallas Teacher Center Professional Semester TX
CIJE: 0 RIE: 1 CAT: 17

Dalton Junior College GA
CIJE: 1 RIE: 3 CAT: 17

Dalton Law
CIJE: 1 RIE: 0 CAT: 20

Dalton Plan
CIJE: 4 RIE: 2 CAT: 15

Daly (Mary)
CIJE: 1 RIE: 1 CAT: 18

Dame Schools
CIJE: 2 RIE: 0 CAT: 05

Dampproofing
CIJE: 0 RIE: 1 CAT: 20

Dams
CIJE: 1 RIE: 1 CAT: 20

Dan
CIJE: 0 RIE: 1 CAT: 13

Dana Corporation
CIJE: 0 RIE: 1 CAT: 17

Dana Hall School MA
CIJE: 0 RIE: 1 CAT: 17

Dance Companies
CIJE: 3 RIE: 4 CAT: 05

Dandelions
CIJE: 5 RIE: 0 CAT: 20

Danforth Foundation
CIJE: 12 RIE: 13 CAT: 17

Danforth Junior College Program
CIJE: 0 RIE: 2 CAT: 19

Danforth Preparation of School Principals Program
CIJE: 0 RIE: 3 CAT: 19

Danger Above and Below
CIJE: 0 RIE: 1 CAT: 22

Dangerous Liaisons (Film)
CIJE: 0 RIE: 1 CAT: 22

Dani (Tribe)
CIJE: 0 RIE: 1 CAT: 08

Daniels (Lloyd)
CIJE: 0 RIE: 1 CAT: 18

Daniels (Sarah)
CIJE: 0 RIE: 1 CAT: 18

Danish Americans
CIJE: 4 RIE: 0 CAT: 08

Danish Family Planning Association
CIJE: 0 RIE: 1 CAT: 17

Danish Folk Schools
CIJE: 4 RIE: 1 CAT: 05

Danish Higher Preparatory Examination
CIJE: 0 RIE: 1 CAT: 21

Danish Institute for Educational Research
CIJE: 1 RIE: 4 CAT: 17

Danish Universities Centres
CIJE: 0 RIE: 1 CAT: 05

Dante (Alighieri)
CIJE: 16 RIE: 3 CAT: 18

DANTES Project (DoD)
USE Defense Activity Non Traditional Education Support

Danville City School District VA
CIJE: 0 RIE: 2 CAT: 17

Danville Community College VA
CIJE: 0 RIE: 1 CAT: 17

Danville Public School District IL
CIJE: 1 RIE: 2 CAT: 17

Daphnia
CIJE: 2 RIE: 0 CAT: 20

DARCEE Program
CIJE: 1 RIE: 5 CAT: 19

Dardic Languages
CIJE: 0 RIE: 1 CAT: 13

Dare County School District NC
CIJE: 0 RIE: 0 CAT: 17

DARE Dictionary
USE Dictionary of American Regional English

Dare Phenomenon
CIJE: 1 RIE: 0 CAT: 11

DARE Program CA
USE Drug Abuse Resistance Education Program

DARE Program ON
USE Development through Adventure Resp and Educ

DARE Program SD
USE Developing Adult Resources through Education

Dari
CIJE: 0 RIE: 11 CAT: 13

Darien Public Schools CT
CIJE: 1 RIE: 0 CAT: 17

Dario (Ruben)
CIJE: 13 RIE: 0 CAT: 18

Darkrooms
CIJE: 3 RIE: 2 CAT: 05

Darling Downs Inst of Advanced Educ (Australia)
CIJE: 0 RIE: 1 CAT: 17

Darling Taxonomy of Administrative Problems
CIJE: 0 RIE: 1 CAT: 15

Darlington County School District SC
CIJE: 2 RIE: 1 CAT: 17

Darmstaadt Career Center
CIJE: 1 RIE: 0 CAT: 17

Darmstadt Adjective Check List
CIJE: 0 RIE: 1 CAT: 21

Darrow (Clarence)
CIJE: 4 RIE: 1 CAT: 18

DART Programing Language
CIJE: 1 RIE: 1 CAT: 04

Dartmouth College Case
USE Trustees of Dartmouth College v Woodward

Dartmouth College NH
CIJE: 49 RIE: 39 CAT: 17

Dartmouth Medical School NH
CIJE: 6 RIE: 1 CAT: 17

Dartmouth Rassias Method
CIJE: 9 RIE: 9 CAT: 15

Dartmouth Secondary School Project
CIJE: 0 RIE: 1 CAT: 19

Dartmouth Seminar on the Teaching of English
CIJE: 15 RIE: 32 CAT: 02

Darts (Clothing)
CIJE: 0 RIE: 1 CAT: 16

DARTTS
USE Diagnostic Assess Reading Trial Teach Strategies

Darwin (Charles)
CIJE: 45 RIE: 7 CAT: 18

Darwin (J H)
CIJE: 0 RIE: 1 CAT: 18

Das (J P)
CIJE: 0 RIE: 1 CAT: 18

DASA Microfiche Reader PMR 50
CIJE: 0 RIE: 1 CAT: 04

DAT Cassettes
USE Digital Audiotape

Data Abstraction
CIJE: 1 RIE: 2 CAT: 04

Data Administration
CIJE: 2 RIE: 2 CAT: 16

Data Based Educational Planning Systems
CIJE: 2 RIE: 0 CAT: 15

Data Based Gymnasium Model
CIJE: 0 RIE: 1 CAT: 15

Data Based Instruction
CIJE: 4 RIE: 2 CAT: 15

Data Based Program Development
CIJE: 0 RIE: 2 CAT: 15

Data Based Program Modification
CIJE: 3 RIE: 3 CAT: 15

Data Based Staff Development Program
CIJE: 0 RIE: 1 CAT: 19

Data Box
CIJE: 2 RIE: 2 CAT: 21

Data Collector (Hypercard Computer Program)
CIJE: 0 RIE: 1 CAT: 04

Data Compression
CIJE: 27 RIE: 3 CAT: 20

Data Crosswalk Codes
CIJE: 0 RIE: 1 CAT: 15

Data Demodulation
CIJE: 0 RIE: 1 CAT: 20

Data Dependence
CIJE: 0 RIE: 1 CAT: 20

Data Desk Professional
CIJE: 0 RIE: 1 CAT: 04

Data Dictionary Systems
CIJE: 3 RIE: 1 CAT: 04

Data Display
CIJE: 5 RIE: 8 CAT: 16

Data Editing
CIJE: 1 RIE: 5 CAT: 20

Data Elements
CIJE: 2 RIE: 1 CAT: 04

Data Entry
CIJE: 6 RIE: 4 CAT: 20

Data Envelopment Analysis
CIJE: 9 RIE: 2 CAT: 15

Data Envelopment Analysis Model
CIJE: 0 RIE: 1 CAT: 15

Data Files
CIJE: 10 RIE: 16 CAT: 16

Data General Nova Computer
CIJE: 0 RIE: 1 CAT: 04

Data General Nova Minicomputer
CIJE: 0 RIE: 1 CAT: 04

Data Generation
CIJE: 6 RIE: 0 CAT: 20

Data Ink Ratio Theory
CIJE: 0 RIE: 1 CAT: 15

Data Integrity
CIJE: 0 RIE: 1 CAT: 20

Data Management
CIJE: 12 RIE: 9 CAT: 20

Data Maps
CIJE: 0 RIE: 1 CAT: 16

Data Models
CIJE: 6 RIE: 1 CAT: 15

Data Organization
CIJE: 7 RIE: 4 CAT: 16

Data Pool
CIJE: 2 RIE: 0 CAT: 16

Data Protection
CIJE: 4 RIE: 2 CAT: 16
SN See also "Data Security"

Data Quality
CIJE: 1 RIE: 2 CAT: 16

Data Reduction Methods
CIJE: 5 RIE: 2 CAT: 15

Data Security
CIJE: 2 RIE: 2 CAT: 16
SN See also "Data Protection" and the Desc "Computer Security"
UF Security of Data

Data Sets
CIJE: 14 RIE: 17 CAT: 04

Data Systems Center MI
CIJE: 0 RIE: 1 CAT: 17

Data Tests
CIJE: 1 RIE: 0 CAT: 21

Data Transmission
CIJE: 17 RIE: 9 CAT: 20

Data Truncation
CIJE: 0 RIE: 1 CAT: 15
UF Truncated Data Distributions

Database and School Profiling Program
CIJE: 0 RIE: 1 CAT: 19

Database Development
CIJE: 53 RIE: 6 CAT: 20

Database Integration
CIJE: 0 RIE: 1 CAT: 20

Database Overlap
CIJE: 5 RIE: 1 CAT: 16

Database Translation
CIJE: 1 RIE: 1 CAT: 20

Databased Course Assessment Method
CIJE: 0 RIE: 2 CAT: 15
UF DCAM

Datafax
CIJE: 0 RIE: 1 CAT: 04

Datamaker (Computer Program)
CIJE: 0 RIE: 1 CAT: 04

DataRelator
CIJE: 0 RIE: 1 CAT: 04

Datasearch (Computer Program)
CIJE: 0 RIE: 1 CAT: 04

DATASIM (Computer Software)
CIJE: 0 RIE: 1 CAT: 04

Date Rape
CIJE: 15 RIE: 13 CAT: 16
SN See also "Dating Violence"

Dating Experiences Questionnaire
CIJE: 0 RIE: 1 CAT: 21

Dating Violence
CIJE: 0 RIE: 3 CAT: 16

DAVID
USE Digital And Video Interactive Device

David and Lisa
CIJE: 0 RIE: 2 CAT: 22

David D Henry Lecture Series
CIJE: 0 RIE: 1 CAT: 03

David Douglas School District OR
CIJE: 2 RIE: 5 CAT: 17

Davids Hyperkinetic Rating Scale
CIJE: 1 RIE: 0 CAT: 21

Davids Word Association and Sentence Completion
CIJE: 1 RIE: 0 CAT: 21

Davidson (Donald)
CIJE: 5 RIE: 1 CAT: 18

Davidson (Madelyn)
CIJE: 1 RIE: 0 CAT: 18

Davidson (Thomas)
CIJE: 1 RIE: 0 CAT: 18

Davidson County Community College NC
CIJE: 3 RIE: 1 CAT: 17

Davidson County School District NC
CIJE: 0 RIE: 1 CAT: 17

Davies (Robertson)
CIJE: 0 RIE: 1 CAT: 18

Davies Brickell Loop
CIJE: 1 RIE: 1 CAT: 04

Davies Speeded Reading Test English Language Prof
CIJE: 0 RIE: 1 CAT: 21

Daviess County School System KY
CIJE: 0 RIE: 1 CAT: 17

Davis (Angela)
CIJE: 1 RIE: 0 CAT: 18

Davis (Frank Marshall)
CIJE: 0 RIE: 1 CAT: 18

Davis (Lawrence M)
CIJE: 2 RIE: 0 CAT: 18

Davis (Miles)
CIJE: 1 RIE: 0 CAT: 18

Davis (William Morris)
CIJE: 0 RIE: 1 CAT: 18

Davis and Elkins College WV
CIJE: 0 RIE: 2 CAT: 17

Davis Bacon Act
CIJE: 1 RIE: 3 CAT: 14

Davis Eells Test of General Intelligence
CIJE: 1 RIE: 1 CAT: 21

Davis Monthan Air Force Base AZ
CIJE: 0 RIE: 1 CAT: 17

Davis Reading Test
CIJE: 4 RIE: 3 CAT: 21

Davis School District UT
CIJE: 0 RIE: 2 CAT: 17

Dawes (Richard)
CIJE: 1 RIE: 0 CAT: 18

Dawes Allotment Act 1887
CIJE: 1 RIE: 3 CAT: 14

Dawkins (John)
CIJE: 2 RIE: 2 CAT: 18

Dawn of Fear
CIJE: 1 RIE: 0 CAT: 22

Dawson College PQ
CIJE: 0 RIE: 2 CAT: 17

Dawson Community College MT
CIJE: 0 RIE: 1 CAT: 17

Day
CIJE: 0 RIE: 0 CAT: 20

Day (Dorothy)
CIJE: 0 RIE: 2 CAT: 18

Day After (The)
CIJE: 2 RIE: 11 CAT: 22

Day Care Environmental Inventory
CIJE: 1 RIE: 2 CAT: 21

Day Care Facilities Loan Guarantee Fund
CIJE: 0 RIE: 1 CAT: 14

Day Care Information Services
CIJE: 0 RIE: 2 CAT: 16

Day Care Licensing
CIJE: 7 RIE: 17 CAT: 15

Day Care Licensing Agencies
CIJE: 0 RIE: 0 CAT: 05

Day Care Quality Assessment Instrument
CIJE: 0 RIE: 1 CAT: 21

Day Care Registration
CIJE: 1 RIE: 1 CAT: 16

Day Care Regulations
CIJE: 1 RIE: 6 CAT: 14

Day Care Selection
CIJE: 10 RIE: 17 CAT: 16
SN See also "Preschool Selection"

Day Care Vendor Voucher System
CIJE: 0 RIE: 1 CAT: 15

Day Language Screen
CIJE: 0 RIE: 2 CAT: 21

Day of the Dead
USE Dia de los Muertos

Daybreak Star Preschool WA
CIJE: 0 RIE: 1 CAT: 17

Daydreaming
CIJE: 21 RIE: 1 CAT: 11

Daylight Savings Time
CIJE: 2 RIE: 0 CAT: 20

Days of the Dead
USE Dia de los Muertos

Dayton (Jonathan)
CIJE: 0 RIE: 1 CAT: 18

Dayton Board of Education v Brinkman
CIJE: 2 RIE: 1 CAT: 14

Dayton Journal Herald OH
CIJE: 0 RIE: 1 CAT: 17

Dayton Miami Valley Consortium OH
CIJE: 0 RIE: 1 CAT: 17

Dayton Public Opinion Center
CIJE: 0 RIE: 1 CAT: 17

Dayton Public Schools OH
CIJE: 7 RIE: 7 CAT: 17

Dayton Study
CIJE: 1 RIE: 1 CAT: 21

Dayton Women Working
CIJE: 0 RIE: 1 CAT: 17

Daytona Beach Community College FL
CIJE: 4 RIE: 5 CAT: 17

Daytona Beach Junior College FL
CIJE: 1 RIE: 1 CAT: 17

dBase
CIJE: 3 RIE: 2 CAT: 04

dBase II
CIJE: 4 RIE: 5 CAT: 04

dBase III
CIJE: 14 RIE: 0 CAT: 04

dBase III Plus
CIJE: 1 RIE: 3 CAT: 04

dBase IV
CIJE: 0 RIE: 2 CAT: 04

DCAM
USE Databased Course Assessment Method

De Anza College CA
CIJE: 3 RIE: 12 CAT: 17

De Anza Reading Center CA
CIJE: 0 RIE: 2 CAT: 17

de Beauvoir (Simone)
USE Beauvoir (Simone de)

De Bello Civili
CIJE: 2 RIE: 0 CAT: 22

De Borda (Jean Charles)
CIJE: 0 RIE: 1 CAT: 18

de Carlo (Giancarlo)
CIJE: 3 RIE: 0 CAT: 18

De Coteau (Clara Blackbird)
CIJE: 0 RIE: 1 CAT: 18

De Gaulle (Charles A)
CIJE: 2 RIE: 0 CAT: 18

De Hirsch Predictive Reading Index
CIJE: 1 RIE: 1 CAT: 21

De La Salle Vocational Day Treatment Center PA
CIJE: 0 RIE: 2 CAT: 17

de Lange Syndrome
CIJE: 5 RIE: 1 CAT: 11
UF Cornelia de Lange Syndrome; De-Langes Syndrome

De Mesquita (Julio)
CIJE: 0 RIE: 1 CAT: 18

De Orilla a Orilla
USE ORILLAS Network

De Paul University IL
CIJE: 14 RIE: 11 CAT: 17

De Quincey (Thomas)
CIJE: 2 RIE: 1 CAT: 18

De Saint Exupery (Antoine)
CIJE: 0 RIE: 1 CAT: 18

De Soto County Schools MS
USE DeSoto County School District MS

De Vinne (Theodore)
CIJE: 1 RIE: 0 CAT: 18

De Vive Voix
CIJE: 0 RIE: 1 CAT: 03
SN "By Word of Mouth" — an audiovisual course for learning French

Deacidification (Paper)
USE Paper Deacidification

Deacons
CIJE: 0 RIE: 3 CAT: 10

Dead Birds (Title)
CIJE: 0 RIE: 1 CAT: 22

Dead Languages
USE Extinct Languages

Dead Sea Scrolls
CIJE: 5 RIE: 0 CAT: 22

Deadlines (News Media)
CIJE: 2 RIE: 0 CAT: 16

Deaf Blind Program and Ability Screening Test
CIJE: 1 RIE: 0 CAT: 21

Deaf Community
CIJE: 9 RIE: 1 CAT: 10

DeafCAN
CIJE: 0 RIE: 1 CAT: 19
SN CAN = College Access Network

Deafness Management Quotient
CIJE: 1 RIE: 0 CAT: 21

Deafness Research Foundation
CIJE: 2 RIE: 0 CAT: 17

Deafnet
CIJE: 1 RIE: 2 CAT: 04

Deafsign Project
CIJE: 1 RIE: 0 CAT: 19

Deakin University (Australia)
CIJE: 7 RIE: 17 CAT: 17

Dean Alienation Scale
CIJE: 1 RIE: 2 CAT: 21

Dean Laterality Preference Schedule
CIJE: 1 RIE: 0 CAT: 21

Dean Miholasky Precognition Test
CIJE: 0 RIE: 1 CAT: 21

Deans Grant Project
CIJE: 4 RIE: 29 CAT: 19

Deans Grants Program
CIJE: 10 RIE: 9 CAT: 19

Deans List
CIJE: 0 RIE: 1 CAT: 16

Dear Abby
USE Van Buren (Abigail)

Dearborn Public Schools MI
CIJE: 0 RIE: 1 CAT: 17

Dearden (R F)
CIJE: 5 RIE: 1 CAT: 18

Death and the Kings Horseman
CIJE: 1 RIE: 0 CAT: 22

Death Anxiety
CIJE: 13 RIE: 2 CAT: 11

Death Anxiety Scale
CIJE: 11 RIE: 2 CAT: 21
UF Templer Death Anxiety Scale

Death of the Ball Turret Gunner
CIJE: 0 RIE: 0 CAT: 22

Death Penalty
USE Capital Punishment

Death Records
CIJE: 4 RIE: 1 CAT: 14

Death Related Occupations
CIJE: 1 RIE: 0 CAT: 09

Death Threat Index
CIJE: 3 RIE: 0 CAT: 21

Debabaon
USE Dibabawon

Debate Coaches
CIJE: 7 RIE: 56 CAT: 09
UF Forensic Coaches

Debate Delivery
CIJE: 0 RIE: 1 CAT: 16

Debate Ethics
CIJE: 1 RIE: 7 CAT: 16

Debate Handbooks
CIJE: 0 RIE: 1 CAT: 16

Debate Strategies
CIJE: 26 RIE: 30 CAT: 15

Debate Theory
CIJE: 44 RIE: 32 CAT: 15

Debate Tournaments
CIJE: 13 RIE: 105 CAT: 16
UF Forensics Tournaments

Debra P v Turlington
CIJE: 13 RIE: 7 CAT: 14

Debriefing
CIJE: 25 RIE: 3 CAT: 15

Debs (Eugene V)
CIJE: 2 RIE: 1 CAT: 18

Debt (Financial)
CIJE: 49 RIE: 60 CAT: 16
SN See also "External Debt," "National Debt," "International Debt," etc.

Debt Collection
CIJE: 0 RIE: 3 CAT: 16

Debt Financing
CIJE: 2 RIE: 2 CAT: 16

Debtors
CIJE: 0 RIE: 4 CAT: 10

Debtors Anonymous
CIJE: 1 RIE: 0 CAT: 17

Debugging Aids
CIJE: 2 RIE: 6 CAT: 04

DEC PDP 1 Computer
CIJE: 0 RIE: 1 CAT: 04

DEC PDP 4 Computer
CIJE: 0 RIE: 2 CAT: 04

DEC PDP 7 Computer
CIJE: 0 RIE: 2 CAT: 04

DEC PDP 8 Computer
CIJE: 0 RIE: 1 CAT: 04

DEC PDP 10 Computer
CIJE: 0 RIE: 3 CAT: 04

DEC PDP 11 Computer
CIJE: 0 RIE: 4 CAT: 04

DEC PDP 12 Computer
CIJE: 0 RIE: 2 CAT: 04

DEC PDP 15 Computer
CIJE: 0 RIE: 1 CAT: 04

Decade Study Test
CIJE: 0 RIE: 4 CAT: 21

Decalage
CIJE: 6 RIE: 3 CAT: 11
SN Discrepant or uneven cognition — use a more specific term if possible, e.g., "Family Decalage," "Horizontal Decalage"

Decambering Mill Operators
CIJE: 0 RIE: 1 CAT: 09

Decatur High School WA
CIJE: 0 RIE: 1 CAT: 17

Decatur Memorial Hospital IL
CIJE: 0 RIE: 1 CAT: 17

Decatur Public Schools IL
CIJE: 1 RIE: 0 CAT: 17

Decatur Study
CIJE: 0 RIE: 1 CAT: 19

Decay (Biology)
USE Biodegradation

Decennial Census Procedures
CIJE: 0 RIE: 4 CAT: 15

Decentering (Psychological)
CIJE: 5 RIE: 4 CAT: 11

Decentering (Psychology)
CIJE: 4 RIE: 2 CAT: 11

Decentralized Counseling
CIJE: 0 RIE: 1 CAT: 11

Decentralized District Projects
CIJE: 0 RIE: 1 CAT: 19

Decentration
CIJE: 12 RIE: 2 CAT: 15

Deciding Program
CIJE: 0 RIE: 1 CAT: 19

Decimal Classification
CIJE: 0 RIE: 3 CAT: 15

Decision Adoption Model
CIJE: 0 RIE: 1 CAT: 15

Decision Aids
CIJE: 0 RIE: 1 CAT: 16

Decision Analysis
CIJE: 14 RIE: 5 CAT: 21

Decision Analysis Technique
CIJE: 1 RIE: 3 CAT: 15

Decision Based Drama
CIJE: 0 RIE: 1 CAT: 15

Decision Counseling
CIJE: 1 RIE: 0 CAT: 11

Decision Grid
CIJE: 1 RIE: 0 CAT: 16

Decision Latency (Learning)
CIJE: 4 RIE: 1 CAT: 11

Decision Making Interview
CIJE: 0 RIE: 2 CAT: 21

Decision Making Rationale for Educational Testing
CIJE: 0 RIE: 1 CAT: 21

Decision Models
CIJE: 15 RIE: 5 CAT: 15

Decision Quality
CIJE: 3 RIE: 1 CAT: 15

Decision Rule Instruction
CIJE: 1 RIE: 0 CAT: 15

Decision Rules
CIJE: 7 RIE: 4 CAT: 15

Decision Science Techniques
CIJE: 2 RIE: 1 CAT: 15

Decision Seminars
CIJE: 1 RIE: 3 CAT: 02

Decision Tables
CIJE: 3 RIE: 1 CAT: 15

Decision Theoretic Testing
CIJE: 0 RIE: 4 CAT: 21

Decision Theory
CIJE: 28 RIE: 22 CAT: 15

Decision Trees
CIJE: 9 RIE: 5 CAT: 15

Decisions
CIJE: 9 RIE: 8 CAT: 16

Decker (Sarah P)
CIJE: 0 RIE: 1 CAT: 18

Declaration of Independence
CIJE: 23 RIE: 7 CAT: 22

Declaration of Persepolis
CIJE: 1 RIE: 0 CAT: 22

Declaration of the Rights of the Child
CIJE: 1 RIE: 7 CAT: 22

Declaration on the Human Environment
CIJE: 1 RIE: 0 CAT: 22

Declarative Forms (Language)
CIJE: 1 RIE: 1 CAT: 13

Declassified Students
CIJE: 1 RIE: 2 CAT: 10

Declining Communities
CIJE: 2 RIE: 5 CAT: 10

Declining Population
CIJE: 1 RIE: 1 CAT: 16

Decoding (Behavior)
CIJE: 3 RIE: 2 CAT: 11

Decoding (Oppositional)
USE Oppositional Decoding

Decoding (Psychology)
CIJE: 3 RIE: 1 CAT: 11

Decoding (Speech)
CIJE: 4 RIE: 4 CAT: 13

Decoding Skills Test
CIJE: 2 RIE: 2 CAT: 21

Decomposition Analysis (Statistics)
CIJE: 6 RIE: 4 CAT: 21

Deconstruction
CIJE: 36 RIE: 14 CAT: 16
UF Deconstructionism; Deconstructionist Theory; Deconstructive Analysis

Deconstructionism
USE Deconstruction

Deconstructionist Theory
USE Deconstruction

Deconstructive Analysis
USE Deconstruction

Deletion (Linguistic)
CIJE: 6 RIE: 5 CAT: 13

Delgado College LA
CIJE: 2 RIE: 3 CAT: 17

Delgado Community College LA
CIJE: 1 RIE: 4 CAT: 17

Delhi School Television Project
CIJE: 0 RIE: 1 CAT: 19

Delibes (Miguel)
CIJE: 1 RIE: 0 CAT: 18

Delinquency Study and Youth Development Project
CIJE: 0 RIE: 2 CAT: 19

Delinquent Handicapped
CIJE: 0 RIE: 1 CAT: 10

Deliverance
CIJE: 1 RIE: 0 CAT: 22

Della Vos (Victor Karlovich)
CIJE: 0 RIE: 1 CAT: 18

Delta Coefficient
CIJE: 0 RIE: 1 CAT: 20

Delta College MI
CIJE: 5 RIE: 6 CAT: 17

Delta Plot Method
CIJE: 0 RIE: 2 CAT: 15

Delta Project GA
CIJE: 0 RIE: 1 CAT: 19

Delta Scale
CIJE: 0 RIE: 1 CAT: 21

Delta School District 37 BC
CIJE: 0 RIE: 1 CAT: 17

Delta Sigma Theta Sorority
CIJE: 1 RIE: 2 CAT: 17

Delta State University MS
CIJE: 0 RIE: 2 CAT: 17

Delta Vocabulary Test
CIJE: 4 RIE: 2 CAT: 21

Delusions
CIJE: 2 RIE: 0 CAT: 11

Demagoguery
CIJE: 1 RIE: 2 CAT: 15

Demand
CIJE: 11 RIE: 7 CAT: 16

Demand Elasticity
USE Elasticity of Demand

Demand Processing
CIJE: 0 RIE: 2 CAT: 15

Demanding Behavior
CIJE: 0 RIE: 1 CAT: 11

Demands (Speech Acts)
CIJE: 0 RIE: 1 CAT: 13

Demby (William)
CIJE: 1 RIE: 0 CAT: 18

Dementia
CIJE: 11 RIE: 0 CAT: 11
SN See also "Senile Dementia"

Demiashkevich (Michael John)
CIJE: 1 RIE: 0 CAT: 18

Deming (W Edwards)
CIJE: 24 RIE: 4 CAT: 18

Deming Management Method
CIJE: 4 RIE: 8 CAT: 15

Deming School District NM
CIJE: 0 RIE: 1 CAT: 17

Democracy Simulation Game (Coleman)
CIJE: 0 RIE: 1 CAT: 21

Democratic Communication
CIJE: 3 RIE: 3 CAT: 16

Democratic Party
CIJE: 25 RIE: 10 CAT: 17

Democratic Socialism
CIJE: 1 RIE: 1 CAT: 16

Democratic Yemen
CIJE: 0 RIE: 1 CAT: 07
SN Merged with "Yemen" (q.v.), May90
UF South Yemen

Demographic Computer Library
CIJE: 0 RIE: 1 CAT: 17

Demographic Planning Model
CIJE: 0 RIE: 1 CAT: 15

Demographic Projections
CIJE: 4 RIE: 10 CAT: 16

Demographic Transition Model
CIJE: 0 RIE: 1 CAT: 15

Demolinguistics
CIJE: 1 RIE: 0 CAT: 13

Demolition Procedures
CIJE: 0 RIE: 1 CAT: 20

Demonstration and Research Ctr Early Child Educ
CIJE: 0 RIE: 19 CAT: 17

Demonstration Cities Act
CIJE: 0 RIE: 1 CAT: 14

Demonstration Guidance Project
CIJE: 0 RIE: 4 CAT: 19

Demonstration Infant Program
CIJE: 0 RIE: 1 CAT: 19

Demonstration Programs School Improve Network TX
CIJE: 0 RIE: 1 CAT: 17

Demonstration Project Group Care of Infants
CIJE: 0 RIE: 2 CAT: 19

Demonstration School for Adults CA
CIJE: 2 RIE: 0 CAT: 17

Demonstration Schools
CIJE: 0 RIE: 3 CAT: 05

Demonstratives
CIJE: 2 RIE: 0 CAT: 13

Demosthenes
CIJE: 0 RIE: 1 CAT: 18
SN Greek orator — 384?-322 B.C.

Demotic
CIJE: 0 RIE: 1 CAT: 13

Demotion (Occupational)
CIJE: 0 RIE: 1 CAT: 16

Demotivation
CIJE: 2 RIE: 1 CAT: 11

Dene (Nation)
CIJE: 2 RIE: 8 CAT: 08

Dene Languages
USE Na Dene

Denervation
CIJE: 1 RIE: 0 CAT: 11

Denial (Psychology)
CIJE: 33 RIE: 11 CAT: 11

Denison Public Schools TX
CIJE: 1 RIE: 0 CAT: 17

Denison University OH
CIJE: 7 RIE: 9 CAT: 17

Denman College (England)
CIJE: 0 RIE: 1 CAT: 17

Denmark
CIJE: 279 RIE: 367 CAT: 07

Denmark Self Concept Test
CIJE: 0 RIE: 1 CAT: 21

Dennis (Wayne)
CIJE: 0 RIE: 2 CAT: 18

Dennis Infracommunication Analysis Device
CIJE: 0 RIE: 1 CAT: 04

Denny (George V)
CIJE: 1 RIE: 1 CAT: 18

Denny Doodlebug Problem
CIJE: 0 RIE: 1 CAT: 21

Denny Rusch Ives Classroom Observation Schedule
CIJE: 0 RIE: 1 CAT: 21

Density
CIJE: 33 RIE: 13 CAT: 20
SN Use a more specific term if possible, e.g., following such initial words as Contour, Group, Item, Lexical, Population, Space, Syntactic, Text, and Texture

Density (Social)
USE Social Density

Densmore (Frances)
CIJE: 0 RIE: 3 CAT: 18

Dental Admission Testing Program
CIJE: 6 RIE: 2 CAT: 21

Dental Appliances
CIJE: 0 RIE: 1 CAT: 04

Dental Auxiliary Education Project
CIJE: 0 RIE: 2 CAT: 19

Dental Auxiliary Utilization Programs
CIJE: 0 RIE: 1 CAT: 19

Dental Charting
CIJE: 0 RIE: 2 CAT: 11

Dental Equipment
CIJE: 1 RIE: 8 CAT: 04

Dental Hygiene Education Program
CIJE: 0 RIE: 1 CAT: 19

Dental Nursing
CIJE: 1 RIE: 0 CAT: 09

Dental Practice Act (Michigan)
CIJE: 0 RIE: 2 CAT: 14

Dental Therapy Assistants
CIJE: 0 RIE: 4 CAT: 09

Denver Articulation Screening Exam
CIJE: 2 RIE: 0 CAT: 21

Denver Auditory Phoneme Sequencing Test (Part 2)
CIJE: 1 RIE: 0 CAT: 21

Denver Auraria Community College CO
CIJE: 0 RIE: 1 CAT: 17

Denver Catholic High Schools CO
CIJE: 1 RIE: 0 CAT: 17

Denver Classroom Teachers Association CO
CIJE: 0 RIE: 1 CAT: 17

Denver Community College CO
CIJE: 1 RIE: 1 CAT: 17

Denver Developmental Screening Test
CIJE: 18 RIE: 15 CAT: 21
SN See also "Revised Denver Developmental Screening Test"

Denver Developmental Screening Test (Japan)
CIJE: 0 RIE: 1 CAT: 21
UF JDDST

Denver Free University CO
CIJE: 0 RIE: 1 CAT: 17

Denver Prescreening Developmental Questionnaire
CIJE: 1 RIE: 1 CAT: 21

Denver Public Library CO
CIJE: 5 RIE: 1 CAT: 17

Denver Public Schools CO
CIJE: 13 RIE: 17 CAT: 17

Denver Regional Council of Governments CO
CIJE: 1 RIE: 0 CAT: 17

Denver Research Institute CO
CIJE: 0 RIE: 1 CAT: 17

Denver Stanford Project
CIJE: 0 RIE: 10 CAT: 19

Denver Uplink Terminal
CIJE: 0 RIE: 2 CAT: 04

Department Image
CIJE: 1 RIE: 1 CAT: 16

Department of Agriculture
CIJE: 44 RIE: 78 CAT: 17

Department of Audiovisual Instruction (NEA)
CIJE: 15 RIE: 4 CAT: 17

Department of Audiovisual Instruction (NEA) Conven
CIJE: 15 RIE: 1 CAT: 02

Department of Classroom Teachers (NEA)
CIJE: 0 RIE: 1 CAT: 17

Department of Commerce
CIJE: 7 RIE: 20 CAT: 17

Department of Defense
CIJE: 38 RIE: 89 CAT: 17
UF DoD

Department of Defense Authorization Act 1983
CIJE: 1 RIE: 1 CAT: 14

Department of Defense Overseas Dep Schools
USE Dependents Schools

Department of Education
CIJE: 167 RIE: 241 CAT: 17

Department of Education (Proposed)
CIJE: 3 RIE: 3 CAT: 17

Department of Education and Science (England)
CIJE: 14 RIE: 1 CAT: 17

Department of Education Educ Research Library
USE Educational Research Library DC

Department of Education Regional Offices
CIJE: 0 RIE: 2 CAT: 17

Department of Energy
CIJE: 21 RIE: 23 CAT: 17

Department of Equal Educational Opportunities
CIJE: 0 RIE: 1 CAT: 17

Department of Health and Human Services
CIJE: 20 RIE: 29 CAT: 17

Department of Health Education and Welfare
CIJE: 49 RIE: 93 CAT: 17

Department of Housing and Urban Development
CIJE: 16 RIE: 32 CAT: 17

Department of Indian Affairs N Devel (Canada)
CIJE: 6 RIE: 0 CAT: 17

Department of Justice
CIJE: 15 RIE: 27 CAT: 17

Department of Labor
CIJE: 32 RIE: 63 CAT: 17

Department of Labor Contract Comp v Reg Univ Calif
CIJE: 2 RIE: 0 CAT: 14
SN Department of Labor, Office of Federal Contract Compliance Programs v Regents of University of California

Department of State
CIJE: 6 RIE: 11 CAT: 17

Department of the Interior
CIJE: 1 RIE: 15 CAT: 17

Department of the Treasury
CIJE: 3 RIE: 3 CAT: 17

Department of Transportation
CIJE: 3 RIE: 10 CAT: 17

Department of Veterans Affairs
CIJE: 6 RIE: 3 CAT: 17
SN Changed from "Veterans Administration," Mar89

Department of War
CIJE: 2 RIE: 1 CAT: 17

Department Stores
CIJE: 2 RIE: 2 CAT: 05

Department Workload
CIJE: 0 RIE: 1 CAT: 16

Departmental Examination System
CIJE: 1 RIE: 0 CAT: 15

DePauw University IN
CIJE: 8 RIE: 10 CAT: 17

Dependability Index (Kane and Brennan)
CIJE: 1 RIE: 0 CAT: 21

Dependency (Economics)
CIJE: 7 RIE: 2 CAT: 16
UF Economic Dependency

Dependent Care Assistance Plans
CIJE: 1 RIE: 2 CAT: 15

Dependent Care Services
CIJE: 0 RIE: 4 CAT: 05

Dependent Care Tax Credit
CIJE: 3 RIE: 0 CAT: 14

Dependent Variables
CIJE: 23 RIE: 5 CAT: 21

Dependents Schools
CIJE: 13 RIE: 88 CAT: 05
UF American Sponsored Overseas Schools; Department of Defense Overseas Dep Schools; DoDDS; Overseas Schools

Dependents Schools European Area
CIJE: 1 RIE: 0 CAT: 17

Dependents Schools Pacific Region
CIJE: 0 RIE: 1 CAT: 17

Dependents Schools Systemwide Testing Program
CIJE: 0 RIE: 1 CAT: 19

Deployment (Military Personnel)
USE Military Deployment

Deportation
CIJE: 9 RIE: 7 CAT: 14

Deposit Collections
CIJE: 1 RIE: 2 CAT: 16

Depository Institutions Deregulation Act 1980
CIJE: 1 RIE: 0 CAT: 14

Depository Library Act 1962
CIJE: 1 RIE: 1 CAT: 14

Depoyster Need Assessment Scale (1971)
CIJE: 1 RIE: 0 CAT: 21

Depreciation
CIJE: 3 RIE: 2 CAT: 16

Depreciation Accounting
CIJE: 3 RIE: 0 CAT: 16

Depression (Economic 1929)
CIJE: 48 RIE: 42 CAT: 12

Depression Adjective Checklists
CIJE: 15 RIE: 1 CAT: 21

Depression Coping Questionnaire
CIJE: 0 RIE: 1 CAT: 21

Depression Proneness Rating Scale
CIJE: 0 RIE: 1 CAT: 21

Depressive Symptoms Questionnaire
CIJE: 0 RIE: 1 CAT: 21

Deprivation Index
CIJE: 0 RIE: 1 CAT: 21

Deprograming (Religion)
CIJE: 0 RIE: 0 CAT: 15

Depth of Delinquency Index
CIJE: 1 RIE: 0 CAT: 21

Deracialization
CIJE: 1 RIE: 0 CAT: 15

Deregulation
CIJE: 35 RIE: 47 CAT: 14
SN See also "Conditional Deregulation" and "Media Deregulation"

Derivational Theory of Complexity
CIJE: 0 RIE: 1 CAT: 15

Derivative Works
CIJE: 2 RIE: 1 CAT: 16

DERIVE Computer Algebra System
CIJE: 2 RIE: 1 CAT: 04

Dermatology
CIJE: 11 RIE: 2 CAT: 11

Derrida (Jacques)
CIJE: 17 RIE: 7 CAT: 18

DES (Drug)
USE Diethylstilbestrol

DES Education and Research Amendments 1992
CIJE: 0 RIE: 1 CAT: 14
UF Public Law 102 409

Des Jarlait (Patrick)
CIJE: 0 RIE: 1 CAT: 18

Des Moines Area Community College IA
CIJE: 7 RIE: 2 CAT: 17

Des Moines Community Corrections Program IA
CIJE: 0 RIE: 1 CAT: 19

Des Moines Plan for Student Success
CIJE: 0 RIE: 2 CAT: 19

Des Moines Public Schools IA
CIJE: 6 RIE: 64 CAT: 17

Desalination
CIJE: 3 RIE: 3 CAT: 20

Descartes (Rene)
CIJE: 11 RIE: 2 CAT: 18

Deschooling
CIJE: 15 RIE: 8 CAT: 16

Describe Your School Inventory (Hoyt)
CIJE: 3 RIE: 2 CAT: 21

Descriptive Cataloging
CIJE: 10 RIE: 8 CAT: 16

Descriptive Cataloging Committee
CIJE: 1 RIE: 0 CAT: 17

Descriptive Discriminant Analysis
CIJE: 0 RIE: 2 CAT: 15

Descriptive Method
CIJE: 3 RIE: 3 CAT: 15

Descriptive Research
CIJE: 17 RIE: 35 CAT: 15

Descriptive Test of English Skills
CIJE: 1 RIE: 1 CAT: 21

Descriptive Test of Mathematics Skills
CIJE: 1 RIE: 2 CAT: 21

Descriptive Tests of Language Skills
CIJE: 4 RIE: 3 CAT: 21

Descriptive Tests of Mathematics Skills
CIJE: 3 RIE: 3 CAT: 21

Descriptor for Individualized Instruction
CIJE: 0 RIE: 3 CAT: 16

Desegregation Advisory Project
CIJE: 0 RIE: 1 CAT: 19

Desegregation Aid
CIJE: 1 RIE: 1 CAT: 14

Deseret Alphabet
CIJE: 0 RIE: 2 CAT: 13

Desert Community College District CA
CIJE: 0 RIE: 2 CAT: 17

Desert Research Institute NV
CIJE: 0 RIE: 1 CAT: 17

Desert Shield
USE Gulf War

Desert Storm
USE Gulf War

Desertification
CIJE: 2 RIE: 2 CAT: 20

Deserts
CIJE: 22 RIE: 7 CAT: 20

Design (Engineering)
CIJE: 21 RIE: 4 CAT: 20

Design Experiments
CIJE: 0 RIE: 1 CAT: 15

Design for School Excellence
CIJE: 0 RIE: 5 CAT: 15

Design for Thinking
CIJE: 0 RIE: 1 CAT: 22

Design History
CIJE: 2 RIE: 1 CAT: 12

Design Judgment (Maitland Graves)
USE Maitland Graves Design Judgment Test

Design Methodology
CIJE: 25 RIE: 4 CAT: 15

Design of Training Systems
CIJE: 0 RIE: 8 CAT: 03

Design Option Decision Trees
CIJE: 0 RIE: 2 CAT: 15

Design Research
CIJE: 13 RIE: 3 CAT: 20

Design Studios
CIJE: 8 RIE: 0 CAT: 05

Design Technology
CIJE: 3 RIE: 2 CAT: 20

Designated Vocational Instruction
CIJE: 2 RIE: 2 CAT: 15

Designation Theory
CIJE: 1 RIE: 0 CAT: 15

Desire
CIJE: 4 RIE: 4 CAT: 16

Desists
CIJE: 0 RIE: 1 CAT: 11
SN Actions directed at stopping misbehaviors

Deskilling
CIJE: 6 RIE: 3 CAT: 15
SN The process of mechanizing or breaking down jobs so that performance may require little or no skills

Desktop Typesetting
CIJE: 1 RIE: 0 CAT: 20

Desorption Ionization
CIJE: 1 RIE: 0 CAT: 20

DeSoto County Public Schools FL
CIJE: 0 RIE: 0 CAT: 17

DeSoto County School District MS
CIJE: 0 RIE: 1 CAT: 17
UF De Soto County Schools MS

Destructive Dialog
CIJE: 0 RIE: 0 CAT: 13

Desulfurization
CIJE: 1 RIE: 0 CAT: 20

Desuperimposition
CIJE: 1 RIE: 3 CAT: 15

Detailers
CIJE: 0 RIE: 1 CAT: 09

Detective Stories
CIJE: 21 RIE: 5 CAT: 16

Detente
CIJE: 2 RIE: 3 CAT: 16

Detention
CIJE: 7 RIE: 16 CAT: 14

Detention (After School)
USE After School Detention

Detergents
CIJE: 13 RIE: 0 CAT: 20

Deterioration (Books)
CIJE: 1 RIE: 10 CAT: 20
UF Book Deterioration

Deterioration (Film)
CIJE: 0 RIE: 2 CAT: 20
UF Film Deterioration

Deterioration (Food)
USE Food Deterioration

Deterioration (Paper)
USE Paper Deterioration

Deterioration Quotient
CIJE: 1 RIE: 0 CAT: 15

Determinant Interaction (Psychology)
CIJE: 1 RIE: 0 CAT: 11

Determinants (Mathematics)
CIJE: 7 RIE: 0 CAT: 20

Determining Instructional Purposes Program
CIJE: 0 RIE: 4 CAT: 19

Detoxification Centers
CIJE: 1 RIE: 3 CAT: 05

Detroit Archdiocesan Multimedia Center MI
CIJE: 1 RIE: 0 CAT: 17

Detroit Childrens Museum MI
CIJE: 1 RIE: 0 CAT: 17

Detroit City School Series
CIJE: 0 RIE: 1 CAT: 22

Detroit College of Business MI
CIJE: 0 RIE: 1 CAT: 17

Detroit Dialect Study
CIJE: 0 RIE: 6 CAT: 19

Detroit Edison v National Labor Relations Board
CIJE: 0 RIE: 1 CAT: 14

Detroit Education Task Force MI
CIJE: 0 RIE: 1 CAT: 17

Detroit General Intelligence Examination
CIJE: 0 RIE: 1 CAT: 21

Detroit Great Cities Project
CIJE: 0 RIE: 2 CAT: 19

Detroit Great Cities Reading
CIJE: 0 RIE: 1 CAT: 19

Detroit Institute of Technology MI
CIJE: 2 RIE: 1 CAT: 17

Detroit Language Study
CIJE: 0 RIE: 3 CAT: 19

Detroit Medical Library Group MI
CIJE: 0 RIE: 1 CAT: 17

Detroit Metropolitan Library MI
CIJE: 3 RIE: 3 CAT: 17

Detroit Objective Referenced Testing Program
CIJE: 1 RIE: 1 CAT: 19

Detroit Public Schools Management Academy MI
CIJE: 0 RIE: 1 CAT: 17

Detroit Public Schools MI
CIJE: 29 RIE: 93 CAT: 17

Detroit Tests of Learning Aptitude
CIJE: 14 RIE: 3 CAT: 21

Detroit Word Recognition Test
CIJE: 0 RIE: 1 CAT: 21

Deuel Vocational Institution CA
CIJE: 2 RIE: 0 CAT: 17

Deuterium
CIJE: 1 RIE: 0 CAT: 20

Deuterons
CIJE: 1 RIE: 0 CAT: 20

Deutsch (Martin)
CIJE: 0 RIE: 1 CAT: 18

Deutsches Institut fur Fernstudien (West Germany)
CIJE: 2 RIE: 0 CAT: 17

Devaluation (Money)
USE Currency Devaluation

Devaluation (Social)
USE Social Devaluation

Devanagari
CIJE: 1 RIE: 10 CAT: 13

Developing a Curriculum Process
USE DACUM Process

Developing Adult Resources through Education
CIJE: 2 RIE: 0 CAT: 19
UF DARE Program SD

Developing Character Transmitting Knowledge
CIJE: 0 RIE: 1 CAT: 22

Developing Cognitive Abilities Test
CIJE: 2 RIE: 2 CAT: 21

Developing Exceptional Educational Potential
CIJE: 0 RIE: 1 CAT: 15

Developing Mathematical Processes
CIJE: 1 RIE: 27 CAT: 15

Developing Mature Interpersonal Relationships Task
CIJE: 0 RIE: 1 CAT: 15

Developing Understanding of Self and Others
CIJE: 5 RIE: 4 CAT: 19

Development Capital
CIJE: 2 RIE: 3 CAT: 16

Development Committees
CIJE: 0 RIE: 1 CAT: 10
UF College Development Committees

Development Directors
USE Development Officers

Development Dissemination and Adoption
CIJE: 1 RIE: 0 CAT: 15

Development Education
CIJE: 25 RIE: 40 CAT: 16

Development Journalism
CIJE: 0 RIE: 4 CAT: 16

Development of Higher Level Thinking Abilities
CIJE: 0 RIE: 1 CAT: 16

Development of Reasoning in Science Project
CIJE: 0 RIE: 1 CAT: 19

Development Officers
CIJE: 2 RIE: 2 CAT: 09
SN If appropriate, use "Development Officers (College)"
UF Development Directors

Development Officers (College)
CIJE: 7 RIE: 3 CAT: 09
UF College Development Officers

Development through Adventure Resp and Educ
CIJE: 1 RIE: 0 CAT: 19
SN Model outdoor experiential program, originally developed for troubled youth by the Ontario Ministry of Community and Social Services
UF DARE Program ON; Project DARE (Outdoor Educ)

Development Training Forum
CIJE: 0 RIE: 1 CAT: 02

Developmental Academic Advising
CIJE: 0 RIE: 1 CAT: 15

Developmental Articulation Test (Hejna)
CIJE: 0 RIE: 1 CAT: 21

Developmental Arts Program
CIJE: 0 RIE: 1 CAT: 19

Developmental Assessment
CIJE: 4 RIE: 5 CAT: 11

Developmental Assessment of Spanish Grammar
CIJE: 1 RIE: 0 CAT: 21

Developmental Assessment Wheel
CIJE: 0 RIE: 1 CAT: 21

Developmental Behavior Checklist
CIJE: 0 RIE: 1 CAT: 21

Developmental Behavioral Biology
CIJE: 0 RIE: 1 CAT: 11

Developmental Behavioral Genetics
CIJE: 14 RIE: 0 CAT: 11

Developmental Biology
CIJE: 3 RIE: 2 CAT: 20

Developmental Bypass Instructional Technology
CIJE: 1 RIE: 0 CAT: 15

Developmental Career Guidance Project
CIJE: 2 RIE: 3 CAT: 19

Developmental Contingency Tables
CIJE: 0 RIE: 1 CAT: 21

Developmental Curriculum
CIJE: 7 RIE: 10 CAT: 03

Developmental Decline
CIJE: 9 RIE: 1 CAT: 11

Developmental Disabil Servs and Facil Constr Act
CIJE: 0 RIE: 0 CAT: 14
UF Public Law 91 517

Developmental Disabilities Act
CIJE: 2 RIE: 3 CAT: 14

Developmental Disabilities Amendments 1978
CIJE: 0 RIE: 0 CAT: 14
UF Public Law 95 602

Developmental Disabilities Assist Bill of Rights
USE Developmental Disabled Assist Bill of Rights Act

Developmental Disabilities Councils
CIJE: 2 RIE: 4 CAT: 10

Developmental Disabled Assist Bill of Rights Act
CIJE: 0 RIE: 13 CAT: 14
UF Developmental Disabilities Assist Bill of Rights; Developmentally Disabled Assist Bill of Rights; Public Law 94 103; Public Law 100 146

Developmental Economic Education Program
CIJE: 14 RIE: 19 CAT: 19

Developmental Education Birth Through Two
CIJE: 3 RIE: 2 CAT: 19

Developmental Evaluation Services for Children
CIJE: 0 RIE: 4 CAT: 17

Developmental Indicators Assessment Learning
CIJE: 7 RIE: 4 CAT: 21

Developmental Indicators Assessment Learning Rev
CIJE: 3 RIE: 3 CAT: 21

Developmental Interdependence Hypothesis
CIJE: 1 RIE: 1 CAT: 15

Developmental Inventory of Sources of Stress
CIJE: 1 RIE: 1 CAT: 21

Developmental Kindergarten (Extra Year Programs)
USE Extra Year Programs (Kindergarten)

Developmental Knowledge Management Practices Scale
CIJE: 0 RIE: 1 CAT: 21

Developmental Lag Hypothesis
CIJE: 2 RIE: 0 CAT: 15

Developmental Placement
CIJE: 6 RIE: 5 CAT: 15

Developmental Play
CIJE: 1 RIE: 4 CAT: 15

Developmental Profile (Alpern and Boll)
USE Alpern Boll Developmental Profile

Developmental Profile (Bessell and Palomargs)
CIJE: 0 RIE: 1 CAT: 21

Developmental Programing Infants Young Children
CIJE: 0 RIE: 1 CAT: 03
SN "Developmental Programming for Infants and Young Children"

Developmental Psychopathology
CIJE: 22 RIE: 4 CAT: 11

Developmental Quotient
CIJE: 5 RIE: 1 CAT: 21

Developmental Readiness
CIJE: 0 RIE: 1 CAT: 11

Developmental Reading Lesson Schedule
CIJE: 0 RIE: 1 CAT: 15

Developmental Record for Infants Young Children
CIJE: 0 RIE: 1 CAT: 21

Developmental Referenced Tests
CIJE: 1 RIE: 0 CAT: 21

Developmental Screening
CIJE: 2 RIE: 6 CAT: 15

Developmental Sentence Scoring
CIJE: 8 RIE: 4 CAT: 21

Developmental Sentence Types
CIJE: 0 RIE: 1 CAT: 15

Developmental Sequences
CIJE: 8 RIE: 4 CAT: 15

Developmental Speech Sequence Model
CIJE: 0 RIE: 1 CAT: 15

Developmental Structuralist Approach
CIJE: 1 RIE: 2 CAT: 15

Developmental Students
CIJE: 2 RIE: 1 CAT: 10

Developmental Supervisory Competency Assessment
CIJE: 0 RIE: 1 CAT: 21

Developmental Teacher Education Program
CIJE: 0 RIE: 0 CAT: 19

Developmental Teacher Evaluation Kit
CIJE: 0 RIE: 3 CAT: 15

Developmental Test of Visual Motor Integration
CIJE: 12 RIE: 12 CAT: 21

Developmental Testing
CIJE: 5 RIE: 2 CAT: 21

Developmental Tests of Visual Motor Association
CIJE: 1 RIE: 0 CAT: 21

Developmental Theory
CIJE: 65 RIE: 31 CAT: 15

Developmental Therapy
CIJE: 6 RIE: 5 CAT: 11

Developmental Vocational Education Program
CIJE: 0 RIE: 5 CAT: 19

Developmental Writing Program
CIJE: 1 RIE: 2 CAT: 19

Developmentally Appropriate Practices
USE Developmentally Appropriate Programs

Developmentally Appropriate Programs
CIJE: 179 RIE: 213 CAT: 19
UF Developmentally Appropriate Practices

Developmentally Disabled Assist Bill of Rights
USE Developmental Disabled Assist Bill of Rights Act

Devereux Elementary School Behavior Rating Scale
CIJE: 9 RIE: 12 CAT: 21

Devereux Model
CIJE: 0 RIE: 1 CAT: 15
SN Intensive intervention with children for competency and life enhancement

Devereux Model 50 Teaching Aid
CIJE: 0 RIE: 1 CAT: 04

Devereux Schools PA
CIJE: 0 RIE: 2 CAT: 17

Deviance
CIJE: 25 RIE: 7 CAT: 11

Deviant Case Analysis
CIJE: 1 RIE: 2 CAT: 15

Deviations from Lesson Plans
CIJE: 0 RIE: 1 CAT: 16

Device Effectiveness Forecasting Technique
CIJE: 0 RIE: 2 CAT: 04
UF DEFT Computer Program

Devoicing
CIJE: 1 RIE: 0 CAT: 13

DeVry Institute of Technology IL
CIJE: 1 RIE: 3 CAT: 17

Dewey (Evelyn)
CIJE: 1 RIE: 0 CAT: 18

Dewey (John)
CIJE: 337 RIE: 132 CAT: 18

Dewey (Melvil)
CIJE: 9 RIE: 0 CAT: 18

Dewey Center Community Writing Project MI
CIJE: 0 RIE: 1 CAT: 19

Dewey Decimal Classification
CIJE: 64 RIE: 44 CAT: 15

Dewey Meiswinkel Discussion Schema
CIJE: 0 RIE: 1 CAT: 15

Dewey Model
CIJE: 2 RIE: 4 CAT: 15

Deweys Experimentalism
CIJE: 0 RIE: 5 CAT: 15

Dexter (Franklin B)
CIJE: 0 RIE: 1 CAT: 18

Dey
CIJE: 0 RIE: 1 CAT: 13

Dhangar Kurux
CIJE: 0 RIE: 2 CAT: 13

Dhimotiki
CIJE: 0 RIE: 1 CAT: 13

Di Donato (Pietro)
CIJE: 0 RIE: 1 CAT: 18

Dia de dar Gracias
CIJE: 0 RIE: 1 CAT: 12

Dia de la Raza
CIJE: 0 RIE: 1 CAT: 12

Dia de los Muertos
CIJE: 1 RIE: 4 CAT: 12
UF Day of the Dead; Days of the Dead; Dias de los Muertos

Diabetes Opinion Survey
CIJE: 0 RIE: 1 CAT: 21

Diablo Valley College CA
CIJE: 0 RIE: 3 CAT: 17

Diablo Valley Education Project
CIJE: 0 RIE: 6 CAT: 19

Diacritical Marking Medium
CIJE: 1 RIE: 0 CAT: 15

Diagnosis Related Groups
CIJE: 3 RIE: 1 CAT: 14
UF Diagnostic Related Groups

Diagnostic Achievement Battery
CIJE: 1 RIE: 0 CAT: 21

Diagnostic Achievement Test for Adolescents (DATA)
CIJE: 1 RIE: 0 CAT: 21

Diagnostic Achievement Tests
CIJE: 0 RIE: 1 CAT: 21

Diagnostic and Prescriptive Mathematics
CIJE: 0 RIE: 1 CAT: 20

Diagnostic Appraisal Systems
CIJE: 1 RIE: 2 CAT: 15

Diagnostic Assess Reading Trial Teach Strategies
CIJE: 0 RIE: 2 CAT: 21
UF DARTTS; Diagnostic Assessments of Reading Trial Teaching

Diagnostic Assessment School Principal Effect
CIJE: 0 RIE: 1 CAT: 15

Diagnostic Assessments of Reading Trial Teaching
USE Diagnostic Assess Reading Trial Teach Strategies

Diagnostic Conference Approach
CIJE: 0 RIE: 1 CAT: 15

Diagnostic Consultation Systems
CIJE: 0 RIE: 3 CAT: 04

Diagnostic Development Project
CIJE: 0 RIE: 1 CAT: 19

Diagnostic Developmental Method
CIJE: 1 RIE: 0 CAT: 15

Diagnostic Educational Grouping Project
CIJE: 1 RIE: 0 CAT: 19

Diagnostic Imaging (Medicine)
USE Medical Imaging

Diagnostic Index
CIJE: 0 RIE: 1 CAT: 11

Diagnostic Instrument of Supervision
CIJE: 0 RIE: 1 CAT: 21

Diagnostic Interview for Children and Adolescents
CIJE: 0 RIE: 1 CAT: 21

Diagnostic Interview Schedule
CIJE: 2 RIE: 1 CAT: 21

Diagnostic Interview Schedule for Children
CIJE: 1 RIE: 0 CAT: 21

Diagnostic Interviews
CIJE: 7 RIE: 4 CAT: 15

Diagnostic Learning Center IL
CIJE: 2 RIE: 0 CAT: 17

Diagnostic Maps
USE DIAMAPs

Diagnostic Mathematics Inventory
CIJE: 0 RIE: 2 CAT: 21

Diagnostic Prescriptive Approach
CIJE: 4 RIE: 14 CAT: 15

Diagnostic Reading Instruction Project
CIJE: 0 RIE: 1 CAT: 19

Diagnostic Reading Scales (Spache)
CIJE: 2 RIE: 4 CAT: 21

Diagnostic Reading Test
CIJE: 1 RIE: 3 CAT: 21

Diagnostic Related Groups
USE Diagnosis Related Groups

Diagnostic Reliability
CIJE: 0 RIE: 1 CAT: 15

Diagnostic Research
CIJE: 1 RIE: 2 CAT: 15

Diagnostic Skills
CIJE: 6 RIE: 3 CAT: 16

Diagnostic Statistical Manual of Mental Disorders
CIJE: 50 RIE: 19 CAT: 15

Diagnostic Supervision
CIJE: 0 RIE: 2 CAT: 15

Diagnostic Systems Approach
CIJE: 0 RIE: 1 CAT: 15

Diagnostic Teaching Cycle
CIJE: 0 RIE: 1 CAT: 15

Diagnostic Test of Word Attack Skills
CIJE: 0 RIE: 1 CAT: 21

Diagnostic Testing System
CIJE: 0 RIE: 0 CAT: 04

Diagonal Linear Adjustment
CIJE: 0 RIE: 1 CAT: 21

Dial a Career
CIJE: 2 RIE: 0 CAT: 15

Dial a Tape
CIJE: 1 RIE: 0 CAT: 04

Dial a Teacher Assistance Program
CIJE: 0 RIE: 1 CAT: 19

Dialcom
CIJE: 1 RIE: 1 CAT: 04

Dialect Differentiation Measure
CIJE: 0 RIE: 1 CAT: 21

Dialect Readers
CIJE: 0 RIE: 3 CAT: 04

Dialectic (Concept)
CIJE: 24 RIE: 6 CAT: 15

Dialectic Information Systems
CIJE: 2 RIE: 0 CAT: 15

Dialectical Enjoinment
CIJE: 0 RIE: 1 CAT: 13

Dialectical Reasoning
CIJE: 27 RIE: 25 CAT: 15

Dialectical Thought
CIJE: 14 RIE: 8 CAT: 15

DIALMAIL
CIJE: 0 RIE: 1 CAT: 04

DIALOG
CIJE: 107 RIE: 54 CAT: 17
UF DIALOG Information Services

Dialog Day
CIJE: 0 RIE: 1 CAT: 15

DIALOG Information Services
USE DIALOG

DIALOG OnDisc
CIJE: 4 RIE: 2 CAT: 04

Dialogic Communication
CIJE: 20 RIE: 18 CAT: 15

Dialogic Education
CIJE: 15 RIE: 8 CAT: 15

Dialogical Reasoning
USE Dialogical Thinking

Dialogical Thinking
CIJE: 1 RIE: 1 CAT: 11
UF Dialogical Reasoning

Dialogics
CIJE: 12 RIE: 4 CAT: 15

Dialogue Analysis
CIJE: 5 RIE: 3 CAT: 15

Dialogue Boxes
CIJE: 0 RIE: 1 CAT: 15

Dialogue Concerning Education
CIJE: 1 RIE: 0 CAT: 22

Dialysis
CIJE: 4 RIE: 3 CAT: 11
SN If possible, use the more specific term "Hemodialysis"

DIAMAPs
CIJE: 0 RIE: 1 CAT: 21
UF Diagnostic Maps

Diamond (Robert M)
CIJE: 1 RIE: 0 CAT: 18

Diamond Cutters
CIJE: 1 RIE: 0 CAT: 09

Diamond Drilling
CIJE: 0 RIE: 1 CAT: 20

Diamonds
CIJE: 2 RIE: 1 CAT: 20

Diapering
CIJE: 1 RIE: 2 CAT: 11

Diapers
CIJE: 2 RIE: 1 CAT: 16

Diarrhea
CIJE: 8 RIE: 9 CAT: 11

Diary of a Young Girl
CIJE: 0 RIE: 1 CAT: 22

Diary of Anne Frank
CIJE: 2 RIE: 0 CAT: 22

Dias de los Muertos
USE Dia de los Muertos

Diatest Responder System
CIJE: 0 RIE: 2 CAT: 04

Diathesis
CIJE: 1 RIE: 0 CAT: 13

DIATOM
CIJE: 0 RIE: 1 CAT: 04

Diatoms
CIJE: 6 RIE: 2 CAT: 20

Diatype Analyzer
CIJE: 1 RIE: 0 CAT: 04

Diaz del Castillo (Bernal)
CIJE: 1 RIE: 0 CAT: 18

Diazo Film
CIJE: 4 RIE: 0 CAT: 04

Dibabawon
CIJE: 0 RIE: 0 CAT: 13
SN A Northwest Austronesian (Philippine) language
UF Debabaon; Manobo (Dibabawon)

Dice
CIJE: 7 RIE: 0 CAT: 04

Dichloroethane
CIJE: 1 RIE: 0 CAT: 20

Dichotic Listening
CIJE: 27 RIE: 14 CAT: 11

Dichotomic Analysis
CIJE: 4 RIE: 4 CAT: 15

Dichotomies
CIJE: 1 RIE: 2 CAT: 16

Dichotomous Choice
CIJE: 2 RIE: 0 CAT: 16

Dichotomous Decisions
CIJE: 3 RIE: 1 CAT: 21

Dichotomous Keys
CIJE: 10 RIE: 2 CAT: 15

Dichotomous Responses
CIJE: 7 RIE: 0 CAT: 21

Dichotomous Scoring
CIJE: 3 RIE: 3 CAT: 21

Dichotomous Search Strategies
CIJE: 0 RIE: 1 CAT: 15

Dichotomous Variables
CIJE: 20 RIE: 17 CAT: 21

Dick and Jane Readers
CIJE: 2 RIE: 1 CAT: 22

Dickens (Charles)
CIJE: 15 RIE: 9 CAT: 18

Dickey (James)
CIJE: 3 RIE: 3 CAT: 18

Dickinson (Emily)
CIJE: 6 RIE: 6 CAT: 18

Dickinson (John)
CIJE: 2 RIE: 1 CAT: 18

Dickinson (Peter)
CIJE: 1 RIE: 0 CAT: 18

Dickinson Classification
CIJE: 1 RIE: 0 CAT: 15

Dickinson College PA
CIJE: 19 RIE: 3 CAT: 17

Dickinson Naylor Taxonomy
CIJE: 1 RIE: 0 CAT: 15

DICSIE Model
CIJE: 0 RIE: 1 CAT: 15
SN "Describe, Interact, Control, Select, Instruct, Evaluate"

Dicta Typing
CIJE: 0 RIE: 1 CAT: 16

Dictionary of American Regional English
CIJE: 3 RIE: 2 CAT: 22
UF DARE Dictionary; Project DARE (Dictionary)

Dictionary of Occupational Titles
CIJE: 22 RIE: 62 CAT: 22

Dictionary Skills
CIJE: 0 RIE: 1 CAT: 16

Dictionnaire d Eloquence Sacree (Nadal)
CIJE: 0 RIE: 1 CAT: 22

Dicto Comp Exercises
CIJE: 1 RIE: 1 CAT: 15

Dicyandiamide
CIJE: 1 RIE: 0 CAT: 20

DIDACTA
CIJE: 3 RIE: 0 CAT: 02

Didactic Games
CIJE: 0 RIE: 1 CAT: 16

Didactic Teaching
CIJE: 12 RIE: 7 CAT: 15

Didactic Training
CIJE: 6 RIE: 2 CAT: 15

Diderot (Denis)
CIJE: 4 RIE: 0 CAT: 18

Didsbury College of Education (England)
CIJE: 3 RIE: 0 CAT: 17

Die Casting Machine Operators
CIJE: 0 RIE: 1 CAT: 09

Die Cutting
CIJE: 2 RIE: 2 CAT: 20

Diebold Literacy Project
CIJE: 0 RIE: 14 CAT: 19

Diederich Rating Scale for Essays
CIJE: 3 RIE: 5 CAT: 21

Diehl Mikulecky Job Literacy Survey
CIJE: 0 RIE: 1 CAT: 21

Dienes (Zoltan)
CIJE: 3 RIE: 0 CAT: 18

Dienes Multibase Arithmetic Blocks
CIJE: 0 RIE: 1 CAT: 15

Diet Therapy
CIJE: 1 RIE: 9 CAT: 11

Dietary Guidelines (USA)
USE United States Dietary Guidelines

Dietary Sodium Intake
USE Salt Intake

Diethylstilbestrol
CIJE: 2 RIE: 1 CAT: 11
UF DES (Drug)

Diff rent Strokes
CIJE: 0 RIE: 0 CAT: 22
UF Different Strokes

Difference (Concept)
CIJE: 5 RIE: 4 CAT: 15
UF Difference Relations

Difference Indicator
CIJE: 0 RIE: 1 CAT: 15

Difference Model
CIJE: 0 RIE: 1 CAT: 15

Difference Relations
USE Difference (Concept)

Difference Scores
CIJE: 21 RIE: 4 CAT: 21

Different Situations Inventory
CIJE: 1 RIE: 0 CAT: 21

Different Strokes
USE Diff rent Strokes

Differential Ability Scales
USE Differential Ability Tests

Differential Ability Tests
CIJE: 0 RIE: 2 CAT: 21
UF Differential Ability Scales

Differential Aptitude Spatial Relations Test
CIJE: 1 RIE: 1 CAT: 21

Differential Aptitude Test
CIJE: 7 RIE: 3 CAT: 21

Differential Aptitude Tests
CIJE: 23 RIE: 31 CAT: 21

Differential Association Theory
CIJE: 4 RIE: 1 CAT: 15

Differential Calculus
CIJE: 3 RIE: 0 CAT: 20

Differential Diagnosis
CIJE: 5 RIE: 1 CAT: 11

Differential Diplomas
CIJE: 0 RIE: 1 CAT: 16

Differential Effects Hypothesis
CIJE: 0 RIE: 1 CAT: 15

Differential Guidance for Gifted Model
CIJE: 1 RIE: 0 CAT: 15

Differential Imagery Questionnaire
CIJE: 0 RIE: 1 CAT: 21

Differential Interest Test
CIJE: 0 RIE: 1 CAT: 21

Differential Personality Inventory
CIJE: 2 RIE: 0 CAT: 21

Differential Readiness Model
CIJE: 1 RIE: 0 CAT: 15

Differential Reinforcement
CIJE: 29 RIE: 2 CAT: 15

Differential Reinforcement of Other Behaviors
CIJE: 8 RIE: 2 CAT: 15

Differential Utility
CIJE: 1 RIE: 0 CAT: 21

Differential Value Profile
CIJE: 1 RIE: 0 CAT: 21

Differential Values Inventory
CIJE: 1 RIE: 3 CAT: 21

Differential Weighting
CIJE: 0 RIE: 0 CAT: 21

Differentiated Additive Androgyny Model
CIJE: 0 RIE: 1 CAT: 15
SN Relates masculinity/femininity and multiple dimensions of self-concept

Differentiated Child Behavior Observational System
CIJE: 1 RIE: 1 CAT: 21

Differentiated Curriculum (Gifted)
CIJE: 6 RIE: 7 CAT: 03

Differentiated Oral Visual Aural Computerized Kine
CIJE: 0 RIE: 1 CAT: 15

Differentiated School Norms
CIJE: 0 RIE: 1 CAT: 21

Differentiated Support Option
CIJE: 0 RIE: 1 CAT: 19

Differentiation
CIJE: 47 RIE: 18 CAT: 15

Differentiation Hypothesis
CIJE: 1 RIE: 1 CAT: 15

Differentiation Integration Contingency Theory
CIJE: 0 RIE: 1 CAT: 15

Differentiation of Self Inventory
CIJE: 0 RIE: 1 CAT: 21

Diffraction
CIJE: 5 RIE: 0 CAT: 20

Diffusion Networks
CIJE: 0 RIE: 1 CAT: 05

Diffusion of Innovations Model
CIJE: 5 RIE: 3 CAT: 15

Diffusion of Innovations Research
CIJE: 2 RIE: 4 CAT: 15

Digeorge Syndrome
CIJE: 1 RIE: 0 CAT: 11

Digest of Education Statistics
CIJE: 0 RIE: 1 CAT: 22

Digestive System
CIJE: 4 RIE: 11 CAT: 11

Digestive System Diseases
CIJE: 0 RIE: 1 CAT: 11

Digestor Gas Analysis
CIJE: 0 RIE: 1 CAT: 20

Digicolor Systems
CIJE: 0 RIE: 1 CAT: 04

Digit Span Tasks
CIJE: 6 RIE: 2 CAT: 11

Digit Span Test (Case and Kurland)
CIJE: 0 RIE: 1 CAT: 21

Digital Analog Interfaces
USE Analog Digital Interfaces

Digital Analog Logic Modules
CIJE: 0 RIE: 1 CAT: 04

Digital Analysis
CIJE: 4 RIE: 0 CAT: 15

Digital And Video Interactive Device
CIJE: 0 RIE: 1 CAT: 04
UF DAVID

Digital Audio Tapes
USE Digital Audiotape

Digital Audiotape
CIJE: 2 RIE: 1 CAT: 04
UF DAT Cassettes; Digital Audio Tapes

Digital Avionics Information System
CIJE: 0 RIE: 9 CAT: 04

Digital Data
CIJE: 48 RIE: 3 CAT: 04

Digital Data Signals
CIJE: 3 RIE: 2 CAT: 20

Digital Equipment Corporation
CIJE: 14 RIE: 9 CAT: 17

Digital Filter Design
CIJE: 0 RIE: 1 CAT: 20

Digital Imagery
CIJE: 18 RIE: 18 CAT: 20
UF Digital Imaging; Image Processing (Digital Techniques)

Digital Imaging
USE Digital Imagery

Digital Information Services
CIJE: 0 RIE: 1 CAT: 20

Digital Logic
CIJE: 0 RIE: 3 CAT: 20

Digital Research Company
CIJE: 1 RIE: 0 CAT: 17

Digital Retouching (Photography)
CIJE: 0 RIE: 6 CAT: 20

Digital Scanning
CIJE: 0 RIE: 1 CAT: 20

Digital Signal Processing
CIJE: 3 RIE: 1 CAT: 20
UF Signal Processing (Digital)

Digital Technology
CIJE: 10 RIE: 4 CAT: 20

Digital Transmission Systems
CIJE: 7 RIE: 7 CAT: 04

Digital Video Interactive
CIJE: 7 RIE: 2 CAT: 20
UF DVI Technology

Digitek Optical Scanner
CIJE: 0 RIE: 1 CAT: 04

Digitizing
CIJE: 14 RIE: 9 CAT: 20

Digoxin
CIJE: 0 RIE: 1 CAT: 11

Digraphs
CIJE: 6 RIE: 3 CAT: 13

Diguet
USE Gaviao

Dilemma Discussion Approach
CIJE: 4 RIE: 29 CAT: 15

Dilemmas of Schooling
CIJE: 2 RIE: 3 CAT: 15

Dilenowisco Educational Cooperative
CIJE: 1 RIE: 1 CAT: 17

Dillard (J L)
CIJE: 1 RIE: 0 CAT: 18

Dillard University LA
CIJE: 1 RIE: 2 CAT: 17

Dillingham City School District AK
CIJE: 0 RIE: 1 CAT: 17

Dillingham Foreign Study Program
CIJE: 0 RIE: 1 CAT: 19

Dillon (John Talbot)
CIJE: 1 RIE: 0 CAT: 18

Dilt (Robert)
CIJE: 0 RIE: 1 CAT: 18

Dilthey (Wilhelm)
CIJE: 3 RIE: 1 CAT: 18

Dilworth (Richardson)
CIJE: 1 RIE: 0 CAT: 18

Dimensional Analysis
CIJE: 20 RIE: 16 CAT: 15

Dimensional Representation
CIJE: 0 RIE: 1 CAT: 15

Dimensional Values (Psychology)
CIJE: 2 RIE: 0 CAT: 11

Dimensionality (Tests)
CIJE: 9 RIE: 10 CAT: 21
SN See also "Multidimensionality (Tests)" and "Unidimensionality (Tests)"

Dimensioning (Mechanical Drawing)
CIJE: 3 RIE: 8 CAT: 20

Dimensions of Excellence Scales
CIJE: 0 RIE: 1 CAT: 21

Dimensions of Schooling Questionnaire
CIJE: 2 RIE: 2 CAT: 21

Dimensions of Self Concept
CIJE: 20 RIE: 2 CAT: 21

Dimensions of Teacher Relationships
CIJE: 0 RIE: 1 CAT: 15

Dimensions of Temperament Survey
CIJE: 4 RIE: 1 CAT: 21

Dimethylbutane
CIJE: 1 RIE: 0 CAT: 20

Diminutives
CIJE: 1 RIE: 2 CAT: 13

DIMTEST (Computer Program)
CIJE: 3 RIE: 7 CAT: 04

DINE Project
CIJE: 3 RIE: 2 CAT: 19

Dining Room Attendants
CIJE: 0 RIE: 2 CAT: 09

Dinka
CIJE: 0 RIE: 1 CAT: 13
SN A Nilotic language of the Eastern Sudanic group

Dinky Hocker Shoots Smack
CIJE: 1 RIE: 0 CAT: 22

Dinnan (James A)
CIJE: 2 RIE: 2 CAT: 18

Dinner at the Homesick Restaurant (Book)
CIJE: 2 RIE: 0 CAT: 22

Diocesan Adult Training Center
CIJE: 1 RIE: 0 CAT: 17

Diocesan Directors of Religious Education
CIJE: 0 RIE: 1 CAT: 09

Diogenes
CIJE: 1 RIE: 0 CAT: 18

Diola
CIJE: 0 RIE: 1 CAT: 13

Dionysianism
CIJE: 0 RIE: 1 CAT: 15

Diophantine Equations
CIJE: 3 RIE: 0 CAT: 20

Dioramas
CIJE: 2 RIE: 3 CAT: 04

Diotima
CIJE: 0 RIE: 1 CAT: 18
SN Socrates' teacher

Dioxin
CIJE: 0 RIE: 2 CAT: 11

Diphenylhydantoin
CIJE: 2 RIE: 0 CAT: 11

Diphthongs
CIJE: 5 RIE: 3 CAT: 13

Dipietro (Robert)
CIJE: 1 RIE: 0 CAT: 18

Diploma in Management Studies
CIJE: 0 RIE: 1 CAT: 16

Diploma Mills
CIJE: 4 RIE: 5 CAT: 16

Diploma of Higher Education
CIJE: 2 RIE: 0 CAT: 16

Diplomat Game
CIJE: 0 RIE: 1 CAT: 21

Diplomatic Immunity
CIJE: 1 RIE: 0 CAT: 14

Diplomatic Services
CIJE: 1 RIE: 1 CAT: 16

Dipole Oscillator
CIJE: 1 RIE: 0 CAT: 04

Dirac (Paul)
CIJE: 2 RIE: 0 CAT: 18

Direct Access Project
CIJE: 0 RIE: 3 CAT: 19

Direct Action for Rehabilitation and Employment
CIJE: 1 RIE: 0 CAT: 19

Direct Assessment
CIJE: 13 RIE: 15 CAT: 21

Direct Broadcast Satellite Systems
USE Direct Satellite Broadcasting

Direct Costs
CIJE: 2 RIE: 3 CAT: 16

Direct Current
CIJE: 1 RIE: 6 CAT: 20

Direct Grant System
CIJE: 0 RIE: 3 CAT: 15

Direct Instruction
CIJE: 195 RIE: 81 CAT: 15

Direct Instruction Follow Through Project
CIJE: 2 RIE: 8 CAT: 19

Direct Instruction Model
CIJE: 25 RIE: 20 CAT: 15

Direct Interventionist Approach
CIJE: 0 RIE: 1 CAT: 15

Direct Legislation
CIJE: 0 RIE: 1 CAT: 14

Direct Lending
CIJE: 0 RIE: 10 CAT: 16

Direct Line Authority
CIJE: 0 RIE: 1 CAT: 15

Direct Mail
CIJE: 15 RIE: 6 CAT: 16

Direct Mail Advertising
CIJE: 17 RIE: 10 CAT: 16

Direct Mail Campaigns
CIJE: 5 RIE: 9 CAT: 16

Direct Manipulation Interface
CIJE: 3 RIE: 1 CAT: 20

Direct Objects
CIJE: 2 RIE: 1 CAT: 13

Direct Pure Piecemeal and Complete Method
CIJE: 1 RIE: 0 CAT: 15

Direct Questioning (Car Test)
CIJE: 0 RIE: 1 CAT: 21

Direct Quotation
CIJE: 1 RIE: 1 CAT: 15

Direct Response Marketing
CIJE: 1 RIE: 1 CAT: 15

Direct Satellite Broadcasting
CIJE: 1 RIE: 1 CAT: 20
UF Direct Broadcast Satellite Systems

Direct Standard Setting Method
CIJE: 0 RIE: 2 CAT: 21

Direct Teaching Model
CIJE: 1 RIE: 2 CAT: 15

Direct Verbal Instruction
CIJE: 0 RIE: 4 CAT: 15

Direct Writing Assessment
CIJE: 3 RIE: 1 CAT: 21

Directed Graphs
CIJE: 1 RIE: 1 CAT: 15

Directed Imagination Technique
CIJE: 1 RIE: 1 CAT: 21

Directed Overt Activity Strategy
CIJE: 0 RIE: 1 CAT: 15

Directed Reading Thinking Activities
CIJE: 24 RIE: 20 CAT: 15

Directed Reading Writing Activities
CIJE: 1 RIE: 1 CAT: 15

Directed Response Training
CIJE: 0 RIE: 1 CAT: 15
UF Response Training

Directing (Theater)
CIJE: 11 RIE: 7 CAT: 15

Direction Following
CIJE: 10 RIE: 8 CAT: 15

Direction Service Centers
CIJE: 0 RIE: 1 CAT: 05

Directional Transactions
CIJE: 1 RIE: 2 CAT: 16

Directionality
CIJE: 9 RIE: 5 CAT: 16

Directions
CIJE: 30 RIE: 15 CAT: 16

Directive Speech
CIJE: 10 RIE: 9 CAT: 13

Directive Teaching
CIJE: 7 RIE: 2 CAT: 15

Directors (Theater)
CIJE: 12 RIE: 8 CAT: 09
SN See also "Film Directors"

Directors of Religious Education
CIJE: 1 RIE: 1 CAT: 09
SN See also "Diocesan Directors of Religious Education"
UF DREs; Parish Directors of Religious Education

Directory of Self Instructional Materials
CIJE: 0 RIE: 2 CAT: 22

Directory of Unpublished Experimental Mental Meas
CIJE: 0 RIE: 0 CAT: 22

Directory Sampling
CIJE: 0 RIE: 1 CAT: 21
UF Telephone Directory Sampling

Disabilities Awareness Curriculum
CIJE: 1 RIE: 1 CAT: 03

Disability Awareness Day
CIJE: 0 RIE: 1 CAT: 12

Disability Management
CIJE: 0 RIE: 1 CAT: 11
UF Managing Disabilities

Disability Opinion Survey (Greer et al)
CIJE: 0 RIE: 1 CAT: 21

Disability Payments
CIJE: 5 RIE: 19 CAT: 14

Disabled Childrens Project TX
CIJE: 0 RIE: 0 CAT: 19

Disabled Employees
USE Employees with Disabilities

Disabled Infants Project
CIJE: 0 RIE: 1 CAT: 19

Disabled Parents
CIJE: 25 RIE: 11 CAT: 10

Disabled Students as Tutors
CIJE: 0 RIE: 1 CAT: 10

Disabled Teachers
CIJE: 14 RIE: 5 CAT: 10

Disadvantaged Country Areas Program (Australia)
CIJE: 0 RIE: 2 CAT: 19

Disadvantaged Pupil Program Fund OH
USE Ohio Disadvantaged Pupil Program Fund

Disadvantaged Schools Program (Australia)
CIJE: 0 RIE: 6 CAT: 19

Disaggregated Analysis
CIJE: 0 RIE: 8 CAT: 15

Disaggregation (Data)
CIJE: 3 RIE: 7 CAT: 21

Disappearing Text Technique
CIJE: 0 RIE: 1 CAT: 13

Disaster Planning
CIJE: 9 RIE: 18 CAT: 15

Disasters
CIJE: 2 RIE: 3 CAT: 16
SN Use a more specific term if possible, e.g., the Descriptor "Natural Disasters" or such Identifiers as "Aircraft Disasters," "Technological Disasters," etc.

Discharge (from Treatment)
CIJE: 0 RIE: 2 CAT: 11

Discharge Planning
CIJE: 11 RIE: 3 CAT: 11

Discharged Patients
CIJE: 1 RIE: 0 CAT: 10

Disciples of Christ
CIJE: 0 RIE: 2 CAT: 17

Disciplinary Referrals
CIJE: 1 RIE: 0 CAT: 15

Disciplinary Styles
CIJE: 5 RIE: 2 CAT: 15
SN See also "Parenting Styles"

Discipline Based Geography Education
CIJE: 0 RIE: 1 CAT: 03

Discipline Based Research
CIJE: 0 RIE: 2 CAT: 15

Discipline Based Teaching Theory
CIJE: 1 RIE: 1 CAT: 15

Discipline Helpline
CIJE: 0 RIE: 1 CAT: 19

Disclaimers
CIJE: 4 RIE: 2 CAT: 16

Disclosure Free Evaluation
CIJE: 1 RIE: 0 CAT: 15

Disclosure II
CIJE: 0 RIE: 1 CAT: 04

Disclosure Models
CIJE: 0 RIE: 1 CAT: 15

Disco Dancing
CIJE: 2 RIE: 1 CAT: 16

Discontinuity
CIJE: 11 RIE: 6 CAT: 15

Discounting Principle
CIJE: 7 RIE: 1 CAT: 15

Discourse
CIJE: 68 RIE: 36 CAT: 13

Discourse Accent
CIJE: 0 RIE: 1 CAT: 13

Discourse Aims
CIJE: 20 RIE: 16 CAT: 13

Discourse Based Teaching
CIJE: 0 RIE: 1 CAT: 15

Discourse Communities
CIJE: 24 RIE: 61 CAT: 10

Discourse Comprehension Abilities Test
CIJE: 0 RIE: 1 CAT: 21

Discourse Conventions
CIJE: 0 RIE: 1 CAT: 13
SN Discourse used in its dominant or most familiar sense

Discourse Markers
CIJE: 1 RIE: 1 CAT: 13

Discourse Organization
CIJE: 16 RIE: 9 CAT: 13

Discourse Synthesis
CIJE: 3 RIE: 3 CAT: 15

DISCOVER AL System
USE DISCOVER for Adult Learners

Discover Art (Textbook Series)
CIJE: 0 RIE: 1 CAT: 22

DISCOVER for Adult Learners
CIJE: 1 RIE: 4 CAT: 04
UF DISCOVER AL System

DISCOVER System
CIJE: 14 RIE: 18 CAT: 04

Discrepancy Analysis
CIJE: 32 RIE: 22 CAT: 15

Discrepancy Evaluation Model
CIJE: 6 RIE: 15 CAT: 15
SN See also "Provus Discrepancy Evaluation Model"

Discrepancy Formulas
CIJE: 2 RIE: 1 CAT: 15
SN Ways of measuring the discrepancy between aptitude (ability) and achievement to identify learning disabilities
UF Discrepancy Measure (Learning Disabled)

Discrepancy Measure
CIJE: 4 RIE: 4 CAT: 21

Discrepancy Measure (Learning Disabled)
USE Discrepancy Formulas

Discrepancy Model
CIJE: 28 RIE: 6 CAT: 15

Discrepant Case Analysis
CIJE: 0 RIE: 1 CAT: 15

Discrepant Events (Science)
CIJE: 7 RIE: 6 CAT: 20

Discrepant Messages
CIJE: 2 RIE: 2 CAT: 15
UF Message Discrepancy

Discrete Mathematics
CIJE: 41 RIE: 15 CAT: 20

Discrete Variables
CIJE: 4 RIE: 3 CAT: 20

Discretionary Programs
CIJE: 1 RIE: 6 CAT: 14

Discretionary Situations
CIJE: 3 RIE: 1 CAT: 15

Discriminant Function Index
CIJE: 4 RIE: 1 CAT: 21

Discriminant Validity
CIJE: 26 RIE: 8 CAT: 21

Discrimination against Children
CIJE: 0 RIE: 1 CAT: 14

Discrimination by Identification of Pictures
CIJE: 0 RIE: 3 CAT: 21

Discrimination Complaints
CIJE: 1 RIE: 2 CAT: 14

Discrimination Index
CIJE: 3 RIE: 3 CAT: 21

Discrimination Indices
CIJE: 2 RIE: 2 CAT: 21

Discrimination Learning Test (Arima)
CIJE: 0 RIE: 1 CAT: 21

Discrimination of Recency
CIJE: 0 RIE: 1 CAT: 11

Discrimination Programing
CIJE: 0 RIE: 1 CAT: 15

Discrimination Training
CIJE: 7 RIE: 0 CAT: 15

Discriminative Stimulus
CIJE: 4 RIE: 0 CAT: 11

Discussion Skills Project (Scotland)
CIJE: 0 RIE: 1 CAT: 19
UF Scottish Discussion Skills Project

Disengagement (Gerontology)
CIJE: 5 RIE: 2 CAT: 11

Disfluencies
CIJE: 4 RIE: 1 CAT: 13

Disfunctional Family
USE Dysfunctional Family

Disguised Test Items
CIJE: 0 RIE: 0 CAT: 21
UF Item Disguise

Disinhibition
CIJE: 0 RIE: 1 CAT: 11

Disintegration (Social)
USE Social Disintegration

Disjunction
CIJE: 2 RIE: 1 CAT: 20

Disjunctive Concepts
CIJE: 1 RIE: 1 CAT: 11

Disjunctive Item Response Functions
CIJE: 0 RIE: 1 CAT: 21

Disjunctive Syllogisms
CIJE: 2 RIE: 1 CAT: 15

Disjunctive Tasks
CIJE: 1 RIE: 1 CAT: 11

Disk Formatting
CIJE: 0 RIE: 2 CAT: 20

Disk Jockeys
CIJE: 0 RIE: 1 CAT: 09

Disk Operating Systems
CIJE: 13 RIE: 5 CAT: 04
SN See also "MS DOS"
UF DOS

Disliked Children
CIJE: 1 RIE: 1 CAT: 10

Dislocated Workers Education Training Program
CIJE: 0 RIE: 1 CAT: 19

Disney (Walt)
CIJE: 8 RIE: 3 CAT: 18

Disneyland CA
CIJE: 0 RIE: 1 CAT: 17

Disneyworld FL
CIJE: 1 RIE: 1 CAT: 17

Disorder in Our Public Schools
CIJE: 2 RIE: 1 CAT: 22
UF Bauer Report

Disparate Impact Theory
CIJE: 1 RIE: 1 CAT: 15

Dispatchers
CIJE: 0 RIE: 4 CAT: 09
SN See also "Aircraft Dispatchers"

Displaced Homemakers Self Suff Assist Act 1990
CIJE: 0 RIE: 1 CAT: 14
UF Public Law 101 554

Displacement (Psychology)
CIJE: 7 RIE: 1 CAT: 11

Disposable Income
CIJE: 0 RIE: 1 CAT: 16

Disruption
CIJE: 10 RIE: 7 CAT: 16

Disruptive Behavior
CIJE: 17 RIE: 28 CAT: 11

Disruptive Behavior Inventory
CIJE: 0 RIE: 1 CAT: 21

Disruptive Effect (Reading)
CIJE: 1 RIE: 2 CAT: 16

Dissatisfaction Theory
CIJE: 7 RIE: 6 CAT: 15

Dissection
CIJE: 50 RIE: 7 CAT: 20

Dissemination Analysis Group Model
CIJE: 0 RIE: 1 CAT: 15

Dissemination Model Assistance Project
CIJE: 0 RIE: 1 CAT: 19

Dissertation Abstracts International Index
CIJE: 7 RIE: 4 CAT: 22

Dissertation Alternatives
CIJE: 0 RIE: 1 CAT: 16

Dissertations in Progress
CIJE: 0 RIE: 1 CAT: 16

Dissident Literature
CIJE: 0 RIE: 1 CAT: 16

Dissipative Structures Theory
CIJE: 1 RIE: 1 CAT: 15

Dissociation
CIJE: 15 RIE: 5 CAT: 11

Dissociation Energy
CIJE: 1 RIE: 0 CAT: 20

Dissonance Reduction
CIJE: 1 RIE: 2 CAT: 11

Distance Education Centers
CIJE: 1 RIE: 2 CAT: 05

Distance from Origins Index
CIJE: 0 RIE: 1 CAT: 21

Distance Learning Project North AB
CIJE: 0 RIE: 1 CAT: 19

Distance University (West Germany)
CIJE: 0 RIE: 2 CAT: 17

Distance University Education via Television
CIJE: 1 RIE: 2 CAT: 19
UF DUET Videoconferencing Program

Distancing Model (Sigel)
CIJE: 1 RIE: 7 CAT: 15

Distant Study Systems
CIJE: 1 RIE: 1 CAT: 15

Distar
CIJE: 21 RIE: 21 CAT: 03
SN Instructional System

Distar Reading Program
CIJE: 6 RIE: 17 CAT: 19

Distillation (Science)
CIJE: 3 RIE: 4 CAT: 20

Distinguished Achievement Awards Entry
CIJE: 0 RIE: 216 CAT: 19

Distinguished Professorship Programs
CIJE: 0 RIE: 1 CAT: 19

Distinguished Service in Trusteeship Award
CIJE: 1 RIE: 0 CAT: 16

Distractibility
CIJE: 9 RIE: 10 CAT: 11

Distractibility (Reading)
CIJE: 1 RIE: 1 CAT: 15

Distraction
CIJE: 29 RIE: 17 CAT: 16

Distractor Technique
CIJE: 0 RIE: 2 CAT: 15

Distress
CIJE: 22 RIE: 5 CAT: 11
SN Use a more specific term if possible, e.g., "Emotional Distress," "Infant Distress"

Distributed Cognition
CIJE: 0 RIE: 1 CAT: 11

Distributed Computer Systems
USE Distributed Computing

Distributed Computing
CIJE: 22 RIE: 3 CAT: 20
UF Distributed Computer Systems; Distributive Computing

Distributed Data Processing Systems
CIJE: 8 RIE: 5 CAT: 04

Distributed Network Learning Framework
CIJE: 0 RIE: 1 CAT: 19

Distributed Office Support System
CIJE: 0 RIE: 1 CAT: 04

Distributed Practice
CIJE: 10 RIE: 1 CAT: 15

Distributed Processing Systems
CIJE: 7 RIE: 2 CAT: 04

Distribution Of Associations Model
CIJE: 2 RIE: 1 CAT: 15

Distribution of Schools
CIJE: 0 RIE: 1 CAT: 16
UF School Distribution

Distributive Computing
USE Distributed Computing

Distributive Education Clubs of America
CIJE: 13 RIE: 44 CAT: 17

Distributive Education Training Project
CIJE: 0 RIE: 1 CAT: 19

Distributive Industry Training Board (England)
CIJE: 1 RIE: 0 CAT: 17

Distributive Justice
CIJE: 24 RIE: 8 CAT: 15

Distributive Justice Scale
CIJE: 1 RIE: 1 CAT: 21

Distributive Law
CIJE: 1 RIE: 1 CAT: 20

Distributive Programs
CIJE: 1 RIE: 1 CAT: 19

Distributive Property
CIJE: 3 RIE: 1 CAT: 20

District Facilitator Project DC
CIJE: 0 RIE: 2 CAT: 19
UF Facilitator Project DC

District Incentive Grants Program NY
CIJE: 1 RIE: 1 CAT: 19

District Media Programs
CIJE: 0 RIE: 1 CAT: 19

District of Columbia
CIJE: 133 RIE: 923 CAT: 07

District of Columbia (Anacostia)
CIJE: 0 RIE: 14 CAT: 07

District of Columbia (Mount Vernon Square)
CIJE: 1 RIE: 0 CAT: 07

District of Columbia Public Library
CIJE: 1 RIE: 1 CAT: 17

District of Columbia Public Schools
CIJE: 23 RIE: 149 CAT: 17

District Personnel
USE School District Personnel

District Power Equalization
CIJE: 9 RIE: 8 CAT: 15

District School Relationship
CIJE: 2 RIE: 3 CAT: 15

District Secondary School Study
CIJE: 0 RIE: 1 CAT: 19

Districtwide Testing Program (California)
CIJE: 0 RIE: 2 CAT: 19

Ditellurium Decafluoride
CIJE: 1 RIE: 0 CAT: 20

Ditto Masters
CIJE: 1 RIE: 49 CAT: 16

Diuretics
CIJE: 1 RIE: 2 CAT: 11

Diurnal Variations
CIJE: 0 RIE: 0 CAT: 11

Divergent Production Battery
CIJE: 0 RIE: 1 CAT: 21

Divergent Questioning
CIJE: 2 RIE: 1 CAT: 21

Divergent Validation
CIJE: 3 RIE: 1 CAT: 21

Diversification
CIJE: 10 RIE: 5 CAT: 15
SN Use a more specific term if possible, e.g., "Economic Diversification," "Revenue Diversification"

Diversified Cooperative Training
CIJE: 0 RIE: 2 CAT: 15

Diversified Educational Experience Program
CIJE: 0 RIE: 1 CAT: 19

Diversified Educational Experiences Program
CIJE: 0 RIE: 1 CAT: 19

Diversified Occupations
CIJE: 1 RIE: 1 CAT: 09

Diversion (Judicial)
CIJE: 7 RIE: 8 CAT: 14
SN See also "Juvenile Diversion"

Diversionary Agencies
CIJE: 0 RIE: 1 CAT: 16

Diversity (Faculty)
CIJE: 20 RIE: 23 CAT: 15

Diversity (Groups)
CIJE: 43 RIE: 43 CAT: 16

Diversity (Socioeconomic)
USE Socioeconomic Diversity

Diversity (Student)
CIJE: 189 RIE: 241 CAT: 15

Diversity Concept
CIJE: 12 RIE: 22 CAT: 15

Divestiture
CIJE: 8 RIE: 8 CAT: 16
UF Corporate Divestiture; Divestment

Divestment
USE Divestiture

Divine Comedy
CIJE: 4 RIE: 1 CAT: 22

Division Hashing Function (Directory Structuring)
CIJE: 1 RIE: 0 CAT: 15

Division of Associated Health Professions
CIJE: 0 RIE: 1 CAT: 17

Division of Labor (Automation)
CIJE: 2 RIE: 1 CAT: 16

Division of Labor (Household)
CIJE: 42 RIE: 8 CAT: 15

Divorce Mediation
CIJE: 2 RIE: 2 CAT: 15

Dix (Marion Quin)
CIJE: 0 RIE: 1 CAT: 18

Dixon (John)
CIJE: 2 RIE: 0 CAT: 18

Dixwell Legal Rights Association CT
CIJE: 0 RIE: 1 CAT: 17

Djajapura Centre (Indonesia)
CIJE: 0 RIE: 1 CAT: 17

Djinang
CIJE: 0 RIE: 1 CAT: 13
SN A Murngic language (Australian Aborigine)
UF Jandjinung

DMI Mathematics Systems
CIJE: 0 RIE: 2 CAT: 21

Do It Now Foundation CA
CIJE: 1 RIE: 0 CAT: 17

Do It Yourself Method
CIJE: 3 RIE: 0 CAT: 15

Do the Right Thing (Film)
CIJE: 0 RIE: 1 CAT: 22

Doane College NE
CIJE: 5 RIE: 4 CAT: 17

DOBIS System
CIJE: 3 RIE: 4 CAT: 04
UF Dortmunder Bibliothekssystem

Docents
CIJE: 4 RIE: 2 CAT: 09

Dockrell (W Bryan)
CIJE: 0 RIE: 1 CAT: 18

Doctor of Education Degrees
CIJE: 1 RIE: 1 CAT: 16
SN See also "External Doctor of Education Degrees"
UF Ed D

Doctor of Philosophy in Education Degrees
CIJE: 1 RIE: 1 CAT: 22
UF Ph D in Education

Doctor Seuss
CIJE: 4 RIE: 2 CAT: 22

Doctor Zhivago
CIJE: 1 RIE: 0 CAT: 22

Docudramas
CIJE: 0 RIE: 4 CAT: 16

Document Action
CIJE: 0 RIE: 1 CAT: 16

Document Analysis
CIJE: 16 RIE: 4 CAT: 15

Document Delivery
CIJE: 66 RIE: 15 CAT: 16
UF Full Text Document Delivery

Document Delivery Service
CIJE: 20 RIE: 11 CAT: 16

Document Delivery Services
CIJE: 28 RIE: 4 CAT: 05

Document Delivery Systems
CIJE: 17 RIE: 5 CAT: 15

Document Delivery Test
CIJE: 1 RIE: 1 CAT: 21

Document Design Center DC
CIJE: 3 RIE: 1 CAT: 17

Document Design Project
CIJE: 2 RIE: 21 CAT: 19

Document Handling
CIJE: 6 RIE: 4 CAT: 15

Document Literacy Skills
CIJE: 0 RIE: 1 CAT: 16

Document Location
CIJE: 0 RIE: 1 CAT: 16

Document Origination Processes
CIJE: 0 RIE: 1 CAT: 15

Document Security
CIJE: 0 RIE: 1 CAT: 20

Document Structure
CIJE: 1 RIE: 1 CAT: 16

Document Supply
CIJE: 0 RIE: 1 CAT: 16

Documentalists
CIJE: 2 RIE: 0 CAT: 09

Documentary Heritage Program NY
CIJE: 0 RIE: 1 CAT: 19

Documentation and Technical Assistance Project
CIJE: 2 RIE: 38 CAT: 19

Documentation Coordination and Research Incentive
CIJE: 0 RIE: 1 CAT: 19

Documentation Research and Training Centre (India)
CIJE: 0 RIE: 1 CAT: 17

Documents Expediting Project
CIJE: 1 RIE: 0 CAT: 19

DoD
USE Department of Defense

DoDDS
USE Dependents Schools

Dodge (Mary Mapes)
CIJE: 0 RIE: 2 CAT: 18

Doe v Plyler
CIJE: 7 RIE: 0 CAT: 14

Doe v Renfrow
CIJE: 2 RIE: 1 CAT: 14

Dogmatism Scale (Rokeach Hebrew)
CIJE: 0 RIE: 0 CAT: 21

Dogmatism Scale (Rokeach)
CIJE: 11 RIE: 7 CAT: 21

Dogrib
CIJE: 0 RIE: 0 CAT: 13
SN An Athapascan-Eyak language
UF Thlingchadinne

Dogrib (Tribe)
CIJE: 0 RIE: 6 CAT: 08

Dogs
CIJE: 7 RIE: 4 CAT: 20
SN See also "Guide Dogs"

Dolan Home Educational Environment Scale
CIJE: 0 RIE: 1 CAT: 21
UF Home Educational Environment Index (Dolan)

Dolch Basic Sight Vocabulary
CIJE: 12 RIE: 11 CAT: 21

Dole (Elizabeth)
CIJE: 0 RIE: 1 CAT: 18

Doll Choice Task
CIJE: 1 RIE: 3 CAT: 21

Doll Play Technique
CIJE: 3 RIE: 1 CAT: 15

Doll Self Point Task
CIJE: 0 RIE: 1 CAT: 21

Dollmaker (The)
CIJE: 1 RIE: 1 CAT: 22

Dolls
CIJE: 14 RIE: 5 CAT: 16
SN See also "Anatomically Correct Dolls"

Dolphins
CIJE: 2 RIE: 3 CAT: 20

Domain Analysis
CIJE: 17 RIE: 12 CAT: 15

Domain Knowledge
CIJE: 12 RIE: 6 CAT: 15
UF Domain Specific Knowledge

Domain Placement
CIJE: 0 RIE: 1 CAT: 16

Domain Projects
CIJE: 0 RIE: 1 CAT: 19

Domain Referenced Testing
CIJE: 3 RIE: 11 CAT: 21

Domain Referenced Tests
CIJE: 27 RIE: 58 CAT: 21

Domain Score Strategy
CIJE: 1 RIE: 0 CAT: 21

Domain Specific Knowledge
USE Domain Knowledge

Domain Specific Thinking
CIJE: 3 RIE: 2 CAT: 15

Domain Specifications
CIJE: 19 RIE: 15 CAT: 15

Domain Validity
CIJE: 2 RIE: 0 CAT: 21

Doman (Glenn)
CIJE: 1 RIE: 0 CAT: 18

Doman Delacato Developmental Profile
CIJE: 0 RIE: 2 CAT: 21

Doman Delacato Method
CIJE: 5 RIE: 3 CAT: 21

Domesday Project (United Kingdom)
CIJE: 0 RIE: 1 CAT: 19

Domestic Volunteer Service Act
CIJE: 0 RIE: 4 CAT: 14

Domian Report
CIJE: 0 RIE: 1 CAT: 22

Dominance Hierarchies
CIJE: 17 RIE: 6 CAT: 21

Dominant Activities
CIJE: 0 RIE: 1 CAT: 16

Dominant Behavior
CIJE: 24 RIE: 16 CAT: 11

Dominant Language
CIJE: 4 RIE: 0 CAT: 13

Dominica
CIJE: 2 RIE: 4 CAT: 07

Dominican College of San Rafael CA
CIJE: 3 RIE: 3 CAT: 17

Dominican Republic
CIJE: 32 RIE: 40 CAT: 07

Dominion Achievement Test in Silent Reading
CIJE: 1 RIE: 0 CAT: 21

Dominion Group Achievement Tests
CIJE: 1 RIE: 0 CAT: 21

Dominion Group Test of Learning Capacity
CIJE: 1 RIE: 0 CAT: 21

Dominion Group Test of Reading Readiness
CIJE: 0 RIE: 1 CAT: 21

Dominion Vocabulary Test
CIJE: 1 RIE: 0 CAT: 21

Don Juan in Hell
CIJE: 0 RIE: 1 CAT: 22

Don Quixote
CIJE: 9 RIE: 2 CAT: 22

Dona Ana Branch Community College NM
USE New Mexico State University Dona Ana Branch

Donahoe Act
CIJE: 0 RIE: 1 CAT: 14

Donahue (Phil)
CIJE: 2 RIE: 2 CAT: 18

Donating Behavior
CIJE: 5 RIE: 1 CAT: 11

Donne (John)
CIJE: 5 RIE: 2 CAT: 18

Donnelly College KS
CIJE: 0 RIE: 4 CAT: 17

Donor Characteristics
CIJE: 0 RIE: 1 CAT: 16
SN i.e., financial donor characteristics

Doolittle (Hilda)
CIJE: 2 RIE: 0 CAT: 18

Doolittle Family Education Center IL
CIJE: 0 RIE: 3 CAT: 17

Doolittle Method
CIJE: 0 RIE: 1 CAT: 15

Doonesbury
CIJE: 0 RIE: 1 CAT: 22

Door (Youth Center) NY
CIJE: 0 RIE: 0 CAT: 17

Door to Door Solicitation
CIJE: 0 RIE: 1 CAT: 16

Doppler Effect
CIJE: 14 RIE: 0 CAT: 20

Doren Diagnostic Reading Test
CIJE: 1 RIE: 0 CAT: 21

Dormitory Aides
CIJE: 0 RIE: 1 CAT: 10

Dormitory Size
CIJE: 0 RIE: 1 CAT: 16

Dorr (Rheta C)
CIJE: 0 RIE: 1 CAT: 18

Dorset Institute of Higher Education (England)
CIJE: 0 RIE: 1 CAT: 17

Dorsett Educational Systems
CIJE: 1 RIE: 0 CAT: 15

Dortmunder Bibliothekssystem
USE DOBIS System

DOS
USE Disk Operating Systems

Dos Amigos Verbal Language Scale
CIJE: 1 RIE: 2 CAT: 21

Dos Passos (John)
CIJE: 1 RIE: 0 CAT: 18

Doshisha University (Japan)
CIJE: 0 RIE: 2 CAT: 17

Dosimeters
CIJE: 0 RIE: 2 CAT: 04

Dostoevsky (Fyodor)
CIJE: 4 RIE: 1 CAT: 18

Dot Matrix Printing
CIJE: 1 RIE: 0 CAT: 20

DOTSYS III
CIJE: 0 RIE: 1 CAT: 04

Double ABCX Model
CIJE: 6 RIE: 4 CAT: 15

Double Alternation Learning
CIJE: 1 RIE: 0 CAT: 15

Double Base Transformations
CIJE: 0 RIE: 2 CAT: 20

Double Bind Hypothesis
CIJE: 2 RIE: 2 CAT: 15

Double Bind Theory
CIJE: 1 RIE: 1 CAT: 15

Double Classification Skills
CIJE: 1 RIE: 0 CAT: 15

Double Criterion Technique
CIJE: 1 RIE: 0 CAT: 21

Double Cross Validation
CIJE: 0 RIE: 1 CAT: 21

Double Entry Journals
CIJE: 1 RIE: 1 CAT: 16

Double Exponential Smoothing
CIJE: 0 RIE: 1 CAT: 15

Double Extrapolation Technique
CIJE: 0 RIE: 1 CAT: 21

Double I Game
CIJE: 1 RIE: 0 CAT: 21

Double Jeopardy
CIJE: 3 RIE: 0 CAT: 14

Double Majors
CIJE: 2 RIE: 2 CAT: 03

Double Standard
CIJE: 6 RIE: 0 CAT: 16

Double Standardized Scoring
CIJE: 1 RIE: 0 CAT: 21

Double Stimulation Method (Vygotsky)
CIJE: 0 RIE: 1 CAT: 15

Doubleday Multimedia CA
CIJE: 0 RIE: 1 CAT: 17

Doublespeak
CIJE: 35 RIE: 16 CAT: 13

Doublespeak (Public)
CIJE: 19 RIE: 13 CAT: 13

Douglas (Gavin)
CIJE: 1 RIE: 0 CAT: 18

Douglas (William O)
CIJE: 6 RIE: 6 CAT: 18

Douglas College BC
CIJE: 0 RIE: 2 CAT: 17

Douglas County School District CO
CIJE: 2 RIE: 0 CAT: 17

Douglas County School District NV
CIJE: 0 RIE: 1 CAT: 17

Douglas Management Institute MO
CIJE: 1 RIE: 0 CAT: 17

Douglass (Frederick)
CIJE: 9 RIE: 7 CAT: 18

Douglass College NJ
USE Rutgers The State University Douglass College NJ

Douglass Psychology Child Study Center
CIJE: 0 RIE: 1 CAT: 17

Doukhobors
CIJE: 1 RIE: 0 CAT: 08

Dove Test of Mental Aptitude
CIJE: 1 RIE: 0 CAT: 21

Dover Educational Television Ctr (Great Britain)
CIJE: 1 RIE: 0 CAT: 17

Dover Public Schools NJ
CIJE: 2 RIE: 0 CAT: 17

Doves Press
CIJE: 1 RIE: 0 CAT: 17

Dow Chemical Company
CIJE: 2 RIE: 0 CAT: 17

Dowling College NY
CIJE: 1 RIE: 7 CAT: 17

Down These Mean Streets
CIJE: 2 RIE: 0 CAT: 22

Downey Model of the Secondary Phase of Education
CIJE: 0 RIE: 1 CAT: 15

Downey Quality Fit Framework
CIJE: 0 RIE: 1 CAT: 15

Downgrading (Linguistics)
CIJE: 0 RIE: 1 CAT: 13

Downriver Learning Disability Center
CIJE: 1 RIE: 0 CAT: 17

Downs (Anthony)
CIJE: 1 RIE: 0 CAT: 18

Downtown Revitalization
CIJE: 2 RIE: 1 CAT: 16

Downward Mobility
CIJE: 0 RIE: 1 CAT: 16

Doxiadis (Constantine)
CIJE: 1 RIE: 0 CAT: 18

Doyle (Denis)
CIJE: 1 RIE: 0 CAT: 18

Drachler (Norman)
CIJE: 1 RIE: 0 CAT: 18

Draft
CIJE: 2 RIE: 9 CAT: 14

Draft Counseling
CIJE: 1 RIE: 2 CAT: 11

Draft Lottery
CIJE: 1 RIE: 1 CAT: 14

Draft Registration
CIJE: 3 RIE: 2 CAT: 14

Drafting (Legal)
CIJE: 1 RIE: 0 CAT: 14

Dragons
CIJE: 5 RIE: 0 CAT: 16

Drainage
CIJE: 1 RIE: 2 CAT: 20

Drake (Sir Francis)
CIJE: 0 RIE: 2 CAT: 18

Drake Music Memory Test
CIJE: 1 RIE: 0 CAT: 21

Drake Rhythm Test
CIJE: 1 RIE: 0 CAT: 21

Drake University IA
CIJE: 10 RIE: 10 CAT: 17

Drama in Education
CIJE: 198 RIE: 59 CAT: 03

Drama of Democracy
CIJE: 0 RIE: 1 CAT: 22

Dramakinetics
CIJE: 1 RIE: 0 CAT: 03

Dramatic Improvisational Behavior
CIJE: 1 RIE: 0 CAT: 11

Dramatic Theory
CIJE: 6 RIE: 2 CAT: 15

Dramatistic Criticism
CIJE: 9 RIE: 13 CAT: 16

Dramaturgical Perspective
CIJE: 1 RIE: 0 CAT: 16

Dramaturgical Role
CIJE: 3 RIE: 1 CAT: 16

Dramaturgy
CIJE: 1 RIE: 1 CAT: 16

Draper Correctional Center AL
CIJE: 2 RIE: 17 CAT: 17

Drapery Makers
CIJE: 0 RIE: 6 CAT: 09

Draw a Circle Task
CIJE: 0 RIE: 1 CAT: 21

Draw a Classroom Test
CIJE: 0 RIE: 5 CAT: 21

Draw A Face Test
CIJE: 1 RIE: 0 CAT: 21

Draw a Line Slowly Test
CIJE: 1 RIE: 3 CAT: 21

Draw a Line Task
CIJE: 0 RIE: 3 CAT: 21

Draw a Man Task
CIJE: 0 RIE: 1 CAT: 21

Draw a Man Test
CIJE: 9 RIE: 9 CAT: 21

Draw a Person Test
CIJE: 31 RIE: 19 CAT: 21

Draw a Woman Task
CIJE: 0 RIE: 1 CAT: 21

Drawing Stimulus Strategy Measure (Ball)
CIJE: 0 RIE: 1 CAT: 21

DrawReg Computer Program
CIJE: 0 RIE: 2 CAT: 04

Dreams Not Enough (The)
CIJE: 0 RIE: 2 CAT: 22

Dreikurs (Rudolf)
CIJE: 2 RIE: 2 CAT: 18

DREs
USE Directors of Religious Education

Dressel (P L)
CIJE: 0 RIE: 2 CAT: 18

Dressel (Paul L)
CIJE: 0 RIE: 1 CAT: 18

Dressing Room Slogans
CIJE: 1 RIE: 0 CAT: 16

Drew Elementary School GA
CIJE: 1 RIE: 0 CAT: 17

Drew University NJ
CIJE: 9 RIE: 3 CAT: 17

Drexel Institute of Technology PA
CIJE: 1 RIE: 3 CAT: 17

Drexel University PA
CIJE: 29 RIE: 38 CAT: 17

Dribble File
CIJE: 0 RIE: 1 CAT: 16

Drift (Scoring)
CIJE: 0 RIE: 2 CAT: 21
SN See also "Coder Drift"
UF Scoring Drift

DRILL (Authoring System)
CIJE: 0 RIE: 1 CAT: 04

Drill Sergeants
CIJE: 0 RIE: 1 CAT: 09

Drill Teams
CIJE: 2 RIE: 0 CAT: 10

Drilling Tools
CIJE: 0 RIE: 5 CAT: 04

Drinan (Robert F)
CIJE: 1 RIE: 0 CAT: 18

Drinking Age
USE Legal Drinking Age

Drinking Games
CIJE: 0 RIE: 2 CAT: 16

Drive By Shootings
CIJE: 0 RIE: 1 CAT: 16

Drive Theory
CIJE: 2 RIE: 1 CAT: 15

Drive Trains (Automotive)
CIJE: 0 RIE: 3 CAT: 04
UF Automotive Drive Trains

Driver Examinations
CIJE: 1 RIE: 3 CAT: 21

Driver Improvement Analysis
CIJE: 0 RIE: 1 CAT: 16

Driver Improvement Analysts
CIJE: 0 RIE: 1 CAT: 09

Driver License Examiner Supervisors
CIJE: 0 RIE: 2 CAT: 09

Driver Licensing
CIJE: 7 RIE: 13 CAT: 21

Driver Performance
CIJE: 4 RIE: 8 CAT: 21

Drivers
CIJE: 9 RIE: 8 CAT: 09

Driving
CIJE: 3 RIE: 6 CAT: 16

Driving Records
CIJE: 2 RIE: 3 CAT: 16

Driving Regulations
CIJE: 0 RIE: 2 CAT: 14

Driving Simulators
CIJE: 0 RIE: 1 CAT: 04

Drop Ceilings
CIJE: 1 RIE: 0 CAT: 20

Drop In Centers
CIJE: 2 RIE: 1 CAT: 05

Drop In Child Care
CIJE: 0 RIE: 2 CAT: 11

Dropout Prediction Scale
CIJE: 1 RIE: 1 CAT: 21

Dropout Prevention Program
CIJE: 1 RIE: 15 CAT: 19

Dropout Reduction thru Employ Achieve and Motiv NY
USE Project DREAM NY

Drosophila
CIJE: 12 RIE: 0 CAT: 20

Droste Hulshoff (Annette E)
CIJE: 1 RIE: 0 CAT: 18

Drought
CIJE: 2 RIE: 9 CAT: 20

Drownings
CIJE: 9 RIE: 4 CAT: 11

Drucker (Peter F)
CIJE: 2 RIE: 1 CAT: 18

Drug Abuse Education Act 1970
CIJE: 1 RIE: 1 CAT: 14

Drug Abuse Information Research Project
CIJE: 0 RIE: 8 CAT: 19

Drug Abuse Questionnaire (Ferneau and Mueller)
CIJE: 0 RIE: 1 CAT: 21

Drug Abuse Reporting Program
CIJE: 1 RIE: 1 CAT: 19

Drug Abuse Resistance Education Program
CIJE: 2 RIE: 7 CAT: 19
SN Cooperative drug prevention project begun in 1983 between the Los Angeles Police Dept and the Los Angeles Unified School Dist and now expanded to more than 3,000 communities in all 50 states and beyond
UF DARE Program CA; Project DARE (Drug Educ)

Drug and Alcohol Survey
CIJE: 0 RIE: 4 CAT: 21

Drug Calculations
CIJE: 0 RIE: 1 CAT: 20

Drug Exposed Children
CIJE: 0 RIE: 6 CAT: 10
SN See also "Fetal Drug Exposure"

Drug Extractors
CIJE: 1 RIE: 0 CAT: 04

Drug Free School Recognition Program
CIJE: 0 RIE: 1 CAT: 19

Drug Free School Zones
CIJE: 0 RIE: 1 CAT: 16

Drug Free Schools
CIJE: 1 RIE: 17 CAT: 05
SN See also "Network for Drug Free Colleges"

Drug Free Schools and Communities Act 1986
CIJE: 3 RIE: 8 CAT: 14

Drug Free Schools and Communities Act 1988
USE Anti Drug Abuse Act 1988

Drug Free Workplace Act 1988
CIJE: 1 RIE: 0 CAT: 14

Drug Impact Index
CIJE: 0 RIE: 1 CAT: 21

Drug Infusion Project
CIJE: 0 RIE: 9 CAT: 19
UF Infusion Project (Drug Education)

Drug Legislation (New York)
CIJE: 2 RIE: 0 CAT: 14

Drug Orientation Scale (Frankel)
CIJE: 1 RIE: 0 CAT: 21

Drug Perception Scale
CIJE: 1 RIE: 0 CAT: 21

Drug Policy
CIJE: 1 RIE: 2 CAT: 11

Drug Related Morbidity
CIJE: 1 RIE: 0 CAT: 11

Drug Resistance
CIJE: 0 RIE: 1 CAT: 11
SN Ability of diseases to withstand the effects of drugs

Drug Survey Questionnaire (Webster)
CIJE: 1 RIE: 0 CAT: 21

Drug Trafficking
CIJE: 5 RIE: 9 CAT: 16

Drug Use Forecasting Study
CIJE: 0 RIE: 1 CAT: 21

Drugs
CIJE: 35 RIE: 14 CAT: 11

Drugstores
CIJE: 0 RIE: 2 CAT: 05

Drums along the Mohawk
CIJE: 1 RIE: 0 CAT: 22

Drury College MO
CIJE: 0 RIE: 2 CAT: 17

DRV Bilingual Test
CIJE: 0 RIE: 1 CAT: 21

Dry Ice
CIJE: 2 RIE: 0 CAT: 20

Dryden (John)
CIJE: 2 RIE: 1 CAT: 18

Drying Beds
CIJE: 0 RIE: 1 CAT: 20

Drywall Construction
CIJE: 1 RIE: 11 CAT: 20

Du Bellay (Joachim)
CIJE: 1 RIE: 0 CAT: 18

Du Bois (W E B)
CIJE: 21 RIE: 5 CAT: 18

Du Gard (Roger Martin)
CIJE: 1 RIE: 0 CAT: 18

Du Pont Corporation
CIJE: 1 RIE: 0 CAT: 17
UF DuPont Company; E I DuPont de Nemours and Co

Dual Audio Television Instruction
CIJE: 0 RIE: 7 CAT: 15

Dual Certification
CIJE: 0 RIE: 2 CAT: 15

Dual Coding Hypothesis
USE Dual Coding Theory

Dual Coding Theory
CIJE: 3 RIE: 1 CAT: 15
UF Dual Coding Hypothesis

Dual Degrees
CIJE: 7 RIE: 1 CAT: 16

Dual Diagnosis
CIJE: 17 RIE: 3 CAT: 11

Dual Economy Theory
CIJE: 1 RIE: 2 CAT: 15

Dual Employed Coping Scales
CIJE: 0 RIE: 1 CAT: 21

Dual Function Librarians
CIJE: 0 RIE: 1 CAT: 09

Dual Grading
CIJE: 1 RIE: 1 CAT: 15

Dual Independent Map Encoding
CIJE: 1 RIE: 2 CAT: 20

Dual Labor Market Theory
CIJE: 0 RIE: 3 CAT: 15

Dual Language Text
CIJE: 0 RIE: 3 CAT: 21

Dual Mode Learning
CIJE: 0 RIE: 2 CAT: 15

Dual Personality
CIJE: 1 RIE: 0 CAT: 11

Dual Perspective Approach
CIJE: 0 RIE: 2 CAT: 15

Dual Principalship
CIJE: 2 RIE: 1 CAT: 15

Dual Progress Plan
CIJE: 0 RIE: 2 CAT: 15

Dual Relationships (Counseling)
CIJE: 1 RIE: 0 CAT: 11

Dual Role
CIJE: 3 RIE: 3 CAT: 16

Dual School Districts
CIJE: 2 RIE: 0 CAT: 16

Dual Task Interference
USE Intertask Interference

Dual Tasks
CIJE: 8 RIE: 5 CAT: 21

Dubin Inquiry (Canada)
CIJE: 0 RIE: 1 CAT: 19

Dublin College of Speech Therapy (Ireland)
CIJE: 1 RIE: 0 CAT: 17

Dubliners
CIJE: 0 RIE: 1 CAT: 22

Dubnoff School for Educational Therapy CA
CIJE: 1 RIE: 1 CAT: 17

Dubois (Pierre)
CIJE: 0 RIE: 1 CAT: 18

Ducharme (Rejean)
CIJE: 0 RIE: 1 CAT: 18

Duchesne School District UT
CIJE: 0 RIE: 1 CAT: 17

Duckweed
CIJE: 3 RIE: 0 CAT: 20

Duelo en el Paraiso
CIJE: 1 RIE: 0 CAT: 22

Dues Checkoff
CIJE: 0 RIE: 47 CAT: 16

DUET Videoconferencing Program
USE Distance University Education via Television

DUET Workshops
CIJE: 1 RIE: 0 CAT: 02
SN Development of University English Teaching Project (England)

Dugger Scale
CIJE: 0 RIE: 1 CAT: 21

Duhamel (Georges)
CIJE: 1 RIE: 0 CAT: 18

Dukakis (Michael)
CIJE: 7 RIE: 4 CAT: 18

Duke Ellington School of the Arts DC
CIJE: 0 RIE: 3 CAT: 17

Duke Power Company NC
CIJE: 0 RIE: 1 CAT: 17

Duke University NC
CIJE: 60 RIE: 23 CAT: 17

Duluth Public Schools MN
CIJE: 5 RIE: 4 CAT: 17

Dulwich College (England)
CIJE: 1 RIE: 0 CAT: 17

Dumazedier (Joffre)
CIJE: 1 RIE: 0 CAT: 18

Dumb Waiter (Pinter)
CIJE: 0 RIE: 1 CAT: 22

Dummy Variables
CIJE: 7 RIE: 3 CAT: 21

Dumond (Don E)
CIJE: 0 RIE: 1 CAT: 18

Dunbar (Paul Lawrence)
CIJE: 1 RIE: 0 CAT: 18

Dunbarton College DC
CIJE: 1 RIE: 0 CAT: 17

Duncan (Otis Dudley)
CIJE: 0 RIE: 5 CAT: 18

Duncan Multiple Range Test
CIJE: 6 RIE: 2 CAT: 21

Duncan Socioeconomic Index
CIJE: 5 RIE: 5 CAT: 21

Duncker (Karl)
CIJE: 2 RIE: 0 CAT: 18

Dundalk Community College MD
CIJE: 4 RIE: 0 CAT: 17

Dundee College of Education (Scotland)
CIJE: 2 RIE: 1 CAT: 17

Dundee Institute of Technology (Scotland)
CIJE: 0 RIE: 1 CAT: 17

Dundee School CO
CIJE: 0 RIE: 1 CAT: 17

Dunlap (John)
CIJE: 1 RIE: 0 CAT: 18

Dunlap (William S)
CIJE: 0 RIE: 1 CAT: 18

Dunn Object Sorting Task
CIJE: 0 RIE: 2 CAT: 21

Dunn Visual Discrimination Task
CIJE: 0 RIE: 1 CAT: 21

Dunnett Test
CIJE: 1 RIE: 1 CAT: 21

Dunns Marriage Role Expectation Inventory
CIJE: 1 RIE: 0 CAT: 21

Dunwoody Industrial Institute MN
CIJE: 1 RIE: 2 CAT: 17

Duopoly Game
CIJE: 1 RIE: 0 CAT: 21

DuPage High School District IL
CIJE: 0 RIE: 2 CAT: 17

Duplex Design
CIJE: 1 RIE: 4 CAT: 21

Duplicate Items (Information)
CIJE: 9 RIE: 0 CAT: 04

Duplicating Equipment
CIJE: 1 RIE: 5 CAT: 04

DuPonceau (Peter Stephen)
CIJE: 0 RIE: 1 CAT: 18

DuPont Company
USE Du Pont Corporation

Duquesne University PA
CIJE: 8 RIE: 10 CAT: 17

Duras (Marguerite)
CIJE: 1 RIE: 0 CAT: 18

Durham (John)
CIJE: 0 RIE: 1 CAT: 18

Durham City School District NC
CIJE: 0 RIE: 1 CAT: 17

Durham College of Applied Arts and Technology ON
CIJE: 0 RIE: 1 CAT: 17

Durham County School District NC
CIJE: 0 RIE: 2 CAT: 17

Durham Education Improvement Program
CIJE: 1 RIE: 13 CAT: 19

Durham Middlefield School District CT
CIJE: 1 RIE: 0 CAT: 17

Durham Summer School (England)
CIJE: 1 RIE: 0 CAT: 17

Durkheim (Emile)
CIJE: 35 RIE: 3 CAT: 18

Durkin (Dolores)
CIJE: 2 RIE: 3 CAT: 18

Durkin (Kevin)
CIJE: 0 RIE: 1 CAT: 18

Durrell Analysis of Reading Difficulty
CIJE: 1 RIE: 7 CAT: 21

Durrell Listening Reading Series
CIJE: 3 RIE: 3 CAT: 22

Durrenmatt (Friedrich)
CIJE: 7 RIE: 1 CAT: 18

Dushane Emergency Fund
CIJE: 1 RIE: 0 CAT: 17

Dushkin (Alexander)
CIJE: 1 RIE: 0 CAT: 18

DUSO Affectivity Assessment Device
CIJE: 2 RIE: 1 CAT: 21

Dutch Identity (Testing)
CIJE: 1 RIE: 1 CAT: 21

Dutch Modern Language Association
CIJE: 0 RIE: 1 CAT: 17

Dutch Speaking
CIJE: 0 RIE: 0 CAT: 08

Dutchess Community College NY
CIJE: 1 RIE: 7 CAT: 17

Dutemple Elementary School
CIJE: 0 RIE: 1 CAT: 17

Dutschke (Rudi)
CIJE: 2 RIE: 0 CAT: 18

Dutton Mathematics Attitude Scale
CIJE: 3 RIE: 3 CAT: 21

Duval County Public Schools FL
CIJE: 4 RIE: 7 CAT: 17

Duval County School Board FL
CIJE: 1 RIE: 18 CAT: 17

DV Child Development Inventory
CIJE: 0 RIE: 1 CAT: 21

DVI Technology
USE Digital Video Interactive

Dvorine Color Blindness Tests
CIJE: 1 RIE: 0 CAT: 21

Dwight D Eisenhower Math and Science Educ Program
CIJE: 2 RIE: 10 CAT: 19
UF Eisenhower Math and Science Educ Program

Dworkin (Andrea)
CIJE: 0 RIE: 1 CAT: 18

Dworkin (Ronald)
CIJE: 2 RIE: 0 CAT: 18

DX Diagnostic Testing System
CIJE: 0 RIE: 2 CAT: 04

Dyadic Adjustment Scale
CIJE: 6 RIE: 0 CAT: 21

Dyadic Consensus
CIJE: 1 RIE: 1 CAT: 15

Dyadic Interaction Analysis
CIJE: 42 RIE: 30 CAT: 15

Dyadic Observation System
CIJE: 0 RIE: 1 CAT: 15

Dyadic Parent Child Interaction Coding System
CIJE: 1 RIE: 0 CAT: 21

Dyads
CIJE: 78 RIE: 21 CAT: 11

Dybwad (Gunnar)
CIJE: 1 RIE: 0 CAT: 18

Dyer Act
CIJE: 0 RIE: 1 CAT: 14

Dyes
CIJE: 10 RIE: 3 CAT: 20

Dying
CIJE: 3 RIE: 4 CAT: 11

Dyirbal
CIJE: 1 RIE: 1 CAT: 13
SN A Pama-Nyungan language

Dylan (Bob)
CIJE: 4 RIE: 0 CAT: 18

Dynalevel
CIJE: 1 RIE: 0 CAT: 04

Dynamic Assessment
CIJE: 30 RIE: 13 CAT: 21

Dynamic Concept Analysis
CIJE: 0 RIE: 1 CAT: 15

Dynamic Instructional Planning
CIJE: 0 RIE: 1 CAT: 15
SN See also "Blackboard Instructional Planner"

Dynamic Learning System
CIJE: 1 RIE: 0 CAT: 15

Dynamic Programing
CIJE: 3 RIE: 3 CAT: 20

Dynamic Simulation
CIJE: 0 RIE: 3 CAT: 15

Dynamic Stories
CIJE: 0 RIE: 1 CAT: 16
SN Stories in which readers must make choices about the direction the stories take at pivotal points in the plots

Dynamic Support
CIJE: 0 RIE: 1 CAT: 15
SN Software use in which the amount of assistance provided by the computer is systematically decreased as novices gain expertise

Dynamics
CIJE: 20 RIE: 1 CAT: 20
SN Use of a more specific term is recommended, e.g., "Business Dynamics," "Dynamics (Music)," "Fluid Dynamics," "Instructional Dynamics," "Modern Management Dynamics," "Storage Dynamics (Memory)," "System Dynamics," or the Descriptor "Group Dynamics"

Dynamics (Music)
CIJE: 1 RIE: 0 CAT: 16
SN Variation and gradation in musical loudness or softness — indicated in musical notation by words or signs, e.g., piano, forte, crescendo, diminuendo

Dynamod II
CIJE: 0 RIE: 12 CAT: 04

Dynamometers
CIJE: 8 RIE: 0 CAT: 04
SN See also "Ergometers"

Dysarthria
CIJE: 12 RIE: 2 CAT: 11

Dyscalculia
CIJE: 9 RIE: 6 CAT: 11

Dyscontrol Syndrome
CIJE: 1 RIE: 0 CAT: 11

Dysfunctional Behavior
CIJE: 11 RIE: 9 CAT: 11

Dysfunctional Family
CIJE: 2 RIE: 9 CAT: 11
UF Disfunctional Family

Dysgraphia
CIJE: 10 RIE: 4 CAT: 11

Dyslalia
CIJE: 1 RIE: 0 CAT: 11

Dysmathematics
CIJE: 0 RIE: 1 CAT: 15
SN A term for low achievement in mathematics in the compulsory school according to set standards

Dysmenorrhea
CIJE: 2 RIE: 0 CAT: 11
UF Menstrual Cramps

Dysphagia
CIJE: 1 RIE: 1 CAT: 11
UF Swallowing Difficulties

Dysphagia Paralytica
CIJE: 1 RIE: 0 CAT: 11

Dyssymbolia
CIJE: 0 RIE: 1 CAT: 11

Dystopia
CIJE: 4 RIE: 2 CAT: 16

Dzilth Na O Dith Hle Community School NM
CIJE: 0 RIE: 2 CAT: 17

E 2 Scale (Rimland)
CIJE: 0 RIE: 0 CAT: 21

E Coefficient
CIJE: 3 RIE: 0 CAT: 21

E I DuPont de Nemours and Co
USE Du Pont Corporation

E Prime
CIJE: 21 RIE: 1 CAT: 13
SN Technique for increasing awareness of abstraction through the deliberate deletion of all forms of the verb "to be"

E R Johnstone Center
CIJE: 0 RIE: 1 CAT: 17

E R Snyder Continuation High School CA
CIJE: 1 RIE: 0 CAT: 17

E Z Cassette Player
CIJE: 0 RIE: 1 CAT: 04

EAC Student Ratings Form
CIJE: 0 RIE: 1 CAT: 21

Each in His Own Way
CIJE: 1 RIE: 0 CAT: 22

Each One Reach One Program
CIJE: 0 RIE: 1 CAT: 19

Eager to Learn
CIJE: 0 RIE: 1 CAT: 22

Eagle and the Mole
CIJE: 0 RIE: 1 CAT: 22

Eagle Feathers
CIJE: 0 RIE: 1 CAT: 16

Eagles
CIJE: 3 RIE: 0 CAT: 20

Eagleton (Terry)
CIJE: 3 RIE: 1 CAT: 18

Eagleton (Thomas)
CIJE: 2 RIE: 1 CAT: 18

Eagleville Hospital and Training Center PA
CIJE: 1 RIE: 1 CAT: 17

Eakins (Thomas)
CIJE: 0 RIE: 1 CAT: 18

Ear Hand Coordination
CIJE: 0 RIE: 0 CAT: 11

Ear Infections
CIJE: 0 RIE: 1 CAT: 11
SN See also "Otitis Media"

Ear Order Strategy
CIJE: 1 RIE: 0 CAT: 15

Ear Plugging
USE Earplugs

Earhart (Amelia)
CIJE: 1 RIE: 1 CAT: 18

Earl Warren Legal Training Program Inc NY
CIJE: 0 RIE: 1 CAT: 17

Earle B Wood Junior High School MD
CIJE: 1 RIE: 0 CAT: 17

Earlham College IN
CIJE: 12 RIE: 11 CAT: 17

Early Adolescent Helper Program NY
CIJE: 1 RIE: 0 CAT: 19

Early Adolescent School Role Strain Inventory
CIJE: 0 RIE: 1 CAT: 21

Early Alert Retention System
CIJE: 0 RIE: 2 CAT: 04

Early American Textbook Collection
CIJE: 0 RIE: 2 CAT: 22

EARLY Assessment (Test)
CIJE: 0 RIE: 1 CAT: 21

Early Childhood Assessment Battery
CIJE: 0 RIE: 1 CAT: 21

Early Childhood Assessment Instrument
CIJE: 0 RIE: 1 CAT: 21

Early Childhood Assessment Project MN
CIJE: 1 RIE: 1 CAT: 19

Early Childhood Combination Program NE
CIJE: 0 RIE: 1 CAT: 19

Early Childhood Consortium (ASCD)
CIJE: 0 RIE: 1 CAT: 17
UF ASCD Early Childhood Consortium

Early Childhood Council CT
CIJE: 1 RIE: 0 CAT: 17

Early Childhood Development Act (Missouri 1984)
CIJE: 0 RIE: 1 CAT: 14

Early Childhood Development Programs
CIJE: 0 RIE: 7 CAT: 19

Early Childhood Direction Centers NY
CIJE: 0 RIE: 1 CAT: 05

Early Childhood Educare
USE Educare

Early Childhood Education and Assistance Prog WA
CIJE: 0 RIE: 3 CAT: 19
UF ECEAP WA

Early Childhood Education Learning System
CIJE: 0 RIE: 2 CAT: 15

Early Childhood Education Linkage System
CIJE: 0 RIE: 3 CAT: 19

Early Childhood Education Week
CIJE: 0 RIE: 1 CAT: 19

Early Childhood Environment Rating Scale
CIJE: 5 RIE: 3 CAT: 21

Early Childhood Family Education
CIJE: 0 RIE: 6 CAT: 03

Early Childhood Inventories Project
CIJE: 0 RIE: 1 CAT: 19

Early Childhood Laboratories
CIJE: 0 RIE: 1 CAT: 05

Early Childhood Language Centered Intervention
CIJE: 0 RIE: 1 CAT: 19

Early Childhood Longitudinal Survey
CIJE: 0 RIE: 2 CAT: 21

Early Childhood Observation Form
CIJE: 0 RIE: 1 CAT: 16

Early Childhood Services (Alberta)
CIJE: 1 RIE: 2 CAT: 19

Early Childhood Specialist Library Program
CIJE: 0 RIE: 3 CAT: 19

Early Childhood Transition Program KS
CIJE: 0 RIE: 1 CAT: 19

Early Education Center MO
CIJE: 1 RIE: 0 CAT: 17

Early Education Program for Children with Disabil
CIJE: 0 RIE: 1 CAT: 19

Early Education Screening Test Battery
CIJE: 0 RIE: 2 CAT: 21

Early Eligibility Determination (Financial Aid)
CIJE: 0 RIE: 1 CAT: 16

Early English Composition Assessment Program
CIJE: 0 RIE: 1 CAT: 19

Early Field Experience
CIJE: 2 RIE: 4 CAT: 15

Early Fives Program MI
CIJE: 0 RIE: 1 CAT: 19

Early Formal Education for the Very Young
USE Hothousing of Preschoolers

Early Graduation
CIJE: 0 RIE: 10 CAT: 16

Early Identification
CIJE: 43 RIE: 26 CAT: 11

Early Identification Assessment Battery
CIJE: 0 RIE: 1 CAT: 21

Early Identification Screening Inventory
CIJE: 0 RIE: 1 CAT: 21

Early Intervention Developmental Profile
CIJE: 1 RIE: 0 CAT: 21

Early Intervention Effectiveness Institute UT
CIJE: 1 RIE: 0 CAT: 17

Early Language Development Test
USE Test of Early Language Development

Early Learning Centers
CIJE: 1 RIE: 0 CAT: 05

Early Lifestyle Program
CIJE: 0 RIE: 1 CAT: 19

Early Literacy
USE Emergent Literacy

Early Maturation
CIJE: 3 RIE: 1 CAT: 11

Early Periodic Screening Diagnosis and Treatment
CIJE: 2 RIE: 24 CAT: 11

Early Periodic Screening Diagnosis Treatment Prog
CIJE: 1 RIE: 5 CAT: 19

Early Prevention of School Failure
CIJE: 4 RIE: 7 CAT: 19

Early Provisions for School Success Program HI
CIJE: 0 RIE: 1 CAT: 19

Early Reading Test
CIJE: 0 RIE: 1 CAT: 21

Early Retirement Incentive Program (California)
CIJE: 0 RIE: 2 CAT: 19

Early School Assessment
CIJE: 0 RIE: 1 CAT: 21

Early School Environment Study
CIJE: 1 RIE: 1 CAT: 19

Early School Personality Questionnaire
CIJE: 2 RIE: 1 CAT: 21

Early Screening Profiles
CIJE: 0 RIE: 2 CAT: 21

Early Social Communication Scales
CIJE: 1 RIE: 1 CAT: 21

Early Start Preschool Program
CIJE: 0 RIE: 2 CAT: 19

Early Start to Good Health Curriculum
CIJE: 0 RIE: 1 CAT: 03

Early to Read
CIJE: 0 RIE: 2 CAT: 19

Early Training Center TN
CIJE: 0 RIE: 1 CAT: 17

Early Training Project
CIJE: 4 RIE: 4 CAT: 19

Early Warning Test NJ
CIJE: 0 RIE: 1 CAT: 21

Early Writing
CIJE: 14 RIE: 6 CAT: 13

Earn and Learn Program IL
CIJE: 0 RIE: 1 CAT: 19

Earned Income Tax Credit
CIJE: 0 RIE: 5 CAT: 14

Earning Potential
CIJE: 7 RIE: 4 CAT: 16

Earplugs
CIJE: 0 RIE: 1 CAT: 04
UF Ear Plugging

Earth
CIJE: 17 RIE: 11 CAT: 20

Earth Core
CIJE: 1 RIE: 1 CAT: 20

Earth Day
CIJE: 15 RIE: 2 CAT: 12

Earth Education Program
CIJE: 0 RIE: 1 CAT: 19

Earth Homes
CIJE: 0 RIE: 1 CAT: 20

Earth Lab
CIJE: 0 RIE: 1 CAT: 19
UF Project Earth Lab

Earth Science Curriculum Project
CIJE: 15 RIE: 34 CAT: 19

Earth Science Educational Program
CIJE: 1 RIE: 0 CAT: 19

ECEAP WA
USE Early Childhood Education and Assistance Prog WA

Echo (Krus et al)
CIJE: 1 RIE: 1 CAT: 21

Echo Reading
CIJE: 2 RIE: 0 CAT: 15

Echoic Response Inventory for Children
CIJE: 0 RIE: 2 CAT: 21

ECIA
USE Education Consolidation and Improvement Act 1981

ECIA Chapter 1 Migrant Programs
CIJE: 0 RIE: 24 CAT: 19

ECIA Chapter 1 National Assessment
USE National Assessment of Chapter 1

Eckerd College FL
CIJE: 4 RIE: 4 CAT: 17

Eckerd Wilderness Camp
CIJE: 0 RIE: 4 CAT: 17

Eckstein (Jerome)
CIJE: 1 RIE: 0 CAT: 18

Eclectic Approach
USE Eclecticism

Eclectic Counseling
CIJE: 1 RIE: 0 CAT: 15

Eclectic Examination
CIJE: 1 RIE: 0 CAT: 21
SN See also "Individualized Eclectic Examination"

Eclectic Teaching
CIJE: 1 RIE: 1 CAT: 15

Eclecticism
CIJE: 18 RIE: 1 CAT: 16
UF Eclectic Approach

Eclipses
CIJE: 0 RIE: 1 CAT: 20
SN See also "Solar Eclipses" and "Lunar Eclipses"

Eclogue Tradition
CIJE: 1 RIE: 0 CAT: 13

Eco Maps
CIJE: 0 RIE: 2 CAT: 15
SN Visual drawings of all resources available in a family system, indicating relationships between a person and the various resources or people affecting that person's life

Ecobehavioral Analysis
CIJE: 8 RIE: 2 CAT: 15

Ecobehavioral Counseling
CIJE: 0 RIE: 1 CAT: 11

Ecofeminism
CIJE: 2 RIE: 1 CAT: 15
SN The drawing of parallels between treatment of women and treatment of the planet

Ecogame
CIJE: 1 RIE: 0 CAT: 16

Ecole Centrale de Lyon (France)
CIJE: 0 RIE: 1 CAT: 17

Ecole Superieure de Commerce de Lyon (France)
USE Lyon Graduate School of Business (France)

Ecole Superieure de Commerce de Nantes (France)
USE Nantes Graduate School of Business (France)

Ecological Assessment
CIJE: 18 RIE: 7 CAT: 15

Ecological Communication Model
CIJE: 1 RIE: 1 CAT: 15

Ecological Dissonance
CIJE: 0 RIE: 1 CAT: 16

Ecological Fallacy (Testing)
CIJE: 1 RIE: 1 CAT: 21

Ecological Inventory Strategies
CIJE: 2 RIE: 0 CAT: 15

Ecological Paradigm
CIJE: 14 RIE: 9 CAT: 15

Ecological Perspective
CIJE: 3 RIE: 1 CAT: 15

Ecological Psychology
CIJE: 21 RIE: 12 CAT: 16

Ecological Validity
CIJE: 10 RIE: 10 CAT: 20

Ecomuseum Model
CIJE: 0 RIE: 1 CAT: 15

Economic and Social Council
CIJE: 1 RIE: 0 CAT: 17

Economic and Social Research Council (England)
CIJE: 5 RIE: 4 CAT: 17

Economic and Youth Opportunities Agency
CIJE: 0 RIE: 1 CAT: 17

Economic Awareness
CIJE: 18 RIE: 32 CAT: 20

Economic Commission for Asia and the Far East
CIJE: 0 RIE: 1 CAT: 17

Economic Competitiveness
CIJE: 0 RIE: 2 CAT: 16

Economic Concepts
CIJE: 78 RIE: 17 CAT: 15

Economic Conversion
CIJE: 0 RIE: 3 CAT: 20

Economic Decline
CIJE: 11 RIE: 6 CAT: 16

Economic Dependency
USE Dependency (Economics)

Economic Development Administration
CIJE: 0 RIE: 0 CAT: 17

Economic Dislocation Worker Adjust Assist Act 1988
CIJE: 0 RIE: 10 CAT: 14
SN See also "Worker Adjustment Assistance Programs"

Economic Diversification
CIJE: 0 RIE: 1 CAT: 16

Economic Efficiency
CIJE: 5 RIE: 2 CAT: 20

Economic Equity
CIJE: 9 RIE: 6 CAT: 20

Economic Evaluation
CIJE: 1 RIE: 0 CAT: 15

Economic Growth
CIJE: 17 RIE: 20 CAT: 20

Economic Impact Studies
CIJE: 16 RIE: 60 CAT: 16
SN See also "Impact Studies"

Economic Indicators
CIJE: 2 RIE: 5 CAT: 16

Economic Literacy
CIJE: 9 RIE: 3 CAT: 03

Economic Literature Index
CIJE: 0 RIE: 1 CAT: 22

Economic Opportunities Commissions
CIJE: 0 RIE: 1 CAT: 17

Economic Opportunities Programs and Services
CIJE: 0 RIE: 1 CAT: 17

Economic Opportunity Act 1964
CIJE: 6 RIE: 54 CAT: 14

Economic Opportunity Act Title I
CIJE: 1 RIE: 2 CAT: 14

Economic Opportunity Act Title II
CIJE: 0 RIE: 3 CAT: 14

Economic Opportunity Act Title III
CIJE: 0 RIE: 3 CAT: 14

Economic Opportunity Act Title V
CIJE: 0 RIE: 1 CAT: 14

Economic Opportunity Amendments 1967
CIJE: 0 RIE: 1 CAT: 14

Economic Planning
CIJE: 2 RIE: 7 CAT: 20

Economic Recovery Tax Act 1981
CIJE: 3 RIE: 0 CAT: 14

Economic Research Service
CIJE: 0 RIE: 3 CAT: 17

Economic Revitalization
CIJE: 0 RIE: 7 CAT: 16

Economic Social Commission for Asia and Pacific
CIJE: 1 RIE: 2 CAT: 17

Economic Stabilization
CIJE: 4 RIE: 1 CAT: 20

Economic Theory
CIJE: 37 RIE: 18 CAT: 15

Economic Trends
CIJE: 15 RIE: 18 CAT: 20

Economics a Programmed Text
CIJE: 1 RIE: 0 CAT: 22

Economics of Information
CIJE: 3 RIE: 1 CAT: 03

Economics Values Inventory
CIJE: 2 RIE: 1 CAT: 21

Economies of Scale
CIJE: 18 RIE: 19 CAT: 20

Economist (The)
CIJE: 0 RIE: 2 CAT: 22

Economy Food Plan
CIJE: 0 RIE: 1 CAT: 19

Ecosphere
CIJE: 1 RIE: 0 CAT: 20

Ecotherapy
CIJE: 0 RIE: 1 CAT: 11

Ecotran Systems Inc
CIJE: 0 RIE: 1 CAT: 17

Ectomorph
CIJE: 1 RIE: 1 CAT: 11

Ecuador
CIJE: 29 RIE: 55 CAT: 07

Ecumenism
CIJE: 4 RIE: 4 CAT: 16

Ed D
USE Doctor of Education Degrees

Ed Net
CIJE: 0 RIE: 1 CAT: 20
UF Oregon Educational Television Network

Eddington (Arthur Stanley)
CIJE: 1 RIE: 0 CAT: 18

Eddy Currents
CIJE: 1 RIE: 2 CAT: 20

Edelman (Marian Wright)
CIJE: 3 RIE: 0 CAT: 18

Edes (Benjamin)
CIJE: 1 RIE: 0 CAT: 18

Edge Cities
CIJE: 2 RIE: 2 CAT: 07
SN Areas on the outskirts of urban cores

Edge Hill College of Education (England)
CIJE: 1 RIE: 0 CAT: 17

Edge Notched Cards
CIJE: 1 RIE: 0 CAT: 04

Edgewater Park Township School District NJ
CIJE: 0 RIE: 1 CAT: 17

Edgewood Independent School District TX
CIJE: 2 RIE: 13 CAT: 17

Edgewood Independent School District v Kirby
CIJE: 2 RIE: 4 CAT: 14

Edina Public Schools MN
CIJE: 3 RIE: 3 CAT: 17

Edinboro State College PA
CIJE: 1 RIE: 2 CAT: 17

Edinboro University of Pennsylvania
CIJE: 0 RIE: 3 CAT: 17

Edinburgh Articulation Test
CIJE: 1 RIE: 0 CAT: 21

Edinburgh Handedness Inventory
CIJE: 4 RIE: 0 CAT: 21

Edison (Thomas)
CIJE: 6 RIE: 1 CAT: 18

Edison Community College FL
CIJE: 3 RIE: 4 CAT: 17

Edison Responsive Environment
CIJE: 7 RIE: 9 CAT: 15

Edison State Community College OH
CIJE: 0 RIE: 1 CAT: 17

Edison Township Schools NJ
CIJE: 0 RIE: 1 CAT: 17

Editing Routines (Computer)
CIJE: 3 RIE: 1 CAT: 20

Edition Theory
CIJE: 1 RIE: 0 CAT: 15

Editions
CIJE: 1 RIE: 1 CAT: 16
SN See also "Variant Editions," "Special Editions," "Armed Services Editions"

Editor Role
CIJE: 12 RIE: 9 CAT: 16

Editorial Boards
CIJE: 2 RIE: 3 CAT: 10

Editorial Content
CIJE: 2 RIE: 1 CAT: 16

Editorial Mechanics
CIJE: 1 RIE: 1 CAT: 16

Editorial Omissions
CIJE: 1 RIE: 1 CAT: 16

Editorial Policy
CIJE: 31 RIE: 43 CAT: 16

EDL Reading Versatility Tests
CIJE: 0 RIE: 2 CAT: 21

Edmonds (Ronald R)
CIJE: 0 RIE: 4 CAT: 18

Edmonds (Walter D)
CIJE: 1 RIE: 0 CAT: 18

Edmonds Community College WA
CIJE: 1 RIE: 5 CAT: 17

Edmonds Learning Style Identification Exercise
CIJE: 2 RIE: 1 CAT: 21

Edmonds School District WA
CIJE: 1 RIE: 2 CAT: 17

Edmonton Instructional Materials Center (Canada)
CIJE: 1 RIE: 0 CAT: 17

Edmonton Public Schools (Canada)
CIJE: 4 RIE: 4 CAT: 17

Edmonton Public Schools AB
CIJE: 1 RIE: 7 CAT: 17

EDPA Institute
CIJE: 0 RIE: 1 CAT: 17

EDUCAR Foundation (Brazil)
USE National Foundation Youth and Adult Educ (Brazil)

EduCard
CIJE: 0 RIE: 3 CAT: 04
UF Adult Education Access Card

Educare
CIJE: 4 RIE: 13 CAT: 15
SN Combination of education and care
UF Early Childhood Educare

Educateurs
CIJE: 0 RIE: 1 CAT: 09

Educating Americans for the 21st Century
CIJE: 0 RIE: 4 CAT: 22

Education 2000 (Global Education)
CIJE: 0 RIE: 1 CAT: 19

Education Act 1944 (England)
CIJE: 3 RIE: 0 CAT: 14

Education Act 1968 (Kenya)
CIJE: 0 RIE: 1 CAT: 14

Education Act 1970 (New Jersey)
CIJE: 0 RIE: 1 CAT: 14

Education Act 1981 (England)
CIJE: 16 RIE: 8 CAT: 14

Education Administration Quarterly
CIJE: 0 RIE: 1 CAT: 22

Education Alternatives Inc
CIJE: 3 RIE: 0 CAT: 17

Education Amendment Act 1980 (Ontario)
USE Bill 82 (Ontario)

Education Amendments 1967
CIJE: 0 RIE: 3 CAT: 14
UF Public Law 90 247

Education Amendments 1970
CIJE: 0 RIE: 1 CAT: 14

Education Amendments 1972
CIJE: 10 RIE: 28 CAT: 14

Education Amendments 1972 Title IV
USE Indian Education Act 1972

Education Amendments 1972 Title IX
USE Title IX Education Amendments 1972

Education Amendments 1972 Title VII
USE Emergency School Aid Act 1972

Education Amendments 1974
CIJE: 6 RIE: 257 CAT: 14
UF Public Law 93 380

Education Amendments 1974 Title II
USE Equal Educational Opportunities Act 1974

Education Amendments 1975
CIJE: 0 RIE: 2 CAT: 14

Education Amendments 1976
CIJE: 11 RIE: 64 CAT: 14
UF Public Law 94 482

Education Amendments 1978
CIJE: 4 RIE: 15 CAT: 14
UF Public Law 95 561

Education Amendments 1978 Title XI
USE Title XI Education Amendments 1978

Education Amendments 1980
CIJE: 6 RIE: 6 CAT: 14

Education Amendments 1978 Section 143
USE Migrant Education Section 143 Projects

Education and Community Project (Israel)
CIJE: 0 RIE: 4 CAT: 19
UF Project Education and Community Devel (Israel)

Education and Ecstasy
CIJE: 0 RIE: 1 CAT: 22

Education and Local Development Project
CIJE: 0 RIE: 4 CAT: 19

Education and Social Environment (Netherlands)
USE Onderwijs un Sociaal Milieu (Netherlands)

Education and the Economy Alliance
CIJE: 0 RIE: 1 CAT: 19

Education and Training Amer Competitiveness Act
CIJE: 0 RIE: 0 CAT: 14

Education and Work Councils
CIJE: 0 RIE: 2 CAT: 10

Education and Work Program
CIJE: 0 RIE: 1 CAT: 19

Education and World Affairs NY
CIJE: 0 RIE: 1 CAT: 17

Education Commission (India)
CIJE: 0 RIE: 3 CAT: 17

Education Commission of the States
CIJE: 17 RIE: 7 CAT: 17

Education Commission of the States CO
CIJE: 22 RIE: 17 CAT: 17

Education Consolidation and Improvement Act 1981
CIJE: 9 RIE: 38 CAT: 14
UF ECIA; Education Improvement and Consolidation Act 1981

Education Consolidation Improvement Act Chapter 1
CIJE: 79 RIE: 688 CAT: 14
SN See also under "ECIA Chapter 1..."
UF Chapter 1 ECIA

Education Consolidation Improvement Act Chapter 2
CIJE: 23 RIE: 108 CAT: 14
UF Chapter 2 ECIA

Education Corps (Iran)
CIJE: 0 RIE: 1 CAT: 17

Education Council Act 1991
USE National Council on Educ Standards and Testing Act

Education Data Elements Dictionary
CIJE: 0 RIE: 3 CAT: 22

Education Data Improvement Project
CIJE: 0 RIE: 8 CAT: 19

Education Development Center MA
CIJE: 1 RIE: 3 CAT: 17

Education Economy Relationship
CIJE: 18 RIE: 20 CAT: 15

Education Entrance Examination SC
CIJE: 0 RIE: 1 CAT: 21

Education Finance Act 1990 (Texas)
CIJE: 0 RIE: 0 CAT: 14

Education Financial Planning Model
CIJE: 1 RIE: 0 CAT: 04

Education for All Handicapped Children Act
CIJE: 535 RIE: 699 CAT: 14
SN After 1990, called "Individuals with Disabilities Education Act"
UF Public Law 94 142

Education for Economic Security Act 1984
CIJE: 0 RIE: 8 CAT: 14
UF Public Law 98 377

Education for Employment IL
CIJE: 0 RIE: 0 CAT: 19
UF Illinois Education for Employment Program

Education for Employment Programs
CIJE: 1 RIE: 0 CAT: 19

Education for Employment WI
CIJE: 0 RIE: 0 CAT: 19
UF Wisconsin Education for Employment Program

Education for Independent Living Model Program
CIJE: 0 RIE: 1 CAT: 19

Education for Parenthood Attitude Scale
CIJE: 0 RIE: 1 CAT: 21

Education for Peace Project
CIJE: 2 RIE: 0 CAT: 19

Education for Self Reliance (Tanzania)
CIJE: 1 RIE: 1 CAT: 19

Education for Tomorrows Jobs
CIJE: 0 RIE: 2 CAT: 22

Education for Work Linkage Project
CIJE: 0 RIE: 6 CAT: 19

Education Improvement and Consolidation Act 1981
USE Education Consolidation and Improvement Act 1981

Education Improvement Project
CIJE: 1 RIE: 7 CAT: 19

Education Index
CIJE: 2 RIE: 4 CAT: 22

Education Libraries
CIJE: 5 RIE: 4 CAT: 05

Education Management Information Exchange
CIJE: 0 RIE: 3 CAT: 17

Education North Project
CIJE: 1 RIE: 6 CAT: 19

Education of the Deaf Act 1986
CIJE: 0 RIE: 1 CAT: 14
UF Public Law 99 371

Education of the Deaf Act Amendments 1992
CIJE: 1 RIE: 1 CAT: 14
UF Public Law 102 421

Education of the Handicapped Act 1970
CIJE: 12 RIE: 33 CAT: 14

Education of the Handicapped Act 1970 (Part B)
CIJE: 0 RIE: 2 CAT: 14

Education of the Handicapped Act 1986 (Part H)
CIJE: 23 RIE: 26 CAT: 14
UF Part H 99 457 (Handicapped Infants and Toddlers); Public Law 99 457 Part H

Education of the Handicapped Act 1991
USE Individuals with Disabilities Education Act

Education of the Handicapped Act Amendments 1983
CIJE: 0 RIE: 4 CAT: 14

Education of the Handicapped Act Amendments 1986
CIJE: 49 RIE: 86 CAT: 14
SN See also "Education of the Handicapped Act 1986..."
UF Public Law 99 457

Education of the Handicapped Act Amendments 1990
USE Individuals with Disabilities Education Act

Education Opinion Inventory
CIJE: 0 RIE: 2 CAT: 21

Education Participation Scale
CIJE: 7 RIE: 1 CAT: 21

Education Policies Commission
CIJE: 1 RIE: 0 CAT: 17

Education Policy Research Center NY
CIJE: 1 RIE: 1 CAT: 17

Education Professions Development Act
CIJE: 27 RIE: 77 CAT: 14

Education Reform Act 1988 (England)
CIJE: 21 RIE: 21 CAT: 14
UF British Education Reform Act 1988; Education Reform Act 1988 (Great Britain)

Education Reform Act 1987 (Great Britain)
CIJE: 2 RIE: 0 CAT: 14

Education Reform Act 1988 (Great Britain)
USE Education Reform Act 1988 (England)

Education Reform Efforts
USE Reform Efforts

Education Reform Movement
CIJE: 0 RIE: 1 CAT: 12

Education Reform Reports
CIJE: 7 RIE: 0 CAT: 16
UF Educational Reform Reports

Education Reform Utilization
CIJE: 4 RIE: 0 CAT: 16
UF Educational Reform Utilization

Education Renewal Center CO
CIJE: 1 RIE: 0 CAT: 17

Education Renewal Consortium AR
USE Arkansas Educational Renewal Consortium

Education Research Analysts TX
CIJE: 1 RIE: 0 CAT: 17

Education Resource Center IL
CIJE: 0 RIE: 1 CAT: 17

Education Revitalization
CIJE: 1 RIE: 2 CAT: 16
SN See also "Educational Renewal"
UF Educational Revitalization

Education Satellite Communications Demo DC
CIJE: 0 RIE: 7 CAT: 17

Education Service Center Region 20 TX
CIJE: 0 RIE: 1 CAT: 17

Education Society Relationship
CIJE: 11 RIE: 2 CAT: 16

Education Specialists
CIJE: 0 RIE: 1 CAT: 09

Education Summit 1989 (NGA)
CIJE: 0 RIE: 3 CAT: 02
SN Held Sep89 in Charlottesville, VA — see also "National Education Goals 1990" — also index "National Governors Association" if appropriate

Education Through Inquiry
CIJE: 1 RIE: 0 CAT: 19

Education Through Student Interaction Program
CIJE: 2 RIE: 0 CAT: 19

Education Through Vision
CIJE: 0 RIE: 2 CAT: 19

Education to Work Council of Philadelphia
CIJE: 0 RIE: 1 CAT: 17

Educational Adequacy
CIJE: 11 RIE: 22 CAT: 15

Educational Administration Quarterly
CIJE: 2 RIE: 2 CAT: 22

Educational Administration Skills Inventory
CIJE: 0 RIE: 1 CAT: 21
UF EASI (Douglas Johnson Calabrese)

Educational Advancement Act
CIJE: 1 RIE: 0 CAT: 14

Educational and Career Exploration System
CIJE: 4 RIE: 6 CAT: 15

Educational and Cultural Council of Nationalities
CIJE: 0 RIE: 1 CAT: 17

Educational Assessment of Social Interaction
CIJE: 0 RIE: 1 CAT: 21

Educational Assessment of Student Interaction
CIJE: 0 RIE: 1 CAT: 21
UF EASI (Goetz et al)

Educational Assistance Test Program
CIJE: 0 RIE: 2 CAT: 19
UF Veterans Educational Assistance Test Program

Educational Association of Worcester
CIJE: 1 RIE: 0 CAT: 17

Educational Attitude Survey
CIJE: 2 RIE: 2 CAT: 21

Educational Attitudes Inventory
CIJE: 1 RIE: 0 CAT: 21

Educational Attitudes Scale
CIJE: 1 RIE: 1 CAT: 21

Educational Awareness
CIJE: 2 RIE: 34 CAT: 16

Educational Beliefs System Inventory
CIJE: 0 RIE: 1 CAT: 21

Educational Biotechnology
CIJE: 0 RIE: 1 CAT: 20

Educational Broadcasting Review
CIJE: 1 RIE: 1 CAT: 22

Educational Broadcasting Review (Journal)
CIJE: 0 RIE: 1 CAT: 22

Educational Brokerage
CIJE: 8 RIE: 17 CAT: 15

Educational Career Serv Community Outreach Prog
CIJE: 0 RIE: 1 CAT: 19

Educational Catalyst Organization
CIJE: 0 RIE: 1 CAT: 17

Educational Clinics
CIJE: 1 RIE: 1 CAT: 05

Educational Collaborative for Greater Boston
CIJE: 0 RIE: 1 CAT: 17

Educational Communications and Technology Journal
CIJE: 2 RIE: 2 CAT: 22

Educational Computer Consortium of Ohio
CIJE: 0 RIE: 1 CAT: 17

Educational Computing Organization of Ontario
CIJE: 0 RIE: 1 CAT: 17

Educational Cooperative Serv Unit Marshall MN
USE Southwest and West Central Ed Coop Serv Unit MN

Educational Cooperative Serv Unit Minneapolis MN
USE Metropolitan Twin Cities Educ Coop Service Unit MN

Educational Coordinators
CIJE: 1 RIE: 1 CAT: 09

Educational Council for Foreign Medical Graduates
CIJE: 1 RIE: 1 CAT: 17

Educational Council Stations
CIJE: 0 RIE: 1 CAT: 05

Educational Criticism
CIJE: 27 RIE: 16 CAT: 15

Educational Development Centers
CIJE: 3 RIE: 3 CAT: 05

Educational Development Series
CIJE: 0 RIE: 2 CAT: 21

Educational Diagnostic and Planning Center WY
CIJE: 0 RIE: 2 CAT: 17

Educational Dissemination Studies Program
CIJE: 0 RIE: 3 CAT: 19

Educational Diversity
CIJE: 6 RIE: 6 CAT: 16

Educational Dramatizations
CIJE: 0 RIE: 1 CAT: 16

Educational Employment Relations Act (California)
CIJE: 1 RIE: 3 CAT: 14

Educational Encouragement
CIJE: 9 RIE: 3 CAT: 16

Educational Entitlements
CIJE: 5 RIE: 5 CAT: 16

Educational EQuality Project
USE EQuality Project

Educational Extension Program
CIJE: 0 RIE: 1 CAT: 19

Educational Facilities Center IL
CIJE: 3 RIE: 0 CAT: 17

Educational Facilities Evaluation
CIJE: 6 RIE: 1 CAT: 15

Educational Facilities Laboratories IL
CIJE: 2 RIE: 5 CAT: 17

Educational Film Library Association
CIJE: 0 RIE: 1 CAT: 17

Educational Goals Assessment
CIJE: 0 RIE: 1 CAT: 21

Educational Guidance in Human Love
CIJE: 1 RIE: 0 CAT: 22

Educational Ideologies
CIJE: 6 RIE: 3 CAT: 15

Educational Imagery
CIJE: 1 RIE: 2 CAT: 15

Educational Imagination (The)
CIJE: 1 RIE: 0 CAT: 22

Educational Impacts Model
CIJE: 0 RIE: 1 CAT: 15

Educational Improvement Center South NJ
CIJE: 0 RIE: 2 CAT: 17

Educational Indicators
CIJE: 44 RIE: 137 CAT: 16
SN See also "International Educational Indicators"

Educational Information
CIJE: 25 RIE: 118 CAT: 16

Educational Information Centers
CIJE: 2 RIE: 23 CAT: 05

Educational Information Centers Program
CIJE: 0 RIE: 1 CAT: 19

Educational Information Consultants
CIJE: 1 RIE: 9 CAT: 09

Educational Information Network
CIJE: 0 RIE: 9 CAT: 17

Educational Interest Groups
CIJE: 6 RIE: 1 CAT: 10

Educational Issues
CIJE: 122 RIE: 312 CAT: 16

Educational Journals
CIJE: 9 RIE: 5 CAT: 16

Educational Kinesiology
CIJE: 1 RIE: 2 CAT: 11

Educational Laboratory Theatre Project
CIJE: 3 RIE: 5 CAT: 19

Educational Leadership
CIJE: 23 RIE: 18 CAT: 16

Educational Leadership Test
CIJE: 0 RIE: 1 CAT: 21

Educational Life Skills
CIJE: 0 RIE: 1 CAT: 16
SN Skills for learning to learn

Educational Management Services
CIJE: 0 RIE: 1 CAT: 15

Educational Marketing
CIJE: 30 RIE: 26 CAT: 15

Educational Mass Media Centre (Ethiopia)
CIJE: 1 RIE: 0 CAT: 17

Educational Materials Coordination Unit IL
CIJE: 0 RIE: 1 CAT: 17

Educational Materials Laboratory
CIJE: 0 RIE: 1 CAT: 17

Educational Materials Producers Council
CIJE: 1 RIE: 0 CAT: 17

Educational Media Council NY
CIJE: 0 RIE: 1 CAT: 17

Educational Media Index
CIJE: 0 RIE: 1 CAT: 22

Educational Media Procedures Council
CIJE: 0 RIE: 1 CAT: 17

Educational Media Production Proj Hearing Impaired
CIJE: 0 RIE: 0 CAT: 19

Educational Media Role
CIJE: 8 RIE: 2 CAT: 16
UF Media Role (Educational Media)

Educational Media Use
CIJE: 3 RIE: 0 CAT: 16
UF Media Use (Educational Media)

Educational Native American Network
CIJE: 0 RIE: 1 CAT: 04

Educational Neglect
CIJE: 0 RIE: 1 CAT: 15

Educational Opportunities Program
CIJE: 1 RIE: 4 CAT: 19

Educational Opportunities Programs
CIJE: 0 RIE: 2 CAT: 19

Educational Opportunity Bank
CIJE: 2 RIE: 3 CAT: 17

Educational Opportunity Centers
CIJE: 1 RIE: 5 CAT: 19

Educational Opportunity Fund (New Jersey)
CIJE: 0 RIE: 3 CAT: 14

Educational Opportunity Programs and Services CA
CIJE: 0 RIE: 1 CAT: 19

Educational Orientation Questionnaire
CIJE: 2 RIE: 1 CAT: 21

Educational Participation Scale
CIJE: 1 RIE: 3 CAT: 21

Educational Partnerships Program (OERI)
CIJE: 0 RIE: 3 CAT: 19

Educational Passports
CIJE: 1 RIE: 0 CAT: 16

Educational Planning Committees
CIJE: 0 RIE: 1 CAT: 10

Educational Policies Commission
CIJE: 2 RIE: 2 CAT: 17

Educational Policy Research Center
CIJE: 0 RIE: 5 CAT: 17

Educational Priorities Panel NY
CIJE: 1 RIE: 2 CAT: 17

Educational Priority Area Project
CIJE: 4 RIE: 5 CAT: 19

Educational Production Function
CIJE: 2 RIE: 3 CAT: 16

Educational Products Information Exchange
CIJE: 14 RIE: 11 CAT: 17

Educational Professions Institute
CIJE: 0 RIE: 1 CAT: 17

Educational Program Auditing
CIJE: 1 RIE: 4 CAT: 09

Educational Programming of Cultural Heritage CA
CIJE: 1 RIE: 1 CAT: 17

Educational Quality Indicators Project AB
CIJE: 0 RIE: 2 CAT: 19

Educational Redeployment Service (England)
CIJE: 1 RIE: 0 CAT: 17

Educational Reform Efforts
USE Reform Efforts

Educational Reform Reports
USE Education Reform Reports

Educational Reform Utilization
USE Education Reform Utilization

Educational Renewal
CIJE: 2 RIE: 3 CAT: 16
SN See also "Education Revitalization"

Educational Renewal Consortium AR
USE Arkansas Educational Renewal Consortium

Educational Research and Development Council MN
CIJE: 0 RIE: 1 CAT: 17

Educational Research and Development Report
CIJE: 0 RIE: 1 CAT: 22

Educational Research Council of America
CIJE: 1 RIE: 7 CAT: 17

Educational Research Library DC
CIJE: 0 RIE: 2 CAT: 17
UF Department of Education Educ Research Library

Educational Research Service
CIJE: 18 RIE: 8 CAT: 17

Educational Research Service Survey
CIJE: 0 RIE: 1 CAT: 21

Educational Resource Center on Deafness TX
CIJE: 0 RIE: 1 CAT: 17

Educational Resource Management System
CIJE: 0 RIE: 1 CAT: 15

Educational Resources Access Programs
CIJE: 1 RIE: 1 CAT: 19

Educational Resources Center (India)
CIJE: 1 RIE: 1 CAT: 17

Educational Restructuring
CIJE: 101 RIE: 46 CAT: 16

Educational Results Information System
CIJE: 0 RIE: 1 CAT: 21

Educational Revitalization
USE Education Revitalization

Educational Rights
CIJE: 2 RIE: 3 CAT: 14
SN See also "Right to Education"

Educational Satellite Communication Demonstration
CIJE: 0 RIE: 4 CAT: 19

Educational Satellite Consortium
CIJE: 0 RIE: 1 CAT: 17

Educational Service Unit 18 Lincoln NE
CIJE: 0 RIE: 1 CAT: 17

Educational Services Inc
CIJE: 1 RIE: 1 CAT: 17

Educational Set Scale
CIJE: 1 RIE: 1 CAT: 21

Educational Set Theory
CIJE: 0 RIE: 0 CAT: 15

Educational Sign Skills Evaluation
CIJE: 0 RIE: 1 CAT: 21

Educational Software Evaluation Consortium
CIJE: 1 RIE: 0 CAT: 17

Educational Stratification
CIJE: 1 RIE: 1 CAT: 15

Educational Systems Corporation
CIJE: 0 RIE: 1 CAT: 17

Educational Technologies Database
CIJE: 0 RIE: 1 CAT: 04

Educational Technologists
CIJE: 8 RIE: 2 CAT: 09

Educational Technology Act
CIJE: 3 RIE: 0 CAT: 14

Educational Technology Center MA
CIJE: 1 RIE: 4 CAT: 17

Educational Technology Predisposition Assessment
CIJE: 0 RIE: 2 CAT: 21

Educational Technology Training Program
CIJE: 0 RIE: 1 CAT: 19

Educational Telecommunication System
CIJE: 0 RIE: 2 CAT: 17

Educational Telecommunications for Alaska Project
CIJE: 0 RIE: 8 CAT: 19

Educational Telephone Network WI
CIJE: 3 RIE: 6 CAT: 17

Educational Television Intervention Programs TN
CIJE: 0 RIE: 1 CAT: 19

Educational Television Stations
CIJE: 0 RIE: 4 CAT: 05

Educational Test Research Institute (Japan)
CIJE: 0 RIE: 1 CAT: 17

Educational Testing Act 1979
CIJE: 0 RIE: 3 CAT: 14

Educational Testing Service
CIJE: 98 RIE: 91 CAT: 17
SN See add'l listings under "ETS..."

Educational Transfer
CIJE: 1 RIE: 0 CAT: 16

Educational Uniformity
CIJE: 0 RIE: 1 CAT: 16

Educational Values Assessment Questionnaire
CIJE: 0 RIE: 1 CAT: 21

Educational Values Perception Inventory
CIJE: 0 RIE: 1 CAT: 21

Educational Values Scale
CIJE: 0 RIE: 1 CAT: 21

Educational Vocabulary
CIJE: 1 RIE: 2 CAT: 16

Educational Warranty
CIJE: 1 RIE: 2 CAT: 15
UF Warranty of Education

Educational Writing
CIJE: 0 RIE: 3 CAT: 16

Educator Revitalization
CIJE: 0 RIE: 0 CAT: 16
UF Teacher Revitalization

Educator Role
CIJE: 33 RIE: 7 CAT: 16

Educators
CIJE: 44 RIE: 15 CAT: 09

Educators 2000 Project
CIJE: 0 RIE: 1 CAT: 19

Educators for Social Responsibility
CIJE: 4 RIE: 2 CAT: 17

Educators Forum
CIJE: 0 RIE: 2 CAT: 03

Educators Peer Instructional Consulting Proj
CIJE: 0 RIE: 1 CAT: 19
UF EPIC Project OH

EDUCE Conceptual Analyzer
CIJE: 0 RIE: 1 CAT: 04
SN EDUCE = Explaining Discourse Understanding with Conceptual Expectations

Educological Perspective
USE Educology

Educological Research
CIJE: 0 RIE: 2 CAT: 15

Educology
CIJE: 2 RIE: 8 CAT: 15
UF Educological Perspective

EDUCOM Financial Planning Model System
CIJE: 0 RIE: 2 CAT: 04

Edumetric Properties of Tests
CIJE: 0 RIE: 2 CAT: 21

Edunet
CIJE: 0 RIE: 1 CAT: 17

Edutainment
CIJE: 0 RIE: 1 CAT: 20

EDUTEK Inc
CIJE: 0 RIE: 1 CAT: 17

Edward VII
CIJE: 1 RIE: 0 CAT: 18

Edwardian Era
CIJE: 2 RIE: 1 CAT: 12

Edwards Multiple Categorization Test
CIJE: 0 RIE: 1 CAT: 21

Edwards Personal Preference Schedule
CIJE: 61 RIE: 34 CAT: 21

Edwards Personality Inventory
CIJE: 8 RIE: 1 CAT: 21

Edwards Social Desirability Scale
CIJE: 2 RIE: 0 CAT: 21

Edwin Gould Outdoor Education Centers NY
CIJE: 0 RIE: 1 CAT: 17

EEOC v Mississippi College
CIJE: 1 RIE: 0 CAT: 14

EEOC v University of New Mexico
CIJE: 1 RIE: 0 CAT: 14

Efe People
CIJE: 0 RIE: 0 CAT: 08

Effect Size Estimator (Glass)
CIJE: 1 RIE: 2 CAT: 21

Effect Strength
CIJE: 2 RIE: 0 CAT: 21

Effectance Motivation
CIJE: 8 RIE: 2 CAT: 11

Effectance Motivation Distribution
CIJE: 1 RIE: 0 CAT: 21

Effective Classroom Management (Elementary)
CIJE: 0 RIE: 3 CAT: 15

Effective Classroom Management (Junior High)
CIJE: 0 RIE: 2 CAT: 15

Effective Listening
CIJE: 1 RIE: 0 CAT: 15

Effective Practice Identification
CIJE: 2 RIE: 1 CAT: 15

Effective Professor Scale (Vaughn)
CIJE: 1 RIE: 0 CAT: 21

Effective Reading in Content Areas
CIJE: 0 RIE: 1 CAT: 15

Effective Reading Programs
CIJE: 0 RIE: 98 CAT: 19

Effective Remedial Math Checklist
CIJE: 0 RIE: 1 CAT: 21

Effective School Scale
CIJE: 0 RIE: 1 CAT: 21

Effective Schools Battery
CIJE: 0 RIE: 3 CAT: 21

Effective Schools Improvement Process
CIJE: 0 RIE: 1 CAT: 15

Effective Schools Movement
CIJE: 26 RIE: 4 CAT: 12

Effective Schools Project
CIJE: 1 RIE: 14 CAT: 19
SN Project of Spencerport Central Schools NY
UF More Effective Schools Teaching Project

Effective Schools Projects
CIJE: 2 RIE: 4 CAT: 19

Effective Teacher Training Program NC
CIJE: 0 RIE: 1 CAT: 19

Effective Teacher Training Program NM
CIJE: 0 RIE: 0 CAT: 19

Effective Teaching and Supervision of Instruction
CIJE: 1 RIE: 0 CAT: 19

Effective Teaching Cooperative
CIJE: 0 RIE: 2 CAT: 19

Effective Teaching Institute
CIJE: 1 RIE: 0 CAT: 02

Effective Use of Resources Project
CIJE: 0 RIE: 3 CAT: 19

Effective Use of Time Program
CIJE: 0 RIE: 2 CAT: 19

Effectively Influencing Political Decisions
CIJE: 1 RIE: 0 CAT: 19

Effectiveness Assessment Matrix (Seybert)
CIJE: 0 RIE: 1 CAT: 15

Effectiveness Motivation Scale (Stott and Sharp)
CIJE: 1 RIE: 0 CAT: 21

Effects of Participating in Vocational Education
CIJE: 0 RIE: 1 CAT: 22

Efference
CIJE: 2 RIE: 0 CAT: 11

Efferent Reading
CIJE: 2 RIE: 2 CAT: 03
SN Reading for information

Efficacy
CIJE: 17 RIE: 10 CAT: 15

Efficacy Scale for Creative Productivity
CIJE: 0 RIE: 1 CAT: 21

Efficacy Scale for Overall Creative Productivity
CIJE: 0 RIE: 1 CAT: 21

Efficiency Index
CIJE: 2 RIE: 2 CAT: 21

Efficiency Ratio
CIJE: 0 RIE: 1 CAT: 21

Effort
CIJE: 96 RIE: 40 CAT: 15

Efik
CIJE: 0 RIE: 1 CAT: 13

Efron (Bradley)
CIJE: 0 RIE: 1 CAT: 18

Efron (Edith)
CIJE: 1 RIE: 0 CAT: 18

Efrons Bootstrap
CIJE: 2 RIE: 3 CAT: 21
SN See also "Bootstrap Methods" and "Bootstrap Hypothesis"

Egalitarianism
CIJE: 23 RIE: 8 CAT: 16

Egan (Kieran)
CIJE: 4 RIE: 1 CAT: 18

Egg Candlers
CIJE: 0 RIE: 1 CAT: 09

Egg Incubation
CIJE: 2 RIE: 1 CAT: 20

Egg Incubators
CIJE: 1 RIE: 0 CAT: 20

Egg Production
CIJE: 0 RIE: 1 CAT: 20

Eggs
CIJE: 6 RIE: 3 CAT: 20

Ego Control
CIJE: 2 RIE: 3 CAT: 11

Ego Development
CIJE: 22 RIE: 4 CAT: 11

Ego Development Theory
CIJE: 12 RIE: 8 CAT: 15

Ego Identity
CIJE: 37 RIE: 0 CAT: 11

Ego Identity Scale (Rasmussen)
CIJE: 1 RIE: 2 CAT: 21

Ego Identity Status
USE Identity Status

Ego Resiliency
CIJE: 2 RIE: 5 CAT: 11

Ego Stage Development Model
CIJE: 0 RIE: 1 CAT: 11

Ego Strength
CIJE: 5 RIE: 1 CAT: 11

Ego Strength Scale (Barron)
USE Barron Ego Strength Scale

Ego Syntonic State
CIJE: 0 RIE: 1 CAT: 11

Eguren (Jose Maria)
CIJE: 1 RIE: 0 CAT: 18

Egypt
CIJE: 121 RIE: 152 CAT: 07

Egypt (Cairo)
CIJE: 7 RIE: 1 CAT: 07

Egyptian Languages
CIJE: 3 RIE: 1 CAT: 13

Egyptian Ministry of Education
USE Ministry of Education (Egypt)

Egyptian National Scientific Tech Info Network
CIJE: 0 RIE: 1 CAT: 04
UF ENSTINET

Egyptian School District IL
CIJE: 0 RIE: 1 CAT: 17

Egyptians
CIJE: 4 RIE: 3 CAT: 08

Ehlen (Arlis)
CIJE: 1 RIE: 0 CAT: 18

Ehninger (Douglas)
CIJE: 0 RIE: 1 CAT: 18

Eibl Eibesfeldt (Irenaus)
CIJE: 0 RIE: 1 CAT: 18

Eidos Program NY
CIJE: 0 RIE: 1 CAT: 19

EIDOS System (OCLC)
USE Electronic Information Delivery Online System

EIEM Rating Scale
USE Evaluation Instrument for Experimental Methodology

EIES
USE Electronic Information Exchange System

EIFER Rating Scale
USE Evaluation Instrument for Experimental Research

Eigenvalue Greater Than Unity Rule (Kaiser)
CIJE: 0 RIE: 1 CAT: 21

Eigenvalues
CIJE: 24 RIE: 17 CAT: 20

Eigenvectors
CIJE: 7 RIE: 2 CAT: 20

Eight Block Sorting Task
CIJE: 0 RIE: 1 CAT: 21

Eight College Professors (Yamamoto et al)
CIJE: 1 RIE: 0 CAT: 21

Eight Millimeter Film
CIJE: 8 RIE: 1 CAT: 04

Eight Year Study
CIJE: 3 RIE: 1 CAT: 19
SN 1933-41 U.S. study of the relationship between high school instruction and college success, carried out by the Progressive Education Association

Eighteen Year Old Vote
CIJE: 7 RIE: 3 CAT: 14

Eighteenth Amendment
CIJE: 4 RIE: 1 CAT: 14
UF Prohibition (USA 1920s)

Eighteenth Century
CIJE: 39 RIE: 12 CAT: 12

Einstein (Albert)
CIJE: 39 RIE: 3 CAT: 18

Einstellung Effect
CIJE: 2 RIE: 1 CAT: 11

Eiseley (Loren)
CIJE: 1 RIE: 2 CAT: 18

Eisenberg (Frances)
CIJE: 0 RIE: 1 CAT: 18

Eisenhower (Dwight D)
CIJE: 16 RIE: 9 CAT: 18

Eisenhower (Mamie)
CIJE: 0 RIE: 1 CAT: 18

Eisenhower College NY
CIJE: 4 RIE: 5 CAT: 17

Eisenhower Math and Science Educ Program
USE Dwight D Eisenhower Math and Science Educ Program

Eisenhower National Clearinghouse
CIJE: 0 RIE: 1 CAT: 17

Eisenstein (Herbert)
CIJE: 1 RIE: 0 CAT: 18

Eisenstein (Sergei M)
CIJE: 2 RIE: 2 CAT: 18

Eisner (Elliot W)
CIJE: 14 RIE: 3 CAT: 18

Eisner Art Attitude Inventory
CIJE: 0 RIE: 2 CAT: 21

Ejectives (Phonetics)
CIJE: 0 RIE: 1 CAT: 13

Ekistics
CIJE: 7 RIE: 4 CAT: 20

Ekman (Paul)
CIJE: 0 RIE: 1 CAT: 18

Ekwall (Eldon E)
CIJE: 1 RIE: 0 CAT: 18

Ekwall Reading Inventory
CIJE: 2 RIE: 3 CAT: 21

El Arco Iris Program TX
CIJE: 0 RIE: 1 CAT: 19

El Camino College CA
CIJE: 4 RIE: 20 CAT: 17

El Camino Senior High School CA
CIJE: 1 RIE: 1 CAT: 17

El Centro de la Causa IL
CIJE: 0 RIE: 1 CAT: 17

El Coronel No Tiene Quien le Escriba
CIJE: 0 RIE: 1 CAT: 22

El Dorado County Board of Education CA
CIJE: 1 RIE: 0 CAT: 17

El Paso Articulation Committee
CIJE: 1 RIE: 0 CAT: 17

El Paso Community College TX
CIJE: 3 RIE: 21 CAT: 17

El Paso Independent School District TX
CIJE: 0 RIE: 7 CAT: 17

El Primer Congreso Mexicanista De 1911
CIJE: 1 RIE: 0 CAT: 02

El Salvador
CIJE: 23 RIE: 61 CAT: 07

Elaborated Code (Linguistics)
CIJE: 0 RIE: 2 CAT: 13

Elaboration
CIJE: 49 RIE: 16 CAT: 16

Elaboration Likelihood Model
CIJE: 8 RIE: 6 CAT: 15

Elaboration Theory
CIJE: 29 RIE: 20 CAT: 15

Elaborative Prompts
CIJE: 8 RIE: 3 CAT: 16

Elamite
CIJE: 1 RIE: 0 CAT: 13

Elasticity
CIJE: 16 RIE: 4 CAT: 20

Elasticity of Demand
CIJE: 0 RIE: 1 CAT: 15
UF Demand Elasticity; Price Elasticity of Demand

Elasticity of Substitution (Manpower)
CIJE: 2 RIE: 1 CAT: 15

Elbert County School District GA
CIJE: 0 RIE: 1 CAT: 17

Elbow (Peter)
CIJE: 8 RIE: 5 CAT: 18

Elder Care
CIJE: 3 RIE: 12 CAT: 16
SN If appropriate, use Descriptor "Adult Day Care"
UF Eldercare Programs

Elder Craftsman Shops
CIJE: 3 RIE: 0 CAT: 05

Elder Ed Program
CIJE: 1 RIE: 0 CAT: 19

Elder Neglect
CIJE: 0 RIE: 1 CAT: 11

Eldercare Programs
USE Elder Care

Eldercollege
CIJE: 0 RIE: 1 CAT: 19

Elderhostels
CIJE: 17 RIE: 7 CAT: 05

Elderscholar Program
CIJE: 0 RIE: 1 CAT: 19

Elected Positions
CIJE: 4 RIE: 3 CAT: 16

Election Rhetoric
USE Political Rhetoric

Elective Mutism
CIJE: 6 RIE: 3 CAT: 11

Electoral College
CIJE: 2 RIE: 1 CAT: 10

Electorate
CIJE: 0 RIE: 2 CAT: 10

Electrastatistics
CIJE: 1 RIE: 0 CAT: 20

Electrets
CIJE: 1 RIE: 0 CAT: 20

Electric Company
CIJE: 14 RIE: 59 CAT: 22

Electric Generators
CIJE: 0 RIE: 5 CAT: 04

Electric Humanities Workshop
CIJE: 1 RIE: 0 CAT: 02

Electric Power Generation
CIJE: 7 RIE: 12 CAT: 20

Electric Power Generators
CIJE: 6 RIE: 0 CAT: 20

Electric Power Research Institute
CIJE: 1 RIE: 0 CAT: 17

Electric Response Audiometry
CIJE: 1 RIE: 0 CAT: 20

Electric Utility Instructor Training Consortium
CIJE: 0 RIE: 1 CAT: 17

Electric Utility Marketing Institute
CIJE: 1 RIE: 0 CAT: 17

Electric Vehicles
CIJE: 3 RIE: 1 CAT: 04

Electrical Accessories Assemblers
CIJE: 0 RIE: 4 CAT: 09

Electrical Discharge Machine
CIJE: 2 RIE: 3 CAT: 04

Electrical Emergencies
CIJE: 0 RIE: 1 CAT: 20

Electrical Engineering
CIJE: 28 RIE: 16 CAT: 20

Electrical Insulation
CIJE: 0 RIE: 0 CAT: 20
UF Insulation (Electricity)

Electrical Network Theory
CIJE: 0 RIE: 1 CAT: 15

Electrical Production
CIJE: 2 RIE: 3 CAT: 20

Electrical Sensing Devices
CIJE: 0 RIE: 1 CAT: 04

Electrical Stimulation
CIJE: 0 RIE: 4 CAT: 11

Electrical Technology
CIJE: 0 RIE: 2 CAT: 20

Electrical Wiring
CIJE: 3 RIE: 32 CAT: 20
SN See also "Electronic Wiring," "Industrial Wiring," "Residential Wiring," and "Signal Wiring"
UF Wiring (Electricity)

Electricite de France
CIJE: 0 RIE: 1 CAT: 17

Electrified Perkins Brailler
CIJE: 0 RIE: 1 CAT: 04

Electroacoustic Filters
CIJE: 0 RIE: 1 CAT: 04

Electroanalytical Techniques
CIJE: 2 RIE: 0 CAT: 15

Electrocardiograms
CIJE: 4 RIE: 7 CAT: 11

Electrochemical Engineering
CIJE: 1 RIE: 0 CAT: 20

Electrochemical Grinding
CIJE: 2 RIE: 0 CAT: 20

Electrocommunications
CIJE: 0 RIE: 1 CAT: 20

Electroconvulsive Therapy
CIJE: 1 RIE: 1 CAT: 11

Electrodes
CIJE: 26 RIE: 2 CAT: 20

Electrogoniometers
CIJE: 1 RIE: 0 CAT: 04

Electrohome Character Projector
CIJE: 0 RIE: 1 CAT: 04

Electrolysis
CIJE: 13 RIE: 0 CAT: 20

Electromagnetic Field
CIJE: 16 RIE: 2 CAT: 20

Electromagnetic Theory
CIJE: 7 RIE: 4 CAT: 15

Electromagnets
CIJE: 3 RIE: 1 CAT: 20

Electromechanical Technology Project
CIJE: 1 RIE: 0 CAT: 19

Electromyography
CIJE: 19 RIE: 6 CAT: 11

Electron Affinities
CIJE: 1 RIE: 0 CAT: 20

Electron Beam Lithography
CIJE: 0 RIE: 2 CAT: 20

Electron Configuration
CIJE: 2 RIE: 0 CAT: 20

Electron Microscopes
CIJE: 8 RIE: 0 CAT: 04

Electron Microscopy
CIJE: 5 RIE: 0 CAT: 20

Electron Pair Repulsion
CIJE: 1 RIE: 0 CAT: 20

Electron Spin Resonance
CIJE: 5 RIE: 0 CAT: 20

Electronegativity
CIJE: 10 RIE: 0 CAT: 20

Electronic Blackboards
CIJE: 2 RIE: 10 CAT: 04

Electronic Books
CIJE: 36 RIE: 4 CAT: 16

Electronic Carpets
CIJE: 1 RIE: 0 CAT: 04

Electronic Chalkboards
CIJE: 1 RIE: 2 CAT: 04

Electronic Communications Privacy Act 1986
CIJE: 2 RIE: 1 CAT: 14

Electronic Composition (Computer Data)
CIJE: 0 RIE: 1 CAT: 20

Electronic Counter Measures
CIJE: 0 RIE: 1 CAT: 04

Electronic Dissemination of Information System
CIJE: 0 RIE: 1 CAT: 15

Electronic Document Delivery
CIJE: 18 RIE: 8 CAT: 20

Electronic Fuel Injection Systems
CIJE: 0 RIE: 1 CAT: 04

Electronic Funds Transfer
CIJE: 6 RIE: 3 CAT: 20

Electronic Futures Inc
CIJE: 0 RIE: 1 CAT: 17

Electronic Games
CIJE: 3 RIE: 1 CAT: 04

Electronic Index Card System
CIJE: 0 RIE: 1 CAT: 04

Electronic Information Delivery Online System
CIJE: 1 RIE: 0 CAT: 19
UF EIDOS System (OCLC)

Electronic Information Exchange System
CIJE: 7 RIE: 2 CAT: 04
UF EIES

Electronic Journals
CIJE: 39 RIE: 10 CAT: 16

Electronic Learning Package Factory
CIJE: 0 RIE: 1 CAT: 19

Electronic Libraries
CIJE: 56 RIE: 12 CAT: 05

Electronic Magazines
CIJE: 2 RIE: 0 CAT: 16

Electronic Media
CIJE: 12 RIE: 2 CAT: 20

Electronic Muscle Stimulation
CIJE: 0 RIE: 1 CAT: 11
UF Muscle Stimulation (Electronic)

Electronic Music
CIJE: 15 RIE: 2 CAT: 16

Electronic Networks for Interaction
CIJE: 7 RIE: 4 CAT: 04
UF ENFI; English Natural Form Instruction

Electronic News Gathering
CIJE: 2 RIE: 1 CAT: 16

Electronic Newspapers
CIJE: 6 RIE: 3 CAT: 16

Electronic Organs
CIJE: 1 RIE: 0 CAT: 04

Electronic Performance Support Systems
USE Performance Support Systems

Electronic Principles Inventory
CIJE: 0 RIE: 1 CAT: 21

Electronic Print
CIJE: 2 RIE: 2 CAT: 16

Electronic Response Analyser
CIJE: 0 RIE: 2 CAT: 04

Electronic Response Systems
CIJE: 2 RIE: 0 CAT: 04

Electronic Simon
CIJE: 0 RIE: 1 CAT: 04

Electronic Spirographs
CIJE: 1 RIE: 0 CAT: 04

Electronic Superhighway
USE Information Superhighway

Electronic Surveillance
CIJE: 6 RIE: 0 CAT: 20

Electronic Testing
CIJE: 1 RIE: 1 CAT: 04

Electronic Town Meetings
CIJE: 0 RIE: 1 CAT: 02

Electronic Trading
CIJE: 0 RIE: 2 CAT: 20

Electronic Typesetting
CIJE: 1 RIE: 0 CAT: 20

Electronic Universities
CIJE: 0 RIE: 8 CAT: 05
UF Electronic University Network

Electronic University Network
USE Electronic Universities

Electronic Wiring
CIJE: 1 RIE: 0 CAT: 20

Electronics Assemblers
CIJE: 0 RIE: 8 CAT: 09

Electronics Institute of Japan
CIJE: 1 RIE: 0 CAT: 17

Electrons
CIJE: 11 RIE: 2 CAT: 20

Electrooculography
CIJE: 2 RIE: 1 CAT: 11

Electrophoresis
CIJE: 13 RIE: 0 CAT: 20

Electroplating Emissions
CIJE: 0 RIE: 1 CAT: 20

Electroretinograms
CIJE: 1 RIE: 0 CAT: 11

Electroscopes
CIJE: 5 RIE: 1 CAT: 04

Electrostatic Precipitators
CIJE: 4 RIE: 0 CAT: 04

Electrostatics
CIJE: 17 RIE: 1 CAT: 20

Electrowriters
CIJE: 1 RIE: 3 CAT: 04

Element Analyzers
CIJE: 1 RIE: 0 CAT: 04

Elementary Art Situational Problems Test
CIJE: 0 RIE: 1 CAT: 21

Elementary Beam Theory
CIJE: 0 RIE: 1 CAT: 15

Elementary Cognitive Tasks
CIJE: 4 RIE: 1 CAT: 21

Elementary Economics Project
CIJE: 1 RIE: 2 CAT: 19

Elementary Education Cert Exam (Connecticut)
USE Connecticut Elementary Educ Certification Exam

Elementary Education Study Group
CIJE: 0 RIE: 1 CAT: 17

Elementary Education Voucher Demonstration
CIJE: 0 RIE: 2 CAT: 19

Elementary Industrial Arts Project
CIJE: 1 RIE: 0 CAT: 19

Elementary Inservice Mathematics Program
CIJE: 0 RIE: 1 CAT: 19

Elementary Intern Program
CIJE: 0 RIE: 1 CAT: 19

Elementary Language Study Experiment
CIJE: 1 RIE: 1 CAT: 19

Elementary Law Related Education Program
CIJE: 0 RIE: 1 CAT: 19

Elementary Linkage Analysis
CIJE: 2 RIE: 0 CAT: 15

Elementary Mathematics Concept Test
CIJE: 0 RIE: 1 CAT: 21

Elementary Particles
CIJE: 5 RIE: 1 CAT: 20

Elementary School Counselor Questionnaire
CIJE: 0 RIE: 1 CAT: 21

Elementary School Curriculum Efficacy Program MI
CIJE: 0 RIE: 1 CAT: 19

Elementary School Economics Project
CIJE: 0 RIE: 1 CAT: 19

Elementary School Environment Survey
CIJE: 1 RIE: 4 CAT: 21

Elementary School Health Curriculum Project
CIJE: 1 RIE: 0 CAT: 19

Elementary School Recognition Program
CIJE: 3 RIE: 2 CAT: 19

Elementary School Science Project
CIJE: 3 RIE: 2 CAT: 19

Elementary School Secondary School Relationship
CIJE: 0 RIE: 1 CAT: 16

Elementary School Teaching Project
CIJE: 0 RIE: 2 CAT: 19

Elementary Science Education Institute TN
CIJE: 0 RIE: 0 CAT: 17

Elementary Science Study
CIJE: 27 RIE: 40 CAT: 16

Elementary Science Survey
CIJE: 0 RIE: 1 CAT: 22

Elementary Secondary Education Act
CIJE: 65 RIE: 217 CAT: 14
SN Elementary and Secondary Education Act 1975; See also Elementary Secondary Education Act Title I, etc. for specific subdivisions of ESEA
UF ESEA

Elementary Secondary Education Act Title I
CIJE: 127 RIE: 1855 CAT: 14

Elementary Secondary Education Act Title II
CIJE: 11 RIE: 71 CAT: 14

Elementary Secondary Education Act Title III
CIJE: 54 RIE: 1751 CAT: 14

Elementary Secondary Education Act Title IV
CIJE: 6 RIE: 101 CAT: 14

Elementary Secondary Education Act Title IV B
CIJE: 2 RIE: 2 CAT: 14

Elementary Secondary Education Act Title IV C
CIJE: 4 RIE: 25 CAT: 14

Elementary Secondary Education Act Title IX
USE Ethnic Heritage Studies Program

Elementary Secondary Education Act Title V
CIJE: 3 RIE: 203 CAT: 14

Elementary Secondary Education Act Title VI
CIJE: 3 RIE: 54 CAT: 14

Elementary Secondary Education Act Title VII
CIJE: 30 RIE: 525 CAT: 14

Elementary Secondary Education Act Title VIII
CIJE: 1 RIE: 23 CAT: 14

Elementary Secondary Education Amendments 1967
CIJE: 0 RIE: 2 CAT: 14

Elementary Secondary General Information Survey
CIJE: 0 RIE: 1 CAT: 21
UF ELSEGIS

Elementary Secondary School Improve Amends 1988
USE Hawkins Stafford Act 1988

Elementary Secondary Schools Civil Rights Survey
CIJE: 0 RIE: 4 CAT: 22

Elementary Social Science Education Program
CIJE: 1 RIE: 0 CAT: 19

Elementary Teachers Science Inventory (Lane)
CIJE: 0 RIE: 1 CAT: 21

Elementary Verbal Communicator
CIJE: 0 RIE: 1 CAT: 04

Elements of English Grammar (Van Winkle)
CIJE: 0 RIE: 1 CAT: 22
SN Complete Title: "EEG: Elements of English Grammar: Rules Explained Simply"

Elements of Reasoning
CIJE: 0 RIE: 2 CAT: 11

Elevating the Importance of Teaching
USE National Project III (FIPSE)

Elevators
CIJE: 3 RIE: 2 CAT: 04

Eleven Plus Secondary Selection Exam
CIJE: 2 RIE: 1 CAT: 21

Eleventh Amendment
CIJE: 9 RIE: 3 CAT: 14

Eleventh Century
CIJE: 0 RIE: 1 CAT: 12

Elgin Community College IL
CIJE: 0 RIE: 6 CAT: 17

Elgin Competency Model
CIJE: 0 RIE: 1 CAT: 15

Elgin School District IL
CIJE: 0 RIE: 1 CAT: 17

Elicitation Techniques
CIJE: 5 RIE: 7 CAT: 15

Eligibility Technicians
USE Eligibility Workers

Eligibility Workers
CIJE: 0 RIE: 1 CAT: 09
UF Eligibility Technicians

Elimination Scoring
CIJE: 1 RIE: 2 CAT: 21

Eliot (Charles W)
CIJE: 1 RIE: 3 CAT: 18

Eliot (George)
CIJE: 3 RIE: 3 CAT: 18

Eliot (T S)
CIJE: 5 RIE: 4 CAT: 18

ELISA Programing Language
CIJE: 0 RIE: 1 CAT: 04

Elite Colleges
CIJE: 0 RIE: 2 CAT: 05

Elite Values
CIJE: 3 RIE: 0 CAT: 16

Elites
CIJE: 11 RIE: 4 CAT: 16

Elizabeth City School District NJ
CIJE: 0 RIE: 0 CAT: 17

Elizabeth City State University NC
CIJE: 1 RIE: 3 CAT: 17

Elizabeth Cleaners Street School
CIJE: 1 RIE: 0 CAT: 17

Elizabeth I (England)
CIJE: 2 RIE: 1 CAT: 18

Elizabethan Drama
CIJE: 7 RIE: 3 CAT: 03

Elizabethan Theaters
CIJE: 0 RIE: 1 CAT: 05

Elizabethtown College PA
CIJE: 3 RIE: 3 CAT: 17

Elizabethtown Community College KY
CIJE: 0 RIE: 1 CAT: 17

Elizur Test of Psycho Organicity
CIJE: 1 RIE: 1 CAT: 21

Elk Grove Unified School District CA
CIJE: 0 RIE: 1 CAT: 17

Elkhart Community Schools IN
CIJE: 1 RIE: 2 CAT: 17

Elkind (David)
CIJE: 4 RIE: 1 CAT: 18

Elkonin (D B)
CIJE: 0 RIE: 1 CAT: 18

Ellender Fellowships
USE Allen J Ellender Fellowship Program

Ellenstown School District WA
CIJE: 0 RIE: 1 CAT: 17

Ellipses
CIJE: 7 RIE: 2 CAT: 20

Ellipsis
CIJE: 8 RIE: 9 CAT: 13

Elliptical Gear Construction
CIJE: 1 RIE: 0 CAT: 20

Ellis (Albert)
CIJE: 13 RIE: 5 CAT: 18

Ellis Island
CIJE: 4 RIE: 2 CAT: 07

Ellis v O Hara
CIJE: 0 RIE: 1 CAT: 14

Ellison (Ralph)
CIJE: 15 RIE: 3 CAT: 18

Ellsworth (Maud)
CIJE: 0 RIE: 1 CAT: 18

Ellul (Jacques)
CIJE: 3 RIE: 3 CAT: 18

Elm Place School IL
CIJE: 1 RIE: 0 CAT: 17

Elmhurst College IL
CIJE: 1 RIE: 3 CAT: 17

Elmira City Public Schools NY
CIJE: 0 RIE: 1 CAT: 17

Elmira College NY
CIJE: 2 RIE: 3 CAT: 17

Elmo Roper and Associates
CIJE: 0 RIE: 1 CAT: 17

Elocution
CIJE: 2 RIE: 2 CAT: 16

Elodea
CIJE: 2 RIE: 0 CAT: 20

Elon College Players NC
CIJE: 0 RIE: 1 CAT: 17

Eloy Elementary School AZ
CIJE: 0 RIE: 1 CAT: 17

Elsa Clubs of America
CIJE: 1 RIE: 0 CAT: 17

ELSEGIS
USE Elementary Secondary General Information Survey

Elton (Eunice)
CIJE: 1 RIE: 0 CAT: 18

Elwell Parker Electric Company
CIJE: 1 RIE: 0 CAT: 17

Ely (John Hart)
CIJE: 0 RIE: 1 CAT: 18

Elyria City School District OH
CIJE: 0 RIE: 1 CAT: 17

Elyria Project for Innovative Curriculum
CIJE: 1 RIE: 0 CAT: 19

Elywn Institutes
CIJE: 0 RIE: 1 CAT: 05

EM Algorithm
CIJE: 34 RIE: 16 CAT: 21
SN See also "GEM Algorithm"

Emai
CIJE: 0 RIE: 1 CAT: 13
SN An Edoid language of Nigeria

Emancipation Proclamation
CIJE: 5 RIE: 1 CAT: 14

Emancipatory Theater
CIJE: 0 RIE: 1 CAT: 16

Embalmers
CIJE: 1 RIE: 1 CAT: 09

Embarras River Basin
CIJE: 0 RIE: 1 CAT: 07

Embarrassment
CIJE: 11 RIE: 8 CAT: 11

Embassies
CIJE: 1 RIE: 2 CAT: 05

Embedded Case Studies
CIJE: 0 RIE: 3 CAT: 15

Embedded Characters
CIJE: 0 RIE: 2 CAT: 11

Embedded Figures Test
CIJE: 34 RIE: 14 CAT: 21
SN See also "Childrens Embedded Figures Test," "Finding Embedded Figures Test," "Preschool Embedded Figures Test," and the entries under "Group Embedded Figures Test"

Embedded Intergroup Relations
CIJE: 1 RIE: 0 CAT: 15

Embedded Items
CIJE: 5 RIE: 4 CAT: 21

Embedded Stories
CIJE: 1 RIE: 1 CAT: 16
UF Stories Within Stories

Embedded Training
CIJE: 3 RIE: 3 CAT: 15

Embedding (Grammar)
CIJE: 5 RIE: 7 CAT: 13

Embedding Transformations
CIJE: 0 RIE: 5 CAT: 13

Embroidery
CIJE: 1 RIE: 1 CAT: 16

Embry Riddle Aeronautical University FL
CIJE: 1 RIE: 4 CAT: 17

Emecheta (Buchi)
CIJE: 2 RIE: 1 CAT: 18

Emergencies
CIJE: 12 RIE: 21 CAT: 16

Emergency Committee of Atomic Scientists
CIJE: 0 RIE: 1 CAT: 17

Emergency Employment Act 1971
CIJE: 5 RIE: 7 CAT: 14

Emergency English for Refugees
CIJE: 0 RIE: 1 CAT: 03

Emergency Evacuations
CIJE: 3 RIE: 3 CAT: 16

Emergency Immigrant Education Act 1984
CIJE: 0 RIE: 3 CAT: 14

Emergency Jobs and Unemployment Assistance Act
CIJE: 1 RIE: 0 CAT: 14

Emergency Jobs Appropriations Act 1983
CIJE: 0 RIE: 4 CAT: 14

Emergency Jobs Programs Extension Act 1976
CIJE: 0 RIE: 1 CAT: 14

Emergency Land Fund
CIJE: 0 RIE: 1 CAT: 19

Emergency Medical Coordinators
CIJE: 0 RIE: 1 CAT: 09

Emergency Medical Services
CIJE: 23 RIE: 31 CAT: 11

Emergency Medicine Examination
CIJE: 0 RIE: 1 CAT: 21

Emergency Preparedness
CIJE: 11 RIE: 7 CAT: 16

Emergency Response Services
CIJE: 0 RIE: 1 CAT: 11

Emergency School Aid Act 1972
CIJE: 23 RIE: 143 CAT: 14
UF Education Amendments 1972 Title VII

Emergency Services Research Demonstration Project
CIJE: 0 RIE: 1 CAT: 19

Emergency Shelters
CIJE: 2 RIE: 0 CAT: 05

Emergency Teacher Certification
CIJE: 2 RIE: 3 CAT: 16

Emergency Unemployment Compensation Act
CIJE: 1 RIE: 0 CAT: 14

Emergency Vehicles
CIJE: 0 RIE: 2 CAT: 04

Emergency Veterans Job Training Act 1983
CIJE: 0 RIE: 7 CAT: 14
UF Public Law 98 77; Veterans Job Training Act 1983

Emergent Languages
CIJE: 0 RIE: 2 CAT: 13

Emergent Leadership
CIJE: 2 RIE: 1 CAT: 16

Emergent Literacy
CIJE: 230 RIE: 299 CAT: 16
SN Children's early experiences with reading and writing
UF Early Literacy

Emergent Meaning
CIJE: 1 RIE: 1 CAT: 13

Emergent Reading Levels
CIJE: 1 RIE: 4 CAT: 15

Emerging Order
CIJE: 0 RIE: 1 CAT: 16

Emeritus Professors
CIJE: 5 RIE: 5 CAT: 10
UF Professors Emeriti

Emerson (Harry)
CIJE: 1 RIE: 0 CAT: 18

Emerson (Mary Moody)
CIJE: 0 RIE: 1 CAT: 18

Emerson (P H)
CIJE: 1 RIE: 0 CAT: 18

Emerson (Ralph Waldo)
CIJE: 9 RIE: 7 CAT: 18

Emerson (Thomas)
CIJE: 2 RIE: 0 CAT: 18

Emerson College MA
CIJE: 4 RIE: 1 CAT: 17

Emery Test Anxiety Scale
CIJE: 0 RIE: 1 CAT: 21

Emic Etic Analysis
CIJE: 6 RIE: 2 CAT: 15

Emig (Janet)
CIJE: 2 RIE: 4 CAT: 18
SN "Janet Ann"

Emigrants
CIJE: 3 RIE: 6 CAT: 10

Emigration
CIJE: 15 RIE: 8 CAT: 16

Emil Schwarzhaupt Foundation
CIJE: 0 RIE: 1 CAT: 17

Emile
CIJE: 6 RIE: 1 CAT: 22

Eminent Domain
CIJE: 4 RIE: 3 CAT: 14

Emission Control
CIJE: 3 RIE: 8 CAT: 20

Emission Control Systems
CIJE: 0 RIE: 5 CAT: 20

Emission Theories (Physics)
CIJE: 1 RIE: 0 CAT: 20

Emissions
CIJE: 3 RIE: 8 CAT: 20

Emma
CIJE: 2 RIE: 0 CAT: 22

Emma Willard School NY
CIJE: 1 RIE: 0 CAT: 17

Emmanuel College MA
CIJE: 0 RIE: 2 CAT: 17

Emory and Henry College VA
CIJE: 3 RIE: 0 CAT: 17

Emory University GA
CIJE: 24 RIE: 11 CAT: 17

Emory Word Analysis Skill Inventory
CIJE: 0 RIE: 2 CAT: 21

Emotion Theory
CIJE: 3 RIE: 4 CAT: 15

Emotional Commitment
CIJE: 1 RIE: 1 CAT: 11

Emotional Distress
CIJE: 26 RIE: 7 CAT: 11

Emotional Expression
CIJE: 16 RIE: 2 CAT: 11

Emotional Reactivity
CIJE: 1 RIE: 1 CAT: 11

Emotional Regulation
CIJE: 0 RIE: 2 CAT: 11

Emotional Support
CIJE: 0 RIE: 1 CAT: 11

Emotionality Rationality Activity Model
CIJE: 1 RIE: 0 CAT: 15

Emotions
CIJE: 79 RIE: 38 CAT: 11

Emotions Profile Index
CIJE: 1 RIE: 0 CAT: 21

Empathetic Imagination
CIJE: 0 RIE: 1 CAT: 11

Empathic Learning
CIJE: 0 RIE: 1 CAT: 16

Empathic Listening
CIJE: 1 RIE: 5 CAT: 13

Emphasis on Excellence Program FL
CIJE: 0 RIE: 1 CAT: 19

Emphysema
CIJE: 0 RIE: 1 CAT: 11

Empire Community College
CIJE: 0 RIE: 1 CAT: 17

Empire State College NY
USE State University of New York Empire State Coll

Empirical Analysis
CIJE: 31 RIE: 14 CAT: 15

Empirical Bayes Estimation
CIJE: 3 RIE: 4 CAT: 21

Empirical Case Study
CIJE: 1 RIE: 3 CAT: 15

Empirical Distribution Function
CIJE: 0 RIE: 1 CAT: 21

Empirical Methods
CIJE: 34 RIE: 8 CAT: 15

Empirical Research
CIJE: 169 RIE: 55 CAT: 15

Empirical Transition Matrixes
CIJE: 0 RIE: 1 CAT: 15

Empiricism
CIJE: 45 RIE: 15 CAT: 15

Empleen Ingles Series
CIJE: 0 RIE: 2 CAT: 22

Employability Competency System Appraisal Test
CIJE: 0 RIE: 2 CAT: 21

Employability Development
CIJE: 5 RIE: 10 CAT: 16

Employability Development Plans
CIJE: 0 RIE: 1 CAT: 15

Employability Maturity Interview
CIJE: 0 RIE: 1 CAT: 21

Employability Skills Series
CIJE: 0 RIE: 13 CAT: 22

Employability Support Network of Disabled Youth
CIJE: 0 RIE: 1 CAT: 19

Employed Uninsured
CIJE: 0 RIE: 1 CAT: 10

Employee Aptitude Survey
CIJE: 3 RIE: 1 CAT: 21

Employee Attrition
CIJE: 0 RIE: 3 CAT: 16

Employee Background Checks
USE Background Checks (Employment)

Employee Deviance
CIJE: 0 RIE: 1 CAT: 16

Employee Education Benefits
USE Tuition Benefit Programs

Employee Fitness Programs
CIJE: 23 RIE: 3 CAT: 19

Employee Health
CIJE: 18 RIE: 4 CAT: 11

Employee Leasing
CIJE: 0 RIE: 1 CAT: 16

Employee Misconduct
CIJE: 1 RIE: 1 CAT: 11
SN See also "Academic Misconduct" and "Research Misconduct"

Employee Ownership
CIJE: 2 RIE: 3 CAT: 16

Employee Participation
CIJE: 53 RIE: 8 CAT: 16

Employee Publications
CIJE: 4 RIE: 3 CAT: 16

Employee Readiness
CIJE: 0 RIE: 1 CAT: 16

Employee Retirement Income Security Act
CIJE: 9 RIE: 4 CAT: 14

Employee Right to Know Act 1978 (Michigan)
CIJE: 0 RIE: 1 CAT: 14

Employee Rights
CIJE: 6 RIE: 5 CAT: 16

Employee Stock Ownership Plans
CIJE: 1 RIE: 1 CAT: 15
UF ESOPs

Employee Theft
CIJE: 3 RIE: 3 CAT: 16

Employee Welfare
CIJE: 13 RIE: 5 CAT: 16

Employees with Disabilities
CIJE: 0 RIE: 1 CAT: 10
UF Disabled Employees

Employer Accounts Strategy
CIJE: 0 RIE: 1 CAT: 15

Employer Based Career Education
CIJE: 6 RIE: 18 CAT: 19

Employer Based Health Insurance
CIJE: 0 RIE: 1 CAT: 11

Employer Role
CIJE: 9 RIE: 18 CAT: 16

Employer Sponsored Skill Training
CIJE: 0 RIE: 1 CAT: 03

Employer Supported Parental Involvement in Educ
CIJE: 1 RIE: 1 CAT: 19

Employer Surveys
CIJE: 12 RIE: 47 CAT: 21

Employer Tuition Aid
USE Tuition Benefit Programs

Employment Act 1946
CIJE: 2 RIE: 2 CAT: 14

Employment Agencies
CIJE: 3 RIE: 5 CAT: 05

Employment and Training Administration
CIJE: 1 RIE: 11 CAT: 17

Employment Aptitude Survey
CIJE: 0 RIE: 2 CAT: 21

Employment Contract Termination
CIJE: 2 RIE: 0 CAT: 16

Employment Enhancement Strategies
CIJE: 0 RIE: 1 CAT: 15

Employment Exit Interviews
CIJE: 2 RIE: 0 CAT: 16

Employment Initiatives
CIJE: 0 RIE: 3 CAT: 16

Employment Legislation
CIJE: 2 RIE: 3 CAT: 14

Employment Location
CIJE: 0 RIE: 1 CAT: 16

Employment Opportunities for Disabld Americans Act
CIJE: 0 RIE: 0 CAT: 14
SN ...of 1986
UF Public Law 99 643

Employment Readiness Profile
CIJE: 0 RIE: 1 CAT: 21

Employment Security
CIJE: 5 RIE: 13 CAT: 16

Employment Security Act (Michigan)
CIJE: 0 RIE: 1 CAT: 14

Employment Security System
CIJE: 0 RIE: 1 CAT: 17

Employment Service
CIJE: 5 RIE: 40 CAT: 17
SN See also "USES..."
UF United States Employment Service

Employment Service Agency (England)
CIJE: 1 RIE: 0 CAT: 17

Employment Standards Administration
CIJE: 1 RIE: 0 CAT: 17

Employment Subsidies
CIJE: 0 RIE: 2 CAT: 16

Employment Training Panel CA
USE California Employment Training Panel

Employment Vouchers
CIJE: 0 RIE: 1 CAT: 16

Emporia Public Schools KS
CIJE: 0 RIE: 1 CAT: 17

Emporia State University KS
CIJE: 17 RIE: 10 CAT: 17

Empowerment
CIJE: 497 RIE: 272 CAT: 15

SN Use a more specific term if possible, e.g., "Self Empowerment," "Parent Empowerment," "Teacher Empowerment"
UF Personal Empowerment

Empty Lot
CIJE: 1 RIE: 1 CAT: 22

Empty Nest Syndrome
CIJE: 5 RIE: 2 CAT: 11

Enabler Model
CIJE: 3 RIE: 7 CAT: 15

Enaction Theory
CIJE: 1 RIE: 4 CAT: 15
SN Stresses that thinking is a skill and should be taught like other skills

Enactive Reading Method
CIJE: 0 RIE: 1 CAT: 15

Enamel Solvents
CIJE: 0 RIE: 1 CAT: 20

Enameling
CIJE: 1 RIE: 4 CAT: 20

Encendiendo Una Llama CT
CIJE: 0 RIE: 1 CAT: 19

Encephalomyelopathy
CIJE: 1 RIE: 0 CAT: 11

Enclitics
CIJE: 1 RIE: 1 CAT: 13

Encoder (Banking)
CIJE: 0 RIE: 1 CAT: 20

Encoding Specificity
CIJE: 4 RIE: 4 CAT: 11

ENCORE (Computer System)
CIJE: 0 RIE: 1 CAT: 04

Encounter Groups
CIJE: 16 RIE: 3 CAT: 10

Encouragement
CIJE: 10 RIE: 6 CAT: 11
SN See also "Educational Encouragement"

Encyclopaedia Britannica
CIJE: 3 RIE: 1 CAT: 22

Encyclopedia of Educational Research
CIJE: 3 RIE: 2 CAT: 22

Encyclopedia of Library and Information Science
CIJE: 3 RIE: 0 CAT: 22

End of Cycle Reading Test
CIJE: 0 RIE: 1 CAT: 21

End of Innocence (Music Video)
CIJE: 0 RIE: 1 CAT: 22

End User Statistical Computing
CIJE: 0 RIE: 1 CAT: 20

Endangered Languages
CIJE: 2 RIE: 0 CAT: 13
SN See also "Extinct Languages"

Endangered Species Act 1973
CIJE: 1 RIE: 1 CAT: 14

Endeavor Instructional Rating Form
CIJE: 4 RIE: 1 CAT: 21

Endeavour Training
CIJE: 1 RIE: 0 CAT: 15

Enderud (H G)
CIJE: 0 RIE: 1 CAT: 18

Endicott Report
CIJE: 0 RIE: 2 CAT: 22

Endler Anxiety Scale
CIJE: 1 RIE: 1 CAT: 21

Endocrine Changes
CIJE: 4 RIE: 0 CAT: 11

Endocrine System
CIJE: 7 RIE: 7 CAT: 11

Endodontics
CIJE: 5 RIE: 0 CAT: 11

Endogenous Mental Retardation
CIJE: 1 RIE: 0 CAT: 11

Endorphins
CIJE: 1 RIE: 2 CAT: 11

Endotoxins
CIJE: 1 RIE: 0 CAT: 11

Endowed Chairs
CIJE: 14 RIE: 3 CAT: 16

Endowed Schools Act 1869 (England)
CIJE: 1 RIE: 0 CAT: 14

Endurance
CIJE: 17 RIE: 5 CAT: 11

Enemies
CIJE: 0 RIE: 2 CAT: 10

Energetics
CIJE: 1 RIE: 1 CAT: 20

Energy and Mans Environment Project
CIJE: 1 RIE: 1 CAT: 19

Energy Bibliography and Index
CIJE: 1 RIE: 0 CAT: 04

Energy Conservation and Production Act 1976
CIJE: 0 RIE: 1 CAT: 14

Energy Consumption
CIJE: 15 RIE: 61 CAT: 20

Energy Conversion
CIJE: 7 RIE: 14 CAT: 20

Energy Coordinators
CIJE: 1 RIE: 0 CAT: 09

Energy Crisis
CIJE: 30 RIE: 21 CAT: 20

Energy Data Base
CIJE: 2 RIE: 2 CAT: 04

Energy Development
CIJE: 17 RIE: 39 CAT: 20

Energy Education Curriculum Project
CIJE: 0 RIE: 2 CAT: 19

Energy Environment Simulator
CIJE: 2 RIE: 1 CAT: 04

Energy Extension Tips Service
CIJE: 0 RIE: 1 CAT: 05

Energy Flow
CIJE: 2 RIE: 2 CAT: 20

Energy Impact Scenario Model
CIJE: 0 RIE: 1 CAT: 15

Energy Knowledge Attitudes Mini Assessment (1977)
CIJE: 0 RIE: 0 CAT: 21

Energy Policy
CIJE: 14 RIE: 10 CAT: 20

Energy Policy and Conservation Act 1975
CIJE: 0 RIE: 1 CAT: 14

Energy Policy Project (Ford Foundation)
CIJE: 2 RIE: 0 CAT: 19

Energy Project For Women
CIJE: 0 RIE: 1 CAT: 19

Energy Recovery Wheel
CIJE: 1 RIE: 0 CAT: 04

Energy Requirements
CIJE: 12 RIE: 7 CAT: 20

Energy Research and Development Administration
CIJE: 14 RIE: 13 CAT: 17

Energy Shutdowns
CIJE: 0 RIE: 0 CAT: 20

Energy Sources
CIJE: 9 RIE: 13 CAT: 20

Energy Storage
CIJE: 0 RIE: 1 CAT: 20

Energy Technology and Society
CIJE: 1 RIE: 0 CAT: 03

ENERGYTAX Simulation Model
CIJE: 0 RIE: 2 CAT: 15

ENFI
USE Electronic Networks for Interaction

Enfield Progress Centre (England)
CIJE: 1 RIE: 0 CAT: 17

Engaged Style
CIJE: 1 RIE: 0 CAT: 15
SN See also "Engagement Style" and, additionally, "Client Engagement," "Cognitive Engagement," "Student Engagement," "Task Engagement," "Teacher Engagement," etc.

Engagement Continuum
CIJE: 1 RIE: 0 CAT: 15
SN See note under "Engaged Style"

Engagement Style
CIJE: 2 RIE: 1 CAT: 15
SN See note under "Engaged Style"

Engelmann (Siegfried)
CIJE: 0 RIE: 1 CAT: 18

Engelmann Becker Curriculum
CIJE: 0 RIE: 3 CAT: 03

Engelmann Becker Model
CIJE: 1 RIE: 4 CAT: 15

Engine Modification
CIJE: 2 RIE: 6 CAT: 20

Engineered Classrooms
CIJE: 3 RIE: 1 CAT: 05

Engineering College Administration Council
CIJE: 0 RIE: 1 CAT: 17

Engineering College Faculty Shortage Project
CIJE: 1 RIE: 0 CAT: 19

Engineering College Research Council
CIJE: 1 RIE: 1 CAT: 17

Engineering Concepts Curriculum Project
CIJE: 9 RIE: 4 CAT: 19

Engineering Council for Professional Development
CIJE: 0 RIE: 1 CAT: 17

Engineering Curriculum
CIJE: 110 RIE: 15 CAT: 03

Engineering Design
CIJE: 2 RIE: 2 CAT: 03

Engineering Education Research
CIJE: 21 RIE: 7 CAT: 20

Engineering Executive Program
CIJE: 0 RIE: 1 CAT: 19

Engineering Index
CIJE: 1 RIE: 1 CAT: 22

Engineering Industry Training Board
CIJE: 3 RIE: 3 CAT: 17

Engineering Manpower Commission
CIJE: 8 RIE: 17 CAT: 17

Engineering Mathematics
CIJE: 4 RIE: 0 CAT: 03

Engineering Mechanics
CIJE: 1 RIE: 0 CAT: 20

Engineering Registration
CIJE: 0 RIE: 1 CAT: 20

Engineering Research Centers
CIJE: 4 RIE: 3 CAT: 05

Engineering Shortage
CIJE: 0 RIE: 1 CAT: 16

Engineering Societies Committee Manpower Training
CIJE: 1 RIE: 0 CAT: 17

Engineers Council for Professional Development
CIJE: 0 RIE: 2 CAT: 17

Engineers Joint Council
CIJE: 0 RIE: 7 CAT: 17

England
CIJE: 2585 RIE: 1135 CAT: 07

England (Bath)
CIJE: 1 RIE: 1 CAT: 07

England (Bircham Newton)
CIJE: 1 RIE: 0 CAT: 07

England (Birmingham)
CIJE: 19 RIE: 7 CAT: 07

England (Bradford)
CIJE: 3 RIE: 1 CAT: 07

England (Bristol)
CIJE: 8 RIE: 6 CAT: 07

England (Cambridge)
CIJE: 10 RIE: 1 CAT: 07

England (Cornwall)
CIJE: 0 RIE: 1 CAT: 07

England (Coventry)
CIJE: 9 RIE: 3 CAT: 07

England (Devon)
CIJE: 2 RIE: 2 CAT: 07

England (Essex)
CIJE: 2 RIE: 1 CAT: 07

England (Hackney)
CIJE: 0 RIE: 2 CAT: 07

England (Hertfordshire)
CIJE: 2 RIE: 2 CAT: 07

England (Isle of Wight)
CIJE: 0 RIE: 0 CAT: 07

England (Lancaster)
CIJE: 0 RIE: 1 CAT: 07

England (Leeds)
CIJE: 5 RIE: 0 CAT: 07

England (Leicester)
CIJE: 1 RIE: 2 CAT: 07

England (Leicestershire)
CIJE: 10 RIE: 4 CAT: 07

England (Liverpool)
CIJE: 14 RIE: 16 CAT: 07

England (London)
CIJE: 156 RIE: 68 CAT: 07

England (New Lanark)
CIJE: 1 RIE: 0 CAT: 07

England (Newcastle upon Tyne)
CIJE: 1 RIE: 1 CAT: 07

England (Newport)
CIJE: 1 RIE: 0 CAT: 07

England (Norfolk)
CIJE: 0 RIE: 1 CAT: 07

England (Northamptonshire)
CIJE: 1 RIE: 2 CAT: 07

England (Nottinghamshire)
CIJE: 7 RIE: 2 CAT: 07

England (Oxfordshire)
CIJE: 11 RIE: 1 CAT: 07

England (Reading)
CIJE: 3 RIE: 0 CAT: 07

England (Ridleyshire)
CIJE: 0 RIE: 1 CAT: 07

England (Robert)
CIJE: 0 RIE: 1 CAT: 18

England (Sandwell)
CIJE: 0 RIE: 1 CAT: 07

England (Sheffield)
CIJE: 19 RIE: 4 CAT: 07

England (South Molton)
CIJE: 0 RIE: 1 CAT: 07

England (Surrey)
CIJE: 3 RIE: 2 CAT: 07

England (Sussex)
CIJE: 0 RIE: 1 CAT: 07

England (Swindon)
CIJE: 1 RIE: 2 CAT: 07

England (Walsall)
CIJE: 1 RIE: 0 CAT: 07

England (Wessex)
CIJE: 0 RIE: 1 CAT: 07

England (West Midlands)
CIJE: 4 RIE: 2 CAT: 07

England (West Yorkshire)
CIJE: 2 RIE: 1 CAT: 07

England (Yorkshire)
CIJE: 5 RIE: 2 CAT: 07

Englewood Learning Center IL
CIJE: 0 RIE: 1 CAT: 17

Englewood Public Library CO
CIJE: 0 RIE: 1 CAT: 17

Englewood Public Schools NJ
CIJE: 0 RIE: 2 CAT: 17

Englewood School Development Program
CIJE: 0 RIE: 1 CAT: 19

English (African)
CIJE: 4 RIE: 1 CAT: 13

English (American Indian)
CIJE: 0 RIE: 3 CAT: 13

English (Appalachian)
CIJE: 1 RIE: 4 CAT: 13

English (Australian)
CIJE: 7 RIE: 2 CAT: 13

English (British)
CIJE: 27 RIE: 22 CAT: 13

English (Cajun)
CIJE: 0 RIE: 1 CAT: 13
UF Cajun English

English (Canadian)
CIJE: 6 RIE: 5 CAT: 13

English (Carriacou Creole)
CIJE: 0 RIE: 1 CAT: 13

English (Chicano)
CIJE: 4 RIE: 3 CAT: 13

English (Filipino)
CIJE: 2 RIE: 1 CAT: 13

English (General American)
CIJE: 1 RIE: 3 CAT: 13

English (Gold Coast)
CIJE: 0 RIE: 1 CAT: 13

English (Hawaiian)
CIJE: 2 RIE: 3 CAT: 13

English (Indian)
CIJE: 6 RIE: 9 CAT: 13

English (Irish)
CIJE: 1 RIE: 3 CAT: 13

English (Isletan)
CIJE: 1 RIE: 0 CAT: 13

English (Liberian)
CIJE: 0 RIE: 1 CAT: 13

English (Midwest)
CIJE: 0 RIE: 1 CAT: 13
SN Midwestern USA

English (Native American)
CIJE: 2 RIE: 0 CAT: 13

English (New York City)
CIJE: 0 RIE: 1 CAT: 13

English (Nigerian)
CIJE: 1 RIE: 2 CAT: 13

English (Puerto Rican)
CIJE: 0 RIE: 1 CAT: 13

English (Saskatchewan Spoken)
CIJE: 1 RIE: 0 CAT: 13

English (Scottish)
CIJE: 0 RIE: 1 CAT: 13

English (Singapore)
CIJE: 5 RIE: 2 CAT: 13

English (Southern)
CIJE: 0 RIE: 2 CAT: 13
SN Southern USA

English (Southwest)
CIJE: 0 RIE: 6 CAT: 13
SN Southwestern USA

English (Standard California)
CIJE: 1 RIE: 1 CAT: 13

English Americans
CIJE: 0 RIE: 1 CAT: 08

English as a Second Dialect
CIJE: 3 RIE: 6 CAT: 13

English as a Second Language Assessment Battery
CIJE: 0 RIE: 2 CAT: 21

English as a Second Language Teacher Institute
CIJE: 0 RIE: 1 CAT: 19

English as an International Language
CIJE: 2 RIE: 1 CAT: 13

English Canadians
CIJE: 5 RIE: 12 CAT: 08

English Composition Test
CIJE: 1 RIE: 7 CAT: 21

English Council of California Two Year Colleges
CIJE: 0 RIE: 1 CAT: 17

English Curriculum Study Centers
CIJE: 0 RIE: 1 CAT: 05

English Education Today
CIJE: 1 RIE: 0 CAT: 22

English Entrance Examination
CIJE: 1 RIE: 0 CAT: 21

English Examinations
CIJE: 2 RIE: 45 CAT: 21

English Grammar Schools
CIJE: 0 RIE: 1 CAT: 05

English High School MA
CIJE: 1 RIE: 1 CAT: 17

English History
CIJE: 14 RIE: 12 CAT: 12

English Journal
CIJE: 10 RIE: 2 CAT: 22

English Language Amendment
CIJE: 6 RIE: 4 CAT: 14

English Language Proficiency Study 1982
CIJE: 0 RIE: 1 CAT: 21

English Language Schools
CIJE: 0 RIE: 2 CAT: 05

English Language Skills Assessment
CIJE: 0 RIE: 2 CAT: 21
SN See also "Combined English Language Skills Assessment Test"

English Law
CIJE: 0 RIE: 2 CAT: 14

English Law History
CIJE: 2 RIE: 0 CAT: 12

English Literacy
CIJE: 1 RIE: 5 CAT: 13

English Literacy Grants
CIJE: 0 RIE: 1 CAT: 14

English Majors
CIJE: 10 RIE: 4 CAT: 10

English Microlab Registry
CIJE: 0 RIE: 1 CAT: 04

English Natural Form Instruction
USE Electronic Networks for Interaction

English Only Movement
CIJE: 10 RIE: 21 CAT: 12

English Picture Vocabulary Test
CIJE: 4 RIE: 0 CAT: 21

English Placement Examination
CIJE: 0 RIE: 1 CAT: 21

English Placement Tests
CIJE: 0 RIE: 7 CAT: 21
SN See also narrower "CSUC English Placement Test," "Illinois English Placement Test," "Purdue Placement Test in English," etc.

English Plus Legislation
USE English Plus Movement

English Plus Movement
CIJE: 0 RIE: 2 CAT: 19
UF English Plus Legislation

English Postal College (England)
CIJE: 1 RIE: 0 CAT: 17

English Proficiency Test
CIJE: 2 RIE: 2 CAT: 21

English Qualifying Exam
CIJE: 0 RIE: 3 CAT: 21

English Skills for Algebra
CIJE: 0 RIE: 1 CAT: 22

English Social Studies Opportunity Program
CIJE: 0 RIE: 1 CAT: 19

English Spanish Verbatim Translation Exam
CIJE: 0 RIE: 0 CAT: 21

English Speaking
CIJE: 31 RIE: 37 CAT: 08
UF Native English Speaking

English Study Societies
CIJE: 0 RIE: 1 CAT: 10

English Teacher Preparation Study
CIJE: 1 RIE: 1 CAT: 03

English Teachers
CIJE: 197 RIE: 139 CAT: 09

English Technical Language School PR
CIJE: 0 RIE: 1 CAT: 17

English Valley Elementary School NY
CIJE: 1 RIE: 0 CAT: 17

Engvall Junior High School CA
CIJE: 0 RIE: 1 CAT: 17

Enhanced ACT
CIJE: 0 RIE: 6 CAT: 21
UF ACT Enhanced

Enhanced Normative Systems Model (Terry)
CIJE: 0 RIE: 1 CAT: 15

Enhanced Skills Training Program
CIJE: 0 RIE: 1 CAT: 19

Enhanced Vocational Education
CIJE: 0 RIE: 1 CAT: 15

Enhancement Funding
CIJE: 0 RIE: 0 CAT: 16

Enlace Project CA
CIJE: 0 RIE: 1 CAT: 19

Enlightenment Thought
CIJE: 12 RIE: 4 CAT: 16

Enlistment Screening Test
CIJE: 0 RIE: 2 CAT: 21

Ennis (Robert)
CIJE: 1 RIE: 5 CAT: 18

Ennis Weir Critical Thinking Essay Test
CIJE: 1 RIE: 1 CAT: 21

Enoch Pratt Free Library MD
CIJE: 4 RIE: 1 CAT: 17

Enology
USE Winemaking

Enriched Career Search
CIJE: 0 RIE: 1 CAT: 19

Enrichment of Teacher and Counselor Competencies
CIJE: 0 RIE: 2 CAT: 19

Enrichment Triad Model
CIJE: 24 RIE: 6 CAT: 15

Enriquez (Carlos)
CIJE: 1 RIE: 0 CAT: 18

Enrollee Test Battery (Neighborhood Youth Corps)
CIJE: 0 RIE: 2 CAT: 21

Enrollment Analysis Matrix
CIJE: 0 RIE: 1 CAT: 15

Enrollment and Facilities Projection Program
CIJE: 0 RIE: 1 CAT: 19

Enrollment Ceilings
CIJE: 4 RIE: 3 CAT: 15

Ensenanza Directa (Mexico)
CIJE: 0 RIE: 3 CAT: 17

ENSTINET
USE Egyptian National Scientific Tech Info Network

Entanglement Test (OBrien and Vacca)
CIJE: 0 RIE: 1 CAT: 21

Entebbe Program
CIJE: 1 RIE: 1 CAT: 19

Entelek Incorporated
CIJE: 0 RIE: 1 CAT: 17

Entering Student Questionnaire
CIJE: 0 RIE: 1 CAT: 21

Entering Student Survey
CIJE: 1 RIE: 2 CAT: 21

Enterprise
CIJE: 6 RIE: 2 CAT: 16

Enterprise High Schools MI
CIJE: 0 RIE: 1 CAT: 19

Enterprise Zones
CIJE: 0 RIE: 3 CAT: 15

Entertainers
CIJE: 3 RIE: 0 CAT: 10

Entertainment
CIJE: 44 RIE: 27 CAT: 16

Enthusiasm
CIJE: 12 RIE: 6 CAT: 16
SN See also "Teacher Enthusiasm"

Enthymeme
CIJE: 4 RIE: 7 CAT: 13

Entitlement
CIJE: 5 RIE: 4 CAT: 14
SN See also "Educational Entitlements" and "Social Entitlements"

Entitlement Programs
CIJE: 3 RIE: 8 CAT: 19

Entomological Research Center FL
CIJE: 0 RIE: 1 CAT: 17

Entrepreneurial Development Training Center PA
CIJE: 0 RIE: 1 CAT: 17

Entry Behavior
CIJE: 7 RIE: 3 CAT: 21

Entry Level Mathematics Examination
CIJE: 0 RIE: 1 CAT: 21

Entry Level Skills
CIJE: 5 RIE: 1 CAT: 21

Entry Level Skills Program
CIJE: 0 RIE: 2 CAT: 19

Entry Standards Assessment
CIJE: 0 RIE: 1 CAT: 21

EntryWay
CIJE: 0 RIE: 1 CAT: 04

Enumeration Task
CIJE: 4 RIE: 1 CAT: 11

Enuresis
CIJE: 31 RIE: 4 CAT: 11

Envelope Machine Operators
CIJE: 0 RIE: 1 CAT: 09

Environment and Interest Inventory
CIJE: 0 RIE: 1 CAT: 21

Environmental Action
CIJE: 58 RIE: 25 CAT: 16

Environmental Assessment Technique
CIJE: 12 RIE: 4 CAT: 21

Environmental Attitudes
CIJE: 63 RIE: 27 CAT: 20

Environmental Awareness
CIJE: 134 RIE: 60 CAT: 20

Environmental Beauty Estimation Method
CIJE: 0 RIE: 1 CAT: 15

Environmental Camp for Handicapped and Others MA
CIJE: 0 RIE: 1 CAT: 17

Environmental Catastrophes
CIJE: 4 RIE: 1 CAT: 20

Environmental Chemistry
CIJE: 18 RIE: 0 CAT: 20

Environmental Communications
CIJE: 7 RIE: 12 CAT: 20

Environmental Complexity
CIJE: 3 RIE: 0 CAT: 20

Environmental Concepts
CIJE: 8 RIE: 19 CAT: 20

Environmental Conservation Commission
CIJE: 2 RIE: 0 CAT: 17

Environmental Control
CIJE: 2 RIE: 10 CAT: 20

Environmental Control (Psychological)
CIJE: 0 RIE: 1 CAT: 11

Environmental Defense Fund
CIJE: 2 RIE: 0 CAT: 17

Environmental Deprivation Scale (Pascal Jenkins)
CIJE: 0 RIE: 6 CAT: 21

Environmental Description Scale (Vielhauer)
CIJE: 1 RIE: 0 CAT: 21

Environmental Design
CIJE: 10 RIE: 2 CAT: 20

Environmental Design Professions
CIJE: 0 RIE: 1 CAT: 09

Environmental Docility Hypothesis
CIJE: 1 RIE: 0 CAT: 15

Environmental Economics
CIJE: 6 RIE: 2 CAT: 20

Environmental Education Act 1970
CIJE: 7 RIE: 6 CAT: 14

Environmental Education Centers
CIJE: 9 RIE: 3 CAT: 05

Environmental Education Literacy
CIJE: 0 RIE: 2 CAT: 20

Environmental Education Outdoor School Program CA
CIJE: 0 RIE: 6 CAT: 19

Environmental Education Programs
CIJE: 121 RIE: 54 CAT: 19

Environmental Education Research
CIJE: 183 RIE: 77 CAT: 20

Environmental Energy Technology
CIJE: 2 RIE: 1 CAT: 20

Environmental Engineering
CIJE: 7 RIE: 1 CAT: 20

Environmental Ethic
CIJE: 55 RIE: 16 CAT: 15

Environmental Experience Stipends Program
CIJE: 2 RIE: 0 CAT: 19

Environmental Field Centers
CIJE: 2 RIE: 0 CAT: 05

Environmental Geology
CIJE: 4 RIE: 1 CAT: 20

Environmental Health
CIJE: 57 RIE: 34 CAT: 11

Environmental Health Engineering
CIJE: 1 RIE: 0 CAT: 03

Environmental Health Proficiency Examinations
CIJE: 1 RIE: 0 CAT: 21

Environmental Health Technology
CIJE: 0 RIE: 1 CAT: 03

Environmental Impact
CIJE: 48 RIE: 17 CAT: 20
SN See also "Biological Impact"

Environmental Impact Reports
CIJE: 19 RIE: 5 CAT: 20

Environmental Indexes
CIJE: 4 RIE: 0 CAT: 20

Environmental Issues
CIJE: 196 RIE: 93 CAT: 20

Environmental Law
CIJE: 11 RIE: 7 CAT: 14

Environmental Literacy
CIJE: 14 RIE: 15 CAT: 20

Environmental Management
CIJE: 49 RIE: 50 CAT: 20

Environmental Measures
CIJE: 4 RIE: 2 CAT: 20

Environmental Medicine
CIJE: 0 RIE: 1 CAT: 11

Environmental Monitoring
CIJE: 25 RIE: 3 CAT: 20

Environmental Movement
CIJE: 23 RIE: 4 CAT: 20

Environmental Occupations
CIJE: 2 RIE: 14 CAT: 09

Environmental Pesticide Control Act
CIJE: 1 RIE: 0 CAT: 14

Environmental Planning Education
CIJE: 14 RIE: 1 CAT: 03

Environmental Policy
CIJE: 23 RIE: 6 CAT: 20

Environmental Press
CIJE: 2 RIE: 3 CAT: 19

Environmental Problems
CIJE: 132 RIE: 69 CAT: 20

Environmental Professionals
CIJE: 6 RIE: 3 CAT: 09

Environmental Protection
CIJE: 79 RIE: 50 CAT: 20

Environmental Protection Agency
CIJE: 87 RIE: 60 CAT: 17

Environmental Psychologists
CIJE: 0 RIE: 1 CAT: 09

Environmental Psychology
CIJE: 18 RIE: 5 CAT: 11

Environmental Quality
CIJE: 30 RIE: 24 CAT: 20

Environmental Quality Index
CIJE: 3 RIE: 1 CAT: 21

Environmental Reporting
CIJE: 5 RIE: 8 CAT: 20

Environmental Research Experimental Schools
CIJE: 0 RIE: 1 CAT: 05

Environmental Risk Assessment
CIJE: 10 RIE: 1 CAT: 15

Environmental Robustness
CIJE: 9 RIE: 0 CAT: 15
SN See also "Robustness Semantic Differential"
UF Classroom Robustness; Robustness (Social Interaction); School Robustness

Environmental Robustness Semantic Differential
USE Robustness Semantic Differential

Environmental Science Services Administration
CIJE: 1 RIE: 0 CAT: 17

Environmental Sciences Institute CA
CIJE: 0 RIE: 1 CAT: 17

Environmental Stability Scale (Crawford Reinard)
CIJE: 0 RIE: 1 CAT: 21

Environmental Stressors
CIJE: 0 RIE: 2 CAT: 20

Environmental Studies Project
CIJE: 4 RIE: 2 CAT: 19

Environmental Study Area Program
CIJE: 1 RIE: 0 CAT: 19

Environmental Study Areas
CIJE: 2 RIE: 2 CAT: 20

Environmental Tobacco Smoke
CIJE: 1 RIE: 4 CAT: 11
SN See also "Passive Smoking"
UF Second Hand Tobacco Smoke

Environmental Trends
CIJE: 4 RIE: 6 CAT: 20

Enzensberger (Hans Magnus)
CIJE: 3 RIE: 0 CAT: 18

Epenthesis
CIJE: 1 RIE: 2 CAT: 13

Ephemera
CIJE: 7 RIE: 2 CAT: 16

Epic of Gilgamesh
CIJE: 2 RIE: 1 CAT: 22

EPIC Project MO
USE Experimental Proj in Instruct Concentration

EPIC Project OH
USE Educators Peer Instructional Consulting Proj

EPIC SOCRATES
CIJE: 1 RIE: 0 CAT: 04
SN See also "IBM Socrates"

EPIC Teacher Information Form
CIJE: 0 RIE: 1 CAT: 21

Epideictic Rhetoric
CIJE: 6 RIE: 3 CAT: 13

Epidemic Theory
CIJE: 0 RIE: 1 CAT: 15

Epidermolysis Bullosa
CIJE: 0 RIE: 1 CAT: 11

Epidural Anesthesia
CIJE: 1 RIE: 0 CAT: 11

Epigenesis
CIJE: 11 RIE: 0 CAT: 20

Epilepsy Foundation of America
CIJE: 3 RIE: 2 CAT: 17

Epinephrine
CIJE: 1 RIE: 0 CAT: 11

Episcopal Academy PA
CIJE: 1 RIE: 0 CAT: 17

Episcopal Church
CIJE: 1 RIE: 1 CAT: 17

Episcopal Home for Children DC
CIJE: 0 RIE: 1 CAT: 17

Episodic Communication Channels in Organizations
CIJE: 0 RIE: 2 CAT: 15

Episodic Mapping
CIJE: 0 RIE: 1 CAT: 15

Episodic Memory
CIJE: 15 RIE: 4 CAT: 11

Episodic Organizers
CIJE: 0 RIE: 3 CAT: 11

Epistemic Research
CIJE: 8 RIE: 5 CAT: 16

Epistemic Rhetoric
USE Rhetoric as Epistemic

Epistemic Triangle
CIJE: 0 RIE: 1 CAT: 15

Epithet
CIJE: 0 RIE: 1 CAT: 13

Epogenic Influences
CIJE: 1 RIE: 0 CAT: 11

Eppelsheimer (Hanns Wilhelm)
CIJE: 1 RIE: 0 CAT: 18

Eppse (Merl R)
CIJE: 1 RIE: 1 CAT: 18

Epstein (Herman T)
CIJE: 2 RIE: 2 CAT: 18

Epstein (Jean)
CIJE: 0 RIE: 2 CAT: 18

Epstein (S)
CIJE: 2 RIE: 1 CAT: 18

Epstein Barr Virus
CIJE: 3 RIE: 1 CAT: 11

Equal Access
CIJE: 18 RIE: 7 CAT: 14

Equal Access Act 1984
CIJE: 28 RIE: 6 CAT: 14

Equal Credit Opportunity Act
CIJE: 3 RIE: 2 CAT: 14

Equal Education Opportunity Program PA
CIJE: 0 RIE: 1 CAT: 19

Equal Educational Opportunities Act 1974
CIJE: 6 RIE: 8 CAT: 14
UF Education Amendments 1974 Title II

Equal Employment Opportunities Enforcement Act
CIJE: 1 RIE: 0 CAT: 14

Equal Employment Opportunity Act 1972
CIJE: 14 RIE: 16 CAT: 14

Equal Employment Opportunity Commission
CIJE: 84 RIE: 33 CAT: 17
SN See add'l listings under "EEOC..."

Equal Employment Opportunity Coordinating Council
CIJE: 0 RIE: 1 CAT: 17

Equal Employment Opportunity Training Institute
CIJE: 0 RIE: 1 CAT: 17

Equal Interval Scoring
CIJE: 3 RIE: 4 CAT: 21

Equal Justice Under Law (American Bar Assn)
CIJE: 0 RIE: 1 CAT: 22
SN Full title — "Equal Justice Under Law: The Supreme Court in American Life"

Equal Pay Act 1963
CIJE: 30 RIE: 23 CAT: 14

Equal Results (Law)
CIJE: 0 RIE: 0 CAT: 14

Equal Rights
CIJE: 10 RIE: 6 CAT: 14

Equal Rights Amendment
CIJE: 48 RIE: 37 CAT: 14

Equal Time Doctrine
CIJE: 0 RIE: 5 CAT: 14

Equality (Mathematics)
CIJE: 13 RIE: 4 CAT: 20

Equality (Social)
CIJE: 29 RIE: 10 CAT: 15
UF Social Equality

EQuality Project
CIJE: 3 RIE: 4 CAT: 19
UF College Board Educational EQuality Project; Educational EQuality Project

Equalizer (Television Series)
CIJE: 0 RIE: 1 CAT: 22

EQUALS Program
CIJE: 1 RIE: 4 CAT: 19
UF Project EQUALS

Equals Sign
CIJE: 1 RIE: 0 CAT: 16

Equamax Criterion
CIJE: 1 RIE: 0 CAT: 21

Equations (Chemistry)
CIJE: 4 RIE: 0 CAT: 20

Equifinality
CIJE: 0 RIE: 1 CAT: 15

Equilibrium (Piaget)
CIJE: 12 RIE: 8 CAT: 11

Equilibrium Model
CIJE: 1 RIE: 4 CAT: 15

Equine Management
CIJE: 0 RIE: 2 CAT: 20
UF Horse Management

Equipercentile Assumption
CIJE: 1 RIE: 4 CAT: 21

Equipercentile Equating
CIJE: 27 RIE: 35 CAT: 21
SN See also "Chained Equipercentile Equating"

Equipment Needs
CIJE: 0 RIE: 6 CAT: 16

Equipment Operation
CIJE: 0 RIE: 4 CAT: 20

Equitable Life Assurance Society
CIJE: 0 RIE: 1 CAT: 17

EQUITY 2000
CIJE: 0 RIE: 1 CAT: 19

Equity Materials
CIJE: 0 RIE: 2 CAT: 16

Equity Theory
CIJE: 18 RIE: 7 CAT: 15

Equivalence Conservation
CIJE: 5 RIE: 2 CAT: 11

Equivalence Formation
CIJE: 5 RIE: 2 CAT: 11

Equivalent Instruction Programs
CIJE: 0 RIE: 2 CAT: 14

Equivariance
CIJE: 0 RIE: 1 CAT: 21

Equivocation
CIJE: 0 RIE: 1 CAT: 16

Erasmus (Desiderius)
CIJE: 4 RIE: 0 CAT: 18

ERASMUS Programme
CIJE: 2 RIE: 5 CAT: 19
SN "European Community Action Scheme for the Mobility of University Students"

Erasmus University (Netherlands)
CIJE: 1 RIE: 0 CAT: 17

Eratosthenes Mathematics
CIJE: 2 RIE: 0 CAT: 20

Ercilla (Jose de)
CIJE: 1 RIE: 0 CAT: 18

Ercilla y Zuniga (Alonso de)
CIJE: 2 RIE: 0 CAT: 18

Erdman (Loula Grace)
CIJE: 1 RIE: 0 CAT: 18

Ergativity
CIJE: 1 RIE: 7 CAT: 13

ERGO Procedure
CIJE: 1 RIE: 0 CAT: 21

Ergogenic Aids
CIJE: 1 RIE: 2 CAT: 11

Ergometers
CIJE: 11 RIE: 3 CAT: 04
SN Devices that measure muscle power
UF Bicycle Ergometer Tests

Ergometrics
CIJE: 1 RIE: 3 CAT: 20
SN Psychometrically based work analysis

Ergometry
CIJE: 2 RIE: 0 CAT: 11
SN The study of muscular exertion and stress
UF Arm Ergometry; Leg Ergometry

Ergonomics Inventories
CIJE: 0 RIE: 1 CAT: 21

Erhardt Developmental Vision Assessment
CIJE: 0 RIE: 1 CAT: 21

ERIC
CIJE: 294 RIE: 595 CAT: 17

ERIC Clearinghouse for Junior Colleges
CIJE: 2 RIE: 6 CAT: 17

ERIC Clearinghouse for Science Math Environ Educ
CIJE: 5 RIE: 35 CAT: 17

ERIC Clearinghouse for Social Studies Soc Sci Educ
CIJE: 67 RIE: 1 CAT: 17

ERIC Clearinghouse on Adult Career Vocational Educ
CIJE: 0 RIE: 3 CAT: 17

ERIC Clearinghouse on Adult Education
CIJE: 1 RIE: 2 CAT: 17

ERIC Clearinghouse on Career Education
CIJE: 4 RIE: 3 CAT: 17

ERIC Clearinghouse on Counsel and Personnel Serv
CIJE: 0 RIE: 1 CAT: 17

ERIC Clearinghouse on Early Childhood Education
CIJE: 0 RIE: 1 CAT: 17

ERIC Clearinghouse on Educational Management
CIJE: 0 RIE: 10 CAT: 17

ERIC Clearinghouse on Educational Media and Tech
CIJE: 0 RIE: 5 CAT: 17

ERIC Clearinghouse on Elementary Early Child Educ
CIJE: 1 RIE: 3 CAT: 17

ERIC Clearinghouse on Exceptional Children
CIJE: 2 RIE: 0 CAT: 17

ERIC Clearinghouse on Handicapped and Gifted Child
CIJE: 1 RIE: 2 CAT: 17

ERIC Clearinghouse on Higher Education
CIJE: 2 RIE: 1 CAT: 17

ERIC Clearinghouse on Information Resources
CIJE: 3 RIE: 0 CAT: 17

ERIC Clearinghouse on Library and Information Scis
CIJE: 0 RIE: 2 CAT: 17

ERIC Clearinghouse on Reading
CIJE: 0 RIE: 1 CAT: 17

ERIC Clearinghouse on Reading and Commun Skills
CIJE: 64 RIE: 7 CAT: 17

ERIC Clearinghouse on Rural Educ and Small Schools
CIJE: 0 RIE: 2 CAT: 17

ERIC Clearinghouse on Teacher Education
CIJE: 3 RIE: 2 CAT: 17

ERIC Clearinghouse on Tests Measurement Evaluation
CIJE: 1 RIE: 4 CAT: 17

ERIC Clearinghouse on the Disadvantaged
CIJE: 1 RIE: 6 CAT: 17

ERIC Clearinghouse on the Teaching of English
CIJE: 2 RIE: 0 CAT: 17

ERIC Clearinghouses
CIJE: 3 RIE: 4 CAT: 05

ERIC Digests
CIJE: 3 RIE: 1391 CAT: 19

ERIC Document Reproduction Service
CIJE: 0 RIE: 4 CAT: 17

ERIC Fact Sheets
CIJE: 0 RIE: 1 CAT: 16

ERIC Mini Reviews
CIJE: 2 RIE: 1 CAT: 16

ERIC ONTAP
CIJE: 1 RIE: 1 CAT: 04

ERIC Processing and Reference Facility
CIJE: 0 RIE: 1 CAT: 17

ERIC SilverPlatter
USE SilverPlatter ERIC

ERIC Trends Issues Papers
CIJE: 0 RIE: 5 CAT: 16

Erica Method
CIJE: 1 RIE: 0 CAT: 15

Erickson (Milton H)
CIJE: 3 RIE: 1 CAT: 18

Erie City School District PA
CIJE: 0 RIE: 2 CAT: 17

Erie Community College NY
CIJE: 2 RIE: 5 CAT: 17

Erie County Technical School PA
CIJE: 1 RIE: 2 CAT: 17

Erikson (Erik)
CIJE: 69 RIE: 41 CAT: 18

Erikson Psychosocial Stage Inventory
CIJE: 6 RIE: 1 CAT: 21

Erlangen University
CIJE: 2 RIE: 0 CAT: 17

Eron (L D)
CIJE: 1 RIE: 0 CAT: 18

Erosion
CIJE: 12 RIE: 7 CAT: 20

Eroticism
CIJE: 4 RIE: 0 CAT: 11

Erotophobia
CIJE: 0 RIE: 1 CAT: 11
SN Negative feelings about sexuality

Error Analysis (Mathematics)
CIJE: 21 RIE: 10 CAT: 20

Error Analysis (Statistics)
CIJE: 14 RIE: 17 CAT: 21

Error Detection
CIJE: 46 RIE: 16 CAT: 15

Error Monitoring
CIJE: 12 RIE: 8 CAT: 15

Error Prone Model
CIJE: 0 RIE: 2 CAT: 15

Error Reports
CIJE: 4 RIE: 1 CAT: 16

Errorless Discrimination Training
CIJE: 3 RIE: 4 CAT: 15

Errorless Learning
CIJE: 1 RIE: 2 CAT: 15

Errors and Omissions Insurance
CIJE: 1 RIE: 0 CAT: 14

Errors and Omissions Tests
CIJE: 0 RIE: 1 CAT: 21

ERTL Index
CIJE: 3 RIE: 1 CAT: 21

Erwin Identity Scale
CIJE: 3 RIE: 1 CAT: 21

Esalen Institute CA
CIJE: 2 RIE: 3 CAT: 17

Escala de Inteligencia Wechsler Ninos Revisada
CIJE: 0 RIE: 1 CAT: 21

Escala de Inteligencia Wechsler Para Ninos
CIJE: 1 RIE: 2 CAT: 21

Escalante (Jaime)
CIJE: 2 RIE: 2 CAT: 18

Escalante Math Program
USE Jaime Escalante Math Program

ESCALATE (System)
CIJE: 0 RIE: 0 CAT: 04

Escalona and Corman Object Permanence Scales
CIJE: 0 RIE: 1 CAT: 21

Escambia County Public Schools FL
CIJE: 1 RIE: 0 CAT: 17

Escandon (Jose de)
CIJE: 0 RIE: 1 CAT: 18

Escherichia Coli
CIJE: 2 RIE: 0 CAT: 20

Escola Superior de Guerra
CIJE: 1 RIE: 0 CAT: 17

Escondido Management System
CIJE: 1 RIE: 0 CAT: 15

Escondido Union School District CA
CIJE: 1 RIE: 1 CAT: 17

Escosura (Patricio de la)
CIJE: 1 RIE: 0 CAT: 18

Escuela Agricola Panamericana (Honduras)
CIJE: 0 RIE: 1 CAT: 17

Escuela Moderna Movement
CIJE: 1 RIE: 0 CAT: 12
SN See also "Modern School Movement"

Escuela Normal Veracruzana (Mexico)
CIJE: 0 RIE: 0 CAT: 17

Escuelas en El Campo
CIJE: 1 RIE: 0 CAT: 16

ESEA
USE Elementary Secondary Education Act

ESEA Title I Migrant Programs
CIJE: 0 RIE: 64 CAT: 19

Eseejja
CIJE: 0 RIE: 1 CAT: 13

Eskasoni Indian Reserve NS
CIJE: 0 RIE: 1 CAT: 17

Eskisehir Academy Economic Coml Sciences (Turkey)
CIJE: 0 RIE: 1 CAT: 17

Esophageal Speech
CIJE: 9 RIE: 0 CAT: 11

ESOPs
USE Employee Stock Ownership Plans

Espanola Municipal Schools NM
CIJE: 0 RIE: 1 CAT: 17

Esperanza School NM
CIJE: 0 RIE: 1 CAT: 17

Espionage
CIJE: 8 RIE: 5 CAT: 14

Espionage Act
CIJE: 0 RIE: 3 CAT: 14

Espionage Books
CIJE: 1 RIE: 0 CAT: 16

Esprit (Journal)
CIJE: 0 RIE: 1 CAT: 22

Essay on Criticism
CIJE: 1 RIE: 0 CAT: 22

Essay Topics
CIJE: 8 RIE: 9 CAT: 16

Essentia Project (Essence)
CIJE: 1 RIE: 0 CAT: 19

Essential Early Education Project
CIJE: 0 RIE: 1 CAT: 19

Essential Elements of Effective Instruction
CIJE: 0 RIE: 1 CAT: 19
SN Project of Spencerport Central Schools NY

Essential Elements of Instruction (Hunter)
CIJE: 0 RIE: 1 CAT: 15
SN See also "Hunter Instructional Model"

Essential High School Content Battery
CIJE: 0 RIE: 1 CAT: 21

Essential Independence (Tests)
CIJE: 0 RIE: 1 CAT: 21

Essential Learning Skills (Oregon)
CIJE: 0 RIE: 1 CAT: 03

Essential Schools Movement
CIJE: 1 RIE: 1 CAT: 12
SN See also "Coalition of Essential Schools"

Essential Skills Mathematics Tests
CIJE: 0 RIE: 1 CAT: 21
SN Part of the Michigan Educational Assessment Program
UF MEAP Essential Skills Mathematics Tests

Essential Skills Program
CIJE: 1 RIE: 2 CAT: 19

Essential Undergrad Curr Speech Commun Small Coll
CIJE: 0 RIE: 1 CAT: 03

Essentialism
CIJE: 15 RIE: 7 CAT: 15

Essentials of Instruction (Program)
CIJE: 0 RIE: 1 CAT: 19

Essex Agricultural and Technical Institute MA
CIJE: 2 RIE: 0 CAT: 17

Essex Community College MD
CIJE: 3 RIE: 6 CAT: 17

Essex County College NJ
CIJE: 4 RIE: 7 CAT: 17

Essex County Vocational Technical Schools NJ
CIJE: 0 RIE: 1 CAT: 17

Essexfields Demonstration Project
CIJE: 0 RIE: 1 CAT: 19

Essexfields Group Rehabilitation Center
CIJE: 0 RIE: 1 CAT: 17

ESSO Company
CIJE: 1 RIE: 0 CAT: 17

ESSO Education Foundation NY
CIJE: 1 RIE: 0 CAT: 17

ESSO Repertory Theatre
CIJE: 0 RIE: 1 CAT: 17

Establishment Clause
CIJE: 40 RIE: 6 CAT: 14

Estancia High School CA
CIJE: 1 RIE: 0 CAT: 17

Esterification
CIJE: 3 RIE: 0 CAT: 20

Estes Attitude Scale
CIJE: 7 RIE: 9 CAT: 21

Estimated Learning Potential
CIJE: 10 RIE: 1 CAT: 21

Estimates of Decision Consistency (Huynh)
CIJE: 0 RIE: 1 CAT: 15

Estimation
CIJE: 54 RIE: 19 CAT: 20

Estonia
CIJE: 3 RIE: 4 CAT: 07
SN See also "USSR (Estonia)"

Estonian Americans
CIJE: 0 RIE: 2 CAT: 08

Estrogen
CIJE: 3 RIE: 1 CAT: 11

Eta Sigma Gamma
CIJE: 1 RIE: 1 CAT: 17

Etching
CIJE: 5 RIE: 1 CAT: 03

Ethane
CIJE: 1 RIE: 0 CAT: 20

Ethanol
CIJE: 0 RIE: 5 CAT: 20

Ether
CIJE: 2 RIE: 0 CAT: 20

Ethic of Care Interview
CIJE: 0 RIE: 1 CAT: 21

Ethical Analysis Protocol
CIJE: 1 RIE: 1 CAT: 15

Ethical Communication
CIJE: 1 RIE: 1 CAT: 16

Ethical Culture Schools
CIJE: 0 RIE: 1 CAT: 05

Ethical Judgment Scale (Vabakas)
CIJE: 2 RIE: 0 CAT: 21

Ethical Quest Project
CIJE: 1 RIE: 1 CAT: 19

Ethical Relativism
CIJE: 1 RIE: 0 CAT: 16

Ethics Position Questionnaire (Forsyth)
CIJE: 0 RIE: 1 CAT: 21

Ethiopia
CIJE: 52 RIE: 92 CAT: 07

Ethiopia (Addis Ababa)
CIJE: 1 RIE: 4 CAT: 07

Ethiopian Educational Television Service
CIJE: 1 RIE: 1 CAT: 17

Ethiopians
CIJE: 2 RIE: 8 CAT: 08

Ethnic Differences
CIJE: 11 RIE: 12 CAT: 16

Ethnic Heritage and Language Schools Project
CIJE: 0 RIE: 1 CAT: 19

Ethnic Heritage Studies Program
CIJE: 1 RIE: 145 CAT: 19
UF Elementary Secondary Education Act Title IX

Ethnic Identity Questionnaire
CIJE: 2 RIE: 0 CAT: 21

Ethnic Literature
CIJE: 6 RIE: 23 CAT: 16
SN See also "Multiethnic Literature"

Ethnic Media
CIJE: 0 RIE: 2 CAT: 16

Ethnic Monitoring (Great Britain)
CIJE: 0 RIE: 1 CAT: 19

Ethnic Newspapers
CIJE: 2 RIE: 4 CAT: 16

Ethnic Revitalization
CIJE: 2 RIE: 1 CAT: 15

Ethnic Schools
CIJE: 3 RIE: 4 CAT: 05

Ethnographic Auditing
CIJE: 0 RIE: 0 CAT: 21

Ethnographic Evaluation
CIJE: 3 RIE: 2 CAT: 21

Ethnographic Films
CIJE: 1 RIE: 3 CAT: 16

Ethnographic Monitoring
CIJE: 1 RIE: 2 CAT: 15

Ethnographic Residual Analysis
CIJE: 1 RIE: 0 CAT: 15

Ethnographic Semantics
CIJE: 2 RIE: 4 CAT: 13

Ethnohistory
CIJE: 10 RIE: 2 CAT: 16

Ethnolinguistics
CIJE: 22 RIE: 7 CAT: 13

Ethnomathematics
CIJE: 9 RIE: 4 CAT: 03

Ethnomethodology
CIJE: 14 RIE: 15 CAT: 03

Ethnomusicology
CIJE: 8 RIE: 8 CAT: 03

Ethnorhetoric
CIJE: 1 RIE: 0 CAT: 13

Ethogenics
CIJE: 2 RIE: 0 CAT: 13

Ethos
CIJE: 18 RIE: 7 CAT: 16

Ethos Level
CIJE: 1 RIE: 1 CAT: 16

Ethyl Ethanoate
CIJE: 1 RIE: 0 CAT: 20

Ethylene
CIJE: 4 RIE: 0 CAT: 20

Etiquette
CIJE: 19 RIE: 16 CAT: 16

Etowah County School District AL
CIJE: 0 RIE: 1 CAT: 17

ETS Academic Profile
CIJE: 2 RIE: 0 CAT: 21
UF Academic Profile (ETS)

ETS Enumeration Task
CIJE: 0 RIE: 1 CAT: 21

ETS Factor Kit
CIJE: 0 RIE: 0 CAT: 21

ETS Growth Study
CIJE: 0 RIE: 1 CAT: 21

ETS Matched Pictures Language Comprehension Task
CIJE: 0 RIE: 1 CAT: 21

ETS Speaking Proficiency English Assessment Kit
USE Speaking Proficiency English Assessment Kit

ETS Specialty Area Tests
CIJE: 0 RIE: 1 CAT: 21
SN See also "NTE Specialty Area Tests"
UF Specialty Area Tests (ETS)

ETS Test Collection
USE Test Collection (Educational Testing Service)

ETS Written Exercises
CIJE: 0 RIE: 1 CAT: 21

Etsako
CIJE: 0 RIE: 1 CAT: 13

Etzioni (Amitai)
CIJE: 9 RIE: 3 CAT: 18

Eu (March Fong)
CIJE: 0 RIE: 1 CAT: 18

Euclid
CIJE: 3 RIE: 2 CAT: 18

Euclid English Demonstration Center OH
CIJE: 0 RIE: 9 CAT: 17

Euclidean Geometry
CIJE: 15 RIE: 1 CAT: 20

Euclidean Model
CIJE: 7 RIE: 0 CAT: 15

Euclidean Objects
CIJE: 0 RIE: 1 CAT: 20

EUDISED
CIJE: 3 RIE: 27 CAT: 17
SN See also earlier spelled-out form "European Documentation and Information System"

EUDISED Multilingual Thesaurus
CIJE: 0 RIE: 1 CAT: 22

Eugene Public Schools OR
CIJE: 9 RIE: 29 CAT: 17

Eugenics
CIJE: 27 RIE: 9 CAT: 11

Eugenio Maria de Hostos Community College
CIJE: 1 RIE: 0 CAT: 17

Euglena
CIJE: 1 RIE: 0 CAT: 20

Euler Circuits (Mathematics)
CIJE: 1 RIE: 0 CAT: 20

Eulers Formula
CIJE: 5 RIE: 0 CAT: 20

Eulogies
CIJE: 5 RIE: 3 CAT: 13

Euphemism
CIJE: 13 RIE: 3 CAT: 13

Euphenics
CIJE: 1 RIE: 0 CAT: 11

Eurasia
CIJE: 0 RIE: 3 CAT: 07

Eureka Project
CIJE: 1 RIE: 8 CAT: 19
SN A review of student financial aid in California — do not confuse with "Project EUREKA"

Eurhythmics
CIJE: 8 RIE: 0 CAT: 15

Euripides
CIJE: 4 RIE: 2 CAT: 18

Euro Americans
CIJE: 5 RIE: 14 CAT: 08

Eurocentres Schools (United Kingdom)
CIJE: 0 RIE: 1 CAT: 17

Eurocentrism
CIJE: 27 RIE: 7 CAT: 16

EUROLEX
CIJE: 0 RIE: 1 CAT: 17

EURONET
CIJE: 8 RIE: 3 CAT: 04

Europa TV
CIJE: 0 RIE: 1 CAT: 17

Europe
CIJE: 701 RIE: 783 CAT: 07

Europe (Central)
CIJE: 6 RIE: 6 CAT: 07

Europe (East Central)
CIJE: 14 RIE: 5 CAT: 07

Europe (East)
CIJE: 88 RIE: 89 CAT: 07

Europe (North)
CIJE: 2 RIE: 0 CAT: 07

Europe (South)
CIJE: 4 RIE: 5 CAT: 07

Europe (Southeast)
CIJE: 2 RIE: 3 CAT: 07

Europe (West)
CIJE: 166 RIE: 187 CAT: 07

European Association for Special Education
CIJE: 1 RIE: 2 CAT: 17

European Association of Information Services
CIJE: 0 RIE: 1 CAT: 17
UF EUSIDIC

European Atomic Energy Community (Belgium)
CIJE: 0 RIE: 1 CAT: 17

European Broadcasting Union (Switzerland)
CIJE: 5 RIE: 2 CAT: 17

European Bureau of Adult Education (Netherlands)
CIJE: 1 RIE: 0 CAT: 17

European Centre for Ethnolinguistic Cartography
CIJE: 0 RIE: 1 CAT: 17

European Centre for Leisure Educ (Czechoslovakia)
CIJE: 1 RIE: 0 CAT: 17

European Centre for the Development of Voc Train
CIJE: 0 RIE: 1 CAT: 17

European Centre Further Education Teachers
CIJE: 0 RIE: 1 CAT: 17

European Coal and Steel Community
CIJE: 1 RIE: 1 CAT: 17

European Communities Commission
CIJE: 12 RIE: 16 CAT: 17
UF Commission of the European Communities

European Community
CIJE: 172 RIE: 194 CAT: 17

European Community Action Prog Educ Training Techn
USE COMETT

European Community Course Credit Trans Sys
CIJE: 0 RIE: 2 CAT: 19

European Council for Education by Corr (Belgium)
CIJE: 0 RIE: 2 CAT: 17

European Court of Human Rights
CIJE: 0 RIE: 1 CAT: 17

European Currency Unit
CIJE: 3 RIE: 1 CAT: 16

European Documentation and Information System
CIJE: 1 RIE: 26 CAT: 17
SN "EUDISED" is the currently preferred form of this term

European Economic Community
CIJE: 50 RIE: 27 CAT: 17

European Education Metathesaurus
CIJE: 0 RIE: 1 CAT: 15

European Forum for Educational Administration
CIJE: 0 RIE: 1 CAT: 17

European Geography
CIJE: 1 RIE: 2 CAT: 03

European Home Study Council
CIJE: 0 RIE: 1 CAT: 17

European Influences
CIJE: 0 RIE: 1 CAT: 16

European Jeremiads
CIJE: 0 RIE: 0 CAT: 16

European Organization for Nuclear Research
CIJE: 1 RIE: 0 CAT: 17

European Parliament
CIJE: 0 RIE: 2 CAT: 17

European Peace Research Association
CIJE: 0 RIE: 1 CAT: 17

European Research Group on Management
CIJE: 1 RIE: 0 CAT: 17

European Space Agency
CIJE: 4 RIE: 3 CAT: 17

European Sports Charter
CIJE: 0 RIE: 1 CAT: 14

European Studies
CIJE: 6 RIE: 11 CAT: 03

European Theater
CIJE: 0 RIE: 2 CAT: 16

European Translations Center (Netherlands)
CIJE: 0 RIE: 1 CAT: 17

European Universities
CIJE: 3 RIE: 7 CAT: 17

European University Institute (Italy)
CIJE: 2 RIE: 0 CAT: 17

Europeans
CIJE: 26 RIE: 9 CAT: 08

EUROTECNET
CIJE: 0 RIE: 1 CAT: 19

Eurotra
CIJE: 0 RIE: 1 CAT: 13
SN Machine translation system designed to translate into the nine official languages of the European Economic Community

Eurotrain
CIJE: 0 RIE: 1 CAT: 02

Eurovision News Exchange
CIJE: 2 RIE: 0 CAT: 17

EURYDICE
CIJE: 0 RIE: 6 CAT: 17
SN "Education Information Network in the European Community"

EUSIDIC
USE European Association of Information Services

Euthanasia
CIJE: 40 RIE: 9 CAT: 11

Eutrophication
CIJE: 4 RIE: 2 CAT: 20

Evaluability Assessment
CIJE: 3 RIE: 9 CAT: 21

Evaluation and Prevocational Conditioning Course
CIJE: 2 RIE: 0 CAT: 03

Evaluation Apprehension
CIJE: 1 RIE: 2 CAT: 11

Evaluation Assistance Center (East)
CIJE: 0 RIE: 1 CAT: 17

Evaluation Center Cube
CIJE: 0 RIE: 1 CAT: 15

Evaluation Costs
CIJE: 0 RIE: 2 CAT: 21

Evaluation for Individualized Instruction Project
CIJE: 0 RIE: 17 CAT: 19

Evaluation Improvement Program CA
USE California Evaluation Improvement Program

Evaluation Instrument for Experimental Methodology
CIJE: 0 RIE: 2 CAT: 21
UF EIEM Rating Scale

Evaluation Instrument for Experimental Research
CIJE: 0 RIE: 1 CAT: 21
UF EIFER Rating Scale

Evaluation Modality Test
CIJE: 0 RIE: 2 CAT: 21

Evaluation of Counselors Scale
CIJE: 3 RIE: 0 CAT: 21

Evaluation of Practices Individualized Schooling
CIJE: 0 RIE: 16 CAT: 19

Evaluation Reports
CIJE: 19 RIE: 40 CAT: 16

Evaluation Research Society
CIJE: 9 RIE: 1 CAT: 17

Evaluation Scale for Four Five Year Old Children
CIJE: 0 RIE: 1 CAT: 21

Evaluation Service Center for Occupational Educ
CIJE: 0 RIE: 8 CAT: 17

Evaluation Standards
CIJE: 22 RIE: 16 CAT: 21

Evaluation Task Development Project
CIJE: 0 RIE: 1 CAT: 19

Evaluation Teams
CIJE: 5 RIE: 4 CAT: 10

Evaluation Timeliness
CIJE: 1 RIE: 0 CAT: 21

Evaluations of Classroom Observations Project
CIJE: 0 RIE: 1 CAT: 19

Evaluative Criteria (Coop Study Sec Sch Standards)
CIJE: 1 RIE: 1 CAT: 21

Evaluative Cues
CIJE: 0 RIE: 1 CAT: 21

Evaluative Dimensions
CIJE: 2 RIE: 3 CAT: 21

Evaluative Meaning
CIJE: 0 RIE: 3 CAT: 21

Evaluative Programs for Innovative Curriculums
CIJE: 1 RIE: 2 CAT: 19

Evaluative Programs Innovative Curriculums Ctr AZ
CIJE: 0 RIE: 1 CAT: 17

Evaluator Characteristics
CIJE: 1 RIE: 4 CAT: 21

Evaluator Credibility
CIJE: 0 RIE: 5 CAT: 21

Evaluator Types (Meltsner)
CIJE: 0 RIE: 1 CAT: 21

Evangelical Christians
CIJE: 7 RIE: 10 CAT: 10

Evans (Rupert N)
CIJE: 1 RIE: 0 CAT: 18

Evans (Walker)
CIJE: 1 RIE: 0 CAT: 18

Evanston Early Identification Scale
CIJE: 1 RIE: 0 CAT: 21

Evanston School District IL
CIJE: 1 RIE: 2 CAT: 17

Evanston Township High School IL
CIJE: 3 RIE: 2 CAT: 17

Evansville Vanderburgh School Corporation IN
CIJE: 1 RIE: 2 CAT: 17

Evaporation
CIJE: 8 RIE: 2 CAT: 20

Evelyn Lowe School (England)
CIJE: 1 RIE: 0 CAT: 17

Evelyn Wood Reading Dynamics
CIJE: 0 RIE: 2 CAT: 22

Even Start
CIJE: 2 RIE: 20 CAT: 19

Evening Newspapers
CIJE: 0 RIE: 1 CAT: 16

Event Analysis
CIJE: 13 RIE: 3 CAT: 15

Event Related Potentials
CIJE: 17 RIE: 7 CAT: 11
UF Brain Event Related Potentials

Event Sampling
CIJE: 3 RIE: 2 CAT: 21

Everett (Edward)
CIJE: 0 RIE: 1 CAT: 18

Everett Community College WA
CIJE: 0 RIE: 2 CAT: 17

Everglades
CIJE: 1 RIE: 4 CAT: 07

Evergreen School CA
CIJE: 1 RIE: 0 CAT: 17

Evergreen State College WA
CIJE: 12 RIE: 22 CAT: 17

Evergreen Valley College CA
CIJE: 1 RIE: 10 CAT: 17

Everson Museum of Art NY
CIJE: 1 RIE: 0 CAT: 17

Every Child a Winner
CIJE: 0 RIE: 0 CAT: 19
SN Individualized movement education program — see also earlier name "Health and Optimum Physical Education Project" (Project HOPE)

Every Child Can Succeed Program
CIJE: 0 RIE: 1 CAT: 19

Every Student Succeeds
CIJE: 0 RIE: 1 CAT: 19

Every Student Survey
CIJE: 0 RIE: 4 CAT: 21

Everyday Memory Questionnaire
CIJE: 1 RIE: 1 CAT: 21

Everyday Stressors Index
CIJE: 0 RIE: 1 CAT: 21

Everymans University (Israel)
CIJE: 5 RIE: 6 CAT: 17

Evidence
CIJE: 49 RIE: 20 CAT: 14
SN After Oct94, if appropriate, use the Thesaurus Descriptor "Evidence (Legal)"

Evil
CIJE: 2 RIE: 1 CAT: 16

Evlyn Hone College (Zambia)
CIJE: 0 RIE: 1 CAT: 17

Evoked Brain Potentials
CIJE: 2 RIE: 2 CAT: 11

Evoked Potentials
CIJE: 6 RIE: 0 CAT: 15

Evoked Recall Theory (Schwartz)
USE Resonance Theory of Mass Communication

Evoker System
CIJE: 1 RIE: 0 CAT: 15

Evolutionary Development Program
CIJE: 0 RIE: 1 CAT: 19

Ewondo
CIJE: 0 RIE: 2 CAT: 13

Exact Conditional Tests
CIJE: 0 RIE: 1 CAT: 21

Exaggerated Hearing Level
CIJE: 0 RIE: 1 CAT: 11

Exam Analysis Procedure
CIJE: 0 RIE: 1 CAT: 15

Examination Files
USE Test Files

Examination Persistence
CIJE: 1 RIE: 0 CAT: 21

Examiner Effect
CIJE: 8 RIE: 3 CAT: 21
SN See also "Rater Effects"

Examining the Varieties of Liberal Education
USE National Project IV

Examples
CIJE: 417 RIE: 40 CAT: 21

Excavations
CIJE: 2 RIE: 2 CAT: 20

Excel Computer Program
CIJE: 0 RIE: 1 CAT: 04

EXCEL Program NC
CIJE: 0 RIE: 1 CAT: 19
SN Enrichment program for highly able students in grades K-2

Excellence
CIJE: 35 RIE: 51 CAT: 16

Excellence (Quality)
CIJE: 8 RIE: 11 CAT: 15

EXcellence in Community Elected and apoint Leadrs
USE Project EXCEL (Public Officials)

Excellence in Education Act 1984
CIJE: 0 RIE: 0 CAT: 14
UF Public Law 98 377 Title VI

Exceptional Child Education Resources
CIJE: 3 RIE: 5 CAT: 16

Exceptional Children (Journal)
CIJE: 0 RIE: 2 CAT: 22

Exceptional Parent Magazine
CIJE: 0 RIE: 0 CAT: 22

Exceptionally Gifted
CIJE: 0 RIE: 1 CAT: 10
SN See also "Extremely Gifted" and "Highly Gifted"

Excerpta Medica
CIJE: 6 RIE: 1 CAT: 22

Excerpta Medica Foundation (Netherlands)
CIJE: 1 RIE: 1 CAT: 17

Excess Costs
CIJE: 2 RIE: 1 CAT: 16

Exchange Visitor Program
CIJE: 0 RIE: 2 CAT: 19

Excitation Transfer Theory
CIJE: 0 RIE: 1 CAT: 15

Exclusion Therapy
CIJE: 0 RIE: 1 CAT: 11

Exclusive Representation
CIJE: 5 RIE: 0 CAT: 14

Exclusivity Provision
CIJE: 1 RIE: 1 CAT: 14

Excretory System
CIJE: 0 RIE: 1 CAT: 11

EXECUCOM
CIJE: 0 RIE: 1 CAT: 17

Executive Committees
CIJE: 0 RIE: 1 CAT: 10
UF College Executive Committees

Executive Exchange Prog Voluntary Service Act 1986
CIJE: 0 RIE: 1 CAT: 14
UF Public Law 99 424

Executive Function (Cognition)
CIJE: 0 RIE: 4 CAT: 11

Executive High School Internships Program
CIJE: 2 RIE: 1 CAT: 19

Executive Information Systems
CIJE: 1 RIE: 2 CAT: 15

Executive Internship Program MD
CIJE: 0 RIE: 1 CAT: 19

Executive Mind
CIJE: 0 RIE: 2 CAT: 15

Executive Order 11246
CIJE: 9 RIE: 12 CAT: 14

Executive Order 11375
CIJE: 1 RIE: 3 CAT: 14

Executive Order 11652
CIJE: 0 RIE: 1 CAT: 14

Executive Order 12356
CIJE: 2 RIE: 3 CAT: 14

Executive Orientation Training Package
CIJE: 0 RIE: 1 CAT: 15

Executive Privilege
CIJE: 1 RIE: 2 CAT: 14

Executive Procedures (Cognition)
CIJE: 3 RIE: 2 CAT: 15

Exemplars of Excellence
CIJE: 1 RIE: 22 CAT: 19

Exemplary Center for Reading Instruction UT
CIJE: 3 RIE: 4 CAT: 17

Exemplary Centers for Reading Instruction
CIJE: 1 RIE: 0 CAT: 05

Exemplary In School Demonstration Projects
CIJE: 0 RIE: 1 CAT: 19

Exemplary Project in Vocational Education MT
CIJE: 0 RIE: 5 CAT: 17

Exemplary Rehabilitation Certificate
CIJE: 0 RIE: 1 CAT: 15

Exemplary Schools
CIJE: 0 RIE: 7 CAT: 05

Exercise in Divergent Thinking
CIJE: 0 RIE: 1 CAT: 21

Exeter Conference NH
CIJE: 2 RIE: 0 CAT: 02

Exeter Writing Project NH
CIJE: 1 RIE: 0 CAT: 19

Exhall Grange School (England)
CIJE: 1 RIE: 0 CAT: 17

Exhaustion of Remedies
CIJE: 1 RIE: 1 CAT: 14

Exhaustive Search Method
CIJE: 0 RIE: 1 CAT: 15

Exhortation
CIJE: 0 RIE: 1 CAT: 16

Exit Examinations
CIJE: 10 RIE: 25 CAT: 21

Exit from Programs
USE Program Exit

Exit Interviews
CIJE: 15 RIE: 10 CAT: 15

Exit Surveys
CIJE: 1 RIE: 1 CAT: 15

Exiting Programs
USE Program Exit

Exiting Students
CIJE: 1 RIE: 2 CAT: 10

Exners Comprehensive System
CIJE: 0 RIE: 2 CAT: 21

Exners Developmental Quality
CIJE: 1 RIE: 0 CAT: 21

Exoffenders
CIJE: 18 RIE: 30 CAT: 16

Exoffenders Employment Project
CIJE: 1 RIE: 0 CAT: 19

Exogenous Mental Retardation
CIJE: 1 RIE: 0 CAT: 11

Expanded Child Care Options Demonstration
CIJE: 0 RIE: 1 CAT: 19

Expanded Food and Nutrition Education Program
CIJE: 7 RIE: 17 CAT: 19

Expanded Sociometric Device (Wright Bond Denison)
CIJE: 1 RIE: 0 CAT: 21

Expanded Speech
CIJE: 2 RIE: 2 CAT: 13

Expanding Environment
CIJE: 7 RIE: 3 CAT: 03

Expanding New Horizons Project
CIJE: 0 RIE: 1 CAT: 19

Expatriate Executives
CIJE: 0 RIE: 1 CAT: 10

Expectancy Theory
CIJE: 26 RIE: 11 CAT: 15

Expectancy Value Model of Student Attitudes
CIJE: 3 RIE: 1 CAT: 15

Expectant Mothers
CIJE: 2 RIE: 1 CAT: 10

Expectation States Theory
CIJE: 6 RIE: 2 CAT: 15

Expectations about Counseling Brief Form
CIJE: 2 RIE: 0 CAT: 21

Expectations about Counseling Questionnaire
CIJE: 1 RIE: 0 CAT: 21

Expected Consequences of Aggression Test (Adams)
CIJE: 1 RIE: 0 CAT: 21

Expected Growth
CIJE: 3 RIE: 1 CAT: 15

Expedition Education
CIJE: 3 RIE: 1 CAT: 03

Expensing
CIJE: 1 RIE: 0 CAT: 16

Experience Based Career Education
CIJE: 26 RIE: 187 CAT: 15

Experience Based Collegiate Education
CIJE: 0 RIE: 1 CAT: 15

Experience Compression Laboratory
CIJE: 1 RIE: 0 CAT: 17

Experience Inventory
CIJE: 0 RIE: 1 CAT: 21

Experience of College Questionnaire (McDowell)
CIJE: 1 RIE: 0 CAT: 21

Experience Recall Test
CIJE: 1 RIE: 1 CAT: 21

Experience Recall Test 2
CIJE: 0 RIE: 1 CAT: 21

Experience Sampling Method
CIJE: 2 RIE: 2 CAT: 15

Experienced Teacher Fellowship Program
CIJE: 1 RIE: 8 CAT: 19

Experienced Teachers
CIJE: 10 RIE: 29 CAT: 10

Experienced Writers
CIJE: 2 RIE: 1 CAT: 10

Experiences in English Inventory
CIJE: 0 RIE: 1 CAT: 21

Experiences in Mathematical Ideas
CIJE: 1 RIE: 0 CAT: 03

Experiential Education Evaluation Project
CIJE: 0 RIE: 2 CAT: 19

Experiential Education Questionnaire
CIJE: 0 RIE: 1 CAT: 21

Experiential Taxonomy (Steinaker and Bell)
CIJE: 0 RIE: 1 CAT: 21

Experiential Therapy
CIJE: 1 RIE: 2 CAT: 11

Experiment at Butte
CIJE: 0 RIE: 1 CAT: 19

Experiment in International Living
CIJE: 4 RIE: 1 CAT: 19

Experimental Assemblers
CIJE: 0 RIE: 1 CAT: 09

Experimental Behavior
CIJE: 2 RIE: 0 CAT: 11

Experimental Education Units
CIJE: 1 RIE: 0 CAT: 05

Experimental Elementary Program
CIJE: 1 RIE: 0 CAT: 19

Experimental Films
CIJE: 0 RIE: 2 CAT: 04

Experimental Freshman Year Program
CIJE: 0 RIE: 7 CAT: 19

Experimental Library Management System
CIJE: 2 RIE: 0 CAT: 15

Experimental Manpower Lab for Corrections AL
CIJE: 0 RIE: 2 CAT: 17

Experimental Manpower Laboratory NY
CIJE: 1 RIE: 1 CAT: 17

Experimental Method Test (Grohsmeyer and Johnson)
CIJE: 0 RIE: 1 CAT: 21

Experimental Preparation Program
CIJE: 0 RIE: 1 CAT: 19

Experimental Program for Orientation CO
CIJE: 1 RIE: 1 CAT: 19

Experimental Proj in Instruct Concentration
CIJE: 1 RIE: 0 CAT: 19
UF EPIC Project MO

Experimental Publication System
CIJE: 0 RIE: 1 CAT: 15

Experimental Reasoning
CIJE: 1 RIE: 1 CAT: 11

Experimental Schools Program
CIJE: 5 RIE: 41 CAT: 19

Experimental Television
CIJE: 0 RIE: 1 CAT: 04

Experimental Time Sharing System
CIJE: 0 RIE: 4 CAT: 15

Experimental Volunteer Army Training Program
CIJE: 0 RIE: 1 CAT: 19

Experimental World Literacy Programme
CIJE: 9 RIE: 2 CAT: 19

Experimentalism
CIJE: 1 RIE: 6 CAT: 16

Experimenter Expectancy Cues
CIJE: 2 RIE: 0 CAT: 16

Experimenter Prestige Effect
CIJE: 0 RIE: 1 CAT: 16

Experiments in Computer Electronics and Logic
CIJE: 0 RIE: 1 CAT: 03

Experimentwise Error
CIJE: 1 RIE: 3 CAT: 21

ExperLOGO
CIJE: 0 RIE: 2 CAT: 04

Expert Novice Paradigm
CIJE: 12 RIE: 8 CAT: 15

Expert Novice Problem Solving
CIJE: 9 RIE: 10 CAT: 15

Expert Science Teaching Evaluation Model
CIJE: 0 RIE: 1 CAT: 15

Expert System Shells
CIJE: 2 RIE: 1 CAT: 04

Expert Witness
CIJE: 14 RIE: 10 CAT: 10

Expertise
CIJE: 65 RIE: 32 CAT: 16

Experts
CIJE: 150 RIE: 73 CAT: 10

Explanation (Simulation Game)
CIJE: 1 RIE: 1 CAT: 15

Explanation Based Learning
CIJE: 0 RIE: 2 CAT: 15

Explanations
CIJE: 40 RIE: 23 CAT: 16

Explanatory Speech
CIJE: 3 RIE: 4 CAT: 13

Expletives
CIJE: 4 RIE: 0 CAT: 13

Explicit Instruction
CIJE: 14 RIE: 5 CAT: 15

Explicitness
CIJE: 1 RIE: 2 CAT: 16

Exploitation
CIJE: 17 RIE: 6 CAT: 16

Exploration
CIJE: 2 RIE: 1 CAT: 16

Exploration Questionnaire (Edwards)
CIJE: 0 RIE: 1 CAT: 21

Exploratory Agriculture
CIJE: 0 RIE: 2 CAT: 20

Exploratory Data Analysis
CIJE: 9 RIE: 3 CAT: 15

Exploratory Drilling (Minerals)
CIJE: 2 RIE: 0 CAT: 20

Exploratory Factor Analysis
CIJE: 19 RIE: 17 CAT: 21

Exploratory Foreign Language Program
USE Foreign Language Exploratory Program

Exploratory Language
CIJE: 3 RIE: 0 CAT: 13

Exploratory Studies
CIJE: 14 RIE: 6 CAT: 16

Exploratory Work Experience Project
CIJE: 0 RIE: 1 CAT: 19

Exploratory Writing
CIJE: 1 RIE: 2 CAT: 13

Explorers
CIJE: 8 RIE: 11 CAT: 10

Explorers Club NY
CIJE: 1 RIE: 0 CAT: 17

Exploring Childhood
CIJE: 4 RIE: 1 CAT: 03

Exploring Human Nature Project
CIJE: 1 RIE: 0 CAT: 19

Exploring Our World Regions (Follett)
CIJE: 0 RIE: 1 CAT: 22

Explosive Behavior
CIJE: 0 RIE: 1 CAT: 11

Explosives
CIJE: 1 RIE: 3 CAT: 20

Expo 92
CIJE: 0 RIE: 2 CAT: 12

Exponential Growth
CIJE: 15 RIE: 2 CAT: 15

Exponentiation (Mathematics)
CIJE: 1 RIE: 2 CAT: 20

Exponents (Mathematics)
CIJE: 17 RIE: 5 CAT: 20

Export to Win
CIJE: 0 RIE: 1 CAT: 22
SN A computer simulation used in int'l marketing seminars

Expository Teaching
CIJE: 2 RIE: 7 CAT: 15

Expository Text
CIJE: 77 RIE: 44 CAT: 13

Express Routing Transportation
CIJE: 0 RIE: 1 CAT: 15

Expressed Values Scale
CIJE: 0 RIE: 1 CAT: 21

Expressive Learning
CIJE: 4 RIE: 0 CAT: 15

Expressive Method for Measuring Need Achievement
CIJE: 0 RIE: 2 CAT: 21

Expressive Objectives
CIJE: 0 RIE: 1 CAT: 15

Expressive One Word Picture Vocabulary Test
CIJE: 7 RIE: 1 CAT: 21

Expressive Therapy
CIJE: 0 RIE: 1 CAT: 11

Expressive Writing
CIJE: 30 RIE: 32 CAT: 13

EXRIB System of Analyzing Teaching
CIJE: 0 RIE: 1 CAT: 15
SN EXRIB = Example, Rule Indicator, Behavior

EXSPRT
CIJE: 0 RIE: 2 CAT: 21
SN A combination of expert systems reasoning and sequential probability ratio test stopping rules for Computer-Based Adaptive Mastery Testing

Exstatix
CIJE: 0 RIE: 1 CAT: 04

Extemporaneous Speaking
CIJE: 5 RIE: 6 CAT: 16

Extended Campus
CIJE: 0 RIE: 2 CAT: 15

Extended Campus Library Services
CIJE: 0 RIE: 4 CAT: 05

Extended Caution Index
CIJE: 1 RIE: 4 CAT: 21

Extended Contracts
CIJE: 2 RIE: 3 CAT: 15

Extended Degree Programs
CIJE: 51 RIE: 46 CAT: 19

Extended Discretion Approach
CIJE: 0 RIE: 1 CAT: 15

Extended Learning Program
CIJE: 0 RIE: 2 CAT: 19

Extended Opportunity Programs and Services
CIJE: 3 RIE: 21 CAT: 19

Extending Family Resources Project
CIJE: 0 RIE: 1 CAT: 19

Extension Service
CIJE: 6 RIE: 14 CAT: 17

Extent of Planning Scale
CIJE: 0 RIE: 1 CAT: 21

Exterminators
CIJE: 2 RIE: 2 CAT: 09

External Anchoring (Psychology)
CIJE: 1 RIE: 0 CAT: 11

External Debt
CIJE: 0 RIE: 1 CAT: 16

External Diploma Programs
CIJE: 0 RIE: 2 CAT: 19

External Doctor of Education Degrees
CIJE: 0 RIE: 0 CAT: 16

External Evaluation
CIJE: 29 RIE: 37 CAT: 21

External Examination Program
CIJE: 1 RIE: 2 CAT: 19

External High School Diploma Program NY
CIJE: 2 RIE: 1 CAT: 19

External High School Diploma Program WI
CIJE: 0 RIE: 3 CAT: 19

External Pacing
CIJE: 0 RIE: 1 CAT: 15

External Sensitivity Index (Kosecoff and Klein)
CIJE: 0 RIE: 1 CAT: 21

External Students (Australia)
CIJE: 0 RIE: 2 CAT: 10
SN Postsecondary students enrolled in Australia's distance education programs

External Validity
CIJE: 13 RIE: 4 CAT: 15

Extinct Languages
CIJE: 1 RIE: 1 CAT: 13
SN See also "Endangered Languages"
UF Dead Languages

Extinction (Species)
CIJE: 13 RIE: 4 CAT: 20

Extra Credit
CIJE: 10 RIE: 1 CAT: 03

Extra Year Programs (Kindergarten)
CIJE: 1 RIE: 5 CAT: 19
UF Developmental Kindergarten (Extra Year Programs); Pre First Grade Transitional Programs

Extraclassroom Activity Fund NY
CIJE: 0 RIE: 1 CAT: 17

Extracts
CIJE: 1 RIE: 1 CAT: 16

Extracurricular Activity Funds
USE Student Activity Funds

Extramarital Relationship
CIJE: 10 RIE: 0 CAT: 11

Extraneous Roots (Mathematics)
CIJE: 1 RIE: 0 CAT: 20

Extrapolation
CIJE: 4 RIE: 2 CAT: 15

Extrasensory Perception
CIJE: 6 RIE: 1 CAT: 11

Extrasentential Expressions
CIJE: 0 RIE: 1 CAT: 13

Extraterrestrial Life
CIJE: 8 RIE: 3 CAT: 20

Extremal Properties
CIJE: 1 RIE: 0 CAT: 15

Extremely Gifted
CIJE: 18 RIE: 4 CAT: 10
SN See also "Exceptionally Gifted" and "Highly Gifted"

Extremism
CIJE: 2 RIE: 3 CAT: 16

Extruder Operators
CIJE: 0 RIE: 1 CAT: 09

Exupery (Saint)
CIJE: 1 RIE: 0 CAT: 18

Exxon Education Foundation
CIJE: 5 RIE: 1 CAT: 17

Exxon Research and Engineering Company
CIJE: 5 RIE: 1 CAT: 17

Exxon Valdez Oil Spill
CIJE: 4 RIE: 1 CAT: 12

Eyak
CIJE: 1 RIE: 1 CAT: 13
SN Of the subgroup Athapascan-Eyak in the Na-Dene language group

Eye Infections
CIJE: 1 RIE: 1 CAT: 11

Eye Structure
CIJE: 0 RIE: 1 CAT: 11

Eyeglasses
CIJE: 5 RIE: 1 CAT: 04

Eyelid Conditioning
CIJE: 2 RIE: 0 CAT: 11

Eyes on the Prize
CIJE: 3 RIE: 1 CAT: 22

Eyestrain
CIJE: 3 RIE: 0 CAT: 11

Eyewitnesses
USE Witnesses

Eyewitnesses to Crime
USE Witnesses to Crime

Eynsham County Primary School (England)
CIJE: 2 RIE: 0 CAT: 17

Eysenck (Hans J)
CIJE: 7 RIE: 0 CAT: 18

Eysenck Personality Inventory
CIJE: 38 RIE: 3 CAT: 21

Eysenck Psychoticism Scale
CIJE: 3 RIE: 1 CAT: 21

Eysencks Behavioral Therapy
CIJE: 1 RIE: 1 CAT: 15

Ezekial v Winkley
CIJE: 1 RIE: 0 CAT: 14

F Olsen Limited (Norway)
CIJE: 0 RIE: 1 CAT: 17

F Ratio
CIJE: 4 RIE: 2 CAT: 15

F Sort Categorization
CIJE: 0 RIE: 1 CAT: 15
UF F Sort Task

F Sort Task
USE F Sort Categorization

F Test
CIJE: 24 RIE: 18 CAT: 21

Fabric Filters
CIJE: 4 RIE: 0 CAT: 04

Fabric Services
CIJE: 0 RIE: 1 CAT: 09

Face to Face Communication
CIJE: 23 RIE: 9 CAT: 15

Facebow Transfer Procedure
CIJE: 0 RIE: 1 CAT: 11

Facet Analysis
CIJE: 24 RIE: 13 CAT: 15

Faceted Classification
CIJE: 2 RIE: 0 CAT: 15

FACETS Computer Program
CIJE: 0 RIE: 1 CAT: 04

FACETS Model
CIJE: 1 RIE: 3 CAT: 15
SN A many-faceted Rasch model

Fachhochschulen
CIJE: 0 RIE: 2 CAT: 05

Facial Action Code
CIJE: 1 RIE: 0 CAT: 21

Facial Attractiveness
CIJE: 11 RIE: 0 CAT: 11

Facial Characteristics
CIJE: 19 RIE: 4 CAT: 16

Facial Configuration
CIJE: 9 RIE: 5 CAT: 16

Facial Deformities
USE Facial Disfigurement

Facial Disfigurement
CIJE: 3 RIE: 1 CAT: 11
UF Facial Deformities

Facial Features
CIJE: 23 RIE: 12 CAT: 11

Facial Perception
CIJE: 0 RIE: 1 CAT: 11

Facial Recognition
CIJE: 8 RIE: 1 CAT: 11

Facial Stimuli
CIJE: 3 RIE: 0 CAT: 11

Facies Models
CIJE: 1 RIE: 0 CAT: 15

Facilitated Appraisal for College Executives
CIJE: 0 RIE: 1 CAT: 19

Facilitated Communication
CIJE: 31 RIE: 7 CAT: 11

Facilitative Environments
CIJE: 10 RIE: 10 CAT: 15

Facilitator Project DC
USE District Facilitator Project DC

Facilitator Project NJ
CIJE: 0 RIE: 1 CAT: 19

Facilitator Styles
CIJE: 10 RIE: 3 CAT: 15

Facilitators
CIJE: 49 RIE: 74 CAT: 10
UF Change Facilitators

Facilitators (Personnel Development)
CIJE: 7 RIE: 4 CAT: 09

Facilities Audits
CIJE: 2 RIE: 0 CAT: 15

Facilities Engineering Construction Agency
CIJE: 1 RIE: 0 CAT: 17

Facility Alternatives
CIJE: 1 RIE: 4 CAT: 16

Facility Evaluation
CIJE: 1 RIE: 6 CAT: 15

Facility Management
CIJE: 3 RIE: 4 CAT: 16

Facility Use
CIJE: 2 RIE: 1 CAT: 16

Facing History
CIJE: 5 RIE: 0 CAT: 03

Facsimile Theory
CIJE: 1 RIE: 0 CAT: 15

FACSTRAP Computer Program
CIJE: 0 RIE: 1 CAT: 04

Fact Opinion Distinction
CIJE: 0 RIE: 1 CAT: 14
UF Opinion v Fact

Fact Sheets
CIJE: 2 RIE: 115 CAT: 22

Factfinding
CIJE: 10 RIE: 10 CAT: 15

Factor Computer Program
CIJE: 0 RIE: 1 CAT: 04

Factor Indeterminancy
CIJE: 1 RIE: 0 CAT: 21

Factor Invariance
CIJE: 15 RIE: 5 CAT: 15

Factor Label Method
CIJE: 2 RIE: 1 CAT: 15

Factor Matching
CIJE: 1 RIE: 1 CAT: 21

Factor Referenced Temperament Scales
CIJE: 0 RIE: 1 CAT: 21

Factor Structure Stability
CIJE: 3 RIE: 0 CAT: 21

Factor V Personality Traits
CIJE: 0 RIE: 1 CAT: 11
SN See also "Big Five Markers"

Factorial Designs
CIJE: 10 RIE: 5 CAT: 21

Factorial Modeling
CIJE: 2 RIE: 1 CAT: 21

Factoring (Mathematics)
CIJE: 31 RIE: 8 CAT: 20

Facts About Science Test
CIJE: 0 RIE: 6 CAT: 21

Facts on Aging Quiz (Palmore)
CIJE: 3 RIE: 4 CAT: 21

FACTS Program NY
USE Financial Aid for Colleges and Tech Schools Prog

Factual Perception
CIJE: 5 RIE: 1 CAT: 11

Facultative Lagoons
CIJE: 0 RIE: 2 CAT: 20

Faculty Activity Analysis
CIJE: 2 RIE: 4 CAT: 15

Faculty Appointments
CIJE: 2 RIE: 1 CAT: 16

Faculty Assistance and Computing Educ Services NY
USE Faculty Assistance Computing Education Services NY

Faculty Assistance Computing Education Services NY
CIJE: 0 RIE: 1 CAT: 19
UF Faculty Assistance and Computing Educ Services NY

Faculty at Work Questionnaire
CIJE: 1 RIE: 1 CAT: 21

Faculty Attitudes
CIJE: 7 RIE: 27 CAT: 16

Faculty Consistency
CIJE: 0 RIE: 1 CAT: 16

Faculty Course Questionnaire
CIJE: 1 RIE: 1 CAT: 21

Faculty Development in Nursing Education Project
CIJE: 0 RIE: 1 CAT: 19

Faculty Evaluation Check List
CIJE: 0 RIE: 2 CAT: 21

Faculty Governance
CIJE: 3 RIE: 1 CAT: 16

Faculty Growth Contracting
CIJE: 0 RIE: 1 CAT: 15

Faculty Improvement Program
CIJE: 1 RIE: 0 CAT: 19

Faculty Liaison
CIJE: 0 RIE: 1 CAT: 16

Faculty Opinion Survey Questionnaire
CIJE: 2 RIE: 0 CAT: 21

Faculty Productivity Reports
CIJE: 0 RIE: 2 CAT: 16

Faculty Projection Program
CIJE: 0 RIE: 1 CAT: 19

Faculty Reappointment
CIJE: 1 RIE: 35 CAT: 16

Faculty Reassignment
CIJE: 0 RIE: 13 CAT: 16

Faculty Records
CIJE: 0 RIE: 1 CAT: 16

Faculty Reimbursement Plan
CIJE: 1 RIE: 0 CAT: 15

Faculty Research
CIJE: 26 RIE: 5 CAT: 16
SN Research by, not about, faculty

Faculty Scheduling System
CIJE: 1 RIE: 0 CAT: 04

Faculty Service
CIJE: 2 RIE: 2 CAT: 16
SN Performance by faculty of noncredit instruction or noninstructional activities for the school community and also the public, e.g., curriculum development, student advising, sponsoring student organizations, and consulting with external individuals and groups

Faculty Status
CIJE: 60 RIE: 26 CAT: 16

Faculty Student Committees
CIJE: 0 RIE: 1 CAT: 10

Faculty Vitality
CIJE: 7 RIE: 7 CAT: 16

Fader (Daniel)
CIJE: 1 RIE: 0 CAT: 18

Fadiman (Clifton)
CIJE: 2 RIE: 0 CAT: 18

Fads
CIJE: 2 RIE: 2 CAT: 16

Faerie Queene
CIJE: 2 RIE: 0 CAT: 22

Fahrenheit 451
CIJE: 2 RIE: 0 CAT: 22

Fail Safe Strategies
CIJE: 1 RIE: 1 CAT: 20

Failure Analysis
CIJE: 6 RIE: 3 CAT: 15

Failure Oriented Training
CIJE: 0 RIE: 1 CAT: 15
SN A model for improving the effectiveness of instructional analysis

Fair Comment
CIJE: 0 RIE: 1 CAT: 14

Fair Credit and Reporting Act 1970
CIJE: 0 RIE: 2 CAT: 14

Fair Credit Billing Act
CIJE: 1 RIE: 2 CAT: 14

Fair Dismissal Law (Oregon)
CIJE: 0 RIE: 1 CAT: 14

Fair Employment Legislation
CIJE: 2 RIE: 2 CAT: 14

Fair Employment Practices Act 1953
CIJE: 1 RIE: 0 CAT: 14

Fair Hearings
CIJE: 1 RIE: 3 CAT: 14

Fair Housing Law 1968
CIJE: 1 RIE: 1 CAT: 14

Fair Housing Laws
CIJE: 4 RIE: 6 CAT: 14

Fair Labor Standards Act
CIJE: 15 RIE: 30 CAT: 14

Fair Representation
CIJE: 7 RIE: 2 CAT: 14

Fair Share Agreements
CIJE: 0 RIE: 1 CAT: 15

Fair Start Program
USE Child Survival Fair Start

FAIRAVEN Computer Program
CIJE: 0 RIE: 1 CAT: 04

Fairchild Hiller Corporation
CIJE: 1 RIE: 0 CAT: 17

Fairchild Industries
CIJE: 1 RIE: 0 CAT: 17

Fairfax County Public Library VA
CIJE: 0 RIE: 1 CAT: 17

Fairfax County Schools VA
CIJE: 23 RIE: 19 CAT: 17

Fairfield Public Schools CT
CIJE: 3 RIE: 1 CAT: 17

Fairfield Suisun Unified School District CA
CIJE: 0 RIE: 1 CAT: 17

Fairleigh Dickinson University NJ
CIJE: 4 RIE: 9 CAT: 17

Fairness
CIJE: 58 RIE: 23 CAT: 11

Fairness Committees
CIJE: 0 RIE: 1 CAT: 10

Fairness Doctrine
CIJE: 13 RIE: 23 CAT: 14

FairTest
CIJE: 0 RIE: 3 CAT: 17
UF National Center for Fair and Open Testing

Fairthorne (Robert A)
CIJE: 2 RIE: 0 CAT: 18

Faith Healing
CIJE: 1 RIE: 1 CAT: 11
UF Spiritual Healing

Fake Color Process
CIJE: 1 RIE: 0 CAT: 15

Faking (Testing)
CIJE: 32 RIE: 3 CAT: 21

Falcon Beach School MB
CIJE: 0 RIE: 1 CAT: 17

Falk Laboratory School PA
CIJE: 0 RIE: 1 CAT: 17
UF University of Pittsburgh PA Falk Laboratory School

Falkland Islands
CIJE: 4 RIE: 3 CAT: 07

Fall (Season)
USE Autumn

Fall of the City (MacLeish)
CIJE: 0 RIE: 1 CAT: 22

Fall River Public Schools MA
CIJE: 4 RIE: 0 CAT: 17

Fallacies
CIJE: 9 RIE: 14 CAT: 16

Fallas (Carlos Luis)
CIJE: 1 RIE: 0 CAT: 18

Fallbrook Union School District CA
CIJE: 1 RIE: 1 CAT: 17

Falling Towards England (James)
CIJE: 0 RIE: 1 CAT: 22

Fallout
CIJE: 2 RIE: 1 CAT: 20

Falls Church Public Schools VA
CIJE: 2 RIE: 0 CAT: 17

False Accusations
USE False Allegations

False Allegations
CIJE: 1 RIE: 1 CAT: 16
UF False Accusations

False Belief Tasks
USE False Beliefs

False Belief Understanding
USE False Beliefs

False Beliefs
CIJE: 11 RIE: 3 CAT: 11
UF False Belief Tasks; False Belief Understanding

False Evaluation Data
CIJE: 1 RIE: 1 CAT: 21

Falwell (Jerry)
CIJE: 6 RIE: 3 CAT: 18

Falwell v Flynt
CIJE: 0 RIE: 2 CAT: 14
UF Hustler v Falwell

Familiarization
CIJE: 6 RIE: 2 CAT: 16

Families and Work Institute
CIJE: 0 RIE: 1 CAT: 17

Families First Program CA
CIJE: 0 RIE: 1 CAT: 19

Families First SD
CIJE: 0 RIE: 1 CAT: 19

Families Involved in Schools and Community MN
CIJE: 0 RIE: 1 CAT: 19

Families Play to Grow Program
CIJE: 1 RIE: 0 CAT: 19

Family Adaptability Cohesion Evaluation Scales
CIJE: 7 RIE: 2 CAT: 21

Family Advocacy
CIJE: 2 RIE: 7 CAT: 16

Family and Work Movement
USE Work and Family Movement

Family and Youth Services Bureau
CIJE: 0 RIE: 1 CAT: 17

Family Assistance Plans
CIJE: 9 RIE: 4 CAT: 19

Family Budgets
CIJE: 2 RIE: 3 CAT: 16

Family Businesses
USE Family Owned Businesses

Family Camp Workshop
CIJE: 1 RIE: 0 CAT: 02

Family Career
CIJE: 0 RIE: 1 CAT: 15

Family Choice Education Initiative (California)
CIJE: 1 RIE: 1 CAT: 14

Family Clusters
CIJE: 0 RIE: 1 CAT: 10

Family Communication
CIJE: 37 RIE: 56 CAT: 11

Family Communication Pattern
CIJE: 6 RIE: 7 CAT: 16

Family Concept Q Sort
CIJE: 1 RIE: 0 CAT: 21

Family Consultation Project
CIJE: 0 RIE: 1 CAT: 19

Family Crises
CIJE: 10 RIE: 8 CAT: 11

Family Day Care Providers
CIJE: 6 RIE: 15 CAT: 09

Family Day Care Rating Scale
CIJE: 0 RIE: 0 CAT: 21
UF Harms Clifford Family Day Care Rating Scale

Family Day Care Systems
CIJE: 2 RIE: 4 CAT: 19

Family Decalage
CIJE: 0 RIE: 1 CAT: 15
SN Uneven cognitive development among family members

Family Democracy
CIJE: 0 RIE: 1 CAT: 16

Family Development
CIJE: 7 RIE: 4 CAT: 16

Family Development Parenting Groups
CIJE: 0 RIE: 1 CAT: 10

Family Development Research Program
CIJE: 1 RIE: 1 CAT: 19

Family Distance Doll Placement Technique
CIJE: 0 RIE: 1 CAT: 15

Family Drawing Depression Scale
CIJE: 0 RIE: 1 CAT: 21

Family Education Loan Program
CIJE: 0 RIE: 13 CAT: 14
SN Formerly Stafford Student Loan Program (1992)

Family Education Program NY
CIJE: 0 RIE: 0 CAT: 19

Family Education Program PQ
CIJE: 0 RIE: 0 CAT: 19

Family Educational Rights and Privacy Act 1974
CIJE: 36 RIE: 44 CAT: 14
SN a.k.a. "Buckley Amendment" (q.v.)
UF FERPA

Family English Literacy
CIJE: 4 RIE: 13 CAT: 13
SN Use only for ESL (English as a Second Language) programs — otherwise, use the Identifier "Family Literacy"
UF FELP Programs

Family English Literacy Network
CIJE: 0 RIE: 2 CAT: 19
UF FELN Program

Family Environment Interview Schedule
CIJE: 1 RIE: 0 CAT: 21

Family Environment Scale
CIJE: 21 RIE: 11 CAT: 21

Family Exchange Centers
CIJE: 0 RIE: 1 CAT: 05

Family Farm Program (California)
CIJE: 0 RIE: 1 CAT: 19

Family Farms
CIJE: 12 RIE: 3 CAT: 05

Family Formation
CIJE: 0 RIE: 2 CAT: 16

Family Friends Program
CIJE: 0 RIE: 4 CAT: 19

Family Functioning
CIJE: 4 RIE: 3 CAT: 11

Family Government Partnerships
USE Government Family Partnerships

Family Infant and Preschool Program NC
CIJE: 0 RIE: 1 CAT: 19

Family Infant Toddler Project
CIJE: 0 RIE: 2 CAT: 19

Family Institutes
CIJE: 0 RIE: 1 CAT: 02

Family Integration Index
CIJE: 0 RIE: 1 CAT: 21

Family Interaction Coding System
CIJE: 1 RIE: 1 CAT: 04

Family Interaction Inventory
CIJE: 0 RIE: 1 CAT: 21

Family Intervention
CIJE: 4 RIE: 6 CAT: 16

Family Involvement Communication System
CIJE: 0 RIE: 2 CAT: 16

Family Law
CIJE: 6 RIE: 9 CAT: 14

Family Learning Centers GA
CIJE: 0 RIE: 1 CAT: 17

Family Leave
CIJE: 1 RIE: 4 CAT: 16
SN See also "Parental Leave"

Family Libraries (Home)
USE Personal Libraries

Family Life and Sex Education Questionnaire
CIJE: 0 RIE: 1 CAT: 21

Family Life and Sexual Health Curr WA
USE FLASH Curriculum WA

Family Life Center MD
CIJE: 1 RIE: 0 CAT: 17

Family Life Curriculum Project
CIJE: 0 RIE: 1 CAT: 03

Family Life Cycle
CIJE: 12 RIE: 2 CAT: 16

Family Life Education Program Development Project
CIJE: 2 RIE: 0 CAT: 19

Family Life Span
CIJE: 5 RIE: 1 CAT: 11

Family Literacy
CIJE: 37 RIE: 172 CAT: 13
SN Literacy intervention for the entire family, rather than just for the children or for the adults — use the more specific Identifier "Family English Literacy" for ESL (English as a Second Language) programs
UF Parent Child Literacy

Family Literacy Aprendiendo Mejorando Educando
USE Project FLAME

Family Math
CIJE: 3 RIE: 1 CAT: 19

Family Matters Project
CIJE: 1 RIE: 1 CAT: 19

Family Needs
CIJE: 18 RIE: 17 CAT: 16

Family Needs Survey
CIJE: 2 RIE: 1 CAT: 21

Family Observation Record Keyboard System
CIJE: 0 RIE: 1 CAT: 04

Family of Origin
CIJE: 9 RIE: 3 CAT: 11

Family of Procreation
CIJE: 1 RIE: 1 CAT: 11

Family Oriented Benefits
CIJE: 0 RIE: 1 CAT: 16

Family Oriented Language Dynamics
CIJE: 0 RIE: 1 CAT: 19
UF FOLD Program

Family Oriented Structured Preschool Activity MN
CIJE: 0 RIE: 1 CAT: 19

Family Outings
CIJE: 1 RIE: 1 CAT: 16

Family Owned Businesses
CIJE: 1 RIE: 1 CAT: 16
UF Family Businesses

Family Planning Association
CIJE: 1 RIE: 0 CAT: 17

Family Policy
CIJE: 10 RIE: 33 CAT: 16

Family Practice Act 1970
CIJE: 0 RIE: 1 CAT: 14

Family Preservation Services
CIJE: 10 RIE: 10 CAT: 19

Family Problem Instrument (Baker)
CIJE: 0 RIE: 1 CAT: 21

Family Protection Legislation
CIJE: 0 RIE: 2 CAT: 14

Family Reception Center NY
CIJE: 1 RIE: 0 CAT: 17

Family Reconstruction
CIJE: 3 RIE: 1 CAT: 11

Family Relations Indicator
CIJE: 1 RIE: 0 CAT: 21

Family Relations Inventory
CIJE: 1 RIE: 1 CAT: 21

Family Relations Test
CIJE: 4 RIE: 0 CAT: 21

Family Relationships Grid
CIJE: 0 RIE: 1 CAT: 21

Family Research
CIJE: 1 RIE: 1 CAT: 15

Family Research Project
CIJE: 0 RIE: 1 CAT: 19

Family Resource and Support Programs
CIJE: 1 RIE: 22 CAT: 19

Family Resource Coalition IL
CIJE: 0 RIE: 2 CAT: 17

Family Resource Scale
CIJE: 0 RIE: 1 CAT: 21

Family Responsibility
CIJE: 20 RIE: 9 CAT: 11

Family Rules
CIJE: 0 RIE: 7 CAT: 16

Family Service Association
CIJE: 0 RIE: 1 CAT: 17

Family Service Society of New Orleans LA
CIJE: 1 RIE: 0 CAT: 17

Family Service Workers
CIJE: 0 RIE: 1 CAT: 09

Family Shelter Care Project
CIJE: 0 RIE: 1 CAT: 19

Family Sociology
USE Sociology of the Family

Family Strengths
CIJE: 6 RIE: 0 CAT: 11

Family Support
CIJE: 12 RIE: 56 CAT: 16
SN See also "Family Resource and Support Programs"

Family Support Act 1988
CIJE: 9 RIE: 39 CAT: 14

Family Support Project MI
CIJE: 0 RIE: 2 CAT: 19

Family Support Scale
CIJE: 0 RIE: 1 CAT: 21

Family Systems Approach
USE Family Systems Theory

Family Systems Theory
CIJE: 63 RIE: 20 CAT: 15
UF Family Systems Approach

Family Therapist Coding System
CIJE: 0 RIE: 1 CAT: 15

Family Therapy
CIJE: 62 RIE: 10 CAT: 11

Family Therapy Institute ND
CIJE: 0 RIE: 1 CAT: 17

Family Ties (Television Program)
CIJE: 0 RIE: 2 CAT: 22

Family Triangles
CIJE: 0 RIE: 0 CAT: 11
UF Nuclear Family Triangulation; Triangulation in Family

Family Values
CIJE: 0 RIE: 1 CAT: 16

Family Welfare Centers
CIJE: 0 RIE: 1 CAT: 05

Famine
CIJE: 6 RIE: 8 CAT: 20

Famous Sayings Test (Bass)
CIJE: 3 RIE: 0 CAT: 21

FAMULUS
CIJE: 1 RIE: 1 CAT: 04

Fan Spread Hypothesis
CIJE: 2 RIE: 3 CAT: 15

Fanagalo
CIJE: 0 RIE: 1 CAT: 13

Fanconi Syndrome
CIJE: 1 RIE: 0 CAT: 11

Fancy Stitchers
CIJE: 0 RIE: 1 CAT: 09

Fanon (Frantz)
CIJE: 3 RIE: 0 CAT: 18

Fantasy Reality Dichotomy
CIJE: 1 RIE: 2 CAT: 15

Fantasy Theme Analysis
CIJE: 13 RIE: 15 CAT: 15

Fante
CIJE: 0 RIE: 2 CAT: 13

Far East
CIJE: 5 RIE: 14 CAT: 07

Far Transfer
CIJE: 1 RIE: 1 CAT: 15

Far West Consortium
CIJE: 0 RIE: 1 CAT: 17

Far West Laboratory for Educational R and D CA
CIJE: 10 RIE: 48 CAT: 17

Far West School CA
CIJE: 0 RIE: 8 CAT: 17

Far West Teacher Corps Network WA
CIJE: 0 RIE: 2 CAT: 17

Far Western Philosophy of Education Society
CIJE: 0 RIE: 1 CAT: 17

Faraday Laws
CIJE: 3 RIE: 0 CAT: 20

Farber (Myron)
CIJE: 0 RIE: 1 CAT: 18

Farce
CIJE: 1 RIE: 1 CAT: 16

Farewell to Arms (A)
CIJE: 0 RIE: 1 CAT: 22

Farey Sequences
CIJE: 1 RIE: 1 CAT: 20

Fargo Public Schools ND
CIJE: 1 RIE: 3 CAT: 17

Farm and Home Management Program
CIJE: 0 RIE: 2 CAT: 19

Farm Bureau
CIJE: 2 RIE: 0 CAT: 17

Farm Business Management Analysis
CIJE: 0 RIE: 2 CAT: 15

Farm Crisis
CIJE: 46 RIE: 35 CAT: 20

Farm Foundation IL
CIJE: 0 RIE: 2 CAT: 17

Farm Labor Contractor Registration Act
CIJE: 0 RIE: 1 CAT: 14

Farm Laboratory
CIJE: 1 RIE: 0 CAT: 17

Farm Policy
CIJE: 0 RIE: 6 CAT: 20

Farm Population
CIJE: 0 RIE: 3 CAT: 10

Farm Radio Forum (Canada)
CIJE: 0 RIE: 3 CAT: 17

Farmer (Penelope)
CIJE: 2 RIE: 0 CAT: 18

Farmer Training Centres (Kenya)
CIJE: 0 RIE: 1 CAT: 05

Farmers Alliance
CIJE: 0 RIE: 1 CAT: 17

Farmers Functional Literacy Project
CIJE: 5 RIE: 2 CAT: 19

Farmers Home Administration
CIJE: 2 RIE: 8 CAT: 17

Farmers Markets
CIJE: 0 RIE: 2 CAT: 05

Farmers Week
CIJE: 1 RIE: 0 CAT: 22

Farming Systems Research
CIJE: 1 RIE: 1 CAT: 15

Farming Systems Research and Extension Approach
CIJE: 0 RIE: 1 CAT: 15

Farmington Municipal Schools NM
CIJE: 0 RIE: 1 CAT: 17

Farmington Plan
CIJE: 0 RIE: 4 CAT: 19

Farmington Public Schools CT
CIJE: 2 RIE: 1 CAT: 17

Farmington Public Schools MI
CIJE: 1 RIE: 2 CAT: 17

Farmland
CIJE: 1 RIE: 5 CAT: 05

Farmland Assessment Act
CIJE: 0 RIE: 2 CAT: 14

Farms
CIJE: 12 RIE: 13 CAT: 20

Farms (Educational)
CIJE: 1 RIE: 2 CAT: 05

Farmworker Data Network
CIJE: 0 RIE: 1 CAT: 04

Farnham Diggory Cognitive Synthesis Task
CIJE: 0 RIE: 1 CAT: 21

Farnsworth (D L)
CIJE: 0 RIE: 1 CAT: 18

Farradanes Relational Indexing
CIJE: 1 RIE: 0 CAT: 16

Farrakhan (Louis)
CIJE: 2 RIE: 1 CAT: 18

Farrar (Frederick William)
CIJE: 1 RIE: 0 CAT: 18

Fascell Stone Amendment
CIJE: 0 RIE: 1 CAT: 14

Fascism Scale
CIJE: 0 RIE: 1 CAT: 16

Fashion Institute of Technology NY
CIJE: 4 RIE: 6 CAT: 17

Fashion Models
CIJE: 0 RIE: 5 CAT: 09

Fashion Shows
CIJE: 1 RIE: 2 CAT: 16

Fast Agricultural Communications Terminal
CIJE: 0 RIE: 1 CAT: 04

Fast Announcement Service
CIJE: 0 RIE: 1 CAT: 16

Fast Fitness Circuit Training
CIJE: 0 RIE: 1 CAT: 11

Fast Foods
CIJE: 7 RIE: 10 CAT: 16

Fast Iterative Recursive Macro System
CIJE: 0 RIE: 1 CAT: 04

Fast Mapping
CIJE: 4 RIE: 2 CAT: 15

Fast Plants
CIJE: 0 RIE: 1 CAT: 20
UF Wisconsin Fast Plants

FAST Program HI
USE Foundational Approaches in Science Teaching

Fast Response Survey System
CIJE: 0 RIE: 5 CAT: 21

Fasteners (Machinery)
CIJE: 0 RIE: 2 CAT: 04

Faster Macro Language
CIJE: 0 RIE: 1 CAT: 04

Fat Albert and the Cosby Kids
CIJE: 0 RIE: 1 CAT: 22

Fat Disorders
CIJE: 1 RIE: 0 CAT: 11

Fatalism
CIJE: 8 RIE: 3 CAT: 16

Fataluku
CIJE: 1 RIE: 0 CAT: 13

Father Present Family
CIJE: 0 RIE: 3 CAT: 10

Fathers Day
CIJE: 0 RIE: 2 CAT: 12

Fathy (Hassan)
CIJE: 0 RIE: 1 CAT: 18

Fats
CIJE: 8 RIE: 6 CAT: 20

Fatty Acids
CIJE: 2 RIE: 1 CAT: 11

Faublas Pressoir Orthography
CIJE: 0 RIE: 2 CAT: 13

Faulkner (William)
CIJE: 20 RIE: 8 CAT: 18

Fault Diagnosis
CIJE: 4 RIE: 4 CAT: 21

Fault Management
CIJE: 0 RIE: 1 CAT: 15

Fault Tree Analysis
CIJE: 4 RIE: 8 CAT: 15
SN See also "Sage Analysis"

Faure Report
CIJE: 2 RIE: 0 CAT: 22

Faust
CIJE: 2 RIE: 0 CAT: 22

Favorable Alternate Sites Project
CIJE: 0 RIE: 1 CAT: 19

Fayette County Public Schools KY
CIJE: 0 RIE: 2 CAT: 17

Fayetteville State University NC
CIJE: 2 RIE: 2 CAT: 17

Fayetteville Technical Institute NC
CIJE: 0 RIE: 10 CAT: 17

FCC v Midwest Video Corporation
CIJE: 0 RIE: 1 CAT: 14

FCC v Pacifica Foundation
CIJE: 1 RIE: 3 CAT: 14

FCC v WNCN Listeners Guild
CIJE: 0 RIE: 1 CAT: 14

FEANI UNESCO Seminar
CIJE: 2 RIE: 1 CAT: 02

Fear Appeal Messages
CIJE: 0 RIE: 1 CAT: 16

Fear of Femininity Scale
CIJE: 0 RIE: 1 CAT: 21

Fear of Negative Evaluation Scale (Watson Friend)
CIJE: 3 RIE: 2 CAT: 21

Fear of Spiders
USE Arachnophobia

Fear Survey Schedule
CIJE: 4 RIE: 0 CAT: 21

Feather River College CA
CIJE: 0 RIE: 1 CAT: 17

Featherman Jones Hauser Hypothesis
CIJE: 1 RIE: 1 CAT: 15

Feature Analysis
CIJE: 13 RIE: 5 CAT: 15

Feature Integration
CIJE: 1 RIE: 1 CAT: 11

Feature Selection
CIJE: 1 RIE: 0 CAT: 20

February (Month)
CIJE: 0 RIE: 0 CAT: 16

Federal Advisory Committee Act 1972
CIJE: 0 RIE: 1 CAT: 14

Federal Agencies
CIJE: 20 RIE: 36 CAT: 05

Federal Aid Highway Act
CIJE: 0 RIE: 1 CAT: 14
UF Public Law 93 87

Federal Archeology Program
CIJE: 0 RIE: 1 CAT: 19
SN The wide range of agencies and activities involved in federal archeology at the national, state, and local levels

Federal Archives and Record Centers
CIJE: 2 RIE: 0 CAT: 05

Federal Assistance for Staff Training
CIJE: 0 RIE: 1 CAT: 19

Federal Aviation Administration
CIJE: 3 RIE: 11 CAT: 17

Federal Aviation Regulation Part 147
CIJE: 0 RIE: 1 CAT: 14

Federal Budget
CIJE: 9 RIE: 15 CAT: 14

Federal Bureau of Investigation
CIJE: 22 RIE: 17 CAT: 17

Federal Catalog System
CIJE: 0 RIE: 1 CAT: 15

Federal City College DC
CIJE: 7 RIE: 14 CAT: 17

Federal City College Lorton Project
CIJE: 1 RIE: 0 CAT: 19

Federal Coal Mine Health and Safety Act
CIJE: 0 RIE: 1 CAT: 14

Federal Communications Commission
CIJE: 73 RIE: 301 CAT: 17

Federal Contractors
CIJE: 0 RIE: 5 CAT: 10

Federal Coor Council Sci Engineering Techn
CIJE: 0 RIE: 2 CAT: 17

Federal Cylinder Project
CIJE: 0 RIE: 3 CAT: 19

Federal Deficit
CIJE: 3 RIE: 1 CAT: 14

Federal Deposit Insurance Corporation
CIJE: 1 RIE: 0 CAT: 17

Federal Election Campaign Act
CIJE: 0 RIE: 1 CAT: 14

Federal Election Commission
CIJE: 2 RIE: 0 CAT: 17

Federal Emergency Management Agency
CIJE: 0 RIE: 8 CAT: 17

Federal Employee Part Time Career Employ Act 1978
CIJE: 0 RIE: 1 CAT: 14

Federal Employees
CIJE: 1 RIE: 4 CAT: 09

Federal Energy Administration
CIJE: 2 RIE: 0 CAT: 17

Federal Executive Institute
CIJE: 0 RIE: 2 CAT: 02

Federal Express
CIJE: 1 RIE: 1 CAT: 17

Federal Express Mail
CIJE: 2 RIE: 2 CAT: 16

Federal Forecasters
CIJE: 0 RIE: 2 CAT: 09

Federal Foundation Program
CIJE: 0 RIE: 1 CAT: 19

Federal Highway Administration
CIJE: 0 RIE: 3 CAT: 17

Federal Highway Safety Act 1966
CIJE: 0 RIE: 1 CAT: 14

Federal Home Loan Bank Board
CIJE: 0 RIE: 1 CAT: 17

Federal Housing Administration
CIJE: 2 RIE: 2 CAT: 17

Federal Information Processing Standards
CIJE: 0 RIE: 1 CAT: 15

Federal Installations
CIJE: 1 RIE: 2 CAT: 05

Federal Insured Student Loan Program
CIJE: 0 RIE: 1 CAT: 19

Federal Interagency Committee on Education
CIJE: 2 RIE: 2 CAT: 17

Federal Interagency Day Care Requirements
CIJE: 4 RIE: 25 CAT: 14

Federal Laboratories
CIJE: 2 RIE: 2 CAT: 05

Federal Lands
CIJE: 0 RIE: 1 CAT: 05

Federal Law Enforcement Training Center
CIJE: 0 RIE: 1 CAT: 17

Federal Library Committee
CIJE: 5 RIE: 17 CAT: 17

Federal Mediation and Conciliation Service
CIJE: 2 RIE: 0 CAT: 17

Federal Motor Carrier Safety Regulations Part 398
CIJE: 0 RIE: 1 CAT: 14

Federal Offenders Rehabilitation Program
CIJE: 0 RIE: 5 CAT: 19

Federal Parliament (Yugoslavia)
CIJE: 0 RIE: 1 CAT: 17

Federal Power Commission
CIJE: 1 RIE: 1 CAT: 17

Federal Property
CIJE: 1 RIE: 0 CAT: 16

Federal Quality Control Reviewers
CIJE: 0 RIE: 2 CAT: 09

Federal Radio Commission
CIJE: 0 RIE: 1 CAT: 17
SN Forerunner of the Federal Communications Commission

Federal Records
CIJE: 3 RIE: 1 CAT: 16

Federal Reformatory for Women WV
CIJE: 1 RIE: 0 CAT: 17

Federal Register
CIJE: 8 RIE: 4 CAT: 22

Federal Reserve Bank of Philadelphia
CIJE: 0 RIE: 1 CAT: 17

Federal Reserve System
CIJE: 4 RIE: 15 CAT: 17

Federal Resource Center for Special Education
CIJE: 0 RIE: 1 CAT: 17

Federal Role
CIJE: 10 RIE: 10 CAT: 16

Federal Rule 23
CIJE: 2 RIE: 0 CAT: 14

Federal School District Relationship
CIJE: 3 RIE: 2 CAT: 16

Federal Schools (Canada)
CIJE: 0 RIE: 3 CAT: 05

Federal Service Entrance Examination
CIJE: 0 RIE: 1 CAT: 21

Federal Service Mandates
CIJE: 0 RIE: 1 CAT: 14

Federal Standards
CIJE: 2 RIE: 1 CAT: 14

Federal State Program Congruity
CIJE: 0 RIE: 2 CAT: 19

Federal Supplemental Benefits Program
CIJE: 0 RIE: 1 CAT: 19

Federal Surplus Foods Program
CIJE: 0 RIE: 2 CAT: 19

Federal Telecommunication Standards Program
CIJE: 0 RIE: 1 CAT: 19

Federal Trade Commission
CIJE: 19 RIE: 26 CAT: 17

Federal Trade Commission Act
CIJE: 0 RIE: 2 CAT: 14

Federal Trade Commission Improvement Act 1980
CIJE: 0 RIE: 0 CAT: 14

Federal Water Pollution Control Act Amendments
CIJE: 1 RIE: 0 CAT: 14

Federal Water Pollution Control Administration
CIJE: 0 RIE: 1 CAT: 17

Federal Water Quality Administration
CIJE: 0 RIE: 1 CAT: 17

Federal Way School District WA
CIJE: 0 RIE: 1 CAT: 17

Federal Writers Project
CIJE: 3 RIE: 2 CAT: 19

Federal Young Adult Services Project
CIJE: 1 RIE: 0 CAT: 19

Federal Youth Center
CIJE: 0 RIE: 4 CAT: 17

Federalist Papers
CIJE: 14 RIE: 14 CAT: 22

Federalist Party
USE Federalists

Federalists
CIJE: 9 RIE: 11 CAT: 10
UF Federalist Party

Federated Learning Communities Project
CIJE: 1 RIE: 0 CAT: 19

Federated States of Micronesia
CIJE: 0 RIE: 8 CAT: 07

Federated States of Micronesia (Kosrae)
CIJE: 0 RIE: 1 CAT: 07

Federated Womens Institutes of Canada
CIJE: 0 RIE: 1 CAT: 17

Federation American Societies for Exptl Biology
CIJE: 1 RIE: 1 CAT: 17

Federation for Unified Science Education
CIJE: 3 RIE: 3 CAT: 17

Federation Licensing Examination
CIJE: 2 RIE: 2 CAT: 21
SN A 3-day competency exam for medical licensure
UF FLEX Test

Federation of American Societies for Exptl Biology
CIJE: 0 RIE: 3 CAT: 17

Federation of Greek Orthodox Choirs
CIJE: 0 RIE: 1 CAT: 17

Federation of Korean Womens Organizations
CIJE: 0 RIE: 1 CAT: 17

Federation of Public Programs in the Humanities
CIJE: 0 RIE: 1 CAT: 17

Federation of Rocky Mountain States
CIJE: 1 RIE: 15 CAT: 17

Federation of Saskatchewan Indians
CIJE: 1 RIE: 0 CAT: 17

Federation of State Medical Boards
CIJE: 1 RIE: 0 CAT: 17

Federation of Swiss Watchmakers
CIJE: 1 RIE: 0 CAT: 17

Fee for Service Health Plans
CIJE: 0 RIE: 1 CAT: 19

Feedback Consultation
CIJE: 0 RIE: 1 CAT: 15

Feedback Control
CIJE: 2 RIE: 1 CAT: 20

Feedback Systems Analysis
CIJE: 3 RIE: 1 CAT: 15

Feedback Systems Control
CIJE: 1 RIE: 0 CAT: 15

Feedback to Oral Reading Miscue Analysis System
CIJE: 0 RIE: 1 CAT: 15

Feeder Schools
CIJE: 0 RIE: 1 CAT: 05

Feedforward
CIJE: 3 RIE: 0 CAT: 16

Feeding Problems
CIJE: 0 RIE: 1 CAT: 11

Feeding Skills
CIJE: 3 RIE: 1 CAT: 11

Feeding Techniques
CIJE: 0 RIE: 1 CAT: 11

Feedwater
CIJE: 0 RIE: 2 CAT: 20

Feeling Good
CIJE: 2 RIE: 7 CAT: 22

Feeling of Knowing
CIJE: 5 RIE: 1 CAT: 15

Feeling Words Curriculum
CIJE: 0 RIE: 1 CAT: 03

Feffer Role Taking Test
CIJE: 0 RIE: 1 CAT: 21

Feijoo y Montenegro (Benito Jeronimo)
CIJE: 2 RIE: 0 CAT: 18

Feingold (B F)
CIJE: 8 RIE: 7 CAT: 18

Feingold Diet
CIJE: 8 RIE: 1 CAT: 11

Feldman (E B)
CIJE: 2 RIE: 2 CAT: 18

Feldshers
CIJE: 1 RIE: 1 CAT: 09

Fellegi Sunter Model of Record Linkage
CIJE: 0 RIE: 1 CAT: 15

Fellini (Federico)
CIJE: 2 RIE: 1 CAT: 18

Fellow Life Management Institute
CIJE: 2 RIE: 0 CAT: 17

Fellows in Education Journalism Program
CIJE: 0 RIE: 1 CAT: 19

Fellowship of Concerned University Students
CIJE: 1 RIE: 0 CAT: 17

FELN Program
USE Family English Literacy Network

Felony Cases
CIJE: 2 RIE: 3 CAT: 14

FELP Programs
USE Family English Literacy

Fels Longitudinal Program
CIJE: 5 RIE: 1 CAT: 19

Felt Board Devices
USE Feltboards

Feltboards
CIJE: 0 RIE: 1 CAT: 04
SN See also "Flannel Boards"
UF Felt Board Devices

Female Bonding
CIJE: 0 RIE: 1 CAT: 11

Feminine Development Program
CIJE: 1 RIE: 1 CAT: 19

Femininity
CIJE: 77 RIE: 23 CAT: 11

Feminist Criticism
CIJE: 112 RIE: 70 CAT: 16

Feminist Pedagogy
CIJE: 8 RIE: 21 CAT: 15

Feminist Press
CIJE: 5 RIE: 1 CAT: 17

Feminist Scholarship
CIJE: 88 RIE: 39 CAT: 03

Femoral Hypoplasia
CIJE: 1 RIE: 0 CAT: 11

Fence Building
CIJE: 0 RIE: 4 CAT: 20

Fennema Sherman Mathematics Attitudes Scales
CIJE: 9 RIE: 8 CAT: 21

Fenton (Edwin)
CIJE: 1 RIE: 0 CAT: 18

Ferguson Florissant Reorganized School District MO
CIJE: 1 RIE: 5 CAT: 17

Ferlinghetti (Lawrence)
CIJE: 3 RIE: 1 CAT: 18

Fermat (Pierre de)
CIJE: 3 RIE: 0 CAT: 18

Fermats Last Theorem
CIJE: 0 RIE: 0 CAT: 20

Fermentation
CIJE: 11 RIE: 2 CAT: 20

Fermi (Enrico)
CIJE: 2 RIE: 1 CAT: 18

Fernald Method
CIJE: 1 RIE: 1 CAT: 15

Fernald School CA
CIJE: 1 RIE: 1 CAT: 17

Fernandez (Macedonio)
CIJE: 1 RIE: 0 CAT: 18

Fernandez (Rufo Manuel)
CIJE: 0 RIE: 1 CAT: 18

Ferns
CIJE: 8 RIE: 2 CAT: 20

Fernuniversitat (West Germany)
CIJE: 8 RIE: 12 CAT: 17
UF Open University (West Germany)

FERPA
USE Family Educational Rights and Privacy Act 1974

Ferraro (Geraldine)
CIJE: 5 RIE: 5 CAT: 18

Ferris State College MI
CIJE: 5 RIE: 9 CAT: 17

Ferris State University MI
CIJE: 2 RIE: 5 CAT: 17

Ferrocenes
CIJE: 1 RIE: 0 CAT: 20

Ferroelectric Crystals
CIJE: 1 RIE: 0 CAT: 20

Ferroin Complexes
CIJE: 1 RIE: 0 CAT: 20

Fertility
CIJE: 15 RIE: 10 CAT: 11

Fertility Cults
CIJE: 0 RIE: 1 CAT: 10

Fertility Values
CIJE: 1 RIE: 3 CAT: 16

Fertilization
CIJE: 2 RIE: 1 CAT: 20

Festival International De La Pantomime
CIJE: 1 RIE: 0 CAT: 02

Festival of American Folklife
CIJE: 3 RIE: 0 CAT: 02

Festivals
CIJE: 11 RIE: 5 CAT: 16

Festschrift
CIJE: 3 RIE: 5 CAT: 16

Fetal Behavior
CIJE: 2 RIE: 0 CAT: 11

Fetal Development
CIJE: 8 RIE: 4 CAT: 11
UF Fetal Growth; Prenatal Development

Fetal Drug Exposure
CIJE: 10 RIE: 37 CAT: 11
UF Prenatal Exposure to Drugs

Fetal Growth
USE Fetal Development

Fetal Hydantoin Syndrome
CIJE: 1 RIE: 0 CAT: 11

Fetal Learning
CIJE: 1 RIE: 1 CAT: 11

Fetal Life
CIJE: 1 RIE: 0 CAT: 11

Fetal Position
CIJE: 0 RIE: 1 CAT: 11

Fetal Research
CIJE: 2 RIE: 0 CAT: 15

Fetal Trimethadione Syndrome
CIJE: 1 RIE: 0 CAT: 11

Fettler
CIJE: 0 RIE: 1 CAT: 09

Feudal Nexus (Game)
CIJE: 0 RIE: 1 CAT: 16

Feuer (Lewis S)
CIJE: 1 RIE: 0 CAT: 18

Feuerstein (Reuven)
CIJE: 8 RIE: 15 CAT: 18

Few (William)
CIJE: 0 RIE: 1 CAT: 18

Fey Acceptance of Others Scale
CIJE: 0 RIE: 2 CAT: 21

Feyerabend (Paul)
CIJE: 1 RIE: 1 CAT: 18

Fiat Corporation
CIJE: 0 RIE: 2 CAT: 17

Fiat Power
CIJE: 5 RIE: 3 CAT: 15

Fiber (Food)
CIJE: 5 RIE: 1 CAT: 11

Fiber Optics
CIJE: 34 RIE: 32 CAT: 20

Fiberglass
CIJE: 4 RIE: 5 CAT: 20

Fiberoptic Endoscopy
CIJE: 1 RIE: 0 CAT: 11

Fibers
CIJE: 3 RIE: 2 CAT: 20

Fibonacci Decision Rule
CIJE: 1 RIE: 0 CAT: 15

Fibonacci Sequences
CIJE: 22 RIE: 1 CAT: 20

Ficciones
CIJE: 0 RIE: 1 CAT: 22

Fictive Kinship
CIJE: 0 RIE: 0 CAT: 15

Fidelity of Supervision Scale
CIJE: 0 RIE: 1 CAT: 21

Fidencio (Nino)
CIJE: 0 RIE: 1 CAT: 18

Fidonet
CIJE: 0 RIE: 1 CAT: 04

Fiedler (Fred E)
CIJE: 0 RIE: 0 CAT: 18

Fiedler Contingency Model of Leader Effectiveness
CIJE: 5 RIE: 3 CAT: 15

Fiedler Interpersonal Perception Scale
CIJE: 1 RIE: 0 CAT: 21

Fiedler Least Preferred Coworker Scale
CIJE: 6 RIE: 2 CAT: 21

Fiela se kind (Matthee)
USE Fielas Child (Matthee)

Fielas Child (Matthee)
CIJE: 0 RIE: 1 CAT: 22
UF Fiela se kind (Matthee)

Field Agents
CIJE: 0 RIE: 11 CAT: 09

Field Analysis
CIJE: 1 RIE: 1 CAT: 15

Field Based Implementation Rating Scale
CIJE: 1 RIE: 0 CAT: 21

Field Based Programs
CIJE: 3 RIE: 10 CAT: 19
SN See also "Home Based Programs" and "Center Based Programs"

Field Dynamical Theory
CIJE: 1 RIE: 0 CAT: 15

Field Guides
CIJE: 1 RIE: 1 CAT: 16

Field Initiated Studies
CIJE: 0 RIE: 3 CAT: 19

Field Local School District OH
CIJE: 0 RIE: 1 CAT: 17

Field Museum of Natural History IL
CIJE: 1 RIE: 1 CAT: 17

Field Observation Technique
CIJE: 1 RIE: 1 CAT: 15

Field of Dreams
CIJE: 0 RIE: 1 CAT: 22

Field Program Associates
CIJE: 0 RIE: 1 CAT: 09

Field Reader Evaluation Form
CIJE: 0 RIE: 1 CAT: 21

Field Sensitive Field Independ Behav Observ Instru
CIJE: 0 RIE: 1 CAT: 21

Field Sensitivity (Teaching)
CIJE: 0 RIE: 4 CAT: 15

Field Studies Council (United Kingdom)
CIJE: 0 RIE: 0 CAT: 17

Field Theory
CIJE: 6 RIE: 7 CAT: 15

Field Theory Design
CIJE: 1 RIE: 0 CAT: 15

Fielding (Henry)
CIJE: 0 RIE: 1 CAT: 18

Fielding (Michael)
CIJE: 1 RIE: 0 CAT: 18

Fielding Institute CA
CIJE: 0 RIE: 1 CAT: 17

Fields (Mathematics)
CIJE: 2 RIE: 0 CAT: 20

Fields Type Teaching Tests
CIJE: 0 RIE: 1 CAT: 21

Fieldston Lower School NY
CIJE: 0 RIE: 1 CAT: 17

Fiesta
CIJE: 1 RIE: 0 CAT: 22

Fiesta Bowl
CIJE: 0 RIE: 2 CAT: 12

Fiestaware
CIJE: 0 RIE: 1 CAT: 16
SN Brightly colored dinnerware first introduced in the U.S. in 1936

Fifer (J)
CIJE: 0 RIE: 1 CAT: 18

Fifteenth Amendment
CIJE: 3 RIE: 1 CAT: 14

Fifth Amendment
CIJE: 7 RIE: 1 CAT: 14

Fifth Generation Computers
CIJE: 0 RIE: 1 CAT: 04

Fifty Percent Law (California)
CIJE: 0 RIE: 3 CAT: 14

Fighting Words Doctrine
CIJE: 0 RIE: 1 CAT: 14

Figural Analogies
CIJE: 1 RIE: 2 CAT: 21
SN See also "Analogical Reasoning"

Figural Creativity
CIJE: 0 RIE: 3 CAT: 16

Figural Intersection Test
CIJE: 4 RIE: 1 CAT: 21

Figural Tradition
CIJE: 0 RIE: 1 CAT: 16

Figurative Conditions
CIJE: 1 RIE: 0 CAT: 11

Figurative Operative Distinctions
CIJE: 1 RIE: 1 CAT: 11

Figure Drawing
CIJE: 7 RIE: 1 CAT: 16

Figure Ground
CIJE: 7 RIE: 2 CAT: 11

Figure Location Test
CIJE: 0 RIE: 1 CAT: 21

Fihrist al Ulum
USE Index of the Sciences (Arabic)

Fiji
CIJE: 29 RIE: 30 CAT: 07

Fijians
CIJE: 2 RIE: 0 CAT: 08

File Oriented Interpretive Language
CIJE: 0 RIE: 1 CAT: 04

File Transfer Protocol
CIJE: 20 RIE: 6 CAT: 20

Filial Crisis
CIJE: 0 RIE: 1 CAT: 11

Filipinos
CIJE: 22 RIE: 14 CAT: 08

Filley School District NE
CIJE: 0 RIE: 0 CAT: 17

Filling Machine Operators
CIJE: 0 RIE: 1 CAT: 09

Fillmore (Charles)
CIJE: 4 RIE: 2 CAT: 18

Fillmore Elementary School CO
CIJE: 0 RIE: 1 CAT: 17

Fillmore Street Reference Project
CIJE: 1 RIE: 0 CAT: 19

Film Aesthetics
CIJE: 0 RIE: 7 CAT: 16

Film Analysis Interaction Record
CIJE: 0 RIE: 1 CAT: 21

Film Analyzers
CIJE: 0 RIE: 1 CAT: 04

Film Base
CIJE: 0 RIE: 1 CAT: 20

Film Classics (Hollywood)
USE Classical Hollywood Films

Film Deterioration
USE Deterioration (Film)

Film Directors
CIJE: 3 RIE: 1 CAT: 09
UF Motion Picture Directors; Movie Directors

Film Evaluation Checklist
CIJE: 1 RIE: 1 CAT: 21

Film Festivals
CIJE: 1 RIE: 8 CAT: 16

Film Gates
CIJE: 0 RIE: 1 CAT: 04

Film Genres
CIJE: 5 RIE: 20 CAT: 16

Film History
CIJE: 12 RIE: 22 CAT: 16

Film Modeling Technique
CIJE: 1 RIE: 0 CAT: 15

Film Music
CIJE: 1 RIE: 5 CAT: 16

Film Noir
CIJE: 0 RIE: 1 CAT: 16

Film Program Notes
CIJE: 0 RIE: 1 CAT: 16

Film Programing
CIJE: 7 RIE: 1 CAT: 16

Film Reviews
CIJE: 15 RIE: 16 CAT: 16

Film Stars
CIJE: 3 RIE: 5 CAT: 09
UF Motion Picture Stars; Movie Stars

Film Theory
CIJE: 13 RIE: 9 CAT: 15

Film Viewing
CIJE: 10 RIE: 17 CAT: 16

Filmic Styles
CIJE: 1 RIE: 3 CAT: 16

Films Incorporated
CIJE: 1 RIE: 1 CAT: 17

FILMS NY
CIJE: 0 RIE: 1 CAT: 17

Filter Leaf Test
CIJE: 0 RIE: 1 CAT: 20

Filter Presses
CIJE: 0 RIE: 1 CAT: 04

Filters
CIJE: 6 RIE: 1 CAT: 04

Filtration
CIJE: 2 RIE: 1 CAT: 20

Final Examinations
CIJE: 14 RIE: 14 CAT: 21

Final Free Recall
CIJE: 1 RIE: 0 CAT: 21

Final Offer Arbitration
CIJE: 4 RIE: 0 CAT: 16

Final Reports
CIJE: 3 RIE: 140 CAT: 16

Finance
CIJE: 13 RIE: 9 CAT: 16

Financial Accounting Standards Board
CIJE: 6 RIE: 0 CAT: 17

Financial Aid for Colleges and Tech Schools Prog
CIJE: 0 RIE: 1 CAT: 19
UF FACTS Program NY

Financial Aid Form
CIJE: 0 RIE: 5 CAT: 16

Financial Aid Recipients
CIJE: 5 RIE: 5 CAT: 10

Financial Analysis
CIJE: 12 RIE: 5 CAT: 16

Financial Assets
CIJE: 1 RIE: 2 CAT: 16

Financial Assistance Workers
CIJE: 0 RIE: 1 CAT: 09

Financial Benefits
CIJE: 0 RIE: 3 CAT: 16

Financial Distress Grants
CIJE: 0 RIE: 2 CAT: 14

Financial Indicators
CIJE: 19 RIE: 27 CAT: 16

Financial Planners (Certified)
USE Certified Financial Planners

Financial Planning
CIJE: 7 RIE: 7 CAT: 16

Financial Projection Program
CIJE: 0 RIE: 1 CAT: 19

Financial Records
CIJE: 0 RIE: 2 CAT: 16

Financial Reports
CIJE: 19 RIE: 10 CAT: 16

Financial Systems
CIJE: 0 RIE: 5 CAT: 15

Financing Community Colleges
CIJE: 1 RIE: 0 CAT: 22

Financing Options
CIJE: 0 RIE: 1 CAT: 16
SN See also "Alternative Financing"

Finch College NY
CIJE: 0 RIE: 1 CAT: 17

Find Aid for the Aged Incorporated
CIJE: 1 RIE: 0 CAT: 17

Find and Inform Talent Project
CIJE: 0 RIE: 2 CAT: 19

Finding Aids
CIJE: 2 RIE: 1 CAT: 16

Finding Embedded Figures Test
CIJE: 0 RIE: 4 CAT: 21

Finding Kids with Special Needs
CIJE: 1 RIE: 1 CAT: 21

Finding Out Descubrimiento
CIJE: 0 RIE: 1 CAT: 03

Findlay College OH
CIJE: 4 RIE: 3 CAT: 17

Fine Arts Career Education GA
CIJE: 1 RIE: 0 CAT: 17

Fine Arts Educational Improvement Project
CIJE: 0 RIE: 2 CAT: 19

Fine Finger Dexterity Work Task Unit
CIJE: 0 RIE: 1 CAT: 21

Finger Counting
CIJE: 9 RIE: 6 CAT: 16

Finger Lakes Community College NY
CIJE: 0 RIE: 1 CAT: 17
SN Name changed (May92) from "Community College of the Finger Lakes NY"

Finger Lakes Dislocated Workers Project NY
CIJE: 0 RIE: 1 CAT: 19

Finger Lakes Library System NY
CIJE: 1 RIE: 0 CAT: 17

Finger Lakes Region Supplementary Educ Ctr NY
CIJE: 0 RIE: 1 CAT: 17

Finger Oscillation Test
CIJE: 1 RIE: 0 CAT: 21

Fingernail Biting
USE Nailbiting

Fingerplays
CIJE: 0 RIE: 7 CAT: 16

Fingerprints
CIJE: 6 RIE: 2 CAT: 16

Fingers
CIJE: 3 RIE: 0 CAT: 11

Finite Element Methods
CIJE: 1 RIE: 1 CAT: 15

Finite Fields
CIJE: 1 RIE: 0 CAT: 20

Finite Geometry
CIJE: 3 RIE: 1 CAT: 20

Finite Mathematics
CIJE: 6 RIE: 3 CAT: 20

Finite State Score Theory
CIJE: 0 RIE: 1 CAT: 15

Finke River Mission (Australia)
CIJE: 0 RIE: 1 CAT: 17

Finland
CIJE: 394 RIE: 352 CAT: 07

Finland (Helsinki)
CIJE: 6 RIE: 9 CAT: 07

Finland (Vasa)
CIJE: 2 RIE: 0 CAT: 07

Finley School NY
CIJE: 0 RIE: 1 CAT: 17

Finnish Americans
CIJE: 2 RIE: 2 CAT: 08

Finnish English Dialect
CIJE: 0 RIE: 1 CAT: 13

Finnish Evangelical Lutheran Church
CIJE: 2 RIE: 0 CAT: 17

Finnish Institute for Childrens Literature
CIJE: 1 RIE: 0 CAT: 17

Finnish People
USE Finns

Finnish Speaking
CIJE: 1 RIE: 3 CAT: 08

Finnish Winter War
CIJE: 0 RIE: 1 CAT: 12
SN War between Finland and the Soviet Union during 1939 and 1940

Finnish Youth Institute
CIJE: 1 RIE: 0 CAT: 17

Finns
CIJE: 2 RIE: 0 CAT: 08
UF Finnish People

FIPSE
USE Fund for Improvement of Postsecondary Education

FIPSE Project Teach
USE Project Teach (FIPSE)

Fire Chiefs
CIJE: 0 RIE: 1 CAT: 09

Fire Departments
CIJE: 0 RIE: 3 CAT: 05

Fire Detection
CIJE: 1 RIE: 1 CAT: 20

Fire Drills
CIJE: 3 RIE: 3 CAT: 16

Fire Education and the News Program
CIJE: 0 RIE: 1 CAT: 19

Fire Extinguisher Maintenance Specialists
CIJE: 0 RIE: 1 CAT: 09

Fire Extinguishers
CIJE: 5 RIE: 7 CAT: 04

Fire Hydrants
CIJE: 0 RIE: 2 CAT: 04

Fire Island National Seashore
CIJE: 1 RIE: 0 CAT: 07

Fire Prevention Officers
CIJE: 0 RIE: 1 CAT: 09

Fire Safety Education
CIJE: 1 RIE: 6 CAT: 03

Fire Streams
CIJE: 0 RIE: 2 CAT: 20

Firearms
CIJE: 26 RIE: 17 CAT: 04

Firefighters Local Union 1784 v Stotts
CIJE: 1 RIE: 1 CAT: 14
UF Stotts Decision

Fireplaces
CIJE: 0 RIE: 3 CAT: 04

Fires
CIJE: 11 RIE: 13 CAT: 20

Firesetters
CIJE: 4 RIE: 4 CAT: 09

Fireside Summer Experience Program NH
CIJE: 0 RIE: 1 CAT: 19

Fireworks Assemblers
CIJE: 0 RIE: 1 CAT: 09

Firing Patterns (Physiology)
CIJE: 0 RIE: 1 CAT: 20

FIRO B Scale
CIJE: 3 RIE: 15 CAT: 21
SN See also "Fundamental Interpersonal Relations Orientation," as well as other "FIRO" entries below

FIRO BC Scale
CIJE: 0 RIE: 1 CAT: 21

FIRO F Scale
CIJE: 1 RIE: 0 CAT: 21

FIRST
USE Fund for Improvement Reform of Schools Teaching

First Amendment
CIJE: 339 RIE: 244 CAT: 14

First Amendment Congresses
CIJE: 2 RIE: 0 CAT: 02

First Art Assessment (1975)
CIJE: 0 RIE: 0 CAT: 21

First Career Occup Develop Assess (1974)
CIJE: 0 RIE: 0 CAT: 21

First Circles
CIJE: 0 RIE: 1 CAT: 16
SN Meetings of teacher and students at the beginning of school days

First Citizenship Assessment (1970)
CIJE: 0 RIE: 0 CAT: 21

First Class Mail
CIJE: 0 RIE: 1 CAT: 16
SN See also "Certified Mail"

First Community Village OH
CIJE: 0 RIE: 1 CAT: 17

First Destination Statistics (United Kingdom)
CIJE: 0 RIE: 1 CAT: 15

First Friends Program
CIJE: 0 RIE: 1 CAT: 19

First Generation Students
CIJE: 14 RIE: 2 CAT: 10

First Grade Reading Group Study
CIJE: 0 RIE: 1 CAT: 22

First Grade Screening Test
CIJE: 2 RIE: 1 CAT: 21

First Impressions
CIJE: 9 RIE: 4 CAT: 16

First Independent Trust Company CA
CIJE: 0 RIE: 1 CAT: 17

First International Science Study
CIJE: 1 RIE: 1 CAT: 22

First Ladies (State)
CIJE: 0 RIE: 1 CAT: 10

First Lessons A Report on Elementary Ed in America
CIJE: 2 RIE: 0 CAT: 22

First Literature Assessment (1971)
CIJE: 0 RIE: 0 CAT: 21

First Mathematics Assessment (1973)
CIJE: 0 RIE: 0 CAT: 21

First Music Assessment (1972)
CIJE: 0 RIE: 0 CAT: 21

First National City Bank NY
CIJE: 2 RIE: 0 CAT: 17

First Order Cognitive Analysis
CIJE: 2 RIE: 2 CAT: 15

First Person Discourse
CIJE: 4 RIE: 1 CAT: 13

First Presbyterian Church of Fort Wayne IN
CIJE: 0 RIE: 1 CAT: 17

First Principal Components Method
CIJE: 0 RIE: 1 CAT: 21

First Reading Assessment (1971)
CIJE: 0 RIE: 0 CAT: 21

First Schools (England)
CIJE: 0 RIE: 1 CAT: 05

First Science Assessment (1970)
CIJE: 0 RIE: 1 CAT: 21

First Social Studies Assessment (1972)
CIJE: 0 RIE: 2 CAT: 21

First Street School NY
CIJE: 1 RIE: 0 CAT: 17

First Week of School
CIJE: 7 RIE: 5 CAT: 12

First Writing Assessment (1970)
CIJE: 0 RIE: 0 CAT: 21

First Years Together (Project)
CIJE: 0 RIE: 2 CAT: 19
SN ...of the Wake County Schools NC

FirstSearch
CIJE: 1 RIE: 1 CAT: 04
UF OCLC FirstSearch

Firth (J R)
CIJE: 4 RIE: 1 CAT: 18

Firthian Linguistics
CIJE: 0 RIE: 1 CAT: 13

Fiscal Accountability
CIJE: 1 RIE: 2 CAT: 16

Fiscal Illusion Model
CIJE: 0 RIE: 1 CAT: 15

Fiscal Impact Budgeting Systems
CIJE: 0 RIE: 1 CAT: 15

Fiscal Response
CIJE: 1 RIE: 5 CAT: 14

Fischer (Frank)
CIJE: 0 RIE: 1 CAT: 18

Fish (Stanley)
CIJE: 7 RIE: 2 CAT: 18

Fish and Game Wardens
CIJE: 0 RIE: 2 CAT: 09

Fish and Wildlife Service
CIJE: 0 RIE: 4 CAT: 17

Fish Cutters
CIJE: 0 RIE: 1 CAT: 09

Fish Farming
CIJE: 0 RIE: 3 CAT: 20

Fish Lake
CIJE: 1 RIE: 0 CAT: 07

Fish Ponds
CIJE: 2 RIE: 2 CAT: 20

Fish Products
CIJE: 0 RIE: 2 CAT: 20

Fishbein (Martin)
CIJE: 4 RIE: 2 CAT: 18

Fishbein Model of Attitudes
CIJE: 7 RIE: 7 CAT: 15

Fisher (H A L)
CIJE: 4 RIE: 0 CAT: 18

Fisher (Walter)
CIJE: 1 RIE: 2 CAT: 18

Fisher Branch Centre for Adult Basic Educ (Canada)
CIJE: 1 RIE: 0 CAT: 17

Fisher Discriminant Function
CIJE: 2 RIE: 4 CAT: 15

Fisher Exact Probability Test
CIJE: 6 RIE: 3 CAT: 21

Fisher Junior College MA
CIJE: 1 RIE: 0 CAT: 17

Fisher Tanh(sup minus 1)
CIJE: 1 RIE: 0 CAT: 15
UF Tanh(sup minus 1) Variance

Fisher Yates Exact Test
CIJE: 2 RIE: 0 CAT: 21

Fisheries Adjustment Program NF
CIJE: 0 RIE: 1 CAT: 19

Fisheries Education
CIJE: 1 RIE: 1 CAT: 03

Fishers
CIJE: 6 RIE: 11 CAT: 09

Fishers Z Transformation
CIJE: 10 RIE: 0 CAT: 15

Fishes
CIJE: 14 RIE: 25 CAT: 20

Fishing
CIJE: 16 RIE: 29 CAT: 16

Fishing Industry
CIJE: 4 RIE: 11 CAT: 20

Fishing Nets
CIJE: 0 RIE: 2 CAT: 04

Fishing Rights
CIJE: 11 RIE: 7 CAT: 14

Fishing Rod Assemblers
CIJE: 0 RIE: 1 CAT: 09

Fisk University TN
CIJE: 4 RIE: 10 CAT: 17

Fission
CIJE: 2 RIE: 0 CAT: 20

Fitchburg State College MA
CIJE: 1 RIE: 13 CAT: 17

Fitness Specialists
CIJE: 6 RIE: 0 CAT: 09

Fitton School MA
CIJE: 1 RIE: 0 CAT: 17

Fitzgerald (F Scott)
CIJE: 4 RIE: 2 CAT: 18

FitzGerald (Frances)
CIJE: 5 RIE: 1 CAT: 18

Fitzgerald Method
CIJE: 1 RIE: 0 CAT: 15

Fitzsimons (Thomas)
CIJE: 0 RIE: 1 CAT: 18

Five Associated University Libraries NY
CIJE: 0 RIE: 11 CAT: 17

Five Civilized Tribes
CIJE: 4 RIE: 5 CAT: 08

Five Civilized Tribes Museum
CIJE: 1 RIE: 0 CAT: 17

Five Colleges Incorporated MA
CIJE: 2 RIE: 2 CAT: 17

Five Little Peppers
CIJE: 1 RIE: 0 CAT: 22

Five Minute Observation
CIJE: 0 RIE: 1 CAT: 15

Five Phase Task Force Technique
CIJE: 1 RIE: 0 CAT: 15

Five State Multi Ethnic Training Project
CIJE: 0 RIE: 1 CAT: 19

Five Year College Programs
CIJE: 0 RIE: 1 CAT: 19

Fixed Item Tests
CIJE: 2 RIE: 1 CAT: 21

Fixed Length Testing
CIJE: 0 RIE: 1 CAT: 21

Fixed Parameter Approach
CIJE: 0 RIE: 4 CAT: 21

Fixed Point Iteration
CIJE: 1 RIE: 0 CAT: 20

Flag Day
CIJE: 1 RIE: 0 CAT: 12

Flag Football
CIJE: 0 RIE: 1 CAT: 16
UF Flagball

Flag Method
CIJE: 0 RIE: 1 CAT: 15

Flagball
USE Flag Football

Flags
CIJE: 6 RIE: 5 CAT: 04

Flaherty (Robert)
CIJE: 0 RIE: 1 CAT: 18

Flaim (Paul)
CIJE: 1 RIE: 0 CAT: 18

Flame Cutting
CIJE: 0 RIE: 1 CAT: 20

Flame Reading
CIJE: 0 RIE: 1 CAT: 16

Flamenco
CIJE: 2 RIE: 0 CAT: 16

Flames
CIJE: 3 RIE: 0 CAT: 20

Flaming (Computer Mediated Communication)
CIJE: 0 RIE: 4 CAT: 13

Flanagan Aptitude Classification Tests
CIJE: 1 RIE: 5 CAT: 21

Flanders (Ned A)
CIJE: 1 RIE: 1 CAT: 18

Flanders System of Interaction Analysis
CIJE: 48 RIE: 105 CAT: 21

Flange Detection Cluster Analysis
CIJE: 1 RIE: 0 CAT: 21

Flannel Boards
CIJE: 1 RIE: 5 CAT: 04
SN See also "Feltboards"

Flanner House IN
CIJE: 0 RIE: 1 CAT: 17

Flap Board (Game)
CIJE: 1 RIE: 0 CAT: 16

Flash Cards
CIJE: 17 RIE: 9 CAT: 04

FLASH Curriculum WA
CIJE: 0 RIE: 1 CAT: 03
UF Family Life and Sexual Health Curr WA

Flashback
CIJE: 2 RIE: 1 CAT: 16

Flathead (Tribe)
CIJE: 1 RIE: 3 CAT: 08

Flathead Indian Reservation MT
CIJE: 1 RIE: 2 CAT: 17

Flathead Valley Community College MT
CIJE: 0 RIE: 1 CAT: 17

Flatworms
CIJE: 3 RIE: 0 CAT: 20

Flaubert (Gustave)
CIJE: 2 RIE: 1 CAT: 18

Flavell (J)
CIJE: 4 RIE: 3 CAT: 18

Flawed Items
CIJE: 0 RIE: 2 CAT: 21

Fleet Ballistic Missile School CA
CIJE: 0 RIE: 1 CAT: 17

Fleet Submarine Training Facility
CIJE: 1 RIE: 0 CAT: 17

Fleischman (Doris E)
CIJE: 1 RIE: 0 CAT: 18
UF Bernays (Doris Fleischman)

Fleischmann Commission Report Elem Secondary Educ
CIJE: 4 RIE: 1 CAT: 22

Fleishmans Supervisory Behavior Description
CIJE: 1 RIE: 0 CAT: 22

Fleming (Robert)
CIJE: 1 RIE: 0 CAT: 18

Flemish
CIJE: 9 RIE: 7 CAT: 13

Flemish University (Belgium)
CIJE: 1 RIE: 1 CAT: 17

Flensburg Polytechnic (Germany)
CIJE: 0 RIE: 1 CAT: 17

Flesch (Rudolph)
CIJE: 4 RIE: 0 CAT: 18

Flesch Reading Ease Formula
CIJE: 18 RIE: 5 CAT: 21

Flesch Reading Ease Score
CIJE: 4 RIE: 1 CAT: 21

Fletcher (Harold)
CIJE: 2 RIE: 0 CAT: 18

Flex Ed Reading Readiness Program
CIJE: 0 RIE: 1 CAT: 19

Florida Commission on Social Studies Education
CIJE: 0 RIE: 1 CAT: 17

Florida Community College at Jacksonville
CIJE: 2 RIE: 9 CAT: 17
SN Formerly "Florida Junior College at Jacksonville"

Florida Compensatory Education Act 1977
CIJE: 0 RIE: 1 CAT: 14

Florida Cooperative Extension Service
CIJE: 0 RIE: 4 CAT: 17

Florida Correctional Institution for Women
CIJE: 0 RIE: 1 CAT: 17

Florida Cosmetology Licensure Examination
CIJE: 0 RIE: 1 CAT: 21

Florida Council on Educational Management
CIJE: 0 RIE: 2 CAT: 17

Florida Diagnostic and Learning Resources System
CIJE: 0 RIE: 0 CAT: 19

Florida Education Opinionnaire
CIJE: 0 RIE: 2 CAT: 21

Florida Education Research and Development Program
CIJE: 1 RIE: 1 CAT: 19

Florida Educational Accountability Act 1976
CIJE: 0 RIE: 4 CAT: 14
UF Florida Accountability Program

Florida Educational Leaders Forum
CIJE: 0 RIE: 1 CAT: 17

Florida Educational Research Development Council
CIJE: 0 RIE: 1 CAT: 17

Florida Educational Resources Information Center
CIJE: 1 RIE: 1 CAT: 17

Florida Farmworkers Residential Training Center
CIJE: 0 RIE: 1 CAT: 17

Florida Functional Literacy Test
CIJE: 3 RIE: 8 CAT: 21

Florida Information Resource Network
CIJE: 1 RIE: 2 CAT: 04

Florida Institute for Correctional Educators
CIJE: 0 RIE: 1 CAT: 17

Florida Instructional Program on Evaluation
CIJE: 0 RIE: 1 CAT: 19

Florida International University
CIJE: 15 RIE: 33 CAT: 17

Florida Junior College at Jacksonville
CIJE: 2 RIE: 8 CAT: 17
SN Renamed "Florida Community College at Jacksonville"

Florida Key Scale
CIJE: 1 RIE: 3 CAT: 21

Florida Keys Community College FL
CIJE: 0 RIE: 3 CAT: 17

Florida Language Profile
CIJE: 0 RIE: 3 CAT: 22

Florida Library Information Network
CIJE: 0 RIE: 1 CAT: 04

Florida Linkage System
CIJE: 2 RIE: 4 CAT: 04

Florida Longitudinal Project
CIJE: 1 RIE: 0 CAT: 19

Florida Master Teacher Program
CIJE: 1 RIE: 3 CAT: 19
UF Master Teacher Program FL

Florida Memorial College
CIJE: 2 RIE: 0 CAT: 17

Florida Merit School Program
CIJE: 0 RIE: 1 CAT: 19
UF Meritorious School Act (Florida)

Florida Migrant Education Program
CIJE: 0 RIE: 1 CAT: 19

Florida Migrant Health Project
CIJE: 0 RIE: 2 CAT: 19

Florida Migratory Child Survey Project
CIJE: 1 RIE: 0 CAT: 19

Florida Minimum Student Performance Standards
CIJE: 0 RIE: 4 CAT: 21
UF Minimum Student Performance Standards (Florida)

Florida Ocean Sciences Institute
CIJE: 1 RIE: 0 CAT: 17

Florida Parent Education Program
CIJE: 0 RIE: 3 CAT: 19

Florida Performance Measurement System
CIJE: 6 RIE: 7 CAT: 21

Florida Presbyterian College
CIJE: 1 RIE: 0 CAT: 17

Florida Professional Practices Council
CIJE: 0 RIE: 1 CAT: 17

Florida Resources in Education Exchange
CIJE: 0 RIE: 1 CAT: 17

Florida School Advisory Councils
CIJE: 0 RIE: 1 CAT: 19

Florida School for the Blind
CIJE: 1 RIE: 0 CAT: 17

Florida Schoolhouse Systems
CIJE: 0 RIE: 1 CAT: 17

Florida Science Assessment Project
CIJE: 0 RIE: 1 CAT: 19

Florida Southern College
CIJE: 1 RIE: 1 CAT: 17

Florida State Board of Health
CIJE: 0 RIE: 1 CAT: 17

Florida State Department of Education
CIJE: 2 RIE: 10 CAT: 17

Florida State Library
CIJE: 0 RIE: 3 CAT: 17

Florida State Plan
CIJE: 0 RIE: 5 CAT: 19

Florida State Postsecondary Education Commission
CIJE: 0 RIE: 3 CAT: 17

Florida State Prison
CIJE: 0 RIE: 2 CAT: 17

Florida State Student Assessment Test
CIJE: 2 RIE: 18 CAT: 21
UF SSAT (Florida)

Florida State Student Assessment Test Part II
CIJE: 6 RIE: 8 CAT: 21

Florida State University
CIJE: 81 RIE: 70 CAT: 17

Florida State University System
USE State University System of Florida

Florida Statewide Assessment Program
CIJE: 3 RIE: 21 CAT: 19

Florida Student Assistance Grant Program
CIJE: 0 RIE: 1 CAT: 19

Florida Taxonomy of Affective Behavior
CIJE: 0 RIE: 1 CAT: 15

Florida Taxonomy of Cognitive Behavior
CIJE: 1 RIE: 10 CAT: 15

Florida Teacher Certification Examination
CIJE: 3 RIE: 9 CAT: 21

Florida Teacher Competency Examination
CIJE: 0 RIE: 7 CAT: 21

Florida Teacher Evaluation Project
USE Teacher Evaluation Project FL

Florida Technological University
CIJE: 3 RIE: 8 CAT: 17

Florida Tuition Voucher Program
CIJE: 0 RIE: 1 CAT: 19

Florida Twelfth Grade Test
CIJE: 0 RIE: 3 CAT: 21

Florida VIEW System
USE Florida Vital Information for Education and Work

Florida Vital Information for Education and Work
CIJE: 1 RIE: 1 CAT: 19
UF Florida VIEW System

Florida Vocational Association
CIJE: 0 RIE: 1 CAT: 17

Florida Writing Enhancement Program
USE Writing Enhancement Program (Florida)

Florida Writing Project Student Survey
CIJE: 0 RIE: 1 CAT: 21

Florissant Valley Community College MO
CIJE: 0 RIE: 2 CAT: 17

Florists
CIJE: 1 RIE: 9 CAT: 09

Flotation Thickening
CIJE: 0 RIE: 1 CAT: 20

Flow Characteristics
CIJE: 3 RIE: 1 CAT: 20

FLOW Computer System
CIJE: 0 RIE: 0 CAT: 04

Flow Processes (Manufacturing)
CIJE: 1 RIE: 0 CAT: 20

FLOW Programing Language
CIJE: 0 RIE: 0 CAT: 04

Flow Theory
CIJE: 0 RIE: 1 CAT: 15

Flower (Linda)
CIJE: 7 RIE: 3 CAT: 18

Flower of the Dragon
CIJE: 1 RIE: 0 CAT: 19

Flower Shops
CIJE: 0 RIE: 1 CAT: 05

Flowers
CIJE: 5 RIE: 1 CAT: 20

Flowers for Algernon
CIJE: 2 RIE: 2 CAT: 22

Flowmeters
CIJE: 1 RIE: 0 CAT: 04

Floyd County School District GA
CIJE: 0 RIE: 1 CAT: 17

Fluency First Approach
CIJE: 0 RIE: 1 CAT: 13

Fluency Shaping Therapy
CIJE: 0 RIE: 1 CAT: 11

Fluharty Preschool Speech Language Screening Test
CIJE: 2 RIE: 1 CAT: 21

Fluid Dynamics
CIJE: 3 RIE: 3 CAT: 20

Fluid Flow
CIJE: 1 RIE: 0 CAT: 20

Fluid Intelligence
CIJE: 32 RIE: 11 CAT: 16

Fluid Power Engineering
CIJE: 2 RIE: 0 CAT: 20

Fluids
CIJE: 2 RIE: 2 CAT: 20

Fluorescence
CIJE: 8 RIE: 0 CAT: 20

Fluorescent Lighting
CIJE: 3 RIE: 4 CAT: 04

Fluorine Compounds
CIJE: 5 RIE: 2 CAT: 20

Fluvanna County Public Schools VA
CIJE: 0 RIE: 1 CAT: 17

Fly Test
CIJE: 0 RIE: 1 CAT: 21

Flynn Model Elementary School RI
CIJE: 1 RIE: 0 CAT: 17

Flynt Cooter Informal Reading Inventory
CIJE: 0 RIE: 1 CAT: 21

FM (Modulation)
USE Frequency Modulation

FM Auditory Trainers
USE Frequency Modulation Hearing Aid Systems

Focal Conflict
CIJE: 0 RIE: 1 CAT: 15

FOCAL Programing Language
CIJE: 0 RIE: 2 CAT: 04

Focke (Rudolph)
CIJE: 0 RIE: 1 CAT: 18

Focus Curriculum Program
CIJE: 0 RIE: 1 CAT: 19

FOCUS Database
CIJE: 0 RIE: 1 CAT: 19
SN National database on dropout prevention

Focus Group Assessment
CIJE: 8 RIE: 15 CAT: 15

Focus Groups
CIJE: 6 RIE: 7 CAT: 10

Focus Groups Approach
CIJE: 67 RIE: 74 CAT: 15

Focus Marking
CIJE: 1 RIE: 1 CAT: 13

Focus on Inner City Social Studies
CIJE: 1 RIE: 31 CAT: 19

Focus on Teaching Project (Scotland)
CIJE: 0 RIE: 1 CAT: 19

Focus Scan Learning Strategy
CIJE: 1 RIE: 0 CAT: 15

Focus Supportive Work Program
CIJE: 0 RIE: 1 CAT: 19

Focused Conversation
CIJE: 1 RIE: 1 CAT: 15

Focused Holistic Scoring
CIJE: 0 RIE: 1 CAT: 21

Focused Observation Form (Henderson and Ward)
CIJE: 0 RIE: 1 CAT: 21

Focusing Behavior
CIJE: 8 RIE: 1 CAT: 11

Focusing Strategies
CIJE: 7 RIE: 3 CAT: 11

Fodor (E M)
CIJE: 1 RIE: 0 CAT: 18

Fodor (Jerry A)
CIJE: 4 RIE: 0 CAT: 18

Folate Deficiency
USE Folic Acid Deficiency

FOLD Program
USE Family Oriented Language Dynamics

Folic Acid Deficiency
CIJE: 0 RIE: 0 CAT: 11
UF Folate Deficiency

Folk Dance
CIJE: 1 RIE: 7 CAT: 16

Folk Healing
USE Folk Medicine

Folk High Schools
CIJE: 10 RIE: 5 CAT: 05

Folk Medicine
CIJE: 12 RIE: 18 CAT: 11
SN See also "Curanderismo"
UF Folk Healing

Folk Music
CIJE: 24 RIE: 27 CAT: 16

Folk Rock
CIJE: 1 RIE: 1 CAT: 16

Folk Wisdom
CIJE: 2 RIE: 2 CAT: 16

Folkeskole
CIJE: 3 RIE: 3 CAT: 05

Folklorists
CIJE: 7 RIE: 2 CAT: 09

Folkpatterns
CIJE: 0 RIE: 1 CAT: 19

Folks (Homer)
CIJE: 1 RIE: 0 CAT: 18

Folktales
CIJE: 49 RIE: 64 CAT: 16

Follett (Mary Parker)
CIJE: 1 RIE: 1 CAT: 18

Follman English Mechanics Guide
CIJE: 0 RIE: 1 CAT: 22

Follow Through Services
CIJE: 2 RIE: 11 CAT: 16

Following Directions
CIJE: 10 RIE: 22 CAT: 21

Followup Materials
CIJE: 2 RIE: 4 CAT: 16

Folsom Cordova Unified School District CA
CIJE: 0 RIE: 1 CAT: 17

Folsom Unified School District CA
CIJE: 0 RIE: 1 CAT: 17

Folwell Multiple Variable Program
CIJE: 0 RIE: 1 CAT: 19

Fond du Lac Technical Institute WI
CIJE: 2 RIE: 0 CAT: 17

Fontane (Theodor)
CIJE: 2 RIE: 0 CAT: 18

Fontanet (Joseph)
CIJE: 2 RIE: 0 CAT: 18

Food Addiction
CIJE: 0 RIE: 1 CAT: 11

Food Additives
CIJE: 13 RIE: 13 CAT: 20

Food and Agriculture Act 1965
CIJE: 0 RIE: 1 CAT: 14

Food and Agriculture Act 1977
CIJE: 0 RIE: 1 CAT: 14

Food and Drug Administration
CIJE: 23 RIE: 14 CAT: 17

Food and Nutrition Service
CIJE: 0 RIE: 7 CAT: 17

Food Assistance Programs
CIJE: 0 RIE: 1 CAT: 19

Food Consumption
CIJE: 20 RIE: 17 CAT: 20

Food Deterioration
CIJE: 3 RIE: 1 CAT: 20
UF Deterioration (Food)

Food Distribution Program
CIJE: 0 RIE: 2 CAT: 19

Food Distribution Programs
CIJE: 2 RIE: 17 CAT: 19

Food Donation Program
CIJE: 0 RIE: 2 CAT: 19

Food Drying
CIJE: 0 RIE: 3 CAT: 20

Food Education and Service Training
CIJE: 2 RIE: 1 CAT: 15

Food Faddism
CIJE: 1 RIE: 1 CAT: 11

Food Gathering
CIJE: 0 RIE: 4 CAT: 16

Food Poisoning
CIJE: 3 RIE: 3 CAT: 11

Food Preferences
CIJE: 13 RIE: 7 CAT: 16

Food Preparation
CIJE: 6 RIE: 40 CAT: 20

Food Processing
CIJE: 11 RIE: 9 CAT: 20

Food Production
CIJE: 14 RIE: 33 CAT: 20

Food Refusal
CIJE: 2 RIE: 0 CAT: 11

Food Research and Action Center DC
CIJE: 0 RIE: 2 CAT: 17

Food Scarcity
CIJE: 12 RIE: 5 CAT: 20

Food Security
CIJE: 0 RIE: 1 CAT: 20

Food Security Act 1985
CIJE: 0 RIE: 7 CAT: 14

Food Selection
CIJE: 11 RIE: 21 CAT: 20

Food Stamp Act 1964
CIJE: 0 RIE: 2 CAT: 14

Food Stamp Act 1977
CIJE: 0 RIE: 5 CAT: 14

Food Stamp Employment and Training Program
CIJE: 1 RIE: 1 CAT: 19

Food Stamp Program
CIJE: 16 RIE: 67 CAT: 19

Food Storage
CIJE: 4 RIE: 8 CAT: 20

Food Supplements
CIJE: 6 RIE: 3 CAT: 11

Food Supply
CIJE: 9 RIE: 5 CAT: 20

Food Tabulators
CIJE: 0 RIE: 1 CAT: 09

Food Waste
CIJE: 1 RIE: 1 CAT: 16

Food Webs
CIJE: 10 RIE: 6 CAT: 20

Foote (Horton)
CIJE: 0 RIE: 1 CAT: 18

Foothill College CA
CIJE: 2 RIE: 4 CAT: 17

Foothill de Anza Community College District CA
CIJE: 2 RIE: 2 CAT: 17

Footscray Institute of Technology (Australia)
CIJE: 1 RIE: 1 CAT: 17

For Character Program (Chicago)
CIJE: 0 RIE: 1 CAT: 19

For Profit
USE Profit Making

For Profit Organizations
USE Proprietary Organizations

For Profit Schools
USE Profit Making Schools

Forage Crops
CIJE: 1 RIE: 2 CAT: 20

Forben (Johann)
CIJE: 1 RIE: 0 CAT: 18

Force Structure Analysis
CIJE: 0 RIE: 1 CAT: 15

Force Transformers
CIJE: 0 RIE: 1 CAT: 04

Forced Alternative Random Response Technique
CIJE: 0 RIE: 1 CAT: 15

Forced Choice Scale (Harvill)
CIJE: 0 RIE: 1 CAT: 21

Forced Choice Self Description Inventory (De Jung)
CIJE: 0 RIE: 1 CAT: 21

Forced Compliance
CIJE: 5 RIE: 2 CAT: 16

Forced Discipline
CIJE: 0 RIE: 1 CAT: 15

Forced Inferential Response Mode
CIJE: 0 RIE: 3 CAT: 15

Forced Relations Method
CIJE: 1 RIE: 0 CAT: 15

Forcible Entry
CIJE: 0 RIE: 3 CAT: 20

Forcing Function
CIJE: 0 RIE: 1 CAT: 15

Ford (Ford Madox)
CIJE: 1 RIE: 0 CAT: 18

Ford (Gerald R)
CIJE: 18 RIE: 5 CAT: 18

Ford (Henry)
CIJE: 2 RIE: 1 CAT: 18

Ford (John)
CIJE: 3 RIE: 1 CAT: 18

Ford Foundation
CIJE: 30 RIE: 84 CAT: 17

Ford Foundation Clinical Supervision Program
CIJE: 0 RIE: 2 CAT: 19

Ford Motor Company
CIJE: 11 RIE: 4 CAT: 17

Ford Training and Placement Program
CIJE: 1 RIE: 6 CAT: 19

Fordham Film Media Conference
CIJE: 1 RIE: 0 CAT: 02

Fordham University NY
CIJE: 13 RIE: 13 CAT: 17

Foreclosures
CIJE: 0 RIE: 1 CAT: 16

Foreign Affairs (Journal)
CIJE: 0 RIE: 1 CAT: 22

Foreign Aid
CIJE: 17 RIE: 25 CAT: 16

Foreign Area Materials Center NY
CIJE: 0 RIE: 1 CAT: 17

Foreign Area Specialists
CIJE: 0 RIE: 1 CAT: 09

Foreign Assistance Act 1975 Title XII
CIJE: 0 RIE: 0 CAT: 14
UF Public Law 94 161 Title XII

Foreign Born
CIJE: 10 RIE: 4 CAT: 10

Foreign Broadcast Information Service
CIJE: 1 RIE: 0 CAT: 17

Foreign Car Mechanics
CIJE: 0 RIE: 2 CAT: 09

Foreign Correspondents
CIJE: 0 RIE: 2 CAT: 09

Foreign Currency
CIJE: 4 RIE: 1 CAT: 16

Foreign Educational Credentials
CIJE: 13 RIE: 37 CAT: 16

Foreign Intervention
CIJE: 1 RIE: 2 CAT: 16

Foreign Language Attitude Quest (Jakobvits)
CIJE: 1 RIE: 0 CAT: 21

Foreign Language Attitude Scale (Dufort)
CIJE: 1 RIE: 1 CAT: 21

Foreign Language Careers
CIJE: 0 RIE: 2 CAT: 09

Foreign Language Display Library MI
CIJE: 0 RIE: 1 CAT: 17

Foreign Language Experience Programs
CIJE: 5 RIE: 7 CAT: 19
UF FLEX Programs

Foreign Language Exploratory Program
CIJE: 1 RIE: 8 CAT: 19
UF Exploratory Foreign Language Program

Foreign Language Innovative Curricula Studies
CIJE: 1 RIE: 9 CAT: 19

Foreign Language Majors
CIJE: 0 RIE: 1 CAT: 10

Foreign Language Press
CIJE: 0 RIE: 1 CAT: 13

Foreign Language Schools (Hawaii)
CIJE: 1 RIE: 0 CAT: 05

Foreign Language Teaching Materials Project
CIJE: 0 RIE: 1 CAT: 19

Foreign Language Weeks
CIJE: 0 RIE: 2 CAT: 12

Foreign Medical Schools
CIJE: 1 RIE: 0 CAT: 05

Foreign News
CIJE: 1 RIE: 10 CAT: 16

Foreign News Correspondents
CIJE: 1 RIE: 3 CAT: 09

Foreign News Media
CIJE: 1 RIE: 2 CAT: 16
UF Foreign Press

Foreign Ownership
CIJE: 0 RIE: 1 CAT: 16

Foreign Policy Association
CIJE: 2 RIE: 2 CAT: 17

Foreign Press
USE Foreign News Media

Foreign Science Information Program
CIJE: 1 RIE: 0 CAT: 19

Foreign Service
CIJE: 3 RIE: 3 CAT: 17

Foreign Service Institute DC
CIJE: 11 RIE: 21 CAT: 17

Foreign Service Institute Interview
CIJE: 11 RIE: 9 CAT: 21

Foreign Service Institute VA
CIJE: 1 RIE: 1 CAT: 17

Foreign Students Home Country Reentry
CIJE: 0 RIE: 5 CAT: 16

Foreign Study League UT
CIJE: 2 RIE: 0 CAT: 17

Foreign Visitors
CIJE: 1 RIE: 0 CAT: 10
SN See also "International Visitors"

Foreign Words
CIJE: 0 RIE: 1 CAT: 13

Foreigner Talk
CIJE: 3 RIE: 9 CAT: 13

Forensic Coaches
USE Debate Coaches

Forensic Directors
CIJE: 0 RIE: 5 CAT: 09

Forensic Psychology
CIJE: 4 RIE: 4 CAT: 11

Forensic Science
CIJE: 25 RIE: 8 CAT: 03

Forensic Sociology
CIJE: 1 RIE: 0 CAT: 03

Forensics Tournaments
USE Debate Tournaments

Forers Measurement of Gullibility
CIJE: 1 RIE: 0 CAT: 21

Foresee Approach
CIJE: 0 RIE: 1 CAT: 15

Foresight Club
CIJE: 1 RIE: 0 CAT: 17

Forest Haven DC
CIJE: 0 RIE: 1 CAT: 17

Forest Park Community College MO
CIJE: 3 RIE: 5 CAT: 17

Forest Park Junior College Center MD
CIJE: 0 RIE: 1 CAT: 17

Forest Park Junior High School OH
CIJE: 1 RIE: 0 CAT: 17

Forest Service
CIJE: 9 RIE: 5 CAT: 17

Forest Trail Library Consortium TX
CIJE: 0 RIE: 1 CAT: 17

Forest Valley Outdoor Education Centre ON
CIJE: 0 RIE: 2 CAT: 17

Foresta Institute for Ocean and Mountain Studies
CIJE: 0 RIE: 1 CAT: 17

Forests
CIJE: 8 RIE: 11 CAT: 20
SN See also "National Forests" and "Tropical Rain Forests"

Forests in Schools Project
CIJE: 0 RIE: 1 CAT: 19

Foretaste of Glory
CIJE: 0 RIE: 1 CAT: 22

Forethought
CIJE: 0 RIE: 1 CAT: 11

Forgery
CIJE: 4 RIE: 2 CAT: 14

Forgiveness
CIJE: 7 RIE: 2 CAT: 16

Fork Lift Truck Operators
CIJE: 0 RIE: 3 CAT: 09

Forkner Shorthand
CIJE: 0 RIE: 3 CAT: 13

Form 441 Assurance Compliance Federal Desegration
CIJE: 0 RIE: 1 CAT: 21

Form Attending
CIJE: 2 RIE: 0 CAT: 16

Form Complexity
CIJE: 1 RIE: 1 CAT: 11

Form Diversity
CIJE: 0 RIE: 1 CAT: 16

Form Dominance
CIJE: 2 RIE: 0 CAT: 16

Form Drawing (Geometry)
CIJE: 0 RIE: 1 CAT: 20

Form Errors (Handwriting)
CIJE: 0 RIE: 1 CAT: 13

Form Matching
CIJE: 1 RIE: 1 CAT: 16

Form Naming
CIJE: 1 RIE: 0 CAT: 16

Form PROM (Personnel Analysis)
CIJE: 0 RIE: 1 CAT: 16

Form Recognition
CIJE: 6 RIE: 0 CAT: 16

Form Reproduction Task
CIJE: 0 RIE: 3 CAT: 16

Form Stimuli
CIJE: 6 RIE: 1 CAT: 16

Form Z Test of Testwiseness (Ferrell)
CIJE: 0 RIE: 1 CAT: 21

Formal Education
CIJE: 27 RIE: 11 CAT: 16

Formal Evaluation
CIJE: 5 RIE: 3 CAT: 21

Formal Features
CIJE: 0 RIE: 1 CAT: 16

Formal Language
CIJE: 4 RIE: 4 CAT: 13

Formal Literary Style
CIJE: 1 RIE: 5 CAT: 13

Formal Mathematics
CIJE: 3 RIE: 1 CAT: 03

Formaldehyde
CIJE: 3 RIE: 2 CAT: 20

Formaldehyde Clock Reaction
CIJE: 1 RIE: 0 CAT: 20

Formalization
CIJE: 8 RIE: 1 CAT: 15

Forman (Milos)
CIJE: 0 RIE: 1 CAT: 18

Forman School CT
CIJE: 0 RIE: 1 CAT: 17

FORMAT (Database)
CIJE: 0 RIE: 1 CAT: 04

Format (Reports)
USE Report Format

Format Manipulation System
CIJE: 0 RIE: 1 CAT: 15

Format Recognition
CIJE: 1 RIE: 2 CAT: 15

Format Searching
CIJE: 0 RIE: 0 CAT: 20

Formative Training
CIJE: 2 RIE: 0 CAT: 15

Formatted Print Statement
CIJE: 0 RIE: 1 CAT: 15

Formatting
CIJE: 5 RIE: 0 CAT: 16
SN Use a more specific term if possible—Disk Formatting, Text Formatting, etc.

Former Teachers
CIJE: 0 RIE: 4 CAT: 10

Formerly Married
CIJE: 0 RIE: 1 CAT: 10

Forming Press Operators
CIJE: 0 RIE: 1 CAT: 09

Formosa
CIJE: 3 RIE: 3 CAT: 07

Formosan Languages
CIJE: 0 RIE: 1 CAT: 13

Formula Budgeting
CIJE: 5 RIE: 22 CAT: 15

Formula Fiction
CIJE: 1 RIE: 0 CAT: 16

Formula Funding
CIJE: 9 RIE: 31 CAT: 16

Formula Phonics
CIJE: 0 RIE: 2 CAT: 13

Formula Phonics Videotape Reading Chain Program
CIJE: 0 RIE: 3 CAT: 19

Formula Poetry
CIJE: 0 RIE: 1 CAT: 16

Formula Translating System
CIJE: 0 RIE: 2 CAT: 15

Formulaic Expressions
CIJE: 4 RIE: 3 CAT: 13

Formulaic Speech
CIJE: 2 RIE: 2 CAT: 13

Formulating Hypotheses Test (Frederiksen)
CIJE: 3 RIE: 1 CAT: 21

Formulation of Relevant Creative Environments
CIJE: 1 RIE: 0 CAT: 15

Forsoksgymnaset
CIJE: 0 RIE: 1 CAT: 05

Fort Apache Reservation
CIJE: 0 RIE: 1 CAT: 17

Fort Belknap Reservation MT
CIJE: 1 RIE: 5 CAT: 17

Fort Berthold Indian Reservation
CIJE: 0 RIE: 3 CAT: 17

Fort Bragg High School CA
CIJE: 1 RIE: 0 CAT: 17

Fort Defiance Window Rock Public Schools AZ
CIJE: 0 RIE: 1 CAT: 17

Fort Dodge Community School District IA
CIJE: 0 RIE: 1 CAT: 17

Fort Frye High School OH
CIJE: 1 RIE: 0 CAT: 17

Fort Hall Reservation
CIJE: 2 RIE: 0 CAT: 17

Fort Hays Kansas State College
CIJE: 2 RIE: 6 CAT: 17

Fort Hays State University KS
CIJE: 2 RIE: 3 CAT: 17

Fort Lewis College CO
CIJE: 0 RIE: 4 CAT: 17

Fort McDermitt Indian Reservation
CIJE: 0 RIE: 1 CAT: 17

Fort Myer Elementary School VA
CIJE: 0 RIE: 1 CAT: 17

Fort Peck Indian Reservation MT
CIJE: 0 RIE: 2 CAT: 17

Fort Scott Community College KS
CIJE: 0 RIE: 1 CAT: 17

Fort Sill Indian School OK
CIJE: 0 RIE: 3 CAT: 17

Fort Steilacoom Community College WA
CIJE: 1 RIE: 5 CAT: 17

Fort Wayne Bible College IN
CIJE: 0 RIE: 1 CAT: 17

Fort Wayne Community Schools IN
CIJE: 0 RIE: 2 CAT: 17

Fort Worth Independent School District TX
CIJE: 4 RIE: 34 CAT: 17

Fort Yuma Hydroponic Farming System
CIJE: 0 RIE: 1 CAT: 15

FORTRAN Programing Language
CIJE: 142 RIE: 90 CAT: 04

Fortunata y Jacinta
CIJE: 1 RIE: 0 CAT: 22

Fortune 500
CIJE: 11 RIE: 8 CAT: 16

Forty Eight Item Counseling Evaluation Test
CIJE: 0 RIE: 1 CAT: 21

Forty Plus
CIJE: 3 RIE: 0 CAT: 17

Forum Campaign for Comprehensive Education
CIJE: 1 RIE: 0 CAT: 19

Forums
CIJE: 7 RIE: 17 CAT: 16
SN Use a more specific term if possible, e.g., "AIR Forum," "Business Higher Education Forum," "Public Issue Forums," "Radio Forums"

Forward House (Canada)
CIJE: 1 RIE: 0 CAT: 17

Forward Mapping
CIJE: 0 RIE: 1 CAT: 15

Fossilization (Language)
USE Fossilized Language

Fossilized English
CIJE: 3 RIE: 3 CAT: 13

Fossilized Language
CIJE: 1 RIE: 9 CAT: 13
UF Fossilization (Language)

Foster (Herbert)
CIJE: 0 RIE: 1 CAT: 18

Foster Care Placement
USE Placement (Foster Care)

Foster Child Advocate Services Project
CIJE: 0 RIE: 1 CAT: 19

Foster Elementary School IL
CIJE: 1 RIE: 0 CAT: 17

Foster Family Based Treatment
CIJE: 0 RIE: 2 CAT: 15

Foster Family Based Treatment Association
CIJE: 0 RIE: 1 CAT: 17

Foster Grandparent Program
CIJE: 5 RIE: 9 CAT: 19

Foster Life Indicator
CIJE: 1 RIE: 0 CAT: 21

Fostering Team Approach Career Education
CIJE: 0 RIE: 1 CAT: 19

Fotonovelas
CIJE: 0 RIE: 1 CAT: 16

Foucault (Michel)
CIJE: 32 RIE: 11 CAT: 18

Found Poems
CIJE: 5 RIE: 0 CAT: 16

Foundation Center
CIJE: 4 RIE: 5 CAT: 17

Foundation Directory
CIJE: 1 RIE: 1 CAT: 22

Foundation for Alcohol and Drug Educ (New Zealand)
CIJE: 0 RIE: 1 CAT: 17

Foundation for Teaching Economics CA
CIJE: 0 RIE: 0 CAT: 17

Foundation Program Assessment Improvement System
CIJE: 0 RIE: 1 CAT: 21

Foundation School Program TX
USE Texas Foundation School Program

Foundation Skills
CIJE: 0 RIE: 1 CAT: 03

Foundational Approaches in Science Teaching
CIJE: 3 RIE: 1 CAT: 03
UF FAST Program HI

Foundations for Gerontological Education Project
CIJE: 0 RIE: 0 CAT: 19

Foundations Project
CIJE: 1 RIE: 1 CAT: 19

Founding Fathers of the United States
CIJE: 13 RIE: 15 CAT: 12

Foundry Occupations
CIJE: 0 RIE: 3 CAT: 09

Fountain Servers
CIJE: 0 RIE: 1 CAT: 09

Fountain Valley Post Tests
CIJE: 0 RIE: 1 CAT: 21

Fountain Valley School District CA
CIJE: 0 RIE: 1 CAT: 17

Four Agency Agreement
CIJE: 0 RIE: 1 CAT: 22

Four and One Half Day School Week
CIJE: 0 RIE: 2 CAT: 16

Four Bands Reservation of Hobbema
CIJE: 1 RIE: 0 CAT: 08

Four Champa Trees
CIJE: 0 RIE: 1 CAT: 22

Four Channel Audio
CIJE: 0 RIE: 1 CAT: 15

Four Channel Data Collection
CIJE: 0 RIE: 1 CAT: 15

Four Color Map Theorem
CIJE: 4 RIE: 0 CAT: 20

Four Corners Area
CIJE: 2 RIE: 5 CAT: 07

Four Corners Electric Power Complex
CIJE: 0 RIE: 1 CAT: 17

Four Corners Mental Retardation Project
CIJE: 0 RIE: 1 CAT: 19

Four Corners Regional Project
CIJE: 0 RIE: 1 CAT: 19

Four Day School Week
CIJE: 5 RIE: 17 CAT: 16

Four Dimensional Geometry
CIJE: 1 RIE: 1 CAT: 20

Four Factor Theory Questionnaire
CIJE: 1 RIE: 0 CAT: 21

Four Families
CIJE: 1 RIE: 0 CAT: 22

Four Food Group System
CIJE: 1 RIE: 0 CAT: 15

Four Mode Factor Analysis
CIJE: 1 RIE: 0 CAT: 21

Four Parameter Model
CIJE: 0 RIE: 1 CAT: 15
SN See also "Beta Binomial Test Model"

Four Phase Model (Policy Formation)
CIJE: 0 RIE: 1 CAT: 15

Four States Project
CIJE: 0 RIE: 4 CAT: 19

Four Worlds Development Project (Alberta)
CIJE: 1 RIE: 11 CAT: 19

Fourier Analysis
CIJE: 11 RIE: 2 CAT: 15

Fourier Series
CIJE: 2 RIE: 1 CAT: 22

Fourier Transformation
CIJE: 15 RIE: 3 CAT: 20

Fourteenth Amendment
CIJE: 63 RIE: 55 CAT: 14

Fourteenth Amendment Article IV
CIJE: 1 RIE: 0 CAT: 14

Fourth Amendment
CIJE: 46 RIE: 15 CAT: 14

Fourth Generation Evaluation Theory
CIJE: 0 RIE: 1 CAT: 15

Fourth Grade Computer Project IN
CIJE: 0 RIE: 1 CAT: 19

Fourth Grade Slump
CIJE: 0 RIE: 3 CAT: 16

Fourth Mathematics Assessment (1985)
CIJE: 0 RIE: 1 CAT: 21

Fourth Writing Assessment (1984)
CIJE: 0 RIE: 1 CAT: 21

Foveal Critical Flicker Frequency
CIJE: 1 RIE: 0 CAT: 11

Fowler (James)
CIJE: 3 RIE: 1 CAT: 18

Fowler Stages of Faith
CIJE: 0 RIE: 1 CAT: 15

Fox (Charles James)
CIJE: 1 RIE: 0 CAT: 18

Fox (Tribe)
CIJE: 0 RIE: 3 CAT: 08

Fox Valley Consortium for the Homeless IL
CIJE: 0 RIE: 2 CAT: 17

Fox Valley Technical College WI
CIJE: 1 RIE: 4 CAT: 17

Fox Valley Technical Institute WI
CIJE: 2 RIE: 3 CAT: 17

Foxboro Company
CIJE: 1 RIE: 0 CAT: 17

Foxfire
CIJE: 122 RIE: 23 CAT: 22

Foxhunting
CIJE: 0 RIE: 1 CAT: 16

Fractal Geometry
USE Fractals

Fractals
CIJE: 15 RIE: 5 CAT: 20
UF Fractal Geometry

Fractional Distillation
CIJE: 2 RIE: 0 CAT: 20

Fractionation Scales
CIJE: 0 RIE: 1 CAT: 15

Fraenkel (Jack)
CIJE: 0 RIE: 1 CAT: 18

Fragile Knowledge
CIJE: 0 RIE: 1 CAT: 16

Fragile X Syndrome
CIJE: 29 RIE: 6 CAT: 11
SN A deformity of the X chromosome that causes signs of autism, mental retardation, or behavioral problems

Frame Alignment Theory
CIJE: 0 RIE: 1 CAT: 15

Frame Analysis
CIJE: 1 RIE: 1 CAT: 15

Frame of Reference Measure
CIJE: 1 RIE: 1 CAT: 21

Frame of Reference Model
CIJE: 2 RIE: 2 CAT: 15

Framegames
CIJE: 2 RIE: 1 CAT: 04

Framing (Critical Thinking)
CIJE: 0 RIE: 1 CAT: 11

Framing (Metacognition)
CIJE: 0 RIE: 1 CAT: 11

Framingham Public Schools MA
CIJE: 1 RIE: 1 CAT: 17

Framingham State College MA
CIJE: 0 RIE: 1 CAT: 17

Framingham Type A Behavior Scale
CIJE: 0 RIE: 1 CAT: 21

Francais Radiophonique Authentique
CIJE: 1 RIE: 0 CAT: 04

France
CIJE: 1066 RIE: 604 CAT: 07

France (Alsace)
CIJE: 5 RIE: 2 CAT: 07

France (Anatole)
CIJE: 1 RIE: 0 CAT: 18

France (Beaubourg)
CIJE: 0 RIE: 1 CAT: 07

France (Brittany)
CIJE: 3 RIE: 5 CAT: 07

France (Cannes)
CIJE: 1 RIE: 0 CAT: 07

France (Cassis)
CIJE: 0 RIE: 1 CAT: 07

France (Gascony)
CIJE: 1 RIE: 0 CAT: 07

France (Grenoble)
CIJE: 1 RIE: 1 CAT: 07

France (Lyon)
CIJE: 2 RIE: 1 CAT: 07

France (Marseilles)
CIJE: 2 RIE: 0 CAT: 07

France (Montpellier)
CIJE: 1 RIE: 0 CAT: 07

France (Paris)
CIJE: 36 RIE: 23 CAT: 07

France (Provence)
CIJE: 3 RIE: 1 CAT: 07

France (Strasbourg)
CIJE: 0 RIE: 2 CAT: 07

France (Vendee)
CIJE: 1 RIE: 0 CAT: 07

France Wiseman Educational Program
CIJE: 1 RIE: 0 CAT: 19

Frances Early Approach
CIJE: 0 RIE: 1 CAT: 15

Frances Howell School District MO
CIJE: 0 RIE: 1 CAT: 17

Francis (Robert)
CIJE: 0 RIE: 1 CAT: 18

Francis Marion College SC
CIJE: 1 RIE: 1 CAT: 17

Francis Tuttle Vo Tech Center OK
CIJE: 1 RIE: 2 CAT: 17

Franck Drawing Completion Test
CIJE: 4 RIE: 1 CAT: 21

Franck Report
CIJE: 3 RIE: 0 CAT: 22

Franco (Francisco)
CIJE: 1 RIE: 1 CAT: 18

Franco American Ethnic Heritage Studies Program
CIJE: 0 RIE: 1 CAT: 19

Franco Americans
CIJE: 6 RIE: 30 CAT: 08

Francophone Africa
CIJE: 6 RIE: 7 CAT: 07

Francophone Areas (Non European)
USE Non European Francophone Areas

Francophone Education (Canada)
CIJE: 5 RIE: 16 CAT: 03
SN See also "French Language Schools"

Francophone Literature
CIJE: 2 RIE: 1 CAT: 13

Francophonie
CIJE: 3 RIE: 1 CAT: 13
SN "La Francophonie" — Supranational movement dedicated to the promotion of the French language

Frank (Barney)
CIJE: 0 RIE: 1 CAT: 18

Frank (Philipp)
CIJE: 0 RIE: 1 CAT: 18

Frank (Robert)
CIJE: 1 RIE: 1 CAT: 18

Frank Porter Graham Center NC
CIJE: 0 RIE: 5 CAT: 17

Frankel (Hermann)
CIJE: 1 RIE: 0 CAT: 18

Frankfurt American High School (West Germany)
CIJE: 1 RIE: 0 CAT: 17

Frankfurt School
CIJE: 5 RIE: 6 CAT: 16

Frankl (Victor E)
CIJE: 1 RIE: 0 CAT: 18

Franklin (Benjamin)
CIJE: 20 RIE: 4 CAT: 18

Franklin (James)
CIJE: 0 RIE: 1 CAT: 18

Franklin (John Hope)
CIJE: 5 RIE: 3 CAT: 18

Franklin (Robert J)
CIJE: 0 RIE: 1 CAT: 18

Franklin and Marshall College PA
CIJE: 15 RIE: 7 CAT: 17

Franklin City School District TN
CIJE: 0 RIE: 1 CAT: 17

Franklin College OH
CIJE: 0 RIE: 1 CAT: 17

Franklin County School District MS
CIJE: 0 RIE: 1 CAT: 17

Franklin County School District TN
CIJE: 0 RIE: 1 CAT: 17

Franklin Institute PA
CIJE: 4 RIE: 0 CAT: 17

Franklin Junior High School CA
CIJE: 0 RIE: 1 CAT: 17

Franklin K Lane High School NY
CIJE: 2 RIE: 1 CAT: 17

Franklin Pierce College NH
CIJE: 1 RIE: 1 CAT: 17

Franklin Research Center PA
CIJE: 1 RIE: 0 CAT: 17

Franklin University OH
CIJE: 0 RIE: 2 CAT: 17

Franklin v Gwinnett County Public Schools
CIJE: 6 RIE: 1 CAT: 14

Fransiscan Handmaids of Mary
CIJE: 0 RIE: 0 CAT: 17

Fraser (Berry J)
CIJE: 1 RIE: 0 CAT: 18

Fraser (Malcolm)
CIJE: 0 RIE: 1 CAT: 18

Fraud
CIJE: 66 RIE: 60 CAT: 14

Fraudulent Credentials
CIJE: 0 RIE: 4 CAT: 16

Fraunhofer (Joseph)
CIJE: 1 RIE: 0 CAT: 18

Frederick (Robert W)
CIJE: 1 RIE: 0 CAT: 18

Frederick Community College MD
CIJE: 0 RIE: 2 CAT: 17

Frederick County Outdoor School MD
CIJE: 1 RIE: 1 CAT: 17

Frederick County Public Schools MD
CIJE: 4 RIE: 3 CAT: 17

Frederiksen (Carl)
CIJE: 1 RIE: 1 CAT: 18

FrEdMail
CIJE: 3 RIE: 1 CAT: 19
UF Free Educational Mail

Fredonia High School NY
CIJE: 1 RIE: 0 CAT: 17

Free Abrasive Machining
CIJE: 2 RIE: 0 CAT: 20

Free African Society
CIJE: 0 RIE: 1 CAT: 17

Free Association Norms
CIJE: 0 RIE: 2 CAT: 21

Free Association Vocabulary Test (Tinker et al)
CIJE: 0 RIE: 1 CAT: 21

Free Associations
CIJE: 5 RIE: 6 CAT: 21

Free Balloons (Aviation)
CIJE: 0 RIE: 1 CAT: 20

Free Clinics
CIJE: 0 RIE: 3 CAT: 05

Free Educational Mail
USE FrEdMail

Free Form Games
CIJE: 0 RIE: 1 CAT: 16

Free Forming
CIJE: 1 RIE: 0 CAT: 15

Free Lance Market
CIJE: 3 RIE: 4 CAT: 16

Free Library of Philadelphia PA
CIJE: 6 RIE: 7 CAT: 17

Free Market Plan
CIJE: 1 RIE: 0 CAT: 15

Free Materials
CIJE: 24 RIE: 44 CAT: 16

Free Modifiers
CIJE: 0 RIE: 1 CAT: 13

Free Press Underground MO
CIJE: 1 RIE: 0 CAT: 17

Free Public Library of the Borough of Madison NJ
CIJE: 1 RIE: 0 CAT: 17

Free Response Test Items
CIJE: 17 RIE: 15 CAT: 21

Free Speech Movement
CIJE: 4 RIE: 4 CAT: 12

Free Text Searching
CIJE: 40 RIE: 8 CAT: 20
UF Full Text Information Retrieval

Free Textbook Law (Missouri)
CIJE: 1 RIE: 0 CAT: 14

Free Time
CIJE: 4 RIE: 3 CAT: 16

Free University of Berlin (West Germany)
CIJE: 4 RIE: 1 CAT: 17

Free University of Brussels (Belgium)
CIJE: 3 RIE: 1 CAT: 17

Free University of Iran
CIJE: 3 RIE: 2 CAT: 17

Free Venture Program
CIJE: 0 RIE: 1 CAT: 19

Freebased Cocaine
USE Cocaine Freebase

Freed Hardeman College TN
CIJE: 0 RIE: 1 CAT: 17

Freedman Report
CIJE: 0 RIE: 1 CAT: 22

Freedmans Village VA
CIJE: 0 RIE: 0 CAT: 07

Freedmens Bureau
CIJE: 2 RIE: 2 CAT: 12

Freedom of Assembly
CIJE: 5 RIE: 6 CAT: 14

Freedom of Association
CIJE: 1 RIE: 2 CAT: 14

Freedom of Information Act
CIJE: 31 RIE: 29 CAT: 14

Freedom of Information Center
CIJE: 1 RIE: 2 CAT: 17

Freedom Quilting Bee Cooperative AL
CIJE: 0 RIE: 1 CAT: 17

Freeland Community Schools MI
CIJE: 0 RIE: 1 CAT: 17

Freemans Journal
CIJE: 0 RIE: 1 CAT: 22

Freeport Public Schools NY
CIJE: 0 RIE: 1 CAT: 17

Freestyle (Television Series)
CIJE: 1 RIE: 3 CAT: 22

Freeway to Learning
CIJE: 1 RIE: 0 CAT: 22

Freeze Drying Method
CIJE: 2 RIE: 0 CAT: 20
UF Vacuum Freeze Drying

Freezing Principle
CIJE: 1 RIE: 1 CAT: 13

Freinet (Celestin)
CIJE: 2 RIE: 2 CAT: 18

Freire (Paulo)
CIJE: 113 RIE: 92 CAT: 18

Fremont County School District WY
CIJE: 0 RIE: 1 CAT: 17

Fremont Newark Community College District CA
CIJE: 0 RIE: 1 CAT: 17

Fremont Public Schools NE
CIJE: 1 RIE: 0 CAT: 17

Fremont Union High School District CA
CIJE: 3 RIE: 3 CAT: 17

French (Acadian)
CIJE: 1 RIE: 5 CAT: 13

French (Cajun)
CIJE: 1 RIE: 2 CAT: 13
UF Cajun French

French (Canadian)
CIJE: 9 RIE: 22 CAT: 13

French (Daniel Chester)
CIJE: 2 RIE: 0 CAT: 18

French (Haitian)
CIJE: 1 RIE: 1 CAT: 13

French (J R P)
CIJE: 1 RIE: 1 CAT: 18

French (Marilyn)
CIJE: 0 RIE: 1 CAT: 18

French (Parisian)
CIJE: 5 RIE: 0 CAT: 13

French (Swiss)
CIJE: 0 RIE: 1 CAT: 13

French Academy (France)
CIJE: 0 RIE: 1 CAT: 17

French Africa
CIJE: 2 RIE: 4 CAT: 07

French and Indian War
CIJE: 1 RIE: 1 CAT: 12
SN War in America (1754-60) in which France and its Indian allies opposed England

French Broadcasting System
CIJE: 1 RIE: 0 CAT: 17

French Civilization
CIJE: 4 RIE: 1 CAT: 16

French Creole
CIJE: 1 RIE: 11 CAT: 13

French Cuisine
CIJE: 1 RIE: 0 CAT: 16

French Culture
CIJE: 6 RIE: 16 CAT: 16

French Culture Research Project
CIJE: 0 RIE: 1 CAT: 19

French Guiana
CIJE: 0 RIE: 3 CAT: 07
UF French Guyana

French Guyana
USE French Guiana

French in Action (Video)
CIJE: 1 RIE: 1 CAT: 22

French Language Schools
CIJE: 1 RIE: 6 CAT: 05
SN See also "Francophone Education (Canada)"

French National Educational Institute
CIJE: 1 RIE: 0 CAT: 17

French People
CIJE: 8 RIE: 6 CAT: 08
SN See add'l listings under "Franco..."

French Republicanism
CIJE: 1 RIE: 0 CAT: 16

French Revolution
CIJE: 28 RIE: 9 CAT: 12

French Speaking
CIJE: 25 RIE: 27 CAT: 08
SN See add'l listings under "Francophone..."

French West Africa
CIJE: 0 RIE: 3 CAT: 07

French West Indies
CIJE: 3 RIE: 2 CAT: 07

Frequency (Electronics)
CIJE: 1 RIE: 2 CAT: 20

Frequency Allocation
CIJE: 0 RIE: 3 CAT: 20

Frequency Analysis
CIJE: 16 RIE: 8 CAT: 15

Frequency Data
CIJE: 6 RIE: 5 CAT: 15

Frequency Discrimination (Auditory)
CIJE: 6 RIE: 1 CAT: 11

Frequency Estimation Equipercentile Equating
CIJE: 6 RIE: 2 CAT: 21

Frequency Memory
CIJE: 0 RIE: 1 CAT: 11

Frequency Modulation
CIJE: 6 RIE: 3 CAT: 20
UF FM (Modulation)

Frequency Modulation Hearing Aid Systems
CIJE: 0 RIE: 1 CAT: 04
UF FM Auditory Trainers

Frequency of Measurement
CIJE: 1 RIE: 3 CAT: 21
UF Measurement Frequency

Frequency of Testing
USE Testing Frequency

Frequency Ratio Method
CIJE: 0 RIE: 1 CAT: 15

Frequency Theory (Learning)
CIJE: 9 RIE: 3 CAT: 15

Frequency Transposition (Auditory)
CIJE: 1 RIE: 0 CAT: 11

Fresh Start Minischool DC
CIJE: 0 RIE: 2 CAT: 17

Freshman Admissions Prediction Equation
CIJE: 0 RIE: 1 CAT: 15

Freshman Interest Groups
CIJE: 1 RIE: 2 CAT: 10

Freshman Orientation
CIJE: 1 RIE: 5 CAT: 16

Freshman Seminars
CIJE: 3 RIE: 15 CAT: 03

Freshman Skills Assessment Program
CIJE: 0 RIE: 1 CAT: 19

Freshman Success Courses
CIJE: 0 RIE: 3 CAT: 03

Freshwater Systems
CIJE: 3 RIE: 6 CAT: 20

Fresno Adult School CA
CIJE: 0 RIE: 1 CAT: 17

Fresno Bee
CIJE: 0 RIE: 1 CAT: 22

Fresno City College CA
CIJE: 0 RIE: 17 CAT: 17

Fresno County Department of Education CA
CIJE: 1 RIE: 0 CAT: 17

Fresno County Project
CIJE: 0 RIE: 1 CAT: 19

Fresno Organizing Project CA
CIJE: 0 RIE: 1 CAT: 19

Fresno State College CA
CIJE: 1 RIE: 4 CAT: 17

Freud (Anna)
CIJE: 1 RIE: 0 CAT: 18

Freud (Sigmund)
CIJE: 58 RIE: 38 CAT: 18

Freyberger (Ruth)
CIJE: 0 RIE: 1 CAT: 18

Fricatives
CIJE: 14 RIE: 10 CAT: 13

Fricot Ranch School CA
CIJE: 0 RIE: 1 CAT: 17

Friction
CIJE: 9 RIE: 5 CAT: 20

Friday Night Lights (Bissinger)
CIJE: 0 RIE: 1 CAT: 22
SN "Friday Night Lights: A Town, A Team, and a Dream"

Friedan (Betty)
CIJE: 2 RIE: 4 CAT: 18

Friedel Crafts Reaction (Chemistry)
CIJE: 1 RIE: 0 CAT: 20

Friedenberg (Edgar Z)
CIJE: 0 RIE: 1 CAT: 18

Friederberg (Pedre)
CIJE: 1 RIE: 0 CAT: 18

Friedman (Martin)
CIJE: 1 RIE: 0 CAT: 18

Friedman (Maurice)
CIJE: 0 RIE: 2 CAT: 18

Friedman (Milton)
CIJE: 4 RIE: 2 CAT: 18

Friedman Two Way Analysis of Variance
CIJE: 4 RIE: 1 CAT: 21

Friedmans Developmental Level
CIJE: 1 RIE: 0 CAT: 21

Friendliness
CIJE: 2 RIE: 1 CAT: 11

Friendly (Fred)
CIJE: 1 RIE: 0 CAT: 18

Friends Central School PA
CIJE: 2 RIE: 1 CAT: 17

Friends Council on Education
CIJE: 1 RIE: 0 CAT: 17

Friends Morgan Project
CIJE: 0 RIE: 1 CAT: 19

Friends of Black Children Project
CIJE: 0 RIE: 1 CAT: 19

Friends of the Library
CIJE: 8 RIE: 15 CAT: 10

Friends of the San Francisco Public Library CA
CIJE: 0 RIE: 2 CAT: 17

Friends School MD
CIJE: 1 RIE: 0 CAT: 17

Friends World College NY
CIJE: 0 RIE: 1 CAT: 17

Friendship Assessment Inventory
CIJE: 0 RIE: 1 CAT: 21

Friendship Cliques
USE Cliques

Friendship Formation
CIJE: 9 RIE: 1 CAT: 11

Friendship Quality
USE Quality of Friendship

Friendship Rating Scale (Bailey and Pierce)
CIJE: 1 RIE: 0 CAT: 21

Friendship Termination
USE Termination of Friendship

Fries (C C)
CIJE: 0 RIE: 4 CAT: 18

Fries American English Series
CIJE: 0 RIE: 2 CAT: 22

Fries Linguistic Method
CIJE: 0 RIE: 1 CAT: 13

Friesland College (Netherlands)
CIJE: 0 RIE: 1 CAT: 17

Frigates
CIJE: 0 RIE: 1 CAT: 04

Frisbee
CIJE: 1 RIE: 1 CAT: 16

Frisch (Max)
CIJE: 6 RIE: 0 CAT: 18

Frisi (Paolo)
CIJE: 1 RIE: 0 CAT: 18

Frisian
CIJE: 12 RIE: 5 CAT: 13

Froebel (Friedrich)
CIJE: 25 RIE: 15 CAT: 18

Froebel Training College (Denmark)
CIJE: 1 RIE: 0 CAT: 17

Frog King or Faithful Henry
CIJE: 0 RIE: 0 CAT: 22

Frogs
CIJE: 18 RIE: 2 CAT: 20

From Subject to Citizen
CIJE: 1 RIE: 0 CAT: 22

Fromm (Erich)
CIJE: 5 RIE: 2 CAT: 18

Front Back Concept (Psychology)
CIJE: 2 RIE: 0 CAT: 11

Front End Analysis
CIJE: 31 RIE: 3 CAT: 15

Front End Processors
CIJE: 3 RIE: 0 CAT: 04

Front End Software
CIJE: 6 RIE: 0 CAT: 04

Front End Types (Automotive)
CIJE: 0 RIE: 1 CAT: 04
UF Automotive Front End Types

Front Range Community College CO
CIJE: 0 RIE: 1 CAT: 17

Frontal Lobe
CIJE: 9 RIE: 1 CAT: 11

Fronteras 1976
CIJE: 0 RIE: 2 CAT: 12

Frontier College (Canada)
CIJE: 4 RIE: 2 CAT: 17

Frontier Communities
CIJE: 4 RIE: 2 CAT: 05

Frontier Community College IL
CIJE: 1 RIE: 1 CAT: 17

Frontier History
CIJE: 25 RIE: 15 CAT: 12

Frontiero v Richardson
CIJE: 3 RIE: 0 CAT: 14

Frost (Robert)
CIJE: 12 RIE: 13 CAT: 18

Frost at Midnight
CIJE: 0 RIE: 1 CAT: 22

Frostbite
CIJE: 2 RIE: 1 CAT: 11

Frostburg State College MD
CIJE: 2 RIE: 9 CAT: 17

Frostburg State University MD
CIJE: 0 RIE: 1 CAT: 17

Frostig Developmental Program of Visual Perception
CIJE: 5 RIE: 7 CAT: 21

Frostig Developmental Test of Visual Perception
CIJE: 24 RIE: 25 CAT: 21

Fruge (August)
CIJE: 0 RIE: 1 CAT: 18

Fruit Packers
CIJE: 0 RIE: 1 CAT: 09

Fruit Pickers
CIJE: 0 RIE: 2 CAT: 09

Fruit Sorters
CIJE: 0 RIE: 1 CAT: 09

Fruita Monument High School
CIJE: 1 RIE: 0 CAT: 17

Fruits
CIJE: 8 RIE: 12 CAT: 20

Frustration
CIJE: 36 RIE: 15 CAT: 11

Fry (Roger)
CIJE: 2 RIE: 1 CAT: 18

Fry Readability Formula
CIJE: 18 RIE: 14 CAT: 21

Frye (Northrop)
CIJE: 20 RIE: 3 CAT: 18

Fryeburg Academy ME
CIJE: 0 RIE: 1 CAT: 17

Fryklund (Verne C)
CIJE: 0 RIE: 2 CAT: 18

Frys Phonetically Regular Words Oral Reading Test
CIJE: 0 RIE: 1 CAT: 21

Fuel Shortages
CIJE: 3 RIE: 0 CAT: 20

Fuel Systems
CIJE: 2 RIE: 7 CAT: 04

Fuentes (Carlos)
CIJE: 9 RIE: 0 CAT: 18

Fuentes (Luis)
CIJE: 1 RIE: 0 CAT: 18

Fugitive Literature
CIJE: 2 RIE: 2 CAT: 16

Fugitive Slave Act 1793
CIJE: 1 RIE: 1 CAT: 14

Fugitive Slave Act 1850
CIJE: 0 RIE: 1 CAT: 14

Fukuyama Profile
CIJE: 8 RIE: 1 CAT: 21

Fulani People
USE Fulbe

Fulbe
CIJE: 0 RIE: 0 CAT: 08
UF Fulani People

Fulbright (J William)
CIJE: 2 RIE: 0 CAT: 18

Fulbright Exchange Program
CIJE: 17 RIE: 18 CAT: 19

Fulbright Hays Act
CIJE: 3 RIE: 16 CAT: 14
UF Mutual Education and Cultural Exchange Act

Fulbright Hays Seminars Abroad Program
CIJE: 0 RIE: 9 CAT: 19

Fulbright Teacher Exchange Program
CIJE: 0 RIE: 6 CAT: 19

Full Employment Act 1972
CIJE: 0 RIE: 1 CAT: 14

Full Employment and Balanced Growth Act 1978
CIJE: 1 RIE: 3 CAT: 14

Full Employment Bill 1945
CIJE: 1 RIE: 0 CAT: 14

Full Faith and Credit Policy
CIJE: 0 RIE: 1 CAT: 16
SN Agreements between higher education institutions to accept student credits and transfers

Full Information Factor Analysis
CIJE: 1 RIE: 4 CAT: 15

Full Range Picture Vocabulary Test (Ammons)
CIJE: 1 RIE: 7 CAT: 21

Full Rank Linear Model
CIJE: 1 RIE: 1 CAT: 15

Full Rank Multivariate Linear Model
CIJE: 1 RIE: 1 CAT: 15

Full Service School Model
CIJE: 1 RIE: 2 CAT: 15

Full Spectrum Lighting
CIJE: 2 RIE: 0 CAT: 20

Full Text Document Delivery
USE Document Delivery

Full Text Indexing
CIJE: 3 RIE: 0 CAT: 15

Full Text Information Retrieval
USE Free Text Searching

Full Time Employment
CIJE: 3 RIE: 1 CAT: 16

Fuller (Buckminster)
CIJE: 7 RIE: 2 CAT: 18

Fuller Reading System
CIJE: 1 RIE: 2 CAT: 15
SN See also "Ball Stick Bird Reading Method"

Fuller Teacher Concerns Theory
USE Teacher Concerns Theory (Fuller)

Fullerton College CA
CIJE: 0 RIE: 7 CAT: 17

Fullerton Junior College CA
CIJE: 2 RIE: 0 CAT: 17

Fullerton Language Test for Adolescents
CIJE: 1 RIE: 1 CAT: 21

Fullilove Case
CIJE: 1 RIE: 1 CAT: 14

Fulton County Public Schools GA
CIJE: 0 RIE: 3 CAT: 17

Fulton High School TN
CIJE: 1 RIE: 0 CAT: 17

Fulton Montgomery Community College NY
CIJE: 0 RIE: 3 CAT: 17

Fumaric Acid
CIJE: 1 RIE: 0 CAT: 20

Fun Fitness Trail
CIJE: 1 RIE: 0 CAT: 15

Fun in Childhood
USE Childhood Fun

Function Based Curriculum
CIJE: 11 RIE: 2 CAT: 03

Function Concept
CIJE: 2 RIE: 2 CAT: 15

Function of Criticism at the Present Time
CIJE: 0 RIE: 1 CAT: 22

Function Probe
CIJE: 0 RIE: 1 CAT: 04

Function Specific Assessment
CIJE: 0 RIE: 1 CAT: 15

Function Supposer
CIJE: 0 RIE: 1 CAT: 04

Functional Ability Rating Scale
CIJE: 0 RIE: 1 CAT: 21

Functional Academic Skills Tests
CIJE: 0 RIE: 1 CAT: 21

Functional Age
CIJE: 0 RIE: 2 CAT: 11

Functional Analysis of Classroom Tasks
CIJE: 0 RIE: 2 CAT: 15

Functional Assessment Inventory
CIJE: 0 RIE: 2 CAT: 21

Functional Basic Reading Series
CIJE: 0 RIE: 1 CAT: 22

Functional Basic Word List for Special Pupils
CIJE: 0 RIE: 2 CAT: 22

Functional Behaviors (Retardation)
CIJE: 0 RIE: 1 CAT: 11

Functional Communication
CIJE: 1 RIE: 3 CAT: 16

Functional Community
CIJE: 0 RIE: 1 CAT: 16

Functional Context
CIJE: 8 RIE: 5 CAT: 15

Functional Context Education
CIJE: 0 RIE: 4 CAT: 15
SN The teaching of reading and mathematics skills in contexts that are relevant to the learner

Functional Ecology of Development
CIJE: 1 RIE: 0 CAT: 16

Functional Fixedness
CIJE: 1 RIE: 0 CAT: 11

Functional Flow Diagrams
CIJE: 0 RIE: 1 CAT: 15

Functional Group Interconversions (Chemistry)
CIJE: 1 RIE: 0 CAT: 20

Functional Independence Measure (Forer et al)
CIJE: 0 RIE: 1 CAT: 15
SN A measure used in rehabilitation medicine for the assessment of disability

Functional Integration
CIJE: 2 RIE: 2 CAT: 15

Functional Job Analysis
CIJE: 3 RIE: 1 CAT: 15

Functional Learning Environments
CIJE: 2 RIE: 4 CAT: 15

Functional Linguistics
CIJE: 23 RIE: 16 CAT: 13

Functional Literacy Examination MS
CIJE: 0 RIE: 0 CAT: 21

Functional Literacy for the National Guard
CIJE: 0 RIE: 1 CAT: 19

Functional Literacy Mini Assessment (1975)
CIJE: 0 RIE: 0 CAT: 21

Functional Literacy Program (DoD)
USE Project FLIT

Functional Literacy Project (India)
CIJE: 0 RIE: 1 CAT: 19

Functional Load
CIJE: 1 RIE: 1 CAT: 13

Functional Mainstreaming for Success Project
CIJE: 0 RIE: 4 CAT: 19

Functional Marking
CIJE: 0 RIE: 1 CAT: 15

Functional Motion Test
CIJE: 1 RIE: 0 CAT: 21

Functional Objectives of Language Learning Project
CIJE: 0 RIE: 1 CAT: 19

Functional Play
CIJE: 4 RIE: 2 CAT: 16

Functional Potential Model
CIJE: 0 RIE: 1 CAT: 15

Functional Properties
CIJE: 5 RIE: 7 CAT: 04

Functional Sentence Perspective
CIJE: 2 RIE: 1 CAT: 13

Functional Similarity
CIJE: 2 RIE: 1 CAT: 11

Functional Speech and Language Training Program
CIJE: 0 RIE: 2 CAT: 19

Functional Unification Grammar
CIJE: 0 RIE: 1 CAT: 13

Functional Visualization
CIJE: 1 RIE: 0 CAT: 11

Functionalism
CIJE: 38 RIE: 13 CAT: 15

Functionally Remote Associates Test
CIJE: 1 RIE: 0 CAT: 21

Functioning Level Testing
CIJE: 1 RIE: 1 CAT: 21

Functionplane Criterion
CIJE: 1 RIE: 0 CAT: 16

Fund Accounting
CIJE: 6 RIE: 4 CAT: 15

Fund Application
CIJE: 3 RIE: 1 CAT: 14

Fund for Adult Education
CIJE: 0 RIE: 6 CAT: 17

Fund for Improvement of Postsecondary Education
CIJE: 18 RIE: 44 CAT: 17
SN See also "FIPSE..." and "National Project I...IV"
UF FIPSE

Fund for Improvement Reform of Schools Teaching
CIJE: 0 RIE: 1 CAT: 17
SN "Fund for the Improvement and Reform of Schools and Teaching"
UF FIRST

Fund for the Advancement of Education
CIJE: 0 RIE: 4 CAT: 17

Fund for the City of New York
CIJE: 0 RIE: 1 CAT: 17

Fundacion Gran Mariscal de Ayacucho (Venezuela)
CIJE: 0 RIE: 1 CAT: 17

Fundamental Academic Skills Test
CIJE: 0 RIE: 1 CAT: 21

Fundamental Achievement Series (Form Xb)
CIJE: 0 RIE: 1 CAT: 22

Fundamental Education Centre Community Development
CIJE: 1 RIE: 0 CAT: 17

Fundamental Graphic Act
CIJE: 0 RIE: 1 CAT: 15

Fundamental Interpersonal Relations Orientation
CIJE: 8 RIE: 9 CAT: 21
SN See also entries under "FIRO"

Fundamental Pedagogics
CIJE: 0 RIE: 1 CAT: 15
SN Afrikaans philosophy of education

Fundamental Schools
CIJE: 11 RIE: 8 CAT: 05

Funding Formulas
CIJE: 25 RIE: 52 CAT: 16

Funds Flow Statements
CIJE: 2 RIE: 0 CAT: 16

Funeral Directors
CIJE: 7 RIE: 2 CAT: 09

Funeral Orations
CIJE: 0 RIE: 1 CAT: 16

Funerals
CIJE: 18 RIE: 10 CAT: 16

Fur Trade
CIJE: 7 RIE: 4 CAT: 20

Furbearing Animals
CIJE: 0 RIE: 1 CAT: 20

Furman University SC
CIJE: 7 RIE: 7 CAT: 17

Furniture Arrangement Floorplan Test
CIJE: 1 RIE: 0 CAT: 21

Furniture Refinishing
CIJE: 0 RIE: 4 CAT: 03

Furniture Repair
CIJE: 0 RIE: 1 CAT: 16

Furno Cost of Education Index
CIJE: 0 RIE: 1 CAT: 15

Furth (Hans G)
CIJE: 0 RIE: 1 CAT: 18

Further Education Unit (England)
CIJE: 0 RIE: 5 CAT: 17

Fusion
CIJE: 6 RIE: 1 CAT: 20

Futuna Islands
USE Wallis and Futuna Islands

Future Business Leaders of America
CIJE: 7 RIE: 13 CAT: 17

Future Cognition
CIJE: 3 RIE: 3 CAT: 16

Future Extension
CIJE: 1 RIE: 1 CAT: 16

Future Farmers of America
CIJE: 195 RIE: 119 CAT: 17

Future Farmers of America IL
CIJE: 1 RIE: 0 CAT: 17

Future Farmers of Colombia
CIJE: 1 RIE: 0 CAT: 17

Future Farmers of Japan
CIJE: 1 RIE: 0 CAT: 17

Future Generations
CIJE: 0 RIE: 1 CAT: 10

Future Homemakers of America
CIJE: 16 RIE: 59 CAT: 17

Future Learning
CIJE: 0 RIE: 1 CAT: 11

Future Markets
CIJE: 0 RIE: 1 CAT: 16

Future Orientation Questionnaire
CIJE: 0 RIE: 1 CAT: 21

Future Problem Solving Program
CIJE: 21 RIE: 2 CAT: 15

Future Scientists of America Foundation
CIJE: 0 RIE: 1 CAT: 17

Future Shock
CIJE: 6 RIE: 4 CAT: 22

Future Teacher Institute CA
CIJE: 0 RIE: 1 CAT: 19

Future Teachers of America
CIJE: 2 RIE: 3 CAT: 17

Future Tense
CIJE: 8 RIE: 1 CAT: 13

Future World Perspective Values Scale
CIJE: 0 RIE: 1 CAT: 21

Futures Markets
CIJE: 2 RIE: 1 CAT: 16

Futures Research
CIJE: 1 RIE: 6 CAT: 15

FUTURES with Jaime Escalante
CIJE: 0 RIE: 1 CAT: 22

Fuzzy Concepts
CIJE: 11 RIE: 5 CAT: 15

Fuzzy Logic
CIJE: 0 RIE: 2 CAT: 15

Fuzzy Set Theory
CIJE: 36 RIE: 6 CAT: 15

Fuzzy Time Series
CIJE: 0 RIE: 2 CAT: 15

FYCSP Word Attack Test
CIJE: 0 RIE: 1 CAT: 21

G Analysis
CIJE: 10 RIE: 2 CAT: 21

G Analysis Weighted G Analysis
CIJE: 1 RIE: 0 CAT: 15

G I Bill
CIJE: 11 RIE: 61 CAT: 14
UF GI Bill (USA)

G I Bill 1984
CIJE: 0 RIE: 1 CAT: 14

G I Bill Improvement Act 1977
CIJE: 0 RIE: 1 CAT: 14

G Index of Agreement
CIJE: 16 RIE: 0 CAT: 21

G P L Viewfinder 900 Videcon Camera
CIJE: 0 RIE: 1 CAT: 04

G Phenomenon (Intelligence)
USE General Intelligence

G SOME Teacher Decision Making Model
CIJE: 0 RIE: 1 CAT: 15

Ga dang
USE Gaddang

Gaberina (Peter)
CIJE: 1 RIE: 0 CAT: 18

Gable Roberts Attitude Towards School Subjects
CIJE: 1 RIE: 1 CAT: 21

Gabler (Mel)
CIJE: 9 RIE: 3 CAT: 18

Gabler (Norma)
CIJE: 9 RIE: 3 CAT: 18

Gabon
CIJE: 1 RIE: 9 CAT: 07

Gabor (Dennis)
CIJE: 0 RIE: 1 CAT: 18

Gadamer (Hans Georg)
CIJE: 5 RIE: 7 CAT: 18

Gadda (Carlo Emilio)
CIJE: 1 RIE: 0 CAT: 18

Gaddang
CIJE: 0 RIE: 0 CAT: 13
SN A Northwest Austronesian (Philippine) language
UF Ga dang

Gadden (Gunnar)
CIJE: 0 RIE: 1 CAT: 18

Gadiel (Clarissa)
CIJE: 0 RIE: 1 CAT: 18

Gadna Youth Corps (Israel)
CIJE: 0 RIE: 1 CAT: 17

Gadsden Independent Schools NM
CIJE: 0 RIE: 0 CAT: 17

Gadsden State Junior College AL
CIJE: 0 RIE: 1 CAT: 17

GAEL Simple Sentence Level Test
USE Grammatical Analysis of Elicited Language

Gafarian (A V)
CIJE: 0 RIE: 1 CAT: 18

Gafuku
USE Gahuku

Gagne (Robert M)
CIJE: 46 RIE: 24 CAT: 18

Gagnes Taxonomy
CIJE: 3 RIE: 8 CAT: 15

Gahagen Bernstein Educational Program
CIJE: 0 RIE: 1 CAT: 19

Gahuku
CIJE: 0 RIE: 1 CAT: 13
SN An East New Guinea Highlands language (East Central group)
UF Gafuku

Gaia Hypothesis
CIJE: 3 RIE: 1 CAT: 20
SN James Lovelock's view of the Earth and everything on it as a unified, self-regulating system

Gain Analysis
CIJE: 2 RIE: 0 CAT: 21

Gain Effective Time Constant Product
CIJE: 0 RIE: 1 CAT: 15

Gain Scores
CIJE: 9 RIE: 8 CAT: 21

Gaines v Anderson
CIJE: 1 RIE: 1 CAT: 14

Gainesville College GA
CIJE: 0 RIE: 1 CAT: 17

Gainsharing
CIJE: 2 RIE: 2 CAT: 16

Gala (Antonio)
CIJE: 1 RIE: 0 CAT: 18

Galactosemia
CIJE: 5 RIE: 1 CAT: 11

Galapagos Islands
CIJE: 1 RIE: 1 CAT: 07

Galax City School District VA
CIJE: 0 RIE: 1 CAT: 17

Galaxy Conference on Adult Education
CIJE: 3 RIE: 3 CAT: 02

Galbahe Language Tests
CIJE: 0 RIE: 1 CAT: 21
SN Tests for measuring Spanish language proficiency and Basque language achievement

Galbraith (John Kenneth)
CIJE: 2 RIE: 1 CAT: 18

Gale Research Company
CIJE: 3 RIE: 0 CAT: 17

Galesburg Public Library IL
CIJE: 0 RIE: 1 CAT: 17

Galice
CIJE: 1 RIE: 0 CAT: 13

Galileo
CIJE: 21 RIE: 3 CAT: 18

Galileo System
CIJE: 1 RIE: 1 CAT: 15

Gallagher Aschner Questioning Category System
CIJE: 0 RIE: 1 CAT: 15

Gallaudet (Thomas Hopkins)
CIJE: 3 RIE: 0 CAT: 18

Gallaudet College DC
CIJE: 21 RIE: 35 CAT: 17

Gallaudet Research Institute DC
CIJE: 0 RIE: 2 CAT: 17

Gallaudet University DC
CIJE: 36 RIE: 16 CAT: 17

Galls (Mechanical)
CIJE: 1 RIE: 0 CAT: 20

Gallup Award
CIJE: 1 RIE: 0 CAT: 16

Gallup Evaluation Model
CIJE: 0 RIE: 1 CAT: 15

Gallup McKinley School District NM
CIJE: 0 RIE: 1 CAT: 17

Gallup Organization
CIJE: 1 RIE: 1 CAT: 17

Gallup Poll
CIJE: 43 RIE: 27 CAT: 16

Galois (Evariste)
CIJE: 2 RIE: 0 CAT: 18

Galois Fields
CIJE: 1 RIE: 0 CAT: 20

Galotti (Emilia)
CIJE: 1 RIE: 0 CAT: 18

Galperin (P J)
CIJE: 3 RIE: 0 CAT: 18

Galton (Sir Francis)
CIJE: 5 RIE: 1 CAT: 18

Galtung (Johan)
CIJE: 0 RIE: 2 CAT: 18

Galvanic Skin Response
CIJE: 16 RIE: 7 CAT: 11

Gambia
CIJE: 8 RIE: 18 CAT: 07

Gambling
CIJE: 18 RIE: 9 CAT: 16

Game Animals
CIJE: 1 RIE: 1 CAT: 20

Game Birds
CIJE: 0 RIE: 1 CAT: 20

Games Analysis System
CIJE: 0 RIE: 2 CAT: 15

Gamesmanship
CIJE: 2 RIE: 3 CAT: 16

Gamma Coefficient
CIJE: 1 RIE: 0 CAT: 21

Gamma Rays
CIJE: 2 RIE: 1 CAT: 20

Gamma Statistical Method
CIJE: 3 RIE: 3 CAT: 15

Ganado Language Arts Development Project AZ
CIJE: 0 RIE: 1 CAT: 19
UF GLAD Project AZ

Ganado Primary School AZ
CIJE: 2 RIE: 2 CAT: 17

Ganado Public School District AZ
USE Ganado School District AZ

Ganado Public Schools Bilingual Education Project
CIJE: 0 RIE: 1 CAT: 19

Ganado School District AZ
CIJE: 2 RIE: 4 CAT: 17
UF Ganado Public School District AZ

Gandhi (Indira)
CIJE: 0 RIE: 3 CAT: 18

Gandhi (Mahatma)
CIJE: 19 RIE: 20 CAT: 18

Gang Membership Inventory
CIJE: 0 RIE: 1 CAT: 21

Gang Rape
CIJE: 0 RIE: 1 CAT: 16

Gangs
CIJE: 16 RIE: 17 CAT: 10

Gann Committee (Great Britain)
CIJE: 1 RIE: 0 CAT: 17

Gannet (Deborah Sampson)
CIJE: 0 RIE: 1 CAT: 18

Gannett Company
CIJE: 0 RIE: 1 CAT: 17
UF Gannett Newspapers

Gannett Foundation
CIJE: 1 RIE: 2 CAT: 17

Gannett Newspapers
USE Gannett Company

Gannon College PA
CIJE: 1 RIE: 0 CAT: 17

Gannon University PA
CIJE: 1 RIE: 1 CAT: 17

Gans (Herbert J)
CIJE: 1 RIE: 0 CAT: 18

Gans (Roma)
CIJE: 1 RIE: 0 CAT: 18

Gap Reduction Model
CIJE: 1 RIE: 1 CAT: 15

Garbage Can Theory
CIJE: 4 RIE: 3 CAT: 15

Garber (LeRoy)
CIJE: 2 RIE: 0 CAT: 18

Garber (Sharon)
CIJE: 1 RIE: 0 CAT: 18

Garcia (Tilin)
CIJE: 1 RIE: 0 CAT: 18

Garcia Lorca (Federico)
CIJE: 13 RIE: 1 CAT: 18

Garcia Marquez (Gabriel)
CIJE: 5 RIE: 2 CAT: 18

Garcia Monge (Joaquin)
CIJE: 1 RIE: 0 CAT: 18

Garden Center Employees
CIJE: 0 RIE: 1 CAT: 09

Garden Cities
CIJE: 1 RIE: 0 CAT: 05

Garden State Graduate Fellowship Program NJ
CIJE: 0 RIE: 1 CAT: 19

Gardening
CIJE: 28 RIE: 28 CAT: 16

Gardens
CIJE: 9 RIE: 2 CAT: 20

Gardiner (Robert)
CIJE: 0 RIE: 1 CAT: 18

Gardner (Alexander)
CIJE: 1 RIE: 0 CAT: 18

Gardner (Dwayne E)
CIJE: 1 RIE: 0 CAT: 18

Gardner (Howard)
CIJE: 20 RIE: 8 CAT: 18

Gardner (John)
CIJE: 7 RIE: 1 CAT: 18

Gardner (Martin)
CIJE: 3 RIE: 0 CAT: 18

Gardner Denver Case
CIJE: 1 RIE: 0 CAT: 14

Gardner Task Force on Education
CIJE: 1 RIE: 0 CAT: 17

Garfield Educational Complex CA
CIJE: 0 RIE: 1 CAT: 17

Garfield Options for Leadership Development
CIJE: 0 RIE: 1 CAT: 19
UF Project GOLD VA

Garfield School District WA
CIJE: 0 RIE: 1 CAT: 17

Garibaldi (Giuseppe)
CIJE: 0 RIE: 1 CAT: 18

Garland (Hamlin)
CIJE: 2 RIE: 1 CAT: 18

Garland Assessment of Graduation Expectations
CIJE: 0 RIE: 1 CAT: 21

Garland Independent School District TX
CIJE: 0 RIE: 2 CAT: 17

Garland Junior College MA
CIJE: 1 RIE: 1 CAT: 17

Garment Design and Construction Certificate
CIJE: 0 RIE: 1 CAT: 16

Garment Inspectors
CIJE: 0 RIE: 1 CAT: 09

Garment Loopers
CIJE: 0 RIE: 1 CAT: 09

Garment Packers
CIJE: 0 RIE: 1 CAT: 09

Garner (Alan)
CIJE: 2 RIE: 0 CAT: 18

Garnett College (England)
CIJE: 1 RIE: 0 CAT: 17

Garnica (Olga)
CIJE: 0 RIE: 1 CAT: 18

Garnishment
CIJE: 0 RIE: 2 CAT: 14

Garrison (Roger)
CIJE: 2 RIE: 1 CAT: 18

Garrison (William Lloyd)
CIJE: 1 RIE: 2 CAT: 18

Garrison Method
CIJE: 0 RIE: 1 CAT: 15

Garvey (Marcus)
CIJE: 5 RIE: 0 CAT: 18

Garvey School District CA
CIJE: 0 RIE: 1 CAT: 17

Garvin (A D)
CIJE: 0 RIE: 1 CAT: 18

Gary E Widmar Et Al v Clark Vincent Et Al
CIJE: 0 RIE: 1 CAT: 14

Gary Public Schools IN
CIJE: 6 RIE: 1 CAT: 17

Gas
USE Gases

Gas Absorption
CIJE: 0 RIE: 1 CAT: 20

Gas Chromatography
CIJE: 4 RIE: 0 CAT: 20

Gas Detectors
CIJE: 1 RIE: 2 CAT: 04

Gas Engines
USE Gasoline Engines

Gas Flow
CIJE: 1 RIE: 1 CAT: 20

Gas Laws (Physics)
CIJE: 7 RIE: 1 CAT: 20

Gas Station Attendants
CIJE: 0 RIE: 5 CAT: 09
UF Automobile Service Station Attendants; Automotive Service Attendants; Service Station Operators

Gas Stations
CIJE: 1 RIE: 0 CAT: 05
UF Service Stations

Gas Technicians
CIJE: 1 RIE: 0 CAT: 09
UF Natural Gas Technicians

Gascon
CIJE: 2 RIE: 1 CAT: 13

Gases
CIJE: 26 RIE: 6 CAT: 20
UF Gas

Gasohol
CIJE: 2 RIE: 3 CAT: 20

Gasoline Engine Assemblers
CIJE: 0 RIE: 1 CAT: 09

Gasoline Engines
CIJE: 0 RIE: 1 CAT: 20
SN See also "Small Gasoline Engines"
UF Gas Engines

Gaston (E Thayer)
CIJE: 1 RIE: 0 CAT: 18

Gaston College NC
CIJE: 0 RIE: 2 CAT: 17

Gaston County School District NC
CIJE: 1 RIE: 2 CAT: 17

Gastroenterology Assistants
CIJE: 0 RIE: 1 CAT: 09

Gastrointestinal Diseases
CIJE: 1 RIE: 2 CAT: 11

Gastrointestinal System
CIJE: 3 RIE: 9 CAT: 11

GATE Project
CIJE: 0 RIE: 1 CAT: 19
UF Guaranteed Accommodation and Training for Employ

Gatekeeper Role
CIJE: 29 RIE: 22 CAT: 16

Gates (Doris)
CIJE: 1 RIE: 0 CAT: 18

Gates Basic Reading Tests
CIJE: 1 RIE: 1 CAT: 21

Gates MacGinitie Readiness Skills Test
CIJE: 2 RIE: 8 CAT: 21

Gates MacGinitie Reading Tests
CIJE: 18 RIE: 73 CAT: 21

GateWay Community College AZ
CIJE: 0 RIE: 1 CAT: 17

Gateway Information System (DoD)
CIJE: 2 RIE: 1 CAT: 04

Gateway Technical Institute WI
CIJE: 0 RIE: 4 CAT: 17

Gateway Vocational Technical School AR
CIJE: 0 RIE: 1 CAT: 17

Gateway Writing Project
CIJE: 1 RIE: 3 CAT: 19

Gatorball
CIJE: 0 RIE: 1 CAT: 16

Gattegno (Caleb)
CIJE: 1 RIE: 4 CAT: 18

Gault v Garrison
CIJE: 1 RIE: 0 CAT: 14

Gauss (Johann Carl Friedrich)
CIJE: 2 RIE: 0 CAT: 18

Gauss Law
CIJE: 1 RIE: 1 CAT: 15

Gaussian Distribution
CIJE: 5 RIE: 0 CAT: 15

Gaussian Poisson Distribution
CIJE: 2 RIE: 1 CAT: 15
UF Poisson Gaussian Distribution

Gaussian Quadrature
CIJE: 1 RIE: 1 CAT: 15

Gautier (Theophile)
CIJE: 2 RIE: 0 CAT: 18

Gaviao
CIJE: 0 RIE: 1 CAT: 13
SN A Monde language of the Tupi family in Brazil
UF Diguet

Gavilan College CA
CIJE: 3 RIE: 1 CAT: 17

Gawboy (Carl)
CIJE: 0 RIE: 1 CAT: 18

Gay (Joyce)
CIJE: 0 RIE: 1 CAT: 18

Gay Liberation Front
CIJE: 1 RIE: 1 CAT: 17

Gay Literature
USE Homosexual Literature

Gay Parents
USE Homosexual Parents

Gay Students Organization v Bonner
CIJE: 2 RIE: 0 CAT: 14

Gay Teachers
USE Homosexual Teachers

Gaya (Ramon)
CIJE: 1 RIE: 0 CAT: 18

Gaza Strip
CIJE: 3 RIE: 4 CAT: 07

Gaze Duration
CIJE: 3 RIE: 2 CAT: 11

Gaze Patterns
CIJE: 16 RIE: 11 CAT: 11

Gbandi
CIJE: 0 RIE: 1 CAT: 13

GEARS Model
CIJE: 0 RIE: 1 CAT: 15
UF Guiding Education toward Adult Roles for Success

Geary County Unified School District KS
CIJE: 0 RIE: 1 CAT: 17
UF Junction City Unified School District 475 KS

GED Writing Skills Test
CIJE: 0 RIE: 0 CAT: 21
UF Writing Skills Test (GED)

Geduldig v Aiello
CIJE: 5 RIE: 0 CAT: 14

Geertz (Clifford)
CIJE: 3 RIE: 3 CAT: 18

Geiger Counters
CIJE: 2 RIE: 1 CAT: 04

Geisel (Theodor Seuss)
CIJE: 1 RIE: 1 CAT: 18

Geisinger Medical Center
CIJE: 1 RIE: 1 CAT: 17

Geist Picture Interest Inventory
CIJE: 1 RIE: 3 CAT: 21

Geist Picture Interest Inventory Deaf Form
CIJE: 1 RIE: 0 CAT: 21

GEM Algorithm
CIJE: 0 RIE: 1 CAT: 21
UF General EM Algorithm

Gem Cutters (Jewelry)
CIJE: 1 RIE: 1 CAT: 09

Gem Cutting
CIJE: 1 RIE: 1 CAT: 20

Gembu
CIJE: 1 RIE: 0 CAT: 13

Gemeinschaft Gesellschaft Value Scale
CIJE: 0 RIE: 1 CAT: 21

Gemini Blackboard
CIJE: 0 RIE: 1 CAT: 04

Gemini System
CIJE: 1 RIE: 0 CAT: 15

Gender (Language)
CIJE: 50 RIE: 41 CAT: 13

Gender Aware Therapy
CIJE: 1 RIE: 1 CAT: 11

Gender Balancing (Curriculum)
CIJE: 2 RIE: 1 CAT: 15

Gender Communication Scale
CIJE: 0 RIE: 1 CAT: 21

Gender Constancy
CIJE: 19 RIE: 10 CAT: 11

Gender Expectations Student Achievement Program
CIJE: 0 RIE: 2 CAT: 19

Gender Gap
CIJE: 1 RIE: 1 CAT: 16

Gender Issues
CIJE: 5 RIE: 4 CAT: 16

Gender Mix
CIJE: 2 RIE: 0 CAT: 15
SN See also "Mixed Sex Dyads"

Gender Role Assignment Scale
CIJE: 0 RIE: 1 CAT: 21

Gender Schema Theory
CIJE: 19 RIE: 15 CAT: 15

General Ability Battery
CIJE: 0 RIE: 1 CAT: 21

General Academic Assessment
CIJE: 1 RIE: 15 CAT: 21

General Academic Simulation Program
CIJE: 0 RIE: 1 CAT: 19

General Accounting Office
CIJE: 26 RIE: 37 CAT: 17

General Adaptation Syndrome
CIJE: 2 RIE: 0 CAT: 16

General Agreement on Tariffs and Trade
CIJE: 4 RIE: 1 CAT: 14

General American Symbols
CIJE: 1 RIE: 0 CAT: 13

General Anxiety Questionnaire (Yasgur and Carnen)
CIJE: 0 RIE: 1 CAT: 21

General Anxiety Scale (Sarason)
CIJE: 1 RIE: 0 CAT: 21

General Anxiety Scale for Children (Sarason)
CIJE: 1 RIE: 2 CAT: 21

General Aptitude Test Battery
CIJE: 34 RIE: 530 CAT: 21

General Association of Teaching Professions
CIJE: 0 RIE: 1 CAT: 17

General Attitude Institutional Authority Question
CIJE: 0 RIE: 0 CAT: 21

General Attitudes Toward Rape Scale
CIJE: 0 RIE: 1 CAT: 21

General Aviation
CIJE: 0 RIE: 2 CAT: 20

General Aviation Manufacturers Association
CIJE: 0 RIE: 1 CAT: 17

General Case Programing
CIJE: 3 RIE: 0 CAT: 15

General Certificate of Education
CIJE: 18 RIE: 5 CAT: 16

General Cognitive Index
CIJE: 3 RIE: 0 CAT: 21

General Cognitive Operations
CIJE: 0 RIE: 1 CAT: 11

General College Pilot Education Program
CIJE: 0 RIE: 1 CAT: 19

General College Program Assessment Project
CIJE: 0 RIE: 1 CAT: 19

General Concerns Inventory
CIJE: 0 RIE: 1 CAT: 21

General Conference Mennonites
CIJE: 0 RIE: 1 CAT: 08

General Culture Test
CIJE: 1 RIE: 2 CAT: 21

General Dynamics Convair
CIJE: 0 RIE: 1 CAT: 17

General Education Board
CIJE: 1 RIE: 2 CAT: 17
SN Private foundation, established by John D. Rockefeller, which provided major support for educational improvement during the first half of the 20th century

General Education Performance Index
CIJE: 2 RIE: 1 CAT: 21
UF GEPI

General Education Provisions Act 1968
CIJE: 1 RIE: 1 CAT: 14

General Education Provisions Act 1974
CIJE: 0 RIE: 3 CAT: 14

General Education Provisions Act Section 405f
CIJE: 0 RIE: 1 CAT: 14

General Educational Development Tests
CIJE: 48 RIE: 223 CAT: 21
SN See also under "GED..."

General Electric Company
CIJE: 15 RIE: 8 CAT: 17

General Electric Computers
CIJE: 0 RIE: 4 CAT: 04

General Electric Foundation
CIJE: 1 RIE: 1 CAT: 17

General EM Algorithm
USE GEM Algorithm

General Equilibrium System
CIJE: 0 RIE: 1 CAT: 15

General Event Representation
CIJE: 0 RIE: 2 CAT: 11

General Factor (Intelligence)
CIJE: 20 RIE: 8 CAT: 11

General Federation of Womens Clubs
CIJE: 2 RIE: 2 CAT: 17

General Impression Scoring
CIJE: 0 RIE: 1 CAT: 21

General Information Processing System
CIJE: 1 RIE: 1 CAT: 15

General Information Programme
CIJE: 3 RIE: 9 CAT: 19

General Information Test (Hart)
CIJE: 0 RIE: 1 CAT: 21

General Intellectual Skills Assessment
CIJE: 1 RIE: 1 CAT: 21

General Intelligence
CIJE: 12 RIE: 3 CAT: 11
SN See also "General Factor (Intelligence)"
UF G Phenomenon (Intelligence)

General Land Allotment Act of 1887
CIJE: 2 RIE: 0 CAT: 14

General Learning Ability Score
CIJE: 0 RIE: 1 CAT: 21

General Learning Corporation
CIJE: 1 RIE: 2 CAT: 17

General Linear Model
CIJE: 7 RIE: 12 CAT: 15

General Living Systems Theory
CIJE: 0 RIE: 1 CAT: 15

General Management In Basket
CIJE: 0 RIE: 1 CAT: 15

General Model of Instruction
CIJE: 0 RIE: 1 CAT: 15

General Motors Corporation
CIJE: 15 RIE: 7 CAT: 17

General Motors Institute
CIJE: 1 RIE: 4 CAT: 17

General Music Corporation
CIJE: 1 RIE: 0 CAT: 17

General Open Systems Theory
CIJE: 0 RIE: 2 CAT: 15

General Policy Systems Theory
CIJE: 0 RIE: 1 CAT: 15

General Practitioners
CIJE: 2 RIE: 1 CAT: 09

General Purpose Display System
CIJE: 0 RIE: 1 CAT: 15

General Purpose Grants
CIJE: 0 RIE: 1 CAT: 14

General Purpose Simulation System
CIJE: 0 RIE: 3 CAT: 15

General Revenue Sharing Act 1972
CIJE: 0 RIE: 0 CAT: 14

General School Characteristics Questionnaire
CIJE: 0 RIE: 1 CAT: 21

General Secondary Educ Certificate Exam (Jordan)
CIJE: 0 RIE: 1 CAT: 21
UF Jordanian GSECE

General Semantics Competency Opinion Test (Ralph)
CIJE: 1 RIE: 0 CAT: 21

General Semantics Paradigm (Korzybski)
CIJE: 1 RIE: 9 CAT: 15

General Services Administration
CIJE: 1 RIE: 6 CAT: 17

General Social Distance Scale
CIJE: 1 RIE: 0 CAT: 21

General Social Survey
CIJE: 20 RIE: 6 CAT: 21

General Systems Theory
CIJE: 24 RIE: 15 CAT: 15

General Teaching Council (Scotland)
CIJE: 2 RIE: 0 CAT: 17

General Telephone Company
CIJE: 2 RIE: 0 CAT: 17

General Theological Library MA
CIJE: 1 RIE: 0 CAT: 17

General Training System
CIJE: 0 RIE: 1 CAT: 15

General Variable Skill
CIJE: 0 RIE: 1 CAT: 20

Generalist Teaching
CIJE: 1 RIE: 1 CAT: 03

Generalists
CIJE: 12 RIE: 11 CAT: 10

Generality
CIJE: 1 RIE: 4 CAT: 15
SN See also "Question Generality"

Generalizable Skills
CIJE: 9 RIE: 2 CAT: 16

Generalizable Skills Importance Questionnaire
CIJE: 0 RIE: 1 CAT: 21

Generalized Academic Simulation Program
CIJE: 0 RIE: 1 CAT: 19

Generalized Approximate Procedure
CIJE: 0 RIE: 1 CAT: 21

Generalized Bogus Pipeline
USE Bogus Pipeline Technique

Generalized Classification Technique
CIJE: 1 RIE: 0 CAT: 15

Generalized Compliance Training
CIJE: 0 RIE: 1 CAT: 11

Generalized Empirical Method
CIJE: 0 RIE: 1 CAT: 15

Generalized Expectancy for Success Scale
CIJE: 1 RIE: 0 CAT: 21

Generalized Imitation
CIJE: 2 RIE: 0 CAT: 15

Generalized Information System
CIJE: 0 RIE: 1 CAT: 15

Generalized InService Training Project
CIJE: 0 RIE: 1 CAT: 19
UF GIST Project WA

Generalized Interpreter
CIJE: 0 RIE: 1 CAT: 15

Generalized Learning Curve Method
CIJE: 0 RIE: 1 CAT: 15

Generalized Response Expectancies
CIJE: 0 RIE: 1 CAT: 11

Generalized Symmetric Means
CIJE: 1 RIE: 0 CAT: 20

Generation Effect
CIJE: 2 RIE: 2 CAT: 11

Generation X
CIJE: 1 RIE: 1 CAT: 10

Generations Together Program
CIJE: 1 RIE: 2 CAT: 19

Generative Computer Assisted Instruction
CIJE: 2 RIE: 5 CAT: 15

Generative Memory Model
CIJE: 1 RIE: 0 CAT: 15

Generative Processes
CIJE: 18 RIE: 10 CAT: 16

Generative Rhetoric
CIJE: 1 RIE: 2 CAT: 13

Generative Semantics
CIJE: 7 RIE: 7 CAT: 13

Generative Transmission
CIJE: 2 RIE: 0 CAT: 11

Generativity
CIJE: 7 RIE: 6 CAT: 15

Generator Test Process
CIJE: 0 RIE: 1 CAT: 15

Generic Affective Competencies Model
CIJE: 0 RIE: 1 CAT: 15

Generic Argument
CIJE: 0 RIE: 1 CAT: 16

Generic Argument (Debate)
CIJE: 0 RIE: 1 CAT: 16

Generic Baccalaureate Nursing Data Project
CIJE: 1 RIE: 0 CAT: 19

Generic Certificates (Agriculture)
CIJE: 0 RIE: 1 CAT: 16

Generic Design
CIJE: 0 RIE: 1 CAT: 15

Generic Evaluation
CIJE: 0 RIE: 1 CAT: 15

GENeric Evaluation SYStem TX
USE GENESYS TX

Generic Nominals
CIJE: 0 RIE: 1 CAT: 13

Generic Organizational Model
CIJE: 0 RIE: 2 CAT: 15

Generic Pharmaceutical Training Institute NY
CIJE: 0 RIE: 1 CAT: 17

Generic Products
CIJE: 0 RIE: 1 CAT: 16

Generic Pronouns
CIJE: 0 RIE: 1 CAT: 13

Generic Skills
CIJE: 2 RIE: 6 CAT: 15

Generic Skills Project
CIJE: 0 RIE: 1 CAT: 19

Generic Technical Competencies
CIJE: 0 RIE: 1 CAT: 15

Generosity
CIJE: 14 RIE: 1 CAT: 16

Genesee Community College NY
CIJE: 2 RIE: 9 CAT: 17

Genesee Finger Lakes Regional Planning Board NY
CIJE: 0 RIE: 1 CAT: 17

Genesee Valley School Development Association NY
CIJE: 0 RIE: 1 CAT: 17

Genesis
CIJE: 2 RIE: 0 CAT: 22

GENESYS TX
CIJE: 0 RIE: 3 CAT: 19
UF GENeric Evaluation SYStem TX

Genetic Code
CIJE: 3 RIE: 0 CAT: 11

Genetic Diseases
CIJE: 3 RIE: 0 CAT: 11
UF Genetic Disorders; Hereditary Diseases

Genetic Disorders
USE Genetic Diseases

Genetic Engineering Company
CIJE: 1 RIE: 0 CAT: 17

Genetic Epistemology
CIJE: 3 RIE: 1 CAT: 15

Genetic Mapping
CIJE: 5 RIE: 0 CAT: 11

Geneva Academy (Switzerland)
CIJE: 0 RIE: 1 CAT: 17

Geneva Community Unit School District 304 IL
CIJE: 0 RIE: 1 CAT: 17

Geneva Disarmament Committee
CIJE: 1 RIE: 0 CAT: 17

Geneva Park Leadership and Training Ctr (Canada)
CIJE: 0 RIE: 1 CAT: 17

Geneva Protocol 1925
CIJE: 0 RIE: 0 CAT: 12

Geneva Public Schools NY
CIJE: 0 RIE: 3 CAT: 17

GENIP
USE Geographic Educ National Implementation Project

Genital Herpes
USE Herpes Simplex

Genitives
CIJE: 3 RIE: 1 CAT: 13

Genito Urinary Technicians
CIJE: 0 RIE: 1 CAT: 09

Genitourinary System
CIJE: 1 RIE: 3 CAT: 11

GENMOD Computer Program
CIJE: 0 RIE: 2 CAT: 04

Genocide
CIJE: 68 RIE: 12 CAT: 16

Genograms
CIJE: 12 RIE: 2 CAT: 11

GENOVA (Computer Program)
CIJE: 0 RIE: 1 CAT: 04

Genre Studies
CIJE: 6 RIE: 6 CAT: 03

Gentele (Goeran)
CIJE: 1 RIE: 0 CAT: 18

Gentile (Giovanni)
CIJE: 1 RIE: 0 CAT: 18

Gentle Spirit
CIJE: 1 RIE: 0 CAT: 22

Gentle Teaching
CIJE: 4 RIE: 0 CAT: 15

Gentrification
CIJE: 9 RIE: 3 CAT: 15

Gentry (Castelle G)
CIJE: 1 RIE: 0 CAT: 18

Gentzels Thelen Model
CIJE: 1 RIE: 0 CAT: 15

Geobased Information Systems
CIJE: 1 RIE: 1 CAT: 04

Geoboards
CIJE: 44 RIE: 3 CAT: 04

Geocoding
CIJE: 2 RIE: 4 CAT: 03

Geodesic Domes
CIJE: 8 RIE: 0 CAT: 04

Geodynamics Project
CIJE: 2 RIE: 0 CAT: 19

Geographic Displacement
CIJE: 1 RIE: 1 CAT: 16

Geographic Educ National Implementation Project
CIJE: 13 RIE: 1 CAT: 19
UF GENIP

Geographic Information Systems
CIJE: 14 RIE: 1 CAT: 16

Geographic Literacy
CIJE: 12 RIE: 4 CAT: 15

Geography Awareness Week
CIJE: 1 RIE: 1 CAT: 12
SN See also "National Geography Awareness Week"

Geography Curriculum Project
CIJE: 1 RIE: 16 CAT: 19

Geography Education Standards Project
CIJE: 1 RIE: 1 CAT: 19

Geolinguistics
CIJE: 1 RIE: 19 CAT: 13

Geologic Time
CIJE: 5 RIE: 1 CAT: 20

Geological Society of America
CIJE: 2 RIE: 0 CAT: 17

Geological Survey
CIJE: 6 RIE: 2 CAT: 17

Geometric Dictionary
CIJE: 0 RIE: 2 CAT: 22

Geometric Family
CIJE: 0 RIE: 1 CAT: 10
SN A family in which there are both sons and daughters — see also "Tilted Family"

Geometric Figures Test (Kannegieter)
CIJE: 0 RIE: 1 CAT: 21

Geometric Forms
CIJE: 4 RIE: 2 CAT: 20

Geometric Inventory (Carpenter et al)
CIJE: 0 RIE: 1 CAT: 21

Geometric Mean
CIJE: 4 RIE: 0 CAT: 20

Geometric Programing
CIJE: 2 RIE: 0 CAT: 20

Geometric Rigidity
CIJE: 1 RIE: 0 CAT: 20

Geometric Supposer
CIJE: 7 RIE: 3 CAT: 20

Geometry Proof Tutor
CIJE: 0 RIE: 1 CAT: 04

Geophysical Monitoring for Climatic Change
CIJE: 1 RIE: 0 CAT: 15

Geopolitical Change
CIJE: 1 RIE: 1 CAT: 15

Geopolitics
CIJE: 15 RIE: 4 CAT: 03

Georg August University (West Germany)
USE University of Goettingen (West Germany)

George (Chief Dan)
CIJE: 0 RIE: 1 CAT: 18

George (Jean Craighead)
CIJE: 1 RIE: 0 CAT: 18

George (Stefan)
CIJE: 1 RIE: 0 CAT: 18

George Brown College ON
CIJE: 0 RIE: 1 CAT: 17

George C Marshall Space Flight Center
CIJE: 1 RIE: 0 CAT: 17

George C Wallace Community College AL Selma
USE Wallace Community College AL Selma

George C Wallace State Comm Coll AL Hanceville
USE Wallace State Community College AL Hanceville

George I Sanchez Junior Senior High School TX
CIJE: 0 RIE: 1 CAT: 17

George III
CIJE: 1 RIE: 0 CAT: 18

George Mason University VA
CIJE: 21 RIE: 20 CAT: 17

George Peabody College for Teachers TN
CIJE: 13 RIE: 11 CAT: 17

George Washington High School NY
CIJE: 1 RIE: 0 CAT: 17

George Washington Univ Medical Center DC
CIJE: 0 RIE: 1 CAT: 17

George Washington University DC
CIJE: 37 RIE: 25 CAT: 17

George Williams College IL
CIJE: 0 RIE: 1 CAT: 17

Georgetown Day Care Center DC
CIJE: 0 RIE: 1 CAT: 17

Georgetown University DC
CIJE: 30 RIE: 24 CAT: 17

Georgetown University Medical Center DC
CIJE: 1 RIE: 1 CAT: 17

Georgia
CIJE: 283 RIE: 921 CAT: 07
SN For the west Asian nation, use "Georgia Republic"

Georgia (Americus)
CIJE: 1 RIE: 3 CAT: 07

Georgia (Athens)
CIJE: 7 RIE: 4 CAT: 07

Georgia (Atlanta Metropolitan Area)
CIJE: 1 RIE: 1 CAT: 07

Georgia (Atlanta)
CIJE: 67 RIE: 182 CAT: 07

Georgia (Augusta)
CIJE: 2 RIE: 2 CAT: 07

Georgia (Bibb County)
CIJE: 0 RIE: 1 CAT: 07

Georgia (Carroll County)
CIJE: 1 RIE: 4 CAT: 07

Georgia (Carrollton)
CIJE: 2 RIE: 0 CAT: 07

Georgia (Central)
CIJE: 0 RIE: 1 CAT: 07

Georgia (Clarke County)
CIJE: 0 RIE: 2 CAT: 07

Georgia (Clayton County)
CIJE: 0 RIE: 1 CAT: 07

Georgia (Cobb County)
CIJE: 3 RIE: 0 CAT: 07

Georgia (Columbia County)
CIJE: 1 RIE: 4 CAT: 07

Georgia (Columbus)
CIJE: 1 RIE: 1 CAT: 07

Georgia (Crisp County)
CIJE: 0 RIE: 1 CAT: 07

Georgia (DeKalb County)
CIJE: 2 RIE: 5 CAT: 07

Georgia (Fort Gordon)
CIJE: 0 RIE: 3 CAT: 07

Georgia (Fulton County)
CIJE: 2 RIE: 2 CAT: 07

Georgia (Gainesville)
CIJE: 0 RIE: 1 CAT: 07

Georgia (Hancock County)
CIJE: 0 RIE: 1 CAT: 07

Georgia (Harris County)
CIJE: 0 RIE: 1 CAT: 07

Georgia (Liberty County)
CIJE: 0 RIE: 1 CAT: 07

Georgia (Morgan County)
CIJE: 0 RIE: 1 CAT: 07

Georgia (Murray County)
CIJE: 0 RIE: 1 CAT: 07

Georgia (North)
CIJE: 1 RIE: 1 CAT: 07

Georgia (Northwest)
CIJE: 0 RIE: 1 CAT: 07

Georgia (Savannah)
CIJE: 3 RIE: 6 CAT: 07

Georgia (Statesboro)
CIJE: 1 RIE: 0 CAT: 07

Georgia (Sumter County)
CIJE: 1 RIE: 0 CAT: 07

Georgia (Valdosta)
CIJE: 0 RIE: 1 CAT: 07

Georgia (Wilkes County)
CIJE: 0 RIE: 2 CAT: 07

Georgia Academy for the Blind
CIJE: 0 RIE: 1 CAT: 17

Georgia Appalachian Outreach Project
CIJE: 0 RIE: 1 CAT: 19

Georgia Assessment of Teacher Effectiveness
CIJE: 0 RIE: 4 CAT: 21

Georgia Assessment Project
CIJE: 0 RIE: 1 CAT: 19

Georgia Basic Curriculum
CIJE: 0 RIE: 1 CAT: 03

Georgia Basic Skills Test
CIJE: 0 RIE: 2 CAT: 21

Georgia Basic Skills Writing Test
CIJE: 0 RIE: 1 CAT: 21

Georgia Career Information System
CIJE: 0 RIE: 1 CAT: 17

Georgia Center for Continuing Education
CIJE: 0 RIE: 1 CAT: 17

Georgia Center for the Multihandicapped
CIJE: 0 RIE: 1 CAT: 17

Georgia College
CIJE: 0 RIE: 2 CAT: 17

Georgia College Preparatory Curriculum
USE College Preparatory Curriculum GA

Georgia Community Continuing Education Service
CIJE: 0 RIE: 1 CAT: 17

Georgia Comprehensive Evaluation System
CIJE: 0 RIE: 2 CAT: 21
UF Comprehensive Evaluation System GA

Georgia Comprehensive Guidance Model
CIJE: 0 RIE: 3 CAT: 15

Georgia Cooperative Extension Service
CIJE: 0 RIE: 1 CAT: 17

Georgia Criterion Referenced Tests
CIJE: 0 RIE: 6 CAT: 21

Georgia Educational Television Network
CIJE: 2 RIE: 1 CAT: 17

Georgia Governors Committee on Postsecondary Educ
USE Governors Committee on Postsecondary Education GA

Georgia Governors Honors Program
CIJE: 3 RIE: 10 CAT: 19

Georgia Governors Remediation Initiative
CIJE: 0 RIE: 0 CAT: 19

Georgia Information Dissemination Center
CIJE: 1 RIE: 0 CAT: 17

Georgia Institute of Technology
CIJE: 25 RIE: 15 CAT: 17

Georgia Instructor Academy
CIJE: 1 RIE: 1 CAT: 17

Georgia Interactive Network
CIJE: 0 RIE: 1 CAT: 17

Georgia Labor Mobility Demonstration Project
CIJE: 0 RIE: 1 CAT: 19

Georgia Library Information Network
CIJE: 0 RIE: 2 CAT: 17

Georgia Media Specialist Evaluation Program
CIJE: 0 RIE: 1 CAT: 19

Georgia Online Database
CIJE: 0 RIE: 1 CAT: 04
UF GOLD Database

Georgia Regents Testing Program
CIJE: 1 RIE: 0 CAT: 19

Georgia Republic
CIJE: 0 RIE: 1 CAT: 07
SN For the U.S. State, use "Georgia"

Georgia Retardation Center
CIJE: 0 RIE: 1 CAT: 17

Georgia Southern College
CIJE: 3 RIE: 5 CAT: 17

Georgia Southern University
CIJE: 4 RIE: 2 CAT: 17

Georgia Southwestern College
CIJE: 2 RIE: 0 CAT: 17

Georgia State Board Postsecondary Vocational Ed
CIJE: 0 RIE: 1 CAT: 17

Georgia State College
CIJE: 0 RIE: 1 CAT: 17

Georgia State Department of Education
CIJE: 0 RIE: 4 CAT: 17

Georgia State University
CIJE: 23 RIE: 47 CAT: 17

Georgia Statewide Testing Program
CIJE: 0 RIE: 3 CAT: 19

Georgia Teacher Certification Testing Program
CIJE: 3 RIE: 32 CAT: 19

Georgia Teacher Evaluation Program
CIJE: 0 RIE: 1 CAT: 19

Georgia Teacher Performance Assessment Instrument
CIJE: 0 RIE: 0 CAT: 21

Georgia University System
CIJE: 1 RIE: 9 CAT: 17

Georgian Court College NJ
CIJE: 0 RIE: 2 CAT: 17

Geosystems
CIJE: 0 RIE: 1 CAT: 20

Geotropism
CIJE: 5 RIE: 0 CAT: 20

Gephart (Robert P Jr)
CIJE: 0 RIE: 0 CAT: 18

GEPI
USE General Education Performance Index

Geraldine R Dodge Foundation
CIJE: 0 RIE: 1 CAT: 17

Gerber (Magda)
CIJE: 0 RIE: 1 CAT: 18

Gerbils
CIJE: 3 RIE: 0 CAT: 20

Gerbner Study
CIJE: 12 RIE: 2 CAT: 22

Gergen and Black Hypothesis
CIJE: 1 RIE: 0 CAT: 15

Gergen Morse Self Consistency Scale
CIJE: 0 RIE: 1 CAT: 21

Geriatric Assessment Units
CIJE: 0 RIE: 1 CAT: 05

Geriatric Education Centers
CIJE: 0 RIE: 2 CAT: 05

Geriatric Workers
CIJE: 0 RIE: 2 CAT: 09

German (Low)
CIJE: 0 RIE: 1 CAT: 13

German (Middle High)
CIJE: 0 RIE: 1 CAT: 13

German (Old High)
CIJE: 3 RIE: 0 CAT: 13

German (Pfaelzisch)
CIJE: 0 RIE: 0 CAT: 13

German (Swiss)
CIJE: 3 RIE: 5 CAT: 13

German American Partnership Program
CIJE: 1 RIE: 1 CAT: 19

German Americans
CIJE: 3 RIE: 19 CAT: 08

German by Satellite
CIJE: 1 RIE: 3 CAT: 19

German Canadians
CIJE: 0 RIE: 2 CAT: 08

German Childrens Protection Federation
CIJE: 0 RIE: 1 CAT: 17

German Culture
CIJE: 6 RIE: 9 CAT: 16

German Federal Armed Forces
CIJE: 0 RIE: 1 CAT: 17
UF West German Armed Forces

German Federation of Adult Education Centers
CIJE: 1 RIE: 0 CAT: 17

German Foundation for Developing Countries
CIJE: 0 RIE: 2 CAT: 17

German History
CIJE: 11 RIE: 4 CAT: 12

German Institute for Academic Home Study
CIJE: 1 RIE: 0 CAT: 17

German Peasant Revolt
CIJE: 1 RIE: 0 CAT: 12

German Psychology
CIJE: 1 RIE: 0 CAT: 15

German Russians
CIJE: 0 RIE: 3 CAT: 08

German Speaking Countries
CIJE: 0 RIE: 1 CAT: 07

German Vocabulary Inventory
CIJE: 3 RIE: 0 CAT: 13

Germanic Languages
CIJE: 6 RIE: 3 CAT: 13

Germans
CIJE: 13 RIE: 11 CAT: 08

Germany
CIJE: 760 RIE: 411 CAT: 07
SN See "West Germany" and "East Germany" for the 1945-1990 time frame

Germany (Berlin)
CIJE: 8 RIE: 3 CAT: 07
SN See also "West Germany (Berlin)"

Germany (Bremen)
CIJE: 0 RIE: 1 CAT: 07
SN See also "West Germany (Bremen)"

Germany (Paderborn)
CIJE: 0 RIE: 1 CAT: 07

Germination
CIJE: 8 RIE: 4 CAT: 20

Germs
CIJE: 1 RIE: 2 CAT: 11

Geronimo
CIJE: 1 RIE: 1 CAT: 18
SN Apache leader, 1829-1909

Gerontocide
CIJE: 0 RIE: 1 CAT: 16

Gerontological Counseling
CIJE: 0 RIE: 2 CAT: 11

Gerontological Information Program
CIJE: 2 RIE: 4 CAT: 19

Gerontology Alcohol Project
CIJE: 1 RIE: 1 CAT: 19

Gerontology Manpower Development Project
CIJE: 1 RIE: 0 CAT: 19

Gerontology Research Instructional Program
CIJE: 0 RIE: 1 CAT: 19

Gerrymandering
CIJE: 3 RIE: 1 CAT: 14

Gerstmann Syndrome
CIJE: 1 RIE: 0 CAT: 11

Gertz v Robert Welch Inc
CIJE: 3 RIE: 5 CAT: 14

Gesell (Arnold)
CIJE: 5 RIE: 5 CAT: 18

Gesell Developmental Schedules
CIJE: 3 RIE: 3 CAT: 21

Gesell Developmental Tests
CIJE: 12 RIE: 11 CAT: 21

Gesell Institute of Child Development CT
CIJE: 3 RIE: 2 CAT: 17

Gesell School Readiness Test
CIJE: 8 RIE: 8 CAT: 21

Gesellschaft fur Deutsche Sprache
CIJE: 1 RIE: 0 CAT: 17

Gesellschaft fur Information und Dokumentation
CIJE: 0 RIE: 2 CAT: 17

Gestalt Personal Homeostasis Inventory
CIJE: 0 RIE: 1 CAT: 21

Gestalt Psychology
CIJE: 32 RIE: 19 CAT: 15

Gestational Age
CIJE: 3 RIE: 1 CAT: 11
SN See also "Conceptional Age"

Gestational Diabetes
CIJE: 0 RIE: 1 CAT: 11
SN Type of diabetes in which onset or recognition of impaired glucose tolerance occurs during pregnancy

Gestational Stress
CIJE: 1 RIE: 0 CAT: 11

Gestural Representation
CIJE: 10 RIE: 2 CAT: 11

Get Set Program
CIJE: 0 RIE: 14 CAT: 19

Getty Center for Education in the Arts
CIJE: 29 RIE: 8 CAT: 17

Getty Institutes for Educators on the Visual Arts
CIJE: 1 RIE: 0 CAT: 02

Gettysburg College PA
CIJE: 3 RIE: 2 CAT: 17

Getzels and Guba Social Systems Model
CIJE: 1 RIE: 5 CAT: 15

Gewirth (Alan)
CIJE: 1 RIE: 0 CAT: 18

Geysers
CIJE: 0 RIE: 1 CAT: 20

Ghana
CIJE: 81 RIE: 102 CAT: 07

Ghana Schools Television Service
CIJE: 1 RIE: 0 CAT: 17

Ghazel
CIJE: 0 RIE: 1 CAT: 13

Ghetto Simulation Game
CIJE: 0 RIE: 6 CAT: 15

Ghibu (Onisifor)
CIJE: 0 RIE: 1 CAT: 18

Ghiselli Self Description Inventory
CIJE: 4 RIE: 1 CAT: 21

Ghost Dance Movement
CIJE: 3 RIE: 1 CAT: 12

Ghost Stories
CIJE: 3 RIE: 6 CAT: 16

Ghost Towns
CIJE: 1 RIE: 1 CAT: 16

Ghostwriting
CIJE: 16 RIE: 6 CAT: 16

GI Bill (USA)
USE G I Bill

Giannini (Vittorio)
CIJE: 1 RIE: 0 CAT: 18

Giannini Foundation of Agricultural Economics CA
CIJE: 0 RIE: 1 CAT: 17

Gibb (Jack)
CIJE: 0 RIE: 1 CAT: 18

Gibberellic Acid
CIJE: 3 RIE: 0 CAT: 20

Gibbons (James)
CIJE: 0 RIE: 1 CAT: 18

Gibbs Helmholtz Equations
CIJE: 1 RIE: 0 CAT: 20

Gibbs Sampling
CIJE: 1 RIE: 1 CAT: 21

Gibraltar
CIJE: 0 RIE: 1 CAT: 07

Giddings (Franklin Henry)
CIJE: 1 RIE: 0 CAT: 18

Gide (Andre)
CIJE: 6 RIE: 0 CAT: 18

Giebenrath (Hans)
CIJE: 1 RIE: 0 CAT: 18

Giffin Trust Scale
CIJE: 0 RIE: 2 CAT: 21

Gift Clubs
CIJE: 6 RIE: 2 CAT: 16

Gifted and Talented Childrens Education Act 1978
CIJE: 0 RIE: 1 CAT: 14

Gifted and Talented Education Program CA
CIJE: 0 RIE: 2 CAT: 19

Gifted Education Module System
CIJE: 1 RIE: 1 CAT: 11

Gifted Science Project Resource File
CIJE: 0 RIE: 1 CAT: 16

Gifted Self Understanding Assessment Battery
CIJE: 1 RIE: 0 CAT: 21

Gifts
CIJE: 12 RIE: 11 CAT: 16

Gifts and Exchange Functions
CIJE: 1 RIE: 2 CAT: 16

Gila River Reservation AZ
CIJE: 0 RIE: 3 CAT: 17

Gilaki
CIJE: 0 RIE: 1 CAT: 13

Gilbert (Thomas)
CIJE: 0 RIE: 1 CAT: 18
SN "Thomas F"

Gilbert and Ellice Islands
CIJE: 1 RIE: 0 CAT: 07
SN Former British colony—separated into Kiribati and Tuvalu in the 1970s

Gilbert Islands
CIJE: 1 RIE: 4 CAT: 07

Gilbert Youth Research
CIJE: 1 RIE: 0 CAT: 17

Gilder (George)
CIJE: 1 RIE: 0 CAT: 18

Gilford Middle High School NH
CIJE: 0 RIE: 1 CAT: 17

Gill School NY
CIJE: 2 RIE: 0 CAT: 17

Gillberg (Bjorn)
CIJE: 1 RIE: 0 CAT: 18

Gilles De La Tourette Syndrome
USE Tourette Syndrome

Gilligan (Carol)
CIJE: 31 RIE: 12 CAT: 18

Gilliland Learning Potential Examination
CIJE: 0 RIE: 1 CAT: 21

Gilman (Charlotte Perkins)
CIJE: 1 RIE: 5 CAT: 18

Gilman (Daniel Coit)
CIJE: 1 RIE: 0 CAT: 18

Gilman (Nicholas)
CIJE: 0 RIE: 1 CAT: 18

Gilmer County School District GA
CIJE: 0 RIE: 1 CAT: 17

Gilmore Oral Reading Test
CIJE: 3 RIE: 3 CAT: 21

Gilroy Unified School District CA
CIJE: 0 RIE: 2 CAT: 17

Gilruth (Robert)
CIJE: 1 RIE: 0 CAT: 18

Gilson (Jamie)
CIJE: 1 RIE: 0 CAT: 18

Gilson (Mary Barnett)
CIJE: 0 RIE: 1 CAT: 18

Gingival Fibromatosis
CIJE: 1 RIE: 0 CAT: 11

Gingras (Louie)
CIJE: 0 RIE: 1 CAT: 18

Gini Coefficient
CIJE: 12 RIE: 2 CAT: 15

GINI Index of Dissimilarity
CIJE: 1 RIE: 3 CAT: 21

Gini Mean Difference
CIJE: 1 RIE: 0 CAT: 21

Ginn 360 Series
CIJE: 1 RIE: 4 CAT: 22

Ginn Diagnostic Vocabulary Test
CIJE: 0 RIE: 1 CAT: 21

Ginn Reading 720 Series
CIJE: 2 RIE: 6 CAT: 22

Gintis (Herbert)
CIJE: 2 RIE: 1 CAT: 18

Ginzberg (Eli)
CIJE: 1 RIE: 2 CAT: 18

Ginzburg (Natalia)
CIJE: 1 RIE: 0 CAT: 18

Gio
CIJE: 0 RIE: 1 CAT: 13

Giono (Jean)
CIJE: 1 RIE: 0 CAT: 18

Gippsland Institute of Advanced Educ (Australia)
CIJE: 0 RIE: 2 CAT: 17

GIRAFFE (Computer Program)
CIJE: 0 RIE: 1 CAT: 04
SN GIRAFFE = General Information Retrieval All Faculties For Bibliographic Education

Girl Guides Association
CIJE: 0 RIE: 2 CAT: 17

Girl Scouts of the USA
CIJE: 13 RIE: 20 CAT: 17

Girls Clubs of America
CIJE: 2 RIE: 8 CAT: 17

Girls into Science and Technology (England)
CIJE: 0 RIE: 1 CAT: 19

Girls into Science and Technology Project
CIJE: 2 RIE: 4 CAT: 19

Giroud (Francoise)
CIJE: 1 RIE: 0 CAT: 18

Giroux (Henry)
CIJE: 5 RIE: 2 CAT: 18

Gissing (George)
CIJE: 0 RIE: 1 CAT: 18

GIST Project WA
USE Generalized InService Training Project

Gitlow v New York
CIJE: 0 RIE: 1 CAT: 14

Gitt (Josiah W)
CIJE: 0 RIE: 1 CAT: 18

Gittinger Personality Assessment System
CIJE: 0 RIE: 1 CAT: 21

Give and Take (Economics Series)
CIJE: 1 RIE: 2 CAT: 03

Given Names
CIJE: 1 RIE: 1 CAT: 13

Giving Rural Adults a Study Program
CIJE: 0 RIE: 1 CAT: 19
UF Project GRASP

Glaciers
CIJE: 10 RIE: 1 CAT: 20

GLAD Project AZ
USE Ganado Language Arts Development Project AZ

Glades Correctional Institution FL
CIJE: 0 RIE: 1 CAT: 17

Gladstone (William)
CIJE: 0 RIE: 1 CAT: 18

Glaser (Barney G)
CIJE: 1 RIE: 0 CAT: 18

Glaser (Robert)
CIJE: 2 RIE: 1 CAT: 18

Glasgow (Ellen)
CIJE: 0 RIE: 1 CAT: 18

Glasgow Corporation Educ TV Service (Scotland)
CIJE: 1 RIE: 0 CAT: 17

Glasgow Retirement Council (Scotland)
CIJE: 1 RIE: 0 CAT: 17

Glasnost
CIJE: 21 RIE: 10 CAT: 12
SN Soviet reform policy of increased "openness," initiated by General Secretary Mikhail Gorbachev in 1986

Glass (G V)
CIJE: 2 RIE: 6 CAT: 18

Glass Analysis Method
CIJE: 2 RIE: 1 CAT: 15

Glass Analysis Program
CIJE: 1 RIE: 0 CAT: 19

Glass Blowers
CIJE: 0 RIE: 2 CAT: 09

Glass Box Theories
CIJE: 1 RIE: 0 CAT: 15

Glass Ceiling
CIJE: 3 RIE: 7 CAT: 15

Glass Cutters
CIJE: 0 RIE: 1 CAT: 09

Glass Inspectors
CIJE: 0 RIE: 1 CAT: 09

Glass Packers
CIJE: 0 RIE: 1 CAT: 09

Glassboro Public Schools NJ
CIJE: 2 RIE: 0 CAT: 17

Glassboro State College NJ
CIJE: 3 RIE: 13 CAT: 17

Glasser (Theodore L)
CIJE: 0 RIE: 1 CAT: 18

Glasser (William)
CIJE: 17 RIE: 19 CAT: 18

Glassow (Patricia)
CIJE: 0 RIE: 1 CAT: 18

Glaucoma
CIJE: 6 RIE: 1 CAT: 11

Glazer (Nathan)
CIJE: 2 RIE: 0 CAT: 18

Gleazer (Edmund J)
CIJE: 1 RIE: 1 CAT: 18

Glen Canyon Dam
CIJE: 0 RIE: 1 CAT: 05

Glen Ellyn Junior High School IL
CIJE: 0 RIE: 1 CAT: 17

Glen Oaks Community College MI
CIJE: 0 RIE: 1 CAT: 17

Glendale Community College AZ
CIJE: 3 RIE: 3 CAT: 17

Glendale Community College CA
CIJE: 1 RIE: 3 CAT: 17

Glendale Community College District CA
CIJE: 0 RIE: 1 CAT: 17

Glendale Elementary School District 40 AZ
CIJE: 0 RIE: 0 CAT: 17

Glendale Public Library CA
CIJE: 0 RIE: 5 CAT: 17

Glendale Unified School District CA
CIJE: 0 RIE: 1 CAT: 17

Glendale Union High School District AZ
CIJE: 2 RIE: 3 CAT: 17

Glenny (Lyman A)
CIJE: 0 RIE: 1 CAT: 18

Glens Falls City School District NY
CIJE: 0 RIE: 1 CAT: 17

Glenview Public Schools IL
CIJE: 1 RIE: 3 CAT: 17

Glenville State College WV
CIJE: 0 RIE: 2 CAT: 17

Glides (Phonology)
CIJE: 2 RIE: 2 CAT: 13

GLISP Programing Language
CIJE: 0 RIE: 2 CAT: 04

Global 2000 Report
CIJE: 1 RIE: 1 CAT: 22

Global Atmospheric Research Program
CIJE: 1 RIE: 0 CAT: 19

Global Awareness
CIJE: 4 RIE: 3 CAT: 16

Global Change
CIJE: 4 RIE: 5 CAT: 16

Global Essay Instruments
CIJE: 0 RIE: 1 CAT: 04

Global Issues
CIJE: 1 RIE: 2 CAT: 16

Global Markets
CIJE: 3 RIE: 1 CAT: 16

Global Method of Structural Analysis
CIJE: 0 RIE: 1 CAT: 15

Global Perspectives
USE World Views

Global Perspectives in Education
CIJE: 6 RIE: 3 CAT: 03

Global Rating Scale (Morrison)
CIJE: 1 RIE: 1 CAT: 21

Global Studies
CIJE: 15 RIE: 34 CAT: 15
SN Research on global matters (Note: Prior to Oct94, this term was not scoped and was sometimes used for the Desc "Global Education")
UF World Studies

Global Survival
CIJE: 5 RIE: 4 CAT: 16

Global TELEclass
CIJE: 0 RIE: 1 CAT: 19
SN TELE = "Telecommunication Enriches Language Experience"

Globes
CIJE: 6 RIE: 6 CAT: 04

Globus Hystericus
CIJE: 0 RIE: 1 CAT: 11

Glomar Challenger
CIJE: 2 RIE: 0 CAT: 20

Gloria and David Bilingual Oral Lang Assessment
CIJE: 0 RIE: 2 CAT: 21

Glossectomy
CIJE: 3 RIE: 0 CAT: 11

Glossematics
CIJE: 2 RIE: 1 CAT: 13

Glossing
CIJE: 8 RIE: 7 CAT: 15

Glossolalia
CIJE: 2 RIE: 1 CAT: 13

Glossynography
CIJE: 1 RIE: 0 CAT: 11

Glottal Stops
CIJE: 1 RIE: 4 CAT: 13

Gloucester County College NJ
CIJE: 2 RIE: 1 CAT: 17

Gloucester Urban Studies Centre
CIJE: 1 RIE: 0 CAT: 17

Gloucestershire College of Arts and Tech (England)
CIJE: 0 RIE: 1 CAT: 17

Glove Sewers
CIJE: 0 RIE: 1 CAT: 09

Glover (Sarah)
CIJE: 2 RIE: 0 CAT: 18

Gloves
CIJE: 0 RIE: 1 CAT: 04

Gluck (Ernst)
CIJE: 1 RIE: 0 CAT: 18

Glucose
CIJE: 4 RIE: 0 CAT: 20

Glucuronidase Deficiency
CIJE: 1 RIE: 0 CAT: 11

Glue Sniffing
CIJE: 2 RIE: 2 CAT: 16

Gluing Machine Operators
CIJE: 0 RIE: 1 CAT: 09

Glutamic Acid
CIJE: 1 RIE: 0 CAT: 20

Glycogens
CIJE: 1 RIE: 0 CAT: 20

Gnanadesikan (R)
CIJE: 1 RIE: 0 CAT: 18

Go Down Moses
CIJE: 1 RIE: 1 CAT: 22

Go Out and Look
CIJE: 1 RIE: 0 CAT: 15

Goal Analysis
CIJE: 6 RIE: 4 CAT: 15

Goal Attainment Scale
CIJE: 1 RIE: 1 CAT: 21

Goal Attainment Scaling
CIJE: 19 RIE: 16 CAT: 15

Goal Based Education
CIJE: 0 RIE: 6 CAT: 15

Goal Based Evaluation
CIJE: 3 RIE: 4 CAT: 15

Goal Based Planning
CIJE: 3 RIE: 5 CAT: 15

Goal Clarity
CIJE: 0 RIE: 1 CAT: 15

Goal Deflection
CIJE: 0 RIE: 2 CAT: 15

Goal Development
CIJE: 7 RIE: 4 CAT: 15

Goal Directed Behavior
CIJE: 8 RIE: 3 CAT: 11

Goal Free Evaluation
CIJE: 6 RIE: 5 CAT: 15

Goal Incompatibility
CIJE: 1 RIE: 1 CAT: 15

Goal Instability Scale
CIJE: 2 RIE: 0 CAT: 21

GOAL ONE Project (NAEYC)
CIJE: 0 RIE: 1 CAT: 19
SN NAEYC = National Association for the Education of Young Children

Goal Oriented Approach to Learning
CIJE: 1 RIE: 1 CAT: 15

Goal Programming
CIJE: 5 RIE: 4 CAT: 15

Goal Setting
CIJE: 98 RIE: 101 CAT: 15

Goal Structures
CIJE: 1 RIE: 0 CAT: 15
UF Competitive Goal Structures; Cooperative Goal Structures; Individual Goal Structures

Goal Theory
CIJE: 1 RIE: 1 CAT: 15

Goal Values
CIJE: 0 RIE: 0 CAT: 16

Goals 2000
CIJE: 16 RIE: 23 CAT: 14
SN President Clinton's strategy to speed progress toward systemic educational reform, based on the "National Education Goals 1990" (q.v.) and signed into law Mar94
UF Goals 2000 Educate America Act; Public Law 103 227

Goals 2000 Educate America Act
USE Goals 2000

Goals Exploration (Students)
USE Student Goals Exploration

GOAT Effect
CIJE: 1 RIE: 0 CAT: 21

God (Concept)
CIJE: 19 RIE: 6 CAT: 16

Godard (Jean Luc)
CIJE: 3 RIE: 2 CAT: 18

Goddard (H H)
CIJE: 2 RIE: 1 CAT: 18

Goddard (Robert)
CIJE: 2 RIE: 0 CAT: 18

Goddard College VT
CIJE: 3 RIE: 2 CAT: 17

Goddard Library MA
CIJE: 1 RIE: 0 CAT: 17

Goddard Research Engineering Management Exercise
CIJE: 1 RIE: 0 CAT: 15

Goddard Space Flight Center MD
CIJE: 1 RIE: 1 CAT: 17

Godfather (The)
CIJE: 0 RIE: 1 CAT: 22

Godkin (Edward L)
CIJE: 0 RIE: 1 CAT: 18

Gods Must Be Crazy (The)
CIJE: 0 RIE: 1 CAT: 22

Godspell
CIJE: 1 RIE: 0 CAT: 22

Godwin (Mary)
USE Shelley (Mary)

Godwin (William)
CIJE: 2 RIE: 1 CAT: 18

Goethe (Johann Wolfgang von)
CIJE: 16 RIE: 3 CAT: 18

Goethe Institute (West Germany)
CIJE: 3 RIE: 3 CAT: 17

Goettinger Teachers College (West Germany)
CIJE: 1 RIE: 0 CAT: 17

Goffman (E)
CIJE: 4 RIE: 3 CAT: 18

Goffman (Erving)
CIJE: 4 RIE: 5 CAT: 18

Goffman Model
CIJE: 0 RIE: 3 CAT: 15

Goffmans Indirect Method
CIJE: 3 RIE: 0 CAT: 15

Gogebic Community College MI
CIJE: 0 RIE: 1 CAT: 17

Gogh (Vincent van)
USE Van Gogh (Vincent)

Gogo
CIJE: 0 RIE: 1 CAT: 13

Gogol (Nikolai Vasilievich)
CIJE: 4 RIE: 0 CAT: 18

Going Places Program CA
CIJE: 0 RIE: 0 CAT: 19

Going to Scale
CIJE: 0 RIE: 1 CAT: 15

Gola
CIJE: 0 RIE: 1 CAT: 13

GOLD Database
USE Georgia Online Database

Goldberg (Gertrude S)
CIJE: 0 RIE: 1 CAT: 18

Goldberg (Moses)
CIJE: 1 RIE: 0 CAT: 18

Goldberg Misogyny Test
CIJE: 1 RIE: 1 CAT: 21

Goldberg Scale of Vocational Development
CIJE: 1 RIE: 0 CAT: 21

Golden Olympics
CIJE: 1 RIE: 0 CAT: 12

Golden Ratio (Mathematics)
CIJE: 7 RIE: 0 CAT: 20

Golden Rule (Testing)
CIJE: 8 RIE: 2 CAT: 21

Golden Section Search Strategies
CIJE: 0 RIE: 1 CAT: 15

Golden State Examination Program CA
CIJE: 0 RIE: 1 CAT: 21

Golden West College CA
CIJE: 4 RIE: 26 CAT: 17

Goldenhar Syndrome
CIJE: 1 RIE: 0 CAT: 11

Goldenrod
CIJE: 1 RIE: 0 CAT: 20

Golding (William)
CIJE: 4 RIE: 1 CAT: 18

Goldman (Emma)
CIJE: 2 RIE: 2 CAT: 18

Goldman Fristoe Test of Articulation
CIJE: 2 RIE: 2 CAT: 21

Goldman Fristoe Woodcock Test Auditory Discrim
CIJE: 3 RIE: 1 CAT: 21

Goldsboro Christian Schools Inc v United States
CIJE: 0 RIE: 1 CAT: 14

Goldsboro City Schools NC
CIJE: 0 RIE: 1 CAT: 17

Goldsmith (Oliver)
CIJE: 2 RIE: 0 CAT: 18

Goldsmiths College (England)
CIJE: 2 RIE: 0 CAT: 17

Goldstein (Kurt)
CIJE: 0 RIE: 1 CAT: 18

Goldstein Sheerer Tests Abstract Concrete Think
CIJE: 0 RIE: 1 CAT: 21

Golf Courses
CIJE: 4 RIE: 1 CAT: 05

Gomez de la Serna (Ramon)
CIJE: 1 RIE: 0 CAT: 18

Gompers (Samuel)
CIJE: 2 RIE: 0 CAT: 18

Gongora y Argote (Luis de)
CIJE: 2 RIE: 0 CAT: 18

Gonococcal Ophthalmia Neonatorum
CIJE: 1 RIE: 0 CAT: 11

Gonzaga University WA
CIJE: 2 RIE: 4 CAT: 17

Gonzales (Rodolfo)
CIJE: 1 RIE: 0 CAT: 18

Gonzalez Acilu (Agustin)
CIJE: 1 RIE: 0 CAT: 18

Gooch (Steve)
CIJE: 0 RIE: 1 CAT: 18

Good (Harry Gehman)
CIJE: 1 RIE: 0 CAT: 18

Good Counsel College NY
CIJE: 1 RIE: 0 CAT: 17

Good Faith Requirements
CIJE: 0 RIE: 1 CAT: 16
SN See also "Bargaining in Good Faith"

Good Housekeeping Seal of Approval
CIJE: 0 RIE: 1 CAT: 16

Good Morning Miss Dove
CIJE: 1 RIE: 0 CAT: 22

Good Neighbor Commission
CIJE: 0 RIE: 3 CAT: 17

Good Night Mr Tom
CIJE: 0 RIE: 1 CAT: 22

Good Schools Project (Kappa Delta Pi)
CIJE: 0 RIE: 4 CAT: 19

Good Shepherd Home and Rehabilitation Center PA
CIJE: 1 RIE: 0 CAT: 17

Goodenough Draw a Man Test
CIJE: 2 RIE: 16 CAT: 21

Goodenough Harris Drawing Test
CIJE: 18 RIE: 14 CAT: 21

Goodlad (John I)
CIJE: 30 RIE: 22 CAT: 18

Goodman (Ellen)
CIJE: 1 RIE: 0 CAT: 18

Goodman (Kenneth)
CIJE: 10 RIE: 8 CAT: 18

Goodman (Nelson)
CIJE: 1 RIE: 2 CAT: 18

Goodman (Paul)
CIJE: 5 RIE: 4 CAT: 18

Goodman (Robert)
CIJE: 0 RIE: 1 CAT: 18

Goodman Model of Reading
CIJE: 0 RIE: 1 CAT: 15

Goodman Multiplicative Association Models
CIJE: 0 RIE: 1 CAT: 21

Goodman Reading Miscue Inventory
CIJE: 1 RIE: 0 CAT: 21

Goodrich (Lois)
CIJE: 1 RIE: 0 CAT: 18

Goodwill Industries of America
CIJE: 2 RIE: 9 CAT: 17

Goodwin (Edward Lawrence)
CIJE: 0 RIE: 1 CAT: 18

Goodyear Tire and Rubber Company
CIJE: 1 RIE: 1 CAT: 17

Goonies (The)
CIJE: 0 RIE: 1 CAT: 22

Gope
USE Kope

Gorbachev (Mikhail)
CIJE: 14 RIE: 12 CAT: 18

Gorbachevich (K S)
CIJE: 3 RIE: 0 CAT: 18

Gordon (Ira)
CIJE: 2 RIE: 2 CAT: 18

Gordon (Peg)
CIJE: 1 RIE: 0 CAT: 18

Gordon (Thomas)
CIJE: 4 RIE: 1 CAT: 18

Gordon Brock Infant School (England)
CIJE: 0 RIE: 1 CAT: 17

Gordon College MA
CIJE: 1 RIE: 6 CAT: 17

Gordon Diagnostic System
CIJE: 1 RIE: 2 CAT: 21

Gordon Personal Inventory
CIJE: 1 RIE: 2 CAT: 21

Gordon Personal Profile
CIJE: 3 RIE: 6 CAT: 21

Gordon Research Conference (1972)
CIJE: 2 RIE: 0 CAT: 02

Gordon Teachers Training College (Israel)
CIJE: 0 RIE: 1 CAT: 17

Gordon v Committee on Character and Fitness
CIJE: 1 RIE: 0 CAT: 14

Gordons Parent Effectiveness Training 1970
CIJE: 1 RIE: 0 CAT: 02

Gore (Tipper)
CIJE: 0 RIE: 1 CAT: 18

Gorelik (Mordecai)
CIJE: 0 RIE: 1 CAT: 18

Gorgias of Leontini
CIJE: 1 RIE: 2 CAT: 18
SN Greek sophist and rhetorician (483-375 B.C.)

Gorum
CIJE: 1 RIE: 1 CAT: 13

Goshen College IN
CIJE: 1 RIE: 6 CAT: 17

Goshute (Tribe)
CIJE: 0 RIE: 1 CAT: 08

Gospel Music
CIJE: 8 RIE: 1 CAT: 16

Gospels
USE New Testament

Goss Formula
CIJE: 1 RIE: 0 CAT: 15

Goss v Lopez
CIJE: 25 RIE: 18 CAT: 14

Gossip
CIJE: 12 RIE: 3 CAT: 16

Gothic
CIJE: 3 RIE: 1 CAT: 13

Gottfredson (L S)
CIJE: 9 RIE: 1 CAT: 18

Gottheil Scale
CIJE: 1 RIE: 0 CAT: 21

Gottschalk (Louis Moreau)
CIJE: 2 RIE: 0 CAT: 18

Gottschalk Hidden Figures Test
CIJE: 0 RIE: 1 CAT: 21

Gottsched (Johann Christoph)
CIJE: 1 RIE: 0 CAT: 18

Goucher College MD
CIJE: 7 RIE: 4 CAT: 17

Gough Sanford Rigidity Scale
CIJE: 0 RIE: 1 CAT: 21

Gould (Stephen Jay)
CIJE: 2 RIE: 1 CAT: 18

Gouldner (Alvin)
CIJE: 2 RIE: 0 CAT: 18

Governesses
CIJE: 0 RIE: 0 CAT: 09

Governeur Central School District NY
CIJE: 0 RIE: 1 CAT: 17

Governing Board Role
CIJE: 1 RIE: 2 CAT: 16

Government Affairs Awareness Program
CIJE: 1 RIE: 0 CAT: 19

Government Business Cooperation
CIJE: 4 RIE: 1 CAT: 16

Government Business Relationship
CIJE: 20 RIE: 5 CAT: 16

Government Citizen Relationship
CIJE: 5 RIE: 8 CAT: 15

Government Contractors
CIJE: 5 RIE: 2 CAT: 10

Government Employees Training Act
CIJE: 0 RIE: 2 CAT: 14

Government Family Partnerships
CIJE: 1 RIE: 0 CAT: 15
UF Family Government Partnerships; Parent Government Partnerships

Government Industry Relationship
CIJE: 15 RIE: 13 CAT: 16

Government Information
CIJE: 82 RIE: 10 CAT: 16

Government Lands
CIJE: 0 RIE: 1 CAT: 05

Government Media Relationship
USE Media Government Relationship

Government Printing Office
CIJE: 69 RIE: 33 CAT: 17

Government Records
CIJE: 8 RIE: 8 CAT: 16

Government Regulation
CIJE: 17 RIE: 6 CAT: 14

Government Reports Announcements and Index
CIJE: 1 RIE: 1 CAT: 22

Government Responsiveness
USE Responsiveness (Government)

Government Schools (Australia)
CIJE: 0 RIE: 1 CAT: 05

Government Spending
CIJE: 15 RIE: 3 CAT: 16

Government Spending (Waste in)
USE Waste in Government Spending

Government Subsidies
CIJE: 2 RIE: 5 CAT: 16

Government Training Centers
CIJE: 1 RIE: 0 CAT: 05

Government Univ Industry Research Roundtable
CIJE: 0 RIE: 2 CAT: 17

Governmental Immunity
CIJE: 6 RIE: 18 CAT: 14

Governor Thomas Johnson High School MD
CIJE: 1 RIE: 0 CAT: 17

Governors Committee on Postsecondary Education GA
CIJE: 0 RIE: 1 CAT: 17
UF Georgia Governors Committee on Postsecondary Educ

Governors Conference Library Info Services IN
CIJE: 0 RIE: 1 CAT: 02
UF Indiana Governors Conference Lib Info Servs

Governors Conference Library Info Services MD
CIJE: 0 RIE: 0 CAT: 02
UF Maryland Governors Conference Lib Info Serv

Governors Conference Library Info Services MO
CIJE: 0 RIE: 1 CAT: 02
UF Missouri Governors Conference Lib Info Serv

Governors Conference Library Info Services MT
CIJE: 0 RIE: 1 CAT: 02
UF Montana Governors Conference Lib Info Serv

Governors Conference Library Info Services ND
CIJE: 0 RIE: 1 CAT: 02
UF North Dakota Governors Conference Lib Info Serv

Governors Conference Library Info Services NE
CIJE: 0 RIE: 1 CAT: 02

UF Nebraska Governors Conference Lib Info Serv

Governors Conference Library Info Services NY
CIJE: 0 RIE: 0 CAT: 02
UF New York Governors Conference Library Info Serv

Governors Conference Library Info Services PA
CIJE: 0 RIE: 0 CAT: 02
UF Pennsylvania Governors Conference Libr Info Serv

Governors Grants
CIJE: 0 RIE: 3 CAT: 14

Governors Honors Programs
CIJE: 2 RIE: 0 CAT: 19

Governors School of North Carolina
CIJE: 1 RIE: 2 CAT: 17
UF North Carolina Governors School

Governors Schools
CIJE: 16 RIE: 1 CAT: 05
SN If appropriate, use a more specific term, e.g., "Arkansas Governors School," "New Jersey Governors School," "Governors School of North Carolina," "Pennsylvania Governors School for the Arts"

Governors State University IL
CIJE: 7 RIE: 10 CAT: 17

Governors Task Force on Voc and Tech Educ OH
CIJE: 0 RIE: 1 CAT: 17
UF Ohio Governors Task Force on Voc and Tech Educ

Gow School NY
CIJE: 0 RIE: 1 CAT: 17

Gowin (D B)
CIJE: 1 RIE: 1 CAT: 18

Gowins V Mapping
CIJE: 4 RIE: 1 CAT: 15

Goya y Lucientes (Francisco Jose de)
CIJE: 1 RIE: 0 CAT: 18

Goytisolo (Juan)
CIJE: 1 RIE: 0 CAT: 18

GPSA Questionnaires
USE Graduate Program Self Assessment

Grace Doherty Library KY
CIJE: 1 RIE: 0 CAT: 17

Graceland College IA
CIJE: 1 RIE: 2 CAT: 17

Gracian y Morales (Baltasar)
CIJE: 1 RIE: 0 CAT: 18

GRAD II (Computer Program)
CIJE: 1 RIE: 0 CAT: 04

Grade 12 Diploma Examinations Program AB
USE Alberta Grade Twelve Diploma Examinations

Grade Anxiety
CIJE: 2 RIE: 1 CAT: 16

Grade Appeal Hearings
CIJE: 1 RIE: 1 CAT: 16

Grade Development Scale
CIJE: 0 RIE: 1 CAT: 21

Grade Differential Statistic
CIJE: 0 RIE: 1 CAT: 21

Grade Level Evaluation
CIJE: 0 RIE: 1 CAT: 21

Grade Success Rate
CIJE: 0 RIE: 1 CAT: 21

Graded Mark Point Scoring
CIJE: 0 RIE: 1 CAT: 21

Graded Objectives in Modern Lang (Great Britain)
CIJE: 0 RIE: 1 CAT: 21

Graded Response Model
CIJE: 13 RIE: 16 CAT: 15

Graded Word Reading Tests
CIJE: 0 RIE: 2 CAT: 21

Gradients (Mathematics)
CIJE: 2 RIE: 0 CAT: 20

GRADS Program OH
USE Graduation Reality and Dual Role Skills Program

Gradual Refinement Approach (Kean et al)
CIJE: 1 RIE: 0 CAT: 15

Graduate (The)
CIJE: 1 RIE: 1 CAT: 22

Graduate Career Development Center TX
CIJE: 1 RIE: 0 CAT: 17

Graduate Career Opportunities Program
CIJE: 0 RIE: 1 CAT: 19

Graduate Education for Librarianship Ohio Project
CIJE: 0 RIE: 4 CAT: 19

Graduate Education Questionnaire
CIJE: 1 RIE: 0 CAT: 21

Graduate Engineering Education System
CIJE: 0 RIE: 1 CAT: 15

Graduate Management Admission Test
CIJE: 7 RIE: 24 CAT: 21

Graduate Program Self Assessment
CIJE: 1 RIE: 0 CAT: 21
UF GPSA Questionnaires

Graduate Record Examinations
CIJE: 91 RIE: 142 CAT: 21
SN See add'l listings under "GRE..."

Graduate Research Assistants
CIJE: 2 RIE: 2 CAT: 09

Graduate School Foreign Language Tests
CIJE: 1 RIE: 2 CAT: 21

Graduate Student Satisfaction Questionnaire
CIJE: 1 RIE: 0 CAT: 21

Graduate Training Program in Community Educ
CIJE: 0 RIE: 2 CAT: 19

Graduated Guidance
CIJE: 2 RIE: 1 CAT: 15

Graduated Scales
CIJE: 1 RIE: 0 CAT: 20

Graduated Tuition
CIJE: 2 RIE: 0 CAT: 16

Graduated Work Incentive Experiment
CIJE: 6 RIE: 2 CAT: 19

Graduation Exit Exam LA
CIJE: 0 RIE: 1 CAT: 21

Graduation Reality and Dual Role Skills Program
CIJE: 0 RIE: 2 CAT: 19
UF GRADS Program OH

Grady (Henry)
CIJE: 0 RIE: 1 CAT: 18

Grady (Roosevelt)
CIJE: 1 RIE: 0 CAT: 18

Graffiti
CIJE: 28 RIE: 7 CAT: 16

Graflex Audio Graphic Instructor
CIJE: 0 RIE: 1 CAT: 04

Graham (Billy)
CIJE: 0 RIE: 3 CAT: 18

Graham (Lorenz)
CIJE: 2 RIE: 0 CAT: 18

Graham (Sylvester)
CIJE: 1 RIE: 0 CAT: 18

Graham Elementary School MI
CIJE: 0 RIE: 1 CAT: 17

Graham Law of Diffusion
CIJE: 2 RIE: 0 CAT: 20

Graham Plan
CIJE: 0 RIE: 1 CAT: 19

Grain Drills
CIJE: 0 RIE: 1 CAT: 04

Grain Silos
CIJE: 1 RIE: 1 CAT: 04

Grambling College LA
CIJE: 1 RIE: 6 CAT: 17

Grambling State University LA
CIJE: 5 RIE: 10 CAT: 17

Gramm Rudman Hollings Balanced Budget Amendment
CIJE: 2 RIE: 3 CAT: 14

Grammar of Action
CIJE: 2 RIE: 1 CAT: 13

Grammarians
CIJE: 1 RIE: 2 CAT: 10

Grammatical Analysis of Elicited Language
CIJE: 1 RIE: 2 CAT: 21
UF GAEL Simple Sentence Level Test

Grammatical Categories
CIJE: 5 RIE: 2 CAT: 13

Grammatical Consciousness Raising
CIJE: 0 RIE: 1 CAT: 13

Grammatical Constraint Hypothesis
CIJE: 0 RIE: 1 CAT: 13

Grammatical Junctures
CIJE: 1 RIE: 0 CAT: 13

Grammatical Mapping
CIJE: 1 RIE: 1 CAT: 13

Grammatical Terminology
CIJE: 6 RIE: 3 CAT: 13

Grammatical Transfer
CIJE: 0 RIE: 1 CAT: 13

Grammaticality
CIJE: 11 RIE: 3 CAT: 13

Gramsci (Antonio)
CIJE: 10 RIE: 1 CAT: 18

Granada Lectures
CIJE: 1 RIE: 0 CAT: 22

Grand Blanc School District MI
CIJE: 1 RIE: 2 CAT: 17

Grand Canyon College AZ
CIJE: 1 RIE: 0 CAT: 17

Grand Forks School District ND
CIJE: 2 RIE: 0 CAT: 17

Grand Rapids Junior College MI
CIJE: 2 RIE: 3 CAT: 17

Grand Rapids Public Schools MI
CIJE: 1 RIE: 2 CAT: 17

Grand Rapids School District MN
CIJE: 0 RIE: 0 CAT: 17

Grand Valley State Colleges MI
CIJE: 1 RIE: 16 CAT: 17

Grand Valley State University MI
CIJE: 0 RIE: 1 CAT: 17

Grand View College IA
CIJE: 0 RIE: 2 CAT: 17

Grandchild Grandparent Relationship
USE Grandparent Grandchild Relationship

Grandletters
CIJE: 0 RIE: 1 CAT: 19

Grandparent Grandchild Relationship
CIJE: 2 RIE: 2 CAT: 16
UF Grandchild Grandparent Relationship

Grandparent Responsibility
CIJE: 4 RIE: 1 CAT: 16

Grandpeople Project
CIJE: 1 RIE: 0 CAT: 19

Granite School District UT
CIJE: 6 RIE: 1 CAT: 17

Grant (Ulysses S)
CIJE: 3 RIE: 4 CAT: 18

Grant MacEwan Community College AB
CIJE: 0 RIE: 2 CAT: 17

Grant Maintained Schools (Great Britain)
CIJE: 1 RIE: 1 CAT: 05

Grant Middle School IL
CIJE: 1 RIE: 0 CAT: 17

Grant Recipients
CIJE: 0 RIE: 1 CAT: 10

Grant School CA
CIJE: 0 RIE: 1 CAT: 17

Grant Simplification
CIJE: 1 RIE: 1 CAT: 14

Grant Union High School District CA
CIJE: 0 RIE: 2 CAT: 17

Grant Wood Area Education Agency IA
CIJE: 0 RIE: 1 CAT: 17

Grants Consolidation
CIJE: 0 RIE: 1 CAT: 15

Granuloma
CIJE: 1 RIE: 0 CAT: 11

Granville Central School District NY
CIJE: 0 RIE: 1 CAT: 17

Granville County Public Schools NC
CIJE: 1 RIE: 0 CAT: 17

Grapes
CIJE: 0 RIE: 1 CAT: 20
SN See also "Viticulture"

GRAPES Production System Model
CIJE: 0 RIE: 1 CAT: 15

Grapevines (Communication)
CIJE: 3 RIE: 2 CAT: 13

Graph Theory
CIJE: 19 RIE: 6 CAT: 15

Graphemic Options Test (Moretz)
CIJE: 0 RIE: 1 CAT: 21

Graphic Arts Industries
CIJE: 0 RIE: 1 CAT: 05

Graphic Character Sets
CIJE: 0 RIE: 1 CAT: 15

Graphic Communication
CIJE: 20 RIE: 12 CAT: 13

Graphic Novels
CIJE: 2 RIE: 1 CAT: 16

Graphic Organizers
CIJE: 39 RIE: 32 CAT: 15

Graphic Postorganizers
CIJE: 2 RIE: 3 CAT: 13

Graphic Records
CIJE: 1 RIE: 1 CAT: 16

Graphic Representation
CIJE: 61 RIE: 28 CAT: 16

Graphic Synthesizers
CIJE: 0 RIE: 1 CAT: 04

Graphical Evaluation and Review Technique
CIJE: 2 RIE: 1 CAT: 15

Graphical Kinematics
CIJE: 0 RIE: 1 CAT: 20

Graphical User Interfaces
CIJE: 17 RIE: 5 CAT: 04
UF GUIs

Graphics Expression Reading Improvement System
CIJE: 0 RIE: 4 CAT: 15

Graphing (Mathematics)
CIJE: 129 RIE: 38 CAT: 20

Graphing Utilities
CIJE: 11 RIE: 5 CAT: 20

Grapho Linguistics
CIJE: 2 RIE: 1 CAT: 13

Graphology
CIJE: 5 RIE: 3 CAT: 20

Graphonemes
CIJE: 2 RIE: 1 CAT: 13

Graphotherapy
CIJE: 1 RIE: 1 CAT: 20

Grasha Riechmann Student Learning Style Scales
CIJE: 2 RIE: 1 CAT: 21

Grasmere School CT
CIJE: 1 RIE: 0 CAT: 17

Grason Stadler E800 Audiometer
CIJE: 0 RIE: 1 CAT: 04

Grason Stadler Operant Conditioning Apparatus
CIJE: 0 RIE: 1 CAT: 04

Grass (Gunter)
CIJE: 3 RIE: 0 CAT: 18

Grass Roots Alternative Diploma Study
CIJE: 0 RIE: 0 CAT: 19
UF Project GRADS

Grasshoppers
CIJE: 1 RIE: 0 CAT: 20

Grassi Block Substitution Test
CIJE: 1 RIE: 0 CAT: 21

Grasslands
CIJE: 1 RIE: 1 CAT: 20

Grassroots Educare Trust (South Africa)
CIJE: 0 RIE: 1 CAT: 17

Grateful Dead
CIJE: 0 RIE: 1 CAT: 22

GRATEFUL MED
CIJE: 0 RIE: 1 CAT: 04
SN The microcomputer-based software that provides a user-friendly interface to most National Library of Medicine databases — see also "MEDLINE"

Gratifications Obtained
CIJE: 3 RIE: 4 CAT: 16

Gratifications Sought
CIJE: 3 RIE: 4 CAT: 16

Gratuities
CIJE: 5 RIE: 1 CAT: 16

Gravel
CIJE: 0 RIE: 1 CAT: 20

Graves (Clare W)
CIJE: 1 RIE: 0 CAT: 18

Graves (Donald)
CIJE: 4 RIE: 5 CAT: 18

Graves (Robert)
CIJE: 1 RIE: 0 CAT: 18

Graves Disease
CIJE: 1 RIE: 0 CAT: 11

Gravez (Margerite)
CIJE: 1 RIE: 0 CAT: 18

Gravimetric Analysis
CIJE: 1 RIE: 0 CAT: 15

Gravity Thickening
CIJE: 0 RIE: 1 CAT: 20

Gravy
CIJE: 0 RIE: 1 CAT: 20

Gray (Asa)
CIJE: 2 RIE: 0 CAT: 18

Gray (Hannah Holborn)
CIJE: 1 RIE: 0 CAT: 18

Gray (James)
CIJE: 1 RIE: 0 CAT: 18

Gray (S Simpson)
CIJE: 0 RIE: 1 CAT: 18
SN See also "S Simpson Gray v Board of Educ City of New York"

Gray (William S)
CIJE: 3 RIE: 3 CAT: 18

Gray Oral Reading Test
CIJE: 6 RIE: 0 CAT: 21

Gray Panthers
CIJE: 4 RIE: 0 CAT: 17

Gray Scales
CIJE: 0 RIE: 1 CAT: 15

Graylands Teachers College (Australia)
CIJE: 0 RIE: 1 CAT: 17

Grays Harbor College WA
CIJE: 0 RIE: 2 CAT: 17

Grazdanka
CIJE: 0 RIE: 1 CAT: 13

GRE Background Questionnaire
CIJE: 0 RIE: 0 CAT: 21

GRE Board
CIJE: 0 RIE: 0 CAT: 17

GRE Cooperative Validity Studies Project
CIJE: 0 RIE: 1 CAT: 19

GRE Validity Study Service
CIJE: 0 RIE: 2 CAT: 17

Great American Family Program
CIJE: 0 RIE: 1 CAT: 19

Great Basin
CIJE: 2 RIE: 5 CAT: 07

Great Bird of Love
CIJE: 0 RIE: 1 CAT: 22

Great Books Curriculum
CIJE: 13 RIE: 8 CAT: 03

Great Britain
CIJE: 4324 RIE: 1433 CAT: 07

Great Cities Program
CIJE: 3 RIE: 82 CAT: 19

Great Cities Research Council IL
CIJE: 0 RIE: 1 CAT: 17

Great Decisions Program
CIJE: 1 RIE: 3 CAT: 19

Great Education Reform Bill 1987 (United Kingdom)
CIJE: 0 RIE: 1 CAT: 14

Great Expectations
CIJE: 4 RIE: 2 CAT: 22

Great Explorations in Math and Science
CIJE: 0 RIE: 1 CAT: 19

Great Falls Precision Teaching Project
CIJE: 0 RIE: 1 CAT: 19

Great Falls Public Schools MT
CIJE: 4 RIE: 1 CAT: 17

Great Gatsby
CIJE: 4 RIE: 4 CAT: 22

Great God Brown
CIJE: 1 RIE: 0 CAT: 22

Great Grandparents
CIJE: 2 RIE: 1 CAT: 10

Great Ideas Curriculum
CIJE: 0 RIE: 1 CAT: 03

Great Lakes
CIJE: 8 RIE: 34 CAT: 07

Great Lakes Apprenticeship Center WI
CIJE: 0 RIE: 1 CAT: 17

Great Lakes Colleges Association
CIJE: 4 RIE: 7 CAT: 17

Great Lakes Intertribal Council Education Comm WI
CIJE: 1 RIE: 0 CAT: 17

Great Lakes Intertribal Council WI
CIJE: 0 RIE: 1 CAT: 17

Great Lakes Naval Training Center IL
CIJE: 0 RIE: 1 CAT: 17

Great Lakes Regional Resource Center
CIJE: 1 RIE: 1 CAT: 17

Great Lakes Water Quality Agreement
CIJE: 0 RIE: 1 CAT: 14

Great Leap Forward (China)
CIJE: 1 RIE: 0 CAT: 12

Great Leap Theory (Literacy)
CIJE: 0 RIE: 1 CAT: 13

Great Neck Adult Learning Centers NY
CIJE: 0 RIE: 1 CAT: 17

Great Oaks Joint Vocational School District OH
CIJE: 2 RIE: 3 CAT: 17

Great Plains (North)
CIJE: 1 RIE: 0 CAT: 07

Great Plains National Instructional TV Library NE
CIJE: 0 RIE: 2 CAT: 17

Great Plains School District Organization Project
CIJE: 0 RIE: 1 CAT: 19

Great Smoky Mountains National Park
CIJE: 0 RIE: 2 CAT: 07

Great Society
CIJE: 4 RIE: 4 CAT: 12

Great Soviet Encyclopedia
CIJE: 1 RIE: 0 CAT: 22

Great Towns Program
CIJE: 0 RIE: 1 CAT: 19

Greater Amsterdam School District
CIJE: 1 RIE: 0 CAT: 17

Greater Avenues for Independence
CIJE: 1 RIE: 13 CAT: 19
SN California welfare-to-work initiative

Greater Cleveland Educational Develop Center OH
CIJE: 0 RIE: 1 CAT: 17

Greater Cleveland Social Studies Project
CIJE: 1 RIE: 1 CAT: 19

Greater Hartford Alliance for Literacy CT
CIJE: 0 RIE: 1 CAT: 19

Greater Hartford Community College CT
CIJE: 0 RIE: 1 CAT: 17

Greater Johnstown Area Vocational Tech School PA
CIJE: 0 RIE: 1 CAT: 17

Greater Lawrence Guidance Center MA
CIJE: 0 RIE: 1 CAT: 17

Greater Pittsburgh Literacy Council PA
CIJE: 0 RIE: 1 CAT: 17

Greater Saint Louis Ad Hoc Committee on ETV MO
CIJE: 0 RIE: 1 CAT: 17

Greatest Common Divisor (Mathematics)
CIJE: 2 RIE: 0 CAT: 20

Greatest Common Factor (Mathematics)
CIJE: 2 RIE: 1 CAT: 20

Greatest Love of All (The)
CIJE: 0 RIE: 1 CAT: 22

Greece
CIJE: 155 RIE: 132 CAT: 07

Greece (Ancient)
CIJE: 17 RIE: 7 CAT: 07

Greece (Athens)
CIJE: 13 RIE: 2 CAT: 07

Greece Central School District NY
CIJE: 9 RIE: 2 CAT: 17

Greek (Koine)
CIJE: 0 RIE: 2 CAT: 13

Greek Australians
CIJE: 3 RIE: 3 CAT: 08

Greek Culture
CIJE: 3 RIE: 5 CAT: 16

Greek Mythology
CIJE: 0 RIE: 3 CAT: 16

Greek Myths (Title)
CIJE: 0 RIE: 0 CAT: 22

Greek Orthodox Church
CIJE: 0 RIE: 3 CAT: 17
UF Orthodox Eastern Church (Greek)

Greek Speaking
CIJE: 0 RIE: 3 CAT: 08

Greek Theory
CIJE: 0 RIE: 2 CAT: 15

Greeks
CIJE: 13 RIE: 14 CAT: 08

Greeley (Andrew)
CIJE: 1 RIE: 1 CAT: 18

Greeley (Horace)
CIJE: 1 RIE: 2 CAT: 18

Greeley Parent Child Center CO
CIJE: 0 RIE: 1 CAT: 17

Green (Edith)
CIJE: 1 RIE: 0 CAT: 18

Green (Thomas)
CIJE: 2 RIE: 1 CAT: 18

Green Bay
CIJE: 1 RIE: 0 CAT: 07

Green Bay Public Schools WI
CIJE: 4 RIE: 2 CAT: 17

Green Chimneys School NY
CIJE: 2 RIE: 2 CAT: 17

Green County Technical High School AR
CIJE: 1 RIE: 0 CAT: 17

Green Function
CIJE: 1 RIE: 0 CAT: 20

Green Is Like a Meadow of Grass
CIJE: 1 RIE: 0 CAT: 22

Green Lakes Outdoor Education Center
CIJE: 1 RIE: 0 CAT: 17

Green Mountain College VT
CIJE: 0 RIE: 1 CAT: 17

Green Pages Concept
CIJE: 0 RIE: 1 CAT: 16

Green Revolution
CIJE: 9 RIE: 2 CAT: 12

Green River Community College WA
CIJE: 1 RIE: 2 CAT: 17

Green River Opportunities for Work KY
USE Project GROW

Green Thumb Green Light Program
CIJE: 0 RIE: 2 CAT: 19

Green Thumb Program
CIJE: 1 RIE: 1 CAT: 19

Green Thumb Project
CIJE: 0 RIE: 1 CAT: 19

Green Turnip Survival Systems
CIJE: 1 RIE: 0 CAT: 15

Green v City of Gadsden
CIJE: 0 RIE: 1 CAT: 14

Green Valley Area Educational Agency 14 IA
CIJE: 0 RIE: 1 CAT: 17

Greenberg (Joseph H)
CIJE: 2 RIE: 1 CAT: 18

Greenberg and Jenkins Linguistic Scale
CIJE: 3 RIE: 0 CAT: 21

Greenberg Law
CIJE: 1 RIE: 0 CAT: 14

Greenbook System
CIJE: 0 RIE: 8 CAT: 15

Greenburgh School District NY
CIJE: 0 RIE: 3 CAT: 17

Greene (Graham)
CIJE: 0 RIE: 1 CAT: 18

Greene (Maxine)
CIJE: 5 RIE: 1 CAT: 18

Greene County Career Center OH
CIJE: 0 RIE: 1 CAT: 17

Greene Joint Vocational School OH
CIJE: 0 RIE: 1 CAT: 17

Greenfield (Thomas)
CIJE: 5 RIE: 3 CAT: 18
SN "Thomas Barr"

Greenfield Community College MA
CIJE: 4 RIE: 0 CAT: 17

Greenfield High School TN
CIJE: 0 RIE: 1 CAT: 17

Greenfield Public Schools MA
CIJE: 1 RIE: 1 CAT: 17

Greenfield Secondary Schools Project
CIJE: 1 RIE: 0 CAT: 19

Greenhill School TX
CIJE: 0 RIE: 1 CAT: 17

Greening of America
CIJE: 2 RIE: 0 CAT: 22

Greenland
CIJE: 3 RIE: 17 CAT: 07

Greenleaf (Robert)
CIJE: 1 RIE: 0 CAT: 18

Greensboro City Public Schools NC
CIJE: 0 RIE: 0 CAT: 17

Greensboro Tri College Consortium NC
CIJE: 0 RIE: 1 CAT: 17

Greensville County School District VA
CIJE: 1 RIE: 2 CAT: 17

Greenville City Schools NC
CIJE: 0 RIE: 1 CAT: 17

Greenville College IL
CIJE: 1 RIE: 1 CAT: 17

Greenville County School District SC
CIJE: 0 RIE: 2 CAT: 17

Greenwich Public Schools CT
CIJE: 2 RIE: 2 CAT: 17

Greenwich Teachers Center CT
CIJE: 1 RIE: 0 CAT: 17

Greenwood School District 50 SC
CIJE: 0 RIE: 0 CAT: 17

Greet (Sir Philip Ben)
CIJE: 1 RIE: 0 CAT: 18

Greeting Cards
CIJE: 4 RIE: 1 CAT: 16

Greetings
CIJE: 3 RIE: 1 CAT: 16

Gregg Shorthand
CIJE: 9 RIE: 12 CAT: 15

Gregorc Style Delineator
CIJE: 4 RIE: 6 CAT: 21
UF Style Delineator (Gregorc)

Gregory (of Tours)
CIJE: 1 RIE: 0 CAT: 18

Gregory Academic Interest Inventory
CIJE: 1 RIE: 0 CAT: 21

Greimas (A J)
CIJE: 2 RIE: 0 CAT: 18

Grenada
CIJE: 14 RIE: 9 CAT: 07

Grendel
CIJE: 0 RIE: 1 CAT: 22

Gresham Grade School District 4 OR
CIJE: 0 RIE: 1 CAT: 17

Grey (Zane)
CIJE: 1 RIE: 0 CAT: 18

Grice (H P)
CIJE: 9 RIE: 8 CAT: 18

Grid Operators
CIJE: 0 RIE: 1 CAT: 09

Gridley Elementary School District CA
CIJE: 0 RIE: 1 CAT: 17

Gridley Farm Labor Camp CA
CIJE: 0 RIE: 1 CAT: 17

Grids
CIJE: 7 RIE: 6 CAT: 20

Grierson (John)
CIJE: 1 RIE: 1 CAT: 18

Grievance Arbitration
CIJE: 3 RIE: 1 CAT: 14

Grieve Report
CIJE: 0 RIE: 1 CAT: 22

Griffin (Dean)
CIJE: 1 RIE: 0 CAT: 18

Griffin (Leland)
CIJE: 0 RIE: 1 CAT: 18

Griffin Ford Model
CIJE: 0 RIE: 1 CAT: 15
SN ...of Latin American city structure

Griffin v County School Board
CIJE: 2 RIE: 0 CAT: 14

Griffiss Air Force Base NY
CIJE: 0 RIE: 1 CAT: 17

Griffith (D W)
CIJE: 2 RIE: 2 CAT: 18

Griffith University (Australia)
CIJE: 5 RIE: 2 CAT: 17

Griffiths (Daniel)
CIJE: 1 RIE: 1 CAT: 18

Griffiths Mental Development Scales
CIJE: 1 RIE: 1 CAT: 21

Griggs v Duke Power Company
CIJE: 5 RIE: 5 CAT: 14

Grignon (Claude)
CIJE: 1 RIE: 0 CAT: 18

Grimke (Angelina Weld)
CIJE: 0 RIE: 0 CAT: 18

Grimm (Jacob)
CIJE: 3 RIE: 2 CAT: 18

Grimm (Wilhelm)
CIJE: 3 RIE: 2 CAT: 18

Grimmelshausen (Hans Jakob Christoffel von)
CIJE: 1 RIE: 0 CAT: 18

Grinnell College IA
CIJE: 3 RIE: 4 CAT: 17

Grinnell Corporation
CIJE: 0 RIE: 1 CAT: 17

Grip Classification
CIJE: 1 RIE: 0 CAT: 11

GRIP Observation Instrument
USE Group Reading Interaction Pattern Observation Ins

Grips Theatre
CIJE: 0 RIE: 1 CAT: 17

Grito de Dolores
CIJE: 0 RIE: 1 CAT: 12

Grocery Checkers
CIJE: 0 RIE: 4 CAT: 09

Grolier Survey
CIJE: 0 RIE: 1 CAT: 22

Groliers Modern English Series Spelling
CIJE: 0 RIE: 1 CAT: 22

Grooved Pegboard Test
CIJE: 1 RIE: 0 CAT: 21

Gros Ventre (North Dakota)
USE Hidatsa

Gros Ventre (North Dakota) (Tribe)
USE Hidatsa (Tribe)

Gros Ventre (Wyoming)
USE Arapaho

Gros Ventre (Wyoming) (Tribe)
USE Arapaho (Tribe)

Gross (Theodore)
CIJE: 1 RIE: 0 CAT: 18

Gross National Product
CIJE: 18 RIE: 25 CAT: 16

Gross Product Originating Series
CIJE: 0 RIE: 1 CAT: 22

Grosse Pointe Public School System MI
CIJE: 1 RIE: 1 CAT: 17

Grossmont College CA
CIJE: 5 RIE: 5 CAT: 17

Grossmont Union High School District CA
CIJE: 0 RIE: 2 CAT: 17

Groteluesch en Model
CIJE: 0 RIE: 1 CAT: 15

Groton Public Schools CT
CIJE: 0 RIE: 1 CAT: 17

Grotowski (Jerzy)
CIJE: 1 RIE: 0 CAT: 18

Ground Station Receivers
CIJE: 0 RIE: 2 CAT: 04

Grounded Theory
CIJE: 28 RIE: 29 CAT: 15

Group Assessment of Interpersonal Traits
CIJE: 2 RIE: 2 CAT: 21

Group Assessment of Logical Thinking
CIJE: 3 RIE: 9 CAT: 21

Group Atmosphere Scale
CIJE: 1 RIE: 0 CAT: 21

Group Attitudes
CIJE: 7 RIE: 9 CAT: 16

Group Characteristics
CIJE: 8 RIE: 17 CAT: 16

Group Cohesion
CIJE: 8 RIE: 10 CAT: 16

Group Consensus Examinations
CIJE: 1 RIE: 1 CAT: 21

Group Conversation Method
CIJE: 0 RIE: 1 CAT: 15

Group Data
CIJE: 3 RIE: 3 CAT: 16

Group Day Care
CIJE: 1 RIE: 11 CAT: 16

Group Density
CIJE: 0 RIE: 1 CAT: 11

Group Description Scale (Narikawa et al)
CIJE: 0 RIE: 1 CAT: 21

Group Development
CIJE: 24 RIE: 4 CAT: 15

Group Embedded Figures Test
CIJE: 18 RIE: 16 CAT: 21
SN See from "Embedded Figures Test" — use either the Oltman entry or Witkin entry (below), if appropriate

Group Embedded Figures Test (Oltman et al)
CIJE: 7 RIE: 0 CAT: 21

Group Embedded Figures Test (Witkin)
CIJE: 17 RIE: 9 CAT: 21
SN Use "Embedded Figures Test" for the individually administered, perceptual test by Witkin et al

Group Facilitation
CIJE: 0 RIE: 1 CAT: 15

Group for the Advancement of Psychiatry
CIJE: 1 RIE: 0 CAT: 17

Group Insurance
CIJE: 0 RIE: 4 CAT: 16

Group Interaction Scale
CIJE: 0 RIE: 1 CAT: 21

Group Interview Guide
CIJE: 0 RIE: 1 CAT: 22

Group Interviews
CIJE: 7 RIE: 3 CAT: 15

Group Inventory for Finding Creative Talent
CIJE: 5 RIE: 3 CAT: 21

Group Inventory for Finding Interests
CIJE: 3 RIE: 0 CAT: 21

Group Leaders
CIJE: 9 RIE: 7 CAT: 10

Group Level Item Response Models
CIJE: 0 RIE: 1 CAT: 21

Group Longevity
CIJE: 1 RIE: 0 CAT: 15

Group Mapping Activity
CIJE: 1 RIE: 1 CAT: 15

Group Oral Review
CIJE: 0 RIE: 1 CAT: 15

Group Personality Projective Test
CIJE: 3 RIE: 0 CAT: 21

Group Preparation
CIJE: 3 RIE: 0 CAT: 15

Group Process Categories
CIJE: 1 RIE: 0 CAT: 15

Group Process Training
CIJE: 3 RIE: 0 CAT: 15

Group Projects Abroad Program
CIJE: 1 RIE: 0 CAT: 19

Group Reading Interaction Pattern Observation Ins
CIJE: 0 RIE: 2 CAT: 15
UF GRIP Observation Instrument

Group Reliable Measures
CIJE: 0 RIE: 1 CAT: 21

Group Selection
CIJE: 3 RIE: 3 CAT: 15

Group Shadow
CIJE: 1 RIE: 0 CAT: 11

Group Size
CIJE: 18 RIE: 8 CAT: 16

Group Test of Creativity
CIJE: 0 RIE: 1 CAT: 21

Group Theory
CIJE: 33 RIE: 12 CAT: 15

Group Therapist Orientation Scale
CIJE: 1 RIE: 0 CAT: 21

Grouping (Cognitive Psychology)
CIJE: 2 RIE: 1 CAT: 11

Groups (Mathematics)
CIJE: 9 RIE: 0 CAT: 20

Groupthink
CIJE: 4 RIE: 2 CAT: 16

Groupware
CIJE: 3 RIE: 1 CAT: 04

Grove City College PA
CIJE: 2 RIE: 4 CAT: 17

Grove City College v Bell
CIJE: 5 RIE: 12 CAT: 14

Grove Park Institute
CIJE: 3 RIE: 0 CAT: 17

Groveton High School VA
CIJE: 1 RIE: 0 CAT: 17

Growing Thinkers Program
CIJE: 0 RIE: 1 CAT: 19
SN A Houston ISD TX program

Growing Up Strong Program
CIJE: 0 RIE: 8 CAT: 19

Growth Accounting
CIJE: 0 RIE: 1 CAT: 15

Growth Centers
CIJE: 1 RIE: 3 CAT: 05

Growth Charts (Children)
USE Child Growth Charts

Growth Curve Analysis
CIJE: 9 RIE: 5 CAT: 15

Growth Through Art and Museum Experience
CIJE: 1 RIE: 0 CAT: 22

Growth Through English
CIJE: 4 RIE: 0 CAT: 22

Growth Units
CIJE: 1 RIE: 0 CAT: 15

Gruen Korte Stephens Internal External Scale
CIJE: 0 RIE: 1 CAT: 21

Grumman Aerospace Corp
CIJE: 1 RIE: 0 CAT: 17

Grundgesetz (West Germany)
USE Basic Law (West Germany)

Grundtvig (Nicolai)
CIJE: 6 RIE: 4 CAT: 18

Grundy (Shirley)
CIJE: 0 RIE: 1 CAT: 18

Grunig (James E)
CIJE: 0 RIE: 1 CAT: 18

Gruppen foer Pedagogisk Elektronik (Sweden)
CIJE: 0 RIE: 1 CAT: 17

Guahibo
CIJE: 0 RIE: 1 CAT: 13

Guajiro
CIJE: 0 RIE: 1 CAT: 13

Guam
CIJE: 14 RIE: 103 CAT: 07

Guam (Agana)
CIJE: 0 RIE: 2 CAT: 07

Guam Community College
CIJE: 0 RIE: 10 CAT: 17

Guam Educators Test of English Proficiency
CIJE: 0 RIE: 1 CAT: 21

Guanano
CIJE: 0 RIE: 1 CAT: 13

Guang Yun
CIJE: 0 RIE: 1 CAT: 22

Guarantee Agencies
USE Guaranty Agencies

Guaranteed Accommodation and Training for Employ
USE GATE Project

Guaranteed Guidance and Counseling Services
CIJE: 0 RIE: 1 CAT: 19
SN Program of Portland School District OR

Guaranteed Student Loan Program
CIJE: 39 RIE: 181 CAT: 14
SN Changed in 1988 to Stafford Student Loan Program

Guaranteed Tax Base Plan
CIJE: 1 RIE: 2 CAT: 19

Guaranteed Tuition Plans
USE Tuition Guarantee Programs

Guaranty Agencies
CIJE: 1 RIE: 9 CAT: 05
UF Guarantee Agencies

Guardian Ad Litem
CIJE: 3 RIE: 2 CAT: 14

Guardianship
CIJE: 16 RIE: 18 CAT: 16

Guare (John)
CIJE: 0 RIE: 1 CAT: 18

Guatemala
CIJE: 68 RIE: 78 CAT: 07

Guatemala (El Jocote)
CIJE: 0 RIE: 1 CAT: 07

Guba (Egon)
CIJE: 5 RIE: 1 CAT: 18

Guba Clark Model
CIJE: 0 RIE: 1 CAT: 15

Guba Stufflebeam CIPP Model
USE Context Input Process Product Evaluation Model

Gubernatorial Elections
CIJE: 2 RIE: 2 CAT: 16

Gude
CIJE: 1 RIE: 1 CAT: 13

Guelph Public Library ON
CIJE: 0 RIE: 0 CAT: 17

Guelph Rural Development Outreach Project
CIJE: 0 RIE: 2 CAT: 19

Guerin Method
CIJE: 0 RIE: 1 CAT: 15

Guess My Bag (Computer Program)
CIJE: 0 RIE: 1 CAT: 04

Guess My Strategy (Computer Program)
CIJE: 0 RIE: 1 CAT: 04

Guest Artist Program
CIJE: 1 RIE: 1 CAT: 19

Guest Speakers
CIJE: 20 RIE: 4 CAT: 10

Guest Workers
CIJE: 1 RIE: 5 CAT: 10

Gugu Yalanji
USE Kuku Yalanji

Guiberto (Giovanni di)
CIJE: 1 RIE: 0 CAT: 18

Guidance Associates
CIJE: 1 RIE: 0 CAT: 09

Guidance Examination (Los Angeles City College)
CIJE: 0 RIE: 2 CAT: 21

Guidance Information System
CIJE: 3 RIE: 6 CAT: 15

Guidance Learning Rate Scale (Keat)
CIJE: 1 RIE: 0 CAT: 21

Guidance Materials
CIJE: 0 RIE: 1 CAT: 16

Guidance Opportunities for Affective Learning
CIJE: 0 RIE: 1 CAT: 19
UF Project GOAL

Guidance Program Questionnaire
CIJE: 0 RIE: 1 CAT: 21

Guidance Testing Assoc Inter American Test Reading
CIJE: 0 RIE: 1 CAT: 21

Guide Dogs
CIJE: 9 RIE: 2 CAT: 20

Guide for College Visits and Reporting
CIJE: 0 RIE: 1 CAT: 22

Guide for Industrial Arts Education in Oklahoma
CIJE: 0 RIE: 1 CAT: 22

Guide for Occupational Exploration
CIJE: 4 RIE: 1 CAT: 21

Guide to Improving Instruction in Industrial Arts
CIJE: 1 RIE: 0 CAT: 22

Guide to Microforms in Print
CIJE: 1 RIE: 0 CAT: 22

Guide to Selecting Basal Reading Programs
CIJE: 0 RIE: 1 CAT: 22

Guided Assignments
CIJE: 0 RIE: 1 CAT: 15

Guided Autobiography
CIJE: 0 RIE: 1 CAT: 03

Guided Discovery Approach
CIJE: 6 RIE: 7 CAT: 15

Guided Fantasy
CIJE: 1 RIE: 1 CAT: 15

Guided Imagery
CIJE: 13 RIE: 4 CAT: 11

Guided Occupational Orientation Program
CIJE: 0 RIE: 4 CAT: 19

Guided Practice
CIJE: 2 RIE: 2 CAT: 15

Guided Readers
CIJE: 0 RIE: 1 CAT: 16

Guided Reading Procedure
CIJE: 9 RIE: 5 CAT: 15

Guided Self Analysis System
CIJE: 1 RIE: 2 CAT: 15

Guided Story Invention
CIJE: 0 RIE: 1 CAT: 15

Guided Writing
CIJE: 2 RIE: 1 CAT: 13

Guided Writing Procedure
CIJE: 1 RIE: 0 CAT: 15

Guidelines for Preparing Teachers of English
CIJE: 1 RIE: 0 CAT: 22

Guidelines in Vocations and Education
CIJE: 0 RIE: 1 CAT: 22

Guides for Better Living
CIJE: 1 RIE: 0 CAT: 03

Guiding Creative Talent
CIJE: 1 RIE: 0 CAT: 22

Guiding Education toward Adult Roles for Success
USE GEARS Model

Guiding Ones Own Development
CIJE: 0 RIE: 1 CAT: 22

GUIDON Program
CIJE: 0 RIE: 2 CAT: 04

Guilford (J P)
CIJE: 11 RIE: 13 CAT: 18

Guilford College NC
CIJE: 6 RIE: 3 CAT: 17

Guilford County School District NC
CIJE: 0 RIE: 1 CAT: 17

Guilford Creativity Test Battery
CIJE: 1 RIE: 3 CAT: 21

Guilford Hoepfner Measures of Intellectual Ability
CIJE: 0 RIE: 1 CAT: 21

Guilford Schneidman Zimmerman Interest Survey
CIJE: 0 RIE: 1 CAT: 21

Guilford Technical Community College NC
CIJE: 0 RIE: 1 CAT: 17

Guilford Zimmerman Aptitude Survey
CIJE: 1 RIE: 1 CAT: 21

Guilford Zimmerman Temperament Survey
CIJE: 7 RIE: 9 CAT: 21

Guilfords Structure of Intellect
CIJE: 26 RIE: 33 CAT: 15

Guilfords Theory of Creativity
CIJE: 3 RIE: 1 CAT: 21

Guillain Barre Polyneuritis
CIJE: 1 RIE: 0 CAT: 11

Guillen (Jorge)
CIJE: 5 RIE: 0 CAT: 18

Guillen (Nicolas)
CIJE: 1 RIE: 0 CAT: 18

Guilloux (Louis)
CIJE: 1 RIE: 0 CAT: 18

Guimaraes Rosa (Joao)
CIJE: 1 RIE: 0 CAT: 18

Guinaang Kalinga
USE Kalinga

Guinea
CIJE: 3 RIE: 4 CAT: 07

Guinea Pigs
CIJE: 3 RIE: 0 CAT: 20

Guiney (Louise)
CIJE: 0 RIE: 1 CAT: 18

Guiraldes (Ricardo)
CIJE: 2 RIE: 0 CAT: 18

GUIs
USE Graphical User Interfaces

Guitars
CIJE: 9 RIE: 4 CAT: 04

Gulf Coast Community College FL
CIJE: 3 RIE: 1 CAT: 17

Gulf Coast Junior College FL
CIJE: 1 RIE: 0 CAT: 17

Gulf County School District FL
CIJE: 0 RIE: 1 CAT: 17

Gulf Language Family
CIJE: 1 RIE: 0 CAT: 13

Gulf of Maine
CIJE: 0 RIE: 4 CAT: 07

Gulf of Mexico
CIJE: 0 RIE: 3 CAT: 07

Gulf Oil Corporation
CIJE: 2 RIE: 0 CAT: 17

Gulf Universities Research Consortium
CIJE: 2 RIE: 0 CAT: 17

Gulf War
CIJE: 49 RIE: 26 CAT: 12
SN 1990-91 (see also "Iran Iraq War")
UF Desert Shield; Desert Storm; Operation Desert Storm; Persian Gulf Crisis 1990 1991

Gulfport Project
CIJE: 1 RIE: 1 CAT: 19

Gullette Hatfield Test of Library Study Skills
CIJE: 1 RIE: 1 CAT: 21

Gulliksen Wilks Regression Tests
CIJE: 0 RIE: 1 CAT: 21

Gulliksens Matched Random Subtests Method
CIJE: 0 RIE: 1 CAT: 21

Gulls
CIJE: 2 RIE: 0 CAT: 20

GUME Project
CIJE: 1 RIE: 3 CAT: 19

Gumperz (John J)
CIJE: 0 RIE: 1 CAT: 18

Gumpgookies Test
CIJE: 2 RIE: 7 CAT: 21

Gun Control
CIJE: 14 RIE: 8 CAT: 14

Gunn (Hartford)
CIJE: 2 RIE: 0 CAT: 18

Gunners Mates
CIJE: 0 RIE: 2 CAT: 09

Gunning Fog Index
CIJE: 7 RIE: 4 CAT: 21

Guns
CIJE: 2 RIE: 4 CAT: 04
SN See also "Toy Guns"

Gunsmithing
CIJE: 0 RIE: 1 CAT: 09

Gurung
CIJE: 0 RIE: 3 CAT: 13

Gusii
CIJE: 8 RIE: 1 CAT: 08

Gussow (Joan)
CIJE: 0 RIE: 1 CAT: 18

Gustatory Sense
CIJE: 5 RIE: 0 CAT: 11

Gustavus Adolphus College MN
CIJE: 4 RIE: 5 CAT: 17

Gusti (Dimitrie)
CIJE: 0 RIE: 1 CAT: 18

Guthrie (James W)
CIJE: 0 RIE: 1 CAT: 18

Guthrie (Tyrone)
CIJE: 1 RIE: 0 CAT: 18

Guthrie (Woody)
CIJE: 0 RIE: 1 CAT: 18

Gutman Library MA
CIJE: 0 RIE: 2 CAT: 17

Gutmann (Amy)
CIJE: 0 RIE: 1 CAT: 18

Guttman Jordan Facet Design
CIJE: 1 RIE: 1 CAT: 21

Guttman Scales
CIJE: 22 RIE: 16 CAT: 21

Guttman Simplex Analysis
CIJE: 6 RIE: 2 CAT: 15

Guttman Weighting Procedure
CIJE: 2 RIE: 2 CAT: 21

Guyana
CIJE: 29 RIE: 25 CAT: 07
SN Formerly British Guiana

Guyanese Creole
CIJE: 3 RIE: 2 CAT: 13

Gwinnett County School System GA
CIJE: 1 RIE: 6 CAT: 17

Gwynedd Mercy College PA
CIJE: 0 RIE: 2 CAT: 17

Gymnastics Meets
CIJE: 0 RIE: 1 CAT: 16

Gynecomastia
CIJE: 1 RIE: 0 CAT: 11

GYNS AT WRK
CIJE: 1 RIE: 0 CAT: 22

Gypsies
CIJE: 17 RIE: 11 CAT: 08
SN See also "Roma"

Gypsy Language
USE Romany

Gypsy Moths
CIJE: 3 RIE: 1 CAT: 20

Gysbers Model
USE Comprehensive Guidance Program Model (Gysbers)

H 2 Immigration Program
CIJE: 0 RIE: 1 CAT: 19

H R 77 (94th Cong 1st Sess)
CIJE: 0 RIE: 1 CAT: 14

H R 4563 (94th Cong 1st Sess)
CIJE: 0 RIE: 1 CAT: 14

H R 5901 (94th Cong 1st Sess)
CIJE: 0 RIE: 1 CAT: 14

H R 8677 (93d Cong 1st Sess)
CIJE: 0 RIE: 1 CAT: 14

H R 9730 (93d Cong 1st Sess)
CIJE: 1 RIE: 0 CAT: 14

H R 12257 (93d Cong 2d Sess)
CIJE: 0 RIE: 1 CAT: 14

H R 15045 (90th Cong 2d Sess)
CIJE: 0 RIE: 1 CAT: 14

H W Wilson Co
CIJE: 12 RIE: 0 CAT: 17

Ha
CIJE: 0 RIE: 1 CAT: 13

Habeas Corpus
CIJE: 1 RIE: 1 CAT: 14

Habermas (Jurgen)
CIJE: 31 RIE: 22 CAT: 18

Habilitation
CIJE: 10 RIE: 5 CAT: 16

Habilitative Aids
CIJE: 1 RIE: 4 CAT: 04

Habitability Data Base
CIJE: 0 RIE: 1 CAT: 15

Habitat Destruction
CIJE: 0 RIE: 2 CAT: 20

Habitat for Humanity International
CIJE: 1 RIE: 0 CAT: 17

Habits
CIJE: 2 RIE: 2 CAT: 11

Habits of the Heart
CIJE: 2 RIE: 1 CAT: 22

Hablar et Parler
CIJE: 0 RIE: 1 CAT: 19

Haby (Rene)
CIJE: 2 RIE: 1 CAT: 18

Hacettepe University (Turkey)
CIJE: 2 RIE: 0 CAT: 17

Hackensack Career Development Center NJ
CIJE: 0 RIE: 1 CAT: 17

Hackensack Public Schools NJ
CIJE: 1 RIE: 0 CAT: 17

Hackers (Computers)
USE Computer Hackers

Hackman Gaither Vocational Interest Inventory
CIJE: 1 RIE: 1 CAT: 21

Hadiyya
CIJE: 0 RIE: 1 CAT: 13

Hadley School for the Blind IL
CIJE: 1 RIE: 0 CAT: 17

Haemophilus Influenzae Type B
USE Hemophilus Influenza Type B

Haemophilus Influenzae Type B Vaccine
USE Hemophilus Vaccines

Haga (W J)
CIJE: 0 RIE: 1 CAT: 18

Hagen Central Incidental Recall Paradigm
CIJE: 0 RIE: 1 CAT: 13

Hagerman Schools ID
CIJE: 2 RIE: 0 CAT: 17

Hagerstown Junior College MD
CIJE: 5 RIE: 19 CAT: 17

Haggerty Olson Wickman Behavior Rating Schedules
CIJE: 0 RIE: 1 CAT: 21

Haggerty Reading Examination
CIJE: 0 RIE: 1 CAT: 21

Hahn (Kurt)
CIJE: 7 RIE: 3 CAT: 18

Hahnemann Medical College and Hospital PA
CIJE: 5 RIE: 3 CAT: 17

Hahnemann Medical Practice Plan
CIJE: 1 RIE: 0 CAT: 11

Hahnemann School of Respiratory Therapy PA
CIJE: 0 RIE: 1 CAT: 17

Hahnemann University PA
CIJE: 3 RIE: 0 CAT: 17

Haida
CIJE: 4 RIE: 5 CAT: 13
SN Of the Na-Dene language group
UF Skittagetan

Haida (Tribe)
CIJE: 1 RIE: 15 CAT: 08

Haifa University (Israel)
CIJE: 6 RIE: 3 CAT: 17

Haight Ashbury Childrens Center CA
CIJE: 0 RIE: 1 CAT: 17

Haile Selassie
CIJE: 1 RIE: 1 CAT: 18

Haile Selassie University (Ethiopia)
CIJE: 0 RIE: 1 CAT: 17

Hailmann (William N)
CIJE: 1 RIE: 1 CAT: 18

Haiman (Franklyn)
CIJE: 0 RIE: 1 CAT: 18

Hair
CIJE: 10 RIE: 3 CAT: 11

Hair Length
CIJE: 4 RIE: 1 CAT: 16

Hair Mineral Levels
CIJE: 1 RIE: 0 CAT: 11

Hair Pulling
CIJE: 1 RIE: 1 CAT: 11
UF Trichotillomania

Hairstyles
CIJE: 3 RIE: 0 CAT: 16

Hairy Ape (the)
CIJE: 1 RIE: 0 CAT: 22

Haiti
CIJE: 30 RIE: 40 CAT: 07

Haitian American Training Institute
CIJE: 0 RIE: 1 CAT: 17

Haitian Culture
CIJE: 0 RIE: 1 CAT: 16

Haitian Parent and Teacher Training Program NY
CIJE: 0 RIE: 4 CAT: 19

Haitian Perinatal Intervention Program
CIJE: 0 RIE: 1 CAT: 19

Haj (Uris)
CIJE: 0 RIE: 1 CAT: 22

Hakka Dialect
CIJE: 2 RIE: 1 CAT: 13

Halakhah
USE Jewish Law

Halbi
CIJE: 0 RIE: 2 CAT: 13

Hale Reaction Performance Timer
CIJE: 1 RIE: 0 CAT: 04

Hale Report
CIJE: 1 RIE: 0 CAT: 22

Hales Exponential Method Evaluating Improvement
CIJE: 1 RIE: 0 CAT: 21

Haley (Margaret A)
CIJE: 0 RIE: 1 CAT: 18

Halftime Shows
CIJE: 1 RIE: 1 CAT: 16

Halftones (Graphic Arts)
CIJE: 2 RIE: 0 CAT: 20

Halia
CIJE: 1 RIE: 0 CAT: 13

Halides
CIJE: 1 RIE: 0 CAT: 20

Hall (D T)
CIJE: 2 RIE: 0 CAT: 18

Hall (Edward T)
CIJE: 2 RIE: 0 CAT: 18

Hall (G Stanley)
CIJE: 8 RIE: 1 CAT: 18

Hall (Joseph Sargent)
CIJE: 0 RIE: 1 CAT: 18

Hall (Richard)
CIJE: 1 RIE: 0 CAT: 18

Hall Dennis Report
CIJE: 0 RIE: 1 CAT: 22

Hall Elementary School
CIJE: 0 RIE: 1 CAT: 17

Hall Occupational Orientation Inventory
CIJE: 0 RIE: 2 CAT: 21

Hall Professionalization Scales
CIJE: 2 RIE: 2 CAT: 21

Halle (Morris)
CIJE: 5 RIE: 3 CAT: 18

Hallermann Streiff Syndrome
CIJE: 2 RIE: 0 CAT: 11

Halleys Comet
CIJE: 3 RIE: 3 CAT: 20

Halliday (M A K)
CIJE: 13 RIE: 3 CAT: 18

Halliwick Method
CIJE: 0 RIE: 1 CAT: 15

Halloween
CIJE: 27 RIE: 9 CAT: 12

Hallucinations
CIJE: 4 RIE: 1 CAT: 11

Hallucinogenic Drugs
CIJE: 0 RIE: 2 CAT: 11

Hallucinogens
CIJE: 3 RIE: 3 CAT: 11

Halo Effect
CIJE: 32 RIE: 11 CAT: 21

Halogenation
CIJE: 1 RIE: 0 CAT: 20

Halogens
CIJE: 7 RIE: 2 CAT: 20

Haloperidol
CIJE: 5 RIE: 0 CAT: 11

Halpin Leader Behavior Description Questionnaire
CIJE: 0 RIE: 1 CAT: 21

Halstead Category Test
CIJE: 1 RIE: 1 CAT: 21

Halstead Higher Education Price Index
CIJE: 0 RIE: 1 CAT: 15

Halstead Public Schools KS
CIJE: 0 RIE: 0 CAT: 17

Halstead Reitan Neuropsychological Tests
CIJE: 14 RIE: 5 CAT: 21

Halvorsen (Ruth Elise)
CIJE: 0 RIE: 1 CAT: 18

Ham Radio
CIJE: 2 RIE: 3 CAT: 04

Hambleton (Ron K)
CIJE: 0 RIE: 2 CAT: 18

Hamburg Central School District NY
CIJE: 1 RIE: 0 CAT: 17

Hamer (Fannie Lou)
CIJE: 1 RIE: 1 CAT: 18

Hamilton (Alexander)
CIJE: 4 RIE: 2 CAT: 18

Hamilton (Elizabeth)
CIJE: 1 RIE: 0 CAT: 18

Hamilton (Milo)
CIJE: 1 RIE: 0 CAT: 18

Hamilton (Virginia)
CIJE: 5 RIE: 0 CAT: 18

Hamilton (W D)
CIJE: 1 RIE: 0 CAT: 18

Hamilton (William Rowan)
CIJE: 1 RIE: 0 CAT: 18

Hamilton College NY
CIJE: 5 RIE: 1 CAT: 17

Hamilton Community Consolidated School District IL
CIJE: 0 RIE: 1 CAT: 17

Hamilton County Public Schools TN
CIJE: 0 RIE: 2 CAT: 17

Hamilton Nuclear Threat Philosophy Scale
CIJE: 0 RIE: 1 CAT: 21

Hamilton Principle
CIJE: 3 RIE: 0 CAT: 20

Hamilton Rating Scale for Depression
CIJE: 2 RIE: 1 CAT: 21

Hamilton Township Schools NJ
CIJE: 0 RIE: 0 CAT: 17

Hamilton Wenham Regional High School MA
CIJE: 1 RIE: 2 CAT: 17

Hamilton Wentworth Roman Catholic Sep Sch Bd ON
CIJE: 0 RIE: 0 CAT: 17

Hamlet
CIJE: 23 RIE: 8 CAT: 22

Hamlin (Hannibal)
CIJE: 0 RIE: 1 CAT: 18

Hamline University MN
CIJE: 3 RIE: 10 CAT: 17

Hammarskjold (Dag)
CIJE: 2 RIE: 0 CAT: 18

Hammill and Irwin Abstraction Test
CIJE: 1 RIE: 0 CAT: 21

Hammond Public Schools IN
CIJE: 1 RIE: 3 CAT: 17

Hammonds (Carsie)
CIJE: 1 RIE: 0 CAT: 18

Hampden Sydney College VA
CIJE: 1 RIE: 1 CAT: 17

Hampshire College MA
CIJE: 34 RIE: 11 CAT: 17

Hampshire Interlibrary Center MA
CIJE: 0 RIE: 1 CAT: 17

Hampton City School District VA
CIJE: 0 RIE: 1 CAT: 17

Hampton Institute VA
CIJE: 14 RIE: 10 CAT: 17

Hampton University VA
CIJE: 1 RIE: 2 CAT: 17
SN Formerly Hampton Institute VA

Han (Athapascan Language)
CIJE: 0 RIE: 0 CAT: 13
SN Language of American Indians in the Yukon River drainage basin

Han (Chinese People)
CIJE: 0 RIE: 0 CAT: 08
SN The distinctly Chinese ethnic population, i.e., those not of Mongol, Manchu, Tibetan, or other non-Chinese extraction

Hand Dynamometer Task
CIJE: 1 RIE: 0 CAT: 21

Hand Finishers
CIJE: 0 RIE: 1 CAT: 09

Hand Function
CIJE: 6 RIE: 1 CAT: 11

Hand Is on the Gate
CIJE: 1 RIE: 0 CAT: 22

Hand Labelers
CIJE: 0 RIE: 1 CAT: 09

Hand Sewers
CIJE: 0 RIE: 1 CAT: 09

Hand Test
CIJE: 14 RIE: 1 CAT: 21

Hand Washing Practices
USE Handwashing

Handbook of Cooperative Education
CIJE: 0 RIE: 1 CAT: 22

Handbook of Human Intelligence (Sternberg)
CIJE: 0 RIE: 1 CAT: 22

Handbook of Latin American Studies
CIJE: 1 RIE: 2 CAT: 22

Handedness Test (Kannegieter)
CIJE: 0 RIE: 1 CAT: 21

Handgame
CIJE: 1 RIE: 0 CAT: 21

Handicap Abuse
USE Abuse (of Disabled)

Handicap Parking Spaces
CIJE: 0 RIE: 1 CAT: 05
UF Handicapped Parking

Handicap Problems Inventory
CIJE: 0 RIE: 1 CAT: 21

Handicapism
CIJE: 4 RIE: 2 CAT: 16

Handicapped Advocacy
CIJE: 0 RIE: 0 CAT: 11

Handicapped Children as Tutors (Project)
CIJE: 0 RIE: 1 CAT: 19

Handicapped Children Model Programs
CIJE: 1 RIE: 1 CAT: 19

Handicapped Childrens Early Educ Assist Act 1968
CIJE: 1 RIE: 1 CAT: 14

Handicapped Childrens Early Education Program
CIJE: 8 RIE: 60 CAT: 19

Handicapped Childrens Protection Act 1986
CIJE: 13 RIE: 6 CAT: 14
UF Public Law 99 372

Handicapped Delinquents
CIJE: 0 RIE: 1 CAT: 10

Handicapped Parking
USE Handicap Parking Spaces

Handicapped Unbound Program AZ
CIJE: 0 RIE: 1 CAT: 19

Handicappers Civil Rights Act 1976 (Michigan)
CIJE: 0 RIE: 1 CAT: 14

Handke (Peter)
CIJE: 1 RIE: 1 CAT: 18

Handler (Philip)
CIJE: 1 RIE: 0 CAT: 18

Hazards
CIJE: 20 RIE: 29 CAT: 16

Hazelwood School District MO
CIJE: 1 RIE: 1 CAT: 17

Hazelwood School District v Kuhlmeier
CIJE: 70 RIE: 21 CAT: 14
UF Kuhlmeier v Hazelwood School District MO

Hazelwood School District v United States
CIJE: 1 RIE: 1 CAT: 14

Hazing
CIJE: 15 RIE: 7 CAT: 16

Hazleton Area School District PA
CIJE: 2 RIE: 0 CAT: 17

Hazlitt (William)
CIJE: 2 RIE: 0 CAT: 18

HBJ Writer
CIJE: 1 RIE: 1 CAT: 04

HDL Cholesterol
USE High Density Lipoprotein Cholesterol

HDTV
USE High Definition Television

Head (David)
CIJE: 1 RIE: 0 CAT: 18

Head Injury Re Entry Project
USE Project HIRe (Head Injuries)

Head Librarians
CIJE: 1 RIE: 1 CAT: 09

Head Lice
CIJE: 4 RIE: 2 CAT: 11

Head Movements
CIJE: 10 RIE: 5 CAT: 11

Head Start
USE Project Head Start

Head Start Arithmetic Test
CIJE: 0 RIE: 1 CAT: 21

Head Start Behavior Inventory (Ziegler)
CIJE: 0 RIE: 3 CAT: 21

Head Start Evaluation Synthesis and Utilization
CIJE: 0 RIE: 1 CAT: 19

Head Start Expansion and Improvement Act 1990
CIJE: 0 RIE: 1 CAT: 14
UF Public Law 101 501

Head Start Improvement Act 1992
CIJE: 0 RIE: 1 CAT: 14
UF Public Law 102 401

Head Start Measures Battery
CIJE: 1 RIE: 1 CAT: 21

Head Start Program Performance Standards
CIJE: 2 RIE: 2 CAT: 21

Head Start Supplementary Training Program
CIJE: 7 RIE: 11 CAT: 19

Head Start Test Collection
CIJE: 0 RIE: 11 CAT: 21

Head Teachers
CIJE: 16 RIE: 9 CAT: 09

Head Wrap (Grammar)
CIJE: 0 RIE: 1 CAT: 13

Headaches
CIJE: 19 RIE: 3 CAT: 11

Headings
CIJE: 14 RIE: 17 CAT: 16

Headmasters
CIJE: 3 RIE: 1 CAT: 09
SN See also the Descriptor "Principals"
UF Headmistresses

Headmistresses
USE Headmasters

Heads of State
CIJE: 0 RIE: 1 CAT: 10

Healing
CIJE: 4 RIE: 7 CAT: 11

Healing Effect
CIJE: 4 RIE: 2 CAT: 11

Health Advocacy Training Project
CIJE: 1 RIE: 1 CAT: 19

Health Aides
CIJE: 1 RIE: 5 CAT: 09

Health and Nutrition Examination Survey
CIJE: 1 RIE: 5 CAT: 22

Health and Optimum Physical Education Project
CIJE: 1 RIE: 0 CAT: 19
SN See also later name "Every Child a Winner"
UF Project HOPE (Physical Education)

Health and Safety at Work Act 1974 (England)
CIJE: 1 RIE: 1 CAT: 14

Health and Science Action Learning Project
CIJE: 0 RIE: 1 CAT: 19

Health Attitudes
CIJE: 21 RIE: 19 CAT: 11

Health Awareness Mini Assessment (1977)
CIJE: 0 RIE: 0 CAT: 21

Health Behavior
CIJE: 96 RIE: 14 CAT: 11

Health Behavior Inventory
CIJE: 1 RIE: 1 CAT: 21

Health Belief Model
CIJE: 13 RIE: 3 CAT: 15

Health Care Assistants
USE Patient Care Assistants

Health Care Economics
CIJE: 1 RIE: 4 CAT: 03

Health Care Financing Administration
CIJE: 1 RIE: 2 CAT: 17

Health Care Partnerships
USE Partnerships in Health Care

Health Care Reform
CIJE: 31 RIE: 3 CAT: 11

Health Care Teams
CIJE: 0 RIE: 4 CAT: 09

Health Careers Information System
CIJE: 1 RIE: 0 CAT: 15

Health Careers Opportunity Program
CIJE: 0 RIE: 5 CAT: 19

Health Careers Summer Program
CIJE: 0 RIE: 3 CAT: 19

Health Communication
CIJE: 27 RIE: 44 CAT: 11

Health Consumer Education Program
CIJE: 0 RIE: 1 CAT: 19

Health Counseling
CIJE: 7 RIE: 2 CAT: 11

Health Decision Making Index
CIJE: 0 RIE: 1 CAT: 21

Health Delivery Systems
CIJE: 11 RIE: 25 CAT: 11

Health Education Assistance Loan Program
CIJE: 0 RIE: 2 CAT: 19

Health Education Consortium
CIJE: 0 RIE: 4 CAT: 17

Health Education Council
CIJE: 1 RIE: 0 CAT: 17

Health Education Journals
CIJE: 1 RIE: 1 CAT: 11

Health Education Paraprofessionals Program NY
CIJE: 0 RIE: 1 CAT: 19

Health Education Research
CIJE: 12 RIE: 1 CAT: 15

Health Education Telecommunications Experiment
CIJE: 0 RIE: 10 CAT: 19

Health Education Tests
CIJE: 0 RIE: 1 CAT: 21

Health Educators
CIJE: 26 RIE: 8 CAT: 09

Health Employee Learning Program
CIJE: 1 RIE: 0 CAT: 19

Health Examination Survey
CIJE: 0 RIE: 11 CAT: 15

Health Fairs
CIJE: 7 RIE: 3 CAT: 11

Health Foods
CIJE: 0 RIE: 1 CAT: 11

Health for All by the Year 2000
CIJE: 1 RIE: 6 CAT: 19
SN World Health Organization initiative — see also "Healthy People 2000"

Health Hazard Appraisal
CIJE: 3 RIE: 1 CAT: 11

Health Hazards
CIJE: 42 RIE: 15 CAT: 11

Health Ideation Pictures
CIJE: 1 RIE: 0 CAT: 11

Health Information
CIJE: 19 RIE: 4 CAT: 11
SN See also "Health Sciences Information"
UF Consumer Health Information

Health Instruction Exchange
CIJE: 0 RIE: 42 CAT: 19

Health Insurance Study
CIJE: 0 RIE: 1 CAT: 22

Health Maintenance Organization Act 1973
CIJE: 1 RIE: 1 CAT: 14

Health Maintenance Organizations
CIJE: 52 RIE: 29 CAT: 05

Health Manpower Act 1968
CIJE: 0 RIE: 5 CAT: 14

Health Manpower Act 1975
CIJE: 0 RIE: 1 CAT: 14

Health Manpower Shortage Areas
CIJE: 0 RIE: 8 CAT: 11
SN See also "Health Personnel Shortage"

Health Motivation
CIJE: 5 RIE: 3 CAT: 11

Health Network Curriculum
CIJE: 0 RIE: 1 CAT: 03

Health Occupations Students of America
CIJE: 3 RIE: 14 CAT: 17

Health Periodicals Database
CIJE: 0 RIE: 1 CAT: 04

Health Personnel Shortage
CIJE: 0 RIE: 1 CAT: 11
SN See also "Health Manpower Shortage Areas"

Health Policy
CIJE: 12 RIE: 5 CAT: 11

Health Professions Capitation Grant
CIJE: 1 RIE: 0 CAT: 19

Health Professions Educ Exten Amendments 1992
CIJE: 0 RIE: 1 CAT: 14
UF Public Law 102 408

Health Professions Education and Distribution Act
CIJE: 0 RIE: 1 CAT: 14

Health Professions Educational Assistance Act
CIJE: 3 RIE: 10 CAT: 14

Health Professions Student Loan Program
CIJE: 1 RIE: 3 CAT: 19

Health Psychology
CIJE: 17 RIE: 3 CAT: 11

Health Resources Administration
CIJE: 1 RIE: 2 CAT: 17

Health Resources and Services Administration
CIJE: 2 RIE: 3 CAT: 17

Health Resources Information
CIJE: 2 RIE: 2 CAT: 11

Health Resources Inventory
CIJE: 1 RIE: 1 CAT: 21

Health Resources Utilization
CIJE: 1 RIE: 4 CAT: 11

Health Risk Appraisal
CIJE: 17 RIE: 6 CAT: 11

Health Risk Susceptibility
CIJE: 0 RIE: 3 CAT: 11

Health Sciences
CIJE: 24 RIE: 5 CAT: 11

Health Sciences Information
CIJE: 11 RIE: 2 CAT: 11

Health Services and Mental Health Administration
CIJE: 0 RIE: 1 CAT: 17

Health Spas
CIJE: 0 RIE: 3 CAT: 05

Health Standards
CIJE: 8 RIE: 1 CAT: 11

Health Start Program
CIJE: 0 RIE: 5 CAT: 19

Health Status
CIJE: 19 RIE: 26 CAT: 11

Health Surveys
CIJE: 6 RIE: 4 CAT: 21

Health Systems Agencies
CIJE: 3 RIE: 2 CAT: 10

Healthy Mothers Healthy Fathers Healthy Babies MO
CIJE: 0 RIE: 1 CAT: 19

Healthy People 2000
CIJE: 8 RIE: 6 CAT: 19
SN National U.S. health promotion and disease prevention initiative targeted to-

ward the year 2000 — see also "Health for All by the Year 2000"

Healthy Thats ME
CIJE: 1 RIE: 1 CAT: 22

HEAR Foundation
CIJE: 0 RIE: 1 CAT: 17

Hearing Ear Dogs
CIJE: 0 RIE: 0 CAT: 11

Hearing Officers
CIJE: 3 RIE: 11 CAT: 09

Hearn (Lafcadio)
CIJE: 0 RIE: 1 CAT: 18

Hearst (Patricia) Trial
CIJE: 0 RIE: 1 CAT: 12

Hearst (William Randolph)
CIJE: 2 RIE: 1 CAT: 18

Heart
CIJE: 5 RIE: 9 CAT: 11
UF Human Heart

Heart Health Program
CIJE: 2 RIE: 4 CAT: 19

Heart Is a Lonely Hunter
CIJE: 1 RIE: 0 CAT: 22

Heart of Darkness
CIJE: 2 RIE: 2 CAT: 22

Heart of the Dragon
CIJE: 0 RIE: 2 CAT: 22

Heart of the Earth Survival School MN
CIJE: 0 RIE: 1 CAT: 17

Heart Smart
CIJE: 1 RIE: 0 CAT: 19
SN A cardiovascular intervention program for elementary students

Heart Smart Cognitive Tests
CIJE: 0 RIE: 1 CAT: 21

Heart Start
CIJE: 0 RIE: 1 CAT: 22
SN Full title: "Heart Start: The Emotional Foundations of School Readiness"

Heart Transplants
CIJE: 1 RIE: 0 CAT: 11

Heartbeat Simulation
CIJE: 1 RIE: 0 CAT: 11

Heartland Community College IL
CIJE: 0 RIE: 1 CAT: 17

Heartsmart Adventures
CIJE: 0 RIE: 1 CAT: 03
SN An interpersonal skills curriculum

Heartwood Program
CIJE: 0 RIE: 2 CAT: 03
SN Ethics curriculum for children

Heat Injuries
CIJE: 0 RIE: 1 CAT: 11

Heat Loss
CIJE: 1 RIE: 1 CAT: 20

Heat Pumps
CIJE: 0 RIE: 5 CAT: 04

Heat Storage
CIJE: 1 RIE: 1 CAT: 20

Heat Transfer
CIJE: 4 RIE: 1 CAT: 20

Heat Treatment (Metals)
CIJE: 0 RIE: 1 CAT: 20

Heater Operators
CIJE: 0 RIE: 1 CAT: 09

Heaters
CIJE: 0 RIE: 1 CAT: 04

HEATH Closer Look
USE Project HEATH

Heath Elementary Mathematics Series
CIJE: 0 RIE: 2 CAT: 22

Heathcote (Dorothy)
CIJE: 9 RIE: 2 CAT: 18

Heating Mechanics
CIJE: 0 RIE: 1 CAT: 09

Heavy Equipment Mechanics
CIJE: 0 RIE: 10 CAT: 09

Heavy Equipment Operators
CIJE: 1 RIE: 19 CAT: 09

Heavy Metals
CIJE: 3 RIE: 1 CAT: 20

Hebb (D O)
CIJE: 2 RIE: 1 CAT: 18

Hebbel (Christian Friedrich)
CIJE: 1 RIE: 0 CAT: 18

Hebel (Johann Peter)
CIJE: 2 RIE: 0 CAT: 18

Hebrew Academy of Nassau County NY
CIJE: 1 RIE: 0 CAT: 17

Hebrew Language Council
CIJE: 1 RIE: 0 CAT: 17

Hebrew Technical Institute CA
CIJE: 0 RIE: 1 CAT: 17

Hebrew University of Jerusalem (Israel)
CIJE: 9 RIE: 7 CAT: 17

Heckling
CIJE: 2 RIE: 2 CAT: 16

Heckman (J J)
CIJE: 0 RIE: 1 CAT: 18

Hectograph Process
CIJE: 0 RIE: 1 CAT: 20

Hedges (Linguistics)
CIJE: 0 RIE: 2 CAT: 13

Hedges (Reading)
CIJE: 0 RIE: 1 CAT: 15

Hedges (Search Technique)
CIJE: 1 RIE: 0 CAT: 15

Hedman Stenotype
CIJE: 1 RIE: 0 CAT: 04

Hedonism
CIJE: 8 RIE: 2 CAT: 16

Heermann (Barry)
CIJE: 0 RIE: 1 CAT: 18

Hefner (Hugh)
CIJE: 1 RIE: 0 CAT: 18

Hegel (Georg Wilhelm Friedrich)
CIJE: 14 RIE: 5 CAT: 18

Hegeler Foundation
CIJE: 0 RIE: 1 CAT: 17

Hegeler Project Reading Study
CIJE: 0 RIE: 1 CAT: 19

Hegemony
CIJE: 10 RIE: 4 CAT: 16

HEGIS
USE Higher Education General Information Survey

HEGIS Data Quality Project
CIJE: 0 RIE: 4 CAT: 19

Hehe
CIJE: 0 RIE: 1 CAT: 13

Heidegger (Martin)
CIJE: 15 RIE: 5 CAT: 18

Heidelberg College OH
CIJE: 1 RIE: 3 CAT: 17

Heider (F N)
CIJE: 3 RIE: 3 CAT: 18

Heider (Karl)
CIJE: 0 RIE: 1 CAT: 18

Heifer Project International
CIJE: 2 RIE: 0 CAT: 19

Heilbron (Louis H)
CIJE: 0 RIE: 1 CAT: 18

Heilprin (Lawrence B)
CIJE: 0 RIE: 1 CAT: 18

Heiltsuk
CIJE: 1 RIE: 0 CAT: 13

Heimlich Maneuver
CIJE: 0 RIE: 3 CAT: 11

Heine (Heinrich)
CIJE: 3 RIE: 0 CAT: 18

Heinicke (Samuel)
CIJE: 1 RIE: 0 CAT: 18

Heinlein (Robert)
CIJE: 0 RIE: 2 CAT: 18

Helburn (Suzanne Wiggins)
CIJE: 0 RIE: 2 CAT: 18

HELDS Project
USE Higher Education for Learning Disabled Students

Helen Keller National Center Act
CIJE: 1 RIE: 2 CAT: 14
UF Keller National Center Act

Helical Thought
CIJE: 0 RIE: 1 CAT: 15

Helicon Waves
CIJE: 1 RIE: 0 CAT: 20

Helicopters
CIJE: 1 RIE: 8 CAT: 04

Heliotrope Free University CA
CIJE: 1 RIE: 0 CAT: 17

Helium
CIJE: 3 RIE: 0 CAT: 20

Helixes
CIJE: 1 RIE: 0 CAT: 20

Hellman (Lillian)
CIJE: 0 RIE: 1 CAT: 18

Helmers (Hermann)
CIJE: 1 RIE: 0 CAT: 18

Helmholtz Theory of Visual Direction
CIJE: 1 RIE: 0 CAT: 15

Help Communities Help Themselves
CIJE: 0 RIE: 3 CAT: 19

Help Elderly Locate Positions
CIJE: 0 RIE: 1 CAT: 19

HELP Information Retrieval System
CIJE: 0 RIE: 1 CAT: 04

Help Systems
CIJE: 26 RIE: 3 CAT: 16

Helper Therapy
CIJE: 1 RIE: 0 CAT: 11

Helpful Entry Level Skills Checklist
CIJE: 0 RIE: 1 CAT: 21

Helpful Opportunities for Pupil Enrichment NY
USE Project HOPE NY

Helping Hand Programs
CIJE: 0 RIE: 2 CAT: 19

Helping Individuals Regain Employment
CIJE: 1 RIE: 0 CAT: 19

Helping One Student To Succeed
CIJE: 0 RIE: 4 CAT: 19
UF HOSTS Program

Helping Relationship Inventory
CIJE: 3 RIE: 1 CAT: 21

Helping Teacher Program
CIJE: 0 RIE: 1 CAT: 19

Helping Underachieving Gifted Students OH
USE HUGS Project OH

Helsinki Final Act
CIJE: 0 RIE: 3 CAT: 14

Helsinki Test
CIJE: 0 RIE: 1 CAT: 21

Heltwate School (England)
CIJE: 0 RIE: 0 CAT: 17

Hemangiomas
CIJE: 0 RIE: 1 CAT: 11

Hematology
CIJE: 3 RIE: 8 CAT: 11

Hemet Unified School District CA
CIJE: 1 RIE: 1 CAT: 17

Hemingway (Ernest)
CIJE: 26 RIE: 11 CAT: 18

Hemispheric Routing TAKv
CIJE: 1 RIE: 0 CAT: 11

Hemispheric Studies Center
CIJE: 0 RIE: 1 CAT: 17

Hemodialysis
CIJE: 4 RIE: 0 CAT: 11
UF Kidney Dialysis; Renal Dialysis

Hemoglobin
CIJE: 12 RIE: 2 CAT: 11

Hemophilia
CIJE: 19 RIE: 7 CAT: 11

Hemophilus Influenza Type B
CIJE: 0 RIE: 0 CAT: 11
UF Haemophilus Influenzae Type B; HiB Disease; Meningitis (Hemophilus)

Hemophilus Vaccines
CIJE: 0 RIE: 0 CAT: 11
UF Haemophilus Influenzae Type B Vaccine; HiB Vaccine

Hempstead High School NY
CIJE: 1 RIE: 0 CAT: 17

Henderson (Algo D)
CIJE: 0 RIE: 1 CAT: 18

Henderson Environmental Learning Process Scale
CIJE: 1 RIE: 1 CAT: 21

Henderson State University AR
CIJE: 2 RIE: 3 CAT: 17

Hendrick Hendrick Love Attitudes Scale
CIJE: 0 RIE: 1 CAT: 21

Hendrick Hendrick Love Instrument
CIJE: 1 RIE: 1 CAT: 21

Hendricks v Carroll
CIJE: 0 RIE: 1 CAT: 14

Henley (Don)
CIJE: 0 RIE: 1 CAT: 18

Henmon Nelson Tests of Mental Ability
CIJE: 3 RIE: 8 CAT: 21

Hennepin County Library System MN
CIJE: 0 RIE: 0 CAT: 17

Henrico County Public Schools VA
CIJE: 0 RIE: 1 CAT: 17

Henrietta Szold Institute (Israel)
CIJE: 0 RIE: 3 CAT: 17

Henry (George W)
CIJE: 0 RIE: 1 CAT: 18

Henry (Joseph)
CIJE: 1 RIE: 0 CAT: 18

Henry Chauncey Conference Center NJ
CIJE: 0 RIE: 1 CAT: 17

Henry County Public Schools IA
CIJE: 0 RIE: 2 CAT: 17

Henry E Huntington Library OR
CIJE: 0 RIE: 1 CAT: 17

Henry Elementary School MO
CIJE: 1 RIE: 0 CAT: 17

Henry Ford Community College MI
CIJE: 1 RIE: 3 CAT: 17

Henry Sibley Senior High School MN
CIJE: 0 RIE: 1 CAT: 17

Henry V
CIJE: 2 RIE: 3 CAT: 22

HEP CAMP National Evaluation Project
CIJE: 0 RIE: 4 CAT: 19

Hepatitis
CIJE: 20 RIE: 10 CAT: 11

Hepatitis B
CIJE: 2 RIE: 1 CAT: 11

Hepburn Romanization
CIJE: 0 RIE: 1 CAT: 13

Her Majesty Industries Incorporated
CIJE: 1 RIE: 0 CAT: 17

Herald Telephone
CIJE: 0 RIE: 1 CAT: 22

Herbal Medicine
CIJE: 1 RIE: 2 CAT: 11

Herbart (Johann Friedrich)
CIJE: 9 RIE: 4 CAT: 18

Herbartian Movement
CIJE: 0 RIE: 1 CAT: 12

Herbert Lehman High School NY
CIJE: 1 RIE: 0 CAT: 17

Herbs
CIJE: 5 RIE: 4 CAT: 20

Herbst (Josephine)
CIJE: 0 RIE: 1 CAT: 18

Hereditary Diseases
USE Genetic Diseases

Hereford Parental Attitude Survey Forms
CIJE: 2 RIE: 1 CAT: 21

Heres Looking at You
CIJE: 1 RIE: 1 CAT: 03

Heriot Watt University (Scotland)
CIJE: 1 RIE: 3 CAT: 17

Heritage Center NC
CIJE: 0 RIE: 1 CAT: 17

Heritage College WA
CIJE: 0 RIE: 2 CAT: 17

Heritage Consistency
CIJE: 0 RIE: 1 CAT: 16

Heritage Foundation
CIJE: 2 RIE: 1 CAT: 17

Heritage Language
CIJE: 2 RIE: 8 CAT: 13
UF Ancestral Language

Herkimer County Community College NY
CIJE: 0 RIE: 2 CAT: 17

Herman (Alexis)
CIJE: 1 RIE: 0 CAT: 18

Hermes Satellite
CIJE: 0 RIE: 2 CAT: 20

Hermods Correspondence School (Sweden)
CIJE: 0 RIE: 1 CAT: 17

Hernandez (Jose)
CIJE: 3 RIE: 1 CAT: 18

Hernandez (Miguel)
CIJE: 1 RIE: 0 CAT: 18

Herndon (James)
CIJE: 1 RIE: 1 CAT: 18

Hernia
CIJE: 1 RIE: 0 CAT: 11

Herodotus
CIJE: 2 RIE: 0 CAT: 18

Heroes
CIJE: 56 RIE: 27 CAT: 10

Heroines
CIJE: 8 RIE: 4 CAT: 10

Herpes
CIJE: 6 RIE: 1 CAT: 11

Herpes Encephalitis
CIJE: 2 RIE: 0 CAT: 11

Herpes Simplex
CIJE: 3 RIE: 4 CAT: 11
UF Genital Herpes

Herpetology
CIJE: 4 RIE: 1 CAT: 20

Herrera y Reissig (Julio)
CIJE: 1 RIE: 0 CAT: 18

Herrick (Genevieve Forbes)
CIJE: 0 RIE: 1 CAT: 18

Herrmann Brain Dominance Survey
CIJE: 0 RIE: 2 CAT: 21

Herrnstein (Richard)
CIJE: 3 RIE: 1 CAT: 18

Hersey Blanchard Changing Skills Model
CIJE: 0 RIE: 1 CAT: 15

Hersey Blanchard Situational Leadership Model
CIJE: 7 RIE: 10 CAT: 15
UF Situational Leadership Mdl (Hersey and Blanchard)

Hershey Museum PA
CIJE: 0 RIE: 1 CAT: 17

Hershey Public Library PA
CIJE: 1 RIE: 0 CAT: 17

Hershey Video Training Courses
CIJE: 1 RIE: 0 CAT: 03

Herskovits (Melville Jean)
CIJE: 4 RIE: 1 CAT: 18

Hertfordshire Advisory Council Educational Tech
CIJE: 0 RIE: 1 CAT: 17

Hervey Law
CIJE: 1 RIE: 0 CAT: 20

Herzberg (Frederick)
CIJE: 21 RIE: 9 CAT: 18

Hesburgh (Theodore M)
CIJE: 1 RIE: 1 CAT: 18

Hesitation (Speech)
CIJE: 9 RIE: 5 CAT: 13

Hesquiat Project
CIJE: 1 RIE: 0 CAT: 19

Hess School Readiness Scale
CIJE: 1 RIE: 0 CAT: 21

Hesse (Hermann)
CIJE: 7 RIE: 3 CAT: 18

Hester (Al)
CIJE: 0 RIE: 1 CAT: 18

Hester (James M)
CIJE: 1 RIE: 0 CAT: 18

Hestian Feminism
CIJE: 0 RIE: 2 CAT: 15

Hestian Hermeneutics
CIJE: 0 RIE: 1 CAT: 13

Heterogeneity of Irrelevancy Assumption
CIJE: 0 RIE: 1 CAT: 15

Heterogeneity of Variance
CIJE: 8 RIE: 3 CAT: 20

Heterogeneous Classrooms
CIJE: 0 RIE: 4 CAT: 15

Heteroscedasticity (Statistics)
CIJE: 6 RIE: 2 CAT: 21

Heterosexuality
CIJE: 8 RIE: 4 CAT: 11

Heterosocial Competence
CIJE: 0 RIE: 1 CAT: 11

Hettinger Strength Chair
CIJE: 1 RIE: 0 CAT: 04

Heuristic Evaluation Problem Programer
CIJE: 1 RIE: 0 CAT: 04

Heuristic Procedure Modification
CIJE: 0 RIE: 1 CAT: 15

Heuristic Program Theory
USE Program Theory

Hewett (Frank)
CIJE: 3 RIE: 1 CAT: 18

Hewlett Packard Company
CIJE: 1 RIE: 0 CAT: 17

Hewlett Packard System
CIJE: 4 RIE: 3 CAT: 04

Hewlett Woodmere Public Library NY
CIJE: 0 RIE: 1 CAT: 17

Heym (Georg)
CIJE: 3 RIE: 0 CAT: 18

Heywood Cases
CIJE: 5 RIE: 1 CAT: 21

HH 3F Helicopter
CIJE: 0 RIE: 2 CAT: 04

HiB Disease
USE Hemophilus Influenza Type B

HiB Vaccine
USE Hemophilus Vaccines

Hibbing Community College MN
CIJE: 0 RIE: 1 CAT: 17

Hickok (Lorena A)
CIJE: 1 RIE: 1 CAT: 18

Hickory City School District NC
CIJE: 0 RIE: 0 CAT: 17

Hickory Township High School PA
CIJE: 1 RIE: 0 CAT: 17

Hicks (Thomas Holliday)
CIJE: 1 RIE: 0 CAT: 18

Hicks Cloze Reading Test
CIJE: 0 RIE: 1 CAT: 21

Hicksville Public Schools NY
CIJE: 0 RIE: 2 CAT: 17

HICOMP PreSchool Curriculum
CIJE: 0 RIE: 1 CAT: 03
SN HICOMP = "Higher Competencies in Communication, Own Care, Motor and Problem Solving"
UF Project HICOMP

Hidalgo Starr Adult Education Coop TX
CIJE: 0 RIE: 1 CAT: 17

Hidatsa
CIJE: 0 RIE: 2 CAT: 13
SN A Siouan language
UF Gros Ventre (North Dakota)

Hidatsa (Tribe)
CIJE: 2 RIE: 5 CAT: 08
UF Gros Ventre (North Dakota) (Tribe)

Hidden Figures Test
CIJE: 14 RIE: 12 CAT: 21

Hierarchical Analysis
CIJE: 29 RIE: 15 CAT: 21

Hierarchical Cluster Analysis
CIJE: 16 RIE: 6 CAT: 21
SN See also "Wards Hierarchical Cluster Analysis"

Hierarchical Cluster Structure
CIJE: 2 RIE: 2 CAT: 13

Hierarchical Control
CIJE: 2 RIE: 5 CAT: 16

Hierarchical Decision Models
CIJE: 4 RIE: 3 CAT: 15

Hierarchical Facet Model of Self Concept
USE Self Concept Model (Shavelson)

Hierarchical Focusing
CIJE: 1 RIE: 0 CAT: 15

Hierarchical Learning
CIJE: 19 RIE: 7 CAT: 11

Hierarchical Linear Modeling
CIJE: 9 RIE: 19 CAT: 15

Hierarchical Models
CIJE: 1 RIE: 1 CAT: 15

Hierarchical Structural Analysis
CIJE: 11 RIE: 3 CAT: 15

Higgins Wertman Test Threshold of Visual Closure
CIJE: 1 RIE: 1 CAT: 21

Higginsville State Sch Hospital Behavioral Scale
CIJE: 0 RIE: 1 CAT: 21

High Definition Television
CIJE: 1 RIE: 15 CAT: 20
UF HDTV

High Density Lipoprotein Cholesterol
CIJE: 1 RIE: 2 CAT: 11
SN See also "Low Density Lipoprotein Cholesterol"
UF Cholesterol HDL; HDL Cholesterol; Lipoproteins (HDL Cholesterol)

High Expectations Reading Program
CIJE: 0 RIE: 1 CAT: 19

High Fat Diet
CIJE: 0 RIE: 1 CAT: 11

High Fidelity Sound
CIJE: 1 RIE: 1 CAT: 20

High Intensity Learning Centers
CIJE: 0 RIE: 3 CAT: 05

High John Library MD
CIJE: 2 RIE: 2 CAT: 17

High Jump
CIJE: 1 RIE: 1 CAT: 16

High Level Figure Classification Test
CIJE: 0 RIE: 1 CAT: 21

High Performance Computing
CIJE: 1 RIE: 23 CAT: 20
SN See also "Supercomputers"

High Performance Computing Act 1991
CIJE: 1 RIE: 9 CAT: 14
UF Public Law 102 194

High Performance Computing and Commun Program
CIJE: 0 RIE: 2 CAT: 19

High Performance Manufacturing
CIJE: 0 RIE: 1 CAT: 20

High Performance Skills
CIJE: 1 RIE: 2 CAT: 16

High Performance Work Organizations
CIJE: 0 RIE: 1 CAT: 09

High Point City School District NC
CIJE: 0 RIE: 0 CAT: 17

High Point College NC
CIJE: 0 RIE: 2 CAT: 17

High Potential Program
CIJE: 1 RIE: 2 CAT: 19

High Pressure Sodium Lighting
CIJE: 1 RIE: 0 CAT: 20

High Priority Location Stipend Program FL
CIJE: 0 RIE: 0 CAT: 19

High Reliability Organizations
CIJE: 0 RIE: 1 CAT: 16

High Rise Buildings
CIJE: 3 RIE: 1 CAT: 05

High Risk Courses
CIJE: 0 RIE: 1 CAT: 03

High Risk Registry
CIJE: 0 RIE: 2 CAT: 11

High Risk Situations
CIJE: 6 RIE: 1 CAT: 11

High Roads Project
CIJE: 0 RIE: 1 CAT: 19

High School (Film)
CIJE: 0 RIE: 1 CAT: 22

High School A Report on Secondary Educ in America
CIJE: 1 RIE: 5 CAT: 22

High School Academies
CIJE: 1 RIE: 6 CAT: 19

High School and Beyond (NCES)
CIJE: 128 RIE: 254 CAT: 19

High School Awards Program
CIJE: 1 RIE: 0 CAT: 19

High School Characteristics Index
CIJE: 7 RIE: 3 CAT: 21
UF Stems High School Characteristics Index

High School Curriculum Center in Government IN
CIJE: 2 RIE: 0 CAT: 17

High School Entrance Examinations
CIJE: 3 RIE: 1 CAT: 21

High School Evening Institute (New Zealand)
CIJE: 1 RIE: 0 CAT: 17

High School for Health Professions TX
CIJE: 4 RIE: 0 CAT: 17

High School Geography Project
CIJE: 21 RIE: 39 CAT: 19

High School Graduation Requirements Law (NJ)
CIJE: 0 RIE: 0 CAT: 14
UF Chapter 241 (New Jersey)

High School Holding Power Index
CIJE: 0 RIE: 1 CAT: 21

High School Improvement Project MI
CIJE: 0 RIE: 3 CAT: 19

High School Independent Press Service
CIJE: 2 RIE: 0 CAT: 17

High School Juniors
CIJE: 7 RIE: 8 CAT: 10

High School Labor Studies Program
CIJE: 0 RIE: 1 CAT: 19

High School on TV
CIJE: 0 RIE: 1 CAT: 22

High School Personality Questionnaire
CIJE: 18 RIE: 2 CAT: 21

High School Political Science Curriculum Project
CIJE: 2 RIE: 31 CAT: 19

High School Psychology
CIJE: 0 RIE: 1 CAT: 03

High School Rank
CIJE: 0 RIE: 1 CAT: 15

High School Sophomores
CIJE: 3 RIE: 19 CAT: 10

High School Student Opinion Survey
CIJE: 0 RIE: 1 CAT: 21
UF ACT High School Student Opinion Survey

High School Study (University of Texas Austin)
CIJE: 0 RIE: 0 CAT: 19

High School Survey on Drugs
CIJE: 0 RIE: 1 CAT: 21

High School Transcript Study 1987
CIJE: 0 RIE: 6 CAT: 19
UF National Assessment of Educ Prog Transcrpt Stdy 87

High School Transcript Study 1990
CIJE: 0 RIE: 2 CAT: 19

High Schools That Work
CIJE: 0 RIE: 1 CAT: 19

High Scope Demonstration Preschool Project
CIJE: 11 RIE: 2 CAT: 19

High Scope Educational Research Foundation MI
CIJE: 1 RIE: 10 CAT: 17

High Scope Model
CIJE: 0 RIE: 2 CAT: 15

High Scope Open Framework
USE Open Framework Curriculum

High Scope Preschool Curriculum Study
CIJE: 3 RIE: 2 CAT: 19

High Scope Summer Workshop for Teenagers
CIJE: 1 RIE: 0 CAT: 02

High Stakes Testing
USE High Stakes Tests

High Stakes Tests
CIJE: 11 RIE: 21 CAT: 21
SN Tests with severe consequences for individual pupils, such as nonpromotion, or those used to rank schools and districts in the media
UF High Stakes Testing

High Success Program
CIJE: 0 RIE: 1 CAT: 19

High Sugar Foods
CIJE: 1 RIE: 0 CAT: 11

High Tech Centers (Disabled)
CIJE: 0 RIE: 1 CAT: 05

High Unemployment Areas
CIJE: 0 RIE: 1 CAT: 16

Highbury Technical College (England)
CIJE: 1 RIE: 0 CAT: 17

Higher Competencies Commun Own Care Motor Problem
CIJE: 0 RIE: 1 CAT: 03
SN "Higher Competencies in Communication, Own Care, Motor and Problem Solving"

Higher Educ Task Force on Imp and Reform Am Educ
CIJE: 1 RIE: 2 CAT: 17

Higher Education Achievement Program
CIJE: 1 RIE: 4 CAT: 19

Higher Education Act 1965
CIJE: 29 RIE: 152 CAT: 14

Higher Education Act 1980
CIJE: 5 RIE: 11 CAT: 14

Higher Education Act Amendments 1972
CIJE: 0 RIE: 1 CAT: 14
UF Public Law 92 318

Higher Education Act Amendments 1976
CIJE: 2 RIE: 4 CAT: 14

Higher Education Act Amendments 1981
CIJE: 0 RIE: 1 CAT: 14

Higher Education Act Amendments 1986
CIJE: 6 RIE: 9 CAT: 14
UF Public Law 99 498

Higher Education Act Amendments 1992
CIJE: 4 RIE: 10 CAT: 14
UF Public Law 102 325

Higher Education Act Title I
CIJE: 0 RIE: 57 CAT: 14

Higher Education Act Title II
CIJE: 6 RIE: 28 CAT: 14

Higher Education Act Title II B
CIJE: 0 RIE: 2 CAT: 14

Higher Education Act Title II D
CIJE: 0 RIE: 2 CAT: 14

Higher Education Act Title III
CIJE: 5 RIE: 41 CAT: 14
UF Institutional Aid Program Title III

Higher Education Act Title IV
CIJE: 6 RIE: 59 CAT: 14

Higher Education Act Title V
CIJE: 2 RIE: 4 CAT: 14

Higher Education Act Title VI
CIJE: 1 RIE: 10 CAT: 14

Higher Education Act Title VII
CIJE: 0 RIE: 2 CAT: 14

Higher Education Act Title VIII
CIJE: 3 RIE: 3 CAT: 14

Higher Education Act Title IX
CIJE: 1 RIE: 5 CAT: 14

Higher Education Act Title X
CIJE: 0 RIE: 1 CAT: 14

Higher Education Act Title XI
CIJE: 0 RIE: 2 CAT: 14
SN See also "Urban Grant University Program"

Higher Education Act Title XII 1972
CIJE: 0 RIE: 3 CAT: 14

Higher Education Amendments 1968
CIJE: 0 RIE: 1 CAT: 14

Higher Education Amendments 1979
CIJE: 0 RIE: 1 CAT: 14

Higher Education and the Handicapped
USE Project HEATH

Higher Education Assistance Foundation
CIJE: 2 RIE: 7 CAT: 17

Higher Education Career Questionnaire
CIJE: 0 RIE: 1 CAT: 21

Higher Education CETA Project
CIJE: 0 RIE: 10 CAT: 19

Higher Education Cooperation Act (Illinois)
CIJE: 2 RIE: 3 CAT: 14

Higher Education Facilities Act 1963
CIJE: 2 RIE: 4 CAT: 14

Higher Education for Adult Mental Health Project
CIJE: 1 RIE: 1 CAT: 19

Higher Education for Learning Disabled Students
CIJE: 0 RIE: 17 CAT: 19
UF HELDS Project

Higher Education General Information Survey
CIJE: 21 RIE: 105 CAT: 19
SN See add'l listings under "HEGIS..."
UF HEGIS

Higher Education Indicators Project
CIJE: 0 RIE: 3 CAT: 19

Higher Education Instructional Television Project
CIJE: 0 RIE: 1 CAT: 19

Higher Education Learning Projects (Physics)
CIJE: 1 RIE: 0 CAT: 19

Higher Education Loan Pool
CIJE: 0 RIE: 1 CAT: 17

Higher Education Location Program
CIJE: 0 RIE: 1 CAT: 19

Higher Education Long Range Planning Program
CIJE: 0 RIE: 1 CAT: 19

Higher Education Management Institute
CIJE: 2 RIE: 2 CAT: 17

Higher Education Opportunity Act 1970
CIJE: 1 RIE: 0 CAT: 14

Higher Education Opportunity Program
CIJE: 0 RIE: 34 CAT: 19

Higher Education Panel
CIJE: 0 RIE: 1 CAT: 17

Higher Education Personnel Training Programs
CIJE: 0 RIE: 1 CAT: 19

Higher Education Price Index
CIJE: 3 RIE: 13 CAT: 22

Higher Education Prison Program
CIJE: 0 RIE: 1 CAT: 19

Higher Education Research Institute
CIJE: 4 RIE: 1 CAT: 17

Higher Education Resource Service
CIJE: 3 RIE: 1 CAT: 17

Higher Education Utilization Study
CIJE: 2 RIE: 1 CAT: 19

Higher Educational Learning Program Survey
CIJE: 1 RIE: 0 CAT: 19

Higher Horizons Program
CIJE: 4 RIE: 34 CAT: 19

Higher Learning in America (Hutchins)
CIJE: 0 RIE: 1 CAT: 22

Higher National Certificate in Applied Physics
CIJE: 1 RIE: 0 CAT: 15

Higher Order Learning
CIJE: 27 RIE: 26 CAT: 11

Higher Order Need Strength Measure B
CIJE: 2 RIE: 0 CAT: 21

Higher Order Thinking Skills Model (McREL)
CIJE: 0 RIE: 0 CAT: 15
UF McREL Higher Order Thinking Skills Model

Highfield Program
CIJE: 0 RIE: 1 CAT: 19

Highland Community College IL
CIJE: 1 RIE: 2 CAT: 17

Highland Park Free School MA
CIJE: 1 RIE: 0 CAT: 17

Highland Park Project
CIJE: 0 RIE: 1 CAT: 19

Highland Park Township High School District IL
CIJE: 2 RIE: 0 CAT: 17

Highland Public Schools IN
CIJE: 0 RIE: 1 CAT: 17

Highland School CT
CIJE: 1 RIE: 0 CAT: 17

Highlander Folk School TN
CIJE: 12 RIE: 8 CAT: 17

Highlighting (Text)
CIJE: 0 RIE: 1 CAT: 16

Highline Community College WA
CIJE: 0 RIE: 2 CAT: 17

Highline Indian Tutoring Program WA
CIJE: 0 RIE: 1 CAT: 19

Highline Public Schools WA
CIJE: 0 RIE: 4 CAT: 17

Highline School District WA
CIJE: 3 RIE: 4 CAT: 17

Highly Gifted
CIJE: 1 RIE: 1 CAT: 10
SN See also "Extremely Gifted" and "Exceptionally Gifted"

Highway Maintenance
CIJE: 0 RIE: 11 CAT: 16

Highway Safety
CIJE: 2 RIE: 26 CAT: 16

Highway Surveying
CIJE: 0 RIE: 1 CAT: 09

Highways
CIJE: 1 RIE: 6 CAT: 20

Hijazi (Urban Dialect)
CIJE: 0 RIE: 1 CAT: 13

Hiking
CIJE: 13 RIE: 14 CAT: 16

Hiligaynon
CIJE: 0 RIE: 3 CAT: 13

Hill (Adams Sherman)
CIJE: 1 RIE: 0 CAT: 18

Hill (Joseph)
CIJE: 1 RIE: 3 CAT: 18

Hill Cognitive Style Mapping Inventory
CIJE: 4 RIE: 2 CAT: 21

Hill Counselor Verbal Response Category System
CIJE: 1 RIE: 0 CAT: 21

Hill School PA
CIJE: 1 RIE: 0 CAT: 17

Hill Street Blues
CIJE: 1 RIE: 1 CAT: 22

Hill Top Preparatory School PA
CIJE: 1 RIE: 1 CAT: 17

Hillcrest High School NY
CIJE: 2 RIE: 0 CAT: 17

Hillcroft College
CIJE: 1 RIE: 0 CAT: 17

Hillsboro Deering Cooperative School District NH
CIJE: 0 RIE: 1 CAT: 17

Hillsborough Community College FL
CIJE: 1 RIE: 2 CAT: 17

Hillsborough County Public Schools FL
CIJE: 1 RIE: 10 CAT: 17

Hillsborough Early Rating Scale
CIJE: 0 RIE: 1 CAT: 21

Hillsdale College MI
CIJE: 4 RIE: 3 CAT: 17

Hillside Outdoor Education Center NY
CIJE: 0 RIE: 1 CAT: 17

Hillside Public Library NY
CIJE: 0 RIE: 1 CAT: 17

Hilprecht (Herman)
CIJE: 0 RIE: 1 CAT: 18

Hilroy Fellowship Program
CIJE: 0 RIE: 1 CAT: 19

Hilson Adolescent Profile
CIJE: 0 RIE: 1 CAT: 21

Hilton United Corporation
CIJE: 0 RIE: 1 CAT: 17

Hinckley College of Further Education (England)
CIJE: 0 RIE: 1 CAT: 17

Hinckleys Attitude Toward the Negro Scale
CIJE: 0 RIE: 1 CAT: 21

Hindi (Literary)
CIJE: 1 RIE: 2 CAT: 13

Hindi (Suddh)
CIJE: 1 RIE: 2 CAT: 13

Hindi Speaking
CIJE: 4 RIE: 0 CAT: 08

Hinds (John)
CIJE: 0 RIE: 1 CAT: 18

Hinds County School District MS
CIJE: 0 RIE: 1 CAT: 17

Hindu Creativity Theory
CIJE: 1 RIE: 0 CAT: 15

Hinduism
CIJE: 7 RIE: 25 CAT: 16

Hindustani
CIJE: 0 RIE: 4 CAT: 13

Hine (Lewis Wickes)
CIJE: 1 RIE: 1 CAT: 18

Hinsdale School Districts IL
CIJE: 3 RIE: 0 CAT: 17

Hinting
CIJE: 1 RIE: 1 CAT: 11

Hip Flexion
CIJE: 2 RIE: 1 CAT: 11

Hip Hop Generation
CIJE: 0 RIE: 1 CAT: 10

Hippies
CIJE: 9 RIE: 6 CAT: 10

HIPPS Method
CIJE: 0 RIE: 1 CAT: 15
SN HIPPS = Hypothesis, Involvement, Participation, Practice, and Sharing

Hiptionary
CIJE: 0 RIE: 1 CAT: 13

Hiram College OH
CIJE: 0 RIE: 7 CAT: 17

Hire the Handicapped Law (Michigan)
CIJE: 0 RIE: 1 CAT: 14

Hired Farm Working Force Survey
CIJE: 0 RIE: 1 CAT: 22

Hiroshima No Pika (Maruki)
CIJE: 0 RIE: 1 CAT: 22

Hiroshima University (Japan)
CIJE: 1 RIE: 1 CAT: 17

Hirsch (E D)
CIJE: 67 RIE: 15 CAT: 18
SN "E.D., Jr."

Hirschi (Travis)
CIJE: 3 RIE: 0 CAT: 18

Hirschman (Albert)
CIJE: 1 RIE: 0 CAT: 18

Hirst (Paul)
CIJE: 13 RIE: 2 CAT: 18

His Enemy His Friend
CIJE: 1 RIE: 0 CAT: 22

Hishkaryana
USE Hixkaryana

Hiskey Nebraska Test of Learning Aptitude
CIJE: 9 RIE: 4 CAT: 21

Hispanic American Achievement
CIJE: 1 RIE: 8 CAT: 16

Hispanic American Education
CIJE: 0 RIE: 14 CAT: 16

Hispanic American Students
CIJE: 11 RIE: 142 CAT: 10

Hispanic American Teachers
CIJE: 1 RIE: 1 CAT: 09

Hispanic American Youth
CIJE: 3 RIE: 0 CAT: 10

Hispanic Arts
CIJE: 0 RIE: 1 CAT: 16

Hispanic Association of Colleges and Universities
CIJE: 4 RIE: 0 CAT: 17

Hispanic Foundation
CIJE: 0 RIE: 1 CAT: 17

Hispanic Heritage Week
CIJE: 0 RIE: 1 CAT: 12

Hispanic Higher Education Coalition
CIJE: 3 RIE: 0 CAT: 17

Hispanic Languages
CIJE: 1 RIE: 1 CAT: 13

Hispanic Literature
CIJE: 3 RIE: 3 CAT: 16

Hispanic Research Center NY
CIJE: 0 RIE: 1 CAT: 17

Hispanic Urban Center Inservice Program
CIJE: 0 RIE: 1 CAT: 19

Hiss (Alger)
CIJE: 0 RIE: 2 CAT: 18

Histiocytosis X
CIJE: 1 RIE: 0 CAT: 11

Histograms
CIJE: 3 RIE: 1 CAT: 15

Histology
CIJE: 3 RIE: 6 CAT: 20

Historians
CIJE: 87 RIE: 14 CAT: 09

Historias de la Artamila
CIJE: 0 RIE: 1 CAT: 22

Historic Sites
CIJE: 21 RIE: 43 CAT: 12
UF Historical Sites

Historical Background
CIJE: 357 RIE: 169 CAT: 16

Historical Bibliography
CIJE: 5 RIE: 8 CAT: 16

Historical Distortion
CIJE: 10 RIE: 1 CAT: 16

Historical Explanation
CIJE: 12 RIE: 12 CAT: 19

Historical Fiction
CIJE: 66 RIE: 20 CAT: 16

Historical Geology
CIJE: 4 RIE: 0 CAT: 03

Historical Influences
CIJE: 54 RIE: 12 CAT: 12

Historical Interpretation
CIJE: 19 RIE: 4 CAT: 15

Historical Landmarks
CIJE: 7 RIE: 23 CAT: 12
SN See also "National Historic Landmarks Program"

Historical Materials
CIJE: 55 RIE: 26 CAT: 16

Historical Methods
CIJE: 70 RIE: 22 CAT: 15

Historical Novels
CIJE: 16 RIE: 1 CAT: 16

Historical Present Tense
CIJE: 2 RIE: 0 CAT: 13

Historical Preservation
CIJE: 4 RIE: 3 CAT: 16

Historical Research
CIJE: 52 RIE: 5 CAT: 15

Historical Rhetoric
CIJE: 20 RIE: 5 CAT: 13

Historical Sites
USE Historic Sites

Historical Societies
CIJE: 5 RIE: 3 CAT: 05

Historical Trends State Educ Facts 1969 to 1989
CIJE: 0 RIE: 1 CAT: 22

History Education Project
CIJE: 1 RIE: 5 CAT: 19

History of British Primary Schools
CIJE: 0 RIE: 1 CAT: 22

History of King Richard III
CIJE: 1 RIE: 0 CAT: 22

Hit Steer System
CIJE: 0 RIE: 1 CAT: 15

Hitchcock (Alfred)
CIJE: 4 RIE: 1 CAT: 18

Hitchcock (Orra White)
CIJE: 0 RIE: 1 CAT: 18

Hitchhiking
CIJE: 2 RIE: 0 CAT: 16

Hitler (Adolf)
CIJE: 21 RIE: 8 CAT: 18

Hitting Behavior (Aggression)
CIJE: 1 RIE: 0 CAT: 11

Hiwassee College TN
CIJE: 1 RIE: 0 CAT: 17

Hixkaryana
CIJE: 0 RIE: 1 CAT: 13
SN Language spoken on the Nhamunda River, northern Brazil
UF Hishkaryana

Hiz (Henri)
CIJE: 1 RIE: 0 CAT: 18

HLM Computer Program
CIJE: 0 RIE: 2 CAT: 04

Hoarseness
CIJE: 1 RIE: 0 CAT: 11

Hobbes (Thomas)
CIJE: 7 RIE: 6 CAT: 18

Hobbit
CIJE: 2 RIE: 0 CAT: 22

Hobbs (N)
CIJE: 3 RIE: 0 CAT: 18

Hobby Accomplishment Information Questionnaire
CIJE: 0 RIE: 1 CAT: 21

Hobson (Julius)
CIJE: 0 RIE: 3 CAT: 18

Hobson (Peter)
CIJE: 1 RIE: 0 CAT: 18

Hobson v Hansen
CIJE: 3 RIE: 7 CAT: 14

Hodgkinson (Harold L)
CIJE: 0 RIE: 1 CAT: 18

Hoechst A G
CIJE: 0 RIE: 1 CAT: 17

Hoegskolan (Kungliga Tekniska)
CIJE: 0 RIE: 1 CAT: 18

Hoffer (Eric)
CIJE: 1 RIE: 0 CAT: 18

Hoffer (Thomas)
CIJE: 0 RIE: 1 CAT: 18

Hoffman (Abbie)
CIJE: 2 RIE: 0 CAT: 18

Hoffman (David)
CIJE: 1 RIE: 0 CAT: 18

Hoffman (Malvina)
CIJE: 0 RIE: 1 CAT: 18

Hoffman Bilingual Schedule
CIJE: 0 RIE: 1 CAT: 21

Hoffman Mathematics System
CIJE: 0 RIE: 1 CAT: 19

Hoffmann (Ernst Theodor Amadeus)
CIJE: 4 RIE: 0 CAT: 18

Hoffmann (Hans G)
CIJE: 3 RIE: 0 CAT: 18

Hofman (A W)
CIJE: 1 RIE: 0 CAT: 18

Hofmannsthal (Hugo von)
CIJE: 3 RIE: 0 CAT: 18

Hofstadter (Richard)
CIJE: 3 RIE: 1 CAT: 18

Hofstede (Geert)
CIJE: 0 RIE: 1 CAT: 18

Hofstra University NY
CIJE: 15 RIE: 50 CAT: 17

Hogan Empathy Scale
CIJE: 0 RIE: 3 CAT: 21

Hoge (Moses Drury)
CIJE: 0 RIE: 1 CAT: 18

Hogg Foundation for Mental Health TX
CIJE: 0 RIE: 1 CAT: 17

Hogs
CIJE: 0 RIE: 8 CAT: 20

Hoists
CIJE: 0 RIE: 1 CAT: 04

Hokulea
CIJE: 0 RIE: 2 CAT: 12
SN Famous voyaging canoe

Holborn Reading Analysis Test
CIJE: 0 RIE: 1 CAT: 21

Holbrook (Josiah)
CIJE: 0 RIE: 1 CAT: 18

Holdaway (Don)
CIJE: 0 RIE: 1 CAT: 18

Holdeman Mennonites
CIJE: 1 RIE: 0 CAT: 08

Holden (Matthew)
CIJE: 0 RIE: 1 CAT: 18

Holderlin (Friedrich)
CIJE: 3 RIE: 0 CAT: 18

Holding of Infants
CIJE: 2 RIE: 2 CAT: 11
UF Infant Holding

Holding Power Project
CIJE: 0 RIE: 2 CAT: 19

Holdings Statements
CIJE: 1 RIE: 1 CAT: 16

Holiday Art Lessons
CIJE: 2 RIE: 0 CAT: 16

Holism
CIJE: 7 RIE: 2 CAT: 15

Holistic Construal Validation Method
CIJE: 1 RIE: 0 CAT: 15

Holistic Education
CIJE: 16 RIE: 8 CAT: 03

Holland
USE Netherlands

Holland (John L)
CIJE: 23 RIE: 18 CAT: 18

Holland (Milton M)
CIJE: 0 RIE: 1 CAT: 18

Holland (Norman)
CIJE: 4 RIE: 0 CAT: 18

Holland College (Canada)
CIJE: 5 RIE: 1 CAT: 17

Holland Day Care Center MI
CIJE: 0 RIE: 1 CAT: 17

Holland Land Company
CIJE: 0 RIE: 2 CAT: 17

Holland Occupational Classification System
CIJE: 1 RIE: 1 CAT: 15

Holland Park School (England)
CIJE: 1 RIE: 0 CAT: 17

Holland Self Directed Search
CIJE: 31 RIE: 10 CAT: 21

Holland Skinner Psychology Course
CIJE: 0 RIE: 1 CAT: 03

Holland Theory of Occupational Choice
USE Hollands Theory of Occupational Choice

Holland Vocational Preference Inventory
CIJE: 76 RIE: 29 CAT: 21

Hollander (Lorin)
CIJE: 1 RIE: 0 CAT: 18

Hollands Hexagonal Model
CIJE: 14 RIE: 6 CAT: 15

Hollands Theory of Occupational Choice
CIJE: 61 RIE: 28 CAT: 15
UF Holland Theory of Occupational Choice

Hollingshead Social Economic Status Measures
CIJE: 2 RIE: 8 CAT: 21

Hollingshead Two Factor Index of Social Position
CIJE: 5 RIE: 3 CAT: 21

Hollingworth (Leta Stetter)
CIJE: 24 RIE: 2 CAT: 18

Hollins College VA
CIJE: 2 RIE: 4 CAT: 17

Hollywood Film Classics
USE Classical Hollywood Films

Hollywood Perspective Method
CIJE: 1 RIE: 0 CAT: 15

Holmes Group
CIJE: 41 RIE: 21 CAT: 17

Holmes Group Report
CIJE: 69 RIE: 20 CAT: 22
UF Tomorrows Teachers

Holmes Readjustment Rating Scale
CIJE: 2 RIE: 1 CAT: 21

Holmesburg Project
CIJE: 6 RIE: 0 CAT: 19

Holocaust
CIJE: 113 RIE: 45 CAT: 12

Holocaust Literature
CIJE: 13 RIE: 6 CAT: 16

Holocaust Survivors
USE Survivors of Nazi Persecution

Holst (Gustav)
CIJE: 1 RIE: 0 CAT: 18

Holt (John)
CIJE: 6 RIE: 3 CAT: 18

Holt Basic Reading System
CIJE: 0 RIE: 2 CAT: 22

Holt Mathematics Series
CIJE: 0 RIE: 1 CAT: 22

Holt Rinehart Winston Company
CIJE: 2 RIE: 2 CAT: 17

Holtville High School AL
CIJE: 0 RIE: 1 CAT: 17

Holtzman Inkblot Technique
CIJE: 9 RIE: 3 CAT: 21

Holtzman Project
CIJE: 5 RIE: 1 CAT: 19

Holyoke Public Schools MA
CIJE: 0 RIE: 2 CAT: 17

Holz (J C)
CIJE: 1 RIE: 0 CAT: 18

Hombitzer (E)
CIJE: 1 RIE: 0 CAT: 18

Homburg (Prinz Friedrich von)
CIJE: 1 RIE: 0 CAT: 18

Home and School (Canada)
CIJE: 1 RIE: 0 CAT: 17

Home and School Association
CIJE: 1 RIE: 0 CAT: 17

Home and School Institute DC
CIJE: 2 RIE: 0 CAT: 17

Home Based Employment
CIJE: 14 RIE: 12 CAT: 16

Home Based Programs
CIJE: 14 RIE: 13 CAT: 19
SN See also "Center Based Programs" and "Field Based Programs"

Home Bilingual Usage Estimate
CIJE: 0 RIE: 3 CAT: 21

Home Builders Institute
CIJE: 0 RIE: 1 CAT: 17

Home Care (Adults)
USE Home Health Care

Home Care (Children)
USE Home Child Care

Home Child Care
CIJE: 15 RIE: 16 CAT: 11
UF Home Care (Children)

Home Child Care Training Project
CIJE: 1 RIE: 0 CAT: 19

Home Community Based Model
CIJE: 1 RIE: 0 CAT: 15

Home Computer Based Learning Systems
CIJE: 2 RIE: 1 CAT: 04

Home Computers
CIJE: 32 RIE: 6 CAT: 04

Home Curriculum
CIJE: 0 RIE: 3 CAT: 03

Home Economics Education Association
CIJE: 0 RIE: 2 CAT: 17

Home Economics Related Occupations
CIJE: 4 RIE: 21 CAT: 09

Home Economics Rural Service NM
CIJE: 0 RIE: 1 CAT: 17

Home Economists
CIJE: 32 RIE: 2 CAT: 09

Home Economists Assistants
CIJE: 0 RIE: 1 CAT: 09

Home Economists in Homemaking
CIJE: 2 RIE: 0 CAT: 17

Home Education Livelihood Program
CIJE: 1 RIE: 1 CAT: 19

Home Educational Environment Index (Dolan)
USE Dolan Home Educational Environment Scale

Home Entertainment Equipment
CIJE: 2 RIE: 1 CAT: 04

Home Environment Review
CIJE: 0 RIE: 1 CAT: 21

Home Environment Review (Garber)
CIJE: 2 RIE: 2 CAT: 21

Home Environmental Process Interview
CIJE: 1 RIE: 0 CAT: 21

Home Equity Conversion
CIJE: 2 RIE: 6 CAT: 16

Home Equity Conversion Project
CIJE: 0 RIE: 1 CAT: 19

Home Evaluation Questionnaires
CIJE: 0 RIE: 1 CAT: 21

Home Health Aide Pilot Training Project
CIJE: 0 RIE: 2 CAT: 19

Home Health Care
CIJE: 9 RIE: 7 CAT: 11
UF Home Care (Adults)

Home Improvement
CIJE: 0 RIE: 6 CAT: 03

Home Index
CIJE: 2 RIE: 0 CAT: 21

Home Industry
USE Cottage Industry

Home Information Scale
CIJE: 1 RIE: 0 CAT: 21

Home Information Systems
CIJE: 1 RIE: 2 CAT: 04

Home Instruction Program Preschool Youngsters
CIJE: 1 RIE: 3 CAT: 19

Home Integrative Communications Systems
CIJE: 0 RIE: 1 CAT: 04

Home Language Survey
CIJE: 0 RIE: 2 CAT: 21

Home Learning Center IN
CIJE: 0 RIE: 1 CAT: 17

Home Learning Center Project
CIJE: 0 RIE: 1 CAT: 19

Home Learning Environment Profile
CIJE: 0 RIE: 1 CAT: 21

Home Libraries
USE Personal Libraries

Home Life Scale Adapted for University Men
CIJE: 1 RIE: 0 CAT: 21

Home Market
CIJE: 1 RIE: 1 CAT: 16

Home Observation for Measurement of Environment
CIJE: 30 RIE: 5 CAT: 21

Home Oriented Preschool Education Program
CIJE: 0 RIE: 13 CAT: 19
UF Project HOPE (Appalachia)

Home Pregnancy Test Kits
CIJE: 0 RIE: 1 CAT: 11
UF Pregnancy Test Kits (Home)

Home Recording
CIJE: 0 RIE: 1 CAT: 20

Home Repair
CIJE: 2 RIE: 3 CAT: 20

Home Rule Act (District of Columbia)
CIJE: 0 RIE: 1 CAT: 14

Home Scale
CIJE: 0 RIE: 1 CAT: 21

Home School Communication Program
CIJE: 1 RIE: 0 CAT: 19

Home School Community Relations Project
CIJE: 0 RIE: 5 CAT: 19

Home School Community Systems
CIJE: 0 RIE: 3 CAT: 15

Home School Study of Language and Literacy Dev MA
CIJE: 0 RIE: 1 CAT: 19

Home Secrets Program
CIJE: 0 RIE: 2 CAT: 19

Home Security
CIJE: 0 RIE: 1 CAT: 20

Home Start Program
CIJE: 8 RIE: 54 CAT: 19

Home Stimulation Inventory (Caldwell)
CIJE: 0 RIE: 2 CAT: 21

Home Stimulation Scale (Wachs et al)
CIJE: 1 RIE: 0 CAT: 21

Home Study Program Inc
CIJE: 1 RIE: 0 CAT: 17

Home Visitors
CIJE: 12 RIE: 3 CAT: 10

Homebuilders WA
CIJE: 0 RIE: 1 CAT: 19
SN An intensive inhome program to prevent the out-of-home placement of children

Homecoming (Pinter)
CIJE: 0 RIE: 2 CAT: 22

Homeless Shelters
USE Shelters

Homeostasis
CIJE: 6 RIE: 2 CAT: 20

Homer
CIJE: 16 RIE: 6 CAT: 18

Homer Price and the Doughnut Machine
CIJE: 1 RIE: 0 CAT: 22

Homerooms
CIJE: 2 RIE: 4 CAT: 05

Homerton College of Education (England)
CIJE: 1 RIE: 0 CAT: 17

Homesharing Project
CIJE: 0 RIE: 1 CAT: 19

Homesickness
CIJE: 3 RIE: 2 CAT: 11

Homestays
CIJE: 0 RIE: 1 CAT: 16

Homestead Ecology Experience
CIJE: 0 RIE: 1 CAT: 15

Homesteading
CIJE: 2 RIE: 2 CAT: 16

Homeward Bound
CIJE: 0 RIE: 1 CAT: 19

Homewood Flossmoor High School IL
CIJE: 1 RIE: 0 CAT: 17

Homework Assistance Programs
CIJE: 2 RIE: 4 CAT: 19

Homework Helper Program
CIJE: 1 RIE: 7 CAT: 19

Homiletics
CIJE: 2 RIE: 1 CAT: 03

Homogamy
CIJE: 2 RIE: 0 CAT: 20

Homogeneity of Regression
CIJE: 5 RIE: 4 CAT: 16

Homogeneity of Variance
CIJE: 17 RIE: 8 CAT: 16

Homographs
CIJE: 3 RIE: 7 CAT: 13

Homology
CIJE: 5 RIE: 0 CAT: 16

Homomorphisms
CIJE: 1 RIE: 0 CAT: 20

Homonemes
CIJE: 0 RIE: 1 CAT: 13

Homonyms
CIJE: 12 RIE: 12 CAT: 13

Homophily
CIJE: 11 RIE: 9 CAT: 16

Homophones
CIJE: 12 RIE: 8 CAT: 13

Homoscedasticity (Statistics)
CIJE: 4 RIE: 1 CAT: 21

Homosexual Literature
CIJE: 11 RIE: 11 CAT: 16
SN See also "Lesbian Literature"
UF Gay Literature

Homosexual Parents
CIJE: 2 RIE: 3 CAT: 10
UF Gay Parents

Homosexual Teachers
CIJE: 0 RIE: 2 CAT: 10
UF Gay Teachers

Honda of America
CIJE: 1 RIE: 1 CAT: 17

Honduras
CIJE: 10 RIE: 38 CAT: 07

Honesty
CIJE: 45 RIE: 14 CAT: 16

Honeycombs
CIJE: 0 RIE: 1 CAT: 20

Honeywell Computers
CIJE: 3 RIE: 1 CAT: 04

Honeywell Inc
CIJE: 10 RIE: 6 CAT: 17

Hong Kong
CIJE: 233 RIE: 144 CAT: 07

Honig v Doe
CIJE: 9 RIE: 1 CAT: 14

Honolulu Community College HI
USE University of Hawaii Honolulu Community College

Honolulu School District HI
CIJE: 1 RIE: 4 CAT: 17

Honolulu Youth Symphony Concerts HI
CIJE: 0 RIE: 1 CAT: 19

Honor
CIJE: 0 RIE: 1 CAT: 16

Honorary Degrees
CIJE: 4 RIE: 3 CAT: 16

Hood College MD
CIJE: 6 RIE: 3 CAT: 17

Hook Technique
CIJE: 2 RIE: 0 CAT: 15

Hooke (Robert)
CIJE: 2 RIE: 0 CAT: 18

Hooke Law
CIJE: 6 RIE: 0 CAT: 20

hooks (bell)
CIJE: 3 RIE: 2 CAT: 18

Hooks (Benjamin L)
CIJE: 0 RIE: 1 CAT: 18

Hooks (Robert)
CIJE: 1 RIE: 0 CAT: 18

Hoopa
USE Hupa

Hoopa (Tribe)
USE Hupa (Tribe)

Hoover (Herbert)
CIJE: 5 RIE: 1 CAT: 18

Hoover (J Edgar)
CIJE: 1 RIE: 3 CAT: 18

Hoover Institution on War Revolution and Peace
CIJE: 1 RIE: 2 CAT: 17

Hope
CIJE: 13 RIE: 5 CAT: 11

Hope College MI
CIJE: 6 RIE: 8 CAT: 17

Hope Commission Report
CIJE: 0 RIE: 1 CAT: 22

Hope School for Blind Multihandicapped Children IL
CIJE: 0 RIE: 1 CAT: 17

Hopelessness
CIJE: 39 RIE: 5 CAT: 11

Hopelessness Scale
CIJE: 8 RIE: 0 CAT: 21

Hopkins County School District KY
CIJE: 0 RIE: 1 CAT: 17

Hopkins Enhancement Survey
CIJE: 0 RIE: 1 CAT: 21

Hopkins School District MN
CIJE: 1 RIE: 2 CAT: 17

Hopkins Symptom Check List
CIJE: 0 RIE: 1 CAT: 11

Hopkinson (Francis)
CIJE: 1 RIE: 1 CAT: 18

Hopkinsville Community College KY
CIJE: 0 RIE: 2 CAT: 17

Hopper (Edward)
CIJE: 2 RIE: 0 CAT: 18

Horace
CIJE: 3 RIE: 0 CAT: 18

Horace Mann League v Board of Public Works
CIJE: 1 RIE: 0 CAT: 14

Horace Mann Lincoln Inst of School Experimentation
CIJE: 0 RIE: 0 CAT: 17

Horace Mann School for the Deaf MA
CIJE: 0 RIE: 2 CAT: 17

Horaces Compromise
CIJE: 4 RIE: 0 CAT: 22
SN "Horace's Compromise: The Dilemma of the American High School"

HORIZONS Program IL
CIJE: 0 RIE: 1 CAT: 19
SN A program administered by the Illinois Occupational Information Coordinating Committee to provide occupational and education information useful to both youth and adults who are making career decisions

Horizontal Articulation
CIJE: 1 RIE: 0 CAT: 13

Horizontal Decalage
CIJE: 2 RIE: 1 CAT: 11
SN Discrepancy in one's mastery of formally similar tasks

Horizontal Evaluation
CIJE: 4 RIE: 2 CAT: 15

Horizontal Sorting
CIJE: 0 RIE: 1 CAT: 15

Horizontal Vertical Illusion
CIJE: 1 RIE: 0 CAT: 11

Horizontality (Concept)
CIJE: 13 RIE: 7 CAT: 16

Horkheimer (Max)
CIJE: 0 RIE: 1 CAT: 18

Hormone Abnormalities
CIJE: 1 RIE: 0 CAT: 11

Hormones
CIJE: 27 RIE: 5 CAT: 11

Horn (Robert E)
CIJE: 1 RIE: 0 CAT: 18

Horn Book Magazine
CIJE: 5 RIE: 3 CAT: 22

Hornby (A S)
CIJE: 1 RIE: 0 CAT: 18

Horner (Matina)
CIJE: 5 RIE: 3 CAT: 18

Horner (Winifred Bryan)
CIJE: 0 RIE: 1 CAT: 18

Horner Scoring System for Fear of Success
CIJE: 4 RIE: 1 CAT: 21

Horney (Karen)
CIJE: 1 RIE: 2 CAT: 18

Horowitz v Curators of University of Missouri
CIJE: 1 RIE: 0 CAT: 14

Horror Fiction
CIJE: 1 RIE: 1 CAT: 16
UF Horror Stories

Horror Films
CIJE: 18 RIE: 2 CAT: 16

Horror Stories
USE Horror Fiction

Horse Management
USE Equine Management

Horseheads Central School District NY
CIJE: 1 RIE: 0 CAT: 17

Horseshoe Crabs
CIJE: 2 RIE: 0 CAT: 20

Horseshoe Pitching
CIJE: 0 RIE: 1 CAT: 16

Horticultural Growth Tables
CIJE: 1 RIE: 0 CAT: 21

Horticulture Therapy
CIJE: 0 RIE: 3 CAT: 11

Horton (Myles)
CIJE: 5 RIE: 2 CAT: 18

Horton v Goose Creek Independent School District
CIJE: 1 RIE: 0 CAT: 14

Hortonville School Dist v Hortonville Educ Assn
CIJE: 0 RIE: 2 CAT: 14

Horvitz Thompson Estimator
CIJE: 0 RIE: 1 CAT: 21

Hose Makers (Rubber Goods)
CIJE: 0 RIE: 1 CAT: 09

Hoses (Water)
CIJE: 0 RIE: 1 CAT: 04

Hosic (James Fleming)
CIJE: 1 RIE: 0 CAT: 18

Hosiery Workers
CIJE: 0 RIE: 6 CAT: 09

Hoso Bunka Foundation
CIJE: 1 RIE: 0 CAT: 17

Hospice Care
CIJE: 6 RIE: 6 CAT: 11

Hospital Administration
CIJE: 5 RIE: 2 CAT: 11

Hospital Based Corporate Child Care
CIJE: 1 RIE: 1 CAT: 11

Hospital Education Directors
CIJE: 0 RIE: 1 CAT: 09

Hospital Ethics Committees
CIJE: 0 RIE: 2 CAT: 10

Hospital Improvement Program
CIJE: 0 RIE: 1 CAT: 19

Hospital Industries Program ME
CIJE: 0 RIE: 1 CAT: 19

Hospital Literature Index
CIJE: 0 RIE: 1 CAT: 22

Hospital Readmission
CIJE: 1 RIE: 1 CAT: 11

Hospital Therapy
CIJE: 2 RIE: 0 CAT: 11

Hospital Training
CIJE: 0 RIE: 1 CAT: 11

Hospital Ward Administration
CIJE: 0 RIE: 2 CAT: 11

Hospitality Education
CIJE: 1 RIE: 11 CAT: 03

Hospitalization Proneness Scale
CIJE: 1 RIE: 0 CAT: 21

Host Families
CIJE: 0 RIE: 4 CAT: 10

Host Nation Programs
CIJE: 0 RIE: 7 CAT: 19

Host Schools (Tournaments)
USE Tournament Hosts

Host Selling Television Commercials
CIJE: 0 RIE: 2 CAT: 16
SN Television commercials that feature the same primary characters as those in the adjacent program content — see also "Program Length Commercials"

Hostage Negotiations
CIJE: 1 RIE: 0 CAT: 16

Hostage Taking
CIJE: 0 RIE: 1 CAT: 16

Hostels
CIJE: 1 RIE: 4 CAT: 05

Hostos (Eugenio Maria de)
CIJE: 0 RIE: 1 CAT: 18

Hostos Community College NY
USE City University of New York Hostos Community Coll

Hostrop v Board of Junior College District
CIJE: 1 RIE: 1 CAT: 14

Hosts Hostesses
CIJE: 0 RIE: 1 CAT: 09

HOSTS Program
USE Helping One Student To Succeed

Hot Deck Procedures
CIJE: 0 RIE: 1 CAT: 21

Hot Mill Operators
CIJE: 0 RIE: 1 CAT: 09

Hot Springs Project
CIJE: 1 RIE: 0 CAT: 19

Hot Wheels Cars (Game)
CIJE: 1 RIE: 1 CAT: 16

Hotchkiss School CT
CIJE: 0 RIE: 1 CAT: 17

Hotellings t
CIJE: 4 RIE: 5 CAT: 21

Hotevilla Bacavi Community School AZ
CIJE: 0 RIE: 1 CAT: 17

Hothousing of Preschoolers
CIJE: 6 RIE: 3 CAT: 11
UF Early Formal Education for the Very Young; Very Early Intensive Preschool Education

Hough Community Project
CIJE: 0 RIE: 1 CAT: 19

Hough Duncan Observation System
CIJE: 0 RIE: 1 CAT: 21

Houghton Committee (Great Britain)
CIJE: 1 RIE: 0 CAT: 17

Houghton Mifflin Company
CIJE: 0 RIE: 1 CAT: 17

Houghton Mifflin Elementary Mathematics Series
CIJE: 0 RIE: 2 CAT: 22

Houghton Mifflin Informal Reading Inventory
CIJE: 0 RIE: 1 CAT: 21

Houghton Mifflin Reading Series
CIJE: 1 RIE: 8 CAT: 22

Houghton Mifflin Student Progress Survey
CIJE: 0 RIE: 1 CAT: 21

Houle (Cyril O)
CIJE: 8 RIE: 8 CAT: 18

Houma (Tribe)
CIJE: 4 RIE: 1 CAT: 08

Housatonic Community College CT
CIJE: 0 RIE: 2 CAT: 17

Housatonic Regional Community College CT
CIJE: 1 RIE: 0 CAT: 17

House Arrest
CIJE: 2 RIE: 1 CAT: 14

House Bill 72 (Texas 1984)
CIJE: 0 RIE: 6 CAT: 14
UF Texas Education Opportunity Act 1984; Texas Education Reform Bill 1984

House Bill 1187 (Colorado 1985)
CIJE: 0 RIE: 2 CAT: 14

House Bill 1706 (Oklahoma 1981)
CIJE: 1 RIE: 0 CAT: 14

House Bill 2020 (Oregon 1987)
CIJE: 0 RIE: 1 CAT: 14
SN Oregon's school improvement and professional development program

House Care Services
CIJE: 0 RIE: 1 CAT: 16

House Committee on Education and Labor
CIJE: 2 RIE: 5 CAT: 17

House Committee on Post Office and Civil Service
CIJE: 0 RIE: 1 CAT: 17

House Committee on the Judiciary
CIJE: 0 RIE: 0 CAT: 17

House Construction
CIJE: 2 RIE: 2 CAT: 20

House of Representatives
CIJE: 11 RIE: 31 CAT: 17

House of the Good Shepherd MD
CIJE: 0 RIE: 1 CAT: 17

House School
CIJE: 1 RIE: 1 CAT: 17

House Science and Technology Committees
CIJE: 1 RIE: 0 CAT: 17

House Select Subcommittee on Education
CIJE: 1 RIE: 1 CAT: 17

House Select Subcommittee on Labor
CIJE: 0 RIE: 1 CAT: 17

House Tree Person Projective Test
CIJE: 5 RIE: 3 CAT: 21

House Wiring
USE Residential Wiring

Household Employment Assn Reevaluation Training
CIJE: 0 RIE: 5 CAT: 15

Household Products
CIJE: 4 RIE: 3 CAT: 16

Housework
CIJE: 49 RIE: 15 CAT: 16

Housing and Community Development Act 1974
CIJE: 0 RIE: 6 CAT: 14

Housing and Community Development Act Title II
CIJE: 0 RIE: 2 CAT: 14

Housing and Urban Development Act 1968
CIJE: 1 RIE: 3 CAT: 14

Housing Codes
CIJE: 1 RIE: 4 CAT: 14

Housing Market
CIJE: 3 RIE: 5 CAT: 16

Houston Baptist University TX
CIJE: 4 RIE: 6 CAT: 17

Houston Chronicle
CIJE: 0 RIE: 1 CAT: 22

Houston Community College System TX
CIJE: 2 RIE: 5 CAT: 17

Houston Community College TX
CIJE: 2 RIE: 6 CAT: 17

Houston Independent School District TX
CIJE: 23 RIE: 69 CAT: 17

Houston Post
CIJE: 0 RIE: 1 CAT: 22

Houston Public Library TX
CIJE: 5 RIE: 1 CAT: 17

Houston Quality Assurance Program TX
CIJE: 0 RIE: 1 CAT: 19

Houston Teacher Conservation Project TX
CIJE: 0 RIE: 1 CAT: 19

Hovland (Carl)
CIJE: 0 RIE: 1 CAT: 18

How Do I Learn Course (England)
CIJE: 0 RIE: 1 CAT: 03

How I Believe
CIJE: 1 RIE: 0 CAT: 22

How I Feel About Some Other Kids
CIJE: 0 RIE: 1 CAT: 22

How I Feel Test
CIJE: 0 RIE: 1 CAT: 21

How I Feel Towards Others
CIJE: 1 RIE: 0 CAT: 21

How I See Myself Scale
CIJE: 5 RIE: 8 CAT: 21

How I Won the War
CIJE: 1 RIE: 0 CAT: 22

How Is Your Logic Test
CIJE: 0 RIE: 1 CAT: 21

How To Books
CIJE: 1 RIE: 1 CAT: 16

Howard (John)
CIJE: 1 RIE: 0 CAT: 18
SN English philanthropist and prison reformer, 1726-1790

Howard College TX
CIJE: 1 RIE: 0 CAT: 17

Howard Community College MD
CIJE: 1 RIE: 14 CAT: 17

Howard County Public Schools MD
CIJE: 4 RIE: 0 CAT: 17

Howard Maze Test
CIJE: 2 RIE: 0 CAT: 21

Howard Street Tutoring Program
CIJE: 1 RIE: 1 CAT: 19

Howard University DC
CIJE: 31 RIE: 30 CAT: 17

Howard University Preschool Project
CIJE: 0 RIE: 1 CAT: 19

Howards Theory of Meta Games
CIJE: 1 RIE: 0 CAT: 15

Howell (William Dean)
CIJE: 1 RIE: 0 CAT: 18

Howell Cheney Vocational Technical School CT
CIJE: 0 RIE: 1 CAT: 17

Howell Elementary School UT
CIJE: 0 RIE: 1 CAT: 17

Howell Road School NY
CIJE: 1 RIE: 0 CAT: 17

Howells Levels of Competence
CIJE: 0 RIE: 1 CAT: 15

Howitt (William)
CIJE: 1 RIE: 0 CAT: 18

Howland Circulating Library NY
CIJE: 0 RIE: 1 CAT: 17

Hoyt (Cyril)
CIJE: 2 RIE: 0 CAT: 18

Hoyt (Kenneth B)
CIJE: 0 RIE: 2 CAT: 18

Hoyt Scale
CIJE: 0 RIE: 1 CAT: 21

Hualapai
CIJE: 1 RIE: 14 CAT: 13
SN A Pai language of the Yuman family
UF Walapai

Hualapai (Tribe)
CIJE: 0 RIE: 3 CAT: 08

Huarte (Juan)
CIJE: 1 RIE: 0 CAT: 18

Huastec
CIJE: 0 RIE: 3 CAT: 13
UF Huaxtec

Huave
CIJE: 0 RIE: 1 CAT: 13
SN A Penutian language

Huaxtec
USE Huastec

HUB System
CIJE: 0 RIE: 2 CAT: 04

Hubbard (Elbert)
CIJE: 1 RIE: 0 CAT: 18

Hubbell (J L)
CIJE: 1 RIE: 0 CAT: 18

Huckel Molecular Orbital Computer Programs
CIJE: 1 RIE: 0 CAT: 04

Huckleberry Finn
CIJE: 16 RIE: 10 CAT: 22

Huckleberry House OH
CIJE: 0 RIE: 1 CAT: 17

Huddersfield Polytechnic (England)
CIJE: 0 RIE: 1 CAT: 17

Huddle Groups
CIJE: 0 RIE: 1 CAT: 10

Hudson (Marshall A)
CIJE: 0 RIE: 1 CAT: 18

Hudson Bay
CIJE: 2 RIE: 1 CAT: 07

Hudson Bay Company
CIJE: 1 RIE: 0 CAT: 12

Hudson County Community College NJ
CIJE: 0 RIE: 7 CAT: 17

Hudson River
CIJE: 2 RIE: 0 CAT: 07

Hudson River Sloop Clearwater Inc
CIJE: 2 RIE: 0 CAT: 17

Hudson Senior High School WI
CIJE: 1 RIE: 0 CAT: 17

Hudson Valley Community College NY
CIJE: 5 RIE: 4 CAT: 17

Hudspeth Retardation Center MS
CIJE: 0 RIE: 1 CAT: 17

Huegel School WI
CIJE: 0 RIE: 1 CAT: 17

Huei Dialects
CIJE: 0 RIE: 1 CAT: 13

Huerta (Dolores)
CIJE: 0 RIE: 0 CAT: 18

Hughes (James Laughlin)
CIJE: 0 RIE: 1 CAT: 18

Hughes (Langston)
CIJE: 13 RIE: 2 CAT: 18

Hughes (Mearns)
CIJE: 1 RIE: 0 CAT: 18

Hughes (Richard I)
CIJE: 1 RIE: 0 CAT: 18

Hughes Aircraft Company
CIJE: 3 RIE: 0 CAT: 17

Hughes School District AR
CIJE: 0 RIE: 1 CAT: 17

Hughson Project
CIJE: 1 RIE: 0 CAT: 19

Hugo (Richard)
CIJE: 0 RIE: 1 CAT: 18

Hugo (Victor)
CIJE: 6 RIE: 0 CAT: 18

Hugo och Josefin (Gripe)
CIJE: 0 RIE: 1 CAT: 22

HUGS Project OH
CIJE: 0 RIE: 1 CAT: 19
UF Helping Underachieving Gifted Students OH

Huguenots
CIJE: 1 RIE: 2 CAT: 08

Huichol
CIJE: 0 RIE: 1 CAT: 13

Huidobro (Vicente)
CIJE: 2 RIE: 0 CAT: 18

Huling Austin (Leslie)
CIJE: 0 RIE: 1 CAT: 18

Hull (Clark)
CIJE: 1 RIE: 1 CAT: 18

Hull House Association IL
CIJE: 3 RIE: 1 CAT: 17

Hull University (England)
CIJE: 7 RIE: 2 CAT: 17

Hullah (John)
CIJE: 1 RIE: 0 CAT: 18

Human Action Research
CIJE: 0 RIE: 1 CAT: 15

Human Capacity Myth
CIJE: 0 RIE: 1 CAT: 11

Human Capital Theory
CIJE: 17 RIE: 9 CAT: 15

Human Corps Programs CA
CIJE: 0 RIE: 2 CAT: 19

Human Development Degree Programs
CIJE: 0 RIE: 1 CAT: 03

Human Development Program
CIJE: 6 RIE: 16 CAT: 19

Human Ecology
CIJE: 26 RIE: 19 CAT: 20

Human Figure Drawing
CIJE: 17 RIE: 3 CAT: 16

Human Figure Drawing Test
CIJE: 4 RIE: 5 CAT: 21

Human Genome Project
CIJE: 10 RIE: 1 CAT: 19

Human Growth and Development Program
CIJE: 0 RIE: 2 CAT: 19

Human Habitat Study
CIJE: 1 RIE: 0 CAT: 17

Human Heart
USE Heart

Human Information Processing Survey
CIJE: 2 RIE: 0 CAT: 21

Human Mutilation
CIJE: 0 RIE: 2 CAT: 11
SN See also "Sexual Mutilation"
UF Mutilation (Human)

Human Potential
CIJE: 2 RIE: 4 CAT: 16

Human Potential Movement
CIJE: 3 RIE: 7 CAT: 15

Human Potential Seminars
CIJE: 3 RIE: 4 CAT: 02

Human Relations Area Files
CIJE: 1 RIE: 2 CAT: 17

Human Relations Incident
CIJE: 0 RIE: 1 CAT: 21

Human Relations Recertification Program
CIJE: 0 RIE: 1 CAT: 19

Human Resource Accounting
CIJE: 2 RIE: 1 CAT: 15

Human Resource Specialists
CIJE: 3 RIE: 4 CAT: 09

Human Resources Administration
CIJE: 7 RIE: 3 CAT: 17

Human Resources Development Authority (Canada)
CIJE: 1 RIE: 0 CAT: 17

Human Resources Development Institute
CIJE: 3 RIE: 0 CAT: 17

Human Resources Development Program
CIJE: 1 RIE: 7 CAT: 19

Human Resources Development Program NC
CIJE: 0 RIE: 2 CAT: 19

Human Resources Professionals
CIJE: 7 RIE: 6 CAT: 09

Human Resources Research Council (Canada)
CIJE: 6 RIE: 0 CAT: 17

Human Resources Research Office
CIJE: 0 RIE: 6 CAT: 17

Human Resources Research Organization
CIJE: 6 RIE: 23 CAT: 17

Human Resources School NY
CIJE: 3 RIE: 2 CAT: 17

Human Rights and Equal Opp Comm Act (Australia)
CIJE: 0 RIE: 1 CAT: 14

Human Rights Commission
CIJE: 1 RIE: 1 CAT: 17

Human Rights Reporting
CIJE: 0 RIE: 0 CAT: 16
UF Reporting of Human Rights Violations

Human Sciences Program
CIJE: 8 RIE: 14 CAT: 19

Human Sciences Research Inc
CIJE: 0 RIE: 1 CAT: 17

Human Service Educators
USE Human Services Educators

Human Service Institute NY
CIJE: 0 RIE: 1 CAT: 17

Human Services Brokers
CIJE: 0 RIE: 0 CAT: 10

Human Services Drug Abuse Project
CIJE: 0 RIE: 2 CAT: 19

Human Services Educators
CIJE: 2 RIE: 0 CAT: 09
UF Human Service Educators

Human Services Manpower Career Center IL
CIJE: 0 RIE: 6 CAT: 17

Human Services Partnerships
USE Partnerships in Human Services

Human Services Professionals
CIJE: 0 RIE: 1 CAT: 09

Human Services Reauthorization Act 1984
CIJE: 0 RIE: 0 CAT: 14
UF Public Law 98 558

Human Services Reauthorization Act 1990
CIJE: 0 RIE: 1 CAT: 14

Human Sounds
CIJE: 0 RIE: 1 CAT: 11

Human Subject Protection
CIJE: 15 RIE: 8 CAT: 21

Human Systems Approach
CIJE: 0 RIE: 2 CAT: 15

Human Talent Research Program
CIJE: 0 RIE: 1 CAT: 19

Human Values and Technological Change Conference
CIJE: 0 RIE: 1 CAT: 02

Humane Education
CIJE: 92 RIE: 22 CAT: 03

Humane Education Teacher of the Year Award
CIJE: 0 RIE: 0 CAT: 16

Humanistic Approaches Provide Positive Environment
CIJE: 1 RIE: 0 CAT: 22

Humanistic Existentialism
CIJE: 1 RIE: 1 CAT: 15

Humanistic Leadership Model
CIJE: 1 RIE: 0 CAT: 15

Humanistic Patient Care
CIJE: 0 RIE: 5 CAT: 11

Humanistic Psychology
CIJE: 33 RIE: 12 CAT: 16

Humanistic Research
CIJE: 8 RIE: 3 CAT: 16

Humanists
CIJE: 20 RIE: 2 CAT: 10

Humanities Curriculum Project
CIJE: 5 RIE: 3 CAT: 19

Humanities Enrichment Program
CIJE: 0 RIE: 1 CAT: 19

Humanities Research Council of Canada
CIJE: 1 RIE: 0 CAT: 17

Humber College ON
CIJE: 1 RIE: 4 CAT: 17

Humboldt (Alexander von)
USE Von Humboldt (Alexander)

Humboldt (Wilhelm von)
USE Von Humboldt (Wilhelm)

Humboldt State College CA
CIJE: 0 RIE: 2 CAT: 17

Humboldt State University CA
CIJE: 3 RIE: 9 CAT: 17

Hume (David)
CIJE: 4 RIE: 2 CAT: 18

Humor Development
CIJE: 0 RIE: 1 CAT: 11

Humor Preference Inventory (Wenck)
CIJE: 0 RIE: 1 CAT: 21

Humphrey Occupational Resource Center MA
CIJE: 0 RIE: 1 CAT: 17

Hunchback in the Park
CIJE: 1 RIE: 0 CAT: 22

Hundred Board
CIJE: 1 RIE: 0 CAT: 04

Hungarian Americans
CIJE: 1 RIE: 8 CAT: 08

Hungarian National Sociolinguistic Survey
CIJE: 0 RIE: 1 CAT: 21

Hungarians
CIJE: 5 RIE: 7 CAT: 08

Hungary
CIJE: 184 RIE: 125 CAT: 07

Hungary (Budapest)
CIJE: 7 RIE: 1 CAT: 07

Hunger of Memory
CIJE: 0 RIE: 1 CAT: 22

Hunt (Brock)
CIJE: 0 RIE: 1 CAT: 18

Hunt (David E)
CIJE: 0 RIE: 2 CAT: 18

Hunt (Everett Lee)
CIJE: 1 RIE: 1 CAT: 18

Hunt (Holman)
CIJE: 0 RIE: 1 CAT: 18

Hunt (J)
CIJE: 1 RIE: 1 CAT: 18

Hunt (Kellogg)
CIJE: 1 RIE: 1 CAT: 18

Hunt (Leigh)
CIJE: 1 RIE: 0 CAT: 18

Hunt (Richard Morris)
CIJE: 1 RIE: 0 CAT: 18

Hunt Paragraph Completion Method
CIJE: 0 RIE: 1 CAT: 21
UF Paragraph Completion Method (Hunt); Paragraph Completion Test of Conceptual Complexity

Hunter (Albert)
CIJE: 0 RIE: 1 CAT: 18

Hunter (Clementine)
CIJE: 0 RIE: 1 CAT: 18

Hunter (Floyd)
CIJE: 1 RIE: 0 CAT: 18

Hunter (Madeline)
CIJE: 42 RIE: 10 CAT: 18

Hunter (Mandsley)
CIJE: 0 RIE: 1 CAT: 18

Hunter College NY
USE City University of New York Hunter College

Hunter Elementary School NY
CIJE: 1 RIE: 1 CAT: 17

Hunter High School NY
CIJE: 0 RIE: 1 CAT: 17

Hunter Instructional Model
CIJE: 6 RIE: 3 CAT: 15
SN See also "Essential Elements of Instruction (Hunter)"
UF Clinical Teaching Model (Hunter)

Hunter Model of Clinical Supervision
CIJE: 0 RIE: 2 CAT: 15
UF Clinical Supervision Model (Hunter)

Hunter Safety
CIJE: 0 RIE: 5 CAT: 16

Hunter Schmidt Meta Analysis
CIJE: 0 RIE: 1 CAT: 15

Hunter Science Aptitude Test
CIJE: 0 RIE: 1 CAT: 21

Hunter Staff Development Model
CIJE: 2 RIE: 1 CAT: 15

Hunter Wolf A B Rating Scale
CIJE: 0 RIE: 3 CAT: 21

Hunting
CIJE: 8 RIE: 26 CAT: 16

Hunting Ridge Elementary School IL
CIJE: 1 RIE: 0 CAT: 17

Huntington (Charles)
CIJE: 0 RIE: 1 CAT: 18

Huntington Beach Union High School District CA
CIJE: 2 RIE: 1 CAT: 17

Huntington College IN
CIJE: 1 RIE: 0 CAT: 17

Huntington Galleries WV
CIJE: 1 RIE: 0 CAT: 17

Huntington Project
CIJE: 2 RIE: 1 CAT: 19

Huntington Public Library
CIJE: 1 RIE: 0 CAT: 17

Huntoon (Mary)
CIJE: 0 RIE: 1 CAT: 18

Huntsville City School System AL
CIJE: 1 RIE: 2 CAT: 17

Huntsville School District AR
CIJE: 0 RIE: 1 CAT: 17

Hupa
CIJE: 1 RIE: 15 CAT: 13
SN Of the Athapascan language family
UF Hoopa

Hupa (Tribe)
CIJE: 1 RIE: 10 CAT: 08
UF Hoopa (Tribe)

Hurd v City of Buffalo
CIJE: 0 RIE: 1 CAT: 14

Hurder (Paul)
CIJE: 0 RIE: 1 CAT: 18

Hurlers Syndrome
CIJE: 1 RIE: 0 CAT: 11

Huron (Tribe)
CIJE: 1 RIE: 4 CAT: 08

Huron High School SD
CIJE: 1 RIE: 0 CAT: 17

Huron Valley Womens Facility MI
CIJE: 0 RIE: 1 CAT: 17

Hurricane Hugo
CIJE: 1 RIE: 3 CAT: 12

Hurricanes
CIJE: 12 RIE: 6 CAT: 20

Hurried Childhood
CIJE: 2 RIE: 2 CAT: 16

Hurst (J Willard)
CIJE: 1 RIE: 0 CAT: 18

Hurston (Zora Neale)
CIJE: 10 RIE: 2 CAT: 18

Hurtado (Elias)
CIJE: 1 RIE: 0 CAT: 18

Hurwitz (Howard L)
CIJE: 0 RIE: 1 CAT: 18

Husserl (Edmund)
CIJE: 5 RIE: 5 CAT: 18

Husson College ME
CIJE: 1 RIE: 2 CAT: 17

Hustler v Falwell
USE Falwell v Flynt

Huston (John)
CIJE: 1 RIE: 0 CAT: 18

Huston Tillotson College TX
CIJE: 0 RIE: 1 CAT: 17

Hutchings Low Fatigue Addition Algorithm
CIJE: 2 RIE: 0 CAT: 20

Hutchins (Robert)
CIJE: 8 RIE: 6 CAT: 18

Hutchins Commission Report
CIJE: 1 RIE: 0 CAT: 22

Hutchinson Community Junior College KS
CIJE: 0 RIE: 1 CAT: 17

Hutt Adaptation of Bender Gestalt Test
CIJE: 2 RIE: 0 CAT: 21

Hutterite Communal Society
CIJE: 9 RIE: 0 CAT: 17

Hutterites
CIJE: 5 RIE: 7 CAT: 08

Hutton (James)
CIJE: 2 RIE: 0 CAT: 18

Huxley (Aldous)
CIJE: 4 RIE: 2 CAT: 18

Hwalek Sengstock Elder Abuse Screening Protocol
CIJE: 0 RIE: 1 CAT: 21

Hwalek Sengstok Elder Abuse Screening Protocol
CIJE: 0 RIE: 1 CAT: 21

Hybrid Computers
CIJE: 0 RIE: 1 CAT: 04

Hybrid Technologies
CIJE: 2 RIE: 2 CAT: 20

Hybridization
CIJE: 0 RIE: 1 CAT: 20

Hycrocephaly
CIJE: 1 RIE: 0 CAT: 11

Hyde Park Cadre
CIJE: 0 RIE: 1 CAT: 17

Hydra
CIJE: 1 RIE: 0 CAT: 22

Hydra Phenomenon
CIJE: 0 RIE: 1 CAT: 15

Hydrams
CIJE: 0 RIE: 1 CAT: 04

Hydration
CIJE: 2 RIE: 0 CAT: 20

Hydraulic Jumps
CIJE: 1 RIE: 0 CAT: 04

Hydrazines
CIJE: 1 RIE: 0 CAT: 20

Hydrobiology
CIJE: 0 RIE: 1 CAT: 20

Hydrocarbon Emissions
CIJE: 1 RIE: 0 CAT: 20

Hydrocarbons
CIJE: 5 RIE: 1 CAT: 20

Hydrocephalus
CIJE: 8 RIE: 3 CAT: 11

Hydrochloric Acid
CIJE: 2 RIE: 0 CAT: 20

Hydrocortisone
CIJE: 5 RIE: 0 CAT: 11

Icaza (Jorge)
CIJE: 1 RIE: 0 CAT: 18

Ice
CIJE: 7 RIE: 4 CAT: 20

Ice Climbing
CIJE: 0 RIE: 1 CAT: 16

Ice Cream
CIJE: 3 RIE: 0 CAT: 16

ICEIT Project
CIJE: 1 RIE: 0 CAT: 19

Iceland
CIJE: 36 RIE: 37 CAT: 07

Icelandic
CIJE: 7 RIE: 12 CAT: 13

Icelandic (Old)
CIJE: 2 RIE: 0 CAT: 13

Ichabod Crane Central School District NY
CIJE: 1 RIE: 1 CAT: 17

ICHPER International Questionnaire
CIJE: 0 RIE: 1 CAT: 21

Iconic Comparison
CIJE: 2 RIE: 2 CAT: 16

Iconic Representation
CIJE: 16 RIE: 3 CAT: 16

Iconic Storage
CIJE: 1 RIE: 2 CAT: 16

Iconicity
CIJE: 6 RIE: 3 CAT: 16
SN The resemblance between a sign and the object or action it represents
UF Sign Iconicity; Visual Iconicity; Visuality (Language)

ICONS (Simulation)
CIJE: 0 RIE: 1 CAT: 19
UF International Communication and Negotiation Simul

ID Expert
CIJE: 0 RIE: 4 CAT: 04
UF Instructional Design Expert

ID Exploratory Behavior
CIJE: 1 RIE: 0 CAT: 11

Idaho
CIJE: 59 RIE: 314 CAT: 07

Idaho (Bingham County)
CIJE: 0 RIE: 4 CAT: 07

Idaho (Boise)
CIJE: 1 RIE: 8 CAT: 07

Idaho (Idaho Falls)
CIJE: 1 RIE: 2 CAT: 07

Idaho (Pocatello)
CIJE: 0 RIE: 3 CAT: 07

Idaho Extension Service
CIJE: 0 RIE: 1 CAT: 17

Idaho Proficiency Test
CIJE: 0 RIE: 1 CAT: 21

Idaho School District Organization Project
CIJE: 0 RIE: 1 CAT: 19

Idaho School Improvement Act 1984
CIJE: 0 RIE: 1 CAT: 14

Idaho State Department of Education
CIJE: 0 RIE: 2 CAT: 17

Idaho State University
CIJE: 9 RIE: 10 CAT: 17

IDD Advisor
CIJE: 0 RIE: 2 CAT: 04
UF Instructional Design and Development Advisor

IDEA
USE Individuals with Disabilities Education Act

Idea Generation
CIJE: 23 RIE: 11 CAT: 16

Idea Mapping
CIJE: 1 RIE: 2 CAT: 15

IDEA Model
CIJE: 0 RIE: 2 CAT: 15

IDEA OH
USE Institute for Development of Educ Activities OH

IDEA Oral Language Proficiency Test
CIJE: 0 RIE: 1 CAT: 21

IDEA Principals Inservice Program
CIJE: 1 RIE: 0 CAT: 19

Idea Processors
CIJE: 0 RIE: 1 CAT: 04

IDEA Questionnaire
CIJE: 1 RIE: 1 CAT: 21

IDEAL Curriculum and Computer System
CIJE: 0 RIE: 1 CAT: 04

Ideal Displacement
CIJE: 1 RIE: 1 CAT: 21

Ideal Gas Law
CIJE: 10 RIE: 1 CAT: 20

Ideal Oral Language Proficiency Test Spanish
CIJE: 0 RIE: 1 CAT: 21

Ideal Pupil Checklist
CIJE: 4 RIE: 0 CAT: 21

Ideal Student Description Q Sort (Whetstone)
CIJE: 0 RIE: 1 CAT: 21

Ideal Text Project (Quebec)
CIJE: 0 RIE: 1 CAT: 19

Ideal Type Methodology (Weber)
CIJE: 0 RIE: 1 CAT: 15

Idealism
CIJE: 25 RIE: 17 CAT: 16

Idealization
CIJE: 7 RIE: 6 CAT: 11

Ideaphoria
CIJE: 0 RIE: 1 CAT: 21

Ideas
CIJE: 28 RIE: 13 CAT: 16

Ideation
CIJE: 14 RIE: 10 CAT: 15
SN Use the more specific Iden "Suicide Ideation," if possible

Ideational Confrontation
CIJE: 0 RIE: 1 CAT: 11

Ideational Fluency
CIJE: 11 RIE: 3 CAT: 11

Identical Transparency Map Method
CIJE: 1 RIE: 0 CAT: 15

Identification Badges
CIJE: 4 RIE: 0 CAT: 04

Identification Cards
CIJE: 1 RIE: 0 CAT: 04
SN See also "School Identification Cards"

Identification of Maturity Level of Subordinates
CIJE: 0 RIE: 1 CAT: 19

Identification Placement Tracking System
CIJE: 0 RIE: 1 CAT: 04

Identifier Authority List
CIJE: 0 RIE: 2 CAT: 22

Identifying School Behavior Problems Program
CIJE: 0 RIE: 1 CAT: 19

Identity (Psychological)
CIJE: 42 RIE: 6 CAT: 11

Identity Conservation
CIJE: 6 RIE: 1 CAT: 11

Identity Crisis
CIJE: 17 RIE: 4 CAT: 11

Identity Formation
CIJE: 100 RIE: 36 CAT: 11

Identity Models
CIJE: 3 RIE: 4 CAT: 15

Identity Status
CIJE: 31 RIE: 2 CAT: 11
UF Ego Identity Status

Identity Status Interview
CIJE: 4 RIE: 1 CAT: 21

Identity Synthesis
CIJE: 1 RIE: 1 CAT: 11

Ideographs
CIJE: 4 RIE: 4 CAT: 16

Idiodynamic Set
CIJE: 1 RIE: 0 CAT: 21

Idioglossia
CIJE: 0 RIE: 2 CAT: 13
SN Private language created and used among siblings, commonly between twins
UF Twin Speech

Idiographic Analysis
CIJE: 5 RIE: 1 CAT: 16

Idiographic Teaching Style
CIJE: 0 RIE: 1 CAT: 15

Idiom Drama
CIJE: 0 RIE: 1 CAT: 15

IDiom System
CIJE: 0 RIE: 1 CAT: 04
SN ID = Instructional Design

Idiopathic Thrombocytopenic Purpura
CIJE: 1 RIE: 0 CAT: 11

Idiot Savants
CIJE: 7 RIE: 1 CAT: 10

Iditarod Sled Dog Race
CIJE: 0 RIE: 1 CAT: 12

IDRA
USE Intercultural Development Research Association

IEA
USE International Assn Evaluation Educ Achievement

IEA Mathematics Study (2d)
USE Second International Mathematics Study

IEA Preprimary Project
CIJE: 1 RIE: 2 CAT: 19

IEA Science Project
CIJE: 3 RIE: 7 CAT: 19

IEA Science Study (2d)
USE Second International Science Study

IEA Six Subject Survey
CIJE: 0 RIE: 1 CAT: 19

IEA Study of Writing
USE IEA Written Composition Study

IEA Written Composition Study
CIJE: 2 RIE: 6 CAT: 19
UF IEA Study of Writing

IELTS
USE International English Language Testing System

IEP Monitoring Analysis Plan
CIJE: 0 RIE: 2 CAT: 19

IES Test
CIJE: 1 RIE: 0 CAT: 21

If You Had a Visitor
CIJE: 0 RIE: 1 CAT: 22

If You Live in a City Where Do You Live
CIJE: 0 RIE: 1 CAT: 22

If You Were Coming in the Fall
CIJE: 1 RIE: 0 CAT: 22

IFLA
USE International Federation of Library Associations

Ifugao
CIJE: 2 RIE: 0 CAT: 13

Ignaciano
CIJE: 0 RIE: 1 CAT: 13

Ignition Systems
CIJE: 1 RIE: 19 CAT: 20

Igorots
CIJE: 1 RIE: 0 CAT: 08

Ijo
CIJE: 0 RIE: 2 CAT: 13

IJR Behavior Checklist
CIJE: 2 RIE: 0 CAT: 21

Ika
CIJE: 0 RIE: 1 CAT: 13
SN A Nupe-Gbari language

Ikipujung Pandang University (Indonesia)
CIJE: 0 RIE: 1 CAT: 17

ILEA Film Study Course
CIJE: 2 RIE: 0 CAT: 03

Iliad
CIJE: 4 RIE: 4 CAT: 22

Iliaura
USE Alyawarra

Ilin (Ivan)
CIJE: 1 RIE: 0 CAT: 18

Illegal Copying (Software)
USE Software Piracy

Illich (Ivan)
CIJE: 19 RIE: 6 CAT: 18

ILLINET
USE Illinois Library and Information Network

Illinois
CIJE: 702 RIE: 2281 CAT: 07

Illinois (Alexander County)
CIJE: 1 RIE: 1 CAT: 07

Illinois (Alton)
CIJE: 1 RIE: 1 CAT: 07

Illinois (Arlington Heights)
CIJE: 3 RIE: 2 CAT: 07

Illinois (Bloomington)
CIJE: 0 RIE: 1 CAT: 07

Illinois (Boone County)
CIJE: 0 RIE: 1 CAT: 07

Illinois (Bureau County)
CIJE: 1 RIE: 0 CAT: 07

Illinois (Canton)
CIJE: 1 RIE: 0 CAT: 07

Illinois (Carbondale)
CIJE: 2 RIE: 66 CAT: 07

Illinois (Central)
CIJE: 1 RIE: 4 CAT: 07

Illinois (Centralia)
CIJE: 0 RIE: 1 CAT: 07

Illinois (Champaign County)
CIJE: 1 RIE: 1 CAT: 07

Illinois (Champaign Urbana)
CIJE: 3 RIE: 3 CAT: 07

Illinois (Champaign)
CIJE: 7 RIE: 25 CAT: 07

Illinois (Chicago Heights)
CIJE: 1 RIE: 2 CAT: 07

Illinois (Chicago Metropolitan Area)
CIJE: 0 RIE: 7 CAT: 07

Illinois (Chicago)
CIJE: 263 RIE: 649 CAT: 07

Illinois (Cobden)
CIJE: 0 RIE: 1 CAT: 07

Illinois (Cook County)
CIJE: 13 RIE: 19 CAT: 07

Illinois (Crystal Lake)
CIJE: 2 RIE: 0 CAT: 07

Illinois (De Kalb County)
CIJE: 1 RIE: 3 CAT: 07

Illinois (De Kalb)
CIJE: 3 RIE: 11 CAT: 07

Illinois (Decatur)
CIJE: 2 RIE: 2 CAT: 07

Illinois (Deerfield)
CIJE: 1 RIE: 1 CAT: 07

Illinois (DuPage County)
CIJE: 3 RIE: 4 CAT: 07

Illinois (East Chicago)
CIJE: 2 RIE: 2 CAT: 07

Illinois (East Humboldt Park)
CIJE: 0 RIE: 1 CAT: 07

Illinois (East Saint Louis)
CIJE: 4 RIE: 6 CAT: 07

Illinois (Edgewater)
CIJE: 0 RIE: 1 CAT: 07

Illinois (Edwardsville)
CIJE: 0 RIE: 5 CAT: 07

Illinois (Elgin)
CIJE: 0 RIE: 4 CAT: 07

Illinois (Elk Grove Village)
CIJE: 3 RIE: 0 CAT: 07

Illinois (Evanston)
CIJE: 12 RIE: 51 CAT: 07

Illinois (Forest Park)
CIJE: 0 RIE: 1 CAT: 07

Illinois (Glenbrook)
CIJE: 0 RIE: 1 CAT: 07

Illinois (Glenview)
CIJE: 2 RIE: 0 CAT: 07

Illinois (Granite City)
CIJE: 1 RIE: 0 CAT: 07

Illinois (Gurnee)
CIJE: 1 RIE: 1 CAT: 07

Illinois (Harrisburg)
CIJE: 0 RIE: 1 CAT: 07

Illinois (Highland Park)
CIJE: 4 RIE: 1 CAT: 07

Illinois (Joliet)
CIJE: 0 RIE: 5 CAT: 07

Illinois (Kankakee)
CIJE: 2 RIE: 4 CAT: 07

Illinois (Lake County)
CIJE: 1 RIE: 7 CAT: 07

Illinois (Libertyville)
CIJE: 0 RIE: 1 CAT: 07

Illinois (Lockport)
CIJE: 0 RIE: 1 CAT: 07

Illinois (Logan County)
CIJE: 0 RIE: 2 CAT: 07

Illinois (Macomb)
CIJE: 2 RIE: 3 CAT: 07

Illinois (Madison County)
CIJE: 1 RIE: 2 CAT: 07

Illinois (McLean County)
CIJE: 1 RIE: 1 CAT: 07

Illinois (Mount Carmel)
CIJE: 0 RIE: 1 CAT: 07

Illinois (Naperville)
CIJE: 1 RIE: 1 CAT: 07

Illinois (New Trier Township)
CIJE: 1 RIE: 0 CAT: 07

Illinois (Niles)
CIJE: 2 RIE: 0 CAT: 07

Illinois (Normal)
CIJE: 0 RIE: 1 CAT: 07

Illinois (North)
CIJE: 1 RIE: 3 CAT: 07

Illinois (Oak Park)
CIJE: 3 RIE: 1 CAT: 07

Illinois (Palatine)
CIJE: 3 RIE: 1 CAT: 07

Illinois (Palos Park)
CIJE: 0 RIE: 1 CAT: 07

Illinois (Park Forest)
CIJE: 0 RIE: 1 CAT: 07

Illinois (Pekin)
CIJE: 0 RIE: 1 CAT: 07

Illinois (Peoria)
CIJE: 2 RIE: 6 CAT: 07

Illinois (Pope County)
CIJE: 0 RIE: 1 CAT: 07

Illinois (Quincy)
CIJE: 0 RIE: 2 CAT: 07

Illinois (River Forest)
CIJE: 1 RIE: 1 CAT: 07

Illinois (Rock Island)
CIJE: 1 RIE: 0 CAT: 07

Illinois (Rockford)
CIJE: 8 RIE: 12 CAT: 07

Illinois (Saint Clair County)
CIJE: 1 RIE: 3 CAT: 07

Illinois (Saint Peter)
CIJE: 0 RIE: 0 CAT: 07

Illinois (Schaumburg)
CIJE: 1 RIE: 0 CAT: 07

Illinois (Skokie)
CIJE: 4 RIE: 3 CAT: 07

Illinois (South)
CIJE: 3 RIE: 9 CAT: 07

Illinois (Springfield)
CIJE: 7 RIE: 29 CAT: 07

Illinois (Sullivan)
CIJE: 0 RIE: 1 CAT: 07

Illinois (Uptown)
CIJE: 0 RIE: 1 CAT: 07

Illinois (Urbana)
CIJE: 4 RIE: 82 CAT: 07

Illinois (Villa Park)
CIJE: 1 RIE: 0 CAT: 07

Illinois (Waukegan)
CIJE: 1 RIE: 1 CAT: 07

Illinois (Wheaton)
CIJE: 0 RIE: 1 CAT: 07

Illinois (Wheeling)
CIJE: 0 RIE: 1 CAT: 07

Illinois (Wilmette)
CIJE: 2 RIE: 2 CAT: 07

Illinois (Winnebago County)
CIJE: 0 RIE: 1 CAT: 07

Illinois (Winnetka)
CIJE: 4 RIE: 3 CAT: 07

Illinois Area Service Centers
CIJE: 0 RIE: 1 CAT: 17

Illinois Arts Council
CIJE: 1 RIE: 0 CAT: 17

Illinois Association Community and Junior Colleges
CIJE: 0 RIE: 1 CAT: 17

Illinois Association for Education Young Children
CIJE: 0 RIE: 1 CAT: 17

Illinois Association of Legal Secretaries
CIJE: 1 RIE: 0 CAT: 17

Illinois Association of School Boards
CIJE: 0 RIE: 2 CAT: 17

Illinois Association of Teachers of English
CIJE: 0 RIE: 3 CAT: 17

Illinois Audiovisual Association
CIJE: 0 RIE: 1 CAT: 17

Illinois Basic Skills Program
CIJE: 0 RIE: 1 CAT: 19

Illinois Bell Telephone Company
CIJE: 2 RIE: 0 CAT: 17

Illinois Career Education Model
CIJE: 0 RIE: 1 CAT: 15

Illinois Central College
CIJE: 4 RIE: 7 CAT: 17

Illinois Certification Testing System
CIJE: 0 RIE: 1 CAT: 21

Illinois Citizens Education Council
CIJE: 0 RIE: 1 CAT: 17

Illinois College
CIJE: 0 RIE: 2 CAT: 17

Illinois College of Optometry
CIJE: 2 RIE: 0 CAT: 17

Illinois Commission on Children
CIJE: 0 RIE: 1 CAT: 17

Illinois Communication Scale
CIJE: 0 RIE: 2 CAT: 21

Illinois Community Care Program
CIJE: 1 RIE: 1 CAT: 19
UF Community Care Program IL

Illinois Community College Board
CIJE: 1 RIE: 9 CAT: 17

Illinois Community College System
CIJE: 0 RIE: 6 CAT: 17

Illinois Community Unit School District 300
CIJE: 1 RIE: 0 CAT: 17

Illinois Competency Based Adult Education Project
CIJE: 0 RIE: 1 CAT: 19

Illinois Consumer Education Association
CIJE: 1 RIE: 0 CAT: 17

Illinois Cooperative Conservation Program
CIJE: 1 RIE: 1 CAT: 19

Illinois Core Curriculum in Agriculture
CIJE: 0 RIE: 1 CAT: 03

Illinois Core Curriculum Project
CIJE: 0 RIE: 2 CAT: 19

Illinois Course Evaluation Questionnaire
CIJE: 5 RIE: 9 CAT: 21

Illinois Curriculum Program
CIJE: 0 RIE: 1 CAT: 19

Illinois Division Vocational Technical Education
CIJE: 0 RIE: 1 CAT: 17

Illinois Domestic Violence Act
CIJE: 0 RIE: 1 CAT: 14

Illinois Eastern Community Colleges
CIJE: 0 RIE: 1 CAT: 17

Illinois Education for Employment Program
USE Education for Employment IL

Illinois Educational Reform Act 1985
CIJE: 1 RIE: 0 CAT: 14

Illinois English Placement Test
CIJE: 1 RIE: 1 CAT: 21

Illinois Federation of Teachers
CIJE: 0 RIE: 1 CAT: 17

Illinois Gifted Program
CIJE: 1 RIE: 9 CAT: 19

Illinois Goal Assessment Program
CIJE: 0 RIE: 6 CAT: 19

Illinois Higher Education Loan Authority
CIJE: 1 RIE: 0 CAT: 17

Illinois Index of Self Derogation
CIJE: 0 RIE: 1 CAT: 21

Illinois Institute for Public Understanding Law
CIJE: 0 RIE: 1 CAT: 17

Illinois Institute of Technology
CIJE: 13 RIE: 3 CAT: 17

Illinois Inventory of Educational Progress
CIJE: 1 RIE: 21 CAT: 21

Illinois Inventory of Parent Opinion
CIJE: 0 RIE: 1 CAT: 21

Illinois Library and Information Network
CIJE: 11 RIE: 13 CAT: 17
UF ILLINET

Illinois Library Materials Processing Center
CIJE: 0 RIE: 1 CAT: 17

Illinois Mathematics and Science Academy
CIJE: 2 RIE: 2 CAT: 17

Illinois Migrant Council
CIJE: 0 RIE: 1 CAT: 17

Illinois Migrant Program
CIJE: 0 RIE: 1 CAT: 19

Illinois Network Exemplary Occup Educ Prog
CIJE: 0 RIE: 1 CAT: 19

Illinois Occupational Curriculum Project
CIJE: 0 RIE: 9 CAT: 19

Illinois Office of Community Development
CIJE: 0 RIE: 1 CAT: 17

Illinois Plan
CIJE: 0 RIE: 1 CAT: 19

Illinois Planning Council on Develop Disabil
CIJE: 0 RIE: 1 CAT: 17

Illinois Prekindergarten At Risk Program
USE Prekindergarten At Risk Program IL

Illinois Problems Index
CIJE: 0 RIE: 2 CAT: 21

Illinois Project for School Reform
CIJE: 0 RIE: 3 CAT: 17

Illinois Public School Finance Project
CIJE: 0 RIE: 1 CAT: 19

Illinois Quality Schools Index
CIJE: 1 RIE: 1 CAT: 21

Illinois Residential Life Survey
CIJE: 0 RIE: 1 CAT: 21

Illinois Rules of the Road
CIJE: 0 RIE: 1 CAT: 22

Illinois Rural Revitalization Planning Program
CIJE: 0 RIE: 1 CAT: 19

Illinois School for the Deaf
CIJE: 3 RIE: 0 CAT: 17

Illinois School Journal
CIJE: 1 RIE: 0 CAT: 22

Illinois Self Rating Scale for English Teachers
CIJE: 0 RIE: 1 CAT: 21

Illinois Soldiers and Sailors Childrens School
CIJE: 1 RIE: 0 CAT: 17

Illinois Specialized Teacher Evaluation Programs
CIJE: 0 RIE: 1 CAT: 17

Illinois Speech and Theatre Association
CIJE: 1 RIE: 1 CAT: 17

Illinois State Board of Education
CIJE: 9 RIE: 15 CAT: 17

Illinois State Board of Higher Education
CIJE: 4 RIE: 4 CAT: 17

Illinois State Colleges and Universities
CIJE: 0 RIE: 1 CAT: 17

Illinois State Council on Nutrition
CIJE: 0 RIE: 1 CAT: 17

Illinois State Dept of Children and Family Servs
CIJE; 1 RIE: 1 CAT: 17

Illinois State Dept of Corrections
CIJE: 0 RIE: 0 CAT: 17

Illinois State Library
CIJE: 4 RIE: 4 CAT: 17

Illinois State Scholarship Commission
CIJE: 5 RIE: 0 CAT: 17

Illinois State University
CIJE: 40 RIE: 48 CAT: 17

Illinois State University Language Project
CIJE: 0 RIE: 1 CAT: 19

Illinois State Wide Curriculum Study Center
CIJE: 1 RIE: 5 CAT: 17

Illinois Study in Inquiry Training
CIJE: 0 RIE: 1 CAT: 19

Illinois Teacher Evaluation Questionnaire
CIJE: 1 RIE: 2 CAT: 21

Illinois Teacher of Home Economics
CIJE: 0 RIE: 1 CAT: 22

Illinois Teacher Performance Appraisal Scale
CIJE: 0 RIE: 1 CAT: 21

Illinois Teachers College
CIJE: 1 RIE: 0 CAT: 17

Illinois Test of Psycholinguistic Abilities
CIJE: 103 RIE: 102 CAT: 21

Illinois Typological Rating Scale
CIJE: 0 RIE: 1 CAT: 21

Illinois Valley Community College
CIJE: 6 RIE: 4 CAT: 17

Illinois Valley Library System
CIJE: 1 RIE: 4 CAT: 17

Illinois Wesleyan University
CIJE: 2 RIE: 1 CAT: 17

Illinois White House Conference on Children
CIJE: 0 RIE: 2 CAT: 02

Illinois Writing Project
CIJE: 0 RIE: 2 CAT: 19

Illinois Youth Commission
CIJE: 0 RIE: 1 CAT: 17

Illness Adaptation Scale
CIJE: 0 RIE: 1 CAT: 21

Illness Scripts
CIJE: 0 RIE: 2 CAT: 11

Illocutionary Content
CIJE: 1 RIE: 1 CAT: 13

Illocutionary Force
CIJE: 3 RIE: 0 CAT: 13

Illuminated Manuscripts
CIJE: 0 RIE: 1 CAT: 16

Illuminative Evaluation
CIJE: 6 RIE: 6 CAT: 21

Illusionless Man and the Visionary Maid
CIJE: 1 RIE: 0 CAT: 22

Illusions
CIJE: 17 RIE: 4 CAT: 16

Illustration Dependence
CIJE: 0 RIE: 1 CAT: 16

Illustrative Sentences
CIJE: 0 RIE: 1 CAT: 13

Illustrators
CIJE: 34 RIE: 9 CAT: 09

Ilocano
CIJE: 0 RIE: 9 CAT: 13

Ilongot
CIJE: 2 RIE: 0 CAT: 13

Image 4 Seminar
CIJE: 1 RIE: 0 CAT: 02

Image Analysis
CIJE: 34 RIE: 13 CAT: 15

Image of Science and Scientists Scale
CIJE: 2 RIE: 0 CAT: 21

Image Processing (Digital Techniques)
USE Digital Imagery

Image Rotators
CIJE: 0 RIE: 1 CAT: 04

Image Theory
CIJE: 6 RIE: 5 CAT: 15

Image Transmission
CIJE: 4 RIE: 3 CAT: 04
UF Visual Image Transmission

Images and Things
CIJE: 2 RIE: 1 CAT: 22

Imaginal Processes Inventory (Starker)
CIJE: 6 RIE: 0 CAT: 21

Imaginary Audience
CIJE: 4 RIE: 1 CAT: 16

Imaginary Audience Scale
CIJE: 3 RIE: 0 CAT: 21

Imaginary Companions
CIJE: 7 RIE: 3 CAT: 16

Imaginative Educational Cooperation Project
CIJE: 0 RIE: 1 CAT: 19

Imagine That
CIJE: 0 RIE: 1 CAT: 22

Imagined Pain Tolerance Test
CIJE: 1 RIE: 0 CAT: 21

Imagined Practice
CIJE: 1 RIE: 1 CAT: 15

Imaging
CIJE: 27 RIE: 17 CAT: 11

Imaging (Medicine)
USE Medical Imaging

Imaging (MRI)
USE Magnetic Resonance Imaging

Imbricated Program for Information Transfer
CIJE: 1 RIE: 0 CAT: 04

Immaculate Heart College CA
CIJE: 1 RIE: 0 CAT: 17

Immediacy
CIJE: 6 RIE: 2 CAT: 16
SN Use the more specific "Teacher Immediacy," if appropriate

Immediate Adaptive Intelligence
CIJE: 1 RIE: 0 CAT: 16

Immediate Learner Effectiveness
CIJE: 0 RIE: 1 CAT: 15

Immediate Reinforcement and Remediation
CIJE: 1 RIE: 0 CAT: 15

Immersion Approach to Thinking
CIJE: 0 RIE: 1 CAT: 15

Immersion Instructional Model
CIJE: 0 RIE: 2 CAT: 15

Immersion Learning Project
CIJE: 0 RIE: 1 CAT: 19

Immigrant Amnesty
CIJE: 1 RIE: 4 CAT: 14

Immigration Act 1976 (Canada)
CIJE: 0 RIE: 1 CAT: 14
UF Canadian Immigration Act 1976

Immigration and Nationality Act 1965
CIJE: 5 RIE: 12 CAT: 14

Immigration and Nationality Act Amendments
CIJE: 0 RIE: 1 CAT: 14
UF Public Law 97 116

Immigration and Naturalization Service
CIJE: 18 RIE: 31 CAT: 17

Immigration Impact
CIJE: 23 RIE: 29 CAT: 16

Immigration Law
CIJE: 38 RIE: 41 CAT: 14

Immigration Legislation
CIJE: 6 RIE: 19 CAT: 14
UF Refugee Legislation

Immigration Reform and Control Act 1986
CIJE: 13 RIE: 53 CAT: 14
UF Public Law 99 603

Immortality
CIJE: 3 RIE: 0 CAT: 16

Immortality Orientation
CIJE: 1 RIE: 0 CAT: 11

Immunization Injection
USE Vaccination

Immunoglobulin
CIJE: 2 RIE: 0 CAT: 11

Immunology
CIJE: 26 RIE: 5 CAT: 11

IMPAC Program AR
USE Instructional Microcomputer Project Ark Classrooms

Impact
CIJE: 41 RIE: 171 CAT: 16

Impact Aid
CIJE: 7 RIE: 35 CAT: 14

IMPACT Diffusion
CIJE: 0 RIE: 1 CAT: 15
SN IMPACT = Instructional Management by Parents, Community, and Teachers

Impact Evaluation
CIJE: 42 RIE: 21 CAT: 21

Impact Evaluation Model
CIJE: 0 RIE: 7 CAT: 15

IMPACT II
CIJE: 10 RIE: 11 CAT: 19

Impact Magazine
CIJE: 0 RIE: 1 CAT: 22

Impact of a Preschool Interracial Program
CIJE: 0 RIE: 1 CAT: 19

Impact of Event Scale
CIJE: 2 RIE: 0 CAT: 21

Impact Scales
CIJE: 1 RIE: 6 CAT: 21

Impact Statements
CIJE: 0 RIE: 1 CAT: 16

Impact Studies
CIJE: 55 RIE: 183 CAT: 15
SN See also "Economic Impact Studies"

Impact Tester
CIJE: 1 RIE: 0 CAT: 04

Impeachment Proceedings
CIJE: 0 RIE: 2 CAT: 14

Impedance Audiometry
CIJE: 4 RIE: 1 CAT: 11

Impellitteri (Joseph T)
CIJE: 0 RIE: 1 CAT: 18

Imperatives (Grammar)
CIJE: 16 RIE: 4 CAT: 13

Imperfective Aspect (Verbs)
CIJE: 9 RIE: 1 CAT: 13

Imperial (Francisco)
CIJE: 1 RIE: 0 CAT: 18

Imperial Valley College CA
CIJE: 0 RIE: 3 CAT: 17

Impersonalization
CIJE: 4 RIE: 0 CAT: 11

Implementation Analysis
CIJE: 12 RIE: 13 CAT: 15

Implicational Analysis
CIJE: 3 RIE: 4 CAT: 13

Implications
CIJE: 4 RIE: 4 CAT: 16
SN Use a more specific term if possible, e.g., "Policy Implications," "Political Implications"

Implicative Meaning Procedure
CIJE: 1 RIE: 0 CAT: 15

Implicit Associational Responses
CIJE: 4 RIE: 1 CAT: 16

Implicit Communication
CIJE: 0 RIE: 3 CAT: 13

Implicit Contract Theory
CIJE: 0 RIE: 1 CAT: 15

Implicit Theories
CIJE: 4 RIE: 1 CAT: 15

Implicit Verbal Behavior
CIJE: 1 RIE: 2 CAT: 13

Implied Authors
CIJE: 1 RIE: 1 CAT: 16

Implied Consent Law (Pennsylvania)
CIJE: 0 RIE: 1 CAT: 14

Implied Orders Tailored Testing
CIJE: 1 RIE: 0 CAT: 21

Implosive Therapy
CIJE: 6 RIE: 1 CAT: 11

Implosives (Phonetics)
CIJE: 0 RIE: 1 CAT: 13

Importance Inventory
CIJE: 0 RIE: 1 CAT: 21

Imposed Mental Imagery
CIJE: 0 RIE: 1 CAT: 11

Imposter Phenomenon
CIJE: 0 RIE: 2 CAT: 11

Impoundment (Federal Funds)
CIJE: 1 RIE: 1 CAT: 14

Impress Method
CIJE: 2 RIE: 2 CAT: 15

Impression Formation
CIJE: 18 RIE: 2 CAT: 11

Impression Management
CIJE: 11 RIE: 6 CAT: 16

Impression Marking
CIJE: 1 RIE: 0 CAT: 16

Impressionistic Rating Procedures
CIJE: 0 RIE: 1 CAT: 21

Impromptu Speeches
CIJE: 2 RIE: 2 CAT: 13

Impromptu Teaching Model
CIJE: 0 RIE: 1 CAT: 15

Improve Your Written Communication Program
CIJE: 0 RIE: 1 CAT: 19

Improved Authoring Language
CIJE: 0 RIE: 1 CAT: 04

Improved Individual Instruction Program PA
CIJE: 0 RIE: 1 CAT: 19

Improving Citizenship Education Project
CIJE: 3 RIE: 1 CAT: 19

Improving Reading Skills
CIJE: 0 RIE: 1 CAT: 19

Improving Test Taking Skills (Riverside)
CIJE: 0 RIE: 0 CAT: 22

Improving the Efficiency of Educ Systems Project
CIJE: 1 RIE: 2 CAT: 19

Improvisation Test for Individuals
CIJE: 2 RIE: 0 CAT: 21

Impulsive Therapy of Stempfl
CIJE: 1 RIE: 0 CAT: 11

Impulsiveness
CIJE: 32 RIE: 7 CAT: 11

Impulsivity Scale
CIJE: 0 RIE: 1 CAT: 21

Impulsivity Scale for Children (Sutton et al)
CIJE: 1 RIE: 0 CAT: 21

Impulsivity Test (Siegel and Olmsted)
CIJE: 0 RIE: 1 CAT: 21

Impunity Jane
CIJE: 1 RIE: 0 CAT: 22

In Basket Simulation
CIJE: 8 RIE: 18 CAT: 15

In Cold Blood
CIJE: 0 RIE: 1 CAT: 22

In Flight Magazines
CIJE: 0 RIE: 1 CAT: 16

In Our Time
CIJE: 1 RIE: 0 CAT: 22

In School Youth
CIJE: 0 RIE: 1 CAT: 10

In School Youth Work Training Program
CIJE: 0 RIE: 1 CAT: 19

In Search of Excellence
CIJE: 7 RIE: 4 CAT: 22

In the French Body
CIJE: 0 RIE: 1 CAT: 22

In the Primary School Attitude Inventory
CIJE: 0 RIE: 1 CAT: 21

In the White Mans Image
CIJE: 0 RIE: 1 CAT: 22

In Training Evaluation Report
CIJE: 1 RIE: 1 CAT: 19

INA Corporation
CIJE: 0 RIE: 1 CAT: 17

INACAP
USE Instituto Nacional de Capacitacion Prof (Chile)

Inaudible Television
CIJE: 0 RIE: 1 CAT: 15

Inca (Tribe)
CIJE: 4 RIE: 4 CAT: 08

Incarcerated Youth
CIJE: 8 RIE: 9 CAT: 10

Incarnate Word College TX
CIJE: 0 RIE: 2 CAT: 17

Incentives for Improvement Program
CIJE: 0 RIE: 1 CAT: 19

Incentives to Improve Basic Education (Haiti)
CIJE: 0 RIE: 1 CAT: 19
UF PROBED Program (Haiti)

Inchworm
CIJE: 1 RIE: 0 CAT: 20

Incident Reporting
CIJE: 0 RIE: 2 CAT: 15

Incidental Memory
CIJE: 2 RIE: 1 CAT: 11

Incidental Science Experience
CIJE: 2 RIE: 0 CAT: 19

Incinerators
CIJE: 4 RIE: 6 CAT: 04

Inclass Reactive Language Method
CIJE: 0 RIE: 1 CAT: 15

Inclined Planes
CIJE: 4 RIE: 0 CAT: 04

Income Disparities
CIJE: 0 RIE: 1 CAT: 16

Income Distribution
CIJE: 19 RIE: 13 CAT: 16

Income Generation
CIJE: 1 RIE: 5 CAT: 15

Income Groups
CIJE: 0 RIE: 3 CAT: 09

Income Improvement
CIJE: 1 RIE: 4 CAT: 16

Income Level
CIJE: 5 RIE: 8 CAT: 16

Income Maintenance
CIJE: 7 RIE: 10 CAT: 16

Income Security
CIJE: 0 RIE: 5 CAT: 16

Income Survey Development Program 1979
CIJE: 0 RIE: 1 CAT: 19

Income Tax Deductions
CIJE: 7 RIE: 0 CAT: 16

Income Taxes
CIJE: 17 RIE: 31 CAT: 14

Income Transfer Programs
CIJE: 2 RIE: 2 CAT: 19

Income Verification
CIJE: 0 RIE: 5 CAT: 14

Income Withholding
CIJE: 0 RIE: 1 CAT: 16

Incompetence
CIJE: 7 RIE: 4 CAT: 16

Incomplete Designs
CIJE: 3 RIE: 1 CAT: 16

Incomplete Figures Test (Francks)
CIJE: 0 RIE: 1 CAT: 21

Incomplete Grades
CIJE: 0 RIE: 1 CAT: 16
UF I Grades

Incomplete Sample Design
CIJE: 0 RIE: 1 CAT: 21

Incongruence (Psychology)
CIJE: 4 RIE: 2 CAT: 11

Incongruency Discrimination Assessment
CIJE: 1 RIE: 2 CAT: 21

Incongruity Game
CIJE: 0 RIE: 1 CAT: 16

Inconsistency
CIJE: 18 RIE: 4 CAT: 16

Incorporated Association of Assistant Masters
CIJE: 1 RIE: 0 CAT: 17

Incorporation (Linguistics)
USE Linguistic Incorporation

Increasing Enrollment
CIJE: 2 RIE: 2 CAT: 16

Incremental Approach (Instruction)
CIJE: 2 RIE: 1 CAT: 15

Incremental Fit Index
CIJE: 1 RIE: 1 CAT: 21
SN An index for assessing the dimensionality underlying a set of test items

Incremental Space
CIJE: 0 RIE: 1 CAT: 16

Incremental Validity
CIJE: 0 RIE: 1 CAT: 15

Incrementalism (Decision Making)
CIJE: 2 RIE: 2 CAT: 15

Incubators
CIJE: 1 RIE: 0 CAT: 04

Incumbent Defeat
CIJE: 1 RIE: 2 CAT: 16

Incunabula
CIJE: 2 RIE: 3 CAT: 16

Indecisiveness
CIJE: 2 RIE: 1 CAT: 16

Indeophones
CIJE: 0 RIE: 1 CAT: 13

Independence Community College KS
CIJE: 0 RIE: 1 CAT: 17

Independence Day
CIJE: 1 RIE: 1 CAT: 12

Independence Day (Mexico)
CIJE: 0 RIE: 1 CAT: 12

Independence Model
CIJE: 4 RIE: 2 CAT: 15

Independence School District MO
CIJE: 1 RIE: 0 CAT: 17

Independence Training
CIJE: 7 RIE: 3 CAT: 15

Independent Aging Program CA
CIJE: 0 RIE: 1 CAT: 19

Independent Bargaining Agents
CIJE: 0 RIE: 5 CAT: 09

Independent Behavior
CIJE: 29 RIE: 13 CAT: 11

Independent Broadcasting Association
CIJE: 0 RIE: 1 CAT: 17

Independent Broadcasting Authority
CIJE: 4 RIE: 0 CAT: 17

Independent Learning Project
CIJE: 1 RIE: 1 CAT: 19

Independent Living Behavior Checklist
CIJE: 0 RIE: 1 CAT: 21

Independent Living Centers
CIJE: 7 RIE: 5 CAT: 05
SN See also "Centers for Independent Living Program"

Independent Living Subsidy Program
CIJE: 2 RIE: 0 CAT: 19

Independent Miniunit Program
CIJE: 0 RIE: 1 CAT: 19

Independent Samples
CIJE: 1 RIE: 1 CAT: 21

Independent Scholars
CIJE: 0 RIE: 1 CAT: 10

Independent School District 196 MN
CIJE: 1 RIE: 4 CAT: 17

Independent School District TX
CIJE: 1 RIE: 1 CAT: 17

Independent Schools Information Service
CIJE: 1 RIE: 0 CAT: 17

Independent Schools Talent Search Program
CIJE: 2 RIE: 6 CAT: 21

Independent Study in the Humanities Fellowship
CIJE: 0 RIE: 1 CAT: 19

Independent Television
CIJE: 1 RIE: 2 CAT: 04

Independent Television Authority (England)
CIJE: 2 RIE: 3 CAT: 17

Independent Television Stations
CIJE: 2 RIE: 0 CAT: 05

Index Chemicus Registry System
CIJE: 2 RIE: 0 CAT: 15

Index Medicus
CIJE: 7 RIE: 5 CAT: 22

Index of Academic Gains
CIJE: 0 RIE: 1 CAT: 21

Index of Adjustment and Values
CIJE: 2 RIE: 1 CAT: 22

Index Of Dispersion (Categorical Data)
CIJE: 1 RIE: 0 CAT: 21

Index of Dissimilarity
CIJE: 2 RIE: 4 CAT: 21

Index of Evaluative Dominance
CIJE: 1 RIE: 0 CAT: 22

Index of Least Restrictive Employment
CIJE: 0 RIE: 1 CAT: 21

Index of Rhythmicity
CIJE: 0 RIE: 1 CAT: 22

Index of Social Competence
CIJE: 1 RIE: 0 CAT: 21

Index of Spouse Abuse
CIJE: 1 RIE: 0 CAT: 21

Index of the Sciences (Arabic)
CIJE: 0 RIE: 1 CAT: 22
UF Fihrist al Ulum

Index Salary Schedules
CIJE: 0 RIE: 1 CAT: 15

Indexer Consistency
CIJE: 4 RIE: 1 CAT: 16

Indexers
CIJE: 6 RIE: 2 CAT: 09

Indexing and Abstracting Services
USE Abstracting and Indexing Services

India
CIJE: 1024 RIE: 832 CAT: 07

India (Ahmadnagar Fort)
CIJE: 1 RIE: 0 CAT: 07

India (Andhra Pradesh)
CIJE: 0 RIE: 1 CAT: 07

India (Bangalore)
CIJE: 3 RIE: 1 CAT: 07

India (Baroda)
CIJE: 4 RIE: 2 CAT: 07

India (Bengal)
CIJE: 0 RIE: 2 CAT: 07

India (Bihar State)
CIJE: 0 RIE: 2 CAT: 07

India (Bombay State)
CIJE: 0 RIE: 1 CAT: 07

India (Bombay)
CIJE: 7 RIE: 4 CAT: 07

India (Calcutta)
CIJE: 1 RIE: 1 CAT: 07

India (Chandigarh UT)
CIJE: 0 RIE: 1 CAT: 07

India (Chandigarh)
CIJE: 0 RIE: 1 CAT: 07

India (Davangere)
CIJE: 0 RIE: 1 CAT: 07

India (Delhi)
CIJE: 5 RIE: 5 CAT: 07

India (Ernakulam)
CIJE: 0 RIE: 1 CAT: 07

India (Gujarat State)
CIJE: 2 RIE: 2 CAT: 07

India (Gujarat)
CIJE: 2 RIE: 3 CAT: 07

India (Haryana)
CIJE: 3 RIE: 1 CAT: 07

India (Himachal Pradesh)
CIJE: 0 RIE: 1 CAT: 07

India (Jaipur)
CIJE: 1 RIE: 1 CAT: 07

India (Karnataka)
CIJE: 3 RIE: 1 CAT: 07

India (Kerala State)
CIJE: 0 RIE: 2 CAT: 07

India (Lucknow)
CIJE: 2 RIE: 1 CAT: 07

India (Madras State)
CIJE: 3 RIE: 1 CAT: 07

India (Maharashtra)
CIJE: 1 RIE: 9 CAT: 07

India (Manipur)
CIJE: 1 RIE: 1 CAT: 07

India (Mysore State)
CIJE: 1 RIE: 6 CAT: 07

India (New Delhi)
CIJE: 8 RIE: 9 CAT: 07

India (Orissa)
CIJE: 2 RIE: 4 CAT: 07

India (Poona)
CIJE: 1 RIE: 2 CAT: 07

India (Punjab State)
CIJE: 6 RIE: 1 CAT: 07

India (Rajasthan)
CIJE: 6 RIE: 2 CAT: 07

India (South)
CIJE: 4 RIE: 2 CAT: 07

India (Tamil Nadu)
CIJE: 2 RIE: 3 CAT: 07

India (Uttar Pradesh)
CIJE: 2 RIE: 4 CAT: 07

India (West Bengal)
CIJE: 1 RIE: 4 CAT: 07

Indian Adult Education Association (India)
CIJE: 0 RIE: 4 CAT: 17

Indian Arts and Crafts Board Amendments Act 1980
CIJE: 0 RIE: 1 CAT: 14

Indian Bill of Rights
CIJE: 2 RIE: 1 CAT: 14

Indian Child Welfare Act 1978
CIJE: 9 RIE: 23 CAT: 14

Indian Child Welfare Program AZ
CIJE: 0 RIE: 2 CAT: 19

Indian Civil Rights Act 1968
CIJE: 1 RIE: 3 CAT: 14

Indian Claims Commission
CIJE: 6 RIE: 1 CAT: 17

Indian Defense League of America
CIJE: 1 RIE: 0 CAT: 17

Indian Education Act 1972
CIJE: 17 RIE: 55 CAT: 14
UF Education Amendments 1972 Title IV

Indian Education Act 1972 Title IV
CIJE: 0 RIE: 33 CAT: 14

Indian Education Act 1988 Title V
CIJE: 0 RIE: 3 CAT: 14

Indian Education Act Amendments 1987
CIJE: 0 RIE: 4 CAT: 14
UF Indian Education Amendments 1987

Indian Education Amendments 1987
USE Indian Education Act Amendments 1987

Indian Education Centre (Canada)
CIJE: 1 RIE: 0 CAT: 17

Indian Education Committees
CIJE: 0 RIE: 3 CAT: 10

Indian Education Fellowship Program
CIJE: 0 RIE: 1 CAT: 19

Indian Education Program
CIJE: 1 RIE: 3 CAT: 19

Indian Education Research Project
CIJE: 0 RIE: 3 CAT: 19

Indian Education Resources Center NM
CIJE: 0 RIE: 1 CAT: 17

Indian Emergency 1975
USE Indian State of Emergency 1975

Indian Health Care Improvement Act
CIJE: 2 RIE: 8 CAT: 14

Indian Health Program
CIJE: 1 RIE: 1 CAT: 19

Indian Health Service
CIJE: 31 RIE: 58 CAT: 17

Indian Hill Project
CIJE: 0 RIE: 1 CAT: 19

Indian Hills Community College IA
CIJE: 0 RIE: 3 CAT: 17

Indian Institute of Technology (India)
CIJE: 1 RIE: 0 CAT: 17

Indian Literature
CIJE: 0 RIE: 2 CAT: 16
SN Literature of India

Indian Music
CIJE: 2 RIE: 1 CAT: 16

Indian National Committee on Space Research
CIJE: 0 RIE: 1 CAT: 17

Indian National Council of Educational Research
CIJE: 0 RIE: 1 CAT: 17

Indian Nations At Risk Task Force
CIJE: 3 RIE: 13 CAT: 17

Indian Oasis Public School District AZ
CIJE: 0 RIE: 1 CAT: 17

Indian Ocean
CIJE: 2 RIE: 1 CAT: 07

Indian Paraprofessional Services
CIJE: 0 RIE: 1 CAT: 17

Indian Peace Medals
CIJE: 0 RIE: 1 CAT: 16

Indian Reorganization Act 1934
CIJE: 10 RIE: 5 CAT: 14

Indian Resource Development
CIJE: 0 RIE: 0 CAT: 16

Indian Resource Development Program
CIJE: 0 RIE: 2 CAT: 19

Indian Resources Development Internship Program
CIJE: 0 RIE: 4 CAT: 19

Indian River Community College FL
CIJE: 2 RIE: 2 CAT: 17

Indian School Equalization Program
CIJE: 0 RIE: 1 CAT: 19

Indian Self Determination Education Assistance Act
CIJE: 4 RIE: 20 CAT: 14
UF Public Law 93 638

Indian State of Emergency 1975
CIJE: 0 RIE: 1 CAT: 12
SN Declaration by Prime Minister Indira Gandhi
UF Indian Emergency 1975

Indian Students University Programme
CIJE: 0 RIE: 1 CAT: 19

Indian Teacher Training Program
CIJE: 0 RIE: 1 CAT: 19

Indian Valley Colleges Project
CIJE: 0 RIE: 1 CAT: 19

Indian Youth Leadership Camps
CIJE: 1 RIE: 0 CAT: 19
SN See also "National Indian Youth Leadership Model"

Indian Youth of America Camps
CIJE: 1 RIE: 0 CAT: 19

Indian Youth Opportunity Conferences
CIJE: 0 RIE: 1 CAT: 02

Indiana
CIJE: 243 RIE: 813 CAT: 07

Indiana (Bartholomew County)
CIJE: 0 RIE: 1 CAT: 07

Indiana (Bloomington)
CIJE: 2 RIE: 3 CAT: 07

Indiana (Central)
CIJE: 0 RIE: 3 CAT: 07

Indiana (Columbus)
CIJE: 1 RIE: 3 CAT: 07

Indiana (Elkhart County)
CIJE: 0 RIE: 1 CAT: 07

Indiana (Elkhart)
CIJE: 1 RIE: 2 CAT: 07

Indiana (Evansville)
CIJE: 0 RIE: 10 CAT: 07

Indiana (Floyd County)
CIJE: 0 RIE: 2 CAT: 07

Indiana (Fort Wayne)
CIJE: 5 RIE: 11 CAT: 07

Indiana (Gary)
CIJE: 13 RIE: 13 CAT: 07

Indiana (Grant County)
CIJE: 0 RIE: 1 CAT: 07

Indiana (Hammond)
CIJE: 1 RIE: 4 CAT: 07

Indiana (Henry County)
CIJE: 0 RIE: 1 CAT: 07

Indiana (Indianapolis)
CIJE: 40 RIE: 51 CAT: 07

Indiana (Kankakee Valley)
CIJE: 0 RIE: 1 CAT: 07

Indiana (Kokomo)
CIJE: 0 RIE: 1 CAT: 07

Indiana (Lafayette)
CIJE: 2 RIE: 1 CAT: 07

Indiana (Lake County)
CIJE: 0 RIE: 2 CAT: 07

Indiana (Lawrence County)
CIJE: 1 RIE: 1 CAT: 07

Indiana (Logansport)
CIJE: 0 RIE: 1 CAT: 07

Indiana (Marion County)
CIJE: 3 RIE: 3 CAT: 07

Indiana (Michigan City)
CIJE: 2 RIE: 0 CAT: 07

Indiana (Monroe County)
CIJE: 3 RIE: 3 CAT: 07

Indiana (Monticello)
CIJE: 1 RIE: 0 CAT: 07

Indiana (Muncie)
CIJE: 12 RIE: 6 CAT: 07

Indiana (New Albany)
CIJE: 0 RIE: 2 CAT: 07

Indiana (New Harmony)
CIJE: 3 RIE: 6 CAT: 07
UF New Harmony Utopian Society

Indiana (Northeast)
CIJE: 0 RIE: 2 CAT: 07

Indiana (Portage)
CIJE: 0 RIE: 1 CAT: 07

Indiana (Porter County)
CIJE: 0 RIE: 2 CAT: 07

Indiana (Richmond)
CIJE: 0 RIE: 1 CAT: 07

Indiana (Saint Joseph County)
CIJE: 0 RIE: 1 CAT: 07

Indiana (South Bend)
CIJE: 4 RIE: 12 CAT: 07

Indiana (South)
CIJE: 1 RIE: 3 CAT: 07

Indiana (Terre Haute)
CIJE: 3 RIE: 8 CAT: 07

Indiana (Vanderburgh County)
CIJE: 0 RIE: 1 CAT: 07

Indiana (Wabash County)
CIJE: 0 RIE: 1 CAT: 07

Indiana (West Lafayette)
CIJE: 0 RIE: 1 CAT: 07

Indiana (Yorktown)
CIJE: 0 RIE: 1 CAT: 07

Indiana Academy for Science Math and Humanities
CIJE: 0 RIE: 2 CAT: 17

Indiana Adult Literacy Coalition
CIJE: 1 RIE: 1 CAT: 17

Indiana Adult Literacy Initiative
CIJE: 0 RIE: 1 CAT: 19

Indiana Basic Competency Skills Test
CIJE: 0 RIE: 2 CAT: 21

Indiana Broadcasters Association
CIJE: 0 RIE: 2 CAT: 17

Indiana Career Resource Center
CIJE: 0 RIE: 3 CAT: 17

Indiana College Placement and Assessment Center
CIJE: 1 RIE: 1 CAT: 17

Indiana Collegiate Press Association
CIJE: 1 RIE: 0 CAT: 17

Indiana Commission for Higher Education
CIJE: 0 RIE: 13 CAT: 17

Indiana Conference Scheme
CIJE: 0 RIE: 1 CAT: 21

Indiana Congress on Education
CIJE: 0 RIE: 1 CAT: 17

Indiana Council for Continuing Education
CIJE: 0 RIE: 1 CAT: 17

Indiana Council on Economic Education
CIJE: 2 RIE: 0 CAT: 17

Indiana County Area Vocational Technical School PA
CIJE: 0 RIE: 1 CAT: 17

Indiana Dept Public Instruction Div Inst Media
CIJE: 0 RIE: 1 CAT: 17

Indiana Global Education Program
CIJE: 0 RIE: 1 CAT: 19

Indiana Governors Conference Lib Info Servs
USE Governors Conference Library Info Services IN

Indiana Higher Education Telecommunications System
CIJE: 0 RIE: 2 CAT: 17

Indiana Institute of Technology
CIJE: 1 RIE: 0 CAT: 17

Indiana Laborers Training Trust Fund
CIJE: 1 RIE: 0 CAT: 17

Indiana Language Program
CIJE: 0 RIE: 7 CAT: 21

Indiana Least Restrictive Environment Project
CIJE: 0 RIE: 1 CAT: 19

Indiana Manpower Research Association
CIJE: 0 RIE: 1 CAT: 17

Indiana Parent Training Project
CIJE: 0 RIE: 2 CAT: 19

Indiana Performance Assessments
CIJE: 0 RIE: 1 CAT: 21

Indiana Plan for Adult Religious Education
CIJE: 1 RIE: 2 CAT: 19

Indiana Plan Institute
CIJE: 0 RIE: 2 CAT: 17

Indiana Principal Leadership Academy
CIJE: 0 RIE: 3 CAT: 17

Indiana Project
CIJE: 0 RIE: 1 CAT: 19

Indiana Routing System
CIJE: 0 RIE: 1 CAT: 15

Indiana School Library Association
CIJE: 0 RIE: 1 CAT: 17

Indiana State Council
CIJE: 0 RIE: 1 CAT: 17

Indiana State Department of Education
CIJE: 0 RIE: 3 CAT: 17

Indiana State Reformatory
CIJE: 1 RIE: 0 CAT: 17

Indiana State University
CIJE: 29 RIE: 25 CAT: 17

Indiana Statewide Testing for Educ Progress
CIJE: 0 RIE: 3 CAT: 21

Indiana TIME Project
CIJE: 0 RIE: 1 CAT: 19

Indiana Univ Purdue Univ at Fort Wayne
CIJE: 0 RIE: 1 CAT: 17

Indiana Univ Purdue Univ at Indianapolis
CIJE: 9 RIE: 7 CAT: 17

Indiana Univ Purdue Univ at Indianapolis Columbus
CIJE: 0 RIE: 1 CAT: 17

Indiana University
CIJE: 125 RIE: 122 CAT: 17

Indiana University Advance College Project
CIJE: 3 RIE: 2 CAT: 19
UF Advance College Project (Indiana University)

Indiana University Bloomington
CIJE: 15 RIE: 49 CAT: 17

Indiana University East
CIJE: 1 RIE: 2 CAT: 17

Indiana University Fort Wayne
CIJE: 0 RIE: 1 CAT: 17

Indiana University Northwest
CIJE: 2 RIE: 5 CAT: 17

Indiana University of Pennsylvania
CIJE: 14 RIE: 17 CAT: 17

Indiana University School of Music
CIJE: 1 RIE: 0 CAT: 17

Indiana University South Bend
CIJE: 4 RIE: 12 CAT: 17

Indiana University Southeast
CIJE: 1 RIE: 9 CAT: 17

Indiana Vocational Technical College
CIJE: 0 RIE: 4 CAT: 17

Indiana Wesleyan University
CIJE: 0 RIE: 1 CAT: 17

Indiana Youth Employment Training Programs
CIJE: 0 RIE: 1 CAT: 19

Indiana Youth Institute
CIJE: 0 RIE: 1 CAT: 17

Indiana Youth Poll
CIJE: 0 RIE: 1 CAT: 21

Indianapolis Marion County Public Library IN
CIJE: 3 RIE: 2 CAT: 17

Indianapolis Model Cities School Program
CIJE: 1 RIE: 0 CAT: 19

Indianapolis Public Schools IN
CIJE: 8 RIE: 11 CAT: 17

Indianhead Technical Institute WI
CIJE: 1 RIE: 1 CAT: 17

Indians into Medicine
CIJE: 1 RIE: 4 CAT: 19
UF INMED

Indic Languages
CIJE: 0 RIE: 3 CAT: 13

Indicator Verification
CIJE: 0 RIE: 3 CAT: 15

Indicators
CIJE: 34 RIE: 87 CAT: 16

Indicators of Excellence Program FL
CIJE: 0 RIE: 0 CAT: 19

Indicators of Quality Schools
CIJE: 2 RIE: 6 CAT: 21

Indigenous Architecture
CIJE: 0 RIE: 1 CAT: 16

Indigenous Knowledge Systems
CIJE: 2 RIE: 1 CAT: 15

Indigenous Mathematics Project
CIJE: 2 RIE: 16 CAT: 19

Indira Gandhi National Open University (India)
CIJE: 0 RIE: 1 CAT: 17

Indirect Assessment
CIJE: 0 RIE: 2 CAT: 21

Indirect Costs
CIJE: 30 RIE: 18 CAT: 16

Indirect Effects (Causal Modeling)
CIJE: 2 RIE: 1 CAT: 15

Indirect Objects
CIJE: 2 RIE: 4 CAT: 13

Indirect Parent Interview
CIJE: 0 RIE: 1 CAT: 15

Indirect Questioning (Puppet Test)
CIJE: 0 RIE: 1 CAT: 21

Indirect Questions
CIJE: 2 RIE: 0 CAT: 13

Indirect Refusals
CIJE: 0 RIE: 1 CAT: 13

Indirect Speech
CIJE: 5 RIE: 14 CAT: 13
UF Reported Speech

Indirect Suggestion
CIJE: 2 RIE: 1 CAT: 11

Indirect Teaching
CIJE: 8 RIE: 0 CAT: 15

Indium
CIJE: 1 RIE: 0 CAT: 20

Individual Achievement Monitoring System
CIJE: 0 RIE: 2 CAT: 21

Individual Achievement Record
CIJE: 0 RIE: 1 CAT: 21

Individual Career Exploration PACK
CIJE: 1 RIE: 0 CAT: 19

Individual Client Inventory
CIJE: 0 RIE: 1 CAT: 21

Individual Cognitive Demand Schedule (Lynch Ames)
CIJE: 1 RIE: 2 CAT: 21

Individual Communications System
CIJE: 0 RIE: 1 CAT: 15

Individual Consistency Index
CIJE: 1 RIE: 1 CAT: 21

Individual Criterion Referenced Test
CIJE: 2 RIE: 0 CAT: 21

Individual Differences Scaling (INDSCAL)
CIJE: 2 RIE: 3 CAT: 21

Individual Differences Scaling Model
CIJE: 2 RIE: 0 CAT: 15

Individual Events (Forensics)
CIJE: 0 RIE: 11 CAT: 16

Individual Events Competition
CIJE: 0 RIE: 4 CAT: 16
SN See also "National Individual Events Tournaments"

Individual Goal Structures
USE Goal Structures

Individual Learning Contracts
CIJE: 1 RIE: 0 CAT: 16

Individual Marital Therapy
CIJE: 0 RIE: 1 CAT: 11
UF Marital Therapy (Individual)

Individual Opinion Inventory (Hull et al)
CIJE: 1 RIE: 1 CAT: 21

Individual Participant Profile
CIJE: 0 RIE: 1 CAT: 21

Individual Physician Profile
CIJE: 1 RIE: 2 CAT: 11

Individual Progress Method
CIJE: 2 RIE: 0 CAT: 15

Individual Progress Program
CIJE: 0 RIE: 1 CAT: 19

Individual Reading Inventory
CIJE: 1 RIE: 1 CAT: 21

Individual Ready Reservists
CIJE: 0 RIE: 1 CAT: 09

Individual Retirement Accounts
CIJE: 1 RIE: 4 CAT: 16

Individual Scaling Analysis
CIJE: 1 RIE: 0 CAT: 21

Individual Service Plans
USE Individualized Service Plans

Individual Short Term Plan Records
CIJE: 0 RIE: 10 CAT: 16

Individual Sports
CIJE: 2 RIE: 4 CAT: 16

Individual Statistics Project (Sweden)
CIJE: 0 RIE: 1 CAT: 19

Individual Student Profile System
CIJE: 0 RIE: 1 CAT: 04

Individual Test of Creativity
CIJE: 0 RIE: 1 CAT: 21

Individual Training Accounts
CIJE: 0 RIE: 1 CAT: 16

Individual Transition Teams
CIJE: 0 RIE: 0 CAT: 10

Individual Vocational Education Plans
USE Individualized Vocational Education Programs

Individualization of Instruction Scale (Gellman)
CIJE: 1 RIE: 1 CAT: 21

Individualized Audio Tutorial Instruction
CIJE: 0 RIE: 3 CAT: 15

Individualized Bilingual Instruction
CIJE: 0 RIE: 2 CAT: 15

Individualized Bilingual Instruction Program
CIJE: 0 RIE: 5 CAT: 19

Individualized Career Plans
CIJE: 1 RIE: 3 CAT: 15

Individualized Classroom Environment Questionnaire
CIJE: 8 RIE: 6 CAT: 21

Individualized Communication
CIJE: 1 RIE: 0 CAT: 15

Individualized Critical Skills Model
CIJE: 0 RIE: 1 CAT: 15

Individualized Curriculum Sequencing Model
CIJE: 2 RIE: 1 CAT: 03

Individualized Early Learning Model
CIJE: 0 RIE: 1 CAT: 15

Individualized Eclectic Examination
CIJE: 1 RIE: 0 CAT: 21

Individualized Employment Programs
CIJE: 0 RIE: 7 CAT: 19

Individualized Evaluation
CIJE: 3 RIE: 4 CAT: 21

Individualized Funding
CIJE: 0 RIE: 1 CAT: 16

Individualized Inservice Teacher Education Project
CIJE: 0 RIE: 1 CAT: 19

Individualized Instruction for Data Access
CIJE: 4 RIE: 6 CAT: 19

Individualized Instruction Inventory (Campbell)
CIJE: 0 RIE: 1 CAT: 21

Individualized Instruction Scale
CIJE: 0 RIE: 2 CAT: 21

Individualized Language Arts Project
CIJE: 0 RIE: 1 CAT: 19

Individualized Learning Modules
CIJE: 0 RIE: 1 CAT: 15

Individualized Learning Plans
CIJE: 3 RIE: 2 CAT: 03

Individualized Mathematics System
CIJE: 0 RIE: 1 CAT: 19

Individualized Program Plans (Retardation)
CIJE: 0 RIE: 1 CAT: 15

Individualized Quality of Life Scale
CIJE: 0 RIE: 1 CAT: 21

Individualized Reading Program
CIJE: 1 RIE: 1 CAT: 19

Individualized Science Instructional System
CIJE: 6 RIE: 3 CAT: 04

Individualized Secondary Teacher Education Program
CIJE: 0 RIE: 3 CAT: 19

Individualized Service Plans
CIJE: 0 RIE: 1 CAT: 19
UF Individual Service Plans

Individualized Study by Telecommunications
CIJE: 0 RIE: 1 CAT: 19

Individualized Teacher Preparation Program
CIJE: 0 RIE: 1 CAT: 19

Individualized Training Plans
CIJE: 0 RIE: 2 CAT: 15

Individualized Training Programs
CIJE: 0 RIE: 1 CAT: 19

Individualized Transition Plans
CIJE: 3 RIE: 16 CAT: 11

Individualized Trust Scale
CIJE: 0 RIE: 1 CAT: 21

Individualized Vocational Education Programs
CIJE: 0 RIE: 2 CAT: 19
UF Individual Vocational Education Plans

Individualizing Spanish for Speakers of English
CIJE: 0 RIE: 7 CAT: 19

Individually Guided Behavior
CIJE: 0 RIE: 1 CAT: 11

Individually Guided Education
CIJE: 53 RIE: 146 CAT: 19

Individually Prescribed Instruction
CIJE: 24 RIE: 105 CAT: 16

Individuals with Disabilities Education Act
CIJE: 43 RIE: 68 CAT: 14
UF Education of the Handicapped Act 1991; Education of the Handicapped Act Amendments 1990; IDEA; Public Law 101 476

Individuals with Disabilities Education Act Part B
CIJE: 0 RIE: 6 CAT: 14
UF Public Law 101 476 Part B

Individuals with Disabilities Education Act Part H
CIJE: 4 RIE: 36 CAT: 14
UF Part H 101 476 (Infants and Toddlers with Disabil); Public Law 101 476 Part H

Individuation
CIJE: 33 RIE: 15 CAT: 16

Indo Aryan Languages
CIJE: 1 RIE: 3 CAT: 13

Indochina
CIJE: 6 RIE: 10 CAT: 07

Indochinese Culture
CIJE: 0 RIE: 3 CAT: 16

Indoctrination
CIJE: 47 RIE: 10 CAT: 16

Indomethacin
CIJE: 0 RIE: 1 CAT: 11

Indonesia
CIJE: 149 RIE: 239 CAT: 07

Indonesia (Djakarta)
USE Indonesia (Jakarta)

Indonesia (East Java)
CIJE: 0 RIE: 2 CAT: 07

Indonesia (Galang)
CIJE: 0 RIE: 2 CAT: 07

Indonesia (Irian Barat)
CIJE: 0 RIE: 1 CAT: 07

Indonesia (Jakarta)
CIJE: 2 RIE: 2 CAT: 07
UF Indonesia (Djakarta)

Indonesia (Java)
CIJE: 3 RIE: 14 CAT: 07

Indonesia (Sumatra)
CIJE: 0 RIE: 1 CAT: 07

Indonesia Nonformal Educational Project
CIJE: 0 RIE: 1 CAT: 19

Indonesian Americans
CIJE: 0 RIE: 1 CAT: 08

Indonesians
CIJE: 1 RIE: 2 CAT: 08

Indoor Air Quality
CIJE: 5 RIE: 1 CAT: 20

INDSCAL Computer Program
CIJE: 5 RIE: 1 CAT: 04

Induced Affect
CIJE: 3 RIE: 3 CAT: 16

Induced Course Load Matrix
CIJE: 2 RIE: 4 CAT: 16

Induced Mental Imagery
CIJE: 0 RIE: 8 CAT: 13

Induced Moods
USE Mood Induction

Induced Probabilities
CIJE: 0 RIE: 1 CAT: 15

Induction (Electronics)
CIJE: 1 RIE: 2 CAT: 20

Induction Loop Amplification
CIJE: 1 RIE: 0 CAT: 20

Inductive Circuits
CIJE: 0 RIE: 1 CAT: 20

Industrial Arts Career Exploration Program
CIJE: 0 RIE: 1 CAT: 19

Industrial Arts Curriculum Project
CIJE: 8 RIE: 16 CAT: 19

Industrial Arts Interaction Analysis Systems
CIJE: 1 RIE: 0 CAT: 15

Industrial Arts Spring Conference
CIJE: 1 RIE: 0 CAT: 02

Industrial Automation
CIJE: 1 RIE: 0 CAT: 20

Industrial Chemistry
CIJE: 7 RIE: 1 CAT: 03

Industrial Design
CIJE: 8 RIE: 1 CAT: 03

Industrial Development
CIJE: 4 RIE: 9 CAT: 16

Industrial Electricity
CIJE: 0 RIE: 3 CAT: 20

Industrial Engineering
CIJE: 3 RIE: 1 CAT: 03

Industrial Engineering Methods
CIJE: 0 RIE: 2 CAT: 15

Industrial Health
CIJE: 1 RIE: 8 CAT: 11

Industrial Information Officers
CIJE: 0 RIE: 1 CAT: 09

Industrial Libraries
CIJE: 7 RIE: 2 CAT: 05

Industrial Marketing
CIJE: 0 RIE: 1 CAT: 09

Industrial Materials
CIJE: 1 RIE: 8 CAT: 20

Industrial Organic Chemistry
CIJE: 1 RIE: 0 CAT: 20

Industrial Organization Theory
CIJE: 2 RIE: 0 CAT: 15

Industrial Policy
CIJE: 5 RIE: 6 CAT: 16

Industrial Processes
CIJE: 3 RIE: 2 CAT: 15

Industrial Production Occupations
CIJE: 0 RIE: 1 CAT: 09

Industrial Radiography
CIJE: 0 RIE: 2 CAT: 20

Industrial Relations Act 1971 (Great Britain)
CIJE: 1 RIE: 0 CAT: 14

Industrial Relations Centre (Canada)
CIJE: 0 RIE: 1 CAT: 17

Industrial Relations Research Association
CIJE: 0 RIE: 1 CAT: 17

Industrial Revitalization
USE Business Revitalization

Industrial Revolution
CIJE: 12 RIE: 14 CAT: 12

Industrial Schools Committee
CIJE: 1 RIE: 0 CAT: 17

Industrial Sewing Classroom Delivery System
CIJE: 0 RIE: 1 CAT: 03

Industrial Tanning Process
CIJE: 1 RIE: 0 CAT: 15

Industrial Technologists
CIJE: 1 RIE: 3 CAT: 09

Industrial Technology Institute MI
CIJE: 1 RIE: 1 CAT: 17

Industrial Television Society
CIJE: 0 RIE: 1 CAT: 17

Industrial Tools
CIJE: 1 RIE: 0 CAT: 20

Industrial Trainers
CIJE: 0 RIE: 1 CAT: 09

Industrial Training Act 1964
CIJE: 7 RIE: 9 CAT: 14

Industrial Training Boards
CIJE: 8 RIE: 1 CAT: 09

Industrial Training Resources Project
CIJE: 0 RIE: 1 CAT: 19

Industrial Wiring
CIJE: 0 RIE: 2 CAT: 20

Industrial Worker (Title)
CIJE: 0 RIE: 1 CAT: 22

Industrialized Building
CIJE: 0 RIE: 1 CAT: 20

Industrialized Building Systems
CIJE: 0 RIE: 2 CAT: 15

Industriology Project
CIJE: 1 RIE: 4 CAT: 19

Industry Based Skill Standards
CIJE: 0 RIE: 1 CAT: 15

Industry Education Councils
CIJE: 8 RIE: 10 CAT: 09

Industry Needs
CIJE: 2 RIE: 2 CAT: 16

Industry Review Panels
CIJE: 0 RIE: 1 CAT: 10

Industry Role
CIJE: 20 RIE: 10 CAT: 16

Industry Services Training Program FL
CIJE: 0 RIE: 0 CAT: 19

Industry Size
CIJE: 1 RIE: 1 CAT: 16

Industry Trends
CIJE: 10 RIE: 4 CAT: 16

Industry Work Experience Program
CIJE: 0 RIE: 1 CAT: 19

INED
USE International Network for Educational Information

Ineffective Subordinates
CIJE: 1 RIE: 0 CAT: 10

Inequity Theory
CIJE: 3 RIE: 1 CAT: 15

Inertia Paradigm
CIJE: 2 RIE: 1 CAT: 21

iNet
CIJE: 0 RIE: 1 CAT: 04

Inexpensive Book Distribution Program
CIJE: 0 RIE: 1 CAT: 19
SN ...for Reading Motivation — Part of "Education Consolidation Improvement Act Chapter 2"

Inexpensive Equipment
CIJE: 2 RIE: 0 CAT: 04

Inexpensive Materials
CIJE: 33 RIE: 10 CAT: 04

Inexpensive Science Teaching Equipment Project
CIJE: 0 RIE: 3 CAT: 19

Inexperienced Writers
CIJE: 0 RIE: 1 CAT: 10

Infant and Preschool Reinforcement Survey
CIJE: 1 RIE: 0 CAT: 21

Infant Care Survey
CIJE: 0 RIE: 1 CAT: 21

Infant Characteristics Questionnaire (Bates)
CIJE: 2 RIE: 1 CAT: 21

Infant Child Relationship
USE Child Infant Relationship

Infant Development Center ME
CIJE: 0 RIE: 1 CAT: 17

Infant Distress
CIJE: 4 RIE: 1 CAT: 11

Infant Education Research Project
CIJE: 1 RIE: 0 CAT: 19

Infant Feeding
CIJE: 10 RIE: 12 CAT: 11

Infant Formula
CIJE: 4 RIE: 5 CAT: 11

Infant Health and Development Program
CIJE: 1 RIE: 1 CAT: 19

Infant Holding
USE Holding of Infants

Infant Houses (Israel)
CIJE: 0 RIE: 1 CAT: 05

Infant Infant Contact Code
CIJE: 0 RIE: 1 CAT: 16

Infant Parent Education Project CA
CIJE: 0 RIE: 1 CAT: 19

Infant Program for Visually Impaired
CIJE: 0 RIE: 1 CAT: 19

Infant Rocking
CIJE: 2 RIE: 0 CAT: 11

Infant Satellite Nurseries Project
CIJE: 0 RIE: 2 CAT: 19

Infant Simulator 1
CIJE: 0 RIE: 1 CAT: 04

Infant Smiling
CIJE: 6 RIE: 0 CAT: 11

Infant State
CIJE: 3 RIE: 0 CAT: 11

Infant Stimulation
CIJE: 14 RIE: 7 CAT: 11

Infant Temperament Questionnaire
CIJE: 2 RIE: 2 CAT: 21

Infant Tracking System
CIJE: 0 RIE: 2 CAT: 16
UF Tracking System (Infants)

Infant Vocalization
CIJE: 14 RIE: 3 CAT: 13

Infanticide
CIJE: 2 RIE: 1 CAT: 16

Infantile Amnesia
CIJE: 3 RIE: 0 CAT: 11

Infantile Autism
CIJE: 0 RIE: 1 CAT: 11

Inferential Comprehension
CIJE: 0 RIE: 1 CAT: 16

Inferentials (Linguistics)
CIJE: 0 RIE: 2 CAT: 13

Inferno
CIJE: 2 RIE: 0 CAT: 22

Infertility
CIJE: 27 RIE: 10 CAT: 11

Infinitives
CIJE: 14 RIE: 2 CAT: 13

Infinity
CIJE: 14 RIE: 0 CAT: 20

Infinity Factory
CIJE: 0 RIE: 5 CAT: 22

Inflammation
CIJE: 1 RIE: 2 CAT: 11

Inflammation (Computer Program)
CIJE: 0 RIE: 0 CAT: 04

Inflection (Grammar)
CIJE: 11 RIE: 10 CAT: 13

Influence Strategies
CIJE: 11 RIE: 4 CAT: 15

Influenza
CIJE: 8 RIE: 0 CAT: 11

Informal Communications
CIJE: 10 RIE: 4 CAT: 16

Informal Education
CIJE: 99 RIE: 83 CAT: 16

Informal Geometry
CIJE: 2 RIE: 0 CAT: 20

Informal Knowledge
CIJE: 2 RIE: 2 CAT: 16

Informal Language Inventory
CIJE: 1 RIE: 1 CAT: 21

Informal Learning
CIJE: 21 RIE: 19 CAT: 15

Informal Literary Style
CIJE: 1 RIE: 0 CAT: 16

Informal Logic
CIJE: 3 RIE: 1 CAT: 15

Informal Negotiations
CIJE: 1 RIE: 0 CAT: 14

Informal Placement Tests
CIJE: 1 RIE: 0 CAT: 21

Informal Reading Assessment Inventory
CIJE: 1 RIE: 2 CAT: 21

Informal Reading Inventory for Directive Teaching
CIJE: 0 RIE: 2 CAT: 21

Informal Sector
CIJE: 0 RIE: 3 CAT: 16

Informal Theories
CIJE: 0 RIE: 1 CAT: 15

Informants
CIJE: 3 RIE: 3 CAT: 10

Informatics Inc
CIJE: 4 RIE: 1 CAT: 17

Information Age
CIJE: 56 RIE: 36 CAT: 12

Information Analysis
CIJE: 30 RIE: 22 CAT: 16

Information Barriers
USE Barriers to Information

Information Based Evaluation
CIJE: 0 RIE: 4 CAT: 21

Information Behavior Research
CIJE: 16 RIE: 1 CAT: 15

Information Books
CIJE: 14 RIE: 4 CAT: 16

Information Bulletins
CIJE: 0 RIE: 1 CAT: 16

Information Consistency
CIJE: 0 RIE: 1 CAT: 15

Information Consolidation
CIJE: 1 RIE: 2 CAT: 15

Information Consultants
CIJE: 3 RIE: 3 CAT: 09

Information Coordination
CIJE: 0 RIE: 1 CAT: 15

Information Counseling
CIJE: 3 RIE: 2 CAT: 15
UF Information Counselors

Information Counselors
USE Information Counseling

Information Desks
CIJE: 0 RIE: 1 CAT: 05
UF Library Information Desks

Information Discrepancy
CIJE: 2 RIE: 1 CAT: 15

Information Dynamics Corporation
CIJE: 0 RIE: 1 CAT: 17

Information Economy
CIJE: 17 RIE: 4 CAT: 16

Information Equity
CIJE: 12 RIE: 5 CAT: 15

Information Exchange
CIJE: 22 RIE: 5 CAT: 16

Information Exchange Procedures
CIJE: 2 RIE: 20 CAT: 15

Information Feedback Schedules
CIJE: 1 RIE: 0 CAT: 15

Information Focus
CIJE: 1 RIE: 4 CAT: 16

Information for Industry
CIJE: 0 RIE: 1 CAT: 02

Information Format
CIJE: 12 RIE: 3 CAT: 15

Information Function (Tests)
CIJE: 11 RIE: 18 CAT: 21

Information Hypothesis
CIJE: 1 RIE: 1 CAT: 15

Information Impact
CIJE: 4 RIE: 1 CAT: 16

Information Industry Association
CIJE: 6 RIE: 3 CAT: 17

Information Infrastructure
CIJE: 25 RIE: 27 CAT: 20
SN See also "National Information Infrastructure" and "Telecommunications Infrastructure"

Information Integration
CIJE: 11 RIE: 6 CAT: 20

Information Integration Theory
CIJE: 7 RIE: 5 CAT: 15

Information Interchange Codes
CIJE: 1 RIE: 2 CAT: 15

Information Knowledge Research Centre
CIJE: 0 RIE: 1 CAT: 17

Information Leakage
CIJE: 3 RIE: 0 CAT: 20

Information Load
CIJE: 3 RIE: 2 CAT: 20

Information Mapping
CIJE: 17 RIE: 5 CAT: 20

Information Mapping Inc
CIJE: 0 RIE: 1 CAT: 17

Information Message Units
CIJE: 0 RIE: 1 CAT: 15

Information Needed for Occupational Entry
CIJE: 1 RIE: 4 CAT: 16

Information on Demand CA
CIJE: 2 RIE: 0 CAT: 17

Information Oriented Language
CIJE: 0 RIE: 2 CAT: 15

Information Overload
CIJE: 17 RIE: 7 CAT: 16

Information Packaging
CIJE: 0 RIE: 1 CAT: 15

Information Partnership Act
CIJE: 0 RIE: 1 CAT: 14

Information Place
CIJE: 1 RIE: 1 CAT: 22

Information Power (AASL AECT)
CIJE: 18 RIE: 2 CAT: 22
SN "Information Power: Guidelines for School Library Media Programs"

Information Preference Questionnaire
CIJE: 0 RIE: 1 CAT: 21

Information Products
CIJE: 22 RIE: 2 CAT: 16

Information Providers
CIJE: 16 RIE: 4 CAT: 10

Information Science Research
CIJE: 28 RIE: 1 CAT: 20

Information Sector
CIJE: 7 RIE: 7 CAT: 10

Information Selection
CIJE: 2 RIE: 2 CAT: 20

Information Society
CIJE: 44 RIE: 30 CAT: 16

Information Strategies
CIJE: 2 RIE: 4 CAT: 15

Information Studies
CIJE: 0 RIE: 1 CAT: 03

Information Subsidies
CIJE: 1 RIE: 2 CAT: 16

Information Superhighway
CIJE: 3 RIE: 3 CAT: 20
UF Electronic Superhighway

Information System for Vocational Decisions
CIJE: 3 RIE: 25 CAT: 15

Information System Users
CIJE: 2 RIE: 4 CAT: 10

Information Transfer Experimental Center MA
CIJE: 0 RIE: 1 CAT: 17

Information Transfer Experiments Project
CIJE: 0 RIE: 1 CAT: 19

Information Value
CIJE: 36 RIE: 3 CAT: 16

Informational Energy
CIJE: 1 RIE: 0 CAT: 15

Informational Media Guaranty Program
CIJE: 0 RIE: 1 CAT: 19

Informational Resource Questionnaire
CIJE: 0 RIE: 1 CAT: 21

Informational Storybooks
CIJE: 0 RIE: 1 CAT: 16

Informative Training
CIJE: 1 RIE: 0 CAT: 15

Informed Consent
CIJE: 57 RIE: 20 CAT: 16

Informed Strategies for Learning
CIJE: 2 RIE: 1 CAT: 03

Infoschemata
CIJE: 0 RIE: 1 CAT: 16

Infoterm
CIJE: 0 RIE: 1 CAT: 17
UF International Information Centre for Terminology

InfoTrac System
CIJE: 4 RIE: 3 CAT: 04

InfoWindow (IBM)
USE IBM InfoWindow

Infrared Absorption Techniques
CIJE: 2 RIE: 0 CAT: 20

Infrared Detectors
CIJE: 2 RIE: 0 CAT: 04

Infrared Masters
CIJE: 1 RIE: 0 CAT: 20

Infrared Radiation
CIJE: 4 RIE: 0 CAT: 20

Infrared Spectrometers
CIJE: 1 RIE: 0 CAT: 04

Infrared Spectroscopy
CIJE: 13 RIE: 0 CAT: 20

Infrastructure
CIJE: 7 RIE: 10 CAT: 16
SN Use a more specific term if possible, e.g., "Building Infrastructure," "Communications Infrastructure," "Information Infrastructure," "National Information Infrastructure," "Research Infrastructure," "Technological Infrastructure," "Telecommunications Infrastructure," "Urban Infrastructures"

Infrequency Scale (Holland)
CIJE: 0 RIE: 1 CAT: 21

Infusion Project (Drug Education)
USE Drug Infusion Project

Inga
CIJE: 1 RIE: 0 CAT: 13

Ingarden (Roman)
CIJE: 2 RIE: 0 CAT: 18

Ingham (Gertrude)
CIJE: 1 RIE: 0 CAT: 18

Ingham Medical Center MI
CIJE: 1 RIE: 0 CAT: 17

Ingomar Middle School PA
CIJE: 1 RIE: 0 CAT: 17

Ingraham v Wright
CIJE: 11 RIE: 7 CAT: 14

Ingratiation
CIJE: 1 RIE: 0 CAT: 11

Ingratiation Tactics
CIJE: 2 RIE: 0 CAT: 15

INGRES Database Management System
CIJE: 0 RIE: 1 CAT: 04

Inhalants
CIJE: 16 RIE: 9 CAT: 11

InHealth
USE International Health Communication Hotline

Inhelder (Baerbel)
CIJE: 10 RIE: 3 CAT: 18

Inhelder Piaget System
CIJE: 2 RIE: 4 CAT: 11

Inherency
CIJE: 1 RIE: 2 CAT: 16

Inheritance Effects (Television)
CIJE: 0 RIE: 2 CAT: 16
SN The tendency for viewers to continue watching a channel at the conclusion of a program

Inhouse Use
CIJE: 10 RIE: 2 CAT: 16

Initial Certification Program NC
CIJE: 0 RIE: 0 CAT: 19
UF North Carolina Initial Certification Program

Initial Learning in Mainstreaming Project
CIJE: 0 RIE: 9 CAT: 19

Initial Training In Service Education of Teachers
CIJE: 1 RIE: 0 CAT: 19

Initiation Rites
CIJE: 4 RIE: 4 CAT: 16

Initiation to Teaching Project AB
USE Alberta Initiation to Teaching Project

Initiative 7 (Washington DC 1981)
CIJE: 0 RIE: 1 CAT: 17

Injection Molding Machine Tenders
CIJE: 0 RIE: 2 CAT: 09

Injections (Medicine)
CIJE: 2 RIE: 4 CAT: 11

Injustice
CIJE: 0 RIE: 1 CAT: 16

Inks
CIJE: 2 RIE: 2 CAT: 04

Inland Area Writing Project
CIJE: 0 RIE: 1 CAT: 19

Inland Steel Company
CIJE: 0 RIE: 1 CAT: 17

INMED
USE Indians into Medicine

Inner Bremsstrahlung Spectrum
CIJE: 1 RIE: 0 CAT: 20

Inner Child Inventory
CIJE: 0 RIE: 1 CAT: 21

Inner City Consortium IL
CIJE: 0 RIE: 1 CAT: 17

Inner City Inc (Polaroid)
USE Polaroid Inner City Inc

Inner City Mathematics Project
CIJE: 0 RIE: 1 CAT: 19

Inner City Teacher Education Project
CIJE: 0 RIE: 1 CAT: 19

Inner Direction (Psychology)
CIJE: 2 RIE: 1 CAT: 11

Inner London Education Authority (England)
CIJE: 16 RIE: 4 CAT: 17

Innis (Harold Adams)
CIJE: 2 RIE: 4 CAT: 18

Innis (Harold)
CIJE: 3 RIE: 2 CAT: 18

Innis College (Canada)
CIJE: 1 RIE: 0 CAT: 17

Innoculation Theory
CIJE: 1 RIE: 2 CAT: 15

INNOTECH (Singapore)
CIJE: 3 RIE: 3 CAT: 17

Innovation Configurations
CIJE: 2 RIE: 5 CAT: 15

Innovations Configuration
CIJE: 0 RIE: 3 CAT: 21

Innovations Program (Australia)
CIJE: 0 RIE: 1 CAT: 19

Innovative Approaches Research Project
CIJE: 0 RIE: 1 CAT: 19

Innovative Diffusion Center
CIJE: 1 RIE: 0 CAT: 17

Innovative Projects Plan
CIJE: 1 RIE: 0 CAT: 19

Innovative Social Studies Urban Elementary Schools
CIJE: 0 RIE: 0 CAT: 03

Innovators
CIJE: 5 RIE: 5 CAT: 10

Inoculation Theory
CIJE: 6 RIE: 0 CAT: 15

Inplacement (Employment)
CIJE: 0 RIE: 1 CAT: 16

Input Hypothesis
CIJE: 13 RIE: 0 CAT: 13

Inputs Process Outputs Analysis
CIJE: 2 RIE: 2 CAT: 15

Inquiry and Assistance Project
CIJE: 0 RIE: 1 CAT: 19

Inquiry Development Program
CIJE: 2 RIE: 1 CAT: 19

Inquiry Role Approach
CIJE: 5 RIE: 7 CAT: 16

Inquiry Teaching Competency Assessment
CIJE: 0 RIE: 1 CAT: 21

Inquiry Theory
CIJE: 2 RIE: 2 CAT: 15

INROADS Program
CIJE: 0 RIE: 1 CAT: 19

INSCAL Multidimensional Scaling
CIJE: 0 RIE: 1 CAT: 21

Insects
CIJE: 20 RIE: 10 CAT: 20

Insects Production Workers
CIJE: 0 RIE: 1 CAT: 09

Inserted Questions
CIJE: 6 RIE: 0 CAT: 15

Inserters
CIJE: 0 RIE: 2 CAT: 09

Inservice Educ and Training of Teachers (Project)
CIJE: 0 RIE: 1 CAT: 19

Inside Out (Television Series)
CIJE: 0 RIE: 2 CAT: 22

Insightful Arithmetic Test (ETS)
CIJE: 0 RIE: 1 CAT: 21

INSIGHTS Program FL
CIJE: 0 RIE: 1 CAT: 19

Insomnia
CIJE: 9 RIE: 2 CAT: 11

INSPEC
CIJE: 12 RIE: 15 CAT: 17

Inspector (Dental Equipment)
CIJE: 0 RIE: 1 CAT: 04

Inspectors
CIJE: 3 RIE: 7 CAT: 09

InstaCap System
CIJE: 0 RIE: 1 CAT: 04

Instance Probability Analysis
CIJE: 1 RIE: 0 CAT: 15

Instant Analysis
CIJE: 0 RIE: 1 CAT: 15

Instantaneous Durational Feedback
CIJE: 1 RIE: 0 CAT: 15

Instantaneous Report of Judgments
CIJE: 0 RIE: 3 CAT: 15

Instantiation Hypothesis
CIJE: 1 RIE: 0 CAT: 15

INSTEP Project KS
CIJE: 0 RIE: 1 CAT: 19
UF Integrative Network for Sci Teach Explor and Prac

Institut fuer Film und Bild (Sweden)
CIJE: 0 RIE: 1 CAT: 17

Institut fur Deutsche Sprache (West Germany)
CIJE: 2 RIE: 0 CAT: 17

Institute for Academic Technology NC
CIJE: 0 RIE: 1 CAT: 17

Institute for Advanced Study NJ
CIJE: 1 RIE: 0 CAT: 17

Institute for Behavioral Research MD
CIJE: 0 RIE: 1 CAT: 17

Institute for Child Study
CIJE: 1 RIE: 1 CAT: 17

Institute for Communication Research
CIJE: 0 RIE: 3 CAT: 17

Institute for Creative Education
CIJE: 0 RIE: 1 CAT: 19

Institute for Crippled and Disabled
CIJE: 0 RIE: 1 CAT: 17

Institute for Demographic and Economic Studies Inc
CIJE: 0 RIE: 2 CAT: 17

Institute for Development of Educ Activities OH
CIJE: 2 RIE: 1 CAT: 17
UF IDEA OH

Institute for Developmental Studies
CIJE: 1 RIE: 5 CAT: 17

Institute for Education and Technology
CIJE: 0 RIE: 1 CAT: 17

Institute for Educational Leadership DC
CIJE: 5 RIE: 3 CAT: 17

Institute for Emotional Education
CIJE: 2 RIE: 0 CAT: 17

Institute for English Language Education (England)
CIJE: 0 RIE: 1 CAT: 17
SN Located at the University of Leeds

Institute for Environmental Education OH
CIJE: 1 RIE: 4 CAT: 17

Institute for Executive Leadership OR
CIJE: 0 RIE: 1 CAT: 17

Institute for Human Development AZ
CIJE: 0 RIE: 1 CAT: 17

Institute for Instructional Research and Practice
CIJE: 0 RIE: 1 CAT: 17

Institute for Interactive Information Environ CA
CIJE: 0 RIE: 1 CAT: 17

Institute for International Education
CIJE: 0 RIE: 1 CAT: 17

Institute for Juvenile Research IL
CIJE: 1 RIE: 2 CAT: 17

Institute for Juvenile Research Symptom Checklist
CIJE: 1 RIE: 0 CAT: 21

Institute for Learning Disability
CIJE: 0 RIE: 1 CAT: 17

Institute for Local Directors Special Education CA
CIJE: 0 RIE: 1 CAT: 17

Institute for Mathematical Studies in Soc Scis CA
CIJE: 2 RIE: 5 CAT: 17

Institute for Middle School Reform MD
CIJE: 0 RIE: 1 CAT: 19
SN Project of Baltimore City Public Schools

Institute for Minority Business Education DC
CIJE: 0 RIE: 1 CAT: 17

Institute for Native American Development IL
CIJE: 0 RIE: 2 CAT: 17

Institute for Perception Research
CIJE: 1 RIE: 0 CAT: 17

Institute for Personality and Ability Testing CT
CIJE: 1 RIE: 1 CAT: 17

Institute for Policy Analysis (Canada)
CIJE: 0 RIE: 1 CAT: 17

Institute for Research and Training Higher Educ OH
CIJE: 1 RIE: 0 CAT: 17

Institute for Research in History
CIJE: 1 RIE: 0 CAT: 17

Institute for Research on Exceptional Children IL
CIJE: 0 RIE: 1 CAT: 17

Institute for Research on Poverty WI
CIJE: 0 RIE: 2 CAT: 17

Institute for Research on Teaching
CIJE: 2 RIE: 3 CAT: 17

Institute for Retired Professionals NY
CIJE: 4 RIE: 2 CAT: 17

Institute for Science Education (West Germany)
CIJE: 3 RIE: 0 CAT: 17

Institute for Services to Education Inc DC
CIJE: 0 RIE: 10 CAT: 17

Institute for Social Research MI
CIJE: 3 RIE: 1 CAT: 17

Institute for Software Engineering CA
CIJE: 1 RIE: 0 CAT: 17

Institute for the Achievement of Human Potential
CIJE: 0 RIE: 1 CAT: 17

Institute for the Advancement of Math and Sci
CIJE: 0 RIE: 1 CAT: 17

Institute for the Development of Educ Activities
CIJE: 2 RIE: 4 CAT: 17

Institute for the Future
CIJE: 0 RIE: 3 CAT: 17

Institute for the Study of Educational Policy DC
CIJE: 1 RIE: 0 CAT: 17

Institute for the Study of Exceptional Children
CIJE: 0 RIE: 2 CAT: 17

Institute of Adv Archit Studies (Great Britain)
CIJE: 1 RIE: 0 CAT: 17

Institute of Africa
CIJE: 1 RIE: 0 CAT: 17

Institute of Afro American Affairs NY
CIJE: 1 RIE: 0 CAT: 17

Institute of American Indian Arts NM
CIJE: 6 RIE: 7 CAT: 17

Institute of Child Guidance Development (Canada)
CIJE: 1 RIE: 0 CAT: 17

Institute of Child Study ON
CIJE: 0 RIE: 0 CAT: 17

Institute of Child Study Security Test
CIJE: 1 RIE: 1 CAT: 21

Institute of Community Services
CIJE: 2 RIE: 0 CAT: 17

Institute of Educational Technology (England)
CIJE: 2 RIE: 3 CAT: 17

Institute of Electrical and Electronics Engineers
CIJE: 5 RIE: 1 CAT: 17

Institute of Electrical Research (Mexico)
CIJE: 1 RIE: 0 CAT: 17

Institute of Industrial Relations Res Conf 1967
CIJE: 0 RIE: 2 CAT: 02

Institute of International Education NY
CIJE: 7 RIE: 6 CAT: 17

Institute of International Studies DC
CIJE: 2 RIE: 0 CAT: 17

Institute of Library Research CA
CIJE: 0 RIE: 7 CAT: 17

Institute of Lifetime Learning DC
CIJE: 1 RIE: 1 CAT: 17

Institute of Medicine DC
CIJE: 5 RIE: 2 CAT: 17

Institute of Museum Services
CIJE: 1 RIE: 1 CAT: 17

Institute of Nutrition of Central America
CIJE: 1 RIE: 0 CAT: 17

Institute of Personnel Management (England)
CIJE: 1 RIE: 0 CAT: 17

Institute of Prof Librarians of Ontario (Canada)
CIJE: 0 RIE: 1 CAT: 17

Institute of Public Affairs IA
CIJE: 1 RIE: 0 CAT: 17

Institute of Rehabilitation Medicine
CIJE: 1 RIE: 0 CAT: 17

Institute of Study for Older Adults
CIJE: 2 RIE: 1 CAT: 17

Institute of Study for Older Adults NY
CIJE: 0 RIE: 2 CAT: 17

Institute of Technology Higher Education (Mexico)
CIJE: 0 RIE: 1 CAT: 17

Institute of Texas Studies
CIJE: 0 RIE: 1 CAT: 19

Institute of Vocational Training (Japan)
CIJE: 1 RIE: 0 CAT: 17

Institute on Rehabilitation Services PA
CIJE: 0 RIE: 1 CAT: 17

Institute Research Development Occupational Ed NY
CIJE: 0 RIE: 2 CAT: 17

Institutes for Advanced Study in Industrial Arts
CIJE: 0 RIE: 1 CAT: 17

Institutes for the Achievement of Human Potential
CIJE: 2 RIE: 0 CAT: 17

Institution of Electrical Engineers
CIJE: 0 RIE: 2 CAT: 17

Institution of Training Officers (United Kingdom)
CIJE: 1 RIE: 0 CAT: 17

Institution on Chautauqua Lake NY
CIJE: 1 RIE: 0 CAT: 17

Institution on Farm Training
CIJE: 0 RIE: 1 CAT: 17

Institutional Aid Program
CIJE: 0 RIE: 1 CAT: 19

Institutional Aid Program Title III
USE Higher Education Act Title III

Institutional Child Abuse Neglect Prevention Proj
CIJE: 0 RIE: 1 CAT: 19

Institutional Conditions
CIJE: 3 RIE: 2 CAT: 11

Institutional Conservation Program
CIJE: 2 RIE: 2 CAT: 19

Institutional Development Corporation
CIJE: 0 RIE: 1 CAT: 17

Institutional Discrimination
CIJE: 6 RIE: 2 CAT: 16

Institutional Distinctiveness
CIJE: 9 RIE: 1 CAT: 16

Institutional Factbooks
CIJE: 0 RIE: 1 CAT: 16

Institutional Functioning Inventory
CIJE: 8 RIE: 4 CAT: 21

Institutional Goals Inventory
CIJE: 4 RIE: 16 CAT: 21

Institutional History
CIJE: 28 RIE: 35 CAT: 16

Institutional Image
CIJE: 61 RIE: 10 CAT: 16

Institutional Leadership Project
CIJE: 6 RIE: 1 CAT: 19

Institutional Lending
CIJE: 0 RIE: 3 CAT: 16

Institutional Organization Theory
CIJE: 1 RIE: 1 CAT: 15

Institutional Performance Survey
CIJE: 0 RIE: 1 CAT: 21

Institutional Practices
CIJE: 0 RIE: 1 CAT: 16

Institutional Prestige
CIJE: 1 RIE: 3 CAT: 16

Institutional Racism
CIJE: 2 RIE: 7 CAT: 16

Institutional Renewal
CIJE: 31 RIE: 19 CAT: 16
SN See also "Institutional Revitalization"

Institutional Report Forms
CIJE: 0 RIE: 3 CAT: 16

Institutional Research Council of Eleven
CIJE: 0 RIE: 1 CAT: 17

Institutional Responsiveness
CIJE: 1 RIE: 4 CAT: 16

Institutional Revitalization
CIJE: 0 RIE: 1 CAT: 15
SN See also "Institutional Renewal"

Institutional Self Assessment Measure (CBE)
CIJE: 0 RIE: 1 CAT: 15
SN CBE = Competency Based Education

Institutional Vitality
CIJE: 47 RIE: 31 CAT: 15

Institutionalization (of Goals)
CIJE: 0 RIE: 2 CAT: 15

Institutionalization (of Innovations)
CIJE: 8 RIE: 9 CAT: 15

Institutionalized Facilities Program NY
CIJE: 0 RIE: 7 CAT: 19

Institutionen foer Tillaempad Elektronik (Sweden)
CIJE: 0 RIE: 1 CAT: 17

Instituto Caro y Cuervo (Colombia)
CIJE: 0 RIE: 1 CAT: 17

Instituto Centro Amer de Ext Cult (Costa Rica)
CIJE: 1 RIE: 0 CAT: 17

Instituto Nacional de Capacitacion Prof (Chile)
CIJE: 0 RIE: 0 CAT: 17
SN National Vocational Training Institute of Chile
UF INACAP

INSTRUCT Programing Language
CIJE: 0 RIE: 1 CAT: 04

Instruction Curriculum Environment
CIJE: 0 RIE: 13 CAT: 03

Instructional Accomplishment Information Systems
CIJE: 0 RIE: 2 CAT: 04

Instructional Accomplishment Inventories
CIJE: 0 RIE: 1 CAT: 21

Instructional Algorithms
CIJE: 0 RIE: 1 CAT: 03

Instructional Analysis
CIJE: 5 RIE: 6 CAT: 16

Instructional Assistance Program
CIJE: 0 RIE: 3 CAT: 19
SN ...of the Georgia Schools

Instructional Broadcasting Assn (Great Britain)
CIJE: 1 RIE: 0 CAT: 17

Instructional Center Library
CIJE: 0 RIE: 1 CAT: 17

Instructional Clarity
CIJE: 2 RIE: 4 CAT: 16

Instructional Communications Service
CIJE: 0 RIE: 1 CAT: 17

Instructional Computer Cooperative
CIJE: 1 RIE: 0 CAT: 17

Instructional Concepts Inventory
CIJE: 0 RIE: 1 CAT: 21

Instructional Concepts Program
CIJE: 0 RIE: 5 CAT: 19

Instructional Consultant Role
CIJE: 4 RIE: 1 CAT: 15

Instructional Consultation
CIJE: 5 RIE: 2 CAT: 16

Instructional Conversation
CIJE: 1 RIE: 7 CAT: 13

Instructional Decision Model
CIJE: 1 RIE: 4 CAT: 15

Instructional Decision Test (Breit and Butts)
CIJE: 0 RIE: 1 CAT: 21

Instructional Design and Development Advisor
USE IDD Advisor

Instructional Design Data Base
CIJE: 0 RIE: 1 CAT: 04

Instructional Design Expert
USE ID Expert

Instructional Design Professionals
CIJE: 0 RIE: 2 CAT: 09

Instructional Development Effectiveness Assessment
CIJE: 2 RIE: 6 CAT: 21

Instructional Development Institute
CIJE: 2 RIE: 2 CAT: 17

Instructional Dialog Facility
CIJE: 1 RIE: 0 CAT: 04

Instructional Dimensions Study
CIJE: 1 RIE: 11 CAT: 21

Instructional Dynamics
CIJE: 0 RIE: 1 CAT: 15

Instructional Feature Analysis
CIJE: 0 RIE: 1 CAT: 15

Instructional Film Research Program
CIJE: 0 RIE: 2 CAT: 19

Instructional Format
CIJE: 4 RIE: 4 CAT: 16

Instructional Graphics Checklist
CIJE: 0 RIE: 1 CAT: 21

Instructional Hierarchies
CIJE: 3 RIE: 2 CAT: 15

Instructional Improvement Centers
CIJE: 0 RIE: 1 CAT: 05

Instructional Improvement Laboratory MN
CIJE: 1 RIE: 0 CAT: 17

Instructional Improvement Questionnaire
CIJE: 4 RIE: 9 CAT: 21

Instructional Information Systems
CIJE: 3 RIE: 4 CAT: 15

Instructional Innovator (Journal)
CIJE: 0 RIE: 1 CAT: 22

Instructional Management
CIJE: 7 RIE: 4 CAT: 16

Instructional Management Questionnaire
CIJE: 0 RIE: 1 CAT: 21

Instructional Management Systems
CIJE: 13 RIE: 47 CAT: 16

Instructional Materials Motivation Scale
CIJE: 1 RIE: 3 CAT: 21

Instructional Microcomputer Project Ark Classrooms
CIJE: 0 RIE: 1 CAT: 19
UF IMPAC Program AR

Instructional Models
CIJE: 15 RIE: 25 CAT: 15

Instructional Monitoring
CIJE: 1 RIE: 1 CAT: 16

Instructional Objectives Exchange
CIJE: 2 RIE: 14 CAT: 17

Instructional Packages
CIJE: 5 RIE: 3 CAT: 16

Instructional Preparation
CIJE: 1 RIE: 2 CAT: 15

Instructional Procedures Preference Inventory
CIJE: 0 RIE: 1 CAT: 21

Instructional Product Verification and Revision
CIJE: 2 RIE: 0 CAT: 15
SN See also "Learner Verification and Revision"

Instructional Productivity System
CIJE: 0 RIE: 1 CAT: 16

Instructional Program Management System
CIJE: 1 RIE: 0 CAT: 15

Instructional Programming Model
CIJE: 0 RIE: 2 CAT: 15

Instructional Quality Inventory
CIJE: 0 RIE: 2 CAT: 21

Instructional Resources Center (Fredonia New York)
CIJE: 1 RIE: 0 CAT: 17

Instructional Science
CIJE: 2 RIE: 2 CAT: 20

Instructional Sensitivity
CIJE: 4 RIE: 7 CAT: 15

Instructional Set
CIJE: 1 RIE: 1 CAT: 15

Instructional Stimuli
CIJE: 2 RIE: 0 CAT: 15

Instructional Stimulus Response Observation Scale
CIJE: 0 RIE: 1 CAT: 21

Instructional Strategy Diagnostic Profile
CIJE: 3 RIE: 1 CAT: 21

Instructional Strategy Subsystem
CIJE: 0 RIE: 1 CAT: 16

Instructional Support
CIJE: 6 RIE: 6 CAT: 16

Instructional Support and Evaluation System
CIJE: 0 RIE: 1 CAT: 16

Instructional Support Services
CIJE: 2 RIE: 1 CAT: 16

Instructional Support System
CIJE: 0 RIE: 4 CAT: 16

Instructional Support System Occupational Educ
CIJE: 0 RIE: 21 CAT: 19

Instructional System for Reading
CIJE: 1 RIE: 0 CAT: 16

Instructional Systems Analysis and Selection
CIJE: 0 RIE: 1 CAT: 15

Instructional Systems Clearinghouse Inc
CIJE: 1 RIE: 0 CAT: 17

Instructional Systems Design
CIJE: 48 RIE: 12 CAT: 15

Instructional Systems Development
CIJE: 29 RIE: 27 CAT: 04

Instructional Systems Development Model
CIJE: 12 RIE: 19 CAT: 15

Instructional Systems in Teacher Education
CIJE: 0 RIE: 5 CAT: 16

Instructional Systems Technology Program
CIJE: 0 RIE: 1 CAT: 19

Instructional Technology and Media Project
CIJE: 0 RIE: 5 CAT: 19

Instructional Telecommunications Consortium
CIJE: 2 RIE: 0 CAT: 17

Instructional Television Fixed Service
CIJE: 3 RIE: 17 CAT: 04

Instructional Television Fixed System
CIJE: 1 RIE: 4 CAT: 04

Instructional Television Futures Planning Group
USE ITV Futures Planning Group

Instructional Television Information Office
CIJE: 1 RIE: 0 CAT: 17

Instructional Television Library Project
CIJE: 0 RIE: 1 CAT: 19

Instructional Terms
CIJE: 0 RIE: 1 CAT: 16

Instructional Theory
CIJE: 16 RIE: 4 CAT: 15

Instructional Theory into Practice (Hunter)
CIJE: 3 RIE: 2 CAT: 15

Instructional Transaction Theory
CIJE: 0 RIE: 1 CAT: 15

Instructional Transfer Model
CIJE: 0 RIE: 1 CAT: 15

Instructional Variables
CIJE: 12 RIE: 7 CAT: 16

Instructionally Sensitive Psychometrics
CIJE: 0 RIE: 0 CAT: 21

Instructions
CIJE: 53 RIE: 29 CAT: 16

Instructor and Course Evaluation System
CIJE: 1 RIE: 5 CAT: 21

Instructor Course Evaluation Questionnaire
CIJE: 0 RIE: 1 CAT: 21

Instructor Logic Programing Language
CIJE: 0 RIE: 2 CAT: 04

Instructors Computer Utility
CIJE: 0 RIE: 1 CAT: 15

Instructors Diagnostic Aid Feedback in Training
CIJE: 1 RIE: 1 CAT: 15

Instrument Assemblers
CIJE: 0 RIE: 1 CAT: 09

Instrument Based Program Monitoring
CIJE: 0 RIE: 3 CAT: 21

Instrument for Observation of Teaching Activities
CIJE: 2 RIE: 4 CAT: 21

Instrument for the Analysis of Science Teaching
CIJE: 0 RIE: 2 CAT: 21

Instrument Makers
CIJE: 0 RIE: 1 CAT: 09

Instrument Mechanics
CIJE: 0 RIE: 3 CAT: 09

Instrument Repairers
CIJE: 0 RIE: 2 CAT: 09

Instrument Society of America
CIJE: 0 RIE: 2 CAT: 17

Instrumental Activities Inventory
CIJE: 1 RIE: 1 CAT: 21

Instrumental Enrichment
CIJE: 25 RIE: 26 CAT: 15

Instrumental Language Functions
CIJE: 0 RIE: 1 CAT: 15

Instrumental Learning
CIJE: 3 RIE: 0 CAT: 15

Instrumental Learning Theory
CIJE: 0 RIE: 2 CAT: 15

Instrumental Music
CIJE: 40 RIE: 8 CAT: 16

Instrumental Understanding
CIJE: 2 RIE: 0 CAT: 20

Instrumental Values
CIJE: 2 RIE: 0 CAT: 16

Instrumental Variable Methods
CIJE: 3 RIE: 1 CAT: 21

Instrumentalism
CIJE: 7 RIE: 4 CAT: 20

Instrumentation Laboratory Inc
CIJE: 1 RIE: 0 CAT: 17

Instrumented Learning
CIJE: 2 RIE: 0 CAT: 15

Instrumented Team Learning
CIJE: 1 RIE: 0 CAT: 15

Insubordination
CIJE: 5 RIE: 0 CAT: 16

Insulating Machine Operators
CIJE: 0 RIE: 1 CAT: 09

Insulation (Electricity)
USE Electrical Insulation

Insulation Blanket Makers
CIJE: 0 RIE: 1 CAT: 09

Insulation Workers
CIJE: 0 RIE: 1 CAT: 09

Insulin
CIJE: 8 RIE: 6 CAT: 11

Insults
CIJE: 5 RIE: 2 CAT: 16

Insurance Adjusters
CIJE: 1 RIE: 1 CAT: 09

Insurance Agents
CIJE: 3 RIE: 0 CAT: 09

Insurance Industry Training Council
CIJE: 1 RIE: 0 CAT: 17

Insurance Information Institute
CIJE: 1 RIE: 0 CAT: 17

Insurance Reserves
CIJE: 0 RIE: 1 CAT: 16

Intaglio Printing
CIJE: 2 RIE: 1 CAT: 13

Integer Programming
CIJE: 3 RIE: 3 CAT: 20

Integral Transforms
CIJE: 1 RIE: 0 CAT: 16

Integrated Bibliographic Information System (DoD)
CIJE: 0 RIE: 5 CAT: 04

Integrated Career Education and Placement Program
CIJE: 0 RIE: 1 CAT: 19

Integrated Character Education
CIJE: 0 RIE: 1 CAT: 03

Integrated Circuits
CIJE: 4 RIE: 4 CAT: 04
UF Microcircuits

Integrated Concept Language Development Approach
CIJE: 0 RIE: 1 CAT: 15

Integrated Contextual Learning
CIJE: 0 RIE: 1 CAT: 15

Integrated Continuing Care Program MA
CIJE: 0 RIE: 1 CAT: 19

Integrated Databases
CIJE: 2 RIE: 4 CAT: 04

Integrated Day
CIJE: 2 RIE: 4 CAT: 16

Integrated Day Program
CIJE: 0 RIE: 1 CAT: 19

Integrated Functional Learning Theory
CIJE: 0 RIE: 2 CAT: 15

Integrated Macro Package
CIJE: 0 RIE: 1 CAT: 04

Integrated Manufacturing
CIJE: 0 RIE: 3 CAT: 20
SN See also "Computer Integrated Manufacturing" and "Flexible Manufacturing"

Integrated Model Preschool Program
CIJE: 0 RIE: 1 CAT: 19

Integrated Network Systems
CIJE: 9 RIE: 1 CAT: 04

Integrated Occupational Program AB
CIJE: 0 RIE: 0 CAT: 19
UF IOP AB

Integrated Organized Approach (Language Teaching)
CIJE: 0 RIE: 4 CAT: 13

Integrated Performance Support Systems
USE Performance Support Systems

Integrated Pest Management
CIJE: 10 RIE: 7 CAT: 20

Integrated Playground Facilities
CIJE: 0 RIE: 1 CAT: 05

Integrated Postsecondary Education Data System
CIJE: 1 RIE: 35 CAT: 04
UF IPEDS

Integrated Procedures Control
CIJE: 0 RIE: 1 CAT: 16

Integrated Regional Resources Management
CIJE: 0 RIE: 1 CAT: 15

Integrated Scientific Information System
CIJE: 0 RIE: 1 CAT: 04

Integrated Services Digital Networks
CIJE: 13 RIE: 1 CAT: 04
UF ISDNs

Integrated Set of Information Systems
CIJE: 2 RIE: 0 CAT: 04

Integrated Skill Development
CIJE: 8 RIE: 1 CAT: 15

Integrated Skills Method
CIJE: 2 RIE: 1 CAT: 15

Integrated Skills Reinforcement
CIJE: 1 RIE: 1 CAT: 15

Integrated Student Data System
CIJE: 0 RIE: 1 CAT: 04

Integrated Studies Project
CIJE: 0 RIE: 1 CAT: 19

Integrated Subject File
CIJE: 1 RIE: 0 CAT: 04

Integration (Mathematics)
CIJE: 13 RIE: 4 CAT: 20

Integration Maintenance
CIJE: 2 RIE: 1 CAT: 16

Integration Readings
CIJE: 0 RIE: 1 CAT: 22

Integrative Negotiations Concept
CIJE: 0 RIE: 1 CAT: 15

Integrative Network for Sci Teach Explor and Prac
USE INSTEP Project KS

Integrative Organized Approach
CIJE: 0 RIE: 1 CAT: 15

Integrative Processes
CIJE: 17 RIE: 13 CAT: 16

Integrity in the College Curriculum
CIJE: 17 RIE: 6 CAT: 22

Intellective Adjective List (Sciortino)
CIJE: 1 RIE: 0 CAT: 21

Intellectual Achievement Responsibility
CIJE: 7 RIE: 6 CAT: 16

Intellectual Achievement Responsibility Quest
CIJE: 11 RIE: 11 CAT: 21

Intellectual Community
CIJE: 0 RIE: 1 CAT: 16

Intellectual Pragmatism Scale (Yuker and Block)
CIJE: 1 RIE: 0 CAT: 21

Intellectual Property Piracy
USE Piracy of Intellectual Property

Intellectual Realism
CIJE: 2 RIE: 0 CAT: 15

Intellectual Self Confidence
CIJE: 0 RIE: 1 CAT: 16

Intellectual Self Confidence Scale (Hiller)
CIJE: 0 RIE: 1 CAT: 21

Intellectual Tasks
CIJE: 3 RIE: 2 CAT: 16

Intellectuals
CIJE: 23 RIE: 7 CAT: 10

Intelligence Authorization Act 1991 Title VIII
USE National Security Education Act 1991

Intelligent Buildings
CIJE: 2 RIE: 1 CAT: 05

Intelligent Maintenance Training System
CIJE: 0 RIE: 1 CAT: 04

Intelligent Terminals
CIJE: 1 RIE: 1 CAT: 04

Intelligent Videodisks
USE Interactive Videodisks

Intelligibility (Speech)
CIJE: 13 RIE: 1 CAT: 13

Intelsat
CIJE: 1 RIE: 4 CAT: 04

Intensify Downplay Approach
CIJE: 0 RIE: 2 CAT: 15

Intension Extension (Concepts)
CIJE: 1 RIE: 1 CAT: 11

Intensive Business Training
CIJE: 2 RIE: 2 CAT: 03

Intensive Care Nursing
CIJE: 2 RIE: 7 CAT: 11

Intensive Care Units
CIJE: 8 RIE: 4 CAT: 05

Intensive Courses
CIJE: 15 RIE: 9 CAT: 03

Intensive Interdependence
CIJE: 1 RIE: 0 CAT: 16

Intensive Reading Instructional Team
CIJE: 0 RIE: 1 CAT: 19

Intensive Reading Instructional Teams Program CT
CIJE: 0 RIE: 1 CAT: 19

Intensive Scheduling
CIJE: 2 RIE: 1 CAT: 15

Intensive Services Project
CIJE: 0 RIE: 1 CAT: 19

Intensive Teacher Education Program
CIJE: 1 RIE: 0 CAT: 19

Intensive Teacher Training Program
CIJE: 0 RIE: 1 CAT: 19

Intent Structures
CIJE: 1 RIE: 1 CAT: 15

Intent to Discriminate
CIJE: 1 RIE: 2 CAT: 14

Intentional Learning Module
CIJE: 0 RIE: 1 CAT: 15

Inter American Center
CIJE: 0 RIE: 1 CAT: 17

Inter American Committee on Adult Education
CIJE: 0 RIE: 1 CAT: 17

Inter American Congress Educational Administration
CIJE: 0 RIE: 1 CAT: 02

Inter American Court of Human Rights
CIJE: 0 RIE: 1 CAT: 17

Inter American Foundation
CIJE: 1 RIE: 6 CAT: 17

Inter American Indian Congress
CIJE: 0 RIE: 1 CAT: 02

Inter American Indian Institute
CIJE: 0 RIE: 1 CAT: 17

Inter American Press Association
CIJE: 0 RIE: 1 CAT: 17

Inter American Series Test of General Ability
CIJE: 0 RIE: 8 CAT: 21

Inter American Society Educ Leadership Development
CIJE: 0 RIE: 1 CAT: 17

Inter American Society for Educ Administration
CIJE: 0 RIE: 1 CAT: 17

Inter American University PR
CIJE: 1 RIE: 0 CAT: 17

Inter Association Council on Test Reviewing
CIJE: 1 RIE: 0 CAT: 17

Inter Child Classroom System
CIJE: 1 RIE: 0 CAT: 15

Inter Institutional Program Development Project
CIJE: 0 RIE: 1 CAT: 19

Inter Item Correlation Coefficients
CIJE: 1 RIE: 1 CAT: 15

Inter Nation Simulation
CIJE: 4 RIE: 2 CAT: 16

Inter Navex
CIJE: 8 RIE: 0 CAT: 02

Inter Organizational Relationship Model
USE Intriligator IOR Model

Inter Person Perception Test
CIJE: 0 RIE: 1 CAT: 21

Inter Press Service
CIJE: 0 RIE: 2 CAT: 17

Inter TAC Institute
CIJE: 0 RIE: 1 CAT: 17

Inter University Biology Teaching Project
CIJE: 2 RIE: 0 CAT: 19

INTERACT (Computer Program)
CIJE: 0 RIE: 1 CAT: 04

Interaction (Statistical)
CIJE: 9 RIE: 4 CAT: 15

Interaction Analysis Category System
CIJE: 0 RIE: 2 CAT: 15

Interaction Analysis for Vocational Educators
CIJE: 1 RIE: 0 CAT: 15

Interaction Attitude Index
CIJE: 0 RIE: 1 CAT: 21

Interaction Check List
CIJE: 0 RIE: 1 CAT: 21

Interaction Network Instrument (Edwards)
CIJE: 0 RIE: 1 CAT: 21

Interaction of Man and the Biosphere
CIJE: 0 RIE: 2 CAT: 22

Interaction Process Analysis Participation Record
CIJE: 1 RIE: 0 CAT: 15

Interaction Scale (Field)
CIJE: 1 RIE: 0 CAT: 21

Interactional Competency Checklist
CIJE: 1 RIE: 1 CAT: 21

Interactional Disturbance (Psychology)
CIJE: 1 RIE: 2 CAT: 11

Interactionism
CIJE: 2 RIE: 1 CAT: 16
SN See also "Symbolic Interactionism"

Interactive Communication
CIJE: 8 RIE: 13 CAT: 15
SN See also "Two Way Communication"

Interactive Compensatory Model
CIJE: 3 RIE: 0 CAT: 15

Interactive Computer Systems
CIJE: 20 RIE: 32 CAT: 04

Interactive Courseware
CIJE: 1 RIE: 1 CAT: 04

Interactive Decision Making
CIJE: 4 RIE: 2 CAT: 15

Interactive Design Management System
CIJE: 0 RIE: 1 CAT: 20

Interactive Errands
CIJE: 0 RIE: 2 CAT: 15

Interactive Fiction
CIJE: 14 RIE: 7 CAT: 04

Interactive Influence System
CIJE: 2 RIE: 0 CAT: 15

Interactive Language Development Teaching Program
CIJE: 1 RIE: 0 CAT: 19

Interactive Language Instruction Assistance Deaf
CIJE: 0 RIE: 1 CAT: 04

Interactive Learning Process Model
CIJE: 5 RIE: 2 CAT: 15

Interactive Model
CIJE: 6 RIE: 8 CAT: 15

Interactive Radio
CIJE: 1 RIE: 7 CAT: 04
SN See also "Two Way Radio"

Interactive Reading
CIJE: 19 RIE: 10 CAT: 15

Interactive Research and Development on Schooling
CIJE: 0 RIE: 1 CAT: 15

Interactive Satellite Instruction
CIJE: 3 RIE: 9 CAT: 04

Interactive Systems
CIJE: 175 RIE: 71 CAT: 15

Interactive Teaching
CIJE: 16 RIE: 24 CAT: 15

Interactive Theater
CIJE: 0 RIE: 1 CAT: 16

Interactive Video Network ND
CIJE: 0 RIE: 1 CAT: 19
UF North Dakota Interactive Video Network

Interactive Video Science Consortium
CIJE: 0 RIE: 1 CAT: 17

Interactive Videodisc Special Education Technology
CIJE: 0 RIE: 1 CAT: 20

Interactive Videodisks
CIJE: 1 RIE: 5 CAT: 04
UF Intelligent Videodisks

Interactive Videotex Project
CIJE: 0 RIE: 2 CAT: 19

Interagency Child Abuse Network
CIJE: 0 RIE: 1 CAT: 19

Interagency Collaborative Initiative
CIJE: 0 RIE: 1 CAT: 19

Interagency Committee on Handicapped Research
CIJE: 0 RIE: 1 CAT: 17

Interagency Committee on Learning Disabilities
CIJE: 3 RIE: 1 CAT: 17

Interagency Conference on Nursing Statistics
CIJE: 0 RIE: 1 CAT: 02

Interagency Coordinating Council
CIJE: 3 RIE: 4 CAT: 17

Interagency Growth Project
CIJE: 0 RIE: 1 CAT: 19

Interagency Language Roundtable
CIJE: 4 RIE: 10 CAT: 17

Interagency Language Roundtable Oral Interview
CIJE: 4 RIE: 2 CAT: 21
SN See also "ACTFL ILR Oral Proficiency Guidelines"

Interagency Panel on Early Childhood R and D
CIJE: 0 RIE: 1 CAT: 17

Interagency Panel Research Development Adulthood
CIJE: 0 RIE: 1 CAT: 02

Interagency Research Information System
CIJE: 0 RIE: 1 CAT: 04

Interbehavioral Psychology
CIJE: 2 RIE: 2 CAT: 11

Intercampus Information Systems
CIJE: 0 RIE: 2 CAT: 15

InterChange Discussion Program
CIJE: 0 RIE: 1 CAT: 04

Intercity Committee for Action NJ
CIJE: 0 RIE: 1 CAT: 17

INTERCOCTA Conceptual Glossary
CIJE: 0 RIE: 1 CAT: 19
SN INTERCOCTA = "International Cooperation in Conceptual and Terminological Analysis"

Intercollegiate Debate Topic
CIJE: 0 RIE: 4 CAT: 16

Interconcept Consistency
CIJE: 0 RIE: 1 CAT: 15

Interconnection
CIJE: 3 RIE: 5 CAT: 16

Intercultural Behavioral Assessment Indices
CIJE: 0 RIE: 1 CAT: 21

Intercultural Communication Course (USIA)
CIJE: 0 RIE: 0 CAT: 03

Intercultural Counseling
CIJE: 0 RIE: 1 CAT: 11

Intercultural Development Research Association
CIJE: 0 RIE: 1 CAT: 17
UF IDRA

Intercultural Learning Network
CIJE: 1 RIE: 6 CAT: 19
SN International microcomputer network designed to enable students from different cultures to work with one another

Intercultural Social Studies Project
CIJE: 1 RIE: 2 CAT: 19

Intercultural Studies Project
CIJE: 0 RIE: 1 CAT: 19

Intercultural Understanding Project
CIJE: 0 RIE: 2 CAT: 19

Interculture System
CIJE: 0 RIE: 1 CAT: 16

Interdependence
CIJE: 65 RIE: 89 CAT: 16

Interdependent Learning Model
CIJE: 2 RIE: 5 CAT: 15

Interdialect Translatability
CIJE: 0 RIE: 1 CAT: 13

Interdisciplinary Cooperation
CIJE: 25 RIE: 2 CAT: 15

Interdisciplinary Cooperative Educ Curric Manual
CIJE: 0 RIE: 1 CAT: 16

Interdisciplinary Health Teams
CIJE: 1 RIE: 5 CAT: 10

Interdisciplinary Model Program in the Arts
CIJE: 1 RIE: 1 CAT: 19

Interdisciplinary Research Group on Poverty
CIJE: 0 RIE: 1 CAT: 17

Interdomain Influences
CIJE: 0 RIE: 1 CAT: 11

Interest Assessment Scales
CIJE: 0 RIE: 3 CAT: 21

Interest Creating Discovery Module
CIJE: 0 RIE: 1 CAT: 15

Interest Groups
CIJE: 37 RIE: 20 CAT: 10

Interest in the Subject Questionnaire
CIJE: 1 RIE: 0 CAT: 21

Interest Rates
CIJE: 4 RIE: 2 CAT: 16

Interests and Ideas Inventory
CIJE: 0 RIE: 1 CAT: 21

Interethnic Communication
CIJE: 2 RIE: 3 CAT: 16

Interference (Learning)
CIJE: 13 RIE: 6 CAT: 11

Interference Effects
CIJE: 21 RIE: 9 CAT: 11

Interference Theory
CIJE: 5 RIE: 1 CAT: 15

Interferometers
CIJE: 9 RIE: 0 CAT: 04

Interferon
CIJE: 0 RIE: 1 CAT: 20

Intergenerational Analysis
CIJE: 6 RIE: 5 CAT: 15

Intergenerational Attitude Transference
CIJE: 0 RIE: 3 CAT: 11

Intergenerational Conflict
CIJE: 13 RIE: 6 CAT: 11

Intergenerational Continuity
CIJE: 2 RIE: 2 CAT: 11

Intergenerational Factors
CIJE: 20 RIE: 7 CAT: 11

Intergenerational Households
CIJE: 3 RIE: 1 CAT: 10

Intergenerational Learning
CIJE: 9 RIE: 8 CAT: 15

Intergenerational Perception
CIJE: 2 RIE: 0 CAT: 11

Intergenerational Relationship
CIJE: 38 RIE: 9 CAT: 11

Intergenerational Solidarity
CIJE: 3 RIE: 1 CAT: 11

Intergenerational Transmission
CIJE: 8 RIE: 7 CAT: 11

Intergovernmental Advisory Council on Education
CIJE: 1 RIE: 0 CAT: 17

Intergovernmental Committee for Migration
CIJE: 1 RIE: 0 CAT: 17

Intergovernmental Personnel Act
CIJE: 3 RIE: 2 CAT: 14

Intergovernmental Relations
CIJE: 5 RIE: 10 CAT: 16

Intergovernmental Task Force Information Systems
CIJE: 0 RIE: 1 CAT: 17

Intergroup Education Project
CIJE: 0 RIE: 1 CAT: 19

Intergroup Relations Project
CIJE: 0 RIE: 1 CAT: 19

Interim Report on Study of Selected ECE Schools
CIJE: 0 RIE: 1 CAT: 22

Interim Term
CIJE: 8 RIE: 6 CAT: 16

Interjections (Grammar)
CIJE: 3 RIE: 2 CAT: 13

Interlake High School WA
CIJE: 1 RIE: 1 CAT: 17

Interlibrary Communications
CIJE: 0 RIE: 31 CAT: 16

Interlingua
CIJE: 2 RIE: 1 CAT: 13
SN An artificial language developed between 1924 and 1951, based primarily on the Romance languages, and intended mainly as a common international language for scientists

Interlingual Distance
CIJE: 0 RIE: 1 CAT: 13

Interlinguistics
CIJE: 3 RIE: 1 CAT: 13

Interlochen Arts Academy MI
CIJE: 3 RIE: 1 CAT: 17

Intermediaries
CIJE: 12 RIE: 8 CAT: 10

Intermediate Care Facilities
CIJE: 21 RIE: 6 CAT: 05

Intermediate Certificate Examination (Ireland)
CIJE: 0 RIE: 0 CAT: 21

Intermediate English Evaluation Project
CIJE: 0 RIE: 1 CAT: 19

Intermediate English Reading Test
CIJE: 0 RIE: 1 CAT: 21

Intermediate Measures of Music Audiation Rhythm
CIJE: 0 RIE: 1 CAT: 21

Intermediate Mental Alertness Test
CIJE: 0 RIE: 1 CAT: 21

Intermediate School 201 NY
CIJE: 3 RIE: 1 CAT: 17

Intermediate Science Curriculum Study
CIJE: 29 RIE: 124 CAT: 19

Intermediate Size Transposition Paradigm
CIJE: 1 RIE: 0 CAT: 15

Intermittent Information Feedback Schedule
CIJE: 0 RIE: 1 CAT: 16

Intermix Approach
CIJE: 1 RIE: 0 CAT: 15

Intermodal Perception
CIJE: 4 RIE: 3 CAT: 15

Intermodal Transportation Careers
CIJE: 0 RIE: 1 CAT: 09

Intermountain Conference Childrens Literature 5th
CIJE: 1 RIE: 0 CAT: 02

Intermountain School UT
CIJE: 3 RIE: 6 CAT: 17

Intermunicipal Cooperation
CIJE: 0 RIE: 1 CAT: 16

Intern Mentor Program
CIJE: 0 RIE: 3 CAT: 19

Internal Auditing
CIJE: 8 RIE: 0 CAT: 15

Internal Colonialism
CIJE: 4 RIE: 4 CAT: 15

Internal Combustion Engine Assemblers
CIJE: 0 RIE: 1 CAT: 09

Internal Consistency
CIJE: 23 RIE: 25 CAT: 21

Internal Evaluation
CIJE: 17 RIE: 5 CAT: 21

Internal External Frame of Reference Model
CIJE: 4 RIE: 5 CAT: 15

Internal External Scale
CIJE: 4 RIE: 1 CAT: 21

Internal External Social Attributes
CIJE: 3 RIE: 1 CAT: 11

Internal Lexicon
CIJE: 0 RIE: 1 CAT: 13

Internal Representation
CIJE: 2 RIE: 1 CAT: 16

Internal Revenue Code
CIJE: 17 RIE: 6 CAT: 14

Internal Revenue Service
CIJE: 52 RIE: 34 CAT: 17

Internal Sensitivity Index (Kosecoff and Klein)
CIJE: 0 RIE: 1 CAT: 21

Internal Structure Analysis
CIJE: 0 RIE: 1 CAT: 15

Internal Validity
CIJE: 15 RIE: 6 CAT: 15

Internality Externality
CIJE: 9 RIE: 14 CAT: 16

Internalization
CIJE: 32 RIE: 13 CAT: 11

International Agricultural Education
CIJE: 0 RIE: 1 CAT: 03

International Aid
CIJE: 53 RIE: 9 CAT: 16

International Assessment of Educational Progress
CIJE: 7 RIE: 5 CAT: 19

International Assn Evaluation Educ Achievement
CIJE: 56 RIE: 53 CAT: 17
SN See also "IEA..."
UF IEA; International Association for the Eval of Ed Achmt

International Association for the Eval of Ed Achmt
USE International Assn Evaluation Educ Achievement

International Association of Metro City Libraries
CIJE: 17 RIE: 0 CAT: 17

International Association of Music Libraries
CIJE: 2 RIE: 0 CAT: 17

International Association of School Librarianship
CIJE: 4 RIE: 5 CAT: 17

International Association of Universities
CIJE: 2 RIE: 3 CAT: 17

International Audio Visual Aids Exhibition
CIJE: 3 RIE: 0 CAT: 02

International Author Indexes
CIJE: 1 RIE: 0 CAT: 04

International Baccalaureate
CIJE: 30 RIE: 7 CAT: 16

International Baccalaureate Diploma Program
CIJE: 1 RIE: 2 CAT: 19

International Baccalaureate Office
CIJE: 2 RIE: 0 CAT: 17

International Bibliographies
CIJE: 4 RIE: 1 CAT: 16

International Biological Program
CIJE: 6 RIE: 2 CAT: 19

International Board on Books for Young People
CIJE: 5 RIE: 0 CAT: 17

International Book Committee
CIJE: 1 RIE: 0 CAT: 17

International Book Year
CIJE: 7 RIE: 8 CAT: 12

International Broadcast Institute (England)
CIJE: 0 RIE: 2 CAT: 17

International Broadcasting
CIJE: 0 RIE: 4 CAT: 20

International Brotherhood of Electrical Workers
CIJE: 2 RIE: 1 CAT: 17

International Bureau of Education
CIJE: 8 RIE: 8 CAT: 17

International Business
CIJE: 20 RIE: 6 CAT: 16

International Business Education
CIJE: 6 RIE: 7 CAT: 03

International Business Machines
CIJE: 24 RIE: 15 CAT: 17
SN See also "IBM Corporation"

International Center for Culture and Environment
CIJE: 0 RIE: 0 CAT: 19

International Center for Industry and Environment
CIJE: 1 RIE: 0 CAT: 17

International Center for Research on Bilingualism
CIJE: 0 RIE: 1 CAT: 17

International Centre for Theoretical Physics
CIJE: 1 RIE: 0 CAT: 17

International Centre Parliamentary Documentation
CIJE: 0 RIE: 1 CAT: 17

International Child Development Center (Italy)
CIJE: 0 RIE: 2 CAT: 17

International Childrens Villages
CIJE: 1 RIE: 0 CAT: 17

International Civil Aviation Organization
CIJE: 3 RIE: 0 CAT: 17

International Clearinghouse MD
CIJE: 1 RIE: 1 CAT: 17

International Commission on Development of Educ
CIJE: 5 RIE: 0 CAT: 17

International Commission on Illumination
CIJE: 0 RIE: 1 CAT: 17

International Committee Against Racism
CIJE: 0 RIE: 1 CAT: 17

International Communication Agency
CIJE: 6 RIE: 4 CAT: 17

International Communication and Negotiation Simul
USE ICONS (Simulation)

International Communication Association
CIJE: 4 RIE: 6 CAT: 17

International Competence
CIJE: 1 RIE: 4 CAT: 15

International Confederation of Free Trade Unions
CIJE: 1 RIE: 0 CAT: 17

International Conference Manpower Training Devel
CIJE: 0 RIE: 7 CAT: 02

International Conference of Educational Planning
CIJE: 1 RIE: 0 CAT: 02

International Conference on Chemical Education
CIJE: 0 RIE: 0 CAT: 02

International Conference on Education
CIJE: 2 RIE: 4 CAT: 02

International Conference on Education 1977
CIJE: 0 RIE: 1 CAT: 02

International Conference on Educational Technology
CIJE: 1 RIE: 0 CAT: 02

International Conference on Film Television Child
CIJE: 0 RIE: 1 CAT: 02

International Conference on General Semantics 11th
CIJE: 0 RIE: 1 CAT: 02

International Conference on Population
CIJE: 0 RIE: 2 CAT: 02

International Conference Second Language Problems
CIJE: 0 RIE: 2 CAT: 02

International Congress of Psychology
CIJE: 0 RIE: 1 CAT: 02

International Congress on Archives
CIJE: 1 RIE: 0 CAT: 02

International Congress on Documentation
CIJE: 0 RIE: 1 CAT: 02

International Congress on Home Help Services
CIJE: 0 RIE: 1 CAT: 02

International Congress on Mathematical Education
CIJE: 1 RIE: 2 CAT: 02

International Congress on Solar Energy
CIJE: 1 RIE: 0 CAT: 02

International Congress University Adult Education
CIJE: 0 RIE: 1 CAT: 02

International Conventions
CIJE: 1 RIE: 1 CAT: 16

International Cooperation Administration
CIJE: 0 RIE: 1 CAT: 17

International Cooperative Alliance
CIJE: 0 RIE: 1 CAT: 17

International Council for Adult Education
CIJE: 10 RIE: 4 CAT: 17

International Council for Building Research
CIJE: 0 RIE: 1 CAT: 17

International Council for Computers in Education
CIJE: 3 RIE: 1 CAT: 17

International Council for Educational Development
CIJE: 1 RIE: 0 CAT: 17

International Council for Educational Media
CIJE: 21 RIE: 2 CAT: 17

International Council of Scientific Unions
CIJE: 4 RIE: 6 CAT: 17

International Council on Archives
CIJE: 3 RIE: 4 CAT: 17

International Council on Education for Teaching
CIJE: 2 RIE: 3 CAT: 17

International Council Science Education
CIJE: 1 RIE: 0 CAT: 17

International Data Library and Ref Service CA
CIJE: 1 RIE: 0 CAT: 17

International Day (School)
CIJE: 0 RIE: 1 CAT: 12

International Debt
CIJE: 4 RIE: 1 CAT: 16

International Development Education Program
CIJE: 1 RIE: 2 CAT: 19

International Development Research Centre ON
CIJE: 3 RIE: 1 CAT: 17

International Documentation in Chemistry
CIJE: 1 RIE: 0 CAT: 15

International Education Act
CIJE: 2 RIE: 6 CAT: 14

International Education Year
CIJE: 7 RIE: 3 CAT: 12

International Educational Indicators
CIJE: 0 RIE: 0 CAT: 16
UF International Indicators Project (OECD CERI)

International Educational Library
CIJE: 0 RIE: 1 CAT: 17

International Encyclopedia of Higher Education
CIJE: 0 RIE: 1 CAT: 22

International Encyclopedia of the Social Sciences
CIJE: 1 RIE: 0 CAT: 22

International English
CIJE: 1 RIE: 0 CAT: 13

International English Language Testing System
CIJE: 0 RIE: 2 CAT: 21
UF IELTS

International Environmental Education Programme
CIJE: 0 RIE: 8 CAT: 19

International Evaluation Education Achievement
CIJE: 4 RIE: 15 CAT: 21

International Extension College (England)
CIJE: 2 RIE: 3 CAT: 17

International Farm Youth Exchange
CIJE: 0 RIE: 1 CAT: 17

International Fed Plantation Agric Allied Workers
CIJE: 1 RIE: 0 CAT: 17

International Federation for Documentation
CIJE: 1 RIE: 21 CAT: 17

International Federation for Information and Docum
CIJE: 0 RIE: 0 CAT: 17

International Federation of Film Archives
CIJE: 0 RIE: 1 CAT: 17

International Federation of Home Economics
CIJE: 1 RIE: 0 CAT: 17

International Federation of Information Processing
CIJE: 0 RIE: 2 CAT: 17

International Federation of Library Assns 1974
CIJE: 0 RIE: 27 CAT: 02

International Federation of Library Associations
CIJE: 48 RIE: 81 CAT: 17
SN See also "Asian Federation of Library Associations"
UF IFLA

International Federation of Modern Lang Teachers
CIJE: 0 RIE: 1 CAT: 17

International Federation of University Women
CIJE: 2 RIE: 0 CAT: 17

International Film and Television Council
CIJE: 0 RIE: 1 CAT: 17

International Finance
CIJE: 0 RIE: 1 CAT: 03

International Fire Service Training Association
CIJE: 0 RIE: 1 CAT: 17

International Folk High School (Denmark)
CIJE: 1 RIE: 0 CAT: 17

International Geological Congress
CIJE: 1 RIE: 0 CAT: 02

International Geological Correlation Program
CIJE: 1 RIE: 1 CAT: 19

International Geosphere Biosphere Programme
CIJE: 0 RIE: 1 CAT: 19

International Health Communication Hotline
CIJE: 0 RIE: 1 CAT: 19
UF InHealth

International High School NY
CIJE: 1 RIE: 1 CAT: 19
SN Collaborative project of the New York City Board of Education and the City University of New York
UF La Guardia Community College Intl High School NY

International High Schools
CIJE: 1 RIE: 3 CAT: 05
SN If appropriate, use the more specific "International High School NY"

International Indicators Project (OECD CERI)
USE International Educational Indicators

International Information Centre for Terminology
USE Infoterm

International Institute for Adult Literacy Methods
CIJE: 1 RIE: 3 CAT: 17

International Institute for Educational Planning
CIJE: 2 RIE: 15 CAT: 17

International Institute MO
CIJE: 0 RIE: 1 CAT: 17

International Institute on the Community College
CIJE: 0 RIE: 1 CAT: 17

International Intervisitation Program Educ Admin
CIJE: 0 RIE: 1 CAT: 19

International Labour Conference
CIJE: 2 RIE: 1 CAT: 02

International Labour Office
CIJE: 22 RIE: 11 CAT: 17

International Labour Organisation
CIJE: 40 RIE: 10 CAT: 17

International Ladies Garment Workers Union
CIJE: 2 RIE: 9 CAT: 17

International League of Socs Mentally Handicapped
CIJE: 1 RIE: 3 CAT: 17

International Legal Exchange Program
CIJE: 1 RIE: 0 CAT: 19

International Librarianship
CIJE: 1 RIE: 5 CAT: 16

International Linguistic Society
CIJE: 0 RIE: 1 CAT: 17

International Literacy Day
CIJE: 0 RIE: 1 CAT: 12
SN Annual September 8 celebration, begun in 1966

International Literacy Year 1990
CIJE: 2 RIE: 60 CAT: 12

International Living Centers
CIJE: 0 RIE: 1 CAT: 05

International Management Training for Educ Change
CIJE: 0 RIE: 2 CAT: 17

International Manpower Institute
CIJE: 0 RIE: 2 CAT: 17

International Manpower Seminar
CIJE: 0 RIE: 2 CAT: 02

International Mathematics Committee
CIJE: 0 RIE: 2 CAT: 17

International Mathematics Olympiad
CIJE: 11 RIE: 0 CAT: 12
SN See also "Mathematical Olympiad"

International Mathematics Study (IEA 2d)
USE Second International Mathematics Study

International Military Education and Training Prog
CIJE: 0 RIE: 1 CAT: 19

International Network for Educational Information
CIJE: 1 RIE: 0 CAT: 17
UF INED

International News
CIJE: 11 RIE: 16 CAT: 16

International Nuclear Information System
CIJE: 3 RIE: 1 CAT: 15

International Nursing Index
CIJE: 0 RIE: 2 CAT: 22

International Olympic Academy
CIJE: 3 RIE: 0 CAT: 17

International Organization for Standardization
CIJE: 15 RIE: 4 CAT: 17
SN See also under "ISO..."

International Organization of Journalists
CIJE: 0 RIE: 1 CAT: 17

International Organization Science and Tech Educ
CIJE: 0 RIE: 3 CAT: 17
UF IOSTE

International Paper Company
CIJE: 4 RIE: 1 CAT: 17

International Peace Research Association
CIJE: 0 RIE: 1 CAT: 17

International Personnel Management Association
CIJE: 0 RIE: 10 CAT: 17

International Phonetic Alphabet
CIJE: 1 RIE: 7 CAT: 13

International Planned Parenthood Federation
CIJE: 0 RIE: 11 CAT: 17

International Potato Center (Peru)
CIJE: 0 RIE: 1 CAT: 17

International Press Institute Program
CIJE: 1 RIE: 0 CAT: 19

International Program for Agric Knowledge Systems
CIJE: 0 RIE: 0 CAT: 19

International Public Relations
CIJE: 0 RIE: 4 CAT: 16

International Radio Television University
CIJE: 2 RIE: 0 CAT: 17

International Reading Association
CIJE: 33 RIE: 43 CAT: 17

International Regulations
CIJE: 3 RIE: 2 CAT: 14

International Relations Program
CIJE: 0 RIE: 4 CAT: 19

International Research Information Service
CIJE: 0 RIE: 1 CAT: 17

International Resource Center MA
CIJE: 0 RIE: 0 CAT: 17

International Resource Management Program
CIJE: 0 RIE: 1 CAT: 03

International Responsibility
CIJE: 0 RIE: 2 CAT: 16

International Review of Applied Psychology
CIJE: 1 RIE: 0 CAT: 22

International Road Research Documentation System
CIJE: 0 RIE: 1 CAT: 15

International School of Brussels (Belgium)
CIJE: 0 RIE: 1 CAT: 17

International Schoolbook Institute in Brunswick
CIJE: 1 RIE: 0 CAT: 17

International Schools
CIJE: 15 RIE: 8 CAT: 05

International Schools Association
CIJE: 1 RIE: 4 CAT: 17

International Science and Engineering Fair
CIJE: 3 RIE: 7 CAT: 02

International Science Foundation
CIJE: 1 RIE: 0 CAT: 17

International Science Study (IEA 2d)
USE Second International Science Study

International Secretariat for Volunteer Service
CIJE: 0 RIE: 1 CAT: 17

International Seminar on Bilingual Education
USE Seminarro Internacional Sobre la Educ Bilingue

International Serials Data System
CIJE: 4 RIE: 3 CAT: 15

International Service Assn for Health Inc
CIJE: 0 RIE: 0 CAT: 17

International Signs and Symbols
CIJE: 0 RIE: 1 CAT: 16

International Sociological Association
CIJE: 0 RIE: 1 CAT: 17

International Space Center
CIJE: 0 RIE: 1 CAT: 17

International Space Hall of Fame Foundation NM
CIJE: 0 RIE: 1 CAT: 17

International Space Programs
CIJE: 0 RIE: 2 CAT: 19

International Standard Bibliographic Description
CIJE: 19 RIE: 14 CAT: 15

International Standard Book Number
CIJE: 6 RIE: 3 CAT: 16

International Standard Classification of Education
CIJE: 0 RIE: 8 CAT: 16

International Standard Serial Number
CIJE: 6 RIE: 2 CAT: 16

International Standards
CIJE: 22 RIE: 3 CAT: 16

International Student Problem Inventory
CIJE: 0 RIE: 1 CAT: 21

International Studies Association
CIJE: 0 RIE: 2 CAT: 17

International Studies on Educational Achievement
CIJE: 3 RIE: 1 CAT: 22

International Study Group for Math Learning
CIJE: 0 RIE: 1 CAT: 17

International Study of Achievement in Written Comp
CIJE: 1 RIE: 2 CAT: 21

International Surveys
CIJE: 14 RIE: 12 CAT: 19

International Symposium for Literacy (Persepolis)
CIJE: 3 RIE: 0 CAT: 02

International System of Units
CIJE: 14 RIE: 9 CAT: 15

International System Typographic Picture Education
CIJE: 1 RIE: 0 CAT: 15

International Technology Education Association
CIJE: 2 RIE: 1 CAT: 17

International Telecommunication Convention
CIJE: 1 RIE: 0 CAT: 02

International Telecommunication Union
CIJE: 2 RIE: 14 CAT: 17

International Telecommunications Satellite
CIJE: 6 RIE: 11 CAT: 04

International Telephone and Telegraph Corporation
CIJE: 0 RIE: 3 CAT: 17
SN See add'l listings under "ITT..."
UF ITT

International Television
CIJE: 0 RIE: 5 CAT: 20

International Television Association
CIJE: 0 RIE: 1 CAT: 17

International Terminology
CIJE: 0 RIE: 1 CAT: 13

International Thespian Society
CIJE: 1 RIE: 1 CAT: 17

International Translations Centre (Netherlands)
CIJE: 0 RIE: 0 CAT: 17

International Trends
CIJE: 3 RIE: 3 CAT: 16

International Union for Conservation of Nature
CIJE: 3 RIE: 6 CAT: 17

International Union of Biological Sciences
CIJE: 1 RIE: 0 CAT: 17

International Union of Geological Sciences
CIJE: 2 RIE: 0 CAT: 17

International Union of Operating Engineers
CIJE: 0 RIE: 1 CAT: 17

International Union of Pure and Applied Chemistry
CIJE: 4 RIE: 0 CAT: 17

International Union of Pure and Applied Physics
CIJE: 0 RIE: 1 CAT: 17

International University Congress
CIJE: 0 RIE: 1 CAT: 02

International University of Communications DC
CIJE: 0 RIE: 1 CAT: 17

International Visitors
CIJE: 1 RIE: 1 CAT: 10
SN See also "Foreign Visitors"

International Womens Year
CIJE: 7 RIE: 9 CAT: 12

International Word Processing Association
CIJE: 0 RIE: 1 CAT: 17

International Work Group for Indigenous Affairs
CIJE: 0 RIE: 2 CAT: 17

International Year of Disabled Persons
CIJE: 2 RIE: 7 CAT: 12

International Year of the Child
CIJE: 11 RIE: 8 CAT: 12

International Youth Hostel Federation
CIJE: 0 RIE: 1 CAT: 17

International Youth Year
CIJE: 5 RIE: 2 CAT: 12

Internationalism
CIJE: 8 RIE: 10 CAT: 16

Internet
CIJE: 242 RIE: 80 CAT: 04

Internet Worm
CIJE: 1 RIE: 0 CAT: 20

Internment Camps
CIJE: 11 RIE: 2 CAT: 05

Interorganizational Arrangements
CIJE: 2 RIE: 1 CAT: 16

Interorganizational Networks
CIJE: 2 RIE: 1 CAT: 05

Interorganizational Relationships
CIJE: 9 RIE: 8 CAT: 16

Interpersonal Attraction Researchers
CIJE: 0 RIE: 1 CAT: 09

Interpersonal Behavior Inventory
CIJE: 0 RIE: 1 CAT: 21

Interpersonal Behavior Survey
CIJE: 0 RIE: 1 CAT: 21

Interpersonal Check List
CIJE: 3 RIE: 2 CAT: 21

Interpersonal Cognitive Problem Solving
CIJE: 1 RIE: 4 CAT: 11

Interpersonal Communication Inventory
CIJE: 2 RIE: 1 CAT: 21

Interpersonal Communications Model
CIJE: 1 RIE: 0 CAT: 15

Interpersonal Confirmation
CIJE: 0 RIE: 2 CAT: 11

Interpersonal Contact Initiation
CIJE: 0 RIE: 2 CAT: 11

Interpersonal Control
USE Control (Social Behavior)

Interpersonal Discrimination
CIJE: 1 RIE: 1 CAT: 11

Interpersonal Distance
CIJE: 8 RIE: 1 CAT: 11

Interpersonal Growth Scale
CIJE: 0 RIE: 1 CAT: 21

Interpersonal Influence Process
CIJE: 12 RIE: 9 CAT: 11

Interpersonal Judgment Scale
CIJE: 1 RIE: 2 CAT: 21

Interpersonal Manipulation
CIJE: 0 RIE: 1 CAT: 16

Interpersonal Maturity Level Typology
CIJE: 3 RIE: 0 CAT: 15

Interpersonal Negotiation Strategies
CIJE: 4 RIE: 3 CAT: 15

Interpersonal Perception Test
CIJE: 0 RIE: 1 CAT: 21

Interpersonal Process Recall
CIJE: 16 RIE: 10 CAT: 16

Interpersonal Psychotherapy
CIJE: 1 RIE: 1 CAT: 11

Interpersonal Reactivity Index (Davis)
CIJE: 3 RIE: 1 CAT: 21

Interpersonal Relationship Assessment Technique
CIJE: 4 RIE: 0 CAT: 21

Interpersonal Relationship Rating Scale
CIJE: 2 RIE: 0 CAT: 21

Interpersonal Synchrony
CIJE: 1 RIE: 1 CAT: 11

Interpersonal Therapy
CIJE: 2 RIE: 0 CAT: 11

Interpersonal Topical Inventory (Tuckman)
CIJE: 1 RIE: 0 CAT: 21

Interpersonal Verbs
CIJE: 2 RIE: 1 CAT: 13

Interpersonal World of the Infant (Stern)
CIJE: 0 RIE: 1 CAT: 22

Interpolated Silences
CIJE: 1 RIE: 0 CAT: 16

Interpolation
CIJE: 11 RIE: 1 CAT: 16

Interpretation (Environmental)
CIJE: 19 RIE: 15 CAT: 20

Interpretation Analysis (Debate)
CIJE: 0 RIE: 1 CAT: 15
SN See also "Interpretation Analysis (Lambert)"

Interpretation Analysis (Lambert)
CIJE: 0 RIE: 1 CAT: 15

Interpretation of Pupil Answers
CIJE: 0 RIE: 1 CAT: 21

Interpretative Validity
USE Interpretive Validity

Interpreters Theatre
CIJE: 1 RIE: 2 CAT: 16

Interpreting
CIJE: 8 RIE: 1 CAT: 16

Interpretive Communities
CIJE: 12 RIE: 5 CAT: 15

Interpretive Research
CIJE: 29 RIE: 22 CAT: 15

Interpretive Structural Modeling
CIJE: 0 RIE: 2 CAT: 19

Interpretive Validity
CIJE: 5 RIE: 2 CAT: 15
UF Interpretative Validity

Interpretivism
CIJE: 8 RIE: 1 CAT: 15

Interprovincial Red Seal Program (Canada)
CIJE: 0 RIE: 1 CAT: 19

Interracial Children
CIJE: 7 RIE: 4 CAT: 10
SN See more specific "Biracial Children" — see also "Mixed Race Persons"

Interracial Communication
USE Transracial Communication

Interracial Family
CIJE: 3 RIE: 0 CAT: 10
SN See more specific "Biracial Family" — see also "Mixed Race Persons"

Interrelated Data
CIJE: 1 RIE: 1 CAT: 16

Interrelated Mathematics Science Project
CIJE: 1 RIE: 0 CAT: 19

Interrogation
CIJE: 1 RIE: 3 CAT: 16

Interrogation Techniques
CIJE: 0 RIE: 1 CAT: 15

Interrogatives
CIJE: 14 RIE: 13 CAT: 13

Interrupted Behavior Chaining
CIJE: 1 RIE: 1 CAT: 15

Interrupted Time Series Analysis
CIJE: 1 RIE: 0 CAT: 15

Interruption
CIJE: 7 RIE: 5 CAT: 16

Interruption Method (Reading)
CIJE: 0 RIE: 1 CAT: 15

Interruptions
CIJE: 17 RIE: 6 CAT: 16

INTERSECT Observation Form
CIJE: 0 RIE: 1 CAT: 21
SN INTERSECT = Interactions for Sex Equity in Classroom Teaching

Intersegmental Coordinating Council CA
CIJE: 0 RIE: 1 CAT: 17

Intersensory Reading Method
CIJE: 1 RIE: 0 CAT: 15

Intersentential Processes
CIJE: 3 RIE: 0 CAT: 13

Intershelving
CIJE: 0 RIE: 1 CAT: 15
SN Integration of media on library shelves

Interskola
CIJE: 0 RIE: 1 CAT: 02

Interstate Certification Project
CIJE: 1 RIE: 1 CAT: 19

Interstate Child Support
CIJE: 0 RIE: 1 CAT: 14

Interstate Commerce Commission
CIJE: 0 RIE: 1 CAT: 17

Interstate Compact on the Placement of Children
CIJE: 0 RIE: 1 CAT: 14

Interstate Compacts
CIJE: 1 RIE: 4 CAT: 16

Interstate Consortium on Metric Education
CIJE: 2 RIE: 0 CAT: 17

Interstate Cooperation
CIJE: 1 RIE: 4 CAT: 16

Interstate Distributive Educ Curriculum Consortium
CIJE: 1 RIE: 4 CAT: 17

Interstate Distributive Education Curriculum
CIJE: 0 RIE: 6 CAT: 03

Interstate Migrant Education Council
CIJE: 0 RIE: 2 CAT: 17

Interstate Migrant Education Task Force
CIJE: 0 RIE: 4 CAT: 17

Interstate Migrant Secondary Services Program
CIJE: 0 RIE: 3 CAT: 19

Interstate Migrant Teacher Exchange
CIJE: 0 RIE: 1 CAT: 19

Interstate Oratorical Association
CIJE: 0 RIE: 1 CAT: 17

Interstate Transportation
CIJE: 2 RIE: 1 CAT: 16

Interstate Validation Process
CIJE: 0 RIE: 1 CAT: 15

Interstimulus Interval
CIJE: 5 RIE: 0 CAT: 16

Intersubjectivity
CIJE: 12 RIE: 5 CAT: 13

Intertask Interference
CIJE: 6 RIE: 4 CAT: 21
UF Dual Task Interference; Multiple Task Interference

Intertextuality
CIJE: 21 RIE: 10 CAT: 13
SN See also "Textuality"

Intertrial Repetition Units (Psychology)
CIJE: 1 RIE: 0 CAT: 11

Intertype Library Networks
CIJE: 0 RIE: 1 CAT: 15

Interuniversity Communications Council
CIJE: 2 RIE: 7 CAT: 17

Interuniversity Council
CIJE: 0 RIE: 1 CAT: 17

Interuniversity Research Unit (England)
CIJE: 1 RIE: 0 CAT: 17

Interval by Interval Method
CIJE: 0 RIE: 1 CAT: 15

Interval Scales
CIJE: 4 RIE: 5 CAT: 21

Interval Scaling
CIJE: 5 RIE: 1 CAT: 21

Interval Shift Analysis
CIJE: 2 RIE: 0 CAT: 15

Interval Time Sampling
CIJE: 0 RIE: 2 CAT: 21

Intervention Assistance Teams
CIJE: 2 RIE: 3 CAT: 10

Intervention by Prescription Project
CIJE: 0 RIE: 1 CAT: 19

Intervention Coaching Project
CIJE: 0 RIE: 1 CAT: 19

Intervention Codes
CIJE: 0 RIE: 1 CAT: 15

Intervention Education
CIJE: 6 RIE: 6 CAT: 16

Intervention Rating Profile
CIJE: 0 RIE: 1 CAT: 21

Interview Rating Scales (Blocker)
CIJE: 0 RIE: 1 CAT: 21

Interview Schedule for Children
CIJE: 0 RIE: 1 CAT: 21

Interview Test of English as a Second Language
CIJE: 0 RIE: 1 CAT: 21
SN Used within the Adult Migrant Education Program in Australia

Interviewer Effects
CIJE: 4 RIE: 4 CAT: 15

Interviewers
CIJE: 20 RIE: 11 CAT: 09

Intifada
CIJE: 1 RIE: 1 CAT: 12
UF Intifadeh

Intifadeh
USE Intifada

Intolerance
CIJE: 5 RIE: 3 CAT: 16

Intolerance of Ambiguity Scale (Budner)
CIJE: 2 RIE: 0 CAT: 21

Intra Agency Committee on Rural Education
CIJE: 1 RIE: 3 CAT: 17

Intraception
CIJE: 0 RIE: 2 CAT: 11

Intracity Competition
CIJE: 0 RIE: 1 CAT: 16

Intraclass Correlation
CIJE: 9 RIE: 5 CAT: 21

Intracranial Hemorrhage
CIJE: 1 RIE: 0 CAT: 11

Intracultural Communication
CIJE: 7 RIE: 1 CAT: 16

Intradepartmental Committee Child Abuse Neglect
CIJE: 0 RIE: 1 CAT: 17

Intradepartmental Council on Indian Affairs
CIJE: 1 RIE: 0 CAT: 17

Intradimensional Variability
CIJE: 1 RIE: 0 CAT: 15

Intragroup Differences
USE Within Group Differences

Intraindividual Variability
CIJE: 2 RIE: 0 CAT: 11

Intransitive Choice Behavior
CIJE: 3 RIE: 1 CAT: 16

Intraocular Lenses
CIJE: 0 RIE: 1 CAT: 04

Intraocular Pressure
CIJE: 1 RIE: 0 CAT: 11

Intrapartum Perinatology
CIJE: 0 RIE: 1 CAT: 11

Intrapersonal Communication
CIJE: 12 RIE: 27 CAT: 13

Intrapersonal Skills
CIJE: 1 RIE: 4 CAT: 11

Intrapsychic Conflict
CIJE: 3 RIE: 0 CAT: 11

Intrasubject Paired Comparison
CIJE: 0 RIE: 1 CAT: 15

Intrauterine Devices
CIJE: 1 RIE: 1 CAT: 11

Intravenous Therapy
CIJE: 3 RIE: 10 CAT: 11

Intriligator IOR Model
CIJE: 0 RIE: 1 CAT: 15
UF Inter Organizational Relationship Model

Intrinsic Criticism
CIJE: 1 RIE: 0 CAT: 16

Intrinsic Extrinsic Classroom Orientation
CIJE: 3 RIE: 2 CAT: 11

Intrinsic Justification
CIJE: 1 RIE: 2 CAT: 15

Introduction to Applied Chemistry
CIJE: 1 RIE: 0 CAT: 22

Introduction to Computing
CIJE: 0 RIE: 2 CAT: 22

Introduction to Programed Instruction
CIJE: 1 RIE: 0 CAT: 22

Introductory Physical Science
CIJE: 7 RIE: 18 CAT: 02

Introspection
CIJE: 12 RIE: 6 CAT: 11

Introspective Measures
CIJE: 2 RIE: 0 CAT: 21

Intrusiveness
CIJE: 5 RIE: 7 CAT: 11

Intubation (Medicine)
CIJE: 0 RIE: 4 CAT: 11

Intuition (Mathematics)
CIJE: 15 RIE: 3 CAT: 20

Inupiaq (Tribe)
CIJE: 0 RIE: 2 CAT: 08

Inupiat (Tribe)
CIJE: 1 RIE: 3 CAT: 08

Invariance
CIJE: 9 RIE: 10 CAT: 20

Invariance Hypothesis
CIJE: 1 RIE: 1 CAT: 15

Invariance Principle
CIJE: 8 RIE: 21 CAT: 13

Invariant Stages
CIJE: 2 RIE: 1 CAT: 16

Inventive Drawing
CIJE: 1 RIE: 0 CAT: 03

Inventors
CIJE: 5 RIE: 6 CAT: 10

Inventory Control
CIJE: 10 RIE: 9 CAT: 16

Inventory for Client and Agency Planning
CIJE: 0 RIE: 1 CAT: 21
SN A multidimensional measure of behavior to assist in making decisions about residential or day placement programs for adults with developmental disabilities

Inventory Learning Styles Conceptions Orientations
CIJE: 0 RIE: 1 CAT: 21
UF Inventory of Learning Styles Conceptns Orientatns

Inventory Management Specialists
CIJE: 0 RIE: 1 CAT: 09

Inventory Methods
CIJE: 8 RIE: 1 CAT: 15

Inventory of Access Displayed Literacy Stimuli
CIJE: 0 RIE: 1 CAT: 21

Inventory of Affective Aspects of Schooling
CIJE: 0 RIE: 2 CAT: 21

Inventory of Assets
CIJE: 0 RIE: 4 CAT: 16

Inventory of Attitudes on Child Guidance (Kinzie)
CIJE: 0 RIE: 1 CAT: 21

Inventory of Beliefs
CIJE: 0 RIE: 3 CAT: 21

Inventory of Change Proneness
CIJE: 1 RIE: 0 CAT: 21

Inventory of Childrens Preschool Experiences
CIJE: 0 RIE: 1 CAT: 21

Inventory of Classroom Management Styles
CIJE: 0 RIE: 2 CAT: 21

Inventory of Cognitive Skills (Boehm)
CIJE: 0 RIE: 1 CAT: 21

Inventory of Counseling Practices
CIJE: 0 RIE: 1 CAT: 21

Inventory of Counselor Behaviors
CIJE: 0 RIE: 0 CAT: 21

Inventory of Dependent and Independent Behavior
CIJE: 0 RIE: 1 CAT: 21

Inventory of Dramatic Behavior (Lazier et al)
CIJE: 1 RIE: 0 CAT: 21

Inventory of Factors Affecting Test Performance
CIJE: 0 RIE: 2 CAT: 21

Inventory of Feminine Values (Steinmann and Fox)
CIJE: 2 RIE: 1 CAT: 21

Inventory of Home Stimulation
CIJE: 2 RIE: 2 CAT: 21

Inventory of Learning Processes
CIJE: 15 RIE: 3 CAT: 21

Inventory of Learning Processes (Revised)
CIJE: 1 RIE: 1 CAT: 21

Inventory of Learning Styles Conceptns Orientatns
USE Inventory Learning Styles Conceptions Orientations

Inventory of Myself as a Professional
CIJE: 0 RIE: 1 CAT: 21

Inventory of Parent and Peer Attachment
CIJE: 0 RIE: 1 CAT: 21

Inventory of Personal Investment (Braskamp Maehr)
CIJE: 0 RIE: 1 CAT: 21

Inventory of Personal Skills for Achievement
CIJE: 0 RIE: 1 CAT: 21

Inventory of Piaget Developmental Tasks
CIJE: 4 RIE: 1 CAT: 21

Inventory of Readiness for Literacy
CIJE: 0 RIE: 1 CAT: 21

Inventory of Religious Activities and Interests
CIJE: 3 RIE: 0 CAT: 21

Inventory of Research
CIJE: 0 RIE: 1 CAT: 16

Inventory of Science Attitudes
CIJE: 0 RIE: 1 CAT: 21

Inventory of Self Appraisal
CIJE: 0 RIE: 3 CAT: 21

Inventory of Socially Supportive Behaviors
CIJE: 0 RIE: 3 CAT: 21

Inventory of Study Habits and Attitudes
CIJE: 1 RIE: 0 CAT: 21

Inventory of Teacher Knowledge of Reading
CIJE: 2 RIE: 2 CAT: 21

Inventory of Test Use Satisfaction
CIJE: 0 RIE: 1 CAT: 21

Inventory of University Classroom Environment
CIJE: 0 RIE: 1 CAT: 21

Inventory Systems
CIJE: 1 RIE: 2 CAT: 16

Inverse Normal Scores
CIJE: 0 RIE: 1 CAT: 21

Inverse Tutoring
CIJE: 1 RIE: 0 CAT: 15

Inverses (Mathematics)
CIJE: 5 RIE: 1 CAT: 20

Inversive Geometry
CIJE: 2 RIE: 0 CAT: 20

Invertebrates
CIJE: 22 RIE: 4 CAT: 20

Inverted Files
CIJE: 16 RIE: 1 CAT: 04

Inverted U Hypothesis
CIJE: 4 RIE: 0 CAT: 15

Inverted Writing
CIJE: 1 RIE: 0 CAT: 13

Investigating Science with Children
CIJE: 1 RIE: 1 CAT: 22

Investigating the Earth
CIJE: 0 RIE: 2 CAT: 22

Investigative Journalism
CIJE: 4 RIE: 4 CAT: 16

Investigative Learning
CIJE: 1 RIE: 1 CAT: 15

Investigative Photography
CIJE: 0 RIE: 1 CAT: 03

Investigative Reporting
CIJE: 14 RIE: 6 CAT: 03

Investigator Planning Exercise
CIJE: 0 RIE: 1 CAT: 21
SN For the Chicago Police Department IL

Investment in People Program
CIJE: 0 RIE: 1 CAT: 19

Investment Projections
CIJE: 1 RIE: 1 CAT: 16

INVIDO System
CIJE: 1 RIE: 0 CAT: 04

Invisible Colleges
CIJE: 14 RIE: 5 CAT: 16

Invisible Man (The)
CIJE: 7 RIE: 4 CAT: 22

Invisible Writing
CIJE: 1 RIE: 2 CAT: 15

Invitation to Decision
CIJE: 0 RIE: 2 CAT: 16

Invitation to Submit Materials
CIJE: 0 RIE: 2 CAT: 22

Invitational Education
CIJE: 8 RIE: 22 CAT: 16

Invitational Learning (Purkey)
CIJE: 0 RIE: 1 CAT: 15

Invitational Teaching Observation Instrument
CIJE: 0 RIE: 1 CAT: 21

Invitational Teaching Survey
CIJE: 0 RIE: 3 CAT: 21

Invitations
CIJE: 2 RIE: 1 CAT: 16

Invitations to Enquiry
CIJE: 3 RIE: 1 CAT: 22

Invoices
CIJE: 4 RIE: 2 CAT: 16
UF Billing

Involuntary Commitment Laws
USE Commitment Laws

Involuntary Labor
CIJE: 1 RIE: 0 CAT: 16

Involuntary Minorities
CIJE: 0 RIE: 1 CAT: 10

Involuntary Smoking
USE Passive Smoking

Involvement Behavior Questionnaire
CIJE: 1 RIE: 1 CAT: 21

Involvement in Learning
CIJE: 25 RIE: 8 CAT: 22

Involvement Inventory
CIJE: 1 RIE: 1 CAT: 21

Involvement Theory
CIJE: 0 RIE: 1 CAT: 15

Involving the Very Young Program
CIJE: 0 RIE: 2 CAT: 19

Inwald Personality Inventory
CIJE: 0 RIE: 2 CAT: 21

Inwald Survey 3
CIJE: 0 RIE: 1 CAT: 21

Iodine
CIJE: 11 RIE: 1 CAT: 20

Ion Exchange
CIJE: 3 RIE: 3 CAT: 20

Ion Exchange Chromatography
CIJE: 1 RIE: 0 CAT: 20

Iona College NY
CIJE: 10 RIE: 4 CAT: 17

Ionesco (Eugene)
CIJE: 7 RIE: 1 CAT: 18

Ionization
CIJE: 6 RIE: 0 CAT: 20

Ionosphere
CIJE: 3 RIE: 0 CAT: 20

Ions
CIJE: 18 RIE: 0 CAT: 20

IOP AB
USE Integrated Occupational Program AB

IOSTE
USE International Organization Science and Tech Educ

Iowa
CIJE: 246 RIE: 872 CAT: 07

Iowa (Ames)
CIJE: 0 RIE: 13 CAT: 07

Iowa (Black Hawk County)
CIJE: 0 RIE: 1 CAT: 07

Iowa (Buchanan County)
CIJE: 0 RIE: 1 CAT: 07

Iowa (Burlington)
CIJE: 0 RIE: 1 CAT: 07

Iowa (Carroll County)
CIJE: 0 RIE: 1 CAT: 07

Iowa (Cedar Falls)
CIJE: 2 RIE: 7 CAT: 07

Iowa (Cedar Rapids)
CIJE: 7 RIE: 6 CAT: 07

Iowa (Central)
CIJE: 0 RIE: 1 CAT: 07

Iowa (Council Bluffs)
CIJE: 2 RIE: 0 CAT: 07

Iowa (Crawford County)
CIJE: 0 RIE: 1 CAT: 07

Iowa (Davenport)
CIJE: 1 RIE: 1 CAT: 07

Iowa (Decorah)
CIJE: 0 RIE: 1 CAT: 07

Iowa (Des Moines)
CIJE: 6 RIE: 46 CAT: 07

Iowa (Dubuque)
CIJE: 1 RIE: 1 CAT: 07

Iowa (East)
CIJE: 0 RIE: 1 CAT: 07

Iowa (Esterville)
CIJE: 0 RIE: 1 CAT: 07

Iowa (Fort Madison)
CIJE: 0 RIE: 1 CAT: 07

Iowa (Greene County)
CIJE: 0 RIE: 1 CAT: 07

Iowa (Grinnell)
CIJE: 0 RIE: 1 CAT: 07

Iowa (Ida County)
CIJE: 0 RIE: 1 CAT: 07

Iowa (Iowa City)
CIJE: 4 RIE: 34 CAT: 07

Iowa (Iowa Falls)
CIJE: 0 RIE: 1 CAT: 07

Iowa (Jackson County)
CIJE: 0 RIE: 1 CAT: 07

Iowa (Keokuk)
CIJE: 1 RIE: 0 CAT: 07

Iowa (Language)
CIJE: 0 RIE: 1 CAT: 13
SN Dialect of Chiwere, a Siouan language

Iowa (Lohrville)
CIJE: 0 RIE: 3 CAT: 07

Iowa (Mahaska County)
CIJE: 0 RIE: 1 CAT: 07

Iowa (Marshalltown)
CIJE: 2 RIE: 7 CAT: 07

Iowa (Milford)
CIJE: 0 RIE: 2 CAT: 07

Iowa (Polk County)
CIJE: 2 RIE: 1 CAT: 07

Iowa (Prairie City)
CIJE: 0 RIE: 1 CAT: 07

Iowa (Sioux City)
CIJE: 1 RIE: 7 CAT: 07

Iowa (Siouxland)
CIJE: 0 RIE: 1 CAT: 07

Iowa (Terril)
CIJE: 0 RIE: 1 CAT: 07

Iowa (Tribe)
CIJE: 0 RIE: 1 CAT: 08

Iowa (Waterloo)
CIJE: 1 RIE: 3 CAT: 07

Iowa (Webster County)
CIJE: 0 RIE: 1 CAT: 07

Iowa Adult Education Association
CIJE: 0 RIE: 1 CAT: 17

Iowa Aging Inventory
CIJE: 0 RIE: 1 CAT: 21

Iowa Algebra Aptitude Test
CIJE: 2 RIE: 1 CAT: 21

Iowa Area IX Alpine Center
CIJE: 0 RIE: 1 CAT: 17

Iowa Area XI Access Center
CIJE: 0 RIE: 1 CAT: 17

Iowa ASSIST Program
CIJE: 0 RIE: 1 CAT: 19

Iowa Career Education Inventory
CIJE: 0 RIE: 2 CAT: 21

Iowa Career Education Model
USE Iowa Model for Career Education

Iowa City Public Library
CIJE: 1 RIE: 0 CAT: 17

Iowa City School District IA
CIJE: 3 RIE: 0 CAT: 17

Iowa Curriculum Assistance System
CIJE: 0 RIE: 1 CAT: 19

Iowa Drug Information Service
CIJE: 1 RIE: 0 CAT: 17

Iowa Early Learning Assessment
CIJE: 0 RIE: 1 CAT: 21

Iowa Educational Broadcasting Network
CIJE: 2 RIE: 0 CAT: 17

Iowa Energy Policy Council
CIJE: 0 RIE: 1 CAT: 17

Iowa Experimental and Development Project
CIJE: 0 RIE: 1 CAT: 19

Iowa Farm and Rural Life Poll
CIJE: 0 RIE: 1 CAT: 21

Iowa Grammar Information Test
CIJE: 0 RIE: 1 CAT: 21

Iowa High School Curriculum Project
CIJE: 0 RIE: 2 CAT: 19

Iowa Higher Education Association
CIJE: 0 RIE: 1 CAT: 17

Iowa Honors Workshop
CIJE: 0 RIE: 1 CAT: 02

Iowa Humanities Board
CIJE: 0 RIE: 1 CAT: 17

Iowa Lakeside Laboratory
CIJE: 1 RIE: 0 CAT: 17

Iowa Library Information Teletype Exchange
CIJE: 1 RIE: 2 CAT: 17

Iowa Microcomputer Occupational Info Network
CIJE: 0 RIE: 1 CAT: 17

Iowa Model for Career Education
CIJE: 0 RIE: 1 CAT: 15
UF Iowa Career Education Model

Iowa Parent Behavior Inventory
CIJE: 1 RIE: 1 CAT: 21

Iowa Problem Solving Project
CIJE: 0 RIE: 1 CAT: 19

Iowa Project
CIJE: 0 RIE: 1 CAT: 19

Iowa Pupil Inventory
CIJE: 0 RIE: 1 CAT: 21

Iowa Regional Computer Network
CIJE: 1 RIE: 0 CAT: 17

Iowa School for the Deaf
CIJE: 2 RIE: 0 CAT: 17

Iowa Severity Rating Scales
CIJE: 1 RIE: 1 CAT: 21

Iowa Silent Reading Tests
CIJE: 2 RIE: 6 CAT: 21

Iowa Social Competency Scale (Preschool)
CIJE: 1 RIE: 0 CAT: 21

Iowa State Board of Regents
CIJE: 0 RIE: 1 CAT: 17

Iowa State Department of Education
CIJE: 0 RIE: 1 CAT: 17

Iowa State Education Association
CIJE: 2 RIE: 1 CAT: 17

Iowa State Library System
CIJE: 1 RIE: 0 CAT: 17

Iowa State Manpower Development Council
CIJE: 0 RIE: 1 CAT: 17

Iowa State University
CIJE: 69 RIE: 48 CAT: 17

Iowa Test of Preschool Development
CIJE: 1 RIE: 1 CAT: 21

Iowa Testing Programs
CIJE: 2 RIE: 2 CAT: 21

Iowa Tests of Basic Skills
CIJE: 60 RIE: 288 CAT: 21

Iowa Tests of Educational Development
CIJE: 15 RIE: 35 CAT: 21

Iowa Training School for Boys
CIJE: 1 RIE: 0 CAT: 17

Iowa UPSTEP
CIJE: 2 RIE: 1 CAT: 19

Iowa Valley Community College District
CIJE: 0 RIE: 1 CAT: 17

Iowa Vocational Assessment System
CIJE: 0 RIE: 1 CAT: 19

Iowa Wesleyan College
CIJE: 0 RIE: 1 CAT: 17

Iowa Writing Project
CIJE: 1 RIE: 2 CAT: 19

IOX Assessment Associates
CIJE: 0 RIE: 1 CAT: 17

IPAINT
CIJE: 0 RIE: 1 CAT: 04

IPAT Anxiety Scale
CIJE: 4 RIE: 4 CAT: 21

IPAT Childrens Personality Questionnaire
CIJE: 1 RIE: 1 CAT: 21

IPEDS
USE Integrated Postsecondary Education Data System

Ipsative Measurement
CIJE: 13 RIE: 8 CAT: 21

IRA Project CONPASS
CIJE: 4 RIE: 0 CAT: 19

Iran
CIJE: 145 RIE: 156 CAT: 07

Iran (Azarbaiyan)
CIJE: 1 RIE: 1 CAT: 07
UF Iran (Azerbaijan)

Iran (Azerbaijan)
USE Iran (Azarbaiyan)

Iran (Fars Province)
CIJE: 1 RIE: 1 CAT: 07

Iran (Khuzestan Province)
CIJE: 0 RIE: 1 CAT: 07

Iran (Shiraz)
CIJE: 1 RIE: 0 CAT: 07

Iran (Tabriz)
CIJE: 0 RIE: 1 CAT: 07

Iran (Teheran)
USE Iran (Tehran)

Iran (Tehran)
CIJE: 2 RIE: 2 CAT: 07
UF Iran (Teheran)

Iran Contra Affair
CIJE: 5 RIE: 1 CAT: 12

Iran Functional Literacy Project
CIJE: 1 RIE: 0 CAT: 19

Iran Hostage Crisis
CIJE: 3 RIE: 5 CAT: 12

Iran Iraq War
CIJE: 0 RIE: 0 CAT: 12
SN 1980-88 (see also "Gulf War")
UF Iraq Iran War

Iranian Americans
CIJE: 0 RIE: 1 CAT: 08

Iranian Languages
CIJE: 0 RIE: 6 CAT: 13

Iranian Revolution 1979
CIJE: 1 RIE: 0 CAT: 12
UF Islamic Revolution (Iran 1979)

Iranians
CIJE: 18 RIE: 13 CAT: 08

Iraq
CIJE: 29 RIE: 39 CAT: 07

Iraq (Baghdad)
CIJE: 0 RIE: 3 CAT: 07

Iraq Iran War
USE Iran Iraq War

Iraqi Scientific Documentation Centre
CIJE: 1 RIE: 0 CAT: 17

Iraqis
CIJE: 3 RIE: 2 CAT: 08

Ireland
CIJE: 224 RIE: 195 CAT: 07

Ireland (Dublin)
CIJE: 15 RIE: 3 CAT: 07

Irish Americans
CIJE: 14 RIE: 25 CAT: 08

Irish Culture
CIJE: 1 RIE: 4 CAT: 16

Irish Drama
CIJE: 0 RIE: 1 CAT: 16

Irish Literature
CIJE: 2 RIE: 5 CAT: 16

Irish People
CIJE: 5 RIE: 12 CAT: 08

Iron (Metal)
CIJE: 5 RIE: 3 CAT: 20

Iron Deficiency
CIJE: 2 RIE: 0 CAT: 11
UF Nonanemic Iron Deficiency

Iron John A Book About Men
CIJE: 0 RIE: 1 CAT: 22

Iron Man
CIJE: 1 RIE: 1 CAT: 22

Ironbound Community Learning Center NJ
CIJE: 0 RIE: 1 CAT: 17

Ironside (Isaac)
CIJE: 1 RIE: 0 CAT: 18

Ironworkers
CIJE: 0 RIE: 2 CAT: 09

Iroquoian Languages
CIJE: 1 RIE: 1 CAT: 13

Iroquois (Nation)
CIJE: 12 RIE: 6 CAT: 08

Iroquois (Tribe)
CIJE: 17 RIE: 17 CAT: 08

Iroquois Confederacy
CIJE: 8 RIE: 2 CAT: 17

Iroquois League
CIJE: 3 RIE: 5 CAT: 17

Irrational Belief Scale (Ellis)
CIJE: 2 RIE: 0 CAT: 21

Irrational Beliefs
CIJE: 13 RIE: 7 CAT: 11

Irrational Beliefs (Ellis)
CIJE: 0 RIE: 1 CAT: 11

Irrational Numbers
CIJE: 7 RIE: 2 CAT: 20

Irrationality
CIJE: 3 RIE: 3 CAT: 11

Irreparable Harm Standard
CIJE: 0 RIE: 1 CAT: 14

Irrigation
CIJE: 5 RIE: 18 CAT: 20

Irrigation Systems
CIJE: 2 RIE: 8 CAT: 20

Irritability
CIJE: 0 RIE: 1 CAT: 11

Irvine Unified School District CA
CIJE: 4 RIE: 2 CAT: 17

Irvine Valley College CA
CIJE: 0 RIE: 3 CAT: 17

Irving (Washington)
CIJE: 3 RIE: 2 CAT: 18

Irving Independent School District TX
CIJE: 0 RIE: 2 CAT: 17

Ischemic Heart Disease
CIJE: 2 RIE: 1 CAT: 11

ISDNs
USE Integrated Services Digital Networks

Iser (Wolfgang)
CIJE: 3 RIE: 1 CAT: 18

ISES (Instructional Support and Evaluation System)
CIJE: 0 RIE: 1 CAT: 21

ISES Teacher Nursery School Battery
CIJE: 0 RIE: 1 CAT: 21

Ishahara Test for Color Blindness
CIJE: 2 RIE: 1 CAT: 21

Isherwood (Christopher)
CIJE: 1 RIE: 0 CAT: 18

Ishihara Test for Color Blindness
CIJE: 1 RIE: 2 CAT: 21

Isla (Jose Francisco de)
CIJE: 1 RIE: 0 CAT: 18

Islam
CIJE: 37 RIE: 19 CAT: 10

Islamic Art
CIJE: 0 RIE: 1 CAT: 16

Islamic Countries
CIJE: 10 RIE: 5 CAT: 07

Islamic Revolution (Iran 1979)
USE Iranian Revolution 1979

Islamic States Broadcasting Organization
CIJE: 1 RIE: 0 CAT: 17

Island (Novel)
CIJE: 0 RIE: 0 CAT: 22

Island of the Blue Dolphins
CIJE: 1 RIE: 1 CAT: 22

Island Trees Union Free School District v Pico
USE Pico v Island Trees Union Free School District

Islands
CIJE: 6 RIE: 0 CAT: 07

Islands Puzzle
CIJE: 1 RIE: 0 CAT: 21

Isle of Independent Study
CIJE: 1 RIE: 0 CAT: 22

ISO 9000
CIJE: 1 RIE: 1 CAT: 22
SN Quality control standard of the "International Organization for Standardization" (q.v.)

Isocrates
CIJE: 8 RIE: 4 CAT: 18

Isokinetics
CIJE: 6 RIE: 2 CAT: 11

Isoko
CIJE: 0 RIE: 1 CAT: 13

Isolation Effect
CIJE: 4 RIE: 5 CAT: 11
SN Facilitating effect of isolation of distinctive features of an item (e.g., type, face, color) on learning

Isoleucine
CIJE: 1 RIE: 0 CAT: 20

Isomerism
CIJE: 2 RIE: 1 CAT: 20

Isomerization
CIJE: 1 RIE: 0 CAT: 20

Isomers
CIJE: 4 RIE: 0 CAT: 20

Isometric Contraction
CIJE: 6 RIE: 0 CAT: 11

Isometric Endurance
CIJE: 1 RIE: 0 CAT: 11

Isometric Strength
CIJE: 1 RIE: 0 CAT: 11

Isometries
CIJE: 2 RIE: 0 CAT: 20

Isomorphism
CIJE: 6 RIE: 4 CAT: 20

Isopods
CIJE: 2 RIE: 0 CAT: 20

Isothermal Community College NC
CIJE: 0 RIE: 1 CAT: 17

Isotonic Strength
CIJE: 1 RIE: 2 CAT: 11

Isotonic Weight Training
CIJE: 0 RIE: 1 CAT: 11

Isotopes
CIJE: 3 RIE: 1 CAT: 04

Isozaki (Arata)
CIJE: 0 RIE: 1 CAT: 18

Israel
CIJE: 1583 RIE: 570 CAT: 07

Israel (Haifa)
CIJE: 7 RIE: 2 CAT: 07

Israel (Jerusalem)
CIJE: 20 RIE: 14 CAT: 07

Israel (Tel Aviv)
CIJE: 24 RIE: 7 CAT: 07

Israel (Tiberias)
CIJE: 1 RIE: 0 CAT: 07

Israel Elementary Science Project
CIJE: 1 RIE: 0 CAT: 19

Israel Library Association
CIJE: 1 RIE: 0 CAT: 17

Israel Ministry of Education and Culture
USE Ministry of Education and Culture (Israel)

Israeli Arabs
CIJE: 7 RIE: 2 CAT: 08

Israeli Interuniversity Psychometric Ent Test
USE Psychometric Entrance Test (Israel)

Israeli Palestinian Conflict
USE Palestinian Israeli Conflict

Israelis
CIJE: 44 RIE: 13 CAT: 08

Issei
CIJE: 3 RIE: 3 CAT: 08

Issue Advertising
CIJE: 1 RIE: 1 CAT: 16

Issue Centered Education
CIJE: 12 RIE: 1 CAT: 03

Issue Differentiation
CIJE: 3 RIE: 2 CAT: 16

Issue Diversity
CIJE: 0 RIE: 1 CAT: 16

Issue Salience
CIJE: 2 RIE: 11 CAT: 16

Issues Approach
CIJE: 10 RIE: 9 CAT: 15

Issues in Disability Scale
CIJE: 1 RIE: 0 CAT: 21

Issues Management
CIJE: 22 RIE: 8 CAT: 15

It Scale for Children
CIJE: 7 RIE: 5 CAT: 21

Italian (American)
CIJE: 4 RIE: 1 CAT: 13

Italian (Australian)
CIJE: 3 RIE: 0 CAT: 13

Italian (Genoese)
CIJE: 0 RIE: 1 CAT: 13

Italian Australians
CIJE: 0 RIE: 1 CAT: 08

Italian Canadians
CIJE: 5 RIE: 4 CAT: 08

Italian Culture
CIJE: 0 RIE: 5 CAT: 16

Italian Radio and Television Agency
CIJE: 0 RIE: 1 CAT: 17

Italian Speaking
CIJE: 1 RIE: 1 CAT: 08

Italians
CIJE: 12 RIE: 12 CAT: 08

Italic (Handwriting)
USE Italic Writing

Italic Writing
CIJE: 3 RIE: 1 CAT: 13
UF Italic (Handwriting)

Italy
CIJE: 340 RIE: 244 CAT: 07

Italy (Florence)
CIJE: 4 RIE: 1 CAT: 07

Italy (Naples)
CIJE: 2 RIE: 0 CAT: 07

Italy (Padua)
CIJE: 1 RIE: 2 CAT: 07

Italy (Pavia)
CIJE: 0 RIE: 1 CAT: 07

Italy (Reggio Emilia)
CIJE: 15 RIE: 8 CAT: 07

Italy (Rome)
CIJE: 19 RIE: 4 CAT: 07

Italy (Sauris)
CIJE: 0 RIE: 1 CAT: 07

Italy (Sicily)
CIJE: 7 RIE: 1 CAT: 07

Italy (Turin)
CIJE: 0 RIE: 1 CAT: 07

Italy (Venice)
CIJE: 4 RIE: 2 CAT: 07

Itard (Jean)
CIJE: 6 RIE: 2 CAT: 18

Itasca Community College MN
CIJE: 1 RIE: 0 CAT: 17

ITEL Automated Typing System
CIJE: 0 RIE: 1 CAT: 15

Item Bias Detection
CIJE: 0 RIE: 2 CAT: 21

Item Calibration
CIJE: 4 RIE: 15 CAT: 21

Item Characteristic Function
CIJE: 9 RIE: 10 CAT: 21

Item Content Criterion
CIJE: 0 RIE: 1 CAT: 21

Item Deletion
CIJE: 1 RIE: 1 CAT: 21

Item Density
CIJE: 0 RIE: 1 CAT: 21

Item Dependency Model
CIJE: 1 RIE: 2 CAT: 15

Item Dimensionality
CIJE: 2 RIE: 3 CAT: 21

Item Discrimination (Tests)
CIJE: 24 RIE: 39 CAT: 21

Item Disguise
USE Disguised Test Items

Item Efficiency Index (Neill and Jackson)
CIJE: 1 RIE: 0 CAT: 21

Item Hierarchies
CIJE: 2 RIE: 6 CAT: 21

Item Homogeneity
CIJE: 5 RIE: 3 CAT: 21

Item Information
CIJE: 1 RIE: 1 CAT: 21

Item Invariance
CIJE: 1 RIE: 3 CAT: 21

Item Item Curves
CIJE: 0 RIE: 1 CAT: 21

Item Learning
CIJE: 1 RIE: 0 CAT: 15

Item Linking
CIJE: 2 RIE: 1 CAT: 21

Item Parameter Drift
CIJE: 1 RIE: 1 CAT: 21

Item Parameters
CIJE: 57 RIE: 72 CAT: 21

Item Parcels
CIJE: 0 RIE: 1 CAT: 21

Item Pattern Scoring
USE Pattern Scoring

Item Position (Tests)
CIJE: 15 RIE: 20 CAT: 21

Item Rating Scale
CIJE: 0 RIE: 2 CAT: 21

Item Rating Sheet
CIJE: 0 RIE: 1 CAT: 21

Item Review Scale
CIJE: 0 RIE: 1 CAT: 21

Item Shells
CIJE: 0 RIE: 2 CAT: 21

Item Subtest Regression
CIJE: 0 RIE: 1 CAT: 21

Item Variance
CIJE: 0 RIE: 1 CAT: 21

Item Wording
CIJE: 5 RIE: 1 CAT: 21

Iterative Methods
CIJE: 35 RIE: 18 CAT: 15

ITFS What It Is How to Plan
CIJE: 0 RIE: 1 CAT: 22

Ithaca City Schools NY
CIJE: 2 RIE: 0 CAT: 17

Ithaca College NY
CIJE: 7 RIE: 10 CAT: 17

Itinerant Behavior Development Program
CIJE: 0 RIE: 1 CAT: 19

Itinerant Teacher Service (Australia)
CIJE: 0 RIE: 1 CAT: 17

Itinerary Planning
CIJE: 0 RIE: 1 CAT: 16

Itonama
CIJE: 0 RIE: 1 CAT: 13

Itsekiri
CIJE: 0 RIE: 1 CAT: 13

ITT
USE International Telephone and Telegraph Corporation

ITT International Fellowship Program
CIJE: 0 RIE: 1 CAT: 19

ITT Sheraton Hotels HI
CIJE: 0 RIE: 2 CAT: 17

Ittleson Center for Child Research
CIJE: 0 RIE: 1 CAT: 17

ITV Futures Planning Group
CIJE: 0 RIE: 1 CAT: 17
UF Instructional Television Futures Planning Group

Ivanov Smolensky Procedure
CIJE: 0 RIE: 1 CAT: 15

Ivory Coast
CIJE: 16 RIE: 49 CAT: 07

Ivy League Colleges
CIJE: 7 RIE: 5 CAT: 05

Iwaidja
CIJE: 0 RIE: 1 CAT: 13
SN An Australian Aboriginal language

Ixil
CIJE: 0 RIE: 2 CAT: 13
SN A Mayan language of Guatemala

Iyengar (Shanto)
CIJE: 0 RIE: 1 CAT: 18

Izaak Walton League of America
CIJE: 1 RIE: 2 CAT: 17

J C Penney
CIJE: 1 RIE: 1 CAT: 17

J Coefficient
CIJE: 3 RIE: 2 CAT: 15

J Curve
CIJE: 1 RIE: 0 CAT: 21

J Paul Getty Center Library CA
CIJE: 1 RIE: 0 CAT: 17

Japanese Speaking
CIJE: 4 RIE: 4 CAT: 08

Japanese Studies
CIJE: 6 RIE: 12 CAT: 03

Japanese Wrapping Papers
CIJE: 1 RIE: 0 CAT: 16

Jaqi Languages
CIJE: 0 RIE: 1 CAT: 13

Jaques (Elliott)
CIJE: 0 RIE: 1 CAT: 18

Jar Test
CIJE: 0 RIE: 2 CAT: 20

Jarai
CIJE: 1 RIE: 0 CAT: 13

Jaramillo (Don Pedrito)
CIJE: 0 RIE: 2 CAT: 18

Jardine (George)
CIJE: 1 RIE: 3 CAT: 18

Jarema Law
CIJE: 0 RIE: 1 CAT: 14

Jarry (Alfred)
CIJE: 1 RIE: 0 CAT: 18

Jarvis Christian College TX
CIJE: 0 RIE: 1 CAT: 17

Jasin (Alexander)
CIJE: 1 RIE: 0 CAT: 18

Jasper Planning Assistant
CIJE: 0 RIE: 1 CAT: 21

Jasper Woodbury Problem Solving Series
CIJE: 1 RIE: 1 CAT: 22

Jaspers (Karl)
CIJE: 3 RIE: 2 CAT: 18

Jastak System
CIJE: 1 RIE: 0 CAT: 21

Javits Wagner O Day Act 1971
CIJE: 1 RIE: 1 CAT: 14

Jay (John)
CIJE: 1 RIE: 1 CAT: 18

Jay (Sarah Livingston)
CIJE: 0 RIE: 1 CAT: 18

Jay Treaty
CIJE: 2 RIE: 0 CAT: 14

JDDST
USE Denver Developmental Screening Test (Japan)

Jean de Brebeuf College (Canada)
CIJE: 1 RIE: 0 CAT: 17

Jeanneret (Rene)
CIJE: 0 RIE: 1 CAT: 18

Jefferson (Thomas)
CIJE: 43 RIE: 17 CAT: 18

Jefferson Center
CIJE: 2 RIE: 0 CAT: 17

Jefferson College MO
CIJE: 2 RIE: 0 CAT: 17

Jefferson Community College KY
CIJE: 1 RIE: 1 CAT: 17

Jefferson Community College NY
CIJE: 0 RIE: 2 CAT: 17

Jefferson County Adult Reading Program KY
CIJE: 0 RIE: 4 CAT: 19

Jefferson County Open High School CO
CIJE: 2 RIE: 2 CAT: 17

Jefferson County Public Schools KY
CIJE: 12 RIE: 16 CAT: 17

Jefferson County School District CO
CIJE: 9 RIE: 15 CAT: 17
UF Jefferson County Schools CO

Jefferson County School District OR
CIJE: 0 RIE: 2 CAT: 17

Jefferson County Schools AL
CIJE: 0 RIE: 1 CAT: 17

Jefferson County Schools CO
USE Jefferson County School District CO

Jefferson County Unified School District
CIJE: 1 RIE: 0 CAT: 17

Jefferson Medical College PA
CIJE: 13 RIE: 2 CAT: 17

Jefferson Parish Prison
CIJE: 1 RIE: 0 CAT: 17

Jefferson Parish Public Schools LA
CIJE: 1 RIE: 3 CAT: 17

Jefferson Parish Writing Project
CIJE: 0 RIE: 1 CAT: 19

Jefferson School IL
CIJE: 1 RIE: 0 CAT: 17

Jefferson State Community College AL
CIJE: 0 RIE: 3 CAT: 17

Jefferson State Junior College AL
CIJE: 0 RIE: 1 CAT: 17

Jeffersonian Democracy
CIJE: 1 RIE: 1 CAT: 16

Jeffries (Leonard)
CIJE: 1 RIE: 1 CAT: 18

Jellyfish
CIJE: 0 RIE: 1 CAT: 20

Jemez Pueblo (Tribe)
CIJE: 1 RIE: 0 CAT: 08

Jencks (Christopher)
CIJE: 37 RIE: 5 CAT: 18

Jencks Report
CIJE: 1 RIE: 0 CAT: 22

Jenkins (J J)
CIJE: 2 RIE: 0 CAT: 18

Jenkins (Richard L)
CIJE: 0 RIE: 1 CAT: 18

Jenkins Activity Survey
CIJE: 7 RIE: 2 CAT: 21

Jensen (Arthur R)
CIJE: 59 RIE: 27 CAT: 18

Jensen (Gary F)
CIJE: 2 RIE: 0 CAT: 18

Jensen Report
CIJE: 3 RIE: 1 CAT: 22

Jensens Theoretical Model of Intelligence
CIJE: 5 RIE: 1 CAT: 15

Jeremiads
CIJE: 1 RIE: 1 CAT: 16
SN See also "American Jeremiads" and "European Jeremiads"

Jericho Union Free District NY
CIJE: 0 RIE: 1 CAT: 17

Jersey City Public Schools NJ
CIJE: 2 RIE: 2 CAT: 17

Jersey City State College NJ
CIJE: 1 RIE: 5 CAT: 17

Jesness Behavior Checklist
CIJE: 0 RIE: 1 CAT: 21

Jesness Inventory
CIJE: 10 RIE: 2 CAT: 21

Jessamine County School District KY
CIJE: 0 RIE: 0 CAT: 17

Jessie Stanton Developmental Playground NY
CIJE: 1 RIE: 0 CAT: 17

Jesuits
CIJE: 9 RIE: 9 CAT: 10

Jesus Christ
CIJE: 0 RIE: 1 CAT: 18

Jesus Christ Superstar
CIJE: 2 RIE: 0 CAT: 22

Jesus People
CIJE: 1 RIE: 0 CAT: 08

Jet Propulsion Laboratory
CIJE: 3 RIE: 0 CAT: 17

JETS Inc
USE Junior Engineering Technical Society

Jeu de Banque (The Bank Game)
CIJE: 0 RIE: 1 CAT: 16

Jewelry
CIJE: 7 RIE: 3 CAT: 04

Jewelry Making Occupations
CIJE: 0 RIE: 4 CAT: 09

Jewett (Charles Coffin)
CIJE: 0 RIE: 1 CAT: 18

Jewish Board of Guardians
CIJE: 0 RIE: 1 CAT: 17

Jewish Child Care Association of New York
CIJE: 1 RIE: 1 CAT: 17

Jewish Culture
CIJE: 9 RIE: 9 CAT: 16

Jewish Day Schools
CIJE: 4 RIE: 10 CAT: 05

Jewish Employment and Vocational Service System
CIJE: 0 RIE: 6 CAT: 17

Jewish Family Services
CIJE: 0 RIE: 1 CAT: 17

Jewish Languages
CIJE: 1 RIE: 1 CAT: 13

Jewish Law
CIJE: 1 RIE: 1 CAT: 14
UF Halakhah

Jewish National and University Library (Israel)
CIJE: 1 RIE: 0 CAT: 17

Jewish Studies
CIJE: 9 RIE: 15 CAT: 03

Jewish Theological Seminary of America NY
CIJE: 1 RIE: 1 CAT: 17

Jewish Vocational Service
CIJE: 0 RIE: 1 CAT: 17

JFK (Film)
CIJE: 0 RIE: 1 CAT: 22

Ji Yun
CIJE: 0 RIE: 1 CAT: 22

Jicarilla Apache (Tribe)
CIJE: 0 RIE: 12 CAT: 08

Jigsaw II
CIJE: 6 RIE: 4 CAT: 21

Jigsaw Method
CIJE: 21 RIE: 11 CAT: 15

Jimenez (Juan Ramon)
CIJE: 3 RIE: 0 CAT: 18

Jinnah (Mohammad Ali)
CIJE: 0 RIE: 1 CAT: 18

Jirel
CIJE: 0 RIE: 3 CAT: 13

Jivaro (Tribe)
CIJE: 0 RIE: 1 CAT: 08

JMB Applied Chemistry
CIJE: 1 RIE: 0 CAT: 03

JMB Engineering Science
CIJE: 1 RIE: 0 CAT: 03

JNCL Resolutions on Lang in American Education
CIJE: 1 RIE: 0 CAT: 16

Joad (C E M)
CIJE: 1 RIE: 0 CAT: 18

Joan of Arc
CIJE: 1 RIE: 1 CAT: 18

Job Activity Survey
CIJE: 2 RIE: 0 CAT: 21

Job Advancement Training Program
CIJE: 0 RIE: 2 CAT: 19

Job Agents
CIJE: 0 RIE: 2 CAT: 09

Job Aids
CIJE: 34 RIE: 11 CAT: 16

Job Analysis and Interest Measurement
CIJE: 0 RIE: 4 CAT: 15

Job Analysis Survey (NBPTS)
CIJE: 0 RIE: 1 CAT: 21
SN NBPTS = National Board for Professional Teaching Standards

Job Attitude Questionnaire (Williams)
CIJE: 0 RIE: 1 CAT: 21

Job Attitude Scale (Saleh)
CIJE: 0 RIE: 2 CAT: 21

Job Cards
CIJE: 1 RIE: 2 CAT: 16

Job Characteristics
CIJE: 13 RIE: 7 CAT: 16

Job Classification
CIJE: 14 RIE: 7 CAT: 16

Job Clubs
CIJE: 4 RIE: 10 CAT: 09

Job Coaches
CIJE: 14 RIE: 11 CAT: 09

Job Control Language
CIJE: 0 RIE: 2 CAT: 04

Job Corps
CIJE: 53 RIE: 119 CAT: 17

Job Corps Graded Reading Program
CIJE: 0 RIE: 1 CAT: 19

Job Descriptive Index
CIJE: 21 RIE: 17 CAT: 15

Job Designs Project OR
CIJE: 0 RIE: 1 CAT: 19

Job Diagnostic Survey (Hackman and Oldham)
CIJE: 3 RIE: 3 CAT: 21

Job Dimensions
CIJE: 1 RIE: 5 CAT: 15

Job Element Procedure J Scale (Primoff)
CIJE: 0 RIE: 1 CAT: 21

Job Enlargement
CIJE: 1 RIE: 1 CAT: 15

Job Evaluation
CIJE: 20 RIE: 9 CAT: 15

Job Exchange Programs
CIJE: 1 RIE: 1 CAT: 19

Job Expectations
CIJE: 4 RIE: 5 CAT: 16
UF Occupational Expectations

Job Finding Clubs (Canada)
CIJE: 0 RIE: 1 CAT: 19

Job Improvement Service
CIJE: 1 RIE: 0 CAT: 17

Job in General Scale
CIJE: 0 RIE: 0 CAT: 21

Job Information Service
CIJE: 2 RIE: 1 CAT: 17

Job Instruction Training
CIJE: 1 RIE: 1 CAT: 15

Job Involvement
CIJE: 12 RIE: 3 CAT: 16

Job Knowledge
CIJE: 1 RIE: 1 CAT: 16

Job Literacy
CIJE: 9 RIE: 39 CAT: 15
SN See also "Workplace Literacy"
UF Occupational Literacy

Job Loss
CIJE: 2 RIE: 2 CAT: 16

Job Matching Systems
CIJE: 1 RIE: 2 CAT: 15
UF Job Person Match

Job Model
CIJE: 0 RIE: 1 CAT: 15

Job Modification
CIJE: 0 RIE: 3 CAT: 15

Job Opportunities and Basic Skills Program
CIJE: 5 RIE: 55 CAT: 19

Job Opportunities for Bilingual Students
USE Project JOBS NY

Job Opportunities for Youth Project
CIJE: 0 RIE: 1 CAT: 19

Job Opportunities in the Business Sector
CIJE: 15 RIE: 14 CAT: 17

Job Opportunities Through Better Skills IL
CIJE: 0 RIE: 1 CAT: 17

Job Orientation
CIJE: 5 RIE: 3 CAT: 15

Job Oriented Basic Skills Program
CIJE: 0 RIE: 1 CAT: 19

Job Performance Aided Training
CIJE: 0 RIE: 1 CAT: 15

Job Performance Appraisal System
CIJE: 0 RIE: 1 CAT: 15

Job Performance Measurement Project
CIJE: 0 RIE: 2 CAT: 19

Job Person Match
USE Job Matching Systems

Job Previews
CIJE: 3 RIE: 0 CAT: 16

Job Reading Task Tests
CIJE: 0 RIE: 1 CAT: 21

Job Related Literacy
CIJE: 5 RIE: 16 CAT: 15

Job Related Mathematics
CIJE: 0 RIE: 13 CAT: 15

Job Related Reading
CIJE: 9 RIE: 15 CAT: 15

Job Relatedness
CIJE: 0 RIE: 1 CAT: 16
UF Job Relevance

Job Relevance
USE Job Relatedness

Job Replication
CIJE: 0 RIE: 1 CAT: 15

Job Restructuring
CIJE: 3 RIE: 3 CAT: 15

Job Satisfaction Inventory (Muthard and Miller)
CIJE: 2 RIE: 2 CAT: 21

Job Scope
CIJE: 1 RIE: 2 CAT: 16

Job Search Skills Training Program
CIJE: 0 RIE: 7 CAT: 19

Job Security System
CIJE: 0 RIE: 1 CAT: 19

Job Service
CIJE: 0 RIE: 6 CAT: 17

Job Shadowing
CIJE: 1 RIE: 10 CAT: 15
UF Shadowing (Jobs)

Job Simulations
CIJE: 1 RIE: 1 CAT: 15

Job Skills Education Program
CIJE: 3 RIE: 5 CAT: 19

Job Stress
CIJE: 49 RIE: 24 CAT: 16

Job Target Approach
CIJE: 0 RIE: 3 CAT: 15

Job Task Performance Tests
CIJE: 0 RIE: 2 CAT: 21

Job Titles
CIJE: 15 RIE: 5 CAT: 16

Job Training 2000
CIJE: 2 RIE: 1 CAT: 19

Job Training Academies
CIJE: 1 RIE: 0 CAT: 05

Job Training and Tryout
CIJE: 1 RIE: 1 CAT: 19

Job Training Coordinating Councils (States)
USE State Job Training Coordinating Councils

Job Training for the Homeless Demonstration Prog
CIJE: 0 RIE: 2 CAT: 19

Job Training Partnership Act 1982
CIJE: 52 RIE: 571 CAT: 14
SN See also "JTPA Performance Standards"

Job Training Partnership Act 1982 Title IIA
CIJE: 3 RIE: 10 CAT: 14

Job Training Partnership Act 1982 Title III
CIJE: 2 RIE: 4 CAT: 14

Job Training Partnership Act Amendments 1992
CIJE: 0 RIE: 1 CAT: 14
UF Job Training Reform Amendments 1992; Public Law 102 367

Job Training Partnership Amendments 1986
CIJE: 0 RIE: 1 CAT: 14

Job Training Reform Amendments 1992
USE Job Training Partnership Act Amendments 1992

Job Training Scheme (England)
CIJE: 0 RIE: 1 CAT: 19

Job Value Factors
CIJE: 2 RIE: 3 CAT: 15

Jobs and Income
CIJE: 0 RIE: 1 CAT: 16

Jobs Child Care Block Grant
CIJE: 0 RIE: 1 CAT: 14

Jobs for Americas Graduates
CIJE: 2 RIE: 2 CAT: 19

Jobs for Americas Graduates Program
CIJE: 0 RIE: 1 CAT: 19

Jobs for Veterans Program
CIJE: 1 RIE: 0 CAT: 19

Jobs for Youth
CIJE: 0 RIE: 4 CAT: 19

Jobs in Instructional Media Study
CIJE: 4 RIE: 1 CAT: 19

Jobs Now
CIJE: 0 RIE: 5 CAT: 19

Jobs Rallies
CIJE: 0 RIE: 1 CAT: 15

Jobscan
CIJE: 1 RIE: 0 CAT: 04

JOBSTART
CIJE: 0 RIE: 5 CAT: 19

JobStart Training Program
CIJE: 0 RIE: 1 CAT: 19
SN Program of older volunteers helping disabled teens and preteens prepare to enter the world of work

Jobtest 1
CIJE: 0 RIE: 1 CAT: 21

Joe Camel
CIJE: 0 RIE: 2 CAT: 16

Johari Window Model
CIJE: 3 RIE: 3 CAT: 15

John A Logan College IL
CIJE: 0 RIE: 2 CAT: 17

John Abbott College PQ
CIJE: 2 RIE: 2 CAT: 17

John Adams Adult School CA
CIJE: 0 RIE: 1 CAT: 17

John Adams High School OR
CIJE: 10 RIE: 1 CAT: 17

John Birch Society
CIJE: 2 RIE: 2 CAT: 17

John Breuner Company
CIJE: 0 RIE: 1 CAT: 17

John C Calhoun State Community College AL
CIJE: 0 RIE: 6 CAT: 17
UF Calhoun State Community College AL

John C Campbell Folk School
CIJE: 0 RIE: 1 CAT: 17

John Carroll University OH
CIJE: 2 RIE: 2 CAT: 17

John Crerar Library IL
CIJE: 1 RIE: 1 CAT: 17

John Dewey Personal Beliefs Inventory
CIJE: 1 RIE: 0 CAT: 21

John Dewey Society
CIJE: 2 RIE: 0 CAT: 17

John F Kennedy Center for the Performing Arts DC
CIJE: 5 RIE: 1 CAT: 17

John F Kennedy Family Service Center MA
CIJE: 0 RIE: 1 CAT: 17

John F Kennedy Library MA
CIJE: 0 RIE: 1 CAT: 17

John F Kennedy School (West Germany)
CIJE: 0 RIE: 1 CAT: 17

John Hancock Life Insurance Company
CIJE: 0 RIE: 1 CAT: 17

John Hancock Mutual Life Insurance Company
CIJE: 0 RIE: 1 CAT: 17

John Howard Society of Canada
CIJE: 0 RIE: 1 CAT: 17

John Jay College NY
USE City University of New York John Jay College

John M Olin Library
CIJE: 0 RIE: 1 CAT: 17

John Marshall High School NY
CIJE: 1 RIE: 0 CAT: 17

John Paul II (Pope)
CIJE: 1 RIE: 1 CAT: 18
UF Pope John Paul II

John Rimoldi Problem Solving Apparatus
CIJE: 0 RIE: 2 CAT: 04

John Rolfe Museum and Historical Res Ctr VA
CIJE: 0 RIE: 0 CAT: 17

John Tracy Clinic CA
CIJE: 2 RIE: 2 CAT: 17

John Tyler Community College VA
CIJE: 0 RIE: 4 CAT: 17

John Wood Community College IL
CIJE: 5 RIE: 6 CAT: 17

John XXIII (Pope)
CIJE: 0 RIE: 0 CAT: 18

Johns Hopkins Academic Games Project
CIJE: 0 RIE: 1 CAT: 19

Johns Hopkins Center for Res on Elem and Mid Schs
USE Center for Research on Elementary and Middle Schs

Johns Hopkins Perceptual Test
CIJE: 0 RIE: 4 CAT: 21

Johns Hopkins University MD
CIJE: 65 RIE: 11 CAT: 17

Johnson (Andrew)
CIJE: 3 RIE: 1 CAT: 18

Johnson (B Lamar)
CIJE: 1 RIE: 2 CAT: 18

Johnson (Earl S)
CIJE: 1 RIE: 0 CAT: 18

Johnson (Gertrude)
CIJE: 1 RIE: 0 CAT: 18

Johnson (Henry)
CIJE: 3 RIE: 1 CAT: 18

Johnson (James Welden)
CIJE: 1 RIE: 0 CAT: 18

Johnson (Lyndon Baines)
CIJE: 23 RIE: 13 CAT: 18

Johnson (Nicholas)
CIJE: 0 RIE: 1 CAT: 18

Johnson (Samuel)
CIJE: 3 RIE: 1 CAT: 18

Johnson (William)
CIJE: 0 RIE: 1 CAT: 18

Johnson and Wales College RI
CIJE: 1 RIE: 1 CAT: 17

Johnson City Central School District NY
CIJE: 2 RIE: 4 CAT: 17

Johnson City Public Schools TN
CIJE: 0 RIE: 1 CAT: 17

Johnson County Community College KS
CIJE: 9 RIE: 44 CAT: 17

Johnson Home Economics Interest Inventory
CIJE: 0 RIE: 1 CAT: 21

Johnson Neyman Technique
CIJE: 10 RIE: 10 CAT: 15

Johnson O Connor Aptitude Tests
CIJE: 0 RIE: 14 CAT: 21

Johnson O Malley Act
CIJE: 7 RIE: 117 CAT: 14

Johnson State College VT
CIJE: 1 RIE: 4 CAT: 17

Johnson Test of Motor Skill Development
CIJE: 0 RIE: 1 CAT: 21

Johnson Wax Company
CIJE: 1 RIE: 0 CAT: 17

Johnston High School RI
CIJE: 1 RIE: 0 CAT: 17

Johnston Junior High School TX
CIJE: 1 RIE: 0 CAT: 17

Join A School Program
CIJE: 0 RIE: 1 CAT: 19

Join A School Survey
CIJE: 0 RIE: 1 CAT: 19

Joining Forces (NASBE)
CIJE: 0 RIE: 1 CAT: 19
UF NASBE Joining Forces Program

Joining Forces Program
CIJE: 0 RIE: 4 CAT: 19

Joint Action
CIJE: 0 RIE: 2 CAT: 16

Joint Appointments
CIJE: 3 RIE: 0 CAT: 16

Joint Big Decision Committees
CIJE: 0 RIE: 1 CAT: 15

Joint Commission on Mental Health of Children
CIJE: 1 RIE: 2 CAT: 17

Joint Committee on Slavic Studies
CIJE: 0 RIE: 1 CAT: 17

Joint Committee on Standards for Educ Evaluation
CIJE: 9 RIE: 7 CAT: 17

Joint Committee on Testing Practices
CIJE: 1 RIE: 1 CAT: 17

Joint Comprehensive Evaluation System
CIJE: 0 RIE: 3 CAT: 15

Joint Council of Language Associations
CIJE: 1 RIE: 0 CAT: 17

Joint Council on Economic Education
CIJE: 45 RIE: 8 CAT: 17

Joint Council on Educational Telecommunications
CIJE: 1 RIE: 2 CAT: 17

Joint Custody
CIJE: 16 RIE: 11 CAT: 14

Joint Development Project Higher Education
CIJE: 0 RIE: 1 CAT: 19

Joint Dissemination Review Panel
CIJE: 8 RIE: 22 CAT: 17
SN Now known as the "Program Effectiveness Panel" (q.v.)

Joint Enrichment Team Project
CIJE: 1 RIE: 0 CAT: 19

Joint First Stage Achievement Test (Japan)
CIJE: 0 RIE: 1 CAT: 21

Joint Injuries
CIJE: 1 RIE: 1 CAT: 11

Joint Innovative Projects
CIJE: 0 RIE: 0 CAT: 19
SN Series of projects of UNESCO Regional Office for Education in Asia and the Pacific

Joint Operating Agreements (Newspapers)
CIJE: 0 RIE: 6 CAT: 14

Joint Product Processes (Mathematics)
CIJE: 0 RIE: 1 CAT: 20

Joint Serials Control System
CIJE: 0 RIE: 1 CAT: 15

Joint Venture
CIJE: 4 RIE: 5 CAT: 15

Jointly Registered Teacher Education Programs NY
CIJE: 0 RIE: 1 CAT: 19
SN Program that allows minorities to transfer from 2 to 4 year teacher education programs and be eligible for initial state teacher certification upon graduation

Jokers Wild Game
CIJE: 1 RIE: 0 CAT: 16

Jokes
CIJE: 10 RIE: 7 CAT: 16

Joliet Community College IL
CIJE: 0 RIE: 1 CAT: 17

Joliet Junior College IL
CIJE: 10 RIE: 5 CAT: 17

Joliet Junior College Inmate Training Program
CIJE: 1 RIE: 0 CAT: 19

Jonathan Livingston Seagull
CIJE: 2 RIE: 0 CAT: 22

Jones (Clara)
CIJE: 1 RIE: 0 CAT: 18

Jones (James A)
CIJE: 0 RIE: 1 CAT: 18

Jones (LeRoi)
CIJE: 3 RIE: 0 CAT: 18

Jones (William)
CIJE: 1 RIE: 0 CAT: 18

Jones County School District MS
CIJE: 0 RIE: 1 CAT: 17

Jones v Illinois Dept of Rehabilitation Services
CIJE: 0 RIE: 0 CAT: 14

Jonesboro Public Schools AR
CIJE: 0 RIE: 2 CAT: 17

Jonson (Ben)
CIJE: 4 RIE: 1 CAT: 18

Joplin Plan
CIJE: 2 RIE: 3 CAT: 15

Joplin R VIII School District MO
CIJE: 0 RIE: 1 CAT: 17

Jordan
CIJE: 41 RIE: 46 CAT: 07

Jordan (Barbara)
CIJE: 4 RIE: 0 CAT: 18

Jordan (Ramallah)
CIJE: 0 RIE: 1 CAT: 07

Jordan Educational Complex CA
CIJE: 0 RIE: 1 CAT: 17

Jordan Educational Television Service
CIJE: 1 RIE: 1 CAT: 17

Jordanhill College of Education TV
CIJE: 1 RIE: 0 CAT: 17

Jordanian Arabs
CIJE: 1 RIE: 1 CAT: 08

Jordanian GSECE
USE General Secondary Educ Certificate Exam (Jordan)

Joreskog (Karl G)
CIJE: 1 RIE: 5 CAT: 18

Joreskogs Congeneric Test Model
CIJE: 3 RIE: 1 CAT: 21

Jose P v Ambach
CIJE: 3 RIE: 1 CAT: 14

Joseph (Robert)
CIJE: 1 RIE: 0 CAT: 18

Joseph and the Amazing Technicolor Dreamcoat
CIJE: 0 RIE: 1 CAT: 22

Joseph Fels Foundation Inc
CIJE: 0 RIE: 1 CAT: 17

Joseph Klingenstein Summer Institute
CIJE: 0 RIE: 1 CAT: 17

Joseph Lauder Institute PA
USE Lauder Institute of Management Internatl Studies

Joseph P Kennedy Jr Foundation
CIJE: 0 RIE: 1 CAT: 17

Josephine County School District OR
CIJE: 0 RIE: 2 CAT: 17

Josiah Quincy Community School MA
CIJE: 1 RIE: 0 CAT: 17

JOSS Programing Language
CIJE: 0 RIE: 3 CAT: 04

JOSTRAN Programing Language
CIJE: 0 RIE: 1 CAT: 04

Joule (James Prescott)
CIJE: 1 RIE: 0 CAT: 18

Jourard (Sidney)
CIJE: 1 RIE: 0 CAT: 18

Jourard Self Disclosure Inventory
CIJE: 7 RIE: 3 CAT: 21

Journal Articles
CIJE: 91 RIE: 28 CAT: 16

Journal Citation Reports
CIJE: 7 RIE: 3 CAT: 16

Journal Control System
CIJE: 0 RIE: 1 CAT: 15

Journal of Academic Librarianship
CIJE: 0 RIE: 1 CAT: 22

Journal of Agricultural Education
CIJE: 1 RIE: 1 CAT: 22

Journal of American Indian Education
CIJE: 0 RIE: 1 CAT: 22

Journal of Chemical Education
CIJE: 1 RIE: 0 CAT: 22

Journal of College Student Development
CIJE: 1 RIE: 1 CAT: 22

Journal of Communication
CIJE: 0 RIE: 1 CAT: 22

Journal of Consulting and Clinical Psychology
CIJE: 1 RIE: 0 CAT: 22

Journal of Counseling Psychology
CIJE: 12 RIE: 1 CAT: 22

Journal of Education for Librarianship
CIJE: 3 RIE: 1 CAT: 22

Journal of Educational Administration
CIJE: 0 RIE: 1 CAT: 22

Journal of Educational Psychology
CIJE: 2 RIE: 2 CAT: 22

Journal of Educational Research
CIJE: 3 RIE: 1 CAT: 22

Journal of Geography in Higher Education
CIJE: 0 RIE: 1 CAT: 22

Journal of Instructional Development
CIJE: 2 RIE: 1 CAT: 22

Journal of Learning Disabilities
CIJE: 2 RIE: 0 CAT: 22

Journal of Marriage and the Family
CIJE: 1 RIE: 0 CAT: 22

Journal of Medical Education
CIJE: 2 RIE: 0 CAT: 22

Journal of Reading
CIJE: 3 RIE: 2 CAT: 22

Journal of Research in Music Education
CIJE: 3 RIE: 2 CAT: 22

Journal of Research in Science Teaching
CIJE: 1 RIE: 1 CAT: 22

Journal of Social Issues
CIJE: 0 RIE: 1 CAT: 22

Journal of Special Education
CIJE: 1 RIE: 0 CAT: 22

Journal of Teacher Education
CIJE: 1 RIE: 1 CAT: 22

Journal of the American Chemical Society
CIJE: 1 RIE: 0 CAT: 22

Journal of the American Forensics Association
CIJE: 0 RIE: 1 CAT: 22

Journal Supplement Abstract Service
CIJE: 0 RIE: 3 CAT: 22

Journalism Bookshelf Project
CIJE: 0 RIE: 1 CAT: 19

Journalism Computer Assisted Instruction
CIJE: 1 RIE: 3 CAT: 22

Journalism Education Association
CIJE: 16 RIE: 0 CAT: 17

Journalism Libraries
CIJE: 0 RIE: 1 CAT: 05

Journalism Licensing
CIJE: 0 RIE: 2 CAT: 16

Journalism Quarterly
CIJE: 1 RIE: 5 CAT: 22

Journalism Research
CIJE: 205 RIE: 167 CAT: 16

Journalism Schools
CIJE: 19 RIE: 9 CAT: 05

Journalistic Objectivity
CIJE: 19 RIE: 12 CAT: 16

Journalistic Style
CIJE: 10 RIE: 6 CAT: 16

Journalists
CIJE: 91 RIE: 102 CAT: 09
UF News Reporters

Journey Literature
CIJE: 5 RIE: 0 CAT: 16

Journeys Unlimited
CIJE: 0 RIE: 1 CAT: 22

Joyce (Bruce R)
CIJE: 1 RIE: 1 CAT: 18

Joyce (James)
CIJE: 14 RIE: 6 CAT: 18

JTPA Performance Standards
CIJE: 0 RIE: 0 CAT: 21

Juan Morel Campos Bilingual Center IL
CIJE: 1 RIE: 1 CAT: 17

Juarez Lincoln Center TX
CIJE: 0 RIE: 1 CAT: 17

Jubilee (Novel)
CIJE: 0 RIE: 0 CAT: 22

Judea
CIJE: 0 RIE: 1 CAT: 07

Judeo Christian Values
CIJE: 1 RIE: 1 CAT: 16

Judeo Provencal
USE Shuadit

Judge Philosophy Statements
CIJE: 0 RIE: 3 CAT: 16
UF Judging Philosophy Statements

Judging Philosophy Statements
USE Judge Philosophy Statements

Judicial Attitudes
CIJE: 2 RIE: 9 CAT: 14

Judicial Evaluation Approach
CIJE: 10 RIE: 5 CAT: 15

Judicial Review
CIJE: 8 RIE: 7 CAT: 14
UF Court Review

Juilliard Repertory Project
CIJE: 0 RIE: 1 CAT: 19

Juilliard School of Music NY
CIJE: 3 RIE: 0 CAT: 17

Jukeboxes
CIJE: 7 RIE: 1 CAT: 04

Jukus
CIJE: 0 RIE: 1 CAT: 05

Jula
CIJE: 0 RIE: 1 CAT: 13

Julia Dychman Andrus Childrens Home NY
CIJE: 1 RIE: 0 CAT: 17

Julia R Materman School PA
CIJE: 1 RIE: 0 CAT: 17

Julius Caesar
CIJE: 4 RIE: 3 CAT: 22
SN Shakespearean play — see also "Caesar (Julius)"

Jump Roping
CIJE: 2 RIE: 2 CAT: 16
UF Rope Jumping; Rope Skipping; Skipping Rope

Jumping
CIJE: 5 RIE: 4 CAT: 16

Junction City Unified School District 475 KS
USE Geary County Unified School District KS

Juncture
CIJE: 2 RIE: 1 CAT: 13

Juneau Borough School District AK
CIJE: 0 RIE: 1 CAT: 17

Jung (Carl G)
CIJE: 47 RIE: 41 CAT: 18

Jung (S M)
CIJE: 0 RIE: 1 CAT: 18

Juniata College PA
CIJE: 0 RIE: 5 CAT: 17

Junior Academies of Science
CIJE: 0 RIE: 1 CAT: 05

Junior Achievement
CIJE: 16 RIE: 6 CAT: 19

Junior Aptitude Tests (South Africa)
CIJE: 0 RIE: 1 CAT: 21

Junior College Act (Illinois 1965)
CIJE: 0 RIE: 1 CAT: 14

Junior College Attitude Survey
CIJE: 0 RIE: 1 CAT: 21
SN Used in a study of attitudes of 2- and 4-year college administrators in Oklahoma toward community college education

Junior College Environment Scales (Astin)
CIJE: 0 RIE: 1 CAT: 21

Junior College Leadership Program
CIJE: 0 RIE: 3 CAT: 19

Junior College Placement Profile
CIJE: 0 RIE: 1 CAT: 21

Junior College Student Inventory (Hendrix)
CIJE: 0 RIE: 1 CAT: 21

Junior Counselors
CIJE: 0 RIE: 2 CAT: 09

Junior Engineering Technical Society
CIJE: 0 RIE: 1 CAT: 17
UF JETS Inc

Junior Eysenck Personality Inventory
CIJE: 15 RIE: 0 CAT: 21

Junior Faculty
CIJE: 6 RIE: 2 CAT: 09

Junior First Grade
CIJE: 3 RIE: 0 CAT: 03

Junior Great Books Program
CIJE: 7 RIE: 3 CAT: 19

Junior High Classroom Organization Study
CIJE: 1 RIE: 1 CAT: 22

Junior High School Association of Illinois
CIJE: 0 RIE: 1 CAT: 17

Junior High School Management Improvement Study
CIJE: 0 RIE: 1 CAT: 22

Junior High School Network Project
CIJE: 0 RIE: 1 CAT: 19

Junior Index of Motivation
CIJE: 7 RIE: 3 CAT: 21

Junior Kindergartens
CIJE: 2 RIE: 9 CAT: 05

Junior League
CIJE: 1 RIE: 1 CAT: 17
SN Use the more specific "Association of Junior Leagues International" for the nat'l/intn'l organization

Junior MESA Program CA
CIJE: 0 RIE: 1 CAT: 19
SN See also "MESA Program CA"

Junior Reserve Officer Training Corps
CIJE: 1 RIE: 1 CAT: 17

Junior Scholastic Aptitude Test
CIJE: 0 RIE: 1 CAT: 21

Junior School Science Project (Australia)
CIJE: 1 RIE: 0 CAT: 17

Junior Schools (United Kingdom)
CIJE: 6 RIE: 3 CAT: 05

Junior Secondary Science Project
CIJE: 0 RIE: 1 CAT: 19

Junior Self Monitoring Scale
CIJE: 1 RIE: 1 CAT: 21

Juniper Gardens Childrens Project
CIJE: 0 RIE: 2 CAT: 19

Junk Art
CIJE: 2 RIE: 0 CAT: 16

Junk Food
CIJE: 1 RIE: 1 CAT: 16

Junk Mail
CIJE: 2 RIE: 0 CAT: 16

Jupiter (Planet)
CIJE: 2 RIE: 0 CAT: 20

Juridical Liberal Power Theory
CIJE: 0 RIE: 1 CAT: 15

Jurisdiction
CIJE: 10 RIE: 8 CAT: 14

Jurisprudence
CIJE: 11 RIE: 3 CAT: 14

Jurmati
CIJE: 0 RIE: 1 CAT: 13

Jurupa Unified School District CA
CIJE: 0 RIE: 2 CAT: 17

Just Community Approach
CIJE: 14 RIE: 2 CAT: 15

Just World Hypothesis
CIJE: 4 RIE: 2 CAT: 15

Just World Scale (Rubin and Peplau)
CIJE: 1 RIE: 3 CAT: 21

Justice Education Teaching Strategies Program
CIJE: 0 RIE: 1 CAT: 19

Justice Reasoning
CIJE: 2 RIE: 2 CAT: 11

Justification (Logic)
CIJE: 1 RIE: 2 CAT: 15

Justification (Psychology)
CIJE: 14 RIE: 8 CAT: 11

Justificatory Rhetoric
CIJE: 1 RIE: 3 CAT: 15

Jutland Open University (Denmark)
CIJE: 0 RIE: 1 CAT: 17

Juvenile Achievement Center TX
CIJE: 1 RIE: 0 CAT: 17

Juvenile Delinquency Prevention Act 1972
CIJE: 0 RIE: 1 CAT: 14

Juvenile Delinquency Youth Offenses Control Act
CIJE: 0 RIE: 1 CAT: 14

Juvenile Diversion
CIJE: 1 RIE: 1 CAT: 14

Juvenile Justice Delinquency Prev Act Amend 1992
CIJE: 0 RIE: 1 CAT: 14
UF Public Law 102 586

Juvenile Justice Delinquency Prevention Act 1974
CIJE: 2 RIE: 20 CAT: 14
UF Public Law 93 415

Juvenile Justice Delinquency Prevention Office
CIJE: 0 RIE: 3 CAT: 17
UF Office of Juvenile Justice Delinquency Prevention

Juvenile Metachromatic Leukodystrophy
CIJE: 1 RIE: 0 CAT: 11

Juvenile Thyrotoxicosis
CIJE: 1 RIE: 0 CAT: 11

K ABC
USE Kaufman Assessment Battery for Children

K Index (Samejima)
CIJE: 0 RIE: 1 CAT: 21

K1 Rule
CIJE: 0 RIE: 1 CAT: 21
SN Rule stating that factors with eigenvalues of 1 or more should be retained in the factor analysis

Kabiye
CIJE: 0 RIE: 3 CAT: 13

Kabuki
CIJE: 5 RIE: 3 CAT: 16

Kabul Dialect
CIJE: 0 RIE: 1 CAT: 13

Kadazan
CIJE: 0 RIE: 2 CAT: 13

Kaelin (E F)
CIJE: 1 RIE: 0 CAT: 18

Kaelin v Grubbs
CIJE: 0 RIE: 1 CAT: 14

Kafka (Franz)
CIJE: 13 RIE: 1 CAT: 18

Kagan Kalagan
CIJE: 0 RIE: 1 CAT: 13
SN A Northwest Austronesian (Philippine) language
UF Kalagan; Tagakaolo

Kagans Interpersonal Process Recall
CIJE: 1 RIE: 0 CAT: 15

Kagate
CIJE: 0 RIE: 1 CAT: 13
SN Dialect of Central Tibetan (Tibetan group) spoken in Nepal
UF Syuuba

Kahn (Herman)
CIJE: 3 RIE: 2 CAT: 18

Kahn (V Shevin)
CIJE: 5 RIE: 0 CAT: 18

Kahn Intelligence Tests
CIJE: 3 RIE: 1 CAT: 21

Kahn Test of New York City
CIJE: 0 RIE: 1 CAT: 21

Kahn Test of Symbol Arrangement
CIJE: 2 RIE: 0 CAT: 21

Kaike
CIJE: 0 RIE: 1 CAT: 13

Kaimowitz v Department of Mental Health
CIJE: 1 RIE: 0 CAT: 14

Kainah (Tribe)
USE Blood (Nation)

Kaiser Foundation Hospital CA
CIJE: 2 RIE: 0 CAT: 17

Kaiser Image Analysis
CIJE: 0 RIE: 1 CAT: 15

Kaiser Industries
CIJE: 0 RIE: 1 CAT: 17

Kaizen
CIJE: 2 RIE: 1 CAT: 15
SN Japanese management concept of continuous improvement involving everyone

KAL 007
CIJE: 3 RIE: 3 CAT: 12
UF Korean Air Lines 007

Kala Lagaw Ya
CIJE: 0 RIE: 1 CAT: 13
SN A Pama-Maric language (Australian Aborigine)

Kalabari
CIJE: 0 RIE: 1 CAT: 13

Kalabit
USE Kelabit

Kalagan
USE Kagan Kalagan

Kalamazoo College MI
CIJE: 7 RIE: 16 CAT: 17

Kalamazoo Public Schools MI
CIJE: 6 RIE: 5 CAT: 17

Kalamazoo Unconference
CIJE: 1 RIE: 0 CAT: 02

Kalamazoo Valley Community College MI
CIJE: 3 RIE: 9 CAT: 17

Kalapalo
CIJE: 1 RIE: 0 CAT: 13

Kalapuya (Tribe)
CIJE: 1 RIE: 0 CAT: 08

Kalaw Kawaw
CIJE: 0 RIE: 1 CAT: 13
SN Dialect of Kala Lagaw Ya (Australian Aborigine)

Kaleidoscope Childrens Art Program
CIJE: 1 RIE: 0 CAT: 19

Kaleidoscope Youth Development Program
CIJE: 1 RIE: 0 CAT: 19

Kaleidoscopes
CIJE: 1 RIE: 0 CAT: 04

Kaliai
CIJE: 2 RIE: 0 CAT: 08

Kalinga
CIJE: 1 RIE: 4 CAT: 13
SN A Northwest Austronesian (Philippine) language
UF Guinaang Kalinga

Kalispel (Tribe)
CIJE: 0 RIE: 3 CAT: 08

Kall
CIJE: 0 RIE: 1 CAT: 13
SN Secret code spoken in Senegal

Kalman Filtering
CIJE: 1 RIE: 1 CAT: 15

Kaluli
CIJE: 0 RIE: 2 CAT: 13

Kaluli People
CIJE: 0 RIE: 1 CAT: 08

Kaman Mishmi
USE Miju

Kamehameha Early Education Program
CIJE: 10 RIE: 57 CAT: 19

Kamehameha Schools HI
CIJE: 3 RIE: 6 CAT: 17

Kamii (Constance)
CIJE: 2 RIE: 1 CAT: 18

Kammersanger
CIJE: 1 RIE: 0 CAT: 18

Kampf (Louis)
CIJE: 1 RIE: 0 CAT: 18

Kamprath (Werner)
CIJE: 0 RIE: 1 CAT: 18

Kanasi
CIJE: 0 RIE: 2 CAT: 13
SN Language of the Daga branch, spoken in Milne Bay Province of Papua New Guinea

Kanawha County Schools WV
CIJE: 3 RIE: 12 CAT: 17

Kanawha County Teacher Education Center WV
CIJE: 1 RIE: 2 CAT: 17

Kandahar Dialects
CIJE: 0 RIE: 1 CAT: 13

Kandinsky (Wassily)
CIJE: 1 RIE: 1 CAT: 18

Kanet (Kathleen)
CIJE: 0 RIE: 1 CAT: 18

Kangaroo Network (Australia)
CIJE: 0 RIE: 2 CAT: 17

Kanji Script
CIJE: 5 RIE: 3 CAT: 13

Kankakee Community College IL
CIJE: 0 RIE: 1 CAT: 17

Kannada Course
CIJE: 0 RIE: 1 CAT: 03

Kano Dialect
CIJE: 0 RIE: 3 CAT: 13

Kansas
CIJE: 141 RIE: 553 CAT: 07

Kansas (Cherokee County)
CIJE: 0 RIE: 1 CAT: 07

Kansas (Clay Center)
CIJE: 0 RIE: 1 CAT: 07

Kansas (Decatur County)
CIJE: 0 RIE: 1 CAT: 07

Kansas (Dunlap City)
CIJE: 0 RIE: 1 CAT: 07

Kansas (Ellis County)
CIJE: 0 RIE: 1 CAT: 07

Kansas (Emporia)
CIJE: 2 RIE: 13 CAT: 07

Kansas (Johnson County)
CIJE: 0 RIE: 7 CAT: 07

Kansas (Kansas City)
CIJE: 9 RIE: 14 CAT: 07

Kansas (Labette County)
CIJE: 0 RIE: 1 CAT: 07

Kansas (Lawrence)
CIJE: 1 RIE: 6 CAT: 07

Kansas (Manhattan)
CIJE: 3 RIE: 4 CAT: 07

Kansas (Montgomery County)
CIJE: 0 RIE: 1 CAT: 07

Kansas (Parsons)
CIJE: 2 RIE: 1 CAT: 07

Kansas (Pittsburg)
CIJE: 0 RIE: 1 CAT: 07

Kansas (Salina)
CIJE: 2 RIE: 2 CAT: 07

Kansas (Sedgwick County)
CIJE: 0 RIE: 2 CAT: 07

Kansas (Southeast)
CIJE: 0 RIE: 4 CAT: 07

Kansas (Topeka)
CIJE: 1 RIE: 8 CAT: 07

Kansas (Wichita County)
CIJE: 0 RIE: 1 CAT: 07

Kansas (Wichita)
CIJE: 7 RIE: 17 CAT: 07

Kansas Advisory Committee on Hispanic Affairs
CIJE: 0 RIE: 1 CAT: 17

Kansas Arts Resource Training System
CIJE: 0 RIE: 1 CAT: 19

Kansas City Kansas Community College
CIJE: 0 RIE: 4 CAT: 17

Kansas City Metropolitan Council on Child Care KS
CIJE: 0 RIE: 1 CAT: 17

Kansas City Midwest Research Institute
CIJE: 1 RIE: 0 CAT: 17

Kansas City Public Schools MO
CIJE: 7 RIE: 56 CAT: 17

Kansas City Regional Council for Higher Education
CIJE: 1 RIE: 3 CAT: 17

Kansas City School Behavior Project
CIJE: 0 RIE: 3 CAT: 19

Kansas City Womens Jazz Festival
CIJE: 1 RIE: 0 CAT: 12

Kansas Computerized Career Information System
CIJE: 0 RIE: 1 CAT: 04

Kansas Curriculum Materials Dissemination Center
CIJE: 0 RIE: 2 CAT: 17

Kansas Individualized Curriculum Sequencing
CIJE: 0 RIE: 1 CAT: 15

Kansas Industrial Training Program
CIJE: 0 RIE: 0 CAT: 19

Kansas Internship Plan
CIJE: 1 RIE: 4 CAT: 19

Kansas Learner Needs Assessment Study
CIJE: 0 RIE: 1 CAT: 22

Kansas Manpower Utilization System for Training
CIJE: 0 RIE: 2 CAT: 15

Kansas Marital Satisfaction Scale
CIJE: 1 RIE: 1 CAT: 21

Kansas Minimum Competency Testing Program
CIJE: 0 RIE: 2 CAT: 19

Kansas Network Special Education Paraprofessional
CIJE: 0 RIE: 1 CAT: 17

Kansas Reflection Impulsivity Scale
CIJE: 4 RIE: 7 CAT: 21

Kansas Regional Medical Program
CIJE: 1 RIE: 0 CAT: 19

Kansas Research Inst Early Child Educ Handicapped
CIJE: 0 RIE: 1 CAT: 17

Kansas School for the Deaf
CIJE: 1 RIE: 0 CAT: 17

Kansas State Board of Education
CIJE: 0 RIE: 6 CAT: 17

Kansas State College Pittsburg
CIJE: 1 RIE: 3 CAT: 17

Kansas State IDEA Form
CIJE: 1 RIE: 0 CAT: 21

Kansas State Master Planning Commission
CIJE: 0 RIE: 2 CAT: 17

Kansas State Teachers College Emporia
CIJE: 0 RIE: 4 CAT: 17

Kansas State University
CIJE: 44 RIE: 41 CAT: 17

Kansas Supreme Court
CIJE: 1 RIE: 0 CAT: 17

Kansas TELENET
CIJE: 0 RIE: 1 CAT: 17

Kansas Wesleyan University
CIJE: 1 RIE: 1 CAT: 17

Kant (Immanuel)
CIJE: 17 RIE: 8 CAT: 18

Kanter (Rosabeth Moss)
CIJE: 1 RIE: 0 CAT: 18

Kantor (J R)
CIJE: 3 RIE: 1 CAT: 18

Kantor (Paul B)
CIJE: 2 RIE: 0 CAT: 18

Kantors Branching Technique
CIJE: 1 RIE: 0 CAT: 15

Kanuri
CIJE: 0 RIE: 4 CAT: 13

Kapampangan
CIJE: 0 RIE: 3 CAT: 13

Kapiolani Community College HI
USE University of Hawaii Kapiolani Community College

Kaplan (Abraham)
CIJE: 0 RIE: 1 CAT: 18

Kaplan (Robert)
CIJE: 3 RIE: 1 CAT: 18

Kappa Coefficient
CIJE: 32 RIE: 11 CAT: 20

KAPPA Computer Program
CIJE: 0 RIE: 1 CAT: 04

Kappa Index
CIJE: 1 RIE: 0 CAT: 21

Kara
CIJE: 0 RIE: 0 CAT: 13
UF Kera (Chad)

Karakalpak
CIJE: 0 RIE: 2 CAT: 13

Karate
CIJE: 2 RIE: 3 CAT: 16

Karate Katas
CIJE: 1 RIE: 0 CAT: 16

Karenga (Maulana Ron)
CIJE: 1 RIE: 0 CAT: 18

Karitiana
CIJE: 0 RIE: 2 CAT: 13
SN An Arikem language of the Tupi family in Brazil

Kent EGY Test
CIJE: 2 RIE: 0 CAT: 21

Kent Infant Development Scale
CIJE: 1 RIE: 2 CAT: 21

Kent Intermediate School District MI
CIJE: 1 RIE: 1 CAT: 17

Kent Mathematics Project
CIJE: 1 RIE: 0 CAT: 19

Kent Rosanoff Word Association Test
CIJE: 0 RIE: 1 CAT: 21

Kent School of Social Work
CIJE: 1 RIE: 0 CAT: 17

Kent State University OH
CIJE: 47 RIE: 56 CAT: 17

Kent State University OH Regional Campuses
CIJE: 1 RIE: 10 CAT: 17

Kent Study
CIJE: 1 RIE: 0 CAT: 22

Kentucky
CIJE: 216 RIE: 936 CAT: 07

Kentucky (Berea)
CIJE: 1 RIE: 1 CAT: 07

Kentucky (Bowling Green)
CIJE: 0 RIE: 5 CAT: 07

Kentucky (Breathitt County)
CIJE: 0 RIE: 2 CAT: 07

Kentucky (Calloway County)
CIJE: 0 RIE: 1 CAT: 07

Kentucky (Central)
CIJE: 0 RIE: 1 CAT: 07

Kentucky (Covington)
CIJE: 2 RIE: 0 CAT: 07

Kentucky (East)
CIJE: 7 RIE: 16 CAT: 07

Kentucky (Elizabethtown)
CIJE: 0 RIE: 1 CAT: 07

Kentucky (Elliott County)
CIJE: 0 RIE: 1 CAT: 07

Kentucky (Fayette County)
CIJE: 2 RIE: 8 CAT: 07

Kentucky (Fort Thomas)
CIJE: 0 RIE: 1 CAT: 07

Kentucky (Frankfort)
CIJE: 0 RIE: 6 CAT: 07

Kentucky (Hardin County)
CIJE: 1 RIE: 2 CAT: 07

Kentucky (Harlan County)
CIJE: 0 RIE: 2 CAT: 07

Kentucky (Hart County)
CIJE: 0 RIE: 2 CAT: 07

Kentucky (Hopkinsville)
CIJE: 0 RIE: 1 CAT: 07

Kentucky (Jackson County)
CIJE: 0 RIE: 1 CAT: 07

Kentucky (Jefferson County)
CIJE: 10 RIE: 31 CAT: 07

Kentucky (Lee County)
CIJE: 0 RIE: 1 CAT: 07

Kentucky (Letcher County)
CIJE: 2 RIE: 0 CAT: 07

Kentucky (Lexington)
CIJE: 7 RIE: 3 CAT: 07

Kentucky (Logan County)
CIJE: 0 RIE: 1 CAT: 07

Kentucky (Louisville)
CIJE: 22 RIE: 58 CAT: 07

Kentucky (McCreary County)
CIJE: 1 RIE: 0 CAT: 07

Kentucky (Morehead)
CIJE: 0 RIE: 1 CAT: 07

Kentucky (Morgan County)
CIJE: 0 RIE: 1 CAT: 07

Kentucky (North)
CIJE: 0 RIE: 1 CAT: 07

Kentucky (Northern)
CIJE: 0 RIE: 2 CAT: 07

Kentucky (Owensboro)
CIJE: 0 RIE: 1 CAT: 07

Kentucky (Paducah)
CIJE: 1 RIE: 2 CAT: 07

Kentucky (Pike County)
CIJE: 0 RIE: 1 CAT: 07

Kentucky (Pikeville)
CIJE: 0 RIE: 1 CAT: 07

Kentucky (Rowan County)
CIJE: 0 RIE: 1 CAT: 07

Kentucky (Scott County)
CIJE: 0 RIE: 1 CAT: 07

Kentucky (Somerset)
CIJE: 0 RIE: 2 CAT: 07

Kentucky (Sturgis)
CIJE: 0 RIE: 1 CAT: 07

Kentucky (Union County)
CIJE: 1 RIE: 0 CAT: 07

Kentucky (Warren County)
CIJE: 0 RIE: 1 CAT: 07

Kentucky (West)
CIJE: 0 RIE: 3 CAT: 07

Kentucky (Whitley County)
CIJE: 0 RIE: 2 CAT: 07

Kentucky Academic Association
CIJE: 0 RIE: 1 CAT: 17

Kentucky Allied Health Project
CIJE: 0 RIE: 7 CAT: 19

Kentucky Association for Communications and Tech
CIJE: 0 RIE: 2 CAT: 17

Kentucky Association for Institutional Research
CIJE: 0 RIE: 1 CAT: 17

Kentucky Beginning Principal Intern Program
CIJE: 1 RIE: 1 CAT: 19

Kentucky Bureau of School Service
CIJE: 0 RIE: 1 CAT: 17

Kentucky Career Ladder Plan
CIJE: 0 RIE: 7 CAT: 22

Kentucky Career Ladder Project
CIJE: 0 RIE: 2 CAT: 19

Kentucky Child Welfare Research Foundation
CIJE: 0 RIE: 1 CAT: 17

Kentucky Community College System
USE University of Kentucky Community College System

Kentucky Comprehensive Listening Test
CIJE: 1 RIE: 2 CAT: 21

Kentucky Cooperative Extension Service
CIJE: 1 RIE: 0 CAT: 17

Kentucky Council of Teachers of English
CIJE: 0 RIE: 1 CAT: 17

Kentucky Council on School Performance Standards
CIJE: 0 RIE: 1 CAT: 17
UF Council on School Performance Standards KY

Kentucky Council Teacher Education Certification
CIJE: 0 RIE: 1 CAT: 17

Kentucky Development Tech Assist Community Ed Proj
CIJE: 0 RIE: 1 CAT: 19

Kentucky Education Reform Act 1990
CIJE: 18 RIE: 31 CAT: 14
SN A 5-year plan to completely revamp an education system the state supreme court ruled unconstitutional

Kentucky Educational Assessment Program
CIJE: 0 RIE: 5 CAT: 19

Kentucky Educational Research Association
CIJE: 0 RIE: 1 CAT: 17

Kentucky Elderly Need Assessment
CIJE: 0 RIE: 1 CAT: 19

Kentucky Environmental Education Program
CIJE: 0 RIE: 2 CAT: 19

Kentucky Equine Educational Program
CIJE: 1 RIE: 0 CAT: 19

Kentucky Essential Skills Test
CIJE: 0 RIE: 3 CAT: 21

Kentucky Individualized Kindergartens
CIJE: 0 RIE: 1 CAT: 19

Kentucky Institute for Beginning Principals
CIJE: 0 RIE: 1 CAT: 19

Kentucky Instructional Resource Information System
CIJE: 0 RIE: 1 CAT: 19

Kentucky Interlocal Cooperative Act and Agreement
CIJE: 0 RIE: 1 CAT: 14

Kentucky January Project
CIJE: 0 RIE: 1 CAT: 19

Kentucky Library Communications Network
CIJE: 0 RIE: 1 CAT: 17

Kentucky Longitudinal Study
CIJE: 0 RIE: 1 CAT: 22

Kentucky Mental Manpower Commission
CIJE: 1 RIE: 0 CAT: 17

Kentucky Model Center
CIJE: 0 RIE: 1 CAT: 17

Kentucky Needs Assessment Project
CIJE: 0 RIE: 1 CAT: 19

Kentucky Nursing Education Project
CIJE: 0 RIE: 7 CAT: 19

Kentucky Observation Instrument
CIJE: 0 RIE: 1 CAT: 21

Kentucky Ohio Michigan Regional Medical Library
CIJE: 0 RIE: 0 CAT: 17

Kentucky Placement and Followup System
CIJE: 0 RIE: 1 CAT: 04

Kentucky Reception Center
CIJE: 1 RIE: 0 CAT: 17

Kentucky School of Crafts
CIJE: 0 RIE: 1 CAT: 17

Kentucky Social Services Need Assessment Project
CIJE: 0 RIE: 1 CAT: 19

Kentucky Staff Industry Exchange Program
CIJE: 0 RIE: 1 CAT: 19

Kentucky State Department of Education
CIJE: 1 RIE: 8 CAT: 17

Kentucky State Library
CIJE: 0 RIE: 1 CAT: 17

Kentucky State University
CIJE: 2 RIE: 8 CAT: 17

Kentucky Student Achievement Project
CIJE: 0 RIE: 1 CAT: 19

Kentucky Teacher Internship Program
CIJE: 0 RIE: 1 CAT: 19

Kentucky v Rudasill
CIJE: 0 RIE: 1 CAT: 14

Kentucky Voc Educ Placement and Followup System
CIJE: 0 RIE: 1 CAT: 19

Kentucky Vocational Staff Industry Exchange Prog
CIJE: 0 RIE: 1 CAT: 19

Kentucky Youth Research Center
CIJE: 0 RIE: 1 CAT: 17

Kenwood School District OK
CIJE: 0 RIE: 1 CAT: 17

Kenworthy (Leonard S)
CIJE: 0 RIE: 1 CAT: 18

Kenya
CIJE: 189 RIE: 231 CAT: 07

Kenya (Kisumu)
CIJE: 0 RIE: 2 CAT: 07

Kenya (Nairobi)
CIJE: 4 RIE: 4 CAT: 07

Kenya (Nandi)
CIJE: 0 RIE: 1 CAT: 07

Kenya National Youth Service
CIJE: 1 RIE: 0 CAT: 17

Kenya Secretarial Project
CIJE: 1 RIE: 0 CAT: 19

Kenyatta University (Kenya)
CIJE: 0 RIE: 1 CAT: 17

Kenyon College OH
CIJE: 2 RIE: 5 CAT: 17

Kephart (Newell)
CIJE: 0 RIE: 2 CAT: 18

Kephart Training
CIJE: 0 RIE: 1 CAT: 03

Kephart Visual Achievement Forms
CIJE: 0 RIE: 1 CAT: 21

Kephart Walking Board Ability Test
CIJE: 0 RIE: 1 CAT: 21

Kepler (Johannes)
CIJE: 3 RIE: 0 CAT: 18

Kepler Law
CIJE: 5 RIE: 0 CAT: 20

Kera (Chad)
USE Kara

Keres Pueblo (Tribe)
CIJE: 1 RIE: 0 CAT: 08

Keresan
CIJE: 0 RIE: 1 CAT: 13

Kerlinger (Fred N)
CIJE: 1 RIE: 1 CAT: 18

Kerlinger Education Scales
CIJE: 3 RIE: 7 CAT: 21

Kern Art Education Information Inventory
CIJE: 0 RIE: 1 CAT: 21

Kern Community College CA
CIJE: 0 RIE: 1 CAT: 17

Kern Community College District CA
CIJE: 0 RIE: 1 CAT: 17

Kern Eastern Sierra Writing Project
CIJE: 0 RIE: 1 CAT: 19

Kern Union High School District CA
CIJE: 0 RIE: 1 CAT: 17

Kernel Density Estimates
USE Kernel Method

Kernel Method
CIJE: 1 RIE: 2 CAT: 15
SN A method of estimating test score distributions
UF Kernel Density Estimates

Kerner Commission Report
CIJE: 6 RIE: 4 CAT: 22

Kerr (Clark)
CIJE: 5 RIE: 3 CAT: 18

Kerr (M E)
CIJE: 5 RIE: 1 CAT: 18

Kerrigan (John)
CIJE: 1 RIE: 0 CAT: 18

Kesey (Ken)
CIJE: 4 RIE: 0 CAT: 18

Ketchikan Community College AK
CIJE: 0 RIE: 1 CAT: 17

Ketogenic Diet
CIJE: 1 RIE: 1 CAT: 11

Ketones
CIJE: 2 RIE: 0 CAT: 20

Ketotic Hypoglycemia
CIJE: 1 RIE: 0 CAT: 11

Kettering City Schools OH
CIJE: 0 RIE: 1 CAT: 17

Kettering Commission Report
CIJE: 1 RIE: 0 CAT: 22

Kettering Foundation
CIJE: 0 RIE: 5 CAT: 17
UF Charles F Kettering Foundation

Kettering Medical Center OH
CIJE: 2 RIE: 0 CAT: 17

Kettering Project
CIJE: 2 RIE: 0 CAT: 19

Kettering School Climate Instrument
USE CFK Ltd School Climate Profile (Fox et al)

Kettleby Public Schools ON
CIJE: 0 RIE: 1 CAT: 17

Key (V O Jr)
CIJE: 0 RIE: 1 CAT: 18

Key (Wilson Bryan)
CIJE: 0 RIE: 2 CAT: 18

Key Assessment System
CIJE: 1 RIE: 1 CAT: 21

Key Control
CIJE: 1 RIE: 1 CAT: 16

Key Informant Approach
CIJE: 1 RIE: 2 CAT: 15

Key Letter in Context
CIJE: 0 RIE: 2 CAT: 16

Key Tracking Program MA
CIJE: 0 RIE: 1 CAT: 19

Key Vocabulary
CIJE: 6 RIE: 1 CAT: 16

Key Vocabulary Words
CIJE: 2 RIE: 1 CAT: 13

Keyano College AB
CIJE: 0 RIE: 2 CAT: 17

Keyboard Computer Music System
CIJE: 6 RIE: 0 CAT: 04

Keyes v Denver School District Number 1
CIJE: 5 RIE: 3 CAT: 14

Keylist Tests
CIJE: 0 RIE: 1 CAT: 21

Keymath Diagnostic Arithmetic Test
CIJE: 9 RIE: 5 CAT: 21

Keynesian Economics
CIJE: 17 RIE: 8 CAT: 03

Keynote Speakers
CIJE: 0 RIE: 1 CAT: 10

Keypunch Instruction
CIJE: 1 RIE: 0 CAT: 03

Keypunch Operators
CIJE: 1 RIE: 5 CAT: 09

KEYS Project
CIJE: 0 RIE: 22 CAT: 19
UF Knowledge of English Yields Success

Keys to School Boardsmanship Project
CIJE: 0 RIE: 1 CAT: 19

Keyser (Samuel Jay)
CIJE: 2 RIE: 0 CAT: 18

Keyser Industrial Park
CIJE: 1 RIE: 0 CAT: 17

Keysort Requisition System
CIJE: 1 RIE: 0 CAT: 15

Keysort Search Procedure
CIJE: 0 RIE: 1 CAT: 15

Keystone Adolescent Program for Stutterers
CIJE: 0 RIE: 1 CAT: 19

Keystone Central School District PA
CIJE: 0 RIE: 2 CAT: 17

Keystone Telebinocular
CIJE: 0 RIE: 1 CAT: 21

Keystone Visual Screening Tests
CIJE: 0 RIE: 1 CAT: 21

Keystone Visual Survey Tests
CIJE: 0 RIE: 1 CAT: 21

Keystone Writing Project TX
CIJE: 0 RIE: 1 CAT: 19

Keystroke LOGO
CIJE: 0 RIE: 1 CAT: 04

Keystroke Timing (Typing)
CIJE: 0 RIE: 1 CAT: 16

Keyword Method (Language Learning)
CIJE: 15 RIE: 10 CAT: 13

Keyword Method (Second Language Learning)
CIJE: 16 RIE: 6 CAT: 13

Keywords
CIJE: 52 RIE: 21 CAT: 15

Keyworth (George A)
CIJE: 0 RIE: 1 CAT: 18

Khaling
CIJE: 0 RIE: 2 CAT: 13

Khalkha
CIJE: 0 RIE: 3 CAT: 13

Kham
CIJE: 0 RIE: 3 CAT: 13

KHAN DU Project
CIJE: 0 RIE: 2 CAT: 19

Khasi
CIJE: 0 RIE: 1 CAT: 13
SN A Mon-Khmer language of central Assam

Khmer Culture
USE Cambodian Culture

Khmer Republic
CIJE: 2 RIE: 5 CAT: 07

Khomeini (Ayatollah Ruhollah)
CIJE: 0 RIE: 6 CAT: 18

Khowar
CIJE: 0 RIE: 2 CAT: 13

KI Aikido
CIJE: 0 RIE: 1 CAT: 03

Kiamichi Area Vocational Technical Schools OK
CIJE: 0 RIE: 1 CAT: 17

Kiamichi Economic Development District OK
CIJE: 1 RIE: 1 CAT: 17

Kiangsi Soviet Period (Chinese History)
CIJE: 5 RIE: 0 CAT: 12

Kibbutzim
CIJE: 87 RIE: 32 CAT: 05

Kickapoo (Tribe)
CIJE: 4 RIE: 3 CAT: 08

Kickapoo Nation School KS
CIJE: 1 RIE: 1 CAT: 17

Kickball
CIJE: 0 RIE: 1 CAT: 16

KIDCOPE
CIJE: 0 RIE: 1 CAT: 21

Kidd (J Robbins)
CIJE: 0 RIE: 1 CAT: 18
SN "Roby"

Kiddie Farm
CIJE: 1 RIE: 0 CAT: 17

KIDLINK Project (Electronic Mail)
CIJE: 0 RIE: 2 CAT: 19
SN Running on Bitnet Listserv at North Dakota State Univ

Kidmaps
CIJE: 0 RIE: 1 CAT: 21

Kidnapping
CIJE: 3 RIE: 19 CAT: 16
SN See also "Abductions" and "Parent Kidnapping"

Kidney Dialysis
USE Hemodialysis

Kidney Disease
CIJE: 8 RIE: 5 CAT: 11
SN See also "Nephrology"

KIDS 4
CIJE: 0 RIE: 1 CAT: 19

Kids Alive (Television Series)
CIJE: 1 RIE: 0 CAT: 22

Kids Club MN
CIJE: 0 RIE: 1 CAT: 19

KIDS Consortium ME
CIJE: 0 RIE: 1 CAT: 17

Kids In Difficult Situations Program
CIJE: 0 RIE: 1 CAT: 19

Kids Interactive Telecomm Experience by Satellite
CIJE: 0 RIE: 0 CAT: 19
UF KITES (Satellite Telelink)

Kids on Campus Inc
CIJE: 1 RIE: 0 CAT: 17

Kids on the Block Puppets
CIJE: 1 RIE: 1 CAT: 16

KIDSc
USE Kindergarten Inventory Develop Social Competency

Kierkegaard (Soren)
CIJE: 4 RIE: 0 CAT: 18

Kiev Construction Engineering Institute (USSR)
CIJE: 1 RIE: 0 CAT: 17

Kiev Polytechnic Institute (USSR)
CIJE: 0 RIE: 1 CAT: 17

Kikuyu
CIJE: 1 RIE: 6 CAT: 13

Kikuyu People
CIJE: 0 RIE: 0 CAT: 08
SN A Bantu-speaking people of Kenya

Kilander Health Knowledge Test
CIJE: 1 RIE: 0 CAT: 21

Killers (The)
CIJE: 0 RIE: 1 CAT: 22

Kilmann Insight Test
CIJE: 1 RIE: 0 CAT: 21

Kilmer (Joyce)
CIJE: 0 RIE: 1 CAT: 18

Kilns
CIJE: 3 RIE: 1 CAT: 04

Kilpatrick (William Heard)
CIJE: 4 RIE: 1 CAT: 18

Kilson (Martin)
CIJE: 1 RIE: 0 CAT: 18

Kim Anderson Bashaw Child Behavior Scale
CIJE: 1 RIE: 0 CAT: 21

Kimberly Clark Corporation
CIJE: 3 RIE: 4 CAT: 17

Kimbundu
CIJE: 0 RIE: 1 CAT: 13

Kinder Lernen Deutsch Project
CIJE: 0 RIE: 2 CAT: 19
UF Children Learn German Project

Kindergarten Diagnostic Instrument
CIJE: 0 RIE: 1 CAT: 21

Kindergarten Enrichment Program
CIJE: 0 RIE: 1 CAT: 19

Kindergarten Evaluation of Learning Potential
CIJE: 0 RIE: 1 CAT: 21

Kindergarten Experience Comparison
CIJE: 0 RIE: 2 CAT: 19

Kindergarten Extended Day Program
CIJE: 0 RIE: 7 CAT: 19

Kindergarten Instructional Design System
CIJE: 0 RIE: 1 CAT: 15

Kindergarten Inventory (North et al)
CIJE: 0 RIE: 1 CAT: 21

Kindergarten Inventory Develop Social Competency
CIJE: 0 RIE: 1 CAT: 21
UF KIDSc

Kindergarten Language Screening Test
CIJE: 0 RIE: 1 CAT: 21

Kindergarten Mathematic Attitude Instrument
CIJE: 0 RIE: 1 CAT: 21

Kindergarten Oral Language Project
CIJE: 0 RIE: 1 CAT: 19
SN ...of the Los Angeles Unified School District CA

Kindergarten Parents Club IN
CIJE: 1 RIE: 0 CAT: 17

Kindergarten Program Entry Survey (SWRL)
CIJE: 0 RIE: 1 CAT: 21

Kindergarten Questionnaire
CIJE: 0 RIE: 1 CAT: 21

Kindergarten Stories
CIJE: 0 RIE: 1 CAT: 16

Kindergarten Teacher Rating Scale
CIJE: 2 RIE: 0 CAT: 21

Kindling Individual Development Systems Project
CIJE: 1 RIE: 0 CAT: 19

Kinematics
CIJE: 21 RIE: 4 CAT: 20

Kinesiology
CIJE: 18 RIE: 9 CAT: 20
SN See also "Educational Kinesiology" and "Mechanical Kinesiology"

Kinetic Family Drawings
CIJE: 4 RIE: 2 CAT: 15

Kinetic Imagery
CIJE: 3 RIE: 0 CAT: 11

Kinetic School Drawing
CIJE: 5 RIE: 0 CAT: 15

Kinetic Structure
CIJE: 9 RIE: 0 CAT: 11

Kinetograms
CIJE: 1 RIE: 0 CAT: 15

King (Clarence)
CIJE: 0 RIE: 1 CAT: 18

King (Martin Luther Jr)
CIJE: 48 RIE: 30 CAT: 18

King (Rodney)
CIJE: 1 RIE: 1 CAT: 18

King (Rufus)
CIJE: 0 RIE: 1 CAT: 18

King Abdul Aziz University
USE King Abdulaziz University (Saudi Arabia)

King Abdulaziz University (Saudi Arabia)
CIJE: 4 RIE: 0 CAT: 17
UF King Abdul Aziz University

King and Queen County Public Schools VA
CIJE: 0 RIE: 0 CAT: 17

King Arthur
CIJE: 3 RIE: 1 CAT: 16
SN See also "Tales from King Arthur"

King Center NY
CIJE: 1 RIE: 0 CAT: 17

King James Version of the Holy Bible
CIJE: 1 RIE: 3 CAT: 22

King Kong
CIJE: 1 RIE: 0 CAT: 22

King Lear
CIJE: 10 RIE: 4 CAT: 22

King Pre Retirement Checklist
CIJE: 0 RIE: 2 CAT: 21

King Timilty Advisory Council
CIJE: 1 RIE: 0 CAT: 17

Kings College (England)
CIJE: 1 RIE: 2 CAT: 17

Kings College PA
CIJE: 7 RIE: 5 CAT: 17

Kingsborough Community College NY
USE City University of New York Kingsborough Comm Coll

Kingsborough Community College WV
CIJE: 1 RIE: 0 CAT: 17

Kingsbury Center DC
CIJE: 0 RIE: 1 CAT: 17

Kingston College (England)
CIJE: 2 RIE: 0 CAT: 17

Kingsville Independent School District v Cooper
CIJE: 1 RIE: 0 CAT: 14

Kinkeeping
CIJE: 1 RIE: 2 CAT: 16

Kinneavy (James)
CIJE: 6 RIE: 9 CAT: 18

Kinney Shoe Corporation
CIJE: 1 RIE: 0 CAT: 17

Kinsey (Alfred)
CIJE: 3 RIE: 0 CAT: 18

Kintsch (Walter)
CIJE: 4 RIE: 3 CAT: 18

Kiowa
CIJE: 1 RIE: 1 CAT: 13
SN A Tanoan language

Kiowa (Tribe)
CIJE: 3 RIE: 6 CAT: 08

Kiowa Apache (Tribe)
CIJE: 0 RIE: 1 CAT: 08

Kiowa Tanoan Languages
USE Tanoan Languages

Kipling (Rudyard)
CIJE: 6 RIE: 1 CAT: 18

Kipsigis
CIJE: 2 RIE: 2 CAT: 13

Kirchner (Ernst Ludwig)
CIJE: 1 RIE: 0 CAT: 18

Kirchner Physical Fitness Test Battery
CIJE: 0 RIE: 1 CAT: 21

Kirchoff Laws
CIJE: 6 RIE: 1 CAT: 20

Kirghizstan
USE Kirgizstan

Kirgizstan
CIJE: 0 RIE: 0 CAT: 07
SN See also "USSR (Kirgizia)"
UF Kirghizstan

Kiribati
CIJE: 1 RIE: 6 CAT: 07

Kiribati (Gilbertese)
CIJE: 0 RIE: 0 CAT: 13

Kirk (Russell)
CIJE: 1 RIE: 1 CAT: 18

Kirk (Samuel)
CIJE: 2 RIE: 1 CAT: 18

Kirkland College NY
CIJE: 1 RIE: 0 CAT: 17

Kirkwood Community College IA
CIJE: 8 RIE: 8 CAT: 17

Kirkwood School District MO
CIJE: 2 RIE: 1 CAT: 17

Kirlian Photography
CIJE: 2 RIE: 0 CAT: 20

Kirschener Report
CIJE: 1 RIE: 0 CAT: 22

Kirst (Michael W)
CIJE: 1 RIE: 1 CAT: 18

Kirton Adaption Innovation Inventory
CIJE: 4 RIE: 1 CAT: 21

Kissi
CIJE: 0 RIE: 1 CAT: 13

Kissler Report 1980
CIJE: 1 RIE: 0 CAT: 22

Kit of Reference Tests for Cognitive Factors
CIJE: 7 RIE: 11 CAT: 21

Kitaskinaw School AB
CIJE: 2 RIE: 0 CAT: 17

Kitchen Helpers
CIJE: 0 RIE: 2 CAT: 09

Kitchen Utensils
CIJE: 3 RIE: 4 CAT: 04

Kitchens
CIJE: 3 RIE: 5 CAT: 05

Kites
CIJE: 14 RIE: 6 CAT: 16

KITES (Satellite Telelink)
USE Kids Interactive Telecomm Experience by Satellite

Klallam (Tribe)
CIJE: 0 RIE: 1 CAT: 08

Klamath
CIJE: 1 RIE: 3 CAT: 13

Klamath (Tribe)
CIJE: 0 RIE: 1 CAT: 08

Klamath County Schools OR
CIJE: 1 RIE: 0 CAT: 17

Klausmeier (Herbert J)
CIJE: 0 RIE: 1 CAT: 18

Klavan (Gene)
CIJE: 1 RIE: 0 CAT: 18

Klee (Paul)
CIJE: 3 RIE: 3 CAT: 18

Klein (J Theodore)
CIJE: 2 RIE: 0 CAT: 18

Kleinbauer (W Eugene)
CIJE: 0 RIE: 1 CAT: 18

Kleist (Heinrich von)
CIJE: 1 RIE: 0 CAT: 18

Klemetti Institute
CIJE: 1 RIE: 0 CAT: 17

Klerer May System
CIJE: 0 RIE: 1 CAT: 15

KLH Child Development Center MA
CIJE: 0 RIE: 1 CAT: 17

Kline (Peter)
CIJE: 0 RIE: 1 CAT: 18

Klinefelters Syndrome
CIJE: 6 RIE: 0 CAT: 11

Klinger (Friedrich Maximilian)
CIJE: 1 RIE: 0 CAT: 18

Klopstock (Friedrich Gottlieb)
CIJE: 1 RIE: 0 CAT: 18

Kluckhohn Inventory
CIJE: 0 RIE: 1 CAT: 21

Knapp Foundation of North Carolina
CIJE: 1 RIE: 0 CAT: 17

Knapp School Libraries Project
CIJE: 2 RIE: 1 CAT: 19

Knauth (Percy)
CIJE: 1 RIE: 0 CAT: 18

Kneesworth House (England)
CIJE: 1 RIE: 0 CAT: 17

KNI Developmental Scale (Woellhof)
CIJE: 0 RIE: 1 CAT: 21

Knife River Indian Village
CIJE: 0 RIE: 1 CAT: 12
SN Nineteenth-century village in what is now North Dakota

Knight (Sarah Kemble)
CIJE: 0 RIE: 1 CAT: 18

Knight Perceived Influence Scale
CIJE: 0 RIE: 1 CAT: 21

Knight Report on Intercollegiate Athletics
CIJE: 1 RIE: 4 CAT: 22
SN Mar91 report of the Knight Foundation Commission on Intercollegiate Athletics
UF Keeping Faith With the Student Athlete

Knight Ridder
CIJE: 1 RIE: 1 CAT: 17

Knit Goods
CIJE: 0 RIE: 1 CAT: 16

Knitting Lace Net Industry Training Bd (England)
CIJE: 0 RIE: 1 CAT: 17

Knives
CIJE: 0 RIE: 1 CAT: 04

Knobler Perceptual Development Test
CIJE: 0 RIE: 2 CAT: 21

Knot Tying
CIJE: 0 RIE: 3 CAT: 16

KNOW NET WA
USE Knowledge Network of Washington

KNOW NET WI
USE Knowledge Network of Wisconsin

Know Nothing Party
CIJE: 1 RIE: 1 CAT: 17

Knowability
CIJE: 0 RIE: 2 CAT: 15

Knower (Franklin)
CIJE: 0 RIE: 1 CAT: 18

Knowes Report
CIJE: 0 RIE: 1 CAT: 22

Knowledge
CIJE: 157 RIE: 48 CAT: 20

Knowledge Ability Theory
CIJE: 0 RIE: 1 CAT: 15

Knowledge About Science and Scientists
CIJE: 0 RIE: 1 CAT: 16

Knowledge Accessing Modes Inventory
CIJE: 0 RIE: 1 CAT: 21

Knowledge Acquisition
CIJE: 148 RIE: 60 CAT: 15

Knowledge and Control
CIJE: 4 RIE: 0 CAT: 16

Knowledge Bases
CIJE: 41 RIE: 17 CAT: 16

Knowledge Control
CIJE: 5 RIE: 3 CAT: 15

Knowledge Development
CIJE: 44 RIE: 13 CAT: 15

Knowledge Engineering
CIJE: 19 RIE: 4 CAT: 15

Knowledge Engineering for Young Scholars Program
CIJE: 0 RIE: 1 CAT: 19

Knowledge Gap Hypothesis
CIJE: 7 RIE: 6 CAT: 15

Knowledge Index
CIJE: 3 RIE: 3 CAT: 04

Knowledge Linkers
CIJE: 1 RIE: 3 CAT: 16

Knowledge Management
CIJE: 2 RIE: 2 CAT: 15

Knowledge Mapping
USE Knowledge Maps

Knowledge Maps
CIJE: 9 RIE: 5 CAT: 15
UF Knowledge Mapping

Knowledge Network BC
CIJE: 0 RIE: 3 CAT: 17
UF Knowledge Network of the West BC

Knowledge Network of the West BC
USE Knowledge Network BC

Knowledge Network of Washington
CIJE: 0 RIE: 1 CAT: 17
UF KNOW NET WA

Knowledge Network of Wisconsin
CIJE: 0 RIE: 1 CAT: 17
UF KNOW NET WI

Knowledge of Child Development Inventory
CIJE: 1 RIE: 1 CAT: 21

Knowledge of Correct Response
CIJE: 2 RIE: 1 CAT: 21

Knowledge of English Yields Success
USE KEYS Project

Knowledge of Infant Development Scale (Dusewicz)
CIJE: 1 RIE: 0 CAT: 21

Knowledge of the World of Work
CIJE: 2 RIE: 0 CAT: 21

Knowledge Production and Utilization
CIJE: 13 RIE: 13 CAT: 16

Knowledge Sciences
CIJE: 1 RIE: 2 CAT: 03

Knowledge Skills and Abilities Method
CIJE: 0 RIE: 1 CAT: 15

Knowledge Transformation Program
CIJE: 0 RIE: 2 CAT: 19

Knowledge Utilization
CIJE: 73 RIE: 43 CAT: 15

Knowles (John)
CIJE: 5 RIE: 3 CAT: 18

Knowles (Malcolm S)
CIJE: 17 RIE: 19 CAT: 18

Knox (Vicesimus II)
CIJE: 1 RIE: 0 CAT: 18

Knox College IL
CIJE: 7 RIE: 4 CAT: 17

Knox County Schools TN
CIJE: 1 RIE: 9 CAT: 17

Knox Cube Test
CIJE: 1 RIE: 1 CAT: 21

Knox Sporakowski Attitudes Toward Love Scale
CIJE: 1 RIE: 0 CAT: 21
UF Attitudes Toward Love Scale (Knox and Sporakowski)

Knoxville City Schools Proficiency Test Project
CIJE: 0 RIE: 1 CAT: 19

Knoxville City Schools TN
CIJE: 1 RIE: 5 CAT: 17

Knoxville College TN
CIJE: 1 RIE: 1 CAT: 17

Knuth (Donald)
CIJE: 1 RIE: 0 CAT: 18

Knuth Achievement Tests in Music
CIJE: 1 RIE: 1 CAT: 21

Koasati
CIJE: 0 RIE: 2 CAT: 13
SN A Muskogean language — see also "Coushatta (Tribe)"

Koch Postulates
CIJE: 4 RIE: 0 CAT: 20

Kodak Equipment
CIJE: 4 RIE: 2 CAT: 04

Kodak Limited
CIJE: 0 RIE: 1 CAT: 17

Kodak Research Laboratories
CIJE: 1 RIE: 0 CAT: 17

Kodak Skills Enhancement Program
CIJE: 0 RIE: 4 CAT: 19

Kodak Trades Trainee Program
CIJE: 1 RIE: 0 CAT: 19

Kodaly (Zoltan)
CIJE: 6 RIE: 1 CAT: 18

Koestler (Arthur)
CIJE: 2 RIE: 1 CAT: 18

Kogan Attitudes Toward Old People Scale
CIJE: 1 RIE: 2 CAT: 21

Koh
CIJE: 0 RIE: 1 CAT: 13

Kohl (Herbert)
CIJE: 3 RIE: 1 CAT: 18

Kohlberg (Lawrence)
CIJE: 215 RIE: 87 CAT: 18

Kohlberg Moral Judgment Interview
CIJE: 21 RIE: 4 CAT: 21

Kohler Company
CIJE: 1 RIE: 0 CAT: 17

Kohns Behavior Checklist and Competence Scale
CIJE: 0 RIE: 1 CAT: 21

Kohs Block Design Test
CIJE: 3 RIE: 2 CAT: 21

Kohut (Heinz)
CIJE: 3 RIE: 6 CAT: 18

Koko Jelandji
USE Kuku Yalanji

Kokuji
CIJE: 0 RIE: 1 CAT: 13

Kolami
CIJE: 0 RIE: 3 CAT: 13

Kolb (David A)
CIJE: 12 RIE: 6 CAT: 18

Kold (Kristen Mikkelsen)
CIJE: 0 RIE: 2 CAT: 18

Kolko (Gabriel)
CIJE: 1 RIE: 0 CAT: 18

Kolmar (Gertrud)
CIJE: 2 RIE: 0 CAT: 18

Kolmogorov School
CIJE: 1 RIE: 0 CAT: 17

Kolmogorov Smirnov Two Sample Test
CIJE: 10 RIE: 6 CAT: 21

Koluschan Language
USE Tlingit

Komensky (Jan Amos)
USE Comenius (Johann Amos)

Komisar (B Paul)
CIJE: 1 RIE: 0 CAT: 18

Komo (North Eastern Bantu)
USE Kuumu

Komsomal
CIJE: 1 RIE: 0 CAT: 17

Konama School NM
CIJE: 1 RIE: 0 CAT: 17

Kondratieff Waves
CIJE: 4 RIE: 1 CAT: 15

Konig (Karl)
CIJE: 1 RIE: 2 CAT: 18

Konkani
CIJE: 2 RIE: 0 CAT: 13

Koontz Child Developmental Program
CIJE: 0 RIE: 1 CAT: 19

Koori People
CIJE: 0 RIE: 1 CAT: 08

Kootenai (Tribe)
CIJE: 0 RIE: 2 CAT: 08

Kope
CIJE: 0 RIE: 4 CAT: 13
SN Of the Kiwaian language family, Papua New Guinea
UF Gope

Koppitz Adaptation of Bender Gestalt Test
CIJE: 1 RIE: 0 CAT: 21

Koppitz Scale of Emotional Indicators
CIJE: 3 RIE: 1 CAT: 21

Koran
CIJE: 1 RIE: 2 CAT: 22
UF Quran

Korczak (Janusz)
CIJE: 5 RIE: 1 CAT: 18

Korea
CIJE: 126 RIE: 149 CAT: 07

Korea Air and Correspondence University
CIJE: 0 RIE: 1 CAT: 17

Korea Military Advisory Group
CIJE: 0 RIE: 1 CAT: 17

Korea Scientific and Technological Inf Center
CIJE: 1 RIE: 1 CAT: 17

Korean Air Lines 007
USE KAL 007

Korean Educational Development Institute
CIJE: 0 RIE: 3 CAT: 17

Korean Library Association
CIJE: 0 RIE: 1 CAT: 17

Koreans
CIJE: 9 RIE: 15 CAT: 08

Korff (Kurt)
CIJE: 0 RIE: 1 CAT: 18

Korsakov (Rimsky)
CIJE: 0 RIE: 1 CAT: 18

Kortright Centre for Conservation ON
CIJE: 0 RIE: 3 CAT: 17

Korty (John)
CIJE: 1 RIE: 0 CAT: 18

Korzybski (Alfred)
CIJE: 6 RIE: 6 CAT: 18

Kosena
CIJE: 0 RIE: 1 CAT: 13

Kosinski (Jerzy)
CIJE: 1 RIE: 0 CAT: 18

Kothari Report
CIJE: 1 RIE: 1 CAT: 22

Kotia Oriya
CIJE: 0 RIE: 3 CAT: 13

Kounin (Jacob)
CIJE: 2 RIE: 1 CAT: 18

Kourion
CIJE: 2 RIE: 0 CAT: 13

Kovalevsky (Sofya)
CIJE: 1 RIE: 0 CAT: 18

Kownslar (Allan O)
CIJE: 0 RIE: 1 CAT: 18

Koymen (Nusret Kemal)
CIJE: 1 RIE: 0 CAT: 18

Koyuk
USE Koyukon

Koyukon
CIJE: 0 RIE: 2 CAT: 13
SN An Athapascan language
UF Koyuk; Koyukukhotana

Koyukukhotana
USE Koyukon

Kozintsev (Grigori)
CIJE: 1 RIE: 0 CAT: 18

Kozol (Jonathan)
CIJE: 16 RIE: 2 CAT: 18

Kpelle
CIJE: 1 RIE: 4 CAT: 13

Krahn
CIJE: 0 RIE: 1 CAT: 13

Kraner Quantitative Development Scale
CIJE: 1 RIE: 0 CAT: 21

Krashen (Stephen)
CIJE: 19 RIE: 11 CAT: 18

Krathwohl (David R)
CIJE: 1 RIE: 1 CAT: 18

Krathwohls Taxonomy
CIJE: 4 RIE: 5 CAT: 15

Kreb Cycle
CIJE: 1 RIE: 0 CAT: 20

Kreitler (Hans)
CIJE: 1 RIE: 0 CAT: 18

Kreitler (Shulamith)
CIJE: 1 RIE: 0 CAT: 18

Krell SAT Computer Software
CIJE: 0 RIE: 1 CAT: 04

Kreps (Juanita)
CIJE: 1 RIE: 0 CAT: 18

Kriewall Criterion Referenced Test Model
CIJE: 0 RIE: 1 CAT: 21

Kriol
CIJE: 0 RIE: 6 CAT: 13
SN A creole language (Australian Aborigine)

Krishna Religious Sect
CIJE: 1 RIE: 0 CAT: 10

Krishnamurti (Jiddu)
CIJE: 1 RIE: 1 CAT: 18

Kropp Verner Evaluation Scale
CIJE: 0 RIE: 12 CAT: 21

Krotkoff v Goucher College
CIJE: 1 RIE: 0 CAT: 14

Kru
CIJE: 1 RIE: 1 CAT: 13

Kruger (W Stanley)
CIJE: 1 RIE: 0 CAT: 18

Krupskaya (Nadezhda Konstantinovna)
CIJE: 2 RIE: 0 CAT: 18

Krusi (J H H)
CIJE: 1 RIE: 0 CAT: 18
SN "Hermann"

Kruskal Wallis Test
CIJE: 6 RIE: 3 CAT: 21

Kruskal Wallis Test Z Scores
CIJE: 0 RIE: 1 CAT: 21

Ku Klux Klan
CIJE: 4 RIE: 11 CAT: 10

Kuba
CIJE: 0 RIE: 1 CAT: 08
SN A Bantu-speaking people of Zaire — see also "Shoowa"

Kubler Ross (Elisabeth)
CIJE: 8 RIE: 2 CAT: 18

Kubrick (Stanley)
CIJE: 1 RIE: 1 CAT: 18

Kuder (Frederic)
CIJE: 2 RIE: 1 CAT: 18

Kuder General Interest Survey (Form E)
CIJE: 5 RIE: 3 CAT: 21

Kuder Interest Card Sort
CIJE: 0 RIE: 1 CAT: 21

Kuder Occupational Interest Survey
CIJE: 20 RIE: 15 CAT: 21

Kuder Preference Record Occupational
CIJE: 0 RIE: 1 CAT: 21

Kuder Preference Record Vocational
CIJE: 3 RIE: 13 CAT: 21

Kuder Richardson Reliability Formulas
CIJE: 15 RIE: 17 CAT: 21

Kuethe (James L)
CIJE: 0 RIE: 1 CAT: 18

Kuhlen (Raymond G)
CIJE: 0 RIE: 1 CAT: 18

Kuhlmann Anderson Intelligence Tests
CIJE: 0 RIE: 6 CAT: 21

Kuhlmann Binet Intelligence Scale
CIJE: 1 RIE: 0 CAT: 21

Kuhlmeier v Hazelwood School District MO
USE Hazelwood School District v Kuhlmeier

Kuhlthau (Carol)
CIJE: 2 RIE: 0 CAT: 18
SN "Carol Collier"

Kuhlthau Model
CIJE: 1 RIE: 2 CAT: 15
SN Process approach to information seeking in a library setting

Kuhn (Maggie)
CIJE: 1 RIE: 0 CAT: 18

Kuhn (Thomas S)
CIJE: 19 RIE: 4 CAT: 18

Kuku Yalanji
CIJE: 0 RIE: 1 CAT: 13
SN A Pama-Maric language (Australian Aborigine)
UF Gugu Yalanji; Koko Jelandji

Kulhavy (R W)
CIJE: 0 RIE: 1 CAT: 18

Kumon Mathematical Method
CIJE: 0 RIE: 1 CAT: 15

Kumtuks Alternative Rehabilitation Program
CIJE: 0 RIE: 1 CAT: 19

Kumu
USE Kuumu

Kung Bushmen
CIJE: 0 RIE: 0 CAT: 08

Kunibidji
USE Ndjebbana

Kuniyoshi (Obara)
CIJE: 1 RIE: 0 CAT: 18

Kunkel McElhinney Model
CIJE: 0 RIE: 2 CAT: 15

Kuno (Susumu)
CIJE: 1 RIE: 1 CAT: 18

Kupia
CIJE: 0 RIE: 4 CAT: 13

Kurds
CIJE: 0 RIE: 5 CAT: 08

Kuring gai College of Advanced Educ (Australia)
CIJE: 2 RIE: 3 CAT: 17

Kurosawa (Akira)
CIJE: 1 RIE: 1 CAT: 18

Kurtosis
CIJE: 4 RIE: 2 CAT: 21

Kurzweil Reading Machine
CIJE: 4 RIE: 1 CAT: 04

Kusaiean
CIJE: 0 RIE: 3 CAT: 13

Kuskin (Karla)
CIJE: 1 RIE: 1 CAT: 18

Kutchin
CIJE: 0 RIE: 1 CAT: 13
SN An Athapascan-Eyak language — see also "Loucheux"

Kutchin (Tribe)
CIJE: 0 RIE: 1 CAT: 08

Kutztown State College PA
CIJE: 0 RIE: 1 CAT: 17

Kutztown University PA
CIJE: 1 RIE: 7 CAT: 17

Kuumu
CIJE: 0 RIE: 2 CAT: 13
SN A North Eastern Bantu language
UF Komo (North Eastern Bantu); Kumu

Kuwait
CIJE: 28 RIE: 28 CAT: 07

Kuwait University
CIJE: 10 RIE: 1 CAT: 17

Kvaraceus Delinquency Proneness Scale
CIJE: 1 RIE: 3 CAT: 21

Kwa
CIJE: 0 RIE: 1 CAT: 13

Kwakiutl
CIJE: 0 RIE: 1 CAT: 13
SN A language of the Kwakiutlan branch of Wakashan — spoken on the coast of British Columbia and adjacent end of Vancouver Island

Kwakiutl (Tribe)
CIJE: 1 RIE: 6 CAT: 08

Kwalwasser Ruch Test of Musical Accomplishment
CIJE: 1 RIE: 0 CAT: 21

Kwanza
USE Kwanzaa

Kwanzaa
CIJE: 5 RIE: 2 CAT: 12
SN African-American harvest festival celebrated annually from December 26 until January 1
UF Kwanza

Kwashiorkor
CIJE: 2 RIE: 2 CAT: 11

Kwazulu
CIJE: 1 RIE: 2 CAT: 07

Kwoma
CIJE: 1 RIE: 0 CAT: 13

Kymograph Recording
CIJE: 2 RIE: 1 CAT: 13

Kyoto Sangyo University (Japan)
CIJE: 1 RIE: 0 CAT: 17

Kyrene School District AZ
CIJE: 1 RIE: 1 CAT: 17

L Amour (Louis)
CIJE: 1 RIE: 1 CAT: 18

L and J Software Analysis Checklist II
CIJE: 0 RIE: 1 CAT: 21

L Anse Creuse Public Schools MI
CIJE: 0 RIE: 1 CAT: 17

L Engle (Madeleine)
CIJE: 4 RIE: 1 CAT: 18

L Scaling
CIJE: 0 RIE: 2 CAT: 15

L Test
CIJE: 0 RIE: 1 CAT: 21

La Bruyere (Jean de)
CIJE: 1 RIE: 0 CAT: 18

La Dictee
CIJE: 0 RIE: 2 CAT: 15

La Flesche (Susan)
CIJE: 0 RIE: 1 CAT: 18

La Flesche (Susette)
CIJE: 0 RIE: 1 CAT: 18

La Fontaine (Jean de)
CIJE: 5 RIE: 0 CAT: 18

La Grange School District 105 IL
CIJE: 0 RIE: 1 CAT: 17

La Guardia Community College Intl High School NY
USE International High School NY

La Guardia Community College NY
USE City University of New York La Guardia Comm Coll

La Jolla School CA
CIJE: 0 RIE: 1 CAT: 17

La Leche League
CIJE: 1 RIE: 1 CAT: 17

La Presse (Newspaper)
CIJE: 0 RIE: 0 CAT: 22

La Puente Union High School District CA
CIJE: 1 RIE: 0 CAT: 17

La Raza
CIJE: 3 RIE: 6 CAT: 08

La Raza National Council
USE National Council of La Raza

La Raza Unida Party
CIJE: 1 RIE: 1 CAT: 17

La Rochefoucauld (Francois)
CIJE: 1 RIE: 0 CAT: 18

La Salle (Donald)
USE LaSalle (Donald P)

La Salle College PA
CIJE: 3 RIE: 2 CAT: 17

La Salle University PA
CIJE: 3 RIE: 7 CAT: 17

La Symphonie Pastorale
CIJE: 1 RIE: 0 CAT: 22

La Trobe University (Australia)
CIJE: 6 RIE: 0 CAT: 17

La Verne College CA
CIJE: 2 RIE: 1 CAT: 17

Laban (Rudolf)
CIJE: 3 RIE: 1 CAT: 18

Labe (Louise)
CIJE: 1 RIE: 0 CAT: 18

Label Class Method
CIJE: 0 RIE: 1 CAT: 15

Labeled Dependency Trees
CIJE: 0 RIE: 1 CAT: 13

Labeling (of Objects)
CIJE: 31 RIE: 11 CAT: 11

Labette Community College KS
CIJE: 0 RIE: 1 CAT: 17

Labonation
CIJE: 1 RIE: 0 CAT: 16

Labor and Industry Occupational Needs System NJ
CIJE: 0 RIE: 1 CAT: 17

Labor Day
CIJE: 3 RIE: 3 CAT: 12

Labor Education Week
CIJE: 0 RIE: 1 CAT: 12

Labor Force Analysis
CIJE: 2 RIE: 4 CAT: 15

Labor Force Segmentation
CIJE: 2 RIE: 4 CAT: 16

Labor Management Conference
CIJE: 0 RIE: 1 CAT: 02

Labor Management Cooperation
CIJE: 1 RIE: 6 CAT: 16

Labor Market Imbalance
CIJE: 1 RIE: 2 CAT: 16

Labor Market Theory
CIJE: 2 RIE: 2 CAT: 15

Labor Mobility Demonstration Project
CIJE: 0 RIE: 1 CAT: 19

Labor Relations Training Center DC
CIJE: 0 RIE: 1 CAT: 17

Labor Responsibility
CIJE: 0 RIE: 2 CAT: 16

Labor Studies
CIJE: 11 RIE: 16 CAT: 03

Labor Union Militancy
CIJE: 0 RIE: 1 CAT: 16

Laboratory Content
CIJE: 0 RIE: 1 CAT: 15

Laboratory Demonstration Scale (Bloom)
CIJE: 0 RIE: 1 CAT: 21

Laboratory Exploration in Biology
CIJE: 1 RIE: 0 CAT: 22

Laboratory Institute to Facilitate Teaching
CIJE: 1 RIE: 0 CAT: 17

Laboratory Integrators
CIJE: 1 RIE: 0 CAT: 16

Laboratory Interaction Categories
CIJE: 1 RIE: 0 CAT: 21

Laboratory Interfacing
CIJE: 63 RIE: 7 CAT: 04

Laboratory Lecture Scale (Bloom)
CIJE: 0 RIE: 1 CAT: 21

Laboratory Observation Schedule and Record
CIJE: 0 RIE: 1 CAT: 21

Laboratory of Interactive Ed Technologies (Italy)
CIJE: 0 RIE: 1 CAT: 17

Laboratory Organisms
CIJE: 4 RIE: 0 CAT: 20

Laboratory Paraprofessionals
CIJE: 2 RIE: 0 CAT: 09

Laboratory Program for Computer Assisted Learning
CIJE: 2 RIE: 0 CAT: 19

Laboratory Program Variables Inventory
CIJE: 1 RIE: 0 CAT: 21

Labour Party (England)
CIJE: 5 RIE: 2 CAT: 17

Labov (William)
CIJE: 8 RIE: 10 CAT: 18

Labrador
CIJE: 9 RIE: 20 CAT: 07
UF Newfoundland (Labrador)

Lacan (Jacques)
CIJE: 13 RIE: 1 CAT: 18

Lacan (Jean)
CIJE: 0 RIE: 1 CAT: 18

Lackland Air Force Base TX
CIJE: 0 RIE: 1 CAT: 17

Laconia State School NH
CIJE: 0 RIE: 1 CAT: 17

LaConner School District WA
CIJE: 0 RIE: 1 CAT: 17

Lacquer Solvents
CIJE: 0 RIE: 1 CAT: 20

Lactation
CIJE: 1 RIE: 4 CAT: 11

Ladd (Everett C)
CIJE: 0 RIE: 1 CAT: 18

Ladders (Equipment)
CIJE: 1 RIE: 3 CAT: 04

Ladies Home Journal
CIJE: 0 RIE: 4 CAT: 22

Lado (Robert)
CIJE: 1 RIE: 2 CAT: 18

Lado English Language Series
CIJE: 0 RIE: 1 CAT: 22

Lado Fries Materials
CIJE: 0 RIE: 1 CAT: 22

Lado Test of Aural Comprehension
CIJE: 0 RIE: 1 CAT: 21

Ladue School District MO
CIJE: 3 RIE: 1 CAT: 17

Lady of Shalott (The)
CIJE: 0 RIE: 1 CAT: 22

Lady Walking in the Rain
CIJE: 0 RIE: 1 CAT: 21

Laetrile
CIJE: 1 RIE: 1 CAT: 11

Lafayette College PA
CIJE: 8 RIE: 4 CAT: 17

Lafayette Parish Compensatory Remedial Program LA
CIJE: 0 RIE: 0 CAT: 19

Laffite (Jean)
USE Lafitte (Jean)

Lafitte (Jean)
CIJE: 0 RIE: 2 CAT: 18
UF Laffite (Jean)

LAG Computer Program
CIJE: 0 RIE: 1 CAT: 04

Lag Sequential Analysis
CIJE: 2 RIE: 2 CAT: 15

Lagoons
CIJE: 0 RIE: 1 CAT: 20

Lagrange Study
CIJE: 1 RIE: 1 CAT: 19

Laguna (Pueblo)
CIJE: 4 RIE: 2 CAT: 08

Laguna Acoma Combined Junior Senior High Sch NM
CIJE: 0 RIE: 1 CAT: 17

Laguna Beach Unified School District CA
CIJE: 0 RIE: 1 CAT: 17

Laguna Reservation AZ
CIJE: 0 RIE: 1 CAT: 17

Laguna Reservation NM
CIJE: 0 RIE: 1 CAT: 17

Laidlaw Mathematics Series (Elementary)
CIJE: 0 RIE: 1 CAT: 03

Laissez Faire
CIJE: 3 RIE: 0 CAT: 16

Lakatos (Imre)
CIJE: 3 RIE: 2 CAT: 18

Lakatosian Programme
CIJE: 1 RIE: 1 CAT: 19

Lake Area Vocational Technical School SD
CIJE: 1 RIE: 0 CAT: 17

Lake City Community College FL
CIJE: 2 RIE: 6 CAT: 17

Lake Country School MN
CIJE: 0 RIE: 1 CAT: 17

Lake County Area Vocational Technical Center FL
CIJE: 1 RIE: 0 CAT: 17

Lake County Public Schools IL
CIJE: 0 RIE: 1 CAT: 17

Lake Erie
CIJE: 2 RIE: 9 CAT: 07

Lake Forest College IL
CIJE: 4 RIE: 2 CAT: 17

Lake Forest School District DE
CIJE: 3 RIE: 2 CAT: 17

Lake Land College IL
CIJE: 1 RIE: 3 CAT: 17

Lake Manitoba Indian Reserve
CIJE: 0 RIE: 1 CAT: 17

Lake Michigan College MI
CIJE: 0 RIE: 1 CAT: 17

Lake Michigan Federation
CIJE: 0 RIE: 1 CAT: 17

Lake Okoboji Educational Media Leadership Conf
CIJE: 6 RIE: 13 CAT: 02

Lake Oswego School District 7J OR
CIJE: 0 RIE: 2 CAT: 17

Lake Stevens School District WA
CIJE: 0 RIE: 1 CAT: 17

Lake Sumter Community College FL
CIJE: 1 RIE: 1 CAT: 17

Lake Superior
CIJE: 1 RIE: 2 CAT: 07

Lake Superior State College MI
CIJE: 0 RIE: 4 CAT: 17

Lake Superior State University MI
CIJE: 0 RIE: 2 CAT: 17

Lake Tahoe
CIJE: 1 RIE: 1 CAT: 07

Lake Washington School District WA
CIJE: 6 RIE: 3 CAT: 17

Lake Winona
CIJE: 1 RIE: 0 CAT: 07

Lake Wobegon
CIJE: 0 RIE: 0 CAT: 16

Lake Wobegon Effect
USE Lake Wobegon Phenomenon

Lake Wobegon Phenomenon
CIJE: 9 RIE: 4 CAT: 21
SN Consistently testing above the norm, contrary to other achievement indicators — in reference to the mythical town where all children are above average
UF Lake Wobegon Effect

Lakeland Community College OH
CIJE: 1 RIE: 9 CAT: 17

Lakeland High School NY
CIJE: 0 RIE: 1 CAT: 17

Lakeshore Curriculum Study Council WI
CIJE: 0 RIE: 1 CAT: 17

Lakeshore Technical Institute WI
CIJE: 2 RIE: 8 CAT: 17

Lakewood School IL
CIJE: 1 RIE: 0 CAT: 17

Lakoff (G)
CIJE: 2 RIE: 1 CAT: 18

Lakota Higher Education Center SD
CIJE: 0 RIE: 1 CAT: 17

Lakota Tuberculosis and Health Association SD
CIJE: 0 RIE: 1 CAT: 17

Lamar Community College CO
CIJE: 0 RIE: 1 CAT: 17

Lamar School District CO
CIJE: 1 RIE: 0 CAT: 17

Lamar State College of Technology TX
CIJE: 0 RIE: 1 CAT: 17

Lamar University TX
CIJE: 4 RIE: 2 CAT: 17

Lamarckian Inheritance
CIJE: 1 RIE: 0 CAT: 20

Lamb
CIJE: 0 RIE: 1 CAT: 20

Lamb (Charles)
CIJE: 1 RIE: 0 CAT: 18

Lambrecht Shorthand Aptitude Test
CIJE: 0 RIE: 1 CAT: 21

Lambuth College TN
CIJE: 1 RIE: 1 CAT: 17

Laminating
CIJE: 1 RIE: 2 CAT: 20

Lamini
CIJE: 0 RIE: 1 CAT: 13

Lammers Report
CIJE: 1 RIE: 0 CAT: 22

Lamnsok
CIJE: 1 RIE: 0 CAT: 13

LAMP Exercises
USE Linguistic Auditory Memory Patterns

LAMP Project
CIJE: 1 RIE: 0 CAT: 19
SN LAMP = Least Academically Motivated Pupils

Lampedusa (Giuseppe Tomasi di)
CIJE: 1 RIE: 0 CAT: 18

Lamplighter School TX
CIJE: 2 RIE: 0 CAT: 17

Lancaster (Joseph)
CIJE: 4 RIE: 2 CAT: 18

Lancaster Approaches to Studying Inventory
USE Approaches to Studying Inventory

Lancaster City School District OH
CIJE: 0 RIE: 1 CAT: 17

Lancaster Elementary School District CA
CIJE: 0 RIE: 1 CAT: 17

Lancaster School District PA
CIJE: 1 RIE: 8 CAT: 17

Land Administration
CIJE: 1 RIE: 0 CAT: 03

Land and Me
CIJE: 0 RIE: 1 CAT: 22

Land and Water Conservation Fund
CIJE: 0 RIE: 1 CAT: 17

Land Application
CIJE: 0 RIE: 14 CAT: 20

Land Claims
CIJE: 11 RIE: 11 CAT: 14

Land Conversion
CIJE: 0 RIE: 1 CAT: 20

Land Ethos
CIJE: 1 RIE: 4 CAT: 15

Land Laboratories
CIJE: 1 RIE: 1 CAT: 05

Land Laboratories AZ
CIJE: 4 RIE: 0 CAT: 17

Land Laboratory IL
CIJE: 0 RIE: 1 CAT: 17

Land Reclamation
CIJE: 2 RIE: 3 CAT: 16

Land Reform
CIJE: 5 RIE: 3 CAT: 16

Land Remote Sensing Commercialization Act 1984
CIJE: 0 RIE: 1 CAT: 14

Land Rights
CIJE: 1 RIE: 4 CAT: 14

Land Treatment
CIJE: 0 RIE: 2 CAT: 20

Landau Damping
CIJE: 1 RIE: 0 CAT: 20

Landau Kleffner Syndrome
CIJE: 1 RIE: 0 CAT: 11

Landers (Ann)
CIJE: 1 RIE: 0 CAT: 18
UF Ann Landers

Landforms
CIJE: 6 RIE: 1 CAT: 20

Landmarks
CIJE: 9 RIE: 4 CAT: 16

Landsat
CIJE: 9 RIE: 5 CAT: 20

Landsat Satellite Maps
CIJE: 3 RIE: 0 CAT: 04

Landscape Architecture
CIJE: 1 RIE: 1 CAT: 20

Landscapes
CIJE: 5 RIE: 5 CAT: 20

Landslides
CIJE: 0 RIE: 1 CAT: 20

Lane (Homer T)
CIJE: 0 RIE: 1 CAT: 18

Lane Community College OR
CIJE: 6 RIE: 12 CAT: 17

Lane County Youth Project
CIJE: 0 RIE: 2 CAT: 19

Laney College CA
CIJE: 0 RIE: 4 CAT: 17

Langdon (John)
CIJE: 0 RIE: 1 CAT: 18

Langdon (Margaret)
CIJE: 0 RIE: 1 CAT: 18

Langdon Elementary School
CIJE: 1 RIE: 0 CAT: 17

Lange (Dorothea)
CIJE: 0 RIE: 3 CAT: 18

Langer (Susanne)
CIJE: 5 RIE: 5 CAT: 18

Langley Research Center VA
CIJE: 0 RIE: 4 CAT: 17

Langmuir Isotherm
USE Langmuir Model

Langmuir Law
CIJE: 1 RIE: 0 CAT: 20

Langmuir Model
CIJE: 0 RIE: 1 CAT: 20
UF Langmuir Isotherm

Langmuir Oral Direction Test
CIJE: 0 RIE: 1 CAT: 21

Langston University OK
CIJE: 0 RIE: 2 CAT: 17

Language Acquisition Device
CIJE: 6 RIE: 2 CAT: 04

Language Acquisition Resource Center NY
CIJE: 0 RIE: 1 CAT: 17

Language across the Curriculum
CIJE: 19 RIE: 26 CAT: 19

Language Analysis Package
CIJE: 0 RIE: 6 CAT: 15

Language and Cognitive Development Center MA
CIJE: 0 RIE: 1 CAT: 17

Language and Thinking Program
CIJE: 0 RIE: 1 CAT: 19

Language Arts (Journal)
CIJE: 10 RIE: 1 CAT: 22

Language Arts Routing System
CIJE: 0 RIE: 2 CAT: 15

Language Arts Test of Cognitive Functioning
CIJE: 0 RIE: 2 CAT: 21

Language Assessment Battery
CIJE: 1 RIE: 17 CAT: 21

Language Assessment Scales (De Avila and Duncan)
CIJE: 5 RIE: 7 CAT: 21

Language Assessment Tasks (Kellman Flood Yoder)
CIJE: 0 RIE: 1 CAT: 21

Language Assignment Umpire
CIJE: 0 RIE: 1 CAT: 21

Language Attitude Scale
CIJE: 0 RIE: 1 CAT: 21

Language Barriers
CIJE: 12 RIE: 5 CAT: 13

Language Camps
CIJE: 4 RIE: 8 CAT: 05

Language Choice
CIJE: 11 RIE: 5 CAT: 13

Language Communication Skills Task
CIJE: 0 RIE: 1 CAT: 21

Language Contact
CIJE: 33 RIE: 46 CAT: 13

Language Creation
CIJE: 3 RIE: 3 CAT: 13

Language Creativity
CIJE: 2 RIE: 1 CAT: 13

Language Deficit Theory
CIJE: 0 RIE: 1 CAT: 13

Language Delayed
CIJE: 6 RIE: 9 CAT: 13

Language Development Project (Australia)
CIJE: 0 RIE: 0 CAT: 19

Language Development Survey
CIJE: 2 RIE: 1 CAT: 21

Language Diversity
CIJE: 11 RIE: 11 CAT: 13

Language Enrichment Communicative Skills Project
CIJE: 0 RIE: 1 CAT: 19

Language Facility Test
CIJE: 1 RIE: 2 CAT: 21

Language for Optimizing Graphically Ordered System
CIJE: 1 RIE: 1 CAT: 04

Language for Preschool
CIJE: 1 RIE: 1 CAT: 19

Language Free Tests
CIJE: 0 RIE: 1 CAT: 21

Language Functions
CIJE: 30 RIE: 18 CAT: 13

Language Implementor Commands
CIJE: 0 RIE: 1 CAT: 04

Language Imposition
CIJE: 1 RIE: 1 CAT: 13

Language Improvement to Facilitate Education
CIJE: 2 RIE: 7 CAT: 19

Language Information Network Clearinghouse System
CIJE: 0 RIE: 5 CAT: 17

Language Innatism
CIJE: 1 RIE: 0 CAT: 13

Language Inquiry
CIJE: 0 RIE: 3 CAT: 13

Language Instruction Registers
CIJE: 0 RIE: 1 CAT: 04

Language Laboratory Monitoring
CIJE: 1 RIE: 0 CAT: 13

Language Lateralization
CIJE: 1 RIE: 1 CAT: 13

Language Loyalty
CIJE: 1 RIE: 4 CAT: 13

Language Maps
CIJE: 0 RIE: 1 CAT: 13

Language Master
CIJE: 7 RIE: 5 CAT: 04

Language Minorities
CIJE: 50 RIE: 162 CAT: 10
UF Language Minority Students; Linguistic Minorities

Language Minority Students
USE Language Minorities

Language Minority Survey
CIJE: 0 RIE: 1 CAT: 21

Language of Politics
USE Political Rhetoric

Language of the Crib
CIJE: 1 RIE: 0 CAT: 22

Language Pathology
CIJE: 2 RIE: 2 CAT: 13

Language Performance in Schools (APU)
CIJE: 0 RIE: 1 CAT: 22

Language Policy
CIJE: 19 RIE: 6 CAT: 13

Language Proficiency Assessment Committees
CIJE: 0 RIE: 3 CAT: 05

Language Proficiency Guidelines
CIJE: 0 RIE: 1 CAT: 21

Language Proficiency Interview
CIJE: 0 RIE: 2 CAT: 21

Language Proficiency Measure
CIJE: 1 RIE: 0 CAT: 21

Language Proficiency Questionnaire
CIJE: 0 RIE: 1 CAT: 21

Language Reform
CIJE: 5 RIE: 8 CAT: 13

Language Repairs
USE Repairs (Language)

Language Sciences
CIJE: 0 RIE: 6 CAT: 13

Language Sensitivity
CIJE: 5 RIE: 5 CAT: 13

Language Shaping Paradigm
CIJE: 0 RIE: 1 CAT: 13

Language Shift
CIJE: 32 RIE: 13 CAT: 13

Language Simplification
CIJE: 5 RIE: 6 CAT: 13

Language Skilled People
CIJE: 3 RIE: 6 CAT: 10

Language Spoken at Home
CIJE: 0 RIE: 1 CAT: 13

Language Spread
CIJE: 3 RIE: 1 CAT: 13

Language System Diagnostic Test
CIJE: 0 RIE: 1 CAT: 21

Language Teaching Record Scheme
CIJE: 1 RIE: 0 CAT: 15

Language Transfer
USE Cross Language Transfer

Languages for Science and Technology
CIJE: 0 RIE: 14 CAT: 13

Lanier Word Processor
CIJE: 0 RIE: 1 CAT: 04

Lankton First Year Algebra Test
CIJE: 0 RIE: 3 CAT: 21

Lansing Community College MI
CIJE: 4 RIE: 12 CAT: 17

Lansing School District MI
CIJE: 2 RIE: 7 CAT: 17

Lansing Teacher Corps MI
CIJE: 0 RIE: 1 CAT: 17

Lanthanide Salt
CIJE: 1 RIE: 0 CAT: 20

Lantran Chincode System
CIJE: 0 RIE: 1 CAT: 15

Lanyon (Richard I)
CIJE: 1 RIE: 0 CAT: 18

Laos
CIJE: 14 RIE: 45 CAT: 07

Laotian Culture
CIJE: 0 RIE: 2 CAT: 16

Laplace Transforms
CIJE: 1 RIE: 1 CAT: 20

Lapland
CIJE: 3 RIE: 2 CAT: 07

Lapp
USE Lappish

Lappic
USE Lappish

Lappish
CIJE: 1 RIE: 5 CAT: 13
SN A Finno-Ugric language
UF Lapp; Lappic; Saamish; Same; Samis

Lapps
CIJE: 2 RIE: 7 CAT: 08
SN See also "Skolt Lapps"
UF Saami; Sami People

Laptop Computers
CIJE: 16 RIE: 6 CAT: 04

Laramie County School District Number 1 WY
CIJE: 0 RIE: 1 CAT: 17

Laredo Junior College TX
CIJE: 0 RIE: 3 CAT: 17

Large Families
CIJE: 0 RIE: 1 CAT: 10

Large Scale Assessment
CIJE: 1 RIE: 0 CAT: 21

Large Scale Programs
CIJE: 16 RIE: 32 CAT: 19

Large Scale Writing Assessment
CIJE: 0 RIE: 1 CAT: 21

Large School Districts
CIJE: 2 RIE: 6 CAT: 05

Large Schools
CIJE: 2 RIE: 2 CAT: 05

Large Spaced Paper
USE Wide Spaced Paper

Lari v California
CIJE: 1 RIE: 0 CAT: 14

Larkin (Philip)
CIJE: 3 RIE: 0 CAT: 18

Larmor (Joseph)
CIJE: 1 RIE: 0 CAT: 18

Larons Dwarfism
CIJE: 1 RIE: 0 CAT: 11

Larra (Mariano Jose de)
CIJE: 3 RIE: 0 CAT: 18

Larreta (Enrique)
CIJE: 1 RIE: 0 CAT: 18

Larry P v Riles
CIJE: 14 RIE: 9 CAT: 14

Larvae
CIJE: 3 RIE: 1 CAT: 20

Laryngectomees
CIJE: 15 RIE: 1 CAT: 16

Larynx
CIJE: 9 RIE: 1 CAT: 11

Las Casas (Bartolome de)
CIJE: 1 RIE: 1 CAT: 18

Las Cruces Public Schools NM
CIJE: 0 RIE: 5 CAT: 17

Las Cruces Teacher Center NM
CIJE: 0 RIE: 1 CAT: 17

Las Positas College CA
CIJE: 0 RIE: 3 CAT: 17

Las Virgenes Unified School District
CIJE: 1 RIE: 0 CAT: 17

LaSalle (Donald P)
CIJE: 1 RIE: 0 CAT: 18
UF La Salle (Donald)

Laser Learning Project MI
CIJE: 0 RIE: 1 CAT: 19

Laser Printers
CIJE: 4 RIE: 1 CAT: 04

LaserCat
CIJE: 0 RIE: 1 CAT: 04

Laspeyres Formula
CIJE: 1 RIE: 0 CAT: 21

Lassen Community College District CA
CIJE: 0 RIE: 1 CAT: 17

LASSI
USE Learning and Study Strategies Inventory

Lasswell (Harold D)
CIJE: 4 RIE: 1 CAT: 18

Last Born
CIJE: 1 RIE: 0 CAT: 10

Last Day of School Activities
CIJE: 1 RIE: 0 CAT: 16

Last Tango in Paris
CIJE: 1 RIE: 0 CAT: 22

Last Temptation of Christ (The)
CIJE: 0 RIE: 0 CAT: 22

Lasting Benefits Study TN
CIJE: 0 RIE: 6 CAT: 19

Latchaw Motor Achievement Test
CIJE: 0 RIE: 1 CAT: 21

Late Entry Students
CIJE: 0 RIE: 1 CAT: 10

Late Infantile Lipidosis
CIJE: 1 RIE: 0 CAT: 11

Late Parenthood
CIJE: 1 RIE: 1 CAT: 11

Late Positive Component (EEG)
CIJE: 0 RIE: 1 CAT: 11

Latency Age Children
CIJE: 3 RIE: 3 CAT: 10

Latent Ability Distributions
CIJE: 0 RIE: 1 CAT: 21

Latent Class Analysis
CIJE: 20 RIE: 2 CAT: 15

Latent Class Models
CIJE: 24 RIE: 10 CAT: 15

Latent Partition Analysis
CIJE: 8 RIE: 4 CAT: 15

Latent Space
CIJE: 0 RIE: 1 CAT: 21

Latent Structure Analysis
CIJE: 6 RIE: 12 CAT: 15

Latent Structure Models
CIJE: 10 RIE: 2 CAT: 15

Latent Variables
CIJE: 37 RIE: 8 CAT: 21

Lateral Awareness
CIJE: 0 RIE: 3 CAT: 11

Lateral Differences
CIJE: 2 RIE: 0 CAT: 15

Lateral Entry
CIJE: 1 RIE: 1 CAT: 15

Lateral Preference
CIJE: 4 RIE: 2 CAT: 11

Lateral Thinking
CIJE: 4 RIE: 2 CAT: 11

Lateral Transfer Students
CIJE: 1 RIE: 2 CAT: 10

Laterality Discrimination Test (Culver et al)
CIJE: 1 RIE: 0 CAT: 21

Latham (Jean Lee)
CIJE: 1 RIE: 0 CAT: 18

Lathes
CIJE: 0 RIE: 2 CAT: 04

Lathrop E Smith Environmental Education Center MD
CIJE: 0 RIE: 2 CAT: 17

Latin A Structural Approach
CIJE: 1 RIE: 1 CAT: 03

Latin America
CIJE: 387 RIE: 556 CAT: 07

Latin American Curriculum Project
CIJE: 2 RIE: 5 CAT: 19

Latin American Literacy Project
CIJE: 0 RIE: 1 CAT: 19

Latin American Network for Documentation in Educ
USE REDUC

Latin American Scholarship Prog of Amer Univs
CIJE: 0 RIE: 2 CAT: 19

Latin American Studies
CIJE: 5 RIE: 15 CAT: 03

Latin School of Chicago IL
CIJE: 2 RIE: 0 CAT: 17

Latin Squares
CIJE: 1 RIE: 4 CAT: 20

Latinas
CIJE: 1 RIE: 3 CAT: 08

Latino Youth Acculturation Scale
CIJE: 0 RIE: 1 CAT: 21

Latinos
CIJE: 51 RIE: 136 CAT: 08

Latitude
CIJE: 5 RIE: 3 CAT: 20

Lattice Theory
CIJE: 2 RIE: 0 CAT: 15

Latvian Americans
CIJE: 1 RIE: 0 CAT: 08

Lau Center
CIJE: 0 RIE: 1 CAT: 17

Lau Decision
USE Lau v Nichols

Lau Program TX
CIJE: 0 RIE: 1 CAT: 19

Lau Remedies
CIJE: 4 RIE: 4 CAT: 14

Lau Remedies 1975
CIJE: 1 RIE: 4 CAT: 14

Lau v Nichols
CIJE: 22 RIE: 59 CAT: 14
UF Lau Decision

Laubach (Frank C)
CIJE: 0 RIE: 2 CAT: 18

Laubach Literacy Action
CIJE: 1 RIE: 8 CAT: 17

Laubach Literacy Inc
CIJE: 0 RIE: 1 CAT: 17

Laubach Literacy International
CIJE: 5 RIE: 2 CAT: 17

Laubach Literacy Method
USE Laubach Method

Laubach Method
CIJE: 2 RIE: 19 CAT: 15
UF Laubach Literacy Method

Laubach Streamlined Series
CIJE: 0 RIE: 1 CAT: 22

Laubach Way to Reading Series
CIJE: 1 RIE: 1 CAT: 22

Lauder Institute of Management Internatl Studies
CIJE: 0 RIE: 2 CAT: 17
SN ...of the University of Pennsylvania
UF Joseph Lauder Institute PA

Laughing Boy (La Farge)
CIJE: 0 RIE: 1 CAT: 22

Laughter
CIJE: 15 RIE: 8 CAT: 16

Laundry Skills
CIJE: 3 RIE: 0 CAT: 16

Laurel High School PA
CIJE: 1 RIE: 0 CAT: 17

Laurelton Self Concept Scale
CIJE: 0 RIE: 2 CAT: 21

Laurence Moon Biedl Syndrome
CIJE: 1 RIE: 0 CAT: 11

Laurendeau (Monique)
CIJE: 0 RIE: 1 CAT: 21

Laurentian University ON
CIJE: 2 RIE: 2 CAT: 17

Laval University (Canada)
CIJE: 3 RIE: 5 CAT: 17

LaValle Bill
CIJE: 1 RIE: 1 CAT: 14

Lavandera (Beatriz)
CIJE: 0 RIE: 1 CAT: 18

Lavender University CA
CIJE: 1 RIE: 0 CAT: 17

Lavin (Richard J)
CIJE: 0 RIE: 1 CAT: 18

Lavoisier (Antoine Laurent)
CIJE: 1 RIE: 0 CAT: 18

Law and Poverty Project
CIJE: 0 RIE: 1 CAT: 19

Law Clerks
CIJE: 1 RIE: 1 CAT: 09

Law Concept Inventory
CIJE: 1 RIE: 0 CAT: 21

Law Day
CIJE: 4 RIE: 8 CAT: 12

Law Education Goals And Learnings
USE Project LEGAL

Law Encounter Severity Scale
CIJE: 0 RIE: 3 CAT: 21

Law Enforcement Agencies
CIJE: 1 RIE: 2 CAT: 05

Law Enforcement Assistance Administration
CIJE: 0 RIE: 15 CAT: 17

Law Enforcement Education Program
CIJE: 2 RIE: 8 CAT: 19

Law Focus Curriculum Project
CIJE: 0 RIE: 1 CAT: 19

Law in a Free Society Project
CIJE: 7 RIE: 5 CAT: 19

Law in American Society Project
CIJE: 9 RIE: 2 CAT: 19

Law in the Social Studies Project
CIJE: 0 RIE: 1 CAT: 19

Law of the Sea Convention
CIJE: 1 RIE: 1 CAT: 14

Law Offices
CIJE: 0 RIE: 1 CAT: 05

Law Related Education Evaluation Project
CIJE: 0 RIE: 1 CAT: 19

Law Review
CIJE: 7 RIE: 1 CAT: 16

Learning Assessment Retention Consortium CA
CIJE: 0 RIE: 4 CAT: 17

Learning Assistance
CIJE: 5 RIE: 5 CAT: 15

Learning Assistance Centers
CIJE: 0 RIE: 5 CAT: 05

Learning Capacities Approach
CIJE: 1 RIE: 1 CAT: 15

Learning Center for Anthropology
CIJE: 1 RIE: 0 CAT: 17

Learning Center Program HI
CIJE: 0 RIE: 1 CAT: 19

Learning Centers Robbinsdale MN
CIJE: 1 RIE: 0 CAT: 17

Learning Communities
CIJE: 12 RIE: 17 CAT: 15

Learning Curves
CIJE: 7 RIE: 5 CAT: 15

Learning Cycle Teaching Method
CIJE: 0 RIE: 3 CAT: 15

Learning Development Program
CIJE: 0 RIE: 1 CAT: 19

Learning Disabilities Research Institutes
CIJE: 0 RIE: 1 CAT: 05

Learning Disabilities Transition Project MN
USE LD Transition Project MN

Learning Disabled College Writers Project
CIJE: 0 RIE: 6 CAT: 19

Learning Earning and Parenting Program OH
CIJE: 0 RIE: 3 CAT: 19
UF LEAP Program OH

Learning Efficiency Test
CIJE: 2 RIE: 1 CAT: 21

Learning Efficiency Test II
CIJE: 0 RIE: 1 CAT: 21

Learning English through Intergeneratl Friendship
USE Project LEIF

Learning Environment
CIJE: 97 RIE: 56 CAT: 16

Learning Environment Desire Enhance Reading Skills
CIJE: 1 RIE: 0 CAT: 21

Learning Environment Inventory
CIJE: 7 RIE: 5 CAT: 21

Learning Environment Inventory (Anderson et al)
CIJE: 19 RIE: 13 CAT: 21

Learning Environment Inventory for Young Children
CIJE: 0 RIE: 1 CAT: 21

Learning Environments
CIJE: 97 RIE: 36 CAT: 16

Learning Exchange Networks
CIJE: 2 RIE: 2 CAT: 05

Learning Experience Approach
CIJE: 3 RIE: 7 CAT: 15

Learning Experience Module
CIJE: 1 RIE: 1 CAT: 15

Learning for Everyday Living
CIJE: 0 RIE: 5 CAT: 19

Learning for Leadership Program
CIJE: 0 RIE: 1 CAT: 19

Learning from Text Project CA
CIJE: 0 RIE: 2 CAT: 19

Learning Groups
CIJE: 5 RIE: 4 CAT: 10

Learning Hierarchies
CIJE: 39 RIE: 24 CAT: 15

Learning House Tutorial Center
CIJE: 0 RIE: 1 CAT: 17

Learning Impasses
CIJE: 0 RIE: 1 CAT: 16

Learning in Retirement Programs
CIJE: 0 RIE: 1 CAT: 19

Learning in Science Project
CIJE: 4 RIE: 51 CAT: 19

Learning in Science Project (Primary)
CIJE: 0 RIE: 24 CAT: 19

Learning in Transit
CIJE: 1 RIE: 0 CAT: 15

Learning Individualized for Canadians
CIJE: 0 RIE: 3 CAT: 15

Learning Information Exchanges
CIJE: 0 RIE: 2 CAT: 05

Learning Information Networks
CIJE: 0 RIE: 0 CAT: 05

Learning Initiative Teams
CIJE: 0 RIE: 1 CAT: 10

Learning Institute of North Carolina
CIJE: 0 RIE: 3 CAT: 17

Learning Living Information Exchange
CIJE: 0 RIE: 1 CAT: 17

Learning Mastery Systems
CIJE: 0 RIE: 14 CAT: 15

Learning Materials Center
CIJE: 1 RIE: 0 CAT: 17

Learning Organizations
CIJE: 6 RIE: 3 CAT: 10

Learning Partners
CIJE: 1 RIE: 1 CAT: 15
UF Learning Partnerships

Learning Partnerships
USE Learning Partners

Learning Patterns
CIJE: 7 RIE: 3 CAT: 16

Learning Potential Assessment Device
CIJE: 17 RIE: 7 CAT: 21

Learning Potential Tests
CIJE: 1 RIE: 1 CAT: 21

Learning Preference Inventory
CIJE: 3 RIE: 3 CAT: 21

Learning Preference Scale (Students)
CIJE: 0 RIE: 0 CAT: 21

Learning Process Questionnaire (Biggs)
CIJE: 0 RIE: 2 CAT: 21
UF Biggs Learning Process Questionnaire

Learning Productivity Model
CIJE: 0 RIE: 2 CAT: 15

Learning Project Interview
CIJE: 0 RIE: 1 CAT: 15

Learning Referral Centers
CIJE: 0 RIE: 2 CAT: 05

Learning Research and Development Center
CIJE: 1 RIE: 25 CAT: 17

Learning Research Associates
CIJE: 0 RIE: 2 CAT: 17

Learning Resource Aided Instruction
CIJE: 0 RIE: 1 CAT: 15

Learning Resource Program
CIJE: 0 RIE: 1 CAT: 19

Learning Resource Support Program
CIJE: 1 RIE: 0 CAT: 19

Learning Segments
CIJE: 0 RIE: 1 CAT: 15

Learning Sets
CIJE: 2 RIE: 1 CAT: 11

Learning Skills Services
CIJE: 0 RIE: 1 CAT: 19

Learning Society
CIJE: 1 RIE: 2 CAT: 16

Learning Starters
CIJE: 1 RIE: 0 CAT: 15

Learning Strategies Questionnaire
CIJE: 0 RIE: 1 CAT: 21

Learning Strategy Inventory (Dansereau)
CIJE: 0 RIE: 1 CAT: 21

Learning Style Inventory
CIJE: 38 RIE: 25 CAT: 21

Learning Style Inventory (Kolb)
CIJE: 17 RIE: 6 CAT: 21

Learning Style Preference Checklist
CIJE: 0 RIE: 1 CAT: 21

Learning Style Profile (NASSP)
CIJE: 4 RIE: 13 CAT: 21
UF NASSP Learning Style Profile

Learning Styles Inventory
CIJE: 14 RIE: 11 CAT: 21

Learning Styles Inventory (Canfield)
USE Canfield Learning Styles Inventory

Learning Styles Inventory (Renzulli and Smith)
CIJE: 0 RIE: 2 CAT: 21

Learning Systems
CIJE: 24 RIE: 3 CAT: 15

Learning Through Discussion
CIJE: 2 RIE: 2 CAT: 15

Learning Through Teaching
CIJE: 3 RIE: 4 CAT: 15

Learning to Be
CIJE: 6 RIE: 0 CAT: 15

Learning to Read
CIJE: 3 RIE: 0 CAT: 15

Learning to Read and Spell
CIJE: 1 RIE: 2 CAT: 15

Learning to Read Through the Arts Program
CIJE: 3 RIE: 13 CAT: 19

Learning to See
CIJE: 2 RIE: 0 CAT: 15

Learning Together PA
CIJE: 0 RIE: 1 CAT: 19
SN "Learning Together: An Interactive Approach to Tutor Training"

Learning Tomorrow Project
CIJE: 0 RIE: 2 CAT: 19

Learning Tree
CIJE: 1 RIE: 1 CAT: 15

Learning Unlimited IN
CIJE: 0 RIE: 1 CAT: 17

Learning Village
CIJE: 1 RIE: 0 CAT: 17

Learning Webs
CIJE: 1 RIE: 3 CAT: 15

Learning Works Program
CIJE: 0 RIE: 1 CAT: 19

LEARNIT (Computer Program)
CIJE: 1 RIE: 0 CAT: 04

Leary Interpersonal Checklist
CIJE: 4 RIE: 1 CAT: 21

LEASE Project
CIJE: 0 RIE: 1 CAT: 19

Lease Purchase Agreements
CIJE: 3 RIE: 1 CAT: 16

Leasing
CIJE: 18 RIE: 10 CAT: 16

Least Absolute Value Statistics
CIJE: 2 RIE: 0 CAT: 21

Least Effort Principle
CIJE: 1 RIE: 0 CAT: 15

Least Principal Components Analysis
CIJE: 0 RIE: 1 CAT: 15

Least Prompts
CIJE: 2 RIE: 0 CAT: 15
UF System of Least Prompts

Least Restrictive Means Test (First Amendment)
CIJE: 0 RIE: 1 CAT: 14

Leave Sharing
CIJE: 0 RIE: 1 CAT: 16

Leaves (Trees)
CIJE: 1 RIE: 1 CAT: 20

Leaves of Grass
CIJE: 0 RIE: 1 CAT: 22

Leaving Behavior
CIJE: 4 RIE: 1 CAT: 11

Leavis (F R)
CIJE: 5 RIE: 1 CAT: 18

Lebanese
CIJE: 6 RIE: 2 CAT: 08

Lebanon
CIJE: 46 RIE: 24 CAT: 07

Lebanon (Beirut)
CIJE: 7 RIE: 0 CAT: 07

Lebanon Correctional Institution OH
CIJE: 0 RIE: 1 CAT: 17

Lebanon High School MO
CIJE: 1 RIE: 0 CAT: 17

Lechatelier Principle
CIJE: 8 RIE: 1 CAT: 20

Lecithin
CIJE: 1 RIE: 0 CAT: 11

Lecture Characteristics Scale
CIJE: 0 RIE: 1 CAT: 21

Lecturers
CIJE: 5 RIE: 6 CAT: 09

Lee (Don L)
CIJE: 2 RIE: 0 CAT: 18

Lee (George Winthrop)
CIJE: 1 RIE: 0 CAT: 18

Lee (Ivy)
CIJE: 1 RIE: 1 CAT: 18

Lee (Mollie Huston)
CIJE: 1 RIE: 0 CAT: 18

Lee (Robert E)
CIJE: 1 RIE: 0 CAT: 18

Lee (Spike)
CIJE: 0 RIE: 1 CAT: 18

Lee Clark Reading Readiness Test
CIJE: 1 RIE: 13 CAT: 21

Lee Clark Reading Test
CIJE: 1 RIE: 2 CAT: 21

Lee College TX
CIJE: 1 RIE: 3 CAT: 17

Lee County School District FL
CIJE: 0 RIE: 1 CAT: 17

Lee Mental Health Center FL
CIJE: 0 RIE: 1 CAT: 17

Lee v Weisman
CIJE: 11 RIE: 0 CAT: 14

Leech Lake Reservation MN
CIJE: 0 RIE: 1 CAT: 17

Leeds and Northrup Development Institute
CIJE: 1 RIE: 0 CAT: 17

Leeds Polytechnic (England)
CIJE: 2 RIE: 0 CAT: 17

Leeds University (England)
USE University of Leeds (England)

Lees Developmental Sentence Types
CIJE: 0 RIE: 1 CAT: 13

Leeuwenhoek (Anton van)
CIJE: 1 RIE: 0 CAT: 18

Leeward Community College HI
USE University of Hawaii Leeward Community College

Leflore County Schools MS
CIJE: 0 RIE: 1 CAT: 17

Left Book Club
CIJE: 1 RIE: 0 CAT: 17

Left Modifier Grouping
CIJE: 0 RIE: 1 CAT: 13

Left Right Discrimination
CIJE: 7 RIE: 2 CAT: 11

Left Ventricle
CIJE: 0 RIE: 1 CAT: 11

Leg Ergometry
USE Ergometry

Leg Strength
CIJE: 2 RIE: 2 CAT: 11

Legal Audits
CIJE: 2 RIE: 1 CAT: 14

Legal Clinics
CIJE: 1 RIE: 1 CAT: 14

Legal Community
CIJE: 1 RIE: 3 CAT: 14

Legal Defense Fund
CIJE: 3 RIE: 0 CAT: 17

Legal Deposit
CIJE: 0 RIE: 3 CAT: 14

Legal Drinking Age
CIJE: 5 RIE: 3 CAT: 14
UF Drinking Age

Legal History
CIJE: 12 RIE: 10 CAT: 12

Legal Information
CIJE: 41 RIE: 28 CAT: 14

Legal Language
CIJE: 10 RIE: 12 CAT: 13

Legal Precedents
CIJE: 4 RIE: 6 CAT: 14

Legal Procedures
CIJE: 3 RIE: 0 CAT: 14

Legal Reference Materials
CIJE: 14 RIE: 7 CAT: 14

Legal Research
CIJE: 37 RIE: 21 CAT: 14

Legal Rights
CIJE: 14 RIE: 11 CAT: 14

Legal Status
CIJE: 6 RIE: 8 CAT: 14

Legal Structures
CIJE: 1 RIE: 5 CAT: 14

Legal Vocabulary
CIJE: 7 RIE: 6 CAT: 13

Legal Writing
CIJE: 16 RIE: 8 CAT: 13

Legalization (Educational Governance)
CIJE: 1 RIE: 1 CAT: 14

Legibility
CIJE: 12 RIE: 8 CAT: 16

Legislated Learning
CIJE: 0 RIE: 1 CAT: 14

Legislative Commission on Expenditure Review
CIJE: 0 RIE: 1 CAT: 17

Legislative Drafting
CIJE: 2 RIE: 0 CAT: 14

Legislative History
CIJE: 9 RIE: 25 CAT: 12

Legislative Intent
CIJE: 3 RIE: 5 CAT: 14

Legislative Reform
CIJE: 1 RIE: 1 CAT: 14

Legislative Research
CIJE: 0 RIE: 1 CAT: 15

Legislative Sessions
CIJE: 1 RIE: 2 CAT: 14

Legislative Teleconference Network AK
CIJE: 0 RIE: 1 CAT: 17

Legislative Voting
CIJE: 1 RIE: 2 CAT: 14

Legitimacy (of Governments)
CIJE: 1 RIE: 1 CAT: 14
SN See also "Political Legitimacy"

Legitimacy (of Programs)
USE Program Legitimacy

Legitimate Peripheral Participation
CIJE: 0 RIE: 1 CAT: 15

Legs
CIJE: 1 RIE: 1 CAT: 11

Lehigh County Community College PA
CIJE: 1 RIE: 9 CAT: 17

Lehigh University PA
CIJE: 25 RIE: 11 CAT: 17

Lehigh Workshop on Poetry for Children
CIJE: 1 RIE: 0 CAT: 02

Lehman College NY
USE City University of New York Lehman College

Leicester Junior College MA
CIJE: 0 RIE: 1 CAT: 17

Leicestershire County Schools (England)
CIJE: 1 RIE: 2 CAT: 17

Leiden Student Corps (Netherlands)
CIJE: 1 RIE: 0 CAT: 17

Leisure Activities
CIJE: 21 RIE: 5 CAT: 16

Leisure Activity Survey
CIJE: 2 RIE: 2 CAT: 21

Leisure Attitudes
CIJE: 9 RIE: 3 CAT: 16

Leisure Behavior Inventory
CIJE: 1 RIE: 0 CAT: 21

Leisure Ethic
CIJE: 3 RIE: 1 CAT: 15

Leisure Needs
CIJE: 2 RIE: 1 CAT: 16

Leisure Services
CIJE: 3 RIE: 9 CAT: 09

Leiter Adult Intelligence Scale
CIJE: 2 RIE: 0 CAT: 21

Leiter International Performance Scale
CIJE: 14 RIE: 8 CAT: 21

Lekotek Method
USE Lekoteks

Lekoteks
CIJE: 2 RIE: 2 CAT: 05
SN Play libraries that serve as resource centers for children with disabilities and their families
UF Lekotek Method

Lelemi
USE Buem

Lemon DiCenso Decision
CIJE: 1 RIE: 0 CAT: 14

Lemon v Kurtzman
CIJE: 9 RIE: 2 CAT: 14

LeMoyne College TN
CIJE: 0 RIE: 1 CAT: 17

LeMoyne Owen College TN
CIJE: 0 RIE: 1 CAT: 17
UF Le Moyne Owen Coll TN

Lenape
CIJE: 0 RIE: 0 CAT: 13

Lenape (Tribe)
CIJE: 4 RIE: 2 CAT: 08

Lend Me Your Ears
CIJE: 0 RIE: 1 CAT: 03

Lenders (Finance)
CIJE: 0 RIE: 2 CAT: 09

Length
CIJE: 18 RIE: 5 CAT: 16

Length of Hospital Stay
CIJE: 1 RIE: 1 CAT: 11
UF Length of Hospitalization

Length of Hospitalization
USE Length of Hospital Stay

Length of Placement
CIJE: 1 RIE: 0 CAT: 16
UF Length of Placement in Foster Care

Length of Placement in Foster Care
USE Length of Placement

Length of Residence
CIJE: 9 RIE: 5 CAT: 16

Length of Stain Gas Indicator
CIJE: 0 RIE: 1 CAT: 04

Length of Utterance
CIJE: 6 RIE: 4 CAT: 13

Leniency (Tests)
CIJE: 2 RIE: 0 CAT: 21

Leniency Response Bias
CIJE: 7 RIE: 3 CAT: 21

Lenin (Vladimir)
CIJE: 23 RIE: 5 CAT: 18

Lenin Library (USSR)
CIJE: 2 RIE: 2 CAT: 17

Leningrad Institute Railway Trans Engineers (USSR)
CIJE: 0 RIE: 1 CAT: 17

Leningrad University (USSR)
CIJE: 2 RIE: 1 CAT: 17

Leninism
CIJE: 8 RIE: 2 CAT: 16

Lenneberg (Eric)
CIJE: 2 RIE: 0 CAT: 18

Lennox High School CA
CIJE: 0 RIE: 1 CAT: 17

Lennox Industries Inc
CIJE: 0 RIE: 1 CAT: 17

Lenoir City Public Schools TN
CIJE: 0 RIE: 1 CAT: 17

Lenoir Community College NC
CIJE: 0 RIE: 1 CAT: 17

Lenoir Rhyne College NC
CIJE: 3 RIE: 3 CAT: 17

Lens Model Analysis
CIJE: 3 RIE: 1 CAT: 15

Lentczner v Yorktown High School
CIJE: 0 RIE: 1 CAT: 14

Leominster Public School System MA
CIJE: 0 RIE: 1 CAT: 17

Leon County School District FL
CIJE: 2 RIE: 7 CAT: 17

Leonard (George)
CIJE: 0 RIE: 1 CAT: 18

Leonard (Sterling)
CIJE: 0 RIE: 1 CAT: 18

Leonardo da Vinci Society
CIJE: 0 RIE: 1 CAT: 17

Leontief Input Output System
CIJE: 1 RIE: 0 CAT: 15

Leopardi (Giacomo)
CIJE: 1 RIE: 0 CAT: 18

Leopold (Werner F)
CIJE: 0 RIE: 1 CAT: 18

Leoti Community Services KS
CIJE: 0 RIE: 1 CAT: 17

Leprosy
CIJE: 1 RIE: 4 CAT: 11

Lerdahl (Fred)
CIJE: 0 RIE: 1 CAT: 18

Lesbian Literature
CIJE: 1 RIE: 0 CAT: 16

Lesch Nyhan Syndrome
CIJE: 7 RIE: 2 CAT: 11

Leskov (Nicolai)
CIJE: 1 RIE: 0 CAT: 18

Lesley College MA
CIJE: 6 RIE: 4 CAT: 17

Leslie Bureau of Suffrage Education NY
CIJE: 0 RIE: 1 CAT: 17

Lesotho
CIJE: 15 RIE: 28 CAT: 07

Less than Two Year Postsecondary Institutions
CIJE: 0 RIE: 0 CAT: 05

Lessing (Doris)
CIJE: 4 RIE: 2 CAT: 18

Lessing (Gotthold Ephraim)
CIJE: 3 RIE: 0 CAT: 18

Lessinger (Leon)
CIJE: 2 RIE: 1 CAT: 18

Lesson Structure
CIJE: 4 RIE: 9 CAT: 15

Lesson Types
CIJE: 0 RIE: 2 CAT: 16

Lessonware
CIJE: 0 RIE: 0 CAT: 04

Lester (Julius)
CIJE: 2 RIE: 0 CAT: 18

Lester (Richard)
CIJE: 1 RIE: 0 CAT: 18

Lester Hill Corporation
CIJE: 1 RIE: 0 CAT: 17

Lesy (Michael)
CIJE: 1 RIE: 0 CAT: 18

Let Me See (Television Series)
CIJE: 0 RIE: 1 CAT: 22

Lethbridge Catholic Separate School District 9 AB
CIJE: 0 RIE: 1 CAT: 17

Lethbridge Community College AB
CIJE: 0 RIE: 0 CAT: 17

Lethbridge School District AB
CIJE: 0 RIE: 2 CAT: 17

Lets Be Amigos Program
CIJE: 0 RIE: 1 CAT: 19

Lets Be Social Home Program
CIJE: 0 RIE: 1 CAT: 19

Letter Detection
USE Letter Recognition

Letter Naming
USE Letter Recognition

Letter Opening Operators
CIJE: 0 RIE: 1 CAT: 09

Letter Recognition
CIJE: 2 RIE: 0 CAT: 13
UF Letter Detection; Letter Naming

Letter Right Communication System
CIJE: 1 RIE: 0 CAT: 15

Letterforms
CIJE: 4 RIE: 1 CAT: 16

Letterman (David)
CIJE: 1 RIE: 1 CAT: 18

Letterman Army Medical Center CA
CIJE: 1 RIE: 0 CAT: 17

Letters of Recommendation
CIJE: 42 RIE: 5 CAT: 16

Letters to the Editor
CIJE: 6 RIE: 11 CAT: 16

Leucine
CIJE: 1 RIE: 0 CAT: 20

Leukemia
CIJE: 19 RIE: 3 CAT: 11

Leupp Boarding School AZ
CIJE: 0 RIE: 3 CAT: 17

Lev (J)
CIJE: 0 RIE: 1 CAT: 18

Level of Aspiration Indicator
CIJE: 1 RIE: 0 CAT: 21

Level of Aspiration Test (Pierce Jones)
CIJE: 0 RIE: 1 CAT: 21

Level of Parent Involvement Questionnaire
CIJE: 0 RIE: 1 CAT: 21
UF AEL Level of Parent Involvement Questionnaire

Level of Supervision Inventory
CIJE: 0 RIE: 1 CAT: 21

Leveling Sharpening Dimension
CIJE: 1 RIE: 2 CAT: 15

Leveling Sharpening House Test
CIJE: 0 RIE: 1 CAT: 21

Levels of Consciousness
CIJE: 9 RIE: 2 CAT: 11
UF Consciousness Levels

Levels of Processing
CIJE: 9 RIE: 5 CAT: 11
UF Processing Levels

Levels of Use of the Innovation
CIJE: 3 RIE: 18 CAT: 21

Levels of Use Scale (Hall and Louck)
CIJE: 0 RIE: 4 CAT: 21

Levenstein Toy Demonstration Program
CIJE: 0 RIE: 2 CAT: 19

Levers
CIJE: 5 RIE: 1 CAT: 20

Levertov (Denise)
CIJE: 2 RIE: 1 CAT: 18

Levertov Machine
CIJE: 0 RIE: 1 CAT: 15

Levi Strauss (Claude)
CIJE: 9 RIE: 3 CAT: 18

Levin (Ira)
CIJE: 1 RIE: 0 CAT: 18

Levin (Meyer)
CIJE: 1 RIE: 0 CAT: 18

Levine (Arthur)
CIJE: 0 RIE: 1 CAT: 18

Levine (M)
CIJE: 1 RIE: 0 CAT: 18

Levine Equating Method
CIJE: 13 RIE: 5 CAT: 15

Levinson (Daniel J)
CIJE: 1 RIE: 3 CAT: 18

Levinson (Daniel)
CIJE: 1 RIE: 2 CAT: 18

Levinson Research Foundation
CIJE: 0 RIE: 1 CAT: 17

Levitan (Sar)
CIJE: 1 RIE: 0 CAT: 18

Levittown v Nyquist
CIJE: 5 RIE: 3 CAT: 14

Lewin (Kurt)
CIJE: 15 RIE: 12 CAT: 18

Lewis (C S)
CIJE: 5 RIE: 3 CAT: 18

Lewis (D)
CIJE: 0 RIE: 1 CAT: 18

Lewis (Elma)
CIJE: 1 RIE: 0 CAT: 18

Lewis (George H)
CIJE: 0 RIE: 0 CAT: 18

Lewis (Jerry)
CIJE: 0 RIE: 1 CAT: 18

Lewis (Oscar)
CIJE: 0 RIE: 1 CAT: 18

Lewis (Sinclair)
CIJE: 2 RIE: 1 CAT: 18

Lewis (W Arthur)
CIJE: 0 RIE: 1 CAT: 18

Lewis Acids
CIJE: 1 RIE: 0 CAT: 20

Lewis and Clark College OR
CIJE: 10 RIE: 12 CAT: 17

Lewis and Clark Community College IL
CIJE: 1 RIE: 1 CAT: 17

Lewis Clark State College ID
CIJE: 1 RIE: 5 CAT: 17

Lewis County Project
CIJE: 0 RIE: 1 CAT: 19

Lewis Structures
CIJE: 4 RIE: 0 CAT: 20

Lewis University IL
CIJE: 0 RIE: 4 CAT: 17

Lewiston Alternative Vocational Center ME
CIJE: 0 RIE: 1 CAT: 17

Lewiston Independent School District ID
CIJE: 0 RIE: 1 CAT: 17

Lexical Access
CIJE: 10 RIE: 3 CAT: 13

Lexical Ambiguity
CIJE: 3 RIE: 2 CAT: 13

Lexical Availability
CIJE: 2 RIE: 1 CAT: 13

Lexical Collocation
CIJE: 0 RIE: 2 CAT: 13
UF Collocations (Lexical Items)

Lexical Decomposition Strategy
CIJE: 0 RIE: 1 CAT: 13
SN Process for defining unfamiliar words

Lexical Density
CIJE: 2 RIE: 0 CAT: 13

Lexical Functional Grammar
CIJE: 0 RIE: 1 CAT: 13

Lexical Semantics
CIJE: 12 RIE: 4 CAT: 13

Lexical Storage
CIJE: 2 RIE: 0 CAT: 13

Lexicographic Preferences
CIJE: 1 RIE: 2 CAT: 13

Lexicometry
CIJE: 0 RIE: 1 CAT: 13

Lexile Scale of Reading
CIJE: 1 RIE: 0 CAT: 21

Lexington Clinical Research Center KY
CIJE: 1 RIE: 0 CAT: 17

Lexington Development Scale
CIJE: 0 RIE: 1 CAT: 15

Lexington Local School District OH
CIJE: 0 RIE: 1 CAT: 17

Lexington Nursery and Kindergarten School
CIJE: 1 RIE: 0 CAT: 17

Lexington School for the Deaf NY
CIJE: 4 RIE: 4 CAT: 17

LEXIS System
CIJE: 14 RIE: 4 CAT: 04

Lexivisions
CIJE: 0 RIE: 1 CAT: 15

Leyh (George)
CIJE: 0 RIE: 1 CAT: 18

Lezama Lima (Jose)
CIJE: 4 RIE: 0 CAT: 18

Lezotte (Larry)
CIJE: 1 RIE: 1 CAT: 18

LF Movement
CIJE: 0 RIE: 1 CAT: 13

Liability Insurance
CIJE: 10 RIE: 8 CAT: 16

Liaison Administrators
CIJE: 1 RIE: 2 CAT: 09

Liaison Approach (Psychology)
CIJE: 1 RIE: 0 CAT: 15

Liaison Committee on Medical Education
CIJE: 3 RIE: 1 CAT: 17

Liaison Teacher Counselors
CIJE: 0 RIE: 1 CAT: 09

Liaison Teacher Program
CIJE: 1 RIE: 0 CAT: 19

Liaison Teacher Returnee Counselor Project
CIJE: 0 RIE: 1 CAT: 19

Liangong Exercises
CIJE: 0 RIE: 1 CAT: 11

Liard (Louis)
CIJE: 1 RIE: 0 CAT: 18

Liberal Arts Colleges
CIJE: 10 RIE: 8 CAT: 05

Liberal Radicalism
CIJE: 1 RIE: 1 CAT: 15

Liberal Studies Program
CIJE: 1 RIE: 1 CAT: 19

Liberation
CIJE: 20 RIE: 4 CAT: 16

Liberation Theology
CIJE: 8 RIE: 3 CAT: 15

Liberatory Learning
CIJE: 1 RIE: 2 CAT: 15

Liberia
CIJE: 31 RIE: 41 CAT: 07

Libertarian Community
CIJE: 2 RIE: 1 CAT: 16

Liberty Baptist College VA
CIJE: 1 RIE: 4 CAT: 17

Liberty Bell Educational Complex TN
CIJE: 0 RIE: 1 CAT: 17

Liberty High School WA
CIJE: 0 RIE: 1 CAT: 17

Liberty Partnerships Program NY
CIJE: 0 RIE: 1 CAT: 19

Liberty University VA
CIJE: 2 RIE: 2 CAT: 17

Libman (Matthew)
CIJE: 0 RIE: 1 CAT: 18

Librarian Client Behavior
CIJE: 11 RIE: 1 CAT: 16

Librarian Evaluation
CIJE: 9 RIE: 3 CAT: 16

Libraries and the Learning Society
CIJE: 0 RIE: 11 CAT: 19

Libraries of the Missouri Information Network
CIJE: 0 RIE: 2 CAT: 17

Library Access Services
CIJE: 0 RIE: 3 CAT: 05

Library Act 1972 (Great Britain)
CIJE: 2 RIE: 4 CAT: 14

Library Administrative Records
CIJE: 0 RIE: 1 CAT: 16

Library and Information Science Abstracts
CIJE: 17 RIE: 2 CAT: 22
UF LISA

Library and Information Science Today
CIJE: 1 RIE: 0 CAT: 22

Library and Learning Resources Program CA
CIJE: 0 RIE: 1 CAT: 19

Library Archives and Documentation Services
CIJE: 0 RIE: 1 CAT: 17

Library Association of Alberta (Canada)
CIJE: 0 RIE: 1 CAT: 17

Library Association of Australia
CIJE: 7 RIE: 2 CAT: 17

Library Attitudes
CIJE: 0 RIE: 1 CAT: 16
SN Attitudes toward libraries

Library Automation Research and Consulting Assn
CIJE: 0 RIE: 1 CAT: 17

Library Bill of Rights
CIJE: 10 RIE: 11 CAT: 22

Library Binding Institute MA
CIJE: 1 RIE: 1 CAT: 17

Library Buildings Awards Program
CIJE: 3 RIE: 0 CAT: 19

Library Cards
CIJE: 7 RIE: 2 CAT: 04

Library Closings
CIJE: 0 RIE: 1 CAT: 16

Library College Conference 1973
CIJE: 1 RIE: 0 CAT: 02

Library Committees
CIJE: 2 RIE: 3 CAT: 10

Library Computer System
CIJE: 11 RIE: 2 CAT: 04

Library Computer Systems
CIJE: 31 RIE: 5 CAT: 04

Library Construction
CIJE: 0 RIE: 2 CAT: 16

Library Consultants
CIJE: 6 RIE: 1 CAT: 09

Library Directors
CIJE: 42 RIE: 7 CAT: 09

Library Education Experimental Project
CIJE: 0 RIE: 4 CAT: 19

Library Educational Alternatives for Preschoolers
USE Project LEAP OH

Library General Information Survey
CIJE: 1 RIE: 4 CAT: 21

Library Growth
CIJE: 3 RIE: 0 CAT: 16

Library History
CIJE: 15 RIE: 12 CAT: 12

Library Independent Study and Guidance Projects
CIJE: 1 RIE: 0 CAT: 19

Library Information Access Retrieval System
CIJE: 1 RIE: 2 CAT: 15

Library Information Desks
USE Information Desks

Library Information Retrieval System
CIJE: 1 RIE: 1 CAT: 15

Library Inventory
CIJE: 4 RIE: 1 CAT: 21

Library Journal
CIJE: 8 RIE: 1 CAT: 22

Library Journals
CIJE: 5 RIE: 2 CAT: 16

Library Labor Cost Accounting System
CIJE: 0 RIE: 1 CAT: 15

Library Legislation
CIJE: 5 RIE: 2 CAT: 14

Library Literature
CIJE: 55 RIE: 8 CAT: 16

Library Literature (Serial)
CIJE: 0 RIE: 1 CAT: 22

Library Management Information System
CIJE: 1 RIE: 1 CAT: 17

Library Materials Conservation
CIJE: 51 RIE: 22 CAT: 16

Library Moves
CIJE: 0 RIE: 1 CAT: 16

Library of Congress
CIJE: 205 RIE: 197 CAT: 17

Library of Congress Classification
CIJE: 53 RIE: 32 CAT: 15

Library of Congress Subject Headings
CIJE: 60 RIE: 37 CAT: 15

Library of Michigan
CIJE: 0 RIE: 3 CAT: 17
UF Michigan Library

Library Operations
CIJE: 41 RIE: 6 CAT: 16

Library Organization
CIJE: 30 RIE: 1 CAT: 16

Library Orientation Instruction Exchange
CIJE: 4 RIE: 0 CAT: 17

Library Partnerships
USE Partnerships in Library Services

Library Pathfinders
CIJE: 4 RIE: 2 CAT: 16

Library Procedures
CIJE: 9 RIE: 39 CAT: 15

Library Public Services
CIJE: 14 RIE: 5 CAT: 05

Library Publications
CIJE: 3 RIE: 3 CAT: 16

Library Publishing
CIJE: 1 RIE: 1 CAT: 16

Library Quotient
CIJE: 1 RIE: 0 CAT: 21

Library Research and Demonstration Program
CIJE: 2 RIE: 2 CAT: 19

Library Reserve
CIJE: 2 RIE: 1 CAT: 16
SN See also "Reserve Book Collections"

Library Reserve Rooms
USE Reserve Reading Rooms

Library Science Literature
CIJE: 19 RIE: 17 CAT: 16

Library Security
CIJE: 19 RIE: 5 CAT: 16

Library Services and Construction Act
CIJE: 33 RIE: 351 CAT: 14

Library Support Groups
CIJE: 0 RIE: 4 CAT: 10

Library Systems Analysis
CIJE: 4 RIE: 2 CAT: 15

Library Technology Program
CIJE: 2 RIE: 0 CAT: 19

Library Terminology
CIJE: 0 RIE: 1 CAT: 13

Library Tours
CIJE: 1 RIE: 1 CAT: 16

Library User Information Service
CIJE: 1 RIE: 2 CAT: 04

Libya
CIJE: 8 RIE: 37 CAT: 07

License Agreements
CIJE: 42 RIE: 4 CAT: 14

License Fees
CIJE: 5 RIE: 1 CAT: 14

License Plates
CIJE: 2 RIE: 1 CAT: 14

License Plates Test
CIJE: 1 RIE: 0 CAT: 21

License Renewal
CIJE: 0 RIE: 1 CAT: 16
SN See also "Certificate Renewal"

Licensed Parenthood
CIJE: 0 RIE: 1 CAT: 16

Licensed Professional Engineer
CIJE: 3 RIE: 0 CAT: 09

Licensed Programs
CIJE: 3 RIE: 3 CAT: 14

Licensing Programs
CIJE: 5 RIE: 6 CAT: 14

Lichens
CIJE: 8 RIE: 0 CAT: 20

Lick Observatory CA
CIJE: 1 RIE: 0 CAT: 17

Licking County Writing Project OH
CIJE: 0 RIE: 1 CAT: 19

Liddell v Saint Louis Board of Education
CIJE: 0 RIE: 1 CAT: 14

Lie Scale for Children
CIJE: 3 RIE: 2 CAT: 21

Lieberman (Philip)
CIJE: 0 RIE: 1 CAT: 18

Liebig (Justus von)
CIJE: 1 RIE: 0 CAT: 18

Liechtenstein
CIJE: 1 RIE: 1 CAT: 07

Liehow (Elliot)
CIJE: 1 RIE: 0 CAT: 18

Lieven (Dorothea)
CIJE: 1 RIE: 0 CAT: 18

Life Adjustment Movement
CIJE: 0 RIE: 1 CAT: 12

Life Adjustment Program
CIJE: 1 RIE: 0 CAT: 19

Life Career Assessment
CIJE: 0 RIE: 1 CAT: 21

Life Career Game
CIJE: 1 RIE: 5 CAT: 15

Life Centered Career Education
CIJE: 6 RIE: 4 CAT: 03

Life Centered Education
CIJE: 0 RIE: 1 CAT: 03

Life Chances
CIJE: 2 RIE: 18 CAT: 16

Life Change Unit Rating Scale for College Students
CIJE: 1 RIE: 0 CAT: 21

Life Coping Skills
CIJE: 11 RIE: 13 CAT: 16

Life Cycle System Management Model
CIJE: 3 RIE: 6 CAT: 15

Life Cycles
CIJE: 68 RIE: 36 CAT: 16

Life Enhancement Afloat Ashore Program
CIJE: 0 RIE: 1 CAT: 19

Life Enrichment Activity Program
CIJE: 2 RIE: 0 CAT: 19

Life Esteem
CIJE: 0 RIE: 1 CAT: 11

Life Events Academic Performance Questionnaire
CIJE: 0 RIE: 1 CAT: 21

Life Events Checklist
CIJE: 1 RIE: 0 CAT: 21

Life Events Scale
CIJE: 1 RIE: 0 CAT: 21

Life Events Scale Children
CIJE: 0 RIE: 1 CAT: 21

Life Expectancy
CIJE: 28 RIE: 13 CAT: 11

Life Expectancy Inventory (Owens)
CIJE: 0 RIE: 1 CAT: 21

Life Experience Inventory
CIJE: 1 RIE: 0 CAT: 21

Life Experience Studies
CIJE: 3 RIE: 1 CAT: 03

Life Experiences Inc
CIJE: 1 RIE: 0 CAT: 17

Life Experiences Scale
CIJE: 1 RIE: 0 CAT: 21

Life Experiences Survey
CIJE: 2 RIE: 0 CAT: 21

Life Geosystems
CIJE: 1 RIE: 0 CAT: 16

Life Goals
CIJE: 6 RIE: 10 CAT: 11

Life Goals Inventory (Beggs)
CIJE: 0 RIE: 1 CAT: 21

Life History Method
CIJE: 6 RIE: 5 CAT: 15

Life Insurance
CIJE: 6 RIE: 11 CAT: 16

Life Insurance Education
CIJE: 2 RIE: 1 CAT: 03

Life Interpersonal History Enquiry
CIJE: 0 RIE: 1 CAT: 21

Life Involvement Model
CIJE: 0 RIE: 1 CAT: 15

Life Lab Science Program
CIJE: 0 RIE: 1 CAT: 19

Life Magazine
CIJE: 2 RIE: 7 CAT: 22

Life Management Curriculum
CIJE: 1 RIE: 9 CAT: 03

Life Masks
CIJE: 1 RIE: 0 CAT: 16

Life Meaning
CIJE: 0 RIE: 2 CAT: 11

Life Meaning Survey
CIJE: 0 RIE: 1 CAT: 21

Life Office Management Association
CIJE: 1 RIE: 0 CAT: 17

Life Planning
CIJE: 23 RIE: 47 CAT: 15

Life Position
CIJE: 0 RIE: 1 CAT: 11

Life Principles Scale
CIJE: 1 RIE: 0 CAT: 21

Life Review
CIJE: 20 RIE: 9 CAT: 11

Life Review Task
CIJE: 0 RIE: 1 CAT: 21

Life Safety Code
CIJE: 0 RIE: 1 CAT: 14

Life Satisfaction Index
CIJE: 2 RIE: 0 CAT: 21

Life Satisfaction Index A
CIJE: 2 RIE: 2 CAT: 21

Life Science Concept Acquisition Test (Riechard)
CIJE: 0 RIE: 1 CAT: 21

Life Science Concept Test (Butler)
CIJE: 0 RIE: 1 CAT: 21

Life Skills Inventory
CIJE: 1 RIE: 0 CAT: 21

Life Space Interviews
CIJE: 9 RIE: 0 CAT: 15

Life Span
CIJE: 20 RIE: 10 CAT: 11

Life Span Development
CIJE: 54 RIE: 29 CAT: 15

Life Stage Vocational Development
CIJE: 1 RIE: 0 CAT: 16

Life Tasks (Adler)
CIJE: 0 RIE: 1 CAT: 11

Life Threatening Events
CIJE: 6 RIE: 1 CAT: 16

Life Transitions
CIJE: 31 RIE: 15 CAT: 16

Life Week
CIJE: 1 RIE: 0 CAT: 22

Life World
CIJE: 5 RIE: 2 CAT: 22

Life Writing Approach
USE Lifewriting

Lifeguard Training
CIJE: 4 RIE: 1 CAT: 03

Lifeguards
CIJE: 6 RIE: 0 CAT: 09

Lifeline
CIJE: 4 RIE: 1 CAT: 19

Lifelong Career Development
CIJE: 4 RIE: 0 CAT: 15

Lifelong Career Development Model
CIJE: 0 RIE: 2 CAT: 19

Lifelong Learning Communities
CIJE: 0 RIE: 0 CAT: 15

Lifelong Learning Project
CIJE: 2 RIE: 2 CAT: 19

Lifelong Readers
CIJE: 1 RIE: 9 CAT: 10

Lifetime Creativity Scales
CIJE: 0 RIE: 1 CAT: 21

Lifetime Employment
CIJE: 5 RIE: 1 CAT: 16

Lifetime Income
CIJE: 2 RIE: 3 CAT: 16

Lifewriting
CIJE: 0 RIE: 2 CAT: 15
SN The composing of personal stories, anecdotes, and memoirs
UF Life Writing Approach

Liff House Childrens Unit
CIJE: 1 RIE: 0 CAT: 17

Liflanders Model
CIJE: 0 RIE: 1 CAT: 15

Lift Every Voice and Sing
CIJE: 1 RIE: 0 CAT: 22

Lifts (for Disabled)
CIJE: 0 RIE: 1 CAT: 04

Ligaments
CIJE: 1 RIE: 0 CAT: 11

Light Bulb Assemblers
CIJE: 0 RIE: 1 CAT: 09

Light Bulbs
CIJE: 1 RIE: 1 CAT: 04

Light in August
CIJE: 1 RIE: 0 CAT: 22

Light Intensity Matching Test (Watson et al)
CIJE: 1 RIE: 0 CAT: 21

Lighthouse Club Day Camp PA
CIJE: 0 RIE: 1 CAT: 17

Lighthouse Learning Project
CIJE: 2 RIE: 1 CAT: 19

Lighthouses
CIJE: 0 RIE: 1 CAT: 05

Lighting Comparators
CIJE: 1 RIE: 0 CAT: 04

Lighting Designers
CIJE: 2 RIE: 0 CAT: 09

Lightly (W H)
CIJE: 0 RIE: 1 CAT: 18

Lightning
CIJE: 13 RIE: 2 CAT: 20

Lightning Conductors
CIJE: 1 RIE: 0 CAT: 20

Lights Retention Scale
CIJE: 3 RIE: 2 CAT: 21

Lightweight Structures
CIJE: 3 RIE: 1 CAT: 20

Ligru Project (Sweden)
CIJE: 0 RIE: 5 CAT: 19

Likability
CIJE: 2 RIE: 1 CAT: 11

Like School Scale (Combers and Keeves)
CIJE: 1 RIE: 0 CAT: 21

Likelihood Function Estimation
CIJE: 2 RIE: 2 CAT: 21

Likelihood Ratio Criterion
CIJE: 2 RIE: 4 CAT: 15

Likelihood Ratio Tests
CIJE: 9 RIE: 1 CAT: 21

Likert (Rensis)
CIJE: 2 RIE: 3 CAT: 18

Likert Model for Organizational Effectiveness
CIJE: 0 RIE: 3 CAT: 15

Likert Profile of Organizational Characteristics
CIJE: 1 RIE: 0 CAT: 21

Likerts Influence Proposition
CIJE: 1 RIE: 0 CAT: 15

Liking
CIJE: 5 RIE: 7 CAT: 16

Liliuokalani
CIJE: 1 RIE: 0 CAT: 18
UF Queen Liliuokalani

Lilliefors Statistic
CIJE: 0 RIE: 1 CAT: 21

Lilly (Eli) and Company
CIJE: 0 RIE: 0 CAT: 17

Lilly (John)
CIJE: 0 RIE: 1 CAT: 18

Lilly Endowment
CIJE: 3 RIE: 2 CAT: 17

Lilly Postdoctoral Fellowships Program
CIJE: 0 RIE: 1 CAT: 19

Lima (Jorge de)
CIJE: 2 RIE: 0 CAT: 18

Limbic Learning
CIJE: 0 RIE: 2 CAT: 16

Limburg State University (Netherlands)
CIJE: 2 RIE: 2 CAT: 17

Limericks
CIJE: 3 RIE: 1 CAT: 13

Limestone
CIJE: 0 RIE: 1 CAT: 20

Limited Closed Interval Measures
CIJE: 0 RIE: 1 CAT: 21

Limited English Writers
CIJE: 0 RIE: 2 CAT: 10

Limited Partnerships
CIJE: 0 RIE: 1 CAT: 16

Limiting What Students Shall Read
CIJE: 2 RIE: 0 CAT: 22

Limits (Concept)
CIJE: 2 RIE: 0 CAT: 20

Limits (Mathematics)
CIJE: 28 RIE: 5 CAT: 20

Limits (Therapy)
CIJE: 1 RIE: 0 CAT: 11

Limits to Growth
CIJE: 1 RIE: 0 CAT: 22

Limnology
CIJE: 8 RIE: 9 CAT: 20

Limulus Test
CIJE: 2 RIE: 0 CAT: 21

LINC Computer
CIJE: 0 RIE: 1 CAT: 04

Lincer (William)
CIJE: 1 RIE: 0 CAT: 18

Lincoln (Abraham)
CIJE: 24 RIE: 12 CAT: 18

Lincoln (Yvonna S)
CIJE: 1 RIE: 1 CAT: 18

Lincoln Attucks Program
CIJE: 0 RIE: 1 CAT: 19

Lincoln Center Library
CIJE: 1 RIE: 0 CAT: 17

Lincoln Center Student Program
CIJE: 0 RIE: 1 CAT: 19

Lincoln College (New Zealand)
CIJE: 0 RIE: 1 CAT: 17

Lincoln College IL
CIJE: 1 RIE: 0 CAT: 17

Lincoln Community High School
CIJE: 1 RIE: 0 CAT: 17

Lincoln Council on Alcoholism and Drugs NE
CIJE: 0 RIE: 1 CAT: 17

Lincoln County Board of Education ON
CIJE: 0 RIE: 1 CAT: 17

Lincoln County Roman Catholic Separate Sch Bd ON
CIJE: 0 RIE: 1 CAT: 17

Lincoln County School District 2 WY
CIJE: 0 RIE: 1 CAT: 17

Lincoln County School of Technology NC
CIJE: 0 RIE: 1 CAT: 17

Lincoln County Schools OR
CIJE: 0 RIE: 3 CAT: 17

Lincoln County Schools VA
CIJE: 0 RIE: 4 CAT: 17

Lincoln Douglas Debate Style
CIJE: 0 RIE: 3 CAT: 15

Lincoln Filene Center Citizenship Public Affairs
CIJE: 2 RIE: 2 CAT: 17

Lincoln Heights Elementary School OH
CIJE: 0 RIE: 1 CAT: 17

Lincoln High School MO
CIJE: 1 RIE: 2 CAT: 17

Lincoln High School Philadelphia PA
CIJE: 0 RIE: 2 CAT: 17

Lincoln Intermediate Spelling Test
CIJE: 0 RIE: 1 CAT: 21

Lincoln Junior High UT
CIJE: 0 RIE: 1 CAT: 17

Lincoln Land Community College IL
CIJE: 2 RIE: 6 CAT: 17

Lincoln Learning Center MN
CIJE: 1 RIE: 2 CAT: 17

Lincoln Memorial University TN
CIJE: 0 RIE: 1 CAT: 17

Lincoln Neighborhood Service Center NY
CIJE: 0 RIE: 1 CAT: 17

Lincoln Oberetsky Motor Development Scale
CIJE: 1 RIE: 0 CAT: 21

Lincoln Public Library IL
CIJE: 0 RIE: 1 CAT: 17

Lincoln Public Schools NE
CIJE: 5 RIE: 12 CAT: 17

Lincoln School Clinical Module Project
CIJE: 1 RIE: 0 CAT: 19

Lincoln Skills Center MI
CIJE: 0 RIE: 1 CAT: 17

Lincoln Terminal System
CIJE: 0 RIE: 6 CAT: 04

Lincoln Trail College IL
CIJE: 0 RIE: 1 CAT: 17

Lincoln Training System
CIJE: 0 RIE: 16 CAT: 15

Lincoln University MO
CIJE: 0 RIE: 5 CAT: 17

Lincoln University PA
CIJE: 0 RIE: 5 CAT: 17

Lincoln Vocational Center FL
CIJE: 1 RIE: 0 CAT: 17

Lincoln Way High School IL
CIJE: 2 RIE: 0 CAT: 17

Lincolnwood Schools IL
CIJE: 1 RIE: 0 CAT: 17

Lindamood Auditory Conceptualization Test
CIJE: 1 RIE: 0 CAT: 21

Lindbergh (Charles)
CIJE: 1 RIE: 0 CAT: 18

Lindblom (Charles E)
CIJE: 0 RIE: 1 CAT: 18

Lindeman (Eduard)
CIJE: 9 RIE: 2 CAT: 18

Lindenwood College MO
CIJE: 0 RIE: 1 CAT: 17

Lindgren (Astrid)
CIJE: 0 RIE: 1 CAT: 18

Lindgren (Henry Clay)
CIJE: 1 RIE: 0 CAT: 18

Lindquist (E F)
CIJE: 1 RIE: 0 CAT: 18

Lindsay (John V)
CIJE: 0 RIE: 1 CAT: 18

Lindsay (Vachel)
CIJE: 2 RIE: 0 CAT: 18

Lindsey Hopkins Technical Education Center FL
CIJE: 0 RIE: 1 CAT: 17

Line (Visual Arts)
CIJE: 0 RIE: 1 CAT: 16

Line Attendants
CIJE: 0 RIE: 1 CAT: 09

Line Drawings
CIJE: 6 RIE: 5 CAT: 16

Line Fitting (Mathematics)
CIJE: 3 RIE: 0 CAT: 20

Line Match Test (Barton)
CIJE: 1 RIE: 0 CAT: 21

Line Orientation
CIJE: 2 RIE: 0 CAT: 11

Line Repairers
CIJE: 0 RIE: 2 CAT: 09

Lineality
CIJE: 1 RIE: 0 CAT: 16

Linear Algebra
CIJE: 19 RIE: 6 CAT: 20

Linear Classification Function
CIJE: 0 RIE: 1 CAT: 21

Linear Discriminant Function
CIJE: 2 RIE: 5 CAT: 15

Linear Equating Method
CIJE: 21 RIE: 33 CAT: 15

Linear Induction Motor
CIJE: 1 RIE: 0 CAT: 04

Linear Logistic Test Model
CIJE: 3 RIE: 2 CAT: 21

Linear Measurement
CIJE: 2 RIE: 3 CAT: 20

Linear Models
CIJE: 55 RIE: 47 CAT: 15

Linear Nevus Sebaceous Syndrome
CIJE: 1 RIE: 0 CAT: 11

Linear Ordering
CIJE: 5 RIE: 5 CAT: 15

Linear Relationships
CIJE: 13 RIE: 5 CAT: 20

LInear Structural RELationships Analysis
USE LISREL Analysis

LInear Structural RELationships Program
USE LISREL Computer Program

Linear Tests
CIJE: 1 RIE: 2 CAT: 21

Linear Trends
CIJE: 3 RIE: 2 CAT: 21

Linfield College OR
CIJE: 0 RIE: 4 CAT: 17

Ling (Daniel)
CIJE: 1 RIE: 0 CAT: 18

Ling System of Speech Training
CIJE: 0 RIE: 1 CAT: 15

Ling Temco Vought Employment Relocation Project
CIJE: 0 RIE: 1 CAT: 19

Lingua Francas
CIJE: 7 RIE: 9 CAT: 13

LINGUA Programme
CIJE: 1 RIE: 1 CAT: 19

Linguaplan Limbourg
CIJE: 0 RIE: 1 CAT: 19

Linguascope
CIJE: 1 RIE: 0 CAT: 04

Linguistic Ability Test (Frederick et al)
CIJE: 0 RIE: 2 CAT: 21

Linguistic Ambiguity
CIJE: 1 RIE: 2 CAT: 13

Linguistic Analysis
CIJE: 16 RIE: 14 CAT: 13

Linguistic Atlas of the Gulf States
CIJE: 0 RIE: 1 CAT: 22

Linguistic Atlas of the Pacific Coast
CIJE: 1 RIE: 0 CAT: 22

Linguistic Atlas of the United States Project
CIJE: 0 RIE: 1 CAT: 19

Linguistic Atlas of the Upper Midwest
CIJE: 0 RIE: 1 CAT: 22

Linguistic Atlases
CIJE: 1 RIE: 3 CAT: 13

Linguistic Auditory Memory Patterns
CIJE: 0 RIE: 1 CAT: 03
UF LAMP Exercises

Linguistic Bibliography Project
CIJE: 0 RIE: 1 CAT: 19

Linguistic Blindness
CIJE: 0 RIE: 1 CAT: 13

Linguistic Codes
CIJE: 4 RIE: 3 CAT: 13

Linguistic Context
CIJE: 8 RIE: 3 CAT: 13

Linguistic Continuum
CIJE: 1 RIE: 1 CAT: 13

Linguistic Conventions
CIJE: 2 RIE: 1 CAT: 13

Linguistic Drift
CIJE: 2 RIE: 0 CAT: 13

Linguistic Form
CIJE: 2 RIE: 1 CAT: 13

Linguistic Geography
CIJE: 3 RIE: 1 CAT: 13

Linguistic Incorporation
CIJE: 0 RIE: 0 CAT: 13
UF Incorporation (Linguistics)

Linguistic Insecurity
CIJE: 1 RIE: 1 CAT: 13

Linguistic Markers
CIJE: 2 RIE: 3 CAT: 13

Linguistic Minorities
USE Language Minorities

Linguistic Pluralism
CIJE: 3 RIE: 3 CAT: 13

Linguistic Relativity
CIJE: 3 RIE: 4 CAT: 13

Linguistic Society of America
CIJE: 1 RIE: 5 CAT: 17

Linguistic String Analysis
CIJE: 1 RIE: 1 CAT: 13

Linguistic String Project
CIJE: 1 RIE: 0 CAT: 19

Linguistic Structures Repetition Test
CIJE: 0 RIE: 2 CAT: 21

Linguistic Units
CIJE: 2 RIE: 1 CAT: 13

Linguistic Variables
CIJE: 4 RIE: 3 CAT: 13

Linguistics Institute of Ireland
CIJE: 0 RIE: 1 CAT: 17

Linguistics Research and Demonstration Project
CIJE: 0 RIE: 1 CAT: 19

Linguists
CIJE: 2 RIE: 3 CAT: 09

Link Courses
CIJE: 2 RIE: 2 CAT: 03

Link F Test
CIJE: 0 RIE: 1 CAT: 21

Linkage
CIJE: 36 RIE: 99 CAT: 15

Linkage Analysis
CIJE: 6 RIE: 9 CAT: 15

Linkage Model (Havelock)
CIJE: 0 RIE: 1 CAT: 15

Linkage Programs
CIJE: 0 RIE: 1 CAT: 19

Linked Judgment Approach
CIJE: 1 RIE: 0 CAT: 21

Linked Systems Project
CIJE: 15 RIE: 4 CAT: 19

Linking Educational Assessments
CIJE: 0 RIE: 1 CAT: 21

Linking Elements Concept
CIJE: 0 RIE: 1 CAT: 15

Linking Lifetimes Programs
CIJE: 0 RIE: 1 CAT: 19

Linking Methods (Metrics)
USE Linking Metrics

Linking Metrics
CIJE: 2 RIE: 3 CAT: 15
UF Linking Methods (Metrics)

Linking Outcomes to Organizational Planning
CIJE: 0 RIE: 3 CAT: 19
UF LOOP System

Linkoping University (Sweden)
CIJE: 3 RIE: 5 CAT: 17

Links (Communication)
USE Communication Links

Links (Indexing)
CIJE: 10 RIE: 0 CAT: 16

Links Inc
CIJE: 0 RIE: 1 CAT: 17

LinkWay
CIJE: 1 RIE: 2 CAT: 04
UF IBM LinkWay

Linn Benton Community College OR
CIJE: 1 RIE: 2 CAT: 17

Linn Benton Education Service District OR
CIJE: 0 RIE: 2 CAT: 17

Linotype Operators
CIJE: 0 RIE: 1 CAT: 09

LINPROG Computer Program
CIJE: 0 RIE: 1 CAT: 04

Lion of the West (Drama)
CIJE: 0 RIE: 1 CAT: 22

Lionni (Leo)
CIJE: 3 RIE: 0 CAT: 18

Lip Reader Trainer
CIJE: 1 RIE: 0 CAT: 04

Lipids
CIJE: 10 RIE: 0 CAT: 20

Lipman (Matthew)
CIJE: 2 RIE: 1 CAT: 18

Lipoproteins
CIJE: 5 RIE: 0 CAT: 11
SN See also "Apolipoproteins"
UF Plasma Lipoproteins

Lipoproteins (HDL Cholesterol)
USE High Density Lipoprotein Cholesterol

Lipoproteins (LDL Cholesterol)
USE Low Density Lipoprotein Cholesterol

Lippert Cards
CIJE: 1 RIE: 0 CAT: 04

Lippincott Basic Reading Series
CIJE: 0 RIE: 1 CAT: 22

Lippincott Company
CIJE: 0 RIE: 1 CAT: 17

Lippincott Reading Program
CIJE: 1 RIE: 1 CAT: 22

Lippincott Series
CIJE: 0 RIE: 1 CAT: 22

Lippmann (Walter)
CIJE: 2 RIE: 3 CAT: 18

Lipscomb Scale of Teacher Attitudes
CIJE: 1 RIE: 0 CAT: 21

Lipset (Seymour Martin)
CIJE: 2 RIE: 1 CAT: 18

Lipsett (Arthur)
CIJE: 0 RIE: 1 CAT: 18

Lipsyte (Robert)
CIJE: 0 RIE: 1 CAT: 18

Liquefied Gases
CIJE: 1 RIE: 0 CAT: 20

Liquefied Petroleum Gas
CIJE: 0 RIE: 1 CAT: 20

Liquid Conservation
CIJE: 5 RIE: 0 CAT: 20

Liquid Crystal Displays
CIJE: 3 RIE: 2 CAT: 04
UF LCDs

Liquid Crystals
CIJE: 7 RIE: 0 CAT: 20

Liquid Pressing
CIJE: 1 RIE: 0 CAT: 20

Liquids
CIJE: 9 RIE: 5 CAT: 20

Liquids (Language)
CIJE: 1 RIE: 0 CAT: 13

LISA
USE Library and Information Science Abstracts

Lisle Fellowship Program
CIJE: 1 RIE: 0 CAT: 19

Lismer (Arthur)
CIJE: 0 RIE: 1 CAT: 18

LISP Programing Language
CIJE: 11 RIE: 21 CAT: 04

Lisping
CIJE: 5 RIE: 0 CAT: 11

Lisramic
CIJE: 1 RIE: 0 CAT: 13

LISREL Analysis
CIJE: 6 RIE: 5 CAT: 15
UF LInear Structural RELationships Analysis

LISREL Computer Program
CIJE: 101 RIE: 62 CAT: 04
UF LInear Structural RELationships Program

List Differentiation Hypothesis
CIJE: 1 RIE: 1 CAT: 15

List Format Text
CIJE: 0 RIE: 1 CAT: 15

List of Periodicals Reviewing Books
CIJE: 0 RIE: 1 CAT: 22

List Organization
CIJE: 2 RIE: 2 CAT: 15

List Poems
CIJE: 0 RIE: 1 CAT: 16

List Processing
CIJE: 6 RIE: 7 CAT: 15

Lista de Encabezamientos de Materia
CIJE: 0 RIE: 1 CAT: 22

Lista y Aragon (Alberto)
CIJE: 1 RIE: 0 CAT: 18

Listen and Look (Clark)
CIJE: 1 RIE: 0 CAT: 21

Listen and Think Program
CIJE: 0 RIE: 1 CAT: 19

Listen Respond Compare Mode
CIJE: 1 RIE: 0 CAT: 21

Listenability
CIJE: 1 RIE: 1 CAT: 16

Listener Preference Profile
CIJE: 0 RIE: 1 CAT: 21

Listening and Reading Comprehension Program
CIJE: 0 RIE: 1 CAT: 19

Listening Comprehension Test (Graham and Orr)
CIJE: 0 RIE: 1 CAT: 21

Listening Comprehension Test for First Grade
CIJE: 0 RIE: 1 CAT: 21

Listening Inference Test (Stern)
CIJE: 0 RIE: 1 CAT: 21

Listening Rate
CIJE: 3 RIE: 3 CAT: 21

Listening Reading Relationship
CIJE: 2 RIE: 2 CAT: 15
UF Reading Listening Relationship

Listening Research
CIJE: 18 RIE: 23 CAT: 15

Listening Response Test (Stein)
CIJE: 0 RIE: 1 CAT: 21

Listening Skills Program
CIJE: 0 RIE: 2 CAT: 19

Listening Strategies
CIJE: 9 RIE: 14 CAT: 11

Listening Summary Translation Exam Spanish
CIJE: 0 RIE: 1 CAT: 21

Listening Test of Specific Content (Stern Keisler)
CIJE: 0 RIE: 1 CAT: 21

Listening Theory
CIJE: 2 RIE: 8 CAT: 15

Listening Vocabulary
CIJE: 1 RIE: 3 CAT: 13

Lister Empathy Scale
CIJE: 1 RIE: 0 CAT: 21

Lister Hill Center MD
CIJE: 9 RIE: 1 CAT: 17

Listserv Discussion Groups
CIJE: 0 RIE: 1 CAT: 10

LISTSERV System
USE Listservs

Listservs
CIJE: 15 RIE: 5 CAT: 04
UF LISTSERV System

Liszt (Franz)
CIJE: 1 RIE: 0 CAT: 18

Litchfield Park AZ
CIJE: 0 RIE: 1 CAT: 17

Literacy as a Social Process
CIJE: 16 RIE: 40 CAT: 15

Literacy Assessment
CIJE: 4 RIE: 6 CAT: 21

Literacy Assessment Battery
CIJE: 0 RIE: 2 CAT: 21

Literacy Audits
CIJE: 2 RIE: 16 CAT: 15

Literacy Campaigns
CIJE: 26 RIE: 22 CAT: 13

Literacy Consortium of Allegheny County PA
CIJE: 0 RIE: 0 CAT: 17

Literacy Corps
CIJE: 3 RIE: 1 CAT: 17

Literacy Events
CIJE: 62 RIE: 27 CAT: 16

Literacy Exchange Network
CIJE: 0 RIE: 1 CAT: 17

Literacy for Every Adult Project CA
CIJE: 0 RIE: 1 CAT: 19

Literacy Hoax
CIJE: 0 RIE: 1 CAT: 16

Literacy House (India)
CIJE: 2 RIE: 2 CAT: 17

Literacy Impact Program
CIJE: 0 RIE: 1 CAT: 19

Literacy Implements a Vibrant Existence SC
USE Project LIVE SC

Literacy in Science and Social Science Project
CIJE: 0 RIE: 1 CAT: 19

Literacy in the Open Access College
CIJE: 0 RIE: 1 CAT: 22

Literacy Observation Matrix
CIJE: 0 RIE: 1 CAT: 21

Literacy Plus Project CA
CIJE: 0 RIE: 1 CAT: 19

Literacy Retention
CIJE: 1 RIE: 1 CAT: 16

Literacy Tests for Teachers
CIJE: 0 RIE: 1 CAT: 21

Literacy Through Love
CIJE: 0 RIE: 1 CAT: 19

Literacy Volunteers Inc
CIJE: 4 RIE: 6 CAT: 17

Literacy Volunteers of America Inc
CIJE: 4 RIE: 14 CAT: 17
SN Formerly Literacy Volunteers Inc (1972)

Literacy Volunteers of New York City
CIJE: 0 RIE: 2 CAT: 17

Literary Awards
CIJE: 3 RIE: 3 CAT: 16

Literary Canon
CIJE: 53 RIE: 44 CAT: 16

Literary Circles
USE Literature Circles

Literary Collaboration
CIJE: 4 RIE: 1 CAT: 16

Literary Craft Tracking
CIJE: 1 RIE: 0 CAT: 03
UF Tracking (Literary Styles)

Literary Digest
CIJE: 0 RIE: 1 CAT: 22

Literary Gaps
CIJE: 0 RIE: 1 CAT: 16

Literary Magazines
CIJE: 37 RIE: 28 CAT: 16

Literary Models
CIJE: 6 RIE: 4 CAT: 16

Literary Newswriting
CIJE: 2 RIE: 1 CAT: 16

Literary Politics
CIJE: 13 RIE: 2 CAT: 03

Literary Profundity Test (Anderson)
CIJE: 1 RIE: 0 CAT: 21

Literary Quality
CIJE: 9 RIE: 5 CAT: 16

Literary Rating Scale (Tway)
CIJE: 0 RIE: 1 CAT: 21

Literary Response
CIJE: 17 RIE: 15 CAT: 16

Literary Settings
CIJE: 3 RIE: 2 CAT: 16

Literary Societies
CIJE: 1 RIE: 1 CAT: 10

Literary Society Libraries
CIJE: 1 RIE: 0 CAT: 05

Literary Sociology
CIJE: 0 RIE: 1 CAT: 15

Literary Themes
USE Theme (Literary)

Literary Theory
CIJE: 82 RIE: 36 CAT: 15

Literate Environment Approach
CIJE: 1 RIE: 2 CAT: 15

Literature Circles
CIJE: 0 RIE: 1 CAT: 10
UF Literary Circles

Literature Composition Relationship
USE Composition Literature Relationship

Literature in Translation
CIJE: 14 RIE: 12 CAT: 16

Lithium
CIJE: 6 RIE: 0 CAT: 20

Lithium Drifted Germanium Detectors
CIJE: 1 RIE: 0 CAT: 04

Lithographers
CIJE: 0 RIE: 4 CAT: 09

Lithography
CIJE: 4 RIE: 4 CAT: 20

Lithuanian Americans
CIJE: 0 RIE: 1 CAT: 08

Lithuanians
CIJE: 2 RIE: 4 CAT: 08

Litter Education Programs
CIJE: 2 RIE: 4 CAT: 19

Littering
CIJE: 6 RIE: 4 CAT: 16

Little Axe Independent School District OK
CIJE: 0 RIE: 1 CAT: 17

Little Drummer Girl (Le Carre)
CIJE: 0 RIE: 1 CAT: 22

Little Egypt Development Center IL
CIJE: 1 RIE: 0 CAT: 17

Little Hoover Commission
CIJE: 1 RIE: 1 CAT: 17

Little House on the Prairie
CIJE: 0 RIE: 1 CAT: 22

Little Papers (Deaf Community)
CIJE: 0 RIE: 1 CAT: 22

Little Prince
CIJE: 5 RIE: 0 CAT: 22

Little Red Cap
USE Little Red Riding Hood

Little Red Riding Hood
CIJE: 2 RIE: 2 CAT: 22
UF Little Red Cap

Little Rock School District AR
CIJE: 3 RIE: 3 CAT: 17

Little Saskatchewan School MB
CIJE: 0 RIE: 0 CAT: 17

Litton Industries
CIJE: 0 RIE: 1 CAT: 17

Live Aid (Concert)
CIJE: 0 RIE: 1 CAT: 12

Live Boys in the Black Hills
CIJE: 0 RIE: 1 CAT: 22
SN ...or the Young Texan Gold Hunters

Live Boys or Charley and Nasho in Texas
CIJE: 0 RIE: 1 CAT: 22

Live Broadcasts
CIJE: 0 RIE: 2 CAT: 16

Live Oak High School CA
CIJE: 1 RIE: 0 CAT: 17

Live Shop
CIJE: 1 RIE: 0 CAT: 16

Live Television Captioning
USE Real Time Captioning

Liver Disease
CIJE: 1 RIE: 1 CAT: 11

Liveright (A A)
CIJE: 1 RIE: 1 CAT: 18

Liverpool Middle School NY
CIJE: 0 RIE: 1 CAT: 17

Lives of Service (Research)
CIJE: 0 RIE: 1 CAT: 16

Lives on the Boundary (Rose)
CIJE: 0 RIE: 1 CAT: 22

Livestock Breeding
CIJE: 0 RIE: 0 CAT: 20

Livestock Feed
CIJE: 0 RIE: 1 CAT: 20

Livestock Industry
CIJE: 0 RIE: 1 CAT: 05

Livestock Judging
CIJE: 0 RIE: 2 CAT: 20

Livestock Sale Barn Employee Competencies
CIJE: 0 RIE: 1 CAT: 21

Livian Wars Task
CIJE: 0 RIE: 1 CAT: 16

Living (Concept)
CIJE: 1 RIE: 1 CAT: 20

Living Arrangements
CIJE: 7 RIE: 1 CAT: 16
SN See also "Alternative Living Arrangements"

Living Arts Program
CIJE: 0 RIE: 1 CAT: 19

Living Away from Home Allowances (Australia)
CIJE: 0 RIE: 1 CAT: 19

Living Classroom (Hall)
CIJE: 0 RIE: 1 CAT: 15

Living Curriculum
CIJE: 2 RIE: 0 CAT: 03

Living History
CIJE: 2 RIE: 1 CAT: 12

Living Library (Pets)
CIJE: 0 RIE: 1 CAT: 19

Living Planet Program
CIJE: 0 RIE: 1 CAT: 19

Living Room School Cognitive Assessment Inventory
CIJE: 0 RIE: 2 CAT: 21

Living Room School Program
CIJE: 0 RIE: 1 CAT: 19

Living School NY
CIJE: 1 RIE: 0 CAT: 17

Living Stage DC
CIJE: 1 RIE: 1 CAT: 17

Living Systems
CIJE: 1 RIE: 1 CAT: 15

Living Wills
CIJE: 4 RIE: 1 CAT: 14

Livingston (William)
CIJE: 0 RIE: 1 CAT: 18

Livingston College NJ
USE Rutgers the State University Livingston Coll NJ

Livingston School for Girls NY
CIJE: 1 RIE: 1 CAT: 17

Livonia Public Schools MI
CIJE: 1 RIE: 5 CAT: 17

Livy (Titus Livius)
CIJE: 1 RIE: 0 CAT: 18

Lix Readability Formula
CIJE: 1 RIE: 1 CAT: 21

Lizardi (Jose Joaquin Fernandez de)
CIJE: 2 RIE: 0 CAT: 18

Lleras (Antonio Alvarez)
CIJE: 1 RIE: 0 CAT: 18

Llopis (Carlos)
CIJE: 1 RIE: 0 CAT: 18

LNNB
USE Luria Nebraska Neuropsychological Battery

LNNB (Childrens Revision)
USE Luria Nebraska Neuropsychological Battery

Load Demand Control
CIJE: 2 RIE: 1 CAT: 15

Loan Counseling
CIJE: 0 RIE: 1 CAT: 16

Loan Forbearance
CIJE: 0 RIE: 1 CAT: 16

Loan Forgiveness
CIJE: 3 RIE: 6 CAT: 16

Loan Programs
CIJE: 6 RIE: 13 CAT: 19

Loan Video Programs
CIJE: 1 RIE: 1 CAT: 19
UF Video Loan Programs

Lobbyists
CIJE: 2 RIE: 3 CAT: 09

Local Action Teams
CIJE: 0 RIE: 1 CAT: 10

Local Advisory Councils
CIJE: 0 RIE: 1 CAT: 10

Local Arts Agency Development Program
CIJE: 0 RIE: 1 CAT: 19

Local Arts Councils
CIJE: 1 RIE: 1 CAT: 10

Local Autonomy
CIJE: 10 RIE: 6 CAT: 16

Local Composite Index Finance Formula
CIJE: 0 RIE: 1 CAT: 15

Local Control
CIJE: 6 RIE: 8 CAT: 16

Local Control Index
CIJE: 0 RIE: 1 CAT: 15

Local Course Improvement Program
CIJE: 0 RIE: 3 CAT: 19

Local Development Officers
CIJE: 0 RIE: 1 CAT: 09

Local Education Authorities (United Kingdom)
CIJE: 5 RIE: 5 CAT: 05

Local Facilitators
CIJE: 0 RIE: 1 CAT: 10

Local Focus on Youth (The)
CIJE: 0 RIE: 1 CAT: 22

Local Government Services Center
CIJE: 1 RIE: 0 CAT: 17

Local Government Services Program
CIJE: 1 RIE: 0 CAT: 19

Local Guaranteed Yield Program
CIJE: 0 RIE: 2 CAT: 19

Local Independence (Tests)
CIJE: 12 RIE: 6 CAT: 21

Local Information Network Knowledge Educ Renew MA
CIJE: 0 RIE: 1 CAT: 17

Local Learning Systems
CIJE: 0 RIE: 1 CAT: 16

Local Literacies
CIJE: 0 RIE: 1 CAT: 10

Local Media
CIJE: 12 RIE: 12 CAT: 16

Local News
CIJE: 13 RIE: 18 CAT: 16

Local Origination
CIJE: 2 RIE: 7 CAT: 16

Local Planning and Assessment Process
CIJE: 1 RIE: 10 CAT: 15

Local Planning and Budgeting Model
CIJE: 0 RIE: 1 CAT: 15

Local Public Works
CIJE: 0 RIE: 1 CAT: 16

Local School Councils
CIJE: 5 RIE: 9 CAT: 10
SN ... of the Chicago Public Schools IL

Local Special Education Planning Model
CIJE: 0 RIE: 1 CAT: 15

Local Taxes
CIJE: 0 RIE: 1 CAT: 16

Local Television Stations
CIJE: 2 RIE: 3 CAT: 05

Localization (Administrative)
CIJE: 0 RIE: 4 CAT: 16

Localization (Neurological)
CIJE: 4 RIE: 0 CAT: 11

Locally Based Research
CIJE: 2 RIE: 0 CAT: 16

Location (Computer Science)
CIJE: 0 RIE: 1 CAT: 15

Location Allocation Package
CIJE: 1 RIE: 0 CAT: 16

Location Theory
CIJE: 1 RIE: 2 CAT: 15

Locational Analysis
CIJE: 1 RIE: 4 CAT: 15

Locative Inversion
CIJE: 0 RIE: 1 CAT: 13

Locatives
CIJE: 2 RIE: 1 CAT: 13

Lock Haven State College PA
CIJE: 2 RIE: 3 CAT: 17

Locke (E A)
CIJE: 1 RIE: 1 CAT: 18

Locke (John)
CIJE: 21 RIE: 8 CAT: 18

Locke Marital Relationship Inventory
CIJE: 1 RIE: 1 CAT: 21

Locke Wallace Marital Adjustment Scale
CIJE: 5 RIE: 3 CAT: 21

Lockers
CIJE: 4 RIE: 1 CAT: 04

Lockheed
CIJE: 9 RIE: 7 CAT: 17

Lockheed Technology Emphasis Camp
CIJE: 0 RIE: 1 CAT: 19

Locksmiths
CIJE: 1 RIE: 0 CAT: 09

Locus of Authority
CIJE: 3 RIE: 1 CAT: 15

Locus of Control in Three Achievement Domains
CIJE: 2 RIE: 0 CAT: 21

Locus of Control Scales (Levenson)
CIJE: 4 RIE: 0 CAT: 21

Locutionary Expressions
CIJE: 1 RIE: 1 CAT: 13
SN See also "Illocutionary..." and "Perlocutionary..."

Loczy Model of Infant Care
CIJE: 0 RIE: 1 CAT: 15

Lodestar International Student Center
CIJE: 1 RIE: 0 CAT: 17

Loevinger (Jane)
CIJE: 3 RIE: 7 CAT: 18

Loevinger (Lee)
CIJE: 1 RIE: 0 CAT: 18

Loevinger Sentence Completion Test
CIJE: 5 RIE: 3 CAT: 21

Log Buildings
CIJE: 0 RIE: 2 CAT: 05

Log Linear Models
CIJE: 39 RIE: 27 CAT: 15

Log Scalers
CIJE: 0 RIE: 1 CAT: 09

Logan (Chief Tahgahjute)
CIJE: 0 RIE: 1 CAT: 18

Logan Cache County Tutorial Center UT
CIJE: 0 RIE: 1 CAT: 17

Logan City School District UT
CIJE: 1 RIE: 0 CAT: 17

Logbooks
CIJE: 7 RIE: 2 CAT: 04

Logic Circuits
CIJE: 2 RIE: 3 CAT: 20

Logic Gates
CIJE: 0 RIE: 1 CAT: 20

Logic Instruction System
CIJE: 0 RIE: 1 CAT: 15

Logical Analysis Device
CIJE: 0 RIE: 1 CAT: 04

Logical Consequences
CIJE: 1 RIE: 2 CAT: 16

Logical Necessity
CIJE: 3 RIE: 1 CAT: 15

Logical Positivism
CIJE: 13 RIE: 7 CAT: 15

Logical Presupposition
CIJE: 1 RIE: 0 CAT: 15

LOGIMO Computer Program
CIJE: 1 RIE: 1 CAT: 04
SN Software for obtaining maximum likelihood estimates of log-linear models

LOGIST Computer Program
CIJE: 12 RIE: 24 CAT: 04

LOGIST Estimation Procedures
CIJE: 3 RIE: 7 CAT: 21

Logistical Support
CIJE: 0 RIE: 1 CAT: 16

Logit Analysis
CIJE: 19 RIE: 12 CAT: 15

Logits
CIJE: 1 RIE: 2 CAT: 15

Logo Action Research Collaborative
CIJE: 0 RIE: 1 CAT: 17

LOGO Programing Language
CIJE: 375 RIE: 192 CAT: 04
SN See also "ExperLOGO"

LOGO System
CIJE: 29 RIE: 24 CAT: 04

Logographic Writing
CIJE: 2 RIE: 1 CAT: 13

Logographs
CIJE: 3 RIE: 2 CAT: 15

Logoli
CIJE: 1 RIE: 0 CAT: 08

Logos (Theology)
CIJE: 0 RIE: 1 CAT: 16

Logotherapy
CIJE: 2 RIE: 5 CAT: 11

LOGTRUE Computer Program
CIJE: 0 RIE: 1 CAT: 04

Lohrville Career Education Model
CIJE: 0 RIE: 1 CAT: 15

Loko
CIJE: 0 RIE: 1 CAT: 13

Lolita
CIJE: 1 RIE: 0 CAT: 22

Loma Linda University CA
CIJE: 5 RIE: 2 CAT: 17

Lompoc School District CA
CIJE: 1 RIE: 0 CAT: 17

Lomwe
CIJE: 0 RIE: 1 CAT: 13

London (Jack)
CIJE: 3 RIE: 1 CAT: 18

London (Perry)
CIJE: 1 RIE: 0 CAT: 18

London Board of Education ON
CIJE: 1 RIE: 2 CAT: 17

London City Schools OH
CIJE: 0 RIE: 1 CAT: 17

London County Council (England)
CIJE: 1 RIE: 0 CAT: 17

London Education Association
CIJE: 1 RIE: 0 CAT: 17

London Education Classification
CIJE: 1 RIE: 0 CAT: 15

London Educational Authority
CIJE: 2 RIE: 0 CAT: 17

London Hospital Medical College
CIJE: 1 RIE: 0 CAT: 17

London Institution
CIJE: 1 RIE: 0 CAT: 17

London School of Economics
CIJE: 2 RIE: 0 CAT: 17

London Special School
CIJE: 1 RIE: 0 CAT: 17

London Times Higher Education Supplement
CIJE: 0 RIE: 1 CAT: 22

Londonderry Elementary School PA
CIJE: 1 RIE: 0 CAT: 17

Lone Ranger (Television Series)
CIJE: 0 RIE: 1 CAT: 22

Lone Star School District No 101 CO
CIJE: 0 RIE: 0 CAT: 17

Lone Walker
CIJE: 1 RIE: 0 CAT: 16

Loneliness of the Long Distance Runner
CIJE: 0 RIE: 2 CAT: 22

Lonergan (Bernard)
CIJE: 1 RIE: 2 CAT: 18

LONESTAR Student Tracking System
USE Longitudinal Student Tracking Reporting System

Loney Draw a Car Test
CIJE: 1 RIE: 0 CAT: 21

Long (Huey)
CIJE: 2 RIE: 1 CAT: 18

Long (Norton)
CIJE: 0 RIE: 1 CAT: 18

Long Ago and Far Away (Television Series)
CIJE: 0 RIE: 1 CAT: 22

Long Beach City College CA
CIJE: 2 RIE: 9 CAT: 17

Long Beach Schools CA
USE Long Beach Unified School District CA

Long Beach Unified School District CA
CIJE: 0 RIE: 2 CAT: 17
UF Long Beach Schools CA

Long Branch School District NJ
CIJE: 0 RIE: 1 CAT: 17

Long Days Journey Into Night
CIJE: 0 RIE: 1 CAT: 22

Long Distance Learning Network
CIJE: 1 RIE: 0 CAT: 20
UF A T and T Long Distance Learning Network

Long Distance Xerography
CIJE: 0 RIE: 3 CAT: 15

Long Duration Exposure Facility
CIJE: 0 RIE: 1 CAT: 20

Long Haul
CIJE: 0 RIE: 2 CAT: 22

Long Hazleton Process of Public Relations Model
CIJE: 0 RIE: 1 CAT: 15

Long Island Educational Communications Council NY
CIJE: 2 RIE: 0 CAT: 17

Long Island University NY
CIJE: 14 RIE: 12 CAT: 17

Long Jumping
CIJE: 2 RIE: 2 CAT: 16

LONG Project (Sweden)
CIJE: 0 RIE: 1 CAT: 19

Long Range Planning for School Improvement PA
CIJE: 0 RIE: 8 CAT: 19

Long Term Care Facilities
CIJE: 9 RIE: 18 CAT: 05

Long Term Effects
CIJE: 15 RIE: 5 CAT: 16

Long Term Marriages
CIJE: 0 RIE: 2 CAT: 11

Long Term Residents
CIJE: 2 RIE: 10 CAT: 10

Longeot Test of Concrete and Formal Reasoning
CIJE: 3 RIE: 2 CAT: 21

Longevity
CIJE: 16 RIE: 4 CAT: 11

Longfellow (Henry Wadsworth)
CIJE: 2 RIE: 0 CAT: 18

Longfellow Education Center MN
CIJE: 0 RIE: 2 CAT: 17

Longhouses
CIJE: 0 RIE: 1 CAT: 05

Longitude
CIJE: 5 RIE: 3 CAT: 20

Longitudinal Diagnosis
CIJE: 2 RIE: 0 CAT: 15

Longitudinal Intervention Research
CIJE: 0 RIE: 1 CAT: 15

Longitudinal Merges
CIJE: 0 RIE: 1 CAT: 21

Longitudinal Scaling
CIJE: 1 RIE: 0 CAT: 21

Longitudinal Student Tracking Reporting System
CIJE: 0 RIE: 1 CAT: 04
UF LONESTAR Student Tracking System

Longitudinal Studies Program (NCES)
CIJE: 0 RIE: 0 CAT: 19

Longitudinal Study of American Youth
CIJE: 5 RIE: 7 CAT: 19
UF LSAY

Longitudinal Study of Children At Risk IL
CIJE: 1 RIE: 2 CAT: 19

Longitudinal Study of Educational Practices
CIJE: 1 RIE: 13 CAT: 19

Longitudinal Study of Elementary School Effects
CIJE: 0 RIE: 12 CAT: 19

Longley (J W)
CIJE: 0 RIE: 1 CAT: 18

Longman Bibliography of Composition and Rhetoric
CIJE: 0 RIE: 1 CAT: 22

Longman Dictionary of Contemporary English
CIJE: 0 RIE: 0 CAT: 22

Longman Lexicon of Contemporary English
CIJE: 0 RIE: 0 CAT: 22

Longshore Industry
CIJE: 1 RIE: 1 CAT: 09

Longview Community College MO
CIJE: 0 RIE: 1 CAT: 17

Longwood College VA
CIJE: 0 RIE: 3 CAT: 17

Look Homeward Angel
CIJE: 1 RIE: 0 CAT: 22

Lookbacks (Reading)
CIJE: 1 RIE: 2 CAT: 16

Looking Backward (Bellamy)
CIJE: 1 RIE: 0 CAT: 22

Loop College IL
USE City Colleges of Chicago Il Loop College

LOOP System
USE Linking Outcomes to Organizational Planning

Loose Coupling
CIJE: 6 RIE: 1 CAT: 15
SN See also "School Organizational Coupling"

Loose Coupling Theory
CIJE: 1 RIE: 8 CAT: 15

Loosely Coupled Systems
CIJE: 13 RIE: 8 CAT: 15

Lopez (Nancy)
CIJE: 0 RIE: 1 CAT: 18

Lopez Aranda (Ricardo)
CIJE: 1 RIE: 0 CAT: 18

Lopez Quintas (Alfonso)
CIJE: 0 RIE: 1 CAT: 18

Lorain City Schools OH
CIJE: 1 RIE: 1 CAT: 17

Lorain County Community College OH
CIJE: 1 RIE: 3 CAT: 17

Lorain County Public Libraries OH
CIJE: 0 RIE: 1 CAT: 17

Loras College IA
CIJE: 0 RIE: 1 CAT: 17

Lord (Frederic M)
CIJE: 1 RIE: 1 CAT: 18

Lord Fairfax Community College VA
CIJE: 0 RIE: 2 CAT: 17

Lord Jim
CIJE: 2 RIE: 0 CAT: 22

Lord of the Flies
CIJE: 5 RIE: 3 CAT: 22

Lord of the Rings
CIJE: 2 RIE: 0 CAT: 22

Lords Paradox
CIJE: 1 RIE: 1 CAT: 15

Lorentz Transformations
CIJE: 4 RIE: 0 CAT: 20

Lorenz (Konrad)
CIJE: 2 RIE: 0 CAT: 18

Lorenz Curve
CIJE: 7 RIE: 1 CAT: 21

Loretto Heights College CO
CIJE: 3 RIE: 7 CAT: 17

Lorge Thorndike Intelligence Tests
CIJE: 17 RIE: 40 CAT: 21

Lorimer (George Horace)
CIJE: 1 RIE: 0 CAT: 18

Lorma
CIJE: 0 RIE: 3 CAT: 13

Lorr Inpatient Multidimensional Psychiatric Scale
CIJE: 1 RIE: 0 CAT: 21

Lorrs Dimension of Interaction in Group Therapy
CIJE: 0 RIE: 1 CAT: 21

Los Alamos High School NM
CIJE: 2 RIE: 0 CAT: 17

Los Alamos National Laboratory NM
CIJE: 3 RIE: 2 CAT: 17

Los Angeles Alternative School CA
CIJE: 0 RIE: 1 CAT: 17

Los Angeles City College CA
CIJE: 0 RIE: 29 CAT: 17

Los Angeles City Schools CA
CIJE: 19 RIE: 29 CAT: 17

Los Angeles College of Chiropractic CA
CIJE: 1 RIE: 0 CAT: 17

Los Angeles College of Optometry CA
CIJE: 0 RIE: 1 CAT: 17

Los Angeles Community College District CA
CIJE: 4 RIE: 18 CAT: 17

Los Angeles Community Colleges CA
CIJE: 2 RIE: 51 CAT: 17

Los Angeles County Juvenile Camp System CA
CIJE: 0 RIE: 1 CAT: 17

Los Angeles County Probation Department Program
CIJE: 0 RIE: 1 CAT: 19

Los Angeles County Schools CA
CIJE: 6 RIE: 12 CAT: 17

Los Angeles County Science Project
CIJE: 0 RIE: 1 CAT: 19

Los Angeles Harbor College CA
CIJE: 0 RIE: 2 CAT: 17

Los Angeles Metropolitan College CA
CIJE: 0 RIE: 1 CAT: 17

Los Angeles Model Mathematics Project
CIJE: 0 RIE: 1 CAT: 19

Los Angeles Pierce College CA
CIJE: 0 RIE: 2 CAT: 17

Los Angeles Public Library CA
CIJE: 10 RIE: 5 CAT: 17

Los Angeles Southwest College CA
CIJE: 0 RIE: 1 CAT: 17

Los Angeles Study
CIJE: 0 RIE: 1 CAT: 19

Los Angeles Suicide Prevention Center CA
CIJE: 1 RIE: 0 CAT: 17

Los Angeles Times
CIJE: 5 RIE: 12 CAT: 17

Los Angeles Trade and Technical College CA
CIJE: 2 RIE: 0 CAT: 17

Los Angeles Unified School District CA
CIJE: 32 RIE: 131 CAT: 17

Los Angeles Valley College CA
CIJE: 0 RIE: 9 CAT: 17

Los Angeles Womens Job Corps Center CA
CIJE: 0 RIE: 1 CAT: 17

Los Gatos Union School District CA
CIJE: 0 RIE: 1 CAT: 17

Los Lunas School District NM
CIJE: 0 RIE: 1 CAT: 17

Los Medanos College CA
CIJE: 1 RIE: 6 CAT: 17

Los Medanos Community College CA
CIJE: 1 RIE: 0 CAT: 17

Los Meganos Intermediate School CA
CIJE: 1 RIE: 0 CAT: 17

Los Rios Community College District CA
CIJE: 3 RIE: 11 CAT: 17

Losing Ground (Murray)
CIJE: 0 RIE: 1 CAT: 22

Loss
CIJE: 45 RIE: 20 CAT: 11

Loss Function
CIJE: 4 RIE: 4 CAT: 15

Lost Adolescence Syndrome
CIJE: 1 RIE: 0 CAT: 11

Lost Colony
CIJE: 0 RIE: 2 CAT: 12

Lost Persons
CIJE: 1 RIE: 4 CAT: 10

Lotka Law of Scientific Productivity
CIJE: 30 RIE: 1 CAT: 20

Lotka Volterra Predation Equations
CIJE: 0 RIE: 1 CAT: 20

Lottery
CIJE: 12 RIE: 5 CAT: 15

Lotus 1 2 3
CIJE: 24 RIE: 13 CAT: 04

Loucheux
CIJE: 0 RIE: 1 CAT: 13
SN An Athapascan-Eyak language — see also "Kutchin"

Loucheux (Tribe)
CIJE: 0 RIE: 1 CAT: 08

Loudermill v Cleveland Board of Education
CIJE: 1 RIE: 1 CAT: 14
SN See also "Cleveland Board of Education v Loudermill"

Loudness Discrimination Test
CIJE: 0 RIE: 0 CAT: 21

Loudon County School District VA
CIJE: 0 RIE: 3 CAT: 17

Loudspeakers
CIJE: 1 RIE: 0 CAT: 04

Louis (Authur)
CIJE: 0 RIE: 1 CAT: 18

Louis B Mayer Teaching Center
CIJE: 1 RIE: 0 CAT: 17

Louis Lumiere College of Secondary Educ (France)
CIJE: 1 RIE: 0 CAT: 17

Louis XIV
CIJE: 2 RIE: 1 CAT: 18

Louisburg College NC
CIJE: 1 RIE: 0 CAT: 17

Louise Child Care Center PA
CIJE: 0 RIE: 1 CAT: 17

Louise Child Care Scale
CIJE: 0 RIE: 1 CAT: 21
SN "...for Evaluating Home Based Day Care"

Louisiana
CIJE: 160 RIE: 720 CAT: 07

Louisiana (Baton Rouge)
CIJE: 8 RIE: 16 CAT: 07

Louisiana (Caddo Bossier Parish)
CIJE: 0 RIE: 1 CAT: 07

Louisiana (Calcasieu Parish)
CIJE: 1 RIE: 3 CAT: 07

Louisiana (East Baton Rouge)
CIJE: 1 RIE: 1 CAT: 07

Louisiana (Iberia Parish)
CIJE: 0 RIE: 1 CAT: 07

Louisiana (Jefferson Parish)
CIJE: 1 RIE: 1 CAT: 07

Louisiana (Lafayette Parish)
CIJE: 0 RIE: 7 CAT: 07

Louisiana (Lafourche Parish)
CIJE: 0 RIE: 1 CAT: 07

Louisiana (Lake Charles)
CIJE: 1 RIE: 3 CAT: 07

Louisiana (Lincoln Parish)
CIJE: 0 RIE: 1 CAT: 07

Louisiana (Natchitoches Parish)
CIJE: 0 RIE: 4 CAT: 07

Louisiana (Natchitoches)
CIJE: 0 RIE: 1 CAT: 07

Louisiana (New Orleans)
CIJE: 34 RIE: 60 CAT: 07

Louisiana (Saint Landry Parish)
CIJE: 2 RIE: 0 CAT: 07

Louisiana (Saint Martinville)
CIJE: 0 RIE: 2 CAT: 07

Louisiana (Saint Mary Parish)
CIJE: 0 RIE: 2 CAT: 07

Louisiana (Shreveport)
CIJE: 3 RIE: 1 CAT: 07

Louisiana (Southeast)
CIJE: 0 RIE: 1 CAT: 07

Louisiana Agriculture (Journal)
CIJE: 0 RIE: 1 CAT: 22

Louisiana Arts and Science Center
CIJE: 0 RIE: 5 CAT: 17

Louisiana Basic Skills Test
CIJE: 0 RIE: 10 CAT: 21

Louisiana Compensatory Remedial Student Profile
CIJE: 0 RIE: 2 CAT: 21

Louisiana Competency Based Education Law
CIJE: 0 RIE: 1 CAT: 14

Louisiana Cooperative Extension Service
CIJE: 0 RIE: 4 CAT: 17

Louisiana Early Childhood Development Program
CIJE: 0 RIE: 1 CAT: 19

Louisiana Educational Accountability Act
CIJE: 0 RIE: 1 CAT: 14

Louisiana High School Conservation Curriculum
CIJE: 0 RIE: 3 CAT: 03

Louisiana Leadership Academy
CIJE: 0 RIE: 1 CAT: 17

Louisiana School Boards Association
CIJE: 0 RIE: 1 CAT: 17

Louisiana School Effectiveness Study
CIJE: 5 RIE: 5 CAT: 19

Louisiana School for the Visually Impaired
CIJE: 0 RIE: 1 CAT: 17

Louisiana Special Plan Upgrading Reading Project
CIJE: 0 RIE: 2 CAT: 19

Louisiana State Assessment Program
CIJE: 0 RIE: 2 CAT: 19

Louisiana State Department of Public Education
CIJE: 1 RIE: 6 CAT: 17

Louisiana State Funded Prog for Hgh Rsk 4 Yr Olds
USE State Funded Program High Risk Four Year Olds LA

Louisiana State University
CIJE: 43 RIE: 28 CAT: 17

Louisiana State University Alexandria
CIJE: 0 RIE: 1 CAT: 17

Louisiana State University Baton Rouge
CIJE: 0 RIE: 5 CAT: 17

Louisiana State University New Orleans
CIJE: 0 RIE: 0 CAT: 17

Louisiana State University Shreveport
CIJE: 2 RIE: 1 CAT: 17

Louisiana State Youth Opportunities Unlimited
CIJE: 0 RIE: 1 CAT: 17

Louisiana Teacher Internship Program
CIJE: 0 RIE: 1 CAT: 19
UF Teacher Internship Program LA

Louisiana Technological University
CIJE: 2 RIE: 3 CAT: 17

Louisville and Jefferson County Childrens Home KY
CIJE: 0 RIE: 1 CAT: 17

Louisville Free Public Library KY
CIJE: 2 RIE: 0 CAT: 17

Louisville Times
CIJE: 0 RIE: 1 CAT: 22

Love (Ruth B)
CIJE: 2 RIE: 0 CAT: 18

Love Deprivation
CIJE: 1 RIE: 0 CAT: 11

Love for Three Oranges
CIJE: 1 RIE: 0 CAT: 22

Love Medicine
CIJE: 1 RIE: 0 CAT: 22

Love Relationships Scale
CIJE: 0 RIE: 2 CAT: 21

Love Song of J Alfred Prufrock (The)
CIJE: 1 RIE: 0 CAT: 22

Love Story
CIJE: 1 RIE: 1 CAT: 22

Love Withdrawal
CIJE: 1 RIE: 0 CAT: 11

Loveira y Chirino (Carlos)
CIJE: 1 RIE: 0 CAT: 18

Lovejoy (Elijah P)
CIJE: 1 RIE: 1 CAT: 18

Lovett School GA
CIJE: 1 RIE: 0 CAT: 17

Low Achievement Scale (Felton)
CIJE: 1 RIE: 0 CAT: 21

Low Cutoff Method
CIJE: 0 RIE: 1 CAT: 21

Low Density Lipoprotein Cholesterol
CIJE: 0 RIE: 2 CAT: 11
SN See also "High Density Lipoprotein Cholesterol"
UF Cholesterol LDL; LDL Cholesterol; Lipoproteins (LDL Cholesterol)

Low Income Home Energy Assistance Act 1981
CIJE: 0 RIE: 2 CAT: 14

Low Income Home Energy Assistance Program
CIJE: 0 RIE: 1 CAT: 19

Low Power Television
CIJE: 1 RIE: 3 CAT: 20

Low Pressure Sodium Lighting
CIJE: 1 RIE: 0 CAT: 04

Low Saxon
CIJE: 1 RIE: 0 CAT: 13

Low Stakes Testing
USE Low Stakes Tests

Low Stakes Tests
CIJE: 0 RIE: 0 CAT: 21
UF Low Stakes Testing

Low Track Classes
USE Lower Track Students

Low Vision Assistants
CIJE: 1 RIE: 0 CAT: 09

Low Vision Services
CIJE: 0 RIE: 1 CAT: 05

Lowell (A Lawrence)
CIJE: 0 RIE: 1 CAT: 18

Lowell (Robert)
CIJE: 4 RIE: 1 CAT: 18

Lowell Area Council on Interlibrary Networks MA
CIJE: 0 RIE: 1 CAT: 17

Lowell Everywhere School
CIJE: 1 RIE: 0 CAT: 17

Lowell Public Schools MA
CIJE: 6 RIE: 1 CAT: 17

Lowell State College MA
CIJE: 0 RIE: 1 CAT: 17

Lowenfeld (Viktor)
CIJE: 19 RIE: 6 CAT: 18

Lowenfeld Mosaic Test
CIJE: 3 RIE: 1 CAT: 21

Lowenfeld World View Technique
CIJE: 0 RIE: 1 CAT: 15

Lower Asymptotes
CIJE: 1 RIE: 1 CAT: 21

Lower Attaining Pupils Programme (England)
CIJE: 0 RIE: 1 CAT: 19

Lower Brule Sioux Reservation
CIJE: 1 RIE: 0 CAT: 17

Lower Columbia College WA
CIJE: 3 RIE: 6 CAT: 17

Lower Kuskokwim School District AK
CIJE: 0 RIE: 1 CAT: 17

Lower Merion School District PA
CIJE: 0 RIE: 2 CAT: 17

Lower Mississippi Delta
CIJE: 0 RIE: 2 CAT: 07

Lower Predicate Calculus Technique
CIJE: 0 RIE: 1 CAT: 20

Lower Track Students
CIJE: 0 RIE: 2 CAT: 10
UF Low Track Classes

Lowery Projective Test of Attitudes
CIJE: 0 RIE: 1 CAT: 21

Lowes Syndrome
CIJE: 0 RIE: 1 CAT: 11
UF Oculocerebrorenal Syndrome

Lowry Technical Training Center CO
CIJE: 0 RIE: 1 CAT: 17

Loyalty
CIJE: 26 RIE: 7 CAT: 16

Loyola (San Ignacio de)
CIJE: 2 RIE: 1 CAT: 18

Loyola College (Canada)
CIJE: 0 RIE: 1 CAT: 17

Loyola College MD
CIJE: 3 RIE: 7 CAT: 17

Loyola Marymount University CA
CIJE: 0 RIE: 2 CAT: 17

Loyola University IL
CIJE: 11 RIE: 4 CAT: 17

Loyola University LA
CIJE: 2 RIE: 5 CAT: 17

Loyola University of Chicago IL
CIJE: 11 RIE: 7 CAT: 17

LRS Seriation Test
CIJE: 0 RIE: 1 CAT: 21

LSAY
USE Longitudinal Study of American Youth

LSU NASA Shuttle Program
CIJE: 1 RIE: 0 CAT: 19

LSW Industries
CIJE: 1 RIE: 0 CAT: 17

Lu (K H)
CIJE: 1 RIE: 0 CAT: 18

Lu Verne Community School District IA
CIJE: 0 RIE: 1 CAT: 17

Lubbock Civil Liberties Union v Lubbock School
CIJE: 2 RIE: 0 CAT: 14

Lubbock Independent School District TX
CIJE: 2 RIE: 3 CAT: 17

Lubetzky (Seymour)
CIJE: 2 RIE: 0 CAT: 18

Lubicon Lake Indian Band
CIJE: 1 RIE: 1 CAT: 08

Lubit Palatal Exerciser
CIJE: 1 RIE: 0 CAT: 04

Lubrication Systems
CIJE: 0 RIE: 6 CAT: 04

Lucan (Marcus Annaeus Lucanus)
CIJE: 4 RIE: 0 CAT: 18

Lucas (George)
CIJE: 0 RIE: 2 CAT: 18

Luce (Henry)
CIJE: 0 RIE: 1 CAT: 18

Luce (Stephen Bleeker)
CIJE: 0 RIE: 1 CAT: 18

Lucia (David)
CIJE: 1 RIE: 0 CAT: 18

Lucia Mar School District CA
CIJE: 1 RIE: 1 CAT: 17

Luck
CIJE: 11 RIE: 5 CAT: 16

Luckmann (Thomas)
CIJE: 1 RIE: 2 CAT: 18

Lucretia Crocker Program
CIJE: 0 RIE: 1 CAT: 19

Lucretius (Titus Lucretius Carus)
CIJE: 6 RIE: 0 CAT: 18

Ludington Reading Room MI
CIJE: 0 RIE: 2 CAT: 17

Ludlow Community Association OH
CIJE: 1 RIE: 0 CAT: 17

Ludlow Elementary School CA
CIJE: 1 RIE: 0 CAT: 17

Ludlum (Jacqueline)
CIJE: 0 RIE: 1 CAT: 18

Ludwig (Otto)
CIJE: 1 RIE: 0 CAT: 18

Lue Dialect
CIJE: 0 RIE: 1 CAT: 13

Lugand (Tribe)
CIJE: 0 RIE: 1 CAT: 08

Luganda
CIJE: 0 RIE: 2 CAT: 13

Luggage Makers
CIJE: 0 RIE: 1 CAT: 09

Lui (Ben Chieh)
CIJE: 0 RIE: 1 CAT: 18

Luiseno
CIJE: 1 RIE: 0 CAT: 13

Lujan v Colorado State Board of Education
CIJE: 0 RIE: 1 CAT: 14

Lukacs (Georg)
CIJE: 3 RIE: 2 CAT: 18

Lull (Ramon)
CIJE: 0 RIE: 1 CAT: 18

Lumbee (Tribe)
CIJE: 0 RIE: 12 CAT: 08

Lummi (Language)
CIJE: 1 RIE: 1 CAT: 13

Lummi (Tribe)
CIJE: 6 RIE: 4 CAT: 08

Lummi Indian Tribal Enterprise
CIJE: 1 RIE: 0 CAT: 17

Lumni Indian Aquaculture Project
CIJE: 0 RIE: 1 CAT: 19

Lunar Eclipses
CIJE: 1 RIE: 0 CAT: 20

Lunar Landings
CIJE: 2 RIE: 0 CAT: 20

Lunar Mascons
CIJE: 1 RIE: 0 CAT: 20

Lunar Materials
CIJE: 1 RIE: 0 CAT: 20

Lunar Science Conference 5th
CIJE: 2 RIE: 0 CAT: 02

Lunar Science Institute
CIJE: 1 RIE: 0 CAT: 17

Lunar Studies
CIJE: 0 RIE: 1 CAT: 03

Lunchroom Aides
CIJE: 0 RIE: 1 CAT: 09
SN See also "Cafeteria Monitors"

Lund University (Sweden)
CIJE: 2 RIE: 4 CAT: 17
UF University of Lund (Sweden)

Lunda Chokwe
CIJE: 0 RIE: 1 CAT: 13

Lung Diseases
CIJE: 7 RIE: 1 CAT: 11
SN See also "Respiratory Diseases"
UF Pulmonary Diseases

Lungs
CIJE: 8 RIE: 3 CAT: 11

Lungs Unlimited
CIJE: 1 RIE: 0 CAT: 19

Lunin (Mikhail Sergeyevich)
CIJE: 1 RIE: 0 CAT: 18

Lunsford (Andrea A)
CIJE: 0 RIE: 1 CAT: 18

Lurcat Test of Graphical Abilities
CIJE: 1 RIE: 0 CAT: 21

Luri Bakhtiari
CIJE: 0 RIE: 1 CAT: 13

Luria (A R)
CIJE: 19 RIE: 11 CAT: 18

Luria Nebraska Intellectual Processes Scale
CIJE: 2 RIE: 0 CAT: 21

Luria Nebraska Neuropsychological Battery
CIJE: 11 RIE: 6 CAT: 21
UF LNNB; LNNB (Childrens Revision)

Lurias Neuropsychological Investigation
CIJE: 1 RIE: 0 CAT: 14

Lushootseed
CIJE: 0 RIE: 1 CAT: 13

Luso Brazilian
CIJE: 1 RIE: 2 CAT: 13

Luso Brazilian Studies Survey
CIJE: 0 RIE: 1 CAT: 19

Luther (Martin)
CIJE: 5 RIE: 0 CAT: 18

Luther College IA
CIJE: 0 RIE: 6 CAT: 17

Lutheran Church
CIJE: 3 RIE: 2 CAT: 10

Lutheran Church in America
CIJE: 2 RIE: 1 CAT: 17

Lutheran Colleges
CIJE: 0 RIE: 2 CAT: 05

Lutheran Educational Conference of North America
CIJE: 0 RIE: 1 CAT: 17

Lutheran Schools
CIJE: 0 RIE: 14 CAT: 05

Lutheran Settlement House PA
CIJE: 0 RIE: 2 CAT: 17

Lutheran World Information Service
CIJE: 0 RIE: 1 CAT: 17

Luxembourg
CIJE: 10 RIE: 37 CAT: 07

Luzerne County Community College PA
CIJE: 1 RIE: 6 CAT: 17

Lwena
CIJE: 0 RIE: 1 CAT: 13

Lycoming College PA
CIJE: 3 RIE: 1 CAT: 17

Lyden University (Netherlands)
CIJE: 1 RIE: 0 CAT: 17

Lye
CIJE: 0 RIE: 1 CAT: 20

Lyman Memorial High School CT
CIJE: 0 RIE: 1 CAT: 17

Lynbrook Union Free School District NY
CIJE: 0 RIE: 1 CAT: 17

Lynch (Benito)
CIJE: 1 RIE: 0 CAT: 18

Lynch v Donnelly
CIJE: 2 RIE: 0 CAT: 14

Lynchburg College VA
CIJE: 4 RIE: 4 CAT: 17

Lynchings
CIJE: 0 RIE: 1 CAT: 14

Lynd (Staughton)
CIJE: 1 RIE: 0 CAT: 18

Lyndhurst Fellowship Program
CIJE: 1 RIE: 4 CAT: 19

Lyndon B Johnson Presidential Library TX
CIJE: 1 RIE: 0 CAT: 17

Lyon (Harold)
CIJE: 1 RIE: 0 CAT: 18

Lyon (Mary)
CIJE: 2 RIE: 2 CAT: 18

Lyon Graduate School of Business (France)
CIJE: 0 RIE: 1 CAT: 17
UF Ecole Superieure de Commerce de Lyon (France)

Lyons (John)
CIJE: 1 RIE: 0 CAT: 18

Lyons Township High School District IL
CIJE: 3 RIE: 0 CAT: 17

Lyons Township High School IL
CIJE: 1 RIE: 1 CAT: 17

Lyotard (Jean Francois)
CIJE: 1 RIE: 2 CAT: 18

Lyrics
CIJE: 19 RIE: 11 CAT: 16
UF Music Lyrics; Song Lyrics

M Factors
CIJE: 3 RIE: 0 CAT: 15

M Space
CIJE: 4 RIE: 1 CAT: 20

MA 3 Associative Memory Test (French et al)
CIJE: 0 RIE: 1 CAT: 21

Mabie (Hamilton Wright)
CIJE: 1 RIE: 0 CAT: 18

Macalester College MN
CIJE: 11 RIE: 6 CAT: 17

MacAllister Report
CIJE: 0 RIE: 1 CAT: 22

MacAndrew Alcoholism Scale
CIJE: 3 RIE: 1 CAT: 21

Macao
CIJE: 4 RIE: 5 CAT: 07
UF Macau

Macau
USE Macao

Macaulay (Thomas B)
CIJE: 2 RIE: 0 CAT: 18

Macbeth
CIJE: 15 RIE: 8 CAT: 22

MacBride Commission Report
CIJE: 5 RIE: 3 CAT: 22

MACC Behavioral Adjustment Scale
CIJE: 1 RIE: 0 CAT: 21

MacDonald (Jeffrey)
CIJE: 1 RIE: 0 CAT: 18

MacDonald Drive Junior High School (Canada)
CIJE: 1 RIE: 0 CAT: 17

MacDonald Tseng Locus of Control Scale
CIJE: 1 RIE: 2 CAT: 21

MacDowell (Edward)
CIJE: 1 RIE: 0 CAT: 18

Mace (Jean)
CIJE: 1 RIE: 0 CAT: 18

Macedonia
CIJE: 1 RIE: 1 CAT: 07

Macedonian
CIJE: 3 RIE: 9 CAT: 13

Macedorumanians
CIJE: 0 RIE: 2 CAT: 08

Mach Scale (Christie)
CIJE: 2 RIE: 1 CAT: 21

Machado (Antonio)
CIJE: 3 RIE: 0 CAT: 18

Machado de Assis (Joachim Maria)
CIJE: 1 RIE: 0 CAT: 18

Machiavelli (Niccolo)
CIJE: 11 RIE: 4 CAT: 18

Machiavellianism
CIJE: 29 RIE: 12 CAT: 16

Machine Dependence
CIJE: 1 RIE: 0 CAT: 16

Machine Design
CIJE: 0 RIE: 1 CAT: 20

Machine Language
CIJE: 1 RIE: 2 CAT: 20

Machine Language Teaching
CIJE: 0 RIE: 1 CAT: 15

Machine Learning
CIJE: 0 RIE: 6 CAT: 20
SN Ability of a device to improve its performance based on its past performance

Machine Operators
CIJE: 0 RIE: 4 CAT: 09

Machine Readable Data
CIJE: 17 RIE: 24 CAT: 16

Machine Shorthand
CIJE: 3 RIE: 3 CAT: 16

Machine Trades Training Program for Youth OH
CIJE: 0 RIE: 1 CAT: 19

Machine Transcription
CIJE: 10 RIE: 6 CAT: 03

Machine Vision
CIJE: 1 RIE: 1 CAT: 20
SN Image acquisition and analysis by machines, e.g., visual sensing by robots

Machines
CIJE: 2 RIE: 3 CAT: 04
SN Use a more specific term if possible, e.g., "Answering Machines," "Automated Teller Machines," "Mimeograph Machines," "Reading Machines," "Sewing Machines," "X Ray Machines"

Machismo
CIJE: 13 RIE: 8 CAT: 11

Machover Anxiety Scale
CIJE: 1 RIE: 0 CAT: 21

Machover Draw a Person Test
CIJE: 1 RIE: 1 CAT: 21

Macintosh Computers
USE Apple Macintosh

Mack Truck Corporation
CIJE: 0 RIE: 1 CAT: 17

MacKay (Donald M)
CIJE: 1 RIE: 0 CAT: 18

MacKaye (Percy)
CIJE: 0 RIE: 1 CAT: 18

Mackey (M Cecil)
CIJE: 1 RIE: 0 CAT: 18

MacKinnon (Catherine)
CIJE: 0 RIE: 1 CAT: 18

Mackworth Corneal Reflection Apparatus
CIJE: 0 RIE: 1 CAT: 04

MacLeish (Archibald)
CIJE: 5 RIE: 1 CAT: 18

MacMagic Program
CIJE: 0 RIE: 2 CAT: 19

Macmillan Company
CIJE: 0 RIE: 2 CAT: 17

Macmillan Reading Program Series
CIJE: 0 RIE: 1 CAT: 22

Macmillan Tutorial System
CIJE: 0 RIE: 1 CAT: 15

Macmurray (John)
CIJE: 2 RIE: 0 CAT: 18

MacMurray College IL
CIJE: 1 RIE: 0 CAT: 17

Macomb 0 to 3 Regional Project IL
CIJE: 0 RIE: 4 CAT: 19

Macomb Community College MI
CIJE: 1 RIE: 11 CAT: 17

Macomb County Community College MI
CIJE: 7 RIE: 15 CAT: 17

Macomb County Teacher Education Council MI
CIJE: 1 RIE: 0 CAT: 17

Macomb Intermediate School District MI
CIJE: 0 RIE: 1 CAT: 17

Macon College GA
CIJE: 0 RIE: 1 CAT: 17

MacPaint
CIJE: 0 RIE: 1 CAT: 04

MacProof
CIJE: 0 RIE: 1 CAT: 04
UF ALP MacProof

MacQuarie University (Australia)
CIJE: 6 RIE: 7 CAT: 17

Macrame
CIJE: 1 RIE: 1 CAT: 16

Macro Administration
CIJE: 0 RIE: 2 CAT: 15

Macro Cohort Enrollment Forecasting
CIJE: 0 RIE: 1 CAT: 15

Macro Graphic System
CIJE: 0 RIE: 1 CAT: 15

Macro Operators
CIJE: 3 RIE: 1 CAT: 20

Macro Theory
CIJE: 4 RIE: 0 CAT: 15

Macroanalysis
CIJE: 12 RIE: 7 CAT: 15

Macrocomponents (Intelligence)
CIJE: 0 RIE: 1 CAT: 11

Macrodesigns
CIJE: 0 RIE: 2 CAT: 15

Macroism
CIJE: 0 RIE: 1 CAT: 15

Macrophotography
CIJE: 2 RIE: 0 CAT: 15

Macroprocesses
CIJE: 2 RIE: 3 CAT: 15

Macrorie (Ken)
CIJE: 8 RIE: 1 CAT: 18

Macrostructures (Information)
CIJE: 2 RIE: 2 CAT: 13

Macrosystems
CIJE: 3 RIE: 1 CAT: 16

Macroteaching
CIJE: 0 RIE: 1 CAT: 15

MacSkimming Natural Science School (Canada)
CIJE: 1 RIE: 0 CAT: 17

Maculaitis Assessment Program
CIJE: 0 RIE: 1 CAT: 21

Mad Magazine
CIJE: 4 RIE: 0 CAT: 22

Madagascar
CIJE: 6 RIE: 11 CAT: 07

Madame Bovary
CIJE: 1 RIE: 1 CAT: 22

Madame Tussauds Wax Museum
CIJE: 1 RIE: 0 CAT: 17

Madawaska School District ME
CIJE: 0 RIE: 1 CAT: 17

MADD
USE Mothers Against Drunk Driving

Madelung Constants
CIJE: 1 RIE: 0 CAT: 20

Madigan (Elvira)
CIJE: 1 RIE: 0 CAT: 18

Madison (James)
CIJE: 9 RIE: 12 CAT: 18

Madison (Robert Lee)
CIJE: 0 RIE: 1 CAT: 18

Madison Area Project
CIJE: 0 RIE: 23 CAT: 19

Madison College VA
CIJE: 2 RIE: 2 CAT: 17

Madison Elementary School ND
CIJE: 1 RIE: 0 CAT: 17

Madison Junior High School NY
CIJE: 1 RIE: 1 CAT: 17

Madison Mutual Housing Association and Coop WI
CIJE: 0 RIE: 1 CAT: 17

Madison Project
CIJE: 2 RIE: 18 CAT: 19

Madison Project Mathematics
CIJE: 0 RIE: 1 CAT: 15

Madison Public Schools WI
CIJE: 4 RIE: 14 CAT: 17

Madison School District AZ
CIJE: 1 RIE: 2 CAT: 17

Madison Vocational Technical and Adult Schools WI
CIJE: 0 RIE: 1 CAT: 17

Madonna College MI
CIJE: 0 RIE: 6 CAT: 17

Madras System
CIJE: 1 RIE: 1 CAT: 15

Madrid Chamber of Commerce and Industry (Spain)
CIJE: 0 RIE: 1 CAT: 17

Madurai University (India)
CIJE: 1 RIE: 0 CAT: 17

Madurese
CIJE: 0 RIE: 2 CAT: 13
SN A West Indonesian language

Magar
CIJE: 0 RIE: 2 CAT: 13

Magazine Covers
CIJE: 1 RIE: 1 CAT: 16

Magazine Index
CIJE: 4 RIE: 2 CAT: 04

Magazine Publishers Association
CIJE: 0 RIE: 1 CAT: 17

Magazine Subscribers
USE Subscribers (Magazines)

Magazine Surveys
CIJE: 0 RIE: 1 CAT: 21

Magazine Writing
CIJE: 1 RIE: 2 CAT: 16

Magee Secondary School (Canada)
CIJE: 0 RIE: 1 CAT: 17

Mager (Robert)
CIJE: 5 RIE: 1 CAT: 18

Maghreb Countries
CIJE: 4 RIE: 18 CAT: 07

Magic
CIJE: 24 RIE: 13 CAT: 16

Magic Circle
CIJE: 9 RIE: 14 CAT: 16

Magic Crossbow (The)
CIJE: 0 RIE: 1 CAT: 22

Magic Cubes
CIJE: 1 RIE: 0 CAT: 20

Magic Ear
CIJE: 0 RIE: 1 CAT: 22

Magic Squares
CIJE: 27 RIE: 0 CAT: 20

Magic Wand Speaking Reader
CIJE: 0 RIE: 1 CAT: 04

Magical Number Seven Concept (Miller)
CIJE: 0 RIE: 0 CAT: 15

Magnetboards
CIJE: 0 RIE: 1 CAT: 04

Magnetic Information Technology
CIJE: 0 RIE: 1 CAT: 20

Magnetic Particle Testing
CIJE: 0 RIE: 2 CAT: 20

Magnetic Resonance Imaging
CIJE: 7 RIE: 2 CAT: 20
SN See related "Nuclear Magnetic Resonance"
UF Imaging (MRI); NMR Imaging

Magnetic Storage
CIJE: 4 RIE: 0 CAT: 20

Magnetic Tape Selectric Typewriter
CIJE: 4 RIE: 2 CAT: 04

Magnetometers
CIJE: 2 RIE: 0 CAT: 04

Magnetotropisms
CIJE: 1 RIE: 0 CAT: 20

Magnitude Estimates
CIJE: 2 RIE: 2 CAT: 21

Magnitude Estimations
CIJE: 11 RIE: 3 CAT: 15

Magnolia Speech School for the Deaf MS
CIJE: 1 RIE: 0 CAT: 17

Magruder Environmental Therapy Complex
CIJE: 1 RIE: 0 CAT: 15

Magubane (Bernard)
CIJE: 1 RIE: 0 CAT: 18

Maguire (Daniel C)
CIJE: 1 RIE: 0 CAT: 18

Mahabharata
CIJE: 0 RIE: 0 CAT: 22
SN Epic poem of India

Mahalanobis Distance Function
CIJE: 1 RIE: 3 CAT: 21

Maharaja Sayajirao University of Baroda (India)
CIJE: 0 RIE: 0 CAT: 17
UF MS University of Baroda (India)

Maharishi International University IA
CIJE: 4 RIE: 0 CAT: 17

Mahl Speech Disturbance Indices
CIJE: 0 RIE: 1 CAT: 21

Mahler (Margaret S)
CIJE: 0 RIE: 1 CAT: 18

Mahoning Valley Vocational School OH
CIJE: 1 RIE: 0 CAT: 17

Maieutic Pedagogy
CIJE: 0 RIE: 1 CAT: 15

Mail Balloting
CIJE: 1 RIE: 0 CAT: 15

Mail Order
CIJE: 7 RIE: 4 CAT: 16

Mail Order Book Delivery
CIJE: 2 RIE: 3 CAT: 16

Mail Order Libraries
CIJE: 2 RIE: 0 CAT: 05

Mail Processing Equipment Maintenance Personnel
CIJE: 0 RIE: 2 CAT: 09

Mail Registration
CIJE: 0 RIE: 3 CAT: 16
UF Registration by Mail

Mail Room Occupations
CIJE: 1 RIE: 5 CAT: 09

Mail Rooms
CIJE: 1 RIE: 0 CAT: 05

Mail Sorters
CIJE: 0 RIE: 3 CAT: 09

Mailable Copy Rate
CIJE: 1 RIE: 0 CAT: 16

Mailed Intervention
CIJE: 0 RIE: 1 CAT: 15

Mailer (Norman)
CIJE: 1 RIE: 2 CAT: 18

Mailing and Shipping
CIJE: 1 RIE: 3 CAT: 16

Mailing Lists
CIJE: 3 RIE: 7 CAT: 16

Maimonides Early Childhood Health Program
CIJE: 0 RIE: 1 CAT: 19

Maimonides Medical Center NY
CIJE: 0 RIE: 1 CAT: 17

Main Idea
CIJE: 48 RIE: 30 CAT: 16

Main Libraries
CIJE: 11 RIE: 0 CAT: 05

Maine
CIJE: 90 RIE: 339 CAT: 07

Maine (Aroostook County)
CIJE: 1 RIE: 2 CAT: 07

Maine (Augusta)
CIJE: 0 RIE: 1 CAT: 07

Maine (Bangor)
CIJE: 0 RIE: 4 CAT: 07

Maine (Bar Harbor)
CIJE: 1 RIE: 0 CAT: 07

Maine (Bethel)
CIJE: 0 RIE: 1 CAT: 07

Maine (Biddeford)
CIJE: 0 RIE: 1 CAT: 07

Maine (Franklin County)
CIJE: 1 RIE: 1 CAT: 07

Maine (Frenchville)
CIJE: 0 RIE: 1 CAT: 07

Maine (Fryeburg)
CIJE: 0 RIE: 1 CAT: 07

Maine (Guilford)
CIJE: 2 RIE: 0 CAT: 07

Maine (Madawaska)
CIJE: 0 RIE: 3 CAT: 07

Maine (Orland)
CIJE: 0 RIE: 1 CAT: 07

Maine (Portland)
CIJE: 0 RIE: 1 CAT: 07

Maine (York County)
CIJE: 0 RIE: 2 CAT: 07

Maine Academy for School Leaders
CIJE: 0 RIE: 1 CAT: 17

Maine Administrator Action Plan
USE Administrator Action Plan (Maine)

Maine Assessment of Educational Progress
CIJE: 0 RIE: 3 CAT: 19

Maine CITE
CIJE: 0 RIE: 1 CAT: 19
UF Maine Consumer Information and Techn Training Exch

Maine Consumer Information and Techn Training Exch
USE Maine CITE

Maine Drug Education Program
CIJE: 0 RIE: 1 CAT: 19

Maine Educational Assessment
CIJE: 0 RIE: 1 CAT: 19

Maine Health Education Resource Center
CIJE: 1 RIE: 1 CAT: 17

Maine Innovative Education Grant Program
CIJE: 0 RIE: 1 CAT: 19

Maine Public Broadcasting Network
CIJE: 2 RIE: 0 CAT: 17

Maine School Administrative District Number 11
CIJE: 0 RIE: 0 CAT: 17

Maine School Administrative District Number 4
CIJE: 0 RIE: 0 CAT: 17

Maine School Administrative District Number 40
CIJE: 0 RIE: 0 CAT: 17

Maine State Dept of Educ and Cultural Services
CIJE: 0 RIE: 2 CAT: 17

Maine State Library
CIJE: 1 RIE: 5 CAT: 17

Maine Student Incentive Scholarship Program
CIJE: 0 RIE: 1 CAT: 19

Maine Township High Schools IL
CIJE: 2 RIE: 2 CAT: 17

Maine v Thiboutot
CIJE: 1 RIE: 0 CAT: 14

Maine Woods (The)
CIJE: 0 RIE: 1 CAT: 22

Maine Youth Center
CIJE: 0 RIE: 5 CAT: 17

Mainframe Computers
CIJE: 50 RIE: 17 CAT: 04

Mainstream Assistance Team Project
CIJE: 0 RIE: 1 CAT: 19

Mainstream English Language Training Project
CIJE: 0 RIE: 3 CAT: 19

Mainstream Inservice Project NJ
CIJE: 1 RIE: 0 CAT: 19

Mainstream Project TEACH
CIJE: 0 RIE: 1 CAT: 19

Mainstreaming (Non English Speaking)
CIJE: 0 RIE: 4 CAT: 15

Mainstreaming Planning Committees
CIJE: 0 RIE: 1 CAT: 05

Mainstreaming the Disadvantaged
CIJE: 1 RIE: 7 CAT: 15

Maintenance Behavior
CIJE: 9 RIE: 3 CAT: 11

Maintenance Bilingual Education
CIJE: 2 RIE: 1 CAT: 03

Maintenance Bilingual Education Programs
CIJE: 1 RIE: 1 CAT: 19

Maintenance Performance System
CIJE: 0 RIE: 1 CAT: 15

Maithili
CIJE: 0 RIE: 5 CAT: 13

Maitland Graves Design Judgment Test
CIJE: 1 RIE: 2 CAT: 21
UF Design Judgment (Maitland Graves)

Majang
CIJE: 0 RIE: 2 CAT: 13
SN Nilo-Saharan language of southwestern Ethiopia

Majhi Dialect
CIJE: 0 RIE: 1 CAT: 13

Major (Kevin)
CIJE: 0 RIE: 1 CAT: 18

Major Field Achievement Test in Political Science
CIJE: 0 RIE: 1 CAT: 21
UF MFATPS

Major Field of Study Map
CIJE: 0 RIE: 1 CAT: 15

Major Thrust in Elementary School Thinking Project
CIJE: 0 RIE: 1 CAT: 19

Major Urban Resource Libraries
CIJE: 0 RIE: 5 CAT: 19

Majority Groups
CIJE: 1 RIE: 1 CAT: 16

Majority Role
CIJE: 3 RIE: 2 CAT: 16

Majority Rule
CIJE: 2 RIE: 2 CAT: 14

Makah (Language)
CIJE: 0 RIE: 4 CAT: 13

Makah (Tribe)
CIJE: 1 RIE: 3 CAT: 08

Makaton Vocabulary
CIJE: 3 RIE: 2 CAT: 13

Make Something Happen
CIJE: 0 RIE: 1 CAT: 22

Makerere University (Uganda)
CIJE: 2 RIE: 3 CAT: 17

Makeup (Theater Arts)
USE Theatrical Makeup

Making Action Plans (MAPS)
USE McGill Action Planning System

Making of a Decision (Film)
CIJE: 0 RIE: 1 CAT: 22

Making Special Friends Project
CIJE: 0 RIE: 4 CAT: 19

Making the Grade
CIJE: 1 RIE: 3 CAT: 22
SN Report of the Twentieth Century Fund Task Force

Making the Grade Eval and Reporting Student Prog
CIJE: 0 RIE: 1 CAT: 22
SN Report of the Etobicoke (Ontario) Board of Education

Makonde (Language)
CIJE: 0 RIE: 0 CAT: 13

Makonde (Tribe)
CIJE: 0 RIE: 1 CAT: 08

Malabar Street School CA
CIJE: 0 RIE: 2 CAT: 17

Malabsorption
CIJE: 1 RIE: 0 CAT: 15

Maladaptive Behavior Record
CIJE: 0 RIE: 4 CAT: 15

Maladaptive Persistence
CIJE: 0 RIE: 1 CAT: 11

Maladjustive Category
CIJE: 1 RIE: 0 CAT: 15

Malagasy Republic
CIJE: 2 RIE: 2 CAT: 07

Malamud (Bernard)
CIJE: 3 RIE: 0 CAT: 18

Malapropisms
CIJE: 1 RIE: 1 CAT: 13

Malaria
CIJE: 1 RIE: 4 CAT: 11

Malaspina College BC
CIJE: 0 RIE: 1 CAT: 17

Malawi
CIJE: 34 RIE: 39 CAT: 07

Malay Peninsula
CIJE: 1 RIE: 0 CAT: 07

Malayan Americans
CIJE: 0 RIE: 1 CAT: 08

Malayans
CIJE: 6 RIE: 5 CAT: 08

Malaysia
CIJE: 164 RIE: 207 CAT: 07

Malaysia (George Town)
CIJE: 1 RIE: 0 CAT: 07

Malaysia (Kuala Lumpur)
CIJE: 4 RIE: 3 CAT: 07

Malaysia (Malaya)
CIJE: 0 RIE: 2 CAT: 07

Malaysia (North Borneo)
CIJE: 0 RIE: 1 CAT: 07

Malaysia (Peninsular)
USE Malaysia (West)

Malaysia (Sabah)
CIJE: 0 RIE: 2 CAT: 07

Malaysia (Sarawak)
CIJE: 2 RIE: 3 CAT: 07

Malaysia (Selangor State)
CIJE: 0 RIE: 1 CAT: 07

Malaysia (West)
CIJE: 3 RIE: 3 CAT: 07
UF Malaysia (Peninsular)

Malaysians
CIJE: 0 RIE: 9 CAT: 08

Malcolm X
CIJE: 18 RIE: 5 CAT: 18

Malcolm X College IL
USE City Colleges of Chicago Il Malcolm X College

Malcolm X Liberation University NC
CIJE: 1 RIE: 0 CAT: 17

Malcomesius (Neva)
CIJE: 1 RIE: 0 CAT: 18

Maldives
CIJE: 0 RIE: 6 CAT: 07

Male Faculty
CIJE: 1 RIE: 2 CAT: 09

Male Female Relationship
CIJE: 14 RIE: 32 CAT: 16

Male Managerial Model
CIJE: 0 RIE: 1 CAT: 15

Maleic Acid
CIJE: 1 RIE: 0 CAT: 20

Mali
CIJE: 14 RIE: 25 CAT: 07

Malicious Coincidence Model
CIJE: 1 RIE: 0 CAT: 15

Malingering
CIJE: 8 RIE: 0 CAT: 11

Malinke
CIJE: 0 RIE: 2 CAT: 13

Malinowski (Bronislaw)
CIJE: 1 RIE: 2 CAT: 18

Maliseet (Tribe)
CIJE: 1 RIE: 3 CAT: 08

Mallarme (Stephane)
CIJE: 3 RIE: 0 CAT: 18

Mallinckrodt Chemical Works
CIJE: 1 RIE: 0 CAT: 17

Mallinckrodt Inc
CIJE: 0 RIE: 1 CAT: 17

Malloy Catholic College for Women NY
CIJE: 0 RIE: 1 CAT: 17

MALM Tutoring System
CIJE: 0 RIE: 1 CAT: 04

Malmo School of Education (Sweden)
CIJE: 0 RIE: 2 CAT: 17

Malocclusion
CIJE: 3 RIE: 1 CAT: 11

Malraux (Andre)
CIJE: 1 RIE: 0 CAT: 18

Malta
CIJE: 29 RIE: 27 CAT: 07

Maltese
CIJE: 3 RIE: 6 CAT: 13

Maltese Australians
CIJE: 0 RIE: 1 CAT: 08

Maltese Falcon
CIJE: 2 RIE: 0 CAT: 22

Malthus (Thomas Robert)
CIJE: 6 RIE: 1 CAT: 18

Malvern Hills College (England)
CIJE: 1 RIE: 0 CAT: 17

Malwi Dialect
CIJE: 0 RIE: 1 CAT: 13

Mamanua
CIJE: 2 RIE: 2 CAT: 13

Mamaroneck Union Free School District NY
CIJE: 0 RIE: 1 CAT: 17

Mambila
CIJE: 1 RIE: 0 CAT: 13

Mammals
CIJE: 22 RIE: 7 CAT: 20

Mampruli
CIJE: 0 RIE: 1 CAT: 13
SN Language of northeastern Ghana

Man A Course of Study
CIJE: 21 RIE: 46 CAT: 03

Man and the Biosphere
CIJE: 11 RIE: 6 CAT: 19

Man and the Environment Curriculum
CIJE: 1 RIE: 0 CAT: 03

Man Environment Systems
CIJE: 1 RIE: 0 CAT: 15

Man for All Seasons (A)
CIJE: 0 RIE: 1 CAT: 22

Man in the Arctic Program
CIJE: 0 RIE: 1 CAT: 19

Man Machine Function Allocation
CIJE: 0 RIE: 2 CAT: 15

Man Made World
CIJE: 3 RIE: 2 CAT: 22

Man Nature Relationship
CIJE: 2 RIE: 2 CAT: 16

Man Who Lived Underground
CIJE: 1 RIE: 0 CAT: 22

Management Analysis
CIJE: 7 RIE: 6 CAT: 15

Management and Planning System
CIJE: 3 RIE: 0 CAT: 15

Management Assistance Teams
CIJE: 0 RIE: 2 CAT: 10

Management Bargaining Teams
CIJE: 0 RIE: 2 CAT: 10

Management by Information
CIJE: 0 RIE: 2 CAT: 15

Management Consulting Service
CIJE: 2 RIE: 1 CAT: 16

Management Control
CIJE: 5 RIE: 2 CAT: 16

Management Control Theory
CIJE: 2 RIE: 1 CAT: 15

Management Counseling
CIJE: 0 RIE: 1 CAT: 15

Management Educational Resources Systems
CIJE: 0 RIE: 1 CAT: 15

Management Engineered Teacher Education
CIJE: 0 RIE: 1 CAT: 15

Management Evaluation Review Compliance Quality
CIJE: 0 RIE: 1 CAT: 16

Management Implications of Team Teaching Project
CIJE: 0 RIE: 5 CAT: 19
UF Project MITT

Management Information Feedback System
CIJE: 0 RIE: 1 CAT: 15

Management Information System Occupational Educ
CIJE: 0 RIE: 43 CAT: 15
UF MISOE

Management Myth Information Systems
CIJE: 0 RIE: 1 CAT: 15

Management of Metric Implementation
CIJE: 0 RIE: 1 CAT: 15

Management Planning and Control System
CIJE: 1 RIE: 0 CAT: 04

Management Practices
CIJE: 66 RIE: 24 CAT: 15

Management Problem Laboratory
CIJE: 0 RIE: 1 CAT: 15

Management Profile (Erlandson)
CIJE: 2 RIE: 0 CAT: 21

Management Responsibility Guide
CIJE: 1 RIE: 1 CAT: 15

Management Review (Journal)
CIJE: 0 RIE: 1 CAT: 22

Management Review and Analysis Program
CIJE: 3 RIE: 11 CAT: 19

Management Science
CIJE: 24 RIE: 2 CAT: 15

Management Skills
CIJE: 59 RIE: 20 CAT: 15

Management Styles
CIJE: 53 RIE: 23 CAT: 15

Management Systems Inventory
CIJE: 0 RIE: 1 CAT: 15

Manager Rating Scale
CIJE: 0 RIE: 1 CAT: 21

Managerial Attention
CIJE: 1 RIE: 0 CAT: 15
UF Administrative Attention

Managerial Class
CIJE: 0 RIE: 1 CAT: 10

Managerial Communication
CIJE: 26 RIE: 10 CAT: 16

Managerial Ecology
CIJE: 0 RIE: 1 CAT: 15

Managerial Frames of Mind Survey
CIJE: 0 RIE: 1 CAT: 21

Managerial Grid
CIJE: 11 RIE: 4 CAT: 15

Managerial Grid Analysis
CIJE: 0 RIE: 1 CAT: 15

Managerial Work Activity Classification System
CIJE: 0 RIE: 1 CAT: 15

Managerialism
CIJE: 2 RIE: 1 CAT: 15

Managing Academic Tasks Study
CIJE: 0 RIE: 1 CAT: 19

Managing Disabilities
USE Disability Management

Managing Occupational Therapy in Rural Education
CIJE: 0 RIE: 1 CAT: 19

Managing Reading By Objectives
CIJE: 0 RIE: 1 CAT: 19

Manatee County Public Schools FL
CIJE: 2 RIE: 2 CAT: 17

Manatees
CIJE: 0 RIE: 1 CAT: 20

Manchester College IN
CIJE: 0 RIE: 1 CAT: 17

Manchester Community College CT
CIJE: 1 RIE: 3 CAT: 17

Manchester Grammar School (England)
CIJE: 1 RIE: 0 CAT: 17

Manchester Public Libraries
CIJE: 1 RIE: 0 CAT: 17

Manchester Statistical Society
CIJE: 1 RIE: 0 CAT: 17

Manchild in the Promised Land
CIJE: 1 RIE: 0 CAT: 22

Mand Model Procedure
CIJE: 0 RIE: 1 CAT: 15

Mandala
CIJE: 3 RIE: 1 CAT: 13

Mandan (Tribe)
CIJE: 5 RIE: 5 CAT: 08

Mandara
CIJE: 0 RIE: 1 CAT: 13

Mandate Consultant (Computer System)
CIJE: 1 RIE: 2 CAT: 04

Mandated Programs
USE Mandatory Programs

Mandated Tests
CIJE: 17 RIE: 20 CAT: 21

Mandatory Bargaining Issues
CIJE: 1 RIE: 0 CAT: 16

Mandatory Continuing Education
CIJE: 35 RIE: 8 CAT: 16

Mandatory Programs
CIJE: 15 RIE: 28 CAT: 16
UF Mandated Programs

Mandatory Reporting of Abuse
CIJE: 0 RIE: 2 CAT: 16

Mandatory Retirement
CIJE: 51 RIE: 20 CAT: 16

Mandatory Special Education Act (Michigan)
CIJE: 0 RIE: 1 CAT: 14

Mandatory Staggered Attendance Plans
CIJE: 2 RIE: 0 CAT: 16

Mande
CIJE: 1 RIE: 2 CAT: 13

Mandelbrot (Benoit B)
CIJE: 0 RIE: 0 CAT: 18

Mandelbrot Law
CIJE: 2 RIE: 0 CAT: 20

Mandelbrot Set
CIJE: 1 RIE: 1 CAT: 20

Manding (Psychology)
USE Mands

Mandler Sarason Test Anxiety Questionnaire
CIJE: 7 RIE: 9 CAT: 21

Mandragola
CIJE: 1 RIE: 0 CAT: 22

Mands
CIJE: 3 RIE: 0 CAT: 11
SN See also "Tacts"
UF Manding (Psychology)

Manes (Stephen)
CIJE: 0 RIE: 1 CAT: 18

Maneuvering Board Problems
CIJE: 0 RIE: 1 CAT: 15

Manganese
CIJE: 3 RIE: 1 CAT: 20

Mangrove Ecosystem
CIJE: 0 RIE: 1 CAT: 20

Mangroves
CIJE: 1 RIE: 2 CAT: 20

Manhasset Union Free School District NY
CIJE: 2 RIE: 2 CAT: 17

Manhattan College NY
CIJE: 1 RIE: 1 CAT: 17

Manhattan Community College NY
USE City University of New York Manhattan Comm Coll

Manhattan Country School NY
CIJE: 1 RIE: 1 CAT: 17

Manhattan School of Music NY
CIJE: 2 RIE: 0 CAT: 17

Manhattanville College NY
CIJE: 2 RIE: 2 CAT: 17

Manhattanville Music Curriculum Program
CIJE: 3 RIE: 0 CAT: 19

Manic Depression
CIJE: 4 RIE: 2 CAT: 11

Manicuring
CIJE: 0 RIE: 2 CAT: 09

Manifest Anxiety Defensiveness Scale (Millimet)
CIJE: 2 RIE: 0 CAT: 21

Manifest Anxiety Scale
CIJE: 5 RIE: 6 CAT: 21

Manifest Needs Questionnaire
CIJE: 3 RIE: 0 CAT: 21

Manifold Interest Schedule
CIJE: 0 RIE: 1 CAT: 15

Manifolds
CIJE: 1 RIE: 0 CAT: 04

Maninka
CIJE: 0 RIE: 2 CAT: 13

Manipulable Influences
CIJE: 3 RIE: 0 CAT: 16

Manipulable Variables
CIJE: 0 RIE: 1 CAT: 20

Manipulandum Referenced Taxonomy
CIJE: 0 RIE: 1 CAT: 15

Manipulative Play
CIJE: 5 RIE: 1 CAT: 15

Manipuri
USE Meitei

Manito
CIJE: 0 RIE: 1 CAT: 13

Manitoba
CIJE: 70 RIE: 368 CAT: 07

Manitoba (Brandon)
CIJE: 1 RIE: 2 CAT: 07

Manitoba (Easterville)
CIJE: 0 RIE: 1 CAT: 07

Manitoba (Fairford)
CIJE: 0 RIE: 1 CAT: 07

Manitoba (North)
CIJE: 2 RIE: 1 CAT: 07

Manitoba (Winnipeg)
CIJE: 10 RIE: 26 CAT: 07

Manitoba Department of Education
CIJE: 0 RIE: 10 CAT: 17

Manitoba Education Information Access
CIJE: 1 RIE: 0 CAT: 15

Manitoba Frontier School Division
CIJE: 0 RIE: 1 CAT: 17

Manitoba Health Assessment Program
CIJE: 0 RIE: 1 CAT: 19

Manitoba Health Services Commission
CIJE: 1 RIE: 0 CAT: 17

Manitoba Indian Brotherhood
CIJE: 1 RIE: 1 CAT: 17

Manitoba Literacy Office
CIJE: 0 RIE: 1 CAT: 17

Manitoba Longitudinal Study on Aging
CIJE: 1 RIE: 0 CAT: 22

Manitoba Mathematics Assessment Program 1981
CIJE: 0 RIE: 1 CAT: 19

Manitoulin Island
CIJE: 1 RIE: 0 CAT: 07

Manitowoc Technical Institute WI
CIJE: 0 RIE: 1 CAT: 17

Mankato State College MN
CIJE: 5 RIE: 5 CAT: 17

Mankato State University MN
CIJE: 4 RIE: 6 CAT: 17

Mankind Research Unlimited
CIJE: 1 RIE: 0 CAT: 17

Mann (Horace)
CIJE: 11 RIE: 4 CAT: 18

Mann (Margaret)
CIJE: 2 RIE: 0 CAT: 18

Mann (Thomas)
CIJE: 4 RIE: 0 CAT: 18

Mann Suiter Developmental Screening Tests
CIJE: 0 RIE: 1 CAT: 21

Mann Whitney U Test
CIJE: 17 RIE: 15 CAT: 21

Mannheim (Karl)
CIJE: 5 RIE: 4 CAT: 18

Mannheim University (West Germany)
CIJE: 2 RIE: 0 CAT: 17

Manning (Henry Edward)
CIJE: 1 RIE: 0 CAT: 18

Manning Theory
CIJE: 0 RIE: 1 CAT: 15

Mano
CIJE: 0 RIE: 2 CAT: 13

Manobo (Agusan)
USE Agusan Manobo

Manobo (Cotabato)
USE Cotabato Manobo

Manobo (Dibabawon)
USE Dibabawon

Manobo (Sarangani)
CIJE: 1 RIE: 0 CAT: 13

Manometers
CIJE: 2 RIE: 0 CAT: 04

Manometry
CIJE: 1 RIE: 0 CAT: 20

Manon Lescaut
CIJE: 1 RIE: 0 CAT: 22

Manor Junior College PA
CIJE: 0 RIE: 3 CAT: 17

Manpower and Talent Clearinghouse
CIJE: 0 RIE: 1 CAT: 17

Manpower Development and Training Act
CIJE: 27 RIE: 219 CAT: 14

Manpower Development and Training Act Programs
CIJE: 15 RIE: 48 CAT: 19

Manpower Development Corporation
CIJE: 1 RIE: 0 CAT: 17

Manpower Institutional Grant Program
CIJE: 0 RIE: 2 CAT: 19

Manpower Planning
CIJE: 11 RIE: 16 CAT: 16

Manpower Policy
CIJE: 2 RIE: 13 CAT: 14

Manpower Projection Model Project
CIJE: 0 RIE: 1 CAT: 19

Manpower Report of the President
CIJE: 1 RIE: 0 CAT: 22

Manpower Report of the President (1972)
CIJE: 1 RIE: 0 CAT: 22

Manpower Report of the President (1975)
CIJE: 1 RIE: 0 CAT: 22

Manpower Requirements Projection Model
CIJE: 0 RIE: 5 CAT: 15

Manpower Services Commission
CIJE: 8 RIE: 0 CAT: 17

Manpower Substitution
CIJE: 0 RIE: 1 CAT: 16

Manrique (Jorge)
CIJE: 1 RIE: 0 CAT: 18

Mansbridge (Albert)
CIJE: 0 RIE: 1 CAT: 18

Mansfield (Michael)
CIJE: 0 RIE: 1 CAT: 18

Mansfield City Schools OH
CIJE: 0 RIE: 2 CAT: 17

Mansfield State College PA
CIJE: 0 RIE: 1 CAT: 17

Mansfield University PA
CIJE: 1 RIE: 3 CAT: 17

Mansoura University (Egypt)
CIJE: 0 RIE: 1 CAT: 17

Mantel Haenszel Procedure
CIJE: 24 RIE: 36 CAT: 21

Manual Accuracy and Speed Test
CIJE: 1 RIE: 0 CAT: 21

Manual Arts Therapy
CIJE: 1 RIE: 0 CAT: 11

Manual Dexterity
CIJE: 6 RIE: 1 CAT: 11

Manual Response Latency
CIJE: 0 RIE: 1 CAT: 15

Manual Searches
CIJE: 8 RIE: 4 CAT: 20

Manual Skills
CIJE: 3 RIE: 1 CAT: 16

Manual Systems
CIJE: 2 RIE: 3 CAT: 04

Manually Coded English
CIJE: 7 RIE: 3 CAT: 13

Manuel (Don Juan)
CIJE: 1 RIE: 0 CAT: 18

Manufacturers Service Representatives
CIJE: 1 RIE: 1 CAT: 09

Manufacturing Automation Protocols
CIJE: 0 RIE: 0 CAT: 20

Manufacturing Chemists Association
CIJE: 2 RIE: 0 CAT: 17

Manuscript Collections
CIJE: 15 RIE: 12 CAT: 16

Manuscript Illumination
CIJE: 0 RIE: 1 CAT: 16

Manuscript Submission Procedures
CIJE: 7 RIE: 3 CAT: 15

Manuscript Typing
CIJE: 1 RIE: 0 CAT: 16

Manuscripts
CIJE: 31 RIE: 17 CAT: 16

Many Guns (Tom)
CIJE: 0 RIE: 1 CAT: 18

Manzano (Sonia)
CIJE: 0 RIE: 1 CAT: 18

Manzi (Albert)
CIJE: 1 RIE: 0 CAT: 18

Manzoni (Alessandro)
CIJE: 2 RIE: 0 CAT: 18

Mao Tse Tung
USE Mao Zedong

Mao Zedong
CIJE: 4 RIE: 7 CAT: 18
UF Mao Tse Tung

Maoism
CIJE: 6 RIE: 2 CAT: 16

Maori (Language)
CIJE: 10 RIE: 16 CAT: 13

Maori (People)
CIJE: 41 RIE: 52 CAT: 08

MAP AT HOME Program
USE Monitoring Achievement in Pittsburgh

MAP Critical Thinking Project
CIJE: 0 RIE: 1 CAT: 19

Map Displays
CIJE: 0 RIE: 2 CAT: 16

Map Libraries
CIJE: 15 RIE: 9 CAT: 05

Map Processing
CIJE: 3 RIE: 1 CAT: 16

Map Projections
CIJE: 3 RIE: 0 CAT: 16

MAPLE Computer Algebra System
CIJE: 2 RIE: 2 CAT: 04

Maple Sugar
CIJE: 4 RIE: 1 CAT: 20

Maple Syrup Urine Disease
CIJE: 2 RIE: 0 CAT: 11

Mapping
CIJE: 30 RIE: 21 CAT: 15
SN Use a more specific term if possible, e.g., following such initial words as Backward, Collection, Competency, Computer, Concept, Curriculum, Fast, Forward, Genetic, Grammatical, Idea, Program, School, Semantic, Story, Structure, and Topographic Brain

Mapping (Composition)
CIJE: 1 RIE: 1 CAT: 15

Mapping Instruction (Mathematics)
CIJE: 0 RIE: 1 CAT: 20

MAPS (for Including All Children in Schools)
USE McGill Action Planning System

MAPS Placement Research Service
CIJE: 0 RIE: 1 CAT: 19
SN See also "Multiple Assessment Programs and Services"
UF CEEB MAPS Placement Research Service

MAPS Tests
USE Multiple Assessment Programs and Services

Maquiladoras
CIJE: 1 RIE: 2 CAT: 05
SN Factories in Mexico

Marana Junior High School AZ
CIJE: 0 RIE: 1 CAT: 17

Maranon (Gregorio)
CIJE: 5 RIE: 0 CAT: 18

Maranungku
CIJE: 0 RIE: 1 CAT: 13
SN An Australian language

Marasmus
CIJE: 1 RIE: 2 CAT: 07

Marat Sade
CIJE: 1 RIE: 0 CAT: 22

Marathon Groups
CIJE: 11 RIE: 0 CAT: 10

Marathon Running
CIJE: 4 RIE: 3 CAT: 16

Marathon Writing
CIJE: 0 RIE: 1 CAT: 13

Marble Board Test
CIJE: 0 RIE: 1 CAT: 21

Marble Game
CIJE: 0 RIE: 1 CAT: 16

Marblehead Public Schools MA
CIJE: 0 RIE: 1 CAT: 17

Marbles (Game)
CIJE: 0 RIE: 1 CAT: 16

Marbling
CIJE: 1 RIE: 1 CAT: 16

Marburg University (West Germany)
CIJE: 1 RIE: 0 CAT: 17

Marbury v Madison
CIJE: 0 RIE: 1 CAT: 14

MARC
CIJE: 151 RIE: 94 CAT: 04

MARC Data Base
CIJE: 13 RIE: 7 CAT: 04

MARC II
CIJE: 6 RIE: 8 CAT: 04

Marcel (Gabriel)
CIJE: 1 RIE: 1 CAT: 18

March (James G)
CIJE: 0 RIE: 2 CAT: 18

March of Dimes
CIJE: 0 RIE: 2 CAT: 17

Marchi Law
CIJE: 0 RIE: 1 CAT: 14

Marcia (James E)
CIJE: 0 RIE: 0 CAT: 18

Marcia Incomplete Sentences Blank
CIJE: 0 RIE: 1 CAT: 21

Marconi (Guglielmo)
CIJE: 2 RIE: 0 CAT: 18

Marcos (Ferdinand)
CIJE: 2 RIE: 1 CAT: 18

Marcuse (Herbert)
CIJE: 3 RIE: 6 CAT: 18

Marcy Open School MN
CIJE: 0 RIE: 1 CAT: 17

Marengo County School District AL
CIJE: 0 RIE: 1 CAT: 17

Marfan Syndrome
CIJE: 1 RIE: 1 CAT: 11

Margenau (Henry)
CIJE: 0 RIE: 1 CAT: 18

Margi
CIJE: 0 RIE: 1 CAT: 13

Margin in Life Scale
CIJE: 0 RIE: 1 CAT: 21

Marginal Costs
CIJE: 0 RIE: 1 CAT: 16

Marginal Means
CIJE: 1 RIE: 0 CAT: 20

Marginal Notes
CIJE: 2 RIE: 1 CAT: 16

Marginal Productivity
CIJE: 1 RIE: 0 CAT: 15

Marginal Students
CIJE: 3 RIE: 3 CAT: 10

Marginal Teachers
CIJE: 0 RIE: 3 CAT: 10

Marginality
CIJE: 37 RIE: 5 CAT: 15

Mari
CIJE: 0 RIE: 1 CAT: 13

Marianne Frostig Center for Educational Therapy
CIJE: 1 RIE: 0 CAT: 17

Maricopa
CIJE: 0 RIE: 2 CAT: 13

Maricopa (Tribe)
CIJE: 1 RIE: 3 CAT: 08

Maricopa Community Colleges AZ
USE Maricopa County Community College District AZ

Maricopa County Community College AZ
CIJE: 1 RIE: 3 CAT: 17

Maricopa County Community College District AZ
CIJE: 6 RIE: 13 CAT: 17
UF Maricopa Community Colleges AZ; Maricopa County Community College System AZ

Maricopa County Community College System AZ
USE Maricopa County Community College District AZ

Maricopa County Organizing Project
CIJE: 0 RIE: 1 CAT: 19

Maricopa Technical Community College AZ
CIJE: 0 RIE: 0 CAT: 17

Marie Curie Memorial Foundation
CIJE: 1 RIE: 0 CAT: 17

Mariel Cubans
CIJE: 2 RIE: 6 CAT: 08

Marietta College OH
CIJE: 0 RIE: 2 CAT: 17

Marietta Independent School District GA
CIJE: 0 RIE: 0 CAT: 17

Marigny (Ryno de)
CIJE: 1 RIE: 0 CAT: 18

Marin Community Colleges CA
CIJE: 0 RIE: 1 CAT: 17

Marin County Jail CA
CIJE: 0 RIE: 1 CAT: 17

Marin County Office of Education CA
CIJE: 2 RIE: 1 CAT: 17

Marin Social Studies Project
CIJE: 0 RIE: 2 CAT: 19

Marinbata
USE Murinbata

Marine Assignment Preference Schedule
CIJE: 0 RIE: 1 CAT: 15

Marine Corps
CIJE: 7 RIE: 59 CAT: 17

Marine Data Management
CIJE: 0 RIE: 2 CAT: 15

Marine Equipment
CIJE: 0 RIE: 7 CAT: 04

Marine Hoses
CIJE: 0 RIE: 1 CAT: 04

Marine Occupations
CIJE: 2 RIE: 14 CAT: 09
UF Maritime Occupations

Marine Pollution Monitoring Programme
CIJE: 0 RIE: 1 CAT: 19

Marine Science Young Scholars Program
CIJE: 0 RIE: 0 CAT: 19
SN Program of the National Science Foundation

Marine Vocational Technical Institute OR
CIJE: 0 RIE: 1 CAT: 17

Marinetti (Filippo Tommaso)
CIJE: 2 RIE: 0 CAT: 18

Marino (Giambattista)
CIJE: 1 RIE: 0 CAT: 18

Marion Carll School
CIJE: 1 RIE: 0 CAT: 17

Marion Public Schools IN
CIJE: 1 RIE: 1 CAT: 17

Marist College NY
CIJE: 2 RIE: 4 CAT: 17

Marist Sisters College (Australia)
CIJE: 0 RIE: 2 CAT: 17

Maritain (Jacques)
CIJE: 4 RIE: 1 CAT: 18

Marital Adjustment
CIJE: 11 RIE: 3 CAT: 11

Marital Alternatives Scale
CIJE: 1 RIE: 0 CAT: 21

Marital Communication Inventory
CIJE: 2 RIE: 0 CAT: 21

Marital Conventionalization Scale
CIJE: 2 RIE: 0 CAT: 21

Marital Coping Inventory (Zbrowski Berman)
CIJE: 0 RIE: 1 CAT: 21

Marital Discord
CIJE: 10 RIE: 3 CAT: 11

Marital History
CIJE: 0 RIE: 1 CAT: 12

Marital Law
CIJE: 0 RIE: 1 CAT: 14

Marital Observation Coding Systems
CIJE: 0 RIE: 1 CAT: 15

Marital Quality
CIJE: 9 RIE: 1 CAT: 11

Marital Rape
CIJE: 1 RIE: 1 CAT: 14

Marital Satisfaction Inventory
CIJE: 6 RIE: 3 CAT: 21

Marital Satisfaction Scale
CIJE: 1 RIE: 0 CAT: 21

Marital Status Inventory
CIJE: 3 RIE: 0 CAT: 21

Marital Therapy
CIJE: 9 RIE: 1 CAT: 11

Marital Therapy (Behavioral)
USE Behavioral Marital Therapy

Marital Therapy (Individual)
USE Individual Marital Therapy

Maritime Law
CIJE: 1 RIE: 1 CAT: 14

Maritime Occupations
USE Marine Occupations

Maritime Trades Program
CIJE: 0 RIE: 1 CAT: 19

Marivaux (Pierre Carlet de Chamblain de)
CIJE: 2 RIE: 0 CAT: 18

Mark (Jan)
CIJE: 2 RIE: 0 CAT: 18

Mark Capture Technique
CIJE: 1 RIE: 1 CAT: 15

Mark IV
CIJE: 0 RIE: 1 CAT: 04

Mark Sense Forms
CIJE: 0 RIE: 3 CAT: 20

Mark Sense Readers
CIJE: 0 RIE: 4 CAT: 20

Mark Stevenson v Jefferson County Public Schools
CIJE: 0 RIE: 1 CAT: 14
UF Stevenson v Jefferson County Public Schools

Mark Twain School MD
CIJE: 0 RIE: 1 CAT: 17

Mark Twain Staff Development Institute MD
CIJE: 0 RIE: 1 CAT: 17

Mark Twain Teacher Internship Program
CIJE: 0 RIE: 2 CAT: 19

MarkED Model Program
CIJE: 0 RIE: 1 CAT: 19

Markedness
CIJE: 41 RIE: 30 CAT: 13

Markedness Differential Hypothesis
CIJE: 1 RIE: 0 CAT: 13

Marker Tests
CIJE: 1 RIE: 2 CAT: 21

Marker Variable Factor Analysis
CIJE: 3 RIE: 0 CAT: 15

Market Analysis
CIJE: 35 RIE: 16 CAT: 15

Market Equilibrium
CIJE: 0 RIE: 1 CAT: 15

Market Forecasts
CIJE: 0 RIE: 4 CAT: 15

Market Linkage Project
CIJE: 0 RIE: 3 CAT: 19

Market News Network
CIJE: 0 RIE: 1 CAT: 15

Market Profiles
CIJE: 2 RIE: 3 CAT: 15

Market Research
CIJE: 66 RIE: 35 CAT: 15

Market Segmentation
CIJE: 20 RIE: 15 CAT: 15

Market Systems Approach
CIJE: 0 RIE: 1 CAT: 15

Market Value
CIJE: 7 RIE: 3 CAT: 16

Market Value Method
CIJE: 0 RIE: 1 CAT: 15

Market Wage Rates
CIJE: 2 RIE: 0 CAT: 15

Marketing Audits
CIJE: 1 RIE: 1 CAT: 15

Marketing Data Base
CIJE: 0 RIE: 1 CAT: 15

Marketing Mix
CIJE: 1 RIE: 0 CAT: 15

Marketing Plans
CIJE: 2 RIE: 3 CAT: 15

Marketing Research
CIJE: 4 RIE: 3 CAT: 15

Marketing Strategies
CIJE: 7 RIE: 6 CAT: 15

Marketplace of Ideas
CIJE: 4 RIE: 1 CAT: 15

Marking Rules
CIJE: 1 RIE: 1 CAT: 15

Marking Skills
CIJE: 0 RIE: 1 CAT: 15

Markles Flats Junior High School NY
CIJE: 0 RIE: 1 CAT: 17

Markovnikov Rule
CIJE: 3 RIE: 0 CAT: 20

Marland (Sidney P)
CIJE: 1 RIE: 1 CAT: 18

Marlboro Township School District NJ
CIJE: 0 RIE: 1 CAT: 17

Marlborough and Wildenstein Galleries
CIJE: 1 RIE: 0 CAT: 17

Marlowe (Christopher)
CIJE: 2 RIE: 0 CAT: 18

Marlowe Crowne Personal Reaction Inventory
CIJE: 1 RIE: 0 CAT: 21

Marlowe Crowne Social Approval
CIJE: 0 RIE: 1 CAT: 11

Marlowe Crowne Social Desirability Scale
CIJE: 17 RIE: 3 CAT: 21
UF Crowne Marlowe Social Desirability Scale

Marmors Mental Rotation Task
CIJE: 2 RIE: 0 CAT: 21

Marquette Alternative High School MI
CIJE: 0 RIE: 1 CAT: 17

Marquette University WI
CIJE: 11 RIE: 8 CAT: 17

Marriage Education
CIJE: 4 RIE: 1 CAT: 03

Marriage Encounter
CIJE: 7 RIE: 1 CAT: 15

Marriage Enrichment
CIJE: 2 RIE: 2 CAT: 11

Marriage Enrichment Programs
CIJE: 6 RIE: 3 CAT: 19

Marriage Plans
CIJE: 0 RIE: 2 CAT: 16

Marriage Role Expectation Inventory
CIJE: 2 RIE: 0 CAT: 21

Marriott Corporation
CIJE: 3 RIE: 3 CAT: 17

Marriott Hotels
CIJE: 1 RIE: 0 CAT: 17

Marriott School of Management UT
CIJE: 0 RIE: 1 CAT: 17

Mars (Planet)
CIJE: 14 RIE: 11 CAT: 20

Mars Hill College NC
CIJE: 1 RIE: 1 CAT: 17

Mars Public Schools PA
CIJE: 1 RIE: 0 CAT: 17

Marsak (Samuil)
CIJE: 1 RIE: 0 CAT: 18

Marsh Self Report Questionnaire
CIJE: 1 RIE: 1 CAT: 21

Marshall (Thomas William)
CIJE: 1 RIE: 0 CAT: 18

Marshall (Thurgood)
CIJE: 1 RIE: 2 CAT: 18

Marshall High School OR
CIJE: 0 RIE: 2 CAT: 17

Marshall Islands
CIJE: 2 RIE: 3 CAT: 07
SN Republic of the Marshall Islands — formerly under U.S. trusteeship, for which see "Pacific Trust Territory (Marshall Islands)"

Marshall Islands (Enewetak Atoll)
CIJE: 0 RIE: 1 CAT: 07

Marshall Plan
CIJE: 1 RIE: 1 CAT: 12
SN Post-World War II European recovery program

Marshall Space Flight Center
CIJE: 1 RIE: 1 CAT: 17

Marshall University Program
CIJE: 0 RIE: 1 CAT: 19

Marshall University WV
CIJE: 4 RIE: 12 CAT: 17

Marshall v Georgia
CIJE: 1 RIE: 1 CAT: 14

Marshalltown Community College IA
CIJE: 0 RIE: 1 CAT: 17

Marshalltown Community School District IA
CIJE: 0 RIE: 1 CAT: 17

Marsupials
CIJE: 1 RIE: 0 CAT: 20

Marti (Jose Julian)
CIJE: 4 RIE: 1 CAT: 18

Martial (Marcus Valerius)
CIJE: 1 RIE: 3 CAT: 18

Martial Arts
CIJE: 7 RIE: 5 CAT: 03

Martian Chronicles
CIJE: 2 RIE: 1 CAT: 22

Martin (Roscoe)
CIJE: 1 RIE: 0 CAT: 18

Martin Luther King Elementary v Ann Arbor
CIJE: 3 RIE: 2 CAT: 14

Martin Luther King Family Center IL
CIJE: 0 RIE: 2 CAT: 17

Martin Luther King Jr Fellowship Program
CIJE: 0 RIE: 2 CAT: 19

Martin Luther King Junior Health Center
CIJE: 0 RIE: 1 CAT: 17

Martin Luther King Junior Memorial Center
CIJE: 1 RIE: 0 CAT: 17

Martin Luther King Memorial Foundation
CIJE: 1 RIE: 0 CAT: 17

Martin Luther King Program
CIJE: 0 RIE: 6 CAT: 19

Martin Marietta Corporation
CIJE: 1 RIE: 1 CAT: 17

Martin Report
CIJE: 2 RIE: 1 CAT: 22

Martin Santos (Luis)
CIJE: 1 RIE: 0 CAT: 18

Martin Temperament Assessment Battery
CIJE: 1 RIE: 1 CAT: 21

Martineau (Harriet)
CIJE: 5 RIE: 1 CAT: 18

Martinek Zaichkowsky Self Concept Scale Children
USE Self Concept Scale for Children

Martinet (Andre)
CIJE: 1 RIE: 0 CAT: 18

Martinez Estrada (Ezequiel)
CIJE: 1 RIE: 0 CAT: 18

Martinez Sierra (Gregorio)
CIJE: 1 RIE: 0 CAT: 18

Martinique
CIJE: 2 RIE: 1 CAT: 07

Martins Motivational Profile
CIJE: 0 RIE: 1 CAT: 21

Marvelous Me (Preschool Edition)
CIJE: 0 RIE: 2 CAT: 03

Marvin Pittman Laboratory School GA
CIJE: 1 RIE: 1 CAT: 17

Marx (Karl)
CIJE: 51 RIE: 21 CAT: 18

Marxist Aesthetics
CIJE: 1 RIE: 0 CAT: 16

Mary B Martin School OH
CIJE: 1 RIE: 0 CAT: 17

Mary Baldwin College VA
CIJE: 2 RIE: 4 CAT: 17

Mary E Switzer Memorial Seminar
CIJE: 0 RIE: 1 CAT: 02

Mary Holmes College MS
CIJE: 1 RIE: 1 CAT: 17

Mary Hooker School CT
CIJE: 1 RIE: 0 CAT: 17

Mary Louise Aiken School CT
CIJE: 1 RIE: 0 CAT: 17

Mary Washington College VA
CIJE: 0 RIE: 2 CAT: 17

Marycrest College IA
CIJE: 0 RIE: 2 CAT: 17

Maryland
CIJE: 166 RIE: 931 CAT: 07

Maryland (Annapolis)
CIJE: 0 RIE: 1 CAT: 07

Maryland (Anne Arundel County)
CIJE: 3 RIE: 6 CAT: 07

Maryland (Baltimore County)
CIJE: 5 RIE: 10 CAT: 07

Maryland (Baltimore)
CIJE: 69 RIE: 142 CAT: 07

Maryland (Berlin)
CIJE: 1 RIE: 0 CAT: 07

Maryland (Bethesda)
CIJE: 1 RIE: 4 CAT: 07

Maryland (Calvert County)
CIJE: 0 RIE: 1 CAT: 07

Maryland (Caroline County)
CIJE: 2 RIE: 0 CAT: 07

Maryland (Carroll County)
CIJE: 2 RIE: 0 CAT: 07

Maryland (Cecil County)
CIJE: 0 RIE: 1 CAT: 07

Maryland (Charles County)
CIJE: 1 RIE: 2 CAT: 07

Maryland (College Park)
CIJE: 2 RIE: 23 CAT: 07

Maryland (Columbia)
CIJE: 2 RIE: 2 CAT: 07

Maryland (Dorchester County)
CIJE: 0 RIE: 2 CAT: 07

Maryland (East)
CIJE: 0 RIE: 1 CAT: 07

Maryland (Eastern Shore)
CIJE: 0 RIE: 2 CAT: 07

Maryland (Ellicott City)
CIJE: 1 RIE: 1 CAT: 07

Maryland (Essex)
CIJE: 0 RIE: 1 CAT: 07

Maryland (Fort Detrick)
CIJE: 1 RIE: 0 CAT: 07

Maryland (Frederick County)
CIJE: 0 RIE: 38 CAT: 07

Maryland (Frederick)
CIJE: 2 RIE: 1 CAT: 07

Maryland (Garrett County)
CIJE: 1 RIE: 0 CAT: 07

Maryland (Glen Burnie)
CIJE: 0 RIE: 1 CAT: 07

Maryland (Hagerstown)
CIJE: 1 RIE: 6 CAT: 07

Maryland (Harford County)
CIJE: 2 RIE: 0 CAT: 07

Maryland (Howard County)
CIJE: 3 RIE: 4 CAT: 07

Maryland (Jessup)
CIJE: 0 RIE: 1 CAT: 07

Maryland (Kent County)
CIJE: 0 RIE: 1 CAT: 07

Maryland (Laurel)
CIJE: 1 RIE: 0 CAT: 07

Maryland (Montgomery County)
CIJE: 17 RIE: 46 CAT: 07

Maryland (Ocean City)
CIJE: 1 RIE: 0 CAT: 07

Maryland (Oxen Hill)
CIJE: 1 RIE: 0 CAT: 07

Maryland (Potomac)
CIJE: 1 RIE: 0 CAT: 07

Maryland (Prince Georges County)
CIJE: 13 RIE: 21 CAT: 07

Maryland (Princess Anne)
CIJE: 0 RIE: 1 CAT: 07

Maryland (Rockville)
CIJE: 4 RIE: 9 CAT: 07

Maryland (Saint Marys County)
CIJE: 1 RIE: 1 CAT: 07

Maryland (Silver Spring)
CIJE: 2 RIE: 3 CAT: 07

Maryland (Towson)
CIJE: 1 RIE: 4 CAT: 07

Maryland (Upper Marlboro)
CIJE: 0 RIE: 4 CAT: 07

Maryland (Washington County)
CIJE: 3 RIE: 4 CAT: 07

Maryland (West)
CIJE: 1 RIE: 1 CAT: 07

Maryland (Worcester County)
CIJE: 1 RIE: 0 CAT: 07

Maryland Accountability Assessment Program
CIJE: 0 RIE: 12 CAT: 19

Maryland Career Development Project
CIJE: 0 RIE: 3 CAT: 19

Maryland Commission on Values Education
CIJE: 1 RIE: 1 CAT: 17

Maryland Correctional Institution for Women
CIJE: 0 RIE: 1 CAT: 17

Maryland Correctional Training Center
CIJE: 0 RIE: 2 CAT: 17

Maryland Council on Early Childhood Development
USE Council on Early Childhood Development MD

Maryland Day Care Voucher Program
CIJE: 0 RIE: 1 CAT: 19

Maryland Education Microcomputer Network
CIJE: 0 RIE: 1 CAT: 04

Maryland Education Technology Network
CIJE: 0 RIE: 0 CAT: 19

Maryland Elementary Mathematics Inservice Program
CIJE: 1 RIE: 0 CAT: 19

Maryland Equal Rights Amendment
CIJE: 0 RIE: 1 CAT: 14

Maryland Functional Mathematics Test
CIJE: 0 RIE: 6 CAT: 21

Maryland Functional Reading Test
CIJE: 0 RIE: 7 CAT: 21

Maryland Functional Testing Program
CIJE: 0 RIE: 6 CAT: 19

Maryland Functional Writing Test
CIJE: 0 RIE: 4 CAT: 21
UF Maryland Writing Test

Maryland Governors Conference Lib Info Serv
USE Governors Conference Library Info Services MD

Maryland Historical Society
CIJE: 2 RIE: 0 CAT: 17

Maryland Interlibrary Loan Network
CIJE: 1 RIE: 0 CAT: 17

Maryland Interlibrary Organization
CIJE: 2 RIE: 1 CAT: 17

Maryland Legislative Coalition and Network
CIJE: 0 RIE: 1 CAT: 17

Maryland Longitudinal Study
CIJE: 0 RIE: 3 CAT: 19

Maryland Parent Attitude Survey
CIJE: 0 RIE: 2 CAT: 21

Maryland Plan
CIJE: 2 RIE: 3 CAT: 19

Maryland Preschool Self Concept Scale
CIJE: 0 RIE: 1 CAT: 21

Maryland Professional Development Academy
CIJE: 3 RIE: 1 CAT: 19

Maryland Public Broadcasting Center
CIJE: 1 RIE: 0 CAT: 17

Maryland Refutation Proof Procedure System
CIJE: 0 RIE: 1 CAT: 15

Maryland School Performance Assessment Program
CIJE: 1 RIE: 8 CAT: 21
UF MSPAP

Maryland Self Concept as a Learner Scale
CIJE: 0 RIE: 1 CAT: 21

Maryland State Council on Vocational Tech Educ
CIJE: 0 RIE: 1 CAT: 17

Maryland State Department of Education
CIJE: 3 RIE: 16 CAT: 17

Maryland State Library Network
CIJE: 0 RIE: 2 CAT: 17

Maryland State Penitentiary
CIJE: 0 RIE: 1 CAT: 17

Maryland Teacher Education Center
CIJE: 0 RIE: 1 CAT: 17

Maryland Test of Citizenship Skills
CIJE: 1 RIE: 2 CAT: 21

Maryland Writing Test
USE Maryland Functional Writing Test

Marylands Tomorrow Projects
CIJE: 0 RIE: 1 CAT: 19

Marylhurst College for Lifelong Learning OR
CIJE: 2 RIE: 1 CAT: 17

Marylhurst Education Center OR
CIJE: 0 RIE: 0 CAT: 17

Marymount Academy CA
CIJE: 1 RIE: 0 CAT: 17

Marymount College CA
CIJE: 0 RIE: 1 CAT: 17
UF Marymount Palos Verdes College CA

Marymount College NY
CIJE: 3 RIE: 2 CAT: 17

Marymount College of Kansas
CIJE: 1 RIE: 1 CAT: 17

Marymount Manhattan College NY
CIJE: 5 RIE: 4 CAT: 17

Marymount Palos Verdes College CA
USE Marymount College CA

Marymount University VA
CIJE: 0 RIE: 3 CAT: 17

Marynet
CIJE: 0 RIE: 1 CAT: 04

Marysville Joint Unified School District CA
CIJE: 0 RIE: 1 CAT: 17

Maryvale Project
CIJE: 0 RIE: 1 CAT: 19

Maryville College of Sacred Heart MO
CIJE: 2 RIE: 0 CAT: 17

Maryville College TN
CIJE: 4 RIE: 1 CAT: 17

Maryville University of Saint Louis MO
CIJE: 0 RIE: 2 CAT: 17

Marywood College PA
CIJE: 2 RIE: 2 CAT: 17

Mascarene Islands
CIJE: 1 RIE: 0 CAT: 07

Mascoma Valley Regional School District NH
CIJE: 0 RIE: 1 CAT: 17

Mascots (Athletics)
CIJE: 0 RIE: 1 CAT: 16

Masculinity
CIJE: 109 RIE: 37 CAT: 16

Masculinity Femininity Variable
CIJE: 22 RIE: 18 CAT: 16

Masefield (John)
CIJE: 2 RIE: 0 CAT: 18

Masfile Project
CIJE: 0 RIE: 2 CAT: 19

MASH (Television Program)
CIJE: 1 RIE: 1 CAT: 22

Mashpee (Tribe)
CIJE: 0 RIE: 1 CAT: 08

Masking (Audiometric)
CIJE: 6 RIE: 0 CAT: 11

Masking (Auditory)
CIJE: 2 RIE: 0 CAT: 11

Masking (Visual)
CIJE: 5 RIE: 0 CAT: 11

Masking (Voice)
USE Voice Masking

Masks
CIJE: 22 RIE: 4 CAT: 04
SN See also "Life Masks"

Maslach Burnout Inventory
CIJE: 27 RIE: 13 CAT: 21

Maslow (Abraham)
CIJE: 66 RIE: 38 CAT: 18
SN "Abraham H"

Maslow Security Insecurity Inventory
CIJE: 0 RIE: 3 CAT: 21

Maslowian Scale
CIJE: 0 RIE: 1 CAT: 21

Maslows Hierarchy of Needs
CIJE: 34 RIE: 21 CAT: 15

Masochism
CIJE: 1 RIE: 1 CAT: 11

Mass (Leonard Bernstein)
CIJE: 1 RIE: 0 CAT: 22

Mass Centroid Location
CIJE: 1 RIE: 0 CAT: 11

Mass Media Reviews
CIJE: 0 RIE: 1 CAT: 16

Mass Nouns
CIJE: 4 RIE: 2 CAT: 13

Mass Spectrometers
CIJE: 5 RIE: 0 CAT: 04

Mass Spectrometry
CIJE: 2 RIE: 0 CAT: 20

Mass Technology
CIJE: 1 RIE: 0 CAT: 20

Mass Transit
CIJE: 2 RIE: 2 CAT: 20

Massachusetts
CIJE: 264 RIE: 1012 CAT: 07

Massachusetts (Amherst)
CIJE: 7 RIE: 9 CAT: 07

Massachusetts (Andover)
CIJE: 0 RIE: 2 CAT: 07

Massachusetts (Arlington)
CIJE: 2 RIE: 2 CAT: 07

Massachusetts (Attleboro)
CIJE: 1 RIE: 2 CAT: 07

Massachusetts (Berkshire County)
CIJE: 0 RIE: 1 CAT: 07

Massachusetts (Boston Chinatown)
CIJE: 0 RIE: 1 CAT: 07
UF Chinatown Boston

Massachusetts (Boston Metropolitan Area)
CIJE: 1 RIE: 2 CAT: 07

Massachusetts (Boston)
CIJE: 162 RIE: 336 CAT: 07

Massachusetts (Brockton)
CIJE: 3 RIE: 0 CAT: 07

Massachusetts (Brookline)
CIJE: 6 RIE: 10 CAT: 07

Massachusetts (Cambridge)
CIJE: 16 RIE: 11 CAT: 07

Massachusetts (Chelmsford)
CIJE: 1 RIE: 3 CAT: 07

Massachusetts (Chelsea)
CIJE: 4 RIE: 3 CAT: 07

Massachusetts (Chestnut Hill)
CIJE: 0 RIE: 4 CAT: 07

Massachusetts (Concord)
CIJE: 2 RIE: 0 CAT: 07

Massachusetts (East)
CIJE: 0 RIE: 4 CAT: 07

Massachusetts (Fall River)
CIJE: 4 RIE: 4 CAT: 07

Massachusetts (Fitchburg)
CIJE: 0 RIE: 1 CAT: 07

Massachusetts (Framingham)
CIJE: 4 RIE: 1 CAT: 07

Massachusetts (Franklin County)
CIJE: 0 RIE: 1 CAT: 07

Massachusetts (Gloucester)
CIJE: 0 RIE: 2 CAT: 07

Massachusetts (Greenfield)
CIJE: 2 RIE: 1 CAT: 07

Massachusetts (Hamilton)
CIJE: 1 RIE: 1 CAT: 07

Massachusetts (Hampden County)
CIJE: 0 RIE: 3 CAT: 07

Massachusetts (Hampshire County)
CIJE: 1 RIE: 1 CAT: 07

Massachusetts (Hathorne)
CIJE: 1 RIE: 0 CAT: 07

Massachusetts (Holyoke)
CIJE: 6 RIE: 5 CAT: 07

Massachusetts (Kingston)
CIJE: 1 RIE: 0 CAT: 07

Massachusetts (Lawrence)
CIJE: 4 RIE: 7 CAT: 07

Massachusetts (Lexington)
CIJE: 4 RIE: 1 CAT: 07

Massachusetts (Lowell)
CIJE: 6 RIE: 5 CAT: 07

Massachusetts (Medford)
CIJE: 3 RIE: 6 CAT: 07

Massachusetts (Melrose)
CIJE: 0 RIE: 1 CAT: 07

Massachusetts (Merrimack Valley)
CIJE: 1 RIE: 0 CAT: 07

Massachusetts (Mount Hermon)
CIJE: 0 RIE: 1 CAT: 07

Massachusetts (Nantucket)
CIJE: 1 RIE: 1 CAT: 07

Massachusetts (New Bedford)
CIJE: 2 RIE: 3 CAT: 07

Massachusetts (Newton)
CIJE: 6 RIE: 1 CAT: 07

Massachusetts (North Easton)
CIJE: 0 RIE: 1 CAT: 07

Massachusetts (North Reading)
CIJE: 1 RIE: 1 CAT: 07

Massachusetts (Northampton)
CIJE: 2 RIE: 2 CAT: 07

Massachusetts (Norwell)
CIJE: 1 RIE: 0 CAT: 07

Massachusetts (Quincy)
CIJE: 1 RIE: 2 CAT: 07

Massachusetts (Reading)
CIJE: 1 RIE: 1 CAT: 07

Massachusetts (Rockland)
CIJE: 2 RIE: 0 CAT: 07

Massachusetts (South Hadley)
CIJE: 0 RIE: 2 CAT: 07

Massachusetts (Springfield)
CIJE: 17 RIE: 22 CAT: 07

Massachusetts (Tewksbury)
CIJE: 0 RIE: 2 CAT: 07

Massachusetts (Waltham)
CIJE: 0 RIE: 4 CAT: 07

Massachusetts (Waverley)
CIJE: 0 RIE: 1 CAT: 07

Massachusetts (Wellesley)
CIJE: 4 RIE: 2 CAT: 07

Massachusetts (West Roxbury)
CIJE: 0 RIE: 1 CAT: 07

Massachusetts (West)
CIJE: 0 RIE: 1 CAT: 07

Massachusetts (Weston)
CIJE: 2 RIE: 4 CAT: 07

Massachusetts (Weymouth)
CIJE: 0 RIE: 1 CAT: 07

Massachusetts (Williamstown)
CIJE: 2 RIE: 1 CAT: 07

Massachusetts (Winchester)
CIJE: 1 RIE: 4 CAT: 07

Massachusetts (Woods Hole)
CIJE: 1 RIE: 1 CAT: 07

Massachusetts (Worcester)
CIJE: 11 RIE: 15 CAT: 07

Massachusetts Advisory Council on Education
CIJE: 0 RIE: 2 CAT: 17

Massachusetts Advocacy Center
CIJE: 1 RIE: 0 CAT: 17

Massachusetts Basic Skills
USE Basic Skills Improvement Program (Massachusetts)

Massachusetts Basic Skills Inventory
CIJE: 0 RIE: 1 CAT: 21

Massachusetts Basic Skills Testing Program
CIJE: 0 RIE: 2 CAT: 21

Massachusetts Bay Colony
CIJE: 2 RIE: 1 CAT: 12

Massachusetts Bay Community College
CIJE: 0 RIE: 2 CAT: 17

Massachusetts Board of Education
CIJE: 0 RIE: 3 CAT: 17

Massachusetts Board of Regents of Higher Education
CIJE: 0 RIE: 3 CAT: 17

Massachusetts Board of Regional Community Colleges
CIJE: 0 RIE: 2 CAT: 17

Massachusetts Board of Retirement v Murgia
CIJE: 1 RIE: 0 CAT: 14
UF Murgia Decision

Massachusetts Bureau of Institutional Schools
CIJE: 0 RIE: 1 CAT: 17

Massachusetts Coalition for School Improvement
CIJE: 0 RIE: 1 CAT: 17

Massachusetts Coll of Pharmacy Allied Health Sci
CIJE: 2 RIE: 1 CAT: 17

Massachusetts College of Art
CIJE: 0 RIE: 4 CAT: 17

Massachusetts Commission Against Discrimination
CIJE: 1 RIE: 1 CAT: 17

Massachusetts Correctional Institution
CIJE: 0 RIE: 1 CAT: 17

Massachusetts Department of Youth Services
CIJE: 2 RIE: 1 CAT: 17

Massachusetts Early Education Project
CIJE: 0 RIE: 1 CAT: 19

Massachusetts Education Loan Authority
CIJE: 0 RIE: 1 CAT: 17

Massachusetts Educational Assessment Program
CIJE: 0 RIE: 16 CAT: 19

Massachusetts Extension Service
CIJE: 0 RIE: 1 CAT: 17

Massachusetts General Hospital
CIJE: 4 RIE: 3 CAT: 17

Massachusetts Higher Educ Communication Network
CIJE: 0 RIE: 1 CAT: 17

Massachusetts Institute of Technology
CIJE: 64 RIE: 44 CAT: 17

Massachusetts Middle Grade Region Alliance Network
CIJE: 0 RIE: 1 CAT: 19

Massachusetts Music Educators Association
CIJE: 0 RIE: 2 CAT: 17

Massachusetts Office for Children
CIJE: 0 RIE: 1 CAT: 17

Massachusetts Public School Improvement Act 1985
USE Chapter 188 (Massachusetts)

Massachusetts Teachers Association
CIJE: 0 RIE: 6 CAT: 17

Massachusetts Transitional Bilingual Education Act
CIJE: 2 RIE: 0 CAT: 14

Massachusetts v Mellon
CIJE: 0 RIE: 1 CAT: 14

Massachusetts Vocational Curriculum Resource Ctr
CIJE: 0 RIE: 1 CAT: 17

Massachusetts Workplace Education Initiative
CIJE: 0 RIE: 1 CAT: 19

Massad Mimicry Test
CIJE: 0 RIE: 1 CAT: 21

Massage Therapy
USE Massages

Massages
CIJE: 2 RIE: 3 CAT: 11
UF Massage Therapy

Massasoit Community College MA
CIJE: 0 RIE: 1 CAT: 17

Massed Practice
CIJE: 4 RIE: 1 CAT: 15

Massee (May)
CIJE: 1 RIE: 0 CAT: 18

Massive Oral Decoding
CIJE: 1 RIE: 0 CAT: 15

Mast Teaching Machine
CIJE: 0 RIE: 1 CAT: 04

Mastectomy
CIJE: 4 RIE: 3 CAT: 11

Master Antenna Television
CIJE: 0 RIE: 1 CAT: 04

Master Builders of Iowa
CIJE: 1 RIE: 0 CAT: 16

Master of Human Services
CIJE: 1 RIE: 0 CAT: 16

Master Schedules
CIJE: 2 RIE: 2 CAT: 15

Master Teacher Examination TX
USE Texas Master Teacher Examination

Master Teacher Model Training Program
CIJE: 0 RIE: 1 CAT: 19

Master Teacher Program
CIJE: 3 RIE: 4 CAT: 19

Master Teacher Program FL
USE Florida Master Teacher Program

Master Teacher Program TN
USE Tennessee Master Teacher Program

Master Teacher Training Program TX
CIJE: 0 RIE: 1 CAT: 19

Master Technicians
CIJE: 0 RIE: 1 CAT: 09

Masters (Edgar Lee)
CIJE: 1 RIE: 2 CAT: 18

Masters at Arms
CIJE: 0 RIE: 1 CAT: 09

Masters Comprehensive Examination
CIJE: 3 RIE: 0 CAT: 21

Masters of Business Administration
CIJE: 44 RIE: 8 CAT: 16

Masters Only Institutions
CIJE: 0 RIE: 1 CAT: 05

Mastery Evaluation
CIJE: 2 RIE: 2 CAT: 15

Mastery Grading
CIJE: 0 RIE: 1 CAT: 15

Mastery in Learning Project (NEA)
CIJE: 1 RIE: 4 CAT: 19
SN National Education Assn project

Mastery Learning Test Model (Besel)
CIJE: 0 RIE: 2 CAT: 21

Mastery Learning Test Model (Emrick and Adams)
CIJE: 0 RIE: 3 CAT: 21

Mastery Model
CIJE: 6 RIE: 6 CAT: 15

Mastery Motivation
CIJE: 3 RIE: 6 CAT: 11

Mastery Orientation
CIJE: 7 RIE: 4 CAT: 11

Mastery Teaching (Hunter)
CIJE: 0 RIE: 1 CAT: 15

Mastodons
CIJE: 1 RIE: 0 CAT: 20

MAT 6
CIJE: 0 RIE: 1 CAT: 21
UF Metropolitan Achievement Tests Sixth Edition

MAT 6 Writing Test
CIJE: 0 RIE: 1 CAT: 21

Mat Su Math Coop Project
CIJE: 0 RIE: 1 CAT: 19

Matanuska Susitna Borough School District AK
CIJE: 0 RIE: 1 CAT: 17

Match Boxes
CIJE: 0 RIE: 21 CAT: 16

Matched Pair Scoring
CIJE: 3 RIE: 2 CAT: 21

Matching (Teaching to Learners)
CIJE: 4 RIE: 1 CAT: 15

Matching Ability
CIJE: 3 RIE: 1 CAT: 11

Matching Cloze
CIJE: 0 RIE: 1 CAT: 15

Matching Errors
CIJE: 2 RIE: 0 CAT: 11

Matching Familiar Figures Test (Kagan)
CIJE: 74 RIE: 44 CAT: 21

Matching Funds
CIJE: 1 RIE: 3 CAT: 16

Matching Gifts
CIJE: 5 RIE: 4 CAT: 16

Matching Gifts (Finance)
CIJE: 4 RIE: 1 CAT: 16

Matching Grants
CIJE: 3 RIE: 1 CAT: 16

Matching Hypothesis
CIJE: 2 RIE: 1 CAT: 15

Matching Procedures (Cognition)
USE Cognitive Matching

Matching Texts
CIJE: 1 RIE: 0 CAT: 13

Matching to Sample Procedure
CIJE: 6 RIE: 3 CAT: 21

Matchplate Patterns
CIJE: 1 RIE: 0 CAT: 15

Material Analysis
CIJE: 0 RIE: 1 CAT: 20

Material Control
CIJE: 1 RIE: 1 CAT: 15

Material Objects
CIJE: 3 RIE: 2 CAT: 15

Material Reinforcement
CIJE: 1 RIE: 0 CAT: 11

Materialism
CIJE: 16 RIE: 11 CAT: 16

Materials Analysis Inventory
CIJE: 0 RIE: 1 CAT: 21

Materials Development Unit
CIJE: 0 RIE: 1 CAT: 15

Materials Expediters
CIJE: 0 RIE: 3 CAT: 09

Materials Handling
CIJE: 1 RIE: 5 CAT: 20

Materials Processing
CIJE: 2 RIE: 2 CAT: 20

Materials Science
CIJE: 12 RIE: 5 CAT: 03

Materials Technology
CIJE: 6 RIE: 5 CAT: 20

Materials Testing
CIJE: 3 RIE: 1 CAT: 21

Maternal and Child Health Block Grants
CIJE: 1 RIE: 2 CAT: 14

Maternal and Child Health Care Act 1976
CIJE: 0 RIE: 0 CAT: 14

Maternal and Child Health Office
USE Office of Maternal and Child Health

Maternal and Child Health Programs Title V
USE Social Security Act Title V

Maternal and Child Health Services
CIJE: 7 RIE: 6 CAT: 11
SN See also "Child Health Care"

Maternal Attitude Scale (Cohler Weiss Gruenbaum)
CIJE: 2 RIE: 0 CAT: 21

Maternal Attitude Toward Independence Training
CIJE: 0 RIE: 1 CAT: 15

Maternal Behavior Scale
CIJE: 0 RIE: 1 CAT: 21

Maternal Custody
CIJE: 0 RIE: 1 CAT: 14

Maternal Deprivation
CIJE: 6 RIE: 1 CAT: 11

Maternal Directiveness
CIJE: 2 RIE: 2 CAT: 16

Maternal Health
CIJE: 6 RIE: 42 CAT: 11

Maternal Hyperphenylalaninemia
CIJE: 1 RIE: 0 CAT: 11

Maternal Infant Health Outreach Worker Program TN
CIJE: 0 RIE: 3 CAT: 19

Maternal Interaction Structured Situation
CIJE: 0 RIE: 2 CAT: 16

Maternal Medication
CIJE: 1 RIE: 0 CAT: 11

Maternal Mortality
CIJE: 1 RIE: 2 CAT: 11

Maternal Responsiveness
CIJE: 30 RIE: 8 CAT: 11

Maternal Self Concept
CIJE: 2 RIE: 5 CAT: 11

Maternal Sensitivity
CIJE: 3 RIE: 4 CAT: 11

Maternal Speech
CIJE: 2 RIE: 3 CAT: 13

Maternal Teaching Observation Technique
CIJE: 1 RIE: 0 CAT: 15

Maternity Benefits
CIJE: 11 RIE: 14 CAT: 16

Math English Science Technology Education Project
CIJE: 4 RIE: 2 CAT: 19
UF MESTEP

Math In Stride
CIJE: 0 RIE: 2 CAT: 03

Math Network Curriculum Project
CIJE: 0 RIE: 9 CAT: 19

Math Remediation Methods Questionnaire
CIJE: 0 RIE: 1 CAT: 21

Math Science Technology Education Project
CIJE: 0 RIE: 1 CAT: 19

Math Their Way Program
CIJE: 0 RIE: 3 CAT: 19

MATHCO
CIJE: 0 RIE: 6 CAT: 03

Mathemagenic Activities
CIJE: 7 RIE: 13 CAT: 15

Mathemagenics
CIJE: 5 RIE: 16 CAT: 20

Mathemathantic Effects
CIJE: 0 RIE: 1 CAT: 15

Mathematical Ability
CIJE: 6 RIE: 3 CAT: 20

Mathematical Analysis
CIJE: 4 RIE: 2 CAT: 20

Mathematical Analysis of Perception and Preference
CIJE: 0 RIE: 1 CAT: 15

Mathematical Association of America
CIJE: 2 RIE: 16 CAT: 17

Mathematical Association of the United Kingdom
CIJE: 2 RIE: 0 CAT: 17

Mathematical Balance
CIJE: 1 RIE: 0 CAT: 20

Mathematical Category Theory
CIJE: 1 RIE: 0 CAT: 15

Mathematical Communication
CIJE: 4 RIE: 3 CAT: 20

Mathematical Computations
CIJE: 5 RIE: 5 CAT: 20

Mathematical Induction
CIJE: 12 RIE: 0 CAT: 20

Mathematical Notation
CIJE: 8 RIE: 2 CAT: 20

Mathematical Olympiad
CIJE: 6 RIE: 1 CAT: 02
SN See also "International Mathematics Olympiad" and "Mathematics Contests"

Mathematical Posters
CIJE: 2 RIE: 0 CAT: 16

Mathematical Power
CIJE: 0 RIE: 1 CAT: 16

Mathematical Programing
CIJE: 1 RIE: 4 CAT: 15

Mathematical Psychology
CIJE: 1 RIE: 1 CAT: 15

Mathematical Readiness
USE Mathematics Readiness

Mathematical Representations
USE Representations (Mathematics)

Mathematical Reviews
CIJE: 0 RIE: 2 CAT: 16

Mathematical Sciences
CIJE: 0 RIE: 2 CAT: 20

Mathematical Sciences Education Board
CIJE: 2 RIE: 2 CAT: 17

Mathematical Sciences Instructor Evaluation Form
CIJE: 0 RIE: 2 CAT: 21

Mathematical Self Concept Scale (Gourgey)
CIJE: 0 RIE: 1 CAT: 21

Mathematical Simulation
CIJE: 1 RIE: 0 CAT: 20

Mathematical Stories
CIJE: 0 RIE: 1 CAT: 16

Mathematical Structure
CIJE: 8 RIE: 2 CAT: 20

Mathematical Systems
CIJE: 2 RIE: 0 CAT: 20

Mathematical Theory
CIJE: 8 RIE: 1 CAT: 15

Mathematical Thinking
CIJE: 25 RIE: 14 CAT: 20
UF Quantitative Thinking

Mathematically and Scientifically Precocious Youth
CIJE: 2 RIE: 1 CAT: 10

Mathematically Gifted
CIJE: 15 RIE: 3 CAT: 10

Mathematics Achievement Questionnaire
CIJE: 1 RIE: 0 CAT: 21

Mathematics and Communications Skills Prog NC
CIJE: 0 RIE: 1 CAT: 19

Mathematics and Music
CIJE: 2 RIE: 0 CAT: 03

Mathematics and Reading
USE Reading Mathematics Relationship

Mathematics Anxiety Rating Scale
CIJE: 12 RIE: 8 CAT: 21

Mathematics Applied to Novel Situations Test
CIJE: 0 RIE: 8 CAT: 21

Mathematics Assessment (State Level)
USE State Mathematics Assessments

Mathematics Assessment Process Middle Grades
CIJE: 0 RIE: 4 CAT: 19

Mathematics Assessment Questionnaire
CIJE: 0 RIE: 6 CAT: 21

Mathematics Attribution Scale
CIJE: 3 RIE: 3 CAT: 21

Mathematics Careers
CIJE: 2 RIE: 2 CAT: 20

Mathematics Centers
CIJE: 1 RIE: 1 CAT: 05

Mathematics Clubs
CIJE: 4 RIE: 1 CAT: 10

Mathematics Composite (NAEP)
CIJE: 0 RIE: 1 CAT: 21

Mathematics Contests
CIJE: 13 RIE: 9 CAT: 16
SN See also "Mathematical Olympiad"

Mathematics Continuous Progress Laboratory OH
CIJE: 0 RIE: 1 CAT: 17

Mathematics Diagnostic Prescriptive Inventory
CIJE: 0 RIE: 1 CAT: 21

Mathematics Diagnostic Testing Project CA
CIJE: 0 RIE: 2 CAT: 21

Mathematics Education Research
CIJE: 866 RIE: 987 CAT: 20

Mathematics Engineering and Science Achievement CA
USE MESA Program CA

Mathematics Evaluation Materials Package
CIJE: 0 RIE: 4 CAT: 15

Mathematics for the Majority Continuation Project
CIJE: 2 RIE: 0 CAT: 19

Mathematics Framework for Calif Public Schools
CIJE: 0 RIE: 6 CAT: 22
SN "Mathematics Framework for California Public Schools, Kindergarten through Grade Twelve"
UF California Mathematics Framework

Mathematics History
CIJE: 125 RIE: 19 CAT: 12

Mathematics Indicators
CIJE: 0 RIE: 1 CAT: 16

Mathematics Interest Inventory
CIJE: 2 RIE: 0 CAT: 21

Mathematics Interests
CIJE: 1 RIE: 5 CAT: 20

Mathematics Intervention Project Model
CIJE: 0 RIE: 1 CAT: 15

Mathematics Laboratories
CIJE: 6 RIE: 16 CAT: 05

Mathematics Methods Program
CIJE: 0 RIE: 13 CAT: 19

Mathematics Mini Assessment (1976)
CIJE: 0 RIE: 1 CAT: 21

Mathematics of Money
CIJE: 13 RIE: 0 CAT: 03

Mathematics Participation
CIJE: 3 RIE: 3 CAT: 20

Mathematics Pentathlon
CIJE: 0 RIE: 4 CAT: 02

Mathematics Process Skills
CIJE: 3 RIE: 0 CAT: 15

Mathematics Readiness
CIJE: 1 RIE: 7 CAT: 20
UF Mathematical Readiness

Mathematics Resource Project
CIJE: 0 RIE: 1 CAT: 19

Mathematics Science Tech Teacher Training Proj NY
CIJE: 0 RIE: 1 CAT: 19
SN Project of Bank Street College of Education NY

Mathematics Self Concept Scale (Holly et al)
CIJE: 1 RIE: 0 CAT: 21

Mathematics Self Efficacy Scale
CIJE: 0 RIE: 1 CAT: 21

Mathematics Skill Test
CIJE: 2 RIE: 0 CAT: 21

Mathematics Skills Improvement Project
CIJE: 0 RIE: 1 CAT: 19

Mathematics Supervisors
CIJE: 0 RIE: 1 CAT: 09

Mathematics Support Center
CIJE: 0 RIE: 1 CAT: 17

Mathematics Teacher (Journal)
CIJE: 0 RIE: 3 CAT: 22

Mathematics Teacher Beliefs Study
CIJE: 0 RIE: 0 CAT: 19

Mathematics Teacher Education Project (England)
CIJE: 4 RIE: 0 CAT: 19

Mathematics Teaching Inventory (ERB)
CIJE: 0 RIE: 1 CAT: 21

Mather (Cotton)
CIJE: 4 RIE: 0 CAT: 18

Mathetics
CIJE: 1 RIE: 4 CAT: 15

Mathews (David)
CIJE: 2 RIE: 0 CAT: 18

Mathews v Eldridge
CIJE: 1 RIE: 0 CAT: 14

Matriarchy
CIJE: 5 RIE: 4 CAT: 16

Matriculation Aides
CIJE: 0 RIE: 1 CAT: 09

Matriculation Mathematics
CIJE: 0 RIE: 1 CAT: 03

Matrix Analogies Test (Expanded Form)
CIJE: 1 RIE: 1 CAT: 21

Matrix Analogies Test (Short Form)
CIJE: 2 RIE: 0 CAT: 21

Matrix Games
CIJE: 1 RIE: 3 CAT: 15

Matrix Management
CIJE: 6 RIE: 4 CAT: 15

Matrix Management Plan
CIJE: 1 RIE: 0 CAT: 15

Matrix Operations
CIJE: 4 RIE: 5 CAT: 20

Matrix Tasks (Siegel and Kresh)
CIJE: 0 RIE: 2 CAT: 21

Mattaponi Indian Reservation
CIJE: 1 RIE: 0 CAT: 17

Mattatuck Community College CT
CIJE: 0 RIE: 3 CAT: 17

Matteson School District IL
CIJE: 0 RIE: 1 CAT: 17

Matthew Halton High School (Canada)
CIJE: 1 RIE: 0 CAT: 17

Matthew Walker Health Center
CIJE: 0 RIE: 1 CAT: 17

Matthews Youth Test for Health
CIJE: 4 RIE: 5 CAT: 21

Mattlin Junior High School
CIJE: 1 RIE: 0 CAT: 17

Mature Students Qualifying Program
CIJE: 0 RIE: 2 CAT: 19

Matute (Ana Maria)
CIJE: 0 RIE: 1 CAT: 18

Matzke Elementary School TX
CIJE: 1 RIE: 0 CAT: 17

MAUD
USE Multiattribute Utility Decomposition

Maudsley Personality Inventory
CIJE: 2 RIE: 1 CAT: 21

Mauger (Claude)
CIJE: 1 RIE: 0 CAT: 18

Maui Community College HI
USE University of Hawaii Maui Community College

Maultsby Common Trait Inventory
CIJE: 1 RIE: 0 CAT: 21

Maupassant (Guy de)
CIJE: 6 RIE: 1 CAT: 18

Mauriac (Francois)
CIJE: 3 RIE: 0 CAT: 18

Mauritania
CIJE: 2 RIE: 6 CAT: 07

Mauritius
CIJE: 9 RIE: 14 CAT: 07

Maurois (Andre)
CIJE: 3 RIE: 0 CAT: 18

MAUT
USE Multi Attribute Utility Theory

MAVO Project
CIJE: 0 RIE: 1 CAT: 19

Max Headroom
CIJE: 0 RIE: 2 CAT: 22

Max Planck Inst for Human Devel and Educ (Germany)
CIJE: 0 RIE: 0 CAT: 17
UF Max Planck Inst fuer Bildungsforschung (Germany); Planck Institute for Human Devel and Ed (Germany)

Max Planck Inst fuer Bildungsforschung (Germany)
USE Max Planck Inst for Human Devel and Educ (Germany)

Maximin Model
CIJE: 1 RIE: 4 CAT: 21

Maximizing Difference Game
CIJE: 2 RIE: 0 CAT: 15

Maximizing Options in Vocational Education
USE Project MOVE

Maximum Internal Correlation Coefficient
CIJE: 0 RIE: 1 CAT: 15

Maximum Security Facilities
CIJE: 1 RIE: 3 CAT: 05

Maxwell (James)
CIJE: 3 RIE: 0 CAT: 18

Maxwell (W David)
CIJE: 1 RIE: 0 CAT: 18

Maxwell Air Force Base
CIJE: 1 RIE: 0 CAT: 17

Maxwell Demon Bottle
CIJE: 1 RIE: 0 CAT: 04

Maxwell International Development Simulation
CIJE: 0 RIE: 1 CAT: 15

May (Month)
CIJE: 0 RIE: 0 CAT: 16

May Day
CIJE: 2 RIE: 0 CAT: 12

May Wescott Elementary School RI
CIJE: 1 RIE: 0 CAT: 17

Maya (People)
CIJE: 17 RIE: 12 CAT: 08

Mayakovsky (Vladimir)
CIJE: 3 RIE: 0 CAT: 18

Mayan (Quiche)
CIJE: 0 RIE: 2 CAT: 13

Mayan Civilization
CIJE: 7 RIE: 2 CAT: 12

Mayhew (Lewis B)
CIJE: 0 RIE: 1 CAT: 18

Mayo Clinic MN
CIJE: 2 RIE: 0 CAT: 17

Mayo State Vocational Technical School KY
CIJE: 0 RIE: 1 CAT: 17

Mayors Panel on School Decentralization NY
CIJE: 0 RIE: 4 CAT: 17

Mays (Benjamin Elijah)
CIJE: 3 RIE: 0 CAT: 18

Mazandarani
CIJE: 0 RIE: 1 CAT: 13

Mazatec
CIJE: 0 RIE: 2 CAT: 13
SN Language of Oaxaca, Mexico
UF Mazateco

Mazateco
USE Mazatec

Maze Technique
CIJE: 9 RIE: 2 CAT: 15

Mazes
CIJE: 9 RIE: 1 CAT: 15

Mazyck Rating Scale for Paraprofessionals
CIJE: 0 RIE: 2 CAT: 21

Mazzoni Arena Models
CIJE: 0 RIE: 1 CAT: 15

McAdoo (William Gibbs)
CIJE: 1 RIE: 0 CAT: 18

McAllister (Jane Ellen)
CIJE: 1 RIE: 0 CAT: 18

McAndrew (William)
CIJE: 1 RIE: 1 CAT: 18

McAteer Act
CIJE: 0 RIE: 6 CAT: 14

MCATL
USE Minnesota Computerized Adaptive Testing Language

McBee Keysort Card File
CIJE: 0 RIE: 1 CAT: 04

McBride School (Canada)
CIJE: 0 RIE: 3 CAT: 17

McCall (Will)
CIJE: 1 RIE: 0 CAT: 18

McCall Crabbs Standard Test Lessons in Reading
CIJE: 3 RIE: 1 CAT: 21

McCandles Intensity of Involvement Scale
CIJE: 0 RIE: 1 CAT: 21

McCarran (Patrick)
CIJE: 0 RIE: 1 CAT: 18

McCarran Walter Act
CIJE: 4 RIE: 0 CAT: 14

McCarron Dial Work Evaluation System
CIJE: 2 RIE: 0 CAT: 15

McCarthy (Charles)
CIJE: 2 RIE: 0 CAT: 18

McCarthy (Eugene)
CIJE: 1 RIE: 0 CAT: 18

McCarthy (Joseph)
CIJE: 8 RIE: 5 CAT: 18

McCarthy Draw a Child Subtest
CIJE: 1 RIE: 0 CAT: 21

McCarthy Draw a Child Test
CIJE: 2 RIE: 1 CAT: 21

McCarthy Scales of Childrens Abilities
CIJE: 87 RIE: 20 CAT: 21

McCarthy Screening Test
CIJE: 10 RIE: 2 CAT: 21

McCarthyism
CIJE: 9 RIE: 12 CAT: 16

McCawley (J D)
CIJE: 1 RIE: 0 CAT: 18

McClelland Need Achievement Test
CIJE: 2 RIE: 6 CAT: 21

McCluer High School MO
CIJE: 1 RIE: 0 CAT: 17

McClures Magazine
CIJE: 0 RIE: 1 CAT: 22

McClusky (Howard Y)
CIJE: 0 RIE: 3 CAT: 18

McCollouch School IN
CIJE: 1 RIE: 0 CAT: 17

McCollough Effect
CIJE: 2 RIE: 0 CAT: 11

McComb Dobrovolny Study Skills Questionnaire
USE Study Skills Questionnaire (McComb Dobrovolny)

McConnell (T R)
CIJE: 1 RIE: 1 CAT: 18

McConnell Language Devel Cultural Disadvantagement
CIJE: 1 RIE: 0 CAT: 21

McCook Community College NE
CIJE: 0 RIE: 3 CAT: 17

McCook Junior College NE
CIJE: 1 RIE: 1 CAT: 17

McCoy (Rhody)
CIJE: 0 RIE: 1 CAT: 18

McCracken Standard Reading Inventory
CIJE: 1 RIE: 0 CAT: 21

McCracken Word List
CIJE: 0 RIE: 1 CAT: 21

McCullers (Carson)
CIJE: 0 RIE: 1 CAT: 18

McCulloch v Maryland
CIJE: 0 RIE: 1 CAT: 14

McCullough Word Analysis Tests
CIJE: 1 RIE: 0 CAT: 21

McCune Reischauer Romanization
CIJE: 0 RIE: 1 CAT: 13

McDaniel Inferred Self Concept Scale
CIJE: 0 RIE: 2 CAT: 21

McDaniel Piers Young Childrens Self Concept Scale
CIJE: 1 RIE: 2 CAT: 21

McDermott (Gerald)
CIJE: 1 RIE: 1 CAT: 18

McDonalds
CIJE: 7 RIE: 5 CAT: 17

McGee F Scale
CIJE: 0 RIE: 1 CAT: 21

McGill Action Planning System
CIJE: 2 RIE: 1 CAT: 15
UF Making Action Plans (MAPS); MAPS (for Including All Children in Schools)

McGill University (Canada)
CIJE: 26 RIE: 31 CAT: 17

McGovern (George)
CIJE: 6 RIE: 4 CAT: 18

McGrath (Earl J)
CIJE: 1 RIE: 2 CAT: 18

McGraw Hill Basic Skills System Reading Test
CIJE: 1 RIE: 2 CAT: 21

McGraw Hill Information Exchange
USE MIX (Online Service)

McGraw Hill Test of Adult Basic Education
CIJE: 0 RIE: 1 CAT: 21

McGraw Hill Writing Test
CIJE: 0 RIE: 1 CAT: 21

McGregor (Douglas)
CIJE: 2 RIE: 2 CAT: 18

McGuffey (William)
CIJE: 3 RIE: 3 CAT: 18

McGuffey Eclectic Readers
USE McGuffey Readers

McGuffey Readers
CIJE: 5 RIE: 5 CAT: 22
UF McGuffey Eclectic Readers

McGuire (William)
CIJE: 1 RIE: 1 CAT: 18

McGuire and White Social Status Index
CIJE: 0 RIE: 2 CAT: 15

McHenry (James)
CIJE: 0 RIE: 1 CAT: 18

McHenry Community High School District 156 IL
CIJE: 0 RIE: 1 CAT: 17

McHenry County College IL
CIJE: 1 RIE: 0 CAT: 17

McHugh McParland Reading Readiness Test
CIJE: 0 RIE: 1 CAT: 21

McIntyre (Alasdair)
CIJE: 0 RIE: 1 CAT: 18

McKee (Howard Joseph Jr)
CIJE: 0 RIE: 1 CAT: 18

McKee Inventory of Phonetic Skill
CIJE: 1 RIE: 0 CAT: 21

McKeesport Area School District PA
CIJE: 0 RIE: 4 CAT: 17

McKendree College IL
CIJE: 1 RIE: 1 CAT: 17

McKenney (James)
CIJE: 0 RIE: 1 CAT: 18

McKenney Keen Model
CIJE: 1 RIE: 0 CAT: 15

McKeon (Richard)
CIJE: 3 RIE: 0 CAT: 18

McKinley Junior High School MI
CIJE: 0 RIE: 1 CAT: 17

McKinley Project
CIJE: 0 RIE: 1 CAT: 19

McKuen (Rod)
CIJE: 2 RIE: 1 CAT: 18

McLaren (Norman)
CIJE: 0 RIE: 1 CAT: 18

McLaughlin (Barry)
CIJE: 1 RIE: 0 CAT: 18

McLendon v Morton
CIJE: 1 RIE: 0 CAT: 14

McLennan Community College TX
CIJE: 0 RIE: 1 CAT: 17

McLeod (Stuart)
CIJE: 1 RIE: 0 CAT: 18

McLeod Control Structure Description Questionnaire
CIJE: 0 RIE: 1 CAT: 21

McLeod Hawley Index of Professional Orientation
CIJE: 0 RIE: 1 CAT: 21

McLuhan (Marshall)
CIJE: 38 RIE: 25 CAT: 18

McMaster University (Canada)
CIJE: 38 RIE: 8 CAT: 17

McMinnville School District OR
CIJE: 0 RIE: 1 CAT: 17

McMurry College TX
CIJE: 2 RIE: 1 CAT: 17

McMurtrie (Douglas C)
CIJE: 0 RIE: 0 CAT: 18

McNamara (Robert S)
CIJE: 1 RIE: 0 CAT: 18

McNeese State University LA
CIJE: 1 RIE: 5 CAT: 17

McNemar Test of Equality of Correlated Proportion
CIJE: 5 RIE: 0 CAT: 21

McPeck (John)
CIJE: 2 RIE: 2 CAT: 18

McPhail (Peter)
CIJE: 1 RIE: 1 CAT: 18

McPherson College KS
CIJE: 0 RIE: 1 CAT: 17

McRAT Program AR
USE Multicultural Reading and Thinking Program AR

McREL
USE Mid Continent Regional Educational Laboratory

McREL Effective Schools Program
CIJE: 0 RIE: 0 CAT: 19

McREL Higher Order Thinking Skills Model
USE Higher Order Thinking Skills Model (McREL)

McREL Instructional Staff Development Program
CIJE: 0 RIE: 2 CAT: 19

McREL Interaction Analysis
CIJE: 0 RIE: 1 CAT: 15

McREL Middle School Advisement Program
CIJE: 0 RIE: 1 CAT: 19

McREL School Improvement Program
CIJE: 0 RIE: 1 CAT: 19

McSorley (Marty)
CIJE: 0 RIE: 1 CAT: 18

McVey (William)
CIJE: 1 RIE: 0 CAT: 18

McVoys Wants and Satisfaction Scale
CIJE: 0 RIE: 1 CAT: 21

MCW APM
USE Modified Confidence Weighted Admissible Prob Meas

MDT Multiple Digit Testing
USE Multi Digit Tests

MDTs
USE Multidisciplinary Teams

Me Generation
CIJE: 2 RIE: 0 CAT: 12

Mead (George Herbert)
CIJE: 12 RIE: 12 CAT: 18

Mead (Margaret)
CIJE: 11 RIE: 1 CAT: 18

Mediation Techniques
CIJE: 15 RIE: 3 CAT: 15

Mediators
CIJE: 25 RIE: 4 CAT: 16

Medicaid
CIJE: 70 RIE: 129 CAT: 19

Medical Advertising Regulation
CIJE: 0 RIE: 1 CAT: 14

Medical Aides
CIJE: 0 RIE: 2 CAT: 09

Medical Anthropology
CIJE: 2 RIE: 1 CAT: 11

Medical College Admission Test
CIJE: 70 RIE: 35 CAT: 21

Medical College of Georgia
CIJE: 19 RIE: 5 CAT: 17

Medical College of Ohio
CIJE: 7 RIE: 2 CAT: 17

Medical College of Pennsylvania
CIJE: 11 RIE: 1 CAT: 17

Medical College of Virginia
CIJE: 8 RIE: 3 CAT: 17

Medical College of Wisconsin
CIJE: 12 RIE: 3 CAT: 17

Medical Consent Forms
CIJE: 0 RIE: 2 CAT: 11

Medical Corps Personnel
CIJE: 0 RIE: 2 CAT: 09

Medical Dental Education Preparatory Program
CIJE: 0 RIE: 1 CAT: 19
UF MEDPREP

Medical Devices
CIJE: 2 RIE: 2 CAT: 04

Medical Documentation
CIJE: 0 RIE: 1 CAT: 11

Medical Education Financing Policy Analyses
CIJE: 0 RIE: 1 CAT: 16

Medical Education Research Offices
USE Offices of Research in Medical Education

Medical Exclusions
CIJE: 0 RIE: 1 CAT: 11

Medical Facilities
CIJE: 3 RIE: 1 CAT: 05

Medical Group Practice
CIJE: 3 RIE: 1 CAT: 15

Medical Illustration (Occupation)
CIJE: 1 RIE: 0 CAT: 09

Medical Imaging
CIJE: 0 RIE: 0 CAT: 11
SN See also "Magnetic Resonance Imaging"
UF Diagnostic Imaging (Medicine); Imaging (Medicine)

Medical Imaging Occupations
CIJE: 0 RIE: 2 CAT: 09

Medical Information Project
CIJE: 0 RIE: 3 CAT: 19

Medical Information Systems
CIJE: 20 RIE: 11 CAT: 20

Medical Knowledge Tests
CIJE: 0 RIE: 2 CAT: 21

Medical Laboratories
CIJE: 2 RIE: 1 CAT: 05

Medical Leave
CIJE: 0 RIE: 6 CAT: 11

Medical Library Assistance Act
CIJE: 1 RIE: 3 CAT: 14

Medical Library Association
CIJE: 11 RIE: 10 CAT: 17

Medical Library Center of New York
CIJE: 0 RIE: 1 CAT: 17

Medical Model
CIJE: 6 RIE: 1 CAT: 15

Medical Negligence
CIJE: 3 RIE: 1 CAT: 11

Medical Play
CIJE: 0 RIE: 1 CAT: 11

Medical Record
CIJE: 1 RIE: 2 CAT: 15

Medical Records
CIJE: 12 RIE: 4 CAT: 11

Medical Schools Learning Environment Survey
CIJE: 1 RIE: 0 CAT: 21

Medical Search
CIJE: 0 RIE: 1 CAT: 15

Medical Specialist Preference Blank
CIJE: 0 RIE: 1 CAT: 21

Medical Specialty Boards
CIJE: 1 RIE: 2 CAT: 09

Medical Specialty Preference Inventory (Zimny)
CIJE: 2 RIE: 0 CAT: 21

Medical Subject Headings
CIJE: 12 RIE: 5 CAT: 22

Medical Supplies Assemblers
CIJE: 0 RIE: 1 CAT: 09

Medical Technology
CIJE: 6 RIE: 6 CAT: 11

Medical Transcribers
CIJE: 1 RIE: 3 CAT: 09

Medical University of South Carolina
CIJE: 17 RIE: 5 CAT: 17

Medical Utilization
CIJE: 0 RIE: 2 CAT: 11

Medically Fragile
CIJE: 10 RIE: 17 CAT: 10

Medically Underserved Areas
CIJE: 11 RIE: 5 CAT: 11

Medicare
CIJE: 44 RIE: 60 CAT: 19

Medicare Capitation
CIJE: 0 RIE: 1 CAT: 16
UF Capitation of Medicare

Medicare Catastrophic Protection Act 1988
CIJE: 0 RIE: 0 CAT: 14
SN Repealed in 1989
UF Public Law 100 360

Medicare Home Care Benefit
CIJE: 0 RIE: 1 CAT: 19

Medication
CIJE: 10 RIE: 7 CAT: 11

Medication Administration Technicians
USE Medication Technicians

Medication Aides
CIJE: 0 RIE: 3 CAT: 09

Medication Technicians
CIJE: 0 RIE: 2 CAT: 09
UF Medication Administration Technicians

Medications
CIJE: 2 RIE: 3 CAT: 11

Medicine Circle
CIJE: 0 RIE: 1 CAT: 15

Medicine Hat Junior College (Canada)
CIJE: 0 RIE: 1 CAT: 17

Medicine Hat Youth Assessment Center AB
CIJE: 0 RIE: 1 CAT: 17

Medicine Men
CIJE: 5 RIE: 6 CAT: 10

Medicine Shows
CIJE: 1 RIE: 1 CAT: 16

Medicine Today
CIJE: 0 RIE: 1 CAT: 22

Medicine Wheel
CIJE: 7 RIE: 3 CAT: 16

Medieval Period
USE Middle Ages

Medigap Insurance
CIJE: 2 RIE: 1 CAT: 11

Mediterranean Region
CIJE: 5 RIE: 6 CAT: 07

Mediterranean Regional Project
CIJE: 0 RIE: 1 CAT: 19

MEDLARS
CIJE: 35 RIE: 23 CAT: 04

MEDLINE
CIJE: 55 RIE: 17 CAT: 04

MEDPREP
USE Medical Dental Education Preparatory Program

Medvedev (Roy A)
CIJE: 1 RIE: 0 CAT: 18

Meese Commission on Pornography
CIJE: 5 RIE: 5 CAT: 17
UF Attorney Generals Commission on Pornography

Meese v Keene
CIJE: 0 RIE: 1 CAT: 14

Meeting of Experts on Mass Communication Society
CIJE: 0 RIE: 1 CAT: 02

Meeting of Minds
CIJE: 0 RIE: 1 CAT: 22

Meeting Street School Screening Test
CIJE: 3 RIE: 3 CAT: 21

Mega Building
CIJE: 1 RIE: 0 CAT: 15

Mega Proposal
CIJE: 0 RIE: 1 CAT: 15

Megargee (E I)
CIJE: 2 RIE: 0 CAT: 18

MegaSkills Home Curriculum
CIJE: 0 RIE: 1 CAT: 03

Megatrends
CIJE: 10 RIE: 4 CAT: 16

Megavitamin Therapy
CIJE: 5 RIE: 1 CAT: 15

Meharry Medical College TN
CIJE: 8 RIE: 3 CAT: 17

Mehlville School District MO
CIJE: 0 RIE: 1 CAT: 17

Mehrabian Measure of Achieving Tendency Females
CIJE: 0 RIE: 1 CAT: 21

Meier (Deborah)
CIJE: 1 RIE: 0 CAT: 18

Meier (Norman C)
CIJE: 0 RIE: 1 CAT: 18

Meier Art Tests
CIJE: 2 RIE: 2 CAT: 21

Meier Burnout Assessment
CIJE: 0 RIE: 1 CAT: 21

Meiklejohn (Alexander)
CIJE: 6 RIE: 4 CAT: 18

Meillet (Antoine)
CIJE: 0 RIE: 0 CAT: 18

Meiosis
CIJE: 4 RIE: 3 CAT: 20

Meitei
CIJE: 1 RIE: 1 CAT: 13
SN A Tibeto-Burman language
UF Manipuri; Meithei

Meithei
USE Meitei

Melanesia
CIJE: 4 RIE: 3 CAT: 07

Melani v Board of Higher Education
CIJE: 0 RIE: 1 CAT: 14

Melanoma
CIJE: 1 RIE: 0 CAT: 11

MELBORP
CIJE: 1 RIE: 0 CAT: 04

Melbourne High School FL
CIJE: 1 RIE: 3 CAT: 17

Mellaril
CIJE: 1 RIE: 0 CAT: 11

Mellon (John C)
CIJE: 0 RIE: 1 CAT: 18

Melodic Interval Discrimination
CIJE: 2 RIE: 0 CAT: 15
UF Melody Recognition

Melodic Intonation Therapy
CIJE: 2 RIE: 0 CAT: 11

Melody Recognition
USE Melodic Interval Discrimination

Melting Pot
CIJE: 6 RIE: 2 CAT: 16

Melville (Herman)
CIJE: 15 RIE: 7 CAT: 18

Melvindale High School MI
CIJE: 1 RIE: 0 CAT: 17

MELVYL
CIJE: 17 RIE: 7 CAT: 04

Mem ExSpan Accelerative Cognitive Training System
CIJE: 0 RIE: 1 CAT: 15
UF MESACTS

Member of the Wedding (The)
CIJE: 0 RIE: 0 CAT: 22

Member Union Relationship
CIJE: 0 RIE: 1 CAT: 15

Membership Benefits
CIJE: 6 RIE: 1 CAT: 16

Membership Requirements
CIJE: 3 RIE: 7 CAT: 16

Membrane Filtration
CIJE: 2 RIE: 0 CAT: 20

Membrane Structures
CIJE: 5 RIE: 0 CAT: 20

Memes
CIJE: 0 RIE: 2 CAT: 16

Memorial Art Gallery
CIJE: 0 RIE: 1 CAT: 17

Memorial Day
CIJE: 2 RIE: 1 CAT: 12

Memorial Junior High School CA
CIJE: 0 RIE: 1 CAT: 17

Memorial University of Newfoundland (Canada)
CIJE: 10 RIE: 5 CAT: 17

Memory Deficits
CIJE: 2 RIE: 3 CAT: 11

Memory for Designs Test (Graham Kendall)
CIJE: 4 RIE: 0 CAT: 21

Memory Load
CIJE: 3 RIE: 3 CAT: 15

Memory Management
CIJE: 4 RIE: 2 CAT: 15

Memory Operating Characteristics
CIJE: 3 RIE: 2 CAT: 15

Memory Protocols
CIJE: 0 RIE: 1 CAT: 11

Memory Span
CIJE: 16 RIE: 3 CAT: 11

Memory Span Tests (Harris)
CIJE: 2 RIE: 0 CAT: 21

Memory Support
CIJE: 1 RIE: 3 CAT: 15

Memory Tasks
CIJE: 38 RIE: 11 CAT: 11

Memory Training
CIJE: 7 RIE: 6 CAT: 11

Memphis and Shelby County Health Department TN
CIJE: 0 RIE: 1 CAT: 17

Memphis City Schools TN
CIJE: 10 RIE: 22 CAT: 17

Memphis Metro Youth Diversion Project
CIJE: 2 RIE: 0 CAT: 19

Memphis State University Campus School TN
CIJE: 0 RIE: 1 CAT: 17

Memphis State University TN
CIJE: 17 RIE: 49 CAT: 17

Men Faculty
CIJE: 0 RIE: 1 CAT: 10

Menand (Louis)
CIJE: 0 RIE: 1 CAT: 18

Menarche
CIJE: 22 RIE: 1 CAT: 11

Mencius (Master Meng)
CIJE: 1 RIE: 0 CAT: 18

Mende (Tribe)
CIJE: 2 RIE: 0 CAT: 08

Mendel (Gregor)
CIJE: 4 RIE: 1 CAT: 18

Mending Wall
CIJE: 0 RIE: 1 CAT: 22

Mendocino College CA
CIJE: 0 RIE: 2 CAT: 17

Mendocino State Hospital CA
CIJE: 2 RIE: 0 CAT: 17

Mendoza (Antonio de)
CIJE: 0 RIE: 1 CAT: 18

Mendoza (Diego Hurtado de)
CIJE: 1 RIE: 0 CAT: 18

Menendez Pidal (Ramon)
CIJE: 3 RIE: 0 CAT: 18

Menendez y Pelayo (Marcelino)
CIJE: 1 RIE: 0 CAT: 18

Meningitis
CIJE: 7 RIE: 6 CAT: 11

Meningitis (Hemophilus)
USE Hemophilus Influenza Type B

Menkes Kinky Hair Syndrome
CIJE: 1 RIE: 0 CAT: 11

Menlo Park Elementary School District CA
CIJE: 0 RIE: 1 CAT: 17

Menninger Clinic
CIJE: 1 RIE: 0 CAT: 17

Mennonite Central Committee
CIJE: 1 RIE: 0 CAT: 17

Mennonite College of Nursing IL
CIJE: 0 RIE: 0 CAT: 17

Mennonites
CIJE: 13 RIE: 17 CAT: 08
SN See also "Holdeman Mennonites," "General Conference Mennonites"

MENO II
CIJE: 0 RIE: 1 CAT: 04

Menominee
CIJE: 1 RIE: 1 CAT: 13

Menominee (Tribe)
CIJE: 10 RIE: 24 CAT: 08

Menominee Agency WI
CIJE: 0 RIE: 1 CAT: 17

Menomonie Vocational and Adult School WI
CIJE: 0 RIE: 1 CAT: 17

Menopause
CIJE: 20 RIE: 4 CAT: 11

Mens Studies
CIJE: 11 RIE: 1 CAT: 03

Menstrual Cramps
USE Dysmenorrhea

Menstrual Disorders
CIJE: 2 RIE: 0 CAT: 11
SN See also "Amenorrhea" and "Dysmenorrhea"

Menstrual Products
CIJE: 2 RIE: 0 CAT: 11

Mental Animation
CIJE: 0 RIE: 1 CAT: 11

Mental Computation
CIJE: 48 RIE: 18 CAT: 11

Mental Development Scales Birth to Three Years
CIJE: 1 RIE: 1 CAT: 21

Mental Dexterity Test
CIJE: 1 RIE: 0 CAT: 21

Mental Effort
CIJE: 4 RIE: 2 CAT: 11
SN See also "Amount of Invested Mental Effort"

Mental Exercises
CIJE: 0 RIE: 1 CAT: 11

Mental Health Amendments 1990
CIJE: 0 RIE: 0 CAT: 14
UF Public Law 101 639

Mental Health Attitude Survey (Fischer and Turner)
CIJE: 1 RIE: 0 CAT: 21

Mental Imagery
CIJE: 39 RIE: 15 CAT: 11

Mental Measurements Yearbook
CIJE: 2 RIE: 7 CAT: 22

Mental Models
CIJE: 41 RIE: 21 CAT: 15

Mental Practice
CIJE: 7 RIE: 0 CAT: 15

Mental Representation
CIJE: 17 RIE: 9 CAT: 16

Mental Retardation Abstracts
CIJE: 1 RIE: 0 CAT: 22

Mental Retardation Expert System
CIJE: 0 RIE: 1 CAT: 04

Mental Retardation Grants 1968
CIJE: 0 RIE: 1 CAT: 14

Mental Rotation
CIJE: 16 RIE: 2 CAT: 11

Mental Rotation Tests
CIJE: 6 RIE: 3 CAT: 21

Mental Skills
CIJE: 0 RIE: 1 CAT: 11

Mental Status Examination
CIJE: 1 RIE: 0 CAT: 21

Mental Step Hypothesis
CIJE: 1 RIE: 0 CAT: 15

Mental Tracking
CIJE: 1 RIE: 2 CAT: 11
UF Tracking (Mental)

Mentalistic Measures
CIJE: 0 RIE: 1 CAT: 21

Mentalistic Theory
CIJE: 2 RIE: 1 CAT: 15

Mentally Gifted Minors Program CA
USE California Mentally Gifted Minors Program

Mentally Retarded Parents
CIJE: 7 RIE: 4 CAT: 10

Mentally Tough Principles
CIJE: 0 RIE: 1 CAT: 15

MENTOR (SUNY Potsdam Coll)
USE Migrant Educators National Training OutReach

Mentor Academy Program
CIJE: 0 RIE: 1 CAT: 19

Mentor Assisted Enrichment Project
CIJE: 0 RIE: 1 CAT: 19

MENTOR In Education NY
CIJE: 0 RIE: 1 CAT: 19
SN Program designed to interest high school students in pursuing careers in teaching

Mentor Peer Group and Incentive Model
CIJE: 0 RIE: 1 CAT: 19

Mentor Project MA
CIJE: 0 RIE: 0 CAT: 19

Mentor Project NYC
USE Project Mentor NY

Mentor Protege Relationship
USE Protege Mentor Relationship

Mentor Teacher Internship Program NY
USE New York State Mentor Teacher Internship Program

Menu Planning
CIJE: 1 RIE: 23 CAT: 16

Menudo
CIJE: 0 RIE: 2 CAT: 16

Menuhin (Yehudi)
CIJE: 1 RIE: 0 CAT: 18

Menyuk (Paula)
CIJE: 1 RIE: 0 CAT: 18

Mercer County Community College NJ
CIJE: 4 RIE: 15 CAT: 17

Mercer County Public Schools WV
CIJE: 0 RIE: 1 CAT: 17

Mercer County Teacher Education Center
CIJE: 0 RIE: 1 CAT: 17

Merchandise Packers
CIJE: 0 RIE: 1 CAT: 09

Merchandise Turnover
CIJE: 1 RIE: 0 CAT: 16

Merchant Marines
CIJE: 3 RIE: 7 CAT: 17

Merchant of Venice
CIJE: 4 RIE: 4 CAT: 22

Merck Sharp and Dohme Research Laboratories
CIJE: 1 RIE: 0 CAT: 17

MERCOSUR
CIJE: 0 RIE: 1 CAT: 14

Mercury (Metal)
CIJE: 18 RIE: 1 CAT: 20

Mercury (Planet)
CIJE: 1 RIE: 0 CAT: 20

Mercy College MI
CIJE: 1 RIE: 3 CAT: 17

Mercy College NY
CIJE: 1 RIE: 6 CAT: 17

Mere Exposure Theory
CIJE: 2 RIE: 1 CAT: 15

Meredith (James A)
CIJE: 0 RIE: 1 CAT: 18

Meredith College NC
CIJE: 0 RIE: 1 CAT: 17

Meria (Juan de)
CIJE: 1 RIE: 0 CAT: 18

Meriam Report
CIJE: 1 RIE: 1 CAT: 22

Meriden Public Schools CT
CIJE: 0 RIE: 1 CAT: 17

Meridi Extension Unit
CIJE: 0 RIE: 1 CAT: 17

Meridian Instructional Model
CIJE: 0 RIE: 1 CAT: 15

Meridian Joint School District ID
CIJE: 0 RIE: 1 CAT: 17

Meridian Public Schools MS
CIJE: 0 RIE: 1 CAT: 17

Merimee (Prosper)
CIJE: 2 RIE: 0 CAT: 18

Merina Dialect
CIJE: 0 RIE: 2 CAT: 13

Meringue
CIJE: 0 RIE: 1 CAT: 16

Merion Elementary School PA
CIJE: 1 RIE: 0 CAT: 17

Merit
CIJE: 6 RIE: 1 CAT: 16

MERIT Computer Network
CIJE: 1 RIE: 4 CAT: 04

Merit Promotion
CIJE: 0 RIE: 2 CAT: 16

Merit System Tests
CIJE: 1 RIE: 1 CAT: 21

Meritocracy
CIJE: 21 RIE: 5 CAT: 15

Meritorious School Act (Florida)
USE Florida Merit School Program

Merleau Ponty (Maurice)
CIJE: 2 RIE: 4 CAT: 18

MERLIN (Computer System)
CIJE: 0 RIE: 1 CAT: 04

MERLIN (Database)
USE Migrant Ed Resources List and Information Network

Merlin the Magician
CIJE: 1 RIE: 1 CAT: 16

MERMAC System
CIJE: 1 RIE: 2 CAT: 04

Merriam Center Library IL
CIJE: 1 RIE: 1 CAT: 17

Merriam Report
CIJE: 0 RIE: 1 CAT: 22

Merrill (M D)
CIJE: 12 RIE: 3 CAT: 18

Merrill Language Screening Test
CIJE: 0 RIE: 1 CAT: 21

Merrill Lynch
CIJE: 2 RIE: 0 CAT: 17

Merrill Palmer Head Start Questionnaire
CIJE: 0 RIE: 1 CAT: 21

Merrill Palmer Institute MI
CIJE: 0 RIE: 2 CAT: 17

Merrill Palmer Personality Rating Scale
CIJE: 0 RIE: 1 CAT: 21

Merrill Palmer Scale of Mental Tests
CIJE: 2 RIE: 4 CAT: 21

Merrimack College MA
CIJE: 1 RIE: 1 CAT: 17

Merrimack Education Center MA
CIJE: 2 RIE: 7 CAT: 17

Merrimack Valley
CIJE: 0 RIE: 1 CAT: 07

Merritt College CA
CIJE: 2 RIE: 3 CAT: 17

Mersenne Primes
CIJE: 1 RIE: 0 CAT: 20

Merton (Robert K)
CIJE: 9 RIE: 1 CAT: 18

Mesa Action Planning System
CIJE: 0 RIE: 1 CAT: 19

Mesa College CO
CIJE: 2 RIE: 1 CAT: 17

Mesa Community College AZ
CIJE: 0 RIE: 2 CAT: 17

Mesa County Valley School District 51 CO
CIJE: 0 RIE: 1 CAT: 17

MESA MEP Program CA
USE MESA Program CA

MESA Program CA
CIJE: 0 RIE: 1 CAT: 19
SN See also "Junior MESA Program CA"
UF Mathematics Engineering and Science Achievement CA; MESA MEP Program CA

Mesa Public Schools AZ
CIJE: 6 RIE: 26 CAT: 17

Mesa State College CO
CIJE: 0 RIE: 1 CAT: 17

Mesa Verde High School CA
CIJE: 1 RIE: 1 CAT: 17

Mesa Verde National Park
CIJE: 0 RIE: 2 CAT: 07

Mesabi Community College MN
CIJE: 0 RIE: 1 CAT: 17

MESACTS
USE Mem ExSpan Accelerative Cognitive Training System

Mescalero Apache (Tribe)
CIJE: 0 RIE: 2 CAT: 08

Mescaline
CIJE: 1 RIE: 3 CAT: 11

MeSH Tree Structure
CIJE: 1 RIE: 0 CAT: 15

Mesmer (Anton)
CIJE: 0 RIE: 1 CAT: 18

Mesoamerica
CIJE: 11 RIE: 2 CAT: 07

Mesomorph
CIJE: 2 RIE: 1 CAT: 11

Mesopotamia
CIJE: 2 RIE: 4 CAT: 07

Mesopotamians
CIJE: 1 RIE: 0 CAT: 08

Mesquakie (Tribe)
CIJE: 0 RIE: 1 CAT: 08

Mesquite Independent School District TX
CIJE: 2 RIE: 0 CAT: 17

Message Assistant
CIJE: 0 RIE: 1 CAT: 04
SN An electronic mail program

Message Based Performances
CIJE: 0 RIE: 1 CAT: 16

Message Design
CIJE: 41 RIE: 25 CAT: 15

Message Discrepancy
USE Discrepant Messages

Message Distortion
CIJE: 1 RIE: 5 CAT: 15

Message Evaluation Skills
CIJE: 1 RIE: 1 CAT: 15

Message Legitimacy
CIJE: 0 RIE: 0 CAT: 16

Message Perception
CIJE: 27 RIE: 23 CAT: 15

Message Responses
CIJE: 18 RIE: 19 CAT: 15

Message Summaries
CIJE: 0 RIE: 1 CAT: 15

Message Switching
CIJE: 1 RIE: 2 CAT: 15

Message Text Formats
CIJE: 0 RIE: 1 CAT: 04

Message Transmission
CIJE: 12 RIE: 10 CAT: 15

Messiah College PA
CIJE: 2 RIE: 1 CAT: 17

Messick (Samuel)
CIJE: 0 RIE: 1 CAT: 18

MESTEP
USE Math English Science Technology Education Project

Mestizos (People)
CIJE: 1 RIE: 4 CAT: 08
SN Persons of mixed European and American Indian ancestry

Meta Analysis of Field Experience
USE Project MAFEX

Meta Attention
CIJE: 1 RIE: 0 CAT: 11

Meta Ethical Thinking
USE Metaethical Reasoning

Meta Ethnography
CIJE: 0 RIE: 1 CAT: 19

Meta Evaluation
CIJE: 18 RIE: 30 CAT: 21

Meta Modeling
CIJE: 0 RIE: 1 CAT: 15

Meta Research
CIJE: 1 RIE: 1 CAT: 15
SN Research on the research in a particular field
UF Metaresearch Programs

Metachromatic Leukodystrophy
CIJE: 1 RIE: 0 CAT: 11

Metacommunication
CIJE: 20 RIE: 8 CAT: 15

Metacomprehension
CIJE: 22 RIE: 15 CAT: 13

Metacourses
CIJE: 0 RIE: 1 CAT: 03

Metacriticism
CIJE: 3 RIE: 1 CAT: 15

Metadiscourse
CIJE: 11 RIE: 11 CAT: 13

Metaethical Reasoning
CIJE: 0 RIE: 1 CAT: 15
UF Meta Ethical Thinking

Metafiction
CIJE: 1 RIE: 1 CAT: 13

Metainformation
CIJE: 1 RIE: 0 CAT: 15

Metakinesics
CIJE: 0 RIE: 1 CAT: 13

Metal Bonded Repair
CIJE: 0 RIE: 1 CAT: 20

Metal Chair Assemblers
CIJE: 0 RIE: 1 CAT: 09

Metal Complexes
CIJE: 2 RIE: 0 CAT: 04

Metal Inert Gas Welding
CIJE: 0 RIE: 2 CAT: 20

Metalanguages
CIJE: 16 RIE: 3 CAT: 13

Metalibrarianship
CIJE: 0 RIE: 1 CAT: 15

Metamethodology
CIJE: 1 RIE: 2 CAT: 15

Metamorph (Computer Program)
CIJE: 0 RIE: 1 CAT: 04

Metamorphosis
CIJE: 6 RIE: 0 CAT: 20

Metamotivation Leadership
CIJE: 1 RIE: 0 CAT: 15

Metanalysis (Linguistics)
CIJE: 0 RIE: 1 CAT: 13
SN The incorrect determination of word boundaries, e.g., mismeaning "Pulitzer Prize" as "pullet surprise"

Metanarration
CIJE: 1 RIE: 1 CAT: 13

Metaphorical Thought
CIJE: 22 RIE: 18 CAT: 15

Metaphysics
CIJE: 35 RIE: 14 CAT: 15

Metapolicy
CIJE: 0 RIE: 1 CAT: 15
SN Policy on policymaking

Metaresearch Programs
USE Meta Research

Metaresponse
CIJE: 0 RIE: 1 CAT: 15

Metasymbol
CIJE: 0 RIE: 3 CAT: 15

Metatelevision
CIJE: 1 RIE: 1 CAT: 15
SN Television programming that contains hidden references to various elements of popular culture

Metatheory
CIJE: 21 RIE: 7 CAT: 15

Metathesis
CIJE: 0 RIE: 4 CAT: 15

Meter (Poetry)
CIJE: 1 RIE: 0 CAT: 13

Methadone
CIJE: 28 RIE: 11 CAT: 11

Methane
CIJE: 4 RIE: 1 CAT: 20

Methane Digestors
CIJE: 0 RIE: 1 CAT: 20

Methanol
CIJE: 1 RIE: 0 CAT: 20

Methaqualone
CIJE: 1 RIE: 2 CAT: 11

Method of Designing Instructional Alternatives
CIJE: 0 RIE: 10 CAT: 15

Method of Moments
CIJE: 0 RIE: 1 CAT: 15
SN See also "Moment Estimators"

Method of Reciprocal Averages
CIJE: 1 RIE: 0 CAT: 15

Methode Audio Visuelle d Anglais
CIJE: 0 RIE: 1 CAT: 15

Methodist Childrens Home Society
CIJE: 0 RIE: 1 CAT: 17

Methodist Church
CIJE: 4 RIE: 10 CAT: 17

Methodology for Assaying Goals in Education
CIJE: 1 RIE: 2 CAT: 19

Methodology Inventory
CIJE: 0 RIE: 1 CAT: 21

Methylmercury Poisoning
CIJE: 1 RIE: 0 CAT: 11

Methylphenidate
CIJE: 42 RIE: 2 CAT: 11

Metis Betterment Act
CIJE: 0 RIE: 1 CAT: 14

Metonymy
CIJE: 4 RIE: 2 CAT: 13

Metric Multidimensional Scaling
CIJE: 2 RIE: 1 CAT: 21

Metric Spaces
CIJE: 2 RIE: 1 CAT: 20

Metric Study Act 1968
CIJE: 0 RIE: 2 CAT: 14

METRO Achievement Project
CIJE: 0 RIE: 1 CAT: 19

Metro Community College NE
CIJE: 0 RIE: 1 CAT: 17

Metro Education
CIJE: 0 RIE: 1 CAT: 15

Metro High School IL
CIJE: 1 RIE: 4 CAT: 17

Metro School IL
CIJE: 0 RIE: 1 CAT: 17

Metro State College CO
CIJE: 0 RIE: 2 CAT: 17

Metrolina Educational Consortia NC
CIJE: 0 RIE: 1 CAT: 17

Metrology
CIJE: 0 RIE: 2 CAT: 20

Metropolitan Achievement Tests
CIJE: 56 RIE: 228 CAT: 21

Metropolitan Achievement Tests Sixth Edition
USE MAT 6

Metropolitan Applied Research Center
CIJE: 2 RIE: 1 CAT: 17

Metropolitan Area Library Authorities
CIJE: 1 RIE: 0 CAT: 17

Metropolitan Community Attitude Inventory
CIJE: 0 RIE: 1 CAT: 21

Metropolitan Community Colleges MO
CIJE: 4 RIE: 2 CAT: 17

Metropolitan Cooperative Library System
CIJE: 0 RIE: 1 CAT: 17

Metropolitan Council for Educational Opportunity
CIJE: 5 RIE: 4 CAT: 17

Metropolitan Council of the Twin Cities Area
CIJE: 0 RIE: 1 CAT: 17

Metropolitan Desegregation Plans
CIJE: 1 RIE: 1 CAT: 16

Metropolitan Detroit Medical Library Group
CIJE: 0 RIE: 1 CAT: 17

Metropolitan Education Commission MI
CIJE: 0 RIE: 0 CAT: 17

Metropolitan Education Television Association
CIJE: 1 RIE: 0 CAT: 17

Metropolitan Educational Development Research Proj
CIJE: 0 RIE: 1 CAT: 19

Metropolitan Educational Park
CIJE: 1 RIE: 0 CAT: 17

Metropolitan Handwriting Scale
CIJE: 0 RIE: 1 CAT: 21

Metropolitan High School TX
CIJE: 1 RIE: 0 CAT: 17

Metropolitan Kansas City Jr College District MO
CIJE: 0 RIE: 3 CAT: 17

Metropolitan Life Insurance Company
CIJE: 1 RIE: 0 CAT: 17

Metropolitan Meteorological Experiment
CIJE: 2 RIE: 0 CAT: 19

Metropolitan Museum of Art NY
CIJE: 4 RIE: 1 CAT: 17

Metropolitan Open School MN
CIJE: 1 RIE: 0 CAT: 17

Metropolitan Pittsburgh Educational Television
CIJE: 1 RIE: 2 CAT: 17

Metropolitan Planning Project of Greater Boston
CIJE: 0 RIE: 1 CAT: 19

Metropolitan Readiness Tests
CIJE: 45 RIE: 121 CAT: 21

Metropolitan Reading Mathematics Achievement Tests
CIJE: 0 RIE: 2 CAT: 21

Metropolitan Reemployment Project
CIJE: 0 RIE: 1 CAT: 19

Metropolitan School Study Council
CIJE: 1 RIE: 1 CAT: 17

Metropolitan State College CO
CIJE: 4 RIE: 23 CAT: 17

Metropolitan State University MN
CIJE: 3 RIE: 6 CAT: 17

Metropolitan Twin Cities Educ Coop Service Unit MN
CIJE: 0 RIE: 1 CAT: 17
UF Educational Cooperative Serv Unit Minneapolis MN

Mexican Academy of Education
CIJE: 0 RIE: 1 CAT: 17

Mexican American Culture Simulator
CIJE: 1 RIE: 1 CAT: 21

Mexican American Culture Simulator Child Welfare
CIJE: 0 RIE: 0 CAT: 15

Mexican American Education Research Project
CIJE: 1 RIE: 3 CAT: 19

Mexican American Inventory of Receptive Abilities
CIJE: 1 RIE: 0 CAT: 21

Mexican American Legal Defense Educational Fund
CIJE: 2 RIE: 3 CAT: 17

Mexican American Studies
CIJE: 3 RIE: 5 CAT: 03

Mexican American Study Project
CIJE: 0 RIE: 7 CAT: 19

Mexican Arts
CIJE: 0 RIE: 1 CAT: 16

Mexican Attitude Inventory
CIJE: 0 RIE: 1 CAT: 21

Mexican Electric Power Research Institute
CIJE: 0 RIE: 1 CAT: 17

Mexican Telesecundaria
CIJE: 1 RIE: 0 CAT: 16

Mexican War
CIJE: 7 RIE: 3 CAT: 12

Mexico
CIJE: 360 RIE: 386 CAT: 07

Mexico (Acapulco)
CIJE: 0 RIE: 1 CAT: 07

Mexico (Chiapas)
CIJE: 2 RIE: 1 CAT: 07

Mexico (Ciudad Guzman)
CIJE: 0 RIE: 1 CAT: 07

Mexico (Ciudad Juarez)
CIJE: 1 RIE: 0 CAT: 07
UF Mexico (Juarez)

Mexico (Guadalajara)
CIJE: 1 RIE: 2 CAT: 07

Mexico (Guerrero)
CIJE: 0 RIE: 1 CAT: 07

Mexico (Hermosillo)
CIJE: 0 RIE: 1 CAT: 07

Mexico (Huasteca)
CIJE: 0 RIE: 1 CAT: 07

Mexico (Jalisco)
CIJE: 0 RIE: 1 CAT: 07

Mexico (Juarez)
USE Mexico (Ciudad Juarez)

Mexico (Mexico City)
CIJE: 7 RIE: 11 CAT: 07

Mexico (Michoacan)
CIJE: 4 RIE: 1 CAT: 07

Mexico (Oaxaca)
CIJE: 9 RIE: 2 CAT: 07

Mexico (Puebla)
CIJE: 1 RIE: 3 CAT: 07

Mexico (Tamaulipas State)
CIJE: 0 RIE: 1 CAT: 07

Mexico (Tijuana)
CIJE: 2 RIE: 0 CAT: 07

Mexico (Veracruz)
CIJE: 2 RIE: 1 CAT: 07

Mexico (Yucatan)
CIJE: 11 RIE: 1 CAT: 07

Mexico City Binational Center
CIJE: 0 RIE: 1 CAT: 17

Mexico Public Schools MO
CIJE: 1 RIE: 1 CAT: 17

Mexico United States Border
CIJE: 1 RIE: 6 CAT: 07
UF United States Mexico Border

Meyer (Conrad Ferdinand)
CIJE: 2 RIE: 0 CAT: 18

Meyer Childrens Rehabilitation Institute
CIJE: 1 RIE: 1 CAT: 17

Meyer Social Attitude Scale
CIJE: 0 RIE: 1 CAT: 21

Meyer v Nebraska
CIJE: 0 RIE: 2 CAT: 14

Meyers (Phillip Van Ness)
CIJE: 0 RIE: 1 CAT: 18

Meyerson (Lee)
CIJE: 0 RIE: 1 CAT: 18

Mezirow (Jack)
CIJE: 6 RIE: 1 CAT: 18

MFATPS
USE Major Field Achievement Test in Political Science

MFVA
USE Montana Functional Vision Assessment

Mhong Language Council
CIJE: 0 RIE: 1 CAT: 17

Miami (Tribe)
CIJE: 1 RIE: 1 CAT: 08

Miami Bilingual Program
CIJE: 0 RIE: 4 CAT: 19

Miami Dade Community College FL
CIJE: 55 RIE: 86 CAT: 17

Miami Linguistic Readers
CIJE: 1 RIE: 5 CAT: 22

Miami Linguistic Reading Program
CIJE: 0 RIE: 1 CAT: 19

Miami Public Library FL
CIJE: 3 RIE: 0 CAT: 17

Miami Public Schools FL
CIJE: 0 RIE: 2 CAT: 17

Miami Southridge Adult Education Center FL
CIJE: 0 RIE: 1 CAT: 17

Miami University OH
CIJE: 24 RIE: 31 CAT: 17

Miami Urban Coalition
CIJE: 0 RIE: 1 CAT: 17

Miami Vice (Television Series)
CIJE: 0 RIE: 2 CAT: 22

Miccosukee
CIJE: 0 RIE: 2 CAT: 13

Miccosukee (Language)
CIJE: 0 RIE: 2 CAT: 13

Miccosukee (Tribe)
CIJE: 4 RIE: 5 CAT: 08

Mice
CIJE: 6 RIE: 1 CAT: 20

Michael J Owens Technical College OH
CIJE: 0 RIE: 1 CAT: 17

Michael Reese Hospital IL
CIJE: 1 RIE: 1 CAT: 17

Michael Test of Oral English Language
CIJE: 0 RIE: 1 CAT: 21

Michael X
CIJE: 1 RIE: 0 CAT: 18

Michaels Informal Test of Student Ability
CIJE: 0 RIE: 1 CAT: 21

Michels (Robert)
CIJE: 1 RIE: 1 CAT: 18

Michener (James A)
CIJE: 6 RIE: 1 CAT: 18

Michigammes Track Club
CIJE: 1 RIE: 0 CAT: 17

Michigan
CIJE: 366 RIE: 1379 CAT: 07

Michigan (Ann Arbor)
CIJE: 15 RIE: 81 CAT: 07

Michigan (Battle Creek)
CIJE: 3 RIE: 3 CAT: 07

Michigan (Bay City)
CIJE: 2 RIE: 2 CAT: 07

Michigan (Benton Harbor)
CIJE: 2 RIE: 6 CAT: 07

Michigan (Berrien County)
CIJE: 0 RIE: 2 CAT: 07

Michigan (Berrien Springs)
CIJE: 0 RIE: 1 CAT: 07

Michigan (Bloomfield Hills)
CIJE: 1 RIE: 3 CAT: 07

Michigan (Clare County)
CIJE: 0 RIE: 1 CAT: 07

Michigan (Colon)
CIJE: 1 RIE: 0 CAT: 07

Michigan (Comstock)
CIJE: 1 RIE: 0 CAT: 07

Michigan (Dearborn)
CIJE: 1 RIE: 4 CAT: 07

Michigan (Detroit Metropolitan Area)
CIJE: 1 RIE: 6 CAT: 07

Michigan (Detroit)
CIJE: 112 RIE: 253 CAT: 07

Michigan (East Detroit)
CIJE: 1 RIE: 0 CAT: 07

Michigan (East Lansing)
CIJE: 2 RIE: 66 CAT: 07

Michigan (Ferndale)
CIJE: 1 RIE: 3 CAT: 07

Michigan (Flint)
CIJE: 12 RIE: 30 CAT: 07

Michigan (Genesee County)
CIJE: 0 RIE: 2 CAT: 07

Michigan (Genesee)
CIJE: 0 RIE: 1 CAT: 07

Michigan (Grand Rapids)
CIJE: 7 RIE: 11 CAT: 07

Michigan (Grosse Pointe)
CIJE: 2 RIE: 3 CAT: 07

Michigan (Highland Park)
CIJE: 1 RIE: 1 CAT: 07

Michigan (Inkster)
CIJE: 0 RIE: 1 CAT: 07

Michigan (Kalamazoo County)
CIJE: 0 RIE: 4 CAT: 07

Michigan (Kalamazoo)
CIJE: 10 RIE: 24 CAT: 07

Michigan (Lansing)
CIJE: 3 RIE: 30 CAT: 07

Michigan (Lenawee County)
CIJE: 0 RIE: 2 CAT: 07

Michigan (Livonia)
CIJE: 3 RIE: 5 CAT: 07

Michigan (Macomb County)
CIJE: 0 RIE: 7 CAT: 07

Michigan (Marquette)
CIJE: 0 RIE: 2 CAT: 07

Michigan (Menominee)
CIJE: 0 RIE: 1 CAT: 07

Michigan (Midland)
CIJE: 0 RIE: 1 CAT: 07

Michigan (Monroe County)
CIJE: 0 RIE: 1 CAT: 07

Michigan (Monroe)
CIJE: 1 RIE: 1 CAT: 07

Michigan (Mount Pleasant)
CIJE: 0 RIE: 2 CAT: 07

Michigan (Muskegon)
CIJE: 0 RIE: 2 CAT: 07

Michigan (Oakland County)
CIJE: 1 RIE: 7 CAT: 07

Michigan (Orchard Lake)
CIJE: 2 RIE: 0 CAT: 07

Michigan (Osceola County)
CIJE: 0 RIE: 1 CAT: 07

Michigan (Oscoda)
CIJE: 1 RIE: 0 CAT: 07

Michigan (Pontiac)
CIJE: 12 RIE: 20 CAT: 07

Michigan (Rochester)
CIJE: 8 RIE: 0 CAT: 07

Michigan (Saginaw County)
CIJE: 1 RIE: 1 CAT: 07

Michigan (Saginaw)
CIJE: 2 RIE: 27 CAT: 07

Michigan (Sault Sainte Marie)
CIJE: 1 RIE: 4 CAT: 07

Michigan (Shiawassee County)
CIJE: 0 RIE: 1 CAT: 07

Michigan (Sparta)
CIJE: 1 RIE: 0 CAT: 07

Michigan (Washtenaw County)
CIJE: 2 RIE: 1 CAT: 07

Michigan (Waterford)
CIJE: 1 RIE: 0 CAT: 07

Michigan (Wayne County)
CIJE: 3 RIE: 1 CAT: 07

Michigan (Ypsilanti)
CIJE: 0 RIE: 18 CAT: 07

Michigan Accountability System
CIJE: 0 RIE: 4 CAT: 15

Michigan Alcoholism Screening Test
CIJE: 3 RIE: 1 CAT: 21

Michigan Analysis Network General Eval Report
CIJE: 0 RIE: 1 CAT: 15

Michigan Association of Childrens Agencies
CIJE: 1 RIE: 0 CAT: 17

Michigan Association of Higher Education
CIJE: 0 RIE: 1 CAT: 17

Michigan Bell Telephone Company
CIJE: 0 RIE: 1 CAT: 17

Michigan Business Education Association
CIJE: 0 RIE: 1 CAT: 17

Michigan Closed Case Survey
CIJE: 0 RIE: 1 CAT: 19

Michigan Commission on High Schools
CIJE: 0 RIE: 1 CAT: 17

Michigan Consortium Assistive Device Delivery Syst
CIJE: 0 RIE: 1 CAT: 17

Michigan Council of Cooperative Nurseries
CIJE: 0 RIE: 1 CAT: 17

Michigan Curriculum Committee on Instr Materials
CIJE: 0 RIE: 1 CAT: 17

Michigan Early Childhood Educ Preschool Program
CIJE: 0 RIE: 6 CAT: 19

Michigan Education Association
CIJE: 1 RIE: 9 CAT: 17

Michigan Education Trust
CIJE: 1 RIE: 1 CAT: 19
SN Tuition prepayment plan

Michigan Educational Assessment Program
CIJE: 7 RIE: 88 CAT: 19
SN See also "MEAP..."

Michigan Educational Resources Information Center
CIJE: 0 RIE: 0 CAT: 17

Michigan Elementary Geography Test
CIJE: 1 RIE: 0 CAT: 21

Michigan Employability Skills Survey
CIJE: 0 RIE: 1 CAT: 21

Michigan Employment Security Commission
CIJE: 0 RIE: 1 CAT: 17

Michigan English Language Assessment Battery
CIJE: 0 RIE: 1 CAT: 21

Michigan Essential Skills Reading Test
CIJE: 0 RIE: 1 CAT: 21

Michigan Federation of Teachers
CIJE: 0 RIE: 2 CAT: 17

Michigan Institute for Educational Management
CIJE: 1 RIE: 1 CAT: 17

Michigan International Student Problem Inventory
CIJE: 0 RIE: 1 CAT: 21

Michigan Labor Mediation Board
CIJE: 1 RIE: 1 CAT: 17

Michigan Language Program
CIJE: 1 RIE: 0 CAT: 19

Michigan Library
USE Library of Michigan

Michigan Library Association
CIJE: 0 RIE: 1 CAT: 17

Michigan Library Consortium
CIJE: 1 RIE: 2 CAT: 17

Michigan Life Role Competencies Project
CIJE: 0 RIE: 1 CAT: 19

Michigan Lifelong Learning Link
CIJE: 0 RIE: 1 CAT: 19

Michigan Marketing Distributive Educ Core Curr
CIJE: 0 RIE: 1 CAT: 03

Michigan Mathematics Early Placement Test
CIJE: 0 RIE: 1 CAT: 21

Michigan Medical Schools Council of Deans
CIJE: 1 RIE: 0 CAT: 17

Michigan Merit Scholarship Program
CIJE: 0 RIE: 1 CAT: 19

Michigan Occupational Competency Assessment Center
CIJE: 0 RIE: 1 CAT: 17

Michigan Occupational Data Analysis System
CIJE: 0 RIE: 1 CAT: 04
UF MODAS System

Michigan Occupational Information System
CIJE: 2 RIE: 5 CAT: 04

Michigan Ohio Regional Educational Laboratory
CIJE: 2 RIE: 6 CAT: 17

Michigan Oral Language Series
CIJE: 0 RIE: 2 CAT: 15

Michigan Organizational Assessment Questionnaire
CIJE: 0 RIE: 1 CAT: 21

Michigan Panel Study of Income Dynamics
CIJE: 2 RIE: 8 CAT: 22

Michigan Partnership for a New Education
CIJE: 0 RIE: 1 CAT: 19

Michigan Picture Test
CIJE: 0 RIE: 1 CAT: 21

Michigan Professional Personnel Register
CIJE: 0 RIE: 2 CAT: 04

Michigan Pupil Attitude Questionnaire
CIJE: 1 RIE: 0 CAT: 21

Michigan Regional Lib Blind Physically Handicapped
CIJE: 0 RIE: 1 CAT: 17

Michigan Research Corporation
CIJE: 0 RIE: 1 CAT: 17

Michigan Restricted Association Norms
CIJE: 0 RIE: 3 CAT: 21

Michigan School for the Blind
CIJE: 0 RIE: 1 CAT: 17

Michigan School for the Deaf
CIJE: 0 RIE: 1 CAT: 17

Michigan Social Issues Cognitive Category System
CIJE: 0 RIE: 3 CAT: 15

Michigan Social Issues Project
CIJE: 0 RIE: 3 CAT: 19

Michigan Special Education Learning Materials Ctr
CIJE: 0 RIE: 1 CAT: 17

Michigan Speech Association
CIJE: 0 RIE: 8 CAT: 17

Michigan State Bilingual Program
CIJE: 0 RIE: 1 CAT: 19
UF State Bilingual Program MI

Michigan State Board of Education
CIJE: 0 RIE: 6 CAT: 17

Michigan State Department of Education
CIJE: 3 RIE: 15 CAT: 17

Michigan State Department of Labor
CIJE: 0 RIE: 1 CAT: 17

Michigan State Department of Social Services
CIJE: 0 RIE: 1 CAT: 17

Michigan State Housing Authority
CIJE: 0 RIE: 1 CAT: 17

Michigan State M Scales
CIJE: 0 RIE: 2 CAT: 21

Michigan State Self Concept of Abilities Scale
CIJE: 1 RIE: 2 CAT: 21

Michigan State University
CIJE: 108 RIE: 137 CAT: 17

Michigan State University Employees Association
CIJE: 0 RIE: 1 CAT: 17

Michigan Student Information System
CIJE: 0 RIE: 3 CAT: 15
UF MiSIS; Student Information System MI

Michigan Student Questionnaire
CIJE: 1 RIE: 3 CAT: 21

Michigan Successive Discrimination Program
CIJE: 0 RIE: 1 CAT: 19

Michigan Teachers Tenure Act 1964
USE Teacher Tenure Act (Michigan)

Michigan Technological University
CIJE: 8 RIE: 14 CAT: 17

Michigan Terminal System
CIJE: 1 RIE: 2 CAT: 15

Michigan Test Battery
CIJE: 1 RIE: 1 CAT: 21

Michigan Test of Aural Comprehension
CIJE: 0 RIE: 2 CAT: 21

Michigan Test of English Language Proficiency
CIJE: 4 RIE: 7 CAT: 21

Michigan Tracking Program
CIJE: 0 RIE: 1 CAT: 19
UF Tracking Program MI

Michigan Vocational Education Evaluation Project
CIJE: 0 RIE: 1 CAT: 19

Michigan Youth Corps
CIJE: 0 RIE: 1 CAT: 17

Michigan Youth Leadership for Action
CIJE: 0 RIE: 1 CAT: 19

Michigan Youth Services
CIJE: 1 RIE: 0 CAT: 17

Michill Adjective Rating Scale
CIJE: 4 RIE: 1 CAT: 21

Micmac (Tribe)
CIJE: 16 RIE: 12 CAT: 08

Micro Administration
CIJE: 0 RIE: 1 CAT: 15

Micro ISIS Software
USE MicroISIS

Micro Precision Technology
CIJE: 0 RIE: 1 CAT: 20

Micro Social Learning Center
CIJE: 1 RIE: 0 CAT: 17

Micro Unit Learning Module
CIJE: 1 RIE: 0 CAT: 15

MICRO VERS
USE Microcomputer Vocational Education Reporting Sys

Microanalysis
CIJE: 16 RIE: 8 CAT: 15

Microbial Genetics
CIJE: 6 RIE: 0 CAT: 20

MicroCAM
CIJE: 1 RIE: 1 CAT: 04
SN A computer-assisted measurement tool that assesses students' knowledge structures and interrelationships among different types of knowledge in various subject-matter domains

MicroCAT Testing System
CIJE: 3 RIE: 2 CAT: 04

Microcephaly
CIJE: 4 RIE: 0 CAT: 11

Microchips
CIJE: 3 RIE: 1 CAT: 04
UF Computer Chips

Microcircuits
USE Integrated Circuits

Microcomponents (Intelligence)
CIJE: 0 RIE: 2 CAT: 11

Microcomputer Based Laboratories
CIJE: 24 RIE: 6 CAT: 05

Microcomputer Diagnostic Testing Project (Canada)
CIJE: 0 RIE: 1 CAT: 19

Microcomputer Manuals
USE Computer Manuals

Microcomputer Program Oriented Budgeting System
CIJE: 0 RIE: 1 CAT: 04

Microcomputer Software and Info for Teachers
USE MicroSIFT

Microcomputer Student Ratio
CIJE: 0 RIE: 1 CAT: 16

Microcomputer Vocational Education Reporting Sys
CIJE: 0 RIE: 4 CAT: 04
UF MICRO VERS

Microcomputers and Middle School Problem Solving
CIJE: 0 RIE: 1 CAT: 19

Microcosm
CIJE: 2 RIE: 0 CAT: 15

Microcultures
CIJE: 9 RIE: 1 CAT: 20

Microdata
CIJE: 2 RIE: 2 CAT: 16

Microdesigns
CIJE: 0 RIE: 1 CAT: 15

Microelectronics Center of North Carolina
CIJE: 1 RIE: 0 CAT: 19

Microelectronics Education Programme
CIJE: 22 RIE: 4 CAT: 19

Microethnography
CIJE: 4 RIE: 2 CAT: 15

Micrographic Catalog Retrieval System
CIJE: 2 RIE: 0 CAT: 15

Micrographic Splicing
CIJE: 1 RIE: 0 CAT: 20

Microgravity
CIJE: 1 RIE: 1 CAT: 20
SN See also "Weightlessness"

Microholography
CIJE: 1 RIE: 0 CAT: 20

Microintensity Index
CIJE: 0 RIE: 1 CAT: 21
SN A measure of the number of students per computer in a school

MicroISIS
CIJE: 0 RIE: 1 CAT: 04
UF Micro ISIS Software

Microlabs
CIJE: 1 RIE: 2 CAT: 05

Micrologic Assemblers
CIJE: 0 RIE: 1 CAT: 09

Micrometers
CIJE: 0 RIE: 8 CAT: 04

Microminiature Circuits
CIJE: 0 RIE: 1 CAT: 20

MICRON Accounting System
CIJE: 0 RIE: 2 CAT: 15

Micronesia
CIJE: 28 RIE: 48 CAT: 07
SN Do not confuse with the "Federated States of Micronesia," which is an independent country

Micronesian
CIJE: 0 RIE: 4 CAT: 13

Micronesian Achievement Test Series
CIJE: 0 RIE: 1 CAT: 21

Micronesians
CIJE: 2 RIE: 5 CAT: 08

Microorganisms
CIJE: 8 RIE: 3 CAT: 20

MICROPIK Model
CIJE: 0 RIE: 1 CAT: 15

MICROPILOT Programing Language
CIJE: 1 RIE: 0 CAT: 04

Microplanning
CIJE: 0 RIE: 3 CAT: 15

Micropolitics
CIJE: 3 RIE: 6 CAT: 15

Micropolygyria
CIJE: 1 RIE: 0 CAT: 11

Microprogramable Computers
CIJE: 0 RIE: 1 CAT: 04

Microprograming
CIJE: 0 RIE: 3 CAT: 15

Micropublishing
CIJE: 17 RIE: 2 CAT: 16

Microscale Chemistry
CIJE: 11 RIE: 1 CAT: 20
UF Microscale Laboratories

Microscale Laboratories
USE Microscale Chemistry

Microscope Selector Reader
CIJE: 0 RIE: 1 CAT: 04

Microscope Slide Preparations
CIJE: 3 RIE: 0 CAT: 20

Microscope Slides
CIJE: 1 RIE: 0 CAT: 04

MICROsearch
CIJE: 3 RIE: 1 CAT: 04

MicroSIFT
CIJE: 2 RIE: 11 CAT: 17
UF Microcomputer Software and Info for Teachers

Microsimulation
CIJE: 0 RIE: 2 CAT: 15

Microsociolinguistic Analysis
CIJE: 0 RIE: 1 CAT: 15

Microsoft DOS
USE MS DOS

Microsoft Windows
CIJE: 1 RIE: 1 CAT: 04

Microsoft Word
CIJE: 1 RIE: 5 CAT: 04

Microsoft Works
CIJE: 2 RIE: 2 CAT: 04

Microstat (Computer Program)
CIJE: 0 RIE: 1 CAT: 04

Microsupervision
CIJE: 1 RIE: 2 CAT: 15

Microsystems
CIJE: 3 RIE: 1 CAT: 16

Microtechnology
CIJE: 2 RIE: 1 CAT: 20

Microthemes
CIJE: 4 RIE: 1 CAT: 16

Microtherapy
CIJE: 1 RIE: 0 CAT: 11

Microville (Simulation Game)
CIJE: 0 RIE: 3 CAT: 04

Microwave Approach
CIJE: 0 RIE: 8 CAT: 15

Microwave Communications Inc
CIJE: 0 RIE: 1 CAT: 17

Microwave Course
CIJE: 0 RIE: 1 CAT: 03

Microwave Demonstrators
CIJE: 1 RIE: 0 CAT: 09

Microwave Ovens
CIJE: 5 RIE: 3 CAT: 04

Microwave Technology
CIJE: 1 RIE: 2 CAT: 20

Microwave Transmission
CIJE: 1 RIE: 3 CAT: 20

Microwave Tube Assemblers
CIJE: 0 RIE: 1 CAT: 09

Microwaves
CIJE: 10 RIE: 1 CAT: 20

Microwriter
CIJE: 0 RIE: 1 CAT: 04

Mid Alabama Adult and Vocational Education
CIJE: 0 RIE: 1 CAT: 15

Mid America Nazarene College KS
CIJE: 1 RIE: 1 CAT: 17

Mid America Vocational Curriculum Consortium
CIJE: 1 RIE: 2 CAT: 17

Mid Atlantic Multifunctional Resource Center
CIJE: 0 RIE: 1 CAT: 17

Mid Career Teacher Education Study
CIJE: 0 RIE: 1 CAT: 19

Mid Continent Regional Educational Laboratory
CIJE: 0 RIE: 7 CAT: 17
SN See also "McREL..."
UF McREL

Mid Continent Regional Educational Laboratory CO
CIJE: 1 RIE: 5 CAT: 17

Mid Continent Regional Educational Laboratory MO
CIJE: 1 RIE: 5 CAT: 17

Mid Florida Technical Institute
CIJE: 0 RIE: 1 CAT: 17

Mid Iowa Computer Center
CIJE: 0 RIE: 1 CAT: 17

Mid Michigan Community Action Council
CIJE: 0 RIE: 1 CAT: 17

Mid Michigan Community College
CIJE: 0 RIE: 1 CAT: 17

Mid Missouri Small School Computer Consortium
CIJE: 0 RIE: 0 CAT: 17

Mid Ocean Dynamic Experiment
CIJE: 2 RIE: 0 CAT: 19

Mid Plains Technical Community College Area NE
CIJE: 0 RIE: 1 CAT: 17

Mid Prairie Community School District IA
CIJE: 0 RIE: 1 CAT: 17

Mid Primary Screening Battery
CIJE: 0 RIE: 1 CAT: 21

Mid School Year Graduation
CIJE: 0 RIE: 1 CAT: 03

Mid South Educational Research Association
CIJE: 0 RIE: 7 CAT: 17
UF Midsouth Educational Research Assn

Mid State VTAE District WI
CIJE: 0 RIE: 1 CAT: 17

Mid Valley Area Vocational Center IL
CIJE: 1 RIE: 0 CAT: 17

MIDASTA
CIJE: 0 RIE: 1 CAT: 04
SN A Chinese/German/English database

Midcareer Programs
CIJE: 1 RIE: 1 CAT: 19

Middle Ages
CIJE: 11 RIE: 4 CAT: 12
UF Medieval Period

Middle Atlantic Placement Association
CIJE: 1 RIE: 0 CAT: 17

Middle Born
CIJE: 0 RIE: 0 CAT: 10

Middle Children
CIJE: 0 RIE: 1 CAT: 10

Middle College High School CA
CIJE: 0 RIE: 1 CAT: 17

Middle College High School NY
CIJE: 7 RIE: 5 CAT: 17
UF Middle College NY

Middle College High School TN
CIJE: 0 RIE: 1 CAT: 17

Middle College NY
USE Middle College High School NY

Middle Colleges
CIJE: 4 RIE: 3 CAT: 05

Middle Ear Disease
CIJE: 5 RIE: 0 CAT: 11

Middle Ear Infections
USE Otitis Media

Middle East
CIJE: 85 RIE: 114 CAT: 07

Middle East Technical University
CIJE: 2 RIE: 0 CAT: 17

Middle Elementary Teaching Team
CIJE: 1 RIE: 0 CAT: 17

Middle Georgia Technical Institute
CIJE: 0 RIE: 1 CAT: 17

Middle Grade School State Policy Initiative
CIJE: 0 RIE: 1 CAT: 19

Middle Grades Assessment Program
CIJE: 3 RIE: 1 CAT: 19

Middle Grades Integrated Process Skills Test
CIJE: 1 RIE: 1 CAT: 21

Middle Grades Mathematics Project
CIJE: 1 RIE: 2 CAT: 19

Middle Income Student Assistance Act
CIJE: 2 RIE: 10 CAT: 14

Middle Management Center
CIJE: 1 RIE: 2 CAT: 17

Middle School Description Survey
CIJE: 0 RIE: 2 CAT: 21

Middle School Instructional Practices Scale
CIJE: 0 RIE: 1 CAT: 21

Middle School Students
CIJE: 107 RIE: 354 CAT: 10

Middle States Association Commission Higher Educ
USE Middle States Association of Colleges and Schools

Middle States Association of Colleges and Schools
CIJE: 6 RIE: 6 CAT: 17
UF Middle States Association Commission Higher Educ

Middle Tennessee State University
CIJE: 4 RIE: 6 CAT: 17

Middle Track Students
CIJE: 0 RIE: 2 CAT: 10

Middlebury College VT
CIJE: 7 RIE: 7 CAT: 17

Middleman Minority Groups
CIJE: 3 RIE: 1 CAT: 10

Middlesex Community College CT
CIJE: 0 RIE: 6 CAT: 17

Middlesex Community College MA
CIJE: 0 RIE: 2 CAT: 17

Middlesex County College NJ
CIJE: 5 RIE: 5 CAT: 17

Middlesex Distance Learning Consortium CT
CIJE: 0 RIE: 1 CAT: 17

Middlesex Hospital CT
CIJE: 0 RIE: 1 CAT: 17

Middlesex Polytechnic (England)
CIJE: 1 RIE: 1 CAT: 17

Middleton Cross Plains Area School District WI
CIJE: 0 RIE: 1 CAT: 17

Middletown
CIJE: 7 RIE: 1 CAT: 19
SN An ongoing study conducted in Muncie/Delaware County Indiana, originally conducted by Robert and Helen Lynd in the 1920s and '30s

Middletown High School RI
CIJE: 0 RIE: 1 CAT: 17

Middletown Nongraded Program
CIJE: 0 RIE: 1 CAT: 19

Midge Control Laboratory FL
CIJE: 0 RIE: 1 CAT: 17

Midland City Education Association MI
CIJE: 1 RIE: 0 CAT: 17

Midland College TX
CIJE: 2 RIE: 0 CAT: 17

Midland Lutheran College NE
CIJE: 0 RIE: 1 CAT: 17

Midland Mathematical Experiment
CIJE: 1 RIE: 0 CAT: 19

Midland Public Schools MI
CIJE: 1 RIE: 0 CAT: 17

Midland Public Schools TX
CIJE: 0 RIE: 1 CAT: 17

Midland School CA
CIJE: 0 RIE: 1 CAT: 17

Midlands Consortium
CIJE: 0 RIE: 1 CAT: 17

Midlands Technical College SC
CIJE: 3 RIE: 7 CAT: 17

Midnight Cowboy
CIJE: 1 RIE: 0 CAT: 22

Midsouth Educational Research Assn
USE Mid South Educational Research Association

Midsummer Nights Dream
CIJE: 6 RIE: 1 CAT: 22

Midterm Examinations
CIJE: 1 RIE: 1 CAT: 21

Midtown Psychiatric Impairment Index
CIJE: 1 RIE: 0 CAT: 21

Midway College KY
CIJE: 0 RIE: 1 CAT: 17

Midway School NY
CIJE: 0 RIE: 1 CAT: 17

Midwest Academic Librarians Conference
CIJE: 1 RIE: 0 CAT: 02

Midwest College Learning Center Association
CIJE: 0 RIE: 1 CAT: 17

Midwest Community College Leadership Program
CIJE: 0 RIE: 1 CAT: 19

Midwest Library Conference
CIJE: 1 RIE: 0 CAT: 02

Midwest Program on Airborne Television Instruction
CIJE: 1 RIE: 4 CAT: 19

Midwest Regional Library Network
CIJE: 0 RIE: 5 CAT: 17

Midwest Regional Media Center for the Deaf
CIJE: 1 RIE: 0 CAT: 17

Midwest Regional MEDLARS Center
CIJE: 0 RIE: 1 CAT: 17

Midwest Talent Search Project
CIJE: 1 RIE: 1 CAT: 19

Midwest Technical Education Center MO
CIJE: 0 RIE: 1 CAT: 17

Midwest Youth Employment and Training Program IL
CIJE: 0 RIE: 1 CAT: 19

Midwestern Educational Research Association
CIJE: 0 RIE: 1 CAT: 17

Midwestern State University TX
CIJE: 0 RIE: 3 CAT: 17

Midwestern States Educational Information Project
CIJE: 2 RIE: 2 CAT: 19

Midwestern University TX
CIJE: 1 RIE: 2 CAT: 17
SN Old name of Midwestern State University TX

Midwives
CIJE: 2 RIE: 3 CAT: 09
SN See also "Nurse Midwives"

Miegel (Agnes)
CIJE: 1 RIE: 0 CAT: 18

Miel (Alice)
CIJE: 1 RIE: 0 CAT: 18

Mien People
CIJE: 0 RIE: 4 CAT: 08

Mifflin (Thomas)
CIJE: 0 RIE: 1 CAT: 18

Mifflin Curriculum Project
CIJE: 1 RIE: 0 CAT: 19

Miftanim (Vocational Schools)
CIJE: 0 RIE: 1 CAT: 05

Migrant Action Program
CIJE: 0 RIE: 1 CAT: 19

Migrant and Seasonal Farm Worker Project
CIJE: 0 RIE: 2 CAT: 19

Migrant Children Educational Act (Colorado)
CIJE: 0 RIE: 1 CAT: 14

Migrant Citizenship Education Project
CIJE: 0 RIE: 1 CAT: 19

Migrant Dropout Youth Program
CIJE: 0 RIE: 1 CAT: 19

Migrant Early Childhood Education Project
CIJE: 0 RIE: 2 CAT: 19

Migrant Ed Resources List and Information Network
CIJE: 0 RIE: 1 CAT: 04
UF MERLIN (Database)

Migrant Education Amendment
CIJE: 0 RIE: 5 CAT: 14

Migrant Education Center WA
CIJE: 0 RIE: 2 CAT: 17

Migrant Education Goals Task Force
CIJE: 0 RIE: 1 CAT: 17
UF Task Force on Migrant Education Goals

Migrant Education Needs Assessment Evaluation Sys
CIJE: 0 RIE: 1 CAT: 21

Migrant Education Oral Language Skills List
CIJE: 0 RIE: 1 CAT: 21

Migrant Education Program
CIJE: 1 RIE: 32 CAT: 19

Migrant Education Record Transfer System
CIJE: 1 RIE: 1 CAT: 04

Migrant Education Research Project
CIJE: 0 RIE: 1 CAT: 19

Migrant Education Secondary Assistance Project
CIJE: 0 RIE: 8 CAT: 19

Migrant Education Section 143 Projects
CIJE: 0 RIE: 1 CAT: 19
UF Education Amendments 1978 Section 143; Section 143 Migrant Education Projects

Migrant Educators National Training OutReach
CIJE: 0 RIE: 10 CAT: 19
UF MENTOR (SUNY Potsdam Coll)

Migrant Head Start Programs
CIJE: 0 RIE: 4 CAT: 19

Migrant Health Act
CIJE: 1 RIE: 2 CAT: 14

Migrant Health Program
CIJE: 0 RIE: 4 CAT: 19

Migrant Home Base Centers
CIJE: 0 RIE: 1 CAT: 05

Migrant Nutrition Education Project
CIJE: 1 RIE: 0 CAT: 19

Migrant Opportunity Program
CIJE: 0 RIE: 1 CAT: 19

Migrant Seasonal Agric Worker Protection Act
CIJE: 0 RIE: 2 CAT: 14

Migrant Student Record Transfer System
CIJE: 9 RIE: 123 CAT: 15

Migrant Tracking
CIJE: 0 RIE: 2 CAT: 15
UF Tracking (Migrants)

Migrants Incorporated
CIJE: 0 RIE: 1 CAT: 17

Miju
CIJE: 0 RIE: 1 CAT: 13
SN A Gyarung-Mishmi language of north Assam
UF Kaman Mishmi; Miju Mishmi

Miju Mishmi
USE Miju

Mikasuki
CIJE: 1 RIE: 0 CAT: 13

Mikmawey School NS
CIJE: 0 RIE: 0 CAT: 17

Milan Federal Correctional Institution
CIJE: 0 RIE: 1 CAT: 17

Milepost Testing Program
CIJE: 0 RIE: 1 CAT: 19
SN ...of the Los Angeles Unified School District

Miles College AL
CIJE: 2 RIE: 1 CAT: 17

Miles Skills Upgrading Program AL
CIJE: 0 RIE: 1 CAT: 19

Milford Visual Communications Project
CIJE: 0 RIE: 1 CAT: 19

Milgram (Stanley)
CIJE: 4 RIE: 2 CAT: 18

Milieu Teaching
CIJE: 6 RIE: 1 CAT: 15

Militarism
CIJE: 10 RIE: 10 CAT: 16

Military Academy (West Point) NY
CIJE: 14 RIE: 34 CAT: 17

Military Advisers Language Text
CIJE: 0 RIE: 1 CAT: 22

Military Applicant Profile
CIJE: 0 RIE: 1 CAT: 21

Military Assistance Language Training
CIJE: 0 RIE: 1 CAT: 19

Military Assistance Program
CIJE: 0 RIE: 1 CAT: 19

Military Assistance to Safety and Traffic
CIJE: 0 RIE: 1 CAT: 16

Military Aviation
CIJE: 0 RIE: 2 CAT: 20

Military Bases
CIJE: 3 RIE: 2 CAT: 05

Military Combat
CIJE: 1 RIE: 3 CAT: 16

Military Curriculum Materials
CIJE: 0 RIE: 25 CAT: 03

Military Curriculum Project
CIJE: 0 RIE: 210 CAT: 19

Military Day Care
CIJE: 2 RIE: 20 CAT: 05

Military Dependents
CIJE: 4 RIE: 12 CAT: 10

Military Deployment
CIJE: 1 RIE: 1 CAT: 16
UF Deployment (Military Personnel)

Military Draft
CIJE: 3 RIE: 5 CAT: 16

Military Educational Assistance Legislation
CIJE: 0 RIE: 2 CAT: 14

Military Enlistment
CIJE: 1 RIE: 10 CAT: 16

Military History
CIJE: 30 RIE: 16 CAT: 12

Military Ideology Scale (Altman)
CIJE: 0 RIE: 1 CAT: 21

Military Industrial Complex
CIJE: 2 RIE: 2 CAT: 16

Military Justice
CIJE: 0 RIE: 1 CAT: 14

Military Law
CIJE: 0 RIE: 2 CAT: 14

Military Librarians Workshop
CIJE: 0 RIE: 1 CAT: 02

Military Libraries
CIJE: 4 RIE: 6 CAT: 05

Military Life Questionnaire
CIJE: 0 RIE: 1 CAT: 21

Military Maneuver Arms Units
CIJE: 0 RIE: 1 CAT: 09

Military Occupation Specialty
CIJE: 0 RIE: 7 CAT: 15

Military Occupational Data Bank
CIJE: 0 RIE: 1 CAT: 21

Military Occupations
CIJE: 0 RIE: 1 CAT: 09

Military Police School
CIJE: 1 RIE: 2 CAT: 17

Military Power
CIJE: 2 RIE: 3 CAT: 16

Military Recruitment
CIJE: 2 RIE: 5 CAT: 16

Military Reenlistment
CIJE: 0 RIE: 6 CAT: 16

Military Reserves
CIJE: 1 RIE: 1 CAT: 10
SN See also "Army Reserve," "Individual Ready Reservists," "Air Force Reserve"
UF Reserves (Military)

Military Role
CIJE: 4 RIE: 9 CAT: 16

Military Selective Service Act
CIJE: 2 RIE: 1 CAT: 14

Military Spending
CIJE: 1 RIE: 2 CAT: 16

Military Testing Association
CIJE: 0 RIE: 4 CAT: 17

Milk
CIJE: 5 RIE: 3 CAT: 11
SN See also "Breast Milk"

Milk Programs
CIJE: 0 RIE: 5 CAT: 19
SN See also "Special Milk Program" and "School Milk Contracts"

Mill (John Stuart)
CIJE: 31 RIE: 4 CAT: 18

Mill Hill Vocabulary Scale
CIJE: 2 RIE: 2 CAT: 21

Mill Neck Manor School for the Deaf NY
CIJE: 1 RIE: 0 CAT: 17

Millard School District NE
CIJE: 0 RIE: 1 CAT: 17

Millay (Edna Saint Vincent)
CIJE: 0 RIE: 1 CAT: 18

Milledgeville State Hospital GA
CIJE: 0 RIE: 1 CAT: 17

Miller (Arthur)
CIJE: 9 RIE: 2 CAT: 18

Miller (Bertha Mahony)
CIJE: 1 RIE: 0 CAT: 18

Miller (James E)
CIJE: 0 RIE: 1 CAT: 18

Miller (Neal E)
CIJE: 0 RIE: 1 CAT: 18

Miller Analogies Test
CIJE: 16 RIE: 11 CAT: 21

Miller Assessment for Preschoolers
CIJE: 7 RIE: 3 CAT: 21

Miller Coleman Readability Scale
CIJE: 1 RIE: 0 CAT: 21

Miller Composite High School (Canada)
CIJE: 1 RIE: 0 CAT: 17

Miller Fisk Sexual Knowledge Questionnaire
CIJE: 1 RIE: 0 CAT: 21

Miller Motivation Scale
CIJE: 0 RIE: 1 CAT: 21

Miller Unruh Reading Act
CIJE: 0 RIE: 4 CAT: 14

Miller Unruh Reading Center CA
CIJE: 0 RIE: 1 CAT: 17

Miller Unruh Reading Program
CIJE: 0 RIE: 2 CAT: 19

Miller v California
CIJE: 0 RIE: 1 CAT: 14

Millersville University PA
CIJE: 1 RIE: 8 CAT: 17

Millfield School (England)
CIJE: 2 RIE: 1 CAT: 17

Milligan (Frank)
CIJE: 0 RIE: 1 CAT: 18

Milligan (Lambdin)
CIJE: 0 RIE: 2 CAT: 18

Millikan v Board of Directors
CIJE: 1 RIE: 0 CAT: 14

Milliken v Bradley
CIJE: 16 RIE: 15 CAT: 14

Milliken v Green
CIJE: 1 RIE: 0 CAT: 14

Millikin University IL
CIJE: 3 RIE: 5 CAT: 17

Millimeter Scale (Harvill)
CIJE: 0 RIE: 1 CAT: 21

Millman (J)
CIJE: 0 RIE: 1 CAT: 18

Millon Clinical Multiaxial Inventory
CIJE: 7 RIE: 3 CAT: 21

Mills (Don)
CIJE: 0 RIE: 2 CAT: 18

Mills (Theodore)
CIJE: 0 RIE: 1 CAT: 18

Mills College CA
CIJE: 6 RIE: 6 CAT: 17

Mills Learning Methods Test
CIJE: 0 RIE: 2 CAT: 21

Mills v Board of Education
CIJE: 1 RIE: 0 CAT: 14

Millsaps College MS
CIJE: 2 RIE: 1 CAT: 17

Millwright
CIJE: 0 RIE: 1 CAT: 21

Millwrights
CIJE: 0 RIE: 22 CAT: 09

Milpitas Unified School District CA
CIJE: 1 RIE: 1 CAT: 17

Milton (John)
CIJE: 12 RIE: 12 CAT: 18

Milton Academy MA
CIJE: 3 RIE: 0 CAT: 17

Milton College WI
CIJE: 1 RIE: 0 CAT: 17

Milton Hershey School PA
CIJE: 1 RIE: 0 CAT: 17

Milton Keynes Home School Link Project
CIJE: 1 RIE: 0 CAT: 19

Milwaukee Academic Interest Inventory
CIJE: 1 RIE: 0 CAT: 21

Milwaukee Area Technical College WI
CIJE: 16 RIE: 11 CAT: 17

Milwaukee Bilingual Education Program
CIJE: 0 RIE: 3 CAT: 19

Milwaukee Braces
CIJE: 1 RIE: 0 CAT: 04

Milwaukee County Mental Health Center
CIJE: 1 RIE: 0 CAT: 17

Milwaukee Federated Library System
CIJE: 1 RIE: 1 CAT: 17

Milwaukee Institute of Technology WI
CIJE: 0 RIE: 2 CAT: 17

Milwaukee Journal
CIJE: 1 RIE: 1 CAT: 22

Milwaukee Project
CIJE: 5 RIE: 0 CAT: 19

Milwaukee Public Museum
CIJE: 1 RIE: 1 CAT: 17

Milwaukee Public Schools WI
CIJE: 29 RIE: 52 CAT: 17

Milwaukee School Guidance Evaluation Scale
CIJE: 1 RIE: 0 CAT: 21

Milwaukee School Improvement Program WI
CIJE: 1 RIE: 1 CAT: 19

Milwaukee School of Engineering WI
CIJE: 1 RIE: 1 CAT: 17

Milwaukee Teacher Expectation Project WI
CIJE: 0 RIE: 1 CAT: 19

Milwaukee Vocational and Adult School WI
CIJE: 0 RIE: 1 CAT: 17

Mimbres Indians
CIJE: 0 RIE: 1 CAT: 08
UF Mogollon Indians

Mimeograph Machines
CIJE: 0 RIE: 1 CAT: 04

Mimetic Discourse
CIJE: 0 RIE: 1 CAT: 13

Mimetic Documents
CIJE: 4 RIE: 0 CAT: 04

Mimetic Traditions
CIJE: 0 RIE: 1 CAT: 15

Mimicry
CIJE: 3 RIE: 1 CAT: 11

Min Dialect
CIJE: 1 RIE: 1 CAT: 13

Min Max Teaching Machine
CIJE: 0 RIE: 4 CAT: 04

Minamata Disease
CIJE: 0 RIE: 1 CAT: 11
SN A form of methyl-mercury poisoning

Mind Body Problem
CIJE: 1 RIE: 1 CAT: 11

Mind Control
CIJE: 2 RIE: 1 CAT: 11
SN See also "Silva Mind Control" and "Thought Control"

Mind Sets
CIJE: 1 RIE: 0 CAT: 11

Mindpower Week
CIJE: 3 RIE: 0 CAT: 12

Mine Safety and Health Administration
CIJE: 0 RIE: 1 CAT: 17

Miner Sentence Completion Scale
CIJE: 7 RIE: 1 CAT: 21

Minerals (Nutrition)
CIJE: 2 RIE: 2 CAT: 11

Miners
CIJE: 5 RIE: 1 CAT: 09

Mini Economy
CIJE: 0 RIE: 2 CAT: 16

Mini MARC
CIJE: 1 RIE: 2 CAT: 04

Mini Midi Program
CIJE: 0 RIE: 1 CAT: 19

Mini RAT (Remote Associates Test)
CIJE: 0 RIE: 1 CAT: 21

Mini Schools
CIJE: 3 RIE: 14 CAT: 05

Mini Society
CIJE: 1 RIE: 1 CAT: 03

Mini Tests
CIJE: 0 RIE: 3 CAT: 21

Miniature Circuits
CIJE: 0 RIE: 1 CAT: 20

Miniature Golf
CIJE: 1 RIE: 0 CAT: 16

Miniature Linguistic Systems
CIJE: 1 RIE: 1 CAT: 13

Miniature Training and Evaluation Battery
CIJE: 0 RIE: 1 CAT: 21

Miniaturized Total Interaction Analysis System
CIJE: 0 RIE: 3 CAT: 15

Minicolleges
CIJE: 1 RIE: 2 CAT: 05

Minigenerators
CIJE: 2 RIE: 0 CAT: 04

Minigrant Program for the Academically Gifted DC
CIJE: 0 RIE: 1 CAT: 19

Minigrants
CIJE: 2 RIE: 8 CAT: 15

Minimal Effect Size
CIJE: 0 RIE: 1 CAT: 15

Minimal Responses
CIJE: 0 RIE: 1 CAT: 15

Minimax Procedure
CIJE: 1 RIE: 1 CAT: 15

Minimobile
CIJE: 0 RIE: 1 CAT: 04

Minimood
CIJE: 0 RIE: 1 CAT: 21

Minimum Abbreviation of Serial Titles
CIJE: 0 RIE: 1 CAT: 15

Minimum Academic Mastery
CIJE: 0 RIE: 1 CAT: 16

Minimum Average Partial Rule (Velicer)
CIJE: 0 RIE: 2 CAT: 21

Minimum Basic Skills Test
CIJE: 0 RIE: 3 CAT: 21
SN Do not use for "New Jersey Minimum Basic Skills Program"

Minimum Competencies Performance Test
CIJE: 1 RIE: 1 CAT: 21

Minimum Distance Principle
CIJE: 3 RIE: 6 CAT: 15

Minimum English Competency Test
CIJE: 0 RIE: 1 CAT: 21

Minimum Foundation Program
CIJE: 0 RIE: 2 CAT: 19

Minimum Skills Diagnostic Tests (North Carolina)
USE North Carolina Minimum Skills Diagnostic Tests

Minimum Student Performance Standards (Florida)
USE Florida Minimum Student Performance Standards

Minimum Trace Factor Analysis
CIJE: 2 RIE: 0 CAT: 21

Miniprint
CIJE: 1 RIE: 0 CAT: 16

Minister Role
CIJE: 3 RIE: 1 CAT: 16

Ministers Committee on Kindergarten Education
CIJE: 0 RIE: 1 CAT: 17

Ministry Higher Secondary Specialized Ed (USSR)
CIJE: 0 RIE: 1 CAT: 17
UF Soviet Ministry of Higher Secondary Specialized Ed

Ministry of Education (Brazil)
CIJE: 0 RIE: 1 CAT: 17
UF Brazilian Ministry of Education

Ministry of Education (Colombia)
CIJE: 1 RIE: 0 CAT: 17
UF Colombian Ministry of Education

Ministry of Education (Egypt)
CIJE: 0 RIE: 1 CAT: 17
UF Egyptian Ministry of Education

Ministry of Education (Japan)
CIJE: 2 RIE: 2 CAT: 17
UF Japan Ministry of Education

Ministry of Education (USSR)
CIJE: 2 RIE: 1 CAT: 17
UF Soviet Ministry of Education

Ministry of Education and Culture (Israel)
CIJE: 3 RIE: 1 CAT: 17
UF Israel Ministry of Education and Culture

Ministry of Employment (Japan)
CIJE: 0 RIE: 0 CAT: 17
UF Japan Ministry of Employment

Ministry of Higher Education (Poland)
CIJE: 0 RIE: 1 CAT: 17
UF Poland Ministry of Higher Education

Minitab II Programing Language
CIJE: 4 RIE: 2 CAT: 04

Minitel
CIJE: 3 RIE: 5 CAT: 04

MINITEX
USE Minnesota Interlibrary Telecommunications Exchange

Minitran MPS 360
CIJE: 0 RIE: 1 CAT: 04

Mink Network Educational Resources Center
CIJE: 0 RIE: 2 CAT: 17

Mink Scale
CIJE: 0 RIE: 2 CAT: 21

Minkowski Space
CIJE: 1 RIE: 0 CAT: 20

Minneapolis Community College MN
CIJE: 0 RIE: 1 CAT: 17

Minneapolis Multi Ethnic Curriculum Project
CIJE: 0 RIE: 11 CAT: 19

Minneapolis Preschool Screening Instrument
CIJE: 1 RIE: 1 CAT: 21

Minneapolis Press Council
CIJE: 0 RIE: 1 CAT: 17

Minneapolis Public Schools MN
CIJE: 10 RIE: 100 CAT: 17

Minneapolis Special School District 1 MN
CIJE: 0 RIE: 1 CAT: 17

MINNEMAST
CIJE: 4 RIE: 53 CAT: 19

Minnesota
CIJE: 342 RIE: 1069 CAT: 07

Minnesota (Bloomington)
CIJE: 1 RIE: 4 CAT: 07

Minnesota (Dakota County)
CIJE: 1 RIE: 3 CAT: 07

Minnesota (Duluth)
CIJE: 3 RIE: 11 CAT: 07

Minnesota (Excelsior)
CIJE: 0 RIE: 1 CAT: 07

Minnesota (Floodwood)
CIJE: 0 RIE: 1 CAT: 07

Minnesota (Hennepin County)
CIJE: 7 RIE: 3 CAT: 07

Minnesota (Minneapolis)
CIJE: 43 RIE: 243 CAT: 07

Minnesota (Moorhead)
CIJE: 0 RIE: 4 CAT: 07

Minnesota (Northeast)
CIJE: 0 RIE: 2 CAT: 07

Minnesota (Olmsted County)
CIJE: 0 RIE: 1 CAT: 07

Minnesota (Pine County)
CIJE: 1 RIE: 1 CAT: 07

Minnesota (Ramsey County)
CIJE: 0 RIE: 4 CAT: 07

Minnesota (Red Lake Falls)
CIJE: 0 RIE: 2 CAT: 07

Minnesota (Saint Cloud)
CIJE: 2 RIE: 0 CAT: 07

Minnesota (Saint Louis Park)
CIJE: 1 RIE: 2 CAT: 07

Minnesota (Saint Paul Park)
CIJE: 1 RIE: 0 CAT: 07

Minnesota (Saint Paul Summit University Area)
CIJE: 0 RIE: 1 CAT: 07

Minnesota (Saint Paul)
CIJE: 23 RIE: 68 CAT: 07

Minnesota (Saint Peter)
CIJE: 0 RIE: 1 CAT: 07

Minnesota (Sibley County)
CIJE: 0 RIE: 1 CAT: 07

Minnesota (South)
CIJE: 0 RIE: 2 CAT: 07

Minnesota (Southeast)
CIJE: 0 RIE: 1 CAT: 07

Minnesota (Southwest)
CIJE: 1 RIE: 3 CAT: 07

Minnesota (Staples)
CIJE: 1 RIE: 2 CAT: 07

Minnesota (Twin Cities)
CIJE: 3 RIE: 22 CAT: 07

Minnesota (West Central)
CIJE: 0 RIE: 1 CAT: 07

Minnesota (White Bear Lake)
CIJE: 0 RIE: 4 CAT: 07

Minnesota (Winona)
CIJE: 2 RIE: 1 CAT: 07

Minnesota (Wrenshall)
CIJE: 0 RIE: 1 CAT: 07

Minnesota Adaptive Instructional System
CIJE: 3 RIE: 5 CAT: 15

Minnesota Assn Private Postsecondary Schools
CIJE: 0 RIE: 1 CAT: 17

Minnesota Braille Sight Saving School
CIJE: 0 RIE: 1 CAT: 17

Minnesota Chemical Depend Prog for Hear Imp Youth
CIJE: 0 RIE: 0 CAT: 19

Minnesota Child Development Inventory
CIJE: 4 RIE: 5 CAT: 21

Minnesota Clerical Test
CIJE: 0 RIE: 1 CAT: 21

Minnesota College Statewide Testing Program
CIJE: 0 RIE: 1 CAT: 21

Minnesota College Teacher Study
CIJE: 1 RIE: 0 CAT: 22

Minnesota Community College Board
CIJE: 0 RIE: 1 CAT: 17

Minnesota Community College Faculty Association
CIJE: 1 RIE: 1 CAT: 17

Minnesota Community College System
CIJE: 1 RIE: 4 CAT: 17

Minnesota Computer Aided Library System
CIJE: 0 RIE: 1 CAT: 15

Minnesota Computerized Adaptive Testing Language
CIJE: 0 RIE: 1 CAT: 04
UF MCATL

Minnesota Correctional Institution for Women
CIJE: 0 RIE: 1 CAT: 17

Minnesota Council on Family Relations
CIJE: 0 RIE: 2 CAT: 17

Minnesota Counseling Inventory
CIJE: 4 RIE: 1 CAT: 21

Minnesota Couples Communication Program
CIJE: 4 RIE: 1 CAT: 19

Minnesota Dialogue on Education Project
CIJE: 0 RIE: 1 CAT: 19

Minnesota Division of Vocational Rehabilitation
CIJE: 0 RIE: 1 CAT: 17

Minnesota Early Language Development Sequence
CIJE: 1 RIE: 1 CAT: 19

Minnesota Early Learning Design
CIJE: 0 RIE: 1 CAT: 19

Minnesota Education Association
CIJE: 0 RIE: 1 CAT: 17

Minnesota Education Expense Tax Deduction Law
CIJE: 0 RIE: 2 CAT: 14

Minnesota Educational Computing Consortium
CIJE: 11 RIE: 10 CAT: 17

Minnesota Educational Effectiveness Program
CIJE: 0 RIE: 2 CAT: 19

Minnesota Educational Follow Up Study
CIJE: 0 RIE: 1 CAT: 15

Minnesota Experimental City
CIJE: 1 RIE: 2 CAT: 19

Minnesota Extension Service
CIJE: 2 RIE: 4 CAT: 17

Minnesota General College
CIJE: 1 RIE: 2 CAT: 17

Minnesota Governors Council on Rural Development
CIJE: 0 RIE: 1 CAT: 17

Minnesota Higher Education Coordinating Board
CIJE: 0 RIE: 3 CAT: 17

Minnesota Importance Questionnaire
CIJE: 8 RIE: 10 CAT: 21

Minnesota Information and Decision Systems
CIJE: 0 RIE: 2 CAT: 15

Minnesota Interlibrary Telecommunications Exchange
CIJE: 0 RIE: 2 CAT: 17
UF MINITEX; Minnesota Interlibrary Teletype Experiment

Minnesota Interlibrary Teletype Experiment
USE Minnesota Interlibrary Telecommunications Exchange

Minnesota Job Description Questionnaire
CIJE: 3 RIE: 3 CAT: 21

Minnesota Job Requirements Questionnaire
CIJE: 2 RIE: 0 CAT: 21

Minnesota Junior College Faculty Association
CIJE: 1 RIE: 0 CAT: 17

Minnesota Mathematics and Science Teaching Project
CIJE: 4 RIE: 53 CAT: 19

Minnesota Metropolitan State College
CIJE: 3 RIE: 2 CAT: 17

Minnesota Model Small Business Management Program
CIJE: 0 RIE: 1 CAT: 19

Minnesota Multiphasic Personality Inventory
CIJE: 365 RIE: 73 CAT: 21

Minnesota Multiphasic Personality Inventory 168
CIJE: 3 RIE: 0 CAT: 21

Minnesota News Council
CIJE: 1 RIE: 0 CAT: 17
SN Formerly "Minnesota Press Council"

Minnesota Nonverbal Test of Creativity (Torrance)
CIJE: 0 RIE: 1 CAT: 21

Minnesota Percepto Diagnostic Test
CIJE: 7 RIE: 3 CAT: 21

Minnesota Plan
CIJE: 2 RIE: 2 CAT: 19

Minnesota Preschool Scale
CIJE: 1 RIE: 1 CAT: 21

Minnesota Press Council
CIJE: 0 RIE: 1 CAT: 17
SN Became "Minnesota News Council" in 1977

Minnesota Public Interest Research Group
CIJE: 0 RIE: 1 CAT: 17

Minnesota Rate of Manipulation Test
CIJE: 2 RIE: 1 CAT: 21

Minnesota Reading Assessment
CIJE: 2 RIE: 1 CAT: 21

Minnesota Reading Readiness Test
CIJE: 0 RIE: 1 CAT: 21

Minnesota Research and Evaluation Project
CIJE: 1 RIE: 8 CAT: 19

Minnesota Satisfaction Questionnaire
CIJE: 9 RIE: 8 CAT: 21

Minnesota Scale for Paternal Occupations
CIJE: 0 RIE: 1 CAT: 21

Minnesota Scale of Employment Satisfaction
CIJE: 1 RIE: 1 CAT: 21

Minnesota Scholastic Aptitude Test
CIJE: 2 RIE: 9 CAT: 21

Minnesota School Attitude Survey
CIJE: 0 RIE: 1 CAT: 21

Minnesota School Effectiveness Program
CIJE: 0 RIE: 5 CAT: 19

Minnesota School for the Deaf
CIJE: 0 RIE: 1 CAT: 17

Minnesota School Health Education Model
CIJE: 0 RIE: 1 CAT: 19

Minnesota School Improvement Program
CIJE: 0 RIE: 1 CAT: 19

Minnesota Secondary School Followup System
CIJE: 0 RIE: 1 CAT: 21

Minnesota Sex Attitude Survey
CIJE: 0 RIE: 1 CAT: 21

Minnesota State Board of Teaching
CIJE: 0 RIE: 1 CAT: 17

Minnesota State College Common Market
CIJE: 0 RIE: 1 CAT: 17

Minnesota State College System
CIJE: 1 RIE: 1 CAT: 17

Minnesota State Department of Education
CIJE: 0 RIE: 5 CAT: 17

Minnesota State Junior College Board
CIJE: 1 RIE: 0 CAT: 17

Minnesota State University Board
CIJE: 0 RIE: 1 CAT: 17

Minnesota Student Attitude Inventory
CIJE: 0 RIE: 1 CAT: 21

Minnesota Studies of Creative Behavior
CIJE: 0 RIE: 1 CAT: 19

Minnesota Survey of Employment Experiences
CIJE: 0 RIE: 1 CAT: 19

Minnesota Teacher Attitude Inventory
CIJE: 39 RIE: 55 CAT: 21

Minnesota Tests of Creative Thinking (Torrance)
CIJE: 3 RIE: 8 CAT: 21

Minnesota Union List of Serials
CIJE: 1 RIE: 2 CAT: 22

Minnesota Vocational Interest Inventory
CIJE: 2 RIE: 8 CAT: 21

Minnesota Wisconsin Reciprocity Agreement
CIJE: 0 RIE: 2 CAT: 14

Minnesota Work Opportunity Center
CIJE: 0 RIE: 1 CAT: 17

Minnetonka School District MN
CIJE: 0 RIE: 2 CAT: 17

Minoan Civilization
CIJE: 2 RIE: 0 CAT: 12

Minooka Consolidated School District 201 IL
CIJE: 0 RIE: 1 CAT: 17

Minor Physical Anomalies
CIJE: 0 RIE: 2 CAT: 11

Minority Achievement Program
CIJE: 0 RIE: 1 CAT: 19

Minority Allied Health Project (AASCU)
CIJE: 0 RIE: 1 CAT: 19

Minority Assistance Program SC
CIJE: 0 RIE: 1 CAT: 19

Minority Business Enterprise Project
CIJE: 1 RIE: 2 CAT: 19

Minority Businesses
CIJE: 2 RIE: 1 CAT: 16
UF Minority Owned Businesses

Minority Enterprise Small Business Investment Cos
CIJE: 0 RIE: 1 CAT: 19

Minority Female Single Parent Demonstration Proj
CIJE: 0 RIE: 1 CAT: 19

Minority Graduate Education Project
CIJE: 0 RIE: 3 CAT: 19

Minority Information Services Network CA
CIJE: 0 RIE: 1 CAT: 17

Minority Institutions Science Improvement Program
CIJE: 0 RIE: 3 CAT: 19

Minority Mobility Project
CIJE: 0 RIE: 2 CAT: 19

Minority Owned Businesses
USE Minority Businesses

Minority Participation Program
CIJE: 1 RIE: 1 CAT: 19

Minority Rights Group
CIJE: 0 RIE: 1 CAT: 17

Minority Scholarships
CIJE: 0 RIE: 2 CAT: 16

Minority Womens Employment Program
CIJE: 1 RIE: 0 CAT: 19

Minot (Louise)
CIJE: 0 RIE: 1 CAT: 18

Minot State University ND
CIJE: 1 RIE; 1 CAT: 17

Minow (Newton)
CIJE: 0 RIE: 2 CAT: 18

Minres Criterion
CIJE: 3 RIE: 0 CAT: 21

Mintzberg (Henry)
CIJE: 8 RIE: 3 CAT: 18

Minutes of Meetings
CIJE: 2 RIE: 6 CAT: 16

Mira Costa Community College CA
USE MiraCosta College CA

Mira de Amescua (Antonio)
CIJE: 1 RIE: 0 CAT: 18

MIRABILIS
CIJE: 1 RIE: 0 CAT: 04

Miracle Worker
CIJE: 0 RIE: 1 CAT: 22

MiraCosta College CA
CIJE: 0 RIE: 3 CAT: 17
UF Mira Costa Community College CA

Miranda Lux Foundation
CIJE: 0 RIE: 1 CAT: 17

Miranda Warning
CIJE: 2 RIE: 2 CAT: 14

Mirror Image Designs
CIJE: 0 RIE: 1 CAT: 21

Mirror Images
CIJE: 30 RIE: 1 CAT: 20

Mirror Movements
CIJE: 0 RIE: 1 CAT: 11
SN Imitative movements of the opposite side of the body, e.g., as when the voluntary wiggling of the fingers of one hand results in similar involuntary movements of the other
UF Movement Overflow (Hands)

Mirror State Counterplans (Debate)
CIJE: 0 RIE: 2 CAT: 16

Misclassification (Statistics)
CIJE: 2 RIE: 2 CAT: 21

Misinterpretation
CIJE: 3 RIE: 2 CAT: 16

MiSIS
USE Michigan Student Information System

Miskimins Self Goal
CIJE: 1 RIE: 0 CAT: 11

Miskimins Self Goal Other Discrepancy Scale
CIJE: 2 RIE: 0 CAT: 21

Mislevy Histogram Solution
CIJE: 0 RIE: 1 CAT: 15

Mismatch Invisible Underemployment
CIJE: 0 RIE: 1 CAT: 15

MISOE
USE Management Information System Occupational Educ

Misogyny
CIJE: 1 RIE: 1 CAT: 11

Misreporting
CIJE: 3 RIE: 2 CAT: 16

Missing Children Act 1982
CIJE: 1 RIE: 1 CAT: 14

Modern Arithmetic Through Discovery
CIJE: 0 RIE: 2 CAT: 22

Modern Art
CIJE: 8 RIE: 3 CAT: 03

Modern Dance
CIJE: 4 RIE: 1 CAT: 03

Modern European Languages Coordinators Committee
CIJE: 1 RIE: 0 CAT: 17

Modern Humanities Research Association
CIJE: 1 RIE: 0 CAT: 17

Modern Language Aptitude Test
CIJE: 10 RIE: 18 CAT: 21

Modern Language Association
CIJE: 60 RIE: 39 CAT: 17

Modern Language Association of Great Britain
CIJE: 2 RIE: 0 CAT: 17

Modern Language Project
CIJE: 0 RIE: 1 CAT: 19

Modern Management Dynamics
CIJE: 2 RIE: 0 CAT: 15

Modern Music
CIJE: 6 RIE: 2 CAT: 03

Modern Rationalism
CIJE: 0 RIE: 1 CAT: 15

Modern School Movement
CIJE: 1 RIE: 2 CAT: 12
SN See also "Escuela Moderna Movement"

Modernity
CIJE: 14 RIE: 5 CAT: 15

Modes of Thought Courses
CIJE: 0 RIE: 1 CAT: 03

Modesto City Schools CA
CIJE: 2 RIE: 2 CAT: 17

Modesto Junior College CA
CIJE: 0 RIE: 3 CAT: 17

Modesto Multi Occupational Project
CIJE: 0 RIE: 1 CAT: 19

Modesty
CIJE: 2 RIE: 2 CAT: 11

Modified Alphabet Test (Kjeldergaard Frankenstein)
CIJE: 0 RIE: 1 CAT: 21

Modified Bennett Test (Price)
CIJE: 1 RIE: 0 CAT: 21

Modified Caution Index
CIJE: 2 RIE: 3 CAT: 21

Modified Component Disability Checklist
CIJE: 0 RIE: 1 CAT: 21

Modified Component Disability Instrument
CIJE: 0 RIE: 1 CAT: 21

Modified Confidence Weighted Admissible Prob Meas
CIJE: 1 RIE: 0 CAT: 21
UF MCW APM

Modified Desensitization
CIJE: 0 RIE: 1 CAT: 11

Modified Mastery Grading System
CIJE: 0 RIE: 0 CAT: 21

Modified Norm Referenced Grading System
CIJE: 0 RIE: 0 CAT: 21

Modified Peabody Picture Vocabulary Test
CIJE: 0 RIE: 1 CAT: 21

Modified Questionnaire Occup Status of Women
CIJE: 0 RIE: 0 CAT: 21

Modified Rabban Toy Preference Test
CIJE: 0 RIE: 1 CAT: 21

Modified Rhyme Hearing Test
CIJE: 3 RIE: 0 CAT: 21

Modified Role Repertory Test (Bieri)
CIJE: 2 RIE: 0 CAT: 21

Modified Rosenberg Self Esteem Scale
CIJE: 0 RIE: 1 CAT: 21

Modified World Affairs Questionnaire
CIJE: 1 RIE: 1 CAT: 21

Modular Achievement Program
CIJE: 0 RIE: 9 CAT: 19

Modular Audio Visual Multimedia Programming
CIJE: 0 RIE: 1 CAT: 15

Modular Boilers
CIJE: 1 RIE: 0 CAT: 04

Modular Furniture Design
CIJE: 0 RIE: 1 CAT: 15

Modular Multiple Alternatives Program
CIJE: 1 RIE: 1 CAT: 19

Modular Systems
CIJE: 6 RIE: 4 CAT: 15

Modularity
CIJE: 3 RIE: 2 CAT: 15

Modularization
CIJE: 3 RIE: 2 CAT: 15

Modulators (Individuals)
CIJE: 1 RIE: 0 CAT: 10

Module Assemblers (Electronics)
CIJE: 0 RIE: 1 CAT: 09

Module Clusters
CIJE: 0 RIE: 1 CAT: 15

Modules and Monographs in Mathematics
CIJE: 0 RIE: 1 CAT: 19

Modulus of Elasticity
CIJE: 1 RIE: 0 CAT: 20

Moebius Band
USE Mobius Strip

Moffett (James)
CIJE: 12 RIE: 5 CAT: 18

Moghul Empire
USE Mogul Empire

Mogollon Indians
USE Mimbres Indians

Mogul Empire
CIJE: 0 RIE: 0 CAT: 12
SN India, 1526-1857
UF Moghul Empire; Mughal Empire

Mohave County Community College AZ
CIJE: 0 RIE: 1 CAT: 17

Mohawk
CIJE: 2 RIE: 9 CAT: 13

Mohawk (Tribe)
CIJE: 12 RIE: 16 CAT: 08

Mohawk College of Applied Arts and Technology ON
CIJE: 0 RIE: 2 CAT: 17

Mohawk Message Repeater Units
CIJE: 0 RIE: 1 CAT: 04

Mohawk Valley Community College NY
CIJE: 0 RIE: 1 CAT: 17

Mohism
CIJE: 1 RIE: 0 CAT: 15

Mohr (P)
CIJE: 1 RIE: 0 CAT: 18

Mohrmann (G P)
CIJE: 1 RIE: 0 CAT: 18

Mojarro (Tomas)
CIJE: 1 RIE: 0 CAT: 18

Mojave (Tribe)
CIJE: 0 RIE: 1 CAT: 08

Mojave Desert
CIJE: 0 RIE: 1 CAT: 07

Molded Rubber Goods Cutters
CIJE: 0 RIE: 1 CAT: 09

Moldmaking
CIJE: 2 RIE: 6 CAT: 20

Molds (Biology)
CIJE: 2 RIE: 1 CAT: 20

Mole (Chemical)
CIJE: 15 RIE: 1 CAT: 20

Molecular Beams
CIJE: 1 RIE: 0 CAT: 20

Molecular Mechanics
CIJE: 2 RIE: 0 CAT: 20

Molecular Orbital Theory
CIJE: 6 RIE: 0 CAT: 15

Molecules
CIJE: 7 RIE: 0 CAT: 20

Molesters of Children
USE Child Molesters

Molesworth Institute
CIJE: 1 RIE: 0 CAT: 17

Moliere
CIJE: 7 RIE: 1 CAT: 18

Moline Project
CIJE: 1 RIE: 0 CAT: 19

Moline School District IL
CIJE: 0 RIE: 2 CAT: 17

Mollusca
CIJE: 0 RIE: 0 CAT: 20

Molybdenum
CIJE: 5 RIE: 0 CAT: 20

Moment Estimators
CIJE: 0 RIE: 2 CAT: 15
SN See also "Method of Moments"

Moment of Silence
CIJE: 2 RIE: 0 CAT: 16

Momentary Verbs
CIJE: 1 RIE: 0 CAT: 13

MOMM Cartel
CIJE: 0 RIE: 1 CAT: 17
SN MOMM = Minnesota, Ohio State, Maryland, and Missouri

Mon Yough Community Action Committee
CIJE: 0 RIE: 2 CAT: 17

Monadnock Developmental Services Inc NH
CIJE: 0 RIE: 1 CAT: 17

Monash University (Australia)
CIJE: 11 RIE: 16 CAT: 17

Monaural Listening
CIJE: 0 RIE: 1 CAT: 11

Mondale (Walter F)
CIJE: 4 RIE: 2 CAT: 18

Mondrian (Piet)
CIJE: 2 RIE: 0 CAT: 18

Monemes
CIJE: 2 RIE: 0 CAT: 13

Monetarism
CIJE: 6 RIE: 2 CAT: 15

Monetary Concepts Task Test (McCarty)
CIJE: 0 RIE: 1 CAT: 21

Monetary Incentives
CIJE: 8 RIE: 5 CAT: 15

Monetary Reinforcement
CIJE: 1 RIE: 1 CAT: 15

Money
CIJE: 24 RIE: 23 CAT: 16

Money Ethic Scale
CIJE: 0 RIE: 2 CAT: 21

Money Game
CIJE: 0 RIE: 1 CAT: 15

Money Measurement and Time Program
CIJE: 1 RIE: 5 CAT: 19

Money Skills
CIJE: 3 RIE: 6 CAT: 15

Mongolia
CIJE: 4 RIE: 14 CAT: 07

Monguagon School MI
CIJE: 1 RIE: 0 CAT: 17

Moniforms
CIJE: 0 RIE: 2 CAT: 04

Monitor Model
CIJE: 24 RIE: 10 CAT: 15
UF Monitor Theory (Krashen)

Monitor of Student Satisfaction Questionnaire
CIJE: 1 RIE: 0 CAT: 21

Monitor Theory (Krashen)
USE Monitor Model

Monitoring
CIJE: 85 RIE: 92 CAT: 15
SN Use a more specific term if possible, e.g., following such initial words as Automated, Comprehension, Environmental, Error, Ethnographic, Performance, Program, Reality, Self, and Work

Monitoring Achievement in Pittsburgh
CIJE: 2 RIE: 2 CAT: 19
UF MAP AT HOME Program

Monitoring Progress
USE Progress Monitoring

Monitoring the Future
CIJE: 3 RIE: 30 CAT: 19

Monkey Bars
CIJE: 0 RIE: 1 CAT: 16

Monkeys
CIJE: 27 RIE: 7 CAT: 20

Monkeys Paw (The)
CIJE: 0 RIE: 1 CAT: 22

Monmouth College NJ
CIJE: 2 RIE: 7 CAT: 17

Monnier (Henry Bonaventure)
CIJE: 1 RIE: 0 CAT: 18

Mono Operationalization Extraspective Measures
CIJE: 1 RIE: 0 CAT: 21

Monochords
CIJE: 0 RIE: 0 CAT: 16

Monochromators
CIJE: 1 RIE: 0 CAT: 04

Monographs
CIJE: 56 RIE: 26 CAT: 16

Monolingual Students
CIJE: 7 RIE: 4 CAT: 10

Monomethylhydrazine
CIJE: 0 RIE: 1 CAT: 20

Monongahela River Basin
CIJE: 0 RIE: 1 CAT: 07

Monongahela Valley
CIJE: 0 RIE: 1 CAT: 07

Mononucleosis
CIJE: 1 RIE: 1 CAT: 11

Monopoly
CIJE: 22 RIE: 14 CAT: 15

Monopoly (Game)
CIJE: 2 RIE: 0 CAT: 16

Monorails
CIJE: 1 RIE: 0 CAT: 04

Monotone Regression
CIJE: 3 RIE: 0 CAT: 15

Monotone Splines
CIJE: 2 RIE: 1 CAT: 21

Monotone Transformation
CIJE: 2 RIE: 0 CAT: 21

Monotonic Deterministic Test Model
CIJE: 0 RIE: 1 CAT: 15

Monotonic Relationships
CIJE: 2 RIE: 0 CAT: 15

Monotonicity Analysis
CIJE: 4 RIE: 2 CAT: 15

Monotonism
CIJE: 2 RIE: 0 CAT: 11

Monotype Printing
CIJE: 2 RIE: 0 CAT: 15

Monroe Calculators
CIJE: 0 RIE: 1 CAT: 04

Monroe City Simulation
CIJE: 1 RIE: 0 CAT: 15

Monroe Community College NY
CIJE: 5 RIE: 9 CAT: 17

Monroe County Community College MI
CIJE: 1 RIE: 4 CAT: 17

Monroe County Library System NY
CIJE: 0 RIE: 1 CAT: 17

Monroe County Public Library IN
CIJE: 1 RIE: 1 CAT: 17

Monroe County School District FL
CIJE: 0 RIE: 2 CAT: 17

Monroe Middle School IA
CIJE: 0 RIE: 1 CAT: 17

Monroe Model
CIJE: 0 RIE: 1 CAT: 15

Monroe Oral Language Scale
CIJE: 0 RIE: 3 CAT: 21

Mons University (Belgium)
CIJE: 1 RIE: 0 CAT: 17

Monsanto Company
CIJE: 1 RIE: 1 CAT: 17

Monsieur Ouine
CIJE: 0 RIE: 1 CAT: 22

Monsoons
CIJE: 1 RIE: 0 CAT: 20

Montagnais (Athapascan Language)
USE Chipewyan

Montagnais (Cree)
CIJE: 0 RIE: 1 CAT: 13
SN Dialect of Cree, an Algonquian language

Montagnais (Tribe)
CIJE: 2 RIE: 1 CAT: 08

Montague (Richard)
CIJE: 2 RIE: 2 CAT: 18

Montague Riley Test
CIJE: 0 RIE: 1 CAT: 21

Montaigne (Michel Eyquem de)
CIJE: 3 RIE: 6 CAT: 18

Montale (Eugenio)
CIJE: 1 RIE: 0 CAT: 18

Montana
CIJE: 86 RIE: 382 CAT: 07

Montana (Billings)
CIJE: 2 RIE: 2 CAT: 07

Montana (Blaine County)
CIJE: 1 RIE: 1 CAT: 07

Montana (Butte)
CIJE: 1 RIE: 1 CAT: 07

Montana (Gallatin County)
CIJE: 0 RIE: 2 CAT: 07

Montana (Glendive)
CIJE: 0 RIE: 1 CAT: 07

Montana (Great Falls)
CIJE: 4 RIE: 4 CAT: 07

Montana (Hardin)
CIJE: 0 RIE: 1 CAT: 07

Montana (Helena)
CIJE: 0 RIE: 7 CAT: 07

Montana (Hill County)
CIJE: 1 RIE: 1 CAT: 07

Montana (Livingston)
CIJE: 0 RIE: 1 CAT: 07

Montana (Missoula County)
CIJE: 0 RIE: 1 CAT: 07

Montana (Missoula)
CIJE: 1 RIE: 3 CAT: 07

Montana (South Central)
CIJE: 0 RIE: 1 CAT: 07

Montana Educational Telecommunications Network
CIJE: 0 RIE: 1 CAT: 17

Montana Functional Vision Assessment
CIJE: 0 RIE: 1 CAT: 21
UF MFVA

Montana Governors Conference Lib Info Serv
USE Governors Conference Library Info Services MT

Montana State Department of Public Instruction
CIJE: 0 RIE: 2 CAT: 17

Montana State University
CIJE: 13 RIE: 25 CAT: 17

Montana Tribal College Development Program
CIJE: 0 RIE: 1 CAT: 19

Montana University System
CIJE: 0 RIE: 5 CAT: 17

Montclair Public Schools NJ
CIJE: 1 RIE: 2 CAT: 17

Montclair State College NJ
CIJE: 10 RIE: 15 CAT: 17

Monte (Domingo del)
CIJE: 1 RIE: 0 CAT: 18

Montebello Unified School District CA
CIJE: 1 RIE: 1 CAT: 17

Montefiore Hospital NY
CIJE: 1 RIE: 1 CAT: 17

Monteith (John)
CIJE: 0 RIE: 1 CAT: 18

Montemayor (Jorge)
CIJE: 1 RIE: 0 CAT: 18

Montenegro
CIJE: 0 RIE: 1 CAT: 07

Monterey Articulation Program
CIJE: 1 RIE: 0 CAT: 19

Monterey Bay
CIJE: 0 RIE: 1 CAT: 07

Monterey County Library CA
CIJE: 0 RIE: 1 CAT: 17

Monterey Institute of International Studies CA
CIJE: 1 RIE: 1 CAT: 17

Monterey Language Program
CIJE: 2 RIE: 2 CAT: 19

Monterey Peninsula College CA
CIJE: 1 RIE: 1 CAT: 17

Monterey Peninsula Unified School District CA
CIJE: 0 RIE: 2 CAT: 17

Monterrey Institute of Technology (Mexico)
CIJE: 0 RIE: 1 CAT: 17

Montesquieu (Charles Louis de Secondat)
CIJE: 1 RIE: 1 CAT: 18

Montessori (Maria)
CIJE: 27 RIE: 34 CAT: 18

Montessori Preschools
CIJE: 9 RIE: 15 CAT: 05

Montessori Schools
CIJE: 30 RIE: 14 CAT: 05

Montfort (Eugene)
CIJE: 1 RIE: 0 CAT: 18

Montgomery (Robert)
CIJE: 1 RIE: 0 CAT: 18

Montgomery Blair High School MD
CIJE: 1 RIE: 0 CAT: 17

Montgomery College MD
CIJE: 14 RIE: 27 CAT: 17

Montgomery County Community College PA
CIJE: 1 RIE: 6 CAT: 17

Montgomery County Public Schools MD
CIJE: 33 RIE: 132 CAT: 17

Montgomery County Public Schools VA
CIJE: 0 RIE: 1 CAT: 17

Montgomery County Schools PA
CIJE: 1 RIE: 0 CAT: 17

Montgomery County Student Alliance
CIJE: 1 RIE: 0 CAT: 17

Montgomery County Work Release Program MD
CIJE: 0 RIE: 1 CAT: 19

Montgomery Learning Disability Clinic AL
CIJE: 0 RIE: 1 CAT: 17

Montgomery Township Public Schools NJ
CIJE: 1 RIE: 0 CAT: 17

Montherlant (Henry de)
CIJE: 4 RIE: 0 CAT: 18

Monthly Catalog of U S Government Publications
CIJE: 5 RIE: 3 CAT: 22

Monthly Checklist of State Publications
CIJE: 0 RIE: 1 CAT: 22

Monticello College
CIJE: 1 RIE: 0 CAT: 17

Montpelier (Madison Home)
CIJE: 0 RIE: 3 CAT: 07

Montpelier Seminary VT
CIJE: 0 RIE: 1 CAT: 17

Montreal Museum of Fine Arts (Canada)
CIJE: 2 RIE: 0 CAT: 17

Montreux Television Symposium
CIJE: 1 RIE: 0 CAT: 02

Montserrat
CIJE: 0 RIE: 1 CAT: 07

Montville Township School District NJ
CIJE: 1 RIE: 0 CAT: 17

Mood (S M)
CIJE: 0 RIE: 1 CAT: 18

Mood Induction
CIJE: 4 RIE: 5 CAT: 11
UF Induced Moods

Mood Test of Significance
CIJE: 0 RIE: 2 CAT: 21

Moody (Raymond)
CIJE: 1 RIE: 0 CAT: 18

Moon
CIJE: 28 RIE: 13 CAT: 20

Moonan (W J)
CIJE: 0 RIE: 1 CAT: 18

Mooney Problem Check List
CIJE: 3 RIE: 11 CAT: 21

Moonlight Schoolhouse
CIJE: 1 RIE: 0 CAT: 19

Moonquakes
CIJE: 1 RIE: 0 CAT: 20

Moore (Alice)
CIJE: 2 RIE: 0 CAT: 18

Moore (Bessie Boehm)
CIJE: 0 RIE: 1 CAT: 18

Moore (George)
CIJE: 1 RIE: 0 CAT: 18

Moore (Henry)
CIJE: 2 RIE: 0 CAT: 18

Moore (Marianne)
CIJE: 1 RIE: 1 CAT: 18

Moore (O K)
CIJE: 2 RIE: 1 CAT: 18

Moore (T W)
CIJE: 2 RIE: 0 CAT: 18

Moore Assessment Profile
CIJE: 2 RIE: 0 CAT: 21

Moore County School District NC
CIJE: 0 RIE: 0 CAT: 17

Moore Independent School District OK
CIJE: 0 RIE: 2 CAT: 17

Moore Method
CIJE: 1 RIE: 0 CAT: 15

Moorhead Area Vocational Technical Institute MN
CIJE: 1 RIE: 0 CAT: 17

Moorhead State College MN
CIJE: 0 RIE: 2 CAT: 17

Moorpark College CA
CIJE: 0 RIE: 1 CAT: 17

MOOSES Computer Program
CIJE: 0 RIE: 1 CAT: 04
SN MOOSES = Multiple Option Observation System for Experimental Studies

Moot Court
CIJE: 6 RIE: 3 CAT: 14

Moot Courts
CIJE: 2 RIE: 0 CAT: 15

Mopeds
CIJE: 0 RIE: 3 CAT: 04

Moraine Park Technical Institute WI
CIJE: 0 RIE: 6 CAT: 17

Moraine Valley Community College IL
CIJE: 8 RIE: 14 CAT: 17

Moral Action Choice Test (Patterson)
CIJE: 0 RIE: 1 CAT: 21

Moral Behavior
CIJE: 12 RIE: 4 CAT: 11

Moral Behavior Analysis Instrument
CIJE: 0 RIE: 1 CAT: 21

Moral Education
CIJE: 37 RIE: 4 CAT: 16
SN Use Desc "Ethical Instruction" for formal moral education

Moral Judgment Task (Piaget)
CIJE: 2 RIE: 6 CAT: 21

Moral Majority
CIJE: 14 RIE: 4 CAT: 10

Moral Orientation
CIJE: 2 RIE: 1 CAT: 11

Moral Reality
CIJE: 12 RIE: 0 CAT: 16

Moral Rearmament
CIJE: 0 RIE: 1 CAT: 15

Moral Reasoning
CIJE: 108 RIE: 44 CAT: 11
SN See also "Justice Reasoning"

Morality Test for Children
CIJE: 3 RIE: 0 CAT: 21

Moran (Tod)
CIJE: 1 RIE: 0 CAT: 18

Morando (Bernardo)
CIJE: 1 RIE: 0 CAT: 18

Moratin (Leandro Fernandez de)
CIJE: 2 RIE: 0 CAT: 18

Moravia (Alberto)
CIJE: 3 RIE: 0 CAT: 18

Moravian College PA
CIJE: 7 RIE: 4 CAT: 17

Moravians
CIJE: 1 RIE: 0 CAT: 08

Moray House College of Education (Scotland)
CIJE: 1 RIE: 2 CAT: 17

Moray House Verbal Reasoning Tests
CIJE: 2 RIE: 0 CAT: 21

Morbid Curiosity
CIJE: 1 RIE: 1 CAT: 11

Morbidity
CIJE: 10 RIE: 4 CAT: 11

Morbidity and Mortality Weekly Report
CIJE: 1 RIE: 0 CAT: 22

More (Sir Thomas)
CIJE: 7 RIE: 1 CAT: 18

More Alternatives for Students
CIJE: 0 RIE: 0 CAT: 19

More Capable Students Project
CIJE: 0 RIE: 1 CAT: 19

More Effective Schools Program
CIJE: 1 RIE: 24 CAT: 19

More Effective Schools Teaching Project
USE Effective Schools Project

More Perfect Union (A)
CIJE: 0 RIE: 1 CAT: 22
SN Videotape re law-related education

Morehead State University KY
CIJE: 4 RIE: 8 CAT: 17

Morehouse College GA
CIJE: 5 RIE: 6 CAT: 17

Moreno Valley Unified School District CA
CIJE: 0 RIE: 1 CAT: 17

Morgan (Arthur Ernest)
CIJE: 0 RIE: 1 CAT: 18

Morgan (Dodge D)
CIJE: 0 RIE: 1 CAT: 18

Morgan Community College CO
CIJE: 1 RIE: 0 CAT: 17

Morgan Community School
CIJE: 1 RIE: 0 CAT: 17

Morgan Community School Board
CIJE: 1 RIE: 0 CAT: 17

Morgan County School System TN
CIJE: 0 RIE: 2 CAT: 17

Morgan State College MD
CIJE: 4 RIE: 3 CAT: 17

Morgan State University MD
CIJE: 2 RIE: 7 CAT: 17

Morike (Edward)
CIJE: 1 RIE: 0 CAT: 18

Morison (Samuel Eliot)
CIJE: 0 RIE: 1 CAT: 18

Mormons
CIJE: 22 RIE: 28 CAT: 10

Morning Newspapers
CIJE: 0 RIE: 1 CAT: 16

Morning Star Native Teacher Education Program
CIJE: 0 RIE: 3 CAT: 19

Morning Star Program
CIJE: 2 RIE: 0 CAT: 19

Moroccans
CIJE: 1 RIE: 3 CAT: 08

Morocco
CIJE: 29 RIE: 71 CAT: 07

Morocco (C)
CIJE: 1 RIE: 0 CAT: 18

Morphine
CIJE: 2 RIE: 0 CAT: 11

Morphisms
CIJE: 0 RIE: 0 CAT: 16

Morphographemics
CIJE: 0 RIE: 1 CAT: 13

Morphographs
CIJE: 0 RIE: 1 CAT: 13

Morpholexical Phenomena
CIJE: 1 RIE: 1 CAT: 13

Morphology of the Folktale
CIJE: 0 RIE: 1 CAT: 22

Morphotonemics
CIJE: 0 RIE: 1 CAT: 13

Morrill (Justin S)
CIJE: 1 RIE: 1 CAT: 18

Morrill Act 1862
CIJE: 9 RIE: 8 CAT: 14

Morrill Act 1890
CIJE: 5 RIE: 6 CAT: 14

Morrill Committee
CIJE: 1 RIE: 0 CAT: 17

Morris (Charles)
CIJE: 2 RIE: 0 CAT: 18

Morris (Gouverneur)
CIJE: 0 RIE: 1 CAT: 18

Morris (Henry)
CIJE: 2 RIE: 0 CAT: 18

Morris (William)
CIJE: 1 RIE: 0 CAT: 18

Morris (Willie)
CIJE: 1 RIE: 0 CAT: 18

Morris Brown College GA
CIJE: 0 RIE: 1 CAT: 17

Morrison (George H)
CIJE: 0 RIE: 1 CAT: 18

Morrison (George)
CIJE: 0 RIE: 1 CAT: 18

Morrison (Philip)
CIJE: 2 RIE: 0 CAT: 18

Morrison (Toni)
CIJE: 17 RIE: 3 CAT: 18

Morristown College TN
CIJE: 0 RIE: 1 CAT: 17

Morristown School District VT
CIJE: 0 RIE: 1 CAT: 17

Morse (Jedidiah)
CIJE: 1 RIE: 0 CAT: 18

Morse Code
CIJE: 2 RIE: 5 CAT: 20

Morse McCune Test of Critical Thinking
CIJE: 0 RIE: 1 CAT: 21

Mortgage Backed Student Loans
CIJE: 0 RIE: 1 CAT: 16

Mortgages
CIJE: 2 RIE: 5 CAT: 16

Morton (Oliver)
CIJE: 0 RIE: 1 CAT: 18
SN "Oliver P" — Indiana's Civil War Governor

Morton College IL
CIJE: 1 RIE: 2 CAT: 17

Morton v Mancari
CIJE: 1 RIE: 0 CAT: 14

Mortuary Science
CIJE: 0 RIE: 5 CAT: 20

Mosaic Construction Test (Hall)
CIJE: 1 RIE: 0 CAT: 21

Mosaics
CIJE: 8 RIE: 5 CAT: 16

Mosby Assess Test
CIJE: 0 RIE: 4 CAT: 21
UF Assess Test (Mosby)

Moscow Institute of Technology (USSR)
CIJE: 0 RIE: 1 CAT: 17

Moscow Power Engineering Institute (USSR)
CIJE: 0 RIE: 1 CAT: 17

Moscow Printing Institute (USSR)
CIJE: 0 RIE: 1 CAT: 17

Moscow State Pedagogical Institute (USSR)
CIJE: 0 RIE: 1 CAT: 17

Moscow State University (USSR)
CIJE: 4 RIE: 1 CAT: 17

Moseley Law
CIJE: 1 RIE: 0 CAT: 20

Mosenthal (Peter)
CIJE: 0 RIE: 0 CAT: 18

Moses
CIJE: 1 RIE: 0 CAT: 18

Moshavim
CIJE: 1 RIE: 1 CAT: 05

Mosher Forced Choice Guilt Scale
CIJE: 3 RIE: 1 CAT: 21

Moslems
USE Muslims

Mosqueda (Jose)
CIJE: 1 RIE: 0 CAT: 18

Mosqueda (Lawrence)
CIJE: 0 RIE: 1 CAT: 18

Mosquitoes
CIJE: 2 RIE: 3 CAT: 20

Moss
CIJE: 2 RIE: 0 CAT: 20

Mossi People
CIJE: 0 RIE: 0 CAT: 08

Most Like Questionnaire (Landis and Hayman)
CIJE: 1 RIE: 0 CAT: 21

Mother Butler Memorial High School
CIJE: 1 RIE: 0 CAT: 17

Mother Cabrini School NY
CIJE: 0 RIE: 1 CAT: 17

Mother Child Home Program
CIJE: 4 RIE: 5 CAT: 19

Mother Child Picture Test
CIJE: 1 RIE: 0 CAT: 21

Mother Daughter Communication Project
CIJE: 0 RIE: 1 CAT: 19

Mother Goose
CIJE: 10 RIE: 4 CAT: 22

Mother Goose Problems Test
CIJE: 0 RIE: 2 CAT: 21

Mother Infant Literary Knowledge Program
CIJE: 0 RIE: 1 CAT: 19

Mothers Against Drunk Drivers
USE Mothers Against Drunk Driving

Mothers Against Drunk Driving
CIJE: 5 RIE: 2 CAT: 17
UF MADD; Mothers Against Drunk Drivers

Mothers Day
CIJE: 0 RIE: 0 CAT: 12

Motion Media
CIJE: 0 RIE: 1 CAT: 20

Motion Picture Association of America
CIJE: 2 RIE: 2 CAT: 17

Motion Picture Code and Rating Program
CIJE: 2 RIE: 0 CAT: 19

Motion Picture Directors
USE Film Directors

Motion Picture Law
CIJE: 0 RIE: 1 CAT: 14

Motion Picture Ratings
CIJE: 2 RIE: 4 CAT: 16

Motion Picture Stars
USE Film Stars

Motion Stills
CIJE: 1 RIE: 1 CAT: 20

Motivated Strategies for Learning Questionnaire
CIJE: 2 RIE: 4 CAT: 21
UF MSLQ

Motivation Analysis Test (Cattell and Horn)
CIJE: 3 RIE: 1 CAT: 21

Motivation Check Sheet
CIJE: 1 RIE: 0 CAT: 21

Motivation Hygiene Theory
CIJE: 6 RIE: 4 CAT: 15

Motivational Design
CIJE: 2 RIE: 1 CAT: 15

Motivational Interview Strategies
CIJE: 0 RIE: 1 CAT: 15

Motivational Orientation
CIJE: 0 RIE: 2 CAT: 11

Motivational Orientation Scale
CIJE: 0 RIE: 1 CAT: 21

Motivational Skill Training Package
CIJE: 0 RIE: 1 CAT: 19

Motivational Skill Training Program
CIJE: 1 RIE: 0 CAT: 19

Motivational Structure Questionnaire Alcoholics
CIJE: 0 RIE: 1 CAT: 21

Motivic Development
CIJE: 1 RIE: 0 CAT: 15

Motley (Constance Baker)
CIJE: 1 RIE: 0 CAT: 18

Moton Center for Independent Studies DC
CIJE: 1 RIE: 0 CAT: 17

Motor Activity Scale
CIJE: 0 RIE: 1 CAT: 21

Motor Behavior Description Categories
CIJE: 0 RIE: 1 CAT: 21

Motor Free Test of Visual Perception
CIJE: 1 RIE: 1 CAT: 21

Motor Inhibition
CIJE: 3 RIE: 2 CAT: 16

Motor Inhibition Test (Ward)
CIJE: 0 RIE: 2 CAT: 21

Motor Perceptual Diagnostic Inventory
CIJE: 0 RIE: 1 CAT: 21

Motor Restraint
CIJE: 1 RIE: 0 CAT: 11

Motor Vehicle Inspections
CIJE: 0 RIE: 1 CAT: 16

Motor Vehicle Manufacturers Association
CIJE: 1 RIE: 0 CAT: 17

Motor Vehicle Registration
CIJE: 0 RIE: 1 CAT: 16

Motorcycles
CIJE: 5 RIE: 24 CAT: 04

Motoric Expression
CIJE: 1 RIE: 0 CAT: 11

Motoric Ideational Sensory Test (Stein and Lenrow)
CIJE: 1 RIE: 0 CAT: 21

Motoric Imagery
CIJE: 1 RIE: 0 CAT: 11

Motoric Inhibition Test (MacCoby et al)
CIJE: 0 RIE: 1 CAT: 21

Motorola Inc
CIJE: 4 RIE: 3 CAT: 17

Mott (Emma)
CIJE: 0 RIE: 1 CAT: 18

Mott (Lucretia Coffin)
CIJE: 2 RIE: 0 CAT: 18

Mott Basic Language Skills Program
CIJE: 0 RIE: 4 CAT: 19

Mott Camp MI
CIJE: 0 RIE: 1 CAT: 17

Mott Community College MI
CIJE: 1 RIE: 1 CAT: 17

Mott Foundation
CIJE: 2 RIE: 12 CAT: 17

Mott Institute for Community Improvement
CIJE: 0 RIE: 2 CAT: 17

Mounds View Public Schools MN
CIJE: 0 RIE: 1 CAT: 17

Mounier (Emmanuel)
CIJE: 1 RIE: 0 CAT: 18

Mount Anthony Union High School VT
CIJE: 1 RIE: 0 CAT: 17

Mount Carmel Guild Child Study Center
CIJE: 1 RIE: 0 CAT: 17

Mount Carmel High School IL
CIJE: 1 RIE: 0 CAT: 17

Mount Diablo Unified School District CA
CIJE: 3 RIE: 6 CAT: 17

Mount Druitt Early Childhood Project
CIJE: 0 RIE: 16 CAT: 19

Mount Druitt Longitudinal Study
CIJE: 0 RIE: 4 CAT: 22

Mount Greylock Regional High School MA
CIJE: 1 RIE: 0 CAT: 17

Mount Healthy City School District Board v Doyle
CIJE: 2 RIE: 1 CAT: 14

Mount Holyoke College MA
CIJE: 12 RIE: 11 CAT: 17

Mount Hood Community College OR
CIJE: 4 RIE: 3 CAT: 17

Mount Ida College MA
CIJE: 2 RIE: 3 CAT: 17

Mount Ida Junior College MA
CIJE: 1 RIE: 0 CAT: 17
SN Now, Mount Ida College MA

Mount Lebanon School District PA
CIJE: 1 RIE: 1 CAT: 17

Mount Marty College SD
CIJE: 0 RIE: 1 CAT: 17

Mount McKinley National Park
CIJE: 1 RIE: 0 CAT: 07

Mount Royal College AB
CIJE: 1 RIE: 0 CAT: 17

Mount Saint Helens
CIJE: 5 RIE: 5 CAT: 07

Mount Saint Marys College CA
CIJE: 1 RIE: 7 CAT: 17

Mount Saint Vincent University NS
CIJE: 3 RIE: 2 CAT: 17

Mount San Antonio College CA
CIJE: 1 RIE: 10 CAT: 17

Mount San Jacinto College CA
CIJE: 2 RIE: 7 CAT: 17

Mount Scopus College (Australia)
CIJE: 0 RIE: 1 CAT: 17

Mount Sinai School of Medicine NY
USE City University of New York Mt Sinai Sch of Med

Mount Stuart Elementary School WA
CIJE: 1 RIE: 0 CAT: 17

Mount Union College OH
CIJE: 3 RIE: 2 CAT: 17

Mount Vernon College DC
CIJE: 1 RIE: 2 CAT: 17

Mount Vernon High School
CIJE: 2 RIE: 0 CAT: 17

Mount Vernon School Community Center VA
CIJE: 1 RIE: 0 CAT: 17

Mountain Bell Project MT
CIJE: 0 RIE: 1 CAT: 19

Mountain Empire Community College VA
CIJE: 2 RIE: 2 CAT: 17

Mountain Plains Program
CIJE: 0 RIE: 140 CAT: 19

Mountain Plains Regional Resource Center UT
CIJE: 0 RIE: 1 CAT: 17

Mountain Speech
CIJE: 0 RIE: 1 CAT: 13

Mountain States Health Manpower and Education
CIJE: 0 RIE: 7 CAT: 17

Mountain States Regional Medical Program
CIJE: 0 RIE: 1 CAT: 19

Mountain View Center
CIJE: 1 RIE: 1 CAT: 17

Mountain View Intermediate School OR
CIJE: 0 RIE: 2 CAT: 17

Mountain Womens Exchange
CIJE: 0 RIE: 1 CAT: 17

Mountaineering
CIJE: 8 RIE: 8 CAT: 16

Mountains
CIJE: 1 RIE: 2 CAT: 07

Mourning
CIJE: 4 RIE: 2 CAT: 11

Mouth Appearance Pictures
CIJE: 0 RIE: 1 CAT: 11

Mouth Protectors
CIJE: 3 RIE: 0 CAT: 11

Mouthwash
CIJE: 4 RIE: 0 CAT: 11

MOVE (Group)
CIJE: 0 RIE: 1 CAT: 17
SN Radical back-to-nature group founded by John Africa

Movement (Visual Arts)
CIJE: 0 RIE: 1 CAT: 16

Movement Notation
CIJE: 2 RIE: 0 CAT: 15

Movement Organization
CIJE: 3 RIE: 1 CAT: 15

Movement Overflow (Hands)
USE Mirror Movements

Movement Refractoriness
CIJE: 1 RIE: 0 CAT: 11

Movement Skills Test Battery
CIJE: 1 RIE: 1 CAT: 21

Movement Therapy
CIJE: 2 RIE: 3 CAT: 11

Movers
CIJE: 0 RIE: 1 CAT: 09

Movie Attendance
CIJE: 1 RIE: 1 CAT: 16

Movie Directors
USE Film Directors

Movie Palaces
CIJE: 0 RIE: 1 CAT: 05

Movie Stars
USE Film Stars

Moviebus
CIJE: 0 RIE: 1 CAT: 04

Movigenics
CIJE: 0 RIE: 1 CAT: 11

Movima
CIJE: 0 RIE: 1 CAT: 13

Movimento Brasileiro de Alfabetizacao
USE Brazilian Literacy Movement

Mowing Equipment
CIJE: 0 RIE: 1 CAT: 04

Moya (Jesus)
CIJE: 0 RIE: 1 CAT: 18

Moyers (Bill)
CIJE: 2 RIE: 0 CAT: 18

Moynihan (Daniel P)
CIJE: 5 RIE: 3 CAT: 18

Moynihan Report
CIJE: 7 RIE: 5 CAT: 22

Mozambique
CIJE: 13 RIE: 11 CAT: 07

Mozart (Wolfgang A)
CIJE: 2 RIE: 2 CAT: 18

Mozert v Hawkins County Public Schools
CIJE: 7 RIE: 0 CAT: 14

MP M Programing Language
CIJE: 0 RIE: 0 CAT: 04

Mr Cucui
CIJE: 1 RIE: 0 CAT: 21

Mr Sammlers Planet
CIJE: 1 RIE: 0 CAT: 22

Mr Smith Goes to Washington
CIJE: 0 RIE: 0 CAT: 22

MS DOS
CIJE: 2 RIE: 4 CAT: 04
UF Microsoft DOS

Ms Magazine
CIJE: 3 RIE: 2 CAT: 22

MS University of Baroda (India)
USE Maharaja Sayajirao University of Baroda (India)

MSLQ
USE Motivated Strategies for Learning Questionnaire

MSPAP
USE Maryland School Performance Assessment Program

MSRT Tutor
CIJE: 1 RIE: 1 CAT: 04
UF Mobile Subscriber Remote telephone Terminal Tutor

MTTI Program CA
USE Multi District Trainer of Trainers Institute

MTV
CIJE: 6 RIE: 1 CAT: 17
UF Music Television Network

Muckraking
CIJE: 4 RIE: 10 CAT: 16

Mucociliary System
CIJE: 2 RIE: 0 CAT: 20

Mucocutaneous Lymph Node Syndrome
CIJE: 2 RIE: 0 CAT: 11

Mucopolysaccharidosis
CIJE: 1 RIE: 0 CAT: 11

Mudie (Charles Edward)
CIJE: 1 RIE: 0 CAT: 18

Mueller Lyer Illusion
CIJE: 0 RIE: 2 CAT: 11

Mueller v Allen
CIJE: 2 RIE: 2 CAT: 14

Muffoletto (Robert)
CIJE: 0 RIE: 1 CAT: 18

Mug Shots
CIJE: 1 RIE: 1 CAT: 16

Mughal Empire
USE Mogul Empire

Muhlenberg College PA
CIJE: 0 RIE: 2 CAT: 17

Muhlenberg School District PA
CIJE: 1 RIE: 1 CAT: 17

Muinane
CIJE: 0 RIE: 1 CAT: 13

Muir (John)
CIJE: 3 RIE: 0 CAT: 18

Mukilteo School District 36 WA
CIJE: 0 RIE: 1 CAT: 17

Mulattoes
CIJE: 4 RIE: 1 CAT: 08

Mulford Act
CIJE: 0 RIE: 1 CAT: 14

Mulligan Stew
CIJE: 0 RIE: 6 CAT: 22

Mulroney (Brian)
CIJE: 1 RIE: 1 CAT: 18

Multi Activity Zones for Education
CIJE: 0 RIE: 1 CAT: 15

Multi Agency Project for Pre Schoolers
CIJE: 0 RIE: 2 CAT: 19

Multi Attribute Consensus Building
CIJE: 0 RIE: 1 CAT: 15

Multi Attribute Utility Theory
CIJE: 2 RIE: 3 CAT: 21
UF MAUT; Multiattribute Utility Models; Multi Attribution Utility Technology

Multi Attribution Utility Technology
USE Multi Attribute Utility Theory

Multi Cam
CIJE: 0 RIE: 1 CAT: 04

Multi Component Career Education Curriculum Model
CIJE: 0 RIE: 1 CAT: 15

Multi County Planning
CIJE: 0 RIE: 1 CAT: 15

Multi Database Searching
CIJE: 1 RIE: 1 CAT: 16
UF Multiple Database Searching

Multi Digit Number Systems
USE Multidigit Numbers

Multi Digit Tests
CIJE: 1 RIE: 7 CAT: 21
UF MDT Multiple Digit Testing; Multiple Digit Tests

Multi District Trainer of Trainers Institute
CIJE: 1 RIE: 1 CAT: 17
UF MTTI Program CA

Multi Ethnic Literature of the US (MELUS)
USE Multiethnic Literature

Multi Factor Attitude Inventory
CIJE: 1 RIE: 0 CAT: 21

Multi Factor Grading
CIJE: 0 RIE: 1 CAT: 15

Multi Genre Research
USE Multigenre Research Projects

Multi Image Presentations
CIJE: 3 RIE: 6 CAT: 15

Multi Indicator Approach
CIJE: 0 RIE: 1 CAT: 15

Multi Language Time Sharing System
CIJE: 0 RIE: 2 CAT: 15

Multi Media Access Project
CIJE: 1 RIE: 0 CAT: 19

Multi Media Training Van
CIJE: 1 RIE: 0 CAT: 19

Multi Media Treatise on Nuclear War and Peace
CIJE: 1 RIE: 0 CAT: 22

Multi Purpose Academic Departments
USE Multipurpose Academic Units

Multi Purpose College Facilities
USE Multipurpose Colleges

Multi Purpose Occupational Information System
CIJE: 0 RIE: 1 CAT: 19

Multi State Teacher Education Project
CIJE: 0 RIE: 9 CAT: 19

Multi Teacher Departments
CIJE: 8 RIE: 0 CAT: 16

Multi Text Method
USE Multitext Approach

Multiattribute Utility Decomposition
CIJE: 0 RIE: 2 CAT: 04
UF MAUD

Multiattribute Utility Models
USE Multi Attribute Utility Theory

Multibase Arithmetic Blocks
CIJE: 2 RIE: 0 CAT: 04

Multicenter Trials
CIJE: 0 RIE: 1 CAT: 15

Multicertification
CIJE: 0 RIE: 3 CAT: 15

Multicollinearity
CIJE: 8 RIE: 9 CAT: 21

Multicounty Districts
CIJE: 0 RIE: 1 CAT: 05

Multicounty Library Systems
CIJE: 0 RIE: 1 CAT: 05

Multicultural Attitude Questionnaire
CIJE: 1 RIE: 0 CAT: 21

Multicultural Career Intern Program DC
CIJE: 0 RIE: 1 CAT: 19

Multicultural Centers
CIJE: 0 RIE: 1 CAT: 05
UF Multicultural Education Centers

Multicultural Counseling
CIJE: 24 RIE: 5 CAT: 11

Multicultural Education Centers
USE Multicultural Centers

Multicultural Education Quick Assessment Test
CIJE: 0 RIE: 1 CAT: 21

Multicultural Improvement of Cognitive Abilities
CIJE: 0 RIE: 1 CAT: 19

Multicultural Materials
CIJE: 50 RIE: 31 CAT: 16

Multicultural Reading and Thinking Program AR
CIJE: 0 RIE: 3 CAT: 19
UF McRAT Program AR

Multicultural Textbook Survey Eval Instrument
CIJE: 1 RIE: 0 CAT: 21

Multidigit Numbers
CIJE: 5 RIE: 1 CAT: 20
UF Multi Digit Number Systems

Multidimensional Actuarial Classification
CIJE: 2 RIE: 0 CAT: 11

Multidimensional Analysis of Classroom Interaction
CIJE: 3 RIE: 1 CAT: 21

Multidimensional Approach
CIJE: 22 RIE: 26 CAT: 15

Multidimensional Aptitude Battery
CIJE: 8 RIE: 2 CAT: 21

Multidimensional Behavior Rating Scale
CIJE: 0 RIE: 1 CAT: 21

Multidimensional Discrimination
CIJE: 2 RIE: 2 CAT: 21

Multidimensional Fear of Death Scale
CIJE: 2 RIE: 0 CAT: 21

Multidimensional Health Locus of Control Scales
CIJE: 4 RIE: 4 CAT: 21

Multidimensional Internal External Locus Control
CIJE: 1 RIE: 1 CAT: 21
SN Multidimensional Internal-External Locus of Control Reinforcement Scale

Multidimensional Item Difficulty
CIJE: 2 RIE: 1 CAT: 21

Multidimensional Latent Space
CIJE: 0 RIE: 1 CAT: 21

Multidimensional Models
CIJE: 16 RIE: 16 CAT: 15

Multidimensional Motivation Instrument
CIJE: 0 RIE: 1 CAT: 21

Multidimensional Multiattributional Causality Sc
CIJE: 6 RIE: 3 CAT: 21
SN "Multidimensional Multiattributional Causality Scale"

Multidimensional Needs Assessment Framework
CIJE: 1 RIE: 0 CAT: 21

Multidimensional Self Concept Scale
CIJE: 1 RIE: 1 CAT: 21

Multidimensional Stimulus Fluency Measure
CIJE: 2 RIE: 3 CAT: 21

Multidimensional Test of Self Concept
CIJE: 0 RIE: 2 CAT: 21

Multidimensionality (Tests)
CIJE: 6 RIE: 9 CAT: 21
SN See also "Dimensionality (Tests)" and "Unidimensionality (Tests)"

Multidisciplinary Academy of Clinical Education CA
CIJE: 0 RIE: 1 CAT: 17

Multidisciplinary Education
CIJE: 5 RIE: 7 CAT: 03

Multidisciplinary Gerontology Centers
CIJE: 1 RIE: 0 CAT: 05

Multidisciplinary Information Systems
CIJE: 3 RIE: 1 CAT: 15

Multidisciplinary Science Curriculum
CIJE: 1 RIE: 1 CAT: 03

Multidisciplinary Teams
CIJE: 20 RIE: 10 CAT: 10
UF MDTs

Multidisciplinary Training Teams
CIJE: 1 RIE: 1 CAT: 15

Multientry Multiexit Approach
CIJE: 0 RIE: 1 CAT: 15

Multiethnic Literature
CIJE: 0 RIE: 4 CAT: 16
UF Multi Ethnic Literature of the US (MELUS)

Multifactor Leadership Questionnaire
CIJE: 0 RIE: 1 CAT: 21

Multifactor Racial Attitude Inventory (Woodmansee)
CIJE: 1 RIE: 1 CAT: 21

Multifactorial Models
CIJE: 1 RIE: 2 CAT: 15

Multifamily Group Therapy
CIJE: 2 RIE: 0 CAT: 11

Multifeature Vocabulary Analysis Grid
CIJE: 0 RIE: 1 CAT: 21

Multigenerational Relationship
CIJE: 4 RIE: 6 CAT: 11

Multigenre Research Projects
CIJE: 0 RIE: 1 CAT: 15
UF Multi Genre Research

Multilateral Collective Bargaining
CIJE: 1 RIE: 0 CAT: 15

Multilateralism
CIJE: 2 RIE: 1 CAT: 16

Multilevel Analysis
CIJE: 16 RIE: 9 CAT: 15
UF Multilevel Analytic Methods

Multilevel Analytic Methods
USE Multilevel Analysis

Multilevel Evaluation Systems Project
CIJE: 0 RIE: 3 CAT: 19

Multilevel Information System
CIJE: 1 RIE: 1 CAT: 04

Multilinear Formula Scoring
CIJE: 1 RIE: 0 CAT: 21

Multilingual Indexes (Skolnik)
CIJE: 1 RIE: 0 CAT: 21

Multilingual Information Systems
CIJE: 1 RIE: 2 CAT: 15

Multilingual Survival Skills Program NY
CIJE: 0 RIE: 1 CAT: 19

Multilist System
CIJE: 0 RIE: 1 CAT: 15

MULTILOG Computer Program
CIJE: 3 RIE: 2 CAT: 04

Multimedia Centers
CIJE: 1 RIE: 0 CAT: 04

Multimedia Computer Systems
CIJE: 4 RIE: 0 CAT: 20

Multimedia Databases
CIJE: 8 RIE: 0 CAT: 04

Multimedia Information Systems
CIJE: 14 RIE: 0 CAT: 15

Multimedia Performances
CIJE: 1 RIE: 3 CAT: 16

Multimedia Rehabilitation Resources Project
CIJE: 0 RIE: 2 CAT: 19

Multimedia Reviews Index
CIJE: 1 RIE: 0 CAT: 21

Multimedia Technology
CIJE: 29 RIE: 7 CAT: 20

Multimodal Counseling
CIJE: 26 RIE: 3 CAT: 11

Multimodal Methods
CIJE: 13 RIE: 4 CAT: 15

Multinational Corporations
CIJE: 31 RIE: 22 CAT: 05

Multinational States
CIJE: 0 RIE: 1 CAT: 16

Multinomial Models
CIJE: 9 RIE: 2 CAT: 21

Multioption School
CIJE: 0 RIE: 1 CAT: 15

Multipass
CIJE: 1 RIE: 2 CAT: 19

Multiphased Need Assessment for Program Decisions
CIJE: 0 RIE: 1 CAT: 15

Multiplan Spreadsheet Software
CIJE: 0 RIE: 1 CAT: 04

Multiplative Classification
CIJE: 1 RIE: 0 CAT: 15

Multiple Access Scheduling
CIJE: 0 RIE: 1 CAT: 15

Multiple Activities Program
CIJE: 0 RIE: 2 CAT: 19

Multiple Affect Adjective Checklist
CIJE: 5 RIE: 2 CAT: 21

Multiple Alternatives Analysis
CIJE: 0 RIE: 2 CAT: 15

Multiple Alternatives Model
CIJE: 0 RIE: 3 CAT: 15

Multiple Alternatives Program
CIJE: 2 RIE: 3 CAT: 19

Multiple Architect Design
CIJE: 1 RIE: 0 CAT: 15

Multiple Assessment Programs and Services
CIJE: 0 RIE: 6 CAT: 21
SN See also "MAPS Placement Research Service"
UF CEEB MAPS Program; MAPS Tests

Multiple Attending (Psychology)
CIJE: 1 RIE: 0 CAT: 11

Multiple Audio Distribution System
CIJE: 1 RIE: 0 CAT: 15

Multiple Authorship
CIJE: 6 RIE: 3 CAT: 16

Multiple Birth Family
CIJE: 0 RIE: 1 CAT: 10

Multiple Careers Magnet Center TX
CIJE: 0 RIE: 1 CAT: 17

Multiple Caregivers
CIJE: 5 RIE: 1 CAT: 10

Multiple Case Study Approach
CIJE: 0 RIE: 1 CAT: 15

Multiple Categorization Test (Sigel)
CIJE: 0 RIE: 1 CAT: 21

Multiple Classes
CIJE: 0 RIE: 1 CAT: 15

Multiple Classification
CIJE: 7 RIE: 0 CAT: 15

Multiple Classification Analysis
CIJE: 2 RIE: 1 CAT: 21

Multiple Comparison Tests
CIJE: 1 RIE: 1 CAT: 21
UF Multiple Comparisons of Means

Multiple Comparisons
CIJE: 11 RIE: 10 CAT: 21

Multiple Comparisons of Means
USE Multiple Comparison Tests

Multiple Contingency Tables
CIJE: 0 RIE: 1 CAT: 15

Multiple Contracting
CIJE: 1 RIE: 0 CAT: 16

Multiple Contrast Tests
CIJE: 2 RIE: 0 CAT: 21

Multiple Correlation Formula
CIJE: 3 RIE: 2 CAT: 21

Multiple Counting
CIJE: 1 RIE: 1 CAT: 15

Multiple Criteria Utility Theory
CIJE: 1 RIE: 0 CAT: 15

Multiple Cue Learning
CIJE: 2 RIE: 0 CAT: 15

Multiple Cutoff Scores
CIJE: 0 RIE: 1 CAT: 21

Multiple Data Gathering Methods
CIJE: 2 RIE: 2 CAT: 15

Multiple Database Searching
USE Multi Database Searching

Multiple Digit Tests
USE Multi Digit Tests

Multiple Endorsements
CIJE: 0 RIE: 2 CAT: 16

Multiple Entry
CIJE: 0 RIE: 2 CAT: 15

Multiple Entry Multiple Exit
CIJE: 0 RIE: 1 CAT: 19
SN See also "Open Entry Open Exit"

Multiple Evaluations
CIJE: 3 RIE: 3 CAT: 15

Multiple Exemplar Training
CIJE: 0 RIE: 1 CAT: 15

Multiple Exit
CIJE: 0 RIE: 1 CAT: 15

Multiple Group Factor Analysis
CIJE: 1 RIE: 1 CAT: 15

Multiple Impact Therapy
CIJE: 1 RIE: 0 CAT: 11

Multiple Intelligences
CIJE: 38 RIE: 24 CAT: 15

Multiple Linear Regression
CIJE: 4 RIE: 8 CAT: 21

Multiple Linkage Analysis
CIJE: 0 RIE: 2 CAT: 15

Multiple Matrix Sampling
CIJE: 5 RIE: 3 CAT: 21

Multiple Measures Approach
CIJE: 12 RIE: 26 CAT: 15

Multiple Model Preschool Program
CIJE: 0 RIE: 2 CAT: 19

Multiple Moderator Approach
CIJE: 1 RIE: 0 CAT: 15

Multiple Negation
CIJE: 1 RIE: 0 CAT: 13

Multiple Operationalization
CIJE: 1 RIE: 0 CAT: 21

Multiple Option Programming
CIJE: 0 RIE: 2 CAT: 15

Multiple Personality Disorder
CIJE: 11 RIE: 2 CAT: 11

Multiple Progress Plan
CIJE: 0 RIE: 1 CAT: 03

Multiple Rating Items
CIJE: 0 RIE: 1 CAT: 21

Multiple Realities
CIJE: 0 RIE: 1 CAT: 15

Multiple Response Alternative Questionnaires
CIJE: 1 RIE: 0 CAT: 21

Multiple Response Data
CIJE: 1 RIE: 1 CAT: 16

Multiple Roles
CIJE: 3 RIE: 2 CAT: 16

Multiple Scalogram Analysis
CIJE: 1 RIE: 1 CAT: 21

Multiple Sclerosis
CIJE: 14 RIE: 5 CAT: 11

Multiple Set Training
CIJE: 1 RIE: 0 CAT: 15

Multiple Site Studies
CIJE: 6 RIE: 3 CAT: 15

Multiple Source Funding
CIJE: 0 RIE: 1 CAT: 16

Multiple Strategies Model for Effective Teaching
CIJE: 0 RIE: 1 CAT: 15

Multiple Talent Approach to Teaching
CIJE: 6 RIE: 0 CAT: 15

Multiple Task Interference
USE Intertask Interference

Multiple Teacher Factors Survey
CIJE: 2 RIE: 1 CAT: 19

Multiple Testing
CIJE: 1 RIE: 1 CAT: 21

Multiple Trails Plan
CIJE: 1 RIE: 0 CAT: 19

Multiple Transfer Students
CIJE: 0 RIE: 1 CAT: 10

Multiple Wage Earner Program
CIJE: 0 RIE: 1 CAT: 19

Multiplex Programing
CIJE: 1 RIE: 0 CAT: 15

Multiplicative Strategies
CIJE: 2 RIE: 1 CAT: 16

Multiplicity Sampling
CIJE: 0 RIE: 1 CAT: 21

Multiplier Effect
CIJE: 9 RIE: 3 CAT: 16

Multipoint Distribution Service
CIJE: 3 RIE: 0 CAT: 15

Multipurpose Academic Units
CIJE: 0 RIE: 1 CAT: 15
SN Academic units responsible for more than one type of degree or for more than one program under a degree
UF Multi Purpose Academic Departments

Multipurpose Buildings
CIJE: 3 RIE: 0 CAT: 04

Multipurpose Colleges
CIJE: 0 RIE: 1 CAT: 05
UF Multi Purpose College Facilities

Multipurpose Senior Services Program
CIJE: 0 RIE: 1 CAT: 19

Multiracial Education
CIJE: 1 RIE: 1 CAT: 03

Multiscore Depression Inventory
CIJE: 2 RIE: 0 CAT: 21

Multisensory Modality
CIJE: 1 RIE: 1 CAT: 11

Multiskilling
CIJE: 0 RIE: 1 CAT: 15

Multispectral Photography
CIJE: 1 RIE: 0 CAT: 20

Multistate Bar Examination
CIJE: 0 RIE: 3 CAT: 21

Multistate Surveys
CIJE: 3 RIE: 7 CAT: 16

Multitext Approach
CIJE: 0 RIE: 1 CAT: 15
SN See also "Single Text Approach"
UF Multi Text Method

Multitype Library Cooperation
CIJE: 7 RIE: 26 CAT: 15

Multitype Library Networks
CIJE: 13 RIE: 20 CAT: 05

Multiuse Furniture
CIJE: 1 RIE: 0 CAT: 04

Multivariate Normal Distribution
CIJE: 1 RIE: 1 CAT: 15

Multivariate Personality Inventory
CIJE: 3 RIE: 0 CAT: 21

Multivibrators (Electrical Equipment)
CIJE: 0 RIE: 2 CAT: 04

Multivision
CIJE: 1 RIE: 0 CAT: 04

Multiword Speech
CIJE: 1 RIE: 4 CAT: 13

Multnomah County CAPS Project OR
CIJE: 0 RIE: 1 CAT: 19

Multnomah County Intermediate Educ District OR
CIJE: 0 RIE: 3 CAT: 17

Multnomah County Outdoor School OR
CIJE: 0 RIE: 10 CAT: 17

MUM Effect
CIJE: 3 RIE: 0 CAT: 15

Mumford (L Quincy)
CIJE: 1 RIE: 0 CAT: 18

Mumford (Lewis)
CIJE: 2 RIE: 1 CAT: 18

Mumps
CIJE: 2 RIE: 0 CAT: 11

MUMPS Programing Language
CIJE: 0 RIE: 0 CAT: 04

Muncie Community Schools IN
CIJE: 1 RIE: 0 CAT: 17

Mundelein College IL
CIJE: 2 RIE: 2 CAT: 17

Munduruku
CIJE: 1 RIE: 0 CAT: 13

Municipal Annexation
CIJE: 0 RIE: 1 CAT: 14

Municipal Bonds
CIJE: 0 RIE: 5 CAT: 16

Municipal Cooperative Education Program
CIJE: 0 RIE: 1 CAT: 19

Municipal Information System
CIJE: 0 RIE: 1 CAT: 15

Municipal Overburden
CIJE: 6 RIE: 15 CAT: 16

Municipal Regulation
CIJE: 0 RIE: 2 CAT: 14

Municipal Universities
CIJE: 0 RIE: 1 CAT: 05

Munoz (Carlos)
CIJE: 0 RIE: 1 CAT: 18

Munsell Hue Circle
CIJE: 1 RIE: 2 CAT: 15

Murals
CIJE: 32 RIE: 2 CAT: 16

Murano Glass Center
CIJE: 0 RIE: 1 CAT: 17

Murdoch (Rupert)
CIJE: 0 RIE: 2 CAT: 18

Murdoch School NC
CIJE: 0 RIE: 1 CAT: 17

Murdoch University (Australia)
CIJE: 9 RIE: 4 CAT: 17

Murfreesboro City Schools TN
CIJE: 2 RIE: 1 CAT: 17

Murgia Decision
USE Massachusetts Board of Retirement v Murgia

Murguia (Theodore I)
CIJE: 1 RIE: 0 CAT: 18

Murinbata
CIJE: 0 RIE: 2 CAT: 13
SN A Garaman language (Australian Aborigine)
UF Marinbata

Murphy Durrell Diagnostic Reading Readiness Test
CIJE: 0 RIE: 1 CAT: 21

Murphy Durrell Reading Readiness Analysis
CIJE: 0 RIE: 8 CAT: 21

Murray (Donald M)
CIJE: 0 RIE: 2 CAT: 18

Murray (Lindley)
CIJE: 1 RIE: 0 CAT: 18

Murray (Pauli)
CIJE: 0 RIE: 1 CAT: 18

Murray County School District GA
CIJE: 0 RIE: 1 CAT: 17

Murray State University KY
CIJE: 7 RIE: 17 CAT: 17

Murrow (Edward R)
CIJE: 3 RIE: 2 CAT: 18

Muscatine Community College IA
CIJE: 1 RIE: 0 CAT: 17

Muscle Soreness
CIJE: 1 RIE: 0 CAT: 11
SN See also "Delayed Muscle Soreness"

Muscle Stimulation (Electronic)
USE Electronic Muscle Stimulation

Muscle Temperature
CIJE: 1 RIE: 0 CAT: 11

Muscular Disabilities
CIJE: 0 RIE: 1 CAT: 11

Muscular Dystrophy
CIJE: 7 RIE: 3 CAT: 11

Muscular Dystrophy Associations of America
CIJE: 1 RIE: 0 CAT: 17

Muscular Tension
CIJE: 6 RIE: 1 CAT: 11

Musculoskeletal Performance
CIJE: 7 RIE: 0 CAT: 11

Museum Collections
CIJE: 11 RIE: 4 CAT: 15

Museum Computer Network
CIJE: 0 RIE: 4 CAT: 17

Museum Educators
CIJE: 2 RIE: 1 CAT: 09

Museum Libraries
CIJE: 22 RIE: 0 CAT: 05

Museum of Fine Arts TX
CIJE: 0 RIE: 1 CAT: 17

Museum of Modern Art NY
CIJE: 3 RIE: 5 CAT: 17

Museum of Science and Industry IL
CIJE: 5 RIE: 0 CAT: 17

Museum of the Book in the Hague (Netherlands)
CIJE: 1 RIE: 0 CAT: 17

Museum of the Media
CIJE: 0 RIE: 1 CAT: 17

Museum Registrars
CIJE: 0 RIE: 1 CAT: 09

Museum Resource Center NY
CIJE: 0 RIE: 1 CAT: 17

Museum Studies
CIJE: 4 RIE: 6 CAT: 03

Mushroom Inspectors
CIJE: 0 RIE: 1 CAT: 09

Mushrooms
CIJE: 10 RIE: 0 CAT: 20

Music Ability
CIJE: 33 RIE: 8 CAT: 15

Music Aptitude
CIJE: 1 RIE: 0 CAT: 15
UF Musical Aptitude

Music Binding
CIJE: 1 RIE: 1 CAT: 16

Music Braille
CIJE: 0 RIE: 3 CAT: 16

Music Call Out Research
CIJE: 0 RIE: 1 CAT: 16

Music Center of Los Angeles County CA
CIJE: 0 RIE: 1 CAT: 17

Music Code of Ethics
CIJE: 1 RIE: 0 CAT: 22

Music Composers
CIJE: 18 RIE: 7 CAT: 10
UF Composers (Music)

Music Critics
CIJE: 0 RIE: 1 CAT: 09

Music Education Research Council
CIJE: 1 RIE: 0 CAT: 17

Music Educators National Conference
CIJE: 52 RIE: 2 CAT: 02

Music Educators National Conference Conv 1970
CIJE: 1 RIE: 0 CAT: 02

Music Ensembles
CIJE: 5 RIE: 4 CAT: 10

Music Evaluation Kit
CIJE: 0 RIE: 1 CAT: 04

Music Festivals
CIJE: 0 RIE: 2 CAT: 12

Music History
CIJE: 12 RIE: 1 CAT: 12

Music Identification
CIJE: 2 RIE: 1 CAT: 15

Music Libraries
CIJE: 10 RIE: 8 CAT: 05

Music Listening Reaction Scale
CIJE: 1 RIE: 0 CAT: 21

Music Literature
CIJE: 2 RIE: 0 CAT: 16

Music Lyrics
USE Lyrics

Music Notation
CIJE: 11 RIE: 1 CAT: 15

Music Supervisors Journal
CIJE: 1 RIE: 1 CAT: 22

Music Syntax
CIJE: 1 RIE: 2 CAT: 16

Music Television Network
USE MTV

Music Videos
CIJE: 22 RIE: 20 CAT: 16

Musical Academy (Sweden)
CIJE: 1 RIE: 0 CAT: 17

Musical Analysis
CIJE: 14 RIE: 5 CAT: 15

Musical Aptitude
USE Music Aptitude

Musical Aptitude Profile
CIJE: 10 RIE: 0 CAT: 21

Musical Equipment
CIJE: 3 RIE: 1 CAT: 04

Musical Independence
CIJE: 0 RIE: 3 CAT: 15

Musical Instrument Digital Interface
CIJE: 10 RIE: 3 CAT: 20

Musical Performance
CIJE: 4 RIE: 0 CAT: 15

Musical Scores
CIJE: 6 RIE: 7 CAT: 16

Musical Synthesizers
CIJE: 11 RIE: 1 CAT: 04

Musicals
CIJE: 7 RIE: 3 CAT: 16

Musil (Robert)
CIJE: 1 RIE: 0 CAT: 18

Muskegon College of Business and Technology MI
CIJE: 0 RIE: 1 CAT: 17
SN Name changed to "Baker College of Muskegon," Jun90

Muskegon Community College MI
CIJE: 1 RIE: 0 CAT: 17

Muskegon Skill Training Center MI
CIJE: 0 RIE: 1 CAT: 17

Muskhogee (Tribe)
CIJE: 0 RIE: 1 CAT: 08

Muskingum Area Technical College OH
CIJE: 0 RIE: 2 CAT: 17

Muskingum College OH
CIJE: 2 RIE: 3 CAT: 17

Muslims
CIJE: 19 RIE: 22 CAT: 10
UF Moslems

Musset (Alfred de)
CIJE: 1 RIE: 0 CAT: 18

Mussolini (Benito)
CIJE: 2 RIE: 2 CAT: 18

Must Carry Rules (Broadcasting)
CIJE: 0 RIE: 1 CAT: 14

Mutations
CIJE: 7 RIE: 1 CAT: 11

Mutilation (Human)
USE Human Mutilation

Mutiny on the Bounty
CIJE: 0 RIE: 0 CAT: 22

Mutism
CIJE: 18 RIE: 3 CAT: 11

Mutual Adaptation
CIJE: 2 RIE: 3 CAT: 15

Mutual Agreement Programing
CIJE: 1 RIE: 1 CAT: 15

Mutual Aid
CIJE: 1 RIE: 1 CAT: 16

Mutual Assistance Associations
CIJE: 1 RIE: 8 CAT: 10

Mutual Education and Cultural Exchange Act
USE Fulbright Hays Act

Mutual Funds
CIJE: 3 RIE: 0 CAT: 16

Mutual Gains Bargaining
CIJE: 0 RIE: 1 CAT: 15

Mutual Help Groups
CIJE: 2 RIE: 2 CAT: 10

Mutual Instruction
CIJE: 1 RIE: 0 CAT: 15

Mutual Involvement Review Activity
CIJE: 0 RIE: 1 CAT: 15

Mutual Life Assurance Company of Canada
CIJE: 1 RIE: 0 CAT: 17

Mutual Parenting
CIJE: 0 RIE: 1 CAT: 11

Mutuality
CIJE: 9 RIE: 4 CAT: 15

Mutually Aided Learning
CIJE: 1 RIE: 1 CAT: 15

My Antonia
CIJE: 2 RIE: 0 CAT: 22

My Class Inventory (Anderson)
CIJE: 5 RIE: 3 CAT: 21

My Class Inventory (Fisher and Fraser)
CIJE: 5 RIE: 4 CAT: 21

My Country School Diary
CIJE: 1 RIE: 0 CAT: 22

My Dream
CIJE: 1 RIE: 0 CAT: 22

My Education Scale
CIJE: 0 RIE: 1 CAT: 21

My Fair Lady
CIJE: 2 RIE: 0 CAT: 22

My Last Duchess
CIJE: 2 RIE: 2 CAT: 22

My Opinion Survey
CIJE: 0 RIE: 2 CAT: 21

My Vocational Situation
CIJE: 8 RIE: 1 CAT: 21

My Weekly Reader
CIJE: 1 RIE: 0 CAT: 22

Myasthenia Gravis
CIJE: 1 RIE: 0 CAT: 11

Mycenaean Civilization
CIJE: 1 RIE: 0 CAT: 12

Mycoplasma Pneumoniae
CIJE: 1 RIE: 0 CAT: 11

Mycoplasmas
CIJE: 0 RIE: 1 CAT: 20

Myelodysplasia
CIJE: 2 RIE: 0 CAT: 11

Myer Pollack Communication Research Lab PQ
CIJE: 0 RIE: 0 CAT: 17

Myers (Walter Dean)
CIJE: 1 RIE: 1 CAT: 18

Myers Achievement Motivation Scale
CIJE: 1 RIE: 0 CAT: 21

Myers Briggs Type Indicator
CIJE: 118 RIE: 87 CAT: 21

Myers Library AZ
CIJE: 0 RIE: 1 CAT: 17

Myklebust (Helmer)
CIJE: 1 RIE: 0 CAT: 18

Myklebust Learning Quotient Method
CIJE: 1 RIE: 1 CAT: 15

Myrdal (Gunnar)
CIJE: 8 RIE: 1 CAT: 18

Myself as a Teacher Scale
CIJE: 0 RIE: 1 CAT: 21

Mysteries (Literature)
CIJE: 25 RIE: 11 CAT: 16

Mystery of Heroism
CIJE: 1 RIE: 0 CAT: 22

Myth of Sisyphus (Camus)
CIJE: 0 RIE: 1 CAT: 22

Myxomycetes
USE Slime Molds

N Factors Questionnaire (Weiss et al)
CIJE: 0 RIE: 1 CAT: 21

Na Dene
CIJE: 2 RIE: 3 CAT: 13
SN Group of North American Indian languages, comprising the Athapascan family, Eyak, Haida, and Tlingit
UF Dene Languages; Nadene Languages

NABPLEX
USE National Assn Boards of Pharmacy Licensure Exam

NachNaff Scale
CIJE: 2 RIE: 1 CAT: 21

NACME
USE National Action Council for Minorities in Engineer

Nacogdoches High School TX
CIJE: 1 RIE: 0 CAT: 17

NACUA
USE National Assn College University Attorneys

Nadene Languages
USE Na Dene

Nader (Ralph)
CIJE: 6 RIE: 2 CAT: 18

Nader Nairn Report
USE Reign of ETS (Nairn)

Nadler (Leonard)
CIJE: 1 RIE: 1 CAT: 18

NAEB
USE National Association of Educational Broadcasters

NAEB Journal
CIJE: 0 RIE: 1 CAT: 22

NAES College IL
USE Native American Educational Services IL

NAFDC Assessment Profile
CIJE: 0 RIE: 0 CAT: 21

NAFTA
USE North American Free Trade Agreement

Nagari Script
CIJE: 0 RIE: 2 CAT: 13

Naglieri Draw a Person Test
CIJE: 0 RIE: 1 CAT: 21

Nahuatl
CIJE: 8 RIE: 7 CAT: 13

Nahuatl (Classical)
CIJE: 2 RIE: 0 CAT: 13

Naidu
CIJE: 1 RIE: 0 CAT: 13

Nail Biting Habit
USE Nailbiting

Nailbiting
CIJE: 0 RIE: 1 CAT: 11
UF Fingernail Biting; Nail Biting Habit; Onychophagia

Nails
CIJE: 1 RIE: 1 CAT: 04

Nairn Report
USE Reign of ETS (Nairn)

Naisbitt (John)
CIJE: 5 RIE: 2 CAT: 18

Naltrexone
CIJE: 7 RIE: 1 CAT: 11

Naltrexone Hydrochloride
CIJE: 2 RIE: 0 CAT: 11

Nambicuara
USE Nambiquara

Nambiquara
CIJE: 1 RIE: 1 CAT: 13
SN A Brazilian language — Ge-Pano-Carib phylum
UF Nambicuara

Name Authority Files
CIJE: 8 RIE: 5 CAT: 04
UF Authority Files (Names)

Name Derivation
CIJE: 2 RIE: 1 CAT: 13

Name Stereotypes
CIJE: 6 RIE: 6 CAT: 13

Names
CIJE: 81 RIE: 32 CAT: 13

NAMES Project Quilt
CIJE: 0 RIE: 2 CAT: 16

Namibia
CIJE: 7 RIE: 18 CAT: 07

Naming Pictured Objects Test
CIJE: 1 RIE: 0 CAT: 21

Naming Response
CIJE: 13 RIE: 8 CAT: 21

Naming Task
CIJE: 14 RIE: 2 CAT: 21

Nampa School District ID
CIJE: 1 RIE: 0 CAT: 17

Nanaimo School District 68 BC
CIJE: 0 RIE: 5 CAT: 17

Nancowry
CIJE: 0 RIE: 1 CAT: 13

Nancy Drew
CIJE: 6 RIE: 4 CAT: 22

Nancy Ernie Aggression Test
CIJE: 0 RIE: 1 CAT: 21

Nannies
CIJE: 3 RIE: 6 CAT: 09
UF Nursemaids

Nanoammeters
CIJE: 1 RIE: 0 CAT: 04

Nantes Graduate School of Business (France)
CIJE: 0 RIE: 1 CAT: 17
UF Ecole Superieure de Commerce de Nantes (France)

Nantucket Elementary School MA
CIJE: 0 RIE: 1 CAT: 17

Nanus (Burt)
CIJE: 0 RIE: 1 CAT: 18

Nanyang University (Singapore)
CIJE: 2 RIE: 0 CAT: 17

Napa College CA
CIJE: 0 RIE: 3 CAT: 17

Napa County Follow Through Project
CIJE: 2 RIE: 0 CAT: 19
UF Napa Vacaville Follow Through Research Project

Napa Infant Program CA
CIJE: 0 RIE: 1 CAT: 19

Napa Vacaville Follow Through Research Project
USE Napa County Follow Through Project

Napa Valley College CA
CIJE: 0 RIE: 1 CAT: 17

Napa Valley Community College District CA
CIJE: 0 RIE: 1 CAT: 17

Napa Valley Public Schools CA
CIJE: 1 RIE: 1 CAT: 17

Napi
CIJE: 0 RIE: 1 CAT: 18

Napier (John)
CIJE: 1 RIE: 0 CAT: 18

Napier College (Scotland)
CIJE: 1 RIE: 3 CAT: 17

Napier Polytechnic of Edinburgh (Scotland)
CIJE: 0 RIE: 3 CAT: 17

Napolean High School MI
CIJE: 0 RIE: 1 CAT: 17

Narayan (Jayaprakash)
CIJE: 0 RIE: 1 CAT: 18

Narcissism
CIJE: 27 RIE: 6 CAT: 11

Narcotic Antogonists
CIJE: 0 RIE: 1 CAT: 11

Narenji v Civiletti
CIJE: 1 RIE: 0 CAT: 14

Narodna Tehnika (Yugoslavia)
CIJE: 0 RIE: 1 CAT: 17

Narragansett (Tribe)
CIJE: 0 RIE: 3 CAT: 08

Narrative Inquiry
CIJE: 1 RIE: 2 CAT: 15

Narrative of Arthur Gordon Pym
CIJE: 1 RIE: 0 CAT: 22

Narrative Report Cards
CIJE: 2 RIE: 1 CAT: 16

Narrative Test Reporting
CIJE: 1 RIE: 1 CAT: 21

Narrative Text
CIJE: 98 RIE: 60 CAT: 16

Narrative Transcript
CIJE: 1 RIE: 0 CAT: 16

Narrative Verse
CIJE: 2 RIE: 2 CAT: 16

Narratology
CIJE: 3 RIE: 4 CAT: 13

Narrow Fellow in the Grass (A)
CIJE: 1 RIE: 0 CAT: 22

Narrowcasting
CIJE: 1 RIE: 0 CAT: 16

NASA Equal Opportunity Program TX
CIJE: 0 RIE: 1 CAT: 19

NASA Spacelink
CIJE: 1 RIE: 1 CAT: 04

NASA Technology Utilization System
CIJE: 1 RIE: 0 CAT: 15

Nasal Lisp
CIJE: 1 RIE: 0 CAT: 13

Nasality
CIJE: 14 RIE: 8 CAT: 13

NASBE
USE National Association of State Boards of Education

NASBE Joining Forces Program
USE Joining Forces (NASBE)

NASDC
USE New American Schools Development Corporation

Nash (Jay Bryan)
CIJE: 1 RIE: 2 CAT: 18

Nashua Public Schools NH
CIJE: 1 RIE: 0 CAT: 17

Nashville Metropolitan Public Schools TN
CIJE: 0 RIE: 9 CAT: 17

Nashville Reading Center TN
CIJE: 1 RIE: 0 CAT: 17

Nashville State Technical Institute TN
CIJE: 2 RIE: 2 CAT: 17

Nashville Union Catalog
CIJE: 0 RIE: 1 CAT: 22

Naskapi (Tribe)
CIJE: 3 RIE: 1 CAT: 08

Nassau Community College NY
CIJE: 7 RIE: 9 CAT: 17

Nassau Educational Resources Center NY
CIJE: 0 RIE: 1 CAT: 17

Nassau Library System NY
CIJE: 2 RIE: 0 CAT: 17

Nasser (Gamal Abd Al)
CIJE: 2 RIE: 0 CAT: 18

NASSGP
USE National Assn of State Scholarship Grant Programs

Nasson College ME
CIJE: 0 RIE: 1 CAT: 17

NASSP
USE National Association Secondary School Principals

NASSP Administrator Internship Project
USE NASSP Internship Project

NASSP Assessment Center Project
CIJE: 26 RIE: 3 CAT: 19

NASSP Bulletin
CIJE: 0 RIE: 3 CAT: 22

NASSP Internship Project
CIJE: 0 RIE: 1 CAT: 19
UF NASSP Administrator Internship Project

NASSP Learning Style Profile
USE Learning Style Profile (NASSP)

Nat King Cole School IL
CIJE: 1 RIE: 0 CAT: 17

NATAL 74
USE NATAL Programing Language

NATAL Programing Language
CIJE: 1 RIE: 1 CAT: 04
UF NATAL 74; National Author Language

Natchez Adams School District MS
CIJE: 0 RIE: 0 CAT: 17

Natchez Adams Vocational School MS
CIJE: 0 RIE: 1 CAT: 17

Natchitoches Parish School District LA
CIJE: 0 RIE: 1 CAT: 17

Nathan Hale High School WA
CIJE: 1 RIE: 0 CAT: 17

Natick Public Schools MA
CIJE: 1 RIE: 0 CAT: 17

Nation (Journal)
CIJE: 1 RIE: 3 CAT: 22

Nation at Risk (A)
CIJE: 80 RIE: 74 CAT: 22

Nation of Islam
CIJE: 2 RIE: 2 CAT: 17

Nation Prepared (A)
CIJE: 10 RIE: 10 CAT: 22
SN "A Nation Prepared: Teachers for the 21st Century"

Nation Responds (The)
CIJE: 1 RIE: 0 CAT: 22

Nation States
CIJE: 4 RIE: 2 CAT: 16

National Aboriginal Languages Program (Australia)
CIJE: 0 RIE: 1 CAT: 19

National Academic Advising Association
CIJE: 10 RIE: 1 CAT: 17

National Academy for School Executives
CIJE: 2 RIE: 2 CAT: 17

National Academy for Vocational Education OH
CIJE: 0 RIE: 1 CAT: 17

National Academy of Early Childhood Programs
CIJE: 4 RIE: 3 CAT: 19

National Academy of Education
CIJE: 6 RIE: 5 CAT: 17

National Academy of Engineering
CIJE: 4 RIE: 3 CAT: 17

National Academy of Peace and Conflict Resolution
CIJE: 2 RIE: 0 CAT: 17
UF United States Academy of Peace

National Academy of Sciences
CIJE: 42 RIE: 23 CAT: 17

National Accred Coun Agencies Serv Blind
CIJE: 0 RIE: 1 CAT: 19

National Accred Council for Agencies Serving Blind
CIJE: 0 RIE: 1 CAT: 17

National Accrediting Agency Clinical Lab Sciences
CIJE: 1 RIE: 1 CAT: 17

National Achievement Scholarship Program
CIJE: 0 RIE: 6 CAT: 17

National Action Council for Minorities in Engineer
CIJE: 1 RIE: 3 CAT: 17
UF NACME

National Action Group
CIJE: 1 RIE: 0 CAT: 17

National Administrator Research Study
CIJE: 0 RIE: 1 CAT: 22

National Adolescent Student Health Survey
CIJE: 1 RIE: 1 CAT: 21

National Adult Educ Professional Develop Consort
CIJE: 0 RIE: 1 CAT: 17

National Adult Education Centre (Somalia)
CIJE: 0 RIE: 1 CAT: 17

National Adult Education Programme (India)
CIJE: 2 RIE: 4 CAT: 19

National Adult Literacy Project
CIJE: 1 RIE: 26 CAT: 19

National Adult Literacy Survey (NCES)
CIJE: 1 RIE: 5 CAT: 21

National Advertising Division
CIJE: 0 RIE: 1 CAT: 17
SN Part of the Council of Better Business Bureaus

National Advertising Review Board
CIJE: 0 RIE: 1 CAT: 17

National Advisory Board Rural Information Needs
CIJE: 0 RIE: 2 CAT: 17

National Advisory Body Local Authority Higher Educ
CIJE: 0 RIE: 1 CAT: 17

National Advisory Com on Handicapped Children
CIJE: 3 RIE: 3 CAT: 17

National Advisory Commission on Civil Disorders
CIJE: 1 RIE: 3 CAT: 17

National Advisory Commission on Health Manpower
CIJE: 0 RIE: 1 CAT: 17

National Advisory Commission on Libraries
CIJE: 1 RIE: 0 CAT: 17

National Advisory Commission on Rural Poverty
CIJE: 1 RIE: 1 CAT: 17

National Advisory Committee on Accredit Inst Elig
CIJE: 1 RIE: 1 CAT: 17

National Advisory Committee on Black Higher Educ
CIJE: 0 RIE: 2 CAT: 17

National Advisory Committee on Educ for the Deaf
CIJE: 0 RIE: 2 CAT: 17

National Advisory Council for Career Education
CIJE: 1 RIE: 4 CAT: 17

National Advisory Council on Adult Education
CIJE: 0 RIE: 10 CAT: 17

National Advisory Council on Education Professions
CIJE: 1 RIE: 0 CAT: 17

National Advisory Council on Ext and Cont Educ
CIJE: 0 RIE: 1 CAT: 17

National Advisory Council on Indian Education
CIJE: 6 RIE: 21 CAT: 17

National Advisory Council on Migrant Health
CIJE: 0 RIE: 1 CAT: 17

National Advisory Council on Rural Development
CIJE: 0 RIE: 2 CAT: 17

National Advisory Council on Vocational Education
CIJE: 8 RIE: 25 CAT: 17

National Advisory Council on Womens Educ Programs
CIJE: 1 RIE: 0 CAT: 17

National Aeronautics and Space Administration
CIJE: 105 RIE: 161 CAT: 17
SN See add'l listings under "NASA..."

National Affiliation for Literacy Advance
CIJE: 1 RIE: 2 CAT: 17

National Agricultural Library DC
CIJE: 20 RIE: 16 CAT: 17

National Agricultural Library MD
CIJE: 0 RIE: 2 CAT: 17

National Agricultural Workers Survey
CIJE: 0 RIE: 1 CAT: 21

National Agricultural Workers Union
CIJE: 0 RIE: 1 CAT: 17

National Air Pollution Control Administration
CIJE: 9 RIE: 5 CAT: 17

National Air Sampling Network
CIJE: 1 RIE: 0 CAT: 15

National Alliance of Black School Educators
CIJE: 0 RIE: 3 CAT: 17

National Alliance of Business
CIJE: 4 RIE: 7 CAT: 17

National Alliance of Businessmen
CIJE: 13 RIE: 6 CAT: 17

National Ambient Air Quality Standards
CIJE: 1 RIE: 0 CAT: 14

National American Indian Court Judges Association
CIJE: 1 RIE: 0 CAT: 17

National and Community Service Act 1990
CIJE: 1 RIE: 4 CAT: 14
UF Public Law 101 610

National and Community Service Trust Act 1993
CIJE: 0 RIE: 2 CAT: 14
SN President Clinton singed the bill Sept. 21, 1993, dubbing the program "Americorps"
UF Public Law 103 82

National and Grindleys Bank Unlimited
CIJE: 1 RIE: 0 CAT: 17

National Apprenticeship Act 1937
CIJE: 0 RIE: 6 CAT: 14

National Apprenticeship Program
CIJE: 1 RIE: 3 CAT: 19

National Apprenticeship System
CIJE: 0 RIE: 1 CAT: 15

National Architectural Accrediting Board
CIJE: 1 RIE: 0 CAT: 17

National Archives and Records Administration
CIJE: 8 RIE: 7 CAT: 17

National Archives and Records Service
CIJE: 2 RIE: 1 CAT: 17
SN Became National Archives and Records Administration in 1985

National Archives Atlanta Branch GA
CIJE: 0 RIE: 1 CAT: 17

National Archives Chicago Branch IL
CIJE: 0 RIE: 1 CAT: 17

National Archives DC
CIJE: 14 RIE: 21 CAT: 17

National Archives Field Branches
CIJE: 1 RIE: 0 CAT: 05

National Archives Library DC
CIJE: 1 RIE: 1 CAT: 17

National Archives of Canada
CIJE: 1 RIE: 0 CAT: 17

National Art Education Association
CIJE: 30 RIE: 7 CAT: 17

National Arts Center of the Philippines
CIJE: 1 RIE: 0 CAT: 17

National Assembly of Local Arts Agencies
CIJE: 0 RIE: 1 CAT: 17

National Assessment Governing Board
CIJE: 0 RIE: 5 CAT: 17

National Board Examinations Part I
CIJE: 1 RIE: 1 CAT: 21

National Board for Certified Counselors
CIJE: 1 RIE: 1 CAT: 17

National Board for Certified Counselors Exam
CIJE: 0 RIE: 1 CAT: 21

National Board for Professional Teaching Standards
CIJE: 20 RIE: 13 CAT: 17

National Board of Chiropractic Examiners
CIJE: 1 RIE: 0 CAT: 17

National Board of Education (Sweden)
CIJE: 4 RIE: 2 CAT: 17
UF Swedish National Board of Education

National Board of Inquiry on Schools
CIJE: 0 RIE: 1 CAT: 17

National Board of Medical Examiners
CIJE: 55 RIE: 17 CAT: 17
UF NBME

National Board of Osteopathic Medical Examiners
CIJE: 0 RIE: 2 CAT: 17

National Board of Schools (Finland)
CIJE: 0 RIE: 1 CAT: 17

National Book Committee
CIJE: 2 RIE: 1 CAT: 17

National Book Development Council
CIJE: 0 RIE: 2 CAT: 17

National Book League
CIJE: 1 RIE: 0 CAT: 17

National Braille Association
CIJE: 1 RIE: 1 CAT: 17

National Broadcasting Company
CIJE: 7 RIE: 11 CAT: 17

National Broadcasting Training Center Radio TV
CIJE: 1 RIE: 0 CAT: 17

National Bureau of Standards
CIJE: 9 RIE: 9 CAT: 17

National Business Education Association
CIJE: 10 RIE: 3 CAT: 17

National Cable Television Association
CIJE: 2 RIE: 7 CAT: 17

National Cancer Institute
CIJE: 3 RIE: 4 CAT: 17

National Capital Parks Service
CIJE: 1 RIE: 0 CAT: 17

National Captioning Institute
CIJE: 0 RIE: 1 CAT: 17

National Career Development Association
CIJE: 5 RIE: 0 CAT: 17

National Career Development Guidelines
CIJE: 0 RIE: 24 CAT: 03

National Cartographic Information Center
CIJE: 2 RIE: 0 CAT: 17

National Catering Business Game
CIJE: 1 RIE: 0 CAT: 16

National Catholic Conference Interracial Justice
CIJE: 1 RIE: 1 CAT: 02

National Catholic Educational Association
CIJE: 10 RIE: 12 CAT: 17

National CEDA Tournament
CIJE: 0 RIE: 6 CAT: 19

National Census Study (Home Economics)
CIJE: 0 RIE: 1 CAT: 22

National Center Educ Media Materials Handicapped
CIJE: 1 RIE: 4 CAT: 17

National Center for Appropriate Technology
CIJE: 1 RIE: 0 CAT: 17

National Center for Atmospheric Research
CIJE: 1 RIE: 0 CAT: 17

National Center for Career Education
CIJE: 0 RIE: 3 CAT: 17

National Center for Child Advocacy
CIJE: 1 RIE: 1 CAT: 17

National Center for Deaf Blind Youths and Adults
CIJE: 1 RIE: 0 CAT: 17

National Center for Education Statistics
CIJE: 29 RIE: 120 CAT: 17
SN See also former names — "National Center for Educational Statistics" (1970s and earlier) and "Center for Education Statistics" (1986-88)

National Center for Educational Communication
CIJE: 0 RIE: 9 CAT: 17

National Center for Educational Planning
CIJE: 0 RIE: 1 CAT: 17

National Center for Educational Research and Devel
CIJE: 1 RIE: 4 CAT: 17

National Center for Educational Statistics
CIJE: 12 RIE: 13 CAT: 17
SN Former name of "National Center for Education Statistics"

National Center for Educational Technology
CIJE: 1 RIE: 1 CAT: 17

National Center for Fair and Open Testing
USE FairTest

National Center for Family Literacy
CIJE: 1 RIE: 2 CAT: 17

National Center for Health Services R and D
CIJE: 1 RIE: 0 CAT: 17

National Center for Health Statistics
CIJE: 6 RIE: 2 CAT: 17

National Center for Higher Educ Management Systems
CIJE: 5 RIE: 33 CAT: 17

National Center for Higher Education
CIJE: 3 RIE: 3 CAT: 17

National Center for Higher Education Management
CIJE: 0 RIE: 4 CAT: 19

National Center for Lifelong Learning
CIJE: 1 RIE: 0 CAT: 17

National Center for Medical Rehabilitation Res
CIJE: 0 RIE: 1 CAT: 17

National Center for Research on Teacher Learning
CIJE: 0 RIE: 1 CAT: 17

National Center for Research Vocational Educ CA
CIJE: 0 RIE: 1 CAT: 17

National Center for Research Vocational Education
CIJE: 2 RIE: 31 CAT: 17

National Center for Resource Recovery
CIJE: 1 RIE: 0 CAT: 17

National Center for School and College Television
CIJE: 0 RIE: 3 CAT: 17

National Center for School Leadership
CIJE: 3 RIE: 0 CAT: 17

National Center for Science Teaching and Learning
CIJE: 1 RIE: 4 CAT: 17

National Center for State Courts
CIJE: 0 RIE: 1 CAT: 17

National Center for the Improvement of Learning
CIJE: 3 RIE: 0 CAT: 17

National Center for the Study of Black Family Life
CIJE: 0 RIE: 1 CAT: 17

National Center for Urban Ethnic Affairs
CIJE: 1 RIE: 1 CAT: 17

National Center for Urban Partnerships
CIJE: 0 RIE: 1 CAT: 17

National Center for Visual Literacy
CIJE: 0 RIE: 1 CAT: 17

National Center for Vocational Education OH
CIJE: 0 RIE: 2 CAT: 17

National Center Improvement Educational Systems
CIJE: 0 RIE: 7 CAT: 17

National Center on Child Abuse and Neglect
CIJE: 2 RIE: 4 CAT: 17

National Center on Educational Outcomes
CIJE: 1 RIE: 2 CAT: 17

National Center on Effective Secondary Schools
CIJE: 1 RIE: 4 CAT: 17

National Center University Entrance Exam (Japan)
CIJE: 0 RIE: 1 CAT: 17

National Centre of Educ Technology (Hungary)
CIJE: 2 RIE: 0 CAT: 17

National Centre Research Rural Educ (Australia)
CIJE: 0 RIE: 3 CAT: 17

National Certificate (Scotland)
CIJE: 0 RIE: 2 CAT: 21
SN Administered by the Scottish Vocational Education Council

National Certification of Teachers
USE National Teacher Certification

National Certifying Exam Physicians Assistants
CIJE: 0 RIE: 1 CAT: 21

National Chicano Research Network
CIJE: 0 RIE: 1 CAT: 17

National Child Care Staffing Study
CIJE: 3 RIE: 2 CAT: 19

National Child Care Survey 1990
CIJE: 1 RIE: 2 CAT: 21

National Child Development Study
CIJE: 5 RIE: 2 CAT: 19

National Child Nutrition Project
CIJE: 0 RIE: 1 CAT: 19

National Child Research Center DC
CIJE: 0 RIE: 1 CAT: 17

National Childminding Association (England)
CIJE: 0 RIE: 1 CAT: 17

National Childrens Bureau (England)
CIJE: 4 RIE: 1 CAT: 17

National Childrens Dental Health Week
CIJE: 1 RIE: 0 CAT: 12

National Civil Service League
CIJE: 1 RIE: 0 CAT: 17

National Clearinghouse for Alcohol and Drug Info
CIJE: 0 RIE: 0 CAT: 17

National Clearinghouse for Bilingual Education
CIJE: 0 RIE: 1 CAT: 17

National Clearinghouse for Drug Abuse Information
CIJE: 1 RIE: 1 CAT: 17

National Clearinghouse for Smoking and Health
CIJE: 1 RIE: 0 CAT: 17

National Clearinghouse Offender Employment Restr
CIJE: 1 RIE: 0 CAT: 17

National Clinic on Technical Education
CIJE: 1 RIE: 0 CAT: 17

National Cluster Coordination Center
CIJE: 0 RIE: 1 CAT: 17

National Coalition for Campus Child Care Inc
CIJE: 1 RIE: 2 CAT: 17

National Coalition of Advanced Technology Centers
CIJE: 0 RIE: 1 CAT: 17

National Coalition on Television Violence
CIJE: 0 RIE: 1 CAT: 17

National Coalition to Abolish Corp Punish Sch
CIJE: 0 RIE: 1 CAT: 17

National Collaboration for Youth
CIJE: 0 RIE: 2 CAT: 17

National College Entrance Exam (Philippines)
CIJE: 1 RIE: 0 CAT: 21

National College Fairs
USE College Fairs

National College of Education IL
CIJE: 2 RIE: 2 CAT: 17

National College Orientation Workshop
CIJE: 1 RIE: 0 CAT: 02

National Collegiate Alcohol Awareness Week
CIJE: 0 RIE: 1 CAT: 12

National Collegiate Athletic Association
CIJE: 156 RIE: 24 CAT: 17
SN See also under "NCAA..."

National Collegiate Athletic Association Rule 48
CIJE: 9 RIE: 4 CAT: 14

National Collegiate Drug Awareness Week
CIJE: 0 RIE: 1 CAT: 12

National Comm New Tech Uses Copyrighted Works
CIJE: 2 RIE: 3 CAT: 17
UF CONTU

National Comm on Student Financial Assistance
CIJE: 1 RIE: 48 CAT: 17

National Comm on Teacher Educ Professional Stds
CIJE: 0 RIE: 3 CAT: 17

National Commission Employment Unemployment Stats
CIJE: 0 RIE: 1 CAT: 17

National Commission Financing Postsecondary Educ
CIJE: 0 RIE: 2 CAT: 17

National Commission for Employment Policy
CIJE: 0 RIE: 3 CAT: 17

National Commission for Manpower Policy
CIJE: 1 RIE: 2 CAT: 17

National Commission for the Social Studies
CIJE: 1 RIE: 1 CAT: 17

National Commission Libraries Information Science
CIJE: 35 RIE: 100 CAT: 17
UF NCLIS

National Commission on Accreditation
CIJE: 1 RIE: 0 CAT: 17

National Commission on Allied Health Education
CIJE: 2 RIE: 1 CAT: 17

National Commission on Excellence in Education
CIJE: 56 RIE: 141 CAT: 17

National Commission on Excellence in Teacher Educ
CIJE: 0 RIE: 41 CAT: 17

National Commission on Higher Education Issues
CIJE: 1 RIE: 0 CAT: 17

National Commission on Migrant Education
CIJE: 0 RIE: 1 CAT: 17

National Commission on Performance Based Education
CIJE: 1 RIE: 0 CAT: 17

National Commission on Secondary Educ Hispanics
CIJE: 0 RIE: 2 CAT: 17

National Commission on Secondary Vocational Educ
CIJE: 1 RIE: 0 CAT: 17

National Commission on Social Studies in Schools
CIJE: 11 RIE: 2 CAT: 17

National Commission on Testing and Public Policy
CIJE: 2 RIE: 1 CAT: 17

National Commission on Trustee Selection
CIJE: 2 RIE: 0 CAT: 17

National Commission on Working Women
CIJE: 0 RIE: 2 CAT: 17

National Commission Reports
CIJE: 13 RIE: 6 CAT: 16

National Commissions
CIJE: 5 RIE: 1 CAT: 16

National Committee Arts for the Handicapped
CIJE: 1 RIE: 2 CAT: 17

National Committee for Audiovisual Aids
CIJE: 1 RIE: 0 CAT: 17

National Committee for AV Aids in Educ Conference
CIJE: 2 RIE: 0 CAT: 02

National Committee for Citizens in Education
CIJE: 4 RIE: 4 CAT: 17

National Committee for Geochemistry
CIJE: 1 RIE: 0 CAT: 17

National Committee for Support of Public Schools
CIJE: 1 RIE: 0 CAT: 17

National Committee on Educ of Migrant Children
CIJE: 0 RIE: 1 CAT: 17

National Committee on Literacy
CIJE: 0 RIE: 1 CAT: 17

National Committee on Secondary Education
CIJE: 0 RIE: 1 CAT: 17

National Committee on the Employment of Youth
CIJE: 0 RIE: 2 CAT: 17

National Commodity Processing System
CIJE: 0 RIE: 1 CAT: 19

National Community Education Day
CIJE: 0 RIE: 1 CAT: 12

National Community School Education Association
CIJE: 3 RIE: 0 CAT: 17

National Computer Conference
CIJE: 0 RIE: 1 CAT: 02

National Computing Centre Limited (England)
CIJE: 0 RIE: 1 CAT: 17

National Conference Assessment Teaching Engl 1970
CIJE: 1 RIE: 0 CAT: 02

National Conference Diffusion Educational Ideas
CIJE: 0 RIE: 1 CAT: 02

National Conference of Bar Examiners
CIJE: 0 RIE: 2 CAT: 17

National Conference of Professors of Educ Admin
CIJE: 0 RIE: 0 CAT: 17
SN See also "National Council of Professors Educ Administration"

National Conference of State Legislatures
CIJE: 1 RIE: 4 CAT: 17

National Conference on Black Women 1st
CIJE: 1 RIE: 0 CAT: 02

National Conference on Career Education
CIJE: 0 RIE: 2 CAT: 02

National Conference on Consumer Protection
CIJE: 1 RIE: 0 CAT: 02

National Conference on Curriculum Development
CIJE: 0 RIE: 1 CAT: 02

National Conference on Independent Scholarship
CIJE: 0 RIE: 1 CAT: 02

National Conference on Population Education
CIJE: 1 RIE: 0 CAT: 02

National Conference on Poverty in Southwest 1965
CIJE: 0 RIE: 1 CAT: 02

National Conference on Program Planning and Eval
CIJE: 0 RIE: 1 CAT: 02

National Conference on Research
CIJE: 0 RIE: 1 CAT: 02

National Conference on Research in English
CIJE: 0 RIE: 6 CAT: 17

National Conference on Rural Education
CIJE: 0 RIE: 1 CAT: 02

National Conference on Social Welfare
CIJE: 1 RIE: 0 CAT: 17

National Conference on Studies in Reading
CIJE: 0 RIE: 11 CAT: 02

National Conference Visual Information Processing
CIJE: 0 RIE: 1 CAT: 02

National Congress for Puerto Rican Rights
CIJE: 0 RIE: 1 CAT: 17

National Congress of Parents and Teachers
CIJE: 2 RIE: 2 CAT: 17

National Congress on Catholic Schools
CIJE: 0 RIE: 0 CAT: 02
SN ...for the Twenty-First Century

National Congress on Engineering Education
CIJE: 0 RIE: 1 CAT: 02

National Congress on Medical Quackery
CIJE: 1 RIE: 0 CAT: 02

National Consortium for Humanizing Education
CIJE: 1 RIE: 4 CAT: 17

National Cooperative Educ Statistics System Forum
CIJE: 0 RIE: 1 CAT: 19

National Coordinated Cataloging Program
CIJE: 1 RIE: 1 CAT: 19

National Coordinating Council on Drug Education
CIJE: 1 RIE: 0 CAT: 17

National Correspondence College (Zambia)
CIJE: 0 RIE: 1 CAT: 17

National Council Community Services Continuing Ed
CIJE: 2 RIE: 1 CAT: 17
UF National Council on Community Services and Cont Ed

National Council for Accreditation of Teacher Educ
CIJE: 77 RIE: 58 CAT: 17

National Council for Educational Technology
CIJE: 6 RIE: 2 CAT: 17

National Council for Effective Schools
CIJE: 0 RIE: 1 CAT: 17

National Council for Geographic Education
CIJE: 21 RIE: 4 CAT: 17
SN See also "NCGE..."

National Council for Occupational Education
CIJE: 0 RIE: 1 CAT: 17

National Council for Technological Awards
CIJE: 1 RIE: 0 CAT: 17

National Council for the Social Studies
CIJE: 144 RIE: 29 CAT: 17

National Council for the Social Studies Conv
CIJE: 2 RIE: 0 CAT: 02

National Council for Vocational Qualifications
CIJE: 4 RIE: 4 CAT: 17
SN See also "National Vocational Qualifications (England)"

National Council Foreign Lang Intl Studies
CIJE: 2 RIE: 1 CAT: 17

National Council Licensure Exam Registered Nurses
CIJE: 5 RIE: 5 CAT: 21

National Council Licensure Examination
CIJE: 3 RIE: 2 CAT: 21

National Council of American Indians
CIJE: 0 RIE: 1 CAT: 17

National Council of Churches
CIJE: 3 RIE: 6 CAT: 17

National Council of Industrial Management Clubs
CIJE: 0 RIE: 1 CAT: 17

National Council of Jewish Women
CIJE: 0 RIE: 5 CAT: 17

National Council of Juvenile Court Judges
CIJE: 0 RIE: 1 CAT: 17

National Council of La Raza
CIJE: 1 RIE: 2 CAT: 17
UF La Raza National Council

National Council of Negro Women
CIJE: 2 RIE: 4 CAT: 17

National Council of Professors Educ Administration
CIJE: 0 RIE: 2 CAT: 17
SN See also "National Conference of Professors of Educ Admin"

National Council of Senior Citizens
CIJE: 0 RIE: 1 CAT: 17

National Council of State Dirs of Comm Jr Colls
CIJE: 0 RIE: 1 CAT: 17

National Council of States on Inservice Education
CIJE: 0 RIE: 4 CAT: 17

National Council of Teachers of Education
CIJE: 0 RIE: 1 CAT: 17

National Council of Teachers of English
CIJE: 124 RIE: 94 CAT: 17
SN See also "NCTE..."

National Council of Teachers of Mathematics
CIJE: 90 RIE: 73 CAT: 17
SN See also "NCTM..."

National Council on Agricultural Life and Labor
CIJE: 0 RIE: 1 CAT: 17

National Council on Community Services and Cont Ed
USE National Council Community Services Continuing Ed

National Council on Educ Standards and Testing
CIJE: 4 RIE: 3 CAT: 17

National Council on Educ Standards and Testing Act
CIJE: 0 RIE: 0 CAT: 14
UF Education Council Act 1991; Public Law 102 62

National Council on Educational Research
CIJE: 1 RIE: 7 CAT: 17

National Council on Higher Learning
CIJE: 0 RIE: 1 CAT: 17

National Council on Indian Opportunity
CIJE: 0 RIE: 1 CAT: 17

National Council on Measurement in Education
CIJE: 13 RIE: 10 CAT: 17
UF NCME

National Council on Schoolhouse Construction
CIJE: 0 RIE: 1 CAT: 17

National Council on Teacher Retirement
CIJE: 0 RIE: 1 CAT: 17

National Council on the Aging
CIJE: 1 RIE: 3 CAT: 17

National Council on the Arts
CIJE: 0 RIE: 1 CAT: 17

National Council on the Handicapped
CIJE: 0 RIE: 2 CAT: 17

National Crime Information Center
CIJE: 0 RIE: 3 CAT: 17
SN Component of the Federal Bureau of Investigation

National Crime Survey
CIJE: 5 RIE: 6 CAT: 22

National Criminal Justice Reference Service
CIJE: 0 RIE: 1 CAT: 17

National Dairy Council
CIJE: 2 RIE: 1 CAT: 17

National Data Base on Aging
CIJE: 0 RIE: 1 CAT: 17

National Data Resource Center
CIJE: 0 RIE: 1 CAT: 19

National Day Care Home Study
CIJE: 2 RIE: 7 CAT: 22

National Day Care Study
CIJE: 1 RIE: 14 CAT: 22

National Debate Topic
CIJE: 0 RIE: 10 CAT: 16

National Debate Tournament
CIJE: 18 RIE: 18 CAT: 02

National Debt
CIJE: 3 RIE: 0 CAT: 16

National Defense Educ Act Inst Teaching Disad Yout
CIJE: 1 RIE: 3 CAT: 02

National Defense Education Act
CIJE: 26 RIE: 59 CAT: 14
SN See also "NDEA..."

National Defense Education Act English Institutes
CIJE: 0 RIE: 3 CAT: 02

National Defense Education Act Institutes
CIJE: 8 RIE: 17 CAT: 02

National Defense Education Act Language Institutes
CIJE: 2 RIE: 20 CAT: 02

National Defense Education Act Summer Institutes
CIJE: 0 RIE: 2 CAT: 02

National Defense Education Act Title III
CIJE: 3 RIE: 22 CAT: 14

National Defense Education Act Title IV
CIJE: 0 RIE: 1 CAT: 14

National Defense Education Act Title V A
CIJE: 0 RIE: 5 CAT: 14

National Defense Education Act Title VI
CIJE: 0 RIE: 98 CAT: 14

National Defense Education Act Title VII
CIJE: 1 RIE: 7 CAT: 14

National Defense Education Act Title XI
CIJE: 1 RIE: 8 CAT: 14

National Defense Education Act Title XI Institute
CIJE: 0 RIE: 12 CAT: 02

National Defense Student Loan Program
CIJE: 3 RIE: 3 CAT: 14
SN Changed in 1972 to National Direct Student Loan Program

National Dental Association
CIJE: 0 RIE: 1 CAT: 17

National Development
CIJE: 19 RIE: 14 CAT: 16

National Diet Library (Japan)
CIJE: 0 RIE: 1 CAT: 17

National Diffusion Network
CIJE: 37 RIE: 112 CAT: 17

National Diffusion Network Programs
CIJE: 6 RIE: 141 CAT: 19

National Direct Student Loan Program
CIJE: 10 RIE: 78 CAT: 14
SN Changed in 1987 to Perkins Loan Program — formerly National Defense Student Loan Program

National Dissemination Conference
CIJE: 0 RIE: 3 CAT: 02

National Dissemination Project
CIJE: 0 RIE: 8 CAT: 19

National Documentation Centers
CIJE: 0 RIE: 1 CAT: 05

National Dropout Statistics Field Test
CIJE: 0 RIE: 1 CAT: 21

National Drug Policy Board
CIJE: 0 RIE: 1 CAT: 17

National Easter Seal Society for Crippled Children
CIJE: 1 RIE: 1 CAT: 17

National Economic Development Board
CIJE: 1 RIE: 0 CAT: 17

National Education Academy
CIJE: 0 RIE: 1 CAT: 17

National Education Association
CIJE: 175 RIE: 285 CAT: 17
SN See also "NEA..."

National Education Commission on Time and Learning
CIJE: 0 RIE: 12 CAT: 17

National Education Dissemination System
CIJE: 0 RIE: 1 CAT: 19

National Education Federation (France)
CIJE: 0 RIE: 1 CAT: 17

National Education Goals 1990
CIJE: 80 RIE: 253 CAT: 12
SN Six goals for American (U.S.) public education in the year 2000, including school readiness, a 90 percent graduation rate, student competence in basic subjects, world leadership in math and science, universal literacy, and safe and drug-free schools — first articulated at the "Education Summit 1989 (NGA)" (q.v.) and formally announced by the governors and President Bush in Feb90
UF Americas Education Goals 1990

National Education Goals Panel
CIJE: 2 RIE: 20 CAT: 17
UF NEGP

National Education Longitudinal Study 1988
CIJE: 14 RIE: 66 CAT: 19
UF NELS 88

National Education Practice File
CIJE: 0 RIE: 1 CAT: 19
UF Practice File (ERIC)

National Education Report Card
USE National Report Card

National Education Task Force de La Raza
CIJE: 0 RIE: 1 CAT: 17

National Education Trust Fund
CIJE: 2 RIE: 2 CAT: 17

National Educational Computing Conference
CIJE: 1 RIE: 1 CAT: 02

National Educational Finance Project
CIJE: 2 RIE: 6 CAT: 19

National Educational Loan Bank
CIJE: 0 RIE: 1 CAT: 17

National Educational Opportunities Act 1975
CIJE: 0 RIE: 1 CAT: 14

National Educational Radio Network
CIJE: 1 RIE: 2 CAT: 17

National Educational Resources Information Service
CIJE: 0 RIE: 1 CAT: 17

National Educational Television
CIJE: 8 RIE: 6 CAT: 17

National Electrical Code
CIJE: 0 RIE: 1 CAT: 14

National Electronic Injury Surveillance System
CIJE: 1 RIE: 1 CAT: 17

National Electronic Service Dealers Association
CIJE: 0 RIE: 1 CAT: 17

National Employer Supported Child Care Project
CIJE: 0 RIE: 3 CAT: 19

National Endowment for Democracy
CIJE: 0 RIE: 1 CAT: 17

National Endowment for the Arts
CIJE: 49 RIE: 17 CAT: 17

National Endowment for the Humanities
CIJE: 93 RIE: 54 CAT: 17

National Energy Conservation Policy Act
CIJE: 0 RIE: 2 CAT: 14

National Energy Conservation Policy Act 1978
CIJE: 0 RIE: 4 CAT: 14

National Energy Education Development Project
CIJE: 1 RIE: 1 CAT: 19
UF NEED Project (Energy Educ)

National Energy Plan
CIJE: 1 RIE: 2 CAT: 19

National Engineering Education Delivery System
CIJE: 0 RIE: 1 CAT: 19
UF NEEDS System (Engineering Educ)

National English Literacy Dem Prog LEP Adults
CIJE: 0 RIE: 1 CAT: 19

National Entrepreneurship Clearinghouse
CIJE: 0 RIE: 1 CAT: 17

National Environment Education Development
CIJE: 1 RIE: 4 CAT: 19

National Environmental Data Referral Service
CIJE: 0 RIE: 3 CAT: 17

National Environmental Education Act 1990
CIJE: 0 RIE: 2 CAT: 14
UF Public Law 101 619

National Environmental Health Association
CIJE: 3 RIE: 0 CAT: 17

National Environmental Policy Act
CIJE: 15 RIE: 3 CAT: 14

National Environmental Research Center
CIJE: 1 RIE: 0 CAT: 17

National Environmental Study Area
CIJE: 0 RIE: 3 CAT: 17

National Evaluation Systems
CIJE: 1 RIE: 2 CAT: 17

National Expansion
CIJE: 0 RIE: 2 CAT: 16

National Extension College (England)
CIJE: 4 RIE: 6 CAT: 17

National Extension Comm on Clergy Continuing Educ
CIJE: 0 RIE: 1 CAT: 17

National Extension Leadership Development Program
CIJE: 1 RIE: 2 CAT: 19

National Eye Institute
CIJE: 0 RIE: 1 CAT: 17

National Faculty Association
CIJE: 0 RIE: 3 CAT: 17

National Faculty Salary Survey
CIJE: 0 RIE: 4 CAT: 19

National Family Day Care Project
CIJE: 0 RIE: 3 CAT: 19

National Family Violence Survey
CIJE: 2 RIE: 1 CAT: 19

National Farm Labor Union
CIJE: 0 RIE: 1 CAT: 17

National Farmers Alliance and Industrial Union
CIJE: 0 RIE: 1 CAT: 17

National Farmers Union
CIJE: 0 RIE: 1 CAT: 17

National Federation of the Blind
CIJE: 3 RIE: 2 CAT: 17

National Field Directors Forum
CIJE: 0 RIE: 1 CAT: 02

National Film Board of Canada
CIJE: 13 RIE: 6 CAT: 17

National Fire Academy MD
CIJE: 0 RIE: 1 CAT: 17

National Fire Protection Association
CIJE: 1 RIE: 4 CAT: 17

National Football League
CIJE: 8 RIE: 4 CAT: 17

National Foreign Language Center
CIJE: 3 RIE: 1 CAT: 17

National Forensic Association
CIJE: 2 RIE: 6 CAT: 17

National Forests
CIJE: 2 RIE: 1 CAT: 20

National Forum on Education Statistics
CIJE: 0 RIE: 2 CAT: 17

National Forum on Information Literacy
CIJE: 1 RIE: 1 CAT: 17

National Foster Parents Association
CIJE: 2 RIE: 0 CAT: 17

National Foundation for Educational Research
CIJE: 4 RIE: 3 CAT: 17

National Foundation for Higher Education
CIJE: 1 RIE: 2 CAT: 17

National Foundation on Arts Humanities Act 1965
CIJE: 0 RIE: 2 CAT: 14

National Foundation on the Arts and the Humanities
CIJE: 1 RIE: 0 CAT: 17

National Foundation Youth and Adult Educ (Brazil)
CIJE: 0 RIE: 1 CAT: 17
UF EDUCAR Foundation (Brazil)

National Fund for Medical Education
CIJE: 1 RIE: 0 CAT: 17

National Gallery of Art DC
CIJE: 2 RIE: 2 CAT: 17

National Gazettes
CIJE: 0 RIE: 1 CAT: 16

National Geographic
CIJE: 3 RIE: 3 CAT: 22

National Geographic Kids Network
CIJE: 3 RIE: 2 CAT: 19
UF NGS Kids Network

National Geographic Society
CIJE: 28 RIE: 8 CAT: 17

National Geography Awareness Week
CIJE: 1 RIE: 1 CAT: 12
SN See also "Geography Awareness Week"

National Goals
CIJE: 19 RIE: 4 CAT: 16
SN See also "National Education Goals 1990"

National Governors Association
CIJE: 20 RIE: 6 CAT: 17

National Graduate Fellows Program
CIJE: 0 RIE: 1 CAT: 19

National Guard
CIJE: 4 RIE: 2 CAT: 17
SN See also "Air National Guard" and "Army National Guard"

National Gypsy Education Council
CIJE: 1 RIE: 0 CAT: 17

National Head Start Association
CIJE: 3 RIE: 2 CAT: 17

National Health
CIJE: 0 RIE: 1 CAT: 11

National Health Examination Survey
CIJE: 2 RIE: 1 CAT: 21

National Health Insurance
CIJE: 13 RIE: 4 CAT: 16

National Health Planning Information Center
CIJE: 0 RIE: 1 CAT: 17

National Health Service (United Kingdom)
USE British National Health Service

National Health Service Corps
CIJE: 5 RIE: 18 CAT: 17

National Health Service Corps Amendments 1985
CIJE: 0 RIE: 1 CAT: 14

National Health Survey
CIJE: 5 RIE: 1 CAT: 21

National Heart Lung and Blood Institute
CIJE: 4 RIE: 1 CAT: 17

National High School Debate Resolutions
CIJE: 0 RIE: 10 CAT: 16

National High School Postal Art Exhibition
CIJE: 1 RIE: 0 CAT: 12

National Highway Traffic Safety Administration
CIJE: 2 RIE: 8 CAT: 17

National Hispanic Scholar Awards Program
CIJE: 0 RIE: 1 CAT: 19

National Hispanic University
CIJE: 0 RIE: 1 CAT: 17

National Historic Landmarks Program
CIJE: 0 RIE: 1 CAT: 19

National Historic Preservation Act
CIJE: 2 RIE: 0 CAT: 14

National Historical Publications Commission
CIJE: 2 RIE: 0 CAT: 17

National History Day
CIJE: 19 RIE: 6 CAT: 12

National History Project
CIJE: 1 RIE: 2 CAT: 19

National History Standards Project
CIJE: 0 RIE: 2 CAT: 19

National Home Study Council
CIJE: 2 RIE: 10 CAT: 17

National Household Education Survey
CIJE: 0 RIE: 15 CAT: 21

National Humanities Faculty
CIJE: 2 RIE: 3 CAT: 17

National Humanities Series
CIJE: 0 RIE: 1 CAT: 22

National Identity
CIJE: 13 RIE: 3 CAT: 16

National Image
CIJE: 4 RIE: 2 CAT: 16

National Independent Living Skills Assessment
CIJE: 2 RIE: 0 CAT: 19

National Independent Regulatory Agencies
CIJE: 0 RIE: 1 CAT: 17

National Indian Bilingual Education Conference
CIJE: 0 RIE: 1 CAT: 02

National Indian Brotherhood
CIJE: 2 RIE: 0 CAT: 17

National Indian Brotherhood (Canada)
CIJE: 0 RIE: 1 CAT: 17

National Indian Child Conference
CIJE: 0 RIE: 1 CAT: 02

National Indian Council on Aging
CIJE: 0 RIE: 5 CAT: 17

National Indian Cultural Conference 3d
CIJE: 1 RIE: 0 CAT: 02

National Indian Education Association
CIJE: 2 RIE: 12 CAT: 17

National Indian Goals and Progress Act
CIJE: 0 RIE: 1 CAT: 14

National Indian Institute
CIJE: 0 RIE: 1 CAT: 17

National Indian Youth Council
CIJE: 1 RIE: 1 CAT: 17

National Indian Youth Leadership Model
CIJE: 0 RIE: 1 CAT: 15
SN See also "Indian Youth Leadership Camps"

National Individual Events Tournaments
CIJE: 0 RIE: 0 CAT: 19

National Industrial Conference Board
CIJE: 1 RIE: 0 CAT: 17

National Industrial Recovery Act
USE National Recovery Administration

National Industrial Television Association
CIJE: 0 RIE: 1 CAT: 17

National Industries for the Blind
CIJE: 1 RIE: 0 CAT: 17

National Information Center for Educational Media
CIJE: 5 RIE: 18 CAT: 17

National Information Center on Deafness
CIJE: 0 RIE: 2 CAT: 17

National Information Infrastructure
CIJE: 28 RIE: 11 CAT: 20
UF NII

National Information Policy
CIJE: 27 RIE: 12 CAT: 16

National Information Standards Organization
CIJE: 10 RIE: 1 CAT: 17

National Information Systems
CIJE: 11 RIE: 33 CAT: 15

National Inservice Network
CIJE: 1 RIE: 4 CAT: 17

National Inst Curriculum Development (Netherlands)
CIJE: 0 RIE: 1 CAT: 17

National Inst Mental Health Neuro Sciences (India)
CIJE: 0 RIE: 1 CAT: 17

National Institute Advancement Career Education
CIJE: 2 RIE: 0 CAT: 17

National Institute Automotive Service Excellence
CIJE: 2 RIE: 1 CAT: 17

National Institute Child Health Human Development
CIJE: 1 RIE: 5 CAT: 17
SN See also narrower "Pregnancy and Perinatology Branch (NIH)"
UF National Institute of Child Health and Human Devel

National Institute for Educ Research (Japan)
CIJE: 0 RIE: 1 CAT: 17

National Institute for Higher Education (Ireland)
CIJE: 0 RIE: 1 CAT: 17

National Institute for Public Information Officer
CIJE: 0 RIE: 1 CAT: 02

National Institute for Staff Organizational Devel
CIJE: 1 RIE: 1 CAT: 17

National Institute for Technical Training
CIJE: 1 RIE: 1 CAT: 17

National Institute for Testing Evaluation (Israel)
CIJE: 0 RIE: 1 CAT: 17

National Institute for Work and Learning DC
CIJE: 1 RIE: 1 CAT: 17

National Institute Independent Colleges Univs
CIJE: 1 RIE: 1 CAT: 17

National Institute Occupational Safety and Health
CIJE: 4 RIE: 3 CAT: 17

National Institute of Adult Education
CIJE: 2 RIE: 2 CAT: 17

National Institute of Child Health and Human Devel
USE National Institute Child Health Human Development

National Institute of Corrections
CIJE: 0 RIE: 1 CAT: 17

National Institute of Dramatic Art
CIJE: 1 RIE: 0 CAT: 17

National Institute of Education
CIJE: 109 RIE: 302 CAT: 17
SN See also "NIE..."

National Institute of Education (Singapore)
CIJE: 0 RIE: 1 CAT: 17

National Institute of Handicapped Research
CIJE: 2 RIE: 5 CAT: 17

National Institute of Justice
CIJE: 0 RIE: 1 CAT: 17

National Institute of Mental Health
CIJE: 33 RIE: 26 CAT: 17

National Institute of Public Affairs
CIJE: 0 RIE: 1 CAT: 17

National Institute of Senior Centers (NCOA)
CIJE: 0 RIE: 1 CAT: 17

National Institute of Standards and Technology
CIJE: 1 RIE: 1 CAT: 17

National Institute on Aging
CIJE: 2 RIE: 2 CAT: 17

National Institute on Disability Rehab Research
CIJE: 0 RIE: 1 CAT: 17

National Institute on Drug Abuse
CIJE: 1 RIE: 3 CAT: 17

National Institutes Innovative Currs Voc Tech Educ
CIJE: 0 RIE: 1 CAT: 02

National Institutes of Health
CIJE: 69 RIE: 26 CAT: 17

National Instructional Television Center
CIJE: 2 RIE: 9 CAT: 17

National Interest Council
CIJE: 0 RIE: 5 CAT: 17

National Interlibrary Loan Code
CIJE: 2 RIE: 0 CAT: 16

National Intern and Resident Matching Program
CIJE: 7 RIE: 1 CAT: 19

National Intramural Recreational Sports Assn
CIJE: 0 RIE: 1 CAT: 17

National Intramural Sports Council
CIJE: 3 RIE: 0 CAT: 17

National Invitational Meeting on Rural Postsec Ed
CIJE: 0 RIE: 1 CAT: 02

National Issues
CIJE: 3 RIE: 7 CAT: 16

National Issues Forum
CIJE: 11 RIE: 10 CAT: 15

National Joint Committee on Learning Disabilities
CIJE: 12 RIE: 5 CAT: 17

National Junior College Athletic Association
CIJE: 4 RIE: 3 CAT: 17

National Junior Horticultural Association
CIJE: 0 RIE: 1 CAT: 17

National Labor Relations Act
CIJE: 27 RIE: 16 CAT: 14

National Labor Relations Board
CIJE: 50 RIE: 18 CAT: 17

National Labor Relations Board v Yeshiva Univ
CIJE: 31 RIE: 27 CAT: 14

National Laboratory for Advancement of Education
CIJE: 3 RIE: 0 CAT: 17

National Laboratory for Higher Education
CIJE: 0 RIE: 1 CAT: 17

National Laboratory on Early Childhood Education
CIJE: 1 RIE: 7 CAT: 17

National Laboratory System
CIJE: 0 RIE: 2 CAT: 17

National Language Academies
CIJE: 0 RIE: 1 CAT: 05

National Language Arts Program
CIJE: 0 RIE: 1 CAT: 19

National Language Teachers Survey
CIJE: 0 RIE: 1 CAT: 21

National Languages and Literacy Inst (Australia)
CIJE: 0 RIE: 1 CAT: 17

National Languages Institute (Australia)
CIJE: 0 RIE: 2 CAT: 17

National Leadership Camp Curriculum
CIJE: 0 RIE: 1 CAT: 03

National Leadership Conference
CIJE: 0 RIE: 6 CAT: 02

National Leadership Institute
CIJE: 1 RIE: 0 CAT: 17

National League for Nursing
CIJE: 23 RIE: 13 CAT: 17

National League for Nursing Achievement Tests
CIJE: 0 RIE: 2 CAT: 21

National League of Cities v Usery
CIJE: 8 RIE: 2 CAT: 14

National Learner Verification and Rev Task Force
CIJE: 2 RIE: 1 CAT: 17

National Lekotek Center
CIJE: 1 RIE: 0 CAT: 17

National Lending Library of Great Britain
CIJE: 3 RIE: 1 CAT: 17

National Library and Information Services Act
CIJE: 1 RIE: 0 CAT: 14

National Library Network
CIJE: 2 RIE: 1 CAT: 17

National Library Network Project (Canada)
CIJE: 0 RIE: 1 CAT: 19

National Library of Australia
CIJE: 3 RIE: 1 CAT: 17

National Library of Canada
CIJE: 15 RIE: 7 CAT: 17

National Library of Medicine MD
CIJE: 53 RIE: 37 CAT: 17

National Library of Venezuela
CIJE: 0 RIE: 1 CAT: 17

National Library Service
CIJE: 0 RIE: 2 CAT: 17

National Library Service for the Blind
CIJE: 4 RIE: 34 CAT: 17

National Library Services for the Blind
CIJE: 0 RIE: 7 CAT: 17

National Library Week
CIJE: 7 RIE: 0 CAT: 12

National Life Safety Fire Code
CIJE: 0 RIE: 1 CAT: 14

National Literacy Act 1991
CIJE: 2 RIE: 9 CAT: 14
UF Public Law 102 73

National Longitudinal Study High School Class 1972
CIJE: 49 RIE: 211 CAT: 21

National Longitudinal Study Math Abilities
CIJE: 2 RIE: 25 CAT: 21

National Longitudinal Survey Labor Market Ex
CIJE: 2 RIE: 2 CAT: 21

National Longitudinal Survey Mature Women
CIJE: 2 RIE: 2 CAT: 21

National Longitudinal Survey New Youth Cohort
USE National Longitudinal Survey Youth Labor Market Ex

National Longitudinal Survey of Youth
CIJE: 12 RIE: 9 CAT: 21

National Longitudinal Survey Work Exp Mature Men
CIJE: 0 RIE: 4 CAT: 21

National Longitudinal Survey Work Exp Young Men
CIJE: 2 RIE: 1 CAT: 21

National Longitudinal Survey Young Women
CIJE: 2 RIE: 2 CAT: 21

National Longitudinal Survey Youth Labor Market Ex
CIJE: 11 RIE: 19 CAT: 21
UF National Longitudinal Survey New Youth Cohort

National Longitudinal Surveys
CIJE: 17 RIE: 33 CAT: 21

National Longitudinal Transition Study Spec Educ
CIJE: 2 RIE: 18 CAT: 21
SN "National Longitudinal Transition Study of Special Education Students"

National Lottery
CIJE: 1 RIE: 0 CAT: 16

National Manpower Institute
CIJE: 1 RIE: 2 CAT: 17

National Manpower Study
CIJE: 0 RIE: 1 CAT: 22

National Marine Education Association
CIJE: 2 RIE: 2 CAT: 17

National Marine Sanctuary Program
CIJE: 0 RIE: 1 CAT: 19

National Maritime Union
CIJE: 1 RIE: 1 CAT: 17

National Materials and Minerals Policy R and D Act
CIJE: 0 RIE: 1 CAT: 14

National Materials Conservation Symposium
CIJE: 1 RIE: 0 CAT: 02

National Media
CIJE: 0 RIE: 1 CAT: 16

National Medical Association
CIJE: 1 RIE: 0 CAT: 17

National Medical Audiovisual Center
CIJE: 2 RIE: 2 CAT: 17

National Medical Expenditure Survey
CIJE: 0 RIE: 0 CAT: 21

National Merit Scholars
CIJE: 10 RIE: 12 CAT: 10

National Merit Scholarship Corporation
CIJE: 0 RIE: 2 CAT: 17

National Merit Scholarship Program
CIJE: 5 RIE: 9 CAT: 21

National Merit Scholarship Qualifying Test
CIJE: 0 RIE: 17 CAT: 21

National Metric Study Conference on Education
CIJE: 0 RIE: 1 CAT: 02

National Metropolitan Area Study
CIJE: 0 RIE: 1 CAT: 19

National Microfilm Association
CIJE: 0 RIE: 4 CAT: 17

National Middle School Association
CIJE: 1 RIE: 3 CAT: 17

National Middle School Study
CIJE: 0 RIE: 2 CAT: 22

National Music Camp
CIJE: 1 RIE: 0 CAT: 17

National Natality Survey
CIJE: 0 RIE: 1 CAT: 21

National Needs
CIJE: 2 RIE: 3 CAT: 16

National Needs Analysis Design
CIJE: 0 RIE: 1 CAT: 15

National Needs Assess Educ Media Mater Handicap
CIJE: 0 RIE: 9 CAT: 19

National Network for Curr Coord in Voc Tec Educ
CIJE: 0 RIE: 8 CAT: 17

National Network for Early Language Learning
CIJE: 0 RIE: 0 CAT: 17

National Network for Educational Renewal
CIJE: 4 RIE: 7 CAT: 19

National Network of Centers for Bilingual Educ
CIJE: 0 RIE: 1 CAT: 17

National News Council
CIJE: 0 RIE: 2 CAT: 17

National Newspaper Literacy Day
CIJE: 0 RIE: 1 CAT: 12

National Nutrition Survey
CIJE: 0 RIE: 1 CAT: 21

National Observance of Childrens Sabbaths
CIJE: 0 RIE: 1 CAT: 12

National Occupational Competency Project
CIJE: 1 RIE: 0 CAT: 21

National Occupational Competency Testing Institute
CIJE: 3 RIE: 5 CAT: 17

National Occupational Information Coordinating Com
CIJE: 5 RIE: 17 CAT: 17

National Occupational Information Service
CIJE: 0 RIE: 2 CAT: 17

National Oceanic and Atmospheric Admin Library
CIJE: 1 RIE: 0 CAT: 17

National Oceanic and Atmospheric Administration
CIJE: 4 RIE: 8 CAT: 17

National Oceanographic Data Center
CIJE: 0 RIE: 3 CAT: 17

National Office for Research and Special Libraries
CIJE: 1 RIE: 0 CAT: 17

National Open University (Taiwan)
CIJE: 0 RIE: 1 CAT: 17

National Opinion Research Center
CIJE: 14 RIE: 6 CAT: 17

National Organization for Women
CIJE: 12 RIE: 4 CAT: 17

National Organization on Legal Problems of Educ
CIJE: 0 RIE: 3 CAT: 17

National Origin
CIJE: 5 RIE: 6 CAT: 16

National Origin Desegregation Assistance Centers
CIJE: 0 RIE: 15 CAT: 05

National Origin Minority Education NH
CIJE: 0 RIE: 0 CAT: 19

National Outdoor Leadership School
CIJE: 6 RIE: 2 CAT: 17

National Park Service
CIJE: 31 RIE: 12 CAT: 17

National Parks
CIJE: 17 RIE: 10 CAT: 05

National Periodicals Center
CIJE: 3 RIE: 2 CAT: 17

National Plan of Action for Women
CIJE: 0 RIE: 1 CAT: 19

National Planning
CIJE: 2 RIE: 15 CAT: 16

National Policy
CIJE: 44 RIE: 24 CAT: 16

National Policy Board for Educ Administration
CIJE: 2 RIE: 1 CAT: 17

National Policy on Education 1986 (India)
CIJE: 0 RIE: 1 CAT: 14

National Postsecondary Agricultural Student Organ
CIJE: 0 RIE: 0 CAT: 17

National Postsecondary Student Aid Field Test
CIJE: 0 RIE: 2 CAT: 19

National Postsecondary Student Aid Study
CIJE: 3 RIE: 15 CAT: 19

National Prepaid Tuition Program
CIJE: 0 RIE: 0 CAT: 19

National Press Club
CIJE: 0 RIE: 1 CAT: 17

National Press Photographers Association
CIJE: 0 RIE: 1 CAT: 17

National Preventive Dentistry Demonstration Prog
CIJE: 0 RIE: 1 CAT: 19

National Primary Survey (England 1978)
USE Primary Education in England

National Priorities
CIJE: 5 RIE: 3 CAT: 16

National Probability Samples
CIJE: 0 RIE: 0 CAT: 21

National Program for Acquisitions and Cataloging
CIJE: 3 RIE: 1 CAT: 19

National Program for Educational Leadership
CIJE: 1 RIE: 5 CAT: 19

National Program for Library and Information Serv
CIJE: 0 RIE: 12 CAT: 19

National Project I (FIPSE)
CIJE: 0 RIE: 0 CAT: 19
UF Better Information for Student Choice

National Project II (FIPSE)
CIJE: 0 RIE: 2 CAT: 19
UF Alternatives to the Revolving Door

National Project III (FIPSE)
CIJE: 0 RIE: 3 CAT: 19
UF Elevating the Importance of Teaching

National Project in Agricultural Communications
CIJE: 1 RIE: 0 CAT: 19

National Project IV
CIJE: 0 RIE: 3 CAT: 19
UF Examining the Varieties of Liberal Education

National Project on Career Education
CIJE: 1 RIE: 2 CAT: 19

National Project on Ethnic America
CIJE: 0 RIE: 2 CAT: 19

National Project on Violence and Bigotry
CIJE: 1 RIE: 0 CAT: 19

National Project Speech Commun Competencies
CIJE: 0 RIE: 1 CAT: 19

National Public Affairs Center for Television
CIJE: 0 RIE: 2 CAT: 17

National Public Affairs Study
CIJE: 1 RIE: 0 CAT: 22

National Public Education Financial Survey
CIJE: 0 RIE: 1 CAT: 21

National Public Radio
CIJE: 9 RIE: 15 CAT: 17

National Qualifications Framework (New Zealand)
CIJE: 0 RIE: 15 CAT: 21

National Rank
CIJE: 0 RIE: 1 CAT: 16

National Reading Center Foundation
CIJE: 1 RIE: 2 CAT: 17

National Reading Conference (Organization)
CIJE: 1 RIE: 34 CAT: 17

National Reading Difficulty Index
CIJE: 0 RIE: 1 CAT: 21

National Reading Improvement Act
CIJE: 1 RIE: 1 CAT: 14

National Reading Improvement Program
CIJE: 0 RIE: 2 CAT: 19

National Reading Research Center
CIJE: 1 RIE: 1 CAT: 17

National Recovery Administration
CIJE: 1 RIE: 1 CAT: 12
UF National Industrial Recovery Act

National Recreation and Park Association
CIJE: 19 RIE: 1 CAT: 17

National Referral Center
CIJE: 3 RIE: 1 CAT: 17

National Regional Resource Center of Pennsylvania
CIJE: 0 RIE: 2 CAT: 17

National Register of Historic Places
CIJE: 6 RIE: 1 CAT: 17

National Rehabilitation Association
CIJE: 2 RIE: 1 CAT: 17

National Report Card
CIJE: 1 RIE: 3 CAT: 21
SN Annual publication recommended by the National Governors' Association for state-by-state measurement of the educational achievement of both students and schools — do not confuse with the "National Assessment of Educational Progress," a.k.a. the Nation's Report Card
UF National Education Report Card

National Research Act
CIJE: 1 RIE: 1 CAT: 14

National Research and Development Centers
CIJE: 1 RIE: 3 CAT: 05

National Research and Education Network
CIJE: 78 RIE: 46 CAT: 17
UF NREN

National Research Center of the Arts
CIJE: 1 RIE: 0 CAT: 17

National Research Center on Gifted and Talented
CIJE: 1 RIE: 2 CAT: 17

National Research Center on Student Learning
CIJE: 0 RIE: 3 CAT: 17

National Research Council
CIJE: 46 RIE: 18 CAT: 17

National Research Council of Canada
CIJE: 5 RIE: 0 CAT: 17

National Research Development Corporation
CIJE: 1 RIE: 0 CAT: 17

National Research Service Awards
CIJE: 1 RIE: 1 CAT: 19

National Research to Development Network
CIJE: 0 RIE: 1 CAT: 19
SN "...for Public School Programs for the Hearing Impaired"

National Resident Matching Program
CIJE: 17 RIE: 2 CAT: 19

National Resource and Dissemination Center
CIJE: 1 RIE: 0 CAT: 17

National Resources Inventory 1982
CIJE: 0 RIE: 1 CAT: 21

National Restaurant Association
CIJE: 0 RIE: 1 CAT: 17

National Rifle Association
CIJE: 1 RIE: 0 CAT: 17

National Rural Center
CIJE: 1 RIE: 0 CAT: 17

National Rural Education Association
CIJE: 1 RIE: 1 CAT: 17

National Rural Education Research Consortium
CIJE: 0 RIE: 3 CAT: 17

National Rural Independent Living Network
CIJE: 0 RIE: 1 CAT: 17

National Rural Project
CIJE: 1 RIE: 4 CAT: 19

National Rural Research Personnel Preparation Proj
CIJE: 0 RIE: 1 CAT: 19

National Rural Small Schools Task Force
CIJE: 0 RIE: 1 CAT: 17

National Rural Studies Committee
CIJE: 0 RIE: 4 CAT: 17

National Safe School Study
CIJE: 0 RIE: 1 CAT: 22

National Safety Council
CIJE: 6 RIE: 1 CAT: 17

National Scholastic Press Association
CIJE: 1 RIE: 1 CAT: 17

National School Age Child Care Alliance
CIJE: 0 RIE: 1 CAT: 17

National School Boards Association
CIJE: 16 RIE: 12 CAT: 17

National School Boards Association Convention 1972
CIJE: 1 RIE: 0 CAT: 02

National School Food Service Program
CIJE: 0 RIE: 1 CAT: 19

National School for Educational Research
CIJE: 0 RIE: 1 CAT: 17

National School Health Services Program
CIJE: 0 RIE: 1 CAT: 19

National School Lunch Act 1946
CIJE: 5 RIE: 7 CAT: 14

National School Lunch Act 1970
CIJE: 1 RIE: 17 CAT: 14

National School Lunch and Child Nutrition Act 1975
CIJE: 0 RIE: 5 CAT: 14

National School Lunch Week
CIJE: 1 RIE: 0 CAT: 12

National School Public Relations Association
CIJE: 4 RIE: 3 CAT: 17

National School Safety Center
CIJE: 4 RIE: 3 CAT: 17

National School Volunteer Program
CIJE: 3 RIE: 6 CAT: 19

National Science Board
CIJE: 7 RIE: 5 CAT: 17

National Science Board Survey
CIJE: 1 RIE: 0 CAT: 21

National Science Education Standards (NRC)
CIJE: 0 RIE: 0 CAT: 15
SN NRC = National Research Council
UF Nature of Science (NRC Standards)

National Science Foundation
CIJE: 709 RIE: 956 CAT: 17

National Science Library (Canada)
CIJE: 0 RIE: 1 CAT: 17

National Science Network
CIJE: 0 RIE: 1 CAT: 17

National Science Policy
CIJE: 1 RIE: 0 CAT: 16

National Science Supervisors Association
CIJE: 0 RIE: 4 CAT: 17

National Science Teachers Assn Sunoco Sci Seminars
CIJE: 1 RIE: 1 CAT: 02

National Science Teachers Association
CIJE: 52 RIE: 63 CAT: 17

National Second Step Project
CIJE: 0 RIE: 2 CAT: 19

National Secretaries Association
CIJE: 1 RIE: 1 CAT: 17

National Security Agency
CIJE: 4 RIE: 2 CAT: 17

National Security Council
CIJE: 3 RIE: 1 CAT: 17

National Security Education Act 1991
CIJE: 0 RIE: 2 CAT: 14
UF Intelligence Authorization Act 1991 Title VIII; Public Law 102 183 Title VIII

National Security Industrial Association
CIJE: 0 RIE: 1 CAT: 17

National Seminar of American Indian Women
CIJE: 0 RIE: 1 CAT: 02

National Seminar on Vocational Guidance
CIJE: 0 RIE: 3 CAT: 02

National Serial Data System (West Germany)
CIJE: 0 RIE: 1 CAT: 04

National Serials Data Program
CIJE: 3 RIE: 4 CAT: 19

National Service
CIJE: 31 RIE: 18 CAT: 16
SN See also "Community Service" and "National and Community Service..."

National Service Corps (Ghana)
CIJE: 1 RIE: 0 CAT: 17

National Service Program (Nigeria)
CIJE: 0 RIE: 1 CAT: 19

National Service Secretariat
CIJE: 0 RIE: 1 CAT: 17

National Sex Equity Demonstration Project
CIJE: 1 RIE: 1 CAT: 19

National Small Business Training Network
CIJE: 1 RIE: 1 CAT: 17

National Small Government Research Network
CIJE: 0 RIE: 1 CAT: 17

National Society for Autistic Children
CIJE: 2 RIE: 2 CAT: 17

National Society for Performance and Instruction
CIJE: 15 RIE: 1 CAT: 17

National Society for Programmed Instruction
CIJE: 0 RIE: 1 CAT: 17

National Society for the Study of Education
CIJE: 14 RIE: 4 CAT: 17

National Society of Professional Engineers
CIJE: 3 RIE: 3 CAT: 17

National Society of Professors
CIJE: 0 RIE: 1 CAT: 17

National Space Science Data Center
CIJE: 1 RIE: 0 CAT: 17

National Spanish Examination
CIJE: 1 RIE: 1 CAT: 21

National Special Media Institutes Model
CIJE: 0 RIE: 1 CAT: 15

National Speech Communication Learning System
CIJE: 0 RIE: 1 CAT: 17

National Spelling Bee
CIJE: 0 RIE: 1 CAT: 19

National Standard Five Assessment
CIJE: 1 RIE: 0 CAT: 21

National Standard Prog Outdoor Leader Certificate
CIJE: 1 RIE: 0 CAT: 16

National Standard Reference Data System
CIJE: 4 RIE: 2 CAT: 15

National Standards
CIJE: 94 RIE: 50 CAT: 16

National Standards Project in Economics
CIJE: 0 RIE: 1 CAT: 19

National Star Ctr Disabled Youth Coll (England)
CIJE: 1 RIE: 0 CAT: 17

National Statistical Libraries
CIJE: 0 RIE: 1 CAT: 05

National Storehouse Educational Materials Success
CIJE: 0 RIE: 1 CAT: 15

National Strategy for Youth Development
CIJE: 0 RIE: 2 CAT: 15
SN HEW National Strategy for Youth Development Model

National Student Association
CIJE: 3 RIE: 2 CAT: 17

National Student Conference on Health Manpower
CIJE: 0 RIE: 1 CAT: 02

National Student Loan Reform Act 1979
CIJE: 0 RIE: 1 CAT: 14

National Student Lobby
CIJE: 0 RIE: 1 CAT: 17

National Student Recreation and Park Society
CIJE: 1 RIE: 0 CAT: 17

National Student Research Center
CIJE: 0 RIE: 1 CAT: 17

National Student Travel Association
CIJE: 1 RIE: 0 CAT: 17

National Study of Guidance
CIJE: 0 RIE: 2 CAT: 19

National Study of Intercollegiate Athletes
CIJE: 0 RIE: 1 CAT: 19

National Study of Internal Medicine Manpower
CIJE: 1 RIE: 0 CAT: 19

National Study of Local Operations under Chapter 2
CIJE: 0 RIE: 6 CAT: 19

National Study of School Evaluation
CIJE: 2 RIE: 4 CAT: 19

National Study of Secondary School Evaluation
CIJE: 1 RIE: 1 CAT: 19

National Summit on Agricultural Education 1989
CIJE: 0 RIE: 1 CAT: 02

National Supported Work Demonstration
CIJE: 6 RIE: 2 CAT: 19

National Survey Fringe Benefits Public Schools
CIJE: 1 RIE: 3 CAT: 22

National Survey of Black Americans
CIJE: 12 RIE: 1 CAT: 22

National Survey of Children
CIJE: 4 RIE: 0 CAT: 19

National Survey of Children 1981
CIJE: 0 RIE: 1 CAT: 22

National Survey of College Graduates (NSF)
CIJE: 0 RIE: 1 CAT: 21

National Survey of Compensatory Education
CIJE: 0 RIE: 1 CAT: 22

National Survey of Economic Education 1981
CIJE: 0 RIE: 1 CAT: 22

National Survey of Postsecondary Faculty
CIJE: 0 RIE: 1 CAT: 21

National Survey of Science Math and Social Studies
CIJE: 0 RIE: 1 CAT: 22

National Survey Salaries Wages Public Schools
CIJE: 2 RIE: 4 CAT: 22

National Symposia for Professionals Evalu Research
CIJE: 0 RIE: 2 CAT: 02

National Symposium Experimental Higher Education
CIJE: 0 RIE: 1 CAT: 02

National TAFE Clearinghouse (Australia)
CIJE: 0 RIE: 4 CAT: 17

National Taiwan Normal University
CIJE: 0 RIE: 2 CAT: 17

National Task Force on Education and World View
CIJE: 1 RIE: 0 CAT: 17

National Task Force on Political Action
CIJE: 1 RIE: 0 CAT: 17

National Task Force on the Integr of Hear Impd St
USE Task Force on Integration of Hearing Impaired

National Teacher Certification
CIJE: 6 RIE: 2 CAT: 15
UF National Certification of Teachers

National Teacher Examinations
CIJE: 60 RIE: 127 CAT: 21
SN See also "NTE..."

National Teachers Association
CIJE: 1 RIE: 0 CAT: 17

National Technical Information Service
CIJE: 38 RIE: 26 CAT: 17

National Technical Institute for the Deaf
CIJE: 29 RIE: 39 CAT: 17

National Technical Teachers College (Nigeria)
CIJE: 0 RIE: 1 CAT: 17

National Technological University
CIJE: 5 RIE: 6 CAT: 17

National Telecommunications and Information Admin
CIJE: 1 RIE: 0 CAT: 17

National Television System Committee
CIJE: 0 RIE: 1 CAT: 17

National Testing
CIJE: 2 RIE: 0 CAT: 21
SN See also "American Achievement Tests"

National Testing Network in Writing
CIJE: 0 RIE: 1 CAT: 17

National Textbook Program
CIJE: 1 RIE: 0 CAT: 19

National Therapeutic Recreation Society
CIJE: 3 RIE: 1 CAT: 17

National Training Agency
CIJE: 1 RIE: 0 CAT: 17

National Training Boards
CIJE: 0 RIE: 3 CAT: 15

National Training Laboratories
CIJE: 3 RIE: 7 CAT: 17

National Training School for Boys
CIJE: 0 RIE: 5 CAT: 17

National Training System
CIJE: 0 RIE: 1 CAT: 19

National Transportation Study
CIJE: 0 RIE: 1 CAT: 19

National Tribal Chairmens Association
CIJE: 1 RIE: 3 CAT: 17

National Trust for Historic Preservation
CIJE: 9 RIE: 1 CAT: 17

National Tsing Hua University (Taiwan)
CIJE: 0 RIE: 3 CAT: 17

National Union Catalog
CIJE: 6 RIE: 13 CAT: 22

National Union Hospital Health Care Employees
CIJE: 1 RIE: 0 CAT: 17

National Union of School Students (England)
CIJE: 1 RIE: 0 CAT: 17

National Union of Students (England)
CIJE: 0 RIE: 0 CAT: 17

National Union of Teachers
CIJE: 3 RIE: 0 CAT: 17

National Union of Teachers (Israel)
CIJE: 1 RIE: 0 CAT: 17

National Universities Commission (Nigeria)
CIJE: 0 RIE: 2 CAT: 17

National University Consortium Telecomm Teaching
CIJE: 2 RIE: 1 CAT: 17

National University Continuing Education Assn
CIJE: 2 RIE: 7 CAT: 17

National University Extension Association
CIJE: 9 RIE: 19 CAT: 17

National University of Malaysia
CIJE: 0 RIE: 1 CAT: 17

National University of Mexico
USE National Autonomous University of Mexico

National University of Singapore
CIJE: 5 RIE: 1 CAT: 17

National University of Zaire
CIJE: 2 RIE: 0 CAT: 17
UF University of Zaire

National University Teleconference Network
CIJE: 1 RIE: 1 CAT: 17

National Urban Education Goals
CIJE: 0 RIE: 1 CAT: 12

National Urban League
CIJE: 2 RIE: 4 CAT: 17

National Vocational Agricultural Teachers Assn
CIJE: 0 RIE: 0 CAT: 17

National Vocational Facility Planning Conference
CIJE: 0 RIE: 1 CAT: 02

National Vocational Guidance Association
CIJE: 7 RIE: 0 CAT: 17

National Vocational Qualifications (England)
CIJE: 15 RIE: 19 CAT: 21
SN See also "National Council for Vocational Qualifications"

National Vocational Teacher Competency Exams
CIJE: 0 RIE: 1 CAT: 21

National Vocational Technical Teacher
CIJE: 0 RIE: 1 CAT: 02

National War College DC
CIJE: 0 RIE: 2 CAT: 17

National Water Quality Initiative
CIJE: 0 RIE: 1 CAT: 19

National Wealth
CIJE: 0 RIE: 1 CAT: 16

National Welfare Rights Organization
CIJE: 2 RIE: 0 CAT: 17

National Wildlife Federation
CIJE: 5 RIE: 3 CAT: 17

National Womens Employment and Education Project
CIJE: 0 RIE: 1 CAT: 19

National Womens History Month
USE Womens History Month

National Womens History Week
CIJE: 0 RIE: 4 CAT: 12
SN See also "Womens History Week"

National Womens History Week Project
CIJE: 0 RIE: 7 CAT: 19

National Womens Political Caucus
CIJE: 0 RIE: 1 CAT: 17

National Workplace Literacy Program
CIJE: 2 RIE: 13 CAT: 19

National Writing Project
CIJE: 39 RIE: 52 CAT: 19

National Young Farmer Educational Institute
CIJE: 1 RIE: 0 CAT: 02

National Youth Administration
CIJE: 1 RIE: 2 CAT: 17

National Youth Apprenticeship Initiative
CIJE: 0 RIE: 1 CAT: 19

National Youth Clubs of America
CIJE: 0 RIE: 1 CAT: 17

National Youth Conference on Highway Safety
CIJE: 0 RIE: 1 CAT: 02

National Youth in Care Network (Canada)
CIJE: 0 RIE: 1 CAT: 17
UF Youth in Care Network (Canada)

National Youth Leadership Council
CIJE: 0 RIE: 2 CAT: 17

National Youth Service
CIJE: 2 RIE: 0 CAT: 16

National Youth Sports Program
CIJE: 1 RIE: 2 CAT: 19

Nationality Origin System
CIJE: 1 RIE: 0 CAT: 15

Nations Report Card
USE National Assessment of Educational Progress

Nationwide Curriculum
CIJE: 0 RIE: 1 CAT: 03

Nationwide Curriculum for Industrial Arts
CIJE: 0 RIE: 1 CAT: 03

Nationwide Insurance Company
CIJE: 0 RIE: 1 CAT: 17

Nationwide Networks
CIJE: 1 RIE: 2 CAT: 04

Nationwide Planning
CIJE: 0 RIE: 2 CAT: 15

Native American Administrator Program
CIJE: 0 RIE: 1 CAT: 19

Native American Church
CIJE: 1 RIE: 1 CAT: 17

Native American Educational Services IL
CIJE: 0 RIE: 0 CAT: 17
UF NAES College IL

Native American Gifted Program Model
CIJE: 0 RIE: 1 CAT: 19

Native American Languages Act 1992
CIJE: 0 RIE: 2 CAT: 14
UF Public Law 102 524

Native American Programs Act 1974
CIJE: 0 RIE: 2 CAT: 14

Native American Programs Act 1974 Title VIII
CIJE: 0 RIE: 1 CAT: 14

Native American Rights Fund
CIJE: 1 RIE: 4 CAT: 17

Native American Studies
CIJE: 16 RIE: 14 CAT: 03
UF Native Studies (American)

Native Americans
CIJE: 116 RIE: 252 CAT: 08

Native Education Project AB
CIJE: 0 RIE: 1 CAT: 19

Native English Speaking
USE English Speaking

Native Foods
CIJE: 0 RIE: 1 CAT: 16

Native Hawaiian Educational Assessment Project
CIJE: 0 RIE: 1 CAT: 19

Native Indian Teacher Education Program
CIJE: 2 RIE: 2 CAT: 19

Native Indian Youth in Museums Project
CIJE: 0 RIE: 1 CAT: 19

Native Infant Program (Canada)
CIJE: 0 RIE: 1 CAT: 19

Native Intelligence Hypothesis
CIJE: 0 RIE: 1 CAT: 15

Native Language
CIJE: 47 RIE: 20 CAT: 13
UF Vernacular

Native Language Assessment
CIJE: 1 RIE: 1 CAT: 13

Native Son
CIJE: 5 RIE: 2 CAT: 22

Native Students (Nontransfers)
USE Nontransfer Students

Native Studies
CIJE: 1 RIE: 19 CAT: 03
SN Use more specific Identifier "Native American Studies," if possible

Native Studies (American)
USE Native American Studies

Nativism
CIJE: 4 RIE: 3 CAT: 16

Nativistic Movement
CIJE: 3 RIE: 2 CAT: 12

Nativization (Language)
CIJE: 2 RIE: 1 CAT: 13

Natrona County Public Library WY
CIJE: 1 RIE: 1 CAT: 17

Natural Approach (Languages)
CIJE: 14 RIE: 9 CAT: 13

Natural Childbirth
CIJE: 0 RIE: 1 CAT: 11

Natural Family Planning
CIJE: 0 RIE: 2 CAT: 11

Natural Foods
CIJE: 2 RIE: 1 CAT: 20

Natural Gas Technicians
USE Gas Technicians

Natural Helpers
CIJE: 3 RIE: 2 CAT: 10

Natural History
CIJE: 17 RIE: 8 CAT: 12

Natural Knowledge
CIJE: 0 RIE: 1 CAT: 15

Natural Language
CIJE: 76 RIE: 44 CAT: 13

Natural Languages
CIJE: 8 RIE: 9 CAT: 13

Natural Learning
CIJE: 3 RIE: 2 CAT: 15

Natural Literacy Development
CIJE: 0 RIE: 2 CAT: 13

Natural Method (Language Learning)
CIJE: 6 RIE: 2 CAT: 13

Natural Resource Information System
CIJE: 0 RIE: 3 CAT: 15

Natural Resources Council of America
CIJE: 1 RIE: 0 CAT: 17

Natural Resources Management
CIJE: 10 RIE: 7 CAT: 16

Natural Rights
CIJE: 4 RIE: 0 CAT: 16

Natural Selection
CIJE: 30 RIE: 4 CAT: 20

Natural Systems
CIJE: 2 RIE: 3 CAT: 15

Naturalistic Content
CIJE: 1 RIE: 2 CAT: 16

Naturalistic Evaluation
CIJE: 23 RIE: 13 CAT: 21

Naturalistic Research
CIJE: 34 RIE: 51 CAT: 16

Naturalistic Studies
CIJE: 16 RIE: 12 CAT: 16

Naturalization Programs
CIJE: 7 RIE: 19 CAT: 19

Nature
CIJE: 74 RIE: 21 CAT: 20

Nature Books
CIJE: 3 RIE: 0 CAT: 16

Nature Computer Camp DC
CIJE: 0 RIE: 2 CAT: 19

Nature Conservancy
CIJE: 0 RIE: 1 CAT: 17

Nature Method Institute
CIJE: 0 RIE: 1 CAT: 17

Nature of Interpolated Passages
CIJE: 1 RIE: 0 CAT: 15

Nature of Science
CIJE: 26 RIE: 7 CAT: 20

Nature of Science (NRC Standards)
USE National Science Education Standards (NRC)

Nature of Science Scale
CIJE: 3 RIE: 0 CAT: 21

Nature of Scientific Knowledge Scale
CIJE: 3 RIE: 2 CAT: 21

Nature Photography
CIJE: 3 RIE: 0 CAT: 03

Nature Stories
CIJE: 4 RIE: 0 CAT: 16

Nature Study
CIJE: 49 RIE: 15 CAT: 15

Nature Study Movement
CIJE: 3 RIE: 2 CAT: 20

Nature Study Society
CIJE: 3 RIE: 0 CAT: 17

Nature Writing
CIJE: 0 RIE: 2 CAT: 03

Naturopaths
CIJE: 0 RIE: 1 CAT: 11

Naturopathy
CIJE: 1 RIE: 0 CAT: 20

Nautical Science Education
CIJE: 1 RIE: 1 CAT: 20

Nava Nirmana Community Development
CIJE: 1 RIE: 0 CAT: 19

Navaho Rehabilitation Project
CIJE: 0 RIE: 1 CAT: 19

Navajo Area School Board Association
CIJE: 0 RIE: 1 CAT: 17

Navajo Bordertown Dormitory Program
CIJE: 0 RIE: 2 CAT: 19

Navajo Community College AZ
CIJE: 11 RIE: 17 CAT: 17

Navajo Curriculum Center
CIJE: 1 RIE: 1 CAT: 17

Navajo Education Resource Center AZ
CIJE: 0 RIE: 1 CAT: 17

Navajo Health Authority
CIJE: 0 RIE: 5 CAT: 17

Navajo Health Education Project
CIJE: 0 RIE: 1 CAT: 19

Navajo Hopi Long Range Rehabilitation Act 1950
CIJE: 1 RIE: 0 CAT: 14

Navajo Hopi Teacher Corps Program
CIJE: 0 RIE: 1 CAT: 19

Navajo Indian Irrigation Project
CIJE: 2 RIE: 1 CAT: 19

Navajo Mission Academy NM
CIJE: 0 RIE: 1 CAT: 17

Navajo Reservation
CIJE: 20 RIE: 13 CAT: 17

Navajo Special Education Teacher Develop Prog AZ
CIJE: 0 RIE: 1 CAT: 19

Navajo Studies
CIJE: 2 RIE: 3 CAT: 03

Navajo Treaty 1868
USE Treaty with Navajo Indians 1868

Navajo Tribal Education Committee
CIJE: 1 RIE: 2 CAT: 17

Naval Academy MD
CIJE: 5 RIE: 18 CAT: 17
SN See also "USNA..."

Naval Academy Student Response Monitor
CIJE: 1 RIE: 0 CAT: 21

Naval Architecture
CIJE: 0 RIE: 1 CAT: 20

Naval Avionics Facility
CIJE: 0 RIE: 1 CAT: 17

Naval Education and Training Command
CIJE: 0 RIE: 3 CAT: 17

Naval Education and Training System
CIJE: 0 RIE: 5 CAT: 17

Naval Education Training Program Development Ctr
CIJE: 0 RIE: 1 CAT: 17

Naval Electronics School
CIJE: 0 RIE: 2 CAT: 17

Naval Flight Officer Training Program
CIJE: 0 RIE: 1 CAT: 19

Naval History
CIJE: 1 RIE: 3 CAT: 12

Naval Junior Reserve Officers Training Corps
CIJE: 0 RIE: 1 CAT: 17

Naval Medical Training Institute
CIJE: 0 RIE: 1 CAT: 17

Naval Observatory DC
CIJE: 0 RIE: 0 CAT: 17

Naval Occupational Task Analysis Program
CIJE: 0 RIE: 1 CAT: 19

Naval Personnel Training Research Laboratory
CIJE: 0 RIE: 2 CAT: 17

Naval Research Laboratory
CIJE: 2 RIE: 2 CAT: 17

Naval Reserve Officers Training Corps
CIJE: 0 RIE: 3 CAT: 17

Naval Reserves
CIJE: 0 RIE: 0 CAT: 17

Naval Special Projects Office
CIJE: 1 RIE: 0 CAT: 17

Naval Training
CIJE: 6 RIE: 32 CAT: 03

Naval Training Device Center
CIJE: 0 RIE: 3 CAT: 17

Naval Training Research Laboratory
CIJE: 0 RIE: 1 CAT: 17

Naval War College RI
CIJE: 0 RIE: 1 CAT: 17

Navarro (Jose Antonio)
CIJE: 1 RIE: 0 CAT: 18

Navidad
CIJE: 0 RIE: 2 CAT: 12

Navigation (Information Systems)
CIJE: 48 RIE: 1 CAT: 20

Navy
CIJE: 45 RIE: 344 CAT: 17

Navy Basic Test Battery
CIJE: 0 RIE: 5 CAT: 21

Navy Nurse Corps
CIJE: 0 RIE: 1 CAT: 16

Navy Plaque Index
CIJE: 0 RIE: 1 CAT: 16

Navy Science Awards Program
CIJE: 1 RIE: 0 CAT: 19

Navy Vocational Interest Inventory
CIJE: 0 RIE: 4 CAT: 21

Nayarit
CIJE: 0 RIE: 1 CAT: 13

Nazareth College MI
CIJE: 0 RIE: 4 CAT: 17

Nazareth College NY
CIJE: 3 RIE: 0 CAT: 17

NBME
USE National Board of Medical Examiners

NBME Examinations
USE National Board Examinations

NCAA v Board of Regents of University of Oklahoma
CIJE: 1 RIE: 1 CAT: 14

NCGE Competency Based Geography Test
CIJE: 0 RIE: 0 CAT: 21

NCLIS
USE National Commission Libraries Information Science

NCME
USE National Council on Measurement in Education

NCR 250 Electronic Cash Register
CIJE: 0 RIE: 1 CAT: 04

NCR Equipment
CIJE: 0 RIE: 3 CAT: 04

NCTE Centers of Excellence
USE Centers of Excellence in English

NCTE Seminar on Research in English Education
CIJE: 7 RIE: 1 CAT: 02

NCTM Curriculum and Evaluation Standards
CIJE: 80 RIE: 73 CAT: 15
UF Curriculum and Evaluation Standards (NCTM)

NCTM Professional Teaching Standards
CIJE: 23 RIE: 8 CAT: 15
UF Professional Teaching Standards (NCTM)

NDEA Institute State Supervisors English Reading
CIJE: 0 RIE: 1 CAT: 02

Ndebele
CIJE: 0 RIE: 1 CAT: 13

Ndjebbana
CIJE: 0 RIE: 1 CAT: 13
SN An Australian Aboriginal language
UF Kunibidji

NEA Contracts
CIJE: 0 RIE: 117 CAT: 14

NEA Moratorium on Testing
CIJE: 0 RIE: 1 CAT: 19

Neals Dance Attitude Inventory
CIJE: 0 RIE: 1 CAT: 21

Near (Holly)
CIJE: 1 RIE: 1 CAT: 18

Near Death Experiences
CIJE: 7 RIE: 0 CAT: 11

Near Death Research
CIJE: 5 RIE: 1 CAT: 15

Near East
CIJE: 5 RIE: 12 CAT: 07

Near Miss Periodicity
CIJE: 1 RIE: 0 CAT: 15

Nearing (Scott)
CIJE: 0 RIE: 0 CAT: 18

NEB SAT Networks
USE NEBSAT

Nebraska
CIJE: 140 RIE: 469 CAT: 07

Nebraska (Bellevue)
CIJE: 1 RIE: 0 CAT: 07

Nebraska (Boys Town)
USE Boys Town NE

Nebraska (Dawes County)
CIJE: 0 RIE: 2 CAT: 07

Nebraska (Fillmore County)
CIJE: 0 RIE: 1 CAT: 07

Nebraska (Grand Island)
CIJE: 0 RIE: 4 CAT: 07

Nebraska (Gretna)
CIJE: 0 RIE: 1 CAT: 07

Nebraska (Lincoln)
CIJE: 8 RIE: 21 CAT: 07

Nebraska (Milford)
CIJE: 0 RIE: 1 CAT: 07

Nebraska (Omaha)
CIJE: 19 RIE: 19 CAT: 07

Nebraska (Scotts Bluff County)
CIJE: 1 RIE: 1 CAT: 07

Nebraska (Seward)
CIJE: 0 RIE: 1 CAT: 07

Nebraska (West)
CIJE: 0 RIE: 1 CAT: 07

Nebraska Alcohol Information Clearinghouse
CIJE: 1 RIE: 0 CAT: 17

Nebraska Center for Women
CIJE: 0 RIE: 1 CAT: 17

Nebraska Cooperative Extension Service
CIJE: 0 RIE: 1 CAT: 17

Nebraska Curriculum Development Center
CIJE: 0 RIE: 25 CAT: 17

Nebraska Educational TV Council for Higher Educ
CIJE: 0 RIE: 1 CAT: 17

Nebraska English Curriculum
CIJE: 0 RIE: 3 CAT: 03

Nebraska Governors Conference Lib Info Serv
USE Governors Conference Library Info Services NE

Nebraska Indian Community College
CIJE: 1 RIE: 0 CAT: 17

Nebraska Indian Community College Macy
CIJE: 0 RIE: 1 CAT: 17

Nebraska Instrument for Syntactic Analysis
CIJE: 0 RIE: 3 CAT: 21

Nebraska Library Association
CIJE: 0 RIE: 1 CAT: 17

Nebraska Library Commission
CIJE: 0 RIE: 2 CAT: 17

Nebraska Online
CIJE: 0 RIE: 1 CAT: 19

Nebraska Physical Science Project
CIJE: 2 RIE: 1 CAT: 19

Nebraska Principals Leadership Questionnaire
CIJE: 0 RIE: 1 CAT: 21

Nebraska School for the Deaf
CIJE: 3 RIE: 1 CAT: 17

Nebraska Secondary Teacher Education Program
CIJE: 2 RIE: 0 CAT: 19

Nebraska State Board of Trustees
CIJE: 0 RIE: 3 CAT: 17

Nebraska State College Education Association
CIJE: 0 RIE: 1 CAT: 17

Nebraska State Department of Education
CIJE: 2 RIE: 3 CAT: 17

Nebraska State Schools for the Sensory Impaired
CIJE: 0 RIE: 1 CAT: 17

Nebraska Technical Community College Areas
USE Nebraska Technical Community Colleges

Nebraska Technical Community Colleges
CIJE: 0 RIE: 2 CAT: 17
UF Nebraska Technical Community College Areas

Nebraska Test of Learning Aptitude
CIJE: 0 RIE: 1 CAT: 21

Nebraska v Faith Baptist
CIJE: 0 RIE: 1 CAT: 14

Nebraska Vocational Technical School
CIJE: 0 RIE: 2 CAT: 17

Nebraska Wesleyan University
CIJE: 3 RIE: 2 CAT: 17

Nebraska Wisconsin Cognitive Assessment Battery
CIJE: 0 RIE: 2 CAT: 21
UF NEWCAB Measure

Nebrija (Antonio de)
CIJE: 1 RIE: 0 CAT: 18

NEBSAT
CIJE: 0 RIE: 1 CAT: 19
SN Nebraska educational satellite telecommunications program
UF NEB SAT Networks

Neck (Anatomy)
CIJE: 1 RIE: 0 CAT: 11

Nedelsky Method
CIJE: 12 RIE: 28 CAT: 15

Nedlands College (Australia)
CIJE: 0 RIE: 1 CAT: 17

Need Achievement Measure (McClelland et al)
CIJE: 0 RIE: 1 CAT: 21

Need Assessment Questionnaire
CIJE: 1 RIE: 1 CAT: 21

Need for Academic Competence Questionnaire
CIJE: 1 RIE: 0 CAT: 21

Need for Assistance Inventory
CIJE: 0 RIE: 2 CAT: 21

Need for Uniqueness Scale (Snyder and Fromkin)
CIJE: 0 RIE: 1 CAT: 21

NEED Project (Energy Educ)
USE National Energy Education Development Project

Need Satisfaction Schedule
CIJE: 1 RIE: 0 CAT: 21

Needham School District MA
CIJE: 0 RIE: 1 CAT: 17

Needles High School CA
CIJE: 1 RIE: 0 CAT: 17

Needs Assessment Information System
CIJE: 0 RIE: 1 CAT: 15

Needs Assessment Model
CIJE: 1 RIE: 2 CAT: 21

Needs Assessment Project (AEL)
CIJE: 0 RIE: 5 CAT: 19

Needs Assessment Questionnaire (Mohan)
CIJE: 0 RIE: 1 CAT: 21

Needs Assessment Rating Scale
CIJE: 0 RIE: 1 CAT: 21

Needs Based Goal Attainment Scaling
CIJE: 1 RIE: 0 CAT: 15

Needs Press Model
CIJE: 0 RIE: 1 CAT: 15

Needs Sensing
CIJE: 0 RIE: 1 CAT: 21

NEEDS System (Engineering Educ)
USE National Engineering Education Delivery System

Neef (Joseph)
CIJE: 1 RIE: 1 CAT: 17

Negative Affect
CIJE: 28 RIE: 9 CAT: 11

Negative Capability
CIJE: 1 RIE: 0 CAT: 15

Negative Instances
CIJE: 8 RIE: 0 CAT: 15

Negative Moods
CIJE: 1 RIE: 1 CAT: 11

Negative News
CIJE: 9 RIE: 2 CAT: 16

Negative Numbers
CIJE: 13 RIE: 4 CAT: 20

Negative Stipulation
CIJE: 1 RIE: 1 CAT: 15

Negative Transfer
CIJE: 3 RIE: 0 CAT: 15

Negative Transportation Rule
CIJE: 0 RIE: 1 CAT: 15

Negativism
CIJE: 7 RIE: 4 CAT: 11

Negev Desert
CIJE: 0 RIE: 0 CAT: 07

Neglected and Delinquent Pupils Project NY
CIJE: 0 RIE: 1 CAT: 19

Neglected Language Program
CIJE: 0 RIE: 2 CAT: 19

Neglected Languages Materials Conference 1974
CIJE: 0 RIE: 9 CAT: 02

Negotiability
CIJE: 2 RIE: 1 CAT: 15

Negotiable Instruments
CIJE: 0 RIE: 2 CAT: 21

Negotiated Order Model
CIJE: 1 RIE: 3 CAT: 15

Negotiated Tuition
CIJE: 0 RIE: 1 CAT: 15

Negotiation Processes
CIJE: 65 RIE: 52 CAT: 15
UF Negotiation Tactics

Negotiation Tactics
USE Negotiation Processes

Negotiators
CIJE: 20 RIE: 22 CAT: 09

NEGP
USE National Education Goals Panel

Negritude
CIJE: 0 RIE: 1 CAT: 16

Negro College Committee on Adult Education
CIJE: 0 RIE: 2 CAT: 17

Negro Ensemble Company
CIJE: 2 RIE: 0 CAT: 17

Nehru (Jawaharlal)
CIJE: 3 RIE: 1 CAT: 18

Neighbor Attitudes
CIJE: 3 RIE: 3 CAT: 16

Neighborhood Centers Day Care Association
CIJE: 0 RIE: 2 CAT: 17

Neighborhood Characteristics
CIJE: 4 RIE: 2 CAT: 16

Neighborhood Development Plan
CIJE: 2 RIE: 0 CAT: 19

Neighborhood English Scheme (England)
CIJE: 0 RIE: 1 CAT: 17

Neighborhood Facilities Program
CIJE: 0 RIE: 1 CAT: 19

Neighborhood Information Centers Project
CIJE: 2 RIE: 3 CAT: 19

Neighborhood Legal Assistance Foundation
CIJE: 1 RIE: 0 CAT: 17

Neighborhood Medical Care Demonstration
CIJE: 1 RIE: 0 CAT: 19

Neighborhood Service Organization
CIJE: 0 RIE: 1 CAT: 17

Neighborhood Youth Corps
CIJE: 14 RIE: 101 CAT: 17

Neighbors
CIJE: 1 RIE: 3 CAT: 10

Neil McNeil Infants Home
CIJE: 0 RIE: 1 CAT: 17

Neill (A S)
CIJE: 18 RIE: 2 CAT: 18

NELS 88
USE National Education Longitudinal Study 1988

Nelson (Florence)
CIJE: 0 RIE: 1 CAT: 18

Nelson Biology Test
CIJE: 1 RIE: 6 CAT: 21

Nelson County Public Schools VA
CIJE: 0 RIE: 1 CAT: 17

Nelson Denny Reading Tests
CIJE: 14 RIE: 33 CAT: 21

Nelson House Indian Reserve MB
CIJE: 0 RIE: 1 CAT: 17

Nelson Reading Test
CIJE: 4 RIE: 4 CAT: 21

Nelson S Dilworth Elementary School CA
CIJE: 0 RIE: 1 CAT: 17

Nematoda
CIJE: 6 RIE: 0 CAT: 20

Nemeth Code
CIJE: 0 RIE: 4 CAT: 16

Nenets
CIJE: 0 RIE: 2 CAT: 13

Neo Piagetian Theory
CIJE: 9 RIE: 7 CAT: 16

Neo Vygotskian Theory
CIJE: 0 RIE: 1 CAT: 15

Neoclassical Economics
CIJE: 6 RIE: 1 CAT: 15

Neocolonialism
CIJE: 4 RIE: 2 CAT: 16

Neoconservatism
CIJE: 8 RIE: 2 CAT: 16

Neoliteracy
CIJE: 0 RIE: 4 CAT: 13
UF Neoliterates

Neoliterates
USE Neoliteracy

Neologism
CIJE: 40 RIE: 8 CAT: 13

NEOMYCIN (Computer Program)
CIJE: 0 RIE: 1 CAT: 04

Neonatal Behavioral Assessment Scale
CIJE: 8 RIE: 5 CAT: 21

Neorationalism
CIJE: 0 RIE: 1 CAT: 16

Neorealism
CIJE: 1 RIE: 0 CAT: 16

Nepal
CIJE: 53 RIE: 117 CAT: 07

NEPHIS
USE NEsted PHrase Indexing System

Nephrology
CIJE: 2 RIE: 1 CAT: 11
SN See also "Kidney Disease"

Nephrotic Syndrome
CIJE: 2 RIE: 0 CAT: 11

Nepotism
CIJE: 10 RIE: 3 CAT: 16

Neptune (Planet)
CIJE: 0 RIE: 0 CAT: 20

Neptune High School NJ
CIJE: 1 RIE: 0 CAT: 17

Neptune Township Public Schools NJ
CIJE: 0 RIE: 1 CAT: 17

Neruda (Pablo)
CIJE: 10 RIE: 1 CAT: 18

Nerve Impulses
CIJE: 4 RIE: 1 CAT: 11

Nervous System
CIJE: 11 RIE: 13 CAT: 11

Neshaminy School District PA
CIJE: 0 RIE: 3 CAT: 17

Nested Data
CIJE: 4 RIE: 3 CAT: 16

Nested Dependencies
CIJE: 1 RIE: 1 CAT: 13

Nested Loops
CIJE: 0 RIE: 1 CAT: 20

NEsted PHrase Indexing System
CIJE: 1 RIE: 1 CAT: 04
UF NEPHIS

Nested Spiral Approach
CIJE: 0 RIE: 2 CAT: 15

Nestle Corporation
CIJE: 0 RIE: 1 CAT: 17

Net Benefit
CIJE: 1 RIE: 1 CAT: 21

Netherland Universities Council
CIJE: 1 RIE: 0 CAT: 17

Netherlands
CIJE: 727 RIE: 623 CAT: 07
UF Holland

Netherlands (Amsterdam)
CIJE: 8 RIE: 6 CAT: 07

Netherlands (Enschede)
CIJE: 0 RIE: 1 CAT: 07

Netherlands (Friesland)
CIJE: 5 RIE: 3 CAT: 07

Netherlands (Hague)
CIJE: 2 RIE: 1 CAT: 07

Netherlands (Maastricht)
CIJE: 0 RIE: 2 CAT: 07

Netherlands (Nijmegen)
CIJE: 3 RIE: 0 CAT: 07

Netherlands (Rotterdam)
CIJE: 2 RIE: 2 CAT: 07

Netherlands (Utrecht)
CIJE: 2 RIE: 0 CAT: 07

Netherlands (Zuyder Zee)
CIJE: 0 RIE: 1 CAT: 07

Netherlands Antilles
CIJE: 0 RIE: 2 CAT: 07

Netherlands Antilles (Curacao)
CIJE: 3 RIE: 1 CAT: 07

Netherlands Central Society for Rehabilitation
CIJE: 0 RIE: 1 CAT: 17

Netherlands Folk High School Association
CIJE: 1 RIE: 0 CAT: 17

Netherlands Information Service
CIJE: 1 RIE: 0 CAT: 17

Netherlands Organisation for Intl Coop in Highr Ed
USE NUFFIC (Netherlands)

Netherlands Preventie Fonds
CIJE: 0 RIE: 1 CAT: 17

Netherlands Universities Foundation for Intl Coop
USE NUFFIC (Netherlands)

Netprime (Computer Program)
CIJE: 0 RIE: 1 CAT: 04

Netsilik (Tribe)
CIJE: 0 RIE: 1 CAT: 08

Network Access Procedures
CIJE: 1 RIE: 3 CAT: 15

Network Analysis Program
CIJE: 0 RIE: 2 CAT: 19

Network Architecture
CIJE: 5 RIE: 2 CAT: 15

Network Based Approach
CIJE: 4 RIE: 0 CAT: 15

Network for Drug Free Colleges
CIJE: 0 RIE: 38 CAT: 17

Network for Outcome Based Schools
CIJE: 0 RIE: 1 CAT: 17

Network Management
CIJE: 3 RIE: 0 CAT: 15

Network Models
CIJE: 8 RIE: 3 CAT: 15

Network Protocols
CIJE: 3 RIE: 1 CAT: 15

NETWORK SCOTLAND LTD
CIJE: 0 RIE: 1 CAT: 17

Network Therapy
CIJE: 1 RIE: 0 CAT: 11

Networking
CIJE: 45 RIE: 47 CAT: 16

Networking Evaluation
CIJE: 1 RIE: 2 CAT: 21

Networks (Persons)
CIJE: 9 RIE: 9 CAT: 16

Neufeld (John)
CIJE: 0 RIE: 1 CAT: 18

Neugarten Age Norms Inquiry
CIJE: 1 RIE: 0 CAT: 16

Neuman Health Care Systems Model
CIJE: 0 RIE: 1 CAT: 15

Neumann (Erich)
CIJE: 1 RIE: 0 CAT: 18

Neumann College PA
CIJE: 0 RIE: 2 CAT: 17

Neural Efficiency Analyzer
CIJE: 3 RIE: 0 CAT: 04

Neural Net Models
CIJE: 2 RIE: 2 CAT: 15

Neural Networks
CIJE: 1 RIE: 5 CAT: 20
UF Artificial Neural Networks

Neural Transmission
CIJE: 6 RIE: 2 CAT: 11

Neurath (Otto)
CIJE: 2 RIE: 0 CAT: 18

Neuro Developmental Observation
CIJE: 1 RIE: 0 CAT: 11

Neuroanatomy
CIJE: 4 RIE: 1 CAT: 11

Neurobiology
CIJE: 16 RIE: 2 CAT: 11

Neuroblastoma
CIJE: 1 RIE: 0 CAT: 11

Neurodevelopmental Therapy
CIJE: 0 RIE: 1 CAT: 11

Neurodevelopmental Treatment Approach
CIJE: 5 RIE: 1 CAT: 11

Neuroeducators
CIJE: 1 RIE: 0 CAT: 09

Neurolinguistic Mirroring
CIJE: 1 RIE: 1 CAT: 11

Neurolinguistic Programming
CIJE: 20 RIE: 9 CAT: 11

Neurological Examination
CIJE: 1 RIE: 1 CAT: 11

Neurological Impress Method
CIJE: 19 RIE: 13 CAT: 15

Neurological Information Network
CIJE: 1 RIE: 0 CAT: 11

Neuromuscular Skills
CIJE: 10 RIE: 2 CAT: 11

Neuropathology
CIJE: 0 RIE: 1 CAT: 11

Neuropharmacology
CIJE: 0 RIE: 1 CAT: 11

Neuropsychological Measures
CIJE: 8 RIE: 3 CAT: 21

Neurosciences
CIJE: 10 RIE: 3 CAT: 20

Neurosciences Research Program
CIJE: 1 RIE: 0 CAT: 19

Neurosurgery
CIJE: 2 RIE: 0 CAT: 11

Neuroticism Scale Questionnaire
CIJE: 1 RIE: 2 CAT: 21

Neurotoxicology
CIJE: 0 RIE: 1 CAT: 11

Neustadt (Richard E)
CIJE: 0 RIE: 2 CAT: 18

Neutrality
CIJE: 14 RIE: 1 CAT: 15

Neutrality Act 1935
CIJE: 0 RIE: 1 CAT: 14

Neutralization (Phonology)
CIJE: 0 RIE: 1 CAT: 13

Neutralization Theory
CIJE: 2 RIE: 0 CAT: 15
SN ...of Delinquency (Matza)

Neutron Activation
CIJE: 1 RIE: 0 CAT: 20

Neutrons
CIJE: 2 RIE: 0 CAT: 20

Nevada
CIJE: 39 RIE: 257 CAT: 07

Nevada (Carson City)
CIJE: 0 RIE: 12 CAT: 07

Nevada (Churchill County)
CIJE: 1 RIE: 1 CAT: 07

Nevada (Clark County)
CIJE: 0 RIE: 4 CAT: 07

Nevada (Douglas County)
CIJE: 1 RIE: 1 CAT: 07

Nevada (Las Vegas)
CIJE: 6 RIE: 11 CAT: 07

Nevada (Reno)
CIJE: 3 RIE: 4 CAT: 07

Nevada (Washoe County)
CIJE: 2 RIE: 3 CAT: 07

Nevada (Wells)
CIJE: 0 RIE: 2 CAT: 07

Nevada CBAHSD Project
CIJE: 0 RIE: 12 CAT: 19

Nevada Heights School MO
CIJE: 0 RIE: 1 CAT: 17

Nevada High School Proficiency Examinations
CIJE: 0 RIE: 3 CAT: 21

Nevada Indian Agency
CIJE: 0 RIE: 2 CAT: 17

Nevada Proficiency Examination Program
CIJE: 0 RIE: 7 CAT: 21

Nevada Rural School District Alliance
CIJE: 0 RIE: 2 CAT: 17

Nevada State Department of Education
CIJE: 0 RIE: 3 CAT: 17

Nevada University and Community College System
USE University and Community College System of Nevada

Nevil Childrens Center for Sensory Deficits PA
CIJE: 0 RIE: 1 CAT: 17

Neville (Edgar)
CIJE: 1 RIE: 0 CAT: 18

New Aesthetic
CIJE: 1 RIE: 0 CAT: 16

New Age Movement
CIJE: 4 RIE: 2 CAT: 12

New Age Thinking
CIJE: 2 RIE: 1 CAT: 16

New American Schools
CIJE: 0 RIE: 1 CAT: 05

New American Schools Development Corporation
CIJE: 8 RIE: 3 CAT: 17
UF NASDC

New Auteurism
CIJE: 0 RIE: 1 CAT: 15

New Barns School
CIJE: 1 RIE: 0 CAT: 17

New Basics
CIJE: 0 RIE: 2 CAT: 03

New Beacon Learning Center
CIJE: 0 RIE: 1 CAT: 17

New Britain Public Library CT
CIJE: 0 RIE: 1 CAT: 17

New Britain School District CT
CIJE: 0 RIE: 1 CAT: 17

New Brunswick
CIJE: 27 RIE: 52 CAT: 07

New Brunswick (Deer Island)
CIJE: 0 RIE: 1 CAT: 07

New Brunswick (Fredericton)
CIJE: 2 RIE: 2 CAT: 07

New Brunswick Department of Labour (Canada)
CIJE: 0 RIE: 1 CAT: 17

New Brunswick Experiment
CIJE: 0 RIE: 2 CAT: 19

New Canaan Public Schools CT
CIJE: 1 RIE: 1 CAT: 17

New Canadians
CIJE: 0 RIE: 2 CAT: 08

New Careers Programs
CIJE: 5 RIE: 99 CAT: 19

New Castle Area Vocational School IN
CIJE: 0 RIE: 1 CAT: 17

New Castle County School District DE
CIJE: 0 RIE: 4 CAT: 17

New Castle School District PA
CIJE: 0 RIE: 9 CAT: 17

New Center for Learning TX
CIJE: 0 RIE: 1 CAT: 17
UF East Texas State University New Ctr for Learning

New Chance
CIJE: 0 RIE: 5 CAT: 19
SN A national demonstration project designed to help disadvantaged 17 - 21-year-old mothers and their children

New Christian Right
CIJE: 5 RIE: 3 CAT: 10

New City School MN
CIJE: 0 RIE: 1 CAT: 17

New Cloze Test (Hisama Lewis and Woehlke)
CIJE: 0 RIE: 1 CAT: 21

New College FL
CIJE: 1 RIE: 3 CAT: 17

New Colleges
CIJE: 8 RIE: 17 CAT: 05

New Criticism
CIJE: 33 RIE: 5 CAT: 16

New Deal
CIJE: 19 RIE: 10 CAT: 12

New Developmental Reading Tests
CIJE: 1 RIE: 2 CAT: 21

New Elementary Teacher Education Program
CIJE: 0 RIE: 1 CAT: 19

New England
CIJE: 66 RIE: 145 CAT: 07

New England Association of Chemistry Teachers
CIJE: 2 RIE: 0 CAT: 17

New England Association of Schools and Colleges
CIJE: 3 RIE: 2 CAT: 17

New England Board of Higher Education
CIJE: 1 RIE: 4 CAT: 17

New England College NH
CIJE: 0 RIE: 1 CAT: 17

New England Deposit Library MA
CIJE: 0 RIE: 1 CAT: 17

New England Document Conservation Center
CIJE: 0 RIE: 1 CAT: 17

New England Educational Assessment Project
CIJE: 1 RIE: 4 CAT: 19

New England Governors Conference
CIJE: 1 RIE: 0 CAT: 02

New England Library Association
CIJE: 1 RIE: 0 CAT: 17

New England Library Information Network
CIJE: 2 RIE: 12 CAT: 17

New England Materials for Instruction Center
CIJE: 3 RIE: 0 CAT: 17

New England Online Users Group
CIJE: 0 RIE: 1 CAT: 17

New England Program in Teacher Education
CIJE: 2 RIE: 5 CAT: 19

New England Regional Student Program
CIJE: 1 RIE: 6 CAT: 19

New England Research Application Center
CIJE: 1 RIE: 1 CAT: 17

New England School of Law MA
CIJE: 0 RIE: 0 CAT: 17

New England Special Educ Instr Materials Center
CIJE: 0 RIE: 1 CAT: 17

New England Study Abroad Programs
CIJE: 0 RIE: 1 CAT: 19

New Entrants Survey
CIJE: 0 RIE: 3 CAT: 22

New Environmental Paradigm
CIJE: 4 RIE: 0 CAT: 21

New Faculty
CIJE: 0 RIE: 3 CAT: 09

New Friends Program
CIJE: 0 RIE: 2 CAT: 19

New Frontiers (Program)
CIJE: 0 RIE: 1 CAT: 19

New Futures Initiative
CIJE: 1 RIE: 2 CAT: 19
SN Of the Annie E. Casey Foundation

New Futures School NM
CIJE: 0 RIE: 1 CAT: 17

New Grammar
CIJE: 0 RIE: 64 CAT: 13

New Guinea
CIJE: 35 RIE: 21 CAT: 07

New Hampshire
CIJE: 43 RIE: 219 CAT: 07

New Hampshire (Groveton)
CIJE: 0 RIE: 1 CAT: 07

New Hampshire (Keene)
CIJE: 0 RIE: 3 CAT: 07

New Hampshire (Manchester)
CIJE: 2 RIE: 2 CAT: 07

New Hampshire (Nashua)
CIJE: 0 RIE: 4 CAT: 07

New Hampshire (New London)
CIJE: 0 RIE: 1 CAT: 07

New Hampshire (Newport)
CIJE: 0 RIE: 1 CAT: 07

New Hampshire (Strafford County)
CIJE: 0 RIE: 1 CAT: 07

New Hampshire College and University Council
CIJE: 2 RIE: 2 CAT: 17

New Hampshire Mentor Teacher Project
CIJE: 0 RIE: 1 CAT: 19

New Hampshire Network
CIJE: 0 RIE: 1 CAT: 17

New Hampshire State Department of Education
CIJE: 0 RIE: 1 CAT: 17

New Hampshire Statewide Testing Program
CIJE: 0 RIE: 1 CAT: 21

New Hampshire Vocational Technical College
CIJE: 0 RIE: 1 CAT: 17

New Harmony Utopian Society
USE Indiana (New Harmony)

New Haven High School IN
CIJE: 1 RIE: 0 CAT: 17

New Haven Public Schools CT
CIJE: 12 RIE: 7 CAT: 17

New Haven Unified School District CA
CIJE: 1 RIE: 1 CAT: 17

New Hebrides
CIJE: 1 RIE: 1 CAT: 07
SN Became "Vanuatu" Jul80

New Hope School CA
CIJE: 0 RIE: 2 CAT: 17

New Horizons in Adult Education
CIJE: 0 RIE: 1 CAT: 22

New Horizons Program IA
CIJE: 0 RIE: 2 CAT: 19
SN ...of the Des Moines Public Schools IA

New Humanism
CIJE: 1 RIE: 1 CAT: 16

New Hyde Park Public Library NY
CIJE: 0 RIE: 1 CAT: 17

New Information and Communication Technologies
CIJE: 0 RIE: 4 CAT: 20

New Information Technologies
CIJE: 0 RIE: 1 CAT: 20

New International Economic Order
CIJE: 9 RIE: 5 CAT: 15

New Jersey
CIJE: 383 RIE: 1130 CAT: 07

New Jersey (Atlantic City)
CIJE: 3 RIE: 5 CAT: 07

New Jersey (Bayonne)
CIJE: 0 RIE: 2 CAT: 07

New Jersey (Bergen County)
CIJE: 0 RIE: 13 CAT: 07

New Jersey (Bloomfield)
CIJE: 2 RIE: 0 CAT: 07

New Jersey (Bordentown)
CIJE: 0 RIE: 1 CAT: 07

New Jersey (Burlington County)
CIJE: 0 RIE: 4 CAT: 07

New Jersey (Camden County)
CIJE: 1 RIE: 1 CAT: 07

New Jersey (Camden)
CIJE: 3 RIE: 9 CAT: 07

New Jersey (Cherry Hill)
CIJE: 0 RIE: 3 CAT: 07

New Jersey (Clifton)
CIJE: 0 RIE: 1 CAT: 07

New Jersey (Dover)
CIJE: 0 RIE: 0 CAT: 07

New Jersey (East Orange)
CIJE: 2 RIE: 5 CAT: 07

New Jersey (Elizabeth)
CIJE: 1 RIE: 5 CAT: 07

New Jersey (Englewood)
CIJE: 0 RIE: 5 CAT: 07

New Jersey (Fort Monmouth)
CIJE: 1 RIE: 0 CAT: 07

New Jersey (Garwood)
CIJE: 0 RIE: 2 CAT: 07

New Jersey (Glassboro)
CIJE: 0 RIE: 1 CAT: 07

New Jersey (Hackensack)
CIJE: 0 RIE: 3 CAT: 07

New Jersey (Hightstown)
CIJE: 0 RIE: 1 CAT: 07

New Jersey (Hoboken)
CIJE: 0 RIE: 4 CAT: 07

New Jersey (Hudson County)
CIJE: 0 RIE: 2 CAT: 07

New Jersey (Jersey City)
CIJE: 5 RIE: 8 CAT: 07

New Jersey (Kenilworth)
CIJE: 3 RIE: 0 CAT: 07

New Jersey (Maplewood)
CIJE: 0 RIE: 1 CAT: 07

New Jersey (Mercer County)
CIJE: 0 RIE: 3 CAT: 07

New Jersey (Middlesex)
CIJE: 1 RIE: 0 CAT: 07

New Jersey (Midland Park)
CIJE: 0 RIE: 1 CAT: 07

New Jersey (Monmouth County)
CIJE: 2 RIE: 3 CAT: 07

New Jersey (Montclair)
CIJE: 3 RIE: 2 CAT: 07

New Jersey (Morris County)
CIJE: 1 RIE: 2 CAT: 07

New Jersey (Morristown)
CIJE: 2 RIE: 1 CAT: 07

New Jersey (Murray Hill)
CIJE: 0 RIE: 1 CAT: 07

New Jersey (New Brunswick)
CIJE: 1 RIE: 0 CAT: 07

New Jersey (Newark)
CIJE: 12 RIE: 30 CAT: 07

New Jersey (North)
CIJE: 2 RIE: 2 CAT: 07

New Jersey (Passaic County)
CIJE: 0 RIE: 3 CAT: 07

New Jersey (Passaic)
CIJE: 0 RIE: 2 CAT: 07

New Jersey (Paterson)
CIJE: 4 RIE: 14 CAT: 07

New Jersey (Pemberton)
CIJE: 0 RIE: 1 CAT: 07

New Jersey (Pennsauken)
CIJE: 1 RIE: 0 CAT: 07

New Jersey (Perth Amboy)
CIJE: 1 RIE: 1 CAT: 07

New Jersey (Plainfield)
CIJE: 0 RIE: 5 CAT: 07

New Jersey (Princeton)
CIJE: 2 RIE: 28 CAT: 07

New Jersey (Raritan)
CIJE: 0 RIE: 0 CAT: 07

New Jersey (Ringwood)
CIJE: 1 RIE: 0 CAT: 07

New Jersey (Saddle Brook)
CIJE: 0 RIE: 1 CAT: 07

New Jersey (Salem County)
CIJE: 0 RIE: 1 CAT: 07

New Jersey (Sandy Hook)
CIJE: 1 RIE: 0 CAT: 07

New Jersey (Somerset County)
CIJE: 1 RIE: 1 CAT: 07

New Jersey (South Orange)
CIJE: 0 RIE: 1 CAT: 07

New Jersey (South Plainfield)
CIJE: 1 RIE: 1 CAT: 07

New Jersey (South)
CIJE: 1 RIE: 2 CAT: 07

New Jersey (Teaneck)
CIJE: 0 RIE: 3 CAT: 07

New Jersey (Tenafly)
CIJE: 1 RIE: 1 CAT: 07

New Jersey (Trenton)
CIJE: 1 RIE: 4 CAT: 07

New Jersey (Union)
CIJE: 1 RIE: 6 CAT: 07

New Jersey (Weehawken)
CIJE: 1 RIE: 2 CAT: 07

New Jersey (West New York)
CIJE: 0 RIE: 2 CAT: 07

New Jersey (Willingboro)
CIJE: 0 RIE: 1 CAT: 07

New Jersey Administrative Code Education Title 6
CIJE: 0 RIE: 2 CAT: 14

New Jersey Adult Reading Project
CIJE: 0 RIE: 1 CAT: 19

New Jersey Alternate Route Program
CIJE: 0 RIE: 1 CAT: 19

New Jersey Basic Skills Assessment Program
CIJE: 2 RIE: 0 CAT: 19

New Jersey Basic Skills Council
CIJE: 1 RIE: 0 CAT: 17

New Jersey Basic Skills Placement Test
USE New Jersey College Basic Skills Placement Test

New Jersey Bell Telephone Reading Project
CIJE: 0 RIE: 1 CAT: 19

New Jersey Board of Public Utility Commissioners
CIJE: 0 RIE: 2 CAT: 17

New Jersey Center for Educational Technology
CIJE: 0 RIE: 1 CAT: 17

New Jersey Child Care Advisory Council
CIJE: 0 RIE: 1 CAT: 17

New Jersey College Basic Skills Placement Test
CIJE: 4 RIE: 29 CAT: 21
UF Basic Skills Placement Test (New Jersey); New Jersey Basic Skills Placement Test

New Jersey College Outcomes Evaluation Program
CIJE: 0 RIE: 1 CAT: 19

New Jersey Collegiate Press Association
CIJE: 1 RIE: 0 CAT: 17

New Jersey Community Action Training Institute
CIJE: 0 RIE: 1 CAT: 02

New Jersey Correctional System
CIJE: 0 RIE: 1 CAT: 17

New Jersey Department of Education
CIJE: 1 RIE: 10 CAT: 17

New Jersey Department of Public Utilities
CIJE: 0 RIE: 2 CAT: 17

New Jersey Education Association
CIJE: 32 RIE: 5 CAT: 17

New Jersey Educational Assessment Program
CIJE: 0 RIE: 9 CAT: 19
SN See also "New Jersey Statewide Testing System"

New Jersey Employer Employee Relations Act
CIJE: 0 RIE: 1 CAT: 14

New Jersey Governors School
CIJE: 1 RIE: 0 CAT: 17

New Jersey Graduated Work Incentive Experiment
CIJE: 1 RIE: 0 CAT: 19

New Jersey High School Proficiency Test
CIJE: 1 RIE: 25 CAT: 21

New Jersey Institute of Technology
CIJE: 9 RIE: 4 CAT: 17

New Jersey Institute Workmens Compensation Rehab
CIJE: 0 RIE: 1 CAT: 17

New Jersey Library Association
CIJE: 0 RIE: 1 CAT: 17

New Jersey Library Network
CIJE: 0 RIE: 1 CAT: 17

New Jersey Mainstream Inservice Project
CIJE: 0 RIE: 1 CAT: 19

New Jersey Minimum Basic Skills Program
CIJE: 3 RIE: 12 CAT: 19

New Jersey Office of Cable Television
CIJE: 0 RIE: 2 CAT: 17

New Jersey Principals and Supervisors Association
CIJE: 0 RIE: 1 CAT: 17

New Jersey Public Employment Relations Commission
CIJE: 0 RIE: 5 CAT: 17

New Jersey Public School Education Act 1975
CIJE: 0 RIE: 3 CAT: 14

New Jersey Reading Association
CIJE: 0 RIE: 1 CAT: 17

New Jersey School Boards Association
CIJE: 0 RIE: 8 CAT: 17

New Jersey School of Conservation
CIJE: 2 RIE: 0 CAT: 17

New Jersey Special Review Assessment
CIJE: 0 RIE: 1 CAT: 21
UF Special Review Assessment NJ

New Jersey State College System
CIJE: 0 RIE: 2 CAT: 17

New Jersey State Federation of Teachers
CIJE: 0 RIE: 2 CAT: 17

New Jersey Statewide Testing System
CIJE: 0 RIE: 1 CAT: 21
SN See also "New Jersey Educational Assessment Program"

New Jersey v Shelton College
CIJE: 0 RIE: 1 CAT: 14

New Jersey v TLO
CIJE: 20 RIE: 11 CAT: 14
UF TLO v New Jersey

New Jersey Youth Corps Program
CIJE: 0 RIE: 1 CAT: 19

New Junior Maudsley Inventory
CIJE: 2 RIE: 0 CAT: 21

New Leaf Program
CIJE: 0 RIE: 1 CAT: 19

New Left
CIJE: 8 RIE: 6 CAT: 16

New Left Scale (Christie et al)
CIJE: 0 RIE: 1 CAT: 21

New Lexington City Schools OH
CIJE: 0 RIE: 1 CAT: 17

New Literacy (Willinsky)
CIJE: 0 RIE: 1 CAT: 22
SN "The New Literacy: Redefining Reading and Writing in the Schools"

New Literates
CIJE: 0 RIE: 3 CAT: 13

New London School District WI
CIJE: 1 RIE: 0 CAT: 17

New Media
CIJE: 1 RIE: 5 CAT: 16

New Medical College Admission Test
CIJE: 2 RIE: 0 CAT: 21

New Mexico
CIJE: 144 RIE: 603 CAT: 07

New Mexico (Alamogordo)
CIJE: 0 RIE: 1 CAT: 07

New Mexico (Albuquerque)
CIJE: 20 RIE: 55 CAT: 07

New Mexico (Bernalillo County)
CIJE: 0 RIE: 2 CAT: 07

New Mexico (Catron County)
CIJE: 0 RIE: 1 CAT: 07

New Mexico (Chama)
CIJE: 0 RIE: 1 CAT: 07

New Mexico (Clovis)
CIJE: 1 RIE: 11 CAT: 07

New Mexico (Dona Ana County)
CIJE: 1 RIE: 3 CAT: 07

New Mexico (Dulce)
CIJE: 0 RIE: 3 CAT: 07

New Mexico (East)
CIJE: 1 RIE: 3 CAT: 07

New Mexico (Espanola)
CIJE: 1 RIE: 3 CAT: 07

New Mexico (Fairview)
CIJE: 0 RIE: 1 CAT: 07

New Mexico (Fort Sumner)
CIJE: 0 RIE: 1 CAT: 07

New Mexico (Gallup)
CIJE: 0 RIE: 2 CAT: 07

New Mexico (Guadalupe)
CIJE: 0 RIE: 1 CAT: 07

New Mexico (Hagerman)
CIJE: 0 RIE: 1 CAT: 07

New Mexico (Las Cruces)
CIJE: 3 RIE: 12 CAT: 07

New Mexico (Las Vegas)
CIJE: 1 RIE: 2 CAT: 07
UF New Mexico (West Las Vegas)

New Mexico (Los Alamos)
CIJE: 2 RIE: 2 CAT: 07

New Mexico (Los Lunas)
CIJE: 0 RIE: 1 CAT: 07

New Mexico (Mora County)
CIJE: 1 RIE: 3 CAT: 07

New Mexico (North)
CIJE: 2 RIE: 8 CAT: 07

New Mexico (Northwest)
CIJE: 0 RIE: 1 CAT: 07

New Mexico (Portales)
CIJE: 1 RIE: 3 CAT: 07

New Mexico (Ramah)
CIJE: 1 RIE: 3 CAT: 07

New Mexico (Rio Arriba County)
CIJE: 0 RIE: 3 CAT: 07

New Mexico (San Juan County)
CIJE: 0 RIE: 1 CAT: 07

New Mexico (San Miguel County)
CIJE: 0 RIE: 4 CAT: 07

New Mexico (Santa Fe County)
CIJE: 0 RIE: 1 CAT: 07

New Mexico (Santa Fe)
CIJE: 2 RIE: 12 CAT: 07

New Mexico (Shiprock)
CIJE: 0 RIE: 2 CAT: 07

New Mexico (Silver City)
CIJE: 0 RIE: 1 CAT: 07

New Mexico (South)
CIJE: 0 RIE: 3 CAT: 07

New Mexico (Taos County)
CIJE: 0 RIE: 3 CAT: 07

New Mexico (Taos)
CIJE: 4 RIE: 3 CAT: 07

New Mexico (Torrance County)
CIJE: 0 RIE: 1 CAT: 07

New Mexico (Torreon)
CIJE: 0 RIE: 1 CAT: 07

New Mexico (Tortugas)
CIJE: 0 RIE: 1 CAT: 07

New Mexico (Tucumcari)
CIJE: 0 RIE: 1 CAT: 07

New Mexico (West Las Vegas)
USE New Mexico (Las Vegas)

New Mexico Agricultural Extension Service
CIJE: 0 RIE: 1 CAT: 17

New Mexico Articulated Assessment System
CIJE: 0 RIE: 1 CAT: 21

New Mexico Commission on the Status of Women
CIJE: 0 RIE: 1 CAT: 17

New Mexico High School Proficiency Examination
CIJE: 2 RIE: 10 CAT: 21

New Mexico Highlands University
CIJE: 0 RIE: 4 CAT: 17

New Mexico Information System
CIJE: 0 RIE: 1 CAT: 17

New Mexico Institute of Mining and Technology
CIJE: 1 RIE: 2 CAT: 17

New Mexico Junior College
CIJE: 1 RIE: 2 CAT: 17

New Mexico Law Center
CIJE: 1 RIE: 0 CAT: 17

New Mexico Office of Indian Affairs
CIJE: 0 RIE: 2 CAT: 17

New Mexico Portfolio Writing Assessment
CIJE: 0 RIE: 3 CAT: 21

New Mexico Research Study Council
CIJE: 0 RIE: 1 CAT: 17

New Mexico Rural Science Education Project
CIJE: 0 RIE: 2 CAT: 19
UF Rural Science Education Project NM

New Mexico School for the Deaf
CIJE: 1 RIE: 0 CAT: 17

New Mexico Solar Energy Institute
CIJE: 0 RIE: 1 CAT: 17

New Mexico Staff Accountability Plan
CIJE: 0 RIE: 3 CAT: 15

New Mexico State Board of Education
CIJE: 0 RIE: 2 CAT: 17

New Mexico State Department of Education
CIJE: 0 RIE: 4 CAT: 17

New Mexico State University
CIJE: 21 RIE: 34 CAT: 17

New Mexico State University Alamogordo
CIJE: 0 RIE: 5 CAT: 17

New Mexico State University Dona Ana Branch
CIJE: 0 RIE: 2 CAT: 17
UF Dona Ana Branch Community College NM

New Mexico Western States Small Schools Project
CIJE: 0 RIE: 2 CAT: 19

New Milford High School NJ
CIJE: 1 RIE: 0 CAT: 17

New Model Me (The)
CIJE: 0 RIE: 1 CAT: 22

New Netherland
CIJE: 0 RIE: 2 CAT: 07

New Netherland Project
CIJE: 0 RIE: 1 CAT: 19

New Nursery School
CIJE: 0 RIE: 6 CAT: 19

New Opportunities in Vocational Education Project
CIJE: 0 RIE: 2 CAT: 19

New Orleans Education Improvement Project
CIJE: 0 RIE: 1 CAT: 19

New Orleans Effective Schools Project LA
CIJE: 0 RIE: 1 CAT: 19

New Orleans Public Schools LA
CIJE: 7 RIE: 18 CAT: 17

New Oxford English Dictionary
CIJE: 1 RIE: 1 CAT: 22

New Parents
CIJE: 2 RIE: 3 CAT: 10

New Parents as Teachers Program
CIJE: 3 RIE: 1 CAT: 19

New Peak Course
CIJE: 0 RIE: 1 CAT: 03

New Phonics
CIJE: 1 RIE: 0 CAT: 13

New Pioneers Program
CIJE: 0 RIE: 1 CAT: 19

New Plymouth School District ID
CIJE: 0 RIE: 1 CAT: 17

New Primary Approach
CIJE: 0 RIE: 1 CAT: 15

New Primary Grades Reading System
CIJE: 1 RIE: 2 CAT: 19

New Realism
CIJE: 2 RIE: 0 CAT: 16

New Republic (Journal)
CIJE: 1 RIE: 3 CAT: 22

New Revised Standard Version of the Bible
CIJE: 3 RIE: 0 CAT: 22

New Rhetoric
CIJE: 12 RIE: 8 CAT: 16

New Right
CIJE: 21 RIE: 7 CAT: 10

New River Community College VA
CIJE: 1 RIE: 4 CAT: 17

New Rochelle Talent Search Project
CIJE: 0 RIE: 1 CAT: 19

New Salina High School KS
CIJE: 1 RIE: 0 CAT: 17

New School for Social Research NY
CIJE: 8 RIE: 4 CAT: 17

New School of Behavior Studies in Educ Program
CIJE: 2 RIE: 2 CAT: 19

New Social Studies
CIJE: 42 RIE: 16 CAT: 16

New Sociology of Education
CIJE: 1 RIE: 2 CAT: 15

New Standards Project (LRDC)
CIJE: 1 RIE: 4 CAT: 19
SN LRDC = Learning Research and Development Center

New Students
CIJE: 5 RIE: 7 CAT: 16

New Teacher and Teacher Aide Project
CIJE: 0 RIE: 1 CAT: 19

New Teacher Retention Project (San Diego)
CIJE: 0 RIE: 2 CAT: 19

New Teachers
CIJE: 9 RIE: 20 CAT: 09

New Testament
CIJE: 2 RIE: 4 CAT: 22
UF Gospels

New Theater
CIJE: 1 RIE: 0 CAT: 16

New Thing Art and Architecture Center
CIJE: 1 RIE: 0 CAT: 17

New Towns
CIJE: 6 RIE: 4 CAT: 16

New Trier Township Coop Film Library IL
CIJE: 1 RIE: 0 CAT: 17

New University of Ulster (Ireland)
CIJE: 2 RIE: 0 CAT: 17

New Ways to Work Job Sharing in Schools Project
CIJE: 0 RIE: 1 CAT: 19

New World Information Order
CIJE: 10 RIE: 22 CAT: 16

New World Order
CIJE: 1 RIE: 3 CAT: 12

New World School of the Arts FL
CIJE: 1 RIE: 1 CAT: 17

New Year (Holiday)
CIJE: 2 RIE: 2 CAT: 12

New Years Resolutions
CIJE: 0 RIE: 0 CAT: 16

New York
CIJE: 725 RIE: 3147 CAT: 07

New York (Albany)
CIJE: 4 RIE: 126 CAT: 07

New York (Albertson)
CIJE: 1 RIE: 1 CAT: 07

New York (Alfred)
CIJE: 0 RIE: 4 CAT: 07

New York (Amityville)
CIJE: 0 RIE: 5 CAT: 07

New York (Amsterdam)
CIJE: 0 RIE: 1 CAT: 07

New York (Bedford Stuyvesant)
CIJE: 2 RIE: 7 CAT: 07

New York (Binghamton)
CIJE: 2 RIE: 1 CAT: 07

New York (Brockport)
CIJE: 0 RIE: 2 CAT: 07

New York (Bronx)
CIJE: 15 RIE: 117 CAT: 07
SN See also "New York (South Bronx)"

New York (Brooklyn)
CIJE: 30 RIE: 152 CAT: 07

New York (Broome County)
CIJE: 1 RIE: 2 CAT: 07

New York (Buffalo)
CIJE: 30 RIE: 73 CAT: 07

New York (Canandaigua)
CIJE: 0 RIE: 1 CAT: 07

New York (Central)
CIJE: 1 RIE: 10 CAT: 07

New York (Chautauqua County)
CIJE: 1 RIE: 0 CAT: 07

New York (Cincinnatus)
CIJE: 0 RIE: 1 CAT: 07

New York (Clinton County)
CIJE: 0 RIE: 6 CAT: 07

New York (Corlears Hook Community)
CIJE: 0 RIE: 1 CAT: 07

New York (Cortland County)
CIJE: 0 RIE: 2 CAT: 07

New York (Cortland)
CIJE: 3 RIE: 4 CAT: 07

New York (Dutchess County)
CIJE: 1 RIE: 2 CAT: 07

New York (East Harlem)
CIJE: 14 RIE: 13 CAT: 07

New York (East Meadow)
CIJE: 0 RIE: 1 CAT: 07

New York (East Tremont)
CIJE: 0 RIE: 1 CAT: 07

New York (Elmira)
CIJE: 4 RIE: 3 CAT: 07

New York (Erie County)
CIJE: 2 RIE: 3 CAT: 07

New York (Farmingdale)
CIJE: 1 RIE: 2 CAT: 07

New York (Flushing)
CIJE: 0 RIE: 7 CAT: 07

New York (Fredonia)
CIJE: 0 RIE: 1 CAT: 07

New York (Garden City)
CIJE: 2 RIE: 1 CAT: 07

New York (Glen Cove)
CIJE: 2 RIE: 0 CAT: 07

New York (Glens Falls)
CIJE: 0 RIE: 1 CAT: 07

New York (Grandview)
CIJE: 0 RIE: 1 CAT: 07

New York (Great Neck)
CIJE: 3 RIE: 2 CAT: 07

New York (Hamburg)
CIJE: 1 RIE: 1 CAT: 07

New York (Harlem)
CIJE: 17 RIE: 51 CAT: 07
SN See also "New York (East Harlem)"

New York (Hartsdale)
CIJE: 1 RIE: 8 CAT: 07

New York (Hempstead)
CIJE: 1 RIE: 6 CAT: 07

New York (Homer)
CIJE: 1 RIE: 2 CAT: 07

New York (Huntington)
CIJE: 3 RIE: 2 CAT: 07

New York (Ithaca)
CIJE: 0 RIE: 63 CAT: 07

New York (Jamesville)
CIJE: 0 RIE: 1 CAT: 07

New York (Kingston)
CIJE: 1 RIE: 1 CAT: 07

New York (Lewis County)
CIJE: 0 RIE: 2 CAT: 07

New York (Little Sandy Creek)
CIJE: 1 RIE: 0 CAT: 07

New York (Liverpool)
CIJE: 1 RIE: 1 CAT: 07

New York (Long Island)
CIJE: 19 RIE: 17 CAT: 07

New York (Mamaroneck)
CIJE: 1 RIE: 0 CAT: 07

New York (Manhattan)
CIJE: 12 RIE: 27 CAT: 07

New York (Mayfield)
CIJE: 0 RIE: 1 CAT: 07

New York (McGraw)
CIJE: 0 RIE: 1 CAT: 07

New York (Monroe County)
CIJE: 5 RIE: 4 CAT: 07

New York (Morrisville)
CIJE: 1 RIE: 1 CAT: 07

New York (Mount Vernon)
CIJE: 2 RIE: 3 CAT: 07

New York (Nassau County)
CIJE: 6 RIE: 16 CAT: 07

New York (New Paltz)
CIJE: 0 RIE: 3 CAT: 07

New York (New Rochelle)
CIJE: 4 RIE: 15 CAT: 07

New York (New York Chinatown)
CIJE: 1 RIE: 0 CAT: 07
UF Chinatown New York City

New York (New York Metropolitan Area)
CIJE: 9 RIE: 18 CAT: 07

New York (New York)
CIJE: 488 RIE: 1974 CAT: 07

New York (Newburgh)
CIJE: 2 RIE: 2 CAT: 07

New York (Newfield)
CIJE: 0 RIE: 1 CAT: 07

New York (Niagara County)
CIJE: 0 RIE: 2 CAT: 07

New York (Niagara Falls)
CIJE: 2 RIE: 5 CAT: 07

New York (Niskayuna)
CIJE: 0 RIE: 1 CAT: 07

New York (North Country)
CIJE: 1 RIE: 3 CAT: 07

New York (North Hempstead)
CIJE: 0 RIE: 1 CAT: 07

New York (Northport)
CIJE: 0 RIE: 1 CAT: 07

New York (Old Westbury)
CIJE: 2 RIE: 1 CAT: 07

New York (Olean)
CIJE: 0 RIE: 1 CAT: 07

New York (Oneonta)
CIJE: 1 RIE: 4 CAT: 07

New York (Onondaga County)
CIJE: 2 RIE: 5 CAT: 07

New York (Orchard Park)
CIJE: 1 RIE: 0 CAT: 07

New York (Oswego County)
CIJE: 0 RIE: 2 CAT: 07

New York (Oswego)
CIJE: 2 RIE: 2 CAT: 07

New York (Otsego County)
CIJE: 1 RIE: 1 CAT: 07

New York (Plainview)
CIJE: 1 RIE: 1 CAT: 07

New York (Plattsburgh)
CIJE: 0 RIE: 2 CAT: 07

New York (Pleasantville)
CIJE: 1 RIE: 1 CAT: 07

New York (Potsdam)
CIJE: 0 RIE: 1 CAT: 07

New York (Poughkeepsie)
CIJE: 0 RIE: 4 CAT: 07

New York (Putnam County)
CIJE: 0 RIE: 2 CAT: 07

New York (Queens)
CIJE: 11 RIE: 50 CAT: 07

New York (Red Creek)
CIJE: 0 RIE: 1 CAT: 07

New York (Rensselaer County)
CIJE: 0 RIE: 1 CAT: 07

New York (Rochester)
CIJE: 21 RIE: 24 CAT: 07

New York (Rockland County)
CIJE: 1 RIE: 0 CAT: 07

New York (Roslyn)
CIJE: 0 RIE: 2 CAT: 07

New York (Rye)
CIJE: 1 RIE: 0 CAT: 07

New York (Saint Lawrence County)
CIJE: 0 RIE: 2 CAT: 07

New York (Scarsdale)
CIJE: 2 RIE: 3 CAT: 07

New York (Schenectady)
CIJE: 0 RIE: 3 CAT: 07

New York (Schuyler County)
CIJE: 0 RIE: 1 CAT: 07

New York (Schuylerville)
CIJE: 1 RIE: 0 CAT: 07

New York (Sinclairville)
CIJE: 0 RIE: 1 CAT: 07

New York (Slide Mountain)
CIJE: 1 RIE: 0 CAT: 07

New York (South Bronx)
CIJE: 2 RIE: 1 CAT: 07

New York (Spencerport)
CIJE: 0 RIE: 14 CAT: 07

New York (Spring Valley)
CIJE: 0 RIE: 1 CAT: 07

New York (Staten Island)
CIJE: 2 RIE: 14 CAT: 07

New York (Steuben County)
CIJE: 0 RIE: 3 CAT: 07

New York (Stony Brook)
CIJE: 0 RIE: 1 CAT: 07

New York (Suffern)
CIJE: 0 RIE: 2 CAT: 07

New York (Suffolk County)
CIJE: 3 RIE: 9 CAT: 07

New York (Syosset)
CIJE: 4 RIE: 1 CAT: 07

New York (Syracuse Area)
CIJE: 0 RIE: 1 CAT: 07

New York (Syracuse)
CIJE: 11 RIE: 135 CAT: 07

New York (Tompkins County)
CIJE: 1 RIE: 1 CAT: 07

New York (Upper Hudson)
CIJE: 0 RIE: 1 CAT: 07

New York (Upstate)
CIJE: 6 RIE: 10 CAT: 07

New York (Utica)
CIJE: 1 RIE: 3 CAT: 07

New York (Verona)
CIJE: 0 RIE: 1 CAT: 07

New York (Wantagh)
CIJE: 0 RIE: 1 CAT: 07

New York (Washington Heights)
CIJE: 2 RIE: 0 CAT: 07

New York (Wayne County)
CIJE: 0 RIE: 5 CAT: 07

New York (West Queens)
CIJE: 0 RIE: 2 CAT: 07

New York (West)
CIJE: 1 RIE: 7 CAT: 07

New York (Westchester County)
CIJE: 7 RIE: 13 CAT: 07

New York (Westchester)
CIJE: 0 RIE: 3 CAT: 07

New York (White Plains)
CIJE: 1 RIE: 12 CAT: 07

New York (Williamsville)
CIJE: 1 RIE: 0 CAT: 07

New York (Yonkers)
CIJE: 3 RIE: 9 CAT: 07

New York (Yorktown Heights)
CIJE: 1 RIE: 3 CAT: 07

New York Alliance for the Public Schools
CIJE: 1 RIE: 1 CAT: 17

New York Chiropractic College
CIJE: 0 RIE: 1 CAT: 17

New York City Adult Literacy Initiative
CIJE: 0 RIE: 3 CAT: 19

New York City Board of Education
CIJE: 56 RIE: 678 CAT: 17

New York City Board of Education v Aspira
USE Aspira v Board of Education

New York City Board of Examiners
CIJE: 0 RIE: 1 CAT: 17

New York City Board of Higher Education
CIJE: 0 RIE: 1 CAT: 17

New York City Central Labor Council
CIJE: 0 RIE: 1 CAT: 17

New York City Commission on Human Rights
CIJE: 0 RIE: 4 CAT: 17

New York City Community College
USE City University of New York NYC Comm Coll

New York City Department of Employment
CIJE: 0 RIE: 1 CAT: 17

New York City Department of Health
CIJE: 0 RIE: 1 CAT: 17

New York City Department of Hospitals
CIJE: 0 RIE: 1 CAT: 17

New York City Education Network
USE NYCENET

New York City Health Care for the Homeless Program
CIJE: 0 RIE: 0 CAT: 19

New York City Infant Day Care Study
CIJE: 1 RIE: 6 CAT: 19

New York City Manpower Information Bulletins
CIJE: 0 RIE: 1 CAT: 22

New York City Planning Department
CIJE: 1 RIE: 0 CAT: 17

New York City Police Department
CIJE: 0 RIE: 1 CAT: 17

New York City School Volunteer Program
CIJE: 1 RIE: 1 CAT: 19

New York City Technical College
USE City University of New York NYC Technical Coll

New York City Urban Corps
CIJE: 0 RIE: 1 CAT: 17

New York Citywide Mathematics Test
CIJE: 0 RIE: 1 CAT: 21

New York Citywide Reading Test
CIJE: 0 RIE: 2 CAT: 21

New York Civil Liberties Union
CIJE: 1 RIE: 1 CAT: 17

New York College Proficiency Examination Program
CIJE: 0 RIE: 2 CAT: 19

New York Daily News
CIJE: 1 RIE: 1 CAT: 22

New York Educational Opportunity Program
CIJE: 0 RIE: 1 CAT: 19

New York Governors Conference Library Info Serv
USE Governors Conference Library Info Services NY

New York Health Occupations Education Program
CIJE: 0 RIE: 1 CAT: 19

New York Herald
CIJE: 0 RIE: 1 CAT: 22

New York High School Student Union
CIJE: 1 RIE: 0 CAT: 17

New York Institute for the Education of the Blind
CIJE: 0 RIE: 0 CAT: 17

New York Institute of Technology
CIJE: 4 RIE: 18 CAT: 17

New York Magazine or Literary Repository
CIJE: 0 RIE: 1 CAT: 22

New York Medical College
CIJE: 11 RIE: 4 CAT: 17

New York Metropolitan Reference and Research Lib
CIJE: 2 RIE: 1 CAT: 17

New York Office of Extension Studies
CIJE: 0 RIE: 1 CAT: 17

New York Office of Vocational Rehabilitation
CIJE: 1 RIE: 2 CAT: 17

New York Philharmonic
CIJE: 1 RIE: 0 CAT: 17

New York Public Library
CIJE: 32 RIE: 7 CAT: 17

New York Rural Schools Program
CIJE: 0 RIE: 1 CAT: 19

New York State Advisory Council
CIJE: 0 RIE: 1 CAT: 17

New York State Archives
CIJE: 1 RIE: 1 CAT: 17

New York State Basic Competency Test in Reading
CIJE: 0 RIE: 2 CAT: 21

New York State Center for Learning Technologies
USE Center for Learning Technologies NY

New York State College of Human Ecology
CIJE: 2 RIE: 0 CAT: 17

New York State Commission Against Discrimination
CIJE: 0 RIE: 1 CAT: 17

New York State Committee on the Handicapped
CIJE: 0 RIE: 1 CAT: 17

New York State Comprehensive Assessment Report
USE Comprehensive Assessment Report (New York)

New York State Conservation Preservation Grants
CIJE: 0 RIE: 0 CAT: 19
SN New York State Discretionary Grant Program for Conservation and Preservation of Library Research Materials

New York State Council on Languages
CIJE: 0 RIE: 1 CAT: 17

New York State Council on the Arts
CIJE: 1 RIE: 1 CAT: 17

New York State Curriculum Guide
CIJE: 1 RIE: 0 CAT: 22

New York State Department of Labor
CIJE: 0 RIE: 1 CAT: 17

New York State Division For Youth
CIJE: 0 RIE: 5 CAT: 17

New York State Division of Library Development
CIJE: 0 RIE: 1 CAT: 17

New York State Education Department
CIJE: 9 RIE: 46 CAT: 17

New York State Employment Service
CIJE: 1 RIE: 0 CAT: 17

New York State English Council
CIJE: 0 RIE: 1 CAT: 17

New York State External High School Diploma Prog
CIJE: 0 RIE: 1 CAT: 19

New York State Fifth Grade Writing Test
CIJE: 0 RIE: 1 CAT: 21

New York State Interlibrary Loan Network
CIJE: 1 RIE: 7 CAT: 17

New York State Legis Comm on Rural Resources
CIJE: 0 RIE: 2 CAT: 17

New York State Legislature
CIJE: 0 RIE: 2 CAT: 17

New York State Library
CIJE: 6 RIE: 29 CAT: 17

New York State Mentor Teacher Internship Program
CIJE: 0 RIE: 5 CAT: 19
UF Mentor Teacher Internship Program NY

New York State Mentoring Program
CIJE: 0 RIE: 1 CAT: 19

New York State Museum and Science Service
CIJE: 1 RIE: 1 CAT: 17

New York State Office Voc Educ Serv Individ Dis
CIJE: 0 RIE: 2 CAT: 17

New York State Prelim Competency Test in Reading
CIJE: 0 RIE: 1 CAT: 21

New York State Pupil Evaluation Program
CIJE: 0 RIE: 11 CAT: 21

New York State Readiness Tests
CIJE: 0 RIE: 1 CAT: 21

New York State Reading and Readiness Tests
CIJE: 0 RIE: 1 CAT: 21

New York State Regents
CIJE: 0 RIE: 19 CAT: 17

New York State Regents Action Plan
CIJE: 1 RIE: 1 CAT: 19

New York State Regents Competency Tests
CIJE: 0 RIE: 10 CAT: 21

New York State Regents Examinations
CIJE: 7 RIE: 36 CAT: 21

New York State Regents External Degree Exams
USE Regents External Degree Program NY

New York State Regents Scholarship Examinations
CIJE: 0 RIE: 5 CAT: 21

New York State Summer School of the Arts
CIJE: 1 RIE: 0 CAT: 17

New York State Teacher Certification Examinations
CIJE: 0 RIE: 1 CAT: 21

New York State Teachers Association
CIJE: 1 RIE: 0 CAT: 17

New York State Technical Assist Resource Network
CIJE: 0 RIE: 1 CAT: 17

New York State Technology Network Ties
USE Technology Network Ties NY

New York Stock Exchange
CIJE: 3 RIE: 1 CAT: 17

New York Tests of Growth in Reading
CIJE: 0 RIE: 4 CAT: 21

New York Theological Seminary
CIJE: 1 RIE: 0 CAT: 17

New York Times
CIJE: 24 RIE: 38 CAT: 22

New York Times Co v Sullivan
CIJE: 1 RIE: 5 CAT: 14

New York Times Information Bank
CIJE: 5 RIE: 3 CAT: 17

New York Times Sunday Magazine
CIJE: 0 RIE: 1 CAT: 22

New York University
CIJE: 57 RIE: 45 CAT: 17

New York Urban Corps
CIJE: 1 RIE: 0 CAT: 17

New York Urban League
CIJE: 0 RIE: 2 CAT: 17

New Yorker
CIJE: 0 RIE: 1 CAT: 22

New Youth Initiatives in Apprenticeship Study
CIJE: 0 RIE: 4 CAT: 22

New Zambia Primary Course
CIJE: 1 RIE: 0 CAT: 03

New Zealand
CIJE: 530 RIE: 581 CAT: 07

New Zealand (Aotearoa)
CIJE: 0 RIE: 2 CAT: 07

New Zealand (Auckland)
CIJE: 11 RIE: 6 CAT: 07

New Zealand (Christchurch)
CIJE: 2 RIE: 5 CAT: 07

New Zealand (Wellington)
CIJE: 4 RIE: 8 CAT: 07

New Zealand Accident Compensation Act 1972
USE Accident Compensation Act 1972 (New Zealand)

New Zealand Accident Compensation Scheme
CIJE: 1 RIE: 0 CAT: 15
UF Accident Compensation Scheme (New Zealand)

New Zealand Correspondence School
CIJE: 0 RIE: 1 CAT: 17

New Zealand Council for Educational Research
CIJE: 1 RIE: 7 CAT: 17

New Zealand Journal of Educational Studies
CIJE: 0 RIE: 1 CAT: 22

New Zealand Library Association
CIJE: 1 RIE: 0 CAT: 17

New Zealand Literature
CIJE: 0 RIE: 2 CAT: 16

New Zealand Reading Recovery Program
CIJE: 1 RIE: 1 CAT: 19

New Zealand Technical Correspondence Institute
CIJE: 0 RIE: 2 CAT: 17

Newari
CIJE: 0 RIE: 2 CAT: 13

Newark Board of Education NJ
CIJE: 0 RIE: 2 CAT: 17

Newark City School District OH
CIJE: 0 RIE: 2 CAT: 17

Newark City Schools OH
CIJE: 1 RIE: 0 CAT: 17

Newark College of Engineering NJ
CIJE: 2 RIE: 0 CAT: 17

Newark Literacy Campaign NJ
CIJE: 0 RIE: 1 CAT: 19

Newark Public Library NJ
CIJE: 3 RIE: 0 CAT: 17

Newark School for Technology NJ
CIJE: 0 RIE: 1 CAT: 17

Newark School System NJ
CIJE: 1 RIE: 18 CAT: 17

Newark Special School District DE
CIJE: 0 RIE: 1 CAT: 17

Newark State College NJ
CIJE: 0 RIE: 2 CAT: 17

Newark Teacher Center NJ
CIJE: 0 RIE: 1 CAT: 17

Newark Teachers Union
CIJE: 1 RIE: 0 CAT: 17

Newark Uniform Testing Program NJ
CIJE: 0 RIE: 1 CAT: 21

Newbasic Catalyst
CIJE: 0 RIE: 2 CAT: 15

Newberg School District OR
CIJE: 0 RIE: 1 CAT: 17

Newberry College SC
CIJE: 1 RIE: 0 CAT: 17

Newberry Library IL
CIJE: 3 RIE: 5 CAT: 17

Newbery Award
CIJE: 36 RIE: 21 CAT: 19

Newburyport Project for Consumer Education
CIJE: 0 RIE: 1 CAT: 19

NEWCAB Measure
USE Nebraska Wisconsin Cognitive Assessment Battery

Newcastle College of Advanced Educ (Australia)
CIJE: 0 RIE: 1 CAT: 17

Newcastle Kent Board of Education ON
CIJE: 0 RIE: 1 CAT: 17

Newcastle Report (England)
CIJE: 1 RIE: 1 CAT: 22

Newcastle School of Librarianship
CIJE: 1 RIE: 0 CAT: 17

Newcastle upon Tyne Inst of Education (England)
CIJE: 1 RIE: 0 CAT: 17

Newcastle upon Tyne Polytechnic (England)
CIJE: 2 RIE: 3 CAT: 17

Newcomb (Theodore)
CIJE: 3 RIE: 0 CAT: 18

Newcomers
CIJE: 8 RIE: 10 CAT: 10

Newfoundland
CIJE: 44 RIE: 58 CAT: 07

Newfoundland (Labrador)
USE Labrador

Newfoundland (Nain)
CIJE: 1 RIE: 0 CAT: 07

Newgate Program
CIJE: 1 RIE: 2 CAT: 19

Newman (Cardinal John Henry)
CIJE: 4 RIE: 3 CAT: 18

Newman (Richard S)
CIJE: 0 RIE: 0 CAT: 18

Newman Keuls Analyses
CIJE: 1 RIE: 3 CAT: 21

Newman Report
CIJE: 3 RIE: 2 CAT: 22

Newman Report Critique
CIJE: 0 RIE: 1 CAT: 22

Newmark (Peter)
CIJE: 0 RIE: 2 CAT: 18

Newport High School KY
CIJE: 0 RIE: 1 CAT: 17

Newport Mesa Unified School District CA
CIJE: 2 RIE: 4 CAT: 17

Newport Naval Base
CIJE: 1 RIE: 1 CAT: 17

Newport News Public Schools VA
CIJE: 2 RIE: 2 CAT: 17

News Accuracy
CIJE: 10 RIE: 3 CAT: 16

News Agencies
CIJE: 5 RIE: 10 CAT: 05

News Bias
CIJE: 7 RIE: 15 CAT: 16

News Borrowing
CIJE: 1 RIE: 1 CAT: 16

News Commentators
CIJE: 4 RIE: 3 CAT: 09

News Content
CIJE: 1 RIE: 2 CAT: 16

News Councils
CIJE: 1 RIE: 1 CAT: 10
SN See also "Press Councils"

News Directors
CIJE: 1 RIE: 5 CAT: 09

News Exchange
CIJE: 0 RIE: 1 CAT: 16
SN See also "Eurovision News Exchange" and "Television News Exchange"

News Flow
CIJE: 1 RIE: 5 CAT: 16

News Interview Programs
CIJE: 0 RIE: 1 CAT: 16

News Morbidity Scale
CIJE: 0 RIE: 1 CAT: 21

News Perspective Bias
CIJE: 0 RIE: 6 CAT: 15

News Producers
CIJE: 1 RIE: 1 CAT: 09

News Releases
CIJE: 3 RIE: 1 CAT: 16

News Reporters
USE Journalists

News Sentinel (Knoxville TN)
CIJE: 0 RIE: 1 CAT: 22

News Sources
CIJE: 23 RIE: 56 CAT: 16

News Stories
CIJE: 46 RIE: 33 CAT: 16

News Topic Selection
USE Topic Selection

News Topics
CIJE: 20 RIE: 17 CAT: 16

News Values
CIJE: 17 RIE: 14 CAT: 16

Newsday Science Education Series Program
CIJE: 0 RIE: 1 CAT: 19

Newsearch
CIJE: 0 RIE: 1 CAT: 04

Newsletter on Intellectual Freedom
CIJE: 0 RIE: 2 CAT: 22

Newsmagazines
CIJE: 28 RIE: 18 CAT: 16

Newspaper Association of America Foundation
CIJE: 0 RIE: 1 CAT: 17

Newspaper Chains
CIJE: 2 RIE: 3 CAT: 16

Newspaper Circulation
CIJE: 18 RIE: 27 CAT: 16

Newspaper Courses
CIJE: 1 RIE: 5 CAT: 03

Newspaper Dynasties
CIJE: 1 RIE: 2 CAT: 16

Newspaper Graphics
CIJE: 0 RIE: 1 CAT: 16

Newspaper Guild
CIJE: 1 RIE: 2 CAT: 17

Newspaper in Education Program
CIJE: 13 RIE: 34 CAT: 19

Newspaper in the Classroom Project
CIJE: 3 RIE: 4 CAT: 19

Newspaper Index (Database)
CIJE: 0 RIE: 1 CAT: 04

Newspaper Ownership
CIJE: 5 RIE: 11 CAT: 16

Newspaper Preservation Act 1970
CIJE: 2 RIE: 8 CAT: 14

Newspaper Research Council
CIJE: 0 RIE: 1 CAT: 17

Newspaper Subscribers
USE Subscribers (Newspapers)

Newspaper Subscriptions
CIJE: 5 RIE: 7 CAT: 16

Newstart Incorporated
CIJE: 0 RIE: 17 CAT: 17

Newsweek
CIJE: 4 RIE: 5 CAT: 22

Newsweek Magazine
CIJE: 5 RIE: 6 CAT: 22

Newswork
CIJE: 0 RIE: 1 CAT: 16

Newton (Isaac)
CIJE: 30 RIE: 4 CAT: 18

Newton Bulletin Board System
CIJE: 0 RIE: 1 CAT: 04

Newton Community Schools MA
CIJE: 0 RIE: 2 CAT: 17

Newton Creative Arts Center
CIJE: 1 RIE: 0 CAT: 17

Newton Laws of Motion
CIJE: 32 RIE: 3 CAT: 20

Newtonian Mechanics
CIJE: 9 RIE: 2 CAT: 20

Newtons Gravitational Constant
CIJE: 1 RIE: 0 CAT: 15

NEXA Program
CIJE: 1 RIE: 1 CAT: 19

NEXIS System
CIJE: 3 RIE: 1 CAT: 04

Nexpert
CIJE: 0 RIE: 1 CAT: 04

NeXT Computer
CIJE: 1 RIE: 2 CAT: 04

NextStep
CIJE: 0 RIE: 1 CAT: 04
SN IBM computer-assisted learning system to help users with career plans

Neylan Colleges
CIJE: 0 RIE: 1 CAT: 05
SN Catholic colleges founded by or maintaining relationships with religious orders of women

Neylan Minorities Project
CIJE: 0 RIE: 1 CAT: 19

Neyman (J)
CIJE: 0 RIE: 1 CAT: 18

Neyman Pearson Hypothesis Testing
CIJE: 2 RIE: 2 CAT: 21

Nez Perce (Tribe)
CIJE: 6 RIE: 8 CAT: 08

Ngaanyatjarra
CIJE: 0 RIE: 1 CAT: 13
SN A Wati language (Australian Aborigine)

Ngee Ann Polytechnic (Singapore)
CIJE: 0 RIE: 1 CAT: 17

NGOs
USE Nongovernmental Organizations

NGS Kids Network
USE National Geographic Kids Network

Ngukurr Bamyili
USE Roper Creole

NHK Gakuen Senior High School (Japan)
CIJE: 1 RIE: 0 CAT: 17

Niagara College of Applied Arts and Tech (Canada)
CIJE: 1 RIE: 1 CAT: 17

Niagara County Community College NY
CIJE: 3 RIE: 2 CAT: 17

Niagara Falls School System NY
CIJE: 1 RIE: 0 CAT: 17

Niagara South Board of Education ON
CIJE: 0 RIE: 1 CAT: 17

Niagara University NY
CIJE: 3 RIE: 3 CAT: 17

Nicaragua
CIJE: 44 RIE: 67 CAT: 07

Nicaraguans
CIJE: 0 RIE: 1 CAT: 08

Niche Books
CIJE: 0 RIE: 1 CAT: 16

Nicholls State University LA
CIJE: 3 RIE: 1 CAT: 17

Nichols (James O)
CIJE: 0 RIE: 1 CAT: 18

Nichols (Mark)
CIJE: 1 RIE: 0 CAT: 18

Nichols (Robert)
CIJE: 0 RIE: 1 CAT: 18

Nicholson (E B)
CIJE: 1 RIE: 0 CAT: 18

Nickel
CIJE: 3 RIE: 0 CAT: 20

Nickel Complexes
CIJE: 1 RIE: 0 CAT: 20

Nicknames
CIJE: 3 RIE: 5 CAT: 16

Nicobarese Languages
CIJE: 0 RIE: 1 CAT: 13

Nicolet College and Technical Institute WI
CIJE: 0 RIE: 2 CAT: 17

Nicolet Vocational Technical Adult Education Dist
CIJE: 0 RIE: 1 CAT: 17

Nicotine
CIJE: 9 RIE: 1 CAT: 11

NIE Archives
CIJE: 0 RIE: 67 CAT: 17

NIE ECS NAEP Item Development Project
CIJE: 0 RIE: 9 CAT: 19

NIE R and D Centers and Regional Educational Labs
CIJE: 0 RIE: 18 CAT: 05

Niebuhr (Reinhold)
CIJE: 6 RIE: 0 CAT: 18

Niels Brock School Internatl Business (Denmark)
CIJE: 0 RIE: 1 CAT: 17

Nielsen Ratings
CIJE: 0 RIE: 4 CAT: 15

Nielsen Surveys
CIJE: 1 RIE: 4 CAT: 21

Nieman Fellowship
CIJE: 0 RIE: 1 CAT: 19

Nienberge
CIJE: 1 RIE: 0 CAT: 13

Nietzsche (Friedrich)
CIJE: 19 RIE: 4 CAT: 18

Nigel (Computer Program)
CIJE: 0 RIE: 1 CAT: 04

Niger
CIJE: 6 RIE: 20 CAT: 07

Niger Congo Languages
CIJE: 0 RIE: 3 CAT: 13

Nigeria
CIJE: 827 RIE: 304 CAT: 07

Nigeria (Bendel State)
CIJE: 5 RIE: 1 CAT: 07

Nigeria (Biafra)
CIJE: 2 RIE: 0 CAT: 07

Nigeria (Ibadan)
CIJE: 6 RIE: 1 CAT: 07

Nigeria (Imo State)
CIJE: 0 RIE: 1 CAT: 07

Nigeria (Kano State)
CIJE: 0 RIE: 1 CAT: 07

Nigeria (Lagos)
CIJE: 12 RIE: 3 CAT: 07

Nigeria (North)
CIJE: 6 RIE: 2 CAT: 07

Nigeria (South)
CIJE: 2 RIE: 1 CAT: 07

Nigeria (West)
CIJE: 4 RIE: 2 CAT: 07

Nigerian Association Translators and Interpreters
CIJE: 1 RIE: 0 CAT: 17

Nigerian Languages
CIJE: 3 RIE: 2 CAT: 13

Nigerians
CIJE: 4 RIE: 3 CAT: 08

Night
CIJE: 0 RIE: 0 CAT: 20

Night Child Care
CIJE: 0 RIE: 1 CAT: 11

Night Fears
CIJE: 2 RIE: 1 CAT: 11

Night Terrors
USE Sleep Disorders

Nightengale Conant Attitude Change Packages
CIJE: 0 RIE: 1 CAT: 21

Nightingale (Florence)
CIJE: 2 RIE: 1 CAT: 18

Nigro (Georgia)
CIJE: 0 RIE: 0 CAT: 18

Nihilism
CIJE: 12 RIE: 0 CAT: 16

Nihongo Tutorial System
CIJE: 1 RIE: 2 CAT: 04

NII
USE National Information Infrastructure

Nijmegen Dental School (Netherlands)
CIJE: 1 RIE: 0 CAT: 17

Nile River
CIJE: 0 RIE: 1 CAT: 07

Niles Township Federation of Teachers
CIJE: 1 RIE: 0 CAT: 17

Niles Township High School District 219 IL
CIJE: 2 RIE: 0 CAT: 17

Niles Township High School West IL
CIJE: 0 RIE: 1 CAT: 17

Nim Rater (Computer Program)
CIJE: 0 RIE: 1 CAT: 04

Nim Speak (Computer Program)
CIJE: 0 RIE: 1 CAT: 04

Nin (Anais)
CIJE: 1 RIE: 0 CAT: 18

Nineteenth Century
CIJE: 142 RIE: 57 CAT: 12

Nineteenth Century History
CIJE: 24 RIE: 29 CAT: 12

Nineteenth Century Rhetoric
CIJE: 4 RIE: 7 CAT: 13

Ninja Turtles
USE Teenage Mutant Ninja Turtles

Ninth Grade Communication Skills Test
CIJE: 0 RIE: 1 CAT: 21

Ninth Grade Proficiency Test
CIJE: 0 RIE: 6 CAT: 21

Nippon Cataloging Rules
CIJE: 0 RIE: 1 CAT: 22

Niskayuna Central School District NY
CIJE: 2 RIE: 1 CAT: 17

Nisqually (Tribe)
CIJE: 0 RIE: 1 CAT: 08

Nissequogue River State Park NY
CIJE: 0 RIE: 1 CAT: 07

Nitella Axillaris
CIJE: 1 RIE: 0 CAT: 20

Nitrates
CIJE: 3 RIE: 1 CAT: 20

Nitrification
CIJE: 0 RIE: 1 CAT: 20

Nitrogen
CIJE: 8 RIE: 3 CAT: 20

Nitrogen Cycle
CIJE: 4 RIE: 1 CAT: 20

Nitrogen Dioxide
CIJE: 0 RIE: 2 CAT: 20

Nitrogen Fixation
CIJE: 5 RIE: 0 CAT: 20

Nitrogen Oxide
CIJE: 1 RIE: 1 CAT: 20

Nitrogen Oxides
CIJE: 3 RIE: 4 CAT: 20

Nixon (Richard M)
CIJE: 28 RIE: 23 CAT: 18

Nixon Administration
CIJE: 8 RIE: 6 CAT: 12

Niyogi Brahmin
CIJE: 1 RIE: 0 CAT: 13

Nizan (Paul)
CIJE: 2 RIE: 0 CAT: 18

Nkrumah (Kwame)
CIJE: 1 RIE: 0 CAT: 18

NLN Achievement Tests
CIJE: 0 RIE: 2 CAT: 21

NMR Imaging
USE Magnetic Resonance Imaging

NMR Spectroscopy
USE Nuclear Magnetic Resonance

No Fault Marital Dissolution
USE No Fault Marital Divorce

No Fault Marital Divorce
CIJE: 0 RIE: 0 CAT: 14
UF No Fault Marital Dissolution

No Guessing Format
CIJE: 0 RIE: 1 CAT: 21

No Pass No Play Rules
CIJE: 0 RIE: 2 CAT: 16
UF C Average Rule (Access to Extracurriculars); Pass to Play

NOAA ERL Library
CIJE: 1 RIE: 1 CAT: 17

Noahs Ark
CIJE: 2 RIE: 1 CAT: 16

Nobel (Alfred)
CIJE: 2 RIE: 2 CAT: 18

Nobel Laureates
CIJE: 3 RIE: 0 CAT: 10

Nobel Prizes
CIJE: 19 RIE: 9 CAT: 19

Noble Center Team Teaching Plan
CIJE: 0 RIE: 1 CAT: 19

Noble Savage Concept
CIJE: 1 RIE: 1 CAT: 15

Node Acquisition and Integration Technique
CIJE: 2 RIE: 1 CAT: 15

Nodier (Charles)
CIJE: 2 RIE: 0 CAT: 18

Nodoz
CIJE: 1 RIE: 0 CAT: 11

Noether (Emmy)
CIJE: 1 RIE: 1 CAT: 18
SN Amalie Emmy Noether

Noggin Factor
CIJE: 0 RIE: 1 CAT: 15

Noh Theater
CIJE: 1 RIE: 1 CAT: 16

NOHARM Computer Program
CIJE: 0 RIE: 2 CAT: 04

Nomenclator
CIJE: 0 RIE: 1 CAT: 16

Nomenclature
CIJE: 18 RIE: 0 CAT: 13

Nominal Response Model
CIJE: 4 RIE: 4 CAT: 15

Nominating Committees
CIJE: 1 RIE: 1 CAT: 10

Nomograms
USE Nomographs

Nomographs
CIJE: 8 RIE: 8 CAT: 15
UF Nomograms

Nomological Network
CIJE: 0 RIE: 3 CAT: 21

Nomothetic Teaching Style
CIJE: 0 RIE: 1 CAT: 15

Non Catholic Students
CIJE: 0 RIE: 3 CAT: 10

Non Cognitive Questionnaire (NCQ)
USE Noncognitive Questionnaire

Non E Mai Troppo Tardi
CIJE: 1 RIE: 0 CAT: 22

Non European Francophone Areas
CIJE: 5 RIE: 1 CAT: 07
UF Francophone Areas (Non European)

Non Formal Education Center MI
USE Nonformal Education Information Center

Non Khmer
CIJE: 1 RIE: 0 CAT: 16

Non Monetary Economic System
USE Nonmonetary Economy

Non Public Schools Learning Resource Center MI
CIJE: 0 RIE: 1 CAT: 17
UF Nonpublic Schools LRC MI

Non Routine Mathematical Problems
USE Nonroutine Problems

Nonacademic Achievement
CIJE: 3 RIE: 1 CAT: 16

Nonacademic Careers
CIJE: 2 RIE: 2 CAT: 09

Nonacademic Labor Market
CIJE: 0 RIE: 1 CAT: 16

Nonacademic Personnel
CIJE: 1 RIE: 2 CAT: 10

Nonaccredited Colleges
CIJE: 1 RIE: 1 CAT: 05
UF Unaccredited Colleges

Nonachievement Syndrome
CIJE: 1 RIE: 0 CAT: 11

Nonalcoholic Beverages
USE Beverages

Nonanemic Iron Deficiency
USE Iron Deficiency

Nonbehavioral Therapy
CIJE: 0 RIE: 1 CAT: 11

Nonbibliographic Databases
CIJE: 3 RIE: 3 CAT: 04

Noncalculus Physics
CIJE: 2 RIE: 0 CAT: 20

Noncash Benefits
CIJE: 1 RIE: 6 CAT: 16

Noncategorical Education Teacher Certification
CIJE: 0 RIE: 0 CAT: 21

Noncognitive Attributes
CIJE: 23 RIE: 6 CAT: 11

Noncognitive Classroom Behaviors
CIJE: 0 RIE: 1 CAT: 11

Noncognitive Questionnaire
CIJE: 5 RIE: 8 CAT: 21
UF Non Cognitive Questionnaire (NCQ)

Noncommercial Films
CIJE: 1 RIE: 1 CAT: 16

Noncommercial Tests
CIJE: 0 RIE: 1 CAT: 21

Noncommissioned Officers
CIJE: 1 RIE: 1 CAT: 09

Noncompensatory Models
CIJE: 0 RIE: 1 CAT: 15

Nonconforming Materials
CIJE: 0 RIE: 1 CAT: 04

Nonconformity
CIJE: 6 RIE: 1 CAT: 16

Noncontact Sports
CIJE: 1 RIE: 0 CAT: 16

Noncustodial Parents
CIJE: 11 RIE: 8 CAT: 10

Nondarwinian Evolution
CIJE: 1 RIE: 0 CAT: 20

Nondegree Students
CIJE: 6 RIE: 2 CAT: 10

Nondegreed Teachers
CIJE: 5 RIE: 5 CAT: 09

Nondestructive Testing
CIJE: 1 RIE: 6 CAT: 21

Nondirective Play
CIJE: 0 RIE: 1 CAT: 15

Nondirective Tutorial Instruction
CIJE: 0 RIE: 1 CAT: 15

Nondiscriminatory Assessment
CIJE: 2 RIE: 7 CAT: 21

Nondiscriminatory Tests (Handicapped)
CIJE: 4 RIE: 7 CAT: 21

Nonentrenchment
CIJE: 1 RIE: 1 CAT: 11

Nonequivalent Control Groups
CIJE: 5 RIE: 3 CAT: 21

Noneuclidean Geometry
CIJE: 5 RIE: 1 CAT: 20

Nonfarm Population
CIJE: 1 RIE: 11 CAT: 10

Nonfluencies (Language)
CIJE: 2 RIE: 1 CAT: 13

Nonformal Education Information Center
CIJE: 0 RIE: 6 CAT: 17
UF Non Formal Education Center MI

Nongovernmental Organizations
CIJE: 23 RIE: 13 CAT: 05
UF NGOs

Nongraded Primaries in Action
CIJE: 0 RIE: 1 CAT: 19

Nonimmigrant Aliens
CIJE: 0 RIE: 1 CAT: 10

Noninstitutional Furniture
CIJE: 2 RIE: 0 CAT: 04

Noninstructional Staff
CIJE: 21 RIE: 25 CAT: 09
SN See also "Support Personnel"

Nonintellectual Abilities
CIJE: 2 RIE: 1 CAT: 16

Nonlinear Management
CIJE: 1 RIE: 0 CAT: 15

Nonlinear Models
CIJE: 21 RIE: 13 CAT: 15

Nonlinear Transformations
CIJE: 3 RIE: 3 CAT: 15

Nonlinguistic Composition
CIJE: 0 RIE: 1 CAT: 16

Nonmetals
CIJE: 2 RIE: 0 CAT: 20

Nonmetric Factor Analysis
CIJE: 2 RIE: 0 CAT: 21

Nonmetric Multidimensional Scaling
CIJE: 7 RIE: 3 CAT: 21

Nonmetric Temporal Path Analysis
USE Analysis of Patterns in Time

Nonmigrants
CIJE: 6 RIE: 5 CAT: 10

Nonmigration
CIJE: 1 RIE: 0 CAT: 16

Nonmonetary Economy
CIJE: 0 RIE: 1 CAT: 16
UF Non Monetary Economic System

Nonmonotonic Covariates
CIJE: 0 RIE: 1 CAT: 21

Nonnative Speakers
CIJE: 37 RIE: 32 CAT: 10

Nonnormal Distributions
CIJE: 13 RIE: 5 CAT: 21

Nonnormed Tests
CIJE: 1 RIE: 1 CAT: 21

Nonnull Hypothesis
CIJE: 0 RIE: 1 CAT: 21

Nonnumerical Computer Applications
CIJE: 0 RIE: 1 CAT: 21

Nonoperant Conditioning
CIJE: 1 RIE: 0 CAT: 11

Nonorthogonal Analysis of Variance
CIJE: 3 RIE: 1 CAT: 15

Nonorthogonal Variables
CIJE: 0 RIE: 4 CAT: 21

Nonparticipation
CIJE: 3 RIE: 6 CAT: 11

Nonpoint Source Pollution
CIJE: 1 RIE: 4 CAT: 20

Nonpolicy Debate
CIJE: 2 RIE: 2 CAT: 15
SN See also "Policy Debate"

Nonprescription Drugs
CIJE: 5 RIE: 6 CAT: 11

Nonprofit Organization Program
CIJE: 0 RIE: 2 CAT: 19

Nonprofit Sector (Labor Market)
CIJE: 0 RIE: 1 CAT: 16

Nonproprietary Training Programs
CIJE: 0 RIE: 1 CAT: 19

Nonpublic School Survey (NCES)
CIJE: 0 RIE: 2 CAT: 19

Nonpublic Schools LRC MI
USE Non Public Schools Learning Resource Center MI

Nonrandom Selection
CIJE: 2 RIE: 4 CAT: 15

Nonrandomized Design
CIJE: 0 RIE: 5 CAT: 21

Nonreactive Measurement
CIJE: 1 RIE: 1 CAT: 21

Nonreading Aptitude Test Battery
CIJE: 2 RIE: 4 CAT: 21

Nonreferral Unions
CIJE: 0 RIE: 1 CAT: 10

Nonresidents
CIJE: 1 RIE: 1 CAT: 10

Nonrespondents
CIJE: 5 RIE: 8 CAT: 10

Nonresponders
CIJE: 6 RIE: 12 CAT: 21

Nonresponse Bias
CIJE: 2 RIE: 2 CAT: 21

Nonrestrictive Clauses
CIJE: 5 RIE: 0 CAT: 13

Nonrestrictive Relatives
CIJE: 1 RIE: 0 CAT: 13

Nonroutine Problems
CIJE: 0 RIE: 1 CAT: 16
UF Non Routine Mathematical Problems

Nonsense Syllables
CIJE: 1 RIE: 3 CAT: 13

Nonsense Test Items
CIJE: 0 RIE: 1 CAT: 21

Nonsense Words
CIJE: 12 RIE: 8 CAT: 13

Nonsexist Personal Attribute Inventory Children
CIJE: 1 RIE: 0 CAT: 21

Nonsmokers
CIJE: 2 RIE: 0 CAT: 10

Nonstandard Analysis
CIJE: 2 RIE: 1 CAT: 15

Nonstrategic Recall
CIJE: 1 RIE: 0 CAT: 11

Nonstructural Elements (Construction)
CIJE: 0 RIE: 1 CAT: 16

Nonstudents
CIJE: 2 RIE: 3 CAT: 10

Nonsupervisory Employees
CIJE: 0 RIE: 1 CAT: 16

Nonsynchrony
CIJE: 0 RIE: 1 CAT: 15

Nontheatrical Film Distribution
CIJE: 1 RIE: 0 CAT: 16

Nontraditional Community College Project
CIJE: 0 RIE: 1 CAT: 19

Nontraditional Employment for Women Act 1991
CIJE: 0 RIE: 2 CAT: 14
UF Public Law 102 235

Nontraditional Employment Training Project
CIJE: 0 RIE: 2 CAT: 19

Nontraditional Institutions
CIJE: 1 RIE: 5 CAT: 05

Nontraditional Lifestyles
CIJE: 5 RIE: 3 CAT: 16

Nontraditional Medicine
CIJE: 1 RIE: 1 CAT: 11

Nontransfer Students
CIJE: 2 RIE: 5 CAT: 10
SN Students who remain in one school or program until completing the highest grade offered or obtaining a degree
UF Continuing Students (Nontransfers); Native Students (Nontransfers)

Nonverbal Artistic Creativity Instrument (Zambito)
CIJE: 0 RIE: 1 CAT: 21

Nonverbal Behavior Category System
CIJE: 0 RIE: 1 CAT: 16

Nonverbal Clauses
CIJE: 0 RIE: 1 CAT: 13

Nonverbal Curiosity Test (Corlis and Weiss)
CIJE: 0 RIE: 1 CAT: 21

Nonverbal Intelligence
CIJE: 2 RIE: 0 CAT: 11

Nonverbal Stimuli
CIJE: 6 RIE: 3 CAT: 11

Nonviolence
CIJE: 13 RIE: 38 CAT: 16

Nonvocal Communication Systems
CIJE: 1 RIE: 1 CAT: 11

Nonvocational Typing
CIJE: 1 RIE: 0 CAT: 03

Nonwage Labor
CIJE: 0 RIE: 1 CAT: 10

Nonwords
CIJE: 6 RIE: 1 CAT: 13

Noonan Syndrome
CIJE: 3 RIE: 0 CAT: 11

Nootka Elementary School (Canada)
CIJE: 0 RIE: 1 CAT: 17

NORCAL Research Group
CIJE: 1 RIE: 3 CAT: 17

Nordic Committee on Documentation and Information
CIJE: 0 RIE: 1 CAT: 17

Nordic Council
CIJE: 0 RIE: 3 CAT: 17

Nordic Countries
CIJE: 13 RIE: 12 CAT: 07

Nordic Paradise
CIJE: 0 RIE: 1 CAT: 19

Nordwrite Project
CIJE: 0 RIE: 2 CAT: 19

Norfolk City Schools VA
CIJE: 3 RIE: 7 CAT: 17

Norfolk State College VA
CIJE: 1 RIE: 5 CAT: 17

Norfolk State University VA
CIJE: 1 RIE: 5 CAT: 17

Norland Nursery Training College (England)
CIJE: 1 RIE: 0 CAT: 17

Norm Conformity Index (Tatsuoka and Tatsuoka)
CIJE: 2 RIE: 1 CAT: 21

Normal Adolescent Project
CIJE: 0 RIE: 1 CAT: 19

Normal Children
CIJE: 92 RIE: 30 CAT: 10

Normal Curve Equivalent Scores
CIJE: 4 RIE: 43 CAT: 21

Normal Distribution
CIJE: 18 RIE: 5 CAT: 21

Normal Heart (Kramer)
CIJE: 0 RIE: 1 CAT: 22

Normal Ogive Models
CIJE: 1 RIE: 3 CAT: 15

Normal Orthant Probabilities
CIJE: 0 RIE: 1 CAT: 15

Normal Schools
CIJE: 10 RIE: 9 CAT: 05

Normal Scores Test
CIJE: 2 RIE: 1 CAT: 21

Normality Tests
CIJE: 1 RIE: 2 CAT: 21

Normalization Regression Estimation
CIJE: 0 RIE: 6 CAT: 21

Normalizing Transformation
CIJE: 2 RIE: 1 CAT: 15

Norman School District OK
CIJE: 1 RIE: 0 CAT: 17

Norman Window (Mathematics)
CIJE: 1 RIE: 0 CAT: 20

Normandale Community College MN
CIJE: 0 RIE: 1 CAT: 17

Normandy Senior High School OH
CIJE: 1 RIE: 0 CAT: 17

Normans
CIJE: 2 RIE: 0 CAT: 08

Normative Philosophy
CIJE: 5 RIE: 3 CAT: 15

Normative Statements
CIJE: 0 RIE: 2 CAT: 21

Normative Systems Research
CIJE: 1 RIE: 1 CAT: 19

NORRIP
USE Northern Region Rural Integrated Programme (Ghana)

Norse Mythology
CIJE: 0 RIE: 1 CAT: 03

North (Oliver)
CIJE: 0 RIE: 2 CAT: 18

North Adams State College MA
CIJE: 1 RIE: 3 CAT: 17

North Africans
CIJE: 0 RIE: 2 CAT: 08

North Allegheny School District PA
CIJE: 1 RIE: 1 CAT: 17

North America
CIJE: 101 RIE: 93 CAT: 07

North American Association for Environmental Educ
CIJE: 2 RIE: 1 CAT: 17

North American Association of Summer Sessions
CIJE: 2 RIE: 1 CAT: 17

North American Collections Inventory Project
CIJE: 3 RIE: 3 CAT: 19

North American Field Education Directors Assn
CIJE: 0 RIE: 1 CAT: 17

North American Free Trade Agreement
CIJE: 7 RIE: 6 CAT: 14
UF NAFTA

North American Indian Womens Association
CIJE: 0 RIE: 2 CAT: 17

North American Plains Indians (Anthrop Label)
CIJE: 0 RIE: 3 CAT: 08

North American Regional Conference on Automation
CIJE: 0 RIE: 1 CAT: 02

North American Rockwell
CIJE: 1 RIE: 0 CAT: 17

North Atlantic Treaty Organization
CIJE: 6 RIE: 18 CAT: 17

North Bay Cooperative Library System CA
CIJE: 0 RIE: 1 CAT: 17

North Bay Pace Center CA
CIJE: 1 RIE: 0 CAT: 17

North Bend School District OR
CIJE: 0 RIE: 1 CAT: 17

North Boone Community Unit Schools IL
CIJE: 1 RIE: 0 CAT: 17

North Carolina
CIJE: 423 RIE: 1290 CAT: 07

North Carolina (Alamance County)
CIJE: 0 RIE: 1 CAT: 07

North Carolina (Asheville)
CIJE: 2 RIE: 1 CAT: 07

North Carolina (Boone)
CIJE: 0 RIE: 1 CAT: 07

North Carolina (Bradford)
CIJE: 0 RIE: 1 CAT: 07

North Carolina (Buncombe County)
CIJE: 0 RIE: 1 CAT: 07

North Carolina (Caldwell County)
CIJE: 1 RIE: 2 CAT: 07

North Carolina (Carteret County)
CIJE: 0 RIE: 1 CAT: 07

North Carolina (Caswell County)
CIJE: 0 RIE: 1 CAT: 07

North Carolina (Chapel Hill)
CIJE: 4 RIE: 11 CAT: 07

North Carolina (Charlotte)
CIJE: 13 RIE: 16 CAT: 07

North Carolina (Cherryville)
CIJE: 0 RIE: 1 CAT: 07

North Carolina (Duplin County)
CIJE: 0 RIE: 5 CAT: 07

North Carolina (Durham County)
CIJE: 1 RIE: 2 CAT: 07

North Carolina (Durham)
CIJE: 7 RIE: 17 CAT: 07

North Carolina (East)
CIJE: 0 RIE: 3 CAT: 07

North Carolina (Edgecombe County)
CIJE: 0 RIE: 1 CAT: 07

North Carolina (Fort Bragg)
CIJE: 0 RIE: 2 CAT: 07

North Carolina (Gaston County)
CIJE: 0 RIE: 3 CAT: 07

North Carolina (Gastonia)
CIJE: 0 RIE: 1 CAT: 07

North Carolina (Goldsboro)
CIJE: 0 RIE: 3 CAT: 07

North Carolina (Greensboro)
CIJE: 7 RIE: 8 CAT: 07

North Carolina (Greenville)
CIJE: 0 RIE: 2 CAT: 07

North Carolina (Guilford County)
CIJE: 0 RIE: 2 CAT: 07

North Carolina (Halifax County)
CIJE: 0 RIE: 2 CAT: 07

North Carolina (Haywood County)
CIJE: 0 RIE: 2 CAT: 07

North Carolina (High Point)
CIJE: 1 RIE: 2 CAT: 07

North Carolina (Hoke County)
CIJE: 0 RIE: 1 CAT: 07

North Carolina (Hyde County)
CIJE: 1 RIE: 1 CAT: 07

North Carolina (Iredell County)
CIJE: 0 RIE: 1 CAT: 07

North Carolina (Lenoir County)
CIJE: 0 RIE: 1 CAT: 07

North Carolina (Mecklenburg County)
CIJE: 3 RIE: 2 CAT: 07

North Carolina (Moore County)
CIJE: 0 RIE: 3 CAT: 07

North Carolina (Morganton)
CIJE: 0 RIE: 1 CAT: 07

North Carolina (Mount Olive)
CIJE: 0 RIE: 1 CAT: 07

North Carolina (New Hanover County)
CIJE: 0 RIE: 1 CAT: 07

North Carolina (Orange County)
CIJE: 1 RIE: 1 CAT: 07

North Carolina (Outer Banks)
CIJE: 1 RIE: 1 CAT: 07

North Carolina (Pitt County)
CIJE: 0 RIE: 3 CAT: 07

North Carolina (Polk County)
CIJE: 0 RIE: 1 CAT: 07

North Carolina (Princeville)
CIJE: 0 RIE: 1 CAT: 07

North Carolina (Raleigh)
CIJE: 2 RIE: 27 CAT: 07

North Carolina (Randolph County)
CIJE: 0 RIE: 1 CAT: 07

North Carolina (Robeson County)
CIJE: 1 RIE: 7 CAT: 07

North Carolina (Rockingham County)
CIJE: 0 RIE: 1 CAT: 07

North Carolina (Rougemont)
CIJE: 0 RIE: 1 CAT: 07

North Carolina (Scotland County)
CIJE: 0 RIE: 1 CAT: 07

North Carolina (Scotland Neck)
CIJE: 0 RIE: 2 CAT: 07

North Carolina (Southern City)
CIJE: 0 RIE: 1 CAT: 07

North Carolina (Wake County)
CIJE: 3 RIE: 1 CAT: 07

North Carolina (West)
CIJE: 0 RIE: 1 CAT: 07

North Carolina (Winston Salem)
CIJE: 1 RIE: 16 CAT: 07

North Carolina (Zebulon)
CIJE: 0 RIE: 1 CAT: 07

North Carolina Advancement School
CIJE: 0 RIE: 11 CAT: 17

North Carolina Agricultural Extension Service
CIJE: 0 RIE: 2 CAT: 17

North Carolina Agricultural Technical State Univ
CIJE: 3 RIE: 4 CAT: 17

North Carolina Annual Testing Program
CIJE: 0 RIE: 8 CAT: 21

North Carolina Appraisal Instrument
CIJE: 0 RIE: 1 CAT: 21

North Carolina Assn for Institutional Research
CIJE: 0 RIE: 2 CAT: 17

North Carolina Assn of Colleges for Teacher Educ
CIJE: 0 RIE: 1 CAT: 17

North Carolina Basic Educ Summer School Prog
USE North Carolina Basic Education Program

North Carolina Basic Education Program
CIJE: 0 RIE: 1 CAT: 19
UF North Carolina Basic Educ Summer School Prog

North Carolina Board of Higher Education
CIJE: 0 RIE: 1 CAT: 17

North Carolina Career Development Program
CIJE: 0 RIE: 3 CAT: 19

North Carolina Center for Advancement of Teaching
CIJE: 0 RIE: 2 CAT: 17

North Carolina Central University
CIJE: 4 RIE: 16 CAT: 17

North Carolina College
CIJE: 1 RIE: 3 CAT: 17

North Carolina Community College System
CIJE: 1 RIE: 20 CAT: 17

North Carolina Competency Tests
CIJE: 3 RIE: 3 CAT: 21
UF North Carolina High School Competency Tests; North Carolina Minimum Competency Tests

North Carolina Educational Computing Service
CIJE: 2 RIE: 1 CAT: 17

North Carolina Elem Sec Sch Reform Act 1984
CIJE: 0 RIE: 0 CAT: 17

North Carolina End of Course Testing Program
CIJE: 0 RIE: 4 CAT: 21

North Carolina Fund
CIJE: 0 RIE: 1 CAT: 17

North Carolina Governors School
USE Governors School of North Carolina

North Carolina High School Competency Tests
USE North Carolina Competency Tests

North Carolina Initial Certification Program
USE Initial Certification Program NC

North Carolina Internship Office
CIJE: 2 RIE: 0 CAT: 17

North Carolina Leadership Institute for Principals
CIJE: 1 RIE: 2 CAT: 17

North Carolina Manpower Development Corporation
CIJE: 1 RIE: 0 CAT: 17

North Carolina Minimum Competency Tests
USE North Carolina Competency Tests

North Carolina Minimum Skills Diagnostic Tests
CIJE: 0 RIE: 2 CAT: 21
UF Minimum Skills Diagnostic Tests (North Carolina)

North Carolina Mobility Project
CIJE: 0 RIE: 1 CAT: 19

North Carolina Outward Bound School
CIJE: 0 RIE: 2 CAT: 17

North Carolina Pilot Kindergarten Program
CIJE: 0 RIE: 1 CAT: 19

North Carolina Preservation Consortium
CIJE: 0 RIE: 1 CAT: 17

North Carolina School for the Deaf
CIJE: 2 RIE: 1 CAT: 17

North Carolina School of Science and Mathematics
CIJE: 5 RIE: 1 CAT: 17

North Carolina Science Technology Research Center
CIJE: 0 RIE: 1 CAT: 17

North Carolina Science Tests
CIJE: 0 RIE: 4 CAT: 21

North Carolina Social Studies Tests
CIJE: 0 RIE: 3 CAT: 21

North Carolina State Board of Education
CIJE: 0 RIE: 3 CAT: 17

North Carolina State Department Public Instruction
CIJE: 0 RIE: 5 CAT: 17

North Carolina State University
CIJE: 18 RIE: 7 CAT: 17

North Carolina State University Raleigh
CIJE: 17 RIE: 34 CAT: 17

North Carolina Statewide Testing Program
CIJE: 0 RIE: 1 CAT: 21

North Carolina Teacher Performance Assess System
CIJE: 0 RIE: 1 CAT: 21

North Carolina Teaching Performance Appraisal
CIJE: 1 RIE: 3 CAT: 21

North Carolina Test of Chemistry
CIJE: 0 RIE: 1 CAT: 21

North Carolina Test of Geometry
CIJE: 0 RIE: 1 CAT: 21

North Carolina v Califano
CIJE: 0 RIE: 1 CAT: 14

North Central Accrediting Association
CIJE: 3 RIE: 1 CAT: 17

North Central Association of Colleges and Schools
CIJE: 111 RIE: 29 CAT: 17

North Central College IL
CIJE: 1 RIE: 1 CAT: 17

North Central Conference on Summer Schools
CIJE: 0 RIE: 1 CAT: 17

North Central Correctional Institute MA
CIJE: 0 RIE: 1 CAT: 17

North Central Louisiana Model Preschool Program
CIJE: 0 RIE: 1 CAT: 19

North Central Regional Educational Laboratory
CIJE: 1 RIE: 11 CAT: 17

North Central Regional Information Exchange
CIJE: 0 RIE: 1 CAT: 19

North Central Technical College OH
CIJE: 0 RIE: 5 CAT: 17

North Central Technical College WI
CIJE: 1 RIE: 1 CAT: 17

North Central Technical Institute WI
CIJE: 4 RIE: 2 CAT: 17

North Chicago Community High School IL
CIJE: 0 RIE: 1 CAT: 17

North Clackamas School District OR
CIJE: 4 RIE: 4 CAT: 17

North Country Community College NY
CIJE: 3 RIE: 7 CAT: 17

North County Union High School NJ
CIJE: 1 RIE: 0 CAT: 17

North Dakota
CIJE: 70 RIE: 384 CAT: 07

North Dakota (Bismarck)
CIJE: 1 RIE: 7 CAT: 07

North Dakota (Cass County)
CIJE: 0 RIE: 2 CAT: 07

North Dakota (Devils Lake)
CIJE: 0 RIE: 1 CAT: 07

North Dakota (Fargo)
CIJE: 5 RIE: 10 CAT: 07

North Dakota (Grand Forks)
CIJE: 2 RIE: 15 CAT: 07

North Dakota (Mandan)
CIJE: 0 RIE: 1 CAT: 07

North Dakota (Minot)
CIJE: 3 RIE: 2 CAT: 07

North Dakota (West Fargo)
CIJE: 1 RIE: 0 CAT: 07

North Dakota Bureau of Educational Research
CIJE: 0 RIE: 1 CAT: 17

North Dakota Century Code
CIJE: 0 RIE: 1 CAT: 14

North Dakota Close Up
CIJE: 0 RIE: 3 CAT: 19

North Dakota Energy and Power Curriculum Guide
CIJE: 0 RIE: 1 CAT: 22

North Dakota Fact Finding Commission
CIJE: 0 RIE: 1 CAT: 17

North Dakota Governors Conference Lib Info Serv
USE Governors Conference Library Info Services ND

North Dakota Interactive Video Network
USE Interactive Video Network ND

North Dakota Network for Knowledge
CIJE: 0 RIE: 2 CAT: 17

North Dakota Pioneers in Equality Project
CIJE: 0 RIE: 1 CAT: 19

North Dakota Public Employee Retirement System
CIJE: 0 RIE: 1 CAT: 19

North Dakota Research Coordinating Unit
CIJE: 0 RIE: 1 CAT: 17

North Dakota Scholars Program
CIJE: 0 RIE: 1 CAT: 19

North Dakota State Nurses Association
CIJE: 1 RIE: 0 CAT: 17

North Dakota State School of Science
CIJE: 1 RIE: 1 CAT: 17

North Dakota State University
CIJE: 6 RIE: 7 CAT: 17

North Dakota University System
CIJE: 0 RIE: 3 CAT: 17

North Devon College (England)
CIJE: 1 RIE: 0 CAT: 17

North East London Polytechnic (England)
CIJE: 2 RIE: 1 CAT: 17

North Florida Junior College
CIJE: 1 RIE: 3 CAT: 17

North Gibson School Corporation IN
CIJE: 2 RIE: 2 CAT: 17

North Gwent College of Further Education (Wales)
CIJE: 0 RIE: 1 CAT: 17

North Harris College TX
CIJE: 0 RIE: 1 CAT: 17

North Harris County College TX
CIJE: 2 RIE: 2 CAT: 17

North Hatt Scale
CIJE: 0 RIE: 1 CAT: 21

North Haven Board of Education v Bell
CIJE: 2 RIE: 0 CAT: 14

North Haven Board of Education v Hufstedler
CIJE: 1 RIE: 0 CAT: 14

North Haven High School CT
CIJE: 0 RIE: 1 CAT: 17

North Hennepin Community College MN
CIJE: 0 RIE: 1 CAT: 17

North Hudson Jointure Commission
CIJE: 1 RIE: 0 CAT: 17

North Hunterdon Regional High School District NJ
CIJE: 0 RIE: 7 CAT: 17

North Iowa Area Community College
CIJE: 1 RIE: 1 CAT: 17

North Island College BC
CIJE: 0 RIE: 1 CAT: 17

North Kentucky Area Vocational School
CIJE: 1 RIE: 0 CAT: 17

North Kitsap School District WA
CIJE: 1 RIE: 1 CAT: 17

North Korea
CIJE: 8 RIE: 9 CAT: 07

North Lake College TX
CIJE: 0 RIE: 1 CAT: 17

North Louisiana Supplementary Education Center
CIJE: 0 RIE: 1 CAT: 17

North Olmsted City Schools OH
CIJE: 0 RIE: 1 CAT: 17

North Orange County Community College District CA
CIJE: 0 RIE: 2 CAT: 17

North Pacific Experiment
CIJE: 1 RIE: 0 CAT: 19

North Providence High School RI
CIJE: 0 RIE: 1 CAT: 17

North Reading Screen Education Project
CIJE: 1 RIE: 2 CAT: 19

North Ridgeville City School District OH
CIJE: 0 RIE: 2 CAT: 17

North Royalton City Schools OH
CIJE: 1 RIE: 0 CAT: 17

North Seattle Community College WA
CIJE: 3 RIE: 7 CAT: 17

North Shore Child Guidance Center NY
CIJE: 1 RIE: 0 CAT: 17

North Shore Community College MA
CIJE: 2 RIE: 6 CAT: 17

North Slope Borough School District AK
CIJE: 1 RIE: 0 CAT: 17

North Suburban Library System IL
CIJE: 3 RIE: 1 CAT: 17

North Syracuse Central Schools NY
CIJE: 3 RIE: 0 CAT: 17

North Texas State University
CIJE: 14 RIE: 21 CAT: 17
SN Name changed (1988) to "University of North Texas"

North Vietnam
CIJE: 2 RIE: 2 CAT: 07

North Vietnam (Hanoi)
CIJE: 0 RIE: 1 CAT: 07

North West Oklahoma Inservice Cooperative
CIJE: 0 RIE: 2 CAT: 17

North Yemen
USE Yemen

North York Board of Education ON
CIJE: 0 RIE: 9 CAT: 17

North York Self Concept Inventory (Crawford)
CIJE: 0 RIE: 6 CAT: 21

Northampton College of Advanced Tech (England)
CIJE: 1 RIE: 0 CAT: 17

Northampton County Area Community College PA
CIJE: 0 RIE: 6 CAT: 17

Northampton Family Literacy Project MA
CIJE: 0 RIE: 1 CAT: 19

Northampton High School MA
CIJE: 1 RIE: 0 CAT: 17

Northampton Monopoly
CIJE: 0 RIE: 3 CAT: 17

Northcliffe (Alfred Charles)
CIJE: 0 RIE: 1 CAT: 18

Northeast Academic Science Information Center
CIJE: 0 RIE: 12 CAT: 17

Northeast Alabama Consortium Profession Develop
CIJE: 0 RIE: 1 CAT: 17

Northeast Coalition of Educational Leaders
CIJE: 0 RIE: 1 CAT: 17

Northeast Conference Teaching of Foreign Languages
CIJE: 3 RIE: 7 CAT: 17

Northwestern University IL
CIJE: 63 RIE: 40 CAT: 17

Northwestern University Marketing Program
CIJE: 1 RIE: 0 CAT: 19

Northwood Institute MI
CIJE: 1 RIE: 1 CAT: 17

Northwood Junior High School IL
CIJE: 0 RIE: 1 CAT: 17

Norton (Charles Eliot)
CIJE: 2 RIE: 0 CAT: 18

Norton (Mary)
CIJE: 3 RIE: 0 CAT: 18

Norton Anthology of American Literature
CIJE: 0 RIE: 1 CAT: 22

Norton Anthology of English Literature
CIJE: 0 RIE: 0 CAT: 22

Norton Communicator Style Measure
CIJE: 1 RIE: 2 CAT: 21

Norwalk Mentor Program CT
CIJE: 0 RIE: 1 CAT: 19

Norwalk Plan
CIJE: 0 RIE: 1 CAT: 19

Norwalk School District CT
CIJE: 3 RIE: 1 CAT: 17

Norway
CIJE: 250 RIE: 251 CAT: 07

Norway (Drammen)
CIJE: 1 RIE: 0 CAT: 07

Norway (Hemnesberget)
CIJE: 0 RIE: 1 CAT: 07

Norway (Oslo)
CIJE: 6 RIE: 3 CAT: 07

Norway Library Planning
CIJE: 1 RIE: 0 CAT: 15

Norwegian Drama
CIJE: 0 RIE: 1 CAT: 16

Norwegian Regional Colleges
CIJE: 0 RIE: 1 CAT: 05

Norwegian Speaking
CIJE: 0 RIE: 1 CAT: 08

Norwegians
CIJE: 5 RIE: 2 CAT: 08

Norwich University VT
CIJE: 1 RIE: 2 CAT: 17

Nostalgia
CIJE: 11 RIE: 2 CAT: 16

Nota Graph System
CIJE: 0 RIE: 1 CAT: 15

Notary Publics
CIJE: 1 RIE: 0 CAT: 09

Notched Edge Cards
CIJE: 0 RIE: 1 CAT: 04

Notebook Computers
CIJE: 1 RIE: 1 CAT: 04

NOTIS Online Software
CIJE: 3 RIE: 2 CAT: 04

Notre Dame College OH
CIJE: 0 RIE: 1 CAT: 17

Notre Dame University (Philippines)
CIJE: 0 RIE: 1 CAT: 17

Nottingham Obstacle Detector
CIJE: 1 RIE: 0 CAT: 04

Nottingham Programming in Math Project
CIJE: 0 RIE: 1 CAT: 19

Noun Compounds
CIJE: 2 RIE: 1 CAT: 13

Noun Frequency Readability Method
CIJE: 0 RIE: 2 CAT: 15

Noun Modifiers
CIJE: 2 RIE: 1 CAT: 13

NOVA (Television Series)
CIJE: 1 RIE: 1 CAT: 22

Nova Complex Schools
CIJE: 0 RIE: 1 CAT: 17

Nova High School FL
CIJE: 2 RIE: 15 CAT: 17

Nova Plan
CIJE: 1 RIE: 0 CAT: 19

Nova Public Schools FL
CIJE: 2 RIE: 0 CAT: 17

Nova Scotia
CIJE: 47 RIE: 53 CAT: 07

Nova Scotia (Cape Breton)
CIJE: 3 RIE: 0 CAT: 07

Nova Scotia (Louisburg)
CIJE: 1 RIE: 0 CAT: 07

Nova Scotia (Pubnico)
CIJE: 0 RIE: 1 CAT: 07

Nova University FL
CIJE: 15 RIE: 41 CAT: 17

NovaNET
CIJE: 1 RIE: 6 CAT: 04

Novel Maturity Scale
CIJE: 1 RIE: 0 CAT: 21

Novelty Experiencing Scale (Pearson)
CIJE: 3 RIE: 0 CAT: 21

Novice Assisted Research
CIJE: 0 RIE: 1 CAT: 15

Novice Debate Association
CIJE: 0 RIE: 2 CAT: 17

Novice Knowledge Engineering
CIJE: 1 RIE: 2 CAT: 15

Novosel v Nationwide Insurance
CIJE: 0 RIE: 1 CAT: 14

Nowicki Strickland Internal External Scale (Adult)
CIJE: 0 RIE: 2 CAT: 21

Nowicki Strickland Internal External Scale (Child)
CIJE: 1 RIE: 1 CAT: 21

Nowicki Strickland Locus of Control Scale
CIJE: 18 RIE: 18 CAT: 21
UF Nowicki Strickland Personal Reaction Survey

Nowicki Strickland Locus of Control Scale Children
CIJE: 3 RIE: 2 CAT: 21

Nowicki Strickland Personal Reaction Survey
USE Nowicki Strickland Locus of Control Scale

NREN
USE National Research and Education Network

NSFNET
CIJE: 2 RIE: 1 CAT: 17

NTE Core Battery
CIJE: 2 RIE: 8 CAT: 21

NTE Professional Knowledge Examination
USE NTE Test of Professional Knowledge

NTE Specialty Area Tests
CIJE: 0 RIE: 3 CAT: 21
SN See also "ETS Specialty Area Tests"
UF Specialty Area Tests (NTE)

NTE Test of Professional Knowledge
CIJE: 4 RIE: 4 CAT: 21
UF NTE Professional Knowledge Examination; Test of Professional Knowledge (NTE)

Nuclear Anxiety Inventory
CIJE: 0 RIE: 1 CAT: 21

Nuclear Bomb Testing
CIJE: 1 RIE: 0 CAT: 20

Nuclear Deterrence
CIJE: 5 RIE: 8 CAT: 20

Nuclear Education
CIJE: 12 RIE: 7 CAT: 03

Nuclear Energy Commission
CIJE: 1 RIE: 0 CAT: 17

Nuclear Engineering
CIJE: 2 RIE: 6 CAT: 20

Nuclear Family Triangulation
USE Family Triangles

Nuclear Freeze
CIJE: 14 RIE: 12 CAT: 16

Nuclear Fusion
CIJE: 2 RIE: 1 CAT: 20

Nuclear Industry
CIJE: 4 RIE: 8 CAT: 20

Nuclear Likelihood Questionnaire
CIJE: 0 RIE: 1 CAT: 21

Nuclear Locus of Control Scales
CIJE: 0 RIE: 1 CAT: 21

Nuclear Magnetic Resonance
CIJE: 57 RIE: 0 CAT: 20
SN See related "Magnetic Resonance Imaging"
UF NMR Spectroscopy

Nuclear Nonproliferation Theory
CIJE: 1 RIE: 1 CAT: 15

Nuclear Nonproliferation Treaty
CIJE: 3 RIE: 2 CAT: 12

Nuclear Oxyacetylene Welding
CIJE: 0 RIE: 1 CAT: 20

Nuclear Reactions
CIJE: 3 RIE: 1 CAT: 20

Nuclear Reactor Operators
CIJE: 1 RIE: 2 CAT: 09

Nuclear Reactors
CIJE: 16 RIE: 23 CAT: 05

Nuclear Regulatory Commission
CIJE: 5 RIE: 4 CAT: 17

Nuclear Safety Information Center
CIJE: 1 RIE: 3 CAT: 17

Nuclear Science Abstracts
CIJE: 1 RIE: 3 CAT: 22

Nuclear Science Curriculum Project
CIJE: 0 RIE: 2 CAT: 19

Nuclear Wastes
CIJE: 11 RIE: 13 CAT: 20

Nuclear Weapons
CIJE: 29 RIE: 24 CAT: 20
SN See also "Nuclear Bomb Testing"

Nuclear Winter
CIJE: 6 RIE: 1 CAT: 20

Nucleonics
CIJE: 1 RIE: 1 CAT: 20

Nucleophilic Substitution
CIJE: 3 RIE: 0 CAT: 20

Nucleus Testing Committee
CIJE: 0 RIE: 4 CAT: 17

NUDIST Computer Program
CIJE: 0 RIE: 1 CAT: 04
SN NUDIST = Non-numerical Unstructured Data Indexing, Searching, and Theorising

NUFFIC (Netherlands)
CIJE: 0 RIE: 1 CAT: 17
UF Netherlands Organisation for Intl Coop in Highr Ed; Netherlands Universities Foundation for Intl Coop

Nuffield Biology
CIJE: 30 RIE: 1 CAT: 19

Nuffield Chemistry
CIJE: 17 RIE: 0 CAT: 19

Nuffield Combined Science
CIJE: 8 RIE: 3 CAT: 19

Nuffield Foundation
CIJE: 10 RIE: 8 CAT: 17

Nuffield French
CIJE: 1 RIE: 0 CAT: 19

Nuffield German
CIJE: 0 RIE: 1 CAT: 19

Nuffield Humanities
CIJE: 1 RIE: 0 CAT: 19

Nuffield Mathematics
CIJE: 4 RIE: 1 CAT: 19

Nuffield Physics
CIJE: 21 RIE: 1 CAT: 19

Nuffield Project
CIJE: 63 RIE: 20 CAT: 19

Nukespeak
CIJE: 3 RIE: 1 CAT: 13
SN Euphemisms used to describe nuclear war and weapons

Null Hypothesis
CIJE: 14 RIE: 13 CAT: 21

Null Subject Parameter
CIJE: 0 RIE: 2 CAT: 21

Number Combinations
CIJE: 0 RIE: 1 CAT: 20

Number Line
CIJE: 16 RIE: 4 CAT: 15

Number Names
CIJE: 2 RIE: 0 CAT: 20

Number Patterns
CIJE: 10 RIE: 1 CAT: 20

Number Right Scoring
CIJE: 11 RIE: 8 CAT: 21

Number Sense
CIJE: 29 RIE: 7 CAT: 16

Number Sentences
CIJE: 1 RIE: 1 CAT: 20

Number Sequences
CIJE: 11 RIE: 1 CAT: 20

Number Theory
CIJE: 38 RIE: 8 CAT: 15

Number Walks
CIJE: 1 RIE: 0 CAT: 20

Numeration Learning Hierarchy
CIJE: 0 RIE: 1 CAT: 15

Numeration Tasks
CIJE: 7 RIE: 3 CAT: 20

Numeric Data
CIJE: 8 RIE: 1 CAT: 20

Numeric Expressions
CIJE: 1 RIE: 2 CAT: 20

Numerical Analysis
CIJE: 22 RIE: 4 CAT: 20

Numerical Methods
CIJE: 27 RIE: 3 CAT: 20

Numerical Order
CIJE: 0 RIE: 1 CAT: 20

Numerosity Discrimination
CIJE: 6 RIE: 3 CAT: 20

Numismatics
CIJE: 1 RIE: 2 CAT: 16
UF Coin Collecting

Nupe
CIJE: 3 RIE: 3 CAT: 13
SN A Kwa language spoken in Nigeria

Nuremberg War Trials
CIJE: 0 RIE: 2 CAT: 12

Nurse Associates
CIJE: 0 RIE: 2 CAT: 09

Nurse Career Pattern Study
CIJE: 0 RIE: 1 CAT: 19

Nurse Clinicians
CIJE: 2 RIE: 0 CAT: 09
UF Clinical Nurse Specialists

Nurse Education Act 1985
CIJE: 0 RIE: 2 CAT: 14

Nurse Educators
CIJE: 0 RIE: 0 CAT: 09
UF Nursing Educators

Nurse Midwives
CIJE: 7 RIE: 4 CAT: 09

Nurse Patient Relationship
CIJE: 7 RIE: 5 CAT: 11

Nurse Physician Relationship
CIJE: 6 RIE: 2 CAT: 11

Nurse Training Act 1964
CIJE: 0 RIE: 3 CAT: 14

Nurse Training Act 1984
CIJE: 0 RIE: 1 CAT: 14

Nursemaids
USE Nannies

Nurseries in Cross Cultural Education
CIJE: 1 RIE: 4 CAT: 17

Nursery Rhymes
CIJE: 27 RIE: 10 CAT: 16

Nurses Educational Funds Inc
CIJE: 1 RIE: 0 CAT: 17

Nurses Professional Orientation Scale
CIJE: 0 RIE: 2 CAT: 21

Nursing Care Plans
CIJE: 0 RIE: 1 CAT: 11

Nursing Clinical Teacher Effectiveness Inventory
CIJE: 0 RIE: 1 CAT: 21

Nursing Dial Access
CIJE: 2 RIE: 1 CAT: 15

Nursing Directors
CIJE: 4 RIE: 1 CAT: 09

Nursing Education Module Authoring System
CIJE: 0 RIE: 1 CAT: 04

Nursing Educators
USE Nurse Educators

Nursing Home Trainer Program
CIJE: 0 RIE: 3 CAT: 19

Nursing Improvement Programs
CIJE: 1 RIE: 1 CAT: 19

Nursing Inservice Educators Greater Milwaukee Area
CIJE: 1 RIE: 0 CAT: 17

Nursing Observation of Behavior Scales (Craig)
CIJE: 1 RIE: 0 CAT: 21

Nursing Research Conference
CIJE: 0 RIE: 1 CAT: 02

Nursing Schools
CIJE: 21 RIE: 4 CAT: 05

Nursing Shortage
CIJE: 1 RIE: 6 CAT: 16

Nursing Student Loan Program
CIJE: 0 RIE: 5 CAT: 19

Nursing Students
CIJE: 13 RIE: 14 CAT: 10

Nurturance
CIJE: 32 RIE: 30 CAT: 15

Nussbaum (Martha)
CIJE: 0 RIE: 1 CAT: 18

Nut Sorters
CIJE: 0 RIE: 1 CAT: 09

Nutcracker Suite
CIJE: 1 RIE: 0 CAT: 22

Nutrient Deficiencies
USE Nutritional Deficiencies

Nutrient Values
CIJE: 0 RIE: 1 CAT: 11

Nutrients
CIJE: 5 RIE: 4 CAT: 11

Nutrition and Gerontology Services Project
CIJE: 0 RIE: 1 CAT: 19

Nutrition Education and Training Program
CIJE: 3 RIE: 16 CAT: 19

Nutrition Education Program
CIJE: 8 RIE: 6 CAT: 19

Nutrition Education Research
CIJE: 60 RIE: 5 CAT: 16

Nutrition Education Training Project MI
CIJE: 0 RIE: 1 CAT: 19

Nutrition Knowledge Tests
CIJE: 0 RIE: 1 CAT: 21

Nutrition Services
CIJE: 1 RIE: 9 CAT: 05

Nutritional Deficiencies
CIJE: 0 RIE: 1 CAT: 11
UF Nutrient Deficiencies

Nutritional Status
CIJE: 0 RIE: 1 CAT: 11

Nutritional Therapy
CIJE: 4 RIE: 1 CAT: 11

Nutron Stars
CIJE: 0 RIE: 0 CAT: 20

Nuyoricans
CIJE: 1 RIE: 0 CAT: 08

Nyakusa
CIJE: 0 RIE: 1 CAT: 13

Nyamwezi
CIJE: 0 RIE: 1 CAT: 13

Nyberg (David)
CIJE: 0 RIE: 1 CAT: 18

NYC TV Film Distribution Project
CIJE: 0 RIE: 1 CAT: 19

NYCENET
CIJE: 0 RIE: 1 CAT: 04
UF New York City Education Network

Nynorsk
CIJE: 1 RIE: 1 CAT: 13

Nyquist Frequency
CIJE: 1 RIE: 0 CAT: 21

Nyquist v Committee Public Educ and Relig Liberty
CIJE: 2 RIE: 0 CAT: 14

NYU Early Childhood Inventory Test
CIJE: 0 RIE: 1 CAT: 21

Nzema
CIJE: 0 RIE: 1 CAT: 13

O Brien (Robert)
CIJE: 1 RIE: 0 CAT: 18

O Connor (Flannery)
CIJE: 3 RIE: 0 CAT: 18

O Connor (Frank)
CIJE: 1 RIE: 0 CAT: 18

O Connor (Sandra Day)
CIJE: 1 RIE: 1 CAT: 18

O Dell (Scott)
CIJE: 2 RIE: 1 CAT: 18

O Estado de Sao Paulo
CIJE: 0 RIE: 1 CAT: 17

O Hara (R P)
CIJE: 0 RIE: 0 CAT: 18

O Hare (Frank)
CIJE: 0 RIE: 1 CAT: 18

O Hear (Anthony)
CIJE: 0 RIE: 1 CAT: 18

O Hear Ramsey Corrective
USE OR Corrective Technique

O Keefe (Georgia)
CIJE: 4 RIE: 0 CAT: 18

O Neil Meeker Borgers Model Career Decision Making
CIJE: 0 RIE: 1 CAT: 15

O Neil v Baine
CIJE: 0 RIE: 0 CAT: 14

O Neill (James M)
CIJE: 1 RIE: 0 CAT: 18

O Toole (James)
CIJE: 0 RIE: 1 CAT: 18

Oak Drive Elementary School NY
CIJE: 1 RIE: 0 CAT: 17

Oak Glen Youth Camp CA
CIJE: 0 RIE: 1 CAT: 17

Oak Grove Project
CIJE: 0 RIE: 1 CAT: 19

Oak Orchard Community Health Center NY
CIJE: 0 RIE: 1 CAT: 17

Oak Park and River Forest High School IL
CIJE: 2 RIE: 2 CAT: 17

Oak Park Book Processing Center
CIJE: 0 RIE: 1 CAT: 17

Oak Park High School MI
CIJE: 1 RIE: 0 CAT: 17

Oak Park Project
CIJE: 0 RIE: 1 CAT: 19

Oak Park School District IL
CIJE: 1 RIE: 1 CAT: 17

Oak Ridge Associated Universities TN
CIJE: 2 RIE: 5 CAT: 17

Oak Ridge Conference on Technical Training
CIJE: 0 RIE: 1 CAT: 02

Oak Ridge National Laboratory
CIJE: 2 RIE: 1 CAT: 17

Oak Ridge Schools TN
CIJE: 0 RIE: 3 CAT: 17

Oak Ridge Technical Enterprises Corporation
CIJE: 1 RIE: 0 CAT: 17

Oakeshott (Michael)
CIJE: 2 RIE: 2 CAT: 18

Oakland Adult Day and Evening School CA
CIJE: 0 RIE: 2 CAT: 17

Oakland Community Career Educ Resource Center CA
CIJE: 0 RIE: 1 CAT: 17

Oakland Community College MI
CIJE: 3 RIE: 12 CAT: 17

Oakland Cottage School
CIJE: 1 RIE: 0 CAT: 17

Oakland Public Library CA
CIJE: 1 RIE: 1 CAT: 17

Oakland Redevelopment Agency
CIJE: 0 RIE: 1 CAT: 17

Oakland Schools MI
CIJE: 2 RIE: 8 CAT: 17

Oakland Study Center Program
CIJE: 0 RIE: 1 CAT: 19

Oakland Unified School District CA
CIJE: 4 RIE: 21 CAT: 17

Oakland University MI
CIJE: 7 RIE: 18 CAT: 17

Oakland Writing Project MI
CIJE: 0 RIE: 1 CAT: 19

Oakland Youth Work Experience Program
CIJE: 0 RIE: 1 CAT: 19

Oaklea Middle School OR
CIJE: 0 RIE: 1 CAT: 17

Oakleaf Elementary School PA
CIJE: 0 RIE: 1 CAT: 17

Oakleaf Project
CIJE: 0 RIE: 4 CAT: 19

Oaklyn Junior High School NJ
CIJE: 1 RIE: 0 CAT: 17

Oakridge Public Schools OR
CIJE: 0 RIE: 1 CAT: 17

Oakton Community College CA
CIJE: 0 RIE: 1 CAT: 17

Oakton Community College IL
CIJE: 10 RIE: 19 CAT: 17

Oakview Elementary School
CIJE: 1 RIE: 0 CAT: 17

Oakwood School CA
CIJE: 1 RIE: 0 CAT: 17

Oandasan (William)
CIJE: 0 RIE: 1 CAT: 18

OARS Multidimensional Functional Assessment
CIJE: 1 RIE: 2 CAT: 21

Oates (Joyce Carol)
CIJE: 3 RIE: 3 CAT: 18

Oats
CIJE: 1 RIE: 1 CAT: 20

Ob Ugrians
CIJE: 0 RIE: 2 CAT: 08

Oberlin (Jean Frederic)
CIJE: 1 RIE: 1 CAT: 18

Oberlin College OH
CIJE: 16 RIE: 18 CAT: 17

Oberry School NC
CIJE: 0 RIE: 1 CAT: 17

Oberth (Hermann)
CIJE: 1 RIE: 0 CAT: 18

OBIS Program
USE Outdoor Biology Instructional Strategies

Object (Grammar)
CIJE: 6 RIE: 4 CAT: 13

Object Attractiveness
CIJE: 0 RIE: 1 CAT: 11

Object Categorization Test
CIJE: 1 RIE: 3 CAT: 21

Object Child Relationship
CIJE: 2 RIE: 1 CAT: 11
UF Child Object Relationship

Object Concept
CIJE: 4 RIE: 3 CAT: 21

Object Constancy
CIJE: 2 RIE: 0 CAT: 21

Object Initial Languages
CIJE: 0 RIE: 1 CAT: 13

Object Naming Test (French)
CIJE: 1 RIE: 0 CAT: 21

Object Orientation
CIJE: 11 RIE: 3 CAT: 11

Object Oriented Programing
CIJE: 10 RIE: 1 CAT: 15

Object Person Relationship
USE Person Object Relationship

Object Relations
CIJE: 23 RIE: 5 CAT: 21

Object Relocation Tasks
CIJE: 1 RIE: 1 CAT: 21

Object Retrieval
CIJE: 4 RIE: 1 CAT: 11

Object Socialization
CIJE: 1 RIE: 1 CAT: 11

Object Sorting Task (Davidson and Greenberg)
CIJE: 1 RIE: 1 CAT: 21

Object Sorting Task (Dunn)
CIJE: 0 RIE: 1 CAT: 21

Object Sorting Test
CIJE: 1 RIE: 0 CAT: 21

Object Substitution
CIJE: 1 RIE: 1 CAT: 11

Object Teaching
CIJE: 0 RIE: 1 CAT: 15

Object Transformations
CIJE: 1 RIE: 1 CAT: 16

Objectics
CIJE: 0 RIE: 1 CAT: 16

Objective Analysis
CIJE: 5 RIE: 5 CAT: 15

Objective Apperception Test (Stricker)
CIJE: 0 RIE: 1 CAT: 21

Objective Behavior Inventory (Nichols)
CIJE: 0 RIE: 1 CAT: 21

Objective Certification
CIJE: 0 RIE: 1 CAT: 15

Objective Item Congruence
CIJE: 0 RIE: 1 CAT: 21

Objective Marking
CIJE: 1 RIE: 0 CAT: 21

Objective Measure of Assertiveness
CIJE: 1 RIE: 0 CAT: 21

Objective Test Scoring Performance Rating
CIJE: 0 RIE: 1 CAT: 21

Objectively Scoreable Apperception Test
CIJE: 0 RIE: 1 CAT: 21

Objectives Bank
CIJE: 0 RIE: 6 CAT: 21

Objectives Based Evaluation Systems
CIJE: 1 RIE: 1 CAT: 21

Objectivism Scale
CIJE: 0 RIE: 1 CAT: 21

Objectivity
CIJE: 79 RIE: 39 CAT: 15

Oblate Sisters of Providence
CIJE: 1 RIE: 0 CAT: 17

Obligatory Contour Principle
CIJE: 0 RIE: 2 CAT: 13

Obnoxious Jerks (Manes)
CIJE: 0 RIE: 1 CAT: 22

Oboes
CIJE: 1 RIE: 0 CAT: 04

Obscurantism
CIJE: 0 RIE: 1 CAT: 16

Observation Checklist of Hemispheric Style
CIJE: 1 RIE: 0 CAT: 21

Observation Criteria
CIJE: 2 RIE: 3 CAT: 15

Observation Lesson Information
CIJE: 0 RIE: 1 CAT: 16

Observation of Socialization Behavior
CIJE: 0 RIE: 1 CAT: 15

Observation of Student Interaction Participation
CIJE: 0 RIE: 1 CAT: 15

Observation of Substantive Curricular Input
CIJE: 0 RIE: 2 CAT: 15

Observation of Teacher Management Behavior
CIJE: 1 RIE: 2 CAT: 15

Observation Schedule and Record
CIJE: 6 RIE: 17 CAT: 21

Observation Schedule for Physical Space (Prescott)
CIJE: 0 RIE: 1 CAT: 21

Observation Schedules
CIJE: 1 RIE: 2 CAT: 15

Observation Techniques
CIJE: 16 RIE: 7 CAT: 15

Observational Learning Theory
CIJE: 1 RIE: 1 CAT: 15

Observational Studies
CIJE: 14 RIE: 4 CAT: 16

Observatories
CIJE: 3 RIE: 2 CAT: 05

Observed Frequencies (Test)
CIJE: 0 RIE: 1 CAT: 21

Observer Effect
CIJE: 2 RIE: 1 CAT: 21

Observer Rating Scales (McDaniel)
CIJE: 0 RIE: 1 CAT: 21

Observer Ratings of Children (Emmerich)
CIJE: 0 RIE: 1 CAT: 21

Observer Reliability
CIJE: 4 RIE: 3 CAT: 21

Observing Responses
CIJE: 2 RIE: 0 CAT: 15

Obsessive Compulsive Behavior
CIJE: 12 RIE: 3 CAT: 11
SN Use the more specific "Compulsive Handwashing," if appropriate

Obsessive Compulsive Scale
CIJE: 0 RIE: 0 CAT: 21

Obstacle Detectors
CIJE: 0 RIE: 1 CAT: 04

Obstetrical Complications
CIJE: 0 RIE: 1 CAT: 11

Obstetrical Drugs
CIJE: 5 RIE: 2 CAT: 11

Obtrusive Measures
CIJE: 0 RIE: 1 CAT: 16

Obturators
CIJE: 1 RIE: 0 CAT: 04

Occidental College CA
CIJE: 5 RIE: 3 CAT: 17

Occitan
CIJE: 11 RIE: 0 CAT: 13

Occu Sort
CIJE: 2 RIE: 2 CAT: 15

Occultism
CIJE: 7 RIE: 5 CAT: 16

Occupancy in Accommodations
CIJE: 0 RIE: 1 CAT: 16

Occupation Systems Theory
CIJE: 0 RIE: 1 CAT: 15

Occupational Affective Behavior Analysis
CIJE: 1 RIE: 1 CAT: 15

Occupational Age Distribution
CIJE: 0 RIE: 1 CAT: 16

Occupational Analysis Inventory
CIJE: 1 RIE: 14 CAT: 21

Occupational Analysts
CIJE: 0 RIE: 1 CAT: 09

Occupational Aspiration Scale
CIJE: 5 RIE: 7 CAT: 21

Occupational Attitude Questionnaire (Williams)
CIJE: 0 RIE: 1 CAT: 21

Occupational Behavior
CIJE: 3 RIE: 1 CAT: 11

Occupational Changes in a Generation Survey
CIJE: 4 RIE: 2 CAT: 21

Occupational Commitment
CIJE: 2 RIE: 1 CAT: 16

Occupational Competence Assessment
CIJE: 0 RIE: 7 CAT: 21

Occupational Competency Project NJ
CIJE: 0 RIE: 1 CAT: 19

Occupational Competency Testing
CIJE: 4 RIE: 1 CAT: 21

Occupational Congruence
CIJE: 0 RIE: 1 CAT: 16
UF Self Occupational Congruence

Occupational Control
CIJE: 1 RIE: 0 CAT: 16

Occupational Development Centers
CIJE: 0 RIE: 1 CAT: 05

Occupational Distribution
CIJE: 5 RIE: 1 CAT: 16

Occupational Employment Statistics Program
CIJE: 0 RIE: 1 CAT: 19

Occupational English Test
CIJE: 0 RIE: 1 CAT: 21

Occupational Expectations
USE Job Expectations

Occupational Expectations Inven (Hofstrand et al)
CIJE: 0 RIE: 1 CAT: 21

Occupational Identity
CIJE: 3 RIE: 1 CAT: 16

Occupational Images
CIJE: 2 RIE: 2 CAT: 16

Occupational Information Access System
CIJE: 0 RIE: 6 CAT: 15

Occupational Information Systems Grants Program
CIJE: 1 RIE: 0 CAT: 19

Occupational Interest Inventory
CIJE: 1 RIE: 4 CAT: 21

Occupational Inventory (Reardon)
CIJE: 1 RIE: 0 CAT: 21

Occupational Knowledge Testing
CIJE: 0 RIE: 1 CAT: 21

Occupational Literacy
USE Job Literacy

Occupational Math Requirements Assessment
CIJE: 0 RIE: 1 CAT: 21

Occupational Mismatch
CIJE: 1 RIE: 1 CAT: 15

Occupational Models
CIJE: 2 RIE: 2 CAT: 16

Occupational Orientation
CIJE: 2 RIE: 4 CAT: 16

Occupational Outlook Handbook
CIJE: 11 RIE: 5 CAT: 22

Occupational Preparation School PA
CIJE: 1 RIE: 0 CAT: 17

Occupational Proficiency
CIJE: 0 RIE: 3 CAT: 16

Occupational Projection Research Project
CIJE: 0 RIE: 3 CAT: 19

Occupational Reinforcer Patterns
CIJE: 0 RIE: 2 CAT: 21

Occupational Repertory Test (Bingham)
CIJE: 0 RIE: 1 CAT: 21

Occupational Report
CIJE: 0 RIE: 1 CAT: 15
SN Computer-generated report that provides occupational information for planning vocational rehabilitation services

Occupational Research Unit
CIJE: 0 RIE: 1 CAT: 16

Occupational Rewards
CIJE: 1 RIE: 3 CAT: 16

Occupational Role Values
CIJE: 1 RIE: 0 CAT: 16

Occupational Safety and Health Act 1970
CIJE: 35 RIE: 33 CAT: 14

Occupational Safety and Health Administration
CIJE: 25 RIE: 15 CAT: 17

Occupational Segregation
CIJE: 31 RIE: 10 CAT: 15

Occupational Shortages Reporting System
CIJE: 0 RIE: 1 CAT: 15

Occupational Socialization
CIJE: 9 RIE: 2 CAT: 16

Occupational Specialists
CIJE: 2 RIE: 17 CAT: 09

Occupational Stability
CIJE: 2 RIE: 1 CAT: 16

Occupational Status
CIJE: 31 RIE: 7 CAT: 16

Occupational Stereotypes
CIJE: 3 RIE: 5 CAT: 16

Occupational Structure
CIJE: 5 RIE: 1 CAT: 16

Occupational Survival Skills
CIJE: 3 RIE: 2 CAT: 16

Occupational Survival Skills Project
CIJE: 0 RIE: 1 CAT: 19

Occupational Training Families
CIJE: 0 RIE: 1 CAT: 15

Occupational Training Information System
CIJE: 2 RIE: 8 CAT: 15

Occupational Upgrading
CIJE: 1 RIE: 1 CAT: 16

Occupational Values
CIJE: 1 RIE: 2 CAT: 15

Occupational Values Inventory
CIJE: 1 RIE: 2 CAT: 21

Occupational Work Adjustment Program
CIJE: 0 RIE: 4 CAT: 19

Occupational Work Experience Program
CIJE: 0 RIE: 1 CAT: 19

Occurrence at Owl Creek Bridge (An)
CIJE: 0 RIE: 1 CAT: 22

Occutapes
CIJE: 0 RIE: 1 CAT: 04

Ocean Basins
CIJE: 3 RIE: 1 CAT: 07

Ocean Commons
CIJE: 0 RIE: 1 CAT: 20

Ocean County College NJ
CIJE: 0 RIE: 4 CAT: 17

Ocean County Social Studies Project
CIJE: 0 RIE: 1 CAT: 19

Ocean County Vocational Technical School NJ
CIJE: 0 RIE: 2 CAT: 17

Ocean Hill Brownsville School District NY
CIJE: 2 RIE: 3 CAT: 17

Ocean Hill Brownsville School Project
CIJE: 0 RIE: 1 CAT: 19

Ocean Management
CIJE: 0 RIE: 1 CAT: 20

Ocean Related Curriculum Activities
USE Project ORCA

Ocean Territories
CIJE: 0 RIE: 1 CAT: 07

Ocean Township School District NJ
CIJE: 0 RIE: 1 CAT: 17

Ocean View School District CA
CIJE: 1 RIE: 2 CAT: 17

Oceania
CIJE: 6 RIE: 37 CAT: 07

Oceanic Education Activities Great Lakes Schools
CIJE: 0 RIE: 15 CAT: 19

Oceanographic Education Center
CIJE: 1 RIE: 0 CAT: 17

Oceanographic Tables and Standards
CIJE: 0 RIE: 1 CAT: 20

Oceans
CIJE: 2 RIE: 6 CAT: 07

OCLC
CIJE: 240 RIE: 170 CAT: 17
SN Formerly the "Ohio College Library Center" (q.v.)
UF Online Computer Library Center

OCLC FirstSearch
USE FirstSearch

OCLC Search CD450
CIJE: 1 RIE: 1 CAT: 04

Octahedral Complexes
CIJE: 1 RIE: 0 CAT: 20

Octal Response
CIJE: 1 RIE: 0 CAT: 15

Octet Rule
CIJE: 0 RIE: 1 CAT: 20

October (Month)
CIJE: 0 RIE: 0 CAT: 16

Octopuses
CIJE: 1 RIE: 1 CAT: 20

Ocular Motility
CIJE: 1 RIE: 0 CAT: 11

Ocular Motor Apraxia
CIJE: 1 RIE: 0 CAT: 11

Oculocerebrorenal Syndrome
USE Lowes Syndrome

Odawa (Tribe)
CIJE: 0 RIE: 1 CAT: 08

Oddity Learning
CIJE: 11 RIE: 2 CAT: 15

Ode Intimations of Immortality (Wordsworth)
CIJE: 0 RIE: 1 CAT: 22

Oden (Gloria)
CIJE: 1 RIE: 0 CAT: 18

Odenheim v Carlstadt East Rutherford Reg Sch Dist
CIJE: 1 RIE: 0 CAT: 14

Odessa College TX
CIJE: 0 RIE: 2 CAT: 17

Odontography
CIJE: 0 RIE: 1 CAT: 11

Odor Index
CIJE: 1 RIE: 0 CAT: 21

Odor Pollution
CIJE: 1 RIE: 0 CAT: 20

Odors
CIJE: 10 RIE: 5 CAT: 20

Odual
CIJE: 0 RIE: 1 CAT: 13

Odyssey
CIJE: 12 RIE: 8 CAT: 22

Odyssey House
CIJE: 0 RIE: 1 CAT: 17

Oedipal Conflict
CIJE: 6 RIE: 5 CAT: 11

Oedipus Rex
CIJE: 2 RIE: 4 CAT: 22

Oedipus Tyrannus (Sophocles)
CIJE: 0 RIE: 1 CAT: 22

Oenology
USE Winemaking

Oettinger (Anthony)
CIJE: 1 RIE: 0 CAT: 18

Of Mice and Men
CIJE: 0 RIE: 1 CAT: 22

Off Campus Activities
CIJE: 6 RIE: 2 CAT: 03

Off Campus Experiential Learning Program
CIJE: 0 RIE: 1 CAT: 19

Off Campus Students
CIJE: 4 RIE: 3 CAT: 10

Off Farm Employment
CIJE: 11 RIE: 2 CAT: 16
SN Use Descriptor "Off Farm Agricultural Occupations" if employment is agricultural

Off Highway Vehicles
USE Off Road Vehicles

Off Reservation Boarding Schools
CIJE: 0 RIE: 2 CAT: 05

Off Road Vehicles
CIJE: 1 RIE: 0 CAT: 04
SN See also "All Terrain Vehicles"
UF Off Highway Vehicles

Off the Air Recordings
CIJE: 3 RIE: 9 CAT: 16

Offender Literacy Programs
CIJE: 0 RIE: 1 CAT: 19

Offensive Speech
CIJE: 1 RIE: 5 CAT: 16

Offer Self Image Questionnaire
CIJE: 14 RIE: 6 CAT: 21

Office Buildings
CIJE: 0 RIE: 1 CAT: 05

Office de Cooperation Radiophonique
CIJE: 0 RIE: 1 CAT: 17

Office Education Association
CIJE: 2 RIE: 0 CAT: 17

Office Education Clubs of America
CIJE: 1 RIE: 0 CAT: 17

Office for Advanced Research in Hispanic Education
CIJE: 0 RIE: 1 CAT: 17

Office for Advancement of Public Negro Colleges
CIJE: 0 RIE: 1 CAT: 17

Office for Civil Rights
CIJE: 19 RIE: 23 CAT: 17
UF Office of Civil Rights

Office for Civil Rights Guidelines
CIJE: 0 RIE: 2 CAT: 14

Office for Scientific and Technical Information
CIJE: 0 RIE: 2 CAT: 17

Office Laboratory Programs
CIJE: 0 RIE: 1 CAT: 19

Office Landscaping
CIJE: 1 RIE: 0 CAT: 09

Office Machine Servicers
CIJE: 0 RIE: 1 CAT: 09

Office Occupations Teachers Conference
CIJE: 0 RIE: 1 CAT: 02

Office of Adolescent Pregnancy Programs
CIJE: 0 RIE: 1 CAT: 17

Office of Bilingual Educ Minority Lang Affairs
CIJE: 0 RIE: 2 CAT: 17

Office of Career Education
CIJE: 5 RIE: 4 CAT: 17

Office of Child Development
CIJE: 6 RIE: 12 CAT: 17

Office of Civil Defense
CIJE: 0 RIE: 1 CAT: 17

Office of Civil Rights
USE Office for Civil Rights

Office of Economic Opportunity
CIJE: 12 RIE: 36 CAT: 17

Office of Economic Research
CIJE: 0 RIE: 7 CAT: 17

Office of Education
CIJE: 103 RIE: 203 CAT: 17

Office of Educational Research and Improvement
CIJE: 28 RIE: 43 CAT: 17

Office of Environmental Education
CIJE: 2 RIE: 1 CAT: 17

Office of Equal Opportunity
CIJE: 0 RIE: 1 CAT: 17

Office of Federal Contract Compliance Programs
CIJE: 6 RIE: 0 CAT: 17

Office of Higher Education Programs
CIJE: 0 RIE: 1 CAT: 17

Office of Human Development
CIJE: 2 RIE: 2 CAT: 17

Office of Human Development Services
CIJE: 0 RIE: 1 CAT: 17

Office of Indian Education
CIJE: 2 RIE: 6 CAT: 17

Office of Indian Education Programs
CIJE: 0 RIE: 10 CAT: 17

Office of Inspector General
CIJE: 2 RIE: 7 CAT: 17

Office of Intergovernmental Science Programs
CIJE: 0 RIE: 1 CAT: 17

Office of Juvenile Justice Delinquency Prevention
USE Juvenile Justice Delinquency Prevention Office

Office of Management and Budget
CIJE: 29 RIE: 28 CAT: 17
SN See add'l listings under "OMB..."
UF OMB

Office of Manpower Policy Evaluation Research
CIJE: 0 RIE: 4 CAT: 17

Office of Maternal and Child Health
CIJE: 0 RIE: 1 CAT: 17
UF Maternal and Child Health Office

Office of Minority Business Enterprise
CIJE: 3 RIE: 0 CAT: 17

Office of Native American Programs
CIJE: 2 RIE: 0 CAT: 17

Office of Naval Research
CIJE: 1 RIE: 10 CAT: 17

Office of Personnel Management
CIJE: 2 RIE: 9 CAT: 17

Office of Program Evaluation
CIJE: 0 RIE: 1 CAT: 17

Office of Research and Development
CIJE: 0 RIE: 3 CAT: 17

Office of Research Grants
CIJE: 1 RIE: 0 CAT: 17

Office of Revenue Sharing
CIJE: 0 RIE: 1 CAT: 17

Office of Science and Technology
CIJE: 6 RIE: 2 CAT: 17

Office of Science Education
CIJE: 1 RIE: 0 CAT: 17

Office of Science Information Service
CIJE: 1 RIE: 5 CAT: 17

Office of Service Delivery Assessment
CIJE: 1 RIE: 0 CAT: 17

Office of Special Educ Rehabilitative Services
CIJE: 5 RIE: 22 CAT: 17

Office of Special Education
CIJE: 2 RIE: 3 CAT: 17

Office of Special Education Programs
CIJE: 5 RIE: 14 CAT: 17
SN Part of the "Office of Special Educ Rehabilitative Services"
UF Special Education Programs (ED)

Office of Student Financial Assistance
CIJE: 0 RIE: 8 CAT: 17

Office of Technical Assistance and Training
CIJE: 0 RIE: 1 CAT: 17

Office of Technology Assessment
CIJE: 28 RIE: 12 CAT: 17

Office of Telecommunications Policy
CIJE: 2 RIE: 7 CAT: 17

Office of the Assistant Secretary for Education
CIJE: 0 RIE: 2 CAT: 17

Office of University Library Management Studies
CIJE: 0 RIE: 4 CAT: 17

Office of Urban Education
CIJE: 0 RIE: 1 CAT: 17

Office of Workers Compensation Programs
CIJE: 0 RIE: 1 CAT: 17

Office of Youth Programs
CIJE: 0 RIE: 2 CAT: 17

Officer Attitudes
CIJE: 2 RIE: 0 CAT: 15

Officer Career Information and Planning System
CIJE: 0 RIE: 1 CAT: 15

Officer Friendly Program
CIJE: 0 RIE: 1 CAT: 19

Officer Selection Battery
CIJE: 0 RIE: 2 CAT: 21

Officer Vic
CIJE: 0 RIE: 1 CAT: 22

Officers (Social Development)
CIJE: 1 RIE: 0 CAT: 09

Offices of Research in Medical Education
CIJE: 0 RIE: 1 CAT: 05
UF Medical Education Research Offices

Offices of Rural Affairs
CIJE: 0 RIE: 1 CAT: 05
UF Rural Affairs Offices

Official Development Assistance
CIJE: 0 RIE: 1 CAT: 19

Official Languages Act (Canada)
CIJE: 0 RIE: 3 CAT: 14

Offline Printing
CIJE: 2 RIE: 1 CAT: 20

Offline Systems
CIJE: 2 RIE: 5 CAT: 04

Offset Duplication
CIJE: 1 RIE: 2 CAT: 04

Offset Lithography
CIJE: 0 RIE: 4 CAT: 16

Offset Printing
CIJE: 1 RIE: 1 CAT: 16

Offshore Drilling
CIJE: 4 RIE: 5 CAT: 20

Ogai (Mori)
CIJE: 1 RIE: 0 CAT: 18

Ogbia
CIJE: 0 RIE: 1 CAT: 13

Ogbu (John)
CIJE: 5 RIE: 5 CAT: 18

Ogburn Report
CIJE: 0 RIE: 1 CAT: 22
SN 1933 report of the President's Research Committee on Social Trends
UF Recent Social Trends in the United States

Ogden City School District UT
CIJE: 0 RIE: 1 CAT: 17

Ogilvie (Mardel)
CIJE: 0 RIE: 1 CAT: 18

Ogilvie Social Competency Scale
CIJE: 0 RIE: 1 CAT: 21

Oglala Lakota College SD
CIJE: 2 RIE: 2 CAT: 17
SN Formerly Oglala Sioux Community College SD

Oglala Sioux Community College SD
CIJE: 0 RIE: 2 CAT: 17
SN Later changed to Oglala Lakota College SD

Oglala Sioux Education Research Project
CIJE: 0 RIE: 2 CAT: 19

Oglethorpe University GA
CIJE: 2 RIE: 1 CAT: 17

Ogontz Plan for Mutual International Education
CIJE: 0 RIE: 1 CAT: 19

Ohio
CIJE: 424 RIE: 1384 CAT: 07

Ohio (Akron)
CIJE: 12 RIE: 21 CAT: 07

Ohio (Athens County)
CIJE: 0 RIE: 1 CAT: 07

Ohio (Athens)
CIJE: 1 RIE: 0 CAT: 07

Ohio (Belmont County)
CIJE: 0 RIE: 1 CAT: 07

Ohio (Berea)
CIJE: 1 RIE: 2 CAT: 07

Ohio (Canton)
CIJE: 2 RIE: 0 CAT: 07

Ohio (Central)
CIJE: 1 RIE: 3 CAT: 07

Ohio (Champaign County)
CIJE: 0 RIE: 1 CAT: 07

Ohio (Cincinnati)
CIJE: 33 RIE: 100 CAT: 07

Ohio (Clark County)
CIJE: 1 RIE: 2 CAT: 07

Ohio (Clermont County)
CIJE: 0 RIE: 3 CAT: 07

Ohio (Cleveland Heights)
CIJE: 5 RIE: 1 CAT: 07

Ohio (Cleveland Model Cities Area)
CIJE: 1 RIE: 0 CAT: 07

Ohio (Cleveland)
CIJE: 61 RIE: 153 CAT: 07

Ohio (Clinton County)
CIJE: 0 RIE: 1 CAT: 07

Ohio (Columbus)
CIJE: 15 RIE: 51 CAT: 07

Ohio (Coshocton)
CIJE: 0 RIE: 1 CAT: 07

Ohio (Cuyahoga County)
CIJE: 4 RIE: 13 CAT: 07

Ohio (Dayton Miami Valley)
CIJE: 0 RIE: 2 CAT: 07

Ohio (Dayton)
CIJE: 19 RIE: 28 CAT: 07

Ohio (Defiance)
CIJE: 0 RIE: 1 CAT: 07

Ohio (East Cleveland)
CIJE: 0 RIE: 1 CAT: 07

Ohio (Franklin County)
CIJE: 4 RIE: 14 CAT: 07

Ohio (Granville)
CIJE: 0 RIE: 1 CAT: 07

Ohio (Greene County)
CIJE: 0 RIE: 2 CAT: 07

Ohio (Grove City)
CIJE: 1 RIE: 3 CAT: 07

Ohio (Hamilton County)
CIJE: 0 RIE: 9 CAT: 07

Ohio (Hillsboro)
CIJE: 0 RIE: 1 CAT: 07

Ohio (Holmes County)
CIJE: 2 RIE: 2 CAT: 07

Ohio (Hudson)
CIJE: 0 RIE: 1 CAT: 07

Ohio (Kent)
CIJE: 0 RIE: 11 CAT: 07

Ohio (Lawrence County)
CIJE: 0 RIE: 1 CAT: 07

Ohio (Leipsic)
CIJE: 0 RIE: 1 CAT: 07

Ohio (Lucas County)
CIJE: 1 RIE: 1 CAT: 07

Ohio (Ludlow)
CIJE: 1 RIE: 0 CAT: 07

Ohio (Madison County)
CIJE: 0 RIE: 1 CAT: 07

Ohio (Marietta)
CIJE: 0 RIE: 1 CAT: 07

Ohio (Medina)
CIJE: 1 RIE: 0 CAT: 07

Ohio (Montgomery County)
CIJE: 0 RIE: 1 CAT: 07

Ohio (Nelsonville)
CIJE: 1 RIE: 0 CAT: 07

Ohio (New Lexington)
CIJE: 1 RIE: 0 CAT: 07

Ohio (Northeast)
CIJE: 2 RIE: 5 CAT: 07

Ohio (Northwest)
CIJE: 2 RIE: 8 CAT: 07

Ohio (Oberlin)
CIJE: 0 RIE: 2 CAT: 07

Ohio (Parma)
CIJE: 2 RIE: 0 CAT: 07

Ohio (Portage County)
CIJE: 0 RIE: 2 CAT: 07

Ohio (Richland County)
CIJE: 1 RIE: 3 CAT: 07

Ohio (Shaker Heights)
CIJE: 3 RIE: 1 CAT: 07

Ohio (South)
CIJE: 0 RIE: 2 CAT: 07

Ohio (Southeast)
CIJE: 4 RIE: 0 CAT: 07

Ohio (Southwest)
CIJE: 2 RIE: 2 CAT: 07

Ohio (Springfield)
CIJE: 0 RIE: 1 CAT: 07

Ohio (Stark County)
CIJE: 0 RIE: 1 CAT: 07

Ohio (Summit County)
CIJE: 0 RIE: 2 CAT: 07

Ohio (Tipp City)
CIJE: 0 RIE: 1 CAT: 07

Ohio (Toledo)
CIJE: 11 RIE: 18 CAT: 07

Ohio (Union County)
CIJE: 0 RIE: 1 CAT: 07

Ohio (Upper Arlington)
CIJE: 3 RIE: 4 CAT: 07

Ohio (Vermilion)
CIJE: 1 RIE: 0 CAT: 07

Ohio (Warren County)
CIJE: 1 RIE: 2 CAT: 07

Ohio (Warren)
CIJE: 4 RIE: 9 CAT: 07

Ohio (Washington County)
CIJE: 0 RIE: 1 CAT: 07

Ohio (West Carrollton)
CIJE: 1 RIE: 1 CAT: 07

Ohio (Worthington)
CIJE: 4 RIE: 3 CAT: 07

Ohio (Yellow Springs)
CIJE: 0 RIE: 2 CAT: 07

Ohio (Youngstown)
CIJE: 5 RIE: 2 CAT: 07

Ohio Academy of Science
CIJE: 1 RIE: 1 CAT: 17

Ohio Association for Supervision Curriculum Devel
CIJE: 0 RIE: 1 CAT: 17

Ohio Board of Regents
CIJE: 2 RIE: 2 CAT: 17

Ohio Career Development Program
CIJE: 1 RIE: 10 CAT: 19

Ohio Career Information System
CIJE: 0 RIE: 2 CAT: 04

Ohio Central School System
CIJE: 0 RIE: 1 CAT: 17

Ohio College Library Center
CIJE: 29 RIE: 54 CAT: 17
SN "OCLC" (q.v.) is currently preferred name form

Ohio Competency Analysis Profiles
CIJE: 1 RIE: 3 CAT: 21

Ohio Consortium for Portfolio Development
CIJE: 1 RIE: 2 CAT: 17

Ohio Continuing Higher Education Association
CIJE: 0 RIE: 2 CAT: 17

Ohio Cooperative Extension Service
CIJE: 2 RIE: 2 CAT: 17

Ohio Council on Advanced Placement
CIJE: 0 RIE: 1 CAT: 17

Ohio Council on Vocational Education
CIJE: 0 RIE: 2 CAT: 17

Ohio County Schools WV
CIJE: 2 RIE: 0 CAT: 17

Ohio Disadvantaged Pupil Program Fund
CIJE: 0 RIE: 3 CAT: 17
UF Disadvantaged Pupil Program Fund OH

Ohio Dominican College
CIJE: 2 RIE: 7 CAT: 17

Ohio Education Association
CIJE: 1 RIE: 5 CAT: 17

Ohio Education Reform Bill
CIJE: 0 RIE: 1 CAT: 14

Ohio Educational Library Media Association
CIJE: 0 RIE: 1 CAT: 17

Ohio Entrepreneurship File
CIJE: 0 RIE: 1 CAT: 04

Ohio Environmental Protection Agency
CIJE: 1 RIE: 1 CAT: 17

Ohio Faculty Senate
CIJE: 1 RIE: 0 CAT: 17

Ohio Governors Conference on Aging
CIJE: 0 RIE: 0 CAT: 02

Ohio Governors Task Force on Voc and Tech Educ
USE Governors Task Force on Voc and Tech Educ OH

Ohio Innovations Survey
CIJE: 0 RIE: 1 CAT: 19

Ohio Institute of Technology
CIJE: 0 RIE: 2 CAT: 17

Ohio Instructional Grants
CIJE: 0 RIE: 1 CAT: 19

Ohio Library Association
CIJE: 0 RIE: 1 CAT: 17

Ohio Library Development Plan
CIJE: 1 RIE: 0 CAT: 19

Ohio Library Information System
CIJE: 0 RIE: 1 CAT: 04

Ohio Library Trustees Association
CIJE: 0 RIE: 1 CAT: 17

Ohio Model
CIJE: 0 RIE: 6 CAT: 15

Ohio Needs Assessment
CIJE: 0 RIE: 1 CAT: 19

Ohio Network for Information Exchange
CIJE: 0 RIE: 1 CAT: 19

Ohio Northern University
CIJE: 0 RIE: 2 CAT: 17

Ohio Plan
CIJE: 2 RIE: 0 CAT: 19

Ohio Printing Achievement Test
CIJE: 0 RIE: 1 CAT: 21

Ohio Printing Performance Test
CIJE: 0 RIE: 1 CAT: 21

Ohio Reading Recovery Program
CIJE: 1 RIE: 3 CAT: 19

Ohio River
CIJE: 2 RIE: 3 CAT: 07

Ohio School for the Deaf
CIJE: 1 RIE: 0 CAT: 17

Ohio Sea Grant Program
CIJE: 2 RIE: 23 CAT: 19

Ohio Social Acceptance Scale (Raths)
CIJE: 3 RIE: 1 CAT: 21

Ohio State Board of Education
CIJE: 0 RIE: 17 CAT: 17

Ohio State Department of Education
CIJE: 0 RIE: 6 CAT: 17

Ohio State Instructional Preference Scale
CIJE: 0 RIE: 1 CAT: 21

Ohio State Midcareer Program in Educational Admin
CIJE: 0 RIE: 1 CAT: 19

Ohio State Univ Computer Graphics Research Group
USE Computer Graphics Research Group

Ohio State University
CIJE: 199 RIE: 129 CAT: 17

Ohio State University Critical Reading Tests
CIJE: 1 RIE: 0 CAT: 21

Ohio State University Hospitals
CIJE: 0 RIE: 1 CAT: 17

Ohio State University Lima
CIJE: 0 RIE: 2 CAT: 17

Ohio State University Newark
CIJE: 0 RIE: 1 CAT: 17

Ohio Student Inventory of Guidance Awareness
CIJE: 0 RIE: 1 CAT: 21

Ohio Survey Tests
CIJE: 1 RIE: 2 CAT: 21

Ohio Technology Transfer Organization
CIJE: 0 RIE: 2 CAT: 17

Ohio Trade Industrial Education Achievement Tests
CIJE: 1 RIE: 2 CAT: 21

Ohio University
CIJE: 27 RIE: 25 CAT: 17

Ohio Valley (Central)
CIJE: 0 RIE: 1 CAT: 07

Ohio Vocational Achievement Tests
CIJE: 0 RIE: 2 CAT: 21

Ohio Vocational Education Achievement Test Program
CIJE: 1 RIE: 2 CAT: 19

Ohio Vocational Interest Survey
CIJE: 6 RIE: 11 CAT: 21

Ohio Wesleyan University
CIJE: 3 RIE: 7 CAT: 17

Ohio Work Values Inventory
CIJE: 5 RIE: 1 CAT: 21

Ohio Works Program
CIJE: 0 RIE: 1 CAT: 19

Ohio Writing Project
CIJE: 1 RIE: 1 CAT: 19

Ohio Youth Commission
CIJE: 0 RIE: 1 CAT: 17

OhioLINK
CIJE: 4 RIE: 3 CAT: 17

Ohlone College CA
CIJE: 1 RIE: 6 CAT: 17

Ohm Law of Electricity
CIJE: 4 RIE: 9 CAT: 20

Ohmmeters
CIJE: 1 RIE: 1 CAT: 04

Ohwaki Kohs Tactile Block Design Intelligence Test
CIJE: 0 RIE: 1 CAT: 21

Oil Belt Vocational Technical School AR
CIJE: 0 RIE: 1 CAT: 17

Oil Cartels
CIJE: 1 RIE: 0 CAT: 10

Oil Changes
CIJE: 0 RIE: 1 CAT: 20

Oil Pollution
CIJE: 2 RIE: 2 CAT: 20

Oil Refining
CIJE: 1 RIE: 0 CAT: 20

Oil Reserves
CIJE: 0 RIE: 0 CAT: 20

Oil Shale
USE Shale Oil

Oil Spills
CIJE: 6 RIE: 2 CAT: 20
SN See also "Exxon Valdez Oil Spill"

Ojemann (Ralph H)
CIJE: 0 RIE: 1 CAT: 18

OK (Word)
CIJE: 0 RIE: 1 CAT: 13

Okaloosa County Schools FL
CIJE: 0 RIE: 1 CAT: 17

Okaloosa Walton Community College FL
CIJE: 0 RIE: 1 CAT: 17

Okaloosa Walton Junior College FL
CIJE: 3 RIE: 2 CAT: 17

Okeanos Ocean Research Foundation
CIJE: 1 RIE: 0 CAT: 17

Okinawa
USE Japan (Okinawa)

Okinawans
CIJE: 0 RIE: 2 CAT: 08

Oklahoma
CIJE: 150 RIE: 710 CAT: 07

Oklahoma (Altus)
CIJE: 0 RIE: 2 CAT: 07

Oklahoma (Bartlesville)
CIJE: 0 RIE: 2 CAT: 07

Oklahoma (Blanchard)
CIJE: 0 RIE: 1 CAT: 07

Oklahoma (Central)
CIJE: 0 RIE: 2 CAT: 07

Oklahoma (Choctaw County)
CIJE: 0 RIE: 1 CAT: 07

Oklahoma (Durant)
CIJE: 0 RIE: 2 CAT: 07

Oklahoma (East)
CIJE: 0 RIE: 5 CAT: 07

Oklahoma (Glencoe)
CIJE: 0 RIE: 1 CAT: 07

Oklahoma (Muskogee)
CIJE: 2 RIE: 1 CAT: 07

Oklahoma (Norman)
CIJE: 1 RIE: 8 CAT: 07

Oklahoma (Oklahoma City)
CIJE: 5 RIE: 20 CAT: 07

Oklahoma (Pawnee County)
CIJE: 0 RIE: 1 CAT: 07

Oklahoma (Sand Springs)
CIJE: 0 RIE: 2 CAT: 07

Oklahoma (Snyder)
CIJE: 0 RIE: 1 CAT: 07

Oklahoma (Southwest)
CIJE: 0 RIE: 1 CAT: 07

Oklahoma (Stillwater)
CIJE: 0 RIE: 20 CAT: 07

Oklahoma (Sulphur)
CIJE: 1 RIE: 0 CAT: 07

Oklahoma (Tahlequah)
CIJE: 0 RIE: 2 CAT: 07

Oklahoma (Tulsa)
CIJE: 8 RIE: 13 CAT: 07

Oklahoma (Wellston)
CIJE: 1 RIE: 0 CAT: 07

Oklahoma (West)
CIJE: 0 RIE: 2 CAT: 07

Oklahoma Assistive Technology Center
CIJE: 0 RIE: 1 CAT: 17

Oklahoma Baptist University
CIJE: 1 RIE: 0 CAT: 17

Oklahoma Center for Continuing Education
CIJE: 0 RIE: 1 CAT: 17

Oklahoma Christian College
CIJE: 2 RIE: 0 CAT: 17

Oklahoma City Community College
CIJE: 0 RIE: 1 CAT: 17

Oklahoma City Metropolitan Library System
CIJE: 0 RIE: 1 CAT: 17

Oklahoma City Public Schools
CIJE: 6 RIE: 19 CAT: 17

Oklahoma City Public Schools v Dowell
CIJE: 2 RIE: 0 CAT: 14

Oklahoma City University
CIJE: 0 RIE: 1 CAT: 17

Oklahoma Coll of Osteopathic Medicine and Surgery
CIJE: 1 RIE: 0 CAT: 17

Oklahoma College of Liberal Arts
CIJE: 1 RIE: 0 CAT: 17

Oklahoma College Testing Program
CIJE: 0 RIE: 2 CAT: 19

Oklahoma Consortium on Research Development
CIJE: 0 RIE: 3 CAT: 17

Oklahoma County Libraries System
CIJE: 3 RIE: 0 CAT: 17

Oklahoma Cultural Understanding Project
CIJE: 0 RIE: 1 CAT: 19

Oklahoma Curriculum and Instr Materials Center
USE Curriculum and Instructional Materials Center OK

Oklahoma Drug Abuse Education Program
CIJE: 0 RIE: 1 CAT: 19

Oklahoma Eagle
CIJE: 0 RIE: 1 CAT: 22

Oklahoma Indian Education Needs Assessment Project
CIJE: 0 RIE: 4 CAT: 19

Oklahoma Northwest Area Vocational Technical Sch
CIJE: 0 RIE: 1 CAT: 17

Oklahoma Regents Loan Fund
CIJE: 0 RIE: 1 CAT: 17
UF Oklahoma State Regents Loan Fund

Oklahoma Rehabilitation Service
CIJE: 0 RIE: 1 CAT: 17

Oklahoma School Testing Program
CIJE: 0 RIE: 6 CAT: 19

Oklahoma State Department of Education
CIJE: 1 RIE: 2 CAT: 17

Oklahoma State Department of Libraries
CIJE: 0 RIE: 0 CAT: 17

Oklahoma State Faculty Survey
CIJE: 0 RIE: 1 CAT: 19

Oklahoma State Regents
CIJE: 0 RIE: 2 CAT: 17

Oklahoma State Regents Loan Fund
USE Oklahoma Regents Loan Fund

Oklahoma State Tech
CIJE: 1 RIE: 0 CAT: 17

Oklahoma State Univ Technical Branch Okmulgee
CIJE: 0 RIE: 1 CAT: 17

Oklahoma State University
CIJE: 20 RIE: 38 CAT: 17

Oklahoma Talkback Medical Education Network
CIJE: 1 RIE: 0 CAT: 19
UF Talkback Medical Education Network

Oklahoma Talkback Television Instruction
USE Talkback Television Instruction

Oklahoma Teletypewriter Interlibrary System
CIJE: 0 RIE: 1 CAT: 15

Oklahoma Televised Instruction System
CIJE: 1 RIE: 1 CAT: 15

Oklahoma Vocational Association
CIJE: 1 RIE: 0 CAT: 17

Oklahoma Writing Project
CIJE: 0 RIE: 1 CAT: 19

Oklahomans for Indian Opportunity
CIJE: 0 RIE: 2 CAT: 17

Oksapmin
CIJE: 2 RIE: 0 CAT: 08

Olbrechts Tyteca (L)
CIJE: 2 RIE: 3 CAT: 18

Old Age Survivors and Disability Insurance
CIJE: 1 RIE: 0 CAT: 16

Old Dominion University VA
CIJE: 12 RIE: 12 CAT: 17

Old Faithful Geyser
CIJE: 1 RIE: 0 CAT: 07

Old Man and the Sea
CIJE: 2 RIE: 1 CAT: 22

Old National Phonetic Symbols
CIJE: 0 RIE: 1 CAT: 13

Old Norse
CIJE: 1 RIE: 1 CAT: 13

Old Order Amish
USE Amish (Old Order)

Old Saxon
CIJE: 1 RIE: 1 CAT: 13

Old Swinford Hospital School (England)
CIJE: 1 RIE: 0 CAT: 17

Old Testament
CIJE: 6 RIE: 2 CAT: 22

Old Times on the Mississippi
CIJE: 1 RIE: 0 CAT: 22

Old Town San Diego State Historic Park
CIJE: 1 RIE: 0 CAT: 17

Old Town School System ME
CIJE: 0 RIE: 1 CAT: 17

Old Yeller
CIJE: 0 RIE: 1 CAT: 22

Older Adult Project
CIJE: 0 RIE: 1 CAT: 19
SN ...within the Health Promotion Research Program at Northern Illinois University

Older Adults Sharing Important Skills
USE Project OASIS

Older American Volunteer Programs
CIJE: 0 RIE: 3 CAT: 19

Older Americans Act 1965
CIJE: 12 RIE: 42 CAT: 14

Older Americans Act 1965 Title IV A
CIJE: 0 RIE: 1 CAT: 14

Older Americans Act 1965 Title V
CIJE: 0 RIE: 6 CAT: 14

Older Americans Act 1965 Title VI
CIJE: 0 RIE: 1 CAT: 14

Older Americans Act 1984
CIJE: 0 RIE: 1 CAT: 14

Older Americans Act Amendments 1978
CIJE: 0 RIE: 3 CAT: 14

Older Americans Act Amendments 1987
CIJE: 0 RIE: 2 CAT: 14
UF Public Law 100 175

Older Child Adoption
USE Adoption of Older Children

Older Library Materials
CIJE: 0 RIE: 1 CAT: 16

Older Persons Counseling Needs Survey
CIJE: 1 RIE: 0 CAT: 21

Older Workers
CIJE: 58 RIE: 61 CAT: 10

Older Workers Benefit Protection Act 1990
CIJE: 1 RIE: 1 CAT: 14
UF Public Law 101 433

Older Workers Jobs Program
CIJE: 0 RIE: 1 CAT: 19

Olechnowicz (Mscislaw)
CIJE: 1 RIE: 0 CAT: 18

Olfactory Discrimination
CIJE: 2 RIE: 0 CAT: 11

Olfactory Sense
CIJE: 10 RIE: 1 CAT: 11

Olfactory Stimuli
CIJE: 3 RIE: 1 CAT: 11

Oligophrenia
CIJE: 1 RIE: 0 CAT: 11

Olive Harvey College IL
USE City Colleges of Chicago IL Olive Harvey College

Oliver (Grace W)
CIJE: 1 RIE: 0 CAT: 18

Oliver (Margaret)
CIJE: 0 RIE: 1 CAT: 18

Oliver High School PA
CIJE: 3 RIE: 0 CAT: 17

Oliver Twist
CIJE: 1 RIE: 1 CAT: 22

Olivet College MI
CIJE: 3 RIE: 0 CAT: 17

Olivet Nazarene College IL
CIJE: 0 RIE: 1 CAT: 17

Olivetti Equipment
CIJE: 0 RIE: 3 CAT: 04

Olivier (Laurence)
CIJE: 1 RIE: 0 CAT: 18

Oller (John)
CIJE: 1 RIE: 1 CAT: 18

Ollier (Claude)
CIJE: 1 RIE: 0 CAT: 18

Ollman v Evans
CIJE: 0 RIE: 2 CAT: 14

Olmec (People)
CIJE: 1 RIE: 1 CAT: 08

Olmedo (Jose Joaquin de)
CIJE: 1 RIE: 0 CAT: 18

Olmsted (Frederick Law)
CIJE: 1 RIE: 1 CAT: 18

Olney Central College IL
CIJE: 0 RIE: 1 CAT: 17

Olney Project
CIJE: 0 RIE: 1 CAT: 19

Olsen (J P)
CIJE: 0 RIE: 1 CAT: 18

Olsen (Lyle)
CIJE: 1 RIE: 0 CAT: 18

Olsgaard Profile of Authorship
CIJE: 1 RIE: 0 CAT: 15

Olson (Mancur)
CIJE: 0 RIE: 1 CAT: 18

Olympia Community Unit District 16 IL
CIJE: 0 RIE: 1 CAT: 17

Olympia Technical Community College WA
CIJE: 0 RIE: 1 CAT: 17

Olympia Vocational Technical Institute WA
CIJE: 1 RIE: 0 CAT: 17

Olympiad (The)
CIJE: 1 RIE: 0 CAT: 22

Olympic College WA
CIJE: 4 RIE: 3 CAT: 17

Olympic Games Boycotts
CIJE: 0 RIE: 0 CAT: 12

Olympic Swimmers
CIJE: 1 RIE: 0 CAT: 10

Olympics of the Mind
CIJE: 2 RIE: 1 CAT: 19

Omaha
CIJE: 0 RIE: 1 CAT: 13
SN Dialect of Dhegiha, a Siouan language

Omaha (Tribe)
CIJE: 7 RIE: 5 CAT: 08

Omaha Magic Theatre
CIJE: 0 RIE: 1 CAT: 17

Omaha Power District
CIJE: 0 RIE: 1 CAT: 17

Omaha Public Schools NE
CIJE: 1 RIE: 6 CAT: 17

Omaha Teacher Corps Project NE
CIJE: 0 RIE: 1 CAT: 19

Oman
CIJE: 8 RIE: 16 CAT: 07

OMB
USE Office of Management and Budget

OMB Circular A110
CIJE: 0 RIE: 1 CAT: 22

OMB Circular A130
CIJE: 5 RIE: 3 CAT: 22

OMB Circular A21
CIJE: 0 RIE: 0 CAT: 22

OMB Circular A87
CIJE: 0 RIE: 1 CAT: 22

Ombudsman Activities Project
CIJE: 0 RIE: 1 CAT: 19

Omega Scale
CIJE: 0 RIE: 1 CAT: 21

Omega Square Statistical Index
CIJE: 1 RIE: 0 CAT: 21

Omission Training
CIJE: 1 RIE: 0 CAT: 15

Omitted Responses
CIJE: 6 RIE: 2 CAT: 21

Omnibus (Television Series)
CIJE: 0 RIE: 1 CAT: 22

Omnibus Budget Reconciliation Act 1981
CIJE: 3 RIE: 17 CAT: 14
UF Omnibus Reconciliation Act 1981; Public Law 97 35

Omnibus Crime Control and Safe Streets Act
CIJE: 0 RIE: 1 CAT: 14

Omnibus Dental Online Treat Info Control System
CIJE: 0 RIE: 0 CAT: 04

Omnibus Diplomatic Security and Antiterrorism Act
CIJE: 0 RIE: 0 CAT: 14
SN ...of 1986

UF Public Law 99 399

Omnibus Education Reconciliation Act 1981
CIJE: 1 RIE: 0 CAT: 14
SN Part of the Omnibus Budget Reconciliation Act 1981, Public Law 97-35

Omnibus Personality Inventory
CIJE: 24 RIE: 34 CAT: 21

Omnibus Questionnaire (Okorodudu)
CIJE: 0 RIE: 1 CAT: 21

Omnibus Reconciliation Act 1981
USE Omnibus Budget Reconciliation Act 1981

Omnibus Tests
CIJE: 2 RIE: 5 CAT: 21

Omnibus Trade and Competitiveness Act 1988
CIJE: 1 RIE: 1 CAT: 14
SN See also "Super 301"
UF Public Law 100 418

Omniology
CIJE: 0 RIE: 1 CAT: 03

Omotic Languages
CIJE: 2 RIE: 0 CAT: 13

Omphalocele
CIJE: 1 RIE: 0 CAT: 11

On Going Organizations
CIJE: 0 RIE: 6 CAT: 05

On Golden Pond
CIJE: 0 RIE: 0 CAT: 22

On Saturday Afternoon
CIJE: 1 RIE: 0 CAT: 22

On Site Assessment
USE Onsite Evaluation

On Site Child Care
USE Onsite Day Care

On Site Needs Assessment Long Range Planning Model
CIJE: 0 RIE: 1 CAT: 15
UF OSP Model for Sex Equity

On the Job Evaluation
CIJE: 1 RIE: 0 CAT: 21

On the Level
CIJE: 0 RIE: 7 CAT: 03

On the Nature of Things
CIJE: 2 RIE: 0 CAT: 22

On the Origin of Species
CIJE: 1 RIE: 0 CAT: 22

On the Right Track Project
CIJE: 0 RIE: 1 CAT: 19

Onan Corporation
CIJE: 0 RIE: 1 CAT: 17

Onassis (Jacqueline Kennedy)
CIJE: 0 RIE: 1 CAT: 18

Once and Future King
CIJE: 0 RIE: 1 CAT: 22

Onderwijs un Sociaal Milieu (Netherlands)
CIJE: 0 RIE: 1 CAT: 19
UF Education and Social Environment (Netherlands)

One Act Plays
CIJE: 0 RIE: 5 CAT: 16

One Child Family
USE Only Child Family

One Group Posttest Design
CIJE: 0 RIE: 1 CAT: 21
UF One Group Posttest Evaluation Model

One Group Posttest Evaluation Model
USE One Group Posttest Design

One Hundred Good Schools
USE 100 Good Schools

One Minute Manager (The)
CIJE: 1 RIE: 1 CAT: 22

One Nation Indivisible
CIJE: 3 RIE: 0 CAT: 22

One Parameter Model
CIJE: 14 RIE: 33 CAT: 15

One Person Household
USE Single Person Household

One Person Libraries
CIJE: 2 RIE: 1 CAT: 05

One Room Drop In School
CIJE: 0 RIE: 1 CAT: 19

One Third of a Nation
CIJE: 2 RIE: 1 CAT: 22
SN May 1988 report of the American Council on Education and the Education Commission of the States on minority participation in education and American life

One to One Correspondence
CIJE: 4 RIE: 2 CAT: 15

One to One Project
CIJE: 1 RIE: 0 CAT: 19

One Voice The Canadian Seniors Network
CIJE: 0 RIE: 3 CAT: 17

One Way Cognition
USE Oneway Thinking

One Way Communication
CIJE: 0 RIE: 1 CAT: 16

Oneida
CIJE: 0 RIE: 0 CAT: 13
SN An Iroquois language

Oneida (Tribe)
CIJE: 1 RIE: 13 CAT: 08

Oneida Consolidated School District NY
CIJE: 1 RIE: 1 CAT: 17

Oneida Indian Reservation WI
CIJE: 0 RIE: 1 CAT: 17

Onetti (Juan Carlos)
CIJE: 4 RIE: 0 CAT: 18

Oneway Thinking
CIJE: 1 RIE: 0 CAT: 11
UF One Way Cognition

Ong (Walter J)
CIJE: 2 RIE: 2 CAT: 18

Ong Havelock Thesis
CIJE: 0 RIE: 1 CAT: 15

Ong v Tovey
CIJE: 1 RIE: 0 CAT: 14

Onion Corers
CIJE: 0 RIE: 1 CAT: 09

Online Administrative Information System
CIJE: 0 RIE: 2 CAT: 15

Online Computer Library Center
USE OCLC

Online Database Information Network
CIJE: 0 RIE: 1 CAT: 17

Online Reading
CIJE: 0 RIE: 1 CAT: 16

Online Search Skills
CIJE: 21 RIE: 15 CAT: 16

Online User Groups
CIJE: 6 RIE: 3 CAT: 10

Only Child Family
CIJE: 2 RIE: 1 CAT: 10
UF One Child Family; Single Child Family

Only Children
CIJE: 18 RIE: 19 CAT: 10

Onomatopoeia
CIJE: 2 RIE: 0 CAT: 13

Onomatopoeia and Images
CIJE: 9 RIE: 0 CAT: 22

Onondaga
CIJE: 2 RIE: 1 CAT: 13

Onondaga (Tribe)
CIJE: 0 RIE: 3 CAT: 08

Onondaga County Public Library System NY
CIJE: 1 RIE: 1 CAT: 17

Onondaga Valley Oral History Project NY
CIJE: 0 RIE: 1 CAT: 19

Onsite Day Care
CIJE: 1 RIE: 4 CAT: 11
UF On Site Child Care

Onsite Evaluation
CIJE: 0 RIE: 1 CAT: 21
UF On Site Assessment

Onsite Monitoring
CIJE: 0 RIE: 1 CAT: 15

Onsite Pueblo Personnel Training Program
CIJE: 0 RIE: 1 CAT: 19

Ontario
CIJE: 495 RIE: 939 CAT: 07

Ontario (Atikokan)
CIJE: 0 RIE: 1 CAT: 07

Ontario (Carleton)
CIJE: 5 RIE: 5 CAT: 07

Ontario (Erin Township)
CIJE: 0 RIE: 1 CAT: 07

Ontario (Georgian Bay Region)
CIJE: 0 RIE: 4 CAT: 07

Ontario (Huron County)
CIJE: 0 RIE: 1 CAT: 07

Ontario (Kingston)
CIJE: 2 RIE: 3 CAT: 07

Ontario (London)
CIJE: 12 RIE: 28 CAT: 07

Ontario (North York)
CIJE: 7 RIE: 20 CAT: 07

Ontario (Northeast)
CIJE: 1 RIE: 1 CAT: 07

Ontario (Oshawa)
CIJE: 1 RIE: 0 CAT: 07

Ontario (Ottawa)
CIJE: 22 RIE: 36 CAT: 07

Ontario (Peel County)
CIJE: 3 RIE: 3 CAT: 07

Ontario (Peterborough County)
CIJE: 2 RIE: 3 CAT: 07

Ontario (Roseneath)
CIJE: 0 RIE: 1 CAT: 07

Ontario (Scarborough)
CIJE: 3 RIE: 5 CAT: 07

Ontario (Simcoe County)
CIJE: 1 RIE: 2 CAT: 07

Ontario (Sudbury)
CIJE: 3 RIE: 3 CAT: 07

Ontario (Toronto)
CIJE: 106 RIE: 134 CAT: 07

Ontario (Welland)
CIJE: 0 RIE: 1 CAT: 07

Ontario (Windsor)
CIJE: 1 RIE: 4 CAT: 07

Ontario (York County)
CIJE: 3 RIE: 5 CAT: 07

Ontario Assessment Instrument Pool
CIJE: 2 RIE: 1 CAT: 21

Ontario CAI Network (Canada)
CIJE: 0 RIE: 1 CAT: 17

Ontario Camp Leadership Centre
CIJE: 0 RIE: 1 CAT: 17

Ontario Colleges of Applied Arts and Technology
CIJE: 0 RIE: 2 CAT: 17
UF Colleges of Applied Arts and Technology ON

Ontario Council for Leadership Educ Admin Ontario
CIJE: 0 RIE: 1 CAT: 17

Ontario Council on University Affairs
CIJE: 0 RIE: 4 CAT: 17

Ontario Curriculum Institute (Canada)
CIJE: 1 RIE: 3 CAT: 17

Ontario Department of Education (Canada)
CIJE: 0 RIE: 10 CAT: 17

Ontario Department of Labour (Canada)
CIJE: 1 RIE: 1 CAT: 17

Ontario Educ Communications Authority (Canada)
CIJE: 0 RIE: 7 CAT: 17

Ontario Education Amendment Act 1980
USE Bill 82 (Ontario)

Ontario Institute for Studies in Education
CIJE: 16 RIE: 27 CAT: 17

Ontario Ministry of Ed Circular H S 1 1972 73
CIJE: 0 RIE: 4 CAT: 14

Ontario Ministry of Ed H S 1 Circulars
CIJE: 0 RIE: 1 CAT: 16

Ontario Scholastic Aptitude Tests
CIJE: 0 RIE: 1 CAT: 21

Ontario School Ability
CIJE: 0 RIE: 1 CAT: 21

Ontario Science Center (Canada)
CIJE: 1 RIE: 0 CAT: 17

Ontario Test of English Achievement
CIJE: 0 RIE: 1 CAT: 21

Ontario Test of English as a Second Language
CIJE: 0 RIE: 1 CAT: 21

Ontario Test of Intrinsic Motivation
CIJE: 1 RIE: 1 CAT: 21

Ontario Test on Attitude Toward Older People
CIJE: 1 RIE: 0 CAT: 21

Ontario Tests for Admission to Colleges and Univs
CIJE: 2 RIE: 0 CAT: 21

Ontario University System
CIJE: 1 RIE: 3 CAT: 17

Ontogeny
CIJE: 23 RIE: 1 CAT: 20

Ontological Evaluation Model
CIJE: 0 RIE: 1 CAT: 15

Ontology
CIJE: 25 RIE: 10 CAT: 16

Onward to Excellence
CIJE: 0 RIE: 4 CAT: 19

Onychophagia
USE Nailbiting

Oo Za We Kwun Center Inc (Canada)
CIJE: 1 RIE: 0 CAT: 17

Op Art
CIJE: 2 RIE: 0 CAT: 16

Op In Procedure (Cloze)
CIJE: 0 RIE: 1 CAT: 15

Open Access (Teacher Professional Development)
CIJE: 0 RIE: 1 CAT: 15

Open Adoption
CIJE: 11 RIE: 1 CAT: 15

Open and Closed Systems
CIJE: 3 RIE: 3 CAT: 15

Open Bargaining
CIJE: 6 RIE: 0 CAT: 14

Open Birth Record Law (Minnesota)
CIJE: 1 RIE: 0 CAT: 14

Open College Networks (Great Britain)
CIJE: 1 RIE: 3 CAT: 19

Open College of Further Education (Australia)
CIJE: 0 RIE: 1 CAT: 17

Open Competence
CIJE: 0 RIE: 1 CAT: 16

Open Corridor Program
CIJE: 0 RIE: 5 CAT: 19

Open Court Readers
CIJE: 2 RIE: 3 CAT: 22

Open Door Programs
CIJE: 0 RIE: 2 CAT: 19

Open End Leads
CIJE: 1 RIE: 0 CAT: 16

Open Ended Opinionnaire (Johnson)
CIJE: 0 RIE: 1 CAT: 21

Open Ended Questions
CIJE: 47 RIE: 50 CAT: 21

Open Entry Open Exit
CIJE: 12 RIE: 16 CAT: 19
SN See also "Multiple Entry Multiple Exit"

Open Field Test (Ward)
CIJE: 0 RIE: 1 CAT: 21

Open Framework Curriculum
CIJE: 0 RIE: 1 CAT: 15
UF High Scope Open Framework

Open Houses
CIJE: 3 RIE: 2 CAT: 05

Open Learning
CIJE: 2 RIE: 0 CAT: 16

Open Learning Agency BC
CIJE: 0 RIE: 1 CAT: 17

Open Learning Centres
CIJE: 0 RIE: 1 CAT: 05
SN Centers established in Great Britain to provide opportunities for adults and young people to improve basic skills

Open Learning Institute BC
CIJE: 6 RIE: 8 CAT: 17

Open Learning Institute of Hong Kong
CIJE: 0 RIE: 1 CAT: 17

Open Library Network (Netherlands)
CIJE: 0 RIE: 1 CAT: 19

Open Meetings
CIJE: 2 RIE: 14 CAT: 16

Open Plan Communities
CIJE: 1 RIE: 0 CAT: 05

Open Program Structure Index
CIJE: 0 RIE: 1 CAT: 15

Open Public Meetings Act (New Jersey)
CIJE: 0 RIE: 1 CAT: 14

Open Road New Jobs CA
CIJE: 0 RIE: 1 CAT: 19

Open Road Student Involvement Project
CIJE: 0 RIE: 1 CAT: 19

Open Sentences
CIJE: 1 RIE: 3 CAT: 13

Open Society
CIJE: 0 RIE: 3 CAT: 15

Open Spaces
CIJE: 0 RIE: 6 CAT: 05

Open Systems Interconnection
CIJE: 24 RIE: 7 CAT: 04

Open Systems Interconnection Reference Model
CIJE: 4 RIE: 0 CAT: 15

Open Systems Theory
CIJE: 13 RIE: 12 CAT: 15

Open Testing
CIJE: 0 RIE: 3 CAT: 21

Open University (Great Britain)
CIJE: 320 RIE: 220 CAT: 17

Open University (Israel)
CIJE: 3 RIE: 1 CAT: 17

Open University (Netherlands)
CIJE: 6 RIE: 3 CAT: 17

Open University (West Germany)
USE Fernuniversitat (West Germany)

Open University of Sri Lanka
CIJE: 0 RIE: 2 CAT: 17

Open Workshop Learning System
CIJE: 1 RIE: 0 CAT: 15

Openness
CIJE: 8 RIE: 5 CAT: 15
SN Use a more specific term if possible, e.g., "Professional Openness"

Operant Analysis
CIJE: 1 RIE: 1 CAT: 15

Operant Behavior
CIJE: 3 RIE: 1 CAT: 11

Operant Behavior Modification Model
CIJE: 2 RIE: 0 CAT: 15

Operant Methodology
CIJE: 1 RIE: 1 CAT: 15

Operant Vigilance Task (Holland)
CIJE: 1 RIE: 0 CAT: 21

Operating Characteristics Estimation
CIJE: 0 RIE: 5 CAT: 21

Operating Procedures
CIJE: 1 RIE: 4 CAT: 15

Operating Ratios
CIJE: 0 RIE: 1 CAT: 16

Operating Systems (Computers)
USE Computer Operating Systems

Operation Alphabet
CIJE: 1 RIE: 2 CAT: 19

Operation Bookstrap
CIJE: 1 RIE: 0 CAT: 19

Operation Breakthrough
CIJE: 0 RIE: 2 CAT: 19

Operation Bridge
CIJE: 0 RIE: 2 CAT: 19

Operation CHAMP UT
USE Childrens Health and Movement Program

Operation Desert Storm
USE Gulf War

Operation EPIC
CIJE: 1 RIE: 0 CAT: 19

Operation Fair Chance
CIJE: 0 RIE: 2 CAT: 19

Operation Future
CIJE: 0 RIE: 1 CAT: 19

Operation Gap Stop
CIJE: 0 RIE: 3 CAT: 19

Operation GO
CIJE: 0 RIE: 1 CAT: 19

Operation Head Start Workers Attitude Scale
CIJE: 0 RIE: 1 CAT: 21

Operation Hitchhike
CIJE: 1 RIE: 0 CAT: 19

Operation Index
CIJE: 0 RIE: 1 CAT: 19

Operation Mainstream
CIJE: 1 RIE: 7 CAT: 19

Operation Manpower
CIJE: 2 RIE: 0 CAT: 19

Operation MEDIHC
CIJE: 1 RIE: 4 CAT: 19

Operation Moonvigil
CIJE: 0 RIE: 2 CAT: 19

Operation Opportunity
CIJE: 1 RIE: 0 CAT: 19

Operation Pathfinder
CIJE: 0 RIE: 5 CAT: 19

Operation PEP
CIJE: 0 RIE: 14 CAT: 19

Operation PRESENCE
CIJE: 1 RIE: 0 CAT: 19

Operation PROBE
CIJE: 0 RIE: 1 CAT: 19

Operation PROTEACH
CIJE: 0 RIE: 6 CAT: 19

Operation Reading Bases Program
CIJE: 0 RIE: 1 CAT: 19

Operation READS
CIJE: 0 RIE: 1 CAT: 19

Operation Reason
CIJE: 0 RIE: 1 CAT: 19

Operation Recover
CIJE: 0 RIE: 1 CAT: 19

Operation Rescue
CIJE: 1 RIE: 2 CAT: 19

Operation Retrieval
CIJE: 0 RIE: 2 CAT: 19

Operation Return
CIJE: 0 RIE: 1 CAT: 19

Operation SAIL
CIJE: 1 RIE: 0 CAT: 19

Operation School Renewal NJ
CIJE: 0 RIE: 3 CAT: 19

Operation Search
CIJE: 0 RIE: 1 CAT: 19

Operation Second Chance
CIJE: 0 RIE: 1 CAT: 19

Operation SER
CIJE: 1 RIE: 1 CAT: 19

Operation Shadow
CIJE: 0 RIE: 1 CAT: 19

Operation Shirtsleeves
CIJE: 0 RIE: 1 CAT: 19

Operation SMART
CIJE: 0 RIE: 4 CAT: 19
UF Science Math and Relevant Technology Project

Operation Stay in School
CIJE: 0 RIE: 2 CAT: 19

Operation Success
CIJE: 0 RIE: 7 CAT: 19

Operation Turnaround
CIJE: 0 RIE: 1 CAT: 19

Operation Wordpower
CIJE: 0 RIE: 2 CAT: 19

Operation Young Adults
CIJE: 0 RIE: 2 CAT: 19

Operational Audit
CIJE: 1 RIE: 0 CAT: 15

Operational Concepts
CIJE: 8 RIE: 7 CAT: 15

Operational Context Training
CIJE: 1 RIE: 1 CAT: 15

Operational Questions
CIJE: 2 RIE: 1 CAT: 15

Operational Testing
CIJE: 0 RIE: 1 CAT: 21

Operations Consultants
CIJE: 1 RIE: 0 CAT: 09

Operative Conditions
CIJE: 1 RIE: 1 CAT: 15

Operettas
CIJE: 1 RIE: 1 CAT: 16

Ophthalmetron
CIJE: 2 RIE: 0 CAT: 04

Ophthalmoscopes
CIJE: 0 RIE: 0 CAT: 11

Opin Procedure (Reading)
CIJE: 0 RIE: 1 CAT: 15

Opinion Attitude and Interest Survey (Fricke)
CIJE: 4 RIE: 1 CAT: 21

Opinion Leaders
CIJE: 5 RIE: 2 CAT: 10

Opinion Polls
CIJE: 17 RIE: 29 CAT: 21

Opinion Research Corporation
CIJE: 3 RIE: 0 CAT: 17

Opinion Survey for Men and Women (SRA)
CIJE: 0 RIE: 1 CAT: 21

Opinion Survey for Teaching the Disadvantaged
CIJE: 0 RIE: 1 CAT: 21

Opinion v Fact
USE Fact Opinion Distinction

Opinionnaire Political Institutions Participation
CIJE: 0 RIE: 1 CAT: 21

Opinions About Mental Illness Scale
CIJE: 1 RIE: 0 CAT: 21

Opler (Morris)
CIJE: 0 RIE: 1 CAT: 18

Opportunities Centers
CIJE: 0 RIE: 1 CAT: 16
SN See also "Educational Opportunity Centers" and "Youth Opportunity Centers"
UF Opportunity Centers

Opportunities for Youth Creative Arts Project
CIJE: 1 RIE: 0 CAT: 19

Opportunities for Youth in Education
CIJE: 0 RIE: 1 CAT: 19

Opportunities Industrialization Centers
CIJE: 2 RIE: 7 CAT: 17

Opportunities Industrialization Centers of America
CIJE: 0 RIE: 3 CAT: 17

Opportunity Award Program
CIJE: 1 RIE: 0 CAT: 19

Opportunity Centers
USE Opportunities Centers

Opportunity Costs
CIJE: 9 RIE: 5 CAT: 16

Opportunity Funding Corporation
CIJE: 1 RIE: 0 CAT: 17

Opportunity School Program
CIJE: 1 RIE: 0 CAT: 19

Opportunity Structures
CIJE: 1 RIE: 0 CAT: 15

Opportunity to Learn
CIJE: 13 RIE: 10 CAT: 21

Opposite Sex Friendship
USE Cross Sex Friendship

Opposite Sex Interaction
USE Cross Sex Interaction

Opposite Sex Peers
USE Cross Sex Peers

Oppositional Behavior
CIJE: 7 RIE: 2 CAT: 11

Oppositional Decoding
CIJE: 1 RIE: 1 CAT: 16
UF Decoding (Oppositional)

Oppression
CIJE: 25 RIE: 12 CAT: 16

OpScan
CIJE: 0 RIE: 4 CAT: 04

Optacon
CIJE: 11 RIE: 19 CAT: 04

Optel
CIJE: 0 RIE: 1 CAT: 04

Opti Planner
CIJE: 0 RIE: 1 CAT: 04

Optical Barcodes
USE Barcodes

Optical Coincidence Cards
CIJE: 1 RIE: 1 CAT: 04

Optical Data Transmission
CIJE: 2 RIE: 4 CAT: 20

Optical Illusions
CIJE: 14 RIE: 1 CAT: 11

Optical Information Systems
CIJE: 1 RIE: 1 CAT: 20

Optical Isomers
CIJE: 1 RIE: 1 CAT: 20

Optical Rotation
CIJE: 2 RIE: 0 CAT: 11

Optical Technicians
CIJE: 0 RIE: 6 CAT: 09

Opticalmen
CIJE: 0 RIE: 1 CAT: 09

Opticians
CIJE: 2 RIE: 3 CAT: 09

Optimal Appropriateness Measurement
CIJE: 1 RIE: 1 CAT: 21

Optimal Control Theory
CIJE: 0 RIE: 1 CAT: 15

Optimal Level Theory
CIJE: 1 RIE: 1 CAT: 15

Optimal Scaling
CIJE: 12 RIE: 5 CAT: 21

Optimal Stimulation Theory
CIJE: 1 RIE: 1 CAT: 15

Optimal Treatment Approach to Needs Assessment
CIJE: 1 RIE: 0 CAT: 21

Optimation Rapid Reading Course
CIJE: 1 RIE: 0 CAT: 03

Optimism
CIJE: 17 RIE: 7 CAT: 11

Optimism Pessimism Test Instrument
CIJE: 1 RIE: 0 CAT: 21

Optimists Daughter (Welty)
CIJE: 0 RIE: 1 CAT: 22

Optimization
CIJE: 22 RIE: 13 CAT: 15

Optimization of Learning
CIJE: 1 RIE: 1 CAT: 15

Optimum Allocation Analysis
CIJE: 0 RIE: 1 CAT: 15

Option Weighting
CIJE: 1 RIE: 2 CAT: 21

Optional Shift (Grammar)
CIJE: 2 RIE: 0 CAT: 13

Optional Test Questions
CIJE: 0 RIE: 1 CAT: 21

Optiscope Enlarger
CIJE: 1 RIE: 0 CAT: 04

Optometric Assistants
CIJE: 0 RIE: 1 CAT: 09

Optometric Technicians
CIJE: 0 RIE: 1 CAT: 09

Optometric Vision Therapy
USE Vision Therapy

Optouts
CIJE: 0 RIE: 1 CAT: 10

OR Corrective Technique
CIJE: 0 RIE: 1 CAT: 15
UF O Hear Ramsey Corrective

ORACLE Formula
CIJE: 0 RIE: 1 CAT: 15

Oracy
CIJE: 7 RIE: 6 CAT: 16

Oraflex
CIJE: 0 RIE: 1 CAT: 11

Oral Aural Visual Project
CIJE: 1 RIE: 0 CAT: 19

Oral Biology
CIJE: 3 RIE: 0 CAT: 20

Oral Communication Across the Curriculum
CIJE: 2 RIE: 4 CAT: 03
SN See also "Speaking Across the Curriculum"

Oral Composing
CIJE: 1 RIE: 1 CAT: 13

Oral Contraception
CIJE: 0 RIE: 1 CAT: 11

Oral Dependence
CIJE: 1 RIE: 0 CAT: 11

Oral English Language Proficiency Tests
CIJE: 0 RIE: 2 CAT: 21

Oral English Program
CIJE: 0 RIE: 2 CAT: 19

Oral Examinations
CIJE: 15 RIE: 18 CAT: 21

Oral Form Discrimination
CIJE: 2 RIE: 0 CAT: 13

Oral History (Smith)
CIJE: 0 RIE: 1 CAT: 22

Oral History Association Colloquium
CIJE: 0 RIE: 2 CAT: 02

Oral Hygiene
CIJE: 1 RIE: 3 CAT: 11

Oral Interpretation Tournaments
CIJE: 0 RIE: 1 CAT: 16

Oral Journals
CIJE: 0 RIE: 2 CAT: 16

Oral Language Bilingual Educational Program
CIJE: 0 RIE: 1 CAT: 19

Oral Language Proficiency Scale
CIJE: 0 RIE: 2 CAT: 21

Oral Language Program
CIJE: 1 RIE: 5 CAT: 19

Oral Learning
CIJE: 3 RIE: 5 CAT: 15

Oral Literature
CIJE: 16 RIE: 20 CAT: 16

Oral Placement Test (Poczik)
CIJE: 0 RIE: 2 CAT: 21

Oral Placement Test for Adults
CIJE: 0 RIE: 1 CAT: 21

Oral Presentations
CIJE: 18 RIE: 8 CAT: 16

Oral Production Tests (Poczik)
CIJE: 0 RIE: 2 CAT: 21

Oral Proficiency Interviews
USE Oral Proficiency Testing

Oral Proficiency Testing
CIJE: 26 RIE: 23 CAT: 21
UF Oral Proficiency Interviews

Oral Reading Inventory
CIJE: 0 RIE: 1 CAT: 21

Oral Reading Test (Baker)
CIJE: 0 RIE: 1 CAT: 21

Oral Reflexes
CIJE: 1 RIE: 0 CAT: 11

Oral Reports
CIJE: 8 RIE: 2 CAT: 16

Oral Roberts University OK
CIJE: 8 RIE: 3 CAT: 17

Oral Speech Mechanism Screening Examination
CIJE: 0 RIE: 1 CAT: 21

Oral Surgery
CIJE: 0 RIE: 1 CAT: 11

Oral Ulcerations
CIJE: 2 RIE: 0 CAT: 11

Oralingua Interaction Skills Curriculum
CIJE: 1 RIE: 0 CAT: 03

Orality
CIJE: 19 RIE: 20 CAT: 11

Orange Coast College CA
CIJE: 2 RIE: 1 CAT: 17

Orange Coast Junior College District CA
CIJE: 1 RIE: 0 CAT: 17

Orange County Consortium
CIJE: 0 RIE: 2 CAT: 17

Orange County Outdoor School CA
CIJE: 0 RIE: 3 CAT: 17

Orange County Public Libraries CA
CIJE: 3 RIE: 0 CAT: 17

Orange County Public Schools FL
CIJE: 5 RIE: 34 CAT: 17

Orange County Vocational Guidance Project
CIJE: 1 RIE: 0 CAT: 19

Orange Unified School District CA
CIJE: 2 RIE: 3 CAT: 17

Orangeburg School District 5 SC
CIJE: 0 RIE: 1 CAT: 17

Oranges
CIJE: 0 RIE: 1 CAT: 20

Orans (Martin)
CIJE: 1 RIE: 0 CAT: 18

Orators
CIJE: 1 RIE: 8 CAT: 10

Oratory
CIJE: 6 RIE: 13 CAT: 16

ORB Program
CIJE: 0 RIE: 1 CAT: 19

ORBIT
CIJE: 3 RIE: 3 CAT: 17
UF ORBIT Search Service

ORBIT Search Service
USE ORBIT

Orbital Mechanics
CIJE: 5 RIE: 1 CAT: 20

Orchard Management
CIJE: 0 RIE: 4 CAT: 20

Orchard School for Retarded Children IL
CIJE: 0 RIE: 1 CAT: 17

Orchard View Community School MI
CIJE: 1 RIE: 0 CAT: 17

Orchestrated Systems Approach
CIJE: 1 RIE: 1 CAT: 15

Order Analysis
CIJE: 9 RIE: 10 CAT: 15

Order Fillers
CIJE: 0 RIE: 1 CAT: 09

Order of Operations (Mathematics)
CIJE: 3 RIE: 2 CAT: 20

Order of Selection (Rehabilitation Act 1973)
CIJE: 0 RIE: 1 CAT: 14

Order of Woodcraft Chivalry
CIJE: 1 RIE: 0 CAT: 17

Order Out (Game)
CIJE: 1 RIE: 0 CAT: 16

Order Relations
CIJE: 4 RIE: 6 CAT: 16

Ordering Operations
CIJE: 2 RIE: 3 CAT: 20

Ordering Syllogisms
CIJE: 2 RIE: 0 CAT: 13

Ordering Theory
CIJE: 17 RIE: 11 CAT: 15

Orderly Departure Program (Thailand)
CIJE: 0 RIE: 1 CAT: 19

Ordinal Hypotheses
CIJE: 0 RIE: 1 CAT: 15

Ordinal Numbers
CIJE: 4 RIE: 2 CAT: 20

Ordinal Position
CIJE: 2 RIE: 2 CAT: 11

Ordinal Scales
CIJE: 18 RIE: 6 CAT: 21

Ordinances
CIJE: 1 RIE: 3 CAT: 14

Ordinary Level Examinations
CIJE: 1 RIE: 1 CAT: 21

Ordinary National Diploma Courses
CIJE: 1 RIE: 0 CAT: 03

Oregon
CIJE: 212 RIE: 1188 CAT: 07

Oregon (Albany)
CIJE: 0 RIE: 4 CAT: 07

Oregon (Ashland)
CIJE: 0 RIE: 1 CAT: 07

Oregon (Baker County)
CIJE: 0 RIE: 1 CAT: 07

Oregon (Beaverton)
CIJE: 0 RIE: 4 CAT: 07

Oregon (Clackamas County)
CIJE: 0 RIE: 4 CAT: 07

Oregon (Corbett)
CIJE: 0 RIE: 1 CAT: 07

Oregon (Corvallis)
CIJE: 1 RIE: 7 CAT: 07

Oregon (Douglas County)
CIJE: 0 RIE: 2 CAT: 07

Oregon (East)
CIJE: 0 RIE: 2 CAT: 07

Oregon (Eugene)
CIJE: 9 RIE: 236 CAT: 07

Oregon (Forest Grove)
CIJE: 1 RIE: 0 CAT: 07

Oregon (Jackson County)
CIJE: 0 RIE: 3 CAT: 07

Oregon (Jefferson County)
CIJE: 0 RIE: 1 CAT: 07

Oregon (Junction City)
CIJE: 1 RIE: 1 CAT: 07

Oregon (Klamath Falls)
CIJE: 0 RIE: 1 CAT: 07

Oregon (Lane County)
CIJE: 0 RIE: 2 CAT: 07

Oregon (Medford)
CIJE: 1 RIE: 0 CAT: 07

Oregon (Milwaukie)
CIJE: 0 RIE: 1 CAT: 07

Oregon (Monmouth)
CIJE: 0 RIE: 21 CAT: 07

Oregon (North Bend)
CIJE: 0 RIE: 1 CAT: 07

Oregon (Philomath)
CIJE: 0 RIE: 1 CAT: 07

Oregon (Polk County)
CIJE: 0 RIE: 2 CAT: 07

Oregon (Portland)
CIJE: 29 RIE: 87 CAT: 07

Oregon (Salem)
CIJE: 4 RIE: 9 CAT: 07

Oregon (Tigard)
CIJE: 1 RIE: 10 CAT: 07

Oregon (Washington County)
CIJE: 2 RIE: 2 CAT: 07

Oregon (Woodburn)
CIJE: 0 RIE: 1 CAT: 07

Oregon Action Plan for Excellence
CIJE: 0 RIE: 2 CAT: 19

Oregon Adaptive Arts Techniques Project
CIJE: 0 RIE: 1 CAT: 19

Oregon Business Education Council
CIJE: 1 RIE: 0 CAT: 17

Oregon College of Education
CIJE: 2 RIE: 4 CAT: 17

Oregon Community College System
CIJE: 0 RIE: 2 CAT: 17

Oregon Consortium for Student Success
CIJE: 0 RIE: 1 CAT: 17

Oregon Council for Computer Education
CIJE: 1 RIE: 0 CAT: 17

Oregon Council for the Social Studies
CIJE: 0 RIE: 1 CAT: 17

Oregon Curriculum Study Center
CIJE: 0 RIE: 50 CAT: 17

Oregon Education Act for the 21st Century 1991
CIJE: 0 RIE: 5 CAT: 14
UF Oregon Educational Reform Act for the 21st Century

Oregon Educational Media Association
CIJE: 0 RIE: 1 CAT: 17

Oregon Educational Reform Act for the 21st Century
USE Oregon Education Act for the 21st Century 1991

Oregon Educational Television Network
USE Ed Net

Oregon Elementary English Project
CIJE: 0 RIE: 38 CAT: 19

Oregon Health Sciences University
CIJE: 7 RIE: 1 CAT: 17

Oregon Institute of Technology
CIJE: 3 RIE: 3 CAT: 17

Oregon Parent Training Network
CIJE: 0 RIE: 1 CAT: 17

Oregon Preschool Assessment System
CIJE: 0 RIE: 1 CAT: 21

Oregon Preschool Test of Interpersonal Cooperation
CIJE: 0 RIE: 1 CAT: 21

Oregon Revised Statute 339 115
USE ORS 339 115 (Oregon 1989)

Oregon School Finance Plan
CIJE: 1 RIE: 1 CAT: 19

Oregon School Study Council
CIJE: 0 RIE: 3 CAT: 17

Oregon Small Schools Program
CIJE: 0 RIE: 4 CAT: 19

Oregon State Correctional Institution
CIJE: 1 RIE: 1 CAT: 17

Oregon State Department of Education
CIJE: 0 RIE: 14 CAT: 17

Oregon State Library
CIJE: 2 RIE: 4 CAT: 17

Oregon State Prison College
CIJE: 1 RIE: 0 CAT: 17

Oregon State Regional Network
CIJE: 0 RIE: 1 CAT: 17

Oregon State School for the Deaf
CIJE: 1 RIE: 0 CAT: 17

Oregon State System of Higher Education
CIJE: 0 RIE: 7 CAT: 17

Oregon State University
CIJE: 43 RIE: 28 CAT: 17

Oregon Statewide Assessment Program
CIJE: 0 RIE: 7 CAT: 19

Oregon Studies
CIJE: 1 RIE: 1 CAT: 03

Oregon System of Mathematics Education
CIJE: 0 RIE: 2 CAT: 15

Oregon Teacher Standards and Practices Commission
CIJE: 1 RIE: 3 CAT: 17

Oregon Technical Institute
CIJE: 0 RIE: 1 CAT: 17

Oregon v Rajneeshpuram
USE State of Oregon v City of Rajneeshpuram

Oregon Youth Coordinating Council
USE Youth Coordinating Council OR

Orem Public Library UT
CIJE: 0 RIE: 3 CAT: 17

Orendain (Antonio)
CIJE: 0 RIE: 1 CAT: 18

Orff (Carl)
CIJE: 2 RIE: 0 CAT: 18

Organ Culture
CIJE: 1 RIE: 0 CAT: 20

Organ Transplants
CIJE: 9 RIE: 1 CAT: 11
SN See also "Heart Transplants"

Organic Education
CIJE: 0 RIE: 1 CAT: 16

Organic Farming
CIJE: 3 RIE: 3 CAT: 20

Organic Integrity Test
CIJE: 1 RIE: 0 CAT: 21

Organic Model
CIJE: 0 RIE: 1 CAT: 15

Organic Personality Syndrome
CIJE: 0 RIE: 1 CAT: 11

Organic Primers
CIJE: 1 RIE: 0 CAT: 15

Organic Teaching
CIJE: 1 RIE: 1 CAT: 15

Organisation for Economic Cooperation Development
CIJE: 31 RIE: 77 CAT: 17

Organization Charts
CIJE: 1 RIE: 12 CAT: 04

Organization Concerned about Rural Education
CIJE: 1 RIE: 0 CAT: 17

Organization for Rehabilitation Through Training
CIJE: 7 RIE: 2 CAT: 17

Organization Man
CIJE: 1 RIE: 0 CAT: 22

Organization Mapping Analysis
CIJE: 2 RIE: 0 CAT: 15

Organization of African Unity
CIJE: 3 RIE: 1 CAT: 17

Organization of American States
CIJE: 12 RIE: 10 CAT: 17

Organization of Petroleum Exporting Countries
CIJE: 5 RIE: 2 CAT: 17

Organization of Unemployed Teachers
CIJE: 1 RIE: 0 CAT: 17

Organization Set Model
CIJE: 0 RIE: 1 CAT: 15

Organization Theory (Psychology)
CIJE: 3 RIE: 2 CAT: 15

Organizational Alternatives
CIJE: 1 RIE: 1 CAT: 15

Organizational Analysis
CIJE: 27 RIE: 12 CAT: 15

Organizational Bargaining Research
CIJE: 0 RIE: 1 CAT: 15

Organizational Behavior
CIJE: 51 RIE: 22 CAT: 15

Organizational Behavior Describer Survey
CIJE: 0 RIE: 1 CAT: 21

Organizational Climate Description Questionnaire
CIJE: 20 RIE: 21 CAT: 21

Organizational Climate Index
CIJE: 2 RIE: 4 CAT: 21

Organizational Climate Survey
CIJE: 0 RIE: 3 CAT: 21

Organizational Commitment
CIJE: 36 RIE: 7 CAT: 16

Organizational Communication Profile
CIJE: 0 RIE: 1 CAT: 21

Organizational Communication Questionnaire
CIJE: 0 RIE: 1 CAT: 21

Organizational Conflict Inventory
CIJE: 0 RIE: 1 CAT: 21
UF Rahim Organizational Conflict Inventory

Organizational Consensus
CIJE: 1 RIE: 0 CAT: 16

Organizational Coupling (Schools)
USE School Organizational Coupling

Organizational Coupling Structure Inventory
CIJE: 0 RIE: 1 CAT: 21

Organizational Culture
CIJE: 131 RIE: 110 CAT: 15

Organizational Diagnosis Questionnaire
CIJE: 0 RIE: 1 CAT: 21

Organizational Elements Model
CIJE: 7 RIE: 0 CAT: 15

Organizational Excellence
CIJE: 0 RIE: 2 CAT: 16

Organizational Frames
CIJE: 2 RIE: 5 CAT: 15

Organizational Health
CIJE: 9 RIE: 1 CAT: 11

Organizational Health Description Questionnaire
CIJE: 1 RIE: 0 CAT: 21

Organizational History
CIJE: 13 RIE: 8 CAT: 12

Organizational Inventory Meeting
CIJE: 1 RIE: 0 CAT: 02

Organizational Learning
CIJE: 5 RIE: 1 CAT: 15

Organizational Level
CIJE: 1 RIE: 1 CAT: 15

Organizational Mavericks
CIJE: 0 RIE: 1 CAT: 10

Organizational Mortality
CIJE: 1 RIE: 0 CAT: 16

Organizational Needs
CIJE: 7 RIE: 2 CAT: 16

Organizational Process Model
CIJE: 0 RIE: 1 CAT: 15

Organizational Psychology
CIJE: 9 RIE: 5 CAT: 11

Organizational Readiness
CIJE: 1 RIE: 1 CAT: 16

Organizational Reports
CIJE: 1 RIE: 1 CAT: 16

Organizational Research
CIJE: 57 RIE: 32 CAT: 15

Organizational School Psychology
CIJE: 1 RIE: 0 CAT: 03

Organizational Skills
CIJE: 22 RIE: 22 CAT: 16

Organizational Specialists
CIJE: 0 RIE: 2 CAT: 09

Organizational Structure
CIJE: 6 RIE: 1 CAT: 15

Organizational Supervision
CIJE: 1 RIE: 0 CAT: 15

Organizational Technology
CIJE: 4 RIE: 3 CAT: 20

Organizational Termination
CIJE: 1 RIE: 0 CAT: 16

Organizational Training
CIJE: 3 RIE: 1 CAT: 15

Organizers
CIJE: 9 RIE: 5 CAT: 15

Organizing Strategies
CIJE: 12 RIE: 10 CAT: 15

Organs (Musical Instrument)
CIJE: 0 RIE: 1 CAT: 04

ORI Inc
CIJE: 0 RIE: 1 CAT: 17

Orient
CIJE: 0 RIE: 1 CAT: 07

Oriental Art
CIJE: 1 RIE: 0 CAT: 03

Oriental Culture
CIJE: 0 RIE: 2 CAT: 08

Oriental Jews
CIJE: 5 RIE: 0 CAT: 08

Oriental Literature
CIJE: 1 RIE: 1 CAT: 16

Orientation Inventory
CIJE: 1 RIE: 4 CAT: 21

Orientation to the World of Work Program
CIJE: 0 RIE: 2 CAT: 19

Orienting Information
CIJE: 0 RIE: 1 CAT: 16

Orienting Instruction
CIJE: 0 RIE: 1 CAT: 03

Orienting Reflex
CIJE: 1 RIE: 0 CAT: 11

Orienting Response
CIJE: 12 RIE: 5 CAT: 16

Orienting Tasks
CIJE: 7 RIE: 2 CAT: 11

Origami
CIJE: 7 RIE: 2 CAT: 16

Origin of Life
CIJE: 4 RIE: 1 CAT: 20

Original Semantic Differential (Elsworth et al)
CIJE: 0 RIE: 1 CAT: 21

ORILLAS Network
CIJE: 0 RIE: 2 CAT: 19
SN Full name is "De Orilla a Orilla" ("From Shore to Shore")
UF De Orilla a Orilla; Project Orillas

Orillia Public Library (Canada)
CIJE: 0 RIE: 1 CAT: 17

Orion Community PA
CIJE: 0 RIE: 1 CAT: 17

Oriya
CIJE: 1 RIE: 10 CAT: 13
SN Language spoken in India in the northeast of the Bastar District of Madhya Pradesh — see also "Adivasi Oriya"

Orlando (Title)
CIJE: 0 RIE: 1 CAT: 22
SN Historical fantasy by Virginia Woolf

Orlando Regional Medical Center FL
CIJE: 0 RIE: 1 CAT: 17

Orleans Hanna Algebra Prognosis Test
CIJE: 4 RIE: 0 CAT: 21

Orleans Hanna Geometry Prognosis Test
CIJE: 2 RIE: 0 CAT: 21

Orleans Niagara Board Coop Educ Services NY
CIJE: 0 RIE: 1 CAT: 17

Orleans Southwest School District VT
CIJE: 0 RIE: 1 CAT: 17

Ornamental Iron Workers
CIJE: 0 RIE: 3 CAT: 09

Orokaiva
CIJE: 0 RIE: 1 CAT: 13

Oromo
CIJE: 0 RIE: 3 CAT: 13

Orozco (Jose Clemente)
CIJE: 2 RIE: 1 CAT: 18

Orphan in History (Cowan)
CIJE: 0 RIE: 1 CAT: 22

Orphanages
CIJE: 5 RIE: 2 CAT: 05

Orphans
CIJE: 14 RIE: 2 CAT: 10

Orpheus
CIJE: 1 RIE: 0 CAT: 18

ORS 339 115 (Oregon 1989)
CIJE: 0 RIE: 1 CAT: 14
UF Oregon Revised Statute 339 115

ORT ONLY MODEL
CIJE: 0 RIE: 1 CAT: 21

Ortega (Daniel)
CIJE: 0 RIE: 1 CAT: 18

Ortega y Gasset (Jose)
CIJE: 13 RIE: 3 CAT: 18

Ortho Film
CIJE: 1 RIE: 0 CAT: 04

Orthodox Eastern Church
USE Eastern Orthodox Church

Orthodox Eastern Church (Greek)
USE Greek Orthodox Church

Orthodox Jews
CIJE: 2 RIE: 1 CAT: 08

Orthogenetical Principle
CIJE: 0 RIE: 1 CAT: 15

Orthogonal Comparison
CIJE: 7 RIE: 9 CAT: 20

Orthographic Redundancy
CIJE: 0 RIE: 1 CAT: 13

Orthographic Structure
CIJE: 8 RIE: 4 CAT: 13

Orthography
CIJE: 37 RIE: 27 CAT: 13

Orthomolecular Therapy
CIJE: 1 RIE: 1 CAT: 11

Orthopedic Certification Examination
CIJE: 1 RIE: 1 CAT: 21

Orthopedic Surgery
CIJE: 5 RIE: 1 CAT: 11

Orthopedics
CIJE: 7 RIE: 4 CAT: 11

Orthopsychiatry
CIJE: 0 RIE: 1 CAT: 11

Orthoptic Vision
CIJE: 0 RIE: 1 CAT: 11
UF Orthoptics

Orthoptics
USE Orthoptic Vision

Orthostatic Tolerance
CIJE: 1 RIE: 0 CAT: 11

Orthotic Prosthetic Education
CIJE: 1 RIE: 1 CAT: 11

Orthotic Technicians
CIJE: 0 RIE: 2 CAT: 09

Ortiz (Alfonso)
CIJE: 1 RIE: 0 CAT: 18

Ortiz (Simon J)
CIJE: 0 RIE: 1 CAT: 18

Orton (Samuel)
CIJE: 6 RIE: 1 CAT: 18

Orton Gillingham Tutorial Program
CIJE: 8 RIE: 1 CAT: 19

Orwell (George)
CIJE: 48 RIE: 14 CAT: 18

Osage (Tribe)
CIJE: 2 RIE: 5 CAT: 08

Osborn (Michael)
CIJE: 0 RIE: 1 CAT: 18

Osborne 1
CIJE: 2 RIE: 1 CAT: 04

Osburn School NY
CIJE: 2 RIE: 0 CAT: 17

Oscar Rose Junior College OK
CIJE: 2 RIE: 0 CAT: 17

Oscillating System
CIJE: 3 RIE: 0 CAT: 04

Oscillators
CIJE: 4 RIE: 4 CAT: 04

Oscillograms
CIJE: 0 RIE: 2 CAT: 04

Oscilloscopes
CIJE: 13 RIE: 3 CAT: 04

Oseretsky Tests of Motor Proficiency
CIJE: 0 RIE: 1 CAT: 21

Oseretzsky (Lincoln)
CIJE: 0 RIE: 1 CAT: 18

Osgood (C E)
CIJE: 0 RIE: 2 CAT: 18

Osgood Semantic Differential Test
CIJE: 9 RIE: 9 CAT: 21

OSIRIS IV (Computer Program)
CIJE: 0 RIE: 1 CAT: 04

OSIRIS Prototype
CIJE: 0 RIE: 1 CAT: 04

OSIRIS Student Accountability System SC
CIJE: 0 RIE: 1 CAT: 04
UF South Carolina Student Database (OSIRIS)

Osler (William)
CIJE: 1 RIE: 1 CAT: 18

Oslo Work Research Institute (Norway)
CIJE: 0 RIE: 1 CAT: 17

Osmosis
CIJE: 19 RIE: 5 CAT: 20

Osmotic Pumps
CIJE: 1 RIE: 0 CAT: 04

OSP Model for Sex Equity
USE On Site Needs Assessment Long Range Planning Model

Osseo School District MN
CIJE: 0 RIE: 0 CAT: 17

Osteitis Pubis
CIJE: 1 RIE: 0 CAT: 11

Osteogenesis Imperfecta
CIJE: 5 RIE: 5 CAT: 11

Osteomyelitis
CIJE: 1 RIE: 0 CAT: 11

Osteoporosis
CIJE: 21 RIE: 4 CAT: 11

Osterhouse (R A)
CIJE: 1 RIE: 0 CAT: 18

Ostinato
CIJE: 1 RIE: 0 CAT: 16

Oswego Plan for Team Supervision
CIJE: 0 RIE: 1 CAT: 19

Otego Unadillo Central School District NY
CIJE: 0 RIE: 1 CAT: 17

Othello
CIJE: 6 RIE: 3 CAT: 22

Othen v Ann Arbor School Board
CIJE: 1 RIE: 0 CAT: 14

Other Sex Friendship
USE Cross Sex Friendship

Other Sex Interaction
USE Cross Sex Interaction

Other Sex Peers
USE Cross Sex Peers

Otis (Eliza)
CIJE: 1 RIE: 1 CAT: 18

Otis Group Intelligence Scale
CIJE: 0 RIE: 1 CAT: 21

Otis Lennon Mental Ability Test
CIJE: 22 RIE: 22 CAT: 21

Otis Lennon School Ability Test
CIJE: 5 RIE: 5 CAT: 21

Otis Quick Scoring Mental Ability Tests
CIJE: 8 RIE: 14 CAT: 21

Otis Self Administering Tests of Mental Ability
CIJE: 1 RIE: 0 CAT: 21

Otis Spunkmeyer Student Motivation Program
CIJE: 0 RIE: 1 CAT: 19

Otitis Media
CIJE: 53 RIE: 10 CAT: 11
UF Middle Ear Infections

Oto
CIJE: 0 RIE: 1 CAT: 13
SN Dialect of Chiwere, a Siouan language
UF Otoe

Oto Manguean
CIJE: 0 RIE: 1 CAT: 13
SN Group of Middle American languages
UF Otomanguean Languages

Otoacoustic Emissions
CIJE: 1 RIE: 1 CAT: 11

Otoe
USE Oto

Otoe (Tribe)
CIJE: 0 RIE: 2 CAT: 08

Otomanguean Languages
USE Oto Manguean

Otomi
CIJE: 1 RIE: 1 CAT: 13

Ottawa
CIJE: 6 RIE: 10 CAT: 13
SN Dialect of Ojibwa

Ottawa (Tribe)
CIJE: 0 RIE: 4 CAT: 08

Ottawa Board of Education ON
CIJE: 0 RIE: 2 CAT: 17

Ottawa High School IL
CIJE: 0 RIE: 1 CAT: 17

Ottawa Project
CIJE: 1 RIE: 0 CAT: 19

Ottawa Public Library (Canada)
CIJE: 1 RIE: 1 CAT: 17

Ottawa University KS
CIJE: 0 RIE: 2 CAT: 17

Otterbein College OH
CIJE: 1 RIE: 6 CAT: 17

Ottoman Empire
CIJE: 4 RIE: 2 CAT: 07

Ottumwa Community School District IA
CIJE: 0 RIE: 2 CAT: 17

Ottumwa Regional Center IA
CIJE: 0 RIE: 1 CAT: 17

Ouachita Parish School System LA
CIJE: 0 RIE: 1 CAT: 07

Ouchi (William)
CIJE: 2 RIE: 2 CAT: 18

OUNCE Classroom Management Program
CIJE: 1 RIE: 0 CAT: 19

Ounce of Prevention Fund IL
USE Ounce of Prevention Program IL

Ounce of Prevention Program IL
CIJE: 0 RIE: 1 CAT: 19
UF Ounce of Prevention Fund IL

Our Class and Its Work Questionnaire
CIJE: 1 RIE: 3 CAT: 21

Our Economy How It Works
CIJE: 0 RIE: 2 CAT: 22

Our Kind of World
CIJE: 0 RIE: 1 CAT: 22

Our Lady of the Lake College TX
CIJE: 0 RIE: 3 CAT: 17

Our Lady of the Lake University of San Antonio TX
CIJE: 0 RIE: 2 CAT: 17

Our School Building Attitude Inventory
CIJE: 0 RIE: 1 CAT: 21

Our Schools Project
CIJE: 1 RIE: 1 CAT: 19

Our Working World
CIJE: 4 RIE: 1 CAT: 22

Our World
CIJE: 0 RIE: 1 CAT: 22

Our Young Authors (Writing Project)
CIJE: 0 RIE: 1 CAT: 19

Out of District Placements
CIJE: 0 RIE: 1 CAT: 16

Out of Field Classes
CIJE: 0 RIE: 1 CAT: 16
SN Classes taught by teachers not holding the required or recommended certification

Out of Level Testing
CIJE: 8 RIE: 31 CAT: 21

Out of Print Materials
CIJE: 10 RIE: 0 CAT: 16

Out of School Credit Experiences Program
CIJE: 1 RIE: 0 CAT: 19

Out of School Misconduct
CIJE: 1 RIE: 0 CAT: 11

Out of School Youth Program
CIJE: 0 RIE: 4 CAT: 19

Out of Seat Behavior
CIJE: 0 RIE: 1 CAT: 11

Out of State Institutions
CIJE: 0 RIE: 10 CAT: 05

Out of State Placement of Children
CIJE: 0 RIE: 6 CAT: 15

Outboard Motor Assemblers
CIJE: 0 RIE: 1 CAT: 09

Outboard Motors
CIJE: 0 RIE: 3 CAT: 04

Outcome Based Education
CIJE: 102 RIE: 66 CAT: 16
SN Educational system that specifies what the student ought to be able to do once he or she leaves the system

Outcome Based Instructional Systems Approach
CIJE: 0 RIE: 2 CAT: 15

Outcome Oriented Evaluation
CIJE: 0 RIE: 1 CAT: 15

Outcome Oriented Grading
CIJE: 0 RIE: 1 CAT: 15

Outcomes Expectancy
CIJE: 15 RIE: 9 CAT: 15

Outdoor and Conservation Education Program
CIJE: 0 RIE: 1 CAT: 19

Outdoor Biology Instructional Strategies
CIJE: 13 RIE: 12 CAT: 15
UF OBIS Program

Outdoor Education for the Handicapped Project KY
CIJE: 0 RIE: 1 CAT: 19

Outdoor Leadership
CIJE: 22 RIE: 22 CAT: 16

Outdoor Learning Laboratory NY
CIJE: 0 RIE: 1 CAT: 17

Outdoor Mobility
CIJE: 1 RIE: 0 CAT: 11

Outdoor Recreation
CIJE: 18 RIE: 35 CAT: 16

Outdoor Recreation Resources Review Commission
CIJE: 1 RIE: 2 CAT: 17

Outdoor Recreationists
CIJE: 0 RIE: 2 CAT: 10

Outdoor Research Project KS
CIJE: 0 RIE: 1 CAT: 19

Outdoor Safety Committees
CIJE: 1 RIE: 0 CAT: 09

Outerdirectedness
CIJE: 8 RIE: 3 CAT: 11

Outliers
CIJE: 11 RIE: 25 CAT: 16

Outline Graphics
CIJE: 0 RIE: 2 CAT: 15

Outlines
CIJE: 13 RIE: 6 CAT: 16
SN See also the Descriptor "Outlining (Discourse)"

Outlook Nashville Program
CIJE: 0 RIE: 1 CAT: 19

Outmigration
CIJE: 1 RIE: 2 CAT: 16

Outpatient Care
CIJE: 29 RIE: 4 CAT: 11

Outpatient Commitment
CIJE: 0 RIE: 1 CAT: 11
UF Psychiatric Outpatient Commitment

Output Measurements
CIJE: 4 RIE: 2 CAT: 15

Output Measures for Public Libraries
CIJE: 8 RIE: 5 CAT: 22

Output Performance Measures
CIJE: 1 RIE: 1 CAT: 15

Outreach and Technical Assistance Network CA
CIJE: 0 RIE: 2 CAT: 19

Outreach Mobile Delivery System NY
CIJE: 0 RIE: 1 CAT: 17

Outstanding Teachers
CIJE: 2 RIE: 15 CAT: 10

Outward Bound
CIJE: 53 RIE: 100 CAT: 19

Outward Bound Bridging Course (Australia)
CIJE: 0 RIE: 2 CAT: 03

Outward Bound School ME
CIJE: 1 RIE: 0 CAT: 17

Outward Bound Sea School (England)
CIJE: 0 RIE: 1 CAT: 17

Over 60 Counseling and Employment Service
CIJE: 1 RIE: 0 CAT: 17

Over All Agreement Score
CIJE: 0 RIE: 1 CAT: 21

Over Easy (Television Series)
CIJE: 0 RIE: 1 CAT: 22

Over Extension Phenomena
CIJE: 2 RIE: 1 CAT: 13

Overage Students
CIJE: 0 RIE: 2 CAT: 10

Overall and Dalals Formula
CIJE: 1 RIE: 0 CAT: 15

OVERALS Computer Program
USE OVERALS Technique

OVERALS Technique
CIJE: 0 RIE: 3 CAT: 15
UF OVERALS Computer Program

Overattribution
CIJE: 0 RIE: 1 CAT: 16

Overconfidence
CIJE: 1 RIE: 2 CAT: 11

Overcontrolled Hostility Scale
CIJE: 3 RIE: 0 CAT: 21

Overcorrection
CIJE: 34 RIE: 1 CAT: 11

Overdetermination
CIJE: 1 RIE: 1 CAT: 15

Overdue Books
CIJE: 11 RIE: 7 CAT: 16

Overeducation
CIJE: 13 RIE: 4 CAT: 15

Overhaul (Fire Science)
CIJE: 0 RIE: 3 CAT: 20

Overhead Project
CIJE: 0 RIE: 1 CAT: 19

Overjustification
CIJE: 3 RIE: 5 CAT: 15

Overlap Hypothesis
CIJE: 5 RIE: 0 CAT: 15

Overlearning
CIJE: 9 RIE: 2 CAT: 15

Overseas Activities
CIJE: 1 RIE: 5 CAT: 16

Overseas American Colleges
CIJE: 1 RIE: 0 CAT: 05

Overseas Campuses
CIJE: 0 RIE: 1 CAT: 05

Overseas Development Ministry
CIJE: 2 RIE: 0 CAT: 17

Overseas Education Service
CIJE: 1 RIE: 1 CAT: 17

Overseas Refugee Training Program
CIJE: 0 RIE: 7 CAT: 19

Overseas Schools
USE Dependents Schools

Overselectivity
CIJE: 6 RIE: 1 CAT: 16

Oversight Information Systems
CIJE: 0 RIE: 1 CAT: 15

Overt Aggression Scale (Yudofsky)
CIJE: 0 RIE: 1 CAT: 21

Overt Verbalization
CIJE: 2 RIE: 2 CAT: 13

Overton (Anthony)
CIJE: 0 RIE: 1 CAT: 18

Overtraining Reversal Effect
CIJE: 1 RIE: 0 CAT: 15

Overuse Injuries
CIJE: 8 RIE: 1 CAT: 11

Overview Snapshot Observation Technique
CIJE: 0 RIE: 1 CAT: 15

Ovid
CIJE: 1 RIE: 1 CAT: 18

Owego Apalachin Central School District NY
CIJE: 0 RIE: 1 CAT: 17

Owen (Robert)
CIJE: 5 RIE: 5 CAT: 18

Owen (Wilfred)
CIJE: 3 RIE: 0 CAT: 18

Owen Report
CIJE: 1 RIE: 0 CAT: 22

Owen Sound Public Library (Canada)
CIJE: 0 RIE: 1 CAT: 17

Owen v City of Independence
CIJE: 1 RIE: 0 CAT: 14

Owen Withee School District WI
CIJE: 0 RIE: 1 CAT: 17

Owens v Commonwealth
CIJE: 1 RIE: 0 CAT: 14

Owensboro City School System KY
CIJE: 0 RIE: 1 CAT: 17

Owensboro Community College KY
CIJE: 0 RIE: 1 CAT: 17

Owensboro Daviess County Public Library KY
CIJE: 0 RIE: 1 CAT: 17

Owl Service
CIJE: 1 RIE: 1 CAT: 22

Owls
CIJE: 13 RIE: 0 CAT: 20

Ownership Patterns
CIJE: 0 RIE: 1 CAT: 16

Ox Bow Incident
CIJE: 1 RIE: 0 CAT: 22

Oxford Advanced Learners Dictionary
CIJE: 1 RIE: 1 CAT: 22

Oxford American Dictionary
CIJE: 2 RIE: 0 CAT: 22

Oxford Council of Europe Study
CIJE: 1 RIE: 0 CAT: 19

Oxford English Dictionary
CIJE: 7 RIE: 2 CAT: 22

Oxford Hills High School ME
CIJE: 1 RIE: 0 CAT: 17

Oxford Polytechnic (England)
CIJE: 4 RIE: 1 CAT: 17

Oxford Preschool Research Project (England)
CIJE: 0 RIE: 1 CAT: 19

Oxford Secondary English Course for Jordan
CIJE: 1 RIE: 0 CAT: 03

Oxidation Ditches
CIJE: 0 RIE: 2 CAT: 20

Oxides
CIJE: 3 RIE: 0 CAT: 20

Oxley (Lawrence A)
CIJE: 0 RIE: 1 CAT: 18
SN "Lawrence Augustus"

Oxnard College CA
CIJE: 0 RIE: 6 CAT: 17

Oxnard School District CA
CIJE: 2 RIE: 7 CAT: 17

Oxnard Union High School District CA
CIJE: 0 RIE: 1 CAT: 17

Oxygen
CIJE: 14 RIE: 3 CAT: 20

Oxygen Administration
CIJE: 2 RIE: 0 CAT: 11

Oxygen Consumption
CIJE: 25 RIE: 6 CAT: 11

Oxygen Profile Test
CIJE: 0 RIE: 1 CAT: 20

Oxygen Uptake Test
CIJE: 4 RIE: 2 CAT: 20

Oye Willie (Title)
CIJE: 0 RIE: 1 CAT: 22

Oyo Ibadan Dialect
CIJE: 0 RIE: 1 CAT: 13

Oysters
CIJE: 1 RIE: 2 CAT: 20

Ozarka Vocational Technical School AR
CIJE: 0 RIE: 1 CAT: 17

Ozarks
CIJE: 5 RIE: 17 CAT: 07

Ozarks (Central)
CIJE: 0 RIE: 1 CAT: 07

Ozone
CIJE: 30 RIE: 7 CAT: 20

Ozone Depletion
CIJE: 4 RIE: 2 CAT: 20

Ozone Detectors
CIJE: 0 RIE: 1 CAT: 04

P Aminobenzoic Acid
CIJE: 1 RIE: 0 CAT: 11

P K Yonge Laboratory School
CIJE: 2 RIE: 4 CAT: 17

P Values
CIJE: 7 RIE: 7 CAT: 21

P3 Latency
CIJE: 2 RIE: 1 CAT: 11

PACE IV
CIJE: 0 RIE: 0 CAT: 02
UF Positive Approaches to Childrens Education IV

PACE Program KY
USE Parent and Child Education Program KY

PACE Project (Great Britain)
USE Primary Assessment Curric Exper (Great Britain)

PACE Project AZ
USE Parent and Child Education Project AZ

Pace University NY
CIJE: 4 RIE: 7 CAT: 17

PACE VI
CIJE: 0 RIE: 0 CAT: 02
UF Positive Approaches to Childrens Education VI

Pacemakers
CIJE: 1 RIE: 1 CAT: 04

PACER Center MN
CIJE: 0 RIE: 3 CAT: 17
UF Parent Advocacy Coalition for Educational Rights

Paces College Student Experiences Questionnaire
CIJE: 0 RIE: 1 CAT: 21

PACES Model
USE Program Advisory Committee Evaluation System

Pacesetters in Innovation
CIJE: 0 RIE: 4 CAT: 22

Pachisi Game
CIJE: 0 RIE: 0 CAT: 16
UF Parcheesi (Brand); Parchisi

Pachucos
CIJE: 3 RIE: 0 CAT: 08

Pacific Asia
USE Asia Pacific Region

Pacific Basin Countries
CIJE: 4 RIE: 8 CAT: 07

Pacific Circle Consortium
CIJE: 0 RIE: 7 CAT: 17

Pacific Circle Project
CIJE: 0 RIE: 1 CAT: 19

Pacific Community Concept
CIJE: 0 RIE: 1 CAT: 15

Pacific Educational Computer Network
CIJE: 0 RIE: 3 CAT: 17

Pacific High School CA
CIJE: 1 RIE: 0 CAT: 17

Pacific Horizons Reading Scheme
CIJE: 1 RIE: 0 CAT: 15

Pacific Information Center (Fiji)
CIJE: 0 RIE: 1 CAT: 17

Pacific Islanders
CIJE: 6 RIE: 24 CAT: 08

Pacific Islands
CIJE: 30 RIE: 59 CAT: 07

Pacific Islands Literature
CIJE: 1 RIE: 3 CAT: 16

Pacific Lutheran University WA
CIJE: 8 RIE: 8 CAT: 17

Pacific Northwest
CIJE: 21 RIE: 31 CAT: 07

Pacific Northwest Bibliographic Center
CIJE: 1 RIE: 3 CAT: 17

Pacific Northwest Indian Reading and Language Prog
CIJE: 1 RIE: 10 CAT: 19

Pacific Northwest Tribes
CIJE: 3 RIE: 14 CAT: 08

Pacific Oaks College and Childrens School CA
CIJE: 0 RIE: 2 CAT: 17

Pacific Ocean
CIJE: 2 RIE: 6 CAT: 07

Pacific Region
CIJE: 22 RIE: 128 CAT: 07

Pacific Region Educational Laboratory
CIJE: 0 RIE: 0 CAT: 17

Pacific Rim
CIJE: 22 RIE: 26 CAT: 16

Pacific Telecommunications Council
CIJE: 0 RIE: 6 CAT: 17

Pacific Trust Territory
CIJE: 3 RIE: 13 CAT: 07

Pacific Trust Territory (Mariana Islands)
CIJE: 2 RIE: 5 CAT: 07

Pacific Trust Territory (Marshall Islands)
CIJE: 0 RIE: 5 CAT: 07
SN Became a republic in 1980s — use "Marshall Islands" for the independent nation

Pacific Trust Territory (Palau Islands)
USE Palau Islands

Pacific Trust Territory (Ponape)
CIJE: 2 RIE: 2 CAT: 07

Pacific University OR
CIJE: 7 RIE: 2 CAT: 17

Pacifica Foundation
CIJE: 3 RIE: 1 CAT: 17

Pacification
CIJE: 1 RIE: 1 CAT: 15

Pacifism
CIJE: 13 RIE: 2 CAT: 16

Package Assessment Scale
CIJE: 1 RIE: 0 CAT: 21

Packaged Meals
CIJE: 1 RIE: 0 CAT: 20

Packaging
CIJE: 16 RIE: 15 CAT: 20

Packaging Machine Mechanics
CIJE: 0 RIE: 1 CAT: 09

Packers
CIJE: 0 RIE: 7 CAT: 09

Packet Reservation Access Method
CIJE: 0 RIE: 1 CAT: 15

Packet Switched Networks
CIJE: 8 RIE: 10 CAT: 04

PACKS Project (United Kingdom)
CIJE: 0 RIE: 1 CAT: 19
UF Procedural and Conceptual Knowledge in Science

Packwood (Robert W)
CIJE: 0 RIE: 1 CAT: 18

Pacoima Elementary School CA
CIJE: 1 RIE: 1 CAT: 17

PACs
USE Political Action Committees

PACT Plus
USE Preliminary American College Test Plus

Paddington Books
CIJE: 1 RIE: 1 CAT: 22

Paddle to the Sea
CIJE: 0 RIE: 1 CAT: 22

Paddock School (Great Britain)
CIJE: 1 RIE: 0 CAT: 17

PADI
USE Program of Assessment Diagnosis and Instruction MD

Padilla Bay
CIJE: 0 RIE: 3 CAT: 07

Padjadjaran University
USE Pajajaran State University (Indonesia)

Padron (Rodriquez del)
CIJE: 1 RIE: 0 CAT: 18

Paegan (Tribe)
USE Peigan (Nation)

Paez
CIJE: 1 RIE: 0 CAT: 13

Page (Ellis)
CIJE: 2 RIE: 1 CAT: 18

Pageants
CIJE: 0 RIE: 1 CAT: 16

Paget Gorman Sign System
CIJE: 2 RIE: 0 CAT: 11

Paget System
CIJE: 1 RIE: 0 CAT: 13

Paging Devices (Radio)
CIJE: 0 RIE: 1 CAT: 04

Pahlavi (Shah Reza)
CIJE: 0 RIE: 1 CAT: 18

Pahlavi National Library (Iran)
CIJE: 0 RIE: 0 CAT: 17

Pahlavi University (Iran)
CIJE: 2 RIE: 1 CAT: 17

Paideia
CIJE: 1 RIE: 7 CAT: 15

Paideia Problems and Possibilities
CIJE: 1 RIE: 0 CAT: 22

Paideia Proposal
CIJE: 26 RIE: 13 CAT: 03

Paige Compositor
CIJE: 0 RIE: 1 CAT: 20

Pain Apperception Test
CIJE: 1 RIE: 0 CAT: 21

Pain Control
CIJE: 8 RIE: 4 CAT: 11

Pain Experience
CIJE: 0 RIE: 1 CAT: 11

Pain Perception
CIJE: 1 RIE: 1 CAT: 11

Pain Tolerance
CIJE: 5 RIE: 1 CAT: 11

Paine (Thomas)
CIJE: 2 RIE: 2 CAT: 18

Paine College GA
CIJE: 0 RIE: 1 CAT: 17

Paint
CIJE: 1 RIE: 4 CAT: 16

Paint Creek Youth Center OH
CIJE: 0 RIE: 1 CAT: 17

PaintWorks Plus
CIJE: 0 RIE: 1 CAT: 04

Paired Classes
USE Paired Courses

Paired Comparisons
CIJE: 49 RIE: 17 CAT: 15

Paired Courses
CIJE: 1 RIE: 3 CAT: 03
UF Paired Classes

Paired Hands Test
CIJE: 1 RIE: 4 CAT: 21

Paired Reading
CIJE: 24 RIE: 14 CAT: 13

Paired Reinforcement
CIJE: 1 RIE: 0 CAT: 11

Paired Stimuli
CIJE: 3 RIE: 2 CAT: 11

Paired Student Interaction
CIJE: 0 RIE: 1 CAT: 15

Paired Teaching
CIJE: 1 RIE: 1 CAT: 15

Pairing Enrichment Program
CIJE: 1 RIE: 0 CAT: 19

Pairing Machine Operators
CIJE: 0 RIE: 1 CAT: 09

Pairwise Preference Data
CIJE: 2 RIE: 0 CAT: 21

Paite
CIJE: 0 RIE: 1 CAT: 13
SN A Northern Chin language of the Tibeto-Burman group
UF Paithe; Vuite

Paithe
USE Paite

Paiute
CIJE: 2 RIE: 0 CAT: 13

Paiute (Tribe)
CIJE: 5 RIE: 22 CAT: 08
SN See also "Northern Paiute (Tribe)" and "Southern Paiute (Tribe)"

Paivio (A)
CIJE: 4 RIE: 3 CAT: 18

Pajajaran State University (Indonesia)
CIJE: 0 RIE: 1 CAT: 17
UF Padjadjaran University

Pajaro Valley Unified School District CA
CIJE: 2 RIE: 6 CAT: 17

Pakehas (People)
CIJE: 0 RIE: 1 CAT: 08

Pakistan
CIJE: 90 RIE: 223 CAT: 07

Pakistan (Karachi)
CIJE: 3 RIE: 3 CAT: 07

Pakistan (Lahore)
CIJE: 1 RIE: 1 CAT: 07

Pakistan (North West Frontier)
CIJE: 1 RIE: 1 CAT: 07

Pakistan (Skardu)
CIJE: 0 RIE: 1 CAT: 07

Pakistan (Taxila)
CIJE: 1 RIE: 0 CAT: 07

Pakistanis
CIJE: 6 RIE: 9 CAT: 08

Pako Corporation
CIJE: 1 RIE: 0 CAT: 17

Pakula (Alan J)
CIJE: 0 RIE: 1 CAT: 18

PAL Programing Language
CIJE: 0 RIE: 2 CAT: 04

Palatine High School IL
CIJE: 1 RIE: 0 CAT: 17

Palau
CIJE: 2 RIE: 4 CAT: 07
SN Former Pacific Trust Territory, for which use "Palau Islands"
UF Belau

Palau Islands
CIJE: 0 RIE: 2 CAT: 07
SN Became a republic in 1981 — use "Palau" for the independent nation
UF Pacific Trust Territory (Palau Islands)

Palauan
CIJE: 0 RIE: 2 CAT: 13

Paleoecology
CIJE: 3 RIE: 0 CAT: 03

Paleosiberian Languages
CIJE: 0 RIE: 2 CAT: 13

Palermo Jenkins Free Association Norms
CIJE: 0 RIE: 5 CAT: 21

Palestine
CIJE: 11 RIE: 15 CAT: 07

Palestine Liberation Organization
CIJE: 6 RIE: 2 CAT: 17

Palestinian Arabic
USE Arabic (Palestinian)

Palestinian Arabs
CIJE: 2 RIE: 6 CAT: 08

Palestinian Israeli Conflict
CIJE: 6 RIE: 4 CAT: 12
UF Israeli Palestinian Conflict

Palestinians
CIJE: 13 RIE: 6 CAT: 08

Pali
CIJE: 1 RIE: 0 CAT: 13

Palindromes
CIJE: 6 RIE: 0 CAT: 13

Palm Beach County Schools FL
CIJE: 5 RIE: 12 CAT: 17

Palm Beach Junior College FL
CIJE: 1 RIE: 0 CAT: 17

Palmar Sweat Print Method
CIJE: 1 RIE: 1 CAT: 15

Palme (Olof)
CIJE: 2 RIE: 1 CAT: 18

Palmer (Alice Freeman)
CIJE: 1 RIE: 1 CAT: 18

Palmer (Harold E)
CIJE: 5 RIE: 0 CAT: 18

Palmer Handwriting Method
CIJE: 0 RIE: 1 CAT: 15

Palmer Memorial Institute NC
CIJE: 1 RIE: 0 CAT: 17

Palmer v Ticcione
CIJE: 0 RIE: 0 CAT: 14

Palmetto High School FL
CIJE: 0 RIE: 1 CAT: 17

Palo Alto Peer Counseling Program
CIJE: 0 RIE: 1 CAT: 19

Palo Alto Unified School District CA
CIJE: 1 RIE: 6 CAT: 17

Palomar College CA
CIJE: 1 RIE: 4 CAT: 17

PALOS
USE Purdue Academic Learning Opportunity Systems

Palos Hills Consol High School District 230 IL
CIJE: 0 RIE: 0 CAT: 17

Palos Verdes Peninsula Unified School District CA
CIJE: 0 RIE: 1 CAT: 17

Palouse School District WA
CIJE: 0 RIE: 1 CAT: 17

Palpation
CIJE: 0 RIE: 0 CAT: 11

Palspan Project
CIJE: 0 RIE: 1 CAT: 19

Pan African Movement
CIJE: 6 RIE: 3 CAT: 12

Pan American Agricultural Teacher Training Program
CIJE: 0 RIE: 1 CAT: 19

Pan American Federation of Medical Schools
CIJE: 0 RIE: 1 CAT: 17

Pan American Health Organization
CIJE: 3 RIE: 3 CAT: 17

Pan American University TX
CIJE: 5 RIE: 4 CAT: 17
SN See also new name "University of Texas Pan American"

Pan Indianism
CIJE: 6 RIE: 1 CAT: 15

Panama
CIJE: 17 RIE: 24 CAT: 07

Panama Canal
CIJE: 2 RIE: 2 CAT: 07

Panama Canal Treaties
CIJE: 2 RIE: 0 CAT: 12

Panama Nuevo Veranillo Project
CIJE: 0 RIE: 1 CAT: 19

Panare
CIJE: 0 RIE: 1 CAT: 13
SN A Carib language (Northern group)
UF Panari

Panari
USE Panare

Panax Cameras
CIJE: 0 RIE: 1 CAT: 04

Pancreas
CIJE: 2 RIE: 0 CAT: 11

Pandialectal Phonology
CIJE: 0 RIE: 1 CAT: 13

Panel Consensus Technique
CIJE: 1 RIE: 2 CAT: 15

Panel of Consultants on Vocational Education
CIJE: 0 RIE: 4 CAT: 17

Panel on Undergraduate Major Curricula
CIJE: 0 RIE: 1 CAT: 02

Panel Review of Products
CIJE: 0 RIE: 2 CAT: 19

Panel Reviews
CIJE: 0 RIE: 1 CAT: 15

Panel Studies
CIJE: 14 RIE: 10 CAT: 15

Panel Study of Income Dynamics
CIJE: 8 RIE: 4 CAT: 19

Pangaea
CIJE: 0 RIE: 1 CAT: 07

Pangasinan
CIJE: 0 RIE: 1 CAT: 13

Panhandle State University OK
CIJE: 0 RIE: 1 CAT: 17

Panic
CIJE: 5 RIE: 1 CAT: 11

Panjab University (India)
CIJE: 1 RIE: 0 CAT: 17
UF Punjab University

Panjabis
USE Punjabis

Panoan
CIJE: 1 RIE: 0 CAT: 13

Panoramas (Backdrops)
CIJE: 1 RIE: 0 CAT: 04

Panoramic Maps
CIJE: 1 RIE: 0 CAT: 04

Pantin (Gerard)
CIJE: 0 RIE: 1 CAT: 18

Pantographers
CIJE: 0 RIE: 1 CAT: 09

Pantographs
CIJE: 1 RIE: 0 CAT: 04

Pap Smears
CIJE: 2 RIE: 1 CAT: 11

Papago (Tribe)
CIJE: 21 RIE: 31 CAT: 08

Papago Indian Reservation AZ
CIJE: 2 RIE: 1 CAT: 17

Papal Volunteers
CIJE: 1 RIE: 0 CAT: 10

Papandropoulou (I)
CIJE: 0 RIE: 1 CAT: 18

Paper Airplanes (Toys)
CIJE: 0 RIE: 1 CAT: 16

Paper and Pencil Tests
CIJE: 57 RIE: 72 CAT: 21

Paper and Pulp Occupations
CIJE: 0 RIE: 10 CAT: 09

Paper Boats (Toys)
CIJE: 1 RIE: 0 CAT: 16

Paper Deacidification
CIJE: 16 RIE: 18 CAT: 20
UF Deacidification (Paper)

Paper Deterioration
CIJE: 12 RIE: 8 CAT: 20
UF Deterioration (Paper)

Paper Dresses
CIJE: 1 RIE: 0 CAT: 16

Paper Flow System
CIJE: 1 RIE: 0 CAT: 15

Paper Folding
CIJE: 7 RIE: 2 CAT: 15

Paper Industry
CIJE: 6 RIE: 4 CAT: 05

PaperChase Online Catalog
CIJE: 2 RIE: 0 CAT: 04

Paperless Society
CIJE: 4 RIE: 0 CAT: 20

Papert (Seymour)
CIJE: 20 RIE: 5 CAT: 18

Paperwork
CIJE: 7 RIE: 8 CAT: 16

Paperwork Control
CIJE: 5 RIE: 1 CAT: 16

Paperwork Reduction
CIJE: 12 RIE: 6 CAT: 16

Paperwork Reduction Act 1980
CIJE: 4 RIE: 4 CAT: 14
UF Public Law 96 511

Papia Kristang
CIJE: 1 RIE: 0 CAT: 13

Papiamento
CIJE: 1 RIE: 1 CAT: 13

Papier Mache
CIJE: 9 RIE: 0 CAT: 15

Papillomata
CIJE: 1 RIE: 0 CAT: 11

Papish v Board of Curators
CIJE: 1 RIE: 0 CAT: 14

Papua New Guinea
CIJE: 109 RIE: 108 CAT: 07

Papua New Guinea (Manus Island)
CIJE: 0 RIE: 2 CAT: 07

Papua New Guinea (North Solomons)
CIJE: 0 RIE: 0 CAT: 07

Papua New Guinea (Trobriand Islands)
CIJE: 1 RIE: 2 CAT: 07

Papua New Guinea Library Association
CIJE: 0 RIE: 1 CAT: 17

Papua New Guinea University of Technology
CIJE: 2 RIE: 3 CAT: 17
UF University of Technology (Papua New Guinea)

Papuan Languages
CIJE: 3 RIE: 2 CAT: 13

Papuans
CIJE: 1 RIE: 0 CAT: 08

Papy Minicomputer
CIJE: 1 RIE: 1 CAT: 04

PAR Testing System
CIJE: 0 RIE: 1 CAT: 21

Para Professional Training Institute
CIJE: 1 RIE: 0 CAT: 02

Parables
CIJE: 9 RIE: 0 CAT: 16

Parachutes
CIJE: 3 RIE: 4 CAT: 04

Paradigm Argument
CIJE: 12 RIE: 4 CAT: 15

Paradigm Case Analysis
CIJE: 0 RIE: 1 CAT: 15

Paradigm Shifts
CIJE: 86 RIE: 27 CAT: 21

Paradigmatic Responses
CIJE: 2 RIE: 3 CAT: 13

Paradigmatic Syntagmatic Language List
CIJE: 0 RIE: 1 CAT: 13

Paradise Lost
CIJE: 4 RIE: 4 CAT: 22

Paradise Valley Community College Center AZ
CIJE: 0 RIE: 1 CAT: 17

Paradise Valley Unified School District AZ
CIJE: 2 RIE: 0 CAT: 17

Paradiso
CIJE: 1 RIE: 0 CAT: 22

Paradoxical Techniques
CIJE: 11 RIE: 6 CAT: 15

Paragraph Boundaries
CIJE: 1 RIE: 1 CAT: 13

Paragraph Completion Method (Hunt)
USE Hunt Paragraph Completion Method

Paragraph Completion Test (Schroder et al)
CIJE: 3 RIE: 1 CAT: 21

Paragraph Completion Test of Conceptual Complexity
USE Hunt Paragraph Completion Method

Paragraph Meaning
CIJE: 2 RIE: 1 CAT: 13

Paragraph Reading Test (Olson)
CIJE: 0 RIE: 1 CAT: 21

Paraguay
CIJE: 20 RIE: 14 CAT: 07

Parallel Alternate Curriculum
CIJE: 2 RIE: 1 CAT: 03

Parallel Analysis (Horn)
CIJE: 5 RIE: 3 CAT: 21

Parallel Forms Reliability
CIJE: 4 RIE: 7 CAT: 21

Parallel Merit Reliability
CIJE: 0 RIE: 1 CAT: 21

Parallel Pairs Evaluation
CIJE: 0 RIE: 1 CAT: 15

Parallel Play
CIJE: 6 RIE: 1 CAT: 15

Parallel Processes
CIJE: 4 RIE: 4 CAT: 15

Parallel Processing
CIJE: 17 RIE: 3 CAT: 15

Parallel Test Forms
CIJE: 16 RIE: 28 CAT: 21

Parallelogram Scaling Model
CIJE: 2 RIE: 1 CAT: 15

Paramecia
CIJE: 2 RIE: 0 CAT: 20

Parameter Estimation of Sequential Testing
CIJE: 4 RIE: 3 CAT: 21

Parameter Identification
CIJE: 16 RIE: 8 CAT: 15

Parametric Analysis
CIJE: 32 RIE: 35 CAT: 15

Paramilitary Role
CIJE: 2 RIE: 0 CAT: 15

Paramo (Pedro)
CIJE: 1 RIE: 0 CAT: 18

Paramus Public Schools NJ
CIJE: 1 RIE: 1 CAT: 17

Paranormal Beliefs
CIJE: 1 RIE: 1 CAT: 16

Paranormal Experiences
CIJE: 1 RIE: 0 CAT: 16

Paraphrase
CIJE: 28 RIE: 28 CAT: 13

Paraphrastic Analysis
CIJE: 1 RIE: 1 CAT: 13

Paraprofessional as Companion Therapist Program
CIJE: 0 RIE: 1 CAT: 19

Parapsychology
CIJE: 16 RIE: 6 CAT: 11

Paraquat
CIJE: 0 RIE: 1 CAT: 11

Parasitic Infections
CIJE: 10 RIE: 4 CAT: 11

Parasitology
CIJE: 3 RIE: 5 CAT: 20

Parasocial Interaction
CIJE: 4 RIE: 2 CAT: 11
SN Perception of face-to-face relationship between TV viewer and media performer

Parasuicide
CIJE: 3 RIE: 2 CAT: 11

Parataxic Distortion
CIJE: 1 RIE: 0 CAT: 13

Paratransit
CIJE: 0 RIE: 1 CAT: 20
SN Modes of transportation other than mass transit and solo-driven automobiles

Paraveterinary Skills
CIJE: 0 RIE: 2 CAT: 11

Parc Way
CIJE: 0 RIE: 1 CAT: 17

Parcel Factoring
CIJE: 0 RIE: 1 CAT: 21

Parcheesi (Brand)
USE Pachisi Game

Parchisi
USE Pachisi Game

Pardo Bazan (Emilia)
CIJE: 4 RIE: 0 CAT: 18

Parengi
CIJE: 0 RIE: 2 CAT: 13

Parent Adaptability Scale (Cain et al)
CIJE: 0 RIE: 1 CAT: 21

Parent Advisory Committees
CIJE: 0 RIE: 10 CAT: 10

Parent Advisory Council for Exceptional Children
CIJE: 0 RIE: 1 CAT: 17

Parent Advisory Councils
CIJE: 4 RIE: 25 CAT: 10

Parent Advocacy Coalition for Educational Rights
USE PACER Center MN

Parent Aide Programs
CIJE: 0 RIE: 2 CAT: 19

Parent and Child Education Program KY
CIJE: 0 RIE: 2 CAT: 19
UF PACE Program KY

Parent and Child Education Project AZ
CIJE: 0 RIE: 0 CAT: 19
UF PACE Project AZ

Parent as a Teacher Inventory
CIJE: 5 RIE: 0 CAT: 21

Parent as a Teacher Inventory (Strom Greathouse)
CIJE: 5 RIE: 0 CAT: 21

Parent as Reader Scale (Guinagh and Jester)
CIJE: 1 RIE: 0 CAT: 21

Parent Assisted Learning Program
CIJE: 2 RIE: 3 CAT: 19

Parent Attitude Child Expressiveness Scale
CIJE: 0 RIE: 1 CAT: 21
UF Parent Attitude toward Child Expressiveness Scl

Parent Attitude Inquiry
CIJE: 0 RIE: 1 CAT: 21

Parent Attitude Rating Scale (Ausubel)
CIJE: 0 RIE: 1 CAT: 21

Parent Attitude toward Child Expressiveness Scl
USE Parent Attitude Child Expressiveness Scale

Parent Attitudes toward School Effectiveness
CIJE: 2 RIE: 1 CAT: 21

Parent Background Forms
CIJE: 0 RIE: 0 CAT: 16

Parent Behavior Form
CIJE: 2 RIE: 1 CAT: 21

Parent Behavior Progression
CIJE: 1 RIE: 2 CAT: 15

Parent Behavior Rating
CIJE: 4 RIE: 2 CAT: 15
UF Behavior Rating of Parents

Parent Behavior Rating Scales (Baldwin et al)
CIJE: 0 RIE: 1 CAT: 21

Parent Breakfasts (School)
CIJE: 1 RIE: 0 CAT: 16

Parent Caregiver Relationship
CIJE: 7 RIE: 14 CAT: 11

Parent Centers
USE Parent Child Centers

Parent Characteristics
CIJE: 4 RIE: 1 CAT: 16

Parent Child Accomplishment Record
CIJE: 0 RIE: 1 CAT: 15

Parent Child Centers
CIJE: 10 RIE: 30 CAT: 05
UF Child Parent Centers; Parent Centers

Parent Child Development Center TX
CIJE: 1 RIE: 1 CAT: 17

Parent Child Development Centers
CIJE: 3 RIE: 7 CAT: 05

Parent Child Early Education Program
CIJE: 0 RIE: 2 CAT: 19

Parent Child Education Program
CIJE: 0 RIE: 1 CAT: 19

Parent Child Interaction Rating Procedure
CIJE: 0 RIE: 2 CAT: 15

Parent Child Literacy
USE Family Literacy

Parent Child Program
CIJE: 0 RIE: 9 CAT: 19

Parent Child Relations Questionnaire
CIJE: 3 RIE: 2 CAT: 21

Parent Child Separation
CIJE: 10 RIE: 4 CAT: 11

Parent Child Toy Lending Library Program
CIJE: 0 RIE: 2 CAT: 19

Parent Commitment
CIJE: 3 RIE: 3 CAT: 11

Parent Committees
CIJE: 0 RIE: 13 CAT: 10

Parent Community Relationship
CIJE: 0 RIE: 3 CAT: 15

Parent Control
CIJE: 1 RIE: 0 CAT: 16

Parent Cooperative Preschools International
CIJE: 0 RIE: 3 CAT: 17

Parent Cooperatives
CIJE: 1 RIE: 2 CAT: 05

Parent Coordinators
CIJE: 0 RIE: 1 CAT: 09

Parent Developed Materials
CIJE: 0 RIE: 1 CAT: 16

Parent Education Expansion Project
CIJE: 0 RIE: 1 CAT: 19

Parent Education Follow Through Program
CIJE: 1 RIE: 13 CAT: 19

Parent Educator Program
CIJE: 1 RIE: 2 CAT: 19

Parent Educator Weekly Report
CIJE: 0 RIE: 1 CAT: 22

Parent Effectiveness
CIJE: 1 RIE: 1 CAT: 11

Parent Effectiveness Training
CIJE: 10 RIE: 9 CAT: 15

Parent Employment Program
CIJE: 0 RIE: 1 CAT: 19

Parent Empowerment
CIJE: 20 RIE: 23 CAT: 15

Parent Expectations
CIJE: 26 RIE: 25 CAT: 11

Parent Experience
CIJE: 2 RIE: 1 CAT: 16

Parent Express
CIJE: 0 RIE: 1 CAT: 22

Parent Favoritism
CIJE: 0 RIE: 2 CAT: 11

Parent Government Partnerships
USE Government Family Partnerships

Parent Group Project
CIJE: 1 RIE: 0 CAT: 19

Parent Guide to Quality Day Care Centers
CIJE: 1 RIE: 1 CAT: 21

Parent Image Differential
CIJE: 1 RIE: 0 CAT: 15

Parent Implementation Advisory Model
CIJE: 1 RIE: 0 CAT: 15

Parent Infant Early Education Program
CIJE: 0 RIE: 1 CAT: 19

Parent Infant Program
CIJE: 3 RIE: 1 CAT: 19

Parent Infant Resource Systems
CIJE: 0 RIE: 1 CAT: 11

Parent Information Center IN
CIJE: 0 RIE: 1 CAT: 17

Parent Interview
CIJE: 1 RIE: 4 CAT: 21

Parent Interview Schedule
CIJE: 0 RIE: 1 CAT: 15

Parent Involvement Coordinators
CIJE: 0 RIE: 0 CAT: 09

Parent Involvement in Education Project
CIJE: 0 RIE: 3 CAT: 19
UF Project PIEP

Parent Involvement through Parent Education
CIJE: 0 RIE: 1 CAT: 19
UF Project PIPE OH

Parent Kidnapping
CIJE: 3 RIE: 12 CAT: 14
SN See also "Kidnapping"

Parent Learning through Children
USE Parent through Child Learning

Parent Leave
USE Parental Leave

Parent Loans for Undergraduate Students Program
CIJE: 0 RIE: 17 CAT: 19
UF PLUS Program (Loans)

Parent Needs
CIJE: 14 RIE: 4 CAT: 11

Parent Needs Inventory
CIJE: 0 RIE: 1 CAT: 21

Parent Observer Program
CIJE: 1 RIE: 0 CAT: 19

Parent Occupation
CIJE: 4 RIE: 1 CAT: 16

Parent Orientation
CIJE: 4 RIE: 2 CAT: 15

Parent Outreach Program
CIJE: 2 RIE: 2 CAT: 19

Parent Overprotection
CIJE: 0 RIE: 2 CAT: 11

Parent Practices Inventory
CIJE: 0 RIE: 1 CAT: 15

Parent Preschool Resource Centre ON
CIJE: 0 RIE: 1 CAT: 17

Parent Problem Solving Scale
CIJE: 0 RIE: 1 CAT: 21

Parent Professional Preschool Performance Profile
CIJE: 0 RIE: 3 CAT: 21

Parent Project
CIJE: 0 RIE: 2 CAT: 19

Parent Provider Relationship
CIJE: 2 RIE: 4 CAT: 15

Parent Rating Scales (Baumrind)
CIJE: 1 RIE: 1 CAT: 21

Parent Reaction Questionnaire (Belton et al)
CIJE: 0 RIE: 1 CAT: 21

Parent Readers Program
CIJE: 1 RIE: 2 CAT: 19

Parent Readiness Education Project
CIJE: 1 RIE: 2 CAT: 19

Parent Readiness Evaluation of Preschoolers
CIJE: 0 RIE: 1 CAT: 21

Parent Reports
CIJE: 9 RIE: 6 CAT: 21

Parent Resources
CIJE: 12 RIE: 69 CAT: 16

Parent Resources and Education Program NY
USE Project PREP NY

Parent Responsiveness
CIJE: 6 RIE: 10 CAT: 11

Parent Satisfaction Survey (NASSP)
CIJE: 0 RIE: 0 CAT: 21

Parent School Communications Questionnaire
CIJE: 1 RIE: 2 CAT: 21

Parent Services Project CA
CIJE: 0 RIE: 2 CAT: 19

Parent Speaker Program
CIJE: 0 RIE: 1 CAT: 19

Parent Strictness
CIJE: 0 RIE: 1 CAT: 11

Parent Study Groups
CIJE: 0 RIE: 1 CAT: 10

Parent Supervision
USE Parental Supervision

Parent Surveys
CIJE: 3 RIE: 30 CAT: 21

PARENT TALK (Newsletter)
CIJE: 0 RIE: 1 CAT: 22

Parent Teach Attitude Quest (Twillie et al)
CIJE: 0 RIE: 1 CAT: 21

Parent Teacher Association
CIJE: 77 RIE: 25 CAT: 17

Parent Teacher Education Centers
CIJE: 1 RIE: 0 CAT: 05

Parent Teaching Home
CIJE: 1 RIE: 0 CAT: 19

Parent Temperament Questionnaire
CIJE: 0 RIE: 1 CAT: 21

Parent through Child Learning
CIJE: 1 RIE: 2 CAT: 11
UF Parent Learning through Children

Parent to Parent Dissemination Project
CIJE: 0 RIE: 1 CAT: 19

Parent to Parent Model
CIJE: 5 RIE: 1 CAT: 15

Parent to Parent of Florida
CIJE: 0 RIE: 1 CAT: 17

Parent Training Technology
CIJE: 1 RIE: 0 CAT: 15

Parent Visitation
CIJE: 8 RIE: 5 CAT: 11
UF Visitation (by Parents)

Parental Alienation Syndrome
CIJE: 1 RIE: 1 CAT: 11

Parental Approval Index
CIJE: 0 RIE: 1 CAT: 21

Parental Attitude and Behavior Inventory
CIJE: 0 RIE: 1 CAT: 21

Parental Attitude Research Instrument
CIJE: 7 RIE: 4 CAT: 21

Parental Attitude Scale
CIJE: 1 RIE: 0 CAT: 21

Parental Awareness Model (Newberger)
CIJE: 0 RIE: 2 CAT: 15

Parental Behavior Inventory
CIJE: 0 RIE: 1 CAT: 21

Parental Challenge
CIJE: 0 RIE: 1 CAT: 11

Parental Consent for Minors
CIJE: 9 RIE: 5 CAT: 16

Parental Contact Scale (Martin)
CIJE: 1 RIE: 0 CAT: 21

Parental Continuum Scale (Goldstein)
CIJE: 1 RIE: 0 CAT: 21

Parental Dominance
CIJE: 2 RIE: 1 CAT: 15

Parental Heritage
CIJE: 1 RIE: 0 CAT: 11

Parental Involvement Program
CIJE: 1 RIE: 2 CAT: 19

Parental Kidnaping Prevention Act 1980
CIJE: 0 RIE: 1 CAT: 14

Parental Leave
CIJE: 14 RIE: 29 CAT: 16
SN See also "Family Leave"

UF Parent Leave

Parental Nurturance Scale
CIJE: 0 RIE: 1 CAT: 21

Parental Psychopathology
CIJE: 0 RIE: 1 CAT: 11

Parental Response Inventory (Miller)
CIJE: 0 RIE: 1 CAT: 21

Parental Supervision
CIJE: 2 RIE: 0 CAT: 16
SN Supervision by parents
UF Parent Supervision

Parenthood
CIJE: 20 RIE: 15 CAT: 11

Parenting After Divorce Project
CIJE: 0 RIE: 1 CAT: 19

Parenting Alliance Inventory
CIJE: 0 RIE: 1 CAT: 21

Parenting Locus of Control Scale
CIJE: 0 RIE: 1 CAT: 21

Parenting Materials Information Center
CIJE: 0 RIE: 3 CAT: 17

Parenting Questionnaire
CIJE: 0 RIE: 1 CAT: 21

Parenting Resources Implementation Model Project
CIJE: 0 RIE: 1 CAT: 19

Parenting Stress Index
CIJE: 7 RIE: 5 CAT: 21

Parenting Style Survey
CIJE: 1 RIE: 0 CAT: 21

Parenting Styles
CIJE: 18 RIE: 13 CAT: 15
SN See also "Disciplinary Styles"

Parents and Children Together
CIJE: 3 RIE: 2 CAT: 19

Parents and Counselors Together Program
CIJE: 0 RIE: 1 CAT: 19

Parents Anonymous
CIJE: 7 RIE: 4 CAT: 17

Parents Are Teachers Too Program
CIJE: 0 RIE: 3 CAT: 19

Parents as Leaders Program KY
CIJE: 0 RIE: 1 CAT: 19

Parents as Partners as Learners Project PQ
CIJE: 0 RIE: 1 CAT: 19

Parents as Partners in Learning Project NJ
CIJE: 0 RIE: 1 CAT: 19

Parents as Volunteers in Education
CIJE: 1 RIE: 1 CAT: 19

Parents Assuring Student Success Program
CIJE: 0 RIE: 1 CAT: 19

Parents Center Project
CIJE: 2 RIE: 1 CAT: 19

Parents Confidential Statement
CIJE: 2 RIE: 2 CAT: 21

Parents Diabetes Opinion Survey
CIJE: 0 RIE: 1 CAT: 21

Parents Enrich Program
CIJE: 0 RIE: 1 CAT: 19

Parents in Action on Special Education v Hannon
CIJE: 0 RIE: 1 CAT: 14

Parents in Partnership with Educators
CIJE: 0 RIE: 1 CAT: 19
UF Project PIPE PA

Parents Participation Share Plan
CIJE: 0 RIE: 1 CAT: 15

Parents Sharing Books IN
CIJE: 0 RIE: 2 CAT: 19

Parents Too Soon (Project)
CIJE: 0 RIE: 2 CAT: 19

Parents Train Parents Project
CIJE: 0 RIE: 1 CAT: 19

Parents Training Parents Program
CIJE: 0 RIE: 1 CAT: 19

Parents United for the DC Public Schools
CIJE: 0 RIE: 1 CAT: 17

Pareto Diagrams
CIJE: 3 RIE: 1 CAT: 15

Pareto Distribution
CIJE: 0 RIE: 1 CAT: 21

Pareto Law
CIJE: 2 RIE: 0 CAT: 15

Pareto Optimality
CIJE: 2 RIE: 0 CAT: 16

Parini (Giuseppe)
CIJE: 1 RIE: 0 CAT: 18

Paris Chamber of Commerce and Industry (France)
USE Chamber of Commerce and Industry of Paris (France)

Parish (Peggy)
CIJE: 1 RIE: 0 CAT: 18

Parish Directors of Religious Education
USE Directors of Religious Education

Parish Libraries
CIJE: 1 RIE: 0 CAT: 05

Parity
CIJE: 10 RIE: 11 CAT: 16

Parity Equity Model
CIJE: 0 RIE: 2 CAT: 15

Parity Profile Questionnaire
CIJE: 0 RIE: 1 CAT: 21

Park (Robert E)
CIJE: 2 RIE: 1 CAT: 18

Park (Robert)
CIJE: 1 RIE: 1 CAT: 18

Park Achievement Seminar
CIJE: 0 RIE: 1 CAT: 02

Park College MO
CIJE: 1 RIE: 2 CAT: 17

Park Elementary School NE
CIJE: 1 RIE: 1 CAT: 17

Park Investment Co v Board of Tax Appeals
CIJE: 0 RIE: 1 CAT: 14

Park Naturalists
CIJE: 1 RIE: 0 CAT: 09

Park Rangers
CIJE: 2 RIE: 1 CAT: 09

Park Row ID Tools
CIJE: 0 RIE: 1 CAT: 04
SN ID = Instructional Design

Park Senior High School MN
CIJE: 2 RIE: 0 CAT: 17

Parkdale Senior High School MD
CIJE: 1 RIE: 0 CAT: 17

Parker (Ely Spencer)
CIJE: 1 RIE: 0 CAT: 18

Parker (Francis)
CIJE: 4 RIE: 1 CAT: 18

Parker (Quanah)
CIJE: 1 RIE: 0 CAT: 18

Parker Elementary School MA
CIJE: 1 RIE: 0 CAT: 17

Parker High School WI
CIJE: 0 RIE: 1 CAT: 17

Parker Project
CIJE: 0 RIE: 2 CAT: 19

Parker v Levy
CIJE: 0 RIE: 1 CAT: 14

Parkhurst (Helen)
CIJE: 1 RIE: 0 CAT: 18

Parkin (Frank)
CIJE: 0 RIE: 1 CAT: 18

Parkland College IL
CIJE: 3 RIE: 7 CAT: 17

Parkland Regional College SK
CIJE: 0 RIE: 2 CAT: 17

Parkrose High School OR
CIJE: 0 RIE: 1 CAT: 17

Parkrose School District OR
CIJE: 0 RIE: 4 CAT: 17

Parks (Gordon)
CIJE: 1 RIE: 1 CAT: 18

Parks (Rosa)
CIJE: 2 RIE: 2 CAT: 18

Parks and Recreation Professionals
CIJE: 22 RIE: 1 CAT: 10

Parks Job Corps Center
CIJE: 1 RIE: 0 CAT: 17

Parkside Junior High School
CIJE: 0 RIE: 1 CAT: 17

Parkway North High School
CIJE: 2 RIE: 1 CAT: 17

Parkway Program
CIJE: 10 RIE: 9 CAT: 19

Parkway School District MO
CIJE: 2 RIE: 2 CAT: 17

Parliament (United Kingdom)
CIJE: 9 RIE: 2 CAT: 17

Parliamentarians
CIJE: 0 RIE: 6 CAT: 09

Parliamentary Libraries
CIJE: 0 RIE: 2 CAT: 05

Parlons Francais
CIJE: 0 RIE: 3 CAT: 22

Parma School District OH
CIJE: 1 RIE: 0 CAT: 17

Parmenter School MA
CIJE: 0 RIE: 1 CAT: 17

Parole
CIJE: 15 RIE: 8 CAT: 14

Parolees
CIJE: 6 RIE: 5 CAT: 10

Parra (Nicanor)
CIJE: 1 RIE: 0 CAT: 18

Parramatta Test of Developmental Levels
CIJE: 1 RIE: 0 CAT: 21

Parrhesia
CIJE: 0 RIE: 1 CAT: 16
SN A word of Greek origin indicating the right to say anything a person chooses

Parricide
CIJE: 3 RIE: 0 CAT: 14

Parry Report
CIJE: 1 RIE: 0 CAT: 22

Parsimony (Statistics)
CIJE: 2 RIE: 2 CAT: 21

Parsing
CIJE: 52 RIE: 24 CAT: 13

Parsippany High School NJ
CIJE: 1 RIE: 0 CAT: 17

Parsonian Model of Organization
CIJE: 0 RIE: 1 CAT: 15

Parsonian Theory
CIJE: 7 RIE: 2 CAT: 15

Parsons (Talcott)
CIJE: 9 RIE: 4 CAT: 18

Parsons College IA
CIJE: 2 RIE: 1 CAT: 17

Parsons Guided Self Analysis
CIJE: 0 RIE: 1 CAT: 15

Parsons Visual Acuity Test
CIJE: 1 RIE: 1 CAT: 21

Part Form Method
CIJE: 0 RIE: 1 CAT: 15

Part H 99 457 (Handicapped Infants and Toddlers)
USE Education of the Handicapped Act 1986 (Part H)

Part H 101 476 (Infants and Toddlers with Disabil)
USE Individuals with Disabilities Education Act Part H

Part Time Work Experience Program
CIJE: 0 RIE: 2 CAT: 19

Part Whole Percentaging Analysis
CIJE: 2 RIE: 1 CAT: 15

Partial Check (Addition)
CIJE: 1 RIE: 0 CAT: 20

Partial Credit Model
CIJE: 20 RIE: 17 CAT: 21

Partial Knowledge (Tests)
CIJE: 4 RIE: 7 CAT: 21

Partial Reinforcement
CIJE: 0 RIE: 1 CAT: 11

Partial Retirement
CIJE: 4 RIE: 0 CAT: 16

Partial Specific Volume
CIJE: 1 RIE: 0 CAT: 20

Participant Action Plan Approach
CIJE: 2 RIE: 3 CAT: 15

Participant Characteristics Quests (Toronto)
CIJE: 0 RIE: 1 CAT: 21

Participation and Equity Program (Australia)
CIJE: 0 RIE: 2 CAT: 19

Participation Education
CIJE: 3 RIE: 6 CAT: 03

Participation in Adult Education Survey (NCES)
CIJE: 0 RIE: 1 CAT: 19

Participation Rates
CIJE: 6 RIE: 6 CAT: 21

Participation Training
CIJE: 8 RIE: 3 CAT: 15

Participative Evaluation
CIJE: 0 RIE: 4 CAT: 21

Participatory Curriculum
CIJE: 1 RIE: 3 CAT: 03

Participatory Evaluation
CIJE: 8 RIE: 10 CAT: 15

Participatory Planning
CIJE: 3 RIE: 1 CAT: 15

Participatory Sorting Method
CIJE: 1 RIE: 0 CAT: 15

Participles
CIJE: 5 RIE: 3 CAT: 13

Particle Model of Matter
CIJE: 2 RIE: 1 CAT: 20

Particle Size
CIJE: 1 RIE: 1 CAT: 20

Particles
CIJE: 5 RIE: 3 CAT: 20

Particles (Grammar)
CIJE: 7 RIE: 5 CAT: 13

Particulate Pollution
CIJE: 6 RIE: 0 CAT: 20

Particulates
CIJE: 9 RIE: 4 CAT: 20

Parties (Social Gatherings)
CIJE: 3 RIE: 2 CAT: 16

Partisan Elections
CIJE: 3 RIE: 3 CAT: 17

Partitioning Procedures
CIJE: 8 RIE: 5 CAT: 15

Partitive Construction
CIJE: 1 RIE: 1 CAT: 13

Partner Notification (Diseases)
USE Contact Tracing

Partner Schools
CIJE: 2 RIE: 5 CAT: 05
SN See also the Desc "Professional Development Schools"

Partners in Americas Artist in Residence
CIJE: 1 RIE: 0 CAT: 19

Partners in Learning
CIJE: 1 RIE: 4 CAT: 21

Partners in Program Excellence
CIJE: 0 RIE: 1 CAT: 19

Partners of the Americas
CIJE: 1 RIE: 1 CAT: 17

Partners Program CO
CIJE: 0 RIE: 1 CAT: 19

Partnership 2000 CA
CIJE: 0 RIE: 0 CAT: 19

Partnership for Academic and Career Education SC
CIJE: 0 RIE: 5 CAT: 19

Partnership for Environmental Technology Education
CIJE: 0 RIE: 1 CAT: 19

Partnership for Health
CIJE: 0 RIE: 3 CAT: 19

Partnership for Rural Improvement
CIJE: 0 RIE: 20 CAT: 21

Partnership in Research
CIJE: 0 RIE: 1 CAT: 15

Partnership Vocational Education Project
CIJE: 1 RIE: 1 CAT: 19

Partnerships (Public Private)
USE Public Private Partnership Programs

Partnerships (Teachers)
USE Teacher Partnerships

Partnerships in Business
USE Business Partnerships

Partnerships in Health Care
CIJE: 0 RIE: 0 CAT: 11
UF Health Care Partnerships

Partnerships in Human Services
CIJE: 0 RIE: 0 CAT: 10
UF Community Services Partnerships; Human Services Partnerships

Partnerships in Library Services
CIJE: 2 RIE: 1 CAT: 09
UF Library Partnerships

Partnerships in Prevention
CIJE: 0 RIE: 1 CAT: 19

Parts Storekeepers
CIJE: 0 RIE: 4 CAT: 09

Paruresis
CIJE: 1 RIE: 0 CAT: 11

Pasadena City College CA
CIJE: 0 RIE: 14 CAT: 17

Pasadena Unified School District CA
CIJE: 4 RIE: 7 CAT: 17

Pascal (Blaise)
CIJE: 6 RIE: 3 CAT: 18

PASCAL Data Base
CIJE: 2 RIE: 3 CAT: 17

PASCAL Programing Language
CIJE: 51 RIE: 34 CAT: 04

Pascal Triangle
CIJE: 24 RIE: 1 CAT: 20

Pascarella (Ernest T)
CIJE: 0 RIE: 3 CAT: 18

Pasco County School District FL
CIJE: 2 RIE: 3 CAT: 17

Pasco Hernando Community College FL
CIJE: 0 RIE: 1 CAT: 17

Pasco School District WA
CIJE: 3 RIE: 5 CAT: 17

Pascual Leone (Juan)
CIJE: 4 RIE: 0 CAT: 18

PASE v Hannon
CIJE: 3 RIE: 1 CAT: 14

Pashto (Afghan)
CIJE: 0 RIE: 1 CAT: 13

Pashto (Eastern Afghan)
CIJE: 0 RIE: 1 CAT: 13

Pask (Gordon)
CIJE: 0 RIE: 2 CAT: 18

Paso (Alfonso)
CIJE: 1 RIE: 0 CAT: 18

Pasos Adelante AZ
CIJE: 0 RIE: 1 CAT: 19

PASS (Computer Program)
USE Policy Analysis and Simulation System

PASS Cognitive Processes
USE PASS Model (Luria)

PASS Evaluation (Programs for Disabled)
USE Program Analysis of Service Systems

PASS Expert System
CIJE: 0 RIE: 1 CAT: 04
UF Performance Assessment for Self Sufficiency System

Pass Incomplete Grading
CIJE: 1 RIE: 0 CAT: 21

PASS Model (Luria)
CIJE: 0 RIE: 1 CAT: 15
UF PASS Cognitive Processes; Planning Attention Simultaneous Successive Model

PASS Program (Migrant Education)
USE Portable Assisted Study Sequence Program

Pass Rates
CIJE: 0 RIE: 2 CAT: 21
UF Passing Rates

PASS Software
USE Prompt Automated Scheduling System

Pass to Play
USE No Pass No Play Rules

Passage Comprehension Test (Woodcock)
USE Woodcock Passage Comprehension Test

Passage Dependency
CIJE: 6 RIE: 2 CAT: 21

Passage Error Rate
CIJE: 0 RIE: 1 CAT: 21

Passage Independency
CIJE: 1 RIE: 0 CAT: 13

Passage Organization
CIJE: 3 RIE: 1 CAT: 16

Passaic County Community College NJ
CIJE: 3 RIE: 2 CAT: 17

Passaic County Vocational School NJ
CIJE: 1 RIE: 0 CAT: 17

Passamaquoddy (Tribe)
CIJE: 1 RIE: 22 CAT: 08

Passamaquoddy Enterprise Zone Development Project
CIJE: 0 RIE: 1 CAT: 19

Passing Rates
USE Pass Rates

Passive Aggressive Behavior
CIJE: 4 RIE: 2 CAT: 11

Passive Smoking
CIJE: 3 RIE: 3 CAT: 11
SN See also "Environmental Tobacco Smoke"
UF Involuntary Smoking; Sidestream Smoking

Passive Solar Design
CIJE: 7 RIE: 2 CAT: 20

Passive Voice
CIJE: 15 RIE: 11 CAT: 13

Passives
CIJE: 24 RIE: 19 CAT: 13

Passivity
CIJE: 20 RIE: 10 CAT: 11

Passport to English
CIJE: 0 RIE: 1 CAT: 19

Passports
CIJE: 0 RIE: 1 CAT: 14

Past Tense
CIJE: 18 RIE: 2 CAT: 13

Pasternak (Boris)
CIJE: 1 RIE: 0 CAT: 18

Pasters
CIJE: 0 RIE: 1 CAT: 09

Pasteur (Louis)
CIJE: 6 RIE: 0 CAT: 18

Pastoral Councils
CIJE: 0 RIE: 1 CAT: 10

Pastoral Counseling
CIJE: 15 RIE: 2 CAT: 15

Pastoral Industry
CIJE: 0 RIE: 1 CAT: 05

Pastoral Letters
CIJE: 2 RIE: 0 CAT: 16
UF Bishops Pastoral Letters

Pastore (John)
CIJE: 0 RIE: 1 CAT: 18

Patel (Vallabhbhai)
CIJE: 0 RIE: 1 CAT: 18

Patent and Trademark Amendments 1980
CIJE: 1 RIE: 1 CAT: 14

Patent Office
CIJE: 5 RIE: 2 CAT: 17

Pater (Walter)
CIJE: 2 RIE: 0 CAT: 18

Paternalism
CIJE: 8 RIE: 4 CAT: 15

Paternity Adjudication
USE Paternity Establishment

Paternity Establishment
CIJE: 2 RIE: 4 CAT: 21
UF Paternity Adjudication

Paterno (Joe)
CIJE: 1 RIE: 0 CAT: 18

Paterson (Katherine)
CIJE: 12 RIE: 2 CAT: 18

Path Goal Theory
CIJE: 0 RIE: 2 CAT: 15

Path Referenced Tests
CIJE: 0 RIE: 3 CAT: 21

Pathfinders
CIJE: 10 RIE: 11 CAT: 16

Pathological Distortion
CIJE: 1 RIE: 0 CAT: 11

Pathos
CIJE: 2 RIE: 1 CAT: 11

PATHS Curriculum
USE Promoting Alternative Thinking Strategies Curric

Pathway School PA
CIJE: 0 RIE: 1 CAT: 17

PATHWAYS Curriculum
CIJE: 0 RIE: 26 CAT: 03

PATHWAYS Project MI
CIJE: 1 RIE: 0 CAT: 19

Pathways to Employment II
CIJE: 0 RIE: 1 CAT: 19

Pathways to Identity Project
CIJE: 0 RIE: 1 CAT: 19

Patient Activity Checklist (Higgs)
CIJE: 1 RIE: 0 CAT: 21

Patient Activity Coordinators
USE Activity Coordinators (Long Term Care)

Patient Care
CIJE: 7 RIE: 28 CAT: 11

Patient Care Assistants
CIJE: 0 RIE: 1 CAT: 09
UF Health Care Assistants

Patient Dumping
CIJE: 0 RIE: 1 CAT: 11

Patient Education Materials
CIJE: 0 RIE: 1 CAT: 11

Patient Management
CIJE: 30 RIE: 5 CAT: 11

Patient Representatives
CIJE: 1 RIE: 2 CAT: 09

Patients Rights
CIJE: 16 RIE: 16 CAT: 11

Patriarchal Societies
CIJE: 9 RIE: 5 CAT: 10

Patricide
CIJE: 1 RIE: 0 CAT: 11

Patrick Henry Community College VA
CIJE: 1 RIE: 1 CAT: 17

Patron Client Relationship
CIJE: 1 RIE: 1 CAT: 15

Patrons
CIJE: 1 RIE: 1 CAT: 10

PATSEARCH Database
CIJE: 1 RIE: 0 CAT: 04

Pattern Analysis
CIJE: 20 RIE: 6 CAT: 21

Pattern Conformity Index
CIJE: 0 RIE: 1 CAT: 21

Pattern Congruity Method
CIJE: 0 RIE: 1 CAT: 15

Pattern Drawing Test
CIJE: 0 RIE: 2 CAT: 21

Pattern Drills Program
CIJE: 0 RIE: 1 CAT: 19

Pattern Goodness
CIJE: 1 RIE: 1 CAT: 15

Pattern Learning Parser
CIJE: 0 RIE: 2 CAT: 15

Pattern Marking (Data)
CIJE: 0 RIE: 1 CAT: 21

Pattern Matching
CIJE: 7 RIE: 5 CAT: 15

Pattern Meaning
CIJE: 0 RIE: 2 CAT: 13

Pattern Meanings Test (Wallach and Kogan)
CIJE: 1 RIE: 2 CAT: 21

Pattern Notes
CIJE: 2 RIE: 1 CAT: 15

Pattern Organization
CIJE: 4 RIE: 3 CAT: 13

Pattern Practice
CIJE: 1 RIE: 1 CAT: 13

Pattern Scoring
CIJE: 0 RIE: 1 CAT: 21
UF Item Pattern Scoring

Pattern Search and Table Translation Technique
CIJE: 0 RIE: 1 CAT: 21

Pattern Walking Test
CIJE: 0 RIE: 1 CAT: 21

Patterned Evasion
CIJE: 1 RIE: 0 CAT: 15

Patterning (Neurology)
CIJE: 0 RIE: 1 CAT: 11

Patterns (Mathematics)
CIJE: 84 RIE: 24 CAT: 20

Patterns in Arithmetic
CIJE: 1 RIE: 5 CAT: 03

Patterns in Human History
CIJE: 1 RIE: 2 CAT: 03

Patterns of Adaptive Learning Survey
CIJE: 0 RIE: 1 CAT: 21

Patterns of Childrearing
CIJE: 0 RIE: 1 CAT: 03

Patterns of Enquiry Project
CIJE: 0 RIE: 1 CAT: 19

Patterson (Frederick O)
CIJE: 0 RIE: 1 CAT: 18

Pattison Social Network Inventory
CIJE: 1 RIE: 1 CAT: 21

Patton (Frank D)
CIJE: 1 RIE: 0 CAT: 18

Patton Speech Content Exam
CIJE: 0 RIE: 1 CAT: 21

Patton State Hospital
CIJE: 0 RIE: 1 CAT: 17

Paul (Hermann)
CIJE: 1 RIE: 0 CAT: 18

Paul (Richard)
CIJE: 2 RIE: 3 CAT: 18

Paul (Robert)
CIJE: 1 RIE: 0 CAT: 18

Paul (Saint)
CIJE: 0 RIE: 1 CAT: 18

Paul D Camp Community College VA
CIJE: 0 RIE: 1 CAT: 17

Paul Douglas Teacher Scholarship Program
CIJE: 0 RIE: 1 CAT: 19

Paul VI (Pope)
CIJE: 0 RIE: 0 CAT: 18

Paulding (James K)
CIJE: 0 RIE: 1 CAT: 18

Pauley v Bailey
CIJE: 5 RIE: 3 CAT: 14

Pauli (Wolfgang)
CIJE: 1 RIE: 0 CAT: 18

Pauli Exclusion Principle
CIJE: 1 RIE: 0 CAT: 20

Paulus Roberge Conditioned Reasoning Test
CIJE: 1 RIE: 0 CAT: 21

Paumari
CIJE: 0 RIE: 1 CAT: 13
SN Dialect of Purupuru of the Arawakan language family (Brazil)

Paus (Johann Werner)
CIJE: 1 RIE: 0 CAT: 18

Pause Model
CIJE: 0 RIE: 2 CAT: 15

Pause Prompt and Praise
CIJE: 1 RIE: 0 CAT: 15

Pausing (Speech)
CIJE: 22 RIE: 8 CAT: 13

PAVAC (ED)
USE Publication and Audio Visual Advisory Council

Pavese (Cesare)
CIJE: 1 RIE: 0 CAT: 18

Pavlov (Ivan Petrovich)
CIJE: 5 RIE: 0 CAT: 18

Pawnee (Tribe)
CIJE: 2 RIE: 5 CAT: 08

Pawnee Heights School District KS
CIJE: 0 RIE: 1 CAT: 17

Pawtuckaway State Park NH
CIJE: 1 RIE: 0 CAT: 07

Paxton (Mary)
USE Keeley (Mary Paxton)

Pay As You Earn
CIJE: 0 RIE: 1 CAT: 19

Pay Boards
CIJE: 1 RIE: 0 CAT: 10

Pay Television
CIJE: 4 RIE: 12 CAT: 04

Payback Period
CIJE: 2 RIE: 0 CAT: 15

Payne (Ethel L)
CIJE: 0 RIE: 1 CAT: 18

Payne (William H)
CIJE: 1 RIE: 0 CAT: 18

Payoff Operators
CIJE: 0 RIE: 1 CAT: 09

Payroll Clerks
CIJE: 0 RIE: 2 CAT: 09

Paz (Octavio)
CIJE: 26 RIE: 0 CAT: 18

PCAT
USE Pharmacy College Admission Test

PCBs
USE Polychlorinated Biphenyls

PCEN Program NY
USE Pupils with Compensatory Educational Needs

PCP
USE Phencyclidine

PDEM 1 Model
CIJE: 0 RIE: 1 CAT: 15

PDQ Center NJ
CIJE: 0 RIE: 1 CAT: 17

PDQ Project
USE Planning Development Quality Services Schools

Peabody College Early Training Project
CIJE: 0 RIE: 1 CAT: 19

Peabody Developmental Motor Scales
CIJE: 0 RIE: 1 CAT: 21

Peabody Education Fund
CIJE: 1 RIE: 1 CAT: 17

Peabody Individual Achievement Test
CIJE: 51 RIE: 13 CAT: 21

Peabody Institute of Baltimore MD
CIJE: 2 RIE: 1 CAT: 17

Peabody Language Development Kits
CIJE: 8 RIE: 27 CAT: 21

Peabody Mathematics Readiness Test
CIJE: 3 RIE: 2 CAT: 21

Peabody Mobility Kit for Infants
CIJE: 0 RIE: 1 CAT: 15

Peabody Mobility Scale
CIJE: 1 RIE: 2 CAT: 21

Peabody Museum
CIJE: 1 RIE: 1 CAT: 17

Peabody Picture Vocabulary Test
CIJE: 117 RIE: 165 CAT: 21

Peabody Picture Vocabulary Test (Revised)
CIJE: 61 RIE: 13 CAT: 21

Peabody Picture Vocabulary Test Spanish (Dunn)
USE Test de Vocabulario en Imagenes Peabody (Dunn)

Peabody Rebus Reading Program
CIJE: 1 RIE: 1 CAT: 19

Peace Corps
CIJE: 39 RIE: 315 CAT: 17

Peace Corps Stateside Teacher Training Model
CIJE: 0 RIE: 5 CAT: 15

Peace Education
CIJE: 32 RIE: 119 CAT: 03

Peace Psychology
CIJE: 0 RIE: 1 CAT: 11

Peace Studies
CIJE: 12 RIE: 22 CAT: 03

PEACESAT
CIJE: 3 RIE: 3 CAT: 19
SN Pacific Educational And Communication Experiment by SATellite

Peak Communication Experiences
CIJE: 0 RIE: 2 CAT: 15

Peak Experiences
CIJE: 11 RIE: 5 CAT: 16

Peak Performance
CIJE: 0 RIE: 3 CAT: 16

Peaked Ability Tests
CIJE: 0 RIE: 2 CAT: 21

Peale (Norman Vincent)
CIJE: 0 RIE: 1 CAT: 18

Peanuts
CIJE: 2 RIE: 0 CAT: 11

Pearce Center for Professional Communication SC
CIJE: 0 RIE: 1 CAT: 17

Pearl (The)
CIJE: 1 RIE: 1 CAT: 22

Pearl Harbor
CIJE: 0 RIE: 5 CAT: 12

Pearl Poet
CIJE: 1 RIE: 1 CAT: 18

Pearl River School District NY
CIJE: 1 RIE: 1 CAT: 17

Pearson (Adelaide)
CIJE: 0 RIE: 1 CAT: 18

Pearson (Karl)
CIJE: 4 RIE: 0 CAT: 18

Pearson Product Moment Correlation
CIJE: 69 RIE: 52 CAT: 15

Peary (Robert)
CIJE: 1 RIE: 0 CAT: 18

Peasants
CIJE: 14 RIE: 6 CAT: 10

Pease (Howard)
CIJE: 1 RIE: 0 CAT: 18

Peat Marwick Mitchell and Company
CIJE: 1 RIE: 0 CAT: 17

Peavey Company
CIJE: 1 RIE: 2 CAT: 17

Peba Yaguan
USE Yagua

Peck (Richard)
CIJE: 5 RIE: 1 CAT: 18

Peck Veldman Sentence Completion Test
CIJE: 0 RIE: 1 CAT: 21

Pedagogic Drama
CIJE: 3 RIE: 1 CAT: 03

Pedagogical Content Knowledge
CIJE: 31 RIE: 38 CAT: 15
SN See from "Teacher Knowledge" — see also the Desc "Knowledge Base for Teaching"

Pedagogical Grammars
CIJE: 0 RIE: 3 CAT: 13

Pedagogical Intelligence
CIJE: 0 RIE: 1 CAT: 15

Pedagogical University of Caracas (Venezuela)
CIJE: 0 RIE: 1 CAT: 17

Pedestrian Concourses
CIJE: 1 RIE: 0 CAT: 04

Pediatric Cancer Patients
CIJE: 0 RIE: 1 CAT: 10

Pediatric Evaluation of Disabilities Inventory
CIJE: 0 RIE: 0 CAT: 21

Pediatric Examination of Educational Readiness
CIJE: 1 RIE: 1 CAT: 21

Pediatric Language Programs
CIJE: 0 RIE: 3 CAT: 19

Pediatric Nurse Associates
CIJE: 1 RIE: 0 CAT: 17

Pediatric Nurses
CIJE: 0 RIE: 1 CAT: 09

Pediatric Psychology
CIJE: 0 RIE: 2 CAT: 11

Pediatric Social Illness
CIJE: 0 RIE: 2 CAT: 11

Pediatricians
CIJE: 11 RIE: 4 CAT: 09

Pedodontics
CIJE: 8 RIE: 0 CAT: 11

Pedology
CIJE: 0 RIE: 2 CAT: 16

Pedophilia
CIJE: 4 RIE: 2 CAT: 11

PEECH Outreach Project
CIJE: 1 RIE: 2 CAT: 19

Peel (E A)
CIJE: 4 RIE: 0 CAT: 18

Peel Board of Education ON
CIJE: 0 RIE: 4 CAT: 17

Peer Assistance and Review Program
CIJE: 0 RIE: 1 CAT: 19

Peer Assisted Leadership Program
CIJE: 4 RIE: 4 CAT: 19

Peer Attitudes toward the Handicapped Scale
CIJE: 0 RIE: 1 CAT: 21

Peer Coaching
CIJE: 41 RIE: 24 CAT: 15

Peer Comparison
CIJE: 1 RIE: 1 CAT: 15

Peer Consultation (Supervision)
CIJE: 0 RIE: 1 CAT: 15

Peer Evaluation Program
CIJE: 3 RIE: 3 CAT: 19

Peer Facilitators
CIJE: 5 RIE: 4 CAT: 10

Peer Group Learning Units
CIJE: 7 RIE: 1 CAT: 03

Peer Intervention Network
CIJE: 0 RIE: 1 CAT: 17

Peer Mediation
CIJE: 5 RIE: 4 CAT: 15

Peer Modeling
CIJE: 12 RIE: 11 CAT: 15

Peer Perception Inventory
CIJE: 0 RIE: 2 CAT: 21

Peer Prepared Method
CIJE: 0 RIE: 1 CAT: 15

Peer Recruitment
CIJE: 0 RIE: 1 CAT: 16

Peer Resource Programs
CIJE: 0 RIE: 1 CAT: 19

Peer Review Organizations
CIJE: 0 RIE: 1 CAT: 10

Peer Supervision
CIJE: 6 RIE: 6 CAT: 15

Peer Support
CIJE: 1 RIE: 3 CAT: 15

Peer Support Groups
CIJE: 1 RIE: 3 CAT: 10

Peer Teachers as Mirrors and Monitors Project
CIJE: 0 RIE: 3 CAT: 19

PEG Program
CIJE: 1 RIE: 2 CAT: 19

Peigan (Nation)
CIJE: 0 RIE: 1 CAT: 08
UF Paegan (Tribe)

Peirce (Charles S)
CIJE: 10 RIE: 12 CAT: 18

Peirce Junior College PA
CIJE: 0 RIE: 2 CAT: 17

Peking National Library (China)
CIJE: 1 RIE: 0 CAT: 17

Peking Opera (China)
CIJE: 1 RIE: 0 CAT: 17

Peking University (China)
CIJE: 2 RIE: 0 CAT: 17

Pelham Middle School (England)
CIJE: 0 RIE: 1 CAT: 17

Pell (Claiborne)
CIJE: 4 RIE: 0 CAT: 18

Pell Equation
CIJE: 1 RIE: 0 CAT: 20

Pell Grant Program
CIJE: 36 RIE: 147 CAT: 14
SN Formerly Basic Educational Opportunity Grants program

Pelvic Examinations
CIJE: 3 RIE: 0 CAT: 11

Pemberton Township Education Association
CIJE: 1 RIE: 0 CAT: 17

Pembroke State University NC
CIJE: 1 RIE: 1 CAT: 17

Pemoline
CIJE: 3 RIE: 0 CAT: 11

Pen Pals
CIJE: 16 RIE: 8 CAT: 10

Pen Plotters (Computers)
USE Computer Plotters

Penal Reform
CIJE: 0 RIE: 2 CAT: 14

Pencil Holding
CIJE: 3 RIE: 0 CAT: 16

Pencil Shape
CIJE: 0 RIE: 1 CAT: 16

Pencil Size
CIJE: 1 RIE: 1 CAT: 16

Pend d Oreilles (Tribe)
CIJE: 0 RIE: 1 CAT: 08

Pendulums
CIJE: 40 RIE: 1 CAT: 04

Pengo
CIJE: 0 RIE: 2 CAT: 13

Penicillin
CIJE: 2 RIE: 0 CAT: 11

Peninsula Academies Program
CIJE: 2 RIE: 7 CAT: 19

Peninsula College WA
CIJE: 0 RIE: 2 CAT: 17

Peninsula School CA
CIJE: 1 RIE: 2 CAT: 17

Penitentiary of New Mexico
CIJE: 0 RIE: 3 CAT: 17

PENMAS (Indonesia)
CIJE: 0 RIE: 3 CAT: 17

Penn Central Company
CIJE: 0 RIE: 1 CAT: 17

Penn Harris Madison School Corporation IN
CIJE: 0 RIE: 2 CAT: 17

Penn Manor School District PA
CIJE: 0 RIE: 1 CAT: 17

Penn State Great Valley PA
CIJE: 0 RIE: 1 CAT: 17

Penn Valley Community College MO
CIJE: 0 RIE: 1 CAT: 17

Penn Valley School MO
CIJE: 0 RIE: 1 CAT: 17

Pennies
CIJE: 1 RIE: 0 CAT: 16

Pennsylvania
CIJE: 425 RIE: 1648 CAT: 07

Pennsylvania (Abington)
CIJE: 0 RIE: 7 CAT: 07

Pennsylvania (Adams County)
CIJE: 0 RIE: 1 CAT: 07

Pennsylvania (Aliquippa)
CIJE: 0 RIE: 1 CAT: 07

Pennsylvania (Allegheny County)
CIJE: 3 RIE: 10 CAT: 07

Pennsylvania (Allentown)
CIJE: 3 RIE: 1 CAT: 07

Pennsylvania (Altoona)
CIJE: 1 RIE: 4 CAT: 07

Pennsylvania (Ardmore)
CIJE: 0 RIE: 1 CAT: 07

Pennsylvania (Armstrong County)
CIJE: 0 RIE: 4 CAT: 07

Pennsylvania (Bellefonte)
CIJE: 1 RIE: 0 CAT: 07

Pennsylvania (Berks County)
CIJE: 0 RIE: 4 CAT: 07

Pennsylvania (Bethlehem)
CIJE: 3 RIE: 9 CAT: 07

Pennsylvania (Bristol)
CIJE: 0 RIE: 1 CAT: 07

Pennsylvania (Bucks County)
CIJE: 0 RIE: 6 CAT: 07

Pennsylvania (Central)
CIJE: 1 RIE: 5 CAT: 07

Pennsylvania (Centre County)
CIJE: 1 RIE: 2 CAT: 07

Pennsylvania (Cheltenham)
CIJE: 1 RIE: 2 CAT: 07

Pennsylvania (Chester County)
CIJE: 0 RIE: 4 CAT: 07

Pennsylvania (Chester)
CIJE: 1 RIE: 2 CAT: 07

Pennsylvania (Clarion)
CIJE: 1 RIE: 3 CAT: 07

Pennsylvania (Clearfield County)
CIJE: 0 RIE: 2 CAT: 07

Pennsylvania (Coatesville)
CIJE: 0 RIE: 2 CAT: 07

Pennsylvania (Columbia County)
CIJE: 0 RIE: 1 CAT: 07

Pennsylvania (Coraopolis)
CIJE: 0 RIE: 1 CAT: 07

Pennsylvania (Cumberland County)
CIJE: 0 RIE: 3 CAT: 07

Pennsylvania (Danville)
CIJE: 0 RIE: 1 CAT: 07

Pennsylvania (Delaware County)
CIJE: 2 RIE: 2 CAT: 07

Pennsylvania (Doylestown)
CIJE: 0 RIE: 2 CAT: 07

Pennsylvania (East)
CIJE: 0 RIE: 3 CAT: 07

Pennsylvania (Easton)
CIJE: 1 RIE: 0 CAT: 07

Pennsylvania (Ebensburg)
CIJE: 0 RIE: 2 CAT: 07

Pennsylvania (Elkins Park)
CIJE: 0 RIE: 1 CAT: 07

Pennsylvania (Ellsworth)
CIJE: 0 RIE: 1 CAT: 07

Pennsylvania (Erie)
CIJE: 3 RIE: 8 CAT: 07

Pennsylvania (Fayette County)
CIJE: 0 RIE: 3 CAT: 07

Pennsylvania (Fort Indiantown Gap)
CIJE: 0 RIE: 4 CAT: 07

Pennsylvania (Fulton County)
CIJE: 0 RIE: 3 CAT: 07

Pennsylvania (Glenside)
CIJE: 0 RIE: 1 CAT: 07

Pennsylvania (Greene County)
CIJE: 0 RIE: 3 CAT: 07

Pennsylvania (Harrisburg)
CIJE: 4 RIE: 39 CAT: 07

Pennsylvania (Hershey)
CIJE: 1 RIE: 0 CAT: 07

Pennsylvania (Hummelstown)
CIJE: 0 RIE: 1 CAT: 07

Pennsylvania (Indiana County)
CIJE: 1 RIE: 5 CAT: 07

Performance of Process Skills Test
CIJE: 0 RIE: 1 CAT: 21

Performance Oriented Management Techniques
CIJE: 1 RIE: 2 CAT: 15

Performance Rating Theory (Cason and Cason)
CIJE: 0 RIE: 4 CAT: 15

Performance Related Enabling Skills Training Proj
CIJE: 0 RIE: 2 CAT: 19

Performance Studies (Speech)
CIJE: 0 RIE: 3 CAT: 13

Performance Support Systems
CIJE: 14 RIE: 0 CAT: 15
UF Electronic Performance Support Systems; Integrated Performance Support Systems

Performative Analysis
CIJE: 1 RIE: 1 CAT: 21

Performative Language
CIJE: 2 RIE: 1 CAT: 13

Performer Writers
CIJE: 1 RIE: 2 CAT: 09
UF Writer Performers

Perfusion Techniques
CIJE: 1 RIE: 0 CAT: 21

Pericles
CIJE: 0 RIE: 1 CAT: 18

Perimeter (Geometry)
CIJE: 12 RIE: 4 CAT: 20

Perinatal Education
CIJE: 1 RIE: 3 CAT: 03

Periodic Functions
CIJE: 8 RIE: 1 CAT: 20

Periodic Law
CIJE: 2 RIE: 0 CAT: 20

Periodic Table
CIJE: 38 RIE: 3 CAT: 20

Periodontal Index
CIJE: 0 RIE: 1 CAT: 11

Periodontics
CIJE: 11 RIE: 3 CAT: 11

Periodontology
CIJE: 0 RIE: 2 CAT: 11

Peripheral Stimuli
CIJE: 5 RIE: 2 CAT: 11

Peripheral Temperature
CIJE: 0 RIE: 1 CAT: 11

Peripheral Vision
CIJE: 8 RIE: 4 CAT: 11

Perkins (Carl D)
CIJE: 1 RIE: 0 CAT: 18

Perkins (Ralph)
CIJE: 0 RIE: 1 CAT: 18

Perkins Act 1984
USE Carl D Perkins Vocational Education Act 1984

Perkins Act 1990
USE Carl D Perkins Voc and Appl Techn Educ Act 1990

Perkins Binet Tests of Intelligence for the Blind
CIJE: 2 RIE: 0 CAT: 21

Perkins Loan Program
CIJE: 1 RIE: 18 CAT: 14
SN Formerly National Direct Student Loan Program
UF Carl D Perkins Loan Program

Perkins School for the Blind MA
CIJE: 1 RIE: 1 CAT: 17

Perkins School of Theology TX
CIJE: 0 RIE: 1 CAT: 17

Perky Effect
CIJE: 1 RIE: 0 CAT: 11

Perlocutionary Effects
CIJE: 1 RIE: 1 CAT: 13

Perls (Fritz)
CIJE: 8 RIE: 2 CAT: 18

Permanency Planning (for Disabled)
CIJE: 1 RIE: 0 CAT: 11

Permanency Planning (Foster Care)
CIJE: 33 RIE: 18 CAT: 11

Permanent Durable Book Paper
CIJE: 0 RIE: 1 CAT: 04

Permanent Guardianship
CIJE: 1 RIE: 0 CAT: 16

Permanent Part Time Teaching
CIJE: 0 RIE: 2 CAT: 16

Permissiveness
CIJE: 7 RIE: 3 CAT: 11

Permits with Transportation
CIJE: 0 RIE: 1 CAT: 19

Permutation T Test
CIJE: 0 RIE: 1 CAT: 21

Permutations
CIJE: 4 RIE: 2 CAT: 20

Permutations (Mathematics)
CIJE: 11 RIE: 1 CAT: 20

Peron (Isabel)
CIJE: 0 RIE: 1 CAT: 18

PERP Model
USE Positive Employment Relations Program

Perrault (M)
CIJE: 1 RIE: 0 CAT: 18

Perrow (Charles)
CIJE: 0 RIE: 1 CAT: 18

Perrow Technology Construct
CIJE: 1 RIE: 1 CAT: 15

Perry (Matthew C)
CIJE: 0 RIE: 1 CAT: 18

Perry (William G Jr)
CIJE: 7 RIE: 6 CAT: 18

Perry (William)
CIJE: 14 RIE: 15 CAT: 18

Perry Child Development Center MI
CIJE: 0 RIE: 1 CAT: 17

Perry Developmental Scheme
CIJE: 5 RIE: 10 CAT: 21

Perry Educ Assn v Perry Local Educators Assn
CIJE: 1 RIE: 0 CAT: 14

Perry Preschool MI
CIJE: 5 RIE: 0 CAT: 17

Perry Preschool Project
CIJE: 14 RIE: 19 CAT: 19

Perry Scheme of Intellectual Ethical Development
CIJE: 5 RIE: 11 CAT: 15

Perseveration
CIJE: 8 RIE: 4 CAT: 16

Persia
CIJE: 1 RIE: 4 CAT: 07

Persian Eysenck Personality Inventory
CIJE: 1 RIE: 0 CAT: 21

Persian Gulf
CIJE: 0 RIE: 2 CAT: 07

Persian Gulf Crisis 1990 1991
USE Gulf War

Perso Arabic Script
CIJE: 0 RIE: 2 CAT: 13

Person (Grammar)
CIJE: 0 RIE: 1 CAT: 13

Person Centered Society
CIJE: 0 RIE: 1 CAT: 15

Person Centered Therapy
CIJE: 1 RIE: 1 CAT: 11

Person Clusters
CIJE: 0 RIE: 1 CAT: 16

Person Description Instrument
CIJE: 0 RIE: 2 CAT: 21

Person Descriptive Instrument (Harrison)
CIJE: 0 RIE: 1 CAT: 21

Person Environment Congruence (Holland)
CIJE: 3 RIE: 2 CAT: 21

Person Environment Fit
CIJE: 35 RIE: 0 CAT: 15

Person Fit Measures
CIJE: 9 RIE: 13 CAT: 21

Person Object Relationship
CIJE: 1 RIE: 1 CAT: 11
UF Object Person Relationship; PO Relationship

Person Parameters
CIJE: 2 RIE: 3 CAT: 21

Persona
CIJE: 13 RIE: 6 CAT: 16

Personal and Family Financial Planning
CIJE: 0 RIE: 5 CAT: 02

Personal Assessment of Coping Experiences
CIJE: 0 RIE: 1 CAT: 21

Personal Assessment of Life Events
CIJE: 0 RIE: 1 CAT: 21

Personal Assistance (of Disabled)
CIJE: 0 RIE: 2 CAT: 11

Personal Attribute Inventory (Parish et al)
CIJE: 1 RIE: 0 CAT: 21

Personal Attribute Inventory for Children (Parish)
CIJE: 8 RIE: 0 CAT: 21

Personal Attribute Inventory Scale
CIJE: 1 RIE: 0 CAT: 21

Personal Attributes Questionnaire
CIJE: 23 RIE: 7 CAT: 21

Personal Beliefs Inventory
CIJE: 2 RIE: 4 CAT: 21

Personal Biserial Index
CIJE: 1 RIE: 0 CAT: 21

Personal Celebrations
CIJE: 0 RIE: 1 CAT: 16

Personal Charm
CIJE: 0 RIE: 1 CAT: 16

Personal Construct Theory
CIJE: 59 RIE: 6 CAT: 21

Personal Control of Outcomes
USE Control of Outcomes

Personal Data Systems
CIJE: 3 RIE: 0 CAT: 15

Personal Discovery Approach
CIJE: 0 RIE: 1 CAT: 11

Personal Effectiveness
CIJE: 3 RIE: 2 CAT: 11

Personal Empowerment
USE Empowerment

Personal Experience Program
CIJE: 0 RIE: 1 CAT: 19

Personal Experiences
CIJE: 74 RIE: 32 CAT: 16

Personal Fables
CIJE: 2 RIE: 2 CAT: 16

Personal File Management
CIJE: 1 RIE: 1 CAT: 15

Personal Finance
CIJE: 4 RIE: 1 CAT: 16

Personal Finance Training
CIJE: 1 RIE: 5 CAT: 15

Personal Futures Planning
CIJE: 0 RIE: 5 CAT: 15

Personal History
CIJE: 3 RIE: 1 CAT: 12

Personal History and Opinion Inventory
CIJE: 0 RIE: 1 CAT: 21

Personal Independence
CIJE: 16 RIE: 12 CAT: 15

Personal Information Systems
CIJE: 9 RIE: 4 CAT: 15

Personal Injury Trials
CIJE: 1 RIE: 1 CAT: 14

Personal Institutional Task Model
CIJE: 0 RIE: 1 CAT: 21

Personal Integration Inventory
CIJE: 0 RIE: 1 CAT: 21

Personal Involvement
CIJE: 5 RIE: 5 CAT: 11

Personal Liability
CIJE: 1 RIE: 3 CAT: 14

Personal Libraries
CIJE: 2 RIE: 1 CAT: 05
UF Family Libraries (Home); Home Libraries

Personal Loss Inventory
CIJE: 0 RIE: 1 CAT: 21

Personal Major Events
CIJE: 2 RIE: 0 CAT: 16

Personal Media Studio
CIJE: 0 RIE: 1 CAT: 04

Personal Names
CIJE: 13 RIE: 3 CAT: 16

Personal Orientation Inventory
CIJE: 73 RIE: 26 CAT: 21

Personal Perspective Scales
CIJE: 0 RIE: 1 CAT: 21

Personal Practical Knowledge
CIJE: 2 RIE: 1 CAT: 15

Personal Problems
CIJE: 15 RIE: 5 CAT: 16

Personal Problems Checklist Adolescent
CIJE: 0 RIE: 1 CAT: 21

Personal Profile System
CIJE: 2 RIE: 4 CAT: 21

Personal Qualities Project
CIJE: 0 RIE: 2 CAT: 19

Personal Rapid Transit
CIJE: 1 RIE: 0 CAT: 15

Personal Reaction Inventory (Snyder)
CIJE: 0 RIE: 1 CAT: 21

Personal Reaction Scale
CIJE: 2 RIE: 0 CAT: 21

Personal Reactions Inventory
CIJE: 1 RIE: 0 CAT: 21

Personal Reactions Scale (Revised)
CIJE: 0 RIE: 1 CAT: 21

Personal Record of School Experience
CIJE: 1 RIE: 4 CAT: 21

Personal Report of Communication Apprehension
CIJE: 13 RIE: 16 CAT: 21
UF PRCA 24

Personal Report of Confidence as a Speaker
CIJE: 1 RIE: 0 CAT: 21

Personal Reports of Subjective Experiences
CIJE: 0 RIE: 2 CAT: 21

Personal Services Occupations
CIJE: 0 RIE: 2 CAT: 09

Personal Style Indicator
CIJE: 0 RIE: 1 CAT: 21

Personal Testing and Interactive Evaluation System
CIJE: 0 RIE: 1 CAT: 04
UF PETITE (Computer Program)

Personal Values Inventory (Schlesser and Finger)
CIJE: 0 RIE: 2 CAT: 21

Personal Values Project
CIJE: 0 RIE: 1 CAT: 19

Personal Values Questionnaire
CIJE: 1 RIE: 1 CAT: 21

Personal Writing
CIJE: 43 RIE: 36 CAT: 16

Personalism (Tests)
CIJE: 0 RIE: 0 CAT: 21

Personality Assessment System
CIJE: 2 RIE: 0 CAT: 15

Personality Attributes Questionnaire
CIJE: 3 RIE: 3 CAT: 21

Personality Characteristics Inventory (Sciortino)
CIJE: 1 RIE: 0 CAT: 21

Personality Completion Test (Ball)
CIJE: 0 RIE: 1 CAT: 21

Personality Diagnostic Questionnaire (Revised)
CIJE: 0 RIE: 1 CAT: 21

Personality Education Behavior Study
CIJE: 0 RIE: 1 CAT: 21

Personality Integration Reputation Test (Duncan)
CIJE: 1 RIE: 0 CAT: 21

Personality Inventory for Children
CIJE: 14 RIE: 4 CAT: 21

Personality Inventory for Children (Revised)
CIJE: 1 RIE: 1 CAT: 21

Personality Research Form
CIJE: 22 RIE: 5 CAT: 21

Personality Scale for Social Respon (Gough)
CIJE: 1 RIE: 0 CAT: 21

Personality Tests and Reviews (Buros)
CIJE: 1 RIE: 0 CAT: 21

Personality Types
CIJE: 5 RIE: 3 CAT: 11

Personality Types and Occupations Questionnaire
CIJE: 1 RIE: 0 CAT: 21

Personalized Approach to Teaching Reading
CIJE: 0 RIE: 1 CAT: 15

Personalized Instructional Remedial Tutorial Syst
CIJE: 0 RIE: 1 CAT: 15

Personalized Reading
CIJE: 2 RIE: 2 CAT: 15

Personalized Stories
CIJE: 2 RIE: 1 CAT: 16

Personalized System of Instruction
CIJE: 176 RIE: 100 CAT: 15

Personalized Teacher Education Program
CIJE: 1 RIE: 3 CAT: 19

Personalizing Educational Prescriptions
CIJE: 0 RIE: 12 CAT: 15

Personification
CIJE: 5 RIE: 3 CAT: 15

Personnel and Guidance Journal
CIJE: 3 RIE: 0 CAT: 22

Personnel Decision Analysis
CIJE: 1 RIE: 1 CAT: 15

Personnel Files
CIJE: 0 RIE: 88 CAT: 16

Personnel for Parent Development Program
CIJE: 0 RIE: 1 CAT: 19

Personnel Preparation Program (OSEP)
CIJE: 0 RIE: 2 CAT: 19
SN OSEP = Office of Special Education Programs

Personnel Research
CIJE: 4 RIE: 4 CAT: 15

Personnel Selection Inventory
CIJE: 0 RIE: 2 CAT: 21

Personnel Simulator
CIJE: 0 RIE: 1 CAT: 15

Persons and Places
CIJE: 0 RIE: 2 CAT: 21

Perspective (Psychology)
CIJE: 17 RIE: 3 CAT: 11

Perspective Ability Test (Miller)
CIJE: 0 RIE: 1 CAT: 21

Perspective Consciousness
CIJE: 0 RIE: 1 CAT: 11

Perspective Realism
CIJE: 0 RIE: 1 CAT: 15

Perspective Taking Task
CIJE: 6 RIE: 2 CAT: 15

Perspective Text Analysis
CIJE: 0 RIE: 7 CAT: 15

Perspective Transformation
CIJE: 5 RIE: 1 CAT: 15

Perspectives Discrepancy Assessment
CIJE: 0 RIE: 4 CAT: 21

Persuasibility
CIJE: 3 RIE: 2 CAT: 16

Persuasive Communication Model
CIJE: 1 RIE: 1 CAT: 15

Persuasive Strategies
CIJE: 23 RIE: 17 CAT: 16

PERTEX Computer Program
CIJE: 0 RIE: 1 CAT: 04

Perth Amboy School District NJ
CIJE: 0 RIE: 1 CAT: 17

Perth Central School District NY
CIJE: 0 RIE: 1 CAT: 17

Perturbation (Perception)
CIJE: 2 RIE: 0 CAT: 11

Perturbation Theory (Physics)
CIJE: 0 RIE: 0 CAT: 20

Pertussis
CIJE: 1 RIE: 1 CAT: 11

Peru
CIJE: 116 RIE: 119 CAT: 07

Peru (Lima)
CIJE: 7 RIE: 1 CAT: 07

Peru (South Central)
CIJE: 0 RIE: 2 CAT: 07

Peru State College NE
CIJE: 1 RIE: 1 CAT: 17

Peruvian Rural School System (Peru)
CIJE: 0 RIE: 0 CAT: 17

Pervasive Developmental Disorders
CIJE: 14 RIE: 2 CAT: 11

Peshawar Dialects
CIJE: 0 RIE: 1 CAT: 13

Pessimism
CIJE: 14 RIE: 2 CAT: 11

Pessoa (Fernando)
CIJE: 1 RIE: 0 CAT: 18

Pestalozzi (Johann Heinrich)
CIJE: 16 RIE: 8 CAT: 18

PET 2001
CIJE: 1 RIE: 0 CAT: 04

Peter Blau Model of Occupational Choice
CIJE: 0 RIE: 1 CAT: 15

Peter Pan
CIJE: 3 RIE: 1 CAT: 22

Peter Rabbit
CIJE: 3 RIE: 1 CAT: 22

Peterborough Project
CIJE: 0 RIE: 1 CAT: 19

Peters (R S)
CIJE: 13 RIE: 1 CAT: 18

Peters Township High School PA
CIJE: 1 RIE: 0 CAT: 17

Petersen (Peter)
CIJE: 0 RIE: 1 CAT: 18

Peterson (Paul E)
CIJE: 0 RIE: 1 CAT: 18

Peterson Child Problem Checklist
CIJE: 1 RIE: 2 CAT: 21

Peterson Quay Behavior Problem Checklist
CIJE: 2 RIE: 3 CAT: 21

Peterson v Oregon State University
CIJE: 1 RIE: 0 CAT: 14

PETITE (Computer Program)
USE Personal Testing and Interactive Evaluation System

Petitio Fallacy
CIJE: 0 RIE: 1 CAT: 13
SN "Begging the question" in logic

Petitions
CIJE: 5 RIE: 0 CAT: 16

Petrakis (Harry Mark)
CIJE: 0 RIE: 1 CAT: 18

Petrarch (Francesco)
CIJE: 2 RIE: 0 CAT: 18

Petriel Reading Comprehension Test
CIJE: 1 RIE: 0 CAT: 21

Petroglyphs
CIJE: 1 RIE: 2 CAT: 16
SN Informative carvings or inscriptions on rocks

Petroleum Abstracts
CIJE: 1 RIE: 0 CAT: 22

Petroleum Engineering
CIJE: 1 RIE: 1 CAT: 20

Petroleum Seepage
CIJE: 2 RIE: 0 CAT: 20

Petronius (Gaius)
CIJE: 3 RIE: 0 CAT: 18

Petrosky (Anthony R)
CIJE: 0 RIE: 1 CAT: 18

Petrov (Archpriest Avoakum)
CIJE: 1 RIE: 0 CAT: 18

Petrushevskaja (Ljudmila)
CIJE: 0 RIE: 1 CAT: 18

Pets
CIJE: 70 RIE: 21 CAT: 20

Pettigrew (Thomas F)
CIJE: 1 RIE: 2 CAT: 18

Pettigrew Category Width Scale
CIJE: 1 RIE: 1 CAT: 21

Pew Campus Roundtable
CIJE: 0 RIE: 1 CAT: 19

Peyote
CIJE: 7 RIE: 2 CAT: 11

PF Project
CIJE: 0 RIE: 1200 CAT: 19

Pfister (Oskar)
CIJE: 1 RIE: 0 CAT: 18

pfs (Database System)
CIJE: 1 RIE: 1 CAT: 04

pH
CIJE: 29 RIE: 4 CAT: 20

Ph Calculation
CIJE: 2 RIE: 2 CAT: 20

Ph D in Education
USE Doctor of Philosophy in Education Degrees

pH Meters
CIJE: 1 RIE: 0 CAT: 04

Phanat Nikhom Refugee Camp (Thailand)
CIJE: 0 RIE: 1 CAT: 17

Pharmaceutical Libraries
CIJE: 1 RIE: 0 CAT: 05

Pharmacology and Patient Care
CIJE: 1 RIE: 4 CAT: 16

Pharmacy College Admission Test
CIJE: 8 RIE: 1 CAT: 21
UF PCAT

Pharmacy Libraries
CIJE: 0 RIE: 1 CAT: 05

Pharmacy Technicians
CIJE: 2 RIE: 8 CAT: 09

Pharynx
CIJE: 3 RIE: 0 CAT: 11

Phasal Analysis
CIJE: 0 RIE: 1 CAT: 15

Phased Construction
CIJE: 2 RIE: 0 CAT: 20

Phased English Courses
CIJE: 0 RIE: 1 CAT: 13

Phased Retirement
CIJE: 3 RIE: 4 CAT: 15

Phases of Reasoning
CIJE: 0 RIE: 1 CAT: 15

Phedre
CIJE: 2 RIE: 0 CAT: 22

Phelps Stokes Foundation of New York
CIJE: 4 RIE: 0 CAT: 17

Phencyclidine
CIJE: 2 RIE: 2 CAT: 11
UF PCP

Phenomenography
CIJE: 8 RIE: 8 CAT: 16

Phenylketonuria
CIJE: 34 RIE: 10 CAT: 11

Phenylpropanolamine
USE PPA

Pheromones
CIJE: 4 RIE: 0 CAT: 20

Phi Alpha Delta Law Fraternity
CIJE: 0 RIE: 2 CAT: 17

Phi Beta Kappa
CIJE: 1 RIE: 2 CAT: 17

Phi Beta Lambda
CIJE: 3 RIE: 1 CAT: 17

Phi Coefficient
CIJE: 8 RIE: 8 CAT: 15

Phi Delta Kappa
CIJE: 5 RIE: 20 CAT: 17

Phi Delta Kappa Study of Students at Risk
USE Study of Students at Risk (Phi Delta Kappa)

Phi Delta Kappan
CIJE: 1 RIE: 2 CAT: 22

Phi Theta Kappa
CIJE: 1 RIE: 1 CAT: 17

Philadelphia Association for Clinical Trials
CIJE: 0 RIE: 1 CAT: 17

Philadelphia Association of School Administrators
CIJE: 1 RIE: 0 CAT: 17

Philadelphia Business Academies
CIJE: 1 RIE: 1 CAT: 19

Philadelphia City Wide Testing Program
CIJE: 0 RIE: 1 CAT: 21

Philadelphia College of Osteopathic Medicine PA
CIJE: 0 RIE: 1 CAT: 17

Philadelphia College of Textiles and Science PA
CIJE: 2 RIE: 0 CAT: 17

Philadelphia Cooperative Office Education Program
CIJE: 1 RIE: 0 CAT: 19

Philadelphia Cooperative Schools Program
CIJE: 0 RIE: 2 CAT: 19

Philadelphia County Medical Society
CIJE: 2 RIE: 0 CAT: 17

Philadelphia Geriatric Center Morale Scale
CIJE: 1 RIE: 2 CAT: 21

Philadelphia Geriatric Center PA
CIJE: 1 RIE: 0 CAT: 17

Philadelphia Leadership Program
CIJE: 0 RIE: 1 CAT: 19

Philadelphia Museum of Art
CIJE: 3 RIE: 1 CAT: 17

Philadelphia Open Classroom Project
CIJE: 0 RIE: 1 CAT: 19

Philadelphia Project
CIJE: 1 RIE: 0 CAT: 19

Philadelphia Reading Test
CIJE: 0 RIE: 2 CAT: 21

Philadelphia Regional Intro Minorities Engineering
CIJE: 1 RIE: 1 CAT: 19

Philadelphia School District PA
CIJE: 25 RIE: 152 CAT: 17

Philadelphia State Hospital PA
CIJE: 1 RIE: 0 CAT: 17

Philadelphia Student Library Resource Requirements
CIJE: 0 RIE: 2 CAT: 19

Philadelphia Test in Fundamentals in Arithmetic
CIJE: 0 RIE: 1 CAT: 21

Philadelphia Verbal Abilities Test
CIJE: 0 RIE: 2 CAT: 21

Philanthropists
CIJE: 2 RIE: 1 CAT: 10

Philately
CIJE: 9 RIE: 2 CAT: 16

Philco CRT
CIJE: 0 RIE: 1 CAT: 04

Philippine Languages
CIJE: 1 RIE: 7 CAT: 13

Philippine Nonverbal Intelligence Test
CIJE: 1 RIE: 0 CAT: 21

Philippine Refugee Processing Center
CIJE: 1 RIE: 5 CAT: 17

Philippine Rural Reconstruction Movement
CIJE: 0 RIE: 1 CAT: 19

Philippines
CIJE: 193 RIE: 368 CAT: 07

Philippines (Bacolod)
CIJE: 0 RIE: 1 CAT: 07

Philippines (Bataan)
CIJE: 0 RIE: 1 CAT: 07

Philippines (Bicol Peninsula)
CIJE: 0 RIE: 1 CAT: 07

Philippines (Davao del Norte)
CIJE: 0 RIE: 1 CAT: 07

Philippines (Ilocos Sur)
CIJE: 0 RIE: 0 CAT: 07

Philippines (Luzon)
CIJE: 1 RIE: 2 CAT: 07

Philippines (Manila)
CIJE: 4 RIE: 3 CAT: 07

Philippines (Mindanao)
CIJE: 0 RIE: 2 CAT: 07

Philips Interactive Laser Vision Authoring System
CIJE: 1 RIE: 0 CAT: 04
UF PHILVAS

Phillips (Craig)
CIJE: 1 RIE: 0 CAT: 18

Phillips (D C)
CIJE: 0 RIE: 0 CAT: 18

Phillips Academy MA
CIJE: 4 RIE: 0 CAT: 17

Phillips County Community College AR
CIJE: 1 RIE: 2 CAT: 17

Phillips Curve Theory
CIJE: 2 RIE: 1 CAT: 15

Phillips Exeter Academy NH
CIJE: 1 RIE: 15 CAT: 17

Phillips Extended Day Magnet Program
CIJE: 0 RIE: 1 CAT: 19

Phillips Foundation
CIJE: 0 RIE: 1 CAT: 17

Phillips Prognostic Rating Scale
CIJE: 2 RIE: 0 CAT: 21

Phillips University OK
CIJE: 0 RIE: 1 CAT: 17

Philosophers
CIJE: 12 RIE: 9 CAT: 10

Philosophic Mindedness
CIJE: 0 RIE: 2 CAT: 11

Philosophic Mindedness Scale (Felker and Smyth)
CIJE: 0 RIE: 1 CAT: 21

Philosophical Analysis
USE Philosophical Research

Philosophical Dualism
CIJE: 1 RIE: 0 CAT: 15

Philosophical Influences
CIJE: 12 RIE: 9 CAT: 15

Philosophical Psychology
CIJE: 0 RIE: 1 CAT: 11

Philosophical Research
CIJE: 2 RIE: 5 CAT: 15
UF Philosophical Analysis

Philosophical Rules
CIJE: 0 RIE: 1 CAT: 15

Philosophies of Human Nature Scale
CIJE: 1 RIE: 0 CAT: 21

Philosophy for Children (Lipman)
CIJE: 3 RIE: 4 CAT: 19

Philosophy of Adult Education Inventory
CIJE: 2 RIE: 1 CAT: 21

Philosophy of Education Project
CIJE: 0 RIE: 1 CAT: 19

Philosophy of History
CIJE: 1 RIE: 1 CAT: 16

Philosophy of Human Nature Instrument (Wrightsman)
CIJE: 0 RIE: 1 CAT: 21

Philosophy of Science
CIJE: 79 RIE: 15 CAT: 16

PHILVAS
USE Philips Interactive Laser Vision Authoring System

PHINEAS (Computer Program)
CIJE: 0 RIE: 0 CAT: 04

Phineas Banning High School CA
CIJE: 0 RIE: 1 CAT: 17

Phipps Outdoor Education Center
CIJE: 1 RIE: 0 CAT: 17

Phlebotomy
CIJE: 1 RIE: 2 CAT: 11

Phnom Penh Dialect
CIJE: 0 RIE: 1 CAT: 13

Phobia Treatment
CIJE: 21 RIE: 2 CAT: 11

Phobic Children
CIJE: 4 RIE: 0 CAT: 11

PHOENIX (Computer System)
CIJE: 1 RIE: 1 CAT: 04

Phoenix Area Public Health Service AZ
CIJE: 0 RIE: 1 CAT: 17

Phoenix College AZ
CIJE: 1 RIE: 5 CAT: 17

Phoenix Elementary School District 1 AZ
CIJE: 0 RIE: 1 CAT: 17

Phoenix Indian Center AZ
CIJE: 0 RIE: 2 CAT: 17

Phoenix Indian High School AZ
CIJE: 1 RIE: 1 CAT: 17

Phoenix Pilot Drug Program
CIJE: 0 RIE: 1 CAT: 19

Phoenix Project
CIJE: 1 RIE: 1 CAT: 19

Phoenix Union High School District AZ
CIJE: 3 RIE: 29 CAT: 17

Phoenix Urban League
CIJE: 1 RIE: 0 CAT: 17

Phoenix Zoo AZ
CIJE: 1 RIE: 0 CAT: 17

Phoenixville Area School District PA
CIJE: 0 RIE: 1 CAT: 17

Phonathons
CIJE: 22 RIE: 5 CAT: 16

Phonemic Awareness
CIJE: 46 RIE: 20 CAT: 11
SN See also "Phonological Awareness"

Phonetic Preference Inventory (Rychlak)
CIJE: 1 RIE: 0 CAT: 21

Phonetic Realization Rules
CIJE: 0 RIE: 1 CAT: 13

Phonetic Refinement Theory
CIJE: 0 RIE: 1 CAT: 15

Phonetic Spelling Judger
CIJE: 0 RIE: 1 CAT: 21

Phonetic Symbolism
CIJE: 1 RIE: 2 CAT: 13

Phonetic Transcription Profic Test (Dew Jensen)
CIJE: 1 RIE: 0 CAT: 21

Phonetic Variability
USE Phonological Variability

Phonic Literature
CIJE: 1 RIE: 0 CAT: 13

Phonic Transfer Index
CIJE: 0 RIE: 1 CAT: 21

Phonics and Word Power
CIJE: 0 RIE: 1 CAT: 22

Phonographs
CIJE: 3 RIE: 2 CAT: 04

Phonological Awareness
CIJE: 27 RIE: 6 CAT: 11
SN See also "Phonemic Awareness"

Phonological Process Analysis
CIJE: 7 RIE: 2 CAT: 15

Phonological Processing
CIJE: 17 RIE: 4 CAT: 11

Phonological Recoding
CIJE: 8 RIE: 2 CAT: 11

Phonological Transcription Accompanied Text
CIJE: 0 RIE: 1 CAT: 15

Phonological Variability
CIJE: 2 RIE: 1 CAT: 13
UF Phonetic Variability

Phonoscope Communications System
CIJE: 0 RIE: 1 CAT: 04

Phonoviewer
CIJE: 0 RIE: 1 CAT: 04

Phonovisual Reading Method
CIJE: 0 RIE: 2 CAT: 15

Phosphates
CIJE: 3 RIE: 1 CAT: 20

Phosphorescence Decay Rates
CIJE: 1 RIE: 0 CAT: 15

Phosphorus
CIJE: 2 RIE: 1 CAT: 20

Photo Analogies Test
CIJE: 1 RIE: 0 CAT: 21

Photo Classification Test (Livingston et al)
CIJE: 0 RIE: 1 CAT: 21

Photo Identification System
CIJE: 2 RIE: 0 CAT: 04

Photo Interviewing (Tucker et al)
CIJE: 0 RIE: 0 CAT: 15

Photo Optics Instrumentation Technicians
CIJE: 0 RIE: 1 CAT: 09

Photo Sequence Comprehension Test
CIJE: 0 RIE: 1 CAT: 21

Photoanalysis
CIJE: 0 RIE: 1 CAT: 15

Photoconductivity
CIJE: 1 RIE: 0 CAT: 20

Photodiodes
CIJE: 2 RIE: 0 CAT: 20

Photodocuments
CIJE: 0 RIE: 1 CAT: 04

Photoelectric Effect
CIJE: 7 RIE: 0 CAT: 20

Photogrammetric Analysis
CIJE: 2 RIE: 0 CAT: 21

Photogrammetry
CIJE: 0 RIE: 3 CAT: 20

Photograms
CIJE: 3 RIE: 0 CAT: 04

Photograph Finishers
CIJE: 0 RIE: 2 CAT: 09

Photographic Assisted Instruction
CIJE: 1 RIE: 0 CAT: 15

Photographic Collections
CIJE: 3 RIE: 2 CAT: 04

Photographic Engineering Technology
CIJE: 1 RIE: 0 CAT: 20

Photographic Perspective Error
CIJE: 1 RIE: 0 CAT: 15

Photographic Pupillometer
CIJE: 0 RIE: 1 CAT: 04

Photoinstrumentation Technology
CIJE: 0 RIE: 1 CAT: 20

Photolithography
CIJE: 0 RIE: 1 CAT: 20

Photomathematics
CIJE: 1 RIE: 0 CAT: 20

Photometry
CIJE: 5 RIE: 1 CAT: 20

Photonovels
CIJE: 1 RIE: 1 CAT: 16

Photons
CIJE: 2 RIE: 1 CAT: 20

Photoplay Magazine
CIJE: 0 RIE: 1 CAT: 22

Photosketching
CIJE: 4 RIE: 0 CAT: 03

Photosynthetic Pigments
CIJE: 1 RIE: 0 CAT: 20

Phototherapy
CIJE: 2 RIE: 4 CAT: 11

Photovoltaic Power
CIJE: 0 RIE: 1 CAT: 20

Photovoltaic Systems
CIJE: 4 RIE: 4 CAT: 20

Photovoltaics
CIJE: 0 RIE: 3 CAT: 20

Phrasal Verbs
CIJE: 4 RIE: 1 CAT: 13

Phrase Reading
CIJE: 3 RIE: 3 CAT: 13

Phrasebooks
CIJE: 0 RIE: 21 CAT: 13

Phrasing
CIJE: 2 RIE: 3 CAT: 13

Phrenology
CIJE: 2 RIE: 0 CAT: 11

Physiatrists
CIJE: 1 RIE: 1 CAT: 09

Physical Abuse
CIJE: 11 RIE: 9 CAT: 11

Physical and Neurological Examination Soft Signs
CIJE: 1 RIE: 0 CAT: 11

Physical Appearance
CIJE: 4 RIE: 3 CAT: 11

Physical Contact
CIJE: 15 RIE: 5 CAT: 11
SN See also "Touching," "Body Contact"

Physical Education Index
CIJE: 1 RIE: 0 CAT: 22

Physical Education Majors
CIJE: 3 RIE: 2 CAT: 10

Physical Education Sports Index
CIJE: 1 RIE: 0 CAT. 22

Physical Environment Perception Scale
CIJE: 0 RIE: 1 CAT: 21

Physical Estimation and Attraction Scales
CIJE: 1 RIE: 1 CAT: 21

Physical Growth Record
CIJE: 1 RIE: 0 CAT: 21

Physical Medicine
CIJE: 0 RIE: 1 CAT: 11

Physical Modeling
CIJE: 0 RIE: 1 CAT: 16

Physical Performance Test
CIJE: 0 RIE: 2 CAT: 21

Physical Plant Administrators
CIJE: 2 RIE: 2 CAT: 09

Physical Properties
CIJE: 8 RIE: 4 CAT: 20

Physical Proximity
CIJE: 2 RIE: 1 CAT: 11

Physical Resources
CIJE: 1 RIE: 0 CAT: 20

Physical Science for Nonscience Students
CIJE: 8 RIE: 3 CAT: 03

Physical Science II
CIJE: 1 RIE: 0 CAT: 03

Physical Science Study Committee
CIJE: 44 RIE: 37 CAT: 17

Physical Sciences Curriculum Study
CIJE: 1 RIE: 0 CAT: 03

Physical Skills Development Program
CIJE: 0 RIE: 1 CAT: 19

Physical State
CIJE: 3 RIE: 1 CAT: 20

Physically Impaired Association of Michigan
CIJE: 2 RIE: 1 CAT: 17

Physician Performance Rating Scale
CIJE: 0 RIE: 1 CAT: 21

Physician Pharmacist Relationship
CIJE: 1 RIE: 0 CAT: 11

Physician Role
CIJE: 17 RIE: 6 CAT: 11

Physicians Serving Handicapped Children Project
CIJE: 1 RIE: 0 CAT: 19

Physics Abstracts
CIJE: 0 RIE: 2 CAT: 22

Physics Achievement Test (Ahlgren Wahlberg Welch)
CIJE: 0 RIE: 4 CAT: 21

Physics Achievement Test (ATP)
CIJE: 0 RIE: 1 CAT: 21
UF ATP Physics Test

Physics and Astronomy Teaching Survey
CIJE: 0 RIE: 2 CAT: 21

Physics and Technology Project (Netherlands)
CIJE: 0 RIE: 1 CAT: 19

Physics Computer Development Project
CIJE: 1 RIE: 7 CAT: 19

Physics Curriculum Development Project
CIJE: 1 RIE: 1 CAT: 19

Physics Mathematics Astronomy Library
CIJE: 1 RIE: 0 CAT: 17

Physics Tests
CIJE: 0 RIE: 1 CAT: 21

Physiognomic Perception
CIJE: 1 RIE: 1 CAT: 11

Physiological Domain
CIJE: 1 RIE: 2 CAT: 11

Physiological Needs
CIJE: 1 RIE: 1 CAT: 11

Physiological Response
CIJE: 4 RIE: 1 CAT: 11

Physiology of Readiness Program
CIJE: 1 RIE: 0 CAT: 19

Phytoplankton
CIJE: 1 RIE: 1 CAT: 20

Pi (Mathematics)
CIJE: 17 RIE: 3 CAT: 20

Piaget (Jean)
CIJE: 1071 RIE: 668 CAT: 18

Piaget Number Concept Test (Dodwell)
CIJE: 0 RIE: 1 CAT: 21

Piaget Object Scale
CIJE: 0 RIE: 1 CAT: 21

Piaget Perspective Taking Test
CIJE: 0 RIE: 1 CAT: 21

Piaget Physical de Centering Test
CIJE: 0 RIE: 2 CAT: 21

Piagetian Logical Operations Test
CIJE: 1 RIE: 0 CAT: 21

Piagetian Research
CIJE: 38 RIE: 15 CAT: 11

Piagetian Reversibility
CIJE: 3 RIE: 1 CAT: 15
UF Reversibility (Piaget)

Piagetian Task Instrument
CIJE: 1 RIE: 1 CAT: 15

Piagetian Tests
CIJE: 49 RIE: 31 CAT: 21

Piagets Clinical Method
CIJE: 3 RIE: 2 CAT: 15

Pianists
CIJE: 4 RIE: 0 CAT: 09

Piano Instruction
CIJE: 13 RIE: 5 CAT: 03

Pianos
CIJE: 9 RIE: 5 CAT: 04

Piazza (Thomas)
CIJE: 0 RIE: 1 CAT: 18

PIC Program
CIJE: 0 RIE: 1 CAT: 19

Pica Behavior
CIJE: 7 RIE: 2 CAT: 11

Pica Library Automation Network
CIJE: 0 RIE: 0 CAT: 17
UF Project for Integrated Catalogue Automation

Picasso (Pablo)
CIJE: 15 RIE: 3 CAT: 18

Pick Theorem
CIJE: 7 RIE: 0 CAT: 20

Pickens County School District SC
CIJE: 0 RIE: 1 CAT: 17

Pickering (John)
CIJE: 0 RIE: 1 CAT: 18

Pickering v Board of Education
CIJE: 2 RIE: 5 CAT: 14

Pickleball
CIJE: 0 RIE: 1 CAT: 16

PICKUP
CIJE: 0 RIE: 0 CAT: 19
SN 1982 initiative of the U.K.'s Dept of Education and Science to update re-

gional mid-career training and retraining programs
UF Professional Industrial and Commercial Updating

Pico v Island Trees Union Free School District
CIJE: 5 RIE: 5 CAT: 14
UF Island Trees Union Free School District v Pico

Picot Taskforce (New Zealand)
CIJE: 0 RIE: 1 CAT: 19

Pictionary Perfect
CIJE: 0 RIE: 1 CAT: 16

Pictogram System
CIJE: 1 RIE: 1 CAT: 15

Pictograph Sentence Memory Task
CIJE: 2 RIE: 1 CAT: 15

Pictographs
CIJE: 3 RIE: 12 CAT: 16

Pictorial Analogy
CIJE: 4 RIE: 0 CAT: 15

Pictorial Apprenticeship Program
CIJE: 0 RIE: 1 CAT: 19

Pictorial Aural Inventory of Science Knowledge
CIJE: 1 RIE: 1 CAT: 21

Pictorial Self Concept Scale (Bolea)
CIJE: 0 RIE: 1 CAT: 21

Pictorial Self Concept Scale for Children
CIJE: 0 RIE: 3 CAT: 21

Pictorial Test of Intelligence
CIJE: 3 RIE: 3 CAT: 21

Picture Categorization Test
CIJE: 0 RIE: 3 CAT: 21

Picture Category Inventory
CIJE: 1 RIE: 0 CAT: 21

Picture Identification Test
CIJE: 5 RIE: 0 CAT: 21

Picture Interpretation
CIJE: 5 RIE: 1 CAT: 16

Picture Interpretation Test (Aliotti and Blanton)
CIJE: 0 RIE: 1 CAT: 21

Picture Interpretation Test (Torrance and Aliotti)
CIJE: 1 RIE: 0 CAT: 21

Picture Interview (Ammon and Ammon)
CIJE: 1 RIE: 0 CAT: 21

Picture Inventory
CIJE: 1 RIE: 0 CAT: 21

Picture Lady Program
CIJE: 1 RIE: 0 CAT: 19

Picture Libraries
CIJE: 4 RIE: 2 CAT: 05

Picture Motivation Test (Herman)
CIJE: 1 RIE: 0 CAT: 21

Picture Motivator Scale (Haywood)
CIJE: 0 RIE: 1 CAT: 21

Picture Object Matching Tasks (Franklin)
CIJE: 0 RIE: 1 CAT: 21

Picture Pairing Test
CIJE: 1 RIE: 0 CAT: 21

Picture Rating Technique
CIJE: 0 RIE: 1 CAT: 15

Picture Redundancy Task (Berry and Jones)
CIJE: 1 RIE: 0 CAT: 21

Picture Scale (Harvill)
CIJE: 0 RIE: 1 CAT: 21

Picture Stories
CIJE: 5 RIE: 2 CAT: 16

Picture Story Language Test
CIJE: 2 RIE: 2 CAT: 21

Picture Superiority Effect
CIJE: 2 RIE: 0 CAT: 11

Picture Text Relationship
CIJE: 16 RIE: 6 CAT: 15

Picture Vocabulary Story
CIJE: 1 RIE: 0 CAT: 15

Picture Vocabulary Test (Zimiles et al)
CIJE: 0 RIE: 1 CAT: 21

Picture Word Game (Corman and Budoff)
CIJE: 0 RIE: 1 CAT: 21

Pictures
CIJE: 41 RIE: 15 CAT: 04

Picuris
CIJE: 0 RIE: 1 CAT: 08

Pidgin Sign English
USE Pidgin Signed English

Pidgin Signed English
CIJE: 3 RIE: 1 CAT: 13
UF Pidgin Sign English

Piecework
CIJE: 1 RIE: 2 CAT: 16

Pied Piper of Hamelin
CIJE: 1 RIE: 1 CAT: 22

Piedmont Export Expansion Program
CIJE: 1 RIE: 0 CAT: 19

Piedmont Region
CIJE: 2 RIE: 1 CAT: 07

Piedmont Region Model for Family Involvement
CIJE: 1 RIE: 0 CAT: 15

Piedmont Schools Project
CIJE: 0 RIE: 2 CAT: 19

Piedmont Technical College SC
CIJE: 0 RIE: 3 CAT: 17

Piedmont Technical Institute NC
CIJE: 0 RIE: 2 CAT: 17
SN Old name of Piedmont Technical College NC

Piedmont University Center of North Carolina
CIJE: 1 RIE: 0 CAT: 17

Piedmont Virginia Community College
CIJE: 1 RIE: 17 CAT: 17

Pierce (Charles Sanders)
CIJE: 1 RIE: 1 CAT: 18

Pierce College CA
CIJE: 1 RIE: 1 CAT: 17

Pierce Community College District 11 WA
CIJE: 0 RIE: 1 CAT: 17

Pierce v Society of Sisters
CIJE: 0 RIE: 4 CAT: 14

Pierre Indian Learning Center SD
CIJE: 0 RIE: 1 CAT: 17

Pierre Indian School SD
CIJE: 0 RIE: 1 CAT: 17

Piers Harris Childrens Self Concept Scale
CIJE: 44 RIE: 44 CAT: 21

Piers Plowman
CIJE: 0 RIE: 1 CAT: 22

Pietism
CIJE: 1 RIE: 1 CAT: 15

Piezoelectric Effect
CIJE: 5 RIE: 0 CAT: 20

Pigault Lebrun (Charles Antoine)
CIJE: 1 RIE: 0 CAT: 18

Pigeons
CIJE: 4 RIE: 0 CAT: 20

Piggybacking (Early Childhood Education)
CIJE: 0 RIE: 1 CAT: 15

Pigman
CIJE: 0 RIE: 1 CAT: 22

Pijin
CIJE: 0 RIE: 4 CAT: 13

Pike (Kenneth L)
CIJE: 2 RIE: 1 CAT: 18

Pikes Peak Community College CO
CIJE: 0 RIE: 1 CAT: 17

Pikes Peak Library District CO
CIJE: 6 RIE: 0 CAT: 17

Pikeville College KY
CIJE: 2 RIE: 0 CAT: 17

Pilgrim (Billy)
CIJE: 1 RIE: 0 CAT: 18

Pilgrims
CIJE: 7 RIE: 1 CAT: 10

Pilipinos
CIJE: 0 RIE: 1 CAT: 08

Pilkington Report
CIJE: 1 RIE: 0 CAT: 22

Pillais Trace
CIJE: 0 RIE: 1 CAT: 21

Pilot Author Language
CIJE: 5 RIE: 3 CAT: 04
SN See also "SuperPILOT Authoring Language"

Pilot Programing Language
CIJE: 10 RIE: 4 CAT: 04

Pilot State Dissemination Program
CIJE: 2 RIE: 3 CAT: 19

PIM Model
CIJE: 0 RIE: 1 CAT: 15
SN A model of evaluation planning, implementation, and management

Pima
CIJE: 0 RIE: 4 CAT: 13

Pima (Tribe)
CIJE: 5 RIE: 24 CAT: 08

Pima Community College AZ
CIJE: 10 RIE: 19 CAT: 17

Pima Maricopa (Tribe)
CIJE: 1 RIE: 1 CAT: 08

Pima Maricopa Reservation AZ
CIJE: 0 RIE: 1 CAT: 17

Pimlico Comprehensive
CIJE: 1 RIE: 0 CAT: 15

PIMMS
USE Project to Increase Mastery of Math and Science

Pimsleur Language Aptitude Battery
CIJE: 3 RIE: 5 CAT: 21

Pimsleur Reading Comprehension Tests
CIJE: 0 RIE: 1 CAT: 21

Pinckney (Charles Cotesworth)
CIJE: 0 RIE: 1 CAT: 18
SN U.S. statesman, 1746-1825

Pinckney (Charles)
CIJE: 0 RIE: 1 CAT: 18
SN U.S. political leader, 1757-1824

PINDIS (Computer Program)
CIJE: 1 RIE: 0 CAT: 04

Pine Lake
CIJE: 1 RIE: 0 CAT: 07

Pine Manor Junior College MA
CIJE: 1 RIE: 0 CAT: 17

Pine Ridge Boarding School SD
CIJE: 0 RIE: 1 CAT: 17

Pine Ridge Indian Reservation SD
CIJE: 2 RIE: 6 CAT: 17

Pine Ridge Reservation Needs Assessment
CIJE: 0 RIE: 1 CAT: 21

Pine to Prairie Cooperative Center MN
CIJE: 0 RIE: 1 CAT: 17

Pine Trees
CIJE: 2 RIE: 0 CAT: 20

Pine View School FL
CIJE: 1 RIE: 0 CAT: 17

Pinel School CA
CIJE: 0 RIE: 1 CAT: 17

Pinellas County Reading System
CIJE: 0 RIE: 2 CAT: 15

Pinellas County School System FL
CIJE: 4 RIE: 5 CAT: 17

Piney Woods Country Life School MS
CIJE: 0 RIE: 1 CAT: 17

Pinget (Robert)
CIJE: 1 RIE: 0 CAT: 18

Pink Collar Occupations
CIJE: 1 RIE: 2 CAT: 09

Pinocchio
CIJE: 3 RIE: 0 CAT: 22

Pinsetter Mechanics
CIJE: 0 RIE: 1 CAT: 09

Pinter (Harold)
CIJE: 7 RIE: 1 CAT: 18

Pintner Cunningham Primary Test
CIJE: 0 RIE: 6 CAT: 21

Pintner Durost Elementary Test
CIJE: 0 RIE: 2 CAT: 21

Pintner General Ability Tests (Verbal Series)
CIJE: 1 RIE: 1 CAT: 21

Pintupi
CIJE: 1 RIE: 0 CAT: 13

Pinyin (Language)
CIJE: 5 RIE: 9 CAT: 13

Pioneer Life
CIJE: 8 RIE: 17 CAT: 16

Pioneer Mental Health Center NE
CIJE: 0 RIE: 1 CAT: 17

Pioneer Organization
CIJE: 3 RIE: 0 CAT: 17

Pioneer Program (NASA)
CIJE: 0 RIE: 1 CAT: 19

PIP Formula
USE Potential for Improving Performance

Pipe Fitters
CIJE: 0 RIE: 3 CAT: 09

PIPE Project NM
USE Pueblo Infant Parent Education Project NM

Pipe Workers
CIJE: 0 RIE: 3 CAT: 09

Pipelines
CIJE: 0 RIE: 3 CAT: 20

PIPER
USE Prescriptive Instructional Program Educ Readiness

Piracy of Intellectual Property
CIJE: 0 RIE: 0 CAT: 16
SN See also "Computer Piracy" and "Software Piracy"
UF Intellectual Property Piracy

Piraha
CIJE: 0 RIE: 3 CAT: 13
SN Amazonian language of central Brazil (Mura family)

PIRAMID Project
CIJE: 0 RIE: 1 CAT: 19

Pirandello (Luigi)
CIJE: 2 RIE: 1 CAT: 18

Pirate Radio
CIJE: 0 RIE: 1 CAT: 16

Pirate Television
CIJE: 0 RIE: 1 CAT: 16

Pirates
CIJE: 3 RIE: 0 CAT: 10

Pirsig (Robert)
CIJE: 2 RIE: 1 CAT: 18

PISA Project
CIJE: 0 RIE: 1 CAT: 19
UF Performance Improvement through Strategy Analysis

Pitch (Language)
CIJE: 14 RIE: 14 CAT: 13

Pitch (Music)
CIJE: 38 RIE: 4 CAT: 16

Pitch Discrimination Test Worksample 740 A
CIJE: 0 RIE: 1 CAT: 21

Pitchell Report for Higher Education
CIJE: 1 RIE: 0 CAT: 22

Pitjantjatjara
CIJE: 0 RIE: 1 CAT: 13
SN Dialect of Kardutjara, a Wati language

Pitkin (Royce S)
CIJE: 0 RIE: 1 CAT: 18

Pitman (James)
CIJE: 1 RIE: 0 CAT: 18

Pitt (William)
CIJE: 0 RIE: 1 CAT: 18

Pitt County Schools NC
CIJE: 0 RIE: 4 CAT: 17

Pitt Technical Institute NC
CIJE: 1 RIE: 0 CAT: 17

Pittenger (John C)
CIJE: 1 RIE: 0 CAT: 18

Pittsburg State University KS
CIJE: 1 RIE: 13 CAT: 17

Pittsburg Unified School District KS
CIJE: 0 RIE: 1 CAT: 17

Pittsburgh Adjustment Survey Scales
CIJE: 1 RIE: 2 CAT: 21

Pittsburgh Area Center for Teachers PA
CIJE: 0 RIE: 1 CAT: 17

Pittsburgh Chemical Information Center
CIJE: 1 RIE: 0 CAT: 17

Pittsburgh Council of Higher Education PA
CIJE: 0 RIE: 1 CAT: 17

Pittsburgh Courier
CIJE: 0 RIE: 1 CAT: 22

Pittsburgh Playhouse
CIJE: 0 RIE: 1 CAT: 17

Pittsburgh School District PA
CIJE: 11 RIE: 32 CAT: 17

Pittsburghs Research Based Instr Supervisory Model
CIJE: 0 RIE: 1 CAT: 15
UF PRISM Model

Pittsfield School District MA
CIJE: 0 RIE: 2 CAT: 17

Pity
CIJE: 1 RIE: 1 CAT: 11

Piven (Frances Fox)
CIJE: 0 RIE: 1 CAT: 18

Pivot Course
CIJE: 0 RIE: 1 CAT: 03

Pivot Grammar
CIJE: 1 RIE: 0 CAT: 13

PIVOT Program
CIJE: 0 RIE: 1 CAT: 19

PL 1 Programing Language
CIJE: 2 RIE: 9 CAT: 04

PL M Programming Language
CIJE: 0 RIE: 0 CAT: 04

PLACE (Program)
CIJE: 0 RIE: 11 CAT: 19

Place Called School (A)
CIJE: 7 RIE: 4 CAT: 22

Place Identity
CIJE: 2 RIE: 3 CAT: 15

Place Names
CIJE: 7 RIE: 5 CAT: 13
UF Toponyms

Place of Birth
CIJE: 2 RIE: 5 CAT: 16

Place of Doors Television Show
CIJE: 1 RIE: 0 CAT: 22

Placebo Control Program
CIJE: 0 RIE: 1 CAT: 19

Placebo Effect
CIJE: 12 RIE: 6 CAT: 11

Placement (Foster Care)
CIJE: 31 RIE: 9 CAT: 11
UF Foster Care Placement

Placement Prevention
CIJE: 5 RIE: 2 CAT: 15
UF Prevention of Placement

Placement Rate
CIJE: 1 RIE: 1 CAT: 15

Placement Teams (Special Education)
USE Special Education Placement Teams

Placement Tests
CIJE: 12 RIE: 50 CAT: 21
SN See also narrower "Informal Placement Tests," "English Placement Tests," "College Board Computerized Placement Tests," etc.

Places Rated Almanac
CIJE: 0 RIE: 1 CAT: 22

Plague
CIJE: 2 RIE: 0 CAT: 22

Plain English
CIJE: 5 RIE: 1 CAT: 13

Plain English Movement
CIJE: 13 RIE: 4 CAT: 12

Plain Language
CIJE: 1 RIE: 2 CAT: 13

Plain Language Laws
CIJE: 3 RIE: 2 CAT: 14

Plain Public Schools OH
CIJE: 1 RIE: 0 CAT: 17

Plainedge Public Library NY
CIJE: 0 RIE: 2 CAT: 17

Plainedge School District NY
CIJE: 0 RIE: 1 CAT: 17

Plainfield School District NJ
CIJE: 1 RIE: 0 CAT: 17

Plainfield School System NJ
CIJE: 0 RIE: 1 CAT: 17

Plains Indians (Anthropological Label)
CIJE: 17 RIE: 9 CAT: 08

Plains Wars
CIJE: 0 RIE: 1 CAT: 12
SN Wars between the United States and the Plains Indians from 1864-1877

Plan Basico
CIJE: 0 RIE: 1 CAT: 19

Plan for Progress
CIJE: 0 RIE: 1 CAT: 19

Plan of a House Test
CIJE: 0 RIE: 1 CAT: 21

Plan Puebla (Mexico)
CIJE: 0 RIE: 1 CAT: 19

PLAN Social Studies
CIJE: 0 RIE: 1 CAT: 03

Plan Student Observation Scale
CIJE: 0 RIE: 2 CAT: 21

Plan Teacher Observation Scale (Quirk et al)
CIJE: 1 RIE: 1 CAT: 21

Planar Strategies
CIJE: 1 RIE: 1 CAT: 15

Planaria
CIJE: 7 RIE: 0 CAT: 20

Planbox Escalation
CIJE: 0 RIE: 1 CAT: 13
SN A linguistic method of analyzing narrative arguments

Planck Constant
CIJE: 6 RIE: 0 CAT: 20

Planck Institute for Human Devel and Ed (Germany)
USE Max Planck Inst for Human Devel and Educ (Germany)

Planer Jacks
CIJE: 0 RIE: 1 CAT: 04

PLANET Teleconferencing System
CIJE: 0 RIE: 1 CAT: 04

Planetary Geology
CIJE: 2 RIE: 1 CAT: 20

Planetology
CIJE: 1 RIE: 0 CAT: 20

Planets
CIJE: 16 RIE: 7 CAT: 20

PLANIT Programing Language
CIJE: 4 RIE: 12 CAT: 04

Plankton
CIJE: 4 RIE: 1 CAT: 20

Planned Activity Check
CIJE: 0 RIE: 1 CAT: 21

Planned Change
CIJE: 2 RIE: 1 CAT: 16
SN See also "CLER Model"

Planned Comparisons
CIJE: 2 RIE: 12 CAT: 21

Planned Course Statements
CIJE: 0 RIE: 1 CAT: 15

Planned Giving
CIJE: 29 RIE: 2 CAT: 16

Planned Individual Learning Experience
CIJE: 1 RIE: 0 CAT: 15

Planned Parenthood Federation
CIJE: 5 RIE: 5 CAT: 17

Planned Variation
CIJE: 1 RIE: 35 CAT: 15

Planners
CIJE: 6 RIE: 7 CAT: 09

Planning and Changing (Journal)
CIJE: 0 RIE: 1 CAT: 22

Planning and Development Units
CIJE: 0 RIE: 1 CAT: 05

Planning and Management Systems Program
CIJE: 0 RIE: 1 CAT: 19

Planning and Placement Teams
CIJE: 0 RIE: 1 CAT: 15

Planning Attention Simultaneous Successive Model
USE PASS Model (Luria)

Planning Boards
CIJE: 0 RIE: 1 CAT: 10

Planning by Objectives
CIJE: 2 RIE: 1 CAT: 15

Planning Development Quality Services Schools
CIJE: 0 RIE: 2 CAT: 19
SN "Planning and Development of Quality Services in the Schools"
UF PDQ Project

Planning Evaluation and Resource Management Model
CIJE: 0 RIE: 2 CAT: 15

Planning for Child Development Package
CIJE: 0 RIE: 2 CAT: 15

Planning for Guidance Excellence
CIJE: 0 RIE: 1 CAT: 19

Planning Implementing Evaluation Cycles
CIJE: 0 RIE: 2 CAT: 15

Planning Management and Evaluation System
CIJE: 0 RIE: 1 CAT: 04

Planning Management Information System
CIJE: 2 RIE: 2 CAT: 15

Planning Monitoring Implementation Model
CIJE: 0 RIE: 7 CAT: 15

Planning Programming Budgeting Evaluation System
CIJE: 4 RIE: 7 CAT: 15

Planning Programming Budgeting System
CIJE: 81 RIE: 168 CAT: 15

Planning Resources in Minnesota Education
CIJE: 0 RIE: 2 CAT: 19

Planographic Prints
CIJE: 1 RIE: 0 CAT: 04

Plant Breeding
CIJE: 3 RIE: 0 CAT: 20

Plant Closings
USE Plant Shutdown

Plant Communities
CIJE: 1 RIE: 0 CAT: 16

Plant Hardiness
CIJE: 0 RIE: 0 CAT: 20

Plant Histology
CIJE: 1 RIE: 0 CAT: 20

Plant Hormones
CIJE: 2 RIE: 0 CAT: 20

Plant Morphology
CIJE: 2 RIE: 0 CAT: 20

Plant Physiology
CIJE: 14 RIE: 2 CAT: 20

Plant Poisons
CIJE: 2 RIE: 0 CAT: 20

Plant Process Operators
CIJE: 0 RIE: 1 CAT: 09
UF Process Plant Operators

Plant Proteins
CIJE: 2 RIE: 0 CAT: 20

Plant Shutdown
CIJE: 7 RIE: 9 CAT: 16
UF Plant Closings

Plant Uses
CIJE: 1 RIE: 3 CAT: 20

Planters Employee Training Program
CIJE: 0 RIE: 1 CAT: 19

Plaque (Dental)
CIJE: 1 RIE: 0 CAT: 11

Plasma Cortisol
USE Hydrocortisone

Plasma Lipoproteins
USE Lipoproteins

Plasterers
CIJE: 0 RIE: 9 CAT: 09

Plastering
CIJE: 0 RIE: 1 CAT: 20

Plasters
CIJE: 4 RIE: 4 CAT: 04

Plastic Bags
CIJE: 0 RIE: 1 CAT: 04

Plastic Surgery
CIJE: 5 RIE: 0 CAT: 11

Plastics and Composites Technology
CIJE: 0 RIE: 1 CAT: 03

Plate Waste
CIJE: 0 RIE: 1 CAT: 11

Plateau Tonga
CIJE: 1 RIE: 0 CAT: 08

Plater (William)
CIJE: 1 RIE: 0 CAT: 18

Platform Approach (Education)
CIJE: 2 RIE: 0 CAT: 15

Plath (Sylvia)
CIJE: 3 RIE: 3 CAT: 18

PLATO
CIJE: 144 RIE: 235 CAT: 04

PLATO II
CIJE: 0 RIE: 1 CAT: 04

PLATO III
CIJE: 0 RIE: 3 CAT: 04

PLATO IV
CIJE: 23 RIE: 107 CAT: 04

Plato of Athens
CIJE: 43 RIE: 20 CAT: 18

Platonic Solids (Mathematics)
CIJE: 1 RIE: 0 CAT: 20

PLATS Project
CIJE: 0 RIE: 1 CAT: 19

Platte County R III Schools MO
CIJE: 0 RIE: 0 CAT: 17

Plausibility (Tests)
CIJE: 1 RIE: 1 CAT: 21

Plausibility (Texts)
CIJE: 1 RIE: 1 CAT: 16

Plausibility Approach
CIJE: 1 RIE: 2 CAT: 15

Plausibility Rating Scales
CIJE: 1 RIE: 0 CAT: 21

Play Centers
CIJE: 10 RIE: 6 CAT: 05

Play Day Activities
USE Playdays

Play Leaders
CIJE: 2 RIE: 2 CAT: 10

Play Learning
CIJE: 22 RIE: 8 CAT: 16

Play Materials
CIJE: 22 RIE: 7 CAT: 16

Play Schools Association
CIJE: 0 RIE: 1 CAT: 17

Play Session Behavior Scale (Hirsch et al)
CIJE: 0 RIE: 1 CAT: 21

Play Situation Picture Sociometric Test (Boger)
CIJE: 0 RIE: 1 CAT: 21

Play Style
CIJE: 5 RIE: 4 CAT: 16

Play Theory
CIJE: 0 RIE: 0 CAT: 15

Playboy of the Western World
CIJE: 1 RIE: 0 CAT: 22

Playcentres
CIJE: 0 RIE: 1 CAT: 05

Playdays
CIJE: 0 RIE: 1 CAT: 12
UF Play Day Activities

Player (Willa)
CIJE: 2 RIE: 0 CAT: 18

Playful Literacy
CIJE: 0 RIE: 1 CAT: 15

Playfulness
CIJE: 2 RIE: 2 CAT: 16

Playground Design
CIJE: 12 RIE: 4 CAT: 16

Playground Equipment
CIJE: 20 RIE: 8 CAT: 04

Playground Progress Sheet
CIJE: 1 RIE: 0 CAT: 21

Playgroups
CIJE: 21 RIE: 12 CAT: 16

PLAYTEST
CIJE: 1 RIE: 0 CAT: 21

Playwrights
CIJE: 5 RIE: 5 CAT: 09

PlayWrite Program
CIJE: 0 RIE: 1 CAT: 19

Plea Bargaining
CIJE: 3 RIE: 2 CAT: 14

Pleasant Activities Survey
CIJE: 0 RIE: 1 CAT: 21

Pleasant Events Schedule
CIJE: 2 RIE: 0 CAT: 21

Pleasant Hill School IA
CIJE: 0 RIE: 2 CAT: 17

Pleasant View School for the Arts OH
CIJE: 0 RIE: 1 CAT: 17

Pleasantness
CIJE: 1 RIE: 1 CAT: 11

Pledge of Allegiance
CIJE: 12 RIE: 4 CAT: 22

PLESE
USE Program for Leadership in Earth Systems Education

Plessy v Ferguson
CIJE: 6 RIE: 5 CAT: 14

Pliny (The Elder)
CIJE: 0 RIE: 1 CAT: 18

Pliny (The Younger)
CIJE: 1 RIE: 0 CAT: 18

PLISSIT Model
CIJE: 0 RIE: 1 CAT: 15
SN PLISSIT = Permission, Little Information, Some Suggestions, Intensive Therapy

Plosives (Phonology)
CIJE: 1 RIE: 1 CAT: 13

Plot (Fiction)
CIJE: 24 RIE: 6 CAT: 16

Plot Method
CIJE: 0 RIE: 2 CAT: 15

Plot Titles Test
CIJE: 0 RIE: 1 CAT: 21

Plotinus
CIJE: 1 RIE: 0 CAT: 18

Plotters (Computers)
USE Computer Plotters

Plowden Report
CIJE: 32 RIE: 3 CAT: 22
SN 1967 report of the Central Advisory Council for Education (England)
UF Children and Their Primary Schools

Plumbers
CIJE: 1 RIE: 2 CAT: 09

Pluralism
CIJE: 26 RIE: 16 CAT: 16

Pluralistic Education
CIJE: 10 RIE: 2 CAT: 16

Pluralistic Ignorance
CIJE: 1 RIE: 1 CAT: 16

Pluralistic Method
CIJE: 1 RIE: 2 CAT: 16

PLUS Program
CIJE: 0 RIE: 5 CAT: 19

PLUS Program (Literacy)
USE Project Literacy U S

PLUS Program (Loans)
USE Parent Loans for Undergraduate Students Program

Plutarch
CIJE: 1 RIE: 2 CAT: 18

Plutchik Exploratory Interest Questionnaire
CIJE: 0 RIE: 2 CAT: 21

Pluto (Planet)
CIJE: 1 RIE: 0 CAT: 20

Plutonium
CIJE: 4 RIE: 0 CAT: 20

Plymouth Canton Community Schools MI
CIJE: 1 RIE: 0 CAT: 17

Plymouth Polytechnic (England)
CIJE: 2 RIE: 1 CAT: 17

Plymouth State College NH
CIJE: 3 RIE: 4 CAT: 17

Pneudraulics
CIJE: 0 RIE: 2 CAT: 20

Pneumatics
CIJE: 1 RIE: 10 CAT: 20

Pneumonia
CIJE: 2 RIE: 1 CAT: 11

PNGE
USE Pre Nursing and Guidance Examination

Po Pay
CIJE: 0 RIE: 1 CAT: 18

PO Relationship
USE Person Object Relationship

Pockets
CIJE: 0 RIE: 1 CAT: 16

POCO Project (Netherlands)
CIJE: 0 RIE: 1 CAT: 19
SN National educational software development project

Pocono Environmental Education Center PA
CIJE: 2 RIE: 0 CAT: 17

Podiatrists
CIJE: 0 RIE: 2 CAT: 09

Poe (Edgar Allan)
CIJE: 6 RIE: 2 CAT: 18

Poe Inventory of Values
CIJE: 0 RIE: 2 CAT: 21

Poetic Forms
CIJE: 1 RIE: 1 CAT: 16

Poetic Humanism
CIJE: 0 RIE: 1 CAT: 16

Poetics
CIJE: 15 RIE: 5 CAT: 03

Poetics of Music
CIJE: 1 RIE: 0 CAT: 03

Poetry in the Schools
CIJE: 0 RIE: 4 CAT: 03

Poetry Workshops
CIJE: 0 RIE: 2 CAT: 16

Poetrywriter (Computer Program)
CIJE: 0 RIE: 1 CAT: 04

Poets in the Schools
CIJE: 11 RIE: 14 CAT: 19

Poggendorff Illusion
CIJE: 2 RIE: 1 CAT: 20

Poggioli (Renato)
CIJE: 1 RIE: 0 CAT: 18

Poindron Study
CIJE: 1 RIE: 0 CAT: 19

Point and Query Interface
CIJE: 0 RIE: 1 CAT: 04

Point Biserial Correlation
CIJE: 10 RIE: 9 CAT: 15

Point Diffusion Patterns
CIJE: 0 RIE: 1 CAT: 21

Point Loma Nazarene College CA
CIJE: 0 RIE: 1 CAT: 17

Point System
CIJE: 1 RIE: 3 CAT: 15

Pointing (Gesture)
CIJE: 4 RIE: 0 CAT: 16

Pointing Behavior
CIJE: 1 RIE: 4 CAT: 11

Points of View (Writing)
CIJE: 18 RIE: 9 CAT: 15

Poisonous Plants
CIJE: 0 RIE: 1 CAT: 20

Poisson Distribution
CIJE: 19 RIE: 4 CAT: 15

Poisson Gaussian Distribution
USE Gaussian Poisson Distribution

Poisson Probability Distribution
CIJE: 2 RIE: 2 CAT: 20

Poisson Process
CIJE: 12 RIE: 2 CAT: 15

Pok O MacCready Outdoor Education Center NY
CIJE: 0 RIE: 1 CAT: 17

Poland
CIJE: 195 RIE: 214 CAT: 07

Poland (Warsaw)
CIJE: 5 RIE: 1 CAT: 07

Poland Ministry of Higher Education
USE Ministry of Higher Education (Poland)

Polanski (Roman)
CIJE: 2 RIE: 0 CAT: 18

Polanyi (Michael)
CIJE: 12 RIE: 5 CAT: 18

Polar Coordinates
CIJE: 7 RIE: 0 CAT: 20

Polar Regions
CIJE: 1 RIE: 0 CAT: 07

Polaris Project WV
CIJE: 0 RIE: 0 CAT: 19

Polarity
CIJE: 7 RIE: 2 CAT: 20

Polarized Filters
CIJE: 6 RIE: 0 CAT: 04

Polarography
CIJE: 2 RIE: 0 CAT: 20

Polaroid Cameras
CIJE: 5 RIE: 2 CAT: 04

Polaroid Corporation
CIJE: 0 RIE: 2 CAT: 17

Polaroid Inner City Inc
CIJE: 0 RIE: 2 CAT: 17
UF Inner City Inc (Polaroid)

Pole (Thomas)
CIJE: 0 RIE: 1 CAT: 18

Pole Vaulting
CIJE: 1 RIE: 1 CAT: 16

Pole Zero Map Analysis
CIJE: 0 RIE: 1 CAT: 15

Police Abuse
CIJE: 2 RIE: 0 CAT: 14

Police and Citizens Together Against Crime
CIJE: 0 RIE: 1 CAT: 17

Police Background Information Form
CIJE: 0 RIE: 1 CAT: 21

Police Knowledge Test
CIJE: 0 RIE: 1 CAT: 21

Police Liaison Program (British Columbia)
CIJE: 0 RIE: 1 CAT: 19

Police Opinion Questionnaire
CIJE: 0 RIE: 2 CAT: 21

Police Science
CIJE: 1 RIE: 1 CAT: 16

Police Standards Act 1967 (Florida)
CIJE: 0 RIE: 1 CAT: 14

Policies Commission Business Economic Education
CIJE: 6 RIE: 0 CAT: 17

Policy Analysis and Simulation System
CIJE: 0 RIE: 1 CAT: 04
UF PASS (Computer Program)

Policy Capturing Method
CIJE: 0 RIE: 3 CAT: 15

Policy Debate
CIJE: 13 RIE: 3 CAT: 15
SN Activity in debate tournaments — see also "Nonpolicy Debate"

Policy Effectiveness
CIJE: 5 RIE: 6 CAT: 16

Policy Forums on Employability Development
CIJE: 0 RIE: 1 CAT: 02

Policy Goal Percentaging Analysis
CIJE: 2 RIE: 0 CAT: 15

Policy Implementation
CIJE: 31 RIE: 38 CAT: 15

Policy Implications
CIJE: 35 RIE: 24 CAT: 16

Policy Interpretation
CIJE: 3 RIE: 2 CAT: 15

Policy Issue Networks
CIJE: 0 RIE: 1 CAT: 15

Policy Issues
CIJE: 38 RIE: 33 CAT: 16

Policy Making Groups
USE Policymakers

Policy Negotiation Simulation
CIJE: 0 RIE: 2 CAT: 15

Policy Research
CIJE: 24 RIE: 23 CAT: 15

Policy Reviews
CIJE: 1 RIE: 1 CAT: 16

Policymakers
CIJE: 31 RIE: 15 CAT: 10
UF Policy Making Groups

Polier (Justine Wise)
CIJE: 1 RIE: 0 CAT: 18

PoliNet
CIJE: 1 RIE: 1 CAT: 17

Polio Vaccines
CIJE: 0 RIE: 2 CAT: 11

Polish English Contrastive Project
CIJE: 0 RIE: 3 CAT: 19

Polish People
CIJE: 6 RIE: 9 CAT: 08

Polish Proficiency Test
CIJE: 0 RIE: 1 CAT: 21

Politeness
CIJE: 52 RIE: 33 CAT: 11

Political Action
CIJE: 24 RIE: 8 CAT: 16

Political Action Committees
CIJE: 10 RIE: 2 CAT: 10
UF PACs

Political Advertising
CIJE: 19 RIE: 24 CAT: 16
SN See also "Political Commercials"

Political Aides
CIJE: 1 RIE: 2 CAT: 09

Political Analysis
CIJE: 11 RIE: 15 CAT: 15

Political and Economic Planning
CIJE: 1 RIE: 1 CAT: 15

Political Appointments
CIJE: 1 RIE: 0 CAT: 16

Political Bargaining Model
CIJE: 0 RIE: 1 CAT: 15

Political Candidate Image
USE Political Image

Political Cartoonists
CIJE: 4 RIE: 1 CAT: 09

Political Cartoons
CIJE: 16 RIE: 10 CAT: 16

Political Commercials
CIJE: 2 RIE: 0 CAT: 16

Political Communication
CIJE: 33 RIE: 55 CAT: 16

Political Consultants
CIJE: 0 RIE: 1 CAT: 09

Political Correctness
CIJE: 62 RIE: 14 CAT: 16
SN See also "Politically Correct Communication"

Political Criticism
CIJE: 5 RIE: 3 CAT: 16

Political Culture
CIJE: 7 RIE: 7 CAT: 16

Political Economics
CIJE: 19 RIE: 6 CAT: 03

Political Education
CIJE: 36 RIE: 12 CAT: 03

Political Education Project (Canada)
CIJE: 1 RIE: 1 CAT: 19

Political Efficacy
CIJE: 6 RIE: 2 CAT: 16

Political Endorsements
CIJE: 5 RIE: 5 CAT: 16

Political Framing
CIJE: 0 RIE: 1 CAT: 15

Political History
CIJE: 37 RIE: 17 CAT: 12

Political Image
CIJE: 13 RIE: 17 CAT: 16
UF Political Candidate Image

Political Implications
CIJE: 4 RIE: 5 CAT: 16

Political Institutions Simulation Laboratory
CIJE: 1 RIE: 0 CAT: 17

Political Knowledge Test (Patrick)
CIJE: 1 RIE: 0 CAT: 21

Political Language
USE Political Rhetoric

Political Legitimacy
CIJE: 3 RIE: 4 CAT: 16
SN See also "Legitimacy (of Governments)"

Political Literacy
CIJE: 0 RIE: 2 CAT: 15

Political Literature
CIJE: 0 RIE: 1 CAT: 16

Political Messages
USE Political Rhetoric

Political Military Exercises
CIJE: 0 RIE: 1 CAT: 16

Political Party Conventions
CIJE: 7 RIE: 5 CAT: 02

Political Reapportionment
CIJE: 2 RIE: 0 CAT: 14

Political Redistricting
CIJE: 1 RIE: 1 CAT: 14

Political Rhetoric
CIJE: 58 RIE: 38 CAT: 13
UF Election Rhetoric; Language of Politics; Political Language; Political Messages

Political Science Curriculum Project
CIJE: 0 RIE: 1 CAT: 19

Political Science Skills Test (Patrick)
CIJE: 1 RIE: 0 CAT: 21

Political Sociology
CIJE: 2 RIE: 2 CAT: 03

Political Symbols
CIJE: 0 RIE: 1 CAT: 16
UF Symbols (Political)

Political Theories
CIJE: 34 RIE: 6 CAT: 15

Political World Interview
CIJE: 0 RIE: 1 CAT: 22

Political Writing
USE Civic Writing

Politically Correct Communication
CIJE: 19 RIE: 16 CAT: 16
SN See also "Political Correctness," "Hate Speech," "Speech Codes"

Politicians
CIJE: 25 RIE: 9 CAT: 09

Politics and the English Language
CIJE: 2 RIE: 1 CAT: 22

Politics of Education Association
CIJE: 0 RIE: 1 CAT: 17

Polk (James K)
CIJE: 4 RIE: 1 CAT: 18

Polk Community College FL
CIJE: 1 RIE: 8 CAT: 17

Polk County School District FL
CIJE: 1 RIE: 1 CAT: 17

Polk Education Association
CIJE: 1 RIE: 0 CAT: 17

Polka Dot Door
CIJE: 0 RIE: 1 CAT: 22

Poll (Influence)
CIJE: 3 RIE: 4 CAT: 16

Pollack Intersensory Reading Method
CIJE: 0 RIE: 1 CAT: 15

Pollen
CIJE: 8 RIE: 0 CAT: 20

Pollutant Concentrations
CIJE: 2 RIE: 3 CAT: 20

Pollutants
CIJE: 12 RIE: 15 CAT: 20

Pollution Control Center
CIJE: 1 RIE: 0 CAT: 17

Pollution Index
CIJE: 1 RIE: 0 CAT: 16

Polo (Marco)
CIJE: 1 RIE: 1 CAT: 18

Poly Hockey
CIJE: 0 RIE: 0 CAT: 16

Polya (George)
CIJE: 11 RIE: 5 CAT: 18

Polybius
CIJE: 0 RIE: 1 CAT: 18

Polychlorinated Biphenyls
CIJE: 7 RIE: 1 CAT: 20
UF PCBs

Polychotomous Responses
CIJE: 1 RIE: 0 CAT: 21

Polychotomous Scoring
CIJE: 3 RIE: 5 CAT: 21

Polyclinic Medical Center PA
CIJE: 0 RIE: 1 CAT: 17

Polyester
CIJE: 0 RIE: 1 CAT: 20

Polyethylene
CIJE: 2 RIE: 0 CAT: 20

Polyethylene Glycol
CIJE: 2 RIE: 0 CAT: 20

Polygamy
CIJE: 4 RIE: 2 CAT: 16

Polyglot Dyslexia
CIJE: 0 RIE: 1 CAT: 11

Polyhalides
CIJE: 1 RIE: 0 CAT: 20

Polymer Chemistry
CIJE: 31 RIE: 4 CAT: 20

Polynesia
CIJE: 4 RIE: 6 CAT: 07

Polynesian Languages
CIJE: 0 RIE: 1 CAT: 13

Polynesian Literature
CIJE: 0 RIE: 1 CAT: 16

Polynesians
CIJE: 2 RIE: 4 CAT: 08

Polynomial Regression Models
CIJE: 1 RIE: 3 CAT: 15

Polyphasic Values Inventory
CIJE: 1 RIE: 0 CAT: 21

Polyphonic Music
CIJE: 1 RIE: 0 CAT: 16

Polyphony (Linguistics)
CIJE: 0 RIE: 0 CAT: 13
SN The representation of different sounds by the same letter or symbol

Polysemous Words
CIJE: 0 RIE: 2 CAT: 13

Polysemy
CIJE: 5 RIE: 2 CAT: 13

Polyserial Correlation
CIJE: 2 RIE: 1 CAT: 21

Polysynthesis
CIJE: 0 RIE: 1 CAT: 13

Polytechnic Institute of Brooklyn NY
CIJE: 3 RIE: 2 CAT: 17
SN Renamed "Polytechnic Institute of New York"

Polytechnic Institute of New York
CIJE: 3 RIE: 2 CAT: 17
SN Was "Polytechnic Inst of Brooklyn" — Renamed again as "Polytechnic University, Brooklyn Campus"

Polytechnic of Central London (England)
CIJE: 2 RIE: 2 CAT: 17

Polytechnic of North London (England)
CIJE: 2 RIE: 0 CAT: 17

Polytechnic of the South Bank (England)
CIJE: 1 RIE: 0 CAT: 17

Polytechnics
CIJE: 14 RIE: 10 CAT: 16

Polytomous Items
CIJE: 4 RIE: 5 CAT: 21

Polytomous Scoring
CIJE: 4 RIE: 4 CAT: 21

Polytomous Variables
CIJE: 4 RIE: 0 CAT: 15

Polytope (Geometry)
CIJE: 0 RIE: 1 CAT: 20

Polyurethane
CIJE: 3 RIE: 0 CAT: 20

Polywater
CIJE: 3 RIE: 0 CAT: 20

Pomeroy House CA
CIJE: 0 RIE: 1 CAT: 17

Pomfret School CT
CIJE: 1 RIE: 0 CAT: 17

Pomona College CA
CIJE: 6 RIE: 5 CAT: 17

Pomona College Goals Conference Survey
CIJE: 0 RIE: 1 CAT: 21

Ponape Islands Central High School TT
CIJE: 1 RIE: 0 CAT: 17

Ponapean
CIJE: 0 RIE: 15 CAT: 13

Ponca (Tribe)
CIJE: 2 RIE: 5 CAT: 08

Ponce Technological University College PR
USE University of Puerto Rico Ponce Techn Univ Coll

Ponds
CIJE: 10 RIE: 4 CAT: 20

Pontiac Bilingual Program (Michigan)
CIJE: 0 RIE: 1 CAT: 19

Pontiac City School System MI
CIJE: 2 RIE: 3 CAT: 17

Pontiac Objective Referenced Test
CIJE: 0 RIE: 1 CAT: 21

Ponzo Illusion
CIJE: 3 RIE: 1 CAT: 11

Pooh Step by Step Guide
CIJE: 0 RIE: 1 CAT: 22

Poole (Ernest)
CIJE: 0 RIE: 1 CAT: 18

Pooled Least Squares Method
CIJE: 0 RIE: 3 CAT: 21

Poospatuck (Tribe)
CIJE: 0 RIE: 2 CAT: 08

Pop Up Books
CIJE: 7 RIE: 1 CAT: 16

Popcorn
CIJE: 2 RIE: 1 CAT: 20

Popcorn Factory
CIJE: 1 RIE: 0 CAT: 16

Pope (Alexander)
CIJE: 5 RIE: 1 CAT: 18

Pope John Paul II
USE John Paul II (Pope)

Popham (W J)
CIJE: 0 RIE: 1 CAT: 18

Popham (W James)
CIJE: 1 RIE: 1 CAT: 18

Popper (Karl)
CIJE: 10 RIE: 4 CAT: 18
SN "Sir Karl"

POPS Program
USE Power of Positive Students Program

Popular Education
CIJE: 19 RIE: 16 CAT: 03

Popular Music
CIJE: 33 RIE: 22 CAT: 16

Population
CIJE: 12 RIE: 6 CAT: 20
SN Use a more specific term if possible, e.g., "Farm Population," "World Population"

Population Aging
CIJE: 1 RIE: 5 CAT: 16
UF Aging Population

Population Awareness Education
CIJE: 3 RIE: 4 CAT: 03

Population Communication
CIJE: 0 RIE: 1 CAT: 20

Population Control
CIJE: 7 RIE: 17 CAT: 20

Population Council
CIJE: 0 RIE: 1 CAT: 17

Population Curriculum Study
CIJE: 0 RIE: 1 CAT: 03

Population Density
CIJE: 4 RIE: 0 CAT: 20

Population Ecology
CIJE: 5 RIE: 1 CAT: 15

Population Ecology Model
CIJE: 1 RIE: 1 CAT: 15

Population Education Project
CIJE: 0 RIE: 1 CAT: 19

Population Environment Curriculum Study
CIJE: 1 RIE: 0 CAT: 03

Population Information
CIJE: 7 RIE: 12 CAT: 20

Population Parameters
CIJE: 11 RIE: 8 CAT: 21

Population Policies
CIJE: 3 RIE: 9 CAT: 20

Population Projections
CIJE: 3 RIE: 6 CAT: 16

Population Stability
CIJE: 2 RIE: 1 CAT: 16
UF Stability (Population)

Population Validity
CIJE: 3 RIE: 2 CAT: 21

Populism
CIJE: 16 RIE: 7 CAT: 16

Populist Party
CIJE: 1 RIE: 3 CAT: 17

Populorum Progressio
CIJE: 0 RIE: 1 CAT: 22

Porcelain
CIJE: 0 RIE: 1 CAT: 20

Porch Index of Communicative Ability
CIJE: 2 RIE: 1 CAT: 21

Pork
CIJE: 0 RIE: 1 CAT: 20

PORPE Strategy
CIJE: 0 RIE: 2 CAT: 15
SN PORPE = "Predict, Organize, Rehearse, Practice, Evaluate"

Porpoises
CIJE: 0 RIE: 2 CAT: 20

Port Arthur Independent School District TX
CIJE: 0 RIE: 1 CAT: 17

Port Chester Public Schools NY
CIJE: 0 RIE: 1 CAT: 17

Port Huron School District MI
CIJE: 0 RIE: 1 CAT: 17

Port Jefferson High School NY
CIJE: 1 RIE: 0 CAT: 17

Portable Assisted Study Sequence Program
CIJE: 1 RIE: 14 CAT: 19
UF PASS Program (Migrant Education)

Portable Braille Recorder
CIJE: 0 RIE: 3 CAT: 04

Portable Dust Collector
CIJE: 1 RIE: 0 CAT: 04

Portable Laboratory Modules
CIJE: 1 RIE: 0 CAT: 04

Portable Practical Educational Preparation Inc AZ
CIJE: 0 RIE: 4 CAT: 17

Portable Rod and Frame Test
CIJE: 1 RIE: 3 CAT: 21

Portable Software
CIJE: 18 RIE: 1 CAT: 04

Portage Curriculum
CIJE: 0 RIE: 1 CAT: 03

Portage Project
CIJE: 5 RIE: 10 CAT: 19

Portal Schools
CIJE: 3 RIE: 13 CAT: 19

Portapak
CIJE: 3 RIE: 1 CAT: 04

Porter Elementary School NY
CIJE: 0 RIE: 1 CAT: 17

Porter Need Satisfaction Questionnaire
CIJE: 0 RIE: 4 CAT: 21

Porter Project
CIJE: 0 RIE: 1 CAT: 19

Porter Scale of Counselor Attitudes
CIJE: 1 RIE: 1 CAT: 21

Porters
CIJE: 0 RIE: 3 CAT: 09

Porterville College CA
CIJE: 0 RIE: 1 CAT: 17

Porteus Maze Test
CIJE: 4 RIE: 5 CAT: 21

Portion Sizes
CIJE: 1 RIE: 0 CAT: 16

Portis (Charles)
CIJE: 1 RIE: 0 CAT: 18

Portland Basic Skills Achievement Levels Testing
CIJE: 0 RIE: 14 CAT: 21

Portland Career Survey Project
CIJE: 0 RIE: 1 CAT: 19

Portland Cement Association
CIJE: 0 RIE: 7 CAT: 17

Portland Community College OR
CIJE: 2 RIE: 10 CAT: 17

Portland High School TN
CIJE: 1 RIE: 0 CAT: 17

Portland Hot Line Program
CIJE: 0 RIE: 1 CAT: 19

Portland Problem Behavior Checklist
CIJE: 0 RIE: 1 CAT: 21

Portland Project
CIJE: 1 RIE: 16 CAT: 19

Portland Public Schools ME
CIJE: 0 RIE: 3 CAT: 17

Portland Public Schools OR
USE Portland School District OR

Portland School District OR
CIJE: 16 RIE: 101 CAT: 17
UF Portland Public Schools OR

Portland Science Test
CIJE: 0 RIE: 2 CAT: 21

Portland State College OR
CIJE: 0 RIE: 3 CAT: 17

Portland State University OR
CIJE: 15 RIE: 20 CAT: 17

Portraits
CIJE: 13 RIE: 4 CAT: 04

Portrayal (Reporting Method)
CIJE: 1 RIE: 2 CAT: 15

Portsmouth College of Technology (England)
CIJE: 1 RIE: 0 CAT: 17

Portsmouth School Administrative Unit NH
CIJE: 0 RIE: 1 CAT: 17

Portugal
CIJE: 66 RIE: 90 CAT: 07

Portugal (Lisbon)
CIJE: 0 RIE: 1 CAT: 07

Portuguese (Brazilian)
CIJE: 11 RIE: 10 CAT: 13

Portuguese Language Development Group
CIJE: 0 RIE: 1 CAT: 17

Portuguese Literature
CIJE: 1 RIE: 0 CAT: 16

Portuguese People
CIJE: 3 RIE: 3 CAT: 08

Posada (Jose Guadalupe)
CIJE: 0 RIE: 2 CAT: 18

POSIT Tutoring System
CIJE: 0 RIE: 1 CAT: 04
SN Intelligent tutoring system for whole-number subtraction

Position Analysis
CIJE: 1 RIE: 1 CAT: 15

Position Analysis Questionnaire
CIJE: 10 RIE: 13 CAT: 21

Position Classification Inventory
CIJE: 0 RIE: 1 CAT: 15

Position Description Questionnaire
CIJE: 0 RIE: 1 CAT: 21

Positional Visibility
CIJE: 1 RIE: 0 CAT: 16

Positioning (Advertising)
CIJE: 2 RIE: 1 CAT: 16

Positioning (of Disabled)
CIJE: 7 RIE: 3 CAT: 11

Positioning (Patients)
CIJE: 2 RIE: 3 CAT: 11

Positive Adolescents Choices Training Program
CIJE: 0 RIE: 1 CAT: 19

Positive Affect
CIJE: 11 RIE: 6 CAT: 11

Positive Approach to Discipline System
CIJE: 0 RIE: 1 CAT: 15

Positive Approaches to Childrens Education IV
USE PACE IV

Positive Approaches to Childrens Education VI
USE PACE VI

Positive Attitudes
CIJE: 23 RIE: 25 CAT: 16

Positive Attitudes in Tennessee Schools
CIJE: 0 RIE: 3 CAT: 19
SN Tennessee college-school partnership program

Positive Disintegration Theory
CIJE: 1 RIE: 1 CAT: 15
UF Dabrowski Theory of Positive Disintegration

Positive Education Program
CIJE: 0 RIE: 2 CAT: 19

Positive Employment Relations Program
CIJE: 0 RIE: 1 CAT: 19
UF PERP Model

Positive Impact Program
CIJE: 0 RIE: 2 CAT: 19

Positive Instances
CIJE: 4 RIE: 0 CAT: 21

Positive Justice Interview (Damon)
CIJE: 1 RIE: 1 CAT: 21

Positive Peer Influence Program
CIJE: 0 RIE: 1 CAT: 19

Positive Regard Scale (Ross and Walters)
CIJE: 1 RIE: 0 CAT: 21

Positive Reinforcement Observation Schedule
CIJE: 3 RIE: 1 CAT: 21

Positive Resiliency in Special Education
CIJE: 0 RIE: 1 CAT: 03
UF PRISE Curriculum

Positive Stipulation
CIJE: 1 RIE: 0 CAT: 15

Positive Uncertainty
CIJE: 1 RIE: 1 CAT: 11

Positive Wording (Tests)
CIJE: 2 RIE: 0 CAT: 21

Positivism
CIJE: 78 RIE: 25 CAT: 15

Posner Snyder Theory
CIJE: 1 RIE: 0 CAT: 15

Posner Task
CIJE: 0 RIE: 1 CAT: 21

Possession Negotiations
CIJE: 0 RIE: 2 CAT: 11

Possessive Individualism
CIJE: 1 RIE: 1 CAT: 15

Possessives
CIJE: 12 RIE: 11 CAT: 13

Possessor Ascension
CIJE: 0 RIE: 1 CAT: 13

Possessor Omission
CIJE: 0 RIE: 1 CAT: 13

Possible Selves
CIJE: 1 RIE: 2 CAT: 11

Post Adjunct Questioning
CIJE: 2 RIE: 1 CAT: 21

Post Admission Preenrollment Testing
CIJE: 1 RIE: 0 CAT: 21

Post Divorce Parental Conflict Scale
CIJE: 0 RIE: 1 CAT: 21

Post Evaluative Conference Rating Scale
CIJE: 0 RIE: 1 CAT: 21

Post High School Experience
CIJE: 0 RIE: 2 CAT: 16

Post Hoc Block Design
CIJE: 1 RIE: 0 CAT: 21

Post Hoc Methods
CIJE: 13 RIE: 11 CAT: 15

Post Hoc Tests
CIJE: 1 RIE: 5 CAT: 21

Post Instructional Similarity Ratings
CIJE: 0 RIE: 1 CAT: 21

Post Literacy Programs
CIJE: 2 RIE: 11 CAT: 19

Post Maturation Treatment
CIJE: 1 RIE: 0 CAT: 11

Post Occupancy Evaluation
CIJE: 8 RIE: 0 CAT: 20

Post Office
CIJE: 4 RIE: 14 CAT: 17

Post Professional Study Centre
CIJE: 0 RIE: 3 CAT: 17

Post Secondary Education Assistance Prog (Canada)
CIJE: 0 RIE: 1 CAT: 19

Post Structural Criticism
USE Poststructuralism

Post Tenure Review
CIJE: 6 RIE: 2 CAT: 15

Post Traumatic Stress Syndrome
USE Posttraumatic Stress Disorder

Post Vietnam Era Veterans Educational Assistance
CIJE: 0 RIE: 2 CAT: 14

Post Wechsler Memory Scale
CIJE: 1 RIE: 0 CAT: 21

Postage
CIJE: 4 RIE: 2 CAT: 16

Postage Stamps
CIJE: 15 RIE: 4 CAT: 16

Postal Academy Program
CIJE: 0 RIE: 1 CAT: 19

Postal Service
CIJE: 17 RIE: 19 CAT: 17

Postal Workers
CIJE: 2 RIE: 7 CAT: 09

Postcards
CIJE: 9 RIE: 1 CAT: 16

Postcards from America (Novels)
CIJE: 0 RIE: 1 CAT: 22

Postconstructivism
CIJE: 0 RIE: 1 CAT: 15

Postdoctoral Faculty Fellowship Program
CIJE: 0 RIE: 1 CAT: 19

Postelthwait (Samuel N)
CIJE: 0 RIE: 1 CAT: 18

Posters
CIJE: 51 RIE: 15 CAT: 04

Postformal Adult Cognition
CIJE: 0 RIE: 1 CAT: 11

Posthospital Outcome
CIJE: 2 RIE: 1 CAT: 11

Posthypnotic Conflict
CIJE: 1 RIE: 0 CAT: 11

Postindustrial Society
CIJE: 19 RIE: 6 CAT: 16

Postindustrialism
CIJE: 7 RIE: 1 CAT: 16

Postman (Neil)
CIJE: 7 RIE: 2 CAT: 18

Postmodernism
CIJE: 122 RIE: 60 CAT: 15

Postmortem Care
CIJE: 0 RIE: 1 CAT: 11

Postnatal Influences
CIJE: 7 RIE: 13 CAT: 11

Postoperative Care
CIJE: 0 RIE: 1 CAT: 11

Postpartum
CIJE: 7 RIE: 5 CAT: 11

Postpartum Care
CIJE: 2 RIE: 7 CAT: 11

Postpartum Depression
CIJE: 11 RIE: 4 CAT: 11

Postpartum Education for Parents
CIJE: 1 RIE: 2 CAT: 17

Postpartum Services
CIJE: 2 RIE: 0 CAT: 11

Postpositivism
CIJE: 3 RIE: 1 CAT: 15

Postreading Activities
CIJE: 4 RIE: 3 CAT: 16

Postreinforcement Intervals
CIJE: 1 RIE: 0 CAT: 15

Postsecondary Education Council
CIJE: 0 RIE: 1 CAT: 17

Postsecondary Education Transcript Study
CIJE: 0 RIE: 6 CAT: 21
SN A supplement to the National Longitudinal Study of the High School Class of 1972

Postsecondary Enrollment Options Act (Minnesota)
CIJE: 1 RIE: 3 CAT: 14

Poststructuralism
CIJE: 48 RIE: 14 CAT: 15
UF Post Structural Criticism

Posttraumatic Stress Disorder
CIJE: 70 RIE: 33 CAT: 11
UF Post Traumatic Stress Syndrome

Postural Reflex Dysfunction
CIJE: 1 RIE: 0 CAT: 11

Postvention
CIJE: 1 RIE: 2 CAT: 15

Potassium
CIJE: 3 RIE: 0 CAT: 20

Potassium Depletion (Physiology)
CIJE: 1 RIE: 1 CAT: 11

Potassium Hexacyanocobaltate
CIJE: 1 RIE: 0 CAT: 20

Potassium Trioxalatoferrate Trihydrate
CIJE: 1 RIE: 0 CAT: 20

Potawatomi (Tribe)
CIJE: 1 RIE: 10 CAT: 08

Potential Aviator Rating Forms
CIJE: 0 RIE: 1 CAT: 21

Potential Curves
CIJE: 1 RIE: 0 CAT: 15

Potential Evaluation Program (Polster and Rosen)
CIJE: 1 RIE: 0 CAT: 21

Potential for Improving Performance
CIJE: 0 RIE: 1 CAT: 15
UF PIP Formula

Potential Markers
CIJE: 0 RIE: 1 CAT: 21

Potential Revenue Index
CIJE: 1 RIE: 1 CAT: 21

Potocki (Jan)
CIJE: 1 RIE: 0 CAT: 18

Potok (Chaim)
CIJE: 2 RIE: 0 CAT: 18

Potometers
CIJE: 2 RIE: 0 CAT: 04

Pott (Francis Lister)
CIJE: 1 RIE: 0 CAT: 18

Potter (Beatrix)
CIJE: 6 RIE: 1 CAT: 18

Pottery Workers
CIJE: 0 RIE: 1 CAT: 09

Potthoff Technique
CIJE: 0 RIE: 1 CAT: 15

Pottsville Free Public Library PA
CIJE: 0 RIE: 1 CAT: 17

Poudre School District CO
CIJE: 3 RIE: 0 CAT: 17

Poughkeepsie Middle School NY
CIJE: 0 RIE: 1 CAT: 17

Poulet (Georges)
CIJE: 2 RIE: 0 CAT: 18

Poultry
CIJE: 1 RIE: 11 CAT: 20

Poultry Farms
CIJE: 0 RIE: 3 CAT: 05

Pound (Ezra)
CIJE: 3 RIE: 1 CAT: 18

Pourbaix Diagrams
CIJE: 2 RIE: 0 CAT: 15

Poway Unified School District CA
CIJE: 2 RIE: 1 CAT: 17

Powell (John)
CIJE: 2 RIE: 1 CAT: 18

Powell (Lewis)
CIJE: 2 RIE: 1 CAT: 18

Power
CIJE: 62 RIE: 35 CAT: 16

Power (Statistics)
CIJE: 113 RIE: 70 CAT: 15

Power Conversion
CIJE: 0 RIE: 1 CAT: 20

Power Equalization
CIJE: 1 RIE: 5 CAT: 16

Power Failures
CIJE: 0 RIE: 1 CAT: 20

Power Lawn Mower Assemblers
CIJE: 0 RIE: 1 CAT: 09

Power Line Technicians
CIJE: 0 RIE: 1 CAT: 09

Power Load Margin Theory
USE Theory of Margin

Power of Positive Students Program
CIJE: 0 RIE: 1 CAT: 19
UF POPS Program

Power Perception Profile
CIJE: 1 RIE: 3 CAT: 21

Power Plant Operators
CIJE: 0 RIE: 8 CAT: 09

Power Plants
CIJE: 6 RIE: 15 CAT: 05

Power Ratio
CIJE: 0 RIE: 1 CAT: 21

Power Restoration Theory
CIJE: 0 RIE: 1 CAT: 15

Power Scores
CIJE: 0 RIE: 1 CAT: 15

Power Strategies
CIJE: 19 RIE: 7 CAT: 15

Power Struggles
CIJE: 13 RIE: 4 CAT: 16

Power Supplies
CIJE: 3 RIE: 2 CAT: 04

Power Supply Circuits
CIJE: 1 RIE: 1 CAT: 20

Power Tools
CIJE: 1 RIE: 25 CAT: 04

Power Train Unit
CIJE: 1 RIE: 0 CAT: 04

Power Trains
CIJE: 0 RIE: 4 CAT: 20

Power Transmission
CIJE: 1 RIE: 6 CAT: 20

Powered Industrial Trucks
CIJE: 0 RIE: 1 CAT: 04

Powerhouse (Television Series)
CIJE: 0 RIE: 1 CAT: 22

Powhatan
CIJE: 1 RIE: 2 CAT: 18
SN Indian chief of Virginia (c1550-1618) — father of Pocahontas

Powhatan Goals of Education
CIJE: 1 RIE: 0 CAT: 19

Powhatan Indians
CIJE: 0 RIE: 0 CAT: 08
UF Powhatans; Powhatan Tribe

Powhatan Language
CIJE: 0 RIE: 0 CAT: 13

Powhatan Project
CIJE: 0 RIE: 1 CAT: 19

Powhatan Tribe
USE Powhatan Indians

Powhatans
USE Powhatan Indians

PPA
CIJE: 2 RIE: 1 CAT: 11
UF Phenylpropanolamine

PPNSIE
CIJE: 1 RIE: 0 CAT: 21
SN Preschool-Primary Nowicki-Strickland Internal-External Control Scale

PPST
USE Pre Professional Skills Tests

Pracademics
CIJE: 0 RIE: 2 CAT: 15

Practical Bible Training School NY
CIJE: 0 RIE: 3 CAT: 17

Practical Experience Phases
CIJE: 1 RIE: 0 CAT: 15

Practical Knowledge
CIJE: 24 RIE: 4 CAT: 16

Practical Reasoning
CIJE: 11 RIE: 2 CAT: 15

Practical Tests
CIJE: 5 RIE: 1 CAT: 21

Practical Work Orientation Program
CIJE: 2 RIE: 1 CAT: 19

Practical Writing
CIJE: 0 RIE: 1 CAT: 03

Practice File (ERIC)
USE National Education Practice File

Practice Profiles
CIJE: 1 RIE: 3 CAT: 15

Practice Questions
CIJE: 0 RIE: 1 CAT: 16

Practice Tests
CIJE: 7 RIE: 8 CAT: 21

Practitioner Involvement (Research)
CIJE: 2 RIE: 4 CAT: 15

Practitioners
CIJE: 18 RIE: 10 CAT: 10

Prader Willi Syndrome
CIJE: 15 RIE: 2 CAT: 11

Pragmalinguistics
CIJE: 4 RIE: 0 CAT: 13

Pragmatism
CIJE: 45 RIE: 11 CAT: 16

Prairie Elementary School IL
CIJE: 0 RIE: 1 CAT: 17

Prairie Home Companion (A)
CIJE: 1 RIE: 1 CAT: 22

Prairie State 2000
CIJE: 0 RIE: 1 CAT: 19

Prairie State College IL
CIJE: 1 RIE: 2 CAT: 17

Prairie View A and M University TX
CIJE: 4 RIE: 1 CAT: 17

Prairies
CIJE: 0 RIE: 1 CAT: 20

Prang (Mary Dana Hicks)
CIJE: 0 RIE: 1 CAT: 18

Pratt (Caroline)
CIJE: 1 RIE: 1 CAT: 18

Pratt Institute NY
CIJE: 2 RIE: 4 CAT: 17

Pravda
CIJE: 1 RIE: 2 CAT: 22

Praxiology
CIJE: 5 RIE: 3 CAT: 15

Praxis III
CIJE: 1 RIE: 1 CAT: 19

Prayer
CIJE: 17 RIE: 12 CAT: 16

Prayer Books
CIJE: 0 RIE: 1 CAT: 16

Praying Mantises
CIJE: 2 RIE: 0 CAT: 20

PRB (ED)
USE Publications Review Board

PRCA 24
USE Personal Report of Communication Apprehension

Pre Algebra
CIJE: 2 RIE: 6 CAT: 03

Pre Collegiate Education Quality Indicators
CIJE: 0 RIE: 1 CAT: 21

Pre Columbian History
CIJE: 7 RIE: 3 CAT: 16

Pre Doctoral Syndrome (Doctoral Students)
USE PreDoctoral Syndrome

Pre Equating (Tests)
CIJE: 1 RIE: 5 CAT: 21

Pre First Grade Transitional Programs
USE Extra Year Programs (Kindergarten)

Pre Nursing and Guidance Examination
CIJE: 0 RIE: 1 CAT: 21
UF PNGE

Pre Professional Skills Tests
CIJE: 3 RIE: 19 CAT: 21
UF PPST; Preprofessional Skills Test

Pre Reading Plan
CIJE: 0 RIE: 3 CAT: 03
UF PReP Activity; Prereading (PReP)

Pre Retirement Association
CIJE: 1 RIE: 0 CAT: 17

Pre Schoolers Workshop Rating Scale
CIJE: 0 RIE: 1 CAT: 21

Pre Speech Assessment Scale
CIJE: 0 RIE: 1 CAT: 21

Pre Structured Case Studies
USE Prestructured Cases

Pre Veterinary Students
CIJE: 0 RIE: 1 CAT: 10

Preadmission and Classification Examination
CIJE: 2 RIE: 1 CAT: 21

Preadolescent Motivation Inventory
CIJE: 0 RIE: 1 CAT: 21

Preapprenticeship Programs
CIJE: 0 RIE: 91 CAT: 19

Precamping
CIJE: 0 RIE: 2 CAT: 03

Precast Concrete
CIJE: 0 RIE: 1 CAT: 04

Precategorical Acoustic Storage
CIJE: 3 RIE: 0 CAT: 11

PRECEDE Model
CIJE: 6 RIE: 2 CAT: 15

Preceptors
CIJE: 7 RIE: 1 CAT: 09

Prechtl Beintema Neurological Examination
CIJE: 2 RIE: 0 CAT: 11

Precipitation
CIJE: 4 RIE: 3 CAT: 20

PRECIS
CIJE: 19 RIE: 3 CAT: 04

Precis Writing
CIJE: 3 RIE: 1 CAT: 13

Precision (Mathematics)
CIJE: 7 RIE: 4 CAT: 20

Precision Journalism
CIJE: 4 RIE: 2 CAT: 16

Precision Measuring Equipment Specialists
CIJE: 0 RIE: 1 CAT: 09

Precision Optics
CIJE: 0 RIE: 1 CAT: 20

Precision Ratios
CIJE: 2 RIE: 1 CAT: 21

Precision Referral Form (Hilfbrunner and Vasa)
CIJE: 1 RIE: 0 CAT: 21

Preclinical Performance
CIJE: 0 RIE: 1 CAT: 11

Precocious Learners
CIJE: 8 RIE: 2 CAT: 10

Precocious Readers
CIJE: 2 RIE: 1 CAT: 10

Precognition
CIJE: 0 RIE: 2 CAT: 16

Preconceptions
CIJE: 6 RIE: 1 CAT: 16

Preconference on the Recruitment of Minorities
CIJE: 1 RIE: 0 CAT: 02

Precounseling Interviews
CIJE: 1 RIE: 0 CAT: 11

Predation
CIJE: 6 RIE: 0 CAT: 20

Predator Prey Relationship
CIJE: 15 RIE: 0 CAT: 20

Predicate Calculus
CIJE: 1 RIE: 2 CAT: 03

Predicate Grammar
CIJE: 2 RIE: 2 CAT: 13

Predicate Matching
CIJE: 0 RIE: 1 CAT: 13

Predicate Raising
CIJE: 1 RIE: 0 CAT: 13

Predicate Structure
CIJE: 0 RIE: 1 CAT: 13

Predicate Subject Order
CIJE: 1 RIE: 3 CAT: 13

Predicates
CIJE: 11 RIE: 11 CAT: 13

Predicatid
CIJE: 0 RIE: 1 CAT: 13

Predictability (Language)
CIJE: 0 RIE: 1 CAT: 13

Predictable Books
CIJE: 8 RIE: 4 CAT: 16

Prediction Equation
CIJE: 1 RIE: 3 CAT: 15

Prediction Interval
CIJE: 1 RIE: 0 CAT: 21

Prediction with Diagnostic Qualities (Hillerich)
CIJE: 0 RIE: 1 CAT: 21

Predictive Analysis
CIJE: 2 RIE: 2 CAT: 15

Predictive Index (Miller)
CIJE: 1 RIE: 0 CAT: 21

Predictive Models
CIJE: 8 RIE: 10 CAT: 15

Predictive Reading
CIJE: 3 RIE: 2 CAT: 15
SN Making informed guesses about what will happen in a story

Predictive Screening Test of Articulation
CIJE: 4 RIE: 1 CAT: 21

Prediger (Dale J)
CIJE: 0 RIE: 1 CAT: 18

Predischarge Education Program
CIJE: 2 RIE: 3 CAT: 19

PreDoctoral Syndrome
CIJE: 0 RIE: 1 CAT: 11
UF Pre Doctoral Syndrome (Doctoral Students)

Predominantly White Colleges
USE White Colleges

Preemployment Courses
CIJE: 0 RIE: 2 CAT: 03

Preemployment Laboratory Education Program
CIJE: 0 RIE: 5 CAT: 19

Preemployment Skills
CIJE: 0 RIE: 2 CAT: 16

Preengineering Ability Test
CIJE: 1 RIE: 0 CAT: 21

Prefaces
CIJE: 2 RIE: 1 CAT: 16

PrefCalc
CIJE: 0 RIE: 1 CAT: 04

Preference Data
CIJE: 25 RIE: 12 CAT: 16

Preference Models
CIJE: 8 RIE: 0 CAT: 15

Preference Patterns
CIJE: 50 RIE: 20 CAT: 16

Preference Ranking
CIJE: 10 RIE: 2 CAT: 21

Preference Semantics
CIJE: 3 RIE: 0 CAT: 13

Preference Transitivity
CIJE: 3 RIE: 0 CAT: 16

Preference Trees
CIJE: 0 RIE: 1 CAT: 21
UF Pretree Model

Preferential Circles
CIJE: 0 RIE: 1 CAT: 16

Preferred Student Characteristic Scale
CIJE: 1 RIE: 0 CAT: 21

Preformation
CIJE: 1 RIE: 0 CAT: 20

Pregnancy and Perinatology Branch (NIH)
CIJE: 0 RIE: 1 CAT: 17
SN Unit of the National Institute of Child Health and Human Development

Pregnancy Discrimination Act 1978
CIJE: 3 RIE: 3 CAT: 14

Pregnancy Test Kits (Home)
USE Home Pregnancy Test Kits

Pregnant Teachers
CIJE: 6 RIE: 1 CAT: 10

Prehistoric Art
CIJE: 3 RIE: 1 CAT: 16

Prehistoric Times
CIJE: 0 RIE: 1 CAT: 12

Prekindergarten Activity Observation Checklist
CIJE: 0 RIE: 1 CAT: 21

Prekindergarten At Risk Program IL
CIJE: 0 RIE: 2 CAT: 19
UF Illinois Prekindergarten At Risk Program

Prekindergarten Saginaw Objective Reference Test
CIJE: 0 RIE: 3 CAT: 21

Prekindergarten Scale (Flynn)
CIJE: 1 RIE: 3 CAT: 21

Prekindergarten Teacher Problems Checklist
CIJE: 0 RIE: 1 CAT: 21

Prelanguage
CIJE: 3 RIE: 0 CAT: 13

Prelaw Curriculum
CIJE: 4 RIE: 3 CAT: 03

Preliminary American College Test Plus
CIJE: 1 RIE: 4 CAT: 21
UF PACT Plus

Preliminary Chinese Proficiency Test
CIJE: 0 RIE: 1 CAT: 21

Preliminary Scholastic Aptitude Test
CIJE: 6 RIE: 39 CAT: 21
UF PSAT

Preliminary Test of English as a Foreign Language
CIJE: 0 RIE: 1 CAT: 21
UF Preliminary TOEFL

Preliminary TOEFL
USE Preliminary Test of English as a Foreign Language

Prelinguistics
CIJE: 4 RIE: 3 CAT: 13

Preliterate Societies
CIJE: 3 RIE: 7 CAT: 10

Premack (D)
CIJE: 1 RIE: 0 CAT: 18

Premack Principle
CIJE: 3 RIE: 2 CAT: 15

Premackese
CIJE: 1 RIE: 0 CAT: 13

Premarital Abuse
CIJE: 2 RIE: 1 CAT: 11

Premarital Communication
CIJE: 2 RIE: 0 CAT: 11

Premarital Communication Inventory (Bienvena)
CIJE: 1 RIE: 0 CAT: 21

Premarital Counseling
CIJE: 16 RIE: 2 CAT: 16

Premarital Sex
CIJE: 25 RIE: 7 CAT: 11

Premarital Sexual Permissiveness Scale (Reiss)
CIJE: 0 RIE: 1 CAT: 21

Premarital Sexual Standards
CIJE: 2 RIE: 1 CAT: 21

Premature Termination of Treatment
CIJE: 1 RIE: 0 CAT: 11

Premature Termination Scale (Jochim)
CIJE: 1 RIE: 0 CAT: 21

Premedical Curriculum
CIJE: 17 RIE: 1 CAT: 03

Premenstrual Syndrome
CIJE: 9 RIE: 3 CAT: 11

Premorbid Adjustment
CIJE: 1 RIE: 0 CAT: 11

Pren Hall Foundation
CIJE: 0 RIE: 1 CAT: 17

Prenasalization
CIJE: 0 RIE: 1 CAT: 13

Prenatal Development
USE Fetal Development

Prenatal Exposure to Drugs
USE Fetal Drug Exposure

Prenatal Interviews
CIJE: 1 RIE: 1 CAT: 11

Preoperational Thought
CIJE: 3 RIE: 5 CAT: 11

Preoperative Care
CIJE: 0 RIE: 1 CAT: 11

Preordinate Model of Product Development
CIJE: 0 RIE: 1 CAT: 15

PReP Activity
USE Pre Reading Plan

Prep Reports
CIJE: 0 RIE: 2 CAT: 22

PREP Study System
CIJE: 0 RIE: 2 CAT: 15

Prepackaged Instruction
CIJE: 3 RIE: 0 CAT: 15

Prepackaged Lunches
CIJE: 1 RIE: 0 CAT: 16

Prepaid Tuition
USE Tuition Prepayment

Preparation for American Secondary Schools
CIJE: 0 RIE: 1 CAT: 19

Preparation for Employment Program
CIJE: 0 RIE: 1 CAT: 19

Preparation for Raising Educational Performance NY
CIJE: 1 RIE: 2 CAT: 19
UF Program to Raise Educational Performance NY

Preparation of English Teachers
CIJE: 0 RIE: 2 CAT: 19

Preparation through Responsive Educ Programs
CIJE: 0 RIE: 3 CAT: 19

Preparative Evaluation
CIJE: 2 RIE: 1 CAT: 21

Preparatory Studies
CIJE: 6 RIE: 0 CAT: 03

Prepare Educational Planners
CIJE: 0 RIE: 8 CAT: 19

Preparing for Profit
CIJE: 0 RIE: 1 CAT: 19

Preparing for Tomorrows World Program
CIJE: 0 RIE: 22 CAT: 19

Preparing Refugees for Elementary Programs
CIJE: 0 RIE: 2 CAT: 19

Prepayment (Tuition)
USE Tuition Prepayment

Prepayment Plans
CIJE: 12 RIE: 1 CAT: 16
SN See also "National Prepaid Tuition Program"

Preplay Learning Technique
CIJE: 0 RIE: 1 CAT: 15

Prepositional Phrases
CIJE: 4 RIE: 5 CAT: 13

Prepositional Verbs
CIJE: 1 RIE: 1 CAT: 13

Prepprenticeship Programs
CIJE: 0 RIE: 1 CAT: 19

Preprimary Enrollment
CIJE: 0 RIE: 1 CAT: 16

Preprimer
CIJE: 1 RIE: 2 CAT: 22

Preprofessional Skills Test
USE Pre Professional Skills Tests

Prepuberty
CIJE: 2 RIE: 1 CAT: 11

Prepublication Review
CIJE: 1 RIE: 1 CAT: 16

Prereading (PReP)
USE Pre Reading Plan

Prereading Activities
CIJE: 42 RIE: 44 CAT: 16

Prereading Exercises
CIJE: 3 RIE: 3 CAT: 03

Prereading Skills
CIJE: 4 RIE: 5 CAT: 16

Prereading Skills Battery
CIJE: 0 RIE: 2 CAT: 21

Prereading Skills Program
CIJE: 0 RIE: 8 CAT: 21

Prereferral Screening Instrument
CIJE: 0 RIE: 2 CAT: 21

Prerelease Programs
CIJE: 0 RIE: 1 CAT: 19

Prerequisite Principles and Skills (Gagne)
CIJE: 2 RIE: 0 CAT: 21

Prerequisite Waivers
CIJE: 0 RIE: 1 CAT: 16

Preretirement
CIJE: 5 RIE: 3 CAT: 16

Presbyterian Church
CIJE: 4 RIE: 4 CAT: 17

Presbyterian Hospital CA
CIJE: 0 RIE: 1 CAT: 17

Presbyterian Saint Lukes Hospital IL
CIJE: 1 RIE: 0 CAT: 17

Preschool Abilities Test
CIJE: 0 RIE: 1 CAT: 21

Preschool Attainment Record
CIJE: 9 RIE: 6 CAT: 21

Preschool Behavior Q Sort
CIJE: 0 RIE: 1 CAT: 21

Preschool Behavior Quest (Behar and Springfield)
CIJE: 3 RIE: 1 CAT: 21

Preschool Behavioral Classification Project
CIJE: 1 RIE: 1 CAT: 21

Preschool Connected Speech Inventory
CIJE: 0 RIE: 1 CAT: 21

Preschool Demonstration Project for Handicapped
CIJE: 0 RIE: 1 CAT: 19

Preschool Developmental Profile
CIJE: 0 RIE: 1 CAT: 21

Preschool Embedded Figures Test
CIJE: 4 RIE: 2 CAT: 21

Preschool Environment Inventory
CIJE: 0 RIE: 2 CAT: 21

PReschool Interest DEscriptor
CIJE: 2 RIE: 0 CAT: 21
UF PRIDE Inventory

Preschool Interest Inventory
CIJE: 0 RIE: 1 CAT: 21

Preschool Interpersonal Problem Solving Test
CIJE: 1 RIE: 5 CAT: 21

Preschool Inventory (Caldwell)
CIJE: 2 RIE: 38 CAT: 21

Preschool Kindergarten Readiness Inventory (Green)
CIJE: 0 RIE: 1 CAT: 21

Preschool Language Assessment Instrument
CIJE: 2 RIE: 1 CAT: 21

Preschool Language Curriculum
CIJE: 0 RIE: 1 CAT: 03

Preschool Language Project
CIJE: 0 RIE: 4 CAT: 19

Preschool Language Scale
CIJE: 10 RIE: 5 CAT: 21

Preschool Learning Development Program NJ
CIJE: 0 RIE: 1 CAT: 19

Preschool Mental Health Program
CIJE: 0 RIE: 1 CAT: 19

Preschool Outcomes Rating Scale
CIJE: 0 RIE: 1 CAT: 21

Preschool Personality Quest (Cattell Dreger)
CIJE: 1 RIE: 0 CAT: 21

Preschool Playgroups Association
CIJE: 3 RIE: 1 CAT: 17

Preschool Preposition Test
CIJE: 0 RIE: 6 CAT: 21

Preschool Racial Attitude Measure
CIJE: 2 RIE: 11 CAT: 21

Preschool Racial Attitude Measure II
CIJE: 1 RIE: 1 CAT: 21

Preschool Rating Scale
CIJE: 0 RIE: 1 CAT: 21

Preschool Recreation Enrichment Program
CIJE: 0 RIE: 5 CAT: 19

Preschool Reunion Behavior Scale
CIJE: 0 RIE: 1 CAT: 21

Preschool Screening Evaluation
CIJE: 1 RIE: 1 CAT: 21

Preschool Selection
CIJE: 0 RIE: 1 CAT: 16
SN See also "Day Care Selection"

Preschool Speech Production Test (Di Johnson)
CIJE: 0 RIE: 1 CAT: 21

Preschool Vigilance Task
CIJE: 0 RIE: 1 CAT: 21

Prescott Institutions
CIJE: 1 RIE: 0 CAT: 17

Prescription Athletic Turf
CIJE: 2 RIE: 0 CAT: 16

Prescription Drugs
CIJE: 8 RIE: 7 CAT: 11

Prescription Learning System
CIJE: 0 RIE: 3 CAT: 19

Prescription Writing (Medicine)
CIJE: 3 RIE: 1 CAT: 17

Prescriptive Counselor Model
CIJE: 0 RIE: 1 CAT: 15

Prescriptive Evaluation Plans
CIJE: 0 RIE: 1 CAT: 15

Prescriptive Grammar
CIJE: 2 RIE: 0 CAT: 13

Prescriptive Instructional Program Educ Readiness
CIJE: 0 RIE: 1 CAT: 21
UF PIPER

Prescriptive Mathematics Inventory
CIJE: 0 RIE: 2 CAT: 21

Prescriptive Reading Inventory
CIJE: 3 RIE: 16 CAT: 21

Prescriptive Research
CIJE: 3 RIE: 3 CAT: 15

Present Perfect Tense
CIJE: 3 RIE: 1 CAT: 13

Present Tense
CIJE: 2 RIE: 3 CAT: 13

Presentation Mode
CIJE: 17 RIE: 12 CAT: 21

Presentation Order
CIJE: 6 RIE: 0 CAT: 11

Presentation Rates
CIJE: 5 RIE: 0 CAT: 15

Preserved Context Indexing System
CIJE: 5 RIE: 4 CAT: 15

Preservice Educ for Teachers of Minorities HI
CIJE: 0 RIE: 1 CAT: 19

Preservice Stages of Concern Questionnaire
CIJE: 0 RIE: 1 CAT: 21

Preservice Teachers
CIJE: 82 RIE: 198 CAT: 10

Preserving a Quality Environment for Learning
CIJE: 0 RIE: 1 CAT: 02

Preseverational Syntax
CIJE: 1 RIE: 0 CAT: 13

Presidential Awards Excellence in Science and Math
CIJE: 3 RIE: 2 CAT: 20

Presidential Comm on Indian Reservation Economies
CIJE: 0 RIE: 1 CAT: 17

Presidential Initiatives
CIJE: 0 RIE: 4 CAT: 19

Presidential Internships Science and Engineering
CIJE: 0 RIE: 1 CAT: 19

Presidential Libraries
CIJE: 12 RIE: 5 CAT: 05

Presidential Messages
CIJE: 9 RIE: 7 CAT: 16

Presidential Primaries
CIJE: 4 RIE: 8 CAT: 16

Presidential Scholars
CIJE: 3 RIE: 0 CAT: 10

Presidential Task Force on Career Advancement
CIJE: 0 RIE: 1 CAT: 17

Presidential Young Investigators Program
CIJE: 0 RIE: 1 CAT: 19
UF PYI Awards

Presidents Academy
CIJE: 1 RIE: 0 CAT: 17

Presidents Advisory Commission on Rural Poverty
CIJE: 1 RIE: 0 CAT: 17

Presidents Comm Foreign Lang International Studies
CIJE: 13 RIE: 17 CAT: 17

Presidents Commission on Americans Outdoors
CIJE: 0 RIE: 2 CAT: 17

Presidents Committee on Employment of Handicapped
CIJE: 0 RIE: 5 CAT: 17

Presidents Committee on Health Education
CIJE: 1 RIE: 1 CAT: 17

Presidents Committee on Mental Retardation
CIJE: 0 RIE: 7 CAT: 17

Presidents Committee on Migratory Labor
CIJE: 0 RIE: 1 CAT: 17

Presidents Conference on Early Childhood Education
CIJE: 0 RIE: 1 CAT: 02

Presidents Council on Environmental Quality
CIJE: 3 RIE: 0 CAT: 17

Presidents Council on Physical Fitness and Sports
CIJE: 4 RIE: 4 CAT: 17

Presidents Council on Youth Opportunity
CIJE: 0 RIE: 1 CAT: 17

Presidents Day
CIJE: 0 RIE: 1 CAT: 12

Presidents Environmental Merit Awards Program
CIJE: 0 RIE: 1 CAT: 19

Presidents Excellence Club TX
CIJE: 0 RIE: 1 CAT: 19
SN Program of Midwestern State Univ.

Presidents Private Sector Survey on Cost Control
CIJE: 1 RIE: 1 CAT: 19

Presidents Scholars Survey
CIJE: 1 RIE: 0 CAT: 21

Presidents Science Advisory Committee
CIJE: 6 RIE: 3 CAT: 17

Presidents State of Union Message
CIJE: 0 RIE: 2 CAT: 22

Presidents Task Force on Communications Policy
CIJE: 1 RIE: 1 CAT: 17

Press Conferences
CIJE: 6 RIE: 6 CAT: 10

Press Councils
CIJE: 3 RIE: 1 CAT: 10
SN See also "News Councils"

Press Criticism
CIJE: 9 RIE: 7 CAT: 16

Press Enterprise Co v Superior Court
CIJE: 0 RIE: 0 CAT: 14

Press Law
CIJE: 4 RIE: 19 CAT: 14

Press Pools
CIJE: 1 RIE: 1 CAT: 10

Press Releases
CIJE: 12 RIE: 10 CAT: 16

Press Responsibility
CIJE: 8 RIE: 23 CAT: 16

Press Secretaries
CIJE: 1 RIE: 3 CAT: 09

Pressey (Sidney Leavitt)
CIJE: 2 RIE: 4 CAT: 18

Pressley Ridge Youth Development Extension PA
CIJE: 0 RIE: 1 CAT: 17

Pressure Groups
CIJE: 30 RIE: 7 CAT: 10

Prestatie Motivatie Test
CIJE: 2 RIE: 0 CAT: 21

Prestatistics Survey Test
CIJE: 1 RIE: 0 CAT: 21

Prestel
CIJE: 4 RIE: 8 CAT: 04

Presthus (Robert)
CIJE: 1 RIE: 0 CAT: 18

Prestige Forms (Language)
CIJE: 0 RIE: 1 CAT: 13

Prestige Languages
CIJE: 2 RIE: 2 CAT: 13

Preston (Joan)
CIJE: 1 RIE: 0 CAT: 18

Prestonsburg Community College KY
CIJE: 0 RIE: 1 CAT: 17

Prestructured Cases
CIJE: 0 RIE: 1 CAT: 16
UF Pre Structured Case Studies

Presumption (Debate)
CIJE: 0 RIE: 2 CAT: 16

Presupposition
CIJE: 13 RIE: 9 CAT: 13

Pretend Reading
CIJE: 4 RIE: 1 CAT: 16

Pretherapy
CIJE: 3 RIE: 2 CAT: 11

Pretraining
CIJE: 10 RIE: 4 CAT: 03

Pretree Model
USE Preference Trees

Pretrial Discovery Information
CIJE: 0 RIE: 1 CAT: 14

Pretty Eagle School MT
CIJE: 0 RIE: 1 CAT: 17

Prevention by Mail Programs
CIJE: 0 RIE: 1 CAT: 19

Prevention of Placement
USE Placement Prevention

Preventive Education
CIJE: 1 RIE: 1 CAT: 16

Preventive Law
CIJE: 2 RIE: 8 CAT: 14

Preventive Maintenance
CIJE: 10 RIE: 4 CAT: 16

Preverbal Communication
CIJE: 4 RIE: 2 CAT: 13

Prevert (Jacques)
CIJE: 0 RIE: 1 CAT: 18

Preview of Modern Concepts in Engineering
CIJE: 1 RIE: 0 CAT: 03

Previewing (Reading)
CIJE: 9 RIE: 2 CAT: 13

Prevision (Statistics)
CIJE: 0 RIE: 0 CAT: 20

Prevision (Written Composition)
CIJE: 0 RIE: 0 CAT: 15

Prevocational Assessment Screen
CIJE: 0 RIE: 1 CAT: 21

Prevost (Abbe)
CIJE: 1 RIE: 0 CAT: 18

Prevost (Antoine Francois)
CIJE: 1 RIE: 0 CAT: 18

Price
CIJE: 21 RIE: 4 CAT: 16

Price Belland Observation System
CIJE: 0 RIE: 1 CAT: 15

Price Break Analysis
CIJE: 1 RIE: 0 CAT: 15

Price City Library UT
CIJE: 0 RIE: 1 CAT: 17

Price Elasticity of Demand
USE Elasticity of Demand

Price Speech Performance Rating Scale
CIJE: 0 RIE: 1 CAT: 21

Price Supports
CIJE: 0 RIE: 1 CAT: 14

Price Wars
CIJE: 0 RIE: 0 CAT: 16

Price Waterhouse and Company
CIJE: 1 RIE: 0 CAT: 17

Pricing
CIJE: 131 RIE: 22 CAT: 16

Pricing Formulas
CIJE: 15 RIE: 2 CAT: 15

Pride
CIJE: 3 RIE: 1 CAT: 16

Pride and Prejudice
CIJE: 3 RIE: 1 CAT: 22

PRIDE Center TX
CIJE: 0 RIE: 1 CAT: 19
SN PRIDE = Positive Responsible Individuals Desiring an Education

Pride in Performance
CIJE: 2 RIE: 2 CAT: 16

PRIDE Inventory
USE PReschool Interest DEscriptor

PRIDE Project
CIJE: 1 RIE: 3 CAT: 19

Priestley (Joseph)
CIJE: 7 RIE: 1 CAT: 18

Prigogine (Ilya)
CIJE: 1 RIE: 1 CAT: 18

Prima Facie Case
CIJE: 1 RIE: 1 CAT: 14

Primary Academic Sentiment Scale
CIJE: 0 RIE: 1 CAT: 21

Primary Acquisition of Language
CIJE: 0 RIE: 1 CAT: 13

Primary Assessment Curric Exper (Great Britain)
CIJE: 0 RIE: 1 CAT: 19
UF PACE Project (Great Britain)

Primary Assessment Program (Australia)
CIJE: 0 RIE: 2 CAT: 19

Primary Authors Language
CIJE: 1 RIE: 1 CAT: 04

Primary Caregivers
CIJE: 3 RIE: 3 CAT: 10

Primary Correspondence School
CIJE: 0 RIE: 1 CAT: 19

Primary Economic Test
CIJE: 0 RIE: 1 CAT: 21

Primary Education in England
CIJE: 3 RIE: 0 CAT: 22
SN A report of Her Majesty's Inspectorate
UF National Primary Survey (England 1978)

Primary Education Program FL
CIJE: 1 RIE: 2 CAT: 19

Primary Education Project
CIJE: 5 RIE: 8 CAT: 19

Primary Education Project (Britain)
CIJE: 1 RIE: 0 CAT: 19

Primary Evaluation Inputs Model
CIJE: 1 RIE: 0 CAT: 19

Primary Ignition Circuits
CIJE: 0 RIE: 0 CAT: 20

Primary Individualized Reading
CIJE: 0 RIE: 1 CAT: 19

Primary Language Indicator Test (Schutt)
CIJE: 0 RIE: 1 CAT: 21

Primary Language Record
CIJE: 1 RIE: 2 CAT: 15
SN Method of systematically observing elementary students in various aspects of their literacy development

Primary Literature
CIJE: 3 RIE: 8 CAT: 16

Primary Mathematics Education Enhancement Prog
CIJE: 0 RIE: 1 CAT: 19

Primary Mental Abilities Test
CIJE: 7 RIE: 3 CAT: 21

Primary Mental Health Project
CIJE: 7 RIE: 2 CAT: 19

Primary Message Systems (Hall)
CIJE: 0 RIE: 0 CAT: 15

Primary Nursing
CIJE: 1 RIE: 0 CAT: 11

Primary Physicians
CIJE: 0 RIE: 1 CAT: 09

Primary Prevention
CIJE: 17 RIE: 8 CAT: 11

Primary Product Functionplane
CIJE: 1 RIE: 0 CAT: 04

Primary Pupil Reading Attitude Inventory
CIJE: 0 RIE: 1 CAT: 21

Primary Representational System
CIJE: 7 RIE: 1 CAT: 15

Primary Schools (United Kingdom)
CIJE: 19 RIE: 8 CAT: 05

Primary Science Project
CIJE: 1 RIE: 0 CAT: 19

Primary Self Concept Inventory (Torshen)
CIJE: 1 RIE: 1 CAT: 21

Primary Self Concept Scale
CIJE: 2 RIE: 0 CAT: 21

Primary Skills Program
CIJE: 0 RIE: 1 CAT: 19

Primary Teacher Questionnaire
CIJE: 0 RIE: 1 CAT: 21

Primary Test of Economic Understanding
CIJE: 2 RIE: 1 CAT: 21

Primary Tests for Grade One (Larkins and Shaver)
CIJE: 1 RIE: 0 CAT: 21

Primary Trait Scoring
CIJE: 9 RIE: 17 CAT: 21

Prime 0 Tec Reading Method
CIJE: 0 RIE: 1 CAT: 15

Prime Sponsors
CIJE: 3 RIE: 19 CAT: 10

PRIME System
CIJE: 0 RIE: 3 CAT: 15

Prime Time (Computer Program)
CIJE: 0 RIE: 1 CAT: 04

Prime Time Rule
CIJE: 1 RIE: 1 CAT: 14

Prime Time Television
CIJE: 28 RIE: 26 CAT: 04

Priming (Reading Comprehension)
CIJE: 1 RIE: 1 CAT: 16

Priming Effects
CIJE: 10 RIE: 4 CAT: 11

Prince and the Pauper
CIJE: 2 RIE: 0 CAT: 22

Prince Differential Values Inventory
CIJE: 0 RIE: 1 CAT: 21

Prince Edward County School Project
CIJE: 0 RIE: 1 CAT: 19

Prince Edward Island
CIJE: 10 RIE: 20 CAT: 07

Prince Edward Island Newstart
CIJE: 0 RIE: 2 CAT: 19

Prince Georges Community College MD
CIJE: 7 RIE: 54 CAT: 17

Prince Georges County Correctional Center MD
CIJE: 0 RIE: 1 CAT: 17

Prince Georges County Public Schools MD
CIJE: 10 RIE: 18 CAT: 17

Prince System
CIJE: 0 RIE: 2 CAT: 15

Princeton High School NJ
CIJE: 0 RIE: 2 CAT: 17

Princeton Manpower Symposium
CIJE: 0 RIE: 1 CAT: 02

Princeton Plan
CIJE: 0 RIE: 4 CAT: 19

Princeton Rutgers Census Data Project
CIJE: 1 RIE: 0 CAT: 19

Princeton University NJ
CIJE: 39 RIE: 15 CAT: 17

Principal Axis Procedure
CIJE: 0 RIE: 1 CAT: 15

Principal Components Analysis
CIJE: 25 RIE: 14 CAT: 21

Principal Incentive Programs
CIJE: 0 RIE: 0 CAT: 19

Principal Interview Guide
CIJE: 0 RIE: 1 CAT: 21

Principal Leadership as Social Control
CIJE: 0 RIE: 1 CAT: 15

Principal Leadership Profile
CIJE: 0 RIE: 1 CAT: 21

Principal Leadership Style Questionnaire (Utz)
CIJE: 0 RIE: 1 CAT: 21

Principal Rating Score
CIJE: 1 RIE: 0 CAT: 21

Principal Role Expectation Inventory
CIJE: 1 RIE: 1 CAT: 21

Principal Succession
CIJE: 0 RIE: 3 CAT: 15

Principal Superintendent Relationship
CIJE: 0 RIE: 2 CAT: 15

Principal Teacher Interaction Study
CIJE: 2 RIE: 9 CAT: 22
UF PTI Study

Principal Transfer
CIJE: 3 RIE: 1 CAT: 16

Principal Welfare
CIJE: 0 RIE: 1 CAT: 16

Principals Centers
CIJE: 6 RIE: 3 CAT: 05

Principals Computer Network
CIJE: 0 RIE: 1 CAT: 19

Principals Inservice Program
CIJE: 1 RIE: 2 CAT: 19

Principals of Leadership
CIJE: 0 RIE: 1 CAT: 22

Principals Reflective Experiential Prep Prog TX
CIJE: 0 RIE: 1 CAT: 19

Principle of the Alphabet Literacy System
CIJE: 2 RIE: 5 CAT: 04

Principles Approach
CIJE: 6 RIE: 5 CAT: 15

Principles of Adult Learning Scale
CIJE: 3 RIE: 8 CAT: 21

Principles of Sociology
CIJE: 0 RIE: 1 CAT: 03

Principles of Technology
CIJE: 8 RIE: 6 CAT: 03

Print Awareness
CIJE: 53 RIE: 75 CAT: 16
UF Print Exposure

Print Exposure
USE Print Awareness

Print Journalism
CIJE: 0 RIE: 2 CAT: 16

Printed Circuit Boards
CIJE: 0 RIE: 1 CAT: 04

Printed Circuits
CIJE: 1 RIE: 0 CAT: 04

Printing and Publishing Industry Training Board
CIJE: 0 RIE: 1 CAT: 17

Printing and Publishing Occupations
CIJE: 0 RIE: 13 CAT: 09

Printing Performance School Readiness Test
CIJE: 1 RIE: 1 CAT: 21

Printing Presses
CIJE: 2 RIE: 3 CAT: 04

Prior Restraint
CIJE: 6 RIE: 4 CAT: 14
SN Prevention of publication or disclosure

Prior Restraint (Censorship)
CIJE: 7 RIE: 5 CAT: 14

Prior Subject Interest
CIJE: 1 RIE: 0 CAT: 21

Prior Weston School (England)
CIJE: 1 RIE: 0 CAT: 17

Priorities
CIJE: 73 RIE: 26 CAT: 16

Priorities in School Mathematics Project
CIJE: 1 RIE: 2 CAT: 19

Priority Country Area Program (Australia)
CIJE: 0 RIE: 6 CAT: 19

Priority Effect
CIJE: 1 RIE: 1 CAT: 15

Priority Exceptional Students Study (Australia)
CIJE: 0 RIE: 1 CAT: 19

Priority Need Index
CIJE: 0 RIE: 0 CAT: 21

Priority Schools
CIJE: 0 RIE: 3 CAT: 05

PRISE Curriculum
USE Positive Resiliency in Special Education

PRISE Reporter
CIJE: 0 RIE: 1 CAT: 16

PRISM Model
USE Pittsburghs Research Based Instr Supervisory Model

PRISM Pittsburgh Model for Staff Development
CIJE: 0 RIE: 2 CAT: 15

PRISM Programing Language
CIJE: 0 RIE: 2 CAT: 04

Prison Boot Camps
USE Jail Boot Camps

Prison Literacy Project PA
CIJE: 0 RIE: 3 CAT: 19

Prison Reform
CIJE: 9 RIE: 7 CAT: 16

Prisoner Fasting
CIJE: 0 RIE: 1 CAT: 16

Prisoners Dilemma Game
CIJE: 25 RIE: 10 CAT: 15

Prisoners of War
CIJE: 9 RIE: 6 CAT: 10

Prisoners Rights
CIJE: 3 RIE: 2 CAT: 14

Pritchett (Herman)
CIJE: 1 RIE: 0 CAT: 18

Privacy Act 1974
CIJE: 3 RIE: 13 CAT: 14

Privacy Preference Scale (Marshall)
CIJE: 1 RIE: 0 CAT: 21

Privacy Protection Act 1980
CIJE: 1 RIE: 1 CAT: 14

Privacy Protection Commission
CIJE: 0 RIE: 1 CAT: 17

Private Benefits
CIJE: 3 RIE: 1 CAT: 16

Private Employment Agency Abuse
CIJE: 0 RIE: 1 CAT: 16

Private Enterprise
CIJE: 8 RIE: 12 CAT: 16

Private Enterprise Market System
CIJE: 0 RIE: 1 CAT: 17

Private Industry
CIJE: 11 RIE: 20 CAT: 05

Private Industry Councils
CIJE: 15 RIE: 65 CAT: 10

Private Investigators
CIJE: 1 RIE: 0 CAT: 09

Private Language
CIJE: 0 RIE: 1 CAT: 13

Private Libraries
CIJE: 8 RIE: 2 CAT: 05

Private Lives
CIJE: 4 RIE: 2 CAT: 22

Private Police
CIJE: 1 RIE: 7 CAT: 09

Private Practice
CIJE: 20 RIE: 4 CAT: 16

Private Practice (Medicine)
CIJE: 10 RIE: 3 CAT: 11

Private Practice (Professions)
CIJE: 9 RIE: 1 CAT: 16

Private Property
CIJE: 4 RIE: 2 CAT: 14

Private School Questionnaire (NCES)
CIJE: 0 RIE: 1 CAT: 21

Private School Survey (NCES)
CIJE: 0 RIE: 1 CAT: 21

Private Sector Initiative Programs
CIJE: 1 RIE: 11 CAT: 19

Private Sector Involvement Project
CIJE: 0 RIE: 1 CAT: 19

Private Self Consciousness
CIJE: 1 RIE: 4 CAT: 11

Private Speech
CIJE: 18 RIE: 16 CAT: 16

Private Transportation
CIJE: 0 RIE: 4 CAT: 16

PRM 78 Dictation Test (Thostenson)
CIJE: 0 RIE: 1 CAT: 21

Pro Cite
CIJE: 3 RIE: 0 CAT: 04

PRO SEARCH
CIJE: 0 RIE: 1 CAT: 04

Pro Verbs
CIJE: 0 RIE: 1 CAT: 13

Proactive Action Model
CIJE: 0 RIE: 2 CAT: 15

Proactive Interference
CIJE: 13 RIE: 4 CAT: 16

Proactive Planning
CIJE: 13 RIE: 4 CAT: 15

Proactive Teaching
CIJE: 2 RIE: 2 CAT: 15

Probabilistic Causation
CIJE: 0 RIE: 1 CAT: 15

Probabilistic Indexing
CIJE: 5 RIE: 2 CAT: 15

Probabilistic Models
CIJE: 38 RIE: 6 CAT: 15

Probabilistic Reasoning
CIJE: 9 RIE: 2 CAT: 20

Probabilistic Sampling
CIJE: 3 RIE: 1 CAT: 21

Probabilistic Utility Model
CIJE: 1 RIE: 1 CAT: 15

Probability Learning
CIJE: 5 RIE: 0 CAT: 15

Probable Cause
CIJE: 3 RIE: 1 CAT: 14

Probation (Criminal Justice)
CIJE: 20 RIE: 6 CAT: 14

PROBE Model
CIJE: 0 RIE: 0 CAT: 15

PROBE Program
CIJE: 0 RIE: 3 CAT: 19
SN Potential Reentry Opportunities in Business and Education

PROBED Program (Haiti)
USE Incentives to Improve Basic Education (Haiti)

Probeware
CIJE: 2 RIE: 1 CAT: 04

Probit Analysis
CIJE: 4 RIE: 1 CAT: 15

Probits
CIJE: 1 RIE: 1 CAT: 15

Problem Attack Behavior Inventory (Randall)
CIJE: 1 RIE: 0 CAT: 21

Problem Based Learning
CIJE: 17 RIE: 13 CAT: 15

Problem Centered Curriculum
CIJE: 37 RIE: 7 CAT: 03

Problem Check List
CIJE: 0 RIE: 1 CAT: 21

Problem Finding
CIJE: 18 RIE: 3 CAT: 16

Problem Formulation (Mathematics)
CIJE: 5 RIE: 3 CAT: 03

Problem Identification
CIJE: 27 RIE: 13 CAT: 16

Problem Identification Matrix
CIJE: 1 RIE: 0 CAT: 15

Problem Inventory for Adolescent Girls
CIJE: 2 RIE: 0 CAT: 21

Problem Inventory for College Students
CIJE: 1 RIE: 0 CAT: 21

Problem List Questionnaire
CIJE: 1 RIE: 0 CAT: 21

Problem Maintenance Process
CIJE: 0 RIE: 0 CAT: 11

Problem Oriented Education
CIJE: 7 RIE: 1 CAT: 15

Problem Oriented Educational Record
CIJE: 0 RIE: 1 CAT: 21

Problem Oriented Instruction
CIJE: 3 RIE: 4 CAT: 03

Problem Oriented Medical Records
CIJE: 5 RIE: 1 CAT: 21

Problem Oriented Record
CIJE: 3 RIE: 0 CAT: 21

Problem Ownership
CIJE: 1 RIE: 2 CAT: 16

Problem Posing
CIJE: 18 RIE: 8 CAT: 16

Problem Representation
CIJE: 2 RIE: 1 CAT: 16

Problem Situations Test
CIJE: 2 RIE: 0 CAT: 21

Problem Solving Assessment
CIJE: 12 RIE: 5 CAT: 15

Problem Solving in Mathematics Project
CIJE: 0 RIE: 9 CAT: 19

Problem Solving Measure for Conflict
CIJE: 0 RIE: 1 CAT: 21

Problem Solving Teams
CIJE: 3 RIE: 3 CAT: 10

Problem Structure
CIJE: 4 RIE: 3 CAT: 15

Problems of Peace and War in the Modern World
CIJE: 1 RIE: 0 CAT: 03

Problems of Teaching Survey
CIJE: 0 RIE: 2 CAT: 21

Procedural and Conceptual Knowledge in Science
USE PACKS Project (United Kingdom)

Procedural Justice
CIJE: 2 RIE: 5 CAT: 15

Procedural Knowledge
CIJE: 5 RIE: 3 CAT: 15

Procedural Reasoning
CIJE: 5 RIE: 4 CAT: 15

Procedural Steps Conformity Index
CIJE: 0 RIE: 1 CAT: 21

PROcedure to Promote Effect effic Study skills
CIJE: 0 RIE: 1 CAT: 19
UF PROPES

Procedure Tracking
CIJE: 1 RIE: 0 CAT: 15
UF Tracking (Procedures)

Procedures for Adopting Educational Innovations
CIJE: 0 RIE: 2 CAT: 19

Procedures for Identifying Problem Drinkers
CIJE: 0 RIE: 1 CAT: 21

PROCESS (Computer Program)
CIJE: 0 RIE: 1 CAT: 04
SN PROCESS = Program for Research on Operator Control in an Experimental Simulated Setting

Process Analysis
CIJE: 35 RIE: 28 CAT: 15

Process Approach (Writing)
CIJE: 130 RIE: 151 CAT: 15
UF Process Writing; Writing as Process; Writing Process Approach

Process Based Organizations
CIJE: 0 RIE: 1 CAT: 15

Process Coding
CIJE: 0 RIE: 1 CAT: 15

Process Consultants
CIJE: 3 RIE: 1 CAT: 09

Process Consultation
CIJE: 4 RIE: 9 CAT: 15

Process for Assessment of Effective Student Funct
CIJE: 0 RIE: 0 CAT: 21

Process Goals
CIJE: 0 RIE: 3 CAT: 16

Process Groups
CIJE: 2 RIE: 1 CAT: 10

Process Improvement
CIJE: 3 RIE: 1 CAT: 15

Process Individualization Curriculum
CIJE: 0 RIE: 2 CAT: 03

Process Instrumentation
CIJE: 0 RIE: 1 CAT: 15

Process Measures
CIJE: 6 RIE: 6 CAT: 21

Process Models
CIJE: 22 RIE: 9 CAT: 15

Process Option Pedagogy
CIJE: 0 RIE: 2 CAT: 15

Process Plant Operators
USE Plant Process Operators

Process Product Relationship
CIJE: 12 RIE: 4 CAT: 15

Process Product Research
CIJE: 21 RIE: 10 CAT: 15

Process Research
CIJE: 16 RIE: 10 CAT: 15

Process Simulation
CIJE: 0 RIE: 1 CAT: 15

Process Skills
CIJE: 27 RIE: 26 CAT: 15
SN Do not use for the Desc "Science Process Skills" — see also add'l Iden "Mathematics Process Skills"

Process Tracing
CIJE: 1 RIE: 1 CAT: 11

Process Writing
USE Process Approach (Writing)

Processes of Science Test
CIJE: 3 RIE: 12 CAT: 21

Processing Levels
USE Levels of Processing

Procrastination
CIJE: 22 RIE: 13 CAT: 16

Procrustes Rotation
CIJE: 6 RIE: 3 CAT: 15

Procter and Gamble Company
CIJE: 1 RIE: 0 CAT: 17

Procurement Personnel
CIJE: 0 RIE: 3 CAT: 09

Producer Consumer School Concept
CIJE: 1 RIE: 0 CAT: 15

Producing Names on Confrontation Test
CIJE: 1 RIE: 0 CAT: 21

Product Approach (Writing)
CIJE: 11 RIE: 2 CAT: 15
UF Writing as Product; Writing Product Approach

Product Barcodes
USE Barcodes

Product Cycles
CIJE: 0 RIE: 1 CAT: 20

Product Development
CIJE: 29 RIE: 16 CAT: 20

Product Impact Project
CIJE: 0 RIE: 1 CAT: 19

Product Market Analysis Model
CIJE: 1 RIE: 1 CAT: 15

Product Moment Correlation Coefficient
CIJE: 0 RIE: 1 CAT: 15

Product Placement
CIJE: 0 RIE: 1 CAT: 15

Product Recall
CIJE: 0 RIE: 1 CAT: 20
UF Recall of Products

Product Safety
CIJE: 6 RIE: 8 CAT: 20

Production Controls
CIJE: 0 RIE: 1 CAT: 15

Production Implementation Evaluation and Revision
CIJE: 0 RIE: 1 CAT: 21

Production Life Cycle Models
CIJE: 0 RIE: 1 CAT: 15

Production Mechanics
CIJE: 1 RIE: 2 CAT: 09

Production Process Model
CIJE: 1 RIE: 2 CAT: 15

Production Quality
CIJE: 1 RIE: 0 CAT: 21

Production Schedules
CIJE: 1 RIE: 1 CAT: 15

Production System Version G Programing Language
CIJE: 0 RIE: 1 CAT: 04

Production Typing
CIJE: 3 RIE: 0 CAT: 03

Production Writing Assessment
CIJE: 0 RIE: 1 CAT: 21

Productive Competence
CIJE: 2 RIE: 2 CAT: 21

Productive Language Assessment Tasks
CIJE: 0 RIE: 1 CAT: 21

Productive School Model
CIJE: 0 RIE: 1 CAT: 15

Productive Thinking Program
CIJE: 2 RIE: 4 CAT: 19

Productivity Environmental Preference Survey
CIJE: 2 RIE: 0 CAT: 21

Productivity Improvement
CIJE: 5 RIE: 16 CAT: 20

Productivity Projects Studies Program UT
CIJE: 0 RIE: 1 CAT: 19

Productivity Sharing Plans
CIJE: 0 RIE: 1 CAT: 19

Products Liability
CIJE: 3 RIE: 1 CAT: 14

Profanity
CIJE: 7 RIE: 3 CAT: 16

Professional Activities
CIJE: 10 RIE: 6 CAT: 16

Professional Activity Inventory
CIJE: 0 RIE: 1 CAT: 21

Professional Agricultural Workers Conference
CIJE: 0 RIE: 1 CAT: 02

Professional Alternative Consortium for Teachers
CIJE: 0 RIE: 1 CAT: 19

Professional and Administrative Career Exam
CIJE: 2 RIE: 5 CAT: 21

Professional Athletics
CIJE: 11 RIE: 5 CAT: 16

Professional Audiovisual Education Study
CIJE: 1 RIE: 0 CAT: 03

Professional Behavior
CIJE: 22 RIE: 16 CAT: 15

Professional Commitment
CIJE: 1 RIE: 1 CAT: 16

Professional Communication
CIJE: 0 RIE: 1 CAT: 03

Professional Community
CIJE: 5 RIE: 5 CAT: 10

Professional Competence Peer Opinionnaire
CIJE: 0 RIE: 1 CAT: 21

Professional Concerns
CIJE: 64 RIE: 128 CAT: 16

Professional Development and Appraisals Program
CIJE: 1 RIE: 0 CAT: 21

Professional Development Centers
CIJE: 5 RIE: 5 CAT: 05
SN See also the Desc "Professional Development Schools"

Professional Development Priorities Process
CIJE: 0 RIE: 1 CAT: 15

Professional Development Profile (Gregore)
CIJE: 1 RIE: 0 CAT: 21

Professional Differentiation
CIJE: 5 RIE: 2 CAT: 16

Professional Disclosure
CIJE: 3 RIE: 2 CAT: 16

Professional Ethics
CIJE: 69 RIE: 30 CAT: 16

Professional Guidelines
CIJE: 2 RIE: 5 CAT: 16

Professional Identity
CIJE: 30 RIE: 2 CAT: 16

Professional Image
CIJE: 4 RIE: 3 CAT: 16

Professional Improvement Record Systems
CIJE: 1 RIE: 0 CAT: 21

Professional Industrial and Commercial Updating
USE PICKUP

Professional Journals
CIJE: 2 RIE: 2 CAT: 16
SN See also "Association Magazines"

Professional Judgment
CIJE: 10 RIE: 4 CAT: 15

Professional Laboratory Experiences
CIJE: 2 RIE: 0 CAT: 16

Professional Literature
CIJE: 62 RIE: 6 CAT: 16
SN See also "Professional Journals"

Professional Managerial Position Questionnaire
CIJE: 0 RIE: 1 CAT: 21

Professional Meetings
CIJE: 3 RIE: 6 CAT: 02

Professional Openness
CIJE: 0 RIE: 1 CAT: 16

Professional Orientation
CIJE: 1 RIE: 3 CAT: 16

Professional Perspectives
CIJE: 0 RIE: 2 CAT: 16

Professional Role
CIJE: 83 RIE: 27 CAT: 16

Professional Schools Program in India
CIJE: 1 RIE: 0 CAT: 19

Professional Secretaries International
CIJE: 3 RIE: 2 CAT: 17

Professional Self Perception (Elsworth et al)
CIJE: 0 RIE: 1 CAT: 21

Professional Sequence
CIJE: 2 RIE: 2 CAT: 16

Professional Socialization
CIJE: 10 RIE: 3 CAT: 16

Professional Sports
CIJE: 8 RIE: 4 CAT: 16

Professional Staff Congress CUNY
CIJE: 0 RIE: 1 CAT: 17
UF CUNY Professional Staff Congress

Professional Standards Program
CIJE: 1 RIE: 0 CAT: 19

Professional Standards Review Organizations
CIJE: 3 RIE: 1 CAT: 05

Professional Teaching Standards (NCTM)
USE NCTM Professional Teaching Standards

Professional Welfare
CIJE: 0 RIE: 1 CAT: 16

Professional Writing
CIJE: 46 RIE: 23 CAT: 16

Professionalism
CIJE: 418 RIE: 125 CAT: 16

Professionalization
CIJE: 14 RIE: 2 CAT: 15

Professionalization of Teaching
CIJE: 23 RIE: 31 CAT: 15
UF Teacher Professionalization

Professions
CIJE: 2 RIE: 2 CAT: 09

Professor of the City Program
CIJE: 0 RIE: 1 CAT: 19

Professor of the Year
USE Teacher of the Year

Professors Emeriti
USE Emeritus Professors

Proficiency Based Credit Assessment
CIJE: 0 RIE: 2 CAT: 15

Proficiency Distributions
CIJE: 0 RIE: 1 CAT: 21

Proficiency Examination Program (ACT)
USE ACT Proficiency Examination Program

Proficiency Modules
CIJE: 0 RIE: 3 CAT: 21

Profile Analysis Approach
CIJE: 1 RIE: 1 CAT: 15

Profile for Assessment of Leaders
CIJE: 0 RIE: 2 CAT: 21

Profile of a School
CIJE: 3 RIE: 6 CAT: 21

Profile of American Youth
CIJE: 0 RIE: 4 CAT: 19

Profile of Child Care Settings
CIJE: 0 RIE: 1 CAT: 19

Profile of Factors
CIJE: 1 RIE: 0 CAT: 21

Profile of Interaction in the Classroom (Crispin)
CIJE: 0 RIE: 2 CAT: 21

Profile of Mood States
CIJE: 5 RIE: 1 CAT: 21

Profile of Nonverbal Sensitivity (Rosenthal et al)
CIJE: 1 RIE: 1 CAT: 21

Profile of Occupational Interests
CIJE: 0 RIE: 1 CAT: 21

Profile of Organizational Characteristics
CIJE: 1 RIE: 1 CAT: 21

Profile of Real Ideal Scholastic Motivation
CIJE: 0 RIE: 2 CAT: 21

Profile of School Excellence
CIJE: 0 RIE: 3 CAT: 21

Profile Variability
CIJE: 1 RIE: 1 CAT: 21

Profiles of Promise
CIJE: 0 RIE: 43 CAT: 22

Profit Making
CIJE: 17 RIE: 5 CAT: 15
UF For Profit

Profit Making Organizations
USE Proprietary Organizations

Profit Making Programs
CIJE: 3 RIE: 3 CAT: 19

Profit Making Public School Management
CIJE: 0 RIE: 0 CAT: 15
UF Public For Profit School Management; Public Profit Making Schools; Public School Profit Making Ventures

Profit Making Schools
CIJE: 2 RIE: 0 CAT: 05
SN See also the Descriptor "Proprietary Schools" and the Identifier "Profit Making Public School Management"
UF For Profit Schools

Profit Maximization
CIJE: 8 RIE: 14 CAT: 16

Profits
CIJE: 13 RIE: 5 CAT: 16

ProfNet
CIJE: 0 RIE: 1 CAT: 19
SN Cooperative of college and university public information officers linked via Internet

Program ACTION
CIJE: 0 RIE: 1 CAT: 19

Program Adaptation
CIJE: 2 RIE: 5 CAT: 15

Program Advisory Committee Evaluation System
CIJE: 0 RIE: 1 CAT: 15
UF PACES Model

Program Alternatives to Special Education
CIJE: 0 RIE: 2 CAT: 19

Program Analysis and Monitoring in Reading
CIJE: 0 RIE: 1 CAT: 15

Program Analysis and Monitoring in Writing
CIJE: 0 RIE: 1 CAT: 19

Program Analysis of Service Systems
CIJE: 3 RIE: 2 CAT: 15
UF PASS Evaluation (Programs for Disabled)

Program Analysis Questionnaire
CIJE: 0 RIE: 1 CAT: 21

Program Applications
CIJE: 0 RIE: 2 CAT: 19

Program Approval
CIJE: 0 RIE: 5 CAT: 15
UF Approval of Programs

Program Assembly Monitor Execution Learn Applicat
CIJE: 0 RIE: 1 CAT: 16

Program Assessment Pupil Instruction System
CIJE: 0 RIE: 1 CAT: 21

Program Assistance and Approval System LA
CIJE: 0 RIE: 1 CAT: 19

Program Assistance for Neophytes NY
USE Project PAN NY

Program Cancellation
CIJE: 3 RIE: 1 CAT: 16

Program Characteristics
CIJE: 31 RIE: 195 CAT: 16

Program Classification Structure
CIJE: 1 RIE: 5 CAT: 15

Program Completers
CIJE: 0 RIE: 2 CAT: 10

Program Component Research
CIJE: 0 RIE: 1 CAT: 15

Program Course Inventory
CIJE: 0 RIE: 2 CAT: 21

Program Development Evaluation
CIJE: 0 RIE: 2 CAT: 21

Program Development Evaluation Method
CIJE: 0 RIE: 2 CAT: 15

Program Directors (Broadcast)
CIJE: 1 RIE: 1 CAT: 09

Program Discontinuation
CIJE: 0 RIE: 4 CAT: 16

Program Duplication
CIJE: 4 RIE: 8 CAT: 15

Program Effectiveness Panel
CIJE: 1 RIE: 5 CAT: 17
SN Formerly the "Joint Dissemination Review Panel" (q.v.) of the U.S. Department of Education

Program Evaluation and Review Technique
CIJE: 25 RIE: 44 CAT: 15

Program Evaluation at Performance Objective Level
CIJE: 0 RIE: 3 CAT: 15

Program Evaluation Questionnaire
CIJE: 0 RIE: 1 CAT: 21

Program Evaluation Survey
CIJE: 3 RIE: 1 CAT: 21

Program Evaluation Tests NY
CIJE: 0 RIE: 1 CAT: 21

Program Exit
CIJE: 4 RIE: 4 CAT: 16
UF Exit from Programs; Exiting Programs; Program Exit Criteria

Program Exit Criteria
USE Program Exit

Program Expansion
CIJE: 9 RIE: 11 CAT: 15

Program for Academic and Creative Enrichment
CIJE: 1 RIE: 0 CAT: 19

Program for Acquiring Competence Entrepreneurship
CIJE: 0 RIE: 58 CAT: 19

Program for Action by Citizens in Education
CIJE: 2 RIE: 0 CAT: 19

Program for Adolescent and Community Education
CIJE: 1 RIE: 0 CAT: 19

Program for Afloat College Education
CIJE: 1 RIE: 0 CAT: 19

Program for Alternative Comprehensive Education NY
CIJE: 0 RIE: 1 CAT: 19

Program for Assessing Youth Employment Skills
CIJE: 0 RIE: 1 CAT: 19

Program for Effective Teaching
CIJE: 9 RIE: 5 CAT: 19

Program for Effective Teaching and Supervision
CIJE: 0 RIE: 1 CAT: 19

Program for Efficient Teaching
CIJE: 0 RIE: 1 CAT: 19

Program for Improvement IL
CIJE: 0 RIE: 1 CAT: 19

Program for Leadership in Earth Systems Education
CIJE: 0 RIE: 1 CAT: 19
UF PLESE

Program for Learning in Accordance with Needs
CIJE: 5 RIE: 20 CAT: 19

Program for Local Service
CIJE: 1 RIE: 0 CAT: 19

Program for More Able Learners
CIJE: 0 RIE: 2 CAT: 19

Program for Quality Teaching BC
CIJE: 0 RIE: 2 CAT: 19

Program for Severely Profoundly Handicapped
CIJE: 0 RIE: 1 CAT: 19

Program IMPACT
CIJE: 0 RIE: 7 CAT: 19

Program in Linguistics and English Teaching
CIJE: 1 RIE: 0 CAT: 19

Program Legitimacy
CIJE: 0 RIE: 0 CAT: 16
UF Legitimacy (of Programs)

Program Length Commercials
CIJE: 0 RIE: 3 CAT: 16
SN See also "Host Selling Television Commercials" and "Political Commercials"

Program Mapping
CIJE: 0 RIE: 1 CAT: 15

Program Modification
CIJE: 4 RIE: 7 CAT: 16

Program Monitoring
CIJE: 6 RIE: 38 CAT: 15

Program Monitoring System
CIJE: 1 RIE: 1 CAT: 04

Program Objectives
CIJE: 19 RIE: 56 CAT: 15

Program of Assessment Diagnosis and Instruction MD
CIJE: 1 RIE: 0 CAT: 19
UF PADI

Program of International Partnerships
CIJE: 1 RIE: 0 CAT: 19

Program of Research and Eval for Public Schools
CIJE: 2 RIE: 1 CAT: 19

Program of Special Directed Studies
CIJE: 0 RIE: 3 CAT: 19

Program on Information Technologies Public Policy
CIJE: 0 RIE: 1 CAT: 19

Program on Noncollegiate Sponsored Instruction
CIJE: 1 RIE: 1 CAT: 19

Program on Public Conceptions of Science
CIJE: 0 RIE: 5 CAT: 19

Program Overlap
CIJE: 1 RIE: 5 CAT: 15

Program Persons Limited English Speaking Ability
CIJE: 0 RIE: 2 CAT: 19

Program PREPARE
CIJE: 0 RIE: 1 CAT: 19

Program React
CIJE: 1 RIE: 0 CAT: 19

Program Replication
CIJE: 1 RIE: 15 CAT: 15

Program Requirements
CIJE: 2 RIE: 11 CAT: 16

Program Review
CIJE: 13 RIE: 21 CAT: 15

Program Review Extension Procedures
CIJE: 0 RIE: 1 CAT: 15

Program Review in Occupational Education
CIJE: 0 RIE: 1 CAT: 19

Program Specialists
CIJE: 1 RIE: 2 CAT: 09

Program Specific Vocational Locator Tests
CIJE: 0 RIE: 1 CAT: 21

Program Sponsorship
CIJE: 0 RIE: 5 CAT: 16

Program Techniques
CIJE: 0 RIE: 1 CAT: 15

Program Theory
CIJE: 8 RIE: 0 CAT: 15
UF Heuristic Program Theory

Program to Develop Efficiency Visual Functioning
CIJE: 0 RIE: 1 CAT: 19

Program to Raise Educational Performance NY
USE Preparation for Raising Educational Performance NY

Program VITAL
CIJE: 1 RIE: 1 CAT: 19

Programa de Educacion Interamericana
CIJE: 0 RIE: 1 CAT: 19

Programa Regional de Desarrollo Educativo (OAS)
CIJE: 0 RIE: 1 CAT: 19

Programable Automation
CIJE: 0 RIE: 1 CAT: 20

Programable Calculators
CIJE: 11 RIE: 11 CAT: 04

Programable Logic Control
CIJE: 0 RIE: 7 CAT: 20

Programed Student Achievement
CIJE: 5 RIE: 0 CAT: 15

Programmatic Approach to Guidance Excellence
CIJE: 1 RIE: 1 CAT: 15

Programmatic Instructional Development
CIJE: 0 RIE: 1 CAT: 15

Programmatic Research
CIJE: 3 RIE: 2 CAT: 15

Programmatic Research Project
CIJE: 0 RIE: 1 CAT: 19

Programmed Instruction Center for Industry
CIJE: 1 RIE: 0 CAT: 17

Programming for Individualized Education Program
CIJE: 0 RIE: 1 CAT: 04

Programming in the Arts
CIJE: 0 RIE: 1 CAT: 19

Programs for Educational Opportunity
CIJE: 0 RIE: 1 CAT: 17

Programs to Advance Teen Health
CIJE: 0 RIE: 1 CAT: 19

Programs to Excite Potential
CIJE: 0 RIE: 3 CAT: 19

Progress
CIJE: 11 RIE: 5 CAT: 16

Progress Charts
CIJE: 0 RIE: 1 CAT: 16

Progress in Education Survey
CIJE: 0 RIE: 1 CAT: 21

Progress Monitoring
CIJE: 1 RIE: 2 CAT: 21
UF Monitoring Progress

Progress Profiles Project
CIJE: 0 RIE: 1 CAT: 19

Progress Reporting
CIJE: 6 RIE: 42 CAT: 21

Progressive (The)
CIJE: 0 RIE: 1 CAT: 22

Progressive Achievement Test
CIJE: 3 RIE: 2 CAT: 21

Progressive Collaborative Model
CIJE: 0 RIE: 1 CAT: 15

Progressive Elaboration
CIJE: 2 RIE: 0 CAT: 16

Progressive Era
CIJE: 18 RIE: 7 CAT: 12

Progressive Focusing
CIJE: 0 RIE: 1 CAT: 21

Progressive Hearing Loss
CIJE: 2 RIE: 0 CAT: 11

Progressive Muscle Relaxation Training
CIJE: 2 RIE: 1 CAT: 11

Progressive State Paradigm
CIJE: 0 RIE: 1 CAT: 15

Progressive Time Delay
CIJE: 0 RIE: 1 CAT: 15

Progressivism
CIJE: 28 RIE: 9 CAT: 16

Prohibition (USA 1920s)
USE Eighteenth Amendment

Project 18
CIJE: 2 RIE: 2 CAT: 19

Project 30 (Teacher Education)
CIJE: 0 RIE: 4 CAT: 19

Project 80
CIJE: 0 RIE: 3 CAT: 19

Project 81
CIJE: 2 RIE: 2 CAT: 19

Project 1000
CIJE: 0 RIE: 1 CAT: 19

Project 1990
CIJE: 1 RIE: 2 CAT: 19

Project 2000
CIJE: 0 RIE: 7 CAT: 19

Project 2061 (AAAS)
CIJE: 8 RIE: 22 CAT: 19
UF AAAS Project 2061

Project 100000
CIJE: 2 RIE: 20 CAT: 19

Project A Plus Elemen Techn Demonstration Schools
CIJE: 0 RIE: 5 CAT: 19

Project A Warm Welcome NY
CIJE: 0 RIE: 1 CAT: 19

Project ABC AB
USE Project Advancement Based on Competency

Project ABC NY
CIJE: 0 RIE: 4 CAT: 19

Project ABLE
CIJE: 2 RIE: 38 CAT: 19

Project Able Career Development Inventory
CIJE: 0 RIE: 1 CAT: 21

Project About Face TN
CIJE: 0 RIE: 2 CAT: 19

Project ABRAZO
CIJE: 0 RIE: 1 CAT: 19

Project ACCEL NJ
CIJE: 0 RIE: 1 CAT: 19
UF Accelerated Curriculum Classes Emphasizing Learn

Project Access
CIJE: 1 RIE: 14 CAT: 19

Project ACCESS WA
CIJE: 0 RIE: 2 CAT: 19
SN ACCESS = A Community Cooperating for Effective Seattle Schools

Project ACCESS WI
CIJE: 0 RIE: 1 CAT: 19
SN ACCESS = A Curriculum-based Collection Evaluation and Selection System

Project Accommodate
CIJE: 0 RIE: 1 CAT: 19

Project Achieve NY
CIJE: 0 RIE: 2 CAT: 19

Project ACT
CIJE: 2 RIE: 8 CAT: 19

Project ACTIVE
CIJE: 1 RIE: 12 CAT: 19
SN "All Children Totally InVolved Exercising"

Project ADAPT
CIJE: 0 RIE: 7 CAT: 19

Project Adelante NY
CIJE: 0 RIE: 1 CAT: 19

Project ADELANTE PA
CIJE: 0 RIE: 1 CAT: 19
SN ADELANTE = Alliance for Developing and Enhancing Latino Awareness and Needs in Teacher Education

Project ADMIRE
CIJE: 0 RIE: 2 CAT: 19

Project Advance
CIJE: 13 RIE: 16 CAT: 19

Project ADVANCE CA
CIJE: 0 RIE: 1 CAT: 19

Project ADVANCE NY
CIJE: 0 RIE: 1 CAT: 19
SN ADVANCE = Adolescents Developing Valuable And Necessary Channels of Esteem

Project Advancement Based on Competency
CIJE: 0 RIE: 1 CAT: 19
SN Five-year study in three Calgary, Alberta, high schools to explore alternatives to the Carnegie Unit for measuring and awarding academic credit
UF Advancement Based on Competency; Project ABC AB

Project Adventure
CIJE: 2 RIE: 10 CAT: 19

Project Adventure Inc MA
CIJE: 0 RIE: 2 CAT: 17

Project Africa
CIJE: 0 RIE: 11 CAT: 19

Project Agriculture
CIJE: 0 RIE: 1 CAT: 19

Project AHEAD
CIJE: 0 RIE: 2 CAT: 19

Project AID
CIJE: 0 RIE: 2 CAT: 19

Project AIMS
CIJE: 1 RIE: 1 CAT: 19
UF Activities that Integrate Mathematics and Science

Project Alert
CIJE: 2 RIE: 17 CAT: 19

Project ALERT GA
CIJE: 0 RIE: 1 CAT: 19
SN ALERT = Atlantans Learning Employment Responsibilities Together

Project ALIVE
CIJE: 0 RIE: 1 CAT: 19
SN A primary prevention model for adolescent suicide

Project ALLTEL
CIJE: 0 RIE: 1 CAT: 19
UF Assessing Long Distance Learning via Telecommunic

Project ALMA NY
CIJE: 0 RIE: 3 CAT: 19
UF Alternative Learning Methodologies thru Acads NY

Project ALMS
CIJE: 0 RIE: 1 CAT: 19

Project ALPHA
CIJE: 0 RIE: 6 CAT: 19
SN Advanced Learning Program in the Humanities and Arts

Project ALPS
CIJE: 0 RIE: 1 CAT: 19

Project AMERICA NY
CIJE: 0 RIE: 4 CAT: 19

SN "Asian and Arabic Mediated Enrichment Resource and Instructional Career Awareness"

Project AMES
USE Actualization of Mainstream Experience Skills

Project APEC
CIJE: 0 RIE: 1 CAT: 19

Project APEX
CIJE: 1 RIE: 3 CAT: 19

Project Approach (Katz and Chard)
CIJE: 0 RIE: 3 CAT: 15

Project Aprendizaje NY
CIJE: 0 RIE: 4 CAT: 19

Project APT
CIJE: 0 RIE: 8 CAT: 19
SN "Administrators, Parents, and Teachers/Assessment, Programing, and Training"

Project ARISE
CIJE: 1 RIE: 2 CAT: 19

Project ARISTOTLE
CIJE: 0 RIE: 2 CAT: 19

Project Ascend
CIJE: 0 RIE: 1 CAT: 19

Project ASCENT
CIJE: 0 RIE: 1 CAT: 19

Project ASERT
CIJE: 0 RIE: 2 CAT: 19

Project Aspiration
CIJE: 0 RIE: 4 CAT: 19

Project ASPIRE
CIJE: 1 RIE: 4 CAT: 19

Project ASSERT
CIJE: 0 RIE: 3 CAT: 19

Project At Your Service NY
CIJE: 0 RIE: 1 CAT: 19

Project Available Better Careers
CIJE: 1 RIE: 0 CAT: 19

Project AWARE
CIJE: 4 RIE: 4 CAT: 19

Project BABS NY
CIJE: 0 RIE: 2 CAT: 19

Project BACIS NY
CIJE: 0 RIE: 1 CAT: 19

Project BACSTOP
CIJE: 0 RIE: 3 CAT: 19
SN Better Acquisition of Cognitive Skills through Outdoor Programming

Project BAIL OUT
CIJE: 0 RIE: 1 CAT: 19

Project Baseline
CIJE: 2 RIE: 18 CAT: 19

Project BASES NY
CIJE: 0 RIE: 1 CAT: 19
UF Bilingual Academics for Special Educ Students NY

PROJECT BASIC
CIJE: 6 RIE: 6 CAT: 04

Project BASICS
CIJE: 0 RIE: 7 CAT: 19

Project BASICS NY
CIJE: 0 RIE: 1 CAT: 19
UF Bilingual Academic Services and Intgr Career Sy NY

Project BATEY NY
CIJE: 0 RIE: 1 CAT: 19

Project Beacon
CIJE: 2 RIE: 14 CAT: 19

Project BEAM
CIJE: 0 RIE: 1 CAT: 19

Project BEAM NY
CIJE: 0 RIE: 2 CAT: 19
UF Bilingual Education through Architectural Math NY

Project BEAM UP
CIJE: 0 RIE: 1 CAT: 19

Project BECA NY
CIJE: 0 RIE: 2 CAT: 19
UF Bilingual Education and Career Awareness Program

Project BECOME NY
CIJE: 0 RIE: 2 CAT: 19

Project Benchmark
CIJE: 0 RIE: 7 CAT: 19

Project BEST
CIJE: 3 RIE: 55 CAT: 19

Project BEST KS
CIJE: 0 RIE: 1 CAT: 19

Project BEST WI
CIJE: 0 RIE: 1 CAT: 19
SN "Better Educational Systems through Telecommunications"

Project BET
CIJE: 1 RIE: 1 CAT: 19
UF Business and Education Together

Project BETA (Arts)
USE Bilingual Education Through the Arts NY

Project BETA NY
CIJE: 0 RIE: 4 CAT: 19
UF Bilingual Education Talented Academy

Project BICEP
CIJE: 0 RIE: 3 CAT: 19

Project BIG
CIJE: 0 RIE: 1 CAT: 19

Project BIOTECH
CIJE: 2 RIE: 1 CAT: 19

Project BISECT NY
CIJE: 0 RIE: 1 CAT: 19

Project BITEC NY
CIJE: 0 RIE: 2 CAT: 19

Project BLAST NY
CIJE: 0 RIE: 2 CAT: 19
UF Bilingual Language Arts Survival Training

Project BO CEC
CIJE: 3 RIE: 8 CAT: 19

Project BOHST
CIJE: 1 RIE: 1 CAT: 19
UF Bringing Out Head Start Talents

Project Bootstrap
CIJE: 1 RIE: 0 CAT: 19

Project BORN FREE
CIJE: 3 RIE: 24 CAT: 19

Project Brave
CIJE: 0 RIE: 17 CAT: 19

Project Breakthrough
CIJE: 3 RIE: 1 CAT: 19

Project Bridge
CIJE: 0 RIE: 1 CAT: 19

Project BRIDGES NY
CIJE: 0 RIE: 4 CAT: 19
SN "Bilingual Resource Instruction for the Development of Gainful Employment Skills"

Project Build
CIJE: 1 RIE: 2 CAT: 19

Project Business
CIJE: 2 RIE: 1 CAT: 19

Project CABE NY
CIJE: 0 RIE: 1 CAT: 19
UF Content Area Bilingual Education NY

Project CABES
CIJE: 0 RIE: 2 CAT: 19
UF Career Advancement through Bilingual Educ Skills

Project CALA NY
CIJE: 0 RIE: 1 CAT: 19
SN CALA = Cognitive Academic Learning Approaches

Project Camelot
CIJE: 1 RIE: 0 CAT: 19

Project CAMIO
CIJE: 0 RIE: 8 CAT: 19

Project Canada West
CIJE: 4 RIE: 34 CAT: 19

Project CANAL
CIJE: 0 RIE: 12 CAT: 19
SN Project of the Chicago Public Schools IL
UF Creating A New Approach to Learning

Project CAP
CIJE: 0 RIE: 2 CAT: 19

Project CAP (Haitian Hispanic Students)
CIJE: 0 RIE: 1 CAT: 19
SN Career awareness program for bilingual Haitian and Hispanic students in the New York City Schools

Project CAP NY
CIJE: 0 RIE: 3 CAT: 19
SN Career awareness program for Chinese-speaking students, most of limited English proficiency, in the New York City Schools

Project CAPABLE ME
CIJE: 0 RIE: 0 CAT: 19

Project CAPABLE NY
CIJE: 0 RIE: 2 CAT: 19

Project CAPISCO
CIJE: 0 RIE: 1 CAT: 19

Project CAR
CIJE: 0 RIE: 1 CAT: 19

Project CARE
CIJE: 5 RIE: 6 CAT: 19

Project Care III OH
CIJE: 0 RIE: 1 CAT: 19

Project CARE NY
CIJE: 0 RIE: 4 CAT: 19
UF Career Awareness and Resource Education prog NY

Project CAREER
CIJE: 2 RIE: 11 CAT: 19

Project Career WI
CIJE: 0 RIE: 1 CAT: 19

Project CARES NY
CIJE: 0 RIE: 2 CAT: 19
UF Career Awareness Resources for Exceptnl Stdnts NY

Project CASA CA
CIJE: 0 RIE: 1 CAT: 19

Project CASE
CIJE: 0 RIE: 1 CAT: 19

Project CAST
CIJE: 0 RIE: 7 CAT: 19

Project CAST NY
CIJE: 0 RIE: 1 CAT: 19
SN CAST = Comprehensive Approach to Substance abuse prevention Training

Project CATCH
CIJE: 0 RIE: 2 CAT: 19

Project Catch Up
CIJE: 1 RIE: 3 CAT: 19

Project CBE
CIJE: 0 RIE: 33 CAT: 19

Project CDCC
CIJE: 0 RIE: 1 CAT: 19

Project CELIT
CIJE: 0 RIE: 1 CAT: 19

Project CELSIM NY
CIJE: 0 RIE: 1 CAT: 19
UF Career Education and Learning Strat Impl Model NY

Project CERES
CIJE: 0 RIE: 2 CAT: 19

Project Challenge TN
CIJE: 0 RIE: 2 CAT: 19

Project CHAMP NY
CIJE: 0 RIE: 1 CAT: 19
UF CHinese Achievement and Mastery Program

Project Change
CIJE: 3 RIE: 10 CAT: 19

Project Changeover
CIJE: 0 RIE: 1 CAT: 19

Project CHASP NY
CIJE: 0 RIE: 1 CAT: 19

Project CHERISH TX
CIJE: 0 RIE: 1 CAT: 19
SN CHERISH = Children in Home Environments: Regulation to Improve Safety and Health

Project CHILD
CIJE: 3 RIE: 26 CAT: 19

Project Child Care
CIJE: 1 RIE: 2 CAT: 19

Project Child Find Serve TX
CIJE: 0 RIE: 1 CAT: 19

Project Child Watch
CIJE: 0 RIE: 1 CAT: 19

Project CHIME
CIJE: 0 RIE: 1 CAT: 19
SN "Children with Hearing Impairments in Mainstreamed Environments"

Project CHOICE
CIJE: 9 RIE: 96 CAT: 19

Project CHOICE (Choosing Optionl Infusd Career Ed)
USE Choosing Optional Infused Career Education NY

Project CHOICE NY
CIJE: 0 RIE: 2 CAT: 19
UF Chinese Opportunities in Career Education NY

Project CIBE NY
CIJE: 0 RIE: 1 CAT: 19
UF Computers In Bilingual Education

Project CIRCUIT
CIJE: 0 RIE: 1 CAT: 19

Project CITE
CIJE: 0 RIE: 1 CAT: 19
SN Competency Identification for Teacher Education

Project City Science
CIJE: 0 RIE: 3 CAT: 19

Project Citywork
CIJE: 0 RIE: 1 CAT: 19

Project CLASS
CIJE: 1 RIE: 3 CAT: 19

Project Clean Air
CIJE: 0 RIE: 2 CAT: 19

Project CLIMB
CIJE: 1 RIE: 1 CAT: 19

Project CLOVER
CIJE: 0 RIE: 1 CAT: 19
SN Computer Link Offering Variable Educational Records

Project CMYC TX
CIJE: 0 RIE: 1 CAT: 19
UF Catch Me if You Can TX

Project COD
CIJE: 0 RIE: 1 CAT: 19

Project CODE (Drug Education)
CIJE: 0 RIE: 1 CAT: 19
UF Collaborating on Drug Education

Project COEXIST
CIJE: 2 RIE: 3 CAT: 19

Project COFFEE
CIJE: 0 RIE: 1 CAT: 19
UF Cooperative Federation for Educ Experiences

Project COLAMDA
CIJE: 0 RIE: 3 CAT: 19

Project COM TECH NY
CIJE: 0 RIE: 1 CAT: 19
UF Bilingual Academic Computer Technology Oriented P

Project Communicate
CIJE: 0 RIE: 3 CAT: 19

Project Community and School Together
CIJE: 0 RIE: 8 CAT: 19

Project COMPAS
CIJE: 0 RIE: 1 CAT: 19

Project Compugrafia LEP NY
CIJE: 0 RIE: 1 CAT: 19
SN Computer Writing Skills for Limited English Proficient Students Project

Project COMPUOCC LEP NY
CIJE: 0 RIE: 1 CAT: 19
SN Project using computers to teach writing and career education to special education students of limited English proficiency

Project COMPUTE
CIJE: 1 RIE: 2 CAT: 19

Project Concern
CIJE: 3 RIE: 19 CAT: 19

Project Concern CT
CIJE: 0 RIE: 4 CAT: 19

Project CoNECT
USE Collaborative Network for Early Childhood Training

Project CONNECT
CIJE: 0 RIE: 5 CAT: 19

Project Conquest
CIJE: 0 RIE: 2 CAT: 19

Project CONSTRUCT
CIJE: 0 RIE: 1 CAT: 19

Project Construct Assessment System
CIJE: 0 RIE: 1 CAT: 21

Project Consumer Operations Survival Training
CIJE: 0 RIE: 44 CAT: 19

Project Continuing Education for Health Manpower
CIJE: 0 RIE: 5 CAT: 19

Project Continuity NE
CIJE: 0 RIE: 1 CAT: 19

Project Cooperation
CIJE: 0 RIE: 2 CAT: 19
SN Cooperative demonstration project among 10 community colleges for research on instructional effectiveness through outcome measures

Project Coordination
CIJE: 1 RIE: 2 CAT: 19

Project COPE
CIJE: 1 RIE: 1 CAT: 19

Project COPERNICUS
CIJE: 0 RIE: 1 CAT: 19
SN COPERNICUS = Cooperation Programme in Europe for Research on Nature and Industry through Coordinated University Studies

Project COPS
CIJE: 0 RIE: 1 CAT: 19

Project CORES
CIJE: 0 RIE: 2 CAT: 19

Project COULD
CIJE: 0 RIE: 19 CAT: 19

Project CREATE CA
CIJE: 0 RIE: 0 CAT: 19
SN "Center for Research and Evaluation in the Application of Technology to Education"

Project CREATE FL
CIJE: 0 RIE: 0 CAT: 19
SN "Collaborative Resources for Educational Alternatives for Teacher Education"

Project CREATIVE
CIJE: 1 RIE: 0 CAT: 19
SN "Computer Related Enriched And Technologically Inspired Viable Education"

Project CREDIT
CIJE: 0 RIE: 1 CAT: 19
SN Certification Renewal Experiences Designed to Improve Teaching

Project CREEP
CIJE: 0 RIE: 1 CAT: 19

Project CREST
CIJE: 2 RIE: 5 CAT: 19

Project CRISP
CIJE: 0 RIE: 1 CAT: 19
SN Computerized Registration Involving Student Participation

Project Criterion
CIJE: 0 RIE: 2 CAT: 19

Project Crossroads
CIJE: 0 RIE: 3 CAT: 19

Project CUE
CIJE: 1 RIE: 16 CAT: 19

Project Dakota MN
CIJE: 0 RIE: 1 CAT: 19

Project Dale Avenue
CIJE: 0 RIE: 6 CAT: 19

Project DARE (Dictionary)
USE Dictionary of American Regional English

Project DARE (Drug Educ)
USE Drug Abuse Resistance Education Program

Project DARE (Outdoor Educ)
USE Development through Adventure Resp and Educ

Project DART GA
CIJE: 0 RIE: 1 CAT: 19

Project Data Tech NY
CIJE: 0 RIE: 3 CAT: 19

Project DAWN
CIJE: 0 RIE: 1 CAT: 19

Project Daylight AZ
CIJE: 0 RIE: 1 CAT: 19

Project DEAF
CIJE: 1 RIE: 0 CAT: 19

Project DECIDE
CIJE: 2 RIE: 6 CAT: 19

Project Decision 2
CIJE: 0 RIE: 1 CAT: 19

Project DELTA
CIJE: 2 RIE: 3 CAT: 19

Project Design
CIJE: 3 RIE: 2 CAT: 19

Project Developmental Continuity
CIJE: 2 RIE: 27 CAT: 19

Project DIALIB
CIJE: 0 RIE: 7 CAT: 19

Project Dimension
CIJE: 1 RIE: 0 CAT: 19

Project Discovery
CIJE: 6 RIE: 6 CAT: 19

Project DISCUSS
CIJE: 0 RIE: 1 CAT: 19

Project DISTIL
CIJE: 0 RIE: 3 CAT: 19

Project DREAM NY
CIJE: 0 RIE: 2 CAT: 19
UF Dropout Reduction thru Employ Achieve and Motiv NY

Project Drive
CIJE: 0 RIE: 9 CAT: 19

Project Early Aid
CIJE: 0 RIE: 2 CAT: 19

Project Early Help
CIJE: 1 RIE: 0 CAT: 19

Project Early Push
CIJE: 0 RIE: 1 CAT: 19

Project Earth Lab
USE Earth Lab

Project East Woodlawn
CIJE: 0 RIE: 1 CAT: 19

Project Education and Community Devel (Israel)
USE Education and Community Project (Israel)

Project Education for Mankind
CIJE: 1 RIE: 0 CAT: 19

Project Education Reform
CIJE: 0 RIE: 1 CAT: 19

Project Eight
CIJE: 1 RIE: 0 CAT: 19

Project ELITES
CIJE: 0 RIE: 1 CAT: 19

Project Emerge
CIJE: 1 RIE: 2 CAT: 19

Project EMIS
CIJE: 0 RIE: 1 CAT: 19

Project Employability
CIJE: 1 RIE: 12 CAT: 19

Project En Tant Que Femmes
CIJE: 0 RIE: 1 CAT: 19

Project English
CIJE: 4 RIE: 217 CAT: 19

Project ENRICH DC
CIJE: 0 RIE: 1 CAT: 19

Project Enrichment
CIJE: 0 RIE: 1 CAT: 19

Project Ent
CIJE: 1 RIE: 0 CAT: 19

Project EPIC FL
CIJE: 0 RIE: 1 CAT: 19

Project EPIC KY
CIJE: 0 RIE: 1 CAT: 19

Project EPOCH
CIJE: 1 RIE: 4 CAT: 19

Project Equality
CIJE: 3 RIE: 8 CAT: 19

Project EQUALS
USE EQUALS Program

Project Equity
CIJE: 0 RIE: 1 CAT: 19
SN Re sex equity issues and laws

Project ESCAPE
CIJE: 0 RIE: 2 CAT: 19

Project ESL SEDAC NY
CIJE: 0 RIE: 1 CAT: 19

Project Esperanza NY
CIJE: 0 RIE: 1 CAT: 19

Project ESPIRIT
CIJE: 0 RIE: 2 CAT: 19

Project Essay Grade
CIJE: 0 RIE: 2 CAT: 19

Project ESURG NE
CIJE: 0 RIE: 3 CAT: 19

Project ET NY
CIJE: 0 RIE: 1 CAT: 19
SN ET = Effective Transition

Project EUREKA
CIJE: 0 RIE: 3 CAT: 19
SN Development of a career information system for California high schools — do not confuse with "Eureka Project"

Project Europe 2000
CIJE: 0 RIE: 2 CAT: 19

Project Evolve
CIJE: 0 RIE: 2 CAT: 19

Project EXCEL
CIJE: 14 RIE: 7 CAT: 19

Project EXCEL (Public Officials)
CIJE: 0 RIE: 1 CAT: 19
UF EXcellence in Community Elected and apoint Leadrs

Project EXCEL CA
CIJE: 0 RIE: 6 CAT: 19
SN Workplace literacy project for limited English proficient workers

Project Exodus
CIJE: 1 RIE: 2 CAT: 19

Project EXPLORATION
CIJE: 0 RIE: 2 CAT: 19

Project EXPLORE NY
CIJE: 0 RIE: 1 CAT: 19
SN EXPLORE = Examine and Plan for Occupational Requisites and Employment

Project Fair Play
CIJE: 0 RIE: 1 CAT: 19

Project FAITH
CIJE: 0 RIE: 1 CAT: 19

Project Family Link
CIJE: 0 RIE: 1 CAT: 19

Project FAST
CIJE: 0 RIE: 6 CAT: 19

Project FIND
CIJE: 1 RIE: 1 CAT: 19

Project First Chance
CIJE: 0 RIE: 3 CAT: 19

Project First Chance Interactive Outreach Project
CIJE: 0 RIE: 1 CAT: 19

Project FLAME
CIJE: 0 RIE: 1 CAT: 19
UF Family Literacy Aprendiendo Mejorando Educando

Project FLIT
CIJE: 1 RIE: 1 CAT: 19
UF FLIT (Army); Functional Literacy Program (DoD)

Project Focus
CIJE: 0 RIE: 6 CAT: 19

Project Focus SC
CIJE: 0 RIE: 1 CAT: 19

Project Follow Through
CIJE: 78 RIE: 373 CAT: 19

Project Follow Through Expansion Program
CIJE: 0 RIE: 2 CAT: 19

Project Follow Through Resource Center NY
CIJE: 0 RIE: 1 CAT: 17

Project for Academic Motivation
CIJE: 0 RIE: 1 CAT: 19

Project for American Studies in Secondary Schools
CIJE: 0 RIE: 1 CAT: 19

Project for an Energy Enriched Curriculum
CIJE: 2 RIE: 3 CAT: 19

Project for Early Education Exceptional Children
CIJE: 0 RIE: 3 CAT: 19

Project for Improving Reading Language Teaching
CIJE: 0 RIE: 1 CAT: 19

Project for Integrated Catalogue Automation
USE Pica Library Automation Network

Project for Minorities and Women in Research
CIJE: 1 RIE: 0 CAT: 19

Project for Study of Academic Precocity
CIJE: 0 RIE: 1 CAT: 19

Project Ford Foundation Gray Area
CIJE: 0 RIE: 2 CAT: 19

Project ForSight
CIJE: 0 RIE: 1 CAT: 19

Project FREDD
CIJE: 0 RIE: 1 CAT: 19

Project Fresh Start
CIJE: 0 RIE: 1 CAT: 19

Project Frontier
CIJE: 0 RIE: 1 CAT: 19

Project Futureprint
CIJE: 0 RIE: 2 CAT: 19

Project Geography 16 19
CIJE: 0 RIE: 0 CAT: 19

Project GET SET NY
CIJE: 0 RIE: 3 CAT: 19

Project Giant Step NY
CIJE: 0 RIE: 1 CAT: 19

Project Gifted
CIJE: 0 RIE: 1 CAT: 19

Project GIVE
CIJE: 0 RIE: 1 CAT: 19

Project GO
CIJE: 0 RIE: 2 CAT: 19

Project GO FOR IT NY
CIJE: 0 RIE: 2 CAT: 19
SN "Great Opportunities for Optional Resources to Improve the Talents of Gifted Bilingual High School Students"

Project GOAL
USE Guidance Opportunities for Affective Learning

Project GOALS NY
CIJE: 0 RIE: 2 CAT: 19
SN GOALS = Guidance Oriented Acquisition of Learning Skills

Project GOLD VA
USE Garfield Options for Leadership Development

Project GRADS
USE Grass Roots Alternative Diploma Study

Project Grammarama
CIJE: 0 RIE: 1 CAT: 19

Project Grant Information System
CIJE: 0 RIE: 1 CAT: 19

Project GRASP
USE Giving Rural Adults a Study Program

Project GROW
CIJE: 1 RIE: 4 CAT: 19
UF Green River Opportunities for Work KY

Project GROW KY
CIJE: 0 RIE: 1 CAT: 19
SN See related Identifier "Project WORTH"

Project GROW PA
CIJE: 0 RIE: 0 CAT: 19
SN Philadelphia's experimental program in computer-assisted instruction

Project Growth
CIJE: 1 RIE: 3 CAT: 15

Project GUARANTEE (Sweden)
CIJE: 0 RIE: 1 CAT: 19

Project HAITI STARS NY
CIJE: 0 RIE: 2 CAT: 19
SN "Higher Achievement and Improvement Through Instruction with Computers and Scholarly Transition and Resource Systems Program"

Project HAPI
CIJE: 0 RIE: 5 CAT: 19

Project HAPPEN
CIJE: 0 RIE: 1 CAT: 19
SN "Helping Agencies Promote Parent Empowerment through Networking"

Project HAPPIER
CIJE: 0 RIE: 4 CAT: 19

Project Head Start
CIJE: 383 RIE: 1374 CAT: 19
SN See add'l listings under "Head Start..."
UF Head Start

Project Head Start (Home Based)
CIJE: 0 RIE: 1 CAT: 19

Project HEAR
CIJE: 1 RIE: 2 CAT: 19

Project HEATH
CIJE: 0 RIE: 1 CAT: 19
UF HEATH Closer Look; Higher Education And The Handicapped

Project HEED
CIJE: 0 RIE: 6 CAT: 19

Project HEELD
CIJE: 0 RIE: 2 CAT: 19

Project HELP
CIJE: 2 RIE: 4 CAT: 19

Project Heroes
CIJE: 1 RIE: 0 CAT: 19

Project HEVRA
CIJE: 0 RIE: 1 CAT: 19

Project HI CLASS NY
CIJE: 0 RIE: 3 CAT: 19
SN HI CLASS = Harmony in Career Learning and Scholastic System

Project HICOMP
USE HICOMP PreSchool Curriculum

Project Hire
CIJE: 0 RIE: 22 CAT: 19

Project HIRe (Head Injuries)
CIJE: 0 RIE: 1 CAT: 19
UF Head Injury Re Entry Project

Project HOLA NY
CIJE: 0 RIE: 3 CAT: 19

Project Home School and the IEP
CIJE: 0 RIE: 1 CAT: 19

Project Homebound
CIJE: 0 RIE: 5 CAT: 19

Project Homeroom IL
CIJE: 0 RIE: 2 CAT: 19

Project HOPE (Appalachia)
USE Home Oriented Preschool Education Program

Project HOPE (Peru)
CIJE: 0 RIE: 0 CAT: 19
SN Program for graduate preparation of teachers in the field of mental retardation

Project HOPE (Physical Education)
USE Health and Optimum Physical Education Project

Project HOPE AZ
CIJE: 0 RIE: 0 CAT: 19
SN Project of the People-to-People Health Foundation Inc

Project HOPE CA
CIJE: 0 RIE: 0 CAT: 19
SN Program to prepare deaf high school students to enter into employment after graduation

Project HOPE NY
CIJE: 0 RIE: 2 CAT: 19
UF Helpful Opportunities for Pupil Enrichment NY

Project HOT
CIJE: 0 RIE: 1 CAT: 19
SN A project designed to create knowledge about teaching higher order thinking skills in African-American students in urban schools

Project Human Educational Awareness Resource
CIJE: 2 RIE: 0 CAT: 19

Project I CAN
CIJE: 1 RIE: 2 CAT: 19

Project ICE
CIJE: 1 RIE: 48 CAT: 19

Project ICES
CIJE: 3 RIE: 4 CAT: 19

Project Ida (Canada)
CIJE: 0 RIE: 1 CAT: 19

Project IDEA
CIJE: 0 RIE: 3 CAT: 19

Project IDEAL ND
CIJE: 0 RIE: 1 CAT: 19

Project IEL (Liberia)
CIJE: 0 RIE: 1 CAT: 19

Project IMPACT
CIJE: 17 RIE: 32 CAT: 19

Project IMPACT (Philippines)
CIJE: 0 RIE: 1 CAT: 19

Project IMPACT NY
CIJE: 0 RIE: 1 CAT: 19

Project Implode
CIJE: 1 RIE: 1 CAT: 19

Project Improve
CIJE: 1 RIE: 1 CAT: 19

Project IN SLIP
CIJE: 0 RIE: 1 CAT: 19

Project Independence
CIJE: 5 RIE: 1 CAT: 19

Project Information Packages
CIJE: 1 RIE: 21 CAT: 16

Project INFORMS
CIJE: 0 RIE: 1 CAT: 19

Project Infut
CIJE: 0 RIE: 1 CAT: 19

Project Innovation
CIJE: 0 RIE: 1 CAT: 19

Project Input
CIJE: 2 RIE: 0 CAT: 19

Project INREAL
CIJE: 0 RIE: 1 CAT: 19

Project INSERVICE IL
CIJE: 0 RIE: 1 CAT: 19

Project Insight
CIJE: 0 RIE: 2 CAT: 19

Project Insite
CIJE: 2 RIE: 0 CAT: 19

Project INSITE (Deaf Blind)
CIJE: 0 RIE: 1 CAT: 19

Project INSPIRE (Malaysia)
CIJE: 0 RIE: 1 CAT: 19

Project Inspire DC
CIJE: 0 RIE: 0 CAT: 19

Project Inspire PA
CIJE: 0 RIE: 1 CAT: 19

Project INSTEP
CIJE: 0 RIE: 1 CAT: 19

Project Instruct
CIJE: 1 RIE: 3 CAT: 19

Project Inter Action MA
CIJE: 0 RIE: 0 CAT: 19

Project Interact
CIJE: 1 RIE: 8 CAT: 19

Project Interchange
CIJE: 2 RIE: 2 CAT: 19

Project Interdependence CA
CIJE: 0 RIE: 1 CAT: 19

Project INTERFACE
CIJE: 1 RIE: 1 CAT: 19

Project Intergroup
CIJE: 0 RIE: 1 CAT: 19

Project Intrex
CIJE: 4 RIE: 18 CAT: 19

Project Jericho CA
CIJE: 0 RIE: 1 CAT: 19

Project Job Opportunities and Education for Youth
CIJE: 0 RIE: 1 CAT: 19

Project JOBS NY
CIJE: 0 RIE: 1 CAT: 19
UF Job Opportunities for Bilingual Students

Project JOLT
CIJE: 1 RIE: 0 CAT: 19

Project Kaleidoscope
CIJE: 2 RIE: 1 CAT: 19
SN Program to improve science and mathematics teacher education

Project Kamunts
CIJE: 0 RIE: 1 CAT: 19

Project Kanpe
CIJE: 0 RIE: 2 CAT: 19

Project KARE
CIJE: 0 RIE: 6 CAT: 19

Project Kidlink
CIJE: 0 RIE: 1 CAT: 19
SN Preschool education in Topeka, Kansas

Project KIDS
CIJE: 0 RIE: 2 CAT: 19

Project KIND FL
CIJE: 0 RIE: 1 CAT: 19
UF Keeping Interfering Noncompliance Down

Project Know How
CIJE: 0 RIE: 4 CAT: 19

Project Kolehion Mandikike (Guam)
CIJE: 0 RIE: 23 CAT: 19

Project L Ouverture
CIJE: 0 RIE: 1 CAT: 19

Project LAST
CIJE: 0 RIE: 1 CAT: 19
SN "Lowest Achieving Schools, Temporarily" program, Cincinnati Public Schools OH

Project Lead the Way
CIJE: 0 RIE: 1 CAT: 19

Project LEADER
CIJE: 1 RIE: 0 CAT: 19

Project Leadership
CIJE: 0 RIE: 10 CAT: 16

Project Leadership Service Conference
CIJE: 1 RIE: 2 CAT: 02

Project LEAP
CIJE: 1 RIE: 2 CAT: 19

Project LEAP OH
CIJE: 0 RIE: 2 CAT: 19
UF Library Educational Alternatives for Preschoolers

Project Learn
CIJE: 0 RIE: 6 CAT: 19

Project LEARN OH
CIJE: 1 RIE: 1 CAT: 19
SN Community-based adult literacy program in Cleveland (Ohio)

Project Learning Tree
CIJE: 2 RIE: 6 CAT: 19

Project Leer
CIJE: 1 RIE: 2 CAT: 19

Project LEGAL
CIJE: 0 RIE: 0 CAT: 19
UF Law Education Goals And Learnings

Project LEIF
CIJE: 0 RIE: 1 CAT: 19
UF Learning English through Intergeneratl Friendship

Project LEM
CIJE: 0 RIE: 3 CAT: 19

Project LET
CIJE: 0 RIE: 7 CAT: 19

Project LEX
CIJE: 0 RIE: 3 CAT: 19

Project LIFE
CIJE: 3 RIE: 0 CAT: 19

Project Life Lab
CIJE: 0 RIE: 3 CAT: 19

Project Lifelong Learning
CIJE: 0 RIE: 3 CAT: 19

Project LIFT
CIJE: 1 RIE: 0 CAT: 19

Project LINC
CIJE: 1 RIE: 2 CAT: 19

Project LINK
CIJE: 0 RIE: 3 CAT: 19

Project LINK Four
CIJE: 0 RIE: 1 CAT: 19

Project LINKER
CIJE: 0 RIE: 1 CAT: 19

Project Literacy
CIJE: 5 RIE: 21 CAT: 19

Project Literacy U S
CIJE: 0 RIE: 8 CAT: 19
UF PLUS Program (Literacy)

Project LIVE SC
CIJE: 0 RIE: 1 CAT: 19
UF Literacy Implements a Vibrant Existence SC

Project Lodestar
CIJE: 0 RIE: 3 CAT: 19

Project LONGSTEP
CIJE: 1 RIE: 13 CAT: 19

Project LOVE
CIJE: 1 RIE: 0 CAT: 19

Project MAC
CIJE: 0 RIE: 2 CAT: 19

Project MAFEX
CIJE: 0 RIE: 1 CAT: 19
UF Meta Analysis of Field Experience

Project Mainstream
CIJE: 0 RIE: 5 CAT: 19

Project Major Issues Juvenile Justice Info Train
CIJE: 1 RIE: 0 CAT: 19

Project Malvern
CIJE: 0 RIE: 3 CAT: 19

Project Management
CIJE: 18 RIE: 14 CAT: 15

Project Mans Environment
CIJE: 1 RIE: 1 CAT: 19

Project MAP (AIR)
USE Model Accounting Plan

Project MART
USE Project Mathematics Anxiety Reduction Training

Project MAS NY
CIJE: 0 RIE: 1 CAT: 19

Project MASTER NY
CIJE: 0 RIE: 2 CAT: 19
SN MASTER = "Mathematics, Art, Science, Technology, and Education Resources"

Project MATCH
CIJE: 0 RIE: 2 CAT: 19

Project Mathematics Anxiety Reduction Training
CIJE: 0 RIE: 2 CAT: 19
UF Project MART

Project MAVE
CIJE: 1 RIE: 1 CAT: 19

Project MAVIS
CIJE: 0 RIE: 7 CAT: 19

Project Measurement
CIJE: 0 RIE: 1 CAT: 19
SN A project of the Iowa Bureau of Special Education

Project Med Vet
CIJE: 0 RIE: 1 CAT: 19

Project Media
CIJE: 0 RIE: 3 CAT: 19

Project Media Guidelines
CIJE: 1 RIE: 2 CAT: 19

Project MEGSSS
CIJE: 0 RIE: 2 CAT: 19

Project MELD
CIJE: 0 RIE: 1 CAT: 19

Project Memphis
CIJE: 1 RIE: 1 CAT: 19

Project Mentor NY
CIJE: 0 RIE: 1 CAT: 19
SN Law-related program for high schools
UF Mentor Project NYC

Project MER
CIJE: 0 RIE: 6 CAT: 19

Project MET
CIJE: 0 RIE: 18 CAT: 19

Project Metro
CIJE: 0 RIE: 1 CAT: 19

Project Microform
CIJE: 0 RIE: 1 CAT: 19

Project MIDNY
CIJE: 0 RIE: 3 CAT: 19

Project MINERVA
CIJE: 3 RIE: 7 CAT: 19

Project MINI SCORE
CIJE: 0 RIE: 10 CAT: 19

Project Mission
CIJE: 0 RIE: 2 CAT: 19

Project MITT
USE Management Implications of Team Teaching Project

Project MOBILE NY
CIJE: 0 RIE: 2 CAT: 19
SN MOBILE = "Methodologies of Bilingual Instruction in Literacy Education"

Project Mobilization
CIJE: 0 RIE: 1 CAT: 19

Project MODEL
CIJE: 1 RIE: 3 CAT: 19

Project MORE
CIJE: 1 RIE: 16 CAT: 19

Project Motivate
CIJE: 0 RIE: 1 CAT: 19

Project Motivation
CIJE: 0 RIE: 1 CAT: 19

Project MOVE
CIJE: 0 RIE: 5 CAT: 19
UF Maximizing Options in Vocational Education

Project Move Ahead
CIJE: 1 RIE: 0 CAT: 19

Project NAIL
CIJE: 0 RIE: 1 CAT: 19

Project NEED
CIJE: 0 RIE: 2 CAT: 19

Project NEED IT
CIJE: 0 RIE: 1 CAT: 19

Project Neglect
CIJE: 0 RIE: 1 CAT: 19

Project NETWORC NV
CIJE: 0 RIE: 0 CAT: 19
SN "Nevada Educational Television Working Out in Rural Communities"

Project NEW
CIJE: 0 RIE: 2 CAT: 19

Project New Hope
CIJE: 0 RIE: 3 CAT: 19

Project New Horizons NY
USE Proyecto Nuevos Horizontes NY

Project Next Step
CIJE: 0 RIE: 4 CAT: 19

Project Nexus
CIJE: 0 RIE: 1 CAT: 19
SN See also "Community Approach to an Integrated Service System"

Project North Carolina in School Television
CIJE: 0 RIE: 1 CAT: 19

Project Nuevos Horizontes NY
USE Proyecto Nuevos Horizontes NY

Project OASES
CIJE: 0 RIE: 1 CAT: 19
SN OASES = Occupational and Academic Skills for the Employment of Students

Project OASIS
CIJE: 0 RIE: 1 CAT: 19
UF Older Adults Sharing Important Skills

Project OCCUPAC
CIJE: 0 RIE: 3 CAT: 19

Project OMNI
CIJE: 0 RIE: 1 CAT: 19

Project on Achieving Equity for Women Soc Work Ed
CIJE: 0 RIE: 1 CAT: 19

Project on Alternatives in Education
CIJE: 0 RIE: 2 CAT: 19

Project on Applied Contrastive Linguistics
CIJE: 0 RIE: 2 CAT: 19

Project on Cooperative Manpower Planning Spec Educ
CIJE: 0 RIE: 1 CAT: 19

Project on Equal Education Rights
CIJE: 1 RIE: 2 CAT: 19

Project on General Education Models
CIJE: 2 RIE: 2 CAT: 15

Project on Involvement
CIJE: 0 RIE: 1 CAT: 19

Project on Linguistic Analysis
CIJE: 1 RIE: 11 CAT: 19

Project on Noncollegiate Sponsored Instruction
CIJE: 1 RIE: 0 CAT: 19

Project on Reallocation
CIJE: 0 RIE: 2 CAT: 19

Project on Redefining the Baccalaureate Degree
CIJE: 1 RIE: 2 CAT: 19
SN Full name—"Project on Redefining the Meaning and Purpose of the Baccalaureate Degree"

Project on Student Development in Small Colleges
CIJE: 1 RIE: 0 CAT: 19

Project on the Predicament of Mankind
CIJE: 0 RIE: 1 CAT: 19

Project Open
CIJE: 2 RIE: 10 CAT: 19

Project Open Classroom
CIJE: 0 RIE: 1 CAT: 19

Project Open Horizons
CIJE: 0 RIE: 1 CAT: 19

Project Opportunity
CIJE: 1 RIE: 6 CAT: 19

Project OPT
CIJE: 1 RIE: 1 CAT: 19

Project Optimus Outreach
CIJE: 0 RIE: 1 CAT: 19

Project OPTION
CIJE: 0 RIE: 2 CAT: 19

Project ORA
CIJE: 0 RIE: 1 CAT: 19

Project ORCA
CIJE: 0 RIE: 16 CAT: 19
UF Ocean Related Curriculum Activities

Project Orillas
USE ORILLAS Network

Project Outreach
CIJE: 1 RIE: 12 CAT: 19

Project Outreach USA
CIJE: 0 RIE: 1 CAT: 19

Project OVERVIEW
CIJE: 0 RIE: 1 CAT: 19

Project Oz IL
CIJE: 0 RIE: 1 CAT: 17
SN Social service agency in McLean County IL

Project PACCE
CIJE: 0 RIE: 1 CAT: 19

Project Pace
CIJE: 1 RIE: 2 CAT: 19

Project PACESETTER
CIJE: 0 RIE: 6 CAT: 19

Project PADRES
CIJE: 0 RIE: 1 CAT: 19

Project Pamong (Indonesia)
CIJE: 0 RIE: 1 CAT: 19

Project PAN NY
CIJE: 0 RIE: 2 CAT: 19
UF Program Assistance for Neophytes NY

Project PARADE
CIJE: 0 RIE: 1 CAT: 19
SN "Projects Advancing Reading Achievement and Developing Ego-strength"

Project Partnership
CIJE: 0 RIE: 1 CAT: 19

Project PASE
CIJE: 0 RIE: 2 CAT: 19

Project PASS
CIJE: 1 RIE: 3 CAT: 19

Project PAT MN
CIJE: 0 RIE: 1 CAT: 19
SN PAT = "Parents Are Teachers"

Project PATHE
CIJE: 0 RIE: 2 CAT: 19

Project Patrol
CIJE: 0 RIE: 1 CAT: 19

Project PAVE
CIJE: 0 RIE: 2 CAT: 19

Project Perform
CIJE: 0 RIE: 2 CAT: 19
SN Effective schools program of Cleveland Public Schools OH

Project Performance Assess Collaborative for Educ
CIJE: 0 RIE: 1 CAT: 19

Project PERMIT
CIJE: 1 RIE: 0 CAT: 19

Project Physics
CIJE: 16 RIE: 11 CAT: 19

Project PIAGET
CIJE: 0 RIE: 2 CAT: 19
SN Bilingual education project — PIAGET = Promoting Intellectual Adaptation Given Experiential Transforming

Project PIEP
USE Parent Involvement in Education Project

Project Pioneer
CIJE: 0 RIE: 1 CAT: 19
SN PIONEER = Partnerships in Integrating and Operating New Effective Educational Research

Project PIPE OH
USE Parent Involvement through Parent Education

Project PIPE PA
USE Parents in Partnership with Educators

Project PIRLT
CIJE: 0 RIE: 1 CAT: 19

Project PISCES
CIJE: 0 RIE: 1 CAT: 19
SN Pilot Infusion System for Career Experiential Studies

Project PLACE
CIJE: 1 RIE: 0 CAT: 19

Project Planners
CIJE: 2 RIE: 0 CAT: 09

Project PLANTWORK
CIJE: 0 RIE: 1 CAT: 19

Project Playpen
CIJE: 1 RIE: 0 CAT: 19

Project POET
CIJE: 0 RIE: 1 CAT: 19

Project Portage
CIJE: 0 RIE: 1 CAT: 19

Project Porvenir NM
CIJE: 0 RIE: 0 CAT: 19
SN A program to provide rural health care

Project Porvenir NY
CIJE: 0 RIE: 4 CAT: 19
SN A program to provide instruction and support to limited English speaking and native Spanish speaking students in grades 4 to 6 in the Bronx

Project PR
CIJE: 0 RIE: 1 CAT: 19
SN Prevention/Rehabilitation for Truant and Disruptive Students

Project PREP NY
CIJE: 0 RIE: 1 CAT: 19
UF Parent Resources and Education Program NY

Project Prepare
CIJE: 0 RIE: 3 CAT: 19
SN Butte (MT) adult basic education program for disadvantaged parents

Project Prepare OH
CIJE: 0 RIE: 9 CAT: 19
SN Personnel preparation in early childhood special education

Project Prevention
CIJE: 0 RIE: 1 CAT: 19
SN Project of preventive intervention in child and adolescent psychiatry

Project Prevocational
CIJE: 0 RIE: 1 CAT: 19

Project PRICE
CIJE: 1 RIE: 12 CAT: 19

Project PRIDE
CIJE: 0 RIE: 9 CAT: 19

Project Pride NY
CIJE: 0 RIE: 2 CAT: 19
SN English as a second language project for limited English proficient Haitian students

Project PRIME
CIJE: 3 RIE: 8 CAT: 19

Project PRIME AZ
CIJE: 0 RIE: 1 CAT: 19
UF PRoject to Improve Minority Education in AZ

Project PRIMER (Jamaica)
CIJE: 0 RIE: 1 CAT: 19

Project PRIMES
CIJE: 0 RIE: 8 CAT: 19

Project Primetime
CIJE: 1 RIE: 6 CAT: 19

Project PRISE MI
CIJE: 0 RIE: 1 CAT: 19
UF Project to Improve Science Education MI

Project PRISM
CIJE: 0 RIE: 3 CAT: 19

Project PROBE
CIJE: 0 RIE: 13 CAT: 19

Project PROCEED
CIJE: 1 RIE: 2 CAT: 04

Project PROF
CIJE: 0 RIE: 1 CAT: 19

Project Prolexia
CIJE: 1 RIE: 0 CAT: 19

Project Protech
CIJE: 1 RIE: 0 CAT: 19

Project Protection
CIJE: 3 RIE: 1 CAT: 19

Project Pryme
CIJE: 0 RIE: 1 CAT: 19

Project Pulse
CIJE: 0 RIE: 2 CAT: 19

Project QUESST
CIJE: 0 RIE: 1 CAT: 19
SN Quantitative Understanding to Enhance Social Science Teaching Project

Project Quest
CIJE: 0 RIE: 1 CAT: 19

Project QUILL
CIJE: 0 RIE: 2 CAT: 19

Project R 3
CIJE: 0 RIE: 2 CAT: 19

Project RAISE OH
USE Rural America Institute for Special Educators

Project RAND
CIJE: 0 RIE: 8 CAT: 19

Project RAPYHT
USE RAPYHT Project

Project Re Ed (Hobbs)
CIJE: 3 RIE: 0 CAT: 19

Project Reach
CIJE: 9 RIE: 10 CAT: 19

Project REACH CO
CIJE: 0 RIE: 1 CAT: 19

Project Reach ME
CIJE: 0 RIE: 1 CAT: 19
SN Collaborative training initiative in early intervention practices

Project Reach NY
CIJE: 0 RIE: 1 CAT: 19
SN Bilingual education at William H. Taft High School in New York City

Project REACH SC
CIJE: 0 RIE: 2 CAT: 19
SN "Rural Educational Alliance for Collaborative Humanities"

Project Reach TX
CIJE: 0 RIE: 1 CAT: 19
SN Alternative school program for seriously at-risk students

Project READ
CIJE: 3 RIE: 12 CAT: 19

Project READ CA
CIJE: 0 RIE: 0 CAT: 19
UF Reading for Educational Achievement and Devel CA

Project READ OH
CIJE: 0 RIE: 1 CAT: 19
UF Reading Education for Adults in Dayton

Project READS
CIJE: 2 RIE: 1 CAT: 19

Project REAL
CIJE: 1 RIE: 1 CAT: 19
UF Real Educational Activities of Learning

Project REAL DE
CIJE: 0 RIE: 0 CAT: 19
UF Relevant Experiences for Alternative Learning Proj

Project REAL NY
CIJE: 0 RIE: 1 CAT: 19
UF Return to Employment And Learning

Project REALISTIC
CIJE: 1 RIE: 2 CAT: 19

Project REAP IN
CIJE: 0 RIE: 1 CAT: 19
UF Reading Enjoying And Presenting

Project RECURSO NY
CIJE: 0 RIE: 3 CAT: 19

Project REDEAL
CIJE: 1 RIE: 2 CAT: 19

Project Redesign
CIJE: 4 RIE: 2 CAT: 19

Project Redirection
CIJE: 1 RIE: 8 CAT: 19

Project REDY
CIJE: 1 RIE: 10 CAT: 19

Project REED
CIJE: 0 RIE: 1 CAT: 19

Project REFLECT
CIJE: 0 RIE: 1 CAT: 19

Project Refocus Outplacement Service
CIJE: 0 RIE: 0 CAT: 19
SN Specially targeted toward blue-collar workers

Project REFOCUS TX
CIJE: 0 RIE: 1 CAT: 19
SN A program designed to enhance economic self-sufficiency of English-as-a-Second-Language AFDC recipients

Project RELATE
CIJE: 1 RIE: 1 CAT: 19

Project REMEDY
CIJE: 1 RIE: 1 CAT: 19

Project RENEW
CIJE: 0 RIE: 2 CAT: 19

Project RESCATE
CIJE: 0 RIE: 1 CAT: 19

Project RESCATE NY
CIJE: 0 RIE: 1 CAT: 19

Project Rescue
CIJE: 0 RIE: 1 CAT: 19

Project RESCUE GA
CIJE: 0 RIE: 1 CAT: 19
SN "Refer, Evaluate, Support, Coordinate, Uncover, and Educate"

Project Respond MO
CIJE: 0 RIE: 2 CAT: 19

Project RETAP
CIJE: 0 RIE: 1 CAT: 19

Project RETOOL
CIJE: 3 RIE: 4 CAT: 19

Project RHISE
CIJE: 0 RIE: 1 CAT: 19

Project RISE
CIJE: 6 RIE: 6 CAT: 19

Project ROLE NJ
CIJE: 0 RIE: 1 CAT: 19

Project ROME
CIJE: 0 RIE: 8 CAT: 19

Project SABE NY
CIJE: 0 RIE: 1 CAT: 19
UF Systematic Approaches to Bilingual Educ Proj NY

Project SACHEM
CIJE: 0 RIE: 1 CAT: 19

Project SACI
CIJE: 0 RIE: 2 CAT: 19

Project SAFE
CIJE: 1 RIE: 0 CAT: 19
UF Seizure Assimilation for Educators

Project SAG
CIJE: 0 RIE: 1 CAT: 19

Project SAGE
CIJE: 0 RIE: 2 CAT: 19

Project SAIL NY
CIJE: 0 RIE: 1 CAT: 19
SN "Success and Achievement In Learning"

Project SAVE
CIJE: 2 RIE: 3 CAT: 19

Project SCALE
CIJE: 0 RIE: 1 CAT: 19
UF Satellite Centers for Adult Leadership

Project SCAT
CIJE: 0 RIE: 12 CAT: 19

Project School to Work
CIJE: 0 RIE: 1 CAT: 19

Project SCOPE
CIJE: 3 RIE: 1 CAT: 19

Project SCORE
CIJE: 0 RIE: 2 CAT: 19

Project SEALL
CIJE: 0 RIE: 1 CAT: 19
SN "Special Education at the Local Level"

Project SEAR
CIJE: 0 RIE: 1 CAT: 19

Project Search
CIJE: 3 RIE: 14 CAT: 19

Project Search for Preventive Approaches
CIJE: 1 RIE: 0 CAT: 19

Project Seattle
CIJE: 0 RIE: 1 CAT: 19

Project Second Look
CIJE: 0 RIE: 1 CAT: 19

Project Secondary English
CIJE: 0 RIE: 2 CAT: 19

Project SEE
CIJE: 1 RIE: 6 CAT: 19

Project SEED
CIJE: 7 RIE: 11 CAT: 19

Project SEEK
CIJE: 10 RIE: 19 CAT: 19
UF Search for Education Elevation and Knowledge NY; SEEK Program NY

Project SEEK OH
CIJE: 0 RIE: 0 CAT: 19
UF Seventh Grade Eclectic Exploration of Knowledge

Project SEEK OK
CIJE: 0 RIE: 0 CAT: 19
UF Sooner Exchange for Educational Knowledge

Project SEESAW
CIJE: 0 RIE: 1 CAT: 19

Project SEISMIC
CIJE: 0 RIE: 2 CAT: 19

Project SELECT
CIJE: 0 RIE: 6 CAT: 19

Project Self Directive Dramatization
CIJE: 0 RIE: 1 CAT: 19

Project Self Discovery
CIJE: 1 RIE: 2 CAT: 19

Project SELF HELP MD
USE SELF HELP Program MD

Project SENAP
CIJE: 0 RIE: 2 CAT: 19

Project Senior
CIJE: 0 RIE: 1 CAT: 19

Project Seniors Tutor for Educational Progress
CIJE: 0 RIE: 3 CAT: 19

Project SERAPHIM
CIJE: 13 RIE: 6 CAT: 19

Project SERVE
CIJE: 1 RIE: 4 CAT: 19

Project SERVE MN
CIJE: 0 RIE: 1 CAT: 19
SN Special Education Rehabilitation Vocational Education Program

Project SERVICE
CIJE: 0 RIE: 1 CAT: 19

Project SESAME
CIJE: 0 RIE: 2 CAT: 19

Project SEST
CIJE: 0 RIE: 1 CAT: 19

Project SET
CIJE: 0 RIE: 1 CAT: 19

Project SETT UP
CIJE: 0 RIE: 1 CAT: 19

Project SHAL
CIJE: 2 RIE: 4 CAT: 19

Project SHARE
CIJE: 1 RIE: 20 CAT: 19

Project SHARE NY
CIJE: 0 RIE: 1 CAT: 19
UF Staff Helping Attain Relevant Education NY

Project SIGN NC
USE School Improvement Groups Network Project NC

Project Simu School
CIJE: 3 RIE: 24 CAT: 19

Project SISS
CIJE: 0 RIE: 1 CAT: 19

Project SITE
CIJE: 1 RIE: 1 CAT: 19

Project Skill
CIJE: 1 RIE: 4 CAT: 19

Project Skyriver
CIJE: 1 RIE: 1 CAT: 19

Project SLATE
CIJE: 0 RIE: 1 CAT: 19
UF State Leadership Assistance for Technology in Educ

Project SMART
CIJE: 0 RIE: 1 CAT: 19
UF Self Management and Resistance Training Proj CA

Project SMART TX
USE SMART Project TX

Project SMILE
CIJE: 0 RIE: 1 CAT: 19

Project SNACK
CIJE: 0 RIE: 1 CAT: 19

Project SOAR
CIJE: 1 RIE: 5 CAT: 19
SN Three meanings for different projects — "Stress on Analytical Reasoning," "Supply, Output, and Requirements," "Save Our American Resources"

Project Social Studies
CIJE: 3 RIE: 72 CAT: 19

Project SOCRATES
CIJE: 1 RIE: 2 CAT: 19
SN Gifted education program, grades 4-5

Project SOL FA
CIJE: 1 RIE: 0 CAT: 19

Project SOLID START
CIJE: 0 RIE: 1 CAT: 19

Project SOLO
CIJE: 2 RIE: 26 CAT: 19

Project SOS
CIJE: 0 RIE: 1 CAT: 19

Project SOUL
CIJE: 0 RIE: 2 CAT: 19

Project SOUL NJ
CIJE: 0 RIE: 1 CAT: 19
UF Society of Unlimited Learning NJ

Project SPACE
CIJE: 0 RIE: 3 CAT: 19

Project SPAN
CIJE: 3 RIE: 5 CAT: 19

Project Speak
CIJE: 0 RIE: 1 CAT: 19

Project SPEAR
CIJE: 0 RIE: 1 CAT: 19

Project SPECIAL
CIJE: 0 RIE: 1 CAT: 19

Project Specific Education of the Eye
CIJE: 0 RIE: 1 CAT: 19

Project SPECTRE
CIJE: 1 RIE: 1 CAT: 19

Project Spectrum
CIJE: 2 RIE: 1 CAT: 19

Project SPEED NY
CIJE: 0 RIE: 2 CAT: 19

Project SPICE
CIJE: 0 RIE: 17 CAT: 19
SN Special Partnership in Career Education

Project SPIRIT
CIJE: 0 RIE: 1 CAT: 19

Project Springboard
CIJE: 0 RIE: 1 CAT: 19

Project SPRUCE
CIJE: 1 RIE: 5 CAT: 19

Project SPUR
USE Special Plan Upgrading Reading

Project STACI
USE Systems Thinking and Curriculum Innovation Project

Project STAR
CIJE: 12 RIE: 20 CAT: 19

Project STAR I IN
CIJE: 0 RIE: 1 CAT: 19

Project STAR PA
CIJE: 0 RIE: 1 CAT: 19
UF Specialized Training for Adoption Readiness PA

Project STAR TN
USE Student Teacher Achievement Ratio Project TN

Project STARS NY (Retailing)
USE Student Training at Retail Stores Project NY

Project STAY
CIJE: 2 RIE: 1 CAT: 19

Project STEEL
CIJE: 0 RIE: 4 CAT: 19
UF Special Teacher Education and Evaluation Lab

Project Step
CIJE: 0 RIE: 5 CAT: 19

Project Step Up
CIJE: 2 RIE: 4 CAT: 19

Project STEPS KY
CIJE: 0 RIE: 1 CAT: 19
UF Sequenced Transition to Educ in the Public Schls

Project STIR
CIJE: 0 RIE: 1 CAT: 19

Project STITE
CIJE: 0 RIE: 1 CAT: 19

Project STOP NY
CIJE: 0 RIE: 1 CAT: 19

UF Schools Teaching Options for Peace

Project STREAM
CIJE: 2 RIE: 1 CAT: 19

Project STRETCH
CIJE: 0 RIE: 17 CAT: 19

Project Strive
CIJE: 1 RIE: 4 CAT: 19

Project STRIVE IN
CIJE: 0 RIE: 1 CAT: 19

Project SUCCESS
CIJE: 2 RIE: 4 CAT: 19

Project SUCCESS (Computer and Career Educ)
CIJE: 0 RIE: 2 CAT: 19
SN SUCCESS = Students Upgrading through Computer and Career Education Systems Services

Project Success Enrichment
CIJE: 0 RIE: 1 CAT: 19

Project Success Environment
CIJE: 0 RIE: 4 CAT: 19

Project Success GA
CIJE: 0 RIE: 1 CAT: 19
SN Vocational educ project of Decatur County Sch Dist (Bainbridge High School)

Project SUCCESS NY
CIJE: 0 RIE: 2 CAT: 19
SN SUCCESS = Striving Upward through College and Career Education for Spanish Speakers

Project Sunrise
CIJE: 0 RIE: 3 CAT: 19

Project SUPER
CIJE: 0 RIE: 1 CAT: 19

Project Superemos NY
CIJE: 0 RIE: 1 CAT: 19

Project Support CA
CIJE: 0 RIE: 1 CAT: 19
SN Gang/drug prevention program

Project Synapse
CIJE: 0 RIE: 2 CAT: 19

Project SYNERGY
CIJE: 2 RIE: 3 CAT: 19
SN An IBM-funded project providing software support for underprepared college students

Project Synthesis
CIJE: 14 RIE: 9 CAT: 15

Project T and N Bucks
CIJE: 0 RIE: 1 CAT: 19

Project TAARK AR
USE Technology Access for Arkansans

Project TACT
CIJE: 0 RIE: 1 CAT: 19

Project TALENT
CIJE: 37 RIE: 79 CAT: 19

Project Talent Mathematics Test
CIJE: 0 RIE: 1 CAT: 21

Project TAMEC
CIJE: 0 RIE: 1 CAT: 19

Project TAPS
CIJE: 1 RIE: 1 CAT: 19

Project TEACH
CIJE: 2 RIE: 6 CAT: 19

Project Teach (FIPSE)
CIJE: 0 RIE: 2 CAT: 19
UF FIPSE Project Teach

Project TEACH NY
CIJE: 0 RIE: 4 CAT: 19
UF Technological Enrich Achmt Cambodians Hispanics

Project TEACH PA
USE Teaching Environment Awareness to Child of Harvest

Project Teacher Excellence
CIJE: 0 RIE: 1 CAT: 19

Project Team Build
CIJE: 1 RIE: 0 CAT: 19

Project TEAMS NE
CIJE: 0 RIE: 5 CAT: 19

Project TECE
CIJE: 0 RIE: 2 CAT: 19

Project Teen Ager SC
CIJE: 0 RIE: 1 CAT: 19

Project Telepac
CIJE: 0 RIE: 4 CAT: 19

Project THEMIS
CIJE: 0 RIE: 6 CAT: 19

Project THINK
CIJE: 2 RIE: 0 CAT: 19

Project THISTLE
CIJE: 1 RIE: 2 CAT: 19

Project Three Cs NY
CIJE: 0 RIE: 1 CAT: 19
SN Chinese, Career education, and Computer education

Project Thrive
CIJE: 0 RIE: 3 CAT: 19

Project TIDE
CIJE: 0 RIE: 1 CAT: 19

Project TIP NY
CIJE: 0 RIE: 2 CAT: 19
UF Transitional Intervention Project NY

Project TNT
CIJE: 0 RIE: 1 CAT: 19

Project to Enhance Effective Learn (Australia)
CIJE: 0 RIE: 1 CAT: 19

PRoject to Improve Minority Education in AZ
USE Project PRIME AZ

Project to Improve Science Education MI
USE Project PRISE MI

Project to Increase Mastery of Math and Science
CIJE: 0 RIE: 5 CAT: 19
UF PIMMS

Project TOMORROW
CIJE: 0 RIE: 1 CAT: 19

Project TOPS
CIJE: 0 RIE: 1 CAT: 19

Project Torque
CIJE: 0 RIE: 4 CAT: 19

Project TOTAL
CIJE: 0 RIE: 1 CAT: 19

Project TOUCH
CIJE: 0 RIE: 1 CAT: 19

Project TRADE
CIJE: 0 RIE: 1 CAT: 19
UF Teacher Retraining And Directed Exchange

Project TRAIN (Special Education)
CIJE: 0 RIE: 1 CAT: 19
SN TRAIN = Training Rural Area Interventionists to meet Needs

Project Training
CIJE: 0 RIE: 1 CAT: 19

Project Training Jobs
CIJE: 0 RIE: 1 CAT: 19

Project Transition
CIJE: 4 RIE: 4 CAT: 19

Project TREK
CIJE: 0 RIE: 1 CAT: 19

Project TREND
CIJE: 0 RIE: 1 CAT: 19

Project Trident
CIJE: 1 RIE: 1 CAT: 19

Project TRIUNFE NY
CIJE: 0 RIE: 3 CAT: 19

Project TRUE
CIJE: 0 RIE: 3 CAT: 19

Project TRY
CIJE: 0 RIE: 5 CAT: 19

Project TTAP
CIJE: 0 RIE: 1 CAT: 19
UF Technology Team Assessment Process

Project Unidos
CIJE: 0 RIE: 1 CAT: 19

Project Unique
CIJE: 0 RIE: 1 CAT: 19
SN Unique = United Now for Integrated Quality Urban-suburban Education

Project UNIQUE NJ
CIJE: 0 RIE: 1 CAT: 19
SN UNIQUE = Underachievers Needing Individualized Qualitative Unique Education

Project Update
CIJE: 0 RIE: 2 CAT: 19

Project Upgrade
CIJE: 0 RIE: 1 CAT: 19

Project Uplift
CIJE: 3 RIE: 2 CAT: 19

Project Upper Cumberland
CIJE: 1 RIE: 0 CAT: 19

Project UPSTART
CIJE: 0 RIE: 3 CAT: 19

Project Upswing
CIJE: 0 RIE: 5 CAT: 19

Project USHER
CIJE: 1 RIE: 1 CAT: 19

Project USTED
CIJE: 0 RIE: 2 CAT: 19

Project Value
CIJE: 2 RIE: 0 CAT: 19

Project Vectors
CIJE: 0 RIE: 1 CAT: 19

Project VEO
CIJE: 1 RIE: 0 CAT: 19

Project VGIP
CIJE: 0 RIE: 1 CAT: 19

Project VIBE
CIJE: 0 RIE: 3 CAT: 19

Project VIBES NY
CIJE: 0 RIE: 1 CAT: 19

Project VIGOR
CIJE: 0 RIE: 5 CAT: 19

Project VIPP
USE Volunteers in Partnership with Parents

Project VITA
CIJE: 2 RIE: 7 CAT: 19

Project VITAL
CIJE: 0 RIE: 2 CAT: 19
SN "Videotapes for Inservice Training for Active Learning"

Project VOICE
CIJE: 0 RIE: 6 CAT: 19

Project Volunteer Power
CIJE: 1 RIE: 0 CAT: 19

Project VOTE
CIJE: 0 RIE: 1 CAT: 19

Project WAGES
CIJE: 0 RIE: 1 CAT: 19

Project Warrior
CIJE: 0 RIE: 1 CAT: 19

Project Washoe
CIJE: 1 RIE: 0 CAT: 19

Project WAT CAP
USE Waterloo Child Assessment Project

Project Watch a Book
CIJE: 0 RIE: 1 CAT: 19

Project WE CARE
CIJE: 0 RIE: 1 CAT: 19

Project WILD
CIJE: 6 RIE: 8 CAT: 19

Project Woodlawn
CIJE: 0 RIE: 2 CAT: 19

Project Workability
CIJE: 1 RIE: 2 CAT: 19

Project WORTH
CIJE: 1 RIE: 1 CAT: 19
SN See also "Project GROW KY"
UF Work Opportunity Readiness for the Homeless

Project WRITE
CIJE: 2 RIE: 0 CAT: 19

Project Yardstick
CIJE: 1 RIE: 0 CAT: 19

Project Youth
CIJE: 0 RIE: 1 CAT: 19

Project Zero Reject
CIJE: 0 RIE: 1 CAT: 19

Projection (Psychology)
CIJE: 9 RIE: 7 CAT: 11

Projection Research
CIJE: 1 RIE: 5 CAT: 20

Projective Film Test (Morrison)
CIJE: 0 RIE: 1 CAT: 21

Projective Geometry
CIJE: 4 RIE: 0 CAT: 20

Projective Picture Inventory (Sciara)
CIJE: 3 RIE: 0 CAT: 21

Projective Picture Test
CIJE: 0 RIE: 1 CAT: 21

Projective Prejudice Test (Katz and Zalk)
CIJE: 0 RIE: 0 CAT: 21

Projective Transformation
CIJE: 2 RIE: 0 CAT: 21

Projects to Advance Creativity in Education
CIJE: 4 RIE: 38 CAT: 19

Projects with Industry
CIJE: 3 RIE: 4 CAT: 19

Projet SAGE (Canada)
CIJE: 0 RIE: 1 CAT: 19

PROLOG Programing Language
CIJE: 28 RIE: 4 CAT: 04

Prometheus Bound
CIJE: 1 RIE: 0 CAT: 22

Promises
CIJE: 1 RIE: 3 CAT: 16

Promising Practices
CIJE: 3 RIE: 26 CAT: 16

Promising Practices Diffusion Project
CIJE: 0 RIE: 4 CAT: 19

Promoting Achievement in School through Sports
CIJE: 0 RIE: 3 CAT: 03

Promoting Alternative Thinking Strategies Curric
CIJE: 0 RIE: 2 CAT: 03
UF PATHS Curriculum

Promotional Gates Program
CIJE: 2 RIE: 5 CAT: 19

Promotional Gates Program NY
CIJE: 0 RIE: 4 CAT: 19

Prompt Automated Scheduling System
CIJE: 0 RIE: 1 CAT: 04
UF PASS Software

Pronatalism
CIJE: 1 RIE: 2 CAT: 15

Proofreaders
CIJE: 0 RIE: 2 CAT: 09

Proofreading Type Tests
CIJE: 1 RIE: 0 CAT: 21

Propaganda Analysis
CIJE: 4 RIE: 3 CAT: 15

Properties Managers (Theater)
CIJE: 1 RIE: 1 CAT: 09

Property Acquisition
CIJE: 1 RIE: 2 CAT: 16

Property Appraisers
CIJE: 0 RIE: 1 CAT: 09

Property Disposal
CIJE: 0 RIE: 1 CAT: 16

Property Disposition
CIJE: 0 RIE: 8 CAT: 14

Property Insurance
CIJE: 3 RIE: 3 CAT: 14

Property Management
CIJE: 5 RIE: 5 CAT: 15

Property Rights
CIJE: 14 RIE: 10 CAT: 14

Property Space
CIJE: 0 RIE: 0 CAT: 21

Property Values
CIJE: 1 RIE: 7 CAT: 16

Property Wealth
CIJE: 2 RIE: 3 CAT: 14

PROPES
USE PROcedure to Promote Effect effic Study skills

Proportion Appraisal (Johnson O Connor)
CIJE: 0 RIE: 0 CAT: 21

Proportion Correct Score
CIJE: 0 RIE: 1 CAT: 21

Proportional Hazards Models
CIJE: 1 RIE: 1 CAT: 15

Proportional Reasoning
CIJE: 23 RIE: 9 CAT: 20

Proportionality Scheme
CIJE: 3 RIE: 1 CAT: 15

Proposed Legislation
CIJE: 22 RIE: 246 CAT: 14

Proposition 1 (California 1979)
CIJE: 0 RIE: 1 CAT: 14

Proposition 2 and One Half (Massachusetts 1980)
CIJE: 4 RIE: 9 CAT: 14

Proposition 4 (California 1979)
CIJE: 0 RIE: 1 CAT: 14

Proposition 8 (California 1982)
USE Victims Bill of Rights (California 1982)

Proposition 9 (California 1980)
CIJE: 1 RIE: 1 CAT: 14

Proposition 13 (California 1978)
CIJE: 27 RIE: 65 CAT: 14

Proposition 63 (California 1986)
CIJE: 0 RIE: 1 CAT: 14

Proposition Generating Task
CIJE: 0 RIE: 1 CAT: 21

Propositional Abilities
CIJE: 0 RIE: 4 CAT: 16

Propositional Analysis
CIJE: 14 RIE: 5 CAT: 16

Propositional Logic
CIJE: 1 RIE: 2 CAT: 16
SN See also "Binary Propositional Logic"

Propositional Logic Test
CIJE: 1 RIE: 1 CAT: 21

Propositions (Grammar)
CIJE: 0 RIE: 1 CAT: 13

Propp (Vladimir)
CIJE: 0 RIE: 2 CAT: 18

Proprietary Drugs
CIJE: 0 RIE: 2 CAT: 11

Proprietary Hospitals
CIJE: 0 RIE: 1 CAT: 05

Proprietary Organizations
CIJE: 8 RIE: 3 CAT: 05
UF For Profit Organizations; Profit Making Organizations

Proprietary Rehabilitation
CIJE: 0 RIE: 1 CAT: 11

Proprioception Tests
CIJE: 2 RIE: 1 CAT: 21

Proration of Funds
CIJE: 0 RIE: 1 CAT: 15

Prose Learning
CIJE: 32 RIE: 88 CAT: 11

Prose Modeling
CIJE: 0 RIE: 1 CAT: 15

PROSIM 5 Production System Simulator
CIJE: 0 RIE: 1 CAT: 04

Prosocial Aggression Scale
CIJE: 0 RIE: 1 CAT: 21

Prosocial Behaviour Questionnaire
CIJE: 2 RIE: 0 CAT: 21

Prosodic Organization
CIJE: 0 RIE: 1 CAT: 13

Prospect Archives
CIJE: 2 RIE: 0 CAT: 17

Prospective Payment System
CIJE: 5 RIE: 3 CAT: 19

Prosser (Charles)
CIJE: 8 RIE: 0 CAT: 18

Prosser Vocational Center IN
CIJE: 0 RIE: 1 CAT: 17

Proster Theory
CIJE: 8 RIE: 2 CAT: 15

Prosthetic Technicians
CIJE: 1 RIE: 2 CAT: 09

Prostitution
CIJE: 23 RIE: 14 CAT: 16
SN See also "Child Prostitution" and "Teenage Prostitution"

Protagoras
CIJE: 4 RIE: 1 CAT: 18
SN c480-c421 BC, Greek sophist, philosopher

Protected Areas
CIJE: 0 RIE: 1 CAT: 20

Protection and Advocacy Mentally Ill Individ Act
CIJE: 0 RIE: 1 CAT: 14
UF Public Law 99 319

Protection Children Sexual Exploitation Act 1977
CIJE: 0 RIE: 1 CAT: 14

Protection Motivation Theory
CIJE: 1 RIE: 2 CAT: 15

Protective Behavior
CIJE: 6 RIE: 0 CAT: 11

Protective Clothing
CIJE: 1 RIE: 0 CAT: 11

Protective Custody
CIJE: 4 RIE: 0 CAT: 14

Protective Factors
CIJE: 0 RIE: 1 CAT: 11

Protective Mechanisms
CIJE: 3 RIE: 1 CAT: 11

Protective Services
CIJE: 5 RIE: 13 CAT: 05

Protective Vocabulary
CIJE: 0 RIE: 1 CAT: 13

Protege Mentor Relationship
CIJE: 8 RIE: 46 CAT: 16
UF Mentor Protege Relationship

Proteges
CIJE: 5 RIE: 0 CAT: 10

Protein
CIJE: 11 RIE: 4 CAT: 11

Protein Deficiency
CIJE: 3 RIE: 8 CAT: 11

Protein Excess
CIJE: 1 RIE: 1 CAT: 11

Protein Inhibitors
CIJE: 0 RIE: 0 CAT: 20

Proteins
CIJE: 29 RIE: 2 CAT: 20

Protestant Ethic Scale
CIJE: 3 RIE: 1 CAT: 21

Protestant Reformation
CIJE: 4 RIE: 2 CAT: 12

Protestant School Board of Greater Montreal
CIJE: 0 RIE: 3 CAT: 17

Proteus Adult Training Center CA
CIJE: 0 RIE: 1 CAT: 17

Proto Algic
CIJE: 0 RIE: 4 CAT: 13
SN The ancestor of Proto-Algonquian and other languages

Proto Algonquian
CIJE: 0 RIE: 2 CAT: 13

Proto Chadic
CIJE: 0 RIE: 1 CAT: 13

Proto Elamo Dravidian
CIJE: 1 RIE: 0 CAT: 13

Proto Indo European
CIJE: 2 RIE: 0 CAT: 13

Proto RELADES
CIJE: 0 RIE: 1 CAT: 13

Protocol Aided Revision
CIJE: 0 RIE: 2 CAT: 15

Protocol Materials Development Project
CIJE: 0 RIE: 1 CAT: 19

Protocol Materials in English Film Series
CIJE: 0 RIE: 2 CAT: 22

Protocols
CIJE: 4 RIE: 0 CAT: 15
SN Use a more specific term if possible, e.g., "Communications Protocols," "Memory Protocols," "Network Protocols"

Protosynthex III
CIJE: 0 RIE: 2 CAT: 04

Prototype Acquisition
CIJE: 5 RIE: 2 CAT: 11

Prototype Diagnostic Test
CIJE: 0 RIE: 2 CAT: 21

Prototype Testing
CIJE: 6 RIE: 2 CAT: 21

Prototypes
CIJE: 169 RIE: 35 CAT: 15

Prototypic Learner Models
CIJE: 1 RIE: 0 CAT: 15

Prototypic System for Reading Instruction
CIJE: 0 RIE: 1 CAT: 15

Protractors
CIJE: 2 RIE: 1 CAT: 04

Proud Parent Syndrome
CIJE: 0 RIE: 1 CAT: 11

Proust (Marcel)
CIJE: 5 RIE: 1 CAT: 18

Provencal
CIJE: 2 RIE: 4 CAT: 13

Proverbs Test
CIJE: 3 RIE: 2 CAT: 21

Provide Addict Care Today
CIJE: 1 RIE: 0 CAT: 19

Providence School District RI
CIJE: 2 RIE: 2 CAT: 17

Providence Social Studies Curriculum Project
CIJE: 1 RIE: 5 CAT: 19

Providence Youth Interviewers Project
CIJE: 0 RIE: 1 CAT: 19

Provincial Examinations
CIJE: 2 RIE: 9 CAT: 21

Provincialism
CIJE: 1 RIE: 1 CAT: 16

Provisional Analysis
CIJE: 0 RIE: 1 CAT: 15

Provisional Certification
CIJE: 3 RIE: 9 CAT: 16

Provo City School District UT
CIJE: 0 RIE: 1 CAT: 17

Provo Code for Analysis of Teaching
CIJE: 0 RIE: 1 CAT: 21

Provo Experiment
CIJE: 0 RIE: 1 CAT: 19

Provosts
CIJE: 1 RIE: 8 CAT: 09

Provus Discrepancy Evaluation Model
CIJE: 1 RIE: 3 CAT: 15

Proximal Goal
CIJE: 1 RIE: 3 CAT: 15

Proxy Reports
CIJE: 1 RIE: 1 CAT: 16

Proyecto Nuevos Horizontes NY
CIJE: 0 RIE: 2 CAT: 19
UF Project New Horizons NY; Project Nuevos Horizontes NY

Prueba de Analisis Auditivo
CIJE: 2 RIE: 0 CAT: 21

Prueba de Aptitud Academica
CIJE: 1 RIE: 3 CAT: 21

Prueba de Articulacion de Consonantes Semivocales
CIJE: 0 RIE: 1 CAT: 21

Prueba Riverside de Realizacion en Espanol
CIJE: 0 RIE: 2 CAT: 21

Prussia
CIJE: 4 RIE: 0 CAT: 07

Prussian
CIJE: 0 RIE: 2 CAT: 13

Psalms
CIJE: 2 RIE: 0 CAT: 22

PSAT
USE Preliminary Scholastic Aptitude Test

PSB Aptitude Test for Practical Nursing
CIJE: 0 RIE: 1 CAT: 21

Pseudo Evaluation
CIJE: 1 RIE: 0 CAT: 21

Pseudo Likelihood Theory
CIJE: 0 RIE: 1 CAT: 15

Pseudo Morphemes
CIJE: 1 RIE: 0 CAT: 13

Pseudoscience
CIJE: 9 RIE: 3 CAT: 20

PSG Production Systems
CIJE: 0 RIE: 1 CAT: 04

Psilocybin
CIJE: 0 RIE: 1 CAT: 11

PSInet
CIJE: 0 RIE: 1 CAT: 19
SN Teleconferencing network for science and mathematics teachers
UF People Sharing Information Network

PsycALERT
CIJE: 0 RIE: 1 CAT: 04

Psychiatric Epidemiology
CIJE: 4 RIE: 0 CAT: 11

Psychiatric Inpatients
CIJE: 1 RIE: 2 CAT: 10

Psychiatric Nursing
CIJE: 4 RIE: 5 CAT: 11

Psychiatric Outpatient Commitment
USE Outpatient Commitment

Psychiatric Outpatients
CIJE: 1 RIE: 1 CAT: 10

Psychiatric Rehabilitation
CIJE: 3 RIE: 0 CAT: 11

Psychiatric Social Workers
CIJE: 0 RIE: 2 CAT: 09

Psychic Energy
CIJE: 1 RIE: 0 CAT: 11

PSYCHINFO
USE PsycINFO

PSYCHLIT
USE PsycLIT

Psychoactive Drugs
CIJE: 10 RIE: 4 CAT: 11

Psychoanalytic Criticism
CIJE: 5 RIE: 1 CAT: 15

Psychoanalytic Theory
CIJE: 34 RIE: 19 CAT: 15

Psychobiography
CIJE: 2 RIE: 0 CAT: 11

Psychobiology
CIJE: 12 RIE: 3 CAT: 20

Psychodiagnosis
CIJE: 0 RIE: 2 CAT: 11

Psychodiagnostic Clinics
CIJE: 1 RIE: 0 CAT: 05

Psychodrama
CIJE: 16 RIE: 5 CAT: 16

Psychodynamic Child Rating Scale
CIJE: 0 RIE: 1 CAT: 21

Psychodynamics
CIJE: 22 RIE: 5 CAT: 15

Psychoeducational Agency School System Model
CIJE: 0 RIE: 1 CAT: 15

Psychoepistemology
CIJE: 0 RIE: 1 CAT: 15

Psychographic Analysis
CIJE: 2 RIE: 2 CAT: 15

Psychographics
CIJE: 1 RIE: 1 CAT: 16

Psychohistory
CIJE: 8 RIE: 0 CAT: 03

Psychological Abstracts
CIJE: 9 RIE: 10 CAT: 22
SN See also "PsycINFO," "PsycLIT," and "PsycALERT"

Psychological Anthropology
CIJE: 2 RIE: 2 CAT: 03

Psychological Assessment
CIJE: 3 RIE: 2 CAT: 11

Psychological Constructs
CIJE: 5 RIE: 4 CAT: 11

Psychological Corporation
CIJE: 1 RIE: 2 CAT: 17

Psychological Differentiation
CIJE: 9 RIE: 6 CAT: 11

Psychological Distance Scale
CIJE: 1 RIE: 0 CAT: 21

Psychological Distress Inventory
CIJE: 1 RIE: 1 CAT: 21

Psychological Games
CIJE: 3 RIE: 0 CAT: 21

Psychological Gender
CIJE: 0 RIE: 4 CAT: 11

Psychological Influences
CIJE: 31 RIE: 18 CAT: 11

Psychological Modernity
CIJE: 0 RIE: 1 CAT: 11

Psychological Parents
CIJE: 0 RIE: 1 CAT: 10

Psychological Productivity Model
CIJE: 0 RIE: 1 CAT: 21

Psychological Refractory Period
CIJE: 2 RIE: 2 CAT: 11

Psychological Screening Inventory
CIJE: 12 RIE: 2 CAT: 21

Psychological Screening Procedure
CIJE: 0 RIE: 1 CAT: 21

Psychological State
CIJE: 4 RIE: 0 CAT: 11

Psychological Stress Evaluator
CIJE: 1 RIE: 1 CAT: 21

Psychology of Mathematics Education
CIJE: 1 RIE: 10 CAT: 11

Psychology of the Self
CIJE: 1 RIE: 0 CAT: 11

Psychology Referenced Tests
CIJE: 0 RIE: 1 CAT: 21

Psychometric Entrance Test (Israel)
CIJE: 0 RIE: 1 CAT: 21
UF Israeli Interuniversity Psychometric Ent Test

Psychomotor Development
CIJE: 3 RIE: 1 CAT: 11

Psychoneurological Assessment
CIJE: 1 RIE: 2 CAT: 21

Psychophysics
CIJE: 4 RIE: 11 CAT: 16

Psychosexual Content of Play Scale (Borowitz)
CIJE: 0 RIE: 1 CAT: 21

Psychosexual Development
CIJE: 5 RIE: 2 CAT: 11

Psychosocial Adaptation
CIJE: 5 RIE: 4 CAT: 11

Psychosocial Crisis
CIJE: 6 RIE: 1 CAT: 11

Psychosocial Deprivation
CIJE: 0 RIE: 1 CAT: 11

Psychosocial Development
CIJE: 55 RIE: 28 CAT: 11

Psychosocial Factors
CIJE: 99 RIE: 13 CAT: 11

Psychosocial Maturity Scale
CIJE: 2 RIE: 9 CAT: 21

Psychosociology
CIJE: 20 RIE: 2 CAT: 11

Psychosynthesis
CIJE: 5 RIE: 2 CAT: 15

Psychotechnology
CIJE: 2 RIE: 2 CAT: 11

Psychotherapeutic Interaction Scales (Truax)
CIJE: 0 RIE: 1 CAT: 21

Psychotherapy Session Project
CIJE: 1 RIE: 0 CAT: 19

Psychotropic Medication
CIJE: 13 RIE: 2 CAT: 11

Psychovocational Model
CIJE: 0 RIE: 1 CAT: 15

PsycINFO
CIJE: 5 RIE: 6 CAT: 04
UF PSYCHINFO

PsycLIT
CIJE: 3 RIE: 2 CAT: 04
UF PSYCHLIT

PTI Study
USE Principal Teacher Interaction Study

PTS PROMT
CIJE: 0 RIE: 0 CAT: 04

PTS US Time Series
CIJE: 0 RIE: 0 CAT: 04

PTV 3
CIJE: 0 RIE: 1 CAT: 04

Puberty
CIJE: 61 RIE: 26 CAT: 11

Puberty Rites
CIJE: 4 RIE: 1 CAT: 16

Public Access
CIJE: 31 RIE: 39 CAT: 16

Public Access Catalog
CIJE: 1 RIE: 3 CAT: 04

Public Access Television
CIJE: 8 RIE: 7 CAT: 16

Public Act 523 (Connecticut)
CIJE: 0 RIE: 6 CAT: 14
UF Connecticut State Act for Disadvantaged Children

Public and Private Schools (Coleman et al)
CIJE: 28 RIE: 16 CAT: 22

Public Artists
CIJE: 1 RIE: 0 CAT: 09

Public Awareness
CIJE: 10 RIE: 11 CAT: 16

Public Broadcast Laboratory
CIJE: 1 RIE: 0 CAT: 17

Public Broadcasters International
CIJE: 0 RIE: 1 CAT: 17

Public Broadcasting
CIJE: 9 RIE: 28 CAT: 20

Public Broadcasting Act
CIJE: 1 RIE: 4 CAT: 14

Public Broadcasting Environment Center
CIJE: 0 RIE: 1 CAT: 17

Public Broadcasting Service
CIJE: 39 RIE: 42 CAT: 17

Public Choice Model (Economics)
CIJE: 9 RIE: 0 CAT: 15

Public Discourse
CIJE: 2 RIE: 11 CAT: 16

Public Dividend Plan
CIJE: 0 RIE: 1 CAT: 19

Public Domain
CIJE: 6 RIE: 0 CAT: 16

Public Domain Software
CIJE: 13 RIE: 3 CAT: 04

Public Education Fund PA
CIJE: 1 RIE: 1 CAT: 17

Public Education Religious Studies Center
CIJE: 0 RIE: 5 CAT: 17

Public Elementary and Secondary Agency Universe
CIJE: 0 RIE: 2 CAT: 21
SN Public Elementary and Secondary Education Agency Universe

Public Elementary and Secondary School Universe
CIJE: 0 RIE: 2 CAT: 21

Public Employee Relations Act (Pennsylvania)
CIJE: 0 RIE: 4 CAT: 14

Public Employee Relations Act 1970 (Pennsylvania)
CIJE: 4 RIE: 1 CAT: 14

Public Employees Fair Employment Act (New York)
CIJE: 1 RIE: 1 CAT: 14

Public Employment Programs
CIJE: 3 RIE: 6 CAT: 19

Public Employment Relations Act (Alaska 1990)
CIJE: 0 RIE: 1 CAT: 14
UF Alaska Public Employment Relations Act

Public Employment Relations Act (Hawaii)
CIJE: 1 RIE: 0 CAT: 14

Public Employment Relations Act (Michigan)
CIJE: 0 RIE: 1 CAT: 14

Public Employment Relations Board
CIJE: 0 RIE: 4 CAT: 17

Public Employment Relations Boards
CIJE: 0 RIE: 4 CAT: 09

Public For Profit School Management
USE Profit Making Public School Management

Public Good
CIJE: 1 RIE: 1 CAT: 16

Public Health Service
CIJE: 19 RIE: 18 CAT: 17

Public Health Service Act
CIJE: 2 RIE: 28 CAT: 14

Public History
CIJE: 7 RIE: 1 CAT: 12

Public Information
CIJE: 1 RIE: 5 CAT: 16

Public Information Act
CIJE: 1 RIE: 0 CAT: 14

Public Information Campaigns
CIJE: 1 RIE: 3 CAT: 16

Public Information Officers
CIJE: 4 RIE: 2 CAT: 09

Public Information Systems
CIJE: 1 RIE: 1 CAT: 04

Public Interest
CIJE: 26 RIE: 20 CAT: 16

Public Interest Information Network
CIJE: 0 RIE: 1 CAT: 17

Public Interest Law
CIJE: 3 RIE: 3 CAT: 14

Public Interest Law Suits
CIJE: 1 RIE: 0 CAT: 14

Public Interest Research Groups
CIJE: 4 RIE: 1 CAT: 10

Public Issue Forums
CIJE: 1 RIE: 2 CAT: 02

Public Lands
CIJE: 1 RIE: 4 CAT: 05
SN See also "Federal Lands"

Public Language
CIJE: 2 RIE: 3 CAT: 13

Public Law 51 (82d Cong 1st Sess)
CIJE: 0 RIE: 1 CAT: 14

Public Law 85 926
CIJE: 0 RIE: 4 CAT: 14

Public Law 87 276
CIJE: 0 RIE: 1 CAT: 14

Public Law 88 164
CIJE: 0 RIE: 2 CAT: 14

Public Law 88 577
USE Wilderness Act 1964

Public Law 89 136
USE Public Works and Economic Development Act 1965

Public Law 89 239
CIJE: 0 RIE: 1 CAT: 14

Public Law 89 313
CIJE: 2 RIE: 12 CAT: 14
SN Amended ESEA Title I to provide Federal assistance for the education of handicapped children in state-operated and supported schools

Public Law 90 247
USE Education Amendments 1967

Public Law 90 472
CIJE: 0 RIE: 2 CAT: 14

Public Law 91 517
USE Developmental Disabil Servs and Facil Constr Act

Public Law 92 318
USE Higher Education Act Amendments 1972

Public Law 93 87
USE Federal Aid Highway Act

Public Law 93 380
USE Education Amendments 1974

Public Law 93 415
USE Juvenile Justice Delinquency Prevention Act 1974

Public Law 93 638
USE Indian Self Determination Education Assistance Act

Public Law 94 103
USE Developmental Disabled Assist Bill of Rights Act

Public Law 94 142
USE Education for All Handicapped Children Act

Public Law 94 161 Title XII
USE Foreign Assistance Act 1975 Title XII

Public Law 94 482
USE Education Amendments 1976

Public Law 94 502
USE Veterans Education and Employment Assistance Act

Public Law 95 192
USE Soil and Water Resources Conservation Act

Public Law 95 471
USE Tribally Controlled Comm Coll Assist Act 1978

Public Law 95 561
USE Education Amendments 1978

Public Law 95 602
USE Developmental Disabilities Amendments 1978

Public Law 96 374
CIJE: 0 RIE: 3 CAT: 14

Public Law 96 511
USE Paperwork Reduction Act 1980

Public Law 97 35
USE Omnibus Budget Reconciliation Act 1981

Public Law 97 116
USE Immigration and Nationality Act Amendments

Public Law 97 292
USE Missing Children Act 1982

Public Law 98 77
USE Emergency Veterans Job Training Act 1983

Public Law 98 377
USE Education for Economic Security Act 1984

Public Law 98 377 Title VI
USE Excellence in Education Act 1984

Public Law 98 524
USE Carl D Perkins Vocational Education Act 1984

Public Law 98 558
USE Human Services Reauthorization Act 1984

Public Law 98 620
USE State Justice Institute Act 1984

Public Law 98 621
USE Saint Elizabeths and DC Mental Health Services Act

Public Law 99 319
USE Protection and Advocacy Mentally Ill Individ Act

Public Law 99 371
USE Education of the Deaf Act 1986

Public Law 99 372
USE Handicapped Childrens Protection Act 1986

Public Law 99 399
USE Omnibus Diplomatic Security and Antiterrorism Act

Public Law 99 424
USE Executive Exchange Prog Voluntary Service Act 1986

Public Law 99 425
USE Child Development Associate Scholarship Assist Act

Public Law 99 457
USE Education of the Handicapped Act Amendments 1986

Public Law 99 457 Part H
USE Education of the Handicapped Act 1986 (Part H)

Public Law 99 498
USE Higher Education Act Amendments 1986

Public Law 99 570
USE Commercial Motor Vehicle Safety Act 1986

Public Law 99 603
USE Immigration Reform and Control Act 1986

Public Law 99 643
USE Employment Opportunities for Disabld Americans Act

Public Law 100 77
USE Stewart B McKinney Homeless Assistance Act 1987

Public Law 100 146
USE Developmental Disabled Assist Bill of Rights Act

Public Law 100 175
USE Older Americans Act Amendments 1987

Public Law 100 235
USE Computer Security Act 1987

Public Law 100 259
USE Civil Rights Restoration Act 1987

Public Law 100 297
USE Hawkins Stafford Act 1988

Public Law 100 360
USE Medicare Catastrophic Protection Act 1988

Public Law 100 379
USE Worker Adjustment and Retraining Notification Act

Public Law 100 407
USE Technology Related Assistance Individ Disabil Act

Public Law 100 418
USE Omnibus Trade and Competitiveness Act 1988

Public Law 100 570
USE Academic Research Facilities Modernization Act

Public Law 100 694
USE Anti Drug Abuse Act 1988

Public Law 101 336
USE Americans with Disabilities Act 1990

Public Law 101 392
USE Carl D Perkins Voc and Appl Techn Educ Act 1990

Public Law 101 433
USE Older Workers Benefit Protection Act 1990

Public Law 101 437
USE Childrens Television Act 1990

Public Law 101 476
USE Individuals with Disabilities Education Act

Public Law 101 476 Part B
USE Individuals with Disabilities Education Act Part B

Public Law 101 476 Part H
USE Individuals with Disabilities Education Act Part H

Public Law 101 501
USE Head Start Expansion and Improvement Act 1990

Public Law 101 542
USE Student Right to Know and Campus Security Act

Public Law 101 554
USE Displaced Homemakers Self Suff Assist Act 1990

Public Law 101 610
USE National and Community Service Act 1990

Public Law 101 619
USE National Environmental Education Act 1990

Public Law 101 639
USE Mental Health Amendments 1990

Public Law 102 62
USE National Council on Educ Standards and Testing Act

Public Law 102 73
USE National Literacy Act 1991

Public Law 102 127
USE Veterans Educational Assistance Amendments 1991

Public Law 102 166
USE Civil Rights Act 1991

Public Law 102 183 Title VIII
USE National Security Education Act 1991

Public Law 102 194
USE High Performance Computing Act 1991

Public Law 102 235
USE Nontraditional Employment for Women Act 1991

Public Law 102 325
USE Higher Education Act Amendments 1992

Public Law 102 367
USE Job Training Partnership Act Amendments 1992

Public Law 102 401
USE Head Start Improvement Act 1992

Public Law 102 408
USE Health Professions Educ Exten Amendments 1992

Public Law 102 409
USE DES Education and Research Amendments 1992

Public Law 102 421
USE Education of the Deaf Act Amendments 1992

Public Law 102 524
USE Native American Languages Act 1992

Public Law 102 586
USE Juvenile Justice Delinquency Prev Act Amend 1992

Public Law 103 82
USE National and Community Service Trust Act 1993

Public Law 103 93
USE Utah Schools and Lands Improvement Act 1993

Public Law 103 141
USE Religious Freedom Restoration Act 1993

Public Law 103 227
USE Goals 2000

Public Law 280 (83d Cong)
CIJE: 3 RIE: 2 CAT: 14

Public Law 480 (83d Cong)
CIJE: 0 RIE: 2 CAT: 14

Public Law 959 (84th Cong 2d Sess)
CIJE: 0 RIE: 1 CAT: 14

Public Leadership Education Network
CIJE: 0 RIE: 1 CAT: 17

Public Lending Rights
CIJE: 15 RIE: 3 CAT: 14

Public Library Association
CIJE: 27 RIE: 2 CAT: 17

Public Library Cincinnati and Hamilton County OH
CIJE: 1 RIE: 0 CAT: 17

Public Library Effectiveness Study
CIJE: 0 RIE: 1 CAT: 19

Public Library Inquiry
CIJE: 1 RIE: 0 CAT: 21

Public Opinion Quarterly
CIJE: 0 RIE: 1 CAT: 22

Public Policy Education
CIJE: 3 RIE: 5 CAT: 03

Public Private Partnership Programs
CIJE: 2 RIE: 3 CAT: 19
UF Partnerships (Public Private)

Public Private Relationship
CIJE: 11 RIE: 20 CAT: 16

Public Profit Making Schools
USE Profit Making Public School Management

Public Radio
CIJE: 5 RIE: 26 CAT: 04

Public Records
CIJE: 11 RIE: 5 CAT: 16

Public Relations Audits
CIJE: 0 RIE: 1 CAT: 15

Public Relations Journal
CIJE: 0 RIE: 1 CAT: 22

Public Relations Journals
CIJE: 0 RIE: 1 CAT: 16

Public Relations Review
CIJE: 1 RIE: 3 CAT: 22

Public Relations Society of America
CIJE: 3 RIE: 4 CAT: 17

Public Safety
CIJE: 3 RIE: 9 CAT: 16

Public School Change Model
CIJE: 0 RIE: 1 CAT: 15

Public School Contracts Law 1977 (New Jersey)
CIJE: 0 RIE: 1 CAT: 14

Public School Profit Making Ventures
USE Profit Making Public School Management

Public School Questionnaire (NCES)
CIJE: 0 RIE: 1 CAT: 21

Public School Survey (NCES)
CIJE: 0 RIE: 0 CAT: 21

Public Schools Act (Canada)
CIJE: 0 RIE: 1 CAT: 14

Public Schools Energy Conservation Service
CIJE: 1 RIE: 4 CAT: 17

Public Schools Latin Primer
CIJE: 1 RIE: 0 CAT: 22

Public Service Advertising
CIJE: 14 RIE: 39 CAT: 16

Public Service Campaigns
CIJE: 3 RIE: 4 CAT: 16

Public Service Careers Program
CIJE: 1 RIE: 5 CAT: 19

Public Service Commission of Canada
CIJE: 0 RIE: 1 CAT: 17
UF Canadian Public Service Commission

Public Service Employment Programs
CIJE: 0 RIE: 2 CAT: 19

Public Service Internships
CIJE: 1 RIE: 0 CAT: 16

Public Services
CIJE: 5 RIE: 25 CAT: 05

Public Technology
CIJE: 0 RIE: 1 CAT: 20

Public Telecommunications Facilities Program
CIJE: 0 RIE: 1 CAT: 19

Public Telecommunications Review (Journal)
CIJE: 0 RIE: 1 CAT: 22

Public Television Library DC
CIJE: 0 RIE: 5 CAT: 17

Public Transportation
CIJE: 9 RIE: 11 CAT: 20

Public Understanding of Science Program
CIJE: 3 RIE: 2 CAT: 19

Public Works
CIJE: 0 RIE: 1 CAT: 16
SN See also "Local Public Works"

Public Works and Economic Development Act 1965
CIJE: 0 RIE: 1 CAT: 14
UF Public Law 89 136

Public Works Employment Act 1977
CIJE: 0 RIE: 2 CAT: 14

Publication and Audio Visual Advisory Council
CIJE: 0 RIE: 1 CAT: 17
UF PAVAC (ED)

Publications Review Board
CIJE: 0 RIE: 1 CAT: 17
UF PRB (ED)

Published Reading Materials
CIJE: 4 RIE: 2 CAT: 16

Publisher Role
CIJE: 10 RIE: 3 CAT: 15

Publishers Weekly
CIJE: 0 RIE: 1 CAT: 22

Puebla Project
CIJE: 0 RIE: 1 CAT: 19

Pueblo Community College CO
CIJE: 2 RIE: 2 CAT: 17

Pueblo Elementary School AZ
CIJE: 0 RIE: 1 CAT: 17

Pueblo Infant Parent Education Project NM
CIJE: 0 RIE: 1 CAT: 19
UF PIPE Project NM

Pueblo Regional Library CO
CIJE: 0 RIE: 1 CAT: 17

Pueblo Revolt (1680)
CIJE: 0 RIE: 1 CAT: 12

Puente Project CA
CIJE: 0 RIE: 3 CAT: 19

Puerto Rican Community Development Project
CIJE: 0 RIE: 2 CAT: 19

Puerto Rican History
CIJE: 2 RIE: 9 CAT: 12

Puerto Rican Literature
CIJE: 0 RIE: 1 CAT: 16

Puerto Rico
CIJE: 105 RIE: 285 CAT: 07

Puerto Rico (Old San Juan)
CIJE: 0 RIE: 1 CAT: 07

Puerto Rico (Rio Piedras)
CIJE: 1 RIE: 4 CAT: 07

Puerto Rico (San Juan)
CIJE: 3 RIE: 11 CAT: 07

Puerto Rico Discovery Day
CIJE: 0 RIE: 1 CAT: 12

Puffery
CIJE: 2 RIE: 2 CAT: 15

Puget
CIJE: 1 RIE: 0 CAT: 13

Puget Sound Educational Consortium WA
CIJE: 0 RIE: 1 CAT: 17

Puget Sound Professional Development Center WA
CIJE: 0 RIE: 2 CAT: 17

Pugh (George E)
CIJE: 0 RIE: 1 CAT: 18

Pugwash Conferences
CIJE: 2 RIE: 0 CAT: 02
SN See also "Student Pugwash"

Puig (Manuel)
CIJE: 1 RIE: 0 CAT: 18

Pulaar
CIJE: 0 RIE: 2 CAT: 13

Pulaski County Special School District AR
CIJE: 4 RIE: 2 CAT: 17

Pulaski School District WI
CIJE: 0 RIE: 1 CAT: 17

Pulci (Luigi)
CIJE: 1 RIE: 0 CAT: 18

Pulet (Georges)
CIJE: 1 RIE: 0 CAT: 18

Pulitzer (Joseph II)
CIJE: 1 RIE: 3 CAT: 18

Pull Out Method
USE Pullout Programs

Pullout Programs
CIJE: 10 RIE: 11 CAT: 19
UF Pull Out Method

Pulmonary Diseases
USE Lung Diseases

Pulp Magazines
CIJE: 1 RIE: 1 CAT: 16

Pulpwood Harvesting
CIJE: 0 RIE: 1 CAT: 20

Pulsars
CIJE: 2 RIE: 0 CAT: 20

Pulsation Thresholds
CIJE: 0 RIE: 1 CAT: 11

Pulse Program (Boston College)
CIJE: 0 RIE: 2 CAT: 19

Pulsed Tungsten Inert Gas Welding
CIJE: 0 RIE: 1 CAT: 20

Pulsejet Engines
CIJE: 1 RIE: 0 CAT: 04

Pumps
CIJE: 1 RIE: 12 CAT: 04

Pumroy Concentration Test
CIJE: 0 RIE: 1 CAT: 21

Pumsy in Pursuit of Excellence
CIJE: 0 RIE: 1 CAT: 19

Punahou School HI
CIJE: 3 RIE: 0 CAT: 17

PUNCT CAI Course
CIJE: 0 RIE: 1 CAT: 03

Punitive Damages
CIJE: 1 RIE: 2 CAT: 14

Punitive Speech
CIJE: 0 RIE: 1 CAT: 14
SN Court-sanctioned public humiliation such as mandated bumper stickers that proclaim drunk driving convictions

Punjab Agricultural University (India)
CIJE: 1 RIE: 0 CAT: 17

Punjab University
USE Panjab University (India)

Punjabis
CIJE: 4 RIE: 1 CAT: 08
UF Panjabis

Punk Rock
CIJE: 4 RIE: 1 CAT: 16

Punnett Square Method
CIJE: 0 RIE: 3 CAT: 15

Pupil Activity Inventory
CIJE: 0 RIE: 1 CAT: 21

Pupil Appraisal Center TX
CIJE: 1 RIE: 1 CAT: 17

Pupil Attitude Questionnaire
CIJE: 1 RIE: 0 CAT: 21

Pupil Attitude Scale
CIJE: 0 RIE: 1 CAT: 21

Pupil Attitude Survey
CIJE: 0 RIE: 1 CAT: 21

Pupil Attitude Toward School Inventory
CIJE: 0 RIE: 2 CAT: 21

Pupil Behavior Form (Schwartz and Mott)
CIJE: 0 RIE: 2 CAT: 21

Pupil Behavior Inventory
CIJE: 0 RIE: 4 CAT: 21

Pupil Control Behavior Form (Helsel and Willower)
CIJE: 2 RIE: 1 CAT: 21

Pupil Control Ideology
CIJE: 31 RIE: 3 CAT: 15

Pupil Control Ideology Form
CIJE: 14 RIE: 6 CAT: 21

Pupil Description of Teaching
CIJE: 1 RIE: 1 CAT: 15

Pupil Directed Instruction in Spelling
CIJE: 1 RIE: 0 CAT: 15

Pupil Enrichment Resource Center WI
CIJE: 1 RIE: 0 CAT: 17

Pupil Evaluation Measure (Whitney et al)
CIJE: 0 RIE: 1 CAT: 21

Pupil Evaluation Program
CIJE: 1 RIE: 10 CAT: 19

Pupil Evaluation Team (Process)
CIJE: 0 RIE: 1 CAT: 15

Pupil Information and Attitudes Inventory
CIJE: 0 RIE: 1 CAT: 21

Pupil Master File
CIJE: 0 RIE: 1 CAT: 15

Pupil Observation Schedule
CIJE: 0 RIE: 1 CAT: 21

Pupil Observation Survey
CIJE: 1 RIE: 2 CAT: 21

Pupil Observation Survey Report
CIJE: 0 RIE: 1 CAT: 21

Pupil Perceptions Origin Influence Questionnaire
CIJE: 0 RIE: 1 CAT: 21

Pupil Performance Models
USE Student Performance Models

Pupil Personnel Service Development Institute TX
CIJE: 0 RIE: 1 CAT: 17

Pupil Personnel Worker Team Evaluation Form
CIJE: 0 RIE: 1 CAT: 21

Pupil Proficiency Law (California)
CIJE: 0 RIE: 3 CAT: 14
UF California Pupil Proficiency Law

Pupil Rating Scale (Myklebust)
CIJE: 6 RIE: 2 CAT: 21

Pupil Record of School Experience
CIJE: 0 RIE: 1 CAT: 21

Pupil Situational Inventory
CIJE: 1 RIE: 1 CAT: 21

Pupil Team Learning
CIJE: 1 RIE: 0 CAT: 15

Pupillometry
CIJE: 1 RIE: 0 CAT: 11

Pupils with Compensatory Educational Needs
CIJE: 0 RIE: 3 CAT: 19
UF PCEN Program NY

Pupils with Special Educational Needs Program
CIJE: 0 RIE: 2 CAT: 19

Purchasing Agents
CIJE: 3 RIE: 0 CAT: 09

Purdue Academic Learning Opportunity Systems
CIJE: 0 RIE: 1 CAT: 19
UF PALOS

Purdue Academic Student Scheduling
CIJE: 0 RIE: 1 CAT: 19

Purdue Concept Formation Test (Conservation)
CIJE: 0 RIE: 1 CAT: 21

Purdue Course Instructor Evaluation Form
CIJE: 0 RIE: 1 CAT: 21

Purdue Creative Thinking Program
CIJE: 8 RIE: 3 CAT: 19

Purdue Elementary Problem Solving Inventory
CIJE: 5 RIE: 6 CAT: 21

Purdue Home Stimulation Scale
CIJE: 0 RIE: 2 CAT: 21

Purdue Instructor Performance Indicator
CIJE: 0 RIE: 1 CAT: 21

Purdue Master Attitude Scales
CIJE: 6 RIE: 2 CAT: 21

Purdue Opinion Panel
CIJE: 0 RIE: 1 CAT: 19

Purdue Pegboard Test
CIJE: 4 RIE: 3 CAT: 21

Purdue Perceptual Motor Survey
CIJE: 5 RIE: 1 CAT: 21

Purdue Placement Test in English
CIJE: 0 RIE: 2 CAT: 21

Purdue Rating Scale for Instruction
CIJE: 2 RIE: 2 CAT: 21

Purdue Real Time Basic System
CIJE: 0 RIE: 1 CAT: 04

Purdue Social Attitudes Scales
CIJE: 0 RIE: 2 CAT: 21

Purdue Student Teacher Opinionnaire
CIJE: 0 RIE: 5 CAT: 21

Purdue Teacher Opinionaire
CIJE: 6 RIE: 6 CAT: 21

Purdue University Calumet IN
CIJE: 2 RIE: 7 CAT: 17

Purdue University Fort Wayne IN
CIJE: 1 RIE: 1 CAT: 17

Purdue University IN
CIJE: 103 RIE: 74 CAT: 17

Purdy Treatment Center for Women WA
CIJE: 0 RIE: 1 CAT: 17

Pure Line Theory
CIJE: 0 RIE: 1 CAT: 15

Pure Mathematics
CIJE: 2 RIE: 1 CAT: 20

Pure Research
CIJE: 3 RIE: 1 CAT: 16

Puritan Jeremiads
USE American Jeremiads

Puritanism
CIJE: 5 RIE: 5 CAT: 16

Purpose (Composition)
CIJE: 65 RIE: 26 CAT: 16
UF Writing Purpose

Purpose Driven Assessment Program CO
CIJE: 0 RIE: 1 CAT: 19

Purpose in Life Test
CIJE: 12 RIE: 1 CAT: 21

Purpose Process Curriculum Framework
CIJE: 13 RIE: 2 CAT: 03

Purves (Alan)
CIJE: 0 RIE: 1 CAT: 18

Push for Excellence Program
CIJE: 7 RIE: 8 CAT: 19

Pushing Excellence in Pupils
CIJE: 0 RIE: 1 CAT: 19

Pushkin (Alexander)
CIJE: 5 RIE: 1 CAT: 18

Pushups
CIJE: 2 RIE: 0 CAT: 11

Puskin Institute (USSR)
CIJE: 1 RIE: 0 CAT: 17

Put In Bay Public Schools OH
CIJE: 0 RIE: 1 CAT: 17

Putnam Northern Westchester BOCES NY
CIJE: 0 RIE: 3 CAT: 17

Putting (Golf)
CIJE: 1 RIE: 1 CAT: 16

Putting America Back to Work
CIJE: 1 RIE: 4 CAT: 19

Putting Research into Educational Practice
CIJE: 1 RIE: 18 CAT: 19

Pygmalion
CIJE: 7 RIE: 2 CAT: 22

Pygmalion in the Classroom
CIJE: 1 RIE: 3 CAT: 22

PYI Awards
USE Presidential Young Investigators Program

Pyle (Ernie)
CIJE: 1 RIE: 1 CAT: 18

Pyloric Stenosis
CIJE: 0 RIE: 2 CAT: 11

Pynchon (Thomas)
CIJE: 1 RIE: 0 CAT: 18

Pyramid Lake Paiute Projects
CIJE: 0 RIE: 1 CAT: 19

Pyramidal Testing
CIJE: 0 RIE: 1 CAT: 21

Pyramids
CIJE: 3 RIE: 1 CAT: 20

Pyramids (Geometry)
CIJE: 2 RIE: 0 CAT: 20

Pyramids Reading Program
CIJE: 0 RIE: 4 CAT: 19

Pyribenzamine
CIJE: 0 RIE: 1 CAT: 11

Pyridoxal Phosphate
CIJE: 1 RIE: 0 CAT: 20

Pythagoras
CIJE: 5 RIE: 0 CAT: 18

Pythagorean Paper Foldings
CIJE: 1 RIE: 0 CAT: 15

Pythagorean Theorem
CIJE: 30 RIE: 6 CAT: 20

Q Analogies
CIJE: 0 RIE: 2 CAT: 21

Q Index
CIJE: 0 RIE: 1 CAT: 15

Q Statistic
CIJE: 0 RIE: 6 CAT: 15

Qafar
CIJE: 0 RIE: 1 CAT: 13
SN A language of the East Cushitic Group

Qatar
CIJE: 6 RIE: 11 CAT: 07

Qinghua University (China)
CIJE: 3 RIE: 0 CAT: 17

Qoyawayma (Polingaysi)
CIJE: 0 RIE: 1 CAT: 18
UF White (Elizabeth Q)

Quabbin Regional School District
CIJE: 1 RIE: 0 CAT: 17

Quackery
CIJE: 3 RIE: 1 CAT: 16

Quad Cities Technical Advisory Council
CIJE: 1 RIE: 0 CAT: 17

Quadratic Assignment
CIJE: 1 RIE: 1 CAT: 21

Quadratic Equations
CIJE: 37 RIE: 7 CAT: 20

Quadrilaterals
CIJE: 3 RIE: 0 CAT: 20

Quadrimester Program
CIJE: 0 RIE: 1 CAT: 19

Quadruplets
CIJE: 1 RIE: 1 CAT: 10

Quads
CIJE: 0 RIE: 2 CAT: 16

Quakers
CIJE: 16 RIE: 10 CAT: 10

QUAL PRO (Computer Program)
CIJE: 0 RIE: 1 CAT: 04

Qualification Raising Programs (USSR)
CIJE: 0 RIE: 1 CAT: 19

Qualified Citation Indexing
CIJE: 0 RIE: 3 CAT: 16

Qualifiers (Language)
CIJE: 0 RIE: 1 CAT: 13

Qualitative Art Education
CIJE: 1 RIE: 1 CAT: 15

Qualitative Chemical Analysis
CIJE: 2 RIE: 0 CAT: 20

Qualitative Criticism
CIJE: 0 RIE: 1 CAT: 15

Qualitative Data (Measurement)
USE Categorical Data

Qualitative Inventory of Word Knowledge
CIJE: 0 RIE: 1 CAT: 21

Qualitative Social Support
CIJE: 0 RIE: 1 CAT: 15

Quality Assurance
CIJE: 27 RIE: 19 CAT: 16

Quality Assurance Model for Process Evaluation
CIJE: 0 RIE: 1 CAT: 15

Quality Basic Education Act (Georgia)
CIJE: 0 RIE: 5 CAT: 14

Quality Criterion Estimate
CIJE: 1 RIE: 0 CAT: 15

Quality Early Childhood Care Model
CIJE: 0 RIE: 1 CAT: 15

Quality Education Act 1990 (New Jersey)
CIJE: 1 RIE: 2 CAT: 14

Quality Education Commission NJ
CIJE: 0 RIE: 1 CAT: 17

Quality Education Conference III
CIJE: 0 RIE: 1 CAT: 02

Quality Education Initiative PA
CIJE: 0 RIE: 1 CAT: 19

Quality Education Program Study
CIJE: 0 RIE: 25 CAT: 19

Quality Education Project MS
USE Mississippi Quality Education Project

Quality Evaluation of Service Trends
CIJE: 0 RIE: 1 CAT: 21

Quality Function Deployment
CIJE: 1 RIE: 1 CAT: 15

Quality Improvement Prog Plan for Spec Educators
USE QUIPP NY

Quality Indicators
CIJE: 47 RIE: 60 CAT: 16

Quality Measurement Project
CIJE: 0 RIE: 5 CAT: 19

Quality of Circumstances Measure
CIJE: 0 RIE: 1 CAT: 21

Quality of Effort
CIJE: 1 RIE: 1 CAT: 16

Quality of Friendship
CIJE: 1 RIE: 3 CAT: 16
UF Friendship Quality

Quality of Instructional Planning Scale
CIJE: 0 RIE: 1 CAT: 21

Quality of Life Project TX
CIJE: 0 RIE: 1 CAT: 19

Quality of Life Survey
CIJE: 0 RIE: 1 CAT: 21
SN "Quality of Life Community Needs Assessment Survey"

Quality of School Life
CIJE: 3 RIE: 7 CAT: 15

Quality of School Life Scale
CIJE: 4 RIE: 7 CAT: 21

Quality of Teacher Work Life Survey
CIJE: 1 RIE: 1 CAT: 21

Quality Performance Accreditation
CIJE: 0 RIE: 5 CAT: 15

Quality Reading Program Questionnaire
CIJE: 1 RIE: 0 CAT: 21

Quality Services Management
CIJE: 0 RIE: 0 CAT: 15

Quality Time
CIJE: 2 RIE: 3 CAT: 16

QUALTEP Teacher Education Program
CIJE: 0 RIE: 1 CAT: 19

Quantal Bioassay
CIJE: 0 RIE: 1 CAT: 20

Quantification Processes
CIJE: 5 RIE: 4 CAT: 15

Quantification Tasks
CIJE: 4 RIE: 1 CAT: 15

Quantifier Float Constructions (Linguistics)
CIJE: 0 RIE: 1 CAT: 13

Quantifiers
CIJE: 14 RIE: 7 CAT: 13

Quantile Computer Program
CIJE: 0 RIE: 1 CAT: 04

Quantitative Aptitude Test (Abu Sayf and Zarour)
CIJE: 1 RIE: 0 CAT: 21

Quantitative Benefit Analysis
CIJE: 0 RIE: 1 CAT: 15

Quantitative Chemical Analysis
CIJE: 3 RIE: 0 CAT: 20

Quantitative Social Support
CIJE: 0 RIE: 1 CAT: 15

Quantitative Thinking
USE Mathematical Thinking

Quantum Theory
CIJE: 12 RIE: 1 CAT: 20

Quarks
CIJE: 6 RIE: 1 CAT: 20

Quarterly Journal of Speech
CIJE: 2 RIE: 1 CAT: 22

Quarterly Profile Examination
CIJE: 5 RIE: 0 CAT: 21

QUASAR Cognitive Assessment Instrument
CIJE: 0 RIE: 1 CAT: 21

QUASAR Project (Mathematics Education)
CIJE: 1 RIE: 2 CAT: 19
SN QUASAR = Quantitative Understanding Amplifying Student Achievement and Reasoning

Quasars
CIJE: 9 RIE: 1 CAT: 20

Quasi Evaluation
CIJE: 1 RIE: 0 CAT: 21

Quasi Markov Simplex Model
CIJE: 1 RIE: 1 CAT: 15

Quasi Mastery Learning System
CIJE: 0 RIE: 1 CAT: 15

Quasimodo (Salvatore)
CIJE: 0 RIE: 1 CAT: 18

Quay Peterson Behavior Problem Checklist
CIJE: 1 RIE: 1 CAT: 21

Quayle (Dan)
CIJE: 1 RIE: 2 CAT: 18

QUBE System
CIJE: 1 RIE: 1 CAT: 04

Que Deletion
CIJE: 0 RIE: 1 CAT: 13

Quebec
CIJE: 237 RIE: 197 CAT: 07

Quebec (Hull)
CIJE: 0 RIE: 0 CAT: 07

Quebec (Lachute)
CIJE: 1 RIE: 0 CAT: 07

Quebec (Montreal)
CIJE: 69 RIE: 67 CAT: 07

Quebec (North)
CIJE: 3 RIE: 3 CAT: 07

Quebec (Pointe Claire)
CIJE: 0 RIE: 1 CAT: 07

Quebec (Quebec)
CIJE: 6 RIE: 5 CAT: 07

Quebec (Rapid Lake)
CIJE: 0 RIE: 1 CAT: 07

Quebec (Town of Mount Royal)
CIJE: 0 RIE: 1 CAT: 07

Quechan (Tribe)
CIJE: 2 RIE: 1 CAT: 08

Quechua People
CIJE: 0 RIE: 1 CAT: 08
UF Quechuas

Quechuas
USE Quechua People

Queen Bee Syndrome
CIJE: 1 RIE: 0 CAT: 16

Queen Liliuokalani
USE Liliuokalani

Queen Margaret College (Scotland)
CIJE: 0 RIE: 1 CAT: 17

Queen Mary College (England)
CIJE: 2 RIE: 1 CAT: 17

Queens Chinese Korean Bilingual Language Arts NY
CIJE: 0 RIE: 1 CAT: 17

Queens College NY
USE City University of New York Queens College

Queens Field Instruction Center
CIJE: 1 RIE: 0 CAT: 17

Queens Tri School Confederation NY
CIJE: 0 RIE: 1 CAT: 19

Queens University (Ireland)
USE Queens University of Belfast (Northern Ireland)

Queens University of Belfast (Northern Ireland)
CIJE: 1 RIE: 0 CAT: 17
UF Queens University (Ireland)

Queens University of Kingston (Canada)
CIJE: 6 RIE: 14 CAT: 17

Queensborough Community College NY
USE City University of New York Queensborough Comm C

Queensborough Public Library NY
CIJE: 4 RIE: 7 CAT: 17

Queensland Itinerant Teacher Service (Australia)
CIJE: 0 RIE: 1 CAT: 17

Queensland Preschool Correspondence Program
CIJE: 0 RIE: 1 CAT: 19

Queensland Test
CIJE: 2 RIE: 0 CAT: 21

Queensland University Aphasia Test
CIJE: 1 RIE: 0 CAT: 21

Queensland University of Technology (Australia)
CIJE: 2 RIE: 2 CAT: 17

QUEMAC Value
CIJE: 0 RIE: 2 CAT: 21

Quemado Public Schools NM
CIJE: 0 RIE: 1 CAT: 17

Queries n Theories
CIJE: 1 RIE: 0 CAT: 22

QUERY
CIJE: 0 RIE: 9 CAT: 04

Query by Example
CIJE: 1 RIE: 1 CAT: 04

Query Formulations
CIJE: 8 RIE: 1 CAT: 15

Query Languages
CIJE: 3 RIE: 0 CAT: 04

Query Negotiation (Library Science)
CIJE: 40 RIE: 9 CAT: 15

Query Processing
CIJE: 7 RIE: 1 CAT: 20

Quest
CIJE: 9 RIE: 3 CAT: 19

Quest Computer Program
CIJE: 0 RIE: 1 CAT: 04

QUEST Program
CIJE: 9 RIE: 4 CAT: 19

Quest Program MA
CIJE: 0 RIE: 1 CAT: 19

Questing
CIJE: 1 RIE: 0 CAT: 15

Question and Answer Exercises
CIJE: 6 RIE: 8 CAT: 21

Question Answer Reciprocity
CIJE: 7 RIE: 6 CAT: 15

Question Answering
CIJE: 29 RIE: 9 CAT: 16

Question Answering Systems
CIJE: 6 RIE: 3 CAT: 15

Question Banks
CIJE: 3 RIE: 0 CAT: 15

Question Box Techniques
CIJE: 0 RIE: 1 CAT: 15

Question Categorization Instruments
CIJE: 1 RIE: 1 CAT: 15

Question Generality
CIJE: 1 RIE: 1 CAT: 15

Question of Economics (A)
CIJE: 0 RIE: 1 CAT: 22

Question Time
CIJE: 1 RIE: 0 CAT: 15

Question Types
CIJE: 37 RIE: 27 CAT: 15

Questioning Strategies Observation System
CIJE: 1 RIE: 3 CAT: 15

Questionnaire for Interactional Teacher Behavior
CIJE: 0 RIE: 1 CAT: 21

Questionnaire for Parents (Purdue Educ Res Ctr)
CIJE: 0 RIE: 1 CAT: 21

Questionnaire for Parish Leaders
CIJE: 1 RIE: 0 CAT: 21

Questionnaire on Resources and Stress
CIJE: 7 RIE: 1 CAT: 21
SN Use for the Holroyd original as well as adapted shorter versions

Questions
CIJE: 104 RIE: 104 CAT: 16

Queuing Networks
CIJE: 3 RIE: 0 CAT: 04

Queuing Studies
CIJE: 1 RIE: 2 CAT: 15

Queuing Theory
CIJE: 4 RIE: 3 CAT: 15

Quevedo y Villegas (Francisco Gomez de)
CIJE: 4 RIE: 0 CAT: 18

Quick and Dirty Form
CIJE: 1 RIE: 0 CAT: 21

Quick Neurological Screening Test
CIJE: 5 RIE: 2 CAT: 21

Quick Number Test (Corsini and Borgatta)
CIJE: 3 RIE: 0 CAT: 21

Quick Startup Vocational Programs
CIJE: 0 RIE: 2 CAT: 19

Quick Test
CIJE: 13 RIE: 3 CAT: 21

Quick Word Test
CIJE: 6 RIE: 0 CAT: 21

Quickspeak
CIJE: 0 RIE: 1 CAT: 13

Quilcene School District WA
CIJE: 0 RIE: 1 CAT: 17

QUILL (Computer Software)
CIJE: 1 RIE: 7 CAT: 04

Quill and Scroll
CIJE: 0 RIE: 2 CAT: 17

Quill and Scroll Editorial Contest
CIJE: 1 RIE: 0 CAT: 21

Quilting
CIJE: 16 RIE: 3 CAT: 16

Quinault (Tribe)
CIJE: 0 RIE: 5 CAT: 08

Quinault Reservation
CIJE: 0 RIE: 1 CAT: 17

Quincy College IL
CIJE: 0 RIE: 1 CAT: 17

Quincy Grammar School MA
CIJE: 0 RIE: 1 CAT: 17

Quincy Public Schools MA
CIJE: 1 RIE: 1 CAT: 17

Quincy School District WA
CIJE: 0 RIE: 1 CAT: 17

Quinmester Program
CIJE: 2 RIE: 722 CAT: 19

QUIPP NY
CIJE: 0 RIE: 2 CAT: 19
UF Quality Improvement Prog Plan for Spec Educators

Quirk (Randolph)
CIJE: 1 RIE: 1 CAT: 18

Quit Smoking Programs
USE Smoking Cessation

Quo Vadis School of Nursing (Canada)
CIJE: 0 RIE: 1 CAT: 17

Quotations
CIJE: 41 RIE: 11 CAT: 16

Quran
USE Koran

R D Seymour Elementary School CT
CIJE: 1 RIE: 0 CAT: 17

R E Gibson Library
CIJE: 1 RIE: 0 CAT: 17

R Technique Factor Analysis
CIJE: 1 RIE: 3 CAT: 15

R2 Values
CIJE: 0 RIE: 2 CAT: 15

Rabbinical Literature
CIJE: 0 RIE: 0 CAT: 16

Rabbis
CIJE: 1 RIE: 1 CAT: 10

Rabbits
CIJE: 3 RIE: 1 CAT: 20

Rabelais (Francois)
CIJE: 0 RIE: 1 CAT: 18

Rabies
CIJE: 1 RIE: 1 CAT: 11

Rabinowitz Mathematics Attitude Scale
CIJE: 1 RIE: 0 CAT: 21

Race Desegregation Training Institute
CIJE: 0 RIE: 1 CAT: 17

Race Fairness
CIJE: 0 RIE: 6 CAT: 16

Race Institute DC
CIJE: 1 RIE: 0 CAT: 17

Race Relations Act 1968 (Great Britain)
CIJE: 1 RIE: 0 CAT: 14

Race Relations Act 1976 (Great Britain)
CIJE: 0 RIE: 3 CAT: 14

Rachel Carson Project
CIJE: 1 RIE: 8 CAT: 19

Rachmans Spontaneous Remission
CIJE: 1 RIE: 0 CAT: 15

Racial Adjustment Action Society
CIJE: 1 RIE: 0 CAT: 17

Racial Attitude and Cultural Expression Test
CIJE: 0 RIE: 2 CAT: 21

Racial Attitudes Picture Test
CIJE: 0 RIE: 1 CAT: 21

Racial Discrimination Act (Australia)
CIJE: 0 RIE: 1 CAT: 14

Racial Harassment
CIJE: 5 RIE: 2 CAT: 16

Racial Identity Attitude Scale
CIJE: 3 RIE: 1 CAT: 21

Racial Imbalance Act (Massachusetts)
CIJE: 1 RIE: 1 CAT: 14

Racial Preference
CIJE: 3 RIE: 4 CAT: 16

Racial Tension Scale (Bowler)
CIJE: 0 RIE: 1 CAT: 21

Racialistic Incidents Inventory
CIJE: 0 RIE: 1 CAT: 21

Racially Isolated Schools
CIJE: 2 RIE: 2 CAT: 05

Racine (Jean)
CIJE: 5 RIE: 0 CAT: 18

Racine Environment Committee Incorporated
CIJE: 0 RIE: 1 CAT: 17

Racine Feedback and Diagnostic System
CIJE: 0 RIE: 1 CAT: 15

Radar Intercept Observers
CIJE: 0 RIE: 3 CAT: 09

Radar Jamming
CIJE: 0 RIE: 1 CAT: 20

Radcliffe College MA
CIJE: 11 RIE: 4 CAT: 17

Radex
CIJE: 2 RIE: 0 CAT: 21

Radford (William C)
CIJE: 0 RIE: 1 CAT: 18

Radford Career Education Program
CIJE: 0 RIE: 15 CAT: 19

Radford City Schools VA
CIJE: 0 RIE: 3 CAT: 17

Radford College VA
CIJE: 1 RIE: 2 CAT: 17

Radford University VA
CIJE: 5 RIE: 20 CAT: 17

Radial Parcelling
CIJE: 1 RIE: 0 CAT: 15

Radiation Monitors
CIJE: 0 RIE: 5 CAT: 09

Radiation Processing
CIJE: 1 RIE: 0 CAT: 20

Radical Behaviorist Approach
CIJE: 1 RIE: 0 CAT: 15

Radical Critical Theory
CIJE: 3 RIE: 2 CAT: 15

Radical Movements
CIJE: 7 RIE: 4 CAT: 16

Radical Press
CIJE: 0 RIE: 3 CAT: 16

Radicalism
CIJE: 45 RIE: 13 CAT: 16

Radio Act 1927
CIJE: 0 RIE: 1 CAT: 14

Radio and Audio Visual Education Network (Canada)
CIJE: 1 RIE: 1 CAT: 17

Radio and Television Univ for Teachers (Poland)
CIJE: 1 RIE: 0 CAT: 17

Radio and Television Universities (China)
CIJE: 1 RIE: 0 CAT: 05
SN See also "Television Universities (China)"
UF Central Radio and Television University (China)

Radio Animation
CIJE: 0 RIE: 1 CAT: 20

Radio Astronomy
CIJE: 6 RIE: 0 CAT: 20

Radio Australia
CIJE: 0 RIE: 2 CAT: 17

Radio Canada International
CIJE: 0 RIE: 1 CAT: 17

Radio Chatter
CIJE: 0 RIE: 4 CAT: 20

Radio Club Association of Niger
CIJE: 0 RIE: 1 CAT: 17

Radio Corporation of America
CIJE: 4 RIE: 0 CAT: 17

Radio ECCA
CIJE: 0 RIE: 1 CAT: 17

Radio Ecca (Canary Islands)
CIJE: 1 RIE: 0 CAT: 17

Radio Forums
CIJE: 0 RIE: 1 CAT: 02
SN See also "Farm Radio Forum (Canada)"

Radio Frequency Auditory Training Systems
CIJE: 1 RIE: 0 CAT: 15

Radio Frequency Distribution System
CIJE: 0 RIE: 3 CAT: 15

Radio Japan
CIJE: 0 RIE: 1 CAT: 17

Radio Language Arts Project (Kenya)
CIJE: 0 RIE: 3 CAT: 19

Radio Learning Group Campaigns
CIJE: 0 RIE: 1 CAT: 15

Radio London
CIJE: 1 RIE: 0 CAT: 17

Radio Marti
CIJE: 0 RIE: 1 CAT: 17

Radio Mathematics Project
CIJE: 1 RIE: 7 CAT: 19

Radio Moscow
CIJE: 0 RIE: 1 CAT: 17

Radio Netherlands
CIJE: 2 RIE: 1 CAT: 17

Radio Operators
CIJE: 0 RIE: 7 CAT: 09

Radio Plays
CIJE: 1 RIE: 2 CAT: 16

Radio Quebec
CIJE: 1 RIE: 2 CAT: 17

Radio Reading Services
CIJE: 0 RIE: 0 CAT: 05

Radio Receiver Assemblers
CIJE: 0 RIE: 1 CAT: 09

Radio Shack Color Computer
CIJE: 1 RIE: 0 CAT: 04

Radio Solent (England)
CIJE: 1 RIE: 0 CAT: 17

Radio Talk (Radio Program)
CIJE: 0 RIE: 1 CAT: 22

Radio Telemetry
CIJE: 4 RIE: 1 CAT: 20

Radio Television News Directors Association
CIJE: 1 RIE: 1 CAT: 17

Radio Vision
CIJE: 3 RIE: 4 CAT: 16

Radio Waves
CIJE: 2 RIE: 3 CAT: 20

Radioactive Wastes
CIJE: 4 RIE: 4 CAT: 20

Radioactivity
CIJE: 11 RIE: 17 CAT: 20

Radiochemistry
CIJE: 8 RIE: 4 CAT: 20

Radiographic Imaging Systems
CIJE: 0 RIE: 1 CAT: 04

Radiological Monitoring
CIJE: 0 RIE: 1 CAT: 03

Radiological Weapons
CIJE: 0 RIE: 1 CAT: 20

Radiophonic Teaching
CIJE: 0 RIE: 2 CAT: 15

Radioprimaria
CIJE: 0 RIE: 1 CAT: 19

Radiotelephone Third Class Operator Permit
CIJE: 0 RIE: 1 CAT: 16

Radiotelevisone Italiana
CIJE: 0 RIE: 1 CAT: 17

Radius Cutters
CIJE: 0 RIE: 1 CAT: 04

Radon
CIJE: 23 RIE: 12 CAT: 11

Rafael Hernandez Elementary School MA
CIJE: 0 RIE: 1 CAT: 17

Rafferty (Max)
CIJE: 0 RIE: 1 CAT: 18

Rahim Organizational Conflict Inventory
USE Organizational Conflict Inventory

Railroad Brakers
CIJE: 0 RIE: 1 CAT: 09

Railroad Conductors
CIJE: 0 RIE: 2 CAT: 09

Railroad Retirement Board
CIJE: 0 RIE: 1 CAT: 17

Railway Labor Act
CIJE: 5 RIE: 1 CAT: 14

Raimund (Ferdinand)
CIJE: 1 RIE: 0 CAT: 18

Rainbows
CIJE: 9 RIE: 0 CAT: 20

Rainforests
USE Tropical Rain Forests

RAISE Bill (Florida)
CIJE: 1 RIE: 2 CAT: 14

Raisin in the Sun
CIJE: 2 RIE: 1 CAT: 22

Rajender v University of Minnesota
CIJE: 1 RIE: 0 CAT: 14

Rajneesh (Bhagwan Shree)
CIJE: 0 RIE: 0 CAT: 18

Rakow (Theresa G)
CIJE: 1 RIE: 0 CAT: 18

Raku
CIJE: 3 RIE: 1 CAT: 16
UF Raku Pottery

Raku Pottery
USE Raku

Raleigh (Sir Walter)
CIJE: 0 RIE: 1 CAT: 18

Raleigh Research Coordinating Unit
CIJE: 0 RIE: 1 CAT: 17

Ralston Purina
CIJE: 1 RIE: 0 CAT: 17

Ramage (John M)
CIJE: 1 RIE: 0 CAT: 18

Ramah Navaho High School NM
CIJE: 2 RIE: 3 CAT: 17

Ramah Navajo School Board NM
CIJE: 0 RIE: 1 CAT: 17

Ramah Navajos
CIJE: 1 RIE: 2 CAT: 08

Ramak Inventory (Meir and Barak)
CIJE: 3 RIE: 0 CAT: 21

Ramapo (Tribe)
CIJE: 0 RIE: 1 CAT: 08

Ramapo Catskill Library System NY
CIJE: 2 RIE: 1 CAT: 17

Ramapo Central School District NY
CIJE: 1 RIE: 0 CAT: 17

Ramapo College of New Jersey
CIJE: 8 RIE: 16 CAT: 17

Ramayana
CIJE: 0 RIE: 2 CAT: 22
SN Epic poem of India

RAMBOT (Expert System)
CIJE: 0 RIE: 1 CAT: 04

Ramirez (Manuel)
CIJE: 0 RIE: 1 CAT: 18

RAMOS
USE Reading and Mathematics Observation System

Ramsey Multiple Schedule
CIJE: 0 RIE: 1 CAT: 15

Ramsey Plan
CIJE: 0 RIE: 2 CAT: 15

Ramus (Peter)
CIJE: 4 RIE: 1 CAT: 18

Ranching
CIJE: 2 RIE: 6 CAT: 16

Rancho Los Alamitos
CIJE: 0 RIE: 1 CAT: 12

Rancho Los Amigos Hospital CA
CIJE: 0 RIE: 1 CAT: 17

Rancho Plan CA
CIJE: 0 RIE: 1 CAT: 19

Rancho Santiago College CA
CIJE: 1 RIE: 5 CAT: 17

Rancho Santiago Community College District CA
CIJE: 0 RIE: 9 CAT: 17

Rand (Ayn)
CIJE: 2 RIE: 0 CAT: 18

Rand Change Agent Study
CIJE: 2 RIE: 2 CAT: 19

Rand Corporation
CIJE: 10 RIE: 13 CAT: 17

Rand Relational Data File
CIJE: 0 RIE: 1 CAT: 15

Randolph (A Philip)
CIJE: 0 RIE: 1 CAT: 18

Randolph County School District WV
CIJE: 0 RIE: 0 CAT: 17

Randolph Macon College VA
CIJE: 4 RIE: 0 CAT: 17

Randolph Macon Womans College VA
CIJE: 1 RIE: 5 CAT: 17

Randolph Sheppard Act
CIJE: 1 RIE: 1 CAT: 14

Random Access Slide Projectors
CIJE: 0 RIE: 1 CAT: 04

Random Breath Testing
CIJE: 0 RIE: 1 CAT: 21

Random Digit Dialing
CIJE: 0 RIE: 3 CAT: 16

Random Effects
CIJE: 8 RIE: 5 CAT: 21

Random House
CIJE: 2 RIE: 0 CAT: 17

Random House Dictionary of the English Language
CIJE: 1 RIE: 1 CAT: 22

Random Learning
CIJE: 4 RIE: 0 CAT: 15

Random Normal Scores Test
CIJE: 0 RIE: 1 CAT: 21

Random Numbers
CIJE: 21 RIE: 1 CAT: 20

Random Trial Increments Model
CIJE: 0 RIE: 1 CAT: 15

Random Variables
CIJE: 10 RIE: 1 CAT: 20

Randomization
CIJE: 26 RIE: 7 CAT: 15

Randomization (Statistics)
CIJE: 20 RIE: 3 CAT: 21

Randomized Experiments
CIJE: 4 RIE: 2 CAT: 20

Randomized Multiple Choice Tests
CIJE: 0 RIE: 1 CAT: 21

Randomized Response Technique
CIJE: 9 RIE: 4 CAT: 21

Randomly Missing Data (Regression Analyses)
CIJE: 0 RIE: 1 CAT: 21

Ranganathan (S R)
CIJE: 6 RIE: 2 CAT: 18

Range Restriction
CIJE: 9 RIE: 5 CAT: 21

Ranger Junior College TX
CIJE: 0 RIE: 1 CAT: 17

Ranger Ricks Nature Magazine
CIJE: 1 RIE: 1 CAT: 22

Rank Concession Syndrome
CIJE: 1 RIE: 0 CAT: 15

Rank Correlation Coefficient
USE Spearman Rank Correlation Coefficient

Rank Order
CIJE: 63 RIE: 24 CAT: 15

Rank Order Transformation
CIJE: 6 RIE: 3 CAT: 21
UF Rank Transformation Procedure

Rank Reducibility
CIJE: 1 RIE: 0 CAT: 21

Rank Transformation Procedure
USE Rank Order Transformation

Ranked Retrieval Output
CIJE: 20 RIE: 0 CAT: 16

Ranken Technical College MO
CIJE: 0 RIE: 1 CAT: 17

Ranken Technical Institute MO
CIJE: 1 RIE: 0 CAT: 17

Rankine (William John M)
CIJE: 1 RIE: 0 CAT: 18

Ranking
CIJE: 142 RIE: 29 CAT: 15

Ranking Errors
CIJE: 3 RIE: 1 CAT: 15

Ranunculus
CIJE: 1 RIE: 0 CAT: 20

Raoult Law
CIJE: 2 RIE: 0 CAT: 20

Rap Music
CIJE: 14 RIE: 6 CAT: 16

Rap Sessions
CIJE: 1 RIE: 1 CAT: 16

Rape Myths
CIJE: 0 RIE: 2 CAT: 16

Rape Recovery
CIJE: 0 RIE: 2 CAT: 11

Rapid Eye Movements
CIJE: 1 RIE: 1 CAT: 11

Rapid Learning Centers
CIJE: 0 RIE: 1 CAT: 05

Rapin (Rene)
CIJE: 1 RIE: 0 CAT: 18

Rappaccinis Daughter
CIJE: 2 RIE: 1 CAT: 22

RAPYHT Project
CIJE: 0 RIE: 11 CAT: 19
SN "Retrieval and Acceleration of Promising Young Handicapped and Talented"
UF Project RAPYHT; Retrieval and Accel of Young Hndcped and Talented

Raquette Lake
CIJE: 2 RIE: 0 CAT: 07

Raran Model
CIJE: 0 RIE: 1 CAT: 15

Rare Books
CIJE: 38 RIE: 31 CAT: 16

Rare Gases
CIJE: 2 RIE: 0 CAT: 20

Raritan Valley Community College NJ
CIJE: 0 RIE: 1 CAT: 17

Rasch Model
CIJE: 196 RIE: 309 CAT: 15
SN For Rasch Partial Credit Model, coordinate with Identifier "Partial Credit Model"

Rasch PROX Procedure
CIJE: 0 RIE: 1 CAT: 15

Rasch Scaled Scores
CIJE: 2 RIE: 23 CAT: 21

Rashomon
CIJE: 0 RIE: 1 CAT: 22

Raskin (Victor)
CIJE: 0 RIE: 1 CAT: 18

Rasselas
CIJE: 1 RIE: 0 CAT: 22

Rassias Method
CIJE: 1 RIE: 1 CAT: 15

Rastafarianism
CIJE: 1 RIE: 1 CAT: 16

Rate (Mathematics)
CIJE: 7 RIE: 3 CAT: 20

Rate Controlled Speech
CIJE: 6 RIE: 7 CAT: 13

Rate of Completion
CIJE: 2 RIE: 1 CAT: 15

Rate of Learning Score
CIJE: 0 RIE: 1 CAT: 21

Rate of Return
CIJE: 35 RIE: 9 CAT: 15

Rate of Return Regulation
CIJE: 0 RIE: 0 CAT: 14

RATE Project (AACTE)
USE Research About Teacher Education Project

Rater Effects
CIJE: 4 RIE: 3 CAT: 21
SN See also "Examiner Effect"

Rater Ratee Similarity
CIJE: 0 RIE: 1 CAT: 21

Rater Reliability
CIJE: 29 RIE: 19 CAT: 21

Rater Stringency Error
CIJE: 2 RIE: 4 CAT: 21

Raths (Louis)
CIJE: 5 RIE: 2 CAT: 18

Rathus Assertiveness Schedule
CIJE: 5 RIE: 1 CAT: 21

Rating Error Theory
CIJE: 1 RIE: 1 CAT: 15

Rating of the Child Questionnaire
CIJE: 1 RIE: 0 CAT: 21

Rating Ranking Scale of Child Behavior (Cromwell)
CIJE: 0 RIE: 1 CAT: 21

Rating Scale Analysis
CIJE: 1 RIE: 2 CAT: 15

Rating Scale for Curriculum Evaluation (Sperry)
CIJE: 0 RIE: 1 CAT: 21

Rating Scale for Directed Teaching
CIJE: 1 RIE: 0 CAT: 21

Rating Scale for Teachers (Quereshi and Widlar)
CIJE: 0 RIE: 1 CAT: 21

Rating Scale Model
CIJE: 2 RIE: 1 CAT: 15

Ratio Scales
CIJE: 2 RIE: 1 CAT: 21

Rational Behavior Training
CIJE: 1 RIE: 2 CAT: 11

Rational Bureaucracy
CIJE: 1 RIE: 2 CAT: 16

Rational Choice Theory
CIJE: 5 RIE: 1 CAT: 15

Rational Decision Making
CIJE: 4 RIE: 3 CAT: 15

Rational Dialogue
CIJE: 2 RIE: 1 CAT: 15

Rational Emotive Education
CIJE: 6 RIE: 1 CAT: 15

Rational Reasoning Test
CIJE: 0 RIE: 1 CAT: 21

Rational Self Counseling
CIJE: 4 RIE: 0 CAT: 11

Rational Set Generator
CIJE: 3 RIE: 1 CAT: 15

Rationalism
CIJE: 28 RIE: 10 CAT: 15
SN See also "Modern Rationalism"

Rationalistic Evaluation
CIJE: 1 RIE: 2 CAT: 21

Rationality
CIJE: 46 RIE: 19 CAT: 15

Rationalization (Decision Making)
CIJE: 6 RIE: 2 CAT: 15

Ratios (Finance)
CIJE: 3 RIE: 0 CAT: 20

Rauding Scale of Prose Difficulty
CIJE: 5 RIE: 1 CAT: 21

RAV v City of Saint Paul
CIJE: 0 RIE: 1 CAT: 14

Raven (B)
CIJE: 0 RIE: 1 CAT: 18

Raven Advanced Progressive Matrices
CIJE: 3 RIE: 1 CAT: 21

Raven Progressive Matrices
CIJE: 82 RIE: 51 CAT: 21

Raven Test of Logical Operations
CIJE: 2 RIE: 1 CAT: 21

Ravens Coloured Progressive Matrices
CIJE: 11 RIE: 7 CAT: 15

Ravitch (Diane)
CIJE: 7 RIE: 1 CAT: 18

Raw Agreement Index
CIJE: 1 RIE: 0 CAT: 21

Rawas
CIJE: 0 RIE: 1 CAT: 13
SN An Austronesian language spoken in Sumatra

Rawls (John)
CIJE: 14 RIE: 1 CAT: 18

Ray (Satyajit)
CIJE: 1 RIE: 0 CAT: 18

Ray Reading Methods Test
CIJE: 0 RIE: 1 CAT: 21

Ray School IL
CIJE: 1 RIE: 0 CAT: 17

Ray Self Checklist of Quality Voc Tech Programs
CIJE: 0 RIE: 1 CAT: 21

Ray Students Estimate of Teachers Concern
CIJE: 0 RIE: 1 CAT: 21

Ray v School District of DeSoto County
CIJE: 1 RIE: 0 CAT: 14

Rayalaseema Telugu
CIJE: 1 RIE: 0 CAT: 13

Raymond Walters College OH
CIJE: 0 RIE: 1 CAT: 17
UF University of Cincinnati Raymond Walters Coll OH

Rays (Animals)
CIJE: 0 RIE: 1 CAT: 20

Raytown Consolidated School District 2 MO
CIJE: 0 RIE: 1 CAT: 17

Rayuelo
CIJE: 1 RIE: 0 CAT: 22

RCA Spectra Computer
CIJE: 1 RIE: 0 CAT: 04

RCDs
USE Remote Control Devices

Re ED Model
CIJE: 0 RIE: 2 CAT: 15

RE FIT Program OH
USE Rural Economics Farmers in Transition

REACH Center for Global and Multicultural Educ
USE Respecting Ethnic and Cultural Heritage Center

Reach Out to Schools Social Competency Program
CIJE: 0 RIE: 1 CAT: 19

Reaching Behavior
CIJE: 13 RIE: 3 CAT: 11

Reactance (Psychology)
CIJE: 10 RIE: 4 CAT: 11

Reaction English
CIJE: 0 RIE: 1 CAT: 13

Reaction Formation
CIJE: 1 RIE: 1 CAT: 11

Reaction Inventory
CIJE: 1 RIE: 1 CAT: 15

Reaction Symposium (Technique)
CIJE: 0 RIE: 1 CAT: 15

Reaction Time Recognition Memory Paradigm
CIJE: 0 RIE: 1 CAT: 15

Reaction Timing
CIJE: 2 RIE: 1 CAT: 15

Reaction to Group Situation Test
CIJE: 0 RIE: 1 CAT: 21

Read (Herbert)
CIJE: 6 RIE: 4 CAT: 18

Read Along
CIJE: 4 RIE: 4 CAT: 15

Read Explore and Discover Program SC
CIJE: 0 RIE: 1 CAT: 19

Read General Science Test
CIJE: 0 RIE: 2 CAT: 21

Read On Write On Program
CIJE: 0 RIE: 1 CAT: 19

Read Test (Colvin and Root)
CIJE: 0 RIE: 1 CAT: 21

Reader Advisors
CIJE: 6 RIE: 1 CAT: 16

Reader Author Relationship
USE Author Reader Relationship

Reader Development Program
CIJE: 1 RIE: 2 CAT: 19

Reader Expectations
CIJE: 8 RIE: 3 CAT: 16

READER Model
CIJE: 0 RIE: 1 CAT: 15

Reader Preferences
CIJE: 8 RIE: 14 CAT: 16

Reader Response Criticism
CIJE: 20 RIE: 16 CAT: 16

Reader Theories
CIJE: 0 RIE: 1 CAT: 15

Reader Writer Conferencing
CIJE: 0 RIE: 1 CAT: 15

Reader Writer Relationship
CIJE: 5 RIE: 2 CAT: 13

Readers Digest
CIJE: 4 RIE: 3 CAT: 22

Readers Ever Aware Climb Higher
CIJE: 1 RIE: 0 CAT: 19

Readers Guide to Periodical Literature
CIJE: 1 RIE: 3 CAT: 22

Readership Analysis
CIJE: 24 RIE: 47 CAT: 15

READI Project ID
USE Rural Education Adult Development in Idaho

Readimobile Project
CIJE: 0 RIE: 1 CAT: 19

Readiness for Vocational Planning Scales
CIJE: 0 RIE: 1 CAT: 21

Reading (Self Selection)
CIJE: 4 RIE: 2 CAT: 15

Reading Accelerator
CIJE: 0 RIE: 1 CAT: 15

Reading Accuracy
CIJE: 10 RIE: 2 CAT: 16

Reading and Math through Community as Classroom NY
CIJE: 0 RIE: 1 CAT: 19

Reading and Mathematics
USE Reading Mathematics Relationship

Reading and Mathematics Observation System
CIJE: 0 RIE: 2 CAT: 21
UF RAMOS

Reading and Mathematics with Athletics NY
CIJE: 0 RIE: 1 CAT: 19

Reading and Study Skills Inven (Williams Kaman)
CIJE: 0 RIE: 1 CAT: 21

Reading Anxiety
CIJE: 4 RIE: 3 CAT: 15

Reading Appraisal Guide
CIJE: 0 RIE: 1 CAT: 21

Reading Area Community College PA
CIJE: 1 RIE: 4 CAT: 17

Reading Attitude Inventory (Lewis)
CIJE: 0 RIE: 1 CAT: 21

Reading Behavior
CIJE: 85 RIE: 65 CAT: 15

Reading Beliefs Inventory
CIJE: 0 RIE: 1 CAT: 21

Reading Biographer
CIJE: 0 RIE: 2 CAT: 21

Reading by Patterns A Programmed Guide
CIJE: 0 RIE: 1 CAT: 22

Reading Card Snellen Rating
CIJE: 0 RIE: 1 CAT: 21

Reading Comprehension Inventory (Guszak)
CIJE: 0 RIE: 1 CAT: 21

Reading Concepts
CIJE: 3 RIE: 23 CAT: 16

Reading Contests
CIJE: 1 RIE: 2 CAT: 16

Reading Decisions Test
CIJE: 0 RIE: 1 CAT: 21

Reading Diary Studies
CIJE: 1 RIE: 1 CAT: 19

Reading Education for Adults in Dayton
USE Project READ OH

Reading English and Mathematics Test
CIJE: 0 RIE: 1 CAT: 21

Reading Enjoying And Presenting
USE Project REAP IN

Reading Expectancy
CIJE: 4 RIE: 2 CAT: 15

Reading Expectancy Formulas
CIJE: 2 RIE: 1 CAT: 15

Reading Experiences Associated with Partners
CIJE: 0 RIE: 1 CAT: 15

Reading Flexibility
CIJE: 6 RIE: 5 CAT: 15

Reading Fluency
CIJE: 52 RIE: 34 CAT: 16

Reading for a Reason
CIJE: 0 RIE: 1 CAT: 22

Reading for Educational Achievement and Devel CA
USE Project READ CA

Reading Free Vocational Interest Inventory
CIJE: 5 RIE: 1 CAT: 21

Reading Grade Level Scale
CIJE: 0 RIE: 2 CAT: 21

Reading Groups
CIJE: 21 RIE: 9 CAT: 10

Reading Guidance Center Southern California
CIJE: 1 RIE: 0 CAT: 17

Reading Help Program
CIJE: 0 RIE: 1 CAT: 19

Reading Improvement (Journal)
CIJE: 0 RIE: 1 CAT: 22

Reading Improvement Through Art
CIJE: 1 RIE: 2 CAT: 19

Reading in High Gear
CIJE: 0 RIE: 2 CAT: 15

Reading Incentive Programs
CIJE: 0 RIE: 1 CAT: 19

Reading Institute Survey
CIJE: 0 RIE: 1 CAT: 21

Reading Instruction and Pupil Personnel Services
CIJE: 0 RIE: 8 CAT: 19

Reading Inventory of Science Knowledge
CIJE: 1 RIE: 1 CAT: 21

Reading Is Fundamental
CIJE: 13 RIE: 26 CAT: 19

Reading Journals
CIJE: 3 RIE: 4 CAT: 16
SN Scholarly, not student, journals

Reading Listening Relationship
USE Listening Reading Relationship

Reading Lists
CIJE: 4 RIE: 6 CAT: 16

Reading Logs
CIJE: 5 RIE: 4 CAT: 16

Reading Machines
CIJE: 5 RIE: 6 CAT: 04

Reading Management
CIJE: 3 RIE: 54 CAT: 16

Reading Mathematics Relationship
CIJE: 8 RIE: 5 CAT: 15
UF Mathematics and Reading; Reading and Mathematics

Reading Miscue Inventory
CIJE: 12 RIE: 9 CAT: 21

Reading Motivation
CIJE: 156 RIE: 214 CAT: 15

Reading Muhlenberg Vocational School PA
CIJE: 0 RIE: 1 CAT: 17

Reading Proficiency Scale (NAEP)
CIJE: 0 RIE: 1 CAT: 21

Reading Program Management System
CIJE: 0 RIE: 1 CAT: 04

Reading Pronunciation Latency Effect
CIJE: 1 RIE: 0 CAT: 15

Reading Public Schools MA
CIJE: 0 RIE: 1 CAT: 17

Reading Rainbow
CIJE: 0 RIE: 5 CAT: 22

Reading Recovery Projects
CIJE: 38 RIE: 55 CAT: 19
SN See also "CLEAR Reading Recovery Program," "Ohio Reading Recovery Program," "New Zealand Reading Recovery Program"

Reading Reliability
CIJE: 0 RIE: 1 CAT: 15

Reading Research Institute
CIJE: 0 RIE: 1 CAT: 17

Reading Retelling Profile
CIJE: 0 RIE: 1 CAT: 21

Reading School District PA
CIJE: 1 RIE: 1 CAT: 17

Reading Sequence
CIJE: 0 RIE: 1 CAT: 16

Reading Span Test (Daneman and Carpenter)
CIJE: 1 RIE: 1 CAT: 21

Reading Speaking Relationship
CIJE: 5 RIE: 11 CAT: 13

Reading Storage Test
CIJE: 3 RIE: 0 CAT: 21

Reading Student Observation Scale (Quirk)
CIJE: 0 RIE: 1 CAT: 21

Reading Style Inventory (Carbo)
CIJE: 4 RIE: 6 CAT: 21

Reading Teacher (Journal)
CIJE: 8 RIE: 2 CAT: 22

Reading Teacher Observation Scale (Quirk et al)
CIJE: 0 RIE: 1 CAT: 21

Reading Teacher Survey (Askov)
CIJE: 0 RIE: 1 CAT: 21

Reading Theories
CIJE: 24 RIE: 25 CAT: 15

Reading to Learn Model
CIJE: 1 RIE: 6 CAT: 15

Reading Uses
CIJE: 8 RIE: 51 CAT: 16

Reading Versatility Test
CIJE: 1 RIE: 0 CAT: 21

Reading While Listening
CIJE: 13 RIE: 7 CAT: 15

Reading with Symbols
CIJE: 0 RIE: 1 CAT: 15

Reading World (Journal)
CIJE: 0 RIE: 2 CAT: 22

Reading Writing and Arithmetic Development System
CIJE: 0 RIE: 1 CAT: 15
UF REWARD Funding Formula

Readings in the History of Mathematics Education
CIJE: 0 RIE: 1 CAT: 22

READiscover Kentucky
CIJE: 0 RIE: 1 CAT: 19

Ready Set Go
CIJE: 1 RIE: 1 CAT: 22

Reaffirmation of Principle
USE Rhetoric of Reaffirmation

Reagan (Ronald)
CIJE: 90 RIE: 51 CAT: 18

Reagan Administration
CIJE: 166 RIE: 161 CAT: 17

Real Educational Activities of Learning
USE Project REAL

Real English
CIJE: 0 RIE: 5 CAT: 16

REAL Enterprises
CIJE: 0 RIE: 1 CAT: 17
UF Rural Entrepreneurship through Action Learning

Real Estate Brokerage
CIJE: 0 RIE: 2 CAT: 16

Real Estate Development
CIJE: 0 RIE: 1 CAT: 16

Real Estate Inspectors
CIJE: 0 RIE: 1 CAT: 09

Real Life English Placement Survey
CIJE: 0 RIE: 1 CAT: 21

Real Math (Curriculum)
CIJE: 0 RIE: 2 CAT: 03

Real Numbers
CIJE: 5 RIE: 5 CAT: 20

Real Time Captioning
CIJE: 0 RIE: 2 CAT: 20
UF Live Television Captioning

Realistic Assessment Various Educational Strategi
CIJE: 0 RIE: 0 CAT: 21

Reality
CIJE: 41 RIE: 25 CAT: 16
SN See also "Moral Reality," "Perceived Reality," & "Social Reality"

Reality Based Evaluation
CIJE: 2 RIE: 6 CAT: 15

Reality Based Television Programs
CIJE: 0 RIE: 1 CAT: 16

Reality Counseling
CIJE: 1 RIE: 0 CAT: 11

Reality Monitoring
CIJE: 5 RIE: 1 CAT: 15

Reality Orientation
CIJE: 6 RIE: 4 CAT: 11

Reality Research
CIJE: 8 RIE: 5 CAT: 15

Reality Testing
CIJE: 3 RIE: 0 CAT: 21

REAP
CIJE: 1 RIE: 1 CAT: 15
SN Strategy for improving reading/writing/study skills

REAP (Belize)
USE Relevant Education for Agriculture and Production

Reasonable Accommodation
CIJE: 8 RIE: 4 CAT: 14

Reasonable Accommodation (Handicapped)
CIJE: 3 RIE: 7 CAT: 11

Reasoned Action Theory
USE Theory of Reasoned Action

Reasoning Impairment
CIJE: 1 RIE: 0 CAT: 11

Reasoning Tests
CIJE: 5 RIE: 15 CAT: 21

Reasons for Going to College Inventory (Dole)
CIJE: 0 RIE: 2 CAT: 21

Reauthorization Legislation
CIJE: 21 RIE: 159 CAT: 14

Reavis High School IL
CIJE: 1 RIE: 0 CAT: 17

Rebus
CIJE: 8 RIE: 3 CAT: 16

Recall Elections
CIJE: 1 RIE: 0 CAT: 14

Recall of Products
USE Product Recall

RECAP JETS Program
CIJE: 0 RIE: 1 CAT: 19

Recapitulation Theory
CIJE: 4 RIE: 1 CAT: 15

Receipts
CIJE: 1 RIE: 1 CAT: 16

Receive Site Facilitators
CIJE: 0 RIE: 1 CAT: 09

Receiver Apprehension
CIJE: 0 RIE: 1 CAT: 11

Receiver Apprehension Test
CIJE: 0 RIE: 2 CAT: 21

Receiver Operating Characteristic Analysis
CIJE: 4 RIE: 0 CAT: 15

Receiving Clerks
CIJE: 0 RIE: 2 CAT: 09

Recency Effect
CIJE: 12 RIE: 4 CAT: 21

Recency Model
CIJE: 1 RIE: 0 CAT: 15

Recent Alumni Questionnaire
CIJE: 0 RIE: 1 CAT: 21

Recent College Graduates Study 1987 (NCES)
CIJE: 0 RIE: 3 CAT: 21
UF Recent College Graduates Survey 1987 (NCES)

Recent College Graduates Study 1991 (NCES)
CIJE: 0 RIE: 1 CAT: 21

Recent College Graduates Survey 1978 (NCES)
CIJE: 0 RIE: 4 CAT: 21

Recent College Graduates Survey 1987 (NCES)
USE Recent College Graduates Study 1987 (NCES)

Recent Life Changes Questionnaire (Grissom et al)
CIJE: 1 RIE: 0 CAT: 21

Recent Social Trends in the United States
USE Ogburn Report

Recently Published Articles
CIJE: 0 RIE: 1 CAT: 22
SN Part of the periodical current awareness service of the American Historical Association

Reception Classes (England)
CIJE: 0 RIE: 1 CAT: 15

Receptivity to Change
CIJE: 1 RIE: 3 CAT: 16

Receptivity to Change Inventory
CIJE: 0 RIE: 2 CAT: 21

Recession
CIJE: 52 RIE: 25 CAT: 12

Recession (Economic 1975)
CIJE: 0 RIE: 1 CAT: 12

Recidivism (Foster Care)
CIJE: 1 RIE: 0 CAT: 11

Recipes (Food)
CIJE: 8 RIE: 67 CAT: 16

Reciprocal Borrowing
CIJE: 0 RIE: 1 CAT: 16

Reciprocal Category System
CIJE: 1 RIE: 10 CAT: 15

Reciprocal Education Program
CIJE: 1 RIE: 0 CAT: 19

Reciprocal Interdependence
CIJE: 5 RIE: 3 CAT: 15

Reciprocal Questioning Procedure
USE ReQuest

Reciprocal Teacher Certification
USE Teacher Certification Reciprocity

Reciprocals (Languages)
CIJE: 0 RIE: 1 CAT: 13

Reciprocity
CIJE: 46 RIE: 30 CAT: 16
SN Use a more specific term if possible, e.g., "Reciprocity (Communication)," "Question Answer Reciprocity," "Social Reciprocity," "Tuition Reciprocity," "Teacher Certification Reciprocity"

Reciprocity (Communication)
CIJE: 12 RIE: 5 CAT: 13

Recitation
CIJE: 11 RIE: 5 CAT: 13

Reclassification
CIJE: 2 RIE: 5 CAT: 15

Recognition Discrimination (Fletcher et al)
CIJE: 1 RIE: 0 CAT: 21

Recognizing Reliable Observations
CIJE: 0 RIE: 1 CAT: 21

Reconstruction Technique
CIJE: 3 RIE: 1 CAT: 15

Reconstructive Approach
CIJE: 6 RIE: 2 CAT: 15

Reconstructive Memory
CIJE: 10 RIE: 3 CAT: 11

Record Press Tenders
CIJE: 0 RIE: 1 CAT: 09

Record Values
CIJE: 0 RIE: 1 CAT: 16
SN ... of a Pareto Distribution

Recorded Aid for Braille Music
CIJE: 0 RIE: 1 CAT: 04

Recorders (Flutes)
CIJE: 0 RIE: 1 CAT: 04

Recording for the Blind
CIJE: 0 RIE: 1 CAT: 17

Recording Industry
CIJE: 4 RIE: 1 CAT: 05

Recording Rules (Observation)
CIJE: 0 RIE: 1 CAT: 15

Records and Archives Management Programme
CIJE: 0 RIE: 2 CAT: 19

Recovery Inc
CIJE: 1 RIE: 0 CAT: 17

Recreation Advisory Council
CIJE: 0 RIE: 1 CAT: 17

Recreation Aides
CIJE: 0 RIE: 1 CAT: 09

Recreation Center for the Handicapped
CIJE: 1 RIE: 0 CAT: 17

Recreation Industry
CIJE: 0 RIE: 1 CAT: 16

Recreation Instruction Service Enrichment
CIJE: 0 RIE: 1 CAT: 19

Recreation Occupations
CIJE: 0 RIE: 4 CAT: 09

Recreation Occupations Education
CIJE: 0 RIE: 1 CAT: 03

Recreation Support Program
CIJE: 0 RIE: 1 CAT: 19

Recreation Workers
CIJE: 2 RIE: 2 CAT: 09

Recreational Experience Preference Scales
CIJE: 1 RIE: 0 CAT: 21

Recreational Mathematics
CIJE: 6 RIE: 1 CAT: 20

Recreational Vehicles
CIJE: 3 RIE: 5 CAT: 04

ReCreative Psychology
CIJE: 0 RIE: 1 CAT: 11

Recruit Attrition
CIJE: 0 RIE: 1 CAT: 15

Recruiter Role
CIJE: 4 RIE: 3 CAT: 16

Recruiting New Teachers Inc
CIJE: 0 RIE: 1 CAT: 17

Recruiting Trends Survey
CIJE: 0 RIE: 3 CAT: 22

Recruitment and Community Technical Resources Ctrs
CIJE: 0 RIE: 1 CAT: 05

Recruitment and Training Program
CIJE: 0 RIE: 1 CAT: 19

Recruitment Materials
CIJE: 2 RIE: 2 CAT: 16

Rectors Exchange Project
CIJE: 0 RIE: 1 CAT: 19

Recursive Models
CIJE: 1 RIE: 1 CAT: 15

Recursive Programing
CIJE: 10 RIE: 4 CAT: 20

Recursive Thought
CIJE: 8 RIE: 3 CAT: 11

Red Badge of Courage
CIJE: 2 RIE: 3 CAT: 22

Red Balloon
CIJE: 1 RIE: 0 CAT: 22

Red Bank Public Schools NJ
CIJE: 3 RIE: 2 CAT: 17

Red Cloud
CIJE: 0 RIE: 2 CAT: 18
SN Sioux Chief, 1822-1909

Red Cloud (Mitchell Jr)
CIJE: 0 RIE: 1 CAT: 18
SN Winnebago Medal of Honor Recipient, 1924-1950

Red Cloud Indian School
CIJE: 1 RIE: 0 CAT: 17

Red Cloud Reading Test
CIJE: 0 RIE: 1 CAT: 21

Red Cross
CIJE: 8 RIE: 4 CAT: 17
UF American National Red Cross; American Red Cross

Red Deer College AB
CIJE: 1 RIE: 3 CAT: 17

Red Deer Public Schools AB
CIJE: 0 RIE: 0 CAT: 17

Red Fox
CIJE: 0 RIE: 1 CAT: 18

Red Guards
CIJE: 2 RIE: 0 CAT: 10

Red Kite
CIJE: 0 RIE: 1 CAT: 22

Red Lake Reservation MN
CIJE: 0 RIE: 1 CAT: 17

Red Lion Case
CIJE: 1 RIE: 1 CAT: 14

Red Pony
CIJE: 1 RIE: 1 CAT: 22

Red River Community College MB
CIJE: 0 RIE: 2 CAT: 17

Red Rocks Community College CO
CIJE: 0 RIE: 1 CAT: 17

Red School House MN
CIJE: 0 RIE: 1 CAT: 17

Reddie (Cecil)
CIJE: 2 RIE: 0 CAT: 18

Redecision Family Therapy
CIJE: 1 RIE: 0 CAT: 11

Redfern Approach
CIJE: 2 RIE: 2 CAT: 15

Redistributive Programs
CIJE: 4 RIE: 2 CAT: 19

Redl (Fritz)
CIJE: 3 RIE: 0 CAT: 18

Redlands Christian Migrant Association
CIJE: 0 RIE: 3 CAT: 17

Redlands Community College OK
CIJE: 0 RIE: 1 CAT: 17
SN Formerly called El Reno Junior College

Redls Managing Surface Behavior
CIJE: 1 RIE: 0 CAT: 15

Redox Reactions
CIJE: 6 RIE: 0 CAT: 20

Redshirting
CIJE: 1 RIE: 0 CAT: 16
SN See also "Academic Redshirting"

Redstone Scientific Information Center
CIJE: 1 RIE: 1 CAT: 17

REDUC
CIJE: 0 RIE: 1 CAT: 17
UF Latin American Network for Documentation in Educ

Reduced Rank Classification
CIJE: 1 RIE: 1 CAT: 21

Reduced Redundancy Test
CIJE: 1 RIE: 0 CAT: 21

Reduction (Chemistry)
CIJE: 4 RIE: 0 CAT: 20

Reduction (Phonology)
CIJE: 1 RIE: 2 CAT: 13

Reduction Formula (Mathematics)
CIJE: 2 RIE: 0 CAT: 20

REDUNDALS Technique
CIJE: 0 RIE: 1 CAT: 15

Redundancy Analysis
CIJE: 16 RIE: 4 CAT: 21

Redundancy Counseling
CIJE: 1 RIE: 0 CAT: 11

Reduplication (Phonology)
CIJE: 3 RIE: 3 CAT: 13

Redwood City Elementary School District CA
CIJE: 0 RIE: 1 CAT: 17

Redwood City School District CA
CIJE: 1 RIE: 3 CAT: 17

Redwood Employees Protection Plan CA
CIJE: 0 RIE: 2 CAT: 19

Redwood Falls School District MN
CIJE: 0 RIE: 2 CAT: 17

Redwood Records
CIJE: 1 RIE: 1 CAT: 17

Redwood School Test (Hurst et al)
CIJE: 1 RIE: 0 CAT: 21

Redwoods Community College District CA
CIJE: 0 RIE: 1 CAT: 17

Reed (Alma)
CIJE: 0 RIE: 1 CAT: 18

Reed and Kellogg System of Diagramming
CIJE: 0 RIE: 1 CAT: 21

Reed College OR
CIJE: 5 RIE: 6 CAT: 17

ReEd Program
CIJE: 0 RIE: 1 CAT: 19

Reed Science Activity Inventory
CIJE: 1 RIE: 0 CAT: 21

Reed v Reed
CIJE: 2 RIE: 0 CAT: 14

Reedley College CA
CIJE: 0 RIE: 1 CAT: 17

Reedsport School District OR
CIJE: 0 RIE: 1 CAT: 17

Reeducation Treatment
CIJE: 2 RIE: 0 CAT: 15

Reemployment
CIJE: 9 RIE: 6 CAT: 15

Reemployment Education Assistance Program
CIJE: 0 RIE: 1 CAT: 19

Reemployment Rights
CIJE: 0 RIE: 1 CAT: 14

Reentry Adult Student Project NY
CIJE: 0 RIE: 1 CAT: 19

Reese (H W)
CIJE: 0 RIE: 1 CAT: 18

Reese (Lizette)
CIJE: 0 RIE: 1 CAT: 18

Reevaluation Counseling
CIJE: 0 RIE: 2 CAT: 11

Reeves (B)
CIJE: 0 RIE: 1 CAT: 18

Reeves (David)
CIJE: 1 RIE: 0 CAT: 18

Reeves (Floyd Wesley)
CIJE: 1 RIE: 0 CAT: 18

Referees
CIJE: 6 RIE: 4 CAT: 10

Reference and Interlibrary Loan Service OH
CIJE: 1 RIE: 1 CAT: 17

Reference and Research Library Resources Program
CIJE: 1 RIE: 10 CAT: 19

Reference Interviews
CIJE: 1 RIE: 1 CAT: 16

Reference Questions
CIJE: 27 RIE: 5 CAT: 16

Reference Skills
CIJE: 5 RIE: 2 CAT: 16

Reference Tests for Noncognitive Factors
CIJE: 0 RIE: 2 CAT: 21

Reference Transactions
CIJE: 11 RIE: 3 CAT: 16

Referendums
CIJE: 9 RIE: 8 CAT: 14

Referential Communication
CIJE: 73 RIE: 22 CAT: 13

Referential Reality
CIJE: 0 RIE: 1 CAT: 11

Referents (Linguistics)
CIJE: 40 RIE: 57 CAT: 13

Referral Preference Rating Scale
CIJE: 1 RIE: 0 CAT: 21

Refinery Operators
CIJE: 0 RIE: 1 CAT: 09

Reflecting (Communication)
CIJE: 1 RIE: 6 CAT: 13

Reflection Methodology
CIJE: 0 RIE: 4 CAT: 15

Reflection Process
CIJE: 13 RIE: 25 CAT: 11

Reflections (Mathematics)
CIJE: 6 RIE: 1 CAT: 20

Reflective Abstraction
CIJE: 0 RIE: 1 CAT: 11

Reflective Analysis
CIJE: 9 RIE: 9 CAT: 15

Reflective Appraisal of Programs
CIJE: 0 RIE: 1 CAT: 15

Reflective Awareness
CIJE: 1 RIE: 1 CAT: 11

Reflective Children
CIJE: 2 RIE: 0 CAT: 10

Reflective Controversy
CIJE: 0 RIE: 1 CAT: 15

Reflective Inquiry
CIJE: 16 RIE: 21 CAT: 15

Reflective Inquiry Teacher Education
USE RITE Program

Reflective Judgment
CIJE: 4 RIE: 5 CAT: 11

Reflective Judgment Model
CIJE: 6 RIE: 4 CAT: 15

Reflective Practice
CIJE: 42 RIE: 22 CAT: 15

Reflective Reading Thinking Activities
CIJE: 1 RIE: 0 CAT: 15

Reflective Supervision
CIJE: 11 RIE: 3 CAT: 15

Reflective Teaching Instrument
CIJE: 1 RIE: 1 CAT: 21
SN An objective instrument to assess a teacher's perceived engagement in reflective practice

Reflective Thinking
CIJE: 184 RIE: 79 CAT: 15

Reflective Writing
CIJE: 15 RIE: 16 CAT: 13

Reflexes
CIJE: 9 RIE: 5 CAT: 11

Reflexive Abstraction
CIJE: 0 RIE: 2 CAT: 11

Reflexives
CIJE: 16 RIE: 23 CAT: 13

REFOCUS Program MO
CIJE: 0 RIE: 1 CAT: 19
SN "Redefine Efforts: Focus on Change Under Supervision"

Reforestation
CIJE: 3 RIE: 6 CAT: 20
SN See also "Deforestation" and "Forests"

Reform Efforts
CIJE: 292 RIE: 349 CAT: 16
UF Educational Reform Efforts; Education Reform Efforts

Reform Strategies
CIJE: 1 RIE: 4 CAT: 16

REFORMA
CIJE: 0 RIE: 1 CAT: 17

Reforma Conference
CIJE: 0 RIE: 1 CAT: 02

Reformation (Historical Period)
CIJE: 4 RIE: 1 CAT: 12

Refractometers
CIJE: 2 RIE: 0 CAT: 04

Refractometry
CIJE: 3 RIE: 0 CAT: 20

Refractory Disorders
CIJE: 0 RIE: 1 CAT: 11

Refregier (Anton)
CIJE: 1 RIE: 0 CAT: 18

Refugee Act 1980
CIJE: 6 RIE: 10 CAT: 14

Refugee Assistance
CIJE: 3 RIE: 31 CAT: 14

Refugee Assistance Amendments Act 1982
CIJE: 0 RIE: 1 CAT: 14

Refugee Camps
CIJE: 6 RIE: 13 CAT: 05

Refugee Education and Employment Program
CIJE: 0 RIE: 4 CAT: 19

Refugee Education Project AZ
CIJE: 0 RIE: 1 CAT: 19

Refugee Legislation
USE Immigration Legislation

Refugee Mental Health
CIJE: 0 RIE: 20 CAT: 11

Refugee Resettlement
CIJE: 3 RIE: 6 CAT: 16

Refugee Womens Alliance
CIJE: 0 RIE: 1 CAT: 17
UF ReWA

Refuges and Wildlife Cooperative Educ Program
USE Refuges Wildlife Cooperative Education Program

Refuges Wildlife Cooperative Education Program
CIJE: 0 RIE: 1 CAT: 19
UF Refuges and Wildlife Cooperative Educ Program

Refunds
CIJE: 3 RIE: 2 CAT: 16

Refusal of Treatment
CIJE: 1 RIE: 0 CAT: 11
SN See also "Right to Refuse Treatment"

Refusal Skills Program
CIJE: 2 RIE: 0 CAT: 19

Refusals
CIJE: 0 RIE: 2 CAT: 16
SN Use a more specific term if possible, e.g., "Food Refusal," "School Refusal," "Refusal of Treatment"

Refutation Text
CIJE: 1 RIE: 2 CAT: 13

Regents Biology
CIJE: 0 RIE: 2 CAT: 20

Regents Chemistry
CIJE: 0 RIE: 1 CAT: 20

Regents External Degree Program NY
CIJE: 3 RIE: 2 CAT: 21
UF New York State Regents External Degree Exams

Reggae
CIJE: 2 RIE: 3 CAT: 16

Regina Plains Community College SK
CIJE: 0 RIE: 1 CAT: 17

Region 1
CIJE: 0 RIE: 2 CAT: 17

Region 2
CIJE: 0 RIE: 3 CAT: 17

Region 3
CIJE: 0 RIE: 4 CAT: 17

Region 4
CIJE: 2 RIE: 4 CAT: 17

Region 5
CIJE: 1 RIE: 4 CAT: 17

Region 6
CIJE: 2 RIE: 8 CAT: 17

Region 7
CIJE: 0 RIE: 5 CAT: 17

Region 8
CIJE: 0 RIE: 10 CAT: 17

Region 9
CIJE: 0 RIE: 5 CAT: 17

Region 10
CIJE: 0 RIE: 2 CAT: 17

Regional and Urban Information Network
CIJE: 1 RIE: 0 CAT: 17

Regional Center Educ Innovation Tech (Singapore)
CIJE: 0 RIE: 3 CAT: 17

Regional Centers
CIJE: 3 RIE: 4 CAT: 05

Regional Colleges
CIJE: 0 RIE: 1 CAT: 05

Regional Council for International Education
CIJE: 0 RIE: 2 CAT: 17

Regional Cultural Resources Program
CIJE: 0 RIE: 1 CAT: 19

Regional Development
CIJE: 7 RIE: 4 CAT: 16

Regional Directors of Education
CIJE: 0 RIE: 1 CAT: 09

Regional Districts
CIJE: 1 RIE: 0 CAT: 05

Regional Education Laboratory for the Carolinas
CIJE: 0 RIE: 1 CAT: 17

Regional Educational Laboratories
CIJE: 4 RIE: 30 CAT: 05

Regional Educational Resource Agencies
CIJE: 0 RIE: 1 CAT: 05

Regional Educational Service Agencies
CIJE: 12 RIE: 21 CAT: 05

Regional English Language Centre (Singapore)
CIJE: 1 RIE: 7 CAT: 17

Regional Environmental Learning System
CIJE: 0 RIE: 1 CAT: 04

Regional Exchange Programs
CIJE: 0 RIE: 2 CAT: 19

Regional History
CIJE: 2 RIE: 8 CAT: 12

Regional In Service Education (RISE) Teacher Ctr
CIJE: 0 RIE: 1 CAT: 17

Regional Information Centers
CIJE: 0 RIE: 2 CAT: 05

Regional Information Exchange Program
CIJE: 0 RIE: 1 CAT: 19

Regional Institute for Children and Adolescents
CIJE: 0 RIE: 1 CAT: 17

Regional Intervention Preschoolers Parents
CIJE: 0 RIE: 1 CAT: 19
SN Regional Intervention Program for Preschoolers and Parents

Regional Intervention Program Preschoolers Parents
CIJE: 0 RIE: 1 CAT: 19

Regional Laboratory Teacher Recognition Program
CIJE: 0 RIE: 1 CAT: 19

Regional Learning Service NY
CIJE: 0 RIE: 0 CAT: 17

Regional Literature
CIJE: 1 RIE: 3 CAT: 16

Regional Magazines
CIJE: 4 RIE: 5 CAT: 16

Regional Media Centers for the Deaf
CIJE: 3 RIE: 0 CAT: 17

Regional Media Centers Network
CIJE: 1 RIE: 1 CAT: 17

Regional Medical Libraries
CIJE: 2 RIE: 0 CAT: 05

Regional Medical Library Network
CIJE: 0 RIE: 1 CAT: 17
SN A network of the National Library of Medicine

Regional Occupational Centers and Programs
CIJE: 2 RIE: 2 CAT: 17
UF California Assn of Reg Occup Ctrs and Progs

Regional Parenting Survey
CIJE: 0 RIE: 1 CAT: 21

Regional Postsecondary Educ Prog Deaf and Handicap
CIJE: 0 RIE: 1 CAT: 19

Regional Postsecondary Education Program for Deaf
CIJE: 0 RIE: 1 CAT: 19

Regional Program Preschool Handicapped Children
CIJE: 0 RIE: 1 CAT: 19

Regional Rehabilitation Exchange Project
CIJE: 0 RIE: 4 CAT: 19
UF RRX Project

Regional Rehabilitation Research Institute CO
CIJE: 1 RIE: 0 CAT: 17

Regional Resource Centers
CIJE: 2 RIE: 5 CAT: 05

Regional Seminar in Agricultural Education
CIJE: 0 RIE: 1 CAT: 02

Regional Surveys
CIJE: 6 RIE: 22 CAT: 21

Regional Training and Dissemination Centers
CIJE: 0 RIE: 1 CAT: 05

Regional Training and Resource Centre (Kenya)
CIJE: 0 RIE: 0 CAT: 17

Regional Universities
CIJE: 3 RIE: 2 CAT: 05

Regionalism
CIJE: 10 RIE: 9 CAT: 16

Regionalized Education
CIJE: 1 RIE: 1 CAT: 16

Regis College CO
CIJE: 3 RIE: 3 CAT: 17

Regis College MA
CIJE: 3 RIE: 3 CAT: 17

Regis High School NY
CIJE: 0 RIE: 1 CAT: 17

Regis Plan for Individualization
CIJE: 0 RIE: 1 CAT: 15

Regis University CO
CIJE: 1 RIE: 2 CAT: 17

Registered Holistic Scoring Method
CIJE: 0 RIE: 3 CAT: 15

Registers (Linguistics)
CIJE: 25 RIE: 20 CAT: 13

Registration by Mail
USE Mail Registration

Registry of Interpreters for the Deaf Inc
CIJE: 0 RIE: 2 CAT: 17

Regression Correction
CIJE: 0 RIE: 1 CAT: 21

Regression Discontinuity Model
CIJE: 9 RIE: 7 CAT: 15

Regression Effects
CIJE: 4 RIE: 0 CAT: 21

Regression Projection Model
CIJE: 0 RIE: 1 CAT: 15

Regression Toward the Mean
CIJE: 3 RIE: 1 CAT: 21

Regressive Behavior
CIJE: 8 RIE: 9 CAT: 11

Regret Functions
CIJE: 0 RIE: 1 CAT: 15

Regrouping (Mathematics)
CIJE: 3 RIE: 2 CAT: 20

Regular Education Inservice Initiative
CIJE: 2 RIE: 2 CAT: 19

Regular Writing Practice Program
CIJE: 0 RIE: 1 CAT: 19

Regulated Breathing Method
CIJE: 1 RIE: 0 CAT: 11

Regulated Expressiveness
CIJE: 0 RIE: 1 CAT: 11

Regulators (Electrical Equipment)
CIJE: 0 RIE: 5 CAT: 04

Regulatory Agencies
CIJE: 14 RIE: 40 CAT: 05

Regulatory Evaluation
CIJE: 3 RIE: 3 CAT: 21

Regulatory Programs
CIJE: 9 RIE: 18 CAT: 14

Regurgitation
CIJE: 3 RIE: 0 CAT: 11

Rehabilitation Act 1973
CIJE: 64 RIE: 104 CAT: 14

Rehabilitation Act 1973 (Section 502)
CIJE: 0 RIE: 1 CAT: 14

Rehabilitation Act 1973 (Section 503)
CIJE: 2 RIE: 0 CAT: 14

Rehabilitation Act 1973 (Section 504)
CIJE: 72 RIE: 122 CAT: 14

Rehabilitation Act Amendments 1974
CIJE: 0 RIE: 1 CAT: 14

Rehabilitation Act Amendments 1986
CIJE: 1 RIE: 6 CAT: 14

Rehabilitation Act Amendments 1992
CIJE: 1 RIE: 2 CAT: 14

Rehabilitation Aides
CIJE: 0 RIE: 2 CAT: 09

Rehabilitation Careers Project
CIJE: 0 RIE: 1 CAT: 19

Rehabilitation Counselor Education Program
CIJE: 2 RIE: 0 CAT: 19

Rehabilitation Counselor Education Programs
CIJE: 1 RIE: 0 CAT: 19

Rehabilitation Counselors
CIJE: 1 RIE: 1 CAT: 09

Rehabilitation Engineering
CIJE: 0 RIE: 4 CAT: 16

Rehabilitation Engineering Center CA
CIJE: 0 RIE: 1 CAT: 17

Rehabilitation Information and Knowledge Test
CIJE: 0 RIE: 1 CAT: 21

Rehabilitation Need and Status Scale
CIJE: 0 RIE: 1 CAT: 21

Rehabilitation Research and Training Center WI
CIJE: 0 RIE: 1 CAT: 17

Rehabilitation Research and Training Centers
CIJE: 0 RIE: 3 CAT: 05

Rehabilitation Research Foundation AL
CIJE: 1 RIE: 2 CAT: 17

Rehabilitation Services Administration
CIJE: 7 RIE: 9 CAT: 17

Rehabilitation Services and Facilities Program
CIJE: 0 RIE: 1 CAT: 19

Rehabilitation Task Performance Evaluation Scale
CIJE: 0 RIE: 1 CAT: 21

Rehabilitative Optometry
CIJE: 0 RIE: 1 CAT: 11

Rehearsal
CIJE: 19 RIE: 7 CAT: 16

Rehearsal (Learning)
CIJE: 14 RIE: 4 CAT: 15

Rehearsal (Memory)
CIJE: 20 RIE: 13 CAT: 15

Rehearsal Strategies
CIJE: 24 RIE: 21 CAT: 15

Rehearsals (Theater)
CIJE: 4 RIE: 3 CAT: 16

Rehiring
CIJE: 0 RIE: 1 CAT: 16

Rehnquist (William)
CIJE: 6 RIE: 1 CAT: 18
SN "William H"

Reichenberger (Arnold G)
CIJE: 1 RIE: 0 CAT: 18

Reid (Alastair)
CIJE: 0 RIE: 1 CAT: 18

Reid (Thomas)
CIJE: 1 RIE: 1 CAT: 18

Reidland High School KY
CIJE: 0 RIE: 1 CAT: 17

Reidsville City School System NC
CIJE: 0 RIE: 1 CAT: 17

Reign of ETS (Nairn)
CIJE: 0 RIE: 2 CAT: 22
UF Nader Nairn Report; Nairn Report

Reimbursement Programs
CIJE: 11 RIE: 12 CAT: 19

Reimer (Everett)
CIJE: 1 RIE: 0 CAT: 18

Reindustrialization
CIJE: 2 RIE: 12 CAT: 16

Reinforced Concrete
CIJE: 1 RIE: 0 CAT: 04

Reinforced Readiness Requisites Program
CIJE: 0 RIE: 1 CAT: 19

Reinforcement History Questionnaire
CIJE: 0 RIE: 1 CAT: 21

Reinforcement Schedules
CIJE: 8 RIE: 0 CAT: 11

Reinforcement Survey Schedule
CIJE: 1 RIE: 2 CAT: 21

Reinforcer Sampling
CIJE: 1 RIE: 0 CAT: 11

Reinstatement
CIJE: 3 RIE: 1 CAT: 15

Reinstatement (Learning)
CIJE: 1 RIE: 0 CAT: 15

Reinstein Reinforcement Schedule
CIJE: 0 RIE: 1 CAT: 21

Reintegration
CIJE: 6 RIE: 4 CAT: 16

Reisman (David)
CIJE: 0 RIE: 1 CAT: 18

Reiss (Ira)
CIJE: 0 RIE: 1 CAT: 18

Reiss Wheel Theory
CIJE: 1 RIE: 0 CAT: 15

Reissman (Leonard)
CIJE: 1 RIE: 0 CAT: 18

Reitan Neuropsychological Batteries
CIJE: 0 RIE: 1 CAT: 21

Rejang
CIJE: 0 RIE: 1 CAT: 13
SN A West Indonesian language

Relapse
CIJE: 42 RIE: 9 CAT: 11

Relapse Crises
CIJE: 4 RIE: 1 CAT: 11

RELATE Computer Program
CIJE: 0 RIE: 1 CAT: 04

Related Sample Percentages
CIJE: 0 RIE: 1 CAT: 15

Related Services
CIJE: 4 RIE: 10 CAT: 05

Related Subjects Instruction
CIJE: 0 RIE: 13 CAT: 15

Related Vocational Instruction Program GA
CIJE: 0 RIE: 1 CAT: 19

Relatedness Coefficient Matrix Program
CIJE: 0 RIE: 1 CAT: 19

Relating Experientially with Parents and Children
CIJE: 0 RIE: 0 CAT: 19

Relation Definition Theory
CIJE: 0 RIE: 1 CAT: 15

Relation Eduction Index
CIJE: 0 RIE: 1 CAT: 15

Relational Approach (Information Retrieval)
CIJE: 24 RIE: 7 CAT: 15

Relational Communication
CIJE: 8 RIE: 2 CAT: 15

Relational Competence
CIJE: 0 RIE: 1 CAT: 15

Relational Concepts
CIJE: 13 RIE: 5 CAT: 15

Relational Efficacy (Marriage)
CIJE: 0 RIE: 1 CAT: 16

Relational Ethics Scale
CIJE: 1 RIE: 2 CAT: 21

Relational Grammar
CIJE: 0 RIE: 9 CAT: 13

Relational Leadership
CIJE: 0 RIE: 1 CAT: 15

Relational Learning
CIJE: 13 RIE: 3 CAT: 15

Relational Models
CIJE: 9 RIE: 2 CAT: 15

Relational Network Approach
CIJE: 4 RIE: 2 CAT: 15

Relational Propositions
CIJE: 1 RIE: 1 CAT: 16

Relational Understanding
CIJE: 5 RIE: 0 CAT: 20

Relations (Mathematics)
CIJE: 5 RIE: 3 CAT: 20

Relationship Belief Inventory
CIJE: 1 RIE: 0 CAT: 21

Relationship Change Research
CIJE: 1 RIE: 3 CAT: 16

Relationship Enhancement
CIJE: 7 RIE: 1 CAT: 15

Relationship Identification
CIJE: 0 RIE: 1 CAT: 15

Relationship Orientation
CIJE: 0 RIE: 2 CAT: 15

Relationship Psychotherapy
CIJE: 1 RIE: 2 CAT: 11

Relationship Quality
CIJE: 1 RIE: 1 CAT: 16

Relationship Questionnaire (Truax and Carkhuff)
CIJE: 1 RIE: 0 CAT: 21

Relationship Termination
CIJE: 4 RIE: 4 CAT: 11

Relative Autonomy Theory
CIJE: 1 RIE: 1 CAT: 15

Relative Clauses
CIJE: 30 RIE: 23 CAT: 13

Relative Difficulty Ratio
CIJE: 1 RIE: 2 CAT: 21

Relative Preference Index
CIJE: 0 RIE: 1 CAT: 21

Relative Thinking
CIJE: 2 RIE: 1 CAT: 15

Relative Wage Models
CIJE: 0 RIE: 2 CAT: 15

Relativism
CIJE: 40 RIE: 11 CAT: 15

Relativization
CIJE: 1 RIE: 4 CAT: 15

Relaxation
CIJE: 12 RIE: 8 CAT: 11

Relaxation Technique (Benson)
CIJE: 1 RIE: 0 CAT: 15

Relay Circuits
CIJE: 1 RIE: 1 CAT: 04

Relevance (Cultural)
CIJE: 5 RIE: 9 CAT: 15

Relevance (Evaluation)
CIJE: 5 RIE: 5 CAT: 21

Relevance (Personal)
CIJE: 3 RIE: 3 CAT: 11

Relevancy Gap
CIJE: 4 RIE: 2 CAT: 15

Relevant Education for Agriculture and Production
CIJE: 0 RIE: 1 CAT: 19
UF REAP (Belize)

Relevant Educational Applications of Computer Tech
CIJE: 0 RIE: 1 CAT: 03

Relevant Experiences for Alternative Learning Proj
USE Project REAL DE

Relevant Redundant Cues Learning
CIJE: 1 RIE: 0 CAT: 15

Reliability Analysis Center
CIJE: 0 RIE: 1 CAT: 17

Reliability Formulas
CIJE: 5 RIE: 6 CAT: 15

Relief Format Assessment Test
CIJE: 1 RIE: 0 CAT: 21

Relief Teacher Training Institute
CIJE: 1 RIE: 0 CAT: 02

Religion in Elementary Social Studies Project
CIJE: 0 RIE: 9 CAT: 19

Religion News
USE Religious News

Religious Art
CIJE: 1 RIE: 2 CAT: 16

Religious Broadcasting
CIJE: 9 RIE: 15 CAT: 16

Religious Conversion
CIJE: 6 RIE: 1 CAT: 16
SN Adoption of a new religion
UF Conversion (Religious)

Religious Cults
CIJE: 5 RIE: 0 CAT: 10

Religious Denominations
CIJE: 4 RIE: 2 CAT: 10

Religious Exercises
CIJE: 1 RIE: 1 CAT: 16

Religious Experiences
CIJE: 9 RIE: 7 CAT: 16
SN See also "Spiritual Experiences"

Religious Freedom
CIJE: 66 RIE: 28 CAT: 16

Religious Freedom Restoration Act 1993
CIJE: 0 RIE: 1 CAT: 14
UF Public Law 103 141

Religious Fundamentalism
CIJE: 55 RIE: 12 CAT: 16

Religious Landmarks
CIJE: 0 RIE: 1 CAT: 16

Religious Libraries
CIJE: 19 RIE: 5 CAT: 05

Religious Movements
CIJE: 4 RIE: 9 CAT: 16

Religious News
CIJE: 1 RIE: 6 CAT: 16
UF Religion News

Religious Practices
CIJE: 13 RIE: 13 CAT: 16

Religious Publications
CIJE: 8 RIE: 5 CAT: 16

Relinquishment of Control
CIJE: 2 RIE: 0 CAT: 11

Reluctant Learners
CIJE: 2 RIE: 2 CAT: 10

Reluctant Readers
CIJE: 29 RIE: 20 CAT: 10

Remaining Off Alcohol and Drugs Program NB
USE ROAD Program NB

Remarkability Theory
CIJE: 1 RIE: 0 CAT: 15

Remcon 2780 Terminal
CIJE: 0 RIE: 1 CAT: 04

Remedial Decrees
CIJE: 0 RIE: 1 CAT: 14

Remedial Interchanges
CIJE: 2 RIE: 3 CAT: 11

Remedial Intervention
CIJE: 8 RIE: 8 CAT: 11

Remediation Assistance Program WA
CIJE: 0 RIE: 0 CAT: 19
SN State program for students in grades 2-9 with basic skills deficiencies

Remodeling
CIJE: 1 RIE: 6 CAT: 16

Remote Access
CIJE: 23 RIE: 1 CAT: 20

Remote Associates Test
CIJE: 19 RIE: 8 CAT: 21

Remote Control Devices
CIJE: 1 RIE: 2 CAT: 04
UF RCDs

Remote Electronic Access Delivery of Information
CIJE: 6 RIE: 2 CAT: 04

Remote Program Storage
CIJE: 0 RIE: 1 CAT: 20

Remote Scoring (Tests)
CIJE: 0 RIE: 1 CAT: 21

Remote Sensing
CIJE: 36 RIE: 9 CAT: 15

Remote Sensing Systems
CIJE: 3 RIE: 1 CAT: 15

Removal of Information Procedure
CIJE: 2 RIE: 0 CAT: 15

Renaissance
CIJE: 20 RIE: 10 CAT: 12

Renaissance Festivals
CIJE: 1 RIE: 0 CAT: 12

Renaissance Information Management System
CIJE: 0 RIE: 1 CAT: 19

Renal Dialysis
USE Hemodialysis

Renal System
CIJE: 6 RIE: 2 CAT: 11

Renape (Tribe)
CIJE: 0 RIE: 1 CAT: 08

Rend Lake College IL
CIJE: 0 RIE: 1 CAT: 17

Rendell Baker v Kohn
CIJE: 0 RIE: 1 CAT: 14

Rene Descartes University (France)
CIJE: 1 RIE: 0 CAT: 17

Renegotiable Student Contracts
CIJE: 1 RIE: 0 CAT: 15

Renewable Resources
CIJE: 1 RIE: 13 CAT: 20

Renfrew (Baron)
CIJE: 1 RIE: 0 CAT: 18

Renoir (Jean)
CIJE: 2 RIE: 0 CAT: 18

Rensselaer Polytechnic Institute NY
CIJE: 17 RIE: 9 CAT: 17

Rent
CIJE: 5 RIE: 2 CAT: 16

Rent Strikes
CIJE: 1 RIE: 0 CAT: 14

Rental Housing Policies
CIJE: 3 RIE: 4 CAT: 14

Rental Property
CIJE: 4 RIE: 6 CAT: 16

Renton School District WA
CIJE: 0 RIE: 1 CAT: 17

Renton Vocational Technical Institute WA
CIJE: 0 RIE: 2 CAT: 17

Renzulli (Joseph)
CIJE: 8 RIE: 2 CAT: 18

Renzulli Hartman Scale
CIJE: 0 RIE: 1 CAT: 21
SN For determination of gifted placement

Renzulli Key Features Model
CIJE: 1 RIE: 0 CAT: 15

Renzulli Scale for Rating Behav Characteristics
USE Scales for Rating Behav Character Superior Student

Reorganization Act 1969 (Massachusetts)
CIJE: 1 RIE: 0 CAT: 14

Repair Theory
CIJE: 0 RIE: 1 CAT: 15

Repairs (Language)
CIJE: 1 RIE: 7 CAT: 13
UF Language Repairs

Repatriation
CIJE: 5 RIE: 2 CAT: 14

Repeated Measures Design
CIJE: 51 RIE: 38 CAT: 15

Repeated Observations
CIJE: 1 RIE: 1 CAT: 15

Repeated Readings
CIJE: 49 RIE: 13 CAT: 15

Repeated Testing
CIJE: 7 RIE: 7 CAT: 21

Repeating Observing Associating and Memorizing
USE ROAM Method

Repeating Response Tendency
CIJE: 1 RIE: 0 CAT: 21

Repertoire International de la Litterature Musical
CIJE: 1 RIE: 0 CAT: 17

Repertory Companies
CIJE: 1 RIE: 1 CAT: 05

Repertory Grid Technique
CIJE: 17 RIE: 2 CAT: 15

Repertory Grid Tests (Kelly)
CIJE: 4 RIE: 0 CAT: 21

Repetition (Language)
CIJE: 31 RIE: 13 CAT: 13

Repetition Effects
CIJE: 33 RIE: 5 CAT: 15

Repetition Tasks
CIJE: 5 RIE: 1 CAT: 15

Repetitive Strain Injuries
CIJE: 1 RIE: 2 CAT: 11

Repetitor I
CIJE: 0 RIE: 1 CAT: 04

Replacement Air Group
CIJE: 0 RIE: 1 CAT: 17

Replacement Costs
CIJE: 2 RIE: 1 CAT: 16

Replacement Roles
CIJE: 1 RIE: 0 CAT: 15

Replays (Video)
CIJE: 1 RIE: 2 CAT: 20
UF Video Replays

Replicants
CIJE: 0 RIE: 1 CAT: 15

Replicating Success PA
CIJE: 0 RIE: 1 CAT: 19
SN School improvement project in Philadelphia

Replication
CIJE: 28 RIE: 28 CAT: 15
SN Use a more specific term if possible, i.e., "Research Replication," "Program Replication," "Job Replication," etc.

Replication (Research)
USE Research Replication

Report Format
CIJE: 7 RIE: 8 CAT: 16
UF Format (Reports)

Report Generators
CIJE: 8 RIE: 3 CAT: 04

Report Program Generator
USE RPG Programing Language

Reported Speech
USE Indirect Speech

Reporting Evaluation System Occupational Education
CIJE: 0 RIE: 5 CAT: 21

Reporting Laws
CIJE: 8 RIE: 3 CAT: 14
SN See also "Child Abuse and Neglect Reporting"

Reporting of Child Abuse
USE Child Abuse and Neglect Reporting

Reporting of Human Rights Violations
USE Human Rights Reporting

Representational Competence
CIJE: 15 RIE: 21 CAT: 15

Representational Modeling
CIJE: 6 RIE: 2 CAT: 15

Representational Response
CIJE: 10 RIE: 4 CAT: 15

Representational Thinking
CIJE: 21 RIE: 18 CAT: 15

Representations (Mathematics)
CIJE: 85 RIE: 16 CAT: 15
UF Mathematical Representations

Representative Anecdotes
CIJE: 1 RIE: 1 CAT: 15

Representative Tax System
CIJE: 2 RIE: 2 CAT: 14

Representativeness
CIJE: 0 RIE: 1 CAT: 16

Repression
CIJE: 13 RIE: 4 CAT: 11

Repression Sensitization Dimension
CIJE: 3 RIE: 1 CAT: 15

Reprints
CIJE: 28 RIE: 1 CAT: 16

Reproducibility
CIJE: 1 RIE: 1 CAT: 20

Reproductive Rights
CIJE: 1 RIE: 1 CAT: 14

Reproductive Technology
CIJE: 1 RIE: 0 CAT: 11

Reptile Eggs
CIJE: 1 RIE: 0 CAT: 20

Reptiles
CIJE: 7 RIE: 2 CAT: 20

Republic
CIJE: 2 RIE: 1 CAT: 22
SN Philosophical dialog by Plato of Athens

Republic of China
USE Taiwan

Republic of Korea
USE South Korea

Republican Party
CIJE: 13 RIE: 18 CAT: 17

Repurposing
CIJE: 1 RIE: 1 CAT: 20
UF Videodisk Repurposing; Video Repurposing

Reputational Method
CIJE: 0 RIE: 3 CAT: 15

ReQuest
CIJE: 0 RIE: 1 CAT: 15
UF Reciprocal Questioning Procedure

Requests
CIJE: 38 RIE: 18 CAT: 16

Requests for Clarification (Responses)
CIJE: 3 RIE: 1 CAT: 16

Requests for Proposals
CIJE: 18 RIE: 12 CAT: 16

Requiem for a Heavyweight
CIJE: 0 RIE: 1 CAT: 22

Required Computers
CIJE: 0 RIE: 1 CAT: 04

Requisite Antecedent Behavior
CIJE: 1 RIE: 0 CAT: 15

Resampling Techniques
CIJE: 1 RIE: 1 CAT: 21

Rescaled and Adjusted Gains within Stratum
CIJE: 0 RIE: 1 CAT: 21

Research About Teacher Education Project
CIJE: 4 RIE: 4 CAT: 19
UF AACTE RATE Project; RATE Project (AACTE)

Research and Develop Ctr Teacher Quality Effective
CIJE: 0 RIE: 1 CAT: 17
UF Teacher Quality and Effectiveness R and D Center

Research and Development Center on Student Testing
USE Center on Student Testing Evaluation and Standards

Research and Development Exchange
CIJE: 1 RIE: 12 CAT: 17

Research and Development Price Index
CIJE: 0 RIE: 3 CAT: 22

Research and Development Utilization Program
CIJE: 1 RIE: 65 CAT: 19

Research and Documentation on Vocational Training
CIJE: 0 RIE: 1 CAT: 17

Research and Graduate Training Facilities
CIJE: 2 RIE: 7 CAT: 05

Research and Information Services for Education PA
CIJE: 0 RIE: 1 CAT: 17
UF RISE PA

Research Conference Instructional Systems Tech
CIJE: 0 RIE: 1 CAT: 02

Research Consortium of New Jersey Colleges
CIJE: 0 RIE: 1 CAT: 17

Research Corporation
CIJE: 3 RIE: 1 CAT: 17

Research Courses
USE Research Curriculum

Research Curriculum
CIJE: 17 RIE: 7 CAT: 03
UF Research Courses

Research Develop Diffuse Adopt Model
CIJE: 0 RIE: 2 CAT: 15

Research Development and Diffusion Model
CIJE: 0 RIE: 1 CAT: 15

Research Equipment
CIJE: 1 RIE: 1 CAT: 04

Research Ethics
CIJE: 4 RIE: 1 CAT: 16

Research Evaluation and Planning Units
CIJE: 0 RIE: 2 CAT: 05

Research Evaluation Vocational Instructional Syst
CIJE: 0 RIE: 1 CAT: 21

Research for Better Schools Incorporated
CIJE: 4 RIE: 16 CAT: 17

Research Impact Gram
CIJE: 0 RIE: 2 CAT: 15

Research Implementation
CIJE: 8 RIE: 2 CAT: 15

Research in Education
CIJE: 6 RIE: 13 CAT: 22

Research in Progress
CIJE: 1 RIE: 4 CAT: 16

Research in Undergraduate Institutions Program
CIJE: 0 RIE: 1 CAT: 19

Research Infrastructure
CIJE: 0 RIE: 1 CAT: 16

Research Institute Innovation Education (Israel)
CIJE: 0 RIE: 1 CAT: 17

Research Integration
CIJE: 6 RIE: 7 CAT: 15

Research into Practice Project (CSE)
USE CSE Research into Practice Project

Research Libraries Group
CIJE: 41 RIE: 8 CAT: 17

Research Libraries Group Conspectus
CIJE: 6 RIE: 1 CAT: 22

Research Libraries Information Network
CIJE: 57 RIE: 12 CAT: 17
UF RLIN

Research Management Computerized Methods
CIJE: 0 RIE: 1 CAT: 15

Research Misconduct
CIJE: 8 RIE: 1 CAT: 11
SN See also "Academic Misconduct" and "Employee Misconduct"

Research Networks
CIJE: 6 RIE: 1 CAT: 16

Research of Continuity
CIJE: 1 RIE: 0 CAT: 15

Research on Higher Education Program (Sweden)
CIJE: 0 RIE: 1 CAT: 19
UF Swedish Research on Higher Education Program

Research on Science Education Survey
CIJE: 1 RIE: 0 CAT: 21

Research on Teaching
USE Teaching Research

Research on Teaching Mathematics Conference
CIJE: 0 RIE: 1 CAT: 02

Research on the Improvement Process Program
CIJE: 0 RIE: 5 CAT: 19

Research Priorities
CIJE: 20 RIE: 25 CAT: 16

Research Quality
CIJE: 1 RIE: 1 CAT: 16

Research Quarterly
CIJE: 1 RIE: 0 CAT: 22

Research Replication
CIJE: 43 RIE: 45 CAT: 15
UF Replication (Research)

Research Results
CIJE: 41 RIE: 80 CAT: 16

Research Seminar in Vocational Education
CIJE: 0 RIE: 1 CAT: 02

Research Styles
CIJE: 9 RIE: 6 CAT: 16

Research Subject Relationship
CIJE: 7 RIE: 3 CAT: 15

Research Subjects (Students)
USE Students as Subjects

Research Suggestions
CIJE: 28 RIE: 70 CAT: 16

Research Summaries
CIJE: 13 RIE: 21 CAT: 16

Research Synthesis
CIJE: 4 RIE: 16 CAT: 15

Research Team Approach to Learning
CIJE: 2 RIE: 0 CAT: 15

Research Teams
CIJE: 4 RIE: 3 CAT: 10

Research Training
CIJE: 19 RIE: 13 CAT: 15

Research Trends
CIJE: 56 RIE: 50 CAT: 16

Research Utilization in Elementary Teacher Educ
USE ARTE RUETE Study

Research Utilization Project
CIJE: 0 RIE: 1 CAT: 19

Research Utilizing Problem Solving
CIJE: 0 RIE: 2 CAT: 15

Researcher Role
CIJE: 30 RIE: 19 CAT: 16

Researcher Subject Relationship
CIJE: 31 RIE: 18 CAT: 15

Researcher Teacher Cooperation
USE Teacher Researcher Cooperation

Researcher Teacher Relationship
USE Teacher Researcher Relationship

Researchers and Teachers
USE Teacher Researcher Relationship

Reservation Access Project
CIJE: 0 RIE: 2 CAT: 19

Reserve Book Collections
CIJE: 8 RIE: 9 CAT: 16
SN See also "Library Reserve"

Reserve Officers Training Corps
CIJE: 20 RIE: 29 CAT: 17
SN See also Army, Naval, or Air Force Reserve Officers Training Corps
UF ROTC

Reserve Reading Rooms
CIJE: 1 RIE: 1 CAT: 05
UF Library Reserve Rooms

Reserves (Financial)
CIJE: 0 RIE: 1 CAT: 16

Reserves (Military)
USE Military Reserves

Reservoirs
CIJE: 0 RIE: 1 CAT: 05

Resettled Migrants
CIJE: 3 RIE: 5 CAT: 10

RESGEN Computer Program
CIJE: 0 RIE: 1 CAT: 04

RESIA Project
CIJE: 0 RIE: 1 CAT: 19

Residence Hall Libraries
CIJE: 1 RIE: 1 CAT: 05

Resident Assistant Stress Inventory
CIJE: 2 RIE: 0 CAT: 21

Resident Places Survey
CIJE: 0 RIE: 3 CAT: 21

Residential Based Career Education
CIJE: 0 RIE: 1 CAT: 03

Residential Career Education Model
CIJE: 0 RIE: 2 CAT: 15

Residential Construction
CIJE: 0 RIE: 1 CAT: 20

Residential Electricians
CIJE: 0 RIE: 1 CAT: 09

Residential Program in Executive Education
CIJE: 0 RIE: 1 CAT: 19

Residential Remodeling
CIJE: 0 RIE: 3 CAT: 16

Residential Wiring
CIJE: 0 RIE: 2 CAT: 20
UF House Wiring

Residual Scores
CIJE: 4 RIE: 7 CAT: 21

Residuals (Statistics)
CIJE: 15 RIE: 26 CAT: 21

Resignation (Job)
CIJE: 8 RIE: 3 CAT: 16

Resilience (Personality)
CIJE: 12 RIE: 16 CAT: 11

Resin
CIJE: 0 RIE: 1 CAT: 20

Resistance (Physics)
CIJE: 1 RIE: 2 CAT: 20

Resistance to Deviation Test
CIJE: 0 RIE: 1 CAT: 21

Resistance Training
CIJE: 4 RIE: 0 CAT: 11

Resistors (Electrical Equipment)
CIJE: 4 RIE: 6 CAT: 04

Resocialization
CIJE: 2 RIE: 1 CAT: 15

Resolutions
CIJE: 9 RIE: 6 CAT: 16

Resonance (Physics)
CIJE: 8 RIE: 1 CAT: 20

Resonance Theory of Mass Communication
CIJE: 0 RIE: 0 CAT: 15
UF Evoked Recall Theory (Schwartz)

Resource Access Projects
CIJE: 0 RIE: 4 CAT: 19

Resource Allocation Management Program
CIJE: 2 RIE: 1 CAT: 19

Resource and Referral Service
CIJE: 1 RIE: 8 CAT: 17

Resource Approach in Industrial Arts
CIJE: 1 RIE: 0 CAT: 15

Resource Based Learning
CIJE: 19 RIE: 14 CAT: 03

Resource Consulting Teacher Program
CIJE: 0 RIE: 0 CAT: 19

Resource Cost Model
CIJE: 3 RIE: 8 CAT: 15

Resource Development
CIJE: 7 RIE: 9 CAT: 15

Resource Development Projects
CIJE: 0 RIE: 2 CAT: 19

Resource Educators for Directed Devel of Instr
CIJE: 0 RIE: 1 CAT: 17

Resource Management
CIJE: 22 RIE: 16 CAT: 15

Resource Requirements Prediction Model
CIJE: 2 RIE: 7 CAT: 15

Resource Specialist Program
CIJE: 0 RIE: 2 CAT: 19

Resource Theory
CIJE: 1 RIE: 2 CAT: 15

Resource Utilization
CIJE: 21 RIE: 37 CAT: 15

Resources in Computer Education
CIJE: 0 RIE: 5 CAT: 04

Resources in Education
CIJE: 8 RIE: 208 CAT: 22

Respect
CIJE: 48 RIE: 8 CAT: 16

Respecting Ethnic and Cultural Heritage Center
CIJE: 0 RIE: 1 CAT: 17
UF REACH Center for Global and Multicultural Educ

Respiration
CIJE: 33 RIE: 23 CAT: 11

Respirators
CIJE: 0 RIE: 1 CAT: 04

Respiratory Diseases
CIJE: 17 RIE: 14 CAT: 11
SN See also "Lung Diseases"

Respiratory Distress Syndrome
CIJE: 4 RIE: 1 CAT: 11

Respiratory Manipulation Training
CIJE: 0 RIE: 1 CAT: 11

Respiratory Problems
CIJE: 0 RIE: 1 CAT: 11

Respiratory System
CIJE: 7 RIE: 7 CAT: 11

Respirometers
CIJE: 2 RIE: 0 CAT: 04

Respond Until Correct Method
CIJE: 0 RIE: 1 CAT: 21

Respondent Behavior
CIJE: 1 RIE: 5 CAT: 11

Respondent Burden
CIJE: 1 RIE: 3 CAT: 16

Response Activation
CIJE: 3 RIE: 0 CAT: 15

Response Alternation
CIJE: 1 RIE: 0 CAT: 11

Response Based Writing
CIJE: 1 RIE: 6 CAT: 15

Response Centered Classroom
CIJE: 1 RIE: 0 CAT: 15

Response Class Matrix (Mash et al)
CIJE: 0 RIE: 1 CAT: 21

Response Competition
CIJE: 2 RIE: 0 CAT: 11

Response Consistency
CIJE: 6 RIE: 2 CAT: 11
UF Response Stability

Response Content and Dispersion Observation Form
CIJE: 0 RIE: 1 CAT: 21

Response Contingent Stimulation
CIJE: 5 RIE: 1 CAT: 11

Response Cost
CIJE: 10 RIE: 0 CAT: 11

Response Criteria
CIJE: 0 RIE: 2 CAT: 11

Response Function Discrepancies
CIJE: 1 RIE: 2 CAT: 21

Response Hierarchy
CIJE: 1 RIE: 0 CAT: 11

Response Inhibition
CIJE: 4 RIE: 0 CAT: 11

Response Involvement
CIJE: 1 RIE: 0 CAT: 11

Response Learning
CIJE: 5 RIE: 3 CAT: 15

Response Meaningfulness
CIJE: 2 RIE: 2 CAT: 11

Response Model
CIJE: 4 RIE: 5 CAT: 15

Response Opportunities
CIJE: 3 RIE: 1 CAT: 11

Response Pattern Aberrance
USE Aberrance

Response Patterns
CIJE: 28 RIE: 34 CAT: 11

Response Shift
CIJE: 5 RIE: 2 CAT: 21

Response Signal Procedure
CIJE: 1 RIE: 0 CAT: 15

Response Sincerity
USE Sincerity of Responses

Response Stability
USE Response Consistency

Response System with Variable Prescriptions
CIJE: 0 RIE: 10 CAT: 04

Response to Literature
CIJE: 100 RIE: 86 CAT: 22

Response to Power Measure (Sweney)
CIJE: 1 RIE: 0 CAT: 21

Response Training
USE Directed Response Training

Responsibility Center Budgeting
CIJE: 5 RIE: 2 CAT: 15

Responsibility Questionnaire (Johnson et al)
CIJE: 1 RIE: 0 CAT: 21

Responsible Living Environment
CIJE: 0 RIE: 1 CAT: 15

Responsive Autonomy in Cooperative Teaching
CIJE: 0 RIE: 1 CAT: 03

Responsive Care Program
CIJE: 0 RIE: 6 CAT: 19

Responsive Classroom Observation Schedule
CIJE: 2 RIE: 0 CAT: 21

Responsive College Programme (England)
CIJE: 0 RIE: 1 CAT: 19

Responsive Design
CIJE: 0 RIE: 1 CAT: 15

Responsive Education Model
CIJE: 0 RIE: 1 CAT: 15

Responsive Education Prog for Special Needs Kids
CIJE: 1 RIE: 0 CAT: 19

Responsive Education Program
CIJE: 0 RIE: 4 CAT: 19

Responsive Education Project NY
CIJE: 0 RIE: 2 CAT: 19

Responsive Elaboration
CIJE: 1 RIE: 0 CAT: 15

Responsive Environment Early Education Program
CIJE: 0 RIE: 2 CAT: 19

Responsive Environment Model
CIJE: 1 RIE: 20 CAT: 19

Responsive Environment Test
CIJE: 0 RIE: 3 CAT: 21

Responsive Environments Corporation
CIJE: 0 RIE: 1 CAT: 17

Responsive Evaluation
CIJE: 18 RIE: 9 CAT: 21

Responsive Follow Through Program
CIJE: 1 RIE: 1 CAT: 19

Responsive Illuminative Evaluation
CIJE: 1 RIE: 0 CAT: 15

Responsive Interaction Teaching
CIJE: 0 RIE: 1 CAT: 15

Responsive Multicultural Basic Skills Approach
CIJE: 0 RIE: 2 CAT: 15

Responsive Parenting
CIJE: 5 RIE: 1 CAT: 19

Responsive Reading Program
CIJE: 0 RIE: 1 CAT: 19

Responsive Services Variety Practitioners
CIJE: 0 RIE: 2 CAT: 19
UF RSVP Program MA

Responsive Teacher Program VT
CIJE: 1 RIE: 0 CAT: 19

Responsive Therapy
CIJE: 0 RIE: 3 CAT: 11

Responsiveness (Government)
CIJE: 1 RIE: 1 CAT: 16
UF Government Responsiveness

Restating (Communication)
CIJE: 0 RIE: 1 CAT: 13

Restaurant Management
CIJE: 1 RIE: 11 CAT: 03

Restaurant Managers
CIJE: 1 RIE: 2 CAT: 09

Restitution
CIJE: 4 RIE: 9 CAT: 14

Restitution Programs
CIJE: 5 RIE: 2 CAT: 19

Reston (James)
CIJE: 0 RIE: 1 CAT: 18

Restoration
CIJE: 15 RIE: 9 CAT: 16

Restoration Comedy
CIJE: 0 RIE: 1 CAT: 16

Restored Behavior
CIJE: 0 RIE: 1 CAT: 11

Restraint
CIJE: 6 RIE: 1 CAT: 11

Restraint of Trade
CIJE: 3 RIE: 0 CAT: 14

Restricted Association Tests (Riegel)
CIJE: 0 RIE: 2 CAT: 21

Restricted Code (Linguistics)
CIJE: 0 RIE: 2 CAT: 13

Restricted Environmental Stimulation Therapy
CIJE: 1 RIE: 1 CAT: 11

Restricted Factor Analysis
CIJE: 0 RIE: 1 CAT: 21

Restricted Maximum Likelihood Bayes
CIJE: 0 RIE: 1 CAT: 21

Restricted Self Adapted Testing
CIJE: 0 RIE: 1 CAT: 21

Restriction of Range
CIJE: 11 RIE: 3 CAT: 21

Restrictive Clauses
CIJE: 6 RIE: 0 CAT: 13

Restrictive Procedures
CIJE: 4 RIE: 2 CAT: 15

Restrictiveness (Child Rearing)
CIJE: 2 RIE: 1 CAT: 11

Resultant Achievement Motivation
CIJE: 5 RIE: 0 CAT: 15

Retail Food Managers
CIJE: 0 RIE: 1 CAT: 09

Retail Security
CIJE: 0 RIE: 1 CAT: 16

Retail Stores
CIJE: 3 RIE: 5 CAT: 05

Retaliation
CIJE: 4 RIE: 2 CAT: 11

Retarded Infants Services
CIJE: 2 RIE: 0 CAT: 19

Retelling
CIJE: 15 RIE: 13 CAT: 15
UF Story Retelling

Retention Index
CIJE: 1 RIE: 0 CAT: 21

Retesting
CIJE: 23 RIE: 19 CAT: 21

Reticence
CIJE: 22 RIE: 18 CAT: 13

Retinal Detachment
CIJE: 3 RIE: 0 CAT: 11

Retinitis Pigmentosa
CIJE: 8 RIE: 1 CAT: 11

Retinoblastoma
CIJE: 2 RIE: 0 CAT: 11

Retired Persons
CIJE: 4 RIE: 7 CAT: 10

Retired Senior Volunteer Program
CIJE: 4 RIE: 9 CAT: 19

Retirement Communities
CIJE: 5 RIE: 1 CAT: 05

Retirement Descriptive Index (Smith et al)
CIJE: 0 RIE: 1 CAT: 21

Retirement Equity Act 1984
CIJE: 0 RIE: 2 CAT: 14

Retirement Pension Security Act 1974
CIJE: 1 RIE: 0 CAT: 14

Retirement Planning
CIJE: 15 RIE: 10 CAT: 19

Retirement Planning Scale
CIJE: 0 RIE: 1 CAT: 21

Retirement Power in Education Project
CIJE: 1 RIE: 1 CAT: 19

Retraction (Linguistics)
CIJE: 0 RIE: 1 CAT: 13

Retreats
CIJE: 21 RIE: 11 CAT: 02

Retrieval (Memory)
CIJE: 87 RIE: 17 CAT: 11

Retrieval and Accel of Young Hndcped and Talented
USE RAPYHT Project

Retrieval Bargaining
CIJE: 0 RIE: 1 CAT: 14

Retroaction (Psychology)
CIJE: 1 RIE: 0 CAT: 11

Retrofitting
CIJE: 3 RIE: 5 CAT: 20

Retroflexion
CIJE: 0 RIE: 1 CAT: 13

Retrolental Fibroplasia
CIJE: 6 RIE: 2 CAT: 11

Retrospective Analysis
CIJE: 0 RIE: 1 CAT: 15

Retrospective Bibliographies
CIJE: 0 RIE: 3 CAT: 16

Retrospective Conversion Working Task Force
CIJE: 0 RIE: 1 CAT: 17

Retrospective Document Retrieval Systems
CIJE: 0 RIE: 1 CAT: 15

Retrospective Miscue Analysis
CIJE: 0 RIE: 2 CAT: 15

Retrospective Pretesting
CIJE: 7 RIE: 1 CAT: 21

Retrospective Studies (Psychology)
CIJE: 11 RIE: 14 CAT: 15

Rett Syndrome
CIJE: 14 RIE: 4 CAT: 11

Return Migration
CIJE: 15 RIE: 9 CAT: 16

Return of the Native
CIJE: 1 RIE: 0 CAT: 22

Return on Investment
CIJE: 46 RIE: 11 CAT: 16

Return Rates (Books)
CIJE: 0 RIE: 1 CAT: 16
UF Book Return Rates

Return to Employment And Learning
USE Project REAL NY

Return to Nursing
CIJE: 0 RIE: 1 CAT: 03

Returnable Bottles
CIJE: 1 RIE: 0 CAT: 04

Returns to Scale
CIJE: 2 RIE: 0 CAT: 15

Reubens (Beatrice)
CIJE: 1 RIE: 0 CAT: 18

Reunion Behavior
CIJE: 7 RIE: 2 CAT: 11

Reunions
CIJE: 34 RIE: 1 CAT: 02

Revealed Differences Techniques
CIJE: 2 RIE: 0 CAT: 15

Revenge
CIJE: 2 RIE: 1 CAT: 11

Revenue Act 1978
CIJE: 1 RIE: 3 CAT: 14

Revenue Canada
CIJE: 0 RIE: 1 CAT: 19

Revenue Diversification
CIJE: 0 RIE: 2 CAT: 15

Revenue Producing Sports
CIJE: 1 RIE: 1 CAT: 16

Revenue Shortfall
CIJE: 1 RIE: 3 CAT: 14

Reversal Learning
CIJE: 6 RIE: 0 CAT: 15

Reversal Tendency
CIJE: 4 RIE: 1 CAT: 15

Reversal Theory
CIJE: 2 RIE: 1 CAT: 15

Reversals (Reading)
CIJE: 0 RIE: 3 CAT: 15

Reverse Chronology Approach
CIJE: 2 RIE: 0 CAT: 15

Reverse Mainstreaming
CIJE: 4 RIE: 8 CAT: 15

Reverse Role Tutoring
CIJE: 4 RIE: 2 CAT: 15

Reverse Transfer Students
CIJE: 11 RIE: 38 CAT: 10
UF Reverse Transfers

Reverse Transfers
USE Reverse Transfer Students

Reversibility (Piaget)
USE Piagetian Reversibility

Review of Agricultural Education Research
CIJE: 1 RIE: 0 CAT: 22

Review of Educational Research
CIJE: 0 RIE: 3 CAT: 22

Review Panels
CIJE: 6 RIE: 7 CAT: 10

Reviewers
CIJE: 19 RIE: 4 CAT: 09

Reviewing Sources
CIJE: 2 RIE: 4 CAT: 15

Revised Art Scale
CIJE: 0 RIE: 2 CAT: 21

Revised Beta Examination
CIJE: 5 RIE: 1 CAT: 21

Revised Childrens Manifest Anxiety Scale
CIJE: 5 RIE: 0 CAT: 21

Revised Denver Developmental Screening Test
CIJE: 5 RIE: 0 CAT: 21

Revised Learning Strategies Inventory
CIJE: 0 RIE: 1 CAT: 21

Revised Minnesota Paper Form Board Test
CIJE: 0 RIE: 1 CAT: 21

Revised Objective Perceptual Test (Fidel and Ray)
CIJE: 1 RIE: 0 CAT: 21

Revised Observer Schedule and Record Form
CIJE: 0 RIE: 1 CAT: 21

Revised Teacher Aides Program
CIJE: 0 RIE: 1 CAT: 19

Revision Processes
CIJE: 40 RIE: 18 CAT: 15

Revisionism
CIJE: 33 RIE: 13 CAT: 15

Revitalization
CIJE: 3 RIE: 5 CAT: 16
SN Use a more specific term if possible, e.g., following such initial words as Cultural, Downtown, Economic, Education, Ethnic, Institutional, Urban

Revitalizing Rural America Program
CIJE: 0 RIE: 1 CAT: 19

Revivals (Plays)
CIJE: 0 RIE: 1 CAT: 16

Revolt of the Masses
CIJE: 1 RIE: 1 CAT: 22

Revolution in Instruction
CIJE: 0 RIE: 1 CAT: 22

Revolutionary Education
CIJE: 0 RIE: 1 CAT: 15

Revolutionary Nationalism
CIJE: 1 RIE: 0 CAT: 16

Revolving Door Identification Model
CIJE: 9 RIE: 2 CAT: 15

Revolving Door Identification Placement Model
CIJE: 2 RIE: 0 CAT: 15

Revolving Door Model
CIJE: 0 RIE: 0 CAT: 15

ReWA
USE Refugee Womens Alliance

REWARD Funding Formula
USE Reading Writing and Arithmetic Development System

Rewinder Operators
CIJE: 0 RIE: 1 CAT: 09

REXALL (Computer Software)
CIJE: 0 RIE: 1 CAT: 04

Rey Auditory Verbal Learning Test
CIJE: 2 RIE: 1 CAT: 21

Reyes (Alfonso)
CIJE: 2 RIE: 0 CAT: 18

Reyes Syndrome
CIJE: 5 RIE: 0 CAT: 11

Reynell Developmental Language Scales
CIJE: 5 RIE: 0 CAT: 21

Reynolds (Frederick W)
CIJE: 1 RIE: 0 CAT: 18

Reynolds (Joshua)
CIJE: 1 RIE: 0 CAT: 18

Reynolds (Maynard C)
CIJE: 1 RIE: 0 CAT: 18

Rhapsodes
CIJE: 0 RIE: 1 CAT: 13

Rhetoric as Epistemic
CIJE: 17 RIE: 16 CAT: 15
UF Epistemic Rhetoric; Rhetorical Epistemology

Rhetoric Frames
CIJE: 5 RIE: 1 CAT: 21

Rhetoric of Reaffirmation
CIJE: 0 RIE: 1 CAT: 16
UF Reaffirmation of Principle

Rhetoric Review (Journal)
CIJE: 0 RIE: 1 CAT: 22

Rhetorical Community
CIJE: 8 RIE: 11 CAT: 13

Rhetorical Competence
CIJE: 4 RIE: 4 CAT: 13

Rhetorical Devices
CIJE: 44 RIE: 24 CAT: 13

Rhetorical Effectiveness
CIJE: 40 RIE: 22 CAT: 13

Rhetorical Epistemology
USE Rhetoric as Epistemic

Rhetorical Force
CIJE: 4 RIE: 4 CAT: 13

Rhetorical Form
CIJE: 1 RIE: 1 CAT: 13

Rhetorical Genres
CIJE: 7 RIE: 1 CAT: 13

Rhetorical Questions
CIJE: 3 RIE: 2 CAT: 13

Rhetorical Science
CIJE: 1 RIE: 1 CAT: 13

Rhetorical Sensitivity
CIJE: 8 RIE: 10 CAT: 13

Rhetorical Sensitivity Scale
CIJE: 1 RIE: 2 CAT: 21

Rhetorical Situation
CIJE: 2 RIE: 2 CAT: 13

Rhetorical Stance
CIJE: 18 RIE: 24 CAT: 13

Rhetorical Strategies
CIJE: 217 RIE: 117 CAT: 13

Rhetorical Structure
CIJE: 1 RIE: 0 CAT: 13

Rhetorical Structure Theory
CIJE: 1 RIE: 1 CAT: 15

Rheumatic Fever
CIJE: 3 RIE: 1 CAT: 11

Rheumatoid Arthritis
CIJE: 5 RIE: 1 CAT: 11

Rheumatology
CIJE: 3 RIE: 1 CAT: 11

Rhinecliff Union Free School District NY
CIJE: 0 RIE: 1 CAT: 17

Rho Coefficient
USE Spearman Rank Correlation Coefficient

Rhode Island
CIJE: 57 RIE: 215 CAT: 07

Rhode Island (Barrington)
CIJE: 0 RIE: 1 CAT: 07

Rhode Island (Cranston)
CIJE: 2 RIE: 4 CAT: 07

Rhode Island (Kingston)
CIJE: 0 RIE: 1 CAT: 07

Rhode Island (Newport County)
CIJE: 0 RIE: 1 CAT: 07

Rhode Island (Newport)
CIJE: 0 RIE: 1 CAT: 07

Rhode Island (Providence)
CIJE: 13 RIE: 48 CAT: 07

Rhode Island (Warwick)
CIJE: 0 RIE: 6 CAT: 07

Rhode Island Board of Regents
CIJE: 0 RIE: 1 CAT: 17

Rhode Island College
CIJE: 8 RIE: 14 CAT: 17

Rhode Island Council of Community Services
CIJE: 0 RIE: 1 CAT: 17

Rhode Island Education Association
CIJE: 1 RIE: 1 CAT: 17

Rhode Island Junior College
CIJE: 3 RIE: 6 CAT: 17

Rhode Island School of Design
CIJE: 1 RIE: 2 CAT: 17

Rhode Island State Department of Education
CIJE: 0 RIE: 5 CAT: 17

Rhode Island State Standards Council
CIJE: 0 RIE: 1 CAT: 17

Rhode Island Teacher Center
CIJE: 0 RIE: 1 CAT: 17

Rhodes College TN
CIJE: 3 RIE: 2 CAT: 17

Rhodes Scholarships
CIJE: 2 RIE: 1 CAT: 16

Rhodes University (South Africa)
CIJE: 2 RIE: 0 CAT: 17

Rhodesia
CIJE: 12 RIE: 21 CAT: 07

Rhodopsin
CIJE: 1 RIE: 0 CAT: 20

Rhyme
CIJE: 39 RIE: 14 CAT: 13

Rhyme Priming
CIJE: 0 RIE: 1 CAT: 16

Rhythm
CIJE: 55 RIE: 22 CAT: 15
SN Use of a more specific term is recommended, e.g., the Descriptors "Rhythm (Music)" and "Language Rhythm"

Rhythm and Blues
CIJE: 1 RIE: 0 CAT: 16

Rhythmic Gymnastics
CIJE: 0 RIE: 2 CAT: 16

Rhythmicities
CIJE: 3 RIE: 1 CAT: 15

RIBYT Data Base System
CIJE: 0 RIE: 1 CAT: 04

Rice
CIJE: 2 RIE: 4 CAT: 20

Rice (Joseph Mayer)
CIJE: 0 RIE: 1 CAT: 18

Rice University TX
CIJE: 10 RIE: 3 CAT: 17

Rich (Adrienne)
CIJE: 2 RIE: 4 CAT: 18

Rich v Martin Marietta Corp
CIJE: 1 RIE: 0 CAT: 14

Richard Cory
CIJE: 1 RIE: 1 CAT: 22

Richard III
CIJE: 2 RIE: 0 CAT: 22

Richard J Daley College IL
USE City Colleges of Chicago IL Richard J Daley Coll

Richards (I A)
CIJE: 11 RIE: 6 CAT: 18

Richards (Jack C)
CIJE: 1 RIE: 0 CAT: 18

Richards (Mary Helen)
CIJE: 0 RIE: 1 CAT: 18

Richards Education Through Music Method
CIJE: 0 RIE: 1 CAT: 15

Richardson (Elizabeth C)
CIJE: 2 RIE: 0 CAT: 18

Richardson Foundation TX
USE Sid W Richardson Foundation TX

Richardson Independent School District TX
CIJE: 3 RIE: 4 CAT: 17

Richardson Power Profile
CIJE: 0 RIE: 1 CAT: 21

Richardson Study
CIJE: 8 RIE: 2 CAT: 19
UF Sid W Richardson Foundation Study

Richaudeau (Francois)
CIJE: 1 RIE: 0 CAT: 18

Richfield Public Schools MN
CIJE: 0 RIE: 1 CAT: 17

Richland Center High School
CIJE: 1 RIE: 0 CAT: 17

Richland College TX
CIJE: 4 RIE: 3 CAT: 17

Richland Community College IL
CIJE: 0 RIE: 1 CAT: 17

Richland County School District 1 SC
CIJE: 3 RIE: 1 CAT: 17

Richland County School District SC
CIJE: 0 RIE: 1 CAT: 17

Richland Economic Development Corporation
CIJE: 0 RIE: 1 CAT: 17

Richland School District 1 SC
CIJE: 1 RIE: 2 CAT: 17

Richman (Julia)
CIJE: 2 RIE: 0 CAT: 18

Richmond Area Young Scholars Program
CIJE: 0 RIE: 1 CAT: 19

Richmond College NY
USE City University of New York Richmond College

Richmond College of TAFE (Australia)
CIJE: 1 RIE: 1 CAT: 17

Richmond Plan
CIJE: 0 RIE: 6 CAT: 19

Richmond Pretechnical Program
CIJE: 0 RIE: 1 CAT: 19

Richmond Professional Institute VA
CIJE: 0 RIE: 1 CAT: 17

Richmond Public Schools VA
CIJE: 7 RIE: 4 CAT: 17

Richmond Technical Institute NC
CIJE: 0 RIE: 1 CAT: 17

Richmond Unified School District CA
CIJE: 4 RIE: 4 CAT: 17

Richter (Anne)
CIJE: 1 RIE: 0 CAT: 18

Richter (Helmut)
CIJE: 1 RIE: 0 CAT: 18

Ricks College ID
CIJE: 0 RIE: 6 CAT: 17

Ricoeur (Paul)
CIJE: 5 RIE: 2 CAT: 18

Ricoh Synchrofax
CIJE: 1 RIE: 0 CAT: 04

Riddick v School Board of Norfolk
CIJE: 2 RIE: 0 CAT: 14

Riddles
CIJE: 22 RIE: 12 CAT: 16

Rider College NJ
CIJE: 10 RIE: 9 CAT: 17

Ridge Regression Analysis
CIJE: 6 RIE: 13 CAT: 15

Ridge Vocational Technical Center FL
CIJE: 0 RIE: 2 CAT: 17

Ridgewood High School IL
CIJE: 2 RIE: 0 CAT: 17

Ridicule
CIJE: 5 RIE: 1 CAT: 11

Riegers Syndrome
CIJE: 1 RIE: 0 CAT: 11

Riel Rebellion (1885)
CIJE: 0 RIE: 2 CAT: 12

Riemannian Space
CIJE: 1 RIE: 0 CAT: 20

Riesman (David)
CIJE: 8 RIE: 0 CAT: 18

Right Hemisphere Deficit Syndrome
CIJE: 0 RIE: 1 CAT: 11

Right Left Discrimination
CIJE: 5 RIE: 0 CAT: 15

Right of Access
CIJE: 3 RIE: 3 CAT: 14

Right of Publicity
CIJE: 0 RIE: 2 CAT: 14

Right Stuff (Wolfe)
CIJE: 0 RIE: 0 CAT: 22

Right to Die
CIJE: 4 RIE: 5 CAT: 14

Right to Education
CIJE: 8 RIE: 4 CAT: 14
SN See also "Educational Rights"

Right to Petition
CIJE: 0 RIE: 1 CAT: 14

Right to Read
CIJE: 45 RIE: 384 CAT: 19

Right to Read Academy NY
CIJE: 0 RIE: 1 CAT: 17

Right to Refuse Treatment
CIJE: 1 RIE: 0 CAT: 11

Right to Strike Legislation
CIJE: 7 RIE: 0 CAT: 14

Right to Treatment
CIJE: 2 RIE: 2 CAT: 14

Right to Work Laws
CIJE: 1 RIE: 1 CAT: 14

Rights and Formula Scoring
CIJE: 1 RIE: 5 CAT: 21

Rights Only Weighted Test
CIJE: 1 RIE: 1 CAT: 21

Rightwriter
CIJE: 1 RIE: 1 CAT: 04

Rigid Designators
CIJE: 0 RIE: 1 CAT: 13

Rigor (Evaluation)
CIJE: 6 RIE: 2 CAT: 21

Rikar Mounts
CIJE: 1 RIE: 0 CAT: 04

Roberts (P Paul)
CIJE: 0 RIE: 1 CAT: 18

Roberts English Series
CIJE: 6 RIE: 2 CAT: 22

Roberts Rules of Order
CIJE: 5 RIE: 2 CAT: 22

Roberts Wesleyan College NY
CIJE: 0 RIE: 2 CAT: 17

Robertson (Pat)
CIJE: 1 RIE: 1 CAT: 18

Robeson (Paul)
CIJE: 2 RIE: 1 CAT: 18

Robichaux (Kerry Stewart)
CIJE: 0 RIE: 1 CAT: 18

Robin (Paul)
CIJE: 1 RIE: 0 CAT: 18

Robins (Margaret Dreier)
CIJE: 0 RIE: 1 CAT: 18

Robinson (Edwin Arlington)
CIJE: 0 RIE: 3 CAT: 18

Robinson (Jackie)
CIJE: 1 RIE: 1 CAT: 18

Robinson (James Harvey)
CIJE: 2 RIE: 1 CAT: 18

Robinson Hall Reading Tests of History
CIJE: 0 RIE: 2 CAT: 21

Robinson Patman Act
CIJE: 1 RIE: 0 CAT: 14

Robinson Test of Scientific Creativity
CIJE: 0 RIE: 1 CAT: 21

Robinson v Cahill
CIJE: 5 RIE: 9 CAT: 14

Robinsons Measure of Agreement
CIJE: 0 RIE: 1 CAT: 21

Robot Odyssey I
CIJE: 0 RIE: 1 CAT: 04

Robust Regression
CIJE: 1 RIE: 1 CAT: 21

Robustness (Social Interaction)
USE Environmental Robustness

Robustness Semantic Differential
CIJE: 1 RIE: 0 CAT: 21
UF Environmental Robustness Semantic Differential

Rochdale College (Canada)
CIJE: 1 RIE: 0 CAT: 17

Rochester Career Guidance Project
CIJE: 1 RIE: 0 CAT: 19

Rochester City School District NY
CIJE: 5 RIE: 22 CAT: 17

Rochester Community Schools MI
CIJE: 0 RIE: 2 CAT: 17

Rochester Consortium MN
CIJE: 0 RIE: 1 CAT: 17

Rochester Institute of Technology NY
CIJE: 23 RIE: 18 CAT: 17

Rochester Method
CIJE: 3 RIE: 2 CAT: 15

Rochester Public Library NY
CIJE: 0 RIE: 2 CAT: 17

Rochester Public Schools MN
CIJE: 2 RIE: 0 CAT: 17

Rochester School for the Deaf NY
CIJE: 3 RIE: 0 CAT: 17

Rochester Social Problem Solving Skills Program
CIJE: 0 RIE: 1 CAT: 19

Rock Art
CIJE: 0 RIE: 1 CAT: 16
SN See also "Petroglyphs"

Rock Climbing
CIJE: 12 RIE: 11 CAT: 16

Rock Point Community School AZ
CIJE: 4 RIE: 4 CAT: 17

Rock Point Experimental School
CIJE: 1 RIE: 0 CAT: 17

Rock Valley College IL
CIJE: 3 RIE: 4 CAT: 17

Rockbridge County Public Schools VA
CIJE: 0 RIE: 1 CAT: 17

Rockdale County Public Schools GA
CIJE: 0 RIE: 1 CAT: 17

Rockdale County School District v Weil
CIJE: 1 RIE: 0 CAT: 14

Rockefeller (John D)
CIJE: 0 RIE: 1 CAT: 18

Rockefeller (Nelson A)
CIJE: 0 RIE: 1 CAT: 18

Rockefeller Commission on the Humanities
CIJE: 2 RIE: 0 CAT: 17

Rockefeller Foundation
CIJE: 13 RIE: 11 CAT: 17

Rocket Propellants
CIJE: 1 RIE: 2 CAT: 20

Rockets
CIJE: 33 RIE: 7 CAT: 20

Rockford School of Medicine IL
CIJE: 2 RIE: 0 CAT: 17

Rockhurst College MO
CIJE: 0 RIE: 1 CAT: 17

Rockland Community College MD
CIJE: 0 RIE: 1 CAT: 17

Rockland Community College NY
CIJE: 8 RIE: 10 CAT: 17

Rockland County Career Education Program
CIJE: 0 RIE: 3 CAT: 19

Rockland County Center Occupational Education NY
CIJE: 1 RIE: 0 CAT: 17

Rockland County Schools MA
CIJE: 1 RIE: 0 CAT: 17

Rockland Project School NY
CIJE: 0 RIE: 1 CAT: 17

Rocks
CIJE: 24 RIE: 12 CAT: 20

Rockwell (George Lincoln)
CIJE: 0 RIE: 1 CAT: 18

Rockwell (Norman)
CIJE: 1 RIE: 1 CAT: 18

Rockwell International Corporation
CIJE: 1 RIE: 1 CAT: 17

Rocky Boy Reservation MT
CIJE: 0 RIE: 2 CAT: 17

Rocky IV (Movie)
CIJE: 0 RIE: 1 CAT: 22

Rocky Mountain Area Project
CIJE: 0 RIE: 3 CAT: 19

Rocky Mountain Educational Laboratory
CIJE: 0 RIE: 2 CAT: 17

Rocky Mountain Regional Resource Center
CIJE: 0 RIE: 3 CAT: 17

Rocky Mountain Satellite Project
CIJE: 0 RIE: 1 CAT: 19

Rocky Mountain School Study Council
CIJE: 1 RIE: 0 CAT: 17

Rocky Mountain States Education Technology Demo
CIJE: 0 RIE: 1 CAT: 02

Rocky Mountains
CIJE: 5 RIE: 2 CAT: 07

ROCTAPUS Closed Circuit TV Program (Australia)
CIJE: 0 RIE: 1 CAT: 19

Roctapus Program
CIJE: 0 RIE: 1 CAT: 19

Rod and Frame Test
CIJE: 28 RIE: 12 CAT: 21

Rodda Act (California)
CIJE: 1 RIE: 5 CAT: 14

Roddenbery Memorial Library GA
CIJE: 1 RIE: 0 CAT: 17

Rodents
CIJE: 2 RIE: 1 CAT: 20

Rodeos
CIJE: 3 RIE: 1 CAT: 16

Rodman Job Corps Center
CIJE: 1 RIE: 0 CAT: 17

Rodo (Jose Enrique)
CIJE: 2 RIE: 0 CAT: 18

Rodriguez (Manuel Diaz)
CIJE: 2 RIE: 0 CAT: 18

Rodriguez (Richard)
CIJE: 2 RIE: 1 CAT: 18

Rodriguez v Los Angeles Unified School District
CIJE: 0 RIE: 1 CAT: 14

Rodriguez v San Antonio Independent School Dist
CIJE: 27 RIE: 24 CAT: 14

Roe (Anne)
CIJE: 2 RIE: 1 CAT: 18

Roe Occupational Classification
CIJE: 4 RIE: 4 CAT: 15

Roe v Wade
CIJE: 3 RIE: 1 CAT: 14

Roemer v Board of Public Works
CIJE: 0 RIE: 1 CAT: 14

Roethke (Theodore)
CIJE: 1 RIE: 2 CAT: 18

Roger Clark Ballard Memorial School KY
CIJE: 0 RIE: 1 CAT: 17

Roger Ludlow High School CT
CIJE: 1 RIE: 0 CAT: 17

Roger Tory Peterson Institute of Natural History
CIJE: 0 RIE: 1 CAT: 17

Roger Williams College RI
CIJE: 1 RIE: 3 CAT: 17

Rogers (Carl)
CIJE: 51 RIE: 27 CAT: 18

Rogers (Everett M)
CIJE: 1 RIE: 2 CAT: 18

Rogers (M E)
CIJE: 1 RIE: 0 CAT: 18

Rogers (Will)
CIJE: 1 RIE: 1 CAT: 18

Rogers Environmental Education Center NY
CIJE: 0 RIE: 2 CAT: 17

Rogets International Thesaurus
CIJE: 0 RIE: 1 CAT: 22

Rogets Thesaurus
CIJE: 1 RIE: 0 CAT: 22

Rokeach (Milton)
CIJE: 3 RIE: 5 CAT: 18

Rokeach Value Survey
CIJE: 27 RIE: 23 CAT: 21

Rokeachs Belief Congruence Theory
CIJE: 0 RIE: 1 CAT: 15

Role Ambiguity
CIJE: 36 RIE: 7 CAT: 11

Role Analysis Paradigm
CIJE: 1 RIE: 1 CAT: 15

Role Bias
CIJE: 2 RIE: 1 CAT: 11

Role Category Questionnaire (Crockett)
CIJE: 6 RIE: 0 CAT: 21

Role Conflict and Ambiguity Scale
CIJE: 1 RIE: 1 CAT: 21

Role Construct Repertory Test (Kelly)
CIJE: 7 RIE: 4 CAT: 21

Role Coupling
CIJE: 0 RIE: 1 CAT: 15

Role Delineation
CIJE: 3 RIE: 6 CAT: 11

Role Evaluation
CIJE: 6 RIE: 4 CAT: 15

Role Hierarchies
CIJE: 2 RIE: 0 CAT: 15

Role Immersion
CIJE: 0 RIE: 1 CAT: 11

Role Innovators
CIJE: 1 RIE: 1 CAT: 15

Role Loss
CIJE: 2 RIE: 0 CAT: 11

Role of Technology
CIJE: 0 RIE: 1 CAT: 20

Role of the Reader Project
CIJE: 0 RIE: 1 CAT: 19

Role Preparation
CIJE: 3 RIE: 2 CAT: 15

Role Renegotiation
CIJE: 0 RIE: 2 CAT: 15

Role Repertory Technique
CIJE: 2 RIE: 1 CAT: 15

Role Reversal
CIJE: 10 RIE: 6 CAT: 15

Role Satisfaction
CIJE: 10 RIE: 12 CAT: 11

Role Shift
CIJE: 19 RIE: 5 CAT: 15

Role Shock
CIJE: 1 RIE: 0 CAT: 11

Role Status
CIJE: 0 RIE: 1 CAT: 16

Role Strain
CIJE: 5 RIE: 1 CAT: 11

Role Taking Task
CIJE: 0 RIE: 1 CAT: 21

Role Transition
CIJE: 13 RIE: 5 CAT: 11

Role Transmission
CIJE: 1 RIE: 1 CAT: 11

Rolland (Romain)
CIJE: 2 RIE: 0 CAT: 18

Rollins College FL
CIJE: 6 RIE: 4 CAT: 17

Rolls Royce
CIJE: 2 RIE: 0 CAT: 17

Roma
CIJE: 1 RIE: 1 CAT: 08
SN See also "Gypsies"

Romains (Jules)
CIJE: 1 RIE: 0 CAT: 18

Romaji Alphabet
CIJE: 0 RIE: 1 CAT: 13

Roman Catholic Church
CIJE: 17 RIE: 14 CAT: 17

Roman Civilization
CIJE: 9 RIE: 8 CAT: 12

Roman Empire
CIJE: 11 RIE: 8 CAT: 12

Roman Mythology
CIJE: 0 RIE: 1 CAT: 16

Roman Republic
CIJE: 0 RIE: 2 CAT: 12

Roman Virginia
CIJE: 1 RIE: 0 CAT: 22

Romana Riley Elementary School GA
CIJE: 0 RIE: 1 CAT: 17

Romance Novels
CIJE: 12 RIE: 10 CAT: 16

Romancero Gitano
CIJE: 0 RIE: 1 CAT: 22

Romania
CIJE: 8 RIE: 0 CAT: 07
SN Preferred IAL spelling 1980-94 was "Rumania"
UF Roumania; Rumania

Romania (Bucharest)
CIJE: 0 RIE: 0 CAT: 07

Romanian (Moldavian)
CIJE: 0 RIE: 0 CAT: 13

Romanian English Contrastive Analysis Project
CIJE: 0 RIE: 1 CAT: 19

Romanians
CIJE: 0 RIE: 0 CAT: 08

Romansh
CIJE: 0 RIE: 4 CAT: 13

Romantic Relationship
CIJE: 8 RIE: 6 CAT: 11

Romany
CIJE: 2 RIE: 3 CAT: 13
UF Gypsy Language

Romeo and Juliet
CIJE: 14 RIE: 6 CAT: 22

Romero (Jose Ruben)
CIJE: 1 RIE: 0 CAT: 18

Romero (Oscar)
CIJE: 0 RIE: 1 CAT: 18

Romney (George)
CIJE: 1 RIE: 0 CAT: 18

Romper Room
CIJE: 0 RIE: 4 CAT: 22

Rontgen (Wilhelm)
CIJE: 1 RIE: 0 CAT: 18

Room 222
CIJE: 1 RIE: 0 CAT: 22

Room Clerks
CIJE: 0 RIE: 1 CAT: 09

Room Management
CIJE: 2 RIE: 1 CAT: 15

Roommates
CIJE: 41 RIE: 8 CAT: 10

Roosevelt (Eleanor)
CIJE: 10 RIE: 9 CAT: 18

Roosevelt (Franklin D)
CIJE: 31 RIE: 5 CAT: 18

Roosevelt (Theodore)
CIJE: 5 RIE: 4 CAT: 18

Roosevelt High School MN
CIJE: 2 RIE: 2 CAT: 17

Roosevelt Junior High School OR
CIJE: 0 RIE: 1 CAT: 17

Roosevelt Public Schools NY
CIJE: 0 RIE: 1 CAT: 17

Roosevelt University IL
CIJE: 8 RIE: 13 CAT: 17

Root Cause Analysis
CIJE: 0 RIE: 1 CAT: 15

Root Mean Square (Statistics)
CIJE: 3 RIE: 2 CAT: 21

Root Words
CIJE: 4 RIE: 9 CAT: 13

Roots (Haley)
CIJE: 17 RIE: 8 CAT: 22

Rope Courses
CIJE: 8 RIE: 11 CAT: 03

Rope Jumping
USE Jump Roping

Rope Skipping
USE Jump Roping

Roper Creole
CIJE: 0 RIE: 1 CAT: 13
UF Ngukurr Bamyili

Roper Organization
CIJE: 2 RIE: 2 CAT: 17

Roper Research Surveys
CIJE: 1 RIE: 5 CAT: 22

Ropes
CIJE: 1 RIE: 4 CAT: 04

Rorschach Content Analysis
CIJE: 1 RIE: 0 CAT: 15

Rorschach Human Movement
CIJE: 1 RIE: 0 CAT: 15

Rorschach Prognostic Rating Scale (Klopfer)
CIJE: 2 RIE: 0 CAT: 21

Rorschach Test
CIJE: 51 RIE: 17 CAT: 21

Rorty (Richard)
CIJE: 8 RIE: 1 CAT: 18

Rosales (Luis)
CIJE: 9 RIE: 0 CAT: 18

Rosary College IL
CIJE: 1 RIE: 1 CAT: 17

Rosary Hill College NY
CIJE: 2 RIE: 0 CAT: 17

Rosch (Eleanor)
CIJE: 2 RIE: 0 CAT: 18

Rose (Arnold)
CIJE: 2 RIE: 0 CAT: 18

Rose (Richard)
CIJE: 1 RIE: 0 CAT: 18

Rose Hill Junior High School WA
CIJE: 0 RIE: 1 CAT: 17

Rose v Council for Better Education
CIJE: 0 RIE: 1 CAT: 14

Rosebud Reservation
CIJE: 0 RIE: 1 CAT: 17

Rosemary Kennedy Center NY
CIJE: 1 RIE: 0 CAT: 17

Rosemarys Baby
CIJE: 1 RIE: 0 CAT: 22

Rosemont v Random House
CIJE: 1 RIE: 0 CAT: 14

Rosenberg (Morris)
CIJE: 0 RIE: 1 CAT: 18

Rosenberg Foundation
CIJE: 0 RIE: 3 CAT: 17

Rosenberg Self Esteem Scale
CIJE: 7 RIE: 14 CAT: 21

Rosenblatt (Louise)
CIJE: 13 RIE: 1 CAT: 18

Rosenburg Test Factor Standardization
CIJE: 0 RIE: 1 CAT: 21

Rosenstock Huessy (Eugene)
CIJE: 0 RIE: 1 CAT: 18

Rosenthal (Robert)
CIJE: 1 RIE: 2 CAT: 18

Rosenthal Effect
CIJE: 1 RIE: 1 CAT: 15

Rosenzweig (Franz)
CIJE: 0 RIE: 2 CAT: 18

Rosenzweig Picture Frustration Study
CIJE: 6 RIE: 1 CAT: 21

Roseville Area Schools MN
CIJE: 1 RIE: 0 CAT: 17

Rosholt High School WI
CIJE: 1 RIE: 0 CAT: 17

Rosholt Public Schools WI
CIJE: 0 RIE: 1 CAT: 17

Roskilde University Center (Denmark)
CIJE: 1 RIE: 1 CAT: 17

Roslyn High School NY
CIJE: 1 RIE: 0 CAT: 17

Rosner Report
CIJE: 0 RIE: 8 CAT: 22

Rosner Richman Perceptual Survey
CIJE: 0 RIE: 1 CAT: 21

Ross (John)
CIJE: 0 RIE: 2 CAT: 18
SN Cherokee chief

Ross (Murray G)
CIJE: 0 RIE: 1 CAT: 18
SN First president of York University ON

Ross (Sinclair)
CIJE: 0 RIE: 1 CAT: 18

Ross Educational Philosophical Inventory
CIJE: 0 RIE: 1 CAT: 21

Ross Test
CIJE: 0 RIE: 1 CAT: 21

Ross Test of Higher Cognitive Processes
CIJE: 2 RIE: 1 CAT: 21

Rossi Landi (F)
CIJE: 1 RIE: 0 CAT: 18

Rossville Alvin School District IL
CIJE: 0 RIE: 1 CAT: 17

Roster and Rating Method
CIJE: 0 RIE: 1 CAT: 15

Rostock University (East Germany)
CIJE: 1 RIE: 0 CAT: 17

Roswell Chall Diagnostic Reading Test Word Anal
CIJE: 1 RIE: 0 CAT: 21

Roswell Independent School District NM
CIJE: 1 RIE: 1 CAT: 17

Rota Project
CIJE: 0 RIE: 2 CAT: 19

Rotameters
CIJE: 0 RIE: 1 CAT: 04

Rotary Driller Helpers
CIJE: 0 RIE: 1 CAT: 09

Rotary Foundation
CIJE: 2 RIE: 0 CAT: 17

Rotating Biological Contactors
CIJE: 0 RIE: 2 CAT: 20

Rotation Tasks
CIJE: 8 RIE: 2 CAT: 21

Rotations (Factor Analysis)
CIJE: 10 RIE: 4 CAT: 15

Rotator Cuff Disease
CIJE: 0 RIE: 1 CAT: 11

ROTC
USE Reserve Officers Training Corps

Rothbart Infant Behavior Questionnaire
CIJE: 2 RIE: 1 CAT: 21

Rothkopf (E Z)
CIJE: 0 RIE: 1 CAT: 18

Rotorcraft
CIJE: 0 RIE: 1 CAT: 20

Rotrou (Jean de)
CIJE: 1 RIE: 0 CAT: 18

Rotter (Julian B)
CIJE: 5 RIE: 3 CAT: 18

Rotter Incomplete Sentences Blank
CIJE: 4 RIE: 1 CAT: 21

Rotter Internal External Locus of Control Scale
CIJE: 70 RIE: 32 CAT: 21

Rotter Interpersonal Trust Scale
CIJE: 8 RIE: 0 CAT: 21

Rotter Level of Aspiration Board
CIJE: 0 RIE: 2 CAT: 21

Rotterdam Medical Faculty (Netherlands)
CIJE: 1 RIE: 0 CAT: 17

Rotters Social Learning Theory
CIJE: 3 RIE: 4 CAT: 15

Rough Rock Demonstration School AZ
CIJE: 11 RIE: 19 CAT: 17

Roumania
USE Romania

Round Meadow Outdoor Learning Laboratory School MD
CIJE: 0 RIE: 1 CAT: 17

Round Robin Reading
CIJE: 9 RIE: 1 CAT: 15

Round Rock Independent School District TX
CIJE: 1 RIE: 1 CAT: 17

Round Table of Editors of Library Journals
CIJE: 0 RIE: 1 CAT: 17

Round Valley High School CA
CIJE: 1 RIE: 0 CAT: 17

Rounding (Mathematics)
CIJE: 7 RIE: 3 CAT: 20

Roundtable Reports
CIJE: 1 RIE: 2 CAT: 22

Roundworm
CIJE: 3 RIE: 0 CAT: 11

Rouse (Mary Jane)
CIJE: 0 RIE: 2 CAT: 18

Rousseau (Jean Jacques)
CIJE: 40 RIE: 7 CAT: 18

Roussy Levy Syndrome
CIJE: 1 RIE: 0 CAT: 11

Route Learning
CIJE: 3 RIE: 0 CAT: 15

Route Mean Squared Difference Method
CIJE: 0 RIE: 1 CAT: 15

Routine Environments
CIJE: 0 RIE: 2 CAT: 16

Routine Events
CIJE: 1 RIE: 3 CAT: 16

Routine Expertise
CIJE: 0 RIE: 1 CAT: 11

Routing Problems (Traffic)
CIJE: 1 RIE: 1 CAT: 16

Routing Tests
CIJE: 0 RIE: 1 CAT: 21

Roving Leaders Outreach Program
CIJE: 0 RIE: 1 CAT: 19

Row Peterson Readiness Test
CIJE: 1 RIE: 0 CAT: 21

Rowe (Mary P)
CIJE: 0 RIE: 1 CAT: 18

Rowing
CIJE: 3 RIE: 2 CAT: 16

Rowland Unified School District CA
CIJE: 2 RIE: 1 CAT: 17

Rowley v Hendrick Hudson School Dist
CIJE: 2 RIE: 3 CAT: 14

Roxbury Community College MA
CIJE: 0 RIE: 2 CAT: 17

Roxbury Latin School MA
CIJE: 1 RIE: 1 CAT: 17

Roxbury Learning Center MA
CIJE: 1 RIE: 0 CAT: 17

Roy Bose Confidence Intervals
CIJE: 0 RIE: 1 CAT: 15
UF Roy Bose Procedure

Roy Bose Procedure
USE Roy Bose Confidence Intervals

Roy Union Intersection Approach
CIJE: 1 RIE: 0 CAT: 15

Royal Air Force (England)
CIJE: 2 RIE: 0 CAT: 17

Royal Australian Navy
CIJE: 1 RIE: 0 CAT: 17

Royal College of Music at Stockholm (Sweden)
CIJE: 1 RIE: 0 CAT: 17

Royal College of Physicians and Surgeons of Canada
CIJE: 0 RIE: 2 CAT: 17

Royal Danish School of Educ Studies (Denmark)
CIJE: 1 RIE: 0 CAT: 17

Royal Doctor Flying Service (Australia)
CIJE: 1 RIE: 0 CAT: 17

Royal Holloway College (England)
CIJE: 1 RIE: 0 CAT: 17

Royal Institute of Technology (Sweden)
CIJE: 0 RIE: 7 CAT: 17

Royal Institution of Cornwall (England)
CIJE: 1 RIE: 0 CAT: 17

Royal Naval School (England)
CIJE: 1 RIE: 0 CAT: 17

Royal Navy (England)
CIJE: 3 RIE: 0 CAT: 17

Royal New Zealand Foundation for the Blind
CIJE: 1 RIE: 1 CAT: 17

Royal Society Catalogue of Scientific Papers
CIJE: 1 RIE: 0 CAT: 22

Royal Society for Prevention of Cruelty to Animals
CIJE: 1 RIE: 0 CAT: 17

Royal Society of Arts (England)
CIJE: 1 RIE: 0 CAT: 17

Royal Society of Arts Examinations Board (England)
CIJE: 0 RIE: 1 CAT: 17

Royal Spanish Academy
CIJE: 4 RIE: 0 CAT: 17

Royal Typewriter Company
CIJE: 1 RIE: 0 CAT: 17

Royalties
CIJE: 21 RIE: 9 CAT: 16

Roys Largest Root
CIJE: 0 RIE: 1 CAT: 21

Rozewicz (Tadeusz)
CIJE: 1 RIE: 0 CAT: 18

RPG Programing Language
CIJE: 0 RIE: 1 CAT: 04
UF Report Program Generator

RPTIM Model
CIJE: 4 RIE: 2 CAT: 15
SN Readiness, Planning, Training, Implementation, and Maintenance Model

RRX Project
USE Regional Rehabilitation Exchange Project

RSVP Program MA
USE Responsive Services Variety Practitioners

Rubber Bands
CIJE: 1 RIE: 0 CAT: 04

Rubber Goods
CIJE: 1 RIE: 3 CAT: 04

Rubbings (Art)
CIJE: 2 RIE: 0 CAT: 16

Rubiks Cube
CIJE: 6 RIE: 1 CAT: 04

Rubin (Ramon)
CIJE: 1 RIE: 0 CAT: 18

Rubric Transition Process
CIJE: 0 RIE: 1 CAT: 21

Ruchardts Experiment
CIJE: 1 RIE: 0 CAT: 22

Rucker Gable Educational Programming Scale
CIJE: 3 RIE: 1 CAT: 21

Rudeness
CIJE: 1 RIE: 1 CAT: 11

Rueda (Salvador)
CIJE: 1 RIE: 0 CAT: 18

RUETE Study
USE ARTE RUETE Study

Rugby
CIJE: 4 RIE: 1 CAT: 16

Rugg (Earle)
CIJE: 1 RIE: 0 CAT: 18

Rugg (Harold Ordwell)
CIJE: 9 RIE: 6 CAT: 18

Rugs
CIJE: 1 RIE: 1 CAT: 04

Ruhr Universitat (West Germany)
CIJE: 1 RIE: 1 CAT: 17

Ruhr Valley
CIJE: 0 RIE: 2 CAT: 07

Ruiz (Juan)
CIJE: 3 RIE: 0 CAT: 18

Ruiz de Alarcon (Juan)
CIJE: 1 RIE: 0 CAT: 18

Rukai
CIJE: 0 RIE: 1 CAT: 13

Rule Administration Behavior
CIJE: 0 RIE: 1 CAT: 15

Rule Application
CIJE: 36 RIE: 17 CAT: 15

Rule Application Test
CIJE: 0 RIE: 1 CAT: 21

Rule Assessment Approach
CIJE: 4 RIE: 0 CAT: 15

Rule Breaking
CIJE: 8 RIE: 5 CAT: 11

Rule Exceptions
CIJE: 2 RIE: 2 CAT: 15

Rule Governed Behavior
CIJE: 9 RIE: 7 CAT: 11

Rule Learning
CIJE: 46 RIE: 32 CAT: 15

Rule Learning (Mathematics)
CIJE: 5 RIE: 1 CAT: 15

Rule Space
CIJE: 1 RIE: 3 CAT: 21

Rule Space Model
CIJE: 4 RIE: 7 CAT: 15

Rule Transfer
CIJE: 0 RIE: 1 CAT: 11

Ruleg System
CIJE: 0 RIE: 2 CAT: 21

Rulers (Instruments)
CIJE: 1 RIE: 2 CAT: 04

Rules and Regulations
CIJE: 41 RIE: 81 CAT: 15

Rules Based Theory
CIJE: 10 RIE: 5 CAT: 15

Rules of Thumb (Statistics)
CIJE: 0 RIE: 1 CAT: 21
UF Statistical Rules of Thumb

Rules Theory
CIJE: 3 RIE: 3 CAT: 15

Rulfo (Juan)
CIJE: 6 RIE: 0 CAT: 18

Rum River Special Education Cooperative MN
CIJE: 0 RIE: 1 CAT: 17

Rumania
USE Romania

Rumination (Chewing)
CIJE: 2 RIE: 0 CAT: 11
SN Regurgitating small amounts of food to rechew and then reswallow

Rumination (Thinking)
CIJE: 0 RIE: 0 CAT: 11

Rumor Management
CIJE: 1 RIE: 1 CAT: 15

Rumors
CIJE: 4 RIE: 6 CAT: 16

Runaway and Homeless Youth Act 1974
CIJE: 0 RIE: 7 CAT: 14

Runaway and Homeless Youth Program
CIJE: 0 RIE: 2 CAT: 19

Runaway Jerk
CIJE: 0 RIE: 1 CAT: 22

Rundi
CIJE: 1 RIE: 0 CAT: 13

Rungus Dusun
CIJE: 0 RIE: 1 CAT: 13

Runners Studies of Attitude Patterns
CIJE: 0 RIE: 1 CAT: 21

Rural Advisory Service (New Zealand)
CIJE: 0 RIE: 1 CAT: 17

Rural Affairs Offices
USE Offices of Rural Affairs

Rural Alabama Pregnancy and Infant Health Program
CIJE: 0 RIE: 1 CAT: 19

Rural America Institute for Special Educators
CIJE: 0 RIE: 2 CAT: 19
UF Project RAISE OH

Rural America Series
CIJE: 0 RIE: 18 CAT: 22

Rural Animation
CIJE: 1 RIE: 0 CAT: 15

Rural Area Model Preschool Project WA
CIJE: 0 RIE: 1 CAT: 19

Rural Areas Social Services Project
CIJE: 0 RIE: 1 CAT: 19

Rural Art Program 1
CIJE: 1 RIE: 0 CAT: 19

Rural Assistance Councils
CIJE: 0 RIE: 1 CAT: 10

Rural Boarding Home Program
CIJE: 1 RIE: 0 CAT: 19

Rural Career Assistance Program
CIJE: 0 RIE: 1 CAT: 19

Rural Clearinghouse for Lifelong Educ and Dev KS
CIJE: 0 RIE: 0 CAT: 17

Rural Clinical Nurse Placement Center CA
CIJE: 0 RIE: 3 CAT: 17

Rural Communities Educational Cooperative TN
CIJE: 0 RIE: 1 CAT: 17

Rural Connection
CIJE: 0 RIE: 1 CAT: 17

Rural County Computer Related Technology Project
CIJE: 1 RIE: 0 CAT: 19

Rural Craft Training Centers (Kenya)
CIJE: 0 RIE: 1 CAT: 05

Rural Culture
CIJE: 13 RIE: 22 CAT: 16

Rural Development Act 1972
CIJE: 11 RIE: 29 CAT: 14

Rural Development Activity Analysis Planning
CIJE: 0 RIE: 1 CAT: 15

Rural Development Committee
CIJE: 0 RIE: 10 CAT: 17

Rural Development Loan Fund
CIJE: 0 RIE: 1 CAT: 14

Rural Development Policy Act 1980
CIJE: 1 RIE: 0 CAT: 14

Rural Development Research Project
CIJE: 0 RIE: 3 CAT: 19

Rural Economic Development Planning Workshop
CIJE: 0 RIE: 1 CAT: 02

Rural Economics Farmers in Transition
CIJE: 0 RIE: 1 CAT: 19
UF RE FIT Program OH

Rural Education Adult Development in Idaho
CIJE: 0 RIE: 1 CAT: 19
UF READI Project ID

Rural Education and Agriculture Program (Belize)
CIJE: 1 RIE: 2 CAT: 19

Rural Education Association
CIJE: 1 RIE: 9 CAT: 17

Rural Education Centers
CIJE: 1 RIE: 6 CAT: 05

Rural Education Development Project (Paraguay)
CIJE: 0 RIE: 1 CAT: 19

Rural Education Program
CIJE: 1 RIE: 5 CAT: 19

Rural Education Rural Family Ed Policy for the 80s
CIJE: 0 RIE: 4 CAT: 22

Rural Effective Schools Project AK
CIJE: 0 RIE: 1 CAT: 19

Rural Electrification
CIJE: 1 RIE: 3 CAT: 20

Rural Entrepreneurship through Action Learning
USE REAL Enterprises

Rural Family Development Project
CIJE: 1 RIE: 5 CAT: 19

Rural Free Universities
CIJE: 0 RIE: 3 CAT: 05

Rural Futures Development Program
CIJE: 0 RIE: 1 CAT: 19

Rural Futures Development Strategy
CIJE: 0 RIE: 4 CAT: 16

Rural Health Clinics
CIJE: 0 RIE: 4 CAT: 05

Rural Health Initiative Program
CIJE: 0 RIE: 1 CAT: 19

Rural Income Maintenance Experiment
CIJE: 0 RIE: 2 CAT: 21

Rural Indian Education Program
CIJE: 0 RIE: 1 CAT: 19

Rural Information Center
CIJE: 0 RIE: 1 CAT: 19
SN Joint venture between the Extension Service and the National Agricultural Library

Rural Initiative Program
CIJE: 0 RIE: 1 CAT: 19
SN ...of the Regional Educational Laboratories

Rural Intervention Project AZ
CIJE: 0 RIE: 1 CAT: 19

Rural Language
CIJE: 0 RIE: 3 CAT: 13

Rural Libraries
CIJE: 0 RIE: 3 CAT: 05

Rural Libraries and the Humanities Project
CIJE: 0 RIE: 1 CAT: 19

Rural Manpower Service
CIJE: 3 RIE: 1 CAT: 19

Rural Ministry Resources
CIJE: 0 RIE: 1 CAT: 17

Rural Nonfarm Employment
CIJE: 0 RIE: 2 CAT: 16

Rural Planning Specialists
CIJE: 0 RIE: 1 CAT: 09

Rural Policy Centers
CIJE: 0 RIE: 1 CAT: 05

Rural Renaissance
CIJE: 1 RIE: 9 CAT: 16

Rural Restructuring
CIJE: 0 RIE: 1 CAT: 16

Rural Revitalization Initiative
CIJE: 0 RIE: 1 CAT: 19
SN ...of the University of Georgia

Rural Satellite Program
CIJE: 0 RIE: 1 CAT: 19
SN ...of the U.S. Agency for International Development

Rural Schools Assistance Program
CIJE: 0 RIE: 1 CAT: 19

Rural Schools Integrated Curricula Project MT
CIJE: 0 RIE: 4 CAT: 19

Rural Science Education Project NM
USE New Mexico Rural Science Education Project

Rural Sociological Society Meeting
CIJE: 1 RIE: 1 CAT: 02

Rural Sociology (Journal)
CIJE: 5 RIE: 1 CAT: 22

Rural Special Education Outreach Project
CIJE: 0 RIE: 1 CAT: 19

Rural Student Vocational Program AK
CIJE: 0 RIE: 1 CAT: 19

Rural Suburban Differences
CIJE: 4 RIE: 2 CAT: 16
UF Suburban Rural Differences

Rural Transition Center
CIJE: 0 RIE: 1 CAT: 17

Rural Virginia Development Foundation
CIJE: 0 RIE: 1 CAT: 17

Rural Work Education Councils
CIJE: 0 RIE: 1 CAT: 05

Ruralification
CIJE: 0 RIE: 1 CAT: 15

Rurban Areas
CIJE: 1 RIE: 1 CAT: 07

Rurbanization
CIJE: 1 RIE: 1 CAT: 15

Rusden State College (Australia)
CIJE: 1 RIE: 0 CAT: 17

Rush (Benjamin)
CIJE: 4 RIE: 1 CAT: 18

Rush Medical College IL
CIJE: 3 RIE: 1 CAT: 17

Rush Presbyterian Saint Lukes Medical Center IL
CIJE: 1 RIE: 0 CAT: 17

Rush University IL
CIJE: 2 RIE: 0 CAT: 17

Ruskin (John)
CIJE: 7 RIE: 0 CAT: 18

Ruskin College (England)
CIJE: 2 RIE: 1 CAT: 17

Russell (Bertrand)
CIJE: 12 RIE: 2 CAT: 18

Russell (Frank Alden)
CIJE: 0 RIE: 1 CAT: 18
SN Broadcaster who used the pseudonym "Ted Malone"

Russell (James)
CIJE: 1 RIE: 0 CAT: 18

Russell (John)
CIJE: 1 RIE: 0 CAT: 18

Russell (Ken)
CIJE: 1 RIE: 0 CAT: 18

Russell Conwell Middle Magnet School
CIJE: 1 RIE: 0 CAT: 17

Russell County Public Schools VA
CIJE: 0 RIE: 1 CAT: 17

Russell Independent School District 418 MN
CIJE: 0 RIE: 1 CAT: 17

Russell Report
CIJE: 5 RIE: 1 CAT: 22

Russell Sage College NY
CIJE: 1 RIE: 6 CAT: 17

Russell Sage Foundation
CIJE: 2 RIE: 3 CAT: 17

Russia
CIJE: 206 RIE: 103 CAT: 07
SN Before 1917 and after 1991, an independent state — see "USSR (Russia)" for the 1917-1991 time frame

Russia (Moscow)
CIJE: 3 RIE: 1 CAT: 07
SN See also "USSR (Moscow)"

Russian Americans
CIJE: 1 RIE: 11 CAT: 08

Russian Education
CIJE: 8 RIE: 1 CAT: 16

Russian History
CIJE: 11 RIE: 11 CAT: 12

Russian Jews
CIJE: 9 RIE: 17 CAT: 08

Russian Speaking
CIJE: 0 RIE: 1 CAT: 08

Russian Studies
CIJE: 2 RIE: 5 CAT: 03

Russian Studies Center for Secondary Schools
CIJE: 0 RIE: 1 CAT: 17

Russian Theater
CIJE: 1 RIE: 0 CAT: 16

Russians
CIJE: 8 RIE: 13 CAT: 08

Rutgers Conference on School Lunch Programs
CIJE: 1 RIE: 0 CAT: 02

Rutgers Drawing Test
CIJE: 1 RIE: 1 CAT: 21

Rutgers Guidance Conference
CIJE: 0 RIE: 1 CAT: 02

Rutgers Seminar on Educational Equity
CIJE: 0 RIE: 1 CAT: 02

Rutgers the State University Camden NJ
CIJE: 6 RIE: 0 CAT: 17

Rutgers The State University Douglass College NJ
CIJE: 1 RIE: 3 CAT: 17
UF Douglass College NJ

Rutgers the State University Livingston Coll NJ
CIJE: 0 RIE: 1 CAT: 17
UF Livingston College NJ

Rutgers the State University New Brunswick NJ
CIJE: 4 RIE: 10 CAT: 17
SN Rutgers the State University New Brunswick Campus

Rutgers the State University Newark NJ
CIJE: 2 RIE: 4 CAT: 17

Rutgers the State University NJ
CIJE: 55 RIE: 44 CAT: 17

Rutherford (Ernest)
CIJE: 5 RIE: 0 CAT: 18

Rutland Area Vocational Technical Center VT
CIJE: 0 RIE: 1 CAT: 17

Rutland Center GA
CIJE: 2 RIE: 0 CAT: 17

Rutter (Michael)
CIJE: 3 RIE: 1 CAT: 18

Ruzicka (R)
CIJE: 1 RIE: 0 CAT: 18

Rwanda
CIJE: 5 RIE: 7 CAT: 07

Ryan (Thomas S)
CIJE: 1 RIE: 0 CAT: 18

Ryan White v Western School Corporation
CIJE: 0 RIE: 1 CAT: 14

Ryans Classroom Observation Record
CIJE: 0 RIE: 10 CAT: 21

Ryans Teacher Characteristics Schedule
CIJE: 0 RIE: 3 CAT: 21

Rydell (Susan)
CIJE: 1 RIE: 0 CAT: 18

Rydell Rosen Ambiguity Tolerance Scale
CIJE: 1 RIE: 0 CAT: 21

Ryder Lake Elementary School
CIJE: 1 RIE: 0 CAT: 17

Ryerson Polytechnical Institute (Canada)
CIJE: 3 RIE: 2 CAT: 17

Rystroms Dialect Deviation Test
CIJE: 1 RIE: 1 CAT: 21

S 6 (93d Cong 1st Session)
CIJE: 0 RIE: 2 CAT: 14

S 1090 (93d Cong 1st Sess)
CIJE: 0 RIE: 1 CAT: 14

S 1228 (93d Cong 1st Sess)
CIJE: 0 RIE: 1 CAT: 14

S P Curve Theory
CIJE: 0 RIE: 1 CAT: 15

S R Inventory of Anxiousness (Endler et al)
CIJE: 3 RIE: 5 CAT: 21

S R Inventory of General Trait Anxiousness
CIJE: 4 RIE: 0 CAT: 21

S Simpson Gray v Board of Educ City of New York
CIJE: 0 RIE: 1 CAT: 14
SN See also "Gray (S Simpson)"

S2RE
CIJE: 0 RIE: 1 CAT: 15

S4R Method
CIJE: 1 RIE: 1 CAT: 15
UF Survey Read Recite Record Review Method

Saab Scania Plant
CIJE: 1 RIE: 0 CAT: 17

Saami
USE Lapps

Saamish
USE Lappish

Saanich Elementary Internship Program
CIJE: 0 RIE: 1 CAT: 19

Saanich School District BC
CIJE: 0 RIE: 0 CAT: 17

Sabah Murut
CIJE: 0 RIE: 1 CAT: 13

Sabato (Ernesto)
CIJE: 2 RIE: 0 CAT: 18

Sabato (Rafael)
CIJE: 1 RIE: 0 CAT: 18

Sabio (Alfonso el)
CIJE: 1 RIE: 0 CAT: 18

Sac and Fox Reservation IA
CIJE: 0 RIE: 1 CAT: 17

Saccadic Eye Movements
CIJE: 7 RIE: 6 CAT: 11

Saccharopinuria
CIJE: 1 RIE: 0 CAT: 11

Sack Yourman Speed Reading Course
CIJE: 1 RIE: 1 CAT: 03

Sacramento City College CA
CIJE: 1 RIE: 11 CAT: 17

Sacramento City Unified School District CA
CIJE: 2 RIE: 16 CAT: 17

Sacramento County Office of Education CA
CIJE: 0 RIE: 2 CAT: 17

Sacramento State College CA
CIJE: 1 RIE: 2 CAT: 17

Sacs (Tribe)
CIJE: 0 RIE: 3 CAT: 08

SAD (Disorder)
USE Seasonal Affective Disorder

Sadako and the Thousand Paper Cranes
CIJE: 0 RIE: 1 CAT: 22

Sadat (Anwar)
CIJE: 0 RIE: 2 CAT: 18

Saddleback College CA
CIJE: 0 RIE: 11 CAT: 17

Saddleback Community College CA
CIJE: 2 RIE: 4 CAT: 17

Sadhu
CIJE: 0 RIE: 1 CAT: 13

SAFARI On Line Text Processing System
CIJE: 0 RIE: 2 CAT: 04

Safe at Home Curriculum
CIJE: 1 RIE: 1 CAT: 03

Safe Deposit Boxes
CIJE: 0 RIE: 1 CAT: 04

Safe Rides Program
CIJE: 0 RIE: 1 CAT: 19

Safe School Study
CIJE: 5 RIE: 10 CAT: 22

Safe Sex
USE Safe Sex Practices

Safe Sex Practices
CIJE: 3 RIE: 4 CAT: 11
UF Safer Sex; Safe Sex

Safer Sex
USE Safe Sex Practices

Safety Directors
CIJE: 1 RIE: 1 CAT: 09

Safety Equipment
CIJE: 0 RIE: 4 CAT: 04

Safety Harbor Exceptional Student Center FL
CIJE: 0 RIE: 1 CAT: 17

Safety Legislation
CIJE: 3 RIE: 1 CAT: 14

Safran Culture Reduced Intelligence Test
CIJE: 0 RIE: 1 CAT: 21

Safran Students Interest Inventory
CIJE: 0 RIE: 2 CAT: 21

Sagan (Carl)
CIJE: 3 RIE: 0 CAT: 18

Sage Analysis
CIJE: 1 RIE: 1 CAT: 15
SN See also "Fault Tree Analysis"

Sage Developmental Scales
CIJE: 0 RIE: 1 CAT: 21

Sage Hill Camp Program
CIJE: 0 RIE: 2 CAT: 19

SAGES P (Johnsen and Corn)
CIJE: 0 RIE: 1 CAT: 21
UF Screening Assessment for Gifted Elem Stdts Primary

Saginaw City School System MI
CIJE: 1 RIE: 63 CAT: 17

Saginaw Junior College MI
CIJE: 1 RIE: 1 CAT: 17

Saginaw Student Rights Center MI
CIJE: 0 RIE: 1 CAT: 17

Saginaw Successful Schools Project MI
CIJE: 0 RIE: 0 CAT: 19

Saginaw Valley State College MI
CIJE: 0 RIE: 1 CAT: 17

Saginaw Valley State University MI
CIJE: 0 RIE: 4 CAT: 17

Saglouc Community Center (Canada)
CIJE: 0 RIE: 1 CAT: 17

Sahaptin
CIJE: 0 RIE: 3 CAT: 13

Sahel
CIJE: 0 RIE: 2 CAT: 07

Saigon Dialect
CIJE: 0 RIE: 2 CAT: 13

Sainik Schools (India)
CIJE: 1 RIE: 0 CAT: 17

Saint Andrews Presbyterian College NC
CIJE: 1 RIE: 0 CAT: 17

Saint Anselm College NH
CIJE: 4 RIE: 1 CAT: 17

Saint Augustine College NC
CIJE: 0 RIE: 1 CAT: 17

Saint Augustine Community College IL
CIJE: 0 RIE: 3 CAT: 17

Saint Augustine School for the Arts NY
CIJE: 0 RIE: 1 CAT: 17

Saint Augustines Center for American Indians
CIJE: 0 RIE: 1 CAT: 17

Saint Boniface School Division MB
CIJE: 0 RIE: 1 CAT: 17

Saint Cecilia Elementary School CA
CIJE: 1 RIE: 0 CAT: 17

Saint Clair (Harry H)
CIJE: 0 RIE: 1 CAT: 18

Saint Clair County Community College MI
CIJE: 0 RIE: 3 CAT: 17

Saint Clair County Teachers Institute IL
CIJE: 0 RIE: 1 CAT: 17

Saint Cloud Audiovisual Center
CIJE: 1 RIE: 0 CAT: 17

Saint Cloud School District MN
CIJE: 0 RIE: 3 CAT: 17

Saint Cloud State College MN
CIJE: 4 RIE: 1 CAT: 17

Saint Cloud State University MN
CIJE: 5 RIE: 13 CAT: 17

Saint Edwards University TX
CIJE: 1 RIE: 10 CAT: 17

Saint Elizabeth Hospital IN
CIJE: 0 RIE: 1 CAT: 17

Saint Elizabeth Hospital Medical Center OH
CIJE: 0 RIE: 1 CAT: 17

Saint Elizabeths and DC Mental Health Services Act
CIJE: 0 RIE: 1 CAT: 14
UF Public Law 98 621

Saint Elizabeths Hospital DC
CIJE: 2 RIE: 2 CAT: 17

Saint Francis Xavier University (Canada)
CIJE: 3 RIE: 1 CAT: 17

Saint George Writing Project (Australia)
CIJE: 0 RIE: 1 CAT: 19

Saint James Head Start Center WA
CIJE: 0 RIE: 1 CAT: 17

Saint Joan of the Stockyards
CIJE: 1 RIE: 0 CAT: 22

Saint Johns College MD
CIJE: 3 RIE: 4 CAT: 17

Saint Johns College NM
CIJE: 0 RIE: 2 CAT: 17

Saint Johns University MN
CIJE: 2 RIE: 7 CAT: 17

Saint Johns University NY
CIJE: 5 RIE: 7 CAT: 17

Saint Josephs College IN
CIJE: 1 RIE: 6 CAT: 17

Saint Josephs School for the Deaf NY
CIJE: 0 RIE: 1 CAT: 17

Saint Josephs University PA
CIJE: 1 RIE: 1 CAT: 17

Saint Lambert Program
CIJE: 4 RIE: 3 CAT: 19

Saint Lawrence College (Canada)
CIJE: 0 RIE: 1 CAT: 17

Saint Lawrence University NY
CIJE: 13 RIE: 4 CAT: 17

Saint Leo College FL
CIJE: 2 RIE: 1 CAT: 17

Saint Leonards of the Holy Child PA
CIJE: 1 RIE: 0 CAT: 17

Saint Louis Baby Study
CIJE: 0 RIE: 2 CAT: 19

Saint Louis City School District MO
CIJE: 15 RIE: 32 CAT: 17

Saint Louis Community College at Meramec MO
CIJE: 0 RIE: 1 CAT: 17

Saint Louis Community College MO
CIJE: 2 RIE: 5 CAT: 17

Saint Louis Evaluation and Training Center
CIJE: 0 RIE: 1 CAT: 17

Saint Louis Globe Democrat
CIJE: 0 RIE: 1 CAT: 22

Saint Louis Hearing and Speech Center
CIJE: 1 RIE: 0 CAT: 17

Saint Louis Junior College District MO
CIJE: 1 RIE: 3 CAT: 17

Saint Louis Post Dispatch
CIJE: 0 RIE: 3 CAT: 22

Saint Louis Regional Library Network MO
CIJE: 0 RIE: 1 CAT: 17

Saint Louis Spelling Test
CIJE: 0 RIE: 1 CAT: 21

Saint Louis Teacher Workshops
CIJE: 0 RIE: 1 CAT: 02

Saint Louis University MO
CIJE: 21 RIE: 10 CAT: 17

Saint Lucia
CIJE: 2 RIE: 7 CAT: 07

Saint Lucia Mathematics Project
CIJE: 0 RIE: 1 CAT: 19

Saint Lukes College (England)
CIJE: 2 RIE: 0 CAT: 17

Saint Martin Parish School Board LA
CIJE: 0 RIE: 1 CAT: 17

Saint Mary Center for Learning
CIJE: 1 RIE: 0 CAT: 17

Saint Mary College KS
CIJE: 1 RIE: 0 CAT: 17

Saint Mary of the Woods College IN
CIJE: 2 RIE: 3 CAT: 17

Saint Marys Area High School PA
CIJE: 1 RIE: 0 CAT: 17

Saint Marys College IN
CIJE: 3 RIE: 14 CAT: 17

Saint Marys College MN
CIJE: 3 RIE: 3 CAT: 17

Saint Marys College of California
CIJE: 1 RIE: 0 CAT: 17

Saint Marys College of Maryland
CIJE: 3 RIE: 0 CAT: 17

Saint Marys County Public Schools MD
CIJE: 0 RIE: 1 CAT: 17

Saint Marys Dominican College LA
CIJE: 0 RIE: 1 CAT: 17

Saint Marys High School AK
CIJE: 0 RIE: 1 CAT: 17

Saint Marys Hospital AZ
CIJE: 0 RIE: 1 CAT: 17

Saint Marys Junior College MN
CIJE: 4 RIE: 7 CAT: 17

Saint Marys University at Halifax (Canada)
CIJE: 3 RIE: 0 CAT: 17

Saint Marys University NS
CIJE: 0 RIE: 1 CAT: 17

Saint Marys University of San Antonio TX
CIJE: 3 RIE: 4 CAT: 17

Saint Meinrad College IN
CIJE: 1 RIE: 0 CAT: 17

Saint Michael Hospital WI
CIJE: 1 RIE: 0 CAT: 17

Saint Michaels Special School AZ
CIJE: 0 RIE: 1 CAT: 17

Saint Norbert College WI
CIJE: 6 RIE: 4 CAT: 17

Saint Olaf College MN
CIJE: 12 RIE: 13 CAT: 17

Saint Patricks Day
CIJE: 3 RIE: 1 CAT: 12

Saint Paul Open School
CIJE: 2 RIE: 0 CAT: 17

Saint Paul Public Library System MN
CIJE: 1 RIE: 1 CAT: 17

Saint Paul Public Schools MN
CIJE: 4 RIE: 11 CAT: 17

Saint Paul Technical Vocational Institute MN
CIJE: 3 RIE: 1 CAT: 17

Saint Pauls School NH
CIJE: 2 RIE: 0 CAT: 17

Saint Peters College NJ
CIJE: 0 RIE: 0 CAT: 17

Saint Petersburg Independent
CIJE: 0 RIE: 1 CAT: 17

Saint Petersburg Junior College Clearwater FL
CIJE: 0 RIE: 2 CAT: 17

Saint Petersburg Junior College FL
CIJE: 5 RIE: 3 CAT: 17

Saint Petersburg Times
CIJE: 0 RIE: 1 CAT: 22

Saint Philips College TX
CIJE: 0 RIE: 1 CAT: 17

Saint Sebastian Syndrome
CIJE: 0 RIE: 1 CAT: 11

Saint Simon (Louis de Rouvroy)
CIJE: 1 RIE: 0 CAT: 18

Saint Viator High School
CIJE: 1 RIE: 0 CAT: 17

Saint Vincent
CIJE: 0 RIE: 3 CAT: 07
UF Saint Vincent and the Grenadines

Saint Vincent and the Grenadines
USE Saint Vincent

Saint Vrain Valley Public Schools CO
CIJE: 1 RIE: 0 CAT: 17

Sainte Marie (Buffy)
CIJE: 0 RIE: 1 CAT: 18

Saints
CIJE: 3 RIE: 1 CAT: 10

SAIR Conference
CIJE: 0 RIE: 38 CAT: 02

Saisiyat
CIJE: 0 RIE: 1 CAT: 13

Sakau
USE Kava Root

Salad Makers
CIJE: 0 RIE: 2 CAT: 09

Salamanders
CIJE: 3 RIE: 0 CAT: 20

Salary Compression
CIJE: 3 RIE: 2 CAT: 15
SN The shrinking difference of salary paid to newcomers as opposed to the amount paid to experienced regulars with seniority or of higher rank

Salary Reductions
CIJE: 1 RIE: 2 CAT: 16

Salem County Vocational Technical Schools NJ
CIJE: 0 RIE: 1 CAT: 17

Salem Keizer Public Schools OR
USE Salem Public Schools OR

Salem Public Schools MA
CIJE: 0 RIE: 1 CAT: 17

Salem Public Schools OR
CIJE: 2 RIE: 6 CAT: 17
UF Salem Keizer Public Schools OR

Salem State College MA
CIJE: 2 RIE: 3 CAT: 17

Salem Teacher Education Model
CIJE: 0 RIE: 1 CAT: 15

Salem Teikyo University WV
CIJE: 0 RIE: 2 CAT: 17

Salem Witch Trials
CIJE: 4 RIE: 4 CAT: 12

Sales Taxes
CIJE: 1 RIE: 7 CAT: 14

Sales Techniques and Results (Program)
CIJE: 0 RIE: 1 CAT: 19

Sales Transactions
CIJE: 3 RIE: 6 CAT: 16

Salesian Society
CIJE: 1 RIE: 1 CAT: 17

Salesperson Client Relationship
CIJE: 1 RIE: 2 CAT: 16

Salicylates
CIJE: 2 RIE: 1 CAT: 11

Salience
CIJE: 7 RIE: 13 CAT: 21

Salience Effects
CIJE: 4 RIE: 3 CAT: 11

Salience Index (Cattell)
CIJE: 0 RIE: 1 CAT: 21

Salience Inventory
CIJE: 0 RIE: 1 CAT: 21

Salient Issues (Jean et al)
CIJE: 0 RIE: 1 CAT: 21

Salinas (Pedro)
CIJE: 2 RIE: 0 CAT: 18

Salinas (Porfirio)
CIJE: 0 RIE: 1 CAT: 18

Salinas Union High School District CA
CIJE: 1 RIE: 1 CAT: 17

Saline Water
USE Saltwater

Salinger (J D)
CIJE: 4 RIE: 4 CAT: 18

Salinger v Random House
CIJE: 0 RIE: 1 CAT: 14

Salinity
CIJE: 2 RIE: 6 CAT: 20

Salisbury State College MD
CIJE: 1 RIE: 2 CAT: 17
SN Became Salisbury State University in 1988

Salish (Tribe)
CIJE: 2 RIE: 3 CAT: 08
SN See also "Coast Salish (Tribe)"

Salish Kootenai College MT
CIJE: 4 RIE: 1 CAT: 17

Salivary Chromosomes
CIJE: 1 RIE: 0 CAT: 11

Salivary Cortisol
USE Hydrocortisone

Salivation
CIJE: 0 RIE: 1 CAT: 11

Saljo (Roger)
CIJE: 0 RIE: 1 CAT: 18

Salkehatchie Consortium SC
CIJE: 0 RIE: 1 CAT: 17

Sallie Mae
USE Student Loan Marketing Association

Sally Test (McCracken et al)
CIJE: 0 RIE: 1 CAT: 21

Salmasius (Claudius)
CIJE: 1 RIE: 0 CAT: 18

Salt
CIJE: 1 RIE: 1 CAT: 20
UF Sodium Chloride; Table Salt

Salt Intake
CIJE: 3 RIE: 0 CAT: 11
UF Dietary Sodium Intake; Sodium Restricted Diet

Salt Lake City School District UT
CIJE: 4 RIE: 15 CAT: 17

Salt Lake Community College UT
CIJE: 0 RIE: 1 CAT: 17

Salt Lake Community High School UT
CIJE: 0 RIE: 1 CAT: 17

Salt Production
CIJE: 0 RIE: 1 CAT: 20

Salteaux (Tribe)
USE Saulteaux (Tribe)

Salton (Gerard)
CIJE: 2 RIE: 1 CAT: 18

Saltons Magical Automatic Retriever of Texts
CIJE: 0 RIE: 6 CAT: 04

Salts
CIJE: 10 RIE: 5 CAT: 20

Saltus Model
CIJE: 0 RIE: 1 CAT: 15

Saltwater
CIJE: 1 RIE: 0 CAT: 20
UF Saline Water

Saltwater Intrusion
CIJE: 0 RIE: 1 CAT: 20

Salutary Neglect
CIJE: 1 RIE: 0 CAT: 14

Salvadoreans
CIJE: 1 RIE: 4 CAT: 08

Salvage (Fire Science)
CIJE: 1 RIE: 3 CAT: 20

Salvation Army
CIJE: 3 RIE: 6 CAT: 17

Sam Houston State University TX
CIJE: 1 RIE: 7 CAT: 17

Sam Rayburn Library TX
CIJE: 0 RIE: 1 CAT: 17

Sama Bangingi
CIJE: 0 RIE: 1 CAT: 13
SN A Northwest Austronesian (Philippine) language

Samal
CIJE: 0 RIE: 4 CAT: 13

Samaritan Ethic
CIJE: 1 RIE: 1 CAT: 15

Sambali (Tina)
USE Tina Sambal

Same
USE Lappish

Same Age Dyads
CIJE: 1 RIE: 1 CAT: 10

Same Race Hypothesis
CIJE: 1 RIE: 0 CAT: 15

Same Race Placement
CIJE: 0 RIE: 1 CAT: 15

Same Sex Children Family
USE Tilted Family

Same Sex Friendship
CIJE: 5 RIE: 3 CAT: 16
SN See also "Cross Sex Friendship"

Same Sex Interaction
CIJE: 2 RIE: 1 CAT: 11
SN See also "Cross Sex Interaction"

Same Sex Peers
CIJE: 18 RIE: 6 CAT: 10
SN See also "Cross Sex Peers"

Samford University AL
CIJE: 4 RIE: 3 CAT: 17

Sami People
USE Lapps

Samis
USE Lappish

Samish (Tribe)
CIJE: 0 RIE: 1 CAT: 08

Samoa
CIJE: 16 RIE: 14 CAT: 07

Samoans
CIJE: 3 RIE: 12 CAT: 08

Sample Forms
CIJE: 0 RIE: 10 CAT: 04

Sample Free Item Analysis
CIJE: 1 RIE: 0 CAT: 21

Sample Materials
CIJE: 0 RIE: 9 CAT: 04

Sample Reports
CIJE: 0 RIE: 3 CAT: 16

Sample Specificity
CIJE: 0 RIE: 1 CAT: 21

Sample Splitting
CIJE: 0 RIE: 1 CAT: 21

Sampling Error
CIJE: 8 RIE: 16 CAT: 21

Samuels (Frederick)
CIJE: 0 RIE: 1 CAT: 18

San Andreas Cultural Continuity Project
CIJE: 0 RIE: 2 CAT: 19

San Antonio College TX
CIJE: 2 RIE: 4 CAT: 17

San Antonio Independent School District TX
CIJE: 4 RIE: 13 CAT: 17

San Antonio Language Research Project
CIJE: 1 RIE: 7 CAT: 19

San Antonio Urban Educ Development Center TX
CIJE: 0 RIE: 1 CAT: 17

San Bernardino Valley College CA
CIJE: 1 RIE: 2 CAT: 17

San Carlos Apache (Tribe)
CIJE: 0 RIE: 4 CAT: 08

San Carlos Apache Reservation AZ
CIJE: 1 RIE: 3 CAT: 17

San Carlos School District AZ
CIJE: 2 RIE: 0 CAT: 17

San Diego Adult School CA
CIJE: 0 RIE: 1 CAT: 17

San Diego Area Instructional Television Authority
CIJE: 0 RIE: 3 CAT: 17

San Diego City College CA
CIJE: 0 RIE: 1 CAT: 17

San Diego City Schools CA
USE San Diego Unified School District CA

San Diego City Schools Research Cooperative
CIJE: 0 RIE: 1 CAT: 17

San Diego Community College CA
CIJE: 1 RIE: 1 CAT: 17

San Diego Community College District CA
CIJE: 0 RIE: 5 CAT: 17

San Diego Community Colleges CA
CIJE: 3 RIE: 3 CAT: 17

San Diego County Department of Education CA
CIJE: 0 RIE: 4 CAT: 17
UF San Diego County Office of Education CA; San Diego County Schools CA

San Diego County Inventory of Reading Attitude
CIJE: 0 RIE: 3 CAT: 21

San Diego County Office of Education CA
USE San Diego County Department of Education CA

San Diego County Schools CA
USE San Diego County Department of Education CA

San Diego History Research Center
CIJE: 1 RIE: 0 CAT: 17

San Diego Mesa College CA
CIJE: 2 RIE: 0 CAT: 17

San Diego Miramar College CA
CIJE: 0 RIE: 1 CAT: 17

San Diego Quick Assessment
CIJE: 0 RIE: 3 CAT: 21

San Diego State College CA
CIJE: 1 RIE: 2 CAT: 17

San Diego State University CA
CIJE: 28 RIE: 35 CAT: 17

San Diego Unified School District CA
CIJE: 25 RIE: 85 CAT: 17
UF San Diego City Schools CA

San Diego Urban League CA
CIJE: 0 RIE: 0 CAT: 17

San Elizario Independent School District TX
CIJE: 0 RIE: 2 CAT: 17

San Fernando Valley State College CA
CIJE: 2 RIE: 2 CAT: 17

San Francisco Art Institute
CIJE: 2 RIE: 0 CAT: 17

San Francisco Bay
CIJE: 2 RIE: 11 CAT: 07

San Francisco Cable Communications Master Plan
CIJE: 0 RIE: 1 CAT: 19

San Francisco Community College District CA
CIJE: 4 RIE: 10 CAT: 17

San Francisco Consortium CA
CIJE: 0 RIE: 1 CAT: 17

San Francisco Education Fund CA
CIJE: 1 RIE: 0 CAT: 17

San Francisco Neurological Institute CA
CIJE: 0 RIE: 1 CAT: 17

San Francisco Public Library CA
CIJE: 5 RIE: 2 CAT: 17

San Francisco Social Competency Scale
CIJE: 0 RIE: 3 CAT: 21

San Francisco State College CA
CIJE: 15 RIE: 10 CAT: 17

San Francisco State University CA
CIJE: 20 RIE: 29 CAT: 17

San Francisco Unified School District CA
CIJE: 9 RIE: 19 CAT: 17

San Joaquin Delta College CA
CIJE: 3 RIE: 10 CAT: 17

San Joaquin Valley
CIJE: 0 RIE: 1 CAT: 07
UF California (San Joaquin Valley)

San Joaquin Valley Library System CA
CIJE: 1 RIE: 0 CAT: 17

San Jose City College CA
CIJE: 0 RIE: 15 CAT: 17

San Jose Evergreen Community College District CA
CIJE: 0 RIE: 2 CAT: 17

San Jose Public Library CA
CIJE: 2 RIE: 0 CAT: 17

San Jose State College CA
CIJE: 9 RIE: 6 CAT: 17

San Jose State Demonstration Preschool Project
CIJE: 0 RIE: 1 CAT: 19

San Jose State University CA
CIJE: 14 RIE: 13 CAT: 17

San Jose Unified School District CA
CIJE: 5 RIE: 9 CAT: 17

San Juan College NM
CIJE: 1 RIE: 7 CAT: 17

San Juan School District UT
CIJE: 0 RIE: 1 CAT: 17

San Juan School NM
CIJE: 0 RIE: 0 CAT: 17

San Juan Unified School District CA
CIJE: 6 RIE: 10 CAT: 17

San Leandro Unified School District CA
CIJE: 0 RIE: 1 CAT: 17

San Lorenzo Valley Unified School District CA
CIJE: 0 RIE: 1 CAT: 17

San Luis Valley
CIJE: 0 RIE: 1 CAT: 07

San Luis Valley Bilingual Bicultural Program
CIJE: 0 RIE: 1 CAT: 19

San Luis Valley Schools CO
CIJE: 0 RIE: 2 CAT: 17

San Manuel Bueno Martir
CIJE: 0 RIE: 1 CAT: 22

San Marcos Independent School District TX
CIJE: 0 RIE: 1 CAT: 17

San Mateo City Schools CA
CIJE: 2 RIE: 0 CAT: 17

San Mateo Community College District CA
CIJE: 0 RIE: 6 CAT: 17

San Mateo Educational Resources Center CA
CIJE: 0 RIE: 4 CAT: 17

San Mateo Union High School District CA
CIJE: 1 RIE: 2 CAT: 17

San Quentin Prison
CIJE: 2 RIE: 1 CAT: 17

San Rafael City Schools CA
CIJE: 0 RIE: 2 CAT: 17

San Ramon Valley Unified School District CA
CIJE: 1 RIE: 1 CAT: 17

San Ysidro Elementary School District CA
CIJE: 0 RIE: 5 CAT: 17

Sanchez (Jose)
CIJE: 1 RIE: 0 CAT: 18

Sanctuary Movement
CIJE: 2 RIE: 1 CAT: 12

Sanctuary Units
CIJE: 1 RIE: 1 CAT: 15

Sand
CIJE: 7 RIE: 1 CAT: 20

Sand Dollars
CIJE: 1 RIE: 0 CAT: 20

Sand Dunes
CIJE: 2 RIE: 3 CAT: 20

Sand Play
CIJE: 5 RIE: 1 CAT: 16
UF Sandplay Activities

Sand Springs Public Schools OK
CIJE: 0 RIE: 2 CAT: 17

Sandawe
CIJE: 0 RIE: 1 CAT: 13
SN A Khoisan Language, South African Group

Sandburg (Carl)
CIJE: 4 RIE: 1 CAT: 18

Sandcasting
CIJE: 2 RIE: 0 CAT: 20

Sander (Volkmar)
CIJE: 1 RIE: 0 CAT: 18

Sanders and Cunningham Model
CIJE: 0 RIE: 1 CAT: 15

Sanders Associates Inc
CIJE: 0 RIE: 0 CAT: 17

Sandhills Community College NC
CIJE: 0 RIE: 1 CAT: 17

Sandhoffs Disease
CIJE: 1 RIE: 0 CAT: 11

Sandoz (Mari)
CIJE: 3 RIE: 0 CAT: 18

Sandplay Activities
USE Sand Play

Sands Point Country Day School NY
CIJE: 0 RIE: 1 CAT: 17

Sandwich Construction
CIJE: 1 RIE: 0 CAT: 21

Sandwich Courses
CIJE: 11 RIE: 5 CAT: 21

Sandwiches
CIJE: 0 RIE: 2 CAT: 20

Sandy Union High School District 2 OR
CIJE: 0 RIE: 1 CAT: 17

Sanford (Terry)
CIJE: 1 RIE: 0 CAT: 18

Sanford and Son
CIJE: 0 RIE: 2 CAT: 22

Sanford Public Schools ME
CIJE: 1 RIE: 1 CAT: 17

Sangamon State University IL
CIJE: 4 RIE: 7 CAT: 17

Sangir
CIJE: 0 RIE: 0 CAT: 13

Sanitarians
CIJE: 3 RIE: 1 CAT: 09

Sanitary Engineering
CIJE: 0 RIE: 1 CAT: 20

Sanitary Landfills
CIJE: 0 RIE: 1 CAT: 20

Sanitary Surveys
CIJE: 0 RIE: 2 CAT: 20

Sanitation Management
CIJE: 0 RIE: 1 CAT: 09

Sansom (William)
CIJE: 1 RIE: 0 CAT: 18

Santa Ana College CA
CIJE: 1 RIE: 6 CAT: 17

Santa Ana Police Department CA
CIJE: 0 RIE: 1 CAT: 17

Santa Barbara City College CA
CIJE: 1 RIE: 7 CAT: 17

Santa Barbara Community Career Development Council
CIJE: 0 RIE: 1 CAT: 17

Santa Barbara Community College CA
CIJE: 0 RIE: 1 CAT: 17

Santa Barbara County Child Development Center CA
CIJE: 1 RIE: 0 CAT: 17

Santa Barbara County Schools CA
CIJE: 0 RIE: 1 CAT: 17

Santa Barbara Unified School District CA
CIJE: 2 RIE: 1 CAT: 17

Santa Clara County Health Department
CIJE: 1 RIE: 0 CAT: 17

Santa Clara County Library CA
CIJE: 0 RIE: 1 CAT: 17

Santa Clara County Office of Education CA
CIJE: 1 RIE: 1 CAT: 17

Santa Clara Inventory of Developmental Tasks
CIJE: 0 RIE: 2 CAT: 21

Santa Clara Pueblo NM
CIJE: 1 RIE: 1 CAT: 17

Santa Clara Unified School District CA
CIJE: 2 RIE: 3 CAT: 17

Santa Clara University CA
CIJE: 5 RIE: 2 CAT: 17

Santa Clarita Community College District CA
CIJE: 0 RIE: 1 CAT: 17

Santa Claus
CIJE: 1 RIE: 2 CAT: 16

Santa Cruz (Nicomedes)
CIJE: 1 RIE: 0 CAT: 18

Santa Cruz Community Service Television Project
CIJE: 0 RIE: 1 CAT: 19

Santa Fe Community College FL
CIJE: 4 RIE: 11 CAT: 17

Santa Fe Community College NM
CIJE: 1 RIE: 9 CAT: 17

Santa Fe Correctional Farm
CIJE: 0 RIE: 1 CAT: 17

Santa Fe Mountain Center NM
CIJE: 1 RIE: 1 CAT: 17

Santa Lucia
CIJE: 0 RIE: 1 CAT: 07

Santa Monica College CA
CIJE: 1 RIE: 1 CAT: 17

Santa Monica Geography Project
CIJE: 0 RIE: 1 CAT: 19

Santa Monica Hospital Medical Center CA
CIJE: 1 RIE: 0 CAT: 17

Santa Monica Project
CIJE: 0 RIE: 2 CAT: 19

Santa Monica Unified School District CA
CIJE: 0 RIE: 1 CAT: 17

Santa Rosa Junior College CA
CIJE: 0 RIE: 3 CAT: 17

Santali
CIJE: 0 RIE: 2 CAT: 13
SN A Munda language of the Austro-Asiatic group

Santee Sioux (Tribe)
CIJE: 1 RIE: 1 CAT: 08

Santeria
CIJE: 0 RIE: 1 CAT: 16

Santiago Library System CA
CIJE: 0 RIE: 1 CAT: 17

Santillana (Inigo Lopez de Mendoza)
CIJE: 1 RIE: 0 CAT: 18

Sao Tome e Principe
CIJE: 0 RIE: 0 CAT: 07

SAPA Process Instrument
CIJE: 1 RIE: 0 CAT: 21

Sapir (Edward)
CIJE: 5 RIE: 1 CAT: 18

Sappho
CIJE: 0 RIE: 1 CAT: 18
SN Greek lyric poet, c. 600 B.C.

Sapporo University (Japan)
CIJE: 0 RIE: 1 CAT: 17

Sara Ngambay
CIJE: 0 RIE: 3 CAT: 13

Sarah Lawrence College NY
CIJE: 5 RIE: 6 CAT: 17

Saramaccan
CIJE: 0 RIE: 1 CAT: 13
SN English-based Creole language of Surinam
UF Saramakkan

Saramakkan
USE Saramaccan

Sarason Test Anxiety Scale
CIJE: 13 RIE: 13 CAT: 21
UF Test Anxiety Scale (Sarason)

Sarason Test Anxiety Scale for Children
CIJE: 7 RIE: 12 CAT: 21
UF Test Anxiety Scale for Children (Sarason)

Sarasota County Schools FL
CIJE: 1 RIE: 0 CAT: 17

Sarasota County Vocational Technical Center FL
CIJE: 0 RIE: 1 CAT: 17

Sarcoidosis
CIJE: 1 RIE: 0 CAT: 11

Sargent (Dudley Allen)
CIJE: 1 RIE: 2 CAT: 18

Sarmi
CIJE: 1 RIE: 0 CAT: 13

Sarmiento (Domingo Faustino)
CIJE: 1 RIE: 0 CAT: 18

Sarraute (Nathalie)
CIJE: 2 RIE: 0 CAT: 18

Sartre (Jean Paul)
CIJE: 18 RIE: 9 CAT: 18

Sarvodaya Shramadana Movement (Sri Lanka)
CIJE: 1 RIE: 1 CAT: 12

SAS Software
USE Student Administration System

Saskatchewan
CIJE: 66 RIE: 129 CAT: 07

Saskatchewan (La Rouge)
CIJE: 1 RIE: 0 CAT: 07

Saskatchewan (North)
CIJE: 2 RIE: 1 CAT: 07

Saskatchewan (Northeast)
CIJE: 1 RIE: 0 CAT: 07

Saskatchewan (Prince Albert)
CIJE: 0 RIE: 2 CAT: 07

Saskatchewan (Regina)
CIJE: 3 RIE: 7 CAT: 07

Saskatchewan (Saskatoon)
CIJE: 6 RIE: 10 CAT: 07

Saskatchewan Division IV Program
CIJE: 0 RIE: 0 CAT: 19

Saskatchewan Institute of Applied Sci and Techn
CIJE: 0 RIE: 2 CAT: 17

Saskatchewan Literacy Network
CIJE: 0 RIE: 2 CAT: 17

Saskatchewan Penitentiary
CIJE: 1 RIE: 0 CAT: 17

Saskatchewan Urban Native Teacher Education Prog
CIJE: 0 RIE: 1 CAT: 19
UF SUNTEP

Saskatoon Welfare Council
CIJE: 1 RIE: 0 CAT: 17

Sasketchewan Educational Research Association
CIJE: 1 RIE: 0 CAT: 17

Saskmedia
CIJE: 0 RIE: 1 CAT: 16

Sastre (Alfonso)
CIJE: 2 RIE: 0 CAT: 18

Satanic Abuse
CIJE: 6 RIE: 0 CAT: 16

Satanic Cults
USE Satanism

Satanism
CIJE: 17 RIE: 3 CAT: 16
UF Satanic Cults

Satellite Campus Students
USE Satellite Students

Satellite Center Students
USE Satellite Students

Satellite Centers for Adult Leadership
USE Project SCALE

Satellite Communications for Learning
CIJE: 1 RIE: 1 CAT: 17

Satellite Dishes
CIJE: 4 RIE: 3 CAT: 04

Satellite Family Outreach Program IL
CIJE: 0 RIE: 1 CAT: 19

Satellite Foster Home Project
CIJE: 0 RIE: 1 CAT: 19

Satellite Instructional Television Experiment
CIJE: 9 RIE: 6 CAT: 04

Satellite Learning Center Project
CIJE: 0 RIE: 2 CAT: 19

Satellite News Gathering
CIJE: 2 RIE: 2 CAT: 16

Satellite Students
CIJE: 0 RIE: 1 CAT: 10
UF Satellite Campus Students; Satellite Center Students

Satellite Telecommunication Modeling Program
CIJE: 1 RIE: 1 CAT: 19

Satie (Erik)
CIJE: 1 RIE: 0 CAT: 18

Satir (Virginia)
CIJE: 3 RIE: 0 CAT: 18

Satisfaction with Hiram Scales
CIJE: 0 RIE: 1 CAT: 21

Saturation Work Initiative Model
CIJE: 0 RIE: 2 CAT: 19
UF SWIM Demonstration of San Diego County

Saturday Morning Discovery
CIJE: 1 RIE: 0 CAT: 19

Saturday School
CIJE: 7 RIE: 7 CAT: 19

Saturday Seminars for Able and Ambitious Students
CIJE: 1 RIE: 1 CAT: 19
UF Catskill Saturday Seminars

Saturday Studio
CIJE: 1 RIE: 0 CAT: 19

Saturday Subway Ride Program
CIJE: 0 RIE: 1 CAT: 19

Saturn (Planet)
CIJE: 0 RIE: 0 CAT: 20

Sauces
CIJE: 0 RIE: 1 CAT: 20

Saudi Arabia
CIJE: 93 RIE: 51 CAT: 07

Sauk Valley College IL
CIJE: 0 RIE: 5 CAT: 17

Sault Sainte Marie Alternative High School MI
CIJE: 0 RIE: 1 CAT: 17

Saulteaux (Tribe)
CIJE: 1 RIE: 2 CAT: 08
UF Salteaux (Tribe)

Saunas
CIJE: 1 RIE: 1 CAT: 04

Saunders (David R)
CIJE: 0 RIE: 1 CAT: 18

Sausalito Teacher Education Project
CIJE: 0 RIE: 2 CAT: 19

Sausalito Unified School District CA
CIJE: 0 RIE: 3 CAT: 17

Saussure (Ferdinand de)
CIJE: 15 RIE: 2 CAT: 18

Savannah State College GA
CIJE: 1 RIE: 2 CAT: 17

Save Our Sons And Daughters
CIJE: 0 RIE: 1 CAT: 17
UF SOSAD

Save the Children Federation
CIJE: 0 RIE: 1 CAT: 17

Save the Children Fund
CIJE: 1 RIE: 2 CAT: 17

SAVES Project
CIJE: 0 RIE: 3 CAT: 19

SAVI SELPH Program
CIJE: 0 RIE: 1 CAT: 19
SN "Science Activities for the Visually Impaired" (q.v.) (and) "Science Enrichment for Learners with Physical Handicaps"

Saving Schoolhouse Energy Project
CIJE: 0 RIE: 7 CAT: 19

Savings
CIJE: 13 RIE: 10 CAT: 16

Savings Accounts
CIJE: 8 RIE: 7 CAT: 16

Savings Bonds
CIJE: 1 RIE: 5 CAT: 16

SAVY Curriculum
CIJE: 0 RIE: 1 CAT: 03
UF Socially Adept Verbalizations of Youth

Sawmill Workers
CIJE: 0 RIE: 3 CAT: 09

Saxon (John)
CIJE: 2 RIE: 1 CAT: 18

Saxon Mathematics Series
CIJE: 0 RIE: 1 CAT: 22

Saxons
CIJE: 1 RIE: 0 CAT: 08

Say It Straight Prevention Program
CIJE: 0 RIE: 1 CAT: 19

SBIDA
USE Small Business Institute Directors Association

Scabies
CIJE: 1 RIE: 0 CAT: 11

Scaffolding
CIJE: 24 RIE: 26 CAT: 04

Scale Analysis
CIJE: 7 RIE: 3 CAT: 15

Scale Anchoring
CIJE: 1 RIE: 1 CAT: 21

Scale for Evaluation Group Counseling Experiences
CIJE: 1 RIE: 0 CAT: 21

Scale for Rating Behav Character Superior Students
USE Scales for Rating Behav Character Superior Student

Scale Models
CIJE: 6 RIE: 0 CAT: 04

Scale of Aesthetic Judgment (Taylor Helmstadter)
CIJE: 0 RIE: 1 CAT: 21

Scale of Childrens Attitudes toward Handicaps
CIJE: 0 RIE: 1 CAT: 21

Scale of Client Satisfaction (Reagles)
CIJE: 0 RIE: 1 CAT: 21

Scale of Economic Liberalism
CIJE: 1 RIE: 0 CAT: 21

Scale of Noneconomic Liberalism
CIJE: 1 RIE: 0 CAT: 21

Scale of Primary Classroom Practices
CIJE: 0 RIE: 1 CAT: 21

Scale of Rehabilitation Gain (Reagles)
CIJE: 0 RIE: 1 CAT: 21

Scale of Student Teacher Concerns
CIJE: 1 RIE: 1 CAT: 21

Scale on Procedures in Dealing with Children
CIJE: 0 RIE: 1 CAT: 21

Scale Score Strategy
CIJE: 2 RIE: 0 CAT: 21

Scaled Achievement Tests
CIJE: 2 RIE: 1 CAT: 21

Scales for Centripetal Centrifugal Family Style
CIJE: 0 RIE: 1 CAT: 21

Scales for Rating Behav Character Superior Student
CIJE: 1 RIE: 1 CAT: 21
UF Renzulli Scale for Rating Behav Characteristics; Scale for Rating Behav Character Superior Students

Scales of Communicative Interaction
CIJE: 2 RIE: 0 CAT: 21

Scales of Independent Behavior
CIJE: 6 RIE: 3 CAT: 21

Scalia (Antonin)
CIJE: 0 RIE: 1 CAT: 18

Scaling (Maximum Dissemination)
CIJE: 0 RIE: 1 CAT: 15

Scaling (Mechanical Drawing)
CIJE: 0 RIE: 1 CAT: 20

Scaling Models
CIJE: 0 RIE: 2 CAT: 15

Scalogram Analyses
CIJE: 1 RIE: 1 CAT: 21

Scalogram Analysis
CIJE: 8 RIE: 6 CAT: 15

SCAN Computer Program
CIJE: 0 RIE: 1 CAT: 04

Scan Module
CIJE: 0 RIE: 1 CAT: 16

Scandals
CIJE: 0 RIE: 1 CAT: 12

Scandia Plan
CIJE: 0 RIE: 1 CAT: 19

Scandinavia
CIJE: 54 RIE: 81 CAT: 07

Scandinavian Culture
CIJE: 0 RIE: 2 CAT: 16

Scandinavian Heritage Project
CIJE: 0 RIE: 2 CAT: 19

Scandinavian Library Congress
CIJE: 1 RIE: 0 CAT: 02

Scandinavian Literature
CIJE: 1 RIE: 0 CAT: 16

Scandinavians
CIJE: 2 RIE: 9 CAT: 08

Scandura (J M)
CIJE: 1 RIE: 1 CAT: 18

Scanlon Plan
CIJE: 6 RIE: 1 CAT: 16

Scanning
CIJE: 24 RIE: 9 CAT: 11
SN Do not use for the Desc "Environmental Scanning" — see also add'l Iden "Digital Scanning"

Scanning Rate
CIJE: 3 RIE: 0 CAT: 11

Scanning Styles
CIJE: 0 RIE: 1 CAT: 11

Scanzoni Model of Female Status Attainment
CIJE: 1 RIE: 0 CAT: 21

Scapegoat Role
CIJE: 1 RIE: 1 CAT: 11

Scapegoating
CIJE: 16 RIE: 3 CAT: 11

Scarborough Board of Education ON
CIJE: 0 RIE: 10 CAT: 17

Scarborough College (Canada)
CIJE: 2 RIE: 1 CAT: 17

Scarborough School District ME
CIJE: 0 RIE: 1 CAT: 17

Scarcity
CIJE: 4 RIE: 2 CAT: 16

Scarlet Letter
CIJE: 6 RIE: 2 CAT: 22

Scarlett Junior High School MI
CIJE: 0 RIE: 1 CAT: 17

Scarritt College TN
CIJE: 0 RIE: 1 CAT: 17

Scarsdale High School NY
CIJE: 2 RIE: 0 CAT: 17

Scatology
CIJE: 1 RIE: 0 CAT: 11

SCATT Program FL
USE Sun Coast Area Teacher Training Program FL

Scattergrams
CIJE: 9 RIE: 5 CAT: 15
UF Scatterplots

Scatterplots
USE Scattergrams

Scenario Testing
CIJE: 1 RIE: 1 CAT: 21

Scenario Writing
CIJE: 6 RIE: 4 CAT: 15

Scenarios
CIJE: 24 RIE: 16 CAT: 16

Scene Design
CIJE: 0 RIE: 1 CAT: 15

SCETI
USE Stanford Computer Based Educator Train Interv

Schaeffer Behavior Inventory
CIJE: 0 RIE: 3 CAT: 21

Schafer (Wilhelm)
CIJE: 1 RIE: 0 CAT: 18

Schail v Tippecanoe County School Corporation
CIJE: 0 RIE: 1 CAT: 14

Schall v Martin
CIJE: 0 RIE: 1 CAT: 14

Schaller (M Joseph)
CIJE: 1 RIE: 0 CAT: 18

Schank (Roger)
CIJE: 2 RIE: 1 CAT: 18

Scharmbeck (Osterholz)
CIJE: 1 RIE: 0 CAT: 18

Schatz (Alfred)
CIJE: 0 RIE: 1 CAT: 18

Schaumburg Early Education Center IL
CIJE: 0 RIE: 1 CAT: 17

Schechner (Richard)
CIJE: 0 RIE: 1 CAT: 18

Schedule of Interpersonal Concern (Kinnane et al)
CIJE: 0 RIE: 1 CAT: 21

Schedule of Recent Experience
CIJE: 2 RIE: 1 CAT: 21

Schedule of Social Functioning (Heimler)
CIJE: 0 RIE: 1 CAT: 21

Scheele (Carl)
CIJE: 1 RIE: 0 CAT: 18

Scheffes Contrast Test
CIJE: 5 RIE: 2 CAT: 21

Scheffler (Israel)
CIJE: 2 RIE: 0 CAT: 18

Schein (Edgar H)
CIJE: 2 RIE: 1 CAT: 18

Schell (Louis)
CIJE: 0 RIE: 1 CAT: 18

Schema Theory
CIJE: 84 RIE: 89 CAT: 15

Schematic Concept Formation
CIJE: 6 RIE: 3 CAT: 15

Schematic Maps
CIJE: 0 RIE: 1 CAT: 15

Scheme Analysing Behaviour Individual Classrooms
CIJE: 0 RIE: 1 CAT: 15

Schenectady County Community College NY
CIJE: 1 RIE: 5 CAT: 17

Schenectady County Public Library NY
CIJE: 1 RIE: 0 CAT: 17

Schenley High School PA
CIJE: 0 RIE: 2 CAT: 17

Scherer (Klaus R)
CIJE: 0 RIE: 1 CAT: 18

Schermerhorn (Richard A)
CIJE: 1 RIE: 0 CAT: 18

Schiller (Friedrich)
CIJE: 6 RIE: 1 CAT: 18

Schistosomiasis
CIJE: 3 RIE: 0 CAT: 20

Schizophrenia Index
CIJE: 0 RIE: 1 CAT: 21

Schlafly (Phyllis)
CIJE: 4 RIE: 2 CAT: 18

Schlegel (Friedrich von)
CIJE: 1 RIE: 0 CAT: 18

Schleiermacher (Friedrich)
CIJE: 1 RIE: 0 CAT: 18

Schlesinger (I M)
CIJE: 1 RIE: 0 CAT: 18

Schlesinger (John)
CIJE: 1 RIE: 0 CAT: 18

Schmid (P)
CIJE: 0 RIE: 1 CAT: 18

Schmidt VD Knowledge Evaluator
CIJE: 0 RIE: 1 CAT: 21

Schneidman Questionnaire (Attitudes Toward Death)
CIJE: 1 RIE: 0 CAT: 21

Schnitzler (Arthur)
CIJE: 1 RIE: 0 CAT: 18

Schoenberg (Arnold)
CIJE: 1 RIE: 0 CAT: 18

SCHOLAR (Computer System)
CIJE: 0 RIE: 6 CAT: 04

Scholarly Communication
CIJE: 36 RIE: 5 CAT: 16

Scholarly Information Exchange
CIJE: 1 RIE: 1 CAT: 16

Scholarly Journalism
CIJE: 4 RIE: 0 CAT: 03

Scholarly Writing
CIJE: 62 RIE: 36 CAT: 16

Scholars in the Arts Program
CIJE: 0 RIE: 1 CAT: 19

Scholars in the Schools Program
CIJE: 0 RIE: 1 CAT: 19

Scholarship Education Defense Fund Racial Equality
CIJE: 0 RIE: 1 CAT: 17

Scholarship Initiative (School Choice)
CIJE: 0 RIE: 1 CAT: 15

Scholastic Aptitude Test
CIJE: 422 RIE: 428 CAT: 21
SN Renamed the "Scholastic Assessment Tests" in Mar93

Scholastic Journalism
CIJE: 12 RIE: 15 CAT: 03

Scholastic Photography Awards
CIJE: 1 RIE: 0 CAT: 16

Scholastic Press Associations
CIJE: 18 RIE: 4 CAT: 05

Schomburg Collection
CIJE: 1 RIE: 0 CAT: 16

Schon (Donald A)
CIJE: 9 RIE: 0 CAT: 18

School 715 (USSR)
CIJE: 0 RIE: 1 CAT: 17

School Academic Competition Inventory
CIJE: 0 RIE: 1 CAT: 21

School Act 1988 (Alberta)
CIJE: 0 RIE: 1 CAT: 14

School Adjustment Scale (Flynn)
CIJE: 1 RIE: 1 CAT: 21

School Age Criminals
CIJE: 0 RIE: 1 CAT: 10

School Age Parents
CIJE: 3 RIE: 3 CAT: 10

School Aid Act Section III (Michigan)
CIJE: 0 RIE: 1 CAT: 14

School Alternative Vocational Education Project
CIJE: 0 RIE: 1 CAT: 19

School and College Ability Tests
CIJE: 17 RIE: 55 CAT: 21

School Anxiety Questionnaire
CIJE: 0 RIE: 2 CAT: 21

School Anxiety Scale
CIJE: 1 RIE: 0 CAT: 21

School Asbestos Safety Act 1979 (New York)
CIJE: 0 RIE: 1 CAT: 14

School Assessment Survey
CIJE: 1 RIE: 2 CAT: 21

School Assistance in Federally Affected Areas
CIJE: 1 RIE: 2 CAT: 14

School Attendance Act (California)
CIJE: 0 RIE: 1 CAT: 14

School Attendance Review Boards
CIJE: 1 RIE: 3 CAT: 10

School Attitude Measure (Dolan and Enos)
CIJE: 1 RIE: 1 CAT: 21

School Attitude Scale for Children
CIJE: 0 RIE: 2 CAT: 21

School Attitudes Questionnaire (Voorst)
CIJE: 0 RIE: 1 CAT: 21

School Based Career Education
CIJE: 1 RIE: 6 CAT: 15

School Based Child Care Centers
CIJE: 1 RIE: 4 CAT: 05

School Based Clinics
CIJE: 10 RIE: 21 CAT: 05

School Based Curriculum Development
CIJE: 5 RIE: 2 CAT: 03

School Based Development Enterprises
USE School Based Enterprises

School Based Early Childhood Centers
CIJE: 0 RIE: 1 CAT: 05

School Based Enterprises
CIJE: 2 RIE: 8 CAT: 16
UF School Based Development Enterprises

School Based Evaluation
CIJE: 1 RIE: 1 CAT: 16

School Based Examining
CIJE: 2 RIE: 2 CAT: 21

School Based Health Clinics
CIJE: 8 RIE: 13 CAT: 05

School Based Information Systems
CIJE: 0 RIE: 1 CAT: 04

School Based Multidisciplinary Team
CIJE: 3 RIE: 1 CAT: 11

School Based Program Evaluation Manual
CIJE: 0 RIE: 1 CAT: 22

School Based Recovery Support
CIJE: 0 RIE: 1 CAT: 16

School Based Services
CIJE: 4 RIE: 8 CAT: 16

School Based Support Teams
CIJE: 3 RIE: 3 CAT: 10
SN See also "School Leadership Teams" and "School Improvement Teams"

School Based Teacher Educators
CIJE: 0 RIE: 14 CAT: 09

School Behavior Profile (Balow)
CIJE: 0 RIE: 2 CAT: 21

School Behavior Rating Scale (Davidson et al)
CIJE: 0 RIE: 2 CAT: 21

School Behavior Survey
CIJE: 1 RIE: 1 CAT: 21

School Boards Associations
CIJE: 0 RIE: 3 CAT: 10

School Breakfast Program
CIJE: 0 RIE: 14 CAT: 19

School Broadcasting Council (England)
CIJE: 1 RIE: 1 CAT: 17

School Business Management
CIJE: 0 RIE: 3 CAT: 15

School Camping
CIJE: 0 RIE: 2 CAT: 03

School Career and Health Record
CIJE: 0 RIE: 1 CAT: 15

School Census
CIJE: 1 RIE: 1 CAT: 15

School Climate Profile
CIJE: 2 RIE: 3 CAT: 21

School Climate Survey (NASSP)
CIJE: 0 RIE: 1 CAT: 21

School Community Association
CIJE: 1 RIE: 0 CAT: 17

School Community Councils
CIJE: 7 RIE: 5 CAT: 05
UF Community School Councils

School Community Education Program
CIJE: 0 RIE: 8 CAT: 19
SN ...in New York City

School Community Improvement Process
CIJE: 0 RIE: 1 CAT: 15

School Community Questionnaire
CIJE: 0 RIE: 1 CAT: 21

School Community Surveys
CIJE: 0 RIE: 0 CAT: 15
UF Community School Surveys

School Construction Systems Development
CIJE: 4 RIE: 4 CAT: 16

School Context Analysis Form
CIJE: 0 RIE: 1 CAT: 21

School Councils
CIJE: 10 RIE: 2 CAT: 10
SN See also "Local School Councils"

School Counselor Attitude Inventory (Baker)
CIJE: 1 RIE: 1 CAT: 21

School Counselor Classification Categories
CIJE: 0 RIE: 1 CAT: 21

School Coupling
USE School Organizational Coupling

School Court Liaison Program
CIJE: 0 RIE: 1 CAT: 19

School Crime
CIJE: 1 RIE: 1 CAT: 14

School Crime and Misbehavior Project
CIJE: 0 RIE: 1 CAT: 19

School Culture
CIJE: 124 RIE: 96 CAT: 16

School Decentralization Act 1969 (New York)
CIJE: 1 RIE: 0 CAT: 14

School Desegregation Monitors
CIJE: 0 RIE: 1 CAT: 10

School Development Program
CIJE: 14 RIE: 8 CAT: 19

School Discipline Policies Practices Study (NCES)
CIJE: 0 RIE: 1 CAT: 19

School Distribution
USE Distribution of Schools

School District Competency Tests
CIJE: 0 RIE: 1 CAT: 21

School District Dissolution
CIJE: 0 RIE: 1 CAT: 16

School District Isolation
CIJE: 0 RIE: 0 CAT: 16

School District Lawyers
CIJE: 2 RIE: 1 CAT: 09

School District Personnel
CIJE: 0 RIE: 1 CAT: 09
UF District Personnel

School District Questionnaire
CIJE: 0 RIE: 2 CAT: 21

School District Treasurers
USE School Treasurers

School Effectiveness Indices
CIJE: 1 RIE: 3 CAT: 21

School Effectiveness Inventory
CIJE: 0 RIE: 1 CAT: 21

School Effectiveness Structural Components Inven
CIJE: 0 RIE: 0 CAT: 21

School Effectiveness Training Project
CIJE: 0 RIE: 3 CAT: 19

School Effects
CIJE: 12 RIE: 11 CAT: 15

School Employment Procedures Act (Mississippi)
CIJE: 0 RIE: 2 CAT: 14

School Environment Inventory (Stern)
CIJE: 0 RIE: 1 CAT: 21

School Environment Preference Schedule
CIJE: 3 RIE: 1 CAT: 21

School Environment Scale (Grossman)
CIJE: 0 RIE: 1 CAT: 21

School Evaluation Project
CIJE: 0 RIE: 4 CAT: 19

School Finance Act 1983 (Arkansas)
USE Arkansas Act 34

School Finance Equalization Management System
CIJE: 0 RIE: 2 CAT: 04

School Finance Research
CIJE: 2 RIE: 2 CAT: 15

School Food Management System
CIJE: 0 RIE: 1 CAT: 15

School for Contemporary Education VA
CIJE: 0 RIE: 2 CAT: 17

School for International Training VT
CIJE: 5 RIE: 1 CAT: 17

School for the Deaf NY
CIJE: 0 RIE: 1 CAT: 17

School Health Education Study
CIJE: 1 RIE: 0 CAT: 19

School Identification Cards
CIJE: 0 RIE: 1 CAT: 04

School Improvement Councils
CIJE: 0 RIE: 1 CAT: 10

School Improvement Groups Network Project NC
CIJE: 0 RIE: 1 CAT: 19
UF Project SIGN NC

School Improvement Model
CIJE: 3 RIE: 7 CAT: 15

School Improvement Partnership Process
CIJE: 0 RIE: 1 CAT: 19

School Improvement Program CA
USE California School Improvement Program

School Improvement Programme (Aga Khan Foundation)
CIJE: 0 RIE: 1 CAT: 19

School Improvement Project (New York City)
CIJE: 3 RIE: 6 CAT: 19

School Improvement Project (Pittsburgh)
CIJE: 0 RIE: 1 CAT: 19

School Improvement Projects
CIJE: 3 RIE: 5 CAT: 19

School Improvement Survey
CIJE: 0 RIE: 1 CAT: 21

School Improvement Teams
CIJE: 1 RIE: 1 CAT: 10
SN See also "School Based Support Teams" and "School Leadership Teams"

School Improvement Through Instructional Process
CIJE: 0 RIE: 8 CAT: 19

School Incentive Reward Program SC
USE South Carolina School Incentive Reward Program

School Influence
CIJE: 3 RIE: 1 CAT: 16

School Information Management Systems
CIJE: 0 RIE: 3 CAT: 04

School Information Questionnaire
CIJE: 0 RIE: 1 CAT: 21

School Information System
CIJE: 0 RIE: 6 CAT: 15

School Instructional Development Model
CIJE: 1 RIE: 0 CAT: 15

School Inventory (Bell)
CIJE: 0 RIE: 1 CAT: 21

School Leadership Teams
CIJE: 0 RIE: 1 CAT: 10
SN See also "School Based Support Teams" and "School Improvement Teams"
UF Leadership Teams (School)

School Legitimation
CIJE: 0 RIE: 1 CAT: 16

School Level Environment Questionnaire
CIJE: 3 RIE: 1 CAT: 21

School Library Journal
CIJE: 0 RIE: 2 CAT: 22

School Library Manpower Project
CIJE: 5 RIE: 2 CAT: 19

School Library Media Program of the Year Award
CIJE: 1 RIE: 0 CAT: 16

School Life Magazine
CIJE: 0 RIE: 1 CAT: 22

School Lunch Program
CIJE: 16 RIE: 47 CAT: 19

School Mapping
CIJE: 0 RIE: 6 CAT: 16

School Mastery of Reading Test
CIJE: 0 RIE: 2 CAT: 21

School Match Database
USE SchoolMatch

School Mathematics Project
CIJE: 11 RIE: 2 CAT: 19

School Mathematics Study Group
CIJE: 9 RIE: 379 CAT: 17

School Milk Contracts
CIJE: 0 RIE: 1 CAT: 16

School Motivation Analysis Test
CIJE: 4 RIE: 0 CAT: 21

School Nurse Achievement Program
CIJE: 0 RIE: 1 CAT: 19

School Nutrition Programs
CIJE: 1 RIE: 4 CAT: 19

School of Experiential Education (Canada)
CIJE: 0 RIE: 1 CAT: 17

School of New Resources
CIJE: 0 RIE: 1 CAT: 19
SN Adult higher education program of the College of New Rochelle NY

School of the Air (Australia)
CIJE: 2 RIE: 10 CAT: 17

School Openings
CIJE: 1 RIE: 1 CAT: 16

School Opinion Questionnaire (Cohen)
CIJE: 1 RIE: 0 CAT: 21

School Opinion Survey (Shaw and Rector)
CIJE: 0 RIE: 1 CAT: 21

School Organization Inventory
CIJE: 2 RIE: 0 CAT: 21

School Organizational Coupling
CIJE: 1 RIE: 2 CAT: 15
SN See also "Loose Coupling"
UF Organizational Coupling (Schools); School Coupling

School Outliers
CIJE: 0 RIE: 1 CAT: 10

School Perception Scales (Lym and Murray)
CIJE: 0 RIE: 1 CAT: 21

School Personnel Satisfaction Inven (Catherwood)
CIJE: 0 RIE: 1 CAT: 21

School Personnel Utilization Project
CIJE: 0 RIE: 6 CAT: 19

School Planning Evaluation Communication System
CIJE: 1 RIE: 13 CAT: 15

School Plant Managers
CIJE: 0 RIE: 1 CAT: 09

School Political Behavior Research Project
CIJE: 0 RIE: 1 CAT: 19

School Practices Information File
CIJE: 2 RIE: 1 CAT: 04

School Practices Information Network
CIJE: 2 RIE: 1 CAT: 04

School Price Index
CIJE: 0 RIE: 1 CAT: 22

School Problem Area Survey
CIJE: 0 RIE: 2 CAT: 21

School Profiles
CIJE: 2 RIE: 3 CAT: 15

School Program Advancing Career Education
CIJE: 0 RIE: 5 CAT: 19

School Program Bonanza Game
CIJE: 0 RIE: 1 CAT: 19

School Psychology Survey
CIJE: 1 RIE: 1 CAT: 21

School Public Library Cooperation
CIJE: 11 RIE: 3 CAT: 16

School Rating Scale (Birnbaum)
CIJE: 1 RIE: 0 CAT: 21

School Rating Schedule
CIJE: 0 RIE: 1 CAT: 21

School Rating Systems
CIJE: 1 RIE: 2 CAT: 21

School Readiness Evaluation Tests (Ozer)
CIJE: 0 RIE: 1 CAT: 21

School Readiness Program (Hartford Conn)
CIJE: 0 RIE: 1 CAT: 21

School Readiness Survey
CIJE: 1 RIE: 1 CAT: 21

School Readiness Tasks (Bateman)
CIJE: 0 RIE: 1 CAT: 21

School Recognition Programs
CIJE: 2 RIE: 1 CAT: 19
SN See also "Elementary School Recognition Program," "Secondary School Recognition Program," and "Drug Free School Recognition Program"

School Reform Assessment Project
CIJE: 0 RIE: 1 CAT: 19

School Refusal
CIJE: 3 RIE: 4 CAT: 11

School Refusal Assessment Scale
CIJE: 0 RIE: 1 CAT: 21

School Renewal
CIJE: 1 RIE: 5 CAT: 16

School Renewal Network
CIJE: 0 RIE: 4 CAT: 17
SN A national collegium of practitioners engaged in school reform activities

School Resource Center TX
CIJE: 0 RIE: 1 CAT: 17

School Retrofit Design Analysis System
CIJE: 1 RIE: 1 CAT: 04

School Robustness
USE Environmental Robustness

School Rules
CIJE: 11 RIE: 10 CAT: 16

School Safety Patrols
CIJE: 1 RIE: 4 CAT: 10

School Scene Apperception Questionnaire
CIJE: 0 RIE: 1 CAT: 21

School Self Improvement Project NY
CIJE: 0 RIE: 2 CAT: 19

School Sentiment Index
CIJE: 1 RIE: 11 CAT: 21

School Sentiment Inventory
CIJE: 0 RIE: 1 CAT: 21

School Site Budgeting
CIJE: 2 RIE: 2 CAT: 15

School Situation Survey
CIJE: 0 RIE: 1 CAT: 21

School Sorting
CIJE: 1 RIE: 1 CAT: 15

School Special Service Teams
CIJE: 1 RIE: 0 CAT: 10

School Sponsored Day Care
CIJE: 1 RIE: 0 CAT: 05

School Stability
CIJE: 1 RIE: 1 CAT: 16

School Stores
CIJE: 13 RIE: 13 CAT: 05

School Study Councils
CIJE: 3 RIE: 1 CAT: 05

School Subject Inventory (Prince)
CIJE: 0 RIE: 1 CAT: 21

School Subjects Attitude Scales
CIJE: 0 RIE: 3 CAT: 21

School Support Questionnaire
CIJE: 0 RIE: 1 CAT: 21

School Survey (Kaufman)
CIJE: 0 RIE: 1 CAT: 21

School Survey of Interpersonal Relationships
CIJE: 1 RIE: 0 CAT: 21

School Team Approach
CIJE: 2 RIE: 1 CAT: 15

School Technology Assessment Research Model
CIJE: 0 RIE: 1 CAT: 15

School to Employment Program
CIJE: 0 RIE: 12 CAT: 19

School to Work Transition
CIJE: 5 RIE: 8 CAT: 15

School Treasurers
CIJE: 0 RIE: 0 CAT: 09
UF School District Treasurers

School Uniforms
CIJE: 0 RIE: 6 CAT: 04

School University Teacher Education Center NY
CIJE: 1 RIE: 2 CAT: 17

School Utilization Study
CIJE: 0 RIE: 1 CAT: 22

School Vision Inventory
CIJE: 1 RIE: 1 CAT: 21

School Volunteer Program
CIJE: 6 RIE: 5 CAT: 19

School Work Culture Profile
CIJE: 0 RIE: 2 CAT: 21

School Yards
CIJE: 6 RIE: 6 CAT: 05

Schoolcraft College MI
CIJE: 4 RIE: 2 CAT: 17

Schooled Language Competence
CIJE: 0 RIE: 1 CAT: 13

Schoolhouse Energy Efficiency Demonstration
CIJE: 1 RIE: 1 CAT: 19

SchoolMatch
CIJE: 0 RIE: 1 CAT: 17
UF School Match Database

Schools and Hospitals Grant Program
CIJE: 4 RIE: 0 CAT: 19

Schools and Staffing Survey (NCES)
CIJE: 2 RIE: 37 CAT: 21

Schools Council (England)
CIJE: 26 RIE: 10 CAT: 17

Schools Council Bilingual Project
CIJE: 1 RIE: 0 CAT: 19

Schools Council Integrated Science Project
CIJE: 8 RIE: 1 CAT: 19

Schools Council Project on Statistical Education
CIJE: 1 RIE: 0 CAT: 19

Schools Council Social Education Project
CIJE: 0 RIE: 1 CAT: 19

Schools for the Seventies
CIJE: 1 RIE: 1 CAT: 16

Schools Information Center IA
CIJE: 0 RIE: 1 CAT: 17

Schools of Business Administration
CIJE: 0 RIE: 1 CAT: 05

Schools of Choice Programs
CIJE: 0 RIE: 1 CAT: 19

Schools of Public Health
CIJE: 1 RIE: 4 CAT: 05

Schools Reaching Out Project
CIJE: 6 RIE: 8 CAT: 19
UF League of Schools Reaching Out

Schools Teaching Options for Peace
USE Project STOP NY

Schools Within a School Plan (Elementary Educ)
CIJE: 2 RIE: 0 CAT: 19

Schools Without Failure
CIJE: 1 RIE: 17 CAT: 05

Schools Without Walls
CIJE: 3 RIE: 8 CAT: 05

Schoolwatch IL
CIJE: 0 RIE: 2 CAT: 19

Schoolwide Enrichment Model
CIJE: 4 RIE: 1 CAT: 15

Schoolwork Module
CIJE: 0 RIE: 1 CAT: 15

Schoolyear 2000 FL
CIJE: 0 RIE: 1 CAT: 19

Schopenhauer (Arthur)
CIJE: 4 RIE: 2 CAT: 18

Schramm (Wilbur)
CIJE: 5 RIE: 4 CAT: 18

Schreiner College TX
CIJE: 0 RIE: 1 CAT: 17

Schrodinger (Erwin)
CIJE: 2 RIE: 0 CAT: 18

Schrodinger Equation
CIJE: 6 RIE: 0 CAT: 20

Schrodingers Cat
CIJE: 0 RIE: 1 CAT: 15

Schubert Assessment Soc Work Stud Perf Field Work
CIJE: 0 RIE: 1 CAT: 21

Schuh (Hermann)
CIJE: 2 RIE: 0 CAT: 18

Schulman (A I)
CIJE: 0 RIE: 1 CAT: 18

Schultz (Charles)
CIJE: 1 RIE: 0 CAT: 18

Schultz (H Stefan)
CIJE: 1 RIE: 0 CAT: 18

Schultz (Raymond E)
CIJE: 3 RIE: 1 CAT: 18

Schumpeter (Joseph)
CIJE: 2 RIE: 1 CAT: 18

Schutz (Alfred)
CIJE: 1 RIE: 3 CAT: 18

Schutz (Heinrich)
CIJE: 1 RIE: 0 CAT: 18

Schutz (William)
CIJE: 0 RIE: 4 CAT: 18

Schuyler (George S)
CIJE: 3 RIE: 0 CAT: 18

Schuylkill County ATVS PA
CIJE: 0 RIE: 1 CAT: 17

Schuylkill Valley Nature Center PA
CIJE: 1 RIE: 0 CAT: 17

Schwab (Joseph J)
CIJE: 12 RIE: 1 CAT: 18

Schwartz Early Mathematics Inventory
CIJE: 1 RIE: 1 CAT: 21

Schwarzer Self Efficacy Scale
CIJE: 0 RIE: 1 CAT: 21

Schweitzer (Albert)
CIJE: 4 RIE: 0 CAT: 18

Schwirian Science Support Scale
CIJE: 2 RIE: 0 CAT: 21

Sciara Jantz Empathy Towards Poverty Scale
CIJE: 0 RIE: 2 CAT: 21

Science (Journal)
CIJE: 2 RIE: 1 CAT: 22

Science 14 24 Program
CIJE: 0 RIE: 1 CAT: 19

Science 81
CIJE: 0 RIE: 1 CAT: 22

Science A Basic Approach
CIJE: 0 RIE: 1 CAT: 03

Science A Process Approach
CIJE: 55 RIE: 60 CAT: 03

Science Ability
CIJE: 2 RIE: 2 CAT: 20

Science Abstracts
CIJE: 0 RIE: 1 CAT: 22

Science Academy of Austin TX
CIJE: 0 RIE: 2 CAT: 17

Science Achievement
CIJE: 66 RIE: 103 CAT: 20

Science Activities for the Visually Impaired
CIJE: 1 RIE: 0 CAT: 19
SN See also "SAVI SELPH Program"

Science Advisory Board
CIJE: 0 RIE: 1 CAT: 17

Science and Engineering Technician Curriculum
CIJE: 0 RIE: 11 CAT: 03

Science and Environmental Education
CIJE: 0 RIE: 1 CAT: 03

Science and Man in the Americas
CIJE: 1 RIE: 0 CAT: 03

Science and Mathematics Support Teacher Program
CIJE: 0 RIE: 1 CAT: 19

Science and Self Determination Project CO
CIJE: 0 RIE: 1 CAT: 19

Science and Technology Entry Program
CIJE: 0 RIE: 0 CAT: 19

Science Anxiety
CIJE: 17 RIE: 8 CAT: 20

Science Aptitude Test (Ralph)
CIJE: 1 RIE: 0 CAT: 21

Science as a Way of Knowing Project
CIJE: 3 RIE: 4 CAT: 19

Science Assessment Research Project
CIJE: 0 RIE: 1 CAT: 19

Science Attitude Inventory
CIJE: 2 RIE: 0 CAT: 21

Science Attitude Scale (Ralph)
CIJE: 0 RIE: 1 CAT: 21

Science Attitude Scale for Preservice Teachers
CIJE: 0 RIE: 1 CAT: 21

Science Citation Index
CIJE: 13 RIE: 6 CAT: 22

Science Classroom Activities Checklist
CIJE: 0 RIE: 2 CAT: 21

Science Classroom Observation Form (Butt et al)
CIJE: 0 RIE: 1 CAT: 21

Science College Ability Test
CIJE: 0 RIE: 1 CAT: 21

Science Concept Learning Project
CIJE: 0 RIE: 6 CAT: 19

Science Curriculum Assessment System (Matthews)
CIJE: 1 RIE: 1 CAT: 21

Science Curriculum Improvement Study
CIJE: 74 RIE: 74 CAT: 19

Science Development Program
CIJE: 2 RIE: 0 CAT: 19

Science Education Centers
CIJE: 1 RIE: 2 CAT: 05

Science Education Programme for Africa
CIJE: 1 RIE: 3 CAT: 19

Science Education Research
CIJE: 1500 RIE: 899 CAT: 20

Science Facilities Standards Committee
CIJE: 1 RIE: 0 CAT: 17

Science Fiction Libraries
CIJE: 1 RIE: 0 CAT: 05

Science Fiction Research Association
CIJE: 1 RIE: 0 CAT: 17

Science for All Programs
CIJE: 1 RIE: 3 CAT: 19

Science for the Blind PA
CIJE: 0 RIE: 1 CAT: 17

Science Framework for California Public Schools
CIJE: 1 RIE: 0 CAT: 03
UF California Science Framework

Science In a Social CONtext
CIJE: 0 RIE: 1 CAT: 03
UF SISCON

Science in Society Project
CIJE: 1 RIE: 3 CAT: 19

Science Indicators
CIJE: 3 RIE: 13 CAT: 16

Science Majors
CIJE: 6 RIE: 4 CAT: 10

Science Manpower Project
CIJE: 0 RIE: 1 CAT: 19

Science Manpower Series
CIJE: 0 RIE: 1 CAT: 22

Science Math and Relevant Technology Project
USE Operation SMART

Science Math Improvement Project
CIJE: 0 RIE: 1 CAT: 19

Science Motivation Project
CIJE: 0 RIE: 2 CAT: 19

Science Museums
CIJE: 3 RIE: 1 CAT: 05

Science News
CIJE: 9 RIE: 6 CAT: 20

Science Observation System
CIJE: 1 RIE: 0 CAT: 15

Science of Creative Intelligence
CIJE: 3 RIE: 0 CAT: 15

Science Olympiad
CIJE: 9 RIE: 2 CAT: 12

Science Opinion Survey
CIJE: 1 RIE: 2 CAT: 21

SCIENCE ORDERS
CIJE: 0 RIE: 1 CAT: 04

Science Participation
CIJE: 0 RIE: 1 CAT: 16

Science Policy
CIJE: 25 RIE: 30 CAT: 20

Science Practical Test (Kosima)
CIJE: 1 RIE: 0 CAT: 21

Science Process Instrument (AAAS)
CIJE: 0 RIE: 1 CAT: 21

Science Process Measure for Teachers
CIJE: 0 RIE: 1 CAT: 21

Science Proficiency Scale
CIJE: 0 RIE: 1 CAT: 21

Science Quality Education Project
CIJE: 0 RIE: 1 CAT: 19

Science Research Associates
CIJE: 7 RIE: 4 CAT: 17
SN See add'l listings under "SRA..."
UF SRA

Science Skills
CIJE: 9 RIE: 20 CAT: 20
SN Do not use for the Desc "Science Process Skills"

Science Spanish Program
CIJE: 0 RIE: 1 CAT: 19

Science State Trait Anxiety Inventory
CIJE: 0 RIE: 1 CAT: 21

Science Supervisors Technical Skills Inventory
CIJE: 0 RIE: 1 CAT: 21

Science Supervisory Style Inventory (Peruzzi)
CIJE: 0 RIE: 1 CAT: 21

Science Support Scale
CIJE: 2 RIE: 1 CAT: 21

Science Talent Search
CIJE: 5 RIE: 0 CAT: 20
SN See also "Westinghouse Science Talent Search"

Science Talk (Newsletter)
CIJE: 0 RIE: 1 CAT: 22

Science Talks
CIJE: 0 RIE: 1 CAT: 20

Science Teacher Education Project
CIJE: 6 RIE: 9 CAT: 19

Science Teacher Inventory of Need
CIJE: 2 RIE: 1 CAT: 21

Science Teacher Observation Rating Form (Oberlin)
CIJE: 1 RIE: 0 CAT: 21

Science Teachers Adaptable Curriculum
CIJE: 0 RIE: 1 CAT: 03

Science Teachers as Research Scientists Program
CIJE: 0 RIE: 1 CAT: 19
UF STARS Program MO

Science Teachers Network
CIJE: 0 RIE: 1 CAT: 19

Science Teaching Equipment Development Program
CIJE: 0 RIE: 1 CAT: 19

Science Teaching Observation Instrument
CIJE: 0 RIE: 1 CAT: 21

Science Teaching Observation Schedule
CIJE: 4 RIE: 0 CAT: 21

Science Teaching Opinion Survey (Golmon)
CIJE: 0 RIE: 1 CAT: 21

Science Teaching State Trait Anxiety Inventory
CIJE: 0 RIE: 1 CAT: 21

Science Technology and Society Courses
CIJE: 38 RIE: 13 CAT: 03

Science Technology Relationship
CIJE: 1 RIE: 0 CAT: 20
UF Technology and Science

Science Test of Educational Progress
CIJE: 0 RIE: 1 CAT: 21

Science Writing
CIJE: 61 RIE: 19 CAT: 20

UF Scientific Writing

SciencePlus Program (ASCP)
CIJE: 0 RIE: 3 CAT: 19
SN ASCP = Atlantic Science Curriculum Project

ScienceVision (Computer Program)
CIJE: 0 RIE: 1 CAT: 04

Scientific American
CIJE: 3 RIE: 3 CAT: 22

Scientific Attitude Inventory
CIJE: 3 RIE: 2 CAT: 21

Scientific Computer Programs
CIJE: 0 RIE: 1 CAT: 04

Scientific Controversy
CIJE: 9 RIE: 0 CAT: 20

Scientific Curiosity Inventory
CIJE: 1 RIE: 0 CAT: 21

Scientific Essays
CIJE: 4 RIE: 2 CAT: 16

Scientific Expeditions
CIJE: 1 RIE: 1 CAT: 20

Scientific Freedom
CIJE: 5 RIE: 0 CAT: 20

Scientific Management
CIJE: 10 RIE: 8 CAT: 15

Scientific Manpower Commission
CIJE: 0 RIE: 6 CAT: 17

Scientific Notation
CIJE: 6 RIE: 3 CAT: 15

Scientific Research Inst Probs Higher Sch (USSR)
CIJE: 0 RIE: 1 CAT: 17

Scientific Resources Incorporated
CIJE: 0 RIE: 1 CAT: 17

Scientific Revolution
CIJE: 9 RIE: 4 CAT: 12

Scientific Systems
CIJE: 0 RIE: 1 CAT: 20

Scientific Theories
CIJE: 17 RIE: 6 CAT: 20

Scientific Theory Profile
CIJE: 0 RIE: 1 CAT: 15

Scientific Thinking
CIJE: 17 RIE: 5 CAT: 20

Scientific Thinking and Research Skill Test
CIJE: 0 RIE: 1 CAT: 21

Scientific Writing
USE Science Writing

Scientificity of Agriculture Test
CIJE: 1 RIE: 0 CAT: 21

Scientization
CIJE: 0 RIE: 1 CAT: 20

SCILSE Program
CIJE: 0 RIE: 1 CAT: 19

SciMate
CIJE: 0 RIE: 1 CAT: 04

Scintillation Counters
CIJE: 1 RIE: 0 CAT: 04

Scipione McDaniel Paradigm
CIJE: 0 RIE: 1 CAT: 15

SCISEARCH
CIJE: 6 RIE: 1 CAT: 04

Scleroderma
CIJE: 1 RIE: 0 CAT: 11

Scoggin Memorial Collections
CIJE: 1 RIE: 0 CAT: 16

Scoliosis
CIJE: 7 RIE: 11 CAT: 11

Scoliosis Association Inc
CIJE: 0 RIE: 1 CAT: 17

SCOLT
USE Southern Conference on Language Teaching

Scooters (for Disabled)
CIJE: 0 RIE: 1 CAT: 04

Scope and Sequence
CIJE: 2 RIE: 14 CAT: 03
SN The horizontal (scope) and vertical (sequence) organization of curriculum content, i.e., structuring what is taught against when it's taught

SCOPE Outdoor Learning Laboratories
CIJE: 0 RIE: 5 CAT: 17

SCOPE Program
CIJE: 1 RIE: 2 CAT: 19

SCOPE Project (Gallaudet Coll and NTID)
USE Systematic Collaborative Outreach Project Effort

Scope Sequence and Coordination
CIJE: 7 RIE: 5 CAT: 19
SN Project of the National Science Teachers Association

SCOPE Tests
USE Standardized Curriculum Oriented Pupil Evaluation

Scopes Trial
CIJE: 10 RIE: 4 CAT: 12

SCORE ACE Program
CIJE: 0 RIE: 1 CAT: 19

Score Distribution
CIJE: 0 RIE: 3 CAT: 21

Score for College (Program)
CIJE: 0 RIE: 1 CAT: 19

Score Groups
CIJE: 0 RIE: 1 CAT: 21

Score Stability
CIJE: 0 RIE: 2 CAT: 21
UF Test Score Stability

Score Variation
CIJE: 0 RIE: 5 CAT: 21
SN See also "Test Score Variance"

Scorekeeping
CIJE: 0 RIE: 1 CAT: 16

Scoring Drift
USE Drift (Scoring)

Scoring High on the California Achievement Tests
CIJE: 0 RIE: 1 CAT: 21

Scoring Rubrics
CIJE: 0 RIE: 1 CAT: 21

Scorsese (Martin)
CIJE: 0 RIE: 1 CAT: 18

Scotch Irish Americans
CIJE: 0 RIE: 1 CAT: 08

Scotland
CIJE: 510 RIE: 309 CAT: 07

Scotland (Edinburgh)
CIJE: 17 RIE: 3 CAT: 07

Scotland (Glasgow)
CIJE: 17 RIE: 6 CAT: 07

Scotland (Lothian Region)
CIJE: 1 RIE: 2 CAT: 07

SCOTS Schedule
USE System Classroom Observation Teaching Strategies

Scott (Fred Newton)
CIJE: 3 RIE: 1 CAT: 18

Scott Foresman Achievement Test Battery
CIJE: 0 RIE: 1 CAT: 21

Scott Foresman Basal Series
CIJE: 0 RIE: 6 CAT: 22

Scott Foresman Company
CIJE: 0 RIE: 5 CAT: 17

Scott Value Scales
CIJE: 0 RIE: 1 CAT: 21

Scottish Action Plan
CIJE: 0 RIE: 1 CAT: 19

Scottish Americans
CIJE: 0 RIE: 3 CAT: 08

Scottish Certificate of Education
CIJE: 3 RIE: 1 CAT: 16

Scottish Computers in Schools Project
CIJE: 1 RIE: 0 CAT: 19

Scottish Council for Educational Technology
CIJE: 1 RIE: 2 CAT: 17

Scottish Council for Research in Education
CIJE: 3 RIE: 11 CAT: 17
SN See also "SCRE..."

Scottish Discussion Skills Project
USE Discussion Skills Project (Scotland)

Scottish Education Department
CIJE: 2 RIE: 2 CAT: 17

Scottish Environmental Education Council
CIJE: 0 RIE: 1 CAT: 17

Scottish Integrated Science
CIJE: 3 RIE: 2 CAT: 19

Scottish Integrated Science Scheme
CIJE: 1 RIE: 0 CAT: 03

Scottish Mathematics Group
CIJE: 1 RIE: 0 CAT: 17

Scottish Microelectronics Development Programme
CIJE: 0 RIE: 0 CAT: 19

Scottish Pupil Profile Project
CIJE: 0 RIE: 1 CAT: 19

Scottish Science Project
CIJE: 1 RIE: 1 CAT: 19

Scottish Vocational Education Council
CIJE: 0 RIE: 0 CAT: 17
SN See also "National Certificate (Scotland)"

Scottish Wider Access Program
CIJE: 0 RIE: 3 CAT: 19
UF SWAP Program (Scotland)

Scottish Young Peoples Survey
CIJE: 0 RIE: 1 CAT: 21

Scottsdale Adult Learning Center AZ
CIJE: 0 RIE: 1 CAT: 17

Scottsdale Community College AZ
CIJE: 2 RIE: 0 CAT: 17

Scottsdale High School AZ
CIJE: 1 RIE: 0 CAT: 17

Scottsdale Public Library AZ
CIJE: 1 RIE: 0 CAT: 17

Scottsdale Unified School District AZ
CIJE: 0 RIE: 2 CAT: 17

Scouting
CIJE: 5 RIE: 6 CAT: 16

Scoutmasters
CIJE: 0 RIE: 1 CAT: 10

Scrambled Sentence Test (Costin)
CIJE: 2 RIE: 0 CAT: 21

Scranton Report
CIJE: 3 RIE: 0 CAT: 22

Scranton State School for the Deaf PA
CIJE: 0 RIE: 1 CAT: 17

SCRE Profile Assessment System
CIJE: 0 RIE: 1 CAT: 21

Scree Test
CIJE: 11 RIE: 5 CAT: 21

Screen Education Project
CIJE: 1 RIE: 0 CAT: 19

Screen Printing
CIJE: 7 RIE: 2 CAT: 20

Screen Text
CIJE: 1 RIE: 2 CAT: 20

Screening Assessment for Gifted Elem Stdts Primary
USE SAGES P (Johnsen and Corn)

Screening Procedures
CIJE: 21 RIE: 34 CAT: 15

Screening Programs
CIJE: 5 RIE: 25 CAT: 19

Screening Test Auditory Comprehension Language
CIJE: 1 RIE: 0 CAT: 21

Screening Test of Academic Readiness
CIJE: 7 RIE: 0 CAT: 21

Screening Test of Adolescent Language
CIJE: 2 RIE: 0 CAT: 21

Screening Units
CIJE: 1 RIE: 0 CAT: 05

Screenplays
CIJE: 6 RIE: 2 CAT: 16

Screenwriters
CIJE: 4 RIE: 4 CAT: 09

Screws
CIJE: 0 RIE: 2 CAT: 04

Scripps (E W)
CIJE: 0 RIE: 3 CAT: 18

Scripps College CA
CIJE: 2 RIE: 7 CAT: 17

SCRIPSIT
CIJE: 1 RIE: 1 CAT: 04
UF SuperSCRIPSIT

Scriptotherapy
CIJE: 0 RIE: 1 CAT: 11

Scripts (Computers)
USE Computer Scripts

Scripts (Knowledge Structures)
CIJE: 18 RIE: 25 CAT: 11

Scriven (R C)
CIJE: 1 RIE: 2 CAT: 18

Scrubbers
CIJE: 3 RIE: 2 CAT: 04

SDS 940 Computer System
CIJE: 0 RIE: 1 CAT: 04

Sea Farming
CIJE: 1 RIE: 0 CAT: 09

Sea Grant Program
CIJE: 4 RIE: 31 CAT: 19

Sea Islands
CIJE: 6 RIE: 0 CAT: 07
SN See also "South Carolina (Sea Islands)"

Sea Lamprey
CIJE: 0 RIE: 1 CAT: 20

Sea Shell Study
USE Seashells

Sea Turtles
CIJE: 0 RIE: 2 CAT: 20

Seabees
CIJE: 0 RIE: 1 CAT: 17

Seafarers Education Service
CIJE: 0 RIE: 1 CAT: 17

Seafarers International Union
CIJE: 2 RIE: 0 CAT: 17

Seaford School District DE
CIJE: 0 RIE: 3 CAT: 17

Seals (Animals)
CIJE: 3 RIE: 1 CAT: 20

Seals (Colleges)
USE College Seals

Seals (John Henry)
CIJE: 0 RIE: 1 CAT: 18

Seals (Mechanics)
CIJE: 0 RIE: 1 CAT: 04

Seals (Printing)
CIJE: 0 RIE: 2 CAT: 16

Seals Decision
CIJE: 0 RIE: 0 CAT: 14

Sealth (Chief)
CIJE: 0 RIE: 1 CAT: 18

Seams (Clothing)
CIJE: 0 RIE: 1 CAT: 16

Seaports
CIJE: 0 RIE: 0 CAT: 05

SEARCH (Silver and Hagan)
CIJE: 0 RIE: 1 CAT: 21

Search and Rescue Management
CIJE: 0 RIE: 1 CAT: 16

Search and Rescue Missions
CIJE: 0 RIE: 2 CAT: 16

Search Battery (Silver et al)
CIJE: 0 RIE: 1 CAT: 21

Search Behavior
CIJE: 39 RIE: 11 CAT: 15

Search Commands
CIJE: 0 RIE: 3 CAT: 16

Search for Education Elevation and Knowledge NY
USE Project SEEK

Search for Solutions (Film Series)
CIJE: 0 RIE: 1 CAT: 22

Search Keys
CIJE: 8 RIE: 1 CAT: 15

Search Negotiation (Computer Science)
CIJE: 6 RIE: 13 CAT: 15

Search of Associative Memory
CIJE: 6 RIE: 0 CAT: 21

SEARCH Program
USE Statewide Education Activities Rural Colo Health

Search Warrants
CIJE: 1 RIE: 2 CAT: 14

Searches in Depth
CIJE: 0 RIE: 1 CAT: 15

Searching Eye
CIJE: 1 RIE: 0 CAT: 22

Searchlight
CIJE: 0 RIE: 14 CAT: 22

Searcy School District AR
CIJE: 0 RIE: 0 CAT: 17

Searle (Chris)
CIJE: 1 RIE: 0 CAT: 18

Searle (John)
CIJE: 1 RIE: 2 CAT: 18
SN "John R"

Searles MacPherson Social Studies Questionnaire
CIJE: 0 RIE: 1 CAT: 21

Sears (Paul B)
CIJE: 1 RIE: 0 CAT: 18

Sears (Peter)
CIJE: 1 RIE: 0 CAT: 18

Sears Aggression Scales
CIJE: 1 RIE: 0 CAT: 21

Sears List of Subject Headings
CIJE: 3 RIE: 3 CAT: 22

Sears Roebuck Foundation
CIJE: 0 RIE: 1 CAT: 17

Sears Self Concept Inventory
CIJE: 2 RIE: 3 CAT: 21

Seashells
CIJE: 1 RIE: 1 CAT: 20
UF Sea Shell Study; Shells (Sea Animals)

Seashore Ecology
CIJE: 1 RIE: 2 CAT: 20

Seashore Measures of Musical Talents
CIJE: 10 RIE: 2 CAT: 21

Seaside Health Education Conference OR
CIJE: 1 RIE: 1 CAT: 02

Season of Birth
CIJE: 6 RIE: 0 CAT: 16

Seasonal Affective Disorder
CIJE: 0 RIE: 1 CAT: 11
UF SAD (Disorder); Winter Depression

Seasonal Celebrations
CIJE: 3 RIE: 16 CAT: 12

Seasons
CIJE: 19 RIE: 15 CAT: 16

Seastrom (Victor)
CIJE: 1 RIE: 0 CAT: 18

Seat Occupancy
CIJE: 1 RIE: 0 CAT: 16

Seating Assignments
CIJE: 3 RIE: 3 CAT: 16

Seating Capacity
CIJE: 1 RIE: 0 CAT: 16

Seating Preferences
CIJE: 15 RIE: 5 CAT: 16

Seattle Algebra Test
CIJE: 0 RIE: 1 CAT: 21

Seattle Argus (Newspaper)
CIJE: 0 RIE: 1 CAT: 22

Seattle Central Community College WA
CIJE: 5 RIE: 1 CAT: 17

Seattle Community College District WA
CIJE: 0 RIE: 4 CAT: 17

Seattle Community College WA
CIJE: 4 RIE: 5 CAT: 17

Seattle Day Nursery Association WA
CIJE: 1 RIE: 0 CAT: 17

Seattle Denver Income Maintenance Experiment
CIJE: 0 RIE: 0 CAT: 19

Seattle Pacific College WA
CIJE: 1 RIE: 1 CAT: 17

Seattle Pacific University WA
CIJE: 2 RIE: 3 CAT: 17

Seattle Performance Appraisal Guide
CIJE: 0 RIE: 1 CAT: 21

Seattle Public Schools WA
CIJE: 14 RIE: 88 CAT: 17

Seattle University WA
CIJE: 4 RIE: 8 CAT: 17

Seatwork
CIJE: 12 RIE: 5 CAT: 03

Sebenta National Institute (Swaziland)
CIJE: 0 RIE: 1 CAT: 17

Sebestyen (Ouida)
CIJE: 0 RIE: 1 CAT: 18

Sechenov (Ivan Mikhailovich)
CIJE: 1 RIE: 0 CAT: 18

Seclusion
CIJE: 1 RIE: 1 CAT: 11
SN See also "Solitude"

Second Amendment
CIJE: 0 RIE: 1 CAT: 14

Second Art Assessment (1979)
CIJE: 0 RIE: 3 CAT: 21

Second Born
CIJE: 3 RIE: 2 CAT: 10

Second Career Occup Develop Assess
CIJE: 0 RIE: 0 CAT: 21

Second Careers
CIJE: 3 RIE: 11 CAT: 16

Second Chance Programs
CIJE: 2 RIE: 3 CAT: 19

Second Chance to Learn Course (England)
CIJE: 0 RIE: 1 CAT: 03

Second Citizenship Social Studies Assess (1976)
CIJE: 0 RIE: 3 CAT: 21

Second Class Mail
CIJE: 1 RIE: 2 CAT: 16

Second Grade Underachievers Program
CIJE: 0 RIE: 1 CAT: 19

Second Hand Tobacco Smoke
USE Environmental Tobacco Smoke

Second Homes
CIJE: 1 RIE: 2 CAT: 05

Second International Mathematics Study
CIJE: 35 RIE: 47 CAT: 22
UF IEA Mathematics Study (2d); International Mathematics Study (IEA 2d); SIMS (IEA)

Second International Science Study
CIJE: 37 RIE: 15 CAT: 22
UF IEA Science Study (2d); International Science Study (IEA 2d); SISS (IEA)

Second Literature Third Reading Assessment (1980)
CIJE: 0 RIE: 11 CAT: 21

Second Mathematics Assessment (1978)
CIJE: 3 RIE: 7 CAT: 21

Second Mile Plan
CIJE: 1 RIE: 4 CAT: 19

Second Music Assessment (1979)
CIJE: 1 RIE: 3 CAT: 21

Second Order Effects
CIJE: 12 RIE: 7 CAT: 15
UF Second Order Factors

Second Order Factors
USE Second Order Effects

Second Reading Assessment (1975)
CIJE: 0 RIE: 0 CAT: 21

Second Science Assessment (1973)
CIJE: 0 RIE: 1 CAT: 21

Second Stage Sampling
CIJE: 1 RIE: 0 CAT: 21

Second Step Nursing Education
CIJE: 1 RIE: 2 CAT: 19

Second Step Violence Prevention Program
CIJE: 0 RIE: 4 CAT: 19

Second Writing Assessment (1974)
CIJE: 0 RIE: 0 CAT: 21

Secondary Amenorrhea
USE Amenorrhea

Secondary Analysis
CIJE: 33 RIE: 20 CAT: 15

Secondary Care
USE Acute Care

Secondary Credit Exchange
CIJE: 0 RIE: 9 CAT: 15

Secondary Developmental Reading Program (Ohio)
CIJE: 0 RIE: 2 CAT: 19
SN Former name of "Secondary Reading Program OH"

Secondary Education Act (Yugoslavia 1970)
CIJE: 0 RIE: 1 CAT: 14

Secondary Education Act 1963 (Netherlands)
CIJE: 0 RIE: 1 CAT: 14

Secondary Exploration of Technology
CIJE: 2 RIE: 3 CAT: 19

Secondary Ignition Circuits
CIJE: 0 RIE: 0 CAT: 20

Secondary Individualized Learning Center Program
CIJE: 0 RIE: 1 CAT: 19

Secondary Informal Reading Inventory
CIJE: 0 RIE: 1 CAT: 21

Secondary Level English Proficiency Test
CIJE: 1 RIE: 3 CAT: 21

Secondary Migration
CIJE: 1 RIE: 1 CAT: 16

Secondary Onomatopoeia
CIJE: 0 RIE: 1 CAT: 13

Secondary Postsecondary Interface Study
CIJE: 2 RIE: 0 CAT: 19

Secondary Postsecondary Transition Proj LD MN
USE LD Transition Project MN

Secondary Preventive Intervention
CIJE: 1 RIE: 2 CAT: 19

Secondary Reading Program OH
CIJE: 0 RIE: 1 CAT: 19
SN Formerly "Secondary Developmental Reading Program (Ohio)"

Secondary School Admission Test Board
CIJE: 0 RIE: 2 CAT: 17

Secondary School Development Program
CIJE: 0 RIE: 1 CAT: 19

Secondary School Experiential Learning Community
CIJE: 0 RIE: 1 CAT: 19

Secondary School Graduate Followup Prog for Deaf
CIJE: 0 RIE: 3 CAT: 19

Secondary School Improvement Program Survey
CIJE: 0 RIE: 1 CAT: 21
SN Full name: Secondary School Improvement Program Effective Schools Survey (SSIPESS)

Secondary School Math Curriculum Study
CIJE: 2 RIE: 2 CAT: 19

Secondary School Recognition Program
CIJE: 2 RIE: 6 CAT: 19

Secondary School Record
CIJE: 0 RIE: 1 CAT: 16

Secondary Schools Basic Skills Demo Assist Prog
CIJE: 0 RIE: 1 CAT: 19

Secondary Student Teacher Performance Profile
CIJE: 0 RIE: 1 CAT: 21

Secondary Task Method
CIJE: 0 RIE: 1 CAT: 15

Secondary Training for Alaskan Rural Students
CIJE: 0 RIE: 4 CAT: 03

Secondary Victimization
CIJE: 0 RIE: 1 CAT: 16

Secrecy
CIJE: 25 RIE: 6 CAT: 16

Secret Writing
CIJE: 0 RIE: 1 CAT: 15

Secretary of Education Recognition Program
CIJE: 0 RIE: 3 CAT: 19

Secretarys Comm on Achieving Necessary Skills
CIJE: 9 RIE: 7 CAT: 17

Section 143 Migrant Education Projects
USE Migrant Education Section 143 Projects

Section Pre Equating (Tests)
CIJE: 0 RIE: 2 CAT: 21

Sector Analysis
CIJE: 2 RIE: 8 CAT: 15

Secular Humanism
CIJE: 32 RIE: 13 CAT: 16
SN Philosophical orientation unrelated to the concept of God

Secularism
CIJE: 14 RIE: 6 CAT: 16

Securities and Exchange Commission
CIJE: 4 RIE: 4 CAT: 17

Securities Credit
CIJE: 0 RIE: 1 CAT: 16

Securities Industry
CIJE: 1 RIE: 2 CAT: 16

Security Blankets
CIJE: 3 RIE: 1 CAT: 11

Security Classifications
CIJE: 5 RIE: 2 CAT: 16

Security Employee Involvement and Training System
CIJE: 0 RIE: 1 CAT: 15

Security Index Inventory (Maslow)
CIJE: 0 RIE: 1 CAT: 21

Security of Attachment
CIJE: 8 RIE: 1 CAT: 11
UF Attachment Security

Security of Data
USE Data Security

Sedimentology
CIJE: 8 RIE: 0 CAT: 20

Sedition
CIJE: 3 RIE: 5 CAT: 14

Sedlacek (William E)
CIJE: 1 RIE: 0 CAT: 18

SEDMS
USE Special Education Data Management System

Sedro Woolley Project
CIJE: 0 RIE: 11 CAT: 19

Seductive Behavior
CIJE: 3 RIE: 0 CAT: 11

Seebohm Report
CIJE: 0 RIE: 1 CAT: 22

Seed (Patricia)
CIJE: 0 RIE: 1 CAT: 18

Seed Preservation
CIJE: 0 RIE: 1 CAT: 20

Seed Production and Distribution Competencies
CIJE: 0 RIE: 2 CAT: 21

Seedig
CIJE: 0 RIE: 1 CAT: 13

Seeds
CIJE: 5 RIE: 7 CAT: 20

SEEDS Project (NASA)
USE Space Exposed Experiment Developed for Students

SEEK Program NY
USE Project SEEK

SEER Technique
CIJE: 2 RIE: 0 CAT: 15

SEESAW
CIJE: 0 RIE: 1 CAT: 04

Segal (Edith)
CIJE: 1 RIE: 0 CAT: 18

Segal (Erich)
CIJE: 1 RIE: 0 CAT: 18

Segment Three (NBC News)
CIJE: 0 RIE: 1 CAT: 22

Segmentals (Phonology)
CIJE: 10 RIE: 9 CAT: 13
UF Autosegmental Phonology

Segmentation (Verbal)
CIJE: 4 RIE: 7 CAT: 13

Segmentation Skills
CIJE: 16 RIE: 5 CAT: 11

Segmented Print (Reading)
CIJE: 1 RIE: 2 CAT: 15

Segments Research
CIJE: 0 RIE: 1 CAT: 15

Segovia (Andres)
CIJE: 0 RIE: 0 CAT: 18

Segraves v California
CIJE: 2 RIE: 0 CAT: 14

Seguin (Edouard O)
CIJE: 1 RIE: 2 CAT: 18

Seguin Form Board
CIJE: 0 RIE: 1 CAT: 21

Seiches
CIJE: 1 RIE: 0 CAT: 20

SEID
USE Self Employment Investment Demonstration

Seiden (Don)
CIJE: 1 RIE: 0 CAT: 18

SEIG Awards AK
USE State Educational Incentive Grant Program AK

SEINE Computer Program
CIJE: 0 RIE: 1 CAT: 04

Seismological Society of America
CIJE: 0 RIE: 1 CAT: 17

Seizure Assimilation for Educators
USE Project SAFE

Sejour (Victor)
CIJE: 1 RIE: 0 CAT: 18

Selden (Samuel)
CIJE: 1 RIE: 0 CAT: 18

Select Commission Immigration Refugee Policy
CIJE: 0 RIE: 3 CAT: 17

SELECT Programing Language
CIJE: 1 RIE: 0 CAT: 04

Selectavision
CIJE: 1 RIE: 0 CAT: 04

Selection Theory
CIJE: 4 RIE: 2 CAT: 15

Selective Attention
CIJE: 39 RIE: 22 CAT: 16

Selective Attention Test (Wahl)
CIJE: 0 RIE: 1 CAT: 21

Selective Enrichment
CIJE: 0 RIE: 1 CAT: 15

Selective Learning
CIJE: 0 RIE: 1 CAT: 11

Selective Listing in Combinations
CIJE: 1 RIE: 0 CAT: 15

Selective Reenlistment Bonus
CIJE: 0 RIE: 1 CAT: 16

Selective Service
CIJE: 12 RIE: 18 CAT: 14

Selective Testing
CIJE: 2 RIE: 0 CAT: 21

Selenium
CIJE: 1 RIE: 0 CAT: 20

Self Adapted Testing
CIJE: 6 RIE: 7 CAT: 21
SN Testing that allows the examinees to choose the difficulty levels of their items on a computer-based test — see also "Restricted Self Adapted Testing"

Self Adaptors
CIJE: 0 RIE: 1 CAT: 16

Self Administered Student Profile
CIJE: 1 RIE: 0 CAT: 21

Self Advancement Via Education
CIJE: 1 RIE: 0 CAT: 19

Self Advocacy
CIJE: 12 RIE: 28 CAT: 16

Self Affirmation
CIJE: 2 RIE: 3 CAT: 11

Self Allocation
CIJE: 1 RIE: 0 CAT: 15

Self Appraisal Instrument (School Management Inst)
CIJE: 0 RIE: 2 CAT: 21

Self Appraisal Inventory
CIJE: 1 RIE: 4 CAT: 21

Self Appraisal Scale (Davidson)
CIJE: 0 RIE: 1 CAT: 21

Self Assessment Oral Language Proficiency Survey
CIJE: 0 RIE: 1 CAT: 21

Self Assessment Questionnaire
CIJE: 1 RIE: 2 CAT: 21

Self Awareness
CIJE: 54 RIE: 77 CAT: 16

Self Blame
CIJE: 2 RIE: 4 CAT: 11
SN See also the Descriptor "Guilt"

Self Care
CIJE: 16 RIE: 7 CAT: 11

Self Censorship
CIJE: 6 RIE: 2 CAT: 14

Self Charting
CIJE: 2 RIE: 0 CAT: 15

Self Compassion
CIJE: 0 RIE: 1 CAT: 11

Self Completion Theory
CIJE: 0 RIE: 1 CAT: 15

Self Concept as a Learner Scale (Waesten)
CIJE: 2 RIE: 3 CAT: 21

Self Concept as a Writer Questionnaire
CIJE: 0 RIE: 1 CAT: 21

Self Concept Enhancing Activities
CIJE: 0 RIE: 2 CAT: 11

Self Concept Model (Shavelson)
CIJE: 0 RIE: 1 CAT: 15
UF Hierarchical Facet Model of Self Concept

Self Concept of Ability Scale (Brookover)
CIJE: 8 RIE: 11 CAT: 21

Self Concept of Academic Ability Test
CIJE: 1 RIE: 1 CAT: 21

Self Concept Scale
CIJE: 6 RIE: 4 CAT: 21

Self Concept Scale for Children
CIJE: 1 RIE: 1 CAT: 21
UF Martinek Zaichkowsky Self Concept Scale Children

Self Conscious Affect and Attribution Inventory
CIJE: 0 RIE: 0 CAT: 21

Self Consciousness
CIJE: 14 RIE: 5 CAT: 11

Self Consciousness Scale (Fenigstein et al)
CIJE: 6 RIE: 1 CAT: 21

Self Consistency Theory
CIJE: 0 RIE: 1 CAT: 11

Self Contained Academic Learning Environment
CIJE: 1 RIE: 0 CAT: 05

Self Contained Open Classrooms
CIJE: 1 RIE: 0 CAT: 05

Self Control Rating Scale (Kendall Wilcox)
CIJE: 2 RIE: 1 CAT: 21

Self Controlled Interactive Learning Systems
CIJE: 1 RIE: 2 CAT: 15

Self Correction
CIJE: 12 RIE: 3 CAT: 15

Self Correction Strategies
CIJE: 5 RIE: 2 CAT: 15

Self Counseling
CIJE: 0 RIE: 1 CAT: 11
SN See also "Rational Self Counseling"

Self Defeating Behavior
CIJE: 3 RIE: 3 CAT: 11

Self Defense
CIJE: 13 RIE: 5 CAT: 16

Self Definition
CIJE: 5 RIE: 4 CAT: 11

Self Description Blank
CIJE: 1 RIE: 0 CAT: 21

Self Description Form
CIJE: 0 RIE: 1 CAT: 21

Self Description Inventory
CIJE: 5 RIE: 1 CAT: 21

Self Description Questionnaire
CIJE: 20 RIE: 16 CAT: 21

Self Description Questionnaire II
CIJE: 1 RIE: 3 CAT: 21

Self Description Questionnaire III
CIJE: 3 RIE: 6 CAT: 21

Self Descriptive Exploratory Research Inventory
CIJE: 0 RIE: 1 CAT: 21

Self Directed Career Programs
CIJE: 0 RIE: 1 CAT: 19

Self Directed Learning Readiness Scale
CIJE: 10 RIE: 10 CAT: 21

Self Directed Questioning
CIJE: 1 RIE: 2 CAT: 11

Self Directed Rating Scale
CIJE: 1 RIE: 0 CAT: 21

Self Directed Search
CIJE: 85 RIE: 26 CAT: 21

Self Directed Search Form E
CIJE: 4 RIE: 1 CAT: 21

Self Direction
CIJE: 5 RIE: 1 CAT: 16

Self Disclosing Coping Model
CIJE: 1 RIE: 0 CAT: 15

Self Disclosure Inventory for Adolescents (West)
CIJE: 2 RIE: 0 CAT: 21

Self Disclosure Questionnaire
CIJE: 2 RIE: 1 CAT: 21

Self Disclosure Test Assumptions Indic Negativism
CIJE: 1 RIE: 0 CAT: 21

Self Discrepancies
CIJE: 0 RIE: 1 CAT: 11

Self Disparaging Humor
CIJE: 3 RIE: 1 CAT: 16

Self Efficacy for Computer Technologies
CIJE: 0 RIE: 1 CAT: 21

Self Efficacy Scale (Sherer et al)
CIJE: 0 RIE: 1 CAT: 21

Self Employment Investment Demonstration
CIJE: 0 RIE: 1 CAT: 19
UF SEID

Self Empowerment
CIJE: 17 RIE: 11 CAT: 11

Self Esteem A Family Affair (Program)
CIJE: 1 RIE: 1 CAT: 19

Self Esteem Inventory
CIJE: 8 RIE: 3 CAT: 21

Self Evaluation Maintenance Model
CIJE: 0 RIE: 2 CAT: 15

Self Evaluation Scale
CIJE: 0 RIE: 2 CAT: 21

Self Examinations (Physical)
CIJE: 5 RIE: 2 CAT: 11

Self Formative Evaluation
CIJE: 0 RIE: 1 CAT: 15

Self Fulfillment
CIJE: 1 RIE: 0 CAT: 11

Self Gain
CIJE: 1 RIE: 1 CAT: 11

Self Gratification
CIJE: 3 RIE: 1 CAT: 11

Self Handicapping
CIJE: 0 RIE: 3 CAT: 11

Self Help Enterprises
CIJE: 1 RIE: 2 CAT: 17

Self Help Facilities
CIJE: 1 RIE: 2 CAT: 05

SELF HELP Program MD
CIJE: 0 RIE: 1 CAT: 19
UF Project SELF HELP MD

Self Image Evaluation (Deschin)
CIJE: 0 RIE: 1 CAT: 21

Self Image Questionnaire for Young Adolescents
CIJE: 0 RIE: 1 CAT: 21

Self Implosion Therapy
CIJE: 0 RIE: 1 CAT: 16

Self Imposed Study Program
CIJE: 1 RIE: 0 CAT: 21

Self Insight Test
CIJE: 2 RIE: 0 CAT: 21

Self Instructional Language Programs
CIJE: 3 RIE: 0 CAT: 19
SN See also "National Assn of Self Instructional Language Prog"

Self Instructional Media Assisted Learning Unit
CIJE: 2 RIE: 0 CAT: 15

Self Insurance
CIJE: 13 RIE: 4 CAT: 14
UF Self Insurance Programs (Organizations)

Self Insurance Programs (Organizations)
USE Self Insurance

Self Interest
CIJE: 12 RIE: 1 CAT: 11

Self Knowledge Development Theory
CIJE: 0 RIE: 1 CAT: 15

Self Knowledge Inventory Lifelong Learning Strateg
CIJE: 0 RIE: 1 CAT: 21

Self Management and Resistance Training Proj CA
USE Project SMART

Self Management and Responsibility Train Prog FL
CIJE: 0 RIE: 0 CAT: 19
UF SMART Program FL

Self Monitoring
CIJE: 158 RIE: 61 CAT: 11

Self Monitoring Negative Checklist
CIJE: 0 RIE: 1 CAT: 21

Self Monitoring Scales (Snyder)
CIJE: 5 RIE: 3 CAT: 21

Self Motivation Inventory
CIJE: 1 RIE: 1 CAT: 21

Self Observation
CIJE: 8 RIE: 4 CAT: 16

Self Observation Scale (Katzenmeyer and Stenner)
CIJE: 1 RIE: 3 CAT: 21

Self Occupational Congruence
USE Occupational Congruence

Self Paced Physics
CIJE: 0 RIE: 3 CAT: 15

Self Perception in School Inventory (Albert)
CIJE: 0 RIE: 2 CAT: 21

Self Perception Inventory
CIJE: 3 RIE: 4 CAT: 21

Self Perception Theory
CIJE: 5 RIE: 1 CAT: 15

Self Planned Learning
CIJE: 3 RIE: 3 CAT: 15

Self Prediction
CIJE: 1 RIE: 2 CAT: 16

Self Presentations
CIJE: 13 RIE: 11 CAT: 11

Self Processor
CIJE: 0 RIE: 3 CAT: 16

Self Protection
CIJE: 5 RIE: 5 CAT: 11

Self Protection Courses
CIJE: 1 RIE: 1 CAT: 03

Self Psychology
CIJE: 4 RIE: 3 CAT: 11

Self Q Interviewing Technique
CIJE: 0 RIE: 1 CAT: 15

Self Questioning Techniques
CIJE: 5 RIE: 1 CAT: 15
UF Self Questioning Training

Self Questioning Training
USE Self Questioning Techniques

Self Ranking Inventory (Purkey)
CIJE: 0 RIE: 1 CAT: 21

Self Rating of Mastery Schedule
CIJE: 0 RIE: 1 CAT: 21

Self Rating Scale (Hope)
CIJE: 0 RIE: 1 CAT: 21

Self Recognition
CIJE: 13 RIE: 2 CAT: 11

Self Recordings (Audiotape)
CIJE: 0 RIE: 1 CAT: 16

Self Reference (Language)
CIJE: 4 RIE: 6 CAT: 13

Self Reference (Psychology)
CIJE: 3 RIE: 5 CAT: 11

Self Referent Q Sort
CIJE: 0 RIE: 1 CAT: 21

Self Referent Questionnaire (Gezi)
CIJE: 0 RIE: 1 CAT: 21

Self Referral
CIJE: 3 RIE: 0 CAT: 11

Self Reflection
CIJE: 3 RIE: 1 CAT: 11

Self Regulated Learning
CIJE: 5 RIE: 9 CAT: 15

Self Regulation
CIJE: 90 RIE: 50 CAT: 16

Self Regulation (Groups)
CIJE: 7 RIE: 3 CAT: 16

Self Regulation (Industry)
CIJE: 4 RIE: 1 CAT: 14

Self Relevance
CIJE: 1 RIE: 1 CAT: 11

Self Reliance
CIJE: 16 RIE: 11 CAT: 11

Self Renewal
CIJE: 0 RIE: 1 CAT: 16

Self Report Measures
CIJE: 107 RIE: 97 CAT: 21

Self Revitalization
CIJE: 0 RIE: 0 CAT: 11

Self Righteousness
CIJE: 1 RIE: 1 CAT: 11

Self Righteousness Questionnaire
CIJE: 0 RIE: 1 CAT: 21

Self Schedule System
CIJE: 2 RIE: 3 CAT: 15

Self Schemas
CIJE: 4 RIE: 4 CAT: 11

Self Scoring Method
CIJE: 2 RIE: 1 CAT: 21

Self Scoring Tests
CIJE: 2 RIE: 4 CAT: 21

Self Selection (Reading)
CIJE: 7 RIE: 3 CAT: 16

Self Selection Bias
CIJE: 10 RIE: 2 CAT: 21

Self Serving Effect
CIJE: 3 RIE: 1 CAT: 11

Self Social Symbols Tasks
CIJE: 0 RIE: 6 CAT: 21

Self Stability
CIJE: 2 RIE: 0 CAT: 11

Self Statement Modification
CIJE: 0 RIE: 1 CAT: 11

Self Statements
CIJE: 4 RIE: 1 CAT: 11

Self Stimulation
CIJE: 26 RIE: 0 CAT: 16

Self Sufficiency
CIJE: 15 RIE: 20 CAT: 11

Self Sufficient Living
CIJE: 0 RIE: 4 CAT: 11

Self Supervision
CIJE: 0 RIE: 2 CAT: 15

Self Talk
CIJE: 5 RIE: 5 CAT: 11

Self Training and Evaluation Process
CIJE: 2 RIE: 0 CAT: 15

Self Verbalization
CIJE: 26 RIE: 3 CAT: 13

Selinsgrove Area School District PA
CIJE: 0 RIE: 1 CAT: 17

Selkirk College (Canada)
CIJE: 0 RIE: 1 CAT: 17

Selkirk High School NY
CIJE: 1 RIE: 0 CAT: 17

Selkup
CIJE: 0 RIE: 1 CAT: 13

Sellers Memorial Library
CIJE: 1 RIE: 0 CAT: 17

Semantic Abbreviation
CIJE: 1 RIE: 1 CAT: 13

Semantic Bootstrapping Hypothesis (Pinker)
CIJE: 1 RIE: 2 CAT: 15

Semantic Categories
CIJE: 14 RIE: 5 CAT: 13

Semantic Consensus Index (Kanungo and Dutta)
CIJE: 1 RIE: 0 CAT: 21

Semantic Contrasts
CIJE: 4 RIE: 1 CAT: 13

Semantic Differential for Sci Students (Ahlgren)
CIJE: 0 RIE: 2 CAT: 21

Semantic Differential Test for Language Attitudes
CIJE: 0 RIE: 3 CAT: 21

Semantic Differential Test of Teacher Attitudes
CIJE: 2 RIE: 1 CAT: 21

Semantic Elaboration
CIJE: 1 RIE: 1 CAT: 13

Semantic Encoding Hypothesis
CIJE: 4 RIE: 0 CAT: 15

Semantic Feature Analysis
CIJE: 3 RIE: 7 CAT: 13

Semantic Features
CIJE: 14 RIE: 8 CAT: 13

Semantic Generalization
CIJE: 1 RIE: 0 CAT: 13

Semantic Integration
CIJE: 6 RIE: 5 CAT: 13

Semantic Interaction Technique
CIJE: 0 RIE: 1 CAT: 15

Semantic Interference Effect
CIJE: 3 RIE: 1 CAT: 13

Semantic Mapping
CIJE: 40 RIE: 42 CAT: 13

Semantic Memory
CIJE: 25 RIE: 5 CAT: 11

Semantic Networks
CIJE: 6 RIE: 2 CAT: 13

Semantic Organizers
CIJE: 4 RIE: 3 CAT: 13

Semantic Potential Theory of Language
CIJE: 1 RIE: 0 CAT: 13

Semantic Priming
CIJE: 3 RIE: 3 CAT: 13

Semantic Relation Comprehension
CIJE: 1 RIE: 2 CAT: 13

Semantic Relation Test
CIJE: 0 RIE: 2 CAT: 21

Semantic Transformations
CIJE: 1 RIE: 1 CAT: 13

Semantic Webbing
CIJE: 13 RIE: 11 CAT: 13
UF Webbing (Semantic)

Semel Auditory Processing Program
CIJE: 1 RIE: 0 CAT: 19

Semi Independent Living Services
CIJE: 1 RIE: 0 CAT: 11

Semi Infinite Programs
CIJE: 0 RIE: 1 CAT: 15

Semiannual Admission
CIJE: 0 RIE: 1 CAT: 16

Semilingualism
CIJE: 0 RIE: 4 CAT: 13

Seminar Acquisition Latin Amer Library Materials
CIJE: 2 RIE: 1 CAT: 02

Seminar on Family Research 13th
CIJE: 1 RIE: 0 CAT: 02

Seminar on Manpower Policy and Program
CIJE: 0 RIE: 3 CAT: 02

Seminar on Wheels
CIJE: 0 RIE: 1 CAT: 03

Seminar Statistics State Vocational Rehabilitation
CIJE: 0 RIE: 1 CAT: 02

Seminarro Internacional Sobre la Educ Bilingue
CIJE: 0 RIE: 1 CAT: 02
UF International Seminar on Bilingual Education

Seminars for State Leaders Postsec Ed (ECS SHEEO)
CIJE: 0 RIE: 113 CAT: 02

Seminole (Tribe)
CIJE: 13 RIE: 15 CAT: 08

Seminole Community College FL
CIJE: 0 RIE: 6 CAT: 17

Seminole County School District FL
CIJE: 0 RIE: 12 CAT: 17

Seminole Junior College FL
CIJE: 0 RIE: 1 CAT: 17

Semiolinguistics
CIJE: 1 RIE: 1 CAT: 13

Semiparametric Estimation
CIJE: 0 RIE: 1 CAT: 15

Semiparametric Models
CIJE: 1 RIE: 0 CAT: 15

Semiprojective Scales of Institutional Evaluation
CIJE: 1 RIE: 0 CAT: 21

Semistandardized Regression Coefficient
CIJE: 1 RIE: 0 CAT: 21

Semmelweis University of Medicine (Hungary)
CIJE: 0 RIE: 0 CAT: 17

Semple (Jesse B)
CIJE: 1 RIE: 0 CAT: 18

Semprun (Jorge)
CIJE: 1 RIE: 0 CAT: 18

Senate
CIJE: 10 RIE: 29 CAT: 17

Senate Bill 1 (California 1968)
CIJE: 1 RIE: 0 CAT: 14

Senate Bill 28 (California 1967)
CIJE: 0 RIE: 1 CAT: 14

Senate Bill 140 (Ohio 1989)
CIJE: 0 RIE: 1 CAT: 14

Senate Bill 160 (California)
CIJE: 0 RIE: 2 CAT: 14

Senate Bill 249 (Oklahoma 1977)
CIJE: 0 RIE: 1 CAT: 14

Senate Bill 308 (Oklahoma 1981)
CIJE: 0 RIE: 1 CAT: 14

Senate Bill 354 (Oregon 1979)
CIJE: 0 RIE: 1 CAT: 14

Senate Bill 813 (California 1983)
CIJE: 2 RIE: 3 CAT: 14

Senate Bill 1225 (California 1983)
CIJE: 0 RIE: 1 CAT: 14

Senate Committee on Labor and Public Welfare
CIJE: 0 RIE: 2 CAT: 17

Senate Professional Association
CIJE: 0 RIE: 1 CAT: 17

Senate Select Committee on Campaign Practices
CIJE: 0 RIE: 1 CAT: 17

Senate Select Committee on Equal Educ Opportunity
CIJE: 0 RIE: 1 CAT: 17

Senate Select Committee on Indian Affairs
CIJE: 3 RIE: 7 CAT: 17

Senate Select Committee on Nutrition
CIJE: 0 RIE: 1 CAT: 17

Senate Subcommittee on Education
CIJE: 1 RIE: 2 CAT: 17

Senate Subcommittee on the Handicapped
CIJE: 0 RIE: 2 CAT: 17

Sendak (Maurice)
CIJE: 11 RIE: 1 CAT: 18

Sender (Ramon J)
CIJE: 1 RIE: 0 CAT: 18

Sender Freies Berlin
CIJE: 1 RIE: 0 CAT: 17

Seneca (Lucius Annaeus)
CIJE: 8 RIE: 0 CAT: 18

Seneca (Tribe)
CIJE: 9 RIE: 10 CAT: 08

Seneca College of Applied Arts and Technology ON
CIJE: 0 RIE: 1 CAT: 17

Senegal
CIJE: 33 RIE: 50 CAT: 07

Senegal (Dakar)
CIJE: 1 RIE: 4 CAT: 07

Senesh (Lawrence)
CIJE: 0 RIE: 1 CAT: 18

Senile Dementia
CIJE: 11 RIE: 6 CAT: 11
SN See also "Dementia"
UF Senility

Senility
USE Senile Dementia

Senior Adult Education Program
CIJE: 0 RIE: 1 CAT: 19

Senior Adult Volunteer Program MD
CIJE: 0 RIE: 0 CAT: 19

Senior Aide Volunteer Educators
CIJE: 0 RIE: 1 CAT: 19

Senior Citizen Centers
CIJE: 11 RIE: 5 CAT: 05

Senior Citizen Questionnaire
CIJE: 0 RIE: 1 CAT: 21

Senior Citizen School Volunteer Program PA
CIJE: 0 RIE: 1 CAT: 19

Senior Citizens Higher Education Act (Virginia)
CIJE: 1 RIE: 1 CAT: 14

Senior Classical League
CIJE: 1 RIE: 0 CAT: 17

Senior Colleague Advisory Network
CIJE: 0 RIE: 1 CAT: 19

Senior Colleges (Australia)
CIJE: 0 RIE: 1 CAT: 05

Senior Community Service Employment Program
CIJE: 1 RIE: 9 CAT: 19

Senior Community Service Project
CIJE: 2 RIE: 0 CAT: 19

Senior Companions Program
CIJE: 0 RIE: 1 CAT: 19

Senior Employment Program
CIJE: 0 RIE: 1 CAT: 19

Senior Executive Service
CIJE: 0 RIE: 2 CAT: 09

Senior High Assessment of Reading Proficiency
CIJE: 0 RIE: 0 CAT: 21

Senior High Assessment of Reading Progress
CIJE: 1 RIE: 0 CAT: 21

Senior High Assessment Skills Written Composition
CIJE: 0 RIE: 0 CAT: 21

Senior Intensified Program
CIJE: 2 RIE: 0 CAT: 19

Senior Motivators in Learning Education Services
CIJE: 0 RIE: 1 CAT: 19
UF SMILES Program UT

Senior Questionnaire
CIJE: 0 RIE: 1 CAT: 21

Senior Teaching Seniors Project
CIJE: 0 RIE: 2 CAT: 19

Seniors Teaching Seniors Project
CIJE: 0 RIE: 1 CAT: 19

Senoufo
CIJE: 0 RIE: 1 CAT: 13

Sensation Seeking
CIJE: 10 RIE: 3 CAT: 11

Sensation Seeking Scale
CIJE: 20 RIE: 0 CAT: 21

Sensationalism
CIJE: 3 RIE: 1 CAT: 16

Sense Making Approach
CIJE: 4 RIE: 6 CAT: 15

Sense of Autonomy Scale
CIJE: 0 RIE: 1 CAT: 21

Sense of Coherence
CIJE: 1 RIE: 1 CAT: 11

Sense of Community
CIJE: 7 RIE: 4 CAT: 11

Sense of Place
CIJE: 6 RIE: 2 CAT: 11

Sense of Power Scale (Moeller)
CIJE: 1 RIE: 0 CAT: 21

Sense of Reality
USE Perceived Reality

Sense Organs
CIJE: 3 RIE: 2 CAT: 11

Sensible Technology Assessment Research
CIJE: 0 RIE: 1 CAT: 15

Sensitivity Analysis
CIJE: 22 RIE: 7 CAT: 15

Sensitivity Training Impact Model
CIJE: 0 RIE: 1 CAT: 15

Sensitization (Language Learning)
CIJE: 0 RIE: 1 CAT: 13

Sensorimotor Cognitive Assessment Scale
CIJE: 0 RIE: 1 CAT: 21

Sensorimotor Play
CIJE: 0 RIE: 1 CAT: 16
UF Sensory Motor Play

Sensory Dimensional Analysis
CIJE: 1 RIE: 0 CAT: 21

Sensory Metaphors
CIJE: 1 RIE: 1 CAT: 13

Sensory Motor Play
USE Sensorimotor Play

Sensory Perceptual Exam
CIJE: 0 RIE: 1 CAT: 21

Sensory Qualities
CIJE: 1 RIE: 1 CAT: 11

Sensory Quotient Test (Cappon et al)
CIJE: 1 RIE: 0 CAT: 21

Sensory Threshold Determination
CIJE: 1 RIE: 0 CAT: 21

Sentence Completion Form
CIJE: 2 RIE: 1 CAT: 21

Sentence Completion Method
CIJE: 5 RIE: 2 CAT: 21

Sentence Completion Test
CIJE: 8 RIE: 11 CAT: 21

Sentence Comprehension Test (Wheldall et al)
CIJE: 1 RIE: 0 CAT: 21

Sentence Fragments
CIJE: 3 RIE: 3 CAT: 13

Sentence Imitation Test (Ammon and Ammon)
CIJE: 1 RIE: 0 CAT: 21

Sentence Interpretation Test (Little)
CIJE: 0 RIE: 1 CAT: 21

Sentence Repetition Task (Anastasiow and Hanes)
CIJE: 0 RIE: 2 CAT: 21

Sentence Synthesizing Program
CIJE: 0 RIE: 1 CAT: 19

Sentence Verification
CIJE: 14 RIE: 1 CAT: 13

Sentencecraft Program
CIJE: 0 RIE: 1 CAT: 19

Seoul National University (South Korea)
CIJE: 0 RIE: 1 CAT: 17

Separate Peace
CIJE: 4 RIE: 4 CAT: 22

Separate Schools (Canada)
CIJE: 0 RIE: 1 CAT: 05

Separation of Powers
CIJE: 8 RIE: 5 CAT: 14

Separation of Variables Concept
CIJE: 1 RIE: 0 CAT: 15

Separatism
CIJE: 11 RIE: 10 CAT: 16

Sephardic Jews
CIJE: 7 RIE: 9 CAT: 08

September (Month)
CIJE: 2 RIE: 0 CAT: 16

Septic Systems
CIJE: 1 RIE: 2 CAT: 20

Sequence Rules (Chemical Nomenclature)
CIJE: 1 RIE: 0 CAT: 15

Sequenced Inventory of Communication Development
CIJE: 6 RIE: 1 CAT: 21

Sequenced Transition to Educ in the Public Schls
USE Project STEPS KY

Sequences (Mathematics)
CIJE: 59 RIE: 13 CAT: 20

Sequencing Skills
CIJE: 10 RIE: 3 CAT: 15

Sequential Analysis
CIJE: 28 RIE: 10 CAT: 15

Sequential Analysis (Wald)
CIJE: 1 RIE: 0 CAT: 21

Sequential Contiguity
CIJE: 3 RIE: 1 CAT: 20

Sequential Data Analysis
CIJE: 4 RIE: 1 CAT: 21

Sequential Estimation
CIJE: 2 RIE: 1 CAT: 21

Sequential Memory
CIJE: 7 RIE: 4 CAT: 11

Sequential Probability Ratio Test (Wald)
CIJE: 2 RIE: 3 CAT: 21

Sequential Processing
CIJE: 18 RIE: 5 CAT: 11

Sequential Requests
CIJE: 0 RIE: 1 CAT: 16

Sequential Testing
CIJE: 7 RIE: 2 CAT: 21

Sequential Tests of Educational Progress
CIJE: 21 RIE: 114 CAT: 21

Sequentially Rejective Bonferroni Test
CIJE: 0 RIE: 1 CAT: 21

Sequestration (Budgets)
CIJE: 0 RIE: 1 CAT: 16

Sequoia Center for Adv of Teaching and Learning
CIJE: 1 RIE: 0 CAT: 17

Sequoia Union High School District CA
CIJE: 0 RIE: 2 CAT: 17

Sequoyah
CIJE: 0 RIE: 2 CAT: 18

Sequoyah Syllabary
CIJE: 1 RIE: 3 CAT: 13

SER Jobs for Progress
CIJE: 0 RIE: 1 CAT: 19

SER LARS (Information System)
CIJE: 0 RIE: 12 CAT: 04
SN "Special Education Resources Location Analysis and Retrieval System"

Serbia
CIJE: 1 RIE: 2 CAT: 07

Serbian
CIJE: 1 RIE: 1 CAT: 13

Serbian Americans
CIJE: 1 RIE: 2 CAT: 08

Serbians
USE Serbs

Serbs
CIJE: 0 RIE: 1 CAT: 08
UF Serbians

SERD Report
CIJE: 0 RIE: 5 CAT: 22

Serendipity Instructional Materials Center
CIJE: 1 RIE: 0 CAT: 17

Serer
CIJE: 0 RIE: 1 CAT: 13

Serging Machines (Sewing)
CIJE: 0 RIE: 1 CAT: 04

Seri
CIJE: 0 RIE: 5 CAT: 13
SN A Hokan language

Serial Averaging
CIJE: 0 RIE: 1 CAT: 15

Serial Deselection
CIJE: 0 RIE: 1 CAT: 15

Serial Evaluation Activities
CIJE: 1 RIE: 0 CAT: 21

Serial Integration
CIJE: 0 RIE: 1 CAT: 11

Serial Multiple Discrimination Teaching Exams
CIJE: 0 RIE: 1 CAT: 21

Serial Position Effect
CIJE: 6 RIE: 1 CAT: 16

Serials Agents
CIJE: 6 RIE: 0 CAT: 16

Serials Automation
USE Conversion of Serials

Serials Cancellation
CIJE: 5 RIE: 2 CAT: 16

Serials Claiming
CIJE: 4 RIE: 1 CAT: 16

Seriation
CIJE: 16 RIE: 5 CAT: 16

Series (Mathematics)
CIJE: 19 RIE: 0 CAT: 20

Series Learning Potential Test
CIJE: 1 RIE: 2 CAT: 21

Serling (Rod)
CIJE: 0 RIE: 1 CAT: 18

Sermons
CIJE: 8 RIE: 7 CAT: 16

Serology
CIJE: 1 RIE: 3 CAT: 11

Serotonin
CIJE: 10 RIE: 1 CAT: 11

Serrano v Priest
CIJE: 34 RIE: 22 CAT: 14

Serum Uric Acid
CIJE: 2 RIE: 0 CAT: 11

SERVEing Young Children Project
CIJE: 0 RIE: 1 CAT: 19
SN SERVE = SouthEastern Regional Vision for Education

SerVermont
CIJE: 0 RIE: 2 CAT: 19

Service Bureau for Modern Language Teachers
CIJE: 0 RIE: 1 CAT: 17

Service Conditional Loan Programs
CIJE: 1 RIE: 0 CAT: 19

Service Contracts
CIJE: 5 RIE: 2 CAT: 16

Service Corps of Retired Executives
CIJE: 0 RIE: 1 CAT: 17

Service Delivery Areas
CIJE: 3 RIE: 31 CAT: 16

Service Delivery Assessment
CIJE: 70 RIE: 35 CAT: 21

Service Journalism
CIJE: 8 RIE: 1 CAT: 16
SN Journalism focusing on informative, how-to articles, over news and human interest content

Service Learning
CIJE: 49 RIE: 22 CAT: 16

Service Outcome Measurement Form
CIJE: 1 RIE: 1 CAT: 21

Service Providers
CIJE: 11 RIE: 9 CAT: 09

Service Quality
CIJE: 12 RIE: 8 CAT: 16

Service Quantity
CIJE: 1 RIE: 3 CAT: 16

Service Reduction
CIJE: 1 RIE: 1 CAT: 16

Service Station Operators
USE Gas Station Attendants

Service Station Training School IL
CIJE: 0 RIE: 1 CAT: 17

Service Stations
USE Gas Stations

Service Sustainability
USE Sustainability

Service Unit Management
CIJE: 0 RIE: 1 CAT: 03

Service Utilization
CIJE: 45 RIE: 30 CAT: 16

ServiceMaster
CIJE: 0 RIE: 1 CAT: 17

Servicemens Opportunity College Program
CIJE: 2 RIE: 6 CAT: 19

Servicemens Readjustments Act 1944
CIJE: 1 RIE: 2 CAT: 14
SN See also "G I Bill"

Services for Expectant Mothers Project
CIJE: 0 RIE: 1 CAT: 19

Services for Families with Child Prog (Australia)
CIJE: 0 RIE: 1 CAT: 19

Services Inventories
CIJE: 0 RIE: 1 CAT: 16

Servicing Industrial Products
CIJE: 1 RIE: 0 CAT: 03

Servicio Pedagogico De Aztlan
CIJE: 1 RIE: 0 CAT: 15

Servol
CIJE: 1 RIE: 3 CAT: 17

Shared Acquisitions and Retention System
CIJE: 0 RIE: 2 CAT: 15

Shared Bibliographic Input Network (DoD)
CIJE: 0 RIE: 1 CAT: 04

Shared Book Experience
CIJE: 9 RIE: 6 CAT: 15
SN See also "Big Books" and "Shared Reading"
UF Shared Book Reading Activities

Shared Book Reading Activities
USE Shared Book Experience

Shared Heritage Child Care Program
CIJE: 0 RIE: 1 CAT: 19

Shared Housing
CIJE: 2 RIE: 4 CAT: 05

Shared Parenting Family
CIJE: 0 RIE: 2 CAT: 10

Shared Past
CIJE: 0 RIE: 1 CAT: 16

Shared Personnel
CIJE: 1 RIE: 2 CAT: 10

Shared Process Evaluation System
CIJE: 0 RIE: 3 CAT: 15

Shared Reading
CIJE: 10 RIE: 4 CAT: 16
SN See also "Shared Book Experience"

Shared Responsibility Model
CIJE: 0 RIE: 1 CAT: 15

Shared Students
CIJE: 0 RIE: 1 CAT: 10

ShareNet
CIJE: 0 RIE: 1 CAT: 04

Shareware
CIJE: 5 RIE: 1 CAT: 04
SN A freeware user supported program

Sharing Business Success Project
CIJE: 0 RIE: 1 CAT: 19

Sharing Centers
CIJE: 1 RIE: 1 CAT: 05

Sharks
CIJE: 3 RIE: 1 CAT: 20

Sharp (Lloyd Burgess)
CIJE: 1 RIE: 0 CAT: 18

Sharpe Health School
CIJE: 0 RIE: 1 CAT: 17

Sharper Minds Program
CIJE: 0 RIE: 1 CAT: 19

Shasta (Tribe)
CIJE: 0 RIE: 1 CAT: 08

Shasta College CA
CIJE: 2 RIE: 2 CAT: 17

Shatkin Dohner Mathematics Attitude Scale
CIJE: 1 RIE: 0 CAT: 21

Shaughnessy (Mina)
CIJE: 14 RIE: 4 CAT: 18

Shavelson (Richard J)
CIJE: 0 RIE: 0 CAT: 18

Shaver (James P)
CIJE: 1 RIE: 1 CAT: 18

Shaw (George Bernard)
CIJE: 6 RIE: 4 CAT: 18

Shaw Hiehle Computational Skills Test
CIJE: 0 RIE: 1 CAT: 21

Shaw University NC
CIJE: 2 RIE: 0 CAT: 17

Shawano Joint School District 8 WI
CIJE: 0 RIE: 1 CAT: 17

Shawnee
CIJE: 0 RIE: 1 CAT: 13

Shawnee (Tribe)
CIJE: 2 RIE: 7 CAT: 08

Shawnee College IL
CIJE: 1 RIE: 0 CAT: 17

Shawnee Community College IL
CIJE: 0 RIE: 1 CAT: 17

Shawnee Development Council
CIJE: 0 RIE: 1 CAT: 17

Shawnee Mission Public Schools KS
CIJE: 6 RIE: 3 CAT: 17

Shawnee State University OH
CIJE: 0 RIE: 1 CAT: 17

Shaycroft (M F)
CIJE: 0 RIE: 1 CAT: 18

Shaycroft Plane Geometry Test
CIJE: 0 RIE: 1 CAT: 21

Shayer Science Reasoning Task
CIJE: 0 RIE: 1 CAT: 21

Sheboygan Area School District WI
CIJE: 1 RIE: 0 CAT: 17

Shedd (Mark R)
CIJE: 2 RIE: 0 CAT: 18

Sheehan Sentence Completion Test
CIJE: 1 RIE: 0 CAT: 21

Sheehy (Gail)
CIJE: 0 RIE: 2 CAT: 18

Sheep
CIJE: 0 RIE: 5 CAT: 20

Sheep Specialists
CIJE: 0 RIE: 1 CAT: 09

Sheffield City Polytechnic (England)
CIJE: 0 RIE: 2 CAT: 17

Shelby County Schools TN
CIJE: 1 RIE: 1 CAT: 17

Shelby State Community College TN
CIJE: 3 RIE: 7 CAT: 17

Sheldon (Charles M)
CIJE: 1 RIE: 0 CAT: 18

Sheldon (Edward Austin)
CIJE: 0 RIE: 1 CAT: 18

Sheldon Basic Reading Series
CIJE: 0 RIE: 1 CAT: 22

Sheldon Jackson College AK
CIJE: 0 RIE: 14 CAT: 17

Shelf Availability (Libraries)
CIJE: 3 RIE: 0 CAT: 16

Shelf Classification
CIJE: 2 RIE: 1 CAT: 15

Shelf Life
CIJE: 2 RIE: 1 CAT: 20

Shelf List Sample (Libraries)
USE Shelflist Sample

Shelflist Count
CIJE: 4 RIE: 0 CAT: 16

Shelflist Sample
CIJE: 0 RIE: 1 CAT: 16
UF Shelf List Sample (Libraries)

Shell Companies Foundation
CIJE: 0 RIE: 3 CAT: 17

Shell Fishing
CIJE: 0 RIE: 2 CAT: 09

Shell Games (Computer Program)
CIJE: 0 RIE: 0 CAT: 04

Shell Molding Technology
CIJE: 1 RIE: 0 CAT: 20

Shell School Technology Program
CIJE: 1 RIE: 0 CAT: 19

Shell Science Centre (South Africa)
CIJE: 0 RIE: 2 CAT: 17

Shelley (Mary)
CIJE: 1 RIE: 0 CAT: 18
SN "Mary W(ollstonecraft)"
UF Godwin (Mary)

Shelley (Percy Bysshe)
CIJE: 0 RIE: 1 CAT: 18

Shelley Joint School District ID
CIJE: 0 RIE: 1 CAT: 17

Shellfish
CIJE: 2 RIE: 3 CAT: 20

Shells (Sea Animals)
USE Seashells

Shelter Rock Public Library
CIJE: 0 RIE: 1 CAT: 17

Sheltered English
CIJE: 6 RIE: 22 CAT: 13

Shelters
CIJE: 35 RIE: 41 CAT: 05
SN Use the more specific "Emergency Shelters," "Spouse Abuse Shelters," and/or "Womens Shelters," if appropriate
UF Homeless Shelters

Shelton College NJ
CIJE: 0 RIE: 1 CAT: 17

Shelving Practices
CIJE: 9 RIE: 10 CAT: 16

Shenandoah College VA
CIJE: 0 RIE: 1 CAT: 17

Shenandoah Valley
CIJE: 1 RIE: 2 CAT: 07

Shenstone (William)
CIJE: 1 RIE: 0 CAT: 18

Shepard Metzler Mental Rotations Test
CIJE: 1 RIE: 2 CAT: 21

Sheppard School Entry Screening Test
CIJE: 1 RIE: 0 CAT: 21

Shera (Jesse)
CIJE: 1 RIE: 1 CAT: 18

Sherbrooke University (Canada)
CIJE: 2 RIE: 0 CAT: 17

Sheridan (Marion C)
CIJE: 0 RIE: 0 CAT: 18

Sherif (Muzafer)
CIJE: 0 RIE: 2 CAT: 18

Sherif Hovland Nine Statement Scale
CIJE: 1 RIE: 0 CAT: 21

Sherlock Computer Program
CIJE: 0 RIE: 1 CAT: 04

Sherlock Holmes
CIJE: 8 RIE: 1 CAT: 22

Sherman Act
CIJE: 4 RIE: 2 CAT: 14

Sherman Film Evaluation Profile
CIJE: 0 RIE: 1 CAT: 21

Sherpa
CIJE: 0 RIE: 5 CAT: 13

Shewhart Control Chart
CIJE: 1 RIE: 0 CAT: 21

Shibatani (Masayoshi)
CIJE: 0 RIE: 1 CAT: 18

Shibusa
CIJE: 1 RIE: 1 CAT: 15
SN Concept of Japanese aesthetics

Shield Legislation
CIJE: 1 RIE: 3 CAT: 14

Shiffrins Procedure
CIJE: 0 RIE: 1 CAT: 15

Shift Work
CIJE: 11 RIE: 5 CAT: 16

Shilha
CIJE: 0 RIE: 2 CAT: 13

Shina
CIJE: 0 RIE: 2 CAT: 13
SN An Indic language of the northern regions of Pakistan and India
UF Sina

Shine Bower Anova
CIJE: 2 RIE: 0 CAT: 16

Shinnecock (Tribe)
CIJE: 0 RIE: 4 CAT: 08

Shintoism
CIJE: 1 RIE: 5 CAT: 16

Shipboard Computers
CIJE: 0 RIE: 2 CAT: 04

Shipboard Libraries
CIJE: 0 RIE: 1 CAT: 05

Shipbuilders
CIJE: 0 RIE: 1 CAT: 09

Shipbuilding
CIJE: 3 RIE: 4 CAT: 03

Shipbuilding Industry
CIJE: 3 RIE: 2 CAT: 05

Shipfitters
CIJE: 0 RIE: 3 CAT: 09

Shipley Hartford Vocabulary Test
CIJE: 1 RIE: 0 CAT: 21

Shipley Institute of Living Scale
CIJE: 14 RIE: 1 CAT: 21

Shippensburg State College PA
CIJE: 3 RIE: 7 CAT: 17

Shippensburg University PA
CIJE: 1 RIE: 6 CAT: 17

Shipping Industry
CIJE: 1 RIE: 8 CAT: 05

Ships
CIJE: 7 RIE: 7 CAT: 04
SN See also "Cruise Ships" and "Frigates"

Shipyard Training Modernization Program
CIJE: 0 RIE: 1 CAT: 19

Shipyards
CIJE: 0 RIE: 1 CAT: 05

Shivwits
CIJE: 0 RIE: 1 CAT: 08

Shock
CIJE: 4 RIE: 8 CAT: 11

Shock Incarceration
CIJE: 2 RIE: 1 CAT: 15
SN See also "Jail Boot Camps"

Shoe and Allied Trades Research Association
CIJE: 1 RIE: 0 CAT: 17

Shoe and Boot Occupations
CIJE: 0 RIE: 3 CAT: 09

Shoe Turf Interface
CIJE: 2 RIE: 2 CAT: 16

Shoemakers
CIJE: 1 RIE: 1 CAT: 09

Shoes
CIJE: 4 RIE: 2 CAT: 16

Shogun
CIJE: 1 RIE: 4 CAT: 22

Shokleng
CIJE: 0 RIE: 1 CAT: 13

Shooting Sports
CIJE: 0 RIE: 6 CAT: 16

Shoowa
CIJE: 0 RIE: 1 CAT: 08
SN A subgroup of the Kuba people of Zaire

Shop and Laboratory Attitude Inventory (Finch)
CIJE: 0 RIE: 1 CAT: 21

Shop Stewards
CIJE: 8 RIE: 0 CAT: 09

Shopkeepers
CIJE: 2 RIE: 0 CAT: 09

Shoplifting
CIJE: 10 RIE: 16 CAT: 16

Shopping
CIJE: 11 RIE: 6 CAT: 16

Shopping Centers
CIJE: 14 RIE: 8 CAT: 05

Shor (Ira)
CIJE: 2 RIE: 1 CAT: 18

Shore Country Day School MA
CIJE: 1 RIE: 0 CAT: 17

Shoreline Community College WA
CIJE: 1 RIE: 4 CAT: 17

Shoreline School District WA
CIJE: 0 RIE: 2 CAT: 17

Short Answer Tests
CIJE: 5 RIE: 8 CAT: 21

Short Assessment Outline
CIJE: 0 RIE: 1 CAT: 16

Short Cycle Education
CIJE: 10 RIE: 5 CAT: 15

Short Form Test of Academic Aptitude
CIJE: 2 RIE: 8 CAT: 21

Short Happy Life of Francis Macomber
CIJE: 1 RIE: 0 CAT: 22

Short Intelligence Test
CIJE: 2 RIE: 0 CAT: 21

Short Order Cooks
CIJE: 0 RIE: 1 CAT: 09

Short Term Accommodations
CIJE: 0 RIE: 2 CAT: 16

Short Term Counseling
CIJE: 14 RIE: 2 CAT: 11

Short Term Developmental Improvements
CIJE: 0 RIE: 1 CAT: 16

Short Term Effects
CIJE: 6 RIE: 3 CAT: 16

Short Term Evaluation
CIJE: 0 RIE: 1 CAT: 21

Short Term Funding
CIJE: 0 RIE: 1 CAT: 15

Short Term Memory Test (Pezzullo et al)
CIJE: 0 RIE: 1 CAT: 21

Short Term Psychodynamic Psychotherapy
CIJE: 0 RIE: 1 CAT: 11

Short Term Storage
CIJE: 1 RIE: 0 CAT: 16

Short Term Training
CIJE: 6 RIE: 9 CAT: 15

Shortened School Week
CIJE: 1 RIE: 1 CAT: 16

Shortwave Broadcast Services
CIJE: 1 RIE: 1 CAT: 15

Shortwave Radio
CIJE: 7 RIE: 3 CAT: 04

Shortwave Radio Relaying
CIJE: 0 RIE: 1 CAT: 20

Shoshone (Tribe)
CIJE: 2 RIE: 15 CAT: 08

Shoshone Bannock (Tribe)
CIJE: 2 RIE: 2 CAT: 08

Shoshoni
CIJE: 0 RIE: 1 CAT: 13

Shoshoni (Tribe)
CIJE: 1 RIE: 1 CAT: 08

Shostrom (E L)
CIJE: 4 RIE: 2 CAT: 18

Shoulders (Anatomy)
CIJE: 0 RIE: 1 CAT: 11

Show and Tell
CIJE: 9 RIE: 3 CAT: 15

Show Business
CIJE: 0 RIE: 1 CAT: 16

Showcase for Excellence Project
CIJE: 0 RIE: 1 CAT: 19

Showmens Guild (Australasia)
CIJE: 0 RIE: 1 CAT: 17

Shredding
CIJE: 1 RIE: 0 CAT: 16

Shreveport Clinic LA
CIJE: 0 RIE: 1 CAT: 17

Shrewsbury Plan
CIJE: 0 RIE: 1 CAT: 19

Shrimp
CIJE: 0 RIE: 1 CAT: 20

Shriners Hospitals for Crippled Children CA
CIJE: 0 RIE: 1 CAT: 17

Shropshire Mathematics Experiment
CIJE: 1 RIE: 0 CAT: 19

Shrubs
CIJE: 0 RIE: 2 CAT: 20

Shrunken Generalized Distance
CIJE: 1 RIE: 1 CAT: 15

Shuadit
CIJE: 0 RIE: 1 CAT: 13
UF Judeo Provencal

Shultz (George)
CIJE: 0 RIE: 1 CAT: 18

Shuo Wen Chie Tsu
CIJE: 0 RIE: 1 CAT: 22

Shuswap
CIJE: 1 RIE: 1 CAT: 13
SN A Salish language

Shuswap (Tribe)
CIJE: 0 RIE: 1 CAT: 08

Shuwaikh Industrial Training Center (Kuwait)
CIJE: 0 RIE: 1 CAT: 17

Sialic Acid
CIJE: 1 RIE: 0 CAT: 20

Siberia
CIJE: 16 RIE: 8 CAT: 07

Siberia (East)
CIJE: 0 RIE: 1 CAT: 07

Siberia (West)
CIJE: 1 RIE: 2 CAT: 07

Sibilants
CIJE: 2 RIE: 0 CAT: 13

Sibleys Downtown Satellite School NY
CIJE: 0 RIE: 1 CAT: 17

Sibling Age Spacing
USE Sibling Spacing

Sibling Attitudes
CIJE: 2 RIE: 1 CAT: 11

Sibling Birth
CIJE: 0 RIE: 2 CAT: 16

Sibling Care
CIJE: 9 RIE: 2 CAT: 11

Sibling Caregivers
CIJE: 0 RIE: 1 CAT: 10

Sibling Deidentification
CIJE: 3 RIE: 0 CAT: 11

Sibling Inventory of Differential Experience
CIJE: 1 RIE: 0 CAT: 21

Sibling Modeling
CIJE: 2 RIE: 1 CAT: 11

Sibling Rivalry
CIJE: 13 RIE: 5 CAT: 11

Sibling Spacing
CIJE: 0 RIE: 2 CAT: 16
UF Sibling Age Spacing

Sibling Tutoring
CIJE: 1 RIE: 0 CAT: 16

SIBTEST (Computer Program)
CIJE: 1 RIE: 1 CAT: 04

Sick Leave
CIJE: 7 RIE: 7 CAT: 16

Sickle Cell Counselor (Computer Simulation)
CIJE: 0 RIE: 1 CAT: 04

Sid W Richardson Foundation Study
USE Richardson Study

Sid W Richardson Foundation TX
CIJE: 0 RIE: 1 CAT: 17
UF Richardson Foundation TX

Sidamo
CIJE: 0 RIE: 1 CAT: 13

Sidereal Time
CIJE: 1 RIE: 0 CAT: 20

Sidestream Smoking
USE Passive Smoking

Sidewalks
CIJE: 1 RIE: 0 CAT: 04

Sidnell (Robert)
CIJE: 0 RIE: 1 CAT: 18

Sidney Hillman Health Center NY
CIJE: 0 RIE: 1 CAT: 17

Siegel (Donald)
CIJE: 0 RIE: 1 CAT: 18

Siegel (Harvey)
CIJE: 0 RIE: 1 CAT: 18

Siegel Prestige Scale
CIJE: 2 RIE: 0 CAT: 21

Siegel Tukey Test
CIJE: 0 RIE: 1 CAT: 21

Siena College NY
CIJE: 2 RIE: 2 CAT: 17

Siena Heights College MI
CIJE: 1 RIE: 2 CAT: 17

Sierra Club
CIJE: 8 RIE: 2 CAT: 17

Sierra College CA
CIJE: 0 RIE: 3 CAT: 17

Sierra Leone
CIJE: 34 RIE: 44 CAT: 07

Sierra Leone (Freetown)
CIJE: 1 RIE: 1 CAT: 07

Sierra Project
CIJE: 0 RIE: 3 CAT: 19

Sievers (Eduard)
CIJE: 1 RIE: 0 CAT: 18

SIF Project
CIJE: 0 RIE: 1 CAT: 19

Sigel Cognitive Style Test
CIJE: 1 RIE: 3 CAT: 21

Sigel Conceptual Style Sorting Task
CIJE: 0 RIE: 2 CAT: 21

Sigel Object Categorization Test
CIJE: 0 RIE: 2 CAT: 21

Sight Sound Inventory
CIJE: 0 RIE: 1 CAT: 21

Sight Sound System
CIJE: 1 RIE: 0 CAT: 16

SIGI PLUS System
USE System of Interactive Guidance and Info Plus

SIGI System
USE System of Interactive Guidance and Information

Sigma 6 Computer
CIJE: 0 RIE: 1 CAT: 04

Sigma 7 Computer
CIJE: 0 RIE: 4 CAT: 04

Sigma 9 Computer
CIJE: 0 RIE: 1 CAT: 04

Sigma Delta Chi
CIJE: 2 RIE: 0 CAT: 17

Sigma Methods
CIJE: 0 RIE: 1 CAT: 15

Sigma Theta Tau International Research Congress
CIJE: 0 RIE: 2 CAT: 02

Sign Iconicity
USE Iconicity

Sign Talk Childrens Centre MB
CIJE: 0 RIE: 1 CAT: 17

Sign Test
CIJE: 0 RIE: 3 CAT: 21

Signability (of Text)
CIJE: 0 RIE: 1 CAT: 16

Signadou College of Education (Australia)
CIJE: 0 RIE: 0 CAT: 17

Signal Corps
CIJE: 1 RIE: 1 CAT: 17

Signal Detection Analysis
CIJE: 4 RIE: 2 CAT: 15

Signal Detection Theory
CIJE: 22 RIE: 4 CAT: 15

Signal Distortion
CIJE: 0 RIE: 1 CAT: 13

Signal Flag Cards
CIJE: 0 RIE: 1 CAT: 16

Signal Processing (Digital)
USE Digital Signal Processing

Signal Systems (Kounin and Gump)
CIJE: 0 RIE: 1 CAT: 15

Signal Wiring
CIJE: 0 RIE: 1 CAT: 20

Signaled Stopping Technique
CIJE: 0 RIE: 1 CAT: 15
SN Framework for mentally processing and understanding messages, conceived in 1973 by R.F. Carter

Signalers
CIJE: 0 RIE: 1 CAT: 09

Signaling Devices (for Disabled)
CIJE: 0 RIE: 0 CAT: 04

Signals
CIJE: 4 RIE: 1 CAT: 15

Signed English
CIJE: 14 RIE: 2 CAT: 13

Signed Numbers Operations
CIJE: 0 RIE: 3 CAT: 20

Signers of the United States Constitution
CIJE: 0 RIE: 23 CAT: 10
UF United States Constitution Signers

Significant Bilingual Instructional Features Study
CIJE: 0 RIE: 1 CAT: 21

Significant Change Model
CIJE: 0 RIE: 1 CAT: 15

Significant Figures
CIJE: 8 RIE: 0 CAT: 20

Signifying (Rhetorical Strategy)
CIJE: 0 RIE: 0 CAT: 13

Signing Exact English
CIJE: 5 RIE: 3 CAT: 13

Signs of Trouble and Erosion A Report on Grad Educ
CIJE: 0 RIE: 1 CAT: 22

Sikhism
CIJE: 0 RIE: 2 CAT: 16

Sikhs
CIJE: 9 RIE: 1 CAT: 08

Sikkim
CIJE: 1 RIE: 1 CAT: 07

Siksika
USE Blackfoot (Language)

Silberman (Charles E)
CIJE: 2 RIE: 2 CAT: 18

Silence
CIJE: 34 RIE: 3 CAT: 16

Silent Majority
CIJE: 1 RIE: 0 CAT: 16

Silent Period (Language Learning)
CIJE: 0 RIE: 1 CAT: 13

Silent Reading Diagnostic Tests (Bond Clymer Hoyt)
CIJE: 1 RIE: 0 CAT: 21

Silent Way (Gattegno)
CIJE: 5 RIE: 12 CAT: 13

Siletz (Tribe)
CIJE: 1 RIE: 3 CAT: 08

Silhouettes
CIJE: 2 RIE: 1 CAT: 16

Silicon
CIJE: 2 RIE: 0 CAT: 20

Silicon Compounds
CIJE: 1 RIE: 0 CAT: 20

Silicon Valley
CIJE: 1 RIE: 1 CAT: 20

Silk Screen Printing
CIJE: 4 RIE: 1 CAT: 16

Silko (Leslie Marmon)
CIJE: 11 RIE: 0 CAT: 18

Silkworms
CIJE: 0 RIE: 0 CAT: 20

Sillitoe (Alan)
CIJE: 2 RIE: 1 CAT: 18

Sills (Beverly)
CIJE: 1 RIE: 0 CAT: 18

Silva (Antonio Jose da)
CIJE: 1 RIE: 0 CAT: 18

Silva Guimaraes (Bernardo Joaquim)
CIJE: 1 RIE: 0 CAT: 18

Silva Mind Control
CIJE: 4 RIE: 1 CAT: 15

Silvaroli Classroom Reading Inventory
CIJE: 0 RIE: 3 CAT: 21

Silver
CIJE: 2 RIE: 0 CAT: 20

Silver Burdett and Ginn Science Series
CIJE: 0 RIE: 1 CAT: 03

Silver Chromate
CIJE: 1 RIE: 0 CAT: 20

Silver Film
CIJE: 4 RIE: 0 CAT: 04

Silver Lake College WI
CIJE: 1 RIE: 1 CAT: 17

Silver Lake Regional High School MA
CIJE: 1 RIE: 0 CAT: 17

Silver Lake State Recreation Area
CIJE: 1 RIE: 0 CAT: 17

Silver Nitrate
CIJE: 1 RIE: 0 CAT: 20

Silver Test of Cognitive Creative Skills
CIJE: 0 RIE: 2 CAT: 21

Silverdale Experiment
CIJE: 1 RIE: 0 CAT: 19

Silverlake Experiment
CIJE: 0 RIE: 1 CAT: 19

SilverPlatter ERIC
CIJE: 1 RIE: 2 CAT: 04
UF ERIC SilverPlatter

SilverPlatter Information Inc
CIJE: 15 RIE: 9 CAT: 17

Silversmithing
CIJE: 0 RIE: 1 CAT: 09

Sim One Project
CIJE: 1 RIE: 2 CAT: 19

Simard v Board of Education
CIJE: 0 RIE: 1 CAT: 14

Simba Program
CIJE: 0 RIE: 2 CAT: 19

SIMCAT System
USE Simulation in Combined Arms Training

Simcoe County Board of Education ON
CIJE: 0 RIE: 1 CAT: 17

Simenon (Georges)
CIJE: 2 RIE: 0 CAT: 18

Similar Benefits (Rehabilitation)
CIJE: 0 RIE: 5 CAT: 11

Similar Response Analysis
CIJE: 1 RIE: 2 CAT: 21

Similar Structure Hypothesis
CIJE: 2 RIE: 0 CAT: 15

Similar Triangles
CIJE: 3 RIE: 0 CAT: 20

Similarities
CIJE: 14 RIE: 6 CAT: 16

Similarity (Concept)
CIJE: 20 RIE: 5 CAT: 15
UF Similarity Relations

Similarity Attraction Hypothesis
CIJE: 0 RIE: 1 CAT: 15

Similarity Attraction Model (Byrne)
CIJE: 1 RIE: 0 CAT: 15

Similarity Coefficient
CIJE: 6 RIE: 0 CAT: 21

Similarity of Experience
CIJE: 0 RIE: 4 CAT: 11

Similarity Ratings
CIJE: 10 RIE: 6 CAT: 21

Similarity Relations
USE Similarity (Concept)

Similarity Thinking Model
CIJE: 0 RIE: 1 CAT: 15

Similes
CIJE: 17 RIE: 8 CAT: 13

Simmons College MA
CIJE: 8 RIE: 1 CAT: 17

Simmons Market Research Bureau
CIJE: 0 RIE: 1 CAT: 17

Simmons University KY
CIJE: 0 RIE: 1 CAT: 17

SIMNET
USE SIMulation NETworking

Simon (Neil)
CIJE: 1 RIE: 1 CAT: 18

Simon (Sidney)
CIJE: 4 RIE: 1 CAT: 18

Simon Biology Test
CIJE: 0 RIE: 1 CAT: 21

Simon Fraser University (Canada)
CIJE: 17 RIE: 4 CAT: 17

Simon Says Game
CIJE: 0 RIE: 1 CAT: 16

Simons Rock College MA
CIJE: 2 RIE: 2 CAT: 17

Simons Rock Early College MA
CIJE: 0 RIE: 3 CAT: 17

Simons Rock of Bard College MA
CIJE: 0 RIE: 1 CAT: 17

Simple Instructional Monitor
CIJE: 0 RIE: 1 CAT: 15

SIMPLE Programing Language
CIJE: 0 RIE: 3 CAT: 04

Simplex Models
CIJE: 9 RIE: 3 CAT: 15

Simplicity Index
CIJE: 2 RIE: 0 CAT: 21

Simplification (Language)
CIJE: 6 RIE: 38 CAT: 13

Simplified Oral Hygiene Index
CIJE: 0 RIE: 1 CAT: 21

Simpson College IA
CIJE: 1 RIE: 2 CAT: 17

Simpson Mazzoli Bill
CIJE: 2 RIE: 2 CAT: 14

Simpsons (The)
CIJE: 1 RIE: 1 CAT: 22

SIMS (IEA)
USE Second International Mathematics Study

Sims Image Based Organizational Model
CIJE: 0 RIE: 1 CAT: 15

SIMS Software
USE Student Information Management System

Simulated Arithmetic Machine
CIJE: 0 RIE: 1 CAT: 04

Simulated Educational Computer
CIJE: 0 RIE: 1 CAT: 04

Simulated Hypothetical Instructional Computer
CIJE: 1 RIE: 0 CAT: 04

Simulated Lesson Analysis Chart
CIJE: 0 RIE: 1 CAT: 04

Simulated Maintenance Task Environment
CIJE: 0 RIE: 1 CAT: 15

Simulated Minority Admissions Exercise
CIJE: 1 RIE: 0 CAT: 15

Simulated Occupational Choice Game
CIJE: 0 RIE: 1 CAT: 15

Simulated Office Education Techniques
CIJE: 0 RIE: 1 CAT: 15

Simulated Oral Proficiency Interview
CIJE: 2 RIE: 4 CAT: 21

Simulated Patients
CIJE: 2 RIE: 1 CAT: 11

Simulated Social Interaction Test
CIJE: 0 RIE: 1 CAT: 21

Simulated Society
CIJE: 1 RIE: 0 CAT: 15

Simulating Alternative Futures in Education
CIJE: 1 RIE: 0 CAT: 15

Simulation Fidelity
CIJE: 1 RIE: 1 CAT: 20
UF Simulator Fidelity

Simulation Games
CIJE: 51 RIE: 6 CAT: 15

Simulation in Combined Arms Training
CIJE: 0 RIE: 1 CAT: 04
UF SIMCAT System

SIMulation NETworking
CIJE: 0 RIE: 1 CAT: 20
UF SIMNET

Simulation of Labor Market Information
CIJE: 0 RIE: 2 CAT: 15

Simulation Option Model
CIJE: 0 RIE: 2 CAT: 15

Simulation Test Interact Teach Competencies (Hays)
CIJE: 0 RIE: 1 CAT: 21

Simulator Fidelity
USE Simulation Fidelity

Simulator Freeze
CIJE: 0 RIE: 1 CAT: 20

Simultaneous Equations
CIJE: 9 RIE: 5 CAT: 20

Simultaneous Interpretation
CIJE: 2 RIE: 2 CAT: 13

Simultaneous Item Bias Procedure
CIJE: 0 RIE: 5 CAT: 21

Simultaneous Language Acquisition
CIJE: 2 RIE: 1 CAT: 13

Simultaneous Learning
CIJE: 3 RIE: 1 CAT: 11

Simultaneous Processing
CIJE: 20 RIE: 5 CAT: 11

Simultaneous Region Procedure
CIJE: 0 RIE: 1 CAT: 21

Simultaneous Research Replication
CIJE: 0 RIE: 2 CAT: 15

Sina
USE Shina

Sincerity
CIJE: 1 RIE: 0 CAT: 11

Sincerity of Responses
CIJE: 0 RIE: 1 CAT: 11
UF Response Sincerity

Sinclair (H)
CIJE: 1 RIE: 1 CAT: 18

Sinclair (May)
CIJE: 1 RIE: 0 CAT: 18

Sinclair (Upton)
CIJE: 0 RIE: 2 CAT: 18

Sinclair Community College OH
CIJE: 6 RIE: 11 CAT: 17

Sinclair ZX Spectrum
CIJE: 1 RIE: 0 CAT: 04

Sinclair ZX81
CIJE: 1 RIE: 0 CAT: 04

Sindangan Subanun
USE Subanun

Sindhi
CIJE: 0 RIE: 3 CAT: 13
SN An Indic language (Northwest Indic Zone, chiefly of Pakistan)

Sing Sing Correctional Facility NY
CIJE: 0 RIE: 1 CAT: 17

Singapore
CIJE: 142 RIE: 168 CAT: 07

Singapore American School
CIJE: 0 RIE: 1 CAT: 17

Singapore Broadcasting Corporation
CIJE: 0 RIE: 1 CAT: 17

Singapore Educational Media Service
CIJE: 1 RIE: 0 CAT: 17

Singapore Educational Television Service
CIJE: 1 RIE: 0 CAT: 17

Singapore National Bibliography
CIJE: 0 RIE: 1 CAT: 22

Singer Company
CIJE: 1 RIE: 0 CAT: 17

Singer Eyeball Estimate of Readability
CIJE: 1 RIE: 0 CAT: 21

Singer Loomis Inventory of Personality
CIJE: 0 RIE: 1 CAT: 21

Single Adults
CIJE: 12 RIE: 4 CAT: 10
SN See also "Single Persons"
UF Unmarried Adults

Single Article Announcement Service
CIJE: 1 RIE: 0 CAT: 16

Single Base Transformations
CIJE: 0 RIE: 1 CAT: 13

Single by Choice Mothers
CIJE: 0 RIE: 1 CAT: 10

Single Child Family
USE Only Child Family

Single Concept Introductory Mathematics Project
CIJE: 1 RIE: 1 CAT: 19

Single Earner Family
CIJE: 3 RIE: 1 CAT: 10
UF Single Income Family

Single Females
CIJE: 5 RIE: 1 CAT: 10

Single Frame Cinema
CIJE: 0 RIE: 1 CAT: 20

Single Group Design
CIJE: 0 RIE: 1 CAT: 21

Single High School Districts
CIJE: 0 RIE: 1 CAT: 05

Single Income Family
USE Single Earner Family

Single Judge Municipal Court Libraries
CIJE: 0 RIE: 1 CAT: 05

Single Living
USE Single Persons

Single Operator Linear Model
CIJE: 0 RIE: 1 CAT: 15

Single Parent Adoption
CIJE: 0 RIE: 1 CAT: 15

Single Parents
CIJE: 1 RIE: 6 CAT: 10
SN See also "Unmarried Parents"

Single Person Household
CIJE: 1 RIE: 0 CAT: 16
UF One Person Household

Single Persons
CIJE: 2 RIE: 0 CAT: 10
SN See also "Single Adults"
UF Single Living; Unmarried Persons

Single Room Occupancy
CIJE: 6 RIE: 5 CAT: 16

Single Sex Classes
CIJE: 5 RIE: 5 CAT: 16

Single Skill Training Courses
CIJE: 0 RIE: 1 CAT: 03

Single Subject Designs
CIJE: 17 RIE: 11 CAT: 21

Single Subject Research Design
CIJE: 53 RIE: 17 CAT: 15

Single Team Bargaining
CIJE: 0 RIE: 1 CAT: 15

Single Text Approach
CIJE: 0 RIE: 0 CAT: 15
SN See also "Multitext Approach"

Single Unit Module
CIJE: 1 RIE: 0 CAT: 15

Single Word Utterances
CIJE: 1 RIE: 1 CAT: 13

Singleton Decree
CIJE: 0 RIE: 2 CAT: 14

Singletons
CIJE: 8 RIE: 2 CAT: 16

Singular Forms (Grammar)
CIJE: 0 RIE: 2 CAT: 13

Singular Value Decomposition
CIJE: 1 RIE: 1 CAT: 15

Sino Soviet Alliance
CIJE: 1 RIE: 0 CAT: 12

Sinusoidal Oscillations
CIJE: 1 RIE: 0 CAT: 20

Sinusoidal Scan (Display Systems)
CIJE: 0 RIE: 1 CAT: 20

Siouan Languages
CIJE: 0 RIE: 3 CAT: 13
SN Broad family of American Indian languages — use Desc "Dakota" for the language of the Sioux tribe

Sioux City Community School District IA
CIJE: 0 RIE: 1 CAT: 17

Sioux City Public Library IA
CIJE: 2 RIE: 0 CAT: 17

Sioux Falls School District SD
CIJE: 3 RIE: 1 CAT: 17

Siqueiros (David Alfaro)
CIJE: 2 RIE: 0 CAT: 18

SIR Adjusted Index (Mushkin)
CIJE: 0 RIE: 1 CAT: 21

Sir Gawain and the Green Knight
CIJE: 1 RIE: 2 CAT: 22

Sir George Williams University (Canada)
CIJE: 1 RIE: 0 CAT: 17

Sirica (John)
CIJE: 1 RIE: 0 CAT: 18

Siriono
CIJE: 0 RIE: 1 CAT: 13

SIRIUS Programing Language
CIJE: 0 RIE: 1 CAT: 04

SIRS Inc
CIJE: 0 RIE: 1 CAT: 17

SIRS Software
USE Student Information and Records System

SISCON
USE Science In a Social CONtext

SISS (IEA)
USE Second International Science Study

Sisseton Wahpeton Sioux (Tribe)
CIJE: 0 RIE: 1 CAT: 08

Sisters of the Holy Family
CIJE: 1 RIE: 0 CAT: 17

Sisyphus (Greek Mythology)
CIJE: 0 RIE: 0 CAT: 16
SN See also "Myth of Sisyphus (Camus)"

Sit Ups
CIJE: 5 RIE: 0 CAT: 11

Sitcoms
USE Situation Comedies

Site Visits
CIJE: 14 RIE: 65 CAT: 16

Sitka Borough School District AK
CIJE: 0 RIE: 2 CAT: 17

Situated Learning
CIJE: 23 RIE: 3 CAT: 15

Situation Comedies
CIJE: 8 RIE: 8 CAT: 16
UF Sitcoms

Situation Specific Subject Competence Test
CIJE: 0 RIE: 1 CAT: 21

Situational Administrative Decision Making Invent
CIJE: 0 RIE: 1 CAT: 21

Situational Analysis
CIJE: 6 RIE: 10 CAT: 15

Situational Appraisal Inven (Pittel Mendelsohn)
CIJE: 1 RIE: 0 CAT: 21

Situational Attitude Inventory (Eberly)
CIJE: 0 RIE: 1 CAT: 21

Situational Attitude Scale (Adults Children)
CIJE: 0 RIE: 1 CAT: 21

Situational Attitude Scale (Sedlacek and Brooks)
CIJE: 2 RIE: 16 CAT: 21

Situational Attitude Scale for Women
CIJE: 1 RIE: 3 CAT: 21

Situational Attitude Scale Simplified
CIJE: 1 RIE: 1 CAT: 21

Situational Change Typology
CIJE: 1 RIE: 0 CAT: 15

Situational Confidence Measures
CIJE: 0 RIE: 2 CAT: 21

Situational Control
CIJE: 1 RIE: 1 CAT: 15

Situational Decision Making
CIJE: 0 RIE: 1 CAT: 15

Situational Effects
CIJE: 0 RIE: 1 CAT: 11

Situational Factors Checklist
CIJE: 0 RIE: 1 CAT: 15

Situational Fear Inventory
CIJE: 0 RIE: 1 CAT: 21

Situational Functional Approach
CIJE: 1 RIE: 3 CAT: 15

Situational Leadership
CIJE: 12 RIE: 3 CAT: 15

Situational Leadership Mdl (Hersey and Blanchard)
USE Hersey Blanchard Situational Leadership Model

Situational Leadership Theory
CIJE: 6 RIE: 3 CAT: 15

Situational Method
CIJE: 9 RIE: 3 CAT: 15

Situational Regression Technique
CIJE: 0 RIE: 1 CAT: 21

Situational Reinforcement
CIJE: 1 RIE: 4 CAT: 16

Situational Salience
CIJE: 0 RIE: 1 CAT: 16

Situational Theory of Communication
CIJE: 1 RIE: 0 CAT: 15

Situational Theory of Management
CIJE: 6 RIE: 1 CAT: 15

Situational Variables
CIJE: 56 RIE: 30 CAT: 20

Six Institutions Consortium
CIJE: 1 RIE: 0 CAT: 17

Six Item Health Administrators Questionnaire
CIJE: 0 RIE: 1 CAT: 21

Six Suppliers Game
CIJE: 1 RIE: 0 CAT: 16

Sixteen Personality Factor Questionnaire
CIJE: 67 RIE: 29 CAT: 21

Sixteenth Century
CIJE: 8 RIE: 4 CAT: 12

Sixth Amendment
CIJE: 3 RIE: 3 CAT: 14

Sixth Form
CIJE: 8 RIE: 3 CAT: 16

Sixth Year Programs
CIJE: 2 RIE: 2 CAT: 19

Size Estimation
CIJE: 14 RIE: 2 CAT: 15

Size Weight Illusion
CIJE: 1 RIE: 0 CAT: 15

Sizemore (Barbara A)
CIJE: 5 RIE: 0 CAT: 18

Sizer (Theodore R)
CIJE: 5 RIE: 0 CAT: 18

SJTCCs
USE State Job Training Coordinating Councils

Skagit Valley College WA
CIJE: 1 RIE: 12 CAT: 17

Skapa
CIJE: 1 RIE: 0 CAT: 16

Skeels and Dye Study
CIJE: 1 RIE: 0 CAT: 19

Sketching
CIJE: 6 RIE: 11 CAT: 20

Skew Curves
CIJE: 9 RIE: 6 CAT: 20

SKI HI Home Visit Curriculum
CIJE: 0 RIE: 1 CAT: 03

SKI HI Language Development Scale
CIJE: 0 RIE: 1 CAT: 21

SKI HI Program
CIJE: 1 RIE: 4 CAT: 19

Skid Row
CIJE: 5 RIE: 0 CAT: 16

Skidmore College NY
CIJE: 4 RIE: 7 CAT: 17

Skiles Instructional Project
CIJE: 1 RIE: 0 CAT: 19

Skill Clinics
CIJE: 0 RIE: 1 CAT: 05

Skill Development for Self Reliance
CIJE: 0 RIE: 1 CAT: 19

Skill Development in Teaching Model
CIJE: 0 RIE: 1 CAT: 15

Skill Profile
CIJE: 0 RIE: 3 CAT: 21

Skill Qualification Test
CIJE: 0 RIE: 6 CAT: 21

Skill Training Improvement Program
CIJE: 2 RIE: 1 CAT: 19

Skill Training Improvement Programs II
CIJE: 0 RIE: 4 CAT: 19

Skills Assessment Module
CIJE: 0 RIE: 1 CAT: 21

Skills Conversion Project
CIJE: 0 RIE: 17 CAT: 19

Skills Essential to Learning Project
CIJE: 0 RIE: 8 CAT: 19

Skills Fairs
CIJE: 0 RIE: 1 CAT: 02

Skills for Ethical Action Program
CIJE: 1 RIE: 2 CAT: 19

Skills Information System
CIJE: 0 RIE: 3 CAT: 15

Skills Inventory for Teams
CIJE: 0 RIE: 1 CAT: 21

Skills Inventory System
CIJE: 2 RIE: 0 CAT: 04

Skills Management System
CIJE: 2 RIE: 2 CAT: 15

Skills Map
CIJE: 0 RIE: 2 CAT: 15

Skills Monitoring System
CIJE: 0 RIE: 2 CAT: 15

Skills Training and Education Program
CIJE: 0 RIE: 0 CAT: 19

Skimming (Reading)
CIJE: 3 RIE: 5 CAT: 15

Skin
CIJE: 10 RIE: 4 CAT: 11

Skin Color
CIJE: 7 RIE: 3 CAT: 11

Skin Infections
CIJE: 1 RIE: 1 CAT: 11

Skinfold Measurement
CIJE: 3 RIE: 0 CAT: 21

Skinner (B F)
CIJE: 74 RIE: 43 CAT: 18

Skipping (Running)
CIJE: 0 RIE: 1 CAT: 16

Skipping Rope
USE Jump Roping

Skittagetan
USE Haida

Skokie School District 68 IL
CIJE: 1 RIE: 1 CAT: 17

Skokomish (Tribe)
CIJE: 1 RIE: 1 CAT: 08

SKOLE (Journal)
CIJE: 0 RIE: 1 CAT: 22

Skolt Lapps
CIJE: 0 RIE: 1 CAT: 08

SKOOLBOL Programing Language
CIJE: 0 RIE: 1 CAT: 04

Skornia (Harry)
CIJE: 0 RIE: 1 CAT: 18

Sky
CIJE: 1 RIE: 1 CAT: 20

Sky Calendars
CIJE: 8 RIE: 0 CAT: 20

Sky Education
CIJE: 1 RIE: 0 CAT: 03

Sky Sculpture
CIJE: 1 RIE: 0 CAT: 16

Skydiving
CIJE: 0 RIE: 0 CAT: 16

Skylab
CIJE: 5 RIE: 6 CAT: 04

Skylab Education Program
CIJE: 1 RIE: 8 CAT: 19

Skylights
CIJE: 1 RIE: 0 CAT: 04

Skyline Career Development Center TX
CIJE: 3 RIE: 3 CAT: 17

Skyline College CA
CIJE: 2 RIE: 6 CAT: 17

Skyline Wide Educational Plan
CIJE: 2 RIE: 3 CAT: 19

Skynet
CIJE: 0 RIE: 1 CAT: 16

Skywalks
CIJE: 1 RIE: 0 CAT: 05

Slang
CIJE: 35 RIE: 10 CAT: 13

Slatoff (Walter J)
CIJE: 0 RIE: 1 CAT: 18

Slaughterhouse Five
CIJE: 2 RIE: 1 CAT: 22

Slave (Athapascan Language)
USE Slavey

Slavey
CIJE: 0 RIE: 0 CAT: 13
UF Slave (Athapascan Language)

Slavic Canadians
CIJE: 0 RIE: 1 CAT: 08

Slavic Culture
CIJE: 0 RIE: 1 CAT: 16

Slavin (Robert E)
CIJE: 6 RIE: 1 CAT: 18

Slavs
CIJE: 4 RIE: 4 CAT: 08

Sledd (James)
CIJE: 1 RIE: 0 CAT: 18

Sledding
CIJE: 1 RIE: 1 CAT: 16

Sleep Disorders
CIJE: 5 RIE: 1 CAT: 11
UF Night Terrors

Sleep Paralysis
CIJE: 1 RIE: 0 CAT: 11

Sleeping Beauty
CIJE: 2 RIE: 1 CAT: 22

Sleepwalking
CIJE: 0 RIE: 1 CAT: 11
UF Somnambulism

Sleeves (Clothing)
CIJE: 0 RIE: 1 CAT: 16

SLEP Program HI
USE Students of Limited English Proficiency Program

Sleuthing Nursing Pathways Project
CIJE: 0 RIE: 1 CAT: 19

SLIAGs
USE State Legalization Impact Assistance Grants

Slide Collections
CIJE: 1 RIE: 2 CAT: 16

Slide Rules
CIJE: 6 RIE: 0 CAT: 04

Slide Sorting Task (George)
CIJE: 0 RIE: 1 CAT: 21

Slide Tape Programs
CIJE: 2 RIE: 2 CAT: 16
UF Slide Tape Shows

Slide Tape Shows
USE Slide Tape Programs

SLIDES Test
CIJE: 1 RIE: 0 CAT: 21

Sliding Fee Scales
CIJE: 1 RIE: 1 CAT: 16

Slim John
CIJE: 1 RIE: 0 CAT: 22

Slime Molds
CIJE: 5 RIE: 0 CAT: 20
UF Myxomycetes

Slingerland Screening Tests
CIJE: 6 RIE: 1 CAT: 21
SN Slingerland Screening Tests for Children with Specific Language Disability

Slingerland Teaching Methods
CIJE: 1 RIE: 1 CAT: 15

Slings (Equipment)
CIJE: 0 RIE: 1 CAT: 04

Slip Probabilities
CIJE: 0 RIE: 1 CAT: 21

Slippery Rock State College PA
CIJE: 4 RIE: 0 CAT: 17

Slippery Rock University PA
CIJE: 4 RIE: 8 CAT: 17

Slips of the Tongue
CIJE: 2 RIE: 0 CAT: 13

Sloan Commission on Cable Communications
CIJE: 0 RIE: 17 CAT: 17

Sloan Commission on Government and Higher Educ
CIJE: 0 RIE: 3 CAT: 17

Sloan Commission Studies
CIJE: 0 RIE: 48 CAT: 22

Sloan Foundation
CIJE: 4 RIE: 3 CAT: 17

Sloan US Army General Hospital VT
CIJE: 0 RIE: 1 CAT: 17

Sloan v Lemon
CIJE: 1 RIE: 1 CAT: 14

Slogan System Analysis (Komisar and McClellan)
CIJE: 0 RIE: 1 CAT: 21

Slope (Mathematics)
CIJE: 9 RIE: 1 CAT: 20

Slope Estimation
CIJE: 2 RIE: 1 CAT: 15

Slope Homogeneity Test
CIJE: 0 RIE: 1 CAT: 21

Slosson Drawing Coordination Test
CIJE: 1 RIE: 0 CAT: 21

Slosson Intelligence Test
CIJE: 63 RIE: 24 CAT: 21

Slosson Intelligence Test (Revised)
CIJE: 1 RIE: 1 CAT: 21

Slosson Oral Reading Test
CIJE: 2 RIE: 3 CAT: 21

Slote Method
CIJE: 2 RIE: 0 CAT: 15

Slough Experiment
CIJE: 1 RIE: 0 CAT: 21

Slovak
CIJE: 5 RIE: 7 CAT: 13

Slovak Republic
USE Slovakia

Slovakia
CIJE: 0 RIE: 2 CAT: 07
UF Slovak Republic

Slovene Americans
CIJE: 1 RIE: 2 CAT: 08

Slovenes
CIJE: 3 RIE: 1 CAT: 08

Slover School MA
CIJE: 0 RIE: 1 CAT: 17

Slow Scan Television
CIJE: 1 RIE: 18 CAT: 20

Sludge Blanket Finders
CIJE: 0 RIE: 1 CAT: 15

Sludge Lagoons
CIJE: 0 RIE: 1 CAT: 20

Slush Casting
CIJE: 1 RIE: 0 CAT: 20

Small Animal Care
CIJE: 1 RIE: 1 CAT: 20

Small Business Administration
CIJE: 7 RIE: 15 CAT: 17

Small Business Centers
CIJE: 1 RIE: 5 CAT: 05
UF Small Business Development Centers

Small Business Development Centers
USE Small Business Centers

Small Business Incubators
USE Business Incubators

Small Business Institute
CIJE: 4 RIE: 1 CAT: 17

Small Business Institute Directors Association
CIJE: 0 RIE: 1 CAT: 17
UF SBIDA

Small Business Investment Act 1958
CIJE: 0 RIE: 1 CAT: 14

Small Cities
CIJE: 2 RIE: 6 CAT: 16

Small Claims Court
CIJE: 1 RIE: 3 CAT: 14

Small Claims Courts
CIJE: 0 RIE: 1 CAT: 14

Small College Faculty Research Opportunity Award
CIJE: 0 RIE: 1 CAT: 16

Small Community and Rural Development Policy
CIJE: 1 RIE: 0 CAT: 16

Small Countries
CIJE: 0 RIE: 6 CAT: 16

Small Earth
CIJE: 1 RIE: 0 CAT: 22

Small Farm Family Program MO
CIJE: 0 RIE: 0 CAT: 19
UF Missouri Small Farm Family Program

Small Farms
CIJE: 3 RIE: 11 CAT: 05

Small Format Videotape
CIJE: 1 RIE: 1 CAT: 04

Small Gasoline Engines
CIJE: 1 RIE: 1 CAT: 20

Small Grant Program (ADAMHA)
CIJE: 0 RIE: 0 CAT: 19

Small Grant Research Program (USOE)
CIJE: 0 RIE: 0 CAT: 19

Small Group Communication
CIJE: 43 RIE: 55 CAT: 16

Small Group Instructional Diagnosis
CIJE: 1 RIE: 4 CAT: 15

Small Group Interaction System
CIJE: 0 RIE: 1 CAT: 15

Small Group Music Strategies
CIJE: 2 RIE: 0 CAT: 15

Small High Schools Project AK
CIJE: 0 RIE: 1 CAT: 19

Small Libraries
CIJE: 17 RIE: 8 CAT: 05
SN See also "One Person Libraries"

Small Planning Units
CIJE: 0 RIE: 1 CAT: 10

Small Presses (Publishers)
CIJE: 10 RIE: 5 CAT: 10

Small Project Assessment Service
CIJE: 0 RIE: 1 CAT: 19

Small School Districts
CIJE: 15 RIE: 51 CAT: 16

Small School Districts Association CA
USE California Small School Districts Association

Small Schools Career Education Development Project
CIJE: 0 RIE: 1 CAT: 19

Small Step Program
CIJE: 1 RIE: 0 CAT: 19

Small Talk
CIJE: 0 RIE: 1 CAT: 13

Small World Problem
CIJE: 1 RIE: 0 CAT: 15

Smaller Communities Program
CIJE: 0 RIE: 1 CAT: 19

Smallest Space Analysis
CIJE: 14 RIE: 3 CAT: 15

Smallpox
CIJE: 1 RIE: 1 CAT: 11

Smaridge (Norah)
CIJE: 1 RIE: 0 CAT: 18

Smart (Christopher)
CIJE: 0 RIE: 1 CAT: 18

Smart (David A)
CIJE: 0 RIE: 1 CAT: 18

SMART Program FL
USE Self Management and Responsibility Train Prog FL

SMART Project TX
CIJE: 0 RIE: 1 CAT: 19
UF Project SMART TX; Summer Migrants Access Resources through Techn

Smart Schools
CIJE: 0 RIE: 1 CAT: 05

Smart Start
CIJE: 0 RIE: 1 CAT: 14

SMARTLINE
CIJE: 0 RIE: 2 CAT: 19

Smedley (Agnes)
CIJE: 0 RIE: 1 CAT: 18

Smetana (Bedrich)
CIJE: 0 RIE: 1 CAT: 18

Smilanskys Cognitive Play Categories
CIJE: 2 RIE: 2 CAT: 15

SMILES Program UT
USE Senior Motivators in Learning Education Services

Smiley Junior High School CO
CIJE: 0 RIE: 1 CAT: 17

Smiling
CIJE: 22 RIE: 7 CAT: 16

Smirnov (A A)
CIJE: 0 RIE: 1 CAT: 18

Smith (Adam)
CIJE: 13 RIE: 5 CAT: 18

Smith (B Othanel)
CIJE: 0 RIE: 1 CAT: 18

Smith (Carol Hobson)
CIJE: 1 RIE: 0 CAT: 18

Smith (Frank)
CIJE: 6 RIE: 1 CAT: 18

Smith (Henry Holmes)
CIJE: 0 RIE: 1 CAT: 18

Smith (Henry Justin)
CIJE: 3 RIE: 0 CAT: 18

Smith (Logan Pearsall)
CIJE: 0 RIE: 1 CAT: 18

Smith (Nila Banton)
CIJE: 0 RIE: 2 CAT: 18

Smith and Meux Classification System
CIJE: 0 RIE: 1 CAT: 21

Smith College MA
CIJE: 14 RIE: 12 CAT: 17

Smith Experience Inventory
CIJE: 0 RIE: 1 CAT: 21

Smith Hughes Act
CIJE: 15 RIE: 7 CAT: 14

Smith Inventory (To Identify Potential Dropouts)
CIJE: 0 RIE: 1 CAT: 21

Smith Lemli Opitz Syndrome
CIJE: 0 RIE: 0 CAT: 11

Smith Lever Act
CIJE: 2 RIE: 3 CAT: 14

Smith Masculinity Femininity Scale
CIJE: 1 RIE: 0 CAT: 21

Smith Sturgeon Conditional Reasoning Test
CIJE: 0 RIE: 1 CAT: 21

Smith Test
CIJE: 2 RIE: 0 CAT: 21

Smith v Robinson
CIJE: 7 RIE: 1 CAT: 14

Smith v Wade
CIJE: 0 RIE: 1 CAT: 14

Smitherman (Geneva)
CIJE: 0 RIE: 1 CAT: 18

Smithsonian Institution
CIJE: 38 RIE: 14 CAT: 17

Smithsonian Science Information Exchange
CIJE: 3 RIE: 1 CAT: 17

Smithtown Computer Program
CIJE: 0 RIE: 1 CAT: 04

SMOG Readability Formula
CIJE: 6 RIE: 4 CAT: 21

Smoke Detectors
CIJE: 2 RIE: 3 CAT: 04

Smoke Free Schools
CIJE: 3 RIE: 2 CAT: 05
UF Tobacco Free Schools

Smokejumpers
CIJE: 1 RIE: 0 CAT: 09

Smokeless Tobacco
CIJE: 32 RIE: 11 CAT: 11
SN See also "Chewing Tobacco"

Smokey Bear
CIJE: 1 RIE: 1 CAT: 16

Smoking Cessation
CIJE: 23 RIE: 4 CAT: 11
UF Quit Smoking Programs

Smoking Consequences Questionnaire
CIJE: 0 RIE: 1 CAT: 21

Smoothing Methods
CIJE: 12 RIE: 21 CAT: 15

Snacks
CIJE: 1 RIE: 3 CAT: 16

Snails
CIJE: 11 RIE: 0 CAT: 20

Snake Phobia
CIJE: 5 RIE: 0 CAT: 11

Snake River School District ID
CIJE: 0 RIE: 1 CAT: 17

Snakes
CIJE: 11 RIE: 3 CAT: 20

Snap On Tools
CIJE: 0 RIE: 1 CAT: 17

Snap Programing
CIJE: 0 RIE: 1 CAT: 20

SNAP Rating Scale
CIJE: 0 RIE: 1 CAT: 21

Snark Syndrome
CIJE: 0 RIE: 1 CAT: 15
SN A belief that women lack ability in science, from the Lewis Carroll poem "The Hunting of the Snark"

Snead State Junior College AL
CIJE: 0 RIE: 1 CAT: 17

Snedden (David Samuel)
CIJE: 7 RIE: 0 CAT: 18

Snellen Test
CIJE: 0 RIE: 2 CAT: 21

Sneve (Virginia Driving Hawk)
CIJE: 0 RIE: 1 CAT: 18

Snohomish School District 201 WA
CIJE: 0 RIE: 1 CAT: 17

SNOMED System
CIJE: 1 RIE: 1 CAT: 15

Snow
CIJE: 14 RIE: 3 CAT: 20

Snow (C P)
CIJE: 7 RIE: 0 CAT: 18

Snow (Richard E)
CIJE: 0 RIE: 1 CAT: 18

Snow College UT
CIJE: 1 RIE: 0 CAT: 17

Snow Hill Institute AL
CIJE: 0 RIE: 1 CAT: 17

Snowmass (Colorado) Conference on Chemistry
CIJE: 1 RIE: 0 CAT: 02

Snowmobiles
CIJE: 4 RIE: 6 CAT: 04

Snyder (Zilpha Keatley)
CIJE: 1 RIE: 0 CAT: 18

Soap
CIJE: 6 RIE: 2 CAT: 20

Soap Films
CIJE: 8 RIE: 0 CAT: 20

Soar Project
CIJE: 0 RIE: 2 CAT: 19
SN Of Xerox's Palo Alto Research Center

Soar Report
CIJE: 1 RIE: 0 CAT: 22
SN "Problems in Using Pupil Outcomes for Teacher Evaluation"

Soares and Soares Self Concept Scale
CIJE: 0 RIE: 1 CAT: 21

SOBER (Test)
CIJE: 0 RIE: 0 CAT: 21

Sobrante Park Evaluation Project
CIJE: 1 RIE: 0 CAT: 19

Sochiapan
CIJE: 1 RIE: 0 CAT: 13

Social Acceptance
CIJE: 14 RIE: 2 CAT: 11

Social Accounting
CIJE: 1 RIE: 2 CAT: 16

Social Activity Frameworks
CIJE: 0 RIE: 1 CAT: 16

Social Adaptation Theory
CIJE: 1 RIE: 0 CAT: 15

Social Adaptational Status
CIJE: 0 RIE: 2 CAT: 11

Social Administration
CIJE: 2 RIE: 0 CAT: 03

Social Affiliation
CIJE: 4 RIE: 2 CAT: 11

Social Allocation Model
CIJE: 2 RIE: 0 CAT: 15

Social and Prevocational Information Battery
CIJE: 3 RIE: 3 CAT: 21

Social and Rehabilitation Service
CIJE: 1 RIE: 3 CAT: 17

Social Anxiety
CIJE: 6 RIE: 6 CAT: 11

Social Area Analysis
CIJE: 3 RIE: 0 CAT: 15

Social Assets Inventory
CIJE: 0 RIE: 1 CAT: 21

Social Attributes Checklist
CIJE: 1 RIE: 2 CAT: 21

Social Avoidance Distress Scale (Watson Friend)
CIJE: 4 RIE: 3 CAT: 21

Social Barriers
CIJE: 2 RIE: 1 CAT: 16

Social Behavior Rating Scale (Herbert)
CIJE: 1 RIE: 0 CAT: 21

Social Breakdown Syndrome
CIJE: 2 RIE: 0 CAT: 11

Social Capital
CIJE: 10 RIE: 5 CAT: 15

Social Causality
CIJE: 1 RIE: 1 CAT: 15

Social Causation Theory
CIJE: 1 RIE: 0 CAT: 15

Social Choice Theory
CIJE: 0 RIE: 1 CAT: 15

Social Circle School System GA
CIJE: 0 RIE: 1 CAT: 17

Social Class Value Orientation Inventory
CIJE: 0 RIE: 1 CAT: 21

Social Commitment
CIJE: 1 RIE: 1 CAT: 11

Social Comparison
CIJE: 48 RIE: 22 CAT: 16

Social Comparison Theory
CIJE: 10 RIE: 3 CAT: 15

Social Competence Assessment Profile
CIJE: 0 RIE: 1 CAT: 21

Social Conflict
CIJE: 2 RIE: 2 CAT: 16

Social Connectedness
CIJE: 0 RIE: 1 CAT: 16

Social Consequences
CIJE: 5 RIE: 0 CAT: 16

Social Construction
CIJE: 13 RIE: 4 CAT: 16

Social Construction of Reality
CIJE: 14 RIE: 6 CAT: 15

Social Constructionism
USE Social Constructivism

Social Constructivism
CIJE: 67 RIE: 26 CAT: 15
SN A perspective of learning and knowing which holds that meaning is not privately constructed, but is generated by social interaction
UF Social Constructionism

Social Context Activity Literacy Model
CIJE: 0 RIE: 1 CAT: 15

Social Control (Interpersonal)
USE Control (Social Behavior)

Social Conventions
CIJE: 1 RIE: 1 CAT: 16
SN See also "Social Rules"

Social Cost
CIJE: 0 RIE: 2 CAT: 15

Social Costs
CIJE: 6 RIE: 4 CAT: 15

Social Darwinism
CIJE: 16 RIE: 4 CAT: 16

Social Decision Schemes
CIJE: 3 RIE: 1 CAT: 21

Social Democratic Party
CIJE: 2 RIE: 0 CAT: 17

Social Density
CIJE: 0 RIE: 1 CAT: 16
UF Density (Social)

Social Deprivation Scale (Zigler et al)
CIJE: 1 RIE: 0 CAT: 21

Social Devaluation
CIJE: 3 RIE: 1 CAT: 11
UF Devaluation (Social)

Social Disintegration
CIJE: 2 RIE: 1 CAT: 16
UF Disintegration (Social)

Social Disruption
CIJE: 0 RIE: 1 CAT: 16

Social Distance
CIJE: 9 RIE: 8 CAT: 11

Social Distance Index (Katz)
CIJE: 0 RIE: 1 CAT: 21

Social Distance Scale (Bogardus)
USE Bogardus Social Distance Scale

Social Distance Survey (Greer et al)
CIJE: 0 RIE: 1 CAT: 21

Social Distance Test
CIJE: 0 RIE: 1 CAT: 21

Social Distress and Anxiety Scale
CIJE: 1 RIE: 0 CAT: 21

Social Dramatics
CIJE: 1 RIE: 1 CAT: 03

Social Ecology
CIJE: 14 RIE: 9 CAT: 15

Social Education
CIJE: 2 RIE: 3 CAT: 03

Social Education (Journal)
CIJE: 2 RIE: 1 CAT: 22

Social Education Materials Project
CIJE: 2 RIE: 0 CAT: 19

Social Efficiency
CIJE: 3 RIE: 1 CAT: 15

Social Entitlements
CIJE: 1 RIE: 5 CAT: 16

Social Episodes Test
CIJE: 1 RIE: 1 CAT: 21

Social Equality
USE Equality (Social)

Social Events
CIJE: 0 RIE: 1 CAT: 16

Social Experience Inventory
CIJE: 0 RIE: 1 CAT: 21

Social Facilitation
CIJE: 3 RIE: 1 CAT: 16

Social Facilitation Model (Cottrell)
CIJE: 1 RIE: 1 CAT: 15

Social Facilitation Theory
CIJE: 0 RIE: 1 CAT: 15

Social Foundations of Education
CIJE: 0 RIE: 1 CAT: 03

Social Functionalist Theory
CIJE: 0 RIE: 1 CAT: 15

Social Gerontology
CIJE: 3 RIE: 2 CAT: 11

Social Good
CIJE: 1 RIE: 4 CAT: 16

Social Health
CIJE: 1 RIE: 2 CAT: 11

Social Hypothesis Testing
CIJE: 0 RIE: 1 CAT: 21

Social Identity
CIJE: 5 RIE: 0 CAT: 16

Social Impact
CIJE: 23 RIE: 14 CAT: 15

Social Impact Assessment
CIJE: 3 RIE: 6 CAT: 21

Social Inferences
CIJE: 7 RIE: 2 CAT: 16

Social Information Processing
CIJE: 3 RIE: 0 CAT: 15

Social Inquiry Model
CIJE: 0 RIE: 1 CAT: 15

Social Interaction Observation Procedure
CIJE: 1 RIE: 4 CAT: 21

Social Interest
CIJE: 6 RIE: 2 CAT: 11

Social Interests Inventory (Grinder)
CIJE: 1 RIE: 0 CAT: 21

Social Isolates
CIJE: 3 RIE: 1 CAT: 11

Social Issues Resources Series
CIJE: 0 RIE: 2 CAT: 22

Social Judgment Theory
CIJE: 14 RIE: 4 CAT: 15

Social Justice
CIJE: 55 RIE: 14 CAT: 14

Social Learning Curriculum
CIJE: 5 RIE: 21 CAT: 15

Social Learning Theory
CIJE: 49 RIE: 22 CAT: 15

Social Loafing
CIJE: 2 RIE: 3 CAT: 11

Social Mapping
CIJE: 0 RIE: 4 CAT: 15

Social Mapping Matrix Assessment
CIJE: 0 RIE: 1 CAT: 21

Social Marginal Product of Labor
CIJE: 1 RIE: 0 CAT: 16

Social Marketing
CIJE: 4 RIE: 5 CAT: 15

Social Marking
CIJE: 3 RIE: 3 CAT: 15

Social Motivation
CIJE: 1 RIE: 2 CAT: 11

Social Motives
CIJE: 3 RIE: 2 CAT: 11

Social Movements
CIJE: 54 RIE: 26 CAT: 12

Social Needs
CIJE: 16 RIE: 13 CAT: 16

Social Order
CIJE: 7 RIE: 2 CAT: 16

Social Participation
CIJE: 9 RIE: 5 CAT: 16

Social Partners (European Community)
CIJE: 0 RIE: 1 CAT: 10

Social Pathology Model
CIJE: 1 RIE: 0 CAT: 15

Social Performance Indicator
CIJE: 0 RIE: 1 CAT: 16

Social Perspectives Scale
CIJE: 0 RIE: 1 CAT: 21

Social Philosophy
CIJE: 3 RIE: 2 CAT: 16

Social Policy
CIJE: 39 RIE: 40 CAT: 16

Social Power
CIJE: 18 RIE: 7 CAT: 16

Social Power Theory
CIJE: 4 RIE: 1 CAT: 15

Social Problem Solving
CIJE: 8 RIE: 10 CAT: 15

Social Problem Solving Training Programs
CIJE: 2 RIE: 0 CAT: 19

Social Process Model
CIJE: 0 RIE: 2 CAT: 15

Social Promotion
CIJE: 6 RIE: 10 CAT: 16

Social Reaction Inventory (Richardson Tasto)
CIJE: 0 RIE: 1 CAT: 21

Social Reaction Inventory (Rotter)
CIJE: 0 RIE: 4 CAT: 21

Social Reaction Scale
CIJE: 0 RIE: 1 CAT: 21

Social Readjustment Rating Scale (Holmes and Rahe)
CIJE: 1 RIE: 1 CAT: 21

Social Reality
CIJE: 13 RIE: 4 CAT: 16

Social Reasoning
CIJE: 4 RIE: 7 CAT: 16

Social Reciprocity
CIJE: 1 RIE: 3 CAT: 15

Social Referencing
CIJE: 12 RIE: 6 CAT: 11

Social Reinforcement Model
CIJE: 2 RIE: 1 CAT: 15

Social Reinforcement Scale (McDavid)
CIJE: 1 RIE: 0 CAT: 21

Social Rejection
CIJE: 2 RIE: 3 CAT: 11

Social Relations Scale
CIJE: 2 RIE: 1 CAT: 21

Social Reporting
CIJE: 0 RIE: 1 CAT: 16

Social Representations
CIJE: 2 RIE: 1 CAT: 11

Social Reproduction
CIJE: 13 RIE: 0 CAT: 15

Social Responsibility Test
CIJE: 1 RIE: 0 CAT: 21

Social Role Range
CIJE: 0 RIE: 2 CAT: 11

Social Rules
CIJE: 5 RIE: 1 CAT: 16
SN See also "Social Conventions"

Social Scale
CIJE: 0 RIE: 1 CAT: 21

Social Scenarios Scale
CIJE: 0 RIE: 1 CAT: 21

Social Science and Social Education Conference
CIJE: 0 RIE: 1 CAT: 02

Social Science Citation Index
CIJE: 13 RIE: 3 CAT: 22

Social Science Curriculum Study Center
CIJE: 0 RIE: 1 CAT: 17

Social Science Education Consortium
CIJE: 2 RIE: 13 CAT: 17

Social Science Fairs
CIJE: 1 RIE: 1 CAT: 16

Social Science Interchange
CIJE: 0 RIE: 2 CAT: 15

Social Science Observation Record
CIJE: 0 RIE: 4 CAT: 21

Social Science Tests
CIJE: 0 RIE: 1 CAT: 21

Social Science Theory
CIJE: 5 RIE: 1 CAT: 15

Social Sciences Citation Index
CIJE: 10 RIE: 3 CAT: 22

Social Sciences Humanities Research Council Canada
CIJE: 0 RIE: 1 CAT: 17

Social Security
CIJE: 71 RIE: 102 CAT: 14

Social Security Act
CIJE: 6 RIE: 27 CAT: 14

Social Security Act Amendments 1975
CIJE: 0 RIE: 0 CAT: 14

Social Security Act Amendments 1977
CIJE: 0 RIE: 1 CAT: 14

Social Security Act Amendments 1980
CIJE: 0 RIE: 0 CAT: 14

Social Security Act Amendments 1981
CIJE: 0 RIE: 1 CAT: 14

Social Security Act Amendments 1983
CIJE: 2 RIE: 1 CAT: 14

Social Security Act Title II
CIJE: 0 RIE: 1 CAT: 14

Social Security Act Title IV
CIJE: 0 RIE: 11 CAT: 14

Social Security Act Title IV A
CIJE: 0 RIE: 9 CAT: 14

Social Security Act Title IV B
CIJE: 0 RIE: 1 CAT: 14

Social Security Act Title IV D
CIJE: 0 RIE: 4 CAT: 14

Social Security Act Title IV E
CIJE: 3 RIE: 4 CAT: 14

Social Security Act Title V
CIJE: 1 RIE: 6 CAT: 14
UF Maternal and Child Health Programs Title V; State Maternal and Child Health Programs Title V; Title V Maternal and Child Health Programs

Social Security Act Title XIX
CIJE: 1 RIE: 3 CAT: 14

Social Security Act Title XX
CIJE: 0 RIE: 47 CAT: 14

Social Security Administration
CIJE: 3 RIE: 10 CAT: 17

Social Security Benefits
CIJE: 12 RIE: 34 CAT: 14

Social Security Data
CIJE: 0 RIE: 1 CAT: 14

Social Security Disability Insurance
CIJE: 2 RIE: 5 CAT: 14

Social Security Education Benefits
USE Social Security Student Benefits Program

Social Security Numbers
CIJE: 3 RIE: 1 CAT: 14

Social Security Student Benefits Program
CIJE: 1 RIE: 3 CAT: 19
UF Social Security Education Benefits

Social Self Efficacy Scale
CIJE: 1 RIE: 0 CAT: 21

Social Services Act 1974
CIJE: 1 RIE: 3 CAT: 14

Social Services Block Grant Program
CIJE: 0 RIE: 7 CAT: 19

Social Services Teams
CIJE: 0 RIE: 2 CAT: 10

Social Situations Scale
CIJE: 0 RIE: 1 CAT: 21

Social Skills Inventory Scale (Welker and Ginn)
CIJE: 0 RIE: 1 CAT: 21

Social Skills Training
CIJE: 19 RIE: 5 CAT: 15

Social Solutions Curriculum
CIJE: 0 RIE: 1 CAT: 03

Social Stigma
USE Stigma

Social Stimuli
CIJE: 3 RIE: 1 CAT: 11

Social Strategies
CIJE: 1 RIE: 1 CAT: 15

Social Studies Curriculum Center
CIJE: 0 RIE: 2 CAT: 17

Social Studies Implementation Project
CIJE: 0 RIE: 1 CAT: 19

Social Studies Inference Test
CIJE: 1 RIE: 3 CAT: 21

Social Studies Materials Data Book
CIJE: 1 RIE: 0 CAT: 22

Social Studies Teachers
CIJE: 19 RIE: 10 CAT: 09

Social Substantive Schedule
CIJE: 0 RIE: 1 CAT: 16

Social Support Networks Inventory (Flaherty)
CIJE: 0 RIE: 1 CAT: 21

Social Support Questionnaire
CIJE: 0 RIE: 1 CAT: 21
SN See also "Childrens Social Support Questionnaire" and "Youth Social Support Questionnaire"

Social Therapy
CIJE: 0 RIE: 1 CAT: 11

Social Transaction Scale
CIJE: 0 RIE: 1 CAT: 21

Social Transition
CIJE: 1 RIE: 1 CAT: 11

Social Transmission
CIJE: 0 RIE: 1 CAT: 16

Social Utility
CIJE: 5 RIE: 0 CAT: 16

Social Utility Models
CIJE: 0 RIE: 1 CAT: 15

Social Validity
CIJE: 17 RIE: 3 CAT: 15

Social Values Questionnaire (Perloe)
CIJE: 0 RIE: 1 CAT: 21

Social Vocabulary Index Test
CIJE: 0 RIE: 1 CAT: 21

Social Welfare Manpower Project
CIJE: 0 RIE: 1 CAT: 19

Social Work Aides
CIJE: 0 RIE: 0 CAT: 09

Social Work Educators
CIJE: 3 RIE: 4 CAT: 10

Social Work Practice Problems Inventory
CIJE: 0 RIE: 1 CAT: 21

Socialist Countries
CIJE: 3 RIE: 2 CAT: 07

Socially Adept Verbalizations of Youth
USE SAVY Curriculum

Societal Benefits
CIJE: 0 RIE: 2 CAT: 16

Societal Impact
CIJE: 5 RIE: 1 CAT: 16

Societal Needs
CIJE: 10 RIE: 10 CAT: 16

Societe Nouvelle
CIJE: 0 RIE: 1 CAT: 17

Society
CIJE: 5 RIE: 11 CAT: 16

Society for a Coastal Area Network
CIJE: 1 RIE: 0 CAT: 17

Society for College and University Planning MI
CIJE: 3 RIE: 1 CAT: 17

Society for College Science Teachers
CIJE: 2 RIE: 1 CAT: 17

Society for Education in Film and Television
CIJE: 0 RIE: 1 CAT: 17

Society for Popular Culture
CIJE: 4 RIE: 0 CAT: 17

Society for Psychological Study of Social Issues
CIJE: 1 RIE: 0 CAT: 17

Society for Pure English (England)
CIJE: 0 RIE: 1 CAT: 17

Society for the Prevention of Blindness
CIJE: 1 RIE: 0 CAT: 17

Society for the Promotion of Educational Reform
CIJE: 1 RIE: 0 CAT: 17

Society for the Study of Curriculum History
CIJE: 0 RIE: 1 CAT: 17

Society of Associated Teachers
CIJE: 1 RIE: 0 CAT: 17

Society of Brothers
CIJE: 1 RIE: 2 CAT: 17

Society of Industrial Artists and Designers
CIJE: 0 RIE: 1 CAT: 17

Society of Industrial Tutors
CIJE: 1 RIE: 0 CAT: 17

Society of Motion Picture and Television Engineers
CIJE: 0 RIE: 1 CAT: 17

Society of Research Administrators
CIJE: 5 RIE: 0 CAT: 17

Society of Teachers of Speech and Drama
CIJE: 1 RIE: 0 CAT: 17

Society of the Publication Critere
CIJE: 1 RIE: 0 CAT: 17

Society of Unlimited Learning NJ
USE Project SOUL NJ

Socio Dental Research
CIJE: 0 RIE: 1 CAT: 11

Socio Scientific Reasoning Model
CIJE: 0 RIE: 1 CAT: 15

Socio Technical Approach
USE Sociotechnical Systems Approach

Socio Technical Management
USE Sociotechnical Management Theory

Sociocentrism
CIJE: 3 RIE: 0 CAT: 11

Socioeconomic Diversity
CIJE: 3 RIE: 3 CAT: 16
UF Diversity (Socioeconomic)

Socioemotional Development
CIJE: 0 RIE: 1 CAT: 11

Sociolects
CIJE: 0 RIE: 2 CAT: 13

Sociological Abstracts
CIJE: 2 RIE: 4 CAT: 22

Sociological Fallacy
CIJE: 1 RIE: 0 CAT: 15

Sociological Resources for the Social Studies
CIJE: 4 RIE: 10 CAT: 19

Sociologists
CIJE: 42 RIE: 6 CAT: 09

Sociology of Education (Journal)
CIJE: 0 RIE: 0 CAT: 22

Sociology of Knowledge
CIJE: 9 RIE: 4 CAT: 15

Sociology of Leisure and Sport Abstracts
CIJE: 1 RIE: 0 CAT: 22

Sociology of Occupations
CIJE: 3 RIE: 2 CAT: 03

Sociology of Science
CIJE: 11 RIE: 2 CAT: 16

Sociology of the Family
CIJE: 1 RIE: 2 CAT: 03
UF Family Sociology

Sociology of Work
CIJE: 7 RIE: 3 CAT: 03

Sociomedicine
CIJE: 1 RIE: 0 CAT: 11

Sociometric Choice Measure
CIJE: 2 RIE: 1 CAT: 21

Sociometric Isolate
CIJE: 1 RIE: 0 CAT: 15

Sociometric Status
CIJE: 42 RIE: 36 CAT: 16

Sociometric Test
CIJE: 2 RIE: 3 CAT: 21

Sociomoral Reflection Measure
CIJE: 6 RIE: 0 CAT: 21

Sociotechnical Management Theory
CIJE: 0 RIE: 2 CAT: 15
UF Socio Technical Management

Sociotechnical Systems
CIJE: 2 RIE: 1 CAT: 15

Sociotechnical Systems Approach
CIJE: 4 RIE: 1 CAT: 15
UF Socio Technical Approach

Socmaticas
CIJE: 0 RIE: 2 CAT: 19

SocNet
CIJE: 1 RIE: 0 CAT: 17

Socorro Independent School District TX
CIJE: 1 RIE: 1 CAT: 17

Socrates
CIJE: 31 RIE: 10 CAT: 18

SOCRATES Autotutorial System
CIJE: 0 RIE: 0 CAT: 04
SN System for Organizing Content to Review And Teach Educational Subjects

SOCRATES Test Retrieval System
CIJE: 0 RIE: 1 CAT: 04

Socratic Method
CIJE: 53 RIE: 23 CAT: 15

Socratic Non Anacoluthic Programing
CIJE: 0 RIE: 2 CAT: 20

Sod Production
CIJE: 0 RIE: 1 CAT: 20

Sodium
CIJE: 2 RIE: 1 CAT: 20

Sodium Carbonate
CIJE: 1 RIE: 0 CAT: 20

Sodium Chloride
USE Salt

Sodium Restricted Diet
USE Salt Intake

Sodium Salicylate
CIJE: 1 RIE: 0 CAT: 20

Sodium Sulfate
CIJE: 1 RIE: 0 CAT: 20

Sodomy
CIJE: 0 RIE: 1 CAT: 11

Soft Contingency Network
CIJE: 0 RIE: 1 CAT: 16

Soft Skills Systems Engineering
CIJE: 0 RIE: 1 CAT: 20

Soft Systems Methodology
CIJE: 0 RIE: 1 CAT: 15

SOFTSWAP
CIJE: 1 RIE: 0 CAT: 04

Software Automatic Mouth
CIJE: 0 RIE: 1 CAT: 04

Software Copying
CIJE: 18 RIE: 12 CAT: 16

Software Piracy
CIJE: 21 RIE: 8 CAT: 16
SN See also "Computer Piracy" and "Piracy of Intellectual Property"
UF Illegal Copying (Software)

Software Publishers Association
CIJE: 0 RIE: 1 CAT: 17

Software Rental (Computers)
USE Computer Software Rental

Software Tools
CIJE: 2 RIE: 7 CAT: 04

SOI Learning Abilities Test
USE Structure of Intellect Learning Abilities Test

SOI Test of Behavioral Skills
CIJE: 1 RIE: 0 CAT: 21

Soil
CIJE: 11 RIE: 4 CAT: 20

Soil and Water Resources Conservation Act
CIJE: 0 RIE: 1 CAT: 14
UF Public Law 95 192

Soil Conservation District Aides
CIJE: 0 RIE: 1 CAT: 09

Soil Conservation Districts
CIJE: 2 RIE: 0 CAT: 20

Soil Conservation Service
CIJE: 5 RIE: 7 CAT: 17

Soil Conservation Society of America
CIJE: 0 RIE: 1 CAT: 17

Soil Restoration
CIJE: 1 RIE: 2 CAT: 20

Soils
CIJE: 2 RIE: 2 CAT: 20

Sojourners
CIJE: 5 RIE: 2 CAT: 10

Solano Community College CA
CIJE: 0 RIE: 3 CAT: 17

Solar Collectors
CIJE: 0 RIE: 2 CAT: 04

Solar Cooking
CIJE: 0 RIE: 1 CAT: 20

Solar Eclipses
CIJE: 13 RIE: 1 CAT: 20

Solar Energy Systems
CIJE: 1 RIE: 4 CAT: 20

Solar Envelope
CIJE: 2 RIE: 0 CAT: 20

Solar Food Dryers
CIJE: 0 RIE: 2 CAT: 04

Solar Heaters
CIJE: 1 RIE: 3 CAT: 04

Solderers
CIJE: 0 RIE: 2 CAT: 09

Soldering
CIJE: 2 RIE: 20 CAT: 20

Sole Community Hospitals
CIJE: 0 RIE: 1 CAT: 05

Sole Proprietorships
CIJE: 0 RIE: 2 CAT: 16

Solemnity
CIJE: 1 RIE: 0 CAT: 11

Solid Mass Balance
CIJE: 0 RIE: 1 CAT: 20

Solid Propellant Processors (Chemical Industry)
CIJE: 0 RIE: 1 CAT: 09

Solid State (Electronics)
CIJE: 1 RIE: 11 CAT: 20

Solid State Chemistry
CIJE: 18 RIE: 0 CAT: 20

Solids
CIJE: 2 RIE: 2 CAT: 20

Solis y Folch de Cardona (Jose)
CIJE: 1 RIE: 0 CAT: 18

Solitary Play
CIJE: 9 RIE: 4 CAT: 11

Solitude
CIJE: 2 RIE: 1 CAT: 16
SN See also "Seclusion"

Solmi (Sergio)
CIJE: 1 RIE: 0 CAT: 18

Solo Experience
CIJE: 3 RIE: 1 CAT: 15

Solo Mode Learning
CIJE: 0 RIE: 1 CAT: 15

Solo Performance
CIJE: 3 RIE: 1 CAT: 15

SOLO Programing Language
CIJE: 0 RIE: 2 CAT: 04

SOLO Taxonomy
CIJE: 3 RIE: 1 CAT: 15
UF Structure of the Observed Learning Outcome

Solomon and Postman Paradigm
CIJE: 1 RIE: 0 CAT: 15

Solomon Four Group Design
CIJE: 3 RIE: 4 CAT: 15

Solomon Islands
CIJE: 13 RIE: 17 CAT: 07

Solstice De Juin
CIJE: 1 RIE: 0 CAT: 22

Solubility
CIJE: 12 RIE: 0 CAT: 20

Solution Error Response Error Model
CIJE: 0 RIE: 2 CAT: 21

Solution Focused Brief Therapy
CIJE: 1 RIE: 1 CAT: 11

Solution Methods (Mathematics)
CIJE: 27 RIE: 3 CAT: 20

Solvay Process
CIJE: 1 RIE: 0 CAT: 20

Solvent Extraction
CIJE: 1 RIE: 0 CAT: 20

Solvents
CIJE: 10 RIE: 4 CAT: 20

Solzhenitsyn (Alexandr)
CIJE: 0 RIE: 3 CAT: 18

Soma Puzzle
CIJE: 1 RIE: 0 CAT: 20

Somalia
CIJE: 10 RIE: 21 CAT: 07

Somalia (Mogadiscio)
CIJE: 0 RIE: 1 CAT: 07

Somatic Alteration
CIJE: 2 RIE: 0 CAT: 11

Somatomedin C
CIJE: 0 RIE: 1 CAT: 11

Somatotyping
CIJE: 2 RIE: 0 CAT: 11

Somerset Area High School PA
CIJE: 1 RIE: 0 CAT: 17

Somerset County College NJ
CIJE: 1 RIE: 1 CAT: 17

Somerset School WA
CIJE: 1 RIE: 0 CAT: 17

Somerton Demonstration School AZ
CIJE: 0 RIE: 3 CAT: 17

Something Else Press
CIJE: 1 RIE: 0 CAT: 17

Somnambulism
USE Sleepwalking

Son Jarocho
CIJE: 1 RIE: 0 CAT: 16

Sonar Operators
CIJE: 2 RIE: 1 CAT: 09

Sonar Pitch Memory Test
CIJE: 0 RIE: 1 CAT: 21

Song File Data Match
CIJE: 0 RIE: 1 CAT: 21

Song Lyrics
USE Lyrics

Song of Roland
CIJE: 2 RIE: 0 CAT: 22

Songbooks
CIJE: 2 RIE: 4 CAT: 16

Songhai (Language)
CIJE: 0 RIE: 0 CAT: 13

Songhai Empire
CIJE: 0 RIE: 1 CAT: 07

Sonia Shankman Orthogenic School
CIJE: 0 RIE: 1 CAT: 17

Sonicguide
CIJE: 13 RIE: 1 CAT: 20

Soninke
CIJE: 0 RIE: 4 CAT: 13

Sonnys Blues
CIJE: 2 RIE: 0 CAT: 22

Sonoma County Junior College District CA
CIJE: 0 RIE: 1 CAT: 17

Sonoma County Schools CA
CIJE: 1 RIE: 1 CAT: 17

Sonoma State University CA
CIJE: 5 RIE: 3 CAT: 17

Sonoran
CIJE: 0 RIE: 1 CAT: 13

Sonority Cycle
CIJE: 1 RIE: 1 CAT: 13

Sons of Liberty
CIJE: 1 RIE: 0 CAT: 17

Sontag (Susan)
CIJE: 1 RIE: 1 CAT: 18

Sony Equipment
CIJE: 2 RIE: 2 CAT: 04

Sooke
CIJE: 0 RIE: 1 CAT: 13
SN A Northern Straits Salish language

Sooner Exchange for Educational Knowledge
USE Project SEEK OK

Sophisticated Instructional Environment
CIJE: 0 RIE: 3 CAT: 16

Sophistication of Body Concept Test
CIJE: 0 RIE: 1 CAT: 21

Sophistication of Reading Interests Scale
CIJE: 1 RIE: 0 CAT: 21

Sophists
CIJE: 17 RIE: 12 CAT: 10

Sophocles
CIJE: 3 RIE: 4 CAT: 18

Sophomore Operative Dentistry
CIJE: 0 RIE: 1 CAT: 03

Sophrology
CIJE: 1 RIE: 1 CAT: 15

Sor Juana Ines de la Cruz
CIJE: 0 RIE: 2 CAT: 22

Sorbian
CIJE: 1 RIE: 0 CAT: 13

Sorbian (Upper)
CIJE: 1 RIE: 0 CAT: 13

Sorenson Teacher Role Preference Inventory
CIJE: 0 RIE: 1 CAT: 21

Sorting Test (Chambers)
CIJE: 0 RIE: 1 CAT: 21

Sorts Test (Riegel)
CIJE: 0 RIE: 1 CAT: 21

SOSAD
USE Save Our Sons And Daughters

Sosva Dialect
CIJE: 0 RIE: 1 CAT: 13

Sotho (Northern)
CIJE: 0 RIE: 0 CAT: 13

Sotho (Southern)
CIJE: 0 RIE: 0 CAT: 13

Soul Music
CIJE: 1 RIE: 2 CAT: 16

Soul on Ice
CIJE: 2 RIE: 0 CAT: 22

Souls of Black Folk
CIJE: 2 RIE: 0 CAT: 22

Sound and the Fury (Faulkner)
CIJE: 0 RIE: 1 CAT: 22

Sound Bites
CIJE: 0 RIE: 1 CAT: 16

Sound Level Meters
CIJE: 1 RIE: 0 CAT: 04

Sound Localization
CIJE: 4 RIE: 1 CAT: 20

Sound of a Word
CIJE: 3 RIE: 1 CAT: 22

Sound on Slide Projectors
CIJE: 0 RIE: 1 CAT: 04

Sound Page System
CIJE: 1 RIE: 0 CAT: 15

Sound Preferences
CIJE: 2 RIE: 0 CAT: 11

Sound Source Ball
CIJE: 0 RIE: 1 CAT: 16

Sound Technicians
CIJE: 1 RIE: 1 CAT: 09

Sounding (Language)
CIJE: 3 RIE: 2 CAT: 13

Sounds and Images
CIJE: 6 RIE: 1 CAT: 21

Soups
CIJE: 0 RIE: 1 CAT: 20

SOURCE (Information Utility)
CIJE: 0 RIE: 0 CAT: 17
UF THE SOURCE

Source Credibility Rating Scale
CIJE: 0 RIE: 1 CAT: 21

Source of Stress Inventory
CIJE: 2 RIE: 0 CAT: 21

Source Study Movement
CIJE: 0 RIE: 1 CAT: 15

Source Valence
CIJE: 0 RIE: 1 CAT: 15

Sourcebooks
CIJE: 1 RIE: 2 CAT: 16

Sources of Instructional Leadership
CIJE: 1 RIE: 2 CAT: 21

Souster Teacher Opinion of Research in Education
CIJE: 0 RIE: 1 CAT: 21

South Africa
CIJE: 423 RIE: 328 CAT: 07

South Africa (Cape Province)
CIJE: 0 RIE: 3 CAT: 07

South Africa (Capetown)
CIJE: 4 RIE: 2 CAT: 07

South Africa (Durban)
CIJE: 0 RIE: 2 CAT: 07

South Africa (Natal)
CIJE: 7 RIE: 2 CAT: 07

South Africa (Transvaal)
CIJE: 0 RIE: 10 CAT: 07

South Africa (Zululand)
CIJE: 3 RIE: 0 CAT: 07

South African Broadcasting Corporation
CIJE: 2 RIE: 0 CAT: 17

South African Homelands
CIJE: 2 RIE: 1 CAT: 07

South Africans
CIJE: 6 RIE: 3 CAT: 08

South Allegheny School District PA
CIJE: 0 RIE: 2 CAT: 17

South Amboy City School District NJ
CIJE: 0 RIE: 1 CAT: 17

South America
CIJE: 51 RIE: 109 CAT: 07

South American Natives
CIJE: 4 RIE: 0 CAT: 08

South Asian Languages
CIJE: 4 RIE: 3 CAT: 13

South Australian College of Advanced Education
CIJE: 2 RIE: 2 CAT: 17

South Australian Department of Further Education
CIJE: 0 RIE: 1 CAT: 17

South Australian Science Teachers Association
CIJE: 6 RIE: 0 CAT: 17

South Bay Cooperative Library System CA
CIJE: 0 RIE: 1 CAT: 17

South Bay Union School District CA
CIJE: 0 RIE: 2 CAT: 17

South Bend Community Schools IN
CIJE: 1 RIE: 2 CAT: 17

South Boston Orientation Center
CIJE: 0 RIE: 1 CAT: 17

South Brunswick Township School District NJ
CIJE: 1 RIE: 1 CAT: 17

South Burlington School District VT
CIJE: 0 RIE: 2 CAT: 17

South Carolina
CIJE: 185 RIE: 839 CAT: 07

South Carolina (Allendale)
CIJE: 0 RIE: 1 CAT: 07

South Carolina (Anderson County)
CIJE: 0 RIE: 1 CAT: 07

South Carolina (Anderson)
CIJE: 0 RIE: 1 CAT: 07

South Carolina (Charleston)
CIJE: 8 RIE: 8 CAT: 07

South Carolina (Cherokee County)
CIJE: 0 RIE: 1 CAT: 07

South Carolina (Clover)
CIJE: 0 RIE: 0 CAT: 07

South Carolina (Columbia)
CIJE: 5 RIE: 4 CAT: 07

South Carolina (Florence)
CIJE: 1 RIE: 0 CAT: 07

South Carolina (Greenville)
CIJE: 3 RIE: 1 CAT: 07

South Carolina (Harleyville)
CIJE: 0 RIE: 1 CAT: 07

South Carolina (Horry County)
CIJE: 0 RIE: 1 CAT: 07

South Carolina (Lexington County)
CIJE: 0 RIE: 1 CAT: 07

South Carolina (Piedmont)
CIJE: 0 RIE: 2 CAT: 07

South Carolina (Rock Hill)
CIJE: 0 RIE: 1 CAT: 07

South Carolina (Sea Islands)
CIJE: 3 RIE: 0 CAT: 07
SN See also "Sea Islands"

South Carolina (Spartanburg)
CIJE: 2 RIE: 2 CAT: 07

South Carolina (Sumter)
CIJE: 1 RIE: 1 CAT: 07

South Carolina (Union County)
CIJE: 0 RIE: 1 CAT: 07

South Carolina (Williamsburg County)
CIJE: 2 RIE: 8 CAT: 07

South Carolina (York County)
CIJE: 0 RIE: 1 CAT: 07

South Carolina Administrators Leadership Academy
CIJE: 1 RIE: 1 CAT: 17

South Carolina Basic Skills Assessment Program
CIJE: 5 RIE: 37 CAT: 19

South Carolina Classroom Management System
CIJE: 0 RIE: 1 CAT: 19

South Carolina Coping Skills Project
CIJE: 0 RIE: 1 CAT: 19

South Carolina Department of Education
CIJE: 2 RIE: 11 CAT: 17

South Carolina Department of Mental Health
CIJE: 0 RIE: 0 CAT: 17

South Carolina Education Association
CIJE: 0 RIE: 1 CAT: 17

South Carolina Education Finance Act 1977
CIJE: 0 RIE: 2 CAT: 14

South Carolina Education Improvement Act 1984
CIJE: 0 RIE: 14 CAT: 14

South Carolina Educational Television
CIJE: 2 RIE: 9 CAT: 17

South Carolina Educator Improvement Act
CIJE: 1 RIE: 3 CAT: 14

South Carolina Governors Remediation Initiative
CIJE: 0 RIE: 0 CAT: 19

South Carolina Law Enforcement Division
CIJE: 1 RIE: 0 CAT: 17

South Carolina Literacy Association
CIJE: 0 RIE: 1 CAT: 17

South Carolina Needs Assessment Instruments
CIJE: 0 RIE: 1 CAT: 21

South Carolina Norm Referenced Testing Program
CIJE: 0 RIE: 1 CAT: 19

South Carolina School Improvement Process
CIJE: 0 RIE: 1 CAT: 14

South Carolina School Incentive Reward Program
CIJE: 1 RIE: 1 CAT: 19
UF School Incentive Reward Program SC

South Carolina Sea Island Citizenship Schools
CIJE: 0 RIE: 1 CAT: 17

South Carolina State College
CIJE: 2 RIE: 6 CAT: 17

Southern Colorado State College
CIJE: 1 RIE: 0 CAT: 17

Southern Conference on Language Teaching
CIJE: 0 RIE: 1 CAT: 17
UF SCOLT

Southern Connecticut State College
CIJE: 1 RIE: 0 CAT: 17

Southern Council on Collegiate Educ for Nursing
CIJE: 0 RIE: 1 CAT: 17

Southern Early Childhood Association
CIJE: 2 RIE: 0 CAT: 17
SN Formerly "Southern Association on Children Under Six"

Southern Education Foundation
CIJE: 3 RIE: 2 CAT: 17

Southern Education Reporting Service
CIJE: 2 RIE: 0 CAT: 17

Southern Farmers Alliance
CIJE: 2 RIE: 0 CAT: 17

Southern Hills Developmental Services SD
CIJE: 0 RIE: 1 CAT: 17

Southern Historical Association
CIJE: 1 RIE: 0 CAT: 17

Southern Illinois Collegiate Common Market
CIJE: 1 RIE: 1 CAT: 17

Southern Illinois University
CIJE: 65 RIE: 34 CAT: 17

Southern Illinois University Carbondale
CIJE: 40 RIE: 29 CAT: 17

Southern Illinois University Edwardsville
CIJE: 7 RIE: 8 CAT: 17

Southern Illinois University School of Medicine
CIJE: 4 RIE: 4 CAT: 17

Southern Illinois University Springfield
CIJE: 1 RIE: 0 CAT: 17

Southern Independent Television
CIJE: 1 RIE: 0 CAT: 17

Southern Interstate Nuclear Board
CIJE: 0 RIE: 1 CAT: 17

Southern Lehigh School District PA
CIJE: 1 RIE: 1 CAT: 17

Southern Magazine
CIJE: 0 RIE: 1 CAT: 22

Southern Maine Vocational Technical Institute
CIJE: 0 RIE: 2 CAT: 17

Southern Medical School Consortium
CIJE: 0 RIE: 3 CAT: 17

Southern Methodist University TX
CIJE: 29 RIE: 16 CAT: 17

Southern Nazarene University OK
CIJE: 1 RIE: 1 CAT: 17
SN Formerly "Bethany Nazarene College OK"

Southern Nevada Vocational Technical Center
CIJE: 0 RIE: 1 CAT: 17

Southern Newspaper Publishers Association
CIJE: 0 RIE: 1 CAT: 17

Southern Oregon Drug Awareness
CIJE: 0 RIE: 1 CAT: 19

Southern Oregon State College
CIJE: 2 RIE: 2 CAT: 17

Southern Paiute
CIJE: 0 RIE: 0 CAT: 13
SN A Uto-Aztecan language

Southern Paiute (Tribe)
CIJE: 0 RIE: 3 CAT: 08

Southern Plains Indians (Anthropological Label)
CIJE: 1 RIE: 0 CAT: 08

Southern Region Research Conf in Agricultural Educ
CIJE: 0 RIE: 2 CAT: 02

Southern Regional Committee for Family Life
CIJE: 0 RIE: 1 CAT: 17

Southern Regional Council
CIJE: 0 RIE: 2 CAT: 17

Southern Regional Education Board
CIJE: 15 RIE: 49 CAT: 17
SN See add'l listings under "SREB..."
UF SREB

Southern Regional Media Center for the Deaf
CIJE: 1 RIE: 0 CAT: 17

Southern Regional Research Project
CIJE: 0 RIE: 6 CAT: 19

Southern Regional Research Projects
CIJE: 0 RIE: 2 CAT: 19

Southern Research Conference in Agricultural Educ
CIJE: 0 RIE: 1 CAT: 02

Southern Rural Development Center
CIJE: 0 RIE: 9 CAT: 17

Southern Rural Development Center MS
CIJE: 0 RIE: 8 CAT: 17

Southern Sociological Society
CIJE: 1 RIE: 1 CAT: 17

Southern State College AR
CIJE: 0 RIE: 1 CAT: 17

Southern State University AR
CIJE: 0 RIE: 1 CAT: 17

Southern Tenant Farmers Union
CIJE: 0 RIE: 3 CAT: 17

Southern University Group
CIJE: 0 RIE: 1 CAT: 05

Southern University LA
CIJE: 4 RIE: 6 CAT: 17

Southern University New Orleans LA
CIJE: 0 RIE: 2 CAT: 17

Southern Utah State College
CIJE: 1 RIE: 2 CAT: 17

Southern Wisconsin Colony and Training School
CIJE: 0 RIE: 2 CAT: 17

Southern Youth Study
CIJE: 2 RIE: 5 CAT: 22

Southerns Ongoing Support
CIJE: 0 RIE: 1 CAT: 19
UF Missouri Southern State College SOS Plan

Southey (Robert)
CIJE: 1 RIE: 0 CAT: 18

Southfield School District MI
CIJE: 0 RIE: 1 CAT: 17

Southgate Education Association
CIJE: 1 RIE: 0 CAT: 17

Southlands College (England)
CIJE: 2 RIE: 0 CAT: 17

Southwest Advanced Learning System for Adults
CIJE: 0 RIE: 1 CAT: 19

Southwest and West Central Ed Coop Serv Unit MN
CIJE: 1 RIE: 0 CAT: 17
UF Educational Cooperative Serv Unit Marshall MN

Southwest Baptist University MO
CIJE: 0 RIE: 1 CAT: 17

Southwest Council of Foreign Language Teachers
CIJE: 0 RIE: 1 CAT: 17

Southwest Educational Development Laboratory
CIJE: 4 RIE: 29 CAT: 17

Southwest London College (England)
CIJE: 1 RIE: 0 CAT: 17

Southwest Minnesota State College
CIJE: 1 RIE: 0 CAT: 17

Southwest Missouri State College
CIJE: 0 RIE: 2 CAT: 17

Southwest Missouri State University
CIJE: 10 RIE: 7 CAT: 17

Southwest Parent Education Resource Center
CIJE: 0 RIE: 1 CAT: 17

Southwest Park and Recreation Training Institute
CIJE: 0 RIE: 1 CAT: 02

Southwest Region Educational Computer Network
CIJE: 0 RIE: 1 CAT: 17

Southwest Regional Laboratory
CIJE: 3 RIE: 17 CAT: 17
SN See add'l listings under "SWRL..."

Southwest Regional Media Center for the Deaf
CIJE: 1 RIE: 0 CAT: 17

Southwest Regional Resource Center
CIJE: 1 RIE: 2 CAT: 17

Southwest Research Institute TX
CIJE: 1 RIE: 1 CAT: 17

Southwest Saint Louis Community Mental Health Ctr
CIJE: 1 RIE: 0 CAT: 17

Southwest Texas Junior College
CIJE: 1 RIE: 3 CAT: 17

Southwest Texas State College
CIJE: 1 RIE: 1 CAT: 17

Southwest Texas State University
CIJE: 9 RIE: 16 CAT: 17

Southwest Texas Teacher Center
CIJE: 1 RIE: 0 CAT: 17

Southwest Virginia Community College
CIJE: 0 RIE: 1 CAT: 17

Southwestern Adventist College TX
CIJE: 1 RIE: 0 CAT: 17

Southwestern American Literature
CIJE: 1 RIE: 3 CAT: 16

Southwestern at Memphis TN
CIJE: 1 RIE: 1 CAT: 17

Southwestern College CA
CIJE: 0 RIE: 11 CAT: 17

Southwestern College NM
CIJE: 0 RIE: 1 CAT: 17

Southwestern Community Action Council
CIJE: 1 RIE: 0 CAT: 17

Southwestern Cooperative Educational Laboratory
CIJE: 1 RIE: 1 CAT: 17

Southwestern Indian Polytechnic Institute NM
CIJE: 2 RIE: 2 CAT: 17

Southwestern Library Association
CIJE: 1 RIE: 10 CAT: 17

Southwestern Library Interstate Coop Endeavor
CIJE: 0 RIE: 11 CAT: 17

Southwestern Michigan College
CIJE: 1 RIE: 0 CAT: 17

Southwestern Social Science Quarterly
CIJE: 1 RIE: 0 CAT: 22

Southwestern Sociological Society Meetings
CIJE: 0 RIE: 1 CAT: 02

Southwestern States Development Project
CIJE: 0 RIE: 1 CAT: 19

Southwestern University School of Law CA
CIJE: 3 RIE: 1 CAT: 17

Soviet Academy of Sciences
CIJE: 1 RIE: 1 CAT: 17
UF Academy of Sciences (USSR)

Soviet Education
CIJE: 31 RIE: 16 CAT: 16

Soviet History
CIJE: 1 RIE: 1 CAT: 12

Soviet Ministry of Education
USE Ministry of Education (USSR)

Soviet Ministry of Higher Secondary Specialized Ed
USE Ministry Higher Secondary Specialized Ed (USSR)

Soviet Pedagogy
CIJE: 9 RIE: 3 CAT: 16

Soviet Reader
CIJE: 1 RIE: 0 CAT: 22

Soviet Research
CIJE: 10 RIE: 13 CAT: 16

Soviet Sleep Learning
CIJE: 0 RIE: 1 CAT: 15

Soviet Studies
CIJE: 9 RIE: 14 CAT: 03

Soviet Union
USE USSR

Sow Bugs
CIJE: 1 RIE: 0 CAT: 20

Sox Scrubber Sludge
CIJE: 1 RIE: 0 CAT: 20

Soybeans
CIJE: 3 RIE: 6 CAT: 20

Soyinka (Wole)
CIJE: 1 RIE: 1 CAT: 18

Space Age
CIJE: 2 RIE: 3 CAT: 20

Space Analysis Manuals Project
CIJE: 0 RIE: 1 CAT: 19

Space Colonization
CIJE: 6 RIE: 4 CAT: 20

Space Communications Corp
CIJE: 0 RIE: 1 CAT: 17

Space Density
CIJE: 1 RIE: 2 CAT: 20
UF Spatial Density

Space Documentation Service
CIJE: 0 RIE: 1 CAT: 17

Space Exposed Experiment Developed for Students
CIJE: 0 RIE: 1 CAT: 19
UF SEEDS Project (NASA)

Space Photography
CIJE: 0 RIE: 1 CAT: 20

Space Programs
CIJE: 0 RIE: 1 CAT: 19
SN See also "United States Space Program"

Space Shuttle
CIJE: 23 RIE: 27 CAT: 20

Space Shuttle Challenger Disaster
USE Challenger Disaster

Space Travel
CIJE: 9 RIE: 10 CAT: 20

Space Weapons
CIJE: 0 RIE: 1 CAT: 20

Spacecraft
CIJE: 9 RIE: 8 CAT: 20

Spacelab
CIJE: 0 RIE: 10 CAT: 20

SPACES (Television Series)
CIJE: 0 RIE: 0 CAT: 22

Spaceship Earth
CIJE: 5 RIE: 4 CAT: 19

Spacesuits
CIJE: 0 RIE: 2 CAT: 04

Spacewalking
CIJE: 0 RIE: 1 CAT: 20

Spache Diagnostic Reading Scales
CIJE: 2 RIE: 2 CAT: 21

Spache Readability Formula
CIJE: 4 RIE: 7 CAT: 21

Spady (William)
CIJE: 0 RIE: 1 CAT: 18

Spaight (Richard Dobbs)
CIJE: 0 RIE: 1 CAT: 18

Spain
CIJE: 253 RIE: 177 CAT: 07

Spain (Balearic Islands)
CIJE: 1 RIE: 0 CAT: 07

Spain (Barcelona)
CIJE: 9 RIE: 4 CAT: 07

Spain (Basque Provinces)
CIJE: 0 RIE: 3 CAT: 07

Spain (Catalonia)
CIJE: 14 RIE: 4 CAT: 07

Spain (Madrid)
CIJE: 8 RIE: 2 CAT: 07

Spain (Malaga Torremolinos)
CIJE: 1 RIE: 0 CAT: 07

Spain (Ocana)
CIJE: 1 RIE: 0 CAT: 07

Spain (Seville)
CIJE: 1 RIE: 0 CAT: 07

Spain (Valencia)
CIJE: 2 RIE: 0 CAT: 07

Spain and the Western Tradition
CIJE: 1 RIE: 0 CAT: 03

Spalding (John Lancaster)
CIJE: 0 RIE: 2 CAT: 18

Span of Control
CIJE: 1 RIE: 1 CAT: 15

Spaniards
CIJE: 5 RIE: 6 CAT: 08

Spanish (American)
CIJE: 0 RIE: 3 CAT: 13

Spanish (Castilian)
CIJE: 6 RIE: 2 CAT: 13

Spanish (Chicano)
CIJE: 1 RIE: 1 CAT: 13

Spanish (Chilean)
CIJE: 0 RIE: 1 CAT: 13

Spanish (Cuban)
CIJE: 1 RIE: 4 CAT: 13

Spanish (Judeo)
CIJE: 1 RIE: 1 CAT: 13

Spanish (Mexican)
CIJE: 3 RIE: 1 CAT: 13

Spanish (Peruvian)
CIJE: 0 RIE: 1 CAT: 13

Spanish (Puerto Rican)
CIJE: 0 RIE: 1 CAT: 13

Spanish (Texas)
CIJE: 4 RIE: 3 CAT: 13

Spanish (Yanito)
CIJE: 0 RIE: 1 CAT: 13

Spanish American Culture
CIJE: 4 RIE: 3 CAT: 03

Spanish American War
CIJE: 4 RIE: 5 CAT: 12

Spanish Articulation Test
CIJE: 0 RIE: 1 CAT: 21

Spanish Civil War
CIJE: 4 RIE: 0 CAT: 12

Spanish Dame School Project
CIJE: 0 RIE: 1 CAT: 19

Spanish English Verbatim Translation Exam
CIJE: 0 RIE: 1 CAT: 21

Spanish Family Guidance Center FL
CIJE: 0 RIE: 1 CAT: 17

Spanish History
CIJE: 1 RIE: 2 CAT: 12

Spanish International Network
CIJE: 0 RIE: 1 CAT: 17

Spanish Language Only Television
CIJE: 1 RIE: 0 CAT: 04

Spanish Literacy Investigation Project
CIJE: 0 RIE: 1 CAT: 19

Spanish Oral Reading Test
CIJE: 1 RIE: 0 CAT: 21

Spanish Royal Academy
CIJE: 14 RIE: 0 CAT: 17

Spanish Slave Code of 1789
CIJE: 1 RIE: 0 CAT: 14

Spanish Surnamed
CIJE: 7 RIE: 28 CAT: 08

Spanton (William)
CIJE: 1 RIE: 0 CAT: 18

Sparck Jones (Karen)
CIJE: 1 RIE: 0 CAT: 18

Spark Timer
CIJE: 1 RIE: 0 CAT: 04

Sparsely Populated Areas Project
CIJE: 0 RIE: 2 CAT: 19

Sparsity (Population)
CIJE: 0 RIE: 11 CAT: 16

Spartacus Youth League
CIJE: 0 RIE: 1 CAT: 17

Spartanburg Methodist College SC
CIJE: 0 RIE: 1 CAT: 17

Spartanburg Technical College SC
CIJE: 1 RIE: 2 CAT: 17

Spartanburg Technical Education Center SC
CIJE: 1 RIE: 0 CAT: 17

Spasmodicism
CIJE: 1 RIE: 1 CAT: 16

Spatial Apperception Test
CIJE: 1 RIE: 0 CAT: 21

Spatial Arrangements Task
CIJE: 0 RIE: 1 CAT: 21

Spatial Characteristics of Data
CIJE: 2 RIE: 1 CAT: 20

Spatial Context
CIJE: 5 RIE: 3 CAT: 11

Spatial Cues
CIJE: 9 RIE: 1 CAT: 11

Spatial Density
USE Space Density

Spatial Distribution
CIJE: 7 RIE: 1 CAT: 16

Spatial Factors
CIJE: 1 RIE: 1 CAT: 16

Spatial Organizers
CIJE: 2 RIE: 1 CAT: 15

Spatial Planning
CIJE: 1 RIE: 2 CAT: 20

Spatial Relations Test
CIJE: 1 RIE: 1 CAT: 21

Spatial Relationships (Sentences)
CIJE: 3 RIE: 2 CAT: 13

Spatial Tasks
CIJE: 15 RIE: 7 CAT: 21

Spatial Tests
CIJE: 9 RIE: 15 CAT: 21

Spatial Transformation Task
CIJE: 0 RIE: 3 CAT: 21

Spaulding System of Classroom Behavioral Analysis
CIJE: 0 RIE: 1 CAT: 21

Spaulding Teacher Activity Rating Schedule
CIJE: 1 RIE: 6 CAT: 21

SPEAK Tests
USE Speaking Proficiency English Assessment Kit

Speakers Bureaus
CIJE: 7 RIE: 8 CAT: 05

Speakes (Larry)
CIJE: 0 RIE: 1 CAT: 18

Speaking Across the Curriculum
CIJE: 4 RIE: 11 CAT: 03
SN See also "Oral Communication Across the Curriculum"

Speaking and Listening across Disciplines
CIJE: 0 RIE: 1 CAT: 19

Speaking Centers
CIJE: 1 RIE: 1 CAT: 05
UF Speaking Laboratories

Speaking Laboratories
USE Speaking Centers

Speaking Proficiency English Assessment Kit
CIJE: 1 RIE: 2 CAT: 21
UF ETS Speaking Proficiency English Assessment Kit; SPEAK Tests

Speaking Style
CIJE: 0 RIE: 4 CAT: 16

Speaking Thinking Relationship
CIJE: 6 RIE: 11 CAT: 15

Speaking Writing Relationship
CIJE: 53 RIE: 50 CAT: 15

Spearman (Charles)
CIJE: 5 RIE: 3 CAT: 18

Spearman Brown Formula
CIJE: 11 RIE: 4 CAT: 15

Spearman Rank Correlation Coefficient
CIJE: 24 RIE: 6 CAT: 15
UF Rank Correlation Coefficient; Rho Coefficient

Spearmans Two Factor Theory
CIJE: 0 RIE: 2 CAT: 15

Spears (Harold)
CIJE: 0 RIE: 1 CAT: 18

Special Action Office for Drug Abuse Prevention
CIJE: 1 RIE: 0 CAT: 17

Special Agricultural Workers
CIJE: 0 RIE: 0 CAT: 09

Special and General Education Leadership Project
CIJE: 0 RIE: 2 CAT: 19

Special Assistance Early Education Handicapped
CIJE: 0 RIE: 1 CAT: 14

Special Collections (Library)
CIJE: 25 RIE: 8 CAT: 16

Special College Counseling Program
CIJE: 0 RIE: 1 CAT: 19

Special Delinquency Prevention Program NY
CIJE: 0 RIE: 1 CAT: 19

Special Editions
CIJE: 1 RIE: 0 CAT: 16

Special Education Administration Training Program
CIJE: 0 RIE: 3 CAT: 19

Special Education Cooperatives
CIJE: 1 RIE: 3 CAT: 05

Special Education Data Management System
CIJE: 0 RIE: 1 CAT: 04
UF SEDMS

Special Education Directors
CIJE: 3 RIE: 2 CAT: 09

Special Education Instructional Materials Centers
CIJE: 6 RIE: 9 CAT: 05

Special Education Intervention Project
CIJE: 0 RIE: 1 CAT: 19

Special Education Management System
CIJE: 2 RIE: 0 CAT: 04

Special Education Placement Teams
CIJE: 0 RIE: 1 CAT: 09
UF Placement Teams (Special Education)

Special Education Planning Model
CIJE: 0 RIE: 1 CAT: 15

Special Education Program Checklist
CIJE: 0 RIE: 1 CAT: 21

Special Education Programs (ED)
USE Office of Special Education Programs

Special Education Rehabilitation Vocational Educ
CIJE: 0 RIE: 1 CAT: 19

Special Education Research Test (Nash)
CIJE: 0 RIE: 1 CAT: 21

Special Education Student Information Network PA
CIJE: 0 RIE: 1 CAT: 17

Special Education Supervisor Training Project
CIJE: 0 RIE: 18 CAT: 19

Special Education Training and Resource Center NY
CIJE: 0 RIE: 2 CAT: 17

Special Education Training and Resource Centers NY
CIJE: 0 RIE: 0 CAT: 05

Special Educational Opportunities Program
CIJE: 2 RIE: 3 CAT: 19

Special Event Day Care
CIJE: 0 RIE: 1 CAT: 16

Special Events
CIJE: 11 RIE: 1 CAT: 16

Special Events (College)
USE College Special Events

Special Food Service Program for Children
CIJE: 0 RIE: 3 CAT: 19

Special Friends Program
CIJE: 1 RIE: 1 CAT: 19

Special Health Revenue Sharing Act 1975
CIJE: 0 RIE: 2 CAT: 14

Special Impact Program
CIJE: 1 RIE: 1 CAT: 19

Special Incentive Programs NY
CIJE: 0 RIE: 1 CAT: 19
SN ...of the NYC public schools

Special Incomplete Sentences Test
CIJE: 1 RIE: 0 CAT: 21

Special Interest Centers
CIJE: 0 RIE: 1 CAT: 05

Special Interest Groups
CIJE: 40 RIE: 24 CAT: 10

Special Libraries (Journal)
CIJE: 0 RIE: 1 CAT: 22

Special Libraries Association
CIJE: 62 RIE: 7 CAT: 17

Special Media Institutes
CIJE: 1 RIE: 1 CAT: 02

Special Milk Program
CIJE: 0 RIE: 10 CAT: 19

Special Needs Children
CIJE: 24 RIE: 14 CAT: 10

Special Needs Groups
CIJE: 1 RIE: 9 CAT: 10

Special Needs Identification Assessment Project
CIJE: 0 RIE: 10 CAT: 19

Special Needs Individuals
CIJE: 0 RIE: 1 CAT: 10

Special Needs People Improving Vocational Guidance
CIJE: 0 RIE: 1 CAT: 19

Special Partnership in Career Education
CIJE: 0 RIE: 8 CAT: 19

Special Plan Upgrading Reading
CIJE: 0 RIE: 1 CAT: 19
UF Project SPUR

Special Program Schools Scheme
CIJE: 0 RIE: 1 CAT: 19

Special Programs Aimed at Reaching Children
CIJE: 0 RIE: 1 CAT: 19

Special Programs for Individualized Needs
CIJE: 0 RIE: 1 CAT: 19

Special Programs in Citizenship Education
CIJE: 0 RIE: 2 CAT: 19

Special Project for Older Citizens
CIJE: 1 RIE: 0 CAT: 19

Special Review Assessment NJ
USE New Jersey Special Review Assessment

Special Services for Disabled Students
CIJE: 0 RIE: 1 CAT: 19

Special Services for Disadvantaged Students
CIJE: 0 RIE: 13 CAT: 19

Special Student Access to Vocational Ed TN
CIJE: 0 RIE: 1 CAT: 19

Special Student Concerns Projects
CIJE: 0 RIE: 1 CAT: 19

Special Supplemen Food Program Women Infants Child
CIJE: 9 RIE: 24 CAT: 19

Special Teacher Education and Evaluation Lab
USE Project STEEL

Special Teens and Parents Study
CIJE: 0 RIE: 1 CAT: 22

Special Test Administration
CIJE: 0 RIE: 1 CAT: 21

Special Training for Employment Program
CIJE: 0 RIE: 1 CAT: 19

Special Training Schools (Japan)
CIJE: 0 RIE: 1 CAT: 05

Special Volunteer Demonstration Programs
CIJE: 0 RIE: 1 CAT: 19

Special Weapons and Tactics Units
USE SWAT Teams

Specialist Schools
CIJE: 1 RIE: 1 CAT: 05

Specialized Accreditation
CIJE: 2 RIE: 3 CAT: 16

Specialized Facilities
CIJE: 1 RIE: 1 CAT: 05

Specialized Training for Adoption Readiness PA
USE Project STAR PA

SpecialNet
CIJE: 3 RIE: 1 CAT: 17

Specialty Animals
CIJE: 0 RIE: 1 CAT: 20
SN Nontraditional agricultural animals, e.g., crawfish, catfish, pheasant, and rabbits

Specialty Area Tests (ETS)
USE ETS Specialty Area Tests

Specialty Area Tests (NTE)
USE NTE Specialty Area Tests

Species Interaction (Biology)
CIJE: 2 RIE: 0 CAT: 20

Specific Aptitude Test Battery
CIJE: 0 RIE: 1 CAT: 21

Specific Comprehension Strategy
CIJE: 0 RIE: 1 CAT: 15

Specific Fear Index
CIJE: 1 RIE: 0 CAT: 21

Specific Heat
CIJE: 3 RIE: 0 CAT: 20

Specific Language Disability Test
CIJE: 1 RIE: 1 CAT: 21

Specific Literacy
CIJE: 0 RIE: 2 CAT: 13

Specific Resistance Test
CIJE: 0 RIE: 1 CAT: 20

Specification Bias
CIJE: 1 RIE: 2 CAT: 16

Specification Error
CIJE: 8 RIE: 1 CAT: 16
UF Misspecification

Specification Searches
CIJE: 2 RIE: 0 CAT: 15

Specifications for Elementary Teacher Education
CIJE: 0 RIE: 16 CAT: 03

Specificity
CIJE: 19 RIE: 6 CAT: 16
SN Use a more specific term if possible—Age Specificity, Content Specificity, Encoding Specificity, etc.

Specificity Doctrine
CIJE: 0 RIE: 1 CAT: 21

Specimen Records (Behavior)
CIJE: 2 RIE: 1 CAT: 11

Specimens (Science)
CIJE: 5 RIE: 3 CAT: 20

Spectator Sports
CIJE: 4 RIE: 2 CAT: 16

Spectrad Theory
CIJE: 1 RIE: 0 CAT: 15

Spectral Analysis
CIJE: 6 RIE: 2 CAT: 15

Spectrometers
CIJE: 5 RIE: 0 CAT: 04

Spectrometry
CIJE: 11 RIE: 0 CAT: 20

Spectrophotometers
CIJE: 5 RIE: 0 CAT: 04

Spectrophotometry
CIJE: 10 RIE: 0 CAT: 20

Spectroscopes
CIJE: 2 RIE: 0 CAT: 04

Spectrum Healthcare Solutions Inc
CIJE: 0 RIE: 1 CAT: 17

Spectrum of Teaching Styles (Mosston)
CIJE: 5 RIE: 1 CAT: 15

Speculum Mentis
CIJE: 0 RIE: 1 CAT: 22

Speech Accommodation
CIJE: 5 RIE: 5 CAT: 13
SN See also "Accommodation Theory"

Speech and Reading Enrichment Program
CIJE: 0 RIE: 1 CAT: 19

Speech Arts League
CIJE: 0 RIE: 1 CAT: 17

Speech Association of America
CIJE: 3 RIE: 2 CAT: 17

Speech Autoinstructional Device
CIJE: 0 RIE: 2 CAT: 04

Speech Coaching
USE Coaching (Speech)

Speech Codes
CIJE: 0 RIE: 2 CAT: 14
SN See also "Hate Speech" and "Politically Correct Communication"

Speech Communication Association
CIJE: 24 RIE: 39 CAT: 17

Speech Communication Education
CIJE: 40 RIE: 112 CAT: 03

Speech Community
CIJE: 6 RIE: 6 CAT: 13

Speech Convergence
CIJE: 1 RIE: 1 CAT: 13

Speech Departments
CIJE: 5 RIE: 4 CAT: 05

Speech Discrimination
CIJE: 10 RIE: 2 CAT: 13

Speech Events
CIJE: 5 RIE: 8 CAT: 16

Speech Functions
CIJE: 4 RIE: 2 CAT: 13

Speech Identification
CIJE: 2 RIE: 2 CAT: 13

Speech Improvement Project of Philadelphia
CIJE: 1 RIE: 0 CAT: 17

Speech Language Pathology Assessment Instrument
CIJE: 0 RIE: 1 CAT: 21

Speech Melody
CIJE: 1 RIE: 0 CAT: 13

Speech Perception
CIJE: 47 RIE: 18 CAT: 13

Speech Physiology
CIJE: 4 RIE: 1 CAT: 13

Speech Play
CIJE: 2 RIE: 1 CAT: 13

Speech Print Relationship
CIJE: 0 RIE: 1 CAT: 13

Speech Rate
CIJE: 52 RIE: 11 CAT: 13

Speech Reception Threshold
CIJE: 1 RIE: 1 CAT: 13

Speech Recoding
CIJE: 1 RIE: 0 CAT: 13

Speech Recognition
CIJE: 5 RIE: 6 CAT: 20
SN See also "Automatic Speech Recognition" and "Voice Recognition"

Speech Research
CIJE: 10 RIE: 34 CAT: 15

Speech Restrictions (Colleges)
CIJE: 1 RIE: 3 CAT: 14

Speech Thinking
CIJE: 0 RIE: 2 CAT: 13

Speech Through Vision Project
CIJE: 2 RIE: 0 CAT: 19

Speech to Print Phonics
CIJE: 0 RIE: 1 CAT: 15

Speech Tournaments
CIJE: 0 RIE: 3 CAT: 16

Speech Writing
CIJE: 13 RIE: 13 CAT: 16

Speed
CIJE: 7 RIE: 1 CAT: 20

Speed Limits
CIJE: 0 RIE: 1 CAT: 14

Speed Reader II
CIJE: 0 RIE: 1 CAT: 04

Speedball
CIJE: 0 RIE: 2 CAT: 16

SPEEDE ExPRESS Electronic Transcript System
CIJE: 0 RIE: 1 CAT: 04

Speededness (Tests)
CIJE: 13 RIE: 18 CAT: 21

Speededness Quotient
CIJE: 2 RIE: 1 CAT: 21

Speedier Project
CIJE: 0 RIE: 2 CAT: 19

Speeding
CIJE: 0 RIE: 3 CAT: 14

Speedometers
CIJE: 2 RIE: 0 CAT: 04

Speedwriting
CIJE: 0 RIE: 1 CAT: 20

Speleology
CIJE: 5 RIE: 1 CAT: 20

SPELL Programing Language
CIJE: 0 RIE: 1 CAT: 04

Spelling and Writing Patterns
CIJE: 4 RIE: 8 CAT: 22

Spelling Bees
CIJE: 4 RIE: 2 CAT: 16

Spelling Errors
CIJE: 11 RIE: 1 CAT: 13

Spelling Growth
CIJE: 29 RIE: 30 CAT: 22

Spelling Patterns
CIJE: 23 RIE: 20 CAT: 13

Spelling Reform
CIJE: 5 RIE: 5 CAT: 13

Spelman College GA
CIJE: 9 RIE: 4 CAT: 17

Spence (Kenneth)
CIJE: 1 RIE: 1 CAT: 18

Spencer (Herbert)
CIJE: 5 RIE: 1 CAT: 18

Spencer Foundation
CIJE: 1 RIE: 1 CAT: 17

Spencerport Central School District NY
CIJE: 0 RIE: 1 CAT: 17

Spending Patterns
CIJE: 14 RIE: 8 CAT: 16

Speno McCloskey Amendment
CIJE: 0 RIE: 1 CAT: 14

Spens (Sir Patrick)
CIJE: 1 RIE: 0 CAT: 18

Spenser (Edmund)
CIJE: 2 RIE: 0 CAT: 18

SPERI
USE Strategic Planning for Educ Reform and Improvement

Spertus College of Judaica IL
CIJE: 0 RIE: 1 CAT: 17

Spheres (Geometry)
CIJE: 8 RIE: 1 CAT: 20

Sphericity Tests
CIJE: 7 RIE: 7 CAT: 21

SPICE Center WV
CIJE: 0 RIE: 1 CAT: 17

SPICE Program
CIJE: 2 RIE: 0 CAT: 19
SN Stanford Program on International and Cross Cultural Education

Spices
CIJE: 0 RIE: 1 CAT: 20

Spiders
CIJE: 10 RIE: 3 CAT: 20

SPIES Rating Scale
USE Stanford Preschool Internal External Scale

Spin Control
CIJE: 1 RIE: 0 CAT: 15

Spin Doctors
CIJE: 1 RIE: 0 CAT: 10

Spinal Cord Injuries
CIJE: 25 RIE: 17 CAT: 11

SPINDEX System
CIJE: 0 RIE: 1 CAT: 04

SPINE Test
CIJE: 1 RIE: 0 CAT: 21

Spinel
CIJE: 1 RIE: 0 CAT: 20

Spinoza (Baruch)
CIJE: 2 RIE: 0 CAT: 18

Spiral Aftereffects (Psychology)
CIJE: 2 RIE: 0 CAT: 11

Spiral of Silence Theory
CIJE: 1 RIE: 2 CAT: 15

Spirantization
CIJE: 0 RIE: 0 CAT: 13
UF Spirants

Spirants
USE Spirantization

SPIRIT (Writing Aid)
CIJE: 0 RIE: 0 CAT: 04

Spirit Duplication
CIJE: 0 RIE: 1 CAT: 20

Spirit River School Division AB
CIJE: 0 RIE: 1 CAT: 17

Spiritual Development
CIJE: 25 RIE: 13 CAT: 11

Spiritual Experiences
CIJE: 18 RIE: 3 CAT: 16
SN See also "Religious Experiences"

Spiritual Healing
USE Faith Healing

Spiritual Health
CIJE: 7 RIE: 3 CAT: 11

Spiritual Needs
CIJE: 2 RIE: 0 CAT: 16

Spiritual Values
CIJE: 0 RIE: 3 CAT: 16

Spiritual Well Being
CIJE: 0 RIE: 1 CAT: 11

Spiritual Well Being Scale
CIJE: 0 RIE: 1 CAT: 21

Spirituality
CIJE: 60 RIE: 16 CAT: 16

Spirituals
CIJE: 1 RIE: 0 CAT: 16
SN If appropriate, use "Black Spirituals"

Spirogyra
CIJE: 1 RIE: 0 CAT: 20

Spirolaterals
CIJE: 3 RIE: 1 CAT: 20

Spline Function
CIJE: 4 RIE: 1 CAT: 21

Splints
CIJE: 1 RIE: 1 CAT: 04

Split Half Test Reliability
CIJE: 9 RIE: 4 CAT: 21

Split Infinitives
CIJE: 2 RIE: 0 CAT: 13

Split Plot Designs
CIJE: 3 RIE: 1 CAT: 15

Split Vu Reading Readiness Program
CIJE: 1 RIE: 0 CAT: 19

Splitting (Psychology)
CIJE: 0 RIE: 1 CAT: 11

Spock (Benjamin)
CIJE: 0 RIE: 1 CAT: 18

Spodek Early Childhood Education Program Analysis
CIJE: 1 RIE: 0 CAT: 21

Spokan
CIJE: 0 RIE: 1 CAT: 13

Spokane (Tribe)
CIJE: 1 RIE: 5 CAT: 08

Spokane Area Vocational Skills Center WA
CIJE: 0 RIE: 1 CAT: 17

Spokane Community College WA
CIJE: 1 RIE: 5 CAT: 17

Spokane Press
CIJE: 0 RIE: 1 CAT: 22

Spokane Public Schools WA
CIJE: 5 RIE: 0 CAT: 17

Spokane Public Telecommunications Center WA
CIJE: 0 RIE: 1 CAT: 17

Spoken Albanian
CIJE: 0 RIE: 1 CAT: 22

Spondee Recognition Tests
CIJE: 1 RIE: 0 CAT: 21

Sponge Painting
CIJE: 1 RIE: 0 CAT: 03

Sponsored Materials
CIJE: 1 RIE: 4 CAT: 16

Sponsored Research
CIJE: 32 RIE: 37 CAT: 16

Sponsors
CIJE: 16 RIE: 29 CAT: 10

Spontaneous Divergent Academic Test (Ball)
CIJE: 0 RIE: 1 CAT: 21

Spontaneous Generation
CIJE: 1 RIE: 0 CAT: 15

Spontaneous Numerical Correspondence Task
CIJE: 0 RIE: 2 CAT: 21

Spontaneous Recovery
CIJE: 3 RIE: 0 CAT: 11

Spontaneous Remission
CIJE: 1 RIE: 0 CAT: 11

Spontaneous Response Drawing
CIJE: 1 RIE: 0 CAT: 16

Spontaneous Singing
CIJE: 0 RIE: 1 CAT: 16

Spontaneous Speech
CIJE: 27 RIE: 32 CAT: 13

Spoon River Anthology
CIJE: 0 RIE: 2 CAT: 22

Spoon River College IL
CIJE: 2 RIE: 1 CAT: 17

Spoonerisms
CIJE: 7 RIE: 0 CAT: 13

Spores
CIJE: 1 RIE: 0 CAT: 20

Sport Ambassadors
CIJE: 1 RIE: 0 CAT: 16

Sport and Recreation Index
CIJE: 1 RIE: 0 CAT: 22

Sport Arena Management
CIJE: 0 RIE: 1 CAT: 16

Sport Competitiveness
CIJE: 1 RIE: 0 CAT: 16

Sport Competitiveness Inventory
CIJE: 0 RIE: 2 CAT: 21

Sport for All
CIJE: 0 RIE: 1 CAT: 16

Sport History
CIJE: 20 RIE: 9 CAT: 12

Sport Injuries
CIJE: 7 RIE: 1 CAT: 16

SPORT IT (Australia)
CIJE: 0 RIE: 1 CAT: 19

Sport Management
CIJE: 13 RIE: 9 CAT: 16

Sport Sociology
CIJE: 1 RIE: 7 CAT: 03

Sporting Goods
CIJE: 0 RIE: 1 CAT: 04

Sports Attitudes Inventory
CIJE: 0 RIE: 2 CAT: 21

Sports Bras
CIJE: 2 RIE: 2 CAT: 16

Sports Clubs
CIJE: 2 RIE: 0 CAT: 10

Sports Illustrated
CIJE: 1 RIE: 1 CAT: 22

Sports Law
CIJE: 1 RIE: 0 CAT: 14

Sports Literature
CIJE: 5 RIE: 2 CAT: 16

Sports Officials
CIJE: 4 RIE: 10 CAT: 09

Sports Officiating
CIJE: 2 RIE: 3 CAT: 16

Sports Stories
CIJE: 3 RIE: 2 CAT: 16

Spouse Abuse
CIJE: 13 RIE: 4 CAT: 11

Spouse Abuse Shelters
CIJE: 1 RIE: 1 CAT: 05

Stairclimbing
CIJE: 2 RIE: 0 CAT: 16

STAIRS Software Package
CIJE: 2 RIE: 0 CAT: 04

Stake (Robert E)
CIJE: 3 RIE: 3 CAT: 18

Stake Evaluation Model
CIJE: 0 RIE: 1 CAT: 15

Stakeholder Evaluation
CIJE: 34 RIE: 21 CAT: 15

Stakeholder Survey
CIJE: 1 RIE: 4 CAT: 21

Stakeholders
CIJE: 42 RIE: 12 CAT: 10

Stalin (Joseph)
CIJE: 3 RIE: 2 CAT: 18

Stallings Environmentally Based Screen
CIJE: 0 RIE: 1 CAT: 21

Stallings Observation Instrument
CIJE: 2 RIE: 2 CAT: 21

Stallings Observation System
CIJE: 4 RIE: 0 CAT: 21

Stamford High School CT
CIJE: 0 RIE: 1 CAT: 17

Stamp Act
CIJE: 1 RIE: 1 CAT: 14

Stampers
CIJE: 0 RIE: 2 CAT: 09

Standard 17
CIJE: 4 RIE: 0 CAT: 14

Standard Assessment System
CIJE: 1 RIE: 1 CAT: 21

Standard Assessment Tasks (Great Britain)
CIJE: 1 RIE: 1 CAT: 21

Standard Behavior Chart (Pennypacker)
CIJE: 3 RIE: 2 CAT: 21

Standard Deviation
CIJE: 21 RIE: 7 CAT: 15

Standard Educational Intelligence Test
CIJE: 1 RIE: 0 CAT: 21

Standard Industrial Classifications
CIJE: 0 RIE: 6 CAT: 21

Standard Literary Norm
CIJE: 0 RIE: 1 CAT: 13

Standard Metropolitan Statistical Areas
CIJE: 12 RIE: 15 CAT: 21

Standard Minimum Rules for Treatment of Prisoners
CIJE: 0 RIE: 1 CAT: 16

Standard Occupational Classification
CIJE: 2 RIE: 10 CAT: 15

Standard Oil Company
CIJE: 2 RIE: 0 CAT: 17

Standard Oral Reading Paragraph Test
CIJE: 0 RIE: 1 CAT: 21

Standard Progressive Matrices
CIJE: 6 RIE: 8 CAT: 15

Standard Reading Inventory
CIJE: 1 RIE: 1 CAT: 21

Standard Reference Code
CIJE: 1 RIE: 0 CAT: 15

Standard Scores
CIJE: 6 RIE: 4 CAT: 21

Standard Setting
CIJE: 85 RIE: 123 CAT: 21

Standard Training Agreements
CIJE: 0 RIE: 1 CAT: 16

Standard Transformation of Academic Grades
CIJE: 0 RIE: 1 CAT: 16

Standardization
CIJE: 94 RIE: 28 CAT: 21

Standardized Assessment System
CIJE: 1 RIE: 3 CAT: 21

Standardized Curriculum
CIJE: 4 RIE: 2 CAT: 03

Standardized Curriculum Oriented Pupil Evaluation
CIJE: 0 RIE: 8 CAT: 21
UF SCOPE Tests

Standardized Data Reporting System
CIJE: 5 RIE: 2 CAT: 21

Standardized Educational Program Audit
CIJE: 0 RIE: 1 CAT: 21

Standardized Mean Change Measures
CIJE: 0 RIE: 1 CAT: 21

Standardized Mean Difference
CIJE: 3 RIE: 0 CAT: 21

Standardized Morbidity Ratio
CIJE: 0 RIE: 1 CAT: 11

Standardized Regression Coefficients
CIJE: 0 RIE: 1 CAT: 21

Standardized Residuals
CIJE: 1 RIE: 1 CAT: 21

Standardized Tests of Achievement for Fiji
CIJE: 0 RIE: 1 CAT: 21

Standards for Educational and Psychological Tests
CIJE: 13 RIE: 11 CAT: 21

Standards for Evaluation Educ Prog Proj Materials
CIJE: 12 RIE: 20 CAT: 21
SN Standards for Evaluations of Educational Programs, Projects and Materials

Standards for Excellence in Trade Industrial Educ
CIJE: 0 RIE: 0 CAT: 22

Standards for School Media Programs
CIJE: 14 RIE: 3 CAT: 22

Standards for Teacher Competence (AFT NCME NEA)
CIJE: 0 RIE: 1 CAT: 15
SN "Standards for Teacher Competence in Educational Assessment of Students" (1990)

Standards for Two Year Coll and Lower Div Math
CIJE: 0 RIE: 1 CAT: 15

Standards Industrial Arts Education Programs Proj
CIJE: 2 RIE: 0 CAT: 19

Standards of Excellence CO
CIJE: 0 RIE: 3 CAT: 19

Standards of Work Performance (Australia)
CIJE: 0 RIE: 1 CAT: 15
UF Australian Standards of Work Performance

Standing Bear (Luther)
CIJE: 1 RIE: 0 CAT: 18

Standing Conference National University Libraries
CIJE: 1 RIE: 0 CAT: 17

Standing Rock Community College ND
CIJE: 0 RIE: 1 CAT: 17

Standing Rock Sioux Reservation ND
CIJE: 1 RIE: 1 CAT: 17

Stanford Achievement Tests
CIJE: 65 RIE: 229 CAT: 21

Stanford Achievement Tests for Hearing Impaired
CIJE: 5 RIE: 3 CAT: 21

Stanford Artificial Intelligence Project
CIJE: 1 RIE: 1 CAT: 21

Stanford Bank Management Simulation
CIJE: 0 RIE: 1 CAT: 15

Stanford Binet Intelligence Scale
CIJE: 136 RIE: 167 CAT: 21

Stanford Binet Intelligence Scale Fourth Edition
CIJE: 15 RIE: 4 CAT: 21

Stanford Brentwood CAI Project
CIJE: 2 RIE: 5 CAT: 19

Stanford Center for R and D in Teaching CA
CIJE: 2 RIE: 2 CAT: 17

Stanford Collegial Evaluation Program
CIJE: 0 RIE: 1 CAT: 19

Stanford Computer Based Educator Train Interv
CIJE: 0 RIE: 0 CAT: 19
UF SCETI

Stanford Curriculum Study
CIJE: 1 RIE: 4 CAT: 22

Stanford Denver Project
CIJE: 0 RIE: 2 CAT: 19

Stanford Diagnostic Mathematics Test
CIJE: 1 RIE: 4 CAT: 21

Stanford Diagnostic Reading Test
CIJE: 5 RIE: 15 CAT: 21

Stanford Early School Achievement Test
CIJE: 3 RIE: 11 CAT: 21

Stanford Heart Disease Prevention Program
CIJE: 1 RIE: 1 CAT: 19

Stanford Hypnotic Susceptibility Scale
CIJE: 3 RIE: 0 CAT: 21

Stanford Kohs Block Design Test
CIJE: 0 RIE: 1 CAT: 21

Stanford Logic Instructional System
CIJE: 0 RIE: 1 CAT: 15

Stanford PDP One System
CIJE: 0 RIE: 2 CAT: 15

Stanford Physics Information Retrieval System
CIJE: 0 RIE: 4 CAT: 15

Stanford Preschool Internal External Scale
CIJE: 3 RIE: 1 CAT: 21
UF SPIES Rating Scale

Stanford Prison Study
CIJE: 2 RIE: 0 CAT: 19

Stanford Public Information Retrieval System
CIJE: 4 RIE: 6 CAT: 15

Stanford Reading and Television Study
CIJE: 0 RIE: 1 CAT: 22

Stanford Research Institute CA
CIJE: 1 RIE: 3 CAT: 17

Stanford School Scheduling System
CIJE: 0 RIE: 6 CAT: 15

Stanford Schools Collaborative
CIJE: 0 RIE: 1 CAT: 19

Stanford Secondary School Project
CIJE: 0 RIE: 1 CAT: 19

Stanford Teacher Competence Appraisal Guide
CIJE: 0 RIE: 5 CAT: 21

Stanford Teacher Education Program
CIJE: 3 RIE: 4 CAT: 19

Stanford Test of Academic Skills
CIJE: 0 RIE: 10 CAT: 21

Stanford University CA
CIJE: 144 RIE: 149 CAT: 17

Stanford Writing Assessment Program
CIJE: 1 RIE: 2 CAT: 19

Stanfords Environment for Teaching Program
CIJE: 1 RIE: 1 CAT: 19

Stanine Scores
USE Stanines

Stanines
CIJE: 1 RIE: 2 CAT: 21
UF Stanine Scores

Stanislaus County Multioccupational Adult Training
CIJE: 0 RIE: 5 CAT: 19

Stanislavski (Konstantin)
CIJE: 1 RIE: 4 CAT: 18

Stanley v Georgia
CIJE: 1 RIE: 0 CAT: 14

Stanley v Illinois
CIJE: 1 RIE: 0 CAT: 14

Stanly Technical College NC
CIJE: 1 RIE: 1 CAT: 17

Stanton (Edwin)
CIJE: 1 RIE: 1 CAT: 18

Stanton (Elizabeth Cady)
CIJE: 3 RIE: 1 CAT: 18

Staples (Robert)
CIJE: 0 RIE: 1 CAT: 18

Staples Area Vocational Technical School MN
CIJE: 1 RIE: 0 CAT: 17

Staples Governing Board CT
CIJE: 2 RIE: 0 CAT: 17

Staples Teacher Center MN
CIJE: 0 RIE: 1 CAT: 17

Stapol (Simulation Game)
CIJE: 1 RIE: 3 CAT: 15

Star Charts
CIJE: 1 RIE: 2 CAT: 20

STaR Neuro Cognitive Assessment Program
CIJE: 0 RIE: 1 CAT: 04

STaR Neuro Cognitive Reading Program
CIJE: 0 RIE: 1 CAT: 04

STAR Project TN
USE Student Teacher Achievement Ratio Project TN

Star Schools
CIJE: 5 RIE: 10 CAT: 05

Star Spangled Banner
CIJE: 0 RIE: 0 CAT: 22

STAR Test Taking Strategy
CIJE: 0 RIE: 1 CAT: 15

Star Tracker
CIJE: 1 RIE: 0 CAT: 04

Star Trek
CIJE: 5 RIE: 2 CAT: 22

Star Trek the Next Generation
CIJE: 0 RIE: 1 CAT: 22

STAR TV
CIJE: 0 RIE: 2 CAT: 19

Star Wars (Film)
CIJE: 0 RIE: 3 CAT: 22

Star Wars (Strategic Defense)
USE Strategic Defense Initiative

Stark Technical College OH
CIJE: 0 RIE: 1 CAT: 17

Starkweather Originality Test
CIJE: 0 RIE: 3 CAT: 21

STARPAHC Project
CIJE: 0 RIE: 1 CAT: 19

Starr Commonwealth Schools
CIJE: 1 RIE: 2 CAT: 17

Starry Night (van Gogh)
CIJE: 0 RIE: 1 CAT: 22

Stars Case Abstract Vignettes
CIJE: 0 RIE: 1 CAT: 21
UF Case Abstract Vignettes (Star)

STARS Program MO
USE Science Teachers as Research Scientists Program

StarServe
CIJE: 0 RIE: 1 CAT: 19

Start Planning Ahead Now
CIJE: 6 RIE: 6 CAT: 19

Start Teaching All Year
CIJE: 0 RIE: 1 CAT: 19

Starter Approach to Reading
CIJE: 0 RIE: 1 CAT: 15

Starter Techniques (Athletics)
CIJE: 0 RIE: 1 CAT: 15

Starting Early
CIJE: 1 RIE: 1 CAT: 19
SN Alcohol education program (Chicago IL)

Starvation
CIJE: 1 RIE: 2 CAT: 11

Stasis Theory
CIJE: 0 RIE: 1 CAT: 15
SN Element of rhetorical theory

Stat Helper
CIJE: 0 RIE: 1 CAT: 04

State Advisory Councils on Vocational Education
CIJE: 0 RIE: 10 CAT: 05

State Aid Formulas
CIJE: 9 RIE: 31 CAT: 15

State and Local Fiscal Assistance Act 1972
CIJE: 1 RIE: 2 CAT: 14

State Anxiety
CIJE: 12 RIE: 12 CAT: 11

State Archives
CIJE: 0 RIE: 1 CAT: 05

State Assessment of Educational Progress
CIJE: 0 RIE: 1 CAT: 19

State Associations
CIJE: 9 RIE: 3 CAT: 05

State Bilingual Program MI
USE Michigan State Bilingual Program

State Board Test Pool Examination
CIJE: 1 RIE: 3 CAT: 21

State Capacity Building Program
CIJE: 1 RIE: 26 CAT: 19
UF Capacity Building for States

State Capitals
CIJE: 3 RIE: 1 CAT: 16

State Center Community College District CA
CIJE: 0 RIE: 1 CAT: 17

State Central Scientific Medical Library (USSR)
CIJE: 1 RIE: 0 CAT: 17

State Characteristics
CIJE: 0 RIE: 1 CAT: 16

State City Relationship
CIJE: 0 RIE: 4 CAT: 16

State College and University Systems
CIJE: 1 RIE: 16 CAT: 05

State College Area Parks and Recreation Department
CIJE: 1 RIE: 0 CAT: 17

State College Area School District PA
CIJE: 1 RIE: 2 CAT: 17

State College of Iowa
CIJE: 0 RIE: 1 CAT: 17

State College of Victoria (Australia)
CIJE: 2 RIE: 0 CAT: 17

State College of Victoria at Hawthorn (Australia)
CIJE: 0 RIE: 1 CAT: 17

State College Relationship
CIJE: 1 RIE: 3 CAT: 16

State Community College of East Saint Louis IL
CIJE: 0 RIE: 1 CAT: 17

State Competency Tests
CIJE: 2 RIE: 4 CAT: 21

State Competitive Scholarship Program
CIJE: 0 RIE: 1 CAT: 19

State Conference Community College Administration
CIJE: 0 RIE: 1 CAT: 02

State Conferences
CIJE: 2 RIE: 2 CAT: 02

State Consultant Model Program
CIJE: 0 RIE: 1 CAT: 19

State Coordinating Boards
CIJE: 2 RIE: 3 CAT: 05

State Council of Higher Education for Virginia
CIJE: 0 RIE: 3 CAT: 17
UF Virginia State Council of Higher Education

State Councils on Vocational Education
CIJE: 1 RIE: 3 CAT: 10

State Dependent Retention
CIJE: 0 RIE: 1 CAT: 11
SN Tendency to recall something more easily when in the same state as when one first learned it

State Disadvantaged Child Project OR
CIJE: 0 RIE: 3 CAT: 19

State Dissemination Grants Program
CIJE: 0 RIE: 15 CAT: 19

State Economic Areas
CIJE: 0 RIE: 2 CAT: 16

State Education Agencies Symposium
CIJE: 0 RIE: 1 CAT: 02

State Education Associations
CIJE: 2 RIE: 3 CAT: 05

State Education Encyclopedia (Texas)
CIJE: 0 RIE: 1 CAT: 22

State Education Performance Chart
CIJE: 0 RIE: 3 CAT: 22
SN The Department of Education's annual (1983-91) oversize state-by-state ranking of education progress including student performance, per-pupil expenditures, and teacher salaries
UF Wall Chart (ED)

State Educational Incentive Grant Program AK
CIJE: 0 RIE: 1 CAT: 19
UF Alaska State Educational Incentive Grant Program; SEIG Awards AK

State Educational Records and Reports Series
CIJE: 0 RIE: 1 CAT: 22

State Employment and Training Councils
CIJE: 0 RIE: 1 CAT: 05

State Employment Initiatives for Youth
CIJE: 0 RIE: 1 CAT: 19

State Employment Security Service Agency
CIJE: 0 RIE: 2 CAT: 17

State Energy Conservation Program
CIJE: 0 RIE: 1 CAT: 19

State Epistemic Curiosity Scale (Leherissey)
CIJE: 0 RIE: 1 CAT: 21

State Fair Community College MO
CIJE: 0 RIE: 4 CAT: 17

State Funded Program High Risk Four Year Olds LA
CIJE: 0 RIE: 2 CAT: 19
UF Louisiana State Funded Prog for Hgh Rsk 4 Yr Olds

State Governors
CIJE: 34 RIE: 19 CAT: 16

State Guarantee Agencies
CIJE: 0 RIE: 3 CAT: 05

State Guides
CIJE: 0 RIE: 2 CAT: 16
SN If appropriate, use Descriptor "State Curriculum Guides"

State Higher Education Executive Officers Assn
CIJE: 1 RIE: 7 CAT: 17

State Historical Societies
CIJE: 0 RIE: 4 CAT: 05

State Historical Society of Wisconsin
CIJE: 1 RIE: 2 CAT: 17
UF Wisconsin State Historical Society

State Humanities Councils
CIJE: 0 RIE: 4 CAT: 05

State Implementation Grant Conference
CIJE: 0 RIE: 1 CAT: 02

State Implementation Grant Program
CIJE: 1 RIE: 2 CAT: 14

State Initiatives
CIJE: 2 RIE: 6 CAT: 15

State Intergovernmental Education Project
CIJE: 0 RIE: 1 CAT: 19

State Issues
CIJE: 1 RIE: 14 CAT: 15

State Job Training Coordinating Councils
CIJE: 0 RIE: 3 CAT: 10
UF Job Training Coordinating Councils (States); SJTCCs

State Justice Institute Act 1984
CIJE: 0 RIE: 1 CAT: 14
UF Public Law 98 620

State Leadership Assistance for Technology in Educ
USE Project SLATE

State Legalization Impact Assistance Grants
CIJE: 0 RIE: 2 CAT: 19
UF SLIAGs

State Legislators
CIJE: 6 RIE: 6 CAT: 09

State Legislatures
CIJE: 3 RIE: 16 CAT: 05

State Level Information Base
CIJE: 0 RIE: 3 CAT: 19

State Level Textbook Adoption
CIJE: 7 RIE: 10 CAT: 16
UF Textbook Adoption (State Level)

State Liaison Representatives
CIJE: 2 RIE: 1 CAT: 09

State Library of Ohio Union Catalog
CIJE: 0 RIE: 1 CAT: 22

State Local Relationship
CIJE: 10 RIE: 5 CAT: 16

State Maternal and Child Health Programs Title V
USE Social Security Act Title V

State Mathematics Assessments
CIJE: 0 RIE: 42 CAT: 21
UF Mathematics Assessment (State Level)

State Nonfiscal Survey of Public Elem Sec Educ
CIJE: 0 RIE: 1 CAT: 21

State Occupational Information Coordinating Comm
CIJE: 6 RIE: 16 CAT: 17

State of Oregon v City of Rajneeshpuram
CIJE: 0 RIE: 1 CAT: 14
UF Oregon v Rajneeshpuram

State of the World Atlas (The)
CIJE: 0 RIE: 1 CAT: 22

State Pension Plans
CIJE: 0 RIE: 1 CAT: 14

State Policy
CIJE: 1 RIE: 2 CAT: 14

State Registers of Child Abuse
USE Child Abuse Registries

State Responsibility
CIJE: 3 RIE: 9 CAT: 16

State Role
CIJE: 28 RIE: 33 CAT: 16

State School Library Media Supervisors Assn
CIJE: 0 RIE: 1 CAT: 17

State Skills Corporations
CIJE: 0 RIE: 1 CAT: 05
SN Public/private ventures designed to increase the supply of skilled workers in a state

State Student Assessment Prog Database 1992 93
CIJE: 0 RIE: 1 CAT: 21

State Student Incentive Grants
CIJE: 1 RIE: 28 CAT: 14

State Supported Day Care Assistance
CIJE: 0 RIE: 1 CAT: 14

State Takeovers
CIJE: 2 RIE: 1 CAT: 16

State Taxes
CIJE: 2 RIE: 6 CAT: 14

State Technical Institute at Memphis TN
CIJE: 2 RIE: 1 CAT: 17

State Technical Services Act 1965
CIJE: 0 RIE: 2 CAT: 14

State Technical Services Program
CIJE: 0 RIE: 1 CAT: 19

State Textbook Adoption Policies
CIJE: 1 RIE: 5 CAT: 15

State Trait Anxiety Inventory
CIJE: 14 RIE: 4 CAT: 21

State Trait Anxiety Inventory (Spielberger)
CIJE: 35 RIE: 25 CAT: 21

State Trait Anxiety Inventory for Children
CIJE: 12 RIE: 0 CAT: 21

State Trait Anxiety Theory
CIJE: 6 RIE: 5 CAT: 21

State Tribal Relationship
CIJE: 1 RIE: 19 CAT: 16

State University Admissions Examination (New York)
CIJE: 0 RIE: 2 CAT: 21

State University New York Librarians Association
CIJE: 1 RIE: 3 CAT: 17

State University of Ghent (Belgium)
CIJE: 2 RIE: 0 CAT: 17

State University of Leiden (Netherlands)
CIJE: 0 RIE: 1 CAT: 17

State University of Nebraska
CIJE: 5 RIE: 24 CAT: 17

State University of New York
CIJE: 67 RIE: 284 CAT: 17
UF SUNY

State University of New York Albany
CIJE: 35 RIE: 39 CAT: 17

State University of New York Amherst
CIJE: 1 RIE: 0 CAT: 17

State University of New York Binghamton
CIJE: 3 RIE: 3 CAT: 17

State University of New York Buffalo
CIJE: 50 RIE: 51 CAT: 17

State University of New York Coll at Brockport
CIJE: 10 RIE: 12 CAT: 17
UF College at Brockport NY

State University of New York Coll at Buffalo
CIJE: 10 RIE: 6 CAT: 17
SN Do not confuse with State University of New York Buffalo
UF College at Buffalo NY

State University of New York Coll at Cortland
CIJE: 11 RIE: 7 CAT: 17

State University of New York Coll at Fredonia
CIJE: 5 RIE: 10 CAT: 17

State University of New York Coll at Geneseo
CIJE: 1 RIE: 6 CAT: 17

State University of New York Coll at New Paltz
CIJE: 2 RIE: 1 CAT: 17

State University of New York Coll at Old Westbury
CIJE: 5 RIE: 4 CAT: 17

State University of New York Coll at Oneonta
CIJE: 0 RIE: 2 CAT: 17

State University of New York Coll at Oswego
CIJE: 9 RIE: 20 CAT: 17

State University of New York Coll at Plattsburgh
CIJE: 6 RIE: 9 CAT: 17

State University of New York Coll at Potsdam
CIJE: 5 RIE: 8 CAT: 17

State University of New York Coll at Purchase
CIJE: 4 RIE: 1 CAT: 17

State University of New York Empire State Coll
CIJE: 19 RIE: 39 CAT: 17
UF Empire State College NY

State University of New York Stony Brook
CIJE: 32 RIE: 19 CAT: 17

State University of NY Agric Tech Coll Alfred
CIJE: 1 RIE: 2 CAT: 17
UF Agricultural and Technical College at Alfred NY

State University of NY Agric Tech Coll Canton
CIJE: 0 RIE: 1 CAT: 17

State University of NY Agric Tech Coll Delhi
CIJE: 2 RIE: 1 CAT: 17

State University of NY Agric Tech Coll Morrisville
CIJE: 2 RIE: 0 CAT: 17
UF Agricultural and Technical College Morrisville NY

State University of NY Coll of Techn Farmingdale
CIJE: 0 RIE: 0 CAT: 17

State University of NY Inst of Techn at Utica Rome
CIJE: 0 RIE: 0 CAT: 17

State University of Utrecht (Netherlands)
CIJE: 1 RIE: 2 CAT: 17
UF University of Utrecht (Netherlands)

State University Survey
CIJE: 1 RIE: 0 CAT: 21

State University System of Florida
CIJE: 11 RIE: 47 CAT: 17
UF Florida State University System

State Urban Education Program (New York)
CIJE: 0 RIE: 3 CAT: 19

Statements About Schools Inventory
CIJE: 0 RIE: 2 CAT: 21

States (Geopolitical Regions)
CIJE: 12 RIE: 24 CAT: 07

Statewide Assessment of Educational Progress
CIJE: 2 RIE: 1 CAT: 21

Statewide Course Numbering System
CIJE: 0 RIE: 2 CAT: 15

Statewide Education Activities Rural Colo Health
CIJE: 1 RIE: 0 CAT: 19
UF SEARCH Program

Statewide Instructional Computing Network NY
CIJE: 0 RIE: 1 CAT: 17

Statewide Job Placement Service MO
CIJE: 0 RIE: 1 CAT: 17

Statewide Longitudinal Study CA
CIJE: 1 RIE: 12 CAT: 19

Statewide Measures Inventory (NCHEMS)
CIJE: 0 RIE: 1 CAT: 21

Statewide Priorities
CIJE: 1 RIE: 2 CAT: 16

Statewide Student Followup System
CIJE: 0 RIE: 1 CAT: 15

Static Abstractions
CIJE: 0 RIE: 1 CAT: 13

Static Balance
CIJE: 0 RIE: 2 CAT: 16

Statics
CIJE: 9 RIE: 0 CAT: 20

Station CMS TV MO
CIJE: 1 RIE: 0 CAT: 17

Station College Executive Project Adult Learning
CIJE: 1 RIE: 2 CAT: 19

Station KCET TV CA
CIJE: 2 RIE: 0 CAT: 17

Station KCMW FM MO
CIJE: 1 RIE: 0 CAT: 17

Station KDIN TV IA
CIJE: 1 RIE: 0 CAT: 17

Station KETC TV MO
CIJE: 5 RIE: 0 CAT: 17

Station KFME TV ND
CIJE: 1 RIE: 0 CAT: 17

Station KIXE CA
CIJE: 1 RIE: 0 CAT: 17

Station KLRN TX
CIJE: 1 RIE: 1 CAT: 17

Station KMOX TV MO
CIJE: 1 RIE: 0 CAT: 17

Station KOAC TV OR
CIJE: 1 RIE: 1 CAT: 17

Station KOAP TV OR
CIJE: 1 RIE: 0 CAT: 17

Station KOCE TV CA
CIJE: 1 RIE: 1 CAT: 17

Station KPEC WA
CIJE: 1 RIE: 0 CAT: 17

Station KPFT Radio TX
CIJE: 1 RIE: 0 CAT: 17

Station KPTS TV
CIJE: 1 RIE: 0 CAT: 17

Station KQED CA
CIJE: 2 RIE: 2 CAT: 17

Station KSL TV UT
CIJE: 0 RIE: 1 CAT: 17

Station KTCA TV MN
CIJE: 1 RIE: 0 CAT: 17

Station KTCI TV MN
CIJE: 1 RIE: 0 CAT: 17

Station KTWU TV KS
CIJE: 0 RIE: 1 CAT: 17

Station KUAT TV
CIJE: 3 RIE: 0 CAT: 17

Station KWMK TV
CIJE: 1 RIE: 0 CAT: 17

Station Trafficking
CIJE: 0 RIE: 1 CAT: 16

Station WABE FM
CIJE: 1 RIE: 0 CAT: 17

Station WEFM IL
CIJE: 0 RIE: 1 CAT: 17

Station WETA TV DC
CIJE: 3 RIE: 1 CAT: 17

Station WFIL TV
CIJE: 0 RIE: 1 CAT: 17

Station WFIU FM IN
CIJE: 0 RIE: 1 CAT: 17

Station WGBH TV MA
CIJE: 0 RIE: 4 CAT: 17

Station WHDH TV
CIJE: 1 RIE: 0 CAT: 17

Station WHS TV
CIJE: 1 RIE: 0 CAT: 17

Station WJA TV
CIJE: 1 RIE: 0 CAT: 17

Station WKNO TV TN
CIJE: 1 RIE: 0 CAT: 17

Station WKRS IL
CIJE: 1 RIE: 0 CAT: 17

Station WMUL TV WV
CIJE: 0 RIE: 1 CAT: 17

Station WMVS TV
CIJE: 1 RIE: 0 CAT: 17

Station WNDU TV
CIJE: 1 RIE: 0 CAT: 17

Station WNYC NY
CIJE: 0 RIE: 1 CAT: 17

Station WNYE FM NY
CIJE: 0 RIE: 1 CAT: 17

Station WPSX TV PA
CIJE: 1 RIE: 1 CAT: 17

Station WQED TV PA
CIJE: 2 RIE: 3 CAT: 17

Station WSWP TV WV
CIJE: 0 RIE: 1 CAT: 17

Station WTTW TV IL
CIJE: 0 RIE: 1 CAT: 17

Station WVPT TV VA
CIJE: 1 RIE: 0 CAT: 17

Station WWVU TV WV
CIJE: 0 RIE: 1 CAT: 17

Station WXXI TV NY
CIJE: 0 RIE: 1 CAT: 17

Station WYES TV LA
CIJE: 1 RIE: 0 CAT: 17

Stationary Engineering
CIJE: 0 RIE: 24 CAT: 20

Statistical Analysis System
CIJE: 23 RIE: 25 CAT: 04

Statistical Interaction
CIJE: 2 RIE: 1 CAT: 21

Statistical Mechanics
CIJE: 6 RIE: 0 CAT: 15

Statistical Moderation
CIJE: 0 RIE: 1 CAT: 15

Statistical Package for the Social Sciences
CIJE: 21 RIE: 37 CAT: 04
UF SPSS Computer Program

Statistical Package for the Social Sciences PC
CIJE: 2 RIE: 3 CAT: 04
SN Personal computer version

Statistical Packages
CIJE: 11 RIE: 13 CAT: 04

Statistical Process Control
CIJE: 8 RIE: 9 CAT: 15

Statistical Processing System
CIJE: 0 RIE: 1 CAT: 04
UF SPS Computer Program

Statistical Reasoning
CIJE: 1 RIE: 1 CAT: 15

Statistical Rules of Thumb
USE Rules of Thumb (Statistics)

Statistical Simulation
CIJE: 3 RIE: 3 CAT: 15

Statistical Test Item Collection System
CIJE: 0 RIE: 2 CAT: 04

Statistical Typewriting
CIJE: 0 RIE: 1 CAT: 20

Statisticians
CIJE: 2 RIE: 1 CAT: 09

Statue of Liberty
CIJE: 7 RIE: 6 CAT: 16

Status Attainment
CIJE: 4 RIE: 3 CAT: 16

Status Attainment Theory
CIJE: 2 RIE: 2 CAT: 15

Status Characteristic Theory
CIJE: 1 RIE: 1 CAT: 21

Status Delinquents
USE Status Offenders

Status Discrepancy
CIJE: 0 RIE: 1 CAT: 16
SN See also "Status Inconsistency"

Status Equalization
CIJE: 1 RIE: 1 CAT: 15

Status Hierarchies
CIJE: 0 RIE: 1 CAT: 15

Status Inconsistency
CIJE: 2 RIE: 1 CAT: 16
SN See also "Status Discrepancy"

Status of Teachers
USE Teacher Status

Status Offenders
CIJE: 23 RIE: 29 CAT: 10
UF Status Delinquents

Status Projections
CIJE: 0 RIE: 1 CAT: 16

Status Quo
CIJE: 4 RIE: 3 CAT: 16

Status Reports
CIJE: 10 RIE: 30 CAT: 16

STATUS System
CIJE: 1 RIE: 0 CAT: 04

Status Terms (Linguistics)
CIJE: 0 RIE: 1 CAT: 13

Status Testing
CIJE: 0 RIE: 1 CAT: 21

Status Variables
CIJE: 1 RIE: 0 CAT: 15

Statutory Emancipation
CIJE: 0 RIE: 1 CAT: 14

Staudinger (Hermann)
CIJE: 2 RIE: 0 CAT: 18

Stauffer (Russell G)
CIJE: 1 RIE: 0 CAT: 18

Stay In You Win Project AB
CIJE: 0 RIE: 4 CAT: 19

Stayton School District 77J OR
CIJE: 0 RIE: 1 CAT: 17

Steady State
CIJE: 14 RIE: 5 CAT: 20

Steam
CIJE: 0 RIE: 2 CAT: 20

Steam Heating
CIJE: 0 RIE: 1 CAT: 20

Steam Power Plant Operators
CIJE: 0 RIE: 3 CAT: 09

Steel
CIJE: 2 RIE: 0 CAT: 20

Steel Construction
CIJE: 1 RIE: 3 CAT: 20

Steering (Automotive)
CIJE: 0 RIE: 7 CAT: 20

Stefan Boltzmann Law
CIJE: 2 RIE: 0 CAT: 20

Stein and Glenn Story Schema
CIJE: 0 RIE: 1 CAT: 21

Steinbeck (John)
CIJE: 5 RIE: 8 CAT: 18

Steiner (George)
CIJE: 4 RIE: 0 CAT: 18

Steiner (Rudolf)
CIJE: 10 RIE: 12 CAT: 18

Steinitz (Kate)
CIJE: 1 RIE: 0 CAT: 18

Stellar Parallax
CIJE: 1 RIE: 0 CAT: 20

Stem Analysis
CIJE: 3 RIE: 2 CAT: 15

Stem Leaf Plot
CIJE: 2 RIE: 0 CAT: 20

Stenberg (Richard)
CIJE: 1 RIE: 0 CAT: 18

Stencil Design Test
CIJE: 0 RIE: 1 CAT: 21

Stendahl Readability Formula
CIJE: 0 RIE: 1 CAT: 15

Stendhal
CIJE: 5 RIE: 1 CAT: 18

Stenograph
CIJE: 1 RIE: 0 CAT: 04

Step Curriculum Units
CIJE: 1 RIE: 0 CAT: 03

Step Forward Project KY
CIJE: 0 RIE: 1 CAT: 19

Step Observation Schedule
CIJE: 0 RIE: 1 CAT: 21

Stephan F Austin State University TX
CIJE: 0 RIE: 1 CAT: 17

Stephen F Austin State University TX
CIJE: 2 RIE: 0 CAT: 17

Stephens (Beth)
CIJE: 1 RIE: 0 CAT: 18

Stephens College MO
CIJE: 5 RIE: 5 CAT: 17

Stephens Delys Reinforcement Contingency Interview
CIJE: 2 RIE: 1 CAT: 21

Stephens v Bongart
CIJE: 0 RIE: 1 CAT: 14

Stephenson Q Methodology
CIJE: 0 RIE: 4 CAT: 21

Steppe (The)
CIJE: 0 RIE: 1 CAT: 22

Steppenwolf
CIJE: 1 RIE: 0 CAT: 22

Stepping Up (Aetna)
CIJE: 0 RIE: 1 CAT: 19

STEPS (Curriculum)
CIJE: 0 RIE: 2 CAT: 03
SN Surviving Today's Experiences and Problems Successfully

STePS Problem Solving Model
USE Structured Team Problem Solving

STEPS Program MO
CIJE: 0 RIE: 1 CAT: 19
SN Program of Kansas City School District
UF Striving Toward Excellence in the Perform Students

Steps to Maturity Program BC
CIJE: 0 RIE: 1 CAT: 19

Stepwise Canonical Correlation Analysis
CIJE: 0 RIE: 1 CAT: 21

Stepwise Regression
CIJE: 21 RIE: 10 CAT: 21

Stereo Broadcasting
CIJE: 0 RIE: 1 CAT: 20

Stereo Microscopes
CIJE: 0 RIE: 1 CAT: 04

Stereognosis
CIJE: 1 RIE: 0 CAT: 16

Stereographs
CIJE: 0 RIE: 1 CAT: 04

Stereopathy Acquiescence Scales (Stern et al)
CIJE: 1 RIE: 0 CAT: 21

Stereoscopes
CIJE: 3 RIE: 1 CAT: 04

Stereotype Questionnaire (Rosenkrantz)
CIJE: 1 RIE: 1 CAT: 21

Stereotyped Behavior
CIJE: 13 RIE: 3 CAT: 11

Stereotypy (Psychology)
CIJE: 20 RIE: 0 CAT: 11

Sterilization
CIJE: 35 RIE: 10 CAT: 11

Sterling College KS
CIJE: 1 RIE: 2 CAT: 17

Sterling Learning Center DC
CIJE: 1 RIE: 0 CAT: 17

Sterlings Numbers
CIJE: 1 RIE: 0 CAT: 20

Stern Activities Index
CIJE: 4 RIE: 13 CAT: 21

Stern Teacher Preference Schedule
CIJE: 0 RIE: 2 CAT: 21

Stern v Sibley Memorial Hospital
CIJE: 1 RIE: 0 CAT: 14

Sternberg (R J)
USE Sternberg (Robert)

Sternberg (Robert)
CIJE: 6 RIE: 4 CAT: 18
UF Sternberg (R J)

Sternberg (Saul)
CIJE: 2 RIE: 0 CAT: 18

Sternberg Triarchic Abilities Test
CIJE: 1 RIE: 0 CAT: 21
SN See also "Triarchic Theory of Intelligence (Sternberg)"

Sterne (Laurence)
CIJE: 2 RIE: 0 CAT: 18

Sterns High School Characteristics Index
USE High School Characteristics Index

Steroids
CIJE: 23 RIE: 12 CAT: 11
UF Anabolic Steroids

Stethoscopes
CIJE: 0 RIE: 2 CAT: 11

STETS Program
USE Structured Training Employment Transitional Serv

Stetson University FL
CIJE: 6 RIE: 0 CAT: 17

Steuben (Baron Friedrich Wilhelm von)
CIJE: 0 RIE: 0 CAT: 18
UF Von Steuben (Frederick William)

Stevens (Lois Prante)
CIJE: 0 RIE: 1 CAT: 18

Stevens (S S)
CIJE: 1 RIE: 1 CAT: 18

Stevens (Wallace)
CIJE: 4 RIE: 1 CAT: 18

Stevens Institute of Technology NJ
CIJE: 8 RIE: 2 CAT: 17

Stevens Power Law
CIJE: 1 RIE: 0 CAT: 20

Stevens Technical Enrichment Program
CIJE: 2 RIE: 2 CAT: 19

Stevenson (Adlai II)
CIJE: 2 RIE: 3 CAT: 18

Stevenson (Robert Louis)
CIJE: 1 RIE: 3 CAT: 18

Stevenson v Jefferson County Public Schools
USE Mark Stevenson v Jefferson County Public Schools

Stevenson Wydler Technology Innovation Act 1980
CIJE: 0 RIE: 1 CAT: 14

Stever (H Guyford)
CIJE: 1 RIE: 0 CAT: 18

Steward (Julian)
CIJE: 0 RIE: 1 CAT: 18

Stewardship
CIJE: 7 RIE: 5 CAT: 16

Stewardship Model
CIJE: 0 RIE: 1 CAT: 15

Stewart (Alvan)
CIJE: 1 RIE: 0 CAT: 18

Stewart (Maria)
CIJE: 0 RIE: 1 CAT: 18

Stewart (Potter)
CIJE: 2 RIE: 1 CAT: 18

Stewart B McKinney Homeless Assist Act Amend 1990
CIJE: 1 RIE: 7 CAT: 14

Stewart B McKinney Homeless Assistance Act 1987
CIJE: 9 RIE: 80 CAT: 14
UF Public Law 100 77

Stewart Indian School NV
CIJE: 0 RIE: 1 CAT: 17

Sticker Family Game
CIJE: 0 RIE: 2 CAT: 16

Stifter (Adalbert)
CIJE: 1 RIE: 0 CAT: 18

Stigma
CIJE: 30 RIE: 9 CAT: 11
UF Social Stigma

Stigmatized Forms (Language)
CIJE: 0 RIE: 1 CAT: 13

Still Photography
CIJE: 2 RIE: 2 CAT: 20

Stillbirth
CIJE: 9 RIE: 0 CAT: 11

Stillman College AL
CIJE: 1 RIE: 1 CAT: 17

Stillwater City School District OK
CIJE: 1 RIE: 0 CAT: 17

Stillwater State Prison
CIJE: 1 RIE: 0 CAT: 17

Stimulus Alignment
CIJE: 2 RIE: 0 CAT: 11

Stimulus Complexity
CIJE: 12 RIE: 15 CAT: 11

Stimulus Configurations
CIJE: 3 RIE: 1 CAT: 11

Stimulus Control
CIJE: 22 RIE: 1 CAT: 11

Stimulus Discrepancy
CIJE: 1 RIE: 0 CAT: 11

Stimulus Fading
CIJE: 5 RIE: 0 CAT: 11

Stimulus Incongruity
CIJE: 2 RIE: 0 CAT: 11

Stimulus Intensity Modulation
CIJE: 2 RIE: 0 CAT: 11

Stimulus Meaningfulness
CIJE: 2 RIE: 0 CAT: 11

Stimulus Onset Asychrony
CIJE: 2 RIE: 0 CAT: 11

Stimulus Preference
CIJE: 3 RIE: 3 CAT: 11

Stimulus Response Latency
CIJE: 0 RIE: 1 CAT: 21

Stimulus Response Psychology
CIJE: 2 RIE: 1 CAT: 11

Stimulus Response Reinforcement Approach
CIJE: 0 RIE: 1 CAT: 15

Stimulus Response Theory
CIJE: 2 RIE: 2 CAT: 15

Stimulus Satiation
CIJE: 1 RIE: 0 CAT: 11

Stimulus Seeking Behavior
CIJE: 0 RIE: 2 CAT: 11

Stimulus Similarity
CIJE: 3 RIE: 1 CAT: 11

Stimulus Similarity Scale
CIJE: 1 RIE: 0 CAT: 21

Stimulus Structure
CIJE: 1 RIE: 1 CAT: 11

Stimulus Timing
CIJE: 1 RIE: 1 CAT: 11

Stimulus to Rule Linkage
CIJE: 0 RIE: 1 CAT: 11

Stingrays
CIJE: 0 RIE: 1 CAT: 20

Stirling University (Scotland)
CIJE: 2 RIE: 1 CAT: 17

Stitchery
CIJE: 8 RIE: 2 CAT: 03

Stochastic Analysis
CIJE: 32 RIE: 20 CAT: 15

Stochastic Approximation Method
CIJE: 0 RIE: 2 CAT: 15

Stochastic Parallel Computation
CIJE: 0 RIE: 1 CAT: 15

Stock Clerks
CIJE: 1 RIE: 10 CAT: 09

Stock Issues (Debate)
CIJE: 0 RIE: 2 CAT: 15

Stock Market
CIJE: 31 RIE: 8 CAT: 16

Stock Market Quotations
CIJE: 1 RIE: 0 CAT: 16

Stockbridge Munzees (Tribe)
CIJE: 0 RIE: 1 CAT: 08

Stockbrokers
CIJE: 2 RIE: 1 CAT: 09

Stockholders
CIJE: 1 RIE: 2 CAT: 10

Stockholm School of Education (Sweden)
CIJE: 0 RIE: 1 CAT: 17

Stockpiling
CIJE: 0 RIE: 1 CAT: 16

Stocks (Cookery)
CIJE: 0 RIE: 1 CAT: 20

Stockton College
CIJE: 0 RIE: 1 CAT: 17

Stockton State College NJ
CIJE: 8 RIE: 3 CAT: 17

Stockton Unified School District CA
CIJE: 3 RIE: 4 CAT: 17

Stockton Unified School District KS
CIJE: 0 RIE: 1 CAT: 17

Stockwell College of Education (England)
CIJE: 1 RIE: 0 CAT: 17

Stogdill (Ralph M)
CIJE: 1 RIE: 1 CAT: 18

Stoichiometry
CIJE: 27 RIE: 2 CAT: 20

Stomata
CIJE: 1 RIE: 0 CAT: 20

Stone
CIJE: 1 RIE: 1 CAT: 20

Stone (Barton)
CIJE: 0 RIE: 1 CAT: 18

Stone (Lucy)
CIJE: 0 RIE: 1 CAT: 18

Stone (W Clement)
CIJE: 1 RIE: 0 CAT: 18

Stone Coles Multidimensional Scaling Method
CIJE: 1 RIE: 0 CAT: 21

Stone v Graham
CIJE: 0 RIE: 1 CAT: 14

Stonehill College MA
CIJE: 1 RIE: 1 CAT: 17

Stonequist (Everett)
CIJE: 0 RIE: 1 CAT: 18

Stoney Indian Language Project AB
CIJE: 0 RIE: 1 CAT: 19

Stony Acres Inc PA
CIJE: 0 RIE: 1 CAT: 17

Stop Action Video
CIJE: 0 RIE: 1 CAT: 04

Stop ERA
CIJE: 0 RIE: 1 CAT: 19

STOP Program
CIJE: 1 RIE: 0 CAT: 19

Stopwords
CIJE: 0 RIE: 1 CAT: 16

Storage (Memory)
CIJE: 22 RIE: 1 CAT: 11

Storage Dynamics (Memory)
CIJE: 1 RIE: 0 CAT: 20

Storaska (Frederic)
CIJE: 1 RIE: 0 CAT: 18

Store Coupon Collecting
CIJE: 0 RIE: 0 CAT: 16

Store Coupons
CIJE: 1 RIE: 2 CAT: 16
UF Coupons (Store)

Store Managers
CIJE: 0 RIE: 5 CAT: 09

Store Workers
CIJE: 0 RIE: 3 CAT: 09

Storefront Schools
CIJE: 2 RIE: 0 CAT: 16

Storekeeper First Class
CIJE: 0 RIE: 1 CAT: 03

Stories Within Stories
USE Embedded Stories

Storm (Theodor W)
CIJE: 1 RIE: 0 CAT: 18

Storms
CIJE: 1 RIE: 3 CAT: 20

Storms Street School NJ
CIJE: 0 RIE: 0 CAT: 17

Stormwater Control
CIJE: 0 RIE: 1 CAT: 20

Story Boards
CIJE: 15 RIE: 7 CAT: 04

Story Completion
CIJE: 6 RIE: 1 CAT: 13

Story Concepts
CIJE: 17 RIE: 5 CAT: 16

Story Content
CIJE: 24 RIE: 20 CAT: 16

Story Frames
CIJE: 6 RIE: 3 CAT: 15

Story Impressions
CIJE: 6 RIE: 4 CAT: 16

Story Knife Tales
CIJE: 1 RIE: 2 CAT: 16

Story List
CIJE: 0 RIE: 1 CAT: 16

Story Mapping
CIJE: 12 RIE: 7 CAT: 15

Story Maps
CIJE: 12 RIE: 6 CAT: 15

Story Retelling
USE Retelling

Story Schema
CIJE: 10 RIE: 4 CAT: 16

Story Setting
CIJE: 5 RIE: 2 CAT: 13

Story Telling by Children
CIJE: 23 RIE: 33 CAT: 16

Story Telling Test
CIJE: 0 RIE: 1 CAT: 21

Story Themes
CIJE: 13 RIE: 4 CAT: 16

Story Tree
CIJE: 3 RIE: 1 CAT: 04

Story Writing
CIJE: 63 RIE: 31 CAT: 13

Stotts Decision
USE Firefighters Local Union 1784 v Stotts

Stouffer Mathematics Test
CIJE: 1 RIE: 0 CAT: 21

Stoughton Area School District WI
CIJE: 0 RIE: 1 CAT: 17

Stout State University WI
CIJE: 2 RIE: 4 CAT: 17

Stout Vocational Rehabilitation Institute WI
CIJE: 1 RIE: 0 CAT: 17

Stouts Procedure
CIJE: 2 RIE: 8 CAT: 15
SN ...for assessing latent trait unidimensionality

Stoves
CIJE: 0 RIE: 3 CAT: 04
SN See also "Cookstoves"

Stow College of Engineering (England)
CIJE: 1 RIE: 0 CAT: 17

Stowe (Calvin Ellis)
CIJE: 1 RIE: 0 CAT: 18

Stowe (Harriet Beecher)
CIJE: 5 RIE: 2 CAT: 18

Strand Approach to Environmental Education
CIJE: 1 RIE: 1 CAT: 03

Strang (Ruth)
CIJE: 0 RIE: 1 CAT: 18

Strang Diagnostic Record for HS and College Studs
CIJE: 1 RIE: 0 CAT: 21

Strategic Arms Limitation Talks
CIJE: 3 RIE: 4 CAT: 12

Strategic Behavior
CIJE: 24 RIE: 16 CAT: 11

Strategic Competence (Languages)
CIJE: 2 RIE: 3 CAT: 13

Strategic Contingencies Theory
CIJE: 1 RIE: 0 CAT: 15

Strategic Defense Initiative
CIJE: 9 RIE: 12 CAT: 20
UF Star Wars (Strategic Defense)

Strategic Family Therapy
CIJE: 2 RIE: 1 CAT: 11

Strategic Interaction Method
CIJE: 1 RIE: 6 CAT: 15

Strategic Knowledge
CIJE: 2 RIE: 0 CAT: 11

Strategic Planning for Educ Reform and Improvement
CIJE: 0 RIE: 1 CAT: 15
UF SPERI

Strategic Reading
CIJE: 8 RIE: 14 CAT: 16

Strategic Reasoning
USE Strategic Thinking

Strategic Remembering
CIJE: 2 RIE: 1 CAT: 11

Strategic Rite
CIJE: 1 RIE: 0 CAT: 11

Strategic Thinking
CIJE: 5 RIE: 5 CAT: 15
UF Strategic Reasoning

Strategic Weapon System Training Program
CIJE: 1 RIE: 0 CAT: 19

Strategies for Change and Knowledge Utilization
CIJE: 0 RIE: 4 CAT: 19

Strategies for Targeting Early Potential
CIJE: 0 RIE: 1 CAT: 19

Strategies Intervention Model
CIJE: 3 RIE: 1 CAT: 15

Strategy Choice
CIJE: 44 RIE: 17 CAT: 15

Strategy Fading
CIJE: 1 RIE: 1 CAT: 15

Strategy Training
CIJE: 46 RIE: 13 CAT: 15

Stratification
CIJE: 20 RIE: 6 CAT: 16

Stratificational Grammar
CIJE: 1 RIE: 9 CAT: 13

Stratified Sampling
CIJE: 4 RIE: 4 CAT: 21

Stratigraphy
CIJE: 7 RIE: 1 CAT: 20

Stratil Counseling Inventory
CIJE: 0 RIE: 1 CAT: 21

Straub (Jean Marie)
CIJE: 0 RIE: 1 CAT: 18

Straubel (James H)
CIJE: 1 RIE: 0 CAT: 18

Strauss (Alfred A)
CIJE: 1 RIE: 1 CAT: 18

Strauss (Leo)
CIJE: 4 RIE: 1 CAT: 18

Straw (Jack)
CIJE: 1 RIE: 0 CAT: 18

Strayer College DC
CIJE: 0 RIE: 1 CAT: 17

Strayer Haig Equalization Formula
CIJE: 0 RIE: 2 CAT: 15

Strayer Haig Mort Formula
CIJE: 0 RIE: 1 CAT: 15

Stream Channelization
CIJE: 2 RIE: 0 CAT: 20

Streaming (Education)
CIJE: 4 RIE: 2 CAT: 16

Streams
CIJE: 4 RIE: 5 CAT: 20

Street Academies
CIJE: 3 RIE: 6 CAT: 05

Street Academy Program
CIJE: 1 RIE: 0 CAT: 19

Street Crime
CIJE: 0 RIE: 1 CAT: 14

Street Survival Skills Questionnaire
CIJE: 2 RIE: 1 CAT: 21

Street Theater
CIJE: 0 RIE: 2 CAT: 16

Streetcar Named Desire (A)
CIJE: 1 RIE: 0 CAT: 22

StreetWise (Newspaper)
CIJE: 0 RIE: 1 CAT: 22

Streetwork
CIJE: 3 RIE: 2 CAT: 17

Streicher (Julius)
CIJE: 0 RIE: 1 CAT: 18

Strelley Community School (Australia)
CIJE: 0 RIE: 1 CAT: 17

Strength through Wisdom
CIJE: 0 RIE: 1 CAT: 22

Strength Training
CIJE: 1 RIE: 2 CAT: 11

Strengthening Research Library Resources Program
CIJE: 0 RIE: 2 CAT: 19

Streptomyces
CIJE: 1 RIE: 0 CAT: 11

Stress (Biological)
CIJE: 47 RIE: 41 CAT: 11

Stress Challenge Programs
CIJE: 0 RIE: 1 CAT: 19

Stress Distributions
CIJE: 1 RIE: 1 CAT: 21

Stress Immunization
CIJE: 0 RIE: 1 CAT: 11

Stress Inoculation
CIJE: 10 RIE: 4 CAT: 11

Stress Profile for Teachers (Wilson)
USE Wilson Stress Profile for Teachers

Stress Reaction Scale for Reading
CIJE: 0 RIE: 1 CAT: 21

Stress Resistance
CIJE: 1 RIE: 0 CAT: 11

Stress Response Scale (Chandler)
CIJE: 2 RIE: 3 CAT: 21

Stretch Workbook
CIJE: 0 RIE: 1 CAT: 16

Stretten v Wadsworth Veterans Hospital
CIJE: 1 RIE: 0 CAT: 14

Stride Rite Intergenerational Day Care Center MA
CIJE: 0 RIE: 1 CAT: 17

Strindberg (August)
CIJE: 2 RIE: 0 CAT: 18

String
CIJE: 2 RIE: 0 CAT: 16

String Comparator Metrics
CIJE: 0 RIE: 1 CAT: 15

String Processing Languages
CIJE: 6 RIE: 1 CAT: 04

Stringed Instruments
CIJE: 12 RIE: 3 CAT: 04

Strip Mines
CIJE: 1 RIE: 0 CAT: 20

Strive Toward Excellence Program
CIJE: 0 RIE: 2 CAT: 19

Striving Toward Excellence in the Perform Students
USE STEPS Program MO

StRoBe (Measure)
USE Student Record of Behavior

Stroboscopes
CIJE: 3 RIE: 0 CAT: 04

Stroboscopic Photography
CIJE: 1 RIE: 0 CAT: 20

Stroboscopy
CIJE: 1 RIE: 0 CAT: 20

Stroke (Disease)
USE Cerebrovascular Disorders

Stromberg Carlson 4020 Microfilm Recorder
CIJE: 0 RIE: 1 CAT: 04

Stromberg Dexterity Test
CIJE: 0 RIE: 1 CAT: 21

Strong Campbell Interest Inventory
CIJE: 75 RIE: 24 CAT: 21

Strong Vincent Comprehensive High School
CIJE: 0 RIE: 1 CAT: 17

Strong Vocational Interest Blank
CIJE: 82 RIE: 57 CAT: 21

Strongsville Public Schools OH
CIJE: 1 RIE: 1 CAT: 17

Strontium Sulfate
CIJE: 1 RIE: 0 CAT: 20

Stroop Color Word Test
CIJE: 26 RIE: 13 CAT: 21

Stroop Effect
CIJE: 2 RIE: 1 CAT: 11

Structional Analysis
CIJE: 0 RIE: 1 CAT: 15

Structural Affect Theory
CIJE: 1 RIE: 1 CAT: 15

Structural Alignments
CIJE: 0 RIE: 1 CAT: 15

Structural Analysis (Economics)
CIJE: 2 RIE: 3 CAT: 15

Structural Analysis (Psychology)
CIJE: 0 RIE: 2 CAT: 15

Structural Analysis (Sociology)
CIJE: 18 RIE: 5 CAT: 15

Structural Change
CIJE: 5 RIE: 4 CAT: 20

Structural Chemistry
CIJE: 2 RIE: 1 CAT: 20

Structural Communication
CIJE: 5 RIE: 6 CAT: 16

Structural Constituents
CIJE: 5 RIE: 3 CAT: 20

Structural Coupling (Organizations)
CIJE: 0 RIE: 2 CAT: 15

Structural Drafting
CIJE: 0 RIE: 2 CAT: 20

Structural Engineering Systems Solver Program
CIJE: 1 RIE: 0 CAT: 19

Structural Exchange Theory
CIJE: 0 RIE: 1 CAT: 15

Structural Family Theory
CIJE: 1 RIE: 1 CAT: 15

Structural Knowledge
CIJE: 1 RIE: 4 CAT: 15

Structural Learning
CIJE: 11 RIE: 4 CAT: 15

Structural Modeling
CIJE: 1 RIE: 1 CAT: 15

Structural Organizers
CIJE: 3 RIE: 3 CAT: 15

Structural Properties Questionnaire
CIJE: 1 RIE: 3 CAT: 21

Structural Response Instructional Model
CIJE: 0 RIE: 0 CAT: 15

Structural Steel Workers
CIJE: 0 RIE: 2 CAT: 09

Structural Visualization
CIJE: 0 RIE: 3 CAT: 15

Structuralism
CIJE: 50 RIE: 16 CAT: 15

Structuration Theory
CIJE: 0 RIE: 2 CAT: 15

Structure (Mathematics)
CIJE: 14 RIE: 1 CAT: 20

Structure Charts
CIJE: 1 RIE: 0 CAT: 04

Structure Coefficients
CIJE: 2 RIE: 5 CAT: 21

Structure Determinism
CIJE: 0 RIE: 1 CAT: 16

Structure Mapping
CIJE: 7 RIE: 2 CAT: 15

Structure Mapping Engine
CIJE: 0 RIE: 1 CAT: 04

Structure Observation Inventory
CIJE: 0 RIE: 1 CAT: 21

Structure of Instruction Rating Scale
CIJE: 0 RIE: 3 CAT: 21

Structure of Intellect
CIJE: 42 RIE: 22 CAT: 21

Structure of Intellect Institute
CIJE: 1 RIE: 0 CAT: 17

Structure of Intellect Learning Abilities Test
CIJE: 7 RIE: 1 CAT: 21
UF Basic Structure of Intellect Learning Abilits Test; SOI Learning Abilities Test

Structure of Knowledge
CIJE: 30 RIE: 25 CAT: 16

Structure of the Observed Learning Outcome
USE SOLO Taxonomy

Structured Activities
CIJE: 9 RIE: 7 CAT: 16

Structured Case Review Blank (Muthard Miller)
CIJE: 0 RIE: 1 CAT: 21

Structured Conceptualization
CIJE: 0 RIE: 2 CAT: 15

Structured Doll Play Test
CIJE: 0 RIE: 1 CAT: 21

Structured Elicitation Techniques
CIJE: 1 RIE: 1 CAT: 21

Structured Interviews
CIJE: 1 RIE: 3 CAT: 21

Structured Language Improvement Project
CIJE: 0 RIE: 1 CAT: 19

Structured Learning
CIJE: 4 RIE: 0 CAT: 15

Structured Learning Groups
CIJE: 0 RIE: 1 CAT: 10

Structured Learning Time Interval
CIJE: 1 RIE: 0 CAT: 15

Structured Model of Competency Based Instruction
CIJE: 0 RIE: 1 CAT: 15

Structured Objective Rorschach Test
CIJE: 0 RIE: 1 CAT: 21

Structured Overview
CIJE: 5 RIE: 12 CAT: 16

Structured Pediatric Psychosocial Interview
CIJE: 3 RIE: 1 CAT: 21

Structured Planning and Debugging Editor
CIJE: 0 RIE: 3 CAT: 04

Structured Programing
CIJE: 8 RIE: 3 CAT: 20

Structured Team Problem Solving
CIJE: 0 RIE: 1 CAT: 15
UF STePS Problem Solving Model

Structured Training Employment Transitional Serv
CIJE: 0 RIE: 3 CAT: 19
UF STETS Program

Structuro Global Audio Visual Method
CIJE: 11 RIE: 0 CAT: 15

Stuart (Jesse)
CIJE: 3 RIE: 4 CAT: 18

Student Accountability Model
CIJE: 0 RIE: 11 CAT: 15

Student Accountability Model (California)
CIJE: 0 RIE: 1 CAT: 15

Student Accounting System
CIJE: 0 RIE: 1 CAT: 04

Student Activities Inventory (Project Talent)
CIJE: 1 RIE: 1 CAT: 21

Student Activities Questionnaire
CIJE: 1 RIE: 2 CAT: 21

Student Activity Directors
CIJE: 3 RIE: 4 CAT: 09

Student Activity Funds
CIJE: 0 RIE: 1 CAT: 16
UF Extracurricular Activity Funds

Student Adaptation to College Questionnaire
CIJE: 3 RIE: 5 CAT: 21

Student Administration System
CIJE: 0 RIE: 1 CAT: 04
UF SAS Software

Student Administrator Ratio
CIJE: 0 RIE: 5 CAT: 15

Student Administrator Relationship
CIJE: 6 RIE: 4 CAT: 16

Student Advancement Programs
CIJE: 0 RIE: 1 CAT: 19

Student Advisory Board PA
CIJE: 0 RIE: 1 CAT: 17

Student Affirmative Action Outreach Program CA
CIJE: 0 RIE: 1 CAT: 19

Student Aid Recipient Survey
CIJE: 0 RIE: 1 CAT: 19

Student American Medical Association
CIJE: 2 RIE: 0 CAT: 17

Student Assessment and Response System
CIJE: 0 RIE: 1 CAT: 21

Student Assessment Consortium
CIJE: 0 RIE: 1 CAT: 17

Student Assessment of Teaching and Learning
CIJE: 0 RIE: 2 CAT: 21
SN Instrument for evaluating student learning at Louisiana State University Evening School

Student Assistance Amendments 1981
CIJE: 0 RIE: 6 CAT: 14

Student Assistance Programs
CIJE: 5 RIE: 3 CAT: 19

Student Assistants
CIJE: 9 RIE: 21 CAT: 10

Student Athletes
CIJE: 1 RIE: 12 CAT: 10

Student Attitude Inventory
CIJE: 1 RIE: 1 CAT: 21

Student Attitude Toward School Inventory
CIJE: 0 RIE: 1 CAT: 21

Student Attitudinal Outcome Measures
CIJE: 0 RIE: 1 CAT: 21

Student Attribute Study
CIJE: 0 RIE: 3 CAT: 21

Student Awareness Programs
CIJE: 2 RIE: 2 CAT: 19

Student Behavior Index (Parker and French)
CIJE: 1 RIE: 0 CAT: 21

Student Behavior Profile (Greenberger)
CIJE: 0 RIE: 1 CAT: 21

Student Belief Rating Scale
CIJE: 0 RIE: 1 CAT: 21

Student California Teachers Association
CIJE: 0 RIE: 1 CAT: 17

Student Camp Counselors
CIJE: 0 RIE: 1 CAT: 09

Student Census Project
CIJE: 0 RIE: 2 CAT: 19

Student Centered Assessment
CIJE: 8 RIE: 29 CAT: 21

Student Chambers of Commerce
CIJE: 0 RIE: 2 CAT: 16

Student Clinicians
CIJE: 0 RIE: 1 CAT: 09

Student Coalition for Action in Literacy Education
CIJE: 0 RIE: 1 CAT: 17

Student College Fit
USE Student Institution Fit

Student Committees
CIJE: 1 RIE: 1 CAT: 16

Student Computer Ratio
CIJE: 0 RIE: 1 CAT: 16
SN The number of students per computer in a school
UF Computer Student Ratio

Student Congress
CIJE: 0 RIE: 1 CAT: 15

Student Consumerism
CIJE: 1 RIE: 3 CAT: 16

Student Cooperation
CIJE: 6 RIE: 5 CAT: 16

Student Corporations
CIJE: 4 RIE: 0 CAT: 16

Student Course and Teacher Evaluation Program
CIJE: 0 RIE: 1 CAT: 19

Student Course Information Project
CIJE: 0 RIE: 2 CAT: 19

Student Course Load
CIJE: 0 RIE: 6 CAT: 16

Student Crisis Index
CIJE: 0 RIE: 1 CAT: 21

Student Critique Form (Air Training Command)
CIJE: 0 RIE: 1 CAT: 21

Student Descriptive Questionnaire
CIJE: 1 RIE: 16 CAT: 21

Student Development Series
CIJE: 0 RIE: 1 CAT: 22

Student Development Vectors (Chickering)
CIJE: 2 RIE: 1 CAT: 21

Student Developmental Task and Lifestyle Inventory
CIJE: 1 RIE: 2 CAT: 21

Student Developmental Task Inventory
CIJE: 7 RIE: 2 CAT: 21

Student Disengagement
CIJE: 3 RIE: 3 CAT: 16
SN See also "Student Engagement"

Student Editors
CIJE: 13 RIE: 1 CAT: 16

Student Educational Attitude Scale
CIJE: 0 RIE: 1 CAT: 21

Student Educational Outcomes Assessment VA
CIJE: 0 RIE: 1 CAT: 21

Student Eligibility Report
CIJE: 1 RIE: 0 CAT: 15

Student Empowerment
CIJE: 43 RIE: 50 CAT: 15

Student Empowerment Report Card
CIJE: 0 RIE: 1 CAT: 21

Student Engagement
CIJE: 32 RIE: 14 CAT: 16
SN See also "Student Disengagement"

Student Evaluation Form
CIJE: 0 RIE: 2 CAT: 21

Student Evaluation of Achievement
CIJE: 0 RIE: 2 CAT: 21

Student Evaluation of Educational Quality
CIJE: 0 RIE: 1 CAT: 21

Student Evaluation of Teaching (Test)
CIJE: 0 RIE: 1 CAT: 21

Student Expectations
CIJE: 16 RIE: 6 CAT: 16

Student Experience Inventory
CIJE: 0 RIE: 1 CAT: 21

Student Experience Questionnaire
CIJE: 1 RIE: 0 CAT: 21

Student Financial Contribution
CIJE: 1 RIE: 4 CAT: 16

Student Flow
CIJE: 6 RIE: 11 CAT: 15

Student Flow Models
CIJE: 0 RIE: 6 CAT: 15

Student Goal Orientation Questionnaire
CIJE: 0 RIE: 1 CAT: 21

Student Goals Exploration
CIJE: 0 RIE: 2 CAT: 15
UF Goals Exploration (Students)

Student Guidance Information System
CIJE: 0 RIE: 1 CAT: 04

Student Handbooks
CIJE: 0 RIE: 7 CAT: 16

Student Health Organizations
CIJE: 2 RIE: 1 CAT: 05

Student Health Records
CIJE: 1 RIE: 3 CAT: 11

Student Industry Relationship
CIJE: 1 RIE: 0 CAT: 16

Student Information and Records System
CIJE: 0 RIE: 1 CAT: 04
UF SIRS Software

Student Information Form
CIJE: 1 RIE: 11 CAT: 16

Student Information Management System
CIJE: 0 RIE: 1 CAT: 04
UF SIMS Software

Student Information System
CIJE: 15 RIE: 14 CAT: 16

Student Information System MI
USE Michigan Student Information System

Student Information System MS
USE Mississippi Student Information System

Student Information System TX
USE Texas Student Information System

Student Initiated Activities
CIJE: 8 RIE: 3 CAT: 16

Student Institution Fit
CIJE: 1 RIE: 2 CAT: 15
UF Student College Fit; Student School Fit

Student Instructional Report
CIJE: 1 RIE: 4 CAT: 21

Student Integration Model
CIJE: 0 RIE: 1 CAT: 15

Student Judgments
CIJE: 2 RIE: 1 CAT: 16

Student Led Activities
CIJE: 6 RIE: 14 CAT: 16

Student Level Observation of Beginning Reading
CIJE: 3 RIE: 0 CAT: 21

Student Library Assistants
CIJE: 1 RIE: 3 CAT: 09

Student Library Assistants of Wisconsin
CIJE: 0 RIE: 1 CAT: 17

Student Licensing
CIJE: 1 RIE: 0 CAT: 16

Student Life Stress Inventory
CIJE: 0 RIE: 1 CAT: 21

Student Listening Profile
CIJE: 0 RIE: 1 CAT: 21

Student Literacy Corps
CIJE: 0 RIE: 4 CAT: 19

Student Loan Consolidation Program
CIJE: 0 RIE: 1 CAT: 19

Student Loan Insurance Fund
CIJE: 0 RIE: 2 CAT: 17

Student Loan Marketing Association
CIJE: 3 RIE: 13 CAT: 17
UF Sallie Mae

Student Matriculation Models
CIJE: 0 RIE: 1 CAT: 15

Student Misbehavior Survey
CIJE: 0 RIE: 1 CAT: 21

Student Movement
CIJE: 5 RIE: 0 CAT: 12

Student National Education Association
CIJE: 1 RIE: 2 CAT: 17

Student National Medical Association
CIJE: 0 RIE: 1 CAT: 17

Student Nonviolent Coordinating Committee
CIJE: 5 RIE: 2 CAT: 17

Student Observation Form (Lindvall)
CIJE: 0 RIE: 1 CAT: 21

Student Observation Scale
CIJE: 0 RIE: 1 CAT: 21
UF BASC Student Observation Scale

Student Occupational Plan Outline
CIJE: 0 RIE: 1 CAT: 16

Student Operated Radio Stations
CIJE: 0 RIE: 1 CAT: 05

Student Operational Language Assessment Scale
CIJE: 0 RIE: 1 CAT: 21

Student Opinion Attitude Poll (FLA Assess Prog)
CIJE: 0 RIE: 1 CAT: 21

Student Opinion Inventory
CIJE: 2 RIE: 2 CAT: 21

Student Opinion Poll (Jackson and Getzels)
CIJE: 0 RIE: 3 CAT: 21

Student Opinion Questionnaire
CIJE: 1 RIE: 5 CAT: 21

Student Opinion Survey
CIJE: 3 RIE: 5 CAT: 21
SN See also "High School Student Opinion Survey"

Student Opinion Survey in Chemistry
CIJE: 1 RIE: 0 CAT: 21

Student Opinion Survey of Teaching
CIJE: 0 RIE: 1 CAT: 21

Student Opinions About Instructional Procedures
CIJE: 1 RIE: 3 CAT: 21

Student Organizing Project
CIJE: 0 RIE: 1 CAT: 19

Student Orientations Survey (Morstain)
CIJE: 1 RIE: 3 CAT: 21

Student Outcomes Information Service
CIJE: 0 RIE: 2 CAT: 19

Student Outcomes Questionnaire
CIJE: 0 RIE: 5 CAT: 21

Student Parent Socialization Study
CIJE: 0 RIE: 1 CAT: 19

Student Perception of Teacher Influence Scale
CIJE: 0 RIE: 1 CAT: 21

Student Perception of Teacher Style (Tuckman)
CIJE: 1 RIE: 1 CAT: 21

Student Perception of Teaching Effectiveness
CIJE: 0 RIE: 1 CAT: 21

Student Perceptions of Teacher
CIJE: 5 RIE: 3 CAT: 15

Student Perceptions of Teaching (Weerts Whitney)
CIJE: 0 RIE: 1 CAT: 21

Student Performance Models
CIJE: 0 RIE: 0 CAT: 15
UF Pupil Performance Models

Student Performances
CIJE: 7 RIE: 4 CAT: 16

Student Personnel Purpose Q Sort (Terenzini)
CIJE: 1 RIE: 0 CAT: 21

Student Placement Teams
CIJE: 3 RIE: 2 CAT: 10

Student Potential Index
CIJE: 0 RIE: 1 CAT: 21

Student Power
CIJE: 4 RIE: 3 CAT: 16

Student Preferences
CIJE: 36 RIE: 7 CAT: 16

Student Press Law Center DC
CIJE: 6 RIE: 0 CAT: 17

Student Press Service
CIJE: 2 RIE: 0 CAT: 17

Student Principal Communication Instrument
CIJE: 1 RIE: 0 CAT: 21

Student Problem Package
CIJE: 1 RIE: 1 CAT: 04

Student Problems Q Sort (Freeze)
CIJE: 0 RIE: 1 CAT: 21

Student Profile (Form)
CIJE: 1 RIE: 1 CAT: 21

Student Pugwash
CIJE: 2 RIE: 1 CAT: 19
SN See also "Pugwash Conferences"

Student Questions
CIJE: 11 RIE: 2 CAT: 16

Student Rating Form (Davis)
CIJE: 0 RIE: 1 CAT: 21

Student Rating Scale (Harvey)
CIJE: 0 RIE: 1 CAT: 21

Student Record of Behavior
CIJE: 0 RIE: 1 CAT: 21
UF StRoBe (Measure)

Student Reporters
CIJE: 18 RIE: 2 CAT: 09

Student Response System
CIJE: 1 RIE: 4 CAT: 15

Student Right to Know and Campus Security Act
CIJE: 1 RIE: 8 CAT: 14
UF Public Law 101 542

Student Right to Know and Campus Security Title II
USE Crime Awareness and Campus Security Act 1990

Student Safety Education Project
CIJE: 0 RIE: 1 CAT: 19

Student Satisfaction
CIJE: 1 RIE: 3 CAT: 16

Student Satisfaction Survey (NASSP)
CIJE: 0 RIE: 0 CAT: 21

Student School Fit
USE Student Institution Fit

Student Science Training Program
CIJE: 3 RIE: 2 CAT: 19

Student Search Service
CIJE: 2 RIE: 0 CAT: 19
UF College Board Student Search Service

Student Selected Materials
CIJE: 0 RIE: 1 CAT: 16

Student Self Assessment Inventory
CIJE: 0 RIE: 1 CAT: 21

Student Self Management Techniques
CIJE: 0 RIE: 1 CAT: 15

Student Self Report
CIJE: 2 RIE: 5 CAT: 21

Student Strengths
CIJE: 0 RIE: 1 CAT: 16

Student Support Services
CIJE: 16 RIE: 17 CAT: 16

Student Support Teams
CIJE: 0 RIE: 1 CAT: 10

Student Survey and Attitude Inventory (SC)
CIJE: 0 RIE: 3 CAT: 21

Student Suspension Questionnaire
CIJE: 0 RIE: 1 CAT: 21

Student Task Involvement
CIJE: 0 RIE: 1 CAT: 21

Student Teacher Achievement Ratio Project TN
CIJE: 2 RIE: 6 CAT: 19
UF Project STAR TN; STAR Project TN

Student Teacher Characteristics
CIJE: 6 RIE: 5 CAT: 16

Student Teacher Experience Program (Ontario)
CIJE: 0 RIE: 1 CAT: 19

Student Teacher Opinionaire
CIJE: 2 RIE: 0 CAT: 21

Student Teacher Rating Form
CIJE: 1 RIE: 1 CAT: 21

Student Teacher Ratio Project
CIJE: 0 RIE: 1 CAT: 19

Student Teacher Relationship Scale
CIJE: 0 RIE: 1 CAT: 21

Student Teaching Centers
CIJE: 1 RIE: 1 CAT: 05

Student Team Learning
CIJE: 4 RIE: 9 CAT: 15

Student Teams
CIJE: 4 RIE: 3 CAT: 10

Student Teams Achievement Divisions
CIJE: 4 RIE: 6 CAT: 15

Student Tracking Systems
CIJE: 4 RIE: 1 CAT: 15

Student Training at Retail Stores Project NY
CIJE: 0 RIE: 1 CAT: 19
UF Project STARS NY (Retailing)

Student Transportation Moratorium Act
CIJE: 1 RIE: 1 CAT: 14

Student Verbal Participation Questionnaire
CIJE: 1 RIE: 0 CAT: 21

Student Work Experience and Training Program
CIJE: 1 RIE: 2 CAT: 19

Students Against Tobacco TX
CIJE: 0 RIE: 1 CAT: 03

Students as Subjects
CIJE: 14 RIE: 17 CAT: 15
UF Research Subjects (Students)

Students Attitudes Toward Statistics Inventory
CIJE: 0 RIE: 2 CAT: 21
SN Developed by Toto Sutarso

Students Chemical Information Project
CIJE: 0 RIE: 2 CAT: 19

Students Evaluation of Educational Quality
CIJE: 10 RIE: 4 CAT: 21

Students Evaluations of Educational Quality
CIJE: 6 RIE: 4 CAT: 21

Students for a Democratic Society
CIJE: 11 RIE: 5 CAT: 17

Students for Medicine Program
CIJE: 1 RIE: 0 CAT: 19

Students of Limited English Proficiency Program
CIJE: 0 RIE: 1 CAT: 19
UF SLEP Program HI

Students Offering Service
CIJE: 0 RIE: 1 CAT: 19
SN Community service for high school credit program of Pasadena USD CA

Students Perceptions of Teachers Questionnaire
CIJE: 1 RIE: 1 CAT: 21

Students Right to Their Own Language (CCCC)
CIJE: 0 RIE: 1 CAT: 22
SN CCCC = Conference on Coll Composition and Communication

Students T Distribution
USE T Test

Students Taking Action for Recognition
CIJE: 0 RIE: 1 CAT: 19

Students Teach Students
CIJE: 0 RIE: 1 CAT: 19

Students Typewriting Test Number 1
CIJE: 1 RIE: 0 CAT: 21

Students Upgrading Mathematical Achievement
CIJE: 0 RIE: 1 CAT: 19

Students Views of an Ideal Student Questionnaire
CIJE: 0 RIE: 1 CAT: 21

Students Views of Ideal Professor Questionnaire
CIJE: 0 RIE: 1 CAT: 21

Studentship
CIJE: 0 RIE: 1 CAT: 16

Studies in the Nature of Character
CIJE: 1 RIE: 0 CAT: 22

Studies in the Physical Sciences
CIJE: 1 RIE: 0 CAT: 03

Studio in a School NY
CIJE: 0 RIE: 2 CAT: 19

Study Activity Survey
CIJE: 0 RIE: 2 CAT: 21

Study Attitudes and Methods Survey
CIJE: 10 RIE: 1 CAT: 21

Study Behavior Inventory
CIJE: 1 RIE: 2 CAT: 21

Study Behavior Inventory Form D
CIJE: 1 RIE: 1 CAT: 21

Study Circles
CIJE: 9 RIE: 30 CAT: 10

Study Commission on Space Science Education
CIJE: 0 RIE: 1 CAT: 17

Study Curriculum Occupational Preparation and Educ
CIJE: 0 RIE: 3 CAT: 03

Study Groups
CIJE: 16 RIE: 10 CAT: 10

Study Habits Inventory (Wrenn)
CIJE: 1 RIE: 2 CAT: 21

Study of Academic Prediction and Growth
CIJE: 1 RIE: 5 CAT: 22

Study of Allied Health Education
CIJE: 0 RIE: 1 CAT: 19

Study of Dissemination Efforts Support Sch Improv
CIJE: 0 RIE: 5 CAT: 19

Study of Educational Facilities Project (Toronto)
CIJE: 0 RIE: 3 CAT: 19

Study of Educational Growth and Opportunity
CIJE: 0 RIE: 1 CAT: 19

Study of High Schools (A)
CIJE: 1 RIE: 2 CAT: 22

Study of Impact of Student Financial Aid Programs
CIJE: 0 RIE: 1 CAT: 22

Study of Mathematically Precocious Youth
CIJE: 38 RIE: 11 CAT: 19

Study of Schooling (A)
CIJE: 15 RIE: 17 CAT: 22

Study of Stanford and the Schools
CIJE: 2 RIE: 2 CAT: 19

Study of Students at Risk (Phi Delta Kappa)
CIJE: 0 RIE: 5 CAT: 19
UF Phi Delta Kappa Study of Students at Risk

Study of Successful Indicators
USE Successful Indicators Study

Study of Values
CIJE: 5 RIE: 11 CAT: 03

Study of Values (Allport Vernon Lindzey)
CIJE: 10 RIE: 11 CAT: 21

Study of Verbally Gifted Youth
CIJE: 0 RIE: 1 CAT: 19

Study of Work Project
CIJE: 0 RIE: 3 CAT: 19

Study Pace
CIJE: 0 RIE: 1 CAT: 16

Study Process Questionnaire (Biggs)
CIJE: 4 RIE: 5 CAT: 21
UF Biggs Study Process Questionnaire

Study Skills Questionnaire (McComb Dobrovolny)
CIJE: 0 RIE: 1 CAT: 21
UF McComb Dobrovolny Study Skills Questionnaire

Study Talk Project
CIJE: 0 RIE: 1 CAT: 19

Study with a Teacher Program
CIJE: 0 RIE: 1 CAT: 19

Study Work Advisor Program
CIJE: 0 RIE: 2 CAT: 19

StudyWorks Project OH
CIJE: 0 RIE: 1 CAT: 19

Stufflebeam (Daniel L)
CIJE: 1 RIE: 0 CAT: 18

Stufflebeam CIPP Model
USE Context Input Process Product Evaluation Model

Stull (Robert)
CIJE: 1 RIE: 0 CAT: 18

Stull Act
CIJE: 5 RIE: 6 CAT: 14

Sturdivant (Frederick)
CIJE: 1 RIE: 0 CAT: 18

Sturt College of Advanced Education (Australia)
CIJE: 2 RIE: 0 CAT: 17

Stuttering Modification Therapy
CIJE: 0 RIE: 1 CAT: 11

Stycar Vision Tests
CIJE: 0 RIE: 1 CAT: 21

Style Delineator (Gregorc)
USE Gregorc Style Delineator

Style Differentiated Instruction
CIJE: 0 RIE: 1 CAT: 15

Style Guides
CIJE: 3 RIE: 6 CAT: 04

Style Manuals
CIJE: 6 RIE: 5 CAT: 04

Stylistics
CIJE: 37 RIE: 24 CAT: 13

Styrofoam
CIJE: 2 RIE: 0 CAT: 20

Styron (William)
CIJE: 3 RIE: 0 CAT: 18

Suares (Andre)
CIJE: 1 RIE: 0 CAT: 18

Suasory Influence
CIJE: 0 RIE: 1 CAT: 15

Subanun
CIJE: 0 RIE: 1 CAT: 13
UF Sindangan Subanun

Subcontracting
CIJE: 3 RIE: 1 CAT: 16

Subgroups
CIJE: 1 RIE: 1 CAT: 10

Subitizing
CIJE: 2 RIE: 3 CAT: 16

Subjacency
CIJE: 1 RIE: 1 CAT: 13

Subject (Grammar)
CIJE: 5 RIE: 16 CAT: 13

Subject Analysis
CIJE: 12 RIE: 4 CAT: 15

Subject Area Preferences
CIJE: 7 RIE: 2 CAT: 15

Subject Centered Curriculum
CIJE: 5 RIE: 4 CAT: 15

Subject Constraints
CIJE: 1 RIE: 1 CAT: 13

Subject Content Knowledge
CIJE: 56 RIE: 65 CAT: 15
SN See from "Teacher Knowledge" — see also the Desc "Knowledge Base for Teaching"

Subject Field Reference Code
CIJE: 1 RIE: 0 CAT: 15

Subject Level Item Response Models
CIJE: 0 RIE: 1 CAT: 21

Subject Literatures
CIJE: 3 RIE: 0 CAT: 13

Subject Specialists
CIJE: 41 RIE: 4 CAT: 10

Subjective Drug Effects Questionnaire (Katz et al)
CIJE: 0 RIE: 1 CAT: 21

Subjective Evaluation
CIJE: 23 RIE: 11 CAT: 15

Subjective Expected Utility
CIJE: 2 RIE: 1 CAT: 15

Subjective Judgment
CIJE: 4 RIE: 3 CAT: 11

Subjective Magnitude Estimation
CIJE: 0 RIE: 1 CAT: 16

Subjective Probability
CIJE: 3 RIE: 2 CAT: 11

Subjective Response Uncertainty
CIJE: 0 RIE: 1 CAT: 21

Subjective Tests
CIJE: 3 RIE: 3 CAT: 21

Subjective Units of Distress Scale
CIJE: 1 RIE: 0 CAT: 21

Subjective Vitality Questionnaire
CIJE: 6 RIE: 0 CAT: 21

Subjective Warrant
CIJE: 1 RIE: 0 CAT: 11

Subjectivity
CIJE: 51 RIE: 18 CAT: 16

Subkoviak (Michael J)
CIJE: 2 RIE: 1 CAT: 18

Sublanguage Grammars
CIJE: 6 RIE: 0 CAT: 13

Sublimation
CIJE: 1 RIE: 1 CAT: 11

Subliminal Advertising
CIJE: 0 RIE: 2 CAT: 16

Subliminal Perception
CIJE: 5 RIE: 5 CAT: 11

Subliminal Psychodynamic Activation
CIJE: 1 RIE: 1 CAT: 15

Subliminal Stimulation
CIJE: 6 RIE: 2 CAT: 16

Subliminal Suggestion
CIJE: 2 RIE: 3 CAT: 11

Submarines
CIJE: 1 RIE: 2 CAT: 04

Submerged Arc Welding
CIJE: 0 RIE: 2 CAT: 20

Subminimum Wage
CIJE: 0 RIE: 5 CAT: 16

Submissive Behavior
CIJE: 12 RIE: 1 CAT: 11

Subordinate Clauses
CIJE: 6 RIE: 2 CAT: 13

Subordinates (Employees)
CIJE: 6 RIE: 1 CAT: 10

Subordination
CIJE: 9 RIE: 1 CAT: 13

Subroutines (Computer Programing)
CIJE: 1 RIE: 1 CAT: 20

Subroutines (Programing)
CIJE: 5 RIE: 0 CAT: 20

Subscribers (Cable Television)
CIJE: 1 RIE: 0 CAT: 10
UF Cable Television Subscribers

Subscribers (Magazines)
CIJE: 4 RIE: 1 CAT: 10
UF Magazine Subscribers

Subscribers (Newspapers)
CIJE: 2 RIE: 5 CAT: 10
UF Newspaper Subscribers

Subscription Agents
CIJE: 11 RIE: 3 CAT: 09

Subscription Television
CIJE: 0 RIE: 3 CAT: 20

Subset Analysis
CIJE: 0 RIE: 3 CAT: 15

Subset Principle
CIJE: 1 RIE: 1 CAT: 13

Subsidiaries
CIJE: 1 RIE: 1 CAT: 16

Subsidiary Communications Authorization
CIJE: 4 RIE: 6 CAT: 14

Subsidized Child Care Services
CIJE: 3 RIE: 17 CAT: 05

Subsistence Agriculture
USE Subsistence Farming

Subsistence Agriculture Game
CIJE: 1 RIE: 0 CAT: 16

Subsistence Farming
CIJE: 0 RIE: 1 CAT: 16
UF Subsistence Agriculture

Subsistence Lifestyle
CIJE: 4 RIE: 3 CAT: 16

Subskills
CIJE: 3 RIE: 1 CAT: 16

Substance Abuse Specialists in Higher Education
CIJE: 0 RIE: 2 CAT: 09

Substation Operators
CIJE: 0 RIE: 1 CAT: 09

Substitute Care
CIJE: 3 RIE: 4 CAT: 11

Substitute Teacher Education Modules
CIJE: 1 RIE: 0 CAT: 19

Substitutes for Leadership Theory (Kerr)
CIJE: 2 RIE: 1 CAT: 15

Substitution Correlates (Grammar)
CIJE: 0 RIE: 1 CAT: 13

Substrata
CIJE: 0 RIE: 1 CAT: 20

Substrata Factor Theory
CIJE: 1 RIE: 7 CAT: 15

Substratum Theory
CIJE: 0 RIE: 1 CAT: 15

Subtests
CIJE: 15 RIE: 10 CAT: 21

Subtitles (Television)
CIJE: 5 RIE: 4 CAT: 16
UF Television Subtitles

Suburban Intercultural Teacher Education Program
CIJE: 0 RIE: 1 CAT: 19

Suburban Newspapers
CIJE: 1 RIE: 1 CAT: 16

Suburban Rural Differences
USE Rural Suburban Differences

Suburban Transportation Demonstration Project
CIJE: 0 RIE: 1 CAT: 19

Suburban Washington Library Film Service
CIJE: 0 RIE: 1 CAT: 17

Subways
CIJE: 2 RIE: 1 CAT: 05

Success Controlled Optimal Reading Experience
CIJE: 0 RIE: 1 CAT: 19

Success Emulation
CIJE: 0 RIE: 2 CAT: 15

Success for All Program
CIJE: 4 RIE: 14 CAT: 19

Success in Beginning Reading and Writing
CIJE: 0 RIE: 2 CAT: 19

Success in Reading and Writing Program
CIJE: 4 RIE: 6 CAT: 19

Success Rates (College Students)
CIJE: 0 RIE: 1 CAT: 16

Successful Indicators Study
CIJE: 0 RIE: 1 CAT: 19
UF Study of Successful Indicators

Successive Approximation
CIJE: 5 RIE: 0 CAT: 20

Successive Categories Method
CIJE: 1 RIE: 0 CAT: 21

Successive Impressions Test I (Lowenfeld)
CIJE: 0 RIE: 0 CAT: 21

Sucher Allred Reading Placement Inventory
CIJE: 2 RIE: 2 CAT: 21

Sucher Allred Word Recognition Test
CIJE: 0 RIE: 1 CAT: 21

Sucking Behavior
CIJE: 17 RIE: 5 CAT: 11

Sucrose
CIJE: 9 RIE: 0 CAT: 11

Sudan
CIJE: 33 RIE: 41 CAT: 07

Sudan (Khartoum)
CIJE: 4 RIE: 1 CAT: 07

Sudan (North)
CIJE: 1 RIE: 0 CAT: 07

Sudan (South)
CIJE: 1 RIE: 2 CAT: 07

Sudan (West)
CIJE: 1 RIE: 0 CAT: 07

Sudden Fiction
CIJE: 0 RIE: 1 CAT: 16

Sudden Infant Death Syndrome
CIJE: 22 RIE: 18 CAT: 11

Sue Bennett College KY
CIJE: 0 RIE: 3 CAT: 17

Suena
CIJE: 0 RIE: 1 CAT: 13

Suffixes
CIJE: 1 RIE: 7 CAT: 13

Suffolk County Community College NY
CIJE: 3 RIE: 4 CAT: 17

Suffolk County Community College NY Eastern Campus
CIJE: 0 RIE: 1 CAT: 17

Suffolk Law School MA
CIJE: 0 RIE: 1 CAT: 17

Suffolk University MA
CIJE: 2 RIE: 9 CAT: 17

Sugar
CIJE: 4 RIE: 3 CAT: 20

Sugar Beets
CIJE: 0 RIE: 1 CAT: 20

Sugar Cane (Crop)
USE Sugarcane

Sugar Chemistry
CIJE: 1 RIE: 0 CAT: 20

Sugar Excess
CIJE: 0 RIE: 2 CAT: 11

Sugar Identification
CIJE: 1 RIE: 0 CAT: 20

Sugarcane
CIJE: 0 RIE: 1 CAT: 20
UF Sugar Cane (Crop)

Sugarman (Stephen)
CIJE: 0 RIE: 2 CAT: 18

Suggestion
CIJE: 11 RIE: 3 CAT: 16

Suggestology
CIJE: 5 RIE: 13 CAT: 15

Suicide Attempts
CIJE: 26 RIE: 4 CAT: 11

Suicide Awareness Scale
CIJE: 0 RIE: 1 CAT: 21

Suicide Ideation
CIJE: 24 RIE: 1 CAT: 11

Suicide Information and Educ Centre AB
CIJE: 0 RIE: 1 CAT: 17

Suicide Intervention Response Inventory
CIJE: 2 RIE: 0 CAT: 21

Suicide Methods
CIJE: 3 RIE: 0 CAT: 11

Suicide Notes
CIJE: 6 RIE: 0 CAT: 11

Suicide Opinion Questionnaire
CIJE: 3 RIE: 2 CAT: 21

Suicide Potential Scale Revised (Miskimins et al)
CIJE: 1 RIE: 0 CAT: 21

Suicide Prevention
CIJE: 12 RIE: 9 CAT: 11

Suicide Prevention Programs
CIJE: 4 RIE: 4 CAT: 19

Suicide Probability Scale
CIJE: 1 RIE: 3 CAT: 21

Suicide Survivors
CIJE: 6 RIE: 3 CAT: 10
UF Survivors of Suicide

Suinn Test Anxiety Behavior Scale
CIJE: 4 RIE: 1 CAT: 21

Sukhothai Thammathirat Open University (Thailand)
CIJE: 1 RIE: 2 CAT: 17

Suki Agricultural Project
CIJE: 0 RIE: 1 CAT: 19

Sukuma
CIJE: 0 RIE: 2 CAT: 13

Sula (Morrison)
CIJE: 0 RIE: 0 CAT: 22

Sulawesi
CIJE: 1 RIE: 0 CAT: 13

Sulcatol
CIJE: 1 RIE: 0 CAT: 20

Sulfur
CIJE: 9 RIE: 0 CAT: 20

Sulfur Dioxide
CIJE: 16 RIE: 1 CAT: 20

Sulfur Oxide
CIJE: 1 RIE: 0 CAT: 20

Sulfur Oxides
CIJE: 1 RIE: 1 CAT: 20

Sulfuric Acid
CIJE: 3 RIE: 0 CAT: 20

Sullins College VA
CIJE: 0 RIE: 1 CAT: 17

Sullivan (Anne)
CIJE: 2 RIE: 1 CAT: 18

Sullivan (Arthur P)
CIJE: 0 RIE: 1 CAT: 18

Sullivan (Harry Stack)
CIJE: 1 RIE: 3 CAT: 18

Sullivan County Community College NY
CIJE: 1 RIE: 0 CAT: 17

Sullivan Programmed Reading Series
CIJE: 1 RIE: 6 CAT: 22

Sulphur Junior and Senior High School OK
CIJE: 1 RIE: 0 CAT: 17

Sultan Qaboos University (Oman)
CIJE: 5 RIE: 4 CAT: 17

Sum of Differences
CIJE: 0 RIE: 1 CAT: 20

Sum of Squares
CIJE: 1 RIE: 1 CAT: 20

Sumerians
CIJE: 3 RIE: 1 CAT: 08

SUMMA Consortium
CIJE: 0 RIE: 1 CAT: 17
SN SUMMA = Strengthening Underrepresented Minority Mathematics Achievement

Summarization
CIJE: 98 RIE: 54 CAT: 15
UF Summary Writing

Summary Writing
USE Summarization

Summation (Mathematics)
CIJE: 17 RIE: 1 CAT: 20

Summer
CIJE: 5 RIE: 1 CAT: 16

Summer At Home Reading Program
CIJE: 0 RIE: 1 CAT: 19

Summer Bridge Program
CIJE: 1 RIE: 2 CAT: 19

Summer Curr Rev Thru Industrial and Business Exper
CIJE: 0 RIE: 1 CAT: 03

Summer Enrichment and Instruction Project
CIJE: 0 RIE: 1 CAT: 19

Summer Food Service Program
CIJE: 0 RIE: 9 CAT: 19

Summer High School Apprentice Research Program
CIJE: 0 RIE: 1 CAT: 19

Summer Institute of Linguistics
CIJE: 0 RIE: 7 CAT: 17

Summer Institute of Technology for Children
CIJE: 0 RIE: 2 CAT: 02

Summer Institute Survey (Nova University)
CIJE: 0 RIE: 2 CAT: 21

Summer Language Bursary Program (Canada)
CIJE: 1 RIE: 0 CAT: 19

Summer Language Bursary Program Placement Test
CIJE: 0 RIE: 1 CAT: 21

Summer Manpower Research Institute
CIJE: 0 RIE: 1 CAT: 02

Summer Migrants Access Resources through Techn
USE SMART Project TX

Summer of Experience Exploration and Discovery
CIJE: 0 RIE: 1 CAT: 19

Summer Program Economically Disadvantaged Youth
CIJE: 1 RIE: 2 CAT: 19

Summer Reporter Project WI
CIJE: 0 RIE: 1 CAT: 19

Summer Research Opportunity Programs
CIJE: 0 RIE: 1 CAT: 19

Summer School in Action
CIJE: 0 RIE: 1 CAT: 19

Summer Teaching Training Inst in Dental Assisting
CIJE: 0 RIE: 2 CAT: 02

Summer Training and Education Program
CIJE: 1 RIE: 8 CAT: 19

Summer Vacations
CIJE: 22 RIE: 8 CAT: 16

Summer Youth Development Project
CIJE: 1 RIE: 1 CAT: 19

Summer Youth Employment and Training Program
USE Summer Youth Employment Program

Summer Youth Employment Program
CIJE: 0 RIE: 13 CAT: 19
UF Summer Youth Employment and Training Program; Summer Youth Program; SYEP; SYETP

Summer Youth Program
USE Summer Youth Employment Program

Summer Youth Service Corps
CIJE: 0 RIE: 1 CAT: 17

Summer Youth Transportation Program
CIJE: 0 RIE: 1 CAT: 19

Summerhill School
CIJE: 15 RIE: 2 CAT: 17

SummerMath Program
CIJE: 1 RIE: 1 CAT: 19

Summit (Roger)
CIJE: 1 RIE: 0 CAT: 18

Summit Authoring System
CIJE: 0 RIE: 1 CAT: 04

Summit Public Schools NJ
CIJE: 2 RIE: 1 CAT: 17

Sumner (William G)
CIJE: 1 RIE: 0 CAT: 18

Sumter Area Technical College SC
CIJE: 0 RIE: 2 CAT: 17

Sun
CIJE: 22 RIE: 8 CAT: 20

Sun Coast Area Teacher Training Program FL
CIJE: 0 RIE: 1 CAT: 19
UF SCATT Program FL; SunCoast Area Teacher Training

Sun Valley Ski School
CIJE: 1 RIE: 0 CAT: 17

Sunburn
CIJE: 1 RIE: 1 CAT: 11

Sunburst Communications
CIJE: 0 RIE: 1 CAT: 17

SunCoast Area Teacher Training
USE Sun Coast Area Teacher Training Program FL

Sunday Evening String Quartet
CIJE: 1 RIE: 0 CAT: 17

Sunday Newspaper Magazines
CIJE: 1 RIE: 1 CAT: 16

Sunderland Polytechnic (England)
CIJE: 3 RIE: 1 CAT: 17

Sundials
CIJE: 5 RIE: 0 CAT: 04

Sunglasses
CIJE: 4 RIE: 0 CAT: 04

Sunken Meadow State Park NY
CIJE: 0 RIE: 2 CAT: 07

Sunland Training Center FL
CIJE: 0 RIE: 1 CAT: 17

Sunny Side School District AZ
CIJE: 1 RIE: 4 CAT: 17

Sunrise Project for the Blind
CIJE: 1 RIE: 0 CAT: 19

Sunshine Act
CIJE: 0 RIE: 2 CAT: 14

Sunshine Laws
CIJE: 17 RIE: 11 CAT: 14

Sunshine State Skills Program
CIJE: 0 RIE: 1 CAT: 19

Sunspaces
CIJE: 0 RIE: 1 CAT: 05

Sunspots
CIJE: 5 RIE: 0 CAT: 20

SUNTEP
USE Saskatchewan Urban Native Teacher Education Prog

Sunwar
CIJE: 0 RIE: 3 CAT: 13

SUNY
USE State University of New York

Super (Donald E)
CIJE: 6 RIE: 7 CAT: 18

Super 8 Films
CIJE: 3 RIE: 5 CAT: 04

Super 301
CIJE: 0 RIE: 1 CAT: 14
SN Part of the 1988 Omnibus Trade and Competitiveness Act

SUPER CARP (Computer Program)
CIJE: 0 RIE: 1 CAT: 04

Super Collider (Superconducting)
USE Superconducting Super Collider

Supercomputers
CIJE: 9 RIE: 19 CAT: 04
SN See also "High Performance Computing"

Superconducting Super Collider
CIJE: 1 RIE: 0 CAT: 20
UF Super Collider (Superconducting)

Superconducting Super Collider Laboratory
CIJE: 0 RIE: 2 CAT: 17

Superconductivity
CIJE: 21 RIE: 0 CAT: 20

Supercooling
CIJE: 2 RIE: 0 CAT: 20

Superhero Play
CIJE: 3 RIE: 1 CAT: 15

Superheroes
CIJE: 3 RIE: 4 CAT: 16

Superintendent of Documents Classification
CIJE: 5 RIE: 2 CAT: 15

Superintendents of Buildings and Grounds
CIJE: 1 RIE: 0 CAT: 09

Superior and Talented Student Project
CIJE: 0 RIE: 1 CAT: 19

Superior School District WI
CIJE: 0 RIE: 1 CAT: 17

Superior Subordinate Relationship
CIJE: 16 RIE: 11 CAT: 15

Superiority Scale
CIJE: 1 RIE: 0 CAT: 21

Superiority Traits
CIJE: 0 RIE: 0 CAT: 11

SUPERMARC
CIJE: 1 RIE: 0 CAT: 04

Supermarket Discovery Center Demonstration Project
CIJE: 1 RIE: 0 CAT: 19

Superordinate Classes
CIJE: 3 RIE: 0 CAT: 11

Superordinate Relations
CIJE: 1 RIE: 1 CAT: 11

SuperPILOT Authoring Language
CIJE: 2 RIE: 0 CAT: 04

SuperSchool (Ameritech)
CIJE: 0 RIE: 1 CAT: 20

SuperSCRIPSIT
USE SCRIPSIT

Supersonic Transports
CIJE: 1 RIE: 0 CAT: 20

SuperStart Comprehensive Prekindergarten Prog NY
CIJE: 0 RIE: 1 CAT: 19

Superstition
CIJE: 11 RIE: 8 CAT: 16

Superstitious Behavior
CIJE: 2 RIE: 1 CAT: 11

Supervised Family Day Care
CIJE: 0 RIE: 1 CAT: 11

Supervision Questionnaire
CIJE: 0 RIE: 1 CAT: 21

Supervision Questionnaire Revised
CIJE: 0 RIE: 1 CAT: 21

Supervisor Behavior Style Scales (Blumberg et al)
CIJE: 0 RIE: 1 CAT: 21

Supervisor Personal Reaction Scale
CIJE: 0 RIE: 1 CAT: 21

Supervisor Subordinate Relationship
CIJE: 23 RIE: 12 CAT: 15

Supervisor Supervisee Relationship
CIJE: 12 RIE: 17 CAT: 15

Supervisor Supervisor Relationship
CIJE: 0 RIE: 1 CAT: 16

Supervisor Teacher Verbal Interaction Instrument
CIJE: 0 RIE: 1 CAT: 21

Supervisors Rating Scale of Practicum Performance
CIJE: 0 RIE: 1 CAT: 21

Supervisory Behavior Description Questionnaire
CIJE: 0 RIE: 6 CAT: 21

Supervisory Conference Rating Scale
CIJE: 0 RIE: 1 CAT: 21

Supervisory Conference Verbal Behavior Instrument
CIJE: 0 RIE: 1 CAT: 21

Supervisory Conferences
CIJE: 1 RIE: 2 CAT: 02

Supervisory Interaction System (Blumberg)
CIJE: 0 RIE: 1 CAT: 21

Supervisory Rotation
CIJE: 0 RIE: 1 CAT: 15

Supervisory Working Alliance Inventory
CIJE: 1 RIE: 1 CAT: 21
SN See also "Working Alliance" and "Working Alliance Inventory"

Suppes (Patrick)
CIJE: 1 RIE: 3 CAT: 18

Supplemental Educational Opportunity Grants
CIJE: 9 RIE: 66 CAT: 14

Supplemental Income
CIJE: 1 RIE: 8 CAT: 16

Supplemental Loans for Students
USE Supplemental Loans for Students Program

Supplemental Loans for Students Program
CIJE: 1 RIE: 3 CAT: 19
UF Supplemental Loans for Students; Supplemental Student Loans

Supplemental Security Income
USE Supplemental Security Income Program

Supplemental Security Income Program
CIJE: 11 RIE: 27 CAT: 19
UF Supplemental Security Income

Supplemental Student Loans
USE Supplemental Loans for Students Program

Supplemental Teacher Participation (Saginaw MI)
CIJE: 0 RIE: 1 CAT: 19

Supplemental Tuition Assistance Program NY
CIJE: 0 RIE: 2 CAT: 19

Supplementary Kindergarten Intervention Program
CIJE: 1 RIE: 0 CAT: 19

Supplementary Mathematics Materials Tech Society
CIJE: 0 RIE: 1 CAT: 19

Supply Occupations
CIJE: 0 RIE: 2 CAT: 09

Supply Side Economics
CIJE: 5 RIE: 5 CAT: 16

Support Courses
CIJE: 1 RIE: 0 CAT: 03

Support Facilities
CIJE: 0 RIE: 4 CAT: 05

Support of User Records and Files
CIJE: 0 RIE: 1 CAT: 16

Support Personnel
CIJE: 16 RIE: 14 CAT: 09
SN See also "Noninstructional Staff"

Support Ranking Questionnaire
CIJE: 0 RIE: 1 CAT: 21

Support Services
CIJE: 18 RIE: 38 CAT: 16
SN See also beginning with "Academic..," "Instructional..," "Student.."

Support Services Program
CIJE: 0 RIE: 4 CAT: 19

Support Systems
CIJE: 104 RIE: 59 CAT: 15

Supported Housing
CIJE: 0 RIE: 5 CAT: 05

Supported Self Study
CIJE: 1 RIE: 2 CAT: 03

Supporting Diversity in Schools MN
CIJE: 0 RIE: 1 CAT: 19

Supporting Extended Family Members Program
CIJE: 0 RIE: 2 CAT: 19

Supportive Learning Environments
CIJE: 8 RIE: 5 CAT: 16

Supportive Services Program
CIJE: 0 RIE: 5 CAT: 19

Supportive Supervision
CIJE: 2 RIE: 5 CAT: 15

Supranational Communication Research Center
CIJE: 0 RIE: 1 CAT: 17

Supreme Court
CIJE: 734 RIE: 297 CAT: 17
SN Usage restricted to U.S. Supreme Court

Supreme Court of Canada
CIJE: 1 RIE: 1 CAT: 17
UF Canadian Supreme Court

Suquamish (Tribe)
CIJE: 0 RIE: 3 CAT: 08

Surdo Cardiac Syndrome
CIJE: 1 RIE: 0 CAT: 11

Surface Gages
CIJE: 0 RIE: 1 CAT: 04

Surface Warfare Officers School RI
CIJE: 0 RIE: 1 CAT: 17

Surfacing Materials
CIJE: 4 RIE: 1 CAT: 16

Surgeon Generals Report on Television Violence
CIJE: 2 RIE: 13 CAT: 22

Surgeons
CIJE: 3 RIE: 1 CAT: 09

Surgical Facilities
CIJE: 1 RIE: 0 CAT: 05

Surgical Supplies Assemblers
CIJE: 0 RIE: 1 CAT: 09

Surinam
CIJE: 7 RIE: 6 CAT: 07
SN Formerly Dutch Guiana
UF Suriname

Suriname
USE Surinam

Surplus Computing Capacity
CIJE: 0 RIE: 1 CAT: 04

Surplus Space
CIJE: 2 RIE: 3 CAT: 16

Surprise
CIJE: 10 RIE: 4 CAT: 16

Surprise Ending Stories
CIJE: 1 RIE: 1 CAT: 16

Surrey School District 36 BC
CIJE: 0 RIE: 1 CAT: 17

Surrey Schools (England)
CIJE: 1 RIE: 0 CAT: 17

Surrogate Families
CIJE: 2 RIE: 1 CAT: 10

Surrogate Motherhood
CIJE: 1 RIE: 1 CAT: 11

Surrogate Parents
CIJE: 4 RIE: 22 CAT: 10
SN Those providing services, or acquiring them for, children whose parents or guardians are unknown or unavailable

Surrogate Pitchers
CIJE: 1 RIE: 0 CAT: 10

Surrogate Pregnancy
CIJE: 1 RIE: 0 CAT: 11

Surrogate Self
CIJE: 1 RIE: 0 CAT: 11

Surrogate Speakers
CIJE: 0 RIE: 0 CAT: 10

Surrogates (Linguistics)
CIJE: 0 RIE: 3 CAT: 13

Surry Community College NC
CIJE: 0 RIE: 3 CAT: 17

Surveillance Systems
CIJE: 5 RIE: 3 CAT: 15
SN See also "Electronic Surveillance"

Survey Achievement Testing
CIJE: 0 RIE: 2 CAT: 21

Survey Computer Applications School Food Service
CIJE: 0 RIE: 1 CAT: 19

Survey of Administrative Functional Efficiency
CIJE: 0 RIE: 1 CAT: 19

Survey of Adult Learning (Educ Testing Service)
CIJE: 0 RIE: 1 CAT: 21

Survey of Basic Skills (California)
CIJE: 1 RIE: 5 CAT: 21

Survey of Basic Skills (SRA)
USE SRA Survey of Basic Skills

Survey of Beliefs about Parenthood
CIJE: 0 RIE: 1 CAT: 21

Survey of Canadian English
CIJE: 6 RIE: 0 CAT: 21

Survey of Cognitive Skills (Childrens Hospital)
CIJE: 0 RIE: 1 CAT: 21

Survey of College Achievement
CIJE: 0 RIE: 1 CAT: 21

Survey of Compensatory Education
CIJE: 0 RIE: 1 CAT: 21

Survey of Confidence in Teaching Reading
CIJE: 0 RIE: 1 CAT: 21

Survey of Consumer Finances
CIJE: 0 RIE: 1 CAT: 21

Survey of Displayed Literacy Stimuli
CIJE: 0 RIE: 1 CAT: 21

Survey of Doctorate Recipients
CIJE: 1 RIE: 3 CAT: 22

Survey of Earned Doctorates
CIJE: 4 RIE: 2 CAT: 22

Survey of Educational Attitudes (Rosenthal et al)
CIJE: 0 RIE: 2 CAT: 21

Survey of Effective School Processes (IDEA)
CIJE: 0 RIE: 1 CAT: 21

Survey of Elementary Epistemic Motivation
CIJE: 0 RIE: 1 CAT: 21

Survey of English Usage
CIJE: 2 RIE: 0 CAT: 21

Survey of Essential Skills
CIJE: 0 RIE: 5 CAT: 21

Survey of Experienced Scientists and Engineers
CIJE: 0 RIE: 1 CAT: 21

Survey of Federal Support to Univs and Colleges
CIJE: 0 RIE: 1 CAT: 22

Survey of Grading Practices
CIJE: 0 RIE: 1 CAT: 21

Survey of Income and Education
CIJE: 5 RIE: 13 CAT: 22

Survey of Income and Program Participation
CIJE: 3 RIE: 9 CAT: 22

Survey of Interpersonal Values (Gordon)
CIJE: 3 RIE: 6 CAT: 21

Survey of Multicultural Education Concepts
CIJE: 0 RIE: 1 CAT: 21

Survey of Object Visualization (Miller)
CIJE: 0 RIE: 1 CAT: 21

Survey of Opinions on Economic Issues (Dawson)
CIJE: 0 RIE: 1 CAT: 21

Survey of Primary Music Reading Development
CIJE: 1 RIE: 0 CAT: 21

Survey of Public Participation in the Arts
CIJE: 0 RIE: 7 CAT: 22

Survey of Reading Attitudes
CIJE: 11 RIE: 0 CAT: 21

Survey of Reading Skills
CIJE: 0 RIE: 1 CAT: 21

Survey of School Attitudes
CIJE: 2 RIE: 3 CAT: 21

Survey of School Attitudes (Hogan)
CIJE: 1 RIE: 1 CAT: 21

Survey of Student Opinion of Teaching
CIJE: 1 RIE: 2 CAT: 21

Survey of Study Habits and Attitudes
CIJE: 5 RIE: 6 CAT: 21

Survey of Study Reading Habits
CIJE: 0 RIE: 1 CAT: 21

Survey of Supervisory Practices
CIJE: 1 RIE: 2 CAT: 21

Survey of Teacher Characteristics and Activities
CIJE: 0 RIE: 1 CAT: 21

Survey of Teacher Education Perceptions
CIJE: 0 RIE: 1 CAT: 21

Survey of Testing Practices
CIJE: 0 RIE: 1 CAT: 21

Survey of Voluntary Support of Education
CIJE: 0 RIE: 5 CAT: 22

Survey of Work Values (Wollack et al)
CIJE: 2 RIE: 2 CAT: 21

Survey on Economic Attitudes
CIJE: 5 RIE: 1 CAT: 22

Survey on Equality of Educational Opportunity
CIJE: 0 RIE: 1 CAT: 21

Survey Read Recite Record Review Method
USE S4R Method

Survey Research
CIJE: 7 RIE: 9 CAT: 15
SN Research about surveys

Surveying (Construction)
CIJE: 0 RIE: 2 CAT: 09
SN See also "Highway Surveying"

Surveying (Engineering)
CIJE: 0 RIE: 6 CAT: 20

Surveying (Geography)
CIJE: 2 RIE: 2 CAT: 20

Surveyors
CIJE: 2 RIE: 2 CAT: 09

Survival
CIJE: 22 RIE: 13 CAT: 16

Survival Competencies
CIJE: 3 RIE: 32 CAT: 16

Survival Education
CIJE: 6 RIE: 14 CAT: 03

Survival Equipment
CIJE: 0 RIE: 2 CAT: 16

Survival Language
CIJE: 5 RIE: 30 CAT: 13

Survival Ratio Models
CIJE: 0 RIE: 1 CAT: 21

Survival Skills
CIJE: 23 RIE: 52 CAT: 16

Survival Training
CIJE: 3 RIE: 2 CAT: 16

Survivors
CIJE: 6 RIE: 0 CAT: 10
SN Use a more specific term if possible

Survivors of Nazi Persecution
CIJE: 4 RIE: 1 CAT: 10
UF Holocaust Survivors

Survivors of Suicide
USE Suicide Survivors

Susceptibility to Hypnosis
USE Hypnotic Susceptibility

Suspense
CIJE: 4 RIE: 1 CAT: 16

Suspense Stories
CIJE: 2 RIE: 1 CAT: 16

Suspiciousness
CIJE: 1 RIE: 0 CAT: 16

Susquehanna River Basin Project
CIJE: 1 RIE: 0 CAT: 19

Sustainability
CIJE: 8 RIE: 2 CAT: 16
UF Service Sustainability

Sustainable Agriculture
CIJE: 8 RIE: 3 CAT: 20

Sustained Attention
CIJE: 4 RIE: 1 CAT: 11

Sustained Effects Study
USE Sustaining Effects Study

Sustaining Effects Study
CIJE: 4 RIE: 19 CAT: 15
UF Sustained Effects Study

Sutherland (Sid)
CIJE: 1 RIE: 0 CAT: 18

Sutherlin Program in Creativity
CIJE: 0 RIE: 3 CAT: 19

Sutro (Adolph)
CIJE: 0 RIE: 1 CAT: 18

Suvorin (Aleksei)
CIJE: 1 RIE: 0 CAT: 18

Suydam Trueblood Attitude Toward Mathematics Scale
CIJE: 0 RIE: 1 CAT: 21
UF Attitude Toward Math Scale (Suydam Trueblood)

Suzak Binet Intelligence Test
CIJE: 0 RIE: 1 CAT: 21

Suzuki (Shinichi)
CIJE: 5 RIE: 3 CAT: 18

Suzzallo (Henry)
CIJE: 0 RIE: 1 CAT: 18

Sveriges Radio
CIJE: 1 RIE: 1 CAT: 17

Svevo (Italo)
CIJE: 2 RIE: 0 CAT: 18

Swabian
CIJE: 2 RIE: 2 CAT: 13

Swadana Delivery System (Indonesia)
CIJE: 0 RIE: 1 CAT: 19

Swadesh (Morris)
CIJE: 1 RIE: 0 CAT: 18

Swaggart (Jimmy)
CIJE: 0 RIE: 3 CAT: 18

Swallowing
CIJE: 1 RIE: 0 CAT: 11

Swallowing Difficulties
USE Dysphagia

Swallowing Therapy
CIJE: 2 RIE: 1 CAT: 11

Swanson (Austin D)
CIJE: 0 RIE: 1 CAT: 18

SWAP Program (Scotland)
USE Scottish Wider Access Program

Swarthmore Chautauqua
CIJE: 0 RIE: 1 CAT: 02

Swarthmore College PA
CIJE: 13 RIE: 7 CAT: 17

Swassing Barbe Modality Index
CIJE: 2 RIE: 4 CAT: 21

SWAT Teams
CIJE: 0 RIE: 0 CAT: 09
UF Special Weapons and Tactics Units

Swazi People
CIJE: 0 RIE: 0 CAT: 08

Swaziland
CIJE: 15 RIE: 36 CAT: 07

Swaziland Teacher Training Project
CIJE: 0 RIE: 1 CAT: 19

Sweden
CIJE: 707 RIE: 1053 CAT: 07

Sweden (Gothenburg)
CIJE: 0 RIE: 5 CAT: 07

Sweden (Linkoping)
CIJE: 0 RIE: 2 CAT: 07

Sweden (Malmo)
CIJE: 2 RIE: 5 CAT: 07

Sweden (Skovde)
CIJE: 2 RIE: 1 CAT: 07

Sweden (Sodertalje)
CIJE: 1 RIE: 0 CAT: 07

Sweden (Stockholm)
CIJE: 15 RIE: 12 CAT: 07

Sweden (Uppsala)
CIJE: 0 RIE: 3 CAT: 07

Swedish Americans
CIJE: 1 RIE: 2 CAT: 08

Swedish Broadcasting Corporation
CIJE: 1 RIE: 1 CAT: 17

Swedish Institute for Childrens Books
CIJE: 1 RIE: 0 CAT: 17

Swedish International Development Authority
CIJE: 1 RIE: 2 CAT: 17

Swedish Metal Trades Employers Association
CIJE: 0 RIE: 1 CAT: 17

Swedish National Board of Education
USE National Board of Education (Sweden)

Swedish National Parent School Association
CIJE: 0 RIE: 1 CAT: 17

Swedish National Union of Students
CIJE: 1 RIE: 0 CAT: 17

Swedish Parliamentary Library
CIJE: 0 RIE: 1 CAT: 17

Swedish Research on Higher Education Program
USE Research on Higher Education Program (Sweden)

Swedish Speaking
CIJE: 4 RIE: 3 CAT: 16

Sweet Briar College VA
CIJE: 3 RIE: 1 CAT: 17

Sweet Street Academy
CIJE: 0 RIE: 1 CAT: 17

Sweetwater County School District Number 2 WY
CIJE: 0 RIE: 1 CAT: 17

Sweetwater Union High School District CA
CIJE: 0 RIE: 1 CAT: 17

Swick Ross Child Perception Inventory
CIJE: 0 RIE: 1 CAT: 21

Swift (Ernest)
CIJE: 1 RIE: 0 CAT: 18

Swift (Jonathan)
CIJE: 8 RIE: 0 CAT: 18

SWIM Demonstration of San Diego County
USE Saturation Work Initiative Model

Swim for Your Life
CIJE: 0 RIE: 1 CAT: 19

Swindon Record of Personal Achievement
CIJE: 0 RIE: 1 CAT: 21

Swinomish (Tribe)
CIJE: 1 RIE: 1 CAT: 08

Switchboard Operators
CIJE: 0 RIE: 1 CAT: 09

Switches
CIJE: 1 RIE: 2 CAT: 04

Switching Theory
CIJE: 1 RIE: 1 CAT: 15

Switzerland
CIJE: 173 RIE: 138 CAT: 07

Switzerland (Geneva)
CIJE: 11 RIE: 5 CAT: 07

Switzerland (Neuchatel)
CIJE: 1 RIE: 0 CAT: 07

Switzerland (Saint Gallen)
CIJE: 0 RIE: 1 CAT: 07

SWRL Beginning Reading Program Test
CIJE: 0 RIE: 1 CAT: 21

SWRL Composition Skills Test
CIJE: 0 RIE: 1 CAT: 21

SWRL English Language and Concepts Program
CIJE: 0 RIE: 4 CAT: 19

SWRL First Grade Spelling Component
CIJE: 0 RIE: 1 CAT: 21

SWRL Instructional Concepts Program Test
CIJE: 0 RIE: 1 CAT: 21

SWRL Kindergarten Program
CIJE: 0 RIE: 1 CAT: 19

SWRL Learning Mastery System
CIJE: 0 RIE: 1 CAT: 15

SWRL Scoring System
CIJE: 0 RIE: 2 CAT: 21

SWRL Tutorial Program
CIJE: 0 RIE: 1 CAT: 19

Sycamore High School
CIJE: 1 RIE: 0 CAT: 17

Sydney Attribution Scale
CIJE: 4 RIE: 1 CAT: 21

Sydney Public Library (Australia)
CIJE: 0 RIE: 1 CAT: 17

Sydney Teachers College (Australia)
CIJE: 0 RIE: 1 CAT: 17

SYEP
USE Summer Youth Employment Program

SYETP
USE Summer Youth Employment Program

Sylheti
CIJE: 0 RIE: 1 CAT: 13
SN A dialect of Khasi

Syllabaries
CIJE: 1 RIE: 5 CAT: 13

Syllabication Ability
CIJE: 3 RIE: 3 CAT: 13

Syllogisms
CIJE: 11 RIE: 7 CAT: 13

Syllogistic Reasoning
CIJE: 18 RIE: 14 CAT: 16

Symbiosis
CIJE: 12 RIE: 3 CAT: 20

Symbol Accentuation
CIJE: 1 RIE: 0 CAT: 13

Symbol Digit Modalities Test
CIJE: 1 RIE: 2 CAT: 21

Symbol Maps
CIJE: 0 RIE: 1 CAT: 04

Symbol Systems Approach
CIJE: 1 RIE: 2 CAT: 15

Symbol Test of Originality
CIJE: 0 RIE: 1 CAT: 21

Symbolic Action
CIJE: 4 RIE: 4 CAT: 15

Symbolic Analysis
CIJE: 0 RIE: 1 CAT: 15

Symbolic Computer Algebra
CIJE: 2 RIE: 0 CAT: 20

Symbolic Convergence Theory of Communication
CIJE: 1 RIE: 1 CAT: 15

Symbolic Immortality
CIJE: 3 RIE: 0 CAT: 15

Symbolic Interaction
CIJE: 17 RIE: 3 CAT: 15

Symbolic Interactionism
CIJE: 20 RIE: 18 CAT: 13

Symbolic Linguistic Encoding
CIJE: 1 RIE: 1 CAT: 13

Symbolic Play Test (Lowe and Costello)
CIJE: 1 RIE: 0 CAT: 21

Symbolic Representation
CIJE: 28 RIE: 23 CAT: 11

Symbolic Speech
CIJE: 1 RIE: 1 CAT: 16

Symbolic Thinking
CIJE: 8 RIE: 6 CAT: 11

Symbolicity
CIJE: 0 RIE: 1 CAT: 16

Symbology
CIJE: 1 RIE: 1 CAT: 16

Symbols (Cartography)
CIJE: 0 RIE: 2 CAT: 20

Symbols (Political)
USE Political Symbols

SYMLOG Coding System
CIJE: 2 RIE: 3 CAT: 15

Symmetric Regression Procedure
CIJE: 0 RIE: 1 CAT: 21

Symmetry Complementarity Analysis
CIJE: 0 RIE: 1 CAT: 16
UF Complementarity Symmetry Analysis

Sympathy
CIJE: 13 RIE: 3 CAT: 16

Symphony (Computer Software)
CIJE: 0 RIE: 1 CAT: 04

Symposium on Urban Cable Television
CIJE: 0 RIE: 2 CAT: 02

Symptomatic Checklist
CIJE: 0 RIE: 1 CAT: 21

Synaction
CIJE: 0 RIE: 1 CAT: 11

Synaesthesia
CIJE: 5 RIE: 1 CAT: 11
UF Synesthesia

Synaesthetics
CIJE: 2 RIE: 1 CAT: 15
UF Synesthetics

Synagogue Libraries
CIJE: 1 RIE: 13 CAT: 05

Synagogues
CIJE: 0 RIE: 2 CAT: 05

Synanon
CIJE: 5 RIE: 3 CAT: 17

Synanon School
CIJE: 1 RIE: 1 CAT: 17

Synaptic Linking Process
CIJE: 1 RIE: 1 CAT: 11

Synchronized Swimming
CIJE: 2 RIE: 2 CAT: 16

Synchronous Learning
CIJE: 1 RIE: 1 CAT: 11

Synchrony
CIJE: 10 RIE: 8 CAT: 11

Synchrotron Radiation
CIJE: 4 RIE: 0 CAT: 20

Syncope
CIJE: 0 RIE: 2 CAT: 11

Synecdoche
CIJE: 1 RIE: 1 CAT: 13

Synectics
CIJE: 15 RIE: 7 CAT: 16
SN Creative group problem solving, guided by participants' analogies

Synergistic Planning
CIJE: 0 RIE: 1 CAT: 15

Synergogy
CIJE: 1 RIE: 1 CAT: 15

Synergy
CIJE: 33 RIE: 17 CAT: 16

Synesthesia
USE Synaesthesia

Synesthetics
USE Synaesthetics

Synge (John Millington)
CIJE: 2 RIE: 0 CAT: 18

Synomorphy
CIJE: 0 RIE: 2 CAT: 15

Synonyms
CIJE: 33 RIE: 19 CAT: 13

Synophones
CIJE: 1 RIE: 0 CAT: 13

Synopses
CIJE: 1 RIE: 4 CAT: 16

Synopsis Journals
CIJE: 1 RIE: 0 CAT: 16

Synoptics
CIJE: 2 RIE: 0 CAT: 16

Syntactic Bootstrapping
CIJE: 0 RIE: 1 CAT: 13

Syntactic Complexity
CIJE: 21 RIE: 17 CAT: 13

Syntactic Density
CIJE: 3 RIE: 2 CAT: 13

Syntactic Elaboration
CIJE: 0 RIE: 2 CAT: 13

Syntactic Maturity
CIJE: 18 RIE: 20 CAT: 13

Syntactic Processing
CIJE: 16 RIE: 0 CAT: 13

Syntactic Recoding
CIJE: 0 RIE: 1 CAT: 13

Syntactic Trace
CIJE: 1 RIE: 0 CAT: 13

Syntactic Words
CIJE: 2 RIE: 1 CAT: 13

Syntactical Mediation
CIJE: 1 RIE: 0 CAT: 13

Syntagma
CIJE: 5 RIE: 3 CAT: 13

Synthesizers
CIJE: 3 RIE: 3 CAT: 04
SN Use of a more specific term is suggested, e.g., the Descriptor "Speech Synthesizers" or other Identifiers such as "Musical Synthesizers" or "Graphic Synthesizers"

Synthetic Fuels
CIJE: 2 RIE: 1 CAT: 20

Synthetic Geometry
CIJE: 2 RIE: 0 CAT: 20

Synthetic Phonics
CIJE: 0 RIE: 0 CAT: 13

Syntopical Theory (Adler)
CIJE: 0 RIE: 1 CAT: 15

Syosset High School NY
CIJE: 1 RIE: 0 CAT: 17

Syphax School DC
CIJE: 0 RIE: 1 CAT: 17

Syracuse City Schools NY
CIJE: 1 RIE: 12 CAT: 17

Syracuse Model City Agency
CIJE: 0 RIE: 1 CAT: 17

Syracuse Scale for Social Acceptance
CIJE: 0 RIE: 1 CAT: 21

Syracuse Scales of Social Relations
CIJE: 0 RIE: 1 CAT: 21

Syracuse Scholastic Rehabilitation Program
CIJE: 0 RIE: 1 CAT: 19

Syracuse Test of Algebraic Fluency
CIJE: 0 RIE: 1 CAT: 21

Syracuse Univ Publications in Continuing Educ NY
CIJE: 0 RIE: 7 CAT: 19

Syracuse Univ Resources for Educators of Adults NY
CIJE: 0 RIE: 5 CAT: 19

Syracuse University NY
CIJE: 83 RIE: 111 CAT: 17

Syracuse Upgrading Project
CIJE: 1 RIE: 0 CAT: 19

Syracuse Visual Figure Background Test
CIJE: 0 RIE: 3 CAT: 21

Syria
CIJE: 6 RIE: 16 CAT: 07

Syria (Damascus)
CIJE: 0 RIE: 3 CAT: 07

Syringes
CIJE: 7 RIE: 3 CAT: 04

SYS IV Management System
CIJE: 0 RIE: 1 CAT: 04

System 3 Communication Network
CIJE: 0 RIE: 1 CAT: 04

System 80
USE Borg Warner System 80

System 2000
CIJE: 1 RIE: 1 CAT: 04

System Classroom Observation Teaching Strategies
CIJE: 0 RIE: 1 CAT: 15
UF SCOTS Schedule

System Compensation
CIJE: 0 RIE: 1 CAT: 16

System Coupling
CIJE: 1 RIE: 3 CAT: 16

System Development Corporation
CIJE: 7 RIE: 8 CAT: 17

System Dynamics
CIJE: 8 RIE: 5 CAT: 15

System Evaluation
CIJE: 10 RIE: 4 CAT: 15

System for Coding and Analysis
CIJE: 0 RIE: 1 CAT: 15

System for Computer Automated Typesetting
CIJE: 0 RIE: 1 CAT: 04

System for Event Evaluation and Review
CIJE: 0 RIE: 1 CAT: 15

System for Objectives Based Evaluation Reading
CIJE: 1 RIE: 1 CAT: 15

System for Teaching Learning Assessment Review LA
CIJE: 1 RIE: 5 CAT: 21

System of Interactive Guidance and Info Plus
CIJE: 5 RIE: 9 CAT: 04
UF SIGI PLUS System

System of Interactive Guidance and Information
CIJE: 11 RIE: 29 CAT: 04
UF SIGI System

System of Least Prompts
USE Least Prompts

System of Multicultural Pluralistic Assessment
CIJE: 27 RIE: 13 CAT: 21

System Performance Assurance
CIJE: 0 RIE: 1 CAT: 15

System Politics
CIJE: 0 RIE: 1 CAT: 15

System Therapy
CIJE: 1 RIE: 0 CAT: 11

Systematic Analysis of Language Transcripts
CIJE: 1 RIE: 1 CAT: 04

Systematic Approach to Reading Improvement
CIJE: 0 RIE: 1 CAT: 15

Systematic Approaches to Bilingual Educ Proj NY
USE Project SABE NY

Systematic Assessment Parent Attachment Behaviors
CIJE: 1 RIE: 0 CAT: 21

Systematic Biology
CIJE: 0 RIE: 2 CAT: 03

Systematic Classroom Observation Pupil Experience
CIJE: 0 RIE: 1 CAT: 15

Systematic Collaborative Outreach Project Effort
CIJE: 0 RIE: 1 CAT: 19
UF SCOPE Project (Gallaudet Coll and NTID)

Systematic Curriculum and Instructional Develop
CIJE: 0 RIE: 3 CAT: 15

Systematic Employment Counseling Approach
CIJE: 0 RIE: 1 CAT: 15

Systematic Facilitative Approach to Consultation
CIJE: 0 RIE: 1 CAT: 15

Systematic Integrated Teaching Learning Approach
CIJE: 0 RIE: 1 CAT: 15

Systematic Monitoring Process for Learning
CIJE: 1 RIE: 0 CAT: 19

Systematic Multiple Level Observation of Groups
CIJE: 1 RIE: 1 CAT: 15

Systematic Screening for Behavior Disorders
CIJE: 5 RIE: 1 CAT: 21

Systematic Skills Training
CIJE: 1 RIE: 1 CAT: 15

Systematic Student Recruitment Program
CIJE: 0 RIE: 1 CAT: 19

Systematic Teacher Training Model
CIJE: 1 RIE: 2 CAT: 15

Systematic Training for Effective Parenting
CIJE: 6 RIE: 4 CAT: 15

Systematicity
CIJE: 0 RIE: 1 CAT: 16
SN The mapping of systems of mutually constraining relations, such as causal chains or chains of implication

Systematized Nomenclature of Pathology
CIJE: 1 RIE: 0 CAT: 15

Systemic Capacity
CIJE: 0 RIE: 1 CAT: 03

Systemic Change
CIJE: 20 RIE: 12 CAT: 16

Systemic Dialectual Evaluation
CIJE: 0 RIE: 0 CAT: 21

Systemic Educational Reform
CIJE: 0 RIE: 1 CAT: 16

Systemic Evaluation
CIJE: 2 RIE: 9 CAT: 15
UF Systemic Evaluation Project (UCLA CSE)

Systemic Evaluation Project (UCLA CSE)
USE Systemic Evaluation

Systemic Grammar
CIJE: 2 RIE: 3 CAT: 13

Systems Engineering
CIJE: 5 RIE: 1 CAT: 20

Systems Management Analysis
CIJE: 0 RIE: 1 CAT: 15

Systems Modeling
CIJE: 3 RIE: 2 CAT: 15

Systems Program Approaching Nonunemployment
CIJE: 0 RIE: 7 CAT: 19

Systems Thinking and Curriculum Innovation Project
CIJE: 0 RIE: 4 CAT: 19

UF Project STACI

Systolic Blood Pressure
CIJE: 1 RIE: 1 CAT: 11

Syuuba
USE Kagate

T Group Member Ratings (Koile and Draeger)
CIJE: 1 RIE: 0 CAT: 21

T Scope Therapy
CIJE: 1 RIE: 0 CAT: 11

T Shirts
CIJE: 3 RIE: 1 CAT: 16

T Test
CIJE: 40 RIE: 40 CAT: 21
UF Students T Distribution

T Units
CIJE: 21 RIE: 15 CAT: 15

T Values
CIJE: 1 RIE: 3 CAT: 15

TAB Inventory of Science Processes
CIJE: 0 RIE: 1 CAT: 21

Tab Item Procedure
CIJE: 0 RIE: 1 CAT: 15

TAB Science Puzzler
CIJE: 0 RIE: 1 CAT: 21

TAB Science Test
CIJE: 1 RIE: 3 CAT: 21

Taba (Hilda)
CIJE: 9 RIE: 3 CAT: 18

Taba (Hilda) Teaching Strategies
CIJE: 8 RIE: 6 CAT: 15

TABA Curriculum Project
CIJE: 5 RIE: 5 CAT: 19

Tabaru
CIJE: 0 RIE: 1 CAT: 13
SN A Halmahera language, northwest group

Table Alphabeticall
CIJE: 0 RIE: 1 CAT: 22

Table Clinics
CIJE: 0 RIE: 1 CAT: 15

Table Producing Language
CIJE: 1 RIE: 2 CAT: 04

Table Salt
USE Salt

Tables of Contents
CIJE: 7 RIE: 1 CAT: 16

Tabloid Newspapers
CIJE: 7 RIE: 1 CAT: 16

Taboo Terms
CIJE: 1 RIE: 0 CAT: 13

Taboos
CIJE: 2 RIE: 5 CAT: 16

Tabriz
CIJE: 0 RIE: 1 CAT: 13

Tabriz University (Iran)
CIJE: 0 RIE: 1 CAT: 17

Tabula Rasa Approach
CIJE: 3 RIE: 2 CAT: 15

Tabular Display Technique
CIJE: 0 RIE: 1 CAT: 15

Tacana
CIJE: 1 RIE: 1 CAT: 13

Tacit Knowing
CIJE: 1 RIE: 0 CAT: 15

Tacit Knowledge
CIJE: 3 RIE: 1 CAT: 16

Tacitus (Cornelius)
CIJE: 1 RIE: 1 CAT: 18

Tacoma Area Council on Giftedness WA
CIJE: 0 RIE: 0 CAT: 17

Tacoma Community College District 22 WA
CIJE: 0 RIE: 1 CAT: 17

Tacoma Community College WA
CIJE: 1 RIE: 1 CAT: 17

Tacoma Public School District WA
CIJE: 4 RIE: 8 CAT: 17

Taconite
CIJE: 1 RIE: 0 CAT: 20

Tactical Air Command
CIJE: 0 RIE: 2 CAT: 17

Tactical Warfare Analysis and Evaluation System
CIJE: 0 RIE: 1 CAT: 15

TACTICS
CIJE: 5 RIE: 17 CAT: 17
UF Technical Assistance Consortium Improve Coll Serv

Tactics for Thinking
CIJE: 0 RIE: 1 CAT: 15

Tactile Communication
CIJE: 10 RIE: 6 CAT: 13

Tactile Defensiveness
CIJE: 3 RIE: 1 CAT: 11

Tactile Graphics Kit
CIJE: 1 RIE: 0 CAT: 04

Tactile Kinesthetic Form Discrimination Test
CIJE: 1 RIE: 0 CAT: 21

Tactile Preference
CIJE: 1 RIE: 0 CAT: 16

Tacts
CIJE: 1 RIE: 0 CAT: 11
SN See also "Mands"

Tactual Motor Test
CIJE: 0 RIE: 1 CAT: 21

Tadjo (Veronique)
CIJE: 0 RIE: 1 CAT: 18

TADPOLE Program
CIJE: 0 RIE: 2 CAT: 19

TAFE (Australia)
CIJE: 5 RIE: 50 CAT: 03
UF Technical and Further Education (Australia)

TAFE National Centre for Research and Development
CIJE: 0 RIE: 3 CAT: 17

Taffies
USE Technologically Advanced Families

Taft (William Howard)
CIJE: 1 RIE: 1 CAT: 18

Taft College CA
CIJE: 0 RIE: 1 CAT: 17

Taft Hartley Act
CIJE: 2 RIE: 1 CAT: 14

TAG
USE Association for the Gifted (The)

Tag Questions
CIJE: 8 RIE: 4 CAT: 21

Tagabili
CIJE: 0 RIE: 2 CAT: 13
SN A Northwest Austronesian (Philippine) language, Bilic group
UF Tboli

Tagakaolo
USE Kagan Kalagan

Tagatz Information Processing Test
CIJE: 0 RIE: 1 CAT: 21

Tagbanwa
CIJE: 0 RIE: 2 CAT: 13

Tagmatic Differentials
CIJE: 0 RIE: 1 CAT: 16

Tagore (Rabindranath)
CIJE: 3 RIE: 3 CAT: 18

Taguchi Methods
CIJE: 0 RIE: 2 CAT: 15

Tahltan
CIJE: 1 RIE: 0 CAT: 13
SN An Athapascan-Eyak language

Tai Chi Chuan
CIJE: 0 RIE: 2 CAT: 16

Tai Shan Dialect
CIJE: 1 RIE: 1 CAT: 13

Tailored Response Testing
CIJE: 1 RIE: 1 CAT: 21

Taiwan
CIJE: 136 RIE: 198 CAT: 07
UF Republic of China

Taiwan (Taipei)
CIJE: 5 RIE: 6 CAT: 07

Taiwanese
CIJE: 11 RIE: 4 CAT: 13

Tajfel (Henri)
CIJE: 0 RIE: 1 CAT: 18

Take 5 Project WA
CIJE: 0 RIE: 1 CAT: 19

Take a Bite Out of Crime
CIJE: 0 RIE: 1 CAT: 22

Take Home Tests
CIJE: 9 RIE: 3 CAT: 21

Take One Small Seed
CIJE: 0 RIE: 1 CAT: 22

Take Pride in America Program
CIJE: 0 RIE: 3 CAT: 19

Takelma (Language)
CIJE: 1 RIE: 0 CAT: 13

TALAM Scale
USE Teacher Attitudes toward Low Achiev in Math Scale

TALC Program
USE Tutoring Adults through Literacy Councils

Tale of Genji (The)
CIJE: 0 RIE: 1 CAT: 22

Talent Corps
CIJE: 1 RIE: 1 CAT: 17

Talent Education Method
CIJE: 1 RIE: 2 CAT: 15

Talent Education Plan
CIJE: 0 RIE: 1 CAT: 03

Talent Education Summer School (Japan)
CIJE: 1 RIE: 0 CAT: 17

Talent Identification Program NC
CIJE: 4 RIE: 2 CAT: 19

Talent Search
CIJE: 6 RIE: 25 CAT: 19

Talent Search and Development Model Project
CIJE: 0 RIE: 1 CAT: 19

Talented Accomplishments Questionnaire
CIJE: 1 RIE: 0 CAT: 21

Talents Unlimited Program
CIJE: 3 RIE: 4 CAT: 19

Tales from King Arthur
CIJE: 2 RIE: 1 CAT: 22

Tales of the Decameron
CIJE: 1 RIE: 0 CAT: 22

Talese (Gay)
CIJE: 0 RIE: 1 CAT: 18

TALINET Project
CIJE: 0 RIE: 3 CAT: 19

Talk Show Hosts
CIJE: 0 RIE: 1 CAT: 09

Talk Shows
CIJE: 8 RIE: 6 CAT: 16

Talk Time
CIJE: 3 RIE: 0 CAT: 13

Talk with the Angels (Meiring)
CIJE: 0 RIE: 1 CAT: 22

Talk Write Method
CIJE: 6 RIE: 9 CAT: 15

Talkback Medical Education Network
USE Oklahoma Talkback Medical Education Network

Talkback Television Instruction
CIJE: 0 RIE: 1 CAT: 19
UF Oklahoma Talkback Television Instruction

Talker Identity
CIJE: 0 RIE: 1 CAT: 13

Talking Tracks
CIJE: 0 RIE: 1 CAT: 04

Talking Typewriter Center NY
CIJE: 1 RIE: 0 CAT: 17

Talking Typewriters
CIJE: 5 RIE: 10 CAT: 04

Talladega College AL
CIJE: 1 RIE: 3 CAT: 17

Talladega County Schools AL
CIJE: 0 RIE: 1 CAT: 17

Tallahassee Community College FL
CIJE: 0 RIE: 6 CAT: 17

Tallchief (Maria)
CIJE: 0 RIE: 3 CAT: 18
UF Wa Xthe Thonba

Tallent (Norman)
CIJE: 1 RIE: 0 CAT: 18

Taller Than Bandai Mountain
CIJE: 1 RIE: 0 CAT: 22

Talley (Jerry)
CIJE: 1 RIE: 0 CAT: 18

Talleyrand Perigord (Charles Maurice de)
CIJE: 1 RIE: 0 CAT: 18

Talmadge Amendments
CIJE: 0 RIE: 1 CAT: 14

Talmage (Thomas DeWitt)
CIJE: 0 RIE: 1 CAT: 18

Talmudic Study
CIJE: 2 RIE: 1 CAT: 03

Talwin
CIJE: 0 RIE: 1 CAT: 11

Tama General Knowledge Test
CIJE: 0 RIE: 1 CAT: 21

Tamagawa University (Japan)
CIJE: 1 RIE: 0 CAT: 17

Tamalpais Union High School District CA
CIJE: 2 RIE: 0 CAT: 17

Tamang
CIJE: 2 RIE: 4 CAT: 13

Tamaqua Area School District PA
CIJE: 1 RIE: 1 CAT: 17

Tamazight
CIJE: 0 RIE: 4 CAT: 13

Tamburlaine the Great
CIJE: 1 RIE: 0 CAT: 22

Tampa Bay Council for Improving College Teaching
CIJE: 1 RIE: 0 CAT: 17

Tampa College FL
CIJE: 0 RIE: 1 CAT: 17

Tampons
CIJE: 4 RIE: 0 CAT: 04

Tan (Amy)
CIJE: 0 RIE: 1 CAT: 18

Tanganyika
CIJE: 2 RIE: 4 CAT: 07

Tanganyika African National Union
CIJE: 2 RIE: 0 CAT: 17

Tangible Symbol Systems
CIJE: 0 RIE: 1 CAT: 15

Tangrams
CIJE: 10 RIE: 2 CAT: 20

Tanh(sup minus 1) Variance
USE Fisher Tanh(sup minus 1)

Tanizaki (Junichiro)
CIJE: 1 RIE: 0 CAT: 18

Tanka
CIJE: 0 RIE: 1 CAT: 16

Tanoan Languages
CIJE: 0 RIE: 1 CAT: 13
UF Kiowa Tanoan Languages

Tanta University (Egypt)
CIJE: 0 RIE: 2 CAT: 17

Tantalum
CIJE: 1 RIE: 0 CAT: 20

Tantalus Ratio
CIJE: 1 RIE: 0 CAT: 20

Tanzania
CIJE: 110 RIE: 170 CAT: 07

Tanzania (Dar es Salaam)
CIJE: 1 RIE: 2 CAT: 07

Tanzania (Kilimanjaro)
CIJE: 0 RIE: 1 CAT: 07

Tanzania Library Service
CIJE: 1 RIE: 1 CAT: 17

Tanzanian Library Services Board Act
CIJE: 0 RIE: 1 CAT: 14

Tao Te Ching
CIJE: 1 RIE: 1 CAT: 22

Tape Analysis Instrument
CIJE: 1 RIE: 0 CAT: 21

Tapeworm
CIJE: 1 RIE: 0 CAT: 11

Tapping Test
CIJE: 1 RIE: 3 CAT: 21

Tarahumara (Tribe)
CIJE: 2 RIE: 2 CAT: 08

Tarascan
CIJE: 1 RIE: 1 CAT: 13

Tarboro High School NC
CIJE: 0 RIE: 1 CAT: 17

TARC Assessment System
CIJE: 3 RIE: 1 CAT: 21

Tardiness
CIJE: 10 RIE: 9 CAT: 16

Tardive Dyskinesia
CIJE: 3 RIE: 0 CAT: 11

Target 2000 SC
CIJE: 0 RIE: 2 CAT: 19

Target Planning
CIJE: 1 RIE: 6 CAT: 15

Target Populations
CIJE: 23 RIE: 17 CAT: 10

Target Valence
CIJE: 0 RIE: 1 CAT: 21

Targeted Assistance Program
CIJE: 0 RIE: 1 CAT: 19

Targeted Communications Program
CIJE: 0 RIE: 2 CAT: 19

Targeted Dissemination
CIJE: 1 RIE: 1 CAT: 20

Targeted Jobs Demonstration Program
CIJE: 0 RIE: 3 CAT: 19

Targeted Jobs Tax Credit
CIJE: 1 RIE: 15 CAT: 14

Tariffs
CIJE: 1 RIE: 2 CAT: 16

Tarkio College MO
CIJE: 0 RIE: 1 CAT: 17

Tarleton Model for Accelerated Teacher Educ
CIJE: 0 RIE: 1 CAT: 15

Tarleton State University TX
CIJE: 1 RIE: 5 CAT: 17

Tarot Reading
CIJE: 1 RIE: 2 CAT: 16

Tarrant County Junior College TX
CIJE: 11 RIE: 9 CAT: 17

Tartrates
CIJE: 1 RIE: 0 CAT: 20

Tashkent Dialect
CIJE: 0 RIE: 2 CAT: 13

Tashlin (Frank)
CIJE: 0 RIE: 1 CAT: 18

Task Accomplishment Inventories (McAfee)
CIJE: 0 RIE: 1 CAT: 21

Task Attractiveness
CIJE: 2 RIE: 1 CAT: 11

Task Characteristics
CIJE: 15 RIE: 11 CAT: 16

Task Completion Take Your Pick
CIJE: 0 RIE: 1 CAT: 21

Task Definition
CIJE: 5 RIE: 3 CAT: 16

Task Engagement
CIJE: 4 RIE: 0 CAT: 16

Task Environments
CIJE: 0 RIE: 1 CAT: 16

Task for Reporting Interviewing Observing
CIJE: 0 RIE: 1 CAT: 21

Task Force Approach
CIJE: 38 RIE: 65 CAT: 15
UF Task Forces

Task Force on Education for Economic Growth
CIJE: 1 RIE: 2 CAT: 17

Task Force on Graduate Medical Education (AAMC)
CIJE: 6 RIE: 0 CAT: 17

Task Force on Integration of Hearing Impaired
CIJE: 0 RIE: 1 CAT: 17
UF National Task Force on the Integr of Hear Impd St

Task Force on Migrant Education Goals
USE Migrant Education Goals Task Force

Task Force on Women Minorities Handicapped
CIJE: 1 RIE: 13 CAT: 17
SN "The Task Force on Women, Minorities, and the Handicapped in Science and Technology"

Task Force on Youth Development Community Prog
CIJE: 0 RIE: 1 CAT: 17

Task Force Public Private Sector Interaction
CIJE: 1 RIE: 0 CAT: 17

Task Force Student Involvement
CIJE: 0 RIE: 1 CAT: 16

Task Forces
USE Task Force Approach

Task Forecast
CIJE: 0 RIE: 1 CAT: 16

Task Goal Attitudes
CIJE: 1 RIE: 1 CAT: 21

Task Inventories (Lists)
USE Task Lists

Task Inventories (Surveys)
USE Task Surveys

Task Lists
CIJE: 1 RIE: 1 CAT: 16
UF Task Inventories (Lists)

Task Modifications
CIJE: 0 RIE: 2 CAT: 11

Task of Emotional Development Test
CIJE: 1 RIE: 1 CAT: 21

Task of Public Educ Opinionnaire (Downey et al)
CIJE: 0 RIE: 2 CAT: 21

Task Orientation
CIJE: 26 RIE: 13 CAT: 16

Task Oriented Instructions
CIJE: 2 RIE: 2 CAT: 15

Task Perception
CIJE: 0 RIE: 1 CAT: 11

Task Performance Sheets
CIJE: 0 RIE: 1 CAT: 21

Task Persistence
CIJE: 4 RIE: 2 CAT: 11

Task Planning
CIJE: 3 RIE: 2 CAT: 21

Task Sequence
CIJE: 4 RIE: 1 CAT: 21

Task Structure
CIJE: 8 RIE: 1 CAT: 16

Task Structure Design
CIJE: 3 RIE: 1 CAT: 15

Task Surveys
CIJE: 0 RIE: 1 CAT: 21
UF Task Inventories (Surveys)

Task Uncertainty
CIJE: 2 RIE: 1 CAT: 15

Task Value
CIJE: 1 RIE: 1 CAT: 15

Tasks of Emotional Development (Revised)
CIJE: 0 RIE: 1 CAT: 21

Tasso (Torquato)
CIJE: 1 RIE: 0 CAT: 18

Taste Discrimination
CIJE: 6 RIE: 4 CAT: 11

Taste Preference
CIJE: 1 RIE: 3 CAT: 11
SN Re the mouth and palate — do not confuse with the Descriptor "Aesthetic Values"

Tata Institute of Fundamental Research (India)
CIJE: 1 RIE: 0 CAT: 17

Tatana
CIJE: 0 RIE: 1 CAT: 13

Tate System of English Language Instruction
CIJE: 0 RIE: 1 CAT: 15

Tattle Tape
CIJE: 1 RIE: 0 CAT: 04

Tattling
CIJE: 0 RIE: 2 CAT: 16

Tau Equivalence
CIJE: 5 RIE: 3 CAT: 21

Taunton Literacy Corps MA
CIJE: 0 RIE: 1 CAT: 17

Tautologies
CIJE: 2 RIE: 1 CAT: 16

Taverns
CIJE: 1 RIE: 1 CAT: 05

Tavistock Group Relations Conference
CIJE: 1 RIE: 1 CAT: 02

Tavistock Institute of Human Relations (England)
CIJE: 3 RIE: 4 CAT: 17

Tavistock Study Groups
CIJE: 2 RIE: 0 CAT: 05

Tax and Expenditure Limitations
CIJE: 1 RIE: 3 CAT: 16

Tax Bases
CIJE: 2 RIE: 9 CAT: 16

Tax Deferral
CIJE: 1 RIE: 3 CAT: 16

Tax Equity
CIJE: 1 RIE: 16 CAT: 14

Tax Equity and Fiscal Responsibility Act 1982
CIJE: 2 RIE: 2 CAT: 14

Tax Exempt Bonds
CIJE: 0 RIE: 1 CAT: 16

Tax Exemptions
CIJE: 47 RIE: 13 CAT: 16

Tax Incentives
CIJE: 0 RIE: 1 CAT: 16

Tax Limitation Efforts
CIJE: 4 RIE: 13 CAT: 14

Tax Limitations
CIJE: 13 RIE: 17 CAT: 14

Tax Preparation
CIJE: 1 RIE: 2 CAT: 03

Tax Reform Act 1948
CIJE: 1 RIE: 0 CAT: 14

Tax Reform Act 1969
CIJE: 9 RIE: 0 CAT: 14

Tax Reform Act 1976
CIJE: 0 RIE: 0 CAT: 14

Tax Reform Act 1978
CIJE: 0 RIE: 0 CAT: 14

Tax Reform Act 1981
CIJE: 1 RIE: 1 CAT: 14

Tax Reform Act 1984
CIJE: 1 RIE: 0 CAT: 14

Tax Reform Act 1986
CIJE: 34 RIE: 11 CAT: 14

Tax Resistance
CIJE: 1 RIE: 0 CAT: 16

Tax Sheltered Annuities
CIJE: 9 RIE: 1 CAT: 16

Tax Utilization
CIJE: 1 RIE: 1 CAT: 16

Taxicab Drivers
CIJE: 0 RIE: 1 CAT: 09

Taxicabs
CIJE: 0 RIE: 1 CAT: 04

Taxidermy
CIJE: 1 RIE: 1 CAT: 20

Taxographic Space
CIJE: 0 RIE: 1 CAT: 15

Taxonomic Skills Achievement Test in Fractions
CIJE: 0 RIE: 1 CAT: 21

Taxonomy of Educational Objectives (Bloom)
USE Blooms Taxonomy

Taxonomy of Image Provocation Profile
CIJE: 0 RIE: 4 CAT: 21

Taxonomy of Interventions
CIJE: 0 RIE: 1 CAT: 21

Taxpayer Equity
CIJE: 2 RIE: 4 CAT: 14

Taxpayer Revolt
CIJE: 2 RIE: 2 CAT: 16

Tay Sachs Disease
CIJE: 5 RIE: 0 CAT: 11

Taylor (A J P)
CIJE: 2 RIE: 0 CAT: 18

Taylor (Frederick Winslow)
CIJE: 11 RIE: 3 CAT: 18

Taylor (Harold A)
CIJE: 0 RIE: 1 CAT: 18

Taylor (Harold)
CIJE: 2 RIE: 1 CAT: 18

Taylor (Jack)
CIJE: 0 RIE: 1 CAT: 18

Taylor (Paul S)
CIJE: 0 RIE: 1 CAT: 18

Taylor (Philip)
CIJE: 2 RIE: 0 CAT: 18

Taylor (Sam)
CIJE: 1 RIE: 0 CAT: 18

Taylor (W L)
CIJE: 1 RIE: 0 CAT: 18

Taylor (Zachary)
CIJE: 2 RIE: 0 CAT: 18

Taylor Business Institute NY
CIJE: 0 RIE: 1 CAT: 17

Taylor Ellison Biographical Inventory
CIJE: 0 RIE: 2 CAT: 21

Taylor Law
CIJE: 4 RIE: 6 CAT: 14

Taylor Manifest Anxiety Scale
CIJE: 10 RIE: 7 CAT: 21

Taylor Murphy Institute VA
CIJE: 0 RIE: 1 CAT: 17

Taylor Public Schools MI
CIJE: 0 RIE: 0 CAT: 17

Taylor Report
CIJE: 7 RIE: 1 CAT: 22

Taylor University IN
CIJE: 0 RIE: 2 CAT: 17

Taylors Theorem
CIJE: 2 RIE: 1 CAT: 15

Tboli
USE Tagabili

Tchaikovsky (Peter)
CIJE: 0 RIE: 1 CAT: 18

TDDs
USE Telecommunication Devices for the Deaf

Te Kohanga Reo (New Zealand)
CIJE: 0 RIE: 1 CAT: 05

Tea Bag Machine Tenders
CIJE: 0 RIE: 1 CAT: 09

Tea Bag Packers
CIJE: 0 RIE: 1 CAT: 09

Teach for America
CIJE: 5 RIE: 3 CAT: 19

Teach Practice Apply Model
CIJE: 1 RIE: 1 CAT: 15
UF TPA Instruction

Teach Skills Inventory
CIJE: 0 RIE: 1 CAT: 21

Teacher Activity Inventory
CIJE: 0 RIE: 1 CAT: 21

Teacher Adaptability Scale
CIJE: 0 RIE: 1 CAT: 21

Teacher Administrator Ratio
CIJE: 1 RIE: 3 CAT: 15

Teacher Advisor Program (Myrick)
CIJE: 0 RIE: 1 CAT: 19

Teacher Advisors
CIJE: 9 RIE: 5 CAT: 09

Teacher Advisory Centres
CIJE: 0 RIE: 1 CAT: 05

Teacher Affective Sensitivity Scale (Kravas)
CIJE: 1 RIE: 1 CAT: 21

Teacher Aide Evaluation
CIJE: 0 RIE: 3 CAT: 16

Teacher and Pupil Performance Ratings
CIJE: 0 RIE: 1 CAT: 21

Teacher Appearance
CIJE: 3 RIE: 0 CAT: 16

Teacher Appraisal for Improvement
CIJE: 0 RIE: 2 CAT: 19

Teacher Appraisal Instrument
CIJE: 1 RIE: 1 CAT: 21

Teacher Appraisal System TX
USE Texas Teacher Appraisal System

Teacher Apprenticeship Program
CIJE: 0 RIE: 2 CAT: 19

Teacher Approval
CIJE: 2 RIE: 0 CAT: 16

Teacher Assessment and Development System
CIJE: 2 RIE: 2 CAT: 15

Teacher Assessment of Classroom Practices
CIJE: 3 RIE: 2 CAT: 15

Teacher Assessment of Pupil Progress (Coley)
CIJE: 0 RIE: 1 CAT: 21

Teacher Assessment Practices Questionnaire
CIJE: 0 RIE: 1 CAT: 21

Teacher Assessment Prep Practices Questionnaire
CIJE: 0 RIE: 1 CAT: 21

Teacher Assessment Project (Stanford Univ)
CIJE: 2 RIE: 0 CAT: 19

Teacher Assistance Teams
CIJE: 2 RIE: 2 CAT: 10

Teacher Attitude Inventory (Whitmore)
CIJE: 0 RIE: 2 CAT: 21

Teacher Attitude Questionnaire (CERLI)
CIJE: 0 RIE: 1 CAT: 21

Teacher Attitudes Toward Evaluation
CIJE: 1 RIE: 3 CAT: 21

Teacher Attitudes toward Low Achiev in Math Scale
CIJE: 0 RIE: 1 CAT: 21
UF TALAM Scale

Teacher Audio Placement System
CIJE: 1 RIE: 0 CAT: 15

Teacher Autonomy Scale
CIJE: 1 RIE: 1 CAT: 21

Teacher Awareness
CIJE: 8 RIE: 9 CAT: 16

Teacher Behavior Continuum
CIJE: 1 RIE: 1 CAT: 15

Teacher Behavior Description Questionnaire
CIJE: 0 RIE: 1 CAT: 21

Teacher Behavior Form (Schwartz and Mott)
CIJE: 0 RIE: 2 CAT: 21

Teacher Belief Inventory
CIJE: 1 RIE: 0 CAT: 21

Teacher Belief Rating Scale
CIJE: 1 RIE: 0 CAT: 21

Teacher Beliefs Study
CIJE: 7 RIE: 4 CAT: 19
SN See also "Mathematics Teacher Beliefs Study"

Teacher Brinkmanship
CIJE: 0 RIE: 2 CAT: 15

Teacher Cadet Program SC
CIJE: 1 RIE: 1 CAT: 19
UF South Carolina Teacher Cadet Program

Teacher Candidates
CIJE: 44 RIE: 19 CAT: 10

Teacher Career and Promotion Study
CIJE: 0 RIE: 3 CAT: 22

Teacher Centered Instruction
CIJE: 12 RIE: 5 CAT: 15

Teacher Certification Reciprocity
CIJE: 0 RIE: 2 CAT: 15
UF Reciprocal Teacher Certification

Teacher Certification Tests
CIJE: 4 RIE: 4 CAT: 21

Teacher Certification Tests (Georgia)
CIJE: 0 RIE: 1 CAT: 21

Teacher Characteristics Scale (Kellinger)
CIJE: 0 RIE: 1 CAT: 21

Teacher Characteristics Schedule
CIJE: 0 RIE: 2 CAT: 15

Teacher Clarity
CIJE: 22 RIE: 6 CAT: 15

Teacher Classroom Activity Profile
CIJE: 0 RIE: 3 CAT: 21

Teacher Collaboration
CIJE: 49 RIE: 55 CAT: 15

Teacher Commitment
CIJE: 2 RIE: 1 CAT: 16

Teacher Communication Scale
CIJE: 0 RIE: 1 CAT: 21

Teacher Community Relationship
CIJE: 7 RIE: 9 CAT: 15

Teacher Competencies Assessment Questionnaire
CIJE: 0 RIE: 1 CAT: 21

Teacher Competency Inventory (Bain et al)
CIJE: 0 RIE: 1 CAT: 21

Teacher Competency Scale (Resnick and Reinert)
CIJE: 1 RIE: 0 CAT: 21

Teacher Conceptions Educ Process Questionnaire
CIJE: 1 RIE: 1 CAT: 21

Teacher Concern Checklist (Parson and Fuller)
CIJE: 0 RIE: 1 CAT: 21

Teacher Concerns Checklist (Parsons and Fuller)
CIJE: 1 RIE: 3 CAT: 21

Teacher Concerns Model
CIJE: 3 RIE: 1 CAT: 15

Teacher Concerns Questionnaire
CIJE: 3 RIE: 5 CAT: 21

Teacher Concerns Statements (Fuller and Case)
CIJE: 0 RIE: 1 CAT: 21

Teacher Concerns Statements (Fuller and Chase)
CIJE: 0 RIE: 1 CAT: 21

Teacher Concerns Theory (Fuller)
CIJE: 0 RIE: 1 CAT: 15
UF Fuller Teacher Concerns Theory

Teacher Consultants
CIJE: 5 RIE: 3 CAT: 09

Teacher Cooperation
CIJE: 32 RIE: 7 CAT: 16

Teacher Cooperatives
USE Teacher Partnerships

Teacher Corporations
USE Teacher Partnerships

Teacher Corps
CIJE: 57 RIE: 302 CAT: 17

Teacher Counselors
CIJE: 2 RIE: 2 CAT: 09
SN See also "Liaison Teacher Counselors"

Teacher Course Assignment
CIJE: 0 RIE: 2 CAT: 16

Teacher Dedication
CIJE: 1 RIE: 0 CAT: 16

Teacher Demand and Shortage Survey (NCES)
CIJE: 0 RIE: 1 CAT: 21

Teacher Development
CIJE: 15 RIE: 7 CAT: 16
SN Activities to encourage and enhance teacher professional growth

Teacher Development Programs
CIJE: 5 RIE: 5 CAT: 19

Teacher Education Academies
CIJE: 0 RIE: 1 CAT: 05

Teacher Education Alliance for Metro
CIJE: 1 RIE: 0 CAT: 17

Teacher Education and Computer Centers
CIJE: 0 RIE: 3 CAT: 05

Teacher Education and Learning to Teach Study
CIJE: 0 RIE: 1 CAT: 19

Teacher Education and Mathematics Project
CIJE: 0 RIE: 10 CAT: 19

Teacher Education and Media Project
CIJE: 0 RIE: 6 CAT: 19
UF AACTE Media Project

Teacher Education and Mentoring Program GA
CIJE: 0 RIE: 1 CAT: 19

Teacher Education Experiences Program
CIJE: 1 RIE: 0 CAT: 19

Teacher Education Internship Project
CIJE: 0 RIE: 3 CAT: 19

Teacher Education Programs (Five Year)
CIJE: 0 RIE: 2 CAT: 19

Teacher Effectance Motivation Rating
CIJE: 2 RIE: 0 CAT: 21

Teacher Effectiveness Index
CIJE: 0 RIE: 1 CAT: 21

Teacher Effectiveness Questionnaire
CIJE: 0 RIE: 1 CAT: 21

Teacher Effectiveness Training
CIJE: 8 RIE: 2 CAT: 15

Teacher Efficacy Scale
CIJE: 3 RIE: 5 CAT: 21

Teacher Efficacy Study
CIJE: 0 RIE: 3 CAT: 22

Teacher Empowerment
CIJE: 44 RIE: 65 CAT: 15

Teacher Engagement
CIJE: 0 RIE: 3 CAT: 16

Teacher Enthusiasm
CIJE: 5 RIE: 2 CAT: 16

Teacher Errors
CIJE: 2 RIE: 0 CAT: 16

Teacher Evaluation and Assessment Center FL
CIJE: 0 RIE: 0 CAT: 17

Teacher Evaluation Needs Identification Survey
CIJE: 1 RIE: 0 CAT: 21

Teacher Evaluation Project FL
CIJE: 0 RIE: 3 CAT: 19
UF Florida Teacher Evaluation Project

Teacher Evaluation Record
CIJE: 0 RIE: 2 CAT: 21

Teacher Evaluation Scale (Brown)
CIJE: 0 RIE: 3 CAT: 21

Teacher Evaluators
CIJE: 3 RIE: 1 CAT: 09

Teacher Expectation Instrument
CIJE: 1 RIE: 0 CAT: 21

Teacher Expectation Questionnaire
CIJE: 1 RIE: 0 CAT: 21

Teacher Expectations and Student Achievement
CIJE: 0 RIE: 2 CAT: 19
SN Project of Spencerport Central Schools NY

Teacher Explanation
CIJE: 7 RIE: 5 CAT: 16

Teacher Expressiveness
CIJE: 0 RIE: 1 CAT: 11

Teacher Fairs
CIJE: 0 RIE: 1 CAT: 16

Teacher Followup Survey (NCES)
CIJE: 0 RIE: 6 CAT: 19

Teacher Growth Program NY
CIJE: 0 RIE: 1 CAT: 19

Teacher Image Questionnaire
CIJE: 2 RIE: 0 CAT: 21

Teacher Immediacy
CIJE: 8 RIE: 12 CAT: 16

Teacher Impression Instrument
CIJE: 1 RIE: 0 CAT: 21

Teacher Improvement Model
CIJE: 0 RIE: 1 CAT: 15

Teacher Incentives
CIJE: 4 RIE: 6 CAT: 15

Teacher Incentives Pilot Program
CIJE: 0 RIE: 1 CAT: 19
UF Teaching Incentives Pilot Program WI

Teacher Incentives Project
CIJE: 0 RIE: 1 CAT: 19
UF TIPS WA

Teacher Industry Exchange Subprogram (Australia)
CIJE: 0 RIE: 1 CAT: 19

Teacher Initiated Activities
CIJE: 3 RIE: 5 CAT: 15

Teacher Initiated Schools
USE Charter Schools

Teacher Innovation Program
CIJE: 2 RIE: 1 CAT: 19

Teacher Instructional Plans Materials Assess Scale
CIJE: 0 RIE: 1 CAT: 21

Teacher Interactive Computer System
CIJE: 1 RIE: 2 CAT: 04

Teacher Internship Program LA
USE Louisiana Teacher Internship Program

Teacher Involvement Project
CIJE: 1 RIE: 1 CAT: 19

Teacher Isolation
CIJE: 5 RIE: 4 CAT: 16

Teacher Journals
CIJE: 10 RIE: 5 CAT: 16

Teacher Judgments
CIJE: 3 RIE: 1 CAT: 16

Teacher Knowledge
CIJE: 136 RIE: 43 CAT: 15
SN The personal repertoire of skills and information possessed by individual teachers (Note: Vague concept — use a more specific Identifier if possible, e.g., "Pedagogical Content Knowledge," "Subject Content Knowledge" — do not confuse with the Descriptors "Knowledge Base for Teaching" or "Teacher Competencies")

Teacher Knowledge and Beliefs Inventory
CIJE: 0 RIE: 1 CAT: 21

Teacher Language
CIJE: 4 RIE: 2 CAT: 13
SN See also "Teacher Talk"

Teacher Language Instrument
CIJE: 0 RIE: 2 CAT: 21

Teacher Leaders
CIJE: 2 RIE: 1 CAT: 10

Teacher Leadership
CIJE: 4 RIE: 2 CAT: 16

Teacher Librarians
CIJE: 56 RIE: 12 CAT: 09

Teacher Locus of Control Scale
CIJE: 1 RIE: 1 CAT: 21

Teacher Mediated Intervention Model
CIJE: 0 RIE: 1 CAT: 15

Teacher Mobility Study Quest (Orlich et al)
CIJE: 0 RIE: 1 CAT: 21

Teacher Mom Project
CIJE: 1 RIE: 0 CAT: 19

Teacher Needs
CIJE: 35 RIE: 17 CAT: 16

Teacher Networks
CIJE: 1 RIE: 1 CAT: 16

Teacher Nonreappointment
CIJE: 2 RIE: 0 CAT: 16

Teacher Observation Personality Schedule (Cooper)
CIJE: 0 RIE: 1 CAT: 21

Teacher Observation Rating Scale (Johnson)
CIJE: 1 RIE: 0 CAT: 21

Teacher Observation Scale (Crockenberg and Bryant)
CIJE: 0 RIE: 2 CAT: 21

Teacher Observation Scales (Purdue)
CIJE: 0 RIE: 1 CAT: 21

Teacher Observational Item
CIJE: 1 RIE: 0 CAT: 21

Teacher Occupational Stress Factor Questionnaire
CIJE: 3 RIE: 0 CAT: 21

Teacher of the Year
CIJE: 25 RIE: 8 CAT: 16
UF Professor of the Year

Teacher Opinion Inventory (Bowers)
CIJE: 0 RIE: 2 CAT: 21

Teacher Opinion Poll
CIJE: 2 RIE: 1 CAT: 21

Teacher Opinion Questionnaire (Holzmiller)
CIJE: 0 RIE: 1 CAT: 21

Teacher Participation Project
CIJE: 0 RIE: 1 CAT: 19

Teacher Partnerships
CIJE: 1 RIE: 4 CAT: 05
UF Partnerships (Teachers); Teacher Cooperatives; Teacher Corporations

Teacher Pension Plans
CIJE: 0 RIE: 1 CAT: 14

Teacher Perceiver Interview
CIJE: 4 RIE: 2 CAT: 21

Teacher Perceiver Screeners
CIJE: 0 RIE: 1 CAT: 21

Teacher Performance Appraisal Instruments
USE Teacher Performance Assessment Instruments

Teacher Performance Appraisal Scale
CIJE: 0 RIE: 3 CAT: 21

Teacher Performance Appraisal System
CIJE: 1 RIE: 7 CAT: 21

Teacher Performance Assessment Instrument
CIJE: 6 RIE: 8 CAT: 21

Teacher Performance Assessment Instruments
CIJE: 5 RIE: 21 CAT: 21
SN See also "Teaching Performance Tests"
UF Teacher Performance Appraisal Instruments

Teacher Performance Competencies Scale
CIJE: 0 RIE: 1 CAT: 21

Teacher Performance Evaluation (Manatt)
CIJE: 0 RIE: 1 CAT: 21

Teacher Performance Evaluation Scale (Sinha)
CIJE: 0 RIE: 1 CAT: 21

Teacher Planning
CIJE: 10 RIE: 3 CAT: 16

Teacher Plus Program
CIJE: 0 RIE: 1 CAT: 19

Teacher Portfolios
CIJE: 0 RIE: 3 CAT: 16

Teacher Power
CIJE: 9 RIE: 2 CAT: 16

Teacher Practices Inventory
CIJE: 2 RIE: 3 CAT: 21

Teacher Practices Observation Record
CIJE: 3 RIE: 10 CAT: 21

Teacher Practices Questionnaire (Sorenson et al)
CIJE: 0 RIE: 5 CAT: 21

Teacher Preferences
CIJE: 0 RIE: 0 CAT: 16

Teacher Preparation Evaluation Inventory
CIJE: 0 RIE: 1 CAT: 21

Teacher Preparation Evaluation Program
CIJE: 0 RIE: 2 CAT: 19

Teacher Preparation Time
CIJE: 0 RIE: 2 CAT: 16

Teacher Principal Conferences
CIJE: 0 RIE: 1 CAT: 02

Teacher Principal Relationship
CIJE: 1 RIE: 1 CAT: 15

Teacher Problem Inventory
CIJE: 0 RIE: 3 CAT: 21

Teacher Problems Q Sort (Bills)
CIJE: 0 RIE: 1 CAT: 21

Teacher Process Measure
CIJE: 0 RIE: 1 CAT: 21

Teacher Professionalization
USE Professionalization of Teaching

Teacher Pupil Question Inventory
CIJE: 0 RIE: 4 CAT: 21

Teacher Pupil Relationship Scale
CIJE: 0 RIE: 1 CAT: 21

Teacher Quality and Effectiveness R and D Center
USE Research and Develop Ctr Teacher Quality Effective

Teacher Questionnaire (Purdue)
CIJE: 0 RIE: 1 CAT: 21

Teacher Rating Form (Murray)
CIJE: 1 RIE: 0 CAT: 21

Teacher Rating Forms
CIJE: 1 RIE: 0 CAT: 21

Teacher Rating of Academic Performance
CIJE: 1 RIE: 0 CAT: 21

Teacher Rating of Administrator Performance
CIJE: 1 RIE: 0 CAT: 21

Teacher Rating of Social Skills
CIJE: 3 RIE: 0 CAT: 21

Teacher Rating of Student Characteristics
CIJE: 5 RIE: 3 CAT: 21

Teacher Rating Scale
CIJE: 3 RIE: 4 CAT: 21

Teacher Rating Scale (Harvey)
CIJE: 0 RIE: 1 CAT: 21

Teacher Reaction Form (Di Johnson)
CIJE: 0 RIE: 1 CAT: 21

Teacher Reassignment
CIJE: 1 RIE: 0 CAT: 15

Teacher Recertification
CIJE: 2 RIE: 2 CAT: 16
UF Teacher Relicensing

Teacher Recruitment and Internship Prj for Success
USE Teacher Recruitment Internship Project Success

Teacher Recruitment Internship Project Success
CIJE: 0 RIE: 1 CAT: 19
UF Teacher Recruitment and Internship Prj for Success

Teacher Referenced Tests
CIJE: 0 RIE: 1 CAT: 21

Teacher Relicensing
USE Teacher Recertification

Teacher Renewal
CIJE: 4 RIE: 3 CAT: 16

Teacher Report of Treatment of Students
CIJE: 1 RIE: 0 CAT: 15

Teacher Researcher Cooperation
CIJE: 30 RIE: 23 CAT: 15
UF Researcher Teacher Cooperation

Teacher Researcher Relationship
CIJE: 43 RIE: 23 CAT: 15
UF Researchers and Teachers; Researcher Teacher Relationship; Teachers and Researchers

Teacher Researchers
CIJE: 160 RIE: 140 CAT: 10

Teacher Resignation
CIJE: 4 RIE: 3 CAT: 16

Teacher Retraining And Directed Exchange
USE Project TRADE

Teacher Revitalization
USE Educator Revitalization

Teacher Role Q Sort
CIJE: 0 RIE: 1 CAT: 21

Teacher Role Survey
CIJE: 0 RIE: 2 CAT: 21

Teacher Satisfaction
CIJE: 1 RIE: 1 CAT: 16

Teacher Satisfaction Survey (NASSP)
CIJE: 0 RIE: 1 CAT: 21

Teacher Self Analysis Inventory (Beauchamp)
CIJE: 0 RIE: 1 CAT: 21

Teacher Self Assessment of Non Sexist Behaviors
CIJE: 0 RIE: 1 CAT: 21

Teacher Sex Role Perception Inventory
CIJE: 1 RIE: 1 CAT: 21

Teacher Socialization
CIJE: 12 RIE: 8 CAT: 16

Teacher Specialists
CIJE: 1 RIE: 2 CAT: 09

Teacher Staff Ratio
CIJE: 0 RIE: 1 CAT: 16

Teacher Status
CIJE: 22 RIE: 4 CAT: 16
UF Status of Teachers

Teacher Stress
CIJE: 26 RIE: 19 CAT: 11

Teacher Student Conferences
CIJE: 40 RIE: 58 CAT: 15

Teacher Support Groups
CIJE: 14 RIE: 6 CAT: 10

Teacher Surplus
CIJE: 5 RIE: 1 CAT: 16

Teacher Surveys
CIJE: 74 RIE: 155 CAT: 16

Teacher Talk
CIJE: 3 RIE: 3 CAT: 13
SN See also "Teacher Language"

Teacher Task Analysis Questionnaire
CIJE: 0 RIE: 1 CAT: 21

Teacher Temperament Questionnaire
CIJE: 4 RIE: 1 CAT: 21

Teacher Tenure Act (Michigan)
CIJE: 1 RIE: 2 CAT: 14
UF Michigan Teachers Tenure Act 1964

Teacher Testing
CIJE: 6 RIE: 9 CAT: 21
SN Do not use for the Desc "Teacher Competency Testing"

Teacher Thinking
CIJE: 50 RIE: 16 CAT: 11

Teacher Transitions
CIJE: 2 RIE: 0 CAT: 15

Teacher Treatment Inventory (Weinstein et al)
CIJE: 3 RIE: 2 CAT: 21

Teacher Volunteer Relationship
CIJE: 0 RIE: 1 CAT: 15

Teacher Warranty
CIJE: 4 RIE: 1 CAT: 15
UF Warranty of Teachers

Teacher Writers
CIJE: 18 RIE: 9 CAT: 10

Teacher Writing
CIJE: 18 RIE: 14 CAT: 16

Teacher Writing Standards Inventory
CIJE: 0 RIE: 1 CAT: 21

Teachers Abroad Program
CIJE: 0 RIE: 1 CAT: 19

Teachers and Researchers
USE Teacher Researcher Relationship

Teachers and Writers Collaborative
CIJE: 6 RIE: 4 CAT: 17

Teachers as Parents
CIJE: 0 RIE: 1 CAT: 16

Teachers Centers Exchange
CIJE: 1 RIE: 2 CAT: 17

Teachers College Columbia University NY
USE Columbia University NY Teachers College

Teachers College Record
CIJE: 0 RIE: 1 CAT: 22

Teachers College Writing Project
CIJE: 2 RIE: 2 CAT: 19

Teachers Course Book
CIJE: 1 RIE: 0 CAT: 22

Teachers for Alaska Program
CIJE: 1 RIE: 2 CAT: 19
UF Teachers for Rural Alaska

Teachers for Our Nations Schools (Goodlad)
CIJE: 0 RIE: 1 CAT: 22

Teachers for Rural Alaska
USE Teachers for Alaska Program

Teachers for Secondary Schools Program
CIJE: 0 RIE: 2 CAT: 19

Teachers for the Real World
CIJE: 0 RIE: 2 CAT: 22

Teachers Guide to Macmillan Readingtime Books
CIJE: 1 RIE: 0 CAT: 22

Teachers Insurance and Annuity Association
CIJE: 32 RIE: 13 CAT: 17

Teachers Knowledge
CIJE: 0 RIE: 4 CAT: 16

Teachers National Field Task Force
CIJE: 0 RIE: 1 CAT: 17

Teachers Need Teachers Program
CIJE: 0 RIE: 1 CAT: 19

Teachers of English to Speakers of Other Languages
CIJE: 4 RIE: 15 CAT: 17

Teachers of the Deaf
CIJE: 0 RIE: 1 CAT: 09

Teachers on Television Project
CIJE: 0 RIE: 1 CAT: 19

Teachers Rating Questionnaire
CIJE: 0 RIE: 8 CAT: 21

Teachers School Readiness Inventory
CIJE: 0 RIE: 1 CAT: 21

Teachers Teaching Teachers
CIJE: 1 RIE: 8 CAT: 19

Teachers Test of Language Skills
CIJE: 0 RIE: 1 CAT: 21

Teachers Workbook of 30000 Words
CIJE: 0 RIE: 1 CAT: 22

Teaching Activities for Language Knowledge
CIJE: 0 RIE: 1 CAT: 19

Teaching Aid Project
CIJE: 1 RIE: 0 CAT: 19

Teaching and Coursewriting Language
CIJE: 0 RIE: 2 CAT: 04

Teaching and Learning about Aging Project
CIJE: 0 RIE: 7 CAT: 19

Teaching and Learning with Computers (IBM)
CIJE: 0 RIE: 1 CAT: 19

Teaching and Learning with Technology Project MI
CIJE: 0 RIE: 1 CAT: 19

Teaching Anxiety Scale
CIJE: 2 RIE: 2 CAT: 21

Teaching as a Science
CIJE: 0 RIE: 1 CAT: 15

Teaching as an Art
CIJE: 0 RIE: 1 CAT: 15
UF Artistic Teaching; Art of Teaching

Teaching Assessment Blank (Holmes)
CIJE: 1 RIE: 0 CAT: 21

Teaching Assistant Training Project
CIJE: 0 RIE: 53 CAT: 19

Teaching Assistants Association
CIJE: 1 RIE: 0 CAT: 17

Teaching Basic Skills Through Vocational Education
CIJE: 0 RIE: 6 CAT: 19

Teaching Behaviors Questionnaire
CIJE: 0 RIE: 2 CAT: 21

Teaching Behaviours Scale (Soh)
CIJE: 0 RIE: 1 CAT: 21

Teaching Black Children to Read
CIJE: 1 RIE: 0 CAT: 22

Teaching by Objectives
CIJE: 1 RIE: 0 CAT: 15

Teaching Contests
CIJE: 1 RIE: 0 CAT: 16

Teaching Doctorate Degree
CIJE: 0 RIE: 1 CAT: 16

Teaching Education (Journal)
CIJE: 0 RIE: 1 CAT: 22

Teaching Effectiveness Network
CIJE: 1 RIE: 2 CAT: 19

Teaching Environment Awareness to Child of Harvest
CIJE: 0 RIE: 5 CAT: 19
UF Project TEACH PA

Teaching Essential Life Skills NJ
CIJE: 0 RIE: 1 CAT: 03

Teaching Events Stress Inventory
CIJE: 0 RIE: 3 CAT: 21

Teaching Excellence Program
CIJE: 0 RIE: 1 CAT: 19

Teaching Experiment
CIJE: 4 RIE: 2 CAT: 19

Teaching Family Model
CIJE: 2 RIE: 1 CAT: 15

Teaching Film Custodians (Association)
CIJE: 0 RIE: 1 CAT: 17

Teaching for Higher Order Thinking
CIJE: 0 RIE: 0 CAT: 19
UF THOT Program (Peterson et al)

Teaching for Mastery
CIJE: 1 RIE: 1 CAT: 22

Teaching Incentives Pilot Program WI
USE Teacher Incentives Pilot Program

Teaching Individuals Protective Strategies
CIJE: 0 RIE: 1 CAT: 19

Teaching Information Processing System
CIJE: 4 RIE: 6 CAT: 15

Teaching Learning Communities Model
CIJE: 0 RIE: 1 CAT: 15

Teaching Learning Graduate Geography
CIJE: 0 RIE: 1 CAT: 03

Teaching Learning in Graduate Geography Proj
CIJE: 0 RIE: 1 CAT: 19

Teaching Learning Interaction Study
CIJE: 0 RIE: 1 CAT: 19

Teaching Methods Matls Centre (Papua New Guinea)
CIJE: 0 RIE: 1 CAT: 17

Teaching Performance Observation Instrument
CIJE: 1 RIE: 0 CAT: 21

Teaching Performance Tests
CIJE: 3 RIE: 3 CAT: 21
SN See also "Teacher Performance Assessment Instruments"

Teaching Perspectives
CIJE: 5 RIE: 7 CAT: 16

Teaching Principals
CIJE: 2 RIE: 1 CAT: 09

Teaching Research
CIJE: 17 RIE: 15 CAT: 15
UF Research on Teaching

Teaching Research Data Based Classroom Model
CIJE: 1 RIE: 1 CAT: 15

Teaching Research Project (New Zealand)
CIJE: 0 RIE: 1 CAT: 19

Teaching Research Systems
CIJE: 0 RIE: 1 CAT: 15

Teaching Resource Classroom Model
CIJE: 0 RIE: 1 CAT: 19

Teaching Scale (Barnard)
CIJE: 0 RIE: 1 CAT: 21

Teaching Sets
CIJE: 1 RIE: 0 CAT: 16

Teaching Situation Reaction Test
CIJE: 1 RIE: 12 CAT: 21

Teaching Strategies Observation Differential
CIJE: 0 RIE: 1 CAT: 21

Teaching Style Classification Scale (Augenstein)
CIJE: 0 RIE: 1 CAT: 21

Teaching Style Q Sort
CIJE: 1 RIE: 1 CAT: 15

Teaching Styles and Pupil Progress (Bennett)
CIJE: 2 RIE: 0 CAT: 22

Teaching Styles Inventory
CIJE: 2 RIE: 2 CAT: 21

Teaching Techniques Evaluation Form (Patrick)
CIJE: 0 RIE: 1 CAT: 21

Teaching Teen Reading Series
CIJE: 0 RIE: 9 CAT: 22

Teaching Tests
CIJE: 0 RIE: 1 CAT: 21

Teaching the Talented Program
CIJE: 0 RIE: 1 CAT: 19

Teaching to the Test
CIJE: 12 RIE: 22 CAT: 21
UF Backwash (Tests); Washback Effect (Testing)

Teaching Your Child
CIJE: 0 RIE: 5 CAT: 03

Team Accelerated Instruction
CIJE: 1 RIE: 1 CAT: 15

Team Approach to Assessment and Programming
CIJE: 0 RIE: 2 CAT: 19

Team Assembly (Factory)
CIJE: 0 RIE: 1 CAT: 16

Team Assessment
CIJE: 0 RIE: 1 CAT: 21

Team Assisted Individualization
CIJE: 10 RIE: 3 CAT: 15

Team Exercise for Action Management Skills
CIJE: 0 RIE: 1 CAT: 15
UF TEAMS Management Simulation

Team Leader Attitude Scale
CIJE: 0 RIE: 1 CAT: 21

Team Learning Methods
CIJE: 7 RIE: 5 CAT: 15

Team Magazine
CIJE: 1 RIE: 0 CAT: 22

Team Oriented Corrective Reading Program
CIJE: 1 RIE: 1 CAT: 19

Teams Games Tournament
CIJE: 8 RIE: 17 CAT: 15

TEAMS Management Simulation
USE Team Exercise for Action Management Skills

Teamsters Union
CIJE: 1 RIE: 1 CAT: 17

Teasing
CIJE: 4 RIE: 4 CAT: 11

Tech Prep
CIJE: 51 RIE: 147 CAT: 15
SN See also "2 Plus 2..."

TechBac
USE Technological Baccalaureate (England)

Techne
CIJE: 0 RIE: 1 CAT: 20

Technical Adequacy (Tests)
CIJE: 1 RIE: 1 CAT: 21

Technical Admissions Standards
CIJE: 0 RIE: 1 CAT: 16

Technical and Further Education (Australia)
USE TAFE (Australia)

Technical and Vocational Education Initiative
CIJE: 10 RIE: 6 CAT: 03
UF TVEI Schemes

Technical Assistance Centers
CIJE: 2 RIE: 50 CAT: 05

Technical Assistance Consortium Improve Coll Serv
USE TACTICS

Technical Assistance Development System
CIJE: 3 RIE: 17 CAT: 15

Technical Assistance for Special Populations Prog
CIJE: 1 RIE: 1 CAT: 19

Technical Communication
CIJE: 103 RIE: 43 CAT: 16

Technical Cooperation Among Developing Countries
CIJE: 0 RIE: 1 CAT: 15

Technical Education College System
CIJE: 2 RIE: 0 CAT: 17

Technical Education Research Centers
CIJE: 5 RIE: 0 CAT: 05

Technical Educational Research Centers
CIJE: 1 RIE: 0 CAT: 05

Technical Entrepreneurship
CIJE: 0 RIE: 1 CAT: 16

Technical Information Support Activities
CIJE: 0 RIE: 3 CAT: 16

Technical Language
CIJE: 26 RIE: 9 CAT: 13

Technical Notes
CIJE: 0 RIE: 1 CAT: 16

Technical Physics Project
CIJE: 0 RIE: 1 CAT: 19

Technical Report Service
CIJE: 1 RIE: 0 CAT: 17

Technical School of the Air
CIJE: 0 RIE: 1 CAT: 17

Technical Services Automation Phase I
CIJE: 1 RIE: 0 CAT: 15

Technical Skills Project
CIJE: 0 RIE: 1 CAT: 19

Technical Teachers College (Australia)
CIJE: 1 RIE: 0 CAT: 17

Technical Theater
CIJE: 0 RIE: 3 CAT: 16

Technical University of Vienna (Austria)
CIJE: 0 RIE: 2 CAT: 17
UF Technische Universitat Wien

Technician Education Council Programs
CIJE: 0 RIE: 1 CAT: 19

Technikon M L Sultan (South Africa)
CIJE: 0 RIE: 1 CAT: 17

Technion Diagnostic System
CIJE: 1 RIE: 3 CAT: 15

Technion Israel Institute of Technology
CIJE: 2 RIE: 6 CAT: 17

Technische Universitat Wien
USE Technical University of Vienna (Austria)

Technocratic Rationality
CIJE: 0 RIE: 1 CAT: 15

Technological Adaptability
CIJE: 5 RIE: 3 CAT: 20

Technological Applications Project
CIJE: 1 RIE: 2 CAT: 19

Technological Baccalaureate (England)
CIJE: 0 RIE: 1 CAT: 16
UF TechBac

Technological Change
CIJE: 98 RIE: 21 CAT: 20

Technological Demands
CIJE: 5 RIE: 3 CAT: 20

Technological Dependence
USE Technologically Dependent

Technological Development Project
CIJE: 0 RIE: 12 CAT: 19

Technological Disasters
CIJE: 0 RIE: 1 CAT: 20

Technological Enrich Achmt Cambodians Hispanics
USE Project TEACH NY

Technological Forecasting
CIJE: 4 RIE: 3 CAT: 20

Technological Infrastructure
CIJE: 5 RIE: 8 CAT: 20

Technological Methods
CIJE: 0 RIE: 2 CAT: 15

Technological Perspective
CIJE: 7 RIE: 4 CAT: 15

Technologically Advanced Families
CIJE: 0 RIE: 0 CAT: 10
UF Taffies

Technologically Dependent
CIJE: 4 RIE: 2 CAT: 10
SN Those dependent on technological health care devices (e.g., ventilator, dialyzer) for life/health maintenance
UF Technological Dependence; Technologically Supported; Technology Dependence

Technologically Supported
USE Technologically Dependent

Technologists
CIJE: 3 RIE: 0 CAT: 09

Technology Access for Arkansans
CIJE: 0 RIE: 3 CAT: 19
UF Project TAARK AR

Technology Achievement Test
CIJE: 0 RIE: 1 CAT: 21

Technology Adaptation Project
CIJE: 0 RIE: 2 CAT: 19

Technology and Basic Skills in Mathematics
CIJE: 0 RIE: 1 CAT: 19

Technology and Science
USE Science Technology Relationship

Technology and Science Careers for Minorities
CIJE: 0 RIE: 1 CAT: 19

Technology Assessment
CIJE: 9 RIE: 16 CAT: 20

Technology Based Instruction
CIJE: 0 RIE: 1 CAT: 15

Technology Coordinators
CIJE: 0 RIE: 1 CAT: 09

Technology Dependence
USE Technologically Dependent

Technology for Children Program
CIJE: 3 RIE: 5 CAT: 19

Technology for Literacy Project
CIJE: 0 RIE: 2 CAT: 19
SN Project of the Saint Paul Foundation MN

Technology in Curriculum Project
USE Technology in the Curriculum Program

Technology in the Curriculum Program
CIJE: 1 RIE: 2 CAT: 19
UF Technology in Curriculum Project

Technology Information System
CIJE: 0 RIE: 2 CAT: 04
UF TIS Intelligent Gateway

Technology Integrated Educ Delivery System AZ
CIJE: 0 RIE: 1 CAT: 19

Technology Integration
CIJE: 6 RIE: 6 CAT: 20

Technology Mediated Interactive Learning
CIJE: 0 RIE: 1 CAT: 15

Technology Network Ties NY
CIJE: 0 RIE: 1 CAT: 20
UF New York State Technology Network Ties

Technology Plans
CIJE: 3 RIE: 12 CAT: 20

Technology Related Assistance Individ Disabil Act
CIJE: 2 RIE: 9 CAT: 14
SN "Technology-Related Assistance for Individuals with Disabilities Act of 1988"
UF Public Law 100 407

Technology Student Association
CIJE: 0 RIE: 1 CAT: 17
SN Formerly (1988) "American Industrial Arts Student Association"

Technology Team Assessment Process
USE Project TTAP

Technology Users
USE Technology Utilization

Technology Utilization
CIJE: 9 RIE: 15 CAT: 20
UF Technology Users

Technostress
CIJE: 4 RIE: 1 CAT: 11
SN Disease of adaptation caused by an inability to cope with new technologies

Teddy Bear Magazines
CIJE: 0 RIE: 1 CAT: 22

Tedium
USE Boredom

Teen Age Medical Service
CIJE: 0 RIE: 1 CAT: 11

Teen Employment Program
CIJE: 1 RIE: 0 CAT: 19

Teen Scene
CIJE: 1 RIE: 0 CAT: 22

Teen Tutorial Program
CIJE: 1 RIE: 0 CAT: 19

Teenage Health Teaching Modules Program
CIJE: 2 RIE: 16 CAT: 19

Teenage Inventory of Social Skills
CIJE: 0 RIE: 1 CAT: 21

Teenage Mutant Ninja Turtles
CIJE: 4 RIE: 0 CAT: 22
UF Ninja Turtles

Teenage Opportunity Programs
CIJE: 1 RIE: 0 CAT: 19

Teenage Parent Program KY
CIJE: 0 RIE: 1 CAT: 19

Teenage Pregnancy and Parenting Project CA
CIJE: 0 RIE: 2 CAT: 19

Teenage Prostitution
CIJE: 2 RIE: 1 CAT: 16
SN See also "Child Prostitution"

Teenage Suicide
USE Adolescent Suicide

Teens for AIDS Prevention Project
CIJE: 0 RIE: 1 CAT: 19

Teesside Polytechnic (England)
CIJE: 1 RIE: 0 CAT: 17

Teeth
CIJE: 3 RIE: 3 CAT: 11

TEFAP
USE Temporary Emergency Food Assistance

Tejedor (Luis)
CIJE: 1 RIE: 0 CAT: 18

Tektronix Graphic Terminals
CIJE: 1 RIE: 3 CAT: 04

Tel Aviv Public Schools (Israel)
CIJE: 0 RIE: 2 CAT: 17

Tel Aviv University (Israel)
CIJE: 12 RIE: 4 CAT: 17

Tele Cyclopedia
CIJE: 0 RIE: 1 CAT: 04

Tele Universite PQ
CIJE: 0 RIE: 1 CAT: 17

Teleapprenticeships
CIJE: 2 RIE: 1 CAT: 15

Teleclasses
CIJE: 1 RIE: 1 CAT: 16

Telecommunication Demonstration Program (Midwest)
CIJE: 0 RIE: 1 CAT: 19

Telecommunication Devices for the Deaf
CIJE: 3 RIE: 3 CAT: 04
UF TDDs; Telephone Devices for the Deaf

Telecommunications Ad Hoc Task Force IL
CIJE: 0 RIE: 1 CAT: 17

Telecommunications Demonstration Program
CIJE: 0 RIE: 3 CAT: 19

Telecommunications Demonstration Projects
CIJE: 0 RIE: 0 CAT: 19

Telecommunications Education Needs Assessment CA
CIJE: 0 RIE: 1 CAT: 21

Telecommunications Infrastructure
CIJE: 3 RIE: 1 CAT: 20
SN See also "Information Infrastructure"

Telecommunications Policy
CIJE: 4 RIE: 7 CAT: 16

Telecommuting
CIJE: 11 RIE: 6 CAT: 04

Telecomputing
CIJE: 2 RIE: 4 CAT: 20
SN Telecommunications between computers (i.e., computing at a distance)

Telecopier Systems
CIJE: 0 RIE: 2 CAT: 04

Telediagnostic Protocol
CIJE: 1 RIE: 1 CAT: 11

Telegraphic Codes
CIJE: 0 RIE: 1 CAT: 13

Telegraphic Speech
CIJE: 1 RIE: 1 CAT: 13

Telegraphy
CIJE: 1 RIE: 4 CAT: 20

Telelearning Project LA
CIJE: 0 RIE: 1 CAT: 19

Telelectures
CIJE: 5 RIE: 6 CAT: 16

Telelink
CIJE: 0 RIE: 1 CAT: 04

Telemarketing
CIJE: 6 RIE: 5 CAT: 16

Telematics
CIJE: 8 RIE: 3 CAT: 20
SN The combining of computer technology and telecommunications

Telemedicine
CIJE: 1 RIE: 9 CAT: 11

Telemedicine Centre NF
CIJE: 0 RIE: 1 CAT: 17

Telenet
CIJE: 6 RIE: 2 CAT: 04

Telenovelas
CIJE: 0 RIE: 1 CAT: 16

Teleology
CIJE: 13 RIE: 3 CAT: 16

Telepathy
CIJE: 3 RIE: 0 CAT: 20

Telephone Ad Takers
CIJE: 0 RIE: 1 CAT: 09

Telephone Answering and Recording Devices
USE Answering Machines

Telephone Answering Services
USE Answering Services

Telephone Apprehension
CIJE: 1 RIE: 2 CAT: 11

Telephone Calls
CIJE: 6 RIE: 1 CAT: 16

Telephone Conference Network
CIJE: 0 RIE: 1 CAT: 04

Telephone Conversation
CIJE: 3 RIE: 2 CAT: 13

Telephone Courtesy
CIJE: 1 RIE: 4 CAT: 16

Telephone Devices for the Deaf
USE Telecommunication Devices for the Deaf

Telephone Directories
CIJE: 5 RIE: 2 CAT: 16

Telephone Directory Sampling
USE Directory Sampling

Telephone Evaluations
CIJE: 0 RIE: 1 CAT: 15

Telephone Interviews
CIJE: 16 RIE: 3 CAT: 15
SN See also "Computer Assisted Telephone Interviewing"

Telephone Mechanics
CIJE: 0 RIE: 3 CAT: 09

Telephone Operators
CIJE: 0 RIE: 4 CAT: 09

Telephone Pioneer of America
CIJE: 1 RIE: 0 CAT: 17

Telephone Reference Services
CIJE: 2 RIE: 0 CAT: 16

Telephone Registration
CIJE: 2 RIE: 1 CAT: 20
UF Touch Tone Telephone Registration

Telephone Relay Services
CIJE: 0 RIE: 1 CAT: 20

Telephone Usage
CIJE: 1 RIE: 0 CAT: 16

Teleprinter Projectors
CIJE: 0 RIE: 1 CAT: 04

Teleprompter Corporation
CIJE: 0 RIE: 1 CAT: 17

Teleprompters
CIJE: 1 RIE: 2 CAT: 04

Telereference
CIJE: 2 RIE: 0 CAT: 04

Telescopes
CIJE: 24 RIE: 2 CAT: 04

Telescuola
CIJE: 0 RIE: 2 CAT: 22

Telesecundaria
CIJE: 3 RIE: 5 CAT: 16

Teleseminars
CIJE: 0 RIE: 1 CAT: 16

Teletel
CIJE: 0 RIE: 3 CAT: 04

Teletraining
CIJE: 6 RIE: 3 CAT: 15

Teletutoring
CIJE: 0 RIE: 1 CAT: 16

Teletypewriters
CIJE: 8 RIE: 20 CAT: 04

Televangelism
CIJE: 5 RIE: 8 CAT: 16

Televised Interactive Education System
CIJE: 1 RIE: 1 CAT: 04
UF TIE System IA

Televised Proceedings
CIJE: 3 RIE: 3 CAT: 16

Television Access
CIJE: 3 RIE: 11 CAT: 20

Television Aesthetics
CIJE: 1 RIE: 3 CAT: 03

Television Announcers
CIJE: 1 RIE: 0 CAT: 09

Television Criticism
CIJE: 24 RIE: 38 CAT: 16

Television Game Shows
CIJE: 3 RIE: 0 CAT: 16

Television Grammar
CIJE: 0 RIE: 2 CAT: 13

Television History
CIJE: 14 RIE: 17 CAT: 16

Television Information Office
CIJE: 0 RIE: 1 CAT: 17

Television Licensing Center
CIJE: 2 RIE: 0 CAT: 17

Television Literacy
CIJE: 9 RIE: 14 CAT: 16

Television Networks
CIJE: 32 RIE: 41 CAT: 04

Television News
CIJE: 92 RIE: 61 CAT: 16

Television News Exchange
CIJE: 1 RIE: 0 CAT: 17

Television News Magazines
CIJE: 2 RIE: 1 CAT: 16

Television News Photographers
CIJE: 1 RIE: 1 CAT: 09

Television Reading Program
CIJE: 4 RIE: 3 CAT: 19

Television Receivers
CIJE: 0 RIE: 1 CAT: 04

Television Research Committee
CIJE: 0 RIE: 1 CAT: 17

Television Research Evanston
CIJE: 0 RIE: 1 CAT: 17

Television Stations
CIJE: 1 RIE: 2 CAT: 05
SN See also "Educational Television Stations," "Independent Television Stations," and "Local Television Stations"

Television Subtitles
USE Subtitles (Television)

Television Theory
CIJE: 3 RIE: 1 CAT: 15

Television Training Center (West Germany)
CIJE: 1 RIE: 0 CAT: 17

Television Training Institute
CIJE: 1 RIE: 0 CAT: 17

Television Universities (China)
CIJE: 0 RIE: 1 CAT: 05
SN See also "Radio and Television Universities (China)"

Television Writing
CIJE: 2 RIE: 4 CAT: 13

Televote
CIJE: 0 RIE: 3 CAT: 16

Telewriting
CIJE: 2 RIE: 6 CAT: 16

Telex
CIJE: 3 RIE: 2 CAT: 20

Telidon System
CIJE: 10 RIE: 17 CAT: 04

Tell Me A Story Test
CIJE: 3 RIE: 1 CAT: 21

Tell Me That You Love Me Junie Moon (Book)
CIJE: 1 RIE: 0 CAT: 22

Telling Time
USE Time Telling

TELLS Test
USE Testing for Essential Learning and Literacy Skills

Telstar Regional High School ME
CIJE: 1 RIE: 0 CAT: 17

TEMAC Algebra
CIJE: 0 RIE: 1 CAT: 03

TEMAS Thematic Apperception Test
CIJE: 0 RIE: 5 CAT: 21

Temkin Law
CIJE: 1 RIE: 0 CAT: 20

Temne
CIJE: 1 RIE: 1 CAT: 13
SN A Mel language spoken in Sierra Leone

Temper Tantrums
CIJE: 6 RIE: 1 CAT: 11

Tempera Painting
CIJE: 3 RIE: 0 CAT: 03

Temperament and Values Inventory
CIJE: 1 RIE: 0 CAT: 21

Temperature Inversions
CIJE: 1 RIE: 0 CAT: 20

Tempest (the)
CIJE: 3 RIE: 1 CAT: 22

Temple (William)
CIJE: 0 RIE: 1 CAT: 18

Temple Buell College CO
CIJE: 1 RIE: 0 CAT: 17

Temple City Project
CIJE: 0 RIE: 1 CAT: 19

Temple City Unified School District CA
CIJE: 0 RIE: 1 CAT: 17

Temple Israel OH
CIJE: 0 RIE: 1 CAT: 17

Temple Philadelphia Trenton Teacher Corps Program
CIJE: 1 RIE: 1 CAT: 19

Temple University PA
CIJE: 53 RIE: 59 CAT: 17

Templer Death Anxiety Scale
USE Death Anxiety Scale

Templin Darley Tests of Articulation
CIJE: 2 RIE: 7 CAT: 21

Temporal Bone Banks
CIJE: 1 RIE: 0 CAT: 11

Temporal Causal Understanding
CIJE: 2 RIE: 1 CAT: 11

Temporal Lobe
CIJE: 2 RIE: 0 CAT: 11

Temporal Orientation Questionnaire (Wulff)
CIJE: 0 RIE: 1 CAT: 21

Temporal Patterning
CIJE: 5 RIE: 2 CAT: 11

Temporal Recall Strategy
CIJE: 4 RIE: 0 CAT: 15

Temporal Stability
CIJE: 1 RIE: 1 CAT: 11

Temporary Care
CIJE: 0 RIE: 0 CAT: 11

Temporary Child Care
CIJE: 0 RIE: 3 CAT: 11

Temporary Day Care
CIJE: 1 RIE: 0 CAT: 11

Temporary Emergency Child Care
CIJE: 0 RIE: 1 CAT: 19

Temporary Emergency Food Assistance
CIJE: 0 RIE: 1 CAT: 19
UF TEFAP

Temporary Employment
CIJE: 34 RIE: 14 CAT: 16

Temporary Help Service Industry
CIJE: 3 RIE: 2 CAT: 05

Temporomandibular Joint Dysfunction
CIJE: 4 RIE: 1 CAT: 11

TEMPUS
CIJE: 1 RIE: 2 CAT: 19
UF Trans European Mobility Scheme for Univ Studies

Ten Commandments
CIJE: 1 RIE: 0 CAT: 14

Ten Perfect Sentences Approach
CIJE: 1 RIE: 0 CAT: 15

Ten Schools Program CA
CIJE: 0 RIE: 1 CAT: 19
SN ...of the Los Angeles Unified School District

Ten State Nutrition Survey 1968 to 1970
CIJE: 1 RIE: 0 CAT: 19

Tenacity
CIJE: 1 RIE: 0 CAT: 16

Tenafly Public Schools NJ
CIJE: 0 RIE: 1 CAT: 17

Tenant Resource Coordinators
CIJE: 0 RIE: 0 CAT: 09

Tenants
CIJE: 6 RIE: 4 CAT: 10

Tenants Insurance
CIJE: 0 RIE: 1 CAT: 16

Tenants Rights
CIJE: 6 RIE: 3 CAT: 14

Tenderloin Senior Outreach Project
CIJE: 1 RIE: 1 CAT: 19

Tenejapa (Tribe)
CIJE: 1 RIE: 1 CAT: 08

TENET
USE Texas Education Network

Teng Xian Dialect
CIJE: 0 RIE: 1 CAT: 13

Tennent (William)
CIJE: 1 RIE: 0 CAT: 18

Tennessee
CIJE: 237 RIE: 755 CAT: 07

Tennessee (Anderson County)
CIJE: 1 RIE: 0 CAT: 07

Tennessee (Blount County)
CIJE: 1 RIE: 4 CAT: 07

Tennessee (Bradley County)
CIJE: 0 RIE: 1 CAT: 07

Tennessee (Campbell County)
CIJE: 1 RIE: 1 CAT: 07

Tennessee (Central)
CIJE: 0 RIE: 1 CAT: 07

Tennessee (Chattanooga)
CIJE: 6 RIE: 13 CAT: 07

Tennessee (Davidson County)
CIJE: 0 RIE: 4 CAT: 07

Tennessee (East)
CIJE: 6 RIE: 8 CAT: 07

Tennessee (Greene County)
CIJE: 0 RIE: 1 CAT: 07

Tennessee (Hawkins County)
CIJE: 0 RIE: 2 CAT: 07

Tennessee (Haywood County)
CIJE: 0 RIE: 1 CAT: 07

Tennessee (Knox County)
CIJE: 1 RIE: 7 CAT: 07

Tennessee (Knoxville)
CIJE: 6 RIE: 16 CAT: 07

Tennessee (Lauderdale County)
CIJE: 0 RIE: 1 CAT: 07

Tennessee (Loudon County)
CIJE: 0 RIE: 1 CAT: 07

Tennessee (Maury County)
CIJE: 0 RIE: 3 CAT: 07

Tennessee (Memphis)
CIJE: 20 RIE: 47 CAT: 07

Tennessee (Nashville)
CIJE: 17 RIE: 57 CAT: 07

Tennessee (Northeast)
CIJE: 0 RIE: 1 CAT: 07

Tennessee (Oak Ridge)
CIJE: 2 RIE: 2 CAT: 07

Tennessee (Overton County)
CIJE: 0 RIE: 2 CAT: 07

Tennessee (Shelby County)
CIJE: 2 RIE: 1 CAT: 07

Tennessee (Upper Cumberland)
CIJE: 1 RIE: 3 CAT: 07
UF Upper Cumberland Region (Middle TN)

Tennessee (Williamson County)
CIJE: 1 RIE: 1 CAT: 07

Tennessee A and I University
CIJE: 0 RIE: 1 CAT: 17

Tennessee Appalachia Educational Cooperative
CIJE: 1 RIE: 0 CAT: 17

Tennessee Area Vocational Technical Schools
CIJE: 1 RIE: 2 CAT: 17

Tennessee Career Ladder Program
CIJE: 4 RIE: 21 CAT: 19
UF Career Ladder Program TN

Tennessee College Womens Sports Federation
CIJE: 0 RIE: 1 CAT: 17

Tennessee Commissioners Report Card
CIJE: 0 RIE: 1 CAT: 19

Tennessee Comprehensive Assessment Program
CIJE: 0 RIE: 5 CAT: 19

Tennessee Higher Education Commission
CIJE: 3 RIE: 10 CAT: 17

Tennessee Initiative on Employment
CIJE: 0 RIE: 1 CAT: 19

Tennessee Instructional Model
CIJE: 0 RIE: 2 CAT: 15

Tennessee Master Teacher Program
CIJE: 2 RIE: 0 CAT: 19
UF Master Teacher Program TN

Tennessee Nutrition Education and Training Program
CIJE: 0 RIE: 3 CAT: 19

Tennessee Proficiency Test
CIJE: 0 RIE: 2 CAT: 21

Tennessee Re Education Institute
CIJE: 0 RIE: 1 CAT: 17

Tennessee Research Coordinating Unit
CIJE: 2 RIE: 0 CAT: 17

Tennessee School for the Blind
CIJE: 0 RIE: 1 CAT: 17

Tennessee School for the Deaf
CIJE: 0 RIE: 1 CAT: 17

Tennessee School Improvement Project
CIJE: 0 RIE: 1 CAT: 19

Tennessee Self Concept Scale
CIJE: 59 RIE: 55 CAT: 21

Tennessee State Department of Education
CIJE: 2 RIE: 3 CAT: 17

Tennessee State University
CIJE: 6 RIE: 13 CAT: 17

Tennessee Technological University
CIJE: 6 RIE: 32 CAT: 17

Tennessee Tombigbee Waterway
CIJE: 0 RIE: 1 CAT: 07

Tennessee Valley Authority
CIJE: 4 RIE: 13 CAT: 17

Tennessee Wesleyan College
CIJE: 0 RIE: 1 CAT: 17

Tennis Incorporated
CIJE: 1 RIE: 0 CAT: 17

Tennis Tests of Achievement (Digennaro)
CIJE: 1 RIE: 0 CAT: 21

Tennyson (Alfred)
CIJE: 3 RIE: 2 CAT: 18

Tennyson (Robert D)
CIJE: 6 RIE: 0 CAT: 18

Tenore Plan MA
CIJE: 0 RIE: 1 CAT: 15

Tenrikyo
CIJE: 1 RIE: 0 CAT: 16

Tense Switching
CIJE: 2 RIE: 0 CAT: 13

Tensile Strength
CIJE: 1 RIE: 0 CAT: 20

Tensing (Vowels)
CIJE: 0 RIE: 1 CAT: 13
UF Vowel Tensing

Tension
CIJE: 14 RIE: 10 CAT: 11

Tension Ranking Questionnaire
CIJE: 0 RIE: 1 CAT: 21

Tension Reduction Theory
CIJE: 0 RIE: 1 CAT: 15

Tenth Amendment
CIJE: 2 RIE: 2 CAT: 14

Tepehuan
CIJE: 0 RIE: 3 CAT: 13
SN An Uto-Aztecan language, Sonoran group

Teratogens
CIJE: 3 RIE: 0 CAT: 10

Teratology
CIJE: 2 RIE: 6 CAT: 20

Terence Cardinal Cooke Health Care Center NY
CIJE: 0 RIE: 1 CAT: 17

Teresa of Avila (Saint)
CIJE: 1 RIE: 0 CAT: 18

Teribe
CIJE: 0 RIE: 1 CAT: 13
SN A Chibchan language of Panama

Terkel (Studs)
CIJE: 4 RIE: 1 CAT: 18

Term Appointments
CIJE: 2 RIE: 1 CAT: 16

Term Classes
CIJE: 0 RIE: 1 CAT: 16

Term Matching
CIJE: 1 RIE: 0 CAT: 15

Terman (Lewis M)
CIJE: 12 RIE: 4 CAT: 18

Terman Concept Mastery Test
USE Concept Mastery Test (Terman)

Terman Group Test of Mental Ability
CIJE: 0 RIE: 1 CAT: 21

Terman Merrill Intelligence Scale
CIJE: 1 RIE: 1 CAT: 21

Terman Merrill Vocabulary Test
CIJE: 0 RIE: 1 CAT: 21

Terminal Air Blending
CIJE: 1 RIE: 0 CAT: 20

Terminal Performance Objectives
CIJE: 0 RIE: 15 CAT: 15
UF TERMOBS

Termination (Networks)
CIJE: 0 RIE: 2 CAT: 20

Termination of Friendship
CIJE: 2 RIE: 0 CAT: 16
UF Friendship Termination

Termination of Rights
CIJE: 0 RIE: 2 CAT: 14

Termination of Special Tribal Status
CIJE: 3 RIE: 2 CAT: 14

Termination of Tribal Status
CIJE: 0 RIE: 4 CAT: 14

Termination of Welfare Benefits
CIJE: 0 RIE: 0 CAT: 14

Terminator (Movie)
CIJE: 0 RIE: 1 CAT: 22

Terminator Remainer Scale (Lorr et al)
CIJE: 1 RIE: 0 CAT: 21

Terministic Screens
CIJE: 0 RIE: 1 CAT: 13

Termites
CIJE: 2 RIE: 3 CAT: 20

TERMOBS
USE Terminal Performance Objectives

Terp Attitude Scale
CIJE: 0 RIE: 1 CAT: 21

Terra
CIJE: 0 RIE: 1 CAT: 16

Terrariums
CIJE: 10 RIE: 1 CAT: 04

Terraset School VA
CIJE: 3 RIE: 0 CAT: 17

Terrazzo Flooring
CIJE: 1 RIE: 0 CAT: 04

Terre Haute Normal School
CIJE: 1 RIE: 0 CAT: 17

Terrell (Mary Church)
CIJE: 4 RIE: 0 CAT: 18

Territorial Decentration
CIJE: 0 RIE: 1 CAT: 16

Territorial Decentration Test (Stoltman)
CIJE: 0 RIE: 2 CAT: 21

Territoriality
CIJE: 17 RIE: 6 CAT: 16

Terrorist Tactics
CIJE: 2 RIE: 6 CAT: 15

Terry (Ellen)
CIJE: 1 RIE: 0 CAT: 18

Terry (Megan)
CIJE: 0 RIE: 1 CAT: 18

Terse Conclusions
CIJE: 2 RIE: 0 CAT: 16

Tertiary Ammonium Chlorides
CIJE: 1 RIE: 0 CAT: 20

Tertiary Colleges
CIJE: 0 RIE: 2 CAT: 05

Tertiary Education Entrance Project
CIJE: 0 RIE: 1 CAT: 19

Tertiary Response
CIJE: 3 RIE: 0 CAT: 13

Terzulo (C A)
CIJE: 0 RIE: 1 CAT: 18

TESCAM (Test Scoring and Analysis)
CIJE: 1 RIE: 0 CAT: 21

TESL Canada
CIJE: 1 RIE: 1 CAT: 17

TESL Materials Development Center
CIJE: 0 RIE: 1 CAT: 17

Tesla (Nikola)
CIJE: 1 RIE: 0 CAT: 18

Tesniere (Lucien)
CIJE: 1 RIE: 0 CAT: 18

Tess of the D Urbervilles
CIJE: 1 RIE: 1 CAT: 22

Tessellations
CIJE: 24 RIE: 1 CAT: 16

Tesseract Way
CIJE: 2 RIE: 1 CAT: 19

Test Adaptations
CIJE: 11 RIE: 12 CAT: 21

Test Analysis
CIJE: 11 RIE: 4 CAT: 21

Test Anxiety Inventory (Spielberger)
CIJE: 4 RIE: 12 CAT: 21

Test Anxiety Scale (Sarason)
USE Sarason Test Anxiety Scale

Test Anxiety Scale for Adolescents
CIJE: 0 RIE: 1 CAT: 21

Test Anxiety Scale for Children (Sarason)
USE Sarason Test Anxiety Scale for Children

Test Appropriateness
CIJE: 5 RIE: 10 CAT: 21

Test Batteries
CIJE: 28 RIE: 50 CAT: 21

Test Battery for Mentally Handicapped Children
CIJE: 1 RIE: 0 CAT: 21

Test Behavior Observation Guide
CIJE: 1 RIE: 0 CAT: 21

Test Bibliographies
CIJE: 0 RIE: 100 CAT: 21

Test Characteristic Curve
CIJE: 0 RIE: 1 CAT: 21

Test Collection (Educational Testing Service)
CIJE: 1 RIE: 92 CAT: 21
UF ETS Test Collection

Test Cue Inventory (Kermis)
CIJE: 0 RIE: 1 CAT: 21

Test Curriculum Overlap
CIJE: 6 RIE: 18 CAT: 21

Test Customization
CIJE: 6 RIE: 8 CAT: 21
UF Customized Testing

Test de Vocabulario en Imagenes Peabody (Dunn)
CIJE: 1 RIE: 0 CAT: 21
UF Peabody Picture Vocabulary Test Spanish (Dunn)

Test Developers
CIJE: 4 RIE: 3 CAT: 09

Test Development Notebook (NY State Dept of Educ)
CIJE: 0 RIE: 1 CAT: 21

Test Directors
CIJE: 5 RIE: 12 CAT: 09

Test Disclosure
CIJE: 5 RIE: 10 CAT: 21

Test Equivalence
CIJE: 16 RIE: 27 CAT: 21

Test Every Senior Project
CIJE: 0 RIE: 5 CAT: 19

Test Expectancy
CIJE: 5 RIE: 1 CAT: 21

Test Files
CIJE: 1 RIE: 0 CAT: 21
UF Examination Files

Test for Ready Steps
CIJE: 0 RIE: 1 CAT: 21

Test Frequency
USE Testing Frequency

Test Homogeneity
CIJE: 4 RIE: 4 CAT: 21

Test Instructions
CIJE: 13 RIE: 16 CAT: 21

Test Levels
CIJE: 0 RIE: 1 CAT: 21

Test Linking
CIJE: 0 RIE: 10 CAT: 21

Test of Academic Skills
CIJE: 0 RIE: 2 CAT: 21

Test of Adolescent Language
CIJE: 3 RIE: 1 CAT: 21

Test of Adult Basic Education
CIJE: 4 RIE: 9 CAT: 21
SN See also "Tests of Adult Basic Education"

Test of Adult College Aptitude
CIJE: 0 RIE: 1 CAT: 21

Test of Auditory Comprehension of Language
CIJE: 5 RIE: 0 CAT: 21

Test of Auditory Perception (Sabatino)
CIJE: 2 RIE: 0 CAT: 21

Test of Auditory Visual Integration (Kahn et al)
CIJE: 1 RIE: 0 CAT: 21

Test of Basic Concepts (Gonzalez Tamayo)
CIJE: 0 RIE: 1 CAT: 21

Test of Basic Information
CIJE: 0 RIE: 2 CAT: 21

Test of Basic Process Skills in Science
CIJE: 0 RIE: 1 CAT: 21

Test of Behavioral Rigidity
CIJE: 2 RIE: 1 CAT: 21

Test of Cognitive Skills
CIJE: 0 RIE: 5 CAT: 21

Test of Computer Literacy for Science Teachers
CIJE: 0 RIE: 1 CAT: 21

Test of Concept Application
CIJE: 0 RIE: 1 CAT: 21

Test of Consumer Competencies
CIJE: 1 RIE: 0 CAT: 21

Test of Coordination of Perspectives (Fowler)
CIJE: 0 RIE: 1 CAT: 21

Test of Critical Thinking (American Council Educ)
CIJE: 1 RIE: 0 CAT: 21

Test of Critical Thinking Skills Physical Science
CIJE: 0 RIE: 1 CAT: 21

Test of Diagnostic Skills (Rimoldi et al)
CIJE: 0 RIE: 2 CAT: 21

Test of Early Language Development
CIJE: 5 RIE: 0 CAT: 21
UF Early Language Development Test

Test of Economic Literacy
CIJE: 20 RIE: 9 CAT: 21

Test of Economic Understanding
CIJE: 4 RIE: 3 CAT: 21

Test of Effective Academic Motivation
CIJE: 0 RIE: 1 CAT: 21

Test of English as a Foreign Language
CIJE: 35 RIE: 63 CAT: 21
UF TOEFL

Test of English for International Communication
CIJE: 0 RIE: 1 CAT: 21

Test of Essential Learning and Literacy Skills PA
USE Testing for Essential Learning and Literacy Skills

Test of Implied Meanings (Sundberg)
CIJE: 0 RIE: 1 CAT: 21

Test of Independent Sample Proportions
CIJE: 0 RIE: 1 CAT: 21

Test of Individual Needs in Reading
CIJE: 0 RIE: 2 CAT: 21

Test of Inference Ability in Reading Comprehension
CIJE: 0 RIE: 0 CAT: 21

Test of Inference Patterns (Howell)
CIJE: 0 RIE: 1 CAT: 21

Test of Insight (French)
CIJE: 0 RIE: 1 CAT: 21

Test of Integrated Process Skills
CIJE: 1 RIE: 2 CAT: 21

Test of Integrated Science Processes
CIJE: 2 RIE: 0 CAT: 21

Test of Language Development
CIJE: 13 RIE: 1 CAT: 21

Test of Logical Thinking (Gray)
CIJE: 0 RIE: 2 CAT: 21

Test of Logical Thinking (Tobin and Capie)
CIJE: 6 RIE: 12 CAT: 21

Test of Modality Aptitude in Reading (Neville)
CIJE: 0 RIE: 1 CAT: 21

Test of Musicality
CIJE: 2 RIE: 0 CAT: 21

Test of Nonverbal Auditory Discrimination
CIJE: 0 RIE: 1 CAT: 21

Test of Nonverbal Intelligence
CIJE: 5 RIE: 3 CAT: 21
UF TONI

Test of Obscure Knowledge
CIJE: 1 RIE: 0 CAT: 21

Test of Occupational Development
CIJE: 1 RIE: 0 CAT: 21

Test of Perceptual Organization
CIJE: 1 RIE: 0 CAT: 21

Test of Professional Knowledge (NTE)
USE NTE Test of Professional Knowledge

Test of Proficiency in Computational Skills
CIJE: 1 RIE: 0 CAT: 21

Test of Reflectivity Impulsivity in Social Context
CIJE: 0 RIE: 1 CAT: 21

Test of Science Knowledge
CIJE: 0 RIE: 1 CAT: 21

Test of Science Processes (Tannenbaum)
CIJE: 3 RIE: 3 CAT: 21

Test of Science Related Attitudes
CIJE: 5 RIE: 0 CAT: 21

Test of Selected Topics in Physics
CIJE: 0 RIE: 1 CAT: 21

Test of Social Inference (Edmonson et al)
CIJE: 1 RIE: 1 CAT: 21

Test of Spoken English
CIJE: 6 RIE: 5 CAT: 21

Test of Standard Written English
CIJE: 14 RIE: 33 CAT: 21

Test of Syntactic Abilities
CIJE: 3 RIE: 1 CAT: 21

Test of Syntactic Abilities Screening Test
CIJE: 1 RIE: 0 CAT: 21

Test of Testwiseness (Slakter)
CIJE: 0 RIE: 1 CAT: 21

Test of Thought and Language
CIJE: 0 RIE: 1 CAT: 21
SN Acronym: Total

Test of Understanding in College Economics
CIJE: 11 RIE: 3 CAT: 21

Test of Understanding Latin America
CIJE: 0 RIE: 1 CAT: 21

Test of Weight Discrimination
CIJE: 0 RIE: 1 CAT: 21

Test of Written English
CIJE: 5 RIE: 7 CAT: 21

Test of Written Expression
CIJE: 0 RIE: 2 CAT: 21

Test of Written Spelling
CIJE: 2 RIE: 0 CAT: 21

Test on Appraising Observations
CIJE: 3 RIE: 1 CAT: 21

Test on Astronomy Concepts
CIJE: 0 RIE: 1 CAT: 21

Test on Astronomy Facts
CIJE: 0 RIE: 1 CAT: 21

Test on the Historical Development of Science
CIJE: 0 RIE: 1 CAT: 21

Test on the Social Aspects of Science
CIJE: 1 RIE: 2 CAT: 21

Test on Understanding Radioactivity
CIJE: 0 RIE: 1 CAT: 21

Test on Understanding Science
CIJE: 15 RIE: 27 CAT: 21

Test Order
CIJE: 4 RIE: 4 CAT: 21

Test Preparation Program Gifted Talented Sophomore
CIJE: 0 RIE: 1 CAT: 19

Test Publishers
CIJE: 11 RIE: 22 CAT: 09

Test Reactivity
CIJE: 0 RIE: 1 CAT: 21

Test Readiness
CIJE: 0 RIE: 1 CAT: 21

Test Redundancy
CIJE: 3 RIE: 1 CAT: 21

Test Repeaters
CIJE: 2 RIE: 8 CAT: 21

Test Reporting
CIJE: 0 RIE: 22 CAT: 21

Test Rescoring
CIJE: 0 RIE: 2 CAT: 21

Test Retest Reliability
CIJE: 35 RIE: 33 CAT: 21

Test Revision
CIJE: 14 RIE: 24 CAT: 21

Test Scatter
CIJE: 1 RIE: 3 CAT: 21

Test Score Abnormality
CIJE: 0 RIE: 0 CAT: 21
UF Abnormality (Test Scores)

Test Score Enhancing Strategies
CIJE: 0 RIE: 1 CAT: 21

Test Score Growth Measurement
CIJE: 0 RIE: 1 CAT: 21

Test Score Stability
USE Score Stability

Test Score Variance
CIJE: 7 RIE: 7 CAT: 21
SN See also "Score Variation"

Test Security
CIJE: 9 RIE: 22 CAT: 21

Test Sensitivity
CIJE: 4 RIE: 4 CAT: 21

Test Shortening Procedures
CIJE: 0 RIE: 1 CAT: 21

Test Specifications
CIJE: 9 RIE: 37 CAT: 21

Test Trials
CIJE: 1 RIE: 0 CAT: 21

Test Use in Schools Study
CIJE: 0 RIE: 1 CAT: 21

Test Use Project
CIJE: 0 RIE: 1 CAT: 19

Test User Qualifications Working Group
CIJE: 0 RIE: 1 CAT: 17
SN An outgrowth of the "Joint Committee on Testing Practices"

TESTFACT
CIJE: 0 RIE: 3 CAT: 04

Testicular Examination
CIJE: 3 RIE: 2 CAT: 11

Testimonials
CIJE: 3 RIE: 2 CAT: 16

Testimony
CIJE: 31 RIE: 55 CAT: 16

Testing 1 2 3
CIJE: 0 RIE: 1 CAT: 04

Testing Accommodations (Disabilities)
CIJE: 0 RIE: 1 CAT: 21

Testing Apparatus
CIJE: 0 RIE: 2 CAT: 21

Testing Centers
CIJE: 1 RIE: 6 CAT: 05

Testing Conditions
CIJE: 15 RIE: 10 CAT: 21

Testing Effects
CIJE: 12 RIE: 29 CAT: 21

Testing for Essential Learning and Literacy Skills
CIJE: 0 RIE: 4 CAT: 21
SN Administered to all Pennsylvania students in grades 3, 5, and 8 since 1985
UF Pennsylvania Test for Essential Learning Skills; TELLS Test; Test of Essential Learning and Literacy Skills PA

Testing Frequency
CIJE: 4 RIE: 2 CAT: 21
UF Frequency of Testing; Test Frequency

Testing Industry
CIJE: 2 RIE: 15 CAT: 10

Testing Information
CIJE: 0 RIE: 1 CAT: 21

Testing Informing Discussing and Evaluating
CIJE: 0 RIE: 1 CAT: 21

Testing Legislation
CIJE: 6 RIE: 1 CAT: 14

Testing Time
CIJE: 1 RIE: 1 CAT: 21

TESTLEN
CIJE: 0 RIE: 1 CAT: 04

Testlets
CIJE: 10 RIE: 4 CAT: 21

Tests and Measurement Courses
CIJE: 1 RIE: 3 CAT: 21

Tests of Academic Progress
CIJE: 1 RIE: 6 CAT: 21

Tests of Achievement and Proficiency
CIJE: 2 RIE: 30 CAT: 21

Tests of Achievement in Basic Skills Mathematics
CIJE: 2 RIE: 0 CAT: 21

Tests of Adult Basic Education
CIJE: 2 RIE: 11 CAT: 21
SN See also "Test of Adult Basic Education"

Tests of Adult Literacy Skills
CIJE: 0 RIE: 1 CAT: 21

Tests of Basic Experiences
CIJE: 2 RIE: 3 CAT: 21

Tests of Individual Performance
CIJE: 0 RIE: 2 CAT: 21
SN ...of the Portland School District OR

Tests of Reading Inter American Series
CIJE: 1 RIE: 1 CAT: 22

TestSense Program
CIJE: 0 RIE: 1 CAT: 04

TETRA Model
CIJE: 2 RIE: 0 CAT: 15

Tetrachoric Correlation
CIJE: 8 RIE: 10 CAT: 15

Tetreau Trahan Visual Interest Test
CIJE: 0 RIE: 1 CAT: 21

Tewa Pueblo
CIJE: 3 RIE: 3 CAT: 08

Tewksbury (Donald G)
CIJE: 0 RIE: 1 CAT: 18

TEX SIS
USE Texas Student Information System

Texarkana Community College TX
CIJE: 0 RIE: 1 CAT: 17

Texarkana Project
CIJE: 1 RIE: 2 CAT: 19

Texarkana Schools TX
CIJE: 3 RIE: 0 CAT: 17

Texas
CIJE: 611 RIE: 2307 CAT: 07

Texas (Abilene)
CIJE: 2 RIE: 3 CAT: 07

Texas (Allen)
CIJE: 0 RIE: 1 CAT: 07

Texas (Alpine)
CIJE: 0 RIE: 1 CAT: 07

Texas (Amarillo)
CIJE: 0 RIE: 3 CAT: 07

Texas (Anthony)
CIJE: 0 RIE: 1 CAT: 07

Texas (Arlington)
CIJE: 3 RIE: 0 CAT: 07

Texas (Atascosa County)
CIJE: 0 RIE: 1 CAT: 07

Texas (Austin)
CIJE: 22 RIE: 155 CAT: 07

Texas (Bexar County)
CIJE: 1 RIE: 5 CAT: 07

Texas (Big Lake)
CIJE: 0 RIE: 1 CAT: 07

Texas (Big Spring)
CIJE: 0 RIE: 1 CAT: 07

Texas (Brooks County)
CIJE: 0 RIE: 1 CAT: 07

Texas (Brownsville)
CIJE: 0 RIE: 4 CAT: 07

Texas (Caldwell County)
CIJE: 1 RIE: 0 CAT: 07

Texas (Caldwell)
CIJE: 0 RIE: 1 CAT: 07

Texas (Cameron County)
CIJE: 0 RIE: 1 CAT: 07

Texas (Camp Woodland Springs)
CIJE: 0 RIE: 1 CAT: 07

Texas (Canutillo)
CIJE: 0 RIE: 1 CAT: 07

Texas (Canyon)
CIJE: 0 RIE: 2 CAT: 07

Texas (College Station)
CIJE: 0 RIE: 3 CAT: 07

Texas (Collin County)
CIJE: 0 RIE: 1 CAT: 07

Texas (Corpus Christi)
CIJE: 5 RIE: 11 CAT: 07

Texas (Corsicana)
CIJE: 2 RIE: 1 CAT: 07

Texas (Crosby)
CIJE: 0 RIE: 1 CAT: 07

Texas (Crystal City)
CIJE: 6 RIE: 6 CAT: 07

Texas (Dallas County)
CIJE: 1 RIE: 4 CAT: 07

Texas (Dallas)
CIJE: 50 RIE: 81 CAT: 07

Texas (Del Rio)
CIJE: 0 RIE: 3 CAT: 07

Texas (Del Valle)
CIJE: 0 RIE: 1 CAT: 07

Texas (Denton)
CIJE: 1 RIE: 3 CAT: 07

Texas (Eagle Pass)
CIJE: 2 RIE: 0 CAT: 07

Texas (East Austin)
CIJE: 1 RIE: 0 CAT: 07

Texas (East)
CIJE: 1 RIE: 30 CAT: 07

Texas (El Paso)
CIJE: 13 RIE: 50 CAT: 07

Texas (Fayette County)
CIJE: 0 RIE: 1 CAT: 07

Texas (Flour Bluff)
CIJE: 0 RIE: 3 CAT: 07

Texas (Fort Bend County)
CIJE: 1 RIE: 2 CAT: 07

Texas (Fort Worth)
CIJE: 6 RIE: 22 CAT: 07

Texas (Galveston County)
CIJE: 0 RIE: 2 CAT: 07

Texas (Galveston)
CIJE: 2 RIE: 3 CAT: 07

Texas (Grayson County)
CIJE: 0 RIE: 1 CAT: 07

Texas (Harlandale)
CIJE: 0 RIE: 7 CAT: 07

Texas (Harris County)
CIJE: 0 RIE: 2 CAT: 07

Texas (Hidalgo County)
CIJE: 0 RIE: 2 CAT: 07

Texas (Hill Country)
CIJE: 0 RIE: 1 CAT: 07

Texas (Houston)
CIJE: 61 RIE: 110 CAT: 07

Texas (Howard County)
CIJE: 0 RIE: 1 CAT: 07

Texas (La Grulla)
CIJE: 0 RIE: 11 CAT: 07

Texas (Laredo)
CIJE: 2 RIE: 6 CAT: 07

Texas (Lubbock)
CIJE: 2 RIE: 9 CAT: 07

Texas (Nacogdoches)
CIJE: 0 RIE: 1 CAT: 07

Texas (North)
CIJE: 0 RIE: 3 CAT: 07

Texas (Odessa)
CIJE: 0 RIE: 1 CAT: 07

Texas (Panhandle)
CIJE: 0 RIE: 1 CAT: 07

Texas (Panola County)
CIJE: 0 RIE: 2 CAT: 07

Texas (Pecos)
CIJE: 0 RIE: 1 CAT: 07

Texas (Port Arthur)
CIJE: 0 RIE: 1 CAT: 07

Texas (Potter County)
CIJE: 0 RIE: 1 CAT: 07

Texas (Richardson)
CIJE: 1 RIE: 1 CAT: 07

Texas (Round Rock)
CIJE: 2 RIE: 0 CAT: 07

Texas (San Angelo)
CIJE: 1 RIE: 1 CAT: 07

Texas (San Antonio)
CIJE: 24 RIE: 92 CAT: 07

Texas (San Marcos)
CIJE: 2 RIE: 8 CAT: 07

Texas (Sonora)
CIJE: 0 RIE: 1 CAT: 07

Texas (South)
CIJE: 9 RIE: 41 CAT: 07

Texas (Southeast)
CIJE: 0 RIE: 3 CAT: 07

Texas (Texas City)
CIJE: 0 RIE: 2 CAT: 07

Texas (Travis County)
CIJE: 1 RIE: 3 CAT: 07

Texas (Uvalde)
CIJE: 1 RIE: 1 CAT: 07

Texas (Waco)
CIJE: 4 RIE: 7 CAT: 07

Texas (West)
CIJE: 3 RIE: 11 CAT: 07

Texas (Willacy County)
CIJE: 0 RIE: 1 CAT: 07

Texas A and I University
CIJE: 2 RIE: 1 CAT: 17
SN Name changed to "Texas A and M University Kingsville"

Texas A and M University
CIJE: 55 RIE: 34 CAT: 17

Texas A and M University Kingsville
CIJE: 0 RIE: 1 CAT: 17
SN Formerly "Texas A and I University"

Texas Academic Skills Program
CIJE: 2 RIE: 9 CAT: 19

Texas Academy of Family Physicians
CIJE: 2 RIE: 0 CAT: 17

Texas Agricultural Experiment Station
CIJE: 0 RIE: 1 CAT: 17

Texas Agricultural Extension Service
CIJE: 2 RIE: 1 CAT: 17

Texas Assessment of Academic Skills
CIJE: 0 RIE: 15 CAT: 21

Texas Assessment of Basic Skills
CIJE: 1 RIE: 30 CAT: 21

Texas Assessment Project
CIJE: 0 RIE: 10 CAT: 19

Texas Association for Graduate Education Research
CIJE: 1 RIE: 1 CAT: 17

Texas Association of Chicanos in Higher Education
CIJE: 0 RIE: 2 CAT: 17

Texas Association of Community Schools
CIJE: 1 RIE: 0 CAT: 17

Texas Association of Educational Technology
CIJE: 1 RIE: 0 CAT: 17

Texas Central Education Agency
CIJE: 0 RIE: 1 CAT: 17

Texas Chiropractic College
CIJE: 0 RIE: 0 CAT: 17

Texas Christian University
CIJE: 6 RIE: 1 CAT: 17

Texas College and University System
CIJE: 1 RIE: 2 CAT: 17

Texas College of Osteopathic Medicine
CIJE: 3 RIE: 0 CAT: 17

Texas Computer Education Association
CIJE: 0 RIE: 2 CAT: 17

Texas Council on Migrant Labor
CIJE: 0 RIE: 2 CAT: 17

Texas Department of Community Affairs
CIJE: 0 RIE: 2 CAT: 17

Texas Department of Community Affairs v Burdine
CIJE: 2 RIE: 0 CAT: 14

Texas Department of Corrections
CIJE: 1 RIE: 1 CAT: 17

Texas Department of Human Resources
CIJE: 0 RIE: 1 CAT: 17

Texas Education Agency
CIJE: 7 RIE: 34 CAT: 17

Texas Education Code
CIJE: 2 RIE: 0 CAT: 14

Texas Education Computer Cooperative
CIJE: 0 RIE: 1 CAT: 17

Texas Education Desegregation Tech Asst Ctr
CIJE: 1 RIE: 0 CAT: 17

Texas Education Network
CIJE: 2 RIE: 3 CAT: 19
UF TENET

Texas Education Opportunity Act 1984
USE House Bill 72 (Texas 1984)

Texas Education Reform Bill 1984
USE House Bill 72 (Texas 1984)

Texas Educational Assessment of Minimum Skills
CIJE: 1 RIE: 75 CAT: 21

Texas Educational Microwave Project
CIJE: 0 RIE: 4 CAT: 19

Texas Educational Television Association
CIJE: 1 RIE: 0 CAT: 17

Texas Employment Commission
CIJE: 1 RIE: 2 CAT: 17

Texas Examination Current Administrators Teachers
CIJE: 1 RIE: 5 CAT: 21

Texas Features of Emotional Disturbance
CIJE: 0 RIE: 1 CAT: 21

Texas Foundation School Program
CIJE: 0 RIE: 1 CAT: 19
UF Foundation School Program TX

Texas Hill Country Writing Project
CIJE: 0 RIE: 6 CAT: 19

Texas Human Talent Project
CIJE: 0 RIE: 1 CAT: 19

Texas Information Service
CIJE: 0 RIE: 1 CAT: 17

Texas Instruments
CIJE: 8 RIE: 6 CAT: 17

Texas Junior College Teachers Association
CIJE: 0 RIE: 2 CAT: 17

Texas Junior High School Study
CIJE: 3 RIE: 3 CAT: 22

Texas Labor Mobility Project
CIJE: 0 RIE: 1 CAT: 19

Texas Learning Technology Group
CIJE: 0 RIE: 1 CAT: 17

Texas Library System
USE Texas State Library

Texas Master Teacher Examination
CIJE: 0 RIE: 1 CAT: 21
UF Master Teacher Examination TX

Texas Migrant Educational Development Center
CIJE: 0 RIE: 1 CAT: 17

Texas Oral Proficiency Test
CIJE: 0 RIE: 4 CAT: 21
SN A performance-based assessment for certification of Spanish, French, and bilingual education teachers in Texas

Texas Prefreshman Engineering Program
CIJE: 0 RIE: 1 CAT: 19

Texas Preschool Screening Inventory
CIJE: 0 RIE: 1 CAT: 21

Texas Project for Elders
CIJE: 0 RIE: 1 CAT: 19

Texas Reading Club
CIJE: 0 RIE: 8 CAT: 17

Texas School for the Blind
CIJE: 1 RIE: 0 CAT: 17

Texas School for the Deaf
CIJE: 1 RIE: 2 CAT: 17

Texas Schools Inc
CIJE: 0 RIE: 1 CAT: 17

Texas Sesquicentennial
CIJE: 0 RIE: 2 CAT: 12

Texas Small Schools Association
CIJE: 0 RIE: 1 CAT: 17

Texas Small Schools Project
CIJE: 0 RIE: 6 CAT: 17

Texas Social Behavior Inventory
CIJE: 4 RIE: 0 CAT: 21

Texas Southern University
CIJE: 6 RIE: 8 CAT: 17

Texas Southern University School of Pharmacy
CIJE: 1 RIE: 0 CAT: 17

Texas Southmost College
CIJE: 1 RIE: 0 CAT: 17

Texas State Board of Education
CIJE: 1 RIE: 1 CAT: 17

Texas State Library
CIJE: 0 RIE: 15 CAT: 17
UF Texas Library System

Texas State Technical College
CIJE: 0 RIE: 2 CAT: 17
SN Campuses in Waco, Harlingen, Amarillo, and Sweetwater

Texas State Technical College Waco
CIJE: 0 RIE: 4 CAT: 17

Texas State Technical Institute
CIJE: 1 RIE: 1 CAT: 17
SN Name changed to "Texas State Technical College"

Texas State Technical Institute Sweetwater
CIJE: 0 RIE: 1 CAT: 17

Texas Student Information System
CIJE: 0 RIE: 2 CAT: 15
UF Student Information System TX; TEX SIS

Texas System of Higher Education
CIJE: 1 RIE: 1 CAT: 17

Texas Teacher Appraisal Instrument
CIJE: 0 RIE: 2 CAT: 21

Texas Teacher Appraisal System
CIJE: 3 RIE: 16 CAT: 19
UF Teacher Appraisal System TX

Texas Teacher Effectiveness Study
CIJE: 0 RIE: 1 CAT: 19

Texas Tech University
CIJE: 24 RIE: 13 CAT: 17

Texas Technological College
CIJE: 2 RIE: 1 CAT: 17

Texas Telecomputer Grid
CIJE: 0 RIE: 1 CAT: 04

Texas Wesleyan University
CIJE: 0 RIE: 1 CAT: 17

Texas Womans University
CIJE: 6 RIE: 5 CAT: 17

Texas Womens Prison at Goree
CIJE: 1 RIE: 0 CAT: 17

Text Adaptation
CIJE: 4 RIE: 2 CAT: 13

Text Analysis
USE Textual Analysis

Text and Illustration Processing System
CIJE: 0 RIE: 1 CAT: 04

Text Based Interest
CIJE: 0 RIE: 1 CAT: 16
SN How interesting a text is

Text Characteristics
CIJE: 6 RIE: 3 CAT: 13

Text Classification
CIJE: 2 RIE: 1 CAT: 13

Text Coherence
CIJE: 16 RIE: 15 CAT: 13

Text Compression
CIJE: 7 RIE: 1 CAT: 16

Text Condensation
CIJE: 3 RIE: 1 CAT: 16

Text Density
CIJE: 0 RIE: 2 CAT: 16
SN See also "Text Density (Computer Display)"

Text Density (Computer Display)
CIJE: 2 RIE: 1 CAT: 20

Text Design
CIJE: 33 RIE: 23 CAT: 13

Text Factors
CIJE: 143 RIE: 242 CAT: 11

Text Formatting
CIJE: 2 RIE: 2 CAT: 13

Text Generation
CIJE: 10 RIE: 3 CAT: 20

Text Handling
CIJE: 12 RIE: 3 CAT: 04

Text Learning
CIJE: 26 RIE: 18 CAT: 15

Text Legibility
CIJE: 1 RIE: 4 CAT: 13

Text Organization
CIJE: 45 RIE: 14 CAT: 13

Text Patterns
CIJE: 2 RIE: 2 CAT: 13

Text Processing (Reading)
CIJE: 111 RIE: 40 CAT: 13

Text Searching
CIJE: 11 RIE: 1 CAT: 20

Text Sets
CIJE: 1 RIE: 2 CAT: 15

Text Transformation
CIJE: 1 RIE: 1 CAT: 13

Text Types
CIJE: 16 RIE: 8 CAT: 13

Textalk
CIJE: 0 RIE: 1 CAT: 04

Textape
CIJE: 0 RIE: 1 CAT: 04

Textbook Activity Guides
CIJE: 1 RIE: 1 CAT: 04

Textbook Adoption (State Level)
USE State Level Textbook Adoption

Textbook Dependency
CIJE: 6 RIE: 1 CAT: 15

Textbook Design
CIJE: 19 RIE: 10 CAT: 16

Textbook Errors
CIJE: 8 RIE: 5 CAT: 16

Textbook Journals
CIJE: 1 RIE: 0 CAT: 16

Textile Industry
CIJE: 8 RIE: 31 CAT: 05

Textile Information Retrieval Program
CIJE: 0 RIE: 1 CAT: 19

Textile Occupations
CIJE: 2 RIE: 13 CAT: 09

Textiles
CIJE: 7 RIE: 9 CAT: 20

Textlinguistics
CIJE: 11 RIE: 7 CAT: 13

Textual Analysis
CIJE: 63 RIE: 53 CAT: 15
UF Text Analysis

Textuality
CIJE: 5 RIE: 2 CAT: 13
SN See also "Intertextuality"

Texture (Art)
CIJE: 9 RIE: 1 CAT: 16

Texture Density
CIJE: 2 RIE: 0 CAT: 11

Texture Mapping
CIJE: 0 RIE: 1 CAT: 15

TH Role
CIJE: 0 RIE: 1 CAT: 13

THA MASTER
CIJE: 0 RIE: 1 CAT: 19
SN "The Hellman Academy for Mathematics and Science Teacher Education Retraining"

Thacher School CA
CIJE: 1 RIE: 1 CAT: 17

Thackray Reading Readiness Profiles
CIJE: 0 RIE: 1 CAT: 21

Thai People
CIJE: 2 RIE: 7 CAT: 08

Thai Sign Language
CIJE: 0 RIE: 1 CAT: 13

Thailand
CIJE: 184 RIE: 294 CAT: 07

Thailand (Bangkok)
CIJE: 4 RIE: 7 CAT: 07

Thakali
CIJE: 0 RIE: 2 CAT: 13

Thalidomide
CIJE: 1 RIE: 1 CAT: 20

Thanksgiving
CIJE: 14 RIE: 8 CAT: 12

Tharu
CIJE: 0 RIE: 2 CAT: 13

Thatcher (Margaret)
CIJE: 9 RIE: 2 CAT: 18

The Arc
USE Arc (Association for Retarded Citizens)

The Dalles School District OR
CIJE: 0 RIE: 1 CAT: 17

The Research Instruments Project
CIJE: 0 RIE: 101 CAT: 19
UF TRIP Project IL

The School System (Columbia Computing Services)
CIJE: 0 RIE: 1 CAT: 04
UF TSS Software

THE SOURCE
USE SOURCE (Information Utility)

Theater Administration
CIJE: 6 RIE: 1 CAT: 16

Theater Festivals
CIJE: 1 RIE: 1 CAT: 12

Theater for Development
CIJE: 1 RIE: 3 CAT: 15

Theater History
CIJE: 7 RIE: 10 CAT: 12

Theater Management
CIJE: 3 RIE: 3 CAT: 09

Theater of the Absurd
CIJE: 5 RIE: 1 CAT: 03

Theater Research
CIJE: 28 RIE: 12 CAT: 16

Theatre in Education Program
CIJE: 5 RIE: 0 CAT: 19

Theatre of the Grotesque
CIJE: 0 RIE: 1 CAT: 03

Theatrical Makeup
CIJE: 0 RIE: 1 CAT: 16
UF Makeup (Theater Arts); Stage Makeup

Theft Detection System
CIJE: 1 RIE: 1 CAT: 15

Thematic Analysis
CIJE: 13 RIE: 12 CAT: 15

Thematic Apperception Test
CIJE: 55 RIE: 27 CAT: 21

Thematic Apperception Test for Academic Motivation
CIJE: 0 RIE: 1 CAT: 21

Thematic Appreciation Test
CIJE: 1 RIE: 1 CAT: 21

Thematic Elementary Science Individualized Studies
CIJE: 0 RIE: 1 CAT: 19

Thematic Maps
CIJE: 6 RIE: 2 CAT: 04

Thematic Matrix Analysis
CIJE: 0 RIE: 1 CAT: 15

Thematic Organizers
CIJE: 11 RIE: 4 CAT: 16

Thematic Relations
CIJE: 1 RIE: 1 CAT: 11

Thematic Stimuli
CIJE: 4 RIE: 1 CAT: 11

Thematic Studies Program
CIJE: 2 RIE: 2 CAT: 19

Thematization
CIJE: 4 RIE: 0 CAT: 16

Theme (Literary)
CIJE: 28 RIE: 7 CAT: 16
UF Literary Themes

Theme A Day
CIJE: 0 RIE: 1 CAT: 19

Theme Centered Interactional Method
CIJE: 1 RIE: 2 CAT: 15

Theme Parks
CIJE: 1 RIE: 2 CAT: 05

Theme Rheme Articulation
CIJE: 0 RIE: 1 CAT: 13

Themes Concerning Blacks Test
CIJE: 1 RIE: 0 CAT: 21

Theobald (Robert)
CIJE: 1 RIE: 0 CAT: 18

Theological Libraries
CIJE: 4 RIE: 2 CAT: 05

Theology
CIJE: 29 RIE: 9 CAT: 03

Theology Students
CIJE: 3 RIE: 2 CAT: 10

Theophylline
CIJE: 1 RIE: 0 CAT: 11

Theoretic Orientation
CIJE: 1 RIE: 7 CAT: 11

Theoretical Analysis
CIJE: 193 RIE: 46 CAT: 15

Theoretical Orientation
CIJE: 36 RIE: 16 CAT: 21

Theoretical Orientation to Reading Profile
CIJE: 1 RIE: 4 CAT: 21

Theory Based Evaluation
CIJE: 11 RIE: 1 CAT: 21

Theory Development
CIJE: 94 RIE: 102 CAT: 16

Theory of Constructive Operators (Pascual Leone)
CIJE: 1 RIE: 0 CAT: 15

Theory of Margin
CIJE: 4 RIE: 2 CAT: 15
UF Power Load Margin Theory

Theory of Mind
CIJE: 9 RIE: 4 CAT: 15

Theory of Reasoned Action
CIJE: 4 RIE: 4 CAT: 15
UF Reasoned Action Theory

Theory of Violators
CIJE: 0 RIE: 1 CAT: 21

Theory of Work Adjustment
CIJE: 9 RIE: 2 CAT: 15

Theory X
CIJE: 4 RIE: 7 CAT: 15

Theory Y
CIJE: 7 RIE: 9 CAT: 15

Theory Z
CIJE: 19 RIE: 11 CAT: 15

Therapen
CIJE: 0 RIE: 1 CAT: 04

Therapeutic Academics
CIJE: 0 RIE: 1 CAT: 03

Therapeutic Communication
CIJE: 5 RIE: 5 CAT: 11

Therapeutic Conditions Training
CIJE: 0 RIE: 1 CAT: 11

Therapeutic Listening
CIJE: 0 RIE: 1 CAT: 11

Therapeutic Reactance Scale
CIJE: 1 RIE: 1 CAT: 21

Therapists Own Family
CIJE: 1 RIE: 0 CAT: 15

Therapy Outcome Differential
CIJE: 1 RIE: 0 CAT: 11

There Are No Children Here
CIJE: 0 RIE: 1 CAT: 22

Thermal Pollution Control
CIJE: 1 RIE: 0 CAT: 20

Thermal Storage
CIJE: 1 RIE: 0 CAT: 20

Thermal Waves
CIJE: 0 RIE: 0 CAT: 20

Thermoform
CIJE: 0 RIE: 1 CAT: 20

Thermographs
CIJE: 1 RIE: 1 CAT: 20

Thermometers
CIJE: 7 RIE: 7 CAT: 04

Thermonuclear Fusion
CIJE: 1 RIE: 0 CAT: 20

Thermoplastic Resins
CIJE: 1 RIE: 0 CAT: 20

Thermoregulation
CIJE: 3 RIE: 1 CAT: 20

Thermostatic Control
CIJE: 1 RIE: 0 CAT: 20

Thermostats
CIJE: 7 RIE: 3 CAT: 04

Thesaurus of Engineering and Scientific Terms
CIJE: 0 RIE: 1 CAT: 22

Thesaurus of ERIC Descriptors
CIJE: 9 RIE: 6 CAT: 22

Theseus Myth
CIJE: 2 RIE: 0 CAT: 22

Thesis Analysis and Synthesis Key
CIJE: 0 RIE: 1 CAT: 15

Theta Estimates
CIJE: 6 RIE: 6 CAT: 21

Thibault (Jacques Anatole)
CIJE: 1 RIE: 0 CAT: 18

Thick Description Method
CIJE: 3 RIE: 3 CAT: 15

Thin Film Separation
CIJE: 1 RIE: 0 CAT: 20

Things People Do Inventory
CIJE: 0 RIE: 1 CAT: 21

Think Aloud Program
CIJE: 5 RIE: 4 CAT: 19

Think It Through
CIJE: 1 RIE: 1 CAT: 19

Think Tanks
CIJE: 0 RIE: 1 CAT: 10

THINKABOUT
CIJE: 2 RIE: 12 CAT: 19

ThinkAbout (Television Series)
CIJE: 1 RIE: 2 CAT: 22

Thinking About My School
CIJE: 0 RIE: 2 CAT: 22

Thinking Across the Curriculum
CIJE: 6 RIE: 14 CAT: 15

Thinking Approach to Problem Solving
CIJE: 0 RIE: 1 CAT: 15

Thinking Improvement Project
CIJE: 0 RIE: 1 CAT: 19

Thinking in English (Matsumoto)
CIJE: 0 RIE: 1 CAT: 22

Thinking Mathematics Project
CIJE: 0 RIE: 1 CAT: 19

Thinking Orientation Scale
CIJE: 1 RIE: 0 CAT: 21

Thinking Skills Program
CIJE: 1 RIE: 2 CAT: 19

Thinking Writing Relationship
USE Writing Thinking Relationship

Thiokol Chemical Corporation
CIJE: 1 RIE: 0 CAT: 17

Thioridazine
CIJE: 4 RIE: 2 CAT: 11

Thiothixene
CIJE: 0 RIE: 1 CAT: 11

Third Citizenship Social Studies Assess (1982)
CIJE: 0 RIE: 2 CAT: 21

Third Cycle
CIJE: 0 RIE: 2 CAT: 16

Third International Mathematics and Science Study
CIJE: 1 RIE: 1 CAT: 19

Third Mathematics Assessment (1982)
CIJE: 0 RIE: 3 CAT: 21

Third Party Credibility
CIJE: 0 RIE: 1 CAT: 16

Third Party Evaluation
CIJE: 5 RIE: 3 CAT: 21

Third Party Liability
CIJE: 2 RIE: 0 CAT: 14

Third Party Payments
CIJE: 1 RIE: 4 CAT: 16

Third Party Reimbursements
CIJE: 5 RIE: 2 CAT: 16

Third Science Assessment (1977)
CIJE: 4 RIE: 0 CAT: 21

Third Wave (Toffler)
CIJE: 1 RIE: 0 CAT: 22

Third Wave Technologies
CIJE: 0 RIE: 1 CAT: 20

Third World
CIJE: 80 RIE: 71 CAT: 16

Third World Education Systems
CIJE: 10 RIE: 8 CAT: 15

Third World Science Project
CIJE: 0 RIE: 15 CAT: 19

Third World Studies Project
CIJE: 0 RIE: 2 CAT: 19

Third Writing Assessment (1979)
CIJE: 0 RIE: 3 CAT: 21

Thirteen College Curriculum Program
CIJE: 0 RIE: 36 CAT: 19

Thirteenth Amendment
CIJE: 2 RIE: 3 CAT: 14

This I Believe Test (Harvey)
CIJE: 2 RIE: 7 CAT: 21

This Land Is Your Land (Song)
CIJE: 0 RIE: 1 CAT: 22

Thlingchadinne
USE Dogrib

THOG Problem
CIJE: 1 RIE: 0 CAT: 15

Thomas (A M)
CIJE: 0 RIE: 1 CAT: 18

Thomas (Alan)
CIJE: 0 RIE: 1 CAT: 18

Thomas (David)
CIJE: 1 RIE: 0 CAT: 18

Thomas (Dylan)
CIJE: 3 RIE: 1 CAT: 18

Thomas (Lewis)
CIJE: 0 RIE: 1 CAT: 18

Thomas (M Carey)
CIJE: 1 RIE: 1 CAT: 18

Thomas (Piri)
CIJE: 1 RIE: 0 CAT: 18

Thomas (R Murray)
CIJE: 0 RIE: 1 CAT: 18

Thomas (W I)
CIJE: 1 RIE: 0 CAT: 18

Thomas A Edison High School PA
CIJE: 0 RIE: 1 CAT: 17

Thomas and Chess Parent and Teacher Questionnaire
CIJE: 0 RIE: 2 CAT: 21

Thomas County School District GA
CIJE: 0 RIE: 1 CAT: 17

Thomas Edison Elementary School CA
CIJE: 0 RIE: 1 CAT: 17

Thomas Equity Perception Scale
CIJE: 0 RIE: 1 CAT: 21

Thomas Jefferson College MI
CIJE: 1 RIE: 0 CAT: 17

Thomas Jefferson High School FL
CIJE: 1 RIE: 0 CAT: 17

Thomas Jefferson High School PA
CIJE: 1 RIE: 1 CAT: 17

Thomas Jefferson University PA
CIJE: 8 RIE: 1 CAT: 17

Thomas Nelson Community College VA
CIJE: 4 RIE: 8 CAT: 17

Thomas Report
CIJE: 1 RIE: 0 CAT: 22

Thomas Self Concept Values Test
CIJE: 1 RIE: 2 CAT: 21

Thomism
CIJE: 0 RIE: 1 CAT: 15

Thompson (Charles H)
CIJE: 3 RIE: 0 CAT: 18

Thompson (William Hale)
CIJE: 1 RIE: 0 CAT: 18

Thompson v Southwest School District
CIJE: 1 RIE: 0 CAT: 14

Thompson Writing Attitude Survey
CIJE: 0 RIE: 1 CAT: 21

Thomson (Sir Joseph John)
CIJE: 1 RIE: 0 CAT: 18

Thomson Foundation College (England)
CIJE: 4 RIE: 0 CAT: 17

Thoreau (Henry David)
CIJE: 18 RIE: 14 CAT: 18

Thorium
CIJE: 2 RIE: 0 CAT: 20

Thorkildsen (Ron)
CIJE: 1 RIE: 0 CAT: 18

Thorndike (Edward L)
CIJE: 15 RIE: 8 CAT: 18

Thorndike (Robert L)
CIJE: 2 RIE: 0 CAT: 18

Thorndike Lorge Word List
CIJE: 0 RIE: 1 CAT: 21

Thorne (Frederick C)
CIJE: 2 RIE: 1 CAT: 18

Thornlea Secondary School (Canada)
CIJE: 0 RIE: 1 CAT: 17

Thornock v Boise Independent School District
CIJE: 0 RIE: 1 CAT: 14

Thornton Community College IL
CIJE: 2 RIE: 1 CAT: 17

Thornton High School
CIJE: 1 RIE: 0 CAT: 17

Thornton Township High School IL
CIJE: 1 RIE: 0 CAT: 17

Thorpe (Gerald)
CIJE: 1 RIE: 0 CAT: 18

Thorpe (Jim)
CIJE: 4 RIE: 1 CAT: 18

THOT Program (Peterson et al)
USE Teaching for Higher Order Thinking

Thought Control
CIJE: 4 RIE: 0 CAT: 11
SN See also "Mind Control"

Thoughts Concerning Education
CIJE: 1 RIE: 0 CAT: 22

Thousand Oaks Elementary School CA
CIJE: 1 RIE: 0 CAT: 17

Threaders (Electronics)
CIJE: 0 RIE: 1 CAT: 09

Threads
CIJE: 2 RIE: 0 CAT: 16

Threat
CIJE: 23 RIE: 9 CAT: 16

Three Cities Employment Training Program
CIJE: 0 RIE: 1 CAT: 19

Three Four Five Club
CIJE: 1 RIE: 0 CAT: 17

Three Little Pigs
CIJE: 3 RIE: 0 CAT: 22

Three Mile Island
CIJE: 7 RIE: 2 CAT: 12

Three Minute Reasoning Test (Hartley and Holt)
CIJE: 1 RIE: 0 CAT: 21

Three Mode Component Analysis
USE Three Mode Factor Analysis

Three Mode Factor Analysis
CIJE: 6 RIE: 1 CAT: 21
UF Three Mode Component Analysis

Three on Two Approach
CIJE: 1 RIE: 3 CAT: 15

Three Parameter Model
CIJE: 40 RIE: 90 CAT: 15

Three Phase Program for School Administrators
CIJE: 0 RIE: 1 CAT: 19

Three Rivers Community College MO
CIJE: 1 RIE: 0 CAT: 17

Three Rs
USE 3Rs

THREEDE Computer Program
CIJE: 0 RIE: 1 CAT: 04

Threshold Analysis
CIJE: 1 RIE: 1 CAT: 15

Threshold by Identification of Pictures Test
CIJE: 0 RIE: 2 CAT: 21

Threshold Project (South Africa)
CIJE: 0 RIE: 3 CAT: 19

Threshold Traits Analysis
CIJE: 2 RIE: 0 CAT: 15

Thresholds
CIJE: 31 RIE: 6 CAT: 21

Thrifty Food Plan
CIJE: 0 RIE: 2 CAT: 11
SN Diet defined by the USDA as a basis for allocating food stamps

Thriving on Chaos (Peters)
CIJE: 0 RIE: 1 CAT: 22

Thrombocytosis
CIJE: 1 RIE: 0 CAT: 11

Throne of Blood
CIJE: 1 RIE: 1 CAT: 22

Through the Looking Glass
CIJE: 3 RIE: 0 CAT: 22

Throwaway Children
CIJE: 0 RIE: 0 CAT: 10

Throwing
CIJE: 10 RIE: 6 CAT: 16

Thucydides
CIJE: 4 RIE: 0 CAT: 18

Thumbsucking
CIJE: 2 RIE: 1 CAT: 11

Thumin Conservatism Liberalism Scale
CIJE: 1 RIE: 0 CAT: 21

Thunderbird Grad School of Intl Management
CIJE: 1 RIE: 1 CAT: 17

Thurston Temperament Schedule
CIJE: 1 RIE: 1 CAT: 21

Thurstone Box Problem
CIJE: 2 RIE: 0 CAT: 21

Thurstone Closure Flexibility Scale
CIJE: 1 RIE: 1 CAT: 21

Thurstone Dominance
CIJE: 0 RIE: 1 CAT: 15

Thurstone Model
CIJE: 4 RIE: 2 CAT: 15

Thurstone Model III Scaling Procedure
CIJE: 3 RIE: 0 CAT: 21

Thurstone Model V Scaling Procedure
CIJE: 2 RIE: 1 CAT: 21

Thurstone Pattern Copying Test
CIJE: 0 RIE: 1 CAT: 21

Thurstone Primary Mental Abilities Schema
CIJE: 3 RIE: 5 CAT: 21

Thurstone Scale of Attitude Toward Negroes
CIJE: 0 RIE: 1 CAT: 21

Thurstone Scales
CIJE: 17 RIE: 8 CAT: 21

Thurstones Law of Comparative Judgment
CIJE: 1 RIE: 0 CAT: 21

Thurstones Primary Mental Abilities Schema
CIJE: 1 RIE: 1 CAT: 21

Thus I Refute Beelzy
CIJE: 0 RIE: 1 CAT: 22

Thut (I N) World Education Center CT
CIJE: 0 RIE: 1 CAT: 17

Thy Project (Denmark)
CIJE: 0 RIE: 1 CAT: 19

Thycydides
CIJE: 1 RIE: 0 CAT: 18

Thyne (J M)
CIJE: 0 RIE: 1 CAT: 18

Thyroid Function
CIJE: 3 RIE: 1 CAT: 11

TI IN Network TX
CIJE: 3 RIE: 7 CAT: 17

Tiananmen Square Uprising
CIJE: 1 RIE: 2 CAT: 12

Tibeto Burman Languages
CIJE: 0 RIE: 1 CAT: 13

TICCIT Computer System
CIJE: 7 RIE: 33 CAT: 04

Tick Toxicosis
CIJE: 2 RIE: 0 CAT: 11

Ticket Agents
CIJE: 0 RIE: 3 CAT: 09

Ticket Splitting
CIJE: 0 RIE: 1 CAT: 16

Tickets
CIJE: 2 RIE: 0 CAT: 04

Tics
CIJE: 5 RIE: 2 CAT: 11

Tidal Pools
CIJE: 1 RIE: 3 CAT: 20

Tidal Waves
CIJE: 0 RIE: 2 CAT: 20

Tides
CIJE: 8 RIE: 10 CAT: 20

Tidewater Community College VA
CIJE: 3 RIE: 9 CAT: 17

Tie Dyeing
CIJE: 2 RIE: 0 CAT: 03

Tie Dying
CIJE: 0 RIE: 1 CAT: 16

Tie Parameters
CIJE: 0 RIE: 1 CAT: 21

TIE System IA
USE Televised Interactive Education System

Tiebout (Charles)
CIJE: 0 RIE: 1 CAT: 18

Tieck (Ludwig)
CIJE: 4 RIE: 0 CAT: 18

Tiedeman (D V)
CIJE: 2 RIE: 0 CAT: 18

TIES Computer System
CIJE: 0 RIE: 1 CAT: 04

Tiffany Experienced Control Scales
CIJE: 0 RIE: 3 CAT: 21

Tigard School District OR
CIJE: 0 RIE: 1 CAT: 17

TIGER Database File
CIJE: 1 RIE: 2 CAT: 04
SN TIGER = "Topologically Integrated Geographic Encoding and Referencing"

Tigre
CIJE: 0 RIE: 1 CAT: 13
SN A Semitic language, Ethiopic group

Tigrinya
CIJE: 0 RIE: 2 CAT: 13

Tilak (Bal Gangadhar)
CIJE: 0 RIE: 1 CAT: 18

Tilden (Freeman)
CIJE: 1 RIE: 0 CAT: 18

Tile Occupations
CIJE: 0 RIE: 10 CAT: 09

Tilework
CIJE: 0 RIE: 1 CAT: 20

Till (Emmett)
CIJE: 0 RIE: 1 CAT: 18

Tillich (Paul)
CIJE: 1 RIE: 2 CAT: 18

Tilted Family
CIJE: 0 RIE: 1 CAT: 10
SN Family in which all of the children are of the same sex—see also "Geometric Family"
UF Same Sex Children Family

Tilton Project
CIJE: 1 RIE: 0 CAT: 19

Tilton v Richardson
CIJE: 1 RIE: 1 CAT: 14

Timber Production
CIJE: 3 RIE: 1 CAT: 20

Timbre Discrimination
CIJE: 3 RIE: 2 CAT: 13

Time and Motion Studies
CIJE: 2 RIE: 2 CAT: 15

Time Base Corrector
CIJE: 2 RIE: 0 CAT: 04

Time Connectives
CIJE: 1 RIE: 0 CAT: 16

Time Constants
CIJE: 0 RIE: 1 CAT: 20

Time Delay
CIJE: 47 RIE: 4 CAT: 15
SN A response prompting and fading method used in instructional interventions with the disabled — for broader indexing, use the Identifier "Time Lag" — do not confuse with the Descriptor "Wait Time"
UF Constant Time Delay

Time Dependent Fluids
CIJE: 1 RIE: 0 CAT: 20

Time Division Multiplex
CIJE: 0 RIE: 1 CAT: 04

Time Expanded Speech
CIJE: 1 RIE: 0 CAT: 13

Time Expressions
CIJE: 6 RIE: 2 CAT: 13

Time for Results (Governors 1991 Report on Educ)
CIJE: 4 RIE: 8 CAT: 22

Time Lag
CIJE: 13 RIE: 2 CAT: 16
SN Do not confuse with the Identifier "Time Delay" or the Descriptor "Wait Time"

Time Magazine
CIJE: 13 RIE: 12 CAT: 22

Time of Your Life
CIJE: 1 RIE: 0 CAT: 22

Time Oriented Data
CIJE: 12 RIE: 1 CAT: 15

Time Reference Inventory
CIJE: 1 RIE: 1 CAT: 21

Time Sampling
CIJE: 11 RIE: 8 CAT: 20

Time Series Analysis
CIJE: 50 RIE: 42 CAT: 15

Time Series Design
CIJE: 13 RIE: 7 CAT: 21

Time Series Experiments
CIJE: 6 RIE: 6 CAT: 15

Time Shared Automatic Control Laboratory
CIJE: 0 RIE: 2 CAT: 04

Time Sharing Ability
CIJE: 2 RIE: 1 CAT: 15

Time Space and Matter
CIJE: 5 RIE: 0 CAT: 20

Time Span Measurement
CIJE: 4 RIE: 2 CAT: 21

Time Studies
CIJE: 18 RIE: 18 CAT: 15

Time Telling
CIJE: 10 RIE: 8 CAT: 16
UF Telling Time

Time to Degree
CIJE: 5 RIE: 10 CAT: 03
SN The time students take to complete a degree
UF Degree Completion Time

Time to Learn (Title)
CIJE: 3 RIE: 0 CAT: 22

Time Travel
CIJE: 1 RIE: 1 CAT: 20

Time Work Fatigue
CIJE: 1 RIE: 1 CAT: 11

Timed Behavior Checklist
CIJE: 0 RIE: 1 CAT: 21

Timelines
CIJE: 20 RIE: 6 CAT: 16

Timeliness
CIJE: 8 RIE: 6 CAT: 16

Timely Action
CIJE: 1 RIE: 1 CAT: 15

Timers
CIJE: 3 RIE: 0 CAT: 04

Times (London)
CIJE: 2 RIE: 1 CAT: 22

Times Beach Disaster
USE Missouri (Times Beach)

Timing
CIJE: 16 RIE: 2 CAT: 16

Timmons Savings Plan
CIJE: 0 RIE: 1 CAT: 16

Timonium Elementary School MD
CIJE: 1 RIE: 0 CAT: 17

Timor (Portuguese)
CIJE: 2 RIE: 0 CAT: 07

Timucua (Tribe)
CIJE: 0 RIE: 1 CAT: 08

Tina Sambal
CIJE: 0 RIE: 1 CAT: 13
SN A Northwest Austronesian (Philippine) language
UF Sambali (Tina)

Ting An Dialect
CIJE: 0 RIE: 1 CAT: 13

Tinker v Des Moines Independent School District
CIJE: 24 RIE: 23 CAT: 14

Tinto (V)
CIJE: 11 RIE: 4 CAT: 18

Tinto Model
CIJE: 6 RIE: 9 CAT: 15
SN Model of college student withdrawal

Tinto Theory
CIJE: 14 RIE: 20 CAT: 15

Tipp City Public Schools OH
CIJE: 0 RIE: 1 CAT: 17

TIPS WA
USE Teacher Incentives Project

Tires
CIJE: 0 RIE: 10 CAT: 04

Tirso de Molina
CIJE: 2 RIE: 1 CAT: 18

Tiruray
CIJE: 0 RIE: 1 CAT: 13

TIS Intelligent Gateway
USE Technology Information System

Titanium
CIJE: 0 RIE: 1 CAT: 20

Title I Evaluation and Reporting System
CIJE: 16 RIE: 64 CAT: 15

Title I Program Analysis and Monitoring
CIJE: 0 RIE: 3 CAT: 15

Title IX Education Amendments 1972
CIJE: 167 RIE: 330 CAT: 14
UF Education Amendments 1972 Title IX

Title V Maternal and Child Health Programs
USE Social Security Act Title V

Title Words
CIJE: 7 RIE: 1 CAT: 13

Title XI Education Amendments 1978
CIJE: 0 RIE: 4 CAT: 14
UF Education Amendments 1978 Title XI

Titles
CIJE: 37 RIE: 4 CAT: 16

Titration Analysis
CIJE: 12 RIE: 2 CAT: 20

Titration Curves
CIJE: 3 RIE: 0 CAT: 20

Titrimetry
CIJE: 11 RIE: 0 CAT: 20

Tiv
CIJE: 0 RIE: 2 CAT: 13

Tiwi
CIJE: 0 RIE: 2 CAT: 13
SN An Australian Aboriginal language
UF Wunuk

Tlapanec
USE Chocho

Tlingit
CIJE: 2 RIE: 6 CAT: 13
SN Of the Na-Dene language group
UF Koluschan Language

Tlingit (Tribe)
CIJE: 4 RIE: 24 CAT: 08

TLO v New Jersey
USE New Jersey v TLO

TMC Publications
USE Total Market Coverage Publications

TMI Groliers Course in General Science
CIJE: 0 RIE: 2 CAT: 03

TMI Groliers Fundamentals of Algebra
CIJE: 0 RIE: 2 CAT: 03

To an Athlete Dying Young
CIJE: 0 RIE: 1 CAT: 22

To Autumn
CIJE: 2 RIE: 0 CAT: 22

To Build a Fire
CIJE: 1 RIE: 1 CAT: 22

To Improve Learning
CIJE: 1 RIE: 0 CAT: 22

To Kill a Mockingbird
CIJE: 4 RIE: 4 CAT: 22

To Reclaim a Legacy
CIJE: 9 RIE: 1 CAT: 22

To the Lighthouse
CIJE: 1 RIE: 0 CAT: 22

Tobacco Free Schools
USE Smoke Free Schools

Tobacco Industry
CIJE: 11 RIE: 0 CAT: 16

Tobacco Processing Occupations
CIJE: 1 RIE: 2 CAT: 09

Tobacco Producers
CIJE: 1 RIE: 0 CAT: 09

Tobit Model Analysis
CIJE: 7 RIE: 2 CAT: 15

Toby House
CIJE: 1 RIE: 0 CAT: 17

Tocqueville (Alexis de)
CIJE: 8 RIE: 2 CAT: 18

Toddler Behavior Questionnaire
CIJE: 0 RIE: 1 CAT: 21

Toddler Temperament Scale
CIJE: 2 RIE: 1 CAT: 21

Todorov (Tzvetan)
CIJE: 2 RIE: 0 CAT: 18

TOEFL
USE Test of English as a Foreign Language

Toffler (Alvin)
CIJE: 10 RIE: 6 CAT: 18

Together We Can
CIJE: 0 RIE: 5 CAT: 19

Togetherness
CIJE: 1 RIE: 1 CAT: 11

Togo
CIJE: 7 RIE: 21 CAT: 07

Togo (Lome)
CIJE: 0 RIE: 1 CAT: 07

Toilet Training
CIJE: 24 RIE: 14 CAT: 11

Toishan Dialect
CIJE: 0 RIE: 1 CAT: 13

Tojolabal
CIJE: 0 RIE: 1 CAT: 13
SN A Mayan language, Tzeltalan group

Tok Pisin
CIJE: 4 RIE: 4 CAT: 13

Tokelau
CIJE: 0 RIE: 2 CAT: 07

Token Earnings
CIJE: 0 RIE: 1 CAT: 15

Token Reinforcement System
CIJE: 5 RIE: 4 CAT: 15

Token Test (Language)
CIJE: 6 RIE: 0 CAT: 21

Tokyo Christian Mass Communication Center (Japan)
CIJE: 1 RIE: 0 CAT: 17

Tokyo Institute of Technology (Japan)
CIJE: 1 RIE: 1 CAT: 17

Toledo Chemistry Placement Examination
CIJE: 1 RIE: 1 CAT: 21

Toledo Lucas County Public Library OH
CIJE: 1 RIE: 1 CAT: 17

Toledo Museum of Art OH
CIJE: 1 RIE: 1 CAT: 17

Toledo Political Affairs Study
CIJE: 0 RIE: 1 CAT: 19

Toledo Public Schools OH
CIJE: 9 RIE: 13 CAT: 17

Toledo Support Teachers Program OH
CIJE: 0 RIE: 1 CAT: 19

Tolerance
CIJE: 59 RIE: 19 CAT: 16

Tolerance (Engineering)
CIJE: 0 RIE: 0 CAT: 20
UF Tolerancing (Drafting)

Tolerance Intervals (Statistics)
CIJE: 2 RIE: 1 CAT: 21

Tolerancing (Drafting)
USE Tolerance (Engineering)

Tolkien (J R R)
CIJE: 8 RIE: 2 CAT: 18

Toll Gate Metrication Project
CIJE: 1 RIE: 0 CAT: 19

Toller (Ernst)
CIJE: 1 RIE: 0 CAT: 18

Tolley Medal
CIJE: 0 RIE: 2 CAT: 16

Tolman (Edward Chace)
CIJE: 1 RIE: 0 CAT: 18

Tolowa
CIJE: 0 RIE: 2 CAT: 13
SN Of the Athapascan language family

Tolowa (Tribe)
CIJE: 0 RIE: 3 CAT: 08

Tolstoy (Leo Nikolayevich)
CIJE: 14 RIE: 1 CAT: 18

Toluene
CIJE: 1 RIE: 0 CAT: 20

Toluidine Blue
CIJE: 1 RIE: 0 CAT: 20

Tom Green County Library System TX
CIJE: 0 RIE: 1 CAT: 17

Tom Jones
CIJE: 1 RIE: 0 CAT: 22

Tom Sawyer
CIJE: 4 RIE: 1 CAT: 22

Tom Snyder Productions
CIJE: 0 RIE: 1 CAT: 17

Toma (David)
CIJE: 0 RIE: 1 CAT: 18

Toman (Walter)
CIJE: 0 RIE: 2 CAT: 18

Tomatis Method
CIJE: 2 RIE: 3 CAT: 15

Tomato Peelers
CIJE: 0 RIE: 1 CAT: 09

Tombigbee Regional Library MS
CIJE: 0 RIE: 1 CAT: 17

Tomoda (Yasumasa)
CIJE: 1 RIE: 0 CAT: 18

Tomorrow Higher Education Project
CIJE: 2 RIE: 3 CAT: 19

Tomorrows Teachers
USE Holmes Group Report

Tompkins Cortland Community College NY
CIJE: 0 RIE: 2 CAT: 17

Tonal Accents
CIJE: 0 RIE: 1 CAT: 13

Tonal Inflection
CIJE: 1 RIE: 1 CAT: 13

Tonal Memory
CIJE: 1 RIE: 1 CAT: 11

Tonal Spelling
CIJE: 0 RIE: 1 CAT: 13

Tondreau (Narciso)
CIJE: 1 RIE: 0 CAT: 18

Tone (Language)
CIJE: 8 RIE: 4 CAT: 13

Tone Decay
CIJE: 1 RIE: 0 CAT: 13

Tone Sandhi
CIJE: 0 RIE: 2 CAT: 13

Tonemes
CIJE: 0 RIE: 1 CAT: 13

Tonga
CIJE: 6 RIE: 6 CAT: 07

Tongan
CIJE: 3 RIE: 5 CAT: 13

Tongan Americans
CIJE: 0 RIE: 2 CAT: 08

Tonguc (Hakki Ismail)
CIJE: 1 RIE: 0 CAT: 18

Tongue
CIJE: 2 RIE: 0 CAT: 11

Tongue Thrusting
CIJE: 6 RIE: 0 CAT: 16

Tongue Twisters
CIJE: 4 RIE: 3 CAT: 16

Tonguing
CIJE: 1 RIE: 0 CAT: 16

TONI
USE Test of Nonverbal Intelligence

Tonnies (Ferdinand)
CIJE: 0 RIE: 1 CAT: 18

Tonomechanics
CIJE: 0 RIE: 1 CAT: 20

Tonsillectomies
CIJE: 0 RIE: 1 CAT: 11

Tonsillitis
CIJE: 0 RIE: 1 CAT: 11

Tools
CIJE: 6 RIE: 5 CAT: 04

Tools for Change
CIJE: 0 RIE: 3 CAT: 22

Tools for Schools Loan Program
CIJE: 0 RIE: 1 CAT: 19

Toomer (Jean)
CIJE: 2 RIE: 1 CAT: 18

Tooth Size
CIJE: 1 RIE: 0 CAT: 11

Toothbrushing
CIJE: 6 RIE: 2 CAT: 11

Toothkeeper Program
CIJE: 0 RIE: 1 CAT: 19

Top Down Assessment
CIJE: 0 RIE: 1 CAT: 21

Top Level Structure
CIJE: 2 RIE: 0 CAT: 13

Top Man X
CIJE: 0 RIE: 1 CAT: 22

Top of Alabama Regional Council of Governments
CIJE: 1 RIE: 0 CAT: 17

Topic Changes
CIJE: 6 RIE: 3 CAT: 13

Topic Classification System
CIJE: 0 RIE: 3 CAT: 15

Topic Control
CIJE: 7 RIE: 1 CAT: 15

Topic Evaluation Questionnaire
CIJE: 0 RIE: 1 CAT: 21

Topic House NY
CIJE: 0 RIE: 2 CAT: 17

Topic Selection
CIJE: 38 RIE: 21 CAT: 16
UF News Topic Selection

Topic Sentences
CIJE: 10 RIE: 6 CAT: 13

Topic Units
CIJE: 4 RIE: 4 CAT: 13

Topicality
CIJE: 8 RIE: 6 CAT: 16

Topicality Arguments
CIJE: 2 RIE: 2 CAT: 16

Topicalization (Language)
CIJE: 2 RIE: 3 CAT: 13

Topographic Brain Mapping
CIJE: 1 RIE: 3 CAT: 11
UF Brain Topography

Topographic Maps
CIJE: 10 RIE: 6 CAT: 16

Toponyms
USE Place Names

Torah
CIJE: 0 RIE: 1 CAT: 22

Torgerson Multidimensional Scaling Model
CIJE: 0 RIE: 1 CAT: 21

Tornado Protection
CIJE: 4 RIE: 5 CAT: 20

Tornado Warnings
CIJE: 0 RIE: 1 CAT: 20

Tornadoes
CIJE: 8 RIE: 9 CAT: 20

Toronto Board of Education Benchmarks ON
CIJE: 0 RIE: 1 CAT: 03
SN Academic standards in mathematics and language at the end of grades 3, 6, 8, and 10

Toronto Board of Education ON
CIJE: 1 RIE: 20 CAT: 17

Toronto Public Library ON
CIJE: 0 RIE: 0 CAT: 17

Toronto Public Schools ON
CIJE: 1 RIE: 13 CAT: 17

Toronto Research and Environment System
CIJE: 1 RIE: 0 CAT: 04

Torque
CIJE: 10 RIE: 0 CAT: 20

Torrance (E Paul)
CIJE: 7 RIE: 3 CAT: 18

Torrance Creative Motivation Inventory
CIJE: 1 RIE: 0 CAT: 21

Torrance Ideal Pupil Checklist
CIJE: 2 RIE: 0 CAT: 21

Torrance Tests of Creative Thinking
CIJE: 68 RIE: 58 CAT: 21

Torrance Unified School District CA
CIJE: 0 RIE: 5 CAT: 17

Torrance Unusual Uses Test
CIJE: 2 RIE: 1 CAT: 21

Torres Rioseco (Arturo)
CIJE: 1 RIE: 0 CAT: 18

Torres Strait Islands
USE Australia (Torres Strait)

Torsca Multidimensional Scaling Technique
CIJE: 0 RIE: 2 CAT: 21

Torsten Husen Attitude Scales
CIJE: 1 RIE: 0 CAT: 21

Torture
CIJE: 2 RIE: 1 CAT: 16

Torture Victims
CIJE: 1 RIE: 1 CAT: 10
UF Victims of Torture

Tory (Henry Marshall)
CIJE: 0 RIE: 1 CAT: 18

Toskery
CIJE: 1 RIE: 0 CAT: 13

Total Action Against Poverty
CIJE: 0 RIE: 2 CAT: 22

Total Adjustment Scale
CIJE: 0 RIE: 1 CAT: 21

Total Alienation Scale
CIJE: 1 RIE: 0 CAT: 21

Total Area Method
CIJE: 0 RIE: 1 CAT: 15

Total Communication Checklist and Assessment
CIJE: 0 RIE: 1 CAT: 21

Total Guidance Information Support System
CIJE: 0 RIE: 2 CAT: 15

Total Information for Education Systems
CIJE: 2 RIE: 0 CAT: 15

Total Library System
CIJE: 2 RIE: 0 CAT: 04

Total Market Coverage Publications
CIJE: 0 RIE: 1 CAT: 16
UF TMC Publications

Total Objective Plan Officer Procurement System
CIJE: 0 RIE: 1 CAT: 15

Total Person Model
CIJE: 0 RIE: 2 CAT: 15

Total Physical Response
CIJE: 16 RIE: 40 CAT: 11

Total Receptor Access Independent Learning Systems
CIJE: 1 RIE: 0 CAT: 15

Total Return Concept
CIJE: 0 RIE: 1 CAT: 15

Totally Enclosed Modular Environment
CIJE: 0 RIE: 1 CAT: 15

Totally Interactive Testing and Analysis System
CIJE: 0 RIE: 1 CAT: 21

Totonac
CIJE: 0 RIE: 1 CAT: 13

Totter Index
CIJE: 0 RIE: 1 CAT: 21

Toubou
CIJE: 0 RIE: 1 CAT: 13

Touch
CIJE: 10 RIE: 2 CAT: 11

Touch of the Poet
CIJE: 1 RIE: 0 CAT: 22

Touch Terminals
CIJE: 3 RIE: 2 CAT: 04

Touch Tone Telephone Registration
USE Telephone Registration

Touch Tone Telephones
CIJE: 5 RIE: 0 CAT: 04

Touching
CIJE: 17 RIE: 9 CAT: 16
SN See also "Body Contact," "Physical Contact"

Touchstones Program (Great Britain)
CIJE: 0 RIE: 0 CAT: 19

Touchstones Project MD
CIJE: 0 RIE: 0 CAT: 19

Tougaloo College MS
CIJE: 3 RIE: 5 CAT: 17

Tougas Amendment (Massachusetts)
CIJE: 0 RIE: 1 CAT: 14

Tough (Alan)
CIJE: 0 RIE: 2 CAT: 18

Tough (Allen)
CIJE: 4 RIE: 0 CAT: 18

Tough (Joan)
CIJE: 4 RIE: 1 CAT: 18

Tough Love
CIJE: 3 RIE: 1 CAT: 15

Tough Movement Structures
CIJE: 0 RIE: 1 CAT: 13

Toulmin (Stephen)
CIJE: 12 RIE: 7 CAT: 18

Toulmins Model
CIJE: 6 RIE: 6 CAT: 15

Toulouse Lautrec (Henri de)
CIJE: 1 RIE: 1 CAT: 18

Tourette Syndrome
CIJE: 20 RIE: 8 CAT: 11
UF Gilles De La Tourette Syndrome

Tournament Hosts
CIJE: 0 RIE: 1 CAT: 10
UF Host Schools (Tournaments)

Toward Intellectual Excellence
CIJE: 0 RIE: 1 CAT: 22

Toward Teen Health Program
CIJE: 0 RIE: 1 CAT: 19

Towards Arts Assessment Project
CIJE: 0 RIE: 1 CAT: 19

Tower of Hanoi Problem
CIJE: 7 RIE: 5 CAT: 16

Tower System
CIJE: 0 RIE: 1 CAT: 15

Town Affiliation Association of the United States
CIJE: 1 RIE: 0 CAT: 17

Town Meetings
CIJE: 11 RIE: 3 CAT: 16

Township High School District 214 IL
CIJE: 1 RIE: 0 CAT: 17

Townsville Coll of Advanced Education (Australia)
CIJE: 0 RIE: 1 CAT: 17

Towson State University MD
CIJE: 5 RIE: 14 CAT: 17

Toxic Shock Syndrome
CIJE: 5 RIE: 0 CAT: 11

Toxoplasmosis
CIJE: 2 RIE: 0 CAT: 11

Toy Demonstrators
CIJE: 1 RIE: 6 CAT: 09

Toy Guns
CIJE: 4 RIE: 0 CAT: 04

Toy Industry
CIJE: 1 RIE: 3 CAT: 16

Toy Lending Libraries
CIJE: 7 RIE: 12 CAT: 05
SN See also "Lekoteks"

Toy Preference Test
CIJE: 1 RIE: 1 CAT: 21
SN See also "Modified Rabban Toy Preference Test"

Toy Preferences
CIJE: 3 RIE: 2 CAT: 11

Toy Safety
CIJE: 1 RIE: 1 CAT: 11

Toy Talk Contexts
CIJE: 0 RIE: 1 CAT: 15

Toynbee (Arnold J)
CIJE: 3 RIE: 0 CAT: 18

Toyota
CIJE: 1 RIE: 1 CAT: 17

TPA Instruction
USE Teach Practice Apply Model

Trac 4 (Game)
CIJE: 1 RIE: 0 CAT: 04

Trace Conditioning
CIJE: 1 RIE: 0 CAT: 15

Trace Element Medicine
CIJE: 1 RIE: 0 CAT: 11

Trace Elements
CIJE: 5 RIE: 0 CAT: 20

Trace Metals
CIJE: 0 RIE: 1 CAT: 20

Trace Minerals
CIJE: 0 RIE: 1 CAT: 11

TRACE Model
CIJE: 1 RIE: 1 CAT: 15

Trace Observation System
CIJE: 0 RIE: 1 CAT: 15

Trace Transparent Access Module
CIJE: 0 RIE: 1 CAT: 04

Tracer Methodology
CIJE: 0 RIE: 1 CAT: 15

Tracey (William R)
CIJE: 0 RIE: 1 CAT: 18

Tracheostomy Suctioning
CIJE: 2 RIE: 2 CAT: 11

Tracing
CIJE: 7 RIE: 1 CAT: 15

Track and Field Clubs
CIJE: 1 RIE: 0 CAT: 16

Track Record Disclosure Regulations
CIJE: 0 RIE: 1 CAT: 14

Track System (Science)
USE Tracking (Science)

Tracking (Aerospace)
USE Tracking (Science)

Tracking (Career Paths)
CIJE: 0 RIE: 1 CAT: 15

Tracking (Cases)
CIJE: 3 RIE: 2 CAT: 15

Tracking (Clients)
USE Client Tracking

Tracking (Documents)
CIJE: 0 RIE: 1 CAT: 15

Tracking (Literary Styles)
USE Literary Craft Tracking

Tracking (Mental)
USE Mental Tracking

Tracking (Migrants)
USE Migrant Tracking

Tracking (Procedures)
USE Procedure Tracking

Tracking (Science)
CIJE: 1 RIE: 1 CAT: 20
UF Tracking (Aerospace); Track System (Science)

Tracking (Visual Motor)
USE Visual Motor Tracking

Tracking (Visual)
USE Visual Tracking

Tracking (Visuomanual)
USE Visuomanual Tracking

Tracking Program MI
USE Michigan Tracking Program

Tracking System (Infants)
USE Infant Tracking System

Tracks (Environment)
CIJE: 1 RIE: 0 CAT: 20

Tractor Trailer Drivers
CIJE: 0 RIE: 1 CAT: 09

Tracy Correspondence Course
CIJE: 0 RIE: 1 CAT: 03

Trade Act 1974
CIJE: 0 RIE: 1 CAT: 14

Trade Adjustment Assistance Program
CIJE: 0 RIE: 6 CAT: 19

Trade and Develop
CIJE: 0 RIE: 1 CAT: 22

Trade Areas
CIJE: 0 RIE: 1 CAT: 16

Trade Associations
CIJE: 0 RIE: 2 CAT: 05

Trade Books
CIJE: 164 RIE: 130 CAT: 04

Trade Deficits
CIJE: 3 RIE: 1 CAT: 16

Trade Journals
CIJE: 2 RIE: 2 CAT: 16
UF Trade Magazines

Trade Magazines
USE Trade Journals

Trade Names
CIJE: 1 RIE: 0 CAT: 16

Trade Negotiations
CIJE: 1 RIE: 1 CAT: 14

Trade Off Analysis
CIJE: 2 RIE: 0 CAT: 15

Trade Off Games
CIJE: 1 RIE: 1 CAT: 15

Trade Offs (Television Series)
CIJE: 0 RIE: 1 CAT: 22

Trade Protectionism
CIJE: 4 RIE: 2 CAT: 16

Trade Readjustment Act 1974
CIJE: 0 RIE: 1 CAT: 14

Trade Routes
CIJE: 3 RIE: 1 CAT: 16

Trade Secrets
CIJE: 2 RIE: 5 CAT: 16

Trade Shows
CIJE: 1 RIE: 1 CAT: 12

Trade Union Seminar on Active Manpower Policy
CIJE: 0 RIE: 1 CAT: 02

TRADEC
CIJE: 0 RIE: 3 CAT: 19
UF Trades Education System (England)

Trademarks
CIJE: 14 RIE: 3 CAT: 14

Tradeoffs
CIJE: 0 RIE: 1 CAT: 16

Trades Education System (England)
USE TRADEC

Trades Guild of Learning
CIJE: 0 RIE: 1 CAT: 17

Trading Posts
CIJE: 4 RIE: 2 CAT: 05

Traditional Birth Attendants
CIJE: 0 RIE: 3 CAT: 10
SN See also "Midwives" and "Nurse Midwives"
UF Birth Attendants (Traditional)

Traditional Family Ideology Scale
CIJE: 1 RIE: 0 CAT: 21

Traditional Healing
CIJE: 7 RIE: 11 CAT: 11

Traditional Oral Literature
CIJE: 1 RIE: 2 CAT: 13

Traditional Orthography
CIJE: 6 RIE: 7 CAT: 13

Traditionally Underserved Persons
CIJE: 0 RIE: 3 CAT: 10

Traffic Behavior
CIJE: 0 RIE: 2 CAT: 11

Traffic Engineering
CIJE: 2 RIE: 1 CAT: 03

Traffic Engineering Technicians
CIJE: 0 RIE: 2 CAT: 09

Traffic Fatalities
CIJE: 0 RIE: 3 CAT: 16

Traffic Record Analysis
CIJE: 0 RIE: 1 CAT: 15

Traffic Violations
CIJE: 1 RIE: 2 CAT: 14

Trail Making Test (Reitan)
CIJE: 7 RIE: 0 CAT: 21

Trailer Watch Programs
CIJE: 0 RIE: 1 CAT: 19

TRAILS Project MO
CIJE: 0 RIE: 1 CAT: 19
SN Tracking Retention and Academic Integration by Learning Style

TRAILS Project OK
USE Training and Assistance Indian Library Services

Trailside School VT
CIJE: 0 RIE: 1 CAT: 17

Trained Aides as Baby Sitters Program
CIJE: 0 RIE: 1 CAT: 19

Trainee Personal Reaction Scale
CIJE: 0 RIE: 1 CAT: 21

Trainer Role
CIJE: 1 RIE: 1 CAT: 16

Training Abstracts Service
CIJE: 0 RIE: 1 CAT: 15

Training Agreements
CIJE: 1 RIE: 2 CAT: 03

Training Alliances in Health and Education
CIJE: 0 RIE: 1 CAT: 19

Training and Assistance Indian Library Services
CIJE: 0 RIE: 2 CAT: 19
UF TRAILS Project OK

Training and Employment Prerequisites Survey
CIJE: 0 RIE: 1 CAT: 19

Training and Enterprise Councils (Great Britain)
CIJE: 1 RIE: 1 CAT: 05

Training and Placement Councils
CIJE: 0 RIE: 1 CAT: 05

Training and Technology Project
CIJE: 3 RIE: 12 CAT: 19

Training and Visit System
CIJE: 0 RIE: 4 CAT: 15

Training Arithmetic Problem Solving Skills
CIJE: 0 RIE: 1 CAT: 19

Training Benefit Forecasting Method
CIJE: 0 RIE: 5 CAT: 15

Training Capacity
CIJE: 0 RIE: 1 CAT: 16

Training Center for Community Programs
CIJE: 0 RIE: 1 CAT: 17

Training Centers
CIJE: 7 RIE: 4 CAT: 05

Training Computer Exerciser
CIJE: 1 RIE: 0 CAT: 04

Training Credits (Great Britain)
CIJE: 0 RIE: 1 CAT: 16

Training Effectiveness
CIJE: 57 RIE: 15 CAT: 15

Training Effectiveness Cost Effectiveness Predict
CIJE: 1 RIE: 1 CAT: 15

Training Extension Course
CIJE: 2 RIE: 2 CAT: 03

Training Guarantee Act (Australia)
CIJE: 0 RIE: 1 CAT: 14

Training Impact Auditing
CIJE: 0 RIE: 1 CAT: 15

Training in Common
CIJE: 0 RIE: 1 CAT: 15

Training Line Simulator
CIJE: 0 RIE: 1 CAT: 04

Training Materials
CIJE: 30 RIE: 19 CAT: 04

Training Needs
CIJE: 226 RIE: 32 CAT: 16

Training of Trainers Model
CIJE: 1 RIE: 2 CAT: 15

Training Officers
CIJE: 4 RIE: 0 CAT: 09

Training Opportunities Program NY
CIJE: 0 RIE: 1 CAT: 19

Training Opportunities Scheme
CIJE: 1 RIE: 0 CAT: 15

Training Outreach Prevention School
CIJE: 0 RIE: 2 CAT: 17

Training Related Jobs
CIJE: 0 RIE: 2 CAT: 09

Training Research Assistance Cooperative Ext Serv
CIJE: 0 RIE: 1 CAT: 17

Training Research Development Station
CIJE: 0 RIE: 1 CAT: 17

Training School for Boys NJ
CIJE: 1 RIE: 0 CAT: 17

Training Sponsors
CIJE: 2 RIE: 1 CAT: 09

Training Stations
CIJE: 0 RIE: 1 CAT: 05

Training Support System
CIJE: 1 RIE: 1 CAT: 15

Training Teacher Trainers Project
CIJE: 1 RIE: 29 CAT: 19

TRAINVICE Models
CIJE: 0 RIE: 1 CAT: 15

Trait Anxiety
CIJE: 11 RIE: 7 CAT: 21

Trait Ascription Questionnaire (Graham)
CIJE: 0 RIE: 1 CAT: 21

Trait Emotions
CIJE: 0 RIE: 1 CAT: 11

Trait Factor Approach
CIJE: 4 RIE: 3 CAT: 15

Trait Indecisiveness Scale
CIJE: 0 RIE: 1 CAT: 21

Trait State Model
CIJE: 0 RIE: 1 CAT: 15
SN A framework for understanding adult literacy

Trakl (Georg)
CIJE: 1 RIE: 0 CAT: 18

Tramp Dog
CIJE: 0 RIE: 1 CAT: 22

Trampolines
CIJE: 11 RIE: 1 CAT: 04

Trans European Mobility Scheme for Univ Studies
USE TEMPUS

Trans World Airlines
CIJE: 0 RIE: 1 CAT: 17
SN See also "TWA..."

Trans World Airlines v Hardison
CIJE: 1 RIE: 0 CAT: 14

Transaction Accounting System
CIJE: 1 RIE: 0 CAT: 15

Transaction Log Analysis
CIJE: 32 RIE: 4 CAT: 15

Transaction Shells
CIJE: 2 RIE: 1 CAT: 16

Transactional Analysis in Accounting
CIJE: 0 RIE: 2 CAT: 15

Transactional Criticism
CIJE: 3 RIE: 4 CAT: 16

Transactional Curriculum
CIJE: 9 RIE: 0 CAT: 03

Transactional Data Systems
CIJE: 0 RIE: 1 CAT: 04

Transactional Evaluation
CIJE: 7 RIE: 5 CAT: 16

Transactional Self
CIJE: 0 RIE: 1 CAT: 15

Transactional Strategies Instruction
CIJE: 0 RIE: 1 CAT: 15

Transactional Teaching Style
CIJE: 1 RIE: 3 CAT: 15

Transactional Theory
CIJE: 9 RIE: 6 CAT: 15

Transactional Writing
CIJE: 3 RIE: 2 CAT: 16

Transactive Communication
CIJE: 2 RIE: 2 CAT: 15

Transactive Theory
CIJE: 0 RIE: 1 CAT: 15

Transaxles (Automotive)
CIJE: 0 RIE: 1 CAT: 04
UF Automotive Transaxles

Transborder Data Flow
USE Transborder Information Flow

Transborder Information Flow
CIJE: 12 RIE: 11 CAT: 16
UF Transborder Data Flow

Transcendence
CIJE: 12 RIE: 3 CAT: 15

Transcendent Communication
CIJE: 0 RIE: 1 CAT: 16

Transcendentalism
CIJE: 9 RIE: 10 CAT: 15

Transcription
CIJE: 22 RIE: 30 CAT: 16

Transcription Method
CIJE: 9 RIE: 5 CAT: 13

Transcription Services
CIJE: 0 RIE: 1 CAT: 16

Transcutaneous Electrical Nerve Stimulation
CIJE: 0 RIE: 1 CAT: 11

Transdermal Electrostimulation
CIJE: 1 RIE: 0 CAT: 11

Transdisciplinary Approach
CIJE: 7 RIE: 8 CAT: 15

Transducers
CIJE: 11 RIE: 5 CAT: 20

Transductive Theory
CIJE: 0 RIE: 1 CAT: 20

Transect Studies
CIJE: 0 RIE: 1 CAT: 15

Transescents
CIJE: 5 RIE: 8 CAT: 16

Transfer (Art Technique)
CIJE: 1 RIE: 0 CAT: 15

Transfer Alliance Program CA
CIJE: 0 RIE: 2 CAT: 19

Transfer Centers
CIJE: 0 RIE: 5 CAT: 05

Transfer Effect
CIJE: 2 RIE: 1 CAT: 15

Transfer Index
CIJE: 1 RIE: 2 CAT: 15

Transfer Officers
CIJE: 0 RIE: 2 CAT: 10

Transfer Payments
CIJE: 4 RIE: 6 CAT: 16

Transfer Rates (College)
CIJE: 5 RIE: 32 CAT: 16
UF College Transfer Rates

Transfer Shock
CIJE: 2 RIE: 4 CAT: 16

Transfer Studies
CIJE: 4 RIE: 3 CAT: 15

Transfer Tracking System
CIJE: 0 RIE: 1 CAT: 19

Transference
CIJE: 28 RIE: 8 CAT: 11

Transferred Epithets
CIJE: 0 RIE: 1 CAT: 13

Transformation Theory (Adult Learning)
CIJE: 1 RIE: 1 CAT: 15
SN Presented in the book "Transformative Dimensions of Adult Learning" (1991) by Jack Mezirow

Transformational Curriculum
CIJE: 0 RIE: 1 CAT: 03

Transformational Geometry
CIJE: 4 RIE: 2 CAT: 20

Transformational Leadership
CIJE: 22 RIE: 15 CAT: 15

Transformational Phonology
CIJE: 1 RIE: 0 CAT: 13

Transformational Stylistics
CIJE: 1 RIE: 0 CAT: 13

Transformative Curriculum
CIJE: 1 RIE: 0 CAT: 03

Transformative Education
CIJE: 1 RIE: 1 CAT: 16

Transformative Leadership
CIJE: 2 RIE: 0 CAT: 15

Transformative Learning
CIJE: 3 RIE: 1 CAT: 11

Transformative Research
CIJE: 6 RIE: 0 CAT: 15

Transformers
CIJE: 2 RIE: 4 CAT: 04

Transgression Behavior
CIJE: 11 RIE: 3 CAT: 11

Transients
CIJE: 0 RIE: 1 CAT: 10

Transition Assistance Program (Veterans)
CIJE: 1 RIE: 2 CAT: 19

Transition Institute IL
CIJE: 0 RIE: 2 CAT: 17

Transition into Electronics Project
CIJE: 0 RIE: 1 CAT: 19

Transition Management
CIJE: 5 RIE: 4 CAT: 15

Transition Metals
CIJE: 2 RIE: 0 CAT: 20

Transition Observation Instrument
CIJE: 0 RIE: 1 CAT: 21

TRANSITION Program
CIJE: 0 RIE: 2 CAT: 19

Transition Program for Refugee Children
CIJE: 0 RIE: 1 CAT: 19

Transition Rates
CIJE: 3 RIE: 1 CAT: 16

Transition Through the Arts
CIJE: 0 RIE: 1 CAT: 19
SN Project of "Very Special Arts" (q.v.)

Transition Time
CIJE: 10 RIE: 19 CAT: 16

Transition to Work Simulation
CIJE: 0 RIE: 1 CAT: 15

Transitional Activities
CIJE: 17 RIE: 13 CAT: 03

Transitional Bilingual Basic Skills Program FL
CIJE: 0 RIE: 0 CAT: 19

Transitional Bilingual Education
CIJE: 8 RIE: 5 CAT: 03

Transitional Bilingual Education Programs
CIJE: 11 RIE: 31 CAT: 19

Transitional Black Womens Project GA
CIJE: 0 RIE: 4 CAT: 19

Transitional Child Care
CIJE: 0 RIE: 1 CAT: 19
SN Program designed to help families meet their child care needs for 1 year after they lose federal or state financial assistance for income-related reasons

Transitional Employment
CIJE: 3 RIE: 1 CAT: 16

Transitional Intervention Project NY
USE Project TIP NY

Transitional Program for Refugee Children NY
CIJE: 0 RIE: 1 CAT: 19

Transitional Resource Addressing Early Education
CIJE: 0 RIE: 1 CAT: 19

Transitional Service Centers
CIJE: 1 RIE: 2 CAT: 05

Transitional Services Coordination Act (Maine)
CIJE: 0 RIE: 1 CAT: 14

Transitive Inferences
CIJE: 6 RIE: 8 CAT: 13

Transitivity
CIJE: 17 RIE: 14 CAT: 13

Transitivity of Weight
CIJE: 2 RIE: 0 CAT: 20

Transivity
CIJE: 3 RIE: 0 CAT: 11

Transkei
CIJE: 3 RIE: 1 CAT: 07

Translating Research Into Practice TN
CIJE: 0 RIE: 1 CAT: 19
SN Program of Knox County Schools
UF TRIP Program TN

Translators Association of the Philippines
CIJE: 0 RIE: 1 CAT: 17

Transliteration
CIJE: 9 RIE: 10 CAT: 13

Transmissions (Automotive)
CIJE: 0 RIE: 10 CAT: 04
UF Automotive Transmissions

Transmitters
CIJE: 1 RIE: 1 CAT: 04

Transmountain Far West Regional Reading Conference
CIJE: 0 RIE: 1 CAT: 02

Transnational Corporations
CIJE: 2 RIE: 7 CAT: 05

Transparency Theory
CIJE: 0 RIE: 1 CAT: 15

Transparent Models
CIJE: 2 RIE: 0 CAT: 15

Transparent Stimulation
CIJE: 0 RIE: 1 CAT: 15

Transpersonal Psychology
CIJE: 24 RIE: 6 CAT: 11

Transport Aircraft
CIJE: 0 RIE: 1 CAT: 20

Transport Coefficients
USE Transport Phenomena

Transport Phenomena
CIJE: 2 RIE: 0 CAT: 20
UF Transport Coefficients

Transportability
CIJE: 2 RIE: 3 CAT: 15

Transportation Act 1970
CIJE: 1 RIE: 0 CAT: 14

Transportation Education
CIJE: 2 RIE: 5 CAT: 03

Transportation Engineering
CIJE: 0 RIE: 1 CAT: 20

Transportation Information Planning Service
CIJE: 0 RIE: 1 CAT: 15

Transportation Models
CIJE: 1 RIE: 3 CAT: 15

Transportation Supervisors
CIJE: 1 RIE: 1 CAT: 16

Transpose Factor Analysis
CIJE: 1 RIE: 0 CAT: 15

Transposer
CIJE: 1 RIE: 0 CAT: 09

Transposition
CIJE: 10 RIE: 0 CAT: 16

Transracial Communication
CIJE: 0 RIE: 1 CAT: 13
UF Interracial Communication

Transsexuals
CIJE: 3 RIE: 4 CAT: 11

Transverse Patterning
CIJE: 1 RIE: 0 CAT: 15

Transylvania
CIJE: 0 RIE: 2 CAT: 07

Transylvania College KY
CIJE: 0 RIE: 2 CAT: 17

Transylvania University KY
CIJE: 1 RIE: 1 CAT: 17

Trantz (Robert)
CIJE: 0 RIE: 1 CAT: 18

Trap Setting (Psycholinguistics)
CIJE: 0 RIE: 0 CAT: 13

Trapping
CIJE: 2 RIE: 6 CAT: 16

Traps (Animals)
USE Animal Traps

Trapshooting
CIJE: 1 RIE: 0 CAT: 16

Trash Compactors
CIJE: 2 RIE: 0 CAT: 04

Traubel (Horace L)
CIJE: 0 RIE: 1 CAT: 18

Traumas
CIJE: 20 RIE: 15 CAT: 11

Travel Agents
CIJE: 0 RIE: 5 CAT: 09

Travel Industry
CIJE: 3 RIE: 5 CAT: 05

Travelers Insurance
CIJE: 0 RIE: 2 CAT: 17

Travers (Robert)
CIJE: 0 RIE: 1 CAT: 18

Travis Unified School District CA
CIJE: 0 RIE: 1 CAT: 17

Treasure Island
CIJE: 2 RIE: 0 CAT: 22

Treasure Valley Community College OR
CIJE: 0 RIE: 1 CAT: 17

Treatment Alternatives Project
CIJE: 1 RIE: 0 CAT: 19

Treatment Interaction Analysis
CIJE: 4 RIE: 1 CAT: 15

Treatment Verification
CIJE: 1 RIE: 1 CAT: 15

Treaty of Dancing Rabbit Creek
CIJE: 0 RIE: 2 CAT: 12

Treaty of Doaks Stand
CIJE: 0 RIE: 1 CAT: 12

Treaty of Ghent
CIJE: 1 RIE: 0 CAT: 14

Treaty of Waitangi (New Zealand)
CIJE: 0 RIE: 1 CAT: 12
UF Waitangi (Treaty of)

Treaty of Washington City
CIJE: 0 RIE: 1 CAT: 12

Treaty with Navajo Indians 1868
CIJE: 0 RIE: 1 CAT: 12
UF Navajo Treaty 1868

Tree Adjoining Grammar
CIJE: 0 RIE: 1 CAT: 13

Tree City USA
CIJE: 0 RIE: 1 CAT: 19

Tree Climbing
CIJE: 1 RIE: 1 CAT: 16
UF Climbing Trees

Tree Drawing Test
CIJE: 0 RIE: 1 CAT: 21

Tree Identification
CIJE: 2 RIE: 2 CAT: 20

TREET Programming System
CIJE: 0 RIE: 2 CAT: 15

Trempealeau County Kellogg Project
CIJE: 0 RIE: 2 CAT: 19

Trend Line Cost Control Method
CIJE: 1 RIE: 0 CAT: 15

Trend of Reading Standards
CIJE: 1 RIE: 0 CAT: 15

Trent Biotic Index
CIJE: 1 RIE: 0 CAT: 20

Trent Polytechnic (England)
CIJE: 1 RIE: 0 CAT: 17

Trent Valley Center
CIJE: 0 RIE: 1 CAT: 17

Trenton High School MO
CIJE: 0 RIE: 2 CAT: 17

Trenton Public Schools NJ
CIJE: 1 RIE: 9 CAT: 17

Trenton State College NJ
CIJE: 11 RIE: 10 CAT: 17

Tressall (Robert)
CIJE: 0 RIE: 1 CAT: 18

Trevelyan Bill
CIJE: 1 RIE: 0 CAT: 14

Tri College University Libraries ND
CIJE: 0 RIE: 1 CAT: 17

Tri County Course Goal Project
CIJE: 0 RIE: 2 CAT: 19

Tri County Regional Library
CIJE: 1 RIE: 0 CAT: 17

Tri County Technical College SC
CIJE: 0 RIE: 2 CAT: 17

Tri County Technical Institute OH
CIJE: 1 RIE: 0 CAT: 17

Tri Cultural Attitude Scale
CIJE: 0 RIE: 1 CAT: 21

Tri Offer Final Offer Arbitration
CIJE: 1 RIE: 0 CAT: 14

Tri Partite Power Theory
CIJE: 0 RIE: 1 CAT: 15

Tri State Parenting Collaborative
CIJE: 0 RIE: 2 CAT: 17

Tri University Project
CIJE: 0 RIE: 5 CAT: 19

TRIAD Teacher Center IN
CIJE: 0 RIE: 1 CAT: 17

Triadic Interaction Analysis
CIJE: 13 RIE: 1 CAT: 15

Triage Health Care Delivery System
CIJE: 1 RIE: 1 CAT: 11

Trial of Last Error
CIJE: 0 RIE: 1 CAT: 22

Trial State Assessment (NAEP)
CIJE: 2 RIE: 66 CAT: 21

Trials
CIJE: 20 RIE: 8 CAT: 14

Trials to Criterion Testing
CIJE: 0 RIE: 1 CAT: 21

Triandis Behavioral Differential
CIJE: 0 RIE: 1 CAT: 21

Triangle Approach
CIJE: 2 RIE: 0 CAT: 15

Triangle Coalition for Sci and Techn Educ
CIJE: 0 RIE: 1 CAT: 17

Triangle Universities Computation Center
CIJE: 0 RIE: 1 CAT: 17

Triangles
CIJE: 43 RIE: 8 CAT: 20

Triangular Constant Method
CIJE: 1 RIE: 0 CAT: 21

Triangular Grid
CIJE: 1 RIE: 0 CAT: 20

Triangulation in Family
USE Family Triangles

Triangulation Interview Form
CIJE: 1 RIE: 0 CAT: 21

Triarchic Theory of Intelligence (Sternberg)
CIJE: 0 RIE: 3 CAT: 15
SN See also "Sternberg Triarchic Abilities Test"

Tribal Aging Programs
CIJE: 0 RIE: 1 CAT: 19

Tribal American Children Center Schools
CIJE: 1 RIE: 0 CAT: 17

Tribal Citizenship
CIJE: 0 RIE: 2 CAT: 16

Tribal Councils
CIJE: 0 RIE: 4 CAT: 08

Tribal Courts
CIJE: 2 RIE: 4 CAT: 14

Tribal Jurisdiction
CIJE: 1 RIE: 3 CAT: 14

Tribal Law
CIJE: 1 RIE: 6 CAT: 14

Tribal Management
CIJE: 2 RIE: 7 CAT: 16

Tribal Normal School (Iran)
CIJE: 1 RIE: 0 CAT: 17

Tribal Officials
CIJE: 0 RIE: 2 CAT: 10

Tribal Status
CIJE: 1 RIE: 2 CAT: 16

Tribally Controlled Comm Coll Assist Act 1978
CIJE: 2 RIE: 9 CAT: 14
UF Public Law 95 471

Tribes Approach
CIJE: 0 RIE: 0 CAT: 15

Tribology
CIJE: 1 RIE: 1 CAT: 20

Tribune Publishing Co v Curators Univ of Missouri
CIJE: 0 RIE: 1 CAT: 14

Tricameral Board
CIJE: 1 RIE: 0 CAT: 17

Trichotillomania
USE Hair Pulling

Trickling Filters
CIJE: 0 RIE: 8 CAT: 20

Tricksters (Folk Culture)
CIJE: 5 RIE: 1 CAT: 16

Tricyclic Antidepressants
CIJE: 2 RIE: 1 CAT: 11

Tridimensional Filming
CIJE: 2 RIE: 0 CAT: 20

Trigg (Roger)
CIJE: 0 RIE: 1 CAT: 18

Trigger Approach
CIJE: 1 RIE: 0 CAT: 15

Trigger Films
CIJE: 2 RIE: 1 CAT: 16

Triglycine Sulfate
CIJE: 1 RIE: 0 CAT: 20

Trigram Analysis
CIJE: 3 RIE: 0 CAT: 15

TRIIC Curriculum
CIJE: 0 RIE: 1 CAT: 03

Trimboli v Board of Education of County of Wayne
CIJE: 0 RIE: 1 CAT: 14

Trimethylammonium
CIJE: 1 RIE: 0 CAT: 20

Trimmers
CIJE: 0 RIE: 1 CAT: 09

Trimodal Programed Instruction
CIJE: 1 RIE: 0 CAT: 15

Trine Project
CIJE: 0 RIE: 1 CAT: 19

Trinidad and Tobago
CIJE: 36 RIE: 35 CAT: 07

Trinity Area School District PA
CIJE: 1 RIE: 0 CAT: 17

Trinity Christian College IL
CIJE: 0 RIE: 1 CAT: 17

Trinity College (Ireland)
CIJE: 7 RIE: 3 CAT: 17

Trinity College CT
CIJE: 3 RIE: 0 CAT: 17

Trinity College VT
CIJE: 0 RIE: 1 CAT: 17

Trinity University TX
CIJE: 8 RIE: 16 CAT: 17

TRIO Programs
CIJE: 1 RIE: 15 CAT: 19

Trip Planning
CIJE: 3 RIE: 1 CAT: 16

TRIP Program TN
USE Translating Research Into Practice TN

TRIP Project IL
USE The Research Instruments Project

Trip to Bountiful
CIJE: 0 RIE: 1 CAT: 22

Triple Jump
CIJE: 1 RIE: 1 CAT: 16

Triple Mode Test of Categorization (Silverman)
CIJE: 0 RIE: 1 CAT: 21

Triplets
CIJE: 2 RIE: 1 CAT: 10

TRIS
CIJE: 1 RIE: 0 CAT: 20

Trismus Pseudocamptodactyly Syndrome
CIJE: 1 RIE: 0 CAT: 11

Trisomy 18 Syndrome
CIJE: 1 RIE: 0 CAT: 11

Tristan (Flora)
CIJE: 1 RIE: 0 CAT: 18

Triton College IL
CIJE: 11 RIE: 13 CAT: 17

Triumph of the Will
CIJE: 2 RIE: 1 CAT: 22

Triune Brain
CIJE: 6 RIE: 3 CAT: 11

TRIVET Program
CIJE: 0 RIE: 5 CAT: 19
SN TRIVET = Techniques of Responsive Intervention to Validate Effective Teaching

Trivial Pursuit
CIJE: 2 RIE: 3 CAT: 16

Trivialization
CIJE: 0 RIE: 1 CAT: 16

Troop Schools
CIJE: 0 RIE: 1 CAT: 05

Tropical Forests
CIJE: 0 RIE: 1 CAT: 20
SN The green band of land between the tropics of Capricorn and Cancer, including forests variously labeled evergreen (rain), moist, deciduous, and open dry woodlands

Tropical Medicine
CIJE: 1 RIE: 0 CAT: 11

Tropical Rain Forests
CIJE: 25 RIE: 9 CAT: 20
SN See also "Deforestation"
UF Rainforests

Tropics
CIJE: 5 RIE: 8 CAT: 20

Troposphere
CIJE: 2 RIE: 0 CAT: 20

Trouble Shooting Checklist
CIJE: 2 RIE: 4 CAT: 16

Troutner (Leroy F)
CIJE: 1 RIE: 0 CAT: 18

Trow (Martin A)
CIJE: 0 RIE: 1 CAT: 18

Trowbridge House OH
CIJE: 0 RIE: 1 CAT: 17

Troy City School District NY
CIJE: 1 RIE: 0 CAT: 17

Troy State University AL
CIJE: 0 RIE: 6 CAT: 17

Troy State University AL Montgomery
CIJE: 0 RIE: 1 CAT: 17

TRS 80
CIJE: 8 RIE: 12 CAT: 04

TRS 80 Color Computer
CIJE: 1 RIE: 0 CAT: 04

TRS 80 Model I
CIJE: 0 RIE: 3 CAT: 04

TRS 80 Model III
CIJE: 1 RIE: 4 CAT: 04

Trubetzkoy (N S)
CIJE: 1 RIE: 0 CAT: 18

Truck Drivers
CIJE: 5 RIE: 24 CAT: 09

Truck Farming
CIJE: 1 RIE: 0 CAT: 09

Truckee Meadows Community College NV
CIJE: 1 RIE: 3 CAT: 17

Trucking Industry
CIJE: 3 RIE: 5 CAT: 05

Trucks
CIJE: 1 RIE: 7 CAT: 04

Trudeau (Garry)
CIJE: 0 RIE: 1 CAT: 18

Trudeau (Pierre Elliott)
CIJE: 2 RIE: 1 CAT: 18

True Grit
CIJE: 1 RIE: 0 CAT: 22

True Point Dimensioning System
CIJE: 1 RIE: 0 CAT: 15

Trueswells 80 20 Rule
CIJE: 2 RIE: 0 CAT: 15

Truffaut (Francois)
CIJE: 3 RIE: 1 CAT: 18

Truman (Bess)
CIJE: 0 RIE: 1 CAT: 18

Truman (Harry S)
CIJE: 9 RIE: 2 CAT: 18

Truman College IL
USE City Colleges of Chicago IL Truman College

Trump (J Lloyd)
CIJE: 0 RIE: 2 CAT: 18

Trump Plan
CIJE: 1 RIE: 2 CAT: 15

Trumpet Model
CIJE: 0 RIE: 1 CAT: 15

Truncated Data Distributions
USE Data Truncation

Truncated Octahedron
CIJE: 1 RIE: 0 CAT: 20

Truncation (Information Retrieval)
CIJE: 2 RIE: 0 CAT: 15

Trust Agreements CA
CIJE: 0 RIE: 0 CAT: 19

Trustee Recruitment
CIJE: 1 RIE: 2 CAT: 16

Trustee Responsibility
CIJE: 0 RIE: 5 CAT: 16

Trustee Role
CIJE: 7 RIE: 8 CAT: 16

Trustee Selection
CIJE: 2 RIE: 4 CAT: 16

Trustees of Dartmouth College v Woodward
CIJE: 1 RIE: 1 CAT: 14
UF Dartmouth College Case

Truth
CIJE: 35 RIE: 15 CAT: 16

Truth (Sojourner)
CIJE: 3 RIE: 6 CAT: 18

Truth in Leasing
CIJE: 0 RIE: 1 CAT: 14

Truth in Lending
CIJE: 1 RIE: 2 CAT: 14

Truth in Testing
CIJE: 12 RIE: 6 CAT: 21

Truth in Testing Act 1979
CIJE: 2 RIE: 4 CAT: 14

Truth in Testing Legislation
CIJE: 3 RIE: 11 CAT: 14

Truth Love Change Model
CIJE: 1 RIE: 0 CAT: 15

Truth Maintenance Systems
CIJE: 0 RIE: 1 CAT: 15

Truth Tables
CIJE: 7 RIE: 0 CAT: 15

Try Foundation
CIJE: 0 RIE: 1 CAT: 17

Tryon (R C)
CIJE: 1 RIE: 0 CAT: 18

Tryon Cluster Analysis Method
CIJE: 0 RIE: 1 CAT: 15

TS 352 A U Multimeter
CIJE: 0 RIE: 1 CAT: 04

Tsetsauts (Tribe)
CIJE: 0 RIE: 1 CAT: 08

Tsimshian
CIJE: 0 RIE: 0 CAT: 13
SN A Penutian language

Tsimshian (Coast)
CIJE: 2 RIE: 2 CAT: 13

Tsimshian (Southern)
CIJE: 1 RIE: 0 CAT: 13

Tsimshian (Tribe)
CIJE: 0 RIE: 5 CAT: 08

Tsiolkovsky (Konstantin)
CIJE: 1 RIE: 0 CAT: 18

Tsonga
CIJE: 0 RIE: 1 CAT: 13

Tsou
CIJE: 0 RIE: 1 CAT: 13

TSS Software
USE The School System (Columbia Computing Services)

Tsunami Warnings
CIJE: 1 RIE: 1 CAT: 20

Tswana
CIJE: 0 RIE: 1 CAT: 13

Tuba City Boarding School AZ
CIJE: 2 RIE: 1 CAT: 17

Tuba City Elementary School AZ
CIJE: 0 RIE: 1 CAT: 17

Tube Feeding
CIJE: 0 RIE: 2 CAT: 11

Tuberculosis
CIJE: 14 RIE: 3 CAT: 11

Tubman (Harriet)
CIJE: 2 RIE: 1 CAT: 18

Tubutama Mission Church
CIJE: 1 RIE: 0 CAT: 17

Tucano
CIJE: 1 RIE: 2 CAT: 13
SN An Eastern Tucanoan language of Colombia and Brazil

Tucker Common Item Equating Method
CIJE: 12 RIE: 5 CAT: 15

Tuckman Teacher Feedback Form
CIJE: 4 RIE: 3 CAT: 15

Tucson Early Education Model
CIJE: 1 RIE: 22 CAT: 15

Tucson Medical Center
CIJE: 1 RIE: 0 CAT: 17

Tucson Public Library AZ
CIJE: 1 RIE: 0 CAT: 17

Tucson Public Schools AZ
CIJE: 4 RIE: 9 CAT: 17

Tudor (Tasha)
CIJE: 1 RIE: 0 CAT: 18

Tudor Period
CIJE: 6 RIE: 1 CAT: 12

Tuesday Released Time Program
CIJE: 0 RIE: 1 CAT: 19

Tufts (John)
CIJE: 2 RIE: 0 CAT: 18

Tufts University MA
CIJE: 22 RIE: 19 CAT: 17

Tuition Assistance Program NY
CIJE: 2 RIE: 14 CAT: 19

Tuition Benefit Programs
CIJE: 5 RIE: 54 CAT: 19
UF Employee Education Benefits; Employer Tuition Aid

Tuition Deposits
CIJE: 1 RIE: 1 CAT: 16

Tuition Fees and Academic Calendar Survey
CIJE: 0 RIE: 2 CAT: 22

Tuition Formulas
CIJE: 0 RIE: 1 CAT: 16

Tuition Futures
CIJE: 1 RIE: 1 CAT: 16

Tuition Guarantee Programs
CIJE: 0 RIE: 1 CAT: 19
UF Guaranteed Tuition Plans

Tuition Investment Programs
CIJE: 0 RIE: 3 CAT: 19

Tuition Prepayment
CIJE: 12 RIE: 6 CAT: 16
SN See also "Prepayment Plans"
UF Prepaid Tuition; Prepayment (Tuition)

Tuition Reciprocity
CIJE: 0 RIE: 4 CAT: 16

Tuition Reimbursement
CIJE: 1 RIE: 4 CAT: 16

Tuition Savings Plans
CIJE: 6 RIE: 5 CAT: 16

Tuition Tax Credits Legislation
CIJE: 1 RIE: 2 CAT: 14

Tuition Waivers
CIJE: 2 RIE: 10 CAT: 16

Tukey (John)
CIJE: 0 RIE: 1 CAT: 18

Tukey Statistic
CIJE: 4 RIE: 3 CAT: 15

Tukeys Test
CIJE: 2 RIE: 5 CAT: 21

Tulane Nutrition Study
CIJE: 0 RIE: 1 CAT: 19

Tulane University LA
CIJE: 12 RIE: 6 CAT: 17

Tularecito
CIJE: 0 RIE: 1 CAT: 22

Tully (Joan)
CIJE: 1 RIE: 0 CAT: 18

Tuloso Midway Independent School District TX
CIJE: 0 RIE: 2 CAT: 17

Tulsa City County Library System OK
CIJE: 1 RIE: 1 CAT: 17

Tulsa Junior College OK
CIJE: 6 RIE: 2 CAT: 17

Tulsa Public Schools OK
CIJE: 7 RIE: 7 CAT: 17

Tulsa Technology Center OK
CIJE: 0 RIE: 1 CAT: 17

Tumbuka
CIJE: 0 RIE: 1 CAT: 13

Tumor Registrars
CIJE: 0 RIE: 5 CAT: 11

Tundra
CIJE: 1 RIE: 1 CAT: 20

Tune Beyond Us
CIJE: 1 RIE: 0 CAT: 22

Tunebo
CIJE: 0 RIE: 1 CAT: 13
SN Language of Colombia's Eastern Andes

Tungsten Inert Gas Welding
CIJE: 0 RIE: 2 CAT: 20

Tungus
CIJE: 0 RIE: 1 CAT: 13

Tunica (Tribe)
CIJE: 0 RIE: 1 CAT: 08

Tunis (John)
CIJE: 1 RIE: 0 CAT: 18

Tunisia
CIJE: 28 RIE: 63 CAT: 07

Tunisians
CIJE: 3 RIE: 0 CAT: 08

Tunnel Vision
CIJE: 1 RIE: 0 CAT: 15

Tuomela (Raimo)
CIJE: 0 RIE: 0 CAT: 18

Tupelo Public Schools MS
CIJE: 3 RIE: 1 CAT: 17

Tupi Guarani Language Family
CIJE: 1 RIE: 0 CAT: 13

Turbidity
CIJE: 0 RIE: 2 CAT: 20

Turbines
CIJE: 0 RIE: 2 CAT: 04

Turboprop Engines
CIJE: 0 RIE: 2 CAT: 04

TurboScan
CIJE: 0 RIE: 1 CAT: 04

Turgenev (Ivan)
CIJE: 2 RIE: 0 CAT: 18

Turing Machines
CIJE: 3 RIE: 1 CAT: 04

Turkey
CIJE: 104 RIE: 139 CAT: 07

Turkey (Ankara)
CIJE: 1 RIE: 5 CAT: 07

Turkey (Dinar)
CIJE: 0 RIE: 1 CAT: 07

Turkey (Gallipoli)
CIJE: 0 RIE: 1 CAT: 07

Turkey (Istanbul)
CIJE: 5 RIE: 1 CAT: 07

Turkeys
CIJE: 0 RIE: 1 CAT: 20

Turki
CIJE: 0 RIE: 1 CAT: 13

Turkish (Modern)
CIJE: 1 RIE: 3 CAT: 13

Turkish (Ottoman)
CIJE: 0 RIE: 1 CAT: 13

Turkish People
USE Turks

Turkistan
CIJE: 0 RIE: 2 CAT: 07

Turkmen
CIJE: 0 RIE: 5 CAT: 13
UF Turkoman

Turkmenistan
CIJE: 0 RIE: 1 CAT: 07

Turkoman
USE Turkmen

Turks
CIJE: 9 RIE: 7 CAT: 08
UF Turkish People

Turn Around Program
CIJE: 0 RIE: 1 CAT: 19

Turn Taking
CIJE: 44 RIE: 25 CAT: 16

Turnaround Time
CIJE: 7 RIE: 5 CAT: 16

Turnarounds (Debate)
CIJE: 0 RIE: 1 CAT: 16

Turner (Darwin T)
CIJE: 0 RIE: 1 CAT: 18

Turner (Frederick Jackson)
CIJE: 8 RIE: 0 CAT: 18

Turner (Joseph M W)
CIJE: 2 RIE: 0 CAT: 18

Turners Syndrome
CIJE: 7 RIE: 1 CAT: 11

Turning Point Program
CIJE: 0 RIE: 3 CAT: 19

Turnkey Systems (Instruction)
CIJE: 4 RIE: 0 CAT: 04

Turnkey Training Safety Program NY
CIJE: 0 RIE: 1 CAT: 19

Turnstile Program CA
CIJE: 0 RIE: 1 CAT: 19

Turntaking (Instructional)
CIJE: 3 RIE: 1 CAT: 15

Turtle Geometry
USE Turtle Graphics

Turtle Graphics
CIJE: 16 RIE: 7 CAT: 04
UF Turtle Geometry

Turtles
CIJE: 10 RIE: 10 CAT: 20

Turtleworks (Computer Program)
CIJE: 0 RIE: 2 CAT: 04

Tuscaloosa County Board of Education AL
CIJE: 0 RIE: 1 CAT: 17

Tuscarora (Tribe)
CIJE: 1 RIE: 2 CAT: 08

Tuscarora Confederacy
CIJE: 1 RIE: 0 CAT: 17

Tuscola High School IL
CIJE: 1 RIE: 0 CAT: 17

Tuskegee Area Study
CIJE: 0 RIE: 1 CAT: 19

Tuskegee Institute AL
CIJE: 11 RIE: 26 CAT: 17

Tussman (Joseph)
CIJE: 0 RIE: 2 CAT: 18

Tutchone
CIJE: 0 RIE: 1 CAT: 13
SN An Athapascan-Eyak language

Tutelo
CIJE: 0 RIE: 2 CAT: 13
SN A Siouan language (extinct)

Tutor (Computer Program)
CIJE: 2 RIE: 12 CAT: 04

TUTOR Programing Language
CIJE: 0 RIE: 9 CAT: 04

Tutor Role
CIJE: 12 RIE: 19 CAT: 16

Tutor Self Assessment Inventory (Brown)
CIJE: 0 RIE: 1 CAT: 21

Tutor Teacher Relationship
CIJE: 2 RIE: 3 CAT: 11

Tutor Training
CIJE: 13 RIE: 12 CAT: 15

Tutored Video Instruction
CIJE: 1 RIE: 3 CAT: 15

Tutorfilm
CIJE: 0 RIE: 1 CAT: 04

Tutorial Advancement Program
CIJE: 1 RIE: 0 CAT: 19

Tutorial Assistance Program CA
CIJE: 0 RIE: 1 CAT: 19

Tutorial Mode
CIJE: 19 RIE: 18 CAT: 15

Tutorial Outreach Program NY
CIJE: 1 RIE: 0 CAT: 19

Tutoring Adults through Literacy Councils
CIJE: 0 RIE: 0 CAT: 19
UF TALC Program

Tutoring Attitude Questionnaire
CIJE: 1 RIE: 0 CAT: 21

Tutortext
CIJE: 0 RIE: 1 CAT: 04

Tutsi
CIJE: 1 RIE: 0 CAT: 08

Tuva
USE Tuvan

Tuvalu
CIJE: 1 RIE: 2 CAT: 07
SN Formerly the Ellice Islands (1978) — see also "Gilbert and Ellice Islands"

Tuvaluan
CIJE: 0 RIE: 1 CAT: 13
SN Polynesian language of the Gilbert and Ellice Islands

Tuvan
CIJE: 0 RIE: 1 CAT: 13
SN Turkic language of south central Soviet Russia
UF Tuva; Tuvinian

Tuvinian
USE Tuvan

TV Guide
CIJE: 3 RIE: 1 CAT: 22

TV Interactive Toys
CIJE: 0 RIE: 1 CAT: 04

TV Phone
CIJE: 0 RIE: 1 CAT: 04

TVEI Schemes
USE Technical and Vocational Education Initiative

TVOntario
CIJE: 2 RIE: 14 CAT: 17

TVOntario Academy
CIJE: 0 RIE: 1 CAT: 17

TWA Hijacking Incident (1985)
USE TWA Hostage Crisis

TWA Hostage Crisis
CIJE: 3 RIE: 1 CAT: 12
UF TWA Hijacking Incident (1985)

Twain (Mark)
CIJE: 20 RIE: 21 CAT: 18

Twelfth Century
CIJE: 0 RIE: 1 CAT: 12

Twelfth Street School Project
CIJE: 0 RIE: 1 CAT: 19

Twelve Angry Men
CIJE: 0 RIE: 2 CAT: 22

Twelve Minute Run
CIJE: 1 RIE: 0 CAT: 16

Twelve Step Programs
USE 12 Step Programs

Twente University of Technology (Netherlands)
CIJE: 3 RIE: 4 CAT: 17

Twentieth Century
CIJE: 63 RIE: 31 CAT: 12

Twentieth Century Fund
CIJE: 2 RIE: 4 CAT: 17

Twentieth Century Fund Task Force
CIJE: 1 RIE: 1 CAT: 17

Twentieth Century History
CIJE: 20 RIE: 11 CAT: 12

Twenty First Century
CIJE: 22 RIE: 10 CAT: 12

Twenty Statements Test (Kuhn)
CIJE: 4 RIE: 2 CAT: 21

Twi
CIJE: 0 RIE: 4 CAT: 13

Twice Retained Program NJ
CIJE: 0 RIE: 1 CAT: 19

Twin City Institute for Talented Youth MN
CIJE: 1 RIE: 3 CAT: 17

Twin Lakes School Corporation IN
CIJE: 0 RIE: 0 CAT: 17

Twin Speech
USE Idioglossia

Twin Tech PA
CIJE: 1 RIE: 0 CAT: 17

Twin Vision
CIJE: 1 RIE: 0 CAT: 11

Twister Tenders
CIJE: 0 RIE: 1 CAT: 09

Two Bridges
CIJE: 0 RIE: 3 CAT: 22

Two Cone Model
CIJE: 0 RIE: 1 CAT: 15

Two Factor Theory of Job Satisfaction (Herzberg)
CIJE: 3 RIE: 1 CAT: 15

Two Group Test (Leitner Dayton)
CIJE: 0 RIE: 1 CAT: 21

Two Parameter Model
CIJE: 30 RIE: 30 CAT: 15

Two Predictor Validity Curve
CIJE: 0 RIE: 1 CAT: 21

Two Stage Testing
CIJE: 2 RIE: 8 CAT: 21

Two Step Flow
CIJE: 0 RIE: 2 CAT: 15

Two Step Principal Components Procedure
CIJE: 2 RIE: 0 CAT: 15

Two Way Bilingual Education
CIJE: 0 RIE: 19 CAT: 03

Two Way Cable Cascades
CIJE: 0 RIE: 1 CAT: 04

Two Way Cable Communications
CIJE: 1 RIE: 3 CAT: 04

Two Way Communication
CIJE: 0 RIE: 10 CAT: 16
SN See also "Interactive Communication"

Two Way Communication Devices
CIJE: 0 RIE: 1 CAT: 04

Two Way Information Services
CIJE: 0 RIE: 1 CAT: 15

Two Way Radio
CIJE: 1 RIE: 4 CAT: 04
SN See also "Interactive Radio"

Two Year Colleges within Universities
CIJE: 0 RIE: 1 CAT: 05
UF Community Colleges within Universities; University Community Colleges

Tyler (Anne)
CIJE: 2 RIE: 2 CAT: 18

Tyler (Ralph W)
CIJE: 24 RIE: 9 CAT: 18

Tyler Ideal Real Self Q Sort
CIJE: 0 RIE: 1 CAT: 21

Tyler Independent School District 409 MN
CIJE: 0 RIE: 1 CAT: 17

Tyler Independent School District TX
CIJE: 0 RIE: 2 CAT: 17

Tylers Model
CIJE: 3 RIE: 2 CAT: 15

Tymnet
CIJE: 4 RIE: 2 CAT: 04

Tympanometry
CIJE: 8 RIE: 1 CAT: 11

Type I Errors
CIJE: 88 RIE: 59 CAT: 21
UF Alpha Errors

Type I Glycogen Storage Disease
CIJE: 1 RIE: 0 CAT: 11

Type II Errors
CIJE: 7 RIE: 14 CAT: 21
UF Beta Errors

Type III Errors
CIJE: 0 RIE: 1 CAT: 21

Type K Item Format
CIJE: 2 RIE: 0 CAT: 21

Type Token Ratios
CIJE: 5 RIE: 1 CAT: 13

Type VI Errors
CIJE: 1 RIE: 1 CAT: 21

Type X Item Format
CIJE: 1 RIE: 0 CAT: 21

Typee
CIJE: 2 RIE: 0 CAT: 22

Typeface
CIJE: 13 RIE: 15 CAT: 16

Typewriters
CIJE: 9 RIE: 2 CAT: 04

Typing Speed
CIJE: 7 RIE: 1 CAT: 21

Typography
CIJE: 51 RIE: 31 CAT: 16

Typology of Love Styles (Lee)
CIJE: 0 RIE: 1 CAT: 21

Tyranny of Testing
CIJE: 0 RIE: 1 CAT: 21

Tyson Foods
CIJE: 0 RIE: 1 CAT: 17

Tyutchev (Fedor Ivanovich)
CIJE: 1 RIE: 0 CAT: 18

Tzu (Lao)
CIJE: 1 RIE: 0 CAT: 18

U Method
CIJE: 0 RIE: 1 CAT: 21
SN Method used to establish the external validity of discriminant analysis results

U S Air (Company)
USE USAir

U S English
CIJE: 3 RIE: 1 CAT: 17

U S News and World Report
CIJE: 6 RIE: 4 CAT: 22

U S USSR Textbook Study Proj
USE US USSR Textbook Study Project

U3A System
USE Universities of the Third Age

Ubertragung
CIJE: 0 RIE: 1 CAT: 15

UCAPAWA
USE United Cannery Agric Pack Allied Workers America

Uchumataqa
CIJE: 0 RIE: 1 CAT: 13
SN A Chipayan language
UF Uru

UCLA Allied Health Professions Projects
CIJE: 0 RIE: 18 CAT: 19

UCLA Librarians Association
CIJE: 0 RIE: 1 CAT: 17

UCLA Loneliness Scale
CIJE: 9 RIE: 2 CAT: 21

UCLA Temperament Form
CIJE: 0 RIE: 1 CAT: 21

Udall (Stewart)
CIJE: 1 RIE: 0 CAT: 18

Udayana University (Indonesia)
CIJE: 1 RIE: 0 CAT: 17

Uganda
CIJE: 42 RIE: 65 CAT: 07

UHF Television
CIJE: 1 RIE: 2 CAT: 04

Uigur
CIJE: 0 RIE: 2 CAT: 13

Uintah and Ouray Reservation UT
CIJE: 0 RIE: 1 CAT: 17

Uintah School District UT
CIJE: 0 RIE: 2 CAT: 17

UK MARC
CIJE: 2 RIE: 1 CAT: 04

Ukeleles
USE Ukuleles

Ukiah (Tribe)
CIJE: 0 RIE: 1 CAT: 08

Ukraine
CIJE: 4 RIE: 9 CAT: 07
SN See also "USSR (Ukraine)"

Ukrainian Americans
CIJE: 0 RIE: 2 CAT: 08

Ukrainian Canadians
CIJE: 0 RIE: 3 CAT: 08

Ukranian Ministry of Education (USSR)
CIJE: 1 RIE: 0 CAT: 17

Ukuleles
CIJE: 1 RIE: 1 CAT: 04
UF Ukeleles

Ulich (Robert)
CIJE: 1 RIE: 0 CAT: 18

Ulrich Planfiles
CIJE: 1 RIE: 0 CAT: 04

Ulrichs International Periodicals Directory
CIJE: 5 RIE: 0 CAT: 22

Ulster County Community College NY
CIJE: 1 RIE: 4 CAT: 17

Ulster Peoples College (Northern Ireland)
CIJE: 3 RIE: 0 CAT: 17

Ultrasonic Echoencephalography
CIJE: 2 RIE: 0 CAT: 11

Ultrasonics
CIJE: 4 RIE: 0 CAT: 20

Ultraviolet Light
CIJE: 6 RIE: 2 CAT: 20

Ultraviolet Radiation
CIJE: 7 RIE: 1 CAT: 20

Ulysses (Joyce)
CIJE: 0 RIE: 0 CAT: 22

Ulysses (Tennyson)
CIJE: 0 RIE: 1 CAT: 22

Umatilla (Tribe)
CIJE: 0 RIE: 1 CAT: 08

Umatilla County Education Service District OR
CIJE: 0 RIE: 1 CAT: 17
UF Umatilla Intermediate Education District OR

Umatilla Intermediate Education District OR
USE Umatilla County Education Service District OR

Umbundu
CIJE: 0 RIE: 2 CAT: 13

Umm Al Qura University (Saudi Arabia)
CIJE: 0 RIE: 1 CAT: 17

Un Coeur Simple
CIJE: 0 RIE: 1 CAT: 22

Unaccompanied Minors
CIJE: 2 RIE: 1 CAT: 10

Unaccredited Colleges
USE Nonaccredited Colleges

Unamuno (Miguel de)
CIJE: 11 RIE: 2 CAT: 18

Unanimity
CIJE: 3 RIE: 1 CAT: 16

Unary Operations
CIJE: 1 RIE: 0 CAT: 20

Unbalanced Designs
CIJE: 3 RIE: 1 CAT: 21

UNC CH Write
CIJE: 0 RIE: 1 CAT: 04

Uncertainty
CIJE: 69 RIE: 20 CAT: 21

Uncertainty Reduction
CIJE: 19 RIE: 11 CAT: 21

Uncertainty Studies Project
CIJE: 0 RIE: 1 CAT: 19

Uncertified Teachers
CIJE: 2 RIE: 3 CAT: 10

Uncle Remus
CIJE: 2 RIE: 2 CAT: 22

Uncle Toms Cabin
CIJE: 6 RIE: 2 CAT: 22

Unconditioned Stimulus
CIJE: 0 RIE: 1 CAT: 15

Unconscious Intention
CIJE: 2 RIE: 1 CAT: 15

Unconscious Processes
USE Unconscious Processing

Unconscious Processing
CIJE: 7 RIE: 1 CAT: 11
UF Unconscious Processes

Undecided Students
CIJE: 4 RIE: 3 CAT: 10

Undercontrol (Psychology)
CIJE: 0 RIE: 1 CAT: 11

Undercounting
CIJE: 1 RIE: 2 CAT: 15

Underdeterminacy
CIJE: 1 RIE: 1 CAT: 15

Undergraduate Libraries
CIJE: 8 RIE: 11 CAT: 05

Undergraduate Mathematics and Applications Project
CIJE: 0 RIE: 1 CAT: 19

Undergraduate Pilot Training
CIJE: 0 RIE: 4 CAT: 15

Undergraduate Program Field Tests
CIJE: 1 RIE: 1 CAT: 21

Underground Power Lines
CIJE: 1 RIE: 0 CAT: 04

Underground Press
CIJE: 8 RIE: 6 CAT: 05

Underground Railroad
CIJE: 3 RIE: 2 CAT: 12

Underground Storage Tanks
CIJE: 2 RIE: 0 CAT: 04

Underlining
CIJE: 21 RIE: 8 CAT: 16

Underlying Phonological Representations
CIJE: 2 RIE: 0 CAT: 13

Understanding Learning Teaching Proj (New Zealand)
CIJE: 0 RIE: 1 CAT: 19

Underwater Research
CIJE: 1 RIE: 0 CAT: 20

Underwood Postman Hypothesis
CIJE: 1 RIE: 0 CAT: 15

Underwriters (Insurance)
CIJE: 2 RIE: 3 CAT: 09

Undeveloped Land
CIJE: 0 RIE: 1 CAT: 16

Undocumented Students
CIJE: 0 RIE: 6 CAT: 10

Unemployment Insurance Act 1970
CIJE: 0 RIE: 3 CAT: 14

Unemployment Insurance Amendments 1976
CIJE: 1 RIE: 1 CAT: 14

UNESCO
CIJE: 337 RIE: 600 CAT: 17

UNESCO Associated Schools Project in Education
CIJE: 24 RIE: 2 CAT: 19

UNESCO Conference on Adult Education 3d
CIJE: 1 RIE: 0 CAT: 02

UNESCO Institute for Education
CIJE: 0 RIE: 1 CAT: 17

UNESCO Prize for Peace Education
CIJE: 0 RIE: 1 CAT: 19

UNESCO Public Library Manifesto
CIJE: 0 RIE: 2 CAT: 22

UNESCO Regional Seminar Adult Educ Development
CIJE: 0 RIE: 1 CAT: 02

UNESCO Teheran Congress on Literacy
CIJE: 0 RIE: 1 CAT: 02

Unfinished Agenda (The)
CIJE: 2 RIE: 1 CAT: 22
SN 1984 report of the National Commission on Secondary Vocational Education

Unfolding Technique
CIJE: 7 RIE: 2 CAT: 15

Ungaretti (Giuseppe)
CIJE: 1 RIE: 0 CAT: 18

UNICEF
CIJE: 24 RIE: 45 CAT: 17
UF United Nations Childrens Fund

UNICERT
CIJE: 0 RIE: 1 CAT: 03
SN Unified language certificate for German universities

Unicode
CIJE: 0 RIE: 1 CAT: 20

UNICOR
CIJE: 0 RIE: 1 CAT: 17

Unidentified Flying Objects
CIJE: 7 RIE: 2 CAT: 20

Unidimensional Scaling
CIJE: 13 RIE: 21 CAT: 21

Unidimensionality (Tests)
CIJE: 35 RIE: 48 CAT: 21
SN See also "Dimensionality (Tests)" and "Multidimensionality (Tests)"

Unification Church
CIJE: 2 RIE: 1 CAT: 17

Unified Intake Services
CIJE: 0 RIE: 1 CAT: 19

Unified Network of Informatics in Teacher Educ
CIJE: 0 RIE: 4 CAT: 17

Unified Science Approach
CIJE: 0 RIE: 2 CAT: 15

Unified Science Mathematics for Elementary Schools
CIJE: 4 RIE: 51 CAT: 03

Unified Studies Learning Packets
CIJE: 1 RIE: 0 CAT: 22

Unified Technical Concepts Curriculum
CIJE: 0 RIE: 1 CAT: 03

Unified Vocational Preparation
CIJE: 0 RIE: 2 CAT: 03

UNIFON Alphabet
CIJE: 4 RIE: 19 CAT: 13

Uniform Building Code
CIJE: 0 RIE: 1 CAT: 14

Uniform Course Numbering
CIJE: 0 RIE: 1 CAT: 16

Uniform Federal Accessibility Standards
CIJE: 0 RIE: 1 CAT: 15

Uniform Financial Reporting Systems
CIJE: 2 RIE: 1 CAT: 15

Uniform Guidelines Employee Selection Procedures
CIJE: 7 RIE: 4 CAT: 21

Uniform Management of Institutional Funds Act
CIJE: 2 RIE: 1 CAT: 14

Uniform Methodology Model
CIJE: 2 RIE: 2 CAT: 15

Uniform Migrant Student Record Transfer System
CIJE: 0 RIE: 2 CAT: 15

Uniform Notation for Expressing Queries
CIJE: 0 RIE: 1 CAT: 04

Uniform Patent Legislation
CIJE: 1 RIE: 0 CAT: 14

Uniform Price Index Calculation System
CIJE: 0 RIE: 1 CAT: 22

Uniform Probate Code
CIJE: 1 RIE: 0 CAT: 14

Uniform Reciprocal Enforcement of Support Laws
CIJE: 0 RIE: 1 CAT: 14

Uniform Slavic Transliteration Alphabet
CIJE: 0 RIE: 1 CAT: 13

Uniform Socio Economic Reporting System
CIJE: 0 RIE: 1 CAT: 15

Uniform Student Evaluation Survey
CIJE: 0 RIE: 1 CAT: 19

Uniform Vehicle Code
CIJE: 0 RIE: 1 CAT: 14

Uniformed Services Univ of the Health Sciences MD
CIJE: 6 RIE: 0 CAT: 17

Uniforms
CIJE: 0 RIE: 5 CAT: 04
SN See also "School Uniforms"

Unimodal Methods
CIJE: 1 RIE: 0 CAT: 15

Unintelligible Messages
CIJE: 0 RIE: 1 CAT: 16

Union Carbide
CIJE: 1 RIE: 3 CAT: 17

Union College
CIJE: 3 RIE: 0 CAT: 17

Union College NJ
CIJE: 1 RIE: 2 CAT: 17

Union College NY
CIJE: 2 RIE: 3 CAT: 17

Union County College NJ
CIJE: 3 RIE: 3 CAT: 17

Union County Regional School District NJ
CIJE: 0 RIE: 2 CAT: 17

Union County School District NC
CIJE: 0 RIE: 1 CAT: 17

Union County Technical Institute NJ
CIJE: 1 RIE: 2 CAT: 17

Union Dues
CIJE: 0 RIE: 16 CAT: 16

Union Election Campaigns
CIJE: 0 RIE: 1 CAT: 16

Union for Experimenting Colleges and Universities
CIJE: 2 RIE: 1 CAT: 17

Union Graduate School
CIJE: 1 RIE: 1 CAT: 17

Union Leadership
CIJE: 1 RIE: 1 CAT: 16

Union Libraries
CIJE: 0 RIE: 1 CAT: 05

Union Lists of Serials
CIJE: 1 RIE: 1 CAT: 22

Union of Soviet Socialist Republics
USE USSR

Union of the Blind (Yugoslavia)
CIJE: 0 RIE: 1 CAT: 17

Union Recognition
CIJE: 1 RIE: 4 CAT: 16

Union Rights
CIJE: 1 RIE: 97 CAT: 14

Union Security
CIJE: 5 RIE: 3 CAT: 16

Union Theological Seminary NY
CIJE: 0 RIE: 1 CAT: 17

Union Underwear Corporation
CIJE: 0 RIE: 1 CAT: 17

Uniondale Union Free School District NY
CIJE: 0 RIE: 1 CAT: 17

Unipolar Inductor
CIJE: 1 RIE: 0 CAT: 20

Unipolar Scale
CIJE: 0 RIE: 1 CAT: 15

UNIQUE Computer Program
CIJE: 1 RIE: 0 CAT: 04

UNIQUE Physical Fitness Test
CIJE: 0 RIE: 1 CAT: 21

Uniqueness Theory
CIJE: 1 RIE: 1 CAT: 15

Unisex Act Interest Inventory
CIJE: 0 RIE: 4 CAT: 21

Unisex Edition of ACT Interest Inventory IV
CIJE: 0 RIE: 1 CAT: 21

UNISIST
CIJE: 14 RIE: 22 CAT: 17

UNISTAR I IEP Program
CIJE: 0 RIE: 1 CAT: 04

Unit Box Approach
CIJE: 3 RIE: 0 CAT: 15

Unit Credit System
CIJE: 0 RIE: 3 CAT: 15

Unit for the Development of Adult Continuing Educ
CIJE: 0 RIE: 1 CAT: 17

Unit Normal Approximation
CIJE: 0 RIE: 1 CAT: 21

Unit of Analysis Problems
CIJE: 22 RIE: 24 CAT: 21

Unit Record Equipment
CIJE: 0 RIE: 1 CAT: 04

Unit Schools
CIJE: 1 RIE: 3 CAT: 05

Unit Treatment Rehabilitation Program
CIJE: 0 RIE: 1 CAT: 19

Unit Ventilators
CIJE: 2 RIE: 0 CAT: 04

Unitarian Universalist Association
CIJE: 1 RIE: 1 CAT: 17

Unitary Theory
CIJE: 3 RIE: 2 CAT: 15

Unitas Therapeutic Community NY
CIJE: 0 RIE: 2 CAT: 17

United Aircraft Library System CT
CIJE: 2 RIE: 0 CAT: 17

United Arab Emirates
CIJE: 2 RIE: 4 CAT: 07

United Arab Emirates University
CIJE: 0 RIE: 1 CAT: 17

United Arab Republic
CIJE: 9 RIE: 31 CAT: 07

United Auto Workers
CIJE: 9 RIE: 9 CAT: 17

United Campus Ministries
CIJE: 0 RIE: 1 CAT: 17

United Campuses to Prevent Nuclear War
CIJE: 0 RIE: 1 CAT: 17

United Cannery Agric Pack Allied Workers America
CIJE: 0 RIE: 1 CAT: 17
UF UCAPAWA

United Cerebral Palsy Association
CIJE: 0 RIE: 2 CAT: 17

United Cerebral Palsy New York v Board of Educ
CIJE: 0 RIE: 1 CAT: 14

United Church of Canada
CIJE: 0 RIE: 1 CAT: 17

United Church of Christ
CIJE: 0 RIE: 3 CAT: 17

United Electric Controls Corporation
CIJE: 0 RIE: 1 CAT: 17

United Farm Workers
CIJE: 2 RIE: 4 CAT: 17

United Federation of College Teachers
CIJE: 0 RIE: 3 CAT: 17

United Federation of Teachers
CIJE: 20 RIE: 16 CAT: 17

United Gold Coast Convention
CIJE: 1 RIE: 0 CAT: 02

United Kingdom
CIJE: 1877 RIE: 919 CAT: 07

United Kingdom Chemical Information Service
CIJE: 1 RIE: 1 CAT: 17

United Kingdom Ministry Overseas Development
CIJE: 0 RIE: 1 CAT: 17

United Kingdom Reading Association
CIJE: 1 RIE: 4 CAT: 17

United Methodist Church
CIJE: 1 RIE: 10 CAT: 17

United Nations
CIJE: 182 RIE: 217 CAT: 17

United Nations Bibliographic Information System
CIJE: 1 RIE: 0 CAT: 04

United Nations Charter
CIJE: 0 RIE: 1 CAT: 14

United Nations Childrens Fund
USE UNICEF

United Nations Commission on the Status of Women
CIJE: 0 RIE: 5 CAT: 17

United Nations Conference on the Human Environment
CIJE: 5 RIE: 4 CAT: 02

United Nations Conference on the Law of the Sea
CIJE: 1 RIE: 2 CAT: 02

University of British Columbia (Canada)
CIJE: 44 RIE: 31 CAT: 17

University of Caldas (Colombia)
CIJE: 1 RIE: 0 CAT: 17

University of Calgary (Canada)
CIJE: 34 RIE: 29 CAT: 17

University of California
CIJE: 94 RIE: 212 CAT: 17

University of California Berkeley
CIJE: 130 RIE: 118 CAT: 17

University of California Davis
CIJE: 49 RIE: 55 CAT: 17

University of California Irvine
CIJE: 36 RIE: 27 CAT: 17

University of California Los Angeles
CIJE: 147 RIE: 107 CAT: 17
SN See add'l listings under "UCLA..."

University of California Riverside
CIJE: 5 RIE: 11 CAT: 17

University of California San Diego
CIJE: 32 RIE: 19 CAT: 17

University of California San Francisco
CIJE: 33 RIE: 3 CAT: 17

University of California Santa Barbara
CIJE: 33 RIE: 27 CAT: 17

University of California Santa Clara
CIJE: 1 RIE: 1 CAT: 17

University of California Santa Cruz
CIJE: 21 RIE: 12 CAT: 17

University of California Santa Cruz Oakes College
CIJE: 1 RIE: 1 CAT: 17

University of Cambridge (England)
CIJE: 10 RIE: 3 CAT: 17

University of Cambridge Local Exam Synd (England)
CIJE: 0 RIE: 2 CAT: 17
UF Cambridge Local Examinations Syndicate (England)

University of Canterbury (England)
CIJE: 3 RIE: 0 CAT: 17

University of Cape Town (South Africa)
CIJE: 11 RIE: 0 CAT: 17

University of Central Arkansas
CIJE: 1 RIE: 2 CAT: 17

University of Central Florida
CIJE: 12 RIE: 17 CAT: 17

University of Central Queensland (Australia)
CIJE: 0 RIE: 1 CAT: 17

University of Central Texas
CIJE: 0 RIE: 4 CAT: 17

University of Ceylon
CIJE: 2 RIE: 0 CAT: 17

University of Chicago IL
CIJE: 68 RIE: 41 CAT: 17

University of Chicago School Mathematics Project
CIJE: 2 RIE: 1 CAT: 19

University of Chile Santiago
CIJE: 2 RIE: 0 CAT: 17

University of Cincinnati Medical Center OH
CIJE: 0 RIE: 1 CAT: 17

University of Cincinnati OH
CIJE: 52 RIE: 28 CAT: 17

University of Cincinnati OH University College
CIJE: 0 RIE: 1 CAT: 17

University of Cincinnati Raymond Walters Coll OH
USE Raymond Walters College OH

University of Colombia
CIJE: 0 RIE: 0 CAT: 17

University of Colorado
CIJE: 40 RIE: 26 CAT: 17

University of Colorado Boulder
CIJE: 20 RIE: 17 CAT: 17

University of Colorado Colorado Springs
CIJE: 3 RIE: 12 CAT: 17

University of Colorado Denver
CIJE: 8 RIE: 2 CAT: 17

University of Colorado Medical Center
CIJE: 6 RIE: 0 CAT: 17

University of Compiegne (France)
CIJE: 1 RIE: 0 CAT: 17

University of Connecticut
CIJE: 45 RIE: 39 CAT: 17

University of Connecticut Storrs
CIJE: 2 RIE: 2 CAT: 17

University of Copenhagen (Denmark)
CIJE: 1 RIE: 2 CAT: 17

University of Dacca (Bangladesh)
CIJE: 1 RIE: 0 CAT: 17

University of Dallas TX
CIJE: 1 RIE: 0 CAT: 17

University of Dar es Salaam (Tanzania)
CIJE: 2 RIE: 2 CAT: 17

University of Dayton OH
CIJE: 10 RIE: 15 CAT: 17

University of Delaware
CIJE: 35 RIE: 46 CAT: 17

University of Denver CO
CIJE: 25 RIE: 14 CAT: 17

University of Detroit MI
CIJE: 3 RIE: 1 CAT: 17

University of Dijon (France)
CIJE: 0 RIE: 1 CAT: 17

University of Dublin (Ireland)
CIJE: 0 RIE: 1 CAT: 17

University of Dubuque IA
CIJE: 1 RIE: 2 CAT: 17

University of East Africa
CIJE: 0 RIE: 2 CAT: 17

University of East Anglia (England)
CIJE: 1 RIE: 0 CAT: 17

University of Edinburgh (Scotland)
CIJE: 10 RIE: 4 CAT: 17

University of Essex (England)
CIJE: 2 RIE: 2 CAT: 17

University of Europe
CIJE: 2 RIE: 0 CAT: 17

University of Evansville IN
CIJE: 5 RIE: 5 CAT: 17

University of Exeter (England)
CIJE: 3 RIE: 2 CAT: 17

University of Findlay OH
CIJE: 0 RIE: 1 CAT: 17

University of Florida
CIJE: 101 RIE: 67 CAT: 17

University of Genova (Italy)
CIJE: 1 RIE: 0 CAT: 17

University of Georgia
CIJE: 97 RIE: 97 CAT: 17

University of Glasgow (Scotland)
CIJE: 4 RIE: 0 CAT: 17

University of Goettingen (West Germany)
CIJE: 0 RIE: 0 CAT: 17
UF Georg August University (West Germany)

University of Gothenburg (Sweden)
CIJE: 1 RIE: 4 CAT: 17

University of Grenoble (France)
CIJE: 3 RIE: 1 CAT: 17

University of Guelph (Ontario)
CIJE: 15 RIE: 10 CAT: 17

University of Guyana
CIJE: 1 RIE: 0 CAT: 17

University of Halle
CIJE: 1 RIE: 1 CAT: 17

University of Hartford CT
CIJE: 17 RIE: 13 CAT: 17

University of Hawaii
CIJE: 47 RIE: 54 CAT: 17

University of Hawaii Community College System
CIJE: 0 RIE: 3 CAT: 17
UF Hawaii Community College System

University of Hawaii Hawaii Community College
CIJE: 0 RIE: 1 CAT: 17
UF Hawaii Community College

University of Hawaii Hilo
CIJE: 0 RIE: 1 CAT: 17

University of Hawaii Honolulu Community College
CIJE: 1 RIE: 3 CAT: 17
UF Honolulu Community College HI

University of Hawaii Kapiolani Community College
CIJE: 2 RIE: 2 CAT: 17
UF Kapiolani Community College HI

University of Hawaii Kauai Community College
CIJE: 1 RIE: 2 CAT: 17
UF Kauai Community College HI

University of Hawaii Leeward Community College
CIJE: 0 RIE: 4 CAT: 17
UF Leeward Community College HI

University of Hawaii Manoa
CIJE: 6 RIE: 5 CAT: 17

University of Hawaii Maui Community College
CIJE: 2 RIE: 5 CAT: 17
UF Maui Community College HI

University of Heidelberg (West Germany)
CIJE: 3 RIE: 0 CAT: 17

University of Helsinki (Finland)
CIJE: 2 RIE: 2 CAT: 17

University of Honduras
USE Universidad Nacional Autonoma de Honduras

University of Hong Kong
CIJE: 9 RIE: 13 CAT: 17

University of Houston Clear Lake TX
CIJE: 4 RIE: 3 CAT: 17

University of Houston School Univ Research Collab
CIJE: 0 RIE: 1 CAT: 19

University of Houston TX
CIJE: 45 RIE: 31 CAT: 17

University of Houston University Park TX
CIJE: 0 RIE: 1 CAT: 17

University of Houston Victoria TX
CIJE: 1 RIE: 0 CAT: 17

University of Hull (England)
CIJE: 1 RIE: 1 CAT: 17

University of Ibadan (Nigeria)
CIJE: 6 RIE: 3 CAT: 17

University of Idaho
CIJE: 13 RIE: 15 CAT: 17

University of Illinois
CIJE: 114 RIE: 99 CAT: 17

University of Illinois Astronomy Program
CIJE: 0 RIE: 4 CAT: 19

University of Illinois Chicago
CIJE: 27 RIE: 7 CAT: 17

University of Illinois Chicago Circle Campus
CIJE: 6 RIE: 11 CAT: 17

University of Illinois College of Medicine
CIJE: 1 RIE: 1 CAT: 17

University of Illinois Committee on School Math
CIJE: 2 RIE: 3 CAT: 17

University of Illinois Medical Center
CIJE: 9 RIE: 4 CAT: 17

University of Illinois Urbana Champaign
CIJE: 70 RIE: 65 CAT: 17

University of Iowa
CIJE: 107 RIE: 50 CAT: 17

University of Jordan
CIJE: 0 RIE: 1 CAT: 17

University of Judaism Lee College CA
CIJE: 0 RIE: 1 CAT: 17

University of Kansas
CIJE: 40 RIE: 34 CAT: 17

University of Kansas Lawrence
CIJE: 2 RIE: 3 CAT: 17

University of Kassel (West Germany)
CIJE: 0 RIE: 1 CAT: 17

University of Kent at Canterbury (England)
CIJE: 2 RIE: 0 CAT: 17

University of Kentucky
CIJE: 83 RIE: 27 CAT: 17

University of Kentucky Community College System
CIJE: 0 RIE: 16 CAT: 17
UF Kentucky Community College System

University of Khartoum (Sudan)
CIJE: 2 RIE: 1 CAT: 17

University of Klagenfurt (Austria)
CIJE: 0 RIE: 1 CAT: 17

University of La Verne CA
CIJE: 1 RIE: 1 CAT: 17

University of Lagos (Nigeria)
CIJE: 2 RIE: 1 CAT: 17

University of Lancaster (England)
CIJE: 18 RIE: 6 CAT: 17

University of Leeds (England)
CIJE: 14 RIE: 6 CAT: 17
UF Leeds University (England)

University of Leicester (England)
CIJE: 2 RIE: 3 CAT: 17

University of Lethbridge (Canada)
CIJE: 8 RIE: 11 CAT: 17

University of Leuven (Belgium)
CIJE: 1 RIE: 0 CAT: 17

University of Liege (Belgium)
CIJE: 1 RIE: 0 CAT: 17

University of Liverpool (England)
CIJE: 9 RIE: 4 CAT: 17

University of Ljubljana (Yugoslavia)
CIJE: 1 RIE: 0 CAT: 17

University of London (England)
CIJE: 14 RIE: 10 CAT: 17

University of Louisville KY
CIJE: 32 RIE: 34 CAT: 17

University of Louvain (Belgium)
CIJE: 4 RIE: 1 CAT: 17

University of Lowell MA
CIJE: 2 RIE: 6 CAT: 17

University of Lowell MA Instr Telecomm Network
CIJE: 0 RIE: 0 CAT: 17

University of Lund (Sweden)
USE Lund University (Sweden)

University of Madrid (Spain)
USE Universidad Autonoma de Madrid (Spain)

University of Maine
CIJE: 7 RIE: 21 CAT: 17

University of Maine Augusta
CIJE: 0 RIE: 2 CAT: 17

University of Maine Farmington
CIJE: 1 RIE: 3 CAT: 17

University of Maine Orono
CIJE: 3 RIE: 14 CAT: 17

University of Maine Portland Gorham
CIJE: 1 RIE: 3 CAT: 17

University of Maine Presque Isle
CIJE: 0 RIE: 5 CAT: 17

University of Malawi
CIJE: 2 RIE: 0 CAT: 17

University of Malaya (Malaysia)
CIJE: 4 RIE: 4 CAT: 17

University of Manchester (England)
CIJE: 6 RIE: 9 CAT: 17

University of Manila (Philippines)
CIJE: 1 RIE: 0 CAT: 17

University of Manitoba (Canada)
CIJE: 19 RIE: 12 CAT: 17

University of Mary Hardin Baylor TX
CIJE: 0 RIE: 1 CAT: 17

University of Maryland
CIJE: 94 RIE: 75 CAT: 17

University of Maryland Baltimore
CIJE: 24 RIE: 5 CAT: 17

University of Maryland Baltimore County
CIJE: 8 RIE: 14 CAT: 17

University of Maryland College Park
CIJE: 41 RIE: 125 CAT: 17

University of Maryland Dental School
CIJE: 0 RIE: 1 CAT: 17

University of Maryland Eastern Shore
CIJE: 1 RIE: 3 CAT: 17

University of Maryland Professional Schools Campus
CIJE: 0 RIE: 1 CAT: 17

University of Maryland School of Medicine
CIJE: 0 RIE: 1 CAT: 17

University of Maryland System
CIJE: 1 RIE: 2 CAT: 17

University of Maryland University College
CIJE: 2 RIE: 1 CAT: 17

University of Massachusetts
CIJE: 47 RIE: 40 CAT: 17

University of Massachusetts Amherst
CIJE: 44 RIE: 43 CAT: 17

University of Massachusetts Boston
CIJE: 11 RIE: 9 CAT: 17

University of Massachusetts Index
CIJE: 1 RIE: 0 CAT: 21

University of Massachusetts Lowell
CIJE: 0 RIE: 1 CAT: 17

University of Mauritius
CIJE: 1 RIE: 0 CAT: 17

University of Medicine and Dentistry of New Jersey
CIJE: 4 RIE: 2 CAT: 17

University of Melbourne (Australia)
CIJE: 15 RIE: 5 CAT: 17

University of Miami FL
CIJE: 39 RIE: 20 CAT: 17

University of Michigan
CIJE: 171 RIE: 103 CAT: 17

University of Michigan Ann Arbor
CIJE: 13 RIE: 12 CAT: 17

University of Michigan Dearborn
CIJE: 1 RIE: 1 CAT: 17

University of Michigan Flint
CIJE: 2 RIE: 3 CAT: 17

University of Michigan Medical School
CIJE: 1 RIE: 2 CAT: 17

University of Michigan Time Use Study
CIJE: 0 RIE: 1 CAT: 19

University of Mid America NE
CIJE: 9 RIE: 34 CAT: 17

University of Minnesota
CIJE: 160 RIE: 223 CAT: 17

University of Minnesota Crookston
CIJE: 1 RIE: 1 CAT: 17

University of Minnesota Duluth
CIJE: 12 RIE: 4 CAT: 17

University of Minnesota Minneapolis
CIJE: 11 RIE: 15 CAT: 17

University of Minnesota Morris
CIJE: 2 RIE: 2 CAT: 17

University of Minnesota Twin Cities
CIJE: 6 RIE: 3 CAT: 17

University of Minnesota Waseca
CIJE: 3 RIE: 5 CAT: 17

University of Mississippi
CIJE: 26 RIE: 11 CAT: 17

University of Mississippi Medical Center
CIJE: 1 RIE: 2 CAT: 17

University of Mississippi School of Dentistry
CIJE: 0 RIE: 2 CAT: 17

University of Missouri
CIJE: 33 RIE: 38 CAT: 17

University of Missouri Columbia
CIJE: 34 RIE: 29 CAT: 17

University of Missouri Kansas City
CIJE: 37 RIE: 33 CAT: 17

University of Missouri Rolla
CIJE: 2 RIE: 3 CAT: 17

University of Missouri Saint Louis
CIJE: 9 RIE: 14 CAT: 17

University of Montana
CIJE: 9 RIE: 8 CAT: 17

University of Montevallo AL
CIJE: 1 RIE: 10 CAT: 17

University of Montpellier (France)
CIJE: 0 RIE: 0 CAT: 17

University of Montreal (Quebec)
CIJE: 1 RIE: 5 CAT: 17

University of Moratuwa (Sri Lanka)
CIJE: 0 RIE: 1 CAT: 17

University of Mostar (Yugoslavia)
CIJE: 0 RIE: 1 CAT: 17

University of Munich (West Germany)
CIJE: 1 RIE: 0 CAT: 17

University of Munster (West Germany)
CIJE: 0 RIE: 0 CAT: 17

University of Mysore (India)
CIJE: 1 RIE: 0 CAT: 17

University of Nairobi (Kenya)
CIJE: 4 RIE: 2 CAT: 17

University of Nancy (France)
CIJE: 0 RIE: 1 CAT: 17

University of Natal (South Africa)
CIJE: 2 RIE: 1 CAT: 17

University of Nebraska
CIJE: 52 RIE: 23 CAT: 17

University of Nebraska Kearney
CIJE: 1 RIE: 1 CAT: 17

University of Nebraska Lincoln
CIJE: 36 RIE: 27 CAT: 17

University of Nebraska Medical Center
CIJE: 7 RIE: 0 CAT: 17

University of Nebraska Omaha
CIJE: 15 RIE: 16 CAT: 17

University of Neuchatel (Switzerland)
USE Universite de Neuchatel (Switzerland)

University of Nevada
CIJE: 12 RIE: 7 CAT: 17

University of Nevada Las Vegas
CIJE: 7 RIE: 5 CAT: 17

University of Nevada Reno
CIJE: 13 RIE: 15 CAT: 17

University of Nevada System
CIJE: 0 RIE: 9 CAT: 17

University of New Brunswick
CIJE: 0 RIE: 2 CAT: 17

University of New Brunswick (Canada)
CIJE: 10 RIE: 4 CAT: 17

University of New England (Australia)
CIJE: 15 RIE: 5 CAT: 17

University of New Hampshire
CIJE: 17 RIE: 23 CAT: 17

University of New Haven CT
CIJE: 1 RIE: 5 CAT: 17

University of New Mexico
CIJE: 53 RIE: 59 CAT: 17

University of New Mexico Medical Center Library
CIJE: 0 RIE: 1 CAT: 17

University of New Mexico School of Medicine
CIJE: 2 RIE: 1 CAT: 17

University of New Orleans LA
CIJE: 5 RIE: 8 CAT: 17

University of New South Wales (Australia)
CIJE: 17 RIE: 22 CAT: 17

University of Newcastle (Australia)
CIJE: 16 RIE: 4 CAT: 17

University of Nigeria
CIJE: 2 RIE: 2 CAT: 17

University of Nijmegen (Netherlands)
CIJE: 5 RIE: 0 CAT: 17

University of North Alabama
CIJE: 0 RIE: 2 CAT: 17

University of North Carolina
CIJE: 59 RIE: 31 CAT: 17

University of North Carolina Asheville
CIJE: 5 RIE: 7 CAT: 17

University of North Carolina Chapel Hill
CIJE: 43 RIE: 30 CAT: 17

University of North Carolina Charlotte
CIJE: 14 RIE: 29 CAT: 17

University of North Carolina Greensboro
CIJE: 13 RIE: 21 CAT: 17

University of North Carolina Wilmington
CIJE: 4 RIE: 19 CAT: 17

University of North Dakota
CIJE: 16 RIE: 36 CAT: 17

University of North Dakota American College Test
CIJE: 1 RIE: 0 CAT: 21

University of North Dakota Grand Forks
CIJE: 2 RIE: 5 CAT: 17

University of North Florida
CIJE: 4 RIE: 15 CAT: 17

University of North Texas
CIJE: 7 RIE: 2 CAT: 17
SN Formerly "North Texas State University"

University of Northern Colorado
CIJE: 41 RIE: 20 CAT: 17

University of Northern Iowa
CIJE: 12 RIE: 25 CAT: 17

University of Notre Dame IN
CIJE: 27 RIE: 11 CAT: 17

University of Nottingham (England)
CIJE: 13 RIE: 2 CAT: 17

University of Oklahoma
CIJE: 17 RIE: 24 CAT: 17

University of Oklahoma Health Science Center
CIJE: 4 RIE: 3 CAT: 17

University of Oklahoma Norman
CIJE: 1 RIE: 1 CAT: 17

University of Omaha NE
CIJE: 0 RIE: 1 CAT: 17

University of Oregon
CIJE: 52 RIE: 52 CAT: 17

University of Oriente (Venezuela)
CIJE: 0 RIE: 1 CAT: 17

University of Oslo (Norway)
CIJE: 4 RIE: 1 CAT: 17

University of Otago (New Zealand)
CIJE: 3 RIE: 2 CAT: 17

University of Ottawa (Canada)
CIJE: 20 RIE: 11 CAT: 17

University of Oxford (England)
CIJE: 13 RIE: 4 CAT: 17

University of Paderborn (West Germany)
CIJE: 0 RIE: 1 CAT: 17

University of Papua New Guinea
CIJE: 8 RIE: 2 CAT: 17

University of Paris (France)
CIJE: 8 RIE: 5 CAT: 17

University of Pennsylvania
CIJE: 90 RIE: 52 CAT: 17

University of Pennsylvania School Council
CIJE: 0 RIE: 1 CAT: 17

University of Pennsylvania Wharton School
CIJE: 0 RIE: 2 CAT: 17
UF Wharton School PA

University of Phoenix AZ
CIJE: 1 RIE: 4 CAT: 17

University of Pittsburgh Johnstown PA
CIJE: 2 RIE: 0 CAT: 17

University of Pittsburgh PA
CIJE: 71 RIE: 83 CAT: 17

University of Pittsburgh PA Falk Laboratory School
USE Falk Laboratory School PA

University of Portland OR
CIJE: 3 RIE: 9 CAT: 17

University of Puerto Rico
CIJE: 2 RIE: 6 CAT: 17

University of Puerto Rico Cayey University College
CIJE: 0 RIE: 1 CAT: 17
UF Cayey University College PR

University of Puerto Rico Ponce Techn Univ Coll
CIJE: 0 RIE: 0 CAT: 17
UF Ponce Technological University College PR

University of Puget Sound WA
CIJE: 4 RIE: 7 CAT: 17

University of Qatar
CIJE: 0 RIE: 2 CAT: 17

University of Queensland (Australia)
CIJE: 22 RIE: 9 CAT: 17

University of Rajasthan (India)
CIJE: 0 RIE: 1 CAT: 17

University of Reading (England)
CIJE: 2 RIE: 2 CAT: 17

University of Redlands CA
CIJE: 8 RIE: 2 CAT: 17

University of Regina SK
CIJE: 1 RIE: 7 CAT: 17

University of Rhode Island
CIJE: 23 RIE: 25 CAT: 17

University of Rhode Island Foundation
CIJE: 0 RIE: 1 CAT: 17

University of Richmond VA
CIJE: 16 RIE: 3 CAT: 17

University of Riyadh (Saudi Arabia)
CIJE: 1 RIE: 0 CAT: 17

University of Rochester NY
CIJE: 43 RIE: 14 CAT: 17

University of Saint Thomas MN
CIJE: 0 RIE: 3 CAT: 17

University of San Carlos (Philippines)
CIJE: 2 RIE: 0 CAT: 17

University of San Diego CA
CIJE: 2 RIE: 1 CAT: 17

University of San Francisco CA
CIJE: 7 RIE: 17 CAT: 17

University of Santa Clara CA
CIJE: 2 RIE: 1 CAT: 17

University of Santiago (Chile)
CIJE: 0 RIE: 2 CAT: 17

University of Saskatchewan (Canada)
CIJE: 29 RIE: 14 CAT: 17

University of Science and Arts of Oklahoma
CIJE: 1 RIE: 0 CAT: 17

University of Scranton PA
CIJE: 8 RIE: 5 CAT: 17

University of Sheffield (England)
CIJE: 14 RIE: 4 CAT: 17

University of Sherbrooke ON
CIJE: 0 RIE: 1 CAT: 17

University of Singapore
CIJE: 2 RIE: 0 CAT: 17
SN See also "National University of Singapore"

University of Skopje (Yugoslavia)
CIJE: 0 RIE: 1 CAT: 17

University of Sokoto (Nigeria)
CIJE: 0 RIE: 1 CAT: 17

University of South Africa
CIJE: 3 RIE: 15 CAT: 17

University of South Alabama
CIJE: 3 RIE: 12 CAT: 17

University of South Australia
CIJE: 2 RIE: 1 CAT: 17

University of South Carolina
CIJE: 68 RIE: 61 CAT: 17

University of South Carolina Coastal Carolina Coll
CIJE: 0 RIE: 1 CAT: 17
UF Coastal Carolina College SC

University of South Carolina Columbia
CIJE: 4 RIE: 6 CAT: 17

University of South Carolina Salkehatchie
CIJE: 1 RIE: 0 CAT: 17

University of South Dakota
CIJE: 8 RIE: 16 CAT: 17

University of South Florida
CIJE: 33 RIE: 32 CAT: 17

University of South Florida Lakeland
CIJE: 0 RIE: 1 CAT: 17

University of Southampton (England)
CIJE: 5 RIE: 0 CAT: 17

University of Southern California
CIJE: 74 RIE: 51 CAT: 17

University of Southern Colorado
CIJE: 1 RIE: 2 CAT: 17

University of Southern Maine
CIJE: 2 RIE: 9 CAT: 17

University of Southern Mississippi
CIJE: 15 RIE: 11 CAT: 17

University of Southern Queensland (Australia)
CIJE: 1 RIE: 3 CAT: 17

University of Southwestern Louisiana
CIJE: 5 RIE: 4 CAT: 17

University of Stellenbosch (South Africa)
CIJE: 1 RIE: 2 CAT: 17

University of Stockholm (Sweden)
CIJE: 0 RIE: 2 CAT: 17

University of Strathclyde (Scotland)
CIJE: 5 RIE: 1 CAT: 17

University of Surrey (England)
CIJE: 13 RIE: 3 CAT: 17

University of Sussex (England)
CIJE: 8 RIE: 5 CAT: 17

University of Sydney (Australia)
CIJE: 18 RIE: 4 CAT: 17

University of Tampa FL
CIJE: 0 RIE: 2 CAT: 17

University of Tampere (Finland)
CIJE: 2 RIE: 1 CAT: 17

University of Tasmania (Australia)
CIJE: 8 RIE: 0 CAT: 17

University of Technology (Iraq)
CIJE: 1 RIE: 0 CAT: 17

University of Technology (Papua New Guinea)
USE Papua New Guinea University of Technology

University of Technology Sydney (Australia)
CIJE: 0 RIE: 2 CAT: 17

University of Tehran (Iran)
CIJE: 0 RIE: 0 CAT: 17

University of Tennessee
CIJE: 38 RIE: 37 CAT: 17

University of Tennessee Chattanooga
CIJE: 8 RIE: 6 CAT: 17

University of Tennessee Knoxville
CIJE: 43 RIE: 71 CAT: 17

University of Tennessee Martin
CIJE: 3 RIE: 4 CAT: 17

University of Tennessee Memphis
CIJE: 4 RIE: 3 CAT: 17

University of Tennessee Nashville
CIJE: 0 RIE: 2 CAT: 17

University of Texas
CIJE: 53 RIE: 24 CAT: 17

University of Texas Arlington
CIJE: 7 RIE: 6 CAT: 17

University of Texas Austin
CIJE: 43 RIE: 85 CAT: 17

University of Texas Dallas
CIJE: 4 RIE: 1 CAT: 17

University of Texas El Paso
CIJE: 12 RIE: 16 CAT: 17

University of Texas Medical Branch Galveston
CIJE: 10 RIE: 6 CAT: 17

University of Texas Medical School Houston
CIJE: 3 RIE: 0 CAT: 17

University of Texas Pan American
CIJE: 1 RIE: 1 CAT: 17
SN ...at Edinburg — see also former name "Pan American University TX"

University of Texas Permian Basin
CIJE: 4 RIE: 2 CAT: 17

University of Texas San Antonio
CIJE: 17 RIE: 2 CAT: 17

University of Texas System
CIJE: 0 RIE: 1 CAT: 17

University of Texas Tyler
CIJE: 0 RIE: 1 CAT: 17

University of Texas v Camenisch
CIJE: 3 RIE: 1 CAT: 14

University of the Air (India)
CIJE: 0 RIE: 3 CAT: 17

University of the Air (Japan)
CIJE: 2 RIE: 2 CAT: 17

University of the Americas (Mexico)
CIJE: 2 RIE: 1 CAT: 17

University of the Basque Country (Spain)
CIJE: 0 RIE: 2 CAT: 17

University of the District of Columbia
CIJE: 5 RIE: 22 CAT: 17

University of the East (Philippines)
CIJE: 1 RIE: 0 CAT: 17

University of the Negeve (Israel)
CIJE: 1 RIE: 0 CAT: 17

University of the North (South Africa)
CIJE: 1 RIE: 1 CAT: 17

University of the Pacific CA
CIJE: 12 RIE: 5 CAT: 17

University of the Philippines
CIJE: 3 RIE: 3 CAT: 17

University of the Philippines Los Banos
CIJE: 0 RIE: 2 CAT: 17

University of the Ryukyus (Japan)
CIJE: 0 RIE: 2 CAT: 17

University of the Sacred Heart PR
CIJE: 0 RIE: 1 CAT: 17

University of the South Pacific (Fiji)
CIJE: 9 RIE: 10 CAT: 17

University of the South TN
CIJE: 1 RIE: 0 CAT: 17

University of the Third Age Models
USE Universities of the Third Age

University of the Virgin Islands
CIJE: 0 RIE: 1 CAT: 17

University of the West Indies (Jamaica)
CIJE: 5 RIE: 8 CAT: 17

University of the Western Cape (South Africa)
CIJE: 4 RIE: 2 CAT: 17

University of the Witwatersrand (South Africa)
CIJE: 5 RIE: 2 CAT: 17

University of Toledo OH
CIJE: 30 RIE: 40 CAT: 17

University of Toledo Springfield Local Schools Pro
CIJE: 0 RIE: 13 CAT: 19

University of Toronto (Canada)
CIJE: 57 RIE: 24 CAT: 17

University of Toronto Library Automation Systems
CIJE: 5 RIE: 3 CAT: 04
UF UTLAS

University of Tromso (Norway)
CIJE: 0 RIE: 1 CAT: 17

University of Trondheim (Norway)
CIJE: 1 RIE: 1 CAT: 17

University of Tulsa OK
CIJE: 5 RIE: 8 CAT: 17

University of Tulsa School for Gifted Children OK
CIJE: 0 RIE: 3 CAT: 17

University of Turku (Finland)
CIJE: 1 RIE: 1 CAT: 17

University of Ulster (Northern Ireland)
CIJE: 6 RIE: 1 CAT: 17

University of Uppsala (Sweden)
USE Uppsala University (Sweden)

University of Urbino (Italy)
CIJE: 4 RIE: 0 CAT: 17

University of Utah
CIJE: 61 RIE: 49 CAT: 17

University of Utrecht (Netherlands)
USE State University of Utrecht (Netherlands)

University of Vermont
CIJE: 32 RIE: 21 CAT: 17

University of Victoria BC
CIJE: 12 RIE: 13 CAT: 17

University of Virginia
CIJE: 66 RIE: 44 CAT: 17

University of Waikato (New Zealand)
CIJE: 3 RIE: 1 CAT: 17

University of Washington
CIJE: 117 RIE: 117 CAT: 17

University of Waterloo (Ontario)
CIJE: 16 RIE: 14 CAT: 17

University of West Florida
CIJE: 7 RIE: 14 CAT: 17

University of Western Australia
CIJE: 11 RIE: 2 CAT: 17

University of Western Ontario (Canada)
CIJE: 22 RIE: 14 CAT: 17

University of Western Ontario Preschool Program
CIJE: 0 RIE: 1 CAT: 19

University of Windsor (Canada)
CIJE: 7 RIE: 13 CAT: 17

University of Winnipeg (Canada)
CIJE: 2 RIE: 3 CAT: 17

University of Wisconsin
CIJE: 85 RIE: 100 CAT: 17

University of Wisconsin Center Baraboo Sauk County
CIJE: 0 RIE: 1 CAT: 17

University of Wisconsin Center Waukesha County
CIJE: 0 RIE: 1 CAT: 17

University of Wisconsin Eau Claire
CIJE: 7 RIE: 10 CAT: 17

University of Wisconsin Green Bay
CIJE: 8 RIE: 7 CAT: 17

University of Wisconsin La Crosse
CIJE: 6 RIE: 7 CAT: 17

University of Wisconsin Madison
CIJE: 67 RIE: 43 CAT: 17

University of Wisconsin Manitowoc County
CIJE: 0 RIE: 1 CAT: 17

University of Wisconsin Milwaukee
CIJE: 30 RIE: 13 CAT: 17

University of Wisconsin Oshkosh
CIJE: 2 RIE: 20 CAT: 17

University of Wisconsin Parkside
CIJE: 7 RIE: 4 CAT: 17

University of Wisconsin Platteville
CIJE: 1 RIE: 2 CAT: 17

University of Wisconsin River Falls
CIJE: 3 RIE: 2 CAT: 17

University of Wisconsin Sheboygan
CIJE: 0 RIE: 1 CAT: 17

University of Wisconsin Stevens Point
CIJE: 3 RIE: 13 CAT: 17

University of Wisconsin Stout
CIJE: 8 RIE: 9 CAT: 17

University of Wisconsin Superior
CIJE: 2 RIE: 1 CAT: 17

University of Wisconsin System
CIJE: 4 RIE: 21 CAT: 17

University of Wisconsin Whitewater
CIJE: 14 RIE: 8 CAT: 17

University of Wollongong (Australia)
CIJE: 2 RIE: 0 CAT: 17

University of Wyoming
CIJE: 33 RIE: 28 CAT: 17

University of Wyoming University School
CIJE: 0 RIE: 1 CAT: 17

University of York (England)
CIJE: 8 RIE: 1 CAT: 17

University of Zaire
USE National University of Zaire

University of Zambia
CIJE: 7 RIE: 1 CAT: 17

University Poll
CIJE: 0 RIE: 1 CAT: 16

University Presses
CIJE: 16 RIE: 9 CAT: 05

University Reform Law (Spain)
CIJE: 0 RIE: 1 CAT: 14

University Research Corporation CO
CIJE: 0 RIE: 1 CAT: 17

University Residence Environment Scales
CIJE: 10 RIE: 3 CAT: 21

University Residential Building System
CIJE: 1 RIE: 1 CAT: 15

University School of Milwaukee
CIJE: 1 RIE: 0 CAT: 17

University School Shaker Heights OH
CIJE: 1 RIE: 1 CAT: 17

University Structure
CIJE: 2 RIE: 0 CAT: 16

University Student Information System (Canada)
CIJE: 0 RIE: 1 CAT: 15
UF Canadian University Student Information System

University Television Newsletter
CIJE: 0 RIE: 1 CAT: 22

University Urban Schools National Task Force
CIJE: 0 RIE: 2 CAT: 17

University Within Walls AK
CIJE: 0 RIE: 1 CAT: 17

University Year for Action Program
CIJE: 5 RIE: 1 CAT: 19

UNIX Operating System
CIJE: 10 RIE: 2 CAT: 04

Unlearning
CIJE: 2 RIE: 0 CAT: 15

Unmarried Adults
USE Single Adults

Unmarried Parents
CIJE: 6 RIE: 9 CAT: 10
SN See also "Single Parents"

Unmarried Persons
USE Single Persons

Unmet Student Financial Needs
CIJE: 0 RIE: 2 CAT: 16

Unmixed Designs
CIJE: 0 RIE: 1 CAT: 21

Unnumbered Graphic Scales
CIJE: 0 RIE: 1 CAT: 21

Unobtrusive Measures
CIJE: 18 RIE: 12 CAT: 16

Unpaid Labor
CIJE: 1 RIE: 1 CAT: 16

Unpleasant Activities Survey
CIJE: 0 RIE: 1 CAT: 21

Unpleasant Events Schedule
CIJE: 2 RIE: 0 CAT: 21

Unpublished Materials
CIJE: 7 RIE: 17 CAT: 16

Unscheduled Time
CIJE: 1 RIE: 1 CAT: 15

Unwanted Children
CIJE: 2 RIE: 2 CAT: 10

Up and Down Method
CIJE: 0 RIE: 1 CAT: 15

Up from Slavery
CIJE: 3 RIE: 0 CAT: 22

Up with People
CIJE: 1 RIE: 0 CAT: 17

Updike (John)
CIJE: 2 RIE: 2 CAT: 18

Upholsterers
CIJE: 0 RIE: 18 CAT: 09

UPI Newswire
USE United Press International

Upper Arlington City Schools OH
CIJE: 2 RIE: 2 CAT: 17

Upper Asymptote Parameter (Testing)
CIJE: 0 RIE: 1 CAT: 21

Upper Cumberland Development District TN
CIJE: 0 RIE: 1 CAT: 17

Upper Cumberland Development Organization TN
CIJE: 1 RIE: 0 CAT: 17

Upper Cumberland Early Intervention Project
CIJE: 0 RIE: 0 CAT: 19

Upper Cumberland Reading Project
CIJE: 0 RIE: 1 CAT: 19

Upper Cumberland Region (Middle TN)
USE Tennessee (Upper Cumberland)

Upper Extremity Impairments
CIJE: 0 RIE: 1 CAT: 11

Upper Iowa University
CIJE: 0 RIE: 1 CAT: 17

Upper Middle Class
CIJE: 0 RIE: 1 CAT: 10

Upper Midwest Regional Educational Laboratory
CIJE: 1 RIE: 2 CAT: 17

Upper Midwest Small Schools Project
CIJE: 0 RIE: 4 CAT: 19

Upper Peninsula Town Meeting of the Air
CIJE: 1 RIE: 0 CAT: 19

Upper Susquehanna Valley Program
CIJE: 0 RIE: 1 CAT: 19

Upper Volta
CIJE: 5 RIE: 13 CAT: 07
SN Known as "Burkina Faso" as of August 4, 1984

Uppsala University (Sweden)
CIJE: 2 RIE: 2 CAT: 17
UF University of Uppsala (Sweden)

Upsala University NJ
CIJE: 4 RIE: 0 CAT: 17

Upton (Albert)
CIJE: 1 RIE: 1 CAT: 18

Upton (John)
CIJE: 0 RIE: 1 CAT: 18

Upward Bound
CIJE: 28 RIE: 94 CAT: 19

Upward Influence
CIJE: 3 RIE: 1 CAT: 16

Urabayen (Felix)
CIJE: 1 RIE: 0 CAT: 18

Ural Volga Region
USE USSR (Volga Ural Region)

Uranium
CIJE: 6 RIE: 0 CAT: 20

Uranium Industry
CIJE: 1 RIE: 2 CAT: 20

Uranus (Planet)
CIJE: 0 RIE: 0 CAT: 20

Urban Access Project
CIJE: 0 RIE: 1 CAT: 19

Urban Adult Education Institute MI
CIJE: 0 RIE: 1 CAT: 17

Urban Affairs Council
CIJE: 0 RIE: 1 CAT: 17

Urban and Minority Education Fellowship Program
CIJE: 0 RIE: 1 CAT: 19

Urban Bias
CIJE: 1 RIE: 3 CAT: 15

Urban Centers
CIJE: 2 RIE: 1 CAT: 05

Urban Coalition
CIJE: 0 RIE: 5 CAT: 17

Urban Community Coll Transfer Opportunities Prog
CIJE: 0 RIE: 17 CAT: 19
UF Urban Transfer Opportunities Program

Urban Concentric Media Plan
CIJE: 1 RIE: 0 CAT: 19

Urban Conservation Project
CIJE: 0 RIE: 1 CAT: 19

Urban Corps
CIJE: 1 RIE: 1 CAT: 17

Urban Crime Prevention Program
CIJE: 0 RIE: 1 CAT: 19

Urban Demonstration Projects OH
CIJE: 0 RIE: 1 CAT: 19

USSR (Ukraine)
CIJE: 14 RIE: 6 CAT: 07

USSR (Uzbekistan)
CIJE: 0 RIE: 8 CAT: 07

USSR (Volga Ural Region)
CIJE: 0 RIE: 0 CAT: 07
UF Asia (Volga Ural Region); Ural Volga Region; Volga Ural Region

Utah
CIJE: 112 RIE: 570 CAT: 07

Utah (Cedar City)
CIJE: 0 RIE: 2 CAT: 07

Utah (Clearfield)
CIJE: 1 RIE: 0 CAT: 07

Utah (Escalante)
CIJE: 0 RIE: 1 CAT: 07

Utah (Language)
USE Ute

Utah (Logan)
CIJE: 1 RIE: 7 CAT: 07

Utah (Provo)
CIJE: 2 RIE: 12 CAT: 07

Utah (Salt Lake City)
CIJE: 9 RIE: 55 CAT: 07

Utah (Salt Lake County)
CIJE: 0 RIE: 3 CAT: 07

Utah (Tooele County)
CIJE: 0 RIE: 1 CAT: 07

Utah (Uintah Basin)
CIJE: 0 RIE: 1 CAT: 07

Utah (Weber County)
CIJE: 1 RIE: 1 CAT: 07

Utah Career Ladder Program
CIJE: 2 RIE: 1 CAT: 19

Utah Educational Technology Initiative
CIJE: 0 RIE: 1 CAT: 19

Utah Project
CIJE: 0 RIE: 1 CAT: 19

Utah Pupil Teacher Self Concept Program
CIJE: 0 RIE: 2 CAT: 19

Utah Schools and Lands Improvement Act 1993
CIJE: 0 RIE: 1 CAT: 14
UF Public Law 103 93

Utah Schools for the Deaf and the Blind
CIJE: 0 RIE: 2 CAT: 17

Utah Skills Center
CIJE: 0 RIE: 1 CAT: 17

Utah State Board of Education
CIJE: 0 RIE: 6 CAT: 17

Utah State Hospital
CIJE: 1 RIE: 0 CAT: 17

Utah State Industrial School
CIJE: 0 RIE: 2 CAT: 17

Utah State Office of Education
CIJE: 1 RIE: 6 CAT: 17

Utah State University
CIJE: 29 RIE: 33 CAT: 17

Utah State University Classroom Management Program
CIJE: 1 RIE: 0 CAT: 19

Utah State University Protocol Project
CIJE: 2 RIE: 0 CAT: 19

Utah Statewide Educational Assessment Program
CIJE: 0 RIE: 2 CAT: 19

Utah Test of Language Development
CIJE: 2 RIE: 1 CAT: 21

Utah Valley Community College
CIJE: 2 RIE: 1 CAT: 17

Ute
CIJE: 0 RIE: 1 CAT: 13
SN Dialect of Southern Paiute
UF Utah (Language); Yuta; Yutah

Ute (Tribe)
CIJE: 11 RIE: 21 CAT: 08

Ute Mountains
CIJE: 0 RIE: 1 CAT: 07

Utica College NY
CIJE: 3 RIE: 7 CAT: 17

Utica Community School District MI
CIJE: 1 RIE: 3 CAT: 17

Utilitarianism
CIJE: 6 RIE: 2 CAT: 16

Utility Analysis
CIJE: 6 RIE: 4 CAT: 15

Utility Functions
CIJE: 7 RIE: 4 CAT: 21

Utility Test (French et al)
CIJE: 0 RIE: 1 CAT: 21

Utility Theory
CIJE: 21 RIE: 7 CAT: 15
SN See also "Multi Attribute Utility Theory" and "Multiple Criteria Utility Theory"

Utilization Framework (Alkin)
CIJE: 0 RIE: 1 CAT: 15

UTLAS
USE University of Toronto Library Automation Systems

Utopia
CIJE: 23 RIE: 14 CAT: 15

Utopian Literature
CIJE: 28 RIE: 4 CAT: 16

Utopian Societies
CIJE: 3 RIE: 2 CAT: 15

Utvardering Genom Uppfoljning Project
CIJE: 0 RIE: 1 CAT: 19

Uzbekistan
CIJE: 0 RIE: 4 CAT: 07
SN See also "USSR (Uzbekistan)"

Uzgiris Hunt Ordinal Scales of Psychological Devel
CIJE: 7 RIE: 9 CAT: 21

Uznadze (D N)
CIJE: 1 RIE: 1 CAT: 18

V Time
USE Voluntary Reduced Work Time

Vaagri Boli
CIJE: 0 RIE: 1 CAT: 13

Vacant Schools
CIJE: 0 RIE: 1 CAT: 05

Vaccination
CIJE: 8 RIE: 4 CAT: 11
UF Immunization Injection

Vaccine Related Injury
CIJE: 0 RIE: 1 CAT: 11

Vaccines
CIJE: 13 RIE: 6 CAT: 11
SN See also "Polio Vaccines"

Vachek (Josef)
CIJE: 0 RIE: 1 CAT: 18

Vacuum
CIJE: 4 RIE: 0 CAT: 20

Vacuum Distillation
CIJE: 1 RIE: 0 CAT: 20

Vacuum Filtration
CIJE: 0 RIE: 1 CAT: 20

Vacuum Freeze Drying
USE Freeze Drying Method

Vagal Tone
CIJE: 4 RIE: 1 CAT: 11

Vagrancy
CIJE: 1 RIE: 2 CAT: 14

Vah Dialect
CIJE: 0 RIE: 1 CAT: 13

Vai
CIJE: 3 RIE: 1 CAT: 13

Vail (Colorado) Conf Counseling Psychology 1973
CIJE: 2 RIE: 0 CAT: 02

Vaizey (John)
CIJE: 1 RIE: 0 CAT: 18

Valdelomar (Abrahm)
CIJE: 1 RIE: 0 CAT: 18

Valdez (Luis)
CIJE: 1 RIE: 0 CAT: 18

Valdosta State College GA
CIJE: 0 RIE: 1 CAT: 17

Valedictorians
CIJE: 4 RIE: 3 CAT: 10

Valence Theory
CIJE: 11 RIE: 1 CAT: 20

Valencia Community College FL
CIJE: 5 RIE: 18 CAT: 17

Valentines Day
CIJE: 5 RIE: 6 CAT: 12

Valera (Juan de)
CIJE: 2 RIE: 0 CAT: 18

Valery (Paul)
CIJE: 0 RIE: 1 CAT: 18

Valett (Robert)
CIJE: 1 RIE: 0 CAT: 18

Valett Stanford Binet L M Profile
CIJE: 0 RIE: 1 CAT: 21

Validation Verification and Testing Techniques
CIJE: 5 RIE: 20 CAT: 15

Validity Generalization
CIJE: 8 RIE: 7 CAT: 21

Validity Network Schema
CIJE: 0 RIE: 1 CAT: 21

Validity Research
CIJE: 12 RIE: 17 CAT: 15

Validity Sector
CIJE: 0 RIE: 1 CAT: 21

Valle Inclan (Ramon del)
CIJE: 2 RIE: 0 CAT: 18

Vallejo (Cesar)
CIJE: 15 RIE: 0 CAT: 18

Vallejo (Manuel Mejia)
CIJE: 1 RIE: 0 CAT: 18

Vallejo Unified School District CA
CIJE: 1 RIE: 2 CAT: 17

Valley City State College ND
CIJE: 0 RIE: 2 CAT: 17

Valley Falls Branch Library RI
CIJE: 1 RIE: 0 CAT: 17

Valley Forge Christian College v Americans United
CIJE: 1 RIE: 0 CAT: 14

Valley Forge Encampment
CIJE: 1 RIE: 0 CAT: 12
SN Winter headquarters of Washington and the Continental Army 1777-78
UF Pennsylvania (Valley Forge Historic Site)

Valley Forge Military Academy and Junior Coll PA
CIJE: 0 RIE: 1 CAT: 17

Valley Migrant League
CIJE: 0 RIE: 1 CAT: 17

Valley Public Schools NE
CIJE: 0 RIE: 1 CAT: 17

Valley Stream Central High School NY
CIJE: 1 RIE: 0 CAT: 17

Valley View School District IL
CIJE: 2 RIE: 3 CAT: 17

Valley View School OH
CIJE: 1 RIE: 0 CAT: 17

Valley View Youth Center IL
CIJE: 1 RIE: 0 CAT: 17

Valleybrook Lakemont Simulation Game
CIJE: 0 RIE: 4 CAT: 15

Valparaiso University IN
CIJE: 0 RIE: 3 CAT: 17

Valuation Theory
CIJE: 2 RIE: 3 CAT: 15

Value Added
CIJE: 43 RIE: 34 CAT: 15

Value Added Model
CIJE: 16 RIE: 5 CAT: 15

Value Added Tax
CIJE: 2 RIE: 2 CAT: 16

Value Added Testing
CIJE: 5 RIE: 4 CAT: 21

Value Analysis
CIJE: 13 RIE: 4 CAT: 15

Value Climate
CIJE: 0 RIE: 1 CAT: 16

Value Engineering
CIJE: 2 RIE: 3 CAT: 15

Value Interest Dynamics Instrument (Neal)
CIJE: 1 RIE: 0 CAT: 21

Value Orientation Test (Kelley)
CIJE: 0 RIE: 1 CAT: 21

Value Orientations
CIJE: 8 RIE: 10 CAT: 16

Value Orientations Scale
CIJE: 0 RIE: 1 CAT: 21

Value Profile Concept
CIJE: 1 RIE: 0 CAT: 16

Value Proposition Debate
CIJE: 2 RIE: 1 CAT: 13

Value Sharing
CIJE: 2 RIE: 3 CAT: 15

Value Triangles
CIJE: 0 RIE: 1 CAT: 15

Value Vectors Index (Lewis)
CIJE: 1 RIE: 0 CAT: 21

Values Concerning Disadvantaged Pupils Quest
CIJE: 0 RIE: 1 CAT: 21

Values Confrontation
CIJE: 1 RIE: 1 CAT: 15

Values in Concert
CIJE: 0 RIE: 1 CAT: 03

Values Inventory
CIJE: 1 RIE: 1 CAT: 21

Values Inventory for Children
CIJE: 1 RIE: 2 CAT: 21

Values Management
CIJE: 0 RIE: 1 CAT: 15

Values Research
CIJE: 12 RIE: 8 CAT: 15

Values Scale
CIJE: 1 RIE: 1 CAT: 21

Valvar Aortic Stenosis
CIJE: 1 RIE: 0 CAT: 11

Valves
CIJE: 0 RIE: 4 CAT: 04

Van Alstyne Picture Vocabulary Test
CIJE: 1 RIE: 3 CAT: 21

Van Buren (Abigail)
CIJE: 1 RIE: 1 CAT: 18
UF Dear Abby

Van Buren Intermediate School District MI
CIJE: 0 RIE: 2 CAT: 17

Van de Graaff Generator
CIJE: 1 RIE: 0 CAT: 04

Van Der Flier Index
CIJE: 1 RIE: 0 CAT: 21

van Dijk (J)
CIJE: 0 RIE: 1 CAT: 18

van Dijk (T A)
CIJE: 1 RIE: 4 CAT: 18

Van Gennep (Arnold)
CIJE: 0 RIE: 1 CAT: 18

van Gogh (Vincent Willem)
USE Van Gogh (Vincent)

Van Gogh (Vincent)
CIJE: 9 RIE: 3 CAT: 18
UF Gogh (Vincent van); van Gogh (Vincent Willem)

Van Hiele Levels
CIJE: 16 RIE: 9 CAT: 20

Van Leer Foundation
CIJE: 1 RIE: 3 CAT: 17

Van Schyndel Voice Indexing System
CIJE: 0 RIE: 1 CAT: 04

Van Til (Cornelius)
CIJE: 0 RIE: 1 CAT: 18

Van Til (William)
CIJE: 3 RIE: 0 CAT: 18

Van Vogt (A E)
CIJE: 0 RIE: 2 CAT: 18

Van Waganen Reading Scales
CIJE: 1 RIE: 1 CAT: 21

Van Wagenen Rate of Comprehension Test
CIJE: 0 RIE: 1 CAT: 21

Vanadium
CIJE: 3 RIE: 0 CAT: 20

Vance Language Skills Test
CIJE: 0 RIE: 1 CAT: 21

Vance Schlechty Study
CIJE: 0 RIE: 1 CAT: 22

Vancouver Board of School Trustees BC
CIJE: 0 RIE: 3 CAT: 17

Vancouver City College (Canada)
CIJE: 1 RIE: 0 CAT: 17

Vancouver Community College BC
CIJE: 0 RIE: 5 CAT: 17

Vancouver Native Indian Cultural Survival Program
CIJE: 0 RIE: 0 CAT: 19

Vancouver School District WA
CIJE: 2 RIE: 1 CAT: 17

Vandenberg Mental Rotations Test
CIJE: 0 RIE: 1 CAT: 21

Vanderbilt Negative Indicators Scale
CIJE: 1 RIE: 1 CAT: 21

Vanderbilt Summer Research Program
CIJE: 0 RIE: 1 CAT: 19

Vanderbilt University TN
CIJE: 47 RIE: 14 CAT: 17

Vane Kindergarten Test
CIJE: 8 RIE: 2 CAT: 21

Vanguard Instructional Model
CIJE: 0 RIE: 1 CAT: 15

Vanguard Joint Vocational School OH
CIJE: 0 RIE: 1 CAT: 17

Vanguard Program
CIJE: 0 RIE: 1 CAT: 19

Vanier College (Canada)
CIJE: 1 RIE: 1 CAT: 17

Vanity Presses
CIJE: 2 RIE: 0 CAT: 05

Vanuatu
CIJE: 2 RIE: 1 CAT: 07
SN Formerly "New Hebrides" — independent since Jul80

Vapor Liquid Equilibrium Data
CIJE: 1 RIE: 0 CAT: 20

Vapors
CIJE: 0 RIE: 1 CAT: 20

VARCL Computer Program
CIJE: 0 RIE: 3 CAT: 04

Vargas Llosa (Mario)
CIJE: 6 RIE: 1 CAT: 18

Variability
CIJE: 17 RIE: 9 CAT: 20
SN Use a more specific term if possible, e.g., "Behavioral Variability," "Intraindividual Variability," "Phonological Variability"

Variability Measurement
CIJE: 7 RIE: 2 CAT: 15

Variable Course Structuring
CIJE: 0 RIE: 1 CAT: 15

Variable Equalization
CIJE: 0 RIE: 1 CAT: 20

Variable Interval Sequenced Action Camera
CIJE: 0 RIE: 1 CAT: 04

Variable Matching Programs
CIJE: 0 RIE: 1 CAT: 19

Variable Rules
CIJE: 4 RIE: 3 CAT: 15

Variable Scheduling
CIJE: 0 RIE: 4 CAT: 15

Variable Utilization Time Principle
CIJE: 0 RIE: 1 CAT: 15

Variables
CIJE: 31 RIE: 24 CAT: 20

Variables (Mathematics)
CIJE: 21 RIE: 4 CAT: 20

Variance (Statistical)
CIJE: 81 RIE: 74 CAT: 15

Variance Partitioning
CIJE: 0 RIE: 2 CAT: 15

Variant Editions
CIJE: 1 RIE: 0 CAT: 16

Variant Spellings
CIJE: 0 RIE: 1 CAT: 13

Varied Auditory Stimulation
CIJE: 1 RIE: 0 CAT: 21

Varimax Procedures
CIJE: 10 RIE: 7 CAT: 16

Vasarely (Victor)
CIJE: 1 RIE: 0 CAT: 18

Vasconcelos (Jose)
CIJE: 2 RIE: 2 CAT: 18

Vascular Dementia
CIJE: 0 RIE: 1 CAT: 11

Vascular Plants
CIJE: 1 RIE: 0 CAT: 20

Vasectomy
CIJE: 1 RIE: 3 CAT: 11

Vassar Attitude Inventory
CIJE: 0 RIE: 1 CAT: 21

Vassar College NY
CIJE: 20 RIE: 10 CAT: 17

Vater Association
CIJE: 1 RIE: 0 CAT: 17

Vatican City State
CIJE: 6 RIE: 2 CAT: 07

Vatican Councils
CIJE: 9 RIE: 4 CAT: 12

VAULT
CIJE: 0 RIE: 2 CAT: 19

VAX 11 780
CIJE: 1 RIE: 0 CAT: 04

VAX Computers
CIJE: 2 RIE: 3 CAT: 04

Vazquez (Richard)
CIJE: 0 RIE: 1 CAT: 18

Veblen (Thorsten)
CIJE: 1 RIE: 0 CAT: 18

Vector Correlation
CIJE: 2 RIE: 0 CAT: 20

Vector Majorization Technique
CIJE: 0 RIE: 1 CAT: 21

Vector Methods
CIJE: 13 RIE: 1 CAT: 15

Vector Model
CIJE: 11 RIE: 1 CAT: 15

Vector Multiplication
CIJE: 1 RIE: 0 CAT: 20

Vector Planning
CIJE: 0 RIE: 1 CAT: 15

Vector Spaces
CIJE: 13 RIE: 1 CAT: 20

Vector Symbol Phrase Grammar
CIJE: 0 RIE: 1 CAT: 04

Vector Theory
CIJE: 11 RIE: 0 CAT: 15

Vector Variables
CIJE: 1 RIE: 1 CAT: 20

Veda
CIJE: 1 RIE: 2 CAT: 16

Vee Diagramming
CIJE: 5 RIE: 1 CAT: 15

Vee Mapping
CIJE: 8 RIE: 1 CAT: 15

Vega (Garcilaso de la)
CIJE: 3 RIE: 0 CAT: 18

Vega Carpio (Lope Felix de)
CIJE: 5 RIE: 1 CAT: 18

Vegetable Fibers
CIJE: 1 RIE: 0 CAT: 20

Vegetable Gardens
CIJE: 3 RIE: 0 CAT: 05

Vegetable Oils
CIJE: 0 RIE: 0 CAT: 20

Vegetables
CIJE: 4 RIE: 20 CAT: 20

Vegetarianism
CIJE: 6 RIE: 4 CAT: 16

Vegetation
CIJE: 1 RIE: 1 CAT: 20

Veinte Poemas de Amor
CIJE: 0 RIE: 1 CAT: 22

Velar Control
CIJE: 0 RIE: 3 CAT: 11

Velasquez (Peter F)
CIJE: 1 RIE: 0 CAT: 18

Veldmans FORTRAN Program ANAVAR
CIJE: 0 RIE: 1 CAT: 04

Velikovsky (Immanuel)
CIJE: 1 RIE: 1 CAT: 18

Velocity
CIJE: 46 RIE: 4 CAT: 20

Velocity Distribution
CIJE: 1 RIE: 0 CAT: 20

Velton Mood Induction Procedure
CIJE: 2 RIE: 1 CAT: 11

Venda (Language)
CIJE: 0 RIE: 0 CAT: 13

Vending Stand Operators
CIJE: 1 RIE: 0 CAT: 09

Venereal Disease Knowledge Inventory
CIJE: 1 RIE: 0 CAT: 21

Venetian Blind Assemblers
CIJE: 0 RIE: 1 CAT: 09

Venezuela
CIJE: 60 RIE: 90 CAT: 07

Venezuela (Caracas)
CIJE: 1 RIE: 3 CAT: 07

Venezuelans
CIJE: 1 RIE: 2 CAT: 08

Vengeance
CIJE: 1 RIE: 0 CAT: 16

Veniaminov (John)
CIJE: 0 RIE: 1 CAT: 18

Venn Diagrams
CIJE: 21 RIE: 3 CAT: 20

Ventilator Dependence
CIJE: 4 RIE: 5 CAT: 11

Ventura College CA
CIJE: 2 RIE: 2 CAT: 17

Ventura Community College District CA
CIJE: 0 RIE: 2 CAT: 17

Ventura Unified School District CA
CIJE: 1 RIE: 0 CAT: 17

Venture Evaluation Procedures
CIJE: 0 RIE: 1 CAT: 21

Venture Program KY
CIJE: 0 RIE: 1 CAT: 19

Ventureno
CIJE: 1 RIE: 0 CAT: 13

Ventures in Community Improvement Project
CIJE: 0 RIE: 2 CAT: 19

Venus (Planet)
CIJE: 3 RIE: 0 CAT: 20

Venus Packaging Limited
CIJE: 1 RIE: 0 CAT: 17

Verbal Aptitude Test
CIJE: 1 RIE: 1 CAT: 21

Verbal Attitude Scale (Rose)
CIJE: 1 RIE: 0 CAT: 21

Verbal Auditory Screening for Children
CIJE: 2 RIE: 0 CAT: 21

Verbal Clitics
CIJE: 0 RIE: 1 CAT: 13

Verbal Coding
CIJE: 5 RIE: 0 CAT: 15

Verbal Decoding Hypothesis
CIJE: 1 RIE: 0 CAT: 15

Verbal Deductive Technique
CIJE: 1 RIE: 0 CAT: 15

Verbal Discrimination
CIJE: 1 RIE: 2 CAT: 15

Verbal Disembedding Test
CIJE: 0 RIE: 1 CAT: 21

Verbal Elaboration
CIJE: 5 RIE: 1 CAT: 13

Verbal Encoding
CIJE: 4 RIE: 3 CAT: 13

Verbal Expressivity Scale
CIJE: 1 RIE: 0 CAT: 21

Verbal Facilitation Effect
CIJE: 1 RIE: 2 CAT: 21

Verbal Imitation
CIJE: 2 RIE: 1 CAT: 13

Verbal Interaction Category System
CIJE: 1 RIE: 3 CAT: 15

Verbal Interaction Project
CIJE: 1 RIE: 15 CAT: 19

Verbal Labeling
CIJE: 13 RIE: 4 CAT: 16

Verbal Language Development Scale
CIJE: 1 RIE: 0 CAT: 21

Verbal Mediation
CIJE: 8 RIE: 8 CAT: 15

Verbal Modeling
CIJE: 1 RIE: 1 CAT: 13

Verbal Nonverbal Reliance Questionnaire
CIJE: 0 RIE: 1 CAT: 21

Verbal Nouns
CIJE: 1 RIE: 2 CAT: 13

Verbal Output Inventory
CIJE: 0 RIE: 1 CAT: 21

Verbal Reaction Behavior Log (Mork)
CIJE: 0 RIE: 1 CAT: 21

Verbal Reading Arithmetic Skills Program
CIJE: 0 RIE: 1 CAT: 19

Verbal Reasoning Quotients
CIJE: 2 RIE: 0 CAT: 21

Verbal Recall
CIJE: 7 RIE: 1 CAT: 21

Verbal Regulation of Behavior
CIJE: 5 RIE: 2 CAT: 21

Verbal Reinforcement
CIJE: 5 RIE: 1 CAT: 21

Verbal Reticence Scale
CIJE: 0 RIE: 0 CAT: 21

Verbal Routines
CIJE: 0 RIE: 2 CAT: 13

Verbal Rules
CIJE: 2 RIE: 2 CAT: 13

Verbal Satiation
CIJE: 2 RIE: 0 CAT: 21

Verbal Self Instruction
CIJE: 5 RIE: 6 CAT: 16

Verbal Skills Curriculum
CIJE: 1 RIE: 0 CAT: 16

Verbal Social Control
CIJE: 1 RIE: 1 CAT: 11

Verbal Visual Synchrony
USE Visual Verbal Synchrony

Verbalizer Visualizer Questionnaire
CIJE: 1 RIE: 1 CAT: 21

Verbo Tonal Method
CIJE: 9 RIE: 7 CAT: 15

Verbosity
CIJE: 3 RIE: 1 CAT: 16

Verdi (Giuseppe)
CIJE: 1 RIE: 0 CAT: 18

Verdicts
CIJE: 2 RIE: 1 CAT: 14

Verga (Giovanni)
CIJE: 2 RIE: 0 CAT: 18

Vergence
CIJE: 1 RIE: 0 CAT: 11

Vergil
CIJE: 2 RIE: 1 CAT: 18

Verification
CIJE: 12 RIE: 6 CAT: 21

Verified Vocational Counseling Instrument
CIJE: 0 RIE: 1 CAT: 21

Verlaine (Paul)
CIJE: 4 RIE: 0 CAT: 18

Vermilion Local School District OH
CIJE: 0 RIE: 1 CAT: 17

Vermilion Parish Schools LA
CIJE: 0 RIE: 1 CAT: 17

Vermin
CIJE: 1 RIE: 1 CAT: 20

Vermont
CIJE: 81 RIE: 295 CAT: 07

Vermont (Brattleboro)
CIJE: 3 RIE: 0 CAT: 07

Vermont (Burlington)
CIJE: 1 RIE: 9 CAT: 07

Vermont (Derby)
CIJE: 0 RIE: 1 CAT: 07

Vermont (Montpelier)
CIJE: 0 RIE: 1 CAT: 07

Vermont (South Burlington)
CIJE: 0 RIE: 1 CAT: 07

Vermont Adult Basic Education Program
CIJE: 0 RIE: 1 CAT: 19

Vermont College
CIJE: 0 RIE: 1 CAT: 17
SN Merged with Norwich Univ in 1972

Vermont Consulting Teacher Program
CIJE: 2 RIE: 0 CAT: 19

Vermont Family Assistance Plan
CIJE: 0 RIE: 1 CAT: 19

Vermont Higher Education Council
CIJE: 0 RIE: 1 CAT: 17

Vermont Mathematics Portfolio Assessment Program
USE Vermont Portfolio Assessment Program

Vermont Portfolio Assessment Program
CIJE: 0 RIE: 0 CAT: 19
UF Vermont Mathematics Portfolio Assessment Program

Vermont State Colleges
CIJE: 0 RIE: 5 CAT: 17

Vermont State Department of Education
CIJE: 0 RIE: 3 CAT: 17

Vernacular
USE Native Language

Vernacular Education
CIJE: 1 RIE: 0 CAT: 16

Verner (C)
CIJE: 0 RIE: 1 CAT: 18

Vernier Caliper
CIJE: 2 RIE: 0 CAT: 21

Vernier Positioning Technique
CIJE: 0 RIE: 2 CAT: 21

Vernon Graded Arithmetic Test
CIJE: 0 RIE: 1 CAT: 21

Vernon Intermediate School TX
CIJE: 1 RIE: 0 CAT: 17

Vernon Regional Technical College TX
CIJE: 0 RIE: 1 CAT: 17

Vernon Verona Sherrill Central High School NY
CIJE: 0 RIE: 1 CAT: 17

VersaBraille
CIJE: 3 RIE: 0 CAT: 04

Versatile Employment of Health Trained Servicemen
CIJE: 1 RIE: 1 CAT: 19

Verstehen
CIJE: 0 RIE: 1 CAT: 16

Vertical Articulation
CIJE: 1 RIE: 1 CAT: 16

Vertical Blanking Interval
CIJE: 0 RIE: 2 CAT: 20

Vertical Equating
CIJE: 8 RIE: 12 CAT: 21

Vertical Files
CIJE: 10 RIE: 9 CAT: 04

Vertical Jump
CIJE: 1 RIE: 0 CAT: 16

Vertical Process Camera
CIJE: 1 RIE: 0 CAT: 04

Vertical Sorting
CIJE: 0 RIE: 1 CAT: 15

Vertical Thinking
CIJE: 4 RIE: 1 CAT: 16

Verticality (Concept)
CIJE: 5 RIE: 2 CAT: 16

Very Early Intensive Preschool Education
USE Hothousing of Preschoolers

Very High Frequency
CIJE: 0 RIE: 1 CAT: 20

Very Large Scale Integration
CIJE: 0 RIE: 0 CAT: 20
UF VLSI Technology

Very Last First Time
CIJE: 2 RIE: 0 CAT: 22

Very Small Aperture Terminal Technology
CIJE: 0 RIE: 1 CAT: 20
UF VSAT Technology

Very Special Arts
CIJE: 1 RIE: 1 CAT: 17
SN An international organization founded in 1974 by Jean Kennedy Smith

Very Special Arts Festivals
CIJE: 2 RIE: 1 CAT: 12

Vesicular Film
CIJE: 4 RIE: 1 CAT: 04

Vesselovsky (Alexander)
CIJE: 1 RIE: 0 CAT: 18

Vestal Central School District NY
CIJE: 1 RIE: 0 CAT: 17

Vestibular Stimulation
CIJE: 12 RIE: 3 CAT: 21

Vestibule Training
CIJE: 1 RIE: 0 CAT: 21

Vesting
CIJE: 4 RIE: 0 CAT: 16

Veszprem University (Hungary)
CIJE: 1 RIE: 0 CAT: 17

Veterans Administration
CIJE: 26 RIE: 72 CAT: 17
SN Changed to "Department of Veterans Affairs," Mar89

Veterans Administration Lakeside Medical Ctr IL
CIJE: 1 RIE: 0 CAT: 17

Veterans Claims
CIJE: 0 RIE: 1 CAT: 16

Veterans Day
CIJE: 0 RIE: 2 CAT: 12

Veterans Education Amendments 1980
CIJE: 0 RIE: 1 CAT: 14

Veterans Education Amendments 1986
CIJE: 0 RIE: 2 CAT: 14

Veterans Education and Employment Amendments 1984
CIJE: 0 RIE: 1 CAT: 14

Veterans Education and Employment Assistance Act
CIJE: 0 RIE: 4 CAT: 14
UF Public Law 94 502

Veterans Education Outreach Program
CIJE: 0 RIE: 0 CAT: 19

Veterans Education Training Amendments Act 1970
CIJE: 1 RIE: 0 CAT: 14

Veterans Educational Assistance Act 1981
CIJE: 0 RIE: 2 CAT: 14

Veterans Educational Assistance Amendments 1991
CIJE: 0 RIE: 1 CAT: 14
UF Public Law 102 127

Veterans Educational Assistance Program
CIJE: 1 RIE: 14 CAT: 19

Veterans Educational Assistance Test Program
USE Educational Assistance Test Program

Veterans Job Training Act 1983
USE Emergency Veterans Job Training Act 1983

Veterans Outreach
CIJE: 0 RIE: 1 CAT: 19

Veterans Readjustment Appointment
CIJE: 1 RIE: 1 CAT: 19

Veterans Readjustment Assistance Act Section 402
CIJE: 0 RIE: 1 CAT: 14

Veterans Rehabilitation Education Amendments 1980
CIJE: 0 RIE: 2 CAT: 14

Veterans Special Education Program
CIJE: 1 RIE: 0 CAT: 19

Veterans Upward Bound
CIJE: 1 RIE: 1 CAT: 19

Veterans Vocational Rehabilitation Program
CIJE: 0 RIE: 1 CAT: 19

Veysey Act
CIJE: 0 RIE: 1 CAT: 14

VHF Teletype Relay Systems
CIJE: 0 RIE: 1 CAT: 15

Viatel (Australia)
CIJE: 0 RIE: 1 CAT: 17

Vibration (Noise)
CIJE: 1 RIE: 1 CAT: 20

Vibration Technique
CIJE: 2 RIE: 0 CAT: 21

Vibrotactile Method
CIJE: 1 RIE: 0 CAT: 21

Vibrotactile Stimulation
CIJE: 5 RIE: 0 CAT: 21

Vibrotactile Stimulation Aids
CIJE: 2 RIE: 0 CAT: 04

Vicarious Conditioning
CIJE: 8 RIE: 2 CAT: 11

Vicarious Participation
CIJE: 6 RIE: 1 CAT: 11

Vicarious Therapy Pretraining
CIJE: 1 RIE: 0 CAT: 15

Vice Presidential Debates
CIJE: 4 RIE: 3 CAT: 16

Vice Presidents of Academic Affairs
CIJE: 1 RIE: 0 CAT: 09
SN See also "College Vice Presidents"

Vice Presidents of the United States
CIJE: 0 RIE: 0 CAT: 10

Vicens Reddy Speech Recognition System
CIJE: 0 RIE: 1 CAT: 15

Vickery (Brian Campbell)
CIJE: 2 RIE: 0 CAT: 18

Vico (Giambattista)
CIJE: 14 RIE: 1 CAT: 18

Victim and Witness Protection Act 1982
CIJE: 0 RIE: 1 CAT: 14

Victim Assistance
CIJE: 1 RIE: 4 CAT: 16

Victim Compensation
CIJE: 2 RIE: 1 CAT: 16

Victimization
CIJE: 35 RIE: 17 CAT: 11

Victims Bill of Rights (California 1982)
CIJE: 0 RIE: 2 CAT: 14
UF Proposition 8 (California 1982)

Victims of Natural Disasters
CIJE: 1 RIE: 0 CAT: 10

Victims of Torture
USE Torture Victims

Victims of War
CIJE: 2 RIE: 1 CAT: 10
UF War Victims

Victims Rights
CIJE: 1 RIE: 3 CAT: 14

Victor Electrowriter Remote Blackboard
CIJE: 0 RIE: 1 CAT: 04

Victor Valley College CA
CIJE: 0 RIE: 5 CAT: 17

Victoria Certificate of Education (Australia)
USE Victorian Certificate of Education (Australia)

Victoria College (Australia)
CIJE: 2 RIE: 1 CAT: 17

Victoria University of Wellington (New Zealand)
CIJE: 2 RIE: 1 CAT: 17

Victorian Age
USE Victorian Period

Victorian Certificate of Education (Australia)
CIJE: 0 RIE: 1 CAT: 21
UF Victoria Certificate of Education (Australia)

Victorian Council of Adult Education
CIJE: 1 RIE: 1 CAT: 17

Victorian Country Education Project (Australia)
CIJE: 0 RIE: 2 CAT: 19

Victorian Period
CIJE: 13 RIE: 3 CAT: 12
UF Victorian Age

Victorian TAFE Off Campus Network (Australia)
CIJE: 0 RIE: 1 CAT: 17

Victorian Technical Schools Division (Australia)
CIJE: 0 RIE: 1 CAT: 17

Vidal (Gore)
CIJE: 0 RIE: 1 CAT: 18

Vidal Olmos (Fernando)
CIJE: 1 RIE: 0 CAT: 18

Video Arcades
CIJE: 1 RIE: 0 CAT: 05

Video Articulator
CIJE: 0 RIE: 1 CAT: 04

Video Audio Compressed
CIJE: 1 RIE: 3 CAT: 16

Video Criticism
CIJE: 0 RIE: 1 CAT: 16

Video Distribution Systems
CIJE: 2 RIE: 2 CAT: 15

Video Instr Develop Educ Opportunity Prog MO
CIJE: 0 RIE: 2 CAT: 19
UF VIDEO Program MO

Video Loan Programs
USE Loan Video Programs

Video Nova Authoring System
CIJE: 1 RIE: 0 CAT: 04

Video Production
CIJE: 18 RIE: 2 CAT: 20

VIDEO Program MO
USE Video Instr Develop Educ Opportunity Prog MO

Video Reference Services
CIJE: 2 RIE: 0 CAT: 15

Video Replays
USE Replays (Video)

Video Repurposing
USE Repurposing

Video Tape Production
CIJE: 15 RIE: 4 CAT: 20

Video Tape Reviews
CIJE: 3 RIE: 2 CAT: 16

Video Technology
CIJE: 103 RIE: 17 CAT: 20

Video Telecommunications
CIJE: 0 RIE: 1 CAT: 20

Video Teleconferencing
CIJE: 8 RIE: 19 CAT: 20

Video Telephone
CIJE: 0 RIE: 9 CAT: 04

Video Viewing
CIJE: 0 RIE: 3 CAT: 16

Videodisk Industry
CIJE: 3 RIE: 2 CAT: 20

Videodisk Repurposing
USE Repurposing

Videographics Systems
CIJE: 3 RIE: 1 CAT: 15

Videomicroscopy
CIJE: 0 RIE: 1 CAT: 20

Videopublishing
CIJE: 0 RIE: 3 CAT: 16

Videosonic Opticom Application
CIJE: 0 RIE: 1 CAT: 20

Videosonic Teaching Machine
CIJE: 0 RIE: 1 CAT: 04

Videotape Participation System
CIJE: 1 RIE: 0 CAT: 15

Videotape Program Service
CIJE: 1 RIE: 0 CAT: 15

Vidicon Equipment
CIJE: 0 RIE: 2 CAT: 04

Vidoco (Francois Eugene)
CIJE: 1 RIE: 0 CAT: 18

Viejas Reservation
CIJE: 1 RIE: 0 CAT: 17

Vienna Correctional Center IL
CIJE: 2 RIE: 0 CAT: 17

Vienna School Business and World Trade (Austria)
CIJE: 0 RIE: 1 CAT: 17

Vientiane Dialect
CIJE: 0 RIE: 1 CAT: 13

Vietnam
CIJE: 69 RIE: 110 CAT: 07

Vietnam Era Veterans Readjustment Assistance Act
CIJE: 0 RIE: 4 CAT: 14

Vietnam Veterans Leadership Program
CIJE: 0 RIE: 1 CAT: 19

Vietnam Veterans Memorial
CIJE: 5 RIE: 3 CAT: 16

Vietnam War Literature
CIJE: 0 RIE: 3 CAT: 16

Vietnamese Culture
CIJE: 0 RIE: 5 CAT: 16

View Castle School District PA
CIJE: 0 RIE: 1 CAT: 17

VIEWS Faucet Assembly
CIJE: 0 RIE: 1 CAT: 21

Views of Life Scale
CIJE: 0 RIE: 1 CAT: 21

Views on Science Technology Society
CIJE: 0 RIE: 1 CAT: 21

VIEWS Screen Assembly
CIJE: 0 RIE: 1 CAT: 21

Vigilance Performance
CIJE: 9 RIE: 2 CAT: 11

Vigilante Films
CIJE: 0 RIE: 1 CAT: 16

Vigilantes
CIJE: 0 RIE: 1 CAT: 10

Vignettes
CIJE: 18 RIE: 17 CAT: 16

Vigo County Public Library IN
CIJE: 2 RIE: 1 CAT: 17

Vigo County School Corporation IN
CIJE: 0 RIE: 1 CAT: 17

Vikings
CIJE: 3 RIE: 1 CAT: 10

Villa Julie College MD
CIJE: 1 RIE: 2 CAT: 17

Villa Lobos (Heitor)
CIJE: 1 RIE: 0 CAT: 18

Villa Maria High School PA
CIJE: 1 RIE: 0 CAT: 17

Village Colleges (England)
CIJE: 0 RIE: 1 CAT: 05

Village High Schools
CIJE: 0 RIE: 1 CAT: 05

Village Library Project AK
CIJE: 0 RIE: 1 CAT: 19

Village Life
CIJE: 2 RIE: 2 CAT: 16

Village Prose
CIJE: 0 RIE: 1 CAT: 16
SN Russian literary movement, 1950-80

Villages
CIJE: 12 RIE: 5 CAT: 16

Villanova University PA
CIJE: 5 RIE: 4 CAT: 17

Villarreal (Jose A)
CIJE: 0 RIE: 1 CAT: 18

Villena (Enrique de)
CIJE: 1 RIE: 0 CAT: 18

Villon (Francois)
CIJE: 1 RIE: 0 CAT: 18

Vilonia School District AR
CIJE: 0 RIE: 1 CAT: 17

Vinal (William)
CIJE: 4 RIE: 0 CAT: 18

Vincennes Open University (France)
CIJE: 0 RIE: 1 CAT: 17

Vincennes University IN
CIJE: 1 RIE: 4 CAT: 17

Vincent de Beauvais
CIJE: 0 RIE: 1 CAT: 18

Vincent Learning Curves
CIJE: 0 RIE: 1 CAT: 21

Vincent Personal Events Time Scale
CIJE: 0 RIE: 1 CAT: 21

Vine Production
CIJE: 0 RIE: 1 CAT: 20

Vineland Adaptive Behavior Scales
CIJE: 17 RIE: 9 CAT: 21

Vineland Ego Development Profile (Howard Miller)
CIJE: 2 RIE: 0 CAT: 21

Vineland Social Maturity Scale
CIJE: 9 RIE: 7 CAT: 21

Viniculture
USE Viticulture

Vintage Effect (Teaching Profession)
CIJE: 0 RIE: 0 CAT: 15
SN Differences in the quality of teachers hired during different time periods

Vinyl
CIJE: 1 RIE: 0 CAT: 04

Vinyl Asbestos Tile
CIJE: 1 RIE: 0 CAT: 04

Vinyl Chloride
CIJE: 3 RIE: 1 CAT: 20

Violation of Assumptions
CIJE: 9 RIE: 8 CAT: 21

Violence Index (Gerbner and Gross)
CIJE: 0 RIE: 1 CAT: 21

Violin Instruction
CIJE: 7 RIE: 0 CAT: 03

Virgin Islands
CIJE: 15 RIE: 73 CAT: 07

Virgin Islands (Saint Croix)
CIJE: 1 RIE: 8 CAT: 07

Virgin Islands (Saint Thomas)
CIJE: 0 RIE: 2 CAT: 07

Virgin Islands Educational Dissemination System
CIJE: 0 RIE: 1 CAT: 04

Virgin Land the American West as Symbol and Myth
CIJE: 1 RIE: 0 CAT: 22

Virgin Valley High School NV
CIJE: 0 RIE: 4 CAT: 17

Virginia
CIJE: 300 RIE: 954 CAT: 07

Virginia (Albemarle County)
CIJE: 4 RIE: 8 CAT: 07

Virginia (Alexandria)
CIJE: 4 RIE: 10 CAT: 07

Virginia (Arlington County)
CIJE: 2 RIE: 1 CAT: 07

Virginia (Arlington)
CIJE: 12 RIE: 24 CAT: 07

Virginia (Baileys Crossroads)
CIJE: 0 RIE: 1 CAT: 07

Virginia (Blacksburg)
CIJE: 1 RIE: 6 CAT: 07

Virginia (Caroline County)
CIJE: 1 RIE: 0 CAT: 07

Virginia (Central)
CIJE: 0 RIE: 2 CAT: 07

Virginia (Charles City County)
CIJE: 0 RIE: 1 CAT: 17

Virginia (Charlottesville)
CIJE: 1 RIE: 6 CAT: 07

Virginia (Chesapeake)
CIJE: 2 RIE: 1 CAT: 07

Virginia (Eastern Shore)
CIJE: 0 RIE: 1 CAT: 07

Virginia (Emporia)
CIJE: 0 RIE: 1 CAT: 07

Virginia (Fairfax County)
CIJE: 13 RIE: 13 CAT: 07

Virginia (Fairfax)
CIJE: 1 RIE: 2 CAT: 07

Virginia (Gloucester County)
CIJE: 0 RIE: 1 CAT: 07

Virginia (Greene County)
CIJE: 0 RIE: 1 CAT: 07

Virginia (Hampton)
CIJE: 2 RIE: 4 CAT: 07

Virginia (Henrico County)
CIJE: 1 RIE: 1 CAT: 07

Virginia (Jamestown)
CIJE: 1 RIE: 2 CAT: 07

Virginia (Loudoun County)
CIJE: 1 RIE: 1 CAT: 07

Virginia (Lunenburg County)
CIJE: 0 RIE: 1 CAT: 07

Virginia (Lynchburg)
CIJE: 0 RIE: 4 CAT: 07

Virginia (Montgomery County)
CIJE: 1 RIE: 0 CAT: 07

Virginia (Nelson County)
CIJE: 0 RIE: 1 CAT: 07

Virginia (Newport News)
CIJE: 2 RIE: 3 CAT: 07

Virginia (Norfolk)
CIJE: 12 RIE: 20 CAT: 07

Virginia (Pennington Gap)
CIJE: 1 RIE: 0 CAT: 07

Virginia (Petersburg)
CIJE: 2 RIE: 2 CAT: 07

Virginia (Portsmouth)
CIJE: 1 RIE: 0 CAT: 07

Virginia (Prince Edward County)
CIJE: 5 RIE: 7 CAT: 07

Virginia (Prince William County)
CIJE: 1 RIE: 4 CAT: 07

Virginia (Reston)
CIJE: 3 RIE: 1 CAT: 07

Virginia (Richmond)
CIJE: 13 RIE: 19 CAT: 07

Virginia (Roanoke)
CIJE: 4 RIE: 5 CAT: 07

Virginia (Southwest)
CIJE: 3 RIE: 4 CAT: 07

Virginia (Tidewater)
CIJE: 0 RIE: 2 CAT: 07

Virginia (Virginia Beach)
CIJE: 4 RIE: 6 CAT: 07

Virginia (Warren County)
CIJE: 0 RIE: 1 CAT: 07

Virginia (Warrenton)
CIJE: 1 RIE: 1 CAT: 07

Virginia (Williamsburg)
CIJE: 4 RIE: 2 CAT: 07

Virginia (York County)
CIJE: 0 RIE: 2 CAT: 07

Virginia Association for Trade and Industrial Educ
CIJE: 0 RIE: 0 CAT: 17

Virginia Beach Schools VA
CIJE: 4 RIE: 17 CAT: 17

Virginia Beginning Teacher Assistance Program
CIJE: 2 RIE: 0 CAT: 19
UF Beginning Teacher Assistance Program VA

Virginia Commonwealth University
CIJE: 25 RIE: 25 CAT: 17

Virginia Community College System
CIJE: 3 RIE: 24 CAT: 17

Virginia Cooperative Extension Service
CIJE: 0 RIE: 2 CAT: 17

Virginia Council for the Social Studies
CIJE: 0 RIE: 1 CAT: 17

Virginia Department of Education
CIJE: 0 RIE: 1 CAT: 17

Virginia Educational Needs Assessment Program
CIJE: 0 RIE: 2 CAT: 19

Virginia Extension Homemakers Council
CIJE: 0 RIE: 1 CAT: 17

Virginia Governors Schools
CIJE: 1 RIE: 0 CAT: 17

Virginia Higher Education Study Commission
CIJE: 0 RIE: 1 CAT: 17

Virginia Highlands Community College
CIJE: 0 RIE: 2 CAT: 17

Virginia Library Advisory Committee
CIJE: 1 RIE: 0 CAT: 17

Virginia Military Institute
CIJE: 5 RIE: 1 CAT: 17

Virginia Polytechnic Inst and State Univ
CIJE: 60 RIE: 32 CAT: 17

Virginia Public Education Network
CIJE: 0 RIE: 1 CAT: 19

Virginia Public Telecommunication Council
CIJE: 0 RIE: 3 CAT: 17

Virginia Quality Educ in Sciences and Technology
CIJE: 0 RIE: 1 CAT: 19

Virginia Satellite Educational Network
CIJE: 0 RIE: 1 CAT: 19

Virginia Standards of Learning Program
CIJE: 1 RIE: 1 CAT: 19

Virginia State College
CIJE: 1 RIE: 0 CAT: 17

Virginia State Council of Higher Education
USE State Council of Higher Education for Virginia

Virginia State University
CIJE: 2 RIE: 4 CAT: 17

Virginia Student Retention Program
CIJE: 0 RIE: 1 CAT: 19

Virginia Teachers Association
CIJE: 1 RIE: 0 CAT: 17

Virginia Tech Library System
CIJE: 4 RIE: 1 CAT: 04

Virginia Union University
CIJE: 1 RIE: 3 CAT: 17

Virginia Vocational Association
CIJE: 0 RIE: 1 CAT: 17

Virginia Western Community College
CIJE: 0 RIE: 3 CAT: 17

Viroids
CIJE: 0 RIE: 1 CAT: 11

Virology
CIJE: 2 RIE: 1 CAT: 11

Virtual Classrooms
CIJE: 1 RIE: 2 CAT: 05

Virtual Libraries
CIJE: 19 RIE: 6 CAT: 05

Virtual Reality
CIJE: 62 RIE: 24 CAT: 20

Virtues
CIJE: 10 RIE: 3 CAT: 16

Vis U Guide Responder 700
CIJE: 0 RIE: 1 CAT: 04

Visas
CIJE: 8 RIE: 2 CAT: 14

Viscometry
CIJE: 2 RIE: 0 CAT: 20

Visconti (Luchino)
CIJE: 1 RIE: 0 CAT: 18

Viscosity
CIJE: 5 RIE: 0 CAT: 20

Visible Displacement
CIJE: 1 RIE: 0 CAT: 11

VisiCalc
CIJE: 2 RIE: 2 CAT: 04

Vision Educational Foundation
CIJE: 1 RIE: 0 CAT: 17

Vision Quest
CIJE: 2 RIE: 6 CAT: 15
SN An American Indian ritual for gaining psychological or religious insight — see also "Wilderness Vision Quest" — do not confuse with the organizational name "VisionQuest National Ltd"

Vision Therapy
CIJE: 0 RIE: 1 CAT: 11
UF Optometric Vision Therapy

VisionQuest National Ltd
CIJE: 0 RIE: 0 CAT: 17
SN Profit-making organization of Tucson AZ that provides treatment programs for troubled youth

Visions
CIJE: 0 RIE: 1 CAT: 16

Visions for Children
CIJE: 0 RIE: 2 CAT: 19
SN African-American preschool program

Visit (Durrenmatt)
CIJE: 0 RIE: 1 CAT: 22

Visit to a Small Planet
CIJE: 0 RIE: 1 CAT: 22

Visitation (by Parents)
USE Parent Visitation

Visitation Moderation
CIJE: 0 RIE: 1 CAT: 15

Visitation Rights
CIJE: 11 RIE: 8 CAT: 14

Visiting Geological Scientist Program
CIJE: 1 RIE: 0 CAT: 19

Visiting Nurse Association
CIJE: 1 RIE: 0 CAT: 17

Visiting Professor Series
CIJE: 1 RIE: 1 CAT: 16

Visiting Scholars
CIJE: 5 RIE: 4 CAT: 10

Visitor Behavior
CIJE: 2 RIE: 2 CAT: 16

Visitor Control
CIJE: 0 RIE: 1 CAT: 15

Visitors
CIJE: 15 RIE: 1 CAT: 10
SN If possible, use more specific "Classroom Visitors," "Home Visitors," "International Visitors," etc.

Visitors Books
CIJE: 1 RIE: 1 CAT: 16

VISTA
USE Volunteers in Service to America

Vista College CA
CIJE: 2 RIE: 9 CAT: 17

VISTA Literacy Corps
USE Volunteers in Service to America Literacy Corps

Vista System (Bell Canada)
CIJE: 0 RIE: 1 CAT: 04

Vista Unified School District CA
CIJE: 2 RIE: 1 CAT: 17

Visual Aesthetic Sensitivity Test (Gotz)
CIJE: 0 RIE: 1 CAT: 21

Visual Analysis Test (Rosner)
CIJE: 0 RIE: 1 CAT: 21

Visual Analytic Skills Test
CIJE: 0 RIE: 1 CAT: 21

Visual and Ocular Motility Tests
CIJE: 0 RIE: 1 CAT: 21

Visual Aptitude
CIJE: 0 RIE: 4 CAT: 15

Visual Assessment Inventory
CIJE: 0 RIE: 1 CAT: 21

Visual Asymmetry
CIJE: 1 RIE: 1 CAT: 11

Visual Attention
CIJE: 24 RIE: 5 CAT: 11

Visual Auditory Kinesthetic Tactile Instruction
CIJE: 1 RIE: 1 CAT: 15

Visual Auditory Tactile Kinesthetic Approach
CIJE: 0 RIE: 1 CAT: 15

Visual Aural Digit Span Test (Koppitz)
CIJE: 3 RIE: 2 CAT: 21

Visual Cliff Experiment
CIJE: 0 RIE: 1 CAT: 21

Visual Communication
CIJE: 10 RIE: 5 CAT: 16

Visual Communication Education
CIJE: 11 RIE: 5 CAT: 03

Visual Communication Education Program
CIJE: 0 RIE: 1 CAT: 19

Visual Complexity
CIJE: 0 RIE: 3 CAT: 15

Visual Compositions
CIJE: 9 RIE: 1 CAT: 13

Visual Coorientation
CIJE: 1 RIE: 0 CAT: 11

Visual Cues
CIJE: 15 RIE: 9 CAT: 11

Visual Design
CIJE: 20 RIE: 7 CAT: 16

Visual Designs Test (Johnson O Connor)
CIJE: 0 RIE: 1 CAT: 21

Visual Discrimination Inventory (Lombard Stern)
CIJE: 0 RIE: 2 CAT: 21

Visual Discrimination Test
CIJE: 1 RIE: 1 CAT: 21

Visual Displays
CIJE: 18 RIE: 6 CAT: 16

Visual Efficiency Scale
CIJE: 3 RIE: 0 CAT: 21

Visual Evoked Potential
CIJE: 3 RIE: 1 CAT: 11

Visual Excellence
CIJE: 0 RIE: 1 CAT: 15

Visual Haptic Training
CIJE: 2 RIE: 1 CAT: 16

Visual Iconicity
USE Iconicity

Visual Image Transmission
USE Image Transmission

Visual Imagery
CIJE: 20 RIE: 9 CAT: 11

Visual Inference Checklist
CIJE: 1 RIE: 0 CAT: 21

Visual Journalism
CIJE: 5 RIE: 9 CAT: 16

Visual Literacy Project for Migrant Youth
CIJE: 1 RIE: 0 CAT: 19

Visual Literacy Test (Turner)
CIJE: 0 RIE: 1 CAT: 21

Visual Manipulation
CIJE: 0 RIE: 1 CAT: 11

Visual Media Technicians
CIJE: 0 RIE: 1 CAT: 09

Visual Merchandising (Displays)
CIJE: 0 RIE: 2 CAT: 15

Visual Motor Functioning
CIJE: 9 RIE: 2 CAT: 16

Visual Motor Integration Test
CIJE: 1 RIE: 2 CAT: 21

Visual Motor Tracking
CIJE: 1 RIE: 0 CAT: 11
UF Tracking (Visual Motor)

Visual Observational Schedule of Teacher Behaviors
CIJE: 0 RIE: 1 CAT: 21

Visual Occlusion
CIJE: 3 RIE: 1 CAT: 11

Visual Perception Inventory
CIJE: 0 RIE: 1 CAT: 21

Visual Perceptual Deficit Hypothesis
CIJE: 1 RIE: 0 CAT: 11

Visual Perceptual Speed
CIJE: 2 RIE: 1 CAT: 21

Visual Placing Response
CIJE: 2 RIE: 1 CAT: 21

Visual Preference
CIJE: 6 RIE: 3 CAT: 11

Visual Preference Technique
CIJE: 1 RIE: 0 CAT: 15

Visual Processing
CIJE: 11 RIE: 3 CAT: 11

Visual Recall
CIJE: 0 RIE: 1 CAT: 11

Visual Representation
CIJE: 22 RIE: 12 CAT: 15

Visual Response System
CIJE: 6 RIE: 2 CAT: 16

Visual Screening
CIJE: 4 RIE: 0 CAT: 11

Visual Sequencing Task
CIJE: 2 RIE: 1 CAT: 21

Visual Studies Workshop
CIJE: 1 RIE: 0 CAT: 02

Visual Syntax
CIJE: 1 RIE: 1 CAT: 16

Visual Testing
USE Visual Tests

Visual Tests
CIJE: 0 RIE: 1 CAT: 21
UF Visual Testing

Visual Thinking
CIJE: 14 RIE: 21 CAT: 11

Visual Tracking
CIJE: 6 RIE: 3 CAT: 11
UF Tracking (Visual)

Visual Verbal Synchrony
CIJE: 1 RIE: 4 CAT: 16
UF Verbal Visual Synchrony

Visuality (Language)
USE Iconicity

Visually Evoked Responses
CIJE: 3 RIE: 1 CAT: 11

Visualmaker
CIJE: 2 RIE: 0 CAT: 16

Visuomanual Tracking
CIJE: 1 RIE: 0 CAT: 11
UF Tracking (Visuomanual)

VITAL
USE Volunteers in Tutoring Adult Learners

VITAL (Authoring System)
CIJE: 2 RIE: 0 CAT: 04

VITAL Career Information Center
CIJE: 0 RIE: 1 CAT: 17

Vital Information for Education and Work
CIJE: 3 RIE: 13 CAT: 19

Vital Signs (Physiology)
CIJE: 0 RIE: 1 CAT: 11

Vital Statistics
CIJE: 7 RIE: 9 CAT: 16

Vitamin A
CIJE: 0 RIE: 3 CAT: 11

Vitamin C
CIJE: 2 RIE: 2 CAT: 11

Vitamin Deficiency
CIJE: 2 RIE: 2 CAT: 11

Vitamins
CIJE: 21 RIE: 9 CAT: 11

Viticulture
CIJE: 1 RIE: 1 CAT: 20
SN See also "Winemaking"
UF Viniculture

Vittorini (Elio)
CIJE: 1 RIE: 0 CAT: 18

Vitz (Paul C)
CIJE: 0 RIE: 0 CAT: 18

Vives (Amadeo)
CIJE: 1 RIE: 0 CAT: 18

Viviani (P)
CIJE: 0 RIE: 1 CAT: 18

Vivid Information
CIJE: 0 RIE: 2 CAT: 16
UF Vividness of Information

Vividness
CIJE: 1 RIE: 1 CAT: 16

Vividness of Information
USE Vivid Information

Vividness of Visual Imagery Questionnaire
CIJE: 2 RIE: 0 CAT: 21

Vivisection
CIJE: 1 RIE: 0 CAT: 20

Vlandis v Kline
CIJE: 2 RIE: 0 CAT: 14

VLSI Technology
USE Very Large Scale Integration

VM Scale (Morrison)
CIJE: 0 RIE: 1 CAT: 21

Vo Ag Facts
CIJE: 1 RIE: 0 CAT: 22

VOC PLAN (Computer Program)
CIJE: 0 RIE: 1 CAT: 04

Vocabulary Assessment Task
CIJE: 0 RIE: 1 CAT: 21

Vocabulary in Context Exercises
CIJE: 2 RIE: 1 CAT: 21

Vocabulary Search Aids
CIJE: 1 RIE: 0 CAT: 16

Vocabulary Switching Systems
CIJE: 0 RIE: 1 CAT: 04

Vocal Exercises
CIJE: 1 RIE: 1 CAT: 16

Vocal Nodules
CIJE: 6 RIE: 0 CAT: 11

VOCAL Programing Language
CIJE: 1 RIE: 1 CAT: 04

Vocal Qualities
CIJE: 7 RIE: 9 CAT: 13

Vocal Tone
CIJE: 0 RIE: 1 CAT: 11

Vocalization
CIJE: 63 RIE: 18 CAT: 13

Vocalization Latency
CIJE: 1 RIE: 1 CAT: 15

Vocational Academy Project
CIJE: 0 RIE: 1 CAT: 19

Vocational Administrative Management System
CIJE: 0 RIE: 1 CAT: 19
SN Project of the Missouri Board of Education

Vocational Adult Secondary Training Project
CIJE: 0 RIE: 1 CAT: 19

Vocational Agriculture in the Changing Scene
CIJE: 1 RIE: 0 CAT: 02

Vocational and Applied Arts Education
CIJE: 0 RIE: 1 CAT: 03

Vocational and Applied Technology Educ Act 1990
USE Carl D Perkins Voc and Appl Techn Educ Act 1990

Vocational and Occupational Interest Choice Exam
CIJE: 0 RIE: 1 CAT: 21

Vocational Apperception Test
CIJE: 0 RIE: 1 CAT: 21

Vocational Assessment Project
CIJE: 0 RIE: 1 CAT: 19

Vocational Assessment Record
CIJE: 0 RIE: 1 CAT: 21

Vocational Attitude Scale
CIJE: 1 RIE: 1 CAT: 21

Vocational Awareness Index (Currie)
CIJE: 1 RIE: 0 CAT: 21

Vocational Behavior Checklist
CIJE: 0 RIE: 1 CAT: 21

Vocational Capacity Scale
CIJE: 0 RIE: 1 CAT: 21

Vocational Careers Assessment Severely Handicapped
CIJE: 0 RIE: 1 CAT: 21

Vocational Commitment Index (Weis and Hubbard)
CIJE: 1 RIE: 2 CAT: 21

Vocational Competency Achievement Tracking Sys NC
CIJE: 0 RIE: 2 CAT: 04
UF VoCATS NC

Vocational Competency Measures Project
CIJE: 0 RIE: 1 CAT: 19

Vocational Counseling Project NJ
CIJE: 0 RIE: 1 CAT: 19

Vocational Counseling Summer Workshops
CIJE: 0 RIE: 1 CAT: 02

Vocational Decision Making Difficulty Scale
CIJE: 1 RIE: 0 CAT: 21

Vocational Decision Making Interview
CIJE: 1 RIE: 1 CAT: 21

Vocational Development Inventory (Crites)
CIJE: 5 RIE: 6 CAT: 21

Vocational Educ Evaluation and Assessment Process
CIJE: 0 RIE: 1 CAT: 15

Vocational Education Act 1963
CIJE: 30 RIE: 119 CAT: 14

Vocational Education Act 1975
CIJE: 5 RIE: 13 CAT: 14

Vocational Education Act 1981
CIJE: 1 RIE: 3 CAT: 14

Vocational Education Act 1984
USE Carl D Perkins Vocational Education Act 1984

Vocational Education Act 1990
USE Carl D Perkins Voc and Appl Techn Educ Act 1990

Vocational Education Amendments 1968
CIJE: 36 RIE: 123 CAT: 14

Vocational Education Amendments 1969
CIJE: 0 RIE: 1 CAT: 14

Vocational Education Amendments 1974
CIJE: 1 RIE: 4 CAT: 14

Vocational Education Amendments 1976
CIJE: 14 RIE: 78 CAT: 14

Vocational Education Consortium of States
CIJE: 0 RIE: 2 CAT: 17

Vocational Education Curriculum Materials Database
CIJE: 1 RIE: 3 CAT: 04

Vocational Education Curriculum Specialists
CIJE: 1 RIE: 26 CAT: 09

Vocational Education Data Reporting Accounting
CIJE: 0 RIE: 1 CAT: 15

Vocational Education Data System
CIJE: 3 RIE: 13 CAT: 04

Vocational Education Dissemination Conference
CIJE: 0 RIE: 0 CAT: 02

Vocational Education for Special Students Program
CIJE: 0 RIE: 7 CAT: 19

Vocational Education Guidelines 1979
CIJE: 0 RIE: 1 CAT: 14

Vocational Education Information Network
CIJE: 0 RIE: 1 CAT: 04

Vocational Education Leadership Institute
CIJE: 0 RIE: 1 CAT: 02

Vocational Education Personnel Development Project
CIJE: 0 RIE: 1 CAT: 19

Vocational Education Readiness Test
CIJE: 0 RIE: 7 CAT: 21

Vocational Education Study
CIJE: 4 RIE: 21 CAT: 22

Vocational Education Test Battery
CIJE: 0 RIE: 3 CAT: 21

Vocational Education Training Needs Instrument
CIJE: 0 RIE: 2 CAT: 21

Vocational Ethics
CIJE: 0 RIE: 1 CAT: 16

Vocational Exploration Demonstration Project
CIJE: 0 RIE: 1 CAT: 19

Vocational Exploration Groups
CIJE: 6 RIE: 0 CAT: 16

Vocational Exploration in the Private Sector
CIJE: 0 RIE: 1 CAT: 19

Vocational Guidance Center Test
CIJE: 1 RIE: 0 CAT: 21

Vocational Guidance Quarterly
CIJE: 2 RIE: 0 CAT: 22

Vocational History Questionnaire
CIJE: 0 RIE: 1 CAT: 21

Vocational Identity
CIJE: 9 RIE: 4 CAT: 11

Vocational Identity Scale (Holland et al)
CIJE: 0 RIE: 1 CAT: 21

Vocational Industrial Clubs of America
CIJE: 12 RIE: 38 CAT: 17

Vocational Information Reporting System Manual
CIJE: 0 RIE: 1 CAT: 22

Vocational Instructional Management System
CIJE: 0 RIE: 2 CAT: 19
SN Project of the Missouri Board of Education

Vocational Instructional Materials Acquisition Sys
CIJE: 0 RIE: 2 CAT: 04

Vocational Interest and Sophistication Assessment
CIJE: 2 RIE: 0 CAT: 21

Vocational Interest Inventory (Mitchell)
CIJE: 5 RIE: 6 CAT: 21

Vocational Interest Survey
CIJE: 0 RIE: 4 CAT: 21
SN Developed in Australia for Australian users

Vocational Investigation and Placement Project
CIJE: 0 RIE: 5 CAT: 19

Vocational Leadership Development Program
CIJE: 0 RIE: 1 CAT: 19

Vocational Maturity Scale (Westbrook et al)
CIJE: 1 RIE: 0 CAT: 21

Vocational Opinion Index
CIJE: 0 RIE: 2 CAT: 21

Vocational Opportunities Clubs of Texas
CIJE: 0 RIE: 1 CAT: 17

Vocational Orientation Packets
CIJE: 0 RIE: 1 CAT: 03

Vocational Pattern Index (Kummerow and Hummel)
CIJE: 0 RIE: 1 CAT: 21

Vocational Performance Sample
CIJE: 0 RIE: 1 CAT: 21

Vocational Personality Report
CIJE: 0 RIE: 1 CAT: 21

Vocational Preference Inventory
CIJE: 15 RIE: 2 CAT: 21

Vocational Rehabilitation Act 1920
CIJE: 2 RIE: 2 CAT: 14

Vocational Rehabilitation Act 1973
CIJE: 5 RIE: 14 CAT: 14

Vocational Rehabilitation Act Amendments 1968
CIJE: 0 RIE: 1 CAT: 14

Vocational Rehabilitation Administration
CIJE: 0 RIE: 1 CAT: 17

Vocational Rehabilitation Ctr Allegheny County NY
CIJE: 1 RIE: 0 CAT: 17

Vocational Rehabilitation Project
CIJE: 0 RIE: 2 CAT: 19

Vocational Rehabilitation Specialists
CIJE: 1 RIE: 0 CAT: 09

Vocational Resource Educators
CIJE: 1 RIE: 4 CAT: 09

Vocational Rotational Laboratory
CIJE: 1 RIE: 0 CAT: 17

Vocational School Psychology
CIJE: 2 RIE: 0 CAT: 03

Vocational Specialists
CIJE: 1 RIE: 0 CAT: 09

Vocational Stability
CIJE: 1 RIE: 0 CAT: 16

Vocational Student Organizations
CIJE: 0 RIE: 2 CAT: 16

Vocational Technical Adult Education Districts
CIJE: 1 RIE: 7 CAT: 05

Vocational Technical Education Act 1983
CIJE: 0 RIE: 1 CAT: 14

Vocational Technical Education Consortium States
CIJE: 8 RIE: 169 CAT: 17

Vocational Technical Information Program
CIJE: 1 RIE: 0 CAT: 19

Vocational Technical Institute KS
CIJE: 0 RIE: 1 CAT: 17

Vocational Technical Resource Consortia
CIJE: 0 RIE: 1 CAT: 17

Vocational Technical Teacher Institute
CIJE: 0 RIE: 1 CAT: 02

Vocational Technology for Cerebral Palsied Project
CIJE: 0 RIE: 2 CAT: 19

Vocational Theory
CIJE: 5 RIE: 1 CAT: 15

Vocational Training Development Inst (Jamaica)
CIJE: 0 RIE: 1 CAT: 17

Vocational Village
CIJE: 1 RIE: 2 CAT: 19

Vocationalism
CIJE: 23 RIE: 2 CAT: 16

VoCATS NC
USE Vocational Competency Achievement Tracking Sys NC

Vocoders
CIJE: 5 RIE: 3 CAT: 04

Vogue Magazine
CIJE: 0 RIE: 1 CAT: 22

Voice (Rhetoric)
CIJE: 73 RIE: 79 CAT: 13

Voice (Verbs)
CIJE: 9 RIE: 4 CAT: 13

Voice Based Learning System
CIJE: 0 RIE: 1 CAT: 04

Voice Entry Terminal
CIJE: 4 RIE: 0 CAT: 04

Voice Indexing
CIJE: 4 RIE: 1 CAT: 20

Voice Mail
CIJE: 14 RIE: 2 CAT: 20
UF Voice Messaging

Voice Masking
CIJE: 1 RIE: 0 CAT: 20
UF Masking (Voice)

Voice Messaging
USE Voice Mail

Voice of America
CIJE: 4 RIE: 3 CAT: 17

Voice of Free China
CIJE: 0 RIE: 1 CAT: 17

Voice Onset Time
CIJE: 17 RIE: 3 CAT: 20

Voice Qualities
CIJE: 7 RIE: 9 CAT: 13

Voice Recognition
CIJE: 13 RIE: 5 CAT: 20
SN See also "Speech Recognition" and "Automatic Speech Recognition"

Voice Stress Analysis
CIJE: 0 RIE: 3 CAT: 15

Voice Support (Reading)
CIJE: 0 RIE: 1 CAT: 15

Voiced Stops
CIJE: 6 RIE: 0 CAT: 13

Voiceprint Identification
CIJE: 0 RIE: 1 CAT: 20

Voices and Visions (Poetry Video Series)
CIJE: 0 RIE: 1 CAT: 22

Voices for Children MT
CIJE: 0 RIE: 1 CAT: 19

Voices for Illinois Children
CIJE: 0 RIE: 2 CAT: 17

Voicing
CIJE: 10 RIE: 6 CAT: 13

Voir Dire Procedures
CIJE: 0 RIE: 1 CAT: 15

Voix et Images De France
CIJE: 2 RIE: 0 CAT: 22

Volga Finnic Languages
CIJE: 0 RIE: 1 CAT: 13

Volga Ural Region
USE USSR (Volga Ural Region)

Volitional Skills
CIJE: 1 RIE: 2 CAT: 11

Volkshochschulen
CIJE: 0 RIE: 3 CAT: 05

Voltage Controls
CIJE: 0 RIE: 1 CAT: 20

Voltaire
CIJE: 3 RIE: 1 CAT: 18

Voltammetry
CIJE: 7 RIE: 0 CAT: 20

Voltmeters
CIJE: 2 RIE: 1 CAT: 04

Volume (Physics)
CIJE: 6 RIE: 0 CAT: 20

Voluntarism
CIJE: 7 RIE: 6 CAT: 16

Voluntary Action Center
CIJE: 0 RIE: 1 CAT: 17

Voluntary Childlessness
CIJE: 4 RIE: 2 CAT: 11

Voluntary Continuing Education
CIJE: 0 RIE: 1 CAT: 16

Voluntary Equal Employment Opportunity Council
CIJE: 0 RIE: 1 CAT: 17

Voluntary Homework System
CIJE: 0 RIE: 1 CAT: 15

Voluntary Labor Arbitration Rules
CIJE: 0 RIE: 1 CAT: 15

Voluntary Participation
CIJE: 12 RIE: 8 CAT: 16

Voluntary Reduced Work Time
CIJE: 0 RIE: 1 CAT: 16
UF V Time

Voluntary Services Overseas (United Kingdom)
CIJE: 0 RIE: 0 CAT: 17
SN A registered United Kingdom charity sending over 600 volunteers a year to some 40 Third World countries

Voluntary Simplicity
CIJE: 2 RIE: 3 CAT: 16
SN Choosing to live more simply, considering the limited nature of the world's resources

Volunteer Against Illiteracy Campaign
CIJE: 0 RIE: 1 CAT: 19

Volunteer Army
CIJE: 2 RIE: 3 CAT: 09
SN See also "All Volunteer Armed Forces"

Volunteer Grandparent Project
CIJE: 0 RIE: 1 CAT: 19

Volunteer Library League Incorporated
CIJE: 1 RIE: 0 CAT: 17

Volunteer Management
CIJE: 6 RIE: 7 CAT: 15

Volunteer Management Support Program
CIJE: 0 RIE: 1 CAT: 19

Volunteer Military Rejectee Program
CIJE: 1 RIE: 0 CAT: 17

Volunteer Service Credits
CIJE: 0 RIE: 1 CAT: 16

Volunteer Skills Data System
CIJE: 0 RIE: 1 CAT: 19

Volunteer Teaching
CIJE: 0 RIE: 1 CAT: 16

Volunteer The National Center
CIJE: 0 RIE: 1 CAT: 17

Volunteerism
CIJE: 0 RIE: 3 CAT: 16

Volunteers in Education
CIJE: 1 RIE: 5 CAT: 16

Volunteers in Parochial Schools
CIJE: 1 RIE: 0 CAT: 16

Volunteers in Partnership with Parents
CIJE: 0 RIE: 2 CAT: 19
UF Project VIPP

Volunteers in Public Schools Program
CIJE: 1 RIE: 0 CAT: 19

Volunteers in School Program
CIJE: 0 RIE: 1 CAT: 19

Volunteers in Service to America
CIJE: 2 RIE: 22 CAT: 17
UF VISTA

Volunteers in Service to America Literacy Corps
CIJE: 0 RIE: 1 CAT: 17
UF VISTA Literacy Corps

Volunteers in Tutoring Adult Learners
CIJE: 0 RIE: 2 CAT: 19
UF VITAL

Volunteers in Tutoring Arrangements Program
CIJE: 0 RIE: 1 CAT: 19

Volunteers Upholding Education
CIJE: 0 RIE: 1 CAT: 17

Volusia County Schools FL
CIJE: 3 RIE: 2 CAT: 17

Vomiting
CIJE: 0 RIE: 0 CAT: 11

Von Baer (Karl Ernst)
CIJE: 0 RIE: 1 CAT: 18

Von Bertalanffy (Ludwig)
USE Bertalanffy (Ludwig von)

Von Harrison (Grant)
CIJE: 0 RIE: 1 CAT: 18

Von Humboldt (Alexander)
CIJE: 1 RIE: 0 CAT: 18
UF Humboldt (Alexander von)

Von Humboldt (Wilhelm)
CIJE: 2 RIE: 3 CAT: 18
UF Humboldt (Wilhelm von)

Von Neumann (John)
CIJE: 0 RIE: 1 CAT: 18

Von Ranke (Leopold)
CIJE: 1 RIE: 0 CAT: 18

Von Restorff Isolation Effect
CIJE: 3 RIE: 0 CAT: 21

Von Steuben (Frederick William)
USE Steuben (Baron Friedrich Wilhelm von)

Vonnegut (Kurt)
CIJE: 6 RIE: 2 CAT: 18

Vonnegut (Mark)
CIJE: 1 RIE: 0 CAT: 18

Voodoo
CIJE: 2 RIE: 2 CAT: 16

Voorhees College SC
CIJE: 1 RIE: 3 CAT: 17

Vort Behavioral Characteristics Progression
CIJE: 0 RIE: 1 CAT: 21

Vorticella
CIJE: 1 RIE: 0 CAT: 20

Votaw (Carmen Delgado)
CIJE: 0 RIE: 1 CAT: 18

Voter Education
CIJE: 1 RIE: 7 CAT: 03

Voters
CIJE: 13 RIE: 10 CAT: 10

Voting Behavior
CIJE: 33 RIE: 30 CAT: 16

Voting Rights Act 1965
CIJE: 10 RIE: 9 CAT: 14

Voucher Agency for Teachers
CIJE: 1 RIE: 0 CAT: 17

Vowel Duration
CIJE: 2 RIE: 2 CAT: 13

Vowel Harmony
CIJE: 2 RIE: 6 CAT: 13

Vowel Sandhi
CIJE: 0 RIE: 1 CAT: 13

Vowel Shift Rule
CIJE: 0 RIE: 1 CAT: 13

Vowel Tensing
USE Tensing (Vowels)

VOXBOX
CIJE: 0 RIE: 1 CAT: 20
SN A computer-based voice interactive language learning system

Voyage of Rediscovery
CIJE: 0 RIE: 1 CAT: 12
SN Third major voyage of the canoe Hokule'a (1985-87)

Voyage of the Mimi
CIJE: 1 RIE: 3 CAT: 22

Voyager Mission
CIJE: 0 RIE: 2 CAT: 12
SN NASA mission from 1977 to 1986 involving two spacecraft, Voyager I and Voyager II, to explore the planets Jupiter, Saturn, Uranus, and Neptune

Voyaguer Outward Bound School
CIJE: 1 RIE: 1 CAT: 17

Voznesensky (Andrei)
CIJE: 1 RIE: 0 CAT: 18

Vrije University (Netherlands)
CIJE: 1 RIE: 0 CAT: 17

Vroom and Yetton Normative Leadership Model
CIJE: 0 RIE: 1 CAT: 15

Vroom Expectancy Theory
CIJE: 2 RIE: 4 CAT: 15

VSAT Technology
USE Very Small Aperture Terminal Technology

VTR Environmental Rating Scale (Poling)
CIJE: 0 RIE: 1 CAT: 21

VTR Risk Model
CIJE: 0 RIE: 1 CAT: 21

Vuite
USE Paite

Vulnerability
CIJE: 17 RIE: 7 CAT: 11

Vulnerable Age Effect
CIJE: 2 RIE: 1 CAT: 15

Vulnerable Child Committee
CIJE: 1 RIE: 0 CAT: 17

Vulnerable Child Syndrome
CIJE: 0 RIE: 1 CAT: 11
SN Condition in which parents persist in viewing their children as vulnerable following recovery from medical complications

Vulpe Performance Analysis System
CIJE: 0 RIE: 1 CAT: 15

Vygotsky (Lev S)
CIJE: 112 RIE: 100 CAT: 18

W Grades
USE Withdrawal Grades

Wa Xthe Thonba
USE Tallchief (Maria)

Waardenburg Syndrome
CIJE: 0 RIE: 2 CAT: 11

Wabanaki Confederacy
CIJE: 0 RIE: 2 CAT: 08

Wabash College IN
CIJE: 2 RIE: 4 CAT: 17

Wabash Project
CIJE: 0 RIE: 1 CAT: 19

Wabash River Valley
CIJE: 0 RIE: 1 CAT: 07

Wabash Valley Education Center Science Test
CIJE: 0 RIE: 1 CAT: 21

Wabash Valley Supplementary Educational Center
CIJE: 1 RIE: 0 CAT: 17

Waber (Bernard)
CIJE: 1 RIE: 0 CAT: 18

Wacker Process
CIJE: 1 RIE: 0 CAT: 20

Wade Giles Transliterations
CIJE: 1 RIE: 2 CAT: 13

Wadena Public School District MN
CIJE: 0 RIE: 1 CAT: 17

Wadiri
USE Yanyuwa

Wage and Price Controls
CIJE: 5 RIE: 3 CAT: 14

Wage Compliance Standards
CIJE: 0 RIE: 1 CAT: 14

Wage Scales
CIJE: 2 RIE: 0 CAT: 16

Wage Subsidies
CIJE: 4 RIE: 6 CAT: 16

Wagner (Richard)
CIJE: 4 RIE: 0 CAT: 18

Wagner College NY
CIJE: 0 RIE: 1 CAT: 17

Wagner O Day Act 1938
CIJE: 1 RIE: 0 CAT: 14

Wagner Peyser Act
CIJE: 1 RIE: 11 CAT: 14

Wahpeton Indian School ND
CIJE: 0 RIE: 1 CAT: 17

Waikato College of Teacher Education (New Zealand)
CIJE: 0 RIE: 1 CAT: 17

WAIS Protocol
USE Wide Area Information Servers

Waitangi (Treaty of)
USE Treaty of Waitangi (New Zealand)

Waiting
CIJE: 1 RIE: 0 CAT: 16
SN The act of lingering or of being delayed — use the more specific "Wait Time" (a Thesaurus Descriptor), if appropriate

Waiting for Godot
CIJE: 1 RIE: 1 CAT: 22

Waiting Lists
CIJE: 1 RIE: 4 CAT: 16

Waiting Rooms
CIJE: 0 RIE: 0 CAT: 05

Waivers
CIJE: 5 RIE: 5 CAT: 16
SN See also "Tuition Waivers," "Prerequisite Waivers," etc.

Wakashan
CIJE: 1 RIE: 1 CAT: 13

Wake County Public School System NC
CIJE: 0 RIE: 6 CAT: 17

Wake Forest University NC
CIJE: 10 RIE: 2 CAT: 17

Wake Forest University School of Law NC
CIJE: 0 RIE: 0 CAT: 17

Wake Technical College NC
CIJE: 0 RIE: 1 CAT: 17

Wake Up Behavior
CIJE: 1 RIE: 0 CAT: 11

Wakefield Bill (California)
CIJE: 1 RIE: 0 CAT: 14

Waking Suggestion
CIJE: 0 RIE: 1 CAT: 11

Walachia
CIJE: 0 RIE: 0 CAT: 07
UF Wallachia

Walapai
USE Hualapai

Walberg Educational Productivity Model
CIJE: 2 RIE: 1 CAT: 15

Walberg Thomas Observation Scale
CIJE: 0 RIE: 2 CAT: 21

Walberg Thomas Teacher Questionnaire
CIJE: 1 RIE: 2 CAT: 21

Walbridge Academy
CIJE: 0 RIE: 1 CAT: 17

Walbrook High School MD
CIJE: 0 RIE: 2 CAT: 17

Walcott (Derek)
CIJE: 2 RIE: 1 CAT: 18

Walden
CIJE: 3 RIE: 3 CAT: 22

Walden III
CIJE: 1 RIE: 0 CAT: 16

Walden Two (Skinner)
CIJE: 0 RIE: 1 CAT: 22

Walden University FL
CIJE: 0 RIE: 3 CAT: 17

Waldorf Astoria Company
CIJE: 0 RIE: 1 CAT: 17

Waldorf Educational Theory
CIJE: 8 RIE: 1 CAT: 15

Waldorf Schools
CIJE: 13 RIE: 9 CAT: 17

Wales
CIJE: 288 RIE: 191 CAT: 07

Wales (Monmouthshire)
CIJE: 0 RIE: 1 CAT: 07

Wales (South)
CIJE: 14 RIE: 4 CAT: 07

Walk a Line Slowly Task
CIJE: 0 RIE: 2 CAT: 21

Walkabout
CIJE: 13 RIE: 4 CAT: 19

Walker (Alice)
CIJE: 13 RIE: 3 CAT: 18

Walker (H M)
CIJE: 0 RIE: 2 CAT: 18

Walker (John Hunter)
CIJE: 0 RIE: 1 CAT: 18

Walker (Lawrence)
CIJE: 1 RIE: 1 CAT: 18

Walker Art Center MN
CIJE: 1 RIE: 0 CAT: 17

Walker Lev Test Three
CIJE: 0 RIE: 1 CAT: 21

Walker Problem Behavior Identification Checklist
CIJE: 1 RIE: 0 CAT: 21

Walker Readiness Test
CIJE: 0 RIE: 9 CAT: 21

Walker River Paiute Reservation NV
CIJE: 0 RIE: 1 CAT: 07

Walkie Talkies
CIJE: 1 RIE: 0 CAT: 04

Walking
CIJE: 39 RIE: 15 CAT: 16

Walkulla County Schools FL
CIJE: 0 RIE: 1 CAT: 17

Wall Chart (ED)
USE State Education Performance Chart

Wall Framing
CIJE: 0 RIE: 1 CAT: 20

Wall Street Journal
CIJE: 5 RIE: 2 CAT: 22

Wall Street Journal Report
CIJE: 0 RIE: 1 CAT: 22

Walla Walla College WA
CIJE: 0 RIE: 1 CAT: 17

Walla Walla Community College WA
CIJE: 1 RIE: 2 CAT: 17

Wallace (George)
CIJE: 4 RIE: 4 CAT: 18

Wallace (Henry)
CIJE: 2 RIE: 1 CAT: 18
SN "Henry A"

Wallace (Karl R)
CIJE: 1 RIE: 1 CAT: 18

Wallace Community College AL Selma
CIJE: 0 RIE: 0 CAT: 17
UF George C Wallace Community College AL Selma

Wallace Self Concept Scale
CIJE: 0 RIE: 2 CAT: 21

Wallace State Community College AL Hanceville
CIJE: 0 RIE: 0 CAT: 17
UF George C Wallace State Comm Coll AL Hanceville

Wallace v Jaffree
CIJE: 2 RIE: 2 CAT: 14

Wallach and Kogan Creativity Test Battery
CIJE: 6 RIE: 1 CAT: 21

Wallachia
USE Walachia

Wallas (G)
CIJE: 1 RIE: 1 CAT: 18

Wallen School of Language (Canada)
CIJE: 1 RIE: 0 CAT: 17

Waller (Willard)
CIJE: 2 RIE: 1 CAT: 18

Wallin Cutsforth Brief Educ Attainment Scale
CIJE: 1 RIE: 0 CAT: 21

Wallingford Wellness Project
CIJE: 0 RIE: 2 CAT: 19

Wallis and Futuna Islands
CIJE: 0 RIE: 1 CAT: 07
UF Futuna Islands

Wallner Test of Listening Comprehension
CIJE: 1 RIE: 0 CAT: 21

Wallon (Henri)
CIJE: 2 RIE: 0 CAT: 18

Wallpaper
CIJE: 1 RIE: 1 CAT: 04

Wallraff (G)
CIJE: 1 RIE: 0 CAT: 18

Walmatjari
CIJE: 1 RIE: 1 CAT: 13

Walpole Public Schools MA
CIJE: 0 RIE: 1 CAT: 17

Walrus and the Carpenter
CIJE: 1 RIE: 0 CAT: 22

Walser (Martin)
CIJE: 2 RIE: 0 CAT: 18

Walsh College OH
CIJE: 0 RIE: 2 CAT: 17

Walsh Healy Public Contract Act
CIJE: 1 RIE: 1 CAT: 14

Walt Disney Studios
CIJE: 1 RIE: 2 CAT: 17

Walter H Boyd High School CA
CIJE: 1 RIE: 0 CAT: 17

Walters State Community College TN
CIJE: 0 RIE: 2 CAT: 17

Walther von der Vogelweide
CIJE: 1 RIE: 0 CAT: 18

WAMNet Project
CIJE: 0 RIE: 1 CAT: 19
UF Water and Molecular Networks Project

Wampanoag (Tribe)
CIJE: 2 RIE: 1 CAT: 08

WANDAH System
USE Writing Aid and Authors Helper

Wang (Margaret C)
CIJE: 0 RIE: 0 CAT: 18

Wang 700 Programing Calculator
CIJE: 0 RIE: 1 CAT: 04

Wang Institute of Graduate Studies MA
CIJE: 1 RIE: 1 CAT: 17

Wang Laboratories MA
CIJE: 2 RIE: 0 CAT: 17

Wang Marking Conventions
CIJE: 0 RIE: 1 CAT: 15

Wang Yani
CIJE: 0 RIE: 0 CAT: 18

Wankel Engines
CIJE: 1 RIE: 0 CAT: 04

Want Ads
CIJE: 7 RIE: 8 CAT: 16

Wantagh Public Schools NY
CIJE: 0 RIE: 1 CAT: 17

Wantoat
CIJE: 1 RIE: 0 CAT: 13

WAOC Observation Instrument
USE WISC R Administration Observational Checklist

Wapanakamikok (Tribe)
CIJE: 0 RIE: 1 CAT: 08

War Against Drugs
USE War on Drugs

War Against Rape (Pakistan)
CIJE: 0 RIE: 1 CAT: 17
SN Subcommittee of the Women's Action Forum in Pakistan

War and Peace
CIJE: 3 RIE: 1 CAT: 22

War Correspondents
CIJE: 0 RIE: 2 CAT: 09

War Dissenters
CIJE: 3 RIE: 1 CAT: 10

War Games
CIJE: 0 RIE: 1 CAT: 16
SN Use "War Games (Children)," if appropriate

War Games (Children)
CIJE: 0 RIE: 1 CAT: 16
SN See also "War Toys"

War of 1812
CIJE: 3 RIE: 5 CAT: 12

War on Drugs
CIJE: 2 RIE: 3 CAT: 11
UF War Against Drugs

War on Poverty
CIJE: 8 RIE: 10 CAT: 19

War Powers Act
CIJE: 0 RIE: 1 CAT: 14

War Resistance Literature
CIJE: 1 RIE: 0 CAT: 03

War Toys
CIJE: 7 RIE: 3 CAT: 16
SN See also "War Games (Children)"

War Victims
USE Victims of War

Warao (Tribe)
CIJE: 0 RIE: 1 CAT: 08

Waray
CIJE: 0 RIE: 1 CAT: 13

Ward (J H)
CIJE: 1 RIE: 0 CAT: 18

Ward (Theodore)
CIJE: 1 RIE: 0 CAT: 18

Ward (Virgil)
CIJE: 1 RIE: 0 CAT: 18

Ward Atmosphere Scale
CIJE: 0 RIE: 2 CAT: 21

Ward Concept
CIJE: 1 RIE: 1 CAT: 15

Ward Grievance Procedure
CIJE: 0 RIE: 1 CAT: 15

Wardens
CIJE: 0 RIE: 1 CAT: 09

Wardrobe Planning
CIJE: 0 RIE: 1 CAT: 16

Wards Hierarchical Cluster Analysis
CIJE: 0 RIE: 1 CAT: 15

Ware High School
CIJE: 1 RIE: 0 CAT: 17

Wariness
CIJE: 3 RIE: 0 CAT: 11

Waring Intimacy Questionnaire
CIJE: 2 RIE: 0 CAT: 21

Wark Committee
CIJE: 0 RIE: 1 CAT: 17

Warlpiri
CIJE: 3 RIE: 1 CAT: 13
SN An Australian Aboriginal language

Warm Springs Career Exploration Project
CIJE: 0 RIE: 1 CAT: 19

Warm Springs Reservation OR
CIJE: 1 RIE: 1 CAT: 17

Warm Up Decrement
CIJE: 1 RIE: 1 CAT: 11

Warm Up Exercises
CIJE: 9 RIE: 1 CAT: 11

Warner Brothers
CIJE: 0 RIE: 1 CAT: 17

Warner Eddison Associates
CIJE: 1 RIE: 0 CAT: 17

Warner Elementary School
CIJE: 1 RIE: 0 CAT: 17

Warner Index of Social Class
CIJE: 0 RIE: 3 CAT: 21

Warner Meeker Eells Index of Status Characteristic
CIJE: 0 RIE: 1 CAT: 21

Warner Pacific College OR
CIJE: 0 RIE: 3 CAT: 17

Warning
CIJE: 4 RIE: 3 CAT: 16

Warnock Report
CIJE: 18 RIE: 1 CAT: 22

Warrant Officers
CIJE: 0 RIE: 1 CAT: 10

Warranted Uncertainty
CIJE: 1 RIE: 0 CAT: 15

Warranties
CIJE: 7 RIE: 6 CAT: 14
SN Use a more specific term if possible

Warranty of Education
USE Educational Warranty

Warranty of Teachers
USE Teacher Warranty

Warren (Earl)
CIJE: 4 RIE: 2 CAT: 18

Warren (Robert Penn)
CIJE: 3 RIE: 0 CAT: 18

Warren (William Whipple)
CIJE: 0 RIE: 1 CAT: 18

Warren City Schools OH
CIJE: 0 RIE: 1 CAT: 17

Warren County Public Schools NC
CIJE: 0 RIE: 1 CAT: 17

Warren Court
CIJE: 1 RIE: 3 CAT: 14

Warren Education Association
CIJE: 1 RIE: 0 CAT: 17

Warren Science Project
CIJE: 0 RIE: 1 CAT: 19

Warren Township Independent School District IN
CIJE: 0 RIE: 1 CAT: 17
SN "Metropolitan School District of Warren Township IN"

Warren Wilson College NC
CIJE: 4 RIE: 2 CAT: 17

Warsaw Pact
CIJE: 1 RIE: 5 CAT: 14

Wartegg Drawing Test
CIJE: 0 RIE: 1 CAT: 21

Wartella (E)
CIJE: 0 RIE: 1 CAT: 18

Warwick (Frances Greville Countess of)
CIJE: 0 RIE: 1 CAT: 18

Warwick High School VA
CIJE: 1 RIE: 0 CAT: 17

Wascana Institute (Saskatchewan)
CIJE: 0 RIE: 1 CAT: 17

Wasco Public Schools CA
CIJE: 0 RIE: 1 CAT: 17

Wasco Wishrams
CIJE: 0 RIE: 1 CAT: 08

Wase (Christopher)
CIJE: 1 RIE: 0 CAT: 18

WASH Project
USE Water and Sanitation for Health Project

Washback Effect (Testing)
USE Teaching to the Test

Washburn University of Topeka KS
CIJE: 2 RIE: 12 CAT: 17

Washburne (Carleton Wolsey)
CIJE: 3 RIE: 1 CAT: 18

Washington
CIJE: 216 RIE: 1120 CAT: 07

Washington (Bellevue)
CIJE: 2 RIE: 2 CAT: 07

Washington (Bellingham)
CIJE: 1 RIE: 6 CAT: 07

Washington (Booker T)
CIJE: 19 RIE: 11 CAT: 18

Washington (Cheney)
CIJE: 1 RIE: 3 CAT: 07

Washington (Clallam County)
CIJE: 0 RIE: 1 CAT: 07

Washington (Clark County)
CIJE: 0 RIE: 2 CAT: 07

Washington (Colville)
CIJE: 0 RIE: 1 CAT: 07

Washington (East)
CIJE: 3 RIE: 2 CAT: 07

Washington (Ellensburg)
CIJE: 1 RIE: 3 CAT: 07

Washington (Everett)
CIJE: 0 RIE: 2 CAT: 07

Washington (George)
CIJE: 10 RIE: 8 CAT: 18

Washington (Gig Harbor)
CIJE: 0 RIE: 1 CAT: 07

Washington (King County)
CIJE: 2 RIE: 11 CAT: 07

Washington (Lincoln County)
CIJE: 0 RIE: 1 CAT: 07

Washington (Maple Valley)
CIJE: 1 RIE: 0 CAT: 07

Washington (Mukilteo)
CIJE: 0 RIE: 1 CAT: 07

Washington (Olympia)
CIJE: 1 RIE: 25 CAT: 07

Washington (Pierce County)
CIJE: 2 RIE: 5 CAT: 07

Washington (Port Townsend)
CIJE: 0 RIE: 1 CAT: 07

Washington (Puget Sound)
CIJE: 1 RIE: 2 CAT: 07

Washington (Redmond)
CIJE: 1 RIE: 1 CAT: 07

Washington (Seattle)
CIJE: 58 RIE: 133 CAT: 07

Washington (Snohomish County)
CIJE: 1 RIE: 3 CAT: 07

Washington (Southeast)
CIJE: 0 RIE: 1 CAT: 07

Washington (Spangle)
CIJE: 0 RIE: 3 CAT: 07

Washington (Spokane)
CIJE: 5 RIE: 14 CAT: 07

Washington (Stevens County)
CIJE: 0 RIE: 1 CAT: 07

Washington (Tacoma)
CIJE: 4 RIE: 19 CAT: 07

Washington (Vancouver)
CIJE: 1 RIE: 0 CAT: 07

Washington (Walla Walla)
CIJE: 2 RIE: 2 CAT: 07

Washington (Wallingford)
CIJE: 0 RIE: 1 CAT: 07

Washington (Wenatchee)
CIJE: 0 RIE: 1 CAT: 07

Washington (Whitman County)
CIJE: 0 RIE: 1 CAT: 07

Washington (Yakima)
CIJE: 6 RIE: 4 CAT: 07

Washington 2000
CIJE: 0 RIE: 1 CAT: 19

Washington Academy NY
CIJE: 1 RIE: 0 CAT: 17

Washington Administrative Code
CIJE: 0 RIE: 1 CAT: 16

Washington and Jefferson College PA
CIJE: 0 RIE: 1 CAT: 17

Washington and Lee University VA
CIJE: 1 RIE: 1 CAT: 17

Washington Area Peace Studies Network DC
CIJE: 0 RIE: 1 CAT: 17

Washington Award for Vocational Excellence
CIJE: 0 RIE: 1 CAT: 16

Washington Center DC
CIJE: 1 RIE: 2 CAT: 17

Washington College MD
CIJE: 5 RIE: 1 CAT: 17

Washington Colloquium on Science and Society
CIJE: 0 RIE: 2 CAT: 02

Washington Community College Evaluation Model
CIJE: 0 RIE: 1 CAT: 15

Washington Concentrated Employment Program
CIJE: 1 RIE: 0 CAT: 19

Washington Consortium of Universities
CIJE: 1 RIE: 0 CAT: 17

Washington County Childrens Project ME
CIJE: 0 RIE: 1 CAT: 19

Washington County School District TN
CIJE: 0 RIE: 1 CAT: 17

Washington County School District UT
CIJE: 0 RIE: 1 CAT: 17

Washington Education Association
CIJE: 0 RIE: 5 CAT: 17

Washington Federation of Independent Schools
CIJE: 1 RIE: 0 CAT: 17

Washington Foreign Language Program
CIJE: 0 RIE: 1 CAT: 19

Washington High School AZ
CIJE: 1 RIE: 0 CAT: 17

Washington Highland Community School DC
CIJE: 1 RIE: 0 CAT: 17

Washington Hospital School of Nursing
CIJE: 1 RIE: 0 CAT: 17

Washington Integrated Secondary Education Project
CIJE: 0 RIE: 1 CAT: 19

Washington Junior High School WI
CIJE: 0 RIE: 1 CAT: 17

Washington Library Network
CIJE: 12 RIE: 9 CAT: 17

Washington Occupational Information Service
USE Washington Occupational Information System

Washington Occupational Information System
CIJE: 0 RIE: 2 CAT: 17
UF Washington Occupational Information Service

Washington Office of Superintendent of Pub Instr
CIJE: 0 RIE: 4 CAT: 17

Washington Post
CIJE: 7 RIE: 12 CAT: 22

Washington Post Online
CIJE: 0 RIE: 0 CAT: 04

Washington Postsecondary Education Commission
CIJE: 1 RIE: 1 CAT: 17

Washington Precollege Testing Program
CIJE: 5 RIE: 10 CAT: 21

Washington PressText
CIJE: 0 RIE: 2 CAT: 04

Washington Research Foundation
CIJE: 0 RIE: 1 CAT: 17

Washington Research Organization
CIJE: 0 RIE: 1 CAT: 17

Washington State Comm Coll Humanities Project
CIJE: 0 RIE: 1 CAT: 19

Washington State Community College System
CIJE: 0 RIE: 7 CAT: 17

Washington State Educational Assessment Program
CIJE: 0 RIE: 2 CAT: 19
UF Washington Statewide Assessment Program

Washington State Educational Service District 105
CIJE: 0 RIE: 0 CAT: 17

Washington State Library
CIJE: 3 RIE: 0 CAT: 17

Washington State University
CIJE: 42 RIE: 33 CAT: 17

Washington Statewide Assessment Program
USE Washington State Educational Assessment Program

Washington Technical Institute DC
CIJE: 1 RIE: 2 CAT: 17

Washington University MO
CIJE: 40 RIE: 19 CAT: 17

Washington University Sentence Completion Test
CIJE: 8 RIE: 0 CAT: 21

Washington v Davis
CIJE: 7 RIE: 4 CAT: 14

Washington West Resource Center VT
CIJE: 0 RIE: 1 CAT: 17

Washington Work Study Program
CIJE: 0 RIE: 2 CAT: 19

Washkuk
CIJE: 1 RIE: 0 CAT: 13

Washo (Tribe)
CIJE: 0 RIE: 3 CAT: 08

Washoe (Tribe)
CIJE: 1 RIE: 9 CAT: 08

Washoe County School District NV
CIJE: 4 RIE: 1 CAT: 17

Washtenaw Alcohol Safety Action Program
CIJE: 0 RIE: 1 CAT: 19

Washtenaw Community College MI
CIJE: 1 RIE: 3 CAT: 17

Waskaganish Community PQ
CIJE: 0 RIE: 0 CAT: 17
SN A Cree community in Quebec

Wasons Selection Task
CIJE: 0 RIE: 1 CAT: 15

Wasps
CIJE: 2 RIE: 1 CAT: 20

Waste Disposal Sites
USE Waste Repositories

Waste Dumps
USE Waste Repositories

Waste in Government Spending
CIJE: 0 RIE: 1 CAT: 16
UF Government Spending (Waste in)

Waste Repositories
CIJE: 0 RIE: 1 CAT: 05
UF Waste Disposal Sites; Waste Dumps

Waste Water Treatment Plant Personnel
CIJE: 0 RIE: 5 CAT: 09

Watauga County Schools NC
CIJE: 1 RIE: 0 CAT: 17

Watchabook
CIJE: 1 RIE: 1 CAT: 16

Water Accidents
CIJE: 1 RIE: 5 CAT: 16

Water Analysis
CIJE: 3 RIE: 4 CAT: 20

Water and Molecular Networks Project
USE WAMNet Project

Water and Sanitation for Health Project
CIJE: 1 RIE: 1 CAT: 19
UF WASH Project

Water Damaged Books
CIJE: 3 RIE: 5 CAT: 04

Water Distribution
CIJE: 0 RIE: 7 CAT: 20

Water Drops
CIJE: 1 RIE: 0 CAT: 20

Water Exercise
CIJE: 0 RIE: 1 CAT: 11
UF Aqua Aerobics; Aquatic Exercise; Water Resistance Exercise

Water Heritage Project
CIJE: 1 RIE: 0 CAT: 19

Water Learning Programs
CIJE: 1 RIE: 1 CAT: 19

Water Lens
CIJE: 1 RIE: 0 CAT: 04

Water Level Tasks
CIJE: 4 RIE: 1 CAT: 16

Water Play
CIJE: 6 RIE: 0 CAT: 16
UF Waterplay Activities

Water Play Facilities
CIJE: 3 RIE: 0 CAT: 05

Water Pollution Control Amendments
CIJE: 1 RIE: 0 CAT: 14

Water Pollution Control Information Test
CIJE: 1 RIE: 0 CAT: 21

Water Quality Administration
CIJE: 1 RIE: 0 CAT: 17

Water Quality Analysis
CIJE: 9 RIE: 3 CAT: 20

Water Quality Management
CIJE: 2 RIE: 4 CAT: 20

Water Quality Water Sampling Standards
CIJE: 0 RIE: 1 CAT: 20

Water Resistance Exercise
USE Water Exercise

Water Resources Council
CIJE: 1 RIE: 0 CAT: 17

Water Resources Document Reference System
CIJE: 1 RIE: 0 CAT: 15

Water Rights
CIJE: 4 RIE: 7 CAT: 14

Water Safety
CIJE: 11 RIE: 2 CAT: 11

Water Sampler
CIJE: 1 RIE: 0 CAT: 04

Water Sampling Standards
CIJE: 1 RIE: 1 CAT: 20

Water Tanks
CIJE: 1 RIE: 0 CAT: 04

Water Transportation
CIJE: 1 RIE: 1 CAT: 20

Water Treatment Plants
CIJE: 0 RIE: 2 CAT: 20

Water Turbidity
CIJE: 1 RIE: 3 CAT: 20

Water Vapor
CIJE: 2 RIE: 0 CAT: 20

Water Watch Program KY
CIJE: 0 RIE: 1 CAT: 19

Waterbury State Technical College CT
CIJE: 1 RIE: 0 CAT: 17

Watercolor
CIJE: 4 RIE: 2 CAT: 03

Waterford Reading Instructional Management Model
CIJE: 1 RIE: 0 CAT: 15

Waterford School UT
CIJE: 1 RIE: 1 CAT: 17

Waterford Township High School MA
CIJE: 1 RIE: 0 CAT: 17

Watergate
CIJE: 26 RIE: 27 CAT: 12

Watergate Sterling Learning Center IL
CIJE: 1 RIE: 0 CAT: 17

Waterhouse (Ann)
CIJE: 1 RIE: 0 CAT: 18

Waterloo Child Assessment Project
CIJE: 0 RIE: 1 CAT: 19
UF Project WAT CAP

Waterloo County Roman Catholic Sep Sch Bd ON
CIJE: 0 RIE: 0 CAT: 17

Watermans Production Rules
CIJE: 0 RIE: 1 CAT: 15

Waterplay Activities
USE Water Play

Waterproofing
CIJE: 0 RIE: 4 CAT: 20

Waters (Frank)
CIJE: 0 RIE: 1 CAT: 18

Watersheds
CIJE: 4 RIE: 3 CAT: 20

Watership Down
CIJE: 3 RIE: 0 CAT: 22

Watertown Public Schools MA
CIJE: 0 RIE: 1 CAT: 17

Waterville Senior High School ME
CIJE: 1 RIE: 0 CAT: 17

Waterways Project
CIJE: 0 RIE: 1 CAT: 19
SN Literary arts program for at-risk students in New York City

Watseka Community High School IL
CIJE: 1 RIE: 0 CAT: 17

Watson (Fletcher G)
CIJE: 1 RIE: 0 CAT: 18

Watson Analysis Schedule
CIJE: 0 RIE: 3 CAT: 21

Watson Barker Listening Test
CIJE: 0 RIE: 6 CAT: 21

Watson Glaser Critical Thinking Appraisal
CIJE: 25 RIE: 26 CAT: 21

Watson Glaser Test of Critical Thinking
CIJE: 2 RIE: 3 CAT: 21

Watt (Bob)
CIJE: 1 RIE: 0 CAT: 18

Watt (James G)
CIJE: 1 RIE: 0 CAT: 18
SN Secretary of the Interior (1981-83)

Watt (James)
CIJE: 1 RIE: 2 CAT: 18
SN Scottish engineer and inventor

Watt (William)
CIJE: 1 RIE: 0 CAT: 18

Watts Writers Workshop
CIJE: 0 RIE: 1 CAT: 02

Watzlawick (Paul)
CIJE: 1 RIE: 3 CAT: 18

Waubonsee Community College IL
CIJE: 1 RIE: 14 CAT: 17

Waubonsee Hearing Impaired Program
CIJE: 0 RIE: 1 CAT: 19

Waukegan Early Evaluation Program
CIJE: 0 RIE: 1 CAT: 19

Waukegan School District IL
CIJE: 0 RIE: 2 CAT: 17

Waukesha County Technical College WI
CIJE: 3 RIE: 2 CAT: 17

Waukesha County Technical Institute WI
CIJE: 4 RIE: 5 CAT: 17

Waukesha High School WI
CIJE: 1 RIE: 1 CAT: 17

Waukesha School District WI
CIJE: 0 RIE: 1 CAT: 17

Wauneka (Annie)
CIJE: 0 RIE: 0 CAT: 18

Waupun School District WI
CIJE: 0 RIE: 0 CAT: 17

Waupun Strategies in Early Childhood Education
CIJE: 0 RIE: 1 CAT: 21

Wave Generators
CIJE: 4 RIE: 2 CAT: 04

Wave Hill Program
CIJE: 0 RIE: 1 CAT: 19

Wave Processes
CIJE: 2 RIE: 0 CAT: 20

Wave Propagation
CIJE: 5 RIE: 2 CAT: 20

Wave Theory
CIJE: 14 RIE: 5 CAT: 15

Waveform Analysis
CIJE: 2 RIE: 5 CAT: 20

Waves (Water)
CIJE: 4 RIE: 4 CAT: 20

Wax Cylinder Recordings
CIJE: 0 RIE: 4 CAT: 04

Way (Florine)
CIJE: 0 RIE: 1 CAT: 18

Way I Feel About Myself
CIJE: 2 RIE: 1 CAT: 22

Way of the World
CIJE: 1 RIE: 0 CAT: 22

Way To Grow School Readiness Program MN
CIJE: 0 RIE: 1 CAT: 19

Way to Rainy Mountain
CIJE: 1 RIE: 0 CAT: 22

Waycross Independent School System GA
CIJE: 1 RIE: 0 CAT: 17

Wayland High School MA
CIJE: 1 RIE: 0 CAT: 17

Wayne Community College NC
CIJE: 0 RIE: 1 CAT: 17

Wayne County Child Development Center
CIJE: 1 RIE: 0 CAT: 17

Wayne County Community College MI
CIJE: 2 RIE: 1 CAT: 17

Wayne County Intermediate School District MI
CIJE: 4 RIE: 2 CAT: 17

Wayne General and Technical College OH
CIJE: 1 RIE: 0 CAT: 17

Wayne State College NE
CIJE: 1 RIE: 8 CAT: 17

Wayne State Experimental Project
CIJE: 0 RIE: 1 CAT: 19

Wayne State University MI
CIJE: 37 RIE: 50 CAT: 17

Ways of Looking at People
CIJE: 0 RIE: 1 CAT: 22

Ways of Reading (Bartholomae and Petrosky)
CIJE: 0 RIE: 0 CAT: 22
SN Full title — "Ways of Reading: An Anthology for Writers"

Ways of Speaking Taxonomy
CIJE: 0 RIE: 1 CAT: 21

Ways to Improve Education in Desegregated Schools
CIJE: 0 RIE: 5 CAT: 19

Ways to Improve Schools and Education (Project)
CIJE: 0 RIE: 3 CAT: 19

Wayside School for Girls NY
CIJE: 0 RIE: 1 CAT: 17

Wayson School Climate and Context Inventory
CIJE: 0 RIE: 2 CAT: 21

Waystage Level (Languages)
CIJE: 0 RIE: 1 CAT: 13

We Do They Do Model
CIJE: 0 RIE: 1 CAT: 15

We Help Ourselves Program
CIJE: 0 RIE: 3 CAT: 19

We Shall Overcome (Song)
CIJE: 0 RIE: 1 CAT: 22

Wealth
CIJE: 9 RIE: 10 CAT: 16

Weapons
CIJE: 29 RIE: 26 CAT: 04

Wear Attitude Inventory
CIJE: 1 RIE: 1 CAT: 21

Weasels
CIJE: 2 RIE: 0 CAT: 20

Weather Forecasting
CIJE: 10 RIE: 7 CAT: 20

Weather Modification
CIJE: 1 RIE: 0 CAT: 20

Weather Reports
CIJE: 4 RIE: 0 CAT: 20

Weather Satellites
CIJE: 4 RIE: 2 CAT: 04

Weather Vanes
CIJE: 2 RIE: 0 CAT: 04

Weatherford Hammond Mountain Collection
CIJE: 1 RIE: 0 CAT: 17

Weatherization
CIJE: 1 RIE: 8 CAT: 20

Weatherstripping
CIJE: 0 RIE: 1 CAT: 20

WEAVE Program
USE Womens Educational and Vocational Enrichment

Weaver (Richard M)
CIJE: 6 RIE: 5 CAT: 18

Weaver Union Elementary School District CA
CIJE: 0 RIE: 1 CAT: 17

Weavers
CIJE: 2 RIE: 1 CAT: 09

Weaving
CIJE: 24 RIE: 10 CAT: 09

Web of Life Biology Course
CIJE: 1 RIE: 0 CAT: 03

Webb (Walter Prescott)
CIJE: 2 RIE: 0 CAT: 18

Webb School CA
CIJE: 0 RIE: 1 CAT: 17

Webb v Board of Education
CIJE: 0 RIE: 1 CAT: 14

Webbing (Semantic)
USE Semantic Webbing

Webbing (Textiles)
CIJE: 0 RIE: 0 CAT: 16

Webbing (Thematic)
CIJE: 10 RIE: 3 CAT: 13

Weber (Brian F)
CIJE: 1 RIE: 0 CAT: 18

Weber (Lillian)
CIJE: 1 RIE: 1 CAT: 18

Weber (Max)
CIJE: 27 RIE: 13 CAT: 18

Weber Individualized Learning Kits
CIJE: 0 RIE: 1 CAT: 03

Weber School District UT
CIJE: 1 RIE: 0 CAT: 17

Weber State College UT
CIJE: 2 RIE: 6 CAT: 17

Weber v Kaiser Aluminum and Chemical Corporation
CIJE: 7 RIE: 3 CAT: 14

Webern (Anton von)
CIJE: 1 RIE: 0 CAT: 18

Webers Law
CIJE: 2 RIE: 0 CAT: 20

Webster (Daniel)
CIJE: 1 RIE: 1 CAT: 18

Webster (Hutton)
CIJE: 0 RIE: 1 CAT: 18

Webster (Noah)
CIJE: 2 RIE: 3 CAT: 18

Webster College MO
CIJE: 5 RIE: 3 CAT: 17

Webster School DC
CIJE: 0 RIE: 1 CAT: 17

Webster Springs High School WV
CIJE: 0 RIE: 1 CAT: 17

Webster University MO
CIJE: 3 RIE: 1 CAT: 17

Webster v Reproductive Health Services
CIJE: 3 RIE: 0 CAT: 14

Websters Third New International Dictionary
CIJE: 0 RIE: 3 CAT: 22

Wechsler Adult Intelligence Scale
CIJE: 174 RIE: 35 CAT: 21

Wechsler Adult Intelligence Scale (Revised)
CIJE: 88 RIE: 16 CAT: 21

Wechsler Bellevue Intelligence Scale
CIJE: 5 RIE: 5 CAT: 21

Wechsler Intelligence Scale (Chinese Revised)
CIJE: 0 RIE: 1 CAT: 21
SN ...for Children (WISC-CR)

Wechsler Intelligence Scale for Children
CIJE: 216 RIE: 91 CAT: 21

Wechsler Intelligence Scale for Children (Revised)
CIJE: 414 RIE: 98 CAT: 21
SN See also "WISC R..."

Wechsler Intelligence Scale for Children III
CIJE: 3 RIE: 6 CAT: 21

Wechsler Intelligence Scale Profile for Teachers
CIJE: 0 RIE: 1 CAT: 21

Wechsler Intelligence Scales Short Forms
CIJE: 10 RIE: 2 CAT: 21

Wechsler Memory Scale
CIJE: 14 RIE: 1 CAT: 21

Wechsler Memory Scale (Revised)
CIJE: 5 RIE: 1 CAT: 21

Wechsler Preschool Primary Scale of Intell (Rev)
CIJE: 1 RIE: 1 CAT: 21

Wechsler Preschool Primary Scale of Intelligence
CIJE: 46 RIE: 18 CAT: 21

Wechsler Scales Complementary Sheet
CIJE: 0 RIE: 1 CAT: 21

Wedding Photography
CIJE: 0 RIE: 1 CAT: 16

Wedekind (Frank)
CIJE: 2 RIE: 0 CAT: 18

Wedgeworth (Robert)
CIJE: 1 RIE: 0 CAT: 18

Weed Control
CIJE: 0 RIE: 1 CAT: 20

Weekend Programs
CIJE: 0 RIE: 1 CAT: 19

Weekly Activity Record
CIJE: 0 RIE: 1 CAT: 15

Weekly Newspapers
CIJE: 5 RIE: 7 CAT: 16

Weekly Student Contact Hours
CIJE: 0 RIE: 25 CAT: 16

Weekly Subject Index
CIJE: 1 RIE: 0 CAT: 21

Weighing Station Operators
CIJE: 0 RIE: 1 CAT: 09

Weight Loss
CIJE: 37 RIE: 13 CAT: 11

Weight Maintenance
CIJE: 14 RIE: 3 CAT: 11

Weight Management Centers
CIJE: 0 RIE: 1 CAT: 05

Weighted Airman Promotion System
CIJE: 0 RIE: 1 CAT: 15

Weighted Data
CIJE: 27 RIE: 9 CAT: 21

Weighted Grading Systems
CIJE: 4 RIE: 2 CAT: 15

Weighted Harmonic Means Analysis
CIJE: 1 RIE: 0 CAT: 21

Weighted Mean
CIJE: 2 RIE: 0 CAT: 20

Weighted Net Percentage Difference
CIJE: 1 RIE: 0 CAT: 15

Weighted Pupil Method
CIJE: 1 RIE: 2 CAT: 15

Weighted Structural Regression
CIJE: 0 RIE: 1 CAT: 21

Weighted Term Searching
CIJE: 57 RIE: 2 CAT: 20

Weighted Variables
CIJE: 8 RIE: 4 CAT: 21

Weighting (Statistical)
CIJE: 26 RIE: 11 CAT: 21

Weightlessness
CIJE: 3 RIE: 1 CAT: 20
SN See also "Microgravity"

Weights and Measures (Commercial)
CIJE: 3 RIE: 1 CAT: 20

Weigl Color Form Sorting Test
CIJE: 2 RIE: 0 CAT: 21

Weigl Goldstein Scheerer Color Form Test
CIJE: 1 RIE: 0 CAT: 21

Weikart (David)
CIJE: 0 RIE: 3 CAT: 18

Weiner (B)
CIJE: 8 RIE: 1 CAT: 18

Weinhouse (Marilyn)
CIJE: 0 RIE: 1 CAT: 18

Weinrich (Harald)
CIJE: 2 RIE: 0 CAT: 18

Weinzweig (A I)
CIJE: 0 RIE: 1 CAT: 18

West Rowan High School NC
CIJE: 1 RIE: 0 CAT: 17

West Shore Community College MI
CIJE: 0 RIE: 3 CAT: 17

West Side Story
CIJE: 1 RIE: 1 CAT: 22

West Texas State University
CIJE: 2 RIE: 2 CAT: 17

West Valley College CA
CIJE: 1 RIE: 2 CAT: 17

West Valley Mission Community College District CA
CIJE: 0 RIE: 1 CAT: 17

West Valley Occupational Center
CIJE: 1 RIE: 0 CAT: 17

West Vancouver Memorial Library (Canada)
CIJE: 1 RIE: 0 CAT: 17

West Virginia
CIJE: 132 RIE: 486 CAT: 07

West Virginia (Arthurdale)
CIJE: 1 RIE: 1 CAT: 07

West Virginia (Berkeley County)
CIJE: 0 RIE: 3 CAT: 07

West Virginia (Braxton County)
CIJE: 1 RIE: 1 CAT: 07

West Virginia (Brooke County)
CIJE: 0 RIE: 1 CAT: 07

West Virginia (Charleston)
CIJE: 3 RIE: 4 CAT: 07

West Virginia (Doddridge County)
CIJE: 0 RIE: 1 CAT: 07

West Virginia (Hampshire County)
CIJE: 1 RIE: 1 CAT: 07

West Virginia (Harpers Ferry)
CIJE: 1 RIE: 1 CAT: 07

West Virginia (Harrison County)
CIJE: 0 RIE: 1 CAT: 07

West Virginia (Kanawha County)
CIJE: 6 RIE: 11 CAT: 07

West Virginia (Marion County)
CIJE: 0 RIE: 1 CAT: 07

West Virginia (Mason County)
CIJE: 1 RIE: 6 CAT: 07

West Virginia (Mercer County)
CIJE: 0 RIE: 4 CAT: 07

West Virginia (Mingo County)
CIJE: 1 RIE: 1 CAT: 07

West Virginia (Monongalia County)
CIJE: 1 RIE: 2 CAT: 07

West Virginia (Morgantown)
CIJE: 0 RIE: 1 CAT: 07

West Virginia (Ohio County)
CIJE: 1 RIE: 1 CAT: 07

West Virginia (Parkersburg)
CIJE: 0 RIE: 2 CAT: 07

West Virginia (Putnam County)
CIJE: 0 RIE: 2 CAT: 07

West Virginia (Raleigh County)
CIJE: 0 RIE: 3 CAT: 07

West Virginia (Wheeling)
CIJE: 3 RIE: 1 CAT: 07

West Virginia (Wood County)
CIJE: 0 RIE: 1 CAT: 07

West Virginia Arts and Humanities Council
CIJE: 1 RIE: 0 CAT: 17

West Virginia Board of Education v Barnette
CIJE: 0 RIE: 1 CAT: 14
UF West Virginia State Board of Education v Barnette

West Virginia College of Graduate Studies
CIJE: 2 RIE: 2 CAT: 17
SN Name changed to "West Virginia Graduate College"

West Virginia Department of Mental Health
CIJE: 0 RIE: 1 CAT: 17

West Virginia Education Fund
CIJE: 0 RIE: 1 CAT: 17

West Virginia Graduate College
CIJE: 1 RIE: 1 CAT: 17
SN Formerly "West Virginia College of Graduate Studies"

West Virginia Institute of Technology
CIJE: 0 RIE: 1 CAT: 17

West Virginia Library Association
CIJE: 0 RIE: 1 CAT: 17

West Virginia Model Center
CIJE: 0 RIE: 1 CAT: 17

West Virginia Model Schools Project
CIJE: 0 RIE: 1 CAT: 19

West Virginia Network for Educ Telecomputing
CIJE: 0 RIE: 1 CAT: 17

West Virginia Rehabilitation Center
CIJE: 0 RIE: 1 CAT: 17

West Virginia Speech Association
CIJE: 0 RIE: 1 CAT: 17

West Virginia State Board of Education v Barnette
USE West Virginia Board of Education v Barnette

West Virginia State College
CIJE: 3 RIE: 7 CAT: 17

West Virginia State County Testing Program
CIJE: 0 RIE: 1 CAT: 19

West Virginia Student Questionnaire
CIJE: 0 RIE: 1 CAT: 21

West Virginia University
CIJE: 42 RIE: 43 CAT: 17

West Virginia University Parkersburg
CIJE: 1 RIE: 0 CAT: 17

West Virginia University Residency Program
CIJE: 1 RIE: 0 CAT: 19

West Virginia Wesleyan College
CIJE: 2 RIE: 4 CAT: 17

West Virginia Writing Project
CIJE: 2 RIE: 0 CAT: 19

West Virginia Youth in Crisis
CIJE: 1 RIE: 0 CAT: 19

West Virginia Youth Science Camp
CIJE: 1 RIE: 0 CAT: 19

West York Area School District PA
CIJE: 0 RIE: 1 CAT: 17

West Yuma County School District CO
CIJE: 1 RIE: 0 CAT: 17

Westchester Community College NY
CIJE: 3 RIE: 9 CAT: 17

Westcott Problem Solving Scale
CIJE: 0 RIE: 1 CAT: 21

Western Association of Schools and Colleges
CIJE: 8 RIE: 8 CAT: 17

Western Australian College of Advanced Education
CIJE: 0 RIE: 1 CAT: 17

Western Australian Inservice Teacher Educ Project
CIJE: 0 RIE: 1 CAT: 19

Western Australian Institute of Technology
CIJE: 6 RIE: 4 CAT: 17

Western Australian Post Secondary Educ Commission
CIJE: 0 RIE: 0 CAT: 17

Western Australian Writing Research Project
CIJE: 1 RIE: 1 CAT: 19

Western Carolina University NC
CIJE: 7 RIE: 10 CAT: 17

Western College Association
CIJE: 0 RIE: 1 CAT: 17

Western College Reading and Learning Association
CIJE: 0 RIE: 1 CAT: 17
SN Formerly Western College Reading Association

Western College Reading Association
CIJE: 0 RIE: 2 CAT: 17

Western Cooperative College (Canada)
CIJE: 0 RIE: 1 CAT: 17

Western Cooperative for Educ Telecommunications
CIJE: 1 RIE: 3 CAT: 17

Western Council on Higher Education for Nursing
CIJE: 0 RIE: 2 CAT: 17

Western Electric
CIJE: 2 RIE: 1 CAT: 17

Western European Union
CIJE: 1 RIE: 0 CAT: 17

Western Hemisphere
CIJE: 5 RIE: 9 CAT: 07

Western Illinois Univ Evaluation Questionnaire
CIJE: 0 RIE: 1 CAT: 21

Western Illinois University
CIJE: 14 RIE: 23 CAT: 17

Western Institute for Distance Education
CIJE: 0 RIE: 1 CAT: 17

Western Institute for Science and Technology
CIJE: 0 RIE: 1 CAT: 17

Western Interstate Commission for Higher Education
CIJE: 10 RIE: 26 CAT: 17
SN See add'l listings under "WICHE..."
UF WICHE

Western Kentucky University
CIJE: 10 RIE: 19 CAT: 17

Western Library Network
CIJE: 4 RIE: 3 CAT: 17

Western Maryland College
CIJE: 2 RIE: 3 CAT: 17

Western Massachusetts Five Coll Pub Sch Partners
CIJE: 0 RIE: 1 CAT: 17

Western Michigan University
CIJE: 18 RIE: 47 CAT: 17

Western Montana College
CIJE: 0 RIE: 4 CAT: 17

Western Montgomery County Area Voc Tech School PA
CIJE: 1 RIE: 0 CAT: 17

Western Music
CIJE: 2 RIE: 1 CAT: 16

Western Nebraska Technical College
CIJE: 1 RIE: 0 CAT: 17

Western Nevada Community College
CIJE: 0 RIE: 1 CAT: 17

Western New England College MA
CIJE: 2 RIE: 1 CAT: 17

Western New Mexico University
CIJE: 1 RIE: 1 CAT: 17

Western Ontario Field Centre
CIJE: 1 RIE: 0 CAT: 17

Western Oregon State College
CIJE: 2 RIE: 8 CAT: 17

Western Penn Health Preceptorship Program
CIJE: 1 RIE: 0 CAT: 19

Western Piedmont Community College NC
CIJE: 0 RIE: 1 CAT: 17

Western Psychological Association
CIJE: 0 RIE: 1 CAT: 17

Western Regional Council State Leagues of Nursing
CIJE: 0 RIE: 1 CAT: 17

Western Regional Resource Center OR
CIJE: 0 RIE: 1 CAT: 17

Western Research Application Center
CIJE: 1 RIE: 1 CAT: 17

Western Reserve University OH
CIJE: 2 RIE: 1 CAT: 17

Western Riding
CIJE: 0 RIE: 1 CAT: 16

Western Samoa
CIJE: 4 RIE: 13 CAT: 07

Western School Journal
CIJE: 1 RIE: 0 CAT: 22

Western Service Systems Inc
CIJE: 0 RIE: 1 CAT: 17

Western Shoshone (Tribe)
CIJE: 1 RIE: 2 CAT: 08

Western Speech Communication Association
CIJE: 1 RIE: 1 CAT: 17

Western State College CO
CIJE: 2 RIE: 2 CAT: 17

Western State College of Colorado
CIJE: 1 RIE: 1 CAT: 17

Western State Hospital VA
CIJE: 0 RIE: 1 CAT: 17

Western States Small Schools Project
CIJE: 0 RIE: 35 CAT: 19

Western Union Telegraph Company
CIJE: 1 RIE: 2 CAT: 17

Western Washington State College
CIJE: 4 RIE: 9 CAT: 17

Western Washington University
CIJE: 6 RIE: 15 CAT: 17

Western Wind
CIJE: 1 RIE: 0 CAT: 22

Western Wisconsin Technical College
CIJE: 0 RIE: 2 CAT: 17

Western Wisconsin Technical Institute
CIJE: 1 RIE: 0 CAT: 17

Westernization
CIJE: 7 RIE: 8 CAT: 16

Westernport Simulation Exercise
CIJE: 0 RIE: 1 CAT: 21

Westerns (Films)
CIJE: 7 RIE: 0 CAT: 16

Westerns (Novels)
CIJE: 5 RIE: 0 CAT: 16

Westfield Public School District NJ
CIJE: 1 RIE: 1 CAT: 17

Westfield State College MA
CIJE: 2 RIE: 2 CAT: 17

Westinghouse Area Vocational High School IL
CIJE: 1 RIE: 0 CAT: 17

Westinghouse Learning Corporation
CIJE: 3 RIE: 3 CAT: 17

Westinghouse Nuclear Training Center IL
CIJE: 0 RIE: 1 CAT: 17

Westinghouse Ohio Study
CIJE: 3 RIE: 1 CAT: 19

Westinghouse Report
CIJE: 1 RIE: 2 CAT: 22

Westinghouse Science Talent Search
CIJE: 9 RIE: 2 CAT: 20
SN See also "Science Talent Search"

WESTLAW Retrieval System
CIJE: 15 RIE: 2 CAT: 04

Westminster College PA
CIJE: 0 RIE: 2 CAT: 17

Westminster College UT
CIJE: 3 RIE: 3 CAT: 17

Westminster Project Social Studies
CIJE: 1 RIE: 0 CAT: 19

Westmont College CA
CIJE: 2 RIE: 2 CAT: 17

Westmoreland County Community College PA
CIJE: 0 RIE: 1 CAT: 17

Westmoreland County School District VA
CIJE: 0 RIE: 2 CAT: 17

Westport Project
CIJE: 0 RIE: 1 CAT: 19

Westridge School CA
CIJE: 0 RIE: 1 CAT: 17

Westside Area Career Occupation Project
CIJE: 0 RIE: 1 CAT: 19

Westside High School NE
CIJE: 1 RIE: 0 CAT: 17

Westside Preparatory School IL
CIJE: 0 RIE: 1 CAT: 17

Westward Movement (United States)
CIJE: 15 RIE: 5 CAT: 12

Wet Nurses
CIJE: 0 RIE: 1 CAT: 09

Wetaskiwin School District AB
CIJE: 0 RIE: 1 CAT: 17

Wetzel Grid Charts
CIJE: 1 RIE: 0 CAT: 21

Wexell v Scott
CIJE: 1 RIE: 0 CAT: 14

Wh Clauses
CIJE: 0 RIE: 1 CAT: 13

Wh Questions
CIJE: 7 RIE: 17 CAT: 13

Whales
CIJE: 13 RIE: 12 CAT: 20

Whamo Super Ball (Toy)
CIJE: 1 RIE: 0 CAT: 16

Whanau House
CIJE: 0 RIE: 1 CAT: 05

Wharton (Edith)
CIJE: 2 RIE: 1 CAT: 18

Wharton County Junior College TX
CIJE: 0 RIE: 1 CAT: 17

Wharton School PA
USE University of Pennsylvania Wharton School

What Color Is Your Parachute
CIJE: 0 RIE: 1 CAT: 22
SN "...: A Practical Manual for Job Hunters and Career Changers"

What I Like to Do (Interest Scale)
CIJE: 0 RIE: 1 CAT: 21

What I Think of Myself Test (Mathewson and Orton)
CIJE: 0 RIE: 1 CAT: 21

What I Want to Do (Inventory)
CIJE: 0 RIE: 1 CAT: 21

What If Situations Test
CIJE: 1 RIE: 3 CAT: 21

What Kind of a Person Are You Test (Torrance)
CIJE: 3 RIE: 0 CAT: 21

What Work Requires of Schools
CIJE: 0 RIE: 1 CAT: 22
SN 1991 report of the Secretary of Labor's Commission on Achieving Necessary Skills (SCANS)

What Works in Reading (Study)
CIJE: 0 RIE: 1 CAT: 22

Whatcom Community College District 21 WA
CIJE: 0 RIE: 0 CAT: 17

Whatcom Community College WA
CIJE: 1 RIE: 2 CAT: 17

Whately (Richard)
CIJE: 3 RIE: 3 CAT: 18

WHCLIS
USE White House Conference Library Info Services

Wheat
CIJE: 0 RIE: 4 CAT: 20

Wheatley (Phillis)
CIJE: 5 RIE: 0 CAT: 18

Wheatley Cube
CIJE: 0 RIE: 2 CAT: 21

Wheatley School
CIJE: 2 RIE: 0 CAT: 17

Wheaton College IL
CIJE: 4 RIE: 1 CAT: 17

Wheaton College MA
CIJE: 4 RIE: 5 CAT: 17

Wheelchair Athletics
CIJE: 2 RIE: 2 CAT: 16

Wheelchairmanship Project
CIJE: 0 RIE: 1 CAT: 19

Wheeler Rorschach Signs
CIJE: 1 RIE: 0 CAT: 21

Wheelersburg Local School District OH
CIJE: 0 RIE: 1 CAT: 17

Wheeless (L R)
CIJE: 0 RIE: 1 CAT: 18

Wheeling School District 21 IL
CIJE: 0 RIE: 1 CAT: 17

Wheelock College MA
CIJE: 1 RIE: 3 CAT: 17

Wheelwright (Philip)
CIJE: 0 RIE: 1 CAT: 18

When the Legends Die
CIJE: 0 RIE: 1 CAT: 22

Where in Louisiana
CIJE: 0 RIE: 1 CAT: 22

Where in the USA Is Carmen Sandiego
CIJE: 0 RIE: 1 CAT: 22

Where in Time Is Carmen Sandiego
CIJE: 0 RIE: 1 CAT: 22

Wherry Formula
CIJE: 3 RIE: 0 CAT: 21

Whewell (William)
CIJE: 1 RIE: 0 CAT: 18

Which to Discuss Test (Maw and Maw)
CIJE: 1 RIE: 0 CAT: 21

WHIDD Analysis
CIJE: 1 RIE: 0 CAT: 15

Whimbey (Arthur)
CIJE: 1 RIE: 0 CAT: 18

Whimbey Analytical Skills Inventory
CIJE: 1 RIE: 1 CAT: 21

Whinnom (Keith)
CIJE: 1 RIE: 1 CAT: 18

Whiplash Shaken Infant Syndrome
CIJE: 1 RIE: 0 CAT: 11

Whisman Language Tutor Program
CIJE: 1 RIE: 0 CAT: 19

Whistle Blowing
CIJE: 7 RIE: 6 CAT: 14

Whitby Public Library (Canada)
CIJE: 0 RIE: 1 CAT: 17

White (Charles)
CIJE: 2 RIE: 0 CAT: 18

White (Clarence)
CIJE: 0 RIE: 1 CAT: 18
SN American photographer

White (E B)
CIJE: 8 RIE: 1 CAT: 18

White (Elizabeth Q)
USE Qoyawayma (Polingaysi)

White (L T)
CIJE: 0 RIE: 1 CAT: 18

White (R T)
CIJE: 0 RIE: 1 CAT: 18

White (Robert W)
CIJE: 0 RIE: 1 CAT: 18

White (Theodore H)
CIJE: 2 RIE: 1 CAT: 18

White (William Lindsay)
CIJE: 0 RIE: 1 CAT: 18

White Backlash
CIJE: 4 RIE: 1 CAT: 16

White Collar Crime
CIJE: 6 RIE: 4 CAT: 14

White Collar Organizations
CIJE: 1 RIE: 0 CAT: 05

White Colleges
CIJE: 22 RIE: 3 CAT: 05
UF Predominantly White Colleges

White Earth Indian Reservation MN
CIJE: 2 RIE: 1 CAT: 17

White Horse Plain School Division Number 20 MB
CIJE: 0 RIE: 2 CAT: 17

White House Conference for a Drug Free America
CIJE: 0 RIE: 1 CAT: 02

White House Conference Library Info Services
CIJE: 54 RIE: 101 CAT: 02
SN Use for both WHCLIS I (1979) and WHCLIS II (1991)
UF WHCLIS; White House Conference on Libry and Info Services

White House Conference on Aging
CIJE: 2 RIE: 49 CAT: 02

White House Conference on Children
CIJE: 6 RIE: 4 CAT: 02

White House Conference on Children and Youth
CIJE: 2 RIE: 3 CAT: 02

White House Conference on Families
CIJE: 4 RIE: 16 CAT: 02

White House Conference on Food Nutrition Health
CIJE: 2 RIE: 1 CAT: 02

White House Conference on Indian Education
CIJE: 1 RIE: 7 CAT: 02

White House Conference on Libry and Info Services
USE White House Conference Library Info Services

White House Conference on Rural Education
CIJE: 0 RIE: 2 CAT: 02

White House Conference on Small Business
CIJE: 0 RIE: 1 CAT: 02

White House Conference on Youth
CIJE: 0 RIE: 5 CAT: 02

White House Consultation with Rural Women
CIJE: 0 RIE: 1 CAT: 02

White House Fellows
CIJE: 0 RIE: 1 CAT: 17

White House Pre Conf Indian Library Info Services
CIJE: 1 RIE: 1 CAT: 02

White House Workshop on Choice in Education
CIJE: 0 RIE: 1 CAT: 02

White Memorial Foundation
CIJE: 0 RIE: 1 CAT: 17

White Mountain Apache (Tribe)
CIJE: 3 RIE: 7 CAT: 08

White Mountains
CIJE: 1 RIE: 0 CAT: 07

White Noise
CIJE: 4 RIE: 0 CAT: 20

Williamsburg Area Community College PA
CIJE: 1 RIE: 0 CAT: 17

Williamsburg Charter
CIJE: 0 RIE: 3 CAT: 16
SN A 1988 document drafted by representatives of U.S. faiths dealing with religious liberty and the place of religion in public life

Williamsburg County Public Schools SC
CIJE: 0 RIE: 1 CAT: 17

Williamson (E G)
CIJE: 1 RIE: 0 CAT: 18

Williamson (Hugh)
CIJE: 0 RIE: 1 CAT: 18

Williamsport Area Community College PA
CIJE: 5 RIE: 5 CAT: 17

Williamsport Area School District PA
CIJE: 1 RIE: 3 CAT: 17

Williamsville School District NY
CIJE: 1 RIE: 0 CAT: 17

Willie M v Hunt
CIJE: 1 RIE: 2 CAT: 14

Willingboro Schools NJ
CIJE: 1 RIE: 0 CAT: 17

Willingness
CIJE: 0 RIE: 1 CAT: 16

Willingness to Collaborate Trait Scale
CIJE: 0 RIE: 1 CAT: 21

Willingness to Commun Self Scale (Brewer et al)
CIJE: 1 RIE: 0 CAT: 21

Willingness to Communicate
CIJE: 0 RIE: 2 CAT: 16
UF Willingness to Communicate Construct

Willingness to Communicate Construct
USE Willingness to Communicate

Willinsky (John)
CIJE: 0 RIE: 1 CAT: 18

Willis (Ben)
CIJE: 0 RIE: 1 CAT: 18

Willis (Meredith Sue)
CIJE: 1 RIE: 0 CAT: 18

Willis (Nathaniel)
CIJE: 0 RIE: 1 CAT: 18

Willis (Paul)
CIJE: 2 RIE: 1 CAT: 18

Willkie (Wendell)
CIJE: 0 RIE: 1 CAT: 18

Willoughby Haggerty Behavior Rating Scale
CIJE: 0 RIE: 1 CAT: 21

Willoughby Personality Schedule
CIJE: 3 RIE: 0 CAT: 21

Willower (Donald J)
CIJE: 1 RIE: 1 CAT: 18

Wills Auditory Gestalt Test
CIJE: 1 RIE: 0 CAT: 21

Wilmington Operational Mathematics Program
CIJE: 0 RIE: 1 CAT: 19

Wilmington Public Library OH
CIJE: 0 RIE: 1 CAT: 17

Wilmington Public Schools DE
CIJE: 0 RIE: 1 CAT: 17

Wilmot Junior High School IL
CIJE: 1 RIE: 0 CAT: 17

Wilms (Wellford W)
CIJE: 0 RIE: 1 CAT: 18

Wilsearch
CIJE: 0 RIE: 2 CAT: 04

Wilson (August)
CIJE: 0 RIE: 1 CAT: 18

Wilson (Edmund)
CIJE: 5 RIE: 1 CAT: 18

Wilson (Edward Osborne)
CIJE: 4 RIE: 0 CAT: 18

Wilson (G D)
CIJE: 0 RIE: 1 CAT: 18

Wilson (Ida May)
CIJE: 0 RIE: 1 CAT: 18

Wilson (James Q)
CIJE: 1 RIE: 1 CAT: 18

Wilson (John)
CIJE: 7 RIE: 1 CAT: 18

Wilson (Logan)
CIJE: 0 RIE: 1 CAT: 18

Wilson (Pete)
CIJE: 1 RIE: 1 CAT: 18

Wilson (Robert)
CIJE: 0 RIE: 2 CAT: 18

Wilson (Woodrow)
CIJE: 17 RIE: 1 CAT: 18

Wilson College (India)
CIJE: 1 RIE: 0 CAT: 17

Wilson College PA
CIJE: 5 RIE: 3 CAT: 17

Wilson School
CIJE: 1 RIE: 0 CAT: 17

Wilson Stress Profile for Teachers
CIJE: 2 RIE: 1 CAT: 21
UF Stress Profile for Teachers (Wilson)

Wilsondisc
CIJE: 2 RIE: 1 CAT: 04

Wilsonline
CIJE: 5 RIE: 1 CAT: 04

Wilsons Disease
CIJE: 2 RIE: 0 CAT: 11

Wilton Public Schools CT
CIJE: 2 RIE: 0 CAT: 17

Win Win Bargaining
CIJE: 2 RIE: 1 CAT: 15

WIN WIN Program
CIJE: 0 RIE: 1 CAT: 19
SN Third-grade classroom guidance program in conflict resolution and peacemaking

Winans (James A)
CIJE: 1 RIE: 0 CAT: 18

Winans (R Foster)
CIJE: 0 RIE: 1 CAT: 18

Winchester Community School CT
CIJE: 1 RIE: 1 CAT: 17

Wind Chill
CIJE: 1 RIE: 0 CAT: 20

Wind Ensembles
CIJE: 1 RIE: 0 CAT: 10

Wind Erosion
CIJE: 2 RIE: 0 CAT: 20

Wind Generators
CIJE: 1 RIE: 2 CAT: 04

Wind in the Willows
CIJE: 2 RIE: 1 CAT: 22

Wind Instruments
CIJE: 0 RIE: 2 CAT: 16

Wind Tunnels
CIJE: 6 RIE: 0 CAT: 04

Windber Area School District PA
CIJE: 0 RIE: 1 CAT: 17

Windermere School District No 4 BC
CIJE: 0 RIE: 0 CAT: 17

Windham Independent School District TX
CIJE: 1 RIE: 0 CAT: 17

Windham Planning Region
CIJE: 0 RIE: 1 CAT: 17

Windmills
CIJE: 1 RIE: 4 CAT: 04

Windowless Schools
CIJE: 1 RIE: 0 CAT: 05

Windows (Software)
CIJE: 4 RIE: 1 CAT: 20
SN See also "Microsoft Windows"

Windsor Early Identification Project
CIJE: 0 RIE: 1 CAT: 19

Windsor High School CT
CIJE: 1 RIE: 0 CAT: 17

Windsor Hills Elementary School CA
CIJE: 1 RIE: 0 CAT: 17

Windsor Separate School Board ON
CIJE: 0 RIE: 1 CAT: 17

Windward Rating Scale
CIJE: 1 RIE: 1 CAT: 21

Wine Science
CIJE: 1 RIE: 2 CAT: 20

Winebago
USE Winnebago

Winemaking
CIJE: 5 RIE: 2 CAT: 16
SN See also "Viticulture"
UF Enology; Oenology

Winfrey (Oprah)
CIJE: 0 RIE: 2 CAT: 18

Wingate College NC
CIJE: 1 RIE: 1 CAT: 17

Wingspread Conferences
CIJE: 9 RIE: 11 CAT: 02

Wingspread Report on Higher Education
CIJE: 0 RIE: 1 CAT: 22

Winnebago
CIJE: 0 RIE: 2 CAT: 13
SN A Siouan language
UF Winebago

Winnebago (Tribe)
CIJE: 2 RIE: 17 CAT: 08

Winnebago Behavior Analysis Program
CIJE: 0 RIE: 1 CAT: 19

Winnemucca (Sarah)
CIJE: 0 RIE: 1 CAT: 18

Winnetka Plan
CIJE: 0 RIE: 1 CAT: 15

Winnetka Public Schools IL
CIJE: 1 RIE: 0 CAT: 17

Winnicott (Donald W)
CIJE: 0 RIE: 1 CAT: 18

Winnie the Pooh
CIJE: 3 RIE: 0 CAT: 22

Winning
CIJE: 3 RIE: 3 CAT: 16

Winnipeg Bible College MB
CIJE: 0 RIE: 1 CAT: 17

Winnipeg School Division Number 1 MB
CIJE: 0 RIE: 3 CAT: 17

Winona Area Technical School MN
CIJE: 0 RIE: 1 CAT: 17

Winona School District MN
CIJE: 0 RIE: 0 CAT: 17

Winona State College MN
CIJE: 1 RIE: 0 CAT: 17

Winona State University MN
CIJE: 1 RIE: 7 CAT: 17

Winooski Supervisory School District VT
CIJE: 0 RIE: 1 CAT: 17

Winstanley (Gerrard)
CIJE: 1 RIE: 0 CAT: 18

Winston Churchill Library
CIJE: 0 RIE: 1 CAT: 17

Winston Dillard School District OR
CIJE: 0 RIE: 1 CAT: 17

Winston Salem and Forsyth County Schools NC
CIJE: 1 RIE: 2 CAT: 17

Winston Salem State College NC
CIJE: 0 RIE: 1 CAT: 17

Winter
CIJE: 15 RIE: 10 CAT: 16

Winter (D)
CIJE: 0 RIE: 1 CAT: 18

Winter Depression
USE Seasonal Affective Disorder

Winter Programs
CIJE: 3 RIE: 3 CAT: 19

Winterbottom Questionnaire
CIJE: 0 RIE: 1 CAT: 21

Winterhaven Percept Test Train Handbook
CIJE: 0 RIE: 1 CAT: 21

Winterowd (W Ross)
CIJE: 0 RIE: 1 CAT: 18

Winters (Yvor)
CIJE: 1 RIE: 0 CAT: 18

Winters Tale
CIJE: 1 RIE: 0 CAT: 22

Winterthur Museum Library
CIJE: 1 RIE: 0 CAT: 17

Winthrop College Competency Testing Project SC
CIJE: 0 RIE: 1 CAT: 19

Winthrop College SC
CIJE: 6 RIE: 11 CAT: 17

Winton Act
CIJE: 2 RIE: 1 CAT: 14

Wire Sculpture
CIJE: 3 RIE: 0 CAT: 03

Wire Services
CIJE: 18 RIE: 9 CAT: 10

Wired City
CIJE: 0 RIE: 5 CAT: 16

Wired Nation
CIJE: 0 RIE: 4 CAT: 16

Wireless Cable
CIJE: 0 RIE: 1 CAT: 20

Wiretapping
CIJE: 2 RIE: 2 CAT: 16

Wiring (Electricity)
USE Electrical Wiring

Wirt Plan
CIJE: 0 RIE: 1 CAT: 19

Wirtschaftliche Bildung Test
CIJE: 0 RIE: 1 CAT: 21
SN German version of the Test of Economic Literacy

WISC R Administration Observational Checklist
CIJE: 0 RIE: 1 CAT: 21
UF WAOC Observation Instrument

WISCHE Federal Executive Institute
CIJE: 1 RIE: 0 CAT: 03

WisCom
USE Wisconsin Competency Based Occup Curr Data System

Wisconsin
CIJE: 355 RIE: 1431 CAT: 07

Wisconsin (Burnett County)
CIJE: 0 RIE: 1 CAT: 07

Wisconsin (Dane County)
CIJE: 3 RIE: 9 CAT: 07

Wisconsin (Eau Claire County)
CIJE: 1 RIE: 2 CAT: 07

Wisconsin (Eau Claire)
CIJE: 0 RIE: 6 CAT: 07

Wisconsin (Forest County)
CIJE: 0 RIE: 1 CAT: 07

Wisconsin (Green Bay)
CIJE: 3 RIE: 1 CAT: 07

Wisconsin (Janesville)
CIJE: 1 RIE: 4 CAT: 07

Wisconsin (Kenosha)
CIJE: 0 RIE: 3 CAT: 07

Wisconsin (La Crosse)
CIJE: 1 RIE: 1 CAT: 07

Wisconsin (Lodi)
CIJE: 0 RIE: 1 CAT: 07

Wisconsin (Madison)
CIJE: 15 RIE: 14 CAT: 07

Wisconsin (Manitowoc)
CIJE: 0 RIE: 3 CAT: 07

Wisconsin (Marquette County)
CIJE: 0 RIE: 1 CAT: 07

Wisconsin (Menomonie)
CIJE: 0 RIE: 2 CAT: 07

Wisconsin (Milwaukee County)
CIJE: 1 RIE: 4 CAT: 07

Wisconsin (Milwaukee)
CIJE: 75 RIE: 128 CAT: 07

Wisconsin (New Glarus)
CIJE: 0 RIE: 1 CAT: 07

Wisconsin (Oshkosh)
CIJE: 0 RIE: 2 CAT: 07

Wisconsin (Portage)
CIJE: 0 RIE: 1 CAT: 07

Wisconsin (Pulaski)
CIJE: 1 RIE: 1 CAT: 07

Wisconsin (Racine)
CIJE: 11 RIE: 14 CAT: 07

Wisconsin (River Falls)
CIJE: 1 RIE: 1 CAT: 07

Wisconsin (Rock County)
CIJE: 0 RIE: 2 CAT: 07

Wisconsin (Sheboygan)
CIJE: 1 RIE: 5 CAT: 07

Wisconsin (Stevens Point)
CIJE: 0 RIE: 5 CAT: 07

Wisconsin (Sussex)
CIJE: 0 RIE: 1 CAT: 07

Wisconsin (Trempealeau County)
CIJE: 1 RIE: 2 CAT: 07

Wisconsin (Walworth County)
CIJE: 0 RIE: 1 CAT: 07

Wisconsin (Waukesha County)
CIJE: 0 RIE: 1 CAT: 07

Wisconsin (Waukesha)
CIJE: 0 RIE: 1 CAT: 07

Wisconsin (Wausau)
CIJE: 0 RIE: 4 CAT: 07

Wisconsin (Waushara County)
CIJE: 0 RIE: 1 CAT: 07

Wisconsin (West de Pere)
CIJE: 0 RIE: 1 CAT: 07

Wisconsin (West)
CIJE: 0 RIE: 1 CAT: 07

Wisconsin (Whitefish Bay)
CIJE: 1 RIE: 1 CAT: 07

Wisconsin Alumni Association
CIJE: 1 RIE: 0 CAT: 17

Wisconsin Alumni Research Foundation
CIJE: 0 RIE: 1 CAT: 17

Wisconsin Area VTAE Moraine Park
CIJE: 0 RIE: 0 CAT: 17

Wisconsin Association of Academic Librarians
CIJE: 2 RIE: 0 CAT: 17

Wisconsin Audiovisual Association
CIJE: 1 RIE: 0 CAT: 17

Wisconsin Audiovisual Education Demonstration
CIJE: 0 RIE: 1 CAT: 19

Wisconsin Basic Needs Survey
CIJE: 1 RIE: 1 CAT: 21

Wisconsin Card Sorting Test
CIJE: 3 RIE: 0 CAT: 21

Wisconsin Career Information System
CIJE: 1 RIE: 1 CAT: 19

Wisconsin Center for Education Research
CIJE: 0 RIE: 3 CAT: 17

Wisconsin Childrens Treatment Center
CIJE: 1 RIE: 1 CAT: 17

Wisconsin Competency Based Occup Curr Data System
CIJE: 0 RIE: 1 CAT: 04
UF WisCom

Wisconsin Competency Based Testing Program
USE Competency Based Testing Program WI

Wisconsin Council of Teachers of English
CIJE: 0 RIE: 1 CAT: 17

Wisconsin Counselor Education Selection Interview
CIJE: 1 RIE: 0 CAT: 21

Wisconsin Curr for Educable Mentally Retarded
CIJE: 1 RIE: 0 CAT: 03

Wisconsin Department of Audiovisual Instruction
CIJE: 1 RIE: 0 CAT: 17

Wisconsin Department of Public Instruction
CIJE: 1 RIE: 14 CAT: 17

Wisconsin Design for Reading Skill Development
CIJE: 2 RIE: 32 CAT: 19

Wisconsin Division of Vocational Rehabilitation
CIJE: 0 RIE: 1 CAT: 17

Wisconsin Education Association
CIJE: 0 RIE: 1 CAT: 17

Wisconsin Education for Employment Program
USE Education for Employment WI

Wisconsin Education Opportunity Program
CIJE: 0 RIE: 1 CAT: 19

Wisconsin Elementary Teacher Education Project
CIJE: 1 RIE: 0 CAT: 19

Wisconsin Employment Relations Board
CIJE: 0 RIE: 1 CAT: 17

Wisconsin Expanding Inventory Reading Development
CIJE: 0 RIE: 1 CAT: 21

Wisconsin Fast Plants
USE Fast Plants

Wisconsin Foundation Vocational Technical Adult Ed
CIJE: 1 RIE: 1 CAT: 17

Wisconsin General Test Apparatus
CIJE: 3 RIE: 2 CAT: 21

Wisconsin Guide Curriculum Improvement Indust Educ
CIJE: 0 RIE: 1 CAT: 22

Wisconsin Guide Local Curr Improvement Indust Educ
CIJE: 0 RIE: 1 CAT: 22

Wisconsin Hearing Conservation Program
CIJE: 0 RIE: 1 CAT: 19

Wisconsin Heights High School
CIJE: 0 RIE: 1 CAT: 17

Wisconsin Improvement Program
CIJE: 1 RIE: 3 CAT: 19

Wisconsin Inactive Nurse Studies
CIJE: 1 RIE: 0 CAT: 19

Wisconsin Indianhead Technical College
CIJE: 0 RIE: 1 CAT: 17

Wisconsin Information System for Education
CIJE: 0 RIE: 2 CAT: 04
UF WISE

Wisconsin Interlibrary Services
CIJE: 1 RIE: 0 CAT: 17

Wisconsin Inventory of Science Processes
CIJE: 1 RIE: 1 CAT: 21

Wisconsin Item Bank
CIJE: 0 RIE: 1 CAT: 21

Wisconsin Junior Dairymens Association
CIJE: 0 RIE: 1 CAT: 17

Wisconsin Leadership Identification Program
CIJE: 0 RIE: 1 CAT: 19
UF Leadership Identification Program WI

Wisconsin Learner Assessment Program
CIJE: 0 RIE: 4 CAT: 19

Wisconsin Library Network Plan
CIJE: 0 RIE: 1 CAT: 19

Wisconsin Model of Status Attainment
CIJE: 6 RIE: 4 CAT: 15

Wisconsin Model Peace Project
CIJE: 1 RIE: 0 CAT: 19

Wisconsin Nurses Association
CIJE: 1 RIE: 0 CAT: 17

Wisconsin Physics Film Evaluation Project
CIJE: 0 RIE: 1 CAT: 19

Wisconsin Program for Renewal Improvement Sec Educ
CIJE: 0 RIE: 2 CAT: 19

Wisconsin Pupil Assessment Program
CIJE: 0 RIE: 10 CAT: 19

Wisconsin R and D Center for Cognitive Learning
CIJE: 0 RIE: 8 CAT: 17

Wisconsin Recreation Leaders Laboratory
CIJE: 1 RIE: 0 CAT: 17

Wisconsin Rural Reading Improvement Project
CIJE: 0 RIE: 3 CAT: 19

Wisconsin Scale (Otto and Rarick)
CIJE: 0 RIE: 1 CAT: 21

Wisconsin School for Boys
CIJE: 1 RIE: 0 CAT: 17

Wisconsin School for Girls
CIJE: 1 RIE: 0 CAT: 17

Wisconsin School for the Deaf
CIJE: 2 RIE: 0 CAT: 17

Wisconsin School for the Visually Handicapped
CIJE: 1 RIE: 1 CAT: 17

Wisconsin School of the Air
CIJE: 1 RIE: 1 CAT: 17

Wisconsin State Historical Society
USE State Historical Society of Wisconsin

Wisconsin State Reading Association
CIJE: 0 RIE: 1 CAT: 17

Wisconsin Statewide Secondary Voc Program Eval Sys
CIJE: 0 RIE: 1 CAT: 19

Wisconsin Supreme Court
CIJE: 0 RIE: 1 CAT: 17

Wisconsin System for Instructional Management
CIJE: 3 RIE: 7 CAT: 15

Wisconsin Test of Adult Basic Education
CIJE: 0 RIE: 1 CAT: 21

Wisconsin Tests Testimony Reasoning Assessment
CIJE: 0 RIE: 3 CAT: 21

Wisconsin Third Grade Reading Test
CIJE: 0 RIE: 1 CAT: 21

Wisconsin v Yoder
CIJE: 5 RIE: 1 CAT: 14

Wisconsin Vocational Technical Adult Ed Districts
CIJE: 0 RIE: 5 CAT: 17

Wisconsin Writing Project
CIJE: 0 RIE: 30 CAT: 19

Wisconsin Youth Initiative
CIJE: 0 RIE: 2 CAT: 19

Wisdom
CIJE: 11 RIE: 4 CAT: 16
SN See also "Folk Wisdom"

WISE
USE Wisconsin Information System for Education

Wise (Arthur)
CIJE: 2 RIE: 1 CAT: 18

Wise Owl Clubs
CIJE: 1 RIE: 2 CAT: 17

Wiseman (Frederick)
CIJE: 4 RIE: 0 CAT: 18

Wishes
CIJE: 1 RIE: 0 CAT: 16

Wishy (Bernard)
CIJE: 1 RIE: 0 CAT: 18

Wiskobas Project
CIJE: 2 RIE: 0 CAT: 19

Wiswesser Line Notation
CIJE: 13 RIE: 0 CAT: 15

Wit and Humor Appreciation Test (OConnell)
CIJE: 1 RIE: 0 CAT: 21

Witch of Agnesi
CIJE: 1 RIE: 0 CAT: 22

Witchcraft
CIJE: 6 RIE: 3 CAT: 16

Withdrawal Grades
CIJE: 0 RIE: 1 CAT: 16
UF W Grades

Within Category Spacing
CIJE: 1 RIE: 0 CAT: 11

Within Class Regression
CIJE: 1 RIE: 1 CAT: 21

Within Group Differences
CIJE: 4 RIE: 2 CAT: 16
UF Intragroup Differences

Within Group Slopes
CIJE: 0 RIE: 1 CAT: 21

Withrow v Larkin
CIJE: 0 RIE: 1 CAT: 14

Witkin (H A)
CIJE: 2 RIE: 6 CAT: 18

Witness (Film)
CIJE: 0 RIE: 1 CAT: 22

Witnesses
CIJE: 22 RIE: 13 CAT: 10
UF Court Witnesses; Eyewitnesses

Witnesses to Crime
CIJE: 14 RIE: 1 CAT: 10
UF Eyewitnesses to Crime

Witte (Stephen)
CIJE: 0 RIE: 1 CAT: 18

Wittenberg College OH
CIJE: 1 RIE: 2 CAT: 17

Wittenberg University OH
CIJE: 3 RIE: 3 CAT: 17

Witters v Washington Dept of Services for Blind
CIJE: 0 RIE: 1 CAT: 14
SN a.k.a. Witters v Commission for the Blind

Wittgenstein (Ludwig)
CIJE: 10 RIE: 11 CAT: 18

Wizard (Computer Program)
CIJE: 0 RIE: 1 CAT: 04

Wizard of Earthsea
CIJE: 1 RIE: 0 CAT: 22

Wizard of Oz
CIJE: 4 RIE: 4 CAT: 22

Wizards of Work IN
CIJE: 0 RIE: 1 CAT: 19

Wofford College SC
CIJE: 1 RIE: 1 CAT: 17

Woititz (J G)
CIJE: 0 RIE: 1 CAT: 18
SN "Janet"

Wojciechowska (Maja)
CIJE: 1 RIE: 0 CAT: 18

Wojokeso
CIJE: 0 RIE: 1 CAT: 13

Wolayto
CIJE: 0 RIE: 1 CAT: 13

Wolcot (John)
CIJE: 0 RIE: 1 CAT: 18

Wolf (R M)
CIJE: 0 RIE: 1 CAT: 18

Wolf Trap Farm Park
CIJE: 1 RIE: 0 CAT: 17

Wolf Welsh Linkage Methodology
CIJE: 0 RIE: 1 CAT: 15

Wolfe (Thomas)
CIJE: 6 RIE: 2 CAT: 18

Wolfensberger (Wolf)
CIJE: 3 RIE: 0 CAT: 18

Wolfflin (Heinrich)
CIJE: 2 RIE: 0 CAT: 18

Wolfgang (Iser)
CIJE: 1 RIE: 0 CAT: 18

Wollensak Equipment
CIJE: 0 RIE: 2 CAT: 04

Wollstonecraft (Mary)
CIJE: 1 RIE: 3 CAT: 18
SN Author of the 1792 feminist thesis "Vindication of the Rights of Woman" — mother of Mary W. Shelley

Wolof (Tribe)
CIJE: 3 RIE: 0 CAT: 08

Wolpe (Joseph)
CIJE: 0 RIE: 1 CAT: 18

Wolpe Lazarus Assertive Inventory
CIJE: 0 RIE: 1 CAT: 21

Wolsey Hall
CIJE: 1 RIE: 0 CAT: 17

Woman Who Came Back
CIJE: 0 RIE: 1 CAT: 22

Women and Girls Employment Enabling Service
CIJE: 0 RIE: 1 CAT: 17

Women as School District Administrators Survey
CIJE: 0 RIE: 1 CAT: 21

Women Attentive to Childrens Happiness
CIJE: 0 RIE: 1 CAT: 16

Women College Presidents
CIJE: 0 RIE: 1 CAT: 09

Women in Development
CIJE: 0 RIE: 13 CAT: 19

Women in Development Programs
CIJE: 0 RIE: 8 CAT: 19

Women in Literature
CIJE: 4 RIE: 12 CAT: 16

Women in Medical Academia Model
CIJE: 0 RIE: 1 CAT: 15

Women in Nature Program
CIJE: 1 RIE: 0 CAT: 19

Women in Nontraditional Careers Curriculum
CIJE: 0 RIE: 1 CAT: 03

Women in Science
CIJE: 8 RIE: 9 CAT: 16

Women in Wisconsin Apprenticeship
CIJE: 1 RIE: 0 CAT: 19

Women Infants Children Supplemental Food Program
CIJE: 7 RIE: 14 CAT: 19

Women Inquire Into Science and Engineering
CIJE: 0 RIE: 2 CAT: 19

Women Journalists
CIJE: 1 RIE: 7 CAT: 09

Women Offender Apprenticeship Program
CIJE: 0 RIE: 1 CAT: 19

Women Owned Businesses
CIJE: 0 RIE: 3 CAT: 16

Women Reaching Women WI
CIJE: 0 RIE: 1 CAT: 17

Womens Action Program
CIJE: 1 RIE: 0 CAT: 19

Womens Bureau
CIJE: 4 RIE: 8 CAT: 17

Womens Centers
CIJE: 15 RIE: 12 CAT: 05

Womens Educational and Vocational Enrichment
CIJE: 0 RIE: 1 CAT: 19
UF WEAVE Program

Womens Educational Equity Act
CIJE: 10 RIE: 46 CAT: 14

Womens Equity Action League
CIJE: 0 RIE: 2 CAT: 17

Womens History
CIJE: 19 RIE: 3 CAT: 12

Womens History Landmark Project
CIJE: 0 RIE: 1 CAT: 19

Womens History Library
CIJE: 1 RIE: 0 CAT: 17

Womens History Month
CIJE: 2 RIE: 0 CAT: 12
UF National Womens History Month

Womens History Research Center
CIJE: 1 RIE: 0 CAT: 17

Womens History Week
CIJE: 0 RIE: 1 CAT: 12
SN See also entries under "National Womens History Week..."

Womens Information and Referral Service
CIJE: 1 RIE: 0 CAT: 17

Womens Liberation Questionnaire (Bove and Miller)
CIJE: 0 RIE: 1 CAT: 21

Womens Liberation Sappho Collective
CIJE: 1 RIE: 0 CAT: 17

Womens Literature
CIJE: 31 RIE: 22 CAT: 16

Womens Magazines
CIJE: 9 RIE: 12 CAT: 16

Womens Media
CIJE: 2 RIE: 2 CAT: 16

Womens National Basketball Coaches Clinic
CIJE: 1 RIE: 0 CAT: 02

Womens National Press Club
CIJE: 0 RIE: 1 CAT: 17

Womens Organizations
CIJE: 15 RIE: 9 CAT: 05

Womens Room (French)
CIJE: 0 RIE: 1 CAT: 22

Womens Shelters
CIJE: 0 RIE: 1 CAT: 05
SN See also "Spouse Abuse Shelters"

Womens Suffrage
CIJE: 11 RIE: 24 CAT: 12

Womens Talent Corps
CIJE: 0 RIE: 3 CAT: 17

Womens Ways of Knowing
CIJE: 1 RIE: 0 CAT: 22
SN Complete title: "Women's Ways of Knowing: The Development of Self, Voice, & Mind"

WomenVenture
CIJE: 0 RIE: 1 CAT: 19

Wonderland (Title)
CIJE: 1 RIE: 0 CAT: 22

Wonderlic Personnel Test
CIJE: 3 RIE: 6 CAT: 21

Wood (Charles)
CIJE: 1 RIE: 0 CAT: 18

Wood (Evelyn)
CIJE: 1 RIE: 1 CAT: 18

Wood (Fuel)
CIJE: 0 RIE: 1 CAT: 20

Wood (Herbert G)
CIJE: 0 RIE: 1 CAT: 18

Wood County Project
CIJE: 1 RIE: 1 CAT: 19

Wood Expansion Meter
CIJE: 1 RIE: 0 CAT: 04

Wood Plastic Composition
CIJE: 1 RIE: 0 CAT: 20

Wood Preservatives
CIJE: 0 RIE: 1 CAT: 20

Wood Processing
CIJE: 0 RIE: 2 CAT: 20

Wood Science
CIJE: 2 RIE: 0 CAT: 20

Wood Substitutes
CIJE: 0 RIE: 1 CAT: 20

Wood Technology
CIJE: 5 RIE: 1 CAT: 20

Wood v Strickland
CIJE: 13 RIE: 8 CAT: 14

Woodbury County Home IA
CIJE: 0 RIE: 1 CAT: 17

Woodcarving
CIJE: 1 RIE: 1 CAT: 20

Woodcock Johnson Psycho Educational Battery
CIJE: 36 RIE: 10 CAT: 21

Woodcock Johnson Tests of Cognitive Ability
CIJE: 16 RIE: 3 CAT: 21

Woodcock Language Proficiency Battery
CIJE: 2 RIE: 2 CAT: 21

Woodcock Passage Comprehension Test
CIJE: 0 RIE: 0 CAT: 21
UF Passage Comprehension Test (Woodcock)

Woodcock Reading Mastery Test
CIJE: 12 RIE: 10 CAT: 21

Woodcock Word Comprehension Test
CIJE: 2 RIE: 0 CAT: 21

Woodger (Joseph)
CIJE: 0 RIE: 1 CAT: 18

Woodhaven Center PA
CIJE: 3 RIE: 0 CAT: 17

Woodlawn Community Board
CIJE: 1 RIE: 1 CAT: 17

Woodlawn Organization
CIJE: 1 RIE: 4 CAT: 17

Woodlawn Public Library
CIJE: 1 RIE: 0 CAT: 17

Woodridge School CA
CIJE: 1 RIE: 0 CAT: 17

Woodrow Wilson National Fellowship Foundation
CIJE: 2 RIE: 5 CAT: 17

Woods
CIJE: 2 RIE: 2 CAT: 20

Woodson (Carter G)
CIJE: 6 RIE: 1 CAT: 18

Woodstock (Concert)
CIJE: 0 RIE: 1 CAT: 12

Woodwind Choirs
CIJE: 1 RIE: 0 CAT: 16

Woodwind Instruments
CIJE: 2 RIE: 0 CAT: 16

Woolbert (Charles Henry)
CIJE: 1 RIE: 0 CAT: 18

Woolf (Virginia)
CIJE: 10 RIE: 6 CAT: 18

Woolley (Helen Thompson)
CIJE: 0 RIE: 1 CAT: 18

Woolley (Mary)
CIJE: 0 RIE: 1 CAT: 18

Woolman (John)
CIJE: 1 RIE: 0 CAT: 18

Wooster Review (Ohio)
CIJE: 0 RIE: 1 CAT: 22

Wor Wic Technical Community College MD
CIJE: 0 RIE: 1 CAT: 17

Worcester College for the Blind (Great Britain)
CIJE: 0 RIE: 1 CAT: 17

Worcester Consortium for Higher Education
CIJE: 0 RIE: 1 CAT: 17

Worcester Polytechnic Institute MA
CIJE: 10 RIE: 12 CAT: 17

Worcester Public Schools MA
CIJE: 0 RIE: 1 CAT: 17

Worcester State College MA
CIJE: 2 RIE: 2 CAT: 17

Worchel Self Concept Inventory
CIJE: 1 RIE: 0 CAT: 21

Word Analysis and Synthesis
CIJE: 3 RIE: 0 CAT: 13

Word Associated Arousal
CIJE: 1 RIE: 0 CAT: 11

Word Associations
CIJE: 6 RIE: 4 CAT: 13

Word Attack Skills
CIJE: 6 RIE: 10 CAT: 13

Word Banks
CIJE: 2 RIE: 1 CAT: 13

Word Blind Centre for Dyslexic Children
CIJE: 0 RIE: 2 CAT: 17

Word Boundaries
CIJE: 7 RIE: 4 CAT: 13

Word Choice
CIJE: 12 RIE: 6 CAT: 13

Word Context Test
CIJE: 0 RIE: 1 CAT: 21

Word Counts
CIJE: 5 RIE: 4 CAT: 13

Word Derivation
CIJE: 1 RIE: 1 CAT: 13

Word Families
CIJE: 1 RIE: 3 CAT: 13

Word Finding Problems
CIJE: 8 RIE: 1 CAT: 13

Word Form Configuration Test (Sabatino)
CIJE: 0 RIE: 1 CAT: 21

Word Formation
CIJE: 17 RIE: 14 CAT: 13

Word Fragments
CIJE: 4 RIE: 1 CAT: 13

Word Games
CIJE: 13 RIE: 14 CAT: 16

Word Identification Test (Johnson et al)
CIJE: 0 RIE: 2 CAT: 21

Word Knowledge
CIJE: 0 RIE: 1 CAT: 13

Word Learning
CIJE: 11 RIE: 2 CAT: 13

Word Learning Tasks (Barr)
CIJE: 0 RIE: 1 CAT: 21

Word Length
CIJE: 13 RIE: 3 CAT: 13

Word List for the 1970s
CIJE: 0 RIE: 1 CAT: 22

Word Master in Spelling
CIJE: 0 RIE: 1 CAT: 19

Word Naming Technique
CIJE: 1 RIE: 1 CAT: 15

Word Omission
CIJE: 1 RIE: 1 CAT: 13

Word Order
CIJE: 57 RIE: 25 CAT: 13

Word Phrase Comprehension Tests (Shiba)
CIJE: 0 RIE: 1 CAT: 21

Word Pitch
CIJE: 0 RIE: 1 CAT: 13

Word Potency
CIJE: 1 RIE: 2 CAT: 13

Word Preference Inventory (Dunn and Rankin)
CIJE: 0 RIE: 1 CAT: 21

Word Processing Instruction
CIJE: 6 RIE: 1 CAT: 03

Word Reading Test
CIJE: 0 RIE: 4 CAT: 21

Word Realism
CIJE: 1 RIE: 0 CAT: 13

Word Recency Training
CIJE: 0 RIE: 1 CAT: 16

Word Retrieval
CIJE: 1 RIE: 2 CAT: 11

Word Shape
CIJE: 2 RIE: 1 CAT: 13

Word Stems
CIJE: 4 RIE: 0 CAT: 13

Word Strings
CIJE: 4 RIE: 3 CAT: 13

Word Structure
CIJE: 3 RIE: 8 CAT: 13

Word Superiority Effect
CIJE: 6 RIE: 2 CAT: 13

Word Use Test
CIJE: 0 RIE: 1 CAT: 21

Word Weaving Program
CIJE: 0 RIE: 1 CAT: 19

WordMAP Computer Program
CIJE: 0 RIE: 1 CAT: 04

WordNet Database
CIJE: 0 RIE: 1 CAT: 04

WordPerfect
CIJE: 2 RIE: 6 CAT: 04

WORDPLAY Program
CIJE: 0 RIE: 1 CAT: 19

Words
CIJE: 42 RIE: 29 CAT: 13

Words in Color
CIJE: 3 RIE: 5 CAT: 15

Words in Pairs Test (O Donnell)
CIJE: 0 RIE: 1 CAT: 21

WordStar
CIJE: 0 RIE: 2 CAT: 04

Wordsworth (William)
CIJE: 13 RIE: 6 CAT: 18

Wordsworth II
CIJE: 0 RIE: 1 CAT: 04

Work (Alcott)
CIJE: 0 RIE: 1 CAT: 22

Work (Physics)
CIJE: 3 RIE: 2 CAT: 20

Work Ability Program CA
CIJE: 0 RIE: 1 CAT: 19

Work Activity Centers
CIJE: 1 RIE: 3 CAT: 05

Work Adjustment Rating Form
CIJE: 1 RIE: 0 CAT: 21

Work Again Project
CIJE: 1 RIE: 4 CAT: 19

Work and Family Movement
CIJE: 0 RIE: 1 CAT: 16
UF Family and Work Movement

Work Aspect Preference Scale
CIJE: 2 RIE: 1 CAT: 21

Work Association Test (Essex and Liu)
CIJE: 0 RIE: 1 CAT: 21

Work Attitudes Inventory
CIJE: 1 RIE: 1 CAT: 21

Work Autonomy
CIJE: 0 RIE: 4 CAT: 15

Work Based Attendance (School Choice)
CIJE: 0 RIE: 2 CAT: 15

Work Based Projects (England)
CIJE: 0 RIE: 1 CAT: 19

Work Bonus Tax Credit
CIJE: 0 RIE: 1 CAT: 16

Work Centrality
CIJE: 9 RIE: 0 CAT: 16

Work Commitment
CIJE: 9 RIE: 3 CAT: 16

Work Components Study
CIJE: 2 RIE: 1 CAT: 19

Work Disabilities
CIJE: 1 RIE: 2 CAT: 11

Work Disincentives
CIJE: 0 RIE: 1 CAT: 16

Work Education Consortium Project
CIJE: 0 RIE: 4 CAT: 19

Work Education Council Southeastern Michigan
CIJE: 0 RIE: 1 CAT: 17

Work Education Councils
CIJE: 0 RIE: 14 CAT: 10

Work Education Evaluation Project
CIJE: 0 RIE: 4 CAT: 19

Work Environment Preference Schedule
CIJE: 2 RIE: 1 CAT: 21

Work Environment Scale
CIJE: 2 RIE: 4 CAT: 21

Work Experience Career Exploration Program
CIJE: 2 RIE: 4 CAT: 19

Work Experience Liberal Arts Programs
CIJE: 0 RIE: 1 CAT: 19

Work Flow
CIJE: 9 RIE: 6 CAT: 16

Work Flow Patterns
CIJE: 1 RIE: 2 CAT: 16

Work Habits
CIJE: 11 RIE: 11 CAT: 16

Work Inc
CIJE: 0 RIE: 1 CAT: 17

Work Incentive Demonstration Program
CIJE: 0 RIE: 4 CAT: 19

Work Incentive Program
CIJE: 27 RIE: 90 CAT: 19

Work Incentives
CIJE: 3 RIE: 5 CAT: 16

Work Interest Questionnaire
CIJE: 0 RIE: 1 CAT: 21

Work Interruptions
CIJE: 0 RIE: 1 CAT: 16

Work Introduction Courses (England)
CIJE: 0 RIE: 0 CAT: 03

Work Itself Work Environment Questionnaire
CIJE: 0 RIE: 2 CAT: 21

Work Keys (ACT)
CIJE: 0 RIE: 1 CAT: 21
UF ACT Work Keys

Work Load (Individuals)
USE Workload

Work Maturity Skills Training Program
CIJE: 0 RIE: 9 CAT: 19

Work Measurement
CIJE: 3 RIE: 5 CAT: 16

Work Monitoring (Computers)
CIJE: 0 RIE: 0 CAT: 20

Work Opportunity Readiness for the Homeless
USE Project WORTH

Work Order Processing System
CIJE: 1 RIE: 1 CAT: 15

Work Orientation
CIJE: 3 RIE: 6 CAT: 16

Work Oriented Literacy Programs
CIJE: 1 RIE: 2 CAT: 19

Work Overload
CIJE: 4 RIE: 2 CAT: 16

Work Performance Assessment (Test)
CIJE: 0 RIE: 0 CAT: 21

Work Permits
CIJE: 0 RIE: 1 CAT: 14

Work Personality Profile
CIJE: 0 RIE: 0 CAT: 21

Work Personality Profile Self Report
CIJE: 0 RIE: 1 CAT: 21

Work Previews
CIJE: 1 RIE: 0 CAT: 16

Work Related Activities Scale
CIJE: 0 RIE: 1 CAT: 21

Work Relevant Attitudes Scale
CIJE: 0 RIE: 1 CAT: 21

Work Stress Inventory
CIJE: 0 RIE: 1 CAT: 21

Work Supplementation Program
CIJE: 0 RIE: 1 CAT: 19

Work Temperament Inventory
CIJE: 0 RIE: 1 CAT: 21

Work Tests
CIJE: 0 RIE: 3 CAT: 21

Work Unit Tasks
CIJE: 1 RIE: 0 CAT: 15

Work Values
CIJE: 16 RIE: 7 CAT: 16

Work Values Inventory
CIJE: 22 RIE: 9 CAT: 21

Worked Examples (Mathematics)
CIJE: 5 RIE: 1 CAT: 20

Worker Adjustment and Retraining Notification Act
CIJE: 0 RIE: 1 CAT: 14
UF Public Law 100 379

Worker Adjustment Assistance Programs
CIJE: 0 RIE: 0 CAT: 19

Worker Alienation
CIJE: 3 RIE: 1 CAT: 15

Worker Motivation Scale (Wherry and South)
CIJE: 0 RIE: 1 CAT: 21

Worker Trainee Examination (Civil Service)
CIJE: 0 RIE: 1 CAT: 21

Workers Councils
CIJE: 3 RIE: 0 CAT: 10

Workers Defense League
CIJE: 0 RIE: 1 CAT: 17

Workers Disability Compensation Act 1980
CIJE: 0 RIE: 1 CAT: 14

Workers Educational Association
CIJE: 22 RIE: 14 CAT: 17

Workers Photography Movement
CIJE: 0 RIE: 1 CAT: 16

Workers Universities (Yugoslavia)
CIJE: 1 RIE: 1 CAT: 05

Workers University (Switzerland)
CIJE: 1 RIE: 0 CAT: 17

Workfare
CIJE: 10 RIE: 6 CAT: 16
SN Work as a requirement for receipt of welfare benefits

Workforce 2000
CIJE: 8 RIE: 10 CAT: 22

Working (Terkel)
CIJE: 0 RIE: 2 CAT: 22

Working Alliance
CIJE: 6 RIE: 1 CAT: 16
SN See also "Working Alliance Inventory" and "Supervisory Working Alliance Inventory"

Working Alliance Inventory
CIJE: 2 RIE: 0 CAT: 21
SN See also "Working Alliance" and "Supervisory Working Alliance Inventory"

Working Group on Direct Broadcast Satellites
CIJE: 0 RIE: 1 CAT: 17

Working Intelligence
CIJE: 0 RIE: 1 CAT: 11

Working Memory
CIJE: 20 RIE: 2 CAT: 11

Working Mens College (England)
CIJE: 4 RIE: 0 CAT: 17

Working Papers
CIJE: 0 RIE: 3 CAT: 16

Working Parents Project
CIJE: 1 RIE: 3 CAT: 19

Working Poor
CIJE: 2 RIE: 2 CAT: 10

Working Together Toward Excel in Teach Educ HI
CIJE: 0 RIE: 1 CAT: 19

Workjobs
CIJE: 0 RIE: 2 CAT: 15

Workload
CIJE: 6 RIE: 3 CAT: 16
SN If applicable, use the Descriptor "Faculty Workload"
UF Work Load (Individuals)

Workparties
CIJE: 1 RIE: 0 CAT: 10

Workplace Democracy
CIJE: 3 RIE: 4 CAT: 15

Workplace Literacy
CIJE: 72 RIE: 664 CAT: 15
SN See also "Job Literacy"

Workplace Literacy Impact Model
CIJE: 0 RIE: 1 CAT: 15

Workplace Literacy Skills and Training Inventory
CIJE: 0 RIE: 1 CAT: 21

Workplace Security
CIJE: 0 RIE: 0 CAT: 16

Workshop for Coordinated Vocational Academic Educ
CIJE: 0 RIE: 1 CAT: 02

Workshop for Improving Instruction of the Deaf
CIJE: 0 RIE: 3 CAT: 02

Workshop in Self Understanding
CIJE: 1 RIE: 0 CAT: 02

Workshop Institute for Living Learning
CIJE: 1 RIE: 0 CAT: 02

Workshop on Occupational Education and Training
CIJE: 0 RIE: 1 CAT: 02

Workshop Physics PA
CIJE: 0 RIE: 1 CAT: 19

World Administrative Radio Conference
CIJE: 13 RIE: 7 CAT: 02

World Administrative Radio Conference 1979
CIJE: 0 RIE: 1 CAT: 02

World Aluminum Abstracts
CIJE: 2 RIE: 0 CAT: 22

World Assembly on Aging
USE United Nations World Assembly on Aging

World Bank
CIJE: 58 RIE: 42 CAT: 17

World Bank Photo Library
CIJE: 0 RIE: 1 CAT: 17

World Book Company
CIJE: 0 RIE: 1 CAT: 17

World Book Encyclopedia
CIJE: 0 RIE: 2 CAT: 22

World Campus Afloat
CIJE: 1 RIE: 0 CAT: 17

World Citizenship
CIJE: 5 RIE: 1 CAT: 16

World Confederation of Labour
CIJE: 0 RIE: 1 CAT: 17

World Confederation of Orgs of the Teaching Prof
CIJE: 5 RIE: 10 CAT: 17

World Conference for Women
CIJE: 0 RIE: 0 CAT: 02

World Conference on Adult Education
CIJE: 0 RIE: 1 CAT: 02

World Conference on Agricultural Education 1970
CIJE: 1 RIE: 0 CAT: 02

World Conference on Cooperative Education 1981
CIJE: 0 RIE: 1 CAT: 02

World Conference on Education for All
CIJE: 4 RIE: 3 CAT: 02

World Conservation Strategy
CIJE: 5 RIE: 4 CAT: 02

World Council for Gifted and Talented Children
CIJE: 2 RIE: 0 CAT: 17

World Council for the Welfare of the Blind
CIJE: 1 RIE: 0 CAT: 17

World Council of Churches
CIJE: 0 RIE: 5 CAT: 17

World Council of Comparative Education Societies
CIJE: 2 RIE: 0 CAT: 17

World Education Project
CIJE: 0 RIE: 6 CAT: 19

World Energy Data System
CIJE: 0 RIE: 1 CAT: 04

World English
CIJE: 1 RIE: 2 CAT: 13

World Environment and Resources Council
CIJE: 1 RIE: 0 CAT: 17

World Federation for Mental Health
CIJE: 0 RIE: 2 CAT: 17

World Federation of Colleges
CIJE: 1 RIE: 0 CAT: 17

World Federation of the Deaf
CIJE: 1 RIE: 10 CAT: 17

World Fertility Survey
CIJE: 1 RIE: 5 CAT: 22

World Food Conference
CIJE: 1 RIE: 1 CAT: 02

World Food Day
CIJE: 1 RIE: 3 CAT: 12

World Functional Literacy Program
CIJE: 1 RIE: 1 CAT: 19

World Future Society
CIJE: 10 RIE: 2 CAT: 17

World Game
CIJE: 0 RIE: 1 CAT: 16

World Games for the Deaf
CIJE: 3 RIE: 1 CAT: 02

World Government
CIJE: 0 RIE: 1 CAT: 16

World Health Organization
CIJE: 27 RIE: 63 CAT: 17

World Health Organization European Region
CIJE: 2 RIE: 4 CAT: 17

World Health Organization Mediterranean Region
CIJE: 1 RIE: 0 CAT: 17

World History Project
CIJE: 1 RIE: 1 CAT: 19

World Hypotheses (Pepper)
CIJE: 2 RIE: 2 CAT: 15

World Information Order
CIJE: 0 RIE: 1 CAT: 16

World Institute of Computer Assisted Teaching
USE WICAT

World Knowledge
CIJE: 7 RIE: 3 CAT: 16

World Law Fund
CIJE: 2 RIE: 0 CAT: 17

World Meteorological Day
CIJE: 1 RIE: 1 CAT: 12

World Meteorological Organization
CIJE: 4 RIE: 1 CAT: 17

World of Construction (Title)
CIJE: 1 RIE: 5 CAT: 22

World of Inquiry School NY
CIJE: 1 RIE: 1 CAT: 17

World of Music (Textbook Series)
CIJE: 0 RIE: 1 CAT: 22

World of Tomorrow School NY
CIJE: 1 RIE: 0 CAT: 17

World of Work Economic Education Project
CIJE: 7 RIE: 56 CAT: 19

World of Work Map
CIJE: 5 RIE: 1 CAT: 16

World Order
CIJE: 10 RIE: 21 CAT: 16

World Order Methodology
CIJE: 1 RIE: 0 CAT: 16

World Order Studies
CIJE: 3 RIE: 9 CAT: 16

World Organization for Early Childhood Education
CIJE: 8 RIE: 1 CAT: 17

World Organization for Human Potential
CIJE: 2 RIE: 0 CAT: 17

World Plan of Action
CIJE: 0 RIE: 1 CAT: 19

World Political Risk Forecasts
CIJE: 0 RIE: 0 CAT: 22

World Population
CIJE: 0 RIE: 1 CAT: 20

World Population Year
CIJE: 1 RIE: 1 CAT: 12

World Post Day
CIJE: 1 RIE: 1 CAT: 12

World Regions Perception Survey
CIJE: 1 RIE: 0 CAT: 21

World Religions
CIJE: 2 RIE: 2 CAT: 03

World Science Information System
CIJE: 1 RIE: 4 CAT: 15

World Series
CIJE: 0 RIE: 1 CAT: 16

World Studies
USE Global Studies

World Summit for Children 1990
CIJE: 0 RIE: 2 CAT: 02

World University
CIJE: 1 RIE: 3 CAT: 16

World Views
CIJE: 85 RIE: 42 CAT: 16
UF Global Perspectives

World Vision (Relief Organization)
CIJE: 0 RIE: 1 CAT: 17

World Wildlife Fund
CIJE: 4 RIE: 2 CAT: 17

Worlds Fairs
CIJE: 4 RIE: 3 CAT: 12

Worldwide Needs Assessment Model
CIJE: 0 RIE: 1 CAT: 15

Worry
CIJE: 14 RIE: 6 CAT: 11

Worry and Emotionality Questionnaire
CIJE: 0 RIE: 2 CAT: 21

Worry Emotionality Scale (Liebert and Morris)
CIJE: 2 RIE: 4 CAT: 21

Worry Emotionality Scale (Morris Davis Hutchings)
CIJE: 1 RIE: 4 CAT: 21

Worship Services
CIJE: 3 RIE: 1 CAT: 16

Worth
CIJE: 0 RIE: 5 CAT: 16

Worth Commission on Educational Planning
CIJE: 1 RIE: 0 CAT: 17

Worth Report
CIJE: 5 RIE: 0 CAT: 22

Worthington Community College MN
CIJE: 0 RIE: 2 CAT: 17

Wratten Filters
CIJE: 1 RIE: 0 CAT: 04

Wray Behavior Scale
CIJE: 0 RIE: 1 CAT: 21

Wrestlers
CIJE: 0 RIE: 2 CAT: 09

Wright (Beatrice A)
CIJE: 1 RIE: 0 CAT: 18

Wright (Benjamin D)
CIJE: 0 RIE: 1 CAT: 18

Wright (Frank Lloyd)
CIJE: 7 RIE: 0 CAT: 18

Wright (Hamilton)
CIJE: 1 RIE: 0 CAT: 18

Wright (J Skelly)
CIJE: 0 RIE: 1 CAT: 18

Wright (James)
CIJE: 0 RIE: 1 CAT: 18
SN Former House Speaker

Wright (Richard)
CIJE: 17 RIE: 2 CAT: 18

Wright (Stephen J)
CIJE: 1 RIE: 0 CAT: 18

Wright Brothers
CIJE: 3 RIE: 0 CAT: 18

Wright College IL
USE City Colleges of Chicago IL Wright College

Wright Patterson Air Force Base
CIJE: 0 RIE: 2 CAT: 17

Wright Proctor Observational Instrument
CIJE: 0 RIE: 1 CAT: 21

Wright Report
CIJE: 0 RIE: 1 CAT: 22

Wright State University OH
CIJE: 18 RIE: 18 CAT: 17

Wrigley (Philip K)
CIJE: 0 RIE: 1 CAT: 18

Wrist Counter
CIJE: 1 RIE: 0 CAT: 04

Wrist Temperature
CIJE: 0 RIE: 2 CAT: 11

Write a Sentence Test
CIJE: 0 RIE: 1 CAT: 21

Writer (The)
CIJE: 0 RIE: 1 CAT: 04

Writer Performers
USE Performer Writers

Writers Block
CIJE: 9 RIE: 4 CAT: 11
UF Writing Blocks

Writers Conferences
USE Writing Conferences

Writers Helper
CIJE: 1 RIE: 1 CAT: 04

Writers in Schools Program
CIJE: 1 RIE: 0 CAT: 19

Writers Market (Title)
CIJE: 0 RIE: 0 CAT: 22

Writers Workbench (Computer Software)
CIJE: 8 RIE: 4 CAT: 04

Writing about Literature
CIJE: 12 RIE: 19 CAT: 03
UF Writing through Literature Instruction

Writing Across the Curriculum Project (England)
CIJE: 4 RIE: 9 CAT: 19

Writing Aid and Authors Helper
CIJE: 0 RIE: 1 CAT: 04
UF WANDAH System

Writing Apprehension Test (Daly and Miller)
CIJE: 5 RIE: 6 CAT: 21

Writing as a Second Language
CIJE: 0 RIE: 4 CAT: 03

Writing as Process
USE Process Approach (Writing)

Writing as Product
USE Product Approach (Writing)

Writing as Punishment
CIJE: 3 RIE: 2 CAT: 15

Writing Blocks
USE Writers Block

Writing by Children
USE Childrens Writing

Writing Coaches
CIJE: 5 RIE: 5 CAT: 09

Writing Conferences
CIJE: 43 RIE: 33 CAT: 02
UF Writers Conferences

Writing Consultants
CIJE: 3 RIE: 1 CAT: 09

Writing Contests
CIJE: 5 RIE: 7 CAT: 16

Writing Contexts
CIJE: 154 RIE: 334 CAT: 13

Writing Development
CIJE: 232 RIE: 234 CAT: 13

Writing Enhancement Program (Florida)
CIJE: 1 RIE: 1 CAT: 19
UF Florida Writing Enhancement Program

Writing Express
CIJE: 0 RIE: 1 CAT: 19

Writing Folders
CIJE: 6 RIE: 4 CAT: 13

Writing for Children
CIJE: 22 RIE: 8 CAT: 16

Writing for Life
CIJE: 0 RIE: 1 CAT: 03

Writing for Television
CIJE: 2 RIE: 1 CAT: 13

Writing Functions
CIJE: 18 RIE: 25 CAT: 13

Writing Groups
CIJE: 25 RIE: 26 CAT: 10

Writing Habits
CIJE: 14 RIE: 11 CAT: 16

Writing Implements
CIJE: 13 RIE: 12 CAT: 16

Writing Intensive Courses
CIJE: 1 RIE: 1 CAT: 03

Writing Is Thinking
CIJE: 4 RIE: 7 CAT: 04

Writing Models
CIJE: 50 RIE: 44 CAT: 15

Writing Motivation
CIJE: 7 RIE: 2 CAT: 16

Writing Networks
CIJE: 0 RIE: 1 CAT: 16

Writing Partner (Software)
CIJE: 0 RIE: 1 CAT: 04

Writing Patterns
CIJE: 12 RIE: 11 CAT: 13

Writing Process Approach
USE Process Approach (Writing)

Writing Product Approach
USE Product Approach (Writing)

Writing Program Assessment Project
CIJE: 0 RIE: 4 CAT: 19

Writing Prompts
CIJE: 6 RIE: 3 CAT: 16

Writing Purpose
USE Purpose (Composition)

Writing Quality
CIJE: 16 RIE: 4 CAT: 13

Writing Samples
CIJE: 16 RIE: 27 CAT: 13

Writing Skills Assessment Test
CIJE: 0 RIE: 5 CAT: 21
SN ...of the City Univ of New York

Writing Skills Test (GED)
USE GED Writing Skills Test

Writing Speed
CIJE: 1 RIE: 2 CAT: 15

Writing Style
CIJE: 113 RIE: 40 CAT: 13

Writing Tasks
CIJE: 59 RIE: 51 CAT: 16

Writing Test Prompts
CIJE: 5 RIE: 6 CAT: 21

Writing Theory
USE Composition Theory

Writing Therapy
CIJE: 1 RIE: 1 CAT: 11

Writing Thinking Relationship
CIJE: 2 RIE: 23 CAT: 15
UF Thinking Writing Relationship

Writing Threshold
CIJE: 0 RIE: 1 CAT: 16

Writing through Literature Instruction
USE Writing about Literature

Writing to Learn
CIJE: 109 RIE: 72 CAT: 03

Writing to Read
CIJE: 13 RIE: 21 CAT: 03

Writing to Read Program
CIJE: 10 RIE: 27 CAT: 19

Writing to Study
CIJE: 0 RIE: 1 CAT: 03

Writing Topics
CIJE: 58 RIE: 20 CAT: 16

Writing What You Read
CIJE: 0 RIE: 2 CAT: 19

Writings on American History
CIJE: 0 RIE: 1 CAT: 22
SN Part of the periodical current awareness service of the American Historical Association

Written Consent
CIJE: 0 RIE: 1 CAT: 16

Written English Proficiency Test
CIJE: 0 RIE: 1 CAT: 21

Written Instruction Stylistic Evaluation
CIJE: 0 RIE: 1 CAT: 21

Written Language Profile
CIJE: 0 RIE: 1 CAT: 21

Written Literacy Forum
CIJE: 2 RIE: 1 CAT: 02

Wu (Chien Shiung)
CIJE: 0 RIE: 1 CAT: 18

Wu Dialect
CIJE: 0 RIE: 1 CAT: 13

Wumpus
CIJE: 1 RIE: 4 CAT: 04

Wundt (Wilhelm)
CIJE: 2 RIE: 1 CAT: 18

Wunuk
USE Tiwi

Wurtsmith Air Force Base
CIJE: 1 RIE: 0 CAT: 17

Wusor
CIJE: 0 RIE: 1 CAT: 04

Wuthering Heights
CIJE: 1 RIE: 0 CAT: 22

Wyatt v Stickney
CIJE: 2 RIE: 3 CAT: 14

Wyer Subjective Probability Model
CIJE: 0 RIE: 1 CAT: 15

Wylie (Elinor)
CIJE: 0 RIE: 1 CAT: 18

Wylie (Laurence)
CIJE: 2 RIE: 1 CAT: 18

Wyndham Science
CIJE: 0 RIE: 2 CAT: 16

Wynn Experimental Model of Student Teacher Seminar
CIJE: 0 RIE: 1 CAT: 15

Wynne School District KS
CIJE: 0 RIE: 1 CAT: 17

Wyoming
CIJE: 48 RIE: 208 CAT: 07

Wyoming (Casper)
CIJE: 1 RIE: 4 CAT: 07

Wyoming (Cheyenne)
CIJE: 1 RIE: 1 CAT: 07

Wyoming (Goshen County)
CIJE: 0 RIE: 1 CAT: 07

Wyoming (Laramie County)
CIJE: 0 RIE: 2 CAT: 07

Wyoming (Laramie)
CIJE: 1 RIE: 2 CAT: 07

Wyoming (Powell)
CIJE: 0 RIE: 1 CAT: 07

Wyoming Community College System
CIJE: 0 RIE: 1 CAT: 17

Wyoming Resolution
CIJE: 15 RIE: 3 CAT: 16
SN Statement of principles and standards for the postsecondary teaching of writing

Wyoming School for the Deaf
CIJE: 1 RIE: 0 CAT: 17

Wyoming School Study Council
CIJE: 0 RIE: 1 CAT: 17

Wyoming State Library
CIJE: 0 RIE: 3 CAT: 17

Wytheville Community College VA
CIJE: 1 RIE: 3 CAT: 17

X Chromosomal Abnormalities
CIJE: 1 RIE: 1 CAT: 11

X Rated Movies
CIJE: 2 RIE: 1 CAT: 16

X Ray Diffraction
CIJE: 5 RIE: 0 CAT: 20

X Ray Fluorescence
CIJE: 1 RIE: 0 CAT: 20

X Ray Machines
CIJE: 0 RIE: 1 CAT: 04

X Rays
CIJE: 14 RIE: 4 CAT: 20

Xavante
CIJE: 0 RIE: 2 CAT: 13
SN A Ge language spoken in Brazil

Xavier University of Louisiana
CIJE: 5 RIE: 10 CAT: 17

Xavier University OH
CIJE: 4 RIE: 3 CAT: 17

Xenograde Concept System
CIJE: 0 RIE: 1 CAT: 15

Xenon
CIJE: 1 RIE: 0 CAT: 20

Xerophthalmia
CIJE: 0 RIE: 1 CAT: 11
SN Dryness of the eyes

Xerox 660 Optical Scanner
CIJE: 0 RIE: 1 CAT: 04

Xerox Corporation
CIJE: 24 RIE: 8 CAT: 17

Xerox LDX
CIJE: 0 RIE: 2 CAT: 04

Xerox Magnavox Telecopier
CIJE: 0 RIE: 4 CAT: 04

Xhosa
CIJE: 5 RIE: 9 CAT: 13

Xinca
CIJE: 1 RIE: 0 CAT: 13

XPT EASE
CIJE: 0 RIE: 1 CAT: 04

XTREE (Computer Program)
CIJE: 0 RIE: 1 CAT: 04

XXY Syndrome
CIJE: 1 RIE: 0 CAT: 11

XYY Syndrome
CIJE: 5 RIE: 0 CAT: 11

Y S v District of Philadelphia
CIJE: 0 RIE: 1 CAT: 14

Yacanes
USE Yakan

Yagua
CIJE: 1 RIE: 3 CAT: 13
UF Peba Yaguan

Yahow
USE Zahao

Yahtzee
CIJE: 3 RIE: 0 CAT: 16

Yakan
CIJE: 0 RIE: 1 CAT: 13
SN A Northwest Austronesian (Philippine) language
UF Yacanes

Yakima (Nation)
CIJE: 3 RIE: 17 CAT: 08

Yakima Public School District WA
CIJE: 2 RIE: 2 CAT: 17

Yakima Valley
CIJE: 0 RIE: 7 CAT: 07

Yakima Valley Community College District 16 WA
CIJE: 0 RIE: 2 CAT: 17

Yakima Valley Community College WA
CIJE: 1 RIE: 1 CAT: 17

Yale Child Study Center CT
CIJE: 3 RIE: 3 CAT: 17

Yale Conference on Learning
CIJE: 0 RIE: 1 CAT: 02

Yale Linguistic Series
CIJE: 0 RIE: 3 CAT: 22

Yale Music Curriculum Project
CIJE: 0 RIE: 1 CAT: 19

Yale New Haven Teachers Institute CT
CIJE: 0 RIE: 0 CAT: 17

Yale Public Schools MI
CIJE: 0 RIE: 3 CAT: 17

Yale Tuition Postponement
CIJE: 1 RIE: 0 CAT: 19

Yale University CT
CIJE: 94 RIE: 47 CAT: 17

Yamamadi
USE Jamamadi

Yanomamo (Tribe)
CIJE: 2 RIE: 0 CAT: 08

Yantai University (China)
CIJE: 0 RIE: 1 CAT: 17

Yanyula
USE Yanyuwa

Yanyuwa
CIJE: 0 RIE: 1 CAT: 13
SN An Australian Aboriginal language
UF Anyuwa; Wadiri; Yanyula

Yao
CIJE: 0 RIE: 2 CAT: 13

Yao (Tribe)
CIJE: 0 RIE: 1 CAT: 08

Yaqui
CIJE: 0 RIE: 1 CAT: 13

Yaqui (Tribe)
CIJE: 7 RIE: 9 CAT: 08

Yarborough (Ralph)
CIJE: 1 RIE: 0 CAT: 18

Yarmouk University (Jordan)
CIJE: 6 RIE: 1 CAT: 17

Yarmouth Intermediate School ME
CIJE: 1 RIE: 0 CAT: 17

Yarn Test (Lampe)
CIJE: 0 RIE: 1 CAT: 21

Yates (Robert)
CIJE: 0 RIE: 1 CAT: 18

Yavapai
CIJE: 2 RIE: 2 CAT: 13

Yavapai (Tribe)
CIJE: 4 RIE: 5 CAT: 08

Yavapai College AZ
CIJE: 1 RIE: 4 CAT: 17

Year 2000 Computerized Farm Project TX
CIJE: 0 RIE: 1 CAT: 19

Year of the Elementary School
CIJE: 1 RIE: 1 CAT: 12

Year Round Programs
CIJE: 3 RIE: 4 CAT: 19

Yearly Evaluation of Services by Students
CIJE: 0 RIE: 1 CAT: 21

Yeast
CIJE: 4 RIE: 1 CAT: 20

Yeasts
CIJE: 2 RIE: 1 CAT: 20

Yeats (Samuel Butler)
CIJE: 1 RIE: 0 CAT: 18

Yeats (William Butler)
CIJE: 7 RIE: 3 CAT: 18

Yellow Ball Workshop
CIJE: 1 RIE: 2 CAT: 02

Yellow Pages
CIJE: 2 RIE: 0 CAT: 16

Yellowhead School Division AB
CIJE: 0 RIE: 1 CAT: 17

Yellowknife (Tribe)
CIJE: 0 RIE: 1 CAT: 08

Yellowstone Boys and Girls Ranch School MT
CIJE: 0 RIE: 1 CAT: 17

Yellowstone National Park
CIJE: 2 RIE: 4 CAT: 07

Yellowstone Ranch WY
CIJE: 0 RIE: 1 CAT: 17

Yeltsin (Boris)
CIJE: 1 RIE: 0 CAT: 18

Yemen
CIJE: 4 RIE: 17 CAT: 07
SN "Democratic Yemen" (South Yemen) (q.v.) and North Yemen were unified in May90
UF North Yemen; Yemen Arab Republic

Yemen Arab Republic
USE Yemen

Yemenites
CIJE: 2 RIE: 2 CAT: 08

Yeomen
CIJE: 0 RIE: 1 CAT: 09

Yes No Questions
CIJE: 8 RIE: 5 CAT: 21

Yeshiva College NY
CIJE: 2 RIE: 2 CAT: 17

Yeshiva University NY
CIJE: 7 RIE: 9 CAT: 17

Yeshivoth
CIJE: 0 RIE: 1 CAT: 05

Yezierska (Anzia)
CIJE: 0 RIE: 1 CAT: 18

Yiddish Literature
CIJE: 0 RIE: 1 CAT: 16

Yiddish Speaking
CIJE: 1 RIE: 1 CAT: 08

YMCA
USE Young Mens Christian Association

Yo Puedo Program CA
CIJE: 0 RIE: 1 CAT: 19

Yoakam Readability Formula
CIJE: 0 RIE: 2 CAT: 21

Yoga
CIJE: 18 RIE: 12 CAT: 16

Yogurt
CIJE: 3 RIE: 0 CAT: 20

Yokomitsu (Riichi)
CIJE: 1 RIE: 0 CAT: 18

Yokut (Tribe)
CIJE: 3 RIE: 0 CAT: 08

Yom Kippur War
CIJE: 4 RIE: 0 CAT: 12

Yonkers Public Schools NY
CIJE: 0 RIE: 1 CAT: 17

Yonsei University (South Korea)
CIJE: 0 RIE: 2 CAT: 17

York Borough Board of Education ON
CIJE: 0 RIE: 0 CAT: 17

York College NE
CIJE: 0 RIE: 0 CAT: 17

York College NY
USE City University of New York York College

York College PA
CIJE: 0 RIE: 3 CAT: 17

York County Literacy Council PA
CIJE: 0 RIE: 1 CAT: 17

York Educational Software Evaluation Scales
CIJE: 4 RIE: 1 CAT: 21

York Region Board of Education ON
CIJE: 1 RIE: 2 CAT: 17

York Technical College SC
CIJE: 0 RIE: 1 CAT: 17

York University ON
CIJE: 13 RIE: 2 CAT: 17

YorkTalk
CIJE: 0 RIE: 1 CAT: 04

Yoruba (Tribe)
CIJE: 10 RIE: 2 CAT: 08

Yosemite Community College District CA
CIJE: 0 RIE: 2 CAT: 17

Young (Ann Eliza)
CIJE: 0 RIE: 1 CAT: 18

Young (Art)
CIJE: 0 RIE: 1 CAT: 18

Young (Brian)
CIJE: 1 RIE: 0 CAT: 18

Young Abe Lincoln
CIJE: 0 RIE: 1 CAT: 22

Young Adult Assessment 1977
CIJE: 0 RIE: 1 CAT: 21

Young Adult Conservation Corps
CIJE: 1 RIE: 3 CAT: 17

Young Adult Learning Academy NY
CIJE: 0 RIE: 3 CAT: 17

Young Adult Literacy Assessment (NAEP)
CIJE: 0 RIE: 2 CAT: 19

Young Audience Music Programs
CIJE: 1 RIE: 0 CAT: 19

Young Authors
CIJE: 4 RIE: 2 CAT: 10

Young Citizens League
CIJE: 0 RIE: 1 CAT: 17

Young Driver Attitude Scale
CIJE: 0 RIE: 1 CAT: 21

Young Farmers Association
CIJE: 1 RIE: 2 CAT: 17

Young Farmers of America
CIJE: 0 RIE: 1 CAT: 17

Young Film Makers Exchange
CIJE: 0 RIE: 2 CAT: 17

Young Goodman Brown
CIJE: 1 RIE: 1 CAT: 22

Young Homemakers of Virginia
CIJE: 0 RIE: 1 CAT: 17

Young Marketer Program
CIJE: 1 RIE: 0 CAT: 19

Young Mens Christian Association
CIJE: 11 RIE: 24 CAT: 17
UF YMCA

Young Mens Christian Association Canada
CIJE: 0 RIE: 1 CAT: 17

Young Mothers Educational Development Program
CIJE: 0 RIE: 2 CAT: 19

Young Offenders Act 1984 (Canada)
CIJE: 0 RIE: 3 CAT: 14

Young Pioneers
CIJE: 10 RIE: 0 CAT: 17

Young Volunteers in ACTION
CIJE: 1 RIE: 1 CAT: 19

Young Womens Christian Association
CIJE: 1 RIE: 11 CAT: 17
UF YWCA

Younger Adult Worker Study
CIJE: 0 RIE: 1 CAT: 22

Younger Chemists Committee
CIJE: 1 RIE: 0 CAT: 17

Youngstown Federation of Teachers
CIJE: 1 RIE: 0 CAT: 17

Youngstown Public Schools OH
CIJE: 0 RIE: 1 CAT: 17

Youngstown State University OH
CIJE: 9 RIE: 7 CAT: 17

Youngstown Vindicator
CIJE: 0 RIE: 1 CAT: 22

Your School Scale (Bullock)
CIJE: 0 RIE: 1 CAT: 21

Your Style of Learning and Thinking
CIJE: 3 RIE: 1 CAT: 21

Your Word Box
CIJE: 0 RIE: 1 CAT: 22

Youth 2000
CIJE: 0 RIE: 1 CAT: 19

Youth 2000 Week
CIJE: 1 RIE: 0 CAT: 12

Youth Act 1980
CIJE: 1 RIE: 5 CAT: 14

Youth Action Teams
CIJE: 0 RIE: 1 CAT: 10

Youth Advocacy Project
CIJE: 0 RIE: 5 CAT: 19

Youth Advocacy Teacher Corps Program
CIJE: 0 RIE: 1 CAT: 19

Youth Advocate Liaison Service
CIJE: 0 RIE: 1 CAT: 19

Youth and Community Service
USE Youth Community Service

Youth and the Law Project
CIJE: 1 RIE: 0 CAT: 19

Youth Apprenticeship Projects
CIJE: 0 RIE: 4 CAT: 19

Youth Art Month
CIJE: 2 RIE: 0 CAT: 12

Youth Attitude Tracking Survey
CIJE: 0 RIE: 1 CAT: 21

Youth Awareness Program DC
CIJE: 0 RIE: 1 CAT: 19

Youth Career Action Program
CIJE: 0 RIE: 1 CAT: 19

Youth Career Development Program
CIJE: 1 RIE: 4 CAT: 19

Youth Chance
CIJE: 0 RIE: 1 CAT: 19

Youth Community Conservation Improvement Project
CIJE: 0 RIE: 3 CAT: 19

Youth Community Service
CIJE: 16 RIE: 4 CAT: 16
UF Youth and Community Service

Youth Conservation Corps
CIJE: 6 RIE: 23 CAT: 17

Youth Coordinating Council OR
CIJE: 0 RIE: 1 CAT: 17
UF Oregon Youth Coordinating Council

Youth Corps
CIJE: 0 RIE: 1 CAT: 10

Youth Development Centers
CIJE: 0 RIE: 3 CAT: 05

Youth Development Model
CIJE: 0 RIE: 1 CAT: 15

Youth Development Program
CIJE: 0 RIE: 3 CAT: 19
SN Program of the Office of Economic Opportunity DC

Youth Development Project MN
CIJE: 0 RIE: 0 CAT: 19

Youth Educational Services CA
CIJE: 1 RIE: 0 CAT: 17

Youth Employment Act 1979
CIJE: 0 RIE: 3 CAT: 14

Youth Employment Act 1980
CIJE: 0 RIE: 1 CAT: 14

Youth Employment and Demonstration Projects Act
CIJE: 9 RIE: 87 CAT: 14

Youth Employment Questionnaire
CIJE: 0 RIE: 1 CAT: 21

Youth Employment Standards Act 1978 (Michigan)
CIJE: 0 RIE: 1 CAT: 17

Youth Employment Training Program
CIJE: 3 RIE: 11 CAT: 19

Youth Entitlement Incentive Pilot Projects
CIJE: 0 RIE: 3 CAT: 19

Youth Exchanging with Seniors TX
CIJE: 0 RIE: 1 CAT: 19

Youth Guidance Systems
CIJE: 0 RIE: 3 CAT: 15

Youth Impaired Driving Model
CIJE: 0 RIE: 1 CAT: 15

Youth in Adult Courts
CIJE: 0 RIE: 1 CAT: 14

Youth in Care Network (Canada)
USE National Youth in Care Network (Canada)

Youth in Transition Project
CIJE: 7 RIE: 8 CAT: 19

Youth Incentive Entitlement Pilot Projects
CIJE: 2 RIE: 15 CAT: 19

Youth Incentives Incorporated
CIJE: 0 RIE: 1 CAT: 17

Youth Indicators
CIJE: 0 RIE: 1 CAT: 16

Youth Knowledge Development Project
CIJE: 0 RIE: 2 CAT: 19

Youth Leadership Program NM
CIJE: 0 RIE: 1 CAT: 19

Youth Ministers
CIJE: 1 RIE: 1 CAT: 09

Youth Opinion Questionnaire
CIJE: 1 RIE: 2 CAT: 21

Youth Opportunities Foundation
CIJE: 0 RIE: 1 CAT: 17

Youth Opportunities Programme (England)
CIJE: 0 RIE: 1 CAT: 19

Youth Opportunities Unlimited
CIJE: 1 RIE: 0 CAT: 19

Youth Opportunity Campaign
CIJE: 1 RIE: 1 CAT: 16

Youth Opportunity Centers
CIJE: 0 RIE: 5 CAT: 05

Youth Opportunity Program
CIJE: 2 RIE: 1 CAT: 19

Youth Organizations United
CIJE: 1 RIE: 0 CAT: 17

Youth Participation
CIJE: 6 RIE: 9 CAT: 16

Youth Perspectives Project
CIJE: 0 RIE: 2 CAT: 17

Youth Research Survey (Forliti)
CIJE: 1 RIE: 0 CAT: 21

Youth Risk Behavior Survey
CIJE: 1 RIE: 1 CAT: 21

Youth Service
CIJE: 2 RIE: 4 CAT: 16
SN Use a more specific term if possible, e.g., "Youth Community Service," "National Youth Service," "Summer Youth Service Corps"

Youth Service Agency SC
CIJE: 0 RIE: 1 CAT: 17

Youth Service America
CIJE: 0 RIE: 2 CAT: 17

Youth Service Bureaus
CIJE: 0 RIE: 2 CAT: 05

Youth Service Corps MI
CIJE: 0 RIE: 1 CAT: 17

Youth Service Development Council
CIJE: 0 RIE: 1 CAT: 17

Youth Services Center NC
CIJE: 0 RIE: 1 CAT: 17

Youth Services Systems
CIJE: 1 RIE: 5 CAT: 15

Youth Serving Agency Program
CIJE: 1 RIE: 0 CAT: 19

Youth Social Support Questionnaire
CIJE: 0 RIE: 1 CAT: 21

Youth Society Movement (Finland)
CIJE: 3 RIE: 0 CAT: 12

Youth Studies
CIJE: 0 RIE: 2 CAT: 15

Youth Training Scheme
CIJE: 17 RIE: 26 CAT: 19

Youth Transition into the Labour Market
CIJE: 0 RIE: 1 CAT: 19

Youth Tutoring Youth
CIJE: 1 RIE: 5 CAT: 19

Youth Unemployment Act 1979
CIJE: 0 RIE: 1 CAT: 14

Youth Values Project
CIJE: 0 RIE: 2 CAT: 19

Youthpoll
CIJE: 0 RIE: 1 CAT: 21

Youthwork Incorporated
CIJE: 1 RIE: 4 CAT: 17

Youthwork National Policy Study
CIJE: 0 RIE: 9 CAT: 22

Yovits Ernst Model
CIJE: 0 RIE: 1 CAT: 21

Ypsilanti Carnegie Infant Education Project
CIJE: 0 RIE: 1 CAT: 19

Ypsilanti Model
CIJE: 0 RIE: 1 CAT: 15

Ypsilanti Preschool Curriculum Demonstration
CIJE: 0 RIE: 1 CAT: 19

Ypsilanti Public Schools MI
CIJE: 1 RIE: 3 CAT: 17

Ypsilanti Rating Scale
CIJE: 0 RIE: 1 CAT: 21

Ysleta Independent School District TX
CIJE: 0 RIE: 2 CAT: 17

Yuba College CA
CIJE: 0 RIE: 1 CAT: 17

Yuba Community College District CA
CIJE: 0 RIE: 1 CAT: 17

Yucaipa Joint Unified School District CA
CIJE: 1 RIE: 0 CAT: 17

Yucatan Peninsula
CIJE: 2 RIE: 1 CAT: 07

Yucca Plants
CIJE: 1 RIE: 0 CAT: 20

Yuchi
CIJE: 1 RIE: 0 CAT: 13

Yucuna
CIJE: 0 RIE: 1 CAT: 13

Yueh Dialect
CIJE: 0 RIE: 1 CAT: 13

Yugoslavia
CIJE: 113 RIE: 144 CAT: 07
SN After 1991, limited to Montenegro and Serbia

Yugoslavia (Belgrade)
CIJE: 5 RIE: 3 CAT: 07

Yugoslavia (Bosnia)
CIJE: 0 RIE: 2 CAT: 07
SN Independent after 1991, which see "Bosnia and Herzegovina"

Yugoslavia (Croatia)
CIJE: 5 RIE: 5 CAT: 07
SN Independent after 1991, which see "Croatia"

Yugoslavia (Macedonia)
CIJE: 0 RIE: 3 CAT: 07
SN Independent after 1991, which see "Macedonia"

Yugoslavia (Serbia)
CIJE: 0 RIE: 3 CAT: 07

Yugoslavia (Slovenia)
CIJE: 4 RIE: 4 CAT: 07
SN Independent after 1991, which see "Slovenia"

Yukon
CIJE: 4 RIE: 5 CAT: 07

Yukon (Whitehorse)
CIJE: 0 RIE: 1 CAT: 07

Yukon Koyukuk School District AK
CIJE: 2 RIE: 0 CAT: 17

Yukon Territory
CIJE: 1 RIE: 7 CAT: 07

Yuma (Tribe)
CIJE: 1 RIE: 2 CAT: 08

Yuma School District Number 1 AZ
CIJE: 1 RIE: 0 CAT: 17

Yuma Union High School District AZ
CIJE: 0 RIE: 1 CAT: 17

Yuman (Tribe)
CIJE: 1 RIE: 1 CAT: 08

Yuman Languages
CIJE: 2 RIE: 7 CAT: 13

Yunga
CIJE: 1 RIE: 0 CAT: 13

Yupik Eskimos
CIJE: 9 RIE: 10 CAT: 08

Yurok
CIJE: 0 RIE: 9 CAT: 13
SN Of the Algonquian language family

Yurok (Tribe)
CIJE: 1 RIE: 8 CAT: 08

Yuta
USE Ute

Yutah
USE Ute

YWCA
USE Young Womens Christian Association

Yxtaholm School (Sweden)
CIJE: 0 RIE: 1 CAT: 17

Z 100 Microcomputers
USE Zenith Z 100 Microcomputers

Z Scores
CIJE: 6 RIE: 6 CAT: 21

Zacchini v Scripps Howard
CIJE: 0 RIE: 1 CAT: 14

Zahao
CIJE: 0 RIE: 1 CAT: 13
SN A Chin language of northwestern Myanmar (Burma)
UF Yahow

Zaire
CIJE: 29 RIE: 24 CAT: 07

Zaire (Kinshasa)
CIJE: 2 RIE: 2 CAT: 07

Zaire River
CIJE: 0 RIE: 1 CAT: 07
SN Previously called the Congo River

Zajonc (Robert B)
CIJE: 4 RIE: 1 CAT: 18

Zambales Mountains
CIJE: 0 RIE: 2 CAT: 07
SN Of w central Luzon, Philippines

Zambia
CIJE: 73 RIE: 66 CAT: 07

Zambians
CIJE: 1 RIE: 1 CAT: 08

Zamboangueno
CIJE: 2 RIE: 0 CAT: 13
SN A Philippine Creole Spanish dialect
UF Chabacano (Zamboanga City)

Zaner Bloser Method
CIJE: 0 RIE: 5 CAT: 15

Zaparoan Languages
CIJE: 0 RIE: 0 CAT: 13

Zapata (Emiliano)
CIJE: 2 RIE: 0 CAT: 18

Zapata County Independent School District TX
CIJE: 0 RIE: 1 CAT: 17

Zapotec
CIJE: 4 RIE: 5 CAT: 13

Zapotec (Tribe)
CIJE: 1 RIE: 1 CAT: 08

Zaramo (Tribe)
CIJE: 0 RIE: 1 CAT: 08

Zarefsky (David)
CIJE: 0 RIE: 1 CAT: 18

Zeeman Effect
CIJE: 1 RIE: 1 CAT: 20

Zeichner (Kenneth M)
CIJE: 0 RIE: 1 CAT: 18

Zeigarnik Effect
CIJE: 3 RIE: 0 CAT: 11

Zeise Salt
CIJE: 1 RIE: 0 CAT: 20

Zeitgeist
CIJE: 2 RIE: 2 CAT: 16

Zeitlin Early Identification Screening
CIJE: 0 RIE: 1 CAT: 21

Zelan (Karen)
CIJE: 1 RIE: 0 CAT: 18

Zen and the Art of Motorcycle Maintenance
CIJE: 0 RIE: 1 CAT: 22

Zen Buddhism
CIJE: 14 RIE: 10 CAT: 16

Zenger (John Peter)
CIJE: 4 RIE: 2 CAT: 18

Zenith Radio Corporation
CIJE: 2 RIE: 1 CAT: 17

Zenith Z 100 Microcomputers
CIJE: 0 RIE: 0 CAT: 04
UF Z 100 Microcomputers

Zero Base Budgeting
CIJE: 32 RIE: 25 CAT: 16

Zero Energy Use
CIJE: 0 RIE: 1 CAT: 20

Zero Input Tracking Analyzer
CIJE: 1 RIE: 0 CAT: 21

Zero One Programming
CIJE: 0 RIE: 2 CAT: 15

Zero Partial Association
CIJE: 0 RIE: 1 CAT: 15

Zero Population Growth
CIJE: 5 RIE: 7 CAT: 20

Zero Reject Concept
CIJE: 2 RIE: 1 CAT: 15

Zero to Three
CIJE: 0 RIE: 5 CAT: 22
SN Bulletin of the National Center for Clinical Infant Programs

Zertifikat Deutsch als Fremdsprache
CIJE: 2 RIE: 1 CAT: 21
UF Certificate in German as a Foreign Language

Zetetics
CIJE: 0 RIE: 2 CAT: 15

ZGRASS Programing Language
CIJE: 1 RIE: 0 CAT: 04

Zhou Enlai
CIJE: 0 RIE: 1 CAT: 18
UF Chou En lai

Zigler (Edward)
CIJE: 1 RIE: 1 CAT: 18

Zimbabwe
CIJE: 67 RIE: 62 CAT: 07

Zimbabwe (Harare)
CIJE: 0 RIE: 1 CAT: 07

Zimbabwe Secondary School Science Project
CIJE: 0 RIE: 39 CAT: 19

Zimdex
CIJE: 3 RIE: 0 CAT: 16

Zimmer (Paul)
CIJE: 0 RIE: 0 CAT: 18

Zimmerman Preschool Language Quotient
CIJE: 1 RIE: 0 CAT: 21

Zinc
CIJE: 8 RIE: 1 CAT: 20

Zindel (Paul)
CIJE: 4 RIE: 3 CAT: 18

Zip Codes
CIJE: 1 RIE: 1 CAT: 16

Zip Test
CIJE: 1 RIE: 3 CAT: 21

Zipfs Law of Vocabulary Distribution
CIJE: 22 RIE: 0 CAT: 13

Zipoli (Domenico)
CIJE: 0 RIE: 1 CAT: 18

Zippers
CIJE: 0 RIE: 1 CAT: 04

Zitkala Sa
CIJE: 2 RIE: 2 CAT: 18
UF Bonnin (Gertrude Simmons)

Zoellner (Robert)
CIJE: 5 RIE: 2 CAT: 18
SN See also "Talk Write Method"

Zola (Emile)
CIJE: 3 RIE: 0 CAT: 18

Zollinger Ellison Syndrome
CIJE: 1 RIE: 0 CAT: 11

Zolotow (Charlotte)
CIJE: 0 RIE: 1 CAT: 18

Zone of Proximal Development
CIJE: 14 RIE: 19 CAT: 15

Zone Sections
CIJE: 0 RIE: 1 CAT: 16
UF Zoned Newspapers

Zoned Newspapers
USE Zone Sections

Zones of Indifference (Behavior)
CIJE: 0 RIE: 5 CAT: 11

Zoning Inspectors
CIJE: 0 RIE: 1 CAT: 09

Zoom
CIJE: 1 RIE: 0 CAT: 22

Zoomobiles
CIJE: 0 RIE: 1 CAT: 04

Zoroastrianism
CIJE: 0 RIE: 4 CAT: 16

Zulu
CIJE: 4 RIE: 9 CAT: 13

Zung Self Rating Depression Scale
CIJE: 11 RIE: 1 CAT: 21

Zuni
CIJE: 0 RIE: 0 CAT: 13
SN A Penutian language

Zuni (Pueblo)
CIJE: 10 RIE: 18 CAT: 07

Zuni Cultural Education Program
CIJE: 0 RIE: 1 CAT: 19

Identifier Category Display

CATEGORY 02: Conferences / Meetings

AAHE Assessment Forum
Abraham Jacobs Memorial Symposium
Academic Year Institutes
Action Seminar
Adult Education Research Conference
AECT 76
AECT Research and Theory Division Meeting
AERA Research Training Presessions Prog
AIR Forum
Airlie Conference
Airlie House Conference on the Classics
Airlie House Lifelong Learning Leaders Retreat
American Assn Advancement Science Academy Conf
American Convention on Human Rights
American Home Economics Association Convention
American Indian Language Development Institute
American Indian Management Institute
American Library Association Convention
American Personnel Guidance Assn Impact Workshop
American Vocational Association Convention
Anglo American Historians Conference
Arizona Principals Academy
ASHE Annual Meeting
Asolo Theater Festival of Florida
Aspen Program Commun Society Govt Media Workshop
Aspen Workshop on Uses of the Cable
Assembly on University Goals and Governance
Athens Symposium on Child in World of Tomorrow
Atomic Industrial Forum
Australian Family Research Conference
Banff Conference 1977
Basle Seminar Education Welfare of Disadvantaged
Bay Area Academic Forum
Belmont Conference Training Elem Math Sci Teachers
Bergamo Adult Education Conference
Beyond the Looking Glass Conference
Bielefeld Geometry Conference
Biological Disarmament Convention
Black Ministers Teachers Conference
Black Psychology
Broadcast Industry Conference
Brookings Conference on Vocational Education
Brussels Satellite Convention
Callaway Gardens Conference High School Sci Prog
Cambridge Conference on Teacher Training
Cannes International Conference on Video Commun
Caribbean Conference for Adult Education
Case Conferences
CAUSE National Conference
Central State Colleges and Universities Seminar
Charles W Hunt Lecture 10th
Chautauquas
Churchill College Conference
CINTERFOR
Citizens Conference on Man Education and Work
Claremont Reading Conference
Clinic on Library Applications of Data Processing
Colorado Conference on Stereotyping in Education
Colorado Consortium on Research Development
Commonwealth Computer Assisted Instr Consortium
Commonwealth Educational Broadcasting Conference
Commonwealth Fund Demonstration Clinics
Communist Party Congress (USSR)
Conference Alternative Futures Vocational Educ
Conference Council of Associate Degree Programs
Conference for Human Development
Conference for Nursing Instructors
Conference on Day Care Service 1965
Conference on Educ of Disadvantaged (New Mexico)
Conference on Equal Educational Opportunity
Conference on Interdisciplinary Activities
Conference on Manpower Surveys
Conference on Open Learning in Higher Education
Conference on Theatre Research (Princeton Univ)
Conference Work Force Adjustments Private Industry
Constitutional Conventions
Consultants Workshop on Technologies
Convention of American Instructors of the Deaf
Convocation of American Indian Scholars 2d
Convocations
Dartmouth Seminar on the Teaching of English
Decision Seminars
Department of Audiovisual Instruction (NEA) Conven
Development Training Forum
DIDACTA
DUET Workshops
Eastern Stream Conference on Migrant Education 5th
Eastern Stream Conference on Migrant Education 7th
Education Summit 1989 (NGA)
Effective Teaching Institute
El Primer Congreso Mexicanista De 1911
Electric Humanities Workshop
Electronic Town Meetings
Eurotrain
Exeter Conference NH
Family Camp Workshop
Family Institutes
FEANI UNESCO Seminar
Federal Executive Institute
Festival International De La Pantomime
Festival of American Folklife
First Amendment Congresses
Fordham Film Media Conference
Galaxy Conference on Adult Education
Getty Institutes for Educators on the Visual Arts
Gordon Research Conference (1972)
Gordons Parent Effectiveness Training 1970
Governors Conference Library Info Services IN
Governors Conference Library Info Services MD
Governors Conference Library Info Services MO
Governors Conference Library Info Services MT
Governors Conference Library Info Services ND
Governors Conference Library Info Services NE
Governors Conference Library Info Services NY
Governors Conference Library Info Services PA
Harvard Schoolyard Bullying Practicum 1987 MA
High Scope Summer Workshop for Teenagers
Human Potential Seminars
Human Values and Technological Change Conference
Illinois White House Conference on Children
Image 4 Seminar
Indian Youth Opportunity Conferences
Industrial Arts Spring Conference
Information for Industry
Institute of Industrial Relations Res Conf 1967
Inter American Congress Educational Administration
Inter American Indian Congress
Inter Navex
Interagency Conference on Nursing Statistics
Interagency Panel Research Development Adulthood
Intermountain Conference Childrens Literature 5th
International Audio Visual Aids Exhibition
International Conference Manpower Training Devel
International Conference of Educational Planning
International Conference on Chemical Education
International Conference on Education
International Conference on Education 1977
International Conference on Educational Technology
International Conference on Film Television Child
International Conference on General Semantics 11th
International Conference on Population
International Conference Second Language Problems
International Congress of Psychology
International Congress on Archives
International Congress on Documentation
International Congress on Home Help Services
International Congress on Mathematical Education
International Congress on Solar Energy
International Congress University Adult Education
International Federation of Library Assns 1974
International Geological Congress
International Labour Conference
International Manpower Seminar
International Science and Engineering Fair
International Symposium for Literacy (Persepolis)
International Telecommunication Convention
International University Congress
Interskola
Introductory Physical Science
Iowa Honors Workshop
Kalamazoo Unconference
Labor Management Conference
Lake Okoboji Educational Media Leadership Conf
Leadership Development Seminar Vocational Educ
Lehigh Workshop on Poetry for Children
Library College Conference 1973
Lunar Science Conference 5th
Mary E Switzer Memorial Seminar
Mathematical Olympiad
Mathematics Pentathlon
Meeting of Experts on Mass Communication Society
Midwest Academic Librarians Conference
Midwest Library Conference
Military Librarians Workshop
Mitchell High School Senior Seminar CO
MLA ADE ADFL Conference
Montreux Television Symposium
Music Educators National Conference
Music Educators National Conference Conv 1970
National Assn of Student Personnel Admins Conf
National Association Educ of Young Children Conf
National Catholic Conference Interracial Justice
National College Orientation Workshop
National Committee for AV Aids in Educ Conference
National Computer Conference
National Conference Assessment Teaching Engl 1970
National Conference Diffusion Educational Ideas
National Conference on Black Women 1st
National Conference on Career Education
National Conference on Consumer Protection
National Conference on Curriculum Development
National Conference on Independent Scholarship
National Conference on Population Education
National Conference on Poverty in Southwest 1965
National Conference on Program Planning and Eval
National Conference on Research
National Conference on Rural Education
National Conference on Studies in Reading
National Conference Visual Information Processing
National Congress on Catholic Schools
National Congress on Engineering Education
National Congress on Medical Quackery
National Council for the Social Studies Conv
National Debate Tournament
National Defense Educ Act Inst Teaching Disad Yout
National Defense Education Act English Institutes
National Defense Education Act Institutes
National Defense Education Act Language Institutes
National Defense Education Act Summer Institutes
National Defense Education Act Title XI Institute
National Dissemination Conference
National Educational Computing Conference
National Field Directors Forum
National Indian Bilingual Education Conference
National Indian Child Conference
National Indian Cultural Conference 3d
National Institute for Public Information Officer
National Institutes Innovative Currs Voc Tech Educ
National Invitational Meeting on Rural Postsec Ed
National Leadership Conference
National Materials Conservation Symposium
National Metric Study Conference on Education
National School Boards Association Convention 1972
National Science Teachers Assn Sunoco Sci Seminars
National Seminar of American Indian Women
National Seminar on Vocational Guidance
National Student Conference on Health Manpower
National Summit on Agricultural Education 1989
National Symposia for Professionals Evalu Research
National Symposium Experimental Higher Education
National Vocational Facility Planning Conference
National Vocational Technical Teacher
National Young Farmer Educational Institute
National Youth Conference on Highway Safety
NCTE Seminar on Research in English Education
NDEA Institute State Supervisors English Reading
Neglected Languages Materials Conference 1974
New England Governors Conference
New Jersey Community Action Training Institute
North American Regional Conference on Automation
Northern Cross Cultural Education Symposium
Northwest Forensic Conference
Northwest Regional Dissemination Configuration
Nursing Research Conference
Oak Ridge Conference on Technical Training
Office Occupations Teachers Conference
Ohio Governors Conference on Aging
Oral History Association Colloquium
Organizational Inventory Meeting
PACE IV
PACE VI
Panel on Undergraduate Major Curricula
Para Professional Training Institute
Park Achievement Seminar
Personal and Family Financial Planning
Policy Forums on Employability Development
Political Party Conventions
Preconference on the Recruitment of Minorities
Preserving a Quality Environment for Learning
Presidents Conference on Early Childhood Education
Princeton Manpower Symposium
Professional Agricultural Workers Conference
Professional Meetings
Project Leadership Service Conference
Public Issue Forums
Pugwash Conferences
Quality Education Conference III
Radio Forums
Reforma Conference
Regional Seminar in Agricultural Education
Relief Teacher Training Institute
Research Conference Instructional Systems Tech
Research on Teaching Mathematics Conference
Research Seminar in Vocational Education
Retreats
Reunions
Rio Symposium Computer Educ Developing Countries
Robert Andrews Millikan Lecture
Robert Lee Sutherland Seminar
Rocky Mountain States Education Technology Demo
Rural Economic Development Planning Workshop
Rural Sociological Society Meeting
Rutgers Conference on School Lunch Programs
Rutgers Guidance Conference
Rutgers Seminar on Educational Equity
Saint Louis Teacher Workshops
SAIR Conference
Scandinavian Library Congress
Seaside Health Education Conference OR
Seminar Acquisition Latin Amer Library Materials
Seminar on Family Research 13th
Seminar on Manpower Policy and Program
Seminar Statistics State Vocational Rehabilitation
Seminarro Internacional Sobre la Educ Bilingue

Seminars for State Leaders Postsec Ed (ECS SHEEO)
Sigma Theta Tau International Research Congress
Skills Fairs
Snowmass (Colorado) Conference on Chemistry
Social Science and Social Education Conference
Southeast Asian Conference on Math Education
Southeast Asian Studies Summer Institute
Southeast Industrial Arts Conference
Southern Agricultural Education Conference
Southern Region Research Conf in Agricultural Educ
Southern Research Conference in Agricultural Educ
Southwest Park and Recreation Training Institute
Southwestern Sociological Society Meetings
Special Media Institutes
Spring Hill Symposium MN
State Conference Community College Administration
State Conferences
State Education Agencies Symposium
State Implementation Grant Conference
Summer Institute of Technology for Children
Summer Manpower Research Institute
Summer Teaching Training Inst in Dental Assisting
Supervisory Conferences
Swarthmore Chautauqua
Symposium on Urban Cable Television
Tavistock Group Relations Conference
Teacher Principal Conferences
Trade Union Seminar on Active Manpower Policy
Transmountain Far West Regional Reading Conference
UNESCO Conference on Adult Education 3d
UNESCO Regional Seminar Adult Educ Development
UNESCO Teheran Congress on Literacy
United Gold Coast Convention
United Nations Conference on the Human Environment
United Nations Conference on the Law of the Sea
United Nations World Assembly on Aging
Universal Copyright Convention
University Manpower Research Seminars
Vail (Colorado) Conf Counseling Psychology 1973
Visual Studies Workshop
Vocational Agriculture in the Changing Scene
Vocational Counseling Summer Workshops
Vocational Education Dissemination Conference
Vocational Education Leadership Institute
Vocational Technical Teacher Institute
Washington Colloquium on Science and Society
Watts Writers Workshop
West Georgia National Conf Career Exploration
West German Conference of Ministers of Education
White House Conference for a Drug Free America
White House Conference Library Info Services
White House Conference on Aging
White House Conference on Children
White House Conference on Children and Youth
White House Conference on Families
White House Conference on Food Nutrition Health
White House Conference on Indian Education
White House Conference on Rural Education
White House Conference on Small Business
White House Conference on Youth
White House Consultation with Rural Women
White House Pre Conf Indian Library Info Services
White House Workshop on Choice in Education
Wingspread Conferences
Womens National Basketball Coaches Clinic
Workshop for Coordinated Vocational Academic Educ
Workshop for Improving Instruction of the Deaf
Workshop in Self Understanding
Workshop Institute for Living Learning
Workshop on Occupational Education and Training
World Administrative Radio Conference
World Administrative Radio Conference 1979
World Conference for Women
World Conference on Adult Education
World Conference on Agricultural Education 1970
World Conference on Cooperative Education 1981
World Conference on Education for All
World Conservation Strategy
World Food Conference
World Games for the Deaf
World Summit for Children 1990
Writing Conferences
Written Literacy Forum
Yale Conference on Learning
Yellow Ball Workshop

CATEGORY 03: Curriculum Areas

3Rs
ABWA Syllabus for Letter Writing Courses
Accelerated Christian Education
Achievement Based Curriculum
Achieving Dialog
Activity Based Curriculum
Adjunct Courses
Adoption Insights
Adult High School Diploma
Advanced Composition
Advanced Mathematics
Advertising Copywriting
Advertising Education
Aesthetic Reading
Agricultural Literacy
Agricultural Marketing
Agricultural Sciences
AIR BAVTE Curriculum
Air Force Junior ROTC
Airmen Basic Resident Courses
Airway Science Curriculum
Ameliorative Curriculum
American Industrial Arts
American Political Behavior
American Problems
Americanization Classes
Amnesty Education
Analytic Philosophy
Analytical Electrochemistry
Analytical Ethics
Anglo American Relations
Appalachian Studies
Applied Anthropology
Applied Arts
Applied Communication
Applied Humanities
Applied Mathematics
Applied Sociology
Applied Statistics
Arc Ed Curriculum
Architectural Technology
Army War College Nonresident Courses
Arts for the Basic Curriculum
Asian American Studies
Assisted Reading Instruction
Astro Archaeology
Astrology
Audiotutorial Minicourses
Autotronics
Aviation College Minor
Axiology
Basic Education
Basic Skills for Independent Living
Basis for Choice Course
Bereiter Engelmann Curriculum
Berkeley Physics Course
Bible Study
Bibliology
Bilingual Vocational Education
Biological Sciences Curr Study Biology Spec Matl
Biological Sciences Curr Study Blue Version
Biological Sciences Curr Study Green Version
Biological Sciences Curr Study Minicourses
Biological Sciences Curr Study Single Topic Films
Biological Sciences Curr Study Yellow Version
Biological Sciences Curriculum Study
Biomedical Engineering Technology
Black Womens Studies
Block Plan
Bloomington Curriculum Plan
Bridging Courses (England)
Broadcasting Curriculum
Bromley Heath Infant Curriculum
Business and Office Career Education Curriculum
Business and Society
Business Dynamics
Business Finance
Business Law
Business Mathematics
Business Statistics
California English Language Arts Framework
California Model Curriculum Computers in Education
California Visual Performing Arts Framework 1989
Capstone Courses
Cardboard Carpentry
Career Construct
Career Exploration Work Simulation Units
Cashier Checker Training
Century 21 Shorthand
Certificate in Computer Programming
Certificate in Data Processing
Character Education
ChemCom
Chemistry Between Atoms
Chicano Studies
Child Centered Education
Children and Their Natural Environment
Chiropractic Education
CHOICE (Career Education Curriculum)
Choices (Nuclear Issues Curriculum)
Choreography
Circuit Training
CityWorks
CIVITAS
Class Length
Classical Music
Classics
Classics (Literature)
Classroom Business Venture
Clinical Experience (Judicial)
Clinical Sociology
Clinical Teacher Education
Cluster Courses
Cognitive Anthropology
Cognitively Oriented Preschool
College Preparatory Curriculum GA
Columbia Home Study Course
Columbia Seminar of Technology and Social Change
Common Basic Electronics Training
Common Core of Learning (Connecticut)
Common Core of Learning (Kentucky)
Communication Across the Curriculum
Communication Arts
Communication in Societies
Communications Curriculum
COMP LAB Course
Comparative Literature
Comparative Psychology
Competency Based Curriculum
Comprehensive Communication Curriculum
Comprehensive Instructional Management System
Comprehensive School Health Education
Computer Engineering
Computer Ethics
Concentric Curriculum
Concrete Poetry
Conducting (Music)
Conductive Education
Constructive Controversy
Consumer Mathematics
Contact Hours
Continuing Engineering Studies
Contra Costa Social Studies Curriculum
Contract Education
Contract Vocational Education
Cooperative School College Communication Studies
Coordinated Vocational Academic Education
Copernican Plan
Course Approval
Course Development
Course Numbering
Course of Study for Elementary Schools
Course Prerequisites
Course Titles
Courses by Newspaper
Creative Curriculum for Family Child Care
Creative Dance
Criterion Teaching
Critical Ethnography
Critical Writing
Cross Credit Courses
Cross Discipline Education
Cross Role Training
Cryptology
Cultural Anthropology
Cultural Ecology
Cultural Economics
Cultural Training Semester
Culturally Relevant Curriculum
Culturally Responsive Education
Culture Based Curriculum
Culture Based Education
Curricular Debate
Curricular Validity
Curriculum Alignment
Curriculum Balance
Curriculum Choice
Curriculum Compacting
Curriculum Consonance
Curriculum Differentiation
Curriculum Duplication
Curriculum Emphases
Curriculum Implementation
Curriculum Management
Curriculum Management Systems
Curriculum Mapping
Curriculum of Attainments
Curriculum Reduction
Curriculum Standards
Dale Carnegie Course
David D Henry Lecture Series
De Vive Voix
Defensive Driving
Design of Training Systems
Developmental Curriculum
Developmental Programing Infants Young Children
Differentiated Curriculum (Gifted)
Disabilities Awareness Curriculum
Discipline Based Geography Education
Distar
Double Majors
Drama in Education
Dramakinetics
Early Childhood Family Education
Early Start to Good Health Curriculum
Earth Systems Education
Eastern European Studies
ECCP Man Made World
Economic Literacy
Economics of Information
Educators Forum
Efferent Reading
Elizabethan Drama
Emergency English for Refugees
Employer Sponsored Skill Training
Energy Technology and Society
Engelmann Becker Curriculum
Engineering Curriculum
Engineering Design
Engineering Mathematics
English Teacher Preparation Study
Environmental Health Engineering
Environmental Health Technology
Environmental Planning Education
Essential Learning Skills (Oregon)
Essential Undergrad Curr Speech Commun Small Coll
Etching
Ethnomathematics
Ethnomethodology
Ethnomusicology
European Geography
European Studies
Evaluation and Prevocational Conditioning Course
Expanding Environment
Expedition Education
Experiences in Mathematical Ideas
Experiments in Computer Electronics and Logic
Exploring Childhood
Extra Credit
Facing History
Family Life Curriculum Project
Feeling Words Curriculum
Feminist Scholarship
Finding Out Descubrimiento
Fire Safety Education
Fisheries Education
FLASH Curriculum WA
Flight to Hope (Refugee Awareness Program)
Forensic Science
Forensic Sociology
Formal Mathematics
Foundation Skills
Foundational Approaches in Science Teaching
Francophone Education (Canada)
Freshman Seminars
Freshman Success Courses
Function Based Curriculum
Furniture Refinishing
Generalist Teaching

Genre Studies
Geocoding
Geopolitics
Georgia Basic Curriculum
Give and Take (Economics Series)
Global Perspectives in Education
Great Books Curriculum
Great Ideas Curriculum
Guided Autobiography
Guides for Better Living
Hands on Science
Hawaiian Studies
Health Care Economics
Health Network Curriculum
Heartsmart Adventures
Heartwood Program
Heres Looking at You
Hershey Video Training Courses
HICOMP PreSchool Curriculum
High Risk Courses
High School Psychology
Higher Competencies Commun Own Care Motor Problem
Historical Geology
Holistic Education
Holland Skinner Psychology Course
Home Curriculum
Home Improvement
Homiletics
Hospitality Education
How Do I Learn Course (England)
Human Development Degree Programs
Humane Education
I Can Achievement Based Curriculum
ILEA Film Study Course
Illinois Core Curriculum in Agriculture
Individualized Curriculum Sequencing Model
Individualized Learning Plans
Industrial Chemistry
Industrial Design
Industrial Engineering
Industrial Sewing Classroom Delivery System
Information Studies
Informed Strategies for Learning
Innovative Social Studies Urban Elementary Schools
Instruction Curriculum Environment
Instructional Algorithms
Integrated Character Education
Intensive Business Training
Intensive Courses
Intercultural Communication Course (USIA)
International Agricultural Education
International Business Education
International Finance
International Resource Management Program
Interstate Distributive Education Curriculum
Inventive Drawing
Investigative Photography
Investigative Reporting
Issue Centered Education
James Madison Elementary School Curriculum
James Madison High School Curriculum
Japanese Studies
Jewish Studies
JMB Applied Chemistry
JMB Engineering Science
Junior First Grade
Kannada Course
Kephart Training
Keynesian Economics
Keypunch Instruction
KI Aikido
Knowledge Sciences
Labor Studies
Laidlaw Mathematics Series (Elementary)
Land Administration
Latin A Structural Approach
Latin American Studies
Leaf Study
Learning across the Curriculum
Lend Me Your Ears
Life Centered Career Education
Life Centered Education
Life Experience Studies
Life Insurance Education
Life Management Curriculum
Lifeguard Training
Linguistic Auditory Memory Patterns
Link Courses
Literary Craft Tracking
Literary Politics
Living Curriculum
Louisiana High School Conservation Curriculum
Lunar Studies
Machine Transcription
Maintenance Bilingual Education
Man A Course of Study
Man and the Environment Curriculum
Marriage Education
Martial Arts
Marvelous Me (Preschool Edition)
Materials Science
Math In Stride
MATHCO
Mathematics and Music
Mathematics of Money
Matriculation Mathematics
Mechanical Technology
Media Courses
Media Education
MegaSkills Home Curriculum
Mens Studies
Metacourses
Mexican American Studies
Michigan Marketing Distributive Educ Core Curr
Microwave Course
Mid School Year Graduation
Military Curriculum Materials
Mini Society
Model Learner Outcomes
Modern Algebra
Modern Art
Modern Dance
Modern Music
Modes of Thought Courses
Multidisciplinary Education
Multidisciplinary Science Curriculum
Multiple Progress Plan
Multiracial Education
Museum Studies
National Career Development Guidelines
National Leadership Camp Curriculum
Nationwide Curriculum
Nationwide Curriculum for Industrial Arts
Native American Studies
Native Studies
Nature Photography
Nature Writing
Navajo Studies
Naval Training
Nebraska English Curriculum
New Basics
New Peak Course
New Zambia Primary Course
Newspaper Courses
Nonvocational Typing
Norse Mythology
Nuclear Education
Off Campus Activities
Omniology
On the Level
Optimation Rapid Reading Course
Oral Communication Across the Curriculum
Oralingua Interaction Skills Curriculum
Ordinary National Diploma Courses
Oregon Studies
Organizational School Psychology
Oriental Art
Orienting Instruction
Outward Bound Bridging Course (Australia)
Oxford Secondary English Course for Jordan
Paideia Proposal
Paired Courses
Paleoecology
Parallel Alternate Curriculum
Participation Education
Participatory Curriculum
PATHWAYS Curriculum
Patterns in Arithmetic
Patterns in Human History
Patterns of Childrearing
Peace Education
Peace Studies
Pedagogic Drama
Peer Group Learning Units
Pennsylvania Comprehensive Read Commun Arts Plan
Pennsylvania General Curriculum Regulations
Perinatal Education
Photosketching
Physical Science for Nonscience Students
Physical Science II
Physical Sciences Curriculum Study
Piano Instruction
Pivot Course
PLAN Social Studies
Plastics and Composites Technology
Poetics
Poetics of Music
Poetry in the Schools
Political Economics
Political Education
Political Sociology
Popular Education
Population Awareness Education
Population Curriculum Study
Population Environment Curriculum Study
Portage Curriculum
Positive Resiliency in Special Education
Practical Writing
Pre Algebra
Pre Reading Plan
Precamping
Predicate Calculus
Preemployment Courses
Prelaw Curriculum
Premedical Curriculum
Preparatory Studies
Prereading Exercises
Preschool Language Curriculum
Pretraining
Preview of Modern Concepts in Engineering
Principles of Sociology
Principles of Technology
Problem Centered Curriculum
Problem Formulation (Mathematics)
Problem Oriented Instruction
Problems of Peace and War in the Modern World
Process Individualization Curriculum
Production Typing
Professional Audiovisual Education Study
Professional Communication
Promoting Achievement in School through Sports
Promoting Alternative Thinking Strategies Curric
Psychohistory
Psychological Anthropology
Public Policy Education
PUNCT CAI Course
Purpose Process Curriculum Framework
Radiological Monitoring
Real Math (Curriculum)
Recreation Occupations Education
Relevant Educational Applications of Computer Tech
Research Curriculum
Residential Based Career Education
Resource Based Learning
Responsive Autonomy in Cooperative Teaching
Restaurant Management
Return to Nursing
Risk Taking 2
Rope Courses
Russian Studies
Sack Yourman Speed Reading Course
Safe at Home Curriculum
SAVY Curriculum
Scholarly Journalism
Scholastic Journalism
School Based Curriculum Development
School Camping
Science A Basic Approach
Science A Process Approach
Science and Engineering Technician Curriculum
Science and Environmental Education
Science and Man in the Americas
Science Framework for California Public Schools
Science In a Social CONtext
Science Teachers Adaptable Curriculum
Science Technology and Society Courses
Scope and Sequence
Scottish Integrated Science Scheme
Seatwork
Second Chance to Learn Course (England)
Secondary Training for Alaskan Rural Students
Self Protection Courses
Seminar on Wheels
Service Unit Management
Servicing Industrial Products
Shipbuilding
Silver Burdett and Ginn Science Series
Single Skill Training Courses
SKI HI Home Visit Curriculum
Sky Education
Social Administration
Social Dramatics
Social Education
Social Foundations of Education
Social Solutions Curriculum
Sociology of Occupations
Sociology of the Family
Sociology of Work
Sophomore Operative Dentistry
Soviet Studies
Spain and the Western Tradition
Spanish American Culture
Speaking Across the Curriculum
Specifications for Elementary Teacher Education
Speech Communication Education
Sponge Painting
Sport Sociology
Standardized Curriculum
Step Curriculum Units
STEPS (Curriculum)
Stitchery
Storekeeper First Class
Strand Approach to Environmental Education
Students Against Tobacco TX
Studies in the Physical Sciences
Study Curriculum Occupational Preparation and Educ
Study of Values
Summer Curr Rev Thru Industrial and Business Exper
Support Courses
Supported Self Study
Survival Education
Systematic Biology
Systemic Capacity
TAFE (Australia)
Talent Education Plan
Talmudic Study
Tax Preparation
Teaching Essential Life Skills NJ
Teaching Learning Graduate Geography
Teaching Your Child
Technical and Vocational Education Initiative
Television Aesthetics
TEMAC Algebra
Tempera Painting
Theater of the Absurd
Theatre of the Grotesque
Theology
Therapeutic Academics
Tie Dyeing
Time to Degree
TMI Groliers Course in General Science
TMI Groliers Fundamentals of Algebra
Toronto Board of Education Benchmarks ON
Tracy Correspondence Course
Traffic Engineering
Training Agreements
Training Extension Course
Transactional Curriculum
Transformational Curriculum
Transformative Curriculum
Transitional Activities
Transitional Bilingual Education
Transportation Education
TRIIC Curriculum
Two Way Bilingual Education
UNICERT
Unified Science Mathematics for Elementary Schools
Unified Technical Concepts Curriculum
Unified Vocational Preparation
Urban Education Studies
USNA Economic Analysis Course
Values in Concert
Violin Instruction
Visual Communication Education
Vocational and Applied Arts Education
Vocational Orientation Packets
Vocational School Psychology
Voter Education
War Resistance Literature
Watercolor
Web of Life Biology Course
Weber Individualized Learning Kits
Whole Life Factor Curriculum
Wire Sculpture
WISCHE Federal Executive Institute
Wisconsin Curr for Educable Mentally Retarded
Women in Nontraditional Careers Curriculum
Word Processing Instruction
Work Introduction Courses (England)
World Religions
Writing about Literature
Writing as a Second Language
Writing for Life
Writing Intensive Courses
Writing to Learn
Writing to Read
Writing to Study

CATEGORY 04: Equipment (Including Computer Programs)

3RIP Search System
3RIP Text Data Base System
AARON (Artificial Intelligence Symbol System)
Abacuses
ABLEDATA Database
Abrasives
Abstat (Computer Program)
Academic Computing
Academic Progress Report
Accelerometers
ACE Data Bank
ACE Institutional Research File
Acid Free Paper
Acoustic Detectors
Acquisition Cards
Acrylic Materials
Actionmap
Activity Cards
Actometers
Ada (Programing Language)
Administrative Communications Network
ADVOCNET
Aerial Combat Simulators
Aerosols
AgriData Network
Air Cleaners
Air Compressors
Air Rifles
Air Samplers
Air Tracks
Aircraft
Aircraft Environmental Systems
Aircraft Weapon Systems
Aircrew Training Devices
Airman Training Line Simulator
Alabama Resource File
Alaska Knowledge Base System
Alaska Statewide Instructional Support System
Alaska Teleconferencing Network
Alaskan Pipeline
Alden II Docufax
Aldus Pagemaker
ALGAMS Programing Language
ALGOL Programing Languages
Algorithmic Processor Description Language
Alkyd Paints
All Terrain Bicycles
All Terrain Vehicles
Alphabet Boards
Alphabet Cards
Altair System
Altered States of Consciousness Induction Devices
Alternative Assessments in Practice Data Base
Alternators
Ambulance Equipment
America History and Life
American Optical Company Sight Screener
American Optical Kindergarten Chart
American Telephone and Telegraph Long Lines
Amiga
AML Microwave Link
Ammeters
Ammunition
Amperostats
Ampex Computer Products
Ampex Videotape Recorders
Amplified Telephones
Amplifiers
Anaglyphs
Analog Digital Interfaces
Analytical Balances
Anchoring Devices
Anemometers
Animal Traps
Annehurst Curriculum Classification System
Anonymous Audience Response System
Answering Machines
Antennas
Antiaircraft Weapons
AP NEWS
APL Programing Language
Apple (Computer)
Apple I
Apple II
Apple II Plus
Apple IIc
Apple IIe
Apple IIGS
Apple III
Apple Interactive Data Analysis
Apple Macintosh
Apple Microcomputers
Apple Writer
Apple Writer II
AppleLink
Applesoft BASIC
AppleWorks
Application Forms
Application Languages
APTICOM (Computer Program)
ARCH GRAPHIC
Archibald Engine
Architectural Grammars Software
Archive Indexes
Arkansas Occupational Educational Information Syst
Armbands
Armed Forces Vision Tester
Art Connection
Art Multimedia Kit
Art Observation Note Taking Form
Articulated Subject Indexes
Articulation Research System
Artifacts
Artificial Limbs
Artificial Turf
ASCAL Computer Program
Assembler Languages
At Your Service (Computer Program)
Atari
Atari 400
Atari 800
Atariwriter
Atmospheric Contaminant Sensors
ATS 1 Geosynchronous Satellite
Attribute Blocks
Audio Notebook
Audio Reader
Audiocups
Audiographics
Audiolingual Aids
Audiometer Trainer Unit
Audiotutorial Equipment
Aural Records
Australian Education Index Data Base
Australian National Satellite System
AutoCAD
Autocoders
Autoharps
Automated Drafting Board
Automated Teller Machines
Automatic Explanation of Reasoning
Automatic Interaction Detector
Automatic Vocal Transaction Analyzer
Automobile Parts
Automobiles
Automotive Computers
Automotive Cooling Systems
Automotive Electrical Systems
Automotive Exhaust Systems
Automotive Supplies
Automotive Suspension Systems
Autonote
Autotutor
Auxanometers
AVLINE
Axial Curve Rotator
Axles
Backup Systems
Balloons
BALLOTS
Balls
Bank Street Writer
Barcode Readers
Barometers
Baruch Retrieval of Automated Info for Negotiation
BASIC Programing Language
BASIC SKILLS Software Program
Basketballs
Bausch and Lomb Orthorater
Bearings
Beginning Teacher Computer Network
Behavioral Science Programing Language
BETTERAVEN Computer Program
Biblio Link
Bibliofile
BiblioFile Intelligent Catalog
Bibliographic Access and Control System
Bibliographic Structure
BICAL Computer Program
Bicycle Helmets
Bicycles
BIGSTEPS Computer Program
Billboards
BILOG Computer Program
Binoculars
Biomedical Computer Programs
BIOSIS Previews
Blackboard Instructional Planner
Blindstitch Machine (Sewing)
BLISS Programing Language
Bliss Symbols
BlockAIDS
Blocks
Blow Molding
Boats
Boilers
Bombs
Bone Conduction Transducers
Bookmatch
Boomerangs
Borg Warner System 80
Boring Tools
Braille Printers
Braille Tape Reader
Braillemboss
BRAILLOPHON
Brain Link Software
Brainiac
Brakes (Automotive)
Brass Instruments
Breath Analyzers
Breathing Equipment
Breeder Reactors
Bricks
Bridges (Structures)
Broadcast Transmission Equipment
BRS After Dark
Bucknell On Line Circulation System
Bulk Data Input Processor
Bunsen Burners
Burroughs Computers
Button Blanket
CAB Abstracts
CADAPPLE (Computer Program)
CAISYS Programing Language
Calcomp Display
Calendar (Computer Program)
Calendars
California Basic Educational Data System
California Spanish Language Data Base
Calipers
Camelot (Computer System)
CAMEO
Canadian On Line Enquiry
CANALS (Computer Program)
Candles
Canvas
Capacitors
CAPSAS Computer Program
Capsela (Toy)
Captioned Films
Carburetors
Cardboard
Career Key (Microcomputer System)
Career Planning Support System
Career Planning System
Career Survival Skills Kit
CARIS
Carnot Engine
Carrier Current Radio
Cassette Sound Filmstrip Viewers
Cathode Ray Tubes
Cathodoluminescence Apparatus
CAUSE National Database
CC 30 Communications Station
CCC Instructional System
Cement
CENFAC Computer Program
Central Dynamic Store
Central Maine Interactive Telecommunications Sys
Central Processing Units
Centrifugal Analyzers
Centrifuges
Ceramic Tile
Chain Saws
Chains (Mechanics)
Channel 2000
Chapel Hill Alphanumeric Terminal
Chapple Interaction Chronograph
Character Codes
Child Language Data Exchange System
Childrens Films
Chinese Character Code for Information Interchange
CHOICE Courseware
Choropleth Maps
Citation Maps
Citizens Band Radio
Civilian Occupation Planning Estimates System
Clamps
Clarinets
Claris CAD
Classroom Observation Instruments
Classroom Screening Instruments
ClassWorks
Climbing Walls
Clocks
Closed Captioned Television Decoders
Closed Catalogs
Clutches (Automotive)
COBOL Programing Language
Cochlear Implants
CODOC System
Collaborative Activation Based Production System
College Explorer Program
Combined Health Information Database
COMCONF
COMIT Programing Language
Command Language
Commercial Generators
Commercial Update and Retrieval System
Commercially Prepared Materials
Commodore 64
Commodore Microcomputers
Commodore PET
Commodore VIC 20
Common Communication Format
Communication Boards
Community Bulletin Board System
Community Radio
Community Switchboards
Compasses
COMPENDEX
Compilers
COMPNY Library
COMPOSER System
Comprehensive Dissertation Index
Compressed Air Equipment
Compressed Audiotape Recordings
Compressed Gas Equipment
Compressed Motion Pictures
Compressor Style Vertical Filing
Compucorp Model 025 Educator
Compupoem (Computer Program)
Computational Algebraic Language
Computer Animation
Computer Assisted Cataloging
Computer Based Message Switching Network
Computer Controlled Vehicles
Computer Image Generator
Computer Library System Inc
Computer Managed Problem Drill
Computer Operating Systems
Computer Plotters
Computer Tables
Computer Tutors
Computer Writing Network
Computerized Accountability Student Achievement
Computerized Catalogs
Computerized Documentation System
Computerized Educational Career Information Link
Computerized Television
COMTASK Database
Concept Assessment Kit
Concept Networks
Concord VTR600
Condensers
Condoms
Conn Keyboards
CONSER
CONSTRUCT Programing Language
Construction Equipment
Contact Lenses
Contour Maps
Control Data Basic Skills Learning System
Control Data Corporation Computers
Convection Ovens
Conveyors
Cookstoves
Cooling Towers
Cooperative Management Information System
Coordinated Occupational Information Network
Copy Cat Camera
Cornell Farm Account Book
Corporate Occupational Information System
Cosmic Explorer (Computer Program)
Costing and Data Management System
Coursewriter Programing Language
Couzens Machine
CP M Operating System
Cradleboards
Craig Videotape Recorder
Crankcase Breathers
CREATE Computer System
Creches
CRISP Computer Program

Crookes Radiometer
Cruise Ships
CSAR Interactive Item Bank System
CSE Evaluation Kit
CSLX Programing Language
Cuisenaire Materials
Cummings Device
CURMIS
Cutting Tools
Daisy Wheel Printers
DART Programing Language
DASA Microfiche Reader PMR 50
Data Abstraction
Data Collector (Hypercard Computer Program)
Data Desk Professional
Data Dictionary Systems
Data Elements
Data General Nova Computer
Data General Nova Minicomputer
Data Sets
Datafax
Datamaker (Computer Program)
DataRelator
Datasearch (Computer Program)
DATASIM (Computer Software)
Davies Brickell Loop
dBase
dBase II
dBase III
dBase III Plus
dBase IV
Deafnet
Debugging Aids
DEC PDP 1 Computer
DEC PDP 4 Computer
DEC PDP 7 Computer
DEC PDP 8 Computer
DEC PDP 10 Computer
DEC PDP 11 Computer
DEC PDP 12 Computer
DEC PDP 15 Computer
Dedicated Computers
Defense Integrated Data System
Dennis Infracommunication Analysis Device
Dental Appliances
Dental Equipment
Denver Uplink Terminal
DERIVE Computer Algebra System
Devereux Model 50 Teaching Aid
Device Effectiveness Forecasting Technique
Diagnostic Consultation Systems
Diagnostic Testing System
Dial a Tape
Dialcom
Dialect Readers
DIALMAIL
DIALOG OnDisc
Diatest Responder System
DIATOM
Diatype Analyzer
Diazo Film
Dice
Digicolor Systems
Digital Analog Logic Modules
Digital And Video Interactive Device
Digital Audiotape
Digital Avionics Information System
Digital Data
Digital Transmission Systems
Digitek Optical Scanner
DIMTEST (Computer Program)
Dioramas
Dipole Oscillator
Disclosure II
DISCOVER for Adult Learners
DISCOVER System
Disk Operating Systems
Distributed Data Processing Systems
Distributed Office Support System
Distributed Processing Systems
DOBIS System
Dosimeters
DOTSYS III
DrawReg Computer Program
DRILL (Authoring System)
Drilling Tools
Drive Trains (Automotive)
Driving Simulators
Drug Extractors
Duplicate Items (Information)
Duplicating Equipment
DX Diagnostic Testing System
Dynalevel
Dynamod II
Dynamometers
E Z Cassette Player
Early Alert Retention System
Earplugs
Easy English Programing Language
Easy Speak (Computer Program)
Easycoder
Edge Notched Cards
EduCard
Education Financial Planning Model
Educational Native American Network
Educational Technologies Database
EDUCE Conceptual Analyzer
EDUCOM Financial Planning Model System
Egyptian National Scientific Tech Info Network
Eight Millimeter Film
Electric Generators
Electric Vehicles
Electrical Discharge Machine
Electrical Sensing Devices
Electrified Perkins Brailler
Electroacoustic Filters
Electrogoniometers
Electrohome Character Projector
Electron Microscopes
Electronic Blackboards
Electronic Carpets
Electronic Chalkboards
Electronic Counter Measures
Electronic Fuel Injection Systems
Electronic Games
Electronic Index Card System
Electronic Information Exchange System
Electronic Networks for Interaction
Electronic Organs
Electronic Response Analyser
Electronic Response Systems
Electronic Simon
Electronic Spirographs
Electronic Testing
Electroscopes
Electrostatic Precipitators
Electrowriters
Element Analyzers
Elementary Verbal Communicator
Elevators
ELISA Programing Language
Emergency Vehicles
ENCORE (Computer System)
Energy Bibliography and Index
Energy Data Base
Energy Environment Simulator
Energy Recovery Wheel
English Microlab Registry
EntryWay
EPIC SOCRATES
Ergometers
ERIC ONTAP
ESCALATE (System)
EURONET
Excel Computer Program
Experimental Films
Experimental Television
ExperLOGO
Expert System Shells
Exstatix
Eyeglasses
Fabric Filters
FACETS Computer Program
FACSTRAP Computer Program
Factor Computer Program
Faculty Scheduling System
FAIRAVEN Computer Program
Family Interaction Coding System
Family Observation Record Keyboard System
FAMULUS
Farmworker Data Network
Fast Agricultural Communications Terminal
Fast Iterative Recursive Macro System
Fasteners (Machinery)
Faster Macro Language
Feltboards
Fidonet
Fifth Generation Computers
File Oriented Interpretive Language
Film Analyzers
Film Gates
Filter Presses
Filters
Fire Extinguishers
Fire Hydrants
Firearms
Fireplaces
FirstSearch
Fishing Nets
Flags
Flannel Boards
Flash Cards
Flexible Furnishings
Flexowriter
Flip Charts
Florida Information Resource Network
Florida Library Information Network
Florida Linkage System
FLOW Computer System
FLOW Programing Language
Flowmeters
Fluorescent Lighting
FOCAL Programing Language
Force Transformers
FORMAT (Database)
FORTRAN Programing Language
Framegames
Francais Radiophonique Authentique
Frequency Modulation Hearing Aid Systems
Frigates
Front End Processors
Front End Software
Front End Types (Automotive)
Fuel Systems
Function Probe
Function Supposer
Functional Properties
G P L Viewfinder 900 Videcon Camera
Gas Detectors
Gateway Information System (DoD)
Geiger Counters
Gemini Blackboard
General Electric Computers
GENMOD Computer Program
GENOVA (Computer Program)
Geobased Information Systems
Geoboards
Geodesic Domes
Geometry Proof Tutor
Georgia Online Database
GIRAFFE (Computer Program)
GLISP Programing Language
Global Essay Instruments
Globes
Gloves
GRAD II (Computer Program)
Graflex Audio Graphic Instructor
Grain Drills
Grain Silos
Graphic Synthesizers
Graphical User Interfaces
Grason Stadler E800 Audiometer
Grason Stadler Operant Conditioning Apparatus
GRATEFUL MED
Ground Station Receivers
Groupware
Guess My Bag (Computer Program)
Guess My Strategy (Computer Program)
GUIDON Program
Guitars
Guns
Habilitative Aids
Hale Reaction Performance Timer
Ham Radio
Harps
Harris Survey Questions
Hawaii Occupational Information System
HBJ Writer
Health Periodicals Database
Heat Pumps
Heaters
Hedman Stenotype
Helicopters
HELP Information Retrieval System
Hettinger Strength Chair
Heuristic Evaluation Problem Programer
Hewlett Packard System
HH 3F Helicopter
HLM Computer Program
Hoists
Home Computer Based Learning Systems
Home Computers
Home Entertainment Equipment
Home Information Systems
Home Integrative Communications Systems
Honeywell Computers
Hoses (Water)
HUB System
Huckel Molecular Orbital Computer Programs
Hundred Board
Hybrid Computers
Hydrams
Hydraulic Jumps
Hydrographic Survey Ship System
Hydrometers
HyperCard
HyperCAT Computer Program
HyperGlyphs
HyperScreen
HyperTalk
IBM 357 Data Collector
IBM 870 Document Writing System
IBM 2250 Display Unit Model 1
IBM 2314 Discs
IBM 3330 Discs
IBM 3741 3742 Data Entry Station
IBM Coder
IBM Core Grammar
IBM Electronic 75 Typewriter
IBM Guidance Counseling Support System
IBM InfoWindow
IBM Mag Card II Typewriter
IBM Model 1 Display Unit
IBM PC Compatibles
IBM PC Plus
IBM PC XT
IBM Personal Computer
IBM Project Control System
IBM PS 2
IBM Socrates
IBM System 7
IBM System 360 370
IBM System 1000
IBM System 1100
IBM System 1200
IBM System 1400
IBM System 1500
IBM System 1600
IBM System 7000
ID Expert
IDD Advisor
Idea Processors
IDEAL Curriculum and Computer System
Identification Badges
Identification Cards
Identification Placement Tracking System
IDiom System
Image Rotators
Image Transmission
Imbricated Program for Information Transfer
Impact Tester
Improved Authoring Language
Incinerators
Inclined Planes
Incubators
Independent Television
Individual Student Profile System
Individualized Science Instructional System
INDSCAL Computer Program
iNet
Inexpensive Equipment
Inexpensive Materials
Infant Simulator 1
Inflammation (Computer Program)
InfoTrac System
Infrared Detectors
Infrared Spectrometers
INGRES Database Management System
Inks
Inspector (Dental Equipment)
InstaCap System
INSTRUCT Programing Language
Instructional Accomplishment Information Systems
Instructional Design Data Base
Instructional Dialog Facility
Instructional Systems Development
Instructional Television Fixed Service
Instructional Television Fixed System
Instructor Logic Programing Language
Integrated Bibliographic Information System (DoD)
Integrated Circuits
Integrated Databases
Integrated Macro Package
Integrated Network Systems
Integrated Postsecondary Education Data System
Integrated Scientific Information System
Integrated Services Digital Networks
Integrated Set of Information Systems
Integrated Student Data System
Integrated Subject File
Intelligent Maintenance Training System
Intelligent Terminals
Intelsat
INTERACT (Computer Program)
Interactive Computer Systems
Interactive Courseware
Interactive Fiction
Interactive Language Instruction Assistance Deaf
Interactive Radio
Interactive Satellite Instruction
Interactive Videodisks
Interagency Research Information System
InterChange Discussion Program

PRISM Programing Language
Pro Cite
PRO SEARCH
Probeware
PROCESS (Computer Program)
Production System Version G Programing Language
Program Monitoring System
Programable Calculators
Programming for Individualized Education Program
PROJECT BASIC
Project PROCEED
PROLOG Programing Language
Prompt Automated Scheduling System
PROSIM 5 Production System Simulator
Protosynthex III
Protractors
PSG Production Systems
PsycALERT
PsycINFO
PsycLIT
PTS PROMT
PTS US Time Series
PTV 3
Public Access Catalog
Public Domain Software
Public Information Systems
Public Radio
Pulsejet Engines
Pumps
Purdue Real Time Basic System
QUAL PRO (Computer Program)
Quantile Computer Program
QUBE System
QUERY
Query by Example
Query Languages
Quest Computer Program
Queuing Networks
QUILL (Computer Software)
Radio Shack Color Computer
Radiographic Imaging Systems
Radius Cutters
RAMBOT (Expert System)
Random Access Slide Projectors
RCA Spectra Computer
Reading Machines
Reading Program Management System
Recorded Aid for Braille Music
Recorders (Flutes)
Recreational Vehicles
Refractometers
Regional Environmental Learning System
Regulators (Electrical Equipment)
Reinforced Concrete
RELATE Computer Program
Relay Circuits
Remcon 2780 Terminal
Remote Control Devices
Remote Electronic Access Delivery of Information
Repetitor I
Report Generators
Required Computers
Research Equipment
RESGEN Computer Program
Resistors (Electrical Equipment)
Resources in Computer Education
Respirators
Respirometers
Response System with Variable Prescriptions
Returnable Bottles
REXALL (Computer Software)
RIBYT Data Base System
Ricoh Synchrofax
Rightwriter
Rikar Mounts
Ring Oven
Ripple Tanks
Robot Odyssey I
Ropes
Rotameters
RPG Programing Language
Rubber Bands
Rubber Goods
Rubiks Cube
Rugs
Rulers (Instruments)
SAFARI On Line Text Processing System
Safe Deposit Boxes
Safety Equipment
Saltons Magical Automatic Retriever of Texts
Sample Forms
Sample Materials
Satellite Dishes
Satellite Instructional Television Experiment
Saunas
Scaffolding
Scale Models
SCAN Computer Program
SCHOLAR (Computer System)
School Based Information Systems
School Finance Equalization Management System
School Identification Cards
School Information Management Systems
School Practices Information File
School Practices Information Network
School Retrofit Design Analysis System
School Uniforms
SCIENCE ORDERS
ScienceVision (Computer Program)
Scientific Computer Programs
SciMate
Scintillation Counters
SCISEARCH
Scooters (for Disabled)
Screws
SCRIPSIT
Scrubbers
SDS 940 Computer System
Seals (Mechanics)
SEESAW
SEINE Computer Program
SELECT Programing Language
Selectavision
SER LARS (Information System)
Serging Machines (Sewing)
Set Top Converters
Sewers
Sewing Machines
Shadow Puppets
Shared Bibliographic Input Network (DoD)
ShareNet
Shareware
Shell Games (Computer Program)
Sherlock Computer Program
Shipboard Computers
Ships
Shortwave Radio
SIBTEST (Computer Program)
Sickle Cell Counselor (Computer Simulation)
Sidewalks
Sigma 6 Computer
Sigma 7 Computer
Sigma 9 Computer
Signaling Devices (for Disabled)
Silver Film
SilverPlatter ERIC
SIMPLE Programing Language
Simulated Arithmetic Machine
Simulated Educational Computer
Simulated Hypothetical Instructional Computer
Simulated Lesson Analysis Chart
Simulation in Combined Arms Training
Sinclair ZX Spectrum
Sinclair ZX81
SIRIUS Programing Language
Skills Inventory System
SKOOLBOL Programing Language
Skylab
Skylights
Slide Rules
Slings (Equipment)
Small Format Videotape
Smithtown Computer Program
Smoke Detectors
Snowmobiles
SOCRATES Autotutorial System
SOCRATES Test Retrieval System
SOFTSWAP
Software Automatic Mouth
Software Tools
Solar Collectors
Solar Food Dryers
Solar Heaters
SOLO Programing Language
Sony Equipment
Sound Level Meters
Sound on Slide Projectors
Spacesuits
Spanish Language Only Television
Spark Timer
Special Education Data Management System
Special Education Management System
Spectrometers
Spectrophotometers
Spectroscopes
Speech Autoinstructional Device
Speed Reader II
SPEEDE ExPRESS Electronic Transcript System
Speedometers
SPELL Programing Language
SPINDEX System
SPIRIT (Writing Aid)
Splints
Sporting Goods
Spraying Equipment
Sprinkler Systems
Stabilometer
Stained Glass
STAIRS Software Package
STaR Neuro Cognitive Assessment Program
STaR Neuro Cognitive Reading Program
Star Tracker
Stat Helper
Statistical Analysis System
Statistical Package for the Social Sciences
Statistical Package for the Social Sciences PC
Statistical Packages
Statistical Processing System
Statistical Test Item Collection System
STATUS System
Stenograph
Stereo Microscopes
Stereographs
Stereoscopes
Stop Action Video
Story Boards
Story Tree
Stoves
String Processing Languages
Stringed Instruments
Stroboscopes
Stromberg Carlson 4020 Microfilm Recorder
Structure Charts
Structure Mapping Engine
Structured Planning and Debugging Editor
Student Accounting System
Student Administration System
Student Guidance Information System
Student Information and Records System
Student Information Management System
Student Problem Package
Style Guides
Style Manuals
Submarines
Summit Authoring System
Sundials
Sunglasses
Super 8 Films
SUPER CARP (Computer Program)
Supercomputers
SUPERMARC
SuperPILOT Authoring Language
Surface Gages
Surplus Computing Capacity
Switches
Symbol Maps
Symphony (Computer Software)
Synthesizers
Syringes
SYS IV Management System
System 3 Communication Network
System 2000
System for Computer Automated Typesetting
System of Interactive Guidance and Info Plus
System of Interactive Guidance and Information
Systematic Analysis of Language Transcripts
Table Producing Language
Tactile Graphics Kit
Talking Tracks
Talking Typewriters
Tampons
Tattle Tape
Taxicabs
Teacher Interactive Computer System
Teaching and Coursewriting Language
Technology Information System
Tektronix Graphic Terminals
Tele Cyclopedia
Telecommunication Devices for the Deaf
Telecommuting
Telecopier Systems
Telelink
Telenet
Telephone Conference Network
Teleprinter Projectors
Teleprompters
Telereference
Telescopes
Teletel
Teletypewriters
Televised Interactive Education System
Television Networks
Television Receivers
Telidon System
Terrariums
Terrazzo Flooring
TESTFACT
Testing 1 2 3
TESTLEN
TestSense Program
Texas Telecomputer Grid
Text and Illustration Processing System
Text Handling
Textalk
Textape
Textbook Activity Guides
The School System (Columbia Computing Services)
Thematic Maps
Therapen
Thermometers
Thermostats
THREEDE Computer Program
TICCIT Computer System
Tickets
TIES Computer System
TIGER Database File
Time Base Corrector
Time Division Multiplex
Time Shared Automatic Control Laboratory
Timers
Tires
Tools
Toronto Research and Environment System
Total Library System
Touch Terminals
Touch Tone Telephones
Toy Guns
Trac 4 (Game)
Trace Transparent Access Module
Trade Books
Training Computer Exerciser
Training Line Simulator
Training Materials
Trampolines
Transactional Data Systems
Transaxles (Automotive)
Transformers
Transmissions (Automotive)
Transmitters
Trash Compactors
TRS 80
TRS 80 Color Computer
TRS 80 Model I
TRS 80 Model III
Trucks
TS 352 A U Multimeter
Turbines
Turboprop Engines
TurboScan
Turing Machines
Turnkey Systems (Instruction)
Turtle Graphics
Turtleworks (Computer Program)
Tutor (Computer Program)
TUTOR Programing Language
Tutorfilm
Tutortext
TV Interactive Toys
TV Phone
Two Way Cable Cascades
Two Way Cable Communications
Two Way Communication Devices
Two Way Radio
Tymnet
Typewriters
UHF Television
UK MARC
Ukuleles
Ulrich Planfiles
UNC CH Write
Underground Power Lines
Underground Storage Tanks
Uniform Notation for Expressing Queries
Uniforms
UNIQUE Computer Program
UNISTAR I IEP Program
Unit Record Equipment
Unit Ventilators
United Nations Bibliographic Information System
Unitized Vehicles
UNIVAC Computers
University of Toronto Library Automation Systems
UNIX Operating System
USA Today Decisionline
User Aids
Valves
Van de Graaff Generator
Van Schyndel Voice Indexing System
VARCL Computer Program

Variable Interval Sequenced Action Camera
VAX 11 780
VAX Computers
Vector Symbol Phrase Grammar
Veldmans FORTRAN Program ANAVAR
VersaBraille
Vertical Files
Vertical Process Camera
Vesicular Film
Vibrotactile Stimulation Aids
Victor Electrowriter Remote Blackboard
Video Articulator
Video Nova Authoring System
Video Telephone
Videosonic Teaching Machine
Vidicon Equipment
Vinyl
Vinyl Asbestos Tile
Virgin Islands Educational Dissemination System
Virginia Tech Library System
Vis U Guide Responder 700
VisiCalc
Vista System (Bell Canada)
VITAL (Authoring System)
VOC PLAN (Computer Program)
Vocabulary Switching Systems
VOCAL Programing Language
Vocational Competency Achievement Tracking Sys NC
Vocational Education Curriculum Materials Database
Vocational Education Data System
Vocational Education Information Network
Vocational Instructional Materials Acquisition Sys
Vocoders
Voice Based Learning System
Voice Entry Terminal
Voltmeters
Walkie Talkies
Wallpaper
Wang 700 Programing Calculator
Wankel Engines
Washington Post Online
Washington PressText
Water Damaged Books
Water Lens
Water Sampler
Water Tanks
Wave Generators
Wax Cylinder Recordings
Weapons
Weather Satellites
Weather Vanes
Weld Filler Materials
Welding Joints
Wells
WESTLAW Retrieval System
Wideband Cable
Wilsearch
Wilsondisc
Wilsonline
Wind Generators
Wind Tunnels
Windmills
Wisconsin Competency Based Occup Curr Data System
Wisconsin Information System for Education
Wizard (Computer Program)
Wollensak Equipment
Wood Expansion Meter
WordMAP Computer Program
WordNet Database
WordPerfect
WordStar
Wordsworth II
World Energy Data System
Wratten Filters
Wrist Counter
Writer (The)
Writers Helper
Writers Workbench (Computer Software)
Writing Aid and Authors Helper
Writing Is Thinking
Writing Partner (Software)
Wumpus
Wusor
X Ray Machines
Xerox 660 Optical Scanner
Xerox LDX
Xerox Magnavox Telecopier
XPT EASE
XTREE (Computer Program)
YorkTalk
Zenith Z 100 Microcomputers
ZGRASS Programing Language
Zippers
Zoomobiles

CATEGORY 05: Facilities

Aboriginal Schools (Australia)
Academic Cooperatives
Academic Health Centers
Activity Oriented Classrooms
Administrator Associations
Adoption Exchange Services
Adult College Career Employment Support Services
Adult Protective Services
Advanced Technology Centers
Adventure Playgrounds
Advertising Agencies
Agency Shops
American Academies
Amusement Parks
Animal Operant Laboratories
Answering Services
Apartments
Appellate Courts
Aquatic Centers
Architectural Environment
Area Education Agency Media Centers
Area Vocational Technical Institutes
Area Vocational Technical Schools
Army Laboratories
Art Departments
Art Libraries
Art Museums
Athletic Departments
Athletic Facilities
Atriums
Audio Virtual Classrooms
Bar Associations
Basic Skills Brush Up Centers
Basic Skills Centers DC
Bible Colleges
Big Eight Universities
Big Ten Universities
Bilingual School Advisory Committees
Binational Centers
Birdhouses
Blue Ribbon Schools
Boards of Cooperative Educational Services
Book Clubs
Bookstores
Boot Camp
Botanical Gardens
Broadcast Laboratories
Bureau of Indian Affairs Schools
Business Incubators
Business Schools
Cabarets
Cable Access Centers
Cable Libraries
Campus Radio Stations
Career Academies
Career Centers
Career Information Centers
Career Magnet Schools
Career Resource Centers
Carnegie Schools
Casinos
Castles
Cathedrals
Cemeteries
Centers of Excellence in English
Centers of Pedagogy
Centres of Excellence
Chambers of Commerce
Charter Schools
Child Abuse Hotlines
Child Abuse Registries
Child Care Consortia
Child Care Resource Centers
Child Evaluation Centers
Child Protective Services
Child Service Demonstration Centers
Child Study Centres (Canada)
Childrens Homes
Childrens Museums
Childrens Villages
Chiropractic Colleges
Church Libraries
Citizens Learning Networks (Japan)
Civic Institutes
Cluster Districts
Cluster Schools
Coed Dormitories
Coffeehouses
Collective Commune Schools
Colleges of Advanced Education (Australia)
Colleges of Art
Colleges of General and Professional Education PQ
Common Schools
Community Arts Councils
Community Based Organizations
Community Correctional Centers
Community Design Centers
Community Instructional Services
Community Learning Centers
Community Mental Health Centers
Community Oriented Schools
Community Renewal Colleges
Community Resource Centers
Comprehensive Schools (Great Britain)
Comprehensive Universities
Comprehensive Vocational Evaluation Centers
Computation Centers
Computer Based Archives
Computer Based Resource Units
Computer Camps
Computer Departments
Computer Schools
Concentration Camps
Condominiums
Congregate Housing
Conservation Centers
Conservation Field Centres (Canada)
Consumer Organizations
Consumer Services
Contract Schools
Contract Training Centers
Convenience Stores
Converted Facilities
Cooperative Centers (Vocational)
Cooperative Educational Service Agencies
Cooperative Elementary Schools
Cooperative Preschools
Corporate Libraries
Country Schools
Courtyards
Credit Bureaus
Curriculum Coordination Centers
Dame Schools
Dance Companies
Danish Folk Schools
Danish Universities Centres
Darkrooms
Day Care Licensing Agencies
Demonstration Schools
Department Stores
Dependent Care Services
Dependents Schools
Design Studios
Detoxification Centers
Diffusion Networks
Direction Service Centers
Distance Education Centers
Document Delivery Services
Drop In Centers
Drug Free Schools
Drugstores
Early Childhood Direction Centers NY
Early Childhood Laboratories
Early Learning Centers
Earth Stations
Education Libraries
Educational Clinics
Educational Council Stations
Educational Development Centers
Educational Information Centers
Educational Television Stations
Elder Craftsman Shops
Elderhostels
Electronic Libraries
Electronic Universities
Elite Colleges
Elizabethan Theaters
Elywn Institutes
Embassies
Emergency Shelters
Employment Agencies
Energy Extension Tips Service
Engineered Classrooms
Engineering Research Centers
English Curriculum Study Centers
English Grammar Schools
English Language Schools
Environmental Education Centers
Environmental Field Centers
Environmental Research Experimental Schools
ERIC Clearinghouses
Ethical Culture Schools
Ethnic Schools
Exemplary Centers for Reading Instruction
Exemplary Schools
Experimental Education Units
Extended Campus Library Services
Fachhochschulen
Family Exchange Centers
Family Farms
Family Welfare Centers
Farmer Training Centres (Kenya)
Farmers Markets
Farmland
Farms (Educational)
Federal Agencies
Federal Archives and Record Centers
Federal Installations
Federal Laboratories
Federal Lands
Federal Schools (Canada)
Feeder Schools
Fire Departments
First Schools (England)
Flower Shops
Folk High Schools
Folkeskole
Foreign Language Schools (Hawaii)
Foreign Medical Schools
Forsoksgymnaset
Free Clinics
French Language Schools
Frontier Communities
Fundamental Schools
Garden Cities
Gas Stations
Geriatric Assessment Units
Geriatric Education Centers
Glen Canyon Dam
Golf Courses
Government Lands
Government Schools (Australia)
Government Training Centers
Governors Schools
Grant Maintained Schools (Great Britain)
Graphic Arts Industries
Growth Centers
Guaranty Agencies
Handicap Parking Spaces
Health Maintenance Organizations
Health Spas
High Intensity Learning Centers
High Rise Buildings
High Tech Centers (Disabled)
Historical Societies
Homerooms
Hostels
Independent Living Centers
Independent Television Stations
Industrial Libraries
Infant Houses (Israel)
Information Desks
Instructional Improvement Centers
Integrated Playground Facilities
Intelligent Buildings
Intensive Care Units
Intermediate Care Facilities
International High Schools
International Living Centers
International Schools
Internment Camps
Interorganizational Networks
Ivy League Colleges
Jails
Jewish Day Schools
Job Training Academies
Journalism Libraries
Journalism Schools
Jukus
Junior Academies of Science
Junior Kindergartens
Junior Schools (United Kingdom)
Kellogg Center for Adult Learning Research MT
Kibbutzim
Kitchens
Land Laboratories
Language Camps
Language Proficiency Assessment Committees
Large School Districts
Large Schools
Law Enforcement Agencies
Law Offices
Learners Advisory Services
Learning Assistance Centers
Learning Disabilities Research Institutes
Learning Exchange Networks
Learning Information Exchanges
Learning Information Networks
Learning Referral Centers
Lekoteks
Less than Two Year Postsecondary Institutions
Liberal Arts Colleges

Library Access Services
Library Public Services
Lighthouses
Literary Society Libraries
Livestock Industry
Local Education Authorities (United Kingdom)
Local Television Stations
Log Buildings
Long Term Care Facilities
Longhouses
Low Vision Services
Lutheran Colleges
Lutheran Schools
Mail Order Libraries
Mail Rooms
Main Libraries
Mainstreaming Planning Committees
Map Libraries
Maquiladoras
Masters Only Institutions
Mathematics Centers
Mathematics Laboratories
Maximum Security Facilities
Medical Facilities
Medical Laboratories
Microcomputer Based Laboratories
Microlabs
Middle Colleges
Miftanim (Vocational Schools)
Migrant Home Base Centers
Military Bases
Military Day Care
Military Libraries
Mini Schools
Minicolleges
Mission Schools
Mobile Tent Schools
Model Schools
Model Stores
Model Technology Schools
Montessori Preschools
Montessori Schools
Moshavim
Movie Palaces
Multicounty Districts
Multicounty Library Systems
Multicultural Centers
Multidisciplinary Gerontology Centers
Multinational Corporations
Multipurpose Colleges
Multitype Library Networks
Municipal Universities
Museum Libraries
Music Libraries
National Archives Field Branches
National Documentation Centers
National Language Academies
National Origin Desegregation Assistance Centers
National Parks
National Research and Development Centers
National Statistical Libraries
New American Schools
New Colleges
News Agencies
Neylan Colleges
NIE R and D Centers and Regional Educational Labs
Nonaccredited Colleges
Nongovernmental Organizations
Nontraditional Institutions
Normal Schools
Norwegian Regional Colleges
Nuclear Reactors
Nursing Schools
Nutrition Services
Observatories
Occupational Development Centers
Off Reservation Boarding Schools
Office Buildings
Offices of Research in Medical Education
Offices of Rural Affairs
On Going Organizations
One Person Libraries
Open Houses
Open Learning Centres
Open Plan Communities
Open Spaces
Orphanages
Out of State Institutions
Overseas American Colleges
Overseas Campuses
Paper Industry
Parent Child Centers
Parent Child Development Centers
Parent Cooperatives
Parent Teacher Education Centers
Parish Libraries
Parliamentary Libraries
Partner Schools
Pastoral Industry
Peoples Universities
Personal Libraries
Pharmaceutical Libraries
Pharmacy Libraries
Picture Libraries
Planning and Development Units
Play Centers
Playcentres
Poultry Farms
Power Plants
Presidential Libraries
Primary Schools (United Kingdom)
Principals Centers
Priority Schools
Private Industry
Private Libraries
Professional Development Centers
Professional Standards Review Organizations
Profit Making Schools
Proprietary Hospitals
Proprietary Organizations
Protective Services
Psychodiagnostic Clinics
Public Lands
Public Services
Racially Isolated Schools
Radio and Television Universities (China)
Radio Reading Services
Rapid Learning Centers
Recording Industry
Recruitment and Community Technical Resources Ctrs
Refugee Camps
Regional Centers
Regional Colleges
Regional Districts
Regional Educational Laboratories
Regional Educational Resource Agencies
Regional Educational Service Agencies
Regional Information Centers
Regional Medical Libraries
Regional Resource Centers
Regional Training and Dissemination Centers
Regional Universities
Regulatory Agencies
Rehabilitation Research and Training Centers
Related Services
Religious Libraries
Repertory Companies
Research and Graduate Training Facilities
Research Evaluation and Planning Units
Reserve Reading Rooms
Reservoirs
Residence Hall Libraries
Retail Stores
Retirement Communities
Rural Craft Training Centers (Kenya)
Rural Education Centers
Rural Free Universities
Rural Health Clinics
Rural Libraries
Rural Policy Centers
Rural Work Education Councils
Scholastic Press Associations
School Based Child Care Centers
School Based Clinics
School Based Early Childhood Centers
School Based Health Clinics
School Community Councils
School Sponsored Day Care
School Stores
School Study Councils
School Yards
Schools of Business Administration
Schools of Public Health
Schools Without Failure
Schools Without Walls
Science Education Centers
Science Fiction Libraries
Science Museums
Screening Units
Seaports
Second Homes
Self Contained Academic Learning Environment
Self Contained Open Classrooms
Self Help Facilities
Senior Citizen Centers
Senior Colleges (Australia)
Separate Schools (Canada)
Settlement Schools
Seven Sisters Colleges
Sex Desegregation Assistance Centers
Shared Housing
Sharing Centers
Shelters
Shipboard Libraries
Shipbuilding Industry
Shipping Industry
Shipyards
Shopping Centers
Single High School Districts
Single Judge Municipal Court Libraries
Skill Clinics
Skywalks
Small Business Centers
Small Farms
Small Libraries
Smart Schools
Smoke Free Schools
Sole Community Hospitals
Southern University Group
Speakers Bureaus
Speaking Centers
Special Education Cooperatives
Special Education Instructional Materials Centers
Special Education Training and Resource Centers NY
Special Interest Centers
Special Training Schools (Japan)
Specialist Schools
Specialized Facilities
Speech Departments
Spouse Abuse Shelters
Stadiums
Star Schools
State Advisory Councils on Vocational Education
State Archives
State Associations
State College and University Systems
State Coordinating Boards
State Education Associations
State Employment and Training Councils
State Guarantee Agencies
State Historical Societies
State Humanities Councils
State Legislatures
State Skills Corporations
Street Academies
Student Health Organizations
Student Operated Radio Stations
Student Teaching Centers
Subsidized Child Care Services
Subways
Sunspaces
Support Facilities
Supported Housing
Surgical Facilities
Synagogue Libraries
Synagogues
Taverns
Tavistock Study Groups
Te Kohanga Reo (New Zealand)
Teacher Advisory Centres
Teacher Education Academies
Teacher Education and Computer Centers
Teacher Partnerships
Technical Assistance Centers
Technical Education Research Centers
Technical Educational Research Centers
Television Stations
Television Universities (China)
Temporary Help Service Industry
Tertiary Colleges
Testing Centers
Textile Industry
Theme Parks
Theological Libraries
Toy Lending Libraries
Trade Associations
Trading Posts
Training and Enterprise Councils (Great Britain)
Training and Placement Councils
Training Centers
Training Stations
Transfer Centers
Transitional Service Centers
Transnational Corporations
Travel Industry
Troop Schools
Trucking Industry
Two Year Colleges within Universities
Undergraduate Libraries
Underground Press
Union Libraries
Unit Schools
United Nations University Centres
Universal Playgrounds
University Clinics
University Presses
Urban Centers
Urban Libraries
Vacant Schools
Vanity Presses
Vegetable Gardens
Video Arcades
Village Colleges (England)
Village High Schools
Virtual Classrooms
Virtual Libraries
Vocational Technical Adult Education Districts
Volkshochschulen
Waiting Rooms
Waste Repositories
Water Play Facilities
Weight Management Centers
Wesleyan Colleges
Whanau House
White Collar Organizations
White Colleges
Wildlife Refuges
Windowless Schools
Womens Centers
Womens Organizations
Womens Shelters
Work Activity Centers
Workers Universities (Yugoslavia)
Yeshivoth
Youth Development Centers
Youth Opportunity Centers
Youth Service Bureaus

CATEGORY 07: Geographic Locations

Acadia
Adirondack Mountains
Afghanistan
Africa
Africa (Central)
Africa (East)
Africa (North)
Africa (Northeast)
Africa (South)
Africa (Sub Sahara)
Africa (Tropical)
Africa (West)
African Savanna
Alabama
Alabama (Africatown)
Alabama (Alexander City)
Alabama (Auburn)
Alabama (Baldwin County)
Alabama (Birmingham)
Alabama (Bullock County)
Alabama (Cherokee County)
Alabama (Conecuh County)
Alabama (Decatur)
Alabama (Etowah County)
Alabama (Florence)
Alabama (Greene County)
Alabama (Hale County)
Alabama (Huntsville)
Alabama (Macon County)
Alabama (Marengo County)
Alabama (Mobile)
Alabama (Montgomery)
Alabama (Northeast)
Alabama (Opelika)
Alabama (Pike County)
Alabama (Selma)
Alabama (Soul City)
Alabama (Sylacauga)
Alabama (Tuscaloosa County)
Alabama (Tuscaloosa)
Alabama (Tuskegee)
Alabama (Wilcox County)
Alaska
Alaska (Aleutian Islands)
Alaska (Anchorage)
Alaska (Attu)
Alaska (Bethel)
Alaska (Bristol Bay)
Alaska (Chevak)
Alaska (Cordova)
Alaska (Eagle)
Alaska (Fairbanks)
Alaska (Juneau)
Alaska (Ketchikan)
Alaska (Kodiak Island)
Alaska (Koyuk)
Alaska (Manokotak)
Alaska (Nome)
Alaska (Northwest)
Alaska (Pribilof Islands)

California (Whittier)
California (Woodland)
California (Yettem)
California (Yolo County)
California (Yuba County)
Cambodia
Cameroon
Cameroon (East)
Cameroon (West)
Camino Real
Canada
Canada (French Provinces)
Canada (Maritime Provinces)
Canada (North)
Canada (Prairie Provinces)
Canada (West)
Canal Zone
Canary Islands
Cape Hatteras
Cape Verde
Caribbean
Caribbean Islands
Carolinas
Caroline Islands
Catawba River
Central African Republic
Central African Republic (Bossangoa)
Central America
Ceylon
Ceylon (Colombo)
Chad
Cherokee Nation
Chesapeake Bay
Chicago Standard Metropolitan Statistical Area
Chile
Chile (Santiago)
China
China (Beijing)
China (Guangzhou)
China (Inner Mongolia)
China (Manchuria)
China (Nanjing)
China (Shanghai)
China (Shanyang)
China (Sichuan Province)
China (Tibet)
China (Zhuji County)
China Coast
Ciskei
Coastal Zones
Coeur d Alene Reservation ID
Cold Climates
Colombia
Colombia (Armero)
Colombia (Bogota)
Colombia (Cali)
Colombia (Medellin)
Colorado
Colorado (Adams County)
Colorado (Alamosa)
Colorado (Aspen)
Colorado (Boulder County)
Colorado (Boulder)
Colorado (Colorado City)
Colorado (Colorado Springs)
Colorado (Denver)
Colorado (El Paso County)
Colorado (Fort Collins)
Colorado (Fort Lupton)
Colorado (Georgetown)
Colorado (Grand Junction)
Colorado (Greeley)
Colorado (Gunnison)
Colorado (Ignacio)
Colorado (Jefferson County)
Colorado (Lakewood)
Colorado (Littleton)
Colorado (Meeker)
Colorado (Mesa County)
Colorado (Monte Vista)
Colorado (Park County)
Colorado (Pueblo)
Colorado (Rocky Ford)
Colorado (San Luis Valley)
Colorado (San Luis)
Colorado (Sedgwick County)
Colorado (Sheridan)
Colorado (South)
Colorado (Vail)
Colorado (Weld County)
Colorado (West)
Columbia River
Columbia River Gorge
Colville Lake
Comoros
Congo
Congo (Brazzaville)
Connecticut
Connecticut (Bridgeport)
Connecticut (Canterbury)
Connecticut (Cheshire)
Connecticut (Danbury)
Connecticut (East Granby)
Connecticut (East Hartford)
Connecticut (Enfield)
Connecticut (Greenwich)
Connecticut (Hamden)
Connecticut (Hartford)
Connecticut (Lebanon)
Connecticut (Madison)
Connecticut (Meriden)
Connecticut (New Britain)
Connecticut (New Canaan)
Connecticut (New Haven)
Connecticut (New London)
Connecticut (Newington)
Connecticut (Norwalk)
Connecticut (Southbury)
Connecticut (Southwest)
Connecticut (Stamford)
Connecticut (Storrs)
Connecticut (Wallingford)
Connecticut (Wallington)
Connecticut (Waterbury)
Connecticut (Waterford)
Connecticut (West Hartford)
Connecticut (West Haven)
Connecticut (Westport)
Connecticut (Windham)
Connecticut River Valley
Connetquot River State Park NY
Continents
Cook Islands
Costa Rica
Cuba
Cuba (Havana)
Cumberland Plateau
Cumberland Valley
Cuttyhunk Island
Cyprus
Czech Republic
Czechoslovakia
Czechoslovakia (Moravia)
Czechoslovakia (Prague)
Czechoslovakia (Slovakia)
Dahomey
Delaware
Delaware (Kent County)
Delaware (New Castle County)
Delaware (Newark)
Delaware (Seaford)
Delaware (Wilmington)
Democratic Yemen
Denmark
District of Columbia
District of Columbia (Anacostia)
District of Columbia (Mount Vernon Square)
Dominica
Dominican Republic
East Germany
East Pakistan
East Timor
Easter Island
Eastern Hemisphere
Ecuador
Edge Cities
Egypt
Egypt (Cairo)
El Salvador
Ellis Island
Embarras River Basin
England
England (Bath)
England (Bircham Newton)
England (Birmingham)
England (Bradford)
England (Bristol)
England (Cambridge)
England (Cornwall)
England (Coventry)
England (Devon)
England (Essex)
England (Hackney)
England (Hertfordshire)
England (Isle of Wight)
England (Lancaster)
England (Leeds)
England (Leicester)
England (Leicestershire)
England (Liverpool)
England (London)
England (New Lanark)
England (Newcastle upon Tyne)
England (Newport)
England (Norfolk)
England (Northamptonshire)
England (Nottinghamshire)
England (Oxfordshire)
England (Reading)
England (Ridleyshire)
England (Sandwell)
England (Sheffield)
England (South Molton)
England (Surrey)
England (Sussex)
England (Swindon)
England (Walsall)
England (Wessex)
England (West Midlands)
England (West Yorkshire)
England (Yorkshire)
Estonia
Ethiopia
Ethiopia (Addis Ababa)
Eurasia
Europe
Europe (Central)
Europe (East Central)
Europe (East)
Europe (North)
Europe (South)
Europe (Southeast)
Europe (West)
Everglades
Falkland Islands
Far East
Federated States of Micronesia
Federated States of Micronesia (Kosrae)
Fiji
Finland
Finland (Helsinki)
Finland (Vasa)
Fire Island National Seashore
Fish Lake
Florida
Florida (Alachua County)
Florida (Belle Glade)
Florida (Boca Raton)
Florida (Brevard County)
Florida (Broward County)
Florida (Central)
Florida (Charlotte County)
Florida (Clearwater)
Florida (Collier County)
Florida (Coral Gables)
Florida (Dade County)
Florida (Daytona Beach)
Florida (De Land)
Florida (Duval County)
Florida (East Naples)
Florida (Escambia County)
Florida (Flagler County)
Florida (Fort Lauderdale)
Florida (Gadsden County)
Florida (Gainesville)
Florida (Gulf County)
Florida (Hialeah)
Florida (Hillsborough County)
Florida (Jacksonville)
Florida (Largo)
Florida (Lee County)
Florida (Leon County)
Florida (Merritt Island)
Florida (Miami Beach)
Florida (Miami)
Florida (Monroe County)
Florida (Naples)
Florida (North)
Florida (Okaloosa County)
Florida (Orange County)
Florida (Orlando)
Florida (Palm Beach County)
Florida (Palm Beach)
Florida (Pasco County)
Florida (Pensacola)
Florida (Pinellas County)
Florida (Polk County)
Florida (Saint Leo)
Florida (Saint Petersburg)
Florida (Sarasota County)
Florida (Sarasota)
Florida (South)
Florida (Southeast)
Florida (Southwest)
Florida (Tallahassee)
Florida (Tampa)
Florida (Titusville)
Florida (Volusia County)
Florida (Wakulla County)
Florida (Walton County)
Formosa
Four Corners Area
France
France (Alsace)
France (Beaubourg)
France (Brittany)
France (Cannes)
France (Cassis)
France (Gascony)
France (Grenoble)
France (Lyon)
France (Marseilles)
France (Montpellier)
France (Paris)
France (Provence)
France (Strasbourg)
France (Vendee)
Francophone Africa
Freedmans Village VA
French Africa
French Guiana
French West Africa
French West Indies
Gabon
Galapagos Islands
Gambia
Gaza Strip
Georgia
Georgia (Americus)
Georgia (Athens)
Georgia (Atlanta Metropolitan Area)
Georgia (Atlanta)
Georgia (Augusta)
Georgia (Bibb County)
Georgia (Carroll County)
Georgia (Carrollton)
Georgia (Central)
Georgia (Clarke County)
Georgia (Clayton County)
Georgia (Cobb County)
Georgia (Columbia County)
Georgia (Columbus)
Georgia (Crisp County)
Georgia (DeKalb County)
Georgia (Fort Gordon)
Georgia (Fulton County)
Georgia (Gainesville)
Georgia (Hancock County)
Georgia (Harris County)
Georgia (Liberty County)
Georgia (Morgan County)
Georgia (Murray County)
Georgia (North)
Georgia (Northwest)
Georgia (Savannah)
Georgia (Statesboro)
Georgia (Sumter County)
Georgia (Valdosta)
Georgia (Wilkes County)
Georgia Republic
German Speaking Countries
Germany
Germany (Berlin)
Germany (Bremen)
Germany (Paderborn)
Ghana
Gibraltar
Gilbert and Ellice Islands
Gilbert Islands
Great Basin
Great Britain
Great Lakes
Great Plains (North)
Great Smoky Mountains National Park
Greece
Greece (Ancient)
Greece (Athens)
Green Bay
Greenland
Grenada
Guam
Guam (Agana)
Guatemala
Guatemala (El Jocote)
Guinea
Gulf of Maine
Gulf of Mexico
Guyana
Haiti
Hawaii
Hawaii (Anahola)
Hawaii (Hawaii County)
Hawaii (Hilo)
Hawaii (Honolulu)
Hawaii (Kauai)
Hawaii (Maui)
Hawaii (Molokai)
Hawaii (Oahu)

Honduras
Hong Kong
Hudson Bay
Hudson River
Hungary
Hungary (Budapest)
Iberian Peninsula
Iceland
Idaho
Idaho (Bingham County)
Idaho (Boise)
Idaho (Idaho Falls)
Idaho (Pocatello)
Illinois
Illinois (Alexander County)
Illinois (Alton)
Illinois (Arlington Heights)
Illinois (Bloomington)
Illinois (Boone County)
Illinois (Bureau County)
Illinois (Canton)
Illinois (Carbondale)
Illinois (Central)
Illinois (Centralia)
Illinois (Champaign County)
Illinois (Champaign Urbana)
Illinois (Champaign)
Illinois (Chicago Heights)
Illinois (Chicago Metropolitan Area)
Illinois (Chicago)
Illinois (Cobden)
Illinois (Cook County)
Illinois (Crystal Lake)
Illinois (De Kalb County)
Illinois (De Kalb)
Illinois (Decatur)
Illinois (Deerfield)
Illinois (DuPage County)
Illinois (East Chicago)
Illinois (East Humboldt Park)
Illinois (East Saint Louis)
Illinois (Edgewater)
Illinois (Edwardsville)
Illinois (Elgin)
Illinois (Elk Grove Village)
Illinois (Evanston)
Illinois (Forest Park)
Illinois (Glenbrook)
Illinois (Glenview)
Illinois (Granite City)
Illinois (Gurnee)
Illinois (Harrisburg)
Illinois (Highland Park)
Illinois (Joliet)
Illinois (Kankakee)
Illinois (Lake County)
Illinois (Libertyville)
Illinois (Lockport)
Illinois (Logan County)
Illinois (Macomb)
Illinois (Madison County)
Illinois (McLean County)
Illinois (Mount Carmel)
Illinois (Naperville)
Illinois (New Trier Township)
Illinois (Niles)
Illinois (Normal)
Illinois (North)
Illinois (Oak Park)
Illinois (Palatine)
Illinois (Palos Park)
Illinois (Park Forest)
Illinois (Pekin)
Illinois (Peoria)
Illinois (Pope County)
Illinois (Quincy)
Illinois (River Forest)
Illinois (Rock Island)
Illinois (Rockford)
Illinois (Saint Clair County)
Illinois (Saint Peter)
Illinois (Schaumburg)
Illinois (Skokie)
Illinois (South)
Illinois (Springfield)
Illinois (Sullivan)
Illinois (Uptown)
Illinois (Urbana)
Illinois (Villa Park)
Illinois (Waukegan)
Illinois (Wheaton)
Illinois (Wheeling)
Illinois (Wilmette)
Illinois (Winnebago County)
Illinois (Winnetka)
India
India (Ahmadnagar Fort)
India (Andhra Pradesh)
India (Bangalore)
India (Baroda)
India (Bengal)
India (Bihar State)
India (Bombay State)
India (Bombay)
India (Calcutta)
India (Chandigarh UT)
India (Chandigarh)
India (Davangere)
India (Delhi)
India (Ernakulam)
India (Gujarat State)
India (Gujarat)
India (Haryana)
India (Himachal Pradesh)
India (Jaipur)
India (Karnataka)
India (Kerala State)
India (Lucknow)
India (Madras State)
India (Maharashtra)
India (Manipur)
India (Mysore State)
India (New Delhi)
India (Orissa)
India (Poona)
India (Punjab State)
India (Rajasthan)
India (South)
India (Tamil Nadu)
India (Uttar Pradesh)
India (West Bengal)
Indian Ocean
Indiana
Indiana (Bartholomew County)
Indiana (Bloomington)
Indiana (Central)
Indiana (Columbus)
Indiana (Elkhart County)
Indiana (Elkhart)
Indiana (Evansville)
Indiana (Floyd County)
Indiana (Fort Wayne)
Indiana (Gary)
Indiana (Grant County)
Indiana (Hammond)
Indiana (Henry County)
Indiana (Indianapolis)
Indiana (Kankakee Valley)
Indiana (Kokomo)
Indiana (Lafayette)
Indiana (Lake County)
Indiana (Lawrence County)
Indiana (Logansport)
Indiana (Marion County)
Indiana (Michigan City)
Indiana (Monroe County)
Indiana (Monticello)
Indiana (Muncie)
Indiana (New Albany)
Indiana (New Harmony)
Indiana (Northeast)
Indiana (Portage)
Indiana (Porter County)
Indiana (Richmond)
Indiana (Saint Joseph County)
Indiana (South Bend)
Indiana (South)
Indiana (Terre Haute)
Indiana (Vanderburgh County)
Indiana (Wabash County)
Indiana (West Lafayette)
Indiana (Yorktown)
Indochina
Indonesia
Indonesia (East Java)
Indonesia (Galang)
Indonesia (Irian Barat)
Indonesia (Jakarta)
Indonesia (Java)
Indonesia (Sumatra)
Iowa
Iowa (Ames)
Iowa (Black Hawk County)
Iowa (Buchanan County)
Iowa (Burlington)
Iowa (Carroll County)
Iowa (Cedar Falls)
Iowa (Cedar Rapids)
Iowa (Central)
Iowa (Council Bluffs)
Iowa (Crawford County)
Iowa (Davenport)
Iowa (Decorah)
Iowa (Des Moines)
Iowa (Dubuque)
Iowa (East)
Iowa (Esterville)
Iowa (Fort Madison)
Iowa (Greene County)
Iowa (Grinnell)
Iowa (Ida County)
Iowa (Iowa City)
Iowa (Iowa Falls)
Iowa (Jackson County)
Iowa (Keokuk)
Iowa (Lohrville)
Iowa (Mahaska County)
Iowa (Marshalltown)
Iowa (Milford)
Iowa (Polk County)
Iowa (Prairie City)
Iowa (Sioux City)
Iowa (Siouxland)
Iowa (Terril)
Iowa (Waterloo)
Iowa (Webster County)
Iran
Iran (Azarbaiyan)
Iran (Fars Province)
Iran (Khuzestan Province)
Iran (Shiraz)
Iran (Tabriz)
Iran (Tehran)
Iraq
Iraq (Baghdad)
Ireland
Ireland (Dublin)
Islamic Countries
Islands
Israel
Israel (Haifa)
Israel (Jerusalem)
Israel (Tel Aviv)
Israel (Tiberias)
Italy
Italy (Florence)
Italy (Naples)
Italy (Padua)
Italy (Pavia)
Italy (Reggio Emilia)
Italy (Rome)
Italy (Sauris)
Italy (Sicily)
Italy (Turin)
Italy (Venice)
Ivory Coast
Jamaica
Jamaica (Kingston)
James River
Japan
Japan (Hiroshima)
Japan (Kyoto)
Japan (Matsumoto)
Japan (Nagasaki)
Japan (Okinawa)
Japan (Ryukyu Islands)
Japan (Tokyo)
Jordan
Jordan (Ramallah)
Judea
Kansas
Kansas (Cherokee County)
Kansas (Clay Center)
Kansas (Decatur County)
Kansas (Dunlap City)
Kansas (Ellis County)
Kansas (Emporia)
Kansas (Johnson County)
Kansas (Kansas City)
Kansas (Labette County)
Kansas (Lawrence)
Kansas (Manhattan)
Kansas (Montgomery County)
Kansas (Parsons)
Kansas (Pittsburg)
Kansas (Salina)
Kansas (Sedgwick County)
Kansas (Southeast)
Kansas (Topeka)
Kansas (Wichita County)
Kansas (Wichita)
Kazakhstan
Kentucky
Kentucky (Berea)
Kentucky (Bowling Green)
Kentucky (Breathitt County)
Kentucky (Calloway County)
Kentucky (Central)
Kentucky (Covington)
Kentucky (East)
Kentucky (Elizabethtown)
Kentucky (Elliott County)
Kentucky (Fayette County)
Kentucky (Fort Thomas)
Kentucky (Frankfort)
Kentucky (Hardin County)
Kentucky (Harlan County)
Kentucky (Hart County)
Kentucky (Hopkinsville)
Kentucky (Jackson County)
Kentucky (Jefferson County)
Kentucky (Lee County)
Kentucky (Letcher County)
Kentucky (Lexington)
Kentucky (Logan County)
Kentucky (Louisville)
Kentucky (McCreary County)
Kentucky (Morehead)
Kentucky (Morgan County)
Kentucky (North)
Kentucky (Northern)
Kentucky (Owensboro)
Kentucky (Paducah)
Kentucky (Pike County)
Kentucky (Pikeville)
Kentucky (Rowan County)
Kentucky (Scott County)
Kentucky (Somerset)
Kentucky (Sturgis)
Kentucky (Union County)
Kentucky (Warren County)
Kentucky (West)
Kentucky (Whitley County)
Kenya
Kenya (Kisumu)
Kenya (Nairobi)
Kenya (Nandi)
Khmer Republic
Kirgizstan
Kiribati
Korea
Kuwait
Kwazulu
Labrador
Lake Erie
Lake Superior
Lake Tahoe
Lake Winona
Laos
Lapland
Latin America
Lebanon
Lebanon (Beirut)
Lesotho
Liberia
Libya
Liechtenstein
Louisiana
Louisiana (Baton Rouge)
Louisiana (Caddo Bossier Parish)
Louisiana (Calcasieu Parish)
Louisiana (East Baton Rouge)
Louisiana (Iberia Parish)
Louisiana (Jefferson Parish)
Louisiana (Lafayette Parish)
Louisiana (Lafourche Parish)
Louisiana (Lake Charles)
Louisiana (Lincoln Parish)
Louisiana (Natchitoches Parish)
Louisiana (Natchitoches)
Louisiana (New Orleans)
Louisiana (Saint Landry Parish)
Louisiana (Saint Martinville)
Louisiana (Saint Mary Parish)
Louisiana (Shreveport)
Louisiana (Southeast)
Lower Mississippi Delta
Luxembourg
Macao
Macedonia
Madagascar
Maghreb Countries
Maine
Maine (Aroostook County)
Maine (Augusta)
Maine (Bangor)
Maine (Bar Harbor)
Maine (Bethel)
Maine (Biddeford)
Maine (Franklin County)
Maine (Frenchville)
Maine (Fryeburg)
Maine (Guilford)
Maine (Madawaska)
Maine (Orland)
Maine (Portland)
Maine (York County)
Malagasy Republic

Tennessee (Knox County)
Tennessee (Knoxville)
Tennessee (Lauderdale County)
Tennessee (Loudon County)
Tennessee (Maury County)
Tennessee (Memphis)
Tennessee (Nashville)
Tennessee (Northeast)
Tennessee (Oak Ridge)
Tennessee (Overton County)
Tennessee (Shelby County)
Tennessee (Upper Cumberland)
Tennessee (Williamson County)
Tennessee Tombigbee Waterway
Texas
Texas (Abilene)
Texas (Allen)
Texas (Alpine)
Texas (Amarillo)
Texas (Anthony)
Texas (Arlington)
Texas (Atascosa County)
Texas (Austin)
Texas (Bexar County)
Texas (Big Lake)
Texas (Big Spring)
Texas (Brooks County)
Texas (Brownsville)
Texas (Caldwell County)
Texas (Caldwell)
Texas (Cameron County)
Texas (Camp Woodland Springs)
Texas (Canutillo)
Texas (Canyon)
Texas (College Station)
Texas (Collin County)
Texas (Corpus Christi)
Texas (Corsicana)
Texas (Crosby)
Texas (Crystal City)
Texas (Dallas County)
Texas (Dallas)
Texas (Del Rio)
Texas (Del Valle)
Texas (Denton)
Texas (Eagle Pass)
Texas (East Austin)
Texas (East)
Texas (El Paso)
Texas (Fayette County)
Texas (Flour Bluff)
Texas (Fort Bend County)
Texas (Fort Worth)
Texas (Galveston County)
Texas (Galveston)
Texas (Grayson County)
Texas (Harlandale)
Texas (Harris County)
Texas (Hidalgo County)
Texas (Hill Country)
Texas (Houston)
Texas (Howard County)
Texas (La Grulla)
Texas (Laredo)
Texas (Lubbock)
Texas (Nacogdoches)
Texas (North)
Texas (Odessa)
Texas (Panhandle)
Texas (Panola County)
Texas (Pecos)
Texas (Port Arthur)
Texas (Potter County)
Texas (Richardson)
Texas (Round Rock)
Texas (San Angelo)
Texas (San Antonio)
Texas (San Marcos)
Texas (Sonora)
Texas (South)
Texas (Southeast)
Texas (Texas City)
Texas (Travis County)
Texas (Uvalde)
Texas (Waco)
Texas (West)
Texas (Willacy County)
Thailand
Thailand (Bangkok)
Timor (Portuguese)
Togo
Togo (Lome)
Tokelau
Tonga
Transkei
Transylvania
Trinidad and Tobago
Tunisia
Turkey
Turkey (Ankara)
Turkey (Dinar)
Turkey (Gallipoli)
Turkey (Istanbul)
Turkistan
Turkmenistan
Tuvalu
Uganda
Ukraine
United Arab Emirates
United Arab Republic
United Kingdom
United States
United States (Border States)
United States (Central)
United States (Coastal Plains)
United States (Deep South)
United States (East North Central)
United States (East)
United States (Far West)
United States (Frostbelt)
United States (Great Lakes Region)
United States (Great Plains States)
United States (Gulf Coast States)
United States (Intermountain West)
United States (Mid Atlantic States)
United States (Midwest)
United States (Mountain Plains)
United States (North Atlantic States)
United States (North Central)
United States (North)
United States (Northeast)
United States (Northern Great Plains)
United States (Northwest)
United States (Pacific States)
United States (Plains States)
United States (Rocky Mountain States)
United States (South Central)
United States (South)
United States (Southeast)
United States (Southwest)
United States (Sunbelt)
United States (Upper Allegheny Region)
United States (Upper Great Lakes)
United States (Upper Midwest)
United States (West Coast)
United States (West)
Upper Volta
Uruguay
USSR
USSR (Armenia)
USSR (Azerbaijan)
USSR (Bashkiria)
USSR (Buryat Republic)
USSR (Byelorussia)
USSR (Estonia)
USSR (Georgia)
USSR (Kamensk Uralski)
USSR (Kazakhstan)
USSR (Kiev)
USSR (Kirgizia)
USSR (Latvia)
USSR (Leningrad)
USSR (Lithuania)
USSR (Lustdorf bei Odessa)
USSR (Mari Republic)
USSR (Moscow)
USSR (Nizhni Tagil)
USSR (Novosibirsk)
USSR (Russia)
USSR (Syzran)
USSR (Tadzhikistan)
USSR (Tuva)
USSR (Ukraine)
USSR (Uzbekistan)
USSR (Volga Ural Region)
Utah
Utah (Cedar City)
Utah (Clearfield)
Utah (Escalante)
Utah (Logan)
Utah (Provo)
Utah (Salt Lake City)
Utah (Salt Lake County)
Utah (Tooele County)
Utah (Uintah Basin)
Utah (Weber County)
Ute Mountains
Uzbekistan
Vanuatu
Vatican City State
Venezuela
Venezuela (Caracas)
Vermont
Vermont (Brattleboro)
Vermont (Burlington)
Vermont (Derby)
Vermont (Montpelier)
Vermont (South Burlington)
Vietnam
Virgin Islands
Virgin Islands (Saint Croix)
Virgin Islands (Saint Thomas)
Virginia
Virginia (Albemarle County)
Virginia (Alexandria)
Virginia (Arlington County)
Virginia (Arlington)
Virginia (Baileys Crossroads)
Virginia (Blacksburg)
Virginia (Caroline County)
Virginia (Central)
Virginia (Charlottesville)
Virginia (Chesapeake)
Virginia (Eastern Shore)
Virginia (Emporia)
Virginia (Fairfax County)
Virginia (Fairfax)
Virginia (Gloucester County)
Virginia (Greene County)
Virginia (Hampton)
Virginia (Henrico County)
Virginia (Jamestown)
Virginia (Loudoun County)
Virginia (Lunenburg County)
Virginia (Lynchburg)
Virginia (Montgomery County)
Virginia (Nelson County)
Virginia (Newport News)
Virginia (Norfolk)
Virginia (Pennington Gap)
Virginia (Petersburg)
Virginia (Portsmouth)
Virginia (Prince Edward County)
Virginia (Prince William County)
Virginia (Reston)
Virginia (Richmond)
Virginia (Roanoke)
Virginia (Southwest)
Virginia (Tidewater)
Virginia (Virginia Beach)
Virginia (Warren County)
Virginia (Warrenton)
Virginia (Williamsburg)
Virginia (York County)
Wabash River Valley
Walachia
Wales
Wales (Monmouthshire)
Wales (South)
Walker River Paiute Reservation NV
Wallis and Futuna Islands
Washington
Washington (Bellevue)
Washington (Bellingham)
Washington (Cheney)
Washington (Clallam County)
Washington (Clark County)
Washington (Colville)
Washington (East)
Washington (Ellensburg)
Washington (Everett)
Washington (Gig Harbor)
Washington (King County)
Washington (Lincoln County)
Washington (Maple Valley)
Washington (Mukilteo)
Washington (Olympia)
Washington (Pierce County)
Washington (Port Townsend)
Washington (Puget Sound)
Washington (Redmond)
Washington (Seattle)
Washington (Snohomish County)
Washington (Southeast)
Washington (Spangle)
Washington (Spokane)
Washington (Stevens County)
Washington (Tacoma)
Washington (Vancouver)
Washington (Walla Walla)
Washington (Wallingford)
Washington (Wenatchee)
Washington (Whitman County)
Washington (Yakima)
West Bank
West Germany
West Germany (Baden Wuerttemberg)
West Germany (Bavaria)
West Germany (Berlin)
West Germany (Bremen)
West Germany (Cologne)
West Germany (Goettingen)
West Germany (Hamburg)
West Germany (Heidelberg)
West Germany (Herne)
West Germany (Hesse)
West Germany (Hessen)
West Germany (Lower Saxony)
West Germany (Munich)
West Germany (North Rhine Westphalia)
West Germany (Rhineland Palatinate)
West Germany (Saarland)
West Indies
West Pakistan
West Virginia
West Virginia (Arthurdale)
West Virginia (Berkeley County)
West Virginia (Braxton County)
West Virginia (Brooke County)
West Virginia (Charleston)
West Virginia (Doddridge County)
West Virginia (Hampshire County)
West Virginia (Harpers Ferry)
West Virginia (Harrison County)
West Virginia (Kanawha County)
West Virginia (Marion County)
West Virginia (Mason County)
West Virginia (Mercer County)
West Virginia (Mingo County)
West Virginia (Monongalia County)
West Virginia (Morgantown)
West Virginia (Ohio County)
West Virginia (Parkersburg)
West Virginia (Putnam County)
West Virginia (Raleigh County)
West Virginia (Wheeling)
West Virginia (Wood County)
Western Hemisphere
Western Samoa
White Mountains
Willamette River
Wisconsin
Wisconsin (Burnett County)
Wisconsin (Dane County)
Wisconsin (Eau Claire County)
Wisconsin (Eau Claire)
Wisconsin (Forest County)
Wisconsin (Green Bay)
Wisconsin (Janesville)
Wisconsin (Kenosha)
Wisconsin (La Crosse)
Wisconsin (Lodi)
Wisconsin (Madison)
Wisconsin (Manitowoc)
Wisconsin (Marquette County)
Wisconsin (Menomonie)
Wisconsin (Milwaukee County)
Wisconsin (Milwaukee)
Wisconsin (New Glarus)
Wisconsin (Oshkosh)
Wisconsin (Portage)
Wisconsin (Pulaski)
Wisconsin (Racine)
Wisconsin (River Falls)
Wisconsin (Rock County)
Wisconsin (Sheboygan)
Wisconsin (Stevens Point)
Wisconsin (Sussex)
Wisconsin (Trempealeau County)
Wisconsin (Walworth County)
Wisconsin (Waukesha County)
Wisconsin (Waukesha)
Wisconsin (Wausau)
Wisconsin (Waushara County)
Wisconsin (West de Pere)
Wisconsin (West)
Wisconsin (Whitefish Bay)
Wyoming
Wyoming (Casper)
Wyoming (Cheyenne)
Wyoming (Goshen County)
Wyoming (Laramie County)
Wyoming (Laramie)
Wyoming (Powell)
Yakima Valley
Yellowstone National Park
Yemen
Yucatan Peninsula
Yugoslavia
Yugoslavia (Belgrade)
Yugoslavia (Bosnia)
Yugoslavia (Croatia)
Yugoslavia (Macedonia)
Yugoslavia (Serbia)
Yugoslavia (Slovenia)
Yukon
Yukon (Whitehorse)
Yukon Territory

Zaire
Zaire (Kinshasa)
Zaire River
Zambales Mountains
Zambia
Zimbabwe
Zimbabwe (Harare)
Zuni (Pueblo)

CATEGORY 08: Groups (Ethnic)

Acadians
Acoma (Pueblo)
Afghans
Africans
Afrikaners
Afro Amerasians
Afro Asians
Afro Caribbeans
Afro Hispanics
Aguaruna (People)
Ahtna (Tribe)
Ak Chin (Tribe)
Akwesasne Mohawk (Tribe)
Alabama (Tribe)
Aleut (Tribe)
Algonquians
Algonquin (Tribe)
Americans (United States)
Amerindians
Amish (Old Order)
Amuesha (People)
Anasazi (Anthropological Label)
Anglo Saxons
Apache (Tribe)
Appalachian People
Appalachian Whites
Arabic Speaking
Arapaho (Tribe)
Arapahoe (Tribe)
Arikara (Tribe)
Armenian Americans
Armenians
Ashkenazim
Asian Blacks
Asians
Assiniboine (Tribe)
Athapascan (Tribe)
Atitecos
Australians
Azande (Tribe)
Azoreans
Aztec (People)
Bahemba People
Bantu Peoples
Banyankole
Bedouins
Belgians
Blackfeet (Tribe)
Blackfoot (Tribe)
Blackfoot Confederacy
Blood (Nation)
Bororo Indians
British
Burmese Americans
Caboclo (People)
Cahuilla (Tribe)
Cajuns
Canadians
Canoncito Navajos
Cape Verdeans
Caribbean Americans
Caribbean Islanders
Catalans
Catawba (Tribe)
Cayuga (Tribe)
Cayuse (Tribe)
Celts
Chaggas
Chaldean Americans
Chaldeans
Chamorros
Chemehuevi (Tribe)
Cheyenne (Tribe)
Chicanas
Chicanos
Chickasaw (Tribe)
Chileans
Chimariko (Tribe)
Chinese Canadians
Chinese People
Chinese Speaking
Chinook (Tribe)
Chipewyan (Tribe)
Chippewa Cree (Tribe)
Chitimacha (Tribe)
Chumash (Tribe)
Clans
Coast Salish (Tribe)
Coeur d Alene (Tribe)
Colombian Americans
Colombians
Colorado River Indian Tribe
Comanche (Tribe)
Confederated Salish and Kootenai Tribes
Congos of Panama
Corn Culture
Coushatta (Tribe)
Creek (Tribe)
Croatian Americans
Croats
Crow (Tribe)
Cuiva (Tribe)
Cuna (Tribe)
Czech Americans
Czechoslovakians
Dani (Tribe)
Danish Americans
Delaware (Tribe)
Dene (Nation)
Dogrib (Tribe)
Doukhobors
Dutch Speaking
East Indians
Eastern Jews
Efe People
Egyptians
English Americans
English Canadians
English Speaking
Estonian Americans
Ethiopians
Euro Americans
Europeans
Fijians
Filipinos
Finnish Americans
Finnish Speaking
Finns
Five Civilized Tribes
Flathead (Tribe)
Four Bands Reservation of Hobbema
Fox (Tribe)
Franco Americans
French People
French Speaking
Fulbe
General Conference Mennonites
German Americans
German Canadians
German Russians
Germans
Goshute (Tribe)
Greek Australians
Greek Speaking
Greeks
Gusii
Gypsies
Haida (Tribe)
Han (Chinese People)
Hare (Tribe)
Havasupai (Tribe)
Hidatsa (Tribe)
Hindi Speaking
Holdeman Mennonites
Houma (Tribe)
Hualapai (Tribe)
Huguenots
Hungarian Americans
Hungarians
Hupa (Tribe)
Huron (Tribe)
Hutterites
Ibans
Ibo (Tribe)
Igorots
Inca (Tribe)
Indonesian Americans
Indonesians
Inupiaq (Tribe)
Inupiat (Tribe)
Iowa (Tribe)
Iranian Americans
Iranians
Iraqis
Irish Americans
Irish People
Iroquois (Nation)
Iroquois (Tribe)
Israeli Arabs
Israelis
Issei
Italian Australians
Italian Canadians
Italian Speaking
Italians
Jamaicans
Japanese People
Japanese Speaking
Jemez Pueblo (Tribe)
Jesus People
Jicarilla Apache (Tribe)
Jivaro (Tribe)
Jordanian Arabs
Kalapuya (Tribe)
Kaliai
Kalispel (Tribe)
Kaluli People
Karuk (Tribe)
Kashaya Pomo (Tribe)
Kekchis
Keres Pueblo (Tribe)
Kickapoo (Tribe)
Kikuyu People
Kiowa (Tribe)
Kiowa Apache (Tribe)
Klallam (Tribe)
Klamath (Tribe)
Koori People
Kootenai (Tribe)
Koreans
Kuba
Kung Bushmen
Kurds
Kutchin (Tribe)
Kwakiutl (Tribe)
La Raza
Laguna (Pueblo)
Lapps
Latinas
Latinos
Latvian Americans
Lebanese
Lenape (Tribe)
Lithuanian Americans
Lithuanians
Logoli
Loucheux (Tribe)
Lubicon Lake Indian Band
Lugand (Tribe)
Lumbee (Tribe)
Lummi (Tribe)
Macedorumanians
Makah (Tribe)
Makonde (Tribe)
Malayan Americans
Malayans
Malaysians
Maliseet (Tribe)
Maltese Australians
Mandan (Tribe)
Maori (People)
Maricopa (Tribe)
Mariel Cubans
Mashpee (Tribe)
Maya (People)
Mende (Tribe)
Mennonites
Menominee (Tribe)
Mescalero Apache (Tribe)
Mesopotamians
Mesquakie (Tribe)
Mestizos (People)
Miami (Tribe)
Miccosukee (Tribe)
Micmac (Tribe)
Micronesians
Mien People
Mimbres Indians
Missouri (Tribe)
Miwok (Tribe)
Mixtecan (Tribe)
Mohawk (Tribe)
Mojave (Tribe)
Montagnais (Tribe)
Moravians
Moroccans
Mossi People
Mulattoes
Muskhogee (Tribe)
Narragansett (Tribe)
Naskapi (Tribe)
Native Americans
Netsilik (Tribe)
New Canadians
Nez Perce (Tribe)
Nicaraguans
Nigerians
Nisqually (Tribe)
Normans
North Africans
North American Plains Indians (Anthrop Label)
Northern Cheyenne (Tribe)
Northern Paiute (Tribe)
Northern Puget Sound Indians
Northwest Coast Indians
Norwegian Speaking
Norwegians
Nuyoricans
Ob Ugrians
Odawa (Tribe)
Okinawans
Oksapmin
Olmec (People)
Omaha (Tribe)
Oneida (Tribe)
Onondaga (Tribe)
Oriental Culture
Oriental Jews
Orthodox Jews
Osage (Tribe)
Otoe (Tribe)
Ottawa (Tribe)
Pachucos
Pacific Islanders
Pacific Northwest Tribes
Paiute (Tribe)
Pakehas (People)
Pakistanis
Palestinian Arabs
Palestinians
Papago (Tribe)
Papuans
Passamaquoddy (Tribe)
Pawnee (Tribe)
Peigan (Nation)
Pend d Oreilles (Tribe)
Pennsylvania Germans
Penobscot (Tribe)
Picuris
Pilipinos
Pima (Tribe)
Pima Maricopa (Tribe)
Plains Indians (Anthropological Label)
Plateau Tonga
Polish People
Polynesians
Ponca (Tribe)
Poospatuck (Tribe)
Portuguese People
Potawatomi (Tribe)
Powhatan Indians
Punjabis
Quechan (Tribe)
Quechua People
Quinault (Tribe)
Ramah Navajos
Ramapo (Tribe)
Renape (Tribe)
Roma
Romanians
Russian Americans
Russian Jews
Russian Speaking
Russians
Sacs (Tribe)
Salish (Tribe)
Salvadoreans
Samish (Tribe)
Samoans
San Carlos Apache (Tribe)
Santee Sioux (Tribe)
Saulteaux (Tribe)
Saxons
Scandinavians
Scotch Irish Americans
Scottish Americans
Seminole (Tribe)
Seneca (Tribe)
Sephardic Jews
Serbian Americans
Serbs
Shasta (Tribe)
Shawnee (Tribe)
Shinnecock (Tribe)
Shivwits
Shoowa
Shoshone (Tribe)
Shoshone Bannock (Tribe)
Shoshoni (Tribe)
Shuswap (Tribe)
Sikhs
Siletz (Tribe)
Sisseton Wahpeton Sioux (Tribe)
Skokomish (Tribe)
Skolt Lapps
Slavic Canadians

Slavs
Slovene Americans
Slovenes
South Africans
South American Natives
Southeast Asians
Southern Paiute (Tribe)
Southern Plains Indians (Anthropological Label)
Spaniards
Spanish Surnamed
Spokane (Tribe)
Squamish (Tribe)
Stockbridge Munzees (Tribe)
Sumerians
Suquamish (Tribe)
Swazi People
Swedish Americans
Swinomish (Tribe)
Tarahumara (Tribe)
Tenejapa (Tribe)
Tewa Pueblo
Thai People
Timucua (Tribe)
Tlingit (Tribe)
Tolowa (Tribe)
Tongan Americans
Tribal Councils
Tsetsauts (Tribe)
Tsimshian (Tribe)
Tunica (Tribe)
Tunisians
Turks
Tuscarora (Tribe)
Tutsi
Ukiah (Tribe)
Ukrainian Americans
Ukrainian Canadians
Umatilla (Tribe)
Ute (Tribe)
Venezuelans
Wabanaki Confederacy
Wampanoag (Tribe)
Wapanakamikok (Tribe)
Warao (Tribe)
Wasco Wishrams
Washo (Tribe)
Washoe (Tribe)
West Africans
West Indians
Western Shoshone (Tribe)
White Mountain Apache (Tribe)
Wichita (Tribe)
Winnebago (Tribe)
Wolof (Tribe)
Yakima (Nation)
Yanomamo (Tribe)
Yao (Tribe)
Yaqui (Tribe)
Yavapai (Tribe)
Yellowknife (Tribe)
Yemenites
Yiddish Speaking
Yokut (Tribe)
Yoruba (Tribe)
Yuma (Tribe)
Yuman (Tribe)
Yupik Eskimos
Yurok (Tribe)
Zambians
Zapotec (Tribe)
Zaramo (Tribe)

CATEGORY 09: Groups (Occupations)

Academic Planning Officers
Academic Professions
Accident Investigation Technicians
Accompanists
Account Executives
Accounts Receivable Clerks
Activity Coordinators (Long Term Care)
Addiction Specialists
Administrative Assistants
Adult Learning Specialists
Advertising Occupations
Aerographers Mates
Agricultural Specialists
Air Transportation Agents
Airborne Radio Code Operators
Airborne Soldiers
Aircraft Assembly Occupations
Aircraft Dispatchers
Aircrew Survival Equipment Personnel
Airframe Technicians
Airplane Flight Attendants
Alterationists
Alternative Careers
Announcers
Applied Science Occupations
Aquacultural Technicians
Archivists
Armor Crew Personnel
Art Librarians
Art Therapists
Artificial Breeding Technicians
Asparagus Sorters
Assemblers
Assemblers (Dental Equipment)
Assemblers (Dry Cell Battery)
Assistant Professors
Astronauts
Athletic Administrators
Athletic Directors
Athletic Trainers
Atomic Energy Occupations
Auctioneers
Audit Clerks
Auditors
Autoclave Operators
Automobile Painters
Automobile Workers
Automotive Service Advisors
Automotive Trade Association Managers
Aviation Data Analysts
Aviation Occupations
Babysitters
Bag Sealers
Baggers
Bakers
Bakery Products Route Personnel
Balling Machine Operators
Bank Tellers
Bartenders
Baser (Electrical Equipment)
Battery Loader
Beauty Shop Managers
Beekeeping
Bench Carpenters
Bibliographers
Bill Collectors
Bindery Workers
Biologists
Blacksmiths
Boarding Machine Operators
Boatswain Mates
Boilermakers
Book Dealers
Bookkeeping Machine Operators
Booksellers
Braiding Machine Operators
Breath Examiner Specialist Instructors
Bridge Inspectors
Broadcast Announcers
Building Construction Technicians
Building Consultants
Building Inspectors
Building Maintenance Personnel
Building Managers
Burlers (Textile)
Business Careers
Business Communication Teachers
Business Executives
Business Librarians
Business Partnerships
Buyers
Cable Assemblers
Cable Makers
Cacao Farmers
Cafeteria Monitors
Cake Finishers
Campaign Managers
Candy Packers
Candy Wrapping Machine Operators
Cannery Mechanics
Cannery Workers
Capacitor Winders
Carding Machine Operators
Cardiopulmonary Technicians
Career Education Directors
Career Technicians
Cartographic Technicians
Case Coverers
Cashiers
Catalogers
Caterers
CATV Operators
Cement Masons
Cement Sealers
Census Takers
Central Office Administrators
Central Office Repairers
Cereal Packers
Certified Financial Planners
Certified Professional Secretaries
Certified Staff
Char Workers
Checkers (Occupation)
Cheese Wrappers and Packers
Chemical Operators
Chemists
Chief Executive Officers
Chief Financial Officers
Chief Information Officers
Chief Planning Officers
Chief Storekeepers
Chief Student Affairs Officers
Child Life Specialists
Child Mental Health Specialists
Chinese Literati
Chiropractors
Cinematographers
City Managers
Civil Service
Civilian Personnel
Classicists
Classified Staff
Clinical Laboratory Occupations
Clinical Medical Librarians
Clinical Preceptors
Clothing Related Occupations
Clowns
Cocoa Farmers
Code Enforcement Personnel
Coil Assemblers
Coil Opener and Down Ender Operators
Coil Winders
Coin Machine Collectors
Cold Mill Operators
Cold Saw Operators
Cold Sizing Mill Operators
College Vice Presidents
Commercial Drivers
Communication Consultants
Communications Equipment Assemblers
Communications Occupations
Community Aides
Community College Teachers
Community Counselors
Community Development Personnel
Community Development Specialists
Community Health Representatives
Community Outreach Specialists
Compositors (Printing and Publishing)
Comptometer Operators
Computer Coordinators
Computer Manufacturers
Computer Occupations
Computer Related Occupations
Computer Service Occupations
Computer Supervisors
Computer Technicians
Condenser Winders
Conference Moderators
Construction Equipment Mechanics
Container Cappers
Container Fillers
Container Makers
Continuing Education Programmers
Continuing Engineering Education Directors
Contract Officers
Contractors (Construction Industry)
Conveyor Loaders
Conveyor Operators
Cooling Conveyor Operators
Copper Miners
Core Plane Wirers
Corn Cutting Machine Operators
Corn Husking Machine Operators
Coroners
Correctional Officers
Corrugator Operators
Counselor Aides
Counselor Coordinators
Counselor Supervisors
Counter Attendants
Court Interpreters
Court Managers
Covering Machine Operators
Cowboys
Credit Clerks
Credit Collection Agents
Credit Investigation Agents
Criminal Justice Workers
Crisis Teachers
Critics
Crusher Inspectors
Curators
Curriculum Directors
Curriculum Specialists
Custodians
Customer Engineering Specialists
Dairy Products Route Personnel
Death Related Occupations
Debate Coaches
Decambering Mill Operators
Defense Workers
Dental Nursing
Dental Therapy Assistants
Detailers
Development Officers
Development Officers (College)
Diamond Cutters
Die Casting Machine Operators
Dining Room Attendants
Diocesan Directors of Religious Education
Directors (Theater)
Directors of Religious Education
Disk Jockeys
Dispatchers
Diversified Occupations
Docents
Documentalists
Drapery Makers
Drill Sergeants
Driver Improvement Analysts
Driver License Examiner Supervisors
Drivers
Dual Function Librarians
Educateurs
Education Specialists
Educational Coordinators
Educational Information Consultants
Educational Program Auditing
Educational Technologists
Educators
Egg Candlers
Electrical Accessories Assemblers
Electronics Assemblers
Eligibility Workers
Embalmers
Emergency Medical Coordinators
Energy Coordinators
English Teachers
Envelope Machine Operators
Environmental Design Professions
Environmental Occupations
Environmental Professionals
Environmental Psychologists
Experimental Assemblers
Exterminators
Extruder Operators
Fabric Services
Facilitators (Personnel Development)
Family Day Care Providers
Family Service Workers
Fancy Stitchers
Fashion Models
Federal Employees
Federal Forecasters
Federal Quality Control Reviewers
Feldshers
Fettler
Field Agents
Field Program Associates
Filling Machine Operators
Film Directors
Film Stars
Financial Assistance Workers
Fire Chiefs
Fire Extinguisher Maintenance Specialists
Fire Prevention Officers
Firesetters
Fireworks Assemblers
Fish and Game Wardens
Fish Cutters
Fishers
Fishing Rod Assemblers
Fitness Specialists
Flight Engineers
Flight Navigators
Floral Designers
Florists
Folklorists
Food Tabulators
Foreign Area Specialists
Foreign Car Mechanics
Foreign Correspondents
Foreign Language Careers
Foreign News Correspondents
Forensic Directors
Fork Lift Truck Operators
Forming Press Operators
Foundry Occupations
Fountain Servers
Fruit Packers
Fruit Pickers

Fruit Sorters
Funeral Directors
Garden Center Employees
Garment Inspectors
Garment Loopers
Garment Packers
Gas Station Attendants
Gas Technicians
Gasoline Engine Assemblers
Gastroenterology Assistants
Gem Cutters (Jewelry)
General Practitioners
Genito Urinary Technicians
Geriatric Workers
Glass Blowers
Glass Cutters
Glass Inspectors
Glass Packers
Glove Sewers
Gluing Machine Operators
Governesses
Graduate Research Assistants
Grid Operators
Grocery Checkers
Guidance Associates
Gunners Mates
Gunsmithing
Hand Finishers
Hand Labelers
Hand Sewers
Hazardous Materials Technicians
Hazardous Occupations
Head Librarians
Head Teachers
Headmasters
Health Aides
Health Care Teams
Health Educators
Hearing Officers
Heater Operators
Heating Mechanics
Heavy Equipment Mechanics
Heavy Equipment Operators
High Performance Work Organizations
Highway Surveying
Hispanic American Teachers
Historians
Home Economics Related Occupations
Home Economists
Home Economists Assistants
Hose Makers (Rubber Goods)
Hosiery Workers
Hospital Education Directors
Hosts Hostesses
Hot Mill Operators
Human Resource Specialists
Human Resources Professionals
Human Services Educators
Human Services Professionals
Illustrators
Income Groups
Independent Bargaining Agents
Indexers
Individual Ready Reservists
Industrial Information Officers
Industrial Marketing
Industrial Production Occupations
Industrial Technologists
Industrial Trainers
Industrial Training Boards
Industry Education Councils
Information Consultants
Injection Molding Machine Tenders
Insects Production Workers
Inserters
Inspectors
Instructional Design Professionals
Instrument Assemblers
Instrument Makers
Instrument Mechanics
Instrument Repairers
Insulating Machine Operators
Insulation Blanket Makers
Insulation Workers
Insurance Adjusters
Insurance Agents
Intermodal Transportation Careers
Internal Combustion Engine Assemblers
Interpersonal Attraction Researchers
Interviewers
Inventory Management Specialists
Ironworkers
Jewelry Making Occupations
Job Agents
Job Clubs
Job Coaches
Journalists
Junior Counselors
Junior Faculty
Keypunch Operators
Kitchen Helpers
Laboratory Paraprofessionals
Law Clerks
Lead Teachers
Lecturers
Leisure Services
Lenders (Finance)
Letter Opening Operators
Liaison Administrators
Liaison Teacher Counselors
Library Consultants
Library Directors
Licensed Professional Engineer
Lifeguards
Light Bulb Assemblers
Lighting Designers
Line Attendants
Line Repairers
Linguists
Linotype Operators
Lithographers
Lobbyists
Local Development Officers
Locksmiths
Log Scalers
Longshore Industry
Low Vision Assistants
Luggage Makers
Lunchroom Aides
Machine Operators
Mail Processing Equipment Maintenance Personnel
Mail Room Occupations
Mail Sorters
Male Faculty
Manicuring
Manufacturers Service Representatives
Marine Occupations
Master Technicians
Masters at Arms
Materials Expediters
Mathematics Supervisors
Matriculation Aides
Meat Cutters
Medical Aides
Medical Corps Personnel
Medical Illustration (Occupation)
Medical Imaging Occupations
Medical Specialty Boards
Medical Supplies Assemblers
Medical Transcribers
Medication Aides
Medication Technicians
Merchandise Packers
Metal Chair Assemblers
Micrologic Assemblers
Microwave Demonstrators
Microwave Tube Assemblers
Midwives
Military Maneuver Arms Units
Military Occupations
Millwrights
Miners
Model Makers
Module Assemblers (Electronics)
Molded Rubber Goods Cutters
Movers
Museum Educators
Museum Registrars
Mushroom Inspectors
Music Critics
Nannies
Negotiators
Neuroeducators
New Faculty
New Teachers
News Commentators
News Directors
News Producers
Nonacademic Careers
Noncommissioned Officers
Nondegreed Teachers
Noninstructional Staff
Notary Publics
Nuclear Reactor Operators
Nurse Associates
Nurse Clinicians
Nurse Educators
Nurse Midwives
Nursing Directors
Nut Sorters
Occupational Analysts
Occupational Specialists
Office Landscaping
Office Machine Servicers
Officers (Social Development)
Onion Corers
Operations Consultants
Optical Technicians
Opticalmen
Opticians
Optometric Assistants
Optometric Technicians
Order Fillers
Organizational Specialists
Ornamental Iron Workers
Orthotic Technicians
Outboard Motor Assemblers
Outdoor Safety Committees
Packaging Machine Mechanics
Packers
Pairing Machine Operators
Pantographers
Paper and Pulp Occupations
Parent Coordinators
Parent Involvement Coordinators
Park Naturalists
Park Rangers
Parliamentarians
Partnerships in Library Services
Parts Storekeepers
Pasters
Patient Care Assistants
Patient Representatives
Payoff Operators
Payroll Clerks
Pediatric Nurses
Pediatricians
Performer Writers
Personal Services Occupations
Pharmacy Technicians
Photo Optics Instrumentation Technicians
Photograph Finishers
Physiatrists
Physical Plant Administrators
Pianists
Pink Collar Occupations
Pinsetter Mechanics
Pipe Fitters
Pipe Workers
Planners
Plant Process Operators
Plasterers
Playwrights
Plumbers
Podiatrists
Political Aides
Political Cartoonists
Political Consultants
Politicians
Porters
Postal Workers
Pottery Workers
Power Lawn Mower Assemblers
Power Line Technicians
Power Plant Operators
Preceptors
Precision Measuring Equipment Specialists
Press Secretaries
Primary Physicians
Printing and Publishing Occupations
Private Investigators
Private Police
Process Consultants
Procurement Personnel
Production Mechanics
Professions
Program Directors (Broadcast)
Program Specialists
Project Planners
Proofreaders
Properties Managers (Theater)
Property Appraisers
Prosthetic Technicians
Provosts
Psychiatric Social Workers
Public Artists
Public Employment Relations Boards
Public Information Officers
Purchasing Agents
Radar Intercept Observers
Radiation Monitors
Radio Operators
Radio Receiver Assemblers
Railroad Brakers
Railroad Conductors
Real Estate Inspectors
Receive Site Facilitators
Receiving Clerks
Record Press Tenders
Recreation Aides
Recreation Occupations
Recreation Workers
Refinery Operators
Regional Directors of Education
Rehabilitation Aides
Rehabilitation Counselors
Residential Electricians
Restaurant Managers
Retail Food Managers
Reviewers
Rewinder Operators
Room Clerks
Rotary Driller Helpers
Rural Planning Specialists
Safety Directors
Salad Makers
Sanitarians
Sanitation Management
Sawmill Workers
School Based Teacher Educators
School District Lawyers
School District Personnel
School Plant Managers
School Treasurers
Screenwriters
Sea Farming
Senior Executive Service
Service Providers
Sewing Machine Repairers
Sheep Specialists
Shell Fishing
Shipbuilders
Shipfitters
Shoe and Boot Occupations
Shoemakers
Shop Stewards
Shopkeepers
Short Order Cooks
Signalers
Silversmithing
Smokejumpers
Social Studies Teachers
Social Work Aides
Sociologists
Soil Conservation District Aides
Solderers
Solid Propellant Processors (Chemical Industry)
Sonar Operators
Sound Technicians
Special Agricultural Workers
Special Education Directors
Special Education Placement Teams
Sports Officials
Stampers
State Legislators
State Liaison Representatives
Statisticians
Steam Power Plant Operators
Stock Clerks
Stockbrokers
Store Managers
Store Workers
Structural Steel Workers
Student Activity Directors
Student Camp Counselors
Student Clinicians
Student Library Assistants
Student Reporters
Subscription Agents
Substance Abuse Specialists in Higher Education
Substation Operators
Superintendents of Buildings and Grounds
Supply Occupations
Support Personnel
Surgeons
Surgical Supplies Assemblers
Surveying (Construction)
Surveyors
SWAT Teams
Switchboard Operators
Talk Show Hosts
Taxicab Drivers
Tea Bag Machine Tenders
Tea Bag Packers
Teacher Advisors
Teacher Consultants
Teacher Counselors
Teacher Evaluators
Teacher Librarians
Teacher Specialists
Teachers of the Deaf
Teaching Principals
Technologists
Technology Coordinators
Telephone Ad Takers

Telephone Mechanics
Telephone Operators
Television Announcers
Television News Photographers
Tenant Resource Coordinators
Test Developers
Test Directors
Test Publishers
Textile Occupations
Theater Management
Threaders (Electronics)
Ticket Agents
Tile Occupations
Tobacco Processing Occupations
Tobacco Producers
Tomato Peelers
Toy Demonstrators
Tractor Trailer Drivers
Traffic Engineering Technicians
Training Officers
Training Related Jobs
Training Sponsors
Transposer
Travel Agents
Trimmers
Truck Drivers
Truck Farming
Twister Tenders
Underwriters (Insurance)
Universal Tellers
Upholsterers
Urban Planners
Vending Stand Operators
Venetian Blind Assemblers
Vice Presidents of Academic Affairs
Visual Media Technicians
Vocational Education Curriculum Specialists
Vocational Rehabilitation Specialists
Vocational Resource Educators
Vocational Specialists
Volunteer Army
War Correspondents
Wardens
Waste Water Treatment Plant Personnel
Weavers
Weaving
Weighing Station Operators
Welfare Librarianship
Wellness Professionals
Wet Nurses
Women College Presidents
Women Journalists
Wrestlers
Writing Coaches
Writing Consultants
Yeomen
Youth Ministers
Zoning Inspectors

CATEGORY 10: Groups (Other)

Abandoned Children
Academic Affairs Committees
Academic Community
Academic Discourse Communities
Academicians
Active Alert Children
Active Readers
Ad Hoc Groups
Adjudicated Youth
Adjustment Center Management Teams
Adult Children of Alcoholics
Adult New Readers
Adult Service Clubs
Adults Molested as Children
Advertising Industry
Advisers
Agricultural Economics Majors
Albinos
Amana Colonies
American Indian Students
American Indian Task Forces
Antifederalists
Artificial Insemination Donors
Asian American Students
Asian Students
Balance of State Program Contractors
Band Directors
Baptists
Barbarians
Barefoot Doctors
Base Christian Communities
Basic Medical Specialists
Basic Writers
Battered Men
Bedridden Patients
Beginning Administrators
Beginning Principals
Beginning Superintendents
Bilingual Workers
Biracial Children
Biracial Family
Black Congressmen
Black Writers
Blended Families
Booster Clubs
Born Again Christians
Bridge Players
Buberian Learning Groups
Buzz Groups
Cabin Leaders
Campesinos
Campus Community Organizers
Career Guidance Teams
Catholic Bishops
Celebrities
Charitable Remainder Trusts
Child Molesters
Child Prodigies
Child Study Teams
Childbirth Coaches
Children of Alcoholics
Children of Substance Abusers
Chinese Communist Party
Chinese Nationalists
Chiropractic Profession
Christian Democratic Party
Church Members
Circuit Riders
Circuses
Citizens Groups
Classroom Visitors
Cliques
Coached Clients
Coalcoholics
Coalitions
Collaborative Councils
Collateral Informants
College Educated
Collegial Support Groups
Collegial Teams
Communication Directors
Community Action Agencies
Community Boards
Community Councils
Commuting Workers
Computer Clubs
Computer Hackers
Computer Users
Confidential Employees
Conscientious Objectors
Conservationists
Consumers
Contractors
Convalescents
Coordinating Councils
Cornucopians
Corporate Families
Corporate Users
Coworkers
Crack Babies
Cross Sex Peers
Cults
Culturally Different Students
Curriculum Councils
Curriculum Leaders
Deacons
Deaf Community
Debtors
Declassified Students
Declining Communities
Defendants
Delinquent Handicapped
Development Committees
Developmental Disabilities Councils
Developmental Students
Disabled Parents
Disabled Students as Tutors
Disabled Teachers
Discharged Patients
Discourse Communities
Disliked Children
Dormitory Aides
Drill Teams
Drug Exposed Children
Eastern Orthodox Church
Editorial Boards
Education and Work Councils
Educational Interest Groups
Educational Planning Committees
Electoral College
Electorate
Emeritus Professors
Emigrants
Employed Uninsured
Employees with Disabilities
Encounter Groups
Enemies
English Majors
English Study Societies
Entertainers
Evaluation Teams
Evangelical Christians
Exceptionally Gifted
Executive Committees
Exiting Students
Expatriate Executives
Expectant Mothers
Experienced Teachers
Experienced Writers
Expert Witness
Experts
Explorers
External Students (Australia)
Extremely Gifted
Facilitators
Faculty Student Committees
Fairness Committees
Family Clusters
Family Development Parenting Groups
Farm Population
Father Present Family
Federal Contractors
Federalists
Fertility Cults
Financial Aid Recipients
First Generation Students
First Ladies (State)
Focus Groups
Foreign Born
Foreign Language Majors
Foreign Visitors
Former Teachers
Formerly Married
Freshman Interest Groups
Friends of the Library
Future Generations
Gangs
Generalists
Generation X
Geometric Family
Government Contractors
Grammarians
Grant Recipients
Great Grandparents
Group Leaders
Guest Speakers
Guest Workers
Handicapped Delinquents
Heads of State
Health Systems Agencies
Heroes
Heroines
High School Juniors
High School Sophomores
Highly Gifted
Hip Hop Generation
Hippies
Hispanic American Students
Hispanic American Youth
Home Visitors
Homosexual Parents
Homosexual Teachers
Hospital Ethics Committees
Host Families
Huddle Groups
Human Services Brokers
Humanists
Idiot Savants
In School Youth
Incarcerated Youth
Independent Scholars
Indian Education Committees
Individual Transition Teams
Industry Review Panels
Ineffective Subordinates
Inexperienced Writers
Informants
Information Providers
Information Sector
Information System Users
Innovators
Intellectuals
Interdisciplinary Health Teams
Interest Groups
Intergenerational Households
Intermediaries
International Visitors
Interracial Children
Interracial Family
Intervention Assistance Teams
Inventors
Involuntary Minorities
Islam
Jesuits
Keynote Speakers
Krishna Religious Sect
Ku Klux Klan
Language Minorities
Language Skilled People
Large Families
Last Born
Late Entry Students
Latency Age Children
Lateral Transfer Students
Lay Readers
Learning Groups
Learning Initiative Teams
Learning Organizations
Library Committees
Library Support Groups
Lifelong Readers
Limited English Writers
Listserv Discussion Groups
Literary Societies
Literature Circles
Local Action Teams
Local Advisory Councils
Local Arts Councils
Local Facilitators
Local Literacies
Local School Councils
Long Term Residents
Lost Persons
Lower Track Students
Lutheran Church
Management Assistance Teams
Management Bargaining Teams
Managerial Class
Marathon Groups
Marginal Students
Marginal Teachers
Mathematically and Scientifically Precocious Youth
Mathematically Gifted
Mathematics Clubs
Medically Fragile
Medicine Men
Men Faculty
Mentally Retarded Parents
Middle Born
Middle Children
Middle School Students
Middle Track Students
Middleman Minority Groups
Military Dependents
Military Reserves
Missionaries
Mixed Age Dyads
Mixed Exceptionality Classes
Mixed Race Persons
Mixed Sex Dyads
Model Minority Groups
Modulators (Individuals)
Monolingual Students
Moral Majority
Mormons
Multidisciplinary Teams
Multiple Birth Family
Multiple Caregivers
Multiple Transfer Students
Music Composers
Music Ensembles
Muslims
Mutual Assistance Associations
Mutual Help Groups
National Merit Scholars
Natural Helpers
Neighbors
New Christian Right
New Parents
New Right
Newcomers
News Councils
Nobel Laureates
Nominating Committees
Non Catholic Students
Nonacademic Personnel
Noncustodial Parents
Nondegree Students
Nonfarm Population
Nonimmigrant Aliens
Nonmigrants
Nonnative Speakers
Nonreferral Unions
Nonresidents
Nonrespondents

Nonsmokers
Nonstudents
Nontransfer Students
Nonwage Labor
Normal Children
Nursing Students
Off Campus Students
Oil Cartels
Older Workers
Olympic Swimmers
Online User Groups
Only Child Family
Only Children
Opinion Leaders
Optouts
Orators
Organizational Mavericks
Orphans
Outdoor Recreationists
Outstanding Teachers
Overage Students
Papal Volunteers
Parent Advisory Committees
Parent Advisory Councils
Parent Committees
Parent Study Groups
Parks and Recreation Professionals
Parolees
Partnerships in Human Services
Pastoral Councils
Patriarchal Societies
Patrons
Pay Boards
Peasants
Pediatric Cancer Patients
Peer Facilitators
Peer Review Organizations
Peer Support Groups
Pen Pals
Percussion Ensembles
Philanthropists
Philosophers
Physical Education Majors
Pilgrims
Pirates
Planning Boards
Play Leaders
Policymakers
Political Action Committees
Practitioners
Pre Veterinary Students
Precocious Learners
Precocious Readers
Pregnant Teachers
Preliterate Societies
Preservice Teachers
Presidential Scholars
Press Conferences
Press Councils
Press Pools
Pressure Groups
Primary Caregivers
Prime Sponsors
Prisoners of War
Private Industry Councils
Problem Solving Teams
Process Groups
Professional Community
Program Completers
Proteges
Psychiatric Inpatients
Psychiatric Outpatients
Psychological Parents
Public Interest Research Groups
Quadruplets
Quakers
Rabbis
Reading Groups
Red Guards
Referees
Reflective Children
Religious Cults
Religious Denominations
Reluctant Learners
Reluctant Readers
Research Teams
Resettled Migrants
Retired Persons
Reverse Transfer Students
Review Panels
Roommates
Rural Assistance Councils
Saints
Same Age Dyads
Same Sex Peers
Satellite Students
School Age Criminals
School Age Parents
School Attendance Review Boards
School Based Support Teams
School Boards Associations
School Councils
School Desegregation Monitors
School Improvement Councils
School Improvement Teams
School Leadership Teams
School Outliers
School Safety Patrols
School Special Service Teams
Science Majors
Scoutmasters
Second Born
Sex Equity Coordinators
Sex Offenders
Shakers
Shared Parenting Family
Shared Personnel
Shared Students
Sibling Caregivers
Signers of the United States Constitution
Single Adults
Single by Choice Mothers
Single Earner Family
Single Females
Single Parents
Single Persons
Small Planning Units
Small Presses (Publishers)
Social Partners (European Community)
Social Services Teams
Social Work Educators
Sojourners
Sophists
Southern Baptists
Special Interest Groups
Special Needs Children
Special Needs Groups
Special Needs Individuals
Spin Doctors
Sponsors
Sports Clubs
Staff Support Teams
Stakeholders
State Councils on Vocational Education
State Job Training Coordinating Councils
Status Offenders
Stockholders
Structured Learning Groups
Student Assistants
Student Athletes
Student Placement Teams
Student Support Teams
Student Teams
Study Circles
Study Groups
Subgroups
Subject Specialists
Subordinates (Employees)
Subscribers (Cable Television)
Subscribers (Magazines)
Subscribers (Newspapers)
Suicide Survivors
Surrogate Families
Surrogate Parents
Surrogate Pitchers
Surrogate Speakers
Survivors
Survivors of Nazi Persecution
Target Populations
Teacher Assistance Teams
Teacher Candidates
Teacher Leaders
Teacher Researchers
Teacher Support Groups
Teacher Writers
Technologically Advanced Families
Technologically Dependent
Tenants
Teratogens
Testing Industry
Theology Students
Think Tanks
Throwaway Children
Tilted Family
Torture Victims
Tournament Hosts
Traditional Birth Attendants
Traditionally Underserved Persons
Transfer Officers
Transients
Tribal Officials
Triplets
Unaccompanied Minors
Uncertified Teachers
Undecided Students
Undocumented Students
United States Overseas Students
Unmarried Parents
Unwanted Children
Upper Middle Class
User Groups
Valedictorians
Vice Presidents of the United States
Victims of Natural Disasters
Victims of War
Vigilantes
Vikings
Visiting Scholars
Visitors
Voters
War Dissenters
Warrant Officers
Welfare Rights Groups
Welfare Societies
Wind Ensembles
Wire Services
Witnesses
Witnesses to Crime
Work Education Councils
Workers Councils
Working Poor
Workparties
Writing Groups
Young Authors
Youth Action Teams
Youth Corps

CATEGORY 11: Health-Related (Including Psychology)

9p Trisomy
Abdomen
Ability Attributes
Absorption (Psychology)
Abstinence
Abuse (of Disabled)
Academic Misconduct
Academic Orientation
Academic Pressure
Academic Self Concept
Academic Stress
Acceptance
Access to Health Care
Achondrogenesis
Acidosis
Acoupedics
Acoustic Neuroma
Acquainting Process
Action Development
Actor Observer Divergence
Acupressure
Acupuncture
Acute Care
Adaptive Expertise
Addictive Behavior
Adenosine Deaminase Enzyme Deficiency
Adjunctive Psychiatric Therapy
Administrative Stress
Admission Statutes (Hospitalization)
Adolescent Suicide
Adrenal Hyperplasia
Adrenocortical Stress Reactivity
Adult Child Relationship
Adult Developmental Decline
Advance Directives
Advice Seeking
Aerospace Medicine
Affectionate Behavior
Affective Cognitive Consistency
Affective Disorders
Affective Response
Affiliative Behavior
Affinity Seeking Strategies
Agamic Psychology
Agility
Agitated Behavior
Agnosia
Agonistic Behavior
Agoraphobia
Alar Controversy
Albrights Dystrophy
Alcohol Nomograms
Alcohol Related Birth Defects
Alcohol Warning Posters
Alcohol Wellness
Alertness
Aliteracy
Alkalosis
Allo Centered Psychotherapy
Allopathic Medicine
Alpha Behavior (Piaget)
Alpha Feedback Training
Alpha Training
Alternative Community Living Arrangements
Ambivalence (Psychology)
Amblyopia
Ambulatory Health Care
Amenorrhea
Amnesia
Amniocentesis
Amphetamine
Amphetamines
Amylase
Anaerobic Digestion
Anaerobic Power
Analytic Ability
Analytic Interactive Style
Anaphylactic Shock
Androgenic Hormones
Anencephaly
Ankle Strength
Ankyloglossia
Anomia
Anonymous Attribution
Anorexia
Antacids
Anthropocentrism
Anthropometry
Antibodies
Antibody Responses
Anticipation
Anticipatory Guidance
Anticipatory Images
Anticipatory Learning
Antidepressants
Antigen
Antineoplastic Drugs
Apert Syndrome
Aplasia (Red Cell)
Apnea
Apolipoproteins
Apothecaries Measures
Applied Developmental Psychology
Approach Avoidance Conflict
Approval Needs
Aptitude Improvement
Arachnophobia
Argumentativeness
Arm Movements
Arm Positioning
Arm Swing
Arms (Anatomy)
Arrhythmicity
Arsenic Poisoning
Arthritis
Artificial Insemination
Artificial Mastoid
Asepsis
Aspartylglucosaminuria
Aspergers Syndrome
Asphyxia
Aspirin
Assertion
Assertion Structured Therapy
Assertive Discipline
Association Strength
Associative Fluency
Attachment Disorders
Attention Diversion
Attitude Discrepant Behavior
Attitude Strength
Attitudinal Reinforcing Discriminative Stimuli
Attributional Feedback
Atypicality
Audio Cuing
Audioanalgesia
Auditory Acuity
Auditory Closure
Auditory Conceptualization
Auditory Figure Ground
Auditory Sensory Memory
Auscultation
Authoritarian Behavior
Autobiographical Recall
Autogenic Training
Autoimmune Disease
Automatic Perceptual Processes
Automatization
Autonomic Nervous System
Autonomic Responses
Aversion Therapy
Aversive Control
Aversive Events
Aversive Stimuli
Aversive Training
Aviation Medicine

Aviation Psychology
Avoidance Behavior
Avoidance Learning
AZT (Drug)
Babkin Reflex
Back (Human Anatomy)
Bacteriology
Barrier Behavior
Beards
Bedsores
Behavior Codes
Behavior Descriptions
Behavior Genetics
Behavior Management
Behavior Settings
Behavior Strengths
Behavioral Consultation
Behavioral Intention
Behavioral Marital Therapy
Behavioral Medicine
Behavioral Psychology
Behavioral Stability
Behavioral Tracking Deficits
Behavioral Variability
Belief Perseverance
Belongingness
Bereavement
Bidimensional Attention
Bidirectionality
Big Five Markers
Binge Drinking
Binge Eating
Biobehavioral State
Biomedical Model
Biorhythms
Bipolar Traits
Birth Spacing
Birth Timing
Bisexuality
Bisociation
Bites and Stings
Biting
Black Expressive Behavior
Blackbird Vision Screening System
Bladder Control
Blepharisma
Blindisms
Blood
Blood Disorders
Blood Donation
Blood Pressure
Blood Pressure Determination
Blood Tests
Blood Transfusion
Bloodborne Pathogens
Blushing
Boating Safety
Body Articulation
Body Awareness
Body FORTRAN
Body Movement Style
Body Movement Therapy
Bodybuilding
Borderline Personality Disorder
Boredom
Bothsides Thinking
Boundary Expansion (Psychology)
Brain
Brain Activity
Brain Development
Brain Functions
Brain Growth
Brain Research
Brain Size
Brain Waves
Brainstem Auditory Evoked Potential
Brainstem Auditory Evoked Response
Brainstem Dysfunction
Branched Chain Ketoaciduria
Breast Cancer
Breast Examination
Breast Milk
Breast Milk Substitutes
Breath Control Training
Bridging (Reading)
Brief Therapy
Bronchiolitis
Brucellosis
Bullying
Burns (Injuries)
Bylers Disease
Bystander Effect
Caffeine
Caloric Values (Nutrition)
Campus Child Care
Canonicality Effect
Carbohydrate Loading
Cardiac Rehabilitation
Cardioenergetics
Cardiology
Cardiopulmonary Function Testing
Cardiopulmonary Technology
Cardiovascular Diseases
Cardiovascular Technology
Caregiver Behavior
Caregiver Burden
Caregiver Child Ratio
Caregiver Evaluation
Caregiver Response
Caring
Carpal Tunnel Syndrome
Caseworker Client Relationship
Cataracts
Catastrophic Health Care
Catastrophic Health Insurance
Catastrophic Insurance
Categorical Processing (Cognition)
Catheterization (Cardiac)
Catheterization (Urinary)
Cautiousness
Celiac Disease
Central Processing Strategies (Cognition)
Centration
Cerebral Sensory Interaction
Cerebrovascular Disorders
Cervical Disease
Character Constancy
Character Development
Chest X Rays
Chewing Behavior
Chewing Tobacco
Child Behavior Therapy
Child Expectations
Child Influence
Child Life Programs
Child Management
Child Mortality
Child Placement
Child Responsiveness
Child Safety
Child Survival
Childhood Collection Preferences
Childhood Depression
Childhood Illnesses
Childrens Preferences
Childrens Responses
Chinning
Choice Behavior
Choking
Cholesterol
Cholinesterase
Chorea
Chromosome Abnormalities
Chromosomes
Chronemics
Circadian Activity Rhythms
Clerical Perceptual Speed
Client Behavior
Client Centered Counseling
Client Centered Therapy
Client Engagement
Client Identification
Clinical Competence
Clinical Ladder
Clinical Reasoning
Clustering (Learning)
Coca Paste (Drug)
Cocaine Freebase
Codependency
Coercive Behavior
Coffin Lowry Syndrome
Cognitive Aptitude
Cognitive Capacity
Cognitive Competence
Cognitive Conflict
Cognitive Controls
Cognitive Dumping Hypothesis
Cognitive Engagement
Cognitive Entry Behaviors
Cognitive Flexibility
Cognitive Fluency
Cognitive Imaging
Cognitive Integration
Cognitive Level
Cognitive Mediation
Cognitive Mediational Paradigm
Cognitive Preference
Cognitive Research
Cognitive Response Analysis
Cognitive Speed
Cohort Change
Cohort Differences
Coincident Anticipation
Cold Chain
Cold Injuries
Collusion
Color Blindness
Color Discrimination
Color Preferences
Color Stimuli
Combined Immunodeficiency Disease
Commons Dilemma Choices
Communication Behavior
Community Based Rehabilitation
Comparison Process
Compatibility (Social)
Complementary Narcissism Theory
Compliance (Counseling)
Compliance (Medical)
Compliance Gaining
Compliance Gaining Messages
Componential Intelligence
Comprehensive Guidance
Compulsive Handwashing
Computerized Biofeedback Clinical Support System
Conation
Concept Acquisition
Concept Comparisons
Concept Identification
Concept Mapping
Concept Recognition
Concept Switching
Concept Utilization
Conceptional Age
Conceptual Barriers
Conceptual Level
Conciliation
Confidence
Confrontation
Congenital Cytomegalovirus
Congenital Toxoplasmosis
Conjunctivitis
Conscience
Conscientiousness
Conscious Processing
Consciousness
Consciousness (Physiology)
Consciousness Research
Consistency (Behavior)
Contact Action Space
Contact Tracing
Contemplation
Content Learning
Contentment
Contextual Age
Contextual Expectations
Contextual Thinking
Contingency Learning
Contour
Contour Density
Contralateral Limb
Contrast Sensitivity Function
Control (Social Behavior)
Control Perception
Controlled Drinking
Conversion Reaction Syndrome
Cooleys Anemia
Coparenting
Corneal Transplants
Coronary Care
Corpuscular Theory
Cortical Blindness
Cortical Electrical Activity
Cortical Visual Impairments
Cosmetic Surgery
Costs (Surgical)
Counselor Administrator Relationship
Counselor Impairment
Counselor Parent Cooperation
Counselor Reassignment
Counteraggression
Counterattitudinal Behavior
Countertransference
Couple Therapy
Covenant Contracting
Covert Rehearsal
Covert Sensitization
Covert Verbalization
Craniosynostosis
Crawling
Creative Play
Crib Confinement
Crisis Child Care
Critical Errors
Critical Events
Crohns Disease
Cross Cultural Counseling
Cross Race Interaction
Cross Sex Interaction
Crossed Hand Eye Dominance
Crouzon Syndrome
Crowd Behavior
Cryotherapy
Crystallization (Psychology)
Crystallized Intelligence
Cue Controlled Relaxation
Cue Selection
Cuento Therapy
Cultural Translators
Curanderismo
Cutis Verticis Gyrata
Cystic Fibrosis
Cytomegalovirus
Cytotechnology
Dare Phenomenon
Daydreaming
de Lange Syndrome
Death Anxiety
Decalage
Decentering (Psychological)
Decentering (Psychology)
Decentralized Counseling
Decision Counseling
Decision Latency (Learning)
Decoding (Behavior)
Decoding (Psychology)
Deductive Nomological Model
Defamiliarization (Concept)
Defectology
Defense Reactions (Physiology)
Defensiveness
Degraded Imagery
Dehirschs Neurophysiological Immaturity
Dehydration
Deinstitutionalization (of Delinquents)
Deja Connu Phenomenon
Delayed Muscle Soreness
Delayed Parenthood
Delayed Reinforcement
Delayed Retention Effect
Delboeuf Illusion
Delegation of Authority
Delegation of Tasks
Delusions
Demanding Behavior
Dementia
Demotivation
Denervation
Denial (Psychology)
Dental Charting
Dermatology
Desists
Determinant Interaction (Psychology)
Developmental Assessment
Developmental Behavioral Biology
Developmental Behavioral Genetics
Developmental Decline
Developmental Psychopathology
Developmental Readiness
Developmental Therapy
Deviance
Diagnostic Index
Dialogical Thinking
Dialysis
Diapering
Diarrhea
Dichotic Listening
Diet Therapy
Diethylstilbestrol
Differential Diagnosis
Digeorge Syndrome
Digestive System
Digestive System Diseases
Digit Span Tasks
Digoxin
Dimensional Values (Psychology)
Dioxin
Diphenylhydantoin
Disability Management
Discharge (from Treatment)
Discharge Planning
Discrimination of Recency
Discriminative Stimulus
Disengagement (Gerontology)
Disinhibition
Disjunctive Concepts
Disjunctive Tasks
Displacement (Psychology)
Disruptive Behavior
Dissociation
Dissonance Reduction
Distractibility
Distress
Distributed Cognition
Diuretics
Diurnal Variations
Dominant Behavior

Hyperrationalization
Hypnotherapy
Hypnotic Susceptibility
Hypoglycemia
Hyponasality
Hypothermia
Hypothyroidism
Hypoxia
Hysterectomies
Hysterical Conversion Reactions
Hysterical Personalities
Iatrogenic Diseases
ID Exploratory Behavior
Idealization
Ideational Confrontation
Ideational Fluency
Identity (Psychological)
Identity Conservation
Identity Crisis
Identity Formation
Identity Status
Identity Synthesis
Idiopathic Thrombocytopenic Purpura
Illness Scripts
Imaging
Immortality Orientation
Immunoglobulin
Immunology
Impedance Audiometry
Impersonalization
Implosive Therapy
Imposed Mental Imagery
Imposter Phenomenon
Impression Formation
Impulsive Therapy of Stempfl
Impulsiveness
Incidental Memory
Incongruence (Psychology)
Independent Behavior
Indirect Suggestion
Individual Marital Therapy
Individual Physician Profile
Individualized Transition Plans
Individually Guided Behavior
Indomethacin
Industrial Health
Infant Distress
Infant Feeding
Infant Formula
Infant Rocking
Infant Smiling
Infant State
Infant Stimulation
Infantile Amnesia
Infantile Autism
Infertility
Inflammation
Influenza
Ingratiation
Inhalants
Inhelder Piaget System
Injections (Medicine)
Inner Direction (Psychology)
Insomnia
Institutional Conditions
Insulin
Intension Extension (Concepts)
Intensive Care Nursing
Interactional Disturbance (Psychology)
Interbehavioral Psychology
Intercultural Counseling
Interdomain Influences
Interference (Learning)
Interference Effects
Intergenerational Attitude Transference
Intergenerational Conflict
Intergenerational Continuity
Intergenerational Factors
Intergenerational Perception
Intergenerational Relationship
Intergenerational Solidarity
Intergenerational Transmission
Internal External Social Attributes
Internalization
Interpersonal Cognitive Problem Solving
Interpersonal Confirmation
Interpersonal Contact Initiation
Interpersonal Discrimination
Interpersonal Distance
Interpersonal Influence Process
Interpersonal Psychotherapy
Interpersonal Synchrony
Interpersonal Therapy
Intertrial Repetition Units (Psychology)
Intraception
Intracranial Hemorrhage
Intraindividual Variability
Intraocular Pressure
Intrapartum Perinatology
Intrapersonal Skills
Intrapsychic Conflict
Intrauterine Devices
Intravenous Therapy
Intrinsic Extrinsic Classroom Orientation
Introspection
Intrusiveness
Intubation (Medicine)
Iron Deficiency
Irrational Beliefs
Irrational Beliefs (Ellis)
Irrationality
Irritability
Ischemic Heart Disease
Isokinetics
Isolation Effect
Isometric Contraction
Isometric Endurance
Isometric Strength
Isotonic Strength
Isotonic Weight Training
Joint Injuries
Justice Reasoning
Justification (Psychology)
Juvenile Metachromatic Leukodystrophy
Juvenile Thyrotoxicosis
Ketogenic Diet
Ketotic Hypoglycemia
Kidney Disease
Kinetic Imagery
Kinetic Structure
Klinefelters Syndrome
Kwashiorkor
Labeling (of Objects)
Lactation
Laetrile
Landau Kleffner Syndrome
Larons Dwarfism
Larynx
Late Infantile Lipidosis
Late Parenthood
Late Positive Component (EEG)
Lateral Awareness
Lateral Preference
Lateral Thinking
Laurence Moon Biedl Syndrome
Learning Sets
Leaving Behavior
Lecithin
Left Right Discrimination
Left Ventricle
Leg Strength
Legs
Length of Hospital Stay
Leprosy
Lesch Nyhan Syndrome
Leukemia
Levels of Consciousness
Levels of Processing
Liangong Exercises
Life Esteem
Life Expectancy
Life Goals
Life Meaning
Life Position
Life Review
Life Span
Life Tasks (Adler)
Ligaments
Likability
Limits (Therapy)
Line Orientation
Linear Nevus Sebaceous Syndrome
Lipoproteins
Lisping
Listening Strategies
Liver Disease
Localization (Neurological)
Logotherapy
Long Term Marriages
Longevity
Loss
Lost Adolescence Syndrome
Love Deprivation
Love Withdrawal
Low Density Lipoprotein Cholesterol
Lowes Syndrome
Lung Diseases
Lungs
Machismo
Macrocomponents (Intelligence)
Maintenance Behavior
Maladaptive Persistence
Malaria
Malingering
Malocclusion
Mands
Manic Depression
Manual Arts Therapy
Manual Dexterity
Maple Syrup Urine Disease
Marfan Syndrome
Marital Adjustment
Marital Discord
Marital Quality
Marital Therapy
Marlowe Crowne Social Approval
Marriage Enrichment
Masking (Audiometric)
Masking (Auditory)
Masking (Visual)
Masochism
Mass Centroid Location
Massages
Mastectomy
Mastery Motivation
Mastery Orientation
Matching Ability
Matching Errors
Material Reinforcement
Maternal and Child Health Services
Maternal Deprivation
Maternal Health
Maternal Hyperphenylalaninemia
Maternal Medication
Maternal Mortality
Maternal Responsiveness
Maternal Self Concept
Maternal Sensitivity
McCollough Effect
Meal Patterns
Mechanical Kinesiology
Mechanical Restraint Procedures
Media Embedded Interactions
Media Habits
Media Therapy
Mediated Experience
Medical Anthropology
Medical Consent Forms
Medical Documentation
Medical Exclusions
Medical Imaging
Medical Leave
Medical Negligence
Medical Play
Medical Records
Medical Technology
Medical Utilization
Medically Underserved Areas
Medication
Medications
Medigap Insurance
Melanoma
Mellaril
Melodic Intonation Therapy
Memory Deficits
Memory Protocols
Memory Span
Memory Tasks
Memory Training
Menarche
Meningitis
Menkes Kinky Hair Syndrome
Menopause
Menstrual Disorders
Menstrual Products
Mental Animation
Mental Computation
Mental Effort
Mental Exercises
Mental Imagery
Mental Rotation
Mental Skills
Mental Tracking
Mescaline
Mesomorph
Meta Attention
Metachromatic Leukodystrophy
Methadone
Methaqualone
Methylmercury Poisoning
Methylphenidate
Microcephaly
Microcomponents (Intelligence)
Micropolygyria
Microtherapy
Middle Ear Disease
Milk
Mimicry
Minamata Disease
Mind Body Problem
Mind Control
Mind Sets
Minerals (Nutrition)
Minor Physical Anomalies
Mirror Movements
Miskimins Self Goal
Misogyny
Mitral Valve Prolapse
Moderate Disabilities
Modesty
Modified Desensitization
Monaural Listening
Mononucleosis
Monotonism
Mood Induction
Moral Behavior
Moral Orientation
Moral Reasoning
Morbid Curiosity
Morbidity
Morphine
Motivational Orientation
Motor Restraint
Motoric Expression
Motoric Imagery
Mourning
Mouth Appearance Pictures
Mouth Protectors
Mouthwash
Movement Refractoriness
Movement Therapy
Movigenics
Mucocutaneous Lymph Node Syndrome
Mucopolysaccharidosis
Mueller Lyer Illusion
Multicultural Counseling
Multidimensional Actuarial Classification
Multifamily Group Therapy
Multigenerational Relationship
Multimodal Counseling
Multiple Attending (Psychology)
Multiple Impact Therapy
Multiple Personality Disorder
Multiple Sclerosis
Multisensory Modality
Mumps
Muscle Soreness
Muscle Temperature
Muscular Disabilities
Muscular Dystrophy
Muscular Tension
Musculoskeletal Performance
Mutations
Mutism
Mutual Parenting
Myasthenia Gravis
Mycoplasma Pneumoniae
Myelodysplasia
Nailbiting
Naltrexone
Naltrexone Hydrochloride
Narcissism
Narcotic Antogonists
National Health
Natural Childbirth
Natural Family Planning
Naturopaths
Near Death Experiences
Neck (Anatomy)
Negative Affect
Negative Moods
Negativism
Nephrology
Nephrotic Syndrome
Nerve Impulses
Nervous System
Network Therapy
Neural Transmission
Neuro Developmental Observation
Neuroanatomy
Neurobiology
Neuroblastoma
Neurodevelopmental Therapy
Neurodevelopmental Treatment Approach
Neurolinguistic Mirroring
Neurolinguistic Programming
Neurological Examination
Neurological Information Network
Neuromuscular Skills
Neuropathology
Neuropharmacology
Neurosurgery
Neurotoxicology
Nicotine
Night Child Care
Night Fears
Nodoz
Nonachievement Syndrome

Nonbehavioral Therapy
Noncognitive Attributes
Noncognitive Classroom Behaviors
Nonentrenchment
Nonoperant Conditioning
Nonparticipation
Nonprescription Drugs
Nonstrategic Recall
Nontraditional Medicine
Nonverbal Intelligence
Nonverbal Stimuli
Nonvocal Communication Systems
Noonan Syndrome
Nurse Patient Relationship
Nurse Physician Relationship
Nursing Care Plans
Nutrient Values
Nutrients
Nutritional Deficiencies
Nutritional Status
Nutritional Therapy
Object Attractiveness
Object Child Relationship
Object Orientation
Object Retrieval
Object Socialization
Object Substitution
Obsessive Compulsive Behavior
Obstetrical Complications
Obstetrical Drugs
Occupational Behavior
Ocular Motility
Ocular Motor Apraxia
Odontography
Oedipal Conflict
Olfactory Discrimination
Olfactory Sense
Olfactory Stimuli
Oligophrenia
Omphalocele
Oneway Thinking
Onsite Day Care
Operant Behavior
Ophthalmoscopes
Oppositional Behavior
Optical Illusions
Optical Rotation
Optimism
Oraflex
Oral Contraception
Oral Dependence
Oral Hygiene
Oral Reflexes
Oral Surgery
Oral Ulcerations
Orality
Ordinal Position
Organ Transplants
Organic Personality Syndrome
Organizational Health
Organizational Psychology
Orienting Reflex
Orienting Tasks
Orthomolecular Therapy
Orthopedic Surgery
Orthopedics
Orthopsychiatry
Orthoptic Vision
Orthostatic Tolerance
Orthotic Prosthetic Education
Osteitis Pubis
Osteogenesis Imperfecta
Osteomyelitis
Osteoporosis
Otitis Media
Otoacoustic Emissions
Out of School Misconduct
Out of Seat Behavior
Outdoor Mobility
Outerdirectedness
Outpatient Care
Outpatient Commitment
Overconfidence
Overcorrection
Overuse Injuries
Oxygen Administration
Oxygen Consumption
P Aminobenzoic Acid
P3 Latency
Paget Gorman Sign System
Pain Control
Pain Experience
Pain Perception
Pain Tolerance
Paired Reinforcement
Paired Stimuli
Palpation
Pancreas
Panic
Pap Smears
Papillomata
Parapsychology
Paraquat
Parasitic Infections
Parasocial Interaction
Parasuicide
Paraveterinary Skills
Parent Caregiver Relationship
Parent Child Separation
Parent Commitment
Parent Effectiveness
Parent Expectations
Parent Favoritism
Parent Infant Resource Systems
Parent Needs
Parent Overprotection
Parent Responsiveness
Parent Strictness
Parent through Child Learning
Parent Visitation
Parental Alienation Syndrome
Parental Challenge
Parental Heritage
Parental Psychopathology
Parenthood
Partial Reinforcement
Partnerships in Health Care
Paruresis
Passive Aggressive Behavior
Passive Smoking
Passivity
Pathological Distortion
Pathos
Patient Care
Patient Dumping
Patient Education Materials
Patient Management
Patients Rights
Patricide
Patterning (Neurology)
Peace Psychology
Peanuts
Pediatric Psychology
Pediatric Social Illness
Pedodontics
Pedophilia
Pelvic Examinations
Pemoline
Penicillin
Perceived Control
Perceptual Communicative Disorders
Perceptual Deficit Hypothesis
Perceptual Distortion
Perceptual Preference
Perceptual Salience
Perceptual Speed
Perfectionism
Periodontal Index
Periodontics
Periodontology
Peripheral Stimuli
Peripheral Temperature
Peripheral Vision
Perky Effect
Permanency Planning (for Disabled)
Permanency Planning (Foster Care)
Permissiveness
Person Centered Therapy
Person Object Relationship
Personal Assistance (of Disabled)
Personal Discovery Approach
Personal Effectiveness
Personal Involvement
Personality Types
Perspective (Psychology)
Perspective Consciousness
Perturbation (Perception)
Pertussis
Pervasive Developmental Disorders
Pessimism
Peyote
Pharynx
Phencyclidine
Phenylketonuria
Philosophic Mindedness
Philosophical Psychology
Phlebotomy
Phobia Treatment
Phobic Children
Phonemic Awareness
Phonological Awareness
Phonological Processing
Phonological Recoding
Phototherapy
Phrenology
Physical Abuse
Physical and Neurological Examination Soft Signs
Physical Appearance
Physical Contact
Physical Medicine
Physical Proximity
Physician Pharmacist Relationship
Physician Role
Physiognomic Perception
Physiological Domain
Physiological Needs
Physiological Response
Piagetian Research
Pica Behavior
Picture Superiority Effect
Pity
Placebo Effect
Placement (Foster Care)
Plaque (Dental)
Plastic Surgery
Plate Waste
Pleasantness
Pneumonia
Pointing Behavior
Polio Vaccines
Politeness
Polyglot Dyslexia
Ponzo Illusion
Positioning (of Disabled)
Positioning (Patients)
Positive Affect
Positive Uncertainty
Possession Negotiations
Possible Selves
Post Maturation Treatment
Postformal Adult Cognition
Posthospital Outcome
Posthypnotic Conflict
Postmortem Care
Postnatal Influences
Postoperative Care
Postpartum
Postpartum Care
Postpartum Depression
Postpartum Services
Posttraumatic Stress Disorder
Postural Reflex Dysfunction
Potassium Depletion (Physiology)
PPA
Prader Willi Syndrome
Precategorical Acoustic Storage
Prechtl Beintema Neurological Examination
Preclinical Performance
Precounseling Interviews
PreDoctoral Syndrome
Premarital Abuse
Premarital Communication
Premarital Sex
Premature Termination of Treatment
Premenstrual Syndrome
Premorbid Adjustment
Prenatal Interviews
Preoperational Thought
Preoperative Care
Prepuberty
Prescription Drugs
Presentation Order
Pretherapy
Primary Nursing
Primary Prevention
Priming Effects
Private Practice (Medicine)
Private Self Consciousness
Problem Maintenance Process
Process Tracing
Progressive Hearing Loss
Progressive Muscle Relaxation Training
Projection (Psychology)
Proprietary Drugs
Proprietary Rehabilitation
Prose Learning
Protective Behavior
Protective Clothing
Protective Factors
Protective Mechanisms
Protein
Protein Deficiency
Protein Excess
Prototype Acquisition
Proud Parent Syndrome
Psilocybin
Psychiatric Epidemiology
Psychiatric Nursing
Psychiatric Rehabilitation
Psychic Energy
Psychoactive Drugs
Psychobiography
Psychodiagnosis
Psychological Assessment
Psychological Constructs
Psychological Differentiation
Psychological Gender
Psychological Influences
Psychological Modernity
Psychological Refractory Period
Psychological State
Psychology of Mathematics Education
Psychology of the Self
Psychomotor Development
Psychosexual Development
Psychosocial Adaptation
Psychosocial Crisis
Psychosocial Deprivation
Psychosocial Development
Psychosocial Factors
Psychosociology
Psychotechnology
Psychotropic Medication
Puberty
Pulsation Thresholds
Pupillometry
Pushups
Pyloric Stenosis
Pyribenzamine
Rabies
Radon
Rape Recovery
Rapid Eye Movements
Rational Behavior Training
Rational Self Counseling
Reaching Behavior
Reactance (Psychology)
Reaction Formation
Reality Counseling
Reality Orientation
Reasonable Accommodation (Handicapped)
Reasoning Impairment
Receiver Apprehension
Recidivism (Foster Care)
Reconstructive Memory
ReCreative Psychology
Recursive Thought
Redecision Family Therapy
Redundancy Counseling
Reevaluation Counseling
Referential Reality
Reflection Process
Reflective Abstraction
Reflective Awareness
Reflective Judgment
Reflexes
Reflexive Abstraction
Refractory Disorders
Refugee Mental Health
Refusal of Treatment
Regressive Behavior
Regulated Breathing Method
Regulated Expressiveness
Regurgitation
Rehabilitative Optometry
Reinforcement Schedules
Reinforcer Sampling
Relapse
Relapse Crises
Relationship Psychotherapy
Relationship Termination
Relaxation
Relevance (Personal)
Relinquishment of Control
Remedial Interchanges
Remedial Intervention
Renal System
Repetitive Strain Injuries
Repression
Reproductive Technology
Research Misconduct
Resilience (Personality)
Resistance Training
Respiration
Respiratory Diseases
Respiratory Distress Syndrome
Respiratory Manipulation Training
Respiratory Problems
Respiratory System
Respondent Behavior
Response Alternation
Response Competition
Response Consistency
Response Contingent Stimulation
Response Cost
Response Criteria
Response Hierarchy

Response Inhibition
Response Involvement
Response Meaningfulness
Response Opportunities
Response Patterns
Responsive Therapy
Restored Behavior
Restraint
Restricted Environmental Stimulation Therapy
Restrictiveness (Child Rearing)
Retaliation
Retinal Detachment
Retinitis Pigmentosa
Retinoblastoma
Retrieval (Memory)
Retroaction (Psychology)
Retrolental Fibroplasia
Rett Syndrome
Reunion Behavior
Revenge
Reyes Syndrome
Rheumatic Fever
Rheumatoid Arthritis
Rheumatology
Ridicule
Riegers Syndrome
Right Hemisphere Deficit Syndrome
Right to Refuse Treatment
Risk Taking Behavior
Risky Shift
Ritalin
Ritual Behavior
Road Behavior
Role Ambiguity
Role Bias
Role Delineation
Role Immersion
Role Loss
Role Satisfaction
Role Shock
Role Strain
Role Transition
Role Transmission
Romantic Relationship
Rotator Cuff Disease
Roundworm
Roussy Levy Syndrome
Routine Expertise
Rudeness
Rule Breaking
Rule Governed Behavior
Rule Transfer
Rumination (Chewing)
Rumination (Thinking)
Saccadic Eye Movements
Saccharopinuria
Safe Sex Practices
Saint Sebastian Syndrome
Salicylates
Salience Effects
Salivary Chromosomes
Salivation
Salt Intake
Same Sex Interaction
Sandhoffs Disease
Sarcoidosis
Scabies
Scanning
Scanning Rate
Scanning Styles
Scapegoat Role
Scapegoating
Scatology
School Based Multidisciplinary Team
School Refusal
Scleroderma
Scoliosis
Scriptotherapy
Scripts (Knowledge Structures)
Seasonal Affective Disorder
Seclusion
Security Blankets
Security of Attachment
Seductive Behavior
Segmentation Skills
Selective Learning
Self Affirmation
Self Blame
Self Care
Self Compassion
Self Concept Enhancing Activities
Self Consciousness
Self Consistency Theory
Self Counseling
Self Defeating Behavior
Self Definition
Self Directed Questioning
Self Discrepancies
Self Empowerment
Self Examinations (Physical)
Self Fulfillment
Self Gain
Self Gratification
Self Handicapping
Self Interest
Self Monitoring
Self Presentations
Self Protection
Self Psychology
Self Recognition
Self Reference (Psychology)
Self Referral
Self Reflection
Self Relevance
Self Reliance
Self Revitalization
Self Righteousness
Self Schemas
Self Serving Effect
Self Stability
Self Statement Modification
Self Statements
Self Sufficiency
Self Sufficient Living
Self Talk
Semantic Memory
Semi Independent Living Services
Senile Dementia
Sensation Seeking
Sense of Coherence
Sense of Community
Sense of Place
Sense Organs
Sensory Qualities
Sequential Memory
Sequential Processing
Serial Integration
Serology
Serotonin
Serum Uric Acid
Set (Psychological)
Severe Discrepancy Levels
Sex Exploitation
Sex Knowledge
Sexogrophobia
Sexual Adjustment
Sexual Attitudes
Sexual Mutilation
Sexual Orientation
Sexual Permissiveness
Sexual Relationships
Sexual Satisfaction
Sexual Violence
Sexually Transmitted Diseases
Shadow Realities
Shame
Shock
Short Term Counseling
Short Term Psychodynamic Psychotherapy
Shoulders (Anatomy)
Sibling Attitudes
Sibling Care
Sibling Deidentification
Sibling Modeling
Sibling Rivalry
Similar Benefits (Rehabilitation)
Similarity of Experience
Simulated Patients
Simultaneous Learning
Simultaneous Processing
Sincerity
Sincerity of Responses
Sit Ups
Situational Effects
Skin
Skin Color
Skin Infections
Sleep Disorders
Sleep Paralysis
Sleepwalking
Smallpox
Smith Lemli Opitz Syndrome
Smokeless Tobacco
Smoking Cessation
Snake Phobia
Social Acceptance
Social Adaptational Status
Social Affiliation
Social Anxiety
Social Breakdown Syndrome
Social Commitment
Social Devaluation
Social Distance
Social Gerontology
Social Health
Social Interest
Social Isolates
Social Loafing
Social Motivation
Social Motives
Social Referencing
Social Rejection
Social Representations
Social Role Range
Social Stimuli
Social Therapy
Social Transition
Socio Dental Research
Sociocentrism
Socioemotional Development
Sociomedicine
Sodomy
Solemnity
Solitary Play
Solution Focused Brief Therapy
Somatic Alteration
Somatomedin C
Somatotyping
Sound Preferences
Spatial Context
Spatial Cues
Specimen Records (Behavior)
Spinal Cord Injuries
Spiral Aftereffects (Psychology)
Spiritual Development
Spiritual Health
Spiritual Well Being
Splitting (Psychology)
Spontaneous Recovery
Spontaneous Remission
Spouse Abuse
Stability (Personal)
Stability (Social Relationships)
Standardized Morbidity Ratio
Starvation
State Anxiety
State Dependent Retention
Stereotyped Behavior
Stereotypy (Psychology)
Sterilization
Steroids
Stethoscopes
Stigma
Stillbirth
Stimulus Alignment
Stimulus Complexity
Stimulus Configurations
Stimulus Control
Stimulus Discrepancy
Stimulus Fading
Stimulus Incongruity
Stimulus Intensity Modulation
Stimulus Meaningfulness
Stimulus Onset Asychrony
Stimulus Preference
Stimulus Response Psychology
Stimulus Satiation
Stimulus Seeking Behavior
Stimulus Similarity
Stimulus Structure
Stimulus Timing
Stimulus to Rule Linkage
Storage (Memory)
Strategic Behavior
Strategic Family Therapy
Strategic Knowledge
Strategic Remembering
Strategic Rite
Strength Training
Streptomyces
Stress (Biological)
Stress Immunization
Stress Inoculation
Stress Resistance
Stroop Effect
Student Health Records
Stuttering Modification Therapy
Subjective Judgment
Subjective Probability
Subjective Warrant
Sublimation
Subliminal Perception
Subliminal Suggestion
Submissive Behavior
Substitute Care
Sucking Behavior
Sucrose
Sudden Infant Death Syndrome
Sugar Excess
Suicide Attempts
Suicide Ideation
Suicide Methods
Suicide Notes
Suicide Prevention
Sunburn
Superiority Traits
Superordinate Classes
Superordinate Relations
Superstitious Behavior
Supervised Family Day Care
Surdo Cardiac Syndrome
Surrogate Motherhood
Surrogate Pregnancy
Surrogate Self
Sustained Attention
Swallowing
Swallowing Therapy
Symbolic Representation
Symbolic Thinking
Synaction
Synaesthesia
Synaptic Linking Process
Synchronous Learning
Synchrony
Syncope
System Therapy
Systolic Blood Pressure
T Scope Therapy
Tactile Defensiveness
Tacts
Talwin
Tapeworm
Tardive Dyskinesia
Task Attractiveness
Task Modifications
Task Perception
Task Persistence
Taste Discrimination
Taste Preference
Tay Sachs Disease
Teacher Expressiveness
Teacher Stress
Teacher Thinking
Teasing
Technostress
Teen Age Medical Service
Teeth
Telediagnostic Protocol
Telemedicine
Telephone Apprehension
Temper Tantrums
Temporal Bone Banks
Temporal Causal Understanding
Temporal Lobe
Temporal Patterning
Temporal Stability
Temporary Care
Temporary Child Care
Temporary Day Care
Temporomandibular Joint Dysfunction
Tension
Testicular Examination
Text Factors
Texture Density
Thematic Relations
Thematic Stimuli
Theophylline
Theoretic Orientation
Therapeutic Communication
Therapeutic Conditions Training
Therapeutic Listening
Therapy Outcome Differential
Thioridazine
Thiothixene
Thought Control
Thrifty Food Plan
Thrombocytosis
Thumbsucking
Thyroid Function
Tick Toxicosis
Tics
Time Work Fatigue
Togetherness
Toilet Training
Tonal Memory
Tongue
Tonsillectomies
Tonsillitis
Tooth Size
Toothbrushing
Topographic Brain Mapping
Total Physical Response
Touch
Tourette Syndrome
Toxic Shock Syndrome
Toxoplasmosis
Toy Preferences
Toy Safety

Trace Element Medicine
Trace Minerals
Tracheostomy Suctioning
Traditional Healing
Traffic Behavior
Trait Emotions
Transcutaneous Electrical Nerve Stimulation
Transdermal Electrostimulation
Transference
Transformative Learning
Transgression Behavior
Transivity
Transpersonal Psychology
Transsexuals
Traumas
Triage Health Care Delivery System
Tricyclic Antidepressants
Trismus Pseudocamptodactyly Syndrome
Trisomy 18 Syndrome
Triune Brain
Tropical Medicine
Tube Feeding
Tuberculosis
Tumor Registrars
Turners Syndrome
Tutor Teacher Relationship
Twin Vision
Tympanometry
Type I Glycogen Storage Disease
Ultrasonic Echoencephalography
Unconscious Processing
Undercontrol (Psychology)
Universal Precautions
Upper Extremity Impairments
Urinalysis
Urinary System
Urinary Tract Infections
Urology
Usher Syndrome
Ushers Syndrome
Vaccination
Vaccine Related Injury
Vaccines
Vagal Tone
Valvar Aortic Stenosis
Vascular Dementia
Vasectomy
Velar Control
Velton Mood Induction Procedure
Ventilator Dependence
Verbal Social Control
Vergence
Vicarious Conditioning
Vicarious Participation
Victimization
Vigilance Performance
Viroids
Virology
Visible Displacement
Vision Therapy
Visual Asymmetry
Visual Attention
Visual Coorientation
Visual Cues
Visual Evoked Potential
Visual Imagery
Visual Manipulation
Visual Motor Tracking
Visual Occlusion
Visual Perceptual Deficit Hypothesis
Visual Preference
Visual Processing
Visual Recall
Visual Screening
Visual Thinking
Visual Tracking
Visually Evoked Responses
Visuomanual Tracking
Vital Signs (Physiology)
Vitamin A
Vitamin C
Vitamin Deficiency
Vitamins
Vocal Nodules
Vocal Tone
Vocational Identity
Volitional Skills
Voluntary Childlessness
Vomiting
Vulnerability
Vulnerable Child Syndrome
Waardenburg Syndrome
Wake Up Behavior
Waking Suggestion
War on Drugs
Wariness
Warm Up Decrement
Warm Up Exercises
Water Exercise
Water Safety
Weight Loss
Weight Maintenance
Well Child Care
Wellness
Whiplash Shaken Infant Syndrome
Whole Brain Learning
Will Power
Williams Elfin Facies Syndrome
Williams Syndrome
Wilsons Disease
Within Category Spacing
Word Associated Arousal
Word Retrieval
Work Disabilities
Working Intelligence
Working Memory
Worry
Wrist Temperature
Writers Block
Writing Therapy
X Chromosomal Abnormalities
Xerophthalmia
XXY Syndrome
XYY Syndrome
Zeigarnik Effect
Zollinger Ellison Syndrome
Zones of Indifference (Behavior)

CATEGORY 12: Historical / Special Events

1880s
1930s
1960s
1970s
1980s
1990s
Abscam
Adult Learning Week
African Diaspora
Age of Enlightenment
Agricultural History
Alexandrian Library (Antiquity)
Alliance for Progress
American Education Week
American Indian Day
American Indian Movement
Antinuclear Movement
Arbor Day
Arizona Archaeology Week
Asian Pacific American Heritage Week
Autocracy
Bar Mitzvah
Bat Mitzvah
Bicentennial
Birthdays
Black History Month
Boston Massacre
Business History
California Gold Rush
California History
Camp David Peace Accords
Canadian History
Career Days
Career Events
Caribbean History
Catholic Schools Week
Catholic Worker Movement
Celebrate Life Day
Census 1790
Centennial (1876)
Centennial Exhibition of 1876
Ceremonies
Challenger Disaster
Chernobyl Disaster
Chicago Fire 1871
Childrens Book Week
Childrens Day
Christmas
Citizenship Day
Civil Disturbances
Classical Period
Cold War
Columbus Day
Columbus Quincentenary
Commemorative Events
Constitution Week
Constitutional Convention
Continental Congress
Corporate History
Costume History
Cuban Missile Crisis
Cuban Revolution
Cultural Revolution
Cultural Revolution (China)
Depression (Economic 1929)
Design History
Dia de dar Gracias
Dia de la Raza
Dia de los Muertos
Disability Awareness Day
Earth Day
Earth Week
East West Conflict
Easter
Education Reform Movement
Edwardian Era
Effective Schools Movement
Eighteenth Century
Eleventh Century
English History
English Law History
English Only Movement
Escuela Moderna Movement
Essential Schools Movement
Expo 92
Exxon Valdez Oil Spill
Fathers Day
Fiesta Bowl
Finnish Winter War
First Week of School
Flag Day
Foreign Language Weeks
Founding Fathers of the United States
Free Speech Movement
Freedmens Bureau
French and Indian War
French Revolution
Fronteras 1976
Frontier History
Geneva Protocol 1925
Geography Awareness Week
German History
German Peasant Revolt
Ghost Dance Movement
Glasnost
Golden Olympics
Great Leap Forward (China)
Great Society
Green Revolution
Grito de Dolores
Gulf War
Halloween
Hanukkah
Hapsburg Empire
Harlem Renaissance
Hearst (Patricia) Trial
Herbartian Movement
Hispanic Heritage Week
Historic Sites
Historical Influences
Historical Landmarks
Hokulea
Holocaust
Hudson Bay Company
Hurricane Hugo
Iditarod Sled Dog Race
Independence Day
Independence Day (Mexico)
Indian State of Emergency 1975
Industrial Revolution
Information Age
International Book Year
International Day (School)
International Education Year
International Literacy Day
International Literacy Year 1990
International Mathematics Olympiad
International Womens Year
International Year of Disabled Persons
International Year of the Child
International Youth Year
Intifada
Iran Contra Affair
Iran Hostage Crisis
Iran Iraq War
Iranian Revolution 1979
Jacksonian Era
Japanese Relocation Camps
KAL 007
Kansas City Womens Jazz Festival
Kiangsi Soviet Period (Chinese History)
Knife River Indian Village
Kwanzaa
Labor Day
Labor Education Week
Law Day
Legal History
Legislative History
Library History
Life Adjustment Movement
Live Aid (Concert)
Living History
Lost Colony
Marital History
Marshall Plan
Massachusetts Bay Colony
Mathematics History
May Day
Mayan Civilization
Me Generation
Media History
Memorial Day
Mexican War
Middle Ages
Military History
Mindpower Week
Minoan Civilization
Modern School Movement
Mogul Empire
Mothers Day
Music Festivals
Music History
Mycenaean Civilization
National Childrens Dental Health Week
National Collegiate Alcohol Awareness Week
National Collegiate Drug Awareness Week
National Community Education Day
National Education Goals 1990
National Geography Awareness Week
National High School Postal Art Exhibition
National History Day
National Library Week
National Newspaper Literacy Day
National Observance of Childrens Sabbaths
National Recovery Administration
National School Lunch Week
National Urban Education Goals
National Womens History Week
Nativistic Movement
Natural History
Naval History
Navidad
New Age Movement
New Deal
New World Order
New Year (Holiday)
Nineteenth Century
Nineteenth Century History
Nixon Administration
Northwest Ordinance 1787
Nuclear Nonproliferation Treaty
Nuremberg War Trials
Olympic Games Boycotts
Organizational History
Palestinian Israeli Conflict
Pan African Movement
Panama Canal Treaties
Pearl Harbor
Perestroika
Personal History
Plain English Movement
Plains Wars
Playdays
Political History
Prehistoric Times
Presidents Day
Progressive Era
Protestant Reformation
Public History
Pueblo Revolt (1680)
Puerto Rican History
Puerto Rico Discovery Day
Rancho Los Alamitos
Recession
Recession (Economic 1975)
Reformation (Historical Period)
Regional History
Renaissance
Renaissance Festivals
Riel Rebellion (1885)
Risdon Massacre (Australia)
Roman Civilization
Roman Empire
Roman Republic
Russian History
Saint Patricks Day
Salem Witch Trials
Sanctuary Movement
Sarvodaya Shramadana Movement (Sri Lanka)
Scandals
Science Olympiad
Scientific Revolution
Scopes Trial
Seasonal Celebrations
Seventeenth Century
Sino Soviet Alliance
Sixteenth Century

Social Movements
Soviet History
Spanish American War
Spanish Civil War
Spanish History
Sport History
Strategic Arms Limitation Talks
Student Movement
Texas Sesquicentennial
Thanksgiving
Theater Festivals
Theater History
Three Mile Island
Tiananmen Square Uprising
Trade Shows
Treaty of Dancing Rabbit Creek
Treaty of Doaks Stand
Treaty of Waitangi (New Zealand)
Treaty of Washington City
Treaty with Navajo Indians 1868
Tudor Period
TWA Hostage Crisis
Twelfth Century
Twentieth Century
Twentieth Century History
Twenty First Century
Underground Railroad
United Nations Decade for Women
United Nations Decade of Disabled Persons
United Nations Intl Year of the Family 1994
USS Arizona
USS Constitution
Valentines Day
Valley Forge Encampment
Vatican Councils
Very Special Arts Festivals
Veterans Day
Victorian Period
Voyage of Rediscovery
Voyager Mission
War of 1812
Watergate
Westward Movement (United States)
Womens History
Womens History Month
Womens History Week
Womens Suffrage
Woodstock (Concert)
World Food Day
World Meteorological Day
World Population Year
World Post Day
Worlds Fairs
Year of the Elementary School
Yom Kippur War
Youth 2000 Week
Youth Art Month
Youth Society Movement (Finland)

CATEGORY 13: Languages / Linguistics

Abipon
Absurdities
Abwa
Academic Language
Adangme
Address Forms
Adivasi Oriya
Adjunct Aids
Adverbial Modifiers
Adversative Connectives
Affective Voice Quality
Affricates
African Languages (Non Bantu)
Africanisms
After Dinner Speaking
Agaw Languages
Agreement (Grammar)
Agta
Aguaruna
Agusan Manobo
Agutaynen
Ahtna Athapascan
Ainu
Aklanon
Akuapem
Alabama (Language)
Alemannic Dialects
Algonquian Languages
Algonquin
Alliteration
Allophones
Alphabetic Principle
Alphabetic Writing
Alsatian Dialects
Alsea
Alternation (Speech)
Alutiiq
Alyawarra
Amazonian Languages
Ambiguity Detection
American Ind
American Indian Sign
American Preceptor
Americanisms
Amis
Amoy
Amphigory
Amuzgo
Anagrams
Analogies
Analogy
Analphabetic Transcription
Analytical Writing
Anaphora
Andean Languages
Angaataha
Anglicisms
Animacy
Animacy Inanimacy
Anindilyakwa
Annamese
Antecedents
Antigone Constraint
Antonyms
Anyi Baoule
Aphesis
Aphorisms
Apophony
Apraxia (Speech)
Arabic (Cairene)
Arabic (Chad)
Arabic (Classical)
Arabic (Colloquial)
Arabic (Egyptian)
Arabic (Gulf)
Arabic (Iraqi)
Arabic (Levantine)
Arabic (Libyan)
Arabic (Literary)
Arabic (Mauritanian)
Arabic (Modern Literary)
Arabic (Modern Standard)
Arabic (Moroccan)
Arabic (Muslim Baghdad)
Arabic (Palestinian)
Arabic (Saudi)
Arabic (Sudanese)
Arabic (Tunisian)
Arabic Persian Writing System
Arabic Script
Aramaic Languages
Arapaho
Areal Linguistics
Argument Research
Arikara
Articles (Grammar)
Asaro
Ashanti
Asian Languages
Aspect (Verbs)
Aspiration (Speech)
Assiniboine
Asymmetry (Language)
Ateso
Atsugewi
Author Reader Relationship
Author Text Relationship
Auxiliary Verbs
Ayacucho
Aztecan
Babbling Drift Hypothesis
Baby Talk
Bacairi
Backlash Interference
Bahnar
Balangao
Balkan Languages
Balto Finnic Languages
Bambara
Bamileke
Bangkok Dialect
Banton
Bassa
Baure
Beginning Writing
Belle
Bete
Bilingual Catalogs
Bilingual Dictionaries
Bilingual Literature
Bilinguals
Biliteracy
Biloquialism
Binandere Languages
Binding Theory
Biolinguistics
Bishop Lowth Complex
Bitransitive Clauses
Black Communication
Blackfoot (Language)
Blending Skills (Reading)
Bokmal
Bonggi
Bono
Bontok
Bororo
Brahmi Script
Braille Code
Branched Fiction
Bransford Franks Linear Effect
Breton
Bridging Vocabulary
British Sign Language
Buem
Bukidnon
Bunun
Bureaucratic Language
Business Speech
Cacaopera
Caddoan Languages
Cakavian Dialects
Calcutta Standard Dialect
Calo
Cameroonian Pidgin
Camsa
Capanahua
Capeverdean
Careful Speech
Carib
Catalan
Causatives (Grammar)
Celtic Languages
Chacobo
Chado Hamitic
Chaga
Chalit
Chamicuro
Character String Handling
Chepang
Cherology
Chichewa
Chien Ou Dialect
Chien Yang Dialect
Childrens Writing
Chiluba
Chinantecan
Chinese (Classical)
Chinese Phonetic Alphabet
Chinook Jargon
Chinookan (Language)
Chipewyan
Chiwere
Chocho
Chontal
Chorti
Chukchi
Chumash
Church Slavic
Ciluba
Civic Writing
Classical Rhetoric
Classifiers (Language)
Clauses
Clear Text Representation
Cliches
Clinical Linguistics
Clitic Pronouns
Clitics
Clustering (Reading)
Coaching (Speech)
Coaction (Speech)
Coarticulation (Speech)
Cognates
Cognitive Academic Language Proficiency
Cognitive Grammar
Collaborative Composing
Collaborative Writing
Colloquialisms
Colombian Languages
Colons (Grammar)
Comanche (Language)
Commas
Common Sense Narratives
Communication Competencies
Communication Dominance
Communication Satisfaction
Communicative Approach
Community Language Learning
Community Literacy
Comparative Constructions
Comparative Rhetoric
Comparative Sentences
Compensation (Communication)
Complete Linguistic Elements Paradigm
Compliments (Language)
Compound Bilingualism
Compound Nouns
Compound Words
Comprehensible Input
Comprehensible Input PLUS Language Experience
Conceptual Parser
Concreteness (Language)
Conditionals
Conference Terminology
Confluency (Second Language Instruction)
Conjunctions
Conjunctive Transformations
Connectives (Grammar)
Consonance
Consonant Cluster Duration
Consonant Clusters
Consonant Deletion
Consonant Mutation
Consonant Vowel Consonant Combinations
Constraint Dependency Grammar
Contemporary Rhetoric
Content Context Words
Content Structure
Context Dependence
Context Dependent Grammar
Contextual Dissonance
Contextualization
Continuative Verbs
Contractions (Grammar)
Contrastive Analysis Hypothesis
Contrastive Rhetoric
Controlled Compositions
Conversation
Conversation Exercises
Conversational Flow
Conversational Management
Conversational Markers
Conversion (Linguistics)
Cooccurrence (Grammar)
Coordinate Bilingualism
Coos
Copula (Grammar)
Copula Deletion (Grammar)
Core Language
Coreference
Coreguaje
Correlational Grammar
Corsican
Cotabato Chabacano
Cotabato Manobo
Count Nouns
Cowlitz
Critical Languages
Cross Language Transfer
Crosslinguistic Influence
Crow
Cuneiform Writing
Cupeno
Cushitic Languages
Dacca Dialect
Daga
Dagari
Dagomba
Dan
Dardic Languages
Dari
Declarative Forms (Language)
Decoding (Speech)
Decontextualized Language
Definite Articles
Deictics
Deixis
Deletion (Linguistic)
Demands (Speech Acts)
Demolinguistics
Demonstratives
Demotic
Deseret Alphabet
Destructive Dialog
Devanagari
Devoicing
Dey
Dhangar Kurux
Dhimotiki
Dialectical Enjoinment
Diathesis
Dibabawon
Digraphs
Diminutives
Dinka

Diola
Diphthongs
Direct Objects
Directive Speech
Disappearing Text Technique
Discourse
Discourse Accent
Discourse Aims
Discourse Conventions
Discourse Markers
Discourse Organization
Disfluencies
Djinang
Dogrib
Dominant Language
Doublespeak
Doublespeak (Public)
Downgrading (Linguistics)
Dyirbal
E Prime
Early Writing
Eclogue Tradition
Efik
Egyptian Languages
Ejectives (Phonetics)
Elaborated Code (Linguistics)
Elamite
Ellipsis
Emai
Embedding (Grammar)
Embedding Transformations
Emergent Languages
Emergent Meaning
Empathic Listening
Enclitics
Endangered Languages
English (African)
English (American Indian)
English (Appalachian)
English (Australian)
English (British)
English (Cajun)
English (Canadian)
English (Carriacou Creole)
English (Chicano)
English (Filipino)
English (General American)
English (Gold Coast)
English (Hawaiian)
English (Indian)
English (Irish)
English (Isletan)
English (Liberian)
English (Midwest)
English (Native American)
English (New York City)
English (Nigerian)
English (Puerto Rican)
English (Saskatchewan Spoken)
English (Scottish)
English (Singapore)
English (Southern)
English (Southwest)
English (Standard California)
English as a Second Dialect
English as an International Language
English Literacy
Enthymeme
Epenthesis
Epideictic Rhetoric
Epithet
Ergativity
Eseejja
Ethnographic Semantics
Ethnolinguistics
Ethnorhetoric
Ethogenics
Etsako
Eulogies
Euphemism
Eurotra
Ewondo
Expanded Speech
Explanatory Speech
Expletives
Exploratory Language
Exploratory Writing
Expository Text
Expressive Writing
Extinct Languages
Extrasentential Expressions
Eyak
Family English Literacy
Family Literacy
Fanagalo
Fante
Fataluku
Faublas Pressoir Orthography
Finnish English Dialect
First Person Discourse
Firthian Linguistics
Flaming (Computer Mediated Communication)
Flemish
Fluency First Approach
Focus Marking
Foreign Language Press
Foreign Words
Foreigner Talk
Forkner Shorthand
Form Errors (Handwriting)
Formal Language
Formal Literary Style
Formosan Languages
Formula Phonics
Formulaic Expressions
Formulaic Speech
Fossilized English
Fossilized Language
Francophone Literature
Francophonie
Free Modifiers
Freezing Principle
French (Acadian)
French (Cajun)
French (Canadian)
French (Haitian)
French (Parisian)
French (Swiss)
French Creole
Fricatives
Fries Linguistic Method
Frisian
Functional Linguistics
Functional Load
Functional Sentence Perspective
Functional Unification Grammar
Future Tense
Gaddang
Gahuku
Galice
Gascon
Gaviao
Gbandi
Gembu
Gender (Language)
General American Symbols
Generative Rhetoric
Generative Semantics
Generic Nominals
Generic Pronouns
Genitives
Geolinguistics
German (Low)
German (Middle High)
German (Old High)
German (Pfaelzisch)
German (Swiss)
German Vocabulary Inventory
Germanic Languages
Ghazel
Gilaki
Gio
Given Names
Glides (Phonology)
Glossematics
Glossolalia
Glottal Stops
Gogo
Gola
Gorum
Gothic
Grammar of Action
Grammatical Categories
Grammatical Consciousness Raising
Grammatical Constraint Hypothesis
Grammatical Junctures
Grammatical Mapping
Grammatical Terminology
Grammatical Transfer
Grammaticality
Grapevines (Communication)
Graphic Communication
Graphic Postorganizers
Grapho Linguistics
Graphonemes
Grazdanka
Great Leap Theory (Literacy)
Greek (Koine)
Guahibo
Guajiro
Guanano
Gude
Guided Writing
Gulf Language Family
Gurung
Guyanese Creole
Ha
Hadiyya
Hagen Central Incidental Recall Paradigm
Haida
Hakka Dialect
Halbi
Halia
Han (Athapascan Language)
Hangul Script
Hanis
Hanja Script
Hanoi Dialect
Havasupai
Hawaiian Pidgin
Haya
Head Wrap (Grammar)
Hedges (Linguistics)
Hehe
Heiltsuk
Hepburn Romanization
Heritage Language
Hesitation (Speech)
Hestian Hermeneutics
Hidatsa
Hierarchical Cluster Structure
Hijazi (Urban Dialect)
Hiligaynon
Hindi (Literary)
Hindi (Suddh)
Hindustani
Hiptionary
Hispanic Languages
Historical Present Tense
Historical Rhetoric
Hixkaryana
Homographs
Homonemes
Homonyms
Homophones
Horizontal Articulation
Hualapai
Huastec
Huave
Huei Dialects
Huichol
Hupa
Hyperbole
Hypercorrection
Hyperparse
Icelandic
Icelandic (Old)
Idioglossia
Ifugao
Ignaciano
Ijo
Ika
Illocutionary Content
Illocutionary Force
Illustrative Sentences
Ilocano
Ilongot
Imperatives (Grammar)
Imperfective Aspect (Verbs)
Implicational Analysis
Implicit Communication
Implicit Verbal Behavior
Implosives (Phonetics)
Impromptu Speeches
Indeophones
Indic Languages
Indirect Objects
Indirect Questions
Indirect Refusals
Indirect Speech
Indo Aryan Languages
Induced Mental Imagery
Infant Vocalization
Inferentials (Linguistics)
Infinitives
Inflection (Grammar)
Inga
Input Hypothesis
Instructional Conversation
Intaglio Printing
Integrated Organized Approach (Language Teaching)
Intelligibility (Speech)
Interdialect Translatability
Interjections (Grammar)
Interlingua
Interlingual Distance
Interlinguistics
Internal Lexicon
International English
International Phonetic Alphabet
International Terminology
Interpersonal Verbs
Interrogatives
Intersentential Processes
Intersubjectivity
Intertextuality
Intrapersonal Communication
Invariance Principle
Inverted Writing
Iowa (Language)
Iranian Languages
Iroquoian Languages
Isoko
Italian (American)
Italian (Australian)
Italian (Genoese)
Italic Writing
Itonama
Itsekiri
Iwaidja
Ixil
Jamaican Creole
Jamamadi
Japanese (Hawaiian)
Jaqi Languages
Jarai
Jewish Languages
Jirel
Jula
Juncture
Jurmati
Kabiye
Kabul Dialect
Kadazan
Kagan Kalagan
Kagate
Kaike
Kala Lagaw Ya
Kalabari
Kalapalo
Kalaw Kawaw
Kalinga
Kall
Kaluli
Kanasi
Kandahar Dialects
Kanji Script
Kano Dialect
Kanuri
Kapampangan
Kara
Karakalpak
Karitiana
Karuk
Kashubian
Kaska
Katakana
Katharevousa
Kathomilumeni
Kazakh
Kazan
Kekchi
Kelabit
Kenkyusha
Keresan
Key Vocabulary Words
Keyword Method (Language Learning)
Keyword Method (Second Language Learning)
Khaling
Khalkha
Kham
Khasi
Khowar
Kikuyu
Kimbundu
Kiowa
Kipsigis
Kiribati (Gilbertese)
Kissi
Klamath
Koasati
Koh
Kokuji
Kolami
Konkani
Kope
Kosena
Kotia Oriya
Kourion
Koyukon
Kpelle
Krahn
Kriol
Kru
Kuku Yalanji
Kupia
Kusaiean

Kutchin
Kuumu
Kwa
Kwakiutl
Kwoma
Kymograph Recording
Labeled Dependency Trees
Lamini
Lamnsok
Language Barriers
Language Choice
Language Contact
Language Creation
Language Creativity
Language Deficit Theory
Language Delayed
Language Diversity
Language Functions
Language Imposition
Language Innatism
Language Inquiry
Language Laboratory Monitoring
Language Lateralization
Language Loyalty
Language Maps
Language Pathology
Language Policy
Language Reform
Language Sciences
Language Sensitivity
Language Shaping Paradigm
Language Shift
Language Simplification
Language Spoken at Home
Language Spread
Languages for Science and Technology
Lappish
Lees Developmental Sentence Types
Left Modifier Grouping
Legal Language
Legal Vocabulary
Legal Writing
Lenape
Length of Utterance
Letter Recognition
Lexical Access
Lexical Ambiguity
Lexical Availability
Lexical Collocation
Lexical Decomposition Strategy
Lexical Density
Lexical Functional Grammar
Lexical Semantics
Lexical Storage
Lexicographic Preferences
Lexicometry
LF Movement
Library Terminology
Limericks
Lingua Francas
Linguistic Ambiguity
Linguistic Analysis
Linguistic Atlases
Linguistic Blindness
Linguistic Codes
Linguistic Context
Linguistic Continuum
Linguistic Conventions
Linguistic Drift
Linguistic Form
Linguistic Geography
Linguistic Incorporation
Linguistic Insecurity
Linguistic Markers
Linguistic Pluralism
Linguistic Relativity
Linguistic String Analysis
Linguistic Units
Linguistic Variables
Liquids (Language)
Lisramic
Listening Vocabulary
Literacy Campaigns
Locative Inversion
Locatives
Locutionary Expressions
Logographic Writing
Loko
Lomwe
Loma
Loucheux
Low Saxon
Lue Dialect
Luganda
Luiseno
Lummi (Language)
Lunda Chokwe
Luri Bakhtiari
Lushootseed
Luso Brazilian
Lwena
Macedonian
Macrostructures (Information)
Madurese
Magar
Maithili
Majang
Majhi Dialect
Makah (Language)
Makaton Vocabulary
Makonde (Language)
Malapropisms
Malinke
Maltese
Malwi Dialect
Mamanua
Mambila
Mampruli
Mandala
Mandara
Mande
Maninka
Manito
Mano
Manobo (Sarangani)
Manually Coded English
Maori (Language)
Maranungku
Marathon Writing
Margi
Mari
Maricopa
Markedness
Markedness Differential Hypothesis
Mass Nouns
Matching Texts
Maternal Speech
Mayan (Quiche)
Mazandarani
Mazatec
McCune Reischauer Romanization
Meitei
Menominee
Merina Dialect
Metacomprehension
Metadiscourse
Metafiction
Metakinesics
Metalanguages
Metanalysis (Linguistics)
Metanarration
Meter (Poetry)
Metonymy
Miccosukee
Miccosukee (Language)
Micronesian
Miju
Mikasuki
Mimetic Discourse
Min Dialect
Miniature Linguistic Systems
Misumalpan Languages
Mitre Grammar
Mixe
Mixtec
Modal Auxiliary Verbs
Modality (Grammar)
Modals (Verbs)
Mohawk
Momentary Verbs
Monemes
Montagnais (Cree)
Morphographemics
Morphographs
Morpholexical Phenomena
Morphotonemics
Mountain Speech
Movima
Muinane
Multiple Negation
Multiword Speech
Munduruku
Murinbata
Na Dene
Nagari Script
Nahuatl
Nahuatl (Classical)
Naidu
Nambiquara
Name Derivation
Name Stereotypes
Names
Nancowry
Narratology
Nasal Lisp
Nasality
Native Language
Native Language Assessment
Nativization (Language)
Natural Approach (Languages)
Natural Language
Natural Languages
Natural Literacy Development
Natural Method (Language Learning)
Nayarit
Ndebele
Ndjebbana
Nenets
Neoliteracy
Neologism
Nested Dependencies
Neutralization (Phonology)
New Grammar
New Literates
New Phonics
Newari
Ngaanyatjarra
Nicobarese Languages
Nienberge
Niger Congo Languages
Nigerian Languages
Nineteenth Century Rhetoric
Niyogi Brahmin
Nomenclature
Nonfluencies (Language)
Nonrestrictive Clauses
Nonrestrictive Relatives
Nonsense Syllables
Nonsense Words
Nonverbal Clauses
Nonwords
Noun Compounds
Noun Modifiers
Nukespeak
Nupe
Nyakusa
Nyamwezi
Nynorsk
Nzema
Object (Grammar)
Object Initial Languages
Obligatory Contour Principle
Occitan
Odual
Ogbia
OK (Word)
Old National Phonetic Symbols
Old Norse
Old Saxon
Omaha
Omotic Languages
Oneida
Onomatopoeia
Onondaga
Open Sentences
Optional Shift (Grammar)
Oral Composing
Oral Form Discrimination
Ordering Syllogisms
Oriya
Orokaiva
Oromo
Orthographic Redundancy
Orthographic Structure
Orthography
Oto
Oto Manguean
Otomi
Ottawa
Over Extension Phenomena
Overt Verbalization
Oyo Ibadan Dialect
Paez
Paget System
Paired Reading
Paite
Paiute
Palauan
Paleosiberian Languages
Pali
Palindromes
Panare
Pandialectal Phonology
Pangasinan
Panoan
Papia Kristang
Papiamento
Papuan Languages
Paradigmatic Responses
Paradigmatic Syntagmatic Language List
Paragraph Boundaries
Paragraph Meaning
Paraphrase
Paraphrastic Analysis
Parataxic Distortion
Parengi
Parsing
Participles
Particles (Grammar)
Partitive Construction
Pashto (Afghan)
Pashto (Eastern Afghan)
Passage Independency
Passive Voice
Passives
Past Tense
Pattern Meaning
Pattern Organization
Pattern Practice
Paumari
Pausing (Speech)
Pedagogical Grammars
Pengo
Pentadic Analysis
Pequot
Perfect Verb Forms
Performance Studies (Speech)
Performative Language
Perlocutionary Effects
Perso Arabic Script
Person (Grammar)
Peshawar Dialects
Petitio Fallacy
Phased English Courses
Philippine Languages
Phnom Penh Dialect
Phonetic Realization Rules
Phonetic Symbolism
Phonic Literature
Phonological Variability
Phrasal Verbs
Phrase Reading
Phrasebooks
Phrasing
Pidgin Signed English
Pijin
Pima
Pintupi
Pinyin (Language)
Piraha
Pitch (Language)
Pitjantjatjara
Pivot Grammar
Place Names
Plain English
Plain Language
Planbox Escalation
Plosives (Phonology)
Political Rhetoric
Polynesian Languages
Polyphony (Linguistics)
Polysemous Words
Polysemy
Polysynthesis
Ponapean
Portuguese (Brazilian)
Possessives
Possessor Ascension
Possessor Omission
Powhatan Language
Pragmalinguistics
Precis Writing
Predicate Grammar
Predicate Matching
Predicate Raising
Predicate Structure
Predicate Subject Order
Predicates
Predicatid
Predictability (Language)
Preference Semantics
Prelanguage
Prelinguistics
Premackese
Prenasalization
Prepositional Phrases
Prepositional Verbs
Prescriptive Grammar
Present Perfect Tense
Present Tense
Preseverational Syntax
Prestige Forms (Language)
Prestige Languages
Presupposition
Preverbal Communication
Previewing (Reading)
Primary Acquisition of Language
Private Language

Pro Verbs
Propositions (Grammar)
Prosodic Organization
Protective Vocabulary
Proto Algic
Proto Algonquian
Proto Chadic
Proto Elamo Dravidian
Proto Indo European
Proto RELADES
Provencal
Prussian
Pseudo Morphemes
Public Language
Puget
Pulaar
Qafar
Qualifiers (Language)
Quantifier Float Constructions (Linguistics)
Quantifiers
Que Deletion
Quickspeak
Rate Controlled Speech
Rawas
Rayalaseema Telugu
Reaction English
Reader Writer Relationship
Reading Speaking Relationship
Reciprocals (Languages)
Reciprocity (Communication)
Recitation
Reduction (Phonology)
Reduplication (Phonology)
Referential Communication
Referents (Linguistics)
Reflecting (Communication)
Reflective Writing
Reflexives
Refutation Text
Registers (Linguistics)
Rejang
Relational Grammar
Relative Clauses
Repairs (Language)
Repetition (Language)
Restating (Communication)
Restricted Code (Linguistics)
Restrictive Clauses
Reticence
Retraction (Linguistics)
Retroflexion
Rhapsodes
Rhetorical Community
Rhetorical Competence
Rhetorical Devices
Rhetorical Effectiveness
Rhetorical Force
Rhetorical Form
Rhetorical Genres
Rhetorical Questions
Rhetorical Science
Rhetorical Sensitivity
Rhetorical Situation
Rhetorical Stance
Rhetorical Strategies
Rhetorical Structure
Rhyme
Rigid Designators
Romaji Alphabet
Romanian (Moldavian)
Romansh
Romany
Root Words
Roper Creole
Rukai
Rundi
Rungus Dusun
Rural Language
Sabah Murut
Sadhu
Sahaptin
Saigon Dialect
Saisiyat
Sama Bangingi
Samal
Sandawe
Sangir
Santali
Sara Ngambay
Saramaccan
Sarmi
Schooled Language Competence
Secondary Onomatopoeia
Seedig
Segmentals (Phonology)
Segmentation (Verbal)
Self Reference (Language)
Self Verbalization
Selkup
Semantic Abbreviation
Semantic Categories
Semantic Contrasts
Semantic Elaboration
Semantic Feature Analysis
Semantic Features
Semantic Generalization
Semantic Integration
Semantic Interference Effect
Semantic Mapping
Semantic Networks
Semantic Organizers
Semantic Potential Theory of Language
Semantic Priming
Semantic Relation Comprehension
Semantic Transformations
Semantic Webbing
Semilingualism
Semiolinguistics
Senoufo
Sensitization (Language Learning)
Sensory Metaphors
Sentence Fragments
Sentence Verification
Sequoyah Syllabary
Serbian
Serer
Seri
Sesotho
Setswana
Shanghai Dialect
Sharada Script
Shawnee
Sheltered English
Sherpa
Shilha
Shina
Shokleng
Shoshoni
Shuadit
Shuswap
Sibilants
Sidamo
Signal Distortion
Signed English
Signifying (Rhetorical Strategy)
Signing Exact English
Silent Period (Language Learning)
Silent Way (Gattegno)
Similes
Simplification (Language)
Simultaneous Interpretation
Simultaneous Language Acquisition
Sindhi
Single Base Transformations
Single Word Utterances
Singular Forms (Grammar)
Siouan Languages
Siriono
Slang
Slavey
Slips of the Tongue
Slovak
Small Talk
Sochiapan
Sociolects
Songhai (Language)
Soninke
Sonoran
Sonority Cycle
Sooke
Sorbian
Sorbian (Upper)
Sosva Dialect
Sotho (Northern)
Sotho (Southern)
Sounding (Language)
South Asian Languages
Southeast Asian Languages
Southern Paiute
Spanish (American)
Spanish (Castilian)
Spanish (Chicano)
Spanish (Chilean)
Spanish (Cuban)
Spanish (Judeo)
Spanish (Mexican)
Spanish (Peruvian)
Spanish (Puerto Rican)
Spanish (Texas)
Spanish (Yanito)
Spatial Relationships (Sentences)
Specific Literacy
Speech Accommodation
Speech Community
Speech Convergence
Speech Discrimination
Speech Functions
Speech Identification
Speech Melody
Speech Perception
Speech Physiology
Speech Play
Speech Print Relationship
Speech Rate
Speech Reception Threshold
Speech Recoding
Speech Thinking
Spelling Errors
Spelling Patterns
Spelling Reform
Spirantization
Split Infinitives
Spokan
Spontaneous Speech
Spoonerisms
Staging (Text)
Standard Literary Norm
Static Abstractions
Status Terms (Linguistics)
Stigmatized Forms (Language)
Story Completion
Story Setting
Story Writing
Strategic Competence (Languages)
Stratificational Grammar
Stylistics
Subanun
Subjacency
Subject (Grammar)
Subject Constraints
Subject Literatures
Sublanguage Grammars
Subordinate Clauses
Subordination
Subset Principle
Substitution Correlates (Grammar)
Suena
Suffixes
Sukuma
Sulawesi
Sunwar
Surrogates (Linguistics)
Survival Language
Swabian
Sylheti
Syllabaries
Syllabication Ability
Syllogisms
Symbol Accentuation
Symbolic Interactionism
Symbolic Linguistic Encoding
Synecdoche
Synonyms
Synophones
Syntactic Bootstrapping
Syntactic Complexity
Syntactic Density
Syntactic Elaboration
Syntactic Maturity
Syntactic Processing
Syntactic Recoding
Syntactic Trace
Syntactic Words
Syntactical Mediation
Syntagma
Synthetic Phonics
Systemic Grammar
Tabaru
Taboo Terms
Tabriz
Tacana
Tactile Communication
Tagabili
Tagbanwa
Tahltan
Tai Shan Dialect
Taiwanese
Takelma (Language)
Talk Time
Talker Identity
Tamang
Tamazight
Tanoan Languages
Tarascan
Tashkent Dialect
Tatana
Teacher Language
Teacher Talk
Technical Language
Telegraphic Codes
Telegraphic Speech
Telephone Conversation
Television Grammar
Television Writing
Temne
Teng Xian Dialect
Tense Switching
Tensing (Vowels)
Tepehuan
Teribe
Terministic Screens
Tertiary Response
Text Adaptation
Text Characteristics
Text Classification
Text Coherence
Text Design
Text Formatting
Text Legibility
Text Organization
Text Patterns
Text Processing (Reading)
Text Transformation
Text Types
Textlinguistics
Textuality
TH Role
Thai Sign Language
Thakali
Tharu
Theme Rheme Articulation
Tibeto Burman Languages
Tigre
Tigrinya
Timbre Discrimination
Time Expanded Speech
Time Expressions
Tina Sambal
Ting An Dialect
Tiruray
Title Words
Tiv
Tiwi
Tlingit
Toishan Dialect
Tojolabal
Tok Pisin
Tolowa
Tonal Accents
Tonal Inflection
Tonal Spelling
Tone (Language)
Tone Decay
Tone Sandhi
Tonemes
Tongan
Top Level Structure
Topic Changes
Topic Sentences
Topic Units
Topicalization (Language)
Toskery
Totonac
Toubou
Tough Movement Structures
Traditional Oral Literature
Traditional Orthography
Transcription Method
Transferred Epithets
Transformational Phonology
Transformational Stylistics
Transitive Inferences
Transitivity
Transliteration
Transracial Communication
Trap Setting (Psycholinguistics)
Tree Adjoining Grammar
Tsimshian
Tsimshian (Coast)
Tsimshian (Southern)
Tsonga
Tsou
Tswana
Tucano
Tumbuka
Tunebo
Tungus
Tupi Guarani Language Family
Turki
Turkish (Modern)
Turkish (Ottoman)
Turkmen
Tutchone
Tutelo
Tuvaluan
Tuvan
Twi
Type Token Ratios

Uchumataqa
Uigur
Umbundu
Underlying Phonological Representations
UNIFON Alphabet
Uniform Slavic Transliteration Alphabet
Universal Grammar
Universal Symbols
Urdu (Lahori Roman)
Urhobo
Usan
Ute
Vaagri Boli
Vah Dialect
Vai
Value Proposition Debate
Variant Spellings
Venda (Language)
Ventureno
Verbal Clitics
Verbal Elaboration
Verbal Encoding
Verbal Imitation
Verbal Modeling
Verbal Nouns
Verbal Routines
Verbal Rules
Vientiane Dialect
Visual Compositions
Vocal Qualities
Vocalization
Voice (Rhetoric)
Voice (Verbs)
Voice Qualities
Voiced Stops
Voicing
Volga Finnic Languages
Vowel Duration
Vowel Harmony
Vowel Sandhi
Vowel Shift Rule
Wade Giles Transliterations
Wakashan
Walmatjari
Wantoat
Waray
Warlpiri
Washkuk
Waystage Level (Languages)
Webbing (Thematic)
Wen Ch Ang Dialect
Wen Yen
Wes Kos (Pidgin)
Wh Clauses
Wh Questions
Whiz Deletions
Whorfian Hypothesis
Winnebago
Wojokeso
Wolayto
Word Analysis and Synthesis
Word Associations
Word Attack Skills
Word Banks
Word Boundaries
Word Choice
Word Counts
Word Derivation
Word Families
Word Finding Problems
Word Formation
Word Fragments
Word Knowledge
Word Learning
Word Length
Word Omission
Word Order
Word Pitch
Word Potency
Word Realism
Word Shape
Word Stems
Word Strings
Word Structure
Word Superiority Effect
Words
World English
Writing Contexts
Writing Development
Writing Folders
Writing for Television
Writing Functions
Writing Patterns
Writing Quality
Writing Samples
Writing Style
Wu Dialect
Xavante
Xhosa
Xinca
Yagua
Yakan
Yanyuwa
Yao
Yaqui
Yavapai
Yuchi
Yucuna
Yueh Dialect
Yuman Languages
Yunga
Yurok
Zahao
Zamboangueno
Zaparoan Languages
Zapotec
Zipfs Law of Vocabulary Distribution
Zulu
Zuni

CATEGORY 14: Laws / Legislation

AAUP Contracts
Abington v Schempp
Abood v Detroit Board of Education
Academic Research Facilities Modernization Act
Accident Compensation Act 1972 (New Zealand)
Act 84 (Pennsylvania 1986)
Act for Better Child Care Services
Act of Liberty
Adams v Califano
Adams v Richardson
Adequate Prior Notice
Administrator Rights
Adoption Assistance and Child Welfare Act 1980
Adult Education Act
Adult Education Act 1965
Adult Education Act 1966
Adult Education Act 1969
Adult Education Act 1978
Adult Education Act Amendments 1984
Adult Education Act Section 321
Adult Education Amendments 1978
AFT Contracts
Age Discrimination Act 1975
Age Discrimination in Employment Act 1967
Age Discrimination in Employment Act Amend 1978
Age Discrimination in Employment Act Amend 1980
Age Discrimination in Employment Act Amend 1984
Age Discrimination in Employment Act Amend 1986
Aggravated Robbery
Agricultural Appropriations Act 1965
Agriculture and Food Act 1981
Aguilar v Felton
Aid to Families with Dependent Children
Aiken v Lieuallen
Alaska Native Claims Settlement Act 1972
Albemarle Paper Company v Moody
Alcohol and Drug Abuse Education Act
Alimony
Allied Health Professions Personnel Training Act
Alma v Dupree
Alternative Minimum Tax
American Assn of Univ Professors v Bloomfield Coll
American Bar Association Canon 35
American Defense Education Act
American Indian Policy Statement 1983
American Indian Religious Freedom Act 1978
Americans with Disabilities Act 1990
Anarchy
Ann Arbor Decision
Anti Drug Abuse Act 1988
Antitrust Laws
Antitrust Legislation
Antonelli v Hammond
Appalachian Regional Development Act 1965
Appeals (Hearings)
Apportionment (Legislative)
Arbitration Awards
Architectural Barriers Act 1968
Architectural Transportation Barriers Compliance
Area Redevelopment Act 1961
Arizona Agricultural Relations Act 1972
Arizona Civil Rights Act
Arkansas Act 34
Arkansas Act 102
Arkansas Act 590
Armstrong Law
Arrest Records
Arrests
Arson
Articles of Confederation
Artifactual Evidence
Arts Humanities and Cultural Affairs Act 1976
Asbestos Abatement Act 1984 (Illinois)
Asbestos Hazard Emergency Response Act 1986
Asbestos School Hazard Abatement Act 1984
Asbestos School Hazard Detection and Control Act
Aspira v Board of Education
Assembly Bill 1725 (California 1989)
Assembly Resolution 48 (California 1963)
Association of American Medical Colleges v Carey
Asylum
At Will Rule
Automobile Theft
Auxiliary Services Act
Baby Doe Rule
Bail
Baker v Owen
Bakke v Regents of University of California
Bankruptcy
Bankruptcy Reform Act 1978
Bantu Education Act 1953
Barnes v Converse College
Basic Educational Opportunity Grants
Basic Indian Education Act
Basic Law (West Germany)
Basic Skills Improvement Policy (Massachusetts)
Bates v State Bar of Arizona
Bauer v Kincaid
Bender v Williamsport Area School District
Bequests
Bethel School District 403 v Fraser
Better School Building Amendment (West Virginia)
Bilateral Agreements
Bilingual Education Act 1968
Bilingual Education Act 1984
Bilingual Education Act Amendments 1974
Bill 82 (Ontario)
Bill of Human Rights 1960 (Canada)
Bill of Rights
Bill of Rights for Foster Children 1973
Blackwolf Case
Blaubergs v Board of Regents Univ System Georgia
Blue Laws
Board of Education v Allen
Board of Regents v Roth
Board of Trustees Keene State College v Sweeney
Board v Rowley
Bob Jones University v United States
Bolling v Sharpe
Bowers v Hardwick
Bradshaw v Rawlings
Branzburg v Hayes
Braxton v Municipal Court
Brito et al v The Zia Company
Broadcast Access Rights
Broadcast Licensing
Broadcast Regulation
Broadcasting Act (Italy)
Brown Act
Brown v Board of Education
Brown v Glines
Buck v Bell
Buckley Amendment
Buckley v Indianapolis Board School Commissioners
Budget Reconciliation Act
Burden of Proof
Bursley Act
Buy Indian Act 1908
Bylaws
California Administrative Code Title 5
California Child Abuse Reporting Law
California Education Code
California Education Code 1976
California Fair Employment and Housing Act
California School Finance Reform Act
Canada United States Free Trade Agreement 1989
Canadian Charter of Rights and Freedoms
Canadian Human Rights Act
Cannon v University of Chicago
Canon Law
Capital Punishment
Career Education Incentive Act
Career Education Incentive Act 1977
Carl D Perkins Voc and Appl Techn Educ Act 1990
Carl D Perkins Vocational Education Act 1984
Carter v Rand McNally Co
Case Law
Castro v Phoenix Union High School District 210
Censure
Certificate of Need
Certificated Personnel Perf Eval Act (Colorado)
Chance v Board of Examiners
Chandler v Florida
Chapman v Rhodes
Chapter 5 (Pennsylvania)
Chapter 53 (New York)
Chapter 74 (Massachusetts)
Chapter 97 (New Jersey)
Chapter 188 (Massachusetts)
Chapter 622 (Massachusetts)
Chapter 636 (Massachusetts)
Chapter 688 (Massachusetts)
Chapter 720 (New York)
Chapter 766 (Massachusetts)
Charter of the French Language (Quebec)
Child Abuse Amendments 1984
Child Abuse Prevention and Treatment Act
Child Abuse Prevention Treatment Adoptn Reform Act
Child Care Act 1979
Child Care and Development Block Grants
Child Care Legislation
Child Care Linkage Legislation
Child Care Services Entitlement
Child Development Associate Scholarship Assist Act
Child Nutrition Act 1966
Child Pornography
Child Support Enforcement
Child Support Enforcement Amendments 1984
Child Support Enforcement Services
Child Welfare Act (Alberta)
Children with Learning Disabilities Act 1969
Childrens Lobby
Childrens Television Act 1990
City of Madison Joint Sch Dist No 8 v WERC
City of Newport v Fact Concerts Inc
City Taxes
Civil Rights Act 1871
Civil Rights Act 1871 Section 1983
Civil Rights Act 1957
Civil Rights Act 1962 Title VII
Civil Rights Act 1964
Civil Rights Act 1964 Title IV
Civil Rights Act 1964 Title VI
Civil Rights Act 1964 Title VII
Civil Rights Act 1968
Civil Rights Act 1968 Title II
Civil Rights Act 1968 Title VIII
Civil Rights Act 1991
Civil Rights Attorneys Fees Award Act
Civil Rights of Institutionalized Persons Act
Civil Rights Restoration Act 1987
Civil Service Reform Act 1978
Class Action
Class Action Suits
Clayton Act
Clayton v Place
Clean Air Act 1963
Clean Air Amendments 1970
Cleveland Board of Education v Lafleur
Cleveland Board of Education v Loudermill
Code of Hammurabi
Codes of Student Conduct
Cohen v Chesterfield City School Board
Cohoes City School District v Cohoes Teachers Assn
Collateral Bar Rule
Colorado Comprehensive Health Education Act 1990
Columbus Board of Education v Penick
Commercial Motor Vehicle Safety Act 1986
Commitment Laws
Committee Public Educ Religious Liberty v Nyquist
Common Law
Communications Act 1934
Communications Satellite Act 1962
Communications Satellite Act 1969
Community Services Block Grant Act
Comprehensive Child Development Act 1971
Comprehensive Education Reform Act (Tennessee)
Comprehensive Employment and Training Act

Comprehensive Employment and Training Act Title IV
Comprehensive Health Manpower Training Act
Comprehensive Service Amendments 1973
Comprehensive Smoking Prevention Educ Act 1981
Comprehensive Special Education Law (Mass)
Computer Crimes
Computer Matching and Privacy Protection Act 1988
Computer Security Act 1987
Conditional Deregulation
Congressional Bills
Conlan Amendment
Connick v Myers
Consent
Conspiracy
Constitutional Amendments
Constitutional Government
Constitutional Ratification
Constitutions
Consumer Credit Laws
Consumer Law
Consumer Leasing Act
Contempt of Court
Content Regulation (Broadcasting)
Contract Law
Contract Management
Contractors Association v Secretary of Labor
Contributory Negligence
Control of Paperwork Amendments 1978
Cooperative Research Act 1954
Cooperative Research Act 1954 Title VII
Copyright Act (Canada)
Copyright Act 1909
Copyright Act 1978
Copyright Compliance
Copyright Law 1976
Copyright Law Amendments 1980
Copyright Revision Bill
Coser v Moore
County Agricultural Extension Council Law
County of Washington v Gunther
Court Interpreters Act 1978
Court Interpreting
Crawford v Board of Education of Los Angeles
Credit Card Fraud
Crime Awareness and Campus Security Act 1990
Crime Detection
Criminal Investigations
Criminal Justice
Criminal Justice Initiative
Criminal Justice System
Criminal Prosecution
Criminal Records
Cross Examination
Davis Bacon Act
Dawes Allotment Act 1887
Day Care Facilities Loan Guarantee Fund
Day Care Regulations
Dayton Board of Education v Brinkman
Death Records
Debra P v Turlington
Deficit Reduction Act 1984
Defunis v Odegaard
Degree Authorization Act (Colorado 1981)
Delaconte v State of North Carolina
Delaney Clause
Demonstration Cities Act
Dental Practice Act (Michigan)
Department of Defense Authorization Act 1983
Department of Labor Contract Comp v Reg Univ Calif
Dependent Care Tax Credit
Deportation
Depository Institutions Deregulation Act 1980
Depository Library Act 1962
Deregulation
DES Education and Research Amendments 1992
Desegregation Aid
Detention
Detroit Edison v National Labor Relations Board
Developmental Disabil Servs and Facil Constr Act
Developmental Disabilities Act
Developmental Disabilities Amendments 1978
Developmental Disabled Assist Bill of Rights Act
Diagnosis Related Groups
Diplomatic Immunity
Direct Legislation
Disability Payments
Discretionary Programs
Discrimination against Children
Discrimination Complaints
Displaced Homemakers Self Suff Assist Act 1990
Diversion (Judicial)
Doe v Plyler
Doe v Renfrow
Domestic Volunteer Service Act
Donahoe Act
Double Jeopardy
Draft
Draft Lottery
Draft Registration
Drafting (Legal)
Driving Regulations
Drug Abuse Education Act 1970
Drug Free Schools and Communities Act 1986
Drug Free Workplace Act 1988
Drug Legislation (New York)
Dyer Act
Early Childhood Development Act (Missouri 1984)
Earned Income Tax Credit
Economic Dislocation Worker Adjust Assist Act 1988
Economic Opportunity Act 1964
Economic Opportunity Act Title I
Economic Opportunity Act Title II
Economic Opportunity Act Title III
Economic Opportunity Act Title V
Economic Opportunity Amendments 1967
Economic Recovery Tax Act 1981
Edgewood Independent School District v Kirby
Education Act 1944 (England)
Education Act 1968 (Kenya)
Education Act 1970 (New Jersey)
Education Act 1981 (England)
Education Amendments 1967
Education Amendments 1970
Education Amendments 1972
Education Amendments 1974
Education Amendments 1975
Education Amendments 1976
Education Amendments 1978
Education Amendments 1980
Education and Training Amer Competitiveness Act
Education Consolidation and Improvement Act 1981
Education Consolidation Improvement Act Chapter 1
Education Consolidation Improvement Act Chapter 2
Education Finance Act 1990 (Texas)
Education for All Handicapped Children Act
Education for Economic Security Act 1984
Education of the Deaf Act 1986
Education of the Deaf Act Amendments 1992
Education of the Handicapped Act 1970
Education of the Handicapped Act 1970 (Part B)
Education of the Handicapped Act 1986 (Part H)
Education of the Handicapped Act Amendments 1983
Education of the Handicapped Act Amendments 1986
Education Professions Development Act
Education Reform Act 1988 (England)
Education Reform Act 1987 (Great Britain)
Educational Advancement Act
Educational Employment Relations Act (California)
Educational Opportunity Fund (New Jersey)
Educational Rights
Educational Technology Act
Educational Testing Act 1979
EEOC v Mississippi College
EEOC v University of New Mexico
Eighteen Year Old Vote
Eighteenth Amendment
Electronic Communications Privacy Act 1986
Elementary Secondary Education Act
Elementary Secondary Education Act Title I
Elementary Secondary Education Act Title II
Elementary Secondary Education Act Title III
Elementary Secondary Education Act Title IV
Elementary Secondary Education Act Title IV B
Elementary Secondary Education Act Title IV C
Elementary Secondary Education Act Title V
Elementary Secondary Education Act Title VI
Elementary Secondary Education Act Title VII
Elementary Secondary Education Act Title VIII
Elementary Secondary Education Amendments 1967
Eleventh Amendment
Ellis v O Hara
Emancipation Proclamation
Emergency Employment Act 1971
Emergency Immigrant Education Act 1984
Emergency Jobs and Unemployment Assistance Act
Emergency Jobs Appropriations Act 1983
Emergency Jobs Programs Extension Act 1976
Emergency School Aid Act 1972
Emergency Unemployment Compensation Act
Emergency Veterans Job Training Act 1983
Eminent Domain
Employee Retirement Income Security Act
Employee Right to Know Act 1978 (Michigan)
Employment Act 1946
Employment Legislation
Employment Opportunities for Disabld Americans Act
Employment Security Act (Michigan)
Endangered Species Act 1973
Endowed Schools Act 1869 (England)
Energy Conservation and Production Act 1976
Energy Policy and Conservation Act 1975
English Language Amendment
English Law
English Literacy Grants
Entitlement
Environmental Education Act 1970
Environmental Law
Environmental Pesticide Control Act
Equal Access
Equal Access Act 1984
Equal Credit Opportunity Act
Equal Educational Opportunities Act 1974
Equal Employment Opportunities Enforcement Act
Equal Employment Opportunity Act 1972
Equal Pay Act 1963
Equal Results (Law)
Equal Rights
Equal Rights Amendment
Equal Time Doctrine
Equivalent Instruction Programs
Errors and Omissions Insurance
Espionage
Espionage Act
Establishment Clause
European Sports Charter
Evidence
Excellence in Education Act 1984
Exclusive Representation
Exclusivity Provision
Executive Exchange Prog Voluntary Service Act 1986
Executive Order 11246
Executive Order 11375
Executive Order 11652
Executive Order 12356
Executive Privilege
Exhaustion of Remedies
Ezekial v Winkley
Fact Opinion Distinction
Fair Comment
Fair Credit and Reporting Act 1970
Fair Credit Billing Act
Fair Dismissal Law (Oregon)
Fair Employment Legislation
Fair Employment Practices Act 1953
Fair Hearings
Fair Housing Law 1968
Fair Housing Laws
Fair Labor Standards Act
Fair Representation
Fairness Doctrine
Falwell v Flynt
Family Choice Education Initiative (California)
Family Education Loan Program
Family Educational Rights and Privacy Act 1974
Family Law
Family Practice Act 1970
Family Protection Legislation
Family Support Act 1988
Farm Labor Contractor Registration Act
Farmland Assessment Act
Fascell Stone Amendment
FCC v Midwest Video Corporation
FCC v Pacifica Foundation
FCC v WNCN Listeners Guild
Federal Advisory Committee Act 1972
Federal Aid Highway Act
Federal Aviation Regulation Part 147
Federal Budget
Federal Coal Mine Health and Safety Act
Federal Deficit
Federal Election Campaign Act
Federal Employee Part Time Career Employ Act 1978
Federal Highway Safety Act 1966
Federal Interagency Day Care Requirements
Federal Motor Carrier Safety Regulations Part 398
Federal Rule 23
Federal Service Mandates
Federal Standards
Federal Trade Commission Act
Federal Trade Commission Improvement Act 1980
Federal Water Pollution Control Act Amendments
Felony Cases
Fifteenth Amendment
Fifth Amendment
Fifty Percent Law (California)
Fighting Words Doctrine
Financial Distress Grants
Firefighters Local Union 1784 v Stotts
First Amendment
Fiscal Response
Fishing Rights
Florey v Sioux Falls School District
Florian Frederick Chess v Gary E Widmar
Florida Compensatory Education Act 1977
Florida Educational Accountability Act 1976
Food and Agriculture Act 1965
Food and Agriculture Act 1977
Food Security Act 1985
Food Stamp Act 1964
Food Stamp Act 1977
Foreign Assistance Act 1975 Title XII
Forgery
Fourteenth Amendment
Fourteenth Amendment Article IV
Fourth Amendment
Franklin v Gwinnett County Public Schools
Fraud
Free Textbook Law (Missouri)
Freedom of Assembly
Freedom of Association
Freedom of Information Act
Frontiero v Richardson
Fugitive Slave Act 1793
Fugitive Slave Act 1850
Fulbright Hays Act
Full Employment Act 1972
Full Employment and Balanced Growth Act 1978
Full Employment Bill 1945
Fullilove Case
Fund Application
G I Bill
G I Bill 1984
G I Bill Improvement Act 1977
Gaines v Anderson
Gardner Denver Case
Garnishment
Gary E Widmar Et Al v Clark Vincent Et Al
Gault v Garrison
Gay Students Organization v Bonner
Geduldig v Aiello
General Agreement on Tariffs and Trade
General Education Provisions Act 1968
General Education Provisions Act 1974
General Education Provisions Act Section 405f
General Land Allotment Act of 1887
General Purpose Grants
General Revenue Sharing Act 1972
Gerrymandering
Gertz v Robert Welch Inc
Gifted and Talented Childrens Education Act 1978
Gitlow v New York
Goals 2000
Goldsboro Christian Schools Inc v United States
Gordon v Committee on Character and Fitness
Goss v Lopez
Government Employees Training Act
Government Regulation
Governmental Immunity
Governors Grants
Gramm Rudman Hollings Balanced Budget Amendment
Grant Simplification
Great Education Reform Bill 1987 (United Kingdom)
Great Lakes Water Quality Agreement
Green v City of Gadsden
Greenberg Law
Grievance Arbitration
Griffin v County School Board
Griggs v Duke Power Company
Grove City College v Bell
Guaranteed Student Loan Program
Guardian Ad Litem

Gun Control
H R 77 (94th Cong 1st Sess)
H R 4563 (94th Cong 1st Sess)
H R 5901 (94th Cong 1st Sess)
H R 8677 (93d Cong 1st Sess)
H R 9730 (93d Cong 1st Sess)
H R 12257 (93d Cong 2d Sess)
H R 15045 (90th Cong 2d Sess)
Habeas Corpus
Handicapped Childrens Early Educ Assist Act 1968
Handicapped Childrens Protection Act 1986
Handicappers Civil Rights Act 1976 (Michigan)
Hart v Community School Board
Hatch Act
Hatch Amendment
Hate Crime
Hate Speech
Hawkins Stafford Act 1988
Hazelwood School District v Kuhlmeier
Hazelwood School District v United States
Head Start Expansion and Improvement Act 1990
Head Start Improvement Act 1992
Health and Safety at Work Act 1974 (England)
Health Maintenance Organization Act 1973
Health Manpower Act 1968
Health Manpower Act 1975
Health Professions Educ Exten Amendments 1992
Health Professions Education and Distribution Act
Health Professions Educational Assistance Act
Helen Keller National Center Act
Helsinki Final Act
Hendricks v Carroll
High Performance Computing Act 1991
High School Graduation Requirements Law (NJ)
Higher Education Act 1965
Higher Education Act 1980
Higher Education Act Amendments 1972
Higher Education Act Amendments 1976
Higher Education Act Amendments 1981
Higher Education Act Amendments 1986
Higher Education Act Amendments 1992
Higher Education Act Title I
Higher Education Act Title II
Higher Education Act Title II B
Higher Education Act Title II D
Higher Education Act Title III
Higher Education Act Title IV
Higher Education Act Title V
Higher Education Act Title VI
Higher Education Act Title VII
Higher Education Act Title VIII
Higher Education Act Title IX
Higher Education Act Title X
Higher Education Act Title XI
Higher Education Act Title XII 1972
Higher Education Amendments 1968
Higher Education Amendments 1979
Higher Education Cooperation Act (Illinois)
Higher Education Facilities Act 1963
Higher Education Opportunity Act 1970
Hire the Handicapped Law (Michigan)
Hobson v Hansen
Home Rule Act (District of Columbia)
Honig v Doe
Horace Mann League v Board of Public Works
Horowitz v Curators of University of Missouri
Horton v Goose Creek Independent School District
Hortonville School Dist v Hortonville Educ Assn
Hostrop v Board of Junior College District
House Arrest
House Bill 72 (Texas 1984)
House Bill 1187 (Colorado 1985)
House Bill 1706 (Oklahoma 1981)
House Bill 2020 (Oregon 1987)
Housing and Community Development Act 1974
Housing and Community Development Act Title II
Housing and Urban Development Act 1968
Housing Codes
Human Rights and Equal Opp Comm Act (Australia)
Human Services Reauthorization Act 1984
Human Services Reauthorization Act 1990
Hurd v City of Buffalo
Idaho School Improvement Act 1984
Illinois Domestic Violence Act
Illinois Educational Reform Act 1985
Immigrant Amnesty
Immigration Act 1976 (Canada)
Immigration and Nationality Act 1965
Immigration and Nationality Act Amendments
Immigration Law
Immigration Legislation
Immigration Reform and Control Act 1986
Impact Aid
Impeachment Proceedings
Implied Consent Law (Pennsylvania)
Impoundment (Federal Funds)
Income Taxes
Income Verification
Indian Arts and Crafts Board Amendments Act 1980
Indian Bill of Rights
Indian Child Welfare Act 1978
Indian Civil Rights Act 1968
Indian Education Act 1972
Indian Education Act 1972 Title IV
Indian Education Act 1988 Title V
Indian Education Act Amendments 1987
Indian Health Care Improvement Act
Indian Reorganization Act 1934
Indian Self Determination Education Assistance Act
Individuals with Disabilities Education Act
Individuals with Disabilities Education Act Part B
Individuals with Disabilities Education Act Part H
Industrial Relations Act 1971 (Great Britain)
Industrial Training Act 1964
Informal Negotiations
Information Partnership Act
Ingraham v Wright
Intent to Discriminate
Intergovernmental Personnel Act
Internal Revenue Code
International Education Act
International Regulations
Interstate Child Support
Interstate Compact on the Placement of Children
Irreparable Harm Standard
Jacob K Javits Gifted Talented Stdnt Educ Act 1988
Jarema Law
Javits Wagner O Day Act 1971
Jay Treaty
Jewish Law
Job Training Partnership Act 1982
Job Training Partnership Act 1982 Title IIA
Job Training Partnership Act 1982 Title III
Job Training Partnership Act Amendments 1992
Job Training Partnership Amendments 1986
Jobs Child Care Block Grant
Johnson O Malley Act
Joint Custody
Joint Operating Agreements (Newspapers)
Jones v Illinois Dept of Rehabilitation Services
Jose P v Ambach
Judicial Attitudes
Judicial Review
Junior College Act (Illinois 1965)
Jurisdiction
Jurisprudence
Juvenile Delinquency Prevention Act 1972
Juvenile Delinquency Youth Offenses Control Act
Juvenile Diversion
Juvenile Justice Delinquency Prev Act Amend 1992
Juvenile Justice Delinquency Prevention Act 1974
Kaelin v Grubbs
Kaimowitz v Department of Mental Health
Katharine Gibbs School (Inc) v FTC
Katko v Briney
Kelley v Metro County Board of Ed of Nashville
Kentucky Education Reform Act 1990
Kentucky Interlocal Cooperative Act and Agreement
Kentucky v Rudasill
Keyes v Denver School District Number 1
Kingsville Independent School District v Cooper
Krotkoff v Goucher College
Land Claims
Land Remote Sensing Commercialization Act 1984
Land Rights
Lari v California
Larry P v Riles
Lau Remedies
Lau Remedies 1975
Lau v Nichols
LaValle Bill
Law of the Sea Convention
Least Restrictive Means Test (First Amendment)
Lee v Weisman
Legal Audits
Legal Clinics
Legal Community
Legal Deposit
Legal Drinking Age
Legal Information
Legal Precedents
Legal Procedures
Legal Reference Materials
Legal Research
Legal Rights
Legal Status
Legal Structures
Legalization (Educational Governance)
Legislated Learning
Legislative Drafting
Legislative Intent
Legislative Reform
Legislative Sessions
Legislative Voting
Legitimacy (of Governments)
Lemon DiCenso Decision
Lemon v Kurtzman
Lentczner v Yorktown High School
Levittown v Nyquist
Library Act 1972 (Great Britain)
Library Legislation
Library Services and Construction Act
License Agreements
License Fees
License Plates
Licensed Programs
Licensing Programs
Liddell v Saint Louis Board of Education
Life Safety Code
Living Wills
Loudermill v Cleveland Board of Education
Louisiana Competency Based Education Law
Louisiana Educational Accountability Act
Low Income Home Energy Assistance Act 1981
Lubbock Civil Liberties Union v Lubbock School
Lujan v Colorado State Board of Education
Lurias Neuropsychological Investigation
Lynch v Donnelly
Lynchings
Maine v Thiboutot
Majority Rule
Mandatory Special Education Act (Michigan)
Manpower Development and Training Act
Manpower Policy
Marbury v Madison
Marchi Law
Marital Law
Marital Rape
Maritime Law
Mark Stevenson v Jefferson County Public Schools
Marshall v Georgia
Martin Luther King Elementary v Ann Arbor
Maryland Equal Rights Amendment
Massachusetts Board of Retirement v Murgia
Massachusetts Transitional Bilingual Education Act
Massachusetts v Mellon
Maternal and Child Health Block Grants
Maternal and Child Health Care Act 1976
Maternal Custody
Mathews v Eldridge
McAteer Act
McCarran Walter Act
McCulloch v Maryland
McLendon v Morton
Media Deregulation
Media Law
Medical Advertising Regulation
Medical Library Assistance Act
Medicare Catastrophic Protection Act 1988
Meese v Keene
Melani v Board of Higher Education
Mental Health Amendments 1990
Mental Retardation Grants 1968
MERCOSUR
Metis Betterment Act
Metric Study Act 1968
Meyer v Nebraska
Middle Income Student Assistance Act
Migrant Children Educational Act (Colorado)
Migrant Education Amendment
Migrant Health Act
Migrant Seasonal Agric Worker Protection Act
Military Educational Assistance Legislation
Military Justice
Military Law
Military Selective Service Act
Miller Unruh Reading Act
Miller v California
Millikan v Board of Directors
Milliken v Bradley
Milliken v Green
Mills v Board of Education
Minnesota Education Expense Tax Deduction Law
Minnesota Wisconsin Reciprocity Agreement
Miranda Warning
Missing Children Act 1982
Missing Childrens Assistance Act 1983
Missing Childrens Assistance Act 1984
Mississippi Education Reform Act 1982
Mississippi Fair Employment Practices Act 1974
Missouri Excellence in Education Act 1985
Moot Court
Morrill Act 1862
Morrill Act 1890
Morton v Mancari
Motion Picture Law
Mount Healthy City School District Board v Doyle
Mozert v Hawkins County Public Schools
Mueller v Allen
Mulford Act
Municipal Annexation
Municipal Regulation
Must Carry Rules (Broadcasting)
Narenji v Civiletti
National Ambient Air Quality Standards
National and Community Service Act 1990
National and Community Service Trust Act 1993
National Apprenticeship Act 1937
National Collegiate Athletic Association Rule 48
National Council on Educ Standards and Testing Act
National Defense Education Act
National Defense Education Act Title III
National Defense Education Act Title IV
National Defense Education Act Title V A
National Defense Education Act Title VI
National Defense Education Act Title VII
National Defense Education Act Title XI
National Defense Student Loan Program
National Direct Student Loan Program
National Educational Opportunities Act 1975
National Electrical Code
National Energy Conservation Policy Act
National Energy Conservation Policy Act 1978
National Environmental Education Act 1990
National Environmental Policy Act
National Foundation on Arts Humanities Act 1965
National Health Service Corps Amendments 1985
National Historic Preservation Act
National Indian Goals and Progress Act
National Labor Relations Act
National Labor Relations Board v Yeshiva Univ
National League of Cities v Usery
National Library and Information Services Act
National Life Safety Fire Code
National Literacy Act 1991
National Materials and Minerals Policy R and D Act
National Policy on Education 1986 (India)
National Reading Improvement Act
National Research Act
National School Lunch Act 1946
National School Lunch Act 1970
National School Lunch and Child Nutrition Act 1975
National Security Education Act 1991
National Student Loan Reform Act 1979
Native American Languages Act 1992
Native American Programs Act 1974
Native American Programs Act 1974 Title VIII
Navajo Hopi Long Range Rehabilitation Act 1950
NCAA v Board of Regents of University of Oklahoma
NEA Contracts
Nebraska v Faith Baptist
Neutrality Act 1935
New Jersey Administrative Code Education Title 6
New Jersey Employer Employee Relations Act
New Jersey Public School Education Act 1975
New Jersey v Shelton College
New Jersey v TLO

Tanzanian Library Services Board Act
Targeted Jobs Tax Credit
Tax Equity
Tax Equity and Fiscal Responsibility Act 1982
Tax Limitation Efforts
Tax Limitations
Tax Reform Act 1948
Tax Reform Act 1969
Tax Reform Act 1976
Tax Reform Act 1978
Tax Reform Act 1981
Tax Reform Act 1984
Tax Reform Act 1986
Taxpayer Equity
Taylor Law
Teacher Pension Plans
Teacher Tenure Act (Michigan)
Technology Related Assistance Individ Disabil Act
Ten Commandments
Tenants Rights
Tenth Amendment
Termination of Rights
Termination of Special Tribal Status
Termination of Tribal Status
Termination of Welfare Benefits
Testing Legislation
Texas Department of Community Affairs v Burdine
Texas Education Code
Third Party Liability
Thirteenth Amendment
Thompson v Southwest School District
Thornock v Boise Independent School District
Tilton v Richardson
Tinker v Des Moines Independent School District
Title IX Education Amendments 1972
Title XI Education Amendments 1978
Tougas Amendment (Massachusetts)
Track Record Disclosure Regulations
Trade Act 1974
Trade Negotiations
Trade Readjustment Act 1974
Trademarks
Traffic Violations
Training Guarantee Act (Australia)
Trans World Airlines v Hardison
Transitional Services Coordination Act (Maine)
Transportation Act 1970
Treaty of Ghent
Trevelyan Bill
Tri Offer Final Offer Arbitration
Trials
Tribal Courts
Tribal Jurisdiction
Tribal Law
Tribally Controlled Comm Coll Assist Act 1978
Tribune Publishing Co v Curators Univ of Missouri
Trimboli v Board of Education of County of Wayne
Trustees of Dartmouth College v Woodward
Truth in Leasing
Truth in Lending
Truth in Testing Act 1979
Truth in Testing Legislation
Tuition Tax Credits Legislation
Unemployment Insurance Act 1970
Unemployment Insurance Amendments 1976
Uniform Building Code
Uniform Management of Institutional Funds Act
Uniform Patent Legislation
Uniform Probate Code
Uniform Reciprocal Enforcement of Support Laws
Uniform Vehicle Code
Union Rights
United Cerebral Palsy New York v Board of Educ
United Nations Charter
United Nations Convention on Rights of the Child
United States Constitution
United States Constitution (Proposed Amendments)
United States Constitution Article 5
United States Housing Act 1937
United States Soviet Union Environmental Agreement
United States v Fordice
United States v Georgia Power Company
United States v Nixon
United States v Providence Journal
United States v Seeger
United States v South Carolina
United States v State of Texas
United States v The Progressive
Universal Declaration of Human Rights
University Administration Reform Act (Netherlands)
University of Texas v Camenisch
University Reform Law (Spain)
Urban Grant University Program
Urban Mass Transportation Act 1976
Utah Schools and Lands Improvement Act 1993
Vagrancy
Valley Forge Christian College v Americans United
Verdicts
Veterans Education Amendments 1980
Veterans Education Amendments 1986
Veterans Education and Employment Amendments 1984
Veterans Education and Employment Assistance Act
Veterans Education Training Amendments Act 1970
Veterans Educational Assistance Act 1981
Veterans Educational Assistance Amendments 1991
Veterans Readjustment Assistance Act Section 402
Veterans Rehabilitation Education Amendments 1980
Veysey Act
Victim and Witness Protection Act 1982
Victims Bill of Rights (California 1982)
Victims Rights
Vietnam Era Veterans Readjustment Assistance Act
Visas
Visitation Rights
Vlandis v Kline
Vocational Education Act 1963
Vocational Education Act 1975
Vocational Education Act 1981
Vocational Education Amendments 1968
Vocational Education Amendments 1969
Vocational Education Amendments 1974
Vocational Education Amendments 1976
Vocational Education Guidelines 1979
Vocational Rehabilitation Act 1920
Vocational Rehabilitation Act 1973
Vocational Rehabilitation Act Amendments 1968
Vocational Technical Education Act 1983
Voting Rights Act 1965
Wage and Price Controls
Wage Compliance Standards
Wagner O Day Act 1938
Wagner Peyser Act
Wakefield Bill (California)
Wallace v Jaffree
Walsh Healy Public Contract Act
War Powers Act
Warranties
Warren Court
Warsaw Pact
Washington v Davis
Water Pollution Control Amendments
Water Rights
Webb v Board of Education
Weber v Kaiser Aluminum and Chemical Corporation
Webster v Reproductive Health Services
Welsch v Noot
West Virginia Board of Education v Barnette
Wexell v Scott
Whistle Blowing
White Collar Crime
Wicks Law (New York)
Widmar v Vincent
Wilderness Act 1964
Williams and Wilkins Co v United States
Williams v Eaton
Williams v Hamilton
Williams v O Brien
Willie M v Hunt
Winton Act
Wisconsin v Yoder
Withrow v Larkin
Witters v Washington Dept of Services for Blind
Womens Educational Equity Act
Wood v Strickland
Work Permits
Worker Adjustment and Retraining Notification Act
Workers Disability Compensation Act 1980
Wyatt v Stickney
Y S v District of Philadelphia
Young Offenders Act 1984 (Canada)
Youth Act 1980
Youth Employment Act 1979
Youth Employment Act 1980
Youth Employment and Demonstration Projects Act
Youth in Adult Courts
Youth Unemployment Act 1979
Zacchini v Scripps Howard

CATEGORY 15: Methods / Theories

0 1 Linear Programming Model
2 Plus 2 Articulation Plan
3 Phase Version Code Transformation Task
3P COTRAN
4 1 4 Calendar
4MAT System
6 S Paradigm
6PQ Method for Discovery Learning
20 20 Analysis
45 15 Plan
ABC (Approach by Concept) Method
ABC X Model (Hill)
Abductive Reasoning
Ability Achievement Discrepancy
Ability by Treatment Interaction
Abolitionism
Absolute Judgment
Absolute Values
Absolutism
Academic Abstention
Academic Alert System
Academic Building Systems
Academic Development Plans
Academic Discourse Theory
Academic Efficiency
Academic Forgiveness
Accelerated Mental Process
Accelerated Schools
Acceptability Judgments
Accommodation Theory
Account Approach
Accountability Based Learning Environment
Accountability Models
Accounting Systems
Accreditation Plus Model
Achievement Motivation Training
Achievement Standards
Acquisition Behavior
ACT Theory
Action Category System
Action Oriented Therapy
Action Reflection Relationship
Action Theory
Action Training Model
Active Audience
Active Listening
Active Staffing Process
Active Teaching
Active Teaching Behaviors
Activity Analysis
Activity Classification
Activity Code and Text System
Activity Group Guidance
Activity Segment
Activity Structures
Activity Theory
Activity Vector Analysis
Ad Populum Fallacy
Adaptation Concept
Adaptation Effect
Adaptation Style Theory
Adapted Felt Figure Technique
Adapted Group Figure Attitude Technique
Adaptive Capacity
Adaptive Concept Acquisition
Adaptive Evaluation Structure
Adaptive Exercise Sequencing
Adaptive Filtering
Adaptive Instructional Management System
Adaptive Instructional Methods
Adaptive Instructional Models
Adaptive Instructional Systems
Adaptive Learning Environments Model
Additive and Multiplicative Constants
Additive Difference Model
Additive Models
Additive Variance
Adjacency Effect
Adjective Generation Technique
Adjusted Resolution
Adkins Life Skills Structured Inquiry
Adlerian Psychology
Administration by Objectives
Administrative and Organizational Systems Model
Administrative Attribution Theory
Administrative Control
Administrative Management by Objective Apprais Sys
Administrative Q Sort
Administrative Terminal System
Administrator Action Plan (Maine)
Administrator Involvement
Adoption Diffusion Theory (Rogers)
Adult Communication Management
Adult Compacts
Adult Competency Training
Adult Education State Plans
Adult Language Levels Management System
Adult Learning Program Service
Advance Teacher Preparation
Advanced Individual Training
Advanced Instructional System (Air Force)
Advanced Pilot Training
Advanced Study Guide Technique
Adventure Economics
Adversary Instructional Model
Adversary Method
Advisory Approach
Advisory Systems
Advocacy Planning
Advocacy Training
Advocate Counseling Model
Affect Abilities Training
Affect Concepts
Affect Effect Theory
Affirmation Strategy
Affordance (Cognition)
After School Detention
Afterlife
Agam Method of Visual Education
Age Adjustment
Age Appropriateness
Age Differential Hypothesis
Age Grading
Age Integrated Learning
Age Relevance
Age Specificity
Agency Client Contracting
Agency Provider Relationship
Agency Theory
Agenda Control Model
Agent Action Objective Model
Aggregate Model
Agree Disagree Statements
Agricultural Knowledge System (Israel)
Ainsworth Strange Situation Procedure
Air Force Phase II Base Level System
Air Force Specialty Code
Air Gap Phenomenon
Akaike Information Criterion
Alabama Resources Information Systems
Alaska Instructional Diagnostic System
Albuquerque Integration Model
Aldous Simulation of Personality
Alloplastic Orientation
ALOHA System
Alpha Learning Systems
Alphanumeric System
Alternance Training
Alternative Admissions (College)
Alternative Educational Plan
Alternative Futures Approach to Planning Model
Alternative Grading
Alternative Justification Approach
Alternative School Calendars
Alternative Teacher Education
Alternatives to Consolidation
Alternatives to Corporal Punishment
Amiability Tilt
Analog Drawing
Analog Transmission Systems
Analogical Reasoning
Analogue Models
Analogues
Analoguing
Analysis of Concepts by Data Processing
Analytic Approach
Analytic Rotational Methods
Analytic Teaching
Analytical Methods
Analytical Model Technique
Analytical Objectivity
Analytical Philosophy of Education
Anarchism
Anchored Assessment
Anchored Instruction
Andersen Newman Model of Utilization
Anecdotal Analysis
Anecdotal Discipline
Anglin Grid

Angoff Methods
Animadversion Error
Animism
Anomie Theory
Anonymous Feedback System
Antagonistic Cooperation
Anthrogogy
Anthropomaximology
Anticipation Interval
Anticipation Method
Anticipatory Socialization
Apocalypticism
Apollo Simulation Checkout and Training System
Apollonianism
Appleton Century Crofts Portable Laboratory System
Application Level Learning
Applications Transfer System
Applied Behavior Analysis
Apprenticeship of Observation Theory
Approach Technique
Approval Plans
Approved Program Approach
Approximation (Statistics)
Archival Information Dissemination System
ARCS Model
Argumentation Theory
Argyrian Theory
Aristotles Concept of Logos
Arkansas Classroom Management Training Model
Array Transformation
Arrow Capron Model
Articulated Faculty Concept
Artificial Intelligence in Training
As Parents Grow Older Model
Aschner Gallagher Verbal Interaction Technique
Assessment Confrontation Strategizing Model
Assessment Intervention Follow Through
Assessment Interview Process
Assignment Models
Assimilation Theory
Association Consolidation
Associational Montage
Associative Group Analysis
Associative Grouping Strategies
Associative Method of Teaching
Assumed Similarity of Opposites
Asymmetric Relationships
Asymptotic Distribution Theory
Atkinson Theory of Motivation
Attention Interest Desire and Action Approach
Attention Reduction Training
Attention Theory
Attitude Information System
Attribute by Treatment Interaction
Attribute Frequency Model
Attribute Identification
Attributed Responsibility
Attributive Theory of Quality
AUDACIOUS
Audible Multi Imagery
Audience Research
Audience Specification
Audio Intercommunication Systems
Audio Motor Units
Audio Tutorial Instruction
Audio Visual Structural Global Method
Audio Visual Tutorial Method
Audiotutorial System
Audiovisual Contracting
Audit Trails
Audition (Theatrical)
Auditions (Music)
Auditory Icons
Aural Study System
Authors in the Schools
Autocorrelation
Autokinetic Word Writing Technique
Automata Models
Automata Theory
Automated Affirmative Action System
Automated Braille System
Automated Cognitive Modeler
Automated Individualized Diagnosis System
Automated Instructional Management Systems
Automated Instructional Materials Handling System
Automated Instructional System
Automated Management Planning Control Systems
Automated Monitoring
Automated Stimulus Control System
Automated Tutoring
Automatic Content Analysis
Automatic Control Systems
Automaticity Training
Automaton Analysis
Automotive Collision Appraisal
Automotive Tune Up Teaching System
Autonomous Learner Model for Gifted and Talented
Autonomous Learning
Autophotographic Metaphor
Autoplastic Orientation
Autoregressive Integrated Moving Averages
Autotutorial Techniques
Availability Heuristic
Availability Rate
Average Visually Evoked Potentials
Averaged Electroencephalic Audiometry
Averaged Electroencephalic Response
Axiom Systems
Back Propagation Learning
Background Interference Procedure
Backward Conditioning
Backward Mapping
Balance Sheet Technique
Balanced Repeated Replication
Ball Stick Bird Reading Method
Ballantines
Bar Graphs
Barcoding
Bargaining
Barriers to Implementation
Barriers to Innovation
Barriers to Participation
Basal Evaluation Form
Base Engineer Automated Management System
Base Rate Approach
Basic Color Terms
Basic Economics Simulation
Bayes Decision Rule
Bayes Theorem
Bean Metzner Model
Beat Elimination Process
Behavior Alteration Techniques
Behavior Analysis
Behavior Analysis Follow Through
Behavior Control Perception Theory
Behavior Modeling
Behavior Observation Systems
Behavior Oriented Prescriptive Teaching Approach
Behavioral Anchoring
Behavioral Categories
Behavioral Consistency Method
Behavioral Consultation Model (Bergan)
Behavioral Event Analysis
Behavioral Organization
Behavioral Systems Approach
Behaviorally Anchored Supervisor System
Bejar Model
Bekesy Audiometry
Belief Maintenance Systems
Bellack System
Benchmarking
Bender Visual Memory Technique
Benefit Forecasting Method
Benefit Segmentation
Bennett Hierarchical Model
Berlin Model of Intelligence
Bernstein Hypothesis
Best Evidence Synthesis
BEST IDEA (Career Education Model)
Beta Index
Beta Multinomial Test Model
Bi Factor Analysis
Bibliographic Theory
Bibliopsychology
Bicognitive Approach
Big Bang Theory
Biglan Model
Bildung (Concept)
Bilingual Bicultural Model
Bilingual Comprehensive Integrat Reading and Comp
Bimodal Theory
Bimultivariate Redundancy Statistic
Binary Coding
Binary Data Analysis
Binary Measurement Model
Binary Propositional Logic
Binary Relational Model
Binary Search Scheme
Binomial Effect Size Display
Binomial Error Model
Biofunctional Model
Biographical Analysis
Biological Determinism
Biopsychosocial Model
Birnbaum Models
Black Box Theories
Blackout Technique
Blank Trial Method
Blended Sound Sight Method of Learning
Block Scheduling
Blocked Careers
Blocker Doctrine
Blooms Mastery Teaching Strategy
Blooms Taxonomy
Bloxoms Rotation Technique
Blumbergs Category System
Bobath Method
Bobitt Procedure
Bochum Model
Bogdanov Theory of Knowledge
Bogus Pipeline Technique
Boolean Search Strategy
Bootstrap Hypothesis
Bootstrap Methods
Borderline Group Method
Bormuth Literacy Model
Bowles Gintis Correspondence Theory
Box Cox Transformations
Box Jenkins Forecasting Model
Box Test
Brain Based Learning
Brain Flow Writing Technique
Breaching Episodes
Breadth of Perspective
Break Even Analysis
Breakthrough to Literacy Approach
Bridging Analogies
Brody Reading Method
Brophy Good Dyadic Interaction Coding System
Building Block Costing
Bully Pulpit Policy Strategy
Bureaucratic Bargaining (Simulation)
Business Education Learning System
Business Research
Butterfly Catastrophe Model
Buzan Organic Study Method
Caffrey Isaacs Economic Impact Model
California Adult Student Assessment System
California Articulation Number System
California Career Assessment Model
California Comprehensive Assessment System
California Education Information System
California Inquiry Conceptual Model
CaMaPe Models
Cameron Model of Organizational Effectiveness
Campus Effectiveness Model
CAMPUS Simulation Model
Canter Model of Assertive Discipline
Capital Improvements Programming
Captioned Media
Card Sort
Career Accessibility Model
Career Anchors Model
Career and Life Planning Model
Career Area Rotation Model
Career Conscious Individual Career Education Model
Career Development Modules
Career Education Document Information System
Career Lattice Model
Career Options Research and Development
Career Paths
Career Progression Systems
Career Salience
Carkhuff Training Model
Carroll Learning Model
Cascade System of Special Educational Services
Case Analysis
Case Approach (Writing)
Case Flagging
Case Method (Teaching Technique)
Case Processing Systems
Case Review Systems
Case Study Simulation
Case Survey Method
Casework Evaluation
Casual Dating Dissolution
Catastrophe Models
Catastrophe Theory
Categorical Special Education
Category Knowledge
Category Observation Systems
Category Theory
Cattell Horn Fluid and Crystallized Ability Theory
Causal Analysis
Causal Inferences
Causal Reasoning
Cause Maps
CEDARS Model
Cellular Learning Theory
Census Data System
Census Occupational Classification
Centour Analysis
Central Control Model (Typing)
Central Limit Theorem
Central Place Theory
CERLI Verbal Behavior Classification System
Certified Trainer Systems
Chain Indexing
Chain Reaction Forum (Technique)
Challenge Coaching
Change Analysis
Change Models (Havelock)
Change Perspectives
Changing Criterion Design
Chaos Theory
Charge Back Systems
Chart Method
Chartering Process
Charting
Check Technique
Childrens Strategies Assessment System
Chomsky Competence Model
Chomsky Halle Phonological System
Christian National Education
Chronometric Techniques
Chunking
Circle of Concern
Circle Time
Circles of Knowledge
Circular Scaling Technique
Circumplex Model of Marital and Family Systems
CITAR Computer Courseware Evaluation Model
City Game
City Model Computer Simulation
Clarifying Purpose Task
Class (Concept)
Class Inclusion
Class Vicariance
Classical Test Theory
Classroom Based Intervention
Classroom Effectiveness
Classroom Simulation
Classroom Teacher Support System
CLER Model
Client Tracking
Clinical Analysis
Clinical Approach
Clinical Interviews
Close Reading Approach
Closed Captioned Television
Cluster Approach (Vocabulary)
Co Citation Analysis
Coached Practice
Coaching
Cobb Douglas Function
Cockpit Resource Management
Code Alphabet Meaning Emphasis
Code Emphasis Method
Coded Elaborative Outline
Coercion Theory
Cognitive Affective Psychomotor Approach
Cognitive Apprenticeships
Cognitive Artifacts
Cognitive Capacity Engagement
Cognitive Code Learning Theory
Cognitive Complexity
Cognitive Congruence Procedure
Cognitive Continuum Theory (Hammond)
Cognitive Deficit Theory
Cognitive Demands
Cognitive Developmental Grouping
Cognitive Economics
Cognitive Engineering
Cognitive Enhancement
Cognitive Frameworks
Cognitive Instructional Counseling
Cognitive Interaction Analysis System
Cognitive Matching
Cognitive Model for Assessing Portfolios
Cognitive Modeling
Cognitive Models
Cognitive Operation Structure
Cognitive Process Theory of Writing
Cognitive Scripting
Cognitive Strategy Instruction in Writing
Cognitive Stress Inoculation Training
Cognitive Transition
Cognitively Guided Instruction
Cognitively Oriented Curriculum Model
Cohort Defined Tasks

COHORT Model
Cohort Survival Procedures
Cohort Survival Ratio Method
Cohort Theory of Word Recognition
Cold Type Composition (Printing)
Colearning
Collaborative Analysis Action Planning Process
Collaborative Bargaining
Collaborative Inquiry
Collaborative Learning
Collaborative Library Systems Development
Collaborative Talk
Collaborative Teaching
Colleague Consultation
Collection Mapping
Collective Coorientation Model
Collective Gaining
Collective Intent
Collective Interpretation
College Characteristics Analysis
College Classroom Vignettes
College Information System
College Suggestor System
Collegial Coaching
Collegial Evaluation
Collegial Governance Structures
Collegial Learning
Collegial Problem Solving
Collegial Supervision
Collegial Team Learning
Collier Factor
Color Theories
Colorado Individualized Instruction
Coloured Progressive Matrices
Combined File Search Strategy
Combined Motivation Education System
Command Action Planning System
Command Information Processing Systems
Commercial Educational Research
Common Criterion Approach
Common Target Game
Communality Estimates
Communicasting
Communication Channels
Communication Links
Communication Management
Communication Rules
Communication Script Analysis
Communication Strategies
Communications Network Training
Communications Protocols
Communications Research
Communicator Motivation
Communicator Style
Communicology
Community Approach to an Integrated Service System
Community Based Education
Community Based Programing
Community Based Report
Community Centered Learning
Community College Occupational Programs Eval Syst
Community Controlled Education
Community Empowerment
Community Exchange Systems
Community Forum Concept
Community Holding Power
Community Integrated Preschool
Community Land Use Game
Community Living Assessment System
Community Medical Television System
Community of Commitment
Community Policing
Community Portrait Analysis
Community Resource Development
Community Resources Pool
Community Vocational Habilitation Services Model
Comparative Economic Systems
Comparative Librarianship
Comparative Method
Comparative Political Systems
Comparative Reading
Comparative Structures
Comparative Stylistics
Compass Reading
Compatible Time Sharing System
Compensatory Models
Competency Based Guidance
Competency Identification Procedures
Competency Mapping
Competency Needs
Competency Rossville Model
Competency Validation (Occupations)
Competing Values Model
Competitive Argument
Competitive Exclusion
Competitive Values
Complement Abilities Pattern
Complete Procedural Review
Complex Concepts
Complex Instruction
Complex Rule Learning
Compliance Gaining Message Selection
Compliance Gaining Strategies
Compliance Training
Component Display Theory
Component Theory
Composing Aloud
Composite Direct Product Model (Browne)
Composition Theory
Compositional Syntactic Placement
Comprehensible Input Analysis
Comprehensible Output Analysis
Comprehension Monitoring
Comprehensive Adult Student Assessment System
Comprehensive Area Manpower Planning System
Comprehensive Assessment Report (New York)
Comprehensive Career Education Model
Comprehensive Education Process
Comprehensive Elementary Teacher Education Models
Comprehensive Guidance Program Model (Gysbers)
Comprehensive Manpower Development System
Comprehensive Objectives Accounting System
Comprehensive Office Laboratory Training
Comprehensive System for Personnel Development
Comprehensive University Scheduling System
Compromise Model (Hofstee)
Computational Mathematics Monitoring System
Computer Aided Facilities Management
Computer Analysis
Computer Assisted Advising
Computer Assisted Career Guidance
Computer Assisted College Administration
Computer Assisted Counseling
Computer Assisted Distribution and Assignment
Computer Assisted Guidance
Computer Assisted Language Analysis System
Computer Assisted Language Instruction
Computer Assisted Language Learning
Computer Assisted Lesson Service
Computer Assisted Management
Computer Assisted Management System
Computer Assisted Patient Simulation
Computer Assisted Placement
Computer Assisted Problem Solving
Computer Assisted Reading Educational System
Computer Assisted Remedial Education
Computer Assisted Reporting to Parents
Computer Assisted Requisitioning
Computer Assisted Scheduling
Computer Assisted Synthesizer System
Computer Assisted Teacher Training System
Computer Assisted Telephone Interviewing
Computer Assisted Video Instruction
Computer Assisted Vocational Counseling System
Computer Assisted Writing
Computer Augmented Lectures
Computer Augmented Teacher Training
Computer Augmented Teaching and Learning System
Computer Constructed Education
Computer Directed Training Subsystem
Computer Managed Geometry
Computer Managed Information
Computer Mentoring
Computer Models
Computer Presented Social Interactions
Computer Processed Sociogram
Computer Program Selection
Computer Related Learning Environments
Computerized Academic Counseling System
Computerized Accounting
Computerized Facilities Inventory
Computerized Techniques
Computerized Understanding of Morphology Language
Computerized Vocational Information System
Concentration
Concept 6 Calendar
Concept Attainment Strategy
Concept Matrices
Concept of Reading
Concept Paper Approach
Concept Reinforcement
Concept Shift Effect
Concept Structure
Concept Structuring Analysis Technique
Concept Tree Method
Conceptual Abstracting
Conceptual Analysis
Conceptual Approach
Conceptual Change
Conceptual Change Theory of Knowledge
Conceptual Comparator
Conceptual Dependency Theory
Conceptual Equivalency
Conceptual Frameworks
Conceptual Graphs
Conceptual Integration
Conceptual Models
Conceptual Peg Model
Conceptual Systems Theory
Concerns Analysis
Concerns Based Adoption Model
Concerns Report Method
Concession Bargaining
Concurrent Adaptive Measurement
Concurrent Enrollment
Conditional Probability
Confidence Intervals (Statistics)
Configural Frequency Analysis
Configurational Approach
Configurational Theory of Innovation Diffusion
Confirmation (Strategy)
Confirmatory Factor Analysis
Confirmatory Questioning Strategy
Conflict Analysis
Conflict Management
Conflict Management Style
Conflict Matrix
Conflict Theory
Confluence Model
Congruence Analysis Techniques
Conjoint Retention Hypothesis
Conjugate Reinforcement
Conlingual Integrated Approach
Connectionism
Connections (Mathematics)
Conscientisation
Consciousness Education
Consensus
Consensus Models
Consensus Moderation
Consequential Evaluation
Consistency Theory
Constant Comparative Method
Constant Information Model
Constitutive Ethnographic Theory
Constructalog
Constructive Criticism
Constructs
Consumer Validation Process
Contact Hypothesis
Containment Policy
Contemporary Industrial Processes
Contemporary Rhetorical Strategies
Content Analysis System
Content Area Reading Enrichment
Content Area Study Experiences
Content Area Teaching
Content Based Group Assessment Model
Content Module
Context Free Tasks
Context Input Process Product Evaluation Model
Contextual Analysis
Contextual Associative Method
Contextual Interaction Theory
Contextual Module Analysis
Contextualism
Contextualized Apprenticeship Model
Contextualized Instruction
Contiguity Theory of Learning
Contingency Analysis
Contingency Approach
Contingency Coefficient
Contingency Framework Administrator Development
Contingency Management System
Contingency Models
Contingency Tables
Contingency Theories
Contingent Negative Variation
Continuing Motivation
Continuity Analysis
Continuity Theory
Continuous Assessment
Continuous Creation
Continuous Growth Models
Continuous Recording Techniques
Continuum Models
Contract Implementation
Contract Item Analysis
Contract Training
Contractual Risk Transfer
Contrast Coding
Contrasting Groups Method
Control Analysis
Control Oriented Interactive Graphic Anal Design
Control Theory
Controlled Choice
Controlled Composition
Controlled Variable Trigrams
Convergence Technique
Convergence Theory
Convergent Communication
Conversation Theory
Conversational Analysis
Conversational Paradigm
Cooley Lohnes Evaluation Model
Cooperative Community Counseling
Cooperative Eval and Develop of School Systems
Cooperative Monitoring
Cooperative Program Planning and Teaching
Cooperative Purchasing
Coordinated Transfer Application System
Coordination Complexes
Coorientation
Copp Clark Canadian Reading Development Series
Coprincipalship
Copy Theory of Memory
Core Plus Education
Cornell Studies in Intergroup Relations
Corporate Athleticism
Corporatism
Corpsman Advisory System
Corrective Feedback Paradigm
Correlated Proportions
Correspondence Theory
Corridor Approach
Corsini Four R School System
Cosmic Approach
Cost Accounting
Cost Allocation to Program System
Cost and Training Effectiveness Analysis
Cost Containment
Cost of Attaining Personnel Requirements
Cost Plus Pricing
Cost Simulation Model
Costs of Schools Training and Education
Counseling Preparation Techniques
Counselmime
Counselor Effectiveness
Countenance Model (Stake)
Counter Culture Values
Counterpart Theory
Counterproposals
County Surveys
Course Assembly System and Tutorial Environment
Course Charting
Course Evaluation Scheme (Birmingham UK)
Coursework Cluster Analysis Model
Courtroom Procedures
Covariance Structural Analysis
Covariation
Covert Communication
Crayon Resist Technique
Creative Alternative Games
Creative Hypothesizing
Creative Job Search Technique
Creative Problem Solving
Creative Problem Solving for Kids
Creative Problem Solving Model
Creative Teaching Dilemma
Creative Visualization
Crime Causation
Crisis Management
Crisis Theory
Criterial Referent Theory (Kerlinger)
Criterion Referenced Supervision
Critical Decision Method
Critical Inquiry
Critical Pedagogy
Critical Success Factors Method
Critique Circle
Cross Ability Tutoring
Cross Angelo Classroom Assessment Model
Cross Categorical Service Delivery Model
Cross Classification Approaches
Cross Cultural Communication Packet

Cross Cultural Reentry
Cross Cultural Teaching
Cross Generational Studies
Cross Lagged Panel Technique
Cross Level Grouping
Cross National Studies
Cross Over Phenomena
Crossmodal Behavior
Croziers Law
Cube Model of Attributions (Kelley)
Cubism
Cue Attendance
Cue Motor Association Theory
Cultivation Theory (Television)
Cultural Adjustment
Cultural Competence
Cultural Criticism
Cultural Deficit Theory
Cultural Dependency
Cultural Distance Approach
Cultural Framing
Cultural Hegemony
Cultural Indicators Research
Cultural Inversion
Cultural Jurisprudence
Cultural Molding
Cultural Relativism
Cultural Reproduction
Cultural Studies
Cultural Universal Hypothesis of Cognitive Devel
Culture Area Concept
Culture Assimilator
Culture Theory
Cumulative Daily Review Process
Cumulative Deficit
Cumulative Learning
Cumulative Presentation
Cumulative Programing
Currere Method
Curriculum Audits
Curriculum Based Information Support System
Curriculum Based Staffing
Curriculum Construct Systems
Curriculum Engineering Systems
Curriculum Leadership Hierarchy
Curriculum Materials Analysis System
Curriculum Matrix
Curriculum Organization and Program Evaluation
Curriculum Review Development and Implementation
Curriculum Theories
Curve Sketching
Curvo Strategy
Custodial Approach
Customary System
Customized Training
Cutback Management
Cyclic Method
Cyclical Evaluation Model
D Nealian Manuscript
D Nealian Method
DACUM Process
Dadaism
Daily Performance Grades
Dalcroze Method
Dalton Plan
Darling Taxonomy of Administrative Problems
Dartmouth Rassias Method
Data Based Educational Planning Systems
Data Based Gymnasium Model
Data Based Instruction
Data Based Program Development
Data Based Program Modification
Data Crosswalk Codes
Data Envelopment Analysis
Data Envelopment Analysis Model
Data Ink Ratio Theory
Data Models
Data Reduction Methods
Data Truncation
Databased Course Assessment Method
Day Care Licensing
Day Care Vendor Voucher System
Debate Strategies
Debate Theory
Debriefing
Decennial Census Procedures
Decentration
Decimal Classification
Decision Adoption Model
Decision Analysis Technique
Decision Based Drama
Decision Models
Decision Quality
Decision Rule Instruction
Decision Rules
Decision Science Techniques
Decision Tables
Decision Theory
Decision Trees
Decontextualization
Default Analysis
Defense Economic Impact Modeling System
Defensive Structuring
Defensive Teaching (Academics)
Deferred Giving
Deferred Maintenance
Deferred Opportunity Education
Deferred Transcription
Deficit Spending
Deficit Theory
Del Becq Model
Del Mod System
Delay Conditioning
Delay Effect
Delay in Feedback Techniques
Delay Retention Effect
Delayed Auditory Feedback
Delayed Copying
Delta Plot Method
Demagoguery
Demand Processing
Deming Management Method
Demographic Planning Model
Demographic Transition Model
Departmental Examination System
Dependent Care Assistance Plans
Deprograming (Religion)
Deracialization
Derivational Theory of Complexity
Descriptive Discriminant Analysis
Descriptive Method
Descriptive Research
Design Experiments
Design for School Excellence
Design Methodology
Design Option Decision Trees
Designated Vocational Instruction
Designation Theory
Deskilling
Desuperimposition
Deterioration Quotient
Developing Exceptional Educational Potential
Developing Mathematical Processes
Developing Mature Interpersonal Relationships Task
Development Dissemination and Adoption
Developmental Academic Advising
Developmental Bypass Instructional Technology
Developmental Interdependence Hypothesis
Developmental Lag Hypothesis
Developmental Placement
Developmental Play
Developmental Reading Lesson Schedule
Developmental Screening
Developmental Sentence Types
Developmental Sequences
Developmental Speech Sequence Model
Developmental Structuralist Approach
Developmental Teacher Evaluation Kit
Developmental Theory
Devereux Model
Deviant Case Analysis
Dewey Decimal Classification
Dewey Meiswinkel Discussion Schema
Dewey Model
Deweys Experimentalism
Diacritical Marking Medium
Diagnostic Appraisal Systems
Diagnostic Assessment School Principal Effect
Diagnostic Conference Approach
Diagnostic Developmental Method
Diagnostic Interviews
Diagnostic Prescriptive Approach
Diagnostic Reliability
Diagnostic Research
Diagnostic Statistical Manual of Mental Disorders
Diagnostic Supervision
Diagnostic Systems Approach
Diagnostic Teaching Cycle
Dial a Career
Dialectic (Concept)
Dialectic Information Systems
Dialectical Reasoning
Dialectical Thought
Dialog Day
Dialogic Communication
Dialogic Education
Dialogics
Dialogue Analysis
Dialogue Boxes
Dichotomic Analysis
Dichotomous Keys
Dichotomous Search Strategies
Dickinson Classification
Dickinson Naylor Taxonomy
DICSIE Model
Dicto Comp Exercises
Didactic Teaching
Didactic Training
Dienes Multibase Arithmetic Blocks
Difference (Concept)
Difference Indicator
Difference Model
Differential Association Theory
Differential Effects Hypothesis
Differential Guidance for Gifted Model
Differential Readiness Model
Differential Reinforcement
Differential Reinforcement of Other Behaviors
Differentiated Additive Androgyny Model
Differentiated Oral Visual Aural Computerized Kine
Differentiation
Differentiation Hypothesis
Differentiation Integration Contingency Theory
Diffusion of Innovations Model
Diffusion of Innovations Research
Digital Analysis
Dilemma Discussion Approach
Dilemmas of Schooling
Dimensional Analysis
Dimensional Representation
Dimensions of Teacher Relationships
Dionysianism
Direct Grant System
Direct Instruction
Direct Instruction Model
Direct Interventionist Approach
Direct Line Authority
Direct Pure Piecemeal and Complete Method
Direct Quotation
Direct Response Marketing
Direct Teaching Model
Direct Verbal Instruction
Directed Graphs
Directed Overt Activity Strategy
Directed Reading Thinking Activities
Directed Reading Writing Activities
Directed Response Training
Directing (Theater)
Direction Following
Directive Teaching
Disaggregated Analysis
Disaster Planning
Disciplinary Referrals
Disciplinary Styles
Discipline Based Research
Discipline Based Teaching Theory
Disclosure Free Evaluation
Disclosure Models
Discontinuity
Discounting Principle
Discourse Based Teaching
Discourse Synthesis
Discrepancy Analysis
Discrepancy Evaluation Model
Discrepancy Formulas
Discrepancy Model
Discrepant Case Analysis
Discrepant Messages
Discretionary Situations
Discrimination Programing
Discrimination Training
Disjunctive Syllogisms
Disparate Impact Theory
Dissatisfaction Theory
Dissemination Analysis Group Model
Dissipative Structures Theory
Distancing Model (Sigel)
Distant Study Systems
Distractibility (Reading)
Distractor Technique
Distributed Practice
Distribution Of Associations Model
Distributive Justice
District Power Equalization
District School Relationship
Diversification
Diversified Cooperative Training
Diversity (Faculty)
Diversity (Student)
Diversity Concept
Division Hashing Function (Directory Structuring)
Division of Labor (Household)
Divorce Mediation
Do It Yourself Method
Document Analysis
Document Delivery Systems
Document Handling
Document Origination Processes
Doll Play Technique
Domain Analysis
Domain Knowledge
Domain Specific Thinking
Domain Specifications
Doolittle Method
Dorsett Educational Systems
Double ABCX Model
Double Alternation Learning
Double Bind Hypothesis
Double Bind Theory
Double Classification Skills
Double Exponential Smoothing
Double Stimulation Method (Vygotsky)
Downey Model of the Secondary Phase of Education
Downey Quality Fit Framework
Dramatic Theory
Drive Theory
Dual Audio Television Instruction
Dual Certification
Dual Coding Theory
Dual Economy Theory
Dual Grading
Dual Labor Market Theory
Dual Mode Learning
Dual Perspective Approach
Dual Principalship
Dual Progress Plan
Dyadic Consensus
Dyadic Interaction Analysis
Dyadic Observation System
Dynamic Concept Analysis
Dynamic Instructional Planning
Dynamic Learning System
Dynamic Simulation
Dynamic Support
Dysmathematics
Ear Order Strategy
Early Childhood Education Learning System
Early Field Experience
Easy Steps to Reading Independence
Ebacher Method
Ebel Method
Ecco Analysis
Echo Reading
Eclectic Counseling
Eclectic Teaching
Eco Maps
Ecobehavioral Analysis
Ecofeminism
Ecological Assessment
Ecological Communication Model
Ecological Inventory Strategies
Ecological Paradigm
Ecological Perspective
Ecomuseum Model
Economic Concepts
Economic Evaluation
Economic Theory
Edison Responsive Environment
Edition Theory
Educare
Education Economy Relationship
Educational Adequacy
Educational and Career Exploration System
Educational Brokerage
Educational Criticism
Educational Facilities Evaluation
Educational Ideologies
Educational Imagery
Educational Impacts Model
Educational Management Services
Educational Marketing
Educational Neglect
Educational Resource Management System
Educational Set Theory
Educational Stratification
Educational Warranty
Educological Research
Educology
Effective Classroom Management (Elementary)
Effective Classroom Management (Junior High)
Effective Listening
Effective Practice Identification
Effective Reading in Content Areas
Effective Schools Improvement Process
Effectiveness Assessment Matrix (Seybert)
Efficacy
Effort

Ego Development Theory
Elaboration Likelihood Model
Elaboration Theory
Elasticity of Demand
Elasticity of Substitution (Manpower)
Electrical Network Theory
Electroanalytical Techniques
Electromagnetic Theory
Electronic Dissemination of Information System
Elementary Beam Theory
Elementary Linkage Analysis
Elgin Competency Model
Elicitation Techniques
Embedded Case Studies
Embedded Intergroup Relations
Embedded Training
Emergent Reading Levels
Emic Etic Analysis
Emotion Theory
Emotionality Rationality Activity Model
Empirical Analysis
Empirical Case Study
Empirical Methods
Empirical Research
Empirical Transition Matrixes
Empiricism
Employability Development Plans
Employee Stock Ownership Plans
Employer Accounts Strategy
Employment Enhancement Strategies
Empowerment
Enabler Model
Enaction Theory
Enactive Reading Method
Endeavour Training
Energy Impact Scenario Model
ENERGYTAX Simulation Model
Engaged Style
Engagement Continuum
Engagement Style
Engelmann Becker Model
Enhanced Normative Systems Model (Terry)
Enhanced Vocational Education
Enrichment Triad Model
Enrollment Analysis Matrix
Enrollment Ceilings
Enterprise Zones
Environmental Beauty Estimation Method
Environmental Docility Hypothesis
Environmental Ethic
Environmental Risk Assessment
Environmental Robustness
Epidemic Theory
Episodic Communication Channels in Organizations
Episodic Mapping
Epistemic Triangle
Equality (Social)
Equifinality
Equilibrium Model
Equity Theory
Erica Method
Error Detection
Error Monitoring
Error Prone Model
Errorless Discrimination Training
Errorless Learning
Escondido Management System
Essential Elements of Instruction (Hunter)
Essentialism
Estimates of Decision Consistency (Huynh)
Ethical Analysis Protocol
Ethnic Revitalization
Ethnographic Monitoring
Ethnographic Residual Analysis
Euclidean Model
Eurhythmics
European Education Metathesaurus
Evaluation Center Cube
Event Analysis
Evoked Potentials
Evoker System
Exam Analysis Procedure
Excellence (Quality)
Excitation Transfer Theory
Executive Information Systems
Executive Mind
Executive Orientation Training Package
Executive Procedures (Cognition)
Exemplary Rehabilitation Certificate
Exhaustive Search Method
Exit Interviews
Exit Surveys
Expectancy Theory
Expectancy Value Model of Student Attitudes
Expectation States Theory
Expected Growth
Experience Based Career Education
Experience Based Collegiate Education
Experience Sampling Method
Experimental Library Management System
Experimental Publication System
Experimental Time Sharing System
Expert Novice Paradigm
Expert Novice Problem Solving
Expert Science Teaching Evaluation Model
Explanation (Simulation Game)
Explanation Based Learning
Explicit Instruction
Exploratory Data Analysis
Exponential Growth
Expository Teaching
Express Routing Transportation
Expressive Learning
Expressive Objectives
EXRIB System of Analyzing Teaching
Extended Campus
Extended Contracts
Extended Discretion Approach
External Pacing
External Validity
Extrapolation
Extremal Properties
Eysencks Behavioral Therapy
F Ratio
F Sort Categorization
Face to Face Communication
Facet Analysis
Faceted Classification
FACETS Model
Facies Models
Facilitative Environments
Facilitator Styles
Facilities Audits
Facility Evaluation
Facsimile Theory
Factfinding
Factor Invariance
Factor Label Method
Faculty Activity Analysis
Faculty Growth Contracting
Faculty Reimbursement Plan
Failure Analysis
Failure Oriented Training
Fair Share Agreements
Fake Color Process
Family Career
Family Decalage
Family Distance Doll Placement Technique
Family Research
Family Systems Theory
Family Therapist Coding System
Fan Spread Hypothesis
Fantasy Reality Dichotomy
Fantasy Theme Analysis
Far Transfer
Farm Business Management Analysis
Farming Systems Research
Farming Systems Research and Extension Approach
Fast Mapping
Fault Management
Fault Tree Analysis
Featherman Jones Hauser Hypothesis
Feature Analysis
Federal Catalog System
Federal Information Processing Standards
Feedback Consultation
Feedback Systems Analysis
Feedback Systems Control
Feedback to Oral Reading Miscue Analysis System
Feeling of Knowing
Fellegi Sunter Model of Record Linkage
Feminist Pedagogy
Fernald Method
Fetal Research
Fiat Power
Fibonacci Decision Rule
Fictive Kinship
Fiedler Contingency Model of Leader Effectiveness
Field Analysis
Field Dynamical Theory
Field Observation Technique
Field Sensitivity (Teaching)
Field Theory
Field Theory Design
Film Modeling Technique
Film Theory
Financial Systems
Finite Element Methods
Finite State Score Theory
First Destination Statistics (United Kingdom)
First Order Cognitive Analysis
Fiscal Illusion Model
Fiscal Impact Budgeting Systems
Fishbein Model of Attitudes
Fisher Discriminant Function
Fisher Tanh(sup minus 1)
Fishers Z Transformation
Fitzgerald Method
Five Minute Observation
Five Phase Task Force Technique
Flag Method
Flexible Benefit Plans
Flexible Learning
Flexible Manufacturing
Flexible Staffing
Flexible Work Organization
Flooding (Psychology)
Florida Assessment Diffusion System
Florida Climate and Control System
Florida Taxonomy of Affective Behavior
Florida Taxonomy of Cognitive Behavior
Flow Theory
Focal Conflict
Focus Group Assessment
Focus Groups Approach
Focus Scan Learning Strategy
Focused Conversation
Food Education and Service Training
Force Structure Analysis
Forced Alternative Random Response Technique
Forced Discipline
Forced Inferential Response Mode
Forced Relations Method
Forcing Function
Foresee Approach
Formalization
Format Manipulation System
Format Recognition
Formative Training
Formatted Print Statement
Formula Budgeting
Formula Translating System
Formulation of Relevant Creative Environments
Fort Yuma Hydroponic Farming System
Forward Mapping
Foster Family Based Treatment
Four Channel Audio
Four Channel Data Collection
Four Food Group System
Four Parameter Model
Four Phase Model (Policy Formation)
Fourier Analysis
Fourth Generation Evaluation Theory
Fowler Stages of Faith
Fractionation Scales
Frame Alignment Theory
Frame Analysis
Frame of Reference Model
Frances Early Approach
Free Forming
Free Market Plan
Frequency Analysis
Frequency Data
Frequency Ratio Method
Frequency Theory (Learning)
Freshman Admissions Prediction Equation
Front End Analysis
Full Information Factor Analysis
Full Rank Linear Model
Full Rank Multivariate Linear Model
Full Service School Model
Full Text Indexing
Fuller Reading System
Fun Fitness Trail
Function Concept
Function Specific Assessment
Functional Analysis of Classroom Tasks
Functional Context
Functional Context Education
Functional Flow Diagrams
Functional Independence Measure (Forer et al)
Functional Integration
Functional Job Analysis
Functional Learning Environments
Functional Marking
Functional Potential Model
Functionalism
Fund Accounting
Fundamental Graphic Act
Fundamental Pedagogics
Furno Cost of Education Index
Future Problem Solving Program
Futures Research
Fuzzy Concepts
Fuzzy Logic
Fuzzy Set Theory
Fuzzy Time Series
G Analysis Weighted G Analysis
G SOME Teacher Decision Making Model
Gagnes Taxonomy
Gain Effective Time Constant Product
Galileo System
Gallagher Aschner Questioning Category System
Gallup Evaluation Model
Games Analysis System
Gamma Statistical Method
Gap Reduction Model
Garbage Can Theory
Garrison Method
Gauss Law
Gaussian Distribution
Gaussian Poisson Distribution
Gaussian Quadrature
GEARS Model
Gemini System
Gender Balancing (Curriculum)
Gender Mix
Gender Schema Theory
General Case Programing
General Equilibrium System
General Information Processing System
General Linear Model
General Living Systems Theory
General Management In Basket
General Model of Instruction
General Open Systems Theory
General Policy Systems Theory
General Purpose Display System
General Purpose Simulation System
General Semantics Paradigm (Korzybski)
General Systems Theory
General Training System
Generality
Generalized Classification Technique
Generalized Empirical Method
Generalized Imitation
Generalized Information System
Generalized Interpreter
Generalized Learning Curve Method
Generative Computer Assisted Instruction
Generative Memory Model
Generativity
Generator Test Process
Generic Affective Competencies Model
Generic Design
Generic Evaluation
Generic Organizational Model
Generic Skills
Generic Technical Competencies
Genetic Epistemology
Gentle Teaching
Gentrification
Gentzels Thelen Model
Geographic Literacy
Geophysical Monitoring for Climatic Change
Geopolitical Change
Georgia Comprehensive Guidance Model
Gergen and Black Hypothesis
German Psychology
Gestalt Psychology
Getzels and Guba Social Systems Model
Ghetto Simulation Game
Gini Coefficient
Glass Analysis Method
Glass Box Theories
Glass Ceiling
Global Method of Structural Analysis
Global Studies
Glossing
Go Out and Look
Goal Analysis
Goal Attainment Scaling
Goal Based Education
Goal Based Evaluation
Goal Based Planning
Goal Clarity
Goal Deflection
Goal Development
Goal Free Evaluation
Goal Incompatibility
Goal Oriented Approach to Learning
Goal Programming
Goal Setting
Goal Structures
Goal Theory
Goddard Research Engineering Management Exercise
Goffman Model
Goffmans Indirect Method
Going to Scale
Golden Section Search Strategies

Goodman Model of Reading
Goss Formula
Government Citizen Relationship
Government Family Partnerships
Gowins V Mapping
Graded Response Model
Gradual Refinement Approach (Kean et al)
Graduate Engineering Education System
Graduated Guidance
Grants Consolidation
GRAPES Production System Model
Graph Theory
Graphic Character Sets
Graphic Organizers
Graphical Evaluation and Review Technique
Graphics Expression Reading Improvement System
Gravimetric Analysis
Gray Scales
Greek Theory
Green Turnip Survival Systems
Greenbook System
Gregg Shorthand
Griffin Ford Model
Groteluesschen Model
Grounded Theory
Group Conversation Method
Group Development
Group Facilitation
Group Interviews
Group Longevity
Group Mapping Activity
Group Oral Review
Group Preparation
Group Process Categories
Group Process Training
Group Reading Interaction Pattern Observation Ins
Group Selection
Group Theory
Growth Accounting
Growth Curve Analysis
Growth Units
Guba Clark Model
Guerin Method
Guidance Information System
Guided Assignments
Guided Discovery Approach
Guided Fantasy
Guided Practice
Guided Reading Procedure
Guided Self Analysis System
Guided Story Invention
Guided Writing Procedure
Guilfords Structure of Intellect
Guttman Simplex Analysis
Habitability Data Base
Halliwick Method
Halstead Higher Education Price Index
Hands On Experience
Harmony Theory
Harrington O Shea Career Decision Making System
Hartford Instructional Package
Hash Coding
Health Belief Model
Health Careers Information System
Health Education Research
Health Examination Survey
Hedges (Reading)
Hedges (Search Technique)
Helical Thought
Helmholtz Theory of Visual Direction
Hersey Blanchard Changing Skills Model
Hersey Blanchard Situational Leadership Model
Hestian Feminism
Heterogeneity of Irrelevancy Assumption
Heterogeneous Classrooms
Heuristic Procedure Modification
Hierarchical Decision Models
Hierarchical Focusing
Hierarchical Linear Modeling
Hierarchical Models
Hierarchical Structural Analysis
High School Rank
High Scope Model
Higher National Certificate in Applied Physics
Higher Order Thinking Skills Model (McREL)
Hindu Creativity Theory
HIPPS Method
Histograms
Historical Interpretation
Historical Methods
Historical Research
Hit Steer System
Holism
Holistic Construal Validation Method
Holland Occupational Classification System
Hollands Hexagonal Model
Hollands Theory of Occupational Choice
Hollywood Perspective Method
Home Community Based Model
Home School Community Systems
Homestead Ecology Experience
Hook Technique
Horizontal Evaluation
Horizontal Sorting
Household Employment Assn Reevaluation Training
Howards Theory of Meta Games
Howells Levels of Competence
Human Action Research
Human Capital Theory
Human Potential Movement
Human Resource Accounting
Human Systems Approach
Humanistic Existentialism
Humanistic Leadership Model
Hunter Instructional Model
Hunter Model of Clinical Supervision
Hunter Schmidt Meta Analysis
Hunter Staff Development Model
Hydra Phenomenon
Hygiene Motivation Theory (Herzberg)
Hyperbolic Distributions
Hypothesis Test Reading Modules
Idea Mapping
IDEA Model
Ideal Type Methodology (Weber)
Ideation
Identical Transparency Map Method
Identity Models
Idiographic Teaching Style
Idiom Drama
Illinois Career Education Model
Image Analysis
Image Theory
Imagined Practice
Immediate Learner Effectiveness
Immediate Reinforcement and Remediation
Immersion Approach to Thinking
Immersion Instructional Model
IMPACT Diffusion
Impact Evaluation Model
Impact Studies
Implementation Analysis
Implicative Meaning Procedure
Implicit Contract Theory
Implicit Theories
Impress Method
Impromptu Teaching Model
In Basket Simulation
Inaudible Television
Incident Reporting
Inclass Reactive Language Method
Income Generation
Incremental Approach (Instruction)
Incremental Validity
Incrementalism (Decision Making)
Independence Model
Independence Training
Index Chemicus Registry System
Index Salary Schedules
Indiana Routing System
Indicator Verification
Indigenous Knowledge Systems
Indirect Effects (Causal Modeling)
Indirect Parent Interview
Indirect Teaching
Individual Communications System
Individual Differences Scaling Model
Individual Progress Method
Individualized Audio Tutorial Instruction
Individualized Bilingual Instruction
Individualized Career Plans
Individualized Communication
Individualized Critical Skills Model
Individualized Early Learning Model
Individualized Learning Modules
Individualized Program Plans (Retardation)
Individualized Training Plans
Induced Probabilities
Industrial Arts Interaction Analysis Systems
Industrial Engineering Methods
Industrial Organization Theory
Industrial Processes
Industrial Tanning Process
Industrialized Building Systems
Industry Based Skill Standards
Inequity Theory
Influence Strategies
Informal Learning
Informal Logic
Informal Theories
Information Behavior Research
Information Consistency
Information Consolidation
Information Coordination
Information Counseling
Information Discrepancy
Information Equity
Information Exchange Procedures
Information Feedback Schedules
Information Format
Information Hypothesis
Information Integration Theory
Information Interchange Codes
Information Message Units
Information Oriented Language
Information Packaging
Information Strategies
Information System for Vocational Decisions
Informational Energy
Informative Training
Ingratiation Tactics
Innoculation Theory
Innovation Configurations
Inoculation Theory
Inputs Process Outputs Analysis
Inquiry Theory
Inserted Questions
Instance Probability Analysis
Instant Analysis
Instantaneous Durational Feedback
Instantaneous Report of Judgments
Instantiation Hypothesis
Institutional Organization Theory
Institutional Revitalization
Institutional Self Assessment Measure (CBE)
Institutional Vitality
Institutionalization (of Goals)
Institutionalization (of Innovations)
Instructional Consultant Role
Instructional Decision Model
Instructional Dynamics
Instructional Feature Analysis
Instructional Hierarchies
Instructional Information Systems
Instructional Models
Instructional Preparation
Instructional Product Verification and Revision
Instructional Program Management System
Instructional Programming Model
Instructional Sensitivity
Instructional Set
Instructional Stimuli
Instructional Systems Analysis and Selection
Instructional Systems Design
Instructional Systems Development Model
Instructional Theory
Instructional Theory into Practice (Hunter)
Instructional Transaction Theory
Instructional Transfer Model
Instructors Computer Utility
Instructors Diagnostic Aid Feedback in Training
Instrumental Enrichment
Instrumental Language Functions
Instrumental Learning
Instrumental Learning Theory
Instrumented Learning
Instrumented Team Learning
Integrated Concept Language Development Approach
Integrated Contextual Learning
Integrated Functional Learning Theory
Integrated Regional Resources Management
Integrated Skill Development
Integrated Skills Method
Integrated Skills Reinforcement
Integrative Negotiations Concept
Integrative Organized Approach
Intellectual Realism
Intensify Downplay Approach
Intensive Scheduling
Intent Structures
Intentional Learning Module
Inter Child Classroom System
Inter Item Correlation Coefficients
Interaction (Statistical)
Interaction Analysis Category System
Interaction Analysis for Vocational Educators
Interaction Process Analysis Participation Record
Interactive Communication
Interactive Compensatory Model
Interactive Decision Making
Interactive Errands
Interactive Influence System
Interactive Learning Process Model
Interactive Model
Interactive Reading
Interactive Research and Development on Schooling
Interactive Systems
Interactive Teaching
Intercampus Information Systems
Interconcept Consistency
Interdependent Learning Model
Interdisciplinary Cooperation
Interest Creating Discovery Module
Interference Theory
Intergenerational Analysis
Intergenerational Learning
Intermediate Size Transposition Paradigm
Intermix Approach
Intermodal Perception
Internal Auditing
Internal Colonialism
Internal External Frame of Reference Model
Internal Structure Analysis
Internal Validity
International Competence
International Documentation in Chemistry
International Nuclear Information System
International Road Research Documentation System
International Serials Data System
International Standard Bibliographic Description
International System of Units
International System Typographic Picture Education
Interpersonal Communications Model
Interpersonal Maturity Level Typology
Interpersonal Negotiation Strategies
Interpretation Analysis (Debate)
Interpretation Analysis (Lambert)
Interpretive Communities
Interpretive Research
Interpretive Validity
Interpretivism
Interrogation Techniques
Interrupted Behavior Chaining
Interrupted Time Series Analysis
Interruption Method (Reading)
Intersensory Reading Method
Intershelving
Interstate Validation Process
Intertype Library Networks
Interval by Interval Method
Interval Shift Analysis
Intervention Codes
Interviewer Effects
Intradimensional Variability
Intrasubject Paired Comparison
Intriligator IOR Model
Intrinsic Justification
Invariance Hypothesis
Inventory Methods
Inverse Tutoring
Inverted U Hypothesis
Investigative Learning
Invisible Writing
Invitational Learning (Purkey)
Involvement Theory
Iowa Model for Career Education
Issues Approach
Issues Management
ITEL Automated Typing System
Item Dependency Model
Item Learning
Iterative Methods
Ivanov Smolensky Procedure
J Coefficient
J Scale Method
Jab Step
Jackknifing Technique
Jacksons Mill Industrial Arts Curriculum Theory
Jangle Fallacy
Janviers Star Model of Function Understanding
Japanese Management Techniques
Japanese Ringi Method
Jensens Theoretical Model of Intelligence
Jigsaw Method
Job Analysis and Interest Measurement
Job Descriptive Index
Job Dimensions
Job Enlargement
Job Evaluation
Job Instruction Training
Job Literacy
Job Matching Systems
Job Model
Job Modification
Job Orientation
Job Performance Aided Training

Job Performance Appraisal System
Job Related Literacy
Job Related Mathematics
Job Related Reading
Job Replication
Job Restructuring
Job Shadowing
Job Simulations
Job Target Approach
Job Value Factors
Jobs Rallies
Johari Window Model
Johnson Neyman Technique
Joint Big Decision Committees
Joint Comprehensive Evaluation System
Joint Serials Control System
Joint Venture
Joplin Plan
Journal Control System
Judicial Evaluation Approach
Juridical Liberal Power Theory
Just Community Approach
Just World Hypothesis
Justification (Logic)
Justificatory Rhetoric
Kagans Interpersonal Process Recall
Kaiser Image Analysis
Kaizen
Kalman Filtering
Kansas Individualized Curriculum Sequencing
Kansas Manpower Utilization System for Training
Kantors Branching Technique
Keller Plan
Kenan Trust Model
Kernel Method
Key Informant Approach
Keysort Requisition System
Keysort Search Procedure
Keywords
Kindergarten Instructional Design System
Kinetic Family Drawings
Kinetic School Drawing
Kinetograms
Klerer May System
Knowability
Knowledge Ability Theory
Knowledge Acquisition
Knowledge Control
Knowledge Development
Knowledge Engineering
Knowledge Gap Hypothesis
Knowledge Management
Knowledge Maps
Knowledge Skills and Abilities Method
Knowledge Utilization
Kondratieff Waves
Krathwohls Taxonomy
Kuhlthau Model
Kumon Mathematical Method
Kunkel McElhinney Model
L Scaling
La Dictee
Label Class Method
Labor Force Analysis
Labor Market Theory
Laboratory Content
Lag Sequential Analysis
Land Ethos
Language Analysis Package
Language Arts Routing System
Language Teaching Record Scheme
Lantran Chincode System
Latent Class Analysis
Latent Class Models
Latent Partition Analysis
Latent Structure Analysis
Latent Structure Models
Lateral Differences
Lateral Entry
Lattice Theory
Laubach Method
Lawshe Kephart Personnel Comparison System
Layering Techniques
Leach Interrogation Model
Leader Match Model
Leader Member Exchange
Leader Selection
Leader Succession
Leadership Effectiveness
Leadership Excellence Achievement Plan
Leadership Match Theory
Learnability Theory
Learner Based Evaluation Systems
Learner Centered Instruction
Learner Verification and Revision
Learnership Leadership Model
Learnfare
Learning Assistance
Learning Capacities Approach
Learning Communities
Learning Curves
Learning Cycle Teaching Method
Learning Experience Approach
Learning Experience Module
Learning Hierarchies
Learning in Transit
Learning Individualized for Canadians
Learning Mastery Systems
Learning Partners
Learning Productivity Model
Learning Project Interview
Learning Resource Aided Instruction
Learning Segments
Learning Starters
Learning Systems
Learning Through Discussion
Learning Through Teaching
Learning to Be
Learning to Read
Learning to Read and Spell
Learning to See
Learning Tree
Learning Webs
Least Effort Principle
Least Principal Components Analysis
Least Prompts
Legislative Research
Legitimate Peripheral Participation
Leisure Ethic
Lens Model Analysis
Leontief Input Output System
Lesson Structure
Letter Right Communication System
Leveling Sharpening Dimension
Levertov Machine
Levine Equating Method
Lexington Development Scale
Lexivisions
Liaison Approach (Psychology)
Liberal Radicalism
Liberation Theology
Liberatory Learning
Library Information Access Retrieval System
Library Information Retrieval System
Library Labor Cost Accounting System
Library of Congress Classification
Library of Congress Subject Headings
Library Procedures
Library Systems Analysis
Life Career Game
Life Cycle System Management Model
Life History Method
Life Involvement Model
Life Planning
Life Space Interviews
Life Span Development
Lifelong Career Development
Lifelong Learning Communities
Lifewriting
Liflanders Model
Likelihood Ratio Criterion
Likert Model for Organizational Effectiveness
Likerts Influence Proposition
Lincoln Douglas Debate Style
Lincoln Training System
Linear Discriminant Function
Linear Equating Method
Linear Models
Linear Ordering
Ling System of Speech Training
Linkage
Linkage Analysis
Linkage Model (Havelock)
Linking Elements Concept
Linking Metrics
LISREL Analysis
List Differentiation Hypothesis
List Format Text
List Organization
List Processing
Listening Reading Relationship
Listening Research
Listening Theory
Literacy as a Social Process
Literacy Audits
Literary Sociology
Literary Theory
Literate Environment Approach
Living Classroom (Hall)
Living Systems
Load Demand Control
Local Composite Index Finance Formula
Local Control Index
Local Planning and Assessment Process
Local Planning and Budgeting Model
Local Special Education Planning Model
Location (Computer Science)
Location Theory
Locational Analysis
Locus of Authority
Loczy Model of Infant Care
Log Linear Models
Logic Instruction System
Logical Necessity
Logical Positivism
Logical Presupposition
Logit Analysis
Logits
Logographs
Lohrville Career Education Model
London Education Classification
Long Distance Xerography
Long Hazleton Process of Public Relations Model
Longitudinal Diagnosis
Longitudinal Intervention Research
Loose Coupling
Loose Coupling Theory
Loosely Coupled Systems
Lords Paradox
Loss Function
Lottery
Lowenfeld World View Technique
M Factors
Machine Language Teaching
Macmillan Tutorial System
Macro Administration
Macro Cohort Enrollment Forecasting
Macro Graphic System
Macro Theory
Macroanalysis
Macrodesigns
Macroism
Macrophotography
Macroprocesses
Macroteaching
Madison Project Mathematics
Madras System
Magical Number Seven Concept (Miller)
Magnitude Estimations
Magruder Environmental Therapy Complex
Maieutic Pedagogy
Mail Balloting
Mailed Intervention
Mainstreaming (Non English Speaking)
Mainstreaming the Disadvantaged
Maintenance Performance System
Major Field of Study Map
Malabsorption
Maladaptive Behavior Record
Maladjustive Category
Male Managerial Model
Malicious Coincidence Model
Man Environment Systems
Man Machine Function Allocation
Management Analysis
Management and Planning System
Management by Information
Management Control Theory
Management Counseling
Management Educational Resources Systems
Management Engineered Teacher Education
Management Information Feedback System
Management Information System Occupational Educ
Management Myth Information Systems
Management of Metric Implementation
Management Practices
Management Problem Laboratory
Management Responsibility Guide
Management Science
Management Skills
Management Styles
Management Systems Inventory
Managerial Attention
Managerial Ecology
Managerial Grid
Managerial Grid Analysis
Managerial Work Activity Classification System
Managerialism
Mand Model Procedure
Maneuvering Board Problems
Manifold Interest Schedule
Manipulandum Referenced Taxonomy
Manipulative Play
Manitoba Education Information Access
Manning Theory
Manpower Requirements Projection Model
Manual Response Latency
Manuscript Submission Procedures
Mapping
Mapping (Composition)
Marginal Productivity
Marginality
Marine Assignment Preference Schedule
Marine Data Management
Marital Observation Coding Systems
Mark Capture Technique
Marker Variable Factor Analysis
Market Analysis
Market Equilibrium
Market Forecasts
Market News Network
Market Profiles
Market Research
Market Segmentation
Market Systems Approach
Market Value Method
Market Wage Rates
Marketing Audits
Marketing Data Base
Marketing Mix
Marketing Plans
Marketing Research
Marketing Strategies
Marketplace of Ideas
Marking Rules
Marking Skills
Marriage Encounter
Maryland Refutation Proof Procedure System
Maslows Hierarchy of Needs
Massed Practice
Massive Oral Decoding
Master Schedules
Mastery Evaluation
Mastery Grading
Mastery Model
Mastery Teaching (Hunter)
Matching (Teaching to Learners)
Matching Cloze
Matching Hypothesis
Matchplate Patterns
Material Control
Material Objects
Materials Development Unit
Maternal Attitude Toward Independence Training
Maternal Teaching Observation Technique
Mathemagenic Activities
Mathemathantic Effects
Mathematical Analysis of Perception and Preference
Mathematical Category Theory
Mathematical Programing
Mathematical Psychology
Mathematical Theory
Mathematics Evaluation Materials Package
Mathematics Intervention Project Model
Mathematics Process Skills
Mathetics
Matrix Games
Matrix Management
Matrix Management Plan
Maximizing Difference Game
Maximum Internal Correlation Coefficient
Maxwell International Development Simulation
Maze Technique
Mazes
Mazzoni Arena Models
McCarron Dial Work Evaluation System
McGill Action Planning System
McGuire and White Social Status Index
McKenney Keen Model
McREL Interaction Analysis
Mean Age Focus Minus Chronological Age
Meaning Conditions
Meaning Emphasis Method
Meaningful Instruction
Meaningful Learning
Meaningfulness
Means Ends Analysis
Measurement Driven Instruction
Media Analysis
Media Attitude Profile
Media Based Learning
Media Behavior Unit
Media Bias
Media Government Relationship
Media Imperialism
Media Literacy
Median Voter Model
Mediated Instruction
Mediated Interaction Visual Response
Mediated Learning Experience
Mediation
Mediation Techniques

Medical Group Practice
Medical Model
Medical Record
Medical Search
Medicine Circle
Mega Building
Mega Proposal
Megavitamin Therapy
Melodic Interval Discrimination
Mem ExSpan Accelerative Cognitive Training System
Member Union Relationship
Memory Load
Memory Management
Memory Operating Characteristics
Memory Support
Mental Models
Mental Practice
Mental Step Hypothesis
Mentalistic Theory
Mentally Tough Principles
Mere Exposure Theory
Meridian Instructional Model
Meritocracy
MeSH Tree Structure
Message Design
Message Distortion
Message Evaluation Skills
Message Perception
Message Responses
Message Summaries
Message Switching
Message Transmission
Meta Modeling
Meta Research
Metacommunication
Metacriticism
Metaethical Reasoning
Metainformation
Metalibrarianship
Metamethodology
Metamotivation Leadership
Metaphorical Thought
Metaphysics
Metapolicy
Metaresponse
Metasymbol
Metatelevision
Metatheory
Metathesis
Method of Designing Instructional Alternatives
Method of Moments
Method of Reciprocal Averages
Methode Audio Visuelle d Anglais
Metro Education
Mexican American Culture Simulator Child Welfare
Michigan Accountability System
Michigan Analysis Network General Eval Report
Michigan Oral Language Series
Michigan Social Issues Cognitive Category System
Michigan Student Information System
Michigan Terminal System
Micro Administration
Micro Unit Learning Module
Microanalysis
Microcosm
Microdesigns
Microethnography
Micrographic Catalog Retrieval System
MICRON Accounting System
MICROPIK Model
Microplanning
Micropolitics
Microprograming
Microsimulation
Microsociolinguistic Analysis
Microsupervision
Microwave Approach
Mid Alabama Adult and Vocational Education
Migrant Student Record Transfer System
Migrant Tracking
Milieu Teaching
Military Occupation Specialty
Mimetic Traditions
Miniaturized Total Interaction Analysis System
Minigrants
Minimal Effect Size
Minimal Responses
Minimax Procedure
Minimum Abbreviation of Serial Titles
Minimum Distance Principle
Minnesota Adaptive Instructional System
Minnesota Computer Aided Library System
Minnesota Educational Follow Up Study
Minnesota Information and Decision Systems
Mislevy Histogram Solution
Mismatch Invisible Underemployment
Mississippi Performance Based Accreditation Model
Mississippi Student Information System
Missouri Comprehensive Guidance Program Model
Missouri Environmental Studies Approach
Mitigating Circumstances
Mixed Media Network
Mobility Facilitator Units
Mock Trials
Modal Learning Concept
Modality Based Instruction
Mode of Primary Production
Mode of Representation
Model Building
Model Characteristics
Model Development
Model Edspec
Model Experiment in Drug Indexing by Computer
Model for Educational Improvement
Model for Evaluation of Educational Building
Model Minority Thesis
Model Neighborhood Area
Model of Career Choice for Women and Men (Astin)
Model of Conceptual Learning and Development
Model of Mastery
Model United Nations
Models of Teaching Concept
Moderation System (National Qualif Framework)
Moderator Variables
Modern Management Dynamics
Modern Rationalism
Modernity
Modular Audio Visual Multimedia Programming
Modular Furniture Design
Modular Systems
Modularity
Modularization
Module Clusters
Mohism
Molecular Orbital Theory
Moment Estimators
Monetarism
Monetary Incentives
Monetary Reinforcement
Money Game
Money Skills
Monitor Model
Monitoring
Monopoly
Monotone Regression
Monotonic Deterministic Test Model
Monotonic Relationships
Monotonicity Analysis
Monotype Printing
Monroe City Simulation
Monroe Model
Moore Method
Moot Courts
Moral Rearmament
Motivation Hygiene Theory
Motivational Design
Motivational Interview Strategies
Motivic Development
Movement Notation
Movement Organization
Multi Activity Zones for Education
Multi Attribute Consensus Building
Multi Component Career Education Curriculum Model
Multi County Planning
Multi Factor Grading
Multi Image Presentations
Multi Indicator Approach
Multi Language Time Sharing System
Multicenter Trials
Multicertification
Multidimensional Approach
Multidimensional Models
Multidisciplinary Information Systems
Multidisciplinary Training Teams
Multientry Multiexit Approach
Multifactorial Models
Multigenre Research Projects
Multilateral Collective Bargaining
Multilevel Analysis
Multilingual Information Systems
Multilist System
Multimedia Information Systems
Multimodal Methods
Multioption School
Multiphased Need Assessment for Program Decisions
Multiplative Classification
Multiple Access Scheduling
Multiple Alternatives Analysis
Multiple Alternatives Model
Multiple Architect Design
Multiple Audio Distribution System
Multiple Case Study Approach
Multiple Classes
Multiple Classification
Multiple Contingency Tables
Multiple Counting
Multiple Criteria Utility Theory
Multiple Cue Learning
Multiple Data Gathering Methods
Multiple Entry
Multiple Evaluations
Multiple Exemplar Training
Multiple Exit
Multiple Group Factor Analysis
Multiple Intelligences
Multiple Linkage Analysis
Multiple Measures Approach
Multiple Moderator Approach
Multiple Option Programming
Multiple Realities
Multiple Set Training
Multiple Site Studies
Multiple Strategies Model for Effective Teaching
Multiple Talent Approach to Teaching
Multiplex Programing
Multipoint Distribution Service
Multipurpose Academic Units
Multiskilling
Multitext Approach
Multitype Library Cooperation
Multivariate Normal Distribution
MUM Effect
Municipal Information System
Munsell Hue Circle
Museum Collections
Music Ability
Music Aptitude
Music Identification
Music Notation
Musical Analysis
Musical Independence
Musical Performance
Mutual Adaptation
Mutual Agreement Programing
Mutual Gains Bargaining
Mutual Instruction
Mutual Involvement Review Activity
Mutuality
Mutually Aided Learning
Myklebust Learning Quotient Method
Narrative Inquiry
NASA Technology Utilization System
National Air Sampling Network
National Apprenticeship System
National Indian Youth Leadership Model
National Information Systems
National Issues Forum
National Needs Analysis Design
National Science Education Standards (NRC)
National Special Media Institutes Model
National Standard Reference Data System
National Storehouse Educational Materials Success
National Strategy for Youth Development
National Teacher Certification
National Training Boards
Nationality Origin System
Nationwide Planning
Native Intelligence Hypothesis
Natural Knowledge
Natural Learning
Natural Resource Information System
Natural Systems
Nature of Interpolated Passages
Nature Study
NCTM Curriculum and Evaluation Standards
NCTM Professional Teaching Standards
Near Death Research
Near Miss Periodicity
Nedelsky Method
Needs Assessment Information System
Needs Based Goal Attainment Scaling
Needs Press Model
Negative Capability
Negative Instances
Negative Stipulation
Negative Transfer
Negative Transportation Rule
Negotiability
Negotiated Order Model
Negotiated Tuition
Negotiation Processes
Neo Vygotskian Theory
Neoclassical Economics
Nested Spiral Approach
Network Access Procedures
Network Architecture
Network Based Approach
Network Management
Network Models
Network Protocols
Neuman Health Care Systems Model
Neural Net Models
Neurological Impress Method
Neutrality
Neutralization Theory
New Auteurism
New International Economic Order
New Mexico Staff Accountability Plan
New Primary Approach
New Sociology of Education
New Zealand Accident Compensation Scheme
Newbasic Catalyst
News Perspective Bias
Newtons Gravitational Constant
Nielsen Ratings
Noble Savage Concept
Node Acquisition and Integration Technique
Noggin Factor
Nominal Response Model
Nomographs
Nomothetic Teaching Style
Noncompensatory Models
Nondirective Play
Nondirective Tutorial Instruction
Nonlinear Management
Nonlinear Models
Nonlinear Transformations
Nonorthogonal Analysis of Variance
Nonpolicy Debate
Nonrandom Selection
Nonstandard Analysis
Nonsynchrony
Normal Ogive Models
Normal Orthant Probabilities
Normalizing Transformation
Normative Philosophy
Norway Library Planning
Nota Graph System
Noun Frequency Readability Method
Novice Assisted Research
Novice Knowledge Engineering
Nuclear Nonproliferation Theory
Number Line
Number Theory
Numeration Learning Hierarchy
Nursing Dial Access
Nurturance
O Neil Meeker Borgers Model Career Decision Making
Object Oriented Programing
Object Teaching
Objective Analysis
Objective Certification
Objectivity
Observation Criteria
Observation of Socialization Behavior
Observation of Student Interaction Participation
Observation of Substantive Curricular Input
Observation of Teacher Management Behavior
Observation Schedules
Observation Techniques
Observational Learning Theory
Observing Responses
Occu Sort
Occupation Systems Theory
Occupational Affective Behavior Analysis
Occupational Information Access System
Occupational Mismatch
Occupational Report
Occupational Segregation
Occupational Shortages Reporting System
Occupational Training Families
Occupational Training Information System
Occupational Values
Octal Response
Oddity Learning
Officer Attitudes
Officer Career Information and Planning System
Ohio Model
Oklahoma Teletypewriter Interlibrary System
Oklahoma Televised Instruction System
Olsgaard Profile of Authorship

Omission Training
On Site Needs Assessment Long Range Planning Model
One Parameter Model
One to One Correspondence
Ong Havelock Thesis
Online Administrative Information System
Onsite Monitoring
Ontological Evaluation Model
Op In Procedure (Cloze)
Open Access (Teacher Professional Development)
Open Adoption
Open and Closed Systems
Open Framework Curriculum
Open Program Structure Index
Open Society
Open Systems Interconnection Reference Model
Open Systems Theory
Open Workshop Learning System
Openness
Operant Analysis
Operant Behavior Modification Model
Operant Methodology
Operating Procedures
Operational Audit
Operational Concepts
Operational Context Training
Operational Questions
Operative Conditions
Opin Procedure (Reading)
Opportunity Structures
Optimal Control Theory
Optimal Level Theory
Optimal Stimulation Theory
Optimization
Optimization of Learning
Optimum Allocation Analysis
OR Corrective Technique
ORACLE Formula
Oral Learning
Orchestrated Systems Approach
Order Analysis
Ordering Theory
Ordinal Hypotheses
Oregon System of Mathematics Education
Organic Model
Organic Primers
Organic Teaching
Organization Mapping Analysis
Organization Set Model
Organization Theory (Psychology)
Organizational Alternatives
Organizational Analysis
Organizational Bargaining Research
Organizational Behavior
Organizational Culture
Organizational Elements Model
Organizational Frames
Organizational Learning
Organizational Level
Organizational Process Model
Organizational Research
Organizational Structure
Organizational Supervision
Organizational Training
Organizers
Organizing Strategies
Orthogenetical Principle
Out of State Placement of Children
Outcome Based Instructional Systems Approach
Outcome Oriented Evaluation
Outcome Oriented Grading
Outcomes Expectancy
Outdoor Biology Instructional Strategies
Outline Graphics
Output Measurements
Output Performance Measures
Overall and Dalals Formula
OVERALS Technique
Overdetermination
Overeducation
Overjustification
Overlap Hypothesis
Overlearning
Oversight Information Systems
Overtraining Reversal Effect
Overview Snapshot Observation Technique
Pacific Community Concept
Pacific Horizons Reading Scheme
Pacification
Packet Reservation Access Method
Paideia
Paired Comparisons
Paired Student Interaction
Paired Teaching
Palmar Sweat Print Method
Palmer Handwriting Method
Pan Indianism
Panel Consensus Technique
Panel Reviews
Panel Studies
Paper Flow System
Paper Folding
Papier Mache
Paradigm Argument
Paradigm Case Analysis
Paradoxical Techniques
Parallel Pairs Evaluation
Parallel Play
Parallel Processes
Parallel Processing
Parallelogram Scaling Model
Parameter Identification
Parametric Analysis
Paramilitary Role
Parent Behavior Progression
Parent Behavior Rating
Parent Child Accomplishment Record
Parent Child Interaction Rating Procedure
Parent Community Relationship
Parent Effectiveness Training
Parent Empowerment
Parent Image Differential
Parent Implementation Advisory Model
Parent Interview Schedule
Parent Orientation
Parent Practices Inventory
Parent Provider Relationship
Parent to Parent Model
Parent Training Technology
Parental Awareness Model (Newberger)
Parental Dominance
Parenting Styles
Parents Participation Share Plan
Pareto Diagrams
Pareto Law
Parity Equity Model
Parsonian Model of Organization
Parsonian Theory
Parsons Guided Self Analysis
Part Form Method
Part Whole Percentaging Analysis
Participant Action Plan Approach
Participation Training
Participatory Evaluation
Participatory Planning
Participatory Sorting Method
Partitioning Procedures
Partnership in Research
PASS Model (Luria)
Pastoral Counseling
Paternalism
Path Goal Theory
Patron Client Relationship
Pattern Congruity Method
Pattern Goodness
Pattern Learning Parser
Pattern Matching
Pattern Notes
Patterned Evasion
Pause Model
Pause Prompt and Praise
Payback Period
PDEM 1 Model
Peabody Mobility Kit for Infants
Peace Corps Stateside Teacher Training Model
Peak Communication Experiences
Pearson Product Moment Correlation
Pedagogical Content Knowledge
Pedagogical Intelligence
Peer Coaching
Peer Comparison
Peer Consultation (Supervision)
Peer Mediation
Peer Modeling
Peer Prepared Method
Peer Supervision
Peer Support
Pentagonal Principle
People Orientation
Percentile Ranking
Percentile Ranks
Perception of Emotion
Perception Research
Perceptual Categories
Perceptual Sensitisation Hypothesis
Perfective Aspect
Performance Analysis
Performance Based Affective Behav Identification
Performance Based Objectives
Performance Budgeting
Performance by Objectives
Performance Funding
Performance Monitoring
Performance Oriented Management Techniques
Performance Rating Theory (Cason and Cason)
Performance Support Systems
Perrow Technology Construct
Perry Scheme of Intellectual Ethical Development
Person Centered Society
Person Environment Fit
Personal Data Systems
Personal File Management
Personal Finance Training
Personal Futures Planning
Personal Independence
Personal Information Systems
Personal Practical Knowledge
Personal Rapid Transit
Personality Assessment System
Personalized Approach to Teaching Reading
Personalized Instructional Remedial Tutorial Syst
Personalized Reading
Personalized System of Instruction
Personalizing Educational Prescriptions
Personification
Personnel Decision Analysis
Personnel Research
Personnel Simulator
Perspective Realism
Perspective Taking Task
Perspective Text Analysis
Perspective Transformation
Persuasive Communication Model
Peter Blau Model of Occupational Choice
Phasal Analysis
Phased Retirement
Phases of Reasoning
Phi Coefficient
Phillips Curve Theory
Philosophical Dualism
Philosophical Influences
Philosophical Research
Philosophical Rules
Phonetic Refinement Theory
Phonological Process Analysis
Phonological Transcription Accompanied Text
Phonovisual Reading Method
Phosphorescence Decay Rates
Photo Interviewing (Tucker et al)
Photoanalysis
Photographic Assisted Instruction
Photographic Perspective Error
Piagetian Reversibility
Piagetian Task Instrument
Piagets Clinical Method
Pictogram System
Pictograph Sentence Memory Task
Pictorial Analogy
Picture Rating Technique
Picture Text Relationship
Picture Vocabulary Story
Piedmont Region Model for Family Involvement
Pietism
Piggybacking (Early Childhood Education)
PIM Model
Pimlico Comprehensive
Pinellas County Reading System
Pittsburghs Research Based Instr Supervisory Model
Place Identity
Placement Prevention
Placement Rate
Planar Strategies
Planned Course Statements
Planned Individual Learning Experience
Planned Variation
Planning and Placement Teams
Planning by Objectives
Planning Evaluation and Resource Management Model
Planning for Child Development Package
Planning Implementing Evaluation Cycles
Planning Management Information System
Planning Monitoring Implementation Model
Planning Programming Budgeting Evaluation System
Planning Programming Budgeting System
Platform Approach (Education)
Plausibility Approach
Play Theory
Playful Literacy
PLISSIT Model
Plot Method
Point Biserial Correlation
Point System
Points of View (Writing)
Poisson Distribution
Poisson Process
Pole Zero Map Analysis
Policy Capturing Method
Policy Debate
Policy Goal Percentaging Analysis
Policy Implementation
Policy Interpretation
Policy Issue Networks
Policy Negotiation Simulation
Policy Research
Political Analysis
Political and Economic Planning
Political Bargaining Model
Political Framing
Political Literacy
Political Theories
Pollack Intersensory Reading Method
Polynomial Regression Models
Polytomous Variables
Population Ecology
Population Ecology Model
PORPE Strategy
Portrayal (Reporting Method)
Position Analysis
Position Classification Inventory
Positive Approach to Discipline System
Positive Disintegration Theory
Positive Stipulation
Positivism
Posner Snyder Theory
Possessive Individualism
Post Hoc Methods
Post Tenure Review
Postconstructivism
Postmodernism
Postpositivism
Postreinforcement Intervals
Poststructuralism
Postvention
Potential Curves
Potential for Improving Performance
Potthoff Technique
Pourbaix Diagrams
Power (Statistics)
Power Restoration Theory
Power Scores
Power Strategies
Pracademics
Practical Experience Phases
Practical Reasoning
Practice Profiles
Practitioner Involvement (Research)
Praxiology
PRECEDE Model
Prediction Equation
Predictive Analysis
Predictive Models
Predictive Reading
Preference Models
Premack Principle
Preordinate Model of Product Development
PREP Study System
Prepackaged Instruction
Preplay Learning Technique
Prescriptive Counselor Model
Prescriptive Evaluation Plans
Prescriptive Research
Presentation Rates
Preserved Context Indexing System
Prevision (Written Composition)
Price Belland Observation System
Price Break Analysis
Pricing Formulas
Primary Language Record
Primary Message Systems (Hall)
Primary Representational System
Prime 0 Tec Reading Method
PRIME System
Prince System
Principal Axis Procedure
Principal Leadership as Social Control
Principal Succession
Principal Superintendent Relationship
Principles Approach
Priority Effect
PRISM Pittsburgh Model for Staff Development
Prisoners Dilemma Game
Proactive Action Model
Proactive Planning
Proactive Teaching
Probabilistic Causation

Stimulus Response Reinforcement Approach
Stimulus Response Theory
Stochastic Analysis
Stochastic Approximation Method
Stochastic Parallel Computation
Stock Issues (Debate)
Story Frames
Story Mapping
Story Maps
Stouts Procedure
Strategic Contingencies Theory
Strategic Interaction Method
Strategic Planning for Educ Reform and Improvement
Strategic Thinking
Strategies Intervention Model
Strategy Choice
Strategy Fading
Strategy Training
Strayer Haig Equalization Formula
Strayer Haig Mort Formula
String Comparator Metrics
Structional Analysis
Structural Affect Theory
Structural Alignments
Structural Analysis (Economics)
Structural Analysis (Psychology)
Structural Analysis (Sociology)
Structural Coupling (Organizations)
Structural Exchange Theory
Structural Family Theory
Structural Knowledge
Structural Learning
Structural Modeling
Structural Organizers
Structural Response Instructional Model
Structural Visualization
Structuralism
Structuration Theory
Structure Mapping
Structured Conceptualization
Structured Learning
Structured Learning Time Interval
Structured Model of Competency Based Instruction
Structured Team Problem Solving
Structuro Global Audio Visual Method
Student Accountability Model
Student Accountability Model (California)
Student Administrator Ratio
Student Congress
Student Eligibility Report
Student Empowerment
Student Flow
Student Flow Models
Student Goals Exploration
Student Institution Fit
Student Integration Model
Student Matriculation Models
Student Perceptions of Teacher
Student Performance Models
Student Response System
Student Self Management Techniques
Student Team Learning
Student Teams Achievement Divisions
Student Tracking Systems
Students as Subjects
Style Differentiated Instruction
Suasory Influence
Subject Analysis
Subject Area Preferences
Subject Centered Curriculum
Subject Content Knowledge
Subject Field Reference Code
Subjective Evaluation
Subjective Expected Utility
Subliminal Psychodynamic Activation
Subset Analysis
Substitutes for Leadership Theory (Kerr)
Substrata Factor Theory
Substratum Theory
Success Emulation
Suggestology
Summarization
Superhero Play
Superintendent of Documents Classification
Superior Subordinate Relationship
Supervisor Subordinate Relationship
Supervisor Supervisee Relationship
Supervisory Rotation
Support Systems
Supportive Supervision
Surveillance Systems
Survey Research
Sustaining Effects Study
Switching Theory
SWRL Learning Mastery System
Symbol Systems Approach
Symbolic Action
Symbolic Analysis
Symbolic Convergence Theory of Communication
Symbolic Immortality
Symbolic Interaction
SYMLOG Coding System
Synaesthetics
Synergistic Planning
Synergogy
Synomorphy
Syntopical Theory (Adler)
System Classroom Observation Teaching Strategies
System Dynamics
System Evaluation
System for Coding and Analysis
System for Event Evaluation and Review
System for Objectives Based Evaluation Reading
System Performance Assurance
System Politics
Systematic Approach to Reading Improvement
Systematic Classroom Observation Pupil Experience
Systematic Curriculum and Instructional Develop
Systematic Employment Counseling Approach
Systematic Facilitative Approach to Consultation
Systematic Integrated Teaching Learning Approach
Systematic Multiple Level Observation of Groups
Systematic Skills Training
Systematic Teacher Training Model
Systematic Training for Effective Parenting
Systematized Nomenclature of Pathology
Systemic Evaluation
Systems Management Analysis
Systems Modeling
T Units
T Values
Tab Item Procedure
Taba (Hilda) Teaching Strategies
Table Clinics
Tabula Rasa Approach
Tabular Display Technique
Tacit Knowing
Tactical Warfare Analysis and Evaluation System
Tactics for Thinking
Taguchi Methods
Talent Education Method
Talk Write Method
Tangible Symbol Systems
Target Planning
Tarleton Model for Accelerated Teacher Educ
Task Force Approach
Task Oriented Instructions
Task Structure Design
Task Uncertainty
Task Value
Tate System of English Language Instruction
Taxographic Space
Taylors Theorem
Teach Practice Apply Model
Teacher Administrator Ratio
Teacher Assessment and Development System
Teacher Assessment of Classroom Practices
Teacher Audio Placement System
Teacher Behavior Continuum
Teacher Brinkmanship
Teacher Centered Instruction
Teacher Certification Reciprocity
Teacher Characteristics Schedule
Teacher Clarity
Teacher Collaboration
Teacher Community Relationship
Teacher Concerns Model
Teacher Concerns Theory (Fuller)
Teacher Effectiveness Training
Teacher Empowerment
Teacher Improvement Model
Teacher Incentives
Teacher Initiated Activities
Teacher Knowledge
Teacher Mediated Intervention Model
Teacher Principal Relationship
Teacher Reassignment
Teacher Report of Treatment of Students
Teacher Researcher Cooperation
Teacher Researcher Relationship
Teacher Student Conferences
Teacher Transitions
Teacher Volunteer Relationship
Teacher Warranty
Teaching as a Science
Teaching as an Art
Teaching by Objectives
Teaching Family Model
Teaching Information Processing System
Teaching Learning Communities Model
Teaching Research
Teaching Research Data Based Classroom Model
Teaching Research Systems
Teaching Style Q Sort
Team Accelerated Instruction
Team Assisted Individualization
Team Exercise for Action Management Skills
Team Learning Methods
Teams Games Tournament
Tech Prep
Technical Assistance Development System
Technical Cooperation Among Developing Countries
Technical Services Automation Phase I
Technion Diagnostic System
Technocratic Rationality
Technological Methods
Technological Perspective
Technology Based Instruction
Technology Mediated Interactive Learning
Teleapprenticeships
Telephone Evaluations
Telephone Interviews
Teletraining
Television Theory
Temporal Recall Strategy
Ten Perfect Sentences Approach
Tennessee Instructional Model
Tenore Plan MA
Tension Reduction Theory
Term Matching
Terminal Performance Objectives
Terrorist Tactics
TETRA Model
Tetrachoric Correlation
Texas Student Information System
Text Learning
Text Sets
Textbook Dependency
Textual Analysis
Texture Mapping
Theater for Development
Theft Detection System
Thematic Analysis
Thematic Matrix Analysis
Theme Centered Interactional Method
Theoretical Analysis
Theory of Constructive Operators (Pascual Leone)
Theory of Margin
Theory of Mind
Theory of Reasoned Action
Theory of Work Adjustment
Theory X
Theory Y
Theory Z
Therapists Own Family
Thesis Analysis and Synthesis Key
Thick Description Method
Thinking Across the Curriculum
Thinking Approach to Problem Solving
Third World Education Systems
THOG Problem
Thomism
Three on Two Approach
Three Parameter Model
Threshold Analysis
Threshold Traits Analysis
Thurstone Dominance
Thurstone Model
Time and Motion Studies
Time Delay
Time Oriented Data
Time Series Analysis
Time Series Experiments
Time Sharing Ability
Time Studies
Timely Action
Tinto Model
Tinto Theory
Title I Evaluation and Reporting System
Title I Program Analysis and Monitoring
Tobit Model Analysis
Token Earnings
Token Reinforcement System
Tomatis Method
Topic Classification System
Topic Control
Total Area Method
Total Guidance Information Support System
Total Information for Education Systems
Total Objective Plan Officer Procurement System
Total Person Model
Total Receptor Access Independent Learning Systems
Total Return Concept
Totally Enclosed Modular Environment
Tough Love
Toulmins Model
Tower System
Toy Talk Contexts
Trace Conditioning
TRACE Model
Trace Observation System
Tracer Methodology
Tracing
Tracking (Career Paths)
Tracking (Cases)
Tracking (Documents)
Trade Off Analysis
Trade Off Games
Traffic Record Analysis
Training Abstracts Service
Training and Visit System
Training Benefit Forecasting Method
Training Effectiveness
Training Effectiveness Cost Effectiveness Predict
Training Impact Auditing
Training in Common
Training of Trainers Model
Training Opportunities Scheme
Training Support System
TRAINVICE Models
Trait Factor Approach
Trait State Model
Transaction Accounting System
Transaction Log Analysis
Transactional Analysis in Accounting
Transactional Self
Transactional Strategies Instruction
Transactional Teaching Style
Transactional Theory
Transactive Communication
Transactive Theory
Transcendence
Transcendentalism
Transdisciplinary Approach
Transect Studies
Transfer (Art Technique)
Transfer Effect
Transfer Index
Transfer Studies
Transformation Theory (Adult Learning)
Transformational Leadership
Transformative Leadership
Transformative Research
Transition Management
Transition to Work Simulation
Transparency Theory
Transparent Models
Transparent Stimulation
Transportability
Transportation Information Planning Service
Transportation Models
Transpose Factor Analysis
Transverse Patterning
Treatment Interaction Analysis
Treatment Verification
TREET Programming System
Trend Line Cost Control Method
Trend of Reading Standards
Tri Partite Power Theory
Triadic Interaction Analysis
Triangle Approach
Triarchic Theory of Intelligence (Sternberg)
Tribes Approach
Trigger Approach
Trigram Analysis
Trimodal Programed Instruction
True Point Dimensioning System
Trueswells 80 20 Rule
Trump Plan
Trumpet Model
Truncation (Information Retrieval)
Truth Love Change Model
Truth Maintenance Systems
Truth Tables
Tryon Cluster Analysis Method
Tucker Common Item Equating Method
Tuckman Teacher Feedback Form
Tucson Early Education Model
Tukey Statistic
Tunnel Vision

Turntaking (Instructional)
Tutor Training
Tutored Video Instruction
Tutorial Mode
Two Cone Model
Two Factor Theory of Job Satisfaction (Herzberg)
Two Parameter Model
Two Step Flow
Two Step Principal Components Procedure
Two Way Information Services
Tylers Model
Ubertragung
Unconditioned Stimulus
Unconscious Intention
Undercounting
Underdeterminacy
Undergraduate Pilot Training
Underwood Postman Hypothesis
Unfolding Technique
Unified Science Approach
Uniform Federal Accessibility Standards
Uniform Financial Reporting Systems
Uniform Methodology Model
Uniform Migrant Student Record Transfer System
Uniform Socio Economic Reporting System
Unimodal Methods
Unipolar Scale
Uniqueness Theory
Unit Box Approach
Unit Credit System
Unitary Theory
United States Dietary Guidelines
Univariate Analysis
Universal Audience
Universal Bibliographic Control
Universal Decimal Classification
Universal Index Numbers
Universal Relation Theory
Universalism
Universality
Universities of the Third Age
University Consortium CDA Resource Model
University Residential Building System
University Student Information System (Canada)
Unlearning
Unscheduled Time
Up and Down Method
Urban Bias
Urbanism
Usability Edit
USC Faculty Planning Model
User Control
User Training
Uses and Gratifications Research
Utility Analysis
Utility Theory
Utilization Framework (Alkin)
Utopia
Utopian Societies
Validation Verification and Testing Techniques
Validity Research
Valleybrook Lakemont Simulation Game
Valuation Theory
Value Added
Value Added Model
Value Analysis
Value Engineering
Value Sharing
Value Triangles
Values Confrontation
Values Management
Values Research
Vanguard Instructional Model
Variability Measurement
Variable Course Structuring
Variable Rules
Variable Scheduling
Variable Utilization Time Principle
Variance (Statistical)
Variance Partitioning
Vector Methods
Vector Model
Vector Planning
Vector Theory
Vee Diagramming
Vee Mapping
Verbal Coding
Verbal Decoding Hypothesis
Verbal Deductive Technique
Verbal Discrimination
Verbal Interaction Category System
Verbal Mediation
Verbo Tonal Method
Vertical Sorting
VHF Teletype Relay Systems
Vicarious Therapy Pretraining
Vicens Reddy Speech Recognition System
Video Distribution Systems
Video Reference Services
Videographics Systems
Videotape Participation System
Videotape Program Service
Vintage Effect (Teaching Profession)
Vision Quest
Visitation Moderation
Visitor Control
Visual Aptitude
Visual Auditory Kinesthetic Tactile Instruction
Visual Auditory Tactile Kinesthetic Approach
Visual Complexity
Visual Excellence
Visual Merchandising (Displays)
Visual Preference Technique
Visual Representation
Vocalization Latency
Vocational Educ Evaluation and Assessment Process
Vocational Education Data Reporting Accounting
Vocational Theory
Voice Stress Analysis
Voice Support (Reading)
Voir Dire Procedures
Voluntary Homework System
Voluntary Labor Arbitration Rules
Volunteer Management
Vroom and Yetton Normative Leadership Model
Vroom Expectancy Theory
Vulnerable Age Effect
Vulpe Performance Analysis System
Walberg Educational Productivity Model
Waldorf Educational Theory
Wang Marking Conventions
Ward Concept
Ward Grievance Procedure
Wards Hierarchical Cluster Analysis
Warranted Uncertainty
Washington Community College Evaluation Model
Wasons Selection Task
Water Resources Document Reference System
Waterford Reading Instructional Management Model
Watermans Production Rules
Wave Theory
We Do They Do Model
Weekly Activity Record
Weighted Airman Promotion System
Weighted Grading Systems
Weighted Net Percentage Difference
Weighted Pupil Method
Welfare Reform
WHIDD Analysis
Who Are You Time Extension Method
Whole Child Approach
Whole to Part Instructional Approach
Wilderness Vision Quest
Win Win Bargaining
Winnetka Plan
Wisconsin Model of Status Attainment
Wisconsin System for Instructional Management
Wiswesser Line Notation
Wolf Welsh Linkage Methodology
Women in Medical Academia Model
Word Naming Technique
Words in Color
Work Autonomy
Work Based Attendance (School Choice)
Work Order Processing System
Work Unit Tasks
Worker Alienation
Workjobs
Workplace Democracy
Workplace Literacy
Workplace Literacy Impact Model
World Hypotheses (Pepper)
World Science Information System
Worldwide Needs Assessment Model
Writing as Punishment
Writing Models
Writing Speed
Writing Thinking Relationship
Wyer Subjective Probability Model
Wynn Experimental Model of Student Teacher Seminar
Xenograde Concept System
Youth Development Model
Youth Guidance Systems
Youth Impaired Driving Model
Youth Services Systems
Youth Studies
Ypsilanti Model
Zaner Bloser Method
Zero One Programming
Zero Partial Association
Zero Reject Concept
Zetetics
Zone of Proximal Development

CATEGORY 16: Miscellaneous

401(k) Plans
1985 Resolution (American Nurses Association)
Abductions
Ability to Benefit Policy
Abridgments (Text)
Absent without Leave
Abstract Art
Abstracting and Indexing Services
Academic Choice
Academic Competitions
Academic Discourse
Academic Futility
Academic Linkage
Academic Load
Academic Progress Standards
Academic Redshirting
Academic Skills
Academic Structure
Academic Support Services
Academic Tradition
Academy Awards
Access to Computers
Access to Facilities
Access to Persons
Access to Services
Accident Investigation
Accion Cultural Popular
Accounts Receivable
Accreditation Standards
Accuracy
Acquaintance Rape
Acquiescence
Acroclinical Semester
Action Plans
Activity Preferences
Activity Settings
Address Labels
Administrative Routine
Administrative Succession
Administrator Bargaining
Administrator Certification
Administrator Routine
Administrator Supply and Demand
Adolescent Attitudes
Adoption Assistance
Adoption of Older Children
Adult Student Relationship
Advance Notice of Employment Termination
Adventure Games
Adventure Stories
Adversary Culture
Advertisements
Advertising Competitions
Advertising Effectiveness
Advertising Logos
Advice Columns
Advisor Role
Advocacy Communication
Aesthetic Communication
Aesthetic Response
Affective Domain
Afrocentrism
Afternoon Newspapers
Age Bias
Age Segregation
Agency Fees
Agenda Preparation (Meetings)
Agendas
Aging (Library Collections)
Aging Out Process
Agrarianism
Agricultural Change
Agricultural Information
Agricultural Policy
Aircraft Disasters
Airplane Flights
Algae Purification System
Alhambra Palace
All But Dissertation
All News Radio
Allen Plan
Alphabet Books
Alphanumeric Codes
Alternative Communities
Alternative Financing
Alternative Living Arrangements
Alternative Media
Alternative Press
Alternative Publishers
Alternative Television
Alternatives to Suspension
Alumni Administration
Alumni Relations
Amateur Athletics
Amateurism
Amendments
American Dream
American Frontier Myth
American Indian Achievement
American Indian Contributions
American Indian Philosophy
American Jeremiads
American Library Association Filing Rules
American Myths
Americanism
Americanization
Amnesty
Anatomically Correct Dolls
Ancestor Worship
Andres Bello Agreement
Anecdotal Records
Anecdotes
Annual Funds
Annual Housing Survey
Annual Worker Plan
Annuities
Anonymity
Anthropomorphism
Anti Americanism
Antiques
Apologia
Apologies
Appalachian Culture
Appalachian Education
Appalachian Literature
Appointive Positions
Appointment Keeping
Appointments
April (Month)
Aptitude Strategies
Archetypes
Architect Role
Archival Value
Archives Education Services
Argumentative Spots
Arlington House VA
Armed Services Editions
Art Concepts
Art Fairs
Art Films
Art Literacy
Art Preference
Art Publications
Art Reproductions
Artist Residencies
Artistic Performance
Artistic Style
Artistic Thought
Asian American Literature
Assassinations
Assaults
Assay Techniques
Associate in Applied Science Degrees
Association Magazines
Association Role
Atheism
Athletic Ability
Athletic Abuses
Athletic Administration
Athletic Draft
Athletic Scholarships
Atmospheres
Atonal Music
Attitudes toward Disabled
Auctions
Audiation
Audience Education
Audiovisual Archives
August (Month)
Australian Culture
Authentic Materials
Authenticity
Authoritarian Teaching
Authoritative Parenting
Authority
Authority Base
Authority Figures
Authorship
Autographs

Competitiveness
Compilations
Complementarity
Composition (Art)
Composition Literature Relationship
Compromise
Computer Architecture
Computer Equity
Computer Ownership
Computer Piracy
Computer Services
Computer Software Rental
Conant Plan
Concept of Other Sympathy
Concrete Operations
Condemnation (Real Estate)
Conducting
Confessional Poetry
Confidence Envelopes
Confidence in Education
Confined Spaces
Confusion
Congregate Dining
Congressional Medal of Honor
Connect Class
Connectivity
Connotations
Consequences
Consolidated Net Worth Statement
Consortium for Longitudinal Studies
Conspiracy Dramas
Constituency Development
Constitutional Processes
Constraining Experiences
Constraints
Construction Grants
Construction Tasks
Constructive Play
Consultant Role
Consumer Complaints
Consumer Information
Consumer Magazines
Consumer Products
Consumer Skills
Consumption
Contact Literature
Contact Narratives
Contemporaneity
Contemporary Literature
Content Cues
Content Designators
Content Specificity
Contests
Context Adaptation
Contingency Power
Contingent Employment
Continuity
Continuous Improvement
Contract Employment
Contradictions
Control Assemblies
Control Factors (Administrative)
Control Mechanisms (Administrative)
Control of Outcomes
Controversial Materials
Controversial Topics
Controversy
Convenience Foods
Conventionalization
Convergent Production
Conversational Domain
Converted Secondary School Rank
Cooperative Play
Copy Cataloging
Copyfitting
Copying Ability
Copying Speed
Copywriting
Core Collections
Corporate Culture
Corporate Excellence Rubric
Corporate Policy
Corporate Politics
Corporate Television
Cosmetics
Cosmopolitan Local Orientation
Cost Management
Cost of Living
Cost of Living Wage Adjustment
Cost Sharing
Costumes
Costumes (Theatrical)
Cottage Industry
Council of Educators Review
Counter Culture
Counteradvertising
Country Music
County Business Patterns
Courage
Course Load
Course Taking Patterns
Creation
Credit Accrual
Credit Cards
Credit Ratings
Credit Reports
Credit Transfer
Cricket (Sport)
Critical Listening
Critical Period
Critique Sessions
Cross Burning
Cross Country Skiing
Cross Sex Friendship
Crossword Puzzles
Crowd Control
Crystallizing Experience
Cuffs (Clothing)
Cultural Arts
Cultural Capital
Cultural Change
Cultural Content
Cultural Contributions
Cultural Democracy
Cultural Epistemology
Cultural Experience
Cultural Journalism
Cultural Myths
Cultural Nationalism
Cultural Reentry
Cultural Relevance
Cultural Resources
Cultural Sensitivity
Cultural Universals
Cultural Values
Culture of Information
Culture Transmission
Cultures Controversy
Currency Devaluation
Curriculum Reconceptualists
Custodial Contracting
Custodian Attitudes
Custom Publishing
Customer Relations
Customer Satisfaction
Customer Services
Daily Activities
Daily Living Literature
Daily Production Reports
Daily Routines
Daily Work Activities
Darts (Clothing)
Data Administration
Data Display
Data Files
Data Maps
Data Organization
Data Pool
Data Protection
Data Quality
Data Security
Database Overlap
Date Rape
Dating Violence
Day Care Information Services
Day Care Registration
Day Care Selection
Deadlines (News Media)
Deans List
Debate Delivery
Debate Ethics
Debate Handbooks
Debate Tournaments
Debt (Financial)
Debt Collection
Debt Financing
Decision Aids
Decision Grid
Decisions
Declining Population
Deconstruction
Dedication
Defense Contracts
Defense Expenditures
Defense Industrial Base
Defense Preparedness
Deference
Degree Depreciation
Deinstitutionalization (of Legal Offenders)
Delayed Return (Foreign Students)
Delegate Selection
Demand
Democratic Communication
Democratic Socialism
Demographic Projections
Demotion (Occupational)
Department Image
Department Workload
Dependency (Economics)
Deposit Collections
Depreciation
Depreciation Accounting
Derivative Works
Deschooling
Descriptive Cataloging
Descriptor for Individualized Instruction
Desire
Detective Stories
Detente
Development Capital
Development Education
Development Journalism
Development of Higher Level Thinking Abilities
Deviations from Lesson Plans
Diagnostic Skills
Diapers
Dichotomies
Dichotomous Choice
Dicta Typing
Dictionary Skills
Didactic Games
Differential Diplomas
Diploma in Management Studies
Diploma Mills
Diploma of Higher Education
Diplomatic Services
Direct Costs
Direct Lending
Direct Mail
Direct Mail Advertising
Direct Mail Campaigns
Directional Transactions
Directionality
Directions
Disasters
Disclaimers
Disco Dancing
Disposable Income
Disruption
Disruptive Effect (Reading)
Dissertation Alternatives
Dissertations in Progress
Dissident Literature
Distinguished Service in Trusteeship Award
Distraction
Distribution of Schools
Ditto Masters
Diversionary Agencies
Diversity (Groups)
Divestiture
Division of Labor (Automation)
Doctor of Education Degrees
Docudramas
Document Action
Document Delivery
Document Delivery Service
Document Literacy Skills
Document Location
Document Structure
Document Supply
Dolls
Domain Placement
Dominant Activities
Donor Characteristics
Door to Door Solicitation
Dormitory Size
Double Entry Journals
Double Standard
Downtown Revitalization
Downward Mobility
Dragons
Dramatistic Criticism
Dramaturgical Perspective
Dramaturgical Role
Dramaturgy
Dressing Room Slogans
Dribble File
Drinking Games
Drive By Shootings
Driver Improvement Analysis
Driving
Driving Records
Drug Free School Zones
Drug Trafficking
Dual Degrees
Dual Role
Dual School Districts
Dues Checkoff
Dynamic Stories
Dynamics (Music)
Dystopia
Eagle Feathers
Early Childhood Observation Form
Early Eligibility Determination (Financial Aid)
Early Graduation
Earning Potential
Easements
Easy Listening Music
Easy Reading Books
Eclecticism
Ecogame
Ecological Dissonance
Ecological Psychology
Economic Competitiveness
Economic Decline
Economic Diversification
Economic Impact Studies
Economic Indicators
Economic Revitalization
Ecumenism
Editions
Editor Role
Editorial Content
Editorial Mechanics
Editorial Omissions
Editorial Policy
Education Reform Reports
Education Reform Utilization
Education Revitalization
Education Society Relationship
Educational Awareness
Educational Diversity
Educational Dramatizations
Educational Encouragement
Educational Entitlements
Educational Indicators
Educational Information
Educational Issues
Educational Journals
Educational Leadership
Educational Life Skills
Educational Media Role
Educational Media Use
Educational Passports
Educational Production Function
Educational Renewal
Educational Restructuring
Educational Transfer
Educational Uniformity
Educational Vocabulary
Educational Writing
Educator Revitalization
Educator Role
Egalitarianism
Elaboration
Elaborative Prompts
Elder Care
Elected Positions
Electronic Books
Electronic Journals
Electronic Magazines
Electronic Music
Electronic News Gathering
Electronic Newspapers
Electronic Print
Elementary School Secondary School Relationship
Elementary Science Study
Elite Values
Elites
Elocution
Emancipatory Theater
Embedded Stories
Embroidery
Emergencies
Emergency Evacuations
Emergency Preparedness
Emergency Teacher Certification
Emergent Leadership
Emergent Literacy
Emerging Order
Emigration
Empathic Learning
Employability Development
Employee Attrition
Employee Deviance
Employee Leasing
Employee Ownership
Employee Participation
Employee Publications
Employee Readiness
Employee Rights
Employee Theft
Employee Welfare
Employer Role
Employment Contract Termination
Employment Exit Interviews
Employment Initiatives

Employment Location
Employment Security
Employment Subsidies
Employment Vouchers
Endowed Chairs
Engineering Shortage
Enhancement Funding
Enlightenment Thought
Enterprise
Entertainment
Enthusiasm
Environmental Action
Ephemera
Epistemic Research
Equals Sign
Equipment Needs
Equity Materials
Equivocation
ERIC Fact Sheets
ERIC Mini Reviews
ERIC Trends Issues Papers
Error Reports
Escuelas en El Campo
Espionage Books
Essay Topics
Ethical Communication
Ethical Relativism
Ethnic Differences
Ethnic Literature
Ethnic Media
Ethnic Newspapers
Ethnographic Films
Ethnohistory
Ethos
Ethos Level
Etiquette
Eurocentrism
European Currency Unit
European Influences
European Jeremiads
European Theater
Evaluation Reports
Evening Newspapers
Evil
Excellence
Exceptional Child Education Resources
Excess Costs
Exhortation
Exoffenders
Expensing
Experimentalism
Experimenter Expectancy Cues
Experimenter Prestige Effect
Expertise
Explanations
Explicitness
Exploitation
Exploration
Exploratory Studies
Extemporaneous Speaking
External Debt
External Doctor of Education Degrees
Extracts
Extremism
Facial Characteristics
Facial Configuration
Facility Alternatives
Facility Management
Facility Use
Faculty Appointments
Faculty Attitudes
Faculty Consistency
Faculty Governance
Faculty Liaison
Faculty Productivity Reports
Faculty Reappointment
Faculty Reassignment
Faculty Records
Faculty Research
Faculty Service
Faculty Status
Faculty Vitality
Fads
Fallacies
False Allegations
Familiarization
Family Advocacy
Family Budgets
Family Communication Pattern
Family Democracy
Family Development
Family Formation
Family Intervention
Family Involvement Communication System
Family Leave
Family Life Cycle
Family Needs
Family Oriented Benefits
Family Outings
Family Owned Businesses
Family Policy
Family Rules
Family Support
Family Values
Farce
Farradanes Relational Indexing
Fascism Scale
Fashion Shows
Fast Announcement Service
Fast Foods
Fatalism
Fear Appeal Messages
February (Month)
Federal Express Mail
Federal Property
Federal Records
Federal Role
Federal School District Relationship
Feedforward
Feminist Criticism
Fertility Values
Festivals
Festschrift
Feudal Nexus (Game)
Field Guides
Fiestaware
Figural Creativity
Figural Tradition
Figure Drawing
Film Aesthetics
Film Festivals
Film Genres
Film History
Film Music
Film Noir
Film Program Notes
Film Programing
Film Reviews
Film Viewing
Filmic Styles
Final Offer Arbitration
Final Reports
Finance
Financial Aid Form
Financial Analysis
Financial Assets
Financial Benefits
Financial Indicators
Financial Planning
Financial Records
Financial Reports
Financing Options
Finding Aids
Finger Counting
Fingerplays
Fingerprints
Fire Drills
First Circles
First Class Mail
First Impressions
Fiscal Accountability
Fishing
Flag Football
Flame Reading
Flamenco
Flap Board (Game)
Flashback
Flexible Response (Communication)
Flicker Ball
Flood (Tradition)
Floor Hockey
Florence Agreement
Fluid Intelligence
Folk Dance
Folk Music
Folk Rock
Folk Wisdom
Folktales
Follow Through Services
Followup Materials
Food Gathering
Food Preferences
Food Waste
Forced Compliance
Foreclosures
Foreign Aid
Foreign Currency
Foreign Educational Credentials
Foreign Intervention
Foreign News
Foreign News Media
Foreign Ownership
Foreign Students Home Country Reentry
Forgiveness
Form Attending
Form Diversity
Form Dominance
Form Matching
Form Naming
Form PROM (Personnel Analysis)
Form Recognition
Form Reproduction Task
Form Stimuli
Formal Education
Formal Features
Formatting
Formula Fiction
Formula Funding
Formula Poetry
Fortune 500
Forums
Fotonovelas
Found Poems
Four and One Half Day School Week
Four Day School Week
Fourth Grade Slump
Foxhunting
Fragile Knowledge
Frankfurt School
Fraudulent Credentials
Free Form Games
Free Lance Market
Free Materials
Free Time
French Civilization
French Cuisine
French Culture
French Republicanism
Freshman Orientation
Frisbee
Fugitive Literature
Full Faith and Credit Policy
Full Time Employment
Functional Communication
Functional Community
Functional Ecology of Development
Functional Play
Functionplane Criterion
Funding Formulas
Funds Flow Statements
Funeral Orations
Funerals
Furniture Repair
Future Cognition
Future Extension
Future Markets
Futures Markets
Gainsharing
Gallup Award
Gallup Poll
Gambling
Gamesmanship
Gang Rape
Gardening
Garment Design and Construction Certificate
Gatekeeper Role
Gatorball
Gender Gap
Gender Issues
General Adaptation Syndrome
General Certificate of Education
Generalizable Skills
Generative Processes
Generic Argument
Generic Argument (Debate)
Generic Certificates (Agriculture)
Generic Products
Generosity
Genocide
Geographic Displacement
Geographic Information Systems
German Culture
Gerontocide
Ghost Stories
Ghost Towns
Ghostwriting
Gift Clubs
Gifted Science Project Resource File
Gifts
Gifts and Exchange Functions
Global Awareness
Global Change
Global Issues
Global Markets
Global Survival
Glue Sniffing
Goal Values
God (Concept)
Good Faith Requirements
Good Housekeeping Seal of Approval
Gospel Music
Gossip
Governing Board Role
Government Business Cooperation
Government Business Relationship
Government Industry Relationship
Government Information
Government Records
Government Spending
Government Subsidies
Grade Anxiety
Grade Appeal Hearings
Graduated Tuition
Graffiti
Grandparent Grandchild Relationship
Grandparent Responsibility
Graphic Novels
Graphic Records
Graphic Representation
Gratifications Obtained
Gratifications Sought
Gratuities
Greek Culture
Greek Mythology
Green Pages Concept
Greeting Cards
Greetings
Gross National Product
Group Attitudes
Group Characteristics
Group Cohesion
Group Data
Group Day Care
Group Insurance
Group Size
Groupthink
Guardianship
Gubernatorial Elections
Guidance Materials
Guided Readers
Gymnastics Meets
Habilitation
Hair Length
Hairstyles
Haitian Culture
Halftime Shows
Handicapism
Handwashing
Handwriting Speed
Hangman (Game)
Harassment
Harmonic Dictation
Harmonization
Harris Jacobson Core List
Hawaii Kyoiku Kai
Hazardous Student Activities
Hazards
Hazing
Headings
Heckling
Hedonism
Hegemony
Help Systems
Heritage Consistency
Hierarchical Control
High Jump
High Performance Skills
High Reliability Organizations
High Unemployment Areas
Highlighting (Text)
Highway Maintenance
Highway Safety
Hiking
Hinduism
Hispanic American Achievement
Hispanic American Education
Hispanic Arts
Hispanic Literature
Historical Background
Historical Bibliography
Historical Distortion
Historical Fiction
Historical Materials
Historical Novels
Historical Preservation
Hitchhiking
Holdings Statements
Holiday Art Lessons
Holocaust Literature
Home Based Employment
Home Equity Conversion
Home Market
Homestays
Homesteading
Homogeneity of Regression
Homogeneity of Variance
Homology
Homophily

Library Administrative Records
Library Attitudes
Library Closings
Library Construction
Library Growth
Library Journals
Library Literature
Library Materials Conservation
Library Moves
Library Operations
Library Organization
Library Pathfinders
Library Publications
Library Publishing
Library Reserve
Library Science Literature
Library Security
Library Tours
License Renewal
Licensed Parenthood
Life Chances
Life Coping Skills
Life Cycles
Life Geosystems
Life Insurance
Life Masks
Life Stage Vocational Development
Life Threatening Events
Life Transitions
Lifetime Employment
Lifetime Income
Liking
Limbic Learning
Limited Partnerships
Line (Visual Arts)
Line Drawings
Lineality
Links (Indexing)
List Poems
Listenability
Literacy Events
Literacy Hoax
Literacy Retention
Literary Awards
Literary Canon
Literary Collaboration
Literary Gaps
Literary Magazines
Literary Models
Literary Newswriting
Literary Quality
Literary Response
Literary Settings
Literature in Translation
Littering
Live Broadcasts
Live Shop
Lives of Service (Research)
Livian Wars Task
Living Arrangements
Loan Counseling
Loan Forbearance
Loan Forgiveness
Local Autonomy
Local Control
Local Learning Systems
Local Media
Local News
Local Origination
Local Public Works
Local Taxes
Localization (Administrative)
Locally Based Research
Location Allocation Package
Logical Consequences
Logistical Support
Logos (Theology)
Lone Walker
Long Jumping
Long Term Effects
Lookbacks (Reading)
Loyalty
Luck
Lyrics
Machiavellianism
Machine Dependence
Machine Readable Data
Machine Shorthand
Macrame
Macrosystems
Magazine Covers
Magazine Writing
Magic
Magic Circle
Mail Order
Mail Order Book Delivery
Mail Registration
Mailable Copy Rate
Mailing and Shipping
Mailing Lists
Main Idea
Majority Groups
Majority Role
Male Female Relationship
Man Nature Relationship
Management Consulting Service
Management Control
Management Evaluation Review Compliance Quality
Managerial Communication
Mandatory Bargaining Issues
Mandatory Continuing Education
Mandatory Programs
Mandatory Reporting of Abuse
Mandatory Retirement
Mandatory Staggered Attendance Plans
Manipulable Influences
Manpower Planning
Manpower Substitution
Manual Skills
Manuscript Collections
Manuscript Illumination
Manuscript Typing
Manuscripts
Maoism
Map Displays
Map Processing
Map Projections
Marathon Running
Marble Game
Marbles (Game)
Marbling
Marginal Costs
Marginal Notes
Market Value
Marriage Plans
Marxist Aesthetics
Mascots (Athletics)
Masculinity
Masculinity Femininity Variable
Mass Media Reviews
Master Builders of Iowa
Master of Human Services
Masters of Business Administration
Match Boxes
Matching Funds
Matching Gifts
Matching Gifts (Finance)
Matching Grants
Materialism
Maternal Directiveness
Maternal Interaction Structured Situation
Maternity Benefits
Mathematical Posters
Mathematical Power
Mathematical Reviews
Mathematical Stories
Mathematics Contests
Mathematics Indicators
Matriarchy
May (Month)
McCarthyism
Meat Inspection
Media Adoption
Media Appraisal
Media Campaigns
Media Characteristics
Media Coverage
Media Ethics
Media Events
Media Experience
Media Exposure
Media Flow
Media Frames
Media Gratifications
Media Imagery
Media Ownership
Media Psychology
Media Relations
Media Reliance
Media Responsibility
Mediating Factors
Mediating Structures
Mediators
Medical Education Financing Policy Analyses
Medicare Capitation
Medicine Shows
Medicine Wheel
Megatrends
Melting Pot
Membership Benefits
Membership Requirements
Memes
Mental Representation
Menu Planning
Menudo
Merchandise Turnover
Meringue
Merit
Merit Promotion
Merlin the Magician
Message Based Performances
Message Legitimacy
Metropolitan Desegregation Plans
Mexican Arts
Mexican Telesecundaria
Microcomputer Student Ratio
Microdata
Micropublishing
Microsystems
Microthemes
Militarism
Military Assistance to Safety and Traffic
Military Combat
Military Deployment
Military Draft
Military Enlistment
Military Industrial Complex
Military Power
Military Recruitment
Military Reenlistment
Military Role
Military Spending
Mini Economy
Miniature Golf
Minimum Academic Mastery
Miniprint
Minister Role
Minority Businesses
Minority Scholarships
Minutes of Meetings
Mirror State Counterplans (Debate)
Misinterpretation
Misreporting
Missing Data
Mission Orientation
Mobile Service Delivery
Mobilization
Mobilizing Information
Moment of Silence
Money
Monkey Bars
Monochords
Monographs
Monopoly (Game)
Moral Education
Moral Reality
Morning Newspapers
Morphisms
Mortgage Backed Student Loans
Mortgages
Mosaics
Motion Picture Ratings
Motor Inhibition
Motor Vehicle Inspections
Motor Vehicle Registration
Mountaineering
Movement (Visual Arts)
Movie Attendance
Muckraking
Mug Shots
Multi Database Searching
Multi Teacher Departments
Multicultural Materials
Multiethnic Literature
Multilateralism
Multimedia Performances
Multinational States
Multiple Authorship
Multiple Contracting
Multiple Endorsements
Multiple Response Data
Multiple Roles
Multiple Source Funding
Multiplicative Strategies
Multiplier Effect
Multistate Surveys
Municipal Bonds
Municipal Overburden
Murals
Music Binding
Music Braille
Music Call Out Research
Music Literature
Music Syntax
Music Videos
Musical Scores
Musicals
Mutual Aid
Mutual Funds
Mysteries (Literature)
NAMES Project Quilt
Narrative Report Cards
Narrative Text
Narrative Transcript
Narrative Verse
Narrowcasting
Nation States
National Bibliographies
National Catering Business Game
National Commission Reports
National Commissions
National Debate Topic
National Debt
National Development
National Expansion
National Gazettes
National Goals
National Health Insurance
National High School Debate Resolutions
National Identity
National Image
National Information Policy
National Interlibrary Loan Code
National Issues
National Lottery
National Media
National Needs
National Origin
National Planning
National Policy
National Priorities
National Rank
National Science Policy
National Service
National Standard Prog Outdoor Leader Certificate
National Standards
National Wealth
National Youth Service
Native Foods
Nativism
Natural Resources Management
Natural Rights
Naturalistic Content
Naturalistic Research
Naturalistic Studies
Nature Books
Nature Stories
Navy Nurse Corps
Navy Plaque Index
Negative News
Negritude
Neighbor Attitudes
Neighborhood Characteristics
Nemeth Code
Neo Piagetian Theory
Neocolonialism
Neoconservatism
Neorationalism
Neorealism
Nepotism
Nested Data
Networking
Networks (Persons)
Neugarten Age Norms Inquiry
New Aesthetic
New Age Thinking
New Criticism
New Humanism
New Left
New Media
New Realism
New Rhetoric
New Social Studies
New Students
New Theater
New Towns
New World Information Order
New Years Resolutions
New Zealand Literature
News Accuracy
News Bias
News Borrowing
News Content
News Exchange
News Flow
News Interview Programs
News Releases
News Sources
News Stories
News Topics
News Values
Newsmagazines
Newspaper Chains
Newspaper Circulation
Newspaper Dynasties
Newspaper Graphics

Newspaper Ownership
Newspaper Subscriptions
Newswork
Niche Books
Nicknames
Nihilism
No Pass No Play Rules
Noahs Ark
Noh Theater
Nomenclator
Non Khmer
Nonacademic Achievement
Nonacademic Labor Market
Noncash Benefits
Noncommercial Films
Nonconformity
Noncontact Sports
Nonintellectual Abilities
Nonlinguistic Composition
Nonmigration
Nonmonetary Economy
Nonprofit Sector (Labor Market)
Nonroutine Problems
Nonstructural Elements (Construction)
Nonsupervisory Employees
Nontheatrical Film Distribution
Nontraditional Lifestyles
Nonverbal Behavior Category System
Nonviolence
Northwest Coast Indian Art
Norwegian Drama
Nostalgia
Nuclear Freeze
Number Sense
Numismatics
Nursery Rhymes
Nursing Shortage
Nutrition Education Research
Object Transformations
Objectics
Obscurantism
Observation Lesson Information
Observational Studies
Obtrusive Measures
Occultism
Occupancy in Accommodations
Occupational Age Distribution
Occupational Commitment
Occupational Congruence
Occupational Control
Occupational Distribution
Occupational Identity
Occupational Images
Occupational Models
Occupational Orientation
Occupational Proficiency
Occupational Research Unit
Occupational Rewards
Occupational Role Values
Occupational Socialization
Occupational Stability
Occupational Status
Occupational Stereotypes
Occupational Structure
Occupational Survival Skills
Occupational Upgrading
October (Month)
Off Farm Employment
Off the Air Recordings
Offensive Speech
Offset Lithography
Offset Printing
Old Age Survivors and Disability Insurance
Older Library Materials
One Act Plays
One Way Communication
Online Reading
Online Search Skills
Ontario Ministry of Ed H S 1 Circulars
Ontology
Op Art
Open Competence
Open End Leads
Open Learning
Open Meetings
Operating Ratios
Operettas
Opportunities Centers
Opportunity Costs
Oppositional Decoding
Oppression
Oracy
Oral Interpretation Tournaments
Oral Journals
Oral Literature
Oral Presentations
Oral Reports
Oratory
Order Out (Game)
Order Relations
Organic Education
Organizational Commitment
Organizational Consensus
Organizational Excellence
Organizational Mortality
Organizational Needs
Organizational Readiness
Organizational Reports
Organizational Skills
Organizational Termination
Oriental Literature
Orienting Information
Orienting Response
Origami
Ostinato
Out of District Placements
Out of Field Classes
Out of Print Materials
Outcome Based Education
Outdoor Leadership
Outdoor Recreation
Outliers
Outlines
Outmigration
Overattribution
Overdue Books
Overseas Activities
Overselectivity
Ownership Patterns
Pachisi Game
Pacific Islands Literature
Pacific Rim
Pacifism
Pageants
Paint
Paper Airplanes (Toys)
Paper Boats (Toys)
Paper Dresses
Paperwork
Paperwork Control
Paperwork Reduction
Parables
Paranormal Beliefs
Paranormal Experiences
Parent Background Forms
Parent Breakfasts (School)
Parent Characteristics
Parent Control
Parent Developed Materials
Parent Experience
Parent Occupation
Parent Resources
Parental Consent for Minors
Parental Leave
Parental Supervision
Pareto Optimality
Parity
Parrhesia
Partial Retirement
Parties (Social Gatherings)
Passage Organization
Pastoral Letters
Pathfinders
Peak Experiences
Peak Performance
Pedology
Peer Recruitment
Pencil Holding
Pencil Shape
Pencil Size
Pennies
Penny Press
Pension Portability
Pentathlon
Perceived Reality
Percussion Instruments
Performance and Competency Based Student Materials
Performance Based Pay
Performance Legitimacy
Performance Levels
Performance Management and Recognition System
Permanent Guardianship
Permanent Part Time Teaching
Perseveration
Person Clusters
Persona
Personal Celebrations
Personal Charm
Personal Experiences
Personal Fables
Personal Finance
Personal Major Events
Personal Names
Personal Problems
Personal Writing
Personalized Stories
Personnel Files
Persuasibility
Persuasive Strategies
Petitions
Petroglyphs
Pharmacology and Patient Care
Phenomenography
Philately
Philosophy of History
Philosophy of Science
Phonathons
Photonovels
Physical Modeling
Pickleball
Pictionary Perfect
Pictographs
Picture Interpretation
Picture Stories
Piecework
Pioneer Life
Piracy of Intellectual Property
Pirate Radio
Pirate Television
Pitch (Music)
Place of Birth
Planned Change
Planned Giving
Plant Communities
Plant Shutdown
Plausibility (Texts)
Play Learning
Play Materials
Play Style
Playfulness
Playground Design
Playgroups
Plot (Fiction)
Pluralism
Pluralistic Education
Pluralistic Ignorance
Pluralistic Method
Pockets
Poetic Forms
Poetic Humanism
Poetry Workshops
Pointing (Gesture)
Pole Vaulting
Police Science
Policy Effectiveness
Policy Implications
Policy Issues
Policy Reviews
Political Action
Political Advertising
Political Appointments
Political Cartoons
Political Commercials
Political Communication
Political Correctness
Political Criticism
Political Culture
Political Efficacy
Political Endorsements
Political Image
Political Implications
Political Legitimacy
Political Literature
Political Military Exercises
Political Symbols
Politically Correct Communication
Poll (Influence)
Pollution Index
Poly Hockey
Polygamy
Polynesian Literature
Polyphonic Music
Polytechnics
Pop Up Books
Popcorn Factory
Popular Music
Population Aging
Population Projections
Population Stability
Populism
Portion Sizes
Portuguese Literature
Positional Visibility
Positioning (Advertising)
Positive Attitudes
Post High School Experience
Postage
Postage Stamps
Postcards
Postindustrial Society
Postindustrialism
Postreading Activities
Power
Power Equalization
Power Struggles
Practical Knowledge
Practice Questions
Pragmatism
Prayer
Prayer Books
Pre Columbian History
Precision Journalism
Precognition
Preconceptions
Predictable Books
Preemployment Skills
Prefaces
Preference Data
Preference Patterns
Preference Transitivity
Preferential Circles
Prehistoric Art
Premarital Counseling
Prepackaged Lunches
Prepayment Plans
Preprimary Enrollment
Prepublication Review
Prereading Activities
Prereading Skills
Prerequisite Waivers
Preretirement
Preschool Selection
Prescription Athletic Turf
Presidential Messages
Presidential Primaries
Press Criticism
Press Releases
Press Responsibility
Prestructured Cases
Presumption (Debate)
Pretend Reading
Preventive Education
Preventive Maintenance
Price
Price Wars
Pricing
Pride
Pride in Performance
Primary Literature
Priming (Reading Comprehension)
Principal Transfer
Principal Welfare
Print Awareness
Print Journalism
Priorities
PRISE Reporter
Prison Reform
Prisoner Fasting
Private Benefits
Private Employment Agency Abuse
Private Enterprise
Private Practice
Private Practice (Professions)
Private Speech
Private Transportation
Proactive Interference
Problem Finding
Problem Identification
Problem Ownership
Problem Posing
Problem Representation
Process Goals
Procrastination
Profanity
Professional Activities
Professional Athletics
Professional Commitment
Professional Concerns
Professional Differentiation
Professional Disclosure
Professional Ethics
Professional Guidelines
Professional Identity
Professional Image
Professional Journals
Professional Laboratory Experiences
Professional Literature
Professional Openness
Professional Orientation
Professional Perspectives
Professional Role
Professional Sequence
Professional Socialization
Professional Sports
Professional Welfare
Professional Writing

Professionalism
Profit Maximization
Profits
Program Assembly Monitor Execution Learn Applicat
Program Cancellation
Program Characteristics
Program Discontinuation
Program Exit
Program Legitimacy
Program Length Commercials
Program Modification
Program Requirements
Program Sponsorship
Progress
Progress Charts
Progressive Elaboration
Progressivism
Project Information Packages
Project Leadership
Promises
Promising Practices
Property Acquisition
Property Disposal
Property Values
Propositional Abilities
Propositional Analysis
Propositional Logic
Prostitution
Protege Mentor Relationship
Provincialism
Provisional Certification
Proxy Reports
Psychodrama
Psychographics
Psychophysics
Puberty Rites
Public Access
Public Access Television
Public Awareness
Public Discourse
Public Domain
Public Good
Public Information
Public Information Campaigns
Public Interest
Public Private Relationship
Public Records
Public Relations Journals
Public Safety
Public Service Advertising
Public Service Campaigns
Public Service Internships
Public Works
Published Reading Materials
Puerto Rican Literature
Pulp Magazines
Punk Rock
Pure Research
Puritanism
Purpose (Composition)
Putting (Golf)
Quackery
Quads
Qualified Citation Indexing
Quality Assurance
Quality Indicators
Quality of Effort
Quality of Friendship
Quality Time
Queen Bee Syndrome
Question Answering
Questions
Quilting
Quotations
Rabbinical Literature
Race Fairness
Racial Harassment
Racial Preference
Radical Movements
Radical Press
Radicalism
Radio Plays
Radio Vision
Radiotelephone Third Class Operator Permit
Raku
Ranching
Random Digit Dialing
Ranked Retrieval Output
Rap Music
Rap Sessions
Rape Myths
Rare Books
Rastafarianism
Rational Bureaucracy
Reader Advisors
Reader Expectations
Reader Preferences
Reader Response Criticism
Reading Accuracy
Reading Concepts
Reading Contests
Reading Fluency
Reading Journals
Reading Lists
Reading Logs
Reading Management
Reading Sequence
Reading Uses
Real English
Real Estate Brokerage
Real Estate Development
Reality
Reality Based Television Programs
Rebus
Receipts
Receptivity to Change
Recipes (Food)
Reciprocal Borrowing
Reciprocity
Record Values
Recreation Industry
Recruiter Role
Recruitment Materials
Redshirting
Reference Interviews
Reference Questions
Reference Skills
Reference Transactions
Reform Efforts
Reform Strategies
Refugee Resettlement
Refunds
Refusals
Reggae
Regional Development
Regional Literature
Regional Magazines
Regionalism
Regionalized Education
Rehabilitation Engineering
Rehearsal
Rehearsals (Theater)
Rehiring
Reindustrialization
Reintegration
Relational Efficacy (Marriage)
Relational Propositions
Relationship Change Research
Relationship Quality
Religious Art
Religious Broadcasting
Religious Conversion
Religious Exercises
Religious Experiences
Religious Freedom
Religious Fundamentalism
Religious Landmarks
Religious Movements
Religious News
Religious Practices
Religious Publications
Remodeling
Rent
Rental Property
Replacement Costs
Report Format
Representativeness
Reprints
Requests
Requests for Clarification (Responses)
Requests for Proposals
Research Ethics
Research in Progress
Research Infrastructure
Research Networks
Research Priorities
Research Quality
Research Results
Research Styles
Research Suggestions
Research Summaries
Research Trends
Researcher Role
Reserve Book Collections
Reserves (Financial)
Residential Remodeling
Resignation (Job)
Resolutions
Respect
Respondent Burden
Responsiveness (Government)
Restoration
Restoration Comedy
Retail Security
Retrospective Bibliographies
Return Migration
Return on Investment
Return Rates (Books)
Revenue Producing Sports
Revitalization
Revivals (Plays)
Revolutionary Nationalism
Rhetoric of Reaffirmation
Rhodes Scholarships
Rhyme Priming
Rhythm and Blues
Rhythmic Gymnastics
Riddles
Ringdoc
Riot Control
Risk Taking
Risky Recreation
Rites
Rites of Passage
Ritual Abuse
Ritual Theatre
Rituals
River Rafting
Roadside Attractions
Rock Art
Rock Climbing
Rodeos
Role Status
Roman Mythology
Romance Novels
Routine Environments
Routine Events
Routing Problems (Traffic)
Rowing
Royalties
Rubbings (Art)
Rugby
Rumors
Rural Culture
Rural Futures Development Strategy
Rural Nonfarm Employment
Rural Renaissance
Rural Restructuring
Rural Suburban Differences
Russian Education
Russian Theater
Salary Reductions
Sales Transactions
Salesperson Client Relationship
Same Sex Friendship
Sample Reports
Sand Play
Santa Claus
Santeria
Saskmedia
Satanic Abuse
Satanism
Satellite News Gathering
Savings
Savings Accounts
Savings Bonds
Scan Module
Scandinavian Culture
Scandinavian Literature
Scanlon Plan
Scarcity
Scenarios
Scholarly Communication
Scholarly Information Exchange
Scholarly Writing
Scholastic Photography Awards
Schomburg Collection
School Based Enterprises
School Based Evaluation
School Based Recovery Support
School Based Services
School Construction Systems Development
School Culture
School District Dissolution
School District Isolation
School Influence
School Legitimation
School Library Media Program of the Year Award
School Mapping
School Milk Contracts
School Openings
School Public Library Cooperation
School Renewal
School Rules
School Stability
Schools for the Seventies
Science Indicators
Science Participation
Scientific Essays
Scoggin Memorial Collections
Scorekeeping
Scottish Certificate of Education
Scouting
Screenplays
Seals (Printing)
Seams (Clothing)
Search and Rescue Management
Search and Rescue Missions
Search Commands
Season of Birth
Seasons
Seat Occupancy
Seating Assignments
Seating Capacity
Seating Preferences
Second Careers
Second Class Mail
Secondary Migration
Secondary School Record
Secondary Victimization
Secrecy
Secular Humanism
Secularism
Securities Credit
Securities Industry
Security Classifications
Selective Attention
Selective Reenlistment Bonus
Self Adaptors
Self Advocacy
Self Awareness
Self Defense
Self Direction
Self Disparaging Humor
Self Implosion Therapy
Self Observation
Self Prediction
Self Processor
Self Recordings (Audiotape)
Self Regulation
Self Regulation (Groups)
Self Renewal
Self Selection (Reading)
Self Stimulation
Semiannual Admission
Sensationalism
Sensorimotor Play
Separatism
September (Month)
Sequential Requests
Sequestration (Budgets)
Serial Position Effect
Serials Agents
Serials Cancellation
Serials Claiming
Seriation
Sermons
Service Contracts
Service Delivery Areas
Service Journalism
Service Learning
Service Quality
Service Quantity
Service Reduction
Service Utilization
Services Inventories
Set Asides
Seven Period Day
Severance Pay
Sex Bonds
Sexual Humor
Shadowing
Shamanism
Shapes
Shared Past
Shared Reading
Shelf Availability (Libraries)
Shelflist Count
Shelflist Sample
Shelving Practices
Shift Work
Shine Bower Anova
Shintoism
Shoe Turf Interface
Shoes
Shooting Sports
Shoplifting
Shopping
Short Assessment Outline
Short Term Accommodations
Short Term Developmental Improvements
Short Term Effects
Short Term Storage
Shortened School Week
Show Business
Shredding

Sibling Birth
Sibling Spacing
Sibling Tutoring
Sick Leave
Sight Sound System
Signability (of Text)
Signal Flag Cards
Sikhism
Silence
Silent Majority
Silhouettes
Silk Screen Printing
Similarities
Simon Says Game
Single Article Announcement Service
Single Person Household
Single Room Occupancy
Single Sex Classes
Singletons
Sisyphus (Greek Mythology)
Site Visits
Situation Comedies
Situational Reinforcement
Situational Salience
Six Suppliers Game
Sixth Form
Skapa
Skid Row
Skipping (Running)
Sky Sculpture
Skydiving
Skynet
Slavic Culture
Sledding
Sleeves (Clothing)
Slide Collections
Slide Tape Programs
Sliding Fee Scales
Small Cities
Small College Faculty Research Opportunity Award
Small Community and Rural Development Policy
Small Countries
Small Group Communication
Small School Districts
Smiling
Smokey Bear
Snacks
Social Accounting
Social Activity Frameworks
Social Barriers
Social Comparison
Social Conflict
Social Connectedness
Social Consequences
Social Construction
Social Conventions
Social Darwinism
Social Density
Social Disintegration
Social Disruption
Social Entitlements
Social Events
Social Facilitation
Social Good
Social Identity
Social Inferences
Social Marginal Product of Labor
Social Needs
Social Order
Social Participation
Social Performance Indicator
Social Philosophy
Social Policy
Social Power
Social Promotion
Social Reality
Social Reasoning
Social Reporting
Social Rules
Social Science Fairs
Social Substantive Schedule
Social Transmission
Social Utility
Societal Benefits
Societal Impact
Societal Needs
Society
Socioeconomic Diversity
Sociology of Science
Sociometric Status
Soft Contingency Network
Software Copying
Software Piracy
Sole Proprietorships
Solitude
Son Jarocho
Songbooks
Sophisticated Instructional Environment
Soul Music
Sound Bites
Sound Source Ball
Sourcebooks
Southwestern American Literature
Soviet Education
Soviet Pedagogy
Soviet Research
Sparsity (Population)
Spasmodicism
Spatial Distribution
Spatial Factors
Speaking Style
Special Collections (Library)
Special Editions
Special Event Day Care
Special Events
Specialized Accreditation
Specification Bias
Specification Error
Specificity
Spectator Sports
Speech Events
Speech Tournaments
Speech Writing
Speedball
Spelling Bees
Spending Patterns
Spiritual Experiences
Spiritual Needs
Spiritual Values
Spirituality
Spirituals
Sponsored Materials
Sponsored Research
Spontaneous Response Drawing
Spontaneous Singing
Sport Ambassadors
Sport Arena Management
Sport Competitiveness
Sport for All
Sport Injuries
Sport Management
Sports Bras
Sports Literature
Sports Officiating
Sports Stories
Spouse Relocation Assistance
Spread (Debate)
Spring (Season)
Square Dancing
Squatter Settlements
Staff Attendance
Staff Attitudes
Staff Characteristics
Staff Recognition
Staffing Patterns
Staffing Ratio
Stage Fright
Stairclimbing
Standard Minimum Rules for Treatment of Prisoners
Standard Training Agreements
Standard Transformation of Academic Grades
State Capitals
State Characteristics
State City Relationship
State College Relationship
State Economic Areas
State Governors
State Guides
State Level Textbook Adoption
State Local Relationship
State Responsibility
State Role
State Takeovers
State Tribal Relationship
Statewide Priorities
Static Balance
Station Trafficking
Statue of Liberty
Status Attainment
Status Discrepancy
Status Inconsistency
Status Projections
Status Quo
Status Reports
Stereognosis
Stewardship
Sticker Family Game
Stock Market
Stock Market Quotations
Stockpiling
Stopwords
Store Coupon Collecting
Store Coupons
Storefront Schools
Story Concepts
Story Content
Story Impressions
Story Knife Tales
Story List
Story Schema
Story Telling by Children
Story Themes
Strategic Reading
Stratification
Streaming (Education)
Street Theater
Stretch Workbook
String
Structural Communication
Structure Determinism
Structure of Knowledge
Structured Activities
Structured Overview
Student Activity Funds
Student Administrator Relationship
Student Chambers of Commerce
Student Committees
Student Computer Ratio
Student Consumerism
Student Cooperation
Student Corporations
Student Course Load
Student Disengagement
Student Editors
Student Engagement
Student Expectations
Student Financial Contribution
Student Handbooks
Student Industry Relationship
Student Information Form
Student Information System
Student Initiated Activities
Student Judgments
Student Led Activities
Student Licensing
Student Occupational Plan Outline
Student Performances
Student Power
Student Preferences
Student Questions
Student Satisfaction
Student Selected Materials
Student Strengths
Student Support Services
Student Teacher Characteristics
Studentship
Study Pace
Subcontracting
Subitizing
Subjective Magnitude Estimation
Subjectivity
Subliminal Advertising
Subliminal Stimulation
Subminimum Wage
Subsidiaries
Subsistence Agriculture Game
Subsistence Farming
Subsistence Lifestyle
Subskills
Subtitles (Television)
Suburban Newspapers
Success Rates (College Students)
Sudden Fiction
Suggestion
Summer
Summer Vacations
Sunday Newspaper Magazines
Superheroes
Superstition
Supervisor Supervisor Relationship
Supplemental Income
Supply Side Economics
Support of User Records and Files
Support Services
Supportive Learning Environments
Surfacing Materials
Surplus Space
Surprise
Surprise Ending Stories
Survival
Survival Competencies
Survival Equipment
Survival Skills
Survival Training
Suspense
Suspense Stories
Suspiciousness
Sustainability
Swedish Speaking
Syllogistic Reasoning
Symbolic Speech
Symbolicity
Symbology
Symmetry Complementarity Analysis
Sympathy
Synchronized Swimming
Synectics
Synergy
Synopses
Synopsis Journals
Synoptics
System Compensation
System Coupling
Systematicity
Systemic Change
Systemic Educational Reform
T Shirts
Tables of Contents
Tabloid Newspapers
Taboos
Tacit Knowledge
Tactile Preference
Tagmatic Differentials
Tai Chi Chuan
Talk Shows
Tanka
Tardiness
Tariffs
Tarot Reading
Task Characteristics
Task Definition
Task Engagement
Task Environments
Task Force Student Involvement
Task Forecast
Task Lists
Task Orientation
Task Structure
Tattling
Tautologies
Tax and Expenditure Limitations
Tax Bases
Tax Deferral
Tax Exempt Bonds
Tax Exemptions
Tax Incentives
Tax Resistance
Tax Sheltered Annuities
Tax Utilization
Taxpayer Revolt
Teacher Aide Evaluation
Teacher Appearance
Teacher Approval
Teacher Awareness
Teacher Commitment
Teacher Cooperation
Teacher Course Assignment
Teacher Dedication
Teacher Development
Teacher Engagement
Teacher Enthusiasm
Teacher Errors
Teacher Explanation
Teacher Fairs
Teacher Immediacy
Teacher Isolation
Teacher Journals
Teacher Judgments
Teacher Leadership
Teacher Needs
Teacher Networks
Teacher Nonreappointment
Teacher of the Year
Teacher Planning
Teacher Portfolios
Teacher Power
Teacher Preferences
Teacher Preparation Time
Teacher Recertification
Teacher Renewal
Teacher Resignation
Teacher Satisfaction
Teacher Socialization
Teacher Staff Ratio
Teacher Status
Teacher Surplus
Teacher Surveys
Teacher Writing
Teachers as Parents
Teachers Knowledge
Teaching Contests
Teaching Doctorate Degree
Teaching Perspectives
Teaching Sets
Team Assembly (Factory)

Technical Admissions Standards
Technical Communication
Technical Entrepreneurship
Technical Information Support Activities
Technical Notes
Technical Theater
Technological Baccalaureate (England)
Teenage Prostitution
Teleclasses
Telecommunications Policy
Telelectures
Telemarketing
Telenovelas
Teleology
Telephone Calls
Telephone Courtesy
Telephone Directories
Telephone Reference Services
Telephone Usage
Telesecundaria
Teleseminars
Teletutoring
Televangelism
Televised Proceedings
Television Criticism
Television Game Shows
Television History
Television Literacy
Television News
Television News Magazines
Televote
Telewriting
Temporary Employment
Tenacity
Tenants Insurance
Tenrikyo
Term Appointments
Term Classes
Termination of Friendship
Terra
Territorial Decentration
Territoriality
Terse Conclusions
Tessellations
Testimonials
Testimony
Text Based Interest
Text Compression
Text Condensation
Text Density
Textbook Design
Textbook Errors
Textbook Journals
Texture (Art)
Theater Administration
Theater Research
Theatrical Makeup
Thematic Organizers
Thematization
Theme (Literary)
Theory Development
Third Cycle
Third Party Credibility
Third Party Payments
Third Party Reimbursements
Third World
Threads
Threat
Throwing
Ticket Splitting
Tie Dying
Time Connectives
Time Lag
Time Telling
Timelines
Timeliness
Timing
Timmons Savings Plan
Titles
Tobacco Industry
Tolerance
Tolley Medal
Tongue Thrusting
Tongue Twisters
Tonguing
Topic Selection
Topicality
Topicality Arguments
Topographic Maps
Torture
Total Market Coverage Publications
Touching
Tower of Hanoi Problem
Town Meetings
Toy Industry
Track and Field Clubs
Trade Areas
Trade Deficits
Trade Journals
Trade Names
Trade Protectionism
Trade Routes
Trade Secrets
Tradeoffs
Traffic Fatalities
Trainer Role
Training Capacity
Training Credits (Great Britain)
Training Needs
Transaction Shells
Transactional Criticism
Transactional Evaluation
Transactional Writing
Transborder Information Flow
Transcendent Communication
Transcription
Transcription Services
Transescents
Transfer Payments
Transfer Rates (College)
Transfer Shock
Transformative Education
Transition Rates
Transition Time
Transitional Employment
Transportation Supervisors
Transposition
Trapping
Trapshooting
Tree Climbing
Tribal Citizenship
Tribal Management
Tribal Status
Tricksters (Folk Culture)
Trigger Films
Trip Planning
Triple Jump
Trivial Pursuit
Trivialization
Trouble Shooting Checklist
Trustee Recruitment
Trustee Responsibility
Trustee Role
Trustee Selection
Truth
Tuition Deposits
Tuition Formulas
Tuition Futures
Tuition Prepayment
Tuition Reciprocity
Tuition Reimbursement
Tuition Savings Plans
Tuition Waivers
Turn Taking
Turnaround Time
Turnarounds (Debate)
Tutor Role
Twelve Minute Run
Two Way Communication
Typeface
Typography
Unanimity
Underlining
Undeveloped Land
Uniform Course Numbering
Unintelligible Messages
Union Dues
Union Election Campaigns
Union Leadership
Union Recognition
Union Security
United Services for Effective Parenting
United States Presidents
United States Territories
Unitrusts
Units Analysis
University Expenditures
University Poll
University Structure
Unmet Student Financial Needs
Unobtrusive Measures
Unpaid Labor
Unpublished Materials
Upward Influence
Urban Development
Urban Infrastructures
Urban Revitalization
Usage Report
User Benefits
User Characteristics
User Fees
User Guides
User Preferences
Utilitarianism
Utopian Literature
Value Added Tax
Value Climate
Value Orientations
Value Profile Concept
Variant Editions
Varimax Procedures
Veda
Vegetarianism
Vengeance
Verbal Labeling
Verbal Self Instruction
Verbal Skills Curriculum
Verbosity
Vernacular Education
Verstehen
Vertical Articulation
Vertical Jump
Vertical Thinking
Verticality (Concept)
Vesting
Veterans Claims
Vice Presidential Debates
Victim Assistance
Victim Compensation
Video Audio Compressed
Video Criticism
Video Tape Reviews
Video Viewing
Videopublishing
Vietnam Veterans Memorial
Vietnam War Literature
Vietnamese Culture
Vigilante Films
Vignettes
Village Life
Village Prose
Villages
Virtues
Visions
Visiting Professor Series
Visitor Behavior
Visitors Books
Visual Communication
Visual Design
Visual Displays
Visual Haptic Training
Visual Journalism
Visual Motor Functioning
Visual Response System
Visual Syntax
Visual Verbal Synchrony
Visualmaker
Vital Statistics
Vivid Information
Vividness
Vocabulary Search Aids
Vocal Exercises
Vocational Ethics
Vocational Exploration Groups
Vocational Stability
Vocational Student Organizations
Vocationalism
Voluntarism
Voluntary Continuing Education
Voluntary Participation
Voluntary Reduced Work Time
Voluntary Simplicity
Volunteer Service Credits
Volunteer Teaching
Volunteerism
Volunteers in Education
Volunteers in Parochial Schools
Voodoo
Voting Behavior
Wage Scales
Wage Subsidies
Waiting
Waiting Lists
Waivers
Walden III
Walking
Want Ads
War Games
War Games (Children)
War Toys
Wardrobe Planning
Warning
Washington Administrative Code
Washington Award for Vocational Excellence
Waste in Government Spending
Watchabook
Water Accidents
Water Level Tasks
Water Play
Wealth
Webbing (Textiles)
Wedding Photography
Weekly Newspapers
Weekly Student Contact Hours
Welfare State
Western Music
Western Riding
Westernization
Westerns (Films)
Westerns (Novels)
Whamo Super Ball (Toy)
Wheelchair Athletics
White Backlash
White Supremacy
Wide Spaced Paper
Williamsburg Charter
Willingness
Willingness to Communicate
Wind Instruments
Winemaking
Winning
Winter
Wired City
Wired Nation
Wiretapping
Wisdom
Wishes
Witchcraft
Withdrawal Grades
Within Group Differences
Women Attentive to Childrens Happiness
Women in Literature
Women in Science
Women Owned Businesses
Womens Literature
Womens Magazines
Womens Media
Woodwind Choirs
Woodwind Instruments
Word Games
Word Recency Training
Work and Family Movement
Work Bonus Tax Credit
Work Centrality
Work Commitment
Work Disincentives
Work Flow
Work Flow Patterns
Work Habits
Work Incentives
Work Interruptions
Work Measurement
Work Orientation
Work Overload
Work Previews
Work Values
Workers Photography Movement
Workfare
Working Alliance
Working Papers
Workload
Workplace Security
World Citizenship
World Game
World Government
World Information Order
World Knowledge
World of Work Map
World Order
World Order Methodology
World Order Studies
World Series
World University
World Views
Worship Services
Worth
Writing Contests
Writing for Children
Writing Habits
Writing Implements
Writing Motivation
Writing Networks
Writing Prompts
Writing Tasks
Writing Threshold
Writing Topics
Written Consent
Wyndham Science
Wyoming Resolution
X Rated Movies
Yahtzee
Yellow Pages
Yiddish Literature
Yoga
Youth Community Service
Youth Indicators
Youth Opportunity Campaign
Youth Participation

Youth Service
Zeitgeist
Zen Buddhism
Zero Base Budgeting
Zimdex
Zip Codes
Zone Sections
Zoroastrianism

CATEGORY 17: Organizations / Institutions

3M Factory Training Center
4 H Clubs
4 H National Center
1202 Commissions
70001 Ltd
A Better Chance Inc
A M Consolidated Schools TX
A T and T Communications Inc
AAHPERD
Abbey Wood Schools
Abbott House
Abernathy Independent School District TX
ABI INFORM
Abilene Christian University TX
Abington Heights School District PA
Abraham Baldwin Agricultural College GA
Abt Associates
Academic Senate for California Community Colleges
Academy for Career Education PA
Academy for Educational Development
Academy for Effective Schools IL
Academy of Instruction
Academy of International Business
Academy of Pedagogical Sciences (USSR)
Academy of the Hebrew Language
Academy Theatre GA
Acadia University NS
Acadiana Consortium
Acalanes Union High School District CA
ACCESS Data Center
ACCESS ERIC
Accountability Through Evaluation Institute
Accreditation Board for Engineering and Technology
Accreditation Council for Graduate Medical Educ
Accrediting Council Educ Journalism Mass Commun
Accuracy in Academia
Accuracy in Media
Achievement Place
Acoma Reservation NM
ACRL Bibliographic Instruction Section
ACTION (Agency)
Action Committee for Higher Education
Action for Childrens Television
Action Library PA
Action Studies Team Canada
Actors Equity
Ad Hoc Committee on Copyright Revision
Ad Hoc Committee on Grades and Evaluation
Adams County Public Schools CO
Adams School MA
Adams State College CO
Addressograph Multigraph
Adel DeSoto Community School District IA
Adelaide Coll of Arts and Education (Australia)
Adelphi University NY
Adirondack Community College NY
Adirondack North Country Association NY
Adirondack Woodcraft Camps
Administration for Children and Families
Administration for Children Youth and Families
Administration for Native Americans
Administration on Aging
Administration Supervision Natl Field Task Force
Administrative Sciences Institute
Adolescent Crisis Team and Respite House MA
Adoption and Guardianship Reform Organization
Adoption Resource Exchange of North America
Adrian College MI
Adrian Public Library MI
Adult Basic Education Centre ON
Adult Bilingual Experimental School
Adult Education Association of Michigan
Adult Education Association of the USA
Adult Education Interim Steering Committee CA
Adult Learning Research Center
Adult Literacy and Basic Skills Unit
Adult Literacy League FL
Adult Literacy Organization of Zimbabwe
Adult Literacy Resource Agency (England)
Adult Student Personnel Association
Advanced Research Projects Agency
Advanced Study Center OH
Advanced Systems Incorporated
Advancement School NC
Advantage Center LA
Advertising Council
Advisory Commission on Intergovernmental Relations
Advisory Committee on Academic Planning
Advisory Committee on Mexican American Education
Advisory Committee on Voluntary Foreign Aid
Advisory Council on College Chemistry
Aerojet General Corporation
Aerospace Corporation CA
Aerospace Education Foundation
Aerospace Education Resource Center
Aerospace Materials Information Center
AEtna Institute for Corporate Education
AFCENT International School (Netherlands)
AFL CIO
Afram Associates
African Adult Education Association
African American Institute NY
African Association for Literacy and Adult Educ
African Heritage Studies Association
African Medical and Research Foundation
African Methodist Episcopal Church
African Museum of Art Frederick Douglass Institute
African Studies Association
Afro American Instructional Curriculum Laboratory
Afro American Society
Afro American Studies Center CA
AFSCME District Council 37 NY
Afton Junior High School WY
Agency for Instructional Television
Agency for International Development
Agency for Tele Education in Canada
Agnews State Hospital CA
AGRICOLA
Agricultural Education Foundation CA
Agricultural Research Service
Ahfachkee Day School
Ahmednagar College
Aims Community College CO
Ain Shams University (Egypt)
Air Command and Staff College AL
Air Correspondence High School (South Korea)
Air Force
Air Force Academy CO
Air Force Aero Propulsion Laboratory
Air Force Extension Course Institute
Air Force Human Resources Laboratory
Air Force Institute of Technology
Air Force Materials Laboratory
Air Force Museum OH
Air Force Reserve
Air Force Reserve Officers Training Corps
Air Force Rocket Propulsion Laboratory
Air National Guard
Air Training Command TX
Air University AL
Air War College AL
Akron Public Schools OH
Akron Summit County Public Library OH
Al Anon
Al Quds Open University (Jordan)
Alabama A and M University
Alabama Aviation and Technical College
Alabama Commission on Higher Education
Alabama Education Study Commission
Alabama Educational Television Commission
Alabama Judicial College
Alabama Junior College Library Association
Alabama Lib Assn Government Documents Round Table
Alabama Library Information Network
Alabama Lung Association
Alabama Model Center
Alabama Polytechnic Institute
Alabama Public Library Service
Alabama Space and Rocket Center
Alabama State University
Alachua County School District FL
Alamance Community College NC
Alameda County Health Department CA
Alamo Community College District TX
Alaska Advisory Council for Libraries
Alaska Division of State Libraries
Alaska Methodist University
Alaska Native Language Center
Alaska Pacific University
Alaska Public School Fund
Alaska Rural Teacher Training Corps
Alaska Sister Schools Network
Alaska Skills Center
Alaska State Department of Education
Albany Medical College NY
Albany State College GA
Albatros Club (Czechoslovakia)
Alberta Career Develop Employment Resource Ctr
Alberta Catholic Education Association
Alberta Catholic School Trustees Association
Alberta Commission Educational Planning (Canada)
Alberta Department of Education
Alberta Distance Learning Centre
Alberta School for the Deaf
Alberta Vocational Centre (Edmonton)
Alberta Vocational College (Edmonton)
Albertus Magnus College CT
Albion College MI
Albright College PA
Albuquerque Indian School NM
Albuquerque Public Schools NM
Albuquerque Technical Vocational Institute NM
Alcoholics Anonymous
Alcorn Agricultural and Mechanical College MS
Alcorn State University MS
Aleutians East Borough School District AK
Alexander City Schools AL
Alexander Graham Bell Association for the Deaf
Alexandre de Rhodes Educational TV Ctre (Vietnam)
Alexandria Area Technical School MN
Alexandria City Schools VA
Alexandria University (Egypt)
Alfateh University (Libya)
Alford Information Technology Centre (Scotland)
Alfred P Sloan Foundation
Alhambra City School District CA
Alhambra High School District CA
Alice Lloyd College KY
All India Radio
All Indian Long Distance Runners Training Camp
All Indian Pueblo Council NM
All Nations Church of God
All Russia Society for the Blind
All Union Ministry of Public Health (USSR)
All Volunteer Armed Forces
Allama Iqbal Open University (Pakistan)
Allan Hancock Joint Community College District CA
Allegany Community College MD
Allegheny College PA
Allegheny County Schools PA
Allegheny Ludlum Steel Corporation PA
Allen County Community College KS
Allen School MA
Allen University SC
Allentown College of Saint Francis de Sales PA
Allentown School District PA
Allerton House IL
Allerton Park Institute IL
Alliance College PA
Alliance Development Committee
Alliance for Arts Education
Alliance for Better Child Care
Alliance for Career and Vocational Education
Alliance for Environmental Education
Alliance for Excellence
Alliance for Excellence VA
Alliance High School OH
Alliance to Involve Minorities in Mathematics
Allied Health Learning Center
Allstate Insurance Company
Alma College MI
Alpena Community College MI
Alpha Plastics Printing Company
Alpha Tau Alpha
Alternate Living Incorporated MD
Alternative Vocational School CT
Altoona Area School District PA
Altoona Area Vocational Technical School PA
Altus Independent Schools OK
Altus Linguistic Laboratory OK
Alum Rock Union School District CA
Aluminum Association
Alverno College WI
Alvin Ailey American Dance Theater
Alvin Junior College TX
Amador Valley Joint Union School District CA
Amalgamated Builders and Contractors of Louisiana
Amalgamated Clothing and Textile Workers Union
Amalgamated Clothing Workers of America
Amalgamated Day Care Center IL
Amarillo College TX
American Academy of Arts and Sciences
American Academy of Child Psychiatry
American Academy of Family Physicians
American Academy of Orthopaedic Surgeons
American Academy of Pediatrics
American Academy of Physical Education
American Academy of Physician Assistants
American Advertising Federation
American Airlines
American Alumni Council
American Arachnid Society
American Arbitration Association
American Assembly Collegiate Schools of Business
American Assn Coll Registrars Admissions Officers
American Assn College University Business Officers
American Assn of Colleges of Podiatric Medicine
American Association for Adult Education
American Association for Advancement of Science
American Association for Agricultural Education
American Association for Agricultural Engineering
American Association for Counseling and Develop
American Association for Gifted Children
American Association for Higher Education
American Association Health Phys Educ Recreation
American Association Marriage and Family Therapy
American Association of Bible Colleges
American Association of Colleges for Teacher Educ
American Association of Colleges of Nursing
American Association of Colleges of Pharmacy
American Association of Community and Junior Colls
American Association of Community Colleges
American Association of Dental Schools
American Association of Engineering Societies
American Association of Instructors of the Blind
American Association of Jr Coll CH Comm Services
American Association of Junior Colleges
American Association of Law Libraries
American Association of Medical Record Librarians
American Association of Physics Teachers
American Association of Retired Persons
American Association of School Administrators
American Association of School Librarians
American Association of School Personnel Admins
American Association of Schs and Depts Journalism
American Association of State Colleges and Univs
American Association of Teacher Educators in Agr
American Association of Teachers of French
American Association of Teachers of German
American Association of University Administrators
American Association of University Professors
American Association of University Women
American Association on Mental Deficiency
American Association Teachers Slavic E Eur Langs
American Association Teachers Spanish Portuguese
American Astronomical Society
American Ballet Theatre
American Bankers Association
American Baptist Convention
American Bar Association
American Bar Foundation
American Bible Society
American Book Publishers Council
American Broadcasting Company
American Brotherhood for the Blind
American Bureau of Industrial Research
American Business
American Camping Association
American Can Company
American Cancer Society

American Career Training Travel School FL
American Chemical Society
American Child Centers Inc
American Civil Liberties Union
American Classical League
American Coalition of Citizens with Disabilities
American College Health Association
American College of Cardiology
American College of Life Underwriters
American College PA
American College Personnel Association
American College Public Relations Association
American College Testing Program
American Community Schools (Greece)
American Correctional Association
American Council for Construction Education
American Council of Learned Societies
American Council of Life Insurance
American Council of Teachers of Russian
American Council on Education
American Council on Education for Journalism
American Council on Pharmaceutical Education
American Council on Rural Special Education
American Council on the Teaching of Foreign Langs
American Counseling Association
American Cyanamid Company
American Debate Association
American Dental Association
American Dental Hygienists Association
American Diabetes Association
American Dietetic Association
American Documentation Institute
American Economic Association
American Educational Research Association
American Educational Studies Association
American Educational Theatre Association
American Electric Power System
American Electronics Association
American Farm Bureau Federation
American Farm School (Greece)
American Fed State County Municipal Employees
American Federation of Labor
American Federation of Teachers
American Field Service
American Film Institute
American Forensic Association
American Foundation for the Blind
American Friends Service Committee
American Geological Institute
American Geophysical Institute
American Geophysical Union
American Graduate School International Management
American Guidance Service
American Heart Association
American Historical Association
American Home Economics Association
American Home Products Corporation
American Hospital Association
American Independent Party
American Indian Bilingual Education Center NM
American Indian Employment Center MN
American Indian Higher Education Consortium
American Indian Law Students Association
American Indian Policy Review Commission
American Indian Science and Engineering Society
American Industrial Arts Association
American Industrial Arts Student Association
American Institute for Foreign Study
American Institute for Research
American Institute of Aeronautics and Astronautics
American Institute of Architects
American Institute of Biological Sciences
American Institute of Cooperation
American Institute of Instruction
American Institute of Musical Studies
American Institute of Physics
American Institute of Sacred Literature
American Institutes for Research
American International School (India)
American Iron and Steel Institute
American Jewish Committee
American Jewish Congress
American Language Institute
American Legion
American Library (France)
American Library Association
American Library Trustee Association
American Management Association
American Marketing Association
American Mathematical Society
American Medical Association
American Medical College Application Service
American Missionary Association
American Motorcyclist Association
American Museum of Natural History NY
American Musicological Society
American National Metric Council
American National Standards Institute
American Newspaper Publishers Association
American Nicaraguan School
American Nuclear Society
American Nurses Association
American Occupational Therapy Association
American Oil Company
American Open University
American Open University NE
American Optometric Association
American Orthopsychiatric Association
American Parliamentary Debate Association
American Personnel and Guidance Association
American Petroleum Institute
American Physical Society
American Physical Therapy Association
American Physiological Society
American Political Science Association
American Printing House for the Blind
American Production and Inventory Control Society
American Psychiatric Association
American Psychological Association
American Public Health Association
American Reading Forum
American Registry of Radiologic Technologists
American Rehabilitation Counseling Association
American Republic Insurance Company
American Revolution Bicentennial Administration
American Revolution Bicentennial Commission
American River College CA
American Satellite Corporation
American School Counselor Association
American School Food Service Association
American School for the Deaf CT
American School Health Association
American Society for Aerospace Education
American Society for Ecological Education
American Society for Engineering Education
American Society for Information Science
American Society for Medical Technology
American Society for Oceanography
American Society for Testing and Materials
American Society for Training and Development
American Society of Allied Health Professions
American Society of Clinical Pathologists
American Society of Journalism Administrators
American Society of Lubrication Engineers
American Society of Magazine Editors
American Society of Mechanical Engineers
American Society of Medical Technologists
American Society of Newspaper Editors
American Society of Training Directors
American Society of Zoologists
American Sociological Association
American Speech and Hearing Association
American Speech Language Hearing Association
American Standard Code Information Interchange
American Standards Association
American Statistical Association
American Student Media Association
American Studies Association
American Technical Education Association
American Telephone and Telegraph Company
American Textbook Publishers Institute
American Theatre Association
American Theological Library Association
American Tract Society
American Translators Association
American University DC
American University in Cairo (Egypt)
American University of Beirut (Lebanon)
American Vacuum Society
American Vocational Association
American Women in Radio and Television
American Youth Foundation
American Youth Hostels Inc
Americans for Indian Opportunity
Americas Unidas
Ameritech
Ames Community School District IA
Ames Research Center
Amherst College MA
Amidon School DC
Amity School District 4J OR
Amityville Public Schools NY
Amnesty International
Ampex Video Institute CA
Amsterdam News NY
Amumara Girls Secondary School (Nigeria)
Anadolu University (Turkey)
Anatolia College (Greece)
Anatone School District WA
Anchorage Community College AK
Anchorage School District AK
Ancona Montessori School IL
Anderson Adult Education Center SC
Anderson County School District SC
Anderson County Schools TN
Anderson Mental Health Center SC
Anderson Public Library IN
Anderson School CT
Andhra Pradesh Open University (India)
Andover Public Schools MA
Andover West Junior High School MA
Andrew Mellon Foundation
Andrew W Mellon Foundation
Andrews University MI
Andrus Gerontology Center CA
Anglican Church
Anglo American Corporation (Rhodesia)
Anheuser Busch Company
Animal Welfare Institute
Ann Arbor Public Schools MI
Anna Maria College MA
Annan Committee (Great Britain)
Anne Arundel Community College MD
Anne Arundel County Community Action Agency MD
Anne Arundel County Public Schools MD
Anne Sullivan Macy Service Deaf Blind Persons NY
Annehurst School OH
Annenberg School of Communications DC
Annie E Casey Foundation
Annual Creative Problem Solving Institute
Annual Reading Institute
Anoka Hennepin School District MN
Antelope Valley College CA
Antelope Valley High School CA
Antelope Valley Union High School District CA
Anthony Gadsen School District NM
Anti Defamation League
Anti Slavery Society
Antilles Consolidated School System PR
Antioch College OH
Antioch College Washington Baltimore Campus MD
Antioch College West
Antioch School of Law DC
Antioch University WA Seattle
Antipoverty Study Commission
Apollo School LA
Appalachia Educational Laboratory WV
Appalachia Improved Reference Services OH
Appalachian Adult Education Center KY
Appalachian Community Service Network
Appalachian Power Company
Appalachian Regional Commission DC
Appalachian Regional School for Church Leaders
Appalachian State University NC
Appalachian Teachers Network
Appalachian Volunteers
Apple Computer Inc
Apple Valley Rosemount MN
Aquinas College MI
Arab Bureau of Education for the Gulf States
Arab Regional Literacy Organization
Arabian American Oil Company
Arapahoe Community College CO
Arapahoe High School CO
Arapahoe School WY
Arc (Association for Retarded Citizens)
Archaeological Research Center (Denmark)
Archdiocese of Chicago IL
Archdiocese of Cincinnati OH
Archdiocese of Dubuque IA
Archdiocese of New York
Archdiocese of Omaha NE
Archdiocese of Philadelphia PA
Archives and Records Information Coalition
Ardmore School District OK
Area Agency on Aging
Area Centers for Services to Deaf Blind Children
Area Health Education Center CO
Area Health Education Centers
Area Learning Center MI
Area Library Councils
Area Redevelopment Administration CA
Area Vocational Schools MI
Area Wide Planning Organization
Argonne National Laboratory IL
ARIN Adult Learning Center
ARIN Adult Learning Center PA
Arizona Archeological Council
Arizona Bilingual Council
Arizona Center for Early Childhood Education
Arizona Commission of Indian Affairs
Arizona Indian Education Association
Arizona Job Colleges
Arizona Leadership Academy
Arizona State Department of Education
Arizona State University
Arizona State University Tempe
Arkansas College
Arkansas Community Education Development Assn
Arkansas Educational Renewal Consortium
Arkansas Enterprises for the Blind
Arkansas Governors School
Arkansas Rehabilitation Service
Arkansas River Education Service Cooperative
Arkansas State Department of Education
Arkansas State Department of Higher Education
Arkansas State Technical Institute
Arkansas State University
Arlington Public Schools VA
Arlington School District WA
ARMCO Steel Corporation
Armed Forces Institute WI
Armed Forces Staff College VA
Armed Forces University (West Germany)
Armour and Company
Armstrong State College GA
Armstrong World Industries
Army
Army Aviation Center AL
Army Aviation School AL
Army Engineer School VA
Army Infantry School GA
Army Judge Advocate Generals School
Army Map Service
Army Medical Training Center
Army Natick Laboratories
Army National Guard
Army Officer Candidate School
Army Research Institute
Army Reserve
Army Reserve Officers Training Corps
Army Signal Center and School NJ
Army Southeastern Signal Corps School GA
Army Topographic Command Library
Army War College PA
Arrowhead Community College Region MN
Art Research Libraries of Ohio
Arthur Andersen and Company
Arthur D Little Management Education Institute MA
Arthurdale Community School WV
Arts Council of Great Britain
ASAP Consortium
Ascension Academy VA
Ashland City School District OH
Ashland College OH
Ashland Community College KY
Ashland Federal Youth Center KY
Ashland University OH
Asia Pacific Economic Cooperation
Asian Broadcasting Union
Asian Development Bank
Asian Federation of Library Associations
Asian Institute of Technology
Asian Institute of Technology (Thailand)
Asian Network for Biological Sciences
Asian South Pacific Bureau of Adult Education
Asnuntuck Community College CT
Asolo State Theatre Company FL
Aspen Institute for Humanistic Studies CA
Aspen Middle School CO
Aspira Inc
Assabet Regional Vocational Sch Dist MA
Assessment Resource Center TN
Assistant Secretary Policy Evaluation and Research
Associated Colleges of Central Kansas
Associated Colleges of the Midwest
Associated Colleges of the Saint Lawrence Valley
Associated Day Care Services Inc PA
Associated Examining Board (England)
Associated Mid Florida Colleges
Associated Organizations for Teacher Education
Associated Press
Associated Press Managing Editors
Associated Public School Systems
Association Children with Learning Disabilities

Bishopswood School (England)
BITNET
Bittersweet Farms OH
Black Appalachian Commission
Black Child Development Institute DC
Black Crusaders
Black Economic Research Center NY
Black Gold Cooperative Library System PA
Black Hawk College IL
Black Hills Special Services Cooperative SD
Black Hills State College SD
Black Mesa Community School AZ
Black Mountain College NC
Black Panther Party
Black Psychiatrists of America
Black Star Picture Agency
Black Students Union
Black United Front
Blackfeet Indian Reservation
Blackhawk Technical College WI
Blackhawk Technical Institute WI
Blackstone Regional Vocational Sch Dist MA
Blackwater Community School AZ
Blackwell North America
Blair Summer School for Journalism
Block Communities Inc
Bloomfield College NJ
Bloomfield Public Schools NJ
Bloomingdale School MA
Bloomingdales Department Store
Bloomington Public Schools MN
Bloomsburg University PA
Blue Hills Regional Vocational Technical School MA
Blue Mountain Small Schools Consortium WA
Blue Ridge Community College NC
Blue Ridge Consortium DC
Bluefield State College WV
Blythedale Childrens Hospital
Bnai Brith
Board of Foreign Scholarships
Board of Urban Affairs
Board on International Comparative Studies Educ
Boat US
Bob Jones University SC
Bobbs Merrill Company
Boeing Company
Boggs Academy GA
Boise Public Schools ID
Boise State University ID
Bolt Beranek and Newman Inc
Bolton College of Education (England)
Book Exchange
Booker T Washington Elementary School IL
Booker Washington Institute of Liberia
Booth Library IL
Border College Consortium
Border Community College Consortium
Border Early Learning Center (South Africa)
Border Patrol Academy TX
Boreal Institute for Northern Studies AB
Boston Adult Literacy Fund MA
Boston Center for Blind Children MA
Boston Childrens Hospital MA
Boston Childrens Museum MA
Boston City Hospital MA
Boston College MA
Boston Indian Council MA
Boston Network for Better Education MA
Boston Office of Environmental Affairs MA
Boston Public Library MA
Boston Public Schools MA
Boston School for the Deaf MA
Boston State College MA
Boston Teachers Union
Boston Theological Institute MA
Boston TV High School MA
Boston University MA
Boulder Public Library CO
Boulder Valley Area Vocational Technical Center CO
Boulder Valley Public Schools CO
Bournemouth Teacher Center
Bowdoin College ME
Bowen School DC
Bowie State College MD
Bowie State University MD
Bowling Green Schools Adult Learning Center Ky
Bowling Green State University OH
Bowman Gray School of Medicine NC
Boy Scouts of America
Boys Clubs of America
Boys Republic
Boys Town NE
Bradford Academy VT
Bradford College MA
Bradley Center GA
Bradley Commission on History in Schools
Bradley University IL
Brainerd Area Vocational Technical School MN
Bramson ORT Technical Institute NY
Brandeis University MA
Brandon General Hospital MB
Brandon University MB
Brandywine High School DE
Brattleboro Union High School VT
Braxton County School District WV
Brazosport College TX
Brenau College GA
Brentwood School District MO
Brentwood Union School District CA
Brevard Community College FL
Brewton City School District AL
Briar Cliff College IA
Brick Township Public Schools NJ
Bridgewater Raritan Regional School District NJ
Bridgewater State College MA
Brigantine National Wildlife Refuge
Brigham Young University Hawaii Campus
Brigham Young University UT
Bristol College of Science and Technology
Bristol Community College MA
Bristol School (England)
Bristol Township School District PA
British and Foreign Bible Society
British Association Commercial and Industrial Educ
British Association for Applied Linguistics
British Association for the Advancement of Science
British Broadcasting Corporation
British Columbia Institute of Technology
British Columbia Library Network
British Columbia Ministry of Education
British Columbia Telephone Company
British Commonwealth Association of Planners
British Computer Society
British Council
British Educational Administration Society
British European Airways
British Film Institute
British Institute Madrid (Spain)
British Library (England)
British Library Lending Division
British Motor Corporation
British Museum (England)
British Museum Library (England)
British National Coal Board
British National Health Service
British North American Committee
British Office for Training Exchange
British Overseas Airways Corporation
British Press Council
British Schools Council
British Standards Institution
British Universities Film Council
British West Indies Regiment
Broadcast Education Association
Brock University (Canada)
Broken Arrow Elementary School KS
Bromwoods Residential Center MO
Bronson Sonic Power Company
Bronx Zoo NY
Brookdale Community College NJ
Brookings Institution DC
Brookland Cayce Schools SC
Brookline Public Schools MA
Brooklyn Education Task Force NY
Brooklyn Public Library NY
Brooklyn Responsive Learning Center NY
Brookmeade Elementary School TN
Brookside Park Family Life Center MA
Brookwood Labor College NY
Broome Community College NY
Brotherhood of Railway and Airline Clerks
Broughal Junior High School PA
Broward Community College FL
Broward County Instructional Television Center FL
Broward County Public Schools FL
Broward County School Board FL
Brown Open School
Brown University Research Foundation RI
Brown University RI
Brownsville Independent School District TX
BRS Information Technologies
Brunel University (England)
Brunswick County Public Schools VA
Brunswick Junior College GA
BRUSH (Belgium)
Bryan Independent School District TX
Bryant College of Business Administration RI
Bryant Woods Elementary School MD
Bryant Youth Educational Support Center MN
Bryn Mawr College PA
Bucknell University PA
Bucks County Area Vocational School PA
Bucks County Community College PA
Bucks County Public Schools PA
Buena Park High School CA
Buena Vista City Public Schools VA
Buena Vista College IA
Buffalo and Erie County Public Library NY
Buffalo Museum of Science NY
Buffalo Public Schools NY
Building Research Station (England)
Bulloch Memorial Hospital GA
Bunker Hill Community College MA
Bureau d Amenagement de l Est du Quebec (Canada)
Bureau for International Language Coordination
Bureau of Apprenticeship and Training
Bureau of Education for the Handicapped
Bureau of Educational Personnel Development
Bureau of Employment Security
Bureau of Higher Education
Bureau of Immigration
Bureau of Indian Affairs
Bureau of Labor Statistics
Bureau of Land Management
Bureau of Libraries
Bureau of Libraries and Educational Technology
Bureau of Libraries and Learning Resources
Bureau of Mines
Bureau of Occupational and Adult Education
Bureau of Outdoor Recreation
Bureau of Prisons
Bureau of the Budget
Bureau of the Census
Bureau of Urban Programs Evaluation
Bureau Regional pour Education en Afrique
Burger Court
Burger King Corporation
Burke County Board of Education NC
Burlington County College NJ
Burlington County Special Services School Dist NJ
Burnaby School District 41 BC
Burnham Committees (England)
Burnt Hills Ballston Lake Central Schools NY
Burris Laboratory School IN
Burwood Education Centre (Australia)
Busch Gardens
Bush Administration
Bush Foundation
Business and Professional Womens Foundation
Business and Technician Education Council
Business and Technology Education Council
Business Council for Effective Literacy
Business Higher Education Forum
Butler County Community College PA
Butler Family Foundation
Butler Hospital RI
Butler Manufacturing
Butler University IN
Butte Community College CA
Butte County Housing Authority
Butte County Public Library CA
C SPAN
C W Post Center NY
C W Post Collegial Federation NY
Cabell County Schools WV
Cabin John Junior High School MD
Cabinet Committee on Cable Communications
Cable News Network
Cable Television Information Center DC
Cabot College of Applied Arts Techn Cont Educ NF
Cabrillo College CA
Caddo Parish Public Schools LA
Cadet Corps
Cadre School (China)
Cairo School District IL
Cairo University (Egypt)
Calcasieu Parish School System LA
Caldwell College NJ
Caldwell Community College and Technical Inst NC
Calexico Unified School District CA
Calgary Board of Education AB
Calgary Roman Catholic Separate Sch Bd AB
Calhoun Elementary School CA
California (Antelope Valley)
California Agricultural Educ Computer Network
California Agricultural Experiment Station
California Art Education Association
California Association of College Stores
California Association of Independent Schools
California Association of School Librarians
California Association of Services to Children
California Association of Student Councils
California Bureau of Intergroup Relations
California Chamber of Commerce
California Childrens Centers
California Commission on Athletics
California Commission on Teacher Credentialing
California Commission Teacher Prep and Licensing
California Community and Junior Colleges Assn
California Community Colleges
California Conservation Corps
California Cooperative University
California Council on the Education of Teachers
California County Offices of Education
California Educational Research Commission
California Employment Training Advisory Council
California Employment Training Panel
California Faculty Association
California Federation of Teachers
California Indian Education Association
California Institute of Technology
California Institution for Women
California Junior College Association
California Junior College Faculty Association
California League Cooperating Schools
California Library Association
California Maritime Academy
California Medi Corps
California Mini Corps
California Office of Compensatory Education
California Office of Private Postsecondary Educ
California Polytechnic State University
California Roundtable
California School for the Deaf
California School Safety Center
California Small School Districts Association
California Society of Psychiatric Technicians
California Special Education Resource Network
California Speech Communication Association
California State Board of Education
California State College Bakersfield
California State College Dominguez Hills
California State College Long Beach
California State College Los Angeles
California State College PA
California State College San Bernardino
California State Department of Education
California State Department of Mental Health
California State Dept of Developmental Services
California State Dept of the Youth Authority
California State Employees Association
California State Library
California State Polytechnic University Pomona
California State Postsecondary Education Comm
California State Training Division
California State University
California State University and Colleges
California State University Bakersfield
California State University Chico
California State University Dominguez Hills
California State University Fresno
California State University Fullerton
California State University Hayward
California State University Inst for Teach Learn
California State University Long Beach
California State University Los Angeles
California State University Northridge
California State University Sacramento
California State University San Bernardino
California State University San Diego
California State University San Jose
California Statewide Mathematics Advisory Com
California Student Aid Commission
California Supreme Court
California Teachers Association
California Test Bureau
California University of Pennsylvania
California Youth Conservation Camps
Callagy Hall NY
Callendar Park College (England)
Callier Center for Communication Disorders TX
Callier Hearing and Speech Center TX
Calvin College MI
Camarillo Childrens Treatment Center CA
Camarillo State Hospital CA

Camberwell Park Infants School (Canada)
Cambria Community Adult School CA
Cambria County Public Library PA
Cambrian College (Canada)
Cambridge Alternative Public School MA
Cambridge Art Center MA
Cambridge Conference on School Mathematics MA
Cambridge Crystallographic Data Centre
Cambridge Hospital MA
Cambridge House University Settlement (England)
Cambridge Junior High School MN
Cambridge Pilot School
Cambridge Public Schools MA
Cambridge Rindge and Latin School MA
Cambridge School Committee MA
Camden Central School District NY
Camden County College NJ
Camden County School District GA
Camden County Vocational and Technical School NJ
Camden Public Schools NJ
Cameron University OK
Camp Cuyamaca CA
Camp Fire Girls Inc
Camp Fire Inc
Camp Kilmer
Camp Limberlost IL
Camp Logan SC
Camp Miniwanca MI
Camp Nana Mah
Camp Paart CT
Camp Partlow AL
Camp Riverwood MA
Campbell College NC
Campbell River School District BC
Camphill Villages
Campus Free College MA
Campus Safety Committee
Canada College CA
Canada Royal Commission Bilingualism Biculturalism
Canada Studies Foundation
Canadian Association for Adult Education
Canadian Association in Support of Native Peoples
Canadian Association of Research Libraries
Canadian Association of University Teachers
Canadian Broadcasting Corporation
Canadian Centre Info Documentation on Archives
Canadian Child Welfare Association
Canadian Commission for the Community College
Canadian Council for Research in Education
Canadian Council of Ministers of Education
Canadian Council of Teachers of English
Canadian Council on Urban and Regional Research
Canadian Education Association
Canadian Government
Canadian Guidance and Counseling Association
Canadian Higher Education Research Network
Canadian Home and School and Parent Teacher Fed
Canadian Home Economics Association
Canadian Human Rights Commission
Canadian International Development Agency
Canadian Library Association
Canadian Manpower Centres
Canadian Manpower Consultative Service
Canadian Mathematics Education Study Group
Canadian Organization for Development through Educ
Canadian Postal System
Canadian Radio Television Commission
Canadian Society for the Study of Education
Canadian Society for the Study of Higher Education
Canadian Special Committee on Poverty
Canadian Teachers Federation
Canarsie School District NY
Canberra College of Advanced Education (Australia)
Canberra Institute of Technology (Australia)
Canfield Local School District OH
Canisius College NY
Canoncito Navajo Reservation NM
Canton Galva Unified School District KS
Canyon High School CA
Cape Croker Ojibway Indian Reserve
Cape Fear Community College NC
Cape Fear Technical Institute NC
Capilano College BC
Capital Area Career Center
Capital Childrens Museum DC
Capitol Childrens Museum DC
Capitol Region Library Council
Captain Stephen Sanislo Elementary School WA
Captioned Films Loan Service for the Deaf
Capuchino High School CA
Carbon Lehigh Intermediate Unit PA
Cardinal Stritch College WI
Cardozo High School DC
CARE Inc
Career Education Resource Center MO
Career Training Center CA
Caribbean Fishery Development Institute
Caribbean Labour Administration Center
Caribbean News Agency
Carl Albert State College OK
Carl Sandburg College IL
Carleton College MN
Carleton University ON
Carlisle Area Science Advisory Committee PA
Carlisle Indian School SD
Carlisle Institute PA
Carmel Clay Schools IN
Carnarvon School (Canada)
Carnegie Commission on Educational Television
Carnegie Commission on Higher Education
Carnegie Corporation
Carnegie Corporation of New York
Carnegie Council on Adolescent Development
Carnegie Council on Children
Carnegie Council on Policy Studies in Higher Educ
Carnegie Foundation
Carnegie Foundation for Advancement of Teaching
Carnegie Institute of Technology PA
Carnegie Institution of Washington
Carnegie Mellon University PA
Carnegie Museum of Art
Carnegie Unit
Carolina Institute for Research on Early Education
Carolina Population Center
Caroline County Public Library MD
Carpinteria Unified School District CA
Carroll College
Carroll Instructional Television Consortium
Carrollton Farmers Branch Independent Sch Dist TX
Carson Indian Agency
Carter Administration
Carteret County Public Schools NC
Carthage College WI
Carver Elementary School DC
Carver Junior High School
Casa de La Raza
Casa Loma College CA
Case Western Reserve University OH
Cashmere School District WA
Casper College WY
Casper Day Care Center WY
Castleberry School District TX
Castleton State College VT
Caswell School NC
Catalina Foothills School District AZ
Catawba Valley Community College NC
Catawba Valley Technical Institute NC
Caterpillar Tractor Company
Catholic Board of Educ Diocese of Cleveland OH
Catholic Church
Catholic International Union for Social Services
Catholic Interracial Council
Catholic Library Association
Catholic Radio and TV Centre for Great Britain
Catholic Teachers Federation
Catholic University Nijmegen (Netherlands)
Catholic University of America DC
Catholic University of Louvain (Belgium)
Catholic University of Puerto Rico
Catonsville Community College MD
Catskill Area School Boards Institute NY
Catskill Area School Study Council NY
Caudill Rowlett and Scott
CAUSE
Cavendish Laboratory
Cayuga County Community College NY
Cayuga Onondaga Board Coop Educ Services NY
Cazenovia College NY
CBS Incorporated
CBS News
CBS Television
Cebu Normal College (Philippines)
Cecil Community College MD
Cedar Falls Community School District IA
Cedar Grove High School WI
Cedar Rapids Community School District IA
Cedar Valley College TX
Cedars Sinai Medical Center CA
Cedarville College OH
Celanese Research Company
Centennial High School OR
Centennial School District CO
Centennial School District MN
Centennial School District OR
Center Advanced Study Educational Admin OR
Center Environmental Communication Educ Studies WI
Center for Advanced Film Studies CA
Center for African Afro American Affairs NC
Center for Agricultural and Rural Development IA
Center for Analysis of Public Issues NY
Center for Applied Linguistics VA
Center for Applied Research in the Apostolate DC
Center for Assessment Administrative Performance
Center for California Public Affairs
Center for Career and Occupational Education NY
Center for Citizenship Education DC
Center for Cognitive Studies VT
Center for Community Justice DC
Center for Computer Sciences and Technology DC
Center for Consumer Home Economics Education CA
Center for Continuing Education of Women CA
Center for Cooperative Research with Schools PA
Center for Development of Non Formal Education TX
Center for Distance Learning NY
Center for Economic Education NY
Center for Economic Education PA
Center for Education Statistics
Center for Educational Design FL
Center for Educational Policy and Management OR
Center for Educational Policy Research MA
Center for Educational Television (Philippines)
Center for Employment Training
Center for Environmental Intern Programs MA
Center for Excellence in Oral Communication CO
Center for Family Life NY
Center for Gerontological Studies MO
Center for Gifted Education VA
Center for Human Development
Center for Human Resources TX
Center for Improvement of Teaching and Learning
Center for Independent Living
Center for Inner City Studies IL
Center for Innovation in Secondary School NC
Center for Innovation in Teacher Education
Center for Instructional Communication NY
Center for Instructional Development
Center for Interactive Techn Applications Res FL
Center for Intercultural Information (Mexico)
Center for Interdisciplinary Creativity
Center for International Education
Center for International Studies NY
Center for Intl Programs Comparative Studies NY
Center for Invention and Development
Center for Learning Technologies NY
Center for Literacy PA
Center for New Work of Flint MI
Center for Occupational Education NC
Center for Philosophic Exchange NY
Center for Population and Environmental Educ NC
Center for Preventive Psychiatry NY
Center for Preventive Therapy and Rehab DC
Center for Psychological Stud in the Nuc Age MA
Center for R and D on Educational Differences MA
Center for Radio and Television
Center for Research and Devel in Higher Educ CA
Center for Research for Mothers and Children
Center for Research Libraries IL
Center for Research on Educ Account Teacher Eval
Center for Research on Elementary and Middle Schs
Center for Research on Eval Standards Stu Test CA
Center for Research on Learning and Teaching MI
Center for School Improvement
Center for Social Organization of Schools MD
Center for Social Work IN
Center for Special Education Technology VA
Center for Studies in Vocational and Tech Educ
Center for Studies of the Person CA
Center for Study of Educational Innovations MA
Center for Study of Problems of Advanced Societies
Center for Successful Child Development IL
Center for Teacher Education Evaluation TN
Center for Teaching and Learning ND
Center for Teaching International Relations CO
Center for the Humanities AZ
Center for the Learning and Teaching of Literature
Center for the Study of Community Colleges CA
Center for the Study of Democratic Institutions CA
Center for the Study of Evaluation CA
Center for the Study of Higher Education CA
Center for the Study of Instruction DC
Center for the Study of Intergroup Relations CA
Center for the Study of Learning IL
Center for the Study of Liberal Educ for Adults MA
Center for the Study of Public Policy MA
Center for the Study of Reading IL
Center for the Study of Sport in Society MA
Center for the Study of Unemployed Youth NY
Center for the Study of Writing
Center for Urban Education NY
Center for Urban Minority Education FL
Center for Urban Research in Education OR
Center for Vocational and Technical Education OH
Center for Vocational Arts CT
Center for Vocational Education OH
Center for Vocational Technical Adult Education WI
Center for Young Children MD
Center Individually Prescribed Learn Activities PA
Center on Effective Elementary Middle Schools
Center on Innovation in Education
Center on New York City Affairs
Center on Student Testing Evaluation and Standards
Center to Improve Learning and Instruction UT
Centers for Disease Control GA
Central American Inst for Adult Educ (Costa Rica)
Central Arizona College
Central Arizona Inservice Consortium
Central Baptist College AR
Central Carolina Technical Institute NC
Central Christian College OK
Central City Head Start Day Care Center NY
Central College KS
Central Columbia High School PA
Central Committee Members (USSR)
Central Community College NE
Central Community College NE Platte Campus
Central Connecticut Business School
Central Connecticut State College
Central Connecticut State University
Central Cooperative School LA
Central Educational Network
Central Florida Community College
Central High School of Commerce ON
Central High School OK
Central Institute of Educ Technology (India)
Central Institute of Educational Research (China)
Central Institute of the Deaf MO
Central Intelligence Agency
Central Libraries Automated Network NV
Central Luzon State University (Philippines)
Central Michigan University
Central Midwestern Regional Educational Lab MO
Central Minnesota Teacher Education Council
Central Missouri State College
Central Missouri State University
Central Nebraska Technical Foundation
Central New York Library Resources Council
Central Oregon Community College
Central Peel Secondary School (Canada)
Central Piedmont Community College NC
Central State University OH
Central State University OK

Central States College Association
Central States Conference Teaching Foreign Lang
Central States Speech Association
Central Texas College
Central Texas Medical Foundation
Central Treaty Organization (Turkey)
Central Valley Microwave Network CA
Central Virginia Community College
Central Washington State College
Central Washington University
Central YMCA Community College IL
Centralia College WA
Centre College KY
Centre d Initiation au Cinema
Centre for Applied Research in Ed (Great Britain)
Centre for Contemporary Cultural Studies (England)
Centre for Continuing Education (Australia)
Centre for Cultural Resources (India)
Centre for Curriculum Renewal Educ Devel (England)
Centre for Educ Research and Innovation (France)
Centre for Educational Devel Overseas (England)
Centre for Educational TV Overseas (England)
Centre for Gifted Education AB
Centre for Learning and Development (Canada)
Centre for Principal Development ON
Centre for Science Education (England)
Centre for Short Lived Phenomena
Centre for Television Research (England)
Centre of Entrepreneurship for the Northwest
Centre Universitaire de Coop Econ Soc (France)
Centro de Altos Estudios Militares
Centro di Telescuola
Centro Interamericano Libros Academicos (Mexico)
Centro Intercultural de Documentacion (Mexico)
Ceres Unified School District CA
Cerritos College CA
Cerro Coso Community College CA
Certificated Employee Council
Chabot College CA
Chabot Observatory CA
Chadron State College NE
Chaffey Community College CA
Chahta Enterprise MS
Challenge for Change Societe Nouvelle (Canada)
Chalmers University of Technology (Sweden)
Chama Valley School District NM
Chamber of Commerce and Industry of Paris (France)
Chamber of Commerce of the United States
Chamber Theater
Chambers Elementary School OH
Champaign Community Schools IL
Champaign Public Library IL
Champlain Regional College PQ
CHAMPUS Program
Chana High School CA
Chandler High School AZ
Chapel Hill City Schools NC
Chapel Island Indian Reserve NS
Chapman College CA
Chapparal High School KS
Charity Schools (England)
Charles County Community College MD
Charles County Public Schools MD
Charles River School MA
Charles Stewart Mott Community College MI
Charleston County School District SC
Charleston Job Corps Center
Charlotte Florence Crittenden Home NC
Charlotte Mecklenburg Public Schools NC
Charlottesville City School District VA
Chase Manhattan Bank NY
Chatham College PA
Chatsworth Avenue School NY
Chattanooga Hamilton County Speech Hearing Ctr TN
Chattanooga Public Schools TN
Chattanooga State Technical Community College TN
Checotah High School OK
Chelmsford School System MA
Chelsea College of Science and Tech (England)
Chelsea Polytechnic (England)
Chelsea School System MA
Chemeketa Community College OR
Chemical Abstracts Service
Chemical Educational Material Study Institutes
Chemical Propulsion Information Agency
Chenowith School District OR
Cherry Creek School District CO
Cherry Creek Schools CO
Chesapeake Bay Center for Environmental Studies MD
Chesapeake Bay Institute MD
Chesapeake College MD
Chesterfield County Public Schools VA
Chesterfield County School District SC
Chevak Village Youth Association AK
Chevrolet Car Company
Chevy Chase Country Day School DC
Cheyenne River Community College SD
Cheyenne River Sioux Reservation SD
Cheyney State College PA
Cheyney University PA
Chi Corporation
Chi Research NJ
Chiang Mai University (Thailand)
Chicago Bar Association IL
Chicago Catholic School Board IL
Chicago Catholic Science Teachers Association IL
Chicago Child Care Society
Chicago Child Parent Centers IL
Chicago Daily News IL
Chicago Heights School District IL
Chicago Jewish Vocational Service IL
Chicago Latin School IL
Chicago Liberation School for Women IL
Chicago Linguistic Society IL
Chicago Police Department IL
Chicago Public Library IL
Chicago Public Schools IL
Chicago State College IL
Chicago State University IL
Chicago Times IL
Chicago Tribune IL
Chicago TV College IL
Chicago Urban League
Chicago Women in Trades
Chicano Mobile Institutes
Chico State College CA
Child and Family Development Center UT
Child and Family Protective Services
Child Care Action Campaign
Child Care Coordinating Council
Child Care Dallas
Child Care Inc NY
Child Care WORKS MN
Child Center Our Lady of Grace MO
Child Development Associate Consortium
Child Development Group of Mississippi
Child Development Programs Advisory Committee CA
Child Protection Inc
Child Protective Service
Child Psychiatric Day Care Unit of Univ Hosp WA
Child Study Association of America
Child Welfare League of America
Childrens Action Alliance AZ
Childrens Aid Society of Metro Toronto (Canada)
Childrens Aid Society of Pennsylvania
Childrens Art Carnival NY
Childrens Art Lab OR
Childrens Assessment Placement Instruction Ctr OH
Childrens Book Council
Childrens Broadcast Institute
Childrens Bureau
Childrens Center NY
Childrens Community Workshop NY
Childrens Crisis Intervention Service NJ
Childrens Defense Fund
Childrens Diagnostic Center VA
Childrens Film Foundation (England)
Childrens Foundation DC
Childrens Group
Childrens Hospital National Medical Center DC
Childrens Hospital of Eastern Ontario
Childrens Hospital of Los Angeles CA
Childrens Hospital of Michigan
Childrens Television Workshop NY
Childrens Theatre Association MD
Childrens Trust Fund
Chilean Development Corporation
Chillicothe City Schools OH
Chilocco Indian School OK
Chinatown Youth Services and Coordinating Ctr CA
Chinese Academy of Social Sciences
Chinese Culture University (Taiwan)
Chinese Enterprise Management Association
Chinese Language Schools
Chinese University of Hong Kong
Chinook Educational Consortium (Canada)
Chipola Junior College FL
Chitimacha Day School LA
Choate School CT
Choctaw County School District MS
Christ College Irvine CA
Christchurch College of Education (New Zealand)
Christian Action Ministry Academy IL
Christian Brothers
Christian Brothers College (Australia)
Christian Brothers College TN
Christian Brothers Colleges
Christian College Coalition
Christian College Consortium
Christopher Newport College VA
Chrysler Corporation
Chrysler Learning Inc
Chula Vista City School District CA
Chulalongkorn University (Thailand)
Church and Synagogue Library Association PA
Church College of Hawaii
Church of England
Church of God
Church of Jesus Christ of Latter Day Saints
Church Women United
Church World Service
Churches Television Centre
Cincinnati Bible College OH
Cincinnati Council on World Affairs OH
Cincinnati Milacron
Cincinnati Public Schools OH
Cincinnati Technical College OH
Cisco Junior College TX
Citadel Military College of South Carolina
Citizens Advisory Council on Status of Women DC
Citizens Commission on Basic Education PA
Citizens Committee on Public Education PA
Citizens Committee to Save WEFM IL
Citizens Communication Ctr for Responsive Media DC
Citizens Crusade Against Poverty
Citizens Forum
Citrus College CA
Citrus County School District FL
City and Country School NY
City and Guilds of London Institute (England)
City College of San Francisco CA
City Colleges of Chicago IL
City Colleges of Chicago IL Chicago City Wide Coll
City Colleges of Chicago IL Harold Washington Coll
City Colleges of Chicago IL Kennedy King College
City Colleges of Chicago IL Loop College
City Colleges of Chicago IL Malcolm X College
City Colleges of Chicago IL Olive Harvey College
City Colleges of Chicago IL Richard J Daley Coll
City Colleges of Chicago IL Truman College
City Colleges of Chicago IL Wright College
City of London Polytechnic (England)
City Technology Colleges (England)
City University of New York
City University of New York Bernard Baruch College
City University of New York Bronx Community Coll
City University of New York Brooklyn College
City University of New York City College
City University of New York Coll of Staten Island
City University of New York Hostos Community Coll
City University of New York Hunter College
City University of New York John Jay College
City University of New York Kingsborough Comm Coll
City University of New York La Guardia Comm Coll
City University of New York Lehman College
City University of New York Manhattan Comm Coll
City University of New York Mt Sinai Sch of Med
City University of New York NYC Comm Coll
City University of New York NYC Technical Coll
City University of New York Queens College
City University of New York Queensborough Comm C
City University of New York Richmond College
City University of New York York College
Civic Center North
Civil Aeronautics Board
Civil Air Patrol
Civil Service Commission
Civilian Affairs Training School
Civilian Conservation Corps
Clackamas Community College OR
Claremont Colleges CA
Claremont High School CA
Claremont Institute for the Study of Change CA
Claremont Mens College CA
Claremont Univ Ctr and Grad Sch CA
Claremore Junior College OK
Clarion State College PA
Clarion University of Pennsylvania
Clark College GA
Clark College WA
Clark County Community College NV
Clark County School District NV
Clark County Schools AL
Clark State Community College OH
Clark University MA
Clarke College IA
Clarke School for the Deaf MA
Clarkson College of Technology NY
Clarkson University NY
Classification Research Group
Clatsop Community College OR
Claypit Hill School MA
Clayton County Schools GA
Clayton Junior College GA
Clayton School District MO
Clayton State College GA
Clear Creek School District CO
Clearfield County Voc Tech School PA
Clearfield Job Corps Urban Center UT
Clearinghouse on Development Communication
Clearinghouse on Mastery Learning LA
Clement C Maxwell Library MA
Clemson University SC
Cleveland City Normal School OH
Cleveland College OH
Cleveland County School District NC
Cleveland Foundation OH
Cleveland Health Sciences Library OH
Cleveland Institute of Art OH
Cleveland Metropolitan Housing Authority OH
Cleveland Museum of Art OH
Cleveland Public Library OH
Cleveland Public Schools OH
Cleveland State Hospital OH
Cleveland State University OH
Cleveland Urban Learning Community OH
Clinch Powell Educational Cooperative TN
Clinite Center for the Hearing Impaired CA
Clinton Administration
Clinton Community Unit High School IL
Clinton County School District KY
Clinton Pilot Cassette Center MN
Clover Park School District WA
Clover Park Vocational Technical Institute WA
Clovis Unified School District CA
Club 6
Club Mediterrane
Club of Rome
CMS Records
Coahoma Junior College MS
Coalition Concerned with Adolescent Pregnancy
Coalition for Better Television
Coalition for Education in the Outdoors
Coalition for National Service
Coalition for Public Library Research
Coalition of Adult Education Organizations DC
Coalition of Business and Educ Collaboration NY
Coalition of English Associations
Coalition of Essential Schools
Coalition of Indian Controlled School Bds CO
Coalition of Teacher Education Programs
Coast Community College District CA
Coast Guard
Coast Guard Academy CT
Coastal Bend Migrant Council TX
Coastal Carolina Community College NC
Coastline Community College CA
Coatesville Area School District PA
Cobb County Public Schools GA
Coca Cola Company
Coca Cola USA
Cochise College AZ
Cochrane Iroquois Falls Board of Education ON
CODIESEE
Coe College IA
Coffee County School District GA
Cognitive Research Trust

Congress 93rd
Congress 94th
Congress 95th
Congress 96th
Congress 97th
Congress 98th
Congress 99th
Congress 100th
Congress 101st
Congress 102nd
Congress 103rd
Congress of Hispanic Education CO
Congress of Industrial Organizations
Congress of Racial Equality
Congressional Black Caucus
Congressional Research Service
Connecticut (Mansfield)
Connecticut Academy for English Geography History
Connecticut Association for Reading Research
Connecticut College
Connecticut Commission for Higher Education
Connecticut Council on the Family
Connecticut Principals Academy
Connecticut Regional Community Colleges
Connecticut Special Ed Network Software Evaluation
Connecticut State Department of Education
Connecticut State University System
Connecticut Valley Hospital
Connecticut Valley Libraries
Connetquot Central School District NY
Conrad N Hilton Foundation
Conroe Independent School District TX
Conseil des Colleges PQ
Conservation and Environmental Science Center NJ
Conservation Education Association
Conservation Foundation
Consolidated Edison Company
Consortium Committee on Latin American Studies
Consortium Develop Professional Materials Voc Educ
Consortium for Advancement Private Higher Educ
Consortium for International Studies Education
Consortium in Educational Media and Technology
Consortium International Cooperation Higher Ed
Consortium of Professional Associations for Study
Consortium of States
Consortium on Early Childbearing and Childrearing
Consortium on Financing Higher Education
Consortium on Peace Research Education Development
Consortium on Research and Development
Consortium to Develop an Online Catalog
Consortium Training Program TX
Constantine School District MI
Constitutional Heritage Club
Constitutional Rights Foundation
Construction Industry Training Board
Consultants in Total Education
Consumer Education Resource Network
Consumer Product Safety Commission
Consumers Union of the United States
Contemporary Research Inc
Continental Divide Training Center
Continuing Education Council
Continuing Library Education Network and Exchange
Contoocook Valley School District NH
Contra Costa College CA
Contra Costa Community College District CA
Contra Costa County Department of Education CA
Contra Costa County Schools CA
Control Data Corporation
Converse College SC
Conwell Middle Magnet School PA
Cook County Hospital IL
Cook School AZ
Cooper Union NY
Cooperative Center for Social Science OH
Cooperative Data Management Committee
Cooperative Education Association
Cooperative Extension Service
COOR Intermediate School District MI
Coordinating Committee on Research in Voc Ed
Coordinating Council for Fine Arts and Humanities
Coordinating Council on Higher Education
Copper Country Intermediate School District MI
Coppin State College MD
Copyright Clearance Center
Copyright Clearinghouse
Copyright Office
Copyright Royalty Tribunal
Core Knowledge Foundation
Cornell University NY
Cornerstone School NY
Corning Community College NY
Corning Glassworks NY
Corning Museum of Glass NY
Coro Foundation NY
Corona Del Mar High School CA
Corona Unified School District CA
Corporate Community Schools of America
Corporate Higher Education Forum (Canada)
Corporation for Economic and Industrial Research
Corporation for Public Broadcasting
Corporation for Public Television
Corpus Christi Independent School District TX
Corpus Christi Public Library TX
Corpus Christi State University TX
Correctional Education Association
Correctional Industries Association
Corvallis School District 1 MT
Corvallis School District OR
Corwith Wesley Community School District IA
Coshocton Public Library OH
Cossatot Vocational Technical School AR
Cosumnes River College CA
Council Bluffs Community School District IA
Council for Accred of Counsel and Relat Educ Prog
Council for Adult and Experiential Learning
Council for Advancement and Support of Education
Council for Advancement of Experiential Learning
Council for American Private Education
Council for Area Planning of Educational Services
Council for Arts and Humanities MA
Council for Basic Education
Council for Chemical Research
Council for Cultural Cooperation (France)
Council for Development of French in Louisiana
Council for Distributive Teacher Education
Council for Educational Diagnostic Services
Council for Elementary Science International
Council for Exceptional Children
Council for Financial Aid to Education
Council for International Health
Council for Jewish Elderly
Council for Learning Disabilities
Council for Liberal Learning
Council for Mutual Economic Assistance
Council for National Academic Awards
Council for National Academic Awards (England)
Council for Occupational Education
Council for Private Postsecondary Voc Educ CA
Council for Science and Society
Council for the Advancement of Small Colleges
Council for the Development of French in Louisiana
Council for Women in Independent Schools
Council Grove High School KS
Council of Administrators of Special Education
Council of Appalachian Governors
Council of Chief State School Officers
Council of Counseling Psychology Training Programs
Council of Cultural Development (France)
Council of Deans
Council of Energy Resource Tribes
Council of Europe (France)
Council of Graduate Schools
Council of Great City Schools
Council of Independent Colleges
Council of Learned Societies in Education
Council of Ministers (USSR)
Council of National Library and Info Associations
Council of National Organizations
Council of Ontario Universities
Council of Ontario Universities (Canada)
Council of Outdoor Educators of Ontario
Council of Professors of Instruction Supervision
Council of Scientific and Industrial Research
Council of State Science Supervisors
Council of State Social Studies Specialists
Council of Student Personnel Assns in Higher Educ
Council of Teaching Hospitals
Council of Urban Boards of Education
Council of Youth
Council on Anthropology and Education
Council on Appalachian Women
Council on Children Media and Merchandising
Council on Chiropractic Education
Council on Collegiate Education for Nursing
Council on Comprehensive Education
Council on Early Childhood Development MD
Council on Education of the Deaf
Council on Educational Policies and Directions
Council on Educational Priorities PA
Council on Foreign Relations
Council on Graduate Education for Public Admin
Council on Indian Education WI
Council on International Educational Exchange
Council on Interracial Books for Children
Council on Language Teaching Development of Japan
Council on Legal Education Opportunities
Council on Library Resources
Council on Library Technology
Council on Optometric Education
Council on Postsecondary Accreditation
Council on Quality Education
Council on Rehabilitation Education
Council on Social Work Education
Councils of Government
Counseling and Human Development Foundation
Countesthorpe College (England)
Country Life Commission on Rural Poverty
Countryside Council
Countryside Council MN
County College of Morris NJ
County Superintendents Association of California
Court of Veterans Appeals
Court TV
Coventry College of Education (England)
Covington Catholic High School
Covington Junior High School
Crafts Council of Great Britain
Crane Normal Institute of Music
Cranfield Institute of Technology (England)
Cranfield School of Management (England)
Cranford Public Schools NJ
Cransbrook Kingswood School MI
Creation Research Society CA
Creative Problem Solving Institute
Creighton University NE
Creswell Public Schools OR
Crete Monee School District IL
Crosby Independent School District TX
Cross Examination Debate Association
Crossroads Rehabilitation Center IN
Crouse Hinds Company
Crow Applegate Lorane School District OR
Crowleys Ridge Vocational Technical School AR
Crown Woods Comprehensive School (England)
Crownpoint Institute of Technology NM
CSUCS Consortium
Cubans University of Miami FL
Cubberley High School CA
Cuesta College CA
Cultural Education Collaborative MA
Culver City Public Schools CA
Cumberland College KY
Cumberland County College NJ
Cumberland County Extension Service ME
Cunningham Childrens Home IL
CUNY Association of Writing Supervisors
Cupertino Union School District CA
Curriculum and Instructional Materials Center OK
Curriculum Development Centre (Australia)
Curriculum Information Network
Curriculum Research and Development Group
Curry College MA
Cutler Orosi Unified School District CA
Cuyahoga Community College Cleveland OH
Cuyahoga Community College Eastern Campus OH
Cuyahoga Community College OH
Cuyahoga Community College Western Campus OH
Cypress College CA
Cyprus Broadcasting Corporation (Switzerland)
Czechoslovakian Academy of Sciences
D Q University CA
D Youville College NY
Dabney S Lancaster Community College VA
Dade County Public Schools FL
Dade Monroe Teacher Education Center FL
Dag Hammarskjold Foundation (Sweden)
Daggett School District UT
Dahlem Environmental Education Center MI
Dakota Community Colleges
Dakota State College SD
Dakota Wesleyan University SD
Dalhousie University (Nova Scotia)
Dallas Baptist College TX
Dallas Baptist University TX
Dallas County Boys Home TX
Dallas County Community College District TX
Dallas County Community Colleges TX
Dallas Independent School District TX
Dallas Public Library TX
Dallas Skyline Center TX
Dallas Teacher Center Professional Semester TX
Dalton Junior College GA
Dana Corporation
Dana Hall School MA
Danforth Foundation
Danish Family Planning Association
Danish Institute for Educational Research
Danville City School District VA
Danville Community College VA
Danville Public School District IL
Dare County School District NC
Darien Public Schools CT
Darling Downs Inst of Advanced Educ (Australia)
Darlington County School District SC
Darmstaadt Career Center
Dartmouth College NH
Dartmouth Medical School NH
Data Systems Center MI
David Douglas School District OR
Davidson County Community College NC
Davidson County School District NC
Daviess County School System KY
Davis and Elkins College WV
Davis Monthan Air Force Base AZ
Davis School District UT
Dawson College PQ
Dawson Community College MT
Daybreak Star Preschool WA
Dayton Journal Herald OH
Dayton Miami Valley Consortium OH
Dayton Public Opinion Center
Dayton Public Schools OH
Dayton Women Working
Daytona Beach Community College FL
Daytona Beach Junior College FL
De Anza College CA
De Anza Reading Center CA
De La Salle Vocational Day Treatment Center PA
De Paul University IL
Deafness Research Foundation
Deakin University (Australia)
Dearborn Public Schools MI
Debtors Anonymous
Decatur High School WA
Decatur Memorial Hospital IL
Decatur Public Schools IL
DeCordova Museum School MA
Decroly School of Barcelona (Spain)
Deep Springs College CA
Deer School AR
Deere and Company
Defense Ceramic Information Center
Defense Civil Preparedness Agency
Defense Documentation Center VA
Defense Language Institute
Defense Language Institute CA
Defense Language Institute TX
Defense Technical Information Center
Defiance College OH
DeKalb Area Technical School GA
DeKalb Community College GA
DeKalb School District GA
Del Mar College TX
Deland Junior High School FL
Delaware County Community College PA
Delaware Educational Television Network
Delaware Extension Service
Delaware Semi Rural School District
Delaware State College
Delaware State University
Delaware Technical and Community College
Delgado College LA
Delgado Community College LA
Delta College MI
Delta School District 37 BC

Delta Sigma Theta Sorority
Delta State University MS
Deming School District NM
Democratic Party
Demographic Computer Library
Demonstration and Research Ctr Early Child Educ
Demonstration Programs School Improve Network TX
Demonstration School for Adults CA
Denison Public Schools TX
Denison University OH
Denman College (England)
Denver Auraria Community College CO
Denver Catholic High Schools CO
Denver Classroom Teachers Association CO
Denver Community College CO
Denver Free University CO
Denver Public Library CO
Denver Public Schools CO
Denver Regional Council of Governments CO
Denver Research Institute CO
Department of Agriculture
Department of Audiovisual Instruction (NEA)
Department of Classroom Teachers (NEA)
Department of Commerce
Department of Defense
Department of Education
Department of Education (Proposed)
Department of Education and Science (England)
Department of Education Regional Offices
Department of Energy
Department of Equal Educational Opportunities
Department of Health and Human Services
Department of Health Education and Welfare
Department of Housing and Urban Development
Department of Indian Affairs N Devel (Canada)
Department of Justice
Department of Labor
Department of State
Department of the Interior
Department of the Treasury
Department of Transportation
Department of Veterans Affairs
Department of War
DePauw University IN
Dependents Schools European Area
Dependents Schools Pacific Region
Des Moines Area Community College IA
Des Moines Public Schools IA
Descriptive Cataloging Committee
Desert Community College District CA
Desert Research Institute NV
DeSoto County Public Schools FL
DeSoto County School District MS
Detroit Archdiocesan Multimedia Center MI
Detroit Childrens Museum MI
Detroit College of Business MI
Detroit Education Task Force MI
Detroit Institute of Technology MI
Detroit Medical Library Group MI
Detroit Metropolitan Library MI
Detroit Public Schools Management Academy MI
Detroit Public Schools MI
Deuel Vocational Institution CA
Deutsches Institut fur Fernstudien (West Germany)
Developmental Evaluation Services for Children
Devereux Schools PA
DeVry Institute of Technology IL
Diablo Valley College CA
Diagnostic Learning Center IL
DIALOG
Dickinson College PA
Didsbury College of Education (England)
Digital Equipment Corporation
Digital Research Company
Dilenowisco Educational Cooperative
Dillard University LA
Dillingham City School District AK
Diocesan Adult Training Center
Disciples of Christ
Disneyland CA
Disneyworld FL
Distance University (West Germany)
Distributive Education Clubs of America
Distributive Industry Training Board (England)
District of Columbia Public Library
District of Columbia Public Schools
Division of Associated Health Professions
Dixwell Legal Rights Association CT
Djajapura Centre (Indonesia)
Do It Now Foundation CA
Doane College NE
Document Design Center DC
Documentation Research and Training Centre (India)
Dominican College of San Rafael CA
Donnelly College KS
Doolittle Family Education Center IL
Door (Youth Center) NY
Dorset Institute of Higher Education (England)
Doshisha University (Japan)
Doubleday Multimedia CA
Douglas College BC
Douglas County School District CO
Douglas County School District NV
Douglas Management Institute MO
Douglass Psychology Child Study Center
Dover Educational Television Ctr (Great Britain)
Dover Public Schools NJ
Doves Press
Dow Chemical Company
Dowling College NY
Downriver Learning Disability Center
Drake University IA
Draper Correctional Center AL
Drew Elementary School GA
Drew University NJ
Drexel Institute of Technology PA
Drexel University PA
Drury College MO
Du Pont Corporation
Dublin College of Speech Therapy (Ireland)
Dubnoff School for Educational Therapy CA
Duchesne School District UT
Duke Ellington School of the Arts DC
Duke Power Company NC
Duke University NC
Duluth Public Schools MN
Dulwich College (England)
Dunbarton College DC
Dundalk Community College MD
Dundee College of Education (Scotland)
Dundee Institute of Technology (Scotland)
Dundee School CO
Dunwoody Industrial Institute MN
DuPage High School District IL
Duquesne University PA
Durham City School District NC
Durham College of Applied Arts and Technology ON
Durham County School District NC
Durham Middlefield School District CT
Durham Summer School (England)
Dushane Emergency Fund
Dutch Modern Language Association
Dutchess Community College NY
Dutemple Elementary School
Duval County Public Schools FL
Duval County School Board FL
Dzilth Na O Dith Hle Community School NM
E R Johnstone Center
E R Snyder Continuation High School CA
Eagleville Hospital and Training Center PA
Earl Warren Legal Training Program Inc NY
Earle B Wood Junior High School MD
Earlham College IN
Early Childhood Consortium (ASCD)
Early Childhood Council CT
Early Education Center MO
Early Intervention Effectiveness Institute UT
Early Training Center TN
East African Library Association
East African Literature Service
East Asian Libraries
East Baton Rouge Parish School System LA
East Bay Activity Center CA
East Bay Regional Park District
East Brunswick School District NJ
East Carolina University NC
East Central Citizens Organization
East Central College Consortium
East Central College MO
East Central Community College MS
East Central Curriculum Coordination Center IL
East Central Curriculum Management Center IL
East Central University OK
East Central Writing Centers Association
East Chicago Junior Police IN
East Harlem Neighborhood Study Club NY
East Hartford Public Schools CT
East Longmeadow School District MA
East Los Angeles College CA
East Los Angeles Occupational Center CA
East Meadow Union Free District NY
East Orange Public Schools NJ
East Saint Louis Public Library IL
East Saint Louis School District IL
East Technical High School OH
East Tennessee Development District
East Tennessee State University
East Tennessee State University Medical School
East Texas State University
East Texas State University Dallas
East West Center HI
East Windsor Regional School District NJ
Eastchester Public Schools NY
Easter Seal Research Institute ON
Eastern Arizona College
Eastern Community College NF Clarenville Campus
Eastern Connecticut State University
Eastern Illinois School Development Council
Eastern Illinois University
Eastern Iowa Community College
Eastern Iowa Community College District
Eastern Kentucky University
Eastern Lancaster County School District PA
Eastern Mennonite College VA
Eastern Michigan University
Eastern Montana College
Eastern New Mexico University
Eastern New Mexico University Clovis
Eastern Oklahoma Development District
Eastern Oregon State College
Eastern Psychological Association
Eastern Regional Institute for Education NY
Eastern State School and Hospital
Eastern Stream Center on Resources Training NY
Eastern Townships School Board PQ
Eastern Virginia Area Health Education Center
Eastern Washington State College
Eastern Washington University
Eastfield College TX
Eastman Kodak Company
Eastman School of Music NY
Easton Area School District PA
EasyNet
Eckerd College FL
Eckerd Wilderness Camp
Ecole Centrale de Lyon (France)
Economic and Social Council
Economic and Social Research Council (England)
Economic and Youth Opportunities Agency
Economic Commission for Asia and the Far East
Economic Development Administration
Economic Opportunities Commissions
Economic Opportunities Programs and Services
Economic Research Service
Economic Social Commission for Asia and Pacific
Ecotran Systems Inc
Edge Hill College of Education (England)
Edgewater Park Township School District NJ
Edgewood Independent School District TX
Edina Public Schools MN
Edinboro State College PA
Edinboro University of Pennsylvania
Edison Community College FL
Edison State Community College OH
Edison Township Schools NJ
Edmonds Community College WA
Edmonds School District WA
Edmonton Instructional Materials Center (Canada)
Edmonton Public Schools (Canada)
Edmonton Public Schools AB
EDPA Institute
Education Alternatives Inc
Education and World Affairs NY
Education Commission (India)
Education Commission of the States
Education Commission of the States CO
Education Corps (Iran)
Education Development Center MA
Education Management Information Exchange
Education Policies Commission
Education Policy Research Center NY
Education Renewal Center CO
Education Research Analysts TX
Education Resource Center IL
Education Satellite Communications Demo DC
Education Service Center Region 20 TX
Education to Work Council of Philadelphia
Educational and Cultural Council of Nationalities
Educational Association of Worcester
Educational Catalyst Organization
Educational Collaborative for Greater Boston
Educational Computer Consortium of Ohio
Educational Computing Organization of Ontario
Educational Council for Foreign Medical Graduates
Educational Diagnostic and Planning Center WY
Educational Facilities Center IL
Educational Facilities Laboratories IL
Educational Film Library Association
Educational Improvement Center South NJ
Educational Information Network
Educational Mass Media Centre (Ethiopia)
Educational Materials Coordination Unit IL
Educational Materials Laboratory
Educational Materials Producers Council
Educational Media Council NY
Educational Media Procedures Council
Educational Opportunity Bank
Educational Policies Commission
Educational Policy Research Center
Educational Priorities Panel NY
Educational Products Information Exchange
Educational Professions Institute
Educational Programming of Cultural Heritage CA
Educational Redeployment Service (England)
Educational Research and Development Council MN
Educational Research Council of America
Educational Research Library DC
Educational Research Service
Educational Resource Center on Deafness TX
Educational Resources Center (India)
Educational Satellite Consortium
Educational Service Unit 18 Lincoln NE
Educational Services Inc
Educational Software Evaluation Consortium
Educational Systems Corporation
Educational Technology Center MA
Educational Telecommunication System
Educational Telephone Network WI
Educational Test Research Institute (Japan)
Educational Testing Service
Educators for Social Responsibility
Edunet
EDUTEK Inc
Edwin Gould Outdoor Education Centers NY
Egyptian School District IL
Eisenhower College NY
Eisenhower National Clearinghouse
El Camino College CA
El Camino Senior High School CA
El Centro de la Causa IL
El Dorado County Board of Education CA
El Paso Articulation Committee
El Paso Community College TX
El Paso Independent School District TX
Elbert County School District GA
Electric Power Research Institute
Electric Utility Instructor Training Consortium
Electric Utility Marketing Institute
Electricite de France
Electronic Futures Inc
Electronics Institute of Japan
Elementary Education Study Group
Elementary Science Education Institute TN
Elgin Community College IL
Elgin School District IL
Elizabeth City School District NJ
Elizabeth City State University NC
Elizabeth Cleaners Street School
Elizabethtown College PA
Elizabethtown Community College KY
Elk Grove Unified School District CA
Elkhart Community Schools IN
Ellenstown School District WA
Elm Place School IL
Elmhurst College IL
Elmira City Public Schools NY
Elmira College NY
Elmo Roper and Associates
Elon College Players NC
Eloy Elementary School AZ
Elsa Clubs of America
Elwell Parker Electric Company
Elyria City School District OH
Embry Riddle Aeronautical University FL
Emergency Committee of Atomic Scientists
Emerson College MA
Emil Schwarzhaupt Foundation
Emma Willard School NY
Emmanuel College MA
Emory and Henry College VA
Emory University GA
Empire Community College
Employment and Training Administration
Employment Security System
Employment Service
Employment Service Agency (England)

Employment Standards Administration
Emporia Public Schools KS
Emporia State University KS
Energy Research and Development Administration
Enfield Progress Centre (England)
Engineering College Administration Council
Engineering College Research Council
Engineering Council for Professional Development
Engineering Industry Training Board
Engineering Manpower Commission
Engineering Societies Committee Manpower Training
Engineers Council for Professional Development
Engineers Joint Council
Englewood Learning Center IL
Englewood Public Library CO
Englewood Public Schools NJ
English Council of California Two Year Colleges
English High School MA
English Postal College (England)
English Technical Language School PR
English Valley Elementary School NY
Engvall Junior High School CA
Enoch Pratt Free Library MD
Ensenanza Directa (Mexico)
Entelek Incorporated
Entomological Research Center FL
Entrepreneurial Development Training Center PA
Environmental Camp for Handicapped and Others MA
Environmental Conservation Commission
Environmental Defense Fund
Environmental Protection Agency
Environmental Science Services Administration
Environmental Sciences Institute CA
Epilepsy Foundation of America
Episcopal Academy PA
Episcopal Church
Episcopal Home for Children DC
Equal Employment Opportunity Commission
Equal Employment Opportunity Coordinating Council
Equal Employment Opportunity Training Institute
Equitable Life Assurance Society
Erasmus University (Netherlands)
ERIC
ERIC Clearinghouse for Junior Colleges
ERIC Clearinghouse for Science Math Environ Educ
ERIC Clearinghouse for Social Studies Soc Sci Educ
ERIC Clearinghouse on Adult Career Vocational Educ
ERIC Clearinghouse on Adult Education
ERIC Clearinghouse on Career Education
ERIC Clearinghouse on Counsel and Personnel Serv
ERIC Clearinghouse on Early Childhood Education
ERIC Clearinghouse on Educational Management
ERIC Clearinghouse on Educational Media and Tech
ERIC Clearinghouse on Elementary Early Child Educ
ERIC Clearinghouse on Exceptional Children
ERIC Clearinghouse on Handicapped and Gifted Child
ERIC Clearinghouse on Higher Education
ERIC Clearinghouse on Information Resources
ERIC Clearinghouse on Library and Information Scis
ERIC Clearinghouse on Reading
ERIC Clearinghouse on Reading and Commun Skills
ERIC Clearinghouse on Rural Educ and Small Schools
ERIC Clearinghouse on Teacher Education
ERIC Clearinghouse on Tests Measurement Evaluation
ERIC Clearinghouse on the Disadvantaged
ERIC Clearinghouse on the Teaching of English
ERIC Document Reproduction Service
ERIC Processing and Reference Facility
Erie City School District PA
Erie Community College NY
Erie County Technical School PA
Erlangen University
Esalen Institute CA
Escambia County Public Schools FL
Escola Superior de Guerra
Escondido Union School District CA
Escuela Agricola Panamericana (Honduras)
Escuela Normal Veracruzana (Mexico)
Eskasoni Indian Reserve NS
Eskisehir Academy Economic Coml Sciences (Turkey)
Espanola Municipal Schools NM
Esperanza School NM
Essex Agricultural and Technical Institute MA
Essex Community College MD
Essex County College NJ
Essex County Vocational Technical Schools NJ
Essexfields Group Rehabilitation Center
ESSO Company
ESSO Education Foundation NY
ESSO Repertory Theatre
Estancia High School CA
Eta Sigma Gamma
Ethiopian Educational Television Service
Etowah County School District AL
Euclid English Demonstration Center OH
EUDISED
Eugene Public Schools OR
Eugenio Maria de Hostos Community College
Eurocentres Schools (United Kingdom)
EUROLEX
Europa TV
European Association for Special Education
European Association of Information Services
European Atomic Energy Community (Belgium)
European Broadcasting Union (Switzerland)
European Bureau of Adult Education (Netherlands)
European Centre for Ethnolinguistic Cartography
European Centre for Leisure Educ (Czechoslovakia)
European Centre for the Development of Voc Train
European Centre Further Education Teachers
European Coal and Steel Community
European Communities Commission
European Community
European Council for Education by Corr (Belgium)
European Court of Human Rights
European Documentation and Information System
European Economic Community
European Forum for Educational Administration
European Home Study Council
European Organization for Nuclear Research
European Parliament
European Peace Research Association
European Research Group on Management
European Space Agency
European Translations Center (Netherlands)
European Universities
European University Institute (Italy)
Eurovision News Exchange
EURYDICE
Evaluation Assistance Center (East)
Evaluation Research Society
Evaluation Service Center for Occupational Educ
Evaluative Programs Innovative Curriculums Ctr AZ
Evanston School District IL
Evanston Township High School IL
Evansville Vanderburgh School Corporation IN
Evelyn Lowe School (England)
Everett Community College WA
Evergreen School CA
Evergreen State College WA
Evergreen Valley College CA
Everson Museum of Art NY
Everymans University (Israel)
Evlyn Hone College (Zambia)
Excerpta Medica Foundation (Netherlands)
EXECUCOM
Exemplary Center for Reading Instruction UT
Exemplary Project in Vocational Education MT
Exhall Grange School (England)
Experience Compression Laboratory
Experimental Manpower Lab for Corrections AL
Experimental Manpower Laboratory NY
Explorers Club NY
Extension Service
Extraclassroom Activity Fund NY
Exxon Education Foundation
Exxon Research and Engineering Company
Eynsham County Primary School (England)
F Olsen Limited (Norway)
Facilities Engineering Construction Agency
Fairchild Hiller Corporation
Fairchild Industries
Fairfax County Public Library VA
Fairfax County Schools VA
Fairfield Public Schools CT
Fairfield Suisun Unified School District CA
Fairleigh Dickinson University NJ
FairTest
Falcon Beach School MB
Falk Laboratory School PA
Fall River Public Schools MA
Fallbrook Union School District CA
Falls Church Public Schools VA
Families and Work Institute
Family and Youth Services Bureau
Family Learning Centers GA
Family Life Center MD
Family Planning Association
Family Reception Center NY
Family Resource Coalition IL
Family Service Association
Family Service Society of New Orleans LA
Family Therapy Institute ND
Far West Consortium
Far West Laboratory for Educational R and D CA
Far West School CA
Far West Teacher Corps Network WA
Far Western Philosophy of Education Society
Fargo Public Schools ND
Farm Bureau
Farm Foundation IL
Farm Laboratory
Farm Radio Forum (Canada)
Farmers Alliance
Farmers Home Administration
Farmington Municipal Schools NM
Farmington Public Schools CT
Farmington Public Schools MI
Fashion Institute of Technology NY
Fayette County Public Schools KY
Fayetteville State University NC
Fayetteville Technical Institute NC
Feather River College CA
Federal Aviation Administration
Federal Bureau of Investigation
Federal City College DC
Federal Communications Commission
Federal Coor Council Sci Engineering Techn
Federal Deposit Insurance Corporation
Federal Election Commission
Federal Emergency Management Agency
Federal Energy Administration
Federal Express
Federal Highway Administration
Federal Home Loan Bank Board
Federal Housing Administration
Federal Interagency Committee on Education
Federal Law Enforcement Training Center
Federal Library Committee
Federal Mediation and Conciliation Service
Federal Parliament (Yugoslavia)
Federal Power Commission
Federal Radio Commission
Federal Reformatory for Women WV
Federal Reserve Bank of Philadelphia
Federal Reserve System
Federal Resource Center for Special Education
Federal Trade Commission
Federal Water Pollution Control Administration
Federal Water Quality Administration
Federal Way School District WA
Federal Youth Center
Federated Womens Institutes of Canada
Federation American Societies for Exptl Biology
Federation for Unified Science Education
Federation of American Societies for Exptl Biology
Federation of Greek Orthodox Choirs
Federation of Korean Womens Organizations
Federation of Public Programs in the Humanities
Federation of Rocky Mountain States
Federation of Saskatchewan Indians
Federation of State Medical Boards
Federation of Swiss Watchmakers
Fellow Life Management Institute
Fellowship of Concerned University Students
Feminist Press
Ferguson Florissant Reorganized School District MO
Fernald School CA
Fernuniversitat (West Germany)
Ferris State College MI
Ferris State University MI
Fiat Corporation
Field Local School District OH
Field Museum of Natural History IL
Field Studies Council (United Kingdom)
Fielding Institute CA
Fieldston Lower School NY
Filley School District NE
Fillmore Elementary School CO
Films Incorporated
FILMS NY
Financial Accounting Standards Board
Finch College NY
Find Aid for the Aged Incorporated
Findlay College OH
Fine Arts Career Education GA
Finger Lakes Community College NY
Finger Lakes Library System NY
Finger Lakes Region Supplementary Educ Ctr NY
Finke River Mission (Australia)
Finley School NY
Finnish Evangelical Lutheran Church
Finnish Institute for Childrens Literature
Finnish Youth Institute
First Community Village OH
First Independent Trust Company CA
First National City Bank NY
First Presbyterian Church of Fort Wayne IN
First Street School NY
Fish and Wildlife Service
Fisher Branch Centre for Adult Basic Educ (Canada)
Fisher Junior College MA
Fisk University TN
Fitchburg State College MA
Fitton School MA
Five Associated University Libraries NY
Five Civilized Tribes Museum
Five Colleges Incorporated MA
Flanner House IN
Flathead Indian Reservation MT
Flathead Valley Community College MT
Fleet Ballistic Missile School CA
Fleet Submarine Training Facility
Flemish University (Belgium)
Flensburg Polytechnic (Germany)
Flinders University of South Australia
Flint Public Library MI
Flintshire Educational Technology Centre (Wales)
Florida A and M University
Florida Academy for School Leaders
Florida Adult Education Association
Florida Atlantic University
Florida Board of Regents
Florida Bureau of Entomology
Florida Bureau of Laboratories
Florida Bureau of Preventable Diseases
Florida Center for Library Automation
Florida Coalition to Abolish Corp Punish in Sch
Florida Colombia Alliance
Florida Commission on Social Studies Education
Florida Community College at Jacksonville
Florida Cooperative Extension Service
Florida Correctional Institution for Women
Florida Council on Educational Management
Florida Educational Leaders Forum
Florida Educational Research Development Council
Florida Educational Resources Information Center
Florida Farmworkers Residential Training Center
Florida Institute for Correctional Educators
Florida International University
Florida Junior College at Jacksonville
Florida Keys Community College FL
Florida Memorial College
Florida Ocean Sciences Institute
Florida Presbyterian College
Florida Professional Practices Council
Florida Resources in Education Exchange
Florida School for the Blind
Florida Schoolhouse Systems
Florida Southern College
Florida State Board of Health
Florida State Department of Education
Florida State Library
Florida State Postsecondary Education Commission
Florida State Prison
Florida State University
Florida Technological University
Florida Vocational Association
Florissant Valley Community College MO
Floyd County School District GA
Fluvanna County Public Schools VA

Flynn Model Elementary School RI
Folsom Cordova Unified School District CA
Folsom Unified School District CA
Fond du Lac Technical Institute WI
Food and Drug Administration
Food and Nutrition Service
Food Research and Action Center DC
Foothill College CA
Foothill de Anza Community College District CA
Footscray Institute of Technology (Australia)
Ford Foundation
Ford Motor Company
Fordham University NY
Foreign Area Materials Center NY
Foreign Broadcast Information Service
Foreign Language Display Library MI
Foreign Policy Association
Foreign Service
Foreign Service Institute DC
Foreign Service Institute VA
Foreign Study League UT
Foresight Club
Forest Haven DC
Forest Park Community College MO
Forest Park Junior College Center MD
Forest Park Junior High School OH
Forest Service
Forest Trail Library Consortium TX
Forest Valley Outdoor Education Centre ON
Foresta Institute for Ocean and Mountain Studies
Forman School CT
Fort Apache Reservation
Fort Belknap Reservation MT
Fort Berthold Indian Reservation
Fort Bragg High School CA
Fort Defiance Window Rock Public Schools AZ
Fort Dodge Community School District IA
Fort Frye High School OH
Fort Hall Reservation
Fort Hays Kansas State College
Fort Hays State University KS
Fort Lewis College CO
Fort McDermitt Indian Reservation
Fort Myer Elementary School VA
Fort Peck Indian Reservation MT
Fort Scott Community College KS
Fort Sill Indian School OK
Fort Steilacoom Community College WA
Fort Wayne Bible College IN
Fort Wayne Community Schools IN
Fort Worth Independent School District TX
Forty Plus
Forward House (Canada)
Foster Elementary School IL
Foster Family Based Treatment Association
Foundation Center
Foundation for Alcohol and Drug Educ (New Zealand)
Foundation for Teaching Economics CA
Fountain Valley School District CA
Four Corners Electric Power Complex
Fox Valley Consortium for the Homeless IL
Fox Valley Technical College WI
Fox Valley Technical Institute WI
Foxboro Company
Framingham Public Schools MA
Framingham State College MA
Frances Howell School District MO
Francis Marion College SC
Francis Tuttle Vo Tech Center OK
Frank Porter Graham Center NC
Frankfurt American High School (West Germany)
Franklin and Marshall College PA
Franklin City School District TN
Franklin College OH
Franklin County School District MS
Franklin County School District TN
Franklin Institute PA
Franklin Junior High School CA
Franklin K Lane High School NY
Franklin Pierce College NH
Franklin Research Center PA
Franklin University OH
Fransiscan Handmaids of Mary
Frederick Community College MD
Frederick County Outdoor School MD
Frederick County Public Schools MD
Fredonia High School NY
Free African Society
Free Library of Philadelphia PA
Free Press Underground MO
Free Public Library of the Borough of Madison NJ
Free University of Berlin (West Germany)
Free University of Brussels (Belgium)
Free University of Iran
Freed Hardeman College TN
Freedom of Information Center
Freedom Quilting Bee Cooperative AL
Freeland Community Schools MI
Freeport Public Schools NY
Fremont County School District WY
Fremont Newark Community College District CA
Fremont Public Schools NE
Fremont Union High School District CA
French Academy (France)
French Broadcasting System
French National Educational Institute
Fresh Start Minischool DC
Fresno Adult School CA
Fresno City College CA
Fresno County Department of Education CA
Fresno State College CA
Fricot Ranch School CA
Friends Central School PA
Friends Council on Education
Friends of the San Francisco Public Library CA
Friends School MD
Friends World College NY
Friesland College (Netherlands)
Froebel Training College (Denmark)
Front Range Community College CO
Frontier College (Canada)
Frontier Community College IL
Frostburg State College MD
Frostburg State University MD
Fruita Monument High School
Fryeburg Academy ME
Fullerton College CA
Fullerton Junior College CA
Fulton County Public Schools GA
Fulton High School TN
Fulton Montgomery Community College NY
Fund for Adult Education
Fund for Improvement of Postsecondary Education
Fund for Improvement Reform of Schools Teaching
Fund for the Advancement of Education
Fund for the City of New York
Fundacion Gran Mariscal de Ayacucho (Venezuela)
Fundamental Education Centre Community Development
Furman University SC
Further Education Unit (England)
Future Business Leaders of America
Future Farmers of America
Future Farmers of America IL
Future Farmers of Colombia
Future Farmers of Japan
Future Homemakers of America
Future Scientists of America Foundation
Future Teachers of America
Gadna Youth Corps (Israel)
Gadsden Independent Schools NM
Gadsden State Junior College AL
Gainesville College GA
Galax City School District VA
Gale Research Company
Galesburg Public Library IL
Gallaudet College DC
Gallaudet Research Institute DC
Gallaudet University DC
Gallup McKinley School District NM
Gallup Organization
Ganado Primary School AZ
Ganado School District AZ
Gann Committee (Great Britain)
Gannett Company
Gannett Foundation
Gannon College PA
Gannon University PA
Gardner Task Force on Education
Garfield Educational Complex CA
Garfield School District WA
Garland Independent School District TX
Garland Junior College MA
Garnett College (England)
Garvey School District CA
Gary Public Schools IN
Gaston College NC
Gaston County School District NC
GateWay Community College AZ
Gateway Technical Institute WI
Gateway Vocational Technical School AR
Gavilan College CA
Gay Liberation Front
Geary County Unified School District KS
Geisinger Medical Center
General Accounting Office
General Association of Teaching Professions
General Aviation Manufacturers Association
General Dynamics Convair
General Education Board
General Electric Company
General Electric Foundation
General Federation of Womens Clubs
General Learning Corporation
General Motors Corporation
General Motors Institute
General Music Corporation
General Services Administration
General Teaching Council (Scotland)
General Telephone Company
General Theological Library MA
Generic Pharmaceutical Training Institute NY
Genesee Community College NY
Genesee Finger Lakes Regional Planning Board NY
Genesee Valley School Development Association NY
Genetic Engineering Company
Geneva Academy (Switzerland)
Geneva Community Unit School District 304 IL
Geneva Disarmament Committee
Geneva Park Leadership and Training Ctr (Canada)
Geneva Public Schools NY
Geological Society of America
Geological Survey
George Brown College ON
George C Marshall Space Flight Center
George I Sanchez Junior Senior High School TX
George Mason University VA
George Peabody College for Teachers TN
George Washington High School NY
George Washington Univ Medical Center DC
George Washington University DC
George Williams College IL
Georgetown Day Care Center DC
Georgetown University DC
Georgetown University Medical Center DC
Georgia Academy for the Blind
Georgia Career Information System
Georgia Center for Continuing Education
Georgia Center for the Multihandicapped
Georgia College
Georgia Community Continuing Education Service
Georgia Cooperative Extension Service
Georgia Educational Television Network
Georgia Information Dissemination Center
Georgia Institute of Technology
Georgia Instructor Academy
Georgia Interactive Network
Georgia Library Information Network
Georgia Retardation Center
Georgia Southern College
Georgia Southern University
Georgia Southwestern College
Georgia State Board Postsecondary Vocational Ed
Georgia State College
Georgia State Department of Education
Georgia State University
Georgia University System
Georgian Court College NJ
Geraldine R Dodge Foundation
German Childrens Protection Federation
German Federal Armed Forces
German Federation of Adult Education Centers
German Foundation for Developing Countries
German Institute for Academic Home Study
Gesell Institute of Child Development CT
Gesellschaft fur Deutsche Sprache
Gesellschaft fur Information und Dokumentation
Getty Center for Education in the Arts
Gettysburg College PA
Ghana Schools Television Service
Giannini Foundation of Agricultural Economics CA
Gila River Reservation AZ
Gilbert Youth Research
Gilford Middle High School NH
Gill School NY
Gilmer County School District GA
Gilroy Unified School District CA
Gippsland Institute of Advanced Educ (Australia)
Girl Guides Association
Girl Scouts of the USA
Girls Clubs of America
Glades Correctional Institution FL
Glasgow Corporation Educ TV Service (Scotland)
Glasgow Retirement Council (Scotland)
Glassboro Public Schools NJ
Glassboro State College NJ
Glen Ellyn Junior High School IL
Glen Oaks Community College MI
Glendale Community College AZ
Glendale Community College CA
Glendale Community College District CA
Glendale Elementary School District 40 AZ
Glendale Public Library CA
Glendale Unified School District CA
Glendale Union High School District AZ
Glens Falls City School District NY
Glenview Public Schools IL
Glenville State College WV
Gloucester County College NJ
Gloucester Urban Studies Centre
Gloucestershire College of Arts and Tech (England)
Goddard College VT
Goddard Library MA
Goddard Space Flight Center MD
Goethe Institute (West Germany)
Goettinger Teachers College (West Germany)
Gogebic Community College MI
Golden West College CA
Goldsboro City Schools NC
Goldsmiths College (England)
Gonzaga University WA
Good Counsel College NY
Good Neighbor Commission
Good Shepherd Home and Rehabilitation Center PA
Goodwill Industries of America
Goodyear Tire and Rubber Company
Gordon Brock Infant School (England)
Gordon College MA
Gordon Teachers Training College (Israel)
Goshen College IN
Goucher College MD
Governeur Central School District NY
Government Printing Office
Government Univ Industry Research Roundtable
Governor Thomas Johnson High School MD
Governors Committee on Postsecondary Education GA
Governors School of North Carolina
Governors State University IL
Governors Task Force on Voc and Tech Educ OH
Gow School NY
Grace Doherty Library KY
Graceland College IA
Graduate Career Development Center TX
Graham Elementary School MI
Grambling College LA
Grambling State University LA
Grand Blanc School District MI
Grand Canyon College AZ
Grand Forks School District ND
Grand Rapids Junior College MI
Grand Rapids Public Schools MI
Grand Rapids School District MN
Grand Valley State Colleges MI
Grand Valley State University MI
Grand View College IA
Granite School District UT
Grant MacEwan Community College AB
Grant Middle School IL
Grant School CA
Grant Union High School District CA
Grant Wood Area Education Agency IA
Granville Central School District NY
Granville County Public Schools NC
Grasmere School CT
Grassroots Educare Trust (South Africa)
Gray Panthers
Graylands Teachers College (Australia)
Grays Harbor College WA
GRE Board
GRE Validity Study Service
Great Cities Research Council IL
Great Falls Public Schools MT
Great Lakes Apprenticeship Center WI
Great Lakes Colleges Association
Great Lakes Intertribal Council Education Comm WI
Great Lakes Intertribal Council WI
Great Lakes Naval Training Center IL
Great Lakes Regional Resource Center
Great Neck Adult Learning Centers NY
Great Oaks Joint Vocational School District OH
Great Plains National Instructional TV Library NE

Greater Amsterdam School District
Greater Cleveland Educational Develop Center OH
Greater Hartford Community College CT
Greater Johnstown Area Vocational Tech School PA
Greater Lawrence Guidance Center MA
Greater Pittsburgh Literacy Council PA
Greater Saint Louis Ad Hoc Committee on ETV MO
Greece Central School District NY
Greek Orthodox Church
Greeley Parent Child Center CO
Green Bay Public Schools WI
Green Chimneys School NY
Green County Technical High School AR
Green Lakes Outdoor Education Center
Green Mountain College VT
Green River Community College WA
Green Valley Area Educational Agency 14 IA
Greenburgh School District NY
Greene County Career Center OH
Greene Joint Vocational School OH
Greenfield Community College MA
Greenfield High School TN
Greenfield Public Schools MA
Greenhill School TX
Greensboro City Public Schools NC
Greensboro Tri College Consortium NC
Greensville County School District VA
Greenville City Schools NC
Greenville College IL
Greenville County School District SC
Greenwich Public Schools CT
Greenwich Teachers Center CT
Greenwood School District 50 SC
Gresham Grade School District 4 OR
Gridley Elementary School District CA
Gridley Farm Labor Camp CA
Griffiss Air Force Base NY
Griffith University (Australia)
Grinnell College IA
Grinnell Corporation
Grips Theatre
Grosse Pointe Public School System MI
Grossmont College CA
Grossmont Union High School District CA
Groton Public Schools CT
Group for the Advancement of Psychiatry
Grove City College PA
Grove Park Institute
Groveton High School VA
Grumman Aerospace Corp
Gruppen foer Pedagogisk Elektronik (Sweden)
Guam Community College
Guelph Public Library ON
Guilford College NC
Guilford County School District NC
Guilford Technical Community College NC
Gulf Coast Community College FL
Gulf Coast Junior College FL
Gulf County School District FL
Gulf Oil Corporation
Gulf Universities Research Consortium
Gustavus Adolphus College MN
Gutman Library MA
Gwinnett County School System GA
Gwynedd Mercy College PA
H W Wilson Co
Habitat for Humanity International
Hacettepe University (Turkey)
Hackensack Career Development Center NJ
Hackensack Public Schools NJ
Hadley School for the Blind IL
Hagerman Schools ID
Hagerstown Junior College MD
Hahnemann Medical College and Hospital PA
Hahnemann School of Respiratory Therapy PA
Hahnemann University PA
Haifa University (Israel)
Haight Ashbury Childrens Center CA
Haile Selassie University (Ethiopia)
Haitian American Training Institute
Hall Elementary School
Halstead Public Schools KS
Hamburg Central School District NY
Hamilton College NY
Hamilton Community Consolidated School District IL
Hamilton County Public Schools TN
Hamilton Township Schools NJ
Hamilton Wenham Regional High School MA
Hamilton Wentworth Roman Catholic Sep Sch Bd ON
Hamline University MN
Hammond Public Schools IN
Hampden Sydney College VA
Hampshire College MA
Hampshire Interlibrary Center MA
Hampton City School District VA
Hampton Institute VA
Hampton University VA
Hango Agricultural College (Tonga)
Hanover School System MA
Harambee Institutes of Technology (Kenya)
Harambee Schools WI
Harcourt Brace Jovanovich
Harcum Junior College PA
Harding College AR
Harford Cecil Supplementary Education Center MD
Harford Community College MD
Harlem Action Group
Harlem Domestic Peace Corps
Harlem Globetrotters
Harlem Hospital Center NY
Harlem Teams for Self Help NY
Harlem Youth Opportunities Unlimited NY
Harmony School KS
Harnett County School District NC
Harris County Juvenile Detention Center TX
Harris County Public Schools TX
Harris Stowe State College MO
Harrisburg Area Community College PA
Harrisburg City School District PA
Harrison County Schools WV
Harrison District 2 CO
Harrison Library NC
Harry E Wood High School IN
Harry Lundeberg School
Hart County School System KY
Hartford Area Vocational Center CT
Hartford Insurance Group
Hartford Public Schools CT
Hartford State Technical College CT
Hartnell Community College CA
Hartwell Nongraded Primary School MA
Hartwick College NY
Harvard Law School MA
Harvard Principals Center MA
Harvard University MA
Harvard University Medical School MA
Harvey Mudd College CA
Harwell Atomic Energy Research Establishment
Hasanuddin University (Indonesia)
Haskell Indian Junior College KS
Hatch School District NM
Hatfield Polytechnic (England)
Haverford College PA
Haverford Township School District PA
Hawaii Association for Retarded Children
Hawaii Bound School
Hawaii Maritime Center
Hawaii Model Child Service
Hawaii Pacific College
Hawaii State Department of Education
Hawaii State Hospital
Hawaii State Senior Center
Hawaii State Test of Essential Competencies
Hawaii Visitors Bureau
Hawaii Vocational Rehabilitation Services Blind
Hawkeye Institute of Technology IA
Hawthorne Cedar Knolls School NY
Hawthorne Center
Haxtun High School CO
Haystack Teacher Crafts Institute ME
Hayward Public Library CA
Hayward State College CA
Hayward Unified School District CA
Haywood Technical Institute NC
Hazard Community College KY
Hazelwood School District MO
Hazleton Area School District PA
Health Care Financing Administration
Health Education Consortium
Health Education Council
Health Occupations Students of America
Health Resources Administration
Health Resources and Services Administration
Health Services and Mental Health Administration
HEAR Foundation
Heart of the Earth Survival School MN
Heartland Community College IL
Hebrew Academy of Nassau County NY
Hebrew Language Council
Hebrew Technical Institute CA
Hebrew University of Jerusalem (Israel)
Hegeler Foundation
Heidelberg College OH
Heliotrope Free University CA
Heltwate School (England)
Hemet Unified School District CA
Hemispheric Studies Center
Hempstead High School NY
Henderson State University AR
Hennepin County Library System MN
Henrico County Public Schools VA
Henrietta Szold Institute (Israel)
Henry Chauncey Conference Center NJ
Henry County Public Schools IA
Henry E Huntington Library OR
Henry Elementary School MO
Henry Ford Community College MI
Henry Sibley Senior High School MN
Her Majesty Industries Incorporated
Herbert Lehman High School NY
Heriot Watt University (Scotland)
Heritage Center NC
Heritage College WA
Heritage Foundation
Herkimer County Community College NY
Hermods Correspondence School (Sweden)
Hershey Museum PA
Hershey Public Library PA
Hertfordshire Advisory Council Educational Tech
Hewlett Packard Company
Hewlett Woodmere Public Library NY
Hibbing Community College MN
Hickory City School District NC
Hickory Township High School PA
Hicksville Public Schools NY
Hidalgo Starr Adult Education Coop TX
High John Library MD
High Point City School District NC
High Point College NC
High School Curriculum Center in Government IN
High School Evening Institute (New Zealand)
High School for Health Professions TX
High School Independent Press Service
High Scope Educational Research Foundation MI
Highbury Technical College (England)
Higher Educ Task Force on Imp and Reform Am Educ
Higher Education Assistance Foundation
Higher Education Loan Pool
Higher Education Management Institute
Higher Education Panel
Higher Education Research Institute
Higher Education Resource Service
Highland Community College IL
Highland Park Free School MA
Highland Park Township High School District IL
Highland Public Schools IN
Highland School CT
Highlander Folk School TN
Highline Community College WA
Highline Public Schools WA
Highline School District WA
Hill School PA
Hill Top Preparatory School PA
Hillcrest High School NY
Hillcroft College
Hillsboro Deering Cooperative School District NH
Hillsborough Community College FL
Hillsborough County Public Schools FL
Hillsdale College MI
Hillside Outdoor Education Center NY
Hillside Public Library NY
Hilton United Corporation
Hinckley College of Further Education (England)
Hinds County School District MS
Hinsdale School Districts IL
Hiram College OH
Hiroshima University (Japan)
Hispanic Association of Colleges and Universities
Hispanic Foundation
Hispanic Higher Education Coalition
Hispanic Research Center NY
Hiwassee College TN
Hoechst A G
Hofstra University NY
Hogg Foundation for Mental Health TX
Holland College (Canada)
Holland Day Care Center MI
Holland Land Company
Holland Park School (England)
Hollins College VA
Holmes Group
Holt Rinehart Winston Company
Holtville High School AL
Holyoke Public Schools MA
Home and School (Canada)
Home and School Association
Home and School Institute DC
Home Builders Institute
Home Economics Education Association
Home Economics Rural Service NM
Home Economists in Homemaking
Home Learning Center IN
Home Study Program Inc
Homerton College of Education (England)
Homewood Flossmoor High School IL
Honda of America
Honeywell Inc
Honolulu School District HI
Hood College MD
Hoover Institution on War Revolution and Peace
Hope College MI
Hope School for Blind Multihandicapped Children IL
Hopkins County School District KY
Hopkins School District MN
Hopkinsville Community College KY
Horace Mann Lincoln Inst of School Experimentation
Horace Mann School for the Deaf MA
Horseheads Central School District NY
Hoso Bunka Foundation
Hotchkiss School CT
Hotevilla Bacavi Community School AZ
Houghton Committee (Great Britain)
Houghton Mifflin Company
Housatonic Community College CT
Housatonic Regional Community College CT
House Committee on Education and Labor
House Committee on Post Office and Civil Service
House Committee on the Judiciary
House of Representatives
House of the Good Shepherd MD
House School
House Science and Technology Committees
House Select Subcommittee on Education
House Select Subcommittee on Labor
Houston Baptist University TX
Houston Community College System TX
Houston Community College TX
Houston Independent School District TX
Houston Public Library TX
Howard College TX
Howard Community College MD
Howard County Public Schools MD
Howard University DC
Howell Cheney Vocational Technical School CT
Howell Elementary School UT
Howell Road School NY
Howland Circulating Library NY
Huckleberry House OH
Huddersfield Polytechnic (England)
Hudson County Community College NJ
Hudson River Sloop Clearwater Inc
Hudson Senior High School WI
Hudson Valley Community College NY
Hudspeth Retardation Center MS
Huegel School WI
Hughes Aircraft Company
Hughes School District AR
Hull House Association IL
Hull University (England)
Human Habitat Study
Human Relations Area Files
Human Resources Administration
Human Resources Development Authority (Canada)
Human Resources Development Institute
Human Resources Research Council (Canada)
Human Resources Research Office
Human Resources Research Organization
Human Resources School NY
Human Rights Commission
Human Sciences Research Inc
Human Service Institute NY
Human Services Manpower Career Center IL
Humanities Research Council of Canada
Humber College ON
Humboldt State College CA
Humboldt State University CA
Humphrey Occupational Resource Center MA
Hunter Elementary School NY
Hunter High School NY
Hunting Ridge Elementary School IL
Huntington Beach Union High School District CA
Huntington College IN
Huntington Galleries WV
Huntington Public Library
Huntsville City School System AL

Huntsville School District AR
Huron High School SD
Huron Valley Womens Facility MI
Husson College ME
Huston Tillotson College TX
Hutchinson Community Junior College KS
Hutterite Communal Society
Hyde Park Cadre
Hyogo University of Teacher Education (Japan)
IBM Corporation
IBM National Support Ctr for Persons with Disabil
Ichabod Crane Central School District NY
Idaho Extension Service
Idaho State Department of Education
Idaho State University
Ikipujung Pandang University (Indonesia)
Illinois Area Service Centers
Illinois Arts Council
Illinois Association Community and Junior Colleges
Illinois Association for Education Young Children
Illinois Association of Legal Secretaries
Illinois Association of School Boards
Illinois Association of Teachers of English
Illinois Audiovisual Association
Illinois Bell Telephone Company
Illinois Central College
Illinois Citizens Education Council
Illinois College
Illinois College of Optometry
Illinois Commission on Children
Illinois Community College Board
Illinois Community College System
Illinois Community Unit School District 300
Illinois Consumer Education Association
Illinois Division Vocational Technical Education
Illinois Eastern Community Colleges
Illinois Federation of Teachers
Illinois Higher Education Loan Authority
Illinois Institute for Public Understanding Law
Illinois Institute of Technology
Illinois Library and Information Network
Illinois Library Materials Processing Center
Illinois Mathematics and Science Academy
Illinois Migrant Council
Illinois Office of Community Development
Illinois Planning Council on Develop Disabil
Illinois Project for School Reform
Illinois School for the Deaf
Illinois Soldiers and Sailors Childrens School
Illinois Specialized Teacher Evaluation Programs
Illinois Speech and Theatre Association
Illinois State Board of Education
Illinois State Board of Higher Education
Illinois State Colleges and Universities
Illinois State Council on Nutrition
Illinois State Dept of Children and Family Servs
Illinois State Dept of Corrections
Illinois State Library
Illinois State Scholarship Commission
Illinois State University
Illinois State Wide Curriculum Study Center
Illinois Teachers College
Illinois Valley Community College
Illinois Valley Library System
Illinois Wesleyan University
Illinois Youth Commission
Immaculate Heart College CA
Immigration and Naturalization Service
Imperial Valley College CA
INA Corporation
Incarnate Word College TX
Incorporated Association of Assistant Masters
Independence Community College KS
Independence School District MO
Independent Broadcasting Association
Independent Broadcasting Authority
Independent School District 196 MN
Independent School District TX
Independent Schools Information Service
Independent Television Authority (England)
Indian Adult Education Association (India)
Indian Claims Commission
Indian Defense League of America
Indian Education Centre (Canada)
Indian Education Resources Center NM
Indian Health Service
Indian Hills Community College IA
Indian Institute of Technology (India)
Indian National Committee on Space Research
Indian National Council of Educational Research
Indian Nations At Risk Task Force
Indian Oasis Public School District AZ
Indian Paraprofessional Services
Indian River Community College FL
Indiana Academy for Science Math and Humanities
Indiana Adult Literacy Coalition
Indiana Broadcasters Association
Indiana Career Resource Center
Indiana College Placement and Assessment Center
Indiana Collegiate Press Association
Indiana Commission for Higher Education
Indiana Congress on Education
Indiana Council for Continuing Education
Indiana Council on Economic Education
Indiana County Area Vocational Technical School PA
Indiana Dept Public Instruction Div Inst Media
Indiana Higher Education Telecommunications System
Indiana Institute of Technology
Indiana Laborers Training Trust Fund
Indiana Manpower Research Association
Indiana Plan Institute
Indiana Principal Leadership Academy
Indiana School Library Association
Indiana State Council
Indiana State Department of Education
Indiana State Reformatory
Indiana State University
Indiana Univ Purdue Univ at Fort Wayne
Indiana Univ Purdue Univ at Indianapolis
Indiana Univ Purdue Univ at Indianapolis Columbus
Indiana University
Indiana University Bloomington
Indiana University East
Indiana University Fort Wayne
Indiana University Northwest
Indiana University of Pennsylvania
Indiana University School of Music
Indiana University South Bend
Indiana University Southeast
Indiana Vocational Technical College
Indiana Wesleyan University
Indiana Youth Institute
Indianapolis Marion County Public Library IN
Indianapolis Public Schools IN
Indianhead Technical Institute WI
Indira Gandhi National Open University (India)
Industrial Relations Centre (Canada)
Industrial Relations Research Association
Industrial Schools Committee
Industrial Technology Institute MI
Industrial Television Society
Infant Development Center ME
Informatics Inc
Information Dynamics Corporation
Information Industry Association
Information Knowledge Research Centre
Information Mapping Inc
Information on Demand CA
Information Transfer Experimental Center MA
Infoterm
Ingham Medical Center MI
Ingomar Middle School PA
Initiative 7 (Washington DC 1981)
Inland Steel Company
Inner City Consortium IL
Inner London Education Authority (England)
Innis College (Canada)
INNOTECH (Singapore)
Innovative Diffusion Center
INSPEC
Institut fuer Film und Bild (Sweden)
Institut fur Deutsche Sprache (West Germany)
Institute for Academic Technology NC
Institute for Advanced Study NJ
Institute for Behavioral Research MD
Institute for Child Study
Institute for Communication Research
Institute for Crippled and Disabled
Institute for Demographic and Economic Studies Inc
Institute for Development of Educ Activities OH
Institute for Developmental Studies
Institute for Education and Technology
Institute for Educational Leadership DC
Institute for Emotional Education
Institute for English Language Education (England)
Institute for Environmental Education OH
Institute for Executive Leadership OR
Institute for Human Development AZ
Institute for Instructional Research and Practice
Institute for Interactive Information Environ CA
Institute for International Education
Institute for Juvenile Research IL
Institute for Learning Disability
Institute for Local Directors Special Education CA
Institute for Mathematical Studies in Soc Scis CA
Institute for Minority Business Education DC
Institute for Native American Development IL
Institute for Perception Research
Institute for Personality and Ability Testing CT
Institute for Policy Analysis (Canada)
Institute for Research and Training Higher Educ OH
Institute for Research in History
Institute for Research on Exceptional Children IL
Institute for Research on Poverty WI
Institute for Research on Teaching
Institute for Retired Professionals NY
Institute for Science Education (West Germany)
Institute for Services to Education Inc DC
Institute for Social Research MI
Institute for Software Engineering CA
Institute for the Achievement of Human Potential
Institute for the Advancement of Math and Sci
Institute for the Development of Educ Activities
Institute for the Future
Institute for the Study of Educational Policy DC
Institute for the Study of Exceptional Children
Institute of Adv Archit Studies (Great Britain)
Institute of Africa
Institute of Afro American Affairs NY
Institute of American Indian Arts NM
Institute of Child Guidance Development (Canada)
Institute of Child Study ON
Institute of Community Services
Institute of Educational Technology (England)
Institute of Electrical and Electronics Engineers
Institute of Electrical Research (Mexico)
Institute of International Education NY
Institute of International Studies DC
Institute of Library Research CA
Institute of Lifetime Learning DC
Institute of Medicine DC
Institute of Museum Services
Institute of Nutrition of Central America
Institute of Personnel Management (England)
Institute of Prof Librarians of Ontario (Canada)
Institute of Public Affairs IA
Institute of Rehabilitation Medicine
Institute of Study for Older Adults
Institute of Study for Older Adults NY
Institute of Technology Higher Education (Mexico)
Institute of Vocational Training (Japan)
Institute on Rehabilitation Services PA
Institute Research Development Occupational Ed NY
Institutes for Advanced Study in Industrial Arts
Institutes for the Achievement of Human Potential
Institution of Electrical Engineers
Institution of Training Officers (United Kingdom)
Institution on Chautauqua Lake NY
Institution on Farm Training
Institutional Development Corporation
Institutional Research Council of Eleven
Institutionen foer Tillaempad Elektronik (Sweden)
Instituto Caro y Cuervo (Colombia)
Instituto Centro Amer de Ext Cult (Costa Rica)
Instituto Nacional de Capacitacion Prof (Chile)
Instructional Broadcasting Assn (Great Britain)
Instructional Center Library
Instructional Communications Service
Instructional Computer Cooperative
Instructional Development Institute
Instructional Improvement Laboratory MN
Instructional Objectives Exchange
Instructional Resources Center (Fredonia New York)
Instructional Systems Clearinghouse Inc
Instructional Telecommunications Consortium
Instructional Television Information Office
Instrument Society of America
Instrumentation Laboratory Inc
Insurance Industry Training Council
Insurance Information Institute
Inter American Center
Inter American Committee on Adult Education
Inter American Court of Human Rights
Inter American Foundation
Inter American Indian Institute
Inter American Press Association
Inter American Society Educ Leadership Development
Inter American Society for Educ Administration
Inter American University PR
Inter Association Council on Test Reviewing
Inter Press Service
Inter TAC Institute
Interactive Video Science Consortium
Interagency Committee on Handicapped Research
Interagency Committee on Learning Disabilities
Interagency Coordinating Council
Interagency Language Roundtable
Interagency Panel on Early Childhood R and D
Intercity Committee for Action NJ
Intercultural Development Research Association
Interdisciplinary Research Group on Poverty
Intergovernmental Advisory Council on Education
Intergovernmental Committee for Migration
Intergovernmental Task Force Information Systems
Interlake High School WA
Interlochen Arts Academy MI
Intermediate School 201 NY
Intermountain School UT
Internal Revenue Service
International Assn Evaluation Educ Achievement
International Association of Metro City Libraries
International Association of Music Libraries
International Association of School Librarianship
International Association of Universities
International Baccalaureate Office
International Board on Books for Young People
International Book Committee
International Broadcast Institute (England)
International Brotherhood of Electrical Workers
International Bureau of Education
International Business Machines
International Center for Industry and Environment
International Center for Research on Bilingualism
International Centre for Theoretical Physics
International Centre Parliamentary Documentation
International Child Development Center (Italy)
International Childrens Villages
International Civil Aviation Organization
International Clearinghouse MD
International Commission on Development of Educ
International Commission on Illumination
International Committee Against Racism
International Communication Agency
International Communication Association
International Confederation of Free Trade Unions
International Cooperation Administration
International Cooperative Alliance
International Council for Adult Education
International Council for Building Research
International Council for Computers in Education
International Council for Educational Development
International Council for Educational Media
International Council of Scientific Unions
International Council on Archives
International Council on Education for Teaching
International Council Science Education
International Data Library and Ref Service CA
International Development Research Centre ON
International Educational Library
International Extension College (England)
International Farm Youth Exchange
International Fed Plantation Agric Allied Workers
International Federation for Documentation
International Federation for Information and Docum
International Federation of Film Archives
International Federation of Home Economics
International Federation of Information Processing
International Federation of Library Associations
International Federation of Modern Lang Teachers
International Federation of University Women
International Film and Television Council
International Fire Service Training Association

International Folk High School (Denmark)
International Institute for Adult Literacy Methods
International Institute for Educational Planning
International Institute MO
International Institute on the Community College
International Labour Office
International Labour Organisation
International Ladies Garment Workers Union
International League of Socs Mentally Handicapped
International Linguistic Society
International Management Training for Educ Change
International Manpower Institute
International Mathematics Committee
International Network for Educational Information
International Olympic Academy
International Organization for Standardization
International Organization of Journalists
International Organization Science and Tech Educ
International Paper Company
International Peace Research Association
International Personnel Management Association
International Planned Parenthood Federation
International Potato Center (Peru)
International Radio Television University
International Reading Association
International Research Information Service
International Resource Center MA
International School of Brussels (Belgium)
International Schoolbook Institute in Brunswick
International Schools Association
International Science Foundation
International Secretariat for Volunteer Service
International Service Assn for Health Inc
International Sociological Association
International Space Center
International Space Hall of Fame Foundation NM
International Studies Association
International Study Group for Math Learning
International Technology Education Association
International Telecommunication Union
International Telephone and Telegraph Corporation
International Television Association
International Thespian Society
International Translations Centre (Netherlands)
International Union for Conservation of Nature
International Union of Biological Sciences
International Union of Geological Sciences
International Union of Operating Engineers
International Union of Pure and Applied Chemistry
International Union of Pure and Applied Physics
International University of Communications DC
International Word Processing Association
International Work Group for Indigenous Affairs
International Youth Hostel Federation
Intersegmental Coordinating Council CA
Interstate Commerce Commission
Interstate Consortium on Metric Education
Interstate Distributive Educ Curriculum Consortium
Interstate Migrant Education Council
Interstate Migrant Education Task Force
Interstate Oratorical Association
Interuniversity Communications Council
Interuniversity Council
Interuniversity Research Unit (England)
Intra Agency Committee on Rural Education
Intradepartmental Committee Child Abuse Neglect
Intradepartmental Council on Indian Affairs
Iona College NY
Iowa Adult Education Association
Iowa Area IX Alpine Center
Iowa Area XI Access Center
Iowa City Public Library
Iowa City School District IA
Iowa Drug Information Service
Iowa Educational Broadcasting Network
Iowa Energy Policy Council
Iowa Higher Education Association
Iowa Humanities Board
Iowa Lakeside Laboratory
Iowa Library Information Teletype Exchange
Iowa Microcomputer Occupational Info Network
Iowa Regional Computer Network
Iowa School for the Deaf
Iowa State Board of Regents
Iowa State Department of Education
Iowa State Education Association
Iowa State Library System
Iowa State Manpower Development Council
Iowa State University
Iowa Training School for Boys
Iowa Valley Community College District
Iowa Wesleyan College
IOX Assessment Associates
Iraqi Scientific Documentation Centre
Ironbound Community Learning Center NJ
Iroquois Confederacy
Iroquois League
Irvine Unified School District CA
Irvine Valley College CA
Irving Independent School District TX
Islamic States Broadcasting Organization
Isothermal Community College NC
Israel Library Association
Italian Radio and Television Agency
Itasca Community College MN
Ithaca City Schools NY
Ithaca College NY
Itinerant Teacher Service (Australia)
ITT Sheraton Hotels HI
Ittleson Center for Child Research
ITV Futures Planning Group
Izaak Walton League of America
J C Penney
J Paul Getty Center Library CA
J Paul Getty Museum CA
J Sargeant Reynolds Community College VA
Jackhead Indian Reserve MB
Jackson Community College MI
Jackson County Intermediate School District MI
Jackson County School District TN
Jackson Municipal Separate School District MS
Jackson River Vocational Center VA
Jackson State College MS
Jackson State Community College TN
Jackson State University MS
Jacksonville State Hospital IL
Jacksonville State University AL
Jagiellonian University (Poland)
Jamaica Library Service (Kingston)
Jamaican Movement for the Advancement of Literacy
James Barry Robinson Institute VA
James Connally Technical Institute TX
James Cook Univ of North Queensland (Australia)
James Jerome Hill Reference Library MN
James Madison University VA
James Wood High School VA
Jamestown College ND
Jamestown Community College NY
Jamestown Community School RI
Jamestown Public Schools RI
Jane Addams Graduate School of Social Work IL
Janesville Public Schools WI
Janus Pannonius University (Hungary)
Japan Association of Language Teachers
Japan Audiovisual Education Association
Japan Broadcasting Company
Japan English Forensics Association
Japan Medical Library Association
Japan National Christian Council
Japan Pharmaceutical Library Association
Japan Teachers Union
Japan United States Friendship Commission
Japanese Communist Party
Jarvis Christian College TX
Jean de Brebeuf College (Canada)
Jefferson Center
Jefferson College MO
Jefferson Community College KY
Jefferson Community College NY
Jefferson County Open High School CO
Jefferson County Public Schools KY
Jefferson County School District CO
Jefferson County School District OR
Jefferson County Schools AL
Jefferson County Unified School District
Jefferson Medical College PA
Jefferson Parish Prison
Jefferson Parish Public Schools LA
Jefferson School IL
Jefferson State Community College AL
Jefferson State Junior College AL
Jericho Union Free District NY
Jersey City Public Schools NJ
Jersey City State College NJ
Jessamine County School District KY
Jessie Stanton Developmental Playground NY
Jet Propulsion Laboratory
Jewish Board of Guardians
Jewish Child Care Association of New York
Jewish Employment and Vocational Service System
Jewish Family Services
Jewish National and University Library (Israel)
Jewish Theological Seminary of America NY
Jewish Vocational Service
Job Corps
Job Improvement Service
Job Information Service
Job Opportunities in the Business Sector
Job Opportunities Through Better Skills IL
Job Service
John A Logan College IL
John Abbott College PQ
John Adams Adult School CA
John Adams High School OR
John Birch Society
John Breuner Company
John C Calhoun State Community College AL
John C Campbell Folk School
John Carroll University OH
John Crerar Library IL
John Dewey Society
John F Kennedy Center for the Performing Arts DC
John F Kennedy Family Service Center MA
John F Kennedy Library MA
John F Kennedy School (West Germany)
John Hancock Life Insurance Company
John Hancock Mutual Life Insurance Company
John Howard Society of Canada
John M Olin Library
John Marshall High School NY
John Rolfe Museum and Historical Res Ctr VA
John Tracy Clinic CA
John Tyler Community College VA
John Wood Community College IL
Johns Hopkins University MD
Johnson and Wales College RI
Johnson City Central School District NY
Johnson City Public Schools TN
Johnson County Community College KS
Johnson State College VT
Johnson Wax Company
Johnston High School RI
Johnston Junior High School TX
Joint Commission on Mental Health of Children
Joint Committee on Slavic Studies
Joint Committee on Standards for Educ Evaluation
Joint Committee on Testing Practices
Joint Council of Language Associations
Joint Council on Economic Education
Joint Council on Educational Telecommunications
Joint Dissemination Review Panel
Joliet Community College IL
Joliet Junior College IL
Jones County School District MS
Jonesboro Public Schools AR
Joplin R VIII School District MO
Jordan Educational Complex CA
Jordan Educational Television Service
Jordanhill College of Education TV
Joseph Fels Foundation Inc
Joseph Klingenstein Summer Institute
Joseph P Kennedy Jr Foundation
Josephine County School District OR
Josiah Quincy Community School MA
Journalism Education Association
Juan Morel Campos Bilingual Center IL
Juarez Lincoln Center TX
Juilliard School of Music NY
Julia Dychman Andrus Childrens Home NY
Julia R Materman School PA
Juneau Borough School District AK
Juniata College PA
Junior Engineering Technical Society
Junior High School Association of Illinois
Junior League
Junior Reserve Officer Training Corps
Junior School Science Project (Australia)
Jurupa Unified School District CA
Jutland Open University (Denmark)
Juvenile Achievement Center TX
Juvenile Justice Delinquency Prevention Office
Kaiser Foundation Hospital CA
Kaiser Industries
Kalamazoo College MI
Kalamazoo Public Schools MI
Kalamazoo Valley Community College MI
Kamehameha Schools HI
Kanawha County Schools WV
Kanawha County Teacher Education Center WV
Kangaroo Network (Australia)
Kankakee Community College IL
Kansas Advisory Committee on Hispanic Affairs
Kansas City Kansas Community College
Kansas City Metropolitan Council on Child Care KS
Kansas City Midwest Research Institute
Kansas City Public Schools MO
Kansas City Regional Council for Higher Education
Kansas Curriculum Materials Dissemination Center
Kansas Network Special Education Paraprofessional
Kansas Research Inst Early Child Educ Handicapped
Kansas School for the Deaf
Kansas State Board of Education
Kansas State College Pittsburg
Kansas State Master Planning Commission
Kansas State Teachers College Emporia
Kansas State University
Kansas Supreme Court
Kansas TELENET
Kansas Wesleyan University
Karl Marx University (East Germany)
Kaskaskia College IL
Kaufman Independent School District TX
Kean College of New Jersey
Kearney State College NE
Kearns High School UT
Keene State College NH
Keep America Beautiful
Keesler Air Force Base
Keewatin Community College MB
Kellogg Center for Continuing Education MI
Kellogg Community College MI
Kellogg Foundation
Kelly Services Inc
Kenai Peninsula Community College AK
Kenan Colloquium
Kendall College IL
Kendall College of Art and Design MI
Kendall Demonstration Elementary School DC
Kennedy Center Federal Correctional Institution WV
Kennedy Job Training Center IL
Kennedy Memorial Christian Home IN
Kennesaw College GA
Kennesaw State College GA
Kenosha Technical Institute WI
Kensington High School for Girls
Kensington School MO
Kent Intermediate School District MI
Kent School of Social Work
Kent State University OH
Kent State University OH Regional Campuses
Kentucky Academic Association
Kentucky Association for Communications and Tech
Kentucky Association for Institutional Research
Kentucky Bureau of School Service
Kentucky Child Welfare Research Foundation
Kentucky Cooperative Extension Service
Kentucky Council of Teachers of English
Kentucky Council on School Performance Standards
Kentucky Council Teacher Education Certification
Kentucky Educational Research Association
Kentucky Library Communications Network
Kentucky Mental Manpower Commission
Kentucky Model Center
Kentucky Ohio Michigan Regional Medical Library
Kentucky Reception Center
Kentucky School of Crafts
Kentucky State Department of Education
Kentucky State Library
Kentucky State University
Kentucky Youth Research Center
Kenwood School District OK
Kenya National Youth Service
Kenyatta University (Kenya)
Kenyon College OH
Kern Community College CA
Kern Community College District CA
Kern Union High School District CA
Ketchikan Community College AK
Kettering City Schools OH
Kettering Foundation
Kettering Medical Center OH
Kettleby Public Schools ON

Keyano College AB
Keyser Industrial Park
Keystone Central School District PA
Kiamichi Area Vocational Technical Schools OK
Kiamichi Economic Development District OK
Kickapoo Nation School KS
Kiddie Farm
KIDS Consortium ME
Kids on Campus Inc
Kiev Construction Engineering Institute (USSR)
Kiev Polytechnic Institute (USSR)
Kimberly Clark Corporation
Kindergarten Parents Club IN
King Abdulaziz University (Saudi Arabia)
King and Queen County Public Schools VA
King Center NY
King Timilty Advisory Council
Kings College (England)
Kings College PA
Kingsborough Community College WV
Kingsbury Center DC
Kingston College (England)
Kinney Shoe Corporation
Kirkland College NY
Kirkwood Community College IA
Kirkwood School District MO
Kitaskinaw School AB
Klamath County Schools OR
Klemetti Institute
KLH Child Development Center MA
Knapp Foundation of North Carolina
Kneesworth House (England)
Knight Ridder
Knitting Lace Net Industry Training Bd (England)
Know Nothing Party
Knowledge Network BC
Knowledge Network of Washington
Knowledge Network of Wisconsin
Knox College IL
Knox County Schools TN
Knoxville City Schools TN
Knoxville College TN
Kodak Limited
Kodak Research Laboratories
Kohler Company
Kolmogorov School
Komsomal
Konama School NM
Korea Air and Correspondence University
Korea Military Advisory Group
Korea Scientific and Technological Inf Center
Korean Educational Development Institute
Korean Library Association
Kortright Centre for Conservation ON
Kuring gai College of Advanced Educ (Australia)
Kutztown State College PA
Kutztown University PA
Kuwait University
Kyoto Sangyo University (Japan)
Kyrene School District AZ
L Anse Creuse Public Schools MI
La Grange School District 105 IL
La Jolla School CA
La Leche League
La Puente Union High School District CA
La Raza Unida Party
La Salle College PA
La Salle University PA
La Trobe University (Australia)
La Verne College CA
Labette Community College KS
Labor and Industry Occupational Needs System NJ
Labor Relations Training Center DC
Laboratory Institute to Facilitate Teaching
Laboratory of Interactive Ed Technologies (Italy)
Labour Party (England)
Lackland Air Force Base TX
Laconia State School NH
LaConner School District WA
Ladue School District MO
Lafayette College PA
Laguna Acoma Combined Junior Senior High Sch NM
Laguna Beach Unified School District CA
Laguna Reservation AZ
Laguna Reservation NM
Lake Area Vocational Technical School SD
Lake City Community College FL
Lake Country School MN
Lake County Area Vocational Technical Center FL
Lake County Public Schools IL
Lake Forest College IL
Lake Forest School District DE
Lake Land College IL
Lake Manitoba Indian Reserve
Lake Michigan College MI
Lake Michigan Federation
Lake Oswego School District 7J OR
Lake Stevens School District WA
Lake Sumter Community College FL
Lake Superior State College MI
Lake Superior State University MI
Lake Washington School District WA
Lakeland Community College OH
Lakeland High School NY
Lakeshore Curriculum Study Council WI
Lakeshore Technical Institute WI
Lakewood School IL
Lakota Higher Education Center SD
Lakota Tuberculosis and Health Association SD
Lamar Community College CO
Lamar School District CO
Lamar State College of Technology TX
Lamar University TX
Lambuth College TN
Lamplighter School TX
Lancaster City School District OH
Lancaster Elementary School District CA
Lancaster School District PA
Land and Water Conservation Fund
Land Laboratories AZ
Land Laboratory IL
Lane Community College OR
Laney College CA
Langdon Elementary School
Langley Research Center VA
Langston University OK
Language Acquisition Resource Center NY
Language and Cognitive Development Center MA
Language Information Network Clearinghouse System
Lansing Community College MI
Lansing School District MI
Lansing Teacher Corps MI
Laramie County School District Number 1 WY
Laredo Junior College TX
Las Cruces Public Schools NM
Las Cruces Teacher Center NM
Las Positas College CA
Las Virgenes Unified School District
Lassen Community College District CA
Lathrop E Smith Environmental Education Center MD
Latin School of Chicago IL
Lau Center
Laubach Literacy Action
Laubach Literacy Inc
Laubach Literacy International
Lauder Institute of Management Internatl Studies
Laurel High School PA
Laurentian University ON
Laval University (Canada)
Lavender University CA
Law Enforcement Assistance Administration
Law Students Civil Rights Research Council
Lawrence County Joint Vocational School OH
Lawrence High School KS
Lawrence Institute of Technology MI
Lawrence Livermore National Laboratory CA
Lawrence Public Schools NY
Lawrence Radiation Laboratory
Lawrence Township Metropolitan School District IN
Lawrence University WI
Lawson State Community College AL
Lay Faculty Association
Laymen in North Kingstown Schools RI
Leadership Institute for a New Century IA
Leadville County School District CO
League for Innovation in the Community Coll CA
League for Innovation in the Community College
League for the Humanities
League of Cooperating Schools
League of Pioneers
League of Professional Schools GA
League of Schools ID
League of United Latin American Citizens
League of Women Voters
League School NY
Leander Community School
Leander Independent School District TX
Learn Alaska Network
Learning About Learning
Learning and Instructional Resources Center
Learning Assessment Retention Consortium CA
Learning Center for Anthropology
Learning Centers Robbinsdale MN
Learning House Tutorial Center
Learning Institute of North Carolina
Learning Living Information Exchange
Learning Materials Center
Learning Research and Development Center
Learning Research Associates
Learning Unlimited IN
Learning Village
Lebanon Correctional Institution OH
Lebanon High School MO
Lee College TX
Lee County School District FL
Lee Mental Health Center FL
Leech Lake Reservation MN
Leeds and Northrup Development Institute
Leeds Polytechnic (England)
Leflore County Schools MS
Left Book Club
Legal Defense Fund
Legislative Commission on Expenditure Review
Legislative Teleconference Network AK
Lehigh County Community College PA
Lehigh University PA
Leicester Junior College MA
Leicestershire County Schools (England)
Leiden Student Corps (Netherlands)
LeMoyne College TN
LeMoyne Owen College TN
Lenin Library (USSR)
Leningrad Institute Railway Trans Engineers (USSR)
Leningrad University (USSR)
Lennox High School CA
Lennox Industries Inc
Lenoir City Public Schools TN
Lenoir Community College NC
Lenoir Rhyne College NC
Leominster Public School System MA
Leon County School District FL
Leonardo da Vinci Society
Leoti Community Services KS
Lesley College MA
Leslie Bureau of Suffrage Education NY
Lester Hill Corporation
Lethbridge Catholic Separate School District 9 AB
Lethbridge Community College AB
Lethbridge School District AB
Letterman Army Medical Center CA
Leupp Boarding School AZ
Levinson Research Foundation
Lewis and Clark College OR
Lewis and Clark Community College IL
Lewis Clark State College ID
Lewis University IL
Lewiston Alternative Vocational Center ME
Lewiston Independent School District ID
Lexington Clinical Research Center KY
Lexington Local School District OH
Lexington Nursery and Kindergarten School
Lexington School for the Deaf NY
Liaison Committee on Medical Education
Liberty Baptist College VA
Liberty Bell Educational Complex TN
Liberty High School WA
Liberty University VA
Libraries of the Missouri Information Network
Library Archives and Documentation Services
Library Association of Alberta (Canada)
Library Association of Australia
Library Automation Research and Consulting Assn
Library Binding Institute MA
Library Management Information System
Library of Congress
Library of Michigan
Library Orientation Instruction Exchange
Lick Observatory CA
Life Experiences Inc
Life Office Management Association
Liff House Childrens Unit
Lighthouse Club Day Camp PA
Lilly (Eli) and Company
Lilly Endowment
Limburg State University (Netherlands)
Lincoln Center Library
Lincoln College (New Zealand)
Lincoln College IL
Lincoln Community High School
Lincoln Council on Alcoholism and Drugs NE
Lincoln County Board of Education ON
Lincoln County Roman Catholic Separate Sch Bd ON
Lincoln County School District 2 WY
Lincoln County School of Technology NC
Lincoln County Schools OR
Lincoln County Schools VA
Lincoln Filene Center Citizenship Public Affairs
Lincoln Heights Elementary School OH
Lincoln High School MO
Lincoln High School Philadelphia PA
Lincoln Junior High UT
Lincoln Land Community College IL
Lincoln Learning Center MN
Lincoln Memorial University TN
Lincoln Neighborhood Service Center NY
Lincoln Public Library IL
Lincoln Public Schools NE
Lincoln Skills Center MI
Lincoln Trail College IL
Lincoln University MO
Lincoln University PA
Lincoln Vocational Center FL
Lincoln Way High School IL
Lincolnwood Schools IL
Lindenwood College MO
Lindsey Hopkins Technical Education Center FL
Linfield College OR
Linguistic Society of America
Linguistics Institute of Ireland
Linkoping University (Sweden)
Links Inc
Linn Benton Community College OR
Linn Benton Education Service District OR
Lippincott Company
Lister Hill Center MD
Litchfield Park AZ
Literacy Consortium of Allegheny County PA
Literacy Corps
Literacy Exchange Network
Literacy House (India)
Literacy Volunteers Inc
Literacy Volunteers of America Inc
Literacy Volunteers of New York City
Little Axe Independent School District OK
Little Egypt Development Center IL
Little Hoover Commission
Little Rock School District AR
Little Saskatchewan School MB
Litton Industries
Live Oak High School CA
Liverpool Middle School NY
Living School NY
Living Stage DC
Livingston School for Girls NY
Livonia Public Schools MI
Local Government Services Center
Local Information Network Knowledge Educ Renew MA
Lock Haven State College PA
Lockheed
Lodestar International Student Center
Logan Cache County Tutorial Center UT
Logan City School District UT
Logo Action Research Collaborative
Loma Linda University CA
Lompoc School District CA
London Board of Education ON
London City Schools OH
London County Council (England)
London Education Association
London Educational Authority
London Hospital Medical College
London Institution
London School of Economics
London Special School
Londonderry Elementary School PA
Lone Star School District No 101 CO
Long Beach City College CA
Long Beach Unified School District CA
Long Branch School District NJ
Long Island Educational Communications Council NY
Long Island University NY
Longfellow Education Center MN
Longview Community College MO
Longwood College VA
Lorain City Schools OH
Lorain County Community College OH
Lorain County Public Libraries OH
Loras College IA
Lord Fairfax Community College VA
Loretto Heights College CO
Los Alamos High School NM
Los Alamos National Laboratory NM
Los Angeles Alternative School CA
Los Angeles City College CA

Merrimack College MA
Merrimack Education Center MA
Merritt College CA
Mesa College CO
Mesa Community College AZ
Mesa County Valley School District 51 CO
Mesa Public Schools AZ
Mesa State College CO
Mesa Verde High School CA
Mesabi Community College MN
Mesquite Independent School District TX
Messiah College PA
Methodist Childrens Home Society
Methodist Church
Metro Community College NE
Metro High School IL
Metro School IL
Metro State College CO
Metrolina Educational Consortia NC
Metropolitan Applied Research Center
Metropolitan Area Library Authorities
Metropolitan Community Colleges MO
Metropolitan Cooperative Library System
Metropolitan Council for Educational Opportunity
Metropolitan Council of the Twin Cities Area
Metropolitan Detroit Medical Library Group
Metropolitan Education Commission MI
Metropolitan Education Television Association
Metropolitan Educational Park
Metropolitan High School TX
Metropolitan Kansas City Jr College District MO
Metropolitan Life Insurance Company
Metropolitan Museum of Art NY
Metropolitan Open School MN
Metropolitan Pittsburgh Educational Television
Metropolitan School Study Council
Metropolitan State College CO
Metropolitan State University MN
Metropolitan Twin Cities Educ Coop Service Unit MN
Mexican Academy of Education
Mexican American Legal Defense Educational Fund
Mexican Electric Power Research Institute
Mexico City Binational Center
Mexico Public Schools MO
Meyer Childrens Rehabilitation Institute
Mhong Language Council
Miami Dade Community College FL
Miami Public Library FL
Miami Public Schools FL
Miami Southridge Adult Education Center FL
Miami University OH
Miami Urban Coalition
Michael J Owens Technical College OH
Michael Reese Hospital IL
Michigammes Track Club
Michigan Association of Childrens Agencies
Michigan Association of Higher Education
Michigan Bell Telephone Company
Michigan Business Education Association
Michigan Commission on High Schools
Michigan Consortium Assistive Device Delivery Syst
Michigan Council of Cooperative Nurseries
Michigan Curriculum Committee on Instr Materials
Michigan Education Association
Michigan Educational Resources Information Center
Michigan Employment Security Commission
Michigan Federation of Teachers
Michigan Institute for Educational Management
Michigan Labor Mediation Board
Michigan Library Association
Michigan Library Consortium
Michigan Medical Schools Council of Deans
Michigan Occupational Competency Assessment Center
Michigan Ohio Regional Educational Laboratory
Michigan Regional Lib Blind Physically Handicapped
Michigan Research Corporation
Michigan School for the Blind
Michigan School for the Deaf
Michigan Special Education Learning Materials Ctr
Michigan Speech Association
Michigan State Board of Education
Michigan State Department of Education
Michigan State Department of Labor
Michigan State Department of Social Services
Michigan State Housing Authority
Michigan State University
Michigan State University Employees Association
Michigan Technological University
Michigan Youth Corps
Michigan Youth Services
Micro Social Learning Center
MicroSIFT
Microwave Communications Inc
Mid America Nazarene College KS
Mid America Vocational Curriculum Consortium
Mid Atlantic Multifunctional Resource Center
Mid Continent Regional Educational Laboratory
Mid Continent Regional Educational Laboratory CO
Mid Continent Regional Educational Laboratory MO
Mid Florida Technical Institute
Mid Iowa Computer Center
Mid Michigan Community Action Council
Mid Michigan Community College
Mid Missouri Small School Computer Consortium
Mid Plains Technical Community College Area NE
Mid Prairie Community School District IA
Mid South Educational Research Association
Mid State VTAE District WI
Mid Valley Area Vocational Center IL
Middle Atlantic Placement Association
Middle College High School CA
Middle College High School NY
Middle College High School TN
Middle East Technical University
Middle Elementary Teaching Team
Middle Georgia Technical Institute
Middle Management Center
Middle States Association of Colleges and Schools
Middle Tennessee State University
Middlebury College VT
Middlesex Community College CT
Middlesex Community College MA
Middlesex County College NJ
Middlesex Distance Learning Consortium CT
Middlesex Hospital CT
Middlesex Polytechnic (England)
Middleton Cross Plains Area School District WI
Middletown High School RI
Midge Control Laboratory FL
Midland City Education Association MI
Midland College TX
Midland Lutheran College NE
Midland Public Schools MI
Midland Public Schools TX
Midland School CA
Midlands Consortium
Midlands Technical College SC
Midway College KY
Midway School NY
Midwest College Learning Center Association
Midwest Regional Library Network
Midwest Regional Media Center for the Deaf
Midwest Regional MEDLARS Center
Midwest Technical Education Center MO
Midwestern Educational Research Association
Midwestern State University TX
Midwestern University TX
Migrant Education Center WA
Migrant Education Goals Task Force
Migrants Incorporated
Mikmawey School NS
Milan Federal Correctional Institution
Miles College AL
Military Academy (West Point) NY
Military Police School
Military Testing Association
Mill Neck Manor School for the Deaf NY
Millard School District NE
Milledgeville State Hospital GA
Miller Composite High School (Canada)
Miller Unruh Reading Center CA
Millersville University PA
Millfield School (England)
Millikin University IL
Mills College CA
Millsaps College MS
Milpitas Unified School District CA
Milton Academy MA
Milton College WI
Milton Hershey School PA
Milwaukee Area Technical College WI
Milwaukee County Mental Health Center
Milwaukee Federated Library System
Milwaukee Institute of Technology WI
Milwaukee Public Museum
Milwaukee Public Schools WI
Milwaukee School of Engineering WI
Milwaukee Vocational and Adult School WI
Mine Safety and Health Administration
Ministers Committee on Kindergarten Education
Ministry Higher Secondary Specialized Ed (USSR)
Ministry of Education (Brazil)
Ministry of Education (Colombia)
Ministry of Education (Egypt)
Ministry of Education (Japan)
Ministry of Education (USSR)
Ministry of Education and Culture (Israel)
Ministry of Employment (Japan)
Ministry of Higher Education (Poland)
Mink Network Educational Resources Center
Minneapolis Community College MN
Minneapolis Press Council
Minneapolis Public Schools MN
Minneapolis Special School District 1 MN
Minnesota Assn Private Postsecondary Schools
Minnesota Braille Sight Saving School
Minnesota Community College Board
Minnesota Community College Faculty Association
Minnesota Community College System
Minnesota Correctional Institution for Women
Minnesota Council on Family Relations
Minnesota Division of Vocational Rehabilitation
Minnesota Education Association
Minnesota Educational Computing Consortium
Minnesota Extension Service
Minnesota General College
Minnesota Governors Council on Rural Development
Minnesota Higher Education Coordinating Board
Minnesota Interlibrary Telecommunications Exchange
Minnesota Junior College Faculty Association
Minnesota Metropolitan State College
Minnesota News Council
Minnesota Press Council
Minnesota Public Interest Research Group
Minnesota School for the Deaf
Minnesota State Board of Teaching
Minnesota State College Common Market
Minnesota State College System
Minnesota State Department of Education
Minnesota State Junior College Board
Minnesota State University Board
Minnesota Work Opportunity Center
Minnetonka School District MN
Minooka Consolidated School District 201 IL
Minority Information Services Network CA
Minority Rights Group
Minot State University ND
MiraCosta College CA
Miranda Lux Foundation
Mission College CA
Missionary Orientation Center
Mississippi Bend Consortium
Mississippi College
Mississippi County Community College AR
Mississippi Gulf Coast Community College
Mississippi Gulf Coast Jr College Jackson
Mississippi Gulf Coast Jr College Perkinston
Mississippi Labor Mobility Project Star Inc
Mississippi Library Commission
Mississippi Southern College
Mississippi State Department of Education
Mississippi State Penitentiary
Mississippi State University
Mississippi University for Women
Mississippi Valley State University
Missoula Council Child Protect Family Support MT
Missoula Technical Center MT
Missouri Career Association
Missouri General Assembly
Missouri Industrial Information Institutes
Missouri Institute of Psychiatry
Missouri Library Association
Missouri Southern State College
Missouri State Dept Elementary Secondary Education
Missouri Telephone Lecture Network
Missouri Western College
Mitchell College
Mitchell College CT
Mitchell County School District GA
Mitre Corporation
Moanalua High School HI
Mobil Oil Company
Mobile County Public Schools AL
Mobile Creches for Working Mothers Children
Mobilization for Youth
Model Secondary School for the Deaf DC
Modern European Languages Coordinators Committee
Modern Humanities Research Association
Modern Language Association
Modern Language Association of Great Britain
Modesto City Schools CA
Modesto Junior College CA
Mohave County Community College AZ
Mohawk College of Applied Arts and Technology ON
Mohawk Valley Community College NY
Molesworth Institute
Moline School District IL
MOMM Cartel
Mon Yough Community Action Committee
Monadnock Developmental Services Inc NH
Monash University (Australia)
Monguagon School MI
Monmouth College NJ
Monroe Community College NY
Monroe County Community College MI
Monroe County Library System NY
Monroe County Public Library IN
Monroe County School District FL
Monroe Middle School IA
Mons University (Belgium)
Monsanto Company
Montana Educational Telecommunications Network
Montana State Department of Public Instruction
Montana State University
Montana University System
Montclair Public Schools NJ
Montclair State College NJ
Montebello Unified School District CA
Montefiore Hospital NY
Monterey County Library CA
Monterey Institute of International Studies CA
Monterey Peninsula College CA
Monterey Peninsula Unified School District CA
Monterrey Institute of Technology (Mexico)
Montgomery Blair High School MD
Montgomery College MD
Montgomery County Community College PA
Montgomery County Public Schools MD
Montgomery County Public Schools VA
Montgomery County Schools PA
Montgomery County Student Alliance
Montgomery Learning Disability Clinic AL
Montgomery Township Public Schools NJ
Monticello College
Montpelier Seminary VT
Montreal Museum of Fine Arts (Canada)
Montville Township School District NJ
Moore County School District NC
Moore Independent School District OK
Moorhead Area Vocational Technical Institute MN
Moorhead State College MN
Moorpark College CA
Moraine Park Technical Institute WI
Moraine Valley Community College IL
Moravian College PA
Moray House College of Education (Scotland)
Morehead State University KY
Morehouse College GA
Moreno Valley Unified School District CA
Morgan Community College CO
Morgan Community School
Morgan Community School Board
Morgan County School System TN
Morgan State College MD
Morgan State University MD
Morrill Committee
Morris Brown College GA
Morristown College TN
Morristown School District VT
Morton College IL
Moscow Institute of Technology (USSR)
Moscow Power Engineering Institute (USSR)
Moscow Printing Institute (USSR)
Moscow State Pedagogical Institute (USSR)
Moscow State University (USSR)
Mother Butler Memorial High School
Mother Cabrini School NY
Mothers Against Drunk Driving
Motion Picture Association of America
Moton Center for Independent Studies DC
Motor Vehicle Manufacturers Association
Motorola Inc
Mott Camp MI
Mott Community College MI
Mott Foundation
Mott Institute for Community Improvement

Mounds View Public Schools MN
Mount Anthony Union High School VT
Mount Carmel Guild Child Study Center
Mount Carmel High School IL
Mount Diablo Unified School District CA
Mount Greylock Regional High School MA
Mount Holyoke College MA
Mount Hood Community College OR
Mount Ida College MA
Mount Ida Junior College MA
Mount Lebanon School District PA
Mount Marty College SD
Mount Royal College AB
Mount Saint Marys College CA
Mount Saint Vincent University NS
Mount San Antonio College CA
Mount San Jacinto College CA
Mount Scopus College (Australia)
Mount Stuart Elementary School WA
Mount Union College OH
Mount Vernon College DC
Mount Vernon High School
Mount Vernon School Community Center VA
Mountain Empire Community College VA
Mountain Plains Regional Resource Center UT
Mountain States Health Manpower and Education
Mountain View Center
Mountain View Intermediate School OR
Mountain Womens Exchange
MOVE (Group)
MTV
Muhlenberg College PA
Muhlenberg School District PA
Mukilteo School District 36 WA
Multi District Trainer of Trainers Institute
Multidisciplinary Academy of Clinical Education CA
Multiple Careers Magnet Center TX
Multnomah County Intermediate Educ District OR
Multnomah County Outdoor School OR
Muncie Community Schools IN
Mundelein College IL
Murano Glass Center
Murdoch School NC
Murdoch University (Australia)
Murfreesboro City Schools TN
Murray County School District GA
Murray State University KY
Muscatine Community College IA
Muscular Dystrophy Associations of America
Museum Computer Network
Museum of Fine Arts TX
Museum of Modern Art NY
Museum of Science and Industry IL
Museum of the Book in the Hague (Netherlands)
Museum of the Media
Museum Resource Center NY
Music Center of Los Angeles County CA
Music Education Research Council
Musical Academy (Sweden)
Muskegon College of Business and Technology MI
Muskegon Community College MI
Muskegon Skill Training Center MI
Muskingum Area Technical College OH
Muskingum College OH
Mutual Life Assurance Company of Canada
Myer Pollack Communication Research Lab PQ
Myers Library AZ
Nacogdoches High School TX
Nampa School District ID
Nanaimo School District 68 BC
Nantes Graduate School of Business (France)
Nantucket Elementary School MA
Nanyang University (Singapore)
Napa College CA
Napa Valley College CA
Napa Valley Community College District CA
Napa Valley Public Schools CA
Napier College (Scotland)
Napier Polytechnic of Edinburgh (Scotland)
Napolean High School MI
Narodna Tehnika (Yugoslavia)
Nashua Public Schools NH
Nashville Metropolitan Public Schools TN
Nashville Reading Center TN
Nashville State Technical Institute TN
Nassau Community College NY
Nassau Educational Resources Center NY
Nassau Library System NY
Nasson College ME
Nat King Cole School IL
Natchez Adams School District MS
Natchez Adams Vocational School MS
Natchitoches Parish School District LA
Nathan Hale High School WA
Natick Public Schools MA
Nation of Islam
National Academic Advising Association
National Academy for School Executives
National Academy for Vocational Education OH
National Academy of Education
National Academy of Engineering
National Academy of Peace and Conflict Resolution
National Academy of Sciences
National Accred Council for Agencies Serving Blind
National Accrediting Agency Clinical Lab Sciences
National Achievement Scholarship Program
National Action Council for Minorities in Engineer
National Action Group
National Adult Educ Professional Develop Consort
National Adult Education Centre (Somalia)
National Advertising Division
National Advertising Review Board
National Advisory Board Rural Information Needs
National Advisory Body Local Authority Higher Educ
National Advisory Com on Handicapped Children
National Advisory Commission on Civil Disorders
National Advisory Commission on Health Manpower
National Advisory Commission on Libraries
National Advisory Commission on Rural Poverty
National Advisory Committee on Accredit Inst Elig
National Advisory Committee on Black Higher Educ
National Advisory Committee on Educ for the Deaf
National Advisory Council for Career Education
National Advisory Council on Adult Education
National Advisory Council on Education Professions
National Advisory Council on Ext and Cont Educ
National Advisory Council on Indian Education
National Advisory Council on Migrant Health
National Advisory Council on Rural Development
National Advisory Council on Vocational Education
National Advisory Council on Womens Educ Programs
National Aeronautics and Space Administration
National Affiliation for Literacy Advance
National Agricultural Library DC
National Agricultural Library MD
National Agricultural Workers Union
National Air Pollution Control Administration
National Alliance of Black School Educators
National Alliance of Business
National Alliance of Businessmen
National American Indian Court Judges Association
National and Grindleys Bank Unlimited
National Architectural Accrediting Board
National Archives and Records Administration
National Archives and Records Service
National Archives Atlanta Branch GA
National Archives Chicago Branch IL
National Archives DC
National Archives Library DC
National Archives of Canada
National Art Education Association
National Arts Center of the Philippines
National Assembly of Local Arts Agencies
National Assessment Governing Board
National Assn Advancement Black Americans Voc Educ
National Assn College University Attorneys
National Assn College University Business Officers
National Assn for Research in Science Teaching
National Assn for the Accreditation of Teach Educ
National Assn Independent Colleges Universities
National Assn of Physical Plant Admins of Univs
National Assn of Private Nontraditional Sch Coll
National Assn of Self Instructional Language Prog
National Assn of State Dir of Special Educ
National Assn of State Dir of Tchr Educ and Cert
National Assn of State Scholarship Grant Programs
National Assn of State Univ and Land Grant Coll
National Assn of Student Employment Administrators
National Assn of Student Personnel Administrators
National Assn Private Nontraditional Schools Coll
National Assn State Directors Vocational Education
National Association Advancement Colored People
National Association Educ of Young Children
National Association Elementary School Principals
National Association Equal Opportunity Higher Educ
National Association for Adult Education
National Association for Bilingual Education
National Association for Business Teacher Educ
National Association for Continuing Adult Educ
National Association for Core Curriculum
National Association for Family Day Care
National Association for Foreign Student Affairs
National Association for Girls and Women in Sport
National Association for Humanities Education
National Association for Mental Health
National Association for Music Therapy
National Association for Nursery Education
National Association for Public School Adult Educ
National Association for Retarded Children
National Association for Retarded Citizens
National Association for the Teaching of English
National Association of Black Adult Educators
National Association of Boards of Pharmacy
National Association of Broadcasters
National Association of Career Education
National Association of Coll Admissions Counselors
National Association of College Stores
National Association of Dental Laboratories
National Association of Educational Broadcasters
National Association of Educational Secretaries
National Association of Geology Teachers
National Association of Hispanic Elderly
National Association of Independent Schools
National Association of Jazz Educators
National Association of Legal Secretaries
National Association of Manufacturers
National Association of Media Educators
National Association of Partners in Education
National Association of Protection Advocacy Sys
National Association of Psychiatric Technology
National Association of School Psychologists
National Association of Schoolmasters
National Association of Schools of Music
National Association of Schools of Theatre
National Association of Social Workers
National Association of State Boards of Education
National Association of Teachers
National Association of Test Directors
National Association of Trade and Technical School
National Association of Women Deans and Counselors
National Association of Youth Clubs
National Association Secondary School Principals
National Athletic Trainers Association
National Audio Visual Aids Centre (England)
National Audio Visual Association
National Audiovisual Center
National Audubon Society
National Audubon Society Expedition Institute
National Automobile Dealers Association
National Autonomous University of Mexico
National Basketball Association
National Bibliographic Service
National Black Child Development Institute
National Black Health Providers Task Force
National Black Nurses Association
National Board for Certified Counselors
National Board for Professional Teaching Standards
National Board of Chiropractic Examiners
National Board of Education (Sweden)
National Board of Inquiry on Schools
National Board of Medical Examiners
National Board of Osteopathic Medical Examiners
National Board of Schools (Finland)
National Book Committee
National Book Development Council
National Book League
National Braille Association
National Broadcasting Company
National Broadcasting Training Center Radio TV
National Bureau of Standards
National Business Education Association
National Cable Television Association
National Cancer Institute
National Capital Parks Service
National Captioning Institute
National Career Development Association
National Cartographic Information Center
National Catholic Educational Association
National Center Educ Media Materials Handicapped
National Center for Appropriate Technology
National Center for Atmospheric Research
National Center for Career Education
National Center for Child Advocacy
National Center for Deaf Blind Youths and Adults
National Center for Education Statistics
National Center for Educational Communication
National Center for Educational Planning
National Center for Educational Research and Devel
National Center for Educational Statistics
National Center for Educational Technology
National Center for Family Literacy
National Center for Health Services R and D
National Center for Health Statistics
National Center for Higher Educ Management Systems
National Center for Higher Education
National Center for Lifelong Learning
National Center for Medical Rehabilitation Res
National Center for Research on Teacher Learning
National Center for Research Vocational Educ CA
National Center for Research Vocational Education
National Center for Resource Recovery
National Center for School and College Television
National Center for School Leadership
National Center for Science Teaching and Learning
National Center for State Courts
National Center for the Improvement of Learning
National Center for the Study of Black Family Life
National Center for Urban Ethnic Affairs
National Center for Urban Partnerships
National Center for Visual Literacy
National Center for Vocational Education OH
National Center Improvement Educational Systems
National Center on Child Abuse and Neglect
National Center on Educational Outcomes
National Center on Effective Secondary Schools
National Center University Entrance Exam (Japan)
National Centre of Educ Technology (Hungary)
National Centre Research Rural Educ (Australia)
National Chicano Research Network
National Child Research Center DC
National Childminding Association (England)
National Childrens Bureau (England)
National Civil Service League
National Clearinghouse for Alcohol and Drug Info
National Clearinghouse for Bilingual Education
National Clearinghouse for Drug Abuse Information
National Clearinghouse for Smoking and Health
National Clearinghouse Offender Employment Restr
National Clinic on Technical Education

National Cluster Coordination Center
National Coalition for Campus Child Care Inc
National Coalition of Advanced Technology Centers
National Coalition on Television Violence
National Coalition to Abolish Corp Punish Sch
National Collaboration for Youth
National College of Education IL
National Collegiate Athletic Association
National Comm New Tech Uses Copyrighted Works
National Comm on Student Financial Assistance
National Comm on Teacher Educ Professional Stds
National Commission Employment Unemployment Stats
National Commission Financing Postsecondary Educ
National Commission for Employment Policy
National Commission for Manpower Policy
National Commission for the Social Studies
National Commission Libraries Information Science
National Commission on Accreditation
National Commission on Allied Health Education
National Commission on Excellence in Education
National Commission on Excellence in Teacher Educ
National Commission on Higher Education Issues
National Commission on Migrant Education
National Commission on Performance Based Education
National Commission on Secondary Educ Hispanics
National Commission on Secondary Vocational Educ
National Commission on Social Studies in Schools
National Commission on Testing and Public Policy
National Commission on Trustee Selection
National Commission on Working Women
National Committee Arts for the Handicapped
National Committee for Audiovisual Aids
National Committee for Citizens in Education
National Committee for Geochemistry
National Committee for Support of Public Schools
National Committee on Educ of Migrant Children
National Committee on Literacy
National Committee on Secondary Education
National Committee on the Employment of Youth
National Community School Education Association
National Computing Centre Limited (England)
National Conference of Bar Examiners
National Conference of Professors of Educ Admin
National Conference of State Legislatures
National Conference on Research in English
National Conference on Social Welfare
National Congress for Puerto Rican Rights
National Congress of Parents and Teachers
National Consortium for Humanizing Education
National Coordinating Council on Drug Education
National Correspondence College (Zambia)
National Council Community Services Continuing Ed
National Council for Accreditation of Teacher Educ
National Council for Educational Technology
National Council for Effective Schools
National Council for Geographic Education
National Council for Occupational Education
National Council for Technological Awards
National Council for the Social Studies
National Council for Vocational Qualifications
National Council Foreign Lang Intl Studies
National Council of American Indians
National Council of Churches
National Council of Industrial Management Clubs
National Council of Jewish Women
National Council of Juvenile Court Judges
National Council of La Raza
National Council of Negro Women
National Council of Professors Educ Administration
National Council of Senior Citizens
National Council of State Dirs of Comm Jr Colls
National Council of States on Inservice Education
National Council of Teachers of Education
National Council of Teachers of English
National Council of Teachers of Mathematics
National Council on Agricultural Life and Labor
National Council on Educ Standards and Testing
National Council on Educational Research
National Council on Higher Learning
National Council on Indian Opportunity
National Council on Measurement in Education
National Council on Schoolhouse Construction
National Council on Teacher Retirement
National Council on the Aging
National Council on the Arts
National Council on the Handicapped
National Crime Information Center
National Criminal Justice Reference Service
National Dairy Council
National Data Base on Aging
National Dental Association
National Diet Library (Japan)
National Diffusion Network
National Drug Policy Board
National Easter Seal Society for Crippled Children
National Economic Development Board
National Education Academy
National Education Association
National Education Commission on Time and Learning
National Education Federation (France)
National Education Goals Panel
National Education Task Force de La Raza
National Education Trust Fund
National Educational Loan Bank
National Educational Radio Network
National Educational Resources Information Service
National Educational Television
National Electronic Injury Surveillance System
National Electronic Service Dealers Association
National Endowment for Democracy
National Endowment for the Arts
National Endowment for the Humanities
National Entrepreneurship Clearinghouse
National Environmental Data Referral Service
National Environmental Health Association
National Environmental Research Center
National Environmental Study Area
National Evaluation Systems
National Extension College (England)
National Extension Comm on Clergy Continuing Educ
National Eye Institute
National Faculty Association
National Farm Labor Union
National Farmers Alliance and Industrial Union
National Farmers Union
National Federation of the Blind
National Film Board of Canada
National Fire Academy MD
National Fire Protection Association
National Football League
National Foreign Language Center
National Forensic Association
National Forum on Education Statistics
National Forum on Information Literacy
National Foster Parents Association
National Foundation for Educational Research
National Foundation for Higher Education
National Foundation on the Arts and the Humanities
National Foundation Youth and Adult Educ (Brazil)
National Fund for Medical Education
National Gallery of Art DC
National Geographic Society
National Governors Association
National Guard
National Gypsy Education Council
National Head Start Association
National Health Planning Information Center
National Health Service Corps
National Heart Lung and Blood Institute
National Highway Traffic Safety Administration
National Hispanic University
National Historical Publications Commission
National Home Study Council
National Humanities Faculty
National Independent Regulatory Agencies
National Indian Brotherhood
National Indian Brotherhood (Canada)
National Indian Council on Aging
National Indian Education Association
National Indian Institute
National Indian Youth Council
National Industrial Conference Board
National Industrial Television Association
National Industries for the Blind
National Information Center for Educational Media
National Information Center on Deafness
National Information Standards Organization
National Inservice Network
National Inst Curriculum Development (Netherlands)
National Inst Mental Health Neuro Sciences (India)
National Institute Advancement Career Education
National Institute Automotive Service Excellence
National Institute Child Health Human Development
National Institute for Educ Research (Japan)
National Institute for Higher Education (Ireland)
National Institute for Staff Organizational Devel
National Institute for Technical Training
National Institute for Testing Evaluation (Israel)
National Institute for Work and Learning DC
National Institute Independent Colleges Univs
National Institute Occupational Safety and Health
National Institute of Adult Education
National Institute of Corrections
National Institute of Dramatic Art
National Institute of Education
National Institute of Education (Singapore)
National Institute of Handicapped Research
National Institute of Justice
National Institute of Mental Health
National Institute of Public Affairs
National Institute of Senior Centers (NCOA)
National Institute of Standards and Technology
National Institute on Aging
National Institute on Disability Rehab Research
National Institute on Drug Abuse
National Institutes of Health
National Instructional Television Center
National Interest Council
National Intramural Recreational Sports Assn
National Intramural Sports Council
National Joint Committee on Learning Disabilities
National Junior College Athletic Association
National Junior Horticultural Association
National Labor Relations Board
National Laboratory for Advancement of Education
National Laboratory for Higher Education
National Laboratory on Early Childhood Education
National Laboratory System
National Languages and Literacy Inst (Australia)
National Languages Institute (Australia)
National Leadership Institute
National League for Nursing
National Learner Verification and Rev Task Force
National Lekotek Center
National Lending Library of Great Britain
National Library Network
National Library of Australia
National Library of Canada
National Library of Medicine MD
National Library of Venezuela
National Library Service
National Library Service for the Blind
National Library Services for the Blind
National Manpower Institute
National Marine Education Association
National Maritime Union
National Medical Association
National Medical Audiovisual Center
National Merit Scholarship Corporation
National Microfilm Association
National Middle School Association
National Music Camp
National Network for Curr Coord in Voc Tec Educ
National Network for Early Language Learning
National Network of Centers for Bilingual Educ
National News Council
National Occupational Competency Testing Institute
National Occupational Information Coordinating Com
National Occupational Information Service
National Oceanic and Atmospheric Admin Library
National Oceanic and Atmospheric Administration
National Oceanographic Data Center
National Office for Research and Special Libraries
National Open University (Taiwan)
National Opinion Research Center
National Organization for Women
National Organization on Legal Problems of Educ
National Outdoor Leadership School
National Park Service
National Periodicals Center
National Policy Board for Educ Administration
National Postsecondary Agricultural Student Organ
National Press Club
National Press Photographers Association
National Public Affairs Center for Television
National Public Radio
National Reading Center Foundation
National Reading Conference (Organization)
National Reading Research Center
National Recreation and Park Association
National Referral Center
National Regional Resource Center of Pennsylvania
National Register of Historic Places
National Rehabilitation Association
National Research and Education Network
National Research Center of the Arts
National Research Center on Gifted and Talented
National Research Center on Student Learning
National Research Council
National Research Council of Canada
National Research Development Corporation
National Resource and Dissemination Center
National Restaurant Association
National Rifle Association
National Rural Center
National Rural Education Association
National Rural Education Research Consortium
National Rural Independent Living Network
National Rural Small Schools Task Force
National Rural Studies Committee
National Safety Council
National Scholastic Press Association
National School Age Child Care Alliance
National School Boards Association
National School for Educational Research
National School Public Relations Association
National School Safety Center
National Science Board
National Science Foundation
National Science Library (Canada)
National Science Network
National Science Supervisors Association
National Science Teachers Association
National Secretaries Association
National Security Agency
National Security Council
National Security Industrial Association
National Service Corps (Ghana)
National Service Secretariat
National Small Business Training Network
National Small Government Research Network
National Society for Autistic Children
National Society for Performance and Instruction
National Society for Programmed Instruction
National Society for the Study of Education
National Society of Professional Engineers
National Society of Professors
National Space Science Data Center
National Speech Communication Learning System
National Star Ctr Disabled Youth Coll (England)
National Student Association
National Student Lobby
National Student Recreation and Park Society
National Student Research Center
National Student Travel Association
National TAFE Clearinghouse (Australia)
National Taiwan Normal University
National Task Force on Education and World View
National Task Force on Political Action
National Teachers Association
National Technical Information Service
National Technical Institute for the Deaf
National Technical Teachers College (Nigeria)
National Technological University
National Telecommunications and Information Admin

North Carolina Leadership Institute for Principals
North Carolina Manpower Development Corporation
North Carolina Outward Bound School
North Carolina Preservation Consortium
North Carolina School for the Deaf
North Carolina School of Science and Mathematics
North Carolina Science Technology Research Center
North Carolina State Board of Education
North Carolina State Department Public Instruction
North Carolina State University
North Carolina State University Raleigh
North Central Accrediting Association
North Central Association of Colleges and Schools
North Central College IL
North Central Conference on Summer Schools
North Central Correctional Institute MA
North Central Regional Educational Laboratory
North Central Technical College OH
North Central Technical College WI
North Central Technical Institute WI
North Chicago Community High School IL
North Clackamas School District OR
North Country Community College NY
North County Union High School NJ
North Dakota Bureau of Educational Research
North Dakota Fact Finding Commission
North Dakota Network for Knowledge
North Dakota Research Coordinating Unit
North Dakota State Nurses Association
North Dakota State School of Science
North Dakota State University
North Dakota University System
North Devon College (England)
North East London Polytechnic (England)
North Florida Junior College
North Gibson School Corporation IN
North Gwent College of Further Education (Wales)
North Harris College TX
North Harris County College TX
North Haven High School CT
North Hennepin Community College MN
North Hudson Jointure Commission
North Hunterdon Regional High School District NJ
North Iowa Area Community College
North Island College BC
North Kentucky Area Vocational School
North Kitsap School District WA
North Lake College TX
North Louisiana Supplementary Education Center
North Olmsted City Schools OH
North Orange County Community College District CA
North Providence High School RI
North Ridgeville City School District OH
North Royalton City Schools OH
North Seattle Community College WA
North Shore Child Guidance Center NY
North Shore Community College MA
North Slope Borough School District AK
North Suburban Library System IL
North Syracuse Central Schools NY
North Texas State University
North West Oklahoma Inservice Cooperative
North York Board of Education ON
Northampton College of Advanced Tech (England)
Northampton County Area Community College PA
Northampton High School MA
Northampton Monopoly
Northeast Academic Science Information Center
Northeast Alabama Consortium Profession Develop
Northeast Coalition of Educational Leaders
Northeast Conference Teaching of Foreign Languages
Northeast High School PA
Northeast Iowa Community College
Northeast Louisiana University
Northeast Metro Technical College MN
Northeast Missouri State College
Northeast Missouri State University
Northeast Regional Instructional Resource Center
Northeast Regional Media Center for the Deaf
Northeast Regional Resource Center VT
Northeast Texas Community College
Northeast University of Technology (China)
Northeast Vocational Advisory Council WA
Northeastern Educational Research Association
Northeastern Illinois State College
Northeastern Illinois University
Northeastern Junior College CO
Northeastern Local School District OH
Northeastern Ohio Universities College of Medicine
Northeastern Oklahoma A and M College
Northeastern Oklahoma State University
Northeastern Regional Library System
Northeastern State University OK
Northeastern University MA
Northern Arizona Long Distance Corporation
Northern Arizona Univ Center Excellence in Educ
Northern Arizona University
Northern Burlington Co Regional High School NJ
Northern Cheyenne Reservation MT
Northern Colorado Educational Board Coop Services
Northern Essex Community College NY
Northern Illinois University
Northern Illinois University Foundation
Northern Illinois University Taft Campus
Northern Kentucky University
Northern Lights College BC Fort Nelson Campus
Northern Maine Technical College
Northern Michigan University
Northern Montana College
Northern Nevada Community College
Northern New Mexico Community College
Northern Oklahoma Development Association
Northern Rockies Consortium for Higher Education
Northern Science Network
Northern Slope Borough School District AK
Northern State College SD
Northern States Power Company
Northern Telecom
Northern Ute Reservation UT
Northern Virginia Community College
Northern Virginia Technical College
Northland Pioneer College AZ
Northland School Division (Canada)
Northland School Division 61 AB
Northrop Institute of Technology CA
Northwest Alabama Community College
Northwest Alabama State Junior College
Northwest Arctic Inupiat Corporation
Northwest Arctic School District AK
Northwest Area Foundation MN
Northwest Association of Schools and Colleges
Northwest Educational Service District 189 WA
Northwest Environmental Education Center
Northwest Evaluation Association
Northwest Indian Council on Education
Northwest Louisiana Supplementary Education Center
Northwest Missouri State University
Northwest Ohio Regional Resource Center
Northwest Reading Consortium
Northwest Regional Educational Laboratory
Northwest Regional Evaluation Association
Northwest Regional Exchange
Northwest Staff Development Center MI
Northwest Territories Public Library Services
Northwestern College IA
Northwestern Curriculum Center in English
Northwestern High School MI
Northwestern Michigan College
Northwestern Oklahoma State University
Northwestern Regional Library NC
Northwestern State University LA
Northwestern University IL
Northwood Institute MI
Northwood Junior High School IL
Norwalk School District CT
Norwich University VT
Notre Dame College OH
Notre Dame University (Philippines)
Nova Complex Schools
Nova High School FL
Nova Public Schools FL
Nova University FL
Novice Debate Association
NSFNET
Nuclear Energy Commission
Nuclear Regulatory Commission
Nuclear Safety Information Center
Nucleus Testing Committee
NUFFIC (Netherlands)
Nuffield Foundation
Nurseries in Cross Cultural Education
Nurses Educational Funds Inc
Nursing Inservice Educators Greater Milwaukee Area
O Estado de Sao Paulo
Oak Drive Elementary School NY
Oak Glen Youth Camp CA
Oak Orchard Community Health Center NY
Oak Park and River Forest High School IL
Oak Park Book Processing Center
Oak Park High School MI
Oak Park School District IL
Oak Ridge Associated Universities TN
Oak Ridge National Laboratory
Oak Ridge Schools TN
Oak Ridge Technical Enterprises Corporation
Oakland Adult Day and Evening School CA
Oakland Community Career Educ Resource Center CA
Oakland Community College MI
Oakland Cottage School
Oakland Public Library CA
Oakland Redevelopment Agency
Oakland Schools MI
Oakland Unified School District CA
Oakland University MI
Oaklea Middle School OR
Oakleaf Elementary School PA
Oaklyn Junior High School NJ
Oakridge Public Schools OR
Oakton Community College CA
Oakton Community College IL
Oakview Elementary School
Oakwood School CA
Oberlin College OH
Oberry School NC
Oblate Sisters of Providence
Occidental College CA
Occupational Preparation School PA
Occupational Safety and Health Administration
Ocean County College NJ
Ocean County Vocational Technical School NJ
Ocean Hill Brownsville School District NY
Ocean Township School District NJ
Ocean View School District CA
Oceanographic Education Center
OCLC
Odessa College TX
Odyssey House
Office de Cooperation Radiophonique
Office Education Association
Office Education Clubs of America
Office for Advanced Research in Hispanic Education
Office for Advancement of Public Negro Colleges
Office for Civil Rights
Office for Scientific and Technical Information
Office of Adolescent Pregnancy Programs
Office of Bilingual Educ Minority Lang Affairs
Office of Career Education
Office of Child Development
Office of Civil Defense
Office of Economic Opportunity
Office of Economic Research
Office of Education
Office of Educational Research and Improvement
Office of Environmental Education
Office of Equal Opportunity
Office of Federal Contract Compliance Programs
Office of Higher Education Programs
Office of Human Development
Office of Human Development Services
Office of Indian Education
Office of Indian Education Programs
Office of Inspector General
Office of Intergovernmental Science Programs
Office of Management and Budget
Office of Manpower Policy Evaluation Research
Office of Maternal and Child Health
Office of Minority Business Enterprise
Office of Native American Programs
Office of Naval Research
Office of Personnel Management
Office of Program Evaluation
Office of Research and Development
Office of Research Grants
Office of Revenue Sharing
Office of Science and Technology
Office of Science Education
Office of Science Information Service
Office of Service Delivery Assessment
Office of Special Educ Rehabilitative Services
Office of Special Education
Office of Special Education Programs
Office of Student Financial Assistance
Office of Technical Assistance and Training
Office of Technology Assessment
Office of Telecommunications Policy
Office of the Assistant Secretary for Education
Office of University Library Management Studies
Office of Urban Education
Office of Workers Compensation Programs
Office of Youth Programs
Ogden City School District UT
Oglala Lakota College SD
Oglala Sioux Community College SD
Oglethorpe University GA
Ohio Academy of Science
Ohio Association for Supervision Curriculum Devel
Ohio Board of Regents
Ohio Central School System
Ohio College Library Center
Ohio Consortium for Portfolio Development
Ohio Continuing Higher Education Association
Ohio Cooperative Extension Service
Ohio Council on Advanced Placement
Ohio Council on Vocational Education
Ohio County Schools WV
Ohio Disadvantaged Pupil Program Fund
Ohio Dominican College
Ohio Education Association
Ohio Educational Library Media Association
Ohio Environmental Protection Agency
Ohio Faculty Senate
Ohio Institute of Technology
Ohio Library Association
Ohio Library Trustees Association
Ohio Northern University
Ohio School for the Deaf
Ohio State Board of Education
Ohio State Department of Education
Ohio State University
Ohio State University Hospitals
Ohio State University Lima
Ohio State University Newark
Ohio Technology Transfer Organization
Ohio University
Ohio Wesleyan University
Ohio Youth Commission
OhioLINK
Ohlone College CA
Oil Belt Vocational Technical School AR
Okaloosa County Schools FL
Okaloosa Walton Community College FL
Okaloosa Walton Junior College FL
Okeanos Ocean Research Foundation
Oklahoma Assistive Technology Center
Oklahoma Baptist University
Oklahoma Center for Continuing Education
Oklahoma Christian College
Oklahoma City Community College
Oklahoma City Metropolitan Library System
Oklahoma City Public Schools
Oklahoma City University
Oklahoma Coll of Osteopathic Medicine and Surgery
Oklahoma College of Liberal Arts
Oklahoma Consortium on Research Development
Oklahoma County Libraries System
Oklahoma Northwest Area Vocational Technical Sch
Oklahoma Regents Loan Fund
Oklahoma Rehabilitation Service
Oklahoma State Department of Education
Oklahoma State Department of Libraries
Oklahoma State Regents
Oklahoma State Tech
Oklahoma State Univ Technical Branch Okmulgee
Oklahoma State University
Oklahoma Vocational Association
Oklahomans for Indian Opportunity
Old Dominion University VA
Old Swinford Hospital School (England)
Old Town San Diego State Historic Park
Old Town School System ME
Oliver High School PA
Olivet College MI
Olivet Nazarene College IL
Olney Central College IL
Olympia Community Unit District 16 IL
Olympia Technical Community College WA
Olympia Vocational Technical Institute WA
Olympic College WA
Omaha Magic Theatre
Omaha Power District

Omaha Public Schools NE
Onan Corporation
One Voice The Canadian Seniors Network
Oneida Consolidated School District NY
Oneida Indian Reservation WI
Online Database Information Network
Onondaga County Public Library System NY
Ontario CAI Network (Canada)
Ontario Camp Leadership Centre
Ontario Colleges of Applied Arts and Technology
Ontario Council for Leadership Educ Admin Ontario
Ontario Council on University Affairs
Ontario Curriculum Institute (Canada)
Ontario Department of Education (Canada)
Ontario Department of Labour (Canada)
Ontario Educ Communications Authority (Canada)
Ontario Institute for Studies in Education
Ontario Science Center (Canada)
Ontario University System
Oo Za We Kwun Center Inc (Canada)
Open College of Further Education (Australia)
Open Learning Agency BC
Open Learning Institute BC
Open Learning Institute of Hong Kong
Open University (Great Britain)
Open University (Israel)
Open University (Netherlands)
Open University of Sri Lanka
Opinion Research Corporation
Opportunities Industrialization Centers
Opportunities Industrialization Centers of America
Opportunity Funding Corporation
Oral Roberts University OK
Orange Coast College CA
Orange Coast Junior College District CA
Orange County Consortium
Orange County Outdoor School CA
Orange County Public Libraries CA
Orange County Public Schools FL
Orange Unified School District CA
Orangeburg School District 5 SC
ORBIT
Orchard School for Retarded Children IL
Orchard View Community School MI
Order of Woodcraft Chivalry
Oregon Business Education Council
Oregon College of Education
Oregon Community College System
Oregon Consortium for Student Success
Oregon Council for Computer Education
Oregon Council for the Social Studies
Oregon Curriculum Study Center
Oregon Educational Media Association
Oregon Health Sciences University
Oregon Institute of Technology
Oregon Parent Training Network
Oregon School Study Council
Oregon State Correctional Institution
Oregon State Department of Education
Oregon State Library
Oregon State Prison College
Oregon State Regional Network
Oregon State School for the Deaf
Oregon State System of Higher Education
Oregon State University
Oregon Teacher Standards and Practices Commission
Oregon Technical Institute
Orem Public Library UT
Organisation for Economic Cooperation Development
Organization Concerned about Rural Education
Organization for Rehabilitation Through Training
Organization of African Unity
Organization of American States
Organization of Petroleum Exporting Countries
Organization of Unemployed Teachers
ORI Inc
Orillia Public Library (Canada)
Orion Community PA
Orlando Regional Medical Center FL
Orleans Niagara Board Coop Educ Services NY
Orleans Southwest School District VT
Osburn School NY
Oscar Rose Junior College OK
Oslo Work Research Institute (Norway)
Osseo School District MN
Otego Unadillo Central School District NY
Ottawa Board of Education ON
Ottawa High School IL
Ottawa Public Library (Canada)
Ottawa University KS
Otterbein College OH
Ottumwa Community School District IA
Ottumwa Regional Center IA
Our Lady of the Lake College TX
Our Lady of the Lake University of San Antonio TX
Outdoor Learning Laboratory NY
Outdoor Recreation Resources Review Commission
Outreach Mobile Delivery System NY
Outward Bound School ME
Outward Bound Sea School (England)
Over 60 Counseling and Employment Service
Overseas Development Ministry
Overseas Education Service
Owego Apalachin Central School District NY
Owen Sound Public Library (Canada)
Owen Withee School District WI
Owensboro City School System KY
Owensboro Community College KY
Owensboro Daviess County Public Library KY
Oxford Hills High School ME
Oxford Polytechnic (England)
Oxnard College CA
Oxnard School District CA
Oxnard Union High School District CA
Ozarka Vocational Technical School AR
P K Yonge Laboratory School
Pace University NY
PACER Center MN
Pacific Circle Consortium
Pacific Educational Computer Network
Pacific High School CA
Pacific Information Center (Fiji)
Pacific Lutheran University WA
Pacific Northwest Bibliographic Center
Pacific Oaks College and Childrens School CA
Pacific Region Educational Laboratory
Pacific Telecommunications Council
Pacific University OR
Pacifica Foundation
Pacoima Elementary School CA
Paddock School (Great Britain)
Pahlavi National Library (Iran)
Pahlavi University (Iran)
Paine College GA
Paint Creek Youth Center OH
Pajajaran State University (Indonesia)
Pajaro Valley Unified School District CA
Pako Corporation
Palatine High School IL
Palestine Liberation Organization
Palm Beach County Schools FL
Palm Beach Junior College FL
Palmer Memorial Institute NC
Palmetto High School FL
Palo Alto Unified School District CA
Palomar College CA
Palos Hills Consol High School District 230 IL
Palos Verdes Peninsula Unified School District CA
Palouse School District WA
Pan American Federation of Medical Schools
Pan American Health Organization
Pan American University TX
Panel of Consultants on Vocational Education
Panhandle State University OK
Panjab University (India)
Papago Indian Reservation AZ
Papua New Guinea Library Association
Papua New Guinea University of Technology
Paradise Valley Community College Center AZ
Paradise Valley Unified School District AZ
Paramus Public Schools NJ
Parc Way
Parent Advisory Council for Exceptional Children
Parent Child Development Center TX
Parent Cooperative Preschools International
Parent Information Center IN
Parent Preschool Resource Centre ON
Parent Teacher Association
Parent to Parent of Florida
Parenting Materials Information Center
Parents Anonymous
Parents United for the DC Public Schools
Park College MO
Park Elementary School NE
Park Senior High School MN
Parkdale Senior High School MD
Parker Elementary School MA
Parker High School WI
Parkland College IL
Parkland Regional College SK
Parkrose High School OR
Parkrose School District OR
Parks Job Corps Center
Parkside Junior High School
Parkway North High School
Parkway School District MO
Parliament (United Kingdom)
Parma School District OH
Parmenter School MA
Parsippany High School NJ
Parsons College IA
Partisan Elections
Partners of the Americas
Pasadena City College CA
Pasadena Unified School District CA
PASCAL Data Base
Pasco County School District FL
Pasco Hernando Community College FL
Pasco School District WA
Passaic County Community College NJ
Passaic County Vocational School NJ
Patent Office
Pathway School PA
Patrick Henry Community College VA
Patton State Hospital
Paul D Camp Community College VA
Pawnee Heights School District KS
PDQ Center NJ
Peabody Education Fund
Peabody Institute of Baltimore MD
Peabody Museum
Peace Corps
Pearce Center for Professional Communication SC
Pearl River School District NY
Peat Marwick Mitchell and Company
Peavey Company
Pedagogical University of Caracas (Venezuela)
Pediatric Nurse Associates
Peel Board of Education ON
Peer Intervention Network
Peirce Junior College PA
Peking National Library (China)
Peking Opera (China)
Peking University (China)
Pelham Middle School (England)
Pemberton Township Education Association
Pembroke State University NC
Peninsula College WA
Peninsula School CA
Penitentiary of New Mexico
PENMAS (Indonesia)
Penn Central Company
Penn Harris Madison School Corporation IN
Penn Manor School District PA
Penn State Great Valley PA
Penn Valley Community College MO
Penn Valley School MO
Pennsylvania Advancement School
Pennsylvania Association for Higher Education
Pennsylvania Association for Retarded Children
Pennsylvania Association of Colleges and Univs
Pennsylvania Association of School Administrators
Pennsylvania College of Optometry
Pennsylvania College of Technology
Pennsylvania Cooperative Extension Service
Pennsylvania Council on Vocational Education
Pennsylvania Department of Educ Executive Academy
Pennsylvania Department of Education
Pennsylvania Department of Public Welfare
Pennsylvania Earth Science Teachers Society
Pennsylvania Executive Academy
Pennsylvania Governors School for Teaching
Pennsylvania Governors School for the Agric Sci
Pennsylvania Governors School for the Arts
Pennsylvania Library Association
Pennsylvania Museum
Pennsylvania Public Television Network
Pennsylvania Regional Instructional Syst for Educ
Pennsylvania State College
Pennsylvania State Colleges and Universities
Pennsylvania State Education Association
Pennsylvania State Library
Pennsylvania State University
Pennsylvania State University Beaver Campus
Pennsylvania State University Behrend Campus
Pennsylvania State University Hershey Medical Ctr
Pennsylvania State University New Kensington
Pennsylvania State University Ogontz Campus
Pennsylvania State University Schuylkill Campus
Pensacola Junior College FL
Pension Benefit Guaranty Corporation
Penta County Vocational School OH
People for the American Way
People United for Rural Education
Peoples Bicentennial Commission
Peoples Computer Company
Peoples Friendship University (USSR)
Peoples Law School of British Columbia
Peoria Teacher Education Center
Peoria Unified School District AZ
Pepperdine University CA
Peralta Community College District CA
Perkins School for the Blind MA
Perkins School of Theology TX
Perry Child Development Center MI
Perry Preschool MI
Perth Amboy School District NJ
Perth Central School District NY
Peru State College NE
Peruvian Rural School System (Peru)
Peters Township High School PA
Phanat Nikhom Refugee Camp (Thailand)
Phelps Stokes Foundation of New York
Phi Alpha Delta Law Fraternity
Phi Beta Kappa
Phi Beta Lambda
Phi Delta Kappa
Phi Theta Kappa
Philadelphia Association for Clinical Trials
Philadelphia Association of School Administrators
Philadelphia College of Osteopathic Medicine PA
Philadelphia College of Textiles and Science PA
Philadelphia County Medical Society
Philadelphia Geriatric Center PA
Philadelphia Museum of Art
Philadelphia School District PA
Philadelphia State Hospital PA
Philippine Refugee Processing Center
Phillips Academy MA
Phillips County Community College AR
Phillips Exeter Academy NH
Phillips Foundation
Phillips University OK
Phineas Banning High School CA
Phipps Outdoor Education Center
Phoenix Area Public Health Service AZ
Phoenix College AZ
Phoenix Elementary School District 1 AZ
Phoenix Indian Center AZ
Phoenix Indian High School AZ
Phoenix Union High School District AZ
Phoenix Urban League
Phoenix Zoo AZ
Phoenixville Area School District PA
Physical Science Study Committee
Physically Impaired Association of Michigan
Physics Mathematics Astronomy Library
Pica Library Automation Network
Pickens County School District SC
Piedmont Technical College SC
Piedmont Technical Institute NC
Piedmont University Center of North Carolina
Piedmont Virginia Community College
Pierce College CA
Pierce Community College District 11 WA
Pierre Indian Learning Center SD
Pierre Indian School SD
Pikes Peak Community College CO
Pikes Peak Library District CO
Pikeville College KY
Pima Community College AZ
Pima Maricopa Reservation AZ
Pine Manor Junior College MA
Pine Ridge Boarding School SD
Pine Ridge Indian Reservation SD
Pine to Prairie Cooperative Center MN
Pine View School FL
Pinel School CA
Pinellas County School System FL
Piney Woods Country Life School MS
Pioneer Mental Health Center NE
Pioneer Organization
Pitt County Schools NC
Pitt Technical Institute NC
Pittsburg State University KS
Pittsburg Unified School District KS
Pittsburgh Area Center for Teachers PA
Pittsburgh Chemical Information Center
Pittsburgh Council of Higher Education PA
Pittsburgh Playhouse
Pittsburgh School District PA
Pittsfield School District MA
Plain Public Schools OH
Plainedge Public Library NY

Ricks College ID
Rider College NJ
Ridge Vocational Technical Center FL
Ridgewood High School IL
Right to Read Academy NY
Rikers Island Penitentiary NY
Rikkyo University (Japan)
Riksbibliotekjenesten
Rindge and Latin High School MA
Rindge Technical High School MA
Rio Grande City Independent School District TX
Rio Grande College OH
Rio Grande Community College District OH
Rio Hondo College CA
Rio Hondo Junior College District CA
Rio Linda Elementary School District CA
Rio Linda Union School District CA
Rio Salado Community College AZ
Ripon College WI
Ripon School District WI
Rise Incorporated
River Dell Center NJ
River East School Division 9 MB
Riverheights School MB
Riverina College (Australia)
Riverina College of Advanced Education (Australia)
Riverina Murray Inst of Higher Educ (Australia)
Riverside Community College CA
Riverside Community College District CA
Riverside County Schools CA
Riverside Junior College CA
Riverside Research Institute
Riverside Unified School District CA
Road Transport Industry Training Board
Roan Selection Trust
Roane State Community College TN
Roanoke City Schools VA
Roanoke College VA
Roanoke County Schools VA
Robarts School ON
Robbins Committee
Robert C Markham Elementary School FL
Robert Kennedy Youth Center WV
Robert Morris College IL
Robert Morris College PA
Robert R Moton Memorial Institute
Robert W Woodruff Library for Advanced Studies
Robert Wood Johnson Foundation
Roberto Clemente High School IL
Roberts Wesleyan College NY
Rochdale College (Canada)
Rochester City School District NY
Rochester Community Schools MI
Rochester Consortium MN
Rochester Institute of Technology NY
Rochester Public Library NY
Rochester Public Schools MN
Rochester School for the Deaf NY
Rock Point Community School AZ
Rock Point Experimental School
Rock Valley College IL
Rockbridge County Public Schools VA
Rockdale County Public Schools GA
Rockefeller Commission on the Humanities
Rockefeller Foundation
Rockford School of Medicine IL
Rockhurst College MO
Rockland Community College MD
Rockland Community College NY
Rockland County Center Occupational Education NY
Rockland County Schools MA
Rockland Project School NY
Rockwell International Corporation
Rocky Boy Reservation MT
Rocky Mountain Educational Laboratory
Rocky Mountain Regional Resource Center
Rocky Mountain School Study Council
Roddenbery Memorial Library GA
Rodman Job Corps Center
Roger Clark Ballard Memorial School KY
Roger Ludlow High School CT
Roger Tory Peterson Institute of Natural History
Roger Williams College RI
Rogers Environmental Education Center NY
Rollins College FL
Rolls Royce
Roman Catholic Church
Romana Riley Elementary School GA
Roosevelt High School MN
Roosevelt Junior High School OR
Roosevelt Public Schools NY
Roosevelt University IL
Roper Organization
Rosary College IL
Rosary Hill College NY
Rose Hill Junior High School WA
Rosebud Reservation
Rosemary Kennedy Center NY
Rosenberg Foundation
Roseville Area Schools MN
Rosholt High School WI
Rosholt Public Schools WI
Roskilde University Center (Denmark)
Roslyn High School NY
Rossville Alvin School District IL
Rostock University (East Germany)
Roswell Independent School District NM
Rotary Foundation
Rotterdam Medical Faculty (Netherlands)
Rough Rock Demonstration School AZ
Round Meadow Outdoor Learning Laboratory School MD
Round Rock Independent School District TX
Round Table of Editors of Library Journals
Round Valley High School CA
Rowland Unified School District CA
Roxbury Community College MA
Roxbury Latin School MA
Roxbury Learning Center MA
Royal Air Force (England)
Royal Australian Navy
Royal College of Music at Stockholm (Sweden)
Royal College of Physicians and Surgeons of Canada
Royal Danish School of Educ Studies (Denmark)
Royal Doctor Flying Service (Australia)
Royal Holloway College (England)
Royal Institute of Technology (Sweden)
Royal Institution of Cornwall (England)
Royal Naval School (England)
Royal Navy (England)
Royal New Zealand Foundation for the Blind
Royal Society for Prevention of Cruelty to Animals
Royal Society of Arts (England)
Royal Society of Arts Examinations Board (England)
Royal Spanish Academy
Royal Typewriter Company
Ruhr Universitat (West Germany)
Rum River Special Education Cooperative MN
Rural Advisory Service (New Zealand)
Rural Clearinghouse for Lifelong Educ and Dev KS
Rural Clinical Nurse Placement Center CA
Rural Communities Educational Cooperative TN
Rural Connection
Rural Development Committee
Rural Education Association
Rural Ministry Resources
Rural Transition Center
Rural Virginia Development Foundation
Rusden State College (Australia)
Rush Medical College IL
Rush Presbyterian Saint Lukes Medical Center IL
Rush University IL
Ruskin College (England)
Russell Conwell Middle Magnet School
Russell County Public Schools VA
Russell Independent School District 418 MN
Russell Sage College NY
Russell Sage Foundation
Russian Studies Center for Secondary Schools
Rutgers the State University Camden NJ
Rutgers The State University Douglass College NJ
Rutgers the State University Livingston Coll NJ
Rutgers the State University New Brunswick NJ
Rutgers the State University Newark NJ
Rutgers the State University NJ
Rutland Area Vocational Technical Center VT
Rutland Center GA
Ryder Lake Elementary School
Ryerson Polytechnical Institute (Canada)
Saab Scania Plant
Saanich School District BC
Sac and Fox Reservation IA
Sacramento City College CA
Sacramento City Unified School District CA
Sacramento County Office of Education CA
Sacramento State College CA
Saddleback College CA
Saddleback Community College CA
Safety Harbor Exceptional Student Center FL
Saginaw City School System MI
Saginaw Junior College MI
Saginaw Student Rights Center MI
Saginaw Valley State College MI
Saginaw Valley State University MI
Saglouc Community Center (Canada)
Sainik Schools (India)
Saint Andrews Presbyterian College NC
Saint Anselm College NH
Saint Augustine College NC
Saint Augustine Community College IL
Saint Augustine School for the Arts NY
Saint Augustines Center for American Indians
Saint Boniface School Division MB
Saint Cecilia Elementary School CA
Saint Clair County Community College MI
Saint Clair County Teachers Institute IL
Saint Cloud Audiovisual Center
Saint Cloud School District MN
Saint Cloud State College MN
Saint Cloud State University MN
Saint Edwards University TX
Saint Elizabeth Hospital IN
Saint Elizabeth Hospital Medical Center OH
Saint Elizabeths Hospital DC
Saint Francis Xavier University (Canada)
Saint James Head Start Center WA
Saint Johns College MD
Saint Johns College NM
Saint Johns University MN
Saint Johns University NY
Saint Josephs College IN
Saint Josephs School for the Deaf NY
Saint Josephs University PA
Saint Lawrence College (Canada)
Saint Lawrence University NY
Saint Leo College FL
Saint Leonards of the Holy Child PA
Saint Louis City School District MO
Saint Louis Community College at Meramec MO
Saint Louis Community College MO
Saint Louis Evaluation and Training Center
Saint Louis Hearing and Speech Center
Saint Louis Junior College District MO
Saint Louis Regional Library Network MO
Saint Louis University MO
Saint Lukes College (England)
Saint Martin Parish School Board LA
Saint Mary Center for Learning
Saint Mary College KS
Saint Mary of the Woods College IN
Saint Marys Area High School PA
Saint Marys College IN
Saint Marys College MN
Saint Marys College of California
Saint Marys College of Maryland
Saint Marys County Public Schools MD
Saint Marys Dominican College LA
Saint Marys High School AK
Saint Marys Hospital AZ
Saint Marys Junior College MN
Saint Marys University at Halifax (Canada)
Saint Marys University NS
Saint Marys University of San Antonio TX
Saint Meinrad College IN
Saint Michael Hospital WI
Saint Michaels Special School AZ
Saint Norbert College WI
Saint Olaf College MN
Saint Paul Open School
Saint Paul Public Library System MN
Saint Paul Public Schools MN
Saint Paul Technical Vocational Institute MN
Saint Pauls School NH
Saint Peters College NJ
Saint Petersburg Independent
Saint Petersburg Junior College Clearwater FL
Saint Petersburg Junior College FL
Saint Philips College TX
Saint Viator High School
Saint Vrain Valley Public Schools CO
Salem County Vocational Technical Schools NJ
Salem Public Schools MA
Salem Public Schools OR
Salem State College MA
Salem Teikyo University WV
Salesian Society
Salinas Union High School District CA
Salisbury State College MD
Salish Kootenai College MT
Salkehatchie Consortium SC
Salt Lake City School District UT
Salt Lake Community College UT
Salt Lake Community High School UT
Salvation Army
Sam Houston State University TX
Sam Rayburn Library TX
Samford University AL
San Antonio College TX
San Antonio Independent School District TX
San Antonio Urban Educ Development Center TX
San Bernardino Valley College CA
San Carlos Apache Reservation AZ
San Carlos School District AZ
San Diego Adult School CA
San Diego Area Instructional Television Authority
San Diego City College CA
San Diego City Schools Research Cooperative
San Diego Community College CA
San Diego Community College District CA
San Diego Community Colleges CA
San Diego County Department of Education CA
San Diego History Research Center
San Diego Mesa College CA
San Diego Miramar College CA
San Diego State College CA
San Diego State University CA
San Diego Unified School District CA
San Diego Urban League CA
San Elizario Independent School District TX
San Fernando Valley State College CA
San Francisco Art Institute
San Francisco Community College District CA
San Francisco Consortium CA
San Francisco Education Fund CA
San Francisco Neurological Institute CA
San Francisco Public Library CA
San Francisco State College CA
San Francisco State University CA
San Francisco Unified School District CA
San Joaquin Delta College CA
San Joaquin Valley Library System CA
San Jose City College CA
San Jose Evergreen Community College District CA
San Jose Public Library CA
San Jose State College CA
San Jose State University CA
San Jose Unified School District CA
San Juan College NM
San Juan School District UT
San Juan School NM
San Juan Unified School District CA
San Leandro Unified School District CA
San Lorenzo Valley Unified School District CA
San Luis Valley Schools CO
San Marcos Independent School District TX
San Mateo City Schools CA
San Mateo Community College District CA
San Mateo Educational Resources Center CA
San Mateo Union High School District CA
San Quentin Prison
San Rafael City Schools CA
San Ramon Valley Unified School District CA
San Ysidro Elementary School District CA
Sand Springs Public Schools OK
Sanders Associates Inc
Sandhills Community College NC
Sands Point Country Day School NY
Sandy Union High School District 2 OR
Sanford Public Schools ME
Sangamon State University IL
Santa Ana College CA
Santa Ana Police Department CA
Santa Barbara City College CA
Santa Barbara Community Career Development Council
Santa Barbara Community College CA
Santa Barbara County Child Development Center CA
Santa Barbara County Schools CA
Santa Barbara Unified School District CA
Santa Clara County Health Department
Santa Clara County Library CA
Santa Clara County Office of Education CA
Santa Clara Pueblo NM
Santa Clara Unified School District CA
Santa Clara University CA
Santa Clarita Community College District CA
Santa Fe Community College FL
Santa Fe Community College NM
Santa Fe Correctional Farm
Santa Fe Mountain Center NM
Santa Monica College CA
Santa Monica Hospital Medical Center CA
Santa Monica Unified School District CA
Santa Rosa Junior College CA
Santiago Library System CA
Sapporo University (Japan)
Sarah Lawrence College NY
Sarasota County Schools FL

Southern Alberta Institute of Technology
Southern Arkansas University
Southern Assn of Land Grant Colls State Univs
Southern Association for Institutional Research
Southern Association of Colleges and Schools
Southern Association on Children Under Six
Southern California College of Optometry
Southern California Consortium Community Coll TV
Southern California Edison Company
Southern California Regional Occupational Center
Southern Christian Leadership Conference
Southern College of Optometry TN
Southern College of Technology GA
Southern Colorado State College
Southern Conference on Language Teaching
Southern Connecticut State College
Southern Council on Collegiate Educ for Nursing
Southern Early Childhood Association
Southern Education Foundation
Southern Education Reporting Service
Southern Farmers Alliance
Southern Hills Developmental Services SD
Southern Historical Association
Southern Illinois Collegiate Common Market
Southern Illinois University
Southern Illinois University Carbondale
Southern Illinois University Edwardsville
Southern Illinois University School of Medicine
Southern Illinois University Springfield
Southern Independent Television
Southern Interstate Nuclear Board
Southern Lehigh School District PA
Southern Maine Vocational Technical Institute
Southern Medical School Consortium
Southern Methodist University TX
Southern Nazarene University OK
Southern Nevada Vocational Technical Center
Southern Newspaper Publishers Association
Southern Oregon State College
Southern Regional Committee for Family Life
Southern Regional Council
Southern Regional Education Board
Southern Regional Media Center for the Deaf
Southern Rural Development Center
Southern Rural Development Center MS
Southern Sociological Society
Southern State College AR
Southern State University AR
Southern Tenant Farmers Union
Southern University LA
Southern University New Orleans LA
Southern Utah State College
Southern Wisconsin Colony and Training School
Southfield School District MI
Southgate Education Association
Southlands College (England)
Southwest and West Central Ed Coop Serv Unit MN
Southwest Baptist University MO
Southwest Council of Foreign Language Teachers
Southwest Educational Development Laboratory
Southwest London College (England)
Southwest Minnesota State College
Southwest Missouri State College
Southwest Missouri State University
Southwest Parent Education Resource Center
Southwest Region Educational Computer Network
Southwest Regional Laboratory
Southwest Regional Media Center for the Deaf
Southwest Regional Resource Center
Southwest Research Institute TX
Southwest Saint Louis Community Mental Health Ctr
Southwest Texas Junior College
Southwest Texas State College
Southwest Texas State University
Southwest Texas Teacher Center
Southwest Virginia Community College
Southwestern Adventist College TX
Southwestern at Memphis TN
Southwestern College CA
Southwestern College NM
Southwestern Community Action Council
Southwestern Cooperative Educational Laboratory
Southwestern Indian Polytechnic Institute NM
Southwestern Library Association
Southwestern Library Interstate Coop Endeavor
Southwestern Michigan College
Southwestern University School of Law CA
Soviet Academy of Sciences
Space Communications Corp
Space Documentation Service
Spanish Family Guidance Center FL
Spanish International Network
Spanish Royal Academy
Spartacus Youth League
Spartanburg Methodist College SC
Spartanburg Technical College SC
Spartanburg Technical Education Center SC
Special Action Office for Drug Abuse Prevention
Special Education Student Information Network PA
Special Education Training and Resource Center NY
Special Libraries Association
SpecialNet
Spectrum Healthcare Solutions Inc
Speech Arts League
Speech Association of America
Speech Communication Association
Speech Improvement Project of Philadelphia
Spelman College GA
Spencer Foundation
Spencerport Central School District NY
Spertus College of Judaica IL
SPICE Center WV
Spirit River School Division AB
Spokane Area Vocational Skills Center WA
Spokane Community College WA
Spokane Public Schools WA
Spokane Public Telecommunications Center WA
Spoon River College IL
Sprachberatungsdienst
Spring Arbor College MI
Spring Branch Elementary Schools TX
Spring Branch School District TX
Spring Garden Elementary School PA
Spring Hill College AL
Spring Independent School District TX
Springfield Avenue Community School NJ
Springfield City Library MA
Springfield City Schools OH
Springfield Clark Joint Vocational School OH
Springfield College MA
Springfield Day Nursery System MA
Springfield Junior College MA
Springfield Public Schools IL
Springfield Public Schools MA
Springfield Public Schools MO
Squibb College NJ
SREB Vocational Education Consortium
Sri Lanka Institute of Distance Education
Stamford High School CT
Standard Oil Company
Standing Conference National University Libraries
Standing Rock Community College ND
Standing Rock Sioux Reservation ND
Stanford Center for R and D in Teaching CA
Stanford Research Institute CA
Stanford University CA
Stanly Technical College NC
Staples Area Vocational Technical School MN
Staples Governing Board CT
Staples Teacher Center MN
Stark Technical College OH
Starr Commonwealth Schools
State Center Community College District CA
State Central Scientific Medical Library (USSR)
State College Area Parks and Recreation Department
State College Area School District PA
State College of Iowa
State College of Victoria (Australia)
State College of Victoria at Hawthorn (Australia)
State Community College of East Saint Louis IL
State Council of Higher Education for Virginia
State Employment Security Service Agency
State Fair Community College MO
State Higher Education Executive Officers Assn
State Historical Society of Wisconsin
State Occupational Information Coordinating Comm
State School Library Media Supervisors Assn
State Technical Institute at Memphis TN
State University New York Librarians Association
State University of Ghent (Belgium)
State University of Leiden (Netherlands)
State University of Nebraska
State University of New York
State University of New York Albany
State University of New York Amherst
State University of New York Binghamton
State University of New York Buffalo
State University of New York Coll at Brockport
State University of New York Coll at Buffalo
State University of New York Coll at Cortland
State University of New York Coll at Fredonia
State University of New York Coll at Geneseo
State University of New York Coll at New Paltz
State University of New York Coll at Old Westbury
State University of New York Coll at Oneonta
State University of New York Coll at Oswego
State University of New York Coll at Plattsburgh
State University of New York Coll at Potsdam
State University of New York Coll at Purchase
State University of New York Empire State Coll
State University of New York Stony Brook
State University of NY Agric Tech Coll Alfred
State University of NY Agric Tech Coll Canton
State University of NY Agric Tech Coll Delhi
State University of NY Agric Tech Coll Morrisville
State University of NY Coll of Techn Farmingdale
State University of NY Inst of Techn at Utica Rome
State University of Utrecht (Netherlands)
State University System of Florida
Statewide Instructional Computing Network NY
Statewide Job Placement Service MO
Station CMS TV MO
Station KCET TV CA
Station KCMW FM MO
Station KDIN TV IA
Station KETC TV MO
Station KFME TV ND
Station KIXE CA
Station KLRN TX
Station KMOX TV MO
Station KOAC TV OR
Station KOAP TV OR
Station KOCE TV CA
Station KPEC WA
Station KPFT Radio TX
Station KPTS TV
Station KQED CA
Station KSL TV UT
Station KTCA TV MN
Station KTCI TV MN
Station KTWU TV KS
Station KUAT TV
Station KWMK TV
Station WABE FM
Station WEFM IL
Station WETA TV DC
Station WFIL TV
Station WFIU FM IN
Station WGBH TV MA
Station WHDH TV
Station WHS TV
Station WJA TV
Station WKNO TV TN
Station WKRS IL
Station WMUL TV WV
Station WMVS TV
Station WNDU TV
Station WNYC NY
Station WNYE FM NY
Station WPSX TV PA
Station WQED TV PA
Station WSWP TV WV
Station WTTW TV IL
Station WVPT TV VA
Station WWVU TV WV
Station WXXI TV NY
Station WYES TV LA
Stayton School District 77J OR
Stephan F Austin State University TX
Stephen F Austin State University TX
Stephens College MO
Sterling College KS
Sterling Learning Center DC
Stetson University FL
Stevens Institute of Technology NJ
Stewart Indian School NV
Stillman College AL
Stillwater City School District OK
Stillwater State Prison
Stirling University (Scotland)
Stockholm School of Education (Sweden)
Stockton College
Stockton State College NJ
Stockton Unified School District CA
Stockton Unified School District KS
Stockwell College of Education (England)
Stonehill College MA
Stony Acres Inc PA
Storms Street School NJ
Stoughton Area School District WI
Stout State University WI
Stout Vocational Rehabilitation Institute WI
Stow College of Engineering (England)
Strayer College DC
Streetwork
Strelley Community School (Australia)
Stride Rite Intergenerational Day Care Center MA
Strong Vincent Comprehensive High School
Strongsville Public Schools OH
Structure of Intellect Institute
Student Advisory Board PA
Student American Medical Association
Student Assessment Consortium
Student California Teachers Association
Student Coalition for Action in Literacy Education
Student Library Assistants of Wisconsin
Student Loan Insurance Fund
Student Loan Marketing Association
Student National Education Association
Student National Medical Association
Student Nonviolent Coordinating Committee
Student Press Law Center DC
Student Press Service
Students for a Democratic Society
Study Commission on Space Science Education
Sturt College of Advanced Education (Australia)
Suburban Washington Library Film Service
Sue Bennett College KY
Suffolk County Community College NY
Suffolk County Community College NY Eastern Campus
Suffolk Law School MA
Suffolk University MA
Suicide Information and Educ Centre AB
Sukhothai Thammathirat Open University (Thailand)
Sullins College VA
Sullivan County Community College NY
Sulphur Junior and Senior High School OK
Sultan Qaboos University (Oman)
SUMMA Consortium
Summer Institute of Linguistics
Summer Youth Service Corps
Summerhill School
Summit Public Schools NJ
Sumter Area Technical College SC
Sun Valley Ski School
Sunburst Communications
Sunday Evening String Quartet
Sunderland Polytechnic (England)
Sunland Training Center FL
Sunny Side School District AZ
Superconducting Super Collider Laboratory
Superior School District WI
Supranational Communication Research Center
Supreme Court
Supreme Court of Canada
Surface Warfare Officers School RI
Surrey School District 36 BC
Surrey Schools (England)
Surry Community College NC
Sveriges Radio
Swarthmore College PA
Swedish Broadcasting Corporation
Swedish Institute for Childrens Books
Swedish International Development Authority
Swedish Metal Trades Employers Association
Swedish National Parent School Association
Swedish National Union of Students
Swedish Parliamentary Library
Sweet Briar College VA
Sweet Street Academy
Sweetwater County School District Number 2 WY
Sweetwater Union High School District CA
Sycamore High School
Sydney Public Library (Australia)
Sydney Teachers College (Australia)
Synanon
Synanon School
Syosset High School NY
Syphax School DC
Syracuse City Schools NY
Syracuse Model City Agency
Syracuse University NY
System Development Corporation
Tabriz University (Iran)
Tacoma Area Council on Giftedness WA

Tacoma Community College District 22 WA
Tacoma Community College WA
Tacoma Public School District WA
Tactical Air Command
TACTICS
TAFE National Centre for Research and Development
Taft College CA
Talent Corps
Talent Education Summer School (Japan)
Talking Typewriter Center NY
Talladega College AL
Talladega County Schools AL
Tallahassee Community College FL
Tamagawa University (Japan)
Tamalpais Union High School District CA
Tamaqua Area School District PA
Tampa Bay Council for Improving College Teaching
Tampa College FL
Tanganyika African National Union
Tanta University (Egypt)
Tanzania Library Service
Tarboro High School NC
Tarkio College MO
Tarleton State University TX
Tarrant County Junior College TX
Task Force on Education for Economic Growth
Task Force on Graduate Medical Education (AAMC)
Task Force on Integration of Hearing Impaired
Task Force on Women Minorities Handicapped
Task Force on Youth Development Community Prog
Task Force Public Private Sector Interaction
Tata Institute of Fundamental Research (India)
Taunton Literacy Corps MA
Tavistock Institute of Human Relations (England)
Taylor Business Institute NY
Taylor Murphy Institute VA
Taylor Public Schools MI
Taylor University IN
Teacher Corps
Teacher Education Alliance for Metro
Teacher Evaluation and Assessment Center FL
Teachers and Writers Collaborative
Teachers Centers Exchange
Teachers Insurance and Annuity Association
Teachers National Field Task Force
Teachers of English to Speakers of Other Languages
Teaching Assistants Association
Teaching Film Custodians (Association)
Teaching Methods Matls Centre (Papua New Guinea)
Teamsters Union
Technical Education College System
Technical Report Service
Technical School of the Air
Technical Teachers College (Australia)
Technical University of Vienna (Austria)
Technikon M L Sultan (South Africa)
Technion Israel Institute of Technology
Technology Student Association
Teesside Polytechnic (England)
Tel Aviv Public Schools (Israel)
Tel Aviv University (Israel)
Tele Universite PQ
Telecommunications Ad Hoc Task Force IL
Telemedicine Centre NF
Telephone Pioneer of America
Teleprompter Corporation
Television Information Office
Television Licensing Center
Television News Exchange
Television Research Committee
Television Research Evanston
Television Training Center (West Germany)
Television Training Institute
Telstar Regional High School ME
Temple Buell College CO
Temple City Unified School District CA
Temple Israel OH
Temple University PA
Tenafly Public Schools NJ
Tennessee A and I University
Tennessee Appalachia Educational Cooperative
Tennessee Area Vocational Technical Schools
Tennessee College Womens Sports Federation
Tennessee Higher Education Commission
Tennessee Re Education Institute
Tennessee Research Coordinating Unit
Tennessee School for the Blind
Tennessee School for the Deaf
Tennessee State Department of Education
Tennessee State University
Tennessee Technological University
Tennessee Valley Authority
Tennessee Wesleyan College
Tennis Incorporated
Terence Cardinal Cooke Health Care Center NY
Terraset School VA
Terre Haute Normal School
TESL Canada
TESL Materials Development Center
Test User Qualifications Working Group
Texarkana Community College TX
Texarkana Schools TX
Texas A and I University
Texas A and M University
Texas A and M University Kingsville
Texas Academy of Family Physicians
Texas Agricultural Experiment Station
Texas Agricultural Extension Service
Texas Association for Graduate Education Research
Texas Association of Chicanos in Higher Education
Texas Association of Community Schools
Texas Association of Educational Technology
Texas Central Education Agency
Texas Chiropractic College
Texas Christian University
Texas College and University System
Texas College of Osteopathic Medicine
Texas Computer Education Association
Texas Council on Migrant Labor
Texas Department of Community Affairs
Texas Department of Corrections
Texas Department of Human Resources
Texas Education Agency
Texas Education Computer Cooperative
Texas Education Desegregation Tech Asst Ctr
Texas Educational Television Association
Texas Employment Commission
Texas Information Service
Texas Instruments
Texas Junior College Teachers Association
Texas Learning Technology Group
Texas Migrant Educational Development Center
Texas Reading Club
Texas School for the Blind
Texas School for the Deaf
Texas Schools Inc
Texas Small Schools Association
Texas Small Schools Project
Texas Southern University
Texas Southern University School of Pharmacy
Texas Southmost College
Texas State Board of Education
Texas State Library
Texas State Technical College
Texas State Technical College Waco
Texas State Technical Institute
Texas State Technical Institute Sweetwater
Texas System of Higher Education
Texas Tech University
Texas Technological College
Texas Wesleyan University
Texas Womans University
Texas Womens Prison at Goree
Thacher School CA
The Dalles School District OR
Thiokol Chemical Corporation
Thomas A Edison High School PA
Thomas County School District GA
Thomas Edison Elementary School CA
Thomas Jefferson College MI
Thomas Jefferson High School FL
Thomas Jefferson High School PA
Thomas Jefferson University PA
Thomas Nelson Community College VA
Thomson Foundation College (England)
Thornlea Secondary School (Canada)
Thornton Community College IL
Thornton High School
Thornton Township High School IL
Thousand Oaks Elementary School CA
Three Four Five Club
Three Rivers Community College MO
Thunderbird Grad School of Intl Management
Thut (I N) World Education Center CT
TI IN Network TX
Tidewater Community College VA
Tigard School District OR
Timonium Elementary School MD
Tipp City Public Schools OH
Toby House
Tokyo Christian Mass Communication Center (Japan)
Tokyo Institute of Technology (Japan)
Toledo Lucas County Public Library OH
Toledo Museum of Art OH
Toledo Public Schools OH
Tom Green County Library System TX
Tom Snyder Productions
Tombigbee Regional Library MS
Tompkins Cortland Community College NY
Top of Alabama Regional Council of Governments
Topic House NY
Toronto Board of Education ON
Toronto Public Library ON
Toronto Public Schools ON
Torrance Unified School District CA
Tougaloo College MS
Town Affiliation Association of the United States
Township High School District 214 IL
Townsville Coll of Advanced Education (Australia)
Towson State University MD
Toyota
Trades Guild of Learning
Trailside School VT
Training Center for Community Programs
Training Outreach Prevention School
Training Research Assistance Cooperative Ext Serv
Training Research Development Station
Training School for Boys NJ
Trans World Airlines
Transition Institute IL
Translators Association of the Philippines
Transylvania College KY
Transylvania University KY
Travelers Insurance
Travis Unified School District CA
Treasure Valley Community College OR
Trent Polytechnic (England)
Trent Valley Center
Trenton High School MO
Trenton Public Schools NJ
Trenton State College NJ
Tri College University Libraries ND
Tri County Regional Library
Tri County Technical College SC
Tri County Technical Institute OH
Tri State Parenting Collaborative
TRIAD Teacher Center IN
Triangle Coalition for Sci and Techn Educ
Triangle Universities Computation Center
Tribal American Children Center Schools
Tribal Normal School (Iran)
Tricameral Board
Trinity Area School District PA
Trinity Christian College IL
Trinity College (Ireland)
Trinity College CT
Trinity College VT
Trinity University TX
Triton College IL
Trowbridge House OH
Troy City School District NY
Troy State University AL
Troy State University AL Montgomery
Truckee Meadows Community College NV
Try Foundation
Tuba City Boarding School AZ
Tuba City Elementary School AZ
Tubutama Mission Church
Tucson Medical Center
Tucson Public Library AZ
Tucson Public Schools AZ
Tufts University MA
Tulane University LA
Tuloso Midway Independent School District TX
Tulsa City County Library System OK
Tulsa Junior College OK
Tulsa Public Schools OK
Tulsa Technology Center OK
Tupelo Public Schools MS
Tuscaloosa County Board of Education AL
Tuscarora Confederacy
Tuscola High School IL
Tuskegee Institute AL
TVOntario
TVOntario Academy
Twente University of Technology (Netherlands)
Twentieth Century Fund
Twentieth Century Fund Task Force
Twin City Institute for Talented Youth MN
Twin Lakes School Corporation IN
Twin Tech PA
Tyler Independent School District 409 MN
Tyler Independent School District TX
Tyson Foods
U S English
UCLA Librarians Association
Udayana University (Indonesia)
Uintah and Ouray Reservation UT
Uintah School District UT
Ukranian Ministry of Education (USSR)
Ulster County Community College NY
Ulster Peoples College (Northern Ireland)
Umatilla County Education Service District OR
Umm Al Qura University (Saudi Arabia)
UNESCO
UNESCO Institute for Education
UNICEF
UNICOR
Unification Church
Unified Network of Informatics in Teacher Educ
Uniformed Services Univ of the Health Sciences MD
Union Carbide
Union College
Union College NJ
Union College NY
Union County College NJ
Union County Regional School District NJ
Union County School District NC
Union County Technical Institute NJ
Union for Experimenting Colleges and Universities
Union Graduate School
Union of the Blind (Yugoslavia)
Union Theological Seminary NY
Union Underwear Corporation
Uniondale Union Free School District NY
UNISIST
Unit for the Development of Adult Continuing Educ
Unitarian Universalist Association
Unitas Therapeutic Community NY
United Aircraft Library System CT
United Arab Emirates University
United Auto Workers
United Campus Ministries
United Campuses to Prevent Nuclear War
United Cannery Agric Pack Allied Workers America
United Cerebral Palsy Association
United Church of Canada
United Church of Christ
United Electric Controls Corporation
United Farm Workers
United Federation of College Teachers
United Federation of Teachers
United Kingdom Chemical Information Service
United Kingdom Ministry Overseas Development
United Kingdom Reading Association
United Methodist Church
United Nations
United Nations Commission on the Status of Women
United Nations Dag Hammarskjold Library
United Nations Economic and Social Council
United Nations Economic Commission for Africa
United Nations Food and Agriculture Organization
United Nations High Commissioner for Refugees
United Nations Institute for Training and Research
United Nations International School
United Nations International University
United Nations Relief and Works Agency
United Nations Research Institute for Social Devel
United Nations Science Tech Policies Inf Exchange
United Nations University (Japan)
United Negro College Fund
United Neighborhood Centers of America
United Neighborhood Houses
United Parents Association
United Planning Organization
United Presbyterian Church
United Press International
United Progress Incorporated
United States Aid Funds Inc
United States Association of Evening Students
United States Committee for Energy Awareness
United States Information Agency
United States Lawn Tennis Association
United States Steel Foundation
United States Time Company
United Steelworkers of America
United Teaching Profession
United Tribes Technical College ND
United University Professions

United Way
Unity College ME
Unity School of Christianity
Universal Colored Peoples Association
Universal Esperanto Association
Universal Studios
Universidad Autonoma B Juarez de Oaxaca (Mexico)
Universidad Autonoma de Madrid (Spain)
Universidad Centroamericana (Nicaragua)
Universidad de Navarra (Spain)
Universidad de Sevilla (Spain)
Universidad Estatal a Distancia (Costa Rica)
Universidad Nacional Abierta (Venezuela)
Universidad Nacional Autonoma de Honduras
Universidad Nacional Autonoma de Nicaragua
Universidad Nacional de Educ a Distancia (Spain)
Universidad Nacional de La Plata (Argentina)
Universidad Pedagogica Libertador (Venezuela)
Universidad Popular IL
Universidad Simon Bolivar (Venezuela)
Universidad Tecnica del Estado (Chile)
Universitas 45 (Indonesia)
Universitas Terbuka (Indonesia)
Universite de Neuchatel (Switzerland)
Universities Council (Netherlands)
Universities Council for Adult Education (England)
Universities Field Staff International
Universities Industry Joint Council
Universities Research Association Incorporated
University Affiliated Facilities
University and Community College System of Nevada
University Centers for Rational Alternatives
University City Science Center PA
University College of Cape Breton NS
University College of Rhodesia
University College of Swansea (Wales)
University Consortium Center MI
University Council for Educational Administration
University Council for Training and Development
University Council for Vocational Education
University Council on Educ for Public Respon
University Elementary School CA
University for Man KS
University for Peace (Costa Rica)
University for Youth CO
University Grants Committee (Great Britain)
University Hospitals of Cleveland OH
University Microfilms International
University National Oceanographic Lab System
University of Aarhus (Denmark)
University of Aberdeen (Scotland)
University of Adelaide (Australia)
University of Akron OH
University of Alabama
University of Alabama Birmingham
University of Alabama System
University of Alaska
University of Alaska Anchorage
University of Alaska Fairbanks
University of Alaska Southeast
University of Alberta (Canada)
University of Amsterdam (Netherlands)
University of Antwerp (Belgium)
University of Arizona
University of Arizona Tucson
University of Arkansas
University of Arkansas Fayetteville
University of Arkansas for Medical Sciences
University of Arkansas Little Rock
University of Arkansas Monticello
University of Arkansas Pine Bluff
University of Aston (England)
University of Baltimore MD
University of Baroda (India)
University of Bath (England)
University of Beirut (Lebanon)
University of Benin (Nigeria)
University of Birmingham (England)
University of Bombay (India)
University of Botswana
University of Botswana Lesotho and Swaziland
University of Bradford (England)
University of Bremen (West Germany)
University of Bridgeport CT
University of Bristol (England)
University of British Columbia (Canada)
University of Caldas (Colombia)
University of Calgary (Canada)
University of California
University of California Berkeley
University of California Davis
University of California Irvine
University of California Los Angeles
University of California Riverside
University of California San Diego
University of California San Francisco
University of California Santa Barbara
University of California Santa Clara
University of California Santa Cruz
University of California Santa Cruz Oakes College
University of Cambridge (England)
University of Cambridge Local Exam Synd (England)
University of Canterbury (England)
University of Cape Town (South Africa)
University of Central Arkansas
University of Central Florida
University of Central Queensland (Australia)
University of Central Texas
University of Ceylon
University of Chicago IL
University of Chile Santiago
University of Cincinnati Medical Center OH
University of Cincinnati OH
University of Cincinnati OH University College
University of Colombia
University of Colorado
University of Colorado Boulder
University of Colorado Colorado Springs
University of Colorado Denver
University of Colorado Medical Center
University of Compiegne (France)
University of Connecticut
University of Connecticut Storrs
University of Copenhagen (Denmark)
University of Dacca (Bangladesh)
University of Dallas TX
University of Dar es Salaam (Tanzania)
University of Dayton OH
University of Delaware
University of Denver CO
University of Detroit MI
University of Dijon (France)
University of Dublin (Ireland)
University of Dubuque IA
University of East Africa
University of East Anglia (England)
University of Edinburgh (Scotland)
University of Essex (England)
University of Europe
University of Evansville IN
University of Exeter (England)
University of Findlay OH
University of Florida
University of Genova (Italy)
University of Georgia
University of Glasgow (Scotland)
University of Goettingen (West Germany)
University of Gothenburg (Sweden)
University of Grenoble (France)
University of Guelph (Ontario)
University of Guyana
University of Halle
University of Hartford CT
University of Hawaii
University of Hawaii Community College System
University of Hawaii Hawaii Community College
University of Hawaii Hilo
University of Hawaii Honolulu Community College
University of Hawaii Kapiolani Community College
University of Hawaii Kauai Community College
University of Hawaii Leeward Community College
University of Hawaii Manoa
University of Hawaii Maui Community College
University of Heidelberg (West Germany)
University of Helsinki (Finland)
University of Hong Kong
University of Houston Clear Lake TX
University of Houston TX
University of Houston University Park TX
University of Houston Victoria TX
University of Hull (England)
University of Ibadan (Nigeria)
University of Idaho
University of Illinois
University of Illinois Chicago
University of Illinois Chicago Circle Campus
University of Illinois College of Medicine
University of Illinois Committee on School Math
University of Illinois Medical Center
University of Illinois Urbana Champaign
University of Iowa
University of Jordan
University of Judaism Lee College CA
University of Kansas
University of Kansas Lawrence
University of Kassel (West Germany)
University of Kent at Canterbury (England)
University of Kentucky
University of Kentucky Community College System
University of Khartoum (Sudan)
University of Klagenfurt (Austria)
University of La Verne CA
University of Lagos (Nigeria)
University of Lancaster (England)
University of Leeds (England)
University of Leicester (England)
University of Lethbridge (Canada)
University of Leuven (Belgium)
University of Liege (Belgium)
University of Liverpool (England)
University of Ljubljana (Yugoslavia)
University of London (England)
University of Louisville KY
University of Louvain (Belgium)
University of Lowell MA
University of Lowell MA Instr Telecomm Network
University of Maine
University of Maine Augusta
University of Maine Farmington
University of Maine Orono
University of Maine Portland Gorham
University of Maine Presque Isle
University of Malawi
University of Malaya (Malaysia)
University of Manchester (England)
University of Manila (Philippines)
University of Manitoba (Canada)
University of Mary Hardin Baylor TX
University of Maryland
University of Maryland Baltimore
University of Maryland Baltimore County
University of Maryland College Park
University of Maryland Dental School
University of Maryland Eastern Shore
University of Maryland Professional Schools Campus
University of Maryland School of Medicine
University of Maryland System
University of Maryland University College
University of Massachusetts
University of Massachusetts Amherst
University of Massachusetts Boston
University of Massachusetts Lowell
University of Mauritius
University of Medicine and Dentistry of New Jersey
University of Melbourne (Australia)
University of Miami FL
University of Michigan
University of Michigan Ann Arbor
University of Michigan Dearborn
University of Michigan Flint
University of Michigan Medical School
University of Mid America NE
University of Minnesota
University of Minnesota Crookston
University of Minnesota Duluth
University of Minnesota Minneapolis
University of Minnesota Morris
University of Minnesota Twin Cities
University of Minnesota Waseca
University of Mississippi
University of Mississippi Medical Center
University of Mississippi School of Dentistry
University of Missouri
University of Missouri Columbia
University of Missouri Kansas City
University of Missouri Rolla
University of Missouri Saint Louis
University of Montana
University of Montevallo AL
University of Montpellier (France)
University of Montreal (Quebec)
University of Moratuwa (Sri Lanka)
University of Mostar (Yugoslavia)
University of Munich (West Germany)
University of Munster (West Germany)
University of Mysore (India)
University of Nairobi (Kenya)
University of Nancy (France)
University of Natal (South Africa)
University of Nebraska
University of Nebraska Kearney
University of Nebraska Lincoln
University of Nebraska Medical Center
University of Nebraska Omaha
University of Nevada
University of Nevada Las Vegas
University of Nevada Reno
University of Nevada System
University of New Brunswick
University of New Brunswick (Canada)
University of New England (Australia)
University of New Hampshire
University of New Haven CT
University of New Mexico
University of New Mexico Medical Center Library
University of New Mexico School of Medicine
University of New Orleans LA
University of New South Wales (Australia)
University of Newcastle (Australia)
University of Nigeria
University of Nijmegen (Netherlands)
University of North Alabama
University of North Carolina
University of North Carolina Asheville
University of North Carolina Chapel Hill
University of North Carolina Charlotte
University of North Carolina Greensboro
University of North Carolina Wilmington
University of North Dakota
University of North Dakota Grand Forks
University of North Florida
University of North Texas
University of Northern Colorado
University of Northern Iowa
University of Notre Dame IN
University of Nottingham (England)
University of Oklahoma
University of Oklahoma Health Science Center
University of Oklahoma Norman
University of Omaha NE
University of Oregon
University of Oriente (Venezuela)
University of Oslo (Norway)
University of Otago (New Zealand)
University of Ottawa (Canada)
University of Oxford (England)
University of Paderborn (West Germany)
University of Papua New Guinea
University of Paris (France)
University of Pennsylvania
University of Pennsylvania School Council
University of Pennsylvania Wharton School
University of Phoenix AZ
University of Pittsburgh Johnstown PA
University of Pittsburgh PA
University of Portland OR
University of Puerto Rico
University of Puerto Rico Cayey University College
University of Puerto Rico Ponce Techn Univ Coll
University of Puget Sound WA
University of Qatar
University of Queensland (Australia)
University of Rajasthan (India)
University of Reading (England)
University of Redlands CA
University of Regina SK
University of Rhode Island
University of Rhode Island Foundation
University of Richmond VA
University of Riyadh (Saudi Arabia)
University of Rochester NY
University of Saint Thomas MN
University of San Carlos (Philippines)
University of San Diego CA
University of San Francisco CA
University of Santa Clara CA
University of Santiago (Chile)
University of Saskatchewan (Canada)
University of Science and Arts of Oklahoma
University of Scranton PA
University of Sheffield (England)
University of Sherbrooke ON
University of Singapore
University of Skopje (Yugoslavia)
University of Sokoto (Nigeria)
University of South Africa
University of South Alabama
University of South Australia
University of South Carolina
University of South Carolina Coastal Carolina Coll
University of South Carolina Columbia
University of South Carolina Salkehatchie
University of South Dakota
University of South Florida

University of South Florida Lakeland
University of Southampton (England)
University of Southern California
University of Southern Colorado
University of Southern Maine
University of Southern Mississippi
University of Southern Queensland (Australia)
University of Southwestern Louisiana
University of Stellenbosch (South Africa)
University of Stockholm (Sweden)
University of Strathclyde (Scotland)
University of Surrey (England)
University of Sussex (England)
University of Sydney (Australia)
University of Tampa FL
University of Tampere (Finland)
University of Tasmania (Australia)
University of Technology (Iraq)
University of Technology Sydney (Australia)
University of Tehran (Iran)
University of Tennessee
University of Tennessee Chattanooga
University of Tennessee Knoxville
University of Tennessee Martin
University of Tennessee Memphis
University of Tennessee Nashville
University of Texas
University of Texas Arlington
University of Texas Austin
University of Texas Dallas
University of Texas El Paso
University of Texas Medical Branch Galveston
University of Texas Medical School Houston
University of Texas Pan American
University of Texas Permian Basin
University of Texas San Antonio
University of Texas System
University of Texas Tyler
University of the Air (India)
University of the Air (Japan)
University of the Americas (Mexico)
University of the Basque Country (Spain)
University of the District of Columbia
University of the East (Philippines)
University of the Negeve (Israel)
University of the North (South Africa)
University of the Pacific CA
University of the Philippines
University of the Philippines Los Banos
University of the Ryukyus (Japan)
University of the Sacred Heart PR
University of the South Pacific (Fiji)
University of the South TN
University of the Virgin Islands
University of the West Indies (Jamaica)
University of the Western Cape (South Africa)
University of the Witwatersrand (South Africa)
University of Toledo OH
University of Toronto (Canada)
University of Tromso (Norway)
University of Trondheim (Norway)
University of Tulsa OK
University of Tulsa School for Gifted Children OK
University of Turku (Finland)
University of Ulster (Northern Ireland)
University of Urbino (Italy)
University of Utah
University of Vermont
University of Victoria BC
University of Virginia
University of Waikato (New Zealand)
University of Washington
University of Waterloo (Ontario)
University of West Florida
University of Western Australia
University of Western Ontario (Canada)
University of Windsor (Canada)
University of Winnipeg (Canada)
University of Wisconsin
University of Wisconsin Center Baraboo Sauk County
University of Wisconsin Center Waukesha County
University of Wisconsin Eau Claire
University of Wisconsin Green Bay
University of Wisconsin La Crosse
University of Wisconsin Madison
University of Wisconsin Manitowoc County
University of Wisconsin Milwaukee
University of Wisconsin Oshkosh
University of Wisconsin Parkside
University of Wisconsin Platteville
University of Wisconsin River Falls
University of Wisconsin Sheboygan
University of Wisconsin Stevens Point
University of Wisconsin Stout
University of Wisconsin Superior
University of Wisconsin System
University of Wisconsin Whitewater
University of Wollongong (Australia)
University of Wyoming
University of Wyoming University School
University of York (England)
University of Zambia
University Research Corporation CO
University School of Milwaukee
University School Shaker Heights OH
University Urban Schools National Task Force
University Within Walls AK
Up with People
Upper Arlington City Schools OH
Upper Cumberland Development District TN
Upper Cumberland Development Organization TN
Upper Iowa University
Upper Midwest Regional Educational Laboratory
Uppsala University (Sweden)
Upsala University NJ
Urban Adult Education Institute MI
Urban Affairs Council
Urban Coalition
Urban Corps
Urban Education Network
Urban Education Task Force
Urban Educational Center
Urban Indian Development Association
Urban Institute
Urban League
Urban Library Trustees Council
Urban Literacy Network
Urban Mississippi River Eco Center
Urban Teacher Corps
Urbana School District IL
Urbandale Community School District
Ursinus College PA
Ursuline College OH
USAir
USENET
Utah Schools for the Deaf and the Blind
Utah Skills Center
Utah State Board of Education
Utah State Hospital
Utah State Industrial School
Utah State Office of Education
Utah State University
Utah Valley Community College
Utica College NY
Utica Community School District MI
Valdosta State College GA
Valencia Community College FL
Vallejo Unified School District CA
Valley City State College ND
Valley Falls Branch Library RI
Valley Forge Military Academy and Junior Coll PA
Valley Migrant League
Valley Public Schools NE
Valley Stream Central High School NY
Valley View School District IL
Valley View School OH
Valley View Youth Center IL
Valparaiso University IN
Van Buren Intermediate School District MI
Van Leer Foundation
Vancouver Board of School Trustees BC
Vancouver City College (Canada)
Vancouver Community College BC
Vancouver School District WA
Vanderbilt University TN
Vanguard Joint Vocational School OH
Vanier College (Canada)
Vassar College NY
Vater Association
Ventura College CA
Ventura Community College District CA
Ventura Unified School District CA
Venus Packaging Limited
Vermilion Local School District OH
Vermilion Parish Schools LA
Vermont College
Vermont Higher Education Council
Vermont State Colleges
Vermont State Department of Education
Vernon Intermediate School TX
Vernon Regional Technical College TX
Vernon Verona Sherrill Central High School NY
Very Special Arts
Vestal Central School District NY
Veszprem University (Hungary)
Veterans Administration
Veterans Administration Lakeside Medical Ctr IL
Viatel (Australia)
Victor Valley College CA
Victoria College (Australia)
Victoria University of Wellington (New Zealand)
Victorian Council of Adult Education
Victorian TAFE Off Campus Network (Australia)
Victorian Technical Schools Division (Australia)
Viejas Reservation
Vienna Correctional Center IL
Vienna School Business and World Trade (Austria)
View Castle School District PA
Vigo County Public Library IN
Vigo County School Corporation IN
Villa Julie College MD
Villa Maria High School PA
Villanova University PA
Vilonia School District AR
Vincennes Open University (France)
Vincennes University IN
Virgin Valley High School NV
Virginia (Charles City County)
Virginia Association for Trade and Industrial Educ
Virginia Beach Schools VA
Virginia Commonwealth University
Virginia Community College System
Virginia Cooperative Extension Service
Virginia Council for the Social Studies
Virginia Department of Education
Virginia Extension Homemakers Council
Virginia Governors Schools
Virginia Higher Education Study Commission
Virginia Highlands Community College
Virginia Library Advisory Committee
Virginia Military Institute
Virginia Polytechnic Inst and State Univ
Virginia Public Telecommunication Council
Virginia State College
Virginia State University
Virginia Teachers Association
Virginia Union University
Virginia Vocational Association
Virginia Western Community College
Vision Educational Foundation
VisionQuest National Ltd
Visiting Nurse Association
Vista College CA
Vista Unified School District CA
VITAL Career Information Center
Vocational Education Consortium of States
Vocational Industrial Clubs of America
Vocational Opportunities Clubs of Texas
Vocational Rehabilitation Administration
Vocational Rehabilitation Ctr Allegheny County NY
Vocational Rotational Laboratory
Vocational Technical Education Consortium States
Vocational Technical Institute KS
Vocational Technical Resource Consortia
Vocational Training Development Inst (Jamaica)
Voice of America
Voice of Free China
Voices for Illinois Children
Voluntary Action Center
Voluntary Equal Employment Opportunity Council
Voluntary Services Overseas (United Kingdom)
Volunteer Library League Incorporated
Volunteer Military Rejectee Program
Volunteer The National Center
Volunteers in Service to America
Volunteers in Service to America Literacy Corps
Volunteers Upholding Education
Volusia County Schools FL
Voorhees College SC
Voucher Agency for Teachers
Voyaguer Outward Bound School
Vrije University (Netherlands)
Vulnerable Child Committee
Wabash College IN
Wabash Valley Supplementary Educational Center
Wadena Public School District MN
Wagner College NY
Wahpeton Indian School ND
Waikato College of Teacher Education (New Zealand)
Wake County Public School System NC
Wake Forest University NC
Wake Forest University School of Law NC
Wake Technical College NC
Walbridge Academy
Walbrook High School MD
Walden University FL
Waldorf Astoria Company
Waldorf Schools
Walker Art Center MN
Walkulla County Schools FL
Walla Walla College WA
Walla Walla Community College WA
Wallace Community College AL Selma
Wallace State Community College AL Hanceville
Wallen School of Language (Canada)
Walpole Public Schools MA
Walsh College OH
Walt Disney Studios
Walter H Boyd High School CA
Walters State Community College TN
Wang Institute of Graduate Studies MA
Wang Laboratories MA
Wantagh Public Schools NY
War Against Rape (Pakistan)
Ware High School
Wark Committee
Warm Springs Reservation OR
Warner Brothers
Warner Eddison Associates
Warner Elementary School
Warner Pacific College OR
Warren City Schools OH
Warren County Public Schools NC
Warren Education Association
Warren Township Independent School District IN
Warren Wilson College NC
Warwick High School VA
Wascana Institute (Saskatchewan)
Wasco Public Schools CA
Washburn University of Topeka KS
Washington Academy NY
Washington and Jefferson College PA
Washington and Lee University VA
Washington Area Peace Studies Network DC
Washington Center DC
Washington College MD
Washington Consortium of Universities
Washington County School District TN
Washington County School District UT
Washington Education Association
Washington Federation of Independent Schools
Washington High School AZ
Washington Highland Community School DC
Washington Hospital School of Nursing
Washington Junior High School WI
Washington Library Network
Washington Occupational Information System
Washington Office of Superintendent of Pub Instr
Washington Postsecondary Education Commission
Washington Research Foundation
Washington Research Organization
Washington State Community College System
Washington State Educational Service District 105
Washington State Library
Washington State University
Washington Technical Institute DC
Washington University MO
Washington West Resource Center VT
Washoe County School District NV
Washtenaw Community College MI
Waskaganish Community PQ
Watauga County Schools NC
Water Quality Administration
Water Resources Council
Waterbury State Technical College CT
Waterford School UT
Waterford Township High School MA
Watergate Sterling Learning Center IL
Waterloo County Roman Catholic Sep Sch Bd ON
Watertown Public Schools MA
Waterville Senior High School ME
Watseka Community High School IL
Waubonsee Community College IL
Waukegan School District IL
Waukesha County Technical College WI
Waukesha County Technical Institute WI
Waukesha High School WI
Waukesha School District WI
Waupun School District WI
Waycross Independent School System GA
Wayland High School MA
Wayne Community College NC
Wayne County Child Development Center
Wayne County Community College MI
Wayne County Intermediate School District MI

Wayne General and Technical College OH
Wayne State College NE
Wayne State University MI
Wayside School for Girls NY
Weatherford Hammond Mountain Collection
Weaver Union Elementary School District CA
Webb School CA
Weber School District UT
Weber State College UT
Webster College MO
Webster School DC
Webster Springs High School WV
Webster University MO
Weirton Steel
Weizmann Institute of Science (Israel)
Weld County School District CO
Wellesley College MA
Wellesley Public Schools MA
Wellington Polytechnic (New Zealand)
Wellness Council of the Midlands
Wells College NY
Wenatchee Valley College WA
Wennington School
Wentworth Institute of Technology MA
Wescoe Committee
Weslaco Independent School District TX
Wesley College DE
Wesleyan College GA
Wesleyan University CT
West 80th Street Day Care Center NY
West African Examinations Council
West African Library Association
West Bloomfield High School MI
West Bloomfield Schools MI
West Chester School District PA
West Chester State College PA
West Chester University of Pennsylvania
West Essex Extension Center NJ
West Fargo School District ND
West Feliciana Parish School District LA
West Franklin Unified School District KS
West Genesee Central School
West Georgia College
West Hartford Community School CT
West Hartford Public Schools CT
West Haverstraw Rehabilitation Hospital
West Hills Community College CA
West Irondequoit Central School District NY
West Junior High School MI
West Kentucky Education Technology Cooperative
West Kentucky Environmental Educ Consort
West Kern Community College District CA
West Leyden High School IL
West Los Angeles College CA
West Northfield District 31 IL
West Ottawa Public School District MI
West Philadelphia Community Free School PA
West Rowan High School NC
West Shore Community College MI
West Texas State University
West Valley College CA
West Valley Mission Community College District CA
West Valley Occupational Center
West Vancouver Memorial Library (Canada)
West Virginia Arts and Humanities Council
West Virginia College of Graduate Studies
West Virginia Department of Mental Health
West Virginia Education Fund
West Virginia Graduate College
West Virginia Institute of Technology
West Virginia Library Association
West Virginia Model Center
West Virginia Network for Educ Telecomputing
West Virginia Rehabilitation Center
West Virginia Speech Association
West Virginia State College
West Virginia University
West Virginia University Parkersburg
West Virginia Wesleyan College
West York Area School District PA
West Yuma County School District CO
Westchester Community College NY
Western Association of Schools and Colleges
Western Australian College of Advanced Education
Western Australian Institute of Technology
Western Australian Post Secondary Educ Commission
Western Carolina University NC
Western College Association
Western College Reading and Learning Association
Western College Reading Association
Western Cooperative College (Canada)
Western Cooperative for Educ Telecommunications
Western Council on Higher Education for Nursing
Western Electric
Western European Union
Western Illinois University
Western Institute for Distance Education
Western Institute for Science and Technology
Western Interstate Commission for Higher Education
Western Kentucky University
Western Library Network
Western Maryland College
Western Massachusetts Five Coll Pub Sch Partners
Western Michigan University
Western Montana College
Western Montgomery County Area Voc Tech School PA
Western Nebraska Technical College
Western Nevada Community College
Western New England College MA
Western New Mexico University
Western Ontario Field Centre
Western Oregon State College
Western Piedmont Community College NC
Western Psychological Association
Western Regional Council State Leagues of Nursing
Western Regional Resource Center OR
Western Research Application Center
Western Reserve University OH
Western Service Systems Inc
Western Speech Communication Association
Western State College CO
Western State College of Colorado
Western State Hospital VA
Western Union Telegraph Company
Western Washington State College
Western Washington University
Western Wisconsin Technical College
Western Wisconsin Technical Institute
Westfield Public School District NJ
Westfield State College MA
Westinghouse Area Vocational High School IL
Westinghouse Learning Corporation
Westinghouse Nuclear Training Center IL
Westminster College PA
Westminster College UT
Westmont College CA
Westmoreland County Community College PA
Westmoreland County School District VA
Westridge School CA
Westside High School NE
Westside Preparatory School IL
Wetaskiwin School District AB
Wharton County Junior College TX
Whatcom Community College District 21 WA
Whatcom Community College WA
Wheatley School
Wheaton College IL
Wheaton College MA
Wheelersburg Local School District OH
Wheeling School District 21 IL
Wheelock College MA
Whitby Public Library (Canada)
White Earth Indian Reservation MN
White Horse Plain School Division Number 20 MB
White House Fellows
White Memorial Foundation
White Plains School System NY
White River School District WA
White River Vocational Technical School AR
White Shield School ND
Whitehead Biomedical Research Institute
Whiteside Area Vocational Center
Whitman College WA
Whitmer Center
Whittier Union Office Training Center
Whittle Communications Inc
Whitworth College WA
WICAT
Wichita Practical Nursing School KS
Wichita Public Schools KS
Wichita State University KS
Widener University PA
Wilberforce University OH
Wilde Lake High School MD
Wilder School District ID
Wilderness Education Association
Wildfowl Trust
Wildlife Research Center
Wiley College TX
Wilfrid Laurier University OT
Wilkes Barre Area Vocational Technical School PA
Wilkes Barre City Schools PA
Wilkes College PA
Wilkes Community College NC
Wilkes University PA
Will County Jail IL
Willamette University OR
Willamette Valley Education Consortium OR
Willard Elementary School MN
Willcox School District AZ
William Jewell College MO
William Mitchell College of Law MN
William Monroe Trotter School MA
William Paterson State College NJ
William Rainey Harper College IL
William Smith High School CO
Williams College MA
Williamsburg Area Community College PA
Williamsburg County Public Schools SC
Williamsport Area Community College PA
Williamsport Area School District PA
Williamsville School District NY
Willingboro Schools NJ
Wilmington Public Library OH
Wilmington Public Schools DE
Wilmot Junior High School IL
Wilson College (India)
Wilson College PA
Wilson School
Wilton Public Schools CT
Winchester Community School CT
Windber Area School District PA
Windermere School District No 4 BC
Windham Independent School District TX
Windham Planning Region
Windsor High School CT
Windsor Hills Elementary School CA
Windsor Separate School Board ON
Wingate College NC
Winnetka Public Schools IL
Winnipeg Bible College MB
Winnipeg School Division Number 1 MB
Winona Area Technical School MN
Winona School District MN
Winona State College MN
Winona State University MN
Winooski Supervisory School District VT
Winston Churchill Library
Winston Dillard School District OR
Winston Salem and Forsyth County Schools NC
Winston Salem State College NC
Winterthur Museum Library
Winthrop College SC
Wisconsin Alumni Association
Wisconsin Alumni Research Foundation
Wisconsin Area VTAE Moraine Park
Wisconsin Association of Academic Librarians
Wisconsin Audiovisual Association
Wisconsin Center for Education Research
Wisconsin Childrens Treatment Center
Wisconsin Council of Teachers of English
Wisconsin Department of Audiovisual Instruction
Wisconsin Department of Public Instruction
Wisconsin Division of Vocational Rehabilitation
Wisconsin Education Association
Wisconsin Employment Relations Board
Wisconsin Foundation Vocational Technical Adult Ed
Wisconsin Heights High School
Wisconsin Indianhead Technical College
Wisconsin Interlibrary Services
Wisconsin Junior Dairymens Association
Wisconsin Nurses Association
Wisconsin R and D Center for Cognitive Learning
Wisconsin Recreation Leaders Laboratory
Wisconsin School for Boys
Wisconsin School for Girls
Wisconsin School for the Deaf
Wisconsin School for the Visually Handicapped
Wisconsin School of the Air
Wisconsin State Reading Association
Wisconsin Supreme Court
Wisconsin Vocational Technical Adult Ed Districts
Wise Owl Clubs
Wittenberg College OH
Wittenberg University OH
Wofford College SC
Wolf Trap Farm Park
Wolsey Hall
Women and Girls Employment Enabling Service
Women Reaching Women WI
Womens Bureau
Womens Equity Action League
Womens History Library
Womens History Research Center
Womens Information and Referral Service
Womens Liberation Sappho Collective
Womens National Press Club
Womens Talent Corps
Woodbury County Home IA
Woodhaven Center PA
Woodlawn Community Board
Woodlawn Organization
Woodlawn Public Library
Woodridge School CA
Woodrow Wilson National Fellowship Foundation
Wor Wic Technical Community College MD
Worcester College for the Blind (Great Britain)
Worcester Consortium for Higher Education
Worcester Polytechnic Institute MA
Worcester Public Schools MA
Worcester State College MA
Word Blind Centre for Dyslexic Children
Work Education Council Southeastern Michigan
Work Inc
Workers Defense League
Workers Educational Association
Workers University (Switzerland)
Working Group on Direct Broadcast Satellites
Working Mens College (England)
World Bank
World Bank Photo Library
World Book Company
World Campus Afloat
World Confederation of Labour
World Confederation of Orgs of the Teaching Prof
World Council for Gifted and Talented Children
World Council for the Welfare of the Blind
World Council of Churches
World Council of Comparative Education Societies
World Environment and Resources Council
World Federation for Mental Health
World Federation of Colleges
World Federation of the Deaf
World Future Society
World Health Organization
World Health Organization European Region
World Health Organization Mediterranean Region
World Law Fund
World Meteorological Organization
World of Inquiry School NY
World of Tomorrow School NY
World Organization for Early Childhood Education
World Organization for Human Potential
World Vision (Relief Organization)
World Wildlife Fund
Worth Commission on Educational Planning
Worthington Community College MN
Wright Patterson Air Force Base
Wright State University OH
Wurtsmith Air Force Base
Wynne School District KS
Wyoming Community College System
Wyoming School for the Deaf
Wyoming School Study Council
Wyoming State Library
Wytheville Community College VA
Xavier University of Louisiana
Xavier University OH
Xerox Corporation
Yakima Public School District WA
Yakima Valley Community College District 16 WA
Yakima Valley Community College WA
Yale Child Study Center CT
Yale New Haven Teachers Institute CT
Yale Public Schools MI
Yale University CT
Yantai University (China)
Yarmouk University (Jordan)
Yarmouth Intermediate School ME
Yavapai College AZ
Yellowhead School Division AB
Yellowstone Boys and Girls Ranch School MT
Yellowstone Ranch WY
Yeshiva College NY
Yeshiva University NY
Yonkers Public Schools NY
Yonsei University (South Korea)
York Borough Board of Education ON
York College NE

York College PA
York County Literacy Council PA
York Region Board of Education ON
York Technical College SC
York University ON
Yosemite Community College District CA
Young Adult Conservation Corps
Young Adult Learning Academy NY
Young Citizens League
Young Farmers Association
Young Farmers of America
Young Film Makers Exchange
Young Homemakers of Virginia
Young Mens Christian Association
Young Mens Christian Association Canada
Young Pioneers
Young Womens Christian Association
Younger Chemists Committee
Youngstown Federation of Teachers
Youngstown Public Schools OH
Youngstown State University OH
Youth Conservation Corps
Youth Coordinating Council OR
Youth Educational Services CA
Youth Employment Standards Act 1978 (Michigan)
Youth Incentives Incorporated
Youth Opportunities Foundation
Youth Organizations United
Youth Perspectives Project
Youth Service Agency SC
Youth Service America
Youth Service Corps MI
Youth Service Development Council
Youth Services Center NC
Youthwork Incorporated
Ypsilanti Public Schools MI
Ysleta Independent School District TX
Yuba College CA
Yuba Community College District CA
Yucaipa Joint Unified School District CA
Yukon Koyukuk School District AK
Yuma School District Number 1 AZ
Yuma Union High School District AZ
Yxtaholm School (Sweden)
Zapata County Independent School District TX
Zenith Radio Corporation

CATEGORY 18: Personal Names

Abelard (Peter)
Abelson (Robert)
Achebe (Chinua)
Adams (Abigail)
Adams (Adrienne)
Adams (Harriet)
Adams (Henry)
Adams (Herbert Baxter)
Adams (John Quincy)
Adams (John)
Adams (Richard)
Adams (Samuel)
Adams (William T)
Addams (Jane)
Adelson (J)
Adler (Alfred)
Adler (Mortimer)
Adorno (T W)
Aeschylus
Agassiz (Louis)
Agathe (Saint)
Agee (James)
Agnew (Spiro)
Agusti (Ignacio)
Ahl (David H)
Ahyokeh
Aiken (Conrad)
Aiken (George L)
Ainsworth (Mary D)
Akbar
Akhmatova (Anna)
Alain
Alas (Leopoldo)
Albee (Edward)
Alberti (Rafael)
Alcott (Bronson)
Alcott (Louisa May)
Alcuin
Aldhelm
Aleixandre (Vicente)
Alexander (F Matthias)
Alexander (James)
Alexander (Lamar)
Alexander (Lloyd)
Alexander the Great
Alford (Thomas Wildcat)
Alger (Horatio)
Algren (Nelson)
Alinsky (Saul)
Allen (James E Jr)
Allen (Nathaniel T)
Allen (Woody)
Allende (Salvador)
Allport (Gordon W)
Alonso (Damaso)
Althusser (Louis)
Alvares (Fernao)
Amberg (George)
Ampere (Andre)
Andersen (Hans Christian)
Anderson (John R)
Anderson (John)
Anderson (Sherwood)
Andioc (Rene)
Andre (Thomas)
Andric (Ivo)
Angel Valente (Jose)
Angell (James Burrill)
Anouilh (Jean)
Anthony (Susan B)
Anthony (W S)
Antonioni (Michelangelo)
Apel (Karl Otto)
Apollinaire (Guillaume)
Applebee (Arthur)
Apuleius (Lucius)
Aquinas (Saint Thomas)
Aquino (Corazon)
Aragon (Louis)
Archimedes
Arden (John)
Arguedas (Jose Maria)
Aries (Philippe)
Aristophanes
Aristotle
Arlt (Roberto)
Arniches (Carlos)
Arnim (Achim von)
Arnold (Matthew)
Arnold (Thomas)
Arnow (Hariette)
Aronfreed (J)
Arreola (Juan Jose)
Artaud (Antonin)
Arvers (Felix)
Asante (Molefi K)
Asch (Solomon E)
Asensio (Eugenio)
Ashbury (John)
Ashe (Arthur)
Ashton Warner (Sylvia)
Askov (Eunice N)
Astin (Alexander W)
Astor (Nancy)
Asturias (Miguel Angel)
Atkinson (John W)
Atkinson (Richard C)
Atwood (Margaret)
Aub (Max)
Auchiah (James)
Auerbach (Erich)
Augustine (Saint)
Austen (Jane)
Austin (J L)
Ausubel (David P)
Avellaneda (Alonso Fernandez de)
Aydelotte (Frank)
Aydemir (Sevket Sureyya)
Ayllon (Teodoro)
Ayres (Clarence)
Azana (Manuel)
Azorin (Jose Martinez Ruiz)
Azrin (Nathan)
Azuela (Mariano)
Babbitt (Irving)
Bach (Richard)
Bacon (Francis)
Baez (Joan)
Bailey (F Lee)
Bailey (Thomas A)
Bailyn (Bernard)
Bain (Alexander)
Baird (A Craig)
Baker (Gwendolyn Calvert)
Baker (Josephine Turck)
Baker (Perren Earle)
Baker (Ray Stannard)
Bakhtin (Mikhail)
Bakker (Jim)
Baldwin (Abraham)
Baldwin (James Mark)
Baldwin (James)
Baldwin (Simeon E)
Bales (R F)
Balzac (Honore de)
Bandeira (Manuel)
Bandura (Albert)
Banjara (Lamani)
Bannatyne (A)
Bantock (G H)
Baraka (Imamu Amiri)
Baratz (Joan)
Barbu (Ion)
Barea (Arturo)
Bargy (Henry)
Barkan (Manuel)
Barker (Joel A)
Barlach (Ernst)
Barnard (Chester)
Barnard (Henry)
Barnes (Harry Elmer)
Barnett (Ross A)
Barney (Natalie Clifford)
Baroja (Pio)
Barr (A S)
Barr (Robert)
Barrault (Jean Louis)
Barrie (J M)
Barrios (Eduardo)
Barron (Jerome)
Barrows (Alice)
Barstow (Rosemary Shingobe)
Barth (James L)
Barthes (Roland)
Bartholdi (Frederic Auguste)
Bartholomae (David)
Bartlett (F C)
Bartok (Bela)
Bass (Saul)
Bassett (Richard)
Bates (Daisy)
Bates (Richard)
Bates (Robert P)
Bateson (Gregory)
Baudelaire (Charles)
Baudouin de Courtenay (Jan)
Baudrillard (Jean)
Baum (L Frank)
Baumrind (Diana)
Bazan (Emilia Parodo)
Bazarov (Yevgeny)
Bearden (Romare)
Beardsley (Aubrey)
Beardsley (Monroe)
Beaujeu (Renaut de)
Beauvoir (Simone de)
Beaver (Tom)
Beck (A T)
Beck (William)
Becker (Carl Lotus)
Becker (Ernest)
Becker (Gary S)
Becker (Howard S)
Becker (Karl)
Beckett (Samuel)
Beckner (Morton)
Becquer (Gustavo Adolfo)
Bede
Beeby (C E)
Beecher (Catherine E)
Beecher (Henry Ward)
Beer (Stafford)
Beethoven (Ludwig van)
Begi (Bahman)
Begin (Menachem)
Behn (Aphra)
Behn (Harry)
Behrangi (Samad)
Behrhorst (Carroll)
Belknap (Jeremy)
Bell (Alexander Graham)
Bell (Daniel)
Bell (Terrel H)
Bellack (Arno)
Bellamy (Edward)
Bellos (Helen)
Bellow (Saul)
Belsky (Jay)
Bembo (Pietro)
Ben Jochannan (Yosef)
Benavente y Martinez (Jacinto)
Bender (Charles Albert)
Bendix (Edward Herman)
Benet (Stephen Vincent)
Benington (John)
Bennett (Henry Garland)
Bennett (James Gordon)
Bennett (Jay)
Bennett (Kay)
Bennett (Louise)
Bennett (William J)
Bentsen (Lloyd)
Bequer (Gustavo)
Bereday (George Z F)
Bereiter (Carl)
Berger (Emmanuel M)
Berger (Peter)
Bergman (Ingmar)
Bergman (Sherrie)
Bergson (Henri)
Berke (Joel S)
Berko (Jean)
Berlak (A)
Berlak (H)
Berlin (James)
Berliner (Emil)
Berlo (David K)
Berman (Ronald S)
Berman (Sanford)
Bernanos (George)
Bernardin de Saint Pierre (Jacques Henri)
Bernays (Edward L)
Bernoulli (Daniel)
Bernstein (Basil)
Bernstein (Leonard)
Berry (Mary)
Berry (Wendell)
Bertalanffy (Ludwig von)
Berthoff (Ann E)
Berynda (Pamvo)
Bethune (Mary McLeod)
Bettelheim (Bruno)
Bichsel (Peter)
Biglan (Anthony)
Billings (Josh)
Billings (Nathaniel)
Binet (Alfred)
Bing (Rudolf)
Birkbeck (George)
Bissell (Claude)
Bissell (Lewis)
Bitzer (Lloyd)
Bizet (Georges)
Bjorklund (Eskil)
Blachowicz (C Z)
Black (Edwin)
Black (Hugo)
Black Elk
Blackwell (Elizabeth)
Blair (David P)
Blair (Francis Preston)
Blair (Hugh)
Blake (William)
Blanchard (Brand)
Blanchard (Ken)
Blanco (Julian C)
Blaney (Jack)
Blank (Rolf K)
Blasco Ibanez (Vicente)
Blatt (Burton)
Blau (Peter M)
Blaug (Mark)
Bleich (David)
Blinderman (Abraham)
Bliss (Henry)
Bloom (Allan)
Bloom (Benjamin S)
Bloome (David)
Bloomfield (Leonard)
Blouner (Robert)
Blount (William)
Bloustein (Edward J)
Blumberg (Arthur)
Blume (Judy)
Blumer (Herbert)
Blyton (Enid)
Boas (Belle)
Boas (Franz)
Boccaccio (Giovanni)
Bodger (Joan H)
Bogdanovich (Peter)
Boggs (Hale)
Boggs (Lilburn W)
Bohm (David)
Bohr (Niels)
Boileau Despreaux (Nicolas)
Bolinger (Dwight)
Bolivar (Simon)
Boll (Heinrich)
Bolles (Ron)
Bonaparte (Napoleon)
Bond (Edward)
Bond (Horace Mann)
Bond (Michael)
Bone (Robert A)
Bonham (Frank)
Bonser (Frederick)

Bontemps (Ama)
Boorstin (Daniel)
Booth (Andrew)
Booth (David)
Booth (John Wilkes)
Booth (Philip)
Borchert (Wolfgang)
Borges (Jorge Luis)
Borgese (Giuseppe Antonio)
Bork (Robert H)
Borland (Hal)
Bormann (Ernest)
Bormuth (John R)
Borton (Terry)
Bose (Subhas Chandra)
Boshier (Roger W)
Bosquet (Alain)
Botwinick (J)
Boudinot (Elias)
Boulanger (Nadia J)
Boulding (Elise)
Bourbaki (Nicolas)
Bourdieu (Pierre)
Bourdon (Raymond)
Bourke White (Margaret)
Bowdler (Thomas)
Bowen (Howard R)
Bowen (Murray)
Bowlby (John)
Bowles (Samuel)
Bowman (Isaiah)
Boyer (Ernest L)
Boyle (Richard P)
Bradbury (Ray)
Brademas (John)
Bradford (Leland)
Bradford (William)
Bradshaw (Lillian)
Bradstreet (Anne)
Braine (Lila Ghent)
Brandsma (Titus)
Brandwein (Paul)
Bransford (J D)
Braque (Georges)
Brassens (Georges)
Bray (Thomas)
Braybrooke (David)
Brearly (David)
Brecht (Bertolt)
Bredeweg (Frank)
Brekle (Herbert Ernst)
Brennan (William J)
Brentano (Clemens)
Breton (Andre)
Breuer (Hans)
Brezhnev (Leonid)
Brickman (William Wolfgang)
Bridgers (Sue Ellen)
Brigance (William Norwood)
Brigdman (Percy)
Briggs (L)
Brigham (Carl C)
Brik (Osip)
Brill (Moshe)
Britting (George)
Britton (James)
Brocki (A C)
Brockriede (Wayne)
Brodie (Bernard)
Brogden (H E)
Bronfenbrenner (Urie)
Bronnen (Arnolt)
Bronowski (Jacob)
Bronte (Anne)
Bronte (Branwell)
Bronte (Charlotte)
Bronte (Emily)
Brooks (Bryce)
Brooks (Clara Mable)
Brooks (Cleanth)
Brooks (David W)
Brooks (Glenwood C Jr)
Brooks (Gwendolyn)
Brooks (Walter R)
Brothers (Joyce)
Broudy (H S)
Brougham (Henry)
Brower (David)
Brown (Bob B)
Brown (Charlotte Hawkins)
Brown (John)
Brown (Marcia)
Brown (Norman O)
Brown (Richard H)
Browne (Vivian)
Brownell (Baker)
Browning (James)
Browning (Robert)
Bruce (Lenny)
Bruch (Hilde)
Bruening (Stephen)
Bruffee (Kenneth)
Bruner (Jerome S)
Bruno (Giordano)
Brunot (Ferdinand)
Brunswik (Egon)
Bryan (Mary Edwards)
Bryan (William Jennings)
Bryant (Olen)
Bryant (Peter)
Bryson (Lyman)
Buber (Martin)
Buchman (Frank)
Buchner (Georg)
Buchta (J William)
Buck (Gertrude)
Buckley (William F)
Buehler (Ezra Christian)
Buehrer (Huber)
Buero Vallejo (Antonio)
Buhler (Charlotte)
Bull (William)
Bullock (Henry)
Bunche (Ralph)
Bundy (McGeorge)
Bunin (Ivan)
Bunuel (Luis)
Burger (Warren E)
Burke (C J)
Burke (Edmund)
Burke (Fred G)
Burke (Kenneth)
Burke (Yvonne B)
Burns (D C)
Burns (James MacGregor)
Burns (Robert)
Burroughs (John)
Burroughs (Nannie Helen)
Burt (M K)
Bush (George)
Buslayev (Fedor Ivanovich)
Buss (Allen R)
Buss (Arnold H)
Buss (Frances Mary)
Butler (Edith)
Butler (Pierce)
Butler (Samuel)
Butts (R Freeman)
Butts (William)
Buzzard (David B)
Buzzatti (Dino)
Byron (Lord George Gordon)
Cabeza de Baca (Fabiola)
Cable (George W)
Cachola (Shirley)
Cadalso (Jose)
Cadman (Charles Wakefield)
Caesar (Julius)
Caesarius (of Arles)
Caldecott (Randolph)
Calderon de la Barca (Pedro)
Caldwell (Erskine)
Calhoun (John C)
Caliver (Ambrose)
Calvin (John)
Campbell (Alexander)
Campbell (George)
Campbell (Helen)
Campbell (Joseph)
Camus (Albert)
Canton (Ray)
Caplan (Gerald)
Capote (Truman)
Capp (Al)
Cardenas (Victor)
Carkhuff (Robert R)
Carlsen (Robert G)
Carlson (Richard O)
Carlson (Robert)
Carlyle (Thomas)
Carmer (Carl)
Carmichael (Stokely)
Carnegie (Andrew)
Carnot (Hippolyte)
Carnot (Sadi)
Caro (M A)
Carpentier (Alejo)
Carrier (J K)
Carroll (John B)
Carroll (Lewis G)
Carson (Johnny)
Carson (Rachel)
Carter (Elliott)
Carter (Forrest)
Carter (Hodding Jr)
Carter (Jimmy)
Case (R)
Castaneda (Alfredo)
Castro (Americo)
Castro (Fidel)
Castro (Michel del)
Cather (Willa S)
Catherine of Siena (Saint)
Catiline
Catrileo Chiguailaf de Godo (Maria)
Cattell (Raymond B)
Catullus
Caulfield (Holden)
Cavazos (Lauro F)
Cavett (Dick)
Cawdrey (Robert)
Cela (Camilo Jose)
Celan (Paul)
Celaya (Gabriel)
Cellerier (Guy)
Centra (John)
Cervantes (Lorna Dee)
Cervantes Saavedra (Miguel de)
Cesaire (Aime)
Chadwick (H A)
Chafe (Wallace)
Chait (Richard)
Chall (Jeanne)
Challe (Robert)
Chambers (M M)
Chambers (Whittaker)
Champlain (Samuel de)
Chandrasekhar (Subrahmanyan)
Chaplin (Charlie)
Char (Rene)
Chase (Stuart)
Chaucer (Geoffrey)
Chavez (Cesar)
Chekhov (Anton Pavlovich)
Chen (Theodore)
Cherwitz (Richard A)
Chesterton (G K)
Chickering (Arthur W)
Chickering (Arthur)
Childs (John)
Chisholm (Margaret)
Chisholm (Shirley)
Choate (Pat)
Chodziesner (Gertrud)
Chomsky (Noam)
Chopin (Kate)
Chorpenning (Charlotte B)
Christensen (Francis)
Christy (Arthur)
Chu (Paul B J)
Chukovsky (Kornei I)
Cicero
Cioran (E M)
Cisneros (Henry G)
Cizek (Franz)
Clair (Rene)
Clap (Thomas)
Clapp (Elsie Ripley)
Clarendon (Edward Hyde 1st Earl of)
Clark (Ann Nolan)
Clark (Billy Curtis)
Clark (Burton R)
Clark (Eve)
Clark (George Rogers)
Clark (Joe)
Clark (Kenneth B)
Clark (Kenneth)
Clark (Mamie)
Clark (Richard E)
Clark (Solomon Henry)
Clark (Thomas Arkle)
Clark (Walter van Tilburg)
Clarke (Arthur C)
Clarke (Edward H)
Classer (William)
Claudius I
Clay (Marie)
Cleary (Beverly)
Cleaver (Eldridge)
Clemenceau (Georges)
Clifton (Lucille)
Clinton (Bill)
Clinton (Cornelia Tappen)
Cloward (Richard)
Clymer (Theodore)
Coard (Bernard)
Coatsworth (Elizabeth)
Cobb (Stanwood)
Coburn (Charles)
Cocteau (Jean)
Cohen (Felix)
Cohen (Harold L)
Cohen (Harold)
Cohen (Leonard)
Cohen (Michael D)
Cohn (Herman)
Cole (Natalie Robinson)
Coleman (James S)
Coleman (John R)
Coleman (Statis)
Coleridge (Samuel Taylor)
Coles (William)
Colette (Sidonie Gabrielle)
Collier (Jeremy)
Collier (John)
Collings (Ellsworth)
Collingwood (R G)
Collins (Barry)
Collins (Marva)
Columbus (Christopher)
Combs (A W)
Comenius (Johann Amos)
Comer (James P)
Comettant (Oscar)
Comstock (Anthony)
Comte (Auguste)
Conant (James Bryant)
Concepcion Valdez (Gabriel de la)
Condillac (Abbe de)
Condorcet (Marie Jean Antoine Nicolas de Caritat)
Conerly (James)
Conford (Ellen)
Confortes (Claude)
Confucius
Congreve (William)
Conkling (Hilda)
Conrad (Joseph)
Conroy (Frank)
Conti (Haroldo)
Conway (Jill Ker)
Conze (Werner)
Cook Lynn (Elizabeth)
Cooke (Janet)
Cooley (Charles H)
Cooley (William W)
Coolidge (Archibald Cary)
Coolidge (Calvin)
Coons (John)
Cooper (Grant)
Cooper (Kent)
Cooper (Percy)
Cooper (Peter)
Cooper (Susan)
Copernicus
Copland (Aaron)
Coppin (Fanny Jackson)
Coppola (Francis Ford)
Corbett (Ned)
Cormier (Robert)
Corneille (Pierre)
Corominas (Joan)
Corominas (Juan)
Corsini (Raymond J)
Cortazar (Julio)
Cortes (Hernan)
Corwin (Ronald)
Coser (Lewis)
Counts (George S)
Counts (George)
Courlander (Harold)
Courtis (Stuart Appleton)
Cousin (Gabriel)
Cousin (Victor)
Cousins (Margaret)
Cousteau (Jacques)
Covello (Leonard)
Coverdale (Ralph)
Cowan (William)
Cowles (Gardner)
Cowles (John)
Cowper (William)
Crabbe (George)
Crandall (Prudence)
Crane (Hart)
Crane (Julia E)
Crane (Stephen)
Crapsey (Adelaide)
Craven (Margaret)
Creelman (James)
Cremin (Lawrence A)
Criado (Eduardo)
Crick (Francis)
Crilly (Lynn)
Croasmun (Earl)
Croce (Benedetto)
Cronbach (Lee J)
Cronin (Joseph)

Cronkite (Walter)
Cross (K Patricia)
Crothers (Edward)
Crouch (Richard Edwin)
Crowder (Norman)
Cruickshank (Donald R)
Cruikshank (William)
Cruse (Harold)
Cruz (San Juan de la)
Cruz (Sor Juana Ines de la)
Csikszentmihalyi (Mihaly)
Cuervo (R J)
Culkin (John)
Cummings (E E)
Cummins (James)
Cuomo (Mario M)
Curry (S S)
Curwen (John)
Cutter (Charles)
D Aulnoy (Madame)
D Souza (Dinesh)
Dabrowski (Kazimierz)
Dale (Edgar)
Dale (R R)
Daley (Richard)
Daly (Mary)
Daniels (Lloyd)
Daniels (Sarah)
Dante (Alighieri)
Dario (Ruben)
Darrow (Clarence)
Darwin (Charles)
Darwin (J H)
Das (J P)
Davidson (Donald)
Davidson (Madelyn)
Davidson (Thomas)
Davies (Robertson)
Davis (Angela)
Davis (Frank Marshall)
Davis (Lawrence M)
Davis (Miles)
Davis (William Morris)
Dawes (Richard)
Dawkins (John)
Day (Dorothy)
Dayton (Jonathan)
De Borda (Jean Charles)
de Carlo (Giancarlo)
De Coteau (Clara Blackbird)
De Gaulle (Charles A)
De Mesquita (Julio)
De Quincey (Thomas)
De Saint Exupery (Antoine)
De Vinne (Theodore)
Dearden (R F)
Debs (Eugene V)
Decker (Sarah P)
Defoe (Daniel)
Delacato (Carl H)
Delany (Martin)
Delibes (Miguel)
Della Vos (Victor Karlovich)
Demby (William)
Demiashkevich (Michael John)
Deming (W Edwards)
Demosthenes
Dennis (Wayne)
Denny (George V)
Densmore (Frances)
Derrida (Jacques)
Des Jarlait (Patrick)
Descartes (Rene)
Deutsch (Martin)
Dewey (Evelyn)
Dewey (John)
Dewey (Melvil)
Dexter (Franklin B)
Di Donato (Pietro)
Diamond (Robert M)
Diaz del Castillo (Bernal)
Dickens (Charles)
Dickey (James)
Dickinson (Emily)
Dickinson (John)
Dickinson (Peter)
Diderot (Denis)
Dienes (Zoltan)
Dillard (J L)
Dillon (John Talbot)
Dilt (Robert)
Dilthey (Wilhelm)
Dilworth (Richardson)
Dinnan (James A)
Diogenes
Diotima
Dipietro (Robert)
Dirac (Paul)
Disney (Walt)
Dix (Marion Quin)
Dixon (John)
Dockrell (W Bryan)
Dodge (Mary Mapes)
Dole (Elizabeth)
Doman (Glenn)
Donahue (Phil)
Donne (John)
Doolittle (Hilda)
Dorr (Rheta C)
Dos Passos (John)
Dostoevsky (Fyodor)
Douglas (Gavin)
Douglas (William O)
Douglass (Frederick)
Downs (Anthony)
Doxiadis (Constantine)
Doyle (Denis)
Drachler (Norman)
Drake (Sir Francis)
Dreikurs (Rudolf)
Dressel (P L)
Dressel (Paul L)
Drinan (Robert F)
Droste Hulshoff (Annette E)
Drucker (Peter F)
Dryden (John)
Du Bellay (Joachim)
Du Bois (W E B)
Du Gard (Roger Martin)
Dubois (Pierre)
Ducharme (Rejean)
Duhamel (Georges)
Dukakis (Michael)
Dumazedier (Joffre)
Dumond (Don E)
Dunbar (Paul Lawrence)
Duncan (Otis Dudley)
Duncker (Karl)
Dunlap (John)
Dunlap (William S)
DuPonceau (Peter Stephen)
Duras (Marguerite)
Durham (John)
Durkheim (Emile)
Durkin (Dolores)
Durkin (Kevin)
Durrenmatt (Friedrich)
Dushkin (Alexander)
Dutschke (Rudi)
Dworkin (Andrea)
Dworkin (Ronald)
Dybwad (Gunnar)
Dylan (Bob)
Eagleton (Terry)
Eagleton (Thomas)
Eakins (Thomas)
Earhart (Amelia)
Eastman (Charles Alexander)
Eastman (Charles)
Easton (David)
Eaton (Cyrus)
Eaton (John)
Ebbinghaus (H)
Eckstein (Jerome)
Eddington (Arthur Stanley)
Edelman (Marian Wright)
Edes (Benjamin)
Edison (Thomas)
Edmonds (Ronald R)
Edmonds (Walter D)
Edward VII
Efron (Bradley)
Efron (Edith)
Egan (Kieran)
Eguren (Jose Maria)
Ehlen (Arlis)
Ehninger (Douglas)
Eibl Eibesfeldt (Irenaus)
Einstein (Albert)
Eiseley (Loren)
Eisenberg (Frances)
Eisenhower (Dwight D)
Eisenhower (Mamie)
Eisenstein (Herbert)
Eisenstein (Sergei M)
Eisner (Elliot W)
Ekman (Paul)
Ekwall (Eldon E)
Elbow (Peter)
Eliot (Charles W)
Eliot (George)
Eliot (T S)
Elizabeth I (England)
Elkind (David)
Elkonin (D B)
Ellis (Albert)
Ellison (Ralph)
Ellsworth (Maud)
Ellul (Jacques)
Elton (Eunice)
Ely (John Hart)
Emecheta (Buchi)
Emerson (Harry)
Emerson (Mary Moody)
Emerson (P H)
Emerson (Ralph Waldo)
Emerson (Thomas)
Emig (Janet)
Enderud (H G)
Engelmann (Siegfried)
England (Robert)
Ennis (Robert)
Enriquez (Carlos)
Enzensberger (Hans Magnus)
Eppelsheimer (Hanns Wilhelm)
Eppse (Merl R)
Epstein (Herman T)
Epstein (Jean)
Epstein (S)
Erasmus (Desiderius)
Ercilla (Jose de)
Ercilla y Zuniga (Alonso de)
Erdman (Loula Grace)
Erickson (Milton H)
Erikson (Erik)
Eron (L D)
Escalante (Jaime)
Escandon (Jose de)
Escosura (Patricio de la)
Etzioni (Amitai)
Eu (March Fong)
Euclid
Euripides
Evans (Rupert N)
Evans (Walker)
Everett (Edward)
Exupery (Saint)
Eysenck (Hans J)
Fader (Daniel)
Fadiman (Clifton)
Fairthorne (Robert A)
Fallas (Carlos Luis)
Falwell (Jerry)
Fanon (Frantz)
Farber (Myron)
Farmer (Penelope)
Farnsworth (D L)
Farrakhan (Louis)
Farrar (Frederick William)
Fathy (Hassan)
Faulkner (William)
Feijoo y Montenegro (Benito Jeronimo)
Feingold (B F)
Feldman (E B)
Fellini (Federico)
Fenton (Edwin)
Ferlinghetti (Lawrence)
Fermat (Pierre de)
Fermi (Enrico)
Fernandez (Macedonio)
Fernandez (Rufo Manuel)
Ferraro (Geraldine)
Feuer (Lewis S)
Feuerstein (Reuven)
Few (William)
Feyerabend (Paul)
Fidencio (Nino)
Fiedler (Fred E)
Fielding (Henry)
Fielding (Michael)
Fifer (J)
Fillmore (Charles)
Firth (J R)
Fischer (Frank)
Fish (Stanley)
Fishbein (Martin)
Fisher (H A L)
Fisher (Walter)
Fitzgerald (F Scott)
FitzGerald (Frances)
Fitzsimons (Thomas)
Flaherty (Robert)
Flaim (Paul)
Flanders (Ned A)
Flaubert (Gustave)
Flavell (J)
Fleischman (Doris E)
Fleming (Robert)
Flesch (Rudolph)
Fletcher (Harold)
Flexner (Abraham)
Fligner (M A)
Flower (Linda)
Focke (Rudolph)
Fodor (E M)
Fodor (Jerry A)
Folks (Homer)
Follett (Mary Parker)
Fontane (Theodor)
Fontanet (Joseph)
Foote (Horton)
Forben (Johann)
Ford (Ford Madox)
Ford (Gerald R)
Ford (Henry)
Ford (John)
Forman (Milos)
Foster (Herbert)
Foucault (Michel)
Fowler (James)
Fox (Charles James)
Fraenkel (Jack)
France (Anatole)
Francis (Robert)
Franco (Francisco)
Frank (Barney)
Frank (Philipp)
Frank (Robert)
Frankel (Hermann)
Frankl (Victor E)
Franklin (Benjamin)
Franklin (James)
Franklin (John Hope)
Franklin (Robert J)
Fraser (Berry J)
Fraser (Malcolm)
Fraunhofer (Joseph)
Frederick (Robert W)
Frederiksen (Carl)
Freinet (Celestin)
Freire (Paulo)
French (Daniel Chester)
French (J R P)
French (Marilyn)
Freud (Anna)
Freud (Sigmund)
Freyberger (Ruth)
Friedan (Betty)
Friedenberg (Edgar Z)
Friederberg (Pedre)
Friedman (Martin)
Friedman (Maurice)
Friedman (Milton)
Friendly (Fred)
Fries (C C)
Frisch (Max)
Frisi (Paolo)
Froebel (Friedrich)
Fromm (Erich)
Frost (Robert)
Fruge (August)
Fry (Roger)
Frye (Northrop)
Fryklund (Verne C)
Fuentes (Carlos)
Fuentes (Luis)
Fulbright (J William)
Fuller (Buckminster)
Furth (Hans G)
Gaberina (Peter)
Gabler (Mel)
Gabler (Norma)
Gabor (Dennis)
Gadamer (Hans Georg)
Gadda (Carlo Emilio)
Gadden (Gunnar)
Gadiel (Clarissa)
Gafarian (A V)
Gagne (Robert M)
Gala (Antonio)
Galbraith (John Kenneth)
Galileo
Gallaudet (Thomas Hopkins)
Galois (Evariste)
Galotti (Emilia)
Galperin (P J)
Galton (Sir Francis)
Galtung (Johan)
Gandhi (Indira)
Gandhi (Mahatma)
Gannet (Deborah Sampson)
Gans (Herbert J)
Gans (Roma)
Garber (LeRoy)
Garber (Sharon)
Garcia (Tilin)
Garcia Lorca (Federico)
Garcia Marquez (Gabriel)

Garcia Monge (Joaquin)
Gardiner (Robert)
Gardner (Alexander)
Gardner (Dwayne E)
Gardner (Howard)
Gardner (John)
Gardner (Martin)
Garibaldi (Giuseppe)
Garland (Hamlin)
Garner (Alan)
Garnica (Olga)
Garrison (Roger)
Garrison (William Lloyd)
Garvey (Marcus)
Garvin (A D)
Gaston (E Thayer)
Gates (Doris)
Gattegno (Caleb)
Gauss (Johann Carl Friedrich)
Gautier (Theophile)
Gawboy (Carl)
Gay (Joyce)
Gaya (Ramon)
Geertz (Clifford)
Geisel (Theodor Seuss)
Gentele (Goeran)
Gentile (Giovanni)
Gentry (Castelle G)
George (Chief Dan)
George (Jean Craighead)
George (Stefan)
George III
Gephart (Robert P Jr)
Gerber (Magda)
Geronimo
Gesell (Arnold)
Gewirth (Alan)
Ghibu (Onisifor)
Giannini (Vittorio)
Gibb (Jack)
Gibbons (James)
Giddings (Franklin Henry)
Gide (Andre)
Giebenrath (Hans)
Gilbert (Thomas)
Gilder (George)
Gillberg (Bjorn)
Gilligan (Carol)
Gilman (Charlotte Perkins)
Gilman (Daniel Coit)
Gilman (Nicholas)
Gilruth (Robert)
Gilson (Jamie)
Gilson (Mary Barnett)
Gingras (Louie)
Gintis (Herbert)
Ginzberg (Eli)
Ginzburg (Natalia)
Giono (Jean)
Giroud (Francoise)
Giroux (Henry)
Gissing (George)
Gitt (Josiah W)
Gladstone (William)
Glaser (Barney G)
Glaser (Robert)
Glasgow (Ellen)
Glass (G V)
Glasser (Theodore L)
Glasser (William)
Glassow (Patricia)
Glazer (Nathan)
Gleazer (Edmund J)
Glenny (Lyman A)
Glover (Sarah)
Gluck (Ernst)
Gnanadesikan (R)
Godard (Jean Luc)
Goddard (H H)
Goddard (Robert)
Godkin (Edward L)
Godwin (William)
Goethe (Johann Wolfgang von)
Goffman (E)
Goffman (Erving)
Gogol (Nikolai Vasilievich)
Goldberg (Gertrude S)
Goldberg (Moses)
Golding (William)
Goldman (Emma)
Goldsmith (Oliver)
Goldstein (Kurt)
Gomez de la Serna (Ramon)
Gompers (Samuel)
Gongora y Argote (Luis de)
Gonzales (Rodolfo)
Gonzalez Acilu (Agustin)
Gooch (Steve)
Good (Harry Gehman)
Goodlad (John I)
Goodman (Ellen)
Goodman (Kenneth)
Goodman (Nelson)
Goodman (Paul)
Goodman (Robert)
Goodrich (Lois)
Goodwin (Edward Lawrence)
Gorbachev (Mikhail)
Gorbachevich (K S)
Gordon (Ira)
Gordon (Peg)
Gordon (Thomas)
Gore (Tipper)
Gorelik (Mordecai)
Gorgias of Leontini
Gottfredson (L S)
Gottschalk (Louis Moreau)
Gottsched (Johann Christoph)
Gould (Stephen Jay)
Gouldner (Alvin)
Gowin (D B)
Goya y Lucientes (Francisco Jose de)
Goytisolo (Juan)
Gracian y Morales (Baltasar)
Grady (Henry)
Grady (Roosevelt)
Graham (Billy)
Graham (Lorenz)
Graham (Sylvester)
Gramsci (Antonio)
Grant (Ulysses S)
Grass (Gunter)
Graves (Clare W)
Graves (Donald)
Graves (Robert)
Gravez (Margerite)
Gray (Asa)
Gray (Hannah Holborn)
Gray (James)
Gray (S Simpson)
Gray (William S)
Greeley (Andrew)
Greeley (Horace)
Green (Edith)
Green (Thomas)
Greenberg (Joseph H)
Greene (Graham)
Greene (Maxine)
Greenfield (Thomas)
Greenleaf (Robert)
Greet (Sir Philip Ben)
Gregory (of Tours)
Greimas (A J)
Grey (Zane)
Grice (H P)
Grierson (John)
Griffin (Dean)
Griffin (Leland)
Griffith (D W)
Griffiths (Daniel)
Grignon (Claude)
Grimke (Angelina Weld)
Grimm (Jacob)
Grimm (Wilhelm)
Grimmelshausen (Hans Jakob Christoffel von)
Gross (Theodore)
Grotowski (Jerzy)
Grundtvig (Nicolai)
Grundy (Shirley)
Grunig (James E)
Guare (John)
Guba (Egon)
Guiberto (Giovanni di)
Guilford (J P)
Guillen (Jorge)
Guillen (Nicolas)
Guilloux (Louis)
Guimaraes Rosa (Joao)
Guiney (Louise)
Guiraldes (Ricardo)
Gumperz (John J)
Gunn (Hartford)
Gussow (Joan)
Gusti (Dimitrie)
Guthrie (James W)
Guthrie (Tyrone)
Guthrie (Woody)
Gutmann (Amy)
Habermas (Jurgen)
Haby (Rene)
Haga (W J)
Hahn (Kurt)
Haile Selassie
Hailmann (William N)
Haiman (Franklyn)
Haley (Margaret A)
Hall (D T)
Hall (Edward T)
Hall (G Stanley)
Hall (Joseph Sargent)
Hall (Richard)
Halle (Morris)
Halliday (M A K)
Halvorsen (Ruth Elise)
Hambleton (Ron K)
Hamer (Fannie Lou)
Hamilton (Alexander)
Hamilton (Elizabeth)
Hamilton (Milo)
Hamilton (Virginia)
Hamilton (W D)
Hamilton (William Rowan)
Hamlin (Hannibal)
Hammarskjold (Dag)
Hammonds (Carsie)
Handke (Peter)
Handler (Philip)
Hanna (Paul)
Hannah (William)
Hansberry (Lorraine)
Hard (William)
Harding (Warren G)
Hardy (G H)
Hardy (Thomas)
Hare (A M)
Harjo (Joy)
Harless (Joseph)
Harley (William)
Harmsworth (Alfred)
Harper (D G)
Harper (Frances Ellen Watkins)
Harper (Ida Husted)
Harper (William Rainey)
Harrington (Fred Harvey)
Harris (Erwin D)
Harris (Jean)
Harris (Joel Chandler)
Harris (Lauren Jay)
Harris (Patricia Roberts)
Harris (William Torrey)
Harrison (Benjamin)
Harrison (John)
Harste (Jerome C)
Hart (Gary)
Hart (Leslie A)
Hart (Philip)
Hart (W A)
Hartmann von Aue
Harvey (William H)
Hatch (Orrin)
Hatfield (Mark)
Hatfield (W Wilbur)
Hauptmann (Bruno)
Hauptmann (Gerhart)
Havel (Vaclav)
Havelock (Ronald G)
Havighurst (Robert)
Hawthorne (Nathaniel)
Hayakawa (S I)
Hayden (Robert)
Haydn (Franz Joseph)
Hayes (Mary)
Hays (W L)
Haywood (Carolyn)
Hazlitt (William)
Head (David)
Hearn (Lafcadio)
Hearst (William Randolph)
Heathcote (Dorothy)
Hebb (D O)
Hebbel (Christian Friedrich)
Hebel (Johann Peter)
Heckman (J J)
Heermann (Barry)
Hefner (Hugh)
Hegel (Georg Wilhelm Friedrich)
Heidegger (Martin)
Heider (F N)
Heider (Karl)
Hellbron (Louis H)
Heilprin (Lawrence B)
Heine (Heinrich)
Heinicke (Samuel)
Heinlein (Robert)
Helburn (Suzanne Wiggins)
Hellman (Lillian)
Helmers (Hermann)
Hemingway (Ernest)
Henderson (Algo D)
Henley (Don)
Henry (George W)
Henry (Joseph)
Herbart (Johann Friedrich)
Herbst (Josephine)
Herman (Alexis)
Hernandez (Jose)
Hernandez (Miguel)
Herndon (James)
Herodotus
Herrera y Reissig (Julio)
Herrick (Genevieve Forbes)
Hermstein (Richard)
Herskovits (Melville Jean)
Herzberg (Frederick)
Hesburgh (Theodore M)
Hesse (Hermann)
Hester (Al)
Hester (James M)
Hewett (Frank)
Heym (Georg)
Hickok (Lorena A)
Hicks (Thomas Holliday)
Hill (Adams Sherman)
Hill (Joseph)
Hilprecht (Herman)
Hinds (John)
Hine (Lewis Wickes)
Hirsch (E D)
Hirschi (Travis)
Hirschman (Albert)
Hirst (Paul)
Hiss (Alger)
Hitchcock (Alfred)
Hitchcock (Orra White)
Hitler (Adolf)
Hiz (Henri)
Hobbes (Thomas)
Hobbs (N)
Hobson (Julius)
Hobson (Peter)
Hodgkinson (Harold L)
Hoegskolan (Kungliga Tekniska)
Hoffer (Eric)
Hoffer (Thomas)
Hoffman (Abbie)
Hoffman (David)
Hoffman (Malvina)
Hoffmann (Ernst Theodor Amadeus)
Hoffmann (Hans G)
Hofman (A W)
Hofmannsthal (Hugo von)
Hofstadter (Richard)
Hofstede (Geert)
Hoge (Moses Drury)
Holbrook (Josiah)
Holdaway (Don)
Holden (Matthew)
Holderlin (Friedrich)
Holland (John L)
Holland (Milton M)
Holland (Norman)
Hollander (Lorin)
Hollingworth (Leta Stetter)
Holst (Gustav)
Holt (John)
Holz (J C)
Hombitzer (E)
Homburg (Prinz Friedrich von)
Homer
Hooke (Robert)
hooks (bell)
Hooks (Benjamin L)
Hooks (Robert)
Hoover (Herbert)
Hoover (J Edgar)
Hopkinson (Francis)
Hopper (Edward)
Horace
Horkheimer (Max)
Horn (Robert E)
Hornby (A S)
Horner (Matina)
Horner (Winifred Bryan)
Horney (Karen)
Horton (Myles)
Hosic (James Fleming)
Hostos (Eugenio Maria de)
Houle (Cyril O)
Hovland (Carl)
Howard (John)
Howell (William Dean)
Howitt (William)
Hoyt (Cyril)
Hoyt (Kenneth B)
Huarte (Juan)
Hubbard (Elbert)
Hubbell (J L)
Hudson (Marshall A)

Lippmann (Walter)
Lipset (Seymour Martin)
Lipsett (Arthur)
Lipsyte (Robert)
Lismer (Arthur)
Lista y Aragon (Alberto)
Liszt (Franz)
Liveright (A A)
Livingston (William)
Livy (Titus Livius)
Lizardi (Jose Joaquin Fernandez de)
Lleras (Antonio Alvarez)
Llopis (Carlos)
Locke (E A)
Locke (John)
Loevinger (Jane)
Loevinger (Lee)
Logan (Chief Tahgahjute)
London (Jack)
London (Perry)
Lonergan (Bernard)
Long (Huey)
Long (Norton)
Longfellow (Henry Wadsworth)
Longley (J W)
Lopez (Nancy)
Lopez Aranda (Ricardo)
Lopez Quintas (Alfonso)
Lord (Frederic M)
Lorenz (Konrad)
Lorimer (George Horace)
Louis (Authur)
Louis XIV
Love (Ruth B)
Loveira y Chirino (Carlos)
Lovejoy (Elijah P)
Lowell (A Lawrence)
Lowell (Robert)
Lowenfeld (Viktor)
Loyola (San Ignacio de)
Lu (K H)
Lubetzky (Seymour)
Lucan (Marcus Annaeus Lucanus)
Lucas (George)
Luce (Henry)
Luce (Stephen Bleeker)
Lucia (David)
Luckmann (Thomas)
Lucretius (Titus Lucretius Carus)
Ludlum (Jacqueline)
Ludwig (Otto)
Lui (Ben Chieh)
Lukacs (Georg)
Lull (Ramon)
Lunin (Mikhail Sergeyevich)
Lunsford (Andrea A)
Luria (A R)
Luther (Martin)
Lynch (Benito)
Lynd (Staughton)
Lyon (Harold)
Lyon (Mary)
Lyons (John)
Lyotard (Jean Francois)
Mabie (Hamilton Wright)
Macaulay (Thomas B)
MacDonald (Jeffrey)
MacDowell (Edward)
Mace (Jean)
Machado (Antonio)
Machado de Assis (Joachim Maria)
Machiavelli (Niccolo)
MacKay (Donald M)
MacKaye (Percy)
Mackey (M Cecil)
MacKinnon (Catherine)
MacLeish (Archibald)
Macmurray (John)
Macrorie (Ken)
Madigan (Elvira)
Madison (James)
Madison (Robert Lee)
Mager (Robert)
Magubane (Bernard)
Maguire (Daniel C)
Mahler (Margaret S)
Mailer (Norman)
Major (Kevin)
Malamud (Bernard)
Malcolm X
Malcomesius (Neva)
Malinowski (Bronislaw)
Mallarme (Stephane)
Malraux (Andre)
Malthus (Thomas Robert)
Mandelbrot (Benoit B)
Manes (Stephen)
Mann (Horace)
Mann (Margaret)
Mann (Thomas)
Mannheim (Karl)
Manning (Henry Edward)
Manrique (Jorge)
Mansbridge (Albert)
Mansfield (Michael)
Manuel (Don Juan)
Many Guns (Tom)
Manzano (Sonia)
Manzi (Albert)
Manzoni (Alessandro)
Mao Zedong
Maranon (Gregorio)
Marcel (Gabriel)
March (James G)
Marcia (James E)
Marconi (Guglielmo)
Marcos (Ferdinand)
Marcuse (Herbert)
Margenau (Henry)
Marigny (Ryno de)
Marinetti (Filippo Tommaso)
Marino (Giambattista)
Maritain (Jacques)
Marivaux (Pierre Carlet de Chamblain de)
Mark (Jan)
Marland (Sidney P)
Marlowe (Christopher)
Marsak (Samuil)
Marshall (Thomas William)
Marshall (Thurgood)
Marti (Jose Julian)
Martial (Marcus Valerius)
Martin (Roscoe)
Martin Santos (Luis)
Martineau (Harriet)
Martinet (Andre)
Martinez Estrada (Ezequiel)
Martinez Sierra (Gregorio)
Marx (Karl)
Masefield (John)
Maslow (Abraham)
Massee (May)
Masters (Edgar Lee)
Mather (Cotton)
Mathews (David)
Matute (Ana Maria)
Mauger (Claude)
Maupassant (Guy de)
Mauriac (Francois)
Maurois (Andre)
Maxwell (James)
Maxwell (W David)
Mayakovsky (Vladimir)
Mayhew (Lewis B)
Mays (Benjamin Elijah)
McAdoo (William Gibbs)
McAllister (Jane Ellen)
McAndrew (William)
McCall (Will)
McCarran (Patrick)
McCarthy (Charles)
McCarthy (Eugene)
McCarthy (Joseph)
McCawley (J D)
McClusky (Howard Y)
McConnell (T R)
McCoy (Rhody)
McCullers (Carson)
McDermott (Gerald)
McGovern (George)
McGrath (Earl J)
McGregor (Douglas)
McGuffey (William)
McGuire (William)
McHenry (James)
McIntyre (Alasdair)
McKee (Howard Joseph Jr)
McKenney (James)
McKeon (Richard)
McKuen (Rod)
McLaren (Norman)
McLaughlin (Barry)
McLeod (Stuart)
McLuhan (Marshall)
McMurtrie (Douglas C)
McNamara (Robert S)
McPeck (John)
McPhail (Peter)
McSorley (Marty)
McVey (William)
Mead (George Herbert)
Mead (Margaret)
Mearns (Hughes)
Mechanic (D)
Medvedev (Roy A)
Megargee (E I)
Meier (Deborah)
Meier (Norman C)
Meiklejohn (Alexander)
Meillet (Antoine)
Mellon (John C)
Melville (Herman)
Menand (Louis)
Mencius (Master Meng)
Mendel (Gregor)
Mendoza (Antonio de)
Mendoza (Diego Hurtado de)
Menendez Pidal (Ramon)
Menendez y Pelayo (Marcelino)
Menuhin (Yehudi)
Menyuk (Paula)
Meredith (James A)
Meria (Juan de)
Merimee (Prosper)
Merleau Ponty (Maurice)
Merrill (M D)
Merton (Robert K)
Mesmer (Anton)
Messick (Samuel)
Meyer (Conrad Ferdinand)
Meyers (Phillip Van Ness)
Meyerson (Lee)
Mezirow (Jack)
Michael X
Michels (Robert)
Michener (James A)
Miegel (Agnes)
Miel (Alice)
Mifflin (Thomas)
Milgram (Stanley)
Mill (John Stuart)
Millay (Edna Saint Vincent)
Miller (Arthur)
Miller (Bertha Mahony)
Miller (James E)
Miller (Neal E)
Milligan (Frank)
Milligan (Lambdin)
Millman (J)
Mills (Don)
Mills (Theodore)
Milton (John)
Minot (Louise)
Minow (Newton)
Mintzberg (Henry)
Mira de Amescua (Antonio)
Mistral (Gabriela)
Mitchell (George)
Mitchell (Lucy Sprague)
Mitchell (Maria)
Mitchell (Richard)
Mitford (Jessica)
Mitterrand (Francois)
Moffett (James)
Mohr (P)
Mohrmann (G P)
Mojarro (Tomas)
Moliere
Mondale (Walter F)
Mondrian (Piet)
Monnier (Henry Bonaventure)
Montague (Richard)
Montaigne (Michel Eyquem de)
Montale (Eugenio)
Monte (Domingo del)
Monteith (John)
Montemayor (Jorge)
Montesquieu (Charles Louis de Secondat)
Montessori (Maria)
Montfort (Eugene)
Montgomery (Robert)
Montherlant (Henry de)
Mood (S M)
Moody (Raymond)
Moonan (W J)
Moore (Alice)
Moore (Bessie Boehm)
Moore (George)
Moore (Henry)
Moore (Marianne)
Moore (O K)
Moore (T W)
Moran (Tod)
Morando (Bernardo)
Moratin (Leandro Fernandez de)
Moravia (Alberto)
More (Sir Thomas)
Morgan (Arthur Ernest)
Morgan (Dodge D)
Morike (Edward)
Morison (Samuel Eliot)
Morocco (C)
Morrill (Justin S)
Morris (Charles)
Morris (Gouverneur)
Morris (Henry)
Morris (William)
Morris (Willie)
Morrison (George H)
Morrison (George)
Morrison (Philip)
Morrison (Toni)
Morse (Jedidiah)
Morton (Oliver)
Mosenthal (Peter)
Moses
Mosqueda (Jose)
Mosqueda (Lawrence)
Motley (Constance Baker)
Mott (Emma)
Mott (Lucretia Coffin)
Mounier (Emmanuel)
Moya (Jesus)
Moyers (Bill)
Moynihan (Daniel P)
Mozart (Wolfgang A)
Mudie (Charles Edward)
Muffoletto (Robert)
Muir (John)
Mulroney (Brian)
Mumford (L Quincy)
Mumford (Lewis)
Munoz (Carlos)
Murdoch (Rupert)
Murguia (Theodore I)
Murray (Donald M)
Murray (Lindley)
Murray (Pauli)
Murrow (Edward R)
Musil (Robert)
Musset (Alfred de)
Mussolini (Benito)
Myers (Walter Dean)
Myklebust (Helmer)
Myrdal (Gunnar)
Nader (Ralph)
Nadler (Leonard)
Naisbitt (John)
Nanus (Burt)
Napi
Napier (John)
Narayan (Jayaprakash)
Nash (Jay Bryan)
Nasser (Gamal Abd Al)
Navarro (Jose Antonio)
Near (Holly)
Nearing (Scott)
Nebrija (Antonio de)
Nehru (Jawaharlal)
Neill (A S)
Nelson (Florence)
Neruda (Pablo)
Neufeld (John)
Neumann (Erich)
Neurath (Otto)
Neustadt (Richard E)
Neville (Edgar)
Newcomb (Theodore)
Newman (Cardinal John Henry)
Newman (Richard S)
Newmark (Peter)
Newton (Isaac)
Neyman (J)
Nichols (James O)
Nichols (Mark)
Nichols (Robert)
Nicholson (E B)
Niebuhr (Reinhold)
Nietzsche (Friedrich)
Nightingale (Florence)
Nigro (Georgia)
Nin (Anais)
Nixon (Richard M)
Nizan (Paul)
Nkrumah (Kwame)
Nobel (Alfred)
Nodier (Charles)
Noether (Emmy)
North (Oliver)
Northcliffe (Alfred Charles)
Northrop (F S C)
Norton (Charles Eliot)
Norton (Mary)
Nussbaum (Martha)
Nyberg (David)
O Brien (Robert)
O Connor (Flannery)
O Connor (Frank)

O Connor (Sandra Day)
O Dell (Scott)
O Hara (R P)
O Hare (Frank)
O Hear (Anthony)
O Keefe (Georgia)
O Neill (James M)
O Toole (James)
Oakeshott (Michael)
Oandasan (William)
Oates (Joyce Carol)
Oberlin (Jean Frederic)
Oberth (Hermann)
Oden (Gloria)
Oettinger (Anthony)
Ogai (Mori)
Ogbu (John)
Ogilvie (Mardel)
Ojemann (Ralph H)
Olbrechts Tyteca (L)
Olechnowicz (Mscislaw)
Oliver (Grace W)
Oliver (Margaret)
Olivier (Laurence)
Oller (John)
Ollier (Claude)
Olmedo (Jose Joaquin de)
Olmsted (Frederick Law)
Olsen (J P)
Olsen (Lyle)
Olson (Mancur)
Onassis (Jacqueline Kennedy)
Onetti (Juan Carlos)
Ong (Walter J)
Opler (Morris)
Orans (Martin)
Orendain (Antonio)
Orff (Carl)
Orozco (Jose Clemente)
Orpheus
Ortega (Daniel)
Ortega y Gasset (Jose)
Ortiz (Alfonso)
Ortiz (Simon J)
Orton (Samuel)
Orwell (George)
Osborn (Michael)
Oseretzsky (Lincoln)
Osgood (C E)
Osler (William)
Osterhouse (R A)
Otis (Eliza)
Ouchi (William)
Overton (Anthony)
Ovid
Owen (Robert)
Owen (Wilfred)
Oxley (Lawrence A)
Packwood (Robert W)
Padron (Rodriquez del)
Page (Ellis)
Pahlavi (Shah Reza)
Paine (Thomas)
Paivio (A)
Pakula (Alan J)
Palme (Olof)
Palmer (Alice Freeman)
Palmer (Harold E)
Pantin (Gerard)
Papandropoulou (I)
Papert (Seymour)
Paramo (Pedro)
Pardo Bazan (Emilia)
Parini (Giuseppe)
Parish (Peggy)
Park (Robert E)
Park (Robert)
Parker (Ely Spencer)
Parker (Francis)
Parker (Quanah)
Parkhurst (Helen)
Parkin (Frank)
Parks (Gordon)
Parks (Rosa)
Parra (Nicanor)
Parsons (Talcott)
Pascal (Blaise)
Pascarella (Ernest T)
Pascual Leone (Juan)
Pask (Gordon)
Paso (Alfonso)
Pasternak (Boris)
Pasteur (Louis)
Pastore (John)
Patel (Vallabhbhai)
Pater (Walter)
Paterno (Joe)
Paterson (Katherine)
Patterson (Frederick O)
Patton (Frank D)
Paul (Hermann)
Paul (Richard)
Paul (Robert)
Paul (Saint)
Paul VI (Pope)
Paulding (James K)
Pauli (Wolfgang)
Paus (Johann Werner)
Pavese (Cesare)
Pavlov (Ivan Petrovich)
Payne (Ethel L)
Payne (William H)
Paz (Octavio)
Peale (Norman Vincent)
Pearl Poet
Pearson (Adelaide)
Pearson (Karl)
Peary (Robert)
Pease (Howard)
Peck (Richard)
Peel (E A)
Peirce (Charles S)
Pell (Claiborne)
Peplau (H E)
Peraza (Fermin)
Percy (Walker)
Perelman (Chaim)
Peresvetov (Ivan)
Peret (Benjamin)
Perez (Leander)
Perez de Ayala (Ramon)
Perez Galdos (Benito)
Pericles
Perkins (Carl D)
Perkins (Ralph)
Perls (Fritz)
Peron (Isabel)
Perrault (M)
Perrow (Charles)
Perry (Matthew C)
Perry (William G Jr)
Perry (William)
Pessoa (Fernando)
Pestalozzi (Johann Heinrich)
Peters (R S)
Petersen (Peter)
Peterson (Paul E)
Petrakis (Harry Mark)
Petrarch (Francesco)
Petronius (Gaius)
Petrosky (Anthony R)
Petrov (Archpriest Avoakum)
Petrushevskaja (Ljudmila)
Pettigrew (Thomas F)
Pfister (Oskar)
Phillips (Craig)
Phillips (D C)
Piaget (Jean)
Piazza (Thomas)
Picasso (Pablo)
Pickering (John)
Pierce (Charles Sanders)
Pigault Lebrun (Charles Antoine)
Pike (Kenneth L)
Pilgrim (Billy)
Pinckney (Charles Cotesworth)
Pinckney (Charles)
Pinget (Robert)
Pinter (Harold)
Pirandello (Luigi)
Pirsig (Robert)
Pitkin (Royce S)
Pitman (James)
Pitt (William)
Pittenger (John C)
Piven (Frances Fox)
Plater (William)
Plath (Sylvia)
Plato of Athens
Player (Willa)
Pliny (The Elder)
Pliny (The Younger)
Plotinus
Plutarch
Po Pay
Poe (Edgar Allan)
Poggioli (Renato)
Polanski (Roman)
Polanyi (Michael)
Pole (Thomas)
Polier (Justine Wise)
Polk (James K)
Polo (Marco)
Polya (George)
Polybius
Poole (Ernest)
Pope (Alexander)
Popham (W J)
Popham (W James)
Popper (Karl)
Portis (Charles)
Posada (Jose Guadalupe)
Postelthwait (Samuel N)
Postman (Neil)
Potocki (Jan)
Potok (Chaim)
Pott (Francis Lister)
Potter (Beatrix)
Poulet (Georges)
Pound (Ezra)
Powell (John)
Powell (Lewis)
Powhatan
Prang (Mary Dana Hicks)
Pratt (Caroline)
Prediger (Dale J)
Premack (D)
Pressey (Sidney Leavitt)
Presthus (Robert)
Preston (Joan)
Prevert (Jacques)
Prevost (Abbe)
Prevost (Antoine Francois)
Priestley (Joseph)
Prigogine (Ilya)
Pritchett (Herman)
Propp (Vladimir)
Prosser (Charles)
Protagoras
Proust (Marcel)
Pugh (George E)
Puig (Manuel)
Pulci (Luigi)
Pulet (Georges)
Pulitzer (Joseph II)
Purves (Alan)
Pushkin (Alexander)
Pyle (Ernie)
Pynchon (Thomas)
Pythagoras
Qoyawayma (Polingaysi)
Quasimodo (Salvatore)
Quayle (Dan)
Quevedo y Villegas (Francisco Gomez de)
Quirk (Randolph)
Rabelais (Francois)
Racine (Jean)
Radford (William C)
Rafferty (Max)
Raimund (Ferdinand)
Rajneesh (Bhagwan Shree)
Rakow (Theresa G)
Raleigh (Sir Walter)
Ramage (John M)
Ramirez (Manuel)
Ramus (Peter)
Rand (Ayn)
Randolph (A Philip)
Ranganathan (S R)
Rankine (William John M)
Rapin (Rene)
Raskin (Victor)
Raths (Louis)
Raven (B)
Ravitch (Diane)
Rawls (John)
Ray (Satyajit)
Read (Herbert)
Reagan (Ronald)
Red Cloud
Red Cloud (Mitchell Jr)
Red Fox
Reddie (Cecil)
Redl (Fritz)
Reed (Alma)
Reese (H W)
Reese (Lizette)
Reeves (B)
Reeves (David)
Reeves (Floyd Wesley)
Refregier (Anton)
Rehnquist (William)
Reichenberger (Arnold G)
Reid (Alastair)
Reid (Thomas)
Reimer (Everett)
Reisman (David)
Reiss (Ira)
Reissman (Leonard)
Renfrew (Baron)
Renoir (Jean)
Renzulli (Joseph)
Reston (James)
Reubens (Beatrice)
Reyes (Alfonso)
Reynolds (Frederick W)
Reynolds (Joshua)
Reynolds (Maynard C)
Rice (Joseph Mayer)
Rich (Adrienne)
Richards (I A)
Richards (Jack C)
Richards (Mary Helen)
Richardson (Elizabeth C)
Richaudeau (Francois)
Richman (Julia)
Richter (Anne)
Richter (Helmut)
Ricoeur (Paul)
Riesman (David)
Riley (Richard W)
Rilke (Rainer Maria)
Rimbaud (Arthur)
Ringenberg (W C)
Ringer (Barbara)
Rivera (Diego)
Rivera (Jose Eustasio)
Robbe Grillet (Alain)
Roberts (Barbara)
Roberts (Lydia J)
Roberts (Millard)
Roberts (P Paul)
Robertson (Pat)
Robeson (Paul)
Robichaux (Kerry Stewart)
Robin (Paul)
Robins (Margaret Dreier)
Robinson (Edwin Arlington)
Robinson (Jackie)
Robinson (James Harvey)
Rockefeller (John D)
Rockefeller (Nelson A)
Rockwell (George Lincoln)
Rockwell (Norman)
Rodo (Jose Enrique)
Rodriguez (Manuel Diaz)
Rodriguez (Richard)
Roe (Anne)
Roethke (Theodore)
Rogers (Carl)
Rogers (Everett M)
Rogers (M E)
Rogers (Will)
Rokeach (Milton)
Rolland (Romain)
Romains (Jules)
Romero (Jose Ruben)
Romero (Oscar)
Romney (George)
Rontgen (Wilhelm)
Roosevelt (Eleanor)
Roosevelt (Franklin D)
Roosevelt (Theodore)
Rorty (Richard)
Rosales (Luis)
Rosch (Eleanor)
Rose (Arnold)
Rose (Richard)
Rosenberg (Morris)
Rosenblatt (Louise)
Rosenstock Huessy (Eugene)
Rosenthal (Robert)
Rosenzweig (Franz)
Ross (John)
Ross (Murray G)
Ross (Sinclair)
Rossi Landi (F)
Rothkopf (E Z)
Rotrou (Jean de)
Rotter (Julian B)
Rouse (Mary Jane)
Rousseau (Jean Jacques)
Rowe (Mary P)
Rozewicz (Tadeusz)
Rubin (Ramon)
Rueda (Salvador)
Rugg (Earle)
Rugg (Harold Ordwell)
Ruiz (Juan)
Ruiz de Alarcon (Juan)
Rulfo (Juan)
Rush (Benjamin)
Ruskin (John)
Russell (Bertrand)
Russell (Frank Alden)
Russell (James)
Russell (John)
Russell (Ken)

Toulouse Lautrec (Henri de)
Toynbee (Arnold J)
Tracey (William R)
Trakl (Georg)
Trantz (Robert)
Traubel (Horace L)
Travers (Robert)
Tressall (Robert)
Trigg (Roger)
Tristan (Flora)
Troutner (Leroy F)
Trow (Martin A)
Trubetzkoy (N S)
Trudeau (Garry)
Trudeau (Pierre Elliott)
Truffaut (Francois)
Truman (Bess)
Truman (Harry S)
Trump (J Lloyd)
Truth (Sojourner)
Tryon (R C)
Tsiolkovsky (Konstantin)
Tubman (Harriet)
Tudor (Tasha)
Tufts (John)
Tukey (John)
Tully (Joan)
Tunis (John)
Tuomela (Raimo)
Turgenev (Ivan)
Turner (Darwin T)
Turner (Frederick Jackson)
Turner (Joseph M W)
Tussman (Joseph)
Twain (Mark)
Tyler (Anne)
Tyler (Ralph W)
Tyutchev (Fedor Ivanovich)
Tzu (Lao)
Udall (Stewart)
Ulich (Robert)
Unamuno (Miguel de)
Ungaretti (Giuseppe)
Updike (John)
Upton (Albert)
Upton (John)
Urabayen (Felix)
Urey (Harold C)
Urrea (Teresa)
Ushakov (Dmitriy Nikolayevich)
Uznadze (D N)
Vachek (Josef)
Vaizey (John)
Valdelomar (Abrahm)
Valdez (Luis)
Valera (Juan de)
Valery (Paul)
Valett (Robert)
Valle Inclan (Ramon del)
Vallejo (Cesar)
Vallejo (Manuel Mejia)
Van Buren (Abigail)
van Dijk (J)
van Dijk (T A)
Van Gennep (Arnold)
Van Gogh (Vincent)
Van Til (Cornelius)
Van Til (William)
Van Vogt (A E)
Vargas Llosa (Mario)
Vasarely (Victor)
Vasconcelos (Jose)
Vazquez (Richard)
Veblen (Thorsten)
Vega (Garcilaso de la)
Vega Carpio (Lope Felix de)
Velasquez (Peter F)
Velikovsky (Immanuel)
Veniaminov (John)
Verdi (Giuseppe)
Verga (Giovanni)
Vergil
Verlaine (Paul)
Verner (C)
Vesselovsky (Alexander)
Vickery (Brian Campbell)
Vico (Giambattista)
Vidal (Gore)
Vidal Olmos (Fernando)
Vidoco (Francois Eugene)
Villa Lobos (Heitor)
Villarreal (Jose A)
Villena (Enrique de)
Villon (Francois)
Vinal (William)
Vincent de Beauvais
Visconti (Luchino)
Vittorini (Elio)
Vitz (Paul C)
Vives (Amadeo)
Viviani (P)
Voltaire
Von Baer (Karl Ernst)
Von Harrison (Grant)
Von Humboldt (Alexander)
Von Humboldt (Wilhelm)
Von Neumann (John)
Von Ranke (Leopold)
Vonnegut (Kurt)
Vonnegut (Mark)
Votaw (Carmen Delgado)
Voznesensky (Andrei)
Vygotsky (Lev S)
Waber (Bernard)
Wagner (Richard)
Walcott (Derek)
Walker (Alice)
Walker (H M)
Walker (John Hunter)
Walker (Lawrence)
Wallace (George)
Wallace (Henry)
Wallace (Karl R)
Wallas (G)
Waller (Willard)
Wallon (Henri)
Wallraff (G)
Walser (Martin)
Walther von der Vogelweide
Wang (Margaret C)
Wang Yani
Ward (J H)
Ward (Theodore)
Ward (Virgil)
Warren (Earl)
Warren (Robert Penn)
Warren (William Whipple)
Wartella (E)
Warwick (Frances Greville Countess of)
Wase (Christopher)
Washburne (Carleton Wolsey)
Washington (Booker T)
Washington (George)
Waterhouse (Ann)
Waters (Frank)
Watson (Fletcher G)
Watt (Bob)
Watt (James G)
Watt (James)
Watt (William)
Watzlawick (Paul)
Wauneka (Annie)
Way (Florine)
Weaver (Richard M)
Webb (Walter Prescott)
Weber (Brian F)
Weber (Lillian)
Weber (Max)
Webern (Anton von)
Webster (Daniel)
Webster (Hutton)
Webster (Noah)
Wedekind (Frank)
Wedgeworth (Robert)
Weikart (David)
Weiner (B)
Weinhouse (Marilyn)
Weinrich (Harald)
Weinzweig (A I)
Weir (Ruth Hirsch)
Weisgard (Leonard)
Weiss (Peter)
Welch (Finis)
Welch (Robert)
Welles (Orson)
Wells (H G)
Wells (Ida B)
Welty (Eudora)
Wendt (Albert)
Werfel (Franz)
Werner (Abraham)
Werner (Alfred)
Werner (H)
Werner (Heinz)
Wertsch (J V)
Wesker (Arnold)
Wesley (Edgar Bruce)
West (Benjamin)
West (Willis Mason)
Wharton (Edith)
Whately (Richard)
Wheatley (Phillis)
Wheeless (L R)
Wheelwright (Philip)
Whewell (William)
Whimbey (Arthur)
Whinnom (Keith)
White (Charles)
White (Clarence)
White (E B)
White (L T)
White (R T)
White (Robert W)
White (Theodore H)
White (William Lindsay)
Whitebear (Bernie)
Whitehead (Alfred North)
Whitehead (Clay)
Whitfield (R C)
Whitman (Albery A)
Whitman (Walt)
Whitney (William Dwight)
Whorf (Benjamin Lee)
Wichelns (Herbert A)
Wickersham (William)
Wideman (John)
Wildavsky (Aaron)
Wilde (Oscar)
Wilder (Laura Ingalls)
Wilder (Thornton)
Wilkins (R A)
Wilkins (Roy)
Will (George F)
Will (Madeleine)
Willard (Emma Hart)
Williams (Raymond)
Williams (William Carlos)
Williamson (E G)
Williamson (Hugh)
Willinsky (John)
Willis (Ben)
Willis (Meredith Sue)
Willis (Nathaniel)
Willis (Paul)
Willkie (Wendell)
Willower (Donald J)
Wilms (Wellford W)
Wilson (August)
Wilson (Edmund)
Wilson (Edward Osborne)
Wilson (G D)
Wilson (Ida May)
Wilson (James Q)
Wilson (John)
Wilson (Logan)
Wilson (Pete)
Wilson (Robert)
Wilson (Woodrow)
Winans (James A)
Winans (R Foster)
Winfrey (Oprah)
Winnemucca (Sarah)
Winnicott (Donald W)
Winstanley (Gerrard)
Winter (D)
Winterowd (W Ross)
Winters (Yvor)
Wise (Arthur)
Wiseman (Frederick)
Wishy (Bernard)
Witkin (H A)
Witte (Stephen)
Wittgenstein (Ludwig)
Woititz (J G)
Wojciechowska (Maja)
Wolcot (John)
Wolf (R M)
Wolfe (Thomas)
Wolfensberger (Wolf)
Wolfflin (Heinrich)
Wolfgang (Iser)
Wollstonecraft (Mary)
Wolpe (Joseph)
Wood (Charles)
Wood (Evelyn)
Wood (Herbert G)
Woodger (Joseph)
Woodson (Carter G)
Woolbert (Charles Henry)
Woolf (Virginia)
Woolley (Helen Thompson)
Woolley (Mary)
Woolman (John)
Wordsworth (William)
Wright (Beatrice A)
Wright (Benjamin D)
Wright (Frank Lloyd)
Wright (Hamilton)
Wright (J Skelly)
Wright (James)
Wright (Richard)
Wright (Stephen J)
Wright Brothers
Wrigley (Philip K)
Wu (Chien Shiung)
Wundt (Wilhelm)
Wylie (Elinor)
Wylie (Laurence)
Yarborough (Ralph)
Yates (Robert)
Yeats (Samuel Butler)
Yeats (William Butler)
Yeltsin (Boris)
Yezierska (Anzia)
Yokomitsu (Riichi)
Young (Ann Eliza)
Young (Art)
Young (Brian)
Zajonc (Robert B)
Zapata (Emiliano)
Zarefsky (David)
Zeichner (Kenneth M)
Zelan (Karen)
Zenger (John Peter)
Zhou Enlai
Zigler (Edward)
Zimmer (Paul)
Zindel (Paul)
Zipoli (Domenico)
Zitkala Sa
Zoellner (Robert)
Zola (Emile)
Zolotow (Charlotte)

CATEGORY 19: Projects / Programs

2 Plus 2 Plus 2 Plus 1 Programs
2 Plus 2 Plus 2 Programs
2 Plus 2 Plus 2 Tech Prep Programs
2 Plus 2 Tech Prep Associate Degrees
2 Plus 2 Tech Prep Programs
3M Optical Videodisc Project
3Rs Program
4 H Debate Project
4 H Programs
4 Plus 2 Plus 2 Tech Prep Programs
10 Cents To Save a Life
12 Step Programs
21st Century Schools Pilot Project IN
310 Project
353 Project
A T and T Alliance for Tomorrows Teachers
AASCU ERIC Model Programs Inventory Project
ABDs of Reading
ABE Reading Sequential Competency System
ABLE Model Program
ABODE Program
ACA Comprehensive Work Entry Program
Academic Administration Internship Program
Academic and Support Group Model
Academic Assessment and Placement Program TN
Academic Challenge for Excellence
Academic Decathlon
Academic Enrichment for the Gifted in Summer
Academic Equity for Rural Schools Program
Academic Excellence Program
Academic Facilities Loan Program
Academic Internship Program CA
Academic Olympiad
Academic Program Evaluation Project
Academic Remedial Training Program (Navy)
Academic Talent Search Program
Academically Oriented Preschool Program
Academics Plus Program
Accelerated Academic Program for Low Achievers
Accelerated Learning of Spanish by Satellite UT
Accelerated Progressive Choice Reading Program
Accent Extension Programme
Accepting Behaviors for Cultural Diversity Project
ACCESS PENNSYLVANIA
ACE UCLA Freshman Survey
Achievement Competence Training
Achievement Directed Leadership Program
Achievement Goals Program
Achievement Motivation Development Project
Achieving Excellence Program (McREL)
ACT 101 Programs
Action Agenda Project
Action Femmes Project
Action for Boston Community Development Project

Action for Youth
Action Group Counseling
Actualization of Mainstream Experience Skills
Adapting Science Materials for the Blind
Adaptive and Corrective Program Physical Education
Adaptive Computerized Training System
Adaptive Learning Environments Program
Adaptive Physical Education Consortium Project
Add Ventures for Girls
Adelante Program CA
Adkins Life Skills Program
Administering for Change Program
Administration Native American Res Analysis Proj
Administrative Internship Program
Administrative Internship Programs
Administrator and Teacher Survey
Administrator Exchange Programs
Admissions Testing Program
Adolescent Infant Development Program DC
Adolescents in Child Training
Adolph Coors Outward Bound Manpower Challenge Prog
Adopt a Grandchild Program FL
Adopt a School
Adopt a Ship Plan
Adoption Bonding Program
Adult Armchair Education Project
Adult Basic Education Demonstration Project
Adult Basic Education Mobile Van Project
Adult Basic Education Outreach
Adult Basic Education Program
Adult Behavioral Classification Project
Adult Career Education Counseling Project
Adult Career Education Resources Survey
Adult Competency Education Project
Adult Cuban Immigrant Project
Adult Development Enrichment Program
Adult Education Act State Grant Program
Adult Education for the Homeless Program
Adult Education Staff Development Project
Adult Education Survey in Finland (1972 to 1973)
Adult Educator Exchange Program
Adult Functional Reading Study
Adult Independent Learner Project
Adult Learning and Public Broadcasting Project
Adult Literacy Education Program
Adult Literacy Initiative
Adults Health and Physical Developmental Program
Adults Learning Projects
Advanced Courses Development Programme (Scotland)
Advanced Education Projects (IBM)
Advanced Institutional Development Program
Advancement of Librarianship
Adventures in Movement for the Handicapped
Advisement and Graduation Information System FL
Aesthetic Education Program
AFDC Unemployed Fathers Program
Africa South of the Sahara Survey
African American Materials Project
African Primary Science Programme
African Social Studies Program
Ag Horizons GA
AgeLink Project NC
Agricultural Manpower Needs Project
Agriculture Industry Program
Aid for Part Time Study Program
Aircraft Instrument Comprehension Program
Alabama Literacy Project
Alabama Performance Based Career Incentive Prog
Alabama Student Grant Program
Alaska Consortium for Transition Services
Alaska Educational Satellite Demonstration Project
Alaska Effective Schooling Program
Alaska Innovative Technology in Education Project
Alaska Library Network
Alaska Native Core Program
Alaska Research on School Effectiveness Project
Alaska Rural School Project
Alaska School Effectiveness Project
Alaska Statewide Assessment Program
Alaska Student Loan Program
Alaska Writing Program
Alaska Youth Initiative
Alaskan Native Needs Assessment
Albany Librarianship Trainee Program
Alberta Achievement Testing Program
ALBERTA BEST
Alberta Diagnostic Reading Program
Alberta Initiation to Teaching Project
Albuquerque Integration Outreach Project
Alcohol Education Discipline Program
All Indian Pueblo Coun Univ New Mex Teach Ed Prog
Allen J Ellender Fellowship Program
Allyn and Bacon Reading Program
Alternate Learning Project
Alternate Semester Program
Alternate State Policy Mechanism Study
Alternative Child Care Program
Alternative Program PA
Alternative Schools Project
Alternative Training Experiment
Alternative Transportation Program
Alternative Youth Employment Strategies Project
Alternatives Prevention Program NY
America 2000 Library Partnership
American Business Language Education
American History Textbooks Project
American Indian Administrator Training Programs
American Indian Archaeology Program
American Indian Law Program
American Indian Program (Harvard)
American Indian Teacher Training Program
American Indians Into Medicine Program
American Industry Project
American Issues Forum
American Memory Project (Library of Congress)
American Outdoor Education Project
Americas Town Meeting of the Air
Amherst Project
Amigos Program MA
Anacostia Community School Project
Analytical Study of Teaching
Anchor Test Study
Andean Oral History Workshop
Anik B Interactive Instructional TV Project
Animals in the Classroom Project
Annenberg CPB Project
Anthropology Curriculum Project
Anthropology Curriculum Study Project
Antioch Education Abroad
Antioch Program on Interracial Education
APACE Program
Apollo Program
Apollo Soyuz Test Project
Appalachia Preschool Education Program
Appalachian Adolescent Health Education Project
Appalachian Community Impact Project
Appalachian Education Satellite Project
Appalachian Regional Development Program
Apple Classrooms of Tomorrow
Apple Corps (Georgia)
Applied Program of Public Service
Apprenticeship Outreach Program
Appropriate Technology Program KS
Approval Order Programs
Aptitudes Research Project
Archaeology and African Cultures Program NY
Area III Valley Intercultural Program
Area Wage Survey Program
Arizona Career Ladder Program
Arizona State Assessment Programs
Arizona Student Assessment Program
Arkansas Educational Assessment Program
Arkansas Special Youth Project
Arkansas Technology Access Program
Armed Forces Health Prof Scholarship Program
Armed Services Materials Conversion Project
Army Specialized Training Program
Art and the Built Environment Project
Art on the Air
Art Partnership Networks
Art Recognition and Talent Search
ARTE RUETE Study
Artes Latinae
Articulated Campus Field Program
Articulated Instructional Media Program
Articulation for Career Education
Artists in Education Program
Artists in Residence Program
Artists in Schools Program
Arts and Science Public Sch Teleconfer Network OK
Arts for Learning Program
Arts for Transition
Arts from the Inside Out PA
Arts in Education Project
Arts in General Education Program NY
Arts in Schools Basic Education Grants
Arts Partners Program NY
Arts PROPEL
Arts Recognition and Talent Search
ASHE ERIC Higher Education Course Syllabi Project
Asia Pacific Programme of Educ Innovat for Develop
Asia Pacific Programme of Education for All
Asian African Pupil Resource Project
Asian and Pacific Student Leader Project
Asian Newcomer Parent Program
Asian Programme of Educ Innovation for Development
Asian Studies Curriculum Project
Asian Youth Substance Abuse Project CA
AskERIC
Aspen Program on Communications and Society
Aspen Project
Assist a School Program KY
Assistance for Isolated Children (Australia)
Assistance to States for State Equalization Plans
Assistant Plus Program
Assistant Teacher Program MS
Assisted Places Scheme (England)
Associate Community School Director Program
Associate Instructor Teaching Skills Program
Associated Colleges Midwest Urban Semester Program
Associated Schools Project
Associates Program
Astor Program for Gifted Children
At Home Program
At Risk Child Care Program
Athena Language Learning Project
Athletes Coaching Teens (Program)
Atlanta Desegregation Plan
Atlanta Project
Atlanta Student Manpower Project
Atlantic Science Curriculum Project NS
Attendance Improvement Plan
ATTLAS Program
Audio Visual Satellite Instruction
Audioinstructional Programs
Auditory Discrimination in Depth Program
Audubon Conservation Program
Auerbach Badger Discussion Group Program
Aurora PRECIS Project
Austin Longitudinal Research Project
Austin Science and Mathematics Consortium TX
Austin Teacher Program TX
Austin Youth River Watch Program TX
Australian Language Levels Project
Australian Science Education Project
Australian Second Language Learning Program
Australian Studies in Student Performance
Automated Leadership Training Program
Auxiliary Career Program
Auxiliary Loan Program
AVID Program
Bachelor Degrees for Soldiers
Ball State Staff Development for Public Schools
Baltimore Longitudinal Study of Aging
Baltimore Teacher Training Project
Bangalore Communicational Teaching Proj (India)
BankAmerica Foundation Educ Initiatives Program
Banks Model School Project
Banneker School Project
Barrier Resolution Project
Basic Citizenship Competencies Project
Basic Education Development Scheme (England)
Basic Education Student Training Program
Basic Educational Enrichment Program
Basic Educational Skills Project
Basic Educational Skills Tutorial Program
Basic Ideas Program
Basic Instruction Programs
Basic Job Readiness Training Program (Montreal)
Basic Literacy for Adult Development
Basic Occupational Language Training
Basic Skills Assessment Program
Basic Skills Education Program
Basic Skills Improvement Program
Basic Skills Improvement Program (Massachusetts)
Basic Skills Instruction for Secondary Schools
Basic Skills Learning Centers Project
Basic Skills Needs Assessment Project
Basic Trilingual Program NY
Basic Village Education Project (Guatemala)
Battle of the Books
Bay Area and the World Project CA
Bay Area China Education Project
Bay Area Global Education Program CA
Bay Area Literacy Referral Network CA
Bay Area Writing Project
BBC Adult Literacy Project (England)
Beacon College Projects
Becoming a Family Project
Before School Programs
Beginning Teacher Evaluation Study
Beginning Teacher Evaluation Study Phase II
Behavioral Classification Project
Behavioral Science Teacher Education Program
Belle Glade Project
Belmont Group Project
Beltman Multi Media Traffic Safety Program
Benchmarks Project ON
Benedum Project WV
Benedum Study Project
Berkeley Growth Study
Berkeley Guidance Project
Berkeley Project
Berkeley Reading Tests Project
Bethel Diagnostic Prescriptive Reading Program
Bethel Project
Better Schools Program TN
Big Brother Big Sister Programs
Big Cities School Project
Bilingual Academic Career Orientation Program NY
Bilingual Curriculum Content Pilot Project FL
Bilingual Education Fellowship Program
Bilingual Education Through the Arts NY
Bilingual Evaluation Technical Assistance Project
Bilingual Prediction Project
Bilingual Program in Auxiliary Services NY
Bilingual Pupil Services Project NY
Bilingual Testing Program NJ
Biliteracy Skills Development Program NY
Bill Wilkerson Hearing and Speech Center Program
Billy Mills Indian Youth Leadership Program
Binford Individualized Curriculum Analysis Project
Biological Sciences Communication Project
Biomedical Interdisciplinary Curriculum Project
Biomedical Research Support Grants
Biomedical Sciences Preparatory Program AL
BISVUX Project (Sweden)
BIZQUIZ
BKR Training Program
Black Creek Watershed Project IN
Black Executive Exchange Program
Blalock FIRST
Block Program (Indiana University)
Block Programs
Bloomington Normal Black History Project
Blueprint for the Future Program ON
Bluewing Tutorial Project
Book Bridges MB
Book Exposure Project
Books by Mail Program
Books Jobs Program
Boston Northampton Language Arts Program
Boston Six MA
Boswell English as a Second Language Program
Botswana National Literacy Program
Boys Town Common Sense Parenting Program
Boys Town Urban Program
Brackenridge Interns in Teaching
Braille Book Bank
Brazilian Literacy Movement
Brazilian Portuguese Project
Bread Loaf Writing Grants Program
Bridenthal Internship in Teaching Program
Bridge Independent Living Project
BRIDGE Program CT
BRIDGE Program OR
BRIDGE Project
Bridge Youth Advocacy Program PA
BRIDGES Program ON
BRIDGES Project (Harvard University)
BRIDGES Project ND
Bridges to Leadership 2000
Bridging the Gap Program
Bronx Academic Bilingual Career Program
Brookline Early Education Project
Brookline LOGO Project
Brunswick Foundation Small College Program

Buchanan Language Program
Buffalo English Linguistics Project
Building Better Boards Project
Building Communities (AACJC)
Building Our American Community Program
Building Strong Families Program
Building Workers Entering Skilled Trades Project
Bundy Aid Program
Bush Clinical Fellows Program
Bush Public School Executive Fellows Program
Business Management Fellowship Program
Calculators and Mathematics Project CA
Caldecott Award
Calgary Listening Inquiry Project AB
California 200 Project
California Academic Partnership Program
California Assessment Program
California Bill of Rights Project
California Child Care Initiative
California Community College Presidents Study
California Demonstration Program in Mathematics
California Demonstration Program in Reading
California Early Childhood Education Program
California Evaluation Improvement Program
California Guaranteed Student Loan Program
California Human Resources Development Plans
California Literacy Campaign
California Literature Program
California Local Educational Reform Network
California Main Street Program
California Master Plan for Higher Education
California Master Plan for Special Education
California Mathematics Project
California Mentally Gifted Minors Program
California Mentor Teacher Program
California Mexican American Educ Research Project
California New Teacher Project
California Occupational Survey
California School Improvement Program
California Staff Development Study
California State Compensatory Education Program
California State Migrant Master Plan
California State Preschool Program
California Statewide Evaluation of Migrant Educ
California Student Opportunity and Access Program
California Study Methods Survey
California Tomorrow Plan
California Video Resource Project
California Writing Project
CALTAC WILL
Cambridge Job Factory Voucher Experiment MA
Cambridge Lesley Literacy Project MA
Camden Program for Severely Handicapped Preschool
Camp Health Aid Program MI
Campus Governance Project
Campus School Plan
Canada Assistance Plan
Canada China Language Centre
Canada Manpower Training Program
Canadian Awareness Project
Canadian Construction Information System
Canadian Jobs Strategy
Canadian Public Issues Project
Canadian Spelling Program
Canadian University Computer Network Program
Canadian University Services Overseas
Capital City Readout
Capital District Humanities Program NY
Capstone Programs
Capstone Survey
Cardiac Wellness Training Project
CARE Boosters Network
CARE Linkages Project
Career Achievement Skills Training Program
Career Advancement Voucher Demonstration Project
Career Alert Planning Program
Career Alternatives for Handicapped Children
Career and Life Skills Project
Career Awareness Secondary Elem Students Project
Career Beginnings Program
Career Business Skills Program
Career Development for Children Project
Career Development for the Handicapped Project
Career Development Project for Tribal Girls
Career Development Study
Career Education Dissemination Project
Career Education PLUS Program
Career Education Project
Career Exploration Program
Career Guidance Program
Career Information Partnership (Canada)
Career Intern Program
Career Occupational Preference System
Career Opportunities Program
Career Oriented Modules Explore Topics in Science
Career Pathways in Energy Conservation MA
Career Pattern Study
Career Planning Program
Career Related Skills Project
Career Selection Education Project
Career Skills Assessment Program
Career Teacher Grant Program
Career Vocational Student Profile Project
Caribbean Agricultural Extension Project
Caribbean American Scholars Project
Caribbean Basin Initiative
Caribbean Fishery Development Project
CARISPLAN
Carleton Project
Carlson Proposal
Carnegie Mellon University Social Studies Project
Carnegie Philosophy Project
Carolina Abecedarian Project NC
CASE Reporting System
Cash Assistance Programs
CASPAR Database
Cassette Review Program
Cataloging in Source
Catskill Area Project in Small School Design
Causality Approach
CCSSO State Collaborative on Assess and Studt Stan
CDA
CDA Scholarship Assistance Program
CEDAR Project (England)
Census Access Program
Census Mapping Project
Centennial Education Program
Center Based Programs
Centerprise Community Publishing Project
Centers for Independent Living Program
Central American Peace Scholarship Program
Central Cities Project
Central Iowa Low Achiever Mathematics Project
Central New York External High Sch Diploma Program
Centralized Correspondence Studies Program AK
Certified Financial Planner Prof Educ Prog
Cessna Aviation Study
CETA Youth Employment Program
Challenge Squared Program GA
Chamorro Materials Project
Chance Program
Change in Liberal Education Project
Changing Teacher Practice Study
Channel One
Character Education Program
Character Research Project
Charlotte Mecklenburg Career Development Program
Charquin Program CA
Cheche Konnen
Chelmsford Project
CHEM Study
Chemical Addictions Prevention in Schools
Chemical Bond Approach
Chemical Education Materials Study
Chemical Technician Curriculum Project
Cherokee Bilingual Education Program
Cherokee Nation Youth Leadership Program
Chicago Area Project
Chicago Creativity Project
Chicago Early Assessment Remediation Lab Program
Chicago Effective Schools Project IL
Chicago Fertility Census
Chicago Mastery Learning Reading Program
Chicago Project
Chicago Student Health Project
Chicago Youth Development Project
Chicano Cooperative History Project
Chicano Periodical Index Project
Chicken Shed Theatre Workshop (England)
Child Advocacy Program
Child and Adolescent Service System Program
Child and Adult Care Food Program
Child and Family Justice Project
Child and Family Mental Health Project
Child and Family Resource Program
Child Awareness Program MO
Child Care Food Program
Child Care in the Admass Society (Sweden)
Child Centered Inservice Training Project NY
Child Development Associate
Child Development Project
Child Development Trainer Program
Child Find
Child Health Assurance Program
Child Nutrition Education Program
Child Nutrition Labeling Program
Child Nutrition Programs
Child Rearing Study
Child Support Enforcement Program
Child Survival and Development Revolution
Child Survival Fair Start
CHILD to Child Program
Child Welfare Research Program
Childhood and Government Project
Childhood Education Program
Children and the Arts FL
Children at Risk of Educational Failure IL
Children Facing Divorce Program
Children Hearings Project MA
Children of Divorce (Program)
Children of the Future (Sweden)
Children Youth Intensive Case Management Prog NY
Childrens Developmental Play Program AL
Childrens Ethnic Art Project
Childrens Health and Movement Program
Childrens Health Assessment Program
Childrens Hearings Project MA
Childrens Learning in Science Project
Childrens Mental Health Project IL
Childrens Television Fair
Chinese Bilingual Education Program NY
Chinle Agency Summer Special Education Program
CHOICES (Program)
Choosing Optional Infused Career Education NY
Christensen Rhetoric Program
Chrysler Dealer Apprenticeship Program
Chukchi News and Information Service AK
CIRCA Project
Cities in Schools
Citizen Leadership Program WI
Citizen Me Project TX
Citizens Education Project MD
Citizenship in Action
City as School Program
City High School Recognition Program
Civic Achievement Award Program
Civic Education Enhancement Project
Clara Barton High School Bilingual Program NY
Claremont Project in Anthropology and Education
Clarifying Environments Program
Class Loading and Student Scheduling Program
Classical Studies Cambridge Project
Classroom Assistant Program
Classroom on Wheels
Classroom Strategy Study
Clay Boat Project
Clay County Education Program KS
CLEAR Reading Recovery Program
Clerical Sector of Learning Opportunity Program
Clerical Solo Program
Cleveland Major Works Classes
Client Assistance Programs (Rehabilitation)
Climax Programs
Clinch Powell Educ Coop Community Ed Project TN
Clinical Center Associate Program
Clinical Infant Development Program
Clinical Supervision Initiative
Close Up Program
Cloverport Plan
Cluster Concept Program
CNN Newsroom
CO Plus Project
Coaching for Improved Teaching
Coal Employment Project
Coca Cola Hispanic Education Fund
Cognitive Academic Language Learning Approach
Cognitive Enrichment Network
Cognitive Environments Project
Cohort Instructional Programs
Coimbra Community Awareness Project (Portugal)
Colfax Plan
Collaboration for Improvement of Teacher Educ
Collaboration for Improving Teacher Educ SK
Collaborations for Literacy
Collaborative Consultation Support System Program
Collaborative Network for Early Childhood Training
Collaborative Perinatal Research Project
Collaborative Research Programme (Scotland)
College 1
College Adapter Program
College Advanced Placement Program
College Alcohol Survey
College Assistance Migrant Program
College Assistance Program
College Bound Program
College Core Curriculum
College Discovery and Development Program
College Education Achievement Project
College for Kids
College for Living
College Guidance Placement Program
College Housing Loan Program
College Investment Decision Study
College Opinion Survey
College Opportunity Grant Program
College Orientation Program
College Orientation Program for Alaskan Natives
College Outcome Measures Project
College Parallel Program
College Parents Programs
College Placement Council Survey 1988
College Reach Out Program
College Readiness Program
College Reading Study Skills Program
College Science Improvement Programs
College Science Instrumentation Program
College Teacher Preparation Program
College Work Study Program
Collier Macmillan English Program
Colombo Plan
Colorado Elementary Science Project
Colorado Foreign Language Proficiency Sample Proj
Colorado Migrant Education Health Program
Colorado Migrant Health Program
Colorado Program
Colorado Rural Revitalization Project
Colorado Training Institute
Colorado Western States Small Schools Project
Colorado Writing Project
Combined Resources for Editing Automated Teaching
COMETS (Project)
COMETT
COMETT CALLIOPE (Project)
COMEX Project
Comfield Model Teacher Education Program
Committee for Education Programs
Commodity Distribution Program
Common Core of Data Program
Common Education
Communi Link
Communication Program Survey
Communication Skills Centers Project
Communication Skills Through Authorship
Community Aging Project
Community Aide Program
Community and Education Project for Beta Israel
Community Apprentice Program
Community Based Alternatives Program NC
Community Behavioral Services AB
Community Campaigns
Community Centered School Support Program
Community College Leadership Program
Community Communications Project
Community Coordinated Child Care Program
Community Corrections Training Project
Community Development Block Grant Program
Community Education Center Programs
Community Education Planning Project
Community Education Program on Home Rule
Community Family Day Care Project
Community Food and Nutrition Programs
Community Health Center Programs
Community Helper Program
Community Human and Resources Training Program
Community Improvement Program
Community Integrated Training and Education OH

Early to Read
Early Training Project
Earn and Learn Program IL
Earth Education Program
Earth Lab
Earth Science Curriculum Project
Earth Science Educational Program
Earth Science Teacher Preparation Project
Earthwatch Program
East Area Schools News Service OR
East Los Angeles Youth Training Employment Project
East Providence Career Education Project
ECIA Chapter 1 Migrant Programs
Economy Food Plan
Education 2000 (Global Education)
Education and Community Project (Israel)
Education and Local Development Project
Education and the Economy Alliance
Education and Work Program
Education Data Improvement Project
Education for Employment IL
Education for Employment Programs
Education for Employment WI
Education for Independent Living Model Program
Education for Peace Project
Education for Self Reliance (Tanzania)
Education for Work Linkage Project
Education Improvement Project
Education North Project
Education Through Inquiry
Education Through Student Interaction Program
Education Through Vision
Educational Assistance Test Program
Educational Career Serv Community Outreach Prog
Educational Dissemination Studies Program
Educational Extension Program
Educational Information Centers Program
Educational Laboratory Theatre Project
Educational Media Production Proj Hearing Impaired
Educational Opportunities Program
Educational Opportunities Programs
Educational Opportunity Centers
Educational Opportunity Programs and Services CA
Educational Partnerships Program (OERI)
Educational Priority Area Project
Educational Quality Indicators Project AB
Educational Resources Access Programs
Educational Satellite Communication Demonstration
Educational Technology Training Program
Educational Telecommunications for Alaska Project
Educational Television Intervention Programs TN
Educators 2000 Project
Educators Peer Instructional Consulting Proj
Effective Reading Programs
Effective Schools Project
Effective Schools Projects
Effective Teacher Training Program NC
Effective Teacher Training Program NM
Effective Teaching and Supervision of Instruction
Effective Teaching Cooperative
Effective Use of Resources Project
Effective Use of Time Program
Effectively Influencing Political Decisions
Eidos Program NY
Eight Year Study
El Arco Iris Program TX
Elder Ed Program
Eldercollege
Elderscholar Program
Electromechanical Technology Project
Electronic Information Delivery Online System
Electronic Learning Package Factory
Elementary Economics Project
Elementary Education Voucher Demonstration
Elementary Industrial Arts Project
Elementary Inservice Mathematics Program
Elementary Intern Program
Elementary Language Study Experiment
Elementary Law Related Education Program
Elementary School Curriculum Efficacy Program MI
Elementary School Economics Project
Elementary School Health Curriculum Project
Elementary School Recognition Program
Elementary School Science Project
Elementary School Teaching Project
Elementary Social Science Education Program
Elyria Project for Innovative Curriculum
Emergency Land Fund
Emergency Services Research Demonstration Project
Emphasis on Excellence Program FL
Employability Support Network of Disabled Youth
Employee Fitness Programs
Employer Based Career Education
Employer Supported Parental Involvement in Educ
Encendiendo Una Llama CT
Energy and Mans Environment Project
Energy Education Curriculum Project
Energy Policy Project (Ford Foundation)
Energy Project For Women
Engineering College Faculty Shortage Project
Engineering Concepts Curriculum Project
Engineering Executive Program
Englewood School Development Program
English as a Second Language Teacher Institute
English Plus Movement
English Social Studies Opportunity Program
Enhanced Skills Training Program
Enlace Project CA
Enriched Career Search
Enrichment of Teacher and Counselor Competencies
Enrollment and Facilities Projection Program
Entebbe Program
Enterprise High Schools MI
Entitlement Programs
Entry Level Skills Program
Environmental Education Outdoor School Program CA
Environmental Education Programs
Environmental Experience Stipends Program
Environmental Press
Environmental Studies Project
Environmental Study Area Program
Equal Education Opportunity Program PA
EQuality Project
EQUALS Program
EQUITY 2000
ERASMUS Programme
ERIC Digests
ESEA Title I Migrant Programs
Essentia Project (Essence)
Essential Early Education Project
Essential Elements of Effective Instruction
Essential Skills Program
Essentials of Instruction (Program)
Essexfields Demonstration Project
Ethical Quest Project
Ethnic Heritage and Language Schools Project
Ethnic Heritage Studies Program
Ethnic Monitoring (Great Britain)
Eureka Project
European Community Course Credit Trans Sys
EUROTECNET
Evaluation for Individualized Instruction Project
Evaluation of Practices Individualized Schooling
Evaluation Task Development Project
Evaluations of Classroom Observations Project
Evaluative Programs for Innovative Curriculums
Even Start
Every Child a Winner
Every Child Can Succeed Program
Every Student Succeeds
Evolutionary Development Program
EXCEL Program NC
Exchange Visitor Program
Executive High School Internships Program
Executive Internship Program MD
Exemplars of Excellence
Exemplary In School Demonstration Projects
Exeter Writing Project NH
Exoffenders Employment Project
Expanded Child Care Options Demonstration
Expanded Food and Nutrition Education Program
Expanding New Horizons Project
Experienced Teacher Fellowship Program
Experiential Education Evaluation Project
Experiment at Butte
Experiment in International Living
Experimental Elementary Program
Experimental Freshman Year Program
Experimental Preparation Program
Experimental Program for Orientation CO
Experimental Proj in Instruct Concentration
Experimental Schools Program
Experimental Volunteer Army Training Program
Experimental World Literacy Programme
Exploratory Work Experience Project
Exploring Human Nature Project
Extended Degree Programs
Extended Learning Program
Extended Opportunity Programs and Services
Extending Family Resources Project
External Diploma Programs
External Examination Program
External High School Diploma Program NY
External High School Diploma Program WI
Extra Year Programs (Kindergarten)
Facilitated Appraisal for College Executives
Facilitator Project NJ
Faculty Assistance Computing Education Services NY
Faculty Development in Nursing Education Project
Faculty Improvement Program
Faculty Projection Program
Families First Program CA
Families First SD
Families Involved in Schools and Community MN
Families Play to Grow Program
Family Assistance Plans
Family Consultation Project
Family Day Care Systems
Family Development Research Program
Family Education Program NY
Family Education Program PQ
Family English Literacy Network
Family Farm Program (California)
Family Friends Program
Family Infant and Preschool Program NC
Family Infant Toddler Project
Family Life Education Program Development Project
Family Math
Family Matters Project
Family Oriented Language Dynamics
Family Oriented Structured Preschool Activity MN
Family Preservation Services
Family Research Project
Family Resource and Support Programs
Family Shelter Care Project
Family Support Project MI
Farm and Home Management Program
Farmers Functional Literacy Project
Farmington Plan
Favorable Alternate Sites Project
Federal Archeology Program
Federal Assistance for Staff Training
Federal City College Lorton Project
Federal Cylinder Project
Federal Foundation Program
Federal Insured Student Loan Program
Federal Offenders Rehabilitation Program
Federal State Program Congruity
Federal Supplemental Benefits Program
Federal Surplus Foods Program
Federal Telecommunication Standards Program
Federal Writers Project
Federal Young Adult Services Project
Federated Learning Communities Project
Fee for Service Health Plans
Fellows in Education Journalism Program
Fels Longitudinal Program
Feminine Development Program
Field Based Programs
Field Initiated Studies
Fillmore Street Reference Project
Financial Aid for Colleges and Tech Schools Prog
Financial Projection Program
Find and Inform Talent Project
Fine Arts Educational Improvement Project
Finger Lakes Dislocated Workers Project NY
Fire Education and the News Program
Fireside Summer Experience Program NH
First Friends Program
First Years Together (Project)
Fisheries Adjustment Program NF
Five State Multi Ethnic Training Project
Five Year College Programs
Flex Ed Reading Readiness Program
Flexible Calendar Pilot Project CA
Flexible Calendar Program CA
Flexible Learning System
Flexible Services Development Project ON
Fleximode (Australia)
Flexistudy (United Kingdom)
Flint Youth Study
Florida Academic Scholars Program
Florida Adult Migrant Program
Florida Beginning Teacher Program
Florida Diagnostic and Learning Resources System
Florida Education Research and Development Program
Florida Instructional Program on Evaluation
Florida Longitudinal Project
Florida Master Teacher Program
Florida Merit School Program
Florida Migrant Education Program
Florida Migrant Health Project
Florida Migratory Child Survey Project
Florida Parent Education Program
Florida School Advisory Councils
Florida Science Assessment Project
Florida State Plan
Florida Statewide Assessment Program
Florida Student Assistance Grant Program
Florida Tuition Voucher Program
Florida Vital Information for Education and Work
Flower of the Dragon
Focus Curriculum Program
FOCUS Database
Focus on Inner City Social Studies
Focus on Teaching Project (Scotland)
Focus Supportive Work Program
Folkpatterns
Folwell Multiple Variable Program
Food Assistance Programs
Food Distribution Program
Food Distribution Programs
Food Donation Program
Food Stamp Employment and Training Program
Food Stamp Program
For Character Program (Chicago)
Ford Foundation Clinical Supervision Program
Ford Training and Placement Program
Foreign Language Experience Programs
Foreign Language Exploratory Program
Foreign Language Innovative Curricula Studies
Foreign Language Teaching Materials Project
Foreign Science Information Program
Forests in Schools Project
Formula Phonics Videotape Reading Chain Program
Forum Campaign for Comprehensive Education
Foster Child Advocate Services Project
Foster Grandparent Program
Fostering Team Approach Career Education
Foundations for Gerontological Education Project
Foundations Project
Four Corners Mental Retardation Project
Four Corners Regional Project
Four States Project
Four Worlds Development Project (Alberta)
Fourth Grade Computer Project IN
France Wiseman Educational Program
Franco American Ethnic Heritage Studies Program
FrEdMail
Free Venture Program
French Culture Research Project
Freshman Skills Assessment Program
Fresno County Project
Fresno Organizing Project CA
Friends Morgan Project
Friends of Black Children Project
Fulbright Exchange Program
Fulbright Hays Seminars Abroad Program
Fulbright Teacher Exchange Program
Functional Literacy for the National Guard
Functional Literacy Project (India)
Functional Mainstreaming for Success Project
Functional Objectives of Language Learning Project
Functional Speech and Language Training Program
Future Teacher Institute CA
Gahagen Bernstein Educational Program
Ganado Language Arts Development Project AZ
Ganado Public Schools Bilingual Education Project
Garden State Graduate Fellowship Program NJ
Garfield Options for Leadership Development
GATE Project
Gateway Writing Project
Gender Expectations Student Achievement Program
General Academic Simulation Program
General College Pilot Education Program
General College Program Assessment Project
General Information Programme
Generalized Academic Simulation Program

Generalized InService Training Project
Generations Together Program
Generic Baccalaureate Nursing Data Project
Generic Skills Project
GENESYS TX
Geodynamics Project
Geographic Educ National Implementation Project
Geography Curriculum Project
Geography Education Standards Project
Georgia Appalachian Outreach Project
Georgia Assessment Project
Georgia Governors Honors Program
Georgia Governors Remediation Initiative
Georgia Labor Mobility Demonstration Project
Georgia Media Specialist Evaluation Program
Georgia Regents Testing Program
Georgia Statewide Testing Program
Georgia Teacher Certification Testing Program
Georgia Teacher Evaluation Program
German American Partnership Program
German by Satellite
Gerontological Information Program
Gerontology Alcohol Project
Gerontology Manpower Development Project
Gerontology Research Instructional Program
Get Set Program
Gifted and Talented Education Program CA
Girls into Science and Technology (England)
Girls into Science and Technology Project
Giving Rural Adults a Study Program
Glass Analysis Program
Global Atmospheric Research Program
Global TELEclass
GOAL ONE Project (NAEYC)
Going Places Program CA
Good Schools Project (Kappa Delta Pi)
Government Affairs Awareness Program
Governors Honors Programs
Graduate Career Opportunities Program
Graduate Education for Librarianship Ohio Project
Graduate Training Program in Community Educ
Graduated Work Incentive Experiment
Graduation Reality and Dual Role Skills Program
Graham Plan
Grandletters
Grandpeople Project
Grass Roots Alternative Diploma Study
GRE Cooperative Validity Studies Project
Great American Family Program
Great Cities Program
Great Decisions Program
Great Explorations in Math and Science
Great Falls Precision Teaching Project
Great Plains School District Organization Project
Great Towns Program
Greater Avenues for Independence
Greater Cleveland Social Studies Project
Greater Hartford Alliance for Literacy CT
Green Thumb Green Light Program
Green Thumb Program
Green Thumb Project
Greenfield Secondary Schools Project
Group Projects Abroad Program
Growing Thinkers Program
Growing Up Strong Program
Guaranteed Guidance and Counseling Services
Guaranteed Tax Base Plan
Guelph Rural Development Outreach Project
Guest Artist Program
Guidance Opportunities for Affective Learning
Guided Occupational Orientation Program
Gulfport Project
GUME Project
H 2 Immigration Program
Hablar et Parler
Haitian Parent and Teacher Training Program NY
Haitian Perinatal Intervention Program
Handicapped Children as Tutors (Project)
Handicapped Children Model Programs
Handicapped Childrens Early Education Program
Handicapped Unbound Program AZ
Happily Ever After Program
Harbor City Learning Program MD
Harkness Fellowship Program
Harlem Youth Opportunities Project
Hartford Effective Schools Initiative
Hartford Higher Education Hispanic Project
Harvard Boston Summer Program
Harvard Growth Study
Harvard Medicare Project
Harvard Preschool Project
Harvard Project Physics
Harvard Project Zero
Harvard Report on Reading
Harvard Social Studies Project
Harvard Studies of Career Development
Hastings Teacher Corps Project FL
Hatch Project 304
Have a Student Help Program
Hawaii English Program
Hawaii Foundation Program
Hawaii Integration Project
Hawaii Interactive Television System
Hawaii Language Immersion Program
Hawaii Language Skills Program
Hawaii Open Program
Hayden SAT Preparation Program
Head Start Evaluation Synthesis and Utilization
Head Start Supplementary Training Program
Health Advocacy Training Project
Health and Optimum Physical Education Project
Health and Science Action Learning Project
Health Careers Opportunity Program
Health Careers Summer Program
Health Consumer Education Program
Health Education Assistance Loan Program
Health Education Paraprofessionals Program NY
Health Education Telecommunications Experiment
Health Employee Learning Program
Health for All by the Year 2000
Health Instruction Exchange
Health Professions Capitation Grant
Health Professions Student Loan Program
Health Start Program
Healthy Mothers Healthy Fathers Healthy Babies MO
Healthy People 2000
Heart Health Program
Heart Smart
Hegeler Project Reading Study
HEGIS Data Quality Project
Heifer Project International
Help Communities Help Themselves
Help Elderly Locate Positions
Helping Hand Programs
Helping Individuals Regain Employment
Helping One Student To Succeed
Helping Teacher Program
HEP CAMP National Evaluation Project
Hesquiat Project
High Expectations Reading Program
High Performance Computing and Commun Program
High Potential Program
High Priority Location Stipend Program FL
High Roads Project
High School Academies
High School and Beyond (NCES)
High School Awards Program
High School Geography Project
High School Improvement Project MI
High School Labor Studies Program
High School Political Science Curriculum Project
High School Study (University of Texas Austin)
High School Transcript Study 1987
High School Transcript Study 1990
High Schools That Work
High Scope Demonstration Preschool Project
High Scope Preschool Curriculum Study
High Success Program
Higher Education Achievement Program
Higher Education CETA Project
Higher Education for Adult Mental Health Project
Higher Education for Learning Disabled Students
Higher Education General Information Survey
Higher Education Indicators Project
Higher Education Instructional Television Project
Higher Education Learning Projects (Physics)
Higher Education Location Program
Higher Education Long Range Planning Program
Higher Education Opportunity Program
Higher Education Personnel Training Programs
Higher Education Prison Program
Higher Education Utilization Study
Higher Educational Learning Program Survey
Higher Horizons Program
Highfield Program
Highland Park Project
Highline Indian Tutoring Program WA
Hilroy Fellowship Program
Hispanic Urban Center Inservice Program
Historical Explanation
History Education Project
Hoffman Mathematics System
Holding Power Project
Holmesburg Project
Holtzman Project
Home Based Programs
Home Child Care Training Project
Home Education Livelihood Program
Home Equity Conversion Project
Home Health Aide Pilot Training Project
Home Instruction Program Preschool Youngsters
Home Learning Center Project
Home Oriented Preschool Education Program
Home School Communication Program
Home School Community Relations Project
Home School Study of Language and Literacy Dev MA
Home Secrets Program
Home Start Program
Homebuilders WA
Homesharing Project
Homeward Bound
Homework Assistance Programs
Homework Helper Program
Honolulu Youth Symphony Concerts HI
HORIZONS Program IL
Hospital Improvement Program
Hospital Industries Program ME
Host Nation Programs
Hot Springs Project
Hough Community Project
Houston Quality Assurance Program TX
Houston Teacher Conservation Project TX
Howard Street Tutoring Program
Howard University Preschool Project
Hughson Project
HUGS Project OH
Human Corps Programs CA
Human Development Program
Human Genome Project
Human Growth and Development Program
Human Relations Recertification Program
Human Resources Development Program
Human Resources Development Program NC
Human Sciences Program
Human Services Drug Abuse Project
Human Talent Research Program
Humanities Curriculum Project
Humanities Enrichment Program
Huntington Project
I Can Do Program
I Gate Survey of Gifted and Talented Programs
I Have a Dream Program
I TRY Programs
Ibero American Heritage Curriculum Project
IBM California Educational Partnership Prog
IBM Project to Train the Handicapped
ICEIT Project
ICONS (Simulation)
Idaho School District Organization Project
IDEA Principals Inservice Program
Ideal Text Project (Quebec)
Identification of Maturity Level of Subordinates
Identifying School Behavior Problems Program
IEA Preprimary Project
IEA Science Project
IEA Six Subject Survey
IEA Written Composition Study
IEP Monitoring Analysis Plan
Illinois Basic Skills Program
Illinois Community Care Program
Illinois Competency Based Adult Education Project
Illinois Cooperative Conservation Program
Illinois Core Curriculum Project
Illinois Curriculum Program
Illinois Gifted Program
Illinois Goal Assessment Program
Illinois Migrant Program
Illinois Network Exemplary Occup Educ Prog
Illinois Occupational Curriculum Project
Illinois Plan
Illinois Public School Finance Project
Illinois Rural Revitalization Planning Program
Illinois State University Language Project
Illinois Study in Inquiry Training
Illinois Writing Project
Imaginative Educational Cooperation Project
Immersion Learning Project
IMPACT II
Impact of a Preschool Interracial Program
Improve Your Written Communication Program
Improved Individual Instruction Program PA
Improving Citizenship Education Project
Improving Reading Skills
Improving the Efficiency of Educ Systems Project
In School Youth Work Training Program
In Training Evaluation Report
Incentives for Improvement Program
Incentives to Improve Basic Education (Haiti)
Incidental Science Experience
Income Survey Development Program 1979
Income Transfer Programs
Independent Aging Program CA
Independent Learning Project
Independent Living Subsidy Program
Independent Miniunit Program
Independent Study in the Humanities Fellowship
Indian Child Welfare Program AZ
Indian Education Fellowship Program
Indian Education Program
Indian Education Research Project
Indian Health Program
Indian Hill Project
Indian Resource Development Program
Indian Resources Development Internship Program
Indian School Equalization Program
Indian Students University Programme
Indian Teacher Training Program
Indian Valley Colleges Project
Indian Youth Leadership Camps
Indian Youth of America Camps
Indiana Adult Literacy Initiative
Indiana Global Education Program
Indiana Least Restrictive Environment Project
Indiana Parent Training Project
Indiana Plan for Adult Religious Education
Indiana Project
Indiana TIME Project
Indiana University Advance College Project
Indiana Youth Employment Training Programs
Indianapolis Model Cities School Program
Indians into Medicine
Indicators of Excellence Program FL
Indigenous Mathematics Project
Individual Career Exploration PACK
Individual Progress Program
Individual Statistics Project (Sweden)
Individualized Bilingual Instruction Program
Individualized Employment Programs
Individualized Inservice Teacher Education Project
Individualized Instruction for Data Access
Individualized Language Arts Project
Individualized Mathematics System
Individualized Reading Program
Individualized Secondary Teacher Education Program
Individualized Service Plans
Individualized Study by Telecommunications
Individualized Teacher Preparation Program
Individualized Training Programs
Individualized Vocational Education Programs
Individualizing Spanish for Speakers of English
Individually Guided Education
Indonesia Nonformal Educational Project
Industrial Arts Career Exploration Program
Industrial Arts Curriculum Project
Industrial Training Resources Project
Industriology Project
Industry Services Training Program FL
Industry Work Experience Program
Inexpensive Book Distribution Program
Inexpensive Science Teaching Equipment Project
Infant Education Research Project
Infant Health and Development Program
Infant Parent Education Project CA
Infant Program for Visually Impaired
Infant Satellite Nurseries Project
Information Transfer Experiments Project
Informational Media Guaranty Program
Initial Certification Program NC
Initial Learning in Mainstreaming Project
Initial Training In Service Education of Teachers
Inland Area Writing Project
Inner City Mathematics Project
Inner City Teacher Education Project
Innovations Program (Australia)
Innovative Approaches Research Project
Innovative Projects Plan
Inquiry and Assistance Project
Inquiry Development Program
INROADS Program
Inservice Educ and Training of Teachers (Project)

INSIGHTS Program FL
INSTEP Project KS
Institute for Creative Education
Institute for Middle School Reform MD
Institute of Texas Studies
Institutional Aid Program
Institutional Child Abuse Neglect Prevention Proj
Institutional Conservation Program
Institutional Leadership Project
Institutionalized Facilities Program NY
Instructional Assistance Program
Instructional Concepts Program
Instructional Film Research Program
Instructional Microcomputer Project Ark Classrooms
Instructional Support System Occupational Educ
Instructional Systems Technology Program
Instructional Technology and Media Project
Instructional Television Library Project
Integrated Career Education and Placement Program
Integrated Continuing Care Program MA
Integrated Day Program
Integrated Model Preschool Program
Integrated Occupational Program AB
Integrated Studies Project
Intensive Reading Instructional Team
Intensive Reading Instructional Teams Program CT
Intensive Services Project
Intensive Teacher Education Program
Intensive Teacher Training Program
Inter Institutional Program Development Project
Inter University Biology Teaching Project
Interactive Language Development Teaching Program
Interactive Video Network ND
Interactive Videotex Project
Interagency Child Abuse Network
Interagency Collaborative Initiative
Interagency Growth Project
INTERCOCTA Conceptual Glossary
Intercultural Learning Network
Intercultural Social Studies Project
Intercultural Studies Project
Intercultural Understanding Project
Interdisciplinary Model Program in the Arts
Intergroup Education Project
Intergroup Relations Project
Intermediate English Evaluation Project
Intermediate Science Curriculum Study
Intern Mentor Program
International Assessment of Educational Progress
International Baccalaureate Diploma Program
International Biological Program
International Center for Culture and Environment
International Development Education Program
International Environmental Education Programme
International Geological Correlation Program
International Geosphere Biosphere Programme
International Health Communication Hotline
International High School NY
International Intervisitation Program Educ Admin
International Legal Exchange Program
International Military Education and Training Prog
International Press Institute Program
International Program for Agric Knowledge Systems
International Relations Program
International Space Programs
International Surveys
Interpretive Structural Modeling
Interprovincial Red Seal Program (Canada)
Interrelated Mathematics Science Project
Interstate Certification Project
Interstate Migrant Secondary Services Program
Interstate Migrant Teacher Exchange
Intervention by Prescription Project
Intervention Coaching Project
Investment in People Program
Involving the Very Young Program
Iowa ASSIST Program
Iowa Curriculum Assistance System
Iowa Experimental and Development Project
Iowa High School Curriculum Project
Iowa Problem Solving Project
Iowa Project
Iowa UPSTEP
Iowa Vocational Assessment System
Iowa Writing Project
IRA Project CONPASS
Iran Functional Literacy Project
Israel Elementary Science Project
Itinerant Behavior Development Program
ITT International Fellowship Program
Jacksonville Hospitals Education Program
Jaime Escalante Math Program
Japan Study Program
Japan United States Textbook Study Project
Jefferson County Adult Reading Program KY
Jefferson Parish Writing Project
Job Advancement Training Program
Job Corps Graded Reading Program
Job Designs Project OR
Job Exchange Programs
Job Finding Clubs (Canada)
Job Opportunities and Basic Skills Program
Job Opportunities for Youth Project
Job Oriented Basic Skills Program
Job Performance Measurement Project
Job Search Skills Training Program
Job Security System
Job Skills Education Program
Job Training 2000
Job Training and Tryout
Job Training for the Homeless Demonstration Prog
Job Training Scheme (England)
Jobs for Americas Graduates
Jobs for Americas Graduates Program
Jobs for Veterans Program
Jobs for Youth
Jobs in Instructional Media Study
Jobs Now
JOBSTART
JobStart Training Program
Johns Hopkins Academic Games Project
Join A School Program
Join A School Survey
Joining Forces (NASBE)
Joining Forces Program
Joint Development Project Higher Education
Joint Enrichment Team Project
Joint Innovative Projects
Jointly Registered Teacher Education Programs NY
Joliet Junior College Inmate Training Program
Journalism Bookshelf Project
Juilliard Repertory Project
Junior Achievement
Junior College Leadership Program
Junior Great Books Program
Junior High School Network Project
Junior MESA Program CA
Junior Secondary Science Project
Juniper Gardens Childrens Project
Justice Education Teaching Strategies Program
Kaleidoscope Childrens Art Program
Kaleidoscope Youth Development Program
Kamehameha Early Education Program
Kansas Arts Resource Training System
Kansas City School Behavior Project
Kansas Industrial Training Program
Kansas Internship Plan
Kansas Minimum Competency Testing Program
Kansas Regional Medical Program
Katimavik Program (Canada)
Keep Youth in School Program
Keeping America Working Project
Keeping Kids Healthy and Parents at Work IA
Kellog Community Services Leadership Program
Kellogg Farmers Study Program
Kellogg Project NY
Kellogg Public Service Research Program
Kenan Trust Family Literacy Project
Kent Mathematics Project
Kentucky Allied Health Project
Kentucky Beginning Principal Intern Program
Kentucky Career Ladder Project
Kentucky Development Tech Assist Community Ed Proj
Kentucky Educational Assessment Program
Kentucky Elderly Need Assessment
Kentucky Environmental Education Program
Kentucky Equine Educational Program
Kentucky Individualized Kindergartens
Kentucky Institute for Beginning Principals
Kentucky Instructional Resource Information System
Kentucky January Project
Kentucky Needs Assessment Project
Kentucky Nursing Education Project
Kentucky Social Services Need Assessment Project
Kentucky Staff Industry Exchange Program
Kentucky Student Achievement Project
Kentucky Teacher Internship Program
Kentucky Voc Educ Placement and Followup System
Kentucky Vocational Staff Industry Exchange Prog
Kenya Secretarial Project
Kern Eastern Sierra Writing Project
Kettering Project
Key Tracking Program MA
KEYS Project
Keys to School Boardsmanship Project
Keystone Adolescent Program for Stutterers
Keystone Writing Project TX
KHAN DU Project
KIDLINK Project (Electronic Mail)
KIDS 4
Kids Club MN
Kids In Difficult Situations Program
Kids Interactive Telecomm Experience by Satellite
Kinder Lernen Deutsch Project
Kindergarten Enrichment Program
Kindergarten Experience Comparison
Kindergarten Extended Day Program
Kindergarten Oral Language Project
Kindling Individual Development Systems Project
Knapp School Libraries Project
Knowledge Engineering for Young Scholars Program
Knowledge Transformation Program
Knoxville City Schools Proficiency Test Project
Kodak Skills Enhancement Program
Kodak Trades Trainee Program
Koontz Child Developmental Program
Kumtuks Alternative Rehabilitation Program
Labor Mobility Demonstration Project
Laboratory Program for Computer Assisted Learning
Lafayette Parish Compensatory Remedial Program LA
Lagrange Study
Lakatosian Programme
LAMP Project
Lane County Youth Project
Language across the Curriculum
Language and Thinking Program
Language Development Project (Australia)
Language Enrichment Communicative Skills Project
Language for Preschool
Language Improvement to Facilitate Education
Large Scale Programs
Laser Learning Project MI
Lasting Benefits Study TN
Latin American Curriculum Project
Latin American Literacy Project
Latin American Scholarship Prog of Amer Univs
Lau Program TX
Law and Poverty Project
Law Enforcement Education Program
Law Focus Curriculum Project
Law in a Free Society Project
Law in American Society Project
Law in the Social Studies Project
Law Related Education Evaluation Project
Lawrence Childrens Health Project MA
LD Transition Project MN
Leaders for Change
Leadership Development Program
Leadership Development Program (Texas A and M)
Leadership Effectiveness and Development Program
Leadership in Educational Administration Dev
Learncycle
Learner Based Accountability System
Learning Abilities Measurement Program
Learning Action Through Social Education Reading
Learning Center Program HI
Learning Development Program
Learning Disabled College Writers Project
Learning Earning and Parenting Program OH
Learning for Everyday Living
Learning for Leadership Program
Learning from Text Project CA
Learning in Retirement Programs
Learning in Science Project
Learning in Science Project (Primary)
Learning Resource Program
Learning Resource Support Program
Learning Skills Services
Learning to Read Through the Arts Program
Learning Together PA
Learning Tomorrow Project
Learning Works Program
LEASE Project
Lets Be Amigos Program
Lets Be Social Home Program
Levenstein Toy Demonstration Program
Lewis County Project
Liaison Teacher Program
Liaison Teacher Returnee Counselor Project
Liberal Studies Program
Liberty Partnerships Program NY
Libraries and the Learning Society
Library and Learning Resources Program CA
Library Buildings Awards Program
Library Education Experimental Project
Library Independent Study and Guidance Projects
Library Research and Demonstration Program
Library Technology Program
Licking County Writing Project OH
Life Adjustment Program
Life Enhancement Afloat Ashore Program
Life Enrichment Activity Program
Life Lab Science Program
Lifeline
Lifelong Career Development Model
Lifelong Learning Project
Lighthouse Learning Project
Ligru Project (Sweden)
Lilly Postdoctoral Fellowships Program
Lincoln Attucks Program
Lincoln Center Student Program
Lincoln School Clinical Module Project
Ling Temco Vought Employment Relocation Project
LINGUA Programme
Linguaplan Limbourg
Linguistic Atlas of the United States Project
Linguistic Bibliography Project
Linguistic String Project
Linguistics Research and Demonstration Project
Linkage Programs
Linked Systems Project
Linking Lifetimes Programs
Linking Outcomes to Organizational Planning
Lisle Fellowship Program
Listen and Think Program
Listening and Reading Comprehension Program
Listening Skills Program
Literacy for Every Adult Project CA
Literacy Impact Program
Literacy in Science and Social Science Project
Literacy Plus Project CA
Literacy Through Love
Litter Education Programs
Living Arts Program
Living Away from Home Allowances (Australia)
Living Library (Pets)
Living Planet Program
Living Room School Program
Loan Programs
Loan Video Programs
Local Arts Agency Development Program
Local Course Improvement Program
Local Government Services Program
Local Guaranteed Yield Program
Lockheed Technology Emphasis Camp
LONG Project (Sweden)
Long Range Planning for School Improvement PA
Longitudinal Studies Program (NCES)
Longitudinal Study of American Youth
Longitudinal Study of Children At Risk IL
Longitudinal Study of Educational Practices
Longitudinal Study of Elementary School Effects
Los Angeles County Probation Department Program
Los Angeles County Science Project
Los Angeles Model Mathematics Project
Los Angeles Study
Louisiana Early Childhood Development Program
Louisiana School Effectiveness Study
Louisiana Special Plan Upgrading Reading Project
Louisiana State Assessment Program
Louisiana Teacher Internship Program
Low Income Home Energy Assistance Program
Lower Attaining Pupils Programme (England)

LSU NASA Shuttle Program
Lucretia Crocker Program
Lumni Indian Aquaculture Project
Lungs Unlimited
Luso Brazilian Studies Survey
Lyndhurst Fellowship Program
Machine Trades Training Program for Youth OH
MacMagic Program
Macomb 0 to 3 Regional Project IL
Madison Area Project
Madison Project
Maimonides Early Childhood Health Program
Maine Assessment of Educational Progress
Maine CITE
Maine Drug Education Program
Maine Educational Assessment
Maine Innovative Education Grant Program
Maine Student Incentive Scholarship Program
Mainstream Assistance Team Project
Mainstream English Language Training Project
Mainstream Inservice Project NJ
Mainstream Project TEACH
Maintenance Bilingual Education Programs
Major Thrust in Elementary School Thinking Project
Major Urban Resource Libraries
Making Special Friends Project
Man and the Biosphere
Man in the Arctic Program
Management Implications of Team Teaching Project
Management Review and Analysis Program
Managing Academic Tasks Study
Managing Occupational Therapy in Rural Education
Managing Reading By Objectives
Manhattanville Music Curriculum Program
Manitoba Health Assessment Program
Manitoba Mathematics Assessment Program 1981
Manpower Development and Training Act Programs
Manpower Institutional Grant Program
Manpower Projection Model Project
MAP Critical Thinking Project
MAPS Placement Research Service
Maricopa County Organizing Project
Marin Social Studies Project
Marine Pollution Monitoring Programme
Marine Science Young Scholars Program
Maritime Trades Program
Mark Twain Teacher Internship Program
MarkED Model Program
Market Linkage Project
Marriage Enrichment Programs
Marshall University Program
Martin Luther King Jr Fellowship Program
Martin Luther King Program
Maryland Accountability Assessment Program
Maryland Career Development Project
Maryland Day Care Voucher Program
Maryland Education Technology Network
Maryland Elementary Mathematics Inservice Program
Maryland Functional Testing Program
Maryland Longitudinal Study
Maryland Plan
Maryland Professional Development Academy
Marylands Tomorrow Projects
Maryvale Project
Masfile Project
Massachusetts Early Education Project
Massachusetts Educational Assessment Program
Massachusetts Middle Grade Region Alliance Network
Massachusetts Workplace Education Initiative
Master Teacher Model Training Program
Master Teacher Program
Master Teacher Training Program TX
Mastery in Learning Project (NEA)
Mat Su Math Coop Project
Maternal Infant Health Outreach Worker Program TN
Math English Science Technology Education Project
Math Network Curriculum Project
Math Science Technology Education Project
Math Their Way Program
Mathematics and Communications Skills Prog NC
Mathematics Assessment Process Middle Grades
Mathematics for the Majority Continuation Project
Mathematics Methods Program
Mathematics Resource Project
Mathematics Science Tech Teacher Training Proj NY
Mathematics Skills Improvement Project
Mathematics Teacher Beliefs Study
Mathematics Teacher Education Project (England)
Mature Students Qualifying Program
MAVO Project
McKinley Project
McREL Effective Schools Program
McREL Instructional Staff Development Program
McREL Middle School Advisement Program
McREL School Improvement Program
Meal Programs
Meals on Wheels
Mechanicsburg Area Phone Pal Program PA
Media and Disadvantaged Project
Media Now Project
Media Research Panel Project (Sweden)
Medicaid
Medical Dental Education Preparatory Program
Medical Information Project
Medicare
Medicare Home Care Benefit
Mediterranean Regional Project
Memphis Metro Youth Diversion Project
Mentor Academy Program
Mentor Assisted Enrichment Project
MENTOR In Education NY
Mentor Peer Group and Incentive Model
Mentor Project MA
Mesa Action Planning System
MESA Program CA
Meta Ethnography
Methodology for Assaying Goals in Education
METRO Achievement Project
Metropolitan Educational Development Research Proj
Metropolitan Meteorological Experiment
Metropolitan Planning Project of Greater Boston
Metropolitan Reemployment Project
Mexican American Education Research Project
Mexican American Study Project
Miami Bilingual Program
Miami Linguistic Reading Program
Michigan Closed Case Survey
Michigan Early Childhood Educ Preschool Program
Michigan Education Trust
Michigan Educational Assessment Program
Michigan Language Program
Michigan Life Role Competencies Project
Michigan Lifelong Learning Link
Michigan Merit Scholarship Program
Michigan Partnership for a New Education
Michigan Social Issues Project
Michigan State Bilingual Program
Michigan Successive Discrimination Program
Michigan Tracking Program
Michigan Vocational Education Evaluation Project
Michigan Youth Leadership for Action
Microcomputer Diagnostic Testing Project (Canada)
Microcomputers and Middle School Problem Solving
Microelectronics Center of North Carolina
Microelectronics Education Programme
Mid Career Teacher Education Study
Mid Ocean Dynamic Experiment
Midcareer Programs
Middle Grade School State Policy Initiative
Middle Grades Assessment Program
Middle Grades Mathematics Project
Middletown
Middletown Nongraded Program
Midland Mathematical Experiment
Midwest Community College Leadership Program
Midwest Program on Airborne Television Instruction
Midwest Talent Search Project
Midwest Youth Employment and Training Program IL
Midwestern States Educational Information Project
Mifflin Curriculum Project
Migrant Action Program
Migrant and Seasonal Farm Worker Project
Migrant Citizenship Education Project
Migrant Dropout Youth Program
Migrant Early Childhood Education Project
Migrant Education Program
Migrant Education Research Project
Migrant Education Secondary Assistance Project
Migrant Education Section 143 Projects
Migrant Educators National Training OutReach
Migrant Head Start Programs
Migrant Health Program
Migrant Nutrition Education Project
Migrant Opportunity Program
Milepost Testing Program
Miles Skills Upgrading Program AL
Milford Visual Communications Project
Military Assistance Language Training
Military Assistance Program
Military Curriculum Project
Milk Programs
Miller Unruh Reading Program
Milton Keynes Home School Link Project
Milwaukee Bilingual Education Program
Milwaukee Project
Milwaukee School Improvement Program WI
Milwaukee Teacher Expectation Project WI
Mini Midi Program
Minigrant Program for the Academically Gifted DC
Minimum Foundation Program
Minneapolis Multi Ethnic Curriculum Project
MINNEMAST
Minnesota Chemical Depend Prog for Hear Imp Youth
Minnesota Couples Communication Program
Minnesota Dialogue on Education Project
Minnesota Early Language Development Sequence
Minnesota Early Learning Design
Minnesota Educational Effectiveness Program
Minnesota Experimental City
Minnesota Mathematics and Science Teaching Project
Minnesota Model Small Business Management Program
Minnesota Plan
Minnesota Research and Evaluation Project
Minnesota School Effectiveness Program
Minnesota School Health Education Model
Minnesota School Improvement Program
Minnesota Studies of Creative Behavior
Minnesota Survey of Employment Experiences
Minority Achievement Program
Minority Allied Health Project (AASCU)
Minority Assistance Program SC
Minority Business Enterprise Project
Minority Enterprise Small Business Investment Cos
Minority Female Single Parent Demonstration Proj
Minority Graduate Education Project
Minority Institutions Science Improvement Program
Minority Mobility Project
Minority Participation Program
Minority Womens Employment Program
Mission 21 VA
Mississippi Quality Education Project
Mississippi Teacher Educ Program Approval Process
Mississippi Workshop Project
Missouri Cooperative Work Program
Missouri Diagnostic Classification Plan
Missouri Mathematics Effectiveness Project
Missouri Performance Based Teacher Evaluation
Missouri Physical Performance Assessment Program
MIT Research Program on Communication Policy
MIT Sloan School of Management Research Program
MLA Foreign Language Program
Mobile Education Teams Program
Mobile Education Technology Project
Mobile Learning Unit Program
Mobility Assistance Program
Mobilization for Maturity Project
Model 2 Reading Program
Model 3 Communication Skills Program
Model Accounting Plan
Model Adoption Exchange Payment System
Model Builders Project
Model Business and Office Block Program
Model Cities Program
Model Early Childhood Parental Training Prog IL
Model Elementary Teacher Education Project
Model Health Care Programs
Model Preschool Program Handicapped Children LA
Model Schools Project
Model T Project
Model Teacher Induction Project
Model United Nations Program
Model Vision Project
Model Vision Project TN
Moderation and Assessment Project (England)
Modern Aids to Education Project
Modern Language Project
Modesto Multi Occupational Project
Modular Achievement Program
Modular Multiple Alternatives Program
Modules and Monographs in Mathematics
Moline Project
Money Measurement and Time Program
Monitoring Achievement in Pittsburgh
Monitoring the Future
Montana Tribal College Development Program
Monterey Articulation Program
Monterey Language Program
Montgomery County Work Release Program MD
Moonlight Schoolhouse
More Alternatives for Students
More Capable Students Project
More Effective Schools Program
Morning Star Native Teacher Education Program
Morning Star Program
Mother Child Home Program
Mother Daughter Communication Project
Mother Infant Literary Knowledge Program
Motion Picture Code and Rating Program
Motivational Skill Training Package
Motivational Skill Training Program
Mott Basic Language Skills Program
Mount Druitt Early Childhood Project
Mountain Bell Project MT
Mountain Plains Program
Mountain States Regional Medical Program
Multi Agency Project for Pre Schoolers
Multi Media Access Project
Multi Media Training Van
Multi Purpose Occupational Information System
Multi State Teacher Education Project
Multicultural Career Intern Program DC
Multicultural Improvement of Cognitive Abilities
Multicultural Reading and Thinking Program AR
Multilevel Evaluation Systems Project
Multilingual Survival Skills Program NY
Multimedia Rehabilitation Resources Project
Multipass
Multiple Activities Program
Multiple Alternatives Program
Multiple Entry Multiple Exit
Multiple Model Preschool Program
Multiple Teacher Factors Survey
Multiple Trails Plan
Multiple Wage Earner Program
Multipurpose Senior Services Program
Multnomah County CAPS Project OR
Municipal Cooperative Education Program
Napa County Follow Through Project
Napa Infant Program CA
NASA Equal Opportunity Program TX
NASSP Assessment Center Project
NASSP Internship Project
National Aboriginal Languages Program (Australia)
National Academy of Early Childhood Programs
National Accred Coun Agencies Serv Blind
National Adult Education Programme (India)
National Adult Literacy Project
National Apprenticeship Program
National Assessment of Chapter 1
National Assessment of Cooperative Learning
National Assessment of Educational Progress
National Assessment of Vocational Education
National Basic Skills Improvement Program
National CEDA Tournament
National Center for Higher Education Management
National Child Care Staffing Study
National Child Development Study
National Child Nutrition Project
National Commodity Processing System
National Cooperative Educ Statistics System Forum
National Coordinated Cataloging Program
National Data Resource Center
National Diffusion Network Programs
National Dissemination Project
National Education Dissemination System
National Education Longitudinal Study 1988
National Education Practice File

National Educational Finance Project
National Employer Supported Child Care Project
National Energy Education Development Project
National Energy Plan
National Engineering Education Delivery System
National English Literacy Dem Prog LEP Adults
National Environment Education Development
National Extension Leadership Development Program
National Faculty Salary Survey
National Family Day Care Project
National Family Violence Survey
National Geographic Kids Network
National Graduate Fellows Program
National Hispanic Scholar Awards Program
National Historic Landmarks Program
National History Project
National History Standards Project
National Independent Living Skills Assessment
National Individual Events Tournaments
National Intern and Resident Matching Program
National Language Arts Program
National Library Network Project (Canada)
National Marine Sanctuary Program
National Metropolitan Area Study
National Needs Assess Educ Media Mater Handicap
National Network for Educational Renewal
National Origin Minority Education NH
National Plan of Action for Women
National Postsecondary Student Aid Field Test
National Postsecondary Student Aid Study
National Prepaid Tuition Program
National Preventive Dentistry Demonstration Prog
National Program for Acquisitions and Cataloging
National Program for Educational Leadership
National Program for Library and Information Serv
National Project I (FIPSE)
National Project II (FIPSE)
National Project III (FIPSE)
National Project in Agricultural Communications
National Project IV
National Project on Career Education
National Project on Ethnic America
National Project on Violence and Bigotry
National Project Speech Commun Competencies
National Reading Improvement Program
National Research Service Awards
National Research to Development Network
National Resident Matching Program
National Rural Project
National Rural Research Personnel Preparation Proj
National School Food Service Program
National School Health Services Program
National School Volunteer Program
National Second Step Project
National Serials Data Program
National Service Program (Nigeria)
National Sex Equity Demonstration Project
National Spelling Bee
National Standards Project in Economics
National Study of Guidance
National Study of Intercollegiate Athletes
National Study of Internal Medicine Manpower
National Study of Local Operations under Chapter 2
National Study of School Evaluation
National Study of Secondary School Evaluation
National Supported Work Demonstration
National Survey of Children
National Textbook Program
National Training System
National Transportation Study
National Water Quality Initiative
National Womens Employment and Education Project
National Womens History Week Project
National Workplace Literacy Program
National Writing Project
National Youth Apprenticeship Initiative
National Youth Sports Program
Native American Administrator Program
Native American Gifted Program Model
Native Education Project AB
Native Hawaiian Educational Assessment Project
Native Indian Teacher Education Program
Native Indian Youth in Museums Project
Native Infant Program (Canada)
Naturalization Programs
Nature Computer Camp DC
Nava Nirmana Community Development
Navaho Rehabilitation Project
Navajo Bordertown Dormitory Program
Navajo Health Education Project
Navajo Hopi Teacher Corps Program
Navajo Indian Irrigation Project
Navajo Special Education Teacher Develop Prog AZ
Naval Flight Officer Training Program
Naval Occupational Task Analysis Program
Navy Science Awards Program
NEA Moratorium on Testing
Nebraska Online
Nebraska Physical Science Project
Nebraska Secondary Teacher Education Program
NEBSAT
Needs Assessment Project (AEL)
Neglected and Delinquent Pupils Project NY
Neglected Language Program
Neighborhood Development Plan
Neighborhood Facilities Program
Neighborhood Information Centers Project
Neighborhood Medical Care Demonstration
Network Analysis Program
Neurosciences Research Program
Nevada CBAHSD Project
New Brunswick Experiment
New Careers Programs
New Chance
New Elementary Teacher Education Program
New England Educational Assessment Project
New England Program in Teacher Education
New England Regional Student Program
New England Study Abroad Programs
New Friends Program
New Frontiers (Program)
New Futures Initiative
New Hampshire Mentor Teacher Project
New Horizons Program IA
New Jersey Adult Reading Project
New Jersey Alternate Route Program
New Jersey Basic Skills Assessment Program
New Jersey Bell Telephone Reading Project
New Jersey College Outcomes Evaluation Program
New Jersey Educational Assessment Program
New Jersey Graduated Work Incentive Experiment
New Jersey Mainstream Inservice Project
New Jersey Minimum Basic Skills Program
New Jersey Youth Corps Program
New Leaf Program
New Mexico Rural Science Education Project
New Mexico Western States Small Schools Project
New Netherland Project
New Nursery School
New Opportunities in Vocational Education Project
New Orleans Education Improvement Project
New Orleans Effective Schools Project LA
New Parents as Teachers Program
New Pioneers Program
New Primary Grades Reading System
New Rochelle Talent Search Project
New School of Behavior Studies in Educ Program
New Standards Project (LRDC)
New Teacher and Teacher Aide Project
New Teacher Retention Project (San Diego)
New Ways to Work Job Sharing in Schools Project
New York City Adult Literacy Initiative
New York City Health Care for the Homeless Program
New York City Infant Day Care Study
New York City School Volunteer Program
New York College Proficiency Examination Program
New York Educational Opportunity Program
New York Health Occupations Education Program
New York Rural Schools Program
New York State Conservation Preservation Grants
New York State External High School Diploma Prog
New York State Mentor Teacher Internship Program
New York State Mentoring Program
New York State Regents Action Plan
New Zealand Reading Recovery Program
Newark Literacy Campaign NJ
Newbery Award
Newburyport Project for Consumer Education
Newgate Program
Newsday Science Education Series Program
Newspaper in Education Program
Newspaper in the Classroom Project
NEXA Program
Neylan Minorities Project
NIE ECS NAEP Item Development Project
Nieman Fellowship
Nobel Prizes
Noble Center Team Teaching Plan
Nongraded Primaries in Action
Nonprofit Organization Program
Nonproprietary Training Programs
Nonpublic School Survey (NCES)
Nontraditional Community College Project
Nontraditional Employment Training Project
Nordic Paradise
Nordwrite Project
Normal Adolescent Project
Normative Systems Research
North American Collections Inventory Project
North Carolina Basic Education Program
North Carolina Career Development Program
North Carolina Mobility Project
North Carolina Pilot Kindergarten Program
North Central Louisiana Model Preschool Program
North Central Regional Information Exchange
North Dakota Close Up
North Dakota Pioneers in Equality Project
North Dakota Public Employee Retirement System
North Dakota Scholars Program
North Pacific Experiment
North Reading Screen Education Project
Northampton Family Literacy Project MA
Northeast Regional Credential Program
Northeast Tech Asst Ctr Learning Disabil Coll Prog
Northeast Texas Agricultural Literacy Network
NorthEast Texas Writing Project
Northeastern Ohio Regional Medical Program
Northeastern States Citizenship Project
Northern Cheyenne Follow Through Project
Northern Indian California Education Project
Northern Michigan Mobility Project
Northern Native Language Project
Northern New England Marine Education Project
Northern Plains Teacher Corps Project ND
Northern Reading Program
Northern Region Rural Integrated Programme (Ghana)
Northwest Connection
Northwestern University Marketing Program
Norwalk Mentor Program CT
Norwalk Plan
Nottingham Programming in Math Project
Nova Plan
Nuclear Science Curriculum Project
Nuffield Biology
Nuffield Chemistry
Nuffield Combined Science
Nuffield French
Nuffield German
Nuffield Humanities
Nuffield Mathematics
Nuffield Physics
Nuffield Project
Nurse Career Pattern Study
Nursing Home Trainer Program
Nursing Improvement Programs
Nursing Student Loan Program
Nutrition and Gerontology Services Project
Nutrition Education and Training Program
Nutrition Education Program
Nutrition Education Training Project MI
NYC TV Film Distribution Project
Oak Grove Project
Oak Park Project
Oakland Study Center Program
Oakland Writing Project MI
Oakland Youth Work Experience Program
Oakleaf Project
Occupational Competency Project NJ
Occupational Employment Statistics Program
Occupational Information Systems Grants Program
Occupational Projection Research Project
Occupational Survival Skills Project
Occupational Work Adjustment Program
Occupational Work Experience Program
Ocean County Social Studies Project
Ocean Hill Brownsville School Project
Oceanic Education Activities Great Lakes Schools
Off Campus Experiential Learning Program
Offender Literacy Programs
Office Laboratory Programs
Officer Friendly Program
Official Development Assistance
Oglala Sioux Education Research Project
Ogontz Plan for Mutual International Education
Ohio Career Development Program
Ohio Innovations Survey
Ohio Instructional Grants
Ohio Library Development Plan
Ohio Needs Assessment
Ohio Network for Information Exchange
Ohio Plan
Ohio Reading Recovery Program
Ohio Sea Grant Program
Ohio State Midcareer Program in Educational Admin
Ohio Vocational Education Achievement Test Program
Ohio Works Program
Ohio Writing Project
Oklahoma College Testing Program
Oklahoma Cultural Understanding Project
Oklahoma Drug Abuse Education Program
Oklahoma Indian Education Needs Assessment Project
Oklahoma School Testing Program
Oklahoma State Faculty Survey
Oklahoma Talkback Medical Education Network
Oklahoma Writing Project
Older Adult Project
Older American Volunteer Programs
Older Workers Jobs Program
Olney Project
Olympics of the Mind
Omaha Teacher Corps Project NE
Ombudsman Activities Project
On the Right Track Project
Onderwijs un Sociaal Milieu (Netherlands)
One Room Drop In School
One to One Project
Onondaga Valley Oral History Project NY
Onsite Pueblo Personnel Training Program
Onward to Excellence
Open College Networks (Great Britain)
Open Corridor Program
Open Door Programs
Open Entry Open Exit
Open Library Network (Netherlands)
Open Road New Jobs CA
Open Road Student Involvement Project
Operation Alphabet
Operation Bookstrap
Operation Breakthrough
Operation Bridge
Operation EPIC
Operation Fair Chance
Operation Future
Operation Gap Stop
Operation GO
Operation Hitchhike
Operation Index
Operation Mainstream
Operation Manpower
Operation MEDIHC
Operation Moonvigil
Operation Opportunity
Operation Pathfinder
Operation PEP
Operation PRESENCE
Operation PROBE
Operation PROTEACH
Operation Reading Bases Program
Operation READS
Operation Reason
Operation Recover
Operation Rescue
Operation Retrieval
Operation Return
Operation SAIL
Operation School Renewal NJ
Operation Search
Operation Second Chance
Operation SER
Operation Shadow
Operation Shirtsleeves
Operation SMART
Operation Stay in School
Operation Success
Operation Turnaround
Operation Wordpower
Operation Young Adults
Opportunities for Youth Creative Arts Project

Opportunities for Youth in Education
Opportunity Award Program
Opportunity School Program
Oral Aural Visual Project
Oral English Program
Oral Language Bilingual Educational Program
Oral Language Program
Orange County Vocational Guidance Project
ORB Program
Orderly Departure Program (Thailand)
Oregon Action Plan for Excellence
Oregon Adaptive Arts Techniques Project
Oregon Elementary English Project
Oregon School Finance Plan
Oregon Small Schools Program
Oregon Statewide Assessment Program
Orientation to the World of Work Program
ORILLAS Network
Orton Gillingham Tutorial Program
Oswego Plan for Team Supervision
Otis Spunkmeyer Student Motivation Program
Ottawa Project
OUNCE Classroom Management Program
Ounce of Prevention Program IL
Our Schools Project
Our Young Authors (Writing Project)
Out of School Credit Experiences Program
Out of School Youth Program
Outdoor and Conservation Education Program
Outdoor Education for the Handicapped Project KY
Outdoor Research Project KS
Outlook Nashville Program
Outreach and Technical Assistance Network CA
Outward Bound
Overhead Project
Overseas Refugee Training Program
Oxford Council of Europe Study
Oxford Preschool Research Project (England)
Pacific Circle Project
Pacific Northwest Indian Reading and Language Prog
PACKS Project (United Kingdom)
Pairing Enrichment Program
Palo Alto Peer Counseling Program
Palspan Project
Pan American Agricultural Teacher Training Program
Panama Nuevo Veranillo Project
Panel Review of Products
Panel Study of Income Dynamics
Paraprofessional as Companion Therapist Program
Parent Aide Programs
Parent and Child Education Program KY
Parent and Child Education Project AZ
Parent Assisted Learning Program
Parent Child Early Education Program
Parent Child Education Program
Parent Child Program
Parent Child Toy Lending Library Program
Parent Education Expansion Project
Parent Education Follow Through Program
Parent Educator Program
Parent Employment Program
Parent Group Project
Parent Infant Early Education Program
Parent Infant Program
Parent Involvement in Education Project
Parent Involvement through Parent Education
Parent Loans for Undergraduate Students Program
Parent Observer Program
Parent Outreach Program
Parent Project
Parent Readers Program
Parent Readiness Education Project
Parent Services Project CA
Parent Speaker Program
Parent Teaching Home
Parent to Parent Dissemination Project
Parental Involvement Program
Parenting After Divorce Project
Parenting Resources Implementation Model Project
Parents and Children Together
Parents and Counselors Together Program
Parents Are Teachers Too Program
Parents as Leaders Program KY
Parents as Partners as Learners Project PQ
Parents as Partners in Learning Project NJ
Parents as Volunteers in Education
Parents Assuring Student Success Program
Parents Center Project
Parents Enrich Program
Parents in Partnership with Educators
Parents Sharing Books IN
Parents Too Soon (Project)
Parents Train Parents Project
Parents Training Parents Program
Parker Project
Parkway Program
Part Time Work Experience Program
Participation and Equity Program (Australia)
Participation in Adult Education Survey (NCES)
Partners in Americas Artist in Residence
Partners in Program Excellence
Partners Program CO
Partnership 2000 CA
Partnership for Academic and Career Education SC
Partnership for Environmental Technology Education
Partnership for Health
Partnership Vocational Education Project
Partnerships in Prevention
Pasos Adelante AZ
Passamaquoddy Enterprise Zone Development Project
Passport to English
PATHWAYS Project MI
Pathways to Employment II
Pathways to Identity Project
Pattern Drills Program
Patterns of Enquiry Project
Paul Douglas Teacher Scholarship Program
Pay As You Earn
Peabody College Early Training Project
Peabody Rebus Reading Program
PEACESAT
Pediatric Language Programs
PEECH Outreach Project
Peer Assistance and Review Program
Peer Assisted Leadership Program
Peer Evaluation Program
Peer Resource Programs
Peer Teachers as Mirrors and Monitors Project
PEG Program
Peninsula Academies Program
Pennsylvania CBTE Project
Pennsylvania Comprehensive Mathematics Plan
Pennsylvania Day Care Study Project
Pennsylvania Educ Needs Assessment Self Study
Pennsylvania Foreign Language Research Project
Pennsylvania Plan
Pennsylvania Rehabilitation Center Program
Pennsylvania Research Infant Devel Educ Project
Pennsylvania School Improvement Program
Pennsylvania Technical Assistance Program
Pennsylvania Writing Project
PEOPEL Program
People to People Program
Peoria Urban Teacher Education Program
PEPI Project
Perach Tutorial Project
Performance Assistance Program
Performance Indicators in Education Program
Performance Related Enabling Skills Training Proj
Permits with Transportation
Perry Preschool Project
Personal Experience Program
Personal Qualities Project
Personal Values Project
Personalized Teacher Education Program
Personnel for Parent Development Program
Personnel Preparation Program (OSEP)
Peterborough Project
Pew Campus Roundtable
PF Project
Philadelphia Business Academies
Philadelphia Cooperative Office Education Program
Philadelphia Cooperative Schools Program
Philadelphia Leadership Program
Philadelphia Open Classroom Project
Philadelphia Project
Philadelphia Regional Intro Minorities Engineering
Philadelphia Student Library Resource Requirements
Philippine Rural Reconstruction Movement
Phillips Extended Day Magnet Program
Philosophy for Children (Lipman)
Philosophy of Education Project
Phoenix Pilot Drug Program
Phoenix Project
Physical Skills Development Program
Physicians Serving Handicapped Children Project
Physics and Technology Project (Netherlands)
Physics Computer Development Project
Physics Curriculum Development Project
Physiology of Readiness Program
PIC Program
PICKUP
Picot Taskforce (New Zealand)
Pictorial Apprenticeship Program
Picture Lady Program
Piedmont Export Expansion Program
Piedmont Schools Project
Pilot State Dissemination Program
Pioneer Program (NASA)
PIRAMID Project
PISA Project
PIVOT Program
PLACE (Program)
Placebo Control Program
Plan Basico
Plan for Progress
Plan Puebla (Mexico)
Planning and Management Systems Program
Planning Development Quality Services Schools
Planning for Guidance Excellence
Planning Resources in Minnesota Education
Planters Employee Training Program
PLATS Project
PlayWrite Program
PLUS Program
POCO Project (Netherlands)
Poets in the Schools
Poindron Study
Polaris Project WV
Police Liaison Program (British Columbia)
Polish English Contrastive Project
Political Education Project (Canada)
Political Science Curriculum Project
Pontiac Bilingual Program (Michigan)
Population Education Project
Portable Assisted Study Sequence Program
Portage Project
Portal Schools
Porter Project
Portland Career Survey Project
Portland Hot Line Program
Portland Project
Positive Adolescents Choices Training Program
Positive Attitudes in Tennessee Schools
Positive Education Program
Positive Employment Relations Program
Positive Impact Program
Positive Peer Influence Program
Post Literacy Programs
Post Secondary Education Assistance Prog (Canada)
Postal Academy Program
Postdoctoral Faculty Fellowship Program
Power of Positive Students Program
Powhatan Goals of Education
Powhatan Project
Practical Work Orientation Program
Prairie State 2000
Praxis III
Preapprenticeship Programs
Predischarge Education Program
Preemployment Laboratory Education Program
Prekindergarten At Risk Program IL
Preparation for American Secondary Schools
Preparation for Employment Program
Preparation for Raising Educational Performance NY
Preparation of English Teachers
Preparation through Responsive Educ Programs
Prepare Educational Planners
Preparing for Profit
Preparing for Tomorrows World Program
Preparing Refugees for Elementary Programs
Prepprenticeship Programs
Prerelease Programs
Preschool Demonstration Project for Handicapped
Preschool Language Project
Preschool Learning Development Program NJ
Preschool Mental Health Program
Preschool Recreation Enrichment Program
Prescription Learning System
Preservice Educ for Teachers of Minorities HI
Presidential Initiatives
Presidential Internships Science and Engineering
Presidential Young Investigators Program
Presidents Environmental Merit Awards Program
Presidents Excellence Club TX
Presidents Private Sector Survey on Cost Control
Prevention by Mail Programs
PRIDE Center TX
PRIDE Project
Primary Assessment Curric Exper (Great Britain)
Primary Assessment Program (Australia)
Primary Correspondence School
Primary Education Program FL
Primary Education Project
Primary Education Project (Britain)
Primary Evaluation Inputs Model
Primary Individualized Reading
Primary Mathematics Education Enhancement Prog
Primary Mental Health Project
Primary Science Project
Primary Skills Program
Prince Edward County School Project
Prince Edward Island Newstart
Princeton Plan
Princeton Rutgers Census Data Project
Principal Incentive Programs
Principals Computer Network
Principals Inservice Program
Principals Reflective Experiential Prep Prog TX
Priorities in School Mathematics Project
Priority Country Area Program (Australia)
Priority Exceptional Students Study (Australia)
Prison Literacy Project PA
Private Sector Initiative Programs
Private Sector Involvement Project
PROBE Program
Problem Solving in Mathematics Project
PROcedure to Promote Effect effic Study skills
Procedures for Adopting Educational Innovations
Product Impact Project
Productive Thinking Program
Productivity Projects Studies Program UT
Productivity Sharing Plans
Professional Alternative Consortium for Teachers
Professional Schools Program in India
Professional Standards Program
Professor of the City Program
Profile of American Youth
Profile of Child Care Settings
Profit Making Programs
ProfNet
Program ACTION
Program Alternatives to Special Education
Program Analysis and Monitoring in Writing
Program Applications
Program Assistance and Approval System LA
Program for Academic and Creative Enrichment
Program for Acquiring Competence Entrepreneurship
Program for Action by Citizens in Education
Program for Adolescent and Community Education
Program for Afloat College Education
Program for Alternative Comprehensive Education NY
Program for Assessing Youth Employment Skills
Program for Effective Teaching
Program for Effective Teaching and Supervision
Program for Efficient Teaching
Program for Improvement IL
Program for Leadership in Earth Systems Education
Program for Learning in Accordance with Needs
Program for Local Service
Program for More Able Learners
Program for Quality Teaching BC
Program for Severely Profoundly Handicapped
Program IMPACT
Program in Linguistics and English Teaching
Program of Assessment Diagnosis and Instruction MD
Program of International Partnerships
Program of Research and Eval for Public Schools
Program of Special Directed Studies
Program on Information Technologies Public Policy
Program on Noncollegiate Sponsored Instruction
Program on Public Conceptions of Science

Program Persons Limited English Speaking Ability
Program PREPARE
Program React
Program Review in Occupational Education
Program to Develop Efficiency Visual Functioning
Program VITAL
Programa de Educacion Interamericana
Programa Regional de Desarrollo Educativo (OAS)
Programmatic Research Project
Programming in the Arts
Programs to Advance Teen Health
Programs to Excite Potential
Progress Profiles Project
Project 18
Project 30 (Teacher Education)
Project 80
Project 81
Project 1000
Project 1990
Project 2000
Project 2061 (AAAS)
Project 100000
Project A Plus Elemen Techn Demonstration Schools
Project A Warm Welcome NY
Project ABC NY
Project ABLE
Project About Face TN
Project ABRAZO
Project ACCEL NJ
Project Access
Project ACCESS WA
Project ACCESS WI
Project Accommodate
Project Achieve NY
Project ACT
Project ACTIVE
Project ADAPT
Project Adelante NY
Project ADELANTE PA
Project ADMIRE
Project Advance
Project ADVANCE CA
Project ADVANCE NY
Project Advancement Based on Competency
Project Adventure
Project Africa
Project Agriculture
Project AHEAD
Project AID
Project AIMS
Project Alert
Project ALERT GA
Project ALIVE
Project ALLTEL
Project ALMA NY
Project ALMS
Project ALPHA
Project ALPS
Project AMERICA NY
Project APEC
Project APEX
Project Aprendizaje NY
Project APT
Project ARISE
Project ARISTOTLE
Project Ascend
Project ASCENT
Project ASERT
Project Aspiration
Project ASPIRE
Project ASSERT
Project At Your Service NY
Project Available Better Careers
Project AWARE
Project BABS NY
Project BACIS NY
Project BACSTOP
Project BAIL OUT
Project Baseline
Project BASES NY
Project BASICS
Project BASICS NY
Project BATEY NY
Project Beacon
Project BEAM
Project BEAM NY
Project BEAM UP
Project BECA NY
Project BECOME NY
Project Benchmark
Project BEST
Project BEST KS
Project BEST WI
Project BET
Project BETA NY
Project BICEP
Project BIG
Project BIOTECH
Project BISECT NY
Project BITEC NY
Project BLAST NY
Project BO CEC
Project BOHST
Project Bootstrap
Project BORN FREE
Project Brave
Project Breakthrough
Project Bridge
Project BRIDGES NY
Project Build
Project Business
Project CABE NY
Project CABES
Project CALA NY
Project Camelot
Project CAMIO
Project Canada West
Project CANAL
Project CAP
Project CAP (Haitian Hispanic Students)
Project CAP NY
Project CAPABLE ME
Project CAPABLE NY
Project CAPISCO
Project CAR
Project CARE
Project Care III OH
Project CARE NY
Project CAREER
Project Career WI
Project CARES NY
Project CASA CA
Project CASE
Project CAST
Project CAST NY
Project CATCH
Project Catch Up
Project CBE
Project CDCC
Project CELIT
Project CELSIM NY
Project CERES
Project Challenge TN
Project CHAMP NY
Project Change
Project Changeover
Project CHASP NY
Project CHERISH TX
Project CHILD
Project Child Care
Project Child Find Serve TX
Project Child Watch
Project CHIME
Project CHOICE
Project CHOICE NY
Project CIBE NY
Project CIRCUIT
Project CITE
Project City Science
Project Citywork
Project CLASS
Project Clean Air
Project CLIMB
Project CLOVER
Project CMYC TX
Project COD
Project CODE (Drug Education)
Project COEXIST
Project COFFEE
Project COLAMDA
Project COM TECH NY
Project Communicate
Project Community and School Together
Project COMPAS
Project Compugrafia LEP NY
Project COMPUOCC LEP NY
Project COMPUTE
Project Concern
Project Concern CT
Project CONNECT
Project Conquest
Project CONSTRUCT
Project Consumer Operations Survival Training
Project Continuing Education for Health Manpower
Project Continuity NE
Project Cooperation
Project Coordination
Project COPE
Project COPERNICUS
Project COPS
Project CORES
Project COULD
Project CREATE CA
Project CREATE FL
Project CREATIVE
Project CREDIT
Project CREEP
Project CREST
Project CRISP
Project Criterion
Project Crossroads
Project CUE
Project Dakota MN
Project Dale Avenue
Project DART GA
Project Data Tech NY
Project DAWN
Project Daylight AZ
Project DEAF
Project DECIDE
Project Decision 2
Project DELTA
Project Design
Project Developmental Continuity
Project DIALIB
Project Dimension
Project Discovery
Project DISCUSS
Project DISTIL
Project DREAM NY
Project Drive
Project Early Aid
Project Early Help
Project Early Push
Project East Woodlawn
Project Education for Mankind
Project Education Reform
Project Eight
Project ELITES
Project Emerge
Project EMIS
Project Employability
Project En Tant Que Femmes
Project English
Project ENRICH DC
Project Enrichment
Project Ent
Project EPIC FL
Project EPIC KY
Project EPOCH
Project Equality
Project Equity
Project ESCAPE
Project ESL SEDAC NY
Project Esperanza NY
Project ESPIRIT
Project Essay Grade
Project ESURG NE
Project ET NY
Project EUREKA
Project Europe 2000
Project Evolve
Project EXCEL
Project EXCEL (Public Officials)
Project EXCEL CA
Project Exodus
Project EXPLORATION
Project EXPLORE NY
Project Fair Play
Project FAITH
Project Family Link
Project FAST
Project FIND
Project First Chance
Project First Chance Interactive Outreach Project
Project FLAME
Project FLIT
Project Focus
Project Focus SC
Project Follow Through
Project Follow Through Expansion Program
Project for Academic Motivation
Project for American Studies in Secondary Schools
Project for an Energy Enriched Curriculum
Project for Early Education Exceptional Children
Project for Improving Reading Language Teaching
Project for Minorities and Women in Research
Project for Study of Academic Precocity
Project Ford Foundation Gray Area
Project ForSight
Project FREDD
Project Fresh Start
Project Frontier
Project Futureprint
Project Geography 16 19
Project GET SET NY
Project Giant Step NY
Project Gifted
Project GIVE
Project GO
Project GO FOR IT NY
Project GOALS NY
Project Grammarama
Project Grant Information System
Project GROW
Project GROW KY
Project GROW PA
Project GUARANTEE (Sweden)
Project HAITI STARS NY
Project HAPI
Project HAPPEN
Project HAPPIER
Project Head Start
Project Head Start (Home Based)
Project HEAR
Project HEATH
Project HEED
Project HEELD
Project HELP
Project Heroes
Project HEVRA
Project HI CLASS NY
Project Hire
Project HIRe (Head Injuries)
Project HOLA NY
Project Home School and the IEP
Project Homebound
Project Homeroom IL
Project HOPE (Peru)
Project HOPE AZ
Project HOPE CA
Project HOPE NY
Project HOT
Project Human Educational Awareness Resource
Project I CAN
Project ICE
Project ICES
Project Ida (Canada)
Project IDEA
Project IDEAL ND
Project IEL (Liberia)
Project IMPACT
Project IMPACT (Philippines)
Project IMPACT NY
Project Implode
Project Improve
Project IN SLIP
Project Independence
Project INFORMS
Project Infut
Project Innovation
Project Input
Project INREAL
Project INSERVICE IL
Project Insight
Project Insite
Project INSITE (Deaf Blind)
Project INSPIRE (Malaysia)
Project Inspire DC
Project Inspire PA
Project INSTEP
Project Instruct
Project Inter Action MA
Project Interact
Project Interchange
Project Interdependence CA
Project INTERFACE
Project Intergroup
Project Intrex
Project Jericho CA
Project Job Opportunities and Education for Youth
Project JOBS NY
Project JOLT
Project Kaleidoscope
Project Kamunts
Project Kanpe
Project KARE
Project Kidlink
Project KIDS
Project KIND FL
Project Know How
Project Kolehion Mandikike (Guam)
Project L Ouverture
Project LAST
Project Lead the Way
Project LEADER
Project LEAP

Project LEAP OH
Project Learn
Project LEARN OH
Project Learning Tree
Project Leer
Project LEGAL
Project LEIF
Project LEM
Project LET
Project LEX
Project LIFE
Project Life Lab
Project Lifelong Learning
Project LIFT
Project LINC
Project LINK
Project LINK Four
Project LINKER
Project Literacy
Project Literacy U S
Project LIVE SC
Project Lodestar
Project LONGSTEP
Project LOVE
Project MAC
Project MAFEX
Project Mainstream
Project Major Issues Juvenile Justice Info Train
Project Malvern
Project Mans Environment
Project MAS NY
Project MASTER NY
Project MATCH
Project Mathematics Anxiety Reduction Training
Project MAVE
Project MAVIS
Project Measurement
Project Med Vet
Project Media
Project Media Guidelines
Project MEGSSS
Project MELD
Project Memphis
Project Mentor NY
Project MER
Project MET
Project Metro
Project Microform
Project MIDNY
Project MINERVA
Project MINI SCORE
Project Mission
Project MOBILE NY
Project Mobilization
Project MODEL
Project MORE
Project Motivate
Project Motivation
Project MOVE
Project Move Ahead
Project NAIL
Project NEED
Project NEED IT
Project Neglect
Project NETWORC NV
Project NEW
Project New Hope
Project Next Step
Project Nexus
Project North Carolina in School Television
Project OASES
Project OASIS
Project OCCUPAC
Project OMNI
Project on Achieving Equity for Women Soc Work Ed
Project on Alternatives in Education
Project on Applied Contrastive Linguistics
Project on Cooperative Manpower Planning Spec Educ
Project on Equal Education Rights
Project on Involvement
Project on Linguistic Analysis
Project on Noncollegiate Sponsored Instruction
Project on Reallocation
Project on Redefining the Baccalaureate Degree
Project on Student Development in Small Colleges
Project on the Predicament of Mankind
Project Open
Project Open Classroom
Project Open Horizons
Project Opportunity
Project OPT
Project Optimus Outreach
Project OPTION
Project ORA
Project ORCA
Project Outreach
Project Outreach USA
Project OVERVIEW
Project PACCE
Project Pace
Project PACESETTER
Project PADRES
Project Pamong (Indonesia)
Project PAN NY
Project PARADE
Project Partnership
Project PASE
Project PASS
Project PAT MN
Project PATHE
Project Patrol
Project PAVE
Project Perform
Project Performance Assess Collaborative for Educ
Project PERMIT
Project Physics
Project PIAGET
Project Pioneer
Project PIRLT
Project PISCES
Project PLACE
Project PLANTWORK
Project Playpen
Project POET
Project Portage
Project Porvenir NM
Project Porvenir NY
Project PR
Project PREP NY
Project Prepare
Project Prepare OH
Project Prevention
Project Prevocational
Project PRICE
Project PRIDE
Project Pride NY
Project PRIME
Project PRIME AZ
Project PRIMER (Jamaica)
Project PRIMES
Project Primetime
Project PRISE MI
Project PRISM
Project PROBE
Project PROF
Project Prolexia
Project Protech
Project Protection
Project Pryme
Project Pulse
Project QUESST
Project Quest
Project QUILL
Project R 3
Project RAND
Project Re Ed (Hobbs)
Project Reach
Project REACH CO
Project Reach ME
Project Reach NY
Project REACH SC
Project Reach TX
Project READ
Project READ CA
Project READ OH
Project READS
Project REAL
Project REAL DE
Project REAL NY
Project REALISTIC
Project REAP IN
Project RECURSO NY
Project REDEAL
Project Redesign
Project Redirection
Project REDY
Project REED
Project REFLECT
Project Refocus Outplacement Service
Project REFOCUS TX
Project RELATE
Project REMEDY
Project RENEW
Project RESCATE
Project RESCATE NY
Project Rescue
Project RESCUE GA
Project Respond MO
Project RETAP
Project RETOOL
Project RHISE
Project RISE
Project ROLE NJ
Project ROME
Project SABE NY
Project SACHEM
Project SACI
Project SAFE
Project SAG
Project SAGE
Project SAIL NY
Project SAVE
Project SCALE
Project SCAT
Project School to Work
Project SCOPE
Project SCORE
Project SEALL
Project SEAR
Project Search
Project Search for Preventive Approaches
Project Seattle
Project Second Look
Project Secondary English
Project SEE
Project SEED
Project SEEK
Project SEEK OH
Project SEEK OK
Project SEESAW
Project SEISMIC
Project SELECT
Project Self Directive Dramatization
Project Self Discovery
Project SENAP
Project Senior
Project Seniors Tutor for Educational Progress
Project SERAPHIM
Project SERVE
Project SERVE MN
Project SERVICE
Project SESAME
Project SEST
Project SET
Project SETT UP
Project SHAL
Project SHARE
Project SHARE NY
Project Simu School
Project SISS
Project SITE
Project Skill
Project Skyriver
Project SLATE
Project SMART
Project SMILE
Project SNACK
Project SOAR
Project Social Studies
Project SOCRATES
Project SOL FA
Project SOLID START
Project SOLO
Project SOS
Project SOUL
Project SOUL NJ
Project SPACE
Project SPAN
Project Speak
Project SPEAR
Project SPECIAL
Project Specific Education of the Eye
Project SPECTRE
Project Spectrum
Project SPEED NY
Project SPICE
Project SPIRIT
Project Springboard
Project SPRUCE
Project STAR
Project STAR I IN
Project STAR PA
Project STAY
Project STEEL
Project Step
Project Step Up
Project STEPS KY
Project STIR
Project STITE
Project STOP NY
Project STREAM
Project STRETCH
Project Strive
Project STRIVE IN
Project SUCCESS
Project SUCCESS (Computer and Career Educ)
Project Success Enrichment
Project Success Environment
Project Success GA
Project SUCCESS NY
Project Sunrise
Project SUPER
Project Superemos NY
Project Support CA
Project Synapse
Project SYNERGY
Project T and N Bucks
Project TACT
Project TALENT
Project TAMEC
Project TAPS
Project TEACH
Project Teach (FIPSE)
Project TEACH NY
Project Teacher Excellence
Project Team Build
Project TEAMS NE
Project TECE
Project Teen Ager SC
Project Telepac
Project THEMIS
Project THINK
Project THISTLE
Project Three Cs NY
Project Thrive
Project TIDE
Project TIP NY
Project TNT
Project to Enhance Effective Learn (Australia)
Project to Increase Mastery of Math and Science
Project TOMORROW
Project TOPS
Project Torque
Project TOTAL
Project TOUCH
Project TRADE
Project TRAIN (Special Education)
Project Training
Project Training Jobs
Project Transition
Project TREK
Project TREND
Project Trident
Project TRIUNFE NY
Project TRUE
Project TRY
Project TTAP
Project Unidos
Project Unique
Project UNIQUE NJ
Project Update
Project Upgrade
Project Uplift
Project Upper Cumberland
Project UPSTART
Project Upswing
Project USHER
Project USTED
Project Value
Project Vectors
Project VEO
Project VGIP
Project VIBE
Project VIBES NY
Project VIGOR
Project VITA
Project VITAL
Project VOICE
Project Volunteer Power
Project VOTE
Project WAGES
Project Warrior
Project Washoe
Project Watch a Book
Project WE CARE
Project WILD
Project Woodlawn
Project Workability
Project WORTH
Project WRITE
Project Yardstick
Project Youth
Project Zero Reject
Projects to Advance Creativity in Education
Projects with Industry
Projet SAGE (Canada)
Promising Practices Diffusion Project
Promotional Gates Program
Promotional Gates Program NY
Prospective Payment System
Protocol Materials Development Project

Secondary School Math Curriculum Study
Secondary School Recognition Program
Secondary Schools Basic Skills Demo Assist Prog
Secretary of Education Recognition Program
Sedro Woolley Project
Self Advancement Via Education
Self Directed Career Programs
Self Employment Investment Demonstration
Self Esteem A Family Affair (Program)
SELF HELP Program MD
Self Instructional Language Programs
Self Management and Responsibility Train Prog FL
Semel Auditory Processing Program
Senior Adult Education Program
Senior Adult Volunteer Program MD
Senior Aide Volunteer Educators
Senior Citizen School Volunteer Program PA
Senior Colleague Advisory Network
Senior Community Service Employment Program
Senior Community Service Project
Senior Companions Program
Senior Employment Program
Senior Intensified Program
Senior Motivators in Learning Education Services
Senior Teaching Seniors Project
Seniors Teaching Seniors Project
Sentence Synthesizing Program
Sentencecraft Program
SER Jobs for Progress
SERVEing Young Children Project
SerVermont
Service Conditional Loan Programs
Servicemens Opportunity College Program
Services for Expectant Mothers Project
Services for Families with Child Prog (Australia)
SET Research Information for Teachers
Seven Year Study
Sex Equity in Educational Leadership
Seychelles Integrated Science Program
Seymour Plan MD
Share and Take Program TX
SHARE Project
Shared Heritage Child Care Program
Sharing Business Success Project
Sharper Minds Program
Shell School Technology Program
Shipyard Training Modernization Program
Showcase for Excellence Project
Shrewsbury Plan
Shropshire Mathematics Experiment
Sierra Project
SIF Project
Silverdale Experiment
Silverlake Experiment
Sim One Project
Simba Program
Single Concept Introductory Mathematics Project
Sixth Year Programs
Skeels and Dye Study
SKI HI Program
Skiles Instructional Project
Skill Development for Self Reliance
Skill Training Improvement Program
Skill Training Improvement Programs II
Skills Conversion Project
Skills Essential to Learning Project
Skills for Ethical Action Program
Skills Training and Education Program
Skylab Education Program
Skyline Wide Educational Plan
Sleuthing Nursing Pathways Project
Small Farm Family Program MO
Small Grant Program (ADAMHA)
Small Grant Research Program (USOE)
Small High Schools Project AK
Small Project Assessment Service
Small Schools Career Education Development Project
Small Step Program
Smaller Communities Program
SMART Project TX
SMARTLINE
Soar Project
Sobrante Park Evaluation Project
Social Education Materials Project
Social Problem Solving Training Programs
Social Security Student Benefits Program
Social Services Block Grant Program
Social Studies Implementation Project
Social Welfare Manpower Project
Sociological Resources for the Social Studies
Socmaticas
South Carolina Basic Skills Assessment Program
South Carolina Classroom Management System
South Carolina Coping Skills Project
South Carolina Governors Remediation Initiative
South Carolina Norm Referenced Testing Program
South Carolina School Incentive Reward Program
South Carolina Statewide Testing Program
South Dakota Plan for Career Education
South Suburban Health Advocate Regional Exchange
Southeast Alternatives
Southeastern Day Care Project
Southeastern New Mexico Bilingual Program
Southeastern Public Education Program
Southern Anthropological Study
Southern California Answering Network
Southern Oregon Drug Awareness
Southern Regional Research Project
Southern Regional Research Projects
Southerns Ongoing Support
Southwest Advanced Learning System for Adults
Southwestern States Development Project
Space Analysis Manuals Project
Space Exposed Experiment Developed for Students
Space Programs
Spaceship Earth
Spanish Dame School Project
Spanish Literacy Investigation Project
Sparsely Populated Areas Project
Speaking and Listening across Disciplines
Special and General Education Leadership Project
Special College Counseling Program
Special Delinquency Prevention Program NY
Special Education Administration Training Program
Special Education Intervention Project
Special Education Rehabilitation Vocational Educ
Special Education Supervisor Training Project
Special Educational Opportunities Program
Special Food Service Program for Children
Special Friends Program
Special Impact Program
Special Incentive Programs NY
Special Milk Program
Special Needs Identification Assessment Project
Special Needs People Improving Vocational Guidance
Special Partnership in Career Education
Special Plan Upgrading Reading
Special Program Schools Scheme
Special Programs Aimed at Reaching Children
Special Programs for Individualized Needs
Special Programs in Citizenship Education
Special Project for Older Citizens
Special Services for Disabled Students
Special Services for Disadvantaged Students
Special Student Access to Vocational Ed TN
Special Student Concerns Projects
Special Supplemen Food Program Women Infants Child
Special Training for Employment Program
Special Volunteer Demonstration Programs
Speech and Reading Enrichment Program
Speech Through Vision Project
Speedier Project
SPICE Program
Split Vu Reading Readiness Program
SPORT IT (Australia)
Springboards Reading Program
Springfields Trajectory Occupational Program
SREB Computer Science Project
SREB Nursing Curriculum Project
SRI International Study National Diffusion Network
Staff Development for School Improvement Program
Standards Industrial Arts Education Programs Proj
Standards of Excellence CO
Stanford Brentwood CAI Project
Stanford Collegial Evaluation Program
Stanford Computer Based Educator Train Interv
Stanford Denver Project
Stanford Heart Disease Prevention Program
Stanford Prison Study
Stanford Schools Collaborative
Stanford Secondary School Project
Stanford Teacher Education Program
Stanford Writing Assessment Program
Stanfords Environment for Teaching Program
Stanislaus County Multioccupational Adult Training
STAR TV
STARPAHC Project
StarServe
Start Planning Ahead Now
Start Teaching All Year
Starting Early
State Assessment of Educational Progress
State Capacity Building Program
State Competitive Scholarship Program
State Consultant Model Program
State Disadvantaged Child Project OR
State Dissemination Grants Program
State Educational Incentive Grant Program AK
State Employment Initiatives for Youth
State Energy Conservation Program
State Funded Program High Risk Four Year Olds LA
State Intergovernmental Education Project
State Legalization Impact Assistance Grants
State Level Information Base
State Technical Services Program
State Urban Education Program (New York)
Statewide Education Activities Rural Colo Health
Statewide Longitudinal Study CA
Station College Executive Project Adult Learning
Stay In You Win Project AB
Step Forward Project KY
Stepping Up (Aetna)
STEPS Program MO
Steps to Maturity Program BC
Stevens Technical Enrichment Program
Stoney Indian Language Project AB
Stop ERA
STOP Program
Strategic Weapon System Training Program
Strategies for Change and Knowledge Utilization
Strategies for Targeting Early Potential
Street Academy Program
Strengthening Research Library Resources Program
Stress Challenge Programs
Strive Toward Excellence Program
Structural Engineering Systems Solver Program
Structured Language Improvement Project
Structured Training Employment Transitional Serv
Student Advancement Programs
Student Affirmative Action Outreach Program CA
Student Aid Recipient Survey
Student Assistance Programs
Student Awareness Programs
Student Census Project
Student Course and Teacher Evaluation Program
Student Course Information Project
Student Literacy Corps
Student Loan Consolidation Program
Student Organizing Project
Student Outcomes Information Service
Student Parent Socialization Study
Student Pugwash
Student Safety Education Project
Student Science Training Program
Student Search Service
Student Teacher Achievement Ratio Project TN
Student Teacher Experience Program (Ontario)
Student Teacher Ratio Project
Student Training at Retail Stores Project NY
Student Work Experience and Training Program
Students Chemical Information Project
Students for Medicine Program
Students of Limited English Proficiency Program
Students Offering Service
Students Taking Action for Recognition
Students Teach Students
Students Upgrading Mathematical Achievement
Studio in a School NY
Study of Allied Health Education
Study of Dissemination Efforts Support Sch Improv
Study of Educational Facilities Project (Toronto)
Study of Educational Growth and Opportunity
Study of Mathematically Precocious Youth
Study of Stanford and the Schools
Study of Students at Risk (Phi Delta Kappa)
Study of Verbally Gifted Youth
Study of Work Project
Study Talk Project
Study with a Teacher Program
Study Work Advisor Program
StudyWorks Project OH
Substitute Teacher Education Modules
Suburban Intercultural Teacher Education Program
Suburban Transportation Demonstration Project
Success Controlled Optimal Reading Experience
Success for All Program
Success in Beginning Reading and Writing
Success in Reading and Writing Program
Successful Indicators Study
Suicide Prevention Programs
Suki Agricultural Project
Summer At Home Reading Program
Summer Bridge Program
Summer Enrichment and Instruction Project
Summer Food Service Program
Summer High School Apprentice Research Program
Summer Language Bursary Program (Canada)
Summer of Experience Exploration and Discovery
Summer Program Economically Disadvantaged Youth
Summer Reporter Project WI
Summer Research Opportunity Programs
Summer School in Action
Summer Training and Education Program
Summer Youth Development Project
Summer Youth Employment Program
Summer Youth Transportation Program
SummerMath Program
Sun Coast Area Teacher Training Program FL
Sunrise Project for the Blind
Sunshine State Skills Program
Superior and Talented Student Project
Supermarket Discovery Center Demonstration Project
SuperStart Comprehensive Prekindergarten Prog NY
Supplemental Loans for Students Program
Supplemental Security Income Program
Supplemental Teacher Participation (Saginaw MI)
Supplemental Tuition Assistance Program NY
Supplementary Kindergarten Intervention Program
Supplementary Mathematics Materials Tech Society
Support Services Program
Supporting Diversity in Schools MN
Supporting Extended Family Members Program
Supportive Services Program
Survey Computer Applications School Food Service
Survey of Administrative Functional Efficiency
Susquehanna River Basin Project
Sutherlin Program in Creativity
Swadana Delivery System (Indonesia)
Swaziland Teacher Training Project
Swim for Your Life
SWRL English Language and Concepts Program
SWRL Kindergarten Program
SWRL Tutorial Program
Syracuse Scholastic Rehabilitation Program
Syracuse Univ Publications in Continuing Educ NY
Syracuse Univ Resources for Educators of Adults NY
Syracuse Upgrading Project
Systematic Collaborative Outreach Project Effort
Systematic Monitoring Process for Learning
Systematic Student Recruitment Program
Systems Program Approaching Nonunemployment
Systems Thinking and Curriculum Innovation Project
TABA Curriculum Project
TADPOLE Program
Take 5 Project WA
Take Pride in America Program
Talent Identification Program NC
Talent Search
Talent Search and Development Model Project

Talents Unlimited Program
TALINET Project
Talkback Television Instruction
Target 2000 SC
Targeted Assistance Program
Targeted Communications Program
Targeted Jobs Demonstration Program
Teach for America
Teacher Advisor Program (Myrick)
Teacher Appraisal for Improvement
Teacher Apprenticeship Program
Teacher Assessment Project (Stanford Univ)
Teacher Beliefs Study
Teacher Cadet Program SC
Teacher Development Programs
Teacher Education and Learning to Teach Study
Teacher Education and Mathematics Project
Teacher Education and Media Project
Teacher Education and Mentoring Program GA
Teacher Education Experiences Program
Teacher Education Internship Project
Teacher Education Programs (Five Year)
Teacher Evaluation Project FL
Teacher Expectations and Student Achievement
Teacher Followup Survey (NCES)
Teacher Growth Program NY
Teacher Incentives Pilot Program
Teacher Incentives Project
Teacher Industry Exchange Subprogram (Australia)
Teacher Innovation Program
Teacher Involvement Project
Teacher Mom Project
Teacher Participation Project
Teacher Plus Program
Teacher Preparation Evaluation Program
Teacher Recruitment Internship Project Success
Teachers Abroad Program
Teachers College Writing Project
Teachers for Alaska Program
Teachers for Secondary Schools Program
Teachers Need Teachers Program
Teachers on Television Project
Teachers Teaching Teachers
Teaching Activities for Language Knowledge
Teaching Aid Project
Teaching and Learning about Aging Project
Teaching and Learning with Computers (IBM)
Teaching and Learning with Technology Project MI
Teaching Assistant Training Project
Teaching Basic Skills Through Vocational Education
Teaching Effectiveness Network
Teaching Environment Awareness to Child of Harvest
Teaching Excellence Program
Teaching Experiment
Teaching for Higher Order Thinking
Teaching Individuals Protective Strategies
Teaching Learning in Graduate Geography Proj
Teaching Learning Interaction Study
Teaching Research Project (New Zealand)
Teaching Resource Classroom Model
Teaching the Talented Program
Team Approach to Assessment and Programming
Team Oriented Corrective Reading Program
Technical Assistance for Special Populations Prog
Technical Physics Project
Technical Skills Project
Technician Education Council Programs
Technological Applications Project
Technological Development Project
Technology Access for Arkansans
Technology Adaptation Project
Technology and Basic Skills in Mathematics
Technology and Science Careers for Minorities
Technology for Children Program
Technology for Literacy Project
Technology in the Curriculum Program
Technology Integrated Educ Delivery System AZ
Teen Employment Program
Teen Tutorial Program
Teenage Health Teaching Modules Program
Teenage Opportunity Programs
Teenage Parent Program KY
Teenage Pregnancy and Parenting Project CA
Teens for AIDS Prevention Project
Telecommunication Demonstration Program (Midwest)
Telecommunications Demonstration Program
Telecommunications Demonstration Projects
Telelearning Project LA
Television Reading Program
Temple City Project
Temple Philadelphia Trenton Teacher Corps Program
Temporary Emergency Child Care
Temporary Emergency Food Assistance
TEMPUS
Ten Schools Program CA
Ten State Nutrition Survey 1968 to 1970
Tenderloin Senior Outreach Project
Tennessee Career Ladder Program
Tennessee Commissioners Report Card
Tennessee Comprehensive Assessment Program
Tennessee Initiative on Employment
Tennessee Master Teacher Program
Tennessee Nutrition Education and Training Program
Tennessee School Improvement Project
Tertiary Education Entrance Project
Tesseract Way
Test Every Senior Project
Test Preparation Program Gifted Talented Sophomore
Test Use Project
Texarkana Project
Texas Academic Skills Program
Texas Assessment Project
Texas Education Network
Texas Educational Microwave Project
Texas Foundation School Program
Texas Hill Country Writing Project
Texas Human Talent Project
Texas Labor Mobility Project
Texas Prefreshman Engineering Program
Texas Project for Elders
Texas Teacher Appraisal System
Texas Teacher Effectiveness Study
Textile Information Retrieval Program
THA MASTER
The Research Instruments Project
Theatre in Education Program
Thematic Elementary Science Individualized Studies
Thematic Studies Program
Theme A Day
Think Aloud Program
Think It Through
THINKABOUT
Thinking Improvement Project
Thinking Mathematics Project
Thinking Skills Program
Third International Mathematics and Science Study
Third World Science Project
Third World Studies Project
Thirteen College Curriculum Program
Three Cities Employment Training Program
Three Phase Program for School Administrators
Threshold Project (South Africa)
Thy Project (Denmark)
Tilton Project
Together We Can
Toledo Political Affairs Study
Toledo Support Teachers Program OH
Toll Gate Metrication Project
Tomorrow Higher Education Project
Tools for Schools Loan Program
Toothkeeper Program
Touchstones Program (Great Britain)
Touchstones Project MD
Toward Teen Health Program
Towards Arts Assessment Project
Trade Adjustment Assistance Program
TRADEC
Trailer Watch Programs
TRAILS Project MO
Trained Aides as Baby Sitters Program
Training Alliances in Health and Education
Training and Assistance Indian Library Services
Training and Employment Prerequisites Survey
Training and Technology Project
Training Arithmetic Problem Solving Skills
Training Opportunities Program NY
Training Teacher Trainers Project
Transfer Alliance Program CA
Transfer Tracking System
Transition Assistance Program (Veterans)
Transition into Electronics Project
TRANSITION Program
Transition Program for Refugee Children
Transition Through the Arts
Transitional Bilingual Basic Skills Program FL
Transitional Bilingual Education Programs
Transitional Black Womens Project GA
Transitional Child Care
Transitional Program for Refugee Children NY
Transitional Resource Addressing Early Education
Translating Research Into Practice TN
Treatment Alternatives Project
Tree City USA
Trempealeau County Kellogg Project
Tri County Course Goal Project
Tri University Project
Tribal Aging Programs
Trine Project
TRIO Programs
TRIVET Program
Trust Agreements CA
Tuesday Released Time Program
Tuition Assistance Program NY
Tuition Benefit Programs
Tuition Guarantee Programs
Tuition Investment Programs
Tulane Nutrition Study
Turn Around Program
Turning Point Program
Turnkey Training Safety Program NY
Turnstile Program CA
Tuskegee Area Study
Tutorial Advancement Program
Tutorial Assistance Program CA
Tutorial Outreach Program NY
Tutoring Adults through Literacy Councils
Twelfth Street School Project
Twice Retained Program NJ
UCLA Allied Health Professions Projects
Uncertainty Studies Project
Undergraduate Mathematics and Applications Project
Understanding Learning Teaching Proj (New Zealand)
UNESCO Associated Schools Project in Education
UNESCO Prize for Peace Education
Unified Intake Services
Uniform Student Evaluation Survey
Unit Treatment Rehabilitation Program
United Nations Development Program
United Nations Environment Program
United States Japanese Film Exchange Project
United States Metric Study
United States Newspaper Program
United States Science Exhibit
United States Space Program
United States Study of Education in Japan
Universal Availability of Publications
Universal Child Immunization Program
Universal School Lunch Program
Universiti Sains Malaysia
University Affiliated Training Programs
University and College Opportunities Program CA
University Impact Study (Delaware)
University of Chicago School Mathematics Project
University of Houston School Univ Research Collab
University of Illinois Astronomy Program
University of Michigan Time Use Study
University of Toledo Springfield Local Schools Pro
University of Western Ontario Preschool Program
University Year for Action Program
Upper Cumberland Early Intervention Project
Upper Cumberland Reading Project
Upper Midwest Small Schools Project
Upper Peninsula Town Meeting of the Air
Upper Susquehanna Valley Program
Upward Bound
Urban Access Project
Urban and Minority Education Fellowship Program
Urban Community Coll Transfer Opportunities Prog
Urban Concentric Media Plan
Urban Conservation Project
Urban Crime Prevention Program
Urban Demonstration Projects OH
Urban Development Action Grant Program
Urban Education Pilot Project OH
Urban Information Specialist Program
Urban Initiative NJ
Urban Language Series
Urban Mathematics Collaborative Project
Urban Observatory Outreach Project
Urban Observatory Program
Urban Preschool Children Project
Urban Problems Work Study Program
Urban Rural Program
Urban Schools Science and Mathematics Program
Urban Science Intern Teaching Project
Urban Simulation Project
Urban Sites Documentation Tech Assistance Program
Urban Suburban Interdistrict Transfer Program
Urban Teacher Education Program IN
Urban Teacher Preparation Program
Urbana Year Long Project IL
URBANDOC Demonstration Project
US USSR Textbook Study Project
Utah Career Ladder Program
Utah Educational Technology Initiative
Utah Project
Utah Pupil Teacher Self Concept Program
Utah State University Classroom Management Program
Utah State University Protocol Project
Utah Statewide Educational Assessment Program
Utvardering Genom Uppfoljning Project
Vancouver Native Indian Cultural Survival Program
Vanderbilt Summer Research Program
Vanguard Program
Variable Matching Programs
VAULT
Venture Program KY
Ventures in Community Improvement Project
Verbal Interaction Project
Verbal Reading Arithmetic Skills Program
Vermont Adult Basic Education Program
Vermont Consulting Teacher Program
Vermont Family Assistance Plan
Vermont Portfolio Assessment Program
Versatile Employment of Health Trained Servicemen
Veterans Education Outreach Program
Veterans Educational Assistance Program
Veterans Outreach
Veterans Readjustment Appointment
Veterans Special Education Program
Veterans Upward Bound
Veterans Vocational Rehabilitation Program
Victorian Country Education Project (Australia)
Video Instr Develop Educ Opportunity Prog MO
Vietnam Veterans Leadership Program
Village Library Project AK
Virginia Beginning Teacher Assistance Program
Virginia Educational Needs Assessment Program
Virginia Public Education Network
Virginia Quality Educ in Sciences and Technology
Virginia Satellite Educational Network
Virginia Standards of Learning Program
Virginia Student Retention Program
Visions for Children
Visiting Geological Scientist Program
Visual Communication Education Program
Visual Literacy Project for Migrant Youth
Vital Information for Education and Work
Vocational Academy Project
Vocational Administrative Management System
Vocational Adult Secondary Training Project
Vocational Assessment Project
Vocational Competency Measures Project
Vocational Counseling Project NJ
Vocational Education for Special Students Program
Vocational Education Personnel Development Project
Vocational Exploration Demonstration Project
Vocational Exploration in the Private Sector
Vocational Instructional Management System
Vocational Investigation and Placement Project
Vocational Leadership Development Program
Vocational Rehabilitation Project
Vocational Technical Information Program
Vocational Technology for Cerebral Palsied Project
Vocational Village
Voices for Children MT
Volunteer Against Illiteracy Campaign
Volunteer Grandparent Project
Volunteer Management Support Program
Volunteer Skills Data System
Volunteers in Partnership with Parents
Volunteers in Public Schools Program
Volunteers in School Program
Volunteers in Tutoring Adult Learners
Volunteers in Tutoring Arrangements Program

CATEGORY 20: Science & Technology

Direct Manipulation Interface
Direct Satellite Broadcasting
Discrepant Events (Science)
Discrete Mathematics
Discrete Variables
Disjunction
Disk Formatting
Dissection
Dissociation Energy
Distillation (Science)
Distributed Computing
Distributive Law
Distributive Property
Ditellurium Decafluoride
Document Security
Dogs
Dolphins
Doppler Effect
Dot Matrix Printing
Double Base Transformations
Drainage
Drop Ceilings
Drosophila
Drought
Drug Calculations
Dry Ice
Drying Beds
Drywall Construction
Dual Independent Map Encoding
Duckweed
Dyes
Dynamic Programing
Dynamics
Eagles
Earth
Earth Core
Earth Homes
Earthworms
Eclipses
Ecological Validity
Economic Awareness
Economic Conversion
Economic Efficiency
Economic Equity
Economic Growth
Economic Planning
Economic Stabilization
Economic Trends
Economies of Scale
Ecosphere
Ed Net
Eddy Currents
Editing Routines (Computer)
Educational Biotechnology
Edutainment
Egg Incubation
Egg Incubators
Egg Production
Eggs
Eigenvalues
Eigenvectors
Ekistics
Elasticity
Electrastatistics
Electrets
Electric Power Generation
Electric Power Generators
Electric Response Audiometry
Electrical Emergencies
Electrical Engineering
Electrical Insulation
Electrical Production
Electrical Technology
Electrical Wiring
Electrochemical Engineering
Electrochemical Grinding
Electrocommunications
Electrodes
Electrolysis
Electromagnetic Field
Electromagnets
Electron Affinities
Electron Beam Lithography
Electron Configuration
Electron Microscopy
Electron Pair Repulsion
Electron Spin Resonance
Electronegativity
Electronic Composition (Computer Data)
Electronic Document Delivery
Electronic Funds Transfer
Electronic Media
Electronic Surveillance
Electronic Trading
Electronic Typesetting
Electronic Wiring
Electrons
Electrophoresis
Electroplating Emissions
Electrostatics
Elementary Particles
Ellipses
Elliptical Gear Construction
Elodea
Emission Control
Emission Control Systems
Emission Theories (Physics)
Emissions
Enamel Solvents
Enameling
Encoder (Banking)
End User Statistical Computing
Energetics
Energy Consumption
Energy Conversion
Energy Crisis
Energy Development
Energy Flow
Energy Policy
Energy Requirements
Energy Shutdowns
Energy Sources
Energy Storage
Engine Modification
Engineering Education Research
Engineering Mechanics
Engineering Registration
Environmental Attitudes
Environmental Awareness
Environmental Catastrophes
Environmental Chemistry
Environmental Communications
Environmental Complexity
Environmental Concepts
Environmental Control
Environmental Design
Environmental Economics
Environmental Education Literacy
Environmental Education Research
Environmental Energy Technology
Environmental Engineering
Environmental Geology
Environmental Impact
Environmental Impact Reports
Environmental Indexes
Environmental Issues
Environmental Literacy
Environmental Management
Environmental Measures
Environmental Monitoring
Environmental Movement
Environmental Policy
Environmental Problems
Environmental Protection
Environmental Quality
Environmental Reporting
Environmental Stressors
Environmental Study Areas
Environmental Trends
Epigenesis
Equality (Mathematics)
Equations (Chemistry)
Equine Management
Equipment Operation
Eratosthenes Mathematics
Ergometrics
Erosion
Error Analysis (Mathematics)
Escherichia Coli
Esterification
Estimation
Ethane
Ethanol
Ether
Ethyl Ethanoate
Ethylene
Euclidean Geometry
Euclidean Objects
Euglena
Euler Circuits (Mathematics)
Eulers Formula
Eutrophication
Evaporation
Excavations
Exploratory Agriculture
Exploratory Drilling (Minerals)
Explosives
Exponentiation (Mathematics)
Exponents (Mathematics)
Extinction (Species)
Extraneous Roots (Mathematics)
Extraterrestrial Life
Factoring (Mathematics)
Facultative Lagoons
Fail Safe Strategies
Fallout
Famine
Faraday Laws
Farey Sequences
Farm Crisis
Farm Policy
Farms
Fast Plants
Fats
Feature Selection
Feedback Control
Feedwater
Fence Building
Fermats Last Theorem
Fermentation
Ferns
Ferrocenes
Ferroelectric Crystals
Ferroin Complexes
Fertilization
Fiber Optics
Fiberglass
Fibers
Fibonacci Sequences
Fields (Mathematics)
File Transfer Protocol
Film Base
Filter Leaf Test
Filtration
Finite Fields
Finite Geometry
Finite Mathematics
Fire Detection
Fire Streams
Fires
Firing Patterns (Physiology)
Fish Farming
Fish Ponds
Fish Products
Fishes
Fishing Industry
Fission
Fixed Point Iteration
Flame Cutting
Flames
Flatworms
Flies
Flight Protocol
Flight Simulation
Floods
Floor Plans
Flotation Thickening
Flow Characteristics
Flow Processes (Manufacturing)
Flowers
Fluid Dynamics
Fluid Flow
Fluid Power Engineering
Fluids
Fluorescence
Fluorine Compounds
Food Additives
Food Consumption
Food Deterioration
Food Drying
Food Preparation
Food Processing
Food Production
Food Scarcity
Food Security
Food Selection
Food Storage
Food Supply
Food Webs
Forage Crops
Forcible Entry
Forests
Form Drawing (Geometry)
Formaldehyde
Formaldehyde Clock Reaction
Format Searching
Four Color Map Theorem
Four Dimensional Geometry
Fourier Transformation
Fractals
Fractional Distillation
Free Abrasive Machining
Free Balloons (Aviation)
Free Text Searching
Freeze Drying Method
Frequency (Electronics)
Frequency Allocation
Frequency Modulation
Freshwater Systems
Friction
Friedel Crafts Reaction (Chemistry)
Frogs
Fruits
Fuel Shortages
Full Spectrum Lighting
Fumaric Acid
Functional Group Interconversions (Chemistry)
Fur Trade
Furbearing Animals
Fusion
Gaia Hypothesis
Galls (Mechanical)
Galois Fields
Game Animals
Game Birds
Gamma Rays
Gardens
Gas Absorption
Gas Chromatography
Gas Flow
Gas Laws (Physics)
Gases
Gasohol
Gasoline Engines
Gem Cutting
General Aviation
General Variable Skill
Generalized Symmetric Means
Geologic Time
Geometric Forms
Geometric Mean
Geometric Programing
Geometric Rigidity
Geometric Supposer
Geosystems
Geotropism
Gerbils
Germination
Geysers
Gibberellic Acid
Gibbs Helmholtz Equations
Glaciers
Glomar Challenger
Glucose
Glutamic Acid
Glycogens
Golden Ratio (Mathematics)
Goldenrod
Gradients (Mathematics)
Graduated Scales
Graham Law of Diffusion
Grapes
Graphical Kinematics
Graphing (Mathematics)
Graphing Utilities
Graphology
Graphotherapy
Grasshoppers
Grasslands
Gravel
Gravity Thickening
Gravy
Greatest Common Divisor (Mathematics)
Greatest Common Factor (Mathematics)
Green Function
Grids
Groups (Mathematics)
Guide Dogs
Guinea Pigs
Gulls
Gypsy Moths
Habitat Destruction
Halftones (Graphic Arts)
Halides
Halleys Comet
Halogenation
Halogens
Hamilton Principle
Hanna Rudorf Algorithm
Hantzsch Pyridine Synthesis
Hardy Weinberg Formula (Genetics)
Harmonic Mean
Harmonics
Harmonigraph
Hawks (Birds)
Heat Loss
Heat Storage
Heat Transfer
Heat Treatment (Metals)
Heavy Metals
Hectograph Process
Helicon Waves
Helium
Helixes
Herbs
Hermes Satellite
Herpetology
Hervey Law

CATEGORY 21: Tests & Testing

Assessment Tool for Moderately Retarded Students
Assessments for Integration Mainstream Settings
Assessments of Performance in Teaching
Assistive Technology Device Predisposition Assess
Association Test (Otto and Koenke)
Assumption Recognition Index
Assumptions (Testing)
Astin Index
Asymmetric Data
Asymptotic Distributions
Asymptotic Power
Asymptotic Standard Errors
ATE Inventory (Flynn)
Attachment Inventory (Schaefer)
Attention Test
Attenuation Paradox
Attitude and Motivation Test Battery
Attitude Appreciations
Attitude Assessment Inventory
Attitude Behavior Scale Law Education
Attitude Interest Analysis Test
Attitude Inventory
Attitude Problem Questionnaire (Newman)
Attitude Scale
Attitude Story Test (Hohn and Swartz)
Attitude to School Questionnaire (Strickland)
Attitude Toward Blindness Questionnaire
Attitude Toward Cheating Scale
Attitude Toward Disabled Persons Scale
Attitude Toward Educational Research Scale
Attitude Toward Handicapped Individuals Scale
Attitude Toward Inservice Scale (Trueblood et al)
Attitude Toward Programed Instruction Inventory
Attitude Toward Radioactivity Scale
Attitude Toward Reading Scale (Kux)
Attitude Toward School
Attitude Toward School Questionnaire
Attitudes Inventory for Youth
Attitudes of Professional Autonomy Scale
Attitudes to Physical Activity Inventory (Kenyon)
Attitudes to Science Scale
Attitudes Toward AIDS Scale
Attitudes Toward College Inventory
Attitudes Toward Computer Technologies
Attitudes Toward Educational Research Scale
Attitudes Toward Feminist Issues Scale (Elmore)
Attitudes Toward Mainstreaming Scale
Attitudes Toward Men in Society Scale
Attitudes Toward Old People Scale
Attitudes Toward Parents Questionnaire
Attitudes Toward Reading Inventory (Hunt)
Attitudes Toward Reading Scale
Attitudes Toward Science and Scientists Scale
Attitudes Toward Social Issues in Medicine
Attitudes Toward Statistics (Wise)
Attitudes Toward Testing Scale
Attitudes Toward the Elderly Scale
Attitudes Toward Vocational Education Scale
Attitudes Toward Women Scale
Attitudes Toward Work and Money Questionnaire
Attitudes Toward Working Mothers Scale
Attitudes Towards the World of Work Scales
Attitudinal Militancy Scale (Wohnsiedler)
Attribute Characteristic Curves
Attribute Interest Form
Attribute Preference Attribute Description Scale
Attribute Requirement Inventory
Attribution Pattern Variable
Attribution Style Questionnaire
Attributional Style Assessment Test
Atypical Response Scale
Audit Dress Rehearsal
Audit of Principal Effectiveness
Auditory Analysis Test
Auditory Automotive Mechanics Diagnostic Achiev
Auditory Comprehension Test (Green and Kramar)
Auditory Dimensional Preference Task
Auditory Impulsivity Task (Kennedy and Butter)
Auditory Recognition Test (Brickner)
Australian Scholastic Aptitude Tests
Australian Second Language Proficiency Ratings
Australian Sex Role Scale
Authentic Assessment
Authority Social Truth Value Cluster Measure
Autism Attitude Scale for Teachers
Automated Readability Index
Autonomic Perception Questionnaire
Autonomy and Relatedness Inventory
Autonomy Attitudes Inventory (Edgar and Brod)
Available Motions Inventory
Avoidance Responses
Ayers Prognostic Test for Early Childhood Educ
B Values
Baby Behavior Questionnaire
Background Activity Inventory
Background and Experience Questionnaire
Bagrut Examinations
Bakersfield Individualized Process
Balance Tests
Balanced California F Scale (Athanasiou)
Balanced Designs
Balanced Incomplete Block Spiralling
Baldwin Picture Story Measure of Kindness Concept
Bales Interaction Process Analysis
Bales Interpersonal Ratings Questionnaire
Balke Maximum Work Capacity Test
Ball Aptitude Battery
Balthazar Scales of Adaptive Behavior
Bankson Language Screening Test
Bannatyne System
Banta Replacement Puzzle
Bar Examinations
Barber Suggestibility Scale
Barbour Observer Schedule
Barclay Classroom Assessment System
Barclay Classroom Climate Inventory
Barclay Early Childhood Assessment System
Barclay Test
Barranquilla Rapid Survey Intelligence Test
Barrett Lennard Relationship Inventory
Barrett Taxonomy
Barron Ego Strength Scale
Barron Welsh Art Scale
Barth Scale
Barth Shermis Social Studies Preference Scale
Bartletts Test of Significance in Factor Analysis
Bartletts Test of Sphericity
Base Free Measure of Change
Baseball Coaching Technical Questionnaire
Basic Achievement Skills Individual Screener
Basic Arithmetic Skills Evaluation
Basic Concept Inventory (Engelmann)
Basic Concept Test (Gilmer)
Basic Economics Test
Basic Education Test
Basic Educational Skills Test
Basic English Skills Test
Basic English Skills Test Plus Supplement
Basic Inventory of Natural Language
Basic Life Skills Mini Assessment (1977)
Basic Living Skills Pupil Record Form
Basic Math Mastery Tests
Basic Objectives Assessment Tests
Basic Occupational Literacy Test
Basic Personality Inventory
Basic Reading Inventory (Johns)
Basic School Skills Inventory
Basic Science Comprehensive Test
Basic Sight Vocabulary
Basic Skills Assessment Tests
Basic Skills Examination
Basic Skills Inventory
Basic Skills Word List
Bass Stick Test
Battelle Developmental Inventory
Battery of Musical Concept Meas (Andrews Deihl)
Battle Student Attitude Scale
Bayesian M Group Regression
Bayley Mental Development Index
Bayley Psychomotor Development Index
Bayley Scales of Infant Development
Beck Depression Inventory
Beckmann Beal Mathematics Competencies Test
Beery Developmental Test Visual Motor Integration
Beginning Postsecondary Students Long Study
Beginning Teachers Questionnaire
Beginning Work Rating Scale
Behavior and Temperament Survey
Behavior Assessment System for Children
Behavior Classification Checklist
Behavior Classification Proj Behav Checklist
Behavior Description Index
Behavior Dimensions Rating Scale
Behavior Evaluation Scale
Behavior Inventory (Zigler)
Behavior Observation Scale
Behavior Observation Schedule (Tannenbaum)
Behavior Prediction Test (Morrison)
Behavior Predispositions Group Situation Inventory
Behavior Preference Inventory
Behavior Problem Checklist
Behavior Ranking Scale (Institute Devel Studies)
Behavior Rating Instrument for Autistic
Behavior Rating Scale for Junior Senior High Schs
Behavioral Academic Self Esteem Scale
Behavioral Acculturation Scale (Szapocynik)
Behavioral Analysis Instrument for Teachers
Behavioral Assessment
Behavioral Checklist Infant Toddler Care Provider
Behavioral Event Interview
Behavioral Expectations Scale
Behavioral Maturity Scale (White)
Behavioral Measures
Behavioral Objectives Writing Skills Test
Behavioral Observation Schedule Pupils Teachers
Behavioral Observation Scoring System
Behavioral Requirements Analysis Checklist
Behavioral Style Questionnaire
Behavioral Styles Inventory
Behavioral Vignettes Test
Behaviorally Anchored Rating Scales
Behrens Fisher Problem
Belief in Personal Control Scale (Revised)
Beliefs About Computers Scale
Bell Adjustment Inventory
Bell Disability Scale of Adjustment
Bellaks Ego Functioning Scale
Bem Sex Role Inventory
Benchmark Testing
Benchmark Tests
Bender Gestalt Test
Bender Gestalt Test for Young Children
Bender Visual Motor Gestalt Test
Benefit T Score
Benjamin Proverb Test
Bennett Hand Tool Test
Bennett Mechanical Comprehension Test
Bentler Interview Development Scale
Benton Boutwell Reading Attitude Inventory
Benton Visual Retention Test
Bergan Scoring Procedure
Berger Self Acceptance Scale
Berger Self Esteem Scale
Berko Test of Morphology
Berko Wug Test
Berry Talbott Language Tests
Best Interests Standards for Child Custody
Best Liked Least Liked
Best Weight Function Method
Beta Binomial Test Model
Beta Densities
Beta Weights
Between Group Differences
Bialer Cromwell Childrens Locus of Control Scale
Bias in Attitudes Survey
Bigram Strategy
Bilevel Dimensionality of Probability
Bilevel Factor Analysis
Bilingual Education Evaluation System
Bilingual Inventory of Natural Language
Bilingual Oral Language Test
Bilingual Program Surveys
Bilingual Syntax Measure
Biller Rating Scale
Bills Index of Adjustment and Values
Binary Scores
Binet Simon Intelligence Scale
Bing Test
Binge Eating Scale
Binois Pichot Vocabulary Test
Binomial Distribution
Binomial Test
Biographical Information Blank (Cline et al)
Biographical Inventory (Ellison et al)
Biographical Inventory for Medicine
Biological Princepts Test (Shipe)
Biology Achievement Test (Sparks)
Biology Attitude Assessment Scale
Biology Classroom Activity Checklist
Biology Laboratory Activity Checklist
Biology Teacher Behavior Inventory (Evans)
Bipolar Trait Ratings Scales
Bisection Procedures
BK Parental Checklist (Buck and Kennealy)
Black Identity Test
Black Ideology Scale
Black Intelligence Test of Cultural Homogeneity
Blanchard Index of Scholastic Aptitude
Blind Learning Aptitude Test
Blishen Socio Economic Index
Block Child Rearing Practices Report
Block Counting (Bussis and Chittenden)
Block Design Test
Block Sorting (Bussis and Chittenden)
Block Test Mode
Blossers Taxonomy
Blox Test
Blyth Second Year Algebra Test
Body Barrier Score
Body Esteem Scale
Boehm Test of Basic Concepts
Bogardus Social Distance Scale
Bonferroni Procedure
Boone Infant Speech and Language Development Scale
Boshiers Education Participation Scale
Boston Diagnostic Aphasia Examination
Botel Reading Inventory
Bown Self Report Inventory
Box Scale (Harvill)
Box Scheffe Test
Boy Girl Identity Task (Emmerich and Goldman)
Boys Listening Test (Graham and Orr)
Braam Sheldon Flexibility of Reading Test
Bracken Basic Concept Scale
Brand Emotions Scale for Writers
Bratt Attitude Test
Brayfield Rothe Job Satisfaction Index
Brazelton Neonatal Assessment Scale
Brazelton Neonatal Behavioral Assessment Scale
Breskin Rigidity Test
Brief Symptom Inventory
Brief Test of Literacy
Brigance Diagnostic Inventories
Brigance Diagnostic Inventory of Basic Skills
Brigance K and 1 Screen
Brighton Reading Individualized Skills Continuum
Brim Scale
Bringing Up Children Inventory
British Ability Scales
British Columbia Assessment of Written Expression
British Columbia Learning Assessment Program
British Columbia Reading Assessment
British Intelligence Scale
BRL Checklist of Prereading Skills
Broad Range Tailored Test of Verbal Ability
Brockton Battery
Broome Functional Behavior Checklist
Brown Carlsen Listening Comprehension Test
Brown Fraser Bellgui Test of Grammatical Contrasts
Brown Holtzman Survey Study Habits and Attitudes
Brown IDS Self Concept Referents Test
Brown Peterson Distractor Task
Brown Peterson Paradigm
Brown Self Report Inventory
Bruininks Oseretsky Test of Motor Proficiency
Bryngelson Glaspey Test
BSCS Achievement Tests
BSCS Comprehensive Final Examination (Mayer)
Buhler Life Goals Inventory
Building Memory Test (ETS)
Bullen Reading Attitude Measure
Bureaucratic Orientation Scale
Burks Behavior Rating Scale
Burks Behavior Rating Scale Organic Brain Dysfunct
Burnett Reading Series Survey Test
Burt Word Reading Test
Bus Driver Trainee Aptitude Test CA
Bushwell John Vocabulary of Arithmetic Test
Buss Durkee Hostility Inventory
Butler Haigh Q Sort
Byrne Repression Sensitization Scale
Bzoch Diagnostic Articulation Test
Bzoch League Receptive Expressive Emergent Lang
C Tests
CAGE (Screening Test)
Cain Levine Social Competency Scale
Caldwell Inventory of Home Stimulation
Caldwell Soule Preschool Inventory
California Accountability Index
California Achievement Tests
California Basic Educational Skills Test
California Behavior Inventory Nursery School Child
California Child Q Set

Denmark Self Concept Test
Denny Doodlebug Problem
Denny Rusch Ives Classroom Observation Schedule
Dental Admission Testing Program
Denver Articulation Screening Exam
Denver Auditory Phoneme Sequencing Test (Part 2)
Denver Developmental Screening Test
Denver Developmental Screening Test (Japan)
Denver Prescreening Developmental Questionnaire
Dependability Index (Kane and Brennan)
Dependent Variables
Depoyster Need Assessment Scale (1971)
Depression Adjective Checklists
Depression Coping Questionnaire
Depression Proneness Rating Scale
Depressive Symptoms Questionnaire
Deprivation Index
Depth of Delinquency Index
Describe Your School Inventory (Hoyt)
Descriptive Test of English Skills
Descriptive Test of Mathematics Skills
Descriptive Tests of Language Skills
Descriptive Tests of Mathematics Skills
Detroit General Intelligence Examination
Detroit Tests of Learning Aptitude
Detroit Word Recognition Test
Developing Cognitive Abilities Test
Developmental Articulation Test (Hejna)
Developmental Assessment of Spanish Grammar
Developmental Assessment Wheel
Developmental Behavior Checklist
Developmental Contingency Tables
Developmental Indicators Assessment Learning
Developmental Indicators Assessment Learning Rev
Developmental Inventory of Sources of Stress
Developmental Knowledge Management Practices Scale
Developmental Profile (Bessell and Palomargs)
Developmental Quotient
Developmental Record for Infants Young Children
Developmental Referenced Tests
Developmental Sentence Scoring
Developmental Supervisory Competency Assessment
Developmental Test of Visual Motor Integration
Developmental Testing
Developmental Tests of Visual Motor Association
Devereux Elementary School Behavior Rating Scale
Diabetes Opinion Survey
Diagnostic Achievement Battery
Diagnostic Achievement Test for Adolescents (DATA)
Diagnostic Achievement Tests
Diagnostic Assess Reading Trial Teach Strategies
Diagnostic Instrument of Supervision
Diagnostic Interview for Children and Adolescents
Diagnostic Interview Schedule
Diagnostic Interview Schedule for Children
Diagnostic Mathematics Inventory
Diagnostic Reading Scales (Spache)
Diagnostic Reading Test
Diagnostic Test of Word Attack Skills
Diagonal Linear Adjustment
Dialect Differentiation Measure
DIAMAPs
Dichotomous Decisions
Dichotomous Responses
Dichotomous Scoring
Dichotomous Variables
Diederich Rating Scale for Essays
Diehl Mikulecky Job Literacy Survey
Difference Scores
Different Situations Inventory
Differential Ability Tests
Differential Aptitude Spatial Relations Test
Differential Aptitude Test
Differential Aptitude Tests
Differential Imagery Questionnaire
Differential Interest Test
Differential Personality Inventory
Differential Utility
Differential Value Profile
Differential Values Inventory
Differential Weighting
Differentiated Child Behavior Observational System
Differentiated School Norms
Differentiation of Self Inventory
Digit Span Test (Case and Kurland)
Dimensionality (Tests)
Dimensions of Excellence Scales
Dimensions of Schooling Questionnaire
Dimensions of Self Concept
Dimensions of Temperament Survey
Diplomat Game
Direct Assessment
Direct Questioning (Car Test)
Direct Standard Setting Method
Direct Writing Assessment
Directed Imagination Technique
Directory Sampling
Disability Opinion Survey (Greer et al)
Disaggregation (Data)
Discourse Comprehension Abilities Test
Discrepancy Measure
Discriminant Function Index
Discriminant Validity
Discrimination by Identification of Pictures
Discrimination Index
Discrimination Indices
Discrimination Learning Test (Arima)
Disguised Test Items
Disjunctive Item Response Functions
Disruptive Behavior Inventory
Distance from Origins Index
Distributive Justice Scale
Divergent Production Battery
Divergent Questioning
Divergent Validation
DMI Mathematics Systems
Document Delivery Test
Dogmatism Scale (Rokeach Hebrew)
Dogmatism Scale (Rokeach)
Dolan Home Educational Environment Scale
Dolch Basic Sight Vocabulary
Doll Choice Task
Doll Self Point Task
Domain Referenced Testing
Domain Referenced Tests
Domain Score Strategy
Domain Validity
Doman Delacato Developmental Profile
Doman Delacato Method
Dominance Hierarchies
Dominion Achievement Test in Silent Reading
Dominion Group Achievement Tests
Dominion Group Test of Learning Capacity
Dominion Group Test of Reading Readiness
Dominion Vocabulary Test
Doren Diagnostic Reading Test
Dos Amigos Verbal Language Scale
Double Criterion Technique
Double Cross Validation
Double Extrapolation Technique
Double I Game
Double Standardized Scoring
Dove Test of Mental Aptitude
Drake Music Memory Test
Drake Rhythm Test
Draw a Circle Task
Draw a Classroom Test
Draw A Face Test
Draw a Line Slowly Test
Draw a Line Task
Draw a Man Task
Draw a Man Test
Draw a Person Test
Draw a Woman Task
Drawing Stimulus Strategy Measure (Ball)
Drift (Scoring)
Driver Examinations
Driver Licensing
Driver Performance
Dropout Prediction Scale
Drug Abuse Questionnaire (Ferneau and Mueller)
Drug and Alcohol Survey
Drug Impact Index
Drug Orientation Scale (Frankel)
Drug Perception Scale
Drug Survey Questionnaire (Webster)
Drug Use Forecasting Study
DRV Bilingual Test
Dual Employed Coping Scales
Dual Language Text
Dual Tasks
Dugger Scale
Dummy Variables
Duncan Multiple Range Test
Duncan Socioeconomic Index
Dunn Object Sorting Task
Dunn Visual Discrimination Task
Dunnett Test
Dunns Marriage Role Expectation Inventory
Duopoly Game
Duplex Design
Durrell Analysis of Reading Difficulty
DUSO Affectivity Assessment Device
Dutch Identity (Testing)
Dutton Mathematics Attitude Scale
DV Child Development Inventory
Dvorine Color Blindness Tests
Dyadic Adjustment Scale
Dyadic Parent Child Interaction Coding System
Dynamic Assessment
E 2 Scale (Rimland)
E Coefficient
EAC Student Ratings Form
Early Adolescent School Role Strain Inventory
EARLY Assessment (Test)
Early Childhood Assessment Battery
Early Childhood Assessment Instrument
Early Childhood Environment Rating Scale
Early Childhood Longitudinal Survey
Early Education Screening Test Battery
Early Identification Assessment Battery
Early Identification Screening Inventory
Early Intervention Developmental Profile
Early Reading Test
Early School Assessment
Early School Personality Questionnaire
Early Screening Profiles
Early Social Communication Scales
Early Warning Test NJ
Earthquake Information Test
EASI (Buss and Plomin)
Eastern African Survey
Echo (Krus et al)
Echoic Response Inventory for Children
Eclectic Examination
Ecological Fallacy (Testing)
Economics Values Inventory
Edinburgh Articulation Test
Edinburgh Handedness Inventory
EDL Reading Versatility Tests
Edmonds Learning Style Identification Exercise
Education Entrance Examination SC
Education for Parenthood Attitude Scale
Education Opinion Inventory
Education Participation Scale
Educational Administration Skills Inventory
Educational Assessment of Social Interaction
Educational Assessment of Student Interaction
Educational Attitude Survey
Educational Attitudes Inventory
Educational Attitudes Scale
Educational Beliefs System Inventory
Educational Development Series
Educational Goals Assessment
Educational Leadership Test
Educational Orientation Questionnaire
Educational Participation Scale
Educational Research Service Survey
Educational Results Information System
Educational Set Scale
Educational Sign Skills Evaluation
Educational Technology Predisposition Assessment
Educational Values Assessment Questionnaire
Educational Values Perception Inventory
Educational Values Scale
Edumetric Properties of Tests
Edwards Multiple Categorization Test
Edwards Personal Preference Schedule
Edwards Personality Inventory
Edwards Social Desirability Scale
Effect Size Estimator (Glass)
Effect Strength
Effectance Motivation Distribution
Effective Professor Scale (Vaughn)
Effective Remedial Math Checklist
Effective School Scale
Effective Schools Battery
Effectiveness Motivation Scale (Stott and Sharp)
Efficacy Scale for Creative Productivity
Efficacy Scale for Overall Creative Productivity
Efficiency Index
Efficiency Ratio
Efrons Bootstrap
Ego Identity Scale (Rasmussen)
Eigenvalue Greater Than Unity Rule (Kaiser)
Eight Block Sorting Task
Eight College Professors (Yamamoto et al)
Eisner Art Attitude Inventory
Ekwall Reading Inventory
Electronic Principles Inventory
Elementary Art Situational Problems Test
Elementary Cognitive Tasks
Elementary Mathematics Concept Test
Elementary School Counselor Questionnaire
Elementary School Environment Survey
Elementary Secondary General Information Survey
Elementary Teachers Science Inventory (Lane)
Eleven Plus Secondary Selection Exam
Elimination Scoring
Elizur Test of Psycho Organicity
EM Algorithm
Embedded Figures Test
Embedded Items
Emergency Medicine Examination
Emery Test Anxiety Scale
Emory Word Analysis Skill Inventory
Emotions Profile Index
Empirical Bayes Estimation
Empirical Distribution Function
Employability Competency System Appraisal Test
Employability Maturity Interview
Employee Aptitude Survey
Employer Surveys
Employment Aptitude Survey
Employment Readiness Profile
End of Cycle Reading Test
Endeavor Instructional Rating Form
Endler Anxiety Scale
Energy Knowledge Attitudes Mini Assessment (1977)
English as a Second Language Assessment Battery
English Composition Test
English Entrance Examination
English Examinations
English Language Proficiency Study 1982
English Language Skills Assessment
English Picture Vocabulary Test
English Placement Examination
English Placement Tests
English Proficiency Test
English Qualifying Exam
English Spanish Verbatim Translation Exam
Enhanced ACT
Enlistment Screening Test
Ennis Weir Critical Thinking Essay Test
Enrollee Test Battery (Neighborhood Youth Corps)
Entanglement Test (OBrien and Vacca)
Entering Student Questionnaire
Entering Student Survey
Entry Behavior
Entry Level Mathematics Examination
Entry Level Skills
Entry Standards Assessment
Environment and Interest Inventory
Environmental Assessment Technique
Environmental Deprivation Scale (Pascal Jenkins)
Environmental Description Scale (Vielhauer)
Environmental Health Proficiency Examinations
Environmental Quality Index
Environmental Stability Scale (Crawford Reinard)
EPIC Teacher Information Form
Equal Interval Scoring
Equamax Criterion
Equipercentile Assumption
Equipercentile Equating
Equivariance
ERGO Procedure
Ergonomics Inventories
Erhardt Developmental Vision Assessment
Erikson Psychosocial Stage Inventory
Error Analysis (Statistics)
Errors and Omissions Tests
ERTL Index
Erwin Identity Scale
Escala de Inteligencia Wechsler Ninos Revisada
Escala de Inteligencia Wechsler Para Ninos
Escalona and Corman Object Permanence Scales
Essential High School Content Battery
Essential Independence (Tests)
Essential Skills Mathematics Tests
Estes Attitude Scale
Estimated Learning Potential
Ethic of Care Interview
Ethical Judgment Scale (Vabakas)
Ethics Position Questionnaire (Forsyth)
Ethnic Identity Questionnaire
Ethnographic Auditing
Ethnographic Evaluation
ETS Academic Profile
ETS Enumeration Task
ETS Factor Kit
ETS Growth Study

ETS Matched Pictures Language Comprehension Task
ETS Specialty Area Tests
ETS Written Exercises
Evaluability Assessment
Evaluation Costs
Evaluation Instrument for Experimental Methodology
Evaluation Instrument for Experimental Research
Evaluation Modality Test
Evaluation of Counselors Scale
Evaluation Scale for Four Five Year Old Children
Evaluation Standards
Evaluation Timeliness
Evaluative Criteria (Coop Study Sec Sch Standards)
Evaluative Cues
Evaluative Dimensions
Evaluative Meaning
Evaluator Characteristics
Evaluator Credibility
Evaluator Types (Meltsner)
Evanston Early Identification Scale
Event Sampling
Every Student Survey
Everyday Memory Questionnaire
Everyday Stressors Index
Exact Conditional Tests
Examination Persistence
Examiner Effect
Examples
Exercise in Divergent Thinking
Exit Examinations
Exners Comprehensive System
Exners Developmental Quality
Expanded Sociometric Device (Wright Bond Denison)
Expectations about Counseling Brief Form
Expectations about Counseling Questionnaire
Expected Consequences of Aggression Test (Adams)
Experience Inventory
Experience of College Questionnaire (McDowell)
Experience Recall Test
Experience Recall Test 2
Experiences in English Inventory
Experiential Education Questionnaire
Experiential Taxonomy (Steinaker and Bell)
Experimental Method Test (Grohsmeyer and Johnson)
Experimentwise Error
Exploration Questionnaire (Edwards)
Exploratory Factor Analysis
Expressed Values Scale
Expressive Method for Measuring Need Achievement
Expressive One Word Picture Vocabulary Test
EXSPRT
Extended Caution Index
Extent of Planning Scale
External Evaluation
External Sensitivity Index (Kosecoff and Klein)
Eysenck Personality Inventory
Eysenck Psychoticism Scale
F Test
Facial Action Code
Factor Indeterminancy
Factor Matching
Factor Referenced Temperament Scales
Factor Structure Stability
Factorial Designs
Factorial Modeling
Facts About Science Test
Facts on Aging Quiz (Palmore)
Faculty at Work Questionnaire
Faculty Course Questionnaire
Faculty Evaluation Check List
Faculty Opinion Survey Questionnaire
Faking (Testing)
False Evaluation Data
Family Adaptability Cohesion Evaluation Scales
Family Concept Q Sort
Family Day Care Rating Scale
Family Drawing Depression Scale
Family Environment Interview Schedule
Family Environment Scale
Family Integration Index
Family Interaction Inventory
Family Life and Sex Education Questionnaire
Family Needs Survey
Family Problem Instrument (Baker)
Family Relations Indicator
Family Relations Inventory
Family Relations Test
Family Relationships Grid
Family Resource Scale
Family Support Scale
Famous Sayings Test (Bass)
Farnham Diggory Cognitive Synthesis Task
Fast Response Survey System
Fault Diagnosis
Fear of Femininity Scale
Fear of Negative Evaluation Scale (Watson Friend)
Fear Survey Schedule
Federal Service Entrance Examination
Federation Licensing Examination
Feffer Role Taking Test
Fennema Sherman Mathematics Attitudes Scales
Fey Acceptance of Others Scale
Fidelity of Supervision Scale
Fiedler Interpersonal Perception Scale
Fiedler Least Preferred Coworker Scale
Field Based Implementation Rating Scale
Field Reader Evaluation Form
Field Sensitive Field Independ Behav Observ Instru
Fields Type Teaching Tests
Figural Analogies
Figural Intersection Test
Figure Location Test
Film Analysis Interaction Record
Film Evaluation Checklist
Final Examinations
Final Free Recall
Finding Embedded Figures Test
Finding Kids with Special Needs
Fine Finger Dexterity Work Task Unit
Finger Oscillation Test
FIRO B Scale
FIRO BC Scale
FIRO F Scale
First Art Assessment (1975)
First Career Occup Develop Assess (1974)
First Citizenship Assessment (1970)
First Grade Screening Test
First Literature Assessment (1971)
First Mathematics Assessment (1973)
First Music Assessment (1972)
First Principal Components Method
First Reading Assessment (1971)
First Science Assessment (1970)
First Social Studies Assessment (1972)
First Writing Assessment (1970)
Fisher Exact Probability Test
Fisher Yates Exact Test
Fixed Item Tests
Fixed Length Testing
Fixed Parameter Approach
Flanagan Aptitude Classification Tests
Flanders System of Interaction Analysis
Flange Detection Cluster Analysis
Flawed Items
Flesch Reading Ease Formula
Flesch Reading Ease Score
Flexibility of Closure
Flexibility of Reading Test
Flint Infant Security Scale
Florida Basic Skills Test
Florida Cosmetology Licensure Examination
Florida Education Opinionnaire
Florida Functional Literacy Test
Florida Key Scale
Florida Minimum Student Performance Standards
Florida Performance Measurement System
Florida State Student Assessment Test
Florida State Student Assessment Test Part II
Florida Teacher Certification Examination
Florida Teacher Competency Examination
Florida Twelfth Grade Test
Florida Writing Project Student Survey
Fluharty Preschool Speech Language Screening Test
Fly Test
Flynt Cooter Informal Reading Inventory
Focused Holistic Scoring
Focused Observation Form (Henderson and Ward)
Following Directions
Forced Choice Scale (Harvill)
Forced Choice Self Description Inventory (De Jung)
Foreign Language Attitude Quest (Jakobvits)
Foreign Language Attitude Scale (Dufort)
Foreign Service Institute Interview
Forers Measurement of Gullibility
Form 441 Assurance Compliance Federal Desegration
Form Z Test of Testwiseness (Ferrell)
Formal Evaluation
Formulating Hypotheses Test (Frederiksen)
Forty Eight Item Counseling Evaluation Test
Foster Life Indicator
Foundation Program Assessment Improvement System
Fountain Valley Post Tests
Four Factor Theory Questionnaire
Four Mode Factor Analysis
Fourth Mathematics Assessment (1985)
Fourth Writing Assessment (1984)
Frame of Reference Measure
Framingham Type A Behavior Scale
Franck Drawing Completion Test
Free Association Norms
Free Association Vocabulary Test (Tinker et al)
Free Associations
Free Response Test Items
Frequency Estimation Equipercentile Equating
Frequency of Measurement
Friedman Two Way Analysis of Variance
Friedmans Developmental Level
Friendship Assessment Inventory
Friendship Rating Scale (Bailey and Pierce)
Frostig Developmental Program of Visual Perception
Frostig Developmental Test of Visual Perception
Fry Readability Formula
Frys Phonetically Regular Words Oral Reading Test
Fukuyama Profile
Full Range Picture Vocabulary Test (Ammons)
Fullerton Language Test for Adolescents
Functional Ability Rating Scale
Functional Academic Skills Tests
Functional Assessment Inventory
Functional Literacy Examination MS
Functional Literacy Mini Assessment (1975)
Functional Motion Test
Functionally Remote Associates Test
Functioning Level Testing
Fundamental Academic Skills Test
Fundamental Interpersonal Relations Orientation
Furniture Arrangement Floorplan Test
Future Orientation Questionnaire
Future World Perspective Values Scale
FYCSP Word Attack Test
G Analysis
G Index of Agreement
Gable Roberts Attitude Towards School Subjects
Gain Analysis
Gain Scores
Galbahe Language Tests
Gamma Coefficient
Gang Membership Inventory
Garland Assessment of Graduation Expectations
Gates Basic Reading Tests
Gates MacGinitie Readiness Skills Test
Gates MacGinitie Reading Tests
GED Writing Skills Test
Geist Picture Interest Inventory
Geist Picture Interest Inventory Deaf Form
GEM Algorithm
Gemeinschaft Gesellschaft Value Scale
Gender Communication Scale
Gender Role Assignment Scale
General Ability Battery
General Academic Assessment
General Anxiety Questionnaire (Yasgur and Carnen)
General Anxiety Scale (Sarason)
General Anxiety Scale for Children (Sarason)
General Aptitude Test Battery
General Attitude Institutional Authority Question
General Attitudes Toward Rape Scale
General Cognitive Index
General Concerns Inventory
General Culture Test
General Education Performance Index
General Educational Development Tests
General Impression Scoring
General Information Test (Hart)
General Intellectual Skills Assessment
General Learning Ability Score
General School Characteristics Questionnaire
General Secondary Educ Certificate Exam (Jordan)
General Semantics Competency Opinion Test (Ralph)
General Social Distance Scale
General Social Survey
Generalizable Skills Importance Questionnaire
Generalized Approximate Procedure
Generalized Expectancy for Success Scale
Geometric Figures Test (Kannegieter)
Geometric Inventory (Carpenter et al)
Georgia Assessment of Teacher Effectiveness
Georgia Basic Skills Test
Georgia Basic Skills Writing Test
Georgia Comprehensive Evaluation System
Georgia Criterion Referenced Tests
Georgia Teacher Performance Assessment Instrument
Gergen Morse Self Consistency Scale
Gesell Developmental Schedules
Gesell Developmental Tests
Gesell School Readiness Test
Gestalt Personal Homeostasis Inventory
Ghiselli Self Description Inventory
Gibbs Sampling
Giffin Trust Scale
Gifted Self Understanding Assessment Battery
Gilliland Learning Potential Examination
Gilmore Oral Reading Test
GINI Index of Dissimilarity
Gini Mean Difference
Ginn Diagnostic Vocabulary Test
Gittinger Personality Assessment System
Global Rating Scale (Morrison)
Gloria and David Bilingual Oral Lang Assessment
Goal Attainment Scale
Goal Instability Scale
GOAT Effect
Goldberg Misogyny Test
Goldberg Scale of Vocational Development
Golden Rule (Testing)
Golden State Examination Program CA
Goldman Fristoe Test of Articulation
Goldman Fristoe Woodcock Test Auditory Discrim
Goldstein Sheerer Tests Abstract Concrete Think
Goodenough Draw a Man Test
Goodenough Harris Drawing Test
Goodman Multiplicative Association Models
Goodman Reading Miscue Inventory
Gordon Diagnostic System
Gordon Personal Inventory
Gordon Personal Profile
Gottheil Scale
Gottschalk Hidden Figures Test
Gough Sanford Rigidity Scale
Grade Development Scale
Grade Differential Statistic
Grade Level Evaluation
Grade Success Rate
Graded Mark Point Scoring
Graded Objectives in Modern Lang (Great Britain)
Graded Word Reading Tests
Graduate Education Questionnaire
Graduate Management Admission Test
Graduate Program Self Assessment
Graduate Record Examinations
Graduate School Foreign Language Tests
Graduate Student Satisfaction Questionnaire
Graduation Exit Exam LA
Grammatical Analysis of Elicited Language
Graphemic Options Test (Moretz)
Grasha Riechmann Student Learning Style Scales
Grassi Block Substitution Test
Gray Oral Reading Test
GRE Background Questionnaire
Greenberg and Jenkins Linguistic Scale
Gregorc Style Delineator
Gregory Academic Interest Inventory
Griffiths Mental Development Scales
Grooved Pegboard Test
Group Assessment of Interpersonal Traits
Group Assessment of Logical Thinking
Group Atmosphere Scale
Group Consensus Examinations
Group Description Scale (Narikawa et al)
Group Embedded Figures Test
Group Embedded Figures Test (Oltman et al)
Group Embedded Figures Test (Witkin)
Group Interaction Scale
Group Inventory for Finding Creative Talent
Group Inventory for Finding Interests
Group Level Item Response Models
Group Personality Projective Test
Group Reliable Measures
Group Test of Creativity
Group Therapist Orientation Scale
Gruen Korte Stephens Internal External Scale
Guam Educators Test of English Proficiency
Guidance Examination (Los Angeles City College)

Inventory of Access Displayed Literacy Stimuli
Inventory of Affective Aspects of Schooling
Inventory of Attitudes on Child Guidance (Kinzie)
Inventory of Beliefs
Inventory of Change Proneness
Inventory of Childrens Preschool Experiences
Inventory of Classroom Management Styles
Inventory of Cognitive Skills (Boehm)
Inventory of Counseling Practices
Inventory of Counselor Behaviors
Inventory of Dependent and Independent Behavior
Inventory of Dramatic Behavior (Lazier et al)
Inventory of Factors Affecting Test Performance
Inventory of Feminine Values (Steinmann and Fox)
Inventory of Home Stimulation
Inventory of Learning Processes
Inventory of Learning Processes (Revised)
Inventory of Myself as a Professional
Inventory of Parent and Peer Attachment
Inventory of Personal Investment (Braskamp Maehr)
Inventory of Personal Skills for Achievement
Inventory of Piaget Developmental Tasks
Inventory of Readiness for Literacy
Inventory of Religious Activities and Interests
Inventory of Science Attitudes
Inventory of Self Appraisal
Inventory of Socially Supportive Behaviors
Inventory of Study Habits and Attitudes
Inventory of Teacher Knowledge of Reading
Inventory of Test Use Satisfaction
Inventory of University Classroom Environment
Inverse Normal Scores
Investigator Planning Exercise
Invitational Teaching Observation Instrument
Invitational Teaching Survey
Involvement Behavior Questionnaire
Involvement Inventory
Inwald Personality Inventory
Inwald Survey 3
Iowa Aging Inventory
Iowa Algebra Aptitude Test
Iowa Career Education Inventory
Iowa Early Learning Assessment
Iowa Farm and Rural Life Poll
Iowa Grammar Information Test
Iowa Parent Behavior Inventory
Iowa Pupil Inventory
Iowa Severity Rating Scales
Iowa Silent Reading Tests
Iowa Social Competency Scale (Preschool)
Iowa Test of Preschool Development
Iowa Testing Programs
Iowa Tests of Basic Skills
Iowa Tests of Educational Development
IPAT Anxiety Scale
IPAT Childrens Personality Questionnaire
Ipsative Measurement
Irrational Belief Scale (Ellis)
ISES (Instructional Support and Evaluation System)
ISES Teacher Nursery School Battery
Ishahara Test for Color Blindness
Ishihara Test for Color Blindness
Islands Puzzle
Issues in Disability Scale
It Scale for Children
Item Bias Detection
Item Calibration
Item Characteristic Function
Item Content Criterion
Item Deletion
Item Density
Item Dimensionality
Item Discrimination (Tests)
Item Efficiency Index (Neill and Jackson)
Item Hierarchies
Item Homogeneity
Item Information
Item Invariance
Item Item Curves
Item Linking
Item Parameter Drift
Item Parameters
Item Parcels
Item Position (Tests)
Item Rating Scale
Item Rating Sheet
Item Review Scale
Item Shells
Item Subtest Regression
Item Variance
Item Wording
J Curve
Jackson Personality Research Form
Jackson Vocational Interest Survey
Jaeger Method
Jaffa Preschool Mental Scale
James Phares Locus of Control Inventory
James Test
Janis Field Feelings of Inadequacy Scale
Janus Environmental Attitudes Scale
Jasper Planning Assistant
Jastak System
Jenkins Activity Survey
Jesness Behavior Checklist
Jesness Inventory
Jigsaw II
Job Activity Survey
Job Analysis Survey (NBPTS)
Job Attitude Questionnaire (Williams)
Job Attitude Scale (Saleh)
Job Diagnostic Survey (Hackman and Oldham)
Job Element Procedure J Scale (Primoff)
Job in General Scale
Job Reading Task Tests
Job Satisfaction Inventory (Muthard and Miller)
Job Task Performance Tests
Jobtest 1
John Dewey Personal Beliefs Inventory
Johns Hopkins Perceptual Test
Johnson Home Economics Interest Inventory
Johnson O Connor Aptitude Tests
Johnson Test of Motor Skill Development
Joint First Stage Achievement Test (Japan)
Joreskogs Congeneric Test Model
Jourard Self Disclosure Inventory
JTPA Performance Standards
Junior Aptitude Tests (South Africa)
Junior College Attitude Survey
Junior College Environment Scales (Astin)
Junior College Placement Profile
Junior College Student Inventory (Hendrix)
Junior Eysenck Personality Inventory
Junior Index of Motivation
Junior Scholastic Aptitude Test
Junior Self Monitoring Scale
Just World Scale (Rubin and Peplau)
K Index (Samejima)
K1 Rule
Kahn Intelligence Tests
Kahn Test of New York City
Kahn Test of Symbol Arrangement
Kansas Marital Satisfaction Scale
Kansas Reflection Impulsivity Scale
Kansas State IDEA Form
Kappa Index
Katz and Braly Scale
Katz Social Adjustment Scale
Kaufman Assessment Battery for Children
Kaufman Brief Intelligence Test
Kaufman Test of Educational Achievement
Keirsey Temperament Sorter
Kendalls Tau
Kennedy Institute Phonics Test
Kent EGY Test
Kent Infant Development Scale
Kent Rosanoff Word Association Test
Kentucky Comprehensive Listening Test
Kentucky Essential Skills Test
Kentucky Observation Instrument
Kephart Visual Achievement Forms
Kephart Walking Board Ability Test
Kerlinger Education Scales
Kern Art Education Information Inventory
Key Assessment System
Keylist Tests
Keymath Diagnostic Arithmetic Test
Keystone Telebinocular
Keystone Visual Screening Tests
Keystone Visual Survey Tests
KIDCOPE
Kidmaps
Kilander Health Knowledge Test
Kilmann Insight Test
Kim Anderson Bashaw Child Behavior Scale
Kindergarten Diagnostic Instrument
Kindergarten Evaluation of Learning Potential
Kindergarten Inventory (North et al)
Kindergarten Inventory Develop Social Competency
Kindergarten Language Screening Test
Kindergarten Mathematic Attitude Instrument
Kindergarten Program Entry Survey (SWRL)
Kindergarten Questionnaire
Kindergarten Teacher Rating Scale
King Pre Retirement Checklist
Kirchner Physical Fitness Test Battery
Kirton Adaption Innovation Inventory
Kit of Reference Tests for Cognitive Factors
Kluckhohn Inventory
KNI Developmental Scale (Woellhof)
Knight Perceived Influence Scale
Knobler Perceptual Development Test
Knowledge Accessing Modes Inventory
Knowledge of Child Development Inventory
Knowledge of Correct Response
Knowledge of Infant Development Scale (Dusewicz)
Knowledge of the World of Work
Knox Cube Test
Knox Sporakowski Attitudes Toward Love Scale
Knuth Achievement Tests in Music
Kogan Attitudes Toward Old People Scale
Kohlberg Moral Judgment Interview
Kohns Behavior Checklist and Competence Scale
Kohs Block Design Test
Kolmogorov Smirnov Two Sample Test
Koppitz Adaptation of Bender Gestalt Test
Koppitz Scale of Emotional Indicators
Kraner Quantitative Development Scale
Kriewall Criterion Referenced Test Model
Kropp Verner Evaluation Scale
Kruskal Wallis Test
Kruskal Wallis Test Z Scores
Kuder General Interest Survey (Form E)
Kuder Interest Card Sort
Kuder Occupational Interest Survey
Kuder Preference Record Occupational
Kuder Preference Record Vocational
Kuder Richardson Reliability Formulas
Kuhlmann Anderson Intelligence Tests
Kuhlmann Binet Intelligence Scale
Kurtosis
Kvaraceus Delinquency Proneness Scale
Kwalwasser Ruch Test of Musical Accomplishment
L and J Software Analysis Checklist II
L Test
Laboratory Demonstration Scale (Bloom)
Laboratory Interaction Categories
Laboratory Lecture Scale (Bloom)
Laboratory Observation Schedule and Record
Laboratory Program Variables Inventory
Lado Test of Aural Comprehension
Lady Walking in the Rain
Lake Wobegon Phenomenon
Lambrecht Shorthand Aptitude Test
Langmuir Oral Direction Test
Language Arts Test of Cognitive Functioning
Language Assessment Battery
Language Assessment Scales (De Avila and Duncan)
Language Assessment Tasks (Kellman Flood Yoder)
Language Assignment Umpire
Language Attitude Scale
Language Communication Skills Task
Language Development Survey
Language Facility Test
Language Free Tests
Language Minority Survey
Language Proficiency Guidelines
Language Proficiency Interview
Language Proficiency Measure
Language Proficiency Questionnaire
Language System Diagnostic Test
Lankton First Year Algebra Test
Large Scale Assessment
Large Scale Writing Assessment
Laspeyres Formula
Latchaw Motor Achievement Test
Latent Ability Distributions
Latent Space
Latent Variables
Laterality Discrimination Test (Culver et al)
Latino Youth Acculturation Scale
Laurelton Self Concept Scale
Laurendeau (Monique)
Law Concept Inventory
Law Encounter Severity Scale
Law School Admission Test
LAWSEQ
Lawson Test of Formal Reasoning
Le Maistre Pollock Health Behavior Inven
Leader Adaptability and Style Inventory
Leader Attributes Inventory
Leader Authenticity Scale
Leader Behavior Description Questionnaire
Leadership Actions Survey
Leadership and Role Study Questionnaire
Leadership Climate Inventory
Leadership Effectiveness Adaptability Description
Leadership Opinion Questionnaire
Leadership Practices Inventory
Leadership Scale for Sports
Learner Preference System
Learning 100
Learning Accomplishment Profile
Learning Activities Questionnaire
Learning and Study Skills Questionnaire
Learning and Study Strategies Inventory
Learning Efficiency Test
Learning Efficiency Test II
Learning Environment Desire Enhance Reading Skills
Learning Environment Inventory
Learning Environment Inventory (Anderson et al)
Learning Environment Inventory for Young Children
Learning Potential Assessment Device
Learning Potential Tests
Learning Preference Inventory
Learning Preference Scale (Students)
Learning Process Questionnaire (Biggs)
Learning Strategies Questionnaire
Learning Strategy Inventory (Dansereau)
Learning Style Inventory
Learning Style Inventory (Kolb)
Learning Style Preference Checklist
Learning Style Profile (NASSP)
Learning Styles Inventory
Learning Styles Inventory (Renzulli and Smith)
Leary Interpersonal Checklist
Least Absolute Value Statistics
Lecture Characteristics Scale
Lee Clark Reading Readiness Test
Lee Clark Reading Test
Leisure Activity Survey
Leisure Behavior Inventory
Leiter Adult Intelligence Scale
Leiter International Performance Scale
Leniency (Tests)
Leniency Response Bias
Level of Aspiration Indicator
Level of Aspiration Test (Pierce Jones)
Level of Parent Involvement Questionnaire
Level of Supervision Inventory
Leveling Sharpening House Test
Levels of Use of the Innovation
Levels of Use Scale (Hall and Louck)
Lexile Scale of Reading
Library General Information Survey
Library Inventory
Library Quotient
License Plates Test
Lie Scale for Children
Life Career Assessment
Life Change Unit Rating Scale for College Students
Life Events Academic Performance Questionnaire
Life Events Checklist
Life Events Scale
Life Events Scale Children
Life Expectancy Inventory (Owens)
Life Experience Inventory
Life Experiences Scale
Life Experiences Survey
Life Goals Inventory (Beggs)
Life Interpersonal History Enquiry
Life Meaning Survey
Life Principles Scale
Life Review Task
Life Satisfaction Index
Life Satisfaction Index A
Life Science Concept Acquisition Test (Riechard)
Life Science Concept Test (Butler)
Life Skills Inventory
Lifetime Creativity Scales
Light Intensity Matching Test (Watson et al)
Lights Retention Scale
Like School Scale (Combers and Keeves)
Likelihood Function Estimation
Likelihood Ratio Tests
Likert Profile of Organizational Characteristics
Lilliefors Statistic
Limited Closed Interval Measures
Limulus Test
Lincoln Intermediate Spelling Test
Lincoln Oberetsky Motor Development Scale
Lindamood Auditory Conceptualization Test
Line Match Test (Barton)
Linear Classification Function
Linear Logistic Test Model
Linear Tests
Linear Trends
Linguistic Ability Test (Frederick et al)
Linguistic Structures Repetition Test

Link F Test
Linked Judgment Approach
Linking Educational Assessments
Lipscomb Scale of Teacher Attitudes
Listen and Look (Clark)
Listen Respond Compare Mode
Listener Preference Profile
Listening Comprehension Test (Graham and Orr)
Listening Comprehension Test for First Grade
Listening Inference Test (Stern)
Listening Rate
Listening Response Test (Stein)
Listening Summary Translation Exam Spanish
Listening Test of Specific Content (Stern Keisler)
Lister Empathy Scale
Literacy Assessment
Literacy Assessment Battery
Literacy Observation Matrix
Literacy Tests for Teachers
Literary Profundity Test (Anderson)
Literary Rating Scale (Tway)
Livestock Sale Barn Employee Competencies
Living Room School Cognitive Assessment Inventory
Lix Readability Formula
Local Independence (Tests)
Locke Marital Relationship Inventory
Locke Wallace Marital Adjustment Scale
Locus of Control in Three Achievement Domains
Locus of Control Scales (Levenson)
Loevinger Sentence Completion Test
LOGIST Estimation Procedures
Loney Draw a Car Test
Longeot Test of Concrete and Formal Reasoning
Longitudinal Merges
Longitudinal Scaling
Lorenz Curve
Lorge Thorndike Intelligence Tests
Lorr Inpatient Multidimensional Psychiatric Scale
Lorrs Dimension of Interaction in Group Therapy
Loudness Discrimination Test
Louise Child Care Scale
Louisiana Basic Skills Test
Louisiana Compensatory Remedial Student Profile
Love Relationships Scale
Low Achievement Scale (Felton)
Low Cutoff Method
Low Stakes Tests
Lowenfeld Mosaic Test
Lower Asymptotes
Lowery Projective Test of Attitudes
LRS Seriation Test
Lurcat Test of Graphical Abilities
Luria Nebraska Intellectual Processes Scale
Luria Nebraska Neuropsychological Battery
MA 3 Associative Memory Test (French et al)
MacAndrew Alcoholism Scale
MACC Behavioral Adjustment Scale
MacDonald Tseng Locus of Control Scale
Mach Scale (Christie)
Machover Anxiety Scale
Machover Draw a Person Test
Maculaitis Assessment Program
Magazine Surveys
Magnitude Estimates
Mahalanobis Distance Function
Mahl Speech Disturbance Indices
Maitland Graves Design Judgment Test
Major Field Achievement Test in Political Science
Management Profile (Erlandson)
Manager Rating Scale
Managerial Frames of Mind Survey
Mandated Tests
Mandler Sarason Test Anxiety Questionnaire
Manifest Anxiety Defensiveness Scale (Millimet)
Manifest Anxiety Scale
Manifest Needs Questionnaire
Mann Suiter Developmental Screening Tests
Mann Whitney U Test
Mantel Haenszel Procedure
Manual Accuracy and Speed Test
Marble Board Test
Marcia Incomplete Sentences Blank
Margin in Life Scale
Marital Alternatives Scale
Marital Communication Inventory
Marital Conventionalization Scale
Marital Coping Inventory (Zbrowski Berman)
Marital Satisfaction Inventory
Marital Satisfaction Scale
Marital Status Inventory
Marker Tests
Marlowe Crowne Personal Reaction Inventory
Marlowe Crowne Social Desirability Scale
Marmors Mental Rotation Task
Marriage Role Expectation Inventory
Marsh Self Report Questionnaire
Martin Temperament Assessment Battery
Martins Motivational Profile
Maryland Functional Mathematics Test
Maryland Functional Reading Test
Maryland Functional Writing Test
Maryland Parent Attitude Survey
Maryland Preschool Self Concept Scale
Maryland School Performance Assessment Program
Maryland Self Concept as a Learner Scale
Maryland Test of Citizenship Skills
Maslach Burnout Inventory
Maslow Security Insecurity Inventory
Maslowian Scale
Massachusetts Basic Skills Inventory
Massachusetts Basic Skills Testing Program
Massad Mimicry Test
Masters Comprehensive Examination
Mastery Learning Test Model (Besel)
Mastery Learning Test Model (Emrick and Adams)
MAT 6
MAT 6 Writing Test
Matched Pair Scoring
Matching Familiar Figures Test (Kagan)
Matching to Sample Procedure
Materials Analysis Inventory
Materials Testing
Maternal Attitude Scale (Cohler Weiss Gruenbaum)
Maternal Behavior Scale
Math Remediation Methods Questionnaire
Mathematical Sciences Instructor Evaluation Form
Mathematical Self Concept Scale (Gourgey)
Mathematics Achievement Questionnaire
Mathematics Anxiety Rating Scale
Mathematics Applied to Novel Situations Test
Mathematics Assessment Questionnaire
Mathematics Attribution Scale
Mathematics Composite (NAEP)
Mathematics Diagnostic Prescriptive Inventory
Mathematics Diagnostic Testing Project CA
Mathematics Interest Inventory
Mathematics Mini Assessment (1976)
Mathematics Self Concept Scale (Holly et al)
Mathematics Self Efficacy Scale
Mathematics Skill Test
Mathematics Teaching Inventory (ERB)
Matrix Analogies Test (Expanded Form)
Matrix Analogies Test (Short Form)
Matrix Tasks (Siegel and Kresh)
Matthews Youth Test for Health
Maudsley Personality Inventory
Maultsby Common Trait Inventory
Maximin Model
Mazyck Rating Scale for Paraprofessionals
McCall Crabbs Standard Test Lessons in Reading
McCandles Intensity of Involvement Scale
McCarthy Draw a Child Subtest
McCarthy Draw a Child Test
McCarthy Scales of Childrens Abilities
McCarthy Screening Test
McClelland Need Achievement Test
McConnell Language Devel Cultural Disadvantagement
McCracken Standard Reading Inventory
McCracken Word List
McCullough Word Analysis Tests
McDaniel Inferred Self Concept Scale
McDaniel Piers Young Childrens Self Concept Scale
McGee F Scale
McGraw Hill Basic Skills System Reading Test
McGraw Hill Test of Adult Basic Education
McGraw Hill Writing Test
McHugh McParland Reading Readiness Test
McKee Inventory of Phonetic Skill
McLeod Control Structure Description Questionnaire
McLeod Hawley Index of Professional Orientation
McNemar Test of Equality of Correlated Proportion
McVoys Wants and Satisfaction Scale
Meadow Kendall Social Emotional Assessment Invent
Mean Contrasts
Mean Cost Rating
Mean Length of Utterance
Mean Residuals
Mean Response (Tests)
Mean Square Fit
Mean Test Evaluation System
Meaning of Words Inventory
Meaningful Measurement
Means End Test
Means Ends Problem Solving Procedure
Measure of Academic Talent
Measure of Educator Stress
Measure of Epistemological Reflection
Measure of Intellectual Development
Measure of Obscure Medical Information
Measure of Sampling Adequacy
Measurement and Planning System Scales
Measurement Competency Test (Mayo)
Measurement Errors
Measurement Integrity
Measurement of Change
Measurement Problems
Measurement Student Activities
Measures of Association
Measures of Creative Thinking in Music
Measures of Musical Abilities
Mechanical Comprehension Tests
Mechanization Scale (Goldman and Kaplan)
Media Management Grid (Miller)
Median Test
Mediated Ranking Technique
Medical College Admission Test
Medical Knowledge Tests
Medical Schools Learning Environment Survey
Medical Specialist Preference Blank
Medical Specialty Preference Inventory (Zimny)
Meeting Street School Screening Test
Mehrabian Measure of Achieving Tendency Females
Meier Art Tests
Meier Burnout Assessment
Memory for Designs Test (Graham Kendall)
Memory Span Tests (Harris)
Mental Development Scales Birth to Three Years
Mental Dexterity Test
Mental Health Attitude Survey (Fischer and Turner)
Mental Rotation Tests
Mental Status Examination
Mentalistic Measures
Merit System Tests
Merrill Language Screening Test
Merrill Palmer Head Start Questionnaire
Merrill Palmer Personality Rating Scale
Merrill Palmer Scale of Mental Tests
Meta Evaluation
Methodology Inventory
Metric Multidimensional Scaling
Metropolitan Achievement Tests
Metropolitan Community Attitude Inventory
Metropolitan Handwriting Scale
Metropolitan Readiness Tests
Metropolitan Reading Mathematics Achievement Tests
Mexican American Culture Simulator
Mexican American Inventory of Receptive Abilities
Mexican Attitude Inventory
Meyer Social Attitude Scale
Michael Test of Oral English Language
Michaels Informal Test of Student Ability
Michigan Alcoholism Screening Test
Michigan Elementary Geography Test
Michigan Employability Skills Survey
Michigan English Language Assessment Battery
Michigan Essential Skills Reading Test
Michigan International Student Problem Inventory
Michigan Mathematics Early Placement Test
Michigan Organizational Assessment Questionnaire
Michigan Picture Test
Michigan Pupil Attitude Questionnaire
Michigan Restricted Association Norms
Michigan State M Scales
Michigan State Self Concept of Abilities Scale
Michigan Student Questionnaire
Michigan Test Battery
Michigan Test of Aural Comprehension
Michigan Test of English Language Proficiency
Michill Adjective Rating Scale
Microintensity Index
Micronesian Achievement Test Series
Mid Primary Screening Battery
Middle Grades Integrated Process Skills Test
Middle School Description Survey
Middle School Instructional Practices Scale
Midterm Examinations
Midtown Psychiatric Impairment Index
Migrant Education Needs Assessment Evaluation Sys
Migrant Education Oral Language Skills List
Military Applicant Profile
Military Ideology Scale (Altman)
Military Life Questionnaire
Military Occupational Data Bank
Mill Hill Vocabulary Scale
Miller Analogies Test
Miller Assessment for Preschoolers
Miller Coleman Readability Scale
Miller Fisk Sexual Knowledge Questionnaire
Miller Motivation Scale
Millimeter Scale (Harvill)
Millon Clinical Multiaxial Inventory
Mills Learning Methods Test
Millwright
Milwaukee Academic Interest Inventory
Milwaukee School Guidance Evaluation Scale
Miner Sentence Completion Scale
Mini RAT (Remote Associates Test)
Mini Tests
Miniature Training and Evaluation Battery
Minimood
Minimum Average Partial Rule (Velicer)
Minimum Basic Skills Test
Minimum Competencies Performance Test
Minimum English Competency Test
Minimum Trace Factor Analysis
Mink Scale
Minneapolis Preschool Screening Instrument
Minnesota Child Development Inventory
Minnesota Clerical Test
Minnesota College Statewide Testing Program
Minnesota Counseling Inventory
Minnesota Importance Questionnaire
Minnesota Job Description Questionnaire
Minnesota Job Requirements Questionnaire
Minnesota Multiphasic Personality Inventory
Minnesota Multiphasic Personality Inventory 168
Minnesota Nonverbal Test of Creativity (Torrance)
Minnesota Percepto Diagnostic Test
Minnesota Preschool Scale
Minnesota Rate of Manipulation Test
Minnesota Reading Assessment
Minnesota Reading Readiness Test
Minnesota Satisfaction Questionnaire
Minnesota Scale for Paternal Occupations
Minnesota Scale of Employment Satisfaction
Minnesota Scholastic Aptitude Test
Minnesota School Attitude Survey
Minnesota Secondary School Followup System
Minnesota Sex Attitude Survey
Minnesota Student Attitude Inventory
Minnesota Teacher Attitude Inventory
Minnesota Tests of Creative Thinking (Torrance)
Minnesota Vocational Interest Inventory
Minres Criterion
Mirror Image Designs
Misclassification (Statistics)
Miskimins Self Goal Other Discrepancy Scale
Mississippi Teacher Assessment Instruments
Missouri Automated Reinforcer Assessment
Missouri Basic Essential Skills Test
Missouri Childrens Picture Series
Missouri College English Test
Missouri College Placement Test
Missouri Kindergarten Inventory Develop Skills
Missouri Mastery and Achievement Tests
Mitofsky Waksberg Procedure
Mixed Income Testing
Mixed Method Triangulation
MLA ADE Survey of Doctoral Programs in English
MLA Cooperative Foreign Language Proficiency Tests
MLA Cooperative Foreign Language Tests
Modal Profile Analysis
Model Identification Test (McIntyre)
Modern Language Aptitude Test
Modified Alphabet Test (Kjeldergaard Frankenstein)
Modified Bennett Test (Price)
Modified Caution Index
Modified Component Disability Checklist
Modified Component Disability Instrument

Modified Confidence Weighted Admissible Prob Meas
Modified Mastery Grading System
Modified Norm Referenced Grading System
Modified Peabody Picture Vocabulary Test
Modified Questionnaire Occup Status of Women
Modified Rabban Toy Preference Test
Modified Rhyme Hearing Test
Modified Role Repertory Test (Bieri)
Modified Rosenberg Self Esteem Scale
Modified World Affairs Questionnaire
Monetary Concepts Task Test (McCarty)
Money Ethic Scale
Monitor of Student Satisfaction Questionnaire
Mono Operationalization Extraspective Measures
Monotone Splines
Monotone Transformation
Monroe Oral Language Scale
Montague Riley Test
Montana Functional Vision Assessment
Mood Test of Significance
Mooney Problem Check List
Moore Assessment Profile
Moral Action Choice Test (Patterson)
Moral Behavior Analysis Instrument
Moral Judgment Task (Piaget)
Morality Test for Children
Moray House Verbal Reasoning Tests
Morse McCune Test of Critical Thinking
Mosaic Construction Test (Hall)
Mosby Assess Test
Mosher Forced Choice Guilt Scale
Most Like Questionnaire (Landis and Hayman)
Mother Child Picture Test
Mother Goose Problems Test
Motivated Strategies for Learning Questionnaire
Motivation Analysis Test (Cattell and Horn)
Motivation Check Sheet
Motivational Orientation Scale
Motivational Structure Questionnaire Alcoholics
Motor Activity Scale
Motor Behavior Description Categories
Motor Free Test of Visual Perception
Motor Inhibition Test (Ward)
Motor Perceptual Diagnostic Inventory
Motoric Ideational Sensory Test (Stein and Lenrow)
Motoric Inhibition Test (MacCoby et al)
Movement Skills Test Battery
Mr Cucui
Multi Attribute Utility Theory
Multi Digit Tests
Multi Factor Attitude Inventory
Multicollinearity
Multicultural Attitude Questionnaire
Multicultural Education Quick Assessment Test
Multicultural Textbook Survey Eval Instrument
Multidimensional Analysis of Classroom Interaction
Multidimensional Aptitude Battery
Multidimensional Behavior Rating Scale
Multidimensional Discrimination
Multidimensional Fear of Death Scale
Multidimensional Health Locus of Control Scales
Multidimensional Internal External Locus Control
Multidimensional Item Difficulty
Multidimensional Latent Space
Multidimensional Motivation Instrument
Multidimensional Multiattributional Causality Sc
Multidimensional Needs Assessment Framework
Multidimensional Self Concept Scale
Multidimensional Stimulus Fluency Measure
Multidimensional Test of Self Concept
Multidimensionality (Tests)
Multifactor Leadership Questionnaire
Multifactor Racial Attitude Inventory (Woodmansee)
Multifeature Vocabulary Analysis Grid
Multilinear Formula Scoring
Multilingual Indexes (Skolnik)
Multimedia Reviews Index
Multinomial Models
Multiple Affect Adjective Checklist
Multiple Assessment Programs and Services
Multiple Categorization Test (Sigel)
Multiple Classification Analysis
Multiple Comparison Tests
Multiple Comparisons
Multiple Contrast Tests
Multiple Correlation Formula
Multiple Cutoff Scores
Multiple Linear Regression
Multiple Matrix Sampling
Multiple Operationalization
Multiple Rating Items
Multiple Response Alternative Questionnaires
Multiple Scalogram Analysis
Multiple Testing
Multiplicity Sampling
Multiscore Depression Inventory
Multistate Bar Examination
Multivariate Personality Inventory
Murphy Durrell Diagnostic Reading Readiness Test
Murphy Durrell Reading Readiness Analysis
Music Listening Reaction Scale
Musical Aptitude Profile
My Class Inventory (Anderson)
My Class Inventory (Fisher and Fraser)
My Education Scale
My Opinion Survey
My Vocational Situation
Myers Achievement Motivation Scale
Myers Briggs Type Indicator
Myself as a Teacher Scale
N Factors Questionnaire (Weiss et al)
NachNaff Scale
NAFDC Assessment Profile
Naglieri Draw a Person Test
Naming Pictured Objects Test
Naming Response
Naming Task
Nancy Ernie Aggression Test
Narrative Test Reporting
National Adolescent Student Health Survey
National Adult Literacy Survey (NCES)
National Agricultural Workers Survey
National Assessment of College Student Learning
National Assn Boards of Pharmacy Licensure Exam
National Baccalaureate Examinations
National Board Examinations
National Board Examinations Part I
National Board for Certified Counselors Exam
National Certificate (Scotland)
National Certifying Exam Physicians Assistants
National Child Care Survey 1990
National College Entrance Exam (Philippines)
National Council Licensure Exam Registered Nurses
National Council Licensure Examination
National Dropout Statistics Field Test
National Health Examination Survey
National Health Survey
National Household Education Survey
National Language Teachers Survey
National League for Nursing Achievement Tests
National Longitudinal Study High School Class 1972
National Longitudinal Study Math Abilities
National Longitudinal Survey Labor Market Ex
National Longitudinal Survey Mature Women
National Longitudinal Survey of Youth
National Longitudinal Survey Work Exp Mature Men
National Longitudinal Survey Work Exp Young Men
National Longitudinal Survey Young Women
National Longitudinal Survey Youth Labor Market Ex
National Longitudinal Surveys
National Longitudinal Transition Study Spec Educ
National Medical Expenditure Survey
National Merit Scholarship Program
National Merit Scholarship Qualifying Test
National Natality Survey
National Nutrition Survey
National Occupational Competency Project
National Probability Samples
National Public Education Financial Survey
National Qualifications Framework (New Zealand)
National Reading Difficulty Index
National Report Card
National Resources Inventory 1982
National Science Board Survey
National Spanish Examination
National Standard Five Assessment
National Survey of College Graduates (NSF)
National Survey of Postsecondary Faculty
National Teacher Examinations
National Testing
National Vocational Qualifications (England)
National Vocational Teacher Competency Exams
Naturalistic Evaluation
Nature of Science Scale
Nature of Scientific Knowledge Scale
Naval Academy Student Response Monitor
Navy Basic Test Battery
Navy Vocational Interest Inventory
NCGE Competency Based Geography Test
Neals Dance Attitude Inventory
Nebraska Instrument for Syntactic Analysis
Nebraska Principals Leadership Questionnaire
Nebraska Test of Learning Aptitude
Nebraska Wisconsin Cognitive Assessment Battery
Need Achievement Measure (McClelland et al)
Need Assessment Questionnaire
Need for Academic Competence Questionnaire
Need for Assistance Inventory
Need for Uniqueness Scale (Snyder and Fromkin)
Need Satisfaction Schedule
Needs Assessment Model
Needs Assessment Questionnaire (Mohan)
Needs Assessment Rating Scale
Needs Sensing
Negotiable Instruments
Nelson Biology Test
Nelson Denny Reading Tests
Nelson Reading Test
Neonatal Behavioral Assessment Scale
Net Benefit
Networking Evaluation
Neuropsychological Measures
Neuroticism Scale Questionnaire
Nevada High School Proficiency Examinations
Nevada Proficiency Examination Program
New Cloze Test (Hisama Lewis and Woehlke)
New Developmental Reading Tests
New Environmental Paradigm
New Hampshire Statewide Testing Program
New Jersey College Basic Skills Placement Test
New Jersey High School Proficiency Test
New Jersey Special Review Assessment
New Jersey Statewide Testing System
New Junior Maudsley Inventory
New Left Scale (Christie et al)
New Medical College Admission Test
New Mexico Articulated Assessment System
New Mexico High School Proficiency Examination
New Mexico Portfolio Writing Assessment
New York Citywide Mathematics Test
New York Citywide Reading Test
New York State Basic Competency Test in Reading
New York State Fifth Grade Writing Test
New York State Prelim Competency Test in Reading
New York State Pupil Evaluation Program
New York State Readiness Tests
New York State Reading and Readiness Tests
New York State Regents Competency Tests
New York State Regents Examinations
New York State Regents Scholarship Examinations
New York State Teacher Certification Examinations
New York Tests of Growth in Reading
Newark Uniform Testing Program NJ
Newman Keuls Analyses
News Morbidity Scale
Neyman Pearson Hypothesis Testing
Nielsen Surveys
Nightengale Conant Attitude Change Packages
Ninth Grade Communication Skills Test
Ninth Grade Proficiency Test
NLN Achievement Tests
No Guessing Format
Nomological Network
Noncategorical Education Teacher Certification
Noncognitive Questionnaire
Noncommercial Tests
Nondestructive Testing
Nondiscriminatory Assessment
Nondiscriminatory Tests (Handicapped)
Nonequivalent Control Groups
Nonmetric Factor Analysis
Nonmetric Multidimensional Scaling
Nonmonotonic Covariates
Nonnormal Distributions
Nonnormed Tests
Nonnull Hypothesis
Nonnumerical Computer Applications
Nonorthogonal Variables
Nonrandomized Design
Nonreactive Measurement
Nonreading Aptitude Test Battery
Nonresponders
Nonresponse Bias
Nonsense Test Items
Nonsexist Personal Attribute Inventory Children
Nonverbal Artistic Creativity Instrument (Zambito)
Nonverbal Curiosity Test (Corlis and Weiss)
Norm Conformity Index (Tatsuoka and Tatsuoka)
Normal Curve Equivalent Scores
Normal Distribution
Normal Scores Test
Normality Tests
Normalization Regression Estimation
Normative Statements
North Carolina Annual Testing Program
North Carolina Appraisal Instrument
North Carolina Competency Tests
North Carolina End of Course Testing Program
North Carolina Minimum Skills Diagnostic Tests
North Carolina Science Tests
North Carolina Social Studies Tests
North Carolina Statewide Testing Program
North Carolina Teacher Performance Assess System
North Carolina Teaching Performance Appraisal
North Carolina Test of Chemistry
North Carolina Test of Geometry
North Hatt Scale
North York Self Concept Inventory (Crawford)
Northwestern Syntax Screening Test
Norton Communicator Style Measure
Novel Maturity Scale
Novelty Experiencing Scale (Pearson)
Nowicki Strickland Internal External Scale (Adult)
Nowicki Strickland Internal External Scale (Child)
Nowicki Strickland Locus of Control Scale
Nowicki Strickland Locus of Control Scale Children
NTE Core Battery
NTE Specialty Area Tests
NTE Test of Professional Knowledge
Nuclear Anxiety Inventory
Nuclear Likelihood Questionnaire
Nuclear Locus of Control Scales
Null Hypothesis
Null Subject Parameter
Number Right Scoring
Nurses Professional Orientation Scale
Nursing Clinical Teacher Effectiveness Inventory
Nursing Observation of Behavior Scales (Craig)
Nutrition Knowledge Tests
Nyquist Frequency
NYU Early Childhood Inventory Test
OARS Multidimensional Functional Assessment
Object Categorization Test
Object Concept
Object Constancy
Object Naming Test (French)
Object Relations
Object Relocation Tasks
Object Sorting Task (Davidson and Greenberg)
Object Sorting Task (Dunn)
Object Sorting Test
Objective Apperception Test (Stricker)
Objective Behavior Inventory (Nichols)
Objective Item Congruence
Objective Marking
Objective Measure of Assertiveness
Objective Test Scoring Performance Rating
Objectively Scoreable Apperception Test
Objectives Bank
Objectives Based Evaluation Systems
Objectivism Scale
Observation Checklist of Hemispheric Style
Observation Schedule and Record
Observation Schedule for Physical Space (Prescott)
Observed Frequencies (Test)
Observer Effect
Observer Rating Scales (McDaniel)
Observer Ratings of Children (Emmerich)
Observer Reliability
Obsessive Compulsive Scale
Occupational Analysis Inventory
Occupational Aspiration Scale
Occupational Attitude Questionnaire (Williams)
Occupational Changes in a Generation Survey

Rabinowitz Mathematics Attitude Scale
Racial Attitude and Cultural Expression Test
Racial Attitudes Picture Test
Racial Identity Attitude Scale
Racial Tension Scale (Bowler)
Racialistic Incidents Inventory
Radex
Ramak Inventory (Meir and Barak)
Random Breath Testing
Random Effects
Random Normal Scores Test
Randomization (Statistics)
Randomized Multiple Choice Tests
Randomized Response Technique
Randomly Missing Data (Regression Analyses)
Range Restriction
Rank Order Transformation
Rank Reducibility
Rasch Scaled Scores
Rate of Learning Score
Rater Effects
Rater Ratee Similarity
Rater Reliability
Rater Stringency Error
Rathus Assertiveness Schedule
Rating of the Child Questionnaire
Rating Ranking Scale of Child Behavior (Cromwell)
Rating Scale for Curriculum Evaluation (Sperry)
Rating Scale for Directed Teaching
Rating Scale for Teachers (Quereshi and Widlar)
Ratio Scales
Rational Reasoning Test
Rationalistic Evaluation
Rauding Scale of Prose Difficulty
Raven Advanced Progressive Matrices
Raven Progressive Matrices
Raven Test of Logical Operations
Raw Agreement Index
Ray Reading Methods Test
Ray Self Checklist of Quality Voc Tech Programs
Ray Students Estimate of Teachers Concern
Reaction to Group Situation Test
Read General Science Test
Read Test (Colvin and Root)
Readiness for Vocational Planning Scales
Reading and Mathematics Observation System
Reading and Study Skills Inven (Williams Kaman)
Reading Appraisal Guide
Reading Attitude Inventory (Lewis)
Reading Beliefs Inventory
Reading Biographer
Reading Card Snellen Rating
Reading Comprehension Inventory (Guszak)
Reading Decisions Test
Reading English and Mathematics Test
Reading Free Vocational Interest Inventory
Reading Grade Level Scale
Reading Institute Survey
Reading Inventory of Science Knowledge
Reading Miscue Inventory
Reading Proficiency Scale (NAEP)
Reading Retelling Profile
Reading Span Test (Daneman and Carpenter)
Reading Storage Test
Reading Student Observation Scale (Quirk)
Reading Style Inventory (Carbo)
Reading Teacher Observation Scale (Quirk et al)
Reading Teacher Survey (Askov)
Reading Versatility Test
Real Life English Placement Survey
Realistic Assessment Various Educational Strategi
Reality Testing
Reasoning Tests
Reasons for Going to College Inventory (Dole)
Receiver Apprehension Test
Recency Effect
Recent Alumni Questionnaire
Recent College Graduates Study 1987 (NCES)
Recent College Graduates Study 1991 (NCES)
Recent College Graduates Survey 1978 (NCES)
Recent Life Changes Questionnaire (Grissom et al)
Receptivity to Change Inventory
Recognition Discrimination (Fletcher et al)
Recognizing Reliable Observations
Recreational Experience Preference Scales
Red Cloud Reading Test
Reduced Rank Classification
Reduced Redundancy Test
Redundancy Analysis
Redwood School Test (Hurst et al)
Reed and Kellogg System of Diagramming
Reed Science Activity Inventory
Reference Tests for Noncognitive Factors
Referral Preference Rating Scale
Reflective Teaching Instrument
Regents External Degree Program NY
Regional Parenting Survey
Regional Surveys
Regression Correction
Regression Effects
Regression Toward the Mean
Regulatory Evaluation
Rehabilitation Information and Knowledge Test
Rehabilitation Need and Status Scale
Rehabilitation Task Performance Evaluation Scale
Reinforcement History Questionnaire
Reinforcement Survey Schedule
Reinstein Reinforcement Schedule
Reitan Neuropsychological Batteries
Relational Ethics Scale
Relationship Belief Inventory
Relationship Questionnaire (Truax and Carkhuff)
Relative Difficulty Ratio
Relative Preference Index
Relevance (Evaluation)
Relief Format Assessment Test
Remote Associates Test
Remote Scoring (Tests)
Renzulli Hartman Scale
Repeated Testing
Repeating Response Tendency
Repertory Grid Tests (Kelly)
Reporting Evaluation System Occupational Education
Resampling Techniques
Rescaled and Adjusted Gains within Stratum
Research Evaluation Vocational Instructional Syst
Research on Science Education Survey
Resident Assistant Stress Inventory
Resident Places Survey
Residual Scores
Residuals (Statistics)
Resistance to Deviation Test
Respond Until Correct Method
Response Class Matrix (Mash et al)
Response Content and Dispersion Observation Form
Response Function Discrepancies
Response Shift
Response to Power Measure (Sweney)
Responsibility Questionnaire (Johnson et al)
Responsive Classroom Observation Schedule
Responsive Environment Test
Responsive Evaluation
Restricted Association Tests (Riegel)
Restricted Factor Analysis
Restricted Maximum Likelihood Bayes
Restricted Self Adapted Testing
Restriction of Range
Retention Index
Retesting
Retirement Descriptive Index (Smith et al)
Retirement Planning Scale
Retrospective Pretesting
Revised Art Scale
Revised Beta Examination
Revised Childrens Manifest Anxiety Scale
Revised Denver Developmental Screening Test
Revised Learning Strategies Inventory
Revised Minnesota Paper Form Board Test
Revised Objective Perceptual Test (Fidel and Ray)
Revised Observer Schedule and Record Form
Rey Auditory Verbal Learning Test
Reynell Developmental Language Scales
Rhetoric Frames
Rhetorical Sensitivity Scale
Richardson Power Profile
Rights and Formula Scoring
Rights Only Weighted Test
Rigor (Evaluation)
Riley Inventory of Basic Learning Skills
Riley Preschool Developmental Screening Inventory
Rinsland Vocabulary List
Rising Junior Examinations
Risk Assessment Tool
Riskin Family Interaction Scale
Robersons Teacher Self Appraisal
Robinson Hall Reading Tests of History
Robinson Test of Scientific Creativity
Robinsons Measure of Agreement
Robust Regression
Robustness Semantic Differential
Rod and Frame Test
Rokeach Value Survey
Role Category Questionnaire (Crockett)
Role Conflict and Ambiguity Scale
Role Construct Repertory Test (Kelly)
Role Taking Task
Root Mean Square (Statistics)
Rorschach Prognostic Rating Scale (Klopfer)
Rorschach Test
Rosenberg Self Esteem Scale
Rosenburg Test Factor Standardization
Rosenzweig Picture Frustration Study
Rosner Richman Perceptual Survey
Ross Educational Philosophical Inventory
Ross Test
Ross Test of Higher Cognitive Processes
Roswell Chall Diagnostic Reading Test Word Anal
Rotation Tasks
Rothbart Infant Behavior Questionnaire
Rotter Incomplete Sentences Blank
Rotter Internal External Locus of Control Scale
Rotter Interpersonal Trust Scale
Rotter Level of Aspiration Board
Routing Tests
Row Peterson Readiness Test
Roys Largest Root
Rubric Transition Process
Rucker Gable Educational Programming Scale
Rule Application Test
Rule Space
Ruleg System
Rules of Thumb (Statistics)
Runners Studies of Attitude Patterns
Rural Income Maintenance Experiment
Rutgers Drawing Test
Ryans Classroom Observation Record
Ryans Teacher Characteristics Schedule
Rydell Rosen Ambiguity Tolerance Scale
Rystroms Dialect Deviation Test
S R Inventory of Anxiousness (Endler et al)
S R Inventory of General Trait Anxiousness
Safran Culture Reduced Intelligence Test
Safran Students Interest Inventory
Sage Developmental Scales
SAGES P (Johnsen and Corn)
Saint Louis Spelling Test
Salience
Salience Index (Cattell)
Salience Inventory
Salient Issues (Jean et al)
Sally Test (McCracken et al)
Sample Free Item Analysis
Sample Specificity
Sample Splitting
Sampling Error
San Diego County Inventory of Reading Attitude
San Diego Quick Assessment
San Francisco Social Competency Scale
Sandwich Construction
Sandwich Courses
Santa Clara Inventory of Developmental Tasks
SAPA Process Instrument
Sarason Test Anxiety Scale
Sarason Test Anxiety Scale for Children
Satisfaction with Hiram Scales
Scale Anchoring
Scale for Evaluation Group Counseling Experiences
Scale of Aesthetic Judgment (Taylor Helmstadter)
Scale of Childrens Attitudes toward Handicaps
Scale of Client Satisfaction (Reagles)
Scale of Economic Liberalism
Scale of Noneconomic Liberalism
Scale of Primary Classroom Practices
Scale of Rehabilitation Gain (Reagles)
Scale of Student Teacher Concerns
Scale on Procedures in Dealing with Children
Scale Score Strategy
Scaled Achievement Tests
Scales for Centripetal Centrifugal Family Style
Scales for Rating Behav Character Superior Student
Scales of Communicative Interaction
Scales of Independent Behavior
Scalogram Analyses
Scanzoni Model of Female Status Attainment
Scenario Testing
Schaeffer Behavior Inventory
Schedule of Interpersonal Concern (Kinnane et al)
Schedule of Recent Experience
Schedule of Social Functioning (Heimler)
Scheffes Contrast Test
Schizophrenia Index
Schmidt VD Knowledge Evaluator
Schneidman Questionnaire (Attitudes Toward Death)
Scholastic Aptitude Test
School Academic Competition Inventory
School Adjustment Scale (Flynn)
School and College Ability Tests
School Anxiety Questionnaire
School Anxiety Scale
School Assessment Survey
School Attitude Measure (Dolan and Enos)
School Attitude Scale for Children
School Attitudes Questionnaire (Voorst)
School Based Examining
School Behavior Profile (Balow)
School Behavior Rating Scale (Davidson et al)
School Behavior Survey
School Climate Profile
School Climate Survey (NASSP)
School Community Questionnaire
School Context Analysis Form
School Counselor Attitude Inventory (Baker)
School Counselor Classification Categories
School District Competency Tests
School District Questionnaire
School Effectiveness Indices
School Effectiveness Inventory
School Effectiveness Structural Components Inven
School Environment Inventory (Stern)
School Environment Preference Schedule
School Environment Scale (Grossman)
School Improvement Survey
School Information Questionnaire
School Inventory (Bell)
School Level Environment Questionnaire
School Mastery of Reading Test
School Motivation Analysis Test
School Opinion Questionnaire (Cohen)
School Opinion Survey (Shaw and Rector)
School Organization Inventory
School Perception Scales (Lym and Murray)
School Personnel Satisfaction Inven (Catherwood)
School Problem Area Survey
School Psychology Survey
School Rating Scale (Birnbaum)
School Rating Schedule
School Rating Systems
School Readiness Evaluation Tests (Ozer)
School Readiness Program (Hartford Conn)
School Readiness Survey
School Readiness Tasks (Bateman)
School Refusal Assessment Scale
School Scene Apperception Questionnaire
School Sentiment Index
School Sentiment Inventory
School Situation Survey
School Subject Inventory (Prince)
School Subjects Attitude Scales
School Support Questionnaire
School Survey (Kaufman)
School Survey of Interpersonal Relationships
School Vision Inventory
School Work Culture Profile
Schools and Staffing Survey (NCES)
Schubert Assessment Soc Work Stud Perf Field Work
Schwartz Early Mathematics Inventory
Schwarzer Self Efficacy Scale
Schwirian Science Support Scale
Sciara Jantz Empathy Towards Poverty Scale
Science Aptitude Test (Ralph)
Science Attitude Inventory
Science Attitude Scale (Ralph)
Science Attitude Scale for Preservice Teachers
Science Classroom Activities Checklist
Science Classroom Observation Form (Butt et al)
Science College Ability Test
Science Curriculum Assessment System (Matthews)
Science Opinion Survey
Science Practical Test (Kosima)
Science Process Instrument (AAAS)
Science Process Measure for Teachers
Science Proficiency Scale
Science State Trait Anxiety Inventory
Science Supervisors Technical Skills Inventory
Science Supervisory Style Inventory (Peruzzi)
Science Support Scale
Science Teacher Inventory of Need
Science Teacher Observation Rating Form (Oberlin)

Science Teaching Observation Instrument
Science Teaching Observation Schedule
Science Teaching Opinion Survey (Golmon)
Science Teaching State Trait Anxiety Inventory
Science Test of Educational Progress
Scientific Attitude Inventory
Scientific Curiosity Inventory
Scientific Thinking and Research Skill Test
Scientificity of Agriculture Test
Score Distribution
Score Groups
Score Stability
Score Variation
Scoring High on the California Achievement Tests
Scoring Rubrics
Scott Foresman Achievement Test Battery
Scott Value Scales
Scottish Young Peoples Survey
Scrambled Sentence Test (Costin)
SCRE Profile Assessment System
Scree Test
Screening Test Auditory Comprehension Language
Screening Test of Academic Readiness
Screening Test of Adolescent Language
SEARCH (Silver and Hagan)
Search Battery (Silver et al)
Search of Associative Memory
Searles MacPherson Social Studies Questionnaire
Sears Aggression Scales
Sears Self Concept Inventory
Seashore Measures of Musical Talents
Seattle Algebra Test
Seattle Performance Appraisal Guide
Second Art Assessment (1979)
Second Career Occup Develop Assess
Second Citizenship Social Studies Assess (1976)
Second Literature Third Reading Assessment (1980)
Second Mathematics Assessment (1978)
Second Music Assessment (1979)
Second Reading Assessment (1975)
Second Science Assessment (1973)
Second Stage Sampling
Second Writing Assessment (1974)
Secondary Informal Reading Inventory
Secondary Level English Proficiency Test
Secondary School Improvement Program Survey
Secondary Student Teacher Performance Profile
Section Pre Equating (Tests)
Security Index Inventory (Maslow)
Seed Production and Distribution Competencies
Seguin Form Board
Selective Attention Test (Wahl)
Selective Testing
Self Adapted Testing
Self Administered Student Profile
Self Appraisal Instrument (School Management Inst)
Self Appraisal Inventory
Self Appraisal Scale (Davidson)
Self Assessment Oral Language Proficiency Survey
Self Assessment Questionnaire
Self Concept as a Learner Scale (Waesten)
Self Concept as a Writer Questionnaire
Self Concept of Ability Scale (Brookover)
Self Concept of Academic Ability Test
Self Concept Scale
Self Concept Scale for Children
Self Conscious Affect and Attribution Inventory
Self Consciousness Scale (Fenigstein et al)
Self Control Rating Scale (Kendall Wilcox)
Self Description Blank
Self Description Form
Self Description Inventory
Self Description Questionnaire
Self Description Questionnaire II
Self Description Questionnaire III
Self Descriptive Exploratory Research Inventory
Self Directed Learning Readiness Scale
Self Directed Rating Scale
Self Directed Search
Self Directed Search Form E
Self Disclosure Inventory for Adolescents (West)
Self Disclosure Questionnaire
Self Disclosure Test Assumptions Indic Negativism
Self Efficacy for Computer Technologies
Self Efficacy Scale (Sherer et al)
Self Esteem Inventory
Self Evaluation Scale
Self Image Evaluation (Deschin)
Self Image Questionnaire for Young Adolescents
Self Imposed Study Program
Self Insight Test
Self Knowledge Inventory Lifelong Learning Strateg
Self Monitoring Negative Checklist
Self Monitoring Scales (Snyder)
Self Motivation Inventory
Self Observation Scale (Katzenmeyer and Stenner)
Self Perception in School Inventory (Albert)
Self Perception Inventory
Self Ranking Inventory (Purkey)
Self Rating of Mastery Schedule
Self Rating Scale (Hope)
Self Referent Q Sort
Self Referent Questionnaire (Gezi)
Self Report Measures
Self Righteousness Questionnaire
Self Scoring Method
Self Scoring Tests
Self Selection Bias
Self Social Symbols Tasks
Semantic Consensus Index (Kanungo and Dutta)
Semantic Differential for Sci Students (Ahlgren)
Semantic Differential Test for Language Attitudes
Semantic Differential Test of Teacher Attitudes
Semantic Relation Test
Semiprojective Scales of Institutional Evaluation
Semistandardized Regression Coefficient
Senior Citizen Questionnaire
Senior High Assessment of Reading Proficiency
Senior High Assessment of Reading Progress
Senior High Assessment Skills Written Composition
Senior Questionnaire
Sensation Seeking Scale
Sense of Autonomy Scale
Sense of Power Scale (Moeller)
Sensorimotor Cognitive Assessment Scale
Sensory Dimensional Analysis
Sensory Perceptual Exam
Sensory Quotient Test (Cappon et al)
Sensory Threshold Determination
Sentence Completion Form
Sentence Completion Method
Sentence Completion Test
Sentence Comprehension Test (Wheldall et al)
Sentence Imitation Test (Ammon and Ammon)
Sentence Interpretation Test (Little)
Sentence Repetition Task (Anastasiow and Hanes)
Sequenced Inventory of Communication Development
Sequential Analysis (Wald)
Sequential Data Analysis
Sequential Estimation
Sequential Probability Ratio Test (Wald)
Sequential Testing
Sequential Tests of Educational Progress
Sequentially Rejective Bonferroni Test
Serial Evaluation Activities
Serial Multiple Discrimination Teaching Exams
Series Learning Potential Test
Service Delivery Assessment
Service Outcome Measurement Form
Sesame Street Test Battery
Set Correlation
Seventh Grade Social Studies Test (Milwaukee)
Sex for Crack Study
Sex Inventory (Thorne)
Sex Role Attitude Instrument
Sex Role Attitude Scale
Sex Role Egalitarianism Scale
Sex Role Inventory
Sex Role Learning Index
Sex Role Questionnaire (Broverman et al)
Sex Role Stereotype Scale (Burt)
Sex Role Stereotype Scale (Rosenkrantz Broverman)
Sexist Attitudes Toward Women Scale
Sexton Bowerman Conflict Handling Scales
Sexual Compatibility Test
Sexual Experiences Survey
Shadows Task
Shape Labeling Inventory
Shape Name Inventory (Inst Developmental Studies)
Shape Statistics
Shape Type Criteria of Profiles
Shapiro Scale
Sharabany Intimate Friendship Scale
Shatkin Dohner Mathematics Attitude Scale
Shaw Hiehle Computational Skills Test
Shaycroft Plane Geometry Test
Shayer Science Reasoning Task
Sheehan Sentence Completion Test
Shepard Metzler Mental Rotations Test
Sheppard School Entry Screening Test
Sherif Hovland Nine Statement Scale
Sherman Film Evaluation Profile
Shewhart Control Chart
Shipley Hartford Vocabulary Test
Shipley Institute of Living Scale
Shop and Laboratory Attitude Inventory (Finch)
Short Answer Tests
Short Form Test of Academic Aptitude
Short Intelligence Test
Short Term Evaluation
Short Term Memory Test (Pezzullo et al)
Sibling Inventory of Differential Experience
Siegel Prestige Scale
Siegel Tukey Test
Sigel Cognitive Style Test
Sigel Conceptual Style Sorting Task
Sigel Object Categorization Test
Sight Sound Inventory
Sign Test
Significant Bilingual Instructional Features Study
Silent Reading Diagnostic Tests (Bond Clymer Hoyt)
Silvaroli Classroom Reading Inventory
Silver Test of Cognitive Creative Skills
Similar Response Analysis
Similarity Coefficient
Similarity Ratings
Simon Biology Test
Simplicity Index
Simplified Oral Hygiene Index
Simulated Oral Proficiency Interview
Simulated Social Interaction Test
Simulation Test Interact Teach Competencies (Hays)
Simultaneous Item Bias Procedure
Simultaneous Region Procedure
Singer Eyeball Estimate of Readability
Singer Loomis Inventory of Personality
Single Group Design
Single Subject Designs
SIR Adjusted Index (Mushkin)
Situation Specific Subject Competence Test
Situational Administrative Decision Making Invent
Situational Appraisal Inven (Pittel Mendelsohn)
Situational Attitude Inventory (Eberly)
Situational Attitude Scale (Adults Children)
Situational Attitude Scale (Sedlacek and Brooks)
Situational Attitude Scale for Women
Situational Attitude Scale Simplified
Situational Confidence Measures
Situational Fear Inventory
Situational Regression Technique
Six Item Health Administrators Questionnaire
Sixteen Personality Factor Questionnaire
SKI HI Language Development Scale
Skill Profile
Skill Qualification Test
Skills Assessment Module
Skills Inventory for Teams
Skinfold Measurement
Slide Sorting Task (George)
SLIDES Test
Slingerland Screening Tests
Slip Probabilities
Slogan System Analysis (Komisar and McClellan)
Slope Homogeneity Test
Slosson Drawing Coordination Test
Slosson Intelligence Test
Slosson Intelligence Test (Revised)
Slosson Oral Reading Test
Slough Experiment
Smith and Meux Classification System
Smith Experience Inventory
Smith Inventory (To Identify Potential Dropouts)
Smith Masculinity Femininity Scale
Smith Sturgeon Conditional Reasoning Test
Smith Test
SMOG Readability Formula
Smoking Consequences Questionnaire
SNAP Rating Scale
Snellen Test
Soares and Soares Self Concept Scale
SOBER (Test)
Social and Prevocational Information Battery
Social Assets Inventory
Social Attributes Checklist
Social Avoidance Distress Scale (Watson Friend)
Social Behavior Rating Scale (Herbert)
Social Class Value Orientation Inventory
Social Competence Assessment Profile
Social Decision Schemes
Social Deprivation Scale (Zigler et al)
Social Distance Index (Katz)
Social Distance Survey (Greer et al)
Social Distance Test
Social Distress and Anxiety Scale
Social Episodes Test
Social Experience Inventory
Social Hypothesis Testing
Social Impact Assessment
Social Interaction Observation Procedure
Social Interests Inventory (Grinder)
Social Mapping Matrix Assessment
Social Perspectives Scale
Social Reaction Inventory (Richardson Tasto)
Social Reaction Inventory (Rotter)
Social Reaction Scale
Social Readjustment Rating Scale (Holmes and Rahe)
Social Reinforcement Scale (McDavid)
Social Relations Scale
Social Responsibility Test
Social Scale
Social Scenarios Scale
Social Science Observation Record
Social Science Tests
Social Self Efficacy Scale
Social Situations Scale
Social Skills Inventory Scale (Welker and Ginn)
Social Studies Inference Test
Social Support Networks Inventory (Flaherty)
Social Support Questionnaire
Social Transaction Scale
Social Values Questionnaire (Perloe)
Social Vocabulary Index Test
Social Work Practice Problems Inventory
Sociometric Choice Measure
Sociometric Test
Sociomoral Reflection Measure
SOI Test of Behavioral Skills
Solution Error Response Error Model
Sonar Pitch Memory Test
Song File Data Match
Sophistication of Body Concept Test
Sophistication of Reading Interests Scale
Sorenson Teacher Role Preference Inventory
Sorting Test (Chambers)
Sorts Test (Riegel)
Sounds and Images
Source Credibility Rating Scale
Source of Stress Inventory
Sources of Instructional Leadership
Souster Teacher Opinion of Research in Education
South Carolina Needs Assessment Instruments
South Carolina Trade Examinations
Spache Diagnostic Reading Scales
Spache Readability Formula
Spanish Articulation Test
Spanish English Verbatim Translation Exam
Spanish Oral Reading Test
Spatial Apperception Test
Spatial Arrangements Task
Spatial Relations Test
Spatial Tasks
Spatial Tests
Spatial Transformation Task
Spaulding System of Classroom Behavioral Analysis
Spaulding Teacher Activity Rating Schedule
Speaking Proficiency English Assessment Kit
Special Education Program Checklist
Special Education Research Test (Nash)
Special Incomplete Sentences Test
Special Test Administration
Specific Aptitude Test Battery
Specific Fear Index
Specific Language Disability Test
Specificity Doctrine
Speech Language Pathology Assessment Instrument
Speededness (Tests)
Speededness Quotient
Sphericity Tests
SPINE Test

Spiritual Well Being Scale
Spline Function
Split Half Test Reliability
Spodek Early Childhood Education Program Analysis
Spondee Recognition Tests
Spontaneous Divergent Academic Test (Ball)
Spontaneous Numerical Correspondence Task
Sport Competitiveness Inventory
Sports Attitudes Inventory
Spouse Observation Checklist (Wills et al)
Sprigle School Readiness Screening Test
SRA Achievement Series
SRA Assessment Survey
SRA Basic Reading Series
SRA Diagnostic Reading Tests
SRA Junior Inventory
SRA Listening Skills Program
SRA Modern Math Understanding Test
SRA Pictorial Reasoning Test
SRA Primary Mental Abilities Test
SRA Spelling Laboratory
SRA Survey of Basic Skills
SRA Tests of Educational Ability
SRA Tests of General Ability
SRA Writing Skills Tests
SRA Youth Inventory
SRI Classroom Observation Procedure
SRI Observational System
Srole Anomie Scale
Stability of Self Scale
Staff Assessment Questionnaire
Staff Attitude Questionnaire
Staff Burnout Scale for Health Professionals
Staff Member Rating Scale
Staff Sentiment Scale
Stages of Concern
Stages of Concern Questionnaire
Stagewise Protected Procedure
Staggered Spondaic Words Test of Central Auditory
Stakeholder Survey
Stallings Environmentally Based Screen
Stallings Observation Instrument
Stallings Observation System
Standard Assessment System
Standard Assessment Tasks (Great Britain)
Standard Behavior Chart (Pennypacker)
Standard Educational Intelligence Test
Standard Industrial Classifications
Standard Metropolitan Statistical Areas
Standard Oral Reading Paragraph Test
Standard Reading Inventory
Standard Scores
Standard Setting
Standardization
Standardized Assessment System
Standardized Curriculum Oriented Pupil Evaluation
Standardized Data Reporting System
Standardized Educational Program Audit
Standardized Mean Change Measures
Standardized Mean Difference
Standardized Regression Coefficients
Standardized Residuals
Standardized Tests of Achievement for Fiji
Standards for Educational and Psychological Tests
Standards for Evaluation Educ Prog Proj Materials
Stanford Achievement Tests
Stanford Achievement Tests for Hearing Impaired
Stanford Artificial Intelligence Project
Stanford Binet Intelligence Scale
Stanford Binet Intelligence Scale Fourth Edition
Stanford Diagnostic Mathematics Test
Stanford Diagnostic Reading Test
Stanford Early School Achievement Test
Stanford Hypnotic Susceptibility Scale
Stanford Kohs Block Design Test
Stanford Preschool Internal External Scale
Stanford Teacher Competence Appraisal Guide
Stanford Test of Academic Skills
Stanines
Starkweather Originality Test
Stars Case Abstract Vignettes
State Board Test Pool Examination
State Competency Tests
State Epistemic Curiosity Scale (Leherissey)
State Mathematics Assessments
State Nonfiscal Survey of Public Elem Sec Educ
State Student Assessment Prog Database 1992 93
State Trait Anxiety Inventory
State Trait Anxiety Inventory (Spielberger)
State Trait Anxiety Inventory for Children
State Trait Anxiety Theory
State University Admissions Examination (New York)
State University Survey
Statements About Schools Inventory
Statewide Assessment of Educational Progress
Statewide Measures Inventory (NCHEMS)
Statistical Interaction
Status Characteristic Theory
Status Testing
Stein and Glenn Story Schema
Stencil Design Test
Step Observation Schedule
Stephens Delys Reinforcement Contingency Interview
Stephenson Q Methodology
Stepwise Canonical Correlation Analysis
Stepwise Regression
Stereopathy Acquiescence Scales (Stern et al)
Stereotype Questionnaire (Rosenkrantz)
Stern Activities Index
Stern Teacher Preference Schedule
Sternberg Triarchic Abilities Test
Stimulus Response Latency
Stimulus Similarity Scale
Stone Coles Multidimensional Scaling Method
Story Telling Test
Stouffer Mathematics Test
Strang Diagnostic Record for HS and College Studs
Stratified Sampling
Stratil Counseling Inventory
Street Survival Skills Questionnaire
Stress Distributions
Stress Reaction Scale for Reading
Stress Response Scale (Chandler)
Stromberg Dexterity Test
Strong Campbell Interest Inventory
Strong Vocational Interest Blank
Stroop Color Word Test
Structural Properties Questionnaire
Structure Coefficients
Structure Observation Inventory
Structure of Instruction Rating Scale
Structure of Intellect
Structure of Intellect Learning Abilities Test
Structured Case Review Blank (Muthard Miller)
Structured Doll Play Test
Structured Elicitation Techniques
Structured Interviews
Structured Objective Rorschach Test
Structured Pediatric Psychosocial Interview
Student Activities Inventory (Project Talent)
Student Activities Questionnaire
Student Adaptation to College Questionnaire
Student Assessment and Response System
Student Assessment of Teaching and Learning
Student Attitude Inventory
Student Attitude Toward School Inventory
Student Attitudinal Outcome Measures
Student Attribute Study
Student Behavior Index (Parker and French)
Student Behavior Profile (Greenberger)
Student Belief Rating Scale
Student Centered Assessment
Student Crisis Index
Student Critique Form (Air Training Command)
Student Descriptive Questionnaire
Student Development Vectors (Chickering)
Student Developmental Task and Lifestyle Inventory
Student Developmental Task Inventory
Student Educational Attitude Scale
Student Educational Outcomes Assessment VA
Student Empowerment Report Card
Student Evaluation Form
Student Evaluation of Achievement
Student Evaluation of Educational Quality
Student Evaluation of Teaching (Test)
Student Experience Inventory
Student Experience Questionnaire
Student Goal Orientation Questionnaire
Student Instructional Report
Student Level Observation of Beginning Reading
Student Life Stress Inventory
Student Listening Profile
Student Misbehavior Survey
Student Observation Form (Lindvall)
Student Observation Scale
Student Operational Language Assessment Scale
Student Opinion Attitude Poll (FLA Assess Prog)
Student Opinion Inventory
Student Opinion Poll (Jackson and Getzels)
Student Opinion Questionnaire
Student Opinion Survey
Student Opinion Survey in Chemistry
Student Opinion Survey of Teaching
Student Opinions About Instructional Procedures
Student Orientations Survey (Morstain)
Student Outcomes Questionnaire
Student Perception of Teacher Influence Scale
Student Perception of Teacher Style (Tuckman)
Student Perception of Teaching Effectiveness
Student Perceptions of Teaching (Weerts Whitney)
Student Personnel Purpose Q Sort (Terenzini)
Student Potential Index
Student Principal Communication Instrument
Student Problems Q Sort (Freeze)
Student Profile (Form)
Student Rating Form (Davis)
Student Rating Scale (Harvey)
Student Record of Behavior
Student Satisfaction Survey (NASSP)
Student Self Assessment Inventory
Student Self Report
Student Survey and Attitude Inventory (SC)
Student Suspension Questionnaire
Student Task Involvement
Student Teacher Opinionaire
Student Teacher Rating Form
Student Teacher Relationship Scale
Student Verbal Participation Questionnaire
Students Attitudes Toward Statistics Inventory
Students Evaluation of Educational Quality
Students Evaluations of Educational Quality
Students Perceptions of Teachers Questionnaire
Students Typewriting Test Number 1
Students Views of an Ideal Student Questionnaire
Students Views of Ideal Professor Questionnaire
Study Activity Survey
Study Attitudes and Methods Survey
Study Behavior Inventory
Study Behavior Inventory Form D
Study Habits Inventory (Wrenn)
Study of Values (Allport Vernon Lindzey)
Study Process Questionnaire (Biggs)
Study Skills Questionnaire (McComb Dobrovolny)
Stycar Vision Tests
Subject Level Item Response Models
Subjective Drug Effects Questionnaire (Katz et al)
Subjective Response Uncertainty
Subjective Tests
Subjective Units of Distress Scale
Subjective Vitality Questionnaire
Subtests
Successive Categories Method
Successive Impressions Test I (Lowenfeld)
Sucher Allred Reading Placement Inventory
Sucher Allred Word Recognition Test
Suicide Awareness Scale
Suicide Intervention Response Inventory
Suicide Opinion Questionnaire
Suicide Potential Scale Revised (Miskimins et al)
Suicide Probability Scale
Suinn Test Anxiety Behavior Scale
Summer Institute Survey (Nova University)
Summer Language Bursary Program Placement Test
Superiority Scale
Supervision Questionnaire
Supervision Questionnaire Revised
Supervisor Behavior Style Scales (Blumberg et al)
Supervisor Personal Reaction Scale
Supervisor Teacher Verbal Interaction Instrument
Supervisors Rating Scale of Practicum Performance
Supervisory Behavior Description Questionnaire
Supervisory Conference Rating Scale
Supervisory Conference Verbal Behavior Instrument
Supervisory Interaction System (Blumberg)
Supervisory Working Alliance Inventory
Support Ranking Questionnaire
Survey Achievement Testing
Survey of Adult Learning (Educ Testing Service)
Survey of Basic Skills (California)
Survey of Beliefs about Parenthood
Survey of Canadian English
Survey of Cognitive Skills (Childrens Hospital)
Survey of College Achievement
Survey of Compensatory Education
Survey of Confidence in Teaching Reading
Survey of Consumer Finances
Survey of Displayed Literacy Stimuli
Survey of Educational Attitudes (Rosenthal et al)
Survey of Effective School Processes (IDEA)
Survey of Elementary Epistemic Motivation
Survey of English Usage
Survey of Essential Skills
Survey of Experienced Scientists and Engineers
Survey of Grading Practices
Survey of Interpersonal Values (Gordon)
Survey of Multicultural Education Concepts
Survey of Object Visualization (Miller)
Survey of Opinions on Economic Issues (Dawson)
Survey of Primary Music Reading Development
Survey of Reading Attitudes
Survey of Reading Skills
Survey of School Attitudes
Survey of School Attitudes (Hogan)
Survey of Student Opinion of Teaching
Survey of Study Habits and Attitudes
Survey of Study Reading Habits
Survey of Supervisory Practices
Survey of Teacher Characteristics and Activities
Survey of Teacher Education Perceptions
Survey of Testing Practices
Survey of Work Values (Wollack et al)
Survey on Equality of Educational Opportunity
Survival Ratio Models
Suydam Trueblood Attitude Toward Mathematics Scale
Suzak Binet Intelligence Test
Swassing Barbe Modality Index
Swick Ross Child Perception Inventory
Swindon Record of Personal Achievement
SWRL Beginning Reading Program Test
SWRL Composition Skills Test
SWRL First Grade Spelling Component
SWRL Instructional Concepts Program Test
SWRL Scoring System
Sydney Attribution Scale
Symbol Digit Modalities Test
Symbol Test of Originality
Symbolic Play Test (Lowe and Costello)
Symmetric Regression Procedure
Symptomatic Checklist
Syracuse Scale for Social Acceptance
Syracuse Scales of Social Relations
Syracuse Test of Algebraic Fluency
Syracuse Visual Figure Background Test
System for Teaching Learning Assessment Review LA
System of Multicultural Pluralistic Assessment
Systematic Assessment Parent Attachment Behaviors
Systematic Screening for Behavior Disorders
Systemic Dialectual Evaluation
T Group Member Ratings (Koile and Draeger)
T Test
TAB Inventory of Science Processes
TAB Science Puzzler
TAB Science Test
Tactile Kinesthetic Form Discrimination Test
Tactual Motor Test
Tag Questions
Tagatz Information Processing Test
Tailored Response Testing
Take Home Tests
Talented Accomplishments Questionnaire
Tama General Knowledge Test
Tape Analysis Instrument
Tapping Test
TARC Assessment System
Target Valence
Task Accomplishment Inventories (McAfee)
Task Completion Take Your Pick
Task for Reporting Interviewing Observing
Task Goal Attitudes
Task of Emotional Development Test
Task of Public Educ Opinionnaire (Downey et al)
Task Performance Sheets
Task Planning
Task Sequence
Task Surveys
Tasks of Emotional Development (Revised)

Tau Equivalence
Taxonomic Skills Achievement Test in Fractions
Taxonomy of Image Provocation Profile
Taxonomy of Interventions
Taylor Ellison Biographical Inventory
Taylor Manifest Anxiety Scale
Teach Skills Inventory
Teacher Activity Inventory
Teacher Adaptability Scale
Teacher Affective Sensitivity Scale (Kravas)
Teacher and Pupil Performance Ratings
Teacher Appraisal Instrument
Teacher Assessment of Pupil Progress (Coley)
Teacher Assessment Practices Questionnaire
Teacher Assessment Prep Practices Questionnaire
Teacher Attitude Inventory (Whitmore)
Teacher Attitude Questionnaire (CERLI)
Teacher Attitudes Toward Evaluation
Teacher Attitudes toward Low Achiev in Math Scale
Teacher Autonomy Scale
Teacher Behavior Description Questionnaire
Teacher Behavior Form (Schwartz and Mott)
Teacher Belief Inventory
Teacher Belief Rating Scale
Teacher Certification Tests
Teacher Certification Tests (Georgia)
Teacher Characteristics Scale (Kellinger)
Teacher Classroom Activity Profile
Teacher Communication Scale
Teacher Competencies Assessment Questionnaire
Teacher Competency Inventory (Bain et al)
Teacher Competency Scale (Resnick and Reinert)
Teacher Conceptions Educ Process Questionnaire
Teacher Concern Checklist (Parson and Fuller)
Teacher Concerns Checklist (Parsons and Fuller)
Teacher Concerns Questionnaire
Teacher Concerns Statements (Fuller and Case)
Teacher Concerns Statements (Fuller and Chase)
Teacher Demand and Shortage Survey (NCES)
Teacher Effectance Motivation Rating
Teacher Effectiveness Index
Teacher Effectiveness Questionnaire
Teacher Efficacy Scale
Teacher Evaluation Needs Identification Survey
Teacher Evaluation Record
Teacher Evaluation Scale (Brown)
Teacher Expectation Instrument
Teacher Expectation Questionnaire
Teacher Image Questionnaire
Teacher Impression Instrument
Teacher Instructional Plans Materials Assess Scale
Teacher Knowledge and Beliefs Inventory
Teacher Language Instrument
Teacher Locus of Control Scale
Teacher Mobility Study Quest (Orlich et al)
Teacher Observation Personality Schedule (Cooper)
Teacher Observation Rating Scale (Johnson)
Teacher Observation Scale (Crockenberg and Bryant)
Teacher Observation Scales (Purdue)
Teacher Observational Item
Teacher Occupational Stress Factor Questionnaire
Teacher Opinion Inventory (Bowers)
Teacher Opinion Poll
Teacher Opinion Questionnaire (Holzmiller)
Teacher Perceiver Interview
Teacher Perceiver Screeners
Teacher Performance Appraisal Scale
Teacher Performance Appraisal System
Teacher Performance Assessment Instrument
Teacher Performance Assessment Instruments
Teacher Performance Competencies Scale
Teacher Performance Evaluation (Manatt)
Teacher Performance Evaluation Scale (Sinha)
Teacher Practices Inventory
Teacher Practices Observation Record
Teacher Practices Questionnaire (Sorenson et al)
Teacher Preparation Evaluation Inventory
Teacher Problem Inventory
Teacher Problems Q Sort (Bills)
Teacher Process Measure
Teacher Pupil Question Inventory
Teacher Pupil Relationship Scale
Teacher Questionnaire (Purdue)
Teacher Rating Form (Murray)
Teacher Rating Forms
Teacher Rating of Academic Performance
Teacher Rating of Administrator Performance
Teacher Rating of Social Skills
Teacher Rating of Student Characteristics
Teacher Rating Scale
Teacher Rating Scale (Harvey)
Teacher Reaction Form (Di Johnson)
Teacher Referenced Tests
Teacher Role Q Sort
Teacher Role Survey
Teacher Satisfaction Survey (NASSP)
Teacher Self Analysis Inventory (Beauchamp)
Teacher Self Assessment of Non Sexist Behaviors
Teacher Sex Role Perception Inventory
Teacher Task Analysis Questionnaire
Teacher Temperament Questionnaire
Teacher Testing
Teacher Treatment Inventory (Weinstein et al)
Teacher Writing Standards Inventory
Teachers Rating Questionnaire
Teachers School Readiness Inventory
Teachers Test of Language Skills
Teaching Anxiety Scale
Teaching Assessment Blank (Holmes)
Teaching Behaviors Questionnaire
Teaching Behaviours Scale (Soh)
Teaching Events Stress Inventory
Teaching Performance Observation Instrument
Teaching Performance Tests
Teaching Scale (Barnard)
Teaching Situation Reaction Test
Teaching Strategies Observation Differential
Teaching Style Classification Scale (Augenstein)
Teaching Styles Inventory
Teaching Techniques Evaluation Form (Patrick)
Teaching Tests
Teaching to the Test
Team Assessment
Team Leader Attitude Scale
Technical Adequacy (Tests)
Technology Achievement Test
Teenage Inventory of Social Skills
Telecommunications Education Needs Assessment CA
Tell Me A Story Test
TEMAS Thematic Apperception Test
Temperament and Values Inventory
Templin Darley Tests of Articulation
Temporal Orientation Questionnaire (Wulff)
Tennessee Proficiency Test
Tennessee Self Concept Scale
Tennis Tests of Achievement (Digennaro)
Tension Ranking Questionnaire
Terman Group Test of Mental Ability
Terman Merrill Intelligence Scale
Terman Merrill Vocabulary Test
Terminator Remainer Scale (Lorr et al)
Terp Attitude Scale
Territorial Decentration Test (Stoltman)
TESCAM (Test Scoring and Analysis)
Test Adaptations
Test Analysis
Test Anxiety Inventory (Spielberger)
Test Anxiety Scale for Adolescents
Test Appropriateness
Test Batteries
Test Battery for Mentally Handicapped Children
Test Behavior Observation Guide
Test Bibliographies
Test Characteristic Curve
Test Collection (Educational Testing Service)
Test Cue Inventory (Kermis)
Test Curriculum Overlap
Test Customization
Test de Vocabulario en Imagenes Peabody (Dunn)
Test Development Notebook (NY State Dept of Educ)
Test Disclosure
Test Equivalence
Test Expectancy
Test Files
Test for Ready Steps
Test Homogeneity
Test Instructions
Test Levels
Test Linking
Test of Academic Skills
Test of Adolescent Language
Test of Adult Basic Education
Test of Adult College Aptitude
Test of Auditory Comprehension of Language
Test of Auditory Perception (Sabatino)
Test of Auditory Visual Integration (Kahn et al)
Test of Basic Concepts (Gonzalez Tamayo)
Test of Basic Information
Test of Basic Process Skills in Science
Test of Behavioral Rigidity
Test of Cognitive Skills
Test of Computer Literacy for Science Teachers
Test of Concept Application
Test of Consumer Competencies
Test of Coordination of Perspectives (Fowler)
Test of Critical Thinking (American Council Educ)
Test of Critical Thinking Skills Physical Science
Test of Diagnostic Skills (Rimoldi et al)
Test of Early Language Development
Test of Economic Literacy
Test of Economic Understanding
Test of Effective Academic Motivation
Test of English as a Foreign Language
Test of English for International Communication
Test of Implied Meanings (Sundberg)
Test of Independent Sample Proportions
Test of Individual Needs in Reading
Test of Inference Ability in Reading Comprehension
Test of Inference Patterns (Howell)
Test of Insight (French)
Test of Integrated Process Skills
Test of Integrated Science Processes
Test of Language Development
Test of Logical Thinking (Gray)
Test of Logical Thinking (Tobin and Capie)
Test of Modality Aptitude in Reading (Neville)
Test of Musicality
Test of Nonverbal Auditory Discrimination
Test of Nonverbal Intelligence
Test of Obscure Knowledge
Test of Occupational Development
Test of Perceptual Organization
Test of Proficiency in Computational Skills
Test of Reflectivity Impulsivity in Social Context
Test of Science Knowledge
Test of Science Processes (Tannenbaum)
Test of Science Related Attitudes
Test of Selected Topics in Physics
Test of Social Inference (Edmonson et al)
Test of Spoken English
Test of Standard Written English
Test of Syntactic Abilities
Test of Syntactic Abilities Screening Test
Test of Testwiseness (Slakter)
Test of Thought and Language
Test of Understanding in College Economics
Test of Understanding Latin America
Test of Weight Discrimination
Test of Written English
Test of Written Expression
Test of Written Spelling
Test on Appraising Observations
Test on Astronomy Concepts
Test on Astronomy Facts
Test on the Historical Development of Science
Test on the Social Aspects of Science
Test on Understanding Radioactivity
Test on Understanding Science
Test Order
Test Reactivity
Test Readiness
Test Redundancy
Test Repeaters
Test Reporting
Test Rescoring
Test Retest Reliability
Test Revision
Test Scatter
Test Score Abnormality
Test Score Enhancing Strategies
Test Score Growth Measurement
Test Score Variance
Test Security
Test Sensitivity
Test Shortening Procedures
Test Specifications
Test Trials
Test Use in Schools Study
Testing Accommodations (Disabilities)
Testing Apparatus
Testing Conditions
Testing Effects
Testing for Essential Learning and Literacy Skills
Testing Frequency
Testing Information
Testing Informing Discussing and Evaluating
Testing Time
Testlets
Tests and Measurement Courses
Tests of Academic Progress
Tests of Achievement and Proficiency
Tests of Achievement in Basic Skills Mathematics
Tests of Adult Basic Education
Tests of Adult Literacy Skills
Tests of Basic Experiences
Tests of Individual Performance
Tetreau Trahan Visual Interest Test
Texas Assessment of Academic Skills
Texas Assessment of Basic Skills
Texas Educational Assessment of Minimum Skills
Texas Examination Current Administrators Teachers
Texas Features of Emotional Disturbance
Texas Master Teacher Examination
Texas Oral Proficiency Test
Texas Preschool Screening Inventory
Texas Social Behavior Inventory
Texas Teacher Appraisal Instrument
Thackray Reading Readiness Profiles
Thematic Apperception Test
Thematic Apperception Test for Academic Motivation
Thematic Appreciation Test
Themes Concerning Blacks Test
Theoretical Orientation
Theoretical Orientation to Reading Profile
Theory Based Evaluation
Theory of Violators
Therapeutic Reactance Scale
Theta Estimates
Things People Do Inventory
Thinking Orientation Scale
Third Citizenship Social Studies Assess (1982)
Third Mathematics Assessment (1982)
Third Party Evaluation
Third Science Assessment (1977)
Third Writing Assessment (1979)
This I Believe Test (Harvey)
Thomas and Chess Parent and Teacher Questionnaire
Thomas Equity Perception Scale
Thomas Self Concept Values Test
Thompson Writing Attitude Survey
Thorndike Lorge Word List
Three Minute Reasoning Test (Hartley and Holt)
Three Mode Factor Analysis
Threshold by Identification of Pictures Test
Thresholds
Thumin Conservatism Liberalism Scale
Thurston Temperament Schedule
Thurstone Box Problem
Thurstone Closure Flexibility Scale
Thurstone Model III Scaling Procedure
Thurstone Model V Scaling Procedure
Thurstone Pattern Copying Test
Thurstone Primary Mental Abilities Schema
Thurstone Scale of Attitude Toward Negroes
Thurstone Scales
Thurstones Law of Comparative Judgment
Thurstones Primary Mental Abilities Schema
Tie Parameters
Tiffany Experienced Control Scales
Time Reference Inventory
Time Series Design
Time Span Measurement
Timed Behavior Checklist
Toddler Behavior Questionnaire
Toddler Temperament Scale
Token Test (Language)
Toledo Chemistry Placement Examination
Tolerance Intervals (Statistics)
Top Down Assessment
Topic Evaluation Questionnaire
Torgerson Multidimensional Scaling Model
Torrance Creative Motivation Inventory
Torrance Ideal Pupil Checklist
Torrance Tests of Creative Thinking
Torrance Unusual Uses Test
Torsca Multidimensional Scaling Technique
Torsten Husen Attitude Scales
Total Adjustment Scale
Total Alienation Scale
Total Communication Checklist and Assessment
Totally Interactive Testing and Analysis System
Totter Index
Toy Preference Test
Traditional Family Ideology Scale
Trail Making Test (Reitan)
Trainee Personal Reaction Scale

Trait Anxiety
Trait Ascription Questionnaire (Graham)
Trait Indecisiveness Scale
Transition Observation Instrument
Tree Drawing Test
Tri Cultural Attitude Scale
Trial State Assessment (NAEP)
Trials to Criterion Testing
Triandis Behavioral Differential
Triangular Constant Method
Triangulation Interview Form
Triple Mode Test of Categorization (Silverman)
Truth in Testing
Tukeys Test
Tutor Self Assessment Inventory (Brown)
Tutoring Attitude Questionnaire
Twenty Statements Test (Kuhn)
Two Group Test (Leitner Dayton)
Two Predictor Validity Curve
Two Stage Testing
Tyler Ideal Real Self Q Sort
Type I Errors
Type II Errors
Type III Errors
Type K Item Format
Type VI Errors
Type X Item Format
Typing Speed
Typology of Love Styles (Lee)
Tyranny of Testing
U Method
UCLA Loneliness Scale
UCLA Temperament Form
Unbalanced Designs
Uncertainty
Uncertainty Reduction
Undergraduate Program Field Tests
Unidimensional Scaling
Unidimensionality (Tests)
Uniform Guidelines Employee Selection Procedures
UNIQUE Physical Fitness Test
Unisex Act Interest Inventory
Unisex Edition of ACT Interest Inventory IV
Unit Normal Approximation
Unit of Analysis Problems
Universal Criterion Scale
Universal Scale for Grades
University of Massachusetts Index
University of North Dakota American College Test
University Residence Environment Scales
Unmixed Designs
Unnumbered Graphic Scales
Unpleasant Activities Survey
Unpleasant Events Schedule
Upper Asymptote Parameter (Testing)
Urban Employment Survey
Urban Language Study
Urban Teacher Development Questionnaire
Urban Teacher Selection Interview
Use of English Examination (Hong Kong)
Uses for Things Test
USES Interest Check List
USES Specific Aptitude Test Battery
Uses Test of Creativity (Guilford)
Using Evaluation Data Form
Utah Test of Language Development
Utility Functions
Utility Test (French et al)
Uzgiris Hunt Ordinal Scales of Psychological Devel
Valett Stanford Binet L M Profile
Validity Generalization
Validity Network Schema
Validity Sector
Value Added Testing
Value Interest Dynamics Instrument (Neal)
Value Orientation Test (Kelley)
Value Orientations Scale
Value Vectors Index (Lewis)
Values Concerning Disadvantaged Pupils Quest
Values Inventory
Values Inventory for Children
Values Scale
Van Alstyne Picture Vocabulary Test
Van Der Flier Index
Van Waganen Reading Scales
Van Wagenen Rate of Comprehension Test
Vance Language Skills Test
Vandenberg Mental Rotations Test
Vanderbilt Negative Indicators Scale
Vane Kindergarten Test
Varied Auditory Stimulation
Vassar Attitude Inventory
Vector Majorization Technique
Venereal Disease Knowledge Inventory
Venture Evaluation Procedures
Verbal Aptitude Test
Verbal Attitude Scale (Rose)
Verbal Auditory Screening for Children
Verbal Disembedding Test
Verbal Expressivity Scale
Verbal Facilitation Effect
Verbal Language Development Scale
Verbal Nonverbal Reliance Questionnaire
Verbal Output Inventory
Verbal Reaction Behavior Log (Mork)
Verbal Reasoning Quotients
Verbal Recall
Verbal Regulation of Behavior
Verbal Reinforcement
Verbal Reticence Scale
Verbal Satiation
Verbalizer Visualizer Questionnaire
Verification
Verified Vocational Counseling Instrument
Vernier Caliper
Vernier Positioning Technique
Vernon Graded Arithmetic Test
Vertical Equating
Vestibular Stimulation
Vestibule Training
Vibration Technique
Vibrotactile Method
Vibrotactile Stimulation
Victorian Certificate of Education (Australia)
VIEWS Faucet Assembly
Views of Life Scale
Views on Science Technology Society
VIEWS Screen Assembly
Vincent Learning Curves
Vincent Personal Events Time Scale
Vineland Adaptive Behavior Scales
Vineland Ego Development Profile (Howard Miller)
Vineland Social Maturity Scale
Violation of Assumptions
Violence Index (Gerbner and Gross)
Visual Aesthetic Sensitivity Test (Gotz)
Visual Analysis Test (Rosner)
Visual Analytic Skills Test
Visual and Ocular Motility Tests
Visual Assessment Inventory
Visual Aural Digit Span Test (Koppitz)
Visual Cliff Experiment
Visual Designs Test (Johnson O Connor)
Visual Discrimination Inventory (Lombard Stern)
Visual Discrimination Test
Visual Efficiency Scale
Visual Inference Checklist
Visual Literacy Test (Turner)
Visual Motor Integration Test
Visual Observational Schedule of Teacher Behaviors
Visual Perception Inventory
Visual Perceptual Speed
Visual Placing Response
Visual Sequencing Task
Visual Tests
Vividness of Visual Imagery Questionnaire
VM Scale (Morrison)
Vocabulary Assessment Task
Vocabulary in Context Exercises
Vocational and Occupational Interest Choice Exam
Vocational Apperception Test
Vocational Assessment Record
Vocational Attitude Scale
Vocational Awareness Index (Currie)
Vocational Behavior Checklist
Vocational Capacity Scale
Vocational Careers Assessment Severely Handicapped
Vocational Commitment Index (Weis and Hubbard)
Vocational Decision Making Difficulty Scale
Vocational Decision Making Interview
Vocational Development Inventory (Crites)
Vocational Education Readiness Test
Vocational Education Test Battery
Vocational Education Training Needs Instrument
Vocational Guidance Center Test
Vocational History Questionnaire
Vocational Identity Scale (Holland et al)
Vocational Interest and Sophistication Assessment
Vocational Interest Inventory (Mitchell)
Vocational Interest Survey
Vocational Maturity Scale (Westbrook et al)
Vocational Opinion Index
Vocational Pattern Index (Kummerow and Hummel)
Vocational Performance Sample
Vocational Personality Report
Vocational Preference Inventory
Von Restorff Isolation Effect
Vort Behavioral Characteristics Progression
VTR Environmental Rating Scale (Poling)
VTR Risk Model
Wabash Valley Education Center Science Test
Walberg Thomas Observation Scale
Walberg Thomas Teacher Questionnaire
Walk a Line Slowly Task
Walker Lev Test Three
Walker Problem Behavior Identification Checklist
Walker Readiness Test
Wallace Self Concept Scale
Wallach and Kogan Creativity Test Battery
Wallin Cutsforth Brief Educ Attainment Scale
Wallner Test of Listening Comprehension
Ward Atmosphere Scale
Waring Intimacy Questionnaire
Warner Index of Social Class
Warner Meeker Eells Index of Status Characteristic
Wartegg Drawing Test
Washington Precollege Testing Program
Washington University Sentence Completion Test
Water Pollution Control Information Test
Watson Analysis Schedule
Watson Barker Listening Test
Watson Glaser Critical Thinking Appraisal
Watson Glaser Test of Critical Thinking
Waupun Strategies in Early Childhood Education
Ways of Speaking Taxonomy
Wayson School Climate and Context Inventory
Wear Attitude Inventory
Wechsler Adult Intelligence Scale
Wechsler Adult Intelligence Scale (Revised)
Wechsler Bellevue Intelligence Scale
Wechsler Intelligence Scale (Chinese Revised)
Wechsler Intelligence Scale for Children
Wechsler Intelligence Scale for Children (Revised)
Wechsler Intelligence Scale for Children III
Wechsler Intelligence Scale Profile for Teachers
Wechsler Intelligence Scales Short Forms
Wechsler Memory Scale
Wechsler Memory Scale (Revised)
Wechsler Preschool Primary Scale of Intell (Rev)
Wechsler Preschool Primary Scale of Intelligence
Wechsler Scales Complementary Sheet
Weekly Subject Index
Weighted Data
Weighted Harmonic Means Analysis
Weighted Structural Regression
Weighted Variables
Weighting (Statistical)
Weigl Color Form Sorting Test
Weigl Goldstein Scheerer Color Form Test
Welch Procedure
Welch Science Process Inventory
Welsh Figure Preference Test
Welsh Phonological Assessment Procedure
Wepman Auditory Discrimination Test
Wesman Personnel Classification Test
West Africa School Certificate Examination
West Virginia Student Questionnaire
Westcott Problem Solving Scale
Western Illinois Univ Evaluation Questionnaire
Westernport Simulation Exercise
Wetzel Grid Charts
What I Like to Do (Interest Scale)
What I Think of Myself Test (Mathewson and Orton)
What I Want to Do (Inventory)
What If Situations Test
What Kind of a Person Are You Test (Torrance)
Wheatley Cube
Wheeler Rorschach Signs
Wherry Formula
Which to Discuss Test (Maw and Maw)
Whimbey Analytical Skills Inventory
Whitman School In Basket Test
Who Am I Inventory
Who to Whom Observation Worksheet
Wichita Guidance Center Checklist
Wickman Behavior Rating Scale
Wide Range Achievement Test
Wide Range Achievement Test (Revised)
Wide Range Assessment of Memory and Learning
Wide Range Intelligence Scale
Wiener Attitude Scale
Wiggins Interpersonal Adjective Scale
Wiggly Block Test
Wilcoxon Matched Pairs Signed Ranks Test
Wilcoxon Rank Sum Test
Willingness to Collaborate Trait Scale
Willingness to Commun Self Scale (Brewer et al)
Willoughby Haggerty Behavior Rating Scale
Willoughby Personality Schedule
Wills Auditory Gestalt Test
Wilson Stress Profile for Teachers
Windward Rating Scale
Winterbottom Questionnaire
Winterhaven Percept Test Train Handbook
Wirtschaftliche Bildung Test
WISC R Administration Observational Checklist
Wisconsin Basic Needs Survey
Wisconsin Card Sorting Test
Wisconsin Counselor Education Selection Interview
Wisconsin Expanding Inventory Reading Development
Wisconsin General Test Apparatus
Wisconsin Inventory of Science Processes
Wisconsin Item Bank
Wisconsin Scale (Otto and Rarick)
Wisconsin Test of Adult Basic Education
Wisconsin Tests Testimony Reasoning Assessment
Wisconsin Third Grade Reading Test
Wit and Humor Appreciation Test (OConnell)
Within Class Regression
Within Group Slopes
Wolpe Lazarus Assertive Inventory
Women as School District Administrators Survey
Womens Liberation Questionnaire (Bove and Miller)
Wonderlic Personnel Test
Woodcock Johnson Psycho Educational Battery
Woodcock Johnson Tests of Cognitive Ability
Woodcock Language Proficiency Battery
Woodcock Passage Comprehension Test
Woodcock Reading Mastery Test
Woodcock Word Comprehension Test
Worchel Self Concept Inventory
Word Context Test
Word Form Configuration Test (Sabatino)
Word Identification Test (Johnson et al)
Word Learning Tasks (Barr)
Word Phrase Comprehension Tests (Shiba)
Word Preference Inventory (Dunn and Rankin)
Word Reading Test
Word Use Test
Words in Pairs Test (O Donnell)
Work Adjustment Rating Form
Work Aspect Preference Scale
Work Association Test (Essex and Liu)
Work Attitudes Inventory
Work Environment Preference Schedule
Work Environment Scale
Work Interest Questionnaire
Work Itself Work Environment Questionnaire
Work Keys (ACT)
Work Performance Assessment (Test)
Work Personality Profile
Work Personality Profile Self Report
Work Related Activities Scale
Work Relevant Attitudes Scale
Work Stress Inventory
Work Temperament Inventory
Work Tests
Work Values Inventory
Worker Motivation Scale (Wherry and South)
Worker Trainee Examination (Civil Service)
Working Alliance Inventory
Workplace Literacy Skills and Training Inventory
World Regions Perception Survey
Worry and Emotionality Questionnaire
Worry Emotionality Scale (Liebert and Morris)
Worry Emotionality Scale (Morris Davis Hutchings)
Wray Behavior Scale
Wright Proctor Observational Instrument
Write a Sentence Test
Writing Apprehension Test (Daly and Miller)
Writing Skills Assessment Test
Writing Test Prompts
Written English Proficiency Test
Written Instruction Stylistic Evaluation
Written Language Profile

Yarn Test (Lampe)
Yearly Evaluation of Services by Students
Yes No Questions
Yoakam Readability Formula
York Educational Software Evaluation Scales
Young Adult Assessment 1977
Young Driver Attitude Scale
Your School Scale (Bullock)
Your Style of Learning and Thinking
Youth Attitude Tracking Survey
Youth Employment Questionnaire
Youth Opinion Questionnaire
Youth Research Survey (Forliti)
Youth Risk Behavior Survey
Youth Social Support Questionnaire
Youthpoll
Yovits Ernst Model
Ypsilanti Rating Scale
Z Scores
Zeitlin Early Identification Screening
Zero Input Tracking Analyzer
Zertifikat Deutsch als Fremdsprache
Zimmerman Preschool Language Quotient
Zip Test
Zung Self Rating Depression Scale

CATEGORY 22: Titles (Literary & Artistic)

3 2 1 Contact
3 2 1 Contact Extras
60 Minutes (Title)
100 Good Schools
120 Years of American Educ Statistical Portrait
1984 (Title)
2001 A Space Odyssey
AAAS Study Guides on Contemporary Problems
Abe Lincoln in Illinois
Absalom Absalom
Abstracts of Instructional and Research Materials
Abt Study of State and Local Compliance
Academic Preparation for College
ACRL Standards for College Libraries (1975)
ACTFL Proficiency Guidelines
ACTFL Provisional Proficiency Guidelines
Action for Excellence
Active Mathematics Teaching
Adams Chronicles
Administrative Compensation Survey
Administrative Science Quarterly
Adventures of Robinson Crusoe
AEL Regional Exchange
Aeneid
Aesop Fables
African Queen
Agents of Innocence (Ignatius)
Agricultural Education Magazine
Agricultural Work Force Survey
Aida (Opera)
Alabama Interlibrary Catalog
Alabama Union List of Serials
Albemarle Report
Alice in Wonderland
Alicias Diary (Hardy)
All about Letters
All in the Family
All My Children
All the Kings Men
Allen Report
Almanac
Amen Corner
America (Song)
America 2000
America the Beautiful
American Addendum (1980)
American Educational Research Journal
American Heritage Dictionary
American Journal of Medicine
American Journal of Mental Deficiency
American Political Science Review
American Way (Magazine)
Americas Choice High Skills or Low Wages
Americas Competitive Challenge
Amerika (Miniseries)
Ames SDI KWOK Index
Anansi the Spider
Andromeda Strain
Anglo American Cataloging Rules
Angus Journal
Animal Farm
Annual Review Information Science and Technology
Antigone
Apocalyptic Premise (The)
Archives of Environmental Health
Archives of Languages of the World
Area Resource File
Areopagitica
Arithmetic Teacher (Journal)
Arizona Champion Coconino Sun
Army Life 78 Study
Around the Bend
Around the Dial (Journal)
Arrow to the Sun
Arrowsmith
Art and Architecture Thesaurus
Art as Experience
Art in the Mainstream (NAEA)
Arts and Humanities Citation Index
As You Like It
Ascent to Excellence in Catholic Education
Aspects of Language
Aspects of the Theory of Syntax
Associated Press Stylebook
Atcon Report 1961
Atlanta World
Attack on Pearl Harbor Cloud of Mystery
Attacking the Wall
Autobiography of Malcolm X
AV Communication Review
Avery Index to Architectural Periodicals
Bank Street Readers
Barriers to Excellence Our Children at Risk
Basic Education Teaching the Adult (Videotape)
Beast in the Jungle
Becoming a Citizen Series
Becoming a Nation of Readers
Being and Time
Being There
Beloved (Morrison)
Benjamin Bunny
Beowulf
Berkeley Older Generation Study
Best Short Plays (Title)
Betts Basic Readers
Beyond Freedom and Dignity
Beyond Growth Next Stage Lang and Area Studies
Beyond New Forks
Bhagavad Gita
Bible
Bibliography of Agriculture
Billy Budd
Biological Abstracts
Birth of a Nation
Birthday Party (Pinter)
Black in White America
Black Jack Davy (Song)
Black Thunder
Blacky Pictures
Blade Runner (Movie)
Blue Book of the John Birch Society
Blue Book Series
Blue Willow
Blues Poetry
Bobbsey Twins
Bodas de Sangre
Book of Good Love
Book of Job
Book of Mormon
Books for College Libraries
Books for Your Children
Books in Print
Boston Gazette
Boston Recorder
Brain Research Bulletin
Brain Research Journal
Breakfast Club (The)
Bride Comes to Yellow Sky (Crane)
Brief Polytechnic Dictionary
Bristol Social Adjustment Guides
British Journal of Educational Psychology
British Journal of Sociology
British Medical Journal
British National Bibliography
Brown University Corpus of American English
Brownies Book
Bulletin Kejar
Bulletin of Environmental Education
Bullock Report
Bundy Report
Bunkyo Museum of Literature (Interactive Video)
Cabaret
Cagney and Lacey
California Business Education Program Guide
California History Social Science Framework (1981)
California History Social Science Framework (1988)
Call for Change in Teacher Education
Call It Courage
Cambridge Kentucky Educ TV GED Video Series
Canadian Classification Dictionary of Occupations
Canadian Periodical Index
Candid Camera
Cant Buy Me Love (Film)
Cantar de Mio Cid
Canterbury Tales
Canticle for Leibowitz
Canto General
Captain Kangaroo
Captains Courageous
Captive (The)
Captive Voices
Caravans (Michener)
Cardinal Principles Report
Career Data Book
Career Development in Global Community Health
Career Education in the Elementary School
Career Information Search Survey
Carnegie Commission Report
Carrascolendas (Television Series)
Cartoon All Stars to the Rescue
Case Studies in Science Education
Catalog of Virginia Library Resources
Catch 22
Catcher in the Rye
Catholic Worker (The)
Cats Cradle (Vonnegut)
CBS Evening News
CBS Reports
Census 1960
Census 1970
Census 1980
Census 1981 (Canada)
Census 1990
Census of Agriculture 1982
Centralized Correspondence Study AK
Century Magazine
Ceremony (Title)
Challenge of Peace (Bishops Pastoral Letter)
Challenge of the Unknown (Film)
Changing Face of the Soviet Union
Changing Old World
Changing Politics of Education (The)
Character Education Inquiry (Hartshorne and May)
Charlie Brown
Charlottes Web
Cheaper by the Dozen
Cheers (Television Series)
Chemical Abstracts
Chemical Abstracts Condensates
Chicano Thesaurus
Child and the Curriculum
Child Structured Learning in Science
Childrens Artistic Paradise
Childrens Choices (Booklist)
Childrens English and Services Study
China a Handbook (1973)
Choice (Yette)
Chosen
Christabel
Christmas Story (The)
Chronicle of Higher Education
Cien Anos De Soledad
Cinderella
Cities at Work
City of God
Classification of Instructional Programs
Classified Index of Occupations and Industries
Classroom Management Improvement Study
Claybrooks First Order Predicate Calculus
Clifford Books
Clockwork Orange
Closer Look
Closing of the American Mind (Bloom)
Clovis Life Skills Materials
CNN World Report
COBUILD
Cockcroft Report
Code of Ethics of the Education Profession
Code of Ethics of the Library Profession
Code of Student Rights and Responsibilities
Coffe Report
Coleman II
Coleman Report
College and Research Libraries (Journal)
College Composition and Communication (Journal)
College English (Journal)
College Teaching and Learning Collection
College Trustee Study
Color Purple (The)
Columbus Dispatch
Command Post Series
Common Threads (Film)
Community 70 Series
Community Services Handbook
Completed Research Health Physical Ed Recreation
Comprehensive Grammar of the English Language
Conant Report
Concept Books
Concepts in Science
Condition of Education (NCES)
Confessions of Zeno
Confraternity of Christian Doctrine
Congressional Record
Consolidated Program Information Report
Consumer Reports
Consumer Skills Kit (NAEP)
Contender (The)
Content Analysis of Textbooks for Black Students
Contra Costa Social Studies Guides
Conversacion en la Catedral
Cook Books
Cornell Medical Index
Correct English Magazine
Cosby Show
Coup de Grace (The)
Courier Journal (Louisville)
Covenants on Human Rights
Cox Commission Report
Cricket (Magazine)
Crime Against Nature (Pratt)
Crime and Punishment
Critical Needs in International Education
Crow Report
Crucible
Crusader (The)
Cry the Beloved Country
Culture of Poverty
Culturefax
Cumulative Book Index
Cumulative Index Nursing Allied Health Literature
Cure (The)
Current Awareness in Health Education
Current Biography Yearbook
Current Index to Journals in Education
Current Papers in Physics
Current Physics Information
Current Population Survey
Curriculum Development Library
Curriculum for Improving Communications Skills
Currie Report
Curtis Digests
Daily Times (Pekin IL)
Dainton Report
Dale Chall List of 3000 Familiar Words
Dallas (Television Series)
Danger Above and Below
Dangerous Liaisons (Film)
David and Lisa
Dawn of Fear
Day After (The)
De Bello Civili
Dead Birds (Title)
Dead Sea Scrolls
Death and the Kings Horseman
Death of the Ball Turret Gunner
Declaration of Independence
Declaration of Persepolis
Declaration of the Rights of the Child
Declaration on the Human Environment
Deep Space 9
Deer Hunter (The)
Deliverance
Design for Thinking
Detroit City School Series
Developing Character Transmitting Knowledge
Dialogue Concerning Education
Diary of a Young Girl
Diary of Anne Frank
Dick and Jane Readers
Dictionary of American Regional English
Dictionary of Occupational Titles
Dictionnaire d Eloquence Sacree (Nadal)
Diff rent Strokes
Digest of Education Statistics
Dinky Hocker Shoots Smack
Dinner at the Homesick Restaurant (Book)
Directory of Self Instructional Materials
Directory of Unpublished Experimental Mental Meas
Discover Art (Textbook Series)
Disorder in Our Public Schools

Dissertation Abstracts International Index
Divine Comedy
Do the Right Thing (Film)
Doctor of Philosophy in Education Degrees
Doctor Seuss
Doctor Zhivago
Dollmaker (The)
Domian Report
Don Juan in Hell
Don Quixote
Doonesbury
Down These Mean Streets
Drama of Democracy
Dreams Not Enough (The)
Drums along the Mohawk
Dubliners
Duelo en el Paraiso
Dumb Waiter (Pinter)
Durrell Listening Reading Series
Each in His Own Way
Eager to Learn
Eagle and the Mole
Early American Textbook Collection
Easy Rider
Ebony Magazine
Economic Literature Index
Economics a Programmed Text
Economist (The)
Educating Americans for the 21st Century
Education Administration Quarterly
Education and Ecstasy
Education Data Elements Dictionary
Education for Tomorrows Jobs
Education Index
Educational Administration Quarterly
Educational Broadcasting Review
Educational Broadcasting Review (Journal)
Educational Communications and Technology Journal
Educational Guidance in Human Love
Educational Imagination (The)
Educational Media Index
Educational Research and Development Report
Effects of Participating in Vocational Education
El Coronel No Tiene Quien le Escriba
Electric Company
Elementary Science Survey
Elementary Secondary Schools Civil Rights Survey
Elements of English Grammar (Van Winkle)
Emile
Emma
Empleen Ingles Series
Employability Skills Series
Empty Lot
Encyclopaedia Britannica
Encyclopedia of Educational Research
Encyclopedia of Library and Information Science
End of Innocence (Music Video)
Endicott Report
Engineering Index
English Education Today
English Journal
English Skills for Algebra
Epic of Gilgamesh
Equal Justice Under Law (American Bar Assn)
Equalizer (Television Series)
Esprit (Journal)
Essay on Criticism
EUDISED Multilingual Thesaurus
Evelyn Wood Reading Dynamics
Exceptional Children (Journal)
Exceptional Parent Magazine
Excerpta Medica
Exploring Our World Regions (Follett)
Export to Win
Eyes on the Prize
Fact Sheets
Faerie Queene
Fahrenheit 451
Fall of the City (MacLeish)
Falling Towards England (James)
Family Ties (Television Program)
Farewell to Arms (A)
Farmers Week
Fat Albert and the Cosby Kids
Faure Report
Faust
Federal Register
Federalist Papers
Feeling Good
Ficciones
Fielas Child (Matthee)
Field of Dreams
Fiesta
Financing Community Colleges
First Grade Reading Group Study
First International Science Study
First Lessons A Report on Elementary Ed in America
Five Little Peppers
Fleischmann Commission Report Elem Secondary Educ
Fleishmans Supervisory Behavior Description
Florida Language Profile
Flowers for Algernon
Follman English Mechanics Guide
Foreign Affairs (Journal)
Foretaste of Glory
Fortunata y Jacinta
Foundation Directory
Four Agency Agreement
Four Champa Trees
Four Families
Fourier Series
Foxfire
Franck Report
Freedman Report
Freemans Journal
Freestyle (Television Series)
Freeway to Learning
French in Action (Video)
Fresno Bee
Friday Night Lights (Bissinger)
Fries American English Series
Frog King or Faithful Henry
From Subject to Citizen
Frost at Midnight
Function of Criticism at the Present Time
Functional Basic Reading Series
Functional Basic Word List for Special Pupils
Fundamental Achievement Series (Form Xb)
Future Shock
FUTURES with Jaime Escalante
Genesis
Gentle Spirit
Geometric Dictionary
Gerbner Study
Ginn 360 Series
Ginn Reading 720 Series
Global 2000 Report
Go Down Moses
Godfather (The)
Gods Must Be Crazy (The)
Godspell
Good Morning Miss Dove
Good Night Mr Tom
Goonies (The)
Government Reports Announcements and Index
Graduate (The)
Granada Lectures
Grateful Dead
Great Bird of Love
Great Expectations
Great Gatsby
Great God Brown
Great Soviet Encyclopedia
Greatest Love of All (The)
Greek Myths (Title)
Green Is Like a Meadow of Grass
Greening of America
Grendel
Grieve Report
Grolier Survey
Groliers Modern English Series Spelling
Gross Product Originating Series
Group Interview Guide
Growth Through Art and Museum Experience
Growth Through English
Guang Yun
Guide for College Visits and Reporting
Guide for Industrial Arts Education in Oklahoma
Guide to Improving Instruction in Industrial Arts
Guide to Microforms in Print
Guide to Selecting Basal Reading Programs
Guidelines for Preparing Teachers of English
Guidelines in Vocations and Education
Guiding Creative Talent
Guiding Ones Own Development
GYNS AT WRK
Habits of the Heart
Hairy Ape (the)
Haj (Uris)
Hale Report
Hall Dennis Report
Hamlet
Hand Is on the Gate
Handbook of Cooperative Education
Handbook of Human Intelligence (Sternberg)
Handbook of Latin American Studies
Happiness Is a Bill of Sale
Hard Times
Harlequin Romances
Harriet the Spy
Harry Stottelmeiers Discovery (Novel)
Harvard Law Review
Haslegrave Report
Hawaii 2000
Hawaii Educational Leadership Study
Health and Nutrition Examination Survey
Health Insurance Study
Healthy Thats ME
Heart Is a Lonely Hunter
Heart of Darkness
Heart of the Dragon
Heart Start
Heath Elementary Mathematics Series
Henry V
Herald Telephone
High School (Film)
High School A Report on Secondary Educ in America
High School on TV
Higher Education Price Index
Higher Learning in America (Hutchins)
Hill Street Blues
Hired Farm Working Force Survey
Hiroshima No Pika (Maruki)
His Enemy His Friend
Historias de la Artamila
Historical Trends State Educ Facts 1969 to 1989
History of British Primary Schools
History of King Richard III
Hobbit
Holmes Group Report
Holt Basic Reading System
Holt Mathematics Series
Homecoming (Pinter)
Homer Price and the Doughnut Machine
Hope Commission Report
Horaces Compromise
Horn Book Magazine
Hospital Literature Index
Houghton Mifflin Elementary Mathematics Series
Houghton Mifflin Reading Series
Houston Chronicle
Houston Post
How I Believe
How I Feel About Some Other Kids
How I Won the War
Huckleberry Finn
Hugo och Josefin (Gripe)
Humanistic Approaches Provide Positive Environment
Hunchback in the Park
Hunger of Memory
Hutchins Commission Report
Hydra
I Am the Mayor
I Can Project
I Feel Me Feel
I Heard a Fly Buzz When I Died
I Know Why the Caged Bird Sings (Angelou)
Identifier Authority List
If You Had a Visitor
If You Live in a City Where Do You Live
If You Were Coming in the Fall
Iliad
Illinois Rules of the Road
Illinois School Journal
Illinois Teacher of Home Economics
Illusionless Man and the Visionary Maid
Images and Things
Imagine That
Impact Magazine
Improving Test Taking Skills (Riverside)
Impunity Jane
In Cold Blood
In Our Time
In Search of Excellence
In the French Body
In the White Mans Image
Index Medicus
Index of Adjustment and Values
Index of Evaluative Dominance
Index of Rhythmicity
Index of the Sciences (Arabic)
Industrial Worker (Title)
Inferno
Infinity Factory
Information Place
Information Power (AASL AECT)
Inside Out (Television Series)
Instructional Innovator (Journal)
Integration Readings
Integrity in the College Curriculum
Interaction of Man and the Biosphere
Interim Report on Study of Selected ECE Schools
International Encyclopedia of Higher Education
International Encyclopedia of the Social Sciences
International Nursing Index
International Review of Applied Psychology
International Studies on Educational Achievement
Interpersonal World of the Infant (Stern)
Introduction to Applied Chemistry
Introduction to Computing
Introduction to Programed Instruction
Investigating Science with Children
Investigating the Earth
Invisible Man (The)
Invitation to Submit Materials
Invitations to Enquiry
Involvement in Learning
Iron John A Book About Men
Iron Man
Island (Novel)
Island of the Blue Dolphins
Isle of Independent Study
ISO 9000
ITFS What It Is How to Plan
James Report
Japanese Education Today
Jasper Woodbury Problem Solving Series
Jencks Report
Jensen Report
Jesus Christ Superstar
JFK (Film)
Ji Yun
Jonathan Livingston Seagull
Joseph and the Amazing Technicolor Dreamcoat
Journal of Academic Librarianship
Journal of Agricultural Education
Journal of American Indian Education
Journal of Chemical Education
Journal of College Student Development
Journal of Communication
Journal of Consulting and Clinical Psychology
Journal of Counseling Psychology
Journal of Education for Librarianship
Journal of Educational Administration
Journal of Educational Psychology
Journal of Educational Research
Journal of Geography in Higher Education
Journal of Instructional Development
Journal of Learning Disabilities
Journal of Marriage and the Family
Journal of Medical Education
Journal of Reading
Journal of Research in Music Education
Journal of Research in Science Teaching
Journal of Social Issues
Journal of Special Education
Journal of Teacher Education
Journal of the American Chemical Society
Journal of the American Forensics Association
Journal Supplement Abstract Service
Journalism Computer Assisted Instruction
Journalism Quarterly
Journeys Unlimited
Jubilee (Novel)
Julius Caesar
Junior High Classroom Organization Study
Junior High School Management Improvement Study
Kansas Learner Needs Assessment Study
Karmel Report
Keating Report
Kent Study
Kentucky Career Ladder Plan
Kentucky Longitudinal Study
Kerner Commission Report
Kettering Commission Report
Kids Alive (Television Series)
Killers (The)
King James Version of the Holy Bible
King Kong
King Lear
Kirschener Report
Kissler Report 1980
Knight Report on Intercollegiate Athletics
Knowes Report
Koran
Kothari Report
La Presse (Newspaper)
La Symphonie Pastorale
Laboratory Exploration in Biology
Ladies Home Journal
Lado English Language Series
Lado Fries Materials

Lady of Shalott (The)
Lammers Report
Land and Me
Language Arts (Journal)
Language of the Crib
Language Performance in Schools (APU)
Last Tango in Paris
Last Temptation of Christ (The)
Laubach Streamlined Series
Laubach Way to Reading Series
Laughing Boy (La Farge)
Leaps and Bounds (Television Series)
Leaves of Grass
Let Me See (Television Series)
Library and Information Science Abstracts
Library and Information Science Today
Library Bill of Rights
Library Journal
Library Literature (Serial)
Life Magazine
Life Week
Life World
Lift Every Voice and Sing
Light in August
Limiting What Students Shall Read
Limits to Growth
Linguistic Atlas of the Gulf States
Linguistic Atlas of the Pacific Coast
Linguistic Atlas of the Upper Midwest
Lion of the West (Drama)
Lippincott Basic Reading Series
Lippincott Reading Program
Lippincott Series
List of Periodicals Reviewing Books
Lista de Encabezamientos de Materia
Literacy in the Open Access College
Literary Digest
Little Drummer Girl (Le Carre)
Little House on the Prairie
Little Papers (Deaf Community)
Little Prince
Little Red Riding Hood
Live Boys in the Black Hills
Live Boys or Charley and Nasho in Texas
Lives on the Boundary (Rose)
Local Focus on Youth (The)
Lolita
London Times Higher Education Supplement
Lone Ranger (Television Series)
Loneliness of the Long Distance Runner
Long Ago and Far Away (Television Series)
Long Days Journey Into Night
Long Haul
Longman Bibliography of Composition and Rhetoric
Longman Dictionary of Contemporary English
Longman Lexicon of Contemporary English
Look Homeward Angel
Looking Backward (Bellamy)
Lord Jim
Lord of the Flies
Lord of the Rings
Losing Ground (Murray)
Louisiana Agriculture (Journal)
Louisville Times
Love for Three Oranges
Love Medicine
Love Song of J Alfred Prufrock (The)
Love Story
MacAllister Report
Macbeth
MacBride Commission Report
Macmillan Reading Program Series
Mad Magazine
Madame Bovary
Magic Crossbow (The)
Magic Ear
Mahabharata
Maine Woods (The)
Make Something Happen
Making of a Decision (Film)
Making the Grade
Making the Grade Eval and Reporting Student Prog
Maltese Falcon
Man for All Seasons (A)
Man Made World
Man Who Lived Underground
Management Review (Journal)
Manchild in the Promised Land
Mandragola
Manitoba Longitudinal Study on Aging
Manon Lescaut
Manpower Report of the President
Manpower Report of the President (1972)
Manpower Report of the President (1975)
Marat Sade
Martian Chronicles
Martin Report
MASH (Television Program)
Mass (Leonard Bernstein)
Mathematics Framework for Calif Public Schools
Mathematics Teacher (Journal)
Max Headroom
McClures Magazine
McGuffey Readers
Medical Subject Headings
Medicine Today
Meeting of Minds
Member of the Wedding (The)
Mending Wall
Mental Measurements Yearbook
Mental Retardation Abstracts
Merchant of Venice
Meriam Report
Merriam Report
Miami Linguistic Readers
Miami Vice (Television Series)
Michigan Panel Study of Income Dynamics
Midnight Cowboy
Midsummer Nights Dream
Military Advisers Language Text
Milwaukee Journal
Minnesota College Teacher Study
Minnesota Union List of Serials
Miracle Worker
Mission (The)
Mistakes in Teaching (Hughes)
Mister Rogers Neighborhood
Moby Dick
Modern Arithmetic Through Discovery
Monkeys Paw (The)
Monsieur Ouine
Monthly Catalog of U S Government Publications
Monthly Checklist of State Publications
Morbidity and Mortality Weekly Report
More Perfect Union (A)
Morphology of the Folktale
Mother Goose
Mount Druitt Longitudinal Study
Moynihan Report
Mr Sammlers Planet
Mr Smith Goes to Washington
Ms Magazine
Mulligan Stew
Multi Media Treatise on Nuclear War and Peace
Music Code of Ethics
Music Supervisors Journal
Mutiny on the Bounty
My Antonia
My Country School Diary
My Dream
My Fair Lady
My Last Duchess
My Weekly Reader
Mystery of Heroism
Myth of Sisyphus (Camus)
NAEB Journal
Nancy Drew
Narrative of Arthur Gordon Pym
Narrow Fellow in the Grass (A)
Nashville Union Catalog
NASSP Bulletin
Nation (Journal)
Nation at Risk (A)
Nation Prepared (A)
Nation Responds (The)
National Administrator Research Study
National Atlas of United States of America
National Census Study (Home Economics)
National Crime Survey
National Day Care Home Study
National Day Care Study
National Geographic
National Humanities Series
National Manpower Study
National Middle School Study
National Public Affairs Study
National Safe School Study
National Survey Fringe Benefits Public Schools
National Survey of Black Americans
National Survey of Children 1981
National Survey of Compensatory Education
National Survey of Economic Education 1981
National Survey of Science Math and Social Studies
National Survey Salaries Wages Public Schools
National Union Catalog
Native Son
New Entrants Survey
New Horizons in Adult Education
New Literacy (Willinsky)
New Model Me (The)
New Oxford English Dictionary
New Republic (Journal)
New Revised Standard Version of the Bible
New Testament
New York City Manpower Information Bulletins
New York Daily News
New York Herald
New York Magazine or Literary Repository
New York State Curriculum Guide
New York Times
New York Times Sunday Magazine
New Yorker
New Youth Initiatives in Apprenticeship Study
New Zealand Journal of Educational Studies
Newcastle Report (England)
Newman Report
Newman Report Critique
News Sentinel (Knoxville TN)
Newsletter on Intellectual Freedom
Newsweek
Newsweek Magazine
Nippon Cataloging Rules
Non E Mai Troppo Tardi
Normal Heart (Kramer)
North Dakota Energy and Power Curriculum Guide
Norton Anthology of American Literature
Norton Anthology of English Literature
NOVA (Television Series)
Nuclear Science Abstracts
Nutcracker Suite
Obnoxious Jerks (Manes)
Occupational Outlook Handbook
Occurrence at Owl Creek Bridge (An)
Ode Intimations of Immortality (Wordsworth)
Odyssey
Oedipus Rex
Oedipus Tyrannus (Sophocles)
Of Mice and Men
Officer Vic
Ogburn Report
Oklahoma Eagle
Old Man and the Sea
Old Testament
Old Times on the Mississippi
Old Yeller
Oliver Twist
Olympiad (The)
OMB Circular A110
OMB Circular A130
OMB Circular A21
OMB Circular A87
Omnibus (Television Series)
On Golden Pond
On Saturday Afternoon
On the Nature of Things
On the Origin of Species
Once and Future King
One Minute Manager (The)
One Nation Indivisible
One Third of a Nation
Onomatopoeia and Images
Open Court Readers
Optimists Daughter (Welty)
Oral History (Smith)
Organization Man
Orlando (Title)
Orphan in History (Cowan)
Othello
Our Economy How It Works
Our Kind of World
Our Working World
Our World
Output Measures for Public Libraries
Over Easy (Television Series)
Owen Report
Owl Service
Ox Bow Incident
Oxford Advanced Learners Dictionary
Oxford American Dictionary
Oxford English Dictionary
Oye Willie (Title)
Pacesetters in Innovation
Paddington Books
Paddle to the Sea
Paideia Problems and Possibilities
Paradise Lost
Paradiso
Parent Educator Weekly Report
Parent Express
PARENT TALK (Newsletter)
Parlons Francais
Parry Report
Pearl (The)
Pennsylvania Union List of Serials
People and a Spirit
People through the Ages
Pere Goriot
Personnel and Guidance Journal
Peter Pan
Peter Rabbit
Petroleum Abstracts
Phedre
Phi Delta Kappan
Phonics and Word Power
Photoplay Magazine
Physical Education Index
Physical Education Sports Index
Physics Abstracts
Pied Piper of Hamelin
Piers Plowman
Pigman
Pilkington Report
Pinocchio
Pitchell Report for Higher Education
Pittsburgh Courier
Place Called School (A)
Place of Doors Television Show
Places Rated Almanac
Plague
Planning and Changing (Journal)
Playboy of the Western World
Pledge of Allegiance
Plowden Report
Political World Interview
Politics and the English Language
Polka Dot Door
Pooh Step by Step Guide
Populorum Progressio
Postcards from America (Novels)
Powerhouse (Television Series)
Prairie Home Companion (A)
Pravda
Prep Reports
Preprimer
Presidents State of Union Message
Pride and Prejudice
Primary Education in England
Prince and the Pauper
Principal Teacher Interaction Study
Principals of Leadership
Private Lives
Profiles of Promise
Progressive (The)
Prometheus Bound
Protocol Materials in English Film Series
Psalms
Psychological Abstracts
Public and Private Schools (Coleman et al)
Public Opinion Quarterly
Public Relations Journal
Public Relations Review
Public Schools Latin Primer
Public Telecommunications Review (Journal)
Publishers Weekly
Pygmalion
Pygmalion in the Classroom
Quarterly Journal of Speech
Queries n Theories
Question of Economics (A)
Radio Talk (Radio Program)
Raisin in the Sun
Ramayana
Random House Dictionary of the English Language
Ranger Ricks Nature Magazine
Rappaccinis Daughter
Rashomon
Rasselas
Rayuelo
Readers Digest
Readers Guide to Periodical Literature
Reading by Patterns A Programmed Guide
Reading for a Reason
Reading Improvement (Journal)
Reading Rainbow
Reading Teacher (Journal)
Reading World (Journal)
Readings in the History of Mathematics Education
Ready Set Go
Recently Published Articles
Recruiting Trends Survey
Red Badge of Courage
Red Balloon
Red Kite
Red Pony
Reign of ETS (Nairn)
Republic
Requiem for a Heavyweight
Research and Development Price Index

Research in Education
Research Libraries Group Conspectus
Research Quarterly
Resources in Education
Response to Literature
Return of the Native
Review of Agricultural Education Research
Review of Educational Research
Revolt of the Masses
Revolution in Instruction
Rhetoric Review (Journal)
Richard Cory
Richard III
Right Stuff (Wolfe)
Ring and the Book (The)
Ring Toss (Photograph)
Ripples
Rise and Fall of the Great Powers (Kennedy)
Rise of the American Nation (Harcourt Brace World)
Rite of Love and Death (Film)
Road from Coorain (Conway)
Robbins Report (England)
Roberts English Series
Roberts Rules of Order
Rocky IV (Movie)
Rogets International Thesaurus
Rogets Thesaurus
Roman Virginia
Romancero Gitano
Romeo and Juliet
Romper Room
Room 222
Roots (Haley)
Roper Research Surveys
Rosemarys Baby
Rosner Report
Roundtable Reports
Royal Society Catalogue of Scientific Papers
Ruchardts Experiment
Runaway Jerk
Rural America Series
Rural Education Rural Family Ed Policy for the 80s
Rural Sociology (Journal)
Russell Report
Sadako and the Thousand Paper Cranes
Safe School Study
Saint Joan of the Stockyards
Saint Louis Globe Democrat
Saint Louis Post Dispatch
Saint Petersburg Times
San Manuel Bueno Martir
Sanford and Son
Saxon Mathematics Series
Scarlet Letter
School Based Program Evaluation Manual
School Library Journal
School Life Magazine
School Price Index
School Utilization Study
Science (Journal)
Science 81
Science Abstracts
Science Citation Index
Science Manpower Series
Science Talk (Newsletter)
Scientific American
Scott Foresman Basal Series
Scranton Report
Search for Solutions (Film Series)
Searching Eye
Searchlight
Sears List of Subject Headings
Seattle Argus (Newspaper)
Second International Mathematics Study
Second International Science Study
Seebohm Report
Segment Three (NBC News)
Separate Peace
SERD Report
Sesame Street
Seventh Seal
Shadow (Book)
Shane
Sheldon Basic Reading Series
Sherlock Holmes
Shogun
Short Happy Life of Francis Macomber
Shuo Wen Chie Tsu
Signs of Trouble and Erosion A Report on Grad Educ
Simpsons (The)
Singapore National Bibliography
Sir Gawain and the Green Knight
SKOLE (Journal)
Slaughterhouse Five
Sleeping Beauty
Slim John
Sloan Commission Studies
Small Earth
Soar Report
Social Education (Journal)
Social Issues Resources Series
Social Science Citation Index
Social Sciences Citation Index
Social Studies Materials Data Book
Sociological Abstracts
Sociology of Education (Journal)
Sociology of Leisure and Sport Abstracts
Solstice De Juin
Song of Roland
Sonnys Blues
Sor Juana Ines de la Cruz
Soul on Ice
Souls of Black Folk
Sound and the Fury (Faulkner)
Sound of a Word
Southern Magazine
Southern Youth Study
Southwestern Social Science Quarterly
Soviet Reader
SPACES (Television Series)
Special Libraries (Journal)
Special Teens and Parents Study
Speculum Mentis
Spelling and Writing Patterns
Spelling Growth
Spokane Press
Spoken Albanian
Spoon River Anthology
Sport and Recreation Index
Sports Illustrated
Square One TV
Stagecoach (Film)
Standards for Excellence in Trade Industrial Educ
Standards for School Media Programs
Stanford Curriculum Study
Stanford Reading and Television Study
Star Spangled Banner
Star Trek
Star Trek the Next Generation
Star Wars (Film)
Starry Night (van Gogh)
State Education Encyclopedia (Texas)
State Education Performance Chart
State Educational Records and Reports Series
State Library of Ohio Union Catalog
State of the World Atlas (The)
Steppe (The)
Steppenwolf
Streetcar Named Desire (A)
StreetWise (Newspaper)
Strength through Wisdom
Student Development Series
Students Right to Their Own Language (CCCC)
Studies in the Nature of Character
Study of Academic Prediction and Growth
Study of High Schools (A)
Study of Impact of Student Financial Aid Programs
Study of Schooling (A)
Sula (Morrison)
Sullivan Programmed Reading Series
Surgeon Generals Report on Television Violence
Survey of Doctorate Recipients
Survey of Earned Doctorates
Survey of Federal Support to Univs and Colleges
Survey of Income and Education
Survey of Income and Program Participation
Survey of Public Participation in the Arts
Survey of Voluntary Support of Education
Survey on Economic Attitudes
Table Alphabeticall
Take a Bite Out of Crime
Take One Small Seed
Tale of Genji (The)
Tales from King Arthur
Tales of the Decameron
Talk with the Angels (Meiring)
Taller Than Bandai Mountain
Tamburlaine the Great
Tao Te Ching
Taylor Report
Teacher Career and Promotion Study
Teacher Efficacy Study
Teachers College Record
Teachers Course Book
Teachers for Our Nations Schools (Goodlad)
Teachers for the Real World
Teachers Guide to Macmillan Readingtime Books
Teachers Workbook of 30000 Words
Teaching Black Children to Read
Teaching Education (Journal)
Teaching for Mastery
Teaching Styles and Pupil Progress (Bennett)
Teaching Teen Reading Series
Team Magazine
Teddy Bear Magazines
Teen Scene
Teenage Mutant Ninja Turtles
Telescuola
Tell Me That You Love Me Junie Moon (Book)
Tempest (the)
Terminator (Movie)
Tess of the D Urbervilles
Tests of Reading Inter American Series
Texas Junior High School Study
There Are No Children Here
Thesaurus of Engineering and Scientific Terms
Thesaurus of ERIC Descriptors
Theseus Myth
ThinkAbout (Television Series)
Thinking About My School
Thinking in English (Matsumoto)
Third Wave (Toffler)
This Land Is Your Land (Song)
Thomas Report
Thoughts Concerning Education
Three Little Pigs
Thriving on Chaos (Peters)
Throne of Blood
Through the Looking Glass
Thus I Refute Beelzy
Time for Results (Governors 1991 Report on Educ)
Time Magazine
Time of Your Life
Time to Learn (Title)
Times (London)
To an Athlete Dying Young
To Autumn
To Build a Fire
To Improve Learning
To Kill a Mockingbird
To Reclaim a Legacy
To the Lighthouse
Tom Jones
Tom Sawyer
Tools for Change
Top Man X
Torah
Total Action Against Poverty
Touch of the Poet
Toward Intellectual Excellence
Trade and Develop
Trade Offs (Television Series)
Tramp Dog
Treasure Island
Trial of Last Error
Trip to Bountiful
Triumph of the Will
True Grit
Tuition Fees and Academic Calendar Survey
Tularecito
Tune Beyond Us
TV Guide
Twelve Angry Men
Two Bridges
Typee
U S News and World Report
Ulrichs International Periodicals Directory
Ulysses (Joyce)
Ulysses (Tennyson)
Un Coeur Simple
Uncle Remus
Uncle Toms Cabin
UNESCO Public Library Manifesto
Unfinished Agenda (The)
Unified Studies Learning Packets
Uniform Price Index Calculation System
Union Lists of Serials
United Nations Documents Index
University Television Newsletter
Up from Slavery
USA Today
Vance Schlechty Study
Veinte Poemas de Amor
Very Last First Time
Virgin Land the American West as Symbol and Myth
Visit (Durrenmatt)
Visit to a Small Planet
Vo Ag Facts
Vocational Education Study
Vocational Guidance Quarterly
Vocational Information Reporting System Manual
Vogue Magazine
Voices and Visions (Poetry Video Series)
Voix et Images De France
Voyage of the Mimi
Waiting for Godot
Walden
Walden Two (Skinner)
Wall Street Journal
Wall Street Journal Report
Walrus and the Carpenter
War and Peace
Warnock Report
Washington Post
Watership Down
Way I Feel About Myself
Way of the World
Way to Rainy Mountain
Ways of Looking at People
Ways of Reading (Bartholomae and Petrosky)
We Shall Overcome (Song)
Websters Third New International Dictionary
Welcome to English
Wesker Trilogy
West Side Story
Western School Journal
Western Wind
Westinghouse Report
What Color Is Your Parachute
What Work Requires of Schools
What Works in Reading (Study)
When the Legends Die
Where in Louisiana
Where in the USA Is Carmen Sandiego
Where in Time Is Carmen Sandiego
White Paper
Who Gets Ahead
Who Will Teach Our Children
Whole Life Factor
Whos Who Among Students in American Universities
Why Foods Spoil
Williams Committee Report (Australia)
Williams Report (Australia)
Wind in the Willows
Wingspread Report on Higher Education
Winnie the Pooh
Winters Tale
Wisconsin Guide Curriculum Improvement Indust Educ
Wisconsin Guide Local Curr Improvement Indust Educ
Witch of Agnesi
Witness (Film)
Wizard of Earthsea
Wizard of Oz
Woman Who Came Back
Womens Room (French)
Womens Ways of Knowing
Wonderland (Title)
Wooster Review (Ohio)
Word List for the 1970s
Work (Alcott)
Workforce 2000
Working (Terkel)
World Aluminum Abstracts
World Book Encyclopedia
World Fertility Survey
World of Construction (Title)
World of Music (Textbook Series)
World Political Risk Forecasts
Worth Report
Wright Report
Writers Market (Title)
Writings on American History
Wuthering Heights
Yale Linguistic Series
Young Abe Lincoln
Young Goodman Brown
Younger Adult Worker Study
Youngstown Vindicator
Your Word Box
Youthwork National Policy Study
Zen and the Art of Motorcycle Maintenance
Zero to Three
Zoom

VOCABULARY DEVELOPMENT PROGRAM — FLOWCHART

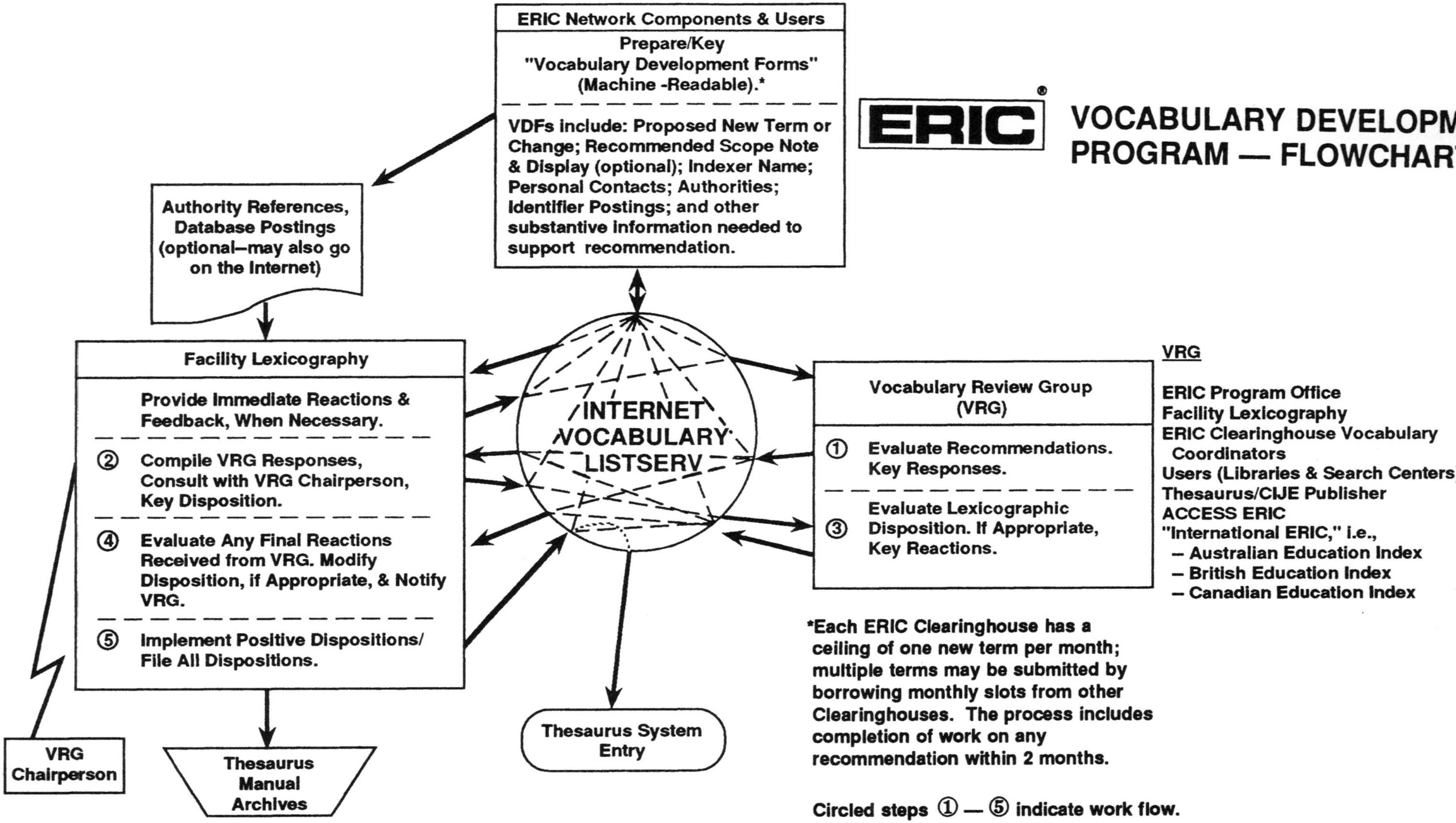

*Each ERIC Clearinghouse has a ceiling of one new term per month; multiple terms may be submitted by borrowing monthly slots from other Clearinghouses. The process includes completion of work on any recommendation within 2 months.

Circled steps ① — ⑤ indicate work flow.

www.ingramcontent.com/pod-product-compliance
Ingram Content Group UK Ltd.
Pitfield, Milton Keynes, MK11 3LW, UK
UKHW050952290926
15470UKWH00005B/1788

9 780897 748902